This new 1981 edition is for

- students who want to do better classwork (and *faster* homework)
- parents who want to answer the thousand-and-one questions their children ask
- executives who need basic facts about business and markets
- *anyone* with curiosity about their world and the people in it.

INFORMATION PLEASE has been "the answer book" for a generation of Americans. This new edition contains more facts—more ideas—than ever before.

If you need to know, turn to

INFORMATION PLEASE!

READER SURVEY

Could we have some information, please?

We want **Information Please** to be as useful as possible to you. The more we know about our readers and their requirements, the better we, in "The Answer Book," can supply the answers you need.

Would you, therefore, take a moment to give *us* some answers, about yourself and the way you use this Almanac? We'll read your replies carefully, and use them to create an even more helpful book for you in future years.

Please check the sections you find most useful:

____ Special articles
____ Election of 1980
____ Current Events
____ Headline History
____ Business and the Economy
____ Energy
____ Environment
____ World and U.S. Statistics
____ Countries of the World
____ Canada
____ Calendar and Holidays
____ Weights and Measures
____ Weather and Climate
____ Science
____ Astronomy and Space
____ Religion
____ Travel
____ Aviation
____ Military
____ Disasters
____ Nutrition and Health
____ Where to Find Out More
____ Writer's Guide
____ Geography and Maps
____ U.S. History & Government
____ Postage
____ U.S. Societies
____ Awards
____ People
____ Guide to Growing Older
____ Taxes
____ Education
____ Sports
____ Entertainment and Culture

Where do you use **Information Please** the most?

___At home ___At work ___In school ___In college

Do you now own

___a dictionary ___an atlas ___a multi-volume encyclopedia

___a one-volume encyclopedia

Your age?

___under 18 ___18–25 ___26–45 ___46–60 ___over 60

Your education?

___now in school ___high school graduate ___some college ___college graduate

Your occupation? ______________________________

We would be very pleased to have you make any other comments you think would be helpful.

Please return this information to the Editor, Information Please Almanac, Simon and Schuster, 1230 Avenue of The Americas, New York, N.Y. 10020.

For convenience, you can remove this page simply by cutting along the dotted line. Or, if you prefer, send us a letter. In either case, we would be grateful for your help.

INFORMATION PLEASE ALMANAC
ATLAS & YEARBOOK
1981
35th EDITION

SIMON AND SCHUSTER
NEW YORK

Editor
Theodore B. Dolmatch
Managing Editor
Otto T. Johnson
Associate Editor
Natalie M. Aust
Senior Editors
Vera J. Dailey
George De Gregorio
Arthur Neuhauser
Arthur P. Reed
Editors
Konrad J. A. Kundig (Science)
Blanche Ormont (Writer's Guide)
Jack Pompan (Business and the Economy)
Jacob Stern (Music)
Sanford Teller (Trivia)
Staff
Editorial Assistants: Barbara Bjelke and Alison Sippel
Cover Design
Al Lichtenberg
Maps
Dyno Lowenstein and Vaughn Gray

The Information Please Almanac invites comments and suggestions from readers. Because of the many letters received, however, it is not possible to respond personally to every correspondent. Nevertheless, all suggestions are most welcome, and the editors will consider them carefully. (Information Please Almanac does not rule on bets or wagers.)

Library of Congress Number: 47–845
ISBN (Hardcover): 0–671–41259–0
ISBN (Paperback): 0–671–41260–4

 Published by Simon and Schuster, a Division of Gulf & Western Corporation, Simon & Schuster Building, Rockefeller Center, 1230 Avenue of the Americas, New York, New York 10020. Manufactured in the United States of America. Library of Congress Cataloging in Publication Data.

INFORMATION PLEASE ALMANAC
Editorial Office
Simon & Schuster
1230 Avenue of the Americas
New York, N.Y., 10020

CONTENTS

INDEX

The Comprehensive Index lists in alphabetical order all the important topics, terms, and names covered and gives the page or pages on which they appear. • To find a fact, date, or idea, begin by looking under the most specific word. For example, to find the population of Des Moines, start by looking for *Des Moines.* But that city is not listed separately. Therefore, the next step is to look under *Iowa* or *Cities, U.S.* Under *Iowa* the designated page gives the latest population of Des Moines. Under *Cities, U.S.* there is a subhead, *Population figures,* with three alternatives: *Largest Cities of U.S.* (of which Des Moines is not one), Largest by state (which refers back to *Iowa*), and *1920-1970* (where Des Moines is listed alphabetically). • For President George Washington, look under *Washington,* before checking *President.* Where general headings (such as *Presidents, U.S.*) are given, they refer to a section where the subject is treated at some length.

INTRODUCTION

What's new *this* year? All the usual things, of course—epitomized by the results of the momentous presidential election of 1980. Here are the data relied upon by so many readers: by journalists and politicians themselves, by all who need to know how many people voted for whom, where.

This information is representative of the updating process that is such a fundamental part of our editors' work. You would be interested, I think, in watching that gleam in the editorial eye which sparkles whenever some new information comes in to us, when the National Academy of Sciences produces research that requires a change in our nutrition tables, when an athlete sets a new record, when a last minute change in the government of some country arrives.

But I take these bits of information—and our editors' precision—for granted by now. After all, such concern for new facts is a basic responsibility of any almanac editor.

What concerns us more is our ability to spot trends—to answer the question that is almost *un*answerable: What *new* information are readers likely to want *next* year?

How well we answer this question is the basic factor in making *Information Please* more useful than any other almanac. So we spend a great deal of time in discussing where the world is heading. This subject is of more than philosophical interest, for if we can anticipate correctly, then we will be able to provide you with the facts that mean more to you than some other facts do.

For example, you will discover in this 1981 edition an article on the economic indicators. We hear so much about the cost of living index, price ratios, interest rates, productivity, etc., that we should really know what these sophisticated measures mean. Therefore, in addition to giving the raw data, we have asked our business editor to define these terms. Even if the economic news is not good, you will be better able to understand what it really means.

Economic factors impinge on us all in ways that are only hinted at by those indicators. And the cost of educating Americans is increasing, affecting everything from our taxes to our children's future. So this year's *Information Please* contains an analysis of those factors which are forcing education costs up.

Energy costs also affect us, so while our last edition expanded our coverage of energy subjects, we felt that still more was required. Therefore, you will find here a new "Solar Energy Primer" which will help you to understand this form of energy better.

Maps give us an opportunity to provide information in a particularly interesting way. That's why we have added maps of Gross National Product (those economic indicators again!), Energy Consumption, Life Expectancy, and Birth Rates.

In our last edition, we furnished data on the "new religions" that blossomed in the 1970s. This year, we face a religious issue that is intertwined with international affairs. The news from Iran and other trouble spots in the Middle East suggests that oil is not the only issue. We must understand the clash of cultures—the differences in points of view which derive from the resurgence of Islamic fundamentalism. So another, international, religious issue deserves attention here—and receives it in a survey of the "culture clash" between Islam and the West.

Not everything in *Information Please* is so deadly serious, however. Our sports section, therefore, has been expanded to include even more "names and numbers," particularly those in the major sports that capture the attention of most Americans. And because sports are sometimes very serious business indeed, we have asked our editors to pay specific attention to the political implications of last year's Moscow Olympics.

All of these changes result from our commitment to give you the information you need. Our latest Reader Survey tells us that we do a pretty good job. But we can never do it perfectly. Please let us know what data *you* feel should be in the next *Information Please.* We will include it if we can, and we will continue to search for other information that our readers want. An almanac should be a living document of our times. I hope you agree that the pages in *Information Please* are alive.

Theodore B. Dolmatch
Editor

SPECIAL FEATURES

American Religious Pluralism

Paul Anthony Schwartz

Assistant Director, Center for the Study of New Religious Movements, Berkeley, California

On the very eve of a new decade, forecasters of national trends were handed a gilt-edged vision of religion in America: on the East Coast, the sight of thousands of young people chanting their welcome to a visiting Roman Pontiff with "JP Two, We Love You!," and at the same instant on the West Coast, the scene of more young people chanting in a slightly different key their homage to one the media was pleased to label "the God-King": his holiness the Fourteenth Dalai Lama, spiritual leader of the exiled Tibetan Buddhists, setting off with beads and bowl to visit his growing American flock.

An omen of the old with the new, this is a vision located somewhere between the keys of Peter and the lotus-jewel. As much as any other, this would make a good snapshot of the present state of religion in America. But the picture remains to be interpreted, some distinctions drawn between light and shadow.

It is hard to imagine a time when religion has been more visible in American life than it is now. At a national conference on "Religion and Energy in the Eighties" held in Washington in January 1980, President Carter urged Americans to recall that they are all "stewards under God's guidance" when it comes to responsible use of the world's dwindling resources. Sponsored by a wide coalition of groups including the National Council of Churches (NCC), the U.S. Catholic Conference (USCC), and the Southern Baptist Convention Sunday School Board, the conference was an apt sign of the increasing interdenominational presence of religious bodies on the political and social scene. Another sign was the "Washington for Jesus" rally held in the capital in April 1980 and attended by some one hundred seventy-five to two hundred thousand evangelicals, Pentecostals, and Charismatic Christians.

At the international level, American consciousness of religious pluralism was broadened as Americans celebrated th consecration of Robert Runcie as the 102n Archbishop of Canterbury, spiritual head o the 65-million-member Anglican (Episcopalian) communion, as well as the designatio of India's Mother Teresa as a Nobel Peac Prize recipient for her work with the destitute and dying in Calcutta's slums.

Exotic religion touched the country mor sharply as the sword of Ayatollah Khomeini' "Islamic Revolution" cut through the veils o a national ignorance about U.S. involvemen in Iranian modernization. The wester media focused on that country as teams o American clergy were granted Christma and Easter visits to the hostages. The composition of these teams again reflected th ecumenical consensus in U.S. religion Thomas Gumbleton, Roman Catholic bisho of Detroit; Dr. William Sloane Coffin, pasto of Riverside Church in New York City; an Rev. William Howard, President of the National Council of Churches.

Finally, in an attempt to probe attitude toward an almost commonplace "ecumenism" among people in the pews, the magazine *U.S. Catholic* collaborated with nin other religious journals in a poll of their readers on intercommunion. Eighty-three per cent of those polled expressed their belie that communion taken in another churc than their own was "as beneficial as" communion in their home church, while 53% reported that they would participate in th communion ritual of another church if the attended a service. By contrast, theologiar and bishops dispute the possibility of authen tic intercommunion.

This suggestion of a division between religious authorities and their flocks points t the continuing conflict between the publi sphere and the authority of various denom national traditions, as the clash betwee "right-to-life" and "pro-choice" group around the issue of abortion illustrates. Th former gathered for a national convention i

Los Angeles in the summer of 1980 to map out strategies for the adoption of a constitutional amendment prohibiting abortion and for the election of anti-abortionists to House and Senate. Meanwhile, "pro-choice" groups questioned the transformation of religious principles into single-issue politics.

Conservative and liberal religion clashed again concerning the role of religion in broadcasting, a topic hotly debated at an "Electronic Church Consultation" sponsored by the NCC in February 1980 in New York in response to a Federal Communications Commission proposal to deregulate radio broadcasting. This is a policy of great interest to the evangelicals (represented by the National Religious Broadcasters) who use the airwaves to generate an estimated $500 million annually. The mainline churches (represented by the USCC and the United Church of Christ) oppose this practice and fear further encroachment upon their traditional sources of funding (the local non-electronic collection plate).

This, as well as the unsettled controversy about the "brainwashing" and "deprogramming" of converts to non-traditional religious groups, raises first Amendment issues, and individual courts and juries continue to wrestle with competing claims. A Mankato, Minn., case recently resulted in an out-of-court payment of $21,000 in damages to a member of the Rama Behera sect who charged a local sheriff and others with kidnapping. The scholarly and legal questions raised by such occurrences will be the focus of a national conference on "Authoritarianism and Legitimate Authority in Religious Groups" to be held at the Graduate Theological Union in Berkeley in June 1981.

Meanwhile, developments in the human and social sciences which would seem to call for a revision of traditional policies have been strongly resisted by religious authorities, who seem as confused by the new demands as many of their faithful. Noteworthy cases include the widespread publicity given to the removal of Roman Catholic theologian Hans Küng from his state university post in Germany on the basis of doctrinal differences with Rome (a move formally protested by a sizeable number of prominent U.S. Catholic theologians), as well as the continuing difficulties of many denominations with the role of sexuality in human living (at least seven major denominations reiterated their opposition to the ordination of homosexuals in the last year) and the role of women in church life (Pope John Paul II's clash with Roman Catholic women in this regard has been widely reported; the Jewish Theological Seminary of America likewise defeated a motion to ordain women rabbis in Conservative synagogues in December 1979).

The presence of both affirmation and real conflict in America's handling of religious issues suggests that Americans, too, participate in the unfolding problematic of the place of religion in the modern world. Rather than forcing some "final solution" of the place of religion in American life, Americans prefer to let the ambiguities remain.

America remains, in its own way, one of the most "religious" nations on the planet. The paradox—and, one suspects, the source of some strength—lies in its ability often to be critical of its own religious accommodation, to continually call into question the forms of its acknowledged religious commitment.

To return to the symbol evoked at the opening of this feature: perhaps what we are meant to focus on between Pope and Lama, new religion and old religion, is the amazing texture and diversity of a still-emerging religious pluralism in the United States. Far from complacent or self-certain, the American religious ethos is unsettled in its search for a sacred vision that embraces the experience of the country in all its complexity. Signs exist, however, that the search does continue.

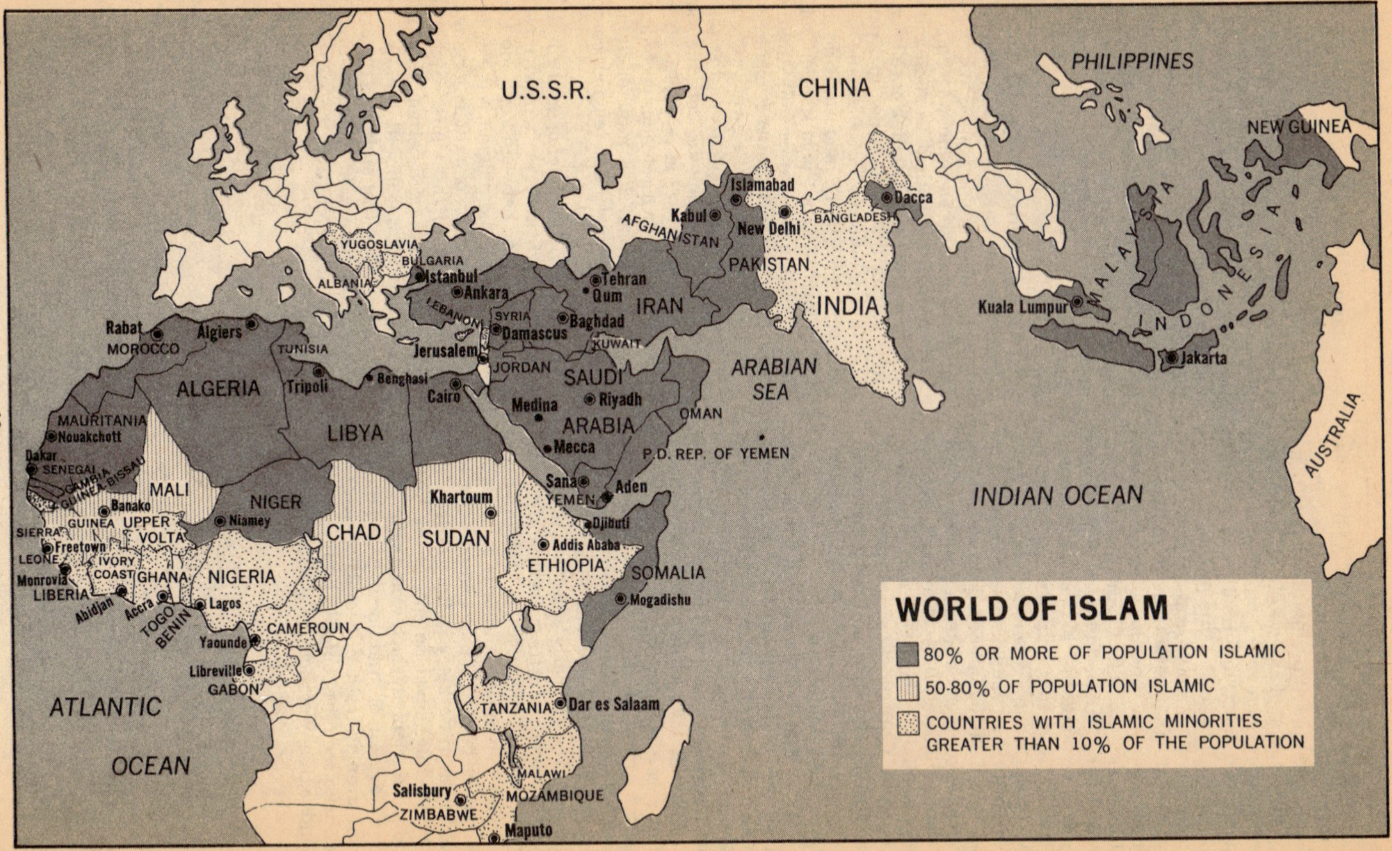
WORLD OF ISLAM
80% OR MORE OF POPULATION ISLAMIC
50-80% OF POPULATION ISLAMIC
COUNTRIES WITH ISLAMIC MINORITIES GREATER THAN 10% OF THE POPULATION
U.S.S.R.
CHINA
PHILIPPINES
NEW GUINEA
MALAYSIA
INDONESIA
Kuala Lumpur
Jakarta
AUSTRALIA
INDIAN OCEAN
Islamabad
Kabul
AFGHANISTAN
New Delhi
PAKISTAN
Dacca
BANGLADESH
INDIA
ARABIAN SEA
YUGOSLAVIA
BULGARIA
ALBANIA
Istanbul
Ankara
LEBANON
SYRIA
Damascus
Baghdad
Tehran
Qum
IRAN
KUWAIT
Jerusalem
JORDAN
SAUDI ARABIA
Riyadh
Medina
Mecca
OMAN
P.D. REP. OF YEMEN
Sana
YEMEN
Aden
Djibuti
Addis Ababa
ETHIOPIA
SOMALIA
Mogadishu
Rabat
MOROCCO
Algiers
TUNISIA
Tripoli
Benghasi
Cairo
ALGERIA
LIBYA
MAURITANIA
Nouakchott
Dakar
SENEGAL
GAMBIA
GUINEA BISSAU
MALI
Banako
GUINEA
UPPER VOLTA
NIGER
Niamey
CHAD
Khartoum
SUDAN
SIERRA LEONE
Freetown
Monrovia
LIBERIA
IVORY COAST
Abidjan
GHANA
Accra
TOGO
BENIN
NIGERIA
Lagos
CAMEROUN
Yaounde
Libreville
GABON
ATLANTIC OCEAN
TANZANIA
Dar es Salaam
MALAWI
MOZAMBIQUE
Salisbury
ZIMBABWE
Maputo

Islam—Culture Clash with the West

Don Shannon

The Iranian revolution, unfolding on the world's television screens with a cast of millions, has probably been the most widely witnessed social upheaval in history. When young revolutionaries seized the U.S. Embassy in Teheran on Nov. 4, 1979, touching off a confrontation with the most powerful Western power, watchers began to learn the meaning of culture clash.

For the first time, Americans and Europeans could see at close range the energy of an eighth-century religion that has not only survived but is now challenging the accepted truths of the secular, high-technology culture of the 20th-century industrialized world. Perhaps more disturbing to Westerners was the evidence that Iranian students in the United States and Europe, many of them engaged in advanced scientific studies, were as captivated by the fanatic old man who had seized power in Iran as were the millions of workers and peasants who flooded into the streets to demonstrate their support for him.

Until he was driven from power by the bizarre revolution of the Ayatollah Ruhollah Khomeini, Shah Mohammed Reza Pahlavi had enshrined modernization as the national goal. Billions of dollars in oil revenues—less the undetermined amounts siphoned off by the imperial family and its favorites—were spent in the pursuit of military and industrial power.

Students who had been selected by the pre-revolutionary regime to become managers of the new Iran inexplicably joined the ranks of a movement aimed at transforming their country into a primitive, xenophobic theocracy. Frequently, the Ayatollah's most urgent concerns appeared to be putting women back in veils and stamping out such infections of the Iranian soul as rock music, alcohol, and mixed bathing.

The Shiite sect, which predominates in Iran, is a fundamentalist minority among the more than half-billion Moslems of the world and, more than almost any other Islamic nation, Iran has retained a rigid and centralized religious structure.

The more numerous followers of the Sunni sect have been compared to Protestant Christians in their belief that salvation is more a matter of the individual's relationship to God. Shiites give a greater place to clerics as intermediaries, to the extent that a messianic figure like Khomeini can gain almost godlike status.

The Iranian clergy were overshadowed in the last 60 years because Shah Reza Mohammed, founder of the Pahlavi line, determined to emulate Turkey's Kemal Ataturk by deliberately suppressing their power. He ordered the shaving of heads and beards of mullahs (priests) who criticized his decrees. Reza's son, the late Shah Mohammed Reza, exiled Khomeini and other holy men who refused to bow to the monarch's insistence that Iran adopt Western ways as the road to progress.

Suppression did not damage the basic organization of the church in Iran. More centralized than in other Islamic states, the training of mullahs took place in the holy city of Qum, which currently functions as Khomeini's capital. The 180,000 mullahs stationed throughout the country formed Khomeini's revolutionary cadre, circulating his statements from exile and organizing the huge demonstrations that eventually overwhelmed the army and forced the Shah to flee in January 1979. The small but growing middle class, which had been fostered by the Shah's vision of the future, was divided and neutralized by the shock of events. Alienated like their counterparts in industrializing societies everywhere, the Iranian middle class welcomed Khomeini's condemnation of corruption and lavish consumption of those close to power. Those who chafed at the refusal of the Shah to share political power were also sympathetic—in the beginning—to the Ayatollah's profession of support for political democracy.

But initial enthusiasm faded when the mullahs showed little aptitude for keeping the national economy running, and the promise of democracy disappeared in a new despotism. Much of the middle class found themselves the targets of hostility because of their real or invented ties to the monarchy, which the revolutionary committees exploited as a weapon to enforce discipline.

Internationally, Iran remained an enigma two years after the revolution's triumph. Soviet penetration had failed to materialize, despite the anarchy that prevailed as the country advanced haltingly toward the construction of a civilian government.

U.S. attempts to retain amicable relations with the new Iran were shattered by the admission of the deposed Shah to New York City for medical treatment despite warnings from Teheran. Washington reacted to the predictable seizure of its embassy with the alternation of unconvincing threats and cajolery, but never offering the apology for past sins that Iran's disorganized new government demanded. Only the Soviet invasion of Afghanistan in December 1979 prevented a wave of pan-Islamic sympathy for Iran from becoming an anti-American tide. The airborne rescue attempt in April ended in burning wreckage on the Iranian desert—a humiliating episode that resulted in the scattering of the hostages and prevented any other such rescue attempts.

The economic cost of the Iranian crisis may never be calculated. U.S. sales of food and manufactured goods to Iran, which totaled $3.7 billion in 1978, fell to just over $1 billion in 1979, when continuing oil imports of $2.7 billion created a $1.7-billion trade deficit in Iran's favor. The ban in all trade except food and medicine reduced trade in 1980 to almost nothing.

By the fall of 1980, conflict spread in Southwest Asia with the border war between Iran and Iraq. Here, too, the battle went beyond the issues of land or economics. Islamic Iraq's culture was almost as heretical to Khomeini as that of the "satanic" Western nations he excoriated. And the threat of Shiite subversion within Iraq, encouraged by Khomeini's exhortations, was answered by a war that threatened to reduce oil reserves throughout the developed world.

The clash between Iran and its Islamic neighbor demonstrated that their argument truly went beyond any national interest. It was a struggle between an autocratic figure rising from the shadows of an ancient past and a world that is, whatever its protestations, becoming increasingly secular.

ELECTION OF 1980

Presidential Campaign Highlights

1979

NOV. 1 Former Gov. John B. Connally of Texas and Sen. Howard H. Baker of Tennessee open Presidential campaigns on Republican ticket.

7 Sen. Edward M. Kennedy of Massachusetts announces Presidential candidacy on Democratic ticket with strong attack on Carter leadership and anti-inflationary policies.

8 Gov. Edmund G. Brown of California enters race for Democratic Presidential nomination.

13 Former Gov. Ronald Reagan of California enters Republican race.

DEC. 4 Jimmy Carter declares candidacy for second term in simple Washington ceremony and asks renomination of Vice President Walter F. Mondale. Carter will continue to "talk sense" to the people. With announcement, there are 17 candidates in all: three Democrats, 10 Republicans, and four minor party.

1980

JAN. 21 George Bush, former CIA chief, wins in Iowa Republican Presidential caucuses over Reagan and others. On Democratic side Carter defeats Kennedy, 2–1, a blow to Senator's national chances. Other candidates in Republican race, in the order in which they finished, were: Sen. Howard H. Baker, Jr., of Tennessee; former Gov. John B. Connally of Texas; Representatives Philip B. Crane and John B. Anderson, both of Illinois, and Sen. Bob Dole of Kansas.

FEB. 7 Kennedy stages mock debate with Carter, using tape recording of a 1978 Presidential news conference.

10 Carter wins modest victory in Maine Democratic caucuses. Kennedy a good second as strength returns. Brown a strong third.

13 Dole drops out of Puerto Rico primary and throws support to Baker.

17 Bush defeats Baker in Puerto Rico primary, first of 1980 Presidential campaign and first in island's history.

26 Carter, with 49% of vote in New Hampshire Democratic primary, defeats Kennedy, with 38%, and Brown, 10%. Reagan wins 50% of vote in field of seven. Bush second, with 23%, Baker third with 13%. Reagan dismisses campaign manager, John P. Sears, long opposed by California conservatives.

MARCH 4 Bush wins Massachusetts GOP primary with 31% of vote, followed closely by Anderson, second, and Reagan, third. In Vermont, Reagan wins, with 31%. Anderson gets 30% and Bush 23%. On the Democratic side, Kennedy wins over Carter, 2–1, in Massachusetts, as expected. Carter takes 3–1 lead in Vermont.

5 Baker first major candidate to drop out of Republican race. Pressure grows for former President Gerald R. Ford to seek nomination.

8 Reagan wins 54% of votes in South Carolina GOP primary, with 30% for Connally and 15% for Bush.

9 Connally drops out of race, ending 14-month campaign.

11 In Florida Democratic primary, Carter wins 61% of vote to 23% for Kennedy and 5% for Brown. On GOP side, Reagan takes 57%, Bush 30%, and Anderson 9%. In Alabama: Carter 82%, Kennedy 13%, Brown 4%, Reagan 70%, Bush 26%. In Georgia: Carter 88%, Kennedy 9%, Brown 2%. Reagan 73%, Bush 13%, Anderson 9%.

15 Former President Gerald R. Ford announces he will not enter Republican nomination race. Dole withdraws from GOP race.

16 Carter narrowly defeats Kennedy in Puerto Rico Democratic primary.

18 Carter wins Illinois Democratic primary with 65% of vote, to 30% for Kennedy and 3% for Brown. In GOP, Reagan wins with 48% to 37% for Anderson and 11% for Bush.

22 Carter overwhelmingly defeats Kennedy in Virginia's Democratic precinct caucuses.

25 Kennedy wins primaries in New York and Connecticut. Reagan wins in New York, Bush in Connecticut.

APRIL 1 Wisconsin primaries: Democratic—Carter 56%; Kennedy 30%; Brown 12%. Republican—Reagan 40%; Bush 31%; Anderson 28%. Kansas primaries—Carter 57%; Kennedy 32%; Brown 5%. Reagan 63%; Anderson 18%; Bush 13%.

5 Carter wins Louisiana primary, 56% to 22% for Kennedy. Reagan, with 74%, defeats Bush, 19%.

12 Some 275 delegates from 30 states form left-wing Citizens Party at Cleveland convention. Dr. Barry Commoner, ecologist, is Presidential candidate and LaDonna Harris, pioneer in native American rights, is running mate.

14 Kennedy is victor in Arizona and Alaska caucuses; makes minor gains in Washington state. Carter gains in South Carolina and maintains hold in Virginia. With caucus victories, Reagan has more than half 998 delegates he needs.

22 Kennedy wins by slim margin in Pennsylvania Democratic primary. Bush GOP victor by comfortable margin. Carter and Reagan make greater gains in delegates.

24 Anderson declares independent candidacy.

26 Kennedy beats Carter by fewer than 300 votes in Michigan caucuses and takes 71–70 edge in state's convention delegates. In Vermont caucuses, Kennedy wins over Carter, 3–2.

30 Carter announces he will lift self-imposed ban on travel and campaigning. Says circumstances that had kept him in White House since hostages were seized in Iran had been "alleviated to some degree."

MAY 3 Reagan and Carter win clear victories over Bush and Kennedy in Texas primaries, but show signs of weakness for general election.

6 Carter and Reagan win triple primary victories. Republican: Indiana, Reagan 74%, Bush 16%; North Carolina, Reagan 67%, Bush 22%; Tennessee, Reagan 74%, Bush 18%. Democratic: Indiana, Carter 68%, Kennedy 32%; North Carolina, Carter 70%, Kennedy 18%; Tennessee, Carter 75%, Kennedy 18%.

13 Reagan and Carter win primaries in Maryland and Nebraska to advance more than nine tenths of way to nominations. Reagan's Nebraska victory a 78% landslide over Bush, and he carries Maryland, 48–41. Carter beats Kennedy 47–38 in both states.

16 Kennedy says he will withdraw from race if Carter debates him and then wins final round of Democratic primaries June 3. But Kennedy says that if he wins the primaries, he will remain for the national convention in August. White House says President will not debate Senator.

17 Carter and Reagan gain delegates in weekend state conventions, despite surprises by rivals. In Maine, Kennedy gets 11–11 split of delegates. In Delaware, Bush wins six, Reagan four, with two uncommitted. Front-runners hold or lengthen commanding leads in Virginia and Hawaii.

20 Bush checks Reagan's drive by winning Michigan Republican primary, 57% to 32%. In Democratic vote, 53% were uncommitted, 34% for Brown. Reagan wins Oregon primary over Bush, 54% to 35%. Carter takes 58% to 32% for Kennedy.

20 Kennedy calls for massive public and private "Marshall Plan" to re-industrialize the country. Charges in Newark, N.J., primary campaign speech that policies of Nixon, Ford, and Carter Administrations have caused "unprecedented" economic disaster.

26 Bush ends active campaigning for Republican Presidential nomination after two years. Asks his delegates at National Convention to vote for Reagan.

27 Results of four primaries: Kentucky—Democratic, Carter 67%, Kennedy 23%; Republican, Reagan, 83%, Bush 7%. Arkansas—Carter 60%, Kennedy 18% (no GOP primary). Nevada—Carter 38%, Kennedy 29%; Reagan 83%, Bush 7%. Idaho—Carter 62%, Kennedy 22%; Reagan 83%, Anderson 10%, Bush 4%.

JUNE 3 Kennedy wins primaries in California, New Jersey, New Mexico, Rhode Island, and South Dakota. Wins 372 delegates for total of 1,239. Carter wins primaries in Ohio, Montana, and West Virginia, getting 321 more delegates for total of 1,964, 298 more than 1,666 needed for nomination. Reagan wins eight primaries in those eight states and in Mississippi. Already assured of nomination.

23 Democratic Platform Committee, meeting at Washington, takes issue with President Carter for first time and adopts pledge to "retire nuclear power plants in an orderly manner."

JULY 1 Anderson ends exploratory phase of independent campaign for Presidency. Says he is "formally announcing my candidacy.

8 Rules Committee of Democratic National Convention rebuffs Kennedy supporters and adopts proposal virtually guaranteeing Carter's renomination. Action requires all delegates to vote on first ballot for candidate they were elected to support.

9 Platform committee of Republican National Committee, meeting at Detroit, abandons party's endorsement of proposed Federal equal rights amendment. Adopts substitute plank saying efforts to ban discrimination against women are "legitimate." Panel opposes "any move which would give the Federal Government more power over families."

10 Mary D. Crisp quits Republican Party convention scene at Detroit after Reagan questions her loyalty and dedication to GOP. She had denounced platform reversal on equal rights amendment and endorsement of constitutional amendment to outlaw abortion.

13 Republican convention Rules Committee votes to reinstate Hispanic, women's, youth, and ethnic groups to executive committee of Republican National Committee. Move reverses National Committee's own Rules Committee.

14 Republican National Convention opens in Detroit. In opening-day address, former President Gerald R. Ford attacks Carter as President who had "sold America short" and had "given up on the Presidency." Reagan buoyant as he arrives at scene and pays call on Ford, celebrating latter's 67th birthday, to symbolize joint effort to cement rival factions.

15 Speakers denounce Carter policies. Former Secretary of State Henry A. Kissinger calls for end of "diplomacy of incoherence" and praises Reagan as "trustee of our hopes."

15 GOP convention adopts conservative platform stressing commitment to economic stimulus, especially in tax cuts. Platform drops support for equal rights amendment and calls for anti-abortion constitutional amendment.

15 Reagan leadership heads off walkout by black delegates by inviting Benjamin L. Hooks, NAACP executive director, to address convention.

16 Ford sets terms for running for Vice President with Reagan. He rejects "figurehead" status and says on national TV he would expect a "meaningful role" in crucial decisions.

16 Convention formally nominates Reagan. In nominating speech, Senator Paul Laxalt of Nevada praises him as one who can unite country.

17 Reagan's acceptance speech bids nation "recapture our destiny" by replacing Carter's "trust me" philosophy. His choice, Bush, accepted as Vice-Presidential running mate as convention ends.

18 Reagan hails Republican unity. Tells National Committee party must appeal to Democrats and independents.

19 Anderson returns from 12-day, 5-nation tour of Europe and Middle East. In London speech he says election of Reagan and Bush would doom strategic arms treaty and touch off new military race with Soviet Union.

31 Reagan discloses details of personal income by releasing copies of Federal tax returns showing adjusted gross income of $515,878 for 1979. He had previously refused to do so, citing right to privacy.

AUG. 3 Tax returns show Anderson is "poorest" of three White House contenders with adjusted gross income of $79,459 for 1979.

4 Kennedy and Anderson address 70th conference of National Urban League in New York. Call for more progress in social conditions of blacks.

5 Reagan, in Urban League conference speech, bids blacks shed any prejudice they might have against him as a "caricatured conservative."

6 Carter addresses Urban League's conference in New York. He assails Reagan's proposed tax cuts as "sugar-coated poison."

11 Democratic National Convention opens in New York's Madison Square Garden. Carter's renomination assured as delegates, 1,936.4 to 1,390.6, approve rule binding them to vote for candidates they are pledged to, thus ending Kennedy's first bid for Presidential nomination.

12 Democratic convention votes to cut off financial and political aid to all party candidates who do not support proposed equal rights amendment to the Constitution. Strong rights plank and one dealing with full employment, one of several changes made in platform over active or passive resistance of the President. Kennedy, in rousing convention speech, throws influence behind party unity and bids Democrats "keep the faith" with their traditional principles.
13 Carter renominated on first ballot with the 1,-989 delegates he had won in primaries and caucuses, well above the 1,666 needed. Carter declines to accept precise language of insurgent economic planks, particularly $12-billion jobs program.
14 Carter says in acceptance speech election offers "stark choice" between rival visions of nation. Praises Kennedy as "tough competitor" and seeks out his support. Senator on platform with Carter but shows coolness toward President, and delegates comment on lack of enthusiasm for unity ritual. Walter F. Mondale nominated as Carter's Vice-Presidential running mate. As convention closes, NBC reports an estimated 90 to 95 million viewers saw all or part of networks' four-day coverage.
14 Anderson announces Mary Crisp, Republican cochairman until ousted in policy dispute, has become national chairman of his independent campaign.
15 President, opening campaign in address to Democratic National Committee, says GOP would hinder civil rights and economic opportunity and enhance risks of war.
20 Reagan, addressing American Legion National Convention in Boston, sticks to military preparedness theme and accuses Administration of falsifying military statistics.
21 President tells Legion convention U.S. could win arms race and that his policies have strengthened nation without risking all-out weapons competition. Kennedy greets President warmly in Boston and pledges campaign support.
23 Anderson charges Reagan bases China policy on "old habits" that could be costly to U.S. Also charges Carter Administration is "playing politics with defense and security policy."
23 In three-day visit to China, Bush tries to reassure officials that Reagan did not really mean his repeated calls for "official" relations with Taiwan. Official Chinese commentator charges Reagan had "insulted one billion Chinese people."
25 Anderson chooses Patrick J. Lucey, 62-year-old liberal Democrat and former Governor of Wisconsin, as Vice-Presidential running mate on independent ticket.
25 Reagan abandons proposal to convert American liaison office on Taiwan into official U.S. Government office. Acknowledges making misstatements on policy toward Taiwan and China.
26 Executive Board of United Automobile Workers endorses Carter despite appeal from Anderson.
27 Leonard Woodcock, U.S. Ambassador to China, warns in Peking that Reagan's statements on Taiwan endanger "delicate" Chinese-American understandings.
30 Anderson platform advocates postponing income tax reduction until Federal budget has been balanced, offers broad range of new tax advantages to individuals and business, and proposes new system of voluntary labor-management wage-price guidelines.

SEPT. 1 Carter opens re-election campaign in Tuscumbia, Ala., in an industrial and farming region of his native South. Denounces Ku Klux Klan.
1 Reagan attacks Carter economic policies in opening his drive with speech at Jersey City. At Detroit he charges that Carter opened campaign in brithplace of Klan. (Pulaski, Tenn., not Tuscumbia, is generally regarded as birthplace of Klan.)
1 Anderson begins National Unity Campaign with Labor Day weekend swing through home state of Illinois and that of running mate, former Gov. Patrick J. Lucey of Wisconsin.
2 Carter, visiting Independence, Mo., accuses Reagan of "slurs and innuendo" in remarks about Klan.
9 Reagan and Anderson accept bid by League of Women Voters to first Presidential debate Sept. 21. Carter declines, insisting that first debate should be two-man encounter between him and Reagan. Brands Anderson candidacy "primarily a creation of the press."
9 Reagan, in major speech in Chicago on economy, outlines five-year program to "balance the budget, reduce tax rates, and restore our defenses." Reiterates call for 30% reduction in Federal income taxes over three years, and says he could cut Government expenditures by at least $195 billion in next five years.
13 New York Liberal Party nominates Anderson for President, declining to support Democrats for first time in 36-year history.
14 Tim Kraft, Carter's campaign manager, quits post following disclosures he was under Federal investigation after allegations that he had used cocaine.
17 Carter, in speech before black Southerners at Atlanta church, says Reagan has turned to racist tactics. President declares, "You've seen in this campaign the stirrings of hate. . . . " Reagan has disavowed use of such tactics.
18 Bush denounces "ugly little insinuations" by Carter in charging Reagan is a racist, and defends Reagan's civil rights record while Governor of California.
20 Carter campaign advertisement charges GOP is trying to defeat him because of his record in aiding blacks. Republicans angrily deny charge.
21 Reagan and Anderson stage first campaign debate, broadcast on nationwide TV from Baltimore. They note Carter's absence after his refusal to join if Anderson is on panel. Reagan and Anderson expound views in reply to group of reporters. Debate sponsored by League of Women Voters.
22 President Carter stages a show of Democratic unity on his first fall campaign visit to California. He is joined by Gov. Edmund G. Brown, Jr., and Sen. Edward M. Kennedy. In Los Angeles, he tells a labor audience that they have the choice in November to determine "whether we have peace or war." In a two-hour stop in Springfield, he tells a student group that his energy plan is "the most exciting single undertaking in the last part of the 20th Century."
27 A New York Times-CBS News poll indicates that Ronald Reagan is the only candidate to benefit significantly from the League of Women Voter debate in Baltimore. It appears that the debate had little effect on Anderson's standing, and that President Carter's refusal to take part apparently hurt him.
29 President Carter stresses his liberal record before almost 1,000 cheering delegates of the International Ladies Garment Workers Union in New York. He tells them that the Republicans have "turned their backs on American women."

OCT. 2 Federal Election Commission says millions in bank loans to Anderson would not necessarily be illegal if he failed to win 5% of popular vote, needed to qualify for retroactive Federal campaign financing. Ruling bolsters his hopes for funds for independent fight. The commission cautioned against "any use of this opinion as a legal sanction for any particular loan transaction."

5 National Organization for Women, at annual convention in San Antonio, Tex., opposed Reagan election because of "medieval stance on women's issues." Endorse Democratic platform on women's rights. The organization decided not to endorse Carter or the independent, John Anderson. But it softened previous rebuff of President.

8 Reagan, in appeal to union members, moves toward center on two key issues. Moderates attack on Occupational Safety and Health Administration and renounces suggestion that unions be made subject to antitrust laws. In appeal to labor, Reagan is making series of increasingly moderate statements on social welfare, the economy, and military affairs. His staff is distributing 250,000 fliers to union people.

9 Carter, in Tennessee speech, tones down criticism of Reagan, saying he might have been "overly enthusiastic" in attacks. But he stands on challenge to Reagan on defense spending, the nuclear arms race, and other issues. Reagan, in Southern swing, defends record on environmental standards after earlier statements indicating willingness to relax them to revive industry.

14 Reagan defends position on equal opportunity for women. Says in Los Angeles news conference that he would name a woman "among the first Supreme Court vacancies in my administration." Replying to what he thinks damaging insinuations by the President, Reagan said he would "use every opportunity" to impress upon women that he considers war "as the last resort. Our mission in the world is to protect the peace." Carter, in Washington speech, charges Reagan's proposals to cut taxes and increase spending would add $130 billion to Federal deficit for fiscal year 1983. He said the cuts would force the dismantling of most Government programs other than the military and Social Security. Carter challenges opponent to specify programs he would eliminate from national budget.

15 Carter attacks Reagan's positions in battle for Massachusetts votes. Ridicules as political his opponent's pledge to put woman on Supreme Court. With Senator Kennedy at his side, Carter presses his attack on Reagan's stand on arms control, Social Security, and other issues. President warns against letting Anderson siphon off votes that would elect the Republican President.

15 Reagan wins endorsement of two black civil rights leaders, Rev. Ralph David Abernathy and Hosea Williams.

18 Reagan reverses stand and agrees to face-to-face debate with President Carter excluding Anderson. League of Women Voters schedules debate for Cleveland on Tuesday, Oct. 28, week before Election Day.

19 Reagan, taking offensive on war-or-peace issue, defends commitment to peace in nationwide TV address. Promises to restore the bipartisan tradition in American national security and foreign policy." Reagan indicates he would appoint Democrats to key foreign and defense policy positions. He says: "The cause of peace knows no party. The cause of peace transcends personal ambition." Carter, in radio address, moves to make strategic arms treaty a major campaign issue. Charges Reagan's attitude on arms control could push nation closer to a "nuclear precipice." Says "peace is my passion." In one of his lengthiest statements on war or peace issue, Carter says the arms control treaty, which Reagan opposes, should be viewed as a "secret weapon" that would improve American security.

OCT. 25 Nancy Reagan, in TV ad, charges "cruel" statements about her husband by President Carter. Says she is "deeply, deeply offended" when Carter "tries to portray him as a warmonger, as a man who would throw the elderly out on the street and cut off their Social Security when, in fact, he never said anything of the kind at any time."

OCT. 28 Carter and Reagan meet in nationally televised Presidential campaign debate in Cleveland sponsored by the League of Women Voters. President, appearing serious, even grim, attacks opponent for criticism of Social Security, minimum wage, equal rights amendment, and health insurance. Reagan, smiling and tossing his head, accuses the President of misrepresenting him. On other issues: They disagree over the economy, the rate of inflation, and the number unemployed. Carter blames Republican predecessors for drop in military spending; Reagan says Carter cut President Ford's budget 38%. Carter says Reagan has "dangerous" attitude on arms control; Reagan says he opposes only SALT II negotiated by Carter and favors real arms reduction.

29 John Anderson criticizes the political activities of some fundamental Protestants and accuses them of advocating "nothing less than an American version of religious intolerance." He spoke before the National Religious Broadcasters Association in Washington.

OCT. 30 Richard V. Allen, chief Reagan foreign policy adviser, quits campaign after public charges that he had used connection with Nixon Administration for personal gain.

How the House of Representatives Elects a President

Should no candidate receive a majority—270 or more—of the electoral votes for President on January 6th, then the members of the House of Representatives would meet immediately to choose a President from among the three highest candidates.

Each state would have only one vote, and a majority of 26 or more votes would be needed to elect a President. If the House of Representatives is unable to elect a winner by Inauguration Day, January 20th, then the Vice-President-elect serves as acting President until the House can decide.

The new Vice-President would be elected separately by the Senate from among the two running-mate candidates who received the most electoral votes. The senators would vote as individuals, with only one vote each.

Should neither the House nor Senate agree on the new President or Vice-President, then the Speaker of the House acts as President until one of them can decide.

The Democratic Platform

Excerpts

The Economy. The Democratic Party will take no action whose effect will be a significant increase in unemployment. . . .

Economic Strength. The Democratic Party is committed to taking the necessary steps to combat the current recession. However, we cannot abandon our fight against inflation.

Solving Our Economic Problems. A Democratic antirecession program must recognize that blacks, Hispanics, other minorities, women, and older workers bear the brunt of recession. We pledge a $12-billion antirecession jobs program, providing at least 800,000 additional jobs, including full funding of the counter-cyclical assistance program for the cities, a major expansion of the youth employment and training program . . . expanded training programs for women and displaced homemakers . . . and new opportunities for the elderly to contribute their talents and skills.

To revive productivity and revitalize our economy, we need a national effort to strengthen the American economy. It must include new tax depreciation rules to stimulate selective capital investment; a simplified tax code to assist business planning; . . . cooperative efforts with labor and management to retool the steel, auto, and shipbuilding industries. . . .

Health. The Democratic Party pledges to seek a national health insurance program with . . . universal coverage, without regard to place of employment, sex, age, marital status, or any other factor; comprehensive medical benefits. . . .

Reproductive Rights. The Democratic Party supports the 1973 Supreme Court decision on abortion rights as the law of the land and opposes any constitutional amendment to restrict or overturn that decision.

Education. The Democratic Party continues to support programs aimed at achieving communities integrated both in terms of race and economic class through constitutional means. Mandatory transportation of students beyond their neighborhoods for the purpose of desegregation remains a judicial tool of last resort.

Equal Rights Amendment. The Democratic Party commits itself to a Constitution, economy, and society open to women on an equal basis with men.

The primary route to that new horizon is ratification of the equal rights amendment. We oppose efforts to rescind E.R.A. in states which have already ratified the amendment, and we shall insist that past recisions are invalid.

The Democratic Party shall withhold financial support and technical campaign assistance from candidates who do not support the E.R.A.

Civil Rights. We oppose efforts to undermine the Supreme Court's historic mandate of school desegregation, and we support affirmative action goals to overturn patterns of discrimination in education and employment.

Tax Reform. We pledge to seek tax reforms which:

Encourage savings by low- and middle-income taxpayers;

Close tax loopholes which benefit only special interests at the expense of the average taxpayer and use the proceeds to bring relief to low- and middle-income Americans;

Curb tax deductions . . . which encourage consumption. . . .

Energy. Our economic security demands that we drastically reduce the massive flow of dollars into the OPEC treasuries and oil company bank accounts at the expense of American consumers and business.

We must establish a massive residential energy conservation grant program.

Major new efforts must be launched to develop synthetic and alternative renewable energy sources.

Defense. We will upgrade the combat readiness of our armed forces. We do not favor a peacetime draft or the exclusion of women from registration.

The MX missile deployment will enhance the survivability of our landbased intercontinental ballistic missile force.

U.S.–Soviet Relations. We stand ready to pursue good-faith negotiations with the Soviet Union at every opportunity on a wide range of issues . . . .

Arms Control. The SALT II Treaty is a vital step in an arms control process that can begin to lift from humanity the shadow of nuclear war.

Human Rights. We support measures designed to restrict trade with the Soviet Union until such time as Soviet emigration policy is made fair and nonrestrictive.

The Middle East. We support Israel's security and will continue to provide generous military and economic aid to that end.

We oppose creation of an independent Palestinian state.

We condemn the Government of Iran for its outrageous conduct in the taking of our diplomatic personnel as hostages.

Europe and Japan. The Democratic Administration will be committed to a strong NATO and a stable military balance in Europe.

The Developing World. The Democratic Administration will work with the Congress to develop and sustain policies and programs of economic cooperation with the developing nations, guided by the test of mutual interest.

Latin America and the Caribbean. We will oppose a spiral of confrontation with Cuba, for its own sake. . . .

Asia. The Democratic Party commits itself to a broadening and deepening of our relationship with China in a way that will benefit both our peoples and the peace and security of the world.

Africa. The Democratic Administration developed a long-term African policy, a policy that is viable on its own merits and does not treat Africa as an appendage to great power competition.

The Republican Platform

Excerpts

Taxes. Substantial tax-rate reductions are needed to offset the massive tax increases facing the working men and women of this country.

The Republican Party believes balancing the budget is essential but opposes the Democrats' attempt to do so through higher taxes. We believe that an essential aspect of balancing the budget is spending restraint by the Federal Government and higher economic growth.

Welfare. For those on welfare, our nation's tax policies provide a penalty for getting a job.

Our nation's welfare problems will not be solved merely by providing increased benefits. By fostering dependency and discouraging self-reliance, the Democratic Party has created a welfare constituency dependent on its continual subsidies. We categorically reject the notion of a guaranteed annual income.

Black Americans. Our fundamental answer to the economic problems of black Americans is the same answer we make to all Americans—full employment without inflation through economic growth.

Hispanic Americans. We pledge to pursue policies that will help to make the opportunities of American life a reality for Hispanics.

Women's Rights. We acknowledge the legitimate efforts of those who support or oppose ratification of the equal rights amendment.

We reaffirm our party's historic commitment to equal rights and equality for women.

The states have a constitutional right to accept or reject a constitutional amendment without Federal interference or pressure.

Republicans must find ways to meet [the child care problems], the working woman's need.

Abortion. While we recognize differing views on this question . . . we affirm our support of a constitutional amendment to restore protection of the right to life for unborn children. We also support the Congressional efforts to restrict the use of taxpayer's dollars for abortion.

Energy. We believe the United States must proceed on a steady and orderly path toward energy self-sufficiency. We believe it is necessary to resume rapid filling of strategic oil reserves.

Republicans advocate the decontrol of the price at wellhead of oil and gas.

We support accelerated use of nuclear energy through technologies that have been proven efficient and safe.

Judiciary. We will work for the appointment of judges at all levels of the judiciary who respect traditional family values and the sanctity of innocent human life.

Inflation. The inflation policies of the Carter Administration have been inconsistent, counterproductive, and tragically inept.

The Republican Party believes inflation can be controlled only by fiscal and monetary restraint, combined with sharp reductions in the tax and regulatory disincentives for savings, investments, and productivity.

Unions. The Republican Party reaffirms its long-standing support for the right of states to enact "right-to-work" laws under section 14(b) of the Taft-Hartley Act.

Grain Embargo. We oppose singling out American farmers to bear the brunt of Carter's ill-conceived, ineffective, and improperly implemented grain embargo.

National Security. Republicans commit themselves to an immediate increase in defense spending to be applied judiciously to critically needed programs. We will build toward a sustained defense expenditure sufficient to close the gap with the Soviets, and ultimately reach the position of military superiority that the American people demand.

Nuclear Forces. In order to counter the problems of ICBM vulnerability, we will propose a number of initiatives to provide the necessary survivability of the ICBM force in as timely and effective a manner as possible.

Conventional Forces. The forces essential to the support of [a global maneuver] strategy must include a much-improved Navy, the force most suitable for maintaining U.S. presence in threatened areas and protecting sea lines of communication.

The Draft. The Republican Party is not prepared to accept a peacetime draft at this time.

U.S.–Soviet Relations. A Republican Administration will continue to seek to negotiate arms reductions in Soviet strategic weapons, in Soviet-bloc force levels in Central Europe, and in other areas that may be amenable to reductions or limitations.

NATO and Europe. We categorically reject unilaterial moratoria on the deployment by the U.S. and NATO of theater nuclear weapons.

In pledging renewed United States leadership, cooperation, and consultation, Republicans assert their expectation that each of the allies will bear a fair share of the common defense effort.

Middle East. With respect to an ultimate peace settlement, Republicans reject any call for involvement of the P.L.O. as not in keeping with the long-term interests of either Israel or the Palestinian Arabs.

The sovereignty, security, and integrity of the State of Israel is a moral imperative and serves the strategic interests of the United States. Republicans reaffirm our fundamental and enduring commitment to this principle.

The Americas. We do not support United States assistance to any Marxist government in this hemisphere, and we oppose the Carter Administration aid program for the Government of Nicaragua.

Asia and the Pacific. A new Republican Administration will restore a strong American role in Asia and the Pacific.

We will strive for the creation of conditions that will foster the peaceful elaboration of our relationship with the People's Republic of China.

. . . we deplore the Carter Administration's treatment of Taiwan, our longtime ally and friend.

James Earl Carter, Jr.

President Carter fought a hard, uphill battle in the 1980 campaign for re-election. As President, he had fought equally hard for his programs in the face of resistance from an independent-minded Democratic Congress, with mixed success, and with fluctuating favor with the public.

In the Democratic nomination and election campaigns, Carter first vanquished Senator Edward M. Kennedy of Massachusetts, who in 1979 had a 2–1 lead in public opinion polls as the choice of Democratic voters. Then, within days of his renomination in August 1980, Carter rose in the Gallup Poll from far behind up to a virtual par with the Republicans' popular Ronald Reagan. It had been much the same story in his first race in 1976, when Carter won election after a dramatic rise from obscurity as Georgia peanut farmer-politician.

James Earl Carter, Jr., was born in the tiny village of Plains, Ga., Oct. 1, 1924, and grew up on the family farm at nearby Archery. Both parents were fifth-generation Georgians. Although his father, who died in 1953, was a segregationist, he treated his black and white workers equally, and was known for his lenient credit policies to the black families who comprised most of the customers of his store in Archery. Carter's mother, Lillian Gordy, now 82, a matriarchal presence in family and community, defied the prevailing racial mores in her home and work as a registered nurse. Jimmy Carter was baptized in 1935 in the conservative Southern Baptist Church and speaks often of being a "born again" Christian. However, he is committed to the separation of church and state.

Carter married Rosalynn Smith, a neighbor, in 1946. Their first child, John William, was born a year later in Portsmouth, Va. Their other children are James Earl III, born in Honolulu in 1950; Donnel Jeffrey, born in New London, Conn., in 1952, and Amy Lynn, born in Plains in 1967.

In 1946 Carter was graduated from the U.S. Naval Academy at Annapolis and served in the nuclear-submarine program under Adm. Hyman G. Rickover. In 1954, after his father's death, he resigned from the Navy to take over the family business, which flourished as a warehouse and cotton gin, with several thousand acres for growing seed peanuts.

Entering politics, Carter was elected to the Georgia Senate in 1962. In 1966 he ran for Governor and lost, but was elected in 1970. During his term a state government reorganization increased economy and efficiency, and new social programs were introduced, all with no general tax increase.

In 1972 Carter began his efforts to become President, and in 1974 criss-crossed the country as chairman of the Democratic Campaign Committee, while building a base for himself.

One campaign problem, Carter's image as the typical Southern white, was erased in 1975 when he won the support of most of the old Southern civil-rights coalition after endorsement by Rep. Andrew Young, black Democrat from Atlanta, closest aide to the Rev. Martin Luther King, Jr. At Carter's 1971 inauguration as Governor, he had called for an end to all forms of racial discrimination in Georgia and had hung a portrait of Dr. King in the state Capitol.

In the 1976 spring primaries, in which he won 19 out of 31, Carter set forth his position in his soft Southern voice, and his electric-blue stare faced down campaign skeptics who joked about "Jimmy who?" His toothy smile became his trademark.

Carter was nominated on the first roll-call vote of the 1976 Democratic convention in New York, and his choice of Walter F. Mondale for Vice President was enthusiastically endorsed. Likewise, in 1980 he was renominated the first ballot after Kennedy forces suffered defeat in their attempt to block a party rule that bound a large majority of pledged delegates to vote for Carter on this ballot. Subsequently the Kennedy camp agreed to support the President's fight despite early indications of coolness.

Carter's victory over Kennedy came from his own hard work and his opponents' errors, also to a great extent from exploiting such events as Iran's seizure of American hostages and the Soviet invasion of Afghanistan. In the "Rose Garden" strategy, Carter ignored the Senator through much of the primary campaign. The President pitched his election campaign to an attack on his rivals, Republican Ronald Reagan and John B. Anderson, Independent. He warned that the Republicans would heighten the risk of war and impede civil rights and economic opportunity.

In assessing his first term, Carter supporters count as successes his foreign policy, particularly the Panama Canal and Middle East Treaties, and the increased rapport with China, all of which won public approval. Generally speaking, observers rate as failures plans for tax and welfare changes and government reorganization, and energy and economic policies concomitant with recession and inflation. The abortive attempt to rescue the Iran hostages also reflected negatively on the Administration. Carter did, however, deflect criticism resulting from the activities of his brother, Billy.

Many pet projects were frustrated by a balky Congress, despite strong Democratic majorities, although only two of his vetoes were overriden. Many of the President's difficulties have been traced to his and his aides' brusqueness in dealing with Capitol Hill and insensitivity to Congressional feelings and tradition. His circle, composed mostly of Georgians, are viewed as outsiders in Washington. Carter's closest aides are Hamilton Jordan and Jody Powell, young Georgians who served in his first Presidential campaign. Other close advisers are his wife; Charles. H. Kirbo, an Atlanta lawyer; and the White House counsel, Lloyd N. Cutler, an experienced Washington lawyer.

Carter, a reserved man, shuns Washington's social life and confines himself to the world of the White House and to Camp David on weekends. He is systematic and disciplined, arising at 6 a.m. and often beginning his work day with a 7 a.m. appointment. He is likely to end that day with a jog about the South Lawn or a swim with his wife.

The evenings are often spent watching movies in the White House family theater, possibly with a few guests, usually members of Congress and their wives.

Despite the facial lines and grey hairs that his first term has brought, Carter and his aides campaigned in 1980 with their usual buoyant energy.

Ronald Reagan

Ronald Reagan, actor turned politician, New Dealer turned conservative, won the 1980 Republican nomination after two previous failures. He rode a tide of resurgent right-wing sentiment among an electorate battered by the winds of unwanted change, longing for a distant simpler era. His nomination and election campaign followed a short but turbulent public career marked by a shrewd tempering of rightist principles to welfare-state realities. And the campaign evinced an effort to broaden his appeal by espousing moderate policies.

Reagan came from a middle-class, Middle West, thoroughly Middle-America environment. He was born in Tampico, Ill., Feb. 6, 1911, the second son of John Edward Reagan, a first-generation Irish-American who was a shop clerk and merchant. It was an impoverished family; Ronald sold home-made popcorn at high-school games and worked as a lifeguard to earn money for his college tuition. When the father got a New Deal WPA job, the youth became an ardent Roosevelt Democrat.

Reagan won his A.B. degree in 1932 from Eureka (Ill.) College, where a photographic memory aided him in his studies and in debating and college theatricals. He also played football and his easy charm led to a pleasant fraternity life. He became a sports announcer for radio station WHO in Des Moines from 1932 to 1937. His career as a film and TV actor stretched from 1937 to 1966.

In service as a World War II captain in an Army film studio, Reagan recoiled from what he saw as the laziness of Civil Service workers. Soon he had moved to the Right, raged against the government's tax bite, and, as president of the Screen Actors Guild, resisted what he considered a Communist plot to subvert the cinema industry. With advancing age, Reagan was eased out of leading-man roles, and in 1954 became a television spokesman for the General Electric Company at $150,000 a year. Eight years later, he had become a nationally known conservative commentator and herald of the old-fashioned virtues; he was pro-business and anti-government to the point where a skittish G.E. tried to cut down on his speaking engagements, and he left the company. He became an active Republican, and in 1964 made a dramatic speech supporting Senator Barry Goldwater, who became the party's nominee. In 1966, California enthusiastically elected Reagan governor by almost a million votes over the political veteran, Democratic Gov. Edmund G. Brown, father of the present Governor, after a draft movement led by wealthy businessmen and keyed to spending cuts. But, bowing to the reality of an impoverished state treasury, he sponsored a billion-dollar tax increase, then the largest state tax rise in U.S. history. (But over the next eight years he sponsored a property tax rebate of $6 billion.) At the end of his second term in 1974, the state budget had grown by $6 billion.

In 1968 Reagan was nosed out by Richard M. Nixon for the G.O.P. nomination and in 1976 by Gerald Ford. In 1980 he won the nomination after a more aggressively conservative campaign.

Reagan was a solid favorite as he entered the protracted primary campaign. After losing the January Iowa caucuses to George Bush of Texas, who became the Vice-Presidential nominee, he took the offensive and scored a smashing victory in the New Hampshire primary. Senator Howard Baker soon dropped out of the race and on March 8 Reagan eliminated former Gov. John B. Connally of Texas in a South Carolina showdown. Soon Reagan outran Bush despite losses in Connecticut, Massachusetts, Pennsylvania, and Michigan.

Much of his success came from cross-over votes from disaffected Democrats and blue-collar workers. This reflected the pattern of his two election victories in California, where he won a large blue-collar and Hispanic vote. And in the election campaign proper, Reagan sought a broad appeal to moderates in the Republican Party and, in a conciliatory convention acceptance speech, expressed a concern for the poor and urged an end to discrimination against women. This he began doing at the Detroit convention in July without betraying his solid core of conservative supporters in what has become known as "Reagan country."

His selection of Bush, a relative moderate, and overtures to former President Ford to run for the Vice Presidency were taken as tokens of his outreach to a wider audience. In one suspenseful period of the convention, Ford sought in negotiations with Reagan a wider role for the Vice President that many thought was impractical and counter to the Constitution.

Reagan's supporters also noted his appeal to the black vote in a rare appearance before a minority group, the New York annual convention of the Urban League. Earlier he had drawn criticism for failing to address the National Association for the Advancement of Colored People.

In general, the Reagan camp refused to go on the defensive, making Carter's record as President the campaign issue. In his own battle, Reagan strove to convince the skeptical that he could fulfill his promises of a $36-billion tax cut along with a balanced budget and stepped-up defense spending. He also had to overcome what many felt was a tendency to lack a grasp of key issues, such as understanding farm parity or automobile industry regulations.

One troublesome issue arose after his nomination with the revival of the topic of Taiwan-U.S. relations. Reagan had repeatedly promised to restore "official" links to Taiwan. In a visit to China, Bush sought to explain Reagan references to Taiwan as the "free Republic of China" as the result of habit, not of deep conviction. The Chinese, however, censured Reagan and said the statements undermined U.S.-China relations and that Reagan had "insulted one billion Chinese people."

Another strong statement that his critics seized upon was Reagan's reference to the Vietnam war as "a noble cause."

Reagan is devoted to his wife, Nancy, whom he married after his divorce from Jane Wyman, the actress. The Reagans spend much time together at their California home and ranch near Santa Barbara when campaign duties do not interfere. Reagan likes to relax with his horses and ranch chores, and is a connoisseur of fine wines. The children of the first marriage are Maureen, his 39-year-old daughter by Miss Wyman, and Michael, 35, an adopted son. In the present marriage the children are Patricia, 27, and Ronald, 22.

Walter Frederick Mondale

Democratic Vice-Presidential Candidate

Vice President Walter F. Mondale, an insider in the White House as he had been an insider in 12 years in the Senate, was Jimmy Carter's running mate in both 1976 and 1980. As a close and influential adviser to the President, pushing for liberal approaches, he found himself a congenial colleague despite the occasional disagreements that he never tried to hide. In the 1980 primary campaign he logged 125,000 miles seeking the Carter renomination and continued the fight after the convention. He preached fiscal restraint and military preparedness, although he had been one of a band of Senate liberals and an ally of Senator Edward M. Kennedy of Massachusetts. And as Carter's popularity fell, Mondale had to block efforts to nominate himself for the No. 1 spot.

As Carter's partner in many policy areas, Mondale helped fashion the package that saved the Chrysler Corporation, opposed a budget compromise that would have escalated defense spending, and was the first in the Administration to urge a boycott of the Moscow Olympic Games. Mr. Carter early assigned Mondale to monitor relations with Africa, and since then with other areas of the world. Mondale headed the joint-agency panel that shaped the President's $2-billion youth employment program in 1980.

Walter Frederick Mondale was born January 5, 1928, in Ceylon, Minn., one of seven children of a minister of Norwegian descent devoted to the social gospel. "Fritz" Mondale attended Macalester College at St. Paul. After two years as an Army corporal in Korea, Mondale entered the University of Minnesota Law School and practiced law for four years. Gov. Orville L. Freeman appointed him State Attorney General in 1960, and in the same year he was elected in his own right and later reelected. In 1964 Mondale was appointed to Humphrey's Senate seat when the latter became Vice President. As a Senator, he fought for civil rights and liberal legislation, such as open housing, Indian education, improved migrant workers' conditions, and child nutrition.

In his first years as Vice President, Mondale remained close to Kennedy and his erstwhile fellow liberals. But the alliance was strained when Mondale supported Carter's policy of fighting inflation by balancing the budget and cutting some domestic programs. Further friction with Kennedy developed over such foreign policy disputes as the Massachusetts Senator's opposition to the restriction on grain exports to the Soviet Union.

Mondale married Joan Adams of St. Paul in 1955. She is a leading advocate of government support for the arts. They have three children: Theodore, 22, a student at the University of Minnesota; Eleanor Jane, 20, a student at St. Lawrence College, Canton, N.Y., and William, 18, who has entered Brown University.

George Bush

Republican Vice-Presidential Candidate

George Bush, although a relative moderate, was Ronald Reagan's running mate on the 1980 Republican ticket. It was the fourth time he had been considered for the Vice-Presidential nomination. Although he boasts impeccable conservative credentials, many on the right wing of the G.O.P. were dismayed to learn that second place had gone to Bush, a product of the Northeast Republican establishment, a member of the hated Trilateral Commission[1], a supporter of the proposed equal rights amendment, and an opponent of a constitutional ban on abortions.

But Bush, a two-term Congressman from Texas, his adopted state, won favorable ratings from the conservative Americans for Constitutional Action for his legislative record. He is a former Director of Central Intelligence and a World War II Navy pilot decorated for heroism after having been shot down in the Pacific.

The nominee was born June 12, 1924, in Milton, Mass., to Prescott and Dorothy Bush. The family later lived in Greenwich, Conn. He attended Phillips Academy at Andover, Mass., and served in the Navy from 1942 to 1945. After the war he earned an economics degree and Phi Beta Kappa key at Yale in 2½ years.

In 1945 he married Barbara Pierce, and in 1948 they left Connecticut for a Texas business career. Bush was co-founder of the Zapata Off-Shore Company, a pioneer in offshore drilling equipment. In 1980 he reported estimated wealth of some $1.4 million.

After Bush's second unsuccessful Senate race, President Nixon appointed him U.S. delegate to the United Nations with the rank of ambassador, and later he became Republican National Chairman. President Ford named him head of the U.S. liaison office in Peking, where he served a year before becoming Director of Central Intelligence.

Entering the 1980 Presidential campaign, Bush lost decisively in the early New Hampshire primary. His hopes were bolstered by victory in the Pennsylvania "beauty" contest and in Massachusetts, Connecticut, and Michigan, but in May he dropped out of the race, short of delegates and money.

At the Detroit convention, he accepted Reagan's telephoned offer of the No. 2 position with alacrity despite his own previous support of the equal rights amendment and opposition to the ban on abortion. But he pledged support of the G.O.P. platform on these and other issues and minimized his differences with Reagan. Dismayed extreme conservatives finally accepted Bush as a pragmatic measure to win votes in the Northeast.

Bush and his wife, Barbara, have lived in 17 cities and 28 homes and have traveled in 26 countries. Mrs. Bush was the "matriarch" of a family of four boys and a girl in the frequent absences of her husband.

1. The Trilateral Commission consists of businessmen, scholars, and public officials in North America, Japan, and Western Europe who discuss economic and foreign policy issues. It was organized by David Rockefeller. Conservatives loathe it as elitist and internationalist.

Presidential Election of 1980

Principal Candidates for President and Vice President
Democratic: Jimmy Carter; Walter F. Mondale
Republican: Ronald Reagan; George Bush
Independent: John B. Anderson; Patrick J. Lucey

State	Total	Carter	Per-	Reagan	Per-	Anderson	Per-	Plurality	Electoral vote		
		Dem.	cent	Rep.	cent	Independent	cent		D	R	I
Alabama	1,297,832	627,808	48	641,609	49	15,855	1	13,801 R	—	9	—
Alaska	120,860	31,408	26	66,874	55	8,091	7	35,466 R	—	3	—
Arizona	861,177	243,498	28	523,124	61	75,805	9	279,646 R	—	6	—
Arkansas	821,025	392,404	48	396,689	48	21,057	3	4,285 R	—	6	—
California	8,422,589	3,040,600	36	4,447,266	53	727,871	9	1,406,666 R	—	45	—
Colorado	1,180,567	367,966	31	650,786	55	130,579	11	282,820	—	7	—
Connecticut	1,392,543	537,407	39	672,648	48	168,260	12	135,231 R	—	8	—
Delaware	236,611	106,650	45	111,631	47	16,344	7	4,981 R	—	3	—
D.C.	163,835	124,376	76	21,765	13	14,971	9	102,611 D	3	—	—
Florida	3,520,914	1,369,120	39	1,943,989	55	178,483	5	574,869 R	—	17	—
Georgia	1,577,649	882,785	56	644,691	41	34,912	2	238,094 D	12	—	—
Hawaii	302,829	135,879	45	130,112	43	32,021	11	5,767 D	4	—	—
Idaho	434,803	109,410	25	289,789	67	27,142	6	180,379 R	—	4	—
Illinois	4,659,439	1,951,073	42	2,335,806	50	344,836	7	384,733 R	—	26	—
Indiana	2,195,004	832,213	38	1,232,764	56	107,729	5	400,551 R	—	13	—
Iowa	1,314,395	508,735	39	676,556	51	114,589	9	167,821 R	—	8	—
Kansas	969,446	324,974	34	562,848	58	67,535	7	237,874 R	—	7	—
Kentucky	1,268,045	605,876	48	626,072	49	29,428	2	20,196 R	—	9	—
Louisiana	1,540,364	707,981	46	796,240	52	26,198	2	88,259 R	—	10	—
Maine	521,571	220,387	42	238,156	46	53,450	10	17,769 R	—	4	—
Maryland	1,489,958	706,327	47	656,255	44	113,452	8	50,072 D	10	—	—
Massachusetts	2,512,026	1,051,104	42	1,054,562	42	382,044	15	3,458 R	—	14	—
Michigan	3,899,864	1,659,208	43	1,914,559	49	272,948	7	255,351 R	—	21	—
Minnesota	1,977,766	924,770	47	844,459	43	169,960	9	80,311 D	10	—	—
Mississippi	887,257	429,988	48	440,747	50	11,871	1	10,759 R	—	7	—
Missouri	2,063,641	917,663	44	1,055,355	51	76,488	4	137,692 R	—	12	—
Montana	232,563	111,972	32	195,108	57	27,919	8	83,136 R	—	4	—
Nebraska	630,623	164,276	26	413,401	66	44,025	7	249,125 R	—	5	—
Nevada	242,964	66,468	27	154,570	64	17,580	7	88,102 R	—	3	—
New Hampshire	383,485	109.080	28	221,771	58	49,295	13	112,691 R	—	4	—
New Jersey	2,878,045	1,119,576	39	1,506,437	52	224,173	8	386,861 R	—	17	—
New Mexico	445,598	165,054	37	245,433	55	28,404	6	80,379 R	—	4	—
New York	5,939,953	2,632,099	44	2,797,684	47	440,480	7	165,585 R	—	41	—
North Carolina	1,854,245	875,776	47	913,898	49	52,364	3	38,122 R	—	13	—
North Dakota	290,321	76,533	26	187,483	65	22,390	8	110,950 R	—	3	—
Ohio	4,259,945	1,743,829	41	2,201,864	52	255,521	6	458,035 R	—	25	—
Oklahoma	1,136,792	399,292	35	683,807	60	38,051	3	284,515 R	—	8	—
Oregon	1,151,492	446,721	39	557,381	48	109,621	10	110,660 R	—	6	—
Pennsylvania	4,515,178	1,932,336	43	2,252,260	50	288,704	6	319,924 R	—	27	—
Rhode Island	389,516	185,319	48	145,576	37	56,213	14	39,743 D	4	—	—
South Carolina	857,659	417,633	49	421,117	49	13,990	2	3,484 R	—	8	—
South Dakota	327,192	103,909	32	198,102	61	21,342	7	94,193 R	—	4	—
Tennessee	1,612,560	781,512	48	787,244	49	35,921	2	5,732 R	—	10	—
Texas	4,530,025	1,844,349	41	2,539,144	56	109,707	2	694,795 R	—	26	—
Utah	598,514	123,447	21	435,839	73	30,191	5	313,392 R	—	4	—
Vermont	210,822	81,421	39	93,554	44	31,671	15	12,133 R	—	3	—
Virginia	1,851,985	748,638	40	983,311	53	93,813	5	234,673 R	—	12	—
Washington	1,547,722	583,596	38	764,393	49	165,443	11	180,797 R	—	9	—
West Virginia	714,911	353,508	49	326,645	46	30,499	4	26,863 D	6	—	—
Wisconsin	2,274,755	988,255	43	1,089,750	48	159,793	7	101,495 R	—	11	—
Wyoming	176,263	49,123	28	110,096	62	12,350	7	60,973 R	—	8	—
Total	**84,798,626**	**34,913,332**	**41**	**43,201,220**	**51**	**5,581,379**	**7**	**8,287,888 R**	**49**	**489**	**—**

NOTE: Results are 99% complete. NATIONAL TOTALS OF OTHER CANDIDATES: Ed Clark, Libertarian Party, 881,612; Barry Commoner, Citizens Party, 221,083. *Source:* Wide World Photos.

The Ninety-Seventh Congress

Composition of 96th and 97th Congresses

	96th Congress				97th Congress			
	Dem.	Rep.	Male	Female	Dem.	Rep.	Male	Female
Senate	59[1]	41	99	1	47[1]	53	98	2
House	276	159	418	16	243[2]	192	416	19

1. Includes one Independent (Byrd of Virginia). 2. Includes one unaffiliated (Foglietta of Pennsylvania).

The Senate

Senior Senator is listed first. The dates in the first column indicate period of service. The date given in parentheses after the Senator's name is year of birth. All terms are for six years and expire in January. Mailing address of Senators: The Senate, Washington, D.C. 20510.

ALABAMA
1979–85 Howell T. Heflin, D (1921)
1981–87 Jeremiah Denton, R (1924)
ALASKA
1968–85 Ted Stevens, R (1923)
1981–87 Frank H. Murkowski, R (1933)
ARIZONA
1969–87 Barry Goldwater, R (1909)
1977–83 Dennis DeConcini, D (1937)
ARKANSAS
1975–87 Dale Bumpers, D (1925)
1979–85 David H. Pryor, D (1934)
CALIFORNIA
1969–87 Alan Cranston, D (1914)
1977–83 S. I. Hayakawa, R (1906)
COLORADO
1975–87 Gary W. Hart, D (1937)
1979–85 William L. Armstrong, R (1937)
CONNECTICUT
1971–83 Lowell P. Weicker, Jr., R (1931)
1981–87 Christopher J. Dodd, D (1944)
DELAWARE
1971–83 William V. Roth, Jr., R (1921)
1973–85 Joseph R. Biden, Jr., D (1942)
FLORIDA
1971–83 Lawton Chiles, D (1930)
1981–87 Paula Hawkins, R (1927)
GEORGIA
1973–85 Sam Nunn, D (1938)
1981–87 Mack Mattingly, R (1931)
HAWAII
1963–87 Daniel K. Inouye, D (1924)
1977–83 Spark M. Matsunaga, D (1916)
IDAHO
1973–85 James A. McClure, R (1924)
1981–87 Steven D. Symms, R (1938)
ILLINOIS
1967–85 Charles H. Percy, R (1919)
1981–87 Alan J. Dixon, D (1927)
INDIANA
1977–83 Richard G. Lugar, R (1932)
1981–87 Dan Quayle, R (1947)
IOWA
1979–85 Roger W. Jepsen, R (1928)
1981–87 Charles E. Grassley, R (1933)
KANSAS
1969–87 Robert J. Dole, R (1923)
1979–85 Nancy Landon Kassebaum, R (1932)
KENTUCKY
1973–85 Walter Huddleston, D (1926)
1975–87 Wendell H. Ford, D (1924)
LOUISIANA
1948–87 Russell B. Long, D (1918)
1973–85 J. Bennett Johnston, D (1932)
MAINE
1980–83 George D. Mitchell, D (1933)
1979–85 William S. Cohen, R (1940)
MARYLAND
1969–87 Charles McC. Mathias, Jr., R (1922)
1977–83 Paul S. Sarbanes, D (1933)
MASSACHUSETTS
1962–83 Edward M. Kennedy, D (1932)
1979–85 Paul E. Tsongas, D (1941)
MICHIGAN
1977–83 Donald W. Riegle, Jr., D (1938)
1979–85 Carl Levin, D (1934)
MINNESOTA
1978–83 David F. Durenberger, R (1934)
1979–85 Rudy Boschwitz, R (1930)
MISSISSIPPI
1947–83 John C. Stennis, D (1901)
1978–85 Thad Cochran, R (1937)

A Voting Majority Never Elected a President

In the 1964 election, Lyndon B. Johnson became the only President to almost succeed in receiving a majority of votes. He got 43,130,000 votes or 37.8% of those who were eligible to vote. The number of Americans of voting age who did not vote that year was 43,445,000 or 38.1%.

The President who received the smallest share of votes from eligible Americans was Martin Van Buren, who obtained 11.4% of the ballots from voting-age Americans.

Since universal suffrage was enacted, Calvin Coolidge claimed the smallest percentage by receiving only 23.7% of the ballots from voting-age citizens.

MISSOURI
1968–87 Thomas F. Eagleton, D (1929)
1977–83 John C. Danforth, R (1936)
MONTANA
1977–83 John Melcher, D (1924)
1979–85 Max Baucus, D (1941)
NEBRASKA
1977–83 Edward Zorinsky, D (1928)
1979–85 J. James Exon, D (1921)
NEVADA
1959–83 Howard W. Cannon, D (1912)
1975–87 Paul Laxalt, R (1922)
NEW HAMPSHIRE
1979–85 Gordon J. Humphrey, R (1940)
1981–87 Warren Rudman, R (1930)
NEW JERSEY
1959–83 Harrison A. Williams, Jr., D (1919)
1979–85 Bill Bradley, D (1943)
NEW MEXICO
1973–85 Pete V. Domenici, R (1932)
1977–83 Harrison H. Schmitt, R (1935)
NEW YORK
1977–83 Daniel P. Moynihan, D (1927)
1981–87 Alfonse D'Amato, R (1937)
NORTH CAROLINA
1973–85 Jesse Helms, R (1921)
1981–87 John P. East, R (1931)
NORTH DAKOTA
1960–83 Quentin N. Burdick, D (1908)
1981–87 Mark Andrews, R (1926)
OHIO
1975–87 John H. Glenn, Jr., D (1921)
1977–83 Howard M. Metzenbaum, D (1917)
OKLAHOMA
1979–85 David L. Boren, D (1941)
1981–87 Don Nickles, R (1949)
OREGON
1967–85 Mark O. Hatfield, R (1922)
1969–87 Bob Packwood, R (1932)
PENNSYLVANIA
1977–83 H. John Heinz III, R (1938)
1981–87 Arlen Specter, R (1930)
RHODE ISLAND
1961–85 Claiborne Pell, D (1918)
1977–83 John H. Chafee, R (1922)
SOUTH CAROLINA
1956–85 Strom Thurmond, R (1902)
1966–87 Ernest F. Hollings, D (1922)
SOUTH DAKOTA
1979–85 Larry Pressler, R (1942)
1981–87 James Abdnor, R (1923)
TENNESSEE
1967–85 Howard H. Baker, Jr., R (1925)
1977–83 James R. Sasser, D (1936)
TEXAS
1961–85 John G. Tower, R (1925)
1971–83 Lloyd M. Bentsen, D (1921)
UTAH
1975–87 E. J. (Jake) Garn, R (1932)
1977–83 Orrin G. Hatch, R (1934)
VERMONT
1971–83 Robert T. Stafford, R (1913)
1975–87 Patrick J. Leahy, D (1940)
VIRGINIA
1965–83 Harry F. Byrd, Jr., I[1] (1914)
1979–85 John W. Warner, R (1927)
WASHINGTON
1953–83 Henry M. Jackson, D (1912)
1981–87 Slade Gorton, R (1928)
WEST VIRGINIA
1958–85 Jennings Randolph, D (1902)
1959–83 Robert C. Byrd, D (1918)
WISCONSIN
1957–83 William Proxmire, D (1915)
1981–87 Robert W. Kasten, Jr., R (1942)
WYOMING
1977–83 Malcolm Wallop, R (1933)
1979–85 Alan K. Simpson, R (1931)

1. Independent.

The House of Representatives

The numerals indicate the Congressional Districts of the states; the designation AL means At-Large. All terms end January 1983. Mailing address of Representatives; House of Representatives, Washington, D.C. 20515.

ALABAMA
(7 Representatives)
1. Jack Edwards, R
2. William L. Dickinson, R
3. William Nichols, D
4. Tom Bevill, D
5. Ronnie G. Flippo, D
6. Albert L. Smith, Jr., R
7. Richard C. Shelby, D

ALASKA
(1 Representative)
AL Don E. Young, R

ARIZONA
(4 Representatives)
1. John J. Rhodes, R
2. Morris K. Udall, D
3. Bob Stump, D
4. Eldon Rudd, R

ARKANSAS
(4 Representatives)
1. Bill Alexander, D
2. Edwin R. Bethune, Jr., R
3. John P. Hammerschmidt, R
4. Beryl F. Anthony, Jr., D

CALIFORNIA
(43 Representatives)
1. Eugene A. Chappie, R
2. Don H. Clausen, R
3. Robert T. Matsui, D
4. Vic Fazio, D
5. John L. Burton, D
6. Phillip Burton, D
7. George Miller, D
8. Ronald V. Dellums, D
9. Fortney H. Stark, D
10. Don Edwards, D
11. Tom Lantos, D
12. Paul N. McCloskey, Jr., R
13. Norman Y. Mineta, D
14. Norman D. Shumway, R
15. Tony Coelho, D
16. Leon E. Panetta, D
17. Charles Pashayan, Jr., R
18. William M. Thomas, R
19. Robert J. Lagomarsino, R
20. Barry M. Goldwater Jr., R
21. Bobbi Fiedler, R
22. Carlos J. Moorhead, R
23. Anthony C. Beilenson, D
24. Henry A. Waxman, D
25. Edward R. Roybal, D
26. John H. Rousselot, R
27. Robert K. Dornan, R
28. Julian C. Dixon, D
29. Augustus F. Hawkins, D
30. George E. Danielson, D
31. Mervyn M. Dymally, D
32. Glenn M. Anderson, D
33. Wayne R. Grisham, R
34. Dan E. Lungren, R
35. Dave Dreier, R

36. George E. Brown, Jr., D
37. Jerry Lewis, R
38. Jerry M. Patterson, D
39. William E. Dannemeyer, R
40. Robert E. Badham, R
41. William Lowery, R
42. Duncan L. Hunter, R
43. Clair W. Burgener, R

COLORADO
(5 Representatives)
1. Patricia Schroeder, D
2. Timothy E. Wirth, D
3. Raymond P. Kogovsek, D
4. Hank Brown, R
5. Kenneth B. Kramer, R

CONNECTICUT
(6 Representatives)
1. William R. Cotter, D
2. Samuel Gejdenson, D
3. Lawrence J. DeNardis, R
4. Stewart B. McKinney, R
5. William R. Ratchford, D
6. Toby Moffett, D

DELAWARE
(1 Representative)
AL Thomas B. Evans, Jr., R

FLORIDA
(15 Representatives)
1. Earl D. Hutto, D
2. Don Fuqua, D
3. Charles E. Bennett, D
4. William V. Chappell, Jr., D
5. William McCollum, R
6. C. W. Bill Young, R
7. Sam M. Gibbons, D
8. Andrew P. Ireland, D
9. Bill Nelson, D
10. L. A. Bafalis, R
11. Daniel A. Mica, D
12. Clay Shaw, R
13. William Lehman, D
14. Claude D. Pepper, D
15. Dante B. Fascell, D

GEORGIA
(10 Representatives)
1. Bo Ginn, D
2. Charles F. Hatcher, D
3. Jack T. Brinkley, D
4. Elliott H. Levitas, D
5. Wyche Fowler, Jr., D
6. Newt Gingrich, R
7. Lawrence P. McDonald, D
8. Billy Lee Evans, D
9. Edgar L. Jenkins, D
10. D. Douglas Barnard, Jr., D

HAWAII
(2 Representatives)
1. Cecil Heftel, D
2. Daniel K. Akaka, D

IDAHO
(2 Representatives)
1. Larry Craig, R
2. George V. Hansen, R

ILLINOIS
(24 Representatives)
1. Harold Washington, D
2. Gus Savage, D
3. Marty Russo, D
4. Edward J. Derwinski, R
5. John G. Fary, D
6. Henry J. Hyde, R
7. Cardiss Collins, D
8. Dan Rostenkowski, D
9. Sidney R. Yates, D
10. John E. Porter, R
11. Frank Annunzio, D
12. Philip M. Crane, R
13. Robert McClory, R
14. John N. Erlenborn, R
15. Tom Corcoran, R
16. Lynn M. Martin, R
17. George M. O'Brien, R
18. Robert H. Michel, R
19. Thomas F. Railsback, R
20. Paul Findley, R
21. Edward R. Madigan, R
22. Daniel B. Crane, R
23. Melvin Price, D
24. Paul Simon, D

INDIANA
(11 Representatives)
1. Adam Benjamin, Jr., D
2. Floyd J. Fithian, D
3. John P. Hiler, R
4. Daniel R. Coats, R
5. Elwood H. Hillis, R
6. David W. Evans, D
7. John T. Myers, R
8. H. Joel Deckard, R
9. Lee H. Hamilton, D
10. Philip R. Sharp, D
11. Andrew Jacobs, Jr., D

IOWA
(6 Representatives)
1. Jim Leach, R
2. Thomas J. Tauke, R
3. Cooper Evans, R
4. Neal Smith, D
5. Thomas R. Harkin, D
6. Berkley W. Bedell, D

KANSAS
(5 Representatives)
1. Pat Roberts, R
2. James E. Jeffries, R
3. Larry Winn, Jr., R
4. Dan Glickman, D
5. Robert Whittaker, R

KENTUCKY
(7 Representatives)
1. Carroll Hubbard, Jr., D
2. William H. Natcher, D
3. Romano L. Mazzoli, D
4. Gene Snyder, R
5. Harold Rogers, R
6. Larry J. Hopkins, R
7. Carl D. Perkins, D

LOUISIANA
(8 Representatives)
1. Robert L. Livingston, R
2. Corinne C. (Lindy) Boggs, D
3. William J. Tauzin, D
4. Buddy Roemer, R
5. Thomas J. Huckaby, D
6. W. Henson Moore, R
7. John B. Breaux, D
8. Gillis W. Long, D

MAINE
(2 Representatives)
1. David F. Emery, R
2. Olympia J. Snowe, R

MARYLAND
(8 Representatives)
1. Roy Dyson, D
2. Clarence D. Long, D
3. Barbara A. Mikulski, D
4. Marjorie S. Holt, R
5. Gladys Noon Spellman, D
6. Beverly B. Byron, D
7. Parren J. Mitchell, D
8. Michael D. Barnes, D

MASSACHUSETTS
(12 Representatives)
1. Silvio O. Conte, R
2. Edward P. Boland, D
3. Joseph D. Early, D
4. Barney Frank, D
5. James M. Shannon, D
6. Nicholas Mavroules, D
7. Edward J. Markey, D
8. Thomas P. O'Neill, Jr., D
9. John J. Moakley, D
10. Margaret M. Heckler, R
11. Brian J. Donnelly, D
12. Gerry E. Studds, D

MICHIGAN
(19 Representatives)
1. John Conyers, Jr., D
2. Carl D. Pursell, R
3. Howard E. Wolpe, D
4. David A. Stockman, R
5. Harold S. Sawyer, R
6. James Dunn, R
7. Dale E. Kildee, D
8. Bob Traxler, D
9. Guy Vander Jagt, R
10. Donald J. Albosta, D
11. Robert W. Davis, R
12. David E. Bonior, D
13. George W. Crockett, Jr., D
14. Dennis M. Hertel, D
15. William D. Ford, D
16. John D. Dingell, D

17. William M. Brodhead, D
18. James J. Blanchard, D
19. William S. Broomfield, R

MINNESOTA
(8 Representatives)
1. Arlen Erdahl, R
2. Thomas M. Hagedorn, R
3. Bill Frenzel, R
4. Bruce F. Vento, D
5. Martin Olav Sabo, D
6. Vincent Weber, R
7. Arlan Stangeland, R
8. James L. Oberstar, D

MISSISSIPPI
(5 Representatives)
1. Jamie L. Whitten, D
2. David R. Bowen, D
3. G. V. (Sonny) Montgomery, D
4. Jon C. Hinson, R
5. Trent Lott, R

MISSOURI
(10 Representatives)
1. William L. Clay, D
2. Robert A. Young, D
3. Richard A. Gephardt, D
4. Ike Skelton, D
5. Richard Bolling, D
6. E. Thomas Coleman, R
7. Gene Taylor, R
8. Wendell Bailey, R
9. Harold L. Volkmer, D
10. William Emerson, R

MONTANA
(2 Representatives)
1. Pat Williams, D
2. Ron Marlenee, R

NEBRASKA
(3 Representatives)
1. Douglas K. Bereuter, R
2. Hal Daub, R
3. Virginia Smith, R

NEVADA
(1 Representative)
AL James D. Santini, D

NEW HAMPSHIRE
(2 Representatives)
1. Norman E. D'Amours, D
2. Judd Gregg, R

NEW JERSEY
(15 Representatives)
1. James J. Florio, D
2. William J. Hughes, D
3. James J. Howard, D
4. Christopher H. Smith, R
5. Millicent Fenwick, R
6. Edwin B. Forsythe, R
7. Marge Roukema, R
8. Robert A. Roe, D
9. Harold C. Hollenbeck, R
10. Peter W. Rodino, Jr., D
11. Joseph G. Minish, D
12. Matthew J. Rinaldo, R
13. James A. Courter, R
14. Frank J. Guarini, D
15. Bernard J. Dwyer, D

NEW MEXICO
(2 Representatives)
1. Manuel Lujan, Jr., R
2. Joseph Skeen, R

NEW YORK
(39 Representatives)
1. William Carney, R
2. Thomas J. Downey, D
3. Gregory W. Carman, R
4. Norman F. Lent, R
5. Raymond McGrath, R
6. John LeBoutillier, R
7. Joseph P. Addabbo, D
8. Benjamin S. Rosenthal, D
9. Geraldine A. Ferraro, D
10. Mario Biaggi, D
11. James H. Scheuer, D
12. Shirley Chisholm, D
13. Stephen J. Solarz, D
14. Frederick W. Richmond, D
15. Leo C. Zeferetti, D
16. Charles E. Schumer, D
17. Guy Molinari, R
18. S. William Green, R
19. Charles B. Rangel, D
20. Ted Weiss, D
21. Robert Garcia, D
22. Jonathan B. Bingham, D
23. Peter A. Peyser, D
24. Richard L. Ottinger, D
25. Hamilton Fish, Jr., R
26. Benjamin A. Gilman, R
27. Matthew F. McHugh, D
28. Samuel S. Stratton, D
29. Gerald B. Solomon, R
30. David O'B. Martin, R
31. Donald J. Mitchell, R
32. George Wortley, R
33. Gary A. Lee, R
34. Frank Horton, R
35. Barber B. Conable, Jr., R
36. John J. LaFalce, D
37. Henry J. Nowak, D
38. Jack F. Kemp, R
39. Stanley N. Lundine, D

NORTH CAROLINA
(11 Representatives)
1. Walter B. Jones, D
2. L. H. Fountain, D
3. Charles O. Whitley, D
4. Ike F. Andrews, D
5. Stephen L. Neal, D
6. Eugene Johnston, R
7. Charles Rose, D
8. W. G. Hefner, D
9. James G. Martin, R
10. James T. Broyhill, R
11. William M. Hendon, R

NORTH DAKOTA
(1 Representative)
AL Byron L. Dorgan, D

OHIO
(23 Representatives)
1. Willis D. Gradison, Jr., R
2. Thomas A. Luken, D
3. Tony P. Hall, D
4. Tennyson Guyer, R
5. Delbert L. Latta, R
6. Robert McEwen, R
7. Clarence J. Brown, R
8. Thomas N. Kindness, R
9. Ed Weber, R
10. Clarence E. Miller, R
11. J. William Stanton, R
12. Robert Shamansky, D
13. Donald J. Pease, D
14. John F. Seiberling, D
15. Chalmers P. Wylie, R
16. Ralph S. Regula, R
17. John M. Ashbrook, R
18. Douglas Applegate, D
19. Lyle Williams, R
20. Mary Rose Oakar, D
21. Louis Stokes, D
22. Dennis E. Eckart, D
23. Ronald M. Mottl, D

OKLAHOMA
(6 Representatives)
1. James R. Jones, D
2. Michael L. Synar, D
3. Wesley W. Watkins, D
4. David McCurdy, D
5. Mickey Edwards, R
6. Glenn English, D

OREGON
(4 Representatives)
1. Les AuCoin, D
2. Denny Smith, R
3. Ron Wyden, D
4. James H. Weaver, D

PENNSYLVANIA
(25 Representatives)
1. Thomas M. Foglietta[1]
2. William H. Gray III, D
3. Raymond F. Lederer, D
4. Charles F. Dougherty, R
5. Richard T. Schulze, R
6. Gus Yatron, D
7. Robert W. Edgar, D
8. James K. Coyne, R
9. E. G. (Bud) Shuster, R
10. Joseph M. McDade, R
11. James L. Nelligan, R
12. John P. Murtha, D
13. Lawrence Coughlin, R
14. William J. Coyne, D
15. Donald L. Ritter, R
16. Robert S. Walker, R
17. Allen E. Ertel, D
18. Doug Walgren, D
19. William F. Goodling, R
20. Joseph M. Gaydos, D
21. Donald A. Bailey, D
22. Austin J. Murphy, D
23. William F. Clinger, Jr., R
24. Marc L. Marks, R
25. Eugene V. Atkinson, D

RHODE ISLAND
(2 Representatives)
1. Fernand J. St. Germain, D
2. Claudine Schneider, R

SOUTH CAROLINA
(6 Representatives)
1. Thomas F. Hartnett, R

2. Floyd D. Spence, R
3. Butler C. Derrick, Jr., D
4. Carroll A. Campbell, Jr., R
5. Kenneth L. Holland, D
6. John L. Napier, R

SOUTH DAKOTA
(2 Representatives)
1. Thomas A. Daschle, D
2. Clint Roberts, R

TENNESSEE
(8 Representatives)
1. James H. Quillen, R
2. John J. Duncan, R
3. Marilyn Lloyd Bouquard, D
4. Albert A. Gore, Jr., D
5. William H. Boner, D
6. Robin L. Beard, R
7. Ed Jones, D
8. Harold E. Ford, D

TEXAS
(24 Representatives)
1. Sam B. Hall, Jr., D
2. Charles Wilson, D
3. James M. Collins, R
4. Ralph M. Hall, D
5. James A. Mattox, D
6. Phil Gramm, D
7. Bill Archer, R
8. Jack Fields, R
9. Jack Brooks, D
10. J. J. (Jake) Pickle, D
11. Marvin Leath, D
12. James C. Wright, Jr., D
13. Jack E. Hightower, D
14. William Patman, D
15. E. (Kika) de la Garza, D
16. Richard C. White, D
17. Charles W. Stenholm, D
18. George T. (Mickey) Leland, D
19. Kent R. Hance, D
20. Henry B. Gonzalez, D
21. Thomas G. Loeffler, R
22. Ronald E. Paul, R
23. Abraham Kazen, Jr., D
24. Martin Frost, D

UTAH
(2 Representatives)
1. James V. Hansen, R
2. David D. Marriott, R

VERMONT
(1 Representative)
AL James M. Jeffords, R

VIRGINIA
(10 Representatives)
1. Paul S. Trible, Jr., R
2. G. William Whitehurst, R
3. Thomas J. Bliley, Jr., R
4. Robert W. Daniel, Jr., R
5. W. E. (Dan) Daniel, D
6. M. Caldwell Butler, R
7. J. Kenneth Robinson, R
8. Stanford E. Parris, R
9. William C. Wampler, R
10. Frank R. Wolf, R

WASHINGTON
(7 Representatives)
1. Joel Pritchard, R
2. Al Swift, D
3. Don L. Bonker, D
4. Sid Morrison, R
5. Thomas S. Foley, D
6. Norman D. Dicks, D
7. Mike Lowry, D

WEST VIRGINIA
(4 Representatives)
1. Robert H. Mollohan, D
2. Cleve Benedict, R
3. Mick Staton, R
4. Nick J. Rahall II, D

WISCONSIN
(9 Representatives)
1. Les Aspin, D
2. Robert W. Kastenmeier, D
3. Steven Gunderson, R
4. Clement J. Zablocki, D
5. Henry S. Reuss, D
6. Thomas E. Petri, R
7. David R. Obey, D
8. Toby A. Roth, R
9. F. James Sensenbrenner, Jr., R

WYOMING
(1 Representative)
AL Richard B. Cheney, R

1. Not affiliated with any party. NOTE: The District of Columbia is represented by a non-voting delegate. Puerto Rico has a resident commissioner in the House and Guam and the Virgin Islands have one delegate each.

The Governors of the Fifty States

State	Governor	Year of birth	Current term[1]	State	Governor	Year of birth	Current term[1]
Ala.	Forrest James, Jr., D	1936	1979–83	Mont.	Ted Schwinden, D	1925	1981–85
Alaska	Jay S. Hammond, R	1922	1978–82[2]	Neb.	Charles Thone, R	1924	1979–83
Ariz.	Bruce E. Babbitt, D	1938	1979–83	Nev.	Robert F. List, R	1936	1979–83
Ark.	Frank D. White, R	1934	1981–83	N.H.	Hugh J. Gallen, D	1924	1981–83
Calif.	Edmund G. Brown, Jr., D	1938	1979–83	N.J.	Brendan T. Byrne, D	1924	1978–82
Colo.	Richard D. Lamm, D	1935	1979–83	N.M.	Bruce King, D	1924	1979–83
Conn.	Ella T. Grasso, D	1919	1979–83	N.Y.	Hugh L. Carey, D	1919	1979–83
Del.	Pierre S. du Pont, IV, R	1935	1981–85	N.C.	James B. Hunt, Jr., D	1937	1981–85
Fla.	Robert Graham, D	1936	1979–83	N.D.	Allen I. Olson, R	1938	1981–85
Ga.	George Busbee, D	1927	1979–83	Ohio	James A. Rhodes, R	1909	1979–83
Hawaii	George R. Ariyoshi, D	1926	1978–82[2]	Okla.	George P. Nigh, D	1927	1979–83
Idaho	John V. Evans, D	1925	1979–83	Ore.	Victor G. Atiyeh, R	1923	1979–83
Ill.	James R. Thompson, R	1936	1979–83	Pa.	Richard L. Thornburgh, R	1932	1979–83
Ind.	Robert D. Orr, R	1917	1981–85	R.I.	J. Joseph Garrahy, D	1931	1981–83
Iowa	Robert D. Ray, R	1928	1979–83	S.C.	Richard W. Riley, D	1933	1979–83
Kan.	John W. Carlin, D	1940	1979–83	S.D.	William J. Janklow, R	1939	1979–83
Ky.	John Y. Brown, Jr., D	1934	1979–83[2]	Tenn.	Lamar Alexander, R	1940	1979–83
La.	David C. Treen, R	1928	1980–84[3]	Tex.	Bill Clements, R	1917	1979–83
Me.	Joseph E. Brennan, D	1934	1979–83	Utah	Scott M. Matheson, D	1929	1981–85
Md.	Harry R. Hughes, D	1926	1979–83	Vt.	Richard A. Snelling, R	1928	1981–83
Mass.	Edward J. King, D	1925	1979–83	Va.	John N. Dalton, R	1931	1978–82
Mich.	William G. Milliken, R	1922	1979–83	Wash.	John Spellman, R	1927	1981–85
Minn.	Albert H. Quie, R	1923	1979–83	W.Va.	John D. Rockefeller IV, D	1937	1981–85
Miss.	William F. Winter, D	1923	1980–84	Wis.	Lee Sherman Dreyfus, R	1926	1979–83
Mo.	Christopher S. Bond, R	1939	1981–85	Wyo.	Ed C. Herschler, D	1918	1979–83

1. Except where indicated, all terms begin in January. 2. December. 3. March.

CURRENT EVENTS

What Happened in 1979–80

The important events of the year, from November 1979 to October 1980, organized for easy reference:

The Countries of the World section (starting on page 142) covers specific international events, country by country. Special commentaries on Business and the Economy, Energy, Medicine, Religion, Space, and Travel appear in the appropriate sections (*see* Index).

Major Events—October 1980

1980 Nobel Prize Winners

Peace: Adolfo Pérez Esquivel, an Argentine rights activist, for his work as leader of an organization promoting human rights in Latin America.

Medicine: Dr. Baruj Benacerraf, chairman of the Pathology Department of the Harvard Medical School; Dr. George D. Snell, staff scientist at the Jackson Laborabory; and Dr. Jean Dausset, head of the Department of Immunology at the University of Paris, for discoveries that helped to explain how the structure of cells relates to diseases and organ transplants.

Economics: Lawrence R. Klein of the University of Pennsylvania for his work in the development of models for forecasting economic trends and the designing of policies to deal with them.

Physics: Dr. James W. Cronin, University of Chicago, and Dr. Val L. Fitch, Princeton University, for their discoveries concerning the symmetry of subatomic particles.

Chemistry: Dr. Paul Berg, Stanford University, Dr. Walter Gilbert, Harvard University, and Dr. Frederick Sanger, an Englishman, Cambridge University, for the development of methods that make it possible to map in considerable detail the structure and function of DNA.

Literature: Czeslaw Milosz, Polish émigré poet and novelist, now an American citizen.

House Ousts Pennsylvania Democrat Over Bribe (Oct. 2): Expels Michael J. Myers by 376–30 vote. Myers, 37, convicted in Abscam investigation. Expulsion first such since Civil War. **(Oct. 7):** Rep. John W. Jenrette, Jr., 44, South Carolina Democrat, second Congressman convicted in Abscam investigation.

Helmut Schmidt Coalition Increases Majority (Oct. 5): Social Democrats and Free Democrats returned to power in national West German elections with strengthened majority of more than 40 seats in lower house of Parliament. Christian Democrats and affiliate lose heavily.

2 Earthquakes in Algeria Kill Thousands (Oct. 10): Destroy most of city of Al Asnam in northwest. Algerian Red Crescent puts toll at from 5,000 to 20,000, with tens of thousands injured.

2 Soviet Astronauts Return After Record Flight (Oct. 11): Leonid I. Popov and Valery V. Ryumin set record of 185 days in space aboard orbiting station *Salyut 6*. Land in Central Asia steppe aboard *Soyuz 37* space capsule; both "feel well."

British Labor Party Faces Leadership Struggle (Oct. 15): Former Prime Minister James Callaghan, 68, resigns as leader after 30 years in center of politics, touching off battle between right and left wings of party over method of choosing successor.

Australian Coalition Survives Election Challenge (Oct. 19): Ballot sharply reduces Parliamentary majority of Prime Minister Malcolm Fraser's Liberal and National Country Parties as opposition Labor Party gains.

Greece Returns to NATO Military Wing (Oct. 20): Ends six-year absence in move consolidating alliance's vital southeastern flank.

U.S. and China Sign Grain Agreement (Oct. 22): Pact commits Peking to buy six to eight million metric tons of American wheat and corn a year for four years. Expected to stabilize trade volume.

Ailing Soviet Prime Minister Resigns (Oct. 23): Aleksei N. Kosygin, 76, quits after 16 years in post. First Premier in 63 years to resign while still in favor, except for wartime action by Vyacheslav M. Molotov. First Deputy, Nikolai A. Tikhonov, 75, succeeds him.

New Italian Government Formed (Oct. 25): Prime Minister Arnaldo Forlani heads four-party coalition, with larger parliamentary majority than virtually all 39 post-World War II governments.

Discover Two More Saturnian Moons (Oct. 28): Voyager 1 photographed a previously undetected 13th and 14th moon in close orbits around the planet's "F" ring.

Labor Party Wins Jamaica Election (Oct. 30): Edward Seaga was elected as the new Prime Minister of Jamaica.

Iran Gives Terms for Freeing Hostages (Nov. 2): President Carter says conditions appear to offer "positive basis" for settling year-long crisis. Iran's Parliament calls for noninterference by U.S. in Iranian affairs, and unfreezing of assets held in U.S.

1979–80

Business and the Economy

1979

Congress Votes Stand-by Gasoline Rationing (Oct. 23): House, 301–112, gives President authority to draft and implement plan if shortage occurs. First important energy measure to clear Congress since President's appeal in previous July.

Union Accord to Save Chrysler Millions (Oct. 25): UAW and corporation agree on three-year contract saving ailing auto company $203 million in two years. Douglas A. Fraser, union president, to sit on company's board.

Times of London Resumes Publication (Nov. 13): Published after shutdown of nearly a year. Cost to International Thomson, Canadian publishers, put at $60 million. Sunday Times also resumes. Papers suspended Nov. 30, 1979, in dispute over manning, technology, and wildcat strikes. Management fails to win goal of computerized typesetting.

Arnold R. Miller Resigns as UMW Head (Nov. 15): Coal miner, 57, named president in 1972 as reformer, quits $42,000-a-year office. In ill health, he had faced move by union officials to depose him. **(Nov. 16):** Sam Church, Jr., 43, another former miner, union vice president, succeeds him as union's 13th president.

Lane Kirkland Succeeds Meany as AFL-CIO Head (Nov. 19): Secretary-treasurer, 57, elected unanimously as second president of federation, succeeding 85-year-old George Meany, retiring. Meany, named AFL-CIO president-emeritus for life, retaining $110,000 annual salary. In policy shift, Kirkland calls upon unions outside federation to rejoin it, addressing its constitutional convention in Washington. **(Jan. 10):** Meany dead of cardiac arrest; had also suffered leukemia. President Carter praises Meany as "an American institution" and "a patriot."

U.S. Steel Closes 15 Plants, Cutting 13,000 Jobs (Nov. 27): Announces shutdown of factories and mills in eight states, affecting production and white-collar workers. Cutback represents about 8% of 166,000 employees at plants representing 5% of 1979 sales.

1980

Exxon Profits Rise to Record $4.26 Billion (Jan. 25): Corporation reports 55.4% increase for 1979 marked by consumer shortages and sharply higher prices. Gross revenues rose 30% to record $84.35 billion; more than any other business had reported for a single year.

Chrysler Reports Record $1.1-Billion Loss for 1979 (Feb. 7): Corporation says fourth quarter $375.8-million deficit brought largest yearly loss in American corporation history.

Amoco Settles Price Violation Suit for $700 Million (Feb. 14): Standard Oil Co. (Indiana) agrees with U.S. Energy Dept. on $300-million reimbursements to customers, payments to government, and cuts in current prices, and for spending $400 million on accelerated investment.

Major Consumer Refund Negotiated (March 4): Federal Trade Commission announces General Motors Acceptance Corp. agrees to pay $2 million to thousands of buyers whose cars and trucks were repossessed. Payments depend on amount company made when vehicles were resold. Commission had charged GMAC conducted "sham" sales of repossessed cars by selling them back to itself at a low price and then reselling for a profit, contrary to state and Federal law.

Chicago Firemen Return After 23-Day Strike, Their First (March 8): Majority of 4,350 accept interim agreement providing broad outlines for written contract, the central issue, after abandoning demand for 10% pay rise. Strikers get partial amnesty from city.

Henry Ford 2nd Quits as Ford Chairman (March 13): Succeeded by Philip Caldwell, chief executive officer. Company left for first time without a Ford at top.

Firestone Tire & Rubber Co. Closing 6 Plants (March 19): Responds to consumer shift to radial tires. Total of 7,265 workers idled.

White House Suspends Protective Pricing on Steel (March 21): Acts after U.S. Steel Corp. files "antidumping" petitions accusing European steel producers of selling to American market at unfairly low prices.

Silver Price Collapse Shakes Hunts' Empire (March 27): Wall Street in turmoil, stock prices depressed as metal closes at $10.80 an ounce, far below January high of $50.05. Nelson Bunker Hunt and W. Herbert Hunt of Dallas forced to raise millions in cash to save $2-billion silver empire. **(March 28):** Silver prices stabilize and all brokerage houses meet obligations. **(March 31):** Hunts dip into oil and gas properties, as well as silver holdings, to cover $400 million in silver losses.

Congress Approves "Windfall" Tax on Oil Profits (March 27): Senate, 66–31, gives final approval, after a year of battles, to $227.3-billion levy over 10 years, one of President Carter's biggest legislative victories. A rider will increase individuals' tax-exemption income from dividends and interest.

New York Tied Up 11 Days by Transit Strike (April 12): Buses and subways resume operation after leaders of city's transit unions reach tentative agreement with Metropolitan Transportation Authority and order 33,000 workers back. Agreement provides more than 20% in pay rises over two years. **(May 12):** Members of two transit unions overwhelmingly accept contract terms.

TV Importers to Pay U.S. $75 Million in Anti-dumping Case (April 28): Commerce Dept. announces settlement involving imports of $2 billion worth of Japanese sets over previous decade at prices alleged to be unfairly low. Importers include Sears, Roebuck & Co., J.C. Penney, and Montgomery Ward.

Unemployment Highest in Nearly Three Years (May 2): Labor Dept. reports rate up to 7% of work force in April from 6.2% in March, biggest one-month increase since January 1975. Hundreds of blue-collar workers laid off as economic activity declines.

$1.5-Billion U.S. Backing for Chrysler Loans Approved (May 10): Loan Guarantee Board rules troubled corporation can qualify, with some conditions, for largest Government rescue package extended to a corporation, with $500 million of guarantees available within 15 days. Company must restructure about $4.4 billion of debt.

Federal Reserve Cuts Back Credit Controls (May 22): Substantial easing of restraints in anti-inflation program designed to make credit easier and less expensive as economy rapidly weakens.

Nation's Recession Declared Official (June 3): National Bureau of Economic Research, arbiter of business cycles, says downturn began in January. Martin Feldstein, president, says "peak has been reached and we are now in deline."

Chrysler Gets First Financing in Bail-out Program (June 24): Chrysler Loan Guarantee Board in Washington authorizes up to $1.5 billion in Federal loan guarantees to beleaguered auto company. In New

York, bankers, lawyers, and Chrysler officials sign documents for immediate $500 million loan to permit Chrysler to pay creditors and avert default.

Carter Approves Deregulation of Bus Lines (July 1): President signs legislation cutting back Government control of $41-billion interstate industry. Says consumers will save as much as $8 billion a year.

Federal Reserve Phases Out Final Credit Controls (July 3): Announces it will remove remaining curbs imposed in March to fight inflation. Since then the recession has worsened and price increases have moderated.

G.M. Reports Record $412-Million Loss (July 24): Setback for second quarter compares with record profit of $1.18 billion in corresponding period of 1979. Recession and competition by Japanese imports blamed.

Ford Reports Record $468-Million Loss (July 29): Poor domestic auto sales bring April-through-June quarter deficit. Profits from overseas operations cut loss.

Chrysler Reports $536.1-Million Loss in Quarter (July 31): Deficit from April through June is largest such deficit ever reported by a U.S. automobile manufacturer. Loss ascribed to plunging sales and cost of retooling to make small cars.

I.C.C. Overturns Collective Setting of Railway Freight Rates (Aug. 13): Interstate Commerce Commission, 5–2, finds practice stifled competition.

Journalists Strike at Times of London (Aug. 22): Seek 21% salary increases in shutting down 195-year-old paper. **(Aug. 29):** Journalists end strike, accepting management offer of 27% pay rise over year and a half. Publication resumes.

Bethlehem Steel Fined $325,000 for Bribery (Aug. 25): Federal judge in Manhattan imposes penalty after corporation's guilty plea to criminal charges that it had paid more than $400,000 from secret funds in bribes to get ship repair business from 1972 to 1976.

Drought Ravages Eastern U.S. (Sept. 11): Agriculture Department reports sharp decline in yields of corn, soybeans, and cotton across much of Eastern half of nation.

Renault to Control American Motors (Sept. 24): The French auto maker would acquire a major interest in A.M.C. under a $200-million agreement. American Motors sought the arrangement in order to financially rescue its auto-making operations.

Carter Offers Aid For Steel Industry (Sept. 30): President Carter announces a package of assistance for the steel industry. The aid package focuses on help in modernizing outdated plants, import protection, and delays on the industry's meeting pollution standards.

The Courts

1979

Court Bars Suit Against Philadelphia Police (Oct. 30): Federal judge William Ditter dismisses major part of civil rights action brought by Justice Dept. against Mayor Frank L. Rizzo and other officials charging they condoned systematic and criminal violence by police. **(Dec. 13):** Judge also dismisses remaining U.S. charge that city officials had practiced racial discrimination in administering federally financed police programs.

Court Allows Veterans to Sue Chemical Makers (Nov. 20): Federal judge in Mineola, L.I., rules 46,000 allegedly injured by defoliant Agent Orange in Vietnam and children born deformed can file Federal actions against five manufacturers for extensive civil damages.

1980

Justices Uphold Military Limitations on Petitions (Jan. 21): Supreme Court, 5–3, rejects challenges to Air Force, Navy, and Marine Corps requirement that armed service members get permission of commanding officers before collecting signatures on complaints to civilian officials. Similar Army regulations not involved.

Justices Uphold CIA Policy on Writings (Feb. 19): Supreme Court, in victory for Government, rules as legally enforceable the agency's contract agreement requiring employees not to publish "any information" about it—classified or not—without specific prior approval. Court holds Frank W. Snepp, 3rd, a former CIA officer, violated his obligations by publishing account of fall of Saigon, and orders him to turn over to Government all earnings from book.

Workers Upheld on Right to Refuse Dangerous Jobs (Feb. 26): Supreme Court rules unanimously that in certain circumstances they can shun tasks they believe pose a danger of death or serious injury. Labor Dept. ruling against employer reprisals is upheld.

Supreme Court Upholds Suits by Prison Inmates (April 22): Decides, 7–2, that Eighth Amendment prohibition against cruel and unusual punishment gives Federal prisoners or survivors right to seek damages against prison officials for mistreatment.

Justices Uphold Right of Petitioning at Shopping Malls (June 9): Supreme Court rules unanimously that states can require owners of private centers to provide access to persons wishing to circulate petitions or otherwise exercise right of free speech.

New Jersey Press Shield Law Upheld (June 9): State's Supreme Court, 6–1, overturns lower court ruling and finds statute protects reporter's confidential notes even from private scrutiny by a judge.

High Court Upholds Patents for New Forms of Life (June 16): Justices, 5–4, affirm award for new bacterium that "digests" oil spills. Decision clears way for growing field of genetic engineering, giving further recognition to revolution in biological research.

Supreme Court Upholds Limits on Federal Aid for Abortions (June 30): Ruling by 5–4 vote revives four-year-old Congressional ban on Medicaid financing for abortions, except in cases of incest or rape or where birth would endanger mother's life.

Justices Affirm Public and Press Right of Access to Criminal Trials (July 2): Decision, 7–1, overturns Virginia Supreme Court ruling, and holds that First Amendment's free speech and free press guarantees afford broad public access to public institutions.

Supreme Court Upholds Affirmative Action (July 2): Approves Federal public works program in which minority contractors get 10% of spending, backing Congress's power to require remedy for racial discrimination. Ruling, 6–3, is first to endorse Federal benefits based on race, but does not establish similar authority for other branches or institutions of Government.

Crime and Violence

1979

Nevada Executes Las Vegas Casino Murderer (Oct. 22): Jesse Walter Bishop, 46, drug addict, dies in gas chamber in state's first execution in 18 years. Prisoner rejects offers of aid and tells of 18 killings for hire.

Scotto and Anastasio Guilty of Waterfront Payoffs (Nov. 15): Federal jury convicts 45-year-old Anthony M. Scotto, politically influential leader of Longshoremen's Association in Brooklyn, of getting more than $200,000 from businessmen by racketeering. Co-defendant, Anthony Anastasio, 50, a union official, convicted of getting more than $50,000. **(Jan. 22):** Judge sentences Scotto to five years in prison, fines him $75,000. **(Jan. 23):** Anastasio sentenced to two years in prison and fined $5,000.

Five Killed in March Against Klan (Nov. 3): Four shot dead, fifth fatally wounded, in Greensboro, N.C., as demonstrators prepare for anti-Klan march. Ten others injured, eight with gunshot wounds. **(Nov. 5):** Fourteen Ku Klux Klansmen arraigned on murder charges. President Carter orders nationwide investigation of Klan activities.

1980

U.S. Paroles Vietnam War Protester in Bombing (Jan. 31): Karleton Armstrong, now 33, leaves Fox Lake, Wis., Correctional Institution eight years after predawn blast at University of Wisconsin Army Mathematics Research Center, in which Robert Fassnacht, physics researcher, was killed.

FBI "Sting" Operation Implicates High Officials (Feb. 2): In two-year undercover operation code-named Abscam (for Arab scam), agents pose as businessmen and Arab sheiks willing to pay bribes for use of influence and position. Meetings surreptitiously videotaped and recorded. FBI reports involvement of Senator Harrison A. Williams, Jr., of New Jersey and five Representatives in Congress. **(Feb. 9):** Abscam operation in Southwest implicates three senior political figures and a leader in organized crime. Political figures named include Jimmy Fitzmorris, Democratic lieutenant governor of Louisiana.

33 Dead in Rioting at New Mexico Prison (Feb. 4): Violence and terror break out when prisoners take 11 guards hostage at State Penitentiary at Santa Fe, where 1,150 were crowded into facility built for 850. Police and National Guardsmen recapture penitentiary after 36 hours. Survivors report wholesale killing and butchery during uprising.

Killer Gets Third Death Sentence in Florida (Feb. 12): Circuit judge dooms Theodore Robert Bundy to electric chair for murder of 12-year-old girl. Bundy, 33, already sentenced for murdering two Florida State University students in 1978.

Former Rep. Daniel J. Flood Pleads Guilty (Feb. 26): Admits guilt on single count of conspiracy to violate Federal campaign laws in taking payoffs from five persons, and is placed on probation for a year. The Pennsylvania Democrat, 76, resigned from House of Representatives Jan. 31 after 31-year career in Congress.

Arizona Court Reverses 2 Convictions in Killing of Reporter (Feb. 26): Supreme bench orders retrials for Max Dunlap, 50, millionaire Phoenix contractor, and James Robison, 57, a plumber. They have spent four years on death row after conviction in car bomb death of Don Bolles, Phoenix reporter. Bolles had written about organized crime and powerful interests in Arizona.

"Scarsdale Diet" Doctor Slain (March 10): Dr. Herman Tarnower, 69, prominent Westchester County, N.Y., physician and author of "The Complete Scarsdale Medical Diet," shot in bedroom of his secluded home at Purchase, N.Y. Jean S. Harris, 56, a long-time friend, charged with killing. She is headmistress of Madeira School for Girls in Virginia.

John Wayne Gacy Convicted in 33 Murders (March 12): Jury in Chicago rejects insanity plea and finds suburban building contractor, 37, guilty of killing boys and young men lured home and then attacked sexually. Deaths are greatest of any previous mass murders in nation. **(March 13):** Judge sentences Gacy to death in electric chair.

Ford Motor Co. Cleared in Three Pinto Deaths (March 13): Indiana jury finds company not guilty on three charges of reckless homicide in 1978 deaths of three young women in fiery rear-end crash involving Pinto car. Verdict ends 10-week trial, first criminal prosecution of a U.S. corporation in case where alleged product defects led to deaths. Ford charged with knowing fuel tanks on Pinto had tendency to explode when struck from behind. **(Aug. 5):** Ford Motor company settles Pinto to action. Agreement reported for $22,500 payment to families of three girls killed when car burst into flames when struck from behind in Indiana. Company was found not guilty of reckless homicide in criminal trial.

Ex-Rep. Allard K. Lowenstein Slain in New York (March 14): Lawyer, 51, antiwar leader and former U.S. Representative, dies after seven shots by deranged former co-worker in civil rights movement in South. Lowenstein led 1968 movement to block election of President Lyndon B. Johnson.

Italian Financier Convicted of Fraud (March 27): Michele Sindona, 59, found guilty in Manhattan Federal Court on charges involving 1974 failure of Franklin National Bank, Long Island, largest bank collapse in U.S. history. Sindona's two-month disappearance in 1979 delayed start of trial. **(June 13):** Sindona gets 25 years in prison and $207,000 fine.

Ex-Governor of Maryland Fails in Final Appeal (April 15): Supreme Court refuses to hear plea by Marvin Mandel to upset conviction of accepting $350,000 in gifts and favors from wealthy friends in return for using office to advance their interest in race track.

Bert Lance Acquitted on 9 Bank Fraud Counts (April 30): Jury in Georgia Federal Court deadlocked on three other charges, resulting in mistrial. Former Federal Budget Director had been accused of hiding debts and making $1 million in questionable loans. Three co-defendants acquitted on most charges. **(June 6):** Justice Department says it will not retry Lance and two co-defendants on remaining charges.

Racial Rioting Flares in Miami; Death Toll 17 (May 17): All-white jury acquits four white former police officers charged with fatal beating of Arthur McDuffie, black Miami insurance man, making it appear an accident. As result, night-long rioting by protesting blacks breaks out, with widespread looting, fires, beatings, and shootings. Hundreds injured. **(May 18):** Shooting, arson, and looting continue. National Guardsmen patrol streets. **(May 19):** Guard reinforced. President Carter sends Attorney General Benjamin R. Civiletti to calm outrage of black community. **(May 20):** Civiletti announces team of 25–30 Federal prosecutors and agents will look into local civil rights abuses. **(June 9):** Angry crowd of several hundred boos Carter as he visits scene of rioting; bottles thrown at President's motorcade. He promises Federal help in rebuilding area and restoring jobs.

Officials Indicted in FBI'S Abscam Inquiry (May 27): U.S. grand jury in Brooklyn files charges against Representative Michael O. Meyers, 35, Democrat of Philadelphia, on charges of bribery, conspiracy to defraud U.S., and interstate travel to aid racketeering. Indictment also names Mayor Angelo J. Errichetti, 50, of Camden and two Philadelphia lawyers, Howard L. Criden, 53, and Louis C. Johanson, 57. Criden and Johanson, a Philadelphia councilman, also under indictment in Philadelphia along with two other councilmen. **(May 28):** Jury indicts Representative Raymond F. Lederer, 42, also of Philadelphia, on similar charges.

Hamilton Jordan Escapes Indictment (May 28): Federal grand jury finds insufficient evidence to accuse White House chief of staff of using cocaine on visit to Manhattan discothèque.

Sniper Wounds Urban League President (May 29): Vernon E. Jordan, 44, prominent civil rights leader, shot in back in Fort Wayne, Ind. parking lot. Jordan was leaving car driven by Martha C. Coleman, board member of local Urban League, whose annual banquet Jordan had addressed earlier. **(June 12):** Jordan transferred to New York hospital. Federal and local police officials report little progress in solving case and determining motive.

Justice Department Refuses to Prosecute Talmadge (May 30): After 22-month investigation, it drops case of Senator Herman E. Talmadge, 66, Georgia Democrat, "denounced" by Senate for mishandling office and campaign finances.

U.S. Jury Indicts Texas Speaker in Fraud Inquiry (June 12): Names Billie Wayne Clayton and three others on conspiracy and racketeering charges growing out of FBI's investigation into organized crime, labor racketeering, and political corruption in Southwest.

South Carolinian Indicted in "Abscam" Inquiry (June 13): Federal grand jury in Washington charges Representative John W. Jenrette, Jr., 44, a Democrat, shared in $50,000 bribery payment.

Reputed Organized Crime Leader Indicted (June 17): Carlos Marcello, 70, charged by Federal grand jury in New Orleans with racketeering, conspiracy, and fraud. Panel accuses Marcello as result of FBI "Brilab" inquiry into scheme to bribe public officials in Louisiana.

Two Representatives Indicted in "Abscam" Inquiry (June 18): Federal grand jury in Brooklyn accuses John M. Murphy of Staten Island and Frank Thompson, Jr., of Trenton, both Democrats, on charges of bribery and conspiracy.

Woman Fugitive Surrenders in "Weatherman" Bombing (July 8): Cathlyn Platt Wilkerson, 35, gives up in office of New York District Attorney. Sought since March 6, 1970, when father's Greenwich Village house blew up during production of dynamite bombs for radical underground group, killing three. **(July 19):** She pleads guilty in Manhattan Criminal Court to unlawful possession of dynamite.

Synanon Founder and Two Aides Guilty in Death Plot (July 15): Charles E. Dederich, 67, founder of drug rehabilitation organization, and others plead no contest to conspiracy to use rattlesnake to attack Paul Morantz, lawyer. Morantz had sued Synanon on behalf of former members and their relatives who had claimed that they were being kept in the group against their will. **(Sept. 3):** Dederich gets five years' probation in plot to kill lawyer. Los Angeles judge cites Dederich's past good works and orders him to cut connection with the drug rehabilitation organization.

Woman Violinist Slain at Metropolitan Opera (July 24): Nude and bound body of Helen Hagnes, 30, playing in orchestra for Berlin Ballet, found in ventilation shaft of New York's Lincoln Center building. **(Aug. 30):** Craig Steven Crimmins, 21, of the Bronx, a Metropolitan Opera stagehand for four years, charged with the killing.

Appeal Upsets Murder Convictions of Former Green Beret Doctor (July 30): Federal Appeals Court in Richmond, Va., reverses verdict for Dr. Jeffrey R. MacDonald, 36, in slayings of wife and two daughters a decade previously at Fort Bragg, N.C. Court finds his right to a speedy trial had been violated.

Bomb Blast Kills 76 in Bologna Train Station (Aug. 2): Nearly 200 injured as explosion demolishes wing of building in north-central Italy. **(Aug. 3):** Investigators suspect neo-Fascist guerrilla gang caused worst terrorist incident in Italian history.

Cabinet Minister Accused in Slaying of Zimbabwe White (Aug. 6): Murder charge filed against Edgar Z. Tekere, 43, Manpower Minister and most radical member in administration of Prime Minister Robert Mugabe. He is held in killing of Gerald William Adams, 68, a white farm manager.

Guard Hunted in $1-Million Brink's Inc. Robbery (Aug. 15): Security agent seizes armored truck in his custody at San Francisco International Airport, commandeers a car, and drives away with bags containing cash.

Four Convicted in First Abscam Trial (Aug. 30): Federal Court jury in Brooklyn finds them guilty of bribery, conspiracy, and interstate travel in aid of a racketeering enterprise. Charges resulted from FBI undercover operation involving agents posing as Arab sheiks. Those guilty are: Rep. Michael J. Myers, Democrat of Philadelphia; Mayor Angelo J. Errichetti of Camden, N.J.; Louis C. Johanson, a Philadelphia city councilman; and Howard L. Criden, a lawyer.

Abbie Hoffman Surrenders After Leaving Hiding (Sept. 4): Counterculture leader of '60s, founder of "Yippies," Youth International Party, now 43, released in own recognizance after giving up in Manhattan. He had jumped bail in 1974 after being charged with sale of three pounds of cocaine to undercover agents. He had been living as "hero" of upstate New York community.

Cuban U.N. Attaché Shot Dead in Queens (Sept. 11): Omega 7, anti-Castro terrorist organization, claims responsibility for killing Felix Garcia Rodriguez, in his 30s, from ambush.

2 Convicted in Philadelphia Abscam Trial (Sept. 16): City Council President George X. Schwartz found guilty in Federal Court of extortion and racketeering. Finance Committee Chairman Harry P. Jannotti guilty of extortion-conspiracy. Video tapes had shown both men accepting $40,000 from undercover agents posing as representatives of bogus Arab sheik.

House Recommends Expulsion of Abscam Figure (Sept. 24): The ethics committee of the House of Representatives voted 10 to 2 to expel Rep. Michael J. Myers, Democrat of Pennsylvania for his bribery conviction in the Abscam scandal.

Disasters

1979

Quake Rocks Southern California (Oct. 15): Tremor in Mexican-border town of Calexico is felt as far north as Los Angeles suburbs and sways buildings in Las Vegas. No injuries reported.

74 Killed in DC-10 Crash at Mexico City (Oct. 31): Plane hits truck and veers out of control as pilot tries to land on runway closed for repairs. Seventy-one of 90 aboard and three on ground dead as aircraft demolishes service building and explodes in flames. No indications of design or maintenance defects.

31 Dead as Two Ships Collide in Gulf (Nov. 1): Freighter *Mimosa* rams tanker *Burmah Agate*, carrying 16.8 million gallons of crude oil; both ships, of Liberian registry, burst into flames five miles south of Galveston, Tex. Crash creates 10-mile long oil spill.

250,000 Flee Chlorine Gas in Ontario (Nov. 12): Evacuated from Mississauga, a Toronto suburb, after derailment of train laden with toxic chemicals. Ninety tons of deadly chlorine slowly leak from ruptured tank car in flaming wreckage of 106-car Canadian Pacific train.

156 Killed in Crash of Pakistani Jetliner (Nov. 26): Pakistan International Airlines Boeing 707 catches fire shortly after takeoff from Jidda Airport in Saudi Arabia. Most of victims were pilgrims returning from Mecca.

257 Killed as DC-10 Crashes Into Antarctic Peak (Nov. 28): New Zealand plane, with 237 passengers, 20 from U.S., and crew of 20, cracks up on sightseeing flight over 12,400-foot Mount Erebus, active volcano, on Ross Island.

11 Rock Fans Killed in Crush at Cincinnati (Dec. 3): At least eight others injured when thousands of young people storm Riverfront Coliseum to get unreserved seats for concert by British group, The Who. **(Dec. 4):** City orders investigation. Deaths raise concern that similar conditions exist at hundreds of other concert halls.

Panel Finds Multiple Causes for DC-10 Crash (Dec. 22): National Transportation Safety Board, 5–0, rules American Airlines; McDonnell Douglas Corp., manufacturer, and Federal Aviation Administration should share blame for disaster in May 1979 at Chicago's O'Hare International Airport in which 275 died. Rules jumbo jet crashed because of combination of improper maintenance and vulnerable design of key structures. Attributes tearing away of left underwing engine to faulty maintenance procedures when engine and its pylon were removed. **(Jan. 23):** FAA calls DC-10 engine mount basically sound but asks modest revision in design to prevent maintenance damage that caused Chicago crash.

Fire Kills 42 at Quebec New Year's Eve Party (Dec. 31): Many bodies packed against rear door of social club near Chapais, copper-mining town about 310 miles north of Montreal. Fifty others suffer burns and smoke inhalation as flames sweep fir-tree decorations.

1980

165 Dead in Bleacher Collapse at Colombia Bullring (Jan. 20): More than 550 injured at annual festival when wooden beams give way under crowd's weight at nation's largest arena at Sincelejo, 200 miles north of Bogotá.

124 Die in Air Crash Northeast of Teheran (Jan. 21): Killed as Iran Air Boeing 727 crashes near mountain village.

23 Coast Guardsmen Killed in Collision (Jan. 28): Coast Guard buoy tender *Blackthorn*, 180-foot cutter, sinks quickly in Tampa Bay, Fla., after crash with 605-foot tanker *Capricorn*. Collision rated worst peacetime disaster in Coast Guard history.

16 Dead in West Coast Storm Crisis (Feb. 19): California Gov. Edmund G. Brown, Jr., declares state of emergency in four counties after week-long storms cause extensive flooding and more than $100 million property damage. Homes destroyed and damaged by mud slides.

36 Dead as Snowstorms Sweep Southeast (March 3): Record low temperatures reported, with two feet of snow in North Carolina and Virginia and flurries as far south as central Florida. Record freeze strikes citrus crop and cripples major cities.

22 U.S. Team Members, Killed in Warsaw Plane Crash (March 14): 14 boxers and 8 officials of U.S. Amateur Athletic Union among 87 victims as Polish jetliner plummets to ground in attempting emergency landing. LOT Airlines Soviet-built Ilyushin 62 was on flight from New York carrying team scheduled to compete against Polish national team.

Volcano Erupts in Southwest Washington State (March 27): Mount St. Helens, dormant 123 years, spews clouds of steam and ash after week of earthquakes. More than 400 loggers, forest rangers, and others evacuated. **(May 19):** Volcano erupts again with 12-mile high drifting column of steam and pumice. Explosion was felt 100 miles away. Some 1300 feet blown off top of mountain. Major perils are drifting ash, forest fires, and flash floods. **(May 20):** Volcanic dust clouds sweep eastward across U.S., spreading fallout as far as 500 miles. **(May 21):** Earth plug formed by slide of dirt, volcanic rock, glacial ice, ash, and debris at outlet of Spirit Lake diminishes fear of catastrophic floods. Death toll estimated at 24, with scores missing. **(May 22):** President Carter flies over volcano. Declares region disaster area, eligible for special Federal aid. **(May 25):** Government officials estimate damage will exceed $1.5 billion. One hundred and 50 square miles of forest laid flat, thousands of miles of roads blocked or impeded, rivers clogged, fish and game killed, crops destroyed, and volcanic ash clouds thrown over cities of Northwest. Eruptions continue.

123 Dead in Capsizing of North Sea Platform (March 28): Helicopters and ships save nearly 100 survivors after one of five huge legs snaps on semisubmersible platform, reportedly from metal fatigue. Phillips Petroleum Co. used "floatel" as rest area for oil field employees.

Tornadoes Strike in 11 States; Four Dead; (April 8): Dozens in "family of storms" injure 100 and cause heavy damage in two-day assault on Arkansas, Illinois, Indiana, Kansas, Michigan, Mississippi, Missouri, Oklahoma, Tennessee, Texas, and Wisconsin. Twisters also reported in Kentucky and Ohio.

146 Britons Perish in Canary Islands Plane Crash (April 25): Chartered Boeing 727 rams mountain six minutes before it was due to land at Los Rodeos Airport outside Santa Cruz de Tenerife. Pilot had given no intimation of anything wrong.

35 Killed as Ship Collapses Bridge in Florida (May 9): Bus, several cars, and pickup truck plummet 140 feet from Sunshine Skyway Bridge into Tampa Bay. The 606-foot phosphate carrier Summit Venture collided with span in driving rainstorm with high winds.

F.A.A. Concludes Year-Long Investigation of DC-10 Airliner (May 17): Relaxes rigorous inspection schedules imposed following May 1979 crash fatal to 275 and requires minor modifications in plane's pylon, structure that attaches engine to wing.

Jamaica Fire Kills 157 Elderly Women (May 20): Sweeps through two-story wooden home for poor in Kingston. Fourteen others missing.

2 Earthquakes Hit California and Nevada (May 25): Set off landslides, buckle roadway, and sway buildings in Sacramento and Los Angeles. At least two persons injured.

Seven Tornadoes Kill 3 in Nebraska Town (June 3): At least 134 injured and more than 250 buildings destroyed in Grand Island.

12 Salvadorans and Smuggler Perish in Arizona Desert (July

5): Succumb to heat and thirst as party of about 30 tries to enter U.S. illegally from Mexico; rest survive. Four smugglers arrested on charges of illegally transporting aliens.

1,265 Dead in U.S. Heat Wave (July 21): Tropical disturbance brings first rain in weeks, giving some relief to Southwest and Middle West.

4,000 Flee as Toxic-Gas Cars Are Derailed in Kentucky (July 26): Four of nine tank cars on Illinois Central freight train catch fire near Fort Knox, and two explode. Residents in four-mile radius evacuated. Three crew members were only ones injured in derailment. Cars contained vinyl chloride, chlorine, acrylonitrile, and toluene, all used in manufacturing.

"Rare" Earthquake Jars 12 States (July 27): Shock centered in northern Kentucky shakes homes and buildings from Michigan to South Carolina and parts of Canada.

272 Known Dead as Hurricane Allen Fades (Aug. 11): Atlantic storm called second strongest of century disappears over Mexico after causing heavy damage in Caribbean Islands. Flooding widespread in Texas, where at least four drown.

281 Reported Dead in Saudi Airliner Crash (Aug. 19): Saudi Arabian Airlines Lockheed Tristar flying to Jidda, Saudi Arabia, goes up in flames after taking off from Riyadh.

Explosion Rocks Nuclear Missile Silo in Arkansas (Sept. 19): Twenty-two Air Force personnel injured, one fatally, as fuel blast shakes underground *Titan 2* structure at Damascus, Ark. Some 1,400 residents are temporarily evacuated. This is third fatal accident involving a missile since 1965. **(Sept. 21):** Military sources confirm that missile carrying a nuclear warhead landed within secured area of missile site. Warhead is described as unarmed. **(Sept. 22):** The Warhead, ejected from the *Titan 2* missile site explosion, is removed without incident and transported to Little Rock Air Force Base, Ark. The 6,000-pound warhead suffered some damage but no radiation leakage.

Education

1979

Judge to Head New Education Department (Oct. 29): Carter to nominate Shirley Mount Hufstedler of California, Federal Appeals Court judge. Judge Hufstedler known as liberal activist.

1980

Columbia University Names 17th President (Jan. 7): Michael I. Sovern, provost for previous year and a former dean of law school, chosen by trustees to succeed William J. McGill, who is leaving after 10 years as head of 17,900-student institution. Sovern, 48, is a specialist in labor relations and employment discrimination.

Saudi Arabia Giving Princeton $5 Million (March 3): University announces gift to expand teaching and research in life sciences. Princeton to help University of Riyadh develop own work in same field.

Court Overturns Massachusetts School-Prayer Law (March 13): Supreme Judicial Court rules six-week-old statute unconstitutional sponsorship of religion.

Anonymous Donor Gives Iowa College $18 Million (May 18): Buena Vista, small liberal arts institution at Storm Lake, gets endowment termed by its president largest per capita gift in history of American philanthropy. School must raise $9 million in matching funds.

Stanford University Selects New President (June 13): Chooses Donald Kennedy, biology researcher, teacher, and administrator, to succeed Richard W. Lyman, who is leaving to head Rockefeller Foundation. Kennedy has served two decades at Stanford, except for two years as national Commissioner of Food and Drugs.

U.S. Strengthens Guidelines for Bilingual Education (Aug. 5): New rules by Department of Education emphasize speedy teaching of English and special instruction for children deficient in English.

Energy

1979

Atomic Panel Calls for Change in Reactor Construction (Oct. 30): President's Commission on Accident at Three Mile Island (Pa.) March 28, 1979, demands fundamental revision in building, operation, and regulation to keep risks of nuclear power "within tolerable limits." Report finds no guarantee that there will be no serious future nuclear accidents. Does not advocate abandonment of nuclear power, but urges ban on new reactors until state and local emergency plans have been approved by U.S. Recommends new, single-head agency to replace Nuclear Regulatory Commission.

1980

Swedes Vote for Limited Increase in Atomic Power (March 23): Nonbinding referendum gives Government coalition of non-Socialist parties mandate to increase number of reactors from 6 to 12. Ballot is first of kind in a nation with advanced nuclear-energy program.

Vermont Bans Uranium Mining (April 14): Companies back down on prospecting plans following passage of bill to prohibit digging for radioactive mineral without approval of Legislature and Governor. Legislators had cited danger to health and farming.

U.S. to Send Atomic Fuel to India (May 7): President Carter decides to provide 40 tons of uranium reactor material although Indian Government refuses assurance that it will stop nuclear tests.

Congress Kills Carter's Oil-Import Fee (June 5): House, 335–34, overrides veto of resolution repealing fee imposed by President as budget-balancing and energy conservation measure. **(June 6):** Senate overrides by 68 to 10. First such setback to a President by Congress controlled by own party since Truman tried to block McCarran-Walter immigration bill in 1952. Congressmen had opposed 10-cent-a-gallon rise in domestic gasoline prices resulting from fee of $4.62 on each barrel of imported oil.

Carter Approves Nuclear Fuel for India (June 19): Backs shipment of 38 tons, reversing Nuclear Regulatory Commission. Deal opposed in Congress because India has refused to accept international safeguards on nuclear facilities.

Congress Votes Synthetic-Fuels Bill (June 26): Completes action on $20-billion program to create Federal corporation to speed distillation of crude oil from tar sands, oil shale, and coal. **(June 30):** President Carter signs measure, declaring "the keystone of our national energy policy is at last being put in place."

House, 232–131, Rejects Carter's Energy Board Plan (June 27): Unexpectedly dooms mobilization project, key element in program to cut oil imports. Liberals join Republicans in killing previously adopted measure.

Radioactive Krypton 85 Gas Vented at Three Mile Island (July 11): Technicians finish clearing damaged nuclear reactor after 13 days, half expected time. Radiation exposure termed no more than 4% of permissible level. Residents who had left homes in Middletown, Pa., area return.

Two U.S. Studies Exonerate Oil Companies in 1979 Shortage (July 17): Justice and Energy Departments blame loss of oil from Iran, declining domestic output, and Government pricing and allocation rules.

Maine Votes to Keep its Nuclear Plant Open (Sept. 23): Maine voters turn out in record numbers and reject by a substantial margin a special referendum to close its 840-megawatt Maine Yankee atomic power plant.

Entertainment and Culture

1979

U.S. Painting Brings Record $2.5 Million (Oct. 25): "Icebergs," long-lost masterpiece by Frederic Edwin Church, 19th century landscape artist, sold in New York for highest price ever paid at public sale for an American painting.

$240,000 Paid for Old Stamp "Cover" (Oct. 30): William Crowe, San Francisco philatelic dealer, buys envelope with three one-cent Benjamin Franklin stamps, each canceled by 1869 "running chicken" device hand-carved by John W. Hill, then Waterbury, Conn., postmaster. The record sum for a U.S. cover was paid at New York auction.

Long-Lost da Vinci Mural Reported Discovered (Nov. 1): Battle scene painted in 1505 believed to have been uncovered under a fresco on wall in Florence's Palazzo Vecchio. Test borings indicate pigment similar to that mixed by artist in two of most famous paintings.

Musical "Grease" Breaks Broadway Record (Dec. 8): Show plays 3,243rd performance at Royale Theater, breaking mark set by "Fiddler on the Roof." "Grease," American production, reported to have grossed $70 million, and it has returned $400,000 for every $10,000 invested.

Seiji Ozawa Leads Peking Orchestra (Dec. 28): Music director of Boston Symphony conducts Beethoven's Ninth Symphony in first performance of it in China in 19 years, given by Peking Central Philharmonic Orchestra before 1,800. Audience astounded by players and singers in Western-style suits or long evening gowns.

1980

Boston Pops Names Arthur Fiedler's Successor (Jan. 10): John Williams, Hollywood composer and conductor known for scores for such films as "Star Wars" and "Jaws," to head unit of Boston Symphony that became national institution under late Mr. Fiedler.

Kennedy Center Names Artistic Director (Feb. 26): Marta Casals Istomin to head programming in performing arts, excluding drama. She is an accomplished cellist; she was married to the late Pablo Casals. Her present husband is Eugene Istomin, the concert pianist.

Art and Antiques Sale Sets $18.9-Million Record (May 24): Garbisch Collection in Cambridge, Md., reaches peak for North America and is world's second most expensive. Exceeded only by $34-million Robert von Hirsch sale in London in 1978.

Crack in Church Wall Endangers "Last Supper" (June 16): Damaged masterpiece by Leonardo da Vinci, 481 years old, further threatened by six-feet long crevice detected in wall of Milan Church of Santa Maria delle Grazie.

Canada Gets a Disputed National Anthem (July 1): Governor General Edward R. Schreyer signs royal proclamation on nation's 113th birthday designating "O Canada" official national anthem. Differences on still-tentative lyrics stem from Canada's political, economic, and cultural divisions.

Two Foundations Save Harper's Magazine (July 9): Literary and political monthly, published for 130 years bought by John D. and Catherine MacArthur Foundation of Chicago and Atlantic Richfield Foundation. Owner, Minneapolis Star and Tribune Company, had announced end of publication, which had been losing at the rate of $1.5 million a year.

F.C.C. Rules Ease Restrictions on Cable TV (July 22): Drops limits on stations relayed from outside franchise areas and ends limits on broadcasting programs also presented by local stations. Cable industry thus almost completely deregulated.

Breakthrough in Nine-Week Screen Actors' Strike (Sept. 17): Their Guild and producers agree to formula for payment in pay-television. Under it, actors would get 4.5% of gross revenues from original programming for pay television after 10 exhibition days on every pay-television system within a year.

New York's Metropolitan Opera Cancels Its Season (Sept. 29): The Metropolitan Opera cancels its 1980–81 season as a result of a month-long labor dispute with musicians. Their union wants to cut work week from five performances to four.

Environment

1980

Interior Secretary Creates Wildlife Refuges in Alaska (Feb. 12): Order by Cecil D. Andrus bars for at least 20 years new oil, gas, and mineral development on 40 million acres, and continues Federal protection of wildlife.

U.S. Issues Rules on Disposal of Hazardous Waste (Feb. 26): Environmental Protection Agency announces new system for materials now virtually unregulated. Businesses that manufacture, transport, or dispose of dangerous chemicals will be required to notify the agency so that a national inventory can be created.

Vermonters Vote Ban on Mining of Uranium (March 4): All but two of 36 central hill towns where issue is on agenda accept argument that exploitation of radioactive ore might present health hazards outweighing economic benefits.

Dumping of Ore Wastes Into Lake Superior Ends (March 17): Reserve Mining Company complies with Federal judge's order to halt discharge of asbestos-laden tailings into world's largest fresh-water lake, ending protracted environmental and public-health dispute. Company had discharged 67,000 tons into lake daily for nearly 25 years. Land-disposal basin will receive wastes under $370-million program.

Mexico Stops World's Worst Oil Spill (March 24): Completes nine-month fight by capping well in Gulf of Mexico that had fouled beaches in southern Texas. Well, 50 miles offshore, had spilled more than 3.1 million barrels of crude since blowing up previous June 3.

Carter Orders Emergency Relief for Pollution Area (May 21): Government to pay for evacuation and temporary housing for 710 families at Love Canal region in Niagara Falls, N.Y., where chemical wastes are buried. Announcement comes four days after test results indicate some residents of area had suffered chromosome damage. Area has become symbol of nationwide problem of finding safe disposal sites for toxic wastes.

Auto Pollution Limits Postponed to 1984 (Sept. 17): Environmental Protection Agency moves to help domestic industry, bringing projected savings for industry to $600 million. Standards originally scheduled for 1983 model year.

House Approves Waste Clean-up Bill (Sept. 23): The House of Representatives votes 351 to 23 to pass a bill to create a $1.2-billion "super-fund" to clean up abandoned toxic waste sites. The bill enables the Federal Government to recover the money from the companies or individuals responsible for the abandoned site.

Health and Medicine

1979

"Laughing Gas" Linked to Diseases in Dental Workers (Oct. 24): Federally financed study finds they have significantly more kidney and liver disease, spontaneous miscarriages, and other serious health problems than those not exposed to nitrous oxide, anesthetic gas. No evidence found of long-term harm to patients.

1980

Court Halves $800,000 Cancer Malpractice Verdict (Feb. 8): Maryland judge rules total excessive for woman misdiagnosed by Dr. Lewis H. Dennis as having cancer. Patient, Helena Blanchfield, 48, had quit job and after five months of chemotherapy, found out that she did not have disease.

3 Studies Find Little Saccharin Link to Cancer (March 5): Contradict previous reports that artificial sweetener played significant role in increased cancer of bladder and urinary tract. Studies conducted by National Cancer Institute, Harvard School of Public Health, and American Health Foundation.

Panel Disagrees With Cholesterol Curbs (May 27): Food and Nutrition Board of National Research Council finds no reason for restriction by average healthy American, a sharp departure from recent dietary recommendations. **(May 31):** Government nutrition and health experts in several agencies challenge report as misleading. One says Americans should seek low-cholesterol diet at least until more evidence is available.

Makers of Tranquillizers Agree to Warning (July 10): Accede to F.D.A. request that physicians be told Valium, Librium, and other minor tranquilizers are not meant to relieve stress of "everyday life."

A.M.A. Eases Code for Doctors (July 22): Simple regulations, substituted for 10 principles of medical ethics, allow physicians to advertise and refer patients to chiropractors.

U.S. Approves Marijuana Use in Cancer Cases (Sept. 10): Sanctions plan for 4,000 specialists to prescribe synthetic marijuana pills to control nausea and vomiting in patients undergoing chemotherapy.

A Tampon Recalled by Manufacturer (Sept. 22): Procter & Gamble voluntarily acts to recall the Rely Tampon after Government studies conclude that its use apparently increases the risk of sometimes fatal toxic shock syndrome.

Experimental Hepatitis Vaccine Shows Great Promise (Sept. 28): An experimental vaccine against Hepatitis B has been shown to be almost totally effective, according to a study made by the New York Blood Center. The Food and Drug Administration will require additional studies before approving the vaccine for the market.

International Affairs

1979

Leading Chinese Dissident Sentenced (Oct. 16): Wei Jingsheng, 20, gets 15 years in jail after conviction for providing military secrets to a foreigner and engaging in counterrevolutionary activities. Mr. Wei had put up wallposter demanding Chinese democracy. **(Oct. 17):** U.S. State Dept. rebukes China over conviction for first time since establishment of diplomatic relations.

Judge Rules Against Carter on Ending Taiwan Treaty (Oct. 17): Federal court in Washington finds President could not terminate mutual defense pact without consent of Congress. Decision by Judge Oliver Gasch comes in lawsuit brought by Sen. Barry Goldwater, Arizona Republican, and other conservatives contending senatorial rights were denied.

Moshe Dayan Quits as Israeli Foreign Minister (Oct. 21): Resigns in disagreement with Prime Minister Menachem Begin's government on self-rule of Palestinians in occupied West Bank and Gaza Strip. Former Defense Minister, 64, had urged moderate stance toward Arabs.

6 Czechoslovakian Dissidents Convicted (Oct. 23): Prison terms of up to five years handed to human-rights activists accused of "subversion of republic." One is Vaclav Havel, playwright, 43, The six are members of Charter 77 human-rights movement. **(Oct. 24):** U.S. denounces Czechoslovakia for "unreasonably harsh sentences" for attempts to exercise "fundamental rights."

Palestine Guerrillas Doomed in Turkey (Oct. 24): Four terrorists condemned to death by military court for raid on Egyptian Embassy in which two Turkish guards were killed in previous July.

South Korean President Assassinated (Oct. 26): Park Chung Hee, 62, ruler for 18 years, slain by chief of Korean Central Intelligence Agency at dinner in a KCIA "safehouse" annex near Presidential Palace. Martial law declared. **(Oct. 28):** Government says the CIA director, Kim Jae Kyu, shot President because of conflict over policy and bitter quarrel with head of President's bodyguards. The bodyguard, Cha Chi Chol, also killed. U.S. sends aircraft carrier and radar warning planes to deter North Korea from taking military advantage. **(Nov. 7):** Investigation charges Kim planned coup. **(Dec. 13):** Security forces arrest Gen. Chung Seung Hwa, martial-law commander, and several other generals. Generals suspected of involvement in President's murder. **(Dec. 14):** Maj. Gen. Chon Too Hwan, security chief, moves to place his men in key government posts. **(Dec. 21):** Choi Kyu Hah takes office as South Korea's fourth president. Indicates shift to democratic rule will be delayed until 1981. Martial law continues.

Iranian Militants Seize U.S. Embassy and Hold Hostages (Nov. 4, 1979): Armed students capture building in Teheran and capture several score Americans employed there. Three others held in Foreign Ministry. Attackers vow to hold Embassy and hostages until deposed Shah, then living, is sent back from New York to face trial in Iran. **(Nov. 5):** U.S. State Department rejects demand that Shah be sent back. **(Nov. 14):** U.S. freezes all official Iranian assets in American banks and blocks Iran from convening U.N. Security Council meeting until all hostages have been freed. **(Nov. 19):** Militants release two black marines and woman secretary. **(Nov. 20):** Ten more hostages released, four women and six black men, leaving 50 held in Embassy and the three at Foreign Ministry. **(April 10, 1980):** Western European nations reject President Carter's appeal to impose economic sanctions against Iran or scale down or close embassies there. **(April 24):** Military effort to rescue hostages fails as three of eight rescue helicopters break down. Mission canceled three hours after task force of helicopters and C-130 transport planes carrying 90-man strike team lands in darkness in desert 250 miles southeast of Teheran. Carter announces eight servicemen were killed when helicopter and transport collided and warns Iran against retaliation for raid. **(April 27):** Charred bodies of those killed are displayed to reporters in U.S. Embassy compound in Teheran. Hostages scattered throughout Iran to balk further rescue attempts. **(July 11):** Richard I. Queen, 28, American consular officer, released because of illness after 250 days as hostage. Flies to Zurich, then home to U.S. Illness diagnosed as multiple sclerosis. **(Sept. 12):** Ayatollah Ruhollah Khomeini lists conditions for release of hostages, omitting demand for U.S. apology for actions in Iran. He wants the U.S. to turn over property of late Shah, cancel claims against Iran, unblock frozen assets, and promise not to intervene politically or militarily in Iran.

Hua Guafeng Tours West Europe (Nov. 6): Chinese Prime Minister leaves Rome after 23-day tour of France, West Germany, Britain, and Italy, first such visit by Chinese head of Government. Economic questions in forefront of discussions.

Fundamentalist Moslems Seize Grand Mosque (Nov. 20): Armed group takes over Islam's holiest shrine at Mecca during morning prayers. Many worshippers trapped, and two are killed. Attackers hold Mosque for two weeks until Saudi Arabia armed forces resume control. **(Jan. 9):** Sixty-three persons beheaded by sword for part in attack, traditional punishment for sacrilege under Islamic law. Forty-one were Saudis, 10 from Egypt, 6 from Southern Yemen, 3 from Kuwait, and one each from Yemen, Sudan, and Iraq. Government says 117 others died as result of siege. Security force's casualties put at 127 dead and 451 wounded.

2 Americans Killed as Pakistani Mob Storms U.S. Embassy (Nov. 21): Marine guard, Cpl. Steven J. Crowley, 19, of Selden, L.I., shot and Chief Warrant Officer Bryan Ellis burned as thousands set fire to embassy compound in Islamabad. Two Pakistani clerks also die. Pakistani helicopters rescue 90 others from roof after they are trapped in a vault for hours. Mob apparently inflamed by inaccurate broadcasts accusing U.S. of complicity in seizure of Great Mosque in Mecca. Other U.S. centers also attacked. Three hundred Americans evacuated.

Irishman, 31, Gets Life in Mountbatten Case (Nov. 23): Justice Ian Hamilton sentences Thomas McMahon of County Monaghan, found guilty by three-judge Dublin tribunal of murdering Earl Mountbatten of Burma Aug. 27 in explosion at sea. Codefendant, Francis McGirl, 24, of County Leitrim, acquitted on murder charge.

Common Market Rejects Britain's Plea for Aid (Nov. 30): Prime Minister Margaret Thatcher fails to persuade partners in European Economic Community to approve $2.2 billion cut in British net contribution in 1980–81.

NATO Approves Installation of U.S. Missiles (Dec. 12): Allies in Brussels meeting decide to accept medium-range nuclear weapons in Europe and to seek talks with Moscow on limiting such weapons. Dutch and Belgians had objected to program. They will delay their acceptance of new missiles.

Rhodesia Wins Independence as Zimbabwe, With Black Majority Rule (Dec. 12, 1979-April 18, 1980): White minority's rebellion against Britain ends as nation returns to legality under Crown. Patriotic Front guerrillas accept British cease-fire plan to end seven-year civil war. Robert Mugabe, leader of largest guerrilla army, wins election, taking 57 of 80 black seats, for absolute majority in Assembly, and becomes Prime Minister.

Four Americans Slain in Istanbul (Dec. 14): Military man and three aircraft company employees shot while returning home from work at Turkish NATO depot. American toll now seven dead in two years of violence; more than 2,400 Turks killed. **(Dec. 15):** Extreme left terrorist group, pro-Moscow Turkish People's Liberation Front-Marxist Leninist Armed Propaganda Union, claims responsibility for attack to expose "American imperialism."

Soviet Invasion of Afghanistan Stirs Protests (Dec. 27): Russian troops reported backing coup in which President Hafizullah Amin is ousted and executed, third Afghan president to be toppled and slain in 20 months. Afghan radio announces Babrak Karmal, former Deputy Prime Minister who had been living in exile in Eastern Europe, is new President and Secretary General of ruling People's Democratic Party. **(Dec. 29):** President Carter reports Soviet troops in Afghanistan now total 20,000 to 25,000. President, in special message, warns Soviet to withdraw forces or face "serious consequences" in relations with U.S. **(Jan. 4, 1980):** Carter announces punitive moves against Soviet, including curtailed grain shipments. **(Jan. 14):** U.N. General Assembly, 104–18, deplores assault and demands Soviet troop withdrawal. **(April 12):** U.S. Olympic Committee bows to President Carter's pressure and agrees to boycott Moscow Games scheduled for summer. President, warning of legal action, says nation does not want to be represented "in a host country that is invading and subjugating another nation." **(June 21):** Soviet announces partial troop withdrawal. **(June 23):** Leonid I. Brezhev, Soviet leader, says imperialist "interventionists" suffered "serious defeat" in Afghanistan; Moscow radio reports a division and 108 tanks being pulled out.

1980

Indira Gandhi Wins Landslide Victory in India (Jan. 6): Her faction of Congress Party assured of two-thirds majority in 542-seat Parliament as 200 million vote. Mrs. Gandhi, 62, who fell from power in 1977 after 20-month rule by decree, is elected in two constituencies and gains support of 20 independents or regional members. **(Jan. 14):** Prime Minister Gandhi and 14 Cabinet ministers sworn in. Most nominees are without national reputation and previous Cabinet experience. **(Jan. 15):** New Delhi special court dismisses two cases arising from her previous regime.

Soviet Arrests Dissident Andrei D. Sakharov (Jan. 22): Sends nuclear physicist and wife, Yelena Bonner, to internal exile in Gorki, industrial city closed to foreigners, because of "subversive activities." Strips nation's foremost rights advocate of title Hero of Socialist Labour and all other Soviet awards. Dr. Sakharov helped develop hydrogen bomb.

Finance Minister Wins Iran Election (Jan. 25): Abolhassan Bani-Sadr is landslide victor in first Presidential balloting. Says he will try to end crisis over Iran's holding of 50 hostages at U.S. Embassy.

Japanese Army Chief Resigns in Spy Inquiry (Jan. 28): Shigato Nakano, ground force chief of staff, quits and 10 other senior officers are disciplined. They take collective responsibility for breach of security in alleged spying by retired major general, Yukihisa Miyanaga, 59, involving Soviet network. The 11 officers were not involved in transfer of documents to Soviet military attaché.

Islamic Nations Censure Soviet and Iran (Jan. 29): Foreign ministers from 34 Moslem countries, meeting at Islamabad, Pakistan, condemn Soviet military intervention in Afghanistan as "a flagrant violation" of international law, and suspend Afghanistan's membership. Islamic Conference also rebukes Iranians for holding 50 American hostages at Teheran.

6 U.S. Embassy Aides Escape From Iran (Jan. 29): Flown out after three months of hiding in Canadian Embassy residences, using Canadian diplomatic passports with Iranian visas forged by CIA. As precaution, small Canadian Embassy staff is evacuated. Americans generally applaud Canada and Canadians for giving the six secret sanctuary.

Queen Juliana Yields Netherlands Throne (Jan. 31): Monarch announces she will abdicate April 30, her 71st birthday, in favor of eldest daughter, Princess Beatrix, 42. Queen's three decades have seen nation's rapid postwar industrial and commercial rebirth. **(April 30)**: Queen Beatrix invested as nation's sixth sovereign in musical and political pageantry in Amsterdam's Nieuwe Kerk. Outside, police skirmish with rioting squatters protesting poor housing.

39 Killed in Attack on Spanish Embassy (Jan. 31): Guatemalan peasants storm building at Guatemala City in protest over their military government, and Guatemalan security forces break in to free diplomats held hostage despite Spanish requests not to intervene. **(Feb. 1)**: Spain breaks relations with Guatemala.

Egypt Ends Participation in Arab Boycott of Israel (Feb. 6): Parliament cancels 1955 law that formally imposed economic sanctions against Israel and any companies dealing with it.

3 Convicted in Major West German War-Crimes Trial (Feb. 11); Cologne court finds former Nazi SS members guilty of complicity in deportation and murder of 50,000 Jews from occupied France. Herbert Hagen, 66, former Nazi police commander in Atlantic region of France, gets 12-year sentence. Kurt Lischka, 70, former chief of Nazi security police in France, gets 10 years, and Ernest Heinrichsohn, 59, SS functionary in Paris, gets six years.

Israel Opens Cairo Embassy, First in an Arab Country (Feb. 18): Unfurls blue-and-white flag from house in Cairo suburb as result of peace treaty with Egypt.

U.S. Vote at U.N. Stirs Controversy (March 1): U.S., in stiffening of policy, joins other 14 Security Council members in rebuking Israel for increasing settlements in Arab territories seized in 1967 war. Vote believed first by U.S. against Israel since settlement expansion began **(March 2)**: President Carter disavows vote. **(March 3)**: Secretary of State Cyrus R. Vance accepts responsibility for "failure of communications." Issue becomes major diplomatic and political embarrassment for Administration. **(March 6)**: In Jerusalem, Prime Minister Menachem Begin dismisses U.N. resolution as "not binding upon us" and says resettlements will continue. **(March 12)**: U.S. criticises Israel for seizing Jerusalem lands. Says expropriation of 1,000 Arab-owned acres for Jewish housing project could harm negotiations on Palestinian self-rule. **(March 20)**: Vance tells Senate committee he refuses to disavow many portions of disputed U.N. resolution. Says U.S. could have endorsed it without problem if references to Jerusalem and dismantling of settlements had been deleted. **(March 21)**: Vance tells House inquiry Carter disavowed U.S. vote because of concern over effect on negotiations for Palestinian self-rule.

Korean Colonel Executed in Murder of President Park Chung Hee (March 6): Pak Hung Ju dies before firing squad. Only serving military officer of six confessed killers, he could not appeal to Supreme Court. **(March 13)**: Gen. Chung Seung Hwa, former Army Chief of Staff and martial-law commander, sentenced to 10 years for alleged role in assassination plot.

First Recipient of Albert Einstein Peace Prize (March 13): Choice of Alva Myrdal, former Swedish ambassador to India and outstanding peace and disarmament advocate, for $50,000 award, announced at U.N. Mrs. Myrdal, 78, is wife of Gunnar Myrdal, Nobel prize-winning economist.

Terrorists Hold Hostages 61 Days in Bogota Embassy (Feb. 27): Armed urban guerrillas capture 80 persons in midday raid on diplomatic reception at Dominican Republic building, including Ambassador Diego C. Asencio of U.S. and 14 other diplomats. **(Feb. 28)**: Terrorists free 13 in exchange for food and supplies. **(March 17)**: Uruguayan ambassador breaks leg escaping in leap from second-story window. Venezuelan envoy suffers heart attack. **(April 27)**: Guerrillas flee to Havana with 12 hostages and release the rest.

Israeli Cabinet Votes Jewish Centers in Occupied Arab City (March 23): Begin's Government approves religious school, or yeshiva, and field school for historical study in Hebron on West Bank. Cabinet cites biblical tie to city and the right of Jews to live anywhere.

Shah Flies to Egypt; Spleen Removed (March 23): Boards chartered airliner in Panama 24 hours before Iran's revolutionary government was to present to Panamanian authorities formal request for extradition. Accepts invitation from President Anwar el-Sadat to live in Egypt, sixth country of refuge since Shah fled Iran early in 1979 at height of Islamic revolution. **(March 24)**: Shah arrives in Egypt. Islamic clerical groups in Iran call for nationwide demonstrations to protest flight. **(March 28)**: Deposed Iranian ruler in satisfactory condition after removal of spleen by team of foreign and Egyptian doctors headed by Dr. Michael E. DeBakey, Houston heart surgeon. **(April 9)**: Shah discharged from hospital and is reported recovered from splenectomy. Flies by helicopter to temporary residence at Kubbeh Palace.

Roman Catholic Prelate Slain in San Salvador (March 24): Archbishop Oscar Arnulfo Romero, 62, who had demanded equality and justice for poor, reportedly murdered by right-wing terrorists as he says mass. **(March 25)**: Leftist guerrillas set off 30 bomb explosions to protest killing. **(March 30)**: Fourteen are killed and 200 injured by explosions and gunfire during Archbishop's funeral on steps of Metropolitan Cathedral.

U.S. Breaks Ties With Iran (April 7): Expels Iranian diplomats and imposes formal embargo on American exports after Ayátollah Ruhollah Khomeini says hostages will remain in hands of militants at U.S. Embassy in Teheran. All entry visas held by Iranians outside U.S. declared null and void.

Thousands of Cubans Find Refuge in U.S. (April 6): Ten thousand jam grounds of Peruvian Embassy in Havana after President Fidel Castro proclaims freedom to leave Cuba if they get foreign visas. **(April 27)**: Wholesale exodus to U.S. under way by sea after regime suspends orderly airlift of exiles to Costa Rica. Thousands start 110-mile journey to Florida from Cuban port of Mariel on small boats provided by Cuban-Americans. **(June 8)**: As exodus dwindles, U.S. Coast Guard reports 112,-118 refugees have arrived from Cuba on 2,427 boats. More than 50,000 reported in Miami area, 5,000 resettled in other cities, and rest await processing at four camps. Hundreds await deportation as criminals. Task of helping new residents begins.

Carter and Sadat End "Constructive" Talks (April 9): In two days, they discuss Israeli settlements and other obstacles to agreement on Palestinian autonomy in West Bank and Gaza Strip. **(April 1)**: Egyptian President leaves for Cairo after condemning Israeli settlements in address to National Press Club.

India's Supreme Court Acquits Sanjay Gandhi and Associate (April 11): Reverses lower court verdict on charges of theft and destruction of film parodying his mother, Prime Minister Indira Gandhi.

President of Liberia Dies in Predawn Army Coup (April 12): Enlisted men, citing "rampant corruption," replace William R. Tolbert, Jr., with Master Sgt. Samuel K. Doe, 28, as head of military government. **(April 22)**: Firing squad executes 13 ministers and other top officials of deposed government as thousands of soldiers and civilians cheer. Military tribunal had convicted them of "high treason and rampant corruption. . . ."

Panel Accuses Argentina of Killing and Torturing Prisoners (April 18): International Human Rights Commission charges Government with "systematic torture and other cruel, inhuman, and degrading practices," and expresses concern about thousands of missing.

Lebanese Kill 2 Irish Soldiers of U.N. (April 18): Armed group also shoots third in reprisal for death of two Moslem youths in clash. Toll of U.N. dead now 41, six of them Irish soldiers.

Carter Attacks Iranians for Exhibiting Bodies (April 28): Accuses officials of violating "all principles of humanity and decency" in publicly exhibiting remains of eight servicemen who died in effort to rescue American hostages in Teheran. **(April 29)**: In news conference, President defends the mission and says U.S. will continue to take "whatever steps are necessary and feasible" to free hostages.

3 Gunmen Seize Iran's Embassy in London (April 30): Hold 19 hostages in demand for more rights for Arab minority in Iran. **(May 5)**: British commandos and police storm embassy and release hostages held 5½ days. Just before raid, two hostages were shot to death inside embassy. No hostages killed in raid. Three of five gunmen holding embassy killed, others captured.

Palestinians Kill 5 Jewish Settlers on West Bank (May 2): Terrorists armed with hand grenades and rifles attack group walking through Hebron, occupied Arab city, after Sabbath prayers. Seventeen wounded. Palestinian commando group in Damascus takes responsibility for attack. **(May 4)**: In retaliation, Israel deports two West Bank Palestinian mayors and an Islamic religious figure to Lebanon. **(May 8)**: With U.S. abstaining, other 14 U.N. Security Council members call on Israel to undo "illegal" deportation of Arab leaders. U.S. deputy chief delegate says measure lacks balance because it lacked reference to terrorist attack.

Tito Buried in Ceremony at Belgrade (May 8): World leaders honor dead President, Croatian peasant's son who created modern Yugoslavia. Among dignitaries are U.S. Vice President Walter F. Mondale, President Leonid I. Brezhnev of Soviet Union, Prime Ministers Hua Guofeng of China, Indira Gandhi of India, and Margaret Thatcher of Britain, and Chancellor Helmut Schmidt of West Germany.

Woman Official in Shah's Regime Executed (May 8): Iran firing squad kills Farrokhrou Parsa, former Education Minister, only woman in former Cabinet and first female member of Iran's Parliament, accused of embezzling Government money.

Quebec Voters Reject Separatist Proposal (May 20): Fifty-eight percent in referendum reject provincial government request for mandate to negotiate sovereignty and special relationship with rest of Canada. Balloting is heavy and peaceful. Majority of French-speaking Quebecers against proposal by nationalist Parti Québécois.

Israel Defense Minister Quits in Military-Budget Dispute (May 25): Ezer Weizman resigns in move taken as symptom of Government attempt to narrow political base, depriving Cabinet of relatively moderate voice. **(June 1)**: Prime Minister Menachem Begin agrees to continue as own Defense Minister, averting showdown on Weizman's successor.

Two Anglican Bishops Arrested in South Africa (May 26): Among 53 church figures, 20 of them ministers, held when armed policemen halt Johannesburg march protesting detention of fellow clergyman for supporting student boycott against school segregation. Marchers held overnight for arraignment on charges of infringing ban on unauthorized open-air gatherings, imposed after nationwide black rioting in 1976.

New Parliament Convenes in Iran (May 28): Revolutionary body hears President Abolhassan Bani-Sadr warn legislators must act swiftly to ease frustrations of people. Islamic clergy form dominant group.

China to Get U.S. Planes and Equipment (May 29): Pentagon announces it will permit sale of air-defense radar, helicopters, and transport aircraft, and authorize American companies to build electronic and helicopter factories in China.

Car Bombs Maim Two Palestinian Mayors (June 2): Injure executives of Nablus and Ramallah in occupied West Bank of Jordan. **(June 3)**: General strike grips West Bank and East Jerusalem in protest. Mayor and City Council of Bethlehem resign as Arab sections grow tense. Israelis investigate on assumption Jewish terrorists were responsible. **(June 5)**: U.N. Security Council, 14–0, criticizes Israel for failing to protect Arab lives. U.S. abstains; delegate condemns crime but complains that Council isolated single outrage.

Agreement Settles Common Market Crisis (June 2): Britain accepts compromise plan for resolving budget dispute threatening Western European economic alliance. Argument revolved about contributions to costs of European Economic Community and agricultural subsidies and trade. **(June 12)**: Nine-nation Venice conference ratifies accord.

Iran Conference Condemns U.S. and Soviet (June 5): Ends with declaration assailing U.S. for role during rule of Shah Riza Pahlevi, and criticizing Soviet intervention in Afghanistan. Delegates include 10 Americans led by former Attorney General Ramsey Clark, attending in defiance of President Carter's ban on travel to Iran.

Tribesmen Massacre Bengali Village in India (June 8): Indian

Army finds 350 bodies of victims slain by guns, spears, swords, scythes, and bows and arrows in village of Mandai. Attack called result of hatred between indigenous tribes and Hindu Bengali immigrants from West Bengal and Bangladesh.

Europeans Back Palestinian Self-Determination (June 13): Venice declaration by nine-nation Economic Community declares Palestinian Liberation Organization should be "associated with" negotiations for Middle East peace settlement.

Many Dead as Police and Demonstrators Clash in South Africa (June 17): Battles around Cape Town erupt into worst violence since year-long upheaval that began at Soweto in 1976 as police and demonstrators fight in mixed-race areas. **(June 18):** Police again fire on demonstrators. Prime Minister pledges to "act relentlessly" to halt stoning, looting, and arson stemming from two-month protest against segregated education. Death toll put as high as 42, although estimates differ; hundreds injured.

Seven-Nation Economic Conference at Venice (June 21): President Carter arrives after meeting with Pope at Vatican and confers with Chancellor Helmut Schmidt of West Germany. The two report agreement on plans of Atlantic alliance to modernize nuclear forces in Western Europe. **(June 23):** Conference ends with pledge by seven leaders of major industrial nations to develop sufficient alternative energy sources by 1990 and to cut oil consumption sharply while allowing economic growth to continue. They envision doubling of coal production and development of nuclear power and synthetic fuels. Carter says he now believes contacts between European and Soviet leaders can be beneficial.

Sanjay Gandhi, 33, Dead in Crash of Small Stunt Plane (June 23): Son of India's Prime Minister Indira Gandhi, her closest adviser and reported heir-apparent, killed with flight instructor at New Delhi in American-built Pitts S-2A biplane.

France Develops Prototype of Neutron Bomb (June 26): President Valéry Giscard d'Estaing announces tests of warhead and says nation will be ready in two or three years to decide on producing weapon that destroys living beings with radiation but avoids major structural damage.

Fighting Halts U.N. Relief Program in Cambodia (June 28): Two-day Vietnam incursion stops international effort to feed 1 million to 1.5 million in famine-stricken nation. A principal problem is flow of men, women, and children across Thai border in search of food.

Four Iranians Stoned to Death in Islamic Execution (July 3): Presiding judge of revolutionary court casts first stone at two men and two women buried up to chests. They had been convicted of sexual offenses.

Carter Honors Late Japanese Prime Minister (July 9): Visits Tokyo for memorial ceremony for Masayoshi Ohira. Confers with Prime Minister Hua Guofeng of China.

Firing Squads Execute 26 in Iran (July 14); General convicted of killings under Shah's rule is among victims, as are two Bahai sect members guilty of espionage. Others executed for sexual, narcotics, and similar offenses.

Armed Forces Stage Coup in Bolivia (July 17): Rebels seize Government Palace in La Paz and capture interim President Lydia Geiler Tejada and top aides in apparent move to block expected choice of leftist in coming ballot.

Iranian Ex-Prime Minister Unhurt in Assassination Attempt (July 18): Armed band raids home in Paris of Shahpur Bakhtiar, last Prime Minister to Shah and an opponent of current regime. Two persons killed and four wounded in attack. Three gunmen captured.

Former Turkish Prime Minister Assassinated (July 19): Nihat Erim, 68, who headed Government in 1971–72, slain by four leftist gunmen near summer home in an Istanbul suburb.

Conservative Named Speaker for Iranian Parliament (July 20): Ayatollah Hashemi Rafsanjani, Islamic clergyman, elected as legislative power passes from Revolutionary Council to Parliament, ending seven weeks of organizational activity.

Gunman Slays Former Syrian Prime Minister (July 21): Salah el-Bitar, 68, opponent of President Hafez al-Assad, assassinated as he is about to enter office of magazine he edited in Paris. Victim a co-founder of Baath Party.

Khomeini Foe Slain in Washington Suburb (July 22): Ali Akbar Tabatabai, press attaché in U.S. during Shah's regime, killed at Bethesda, Md., home by assailant dressed as a postal worker. Tabatabai, 49, was president of the Iran Freedom Foundation, nonprofit corporation dedicated to "secular democracy" in Iran. **(July 23):** Two arrested in killing, one a Washington mail carrier.

Thousands of Turkish Workers Protest Slaying (July 22): Kemal Turkler, head of powerful leftist Metalworkers' Union, assassinated in apparent retaliation for murder of Nihat Erim, former conservative Prime Minister. Right-wing terrorist group takes responsibility. **(July 23):** Thousands of workers in major cities walk off jobs to denounce killing.

Police Chief Is Choice as Iran's Premier (July 26): National official, Mostafa Mir-Salim, 33, a French-trained engineer, designated by President Abolhassan Bani-Sadr in compromise with Fundamentalist Islamic opponents. Mir-Salim, a member of Islamic Republican Party's central council, is regarded as relatively independent.

Deposed Shah of Iran Dead at 60 (July 27): After 18 months of exile, Mohammed Riza Pahlevi succumbs in Cairo military hospital to collapse of circulatory system. Washington statement makes no mention of Shah's nearly 40-year alliance with U.S. Teheran spokesman says, "For us, he has been dead for years." Iranians celebrate in streets. **(July 29):** Shah has elaborate military funeral in Cairo, honored by President Anwar el-Sadat of Egypt, only leader to support him in adversity. Former President Richard M. Nixon and deposed King Constantine of Greece only prominent foreign mourners.

Peru Installs Democratic Government (July 28): Twelve years of military rule ends with inauguration of President Fernando Belaúnde Terry for a five-year term. Rosalynn Carter represents U.S. Also present are democratically elected Presidents of Venezuela, Colombia, and Costa Rica, and Prime Minister Adolf Suárez of Spain.

New Hebrides Gets Full Independence (July 29): Britain and France end 74 years of joint rule of Pacific island group, now known as Vanuatu. Separatists control main town on Espiritu Santo Island.

Israel Affirms Jerusalem as Capital (July 30): Parliament, 69–15, approves bill criticized by Washington and Cairo. Israel annexed eastern, Arab section of city after capturing it from Jordan in 1967 war.

Hard-Liner Becomes Iran's Prime Minister (Aug. 10): President Abolhassan Bani-Sadr criticized in Parliament for wording of nomination of Mohammed Ali Rajai, 46, former mathematics teacher with little government experience, the choice of the Islamic Republican Party. President suggests nominee was foisted on him and is quoted as saying Rajai is incompetent and poorly informed. **(Aug. 11):** Nomination approved in secret Parliament ballot, 153–24.

Communal Rioting Flares in Indian Cities (Aug. 16): New arson attacks, sniper fire, and stabbings reported in northern city of Moradabad, where trouble has sparked Moslem-Hindu conflict in many widely separated areas.

Muskie Rebukes U.N. Security Council (Aug. 20): Secretary of State charges "unbalanced and unrealistic" resolutions damage peace prospects in Middle East. He abstains as council votes, 14–0, for removal of 11 remaining embassies from disputed city of Jerusalem.

Zimbabwe Prime Minister Visits U.S. (Aug. 27): Robert Mugabe tells congressmen of need for expanded help for nation to recover from 15 years of guerrilla warfare. In White House visit, he endorses President Carter for re-election.

U.S. Ambassador Unhurt in Beirut Attack (Aug. 28): John Gunther Dean, 54, career diplomat, ambushed with machine-gun fire by unknown assailant. He had objected to Israeli raid Aug. 19 against Palestinian targets in southern Lebanon.

Rights Group Asks Halt to Iranian Executions (Aug. 28): Amnesty International says at least 1,000 persons were executed in first 18 months of Islamic revolution.

Chinese Adopt Policy Emphasizing Profits and Local Control (Aug. 31): Reshape financial institutions to make profit incentive and local accountability for economic performance the forces behind economic growth. Banks will be run independently, state-owned factories and business will pay interest and taxes, and an income tax will be required for individual entrepreneurs.

Polish Workers End 18-Day Walkout (Sept. 1): Win expanded political and economic concessions from Communist government, including a pledge to restrain censorship and the opening of state-controlled media to a wide variety of opinion. Government recognizes right to form independent unions and to strike, a major change in Soviet-bloc policy. It freed dissidents who had supported protest. **(Sept. 3):** After agreeing to strike settlements, Edward Giereck is replaced as Poland's Communist leader. He is declared ill and hospitalized with a heart ailment. His replacement is Stanislaw Kania, 53, a party professional. **(Sept. 6):** Kania pledges party will honor strike agreement and calls outbreak "a protest not against the principles of socialism but against the mistakes of the party."

Army Officers Keep Power in South Korea (Aug. 27): Chun Doo Hwan, head of military group in control since May 17, endorsed by electoral college. **(Sept. 2):** Officers direct vital functions although President names 20-man cabinet consisting mostly of civilian specialists, including two American-trained ones in key posts.

Chinese Move to Strengthen Leadership (Sept. 7): Hua Guofeng resigns as Prime Minister and asks National Peoples Congress meeting in Peking to replace him with Zhao Ziyang, innovative former provincial party chief. Hua remains as Communist Party chairman. **(Sept. 10):** Congress formally elects Zhao. Appoints three new Deputy Prime Ministers in move to rejuventate aging leadership.

Commonwealth Parley Criticizes Soviet Union and Vietnam (Sept. 8): Five-day conference at New Delhi of Asian and Pacific members votes veiled condemnation of actions in Afghanistan and Cambodia.

Britain Withdraws Diplomats From Teheran Embassy (Sept. 9): Finds risk of their being taken hostage. Government begins to deport Iranian students arrested during violent demonstrations in August.

Syria and Libya Merge Into One State (Sept. 10): Fourteen-point proclamation, issued in Tripoli and Damascus, calls merger "a means of liberating Palestine." Invited other Arab nations to join.

Soviet Union Increasing Aid to Poland (Sept. 11): Agrees to increase delivery of food and goods after first meeting of two nations' leaders since nationwide Polish strike. **(Sept. 12):** President Carter praises "entire Polish nation" and approves $670 million worth of new credit guarantees for grain purchase by Poland.

Military Chiefs Seize Power in Turkish Coup (Sept. 12): After bloodless move, they pledge to wipe out growing extremist violence and restore political stability. Gen. Kenan Evren, 62, armed forces chief, announces formation of National Security Council to rule until new government is formed.

Ottawa Constitutional Conference a Failure (Sept. 13): Canadian Federal and provincial governments fail to agree on compact to replace existing British North America Act of 1867, the present "constitution," with document formulated and amended by Canadians.

Ousted Nicaragua Ruler Assassinated (Sept. 17): Anastasio Somozo Debayle and two aides killed by gunfire in Asuncion, Paraguay capital. Six-man Nicaraguan "hit squad" blamed. The 54-year-old Somoza fled Sandinist guerrillas in July 1979. Family ruled Nicaragua from 1936 until then.

Iraq Seizes 90 Square Miles in Iran (Sept. 19): In two weeks fighting on border, 10,000 Iraq troops take area Iraq considers its own, after canceling border agreement. **(Sept. 20):** Iran calls up several thousand reservists "to defend the integrity of the country" as fighting continues. **(Sept. 21):** Iraq reports forces destroyed five Iranian gunboats. Clashes reported all along 270-mile border.

Turkey Forms Civilian Cabinet (Sept. 21): New Prime Minister Bulent Ulusu, a retired admiral, announces the formation of a 26-member civilian cabinet. The cabinet includes 7 retired generals and 13 former government officials. The remainder are 4 professors, a labor union leader, a journalist, and an industrialist.

Iraq Attacks Iranian Airfields (Sept. 22): Iraqi jets strike 10 Iranian air bases, including Teheran's, as border conflict widens. The United States expresses concern that the hostilities could lead to further fragmentation of Iran and create increased opportunities for Soviet encrouchment in the Persian Gulf area. It is also feared that the hostilities will further delay a settlement of the hostage crisis.

Iraq and Iran Bomb Oil Installations (Sept. 23): Iraq troops invade Iran at several points and its air force bombs oil refinery at Abadan. Iranian planes strike Baghdad and other oil fields. In Washington, President Carter pledges neutrality in the Persian Gulf. The United Nations Security Council holds an emergency meeting to discuss the conflict, appealing to Iran and Iraq to cease fighting.

Gandhi Regime Gets Power to Jail Without Trial (Sept. 23): A new national security law goes into effect giving Prime Minister Gandhi's Government the power to imprison anyone for up to one year without trial. The new law raises fears of a return to detentions carried out by Mrs. Gandhi's 1975–77 emergency rule.

Iraq-Iran Conflict: Historical Background

A.D. 637 Iran (called Persia until 1935) defeated by Arab forces at battle of Qadisiyah. In 1980, President Saddam Hussein of Iraq charged that Iran's recent moves against Iraq are to "avenge Qadisiyah."

A.D. 680 Islam divides into two sects—Sunni and Shiite. Today, Iran is ruled by Shiites; Iraq and most Persian Gulf nations, by Sunni. 55% of Iraq's population is Shiite, and this large group resents Sunni power. Khomeini in 1979–80 urged Iraqi Shiites to overthrow their "satanic" government. Iraqi government sees Iranian government as threat.

1534 Iraq (called Mesopotamia until 1921) conquered by Ottoman Turks. Long enmity between Turkey and Iran extends to Iraqi area, too.

1932 Iraq becomes independent nation.

1934 Iraq appeals to League of Nations on border dispute with Iran.

1937 Border agreement signed. Iran was allowed to use Shatt al Arab waterway but not given a border down the middle.

1958 Iraqi monarchy overthrown.

1961 All shipping on Shatt al Arab stopped because of border disputes.

1968 Baath party takes control of Iraq.

1972 Iraq signs treaty of friendship with Soviet Union. By mid 1960s Iraq was receiving huge amounts of Soviet aid while Iran, under Shah, was pro-Western.

1975 Iran agrees to stop aiding Kurdish tribesmen, who inhabit the mountains of northern Iraq, in their rebellion against Iraqi domination, in exchange for boundary between the two countries being set in middle of Shatt al Arab. Iraq also dropped claim to Arabistan (known in Iran as Khuzistan), an oil-rich province of Iran.

1978 Iraq becomes less radical, executes 21 Communist Party members accused of pro-Soviet political activities.

1979 After fall of Shah, and Iranian disorders, Iraq reasserts power and reclaims disputed border territories.

1980 Armed fighting begins as dispute becomes more ideological, pitting secular Iraq's vision of pan-Arab leadership against the new religious government of Iran's vision of a pan-Islamic union—with the ultimate prize being control of the economically important Persian Gulf. For a more detailed background to the conflict, please see *The Cambridge History of Islam*, 2 volumes (1970), and *The Encyclopedia of Islam*, 4 volumes and supplement (1913–38; new edition, 1960–). The following periodicals, published quarterly, contain more current reports: *The Middle East Journal* (Washington, D.C., since 1947), and *The International Journal of Middle Eastern Studies* (Cambridge, since 1970).

Iraq Troops Push Deeper Into Iran (Sept. 24): Iraq forces seize a 10-mile strip of Iranian territory. Both sides bomb each other's oil installations. Iraq and Iran halt all oil shipments from Persian Gulf, taking about 2.7 million barrels of oil per day out of world market. President Carter says U.S. is discussing oil shipment contingency plans with other nations.

Iraq Troops Continue Advance, Cut Rail Line (Sept. 25): Iraq troops surround important oil port of Khurramshahr and cut rail link between southern oil cities and Iran.

Cuba Stops Boat Exodus (Sept. 26): The Cuban Government officially ends the boatlift that brought 125,000 refugees from Cuba to the United States.

Iraq Halts Oil Exports (Sept. 26): Iraq suspends all oil exports because it has none to ship. Iraq normally ships 3.3 million barrels a day. Its oil refineries have apparently suffered great damage from Iranian attacks.

Italian Coalition Government Resigns (Sept. 27): The three-party coalition Government of Prime Minister Francesco Cossiga resigns after a one-vote defeat over its economic proposals.

Pakistan's President Arrives in Iran for Peace Talks (Sept. 27): President Mohammad Zia ul-Haq of Pakistan arrives in Teheran, acting as a "good will" emissary of the 40-nation Islamic Conference which seeks to end the fighting in the Persian Gulf. Iran's Prime Minister says at a news conference that Iran would not accept mediation in the conflict with Iraq. **(Sept. 28):** President Mohammad Zia ul-Haq mission to Iran unsuccessful.

Bomb Explodes at Munich Oktoberfest (Sept. 27): A bomb explodes near an exit to the Oktoberfest, Munich, West Germany, as crowds are leaving. Twelve people are killed and 114 persons injured. **(Sept. 28):** Six members of the neo-Nazi Defense Sport Group are arrested on suspicion of placing the bomb. **(Sept. 29):** They are released for lack of sufficient evidence.

Iraq's Leader Asks For Peace Talks With Iran (Sept. 28): President Saddam Hussein of Iraq says that his country is ready to negotiate directly with Iran to settle their differences or through any third-party international body or organization that they respect. However, President Hussein again demands territorial concessions that Iran has constantly rejected. **(Sept. 29):** Iraq accepts UN Security Council's appeal for end of fighting and mediation if Iran will agree to a cease-fire. **(Sept. 30):** Ayatollah Khomeini rejects peace proposals; declares that "Iranians will fight against Iraq" to the end.

U.S. to Send Aircraft to Saudis (Sept. 30): The Carter Administration has decided to send four radar Awac (Airborne Warning and Control System) aircraft to Saudi Arabia to provide that country with an early warning system that it lacks.

National Government and Politics

1979

Carter Business Cleared on Campaign Funds (Oct. 16): Special Federal investigator, Paul J. Curran, reports after 7-month investigation "no evidence whatsoever" that profits of family's peanut business had been diverted to Carter's 1976 Presidential campaign. Curran, Republican New York lawyer, reports Gerald Rafshoon advertising agency, which extended credit to campaign, used no money from unknown sources.

Congress Votes $19 Billion for Synthetic Fuels (Nov. 9): In victory for Carter Administration, it gives final approval for setting up domestic synthetics industry to counter dependence on imported oil, and $1.35 billion in emergency heating aid for the poor. Measure includes $1 billion for solar energy and conservation programs.

1980

Carter Warns Soviet Against Persian Gulf Attack (Jan. 23): President's third State of the Union Message to Congress says U.S. will "use any means necessary, including force," to oppose Russian threat to Middle Eastern oil fields. Brands Soviet invasion of Afghanistan attempt "to consolidate a strategic position that poses a grave threat to free movement" of oil. Announces he will seek authority to resume Selective Service registration. **(Jan. 28):** President's budget holds the line on most nonmilitary programs, forecasts mild recess and high unemployment, and omits calls for tax cut. Sets record outlays of $616 billion, revenues of $600 billion, and deficit of $16 billion in 1981 fiscal year. **(Jan. 30):** Administration's Economic

Report to Congress offers gloomy outlook, with persistent inflation and lower growth over next two years. Report concedes officials are perplexed about many problems, including decline in productivity.

Carter Asks Draft Registration of Men and Women (Feb. 8): Proposes demonstration of "our resolve as a nation" to resist further Soviet aggression in Persian Gulf region. Says women would be drafted only for noncombat duty.

Federal Report Says J. Edgar Hoover Barred Klansmen's Trial (Feb. 17): Justice Dept. reveals late director of FBI blocked prosecution of four identified by agents as bombers who killed four black children at Birmingham, Ala., Baptist church in 1963. Report says Hoover called chance of successful prosecution "very remote." As a result, it was 14 years before there was a conviction in church murder. Justice Dept. also reports a suspect in bombing was hired later as an informer despite evidence that he had been involved in crime.

Vote Dooms Plan to Register Women for Draft (March 6): House Armed Services subcommittee rejects Carter proposal as unnecessary.

President Announces $13 Billion Federal Spending Cut (March 14): Carter outlines program of "pain" and "discipline" to curb soaring inflation rate by balancing budget in 1981. Orders immediate oil-import fee to raise gasoline prices 10 cents a gallon. Joins Federal Reserve Board in drastic move to curb consumer credit, including credit card restrictions.

Cyrus R. Vance Resigns as U.S. Secretary of State (April 28): Quits after "anguished debate" in own mind because of inability to support President Carter's decision to try to rescue hostages in Iran. President accepts his "correct decision." **(April 29):** President designates Senator Edmund S. Muskie, Maine Democrat, as successor. **(May 7):** Muskie confirmed by Senate, 94–2. In hearing by Foreign Relations Committee Muskie says U.S. must find out whether it is on "a direct collision course" with the Soviet Union that could result in nuclear war.

Edmund S. Muskie's Successor in Senate Named (May 8): Maine Governor Joseph E. Brennan appoints Federal District Judge George J. Mitchell, 46, to fill remaining 2½ years of term. Mitchell long active in Maine Democratic politics.

H.E.W. Gets New Name and New Functions (May 14): Department of Health, Education, and Welfare becomes Department of Health and Human Services following formation of new Department of Education. New D.H.H.S. consists of Public Health Service, including Food and Drug Administration; Social Security Administration, and Office of Human Development Services.

Rep. Charles C. Diggs, Jr., Resigns (June 3): Michigan Democrat, 57, senior black member of Congress, ends Congressional career of nearly 26 years after Supreme Court refuses to review his October 1978 conviction of mail fraud and falsifying Congressional payrolls.

Three Computer Errors Indicate Soviet Attack (June 3): U.S. strategic bomber crews alerted and missiles are prepared for firing after computer in North American Air Defense Command sets off false signals that Soviet nuclear attack is under way from submarines and Russian land bases. Error is second in seven months. **(June 7):** Same computer sends out another false signal of attack. Error detected within three minutes.

House Censures California Democrat (June 10): Votes to punish Representative Charles H. Wilson, 63, nine-term Congressman, for violating House rules in converting campaign funds to own use and taking money from man with direct interest in pending legislation. Wilson had been defeated in California primary.

Congress Votes Draft-Registration Bill (June 12): Senate, 58–34, approves $13.3 million for program to require 4 million young men to register at post offices. **(June 25):** House, 234–168, gives final approval. In Senate five members of Armed Services Committee warn that military conscription must be renewed if Army fails to get better-quality recruits. **(July 2):** President Carter orders that young men register for possible military conscription.

Billy Carter Settles Charges by U.S. (July 14): President's brother registers as agent of Libya and discloses receipt of $220,000 in payments from African nation. Does not admit or deny charges of violating Foreign Agents Registration Act.

Carter Sends New Marine Force to Indian Ocean (July 16): Orders assault force of 1,800 men and five amphibious warships to underscore U.S. military presence.

Draft Registration Ruled Unconstitutional (July 18): Three-judge Federal Court in Philadelphia cites exclusion of women and permanently enjoins Carter Administration from reviving enrollment of young men. **(July 19):** Supreme Court Justice William F. Brennan, Jr., delays order on Government's appeal and rules registration can begin. **(July 20):** Selective Service System proceeds with plans to register men born in 1960 and 1961. Thousands register despite protests at major-city post offices.

Billy Carter's Action Under Inquiry (July 22): White House discloses request to President's brother to arrange meeting with representative of Libya to ask aid in freeing U.S. hostages in Iran. **(Aug. 4):** President asserts brother had in no way influenced policy toward Libya. Reports to Senate panel investigating controversy over Billy. In news conference, President discusses relations with brother and reveals feeling he could not control brother's actions. **(Aug. 21):** Billy Carter tells Senate panel he had never been asked by Libya to try to influence U.S. policy and had never tried to do so. **(Sept. 5):** Special Senate subcommittee believes Justice Department investigators acted honorably in examining Billy's ties with Libya and his $220,000 loan from Libya, and feels Billy's registration as foreign agent was correct.

Announcement of Radar-Proof Aircraft Becomes Issue (Aug. 22): Defense Secretary Harold Brown discloses "a major technological advance" in Stealth project to develop plane that can evade detection. Secrecy of project in doubt. **(Sept. 9):** Controversy mounts after announcement is criticized in Congress and Reagan accuses Administration of damaging national security by "leaking" project. In Perth Amboy, N.J., speech, Carter denies harm to security and charges Reagan with "cheap politics" and "irresponsible behavior."

Congressional Conferees Kill Key Carter Urban Plan (Sept. 19): Dispute over public works spending dooms measure to provide Federal loans, loan guarantees, and interest subsidies to stimulate private investment in distressed areas.

Senate Approves Selling Atomic Fuel to India (Sept. 24): After seven hours of debate, the Senate votes 48 to 46 to sell 38 tons of enriched uranium to India giving Carter a major policy victory.

1980 Census Ruled Invalid (Sept. 25): Federal Judge, H.W. Gilmore of Detroit, rules that census undercounted blacks and Hispanic Americans, and orders the Government to revise figures upward for those groups throughout the country.

Tax Cut Bid Defeated (Sept. 25): Democrats defeat a Republican attempt to put before Senate a bill proposing $40 billion in tax relief for individuals and businesses next year. Democrats contend that tax cuts should not be considered in an election campaign atmosphere.

New Jersey Imposes Water Rationing (Sept. 27): Governor Byrne orders mandatory water rationing of 25% by users in 114 communities in Northern New Jersey as severe drought continues. Appeals for a concentrated effort to help preserve the dwindling supplies of water throughout the fall and winter.

People, Places, and Things

1979

75,000 March to Demand Homosexual Rights (Oct. 14): Crowd from throughout country parades in Washington to support rights legislation.

U.S. Surgeons Operate on Shah (Oct. 24): Mohammed Riza Pahlevi, deposed leader of Iran, undergoes 2½-hour operation at New York Hospital-Cornell Medical Center for removal of small gallstones and gall bladder. **(Oct. 25):** Doctors report Shah has advanced lymph node cancer and prescribe chemotherapy.

Sale of Bokassa's Homes to Aid U.N. Agency (Oct. 26): Bernard Tapie, 36, French businessman, persuades Jean-Bedel Bokassa, deposed Emperor of Central African Republic, to sell him his vast properties in France. Tapie is offering proceeds from resale, estimated at $10 to $12 million, to United Nations' Children's Fund.

Battle Over Igor Stravinsky's Estate Settled (Dec. 11): Filing of court papers signed in New York, Paris, and Switzerland ends eight-year dispute between composer's 92-year-old widow and children by first wife over estate estimated at $3.5 million.

Haig Gets United Technologies Post (Dec. 26): Corporation chooses retired general Alexander M. Haig, Jr., 55, President Nixon's chief of staff and recent supreme commander of NATO, as president and chief operating officer.

1980

"Born Free" Author Killed in Kenya Jungle (Jan. 3): Joy Adamson, Austrian, aged 69, who wrote of lioness she raised from a cub, found dead near remote camp where she had been studying leopard behavior. At first reported slain by a lion. **(Jan. 11):** Police believe she was murdered and hold three former employees for investigation.

Japanese Deport Paul McCartney on Marijuana Charge (Jan. 16): Thirty-seven-year-old former Beatles singer is arrested at New Tokyo International Airport on charge of smuggling eight ounces into country. **(Jan. 25):** Held 10 days, singer is deported. Tour by the group, Wings, canceled.

Japanese Prince Comes of Age in Ancient Ritual (Feb. 23): Hiro, elder son of Crown Prince Akihito and Crown Princess Michiko, marks 20th birthday in 8th-century court ceremony. He is destined to ascend throne as 126th emperor after father, now 46.

Howard Hughes's Dreamboat Going to Museum (March 6): Summa Corp. decides to donate huge wooden airplane called Spruce Goose, now a white elephant, to museum in either Long Beach, Calif., or San Diego. Aircraft was Hughes's World War II dream of creating military transport made almost entirely of wood.

Senator William Proxmire Apologizes to "Golden Fleece" Winner (March 24): In Senate remarks, he retracts statements about Dr. Donald R. Hutchinson in presenting "award" in 1975 for $500,000 study on aggression in monkeys. Scientist had taken $8-million case to Supreme Court. Proxmire must pay $10,000 of own money. Senate will pay $5,132 court costs. Cost to taxpayers of Proxmire's legal defense set at $124,351.

Most Valuable Stamp in World Auctioned (April 5): Magenta-colored British Guiana 1856 1-cent, one-of-a-kind variety, fetches $850,000, highest price ever paid for a postage stamp. Anonymous collector buys it as New York auction from Irwin R. Weinberg, Wilkes-Barre, Pa., dealer acting for a syndicate that paid $280,000 for the stamp 10 years previously.

British Peer and Vicars Arrested in Raid on Brothel (April 21): London court told that member of Irish Parliament was also among customers trapped by police in $55 establishment.

Margaret Truman Author of Mystery (April 24): Daughter of President Harry S. Truman insists "Murder in the White House" is pure fiction.

Posthumous Medal of Honor for Vietnam War Hero (May 16): Widow of Marine Col. Donald Gilbert Cook receives nation's highest award for bravery at Pentagon ceremony. Colonel Cook died in Vietcong prison. Described as heroic in refusing to give information, he is cited for "conspicuous gallantry and intrepidity at risk of life."

Sight and Hearing Return After Lightning Strikes (June 8): Edwin E. Robinson, 62, of Falmouth, Me., says he can see and hear again after having been struck during storm. He had worked as a long-haul truck driver until he lost faculties in 1971 highway accident.

High-School Band Gets Nixon-Era Uniforms (June 13): Thirty-one gaudy costumes designed for White House security guards go to Meridan-Cleghorn High School organization in Iowa for $10 each. Suits cost $200 each when made in 1970.

Britain Scraps Famous Warship (July 19): *Ark Royal*, fourth bearer of name in Royal Navy history, brings $1.8 million despite efforts to save ship since she was decommissioned in 1978.

Britain Hails Queen Mother on 80th Birthday (Aug. 4): Thousands press close to Elizabeth's palace in London celebration as military jets fly overhead and 21-gun salutes are fired.

Panda Born in Mexico City Zoo; Lives 8 Days (Aug. 12): First giant panda conceived in captivity outside China measures four inches long, weighs just over three ounces. Baby named Xeng-Li, Chinese for success. Conception credited to high altitude, special diet, and keeping parents in same area. **(Aug. 20):** Cub crushed to death by mother, weighing about 270 pounds.

White House Loses 30 Layers of Old Paint (Sept. 7): Workers strip sandstone surface in biggest renovation since Truman Administration.

Ex-Marine Wins Battle for Medal of Honor (Sept. 12): Anthony Casamento, now 59, former corporal, receives highest military badge of courage from President Carter at White House. Veteran had lobbied for medal for 38 years since being severely wounded in Battle of Guadacanal in World War II.

Religion

1979

Pope and Orthodox Ecumenical Patriarch Issue Joint Declaration (Nov. 30): John Paul II and Dimitrios I pledge in Istanbul to "hasten the day of full communion between the Catholic Church and the Orthodox Church." After talks and joint worship, leaders announce joint commission of prelates and theologians to discuss differences remaining after 10 centuries of separation.

Mormons Excommunicate ERA Supporter (Dec. 5): Church bans Sonia Johnson, 43, of Sterling, Va., because of her conflict with leaders over advocacy of equal rights amendment. A fifth-generation Mormon, she feels "betrayed" and will not recant her ERA support.

Vatican Censures Theologian for Liberal Views (Dec. 18): Bars Rev. Hans Küng, a Swiss, professor at University of Tübingen, Germany, from teaching, in move to uphold traditional doctrine. Theologian author of books and papers questioning age-old Roman Catholic tenets. **(April 10):** Küng accepts compromise settlement with university to allow him to remain on faculty without examining candidates for priesthood.

China Permits Public Consecration of Roman Catholic Bishop (Dec. 21): Ceremony for Michael Fu Tieshan at Nantang Cathedral, Peking, shows most open official tolerance toward religion since 1978 Constitution gave Chinese right to believe. Bishop elected by parishioners and induction is not recognized by Vatican.

1980

Poland's Catholics Win Battle with Communist Regime (Feb. 10): Resolve "Battle of Jasna Gora," church-state confrontation over expansion of bumpy road at foot of famous Paulite monastery in Czestochowa, Polish Catholics' holiest shrine. Church had charged 32-foot-wide underground pedestrian passage was too narrow to accommodate pilgrims. State authorities agree to abandon tunnel, close cross street during major pilgrimages, and install a traffic light.

102nd Archibishop of Canterbury Enthroned (March 25): Robert Runcie, war hero, seated as leader of world's 65 million Anglicans in nationally televised service at cathedral in Canterbury, England, attended by Prince Charles, four present and past prime ministers, and ecclesiastical dignitaries from around world.

Huge Crowds Cheer Pope in 10-Day Visit to Africa (May 2): Native dancers, honor guards, and officials greet John Paul II on arrival at Kinshasa, Zaire, on first leg of trip in which he urges Continent's 200 million Christians to participate more vigorously in political life of their countries. **(May 4):** At Kinshasa, seven women and two children are trampled to death and 72 persons are injured as 1.5 million crowd to get into mass celebrated by Pontiff in front of People's Palace. **(May 10):** Abidjan, Ivory Coast, is Pope's last stop before he returns to Rome. On short visit to Upper Volta, one of world's poorest countries, hundreds of thousands acclaim him and he appeals for aid for drought victims.

Vatican Seeks to End "Abuses" in Celebrating Mass (May 23): Ten-page order made public in Rome with approval of Pope John Paul II cites "manipulation of liturgical texts for social and political ends."

Pope Visits France and Is Critical of Church There (May 30): John Paul II, arriving in Paris for four-day trip, is greeted by thousands, by President and Mrs. Valéry d'Estaing, and by the Garde Républicaine. President praises his simplicity and humanity. In reply Pontiff issues what is regarded as rebuke to church in France, where its influence is declining. **(June 2):** Pope ends visit with speech to UNESCO delegates calling on world leaders to "save the family of man" from nuclear war.

Vatican Upholds Condemnation of Euthanasia (June 26): But declaration updating Roman Catholic views on "mercy killing" says individuals have right in some circumstances to reject burdensome life-support systems.

Thousands Acclaim Pope in 12-Day Visit to Brazil (June 30): John Paul II starts "religious and pastoral" visit, but emphasizes nation's social problems. **(July 9):** Three trampled to death and 30 are injured at Fortaleza when crowds storm entrance to soccer stadium to hear Pontiff. **(July 11):** He ends strenuous tour to nation of 120 million, largest Roman Catholic country, after meeting laity and clergy. He supports activist wing of Brazilian church in moves to help the poor, but stresses primacy of the gospel and creed of nonviolence.

Baptists of World Choose Leader (July 10): Rev. Gerhard Claas, West German minister, named general secretary of 30-million member Baptist World Alliance at Toronto convention.

First Woman Bishop in U.S. Named (July 17): Rev. Marjorie S. Matthews, 64, of Traverse City, Mich., a Ph.D., elected by United Methodist Church delegates at North Central regional conference in Dayton, Ohio.

Vatican Rules Married Anglican Priests Can Join Catholic Clergy (Aug. 20): National Conference of Catholic Bishops announces plan affecting persons who, "while wishing to retain some elements of Anglican tradition, fully accept Roman Catholic doctrines and the authority of the Pope and Bishops."

Pope Opens Synod On Family Issues (Sept. 26): Pope John Paul II, after opening a month-long synod of Roman Catholic bishops in Rome, reaffirms his opposition to divorce. He says that "Families must preserve fundamental values of the church."

Science

1979

Scientists Discover Anti-matter from Interstellar Space (Oct. 16): High-altitude balloon carrying ultrasensitive instruments detects stream of first such matter found outside a terrestrial laboratory. Discovery reported by Dr. Robert L. Golden and colleagues at New Mexico University under $5-million NASA program.

First Land Vehicle Breaks Sound Barrier (Dec. 18): Stan Barrett, movie stunt man, drives Budweiser Rocket 739.666 miles an hour at Edwards Air Force Base, Calif. Moves three-wheeled cart-shaped vehicle more than 600 mph with 48,000-hp main engine before cutting in 6,000 pounds of thrust from rocket engine of Sidewinder missile.

1980

Gene-Splicing Produces Natural Virus-Fighting Substance (Jan. 16): Scientists announce production of human interferon with promise of economical commercial use. Believe substance has potential for curing wide variety of virus diseases, including colds. Research carried out by Biogen, S.A., international concern based in Geneva, Switzerland.

Prints of First Accurate Gulf Stream Chart Found (Feb. 5): Scientist at Woods Hole Oceanographic Institution (Mass.) reports discovering original copies of chart prepared in 1769-70 by Benjamin Franklin to speed trans-Atlantic mails. Two of prints, believed lost for nearly 200 years, discovered in Bibliothèque Nationale in Paris and a third at Naval Library in London.

Unmanned Spacecraft Orbited to Study Solar Flares (Feb. 14): *Solar Max* (for Solar Maximum Mission) launched from Kennedy Space Center in Florida carrying seven scientific instruments to study violent eruptions near sun's surface. The 5,100-pound ship is first built to be repaired or retrieved by astronauts on planned space shuttle.

Total Eclipse of Sun Viewed Over Africa (Feb. 16): Teams of scientists study 48th phenomenon of 20th century as it begins over central Atlantic Ocean and darkens wide area. Moon's shadow obscures sun over Atlantic and heads east across Zaire, Tanzania, and Kenya and toward India at 1,200 miles an hour.

Simulated Dive Sets Record (April 2): Three volunteers at Duke University, Durham, N.C., emerge from pressure tank after 28-day test sets world mark simulating a dive to 2,132 feet beneath the sea. Test used novel mixture of breathing gases: helium and oxygen with only 10% nitrogen.

2 Soviet Astronauts Rendezvous with Space Station (April 9): Valery V. Ryumin, 40, civilian flight engineer, and his commander, Air Force Lieut. Col. Leonid I. Popov, 34, launched from Baikonur astrodrome near Leninsk in Soviet Kazakhstan. **(April 10):** They dock *Soyuz 34* space capsule with Salyut laboratory in earth orbit, first difficult phase of a mission in space exploration. Ryumin left Salyut eight months previously after record 175-day mission.

U.S. and Japan Reach 5-year Science Accord (May 1): President Carter and Prime Minister Masayoshi Ohira sign broad agreement for direct collaboration on basic research ranging from earthquake prediction to pest control. Pact a major innovation in international scientific cooperation.

Two Make First Balloon Trip Across Continent (May 12): Maxie L. Anderson, 45, of New Mexico, and son, Kris, 23, land on Gaspé Peninsula of Eastern Canada after four-day voyage from California, first nonstop transcontinental balloon flight.

19 Astronaut Candidates for Space Shuttle Selected (May 29): NASA picks two women, a black, and a Hispanic in second group for project. Agency now has 62 astronauts on flight status.

Soviet Bloc Astronauts Return From Orbiting Link-Up (June 3): Bertalan Farkas, 30, first Hungarian sent into space, and Soviet commander, Valery Kubasov, 45, land in Central Asia after flight May 26 to dock with *Salyut 6* orbiting station, fifth Soviet block Intercosmos mission. Salyut crew is left in space.

Scientists Discover Oldest Biological Cells (June 19): Analysis of fossil remains in ancient rocks of remote northwestern Australia pushes back date at which such relatively advanced forms of microbial life are known to have appeared. This now set at 3.5 billion years ago, about 1.2 billion years earlier than had been previously confirmed.

New Biochemical Test Traces Elephant's Ancestry to Woolly Mammoth (July 10): Reaction in rabbits to albumin solution injection from frozen carcass of prehistoric creature shows kinship conclusively, University of California researchers report. Test hailed as important exploratory tool in fossil genetics.

Soviet-Vietnam Space Team Returns to Earth (July 31): Commander Viktor Gorbatko, of Soviet Union, and Pham Tuan, of Vietnam, spend week in space after launching in sixth "international partnership" mission designed for political impact. They linked up with Soviet orbiting station *Salyut 6* and carried out medical-biological research projects.

Controllers Shut Off Mars-Orbiting Spacecraft (Aug. 7): Silence radio transmitter as *Viking 1* ends mission when it runs out of steering gas after four years exploring planet.

7-Foot Great White Shark Captured on Coast (Aug. 19): Marine biologists elated by good health of specimen put on display in huge tank at San Francisco's Steinhart Aquarium. It is first such shark to be kept alive in captivity.

Ancient Palace Unearthed in Israel (Aug. 22): Archeologists believe it was fortress of King David or King Solomon at Temple Mount, near site of Second Temple, built in sixth century B.C. Report evidence that ancient Israelites worshiped idols.

Scientists Report Transfer of Genes to Mice (Sept. 2): Three at Yale, Dr. Francis H. Ruddle, Dr. Jon Gordon, and Dr. George Scangos, conduct experiments with implications for genetic research. They believe genes from viruses that were successfully injected into newly fertilized mouse egg cells became permanently incorporated with tissues of the growing embryo, altering the animal's fundamental genetic composition.

15 Nations Sign Convention to Protect Marine Life in Antarctic (Sept. 20): Agreement reached in Australia clears way for dealing with mineral resources of continent. Submarine oil and gas deposits also at issue.

Sports

1979

Drugs Bring Ban on 7 Women Athletes (Oct. 25): International Amateur Athletic Federation announces East European track and field athletes, including year's fastest 1,500-meter runners, are barred from international competition until further notice for failing anabolic steroid tests in summer of 1979 at Balkan Games in Athens.

Nolan Ryan to Get $1 Million Record Yearly Salary (Nov. 15): Right-handed pitcher for California Angels, aged 32, agrees to play for Houston Astros and gets signing bonus and retirement payment.

Boxer Dead Five Days After Knockout (Nov. 28): Willie Classen succumbs to irreversible brain damage suffered in fight at New York's Felt Forum Nov. 23. Investigation raises questions about conduct of fight and extent of Classen's injuries in previous fight, Oct. 9 in London. **(Dec. 13):** New York State Athletic Commission halts professional fights pending new safety procedures, reacting to legislative investigation of Classen's death. **(Jan. 12):** New York lifts ban after several safeguards are put into effect, including neurological course for referees and cornermen.

1980

Fourth Boxing Fatality in Two Months (Jan. 18): Harlan Hoosier, 13, of Beauty, Ky., dies of brain concussion in Huntington, W. Va. Taken to hospital after winning all three matches in tournament at Lenore, W. Va.

New York Mets Sold for $21 Million (Jan. 24): Doubleday & Co., New York book publisher, buys controlling interest from Payson family. Price a record for a baseball club and twice what Yankees commanded six years previously. Mets to stay in New York.

Olympic Committee Heeds Carter's Call for Boycott (April 12): U.S. organization votes, 1,604–797, for nonparticipation in Moscow Games scheduled for summer. Action follows appeal by Vice President Walter F. Mondale citing Soviet invasion of Afghanistan.

Runner Captures Third Consecutive Boston Marathon Title (April 21): Bill Rodgers, 32, first in 56 years to do so, with time of 2 hours 12 minutes 11 seconds for 26-mile-385-yard course. Takes fourth crown over-all in field of 5,364 starters in 84th competition.

Former Jockey Guilty of Fixing Nine Races (May 19): Con Errico, 58, convicted in Brooklyn Federal Court of bribing riders at Aqueduct and Saratoga in 1974 and 1975. He had been implicated in testimony by José Amy, 26, jockey whose horses earned more than $2 million in preceding year. Amy also named other well-known jockeys, including Angel Cordero and Jacinto Vasquez, two-time winners of the Kentucky Derby, and Jorge Velasquez, one of top stakes-winning riders. All these jockeys denied the charges. **(June 18):** Errico sentenced to 10 years in prison and is fined $25,000.

Agreement Averts Major League Baseball Strike (May 23): Representatives of club owners and players defer further settlement of critical "free-agent" compensation issue until January. Joint committee to study question.

New Zealand Woman Breaks Atlantic Record (July 3): Dame Naomi James crosses to Newport, R.I., in 25 days 19 hours in *Kritter Lady,* 53-foot sloop, breaking previous woman's record by four days in Single-Handed Trans Atlantic Race.

Miss Goolagong Wins Wimbledon Championship (July 4): Evonne Goolagong Cawley, 28, of Australia, takes women's crown nine years after her first title. Beats longtime rival, Chris Evert Lloyd, for $45,000 first prize and traditional silver plate.

XXII Olympic Games Open With Moscow Sealed Off (July 19): Boycotted by United States, West Germany, Japan, and scores of other countries in protest against Soviet invasion of Afghanistan. Leonid I. Brezhnev opens games in ceremony guarded by thousands of uniformed soldiers and policemen. **(Aug. 3):** Olympic Games in Moscow close with denunciation of boycott by Lord Killanin, outgoing president of International Olympic Committee. Soviet Union scores high in athletic prowess and organizational ability, but fails to win hoped-for world political prestige.

State and Local Governments

1979

Birmingham, Ala., Gets First Black Mayor (Oct. 30): Richard Arrington, 45, educator, elected in city regarded 16 years earlier as most segregated big city in U.S. Ninety percent of whites voted for opponent, Frank Parsons, 38, white lawyer, and virtually all blacks for Arrington.

Woman Re-Elected San Francisco Mayor (Dec. 12): Dianne Feinstein only top office-holder to keep post in ballot that defeats district attorney, sheriff, and four of five county supervisors. She had been appointed by supervisors to complete term of slain George Moscone.

1980

Californians Turn Down Income Tax Slash (June 3): Vote overwhelmingly against Proposition 9, which would have cut state levy in half. Two years previously they had approved Proposition 13 for sharply reduced property taxes.

New York Gets "Toughest Handgun Law in Country" (June 13): Gov. Carey signs drastic measure to restrict plea bargaining and require minimum one-year prison terms for most convictions for carrying unlicensed loaded pistols in public places.

Chattanooga Deploys Black Civilian Patrols (July 25): Withdraws police from area of three nights of racial disorders, where seven police officers were shot from ambush.

Women

1979

First Woman Editor in Chief for Yale Daily News (Oct. 22): Anne Gardner Perkins, 20, a junior from Baltimore, heads distinguished 101-year-old college paper. Predecessors included Supreme Court Justice Potter Stewart.

1980

West Point Women Choose Combat Branches (Jan. 24): More than half of 62 first female graduates of Military Academy assigned at own request. Law bars them from specialities likely to involve close combat.

Woman Firefighter Gives Up Her Job (May 14): Linda Eaton quits in Iowa City, alleging harassment after she won a 16-month legal battle for right to breast-feed her baby at firehouse. Iowa Civil Rights Commission had found she was victim of sex discrimination. Department's only woman firefighter got back pay of $145, $2,000 in damages, and $26,000 in legal fees.

Women Employed by U.S. Win Sex Discrimination Case (May 20): Federal court in Washington awards $6 million in back pay and $10 million in increased future earnings to 324 bindery workers in Government Printing Office. Judge finds office paid women less than men for equal work.

First Women Graduate From Service Academies (May 21): Coast Guard commissions 14 women and 142 men at New London academy's 98th graduation ceremony. **(May 28):** U.S. Military Academy graduates 61 women in class of 809. At Naval Academy 55 women are part of graduating class of 938 midshipmen, and Air Force Academy graduates 97 women and 970 men.

All-Woman Class Graduates as Jersey Troopers (June 27): Thirty survivors of 104 who began grueling 20-week training at Sea Girt camp receive their police badges. Official says they helped state set national example for breaking "barriers of sexism."

Women's Second World Conference Held in Copenhagen (July 14): About 1,000 delegates from 118 countries gather at sessions of United Nations Decade for Women. Speakers report decline in status of women around world since first conference five years previously.

Woman Gets Place on AFL-CIO Executive Board (Aug. 21): Joyce Miller, president of Coalition of Labor Union Women, first of sex to serve on council since federation's formation 25 years previously.

Deaths in 1979–1980

Abrams, Harry N., 74: publisher of art books. Nov. 25, 1979.

Adamson, Joy, 69: conservationist in Africa was author of *Born Free,* story of Elsa the lioness. Jan. 3, 1980.

Ardrey, Robert, 71: author of books on anthropology and evolution of human behavior; also wrote screenplays. Jan. 14, 1980.

Barth, Alan, 73: author of books on civil liberties, former editorial writer for *Washington Post.* Nov. 20, 1979.

Barthes, Roland, 64: French writer and critic. March 25, 1980.

Bartlett, Dewey F., 59: former Republican Senator from Oklahoma. March 1, 1980.

Beaton, Cecil 76: British photographer and designer won film Oscars for *Gigi* and *My Fair Lady.* Jan. 18, 1980.

Bishop, Elizabeth, 68: Pulitzer Prize-winning poet. Oct. 6, 1979.

Blanchard, Paul, 87: writer and critic of Catholic Church. Jan. 27, 1980.

Blondell, Joan, 70: film actress appeared in *The Public Enemy, Gold Diggers of 1933, The Crowd Roars, Three Men on a Horse, The Champ.* Dec. 25, 1979.

Boulanger, Nadia, 92: French teacher of musical composition, whose pupils included Aaron Copland, Roy Harris, and Elliott Carter. Oct. 22, 1979.

Bowman, Lee, 64: screen and TV actor. Dec. 25, 1979.

Britton, Barbara, 59: stage and screen actress. Jan. 17, 1980.

Brown, Virgil, 102: Oklahoma bottler was credited with developing six-pack carton for beverages. Dec. 31, 1979.

Capp, Al, 70: cartoonist drew "L'il Abner" strip for 43 years. Nov. 5, 1979.

Cavanagh, Jerome P., 51: Mayor of Detroit 1962–70, served during 1967 race riot. Nov. 27, 1979.

Cavanaugh, Rev. John J., 80: ex-president of University of Notre Dame. Dec. 28, 1979.

Champion, Gower, 59: dancer, choreographer, and director worked on *Hello, Dolly!, Lend an Ear, Bye Bye Birdie, I Do! I Do!, and 42nd Street,* which opened the day he died. Aug. 25, 1980.

Clurman, Harold, 78: stage director, critic and author; founder of Group Theater. Sept. 9, 1980.

Cochran, Jacqueline, 74: first woman to fly faster than sound, set more than 200 records. Aug. 9, 1980.

Coughlin, Rev. Charles E., 88: "radio priest" of 1930s known for anti-New Deal and anti-Semitic sermons from Shrine of the Little Flower in Royal Oak, Mich. Oct. 27, 1979.

Cromwell, John, 91: actor, producer, and director on stage and screen. Sept. 26, 1979.

Davis, Benny, 84: wrote such hit songs as *Baby Face, Margie, Carolina Moon.* Dec. 20, 1979.

Dionne, Oliva, 76: father of Canadian quintuplets born in 1934. Nov. 15, 1979.

Douglas, William O., 81: Associate Justice of U.S. Supreme Court 1939–1975 served longest term in court's history. Jan. 19, 1980.

Douglas, Helen Gahagan, 79: stage and screen actress; as U.S. Representative from California, she lost to Nixon in bitter 1950 race for Senate; wife of Melvyn Douglas, the actor. June 28, 1980.

Donovan, Arthur, 89: boxing referee officiated at 14 heavyweight title bouts, a record. Sept. 1, 1980.

Dragonette, Jessica, 71(?): soprano started in radio in 1926 and appeared for 22 consecutive years, singing operetta and semi-classical music. March 18, 1980.

Durante, Jimmy, 86: entertainer and comedian for 60 years. Jan. 29, 1980.

Dvorak, Ann, 67: film actress appeared in *Scarface, The Crowd Roars.* Dec. 10, 1979.

Eisenhower, Mamie Doud, 83: widow of Dwight D. Eisenhower, 34th President of the United States. Nov. 1, 1979.

Farkas George, 78: founder of chain of Alexander's department stores. April 5, 1980.

Fields, Gracie, 81: British singer and comedienne. Sept. 27, 1979.

Focke, Heinrich, 88: German aviation pioneer was leading developer of the helicopter. Feb. 25, 1980.

Fitzsimmons, Freddie, 78: knuckleball pitcher with old New York Giants and Brooklyn Dodgers. Nov. 18, 1979.

Finletter, Thomas K., 86: Secretary of Air Force under Truman during Korean War. April 24, 1980.

Fogarty, Anne, 60: fashion designer known for young American look. Jan. 15, 1980.

Frank, Otto, 91: father of Anne, who wrote her famous diary while in a Nazi concentration camp. Aug. 19, 1980.

Fromm, Erich, 79: psychoanalyst and social philospher wrote *The Art of Loving.* March 18, 1980.

Gandhi, Sanjay, 33: son of Prime Minister Indira Gandhi of India and a leading member of Parliament. Killed in plane crash June 23, 1980.

Gardiner, Reginald, 77: character actor appeared on screen in *A Yank in the R.A.F., The Great Dictator, Mr. Hobbs Takes a Vacation.* July 7, 1980.

Guggenheim, Peggy, 81: amassed collection of modern art valued at $30 million. Dec. 23, 1979.

Halas, George, Jr., 54: president of Chicago Bears of National Football League. Dec. 16, 1979.

Harris, Jed, 79: Broadway producer put on *The Front Page, The Royal Family, Our Town, The Heiress.* Nov. 15, 1979.

Haymes, Dick, 61: singer in big-band era of 1940s; played in 35 films. March 28, 1980.

Hébert, F. Edward, 78: former Democratic Representative from Louisiana headed Armed Services Committee. Dec. 29, 1979.

Hitchcock, Alfred, 80: master of suspense films made *Foreign Correspondent, Lifeboat, Suspicion, Notorious, Strangers on a Train, Spellbound,* and *Psycho.* April 29, 1980.

Hollander, Louis, 87: co-founder and ex-vice president of Amalgamated Clothing Workers of America. Jan. 3, 1980.

Iturbi, José, 84: concert pianist also appeared in many movies. June 28, 1980.

Janssen, David, 49: actor appeared on films in *The Green Berets* and on TV in *The Fugitive, Harry O.,* and *Richard Diamond, Private Detective.* Feb. 13, 1980.

Jones, Howard Mumford, 88: historian of American culture won Pulitzer Prize in 1965 for *O Strange New World.* May 11, 1980.

Joseph, Dov, 80: a founder of State of Israel and Military Governor of besieged Jerusalem in 1948 Middle East war. Jan. 6, 1980.

Khama, Sir Seretse, 59: first President of Botswana, since 1966. July 13, 1980.

Kokoschka, Oskar, 93: Austrian artist was a leading figure in Expressionist movement. Feb. 22, 1980.

Kostelanetz, Andre, 78: conductor of classical and popular music. Jan. 14, 1980.

Kuter, Gen. Laurence S., 74: architect of U.S. Air Force and a planner of use of air power in World War II. Nov. 30, 1979.

Lauck, Chester, 78: played Lum in *Lum 'n' Abner* radio show from 1928 to 1952. Feb. 21, 1980.

Levenson, Sam, 68: high school teacher became entertainer and author. Aug. 27, 1980.

Longworth, Alice Roosevelt, 96: last surviving child of Theodore Roosevelt; leading figure in Washington 75 years. Feb. 20, 1980.

Lowenstein, Allard, 51: former Democratic Representative from New York led 1968 anti-Johnson campaign. Shot, March 14, 1980.

Mackey, Bernard, 70: guitarist and singer was member of original Ink Spots quartet. March 5, 1980.

Mantovani, Annunzio, 74: orchestra leader known for his soft, smooth string-oriented style. March 29, 1980.

Marquand, Richard (Rube), 90: National League lefthanded pitcher from 1908 to 1925; his 19 consecutive victories in 1912 with the New York Giants has never been broken. June 1, 1980.

Marx, Zeppo, 78: last of the Marx Brothers. Nov. 30, 1979.

Meany, George, 85: served as first president of AFL–CIO for 25 years. Jan. 10, 1980.

Milestone, Lewis, 84: directed such films as *All Quiet on the Western Front, The Front Page, Of Mice and Men,* and *Walk in the Sun.* Sept. 25, 1980.

Miller, Henry, 88: author of controversial *Tropic of Cancer, Tropic of Capricorn, Sexus, Plexus,* and *Nexus.* June 7, 1980.

Mohammed Reza Pahlavi, 60: deposed Shah of Iran, who ascended throne in 1941 and was overthrown in 1979. July 27, 1980.

Moroney, A.S. Mike, 77: Democratic Senator from Oklahoma 1951–69. Feb. 13, 1980.

Muñoz Marin, Luis, 82: first elected Governor of Puerto Rico served from 1948 to 1964. April 30, 1980.

Mussolini, Rachele, 89: widow of the Italian dictator. Oct. 30, 1979.

Narayan, Jaya Prakash, 76: colleague of Gandhi in fight for Indian independence. Oct. 8, 1979.

Nenni, Pietro, 88: Italian Socialist leader. Jan. 1, 1980.

Nielsen, Arthur Charles, 83: head of giant market-research concern devised TV-ratings system. June 1, 1980.

Oberon, Merle, 68: film actress appeared in *Wuthering Heights, The Private Life of Henry VIII, The Scarlet Pimpernel.* Nov. 23, 1979.

Owens, Jesse, 66: winner of four gold medals in track at 1936 Olympic Games in Berlin. March 31, 1980.

Perelman, S(idney) J(oseph), 75: humorist wrote *Acres and Pains, The Swiss Family Perelman, The Ill Tempered Clavichord, The Rising Gorge.* Oct. 17, 1979.

Park Chung Hee, 62: President of South Korea since 1961. Shot by chief of Korean Central Intelligence Agency Oct. 27, 1979.

Page, Joe, 62: star relief pitcher for New York Yankees from 1944 to 1950. April 21, 1980.

Porter, Katherine Anne, 90: Pulitzer Prize-winning novelist and short-story writer; author of *Pale Horse, Pale Rider,* and *Ship of Fools.* Sept. 18, 1980.

Powers, Lieut. Col. John A. (Shorty), 57: voice of the astronauts during space flights in 1960s. Jan. 1, 1980.

Reed, Stanley F., 95: served on U.S. Supreme Court from 1938 to 1957; lived longest of any Justice in Court's history. April 3, 1980.

Rhine, J.B., 84: psychologist was pioneer in extra sensory perception (ESP); headed Parapsychology Laboratory at Duke University. Feb. 20, 1980.

Rodgers, Richard, 77: composer of Broadway musicals including *Pal Joey, Oklahoma!, Carousel, South Pacific, The King and I, The Sound of Music.* Dec. 30, 1979.

Ronne, Finn, 80: Antarctic explorer was on nine expeditions to region. Jan. 12, 1980.

Roth, Lillian, 69: actress, singer, and author of her autobiography, *I'll Cry Tomorrow.* May 12, 1980.

Rovere, Richard H., 64: writer on American politics, columnist for *The New Yorker* magazine. Nov. 23, 1979.

Rukeyser, Muriel, 66: poet known for verse protesting inhumanity. Feb. 12, 1980.

Sartre, Jean-Paul, 74: existentialist philosopher and writer. April 15, 1980.

Schary, Dore, 74: former chief of production at M-G-M and R.K.O.; screenwriter and playwright was author of *Sunrise at Campobello* on Broadway. July 7, 1980.

Sellers, Peter, 54: British comedian played bumbling Inspector Clouseau in *Pink Panther* films. Also appeared in *I'm All Right, Jack, The Mouse That Roared, Being There.* July 24, 1980.

Seltzer, Louis B., 82: former editor of *The Cleveland Press.* March 2, 1980.

Sheen, Archbishop Fulton J., 84: Roman Catholic cleric conducted *Catholic Hour* on radio and *Life Is Worth Living* program on TV. Dec. 9, 1979.

Sherrill, Henry Knox, 89: Presiding Bishop of the Episcopal Church from 1946 to 1958. May 11, 1980.

Silverheels, Jay, 62: played Tonto in *The Lone Ranger* on TV. March 5, 1980.

Snow C(harles) P(ercy), 74: physicist, novelist, and playwright; wrote *Strangers and Brothers* series and *A Coat of Varnish.* July 1, 1980.

Somoza Debayle, Anastasio, 54: deposed president of Nicaragua; assassinated in Uruguay. Sept. 17, 1980.

Stevens, Dr. Marvin A. (Mal), 79: orthopedic surgeon coached football at Yale and N.Y.U. Dec. 6, 1979.

Stone, Milburn, 75: played Doc Adams for 20 years on *Gunsmoke* on TV. June 12, 1980.

Susskind, Walter, 66: former conductor of St. Louis Symphony and principal guest conductor of Cincinnati Symphony. March 25, 1980.

Tiomkin, Dimitri, 85: won Oscars for film scores for *High Noon, The High and the Mighty, The Alamo, The Old Man and the Sea.* Nov. 11, 1979.

Tito (Josip Broz), 87: leader of Yugoslavia since World War II. May 4, 1980.

Tobias, George, 78: character actor appeared in films in *Strawberry Blonde; My Sister, Eileen; Mildred Pierce; Stalag 17; Marjorie Morningstar;* played neighbor in *Bewitched* on TV. Feb. 28, 1980.

Tolbert, William R., Jr., 66: President of Liberia since 1971. Killed in coup April 12, 1980.

Tolstoy, Alexandra, 95: author and lecturer was last surviving child of Leo Tolstoy. Sept. 26, 1979.

Wright, James, 52: poet won Pulitzer Prize in 1972. March 25, 1980.

Yahya Khan, Agha Mohammad, 63: military leader of Pakistan from 1969 to 1971. Aug. 8, 1980.

Zanuck, Darryl F., 77: film producer turned out *The Snake Pit, The Razor's Edge, All About Eve, The Longest Day, Cleopatra, Patton.* Dec. 22, 1979.

The Year's Top Trivia

Sanford Teller

The 2,000-year-old Great Wall of China began to crumble in 1980. The damage to the wall wasn't caused by shoddy workmanship. The culprits were identified as farmers who were stealing stones from the Great Wall to build pigpens. According to the *Peking Daily*, some 35 miles of the 120 miles of the wall around the Peking region were damaged by the stone thieves.

The paper pointed out that farmers were taking such revolutionary slogans as "Use the Past to serve the present" and "Obtain materials locally" a bit too literally.

●

The government announced a major fringe benefit for seasoned coconut pickers in Northern Malaysia. Each picker who has been engaged in the profession for at least ten years will be given a monkey.

Of course, these aren't your ordinary run-of-the-mill simians. They've been trained to climb tall coconut trees and to harvest the big'n juicy fruits. And their productivity rate is double that of a human coconut picker.

What about those pickers who already have a monkey? Not to worry. The government is giving each of them a bicycle.

●

Maryland state Sen. Howard A. Denis lost his hard-fought battle to get rid of the state's official song, "Maryland, My Maryland." The Senate Constitution and Public Law Committee voted to defeat his bill—which would have stripped the song of its status.

Denis, a former New Yorker, objected to several lyrics, specifically those calling Abraham Lincoln a "despot" and Yankees "Northern scum." He noted that "it is probably" the only state song that advocates the overthrow of the government."

"Maryland, My Maryland" was written by James Ryder Randall, a supporter of the South, in 1861. But it wasn't adopted as the official state song until 1939.

One of the song's strongest advocates, Sen. Thomas V. Mike Miller, Jr., said: "That song is part of our heritage. And now, Denis, who comes from Brooklyn and carpetbagged his way into the state of Maryland, wants to change our history."

●

James Edwards, whose term as governor of South Carolina expired in January, went back to practicing his former occupation.

Prior to his election, Mr. Edwards was a dentist. He was, clearly, delighted to be involved with dentistry again. As he put it: "It's so satisfying to get my fingers back in the saliva!"

●

If you want to minimize the risk of infection, the next time you check into the hospital for surgery be sure to insist that the operation is performed by a surgeon who is female, young—and naked.

That's the conclusion of a report from Stockholm, published in the *Journal of Nordic Medical Associations*.

According to the magazine, naked people usually spread fewer germs than folks wearing clothing. And naked women, at the height of their fertility, will spread significantly fewer germs than birthday-suited men.

John Hamil, co-owner of the Elliott-Hamil Funeral Home in Abilene, Tex., had a bone to pick with the Southwestern Bell Telephone Company.

Hamil had asked for a listing in the Abilene Yellow Page phone directory—and he got one. But his establishment wasn't grouped with the city's other funeral homes. It ended up in another classification. Under "Frozen Food—Wholesale."

A phone company spokeswoman blamed the error on a faulty computer.

●

You can't accuse the U.S. armed forces of sex discrimination.

Early in the year, a couple of attractive servicewomen were officially reprimanded for posing in *Playboy*.

Then a Navy *man* found himself in hot water.

Jeffrey Bandy, a five-year Navy veteran, supplemented his income by moonlighting as a stripper at a nightclub, patronized mostly by women, in Fremont, Calif. His nocturnal activities earned him two demotions in less than a month. He was also ordered to stop stripping out of his Navy uniform.

Bandy's act consisted of going onstage, fully clad, and peeling his uniform off to a record of the Village People's hit song, "In the Navy." The Navy brass also objected to another aspect of Bandy's performance: He had his Good Conduct medal pinned to his shorts.

●

In a stirring demonstration of the good-neighbor policy, residents of Beaver, Okla., came to the aid of contestants in the cow chip toss at the San Diego State Fair.

Heavy rains in Southern California had permeated the local cow chips, making them too moist to get a proper grip on. The California chips were in such poor shape that state fair officials were about ready to substitute Frisbees for them. But the good folks in Beaver, home of the annual World Class Chip Toss, rolled up their sleeves and pitched in by shipping three sacks of dry cow chips to San Diego. They were marked "Fragile" and air expressed as "Meadow Muffins."

A grateful San Diego Fair spokesman, Bill Arbulo, sang the praises of the Oklahoma chips: "They are the best. Some people think the best ones are from Texas, but that's not true. The muffins from Oklahoma are much bigger than California ones. They are more of a challenge to throw."

●

If there's one state where authorities won't tolerate misappropriation of funds—or bananas—it's Maine.

John White, a kitchen worker at a state hospital in Augusta, was fired after being charged with eating a banana he allegedly swiped from a patient's tray.

White maintained that he was completely innocent. He swore that the banana was one he had brought from home. After a formal hearing, White was reinstated. As a spokesman for the State Employees Association noted: "The hearing officer said it wasn't proved beyond a reasonable doubt that he stole a state banana."

But another state employee wasn't as fortunate. He lost his job permanently—for eating one state French fry.

(More Triva follows the Index)

A Basic Guide to Economic Statistics

Jack M. Pompan

As the economy has become a regular and continuing concern for us all, terms which were once encountered only in economics courses or business forecasts now appear daily on the front pages of American newspapers. Yet how many of us really understand what is meant by real gross national product or consumer price index? What is an index of production? How is the rate of unemployment determined? This guide attempts to give a basic understanding of what these economic statistics mean and, perhaps more importantly, some idea of their limitations.

Gross National Product (GNP)

This most fundamental of all economic statistics is an effort, in essence, to answer the question "How's business?" for the country as a whole. It is called *Gross National Product* (GNP) and is the most important among a group of economic statistics measuring the rate of economic activity. Gross National Product is intended to measure the market value of all the goods and services currently produced in the United States.

If you were asked to devise a measure of total economic activity, you might be tempted to add together the sales of all businesses. That method would include the sale of an automobile tire when Firestone sold it to General Motors, add it in again when the car and tires were sold to the dealer, and once more when the dealer sold the car to the consumer. Gross National Product is calculated in a way designed to avoid repetitive inclusions.

Under the *basic* or *output* method of calculating GNP, we begin with the total amount the consumer spent in the marketplace—for durable goods, such as automobiles, and for nondurable goods, such as food and clothing—and for services. To this amount of personal consumption expenditures is added the amount spent not for consumption but for investment, including the investment by business in machinery, plants, and office buildings. Purchase of new residential property is also considered investment, even if the "investor" is going to occupy the house. While we now have totaled consumption and investment sales, all goods produced are not sold in the same period, and business inventories go up and down. We must, therefore, add the amount of change in business inventories to the sales totals.

Since we are attempting to determine a *national* measure of economic activity, we must adjust for the effect of transactions outside the country. If exports exceed imports, the excess must be added to what we have spent, since this excess represents additional production that we have not counted so far. On the other hand, if we have imported more than we have exported, our total consumption and investment expenditures include money spent for things produced in other nations. In that case, we must subtract this amount from our total.

The fourth major factor in determining Gross National Product is the total of expenditures by federal, state, and local government—the third economic group after consumers and business. Government expenditures must be added to consumption expenditures, investment, and net exports to arrive at the total GNP.

Some GNP Difficulties. When we set out to calculate GNP, important practical difficulties are encountered. Because houses serve their buyers over a very long period of time, a serious distortion would result if the entire expenditure by the consumer on the home were included when the house was purchased. To cope with this problem, the designers of the GNP system decided to consider purchase of houses as a business investment rather than as a consumer expenditure. To round out this picture, the system considers that the homeowner in effect "rents" the home to the consumer—even if he is both the owner and the occupier. A rental value is imputed or artificially assigned and calculated for owner-occupied homes and included in consumer expenditures.

The concept of Gross National Product is based on market valuation, but it is impossible to apply this approach to government expenditures—federal, state, and local. When the government buys a ream of paper it is, of course, acting as a consumer and these expenditures could be considered in the same manner as consumer expenditures. However, this is not true with respect to the substantial sums spent on government employees since they are outside the market economy.

The GNP system assumes that the market value of a government service is the amount spent on the service. Thus, government expenditures are included in GNP directly. This, of course, creates the somewhat odd situation where the addition of staff to a government payroll increases Gross National Product regardless of what the staff is doing—not a completely satisfactory solution.

GNP is a measure of economic activity, not of the quality of life or of the standard of living. It does not attempt to evaluate the relative usefulness of various economic activities but uses the valuation of the marketplace. It does not adjust for pollution, traffic jams, or the peace of mind or state of health of the American people. Since it measures market value, it does not attempt to place a value on those important activities which take place outside the market economy, such as housework, home gardening, or voluntary activities.

"National" clearly defines that we are talking about results of the United States, and "Product" indicates that we are measuring production in the economic sense including goods and services, but what does "Gross" mean? It means that the decrease in the value of plant, equipment, and other long-term assets due to wear and tear and the passage of time (what economists call "capital consumption allowances" and what accountants call "depreciation") are not subtracted as they are in the case of *net* national product.

Real GNP and the Deflator. Since the Gross National Product is measured in dollars, it is affected by inflation. If prices go up, the Gross National Product increases even if the amount of economic activity is the same. It was, therefore, important to develop a measure of economic activity unaffected by price changes. To do this, the statisticians establish a base year (currently 1967) and adjust the amount of each segment of the Gross National Product to what it would have been if the prices of the base year had applied. This establishes what is referred to as *"real"* GNP (measured in 1967 dollars) as opposed to the market value GNP, which is referred to as *"nominal." Real* GNP is the single most important economic statistic and changes in real GNP are carefully monitored by economic forecasters and politicians.

The ratio between *nominal GNP* and *real GNP* is called the *implicit GNP deflator* and is viewed by most economists as the best single measure of inflation since it indicates the rate of price change as it affects the economy as a whole.

FRB Index of Industrial Production

In addition to GNP, there are many other measures of economic activity. One of the most important is the *Index of Industrial Production*, published monthly by the Board of Governors of the Federal Reserve System—sometimes called the Federal Reserve Index of Industrial Production.

An index is a method of expressing the relationship between a factor measured in one period and a similar measurement made in a base period. When the index number is prepared, the base period is expressed as 100. The Federal Reserve Board Index measures changes in the physical output of manufacturers, miners, and operators of electric and gas utilities. The index is broken down into four major market segments: consumer goods, business and defense equipment, intermediate products, and materials. Production indexes are calculated for each of these segments and further detailed groups.

Since an index must have a base period, it is important to remember that the measurement is in terms of that base period and *not* in terms of the previous year. For example, the 1978 Federal Reserve Board Index of Production was 145.2 (1967 base year equal to 100). In July 1979 it was 152.1 or 6.9% higher than the 145.2 of the year before. This does not, however, mean a 6.9% increase, but rather an increase of 6.9% of the 1968 level of production. To determine the percentage increase between the years, it is necessary to divide the 1979 index by the 1978 index—152.1 divided by 145.2 yields 104.7%, indicating a 4.7% increase. These relationships are true of all indexes.

The FRB Index covers industries that produce approximately 35% of the value of GNP output in the United States. Since it is concerned with production and not with sales, it is useful in discerning imbalances between manufacturing and sales in given groups of industries.

Rate of Unemployment

It is a serious personal problem and perhaps a tragedy when a person is unable to find work. When this situation is multiplied many times over, the society is faced with major concerns. Because of our concern about our neighbors and ourselves, we look carefully at the report of unemployment. The *rate of unemployment* as reported is intended to reflect the percentage of the people actively in the labor force who are unemployed, *not* a percentage of the total population. It is important, therefore, to understand the definition of work force.

The work force includes all individuals actively looking for work, even if on temporary layoff, plus those who are actively working, including self-employed. Generally, personnel in the armed forces of the United States are excluded from both sets of statistics.

The basic source of this data is work done by the Census Bureau for the Bureau of Labor Statistics. Each month the Census Bureau interviews about 50,000 householders on a controlled sample basis. They ask what each member of the household was doing most of last week—working, keeping house, going to school, or something else. A person is counted as employed if he did any work for pay during that past week, whether it be full-time, part-time, or temporary. An individual who did not work in the last week is asked whether or not he or she had a job from which he or she was temporarily absent or on layoff and, if not, is asked whether he or she has looked for work during the last four weeks and what he or she has been doing to find employment. If the interviewer is satisfied by the householder's reply, then the individual is counted among the people who are actively seeking employment.

This monthly survey compiles data on the size of the work force, the number employed, and the number unemployed, and does this for regions and segments of the population, such as male and female, blacks, teenagers, etc. The resultant statistics are generally reported in the press only in terms of unemployment *rate*. In fact, the United States has enjoyed a spectacular growth in number of employed in recent years—a circumstance which has been largely unnoted in the general press.

Some Problems of Measuring Unemployment. The method of determining unemployment has been criticized for leaving out of the work force those unemployed people who are so discouraged that they no longer actively seek employment. On the other hand, it has also been criticized for counting as unemployed those who report that they have actively sought employment and, in fact, have not or have done so only casually.

And even if this process were to function perfectly, the resulting index of unemployment would not measure the number of people who are underemployed; that is, earning substantially less than they would earn if they were working at their occupations for a full work week, or those who are employed at jobs substantially below their skill levels. The measurement of employment is subject to some statistical uncertainties, and a commission has made a series of recommendations for a major overhaul in this system.

In addition to the survey we have described, an additional survey based on a sampling of employing establishments compiles an independent number of total employed. Since these are data recorded by establishments, there is no indication of the number of people in the total work force. There are, however, from time to time, important discrepancies between the results of the two studies as to the number of employed in the United States, and this second group of data receives little attention.

Unemployment data are based on a statistical sampling method and achieve a high degree of accuracy for the United States as a whole, but not for a smaller measuring unit, such as a city. As a result, fluctuations in data for smaller cities are frequently the result of statistical quirks.

Consumer Price Index (CPI)

Of all economic statistics, the ones guaranteed to grab headlines today are those concerned with inflation—particularly the *Consumer Price Index*, prepared by the U.S. Department of Labor. To calculate this index, a theoretical market basket of goods and services purchased by urban wage earners is priced each month on a comparative basis for various locations throughout the United States. The specific items involved in the index are changed from time to time to reflect changes in consumer living standards and tastes. The price of each of the items in the index is weighted by a factor intended to reflect the average wage earner's purchases of the item.

Complications of the CPI. The task of constructing this index is difficult. An automobile purchased in 1981 is not the same kind of automobile as one purchased in 1971. How are these products made comparable? New products also present complications. Desk calculators, for example, are available today for less than $100 that will perform more than the functions performed by one costing several thousand dollars fifteen years ago and do it quieter and faster. The statisticians of the Department of Labor attempt to adjust for such variations.

Another major complication arises because of the use of fixed weights, that is, the market basket is presumed to be constant. In fact, if the price of a particular commodity rises with respect to others, consumers purchase less of it. If steak gets too expensive, people buy more chicken. The fixed weights of the CPI do not cope with this "law of substitution."

There are other factors that are included in the CPI in the aggregate, such as mortgage rate interests, which do not affect all or even a majority of consumers who will not incur new mortgages this year but will continue to pay on the existing mortgages at the original rate of interest.

CPI and the PCE Deflator. For these reasons many economists believe that the Consumer Price Index, in spite of the fact that it is so frequently referred to by the press, is really not an appropriate index of inflation as it affects individuals. The index that does this best is called the *implicit price deflator for Personal Consumption Expenditures.*

An implicit price deflator is the ratio between a group of expenditures expressed in current dollars and those expenditures expressed in dollars of an earlier period. Current Personal Consumption Expenditures are adjusted by applying an appropriate price index to each segment of expenditures. This expresses the item currently consumed in terms of the earlier price level. The ratio between current expenditures and the price adjusted expenditures is the implicit price deflator for Personal Consumption Expenditures. Since it starts with the expenditures people are making currently, the implicit price deflator for PCE inherently adjusts for changes that people have made in spending as the relative prices of certain commodities have increased.

These differences are often not just technical and certainly not just of interest to economists. In the first quarter of 1980, the CPI increased at a rate of 16.9% annually while the PCE deflator increased at 12.5%. Among the reasons for this 4% spread was the fact that oil and gas have a smaller weight in the PCE deflator because people have been spending less of their incomes for these items. Home ownership costs and space rental costs are also more highly weighted than actual consumption expenditures in the first quarter of 1980.

Interestingly, the existence of the Consumer Price Index itself may be an inflationary factor, since many union contracts are tied to the increase in the CPI, as is automatic escalation of Social Security payments. If inflation is being overstated by the CPI, then the wage rates being given to adjust for the CPI increase are actually higher than necessary and are adding fuel to the inflationary fire.

CPI Revisions. Even in times in which prices and consumption patterns are not changing rapidly, consumption patterns change over time, and this requires periodic revisions of the market basket for a price index.

The CPI was originally designed as an index for urban wage earners and clerical workers, a limited group. Therefore, beginning in January 1978, two indexes were established: one for all wage earners and clerical workers, revised, called *CPI-W*, and a new index intended to cover all urban consumers, *CPI-U*, designed to cover a broader range of consumers. No significant differences have arisen between the indexes so far, but only time will tell whether this change was significant.

Leading Economic Indicators

An index originally developed not by the government but a private institution, the National Bureau of Economic Research, often makes front-page news. It is called the *Index of Leading Economic Indicators*. The National Bureau researched the nature and prediction of business cycles and identified certain economic statistics or indexes which tend to move up or down in advance of the movement of the economy as a whole. These are called "*leading* indicators" compared to the indicators that move with the economy—*coincident* indicators—and those that follow the movements of the general business cycle or "*lagging* indicators."

The index of leading indicators is based on the following factors: the average work week in manufacturing, contracts for new plant and equipment, building permits issued for private housing starts, new business formations, changes in business inventories, changes in prices of raw materials used in industry, common stock prices, monetary aggregates expressed in constant dollars, reports of late deliveries, the rate of layoffs in manufacturing (inverted), and the volume of new orders for consumer goods.

The *Index of Leading Economic Indicators* did not work well in anticipating the 1974–75 recession, and later analysis indicated that several of the factors used, such as corporate profits and changes in consumer debt were confused by rapid increase in prices. The current list is a revision made in 1975 that was intended to eliminate the distortion of the index by inflation. Indexes are prepared for each of the items involved and they are then weighted together. The Index of Leading Economic Indicators has turned *down* on the average about nine months before a recession period, and it has turned *up* about four months ahead of the start of an expansion phase. However, the variations in times are substantial and sometimes give off false signals.

These comments have only been, of course, the briefest of introduction to the most important economic statistics. Most of these statistics and many more are available in publications of the government such as *Survey of Current Business* and the biennial edition of *Business Statistics* and *Business Conditions Digest* (U.S. Government Printing Office).

As we have seen, the job of collecting meaningful, effective economic statistics is not an easy one and must continually accommodate the developing nature of the economy. We have evolved, in the years since the Great Depression, enormously complex and sophisticated machinery for collecting economic data. We have dealt here only with the most commonly reported economic statistics. The measurement of an economy as large and complex as that of the United States cannot be reduced to two or three numbers, and while the headlines at the moment may be limited to that kind of data, understanding what is happening requires understanding what all these numbers are all about.

Consumer Price Indexes

(1967 = 100)

Year	Commodities	Services	Housing	All items	Percent change[1]	Year	Commodities	Services	Housing	All items	Percent change[1]
1940	40.6	43.6	52.4	42.0	1.0	1965	95.7	92.2	94.9	94.5	1.7
1945	56.3	48.2	59.1	53.9	2.3	1970	113.5	121.6	118.9	116.3	5.9
1950	78.8	58.7	72.8	72.1	1.0	1975	158.4	166.6	166.8	161.2	8.9
1955	85.1	70.9	82.3	80.2	−0.4	1978	187.1	210.9	202.8	195.4	7.7
1960	91.5	83.5	90.2	88.7	1.6	1979	208.4	234.2	227.6	217.4	11.3

1. Over previous year. *Source:* Department of Labor, Bureau of Labor Statistics.

Employment and Unemployment

(in millions of persons)

Category	1980[1]	1979	1978	1975	1970	1959	1950	1945	1941	1932	1929
EMPLOYMENT STATUS[2]											
Total noninstitutional population	166.4	163.6	161.1	153.4	140.2	117.9	106.6	105.5	101.5	—	—
Total labor force	107.3	105.0	102.5	94.8	85.9	70.9	63.9	65.3	57.5	51.3	49.4
Percent of population	64.5	64.2	63.7	61.8	61.3	60.2	59.9	61.9	56.7	—	—
Civilian labor force	105.2	102.9	100.4	92.6	82.7	68.4	62.2	53.9	55.9	51.0	49.2
Employed	97.0	96.9	94.4	84.8	78.6	64.6	58.9	52.8	50.4	38.9	47.6
Agriculture	3.3	3.3	3.3	3.4	3.5	5.6	7.2	8.6	9.1	10.2	10.5
Nonagricultural industries	93.7	93.6	91.0	81.4	75.2	59.1	51.8	44.2	41.3	28.8	37.2
Unemployed	8.2	6.0	6.0	7.8	4.1	3.7	3.3	1.0	5.6	12.1	1.6
Percent of labor force	7.8	5.8	6.0	8.5	4.9	5.5	5.3	1.9	9.9	23.6	3.2
Not in labor force	59.1	58.6	58.5	58.7	54.3	47.0	42.8	40.2	44.0	—	—
INDUSTRY											
Total nonagricultural employment	89.8	89.9	86.7	76.9	70.9	53.3	45.2	40.4	36.5	23.6	31.3
Goods-producing industries	25.1	26.5	25.6	22.6	23.6	20.4	18.5	17.5	16.0	8.6	13.3
Mining	1.0	1.0	0.9	0.8	0.6	0.7	0.9	0.8	1.0	0.7	1.1
Construction	4.3	4.5	4.3	3.5	.3.6	3.0	2.4	1.1	1.8	1.0	1.5
Manufacturing: Durable goods	11.8	12.8	12.3	10.7	11.2	9.4	8.1	9.1	7.0	—	—
Nondurable goods	8.0	8.3	8.2	7.6	8.2	7.3	7.1	6.5	6.2	—	—
Services-producing industries	64.7	63.4	61.1	54.3	47.3	32.9	26.7	22.9	20.6	15.0	18.0
Transportation and public utilities	5.1	5.1	5.2	4.5	4.5	4.0	4.0	3.9	3.3	2.8	3.9
Trade: Wholesale	5.2	5.2	5.0	4.4	4.0	3.1	2.6	1.9	2.0	—	—
Retail	15.3	15.1	14.6	12.6	11.0	8.0	6.8	5.4	5.3	—	—
Finance, insurance, and real estate	5.2	5.0	4.7	4.2	3.6	2.5	1.9	1.5	1.5	1.3	1.5
Services	17.7	17.1	16.3	13.9	11.5	7.1	5.4	4.2	3.9	2.9	3.4
Federal government	2.9	2.8	2.7	2.7	2.7	2.2	1.9	2.8	1.3	0.6	0.5
State and local government	13.3	13.1	12.9	11.9	9.8	5.9	4.1	3.1	3.3	2.7	2.5

1. July seasonally adjusted. Industry data are preliminary. 2. For 1929–45, figures on employment status relate to persons 14 years and over; beginning in 1950, 16 years and over. NOTE: Figures may not add to totals because of rounding. *Source:* Department of Labor, Bureau of Labor Statistics.

The Economy in 1980

Monte J. Gordon
Vice President and Director of Research
The Dreyfus Corporation

The major economic issues of 1980 were inflation, recession, and the monetary policy of the Federal Reserve and its effect on interest rates—all against the background of a presidential election year. Further, each of these factors impacted and affected the others, and 1980 was a year which will not soon be forgotten.

The key factor was inflationary pressure, which had begun to take hold in 1979 and which carried strongly into 1980. The rate of inflation soared during the first quarter to an annual rate of 16.9% for the consumer price index, then slipped slightly to an annual rate of 13.7% during the second quarter. In July, the index was unchanged, but this was due only to a sharp decline in housing costs. Other elements in the index rose. Continued inflationary pressures were indicated by the report that an index measuring wholesale prices rose at an annual rate of 20.4% in July. Consumers anticipated still higher prices ahead and so spent aggressively, expanding their debt.

Consumer spending had kept economic activity humming along in 1979, past the point at which most professional observers expected the economy to turn down into 1980. Interest rates rose rapidly. The best example is the prime rate of banks (the interest rate charged to their best corporate customers, relatively few in number). During 1980, in a rapid series of increases, the prime rate rose from 15¾% in January to 20% in April. During the same period, mortgage rates began to climb sharply, reaching levels of 19% in certain areas of the country. The rise in rates was reflected throughout the money markets. Thus the most sensitive short-term rates, Federal Funds (excess reserves held by some banks which are loaned overnight to other banks that need reserves), rose at one point to a level of 25%. A major effect of these developments was a virtual paralysis of the long-term bond market. In March, short-term rates climbed to around 15% for six-month treasury bills and 16½% for 30-day treasury bills, while 30-day commercial paper rose to slightly over 18%. The action of corporations in turning to the short-term debt market reflected their refusal to undertake long-term commitments in a highly inflationary environment.

The Administration and the Federal Reserve became increasingly concerned at this turn of events, particularly with respect to the spiraling inflation rate, which showed no sign of abating. To break the developing inflation psychology, the Federal Reserve announced a number of credit controls on March 14. These were essentially designed to limit new credit extensions above existing levels and affected credit cards and bank loans. They had an immediate impact. Retail sales dropped sharply, led by automobile sales, and housing starts, which were beginning to ease, also fell precipitously. Thus, in April, auto sales fell to 892,000 units compared to 1,103,300 units a year earlier. By mid-April, sales had fallen to an annual rate of 5.7 million units, the lowest rate since mid-April 1975. The Chrysler Corporation faced bankruptcy without government help. This assistance was finally forthcoming in the form of loan guarantees up to $1.5 billion, under the control of a specially appointed board. And while General Motors, Ford, and Chrysler reported deficits totaling about $1.3 billion in the second quarter of 1980, sales of fuel-efficient imports climbed to about 30% of total auto sales.

Housing was affected by the credit controls established by the Federal Reserve board. Single-family new home sales fell to a low of 343,000 units (annual rate seasonally adjusted) in April when record mortgage interest rates discouraged home sales and construction. In June, new home sales rose 16% from May as mortgage rates declined. The June sales of 535,000 units (annual rate) were well below the pace of 698,000 units in June 1979. The average price for homes in June 1980 was $77,900, up from $73,800 in May.

These developments in the housing and auto industry mirrored the recessionary trend which began to grip the whole economy. The National Bureau of Economic Research, (a nonprofit organization specializing in economic research of business cycles) determined that the recession began in February 1980. The recession, which had been widely predicted for 1979, came on with great ferocity in 1980. In the second quarter of 1980, Gross National Product fell 9% in real terms adjusted for inflation, nearly equaling the steepest quarterly decline of 9.1% in the recession of 1974–75.

To many observers, the action of the Federal Reserve in setting up credit controls added considerably to the steepness of the decline. In any event, on May 22, the Federal Reserve eased some of the new controls and then, in early July, eliminated them. This did not mean, however, that the Federal Reserve altered its basic policy of monetary restraint. Indeed, Chairman Volcker of the Federal Reserve was very explicit in stating that moderation of the inflation continued as the primary objective and that the rate of increase in the money supply would be held to a range of between 3½% and 6%. This could slow recovery from the recession but is designed to hold inflationary pressures in check.

The major thrust of the credit controls was directed toward the consumer. Its success was reflected in a steady decline in installment debt. Banks throughout the country restricted personal loans and various major retailers also acted to tighten up their credit. As a consequence, retail trade figures slumped sharply in the early part of the year, with only modest recovery evident as the year moved along.

The effect of reduced consumer spending was reflected in the decline of the production of the nation's factories, utilities, and mines. Industrial production fell 2.2% in April, 2.4% in May, and 2.4% in June. The declines in May and June were the largest since the 3.4% decline in January 1975 during the recession. One of the major effects of the slowdown was the rise in unemployment. In March, unemployment was at a 6.2% level. The level jumped sharply in April to 7% and to 7.8% in

May. It leveled off at about 7.8%, although forecasts suggested it would reach 8.5% by the end of 1980.

As the impact of credit controls began to spread, interest rates began to drop at a virtually unprecedented rate, with the prime rate plummeting from a high of 20% on April 2 to a low of 10¾% during the last week in July, and leveling off at around 11% early in the third quarter. Mortgage rates, which reached a level of about 19%, declined rapidly to about 12½% by mid-year. The decline in interest rates began to encourage the consumer to spend more aggressively. As a result, housing sales began to improve and auto sales showed signs of bottoming out. However, interest rates began to rise, led by mortgage rates. As a consequence, doubts were aroused as to the stamina of the recovery.

On the inflation front, developments were less encouraging. In June, the consumer price index was reported at a 12% annual rate (although statistical factors caused July to report no increase in the index). These are still rather high figures, considering that at the bottom of the recession in 1974–75, the inflation rate fell to around 5%. Hopes for further significant decline were dimmed somewhat as a result of a drought throughout the farm area. The anticipated corn crop was reduced by about 14%.

Higher selling prices for grain could result in higher food costs to consumers. Reduced crop yields (93 bushels per acre compared with 106 bushels in 1979) meant a decline to a production of 6.6 billion bushels of corn. This would fall short of the 7.4 billion bushels which will be used in the U.S. and exported next year. Not only is this likely to deplete our corn inventories, but a reduction of about 2% in corn production usually means an increase of about 3% in farm prices.

In another sector of significance to the problem of inflation, the cost of imported oil, 1980 was somewhat more encouraging. Although the price of oil imports into the U.S. rose as a result of price increases imposed by the Organization of Petroleum Exporting Countries (OPEC), they showed signs of stability and even eased late in the year. According to the Department of Commerce, the cost per barrel of imported oil rose from $26.69 per barrel in January 1980 to $31.00 per barrel in June. At that point, it began to stabilize. Indeed, decreases in oil prices began to appear, with several U.S. companies reducing their prices by from $1.00 to $4.00 per barrel. The combination of a recessionary trend and energy conservation in the U.S. acted to reduce the demand for imported oil by about 25% and build substantial inventories. Saudi Arabia maintained its 9.5 million barrels per day production level to develop a unified price structure for OPEC and end the leapfrogging of price by various members, such as Iran. A sign of lessened demand for gasoline was the fact that refinery operations dropped to a level of around 70% in the U.S. during the third quarter, compared with over 90% a year earlier.

As the year came to a close, the concern mounted that Saudi Arabia would decrease production, an action which could significantly affect the supply of oil and cause higher prices.

The stock market during 1980 was affected to a major degree by the threat of recession and the outlook for inflation—both factors being, in turn, related to the presidential election campaign. During the early months, the stock market declined sharply, recording a low of 759.13 on the Dow Jones Average on April 21. Shortly after the imposition of credit controls, and as the evidence of their effectiveness mounted and the economy and interest rates turned down sharply, investors began to look to recovery late in 1980 and early in 1981. The stock market rose significantly, breaking through the 900 line on the Dow Jones Average after several attempts and surged toward the 1000 mark, sparked by heavy institutional trading.

Consumer Price Index for Urban Wage Earners and Clerical Workers

(1967 = 100)

Effective January 1978, the Consumer Price Index was revised, with two indexes now being produced: A new index for All Urban Consumers covers 80% of the non-institutional population; the other index, the Consumer Price Index for Urban Wage Earners and Clerical Workers, covers about half of those included in the new index and is a major revision of the one that had been published for many years.

	1980[1]	1979	1975	1970	1965	1960	1955	1950	1945
All items	248.0	217.7	161.2	116.3	94.5	88.7	80.2	72.1	53.9
Food total	255.5	234.7	175.4	114.9	94.4	88.0	81.6	—	—
Apparel and upkeep	175.4	166.4	142.3	116.1	93.7	89.6	84.1	79.0	61.5
Housing total	265.1	227.5	166.8	118.9	94.9	90.2	82.3	72.8	59.1
Rent	191.8	175.9	137.3	110.1	96.9	91.7	84.3	70.4	58.8
Gas and electricity	313.5	257.6	169.6	107.3	99.4	98.6	87.5	81.2	79.6
Fuel oil, coal, bottled gas	561.9	403.6	253.3	110.1	94.6	89.2	82.3	72.7	48.0
House operation[2]	203.5	188.9	158.1	113.4	95.3	93.8	89.9	—	—
House Furnishings	172.9	162.6	144.4	111.4	97.1	99.3	99.2	95.5	73.3
Transportation	251.9	212.8	150.6	112.7	95.9	89.6	77.4	68.2	47.8
Medical care	267.8	240.1	168.6	120.6	89.5	79.1	64.8	53.7	42.1
Personal care	213.1	195.5	150.7	113.2	95.2	90.1	77.9	68.3	55.1
Entertainment	204.4	187.6	144.4	113.4	95.9	87.3	76.7	74.4	62.4

1. July. 2. Combines house furnishings and operation. *Source:* Department of Labor, Bureau of Labor Statistics.

Per Capita Personal Income by States

State	1979[1]	1978
Alabama	$6,976	$6,325
Alaska	11,252	10,849
Arizona	8,305	7,385
Arkansas	6,785	6,121
California	9,913	8,916
Colorado	8,945	8,116
Connecticut	9,959	8,915
Delaware	9,537	8,531
D.C.	10,911	9,598
Florida	8,532	7,578
Georgia	7,515	6,779
Hawaii	9,353	8,465
Idaho	7,446	7,074
Illinois	9,823	8,870
Indiana	8,686	7,703
Iowa	8,589	7,856
Kansas	9,055	7,846
Kentucky	7,342	6,605
Louisiana	7,477	6,738
Maine	7,057	6,308
Maryland	9,150	8,348
Massachusetts	8,844	7,926
Michigan	9,269	8,487
Minnesota	8,760	7,904
Mississippi	6,167	5,582
Missouri	8,132	7,287
Montana	7,412	6,915
Nebraska	8,341	7,544
Nevada	10,204	9,377
New Hampshire	8,231	7,378
New Jersey	9,702	8,775
New Mexico	7,294	6,599
New York	9,098	8,230
North Carolina	7,359	6,640
North Dakota	7,774	7,432
Ohio	8,775	7,857
Oklahoma	8,226	7,127
Oregon	8,842	8,076
Pennsylvania	8,559	7,744
Rhode Island	8,266	7,447
South Carolina	7,027	6,292
South Dakota	7,334	6,585
Tennessee	7,299	6,561
Texas	8,649	7,746
Utah	7,185	6,594
Vermont	7,280	6,601
Virginia	8,605	7,721
Washington	9,435	8,553
West Virginia	7,470	6,629
Wisconsin.	8,419	7,532
Wyoming	9,657	8,687
United States	**8,706**	**7,840**

1. Preliminary. *Source:* Department of Commerce, Bureau of Economic Analysis.

Gross National Product or Expenditure
(in billions)

Item	1980[1]	1979	1978	1977	1976	1975	1974	1970	1965	1960	1955	1950	1946	1938	1933	1929
Gross national product	$2,523	$2,369	$2,128	$1,900	$1,702	$1,529	$1,413	$982	$688	$506	$399	$286	$210	$85	$56	$103
GNP in constant (1972) dollars	1,411	1,432	1,399	1,341	1,273	1,202	1,218	1,075	926	737	655	534	477	312	222	315
Personal consumption expenditures	1,628	1,510	1,351	1,210	1,090	980	890	619	430	325	254	192	144	64	46	77
Durable goods	197	213	200	179	157	133	122	85	63	43	39	31	16	6	3	9
Nondurable goods	654	597	531	481	444	409	376	265	189	151	123	98	83	34	22	38
Services	777	700	620	550	489	438	391	269	179	131	92	63	45	24	20	30
Gross private domestic investment	367	387	352	303	243	189	215	141	112	76	68	54	31	6	1	16
Residential structures	89	114	108	92	68	52	54	36	31	24	24	20	7	2	1	4
Nonresidential structures	103	93	77	63	57	53	54	38	26	18	14	9	7	2	1	5
Producers' durable equipment	163	162	145	127	108	96	97	64	46	30	24	18	10	3	1	6
Change in business inventories	12	18	22	22	10	−11	9	4	10	4	6	7	6	−1	−2	2
Net export of goods and services	−1	−5	−10	−10	8	20	6	4	8	4	2	2	8	1	(2)	1
Government purchases	527	476	436	396	361	339	303	219	138	100	75	38	28	13	8	8
Federal	193	167	153	144	130	123	111	96	67	54	44	19	18	5	2	1
National defense	124	108	99	94	86	84	77	74	49	44	38	14	15	n.a.	n.a.	n.a.
Other	69	58	54	50	44	39	34	22	18	9	6	5	3	n.a.	n.a.	n.a.
State and local	335	310	283	252	232	216	192	123	71	47	31	20	10	8	6	7
Implicit price deflator	178[3]	163	150	142	134	127	116	91	74	69	61	54	44	27	25	33

1. Second quarter annual rate (preliminary). 2. Less than $500 million. 3. May. NOTE: n.a. = not available. *Source:* Department of Commerce, Bureau of Economic Analysis.

Shareholders in Public Corporations

Characteristic	1975	1970	1965	1962	1959	1956	1952
Individual shareholders (thousands)	25,270	30,850	20,120	17,010	12,490	8,630	6,490
Owners of shares listed on New York Stock Exchange (thousands)	17,950	18,290	12,430	11,020	8,510	6,880	n.a.
Adult shareowner incidence in population	1 in 6	1 in 4	1 in 6	1 in 6	1 in 8	1 in 12	1 in 16
Median household income	$19,000	$13,500	$9,500	$8,600	$7,000	$6,200	$7,100
Adult shareowners with household income: under $10,000 (thousands)	3,420	8,170	10,080	10,340	9,340	n.a.	n.a.
$10,000 and over (thousands)	19,970	20,130	8,410	5,920	2,740	n.a.	n.a.
Adult female shareowners (thousands)	11,750	14,290	9,430	8,290	6,350	4,260	3,140
Adult male shareowners (thousands)	11,630	14,340	9,060	7,970	5,740	4,020	3,210
Median age	53	48	49	48	49	48	51

NOTE: n.a. = not available. Data are latest available. *Source:* New York Stock Exchange.

What Americans Pay in Personal Taxes[1] and What They Save

(in billions of current dollars)

Item	1980[2]	1975	1970	1965	1960	1955	1950
Gross personal income	$2,078.3	$1,255.5	$808.3	$538.9	$401.0	$310.9	$227.6
Social insurance contributions	86.4	50.5	28.0	13.4	9.3	5.2	2.9
Tax and non-tax payments to governments	324.3	168.8	116.6	65.7	50.9	35.5	20.7
Income available for spending and saving[3]	1,754.0	1,086.7	691.7	473.2	350.0	275.3	206.9
Income available per capita (dollars)	7,892	5,088	3,376	2,436	1,937	1,666	1,364
Personal saving	82.9	83.6	56.2	28.4	17.0	15.8	13.1
Rate of personal saving	4.7%	7.7%	8.1%	6.4%	4.9%	5.4%	6.3%

1. Personal income basis: direct taxes and payments only; corporate taxes and payments, paid by shareholders or customers, and hidden and consumption taxes not included. 2. Second-quarter annual rate (preliminary). 3. Disposable personal income. *Source:* Department of Commerce, Bureau of Economic Analysis.

Interest Rates

Instrument	1980[1]	1979	1978	1977	1976	1975	1974	1973	1972	1970	1967
MONEY MARKET RATES											
Federal funds	8.98	11.20	7.94	5.54	5.05	5.82	10.51	8.74	4.44	7.17	4.22
Prime commercial paper											
3 months	8.68	10.97	7.94	5.54	5.24	6.26	10.05	8.20	4.66	—	—
6 months	8.61	10.91	7.99	5.60	5.35	6.33	9.87	8.15	4.69	7.72	5.10
Prime bankers acceptances, 90 days	8.97	11.04	8.11	5.59	5.19	6.30	9.92	8.08	4.47	7.31	4.75
Certificates of deposit, 3 months, secondary market	8.93	11.22	8.22	5.64	—	—	—	—	—	—	—
U.S. government securities: bills, 6-month yield	8.49	10.06	7.58	5.53	5.26	6.11	7.95	7.20	4.49	6.51	4.61
CAPITAL MARKET RATES											
U.S. Treasury											
Notes and bonds maturing in 3–5 years	—	9.58	8.30	6.85	6.94	7.55	7.81	6.92	5.85	7.37	5.07
5 years	9.92	9.52	8.32	6.99	7.18	7.77	7.80	—	—	—	—
10 years	10.59	9.44	8.41	7.42	7.61	7.99	7.56	—	—	—	—
State and local Moody's series:											
Aaa	8.15	5.92	5.52	5.20	5.66	6.42	5.89	—	—	—	—
Baa	9.30	6.73	6.27	6.12	7.49	7.62	6.53	—	—	—	—
Corporate bonds, seasoned issues:											
Aaa	11.33	9.63	8.73	8.02	8.43	8.83	8.57	—	—	—	—
Aa	11.61	9.94	8.92	8.24	8.75	9.17	8.84	—	—	—	—
A	12.09	10.20	9.12	8.49	9.09	9.65	9.20	—	—	—	—
Baa	12.70	10.69	9.45	8.97	9.75	10.61	9.50	—	—	—	—

1. Week ending Aug. 1. *Source* Federal Reserve Bulletin, August 1980.

Consumer Price Index for All Urban Consumers

(1967 = 100)

Group	July 1980	Percent change Jan.-July
All items	—	11.7
Food	252.9	6.7
Alcoholic beverages	187.0	8.2
Apparel and upkeep	177.9	6.5
Men's and boys' apparel	167.6	3.7
Women's and girls' apparel	153.4	—.1
Footwear	191.0	6.6
Housing, total	265.1	15.0
Rent	192.1	8.9
Gas and electricity	314.3	32.5
Fuel oil, coal, bottled gas	560.4	18.9
House operation[1]	206.4	9.3
House furnishings	175.1	8.2
Transportation	248.6	11.6
Medical care	266.6	10.2
Personal care	214.4	10.2
Tobacco products	203.8	7.3
Entertainment	206.4	11.2
Personal and educational expenses	233.1	7.3

1. Combines house furnishings and operation. *Source:* Department of Labor, Bureau of Labor Statistics.

Per Capita Personal Income

Year	Amount	Year	Amount	Year	Amount	Year	Amount	Year	Amount
1929	$705	1956	$1,980	1962	$2,373	1968	$3,433	1974	$5,428
1935	474	1957	2,050	1963	2,460	1969	3,667	1975	5,851
1940	593	1958	2,074	1964	2,592	1970	3,893	1976	6,402
1945	1,223	1959	2,166	1965	2,773	1971	4,132	1977	7,043
1950	1,501	1960	2,219	1966	2,987	1972	4,493	1978	7,854
1955	1,881	1961	2,269	1967	3,167	1973	4,980	1979	8,773

Source: Department of Commerce, Bureau of Economic Analysis.

Total Family Income

(figures in percent)

Family income	White 1978	White 1975	White 1970	White 1965	Black and other races 1978	Black and other races 1975	Black and other races 1970	Black and other races 1965
Families (thousands)[1]	50,910	49,873	46,535	43,497	6,894	6,372	5,413	4,782
Under $3,000	2.5	3.1	3.6	5.1	8.3	9.5	10.5	14.6
$3,000 to $4,999	4.0	5.2	4.9	6.2	12.2	12.8	11.8	15.3
$5,000 to $6,999	5.6	6.7	6.2	7.1	9.5	11.4	11.0	15.3
$7,000 to $9,999	9.4	11.1	10.4	12.1	13.3	14.2	16.1	18.0
$10,000 to $11,999 } $12,000 to $14,999 }	16.6	7.6	7.8	9.9	17.4	8.8	9.1	9.1
		12.1	13.2	15.5		11.0	11.3	10.3
$15,000 to $24,999	32.5	33.4	34.7	31.3	23.4	22.9	21.7	14.3
$25,000 and over	29.5	20.7	19.3	12.8	16.0	9.4	8.4	3.0
Median income	$18,368	$14,268	$10,236	$7,251	$11,754	$9,321	$6,516	$3,993

1. As of March 1979. *Source:* Department of Commerce, Bureau of the Census. NOTE: Figures are latest available.

Median Earnings of Full-Time Women Workers

(persons 14 years and over)

Major occupation group	1978 earnings	As percent of men's earnings
Professional and technical workers	$12,647	64.1
Nonfarm managers and administrators	10,689	54.4
Clerical workers	9,158	59.9
Sales workers	7,644	45.4
Operatives (including transport)	8,005	58.6
Service workers (except private household)	7,010	63.6
All occupations	**9,350**	**59.4**

Source: Department of Labor, Women's Bureau.

Median Family Income

(in current dollars)

Year	Income	Percent change	Year	Income	Percent change
1960	$ 5,620	—	1974	$12,836	6.5
1970	9,867	—	1975	13,719	6.3
1971	10,285	4.2	1976	14,958	9.0
1972	11,116	8.1	1977	16,009	7.0
1973	12,051	8.4	1978	17,640	10.2

Source: Department of Commerce, Bureau of the Census. NOTE: Figures are latest available.

Annual Budgets for 4-Person Urban Families, Autumn 1979

Item	Lower budget		Intermediate budget		Higher budget	
	Amount	Percent increase 1978–79	Amount	Percent increase 1978–79	Amount	Percent increase 1978–79
Total family consumption	$10,234	9.0	$15,353	9.7	$21,069	9.6
Food	3,911	9.4	5,044	9.4	6,360	9.5
Housing	2,409	7.9	4,594	9.9	6,971	9.9
Transportation	1,004	17.3	1,851	17.7	2,411	18.0
Clothing	866	2.2	1,235	2.2	1,804	2.0
Personal care	323	7.3	433	7.4	613	7.5
Medical Care	1,171	10.0	1,176	9.9	1,227	9.9
Other family consumption	550	6.8	1,021	6.8	1,684	6.7
Other items	539	7.4	877	8.3	1,478	8.3
Personal income taxes	1,032	10.4	3,031	10.7	6,357	10.8
Social security and disability	781	8.6	1,256	17.1	1,413	29.5
Total budget	**12,585**	**9.0**	**20,517**	**10.2**	**30,317**	**10.6**

NOTE: Above budgets illustrate three levels of living based on estimates of costs for goods and services rather than actual expenditures. Totals may not add because of rounding. *Source:* Department of Labor, Bureau of Labor Statistics.

Annual Budgets for a Retired Couple, Autumn 1979

Item	Lower Budget		Intermediate Budget		Higher Budget	
	Amount	Percent increase 1978–79	Amount	Percent increase 1978–79	Amount	Percent increase 1978–79
Total family consumption	$5,763	9.2	$8,047	9.1	$11,719	9.3
Food	1,882	9.1	2,507	9.0	3,149	9.2
Housing	1,996	9.0	2,862	8.4	4,481	8.3
Transportation	420	16.7	820	17.0	1,528	17.6
Clothing	225	2.3	378	2.4	581	2.3
Personal care	169	8.3	247	7.9	362	8.1
Medical care[1]	837	9.4	842	9.5	848	9.6
Other consumption	234	6.4	390	6.6	770	6.6
Other items	259	9.3	515	9.1	950	8.6
Total budget	**6,023**	**9.2[2]**	**8,562**	**9.1[2]**	**12,669**	**9.3[2]**

1. Contains preliminary estimate for out-of-pocket costs for Medicare. 2. Largest increases since 1974. *Source:* Department of Commerce, Bureau of Labor Statistics.

National Income by Type
(in billions of dollars)

Type of share	1980[1]	1980 % of total	1979	1975	1970	1965	1960	1955	1950
National income	$2,035.4	100.0	$1,924.8	$1,215.0	$800.5	$564.3	$414.5	$331.0	$241.1
Compensation of employees	1,555.2	76.4	1,459.2	931.1	603.9	393.8	294.2	224.5	154.6
Wages and salaries	1,303.6	64.0	1,227.4	805.9	542.0	358.9	270.8	211.3	146.8
Supplements to wages and salaries	251.6	12.4	231.8	125.2	61.9	35.0	23.4	13.2	7.8
Proprietors' income	130.0	6.4	130.8	87.0	66.9	57.3	46.2	41.7	37.5
Business and professional	102.3	5.0	98.0	63.5	50.0	42.4	34.2	30.3	24.0
Farm	27.7	1.4	32.8	23.5	16.9	14.8	12.0	11.4	13.5
Rental income of persons	27.0	1.3	26.9	22.4	23.9	19.0	15.8	13.9	9.4
Corporate profits[2]	175.0	8.6	178.2	95.9	69.4	76.1	49.9	46.9	37.7
Net interest	148.1	7.3	129.7	78.6	36.4	18.2	8.4	4.1	2.0

1. First quarter annual rate. 2. Includes inventory valuation adjustment. *Source:* Department of Commerce, Bureau of Economic Analysis.

Federal Reserve Board Indexes of Production
(1967 = 100)

Industry	1980[1]	1979	1975	1970
Total industrial production	138.8	152.2	117.8	106.7
Total manufactures	137.2	153.2	116.3	105.2
Durable manufactures	127.5	146.3	109.3	101.5
Primary metals	83.9	121.2	96.4	106.9
Fabricated metal products	123.5	148.5	109.9	109.4
Machinery	154.2	163.6	125.1	100.3
Transportation equipment	110.6	135.3	97.4	90.4
Instruments and products	166.5[2]	174.9	132.3	110.8
Clay, glass, and stone products	138.2[2]	163.3	117.9	106.4
Lumber and products	103.1[2]	136.9	107.6	106.3
Furniture and fixtures	146.2	161.4	118.2	99.4
Nondurable manufactures	151.2[2]	163.3	126.4	110.6
Textile mill products	129.9[3]	143.8	122.3	106.3
Apparel products	126.9[2]	130.7	107.6	97.8
Leather products	69.3	71.3	76.5	90.8
Rubber and plastics products	241.6[2]	270.0	166.7	115.7
Paper and products	144.8[2]	150.8	116.3	113.3
Printing and publishing	132.7[2]	136.9	113.4	104.1
Chemicals and products	191.7	210.4	147.3	120.3
Petroleum products	132.0[2]	143.6	124.1	112.6
Foods	146.2[3]	147.9	123.4	111.7
Tobacco products	117.2	117.1	111.8	100.0
Mining	131.9	125.3	112.8	109.7
Coal	149.6	133.6	113.4	105.7
Oil and gas extraction	134.5[2]	121.7	113.3	109.7
Metal mining	117.0	126.8	115.8	131.3
Stone and earth minerals	123.6	137.6	107.0	98.8
Utilities	171.6[2]	166.1	146.0	128.3

1. July estimate except where otherwise indicated. 2. June preliminary. 3. May. *Source: Federal Reserve Bulletin,* August 1980.

Producer Price Indexes by Major Commodity Groups
(1967 = 100)

Commodity	1980[1]	1978	1975	1970	1965	1960	1955
All commodities	265.2	209.3	174.9	110.4	96.6	94.9	87.8
Farm products	233.4	212.5	186.7	111.0	98.7	97.2	98.2
Processed foods	233.8	202.6	182.6	112.1	95.5	89.5	85.0
Textile products and apparel	182.4	159.8	137.9	107.1	99.8	99.5	98.7
Hides, skins, and leather products	241.0	200.1	148.5	110.3	94.3	90.8	77.3
Fuels and related products and power	574.8	322.5	245.1	106.2	95.5	96.1	91.2
Chemicals and allied products	261.7	198.8	181.3	102.2	99.0	101.8	98.5
Rubber and plastic products	217.1	174.8	150.2	108.3	95.9	103.1	102.4
Lumber and wood products	279.8	276.0	176.9	113.6	95.9	95.3	97.1
Pulp, paper, and allied products	251.3	195.6	170.4	108.2	96.2	98.1	87.8
Metals and metal products	282.4	227.1	185.6	116.6	96.4	92.4	82.1
Machinery and equipment	238.8	196.1	161.4	111.4	93.9	92.0	75.7
Furniture and household durables	185.3	160.4	139.7	107.5	96.9	99.0	93.3
Nonmetallic mineral products	283.2	222.8	174.0	112.9	97.5	97.2	87.5
Transportation equipment (Dec. 1968 = 100)	202.2	173.5	141.5	104.6	98.5	98.8	—
Miscellaneous products	257.4	184.3	147.7	109.9	95.9	93.0	86.5

1. June. NOTE: Previous to January 1978, above table was known as Wholesale Price Indexes. *Source:* Department of Labor, Bureau of Labor Statistics.

Farm Index
(1967 = 100)

Year	Prices paid by farmers[1]	Prices rec'd by farmers[2]	Ratio
1945	56	83	148
1950	75	103	137
1955	81	93	115
1960	88	95	108
1965	94	98	104
1970	112	110	98
1975	180	185	103
1978	219	210	96
1979	261	250	96

1. Commodities, interest, and taxes, and wage rates. 2. All crops and livestock. *Source:* Department of Agriculture, Economics, Statistics, and Cooperatives Service.

Amount of Life Insurance in Force
(in millions)

As of Dec. 31	Ordinary	Group	Industrial	Credit	Total
1915	$16,650	$ 100	$ 4,279	—	$ 21,029
1945	101,550	22,172	27,675	365	151,762
1950	149,071	47,793	33,415	3,844	234,168
1955	216,812	101,345	39,682	14,493	373,332
1960	341,881	175,903	39,563	29,101	586,448
1965	499,638	308,078	39,818	53,020	900,554
1970	734,730	551,357	38,644	77,392	1,402,123
1975	1,083,421	904,695	39,423	112,032	2,139,571
1978	1,425,095	1,243,994	38,080	163,081	2,870,250
1979	1,585,878	1,419,418	37,794	179,250	3,222,340

Source: American Council of Life Insurance.

Value of New Construction Put in Place
(in millions of dollars)

Activity	1979	1975	1970	1960	1950	1940	1933	1929
Total new construction activity	$228,950	$134,535	$94,855	$54,738	$33,575	$8,682	$2,879	$10,793
New private construction activity	179,948	93,651	66,759	38,875	26,709	5,504	1,231	8,307
Residential	99,030	46,472	31,864	22,975	18,126	2,985	470	3,625
New dwelling units	78,587	34,408	24,272	17,279	15,551	2,560	290	3,040
Additions and alterations	18,236	10,925	6,234	4,831	2,400	335	145	340
Nonhousekeeping	2,206	1,139	1,358	865	175	90	35	245
Nonresidential building, except farm and public utility	47,298	26,407	21,417	10,149	3,904	1,025	406	2,694
Industrial	14,950	8,018	6,538	2,851	1,062	442	176	949
Commercial[1]	24,924	12,806	9,754	4,180	1,415	348	130	1,135
Other	7,424	5,582	5,125	3,118	1,427	235	100	610
Public utility	26,467	17,379	11,020	4,621	3,045	771	261	1,578
Railroads	1,259	514	306	n.a.	n.a.	167	94	510
Telephone and telegraph	6,343	3,683	2,968	1,088	440	122	45	354
Farm construction	5,700	2,325	1,512	849	1,522	240	49	307
New public construction activity	49,003	40,884	28,096	15,863	6,866	3,628	1,648	2,486
Residential	1,211	754	1,107	716	345	200	n.a.	n.a.
Nonresidential building	14,646	14,719	9,550	4,395	2,387	615	230	659
Industrial	1,411	918	499	407	224	164	2	n.a.
Educational	6,903	7,760	5,619	2,818	1,133	156	52	389
Hospital and institutional	1,648	1,745	837	401	499	54	49	101
Other	4,684	4,296	2,595	1,169	531	241	127	169
Military facilities	1,640	1,389	718	1,366	177	385	36	19
Highway	11,915	10,854	9,981	5,437	2,134	1,302	847	1,266
Sewer and water	7,298	6,566	2,638	1,487	659	338	95	253
Conservation and development	4,587	3,257	1,908	1,175	942	528	359	115

1. Warehouses, office and loft buildings; stores, restaurants and garages. NOTE: n.a. = not available. *Source:* Department of Commerce, Bureau of the Census.

Expenditures for New Plant and Equipment[1]
(in millions of dollars)

Year	Manufacturing and mining	Transportation	All other[2]	Total[3]
1945	$4,366	$1,122	$3,204	$8,692
1950	8,230	2,370	9,600	20,210
1955	13,200	2,580	13,770	29,530
1960	16,390	3,120	17,230	36,750
1965	24,900	4,890	24,620	54,420
1970	33,840	6,040	39,830	79,710
1973	40,750	6,030	52,960	99,740
1974	49,190	6,660	56,560	112,400
1975	51,740	7,570	53,470	112,780
1976	56,480	7,450	56,570	120,490
1977	64,660	6,930	64,210	135,800
1978	72,400	8,050	73,370	153,820
1979	84,480	10,120	82,480	177,090

1. Data exclude agriculture. 2. Includes electric and gas utilities, trade, service, communications, construction, and finance. 3. Details may not add up to totals because of rounding. *Source:* Department of Commerce, Bureau of Economic Analysis.

New Housing Starts[1] and Mobile Homes Shipped
(in thousands)

Year	No. of units started	Year	No. of units started	Year	Mobile homes shipped
1900	189	1955	1,646	1965	216
1905	507	1960[1]	1,296	1970	401
1910	387	1965	1,510	1971	497
1915	433	1970	1,469	1972	576
1920	247	1973	2,057	1973	567
1925	937	1974	1,352	1974	329
1930	330	1975	1,171	1975	213
1935	221	1976	1,548	1976	246
1940	603	1977	1,990	1977	265
1945	326	1978	2,023	1978	275
1950	1,952	1979	1,749	1979	276

1. Prior to 1960, starts limited to nonfarm housing; from 1960 on, figures include farm housing. *Sources:* Department of Commerce, Housing Construction Statistics, 1900–1965, and Construction Reports, Housing Starts, 1970–79; Manufactured Housing Institute; National Conference of States on Building Codes and Standards.

Highest Paid Women Executives

The top half dozen highest-paid women employed by public corporations at the beginning of the 1980s are: Jane Cahill Pfeiffer, chairman, NBC, $425,000; Rosemarie Sena, senior vice president, Shearson Hayden Stone, $300,000; Katharine Graham, president, Washington Post Co., $375,000; Olive Ann Beech, chairman, Beech Aircraft, $220,000; Joan Manley, chairman, Time-Life Books, $203,000; and Juliette M. Moran, vice president, GAF, $195,000.

50 Most Active Stocks in 1979

Stock	Share volume
Int'l Business Machines	61,275,900
Caesar's World	57,218,800
Bally Manufacturing	52,417,200
Texaco	51,888,300
Gulf Oil	51,495,100
American Tel. & Tel.	45,387,120
Exxon	42,409,800
Boeing	39,967,000
Charter Company	38,273,700
General Motors	37,554,600
Sears, Roebuck	36,642,300
Occidental Petroleum	36,595,100
Mobil	34,872,000
Howard Johnson	33,789,800
Ramada Inns	33,130,350
Eastman Kodak	32,907,100
Pan American World Airways	29,466,700
Dow Chemical	29,287,800
General Public Utilities	28,507,300
Amerada Hess	28,475,400
Citicorp	28,413,400
Sterling Drug	28,256,900
Phillips Petroleum	28,135,400
NLT	28,038,200
Louisiana Land & Exploration	27,493,000
National Semiconductor	27,125,100
Xerox	26,632,700
Tesoro Petroleum	26,226,000
American Motors	26,071,600
Westinghouse Electric	25,944,300
Mesa Petroleum	25,741,800
International Tel. & Tel.	25,465,500
Storage Technology	25,026,400
American Home Products	24,700,800
Texas International	24,430,700
Warner-Lambert	24,341,500
Polaroid	24,323,800
Southern Company	24,199,800
Conoco	24,055,300
Ralston Purina	23,565,800
General Electric	23,312,000
Atlantic Richfield	23,091,700
RCA	22,856,300
Ford Motor	22,761,500
Standard Oil (Indiana)	22,299,700
Holiday Inns	22,179,500
Gulf & Western Industries	22,117,300
Chrysler	22,009,700
Pepsico	21,921,800
UAL	21,760,000

Source: New York Stock Exchange.

Dow Jones Industrial Stock Averages

Year	High	Low	Close
1915	99.21	54.22	99.15
1916	110.15	84.96	95.00
1917	99.18	65.95	74.38
1918	89.07	73.38	82.20
1919	119.62	79.15	107.97
1920	109.88	66.75	71.95
1921	81.50	63.90	81.10
1922	103.43	78.59	98.73
1923	105.38	85.76	95.52
1924	120.51	88.33	120.51
1925	159.39	115.00	156.66
1926	166.64	135.20	157.20
1927	202.40	152.73	202.40
1928	300.00	191.33	300.00
1929	381.17	198.69	248.48
1930	294.07	157.51	164.58
1931	194.36	73.79	77.90
1932	88.78	41.22	59.93
1933	108.67	50.16	99.90
1934	110.74	85.51	104.04
1935	148.44	96.71	144.13
1936	184.90	143.11	179.90
1937	194.40	113.64	120.85
1938	158.41	98.95	154.76
1939	155.92	121.44	150.24
1940	152.80	111.84	131.13
1941	133.59	106.34	110.96
1942	119.71	92.92	119.40
1943	145.82	119.26	135.89
1944	152.53	134.22	152.32
1945	195.82	151.35	192.91
1946	212.50	163.12	177.20
1947	186.85	163.21	181.16
1948	193.16	165.39	177.30
1949	200.52	161.60	200.13
1950	235.47	196.81	235.41
1951	276.37	238.99	269.23
1952	292.00	256.35	291.90
1953	293.79	255.49	280.90
1954	404.39	279.87	404.39
1955	488.40	388.20	488.40
1956	521.05	462.35	499.47
1957	520.77	419.79	435.69
1958	583.65	436.89	583.65
1959	679.36	574.46	679.36
1960	685.47	566.05	615.89
1961	734.91	610.25	731.14
1962	726.01	535.76	652.10
1963	767.21	646.79	762.95
1964	891.71	766.08	874.13
1965	969.26	840.59	969.26
1966	995.15	744.32	785.69
1967	943.08	786.41	905.11
1968	985.21	825.13	943.75
1969	968.85	769.93	800.36
1970	842.00	631.16	838.92
1971	950.82	797.97	890.20
1972	1036.27	889.15	1020.02
1973	1051.70	788.31	850.86
1974	891.66	577.60	616.24
1975	881.81	632.04	852.41
1976	1014.79	858.71	1004.65
1977	999.75	800.85	835.15
1978	907.74	742.12	805.01
1979	897.67	796.67	838.74
January	859.75	811.42	839.22
February	841.56	807.00	808.82
March	871.36	815.75	862.01
April	879.50	854.90	854.90
May	857.59	822.16	822.33
June	849.10	821.21	841.98
July	852.99	825.51	846.42
August	887.63	846.16	887.63
September	893.94	866.13	878.58
October	897.67	805.46	915.70
November	831.74	796.67	822.35
December	844.62	819.62	838.74
1980	—	—	—
January	891.38	820.31	875.85
February	903.84	854.44	863.14
March	856.48	759.98	785.75
April	811.09	759.13	805.46
May	860.32	805.20	850.85
June	887.54	843.77	867.92
July	936.18	872.27	935.32
August	966.72	929.78	932.59
September	974.57	921.93	932.42

NOTE: The industrial average was composed of 12 stocks before the New York Stock Exchange closed in July 1914 because of World War I. In September 1916, the list was enlarged to 20 industrial stocks and computed back to the opening of the Exchange on Dec. 12, 1914. On Oct. 1, 1928, the number of stocks making up the industrial average was increased to 30, the present number, although individual stocks have been added and deleted.

Record Personal Bankruptcies Filed

It has been estimated that almost 355,000 Americans filed for bankruptcy in 1980. This was 120,000 more persons than in 1975 when the previous record was set.

Business Population

(in thousands of concerns)

Item	1977[1]	1976[1]	1975[1]	1970[1]	1965[1]	1953	1949	1941	1933	1929
Total operating businesses[2]	14,740	14,559	13,979	12,001	11,417	4,188	3,984	3,276	2,782	3,029
Manufacturing	482	467	468	410	408	331	322	230	167	257
Wholesale trade	576	591	587	470	444	283	260	190	142	148
Retail trade	2,459	2,440	2,322	2,210	2,044	1,846	1,783	1,561	1,291	1,327
Service industries	4,043	3,834	3,669	2,964	2,565	750	739	615	575	591
Construction	1,279	1,221	1,144	875	876	405	339	194	185	234
All other[3]	5,901	6,007	5,788	5,072	5,080	573	541	486	422	472
New incorporations	432	376	326	264	204	352	331	290	n.a.	n.a.
Commercial and industrial failures[4]	7.9	9.6	11.4	10.7	13.5	8.9	9.2	11.8	19.9	22.9

1. Data for total operating businesses are now based on tax returns; not comparable with earlier figures. 2. 1929–33, annual average; 1941–53, as of January 1. 3. Includes agriculture, forestry, and fishing; mining; transportation, communication, electric, gas, and sanitary services; finance, insurance, and real estate; wholesale and retail trade not allocable; and nature of business not allocable. 4. Closures resulting in a known loss to creditors. NOTE: New incorporations for 1978 were 477,827; failures, 6,619. n.a. = not available. *Sources:* Departments of Commerce and the Treasury; Dun & Bradstreet.

Largest Businesses, 1979

(in thousands of dollars)

Source: Fortune magazine.

50 LARGEST INDUSTRIAL CORPORATIONS

	Sales	*Assets*
Exxon	$79,106,471	$49,489,964
General Motors	66,311,200	32,215,800
Mobil	44,720,908	27,505,756
Ford Motor	43,513,700	23,524,600
Texaco	38,350,370	22,991,955
Standard Oil of California	29,947,554	18,102,632
Gulf Oil	23,910,000	17,265,000
International Business Machines	22,862,776	24,529,974
General Electric	22,460,600	16,644,500
Standard Oil (Ind.)	18,610,347	17,149,899
International Telephone & Telegraph	17,197,423	15,091,321
Atlantic Richfield	16,233,959	13,833,387
Shell Oil	14,431,211	16,127,016
U.S. Steel	12,929,100	11,029,900
Conoco	12,647,998	9,311,171
E.I. du Pont de Nemours	12,571,800	8,940,200
Chrysler	12,001,900	6,653,100
Tenneco	11,209,000	11,631,000
Western Electric	10,964,075	7,128,324
Sun	10,666,000	7,460,600
Occidental Petroleum	9,554,795	5,560,330
Phillips Petroleum	9,502,775	8,518,709
Procter & Gamble	9,329,306	5,663,627
Dow Chemical	9,255,387	10,251,637
Union Carbide	9,176,500	8,802,600
United Technologies	9,053,358	6,426,123
International Harvester	8,392,042	5,247,475
Goodyear Tire & Rubber	8,238,676	5,371,239
Boeing	8,131,000	4,897,200
Eastman Kodak	8,028,231	7,554,128
LTV	7,996,809	3,864,757
Standard Oil (Ohio)	7,916,023	9,209,001
Caterpillar Tractor	7,613,200	5,403,300
Union Oil of California	7,567,698	6,013,149
Beatrice Foods	7,468,373	3,669,095
RCA	7,454,600	5,990,200
Westinghouse Electric	7,332,000	6,821,500
Bethlehem Steel	7,137,200	5,165,900
R.J. Reynolds Industries	7,133,100	6,421,900
Xerox	7,027,000	6,553,600
Amerada Hess	6,769,941	4,899,237
Esmark	6,743,167	2,389,872
Marathon Oil	6,680,597	4,321,133
Ashland Oil	6,473,867	3,113,214
Rockwell International	6,466,100	4,127,600
Kraft	6,432,900	2,523,300
Cities Service	6,276,500	4,773,000
Monsanto	6,192,600	5,539,100
Philip Morris	6,144,091	6,378,852
General Foods	5,472,456	2,565,312

50 LARGEST RETAILING COMPANIES

	Sales	*Assets*
Sears Roebuck	$17,514,252	$16,421,972
Safeway Stores	13,717,861	3,100,768
K mart	12,858,585	5,642,439
J.C. Penney	11,274,000	5,077,000
Kroger	9,029,315	1,776,111
Great Atlantic & Pacific Tea	7,469,659	1,281,226
F.W. Woolworth	6,785,000	2,927,000
Lucky Stores	5,815,927	1,221,547
Federated Department Stores	5,806,442	3,295,344
Montgomery Ward	5,251,085	3,598,715
Winn-Dixie Stores	4,930,538	857,239
City Products	3,918,800	1,214,600
Southland	3,856,222	1,367,575
American Stores	3,786,332	1,201,934
Jewel Companies	3,764,266	1,012,367
Dayton Hudson	3,384,849	1,832,785
May Department Stores	2,977,190	2,106,936
Albertson's	2,673,848	572,789
Carter Hawley Hale Stores	2,408,028	1,481,249
Grand Union	2,398,944	641,902
Supermarkets General	2,372,574	527,501
Rapid-American	2,312,245	1,587,729
Allied Stores	2,239,749	1,486,611
Wickes	2,095,206	888,267
R.H. Macy	2,058,048	1,197,281
Gamble-Skogmo	2,053,003	1,076,519
Melville	2,022,770	773,357
ARA Services	2,002,389	865,109
McDonald's	1,911,853	2,354,006
Stop & Shop Companies	1,878,864	446,979
Dillon Companies	1,797,104	387,170
Associated Dry Goods	1,783,212	978,704
Food Fair	1,725,307	389,731
Zayre	1,549,729	522,052
Marriott Corp.	1,509,957	1,080,365

Walgreen	1,344,542	402,350
Fisher Foods	1,336,293	332,892
Jack Eckerd	1,325,140	490,137
Wal-Mart Stores	1,252,980	457,879
Tandy	1,215,483	609,589
First National Supermarkets	1,111,691	233,429
Waldbaum	1,103,443	186,759
Giant Food	1,080,842	281,574
Mercantile Stores	1,067,937	586,741
Fred Meyer	1,060,203	406,737
National Tea	1,045,696	251,178
Fed-Mart	975,139	321,332
Revco D.S.	927,533	313,546
Borman's	905,376	142,471
Zale	904,464	609,866

10 LARGEST COMMERCIAL BANKS

	Assets	*Deposits*
BankAmerica Corp.	$108,389,318	$84,984,746
Citicorp	106,370,619	70,290,725
Chase Manhattan Corp.	64,708,018	48,456,210
Manufacturers Hanover Corp.	47,675,446	38,156,078
J.P. Morgan & Co.	43,487,679	30,278,552
Chemical New York Corp.	39,375,293	28,986,820
Continental Illinois Corp.	35,790,119	24,007,200
Bankers Trust New York Corp.	30,952,922	22,436,852
First Chicago Corp.	30,181,800	21,106,060
Western Bancorp.	29,687,134	23,631,073

10 LARGEST LIFE INSURANCE COMPANIES

	Assets	*Premium and annuity income*
Prudential	$54,734,107	$8,007,951
Metropolitan	44,967,563	5,934,722
Equitable Life Assurance	30,839,211	4,576,910
Aetna Life	18,548,768	4,729,187
New York Life	18,479,224	2,598,658
John Hancock Mutual	17,318,502	2,170,657
Connecticut General Life	12,240,721	2,434,535
Travelers	11,816,987	3,642,396
Northwestern Mutual	10,553,947	1,246,917
Massachusetts Mutual	8,340,825	1,222,180

10 LARGEST TRANSPORTATION COMPANIES

	Operating revenues	*Assets*
Trans World Corp.	$4,334,046	$2,806,807
UAL	3,831,523	3,862,449
United Parcel Service	3,359,006	1,067,015
American Airlines	3,252,532	3,182,495
Burlington Northern	3,250,495	4,228,484
Eastern Air Lines	2,881,526	2,453,018
Southern Pacific	2,626,442	5,025,148
Santa Fe Industries	2,555,600	3,883,100
Pan American World Airways	2,484,709	2,676,720
Delta Air Lines	2,380,928	1,788,325

10 LARGEST UTILITIES

	Assets	*Operating revenues*
American Telephone & Telegraph	$113,768,836	$45,408,078
General Telephone & Electronics	18,405,965	9,957,817
Southern Company	10,552,095	3,128,169
Pacific Gas & Electric	10,310,763	4,372,220
Commonwealth Edison	9,172,615	2,720,922
American Electric Power	8,780,368	2,813,691
Consolidated Edison	7,133,210	3,332,786
Southern California Edison	6,977,237	2,563,974
Middle South Utilities	6,503,068	1,823,059
Public Service Electric & Gas	6,104,183	2,416,707

10 LARGEST DIVERSIFIED FINANCIAL COMPANIES

	Assets	*Revenues*
Aetna Life & Casualty	$30,228,463	$11,446,880
Travelers Corp.	19,159,864	7,888,901
American Express	17,108,200	4,666,500
H.F. Ahmanson	12,137,253	1,211,220
Merrill Lynch & Co.	10,556,100	2,051,996
First Charter Financial	9,548,833	846,313
Great Western Financial	9,453,989	878,354
INA	8,987,035	4,551,372
Loews	8,842,683	4,065,475
Transamerica	7,983,535	4,044,647

Estimated Annual Retail and Wholesale Sales by Kind of Business

(in millions of dollars)

Kind of business	1979	1978
Retail trade, total	886,047	800,890
Building materials, hardware, garden supply, and mobile home dealers	52,239	45,892
Automotive dealers	177,714	168,035
Furniture, home furnishings, and equipment stores	41,868	36,719
General merchandise group stores	110,233	101,240
Food stores	191,326	171,997
Gasoline service stations	71,894	59,270
Apparel and accessory stores	43,028	39,413
Eating and drinking places	75,139	69,145
Drug stores and proprietary stores	27,174	24,787
Liquor stores	15,595	13,764
Merchant wholesale trade, total	883,334	754,105
Total, (excluding farm-product raw materials)	785,022	670,902
Durable goods, total	404,286	349,916
Motor vehicles and automotive parts and supplies	76,519	68,298
Furniture and home furnishings	14,055	12,966
Lumber and other construction materials	36,998	32,223
Electrical goods	44,487	38,325
Hardware, plumbing, heating, and supplies	28,875	25,868
Machinery, equipment, supplies	111,843	97,877
Scrap and waste materials	16,818	11,804
Nondurable goods, total	479,048	404,189
Total (excluding farm-product raw materials)	380,736	320,986
Paper and paper products	19,721	17,586
Drugs, drug proprietaries, and druggists' sundries	12,638	11,526
Apparel, piece goods, and notions	27,537	25,076
Groceries and related products	138,635	125,091
Beer, wine, distilled alcoholic beverages	30,648	27,028
Miscellaneous nondurable goods	63,969	52,125
Tobacco and tobacco products	10,203	9,671

Source: Department of Commerce. Bureau of the Census.

50 Companies With Largest Number of Stockholders

Company	Stockholders	Company	Stockholders
American Telephone & Telegraph	2,978,000	Niagara Mohawk Power	209,000
General Motors	1,219,000	E. I. du Pont de Nemours	209,000
International Business Machines	697,000	Chrysler Corporation	207,000
Exxon Corporation	686,000	Northeast Utilities	200,000
General Electric	527,000	Atlantic Richfield	193,000
General Telephone & Electronics	462,000	Southern California Edison	181,000
Texaco Inc.	415,000	Westinghouse Electric	181,000
Gulf Oil	343,000	Standard Oil (Indiana)	176,000
Southern Company	341,000	BankAmerica	174,000
Ford Motor	337,000	Ohio Edison	173,000
Sears, Roebuck	334,000	Union Carbide Corporation	171,000
American Electric Power	295,000	Virginia Electric & Power	170,000
Mobil Corporation	274,000	General Public Utilities	169,000
Philadelphia Electric	260,000	Consumers Power	165,000
U.S. Steel	259,000	Union Electric	158,000
Standard Oil of California	256,000	Occidental Petroleum	156,000
Pacific Gas & Electric	255,000	Pennsylvania Power	155,000
Consolidated Edison	248,000	Columbia Gas System	152,000
Commonwealth Edison	245,000	Long Island Lighting	152,000
Eastman Kodak	242,000	Bethlehem Steel	151,000
RCA	239,000	Middle South Utilities	147,000
Tenneco, Inc.	232,000	Transamerica Corporation	146,000
Detroit Edison	232,000	Greyhound Corporation	146,000
Public Service Electric & Gas	227,000	Pan American World Airways	145,000
International Telephone & Telegraph	220,000	American Motors	145,000

NOTE: As of early 1980. *Source:* New York Stock Exchange.

50 Leading Stocks in Market Value

Stock	Market value (millions)	Listed shares (millions)	Stock	Market value (millions)	Listed shares (millions)
International Business Machines	$ 37,734	583.9	Halliburton Company	$ 5,009	58.9
American Telephone & Telegraph	36,529	700.8	Johnson & Johnson	4,857	61.3
Exxon Corporation	24,983	453.2	Caterpillar Tractor	4,667	86.4
General Motors	14,605	291.4	American Home Products	4,585	168.3
Schlumberger, N.V.	12,524	133.6	Morris (Philip) Inc.	4,484	124.5
Standard Oil (Indiana)	12,002	152.2	Eli Lilly	4,380	73.3
General Electric	11,747	231.5	Teledyne Inc.	4,325	32.3
Mobil Corporation	11,726	212.2	Coca-Cola Company	4,292	124.0
Standard Oil of California	9,638	171.0	Sun Company Inc.	4,194	60.0
Atlantic Richfield	9,208	114.6	Tenneco Inc.	4,110	106.1
Shell Oil	8,376	154.4	Weyerhaeuser Company	4,084	128.6
Texaco Inc.	7,920	274.3	General Telephone & Electronics	4,081	144.5
Eastman Kodak	7,796	161.6	BankAmerica Corporation	4,074	147.5
Phillips Petroleum	7,414	154.4	Union Oil of California	3,877	86.6
Gulf Oil	7,311	211.9	SmithKline Corporation	3,827	60.9
Getty Oil	6,529	88.5	Hewlett-Packard Company	3,500	59.2
Dow Chemical	6,436	200.4	Reynolds (R.J.) Industries	3,478	101.5
Procter & Gamble	6,140	82.7	Union Pacific	3,449	47.7
Minnesota Mining & Manufacturing	5,944	118.0	Ford Motor	3,398	106.2
E. I. du Pont de Nemours	5,886	145.8	Superior Oil	3,366	25.5
Sears, Roebuck	5,844	324.6	Boeing Company	3,294	65.1
Merck & Company	5,501	75.9	Burroughs Corporation	3,223	41.1
Conoco	5,353	113.3	Marathon Oil	3,072	61.4
Standard Oil (Ohio)	5,327	60.3	Citicorp	3,038	128.6
Xerox Corporation	5,098	82.1	International Telephone & Telegraph	2,971	115.9
			Total	**375,206**	**7,508.0**

NOTE: As of Dec. 31, 1979. The 50 leading stocks with the largest market value at the end of 1979 totaled $375 billion, or 40% of the value of all common shares for the 1,536 common stocks on the New York Stock Exchange. The five largest issues were valued at $126 billion, or 14% of the total. Five corporations joined the list in 1979—Conoco, Sun Company Inc., Union Pacific, Superior Oil, and Marathon Oil. *Source:* New York Stock Exchange.

Consumer Credit

(non-installment credit; in millions of dollars)

End of year	Service credit	Charge accounts	Single-payment loans	Total credit outstanding
1945	$ 845	$ 2,687	$ 1,491	$ 5,023
1950	1,638	4,858	3,642	10,138
1955	2,316	6,761	6,002	15,079
1960[1]	3,734	7,235	9,084	20,053
1965	5,545	8,319	15,462	29,326
1970	9,106	9,156	19,323	37,585
1975	12,027	11,739	27,378	51,144
1977	14,811	10,988	32,770	58,569
1978	16,431	12,002	36,255	64,688
1979	18,639	12,763	39,745	70,877

1. Beginning with 1960, data include Alaska and Hawaii. *Source:* Federal Reserve Board.

Terms on Conventional First Mortgages: All Major Types of Lenders

Type of homes and year	Contract rate (percent)	Fees and charges (percent)	Effective rate (percent)	Maturity (years)	Loan amount	Purchase price	Loan-to-price ratio (percent)
New homes: 1980[1]	12.61	2.04	13.00	28.5	$59,300	$82,800	73.5
1979	10.48	1.66	10.77	28.5	53,300	74,400	73.9
1978	9.30	1.39	9.54	28.0	45,900	62,600	75.3
1977	8.80	1.33	9.01	27.9	40,500	54,300	76.3
1975	8.75	1.54	—	26.8	33,300	44,600	76.1
1970	8.27	1.03	—	25.1	25,200	35,500	71.7
Existing homes: 1980[1]	13.21	1.77	13.56	27.0	50,500	71,100	73.3
1979	10.66	1.45	10.92	27.1	46,300	64,600	74.0
1978	9.37	1.26	9.58	26.4	39,400	54,200	75.1
1977	8.83	1.17	9.02	25.8	34,700	47,500	75.1
1975	9.01	1.19	—	24.0	27,400	38,200	73.4
1970	8.20	0.92	—	22.8	21,000	30,000	71.1

1. April. *Source:* Federal Home Loan Bank Board.

National Labor Unions With Membership Over 100,000

Members[1]	Union
1,499,425	Automobile, Aerospace and Agricultural Implement Workers of America, International Union, United (Ind.)
166,858	Bakery and Confectionery Workers' International Union of America
145,500	Boilermakers, Iron Ship Builders, Blacksmiths, Forgers and Helpers, International Brotherhood of
n.a.	Bricklayers and Allied Craftsmen, International Union of
174,932	Bridge and Structural Iron Workers, International Association of
105,000	California State Employees' Association (Ind.)
768,762	Carpenters and Joiners of America, United Brotherhood of
150,000	Classified School Employees, American Association of (Ind.)
501,000	Clothing and Textile Workers Union of North America, Amalgamated
508,063	Communications Workers of America
1,696,469	Education Association, National (Ind.)
255,427	Electrical, Radio and Machine Workers, International Union of
166,000	Electrical, Radio and Machine Workers of America, United (Ind.)
1,011,726	Electrical Workers, International Brotherhood of
176,474	Fire Fighters, International Association of
265,506	Government Employees, American Federation of
200,000	Government Employees, National Association of (Ind.)
403,890	Hotel and Restaurant Employees and Bartenders International Union
610,000	Laborers' International Union of North America
348,380	Ladies' Garment Workers' Union, International
227,005	Letter Carriers of the United States of America, National Association of
920,735	Machinists and Aerospace Workers, International Association of
119,203	Maintenance of Way Employees, Brotherhood of
500,000	Meat Cutters and Butcher Workmen of North America, Amalgamated
307,944	Mine Workers of America, United (Ind.)
330,000	Musicians, American Federation of
187,000	Nurses' Association; American (Ind.)
105,000	Office and Professional Employees International Union

Members[1]	Union
180,000	Oil, Chemical and Atomic Workers International Union
411,860	Operating Engineers, International Union of
190,000	Painters and Allied Trades of the United States and Canada, International Brotherhood of
284,329	Paperworkers International Union, United
337,055	Plumbing and Pipe Fitting Industry of the United States and Canada, United Association of Journeymen and Apprentices of the
140,000	Police, Fraternal Order of (Ind.)
245,826	Postal Workers' Union, American
120,000	Printing and Graphic Communications Union, International
200,083	Railway, Airline and Steamship Clerks, Freight Handlers, Express and Station Employees, Brotherhood of
735,000	Retail Clerks International Association
198,000	Retail, Wholesale and Department Store Union
199,990	Rubber, Cork, Linoleum and Plastic Workers of America, United
625,000	Service Employees' International Union
158,528	Sheet Metal Workers' International Association
1,020,000	State, County and Municipal Employees of America, American Federation of
1,285,740	Steelworkers of America, United
500,000	Teachers, American Federation of
1,923,896	Teamsters, Chauffeurs, Warehousemen and Helpers of America, International Brotherhood of (Ind.)
154,000	Transit Union, Amalgamated
130,000	Transport Workers Union of America
175,500	Transportation Union, United
117,691	Woodworkers of America, International

1. 1978. NOTE: Unless indicated by Ind. (Independent), all unions are affliated with the AFL-CIO. n.a.=not available. *Source:* Department of Labor, Bureau of Labor Statistics.

Strikes and Lockouts

Year	Strikes and lockouts	Workers involved (thousands)	Man-days idle (thousands)	Year	Strikes and lockouts	Workers involved (thousands)	Man-days idle (thousands)
1895	1,255	407	n.a.	1950	4,843	2,410	38,800
1900	1,839	568	n.a.	1955	4,320	2,650	28,200
1905	2,186	302	n.a.	1960	3,333	1,320	19,100
1915	1,593	n.a.	n.a.	1965	3,963	1,550	23,300
1920	3,411	1,463	n.a.	1970	5,716	3,305	66,414
1925	1,301	428	n.a.	1975	5,031	1,746	31,237
1930	637	183	3,320	1977	5,506	2,040	35,822
1935	2,014	1,120	15,500	1978	4,230	1,623	36,992
1940	2,508	577	6,700	1979[2]	4,780	1,720	35,467
1945	4,750	3,470	38,000				

1. First year for which figures include Alaska and Hawaii. 2. Preliminary. NOTE: n.a. = not available. *Source:* Department of Labor, Bureau of Labor Statistics.

Persons in the Labor Force

Year	Working population		Percent of working population in		Year	Working population		Percent of working population in	
	Number (thousands)	%total population aged 10 and over[1]	Farm occupation	Nonfarm occupation		Number (thousands)	%total population aged 10 and over[1]	Farm occupation	Nonfarm occupation
1820	2,881	44.4	71.8	28.2	1900	29,073	50.2	37.5	62.5
1830	3,932	45.5	70.5	29.5	1910	37,371	52.2	31.0	69.0
1840	5,420	46.6	68.6	31.4	1920	42,434	51.3	27.0	73.0
1850	7,697	46.8	63.7	36.3	1930	48,830	49.5	21.4	78.6
1860	10,533	47.0	58.9	41.1	1940	52,966	52.4	17.0	83.0
1870	12,925	44.4	53.0	47.0	1950	59,671	53.4	11.5	88.5
1880	17,392	47.3	49.4	50.6	1960	69,877	55.3	5.9	94.1
1890	23,318	49.2	42.6	57.4	1970	82,897	55.5	2.9	97.1

1. For 1820 to 1930, the data relate to the population and gainful workers at ages 10 and over. For 1940 to 1970, the data relate to the population and labor force at ages 14 and over: the farm and nonfarm percentages relate only to the experienced labor force. *Source:* Department of Commerce, Bureau of the Census.

How Consumers Spend Their Dollar
(in billions)

	1978	1978 % of total	1975	1970	1965	1960	1955	1950	1940	1930
Food	$240.7	17.8	$184.7	$112.1	$85.8	$70.1	$58.1	$46.0	$16.6	$18.0
Tobacco	17.9	1.3	14.7	11.2	8.4	7.0	5.0	4.3	1.9	1.5
Alcohol	30.9	2.3	24.9	17.9	13.0	10.4	9.1	7.9	3.6	n.a.
Clothing, accessories, and jewelry	107.6	8.0	82.0	62.8	43.3	33.0	28.0	23.7	8.9	9.7
Personal care	18.6	1.4	14.2	10.4	7.6	5.3	3.5	2.4	1.0	1.0
Housing	212.2	15.7	150.2	90.9	63.5	46.3	33.7	21.3	9.4	11.1
Household operation	195.0	14.4	142.3	87.4	61.8	46.9	37.3	29.5	10.5	9.6
Medical care	131.0	9.7	89.2	47.4	28.1	19.1	12.8	8.8	3.0	2.8
Personal business	71.1	5.3	51.6	35.3	21.9	15.0	10.0	6.8	3.3	3.7
Transportation	191.3	14.2	125.5	77.8	58.2	43.1	35.6	24.7	7.1	6.1
Recreation	91.2	6.8	66.5	40.7	26.3	18.3	14.1	11.1	3.8	4.0
Private education and research	20.8	1.5	15.5	10.4	5.9	3.7	2.3	1.6	0.6	0.7
Religious and welfare activities	17.2	1.3	13.0	8.6	6.0	4.7	3.3	2.3	1.0	1.2
Foreign travel and other	5.2	0.4	5.0	4.8	3.2	2.2	1.6	0.6	(1)	0.5
Total	**1,350.8**	**100.0**	**979.1**	**617.6**	**432.8**	**325.2**	**254.4**	**191.0**	**70.8**	**69.9**

1. Less than $100 million. *Source:* Department of Commerce, Bureau of Economic Analysis.

Employed Persons 16 Years and Over, by Race and Occupational Groups

Race and occupational group	1979 Number	1979 Percent distribution	1978 Number	1978 Percent distribution	Percent change, 1978–79
WHITE					
White-collar workers	45,203,000	52.5	43,388,000	51.8	4.2
Professional and technical workers	13,714,000	15.9	13,012,000	15.5	5.4
Managers and administrators, except farm	9,945,000	11.6	9,597,000	11.4	3.6
Sales workers	5,861,000	6.8	5,651,000	6.7	3.7
Clerical workers	15,683,000	18.2	15,128,000	18.0	3.7
Blue-collar workers	28,063,000	32.6	27,611,000	32.9	1.6
Craft and kindred workers	11,858,000	13.8	11,460,000	13.7	3.5
Operatives, except transport	9,264,000	10.8	9,242,000	11.0	0.2
Transport equipment operatives	3,089,000	3.6	3,014,000	3.6	2.5
Nonfarm laborers	3,851,000	4.5	3,894,000	4.6	−1.1
Private household workers	728,000	0.8	779,000	0.9	−6.5
Service workers, except private household	9,571,000	11.1	9,518,000	11.4	0.6
Farm Workers	2,460,000	2.9	2,540,000	3.0	−3.1
Total	**86,025,000**	**100.0**	**83,836,000**	**100.0**	**2.6**
BLACK AND OTHER					
White-collar workers	4,140,000	37.9	3,817,000	36.2	8.5
Professional and technical workers	1,336,000	12.2	1,233,000	11.7	8.4
Managers and administrators, except farm	572,000	5.2	508,000	4.8	12.6
Sales workers	302,000	2.8	300,000	2.8	0.7
Clerical workers	1,931,000	17.7	1,776,000	16.9	8.7
Blue-collar workers	4,003,000	36.7	3,920,000	37.2	2.1
Craft and kindred workers	1,022,000	9.4	925,000	8.8	10.5
Operatives, except transport	1,645,000	15.1	1,632,000	15.5	0.8
Transport equipment operatives	523,000	4.8	527,000	5.0	−0.8
Nonfarm laborers	813,000	7.4	835,000	7.9	−2.6
Private household workers	360,000	3.3	383,000	3.6	−6.0
Service workers, except private household	2,175,000	19.9	2,158,000	20.5	0.8
Farm workers	243,000	2.2	258,000	2.4	−5.8
Total	**10,920,000**	**100.0**	**10,537,000**	**100.0**	**3.6**

Source: Department of Labor, Bureau of Labor Statistics.

Women in the Working Population

Year[1]	Number (thousands)	Percent of female population aged 10 and over[1]	Percent of total working population aged 10 and over[1]
1880	2,647	14.7	15.2
1890	4,006	17.4	17.2
1900	5,319	18.8	18.3
1910	7,445	21.5	19.9
1920	8,637	21.4	20.4
1930	10,752	22.0	22.0
1940	12,845	25.4	24.3
1950	18,412	33.9	17.3
1960[2]	23,272	37.8	19.4
1970	31,560	43.4	22.5
1978	42,002	50.1	26.1
1979	43,531	51.1	26.6

1. For 1880–1930; data relate to population and gainful workers at ages 10 and over; for 1940, to ages 14 and over; for 1950–78, to population at ages 16 and over. 2. Beginning in 1960, figures include Alaska and Hawaii. *Sources:* Department of Commerce, Bureau of the Census, and Department of Labor, Bureau of Labor Statistics.

Mothers Participating in Labor Force

(figures in percentage)

Year	Mothers with children: Under 18 years	6 to 17 years	Under 6 years[1]
1950	21.6	32.8	13.6
1955	27.0	38.4	18.2
1965	35.0	45.7	25.3
1975	47.4	54.8	38.9
1976	48.8	56.2	39.7
1977	50.7	58.3	40.9
1978	52.9	60.0	43.7
1979	54.5	61.6	45.4

1. May also have older children. NOTE: For 1950 and 1955, data are for April; for 1965 and 1975–78, data are for March. *Source:* Department of Labor, Women's Bureau.

Employed Persons by Major Occupations, 1979

(in thousands)

Occupations	Total employed	Percent distribution: Female	Black and other
White-collar workers	49,342	52.8	8.4
Professional and technical	15,050	43.3	8.9
Accountants	1,045	32.9	8.4
Architects	84	6.0	9.5
Computer programmers	321	29.0	8.1
Computer systems analysts	177	24.3	7.3
Engineers	1,385	2.9	6.3
Aeronautical and astronautical engineers	64	1.6	4.7
Civil engineers	162	2.5	7.4
Electrical and electronic engineers	356	2.2	7.3
Industrial engineers	245	7.3	6.5
Mechanical engineers	237	1.3	5.1
Lawyers and judges	499	12.4	2.6
Librarians, archivists, and curators	201	78.1	8.5
Life and physical scientists	280	18.9	8.2
Biological scientists	55	36.4	7.3
Chemists	125	15.2	11.2
Operations and systems researchers and analysts	156	21.2	10.3
Personnel and labor relations workers	413	45.5	10.2
Dentists	131	4.6	4.6
Pharmacists	135	24.4	9.6
Physicians, medical and osteopathic	431	10.7	9.5
Registered nurses	1,223	96.8	11.4
Therapists	207	72.9	11.6
Health technologists and technicians	534	69.5	11.4
Religious workers	339	13.3	8.3
Economists	119	24.4	4.2
Psychologists	91	50.5	5.5
Social workers	361	64.3	20.8
Recreation workers	116	52.6	21.6
Teachers, college and university	545	31.6	6.8
Teachers, except college and university	3,118	70.8	10.1
Adult education teachers	76	51.3	7.9
Elementary school teachers	1,374	84.3	12.0
Prekindergarten and kindergarten teachers	234	97.4	14.1
Secondary school teachers	1,213	50.7	8.2
Engineering and science technicians	1,039	15.9	8.2
Airplane pilots	72	—	1.4
Vocational and educational counselors	167	53.3	14.4
Writers, artists, and entertainers	1,243	37.8	5.7
Athletes and kindred workers	105	38.1	4.8
Designers	179	28.5	6.1
Editors and reporters	201	42.3	5.5
Musicians and composers	145	35.9	6.9
Painters and sculptors	189	46.6	5.8
Photographers	107	21.5	6.5
Public relations specialists and publicity writers	130	43.8	3.8
Managers and administrators, except farm	10,516	24.6	5.4
Bank officials and financial managers	620	31.6	5.0

Occupations	Total employed	Percent distribution	
		Female	Black and other
Buyers and purchasing agents	451	30.4	6.0
Buyers, wholesale and retail trade	200	40.0	6.5
Health administrators	185	48.1	7.0
Office managers n.e.c.	416	63.0	2.2
Officials and administrators, public administration n.e.c.	414	26.6	10.1
Restaurant, cafeteria, and bar managers	632	35.4	9.3
Sales managers and department heads, retail trade	339	39.8	4.7
Sales managers, except retail trade	347	8.6	3.5
School administrators, elementary and secondary	299	37.5	11.0
Sales workers	6,163	45.1	4.9
Insurance agents, brokers and underwriters	534	23.8	6.2
Real estate agents and brokers	616	49.4	2.8
Stock and bond sales agents	122	19.7	3.3
Sales representatives, manufacturing industries	398	17.1	3.0
Sales representatives, wholesale trade	904	10.4	3.2
Sales clerks, retail trade	2,362	70.7	6.9
Sales workers, except clerks, retail trade	549	20.0	2.2
Clerical workers	17,613	80.3	11.0
Bank tellers	493	92.9	9.3
Billing clerks	162	90.1	8.6
Bookkeepers	1,910	91.1	5.4
Cashiers	1,477	87.9	10.5
Counter clerks, except food	362	77.9	11.0
File clerks	305	86.6	21.0
Insurance adjusters, examiners, and investigators	173	55.5	12.7
Library attendants and assistants	165	79.4	12.7
Mail carriers, post office	253	10.3	10.7
Computer and peripheral equipment operators	453	61.6	13.0
Key punch operators	274	95.3	23.0
Payroll and timekeeping clerks	236	81.4	8.5
Postal clerks	259	34.4	23.9
Receptionists	600	97.2	8.7
Secretaries	3,729	99.1	6.6
Shipping and receiving clerks	484	21.3	13.6
Statistical clerks	400	78.8	12.3
Stock clerks and storekeepers	529	31.9	14.4
Teachers aids, except school monitors	350	93.4	17.1
Telephone operators	327	91.7	16.8
Typists	1,020	96.7	17.2
Blue-collar workers	**32,066**	**18.4**	**12.5**
Craft and kindred workers	12,880	5.7	7.9
Carpenters	1,276	1.3	5.1
Brickmasons and stonemasons	205	.5	16.1
Electricians	640	1.3	5.6
Excavating, grading, and road machinery operators	444	.5	9.5
Painters, construction and maintenance	483	5.0	10.6
Plumbers and pipefitters	450	.4	9.6
Structural metal craft workers	86	—	7.0
Roofers and slaters	148	—	10.1

Occupations	Total employed	Percent distribution	
		Female	Black and other
Blue-collar worker supervisors n.e.c.	1,739	10.2	7.4
Machinists and job setters	642	3.3	7.9
Metal craft workers, excluding mechanics, machinists, and job setters	649	2.8	7.2
Sheetmetal workers and tinsmiths	158	2.5	5.1
Tool and die makers	184	2.2	3.8
Automobile body repairers	192	.5	8.3
Automobile mechanics	1,081	.6	9.4
Mechanics, except automobiles	2,178	1.9	6.7
Heavy equipment mechanics, including diesel	954	1.2	6.7
Household appliance and accessory installers and mechanics	156	2.6	7.1
Compositors and typesetters	186	29.0	7.0
Printing press operators	192	11.5	9.9
Bakers	140	43.6	12.9
Crane, derrick, and hoist operators	164	1.2	15.9
Decorators and window dressers	129	72.9	3.9
Stationary engineers	192	1.0	8.9
Telephone installers and repairers	302	9.9	7.9
Operatives, except transport	10,909	39.9	15.1
Assemblers	1,289	53.4	15.8
Checkers, examiners and inspectors, manufacturing	746	51.2	12.2
Garage workers and gas station attendants	369	5.4	11.4
Packers and wrappers, excluding meat and produce	626	63.7	19.2
Precision machine operatives	405	13.3	8.9
Sewers and stitchers	810	95.3	18.3
Welders and flame cutters	713	4.5	10.5
Transport equipment operatives	3,612	8.1	14.5
Bus drivers	358	45.5	19.6
Delivery and route workers	580	8.1	9.0
Taxicab drivers and chauffeurs	164	13.4	28.0
Truck drivers	1,965	2.1	13.3
Nonfarm laborers	4,665	11.3	17.4
Service workers	**12,834**	**62.4**	**19.8**
Private households	1,088	97.6	33.1
Service workers, except private households	11,747	59.2	18.5
Cleaning workers	2,450	35.6	28.4
Food service workers	4,300	68.4	13.8
Bartenders	296	43.6	6.8
Cooks	1,251	56.0	19.3
Waiters	1,363	89.4	7.9
Health service workers	1,818	90.4	24.9
Dental assistants	134	97.8	4.5
Health aids, excluding nursing	281	87.5	22.4
Nursing aides, orderlies and attendants	1,024	87.5	30.6
Practical nurses	376	97.9	18.6
Protective service workers	1,406	8.8	12.4
Fire fighters	236	.4	6.4
Guards	569	10.9	17.6
Police and detectives	484	6.0	9.9
Sheriffs and bailiffs	68	7.4	8.8
Farm workers	**2,703**	**18.0**	**9.0**
Farmers and farm managers	1,446	9.6	2.6
Farm laborers, wage workers	930	16.8	20.9
Total employed	**96,945**	**41.7**	**11.3**

NOTE: n.e.c. = "not elsewhere classified" and designates broad categories of occupations that cannot be more specifically identified. *Source:* Department of Labor, Bureau of Labor Statistics.

Percent Unemployed in the Civilian Labor Force

Year	Percent Unemployed	Year	Percent Unemployed
1920	5.2	1974	5.6
1922	6.7	1975	8.5
1924	5.0	1976	7.7
1926	1.8	1977	7.0
1928	4.2	1978	6.0
1930	8.7	1979	5.8
1932	23.6	Jan.	5.8
1934	21.7	Feb.	5.7
1936	16.9	March	5.7
1938	19.0	April	5.8
1940	14.6	May	5.8
1942	4.7	June	5.7
1944	1.2	July	5.7
1946	3.9	Aug.	5.9
1948	3.8	Sept.	5.8
1950	5.3	Oct.	5.9
1952	3.0	Nov.	5.8
1954	5.5	Dec.	5.9
1956	4.1	1980	
1958	6.8	Jan.	6.2
1960	5.5	Feb.	6.0
1962	5.5	March	6.2
1964	5.2	April	7.0
1966	3.8	May	7.8
1968	3.6	June	7.7
1970	4.9	July	7.8
1972	5.6	Aug.	7.6
1973	4.9	Sept.	7.5

NOTE: Estimates prior to 1940 are based on sources other than direct enumeration. *Source:* Department of Labor, Bureau of Labor Statistics.

Unemployment Rate, 1979

Race and age	Women[1]	Men[1]
All races:	6.8	5.1
16 to 19 years	16.4	15.8
20 years and over	5.7	4.1
White	5.9	4.4
16 to 19 years	13.9	13.9
20 years and over	5.0	3.6
Minority races	12.3	10.3
16 to 19 years	35.7	31.5
20 years and over	10.1	8.4

1. Annual averages. *Source:* Department of Labor, Women's Bureau.

Leading Advertising Agencies in World Billings

(in millions of dollars)

Agency	1979	1978
Young & Rubicam	$1,921.1	$1,359.5
J. Walter Thompson Co.	1,693.0	1,476.0
McCann–Erickson	1,670.3	1,407.1
Ogilvy & Mather Intl.	1,392.6	1,131.9
Ted Bates & Co.	1,203.0	904.0
SSC&B	1,021.6	887.6
BBDO International	985.5	817.3
Leo Burnett Co.	950.7	866.1
Foote, Cone, & Belding	918.1	740.5
D'Arcy–MacManus & Masius	853.6	698.8

Source: Reprinted with permission from the March 19, 1980, issue of *Advertising Age*. Copyright 1980 by Crain Communications, Inc.

Advertising Expenditures by Medium

(in billions)

Medium	1979[1] Amt.	1979[1] % of total	1975 Amt.	1975 % of total	1970 Amt.	1970 % of total	1965 Amt.	1965 % of total	1960 Amt.	1960 % of total	1950 Amt.	1950 % of total
Newspapers	$14.6	29.3	$8.4	29.9	$5.8	29.3	$4.5	29.2	$3.7	31.0	$2.1	36.4
Magazines	2.9	5.9	1.5	5.2	1.3	6.8	1.2	7.9	0.9	7.9	0.5	9.0
Business Papers	1.6	3.2	0.9	3.3	0.7	3.8	0.7	4.4	0.6	5.1	0.3	4.4
Radio	3.4	6.8	2.0	7.0	1.3	6.5	0.9	6.0	0.7	5.8	0.6	10.6
Television	10.2	20.5	5.3	18.6	3.7	18.7	2.5	16.5	1.6	13.3	0.2	3.0
Direct mail	6.7	13.3	4.2	14.8	2.7	13.9	2.3	15.2	1.8	15.3	0.8	14.1
Outdoor	0.5	1.1	0.3	1.2	0.2	1.2	0.2	1.2	0.2	1.7	0.1	2.5
Miscellaneous[2]	9.8	19.7	5.6	20.0	3.9	19.8	3.0	19.6	2.4	19.8	1.1	20.0
Total	**49.8**	**100.0**	**28.2**	**100.0**	**19.6**	**100.0**	**15.3**	**100.0**	**11.9**	**100.0**	**5.7**	**100.0**

1. Preliminary. 2. Includes regional farm papers. *Sources:* McCann-Erickson, Inc., and *Advertising Age*.

Annual Railroad Carloadings

Year	Total	Year	Total	Year	Total	Year	Total
1920	33,754,000	1945	41,918,000	1970	27,160,000	1975	23,217,000
1925	34,783,000	1950	38,903,000	1971	25,266,000	1976	23,457,000
1930	30,173,000	1955	37,636,000	1972	26,105,000	1977	23,173,000
1935	22,015,000	1960	30,441,000	1973	27,338,000	1978	23,373,000
1940	36,358,000	1965	29,248,000	1974	26,184,000	1979	23,876,000

Source: Association of American Railroads.

Composition of the Civilian Labor Force and Unemployment

Race, sex, and age	July 1980 Civilian labor force Number (thousands)	Percent distribution	July 1980 Unemployed Number (thousands)	Percent distribution	Rate	July 1979 Civilian labor force Number (thousands)	Percent distribution	July 1979 Unemployed Number (thousands)	Percent distribution	Rate
White	92,456	88.9	6,392	77.9	6.9	90,659	88.0	4,539	76.9	5.0
Men, 20 years and older	49,388	46.9	2,967	36.2	6.0	48,634	47.2	1,761	29.8	3.6
Women, 20 years and older	34,785	33.1	2,042	24.9	5.9	33,604	32.6	1,618	27.4	4.8
Teenagers, 16 to 19 years	8,283	7.9	1,383	16.9	16.7	8,421	8.2	1,160	19.7	13.8
Black and other	12,739	12.1	1,807	22.0	14.2	12,386	12.0	1,363	23.1	11.0
Men, 20 years and older	6,049	5.7	771	9.4	12.7	5,961	5.8	498	8.4	8.4
Women, 20 years and older	5,633	5.3	649	7.9	11.5	5,398	5.2	541	9.2	10.0
Teenagers, 16 to 19 years	1,057	1.0	387	4.7	36.6	1,027	1.0	324	5.5	31.5
All races										
Men, 20 years and older	55,398	52.7	3,730	45.4	6.7	54.579	53.0	2,259	38.3	4.1
Women, 20 years and older	40,471	38.5	2,702	32.9	6.7	39,033	37.8	2,159	36.6	5.5
Teenagers, 16 to 19 years	9,334	8.9	1,774	21.6	19.0	9,481	9.2	1,484	25.1	15.8
Total	**105,203**	**100.0**	**8,207**	**100.0**	**7.8**	**103,045**	**100.0**	**5,902**	**100.0**	**5.7**

NOTE: Totals may not add due to rounding. *Source:* Department of Labor, Bureau of Labor Statistics.

Nonmanufacturing Industries—Gross Average Weekly Earnings and Hours Worked

Industry	1980[1] Earnings	1980[1] Hours worked	1979 Earnings	1979 Hours worked	1975 Earnings	1975 Hours worked	1970 Earnings	1970 Hours worked	1958 Earnings	1958 Hours worked
Bituminous coal and lignite mining	$437.30	39.9	$418.40	41.0	$284.53	39.2[2]	$186.41	40.8	$97.57	33.3
Metal mining	419.63	41.1	381.92	41.2	250.72	42.3	165.68	42.7	94.96	38.6
Nonmetallic minerals	324.82	43.6	310.05	45.0	213.09	43.4	155.11	44.7	88.33	43.3
Telephone communications	339.55	39.9	324.41	40.2	221.18	38.4	131.60	39.4	78.72	38.4
Radio and TV broadcasting	279.65	38.1	262.05	38.2	214.50	39.0	147.45	38.2	100.70	38.0
Electric, gas and sanitary services	367.38	41.7	343.19	41.7	246.79	41.2	172.64	41.5	98.57	40.9
Local and suburban transportation	273.62	39.2	285.23	41.1	196.89	40.1	142.30	42.1	87.29	43.0
Wholesale trade	267.88	38.6	247.93	38.8	188.75	38.6	137.60	40.0	84.02	40.2
Retail trade	146.53	30.4	139.07	30.7	108.22	32.4	82.47	33.8	54.10	38.1
Hotels, tourist courts, motels	138.79	31.4	122.98	30.9	89.64	31.9	68.16	34.6	40.89	39.7
Laundries and dry cleaning plants	151.53	33.9	141.04	34.4	106.05	35.0	77.47	35.7	45.28	38.7
General building contracting	336.72	36.8	309.46	35.9	254.88	36.0	184.40	36.3	96.92	35.5

1. June preliminary. 2. 11-month average. *Source:* Department of Labor, Bureau of Labor Statistics.

Manufacturing Industries—Gross Average Weekly Earnings and Hours Worked

Industry	1980[1] Earnings	1980[1] Hours worked	1979 Earnings	1979 Hours worked	1975 Earnings	1975 Hours worked	1970 Earnings	1970 Hours worked	1958 Earnings	1958 Hours worked	1953 Earnings	1953 Hours worked
All manufacturing[2]	$283.19	38.9	$268.94	40.2	$189.51	39.4	$133.73	39.8	$82.71	39.2	$70.47	40.5
Durable goods	303.41	39.2	290.50	40.8	205.09	39.9	143.07	40.3	89.27	39.5	76.63	41.2
Primary metal industries	378.02	38.3	371.36	41.4	246.80	40.0	159.17	40.5	101.11	38.3	84.46	41.0
Iron and steel foundries	317.15[3]	39.3[3]	316.52	41.0	220.99	40.4	151.03	40.6	86.86	37.6	77.64	41.3
Nonferrous foundries	281.52[3]	39.1[3]	269.73	40.5	190.03	39.1	138.16	39.7	90.85	39.5	79.73	41.1
Fabricated metal products	290.77	39.4	278.26	40.8	201.60	40.0	143.67	40.7	89.78	39.9	76.49	41.8

Industry	1980[1] Earnings	1980[1] Hours worked	1979 Earnings	1979 Hours worked	1975 Earnings	1975 Hours worked	1970 Earnings	1970 Hours worked	1958 Earnings	1958 Hours worked	1953 Earnings	1953 Hours worked
Hardware, cutlery, hand tools	270.27[3]	38.5[3]	260.55	39.9	187.07	39.3	132.33	40.1	82.92	39.3	71.80	41.5
Other hardware	279.17[3]	38.4[3]	266.74	39.4	195.42	39.4	133.46	40.2	84.32	39.4	72.63	41.5
Structural metal products	290.65[3]	40.2[3]	265.32	40.2	202.61	40.2	142.61	40.4	92.63	40.1	79.71	42.4
Electric and electronic equipment	265.27	38.5	254.29	40.3	180.91	39.5	130.54	39.8	83.95	39.6	70.99	40.8
Machinery, except electrical	321.20	40.0	306.39	41.8	219.22	40.9	154.95	41.1	94.33	39.8	82.68	42.4
Transportation equipment	367.88	39.6	351.44	41.2	242.61	40.3	163.22	40.3	100.40	40.0	85.28	41.6
Motor vehicles and equipment	377.71[3]	38.7[3]	373.68	41.2	262.68	40.6	170.07	40.3	101.24	39.7	89.88	42.0
Lumber and wood products	254.89	38.1	240.16	39.5	167.35	39.1	117.51	39.7	69.09	38.6	60.76	39.2
Furniture and fixtures	204.23	37.2	195.32	38.6	142.13	37.9	108.58	39.2	69.95	39.3	62.99	40.9
Nondurable goods	255.15	38.6	235.80	39.3	168.78	38.8	120.43	39.1	74.11	38.8	62.57	39.6
Textile mill products	193.61	38.8	187.80	40.3	133.28	39.2	97.76	39.9	57.51	38.6	53.18	39.1
Apparel and other textile products	156.64	35.2	149.25	35.2	111.97	35.1	84.37	35.3	54.05	35.1	48.74	36.1
Leather and leather products	167.72	36.7	154.40	36.5	120.80	37.4	92.63	37.2	57.25	36.7	50.90	37.7
Food and kindred products	275.22	39.6	250.17	39.9	184.17	40.3	127.98	40.5	79.15	40.8	63.50	41.5
Tobacco manufactures	291.93	35.3	254.22	38.0	171.38	38.0	110.00	37.8	62.17	39.1	47.63	38.1
Paper and allied products	333.60	41.7	303.31	42.6	207.58	41.6	144.14	41.9	87.99	41.9	71.81	43.0
Printing and publishing	278.94	36.8	259.13	37.5	198.32	37.0	147.78	37.7	94.62	38.0	82.29	39.0
Chemicals and allied products	341.52	40.9	317.26	41.8	219.63	40.9	153.50	41.6	93.20	40.7	74.21	41.0
Petroleum and coal products	456.40	43.8	410.41	43.8	267.07	41.6	182.76	42.7	111.66	40.9	90.35	40.7

1. July preliminary. 2. Average weekly earnings in 1919 = \$21.84; 1929 = \$24.76; 1932 = \$16.89; 1939 = \$23.64. Average hours worked per week in 1914 = 49.4; 1929 = 44.2; 1932 = 38.3; 1939 = 37.7. 3. June preliminary. *Source:* Department of Labor, Bureau of Labor Statistics.

Employment by Marital Status and Sex, March, 1979

(in thousands)

Marital status and sex (persons 16 years and over)	Population	Civilian labor force: Number	Labor force participation rate	Employed	Unemployed: Number	Unemployed: Percent of labor force
Men	76,894	58,608	77.0	55,237	3,372	5.8
Never married	21,105	14,895	70.9	13,108	1,787	12.0
Married, wife present	48,255	38,756	81.4	37,514	1,243	3.2
Other ever married	7,534	4,957	66.2	4,615	343	6.9
Married, wife absent	2,117	1,599	76.5	1,470	129	8.1
Widowed	1,945	570	29.3	547	23	4.0
Divorced	3,472	2,789	80.9	2,598	191	6.8
Women	84,686	42,971	50.7	40,150	2,821	6.6
Never married	17,564	11,006	62.7	9,940	1,066	9.7
Married, husband present	48,239	23,832	49.4	22,620	1,212	5.1
Other ever married	18,884	8,133	43.1	7,590	543	6.7
Married, husband absent	3,075	1,808	58.8	1,631	177	9.8
Widowed	10,450	2,358	22.6	2,235	123	5.2
Divorced	5,359	3,967	74.0	3,723	243	6.1
Total: Both sexes	**161,580**	**101,579**	**63.2**	**95,387**	**6.193**	**6.1**

NOTE: Due to rounding, sums of individuals items may not equal total. *Source:* Department of Labor, Bureau of Labor Statistics.

Occupations of Employed Women
(16 years of age and over)

Occupations	1979[1] (percent)	1978[1] (percent)	1977[1] (percent)	1976[1] (percent)
Professional and technical workers	16.1	15.6	15.9	16.0
Managers and administrators (except farm)	6.4	6.1	5.9	5.5
Sales workers	6.9	6.9	6.8	6.7
Clerical workers	35.0	34.6	34.7	34.9
Craft and kindred workers	1.8	1.8	1.6	1.6
Operatives, except transport	10.8	11.1	11.2	11.3
Transport equipment operatives	.7	.7	.6	.6
Nonfarm laborers	1.3	1.3	1.2	1.1
Private household workers	2.6	2.9	3.1	3.1
Service workers	17.2	17.7	17.9	17.9
Farmers and farm managers	.3	.3	.3	.3
Farm laborers and supervisors	.9	1.0	1.0	1.0

1. Annual averages. NOTE: Details may not add up to totals because of rounding. *Source:* Department of Labor, Women's Bureau.

Earnings Distribution of Full-Time Workers, by Sex, 1978
(persons 14 years old and over)

Earnings group	Number (in thousands)		Distribution (percent)		Likelihood of a woman rather than a man to be in each earnings group (percent)
	Women	Men	Women	Men	
Less than $3,000	630	930	3.0	2.4	1.3
$3,000 to $4,999	1,179	834	5.7	2.0	2.9
$5,000 to $6,999	3,642	2,077	17.5	5.1	3.4
$7,000 to $9,999	6,236	4,613	29.8	11.2	2.7
$10,000 to $14,999	6,433	10,043	30.8	24.4	1.3
$15,000 and over	2,793	22,539	13.4	54.9	0.2
Total with earnings	**20,914**	**41,036**	**100.0**	**100.0**	**1.0**

1. Figures obtained by dividing percentages for women by percentages for men. *Source:* Department of Commerce, Bureau of the Census.

Median Income Comparisons of Full-Time Workers by Educational Attainment 1978
(persons 25 years and over)

Years of school completed	Median income		Income gap in dollars	Women's income as a percent of men's	Percent men's income exceeded women's
	Women	Men			
Elementary school:					
Less than 8 years	$6,648	$10,474	$3,826	63.5	57.6
8 years	7,489	12,965	5,476	57.8	73.1
High School:					
1 to 3 years	7,996	14,199	6,203	56.3	77.6
4 years	9,769	16,396	6,627	59.6	67.8
College:					
1 to 3 years	10,634	17,411	6,777	61.1	63.7
4 years or more	13,395	22,095	8,700	60.6	64.9

Source: Department of Commerce, Bureau of the Census.

Women in the Labor Force
(16 years of age and over)

Labor force status	1979 (thousands)	1978 (thousands)	1977 (thousands)	1976 (thousands)
In the labor force:	43,391	41,878	39,952	38,414
16 to 19 years of age	4,481	4,462	4,267	4,138
20 years and over	38,910	37,416	35,685	34,276
Employed	40,446	38,882	36,685	35,095
16 to 19 years of age	3,748	3,702	3,486	3,365
20 years and over	36,698	35,180	33,199	31,730
Unemployed	2,945	2,996	3,267	3,320
16 to 19 years of age	733	760	781	773
20 years and over	2,212	2,236	2,486	2,547
Not in the labor force:	41,692	41,887	42,510	42,789
Women as percent of labor force	42.2	41.7	41.0	40.5
Total civilian population	85,083	83,765	82,462	81,203

Source: Department of Labor, Women's Bureau.

Characteristics of Households With Female Heads, 1978

Characteristics	Number of households
All households	77,330,000
Number with female head	19,987,000
Percent of all households	25.8
Persons per household	2.0
Under 18 years	11,116,000
Percentage under 18 years	28.3
18 years and over	28,120,000
Percentage 18 years and over	71.7
Marital status of female head	
Married, husband absent	23,520,000
Widowed	8,821,000
Divorced	4,379,000
Single	4,436,000

Income bracket	Number of households
Household income of female head	
Under $2,000	1,160,000
$2,000 to $3,999	4,361,600
$4,000 to $5,999	3,169,000
$6,000 to $7,999	2,404,000
$8,000 to $9,999	1,884,000
$10,000 to $14,999	3,305,000
$15,000 to $24,999	2,763,000
$25,000 to $49,999	856,000
$50,000 and over	84,000
Median income	$7,084

Source: Department of Commerce, Bureau of the Census.

Comparison of Median Earnings of Full-Time Workers by Sex
(persons 14 years and over)

Year	Median earnings: Women	Median earnings: Men	Earnings gap in dollars	Women's earnings as a percent of men's	Percent men's earnings exceeded women's	Earnings gap in constant 1978 dollars
1960	$3,257	$5,368	$2,111	60.7	64.8	$4,650
1965	3,828	6,388	2,560	60.0	66.9	5,293
1970	5,323	8,966	3,643	59.4	68.4	6,121
1971	5,593	9,399	3,806	59.5	68.0	6,131
1972	5,903	10,202	4,299	57.9	72.8	6,704
1973	6,335	11,186	4,851	56.6	76.6	7,122
1974	6,970	11,889	4,919	58.6	70.6	6,508
1975	7,504	12,758	5,254	58.8	70.0	6,369
1976	8,099	13,455	5,356	60.2	66.1	6,138
1977	8,618	14,626	6,008	58.9	69.7	6,468
1978	9,350	15,730	6,380	59.4	68.2	—

Source: Department of Commerce, Bureau of the Census.

Homes With Selected Electrical Appliances

(in millions)

Item	1979 Number	1979 Percent	1965 Number	1965 Percent	1960 Number	1960 Percent	1952 Number	1952 Percent
Air conditioners, room	44.1	55.5	13.9	24.2	7.8	15.1	0.6	1.3
Blenders	41.6	52.4	7.5	13.0	4.1	8.0	1.5	3.5
Calculators, electronic	79.3	99.9	n.a.	n.a.	—	—	—	—
Clothes dryers (incl. gas)	48.8	61.5	15.2	26.4	10.1	19.6	1.5	3.6
Clothes washers	61.4	77.3	50.3	87.4	44.1	85.4	32.2	76.2
Coffeemakers	79.3	99.9	41.3	71.7	30.2	58.3	21.6	51.0
Dishwashers	34.2	43.0	7.8	13.5	3.7	7.1	1.3	3.0
Electric blankets	51.0	64.2	20.0	34.7	12.2	23.6	3.6	8.6
Food waste disposers	34.1	43.0	7.9	13.6	5.4	10.5	1.4	3.3
Freezers, home	35.5	44.7	15.7	27.2	12.1	23.4	4.9	11.5
Hair dryers, hand-held	35.0	44.1	n.a.	n.a.	—	—	—	—
Knives, slicing	33.2	41.9	n.a.	n.a.	—	—	—	—
Mixers	73.7	92.8	41.9	72.8	29.0	56.0	12.6	29.7
Radios[1]	79.3	99.9	58.2	99.3	50.3	94.3	43.7	96.2
Ranges, electric	39.7	50.0	24.4	42.3	19.3	37.3	10.2	24.1
Refrigerators	79.2	99.8	57.3	99.5	50.8	98.2	37.8	89.2
Television: Black and white	79.3	99.9	55.9	97.1	46.2	89.4	19.8	46.7
Color	71.3	89.8	5.5	9.5	n.a.	n.a.	n.a.	n.a.
Toasters	79.3	99.9	48.1	83.6	37.2	72.0	30.0	70.9
Vacuum cleaners	79.3	99.9	48.1	83.5	38.4	74.3	25.1	59.4
Total number of wired homes	**79.4**	**100.0**	**57.6**	**100.0**	**51.7**	**100.0**	**42.3**	**100.0**

1. Radio data based on 53,300,000 homes in 1960 and 58,566,000 in 1965. NOTE: Percentages based on total number of homes wired for electricity. n.a. = not available. *Sources:* Gralla Publications, Inc., and *Merchandising Week.*

Government Employment and Payrolls

Year and function	Employees (in thousands) Total	Federal[1]	State	Local	Monthly payrolls (in millions) Total	Federal[1]	State	Local
1940	4,474	1,128	3,346		$566	$177	$389	
1945	6,556	3,375	3,181		1,110	642	468	
1950	6,402	2,117	1,057	3,228	1,528	613	218	96
1955	7,432	2,378	1,199	1,436	2,265	846	326	1,093
1960	8,808	2,421	1,527	4,860	3,333	1,118	524	1,691
1965	10,589	2,588	2,028	5,973	4,884	1,484	849	2,551
1970	13,028	2,881	2,755	7,392	8,334	2,428	1,612	4,294
1972	13,759	2,795	2,957	8,007	9,950	2,710	1,937	5,303
1973	14,139	2,786	3,013	8,339	11,027	3,102	2,158	5,857
1975	14,973	2,890	3,271	8,813	13,224	3,584	2,653	6,987
1976	15,012	2,843	3,343	8,826	13,924	3,565	2,894	7,465
1977	15,614	2,848	3,491	9,274	15,338	3,918	3,195	8,225
1978	15,628	2,885	3,539	9,204	16,483	4,344	3,483	8,656
1979, total	15,971	2,869	3,699	9,403	18,077	4,728	3,869	9,480
National defense and international relations	959	959	(2)	(2)	1,563	1,563	(2)	(2)
Postal service	657	657	(2)	(2)	1,103	1,103	(2)	(2)
Education	6,756	24	1,577	5,156	6,791	34	1,451	5,306
Instructional employees	3,762	(2)	460	3,303	4,778	(2)	671	4,107
Highways	570	5	260	305	622	10	314	298
Health and hospitals	1,625	259	680	686	1,713	391	692	630
Police protection	711	57	74	580	923	109	106	708
Local fire protection	309	(2)	(2)	309	332	(2)	(2)	332
Sewerage and sanitation	229	(2)	(2)	229	229	(2)	(2)	229
Local parks and recreation	226	(2)	(2)	226	165	(2)	(2)	165
Natural resources	509	285	188	36	683	451	200	32
Financial administration	426	108	125	193	477	160	146	172
All other	2,994	513	795	1,685	3,476	909	959	1,608

1. Civilians only. 2. Not applicable. *Source:* Department of Commerce, Bureau of the Census.

Receipts and Outlays of the Federal Government

(in millions of dollars)

From 1789 to 1842, the federal fiscal year ended Dec. 31; from 1844 to 1976, on June 30; and beginning 1977, on Sept. 30.

	Receipts						Outlays					
		Internal revenue										
Year	Customs (including tonnage tax)[1]	Income and profits tax	Other	Miscel-laneous taxes and receipts	Total receipts	Net receipts[2]	Department of Defense (Army, 1789–1950)	Department of the Navy	Interest on public debt	All other	Net outlays[3]	Surplus (+) or deficit (−)
1789–1791	$ 4	—	—	—	$ 4	$ 4	$ 1	—	$ 2	$ 1	$ 4	—
1800	9	—	$ −1	$ 1	11	11	3	$ 3	3	1	11	—
1810	9	—	—	1	9	9	2	2	3	1	8	$ +1
1820	15	—	—	3	18	18	3	4	5	6	18	—
1830	22	—	—	3	25	25	5	3	2	5	15	+10
1840	14	—	—	6	20	20	7	6	—	11	24	−4
1850	40	—	—	4	44	44	9	8	4	18	40	+4
1860	53	—	—	3	56	56	16	12	3	32	63	−7
1865	85	—	209	39	334	334	1,031	123	77	66	1,298	−964
1870	195	—	185	32	411	411	58	22	129	101	310	+101
1880	187	—	124	23	334	334	38	14	96	120	268	+66
1890	230	—	143	31	403	403	45	22	36	215	318	+85
1900	233	—	295	39	567	567	135	56	40	290	521	+46
1910	334	—	290	52	675	675	190	123	21	359	694	−19
1915	210	$ 80	335	72	698	683	202	142	23	379	746	−63
1918	180	2,314	872	299	3,665	3,645	4,870	1,279	190	6,339	12,677	−9,032
1929	602	2,331	607	493	4,033	3,862	426	365	678	1,658	3,127	+734
1933	251	746	858	225	2,080	1,997	435	349	689	3,125	4,598	−2,602
1939	319	2,189	2,972	188	5,668	4,979	695	673	941	6,533	8,841	−3,862
1943	324	16,094	6,050	934	23,402	21,947	42,526	20,888	1,808	14,146	79,368	−57,420
1944	431	34,655	7,030	3,325	45,441	43,563	49,438	26,538	2,609	16,401	94,986	−51,423
1945	355	35,173	8,729	3,494	47,750	44,362	50,490	30,047	3,617	14,149	98,303	−53,941
1950	423	28,263	11,186	1,439	41,311	36,422	5,789	4,130	5,750	23,875	39,544	−3,122
1956[4]	705	56,639	20,564	389	78,297	74,547	35,693	—	6,787	27,981	70,460	+4,087
1960	1,123	67,151	28,266	1,190	97,730	92,492	43,969	—	9,180	39,075	92,223	+269
1965	1,478	79,792	39,996	1,598	122,863	116,833	47,179	—	11,346	59,904	118,430	−1,596
1970	2,494	138,689	65,276	3,424	209,883	193,743	78,360	—	19,304	98,924	196,588	−2,845
1975	3,782	202,146	108,371	6,711	321,010	280,997	87,471	—	32,665	205,969	326,105	−45,108
1977	5,287	246,976	134,383	6,549	393,195	357,762	97,930	—	41,900	262,973	402,802	−45,040
1978	6,729	278,438	148,017	7,414	440,598	401,997	105,677	—	48,695	296,386	450,758	−48,761
1979	7,640	322,995	166,848	9,239	506,721	465,940	117,921	—	59,837	315,462	493,221	−27,281[5]

1. Beginning 1933, tonnage tax is included in "Other receipts." 2. Net receipts equal total receipts less (a) appropriations to federal old-age and survivors' insurance trust fund beginning fiscal year 1939 and (b) refunds of receipts beginning fiscal year 1933. 3. Includes Air Force 1950–65 (in millions): 1950—$3,521; 1956—$16,750; 1960—$19,065; 1965—$18,471. 4. Beginning 1956, computed on unified budget concepts; not strictly comparable with preceding figures. 5. A joint Treasury–Office of Management and Budget press statement, released with the September 1979 Monthly Treasury Statement, adjusted this total to $27.7 billion to include administrative expenses and interest receipts of the Exchange Stabilization Fund. *Source:* Department of the Treasury, Bureau of Government Financial Operations.

Federal Budget—Receipts and Outlays

(in billions of dollars)

Source or function	1980 est.	1981 est.	1982 est.
RECEIPTS			
Individual income taxes	$241.5[1]	$279.9[1]	$326.1[1]
Corporate income taxes	74.2[1]	74.1[1]	81.6[1]
Social insurance taxes and contributions	163.5[1]	188.9[1]	218.3[1]
Employment taxes and contributions	138.6	161.6	—
Unemployment insurance	16.8	18.6	—
Contributions for other insurance and retirement	6.7	7.1	—
Excise taxes	25.2[1]	42.2[1]	51.9[1]
Estate and gift taxes	5.8[1]	6.0[1]	6.5[1]
Customs duties	7.3[1]	7.8[1]	8.2[1]
Miscellaneous receipts	11.5[1]	13.1[1]	14.0[1]
Total budget receipts	**532.4[1]**	**628.0[1]**	**724.8[1]**
OUTLAYS			
National defense	130.4	146.2	165.5
Department of Defense—military	127.4	142.7	161.6
Atomic energy defense activities	3.0	3.4	3.6
International affairs	10.4	9.6	10.2
Foreign economic and financial assistance	6.0	6.2	6.8
Military assistance	.9	.8	.6
Conduct of foreign affairs	1.4	1.5	1.6
Foreign information and exchange activities	.5	.6	.6
International financial programs	1.7	.7	.6
General science, space, and technology	5.9	6.4	6.9
General science and basic research	1.4	1.6	1.6
Space flight	2.7	3.0	3.1
Space science, applications, and technology	1.3	1.4	1.6
Energy	7.8	8.1	11.0
Supply	5.5	4.5	4.5
Conservation	.6	1.2	2.5
Emergency energy preparedness	.8	1.3	2.9
Information, policy, and regulation	.9	1.2	1.2
Natural resources and environment	12.8	12.8	13.7
Water resources	4.2	4.1	4.6
Conservation and land management	2.3	2.2	2.3
Recreation resources	1.5	1.5	1.7
Pollution control and abatement	4.9	5.1	5.4
Other natural resources	1.4	1.5	1.5
Agriculture	4.6	2.8	3.0
Farm income stabilization	3.3	1.4	1.5
Research and services	1.4	1.4	1.5
Commerce and housing credit	5.5	.7	3.2
Mortgage credit and thrift insurance	1.9	−2.8	−.5
Postal Service	1.7	1.6	1.6
Other advancement and regulation of commerce	2.1	2.2	2.2
Transportation	19.6	20.2	21.6
Ground	13.6	13.8	15.0
Air	3.8	4.0	4.1
Water	2.2	2.3	2.4
Other	.1	.1	.1
Community and regional development	8.5	8.8	9.4
Community development	4.5	5.0	5.2
Area and regional development	2.7	3.0	3.4
Disaster relief and insurance	1.3	.9	.8
Education, training, employment, and social services	30.7	32.0	35.0
Elementary, secondary, and vocational education	7.3	7.8	9.2
Higher education	5.5	5.2	5.5
Research and general education aids	1.4	1.4	1.5
Training and employment	10.4	11.3	11.8
Other labor services	.6	.6	.6
Social services	5.5	5.7	6.0
Health	56.6	62.4	70.8
Health care services	51.6	57.3	65.2
Health research	3.3	3.6	3.9
Education and training of health-care work force	.7	.6	.7
Consumer and occupational health and safety	1.0	1.0	1.1
Income security	190.9	220.0	241.7
General retirement and disability insurance	124.6	144.1	161.3
Federal employee retirement and disability	14.6	17.1	19.4
Unemployment compensation	15.6	18.8	17.4
Public assistance and other income supplements	36.1	40.1	43.6
Veterans benefits and services	20.8	21.7	23.2
Income security	11.7	13.0	14.2
Education, training, and rehabilitation	2.2	1.9	1.5
Hospital and medical care	6.4	6.4	6.8
Administration of justice	4.5	4.7	4.9
Law enforcement activities	2.2	2.3	2.3
Litigative and judicial activities	1.4	1.5	1.5
Correctional activities	.3	.4	.4
Criminal justice assistance	.6	.6	.7
General government	4.9	4.9	5.1
Legislative functions	1.1	1.1	1.1
Executive direction and management	.1	.1	.1
Central fiscal operations	2.7	2.8	2.9
General property and records management	.3	.4	.5
Central personnel management	.2	.2	.2
Other general government	.7	.5	.5
General purpose fiscal assistance	8.7	9.6	9.7
General revenue sharing	6.9	6.9	6.9
Other fiscal assistance	1.8	2.8	2.8
Interest	63.3	67.2	68.0
On the public debt	73.3	79.4	82.0
Other interest	−10.0	−12.2	−14.0
Allowances	.1	2.6	9.8
Civilian pay raises	—	1.1	3.3
Contingencies for other requirements	.1	1.5	6.5
Undistributed offsetting receipts	−22.3	−25.1	−26.4
Employer share, employee retirement	−5.9	−6.2	−6.4
Interest received by trust funds	−11.5	−13.0	−14.1
Rents and royalties on the Outer Continental Shelf	−4.8	−6.0	−6.0
Total outlays	**568.9[1]**	**611.5[1]**	**683.3[1]**
Total surplus or deficit (−)	**−36.5[1]**	**16.5[1]**	**41.5[1]**

1. Revised figure. NOTE: The fiscal year is from Oct. 1 to Sept. 30. *Source:* Executive Office of the President, Office of Management and Budget.

Per Capita Social Welfare Expenditures Under Public Programs

Year	Social insurance	Public aid	Health and medical programs	Veterans' programs	Education	Other social welfare	All health and medical care[1]	Total[2]	Total social welfare (in millions)[3]
1950	$ 32	$ 16	$ 13	$44	$ 43	$ 3	$ 20	$ 153	$ 23,421
1955	59	18	19	28	67	4	26	195	32,512
1960	105	22	24	30	96	6	35	285	52,106
1965	142	32	32	30	143	11	48	391	76,929
1970	262	79	48	43	245	20	122	701	145,484
1975	565	188	82	78	373	35	235	1,336	289,349
1976	665	220	88	86	402	42	267	1,519	331,121
1977	730	241	93	86	430	44	307	1,642	360,645
1978	787	269	102	89	457	48	344	1,775	393,188
PERCENTAGE INCREASE FOR 1978 FROM—									
1950	2,346	1,555	661	102	951	1,536	1,623	1,064	1,579
1955	1,240	1,397	450	213	585	1,188	1,200	812	1,109
1960	647	1,098	318	202	374	666	882	522	655
1965	453	742	222	194	220	355	610	354	411
1970	200	239	114	106	86	139	183	153	170
1975	39	43	24	14	22	37	46	33	36
1976	18	22	16	3	14	15	29	17	19
1977	8	12	10	4	6	10	12	8	9

1. Combines health and medical programs with medical services provided in connection with social insurance, public aid, veterans', vocational rehabilitation, and antipoverty programs. 2. Includes housing, not shown. 3. Excludes expenditures abroad for education, veterans' benefits, civil service retirement benefits, and certain other items. Figures are latest available. *Source:* Department of Health, and Human Services. *Social Security Bulletin,* May 1980.

Social Welfare Expenditures Under Public Programs

(in millions of dollars)

Year and source of funds	Social insurance	Public aid	Health and medical programs	Veterans' programs	Education	Housing	Other social welfare	All health and medical care[1]	Total social welfare	Total social welfare as: Percent of gross national product	Percent of total gov't outlays
FEDERAL											
1950	$ 2,103	$ 1,103	$ 604	$ 6,386	$ 157	$ 15	$ 174	$ 1,362	$ 10,541	4.0	26.2
1955	6,385	1,504	1,150	4,772	485	75	252	1,948	14,623	3.9	22.3
1960	14,307	2,117	1,737	5,367	868	144	417	2,918	24,957	5.0	28.1
1965	21,807	3,594	2,781	6,011	2,470	238	812	4,625	37,712	5.7	32.6
1970	45,246	9,649	4,775	8,952	5,876	582	2,259	16,600	77,337	8.1	40.1
1975	99,715	27,205	8,547	16,570	8,629	2,541	4,264	34,126	167,470	11.5	54.0
1977	134,744	35,399	10,067	18,861	9,972	4,006	5,465	46,094	218,514	11.9	56.3
1978[2]	147,324	40,979	11,452	19,569	10,371	4,887	5,872	52,512	240,453	11.8	55.3
STATE AND LOCAL											
1950	2,844	1,393	1,460	480	6,518	([3])	274	1,704	12,967	4.9	59.2
1955	3,450	1,499	1,953	62	10,672	15	367	2,473	18,017	4.7	55.3
1960	4,999	1,984	2,727	112	16,758	33	723	3,478	27,337	5.5	60.1
1965	6,316	2,690	3,466	20	25,638	80	1,254	4,911	39,464	6.0	60.4
1970	9,446	6,839	5,132	127	44,970	120	1,886	8,791	68,519	7.1	64.0
1975	23,298	13,502	9,241	449	72,204	631	3,269	17,110	122,594	8.4	65.0
1977	26,123	17,495	10,371	155	84,448	353	4,094	21,170	143,039	7.8	65.9
1978[2]	27,778	18,641	11,552	174	90,817	337	4,711	23,686	154,010	7.5	63.6
TOTAL											
1950	4,947	2,496	2,064	6,866	6,674	15	448	3,065	23,508	8.9	37.4
1955	9,835	3,003	3,103	4,834	11,157	89	619	4,421	32,640	8.6	32.7
1960	19,307	4,101	4,464	5,479	17,626	177	1,139	6,395	52,293	10.5	38.4
1965	28,123	6,283	6,246	6,031	28,108	318	2,066	9,535	77,175	11.7	42.2
1970	54,691	16,488	9,907	9,078	50,846	701	4,145	25,391	145,856	15.2	48.2
1975	123,013	40,706	17,788	17,019	80,833	3,172	7,533	51,236	290,064	19.9	57.9

Year and source of funds	Social insurance	Public aid	Health and medical programs	Veterans' programs	Education	Housing	Other social welfare	All health and medical care[1]	Total social welfare	Total social welfare as: Percent of gross national product	Percent of total gov't outlays
1977	160,867	53,895	20,438	19,105	94,421	4,358	9,559	67,264	361,553	19.7	59.5
1978[2]	175,101	59,620	23,004	19,742	101,188	5,225	10,582	76,198	394,462	19.3	58.1
PERCENT OF TOTAL, BY TYPE											
1950	21.0	10.6	8.8	29.2	28.4	0.1	1.9	13.0	100.0	(3)	(3)
1955	30.1	9.2	9.5	14.8	34.2	0.3	1.9	13.5	100.0	(3)	(3)
1960	36.9	7.8	8.5	10.5	33.7	0.3	2.2	12.2	100.0	(3)	(3)
1965	36.4	8.1	8.1	7.8	36.4	0.4	2.7	12.4	100.0	(3)	(3)
1970	37.5	11.3	6.7	6.2	34.9	0.5	3.0	17.2	100.0	(3)	(3)
1975	42.4	14.0	6.1	5.9	27.9	1.1	2.6	17.7	100.0	(3)	(3)
1977	44.5	14.9	5.7	5.3	26.1	1.2	2.6	18.6	100.0	(3)	(3)
1978[2]	44.4	15.1	5.8	5.0	25.7	1.3	2.7	19.3	100.0	(3)	(3)
FEDERAL PERCENT OF TOTAL											
1950	42.5	44.2	29.2	93.0	2.3	100.0	38.9	44.4	44.8	(3)	(3)
1955	64.9	50.1	37.1	98.7	4.3	83.7	40.7	44.1	44.8	(3)	(3)
1960	74.1	51.6	38.9	98.0	4.9	81.2	36.6	45.6	47.7	(3)	(3)
1965	77.5	57.2	44.5	99.7	8.8	74.9	39.3	48.5	48.9	(3)	(3)
1970	82.7	58.5	48.2	98.6	11.6	82.9	54.5	65.4	53.0	(3)	(3)
1975	81.1	66.8	49.0	97.4	11.0	78.7	56.6	67.1	58.4	(3)	(3)
1977	83.8	66.9	49.1	99.2	10.6	91.9	57.2	68.6	60.4	(3)	(3)
1978[2]	84.1	68.7	49.0	99.1	10.2	93.5	55.5	68.9	60.9	(3)	(3)

1. Combines health and medical programs with medical services provided in connection with social insurance, public aid, veterans, and other social welfare programs. 2. Preliminary. 3. Not applicable. NOTE: Figures are latest available. *Source:* Department of Health and Human Services. *Social Security Bulletin,* May 1980.

Contributions to International Organizations

(for fiscal year 1979 in millions of dollars)

Organization	Amount[1]
United Nations and Specialized Agencies	$283.29
United Nations	141.10
Food and Agricultural Organization	22.46
International Atomic Energy Agency	18.28
International Civil Aviation Organization	4.43
Joint Financing Program	3.16
International Telecommunications Union	2.77
UNESCO	36.50
World Health Organization	49.20
World Meteorological Organization	4.27
Others	1.12
United Nations Peacekeeping Forces	75.70
United Nations Emergency Force	67.00
United Nations Force in Cyprus	8.70
Inter-American Organizations	69.38
Organization of American States	34.73
Pan American Health Organization	22.70
Inter-American Institute of Agricultural Sciences	9.95
Inter-American Tropical Tuna Commission	1.61
Others	.39
Regional Organizations	27.06
NATO Civilian Headquarters	12.61
Organization for Economic Cooperation and Development	12.94
Others	1.51
Other International Organizations	13.12
Customs Cooperation Council	1.41
General Agreement on Tariffs and Trade	3.33
Intergovernmental Committee for European Migration	2.60
International Institute for Cotton	2.10
Others	3.68
Special Voluntary Programs	563.10
Consultative Group on International Agricultural Research	24.80
Intergovernmental Committee for European Migration—Special Voluntary	53.28
International Atomic Energy Agency—Operational Program	12.00[2]
Ogranization of American States—Special Development Assistance Fund	6.00
Organization of American States—Special Multilateral Fund (education and science)	6.50
United Nations Children Fund	30.00
United Nations Development Program	126.00
United Nations Environment Fund	10.00
UN/FAO World Food Program	95.10
United Nations Fund for Populations Activities	30.00
United Nations High Commissioner for Refugees	34.97
Special Resettlement and Relief Programs	55.84
United Nations Relief and Works Agency	52.00
World Health Organization—	
Special Programs	6.91
Others	19.70
Total	**1,031.65**

1. Estimated. 2. Includes cash, commodities and services and $6.6 million for Safeguard Program. *Source:* Department of State.

The Public Debt

Year	Gross debt: Amount (in millions)	Gross debt: Per capita	Year	Gross debt: Amount (in millions)	Gross debt: Per capita
1800 (Jan. 1)	$ 83	$ 15.87	1950	$256,087[2]	$1,688.30
1860	65	2.06	1955	272,807[2]	1,650.63
1865	2,678	75.01	1960	284,093[2]	1,572.31
1900	1,263	16.60	1965	313,819[2]	1,612.70
1920	24,299	228.23	1970	370,094[2]	1,807.09
1925	20,516	177.12	1975	533,189	2,496.90
1930	16,185	131.51	1976	634,702	2,950.15
1935	28,701	225.55	1977	698,840	3,215.59
1940	42,968	325.23	1978	771,544	3,521.78
1945	258,682	1,848.60	1979[1]	826,519	3,739.92

1. Preliminary, Sept. 30, 1979. 2. Adjusted to exclude issues to the International Monetary Fund and other international lending institutions to conform to the budget presentation. *Source:* Department of the Treasury, Bureau of Government Financial Operations.

Foreign Assistance
(in millions of dollars)

Calendar years	Economic Assistance (net): Net new grants	Net new credits	Net other assistance	Total	Military grants (net)	Net assistance[1]
July 1945–50[2]	$18,413	$ 8,086	—	$ 26,498	$ 1,981	$ 28,479
1951–55	10,459	556	$ 541	11,556	14,464	26,020
1956–60	8,291	1,503	2,226	12,021	11,327	23,348
1961–65	9,384	5,522	576	15,482	7,831	23,313
1966–70	8,808	9,430	−564	17,674	12,028	29,702
1971–75	12,939	7,542	−725	19,738	16,693	36,431
1976	2,268	3,275	−54	5,490	1,339	6,830
1977	2,283	2,861	−39	5,105	766	5,871
1978	2,676	3,691	−52	6,315	817	7,131
1979	3,006	3,323	−69	6,259	910	7,169
Total postwar period[2]	**78,527**	**45,771**	**1,840**	**126,138**	**68,156**	**194,295**

1. Excludes investment in international nonmonetary financial institutions of $6,848 million. 2. Includes transactions after V-J Day (Sept. 2, 1945). NOTE: Detail may not add to total due to rounding. *Source:* Department of Commerce, Bureau of Economic Analysis.

Domestic Freight Traffic by Major Carriers
(in millions of ton-miles)[1]

Year	Railroads: Ton-miles	Railroads: % of total	Inland waterways[2]: Ton-miles	Inland waterways[2]: % of total	Motor trucks: Ton-miles	Motor trucks: % of total	Oil pipelines: Ton-miles	Oil pipelines: % of total	Air carriers: Ton-miles	Air carriers: % of total
1940	379,201	61.3	118,057	19.1	62,043	10.0	59,277	9.6	14	—
1945	690,809	67.3	142,737	13.9	66,948	6.5	126,530	12.3	91	—
1950	596,940	56.2	163,344	15.4	172,860	16.3	129,175	12.1	318	—
1955	631,385	49.5	216,508	17.0	223,254	17.5	203,244	16.0	481	—
1960	579,130	44.1	220,253	16.8	285,483	21.7	228,626	17.4	778	—
1965	708,700	43.3	262,421	16.0	359,218	21.9	306,393	18.7	1,910	0.1
1970	771,168	39.8	318,560	16.4	412,000	21.3	431,000	22.3	3,274	0.2
1975	759,000	36.7	342,210	16.5	454,000	22.0	507,300	24.6	3,732	0.2
1976	799,876	36.3	372,865	16.9	510,000	23.2	515,100	23.4	3,900	0.2
1977	833,994	36.1	368,275	15.9	555,000	24.1	546,000	23.7	4,181	0.2
1978	867,982	35.1	409,316	16.6	602,000	24.4	585,800	23.7	4,630	0.2
1979[3]	920,000	35.7	424,000	16.4	627,000	24.3	604,000	23.4	4,664	0.2

1. Mail and express included, except railroads for 1970. 2. Rivers, canals, and domestic traffic on Great Lakes. 3. Preliminary. *Sources:* Interstate Commerce Commission; Civil Aeronautics Board; Association of American Railroads.

Waterborne Commerce at Selected Ports, 1978

(excluding Great Lakes; in thousands of tons)

	Foreign		Domestic					
			Coastwise		Internal			
Port or harbor	Imports	Exports	Receipts	Ship-ments	Receipts	Ship-ments	Local	Total
Baltimore	17,508	14,339	$ 4,385	843	$ 3,515	1,829	4,390	46,809
Baton Rouge, La.	16,900	11,432	4,443	5,805	13,795	21,142	1,052	74,570
Beaumont, Tex.	25,434	4,192	2,234	9,247	5,041	6,274	349	52,770
Boston	6,712	794	14,670	2,647	120	—	1,238	26,074
Corpus Christi, Tex.	20,463	5,862	345	13,281	1,410	4,444	7,487	46,445
Houston	42,197	20,050	4,178	14,796	11,183	13,839	5,692	111,936
Lake Charles, La.	6,625	1,626	10,796	42,317	90,638	3,573	406	26,606
Long Beach, Calif.	9,286	6,983	11,998	2,082	7,189	306	2,119	31,586
Los Angeles	12,659	3,697	9,659	4,416	4,768	719	1,200	32,827
Marcus Hook, Pa.	15,981	146	5,178	2,427	3,898	4,565	541	32,736
Mobile, Ala.	10,679	5,190	446	1,023	7,327	10,107	1,489	36,261
New Orleans	23,298	40,481	3,009	10,443	53,568	25,564	4,249	160,616
New York	55,923	6,093	34,840	24,536	3,932	15,874	45,535	186,733
Norfolk, Va.	6,027	16,926	2,263	699	3,455	3,983	1,294	34,019
Pascagoula, Miss.	8,237	3,899	777	5,345	1,865	4,878	244	25,244
Paulsboro, N.J.	12,296	102	2,354	2,621	3,529	2,938	1,552	23,994
Philadelphia	26,390	4,338	2,098	4,241	8,962	329	1,501	50,823
Portland, Me.	17,207	17	4,145	615	12	—	169	22,165
Portland, Ore.	2,035	9,596	4,600	294	4,560	2,528	2,960	26,573
Port Arthur, Tex.	17,027	2,163	1,032	7,807	1,499	3,930	16	33,475
Richmond, Calif.	3,426	425	7,362	4,691	1,882	902	2,994	18,986
St. Louis	—	—	3	3	6,363	14,674	1,382	22,425
Tampa, Fla.	4,845	17,058	16,994	7,967	100	43	68	47,077
Texas City, Tex.	14,396	745	1,299	7,188	5,220	5,654	1,553	34,656

Source: Department of Commerce, Bureau of the Census.

Estimated Motor Vehicle Registration, 1978

(in thousands; including publicly owned vehicles except those owned by the military)

State	Autos[1]	Trucks and buses	Motor-cycles	Total	State	Autos[1]	Trucks and buses	Motor-cycles	Total
Alabama	2,105	758	70	2,933	Montana	563	339	61	963
Alaska	168	100	11	279	Nebraska	858	384	51	1,293
Arizona	1,261	515	72	1,848	Nevada	465	166	22	653
Arkansas	999	503	31	1,533	New Hampshire	583	99	47	729
California	12,343	3,630	662	16,635	New Jersey	4,284	478	90	4,852
Colorado	2,021	673	124	2,818	New Mexico	661	387	46	1,094
Connecticut	2,051	178	78	2,307	New York	7,335	1,015	156	8,506
Delaware	322	74	9	405	North Carolina	3,386	1,103	95	4,584
D.C.	212	17	4	233	North Dakota	360	257	28	645
Florida	5,939	1,252	153	7,344	Ohio	6,441	1,700	236	8,377
Georgia	2,975	814	107	3,896	Oklahoma	1,715	827	119	2,661
Hawaii	460	88	6	554	Oregon	1,486	510	75	2,071
Idaho	485	311	50	846	Pennsylvania	5,793	1,105	185	7,083
Illinois	6,080	1,273	257	7,610	Rhode Island	590	84	26	700
Indiana	2,910	968	159	4,037	South Carolina	1,541	443	35	2,019
Iowa	1,786	639	184	2,609	South Dakota	369	230	27	626
Kansas	1,377	601	84	2,062	Tennessee	2,401	620	81	3,102
Kentucky	1,834	814	62	2,710	Texas	7,720	2,961	218	10,899
Louisiana	1,899	779	76	2,754	Utah	684	320	56	1,060
Maine	544	182	40	766	Vermont	305	72	20	397
Maryland	2,331	458	74	2,863	Virginia	2,996	520	73	3,589
Massachusetts	3,295	449	85	3,829	Washington	2,254	859	110	3,223
Michigan	5,300	1,188	256	6,744	West Virginia	863	345	48	1,256
Minnesota	2,012	742	138	2,892	Wisconsin	2,284	614	152	3,050
Mississippi	1,178	470	30	1,678	Wyoming	255	181	19	455
Missouri	2,406	832	86	3,324	**Total**	**120,485**	**33,927**	**4,984**	**159,396**

1. Includes taxicabs. *Source:* Department of Transportation, Federal Highway Administration.

Domestic and Export Factory Sales of Motor Vehicles
(in thousands)

	From plants in United States[1]								
	Passenger cars			Motor trucks and buses			Total motor vehicles		
Year	Total	Domestic	Exports	Total	Domestic	Exports	Total	Domestic	Exports
1965	9,297	9,092	205	1,700	1,564	136	10,997	10,656	341
1970	6,531	6,171	359	1,642	1,515	127	8,173	7,686	486
1975	6,708	6,068	640	2,235	1,966	269	8,943	8,034	909
1976	8,481	7,821	660	2,927	2,682	245	11,408	10,503	905
1977	9,177	8,489	688	3,380	3,117	263	12,557	11,606	951
1978	9,146	8,474	672	3,670	3,379	291	12,816	11,853	963
1979	8,401	7,660	741	3,007	2,712	296	11,408	10,371	1,037

1. Excludes factory sales to all Federal government agencies. *Source:* Motor Vehicle Manufacturers Association of the U.S.

Domestic Passenger Car Sales

Company and model	1979	1978	1977
American Motors	162,057	170,739	184,361
Spirit/Gremlin	54,356	24,412	37,531
Concord/Hornet	85,432	114,764	79,508
Pacer	8,168	20,811	44,874
Matador	—	9,471	22,041
AMX 1978	—	1,281	407
Eagle	14,101	—	—
Chrysler Corp.	942,207	1,146,258	1,219,752
Total Plymouth	325,523	404,371	444,063
Horizon	146,740	118,993	—
Volare	167,091	210,125	306,548
Voyager	8,265	13,895	13,767
Fury	2,681	60,378	92,056
Plymouth	746	980	31,692
Total Chrysler	248,840	298,892	317,012
LeBaron	99,588	125,558	70,037
Cordoba	61,801	105,442	142,619
Chrysler	87,451	67,892	104,356
Total Dodge	367,844	442,995	458,677
Omni	124,378	89,497	—
Aspen	117,777	157,308	244,009
Sportsman	24,917	44,376	45,380
Diplomat	45,131	60,656	40,072
Monaco	2,554	37,594	59,559
Magnum/Charger	24,784	48,326	37,409
Dodge	28,303	5,238	32,248
Ford Motor	2,132,644	2,582,702	2,552,210
Ford Division	1,491,374	1,814,717	1,862,796
Pinto	187,708	167,880	220,775
Mustang	304,053	199,760	170,659
Fairmont	338,819	405,780	167,841
Club Wagon	31,094	45,964	38,761
Granada	141,737	219,026	355,186
LTD II	26,700	138,947	203,922
Thunderbird	215,698	304,430	325,153
Ford	245,565	332,930	380,499
L-M Division	641,270	767,985	689,414
Total Mercury	509,999	579,498	508,132
Bobcat	44,674	30,201	35,481
Zephyr	99,335	120,781	42,234
Monarch	55,347	78,824	106,821
Cougar	3,955	35,251	53,207
XR-7	121,184	159,687	129,779
Capri	90,850	18,035	—
Mercury	94,654	136,719	140,610
Total Lincoln	131,271	188,487	181,282
Versailles	13,586	15,747	13,490
Lincoln	60,797	97,009	92,985
Mark V/VI	56,888	75,731	74,807
General Motors	4,911,875	5,385,282	5,148,131
Buick Division	714,508	781,364	746,394
Skyhawk	18,768	22,221	24,872
Skylark	115,000	97,915	97,196
Century	62,210	74,813	104,786
Regal	249,379	248,543	174,871
LeSabre	129,554	190,414	187,519
Electra	88,195	121,705	136,341
Riviera	51,402	25,753	20,809
Cadillac Division	314,034	350,813	335,785
Seville	45,317	55,721	44,667
Cadillac	206,164	248,825	244,770
Eldorado	62,553	46,267	46,348
Chevrolet Division	2,152,803	2,349,781	2,280,439
Chevette	375,724	247,088	196,218
Monza	141,564	158,127	157,226
Citation/Nova	308,437	248,214	312,135
Sportvan	24,594	43,582	39,609
Camaro	204,742	260,201	208,511
Malibu	344,233	374,124	296,193
Monte Carlo	265,877	355,058	370,825
Chevrolet	449,001	621,140	657,151
Corvette	38,631	42,247	42,571
Oldsmobile Division	949,488	1,006,344	977,046
Starfire	18,611	18,351	19,120
Omega	50,098	42,860	51,724
Cutlass	114,092	113,286	527,939
Supreme	404,068	406,993	—
Oldsmobile 88	223,699	273,384	225,937
Oldsmobile 98	92,075	123,431	123,466
Toronado	46,845	28,039	28,860
Pontiac Division	781,042	896,980	808,467
Sunbird	89,107	91,737	90,483
Phoenix	80,857	58,280	72,520
Firebird	149,211	188,212	137,807
LeMans	114,993	125,020	73,051
Grand Prix	175,573	224,195	235,833
Pontiac	171,301	209,536	198,763
Volkswagen	166,839	23,017	—
Industry total	**8,315,622**	**9,307,998**	**9,104,454**

Source: Automotive News, Jan. 14, 1980.

Passenger Car Production by Makes

Companies and models	1979	1978	1977	1975	1970	1965
American Motors Corporation	184,636	164,351	156,994	323,704	276,127	346,367
Chrysler Corporation	906,675	1,082,274				
Plymouth	368,076	437,441	492,063	443,550	699,031	679,539
Dodge	357,173	408,327	497,232	354,482	405,699	547,531
Chrysler	181,426	236,504	247,064	102,940	158,614	224,061
Imperial	—	—	—	1,930	10,111	16,422
Total	**906,675**	**1,082,274**	**1,236,359**	**902,902**	**1,273,455**	**1,467,553**
Ford Motor Company						
Ford	1,345,427	1,698,136	1,761,373	1,301,414	1,647,918	2,164,902
Mercury	509,450	624,229	583,055	405,104	310,463	355,404
Lincoln	151,960	189,523	211,439	101,520	58,771	45,470
Total	**2,006,837**	**2,511,888**	**2,555,867**	**1,808,038**	**2,017,152**	**2,565,776**
General Motors Corporation						
Chevrolet	2,261,757	2,364,685	2,133,403	1,687,091	1,504,614	2,587,509
Pontiac	731,600	880,594	875,957	523,469	422,212	860,652
Oldsmobile	1,008,249	910,252	1,079,841	654,342	439,632	650,801
Buick	787,123	810,324	801,202	535,820	459,931	653,838
Cadillac	345,831	350,761	369,254	278,404	152,859	196,595
Total	**5,134,560**	**5,316,616**	**5,259,657**	**3,679,126**	**2,979,248**	**4,949,395**
Checker Motors Corporation	4,766	4,225	4,777	3,181	4,146	6,136
Volkswagen of America	173,192	40,194	—	—	—	—
Industry total	**8,410,666**	**9,119,548**	**9,213,654**	**6,716,951**	**6,550,128**	**9,335,227**

Source: Automotive News, Jan. 14, 1980.

Passenger Car Data

	1978	1960	1950	1940
U.S. passenger cars and taxis registered (thousands)	116,575	61,671	40,339	27,466
Total mileage of U.S. passenger cars (millions)	1,171,092	588,083	363,613	249,600
Total fuel consumption of U.S. passenger cars (millions of gallons)	83,312	41,169	24,305	16,323
World registration of cars, trucks, and buses (thousands)	380,020	126,908	70,424	n.a.
U.S. registration of cars, trucks, and buses (thousands)	148,778	73,858	49,162	32,453
U.S. share of world registration of cars, trucks, and buses	39.2%	58.2%	69.8%	n.a.

NOTE: n.a. = not available. *Source:* Motor Vehicle Manufacturers Association of the U.S.

Intercity Passenger Traffic
(in millions of passenger-miles)

	Railroads		Buses		Air carriers		Inland waterways[1]			
Year	Miles	% of total	Miles	% of total	Miles	% of total	Miles	% of total	Total commercial	Private airplanes
1940	24,766	67.1	9,800	26.5	1,052	2.8	1,317	3.6	36,935	—
1945	93,535	74.3	27,027	21.4	3,362	2.7	2,056	1.6	125,980	—
1950	32,481	46.3	26,436	37.7	10,072	14.3	1,190	1.7	70,179	—
1955	28,695	36.5	25,519	32.4	22,741	28.9	1,738	2.2	78,693	—
1960	21,574	28.6	19,327	25.7	31,730	42.1	2,688	3.6	75,319	2,228
1965	17,557	17.9	23,775	24.2	53,719	54.7	3,101	3.2	98,152	4,364
1970	10,903	7.3	25,300	16.9	109,499	73.1	4,000	2.7	149,702	9,101
1975	10,075	5.8	25,000	14.2	136,432	77.7	4,000	2.3	175,507	11,500
1976	11,000	5.8	25,000	13.2	150,000	78.9	4,000	2.1	190,000	13,000
1977	10,400	5.1	25,900	12.7	164,200	80.3	4,000	1.9	204,500	12,100
1978[2]	10,500	4.6	25,400	11.1	189,100	82.6	4,000	1.7	229,000	12,700
1979[2]	11,600	4.6	26,600	10.5	210,300	83.3	4,000	1.6	252,500	13,300

1. Rivers, canals, and Great Lakes. 2. Preliminary. NOTE: Beginning in 1970, data include Alaska and Hawaii. n.a. = not available. *Sources:* Interstate Commerce Commission; Civil Aeronautics Board; Association of American Railroads.

Exports of Leading Commodities
(value in millions of dollars)

Commodity	1979	1978
Food and live animals	$22,245	$18,311
Meat and preparations	1,127	958
Dairy products and eggs	161	190
Grains and preparations	14,450	11,634
Wheat, including wheat flour	5,491	4,532
Rice	850	929
Fruits and nuts	1,525	1,335
Vegetables	605	554
Feed for animals	2,317	1,921
Beverages and tobacco	2,337	2,293
Tobacco and manufactures	2,093	2,107
Beverages and other tobacco	244	186
Crude materials, inedible, except fuels	20,755	15,555
Hides and skins, except fur skins	992	695
Soybeans, other oilseeds, peanuts	6,379	5,864
Synthetic rubber	579	369
Wood in the rough	1,992	1,376
Wood pulp	1,104	817
Textile fibers and wastes	3,047	2,302
Ores and metal scrap	3,325	1,839
Mineral fuels and related materials	5,616	3,881
Coal	3,394	2,046
Petroleum and products	1.914	1,564
Animal and vegetable oils and fats	1,845	1,521
Soybean oil	769	569
Chemicals	17,306	12,623
Chemical elements and compounds	7,704	5,293
Medicines and pharmaceuticals	1,591	1,404
Fertilizers, manufacturer	1,404	1,091
Plastic materials and resins	3,241	2,088
Machinery and transport equipment	70,491	59,268
Machinery	45,914	38,105
Power generating machinery	5,666	4,592
Aircraft engines, parts	1,423	1,142
Automotive engines, parts	1,631	1,364
Agricultural machinery	1,088	844
Tractors and parts	597	493
Office machines	6,475	5,006
Metalworking machinery	1,391	1,188
Textile and leather machinery	629	485
Transport equipment	24,577	21,163
Road motor vehicles and parts	13,904	12,148
Aircraft, parts, and accessories	9,719	8,203
Other manufactured goods	28,879	22,644
Tires and tubes	353	280
Paper and manufactures	1,967	1,597
Nonmetallic mineral manufactures	1,949	1,597
Metals and manufactures	7,505	5,854
Iron and steel-mill products	2,227	1,646
Nonferrous base metals	1,609	1,048
Other manufactures of metals	3,431	3,107
Textiles, other than clothing	3,189	2,225
Clothing	919	650
Scientific instruments	3,611	2,786
Photographic equipment, supplies	1,811	1,564
Printed matter	956	812
Other transactions	9,103	5,030
Total	**$178,578**	**$141,126**

Imports of Leading Commodities
(value in millions of dollars)

Commodity	1979	1978
Food and live animals	$15,171	$13,521
Cattle, except for breeding	236	250
Meat and preparations	2,539	1,856
Cheese	293	270
Fish	2,639	2,212
Grains and feed for animals	298	247
Fruits and nuts	1,324	1,126
Vegetables	737	711
Sugar	974	723
Coffee, green	3,820	3,728
Cocoa or cacao beans	555	667
Tea	126	115
Spices	139	144
Beverages and tobacco	2,566	2,221
Alcoholic beverages	2,013	1,744
Tobacco, unmanufactured	436	396
Crude materials, inedible, except fuels	10,651	9,294
Hides and skins, except fur skins	139	106
Fur skins, undressed	183	142
Rubber, including latex	1,058	840
Lumber	2,910	2,742
Wood pulp	1,506	1,120
Textile fibers and wastes	231	248
Industrial diamonds	116	69
Asbestos, unmanufactured	144	162
Ores and metal scrap	3,247	2,813
Iron ore and concentrates	923	845
Ores and concentrates, nonferrous metals	2,324	1,968
Mineral fuels and related materials	60,061	42,096
Petroleum and products	56,046	39,109
Natural gas	2,765	2,000
Animal and vegetable oils and fats	740	511
Chemicals	7,485	6,430
Organic chemicals	2,159	1,734
Inorganic chemicals	2,059	1,827
Medicinal and pharmaceutical products	441	449
Fertilizers, manufactured	976	869
Machinery and transport equipment	53,678	47,590
Machinery	28,530	24,752
Automotive engines, parts	1,949	2,090
Transport equipment	25,148	22,838
Automobiles and parts	22,053	20,579
Aircraft and parts	1,078	637
Other manufactured goods	51,071	46,296
Wood manufactures, excluding furniture	1,370	1,219
Paper and manufactures	3,356	2,923
Glass, glassware, and pottery	1,097	1,048
Diamonds, excluding industrial	1,862	1,973
Metals and manufactures	17,457	15,714
Pig iron and ferroalloys	702	573
Iron and steel-mill products	6,764	6,687
Platinum group metals	800	430
Nonferrous base metals	4,676	4,367
Textiles, other than clothing	2,216	2,200
Clothing	5,876	5,657
Footwear	2,859	2,585
Furniture	1,035	875
Scientific and photographic apparatus	1,570	1,435
Clocks and watches	946	947
Toys, games, and sporting goods	1,591	1,274
Artworks and antiques	1,487	1,312
Other transactions	4,905	4,018
Total	**$206,327**	**$171,978**

Source: Department of Commerce, Bureau of the Census, Office of International Economic Research.

Exports and General Imports by Countries and Areas

($25 million and over; value in millions)

Area and country	Exports, including re-exports 1979	1970	1960	1950	General imports 1979	1970	1960	1950
NORTH AND SOUTH AMERICA								
Canada	$33,096	$9,079	$3,810	$2,039	$38,099	$11,092	$2,901	$1,960
19 American Republics	26,257	5,695	3,577	2,720	24,782	4,779	3,528	2,910
Argentina	1,890	441	359	148	587	172	98	206
Bolivia	146	46	25	21	222	25	9	35
Brazil	3,442	840	464	365	3,119	670	570	715
Chile	886	300	203	73	440	157	193	160
Colombia	1,409	395	253	237	1,209	269	299	313
Costa Rica	413	94	45	27	389	117	35	25
Dominican Republic	610	143	42	43	667	184	110	38
Ecuador	696	127	57	29	816	109	65	34
El Salvador	352	64	43	33	444	48	32	51
Guatemala	467	100	64	44	413	87	59	54
Haiti	243	34	25	25	222	32	18	23
Honduras	324	89	35	24	415	102	34	20
Mexico	9,847	1,704	831	526	8,813	1,218	443	315
Nicaragua	100	77	30	19	234	61	21	19
Panama	528	208	90	112	191	76	24	10
Paraguay	128	18	9	3	164	11	8	6
Peru	720	214	147	76	1,181	340	183	49
Uruguay	127	41	63	41	91	19	21	106
Venezuela	3,931	759	567	406	5,166	1,082	948	324
OTHER WESTERN HEMISPHERE								
Bahamas	334	173	49	7	1,589	82	8	1
Barbados	120	22	6	1	57	9	1	(1)
Bermuda	121	92	32	10	11	1	2	(1)
Cuba	(1)	(1)	225	464	(1)	(1)	357	406
French West Indies	59	15	4	3	6	9	(1)	(1)
Guyana	74	25	12	3	66	43	11	1
Jamaica	292	218	48	9	375	187	54	2
Leeward and Windward Islands	98	32	6	1	33	6	2	2
Netherlands Antilles	412	126	65	70	1,830	416	265	158
Suriname	114	35	18	7	106	56	30	13
Trinidad and Tobago	462	84	36	6	1,560	232	55	9
EUROPE								
Western Europe	54,331	14,463	7,204	3,280	41,684	11,169	4,187	1,368
Austria	312	74	80	106	380	120	49	16
Belgium and Luxembourg	5,186	1,195	467	291	1,741	696	364	140
Denmark	732	227	146	65	707	284	98	12
Finland	337	99	56	21	449	114	52	35
France	5,587	1,483	699	475	4,771	942	396	132
Germany, West	8,482	2,741	1,272	(2)	10,955	3,127	897	—
Greece	812	203	103	107	183	52	33	17
Iceland	48	13	12	6	225	47	10	4
Ireland	695	112	43	47	323	135	28	2
Italy	4,359	1,353	715	369	4,918	1,316	393	109
Malta	27	6	(2)	(2)	9	1	(2)	(2)
Netherlands	6,907	1,651	817	251	1,852	528	213	85
Norway	688	196	108	95	1,266	142	66	41
Portugal	691	126	45	34	244	92	35	21
Spain	2,507	712	208	46	1,304	353	88	50
Sweden	1,513	543	301	99	1,652	399	170	71
Switzerland	3,660	700	254	130	2,076	459	198	110
Turkey	354	315	178	84	201	70	60	61
United Kingdom	10,635	2,536	1,487	548	8,029	2,194	993	335
Yugoslavia	757	168	88	43	389	96	41	19
Soviet Bloc	5,683	354	194	27	1,865	226	81	81
Bulgaria	57	15	73	857	35	2	1	2
Czechoslovakia	281	22	5	11	51	24	12	27
Germany, East	356	32	4	(2)	36	9	3	(2)
Hungary	78	28	2	3	110	6	2	2
Poland	793	70	143	9	423	98	39	11
Romania	501	66	1	2	328	13	1	(1)
U.S.S.R.	3,607	119	39	1	872	72	23	38
ASIA AND OCEANIA								
Total Asia and Oceania	53,090	11,294	4,700	1,691	69,812	9,103	2,987	1,846

Area and country	Exports, including re-exports 1979	1970	1960	1950	General imports 1979	1970	1960	1950
Near East	11,030	1,423	532	228	14,988	10,515	312	131
Bahrain	160	12	8	7	11	8	3	2
Iran	1,019	326	156	38	2,784	67	51	24
Iraq	442	22	37	10	618	3	27	12
Israel	1,857	592	130	(2)	749	150	27	(2)
Jordan	334	63	20	1	4	(1)	92	8
Kuwait	765	62	41	3	87	25	124	42
Lebanon	227	64	45	28	15	13	3	4
Oman	88	—	—	—	317	—	—	—
Qatar	138	—	—	—	279	—	—	—
Saudi Arabia	4,875	141	46	34	7,983	20	65	24
Syria	229	11	38	11	165	2	7	12
United Arab Emirates	667	—	—	—	1,971	—	—	—
Yemen, People's Dem. Rep. of	14	—	—	—	4	—	—	—
Yemen Arab Republic	214	—	—	—	2	—	—	—
Far East	37,741	8,682	1,979	1	51,371	8,682	2,406	1,360
Bangladesh	204	—	—	—	88	—	—	—
Brunei	51	10[3]	—	—	172	(1 3)	—	—
China	1,724	—	—	37	591	(1)	(1)	146
China (Taiwan)	3,271	527	278	40	5,901	549	20	3
Hong Kong	2,083	406	125	104	4,006	944	139	5
India	1,167	574	642	217	1,038	298	228	259
Indonesia	982	266	100	85	3,621	182	216	156
Japan	17,579	4,652	1,447	418	26,243	5,875	1,149	182
Korea, South	4,191	643	231	(2)	4,047	370	5	(2)
Malaysia[4]	932	67	18	(2)	2,146	270	156	(2)
Pakistan	529	328	170	31	120	80	36	31
Philippines	1,570	373	307	247	1,489	472	307	236
Singapore	2,331	240	42	(2)	1,467	81	19	(2)
Sri Lanka	57	12	14	7	100	26	39	66
Thailand	961	155	71	29	600	100	56	75
Australia	3,617	986	423	115	2,164	611	142	141
New Zealand and Samoa	533	135	78	29	710	222	119	65
Papua New Guinea	33	18	1	(1)	72	12	(1)	—
AFRICA								
Total Africa	6,299	1,425	793	376	24,377	1,067	534	494
Algeria	404	62	28	16	4,940	10	1	5
Angola	92	38	11	7	326	68	26	13
Botswana	6	—	—	—	60	63	—	—
Cameroon	61	19	—	5	202	25	6	—
Canary Islands	113	22	14	6	6	4	(1)	(1)
Congo	14	—	—	—	74	—	—	—
Egypt	1,433	77	151	34	381	23	32	55
Ethiopia	104	26	12	3	109	67	27	12
Gabon	33	7	—	—	320	9	—	—
Ghana	91	59	17	6	225	91	52	61
Guinea	23	7	—	—	63	77	—	—
Ivory Coast	128	36	—	—	363	92	—	—
Kenya	61	34	—	—	50	23	—	—
Liberia	108	46	36	25	136	51	39	21
Libya	468	108	43	(1)	5,256	39	(1)	(1)
Madagascar	61	7[5]	3	4	69	32[5]	13	8
Mauritius	16	—	—	—	39	—	—	—
Morocco	271	89	36	—	40	10	10	—
Mozambique	30	22	10	8	50	18	4	3
Nigeria	632	129	26	6	8,162	71	40	35
Rwanda	6	—	—	—	41	—	—	—
Senegal	32	8	—	—	5	1	—	—
Sierra Leone	16	8	—	—	86	8	—	—
South Africa[6]	1,423	563	288	129	2,623	290	108	142
Tanzania	36	12	—	—	46	24	—	—
Uganda	1	4	—	—	82	48	—	—
Zaire	113	62	27	41	286	41	58	46
Zambia	68	—	—	—	121	—	—	—
Summary:								
Developed countries	110,566	29,877	13,250	6,010	111,514	29,259	8,605	3,858
Developing countries	62,982	12,993	7,131	4,193	92,345	10,442	5,965	4,767
Total[8]	**181,802**	**43,224**	**20,575[7]**	**10,275[7]**	**206,327**	**39,952**	**14,654[7]**	**8,852[7]**

1. Less than $500,000. 2. Not applicable. 3. Includes Bhutan, Maldives, and Portuguese Timor. 4. Excludes Sarawak and

Sabah, which are included with Singpore through 1960. 5. Includes French Indian Ocean areas. 6. South-West Africa, Bechuanaland, and Swaziland included for 1950 and 1960; South-West Africa (Namibia) included for 1970 and 1979. 7. Includes Communist areas in Europe and Asia. *Source:* Department of Commerce, Bureau of the Census, Office of International Economic Research. 8. Includes "special category" merchandise.

Balance of International Payments

(in billions of dollars)

Item	1979	1978	1977	1975	1970	1965	1960	1955	1949
Exports of goods and services (excluding transfers under military grants)	$286.5	$221.0	$184.7	$155.7	$65.7	$41.1	$28.9	$19.9	$15.8
Merchandise adjusted, excluding military	182.1	142.1	120.8	107.1	42.5	26.5	19.7	14.4	12.2
Transfers under U.S. military agency sales contracts	7.2	8.2	7.5	3.9	1.5	0.8	0.3	0.2	n.s.s.
Receipts of income on U.S. investments abroad	66.0	43.0	32.6	25.4	11.8	7.4	4.6	2.6	1.5
Other services	31.3	27.8	23.9	19.3	9.9	6.4	4.3	2.7	2.1
Imports of goods and services	−281.6	−230.2	−194.2	−132.6	−60.0	−32.8	−23.7	−17.8	−9.6
Merchandise, adjusted, excluding military	−211.5	−175.8	−151.7	−98.0	−39.9	−21.5	−14.8	−11.5	−6.9
Direct defense expenditures	−8.5	−7.4	−5.8	−4.8	4.9	−3.0	−3.1	−2.9	−0.6
Payments of income on foreign investments in U.S.	−33.5	−22.1	−14.6	−12.6	−5.5	−2.1	−1.2	−0.5	−0.3
Other services	−28.2	−25.0	−22.1	−17.2	−9.8	−6.2	−4.6	−2.8	−1.8
Unilateral transfers, excluding military grants, net	−5.7	−5.1	−4.6	−4.6	−3.3	−2.9	−2.3	−2.5	−5.6
U.S. Government assets abroad, net	−61.7	−61.2	−35.8	−3.5	−1.6	−1.6	−1.1	−0.3	−0.7
U.S. private assets abroad, net	−56.9	−57.3	−31.7	−35.4	−10.2	−5.3	−5.1	−1.3	−0.6
U.S. assets abroad, official reserve, net	−1.1	0.7	−0.4	−0.6	2.5	1.2	2.1	0.2	−0.3
Foreign assets in U.S., net	37.6	64.1	50.7	15.6	6.4	0.7	2.3	−1.4	0.2
Statistical discrepancy	23.8	11.4	−0.9	5.5	−0.2	−0.5	−1.0	0.4	0.7
Balance on goods and services	4.9	−9.2	−9.5	23.1	5.7	8.3	5.1	2.2	6.2
Balance on goods, services, and remittances	2.7	−11.1	−11.3	21.3	4.1	7.2	4.5	1.6	5.6
Balance on current account	−0.8	−14.3	−14.1	18.4	2.4	5.4	2.8	−0.3	0.6

NOTE: n.s.s. = not shown separately. — denotes debits; sum of credits equals sum of credits. *Source:* Department of Commerce, Bureau of Economic Analysis.

Farm Income

(in millions of dollars)

Year	Cash receipts from marketings: Crops	Cash receipts from marketings: Livestock, livestock products	Government payments	Total cash income
1920	$6,644	$5,956	—	$12,600
1925	5,545	5,476	—	11,021
1930	3,868	5,187	—	9,055
1935	2,977	4,143	$ 573	7,693
1940	3,469	4,913	723	9,105
1945	9,655	12,008	742	22,405
1950	12,356	16,105	283	28,744
1955	13,523	15,967	229	29,719
1960	15,208	18,946	702	34,856
1965	17,392	21,958	2,463	41,813
1970	20,907	29,615	3,717	54,239
1971	22,276	30,583	3,145	56,004
1972	25,520	35,670	3,961	65,151
1973	41,132	45,936	2,607	89,675
1974	51,090	41,359	531	92,980
1975	45,150	43,059	807	89,016
1976	48,668	46,152	734	95,554
1977	48,222	47,432	1,819	97,473
1978	52,051	58,991	3,030	114,072

Source: Department of Agriculture, Economics, Statistics, and Cooperatives Service. NOTE: Figures are latest available.

Consumption of Principal Foods[1]

(in pounds per capita)

Foods	1979	1957–59 avg	1935–39 avg
Red meats	147.2	131.4	109.8
Poultry	59.0	33.5	15.6
Eggs[2]	35.9	45.2	36.4
Fluid milk and cream	283.2	337.0	330.0
Cheese	17.6	7.9	5.6
Butter	4.6	8.2	17.0
Margarine	11.7	8.9	2.9
Fats and oils[3]	44.9	31.5	29.3
Fresh fruits	81.0	95.5	135.5
Processed fruits[4]	n.a.	47.8	25.5
Fresh vegetables	n.a.	104.1	113.2
Processed vegetables	n.a.	49.9	29.5
Potatoes, sweet potatoes[5]	83.4	106.6	139.4
Sugar	91.3	96.1	97.5
Corn products[6]	n.a.	40.1	51.9
Wheat flour	117.0	120.0	160.0
Coffee	8.6	15.7	14.0
Cocoa	2.6	3.5	4.4

1. Civilian consumption, retail equivalent basis. 2. Pounds, not number. 3. Excludes butter and margarine. 4. Pack year. Excludes chilled fruits and juices. 5. Retail weight. 6. Corn used in food products. NOTE: n.a. = not available. *Source:* Department of Agriculture, Economics, Statistics, and Cooperatives Service.

Livestock on Farms
(in thousands)

Type	1980	1979	1975	1970	1965	1960	1955	1950	1945
Cattle[1]	110,961	110,864	132,028	112,369	109,000	96,236	96,592	77,963	85,573
Dairy cows[1]	10,810	10,839	11,220	13,303	16,981	19,527	23,462	23,853	27,770
Sheep[1]	12,513	12,220	14,515	20,423	25,127	33,170	31,582	29,826	39,609
Swine[1]	66,950	60,100	54,693	57,046	56,106	59,026	50,474	58,937	59,373
Chickens[2]	399,676	395,769	384,101	422,000	401,000	369,000	391,000	457,000	516,000
Turkeys[3]	—	3,700	3,014	6,715	6,100	5,633	4,917	5,124	7,082

1. As of Jan. 1. 2. As of Jan. 1 the previous year for 1945–60 and Dec. 1 for 1965–80. 3. Turkey breeder hens for 1975–79 and as of Dec. 1. *Source:* Department of Agriculture, Economics, Statistics, and Cooperatives Service.

Agricultural Output by States, 1979 Crops

State	Corn (1,000 bu)	Wheat (1,000 bu)	Cotton (1,000 ba[1])	Potatoes (1,000 cwt)	Tobacco (1,000 lb)	Cattle[2] (1,000 head)	Swine[3] (1,000 head)
Alabama	30,622	2,470	324	2,552	825	1,730	880
Alaska	—	—	—	—	—	8.4	1.10
Arizona	5,175	9,540	1,347	1,302	—	1,050	149
Arkansas	2,100	14,700	606	—	—	2,000	600
California	30,420	58,200	3,408	20,911	—	4,550	180
Colorado	92,075	70,183	—	13,353	—	2,975	430
Connecticut	—	—	—	418	4,925	104	11.0
Delaware	17,034	1,020	—	1,056	—	30	50
Florida	19,080	—	4	6,008	22,400	2,300	425
Georgia	100,750	5,600	152	—	100,965	1,600	2,280
Hawaii	—	—	—	—	—	213	53
Idaho	3,608	74,140	—	88,200	—	1,860	110
Illinois	1,358,080	55,900	—	447	—	2,700	6,950
Indiana	664,160	44,415	—	1,359	11,895	1,850	4,900
Iowa	1,625,600	2,664	—	231	—	7,150	16,200
Kansas	171,990	410,400	—	—	—	6,100	2,070
Kentucky	132,600	11,020	—	—	343,145	2,700	1,400
Louisiana	2,214	756	690	147	56	1,300	150
Maine	—	—	—	28,750	—	131	13.0
Maryland	58,905	4,218	—	248	26,400	380	235
Massachusetts	—	—	—	748	1,892	103	60
Michigan	237,500	33,755	—	9,548	—	1,310	960
Minnesota	606,000	90,384	—	14,716	—	3,750	4,900
Mississippi	5,720	3,680	1,437	—	—	1,810	440
Missouri	228,660	70,400	157	—	6,013	5,350	4,550
Montana	385	116,475	—	1,800	—	2,645	209
Nebraska	793,500	86,700	—	1,752	—	6,400	4,150
Nevada	—	1,610	2	4,950	—	580	9.0
New Hampshire	—	—	—	—	—	70	9.9
New Jersey	7,380	1,476	—	2,125	—	100	57
New Mexico	8,066	8,756	112	1,210	—	1,600	87
New York	55,250	6,560	—	12,894	—	1,780	139
North Carolina	128,440	7,560	43	2,729	621,368	1,080	2,600
North Dakota	22,040	252,235	—	18,240	—	2,000	370
Ohio	417,450	63,360	—	2,694	14,063	1,925	2,070
Oklahoma	8,250	216,600	522	—	—	5,500	370
Oregon	1,100	57,310	—	25,310	—	1,510	115
Pennsylvania	115,425	8,122	—	6,000	17,696	1,900	840
Rhode Island	—	—	—	897	—	8.0	9.9
South Carolina	40,720	3,597	116	—	117,705	625	650
South Dakota	210,900	60,060	—	1,203	—	4,010	2,000
Tennessee	51,460	10,030	171	387	104,829	2,300	1,400
Texas	132,300	138,000	5,539	3,752	—	13,200	910
Utah	1,504	6,680	—	1,300	—	840	55
Vermont	—	—	—	147	—	340	8.5
Virginia	51,045	6,300	—	3,185	109,603	1,750	850
Washington	12,257	118,000	—	48,925	—	1,579	126
West Virginia	4,543	340	—	—	1,658	545	56
Wisconsin	306,940	2,162	—	17,010	25,644	4,280	1,830
Wyoming	2,523	6,354	—	1,144	—	1,340	32
United States	**7,763,771**	**2,141,732**	**146,230**	**347,648**	**1,531,082**	**110,961**	**66,950**

1. 480-lb net-weight bales. 2. Number on farms as of Jan. 1, 1980. Number on farms as of Dec. 1, 1979. *Source:* Department of Agriculture, Economics, Statistics, and Cooperatives Service.

New Dietary Guidelines for Americans

Sources: U.S. Department of Agriculture and U.S. Department of Health and Social Services

Eat a Variety of Foods

You need about 40 different nutrients to stay healthy. These nutrients are in the foods you normally eat.

However, no single food item supplies all the essential nutrients in the amounts that you need. You should, therefore, eat a variety of foods to assure an adequate diet. Try to select foods each day from each of several major groups: for example, fruits and vegetables; cereals, breads, and grains; meats, poultry, eggs, and fish; kidney beans, lima beans, and black-eyed peas, which are good sources of protein; and milk, cheese, and yogurt.

You will rarely need to take vitamin or mineral supplements if you eat a wide variety of foods. There are a few important exceptions to this general statement:

Women in their childbearing years may need to take iron supplements to replace the iron they lose with menstrual bleeding. Women who are no longer menstruating should not take iron supplements routinely.

Women who are pregnant or who are breastfeeding need more of many nutrients, especially iron, folic acid, vitamin A, calcium, and sources of energy (calories from carbohydrates, proteins, and fats). Detailed advice should come from their physicians or from dieticians.

Infants also have special nutritional needs. Healthy full-term infants should be breastfed unless there are special problems. The nutrients in human breast milk tend to be digested and absorbed more easily than those in cow's milk. In addition, breast milk may serve to transfer immunity to some diseases from mother to the infant.

Normally, most babies do not need solid foods until they are 3 to 6 months old. At that time, other foods can be introduced gradually. Prolonged breast or bottlefeeding—without solid foods or supplemental iron—can result in iron deficiency.

You should not add salt or sugar to the baby's foods—the foods themselves contain enough salt and sugar.

Maintain Ideal Weight

If you are too fat, your chances of developing some chronic disorders are increased. Obesity is associated with high blood pressure, increased levels of blood fats (triglycerides) and cholesterol, and the most common type of diabetes. All of these, in turn, are associated with increased risks of heart attacks and strokes. Thus, you should try to maintain "ideal" weight.

In order to lose weight, you must take in fewer calories than you burn. This means that you must either select foods containing fewer calories or you must increase your activity—or both.

If you need to lose weight, do so gradually. Steady loss of 1 to 2 pounds a week—until you reach your goal—is relatively safe and more likely to be maintained.

Avoid crash diets that are severely restricted in the variety of foods they allow. Diets containing fewer than 800 calories may be hazardous. Some people have developed kidney stones, disturbing psychological changes, and other complications while following such diets. A few people have died suddenly and without warning.

Do not attempt to reduce your weight below the acceptable range. Severe weight loss may be as-

Desirable Weights[1]

Height[2]		Weight[3]			
		Men		Women	
in.	cm	lb	kg	lb	kg
58	147	— —	— —	102 (92–119)	46 (42–54)
60	152	— —	— —	107 (96–125)	49 (44–57)
62	158	123 (112–141)	56 (51–64)	113 (102–131)	51 (46–59)
64	163	130 (118–148)	59 (54–67)	120 (108–138)	55 (49–63)
66	168	136 (124–156)	62 (56–71)	128 (114–146)	58 (52–66)
68	173	145 (132–166)	66 (60–75)	136 (122–154)	62 (55–70)
70	178	154 (140–174)	70 (64–79)	144 (130–163)	65 (59–74)
72	183	162 (148–184)	74 (67–84)	152 (138–173)	69 (63–79)
74	188	171 (156–194)	78 (71–88)	— —	— —
76	193	181 (164–204)	82 (74–93)	— —	— —

1. Desirable weights for men and women of different heights, based on evidence from insurance statistics of weight in relation to longevity. According to the National Center for Health Statistics, the average American male adult is 70 in. tall (178 cm) and the average female is 64 in. tall (163 cm). Accordingly, the average desirable weights are 154 lb (70 kg) and 120 lb (55 kg) throughout adult life. 2. Without shoes. 3. Without clothes. Average weight ranges in parentheses. *Source: Recommended Dietary Allowances,* 9th Edition (1980), with permission of the National Academy of Sciences, Washington, D.C.

sociated with nutrient deficiencies, menstrual irregularities, infertility, hair loss, skin changes, cold intolerance, severe constipation, psychiatric disturbances, and other complications.

Avoid Too Much Fat, Saturated Fat, and Cholesterol

Populations like ours with diets high in saturated fats and cholesterol tend to have high blood cholesterol levels. Individuals within these populations usually have greater risks of having heart attacks than people eating low-fat, low-cholesterol diets.

Eating extra saturated fat and cholesterol will increase blood cholesterol levels in most people. However, there are wide variations among people —related to heredity and the way each person's body uses cholesterol.

There is controversy about what recommendations are appropriate for healthy Americans. But for the U.S. population *as a whole,* reduction in our current intake of total fat, saturated fat, and cholesterol is sensible. This suggestion is especially appropriate for people who have high blood pressure or who smoke.

The recommendations are not meant to prohibit the use of any specific food item or to prevent you from eating a variety of foods. For example, eggs and organ meats (such as liver) contain cholesterol, but they also contain many essential vitamins and minerals, as well as protein. Such items can be eaten in moderation, as long as your over-all cholesterol intake is not excessive.

Eat Foods With Adequate Starch and Fiber

The major sources of energy in the average U.S. diet are carbohydrates and fats. If you limit your fat intake, you should increase your calories from carbohydrates to supply your body's energy needs.

In trying to reduce your weight to "ideal" levels, carbohydrates have an advantage over fats: carbohydrates contain less than half the number of calories per ounce than fats.

Complex carbohydrate foods are better than *simple* carbohydrates in this regard. Simple carbohydrates—such as sugars—provide calories but little else in the way of nutrients. Complex carbohydrate foods—such as beans, peas, nuts, seeds, fruits and vegetables, and whole grain breads, cereals, and products—contain many essential nutrients in addition to calories.

Increasing your consumption of certain complex carbohydrates can also help increase dietary fiber. The average American diet is relatively low in fiber. Eating more foods high in fiber tends to reduce the symptoms of chronic constipation, diverticulosis, and some types of "irritable bowel." There is also concern that low fiber diets might increase the risk of developing cancer of the colon, but whether this is true is not yet known.

Avoid Too Much Sugar

The major hazard from eating too much sugar is tooth decay (dental caries). The risk of caries increases the more frequently you eat sugar and sweets, especially if you eat between meals, and if you eat foods that stick to the teeth.

Obviously, there is more to healthy teeth than avoiding sugars. Careful dental hygiene and exposure to adequate amounts of fluoride in the water are especially important.

Contrary to widespread opinion, too much sugar in your diet does not seem to cause diabetes. The most common type of diabetes is seen in obese adults, and avoiding sugar, without correcting the overweight, will not solve the problem. There is also no convincing evidence that sugar causes heart attacks or blood vessel diseases.

To avoid excessive sugars use less of all sugars, including white sugar, brown sugar, raw sugar, honey, and syrups; eat less of foods containing these sugars, such as candy, soft drinks, ice cream, cakes, cookies; select fresh fruits or fruits canned without sugar and with light syrup rather than heavy syrup; and read food labels for clues on sugar content—if the names sucrose, glucose, maltose, dextrose, lactose, fructose, or syrups appear first, then there is a large amount of sugar. Remember, how often you eat sugar is as important as how much sugar you eat.

Avoid Too Much Sodium

Table salt contains sodium and chloride—both are essential elements.

Sodium is also present in many beverages and

Physicians, Dentists, and Nurses
(numbers in thousands)

Profession	1977	1976	1975	1973	1970	1965	1960	1955
Physicians, number	438	426	409	381	348	305	275	255
Rate per 100,000 resident population[1]	198	194	188	178	166	153	148	150
Active (exc. physicians in Federal serv.)	362	351	338	312	282	255	n.a.	n.a.
Rate per 100,000 resident population[1]	165	161	155	146	135	129	n.a.	n.a.
Doctors of medicine[2]	421	409	394	366	334	292	260	242
Doctors of osteopathy	17[3]	16[3]	15[3]	15[3]	14	13	14	14
Physicians admitted to U.S. as immigrants[4]	7.1	8.1	7.1	7.1	3.2	2.0	1.6	1.0
Dentists, number[5]	118	n.a.	n.a.	122	116	109	103	95
Active (excl. dentists in Federal service)	113	110	108	101	96	86	85	76
Rate per 100,000 resident population[1]	52	52	50	48	47	45	47	47
Nurses, number (active registered)	1,011	961	906	815	700	613	504	430
Rate per 100,000 resident population[1]	465	449	427	390	345	319	282	259

1. Based on Bureau of the Census population estimates. 2. Excludes non-Federal physicians with temporary foreign addresses. 3. Estimated. 4. Immigration and Naturalization Service figures. 5. Beginning 1960, excludes graduates of year stated. NOTE: n.a. = not available. *Source:* Department of Health, Education, and Welfare, National Center for Health Statistics.

foods that we eat, especially in certain processed foods, condiments, sauces, pickled foods, salty snacks, and sandwich meats. Baking soda, baking powder, monosodium glutamate (MSG), soft drinks, and even many medications (many antacids, for instance) contain sodium.

The major hazard of excessive sodium is for persons who have high blood pressure. In populations with low-sodium intakes, high blood pressure is rare. In contrast, in populations with high-sodium intakes, high blood pressure is common. If people with high blood pressure severely restrict their sodium intakes, their blood pressures will *usually* fall—although not always to normal levels.

To avoid too much sodium, learn to enjoy the unsalted flavors of foods; cook with only small amounts of added salt; add little or no salt to food at the table; limit intake of salty foods, such as potato chips, pretzels, salted nuts, and popcorn, condiments (soy sauce, steak sauce, garlic salt), cheese, pickled foods, cured meats; and read food labels carefully to determine the amounts of sodium in processed foods and snack items.

If You Drink Alcohol, Do So In Moderation

Alcoholic beverages tend to be high in calories and low in other nutrients. Even moderate drinkers may need to drink less if they wish to achieve ideal weight.

On the other hand, heavy drinkers may lose their appetites for foods containing essential nutrients. Vitamin and mineral deficiencies occur commonly in heavy drinkers—in part, because alcohol alters the absorption and use of some essential nutrients.

Sustained or excessive alcohol consumption by pregnant women has caused birth defects. Pregnant women should limit alcohol intake to 2 ounces or less on any single day.

Annual Increase in Cost of Medical Care
(in percent)

Year	All consumer prices	Total medical care	Hospital semi-private room charges	Physicians' fees	Dentists' fees
1965	1.7	2.1	5.3	3.1	2.9
1966	2.9	2.9	6.1	3.9	2.9
1967	2.9	6.5	17.3	7.4	4.5
1968	4.2	6.4	15.9	6.1	5.2
1969	5.4	6.5	13.5	6.1	5.8
1970	5.9	6.4	12.8	7.2	6.8
1971	4.3	6.9	13.3	7.5	6.0
1972	3.3	4.7	9.4	5.2	5.7
1973	6.2	3.1	5.0	2.6	3.1
1974	11.0	5.7	6.0	5.0	4.4
1975	9.1	12.5	16.4	12.8	10.8
1976	5.8	10.2	15.2	11.4	7.7
1977	6.5	9.6	11.5	9.3	7.5

Source: Department of Health and Human Services; Social Security Administration. NOTE: Data are most recent available.

Health Care Expenditures Per Person, 1978[1]

		Third-party payments				
Type of expenditure	Direct payments	Private health insurance	Government	Philanthropy and industry	Total	Total
Hospital care	$ 33.79	$119.84	$183.50	$3.81	$307.14	$340.93
Physicians' services	53.87	61.79	42.33	.09	104.21	158.08
Dentists' services	45.80	11.43	2.42	—	13.84	59.64
Other professional services	10.02	4.62	4.36	.18	9.16	19.17
Drugs and drug sundries	56.80	5.07	5.83	—	10.90	69.70
Eyeglasses and appliances	15.60	.20	1.60	—	1.80	17.40
Nursing-home care	32.19	.48	37.48	.48	38.44	70.64
Other health services	—	—	14.16	5.27	19.43	—
Total per person	**248.06**	**203.43**	**291.67**	**9.82**	**504.92**	**752.98**

1. Based on July 1 population estimates including outlying territories, armed forces and federal employees overseas, and their dependents. NOTE: Figures may not add up to totals due to rounding. Data are most recent available. *Sources:* Department of Health and Human Services, Health Care Financing Administration.

Estimated Safe and Adequate Daily Dietary Intakes of Additional Selected Vitamins and Minerals[1]

		Vitamins			Trace Elements[2]						Electrolytes		
	Age (years)	Vitamin K (μg)	Biotin (μg)	Pantothenic Acid (mg)	Copper (mg)	Manganese (mg)	Fluoride (mg)	Chromium (mg)	Selenium (mg)	Molybdenum (mg)	Sodium (mg)	Potassium (mg)	Chloride (mg)
Infants	0–0.5	12	35	2	0.5–0.7	0.5–0.7	0.1–0.5	0.01–0.04	0.01–0.04	0.03–0.06	115–350	350–925	275–700
	0.5–1	10–20	50	3	0.7–1.0	0.7–1.0	0.2–1.0	0.02–0.06	0.02–0.06	0.04–0.08	250–750	425–1275	400–1200
Children	1–3	15–30	65	3	1.0–1.5	1.0–1.5	0.5–1.5	0.02–0.08	0.02–0.08	0.05–0.1	325–975	550–1650	500–1500
and	4–6	20–40	85	3–4	1.5–2.0	1.5–2.0	1.0–2.5	0.03–0.12	0.03–0.12	0.06–0.15	450–1350	775–2325	700–2100
Adolescents	7–10	30–60	120	4–5	2.0–2.5	2.0–3.0	1.5–2.5	0.05–0.2	0.05–0.2	0.1–0.3	600–1800	1000–3000	925–2775
	11+	50–100	100–200	4–7	2.0–3.0	2.5–5.0	1.5–2.5	0.05–0.2	0.05–0.2	0.15–0.5	900–2700	1525–4575	1400–4200
Adults		70–140	100–200	4–7	2.0–3.0	2.5–5.0	1.5–4.0	0.05–0.2	0.05–0.2	0.15–0.5	1100–3300	1875–5625	1700–1500

1. Because there is less information on which to base allowances, these figures are not given in the main table of the RDA and are provided in the form of ranges of recommended intakes. 2. Since the toxic levels for many trace elements may be only several times usual intakes, the upper levels for the trace elements given in this table should not be habitually exceeded. NOTE: μg—microgram; mg—milligram. *Source: Recommended Dietary Allowances,* Ninth Edition (1980), with the permission of the National Academy of Sciences, Washington, D.C.

Recommended Dietary Allowances

The Recommended Dietary Allowances (RDA) given in the tables are the latest established by the National Academy of Sciences Committee on Dietary Allowances as recommendations for the average daily amounts of nutrients for healthy population groups. They should not be confused with requirements for a specific individual.

Differences in the nutrient requirements of individuals are ordinarily unknown. Therefore, RDA (except for energy) are estimated to exceed the requirements of most individuals. Intake below the recommended allowance for a nutrient is not necessarily inadequate, but the risk of its being inadequate is increased if intake falls below the level recommended as safe.

Special needs for nutrients arising from such problems as premature birth, inherited metabolic disorders, infections, chronic diseases, and the use of medications are not covered by the RDA.

These dietary allowances form the basis for the RDA set by the Food and Drug Administration and are found on food labels as "U.S.R.D.A." The nutritional label lists the percentage of the RDA for protein and any of 17 vitamins and minerals found in the product. This does not represent all the required nutrients.

Because individual foods are not nutritionally complete, RDA should be met by eating a wide variety of selected foods in your diet.

Allowance for Energy

The recommended allowances for energy are estimates of the average needs of population groups, not recommended intakes for individuals. These needs vary from person to person and are not easily predictable without detailed information about physical characteristics and activity of the individual. Hence, the average energy needs for each age and sex are provided only as guidelines and are not repeated in the general table of recommended allowances.

Adjustments in RDA

The RDA does not take into account special needs that may require special attention. Some of these considerations are:

Physical Activity. This increases energy expenditure. Here, the increased need for a nutrient that may be related to carbohydrate utilization is generally met by consuming a larger amount of food. Attention must be given to salt and water losses due to sweating, which if prolonged, may lead to a loss of other nutrients.

Climate. There is little evidence that nutrient requirements, other than those for energy, are altered when individuals are exposed to heat or cold. Therefore, adjustments in dietary allowances to compensate for temperature changes are not considered necessary. However, exposures to temperatures that increase sweating will also increase the need for water and salt.

Aging. It is evident from studies of adult populations that body composition changes throughout life, with fat increasing and metabolically active tissues being slowly reduced. This reduction accounts for the fall in basal energy metabolism, often with an even greater reduction in physical activity.

As a result, less food is needed to meet energy requirements, and, unless food choices are made with great care, the amounts of essential nutrients may fall below desirable levels. It is important for older people to make sure that the smaller quantities of food that they eat are selected to provide the needed amounts of essential nutrients.

It is also important that physical activity be continued in adult life and into old age.

Mean Heights and Weights and Recommended Energy Intake

Category	Age (years)	Weight		Height		Energy needs (with range)	
		(lb)	(kg)	(in.)	(cm)	(kcal)	(MJ)
Infants	0.0–0.5	13	6	24	60	kg X 115 (95–145)	kg X .48
	0.5–1.0	20	9	28	71	kg X 105 (80–135)	kg X .44
Children	1–3	29	13	35	90	1300 (900–1800)	5.5
	4–6	44	20	44	112	1700 (1300–2300)	7.1
	7–10	62	28	52	132	2400 (1650–3300)	10.1
Males	11–14	99	45	62	157	2700 (2000–3700)	11.3
	15–18	145	66	69	176	2800 (2100–3900)	11.8
	19–22	154	70	70	177	2900 (2500–3300)	12.2
	23–50	154	70	70	178	2700 (2300–3100)	11.3
	51–75	154	70	70	178	2400 (2000–2800)	10.1
	76 +	154	70	70	178	2050 (1650–2450)	8.6
Females	11–14	101	46	62	157	2200 (1500–3000)	9.2
	15–18	120	55	64	163	2100 (1200–3000)	8.8
	19–22	120	55	64	163	2100 (1700–2500)	8.8
	23–50	120	55	64	163	2000 (1600–2400)	8.4
	51–75	120	55	64	163	1800 (1400–2200)	7.6
	76 +	120	55	64	163	1600 (1200–2000)	6.7
Pregnancy						+ 300	
Lactation						+ 500	

The energy allowances for the young adults are for men and women doing light work. The allowances for the two older age groups represent mean energy needs over these age spans, allowing for a 2% decrease in basal (resting) metabolic rate per decade and a reduction in activity of 200 kcal/day for men and women between 51 and 75 years, 500 kcal for men over 75 years, and 400 kcal for women over 75. The customary range of daily energy output is shown for adults in parentheses, and is based on a variation in energy needs of ± 400 kcal at any one age, emphasizing the wide range of energy intakes appropriate for any group of people. Energy allowances for children through age 18 are based on median energy intakes of children these ages followed in longitudinal growth studies. The values in parentheses are 10th and 90th percentile of energy intake, to indicate the range of energy consumption among children of these ages. NOTE: kg—kilogram; cm—centimeter; kcal—kilocalorie; MJ—megajoule. 1 kcal is equivalent to 4.18 kilojoules. 1 megajoule is equal to 1000 kilojoules. *Source: Recommended Dietary Allowances,* Ninth Edition (1980), with the permission of the National Academy of Sciences, Washington, D.C.

Hospital Facilities, 1978

State	Hospitals[1]	Beds	Admissions during year
Alabama	148	25,242	752,371
Alaska	26	1,697	55,026
Arizona	78	11,339	381,835
Arkansas	96	12,650	437,193
California	613	114,836	3,329,040
Colorado	101	14,666	461,016
Connecticut	64	18,791	453,400
Delaware	15	4,099	83,440
D.C.	19	9,003	206,323
Florida	245	54,211	1,608,248
Georgia	189	31,146	953,571
Hawaii	27	3,813	115,985
Idaho	51	3,737	134,023
Illinois	285	75,484	2,044,793
Indiana	135	33,816	884,030
Iowa	141	21,613	576,577
Kansas	164	18,161	462,395
Kentucky	121	18,815	637,963
Louisiana	159	25,128	765,584
Maine	53	7,324	182,640
Maryland	85	25,210	562,144
Massachusetts	189	45,456	936,260
Michigan	244	50,661	1,475,922
Minnesota	188	31,051	721,385
Mississippi	114	16,234	480,422
Missouri	187	35,437	972,727
Montana	65	5,652	142,825
Nebraska	108	11,674	304,679
Nevada	25	3,234	112,072
New Hampshire	33	4,995	139,011
New Jersey	139	44,157	1,085,874
New Mexico	54	6,503	193,010
New York	368	134,425	2,739,053
North Carolina	158	33,774	922,044
North Dakota	60	5,830	147,421
Ohio	241	64,158	1,846,100
Oklahoma	141	17,482	512,410
Oregon	85	11,568	372,915
Pennsylvania	313	86,474	1,983,899
Rhode Island	21	6,700	146,925
South Carolina	88	16,919	472,960
South Dakota	70	5,676	144,660
Tennessee	160	31,008	933,101
Texas	565	79,071	2,465,947
Utah	41	5,084	204,164
Vermont	19	3,036	76,649
Virginia	135	32,138	794,746
Washington	127	16,138	584,327
West Virginia	80	14,170	395,285
Wisconsin	171	26,630	779,079
Wyoming	31	2,529	69,713
TOTAL	**7,015**	**1,380,645**	**37,243,182**

1. All registered hospitals. Data estimated for nonreporting hospitals. NOTE: Data are latest available. *Source:* American Hospital Association.

Recommended Daily Dietary Allowances[1]

Designed for the maintenance of good nutrition of practically all healthy persons in the U.S. (revised 1979)

						Fat-Soluble Vitamins			Water-Soluble Vitamins							Minerals					
Persons	Age (years)	Wgt. (lbs)	Wgt. (kg)	Hgt. (in.)	Hgt. (cm)	Vitamin A µg R.E.[2]	Vitamin D (µg)[3]	Vitamin E (mgα T.E.)[4]	Ascorbic Acid (mg)	Folacin[3] (µg)	Niacin[5] (mg)	Riboflavin (mg)	Thiamin (mg)	Vitamin B_6 (mg)	Vitamin B_{12} (µg)	Calcium (mg)	Phosphorus (mg)	Iodine (µg)	Iron (mg)	Magnesium (mg)	Zinc (mg)
Infants	0.0–0.5	13	6	24	60	420	10	3	35	30	6	0.4	0.3	0.3	0.5[6]	360	240	40	10	50	3
	0.5–1.0	20	9	28	71	400	10	4	35	45	8	0.6	0.5	0.6	1.5	540	360	50	15	70	5
Children	1–3	29	13	35	90	400	10	5	45	100	9	0.8	0.7	0.9	2.0	800	800	70	15	150	10
	4–6	44	20	44	112	500	10	6	45	200	11	1.1	0.9	1.3	2.5	800	800	90	10	200	10
	7–10	62	28	52	132	700	10	7	45	300	16	1.4	1.2	1.6	3.0	800	800	120	10	250	10
Males	11–14	99	45	62	157	1,000	10	8	50	400	18	1.6	1.4	1.8	3.0	1,200	1,200	150	18	350	15
	15–18	145	66	69	176	1,000	10	10	60	400	18	1.7	1.4	2.0	3.0	1,200	1,200	150	18	400	15
	19–22	154	70	70	177	1,000	7.5	10	60	400	19	1.7		2.2	3.0	800	800	150	10	350	15
	23–50	154	70	70	178	1,000	5	10	60	400	18	1.6	1.4	2.2	3.0	800	800	150	10	350	15
	51+	154	70	70	178	1,000	5	10	60	400	16	1.4	1.2	2.2	3.0	800	800	150	10	350	15
Females	11–14	101	46	62	157	800	10	8	50	400	15	1.3	1.1	1.8	3.0	1,200	1,200	150	18	300	15
	15–18	120	55	64	163	800	10	8	60	400	14	1.3	1.1	2.0	3.0	1,200	1,200	150	18	300	15
	19–22	120	55	64	163	800	7.5	8	60	400	14	1.3	1.1	2.0	3.0	800	800	150	18	300	15
	23–50	120	55	64	163	800	5	8	60	400	13	1.2	1.0	2.0	3.0	800	800	150	18	300	15
	51+	120	55	64	163	800	5	8	60	400	13	1.2	1.0	2.0	3.0	800	800	150	10	300	15
Pregnant	—	—	—	—	—	+200	+5	+2	+20	+400	+2	+0.3	+0.4	+0.6	+1.0	+400	+400	+25	[7]	+150	+5
Lactating	—	—	—	—	—	+400	+5	+3	+40	+100	+5	+0.5	+0.5	+0.5	+1.0	+400	+400	+50	[7]	+150	+10

1. Allowances provide for individual variances among most normal persons living in the United States under usual environmental stresses. 2. Retinol equivalents. 1 Retinol equivalent = 1 µg retinol. 3. As cholecalciferol. 10 µg cholecalciferol = 400 I.U. vitamin D. 4. αtocopherol equivalents. 1 mg d-α-tocopherol = 1 α T.E. 5. Although expressed as niacin, the average 1 mg of niacin is derived from each 60 mg of dietary tryptophan. 6. The RDA for vitamin B12 in infants is based on average concentration of the vitamin in human milk. 7. Cannot be met by ordinary diets: use of supplemental iron is recommended. NOTE: mg—milligram; µg—microgram; IU—International Units; lbs—pounds; Wgt.—Weight; Hgt.—Height. *Source: Recommended Dietary Allowances,* Ninth Edition (1980), with the permission of the National Academy of Sciences, Washington, D.C.

Communicable Diseases

Disease	Incubation period[1]	Period of communicability
Chickenpox (varicella)	2 to 3 weeks	From 5 days before appearance of vesicles to 6 days after
Common Cold	12 to 72 hours; usually 24 hrs	From 1 day before onset to 5 days after
Conjunctivitis	1 to 3 days	During course of active infection
Diphtheria	2 to 5 days	Usually 2 weeks or less; seldom more than 4 weeks
Dysentery, amebic	2 to 4 weeks (varies widely)	During intestinal infection; possibly for years if untreated
Enterobiasis (pinworm)	3 to 6 weeks	Not directly transmitted
Food poisoning: Botulism	12 to 36 hours	Not applicable
Salmonella infection	6 to 72 hours; usually 36	3 days to 3 weeks (extremely variable)
Staphylococcus intoxication	2 to 4 hours	Not applicable
German measles (rubella)	8 to 10 days; usually 14	1 week before and at least 4 days after onset of rash
Gonorrhea	2 to 5 days; sometimes longer	Indefinite unless treated
Hepatitis (serum)	45 to 160 days; usually 80 to 100	Many weeks before onset of symptoms
Herpes Simplex	Up to 2 weeks	As long as 7 weeks after recovery
Impetigo contagiosa	4 to 10 days; sometimes longer	Until lesions are healed
Infectious mononucleosis	Varies 2 to 6 weeks	Unknown
Influenza	Usually 1 to 3 days	Probably limited to 3 days from clinical onset
Measles (rubeola)	10 days (to onset): 14 days (to rash)	From beginning of prodromal period to 4 days after onset of rash
Meningitis, meningococcal	2 to 10 days	Usually 1 day after appropriate medication
Mumps	12 to 26 days; commonly 18	From 6 days before distinctive symptoms up to 9 days after
Pediculosis	Apprx. 2 weeks	While lice remain alive
Pneumonia: Bacterial	Usually 1 to 3 days	Unknown
Viral	Believed to be 1 to 3 days	Unknown
Poliomyelitis	3 to 21 days; commonly 7 to 12	7 to 10 days before and after onset of symptoms
Rabies	2 to 8 weeks or longer	From animals, 3 to 5 days before onset and during course of the disease
Respiratory (acute viral)	Few days to 1 week or more	Duration of active disease
Ringworm (of body)	4 to 10 days	As long as lesions are present
(Athlete's foot)	Unknown	As long as lesions are present
Scarlet fever and streptococcal sore throat	1 to 3 days	Uncomplicated cases apprx. 10 to 21 days; in untreated cases, weeks or months
Smallpox	7 to 17 days; commonly 10 to 12	During first week
Syphilis	10 days to 10 weeks; usually 3 weeks	Variable and indefinite
Tetanus	4 days to 3 weeks	Not applicable
Trichinosis	2 to 28 days after ingestion of infected meat; usually 9 days	Not directly transmitted
Tuberculosis	4 to 12 weeks (to primary phase)	As long as tubercle bacilli are discharged by patient
Typhoid fever	1 to 3 weeks, average 2 weeks	As long as typhoid bacilli appear in excreta; 2 to 5% of patients become permanent carriers
Whooping cough (pertussis)	Commonly 7 days, almost uniformly within 10 days, and not exceeding 21 days	From 7 days after exposure to 3 weeks after onset of typical paroxysms

1. Usual limits. NOTE: This list is incomplete, but includes those diseases that are most common and widespread.

Income: Doctors and Dentists

Year	Self-employed physicians	Self-employed dentists	Male professional and technical workers	All U.S. full-time employees
1955	$16,107	$11,533	$ 5,055	$ 3,923
1967	34,740	22,850	8,882	6,307
1970	43,100	28,100	10,722	7,713
1974	54,140	30,500	13,391	9,991
1976	62,799	35,000	14,400	11,623

Source: Council on Wage and Price Stability. NOTE: Data are most recent available.

Calories, Minerals, and Vitamins of Selected Foods

Food and amount	Energy (calories)	Nutrients: Protein (gm)	Nutrients: Fat (gm)	Minerals: Calcium (mg)	Minerals: Iron (mg)	Vitamins: Vitamin A (IU)	Vitamins: Vitamin B_1 (thiamin) (mg)	Vitamins: Vitamin B_2 (riboflavin) (mg)	Vitamins: Niacin (mg)	Vitamins: Vitamin C (ascorbic acid) (mg)
Apple, 1 medium, raw	80	—	1	10	.4	120	.04	.03	.1	6
Applesauce, 1 cup, canned, unsweetened	100	—	—	10	1.2	100	.05	.02	.1	2
Bacon, 2 slices, crisp	85	4	8	2	.5	—	.08	.05	.8	—
Banana, 1 medium	100	1	—	10	.8	230	.06	.07	.8	12
Beans, snap green, 1 cup cooked	30	2	—	63	.8	680	.09	.11	.6	15
Beans, red kidney, 1 cup canned	230	15	1	74	4.6	10	.13	.10	1.5	—
Beans, baked, pork and molasses, 1 cup	385	16	12	161	5.9	—	.15	.10	1.3	—
Beef cuts, cooked: Chuck, boned, 3 ounces	245	23	16	10	2.9	30	.04	.18	3.6	—
Hamburger, 3 ounces	235	20	17	9	2.6	30	.07	.17	4.4	—
Rib roast, 3 ounces boned	375	17	33	8	2.2	70	.05	.13	3.1	—
Round, 3 ounces boned	220	24	13	10	3.0	20	.07	.19	4.8	—
Sirloin, 3 ounces boned	330	20	27	9	2.5	50	.05	.15	4.0	—
Beef stew with vegetables, 1 cup	220	16	11	29	2.9	2,400	.15	.17	4.7	17
Beets, 1 cup cooked	55	2	—	24	.9	30	.05	.07	.5	10
Breads: Cracked wheat, average slice	65	2	1	22	.5	—	.08	.06	.8	—
Italian, average slice, enriched	85	3	—	5	.7	—	.12	.07	1.0	—
Raisin, average slice enriched	65	2	1	18	.6	—	.09	.06	.6	—
Rye (American), average slice	60	2	—	19	.5	—	.07	.05	.7	—
White, average slice enriched	70	2	1	21	.6	—	.10	.06	.8	—
Whole wheat, average slice	65	3	1	24	.8	—	.09	.03	.8	—
Butter, 1 tbsp	100	—	12	3	—	430	—	—	—	—
Cabbage, 1 cup, raw, coarsely shredded	15	1	—	34	.3	90	.04	.04	.2	33
Cake: Sponge, average slice	195	5	4	20	1.1	300	.09	.14	.6	—
Pound, average slice	160	2	10	6	.5	80	.05	.06	.4	—
Candies: Caramels, 1 ounce	115	1	3	42	.4	—	.01	.05	.1	—
Chocolate, milk, 1 ounce	145	2	9	65	.3	80	.02	.10	.1	—
Cantaloup, ½ melon	80	2	—	38	1.1	9,240	.11	.08	1.6	90
Carrot, raw, 1 average size	30	1	—	27	.5	7,930	.04	.04	.4	6
Catsup, 1 tbsp	15	—	—	3	.1	210	.01	.01	.2	2
Cheese: Cheddar, 1 ounce	115	7	9	204	.2	300	.01	.11	—	—
Cottage, creamed, 1 cup	235	28	10	135	.3	370	.05	.37	.3	—
Cottage, uncreamed, 1 cup	125	25	1	46	.3	40	.04	.21	.2	—
Cream cheese, 1 ounce	100	2	10	23	.3	400	—	.06	—	—
Swiss, natural, 1 ounce	105	8	8	272	—	240	.01	.10	—	—
Swiss, process, 1 ounce	95	7	7	219	.2	230	—	.08	—	—
Chicken, broiled, 3 ounces	115	20	3	8	1.4	80	.05	.16	7.4	—

Chicken, fried, ½ breast, 3.3 ounces	160	26	5	9	1.3	70	.04	.17	11.6	—
Chicken, canned, boned, 3 ounces	170	18	10	18	1.3	200	.03	.11	3.7	3
Clams, raw, 3 ounces	65	11	1	59	5.2	90	.08	.15	1.1	8
Cocoa, 1 cup, homemade	220	9	9	298	.8	320	.10	.44	.4	2
Coffee; black, 1 cup	—	—	—	—	—	—	—	—	—	—
Cola, carbonated, 12 ounces	145	—	—	—	—	—	—	—	—	—
Corn, average ear	70	2	1	2	.5	310	.09	.08	1.1	7
Corn flakes, 1 cup	95	2	—	3	.6	1,180	.29	.35	2.9	9
Crabmeat, canned, 3 ounces	85	15	2	38	.7	—	.07	.07	1.6	—
Crackers, Graham, 4	110	2	3	11	1.0	—	.04	.16	1.0	—
Saltines, 4	50	1	1	2	.5	—	.05	.05	.4	—
Cream: Light, table, 1 cup	470	6	46	231	.1	1,730	.08	.36	.1	2
Heavy, whipping, 1 cup	820	5	88	154	.1	3,500	.05	.26	.1	1
Sour, 1 cup	495	7	48	268	.1	1,820	.08	.34	.2	2
Whipped topping (pressurized), 1 cup	155	2	13	61	—	550	.02	.04	—	—
Doughnut, 1 plain	100	1	5	10	.4	20	.05	.05	.4	—
Egg: Raw or cooked in shell, 1	80	6	6	28	1.0	260	.04	.14	—	—
Omelet, scrambled, 1	95	6	7	47	.9	310	.04	.16	—	—
Frankfurter, 1	170	7	15	3	.8	—	.08	.11	1.4	—
Fruit cocktail, 1 cup canned	195	1	—	23	1.0	360	.05	.03	1.0	5
Grapefruit: Raw, ½	45	1	—	19	.5	10	.05	.02	.2	44
Canned, syrup, 1 cup	180	2	—	33	.8	30	.08	.05	.5	76
Juice, fresh, 1 cup	95	1	—	22	.5	20	.10	.05	.5	93
Haddock, breaded, fried, 3 ounces	140	17	5	34	1.0	—	.03	.06	2.7	2
Honey, strained, 1 tbsp.	65	—	—	1	.1	—	—	.01	.1	—
Ice cream, 1 cup	270	5	14	176	.1	540	.05	.33	.1	1
Jellies, 1 tbsp	50	—	—	4	.3	—	—	.01	—	1
Lamb: Rib chop, boned, 4 ounces	400	25	33	10	1.5	—	.14	.25	5.6	—
Leg roast, 3 ounces, boned	235	22	16	9	1.4	—	.13	.23	4.7	—
Lemon, 1 medium	20	1	—	19	.4	10	.03	.01	.1	39
Liver: Beef, fried, 2 ounces	130	15	6	6	5.0	30,280	.15	2.37	9.4	15
Luncheon meat: Boiled ham, 2 ounces	135	11	10	6	1.6	—	.25	.09	1.5	—
Canned, spiced or unspiced, 2 ounces	165	8	14	5	1.2	—	.18	.12	1.6	—
Macaroni, enriched, 1 cup	155	5	1	11	1.3	—	.20	.11	1.5	—
Macaroni and cheese, 1 cup	430	17	22	362	1.8	860	.20	.40	1.8	—
Margarine, 1 tbsp	100	—	12	3	—	470	—	—	—	—
Mayonnaise, 1 tbsp	100	—	11	3	.1	40	—	.01	—	—
Milk: Whole, 1 cup	150	8	8	291	.1	310	.09	.40	.2	2
Skim (non-fat), 1 cup	85	8	—	302	.1	500	.09	.34	.2	2
Buttermilk, 1 cup	100	8	2	285	.1	80	.08	.38	.1	2
Mushrooms, canned, 1 cup	40	5	—	15	1.2	—	.04	.60	4.8	4
Nuts: Almonds, 1 cup shelled	850	26	77	332	6.7	—	.34	1.31	5.0	—
Peanuts, roasted, 1 cup	840	37	72	107	3.0	—	.46	.19	24.8	—
Oatmeal, 1 cup cooked	130	5	2	22	1.4	—	.19	.05	.2	—
Oils, salad, cooking, 1 tbsp	120	—	14	—	—	—	—	—	—	—
Orange, 1 medium	65	1	—	54	.5	260	.13	.05	.5	66

Food and amount	Energy (calories)	Nutrients: Protein (gm)	Nutrients: Fat (gm)	Minerals: Calcium (mg)	Minerals: Iron (mg)	Vitamins: Vitamin A (IU)	Vitamins: Vitamin B₁ (thiamin) (mg)	Vitamins: Vitamin B₂ (riboflavin) (mg)	Vitamins: Niacin (mg)	Vitamins: Vitamin C (ascorbic acid) (mg)
Orange juice, fresh, 1 cup	110	2	—	27	.5	500	.22	.07	1.0	124
Frozen, diluted with 3 parts water, 1 cup	120	2	—	25	.2	540	.23	.03	.9	120
Oysters, raw, 1 cup	160	20	4	226	13.2	740	.34	.43	6.0	—
Pancake, wheat, 1 average	60	2	2	27	.4	30	.06	.07	.5	—
Peach, raw, 1 medium	40	1	—	9	.5	1,330	.02	.05	1.0	7
Peanut butter, 1 tbsp	95	4	8	9	.3	—	.02	.02	2.4	—
Peas, green, 1 cup	110	8	—	30	3.0	960	.43	.14	2.7	21
Pie: Apple, 4-inch wedge	345	3	15	11	.9	40	.15	.11	1.3	2
Cherry, 4-inch wedge	350	4	15	19	.9	590	.16	.12	1.4	—
Lemon meringue, 4-inch wedge	305	4	12	17	1.0	200	.09	.12	.7	4
Pineapple, raw, 1 cup diced	80	1	—	26	.8	110	.14	.05	.3	26
Pineapple juice, canned, 1 cup	140	1	—	38	.8	130	.13	.05	.5	23
Pizza (cheese), 4¾-inch wedge	145	6	4	86	1.1	230	.16	.18	1.6	4
Pork: Roast, 3 ounces	310	21	24	9	2.7	—	.78	.22	4.8	—
Chop, with bone, 2.7 ounces	305	19	25	9	2.7	—	.75	.22	4.5	—
Potatoes: Baked, 1 medium	145	4	—	14	1.1	—	.15	.07	2.7	31
French fried, deep fat, 10 pieces	135	2	7	8	.7	—	.07	.04	1.6	11
Mashed with milk, 1 cup	135	4	2	50	.8	40	.17	.11	2.1	21
Potato chips, 10	115	1	8	8	.4	—	.04	.01	1.0	3
Prune juice, 1 cup canned	195	1	—	36	1.8	—	.03	.03	1.0	5
Rice: White, enriched, 1 cup cooked	225	4	—	21	1.8	—	.23	.02	2.1	—
Puffed, 1 cup	60	1	—	3	.3	—	.07	.01	.7	—
Salad dressings: Mayonnaise type, 1 tbsp	65	—	6	2	—	30	—	—	—	—
French, 1 tbsp	65	—	6	2	.1	—	—	—	—	—
French, low calorie, 1 tbsp	15	—	1	2	.1	—	—	—	—	—
Salmon: Canned, 3 ounces	120	17	5	167	.7	60	.03	.16	6.8	—
Sardines, canned, 3 ounces	175	20	9	372	2.5	190	.02	.17	4.6	—
Spaghetti, 1 cup cooked	155	5	1	11	1.3	—	.20	.11	1.5	—
Spinach, 1 cup cooked	40	5	1	167	4.0	14,580	.13	.25	.9	50
Sugar, 1 teaspoon	15	—	—	—	—	—	—	—	—	—
Tomato juice, canned, 1 cup	45	2	—	17	2.2	1,940	.12	.07	1.9	39
Tuna fish, 3 ounces	170	24	7	7	1.6	70	.04	.10	10.1	—
Veal, 3-ounce cutlet	185	23	9	9	2.7	—	.06	.21	4.6	—
Yogurt, from lowfat milk, 8-oz. container, plain	145	12	4	415	.2	150	.10	.49	.3	2

NOTE: Gm—gram; Mg—milligram; IU—International Unit. A dash in a column indicates little or no basis for assigning value. *Source:* Department of Agriculture, Science and Education Administration.

HEADLINE HISTORY

In any broad overview of history, arbitrary compartmentalization of facts is self-defeating (and makes locating interrelated people, places, and things that much harder). Therefore, Headline History is designed as a "timeline"—a chronology that highlights both the march of time and interesting, sometimes surprising, juxtapositions.

Also see related sections of *Information Please,* particularly the Statistical History of the United States, Inventions and Discoveries, Countries of the World, etc.

B.C.

Before Christ or Before Common Era (B.C.E.)

4500–3000 B.C. Sumerians in the Tigris and Euphrates valleys develop a city-state civilization; first phonetic writing (**c.3500 B.C.**). Egyptian agriculture develops. Western Europe is neolithic, without metals or written records. Earliest recorded date in Egyptian calendar (**4241 B.C.**). First year of Jewish calendar (**3760 B.C.**). Copper used by Egyptians and Sumerians.

3000–2000 B.C. Pharaonic rule begins in Egypt. Cheops, 4th dynasty (**2700–2675 B.C.**). The Great Sphinx of Giza. Earliest Egyptian mummies. Papyrus. Phoenician settlements on coast of what is now Syria and Lebanon. Semitic tribes settle in Assyria. Sargon, first Akkadian king, builds Mesopotamian empire. The Gilgamesh epic (**c.3000 B.C.**). Abraham leaves Ur (**c.2000 B.C.**). Systematic astronomy in Egypt, Babylon, India, China.

2000–1500 B.C. Hyksos invaders drive Egyptians from Lower Egypt (**17th century B.C.**). Amosis I frees Egypt from Hyksos (**c.1600 B.C.**). Assyrians rise to power—cities of Ashur and Nineveh. Twenty-four-character alphabet in Egypt. Israelites enslaved in Egypt. Cuneiform inscriptions used by Hittites. Peak of Minoan culture on Isle of Crete—earliest form of written Greek. Hammurabi, king of Babylon, develops oldest existing code of laws (**18th century B.C.**). In Britain, Stonehenge erected on some unknown astronomical rationale.

1500–1000 B.C. Ikhnaton develops monotheistic religion in Egypt (**c.1375 B.C.**). His successor, Tutankhamen, returns to earlier gods. Moses leads Israelites out of Egypt into Canaan—Ten Commandments. Greeks destroy Troy (**c.1193 B.C.**). End of Greek civilization in Mycenae with invasion of Dorians. Chinese civilization develops under Shang dynasty. Olmec civilization in Mexico—stone monuments; picture writing.

1000–900 B.C. Solomon succeeds King David, builds Jerusalem temple. After Solomon's death, kingdom divided into Israel and Judah. Hebrew elders begin to write Old Testament books of Bible. Phoenicians colonize Spain with settlement at Cadiz.

900–800 B.C. Phoenicians establish Carthage (**c.810 B.C.**). The *Iliad* and the *Odyssey,* perhaps composed by Greek poet Homer.

800–700 B.C. Prophets Amos, Hosea, Isaiah. First recorded Olympic games (**776 B.C.**). Legendary founding of Rome by Romulus (**753 B.C.**). Assyrian king Sargon II conquers Hittites, Chaldeans, Samaria (end of Kingdom of Israel). Earliest written music. Chariots introduced into Italy by Etruscans.

700–600 B.C. End of Assyrian Empire (**616 B.C.**)—Nineveh destroyed by Chaldeans (Neo-Babylonians) and Medes (**612 B.C.**). Founding of Byzantium by Greeks (**c.660 B.C.**). Building of the Acropolis in Athens. Solon, Greek lawgiver (**640–560 B.C.**). Sappho of Lesbos, Greek poetess. Lao-Tse, Chinese philosopher and founder of Taoism (born **c.604 B.C.**).

600–500 B.C. Babylonian king Nebuchadnezzar builds empire, destroys Jerusalem (**586 B.C.**). Babylonian Captivity of the Jews (starting **587 B.C.**). Hanging Gardens of Babylon. Cyrus the Great of Persia creates great empire, conquers Babylon (**539 B.C.**), frees the Jews. Athenian democracy develops. Aeschylus, Greek dramatist (**525–465 B.C.**). Confucius (**551–479 B.C.**) develops philosophy-religion in China. Buddha (**563–483 B.C.**) founds Buddhism in India.

500–400 B.C. Greeks defeat Persians: battles of Marathon (**490 B.C.**), Thermopylae (**480 B.C.**), Salamis (**480 B.C.**). Peloponnesian Wars between Athens and Sparta (**431–404 B.C.**)—Sparta victorious. Pericles comes to power in Athens (**462**

Some Ancient Civilizations

Name	Approximate dates	Location	Major cities
Akkadian	2350–2230 B.C.	Mesopotamia, parts of Syria, Asia Minor, Iran	Akkad, Ur, Erich
Assyrian	1800–889 B.C.	Mesopotamia, Syria	Assur, Nineveh, Calah
Babylonian	1728–1686 B.C. (old) 625–539 B.C. (new)	Mesopotamia, Syria, Palestine	Babylon
Cimmerian	750–500 B.C.	Caucasus, northern Asia Minor	—
Egyptian	2850–715 B.C.	Nile valley	Thebes, Memphis, Tanis
Etruscan	900–396 B.C.	Northern Italy	—
Greek	900–200 B.C.	Greece	Athens, Sparta, Thebes, Mycenae, Corinth
Hittite	1640–1200 B.C.	Asia Minor, Syria	Hattusas, Nesa
Lydian	700–547 B.C.	Western Asia Minor	Sardis, Miletus
Mede	835–550 B.C.	Iran	Media
Minoan	3000–1100 B.C.	Crete	Knossos
Persian	559–330 B.C.	Iran, Asia Minor, Syria	Persepolis, Pasargadae
Phoenician	1100–332 B.C.	Palestine (colonies: Gibralter, Carthage Sardinia)	Tyre, Sidon, Byblos
Phrygian	1000–547 B.C.	Central Asia Minor	Gordion
Roman	500 B.C.- A.D. 300	Italy, Mediterranean region, Asia Minor, western Europe	Rome, Byzantium
Scythian	800–300 B.C.	Caucasus	—
Sumerian	3200–2360 B.C.	Mesopotamia	Ur, Nippur

B.C.). Flowering of Greek culture during the Age of Pericles (**450–400** B.C.). Sophocles, Greek dramatist (**496–c.406** B.C.). Hippocrates, Greek "Father of Medicine" (born **460** B.C.). Xerxes I, king of Persia (rules **485–465** B.C.).

400–300 B.C. Pentateuch—first five books of the Old Testament evolve in final form. Philip of Macedon assassinated (**336** B.C.) after conquering Greece; succeeded by son, Alexander the Great (**356–323** B.C.), who destroys Thebes (**335** B.C.), conquers Tyre and Jerusalem (**332** B.C.), occupies Babylon (**330** B.C.), invades India, and dies in Babylon. His empire is divided among his generals; one of them, Seleucis I, establishes Middle East empire with capitals at Antioch (Syria) and Seleucia (in Iraq). Trial and execution of Greek philosopher Socrates (**399** B.C.). Dialogues recorded by his student, Plato. Euclid's work on geometry (**323** B.C.). Aristotle, Greek philosopher (**354–322** B.C.). Demosthenes, Greek orator (**384–322** B.C.). Praxiteles, Greek sculptor (**400–330** B.C.).

300–251 B.C. First Punic War (**264–241** B.C.): Rome defeats the Carthaginians and begins its domination of the Mediterranean. Temple of the Sun at Teotihuacan, Mexico (**c.300** B.C.). Invention of Mayan calendar in Yucatán —more exact than older calendars. First Roman gladiatorial games (**264** B.C.). Archimedes, Greek mathematician (**287–212** B.C.).

250–201 B.C. Second Punic War (**219–201** B.C.): Hannibal, Carthaginian general (**246–142** B.C.), crosses the Alps (**218** B.C.), reaches gates of Rome (**211** B.C.), retreats, and is defeated by Scipio Africanus at Zama (**202** B.C.). Great Wall of China built (**c.215** B.C.).

200–151 B.C. Romans defeat Seleucid King Antiochus III at Thermopylae (**191** B.C.)—beginning of Roman world domination. Maccabean revolt against Romans (**167** B.C.).

150–101 B.C. Third Punic War (**149–146** B.C.): Rome destroys Carthage, killing 450,000 and enslaving the remaining 50,000 inhabitants. Roman armies conquer Macedonia, Greece, Turkey, Balearic Islands, and southern France. Venus de Milo (**c.140** B.C.). Cicero, Roman orator (**106–43** B.C.).

100–51 B.C. Julius Caesar (**100–44** B.C.) invades Britain (**55** B.C.) and conquers Gaul (France) (**c.50** B.C.). Spartacus leads slave revolt against Rome (**71** B.C.). Romans conquer Seleucid empire. Roman general Pompey conquers Jerusalem (**63** B.C.). Cleopatra on Egyptian throne (**51–31** B.C.). Chinese develop use of paper (**c.100** B.C.). Virgil, Roman poet (**70–19** B.C.). Horace, Roman poet (**65–8** B.C.).

50–1 B.C. Caesar crosses Rubicon to fight Pompey (**50 B.C.**). Herod made Roman governor of Judea (**47 B.C.**). Caesar murdered (**44 B.C.**). Caesar's nephew, Octavian, defeats Mark Antony and Cleopatra at Battle of Actium (**31 B.C.**), and establishes Roman empire as Emperor Augustus—rules **27 B.C.-A.D. 14**. Birth of Jesus Christ (variously given from **4 B.C.** to **A.D. 7**). Ovid, Roman poet (**43 B.C.-A.D. 18**).

A.D.

The Christian or Common Era (C.E.)

1–49 After Augustus, Tiberius becomes emperor (dies, **37**), succeeded by Caligula (assassinated, **42**), who is followed by Claudius. Crucifixion of Jesus (probably **30**). Han dynasty in China founded by Emperor Kuang Wu Ti. Buddhism introduced to China.

50–99 Claudius poisoned (**54**), succeeded by Nero (commits suicide, **68**). Missionary journeys of Paul the Apostle (**34–60**). Jews revolt against Rome; Jerusalem destroyed (**70**). Roman persecutions of Christians begin (**64**). Colosseum built in Rome (**71–80**). Trajan (rules **98–116**); Roman empire extends to Mesopotamia, Arabia, Balkans. First Gospels of St. Mark, St. John, St. Matthew.

100–149 Hadrian rules Rome (**117–138**); codifies Roman law, establishes postal system, builds wall between England and Scotland. Jews revolt under Bar Kokhba (**122–135**); final *Diaspora* (dispersion) of Jews begins.

150–199 Marcus Aurelius (rules Rome **161–180**). Oldest Mayan temples in Central America (**c.200**). Mayan civilization develops writing, astronomy, mathematics.

200–249 Goths invade Asia Minor (**c.220**). Roman persecutions of Christians increase. Persian (Sassanid) empire re-established. End of Chinese Han dynasty.

250–299 Increasing invasions of the Roman empire by Franks and Goths. Buddhism spreads in China.

300–349 Constantine the Great (rules **312–337**) reunites eastern and western Roman empires, with new capital (Constantinople) on site of Byzantium (**330**); issues Edict of Milan legalizing Christianity (**313**); becomes a Christian on his deathbed (**337**). Council of Nicaea (**325**) defines orthodox Christian doctrine. First Gupta dynasty in India (**c.320**).

350–399 Huns (Mongols) invade Europe (**c.360**). Theodosius the Great (rules **392–395**)—last emperor of a united Roman empire. Roman empire permanently divided in **395**: western empire ruled from Rome; eastern empire ruled from Constantinople.

400–449 Western Roman empire disintegrates under weak emperors. Alaric, king of the Visigoths, sacks Rome (**410**). Attila, Hun chieftain, attacks Roman provinces (**433**). St. Patrick returns to Ireland (**432**). St. Augustine's *City of God* (**411**).

450–499 Vandals destroy Rome (**455**). Western Roman empire ends as Odoacer, German chieftain, overthrows last Roman emperor, Romulus Augustulus, and becomes king of Italy (**476**). Ostrogothic kingdom of Italy established by Theodoric the Great (**493**). Clovis, ruler of the Franks, is converted to Christianity (**496**). First schism between western and eastern churches (**484**). Peak of Mayan culture in Mexico (**c.460**).

500–549 Eastern and western churches reconciled (**519**). Justinian I, the Great (**483–565**), becomes Byzantine emperor (**527**), issues his first code of civil laws (**529**), conquers North Africa, Italy, and part of Spain. Plague spreads through Europe (from **542**). Arthur, semi-legendary king of the Britons (killed, **c.537**). Boëthius, Roman scholar (executed, **524**).

550–599 Beginnings of European silk industry after Justinian's missionaries smuggle silkworms out of China (**553**). Mohammed, founder of Islam (**570–632**). Buddhism in Japan (**c.560**). St. Augustine of Canterbury brings Christianity to Britain (**597**). After killing about half the population, plague in Europe subsides (**594**).

600–649 Mohammed flees from Mecca to Medina (the *Hegira*); first year of the Muslim calendar (**622**). Muslim empire grows (**634**). Arabs conquer Jerusalem (**637**), destroy Alexandrian library (**641**), conquer Persians (**641**). Fatima, Mohammed's daughter (**606–632**).

650–699 Arabs attack North Africa (**670**), destroy Carthage (**697**). Venerable Bede, English monk (**672–735**).

700–749 Arab empire extends from Lisbon to China (by **716**). Charles Martel, Frankish leader, defeats Arabs at Tours/Poitiers, halting Arab advance in Europe (**732**). Charlemagne (**742–814**).

750–799 Caliph Harun al-Rashid rules Arab empire (**786–809**): the "golden age" of Arab culture. Vikings begin attacks on Britain (**790**), land in

Ireland (**795**). Charlemagne becomes king of the Franks (**771**). City of Machu Picchu flourishes in Peru.

800–849 Charlemagne (Charles the Great) crowned first Holy Roman Emperor in Rome (**800**). Arabs conquer Crete, Sicily, and Sardinia (**826–827**). Charlemagne dies (**814**), succeeded by his son, Louis the Pious, who divides France among his sons (**817**).

850–899 Norsemen attack as far south as the Mediterranean but are repulsed (**859**), discover Iceland (**861**). Alfred the Great becomes king of Britain (**871**), defeats Danish invaders (**878**). Russian nation founded by Vikings under Prince Rurik, establishing capital at Novgorod (**855–879**).

900–949 Vikings discover Greenland (**c.900**). Arab Spain under Abd ar-Rahman III becomes center of learning (**912–961**).

950–999 Eric the Red establishes first Viking colony in Greenland (**982**). Mieczyslaw I becomes first ruler of Poland (**960**). Hugh Capet elected King of France in **987**; Capetian dynasty to rule until **1328**. Musical notation systematized (**c.990**). Vikings and Danes attack Britain (**988–999**). Holy Roman Empire founded by Otto I, King of Germany since **936**, crowned by Pope John XII in **962**.

---

c.1000 Hungary and Scandinavia converted to Christianity. Viking raider Leif Ericson discovers North America, calls it *Vinland*. Chinese invent gunpowder. *Beowulf*, Old English epic.

1009 Moslems destroy Holy Sepulchre in Jerusalem.

1013 Danes control England. Canute takes throne (**1016**), conquers Norway (**1028**), dies (**1035**); kingdom divided among his sons: Harold Harefoot (England), Sweyn (Norway), Hardecanute (Denmark).

1040 Macbeth murders Duncan, king of Scotland.

1053 Robert Guiscard, Norman invader, establishes kingdom in Italy, conquers Sicily (**1072**).

1054 Final separation between Eastern (Orthodox) and Western (Roman) churches.

1055 Seljuk Turks, Asian nomads, move west, capture Baghdad, Armenia (**1064**), Syria, and Palestine (**1075**).

1066 William of Normandy invades England, defeats last Saxon king, Harold II, at Battle of Hastings, crowned William I of England ("the Conqueror").

1073 Emergence of strong papacy when Gregory VII is elected. Conflict with English and French kings and German emperors will continue throughout medieval period.

1095 (*See* special material on "The Crusades.")

Omar Khayyám, *Persian poet* (1027?–1123)
El Cid, *Spanish national hero* (1040–1099)
Peter Abelard, *French theologian* (1079–1142)
Judah Halevi, *Jewish poet* (1085–1140)

1150–67 Universities of Paris and Oxford founded in France and England.

1162 Thomas à Becket named Archbishop of Canterbury, murdered by Henry II's men (**1170**). Troubadours (wandering minstrels) glorify romantic concepts of feudalism.

1189 Richard I ("the Lionhearted") succeeds Henry II in England, killed in France (**1199**), succeeded by King John.

1211 Genghis Khan invades China, captures Peking (**1214**), conquers Persia (**1218**), invades Russia (**1223**), dies (**1227**).

1215 King John forced by barons to sign Magna Carta at Runneymede, limiting royal power.

1233 The Inquisition begins as Pope Gregory IX assigns Dominicans responsibility for combatting heresy. Torture used (**1252**). Ferdinand and Isabella establish Spanish Inquisition (**1478**). Tourquemada, Grand Inquisitor, forces conversion or expulsion of Spanish Jews (**1492**). Forced conversion of Moors (**1499**). Inquisition in Portugal (**1531**). First Protestants burned at the stake in Spain (**1543**). Spanish Inquisition abolished (**1834**).

1241 Mongols defeat Germans in Silesia, invade Poland and Hungary, with-

Thomas à Becket, *English prelate and martyr* (1118–1170)
Moses Maimonides, *Jewish philosopher* (1135–1204)
Genghis Khan, *Mongol emperor* (1162–1227)
St. Francis of Assisi, *founder of Franciscans* (1182–1226)
Roger Bacon, *English scientist* (1214–1294)
Kublai Khan, *Mongol ruler* (1216–1294)
St. Thomas Aquinas, *Catholic theologian* (1225–1274)
Marco Polo, *Venetian explorer* (1254–1323)
Dante Alighieri, *Italian poet* (1265–1321)

THE CRUSADES (1096–1291)

In **1095** Pope Urban II calls for war to rescue Holy Land from Moslem infidels at Council of Clermont. *First Crusade* (**1096**)—about 500,000 peasants led by Peter the Hermit prove so troublesome that Byzantine Emperor Alexius ships them to Asia Minor; only 25,000 survive return after massacre by Seljuk Turks. Followed by organized army, led by nobility, which reaches Constantinople (**1097**), conquers Jerusalem (**1099**), Acre (**1104**), establishes Latin Kingdom protected by Knights of St. John the Hospitaller (**1100**), and Knights Templar (**1123**). Seljuk Turks start series of counterattacks (**1144**). *Second Crusade* (**1146**) led by King Louis VIII of France and Emperor Conrad III. Crusaders perish in Asia Minor (**1147**).

Saladin controls Egypt (**1171**), unites Islam in Holy War (*Jihad*) against Christians, recaptures Jerusalem (**1187**). *Third Crusade* (**1189**) under kings of France, England, and Germany fails to reduce Saladin's power. *Fourth Crusade* (**1200–1204**)—French knights sack Greek Christian Constantinople, establish Latin empire in Byzantium. Greeks re-establish Orthodox faith (**1262**).

Children's Crusade (**1212**)—Only 1 of 30,000 French children and about 200 of 20,000 German children survive to return home. Other Crusades—against Egypt (**1217**), *Sixth* (**1228**), *Seventh* (**1248**), *Eighth* (**1270**). Mamelukes conquer Acre; end of the Crusades (**1291**).

draw from Europe after Ughetai, Mongol leader, dies.
1251 Kublai Khan governs China, becomes ruler of Mongols **(1259)**, establishes Yuan dynasty in China **(1280)**, invades Burma **(1287)**, dies **(1294)**.
1271 Marco Polo of Venice travels to China, in court of Kublai Khan **(1275–1292)**, returns to Genoa **(1295)** and writes *Travels*.
1272 English King Edward I conquers Wales and Scotland; Great Britain unified. Summons the Model Parliament in **1295**.

1312–37 Mali Empire reaches its height in Africa under King Mansa Musa.
1337–1453 Hundred Years' War—English and French kings fight for control of France.
c.1325 The beginning of the Renaissance in Italy: writers Dante, Petrarch, Boccaccio; painter Giotto. Development of *No* drama in Japan. Aztecs establish capital on site of modern Mexico City. Peak of Moslem culture in Spain. Small cannon in use.
1347–1351 At least 25 million people die in Europe's "Black Death" (bubonic plague).
1368 Ming dynasty begins in China.
1376–82 John Wycliffe, pre-Reformation religious reformer and followers translate Latin bible into English.
1378 The Great Schism **(to 1417)**—rival popes in Rome and Avignon, France, fight for control of Roman Catholic Church.
c.1387 Chaucer's *Canterbury Tales*.

1415 Henry V defeats French at Agincourt. Jan Hus, Bohemian preacher and follower of Wycliffe, burned at stake in Constance as heretic.
1418–60 Portugal's Prince Henry the Navigator sponsors exploration of Africa's coast.
1428 Joan of Arc leads French against English, captured by Burgundians **(1430)** and turned over to the English, burned at the stake as a witch after ecclesiastical trial **(1431)**.
1438 Inca rule in Peru.
1450 Florence becomes center of Renaissance arts and learning under the Medicis.
1453 Turks conquer Constantinople, end of the Byzantine empire. Hundred Years' War between France and England ends.
1455 The Wars of the Roses, civil wars between rival noble factions, begin in England **(to 1485)**. Having invented printing with movable type at Mainz, Germany, Johann Gutenberg completes first bible.
1462 Ivan the Great rules Russia until **1505** as first czar; ends payment of tribute to Mongols.
1492 Moors conquered in Spain by troops of Ferdinand and Isabella. Columbus discovers Caribbean islands, returns to Spain **(1493)**. Second voyage to Dominica, Jamaica, Puerto Rico **(1493–1496)**. Third voyage to Orinoco **(1498)**. Fourth voyage to Honduras and Panama **(1502–1504)**.
1497 Vasco da Gama sails around Africa and discovers sea route to India **(1498)**. Establishes Portuguese colony in India **(1502)**. John Cabot, employed by England, reaches and explores Canadian coast. Michelangelo's *Bacchus* sculpture.

Leonardo da Vinci, *Renaissance artistic and scientific genius* (1452–1519)
Vasco da Gama, *Portuguese explorer* (1460–1524)
Juan Ponce de León, *Spanish explorer* (1460–1521)
Hans Holbein (the Elder), *German painter* (1465?–1524)
Niccolo Machiavelli, *Italian author* (1468–1527)
Albrecht Dürer, *German painter* (1471–1528)
Nicolaus Copernicus, *Polish scientist* (1473–1543)
Michelangelo Buonarroti, *Italian painter, sculptor, architect* (1475–1564)
Cesare Borgia, *Renaissance prince* (1476–1507)
Titian, *Italian painter* (1477–1576)
Sir Thomas More, *English statesman* (1478–1535)
Lucrezia Borgia, *Italian patron of the arts* (1480–1519)
Ferdinand Magellan, *Portuguese explorer* (1480–1521)
Martin Luther, *German Reformation leader* (1483–1546)
Raphael, *Italian painter* (1483–1520)
Ulrich Zwingli, *Swiss humanist* (1484–1531)
Hernando Cortes, *Spanish Conquistador* (1485–1547)
Andrea del Sarto, *Florentine painter* (1486–1531)
Thomas Cranmer, *English churchman* (1489–1556)
François Rabelais, *French writer* (1490–1553)
Jacques Cartier, *French explorer* (1491–1557)
St. Ignatius de Loyola, *founder of Jesuits* (1491–1556)
Paracelsus, *Swiss physician* (1493–1541)
Correggio, *Italian painter* (1494–1534)
Hans Holbein (the Younger) *German painter* (1497–1543)
Hernando De Soto, *Spanish explorer* (1499–1542)

Duns Scotus, *Scottish theologian* (1265–1308)
Giotto, *Italian painter* (1276–1337)

Guillaume de Machaut, *French composer* (1300–1377)
Petrarch (Francesco Petrarca), *Italian poet* (1304–1374)
Giovanni Boccaccio, *Florentine novelist* (1313–1375)
John Wycliffe, *English church reformer* (1320–1384)
Geoffrey Chaucer, *English writer* (c.1340–1400)
Jan Hus, *Bohemian religious reformer* (c.1369–1415)
Thomas à Kempis, *German mystic* (1380–1471)
Donatello, *Italian sculptor* (1386–1466)
Fra Angelico, *Italian painter* (1387–1455)
Johann Gutenberg, *inventor of movable type* (1398–1468)
Luca della Robbia, *Italian sculptor* (1400–1482)
Guillaume Dufay, *French composer* (c.1400–1474)
Fra Filippo Lippi, *Italian painter* (1406–1469)
Joan of Arc, *French saint and national heroine* (1412–1431)
Tomas de Torquemada, *Spanish Inquisitor* (1420–1498)
Giovanni Bellini, *Italian painter* (1430–1516)
François Villon, *French poet* (1431–1465?)
Sandro Botticelli, *Italian painter* (1444–1510)
Lorenzo de'Medici, *Renaissance ruler* (1449–1492)
Hieronymus Bosch, *Dutch painter* (1450–1516)
Josquin des Prés, *Dutch composer* (1450–1521)
Isabella I, *Queen of Spain* (1451–1504)
Christopher Columbus, *Italian explorer* (1451–1506)
Amerigo Vespucci, *Italian navigator* (1451–1512)
Savonarola, *Italian churchman* (1452–1498)

1501 First black slaves in America brought to Spanish colony of Santo Domingo.

c.1503 Leonardo da Vinci paints the *Mona Lisa.*

1506 St. Peter's Church started in Rome; designed and decorated by such artists and architects as Bramante, Michelangelo, da Vinci, Raphael, and Bernini before its completion in **1626**.

1509 Henry VIII ascends English throne. Michelangelo paints the ceiling of the Sistine Chapel.

1517 Turks conquer Egypt, control Arabia. Martin Luther posts his 95 theses denouncing church abuses on church door in Wittenberg—start of the Reformation in Germany.

1519 Ulrich Zwingli begins Reformation in Switzerland. Hernando Cortes conquers Mexico for Spain. Charles I of Spain is chosen Holy Roman Emperor Charles V. Spanish explorer Fernando Magellan sets out to circumnavigate the globe.

1520 Luther excommunicated by Pope Leo X. Suleiman I ("the Magnificent") becomes Sultan of Turkey, invades Hungary **(1521)**, Rhodes **(1522)**, attacks Austria **(1529)**, annexes Hungary **(1541)**, Tripoli **(1551)**, makes peace with Persia **(1553)**, destroys Spanish fleet **(1560)**, dies **(1566)**. Magellan reaches the Pacific, is killed by Philippine natives **(1521)**. One of his ships under Juan Sebastián del Cano continues around the world, reaches Spain **(1522)**.

1524 Verrazano, sailing under the French flag, explores the New England coast and New York Bay.

1527 Troops of the Holy Roman Empire attack Rome, imprison Pope Clement VII—the end of the Italian Renaissance. Castiglione writes *The Courtier.* The Medici expelled from Florence.

1532 Pizarro marches from Panama to Peru, kills the Inca chieftain, Atahualpa, of Peru **(1533)**. Machiavelli's *Prince* published posthumously.

1535 Reformation begins as Henry VIII makes himself head of English Church after being excommunicated by Pope. Sir Thomas More executed as traitor for refusal to acknowledge king's religious authority. Jacques Cartier sails up the St. Lawrence River, basis of French claims to Canada.

1536 Henry VIII executes second wife, Anne Boleyn. John Calvin establishes Presbyterian form of Protestantism in Switzerland, writes *Institutes of the Christian Religion.* Danish and Norwegian Reformations. Michelangelo's *Last Judgment.*

1541 John Knox leads Reformation in Scotland, establishes Presbyterian church **(1560)**.

1543 Publication of *On the Revolution of Heavenly Bodies* by Polish scholar Nicolaus Copernicus—giving his theory that the earth revolves around the sun.

1545 Council of Trent to meet intermittently until **1563** to define Catholic dogma and doctrine, reiterate papal authority.

1547 Ivan IV ("the Terrible") crowned as Czar of Russia, begins conquest of Astrakhan and Kazan **(1552)**, battles nobles (boyars) for power **(1564)**, kills his son **(1580)**, dies, and is succeeded by a son who gives power to Boris Godunov **(1584)**.

1553 Roman Catholicism restored in England by Queen Mary I, who rules until **1558**. Religious radical Michael Servetus burned as heretic in Geneva by order of John Calvin.

1554 Benvenuto Cellini completes the bronze *Perseus.*

1556 Akbar the Great becomes Mogul emperor of India, conquers Afghanistan **(1581)**, continues wars of conquest (until **1605**).

1558 Queen Elizabeth I ascends the throne (rules to **1603**). Restores Protestantism, establishes state Church of England (Anglicanism). Renaissance will reach height in England—Shakespeare, Marlowe, Spenser.

1561 Persecution of Huguenots in France stopped by Edict of Orleans. French religious wars begin again with massacre of Huguenots at Vassy. St. Bartholomew's Day Massacre—thousands of Huguenots murdered **(1572)**. Amnesty granted **(1573)**. Persecution continues periodically until Edict of Nantes **(1598)** gives Huguenots religious freedom (until **1685**).

1568 Protestant Netherlands revolts against Catholic Spain; independence will be acknowledged by Spain in **1648**. High point of Dutch Renaissance—painters Rubens, Van Dyck, Hals, and Rembrandt.

1570 Japan permits visits of foreign ships. Queen Elizabeth I excommunicated by Pope. Turks attack Cyprus and war on Venice. Turkish fleet defeated at Battle of Lepanto by Spanish and Italian fleets **(1571)**. Peace of Constantinople **(1572)** ends Turkish attacks on Europe.

1580 Francis Drake returns to England after circumnavigating the globe. Knighted by Queen Elizabeth I **(1581)**. Montaigne's *Essays* published.

1583 William of Orange rules The Netherlands; assassinated on orders of Philip II of Spain **(1584)**.

- Benvenuto Cellini, *Florentine sculptor* (1500–1571)
- Nostradamus, *French astrologer* (1503–1566)
- John Knox, *Scottish church reformer* (1505–1572)
- St. Francis Xavier, *Jesuit missionary* (1506–1552)
- John Calvin, *Swiss theologian* (1509–1564)
- Giorgio Vasari, *Italian art historian* (1511–1574)
- Andreas Vesalius, *Dutch anatomist* (1515–1564)
- Andrea Palladio, *Italian architect* (1518–1580)
- Tintoretto (Jacopo Robusti), *Italian painter* (1518–1594)
- Pieter Brueghel (the Elder), *Dutch painter* (1520–1569)
- Pierre de Ronsard, *French poet* (1524–1585)
- Giovanni Palestrina, *Italian composer* (1526–1594)
- Paolo Veronese, *Italian painter* (1528–1588)
- Queen Elizabeth, *English ruler* (1533?–1603)
- Michel de Montaigne, *French author* (1533–1592)
- El Greco, *Spanish-Greek painter* (1542–1614)
- Tycho Brahe, *Danish astronomer* (1546–1601)
- Miguel de Cervantes, *Spanish writer* (1547–1616)
- Giordano Bruno, *Italian philosopher* (1548–1600)
- Sir Walter Raleigh, *English courtier* (1552–1618)
- Edmund Spenser, *English poet* (1552–1599)
- Giovanni Gabrieli, *Italian composer* (c.1557–1612)
- Francis Bacon, *English philosopher* (1561–1626)
- Christopher Marlowe, *English dramatist* (1564–1593)
- Galileo Galilei, *Italian scientist* (1564–1642)
- William Shakespeare, *English dramatist and poet* (1564–1616)
- Michelangelo da Caravaggio, *Italian painter* (c.1565–1609)
- Claudio Monteverdi, *Italian composer* (1567–1643)
- Johannes Kepler, *German astronomer* (1571–1630)
- John Donne, *English poet* (1573–1631)
- Inigo Jones, *English architect* (1573–1652)
- Ben Jonson, *English dramatist* (1573–1637)
- Peter Paul Rubens, *Flemish painter* (1577–1652)
- William Harvey, *English physician and anatomist* (1578–1657)

1587 Mary, Queen of Scots, executed for treason by order of Queen Elizabeth I. Monteverdi's *First Book of Madrigals.*
1588 Defeat of the Spanish Armada by English. Henry, King of Navarre and Protestant leader, recognized as Henry IV, first Bourbon king of France. Converts to Roman Catholicism in **1593** in attempt to end religious wars.
1590 Henry IV enters Paris, wars on Spain (**1595**), marries Maria de Medici (**1600**), assassinated (**1610**). Spenser's *The Faerie Queen.* El Greco's *St. Jerome.* Galileo's experiments with falling objects.
1598 Boris Godunov becomes Russian Czar. Tycho Brahe describes his astronomical experiments.

1600 Giordano Bruno burned as a heretic. Ieyasu rules Japan, moves capital to Edo (Tokyo). Shakespeare's *Hamlet* begins his most productive decade. English East India Company established to develop overseas trade.
1607 Jamestown, Virginia, established—first permanent English colony on American mainland.
1609 Samuel de Champlain establishes French colony of Quebec.
1611 Gustavus Adolphus elected King of Sweden. King James Version of the Bible published in England. Rubens paints his *Descent from the Cross.*
1614 John Napier discovers logarithms.
1618 Start of the Thirty Years' War (to **1648**)—Protestant revolt against Catholic oppression; Denmark, Sweden, and France will invade Germany in later phases of war. Kepler proposes his Third Law of planetary motion.
1620 Pilgrims, after three-month voyage in *Mayflower,* land at Plymouth Rock. Francis Bacon's *Novum Organum.*
1633 Inquisition forces Galileo to recant his belief in Copernican theory.
1642 English Civil War. Cavaliers, supporters of Charles I, against Roundheads, parliamentary forces. Oliver Cromwell defeats Royalists (**1646**). Parliament demands reforms. Charles I offers concessions, brought to trial (**1648**), beheaded (**1649**). Cromwell becomes Lord Protector (**1653**). Rembrandt paints his *Night Watch.*
1644 End of Ming Dynasty in China—Manchus come to power. Descartes' *Principles of Philosophy.* John Milton's *Areopagitica* on the freedom of the press.
1648 End of the Thirty Years' War. German population about half of what it was in **1618** because of war and pestilence.
1658 Cromwell dies; his son, Richard, resigns and Puritan government collapses.
1660 English Parliament calls for the restoration of the monarchy; invites Charles II to return from France.
1661 Charles II is crowned King of England. Louis XIV begins personal rule as absolute monarch; starts to build Versailles.
1664 British take New Amsterdam from the Dutch. English limit "Nonconformity" with re-established Anglican Church. Isaac Newton's experiments with gravity.
1665 Great Plague in London kills 75,000.
1666 Great Fire of London. Molière's *Misanthrope.*
1683 War of European powers against the Turks (to **1699**). Vienna withstands three-month Turkish siege; high point of Turkish advance in Europe.

Frans Hals, *Dutch painter* (1581–1666)
Phineas Fletcher, *English dramatist* (1582–1650)
Francis Beaumont, *English dramatist* (1584–1616)
Cardinal Richelieu, *French prelate* (1585–1642)
Thomas Hobbes, *English philosopher* (1588–1679)
John Winthrop, *first governor of Massachusetts* (1588–1649)
Robert Herrick, *English poet* (1591–1674)
Johann Amos Comenius, *Moravian educational reformer* (1592–1670)
Peter Stuyvesant, *Dutch administrator in America* (1592–1672)
George Herbert, *English poet* (1593–1633)
Izaak Walton, *English biographer* (1593–1683)
Nicola Amati, *Italian violin maker* (1594–1684)
Nicolas Poussin, *French painter* (1594–1665)
Pocahontas, *Indian princess* (1595–1617)
René Descartes, *French philosopher* (1596–1650)
Oliver Cromwell, *English general and statesman* (1599–1658)
Anthony Van Dyck, *Flemish painter* (1599–1641)
Diego Velázquez, *Spanish painter* (1599–1660)
Pedro Calderón de la Barca, *Spanish dramatist* (1600–1681)
Roger Williams, *American religious leader* (1604–1683)
Pierre Corneille, *French dramatist* (1606–1684)
Rembrandt van Rijn, *Dutch painter* (1606–1669)

THE FOUNDING OF THE AMERICAN NATION

Colonization of America begins: Jamestown, Va. (**1607**); Pilgrims in Plymouth (**1620**); Massachusetts Bay Colony (**1630**); New Netherland founded by Dutch West India Company (**1623**), captured by English (**1664**). Delaware established by Swedish trading company (**1638**), absorbed later by Penn family. Proprietorships by royal grants to Lord Baltimore (Maryland, **1632**); Captain John Mason (New Hampshire, **1635**); Sir William Berkeley and Sir George Carteret (New Jersey, **1663**); friends of Charles II (the Carolinas, **1663**); William Penn (Pennsylvania, **1682**); James Oglethorpe and others (Georgia, **1732**).

Increasing conflict between colonists and Britain on western frontier because of royal edict limiting western expansion (**1763**), and regulation of colonial trade and increased taxation of colonies (Writs of Assistance allow search for illegal shipments, **1761**; Sugar Act, **1764**; Currency Act, **1764**; Stamp Act, **1765**; Quartering Act, **1765**; Duty Act, **1767**.) Boston Massacre (**1770**). Lord North attempts conciliation (**1770**). Boston Tea Party (**1773**), followed by punitive measures passed by Parliament—the "Intolerable Acts."

First Continental Congress (**1774**) sends "Declaration of Rights and Grievances" to King, urges colonies to form Continental Association. Paul Revere's Ride and Lexington and Concord battle between Massachusetts minutemen and British (**1775**).

Second Continental Congress (**1775**), while sending "olive branch" to the king, begins to raise army, appoints Washington commander-in-chief, and seeks alliance with France. Some colonial legislatures urge their delegates to vote for independence. Declaration of Independence (**July 4, 1776**).

Major Battles of the Revolutionary War: *Long Island:* Howe defeats Putnam's division of Washington's Army in Brooklyn Heights, but Americans escape across East River (**1776**). *Trenton and Princeton:* Washington defeats Hessians at Trenton, British at Princeton, winters at Morristown (**1776–77**). Howe winters in Philadelphia; Washington at Valley Forge (**1777–78**). Burgoyne surrenders British army to General Gates at *Saratoga* (**1777**).

France recognizes American independence (**1778**). The War moves south: Savannah captured by British (**1778**); Charleston occupied (**1780**); Americans fight successful guerrilla actions under Marion, Pickens, and Sumter. In the West, George Rogers Clark attacks Forts Kaskaskia and Vincennes (**1778–1779**), defeating British in the region. Cornwallis surrenders at *Yorktown,* Virginia (**Oct. 19, 1781**). By **1782**, Britain is eager for peace because of conflicts with European nations. *Peace of Paris* (**1783**): Britain recognizes American independence.

1685 James II succeeds Charles II in England, calls for freedom of conscience (**1687**). Protestants fear restoration of Catholicism and demand "Glorious Revolution." William of Orange invited to England and James II escapes to France (**1688**). William III and his wife, Mary, crowned. In France, Edict of Nantes of 1598, granting freedom of worship to Huguenots (French Protestants), is revoked by Louis XIV; thousands of Protestants flee.

1689 Peter the Great becomes Czar of Russia—attempts to westernize nation and build Russia as military power. Defeats Charles XII of Sweden at Poltava (**1709**). Beginning of the French and Indian Wars (to **1763**), campaigns in America linked to a series of wars between France and England for domination of Europe.

1690 William III of England defeats former King James II and Irish rebels at Battle of the Boyne in Ireland. John Locke's *Human Understanding.*

John Milton, *English poet* (1608–1674)
François de La Rouchefoucauld, *French author* (1613–1680)
Henry More, *English philosopher* (1614–1687)
Cyrano de Bergerac, *French poet* (1619–1655)
Andrew Marvell, *English poet* (1621–1678)
Molière (Jean-Baptiste Poquelin), *French dramatist* (1622–1673)
Blaise Pascal, *French philosopher* (1623–1662)
Robert Boyle, *English scientist* (1627–1691)
John Bunyan, *English author* (1628–1688)
John Dryden, *English dramatist* (1631–1700)
John Locke, *English philosopher* (1631–1704)
Luca Giordano, *Italian painter* (1632–1705)
Anton van Leeuwenhoek, *Dutch zoologist* (1632–1723)

Jan Vermeer, *Dutch painter* (1632–1675)
Baruch Spinoza, *Dutch philosopher* (1632–1677)
Christopher Wren, *English architect* (1632–1723)
Samuel Pepys, *English diarist* (1633–1703)
Jean Baptiste Lully, *French composer* (1639–1687)
Jean Racine, *French dramatist* (1639–1699)
Sir Isaac Newton, *English philosopher and mathematician* (1642–1727)
William Penn, *founder of Pennsylvania* (1644–1718)
Antonio Stradivari, *Italian violin maker* (1644–1737)
Gottfried W. von Leibniz, *German scientist* (1646–1716)
Arcangelo Corelli, *Italian composer* (1653–1713)
Jacques Bernoulli, *Swiss scientist* (1654–1705)

Edmund Halley, *English astronomer* (1656–1742)
Henry Purcell, *English composer* (1658–1695)
Daniel Defoe, *English author* (1659–1731)
Alessandro Scarlatti, *Italian composer* (1659–1725)
Cotton Mather, *Massachusetts churchman* (1663–1728)
François Couperin, *French composer* (1668–1733)
Giovanni Battista Vico, *Italian philosopher* (1668–1744)
William Congreve, *English dramatist* (1670–1730)
Peter the Great, *Russian czar* (1672–1725)
Antonio Vivaldi, *Italian composer* (1678–1741)

George Phillip Telemann, *German composer* (1681–1767)
Jean Philippe Rameau, *French composer* (1683–1764)
Jean Antoine Watteau, *French painter* (1684–1721)
J.S. Bach, *German composer* (1685–1750)
George Frederick Handel, *German-English composer* (1685–1759)
Domenico Scarlatti, *Italian composer* (1685–1757)
Gabriel Fahrenheit, *German physicist* (1686–1736)
Alexander Pope, *English poet* (1688–1744)
Emanuel Swedenborg, *Swedish mystic* (1688–1772)
Baron de Montesquieu, *French philosopher* (1689–1755)
François de Voltaire, *French philosopher* (1694–1778)
Canaletto (Antonio Canale), *Italian painter* (1697–1768)
William Hogarth, *English painter* (1697–1764)

1701 War of the Spanish Succession begins—the last of Louis XIV's wars for domination of the continent. The Peace of Utrecht (**1714**) will end the conflict and mark the rise of the British Empire. Called Queen Anne's War in America, it ends with the British taking New Foundland, Acadia, and Hudson's Bay Territory from France, and Gibraltar and Minorca from Spain.

1704 Deerfield (Conn.) Massacre of English colonists by French and Indians. Bach's first cantata. Jonathan Swift's *Tale of a Tub. Boston News Letter* —first newspaper in America.

1707 United Kingdom of Great Britain formed—England, Wales, and Scotland joined by parliamentary Act of Union.

1729 J. S. Bach's *St. Matthew's Passion.* Isaac Newton's *Principia* translated from Latin into English.

1735 John Peter Zenger, New York editor, acquitted of libel in New York, establishing press freedom.

1740 Capt. Vitus Bering, Dane employed by Russia, discovers Alaska.

1746 British defeat Scots under Stuart Pretender Prince Charles at Culloden Moor. Last battle fought on British soil.

1751 Publication of the *Encyclopédie* begins in France, the "bible" of the Enlightenment.

1755 Samuel Johnson's *Dictionary* first published. Great earthquake in Lisbon, Portugal—over 60,000 die.

1756 Seven Years' War (called French and Indian War in America) (to **1763**), in which Britain and Prussia defeat France, Spain, Austria, and Russia.

François Boucher, *French painter* (1703–1770)
Jonathan Edwards, *American theologian* (1703–1758)
John Wesley, *founder of Methodism* (1703–1791)
Benjamin Franklin, *American statesman* (1706–1790)
Henry Fielding, *English novelist* (1707–1754)
Leonhard Euler, *Swiss mathematician* (1707–1783)
Linnaeus (Carl von Linné), *Swedish botanist* (1707–1778)
Samuel Johnson, *English author* (1709–1784)
William Boyce, *English composer* (1710–1779)
Giovanni Pergolesi, *Italian composer* (1710–1736)
David Hume, *Scottish philosopher* (1711–1776)

France loses North American colonies; Spain cedes Florida to Britain in exchange for Cuba. In India, over 100 British prisoners die in "Black Hole of Calcutta."

1757 Beginning of British Empire in India as Robert Clive, British commander, defeats Nawab of Bengal at Plassey.

1759 British capture Quebec from French. Voltaire's *Candide.* Haydn's *Symphony No. 1.*

1762 Catherine II ("the Great") becomes Czarina of Russia. J. J. Rousseau's *Social Contract.* Mozart tours Europe as six-year-old prodigy.

1769 Sir William Arkwright patents a spinning machine—an early step in the Industrial Revolution.

1772 Joseph Priestley and Daniel Rutherford independently discover nitrogen. Partition of Poland—in **1772, 1793,** and **1795,** Austria, Prussia, and Russia divide land and people of Poland, end its independence.

1775 The American Revolution *(see* "The Founding of the American Nation"). James Watt invents the steam engine. Priestley discovers hydrochloric and sulfuric acids.

1776 Adam Smith's *Wealth of Nations.* Edward Gibbon's *Decline and Fall of the Roman Empire.* Thomas Paine's *Common Sense.* Fragonard's *Washerwoman.* Mozart's *Haffner Serenade.*

1778 Capt. James Cook discovers Hawaii. Franz Mesmer uses hypnotism.

1781 Immanuel Kant's *Critique of Pure Reason.* Herschel discovers Uranus.

1783 End of Revolutionary War *(see* special material on "The Founding of the American Nation"). William Blake's poems. Beethoven's first printed works.

1784 Crimea annexed by Russia. John Wesley's *Deed of Declaration,* the basic work of Methodism.

1785 Russians settle Aleutian Islands.

1787 The Constitution of the United States signed. Lavoisier's work on chemical nomenclature. Mozart's *Don Giovanni.*

1788 French *Parlement* presents grievances to Louis XVI who agrees to convening of Estates-General in **1789**—not called since **1613**. Goethe's *Egmont.* Laplace's *Laws of the Planetary System.*

1789 French Revolution *(see* special material on the "French Revolution"). In U.S., George Washington elected President with all 69 votes of the Electoral College, takes oath of office in New York City. Vice President: John Adams. Secretary of State: Thomas Jefferson. Secretary of Treasury: Alexander Hamilton.

Jean-Jacques Rousseau, *French philosopher* (1712–1778)
Denis Diderot, *French encyclopedist* (1713–1784)
Laurance Sterne, *English novelist* (1713–1768)
K.P.E. Bach, *German composer* (1714–1788)
David Garrick, *English actor* (1717–1779)
Horace Walpole, *English statesman and novelist* (1717–1797)
Thomas Chippendale, *English artisan* (1718?–1779)
Bernardo Canaletto, *Italian painter* (1720–1780)
Giambattista Piranesi, *Italian artist* (1720–1778)
Baron von Münchhausen, *German anecdotist* (1720–1797)
Mme. de Pompadour, *French courtesan* (1721–1764)
Tobias Smollet, *English novelist* (1721–1771)
Samuel Adams, *American patriot* (1722–1803)
Joshua Reynolds, *English painter* (1723–1792)
Adam Smith, *English economist* (1723–1790)
Immanuel Kant, *German philosopher* (1724–1804)
Giovanni Casanova, *Italian adventurer* (1725–1798)
Thomas Gainsborough, *English painter* (1727–1788)
Oliver Goldsmith, *English writer* (1728–1774)
Catherine II (Catherine the Great), *Russian empress* (1729–1796)
Edmund Burke, *English statesman* (1729–1797)
William Cowper, *English poet* (1731–1800)

George Washington, *first American President* (1732–1799)
J.H. Fragonard, *French painter* (1732–1800)
Josef Haydn, *Austrian composer* (1732–1809)
Franz Anton Mesmer, *Austrian hypnotist* (1733–1815)
Joseph Priestley, *English scientist* (1733–1804)
John Adams, *American President* (1735–1836)
Daniel Boone, *American frontiersman* (1735–1820)
Patrick Henry, *American patriot* (1736–1799)
James Watt, *Scottish inventor* (1736–1819)
John S. Copley, *American painter* (1737–1815)
Edward Gibbon, *English historian* (1737–1794)

Thomas Paine, *American author and patriot* (1737–1809)
William Herschel, *English astronomer* (1738–1822)
Prince Potemkin, *Russian statesman* (1739–1791)
James Boswell, *Scottish writer* (1740–1795)
Marquis de Sade, *French libertine and writer* (1741–1814)
Benedict Arnold, *American general and traitor* (1741–1801)
Luigi Boccherini, *Italian composer* (1743–1805)
Antoine Lavoisier, *French chemist* (1743–1794)

Jean-Paul Marat, *French revolutionist* (1743–1793)
Thomas Jefferson, *American President* (1743–1826)
Jean-Baptiste de Lamark, *French scientist* (1744–1829)
Alessandro Volta, *Italian scientist* (1745–1827)
Francisco de Goya, *Spanish painter* (1746–1828)
Johann Pestalozzi, *Swiss educator* (1746–1827)
John Paul Jones, *American naval officer* (1747–1792)
Jeremy Bentham *English economist* (1748–1832)
Jacques David, *French painter* (1748–1825)
Count Casimir Pulaski, *Polish-American patriot* (1748–1779)
Johann Wolfgang von Goethe, *German writer* (1749–1832)

FRENCH REVOLUTION (1789–1799)

Revolution begins when Third Estate (Commons) delegates swear not to disband until France has a constitution. Paris mob storms Bastille, symbol of royal power **(July 14, 1789)**. National Assembly votes for Constitution, Declaration of the Rights of Man, a limited monarchy, and other reforms **(1789–90)**. Legislative Assembly elected, Revolutionary Commune formed, and French Republic proclaimed **(1792)**. War of the First Coalition—Austria, Prussia, Britain, Netherlands, and Spain fight to restore French nobility **(1792–97)**. Start of series of wars between France and European powers that will last, almost without interruption, for 23 years. Louis XVI and Marie Antoinette executed. Committee of Public Safety begins Reign of Terror as political control measure. Interfactional rivalry leads to mass killings. Danton and Robespierre executed. Third French Constitution sets up Directory government **(1795)**.

1790 H.M.S. *Bounty* mutineers settle on Pitcairn Island. Aloisio Galvani experiments on electrical stimulation of the muscles. Philadelphia temporary capital of U.S. as Congress votes to establish new capital on Potomac. U.S. population about 3,929,000, including 698,000 slaves. Lavoisier formulates *Table of 31 chemical elements*.

1791 U.S. Bill of Rights ratified. Boswell's *Life of Johnson*.

1794 Kosciusko's uprising in Poland quelled by the Russians. In U.S., Whiskey Rebellion in Pennsylvania as farmers object to liquor taxes. U.S. Navy and Post Office Department established.

1796 Napoleon Bonaparte, French general, defeats Austrians. In the U.S., Washington's Farewell Address **(Sept. 17)**; John Adams elected President; Thomas Jefferson, Vice President. Edward Jenner introduces smallpox vaccination.

1798 Napoleon extends French conquests to Rome and Egypt.

1799 Napoleon leads coup that overthrows Directory, becomes First Consul —one of three who rule France.

James Madison, *American President* (1751–1836)
Richard Brinsley Sheridan, *Irish dramatist* (1751–1816)
Fanny Burney, *English writer* (1752–1840)
Betsy Ross, *American flagmaker* (1752–1836)
C. de Talleyrand-Périgord, *French statesman* (1754–1838)
Marie Antoinette, *French queen* (1755–1793)
Alexander Hamilton, *American statesman* (1755–1804)
Gilbert Stuart, *American painter* (1755–1828)
Aaron Burr, *American statesman* (1756–1836)
Wolfgang Amadeus Mozart, *Austrian composer* (1756–1791)
William Blake, *English poet* (1757–1827)
Marquis de Lafayette, *French general in America* (1757–1834)
James Monroe, *American President* (1758–1831)
Horatio Nelson, *English admiral* (1758–1805)
Maximilien de Robespierre, *French revolutionist* (1758–1794)
Noah Webster, *American lexicographer* (1758–1843)
Robert Burns, *Scottish poet* (1759–1796)
Katsuhika Hokusai, *Japanese artist* (1760–1849)
Luigi Cherubini, *Italian composer* (1760–1842)
Robert Fulton, *American inventor* (1765–1815)
Eli Whitney, *American inventor* (1765–1825)
John Dalton, *English chemist* (1766–1844)
T. R. Malthus, *English economist* (1766–1834)
John Quincy Adams, *American President* (1767–1848)
Andrew Jackson, *American President* (1767–1845)
Jacques Lafitte, *French pirate* (1767–1844)
Tecumseh, *American Indian chief* (1768?–1813)
Napoleon Bonaparte, *French emperor* (1769–1821)
Duke of Wellington, *English general* (1769–1852)
Ludwig van Beethoven, *German composer* (1770–1827)
G. W. F. Hegel, *German philosopher* (1770–1831)
William Wordsworth, *English writer* (1770–1850)
Robert Owen, *English social reformer* (1771–1858)
Walter Scott, *Scottish novelist* (1771–1832)
Friedrich von Schlegel, *German philosopher* (1772–1829)
Prince K. von Metternich, *Austrian statesman* (1773–1859)
Jane Austen, *English novelist* (1775–1817)
J. W. Turner, *English painter* (1775–1851)
John Constable, *English painter* (1776–1837)
Henry Clay, *American statesman* (1777–1852)
Heinrich von Kleist, *German poet* (1777–1811)
Karl von Clausewitz, *German military strategist* (1780–1831)
J.A. Ingres, *French painter* (1780–1867)
Nicolo Paganini, *Italian composer* (1782–1840)
Daniel Webster, *American statesman* (1782–1852)
Simón Bolívar, *Latin American patriot* (1783–1830)
Washington Irving, *American writer* (1783–1859)
Stendahl (Marie Henri Beyle), *French novelist* (1783–1842)
J. J. Audubon, *American naturalist* (1785–1851)

1800 Napoleon conquers Italy, firmly establishes himself as First Consul in France. In the U.S., Federal Government moves to Washington. Robert Owen's social reforms in England. William Herschel discovers infrared rays. Alessandro Volta produces electricity.

1801 Austria makes temporary peace with France. United Kingdom of Great Britain and Ireland established with one monarch and one parliament; Catholics excluded from voting.

1803 U.S. negotiates Louisiana Purchase from France: For $15 million, U.S. doubles its domain, increasing its territory by 827,000 sq mi. (2,144,500 sq km), from Mississippi River to Rockies and from Gulf of Mexico to British North America.

1804 Haiti declares independence from France; first black nation to gain freedom from European colonial rule. Napoleon proclaims himself emperor of France, systematizes French law under *Code Napoleon*. In the U.S., Alexander Hamilton is mortally wounded in duel with Aaron Burr. Lewis and Clark expedition begins exploration of what is now northwestern U.S.

1805 Lord Nelson defeats the French-Spanish fleets in the Battle of Trafalgar. Napoleon victorious over Austrian and Russian forces at the Battle of Austerlitz.

1807 Robert Fulton makes first successful steamboat trip on *Clermont* between New York City and Albany.

Davy Crockett, *American frontiersman* (1786–1836)
Carl Maria von Weber, *German composer* (1786–1826)
Louis Daguerre, *French photographic pioneer* (1787–1851)
Lord Byron, *English poet* (1788–1824)
Arthur Schopenhauer, *German philosopher* (1788–1860)
James Fenimore Cooper, *American writer* (1789–1851)
Michael Faraday, *English physicist* (1791–1867)
Samuel F. B. Morse, *American inventor* (1791–1872)

1808 French armies occupy Rome and Spain, extending Napoleon's empire. Britain begins aiding Spanish guerrillas against Napoleon in Peninsular War. In the U.S., Congress bars importation of slaves. Beethoven's *Fifth* and *Sixth Symphonies* performed.

1812 Napoleon's Grand Army invades Russia in June. Forced to retreat in winter, most of Napoleon's 600,000 men are lost. In the U.S., war with Britain declared over freedom of the seas for U.S. vessels. U.S.S. *Constitution* sinks British frigate. *(See* special material on the "War of 1812.")

1814 French defeated by allies (Britain, Austria, Russia, Prussia, Sweden, and Portugal) in War of Liberation. Napoleon exiled to Elba, off Italian coast. Bourbon King Louis XVIII takes French throne. George Stephenson builds first practical steam locomotive.

1815 Napoleon returns: "Hundred Days" begin. Napoleon defeated by Wellington at Waterloo, banished again to St. Helena in South Atlantic. Congress of Vienna: victorious allies change the map of Europe.

1817 Simón Bolívar establishes independent Venezuela, as Spain loses hold on South American countries. Bolívar named President of Colombia **(1819)**. Peru, Guatemala, Panama, and Santo Domingo proclaim independence from Spain **(1821)**.

1820 Missouri Compromise—Missouri admitted as slave state but slavery barred in rest of Louisiana Purchase north of 36°30′ N.

1822 Greeks proclaim a republic and independence from Turkey. Turks invade Greece. Russia declares war on Turkey **(1828)**. Greece also aided by France and Britain. War ends and Turks recognize Greek independence **(1829)**. Brazil becomes independent of Portugal. Schubert's *Eighth Symphony* ("The Unfinished").

1823 U.S. Monroe Doctrine warns European nations not to interfere in Western Hemisphere.

1824 Mexico becomes a republic, three years after declaring independence from Spain. Beethoven's *Ninth Symphony.*

1825 First passenger-carrying railroad in England.

1830 French invade Algeria. Louis Philippe becomes "Citizen King" as revolution forces Charles X to abdicate. Mormon church formed in U.S. by Joseph Smith.

1831 Polish revolt against Russia fails. Belgium separates from the Netherlands. In U.S., Nat Turner leads unsuccessful slave rebellion.

1833 Slavery abolished in British Empire.

1834 Charles Babbage invents "analytical engine," precursor of computer. McCormick patents reaper.

1836 Boer farmers start "Great Trek"—Natal, Transvaal, and Orange Free State founded in South Africa. Mexican army besieges Texans in Alamo. Entire garrison, including Davy Crockett and Jim Bowie, wiped out. Texans gain independence from Mexico after winning Battle of San Jacinto. Dickens's *Pickwick Papers.*

1837 Victoria becomes Queen of Great Britain. Mob kills Elijah P. Lovejoy, Illinois abolitionist publisher.

1839 First Opium War (to **1842**) between Britain and China, over importation of drug into China.

1840 Lower and Upper Canada united.

1841 U.S. President Harrison dies **(April 4)** one month after inauguration; John Tyler becomes first Vice President to succeed to Presidency.

1844 Democratic convention calls for annexation of Texas and acquisition of Oregon ("Fifty-four-forty-or-fight"). Five Chinese ports opened to U.S. ships. Samuel F. B. Morse patents telegraph.

1845 Congress adopts joint resolution for annexation of Texas.

1846 Failure of potato crop causes famine in Ireland. U.S. declares war on Mexico. California and New Mexico annexed by U.S. Brigham Young leads Mormons to Great Salt Lake. W. T. Morton uses ether as anesthetic. Sewing machine patented by Elias Howe.

1848 Revolt in Paris: Louis Philippe abdicates; Louis Napoleon elected President of French Republic. Revolutions in Vienna, Venice, Berlin, Milan, Rome, and Warsaw. Put down by royal troops in **1848–49**. U.S.-Mexico War ends; Mexico cedes claims to Texas, California, Arizona, New Mexico, Utah, Nevada. U.S. treaty with Britain sets Oregon Territory boundary at 49th parallel. Karl Marx and Friedrich Engels' *Communist Manifesto.*

1849 California gold rush begins.

Percy Bysshe Shelley, *English poet* (1792–1822)
Gioacchino Rossini, *Italian composer* (1792–1868)
Sam Houston, *Texas political leader* (1793–1863)
John Keats, *English poet* (1795–1821)
Thomas Carlyle, *British historian* (1795–1881)
Heinrich Heine, *German poet* (1797–1856)
Ando Hiroshige, *Japanese painter* (1797–1858)
Franz Schubert, *Austrian composer* (1797–1828)
Adam Mickiewicz, *Polish poet* (1798–1855)
Auguste Comte, *French philosopher* (1798–1857)
Ferdinand Delacroix, *French painter* (1798–1863)
Honoré de Balzac, *French novelist* (1799–1850)
Aleksander Pushkin, *Russian poet* (1799–1837)
John Henry Newman, *English prelate* (1801–1890)
Brigham Young, *Mormon leader* (1801–1877)
Lajos Kossuth, *Hungarian patriot* (1802–1894)
Alexander Dumas, père, *French novelist* (1802–1870)
Victor Hugo, *French novelist* (1802–1885)
Ralph Waldo Emerson, *American philosopher* (1803–1882)
Hector Berlioz, *French composer* (1803–1869)
Benjamin Disraeli, *British statesman* (1804–1881)
Nathaniel Hawthorne, *American novelist* (1804–1864)
George Sand, *French writer* (1804–1876)
Giuseppe Mazzini, *Italian patriot* (1805–1872)
Hans Christian Andersen, *Danish writer* (1805–1875)
Alexis de Tocqueville, *French writer* (1805–1859)
Elizabeth Barrett Browning, *English poet* (1806–1861)
John Stuart Mill, *English philosopher* (1806–1873)
Giuseppe Garibaldi, *Italian patriot* (1807–1882)
Henry Wadsworth Longfellow, *American poet* (1807–1882)
Honoré Daumier, *French artist* (1808–1879)

WAR OF 1812

British interference with American trade, impressment of American seamen, and "War Hawks" drive for western expansion lead to war. American attacks on Canada foiled; U.S. Commodore Perry wins battle of Lake Erie **(1813)**. British capture and burn Washington **(1814)** but fail to take Fort McHenry at Baltimore. Andrew Jackson repulses assault on New Orleans after treaty of Ghent ends war **(1815)**. War settles little but strengthens U.S. as independent nation.

1850 Henry Clay opens great debate on slavery, warns South against secession.

1851 Herman Melville's *Moby Dick.* Harriet Beecher Stowe's *Uncle Tom's Cabin.*

1852 South African Republic established. Louis Napoleon proclaims himself Napoleon III ("Second Empire").

1853 Crimean War begins as Turkey declares war on Russia. Commodore Perry reaches Tokyo.

1854 Britain and France join Turkey in war on Russia. In U.S., Kansas-Nebraska Act permits local option on slavery; rioting and bloodshed. Japanese allow American trade. Antislavery men in Michigan form Republican Party. Tennyson's *Charge of the Light Brigade.* Thoreau's *Walden.*

1855 Armed clashes in Kansas between pro- and anti- slavery forces. Florence Nightingale nurses wounded in Crimea. Walt Whitman's *Leaves of Grass.*

1856 Flaubert's *Madame Bovary.*

1857 Supreme Court, in Dred Scott decision, rules that a slave is not a citizen. Financial crisis in Europe and U.S. Great Mutiny (Sepoy Rebellion) begins in India. India placed under crown rule as a result.

1858 Pro-slavery constitution rejected in Kansas. Abraham Lincoln makes strong antislavery speech in Springfield, Ill.: ". . . this Government cannot endure permanently half slave and half free." Lincoln-Douglas debates. First trans-Atlantic telegraph cable completed by Cyrus W. Field.

1859 John Brown raids Harpers Ferry; is captured and hanged. Work begins on Suez Canal. Unification of Italy starts under leadership of Count Cavour, Sardinian premier. Joined by France in war against Austria. Edward Fitzgerald's *Rubaiyat of Omar Khayyam.* Charles Darwin's *Origin of Species.* J. S. Mill's *On Liberty*

1861 U.S. Civil War begins as attempts at compromise fail *(see* special material on "The Civil War"). Congress creates Colorado, Dakota, and Nevada territories; adopts income tax; Lincoln inaugurated. Serfs emancipated in Russia. Pasteur's theory of germs. Independent Kingdom of Italy proclaimed under Sardinian King Victor Emmanuel II.

1863 French capture Mexico City; proclaim Archduke Maximilian of Austria emperor.

1865 Lincoln fatally shot at Ford's Theater by John Wilkes Booth. Vice President Johnson sworn as successor. Booth caught and dies of gunshot wounds; four conspirators are hanged. Joseph Lister begins antiseptic surgery. Gregor Mendel's Law of Heredity. Lewis Carroll's *Alice's Adventures in Wonderland.*

1866 Alfred Nobel invents dynamite. Seven Weeks' War: Austria defeated by Prussia and Italy.

1867 Austria-Hungary Dual Monarchy established. French leave Mexico; Maximilian executed. Dominion of Canada established. U.S. buys Alaska from Russia for $7,200,000. South African diamond field discovered. Volume I of Marx's *Das Kapital.* Strauss's *Blue Danube.*

1868 Revolution in Spain; Queen Isabella deposed, flees to France. In U.S., Fourteenth Amendment giving civil rights to blacks is ratified. Georgia under military government after legislature expels blacks.

Abraham Lincoln, *American president* (1809–1865)
Nicolai Gogol, *Russian writer* (1809–1852)
Edgar Allan Poe, *American writer* (1809–1849)
Alfred, Lord Tennyson, *English poet* (1809–1892)
William Ewart Gladstone, *British statesman* (1809–1898)
Charles Darwin, *English scientist* (1809–1882)
Felix Mendelssohn, *German composer* (1809–1847)
Louis Braille, *French inventor of touch alphabet for blind* (1809–1852)
Frédéric Chopin, *Polish composer* (1810–1849)
Robert Schumann, *German composer* (1810–1856)
Phineas T. Barnum, *American showman* (1810–1891)
Harriet Beecher Stowe, *American writer* (1811–1896)
William M. Thackeray, *English novelist* (1811–1863)
Franz Liszt, *Hungarian composer* (1811–1896)
Robert Browning, *English poet* (1812–1889)
Charles Dickens, *English novelist* (1812–1870)
Alfred Krupp, *German munitions magnate* (1812–1887)
Sören Kierkegaard, *Danish philosopher* (1813–1855)
Giuseppe Verdi, *Italian composer* (1813–1901)
Richard Wagner, *German composer* (1813–1883)
Otto von Bismarck, *Prussian statesman* (1815–1898)
Charlotte Brontë, *English writer* (1816–1855)

THE CIVIL WAR (1861–1865)
(The War Between the States or the War of the Rebellion)

Apart from the matter of slavery, the Civil War arose out of both the economic and political rivalry between an agrarian South and an industrial North and the issue of the right of states to secede from the Union.

1861 After South Carolina secedes (**Dec. 20, 1860**), Mississippi, Florida, Alabama, Georgia, Louisiana, and Texas follow, forming the Confederate States of America, with Jefferson Davis as president (**Jan.-March**). War begins as Confederates fire on Fort Sumter (**April 12**). Lincoln calls for 75,000 volunteers. Southern ports blockaded by superior Union naval forces. Virginia, Arkansas, Tennessee, and North Carolina secede to complete 11-state Confederacy. Union army advancing on Richmond repulsed at first Battle of Bull Run (**July**).

1862 Edwin M. Stanton named Secretary of War (**Jan.**). Grant wins first important Union victory in West, at Fort Donelson; Nashville falls (**Feb.**). Ironclads, Union's *Monitor* and Confederate's *Virginia (Merrimac)* duel at Hampton Roads (**March**). New Orleans falls to Union fleet under Farragut; city occupied (**April**). Grant's army escapes defeat at Shiloh. Memphis falls as Union gunboats control upper Mississippi (**June**). Confederate general Robert E. Lee victorious at second Battle of Bull Run (**Aug.**). Union army under McClellan halts Lee's attack on Washington in the Battle of Antietam (**Sept.**). Lincoln removes McClellan for lack of aggressiveness. Burnside's drive on Richmond fails at Fredericksburg (**Dec.**). Union forces under Rosecrans chase Bragg through Tennessee; battle of Murfreesboro (**Oct.-Jan. 1863**).

1863 Lee defeats Hooker at Chancellorsville; "Stonewall" Jackson, Confederate general, dies (**May**). Confederate invasion of Pennsylvania stopped at Gettysburg by George Meade—Lee loses 20,000 men—the greatest battle of the War (**July**). It and the Union victory at Vicksburg mark the war's turning point. Union general George H. Thomas, the "Rock of Chickamauga," holds Bragg's forces on Georgia-Tennessee border (**Sept.**). Sherman, Hooker, and Thomas drive Bragg back to Georgia. Tennessee restored to the Union (**Nov.**).

1864 Ulysses S. Grant named commander-in-chief of Union forces (**March**). In the Wilderness campaign, Grant forces Lee's Army of Northern Virginia back toward Richmond (**May-June**). Sherman's Atlanta campaign and "march to the sea" (**May-Sept.**). Farragut's victory at Mobile Bay (**Aug.**). Hood's Confederate army defeated at Nashville. Sherman takes Savannah (**Dec.**).

1865 Sheridan defeats Confederates at Five Forks; Confederates evacuate Richmond (**April**). On **April 9**, Lee surrenders to Grant at Appomattox.

1869 First U.S. transcontinental rail route completed. James Fisk and Jay Gould attempt to control gold market causes Black Friday panic. Suez Canal opened. Mendeleev's periodic table of elements.
1870 Franco-Prussian War (to **1871**): Napoleon III capitulates at Sedan. Revolt in Paris; Third Republic proclaimed.
1871 France surrenders Alsace-Lorraine to Germany; war ends. German Empire proclaimed with Prussian King as Kaiser Wilhelm I. Fighting with Apaches begins in American West. Boss Tweed corruption exposed in New York. The Chicago Fire, with 250 deaths and $196-million damage. Stanley meets Livingston in Africa.
1872 Congress gives amnesty to most Confederates. Jules Verne's *Around the World in 80 Days*.
1873 Economic crisis in Europe. U.S. establishes gold standard.
1875 First Kentucky Derby.
1876 Sioux kill Gen. George A. Custer and 264 troopers at Little Big Horn River. Alexander Graham Bell patents the telephone.
1877 After Presidential election of **1876**, Electoral Commission gives disputed Electoral College votes to Rutherford B. Hayes despite Tilden's popular majority. Russo-Turkish war (ends in **1878** with power of Turkey in Europe broken). Reconstruction ends in the American South. Thomas Edison patents phonograph.
1878 Congress of Berlin revises Treaty of San Stefano ending Russo-Turkish War; makes extensive redivision of southeastern Europe. First commercial telephone exchange opened in New Haven, Conn.
1880 U.S.-China treaty allows U.S. to restrict immigration of Chinese labor.
1881 President Garfield fatally shot by assassin; Vice President Arthur succeeds him. Charles J. Guiteau convicted and executed (in **1882**).
1882 Terrorism in Ireland after land evictions. Britain invades and conquers Egypt. Germany, Austria, and Italy form Triple Alliance. In U.S., Congress adopts Chinese Exclusion Act. Rockefeller's Standard Oil Trust is first industrial monopoly. In Berlin, Robert Koch announces discovery of tuberculosis germ.
1883 Congress creates Civil Service Commission. Brooklyn Bridge and Metropolitan Opera House completed.
1885 British Gen. Charles G. "Chinese" Gordon killed at Khartoum in Egyptian Sudan.
1886 Bombing at Haymarket Square, Chicago, kills seven policemen and injures many others. Eight alleged anarchists accused—three imprisoned, one commits suicide, four hanged. (In **1893**, Illinois Governor Altgeld, critical of trial, pardons three survivors.) Statue of Liberty dedicated. Geronimo, Apache Indian chief, surrenders.
1887 Queen Victoria's Golden Jubilee. Sir Arthur Conan Doyle's first Sherlock Holmes story, "A Study in Scarlet."
1888 Historic March blizzard in Northeast U.S.—many perish, property damage exceeds $25 million. George Eastman's box camera (the Kodak). J.B. Dunlop invents pneumatic tire. Jack the Ripper murders in London.
1889 Second (Socialist) International founded in Paris. Indian Territory in Oklahoma opened to settlement. Thousands die in Johnstown, Pa., flood. Mark Twain's *A Connecticut Yankee in King Arthur's Court*.
1890 Congress votes Sherman Antitrust Act. Sitting Bull killed in Sioux uprising.
1892 Battle between steel strikers and Pinkerton guards at Homestead, Pa.; union defeated after militia intervenes. Silver mine strikers in Idaho fight non-union workers; U.S. troops dispatched. Diesel engine patented.
1894 Sino-Japanese War begins (ends in **1895** with China's defeat). In France, Capt. Alfred Dreyfus convicted on false treason charge (pardoned in **1906**). In U.S., Jacob S. Coxey of Ohio leads "Coxey's Army" of unemployed on Washington. Eugene V. Debs calls general strike of rail workers to support Pullman Company strikers; strike broken, Debs jailed for six months. Thomas A. Edison's kinetoscope given first public showing in New York City.
1895 X-rays discovered by German physicist, Wilhelm Roentgen.
1896 Supreme Court's *Plessy* v. *Ferguson* decision—"separate but equal"

Henry David Thoreau, *American writer* (1817–1862)
Ivan Turgenev, *Russian writer* (1818–1883)
Karl Marx, *German political philosopher* (1818–1883)
Queen Victoria, *British monarch* (1819–1901)
George Eliot, *English novelist* (1819–1880)
Walt Whitman, *American poet* (1819–1892)
Friedrich Engels, *German political philosopher* (1820–1895)
Florence Nightingale, *English nurse* (1820–1910)
Charles Baudelaire, *French poet* (1821–1867)
Feodor Dostoevsky, *Russian writer* (1821–1881)
Gustave Flaubert, *French novelist* (1821–1880)
Mary Baker Eddy, *founder of Christian Science* (1821–1910)
Ulysses S. Grant, *American President* (1822–1885)
Gregor Mendel, *Austrian scientist* (1822–1884)
Louis Pasteur, *French scientist* (1822–1895)
Alexandre Dumas, fils, *French writer* (1824–1895)
Johann Strauss, *Austrian "waltz king"* (1825–1899)
Stephen Foster, *American composer* (1826–1864)
Joseph Lister, *English surgeon* (1827–1912)
Henrik Ibsen, *Norwegian dramatist* (1828–1906)
Leo Tolstoi, *Russian novelist* (1828–1910)
Jules Verne, *French author* (1828–1905)
William Booth, *Salvation Army founder* (1829–1912)
Emily Dickinson, *American poet* (1830–1886)
James Clerk Maxwell, *Scottish astronomer and physicist* (1831–1879)
Louisa May Alcott, *American author* (1832–1888)
Horatio Alger, *American author* (1834–1899)
Lewis Carroll (Charles Lutwidge Dodgson), *English author* (1832–1898)

SPANISH-AMERICAN WAR (1898–1899)

War fires stoked by "jingo journalism" as American people support Cuban rebels against Spain. American business sees economic gain in Cuban trade and resources and American power zones in Latin America. Outstanding events: Submarine mine explodes U.S. battleship *Maine* in Havana Harbor (**Feb. 15**); 260 killed; responsibility never fixed. Congress declares independence of Cuba (**April 19**). Spain declares war on U.S. (**Apr. 24**); Congress (**Apr. 25**) formally declares nation has been at war with Spain since Apr. 21. Commodore George Dewey wins seven-hour battle of Manila Bay (**May 1**). Spanish fleet destroyed off Santiago, Cuba (**July 3**); city surrenders (**July 17**). Treaty of Paris (ratified by Senate in **1899**) ends war. U.S. given Guam and Puerto Rico and agrees to pay Spain $20 million for Philippines. Cuba independent of Spain; under U.S. military control for three years until **May 20, 1902**. Yellow fever is eradicated and political reforms achieved.

doctrine. Alfred Nobel's will establishes prizes for peace, science, and literature. Marconi receives first wireless patent in Britain. William Jennings Bryan delivers "Cross of Gold" speech at Democratic Convention in Chicago. First modern Olympic games held in Athens, Greece.

1898 Chinese "Boxers," anti-foreign organization, established. They stage uprisings against Europeans in **1900**; U.S. and other Western troops relieve Peking legations. Spanish-American War *(see* special material on the "Spanish-American War"). Pierre and Marie Curie discover radium and polonium.

1899 Boer War (or South African War). Conflict between British and Boers (descendants of Dutch settlers of South Africa). Causes rooted in long-standing territorial disputes and in friction over political rights for English and other "uitlanders" following 1886 discovery of vast gold deposits in Transvaal. (British victorious as war ends in **1902**.) Casualties: 5,774 British dead, about 4,000 Boers. Union of South Africa established in **1908** as confederation of colonies; becomes British dominion in **1910**.

1900 Hurricane ravages Galveston, Tex.; 6,000 drown. Sigmund Freud's *The Interpretation of Dreams.*

1901 Queen Victoria dies; succeeded by son, Edward VII. As President McKinley begins second term, he is shot fatally by anarchist Leon Czolgosz. Theodore Roosevelt sworn in as successor.

1902 Enrico Caruso's first gramophone recording.

1903 Wright brothers, Orville and Wilbur, fly first powered, controlled, heavier-than-air plane at Kitty Hawk, N.C. Henry Ford organizes Ford Motor Company.

1904 Russo-Japanese War—competition for Korea and Manchuria: In **1905**, Port Arthur surrenders to Japanese and Russia suffers other defeats; President Roosevelt mediates Treaty of Portsmouth, N.H., ending war with concessions for Japan. *Entente Cordiale:* Britain and France settle their international differences. General theory of radioactivity by Rutherford and Soddy. New York City subway opened.

1905 General strike in Russia; first workers' soviet set up in St. Petersburg. Sailors on battleship *Potemkin* mutiny; reforms including first Duma (parliament) established by Czar's "October Manifesto." Albert Einstein's special theory of relativity and other key theories in physics. Franz Lehar's *Merry Widow.*

1906 San Francisco earthquake and three-day fire; 500 dead. Roald Amundsen, Norwegian explorer, fixes magnetic North Pole.

1907 Second Hague Peace Conference, of 46 nations, adopts 10 conventions on rules of war. Financial panic of **1907** in U.S.

1908 Earthquake kills 150,000 in southern Italy and Sicily. U.S. Supreme Court, in Danbury Hatters' case, outlaws secondary union boycotts.

1909 North Pole reached by American explorers Robert E. Peary and Matthew Henson.

1910 Boy Scouts of America incorporated.

1911 First use of aircraft as offensive weapon in Turkish-Italian War. Italy defeats Turks and annexes Tripoli and Libya. Chinese Republic proclaimed after revolution overthrows Manchu dynasty. Sun Yat-sen named president. Mexican Revolution: Porfirio Diaz, president since 1877, replaced by Francisco Madero. Triangle Shirtwaist Company fire in New York; 145 killed. Richard Strauss's *Der Rosenkavalier.* Irving Berlin's *Alexander's Ragtime Band.* Amundsen reaches South Pole.

1912 Balkan Wars **(1912–13)** resulting from territorial disputes: Turkey defeated by alliance of Bulgaria, Serbia, Greece, and Montenegro; London peace treaty **(1913)** partitions most of European Turkey among the victors. In second war **(1913)**, Bulgaria attacks Serbia and Greece and is defeated after Romania intervenes and Turks recapture Adrianople. *Titanic* sinks on maiden voyage; over 1,500 drown.

1913 Suffragettes demonstrate in London. Garment workers strike in New York and Boston; win pay raise and shorter hours. Sixteenth Amendment (income tax) and 17th (popular election of U.S. senators) adopted. Bill creating U.S. Federal Reserve System becomes law. Stravinsky's *The Rite of Spring.*

1914 World War I begins *(see* special material on "World War I"). Panama Canal officially opened. Congress sets up Federal Trade Commission, passes Clayton Antitrust Act. U.S. Marines occupy Veracruz, Mexico, intervening in civil war to protect American interests.

1915 U.S. protests German submarine actions and British blockade of Germany. U.S. banks lend $500 million to France and Britain. D. W. Griffith's film *Birth of a Nation.* Albert Einstein's *General Theory of Relativity.*

1916 Congress expands armed forces. Tom Mooney arrested for San Francisco bombing (pardoned in **1939**). Pershing fails in raid into Mexico in

Edouard Manet, *French painter* (1832–1883)
Johannes Brahms, *German composer* (1833–1897)
Alfred Nobel, *Swedish industrialist* (1833–1896)
Edgar Dégas, *French painter* (1834–1917)
James McNeill Whistler, *American painter* (1834–1903)
Dmitri Mendeleev, *Russian chemist* (1834–1907)
Mark Twain (Samuel L. Clemens), *American author* (1835–1910)
Camille Saint-Saëns, *French composer* (1835–1910)
Andrew Carnegie, *American industrialist* (1835–1919)
W. S. Gilbert, *English librettist* (1836–1911)
Bret Harte, *American novelist* (1836–1902)
Winslow Homer, *American painter* (1836–1910)
Sitting Bull, *American Indian chief* (1837–1890)
J. P. Morgan, *American financier* (1837–1913)
Georges Bizet, *French composer* (1838–1875)
Paul Cézanne, *French painter* (1839–1906)
John D. Rockefeller, *American industrialist* (1839–1937)
Thomas Hardy, *English novelist* (1840–1928)
Emile Zola, *French novelist* (1840–1902)
Claude Monet, *French painter* (1840–1926)
Pierre Renoir, *French painter* (1840–1919)
Auguste Rodin, *French sculptor* (1840–1917)
Peter Ilich Tchaikovsky, *Russian composer* (1840–1893)
Ambrose Bierce, *American author* (1842–1914)
William James, *American philosopher* (1842–1910)
Arthur Sullivan, *English composer* (1842–1900)
Henry James, *American novelist* (1843–1916)
Edvard Grieg, *Norwegian composer* (1843–1907)
Sarah Bernhardt, *French actress* (1844–1923)
Anatole France (Jacques Anatole Thibault), *French author* (1844–1924)
Gerard Manley Hopkins, *English poet* (1844–1899)
Friedrich Nietzsche, *German philosopher* (1844–1900)
Nikolai Rimski-Korsakov, *Russian composer* (1844–1908)

quest of rebel Pancho Villa. U.S. buys Virgin Islands from Denmark for $25 million. President Wilson re-elected with "he kept us out of war" slogan. "Black Tom" explosion at munitions dock in Jersey City, N.Y., $40,000,000 damages; traced to German saboteurs. Margaret Sanger opens first birth control clinic. Easter Rebellion in Ireland put down by British troops.

1917 First U.S. combat troops in France as U.S. declares war **(April 6)**. Russian Revolution—climax of long unrest under czars. February Revolution—Czar forced to abdicate, liberal government created. Kerensky becomes prime minister and forms provisional government **(July)**. In October Revolution, Bolsheviks seize power in armed coup d'état led by Lenin and Trotsky. Kerensky flees. Revolutionaries execute the czar and his family **(1918)**. Reds set up Third International in Moscow **(1919)**. Balfour Declaration promises Jewish homeland in Palestine. Sigmund Freud's *Introduction to Psychoanalysis*.

1918 Russian Civil War between Reds (Bolsheviks) and Whites (anti-Bolsheviks); Reds win in **1920**. Allied troops (U.S., British, French) intervene **(March)**; leave in **1919**. Japanese hold Vladivostok until 1922. World-wide influenza epidemic strikes; by **1920**, nearly 20 million are dead. In U.S. alone, 500,000 perish.

1919 Third International (Comintern) establishes Soviet control over international Communist movements. Paris peace conference. Versailles Treaty, incorporating Wilson's draft Covenant of League of Nations, signed by Allies and Germany; rejected by U.S. Senate. Congress formally ends war in **1921**. Eighteenth (Prohibition) Amendment adopted. Alcock and Brown make first trans-Atlantic non-stop flight.

1920 League of Nations holds first meeting at Geneva, Switzerland. U.S. Dept. of Justice "red hunt" nets thousands of radicals; aliens deported. Woman suffrage (19th) amendment ratified. First Agatha Christie mystery. Sinclair Lewis's *Main Street*.

1921 Reparations Commission fixes German liability at 132 billion gold marks. German inflation begins. Major treaties signed at Washington Disarmament Conference limit naval tonnage and pledge to respect territorial integrity of China. Irish Free State formed in southern Ireland as self-governing dominion of British Empire. In U.S., Nicola Sacco and Bartolomeo Vanzetti, Italian-born anarchists, convicted of armed robbery murder; case stirs world-wide protests; they are executed in **1927**.

1922 Mussolini marches on Rome; forms Fascist government. Irish Free State officially proclaimed.

1923 Adolf Hitler's "Beer Hall Putsch" in Munich fails; in **1924** he is sentenced to five years in prison where he writes *Mein Kampf;* released after eight months. Occupation of Ruhr by French and Belgian troops to enforce reparations payments. Widespread Ku Klux Klan violence in U.S. George Gershwin's *Rhapsody in Blue*.

1924 Death of Lenin; Stalin wins power struggle, rules as Soviet dictator until death in **1953**. Italian Fascists murder Socialist leader Giacomo Matteotti. Interior Secretary Albert B. Fall and oilmen Harry Sinclair and Edward L. Doheny are charged with conspiracy and bribery in the Teapot Dome scandal, involving fraudulent leases of naval oil reserves. In **1931**,

Wilhelm Conrad Roentgen, *German discoverer of X-rays* (1845–1923)
Gabriel Fauré, *French composer* (1845–1924)
Thomas Alva Edison, *American inventor* (1847–1931)
Alexander Graham Bell, *American inventor* (1847–1922)
Paul Gauguin, *French painter* (1848–1903)
August Strindberg, *Swedish dramatist* (1849–1912)
Luther Burbank, *American horticulturist* (1849–1926)
Guy de Maupassant, *French author* (1850–1893)
Robert Louis Stevenson, *English author* (1850–1894)
Vincent Van Gogh, *Dutch painter* (1853–1890)
George Eastman, *American photographic pioneer* (1854–1932)
George Bernard Shaw, *Irish dramatist* (1856–1950)
Oscar Wilde, *Anglo-Irish author* (1856–1900)
Sigmund Freud, *Austrian founder of psychoanalysis* (1856–1939)
Robert E. Peary, *American explorer* (1856–1920)
Booker T. Washington, *American educator* (1856–1915)
Joseph Conrad, *Anglo-Polish novelist* (1857–1924)
Giacomo Puccini, *Italian composer* (1858–1924)
Theodore Roosevelt, *American President* (1858–1919)
Max Planck, *German physicist* (1858–1947)

WORLD WAR I (1914–1918)

Imperial, territorial, and economic rivalries lead to the "Great War" between the Central Powers (Austria-Hungary, Germany, Bulgaria, and Turkey) and the Allies (U.S., Britain, France, Russia, Belgium, Serbia, Greece, Romania, Montenegro, Portugal, Italy, Japan). About 10 million combatants killed, 20 million wounded.

1914 Austrian Archduke Francis Ferdinand and wife assassinated in Sarajevo by Serbian nationalist, Gavrilo Princip **(June 28)**. Austria declares war on Serbia **(July 28)**. Germany declares war on Russia **(Aug. 1)**, on France **(Aug. 3)**, invades Belgium **(Aug. 4)**. Britain declares war on Germany **(Aug. 4)**. Germans defeat Russians in Battle of Tannenberg on Eastern Front **(Aug.)**. First Battle of the Marne **(Sept.)**. German drive stopped 25 miles from Paris. By end of year, war on the Western Front is "positional" in the trenches.

1915 German submarine blockade of Great Britain begins **(Feb.)**. Dardanelles Campaign—British land in Turkey **(April)**, withdraw from Gallipoli **(Dec. to Jan. 1916)**. Germans use gas at second Battle of Ypres **(April-May)**. *Lusitania* sunk by German submarine—1,198 lost, including 128 Americans **(May 7)**. On Eastern Front, German and Austrian "great offensive" conquers all of Poland and Lithuania; Russians lose 1 million men **(by Sept. 6)**. "Great Fall Offensive" by Allies results in little change from 1914 **(Sept.-Oct.)**. Britain and France declare war on Bulgaria **(Oct. 14)**.

1916 Battle of Verdun—Germans and French each lose about 350,000 men **(Feb.)**. Extended submarine warfare begins **(March)**. British-German sea battle of Jutland **(May)**; British lose more ships, but German fleet never ventures forth again. On Eastern front, the Brusilov offensive demoralizes Russians, costs them 1 million men **(June-Sept.)**. Battle of the Somme—British lose over 400,000; French, 200,000; Germans, about 450,000; all with no strategic results **(July-Nov.)**. Romania declares war on Austria-Hungary **(Aug. 27)**. Bucharest captured **(Dec.)**.

1917 U.S. declares war on Germany **(April 6)**. Submarine warfare at peak **(April)**. On Italian Front, Battle of Caporetto—Italians retreat, losing 600,000 prisoners and deserters **(Oct.-Dec.)**. On Western Front, Battles of Arras, Champagne, Ypres (third battle), etc. First large British tank attack **(Nov.)**. U.S. declares war on Austria-Hungary **(Dec. 7)**. Armistice between new Russian Bolshevik government and Germans **(Dec. 15)**.

1918 Great offensive by Germans **(March-June)**. Americans' first important battle role at Château-Thierry—as they and French stop German advance **(June)**. Second Battle of the Marne **(July-Aug.)**—start of Allied offensive at Amiens, St. Mihiel, etc. Battles of the Argonne and Ypres panic German leadership **(Sept.-Oct.)**. British offensive in Palestine **(Sept.)**. Germans ask for armistice **(Oct. 4)**. British armistice with Turkey **(Oct.)**. German Kaiser abdicates **(Nov.)**. Hostilities cease on Western Front **(Nov. 11)**.

Fall is sentenced to year in prison; Doheny and Sinclair acquitted of bribery. Nellie Tayloe Ross elected governor of Wyoming; first woman governor elected in U.S. Nathan Leopold and Richard Loeb convicted in "thrill killing" of Bobby Franks in Chicago; defended by Clarence Darrow; sentenced to life imprisonment. (Loeb killed by fellow convict in **1936**; Leopold paroled in **1958**, dies in **1971**.)

1925 Locarno conferences seek to secure European peace by mutual guarantees. John T. Scopes convicted and fined for teaching evolution in a public school in Tennessee "Monkey Trial"; sentence set aside. John Logie Baird, Scottish inventor, transmits human features by television. Adolf Hitler publishes Volume I of *Mein Kampf.*

1926 General strike in Britain brings nation's activities to standstill. U.S. marines dispatched to Nicaragua during revolt; they remain until **1933**. Gertrude Ederle of U.S. is first woman to swim English Channel.

1927 German economy collapses. Socialists riot in Vienna; general strike follows acquittal of Nazis for political murder. Trotsky expelled from Russian Communist Party. Charles A. Lindbergh flies first successful solo non-stop flight from New York to Paris. Ruth Snyder and Judd Gray convicted of murder of Albert Snyder; they are executed at Sing Sing prison in **1928**. *The Jazz Singer,* with Al Jolson, first part-talking motion picture.

1928 Kellogg-Briand Pact, outlawing war, signed in Paris by 65 nations. Alexander Fleming discovers penicillin. Richard E. Byrd starts expedition to Antarctic; returns in **1930**.

1929 Trotsky expelled from U.S.S.R. Lateran Treaty establishes independent Vatican City. In U.S., stock market prices collapse, with U.S. securities losing $26 billion—first phase of Depression and world economic crisis. St. Valentine's Day gangland massacre in Chicago.

1930 Britain, U.S., Japan, France, and Italy sign naval disarmament treaty. Nazis gain in German elections. Cyclotron developed by Ernest O. Lawrence, U.S. physicist.

1931 Spain becomes a republic with overthrow of King Alfonso XIII. German industrialists finance 800,000-strong Nazi party. British parliament enacts statute of Westminster, legalizing dominion equality with Britain. Mukden Incident begins Japanese occupation of Manchuria. In U.S., Hoover proposes one-year moratorium of war debts. Harold C. Urey discovers heavy hydrogen. Gangster Al Capone sentenced to 11 years in prison for tax evasion (freed in **1939**; dies in **1947**).

1932 Nazis lead in German election with 230 Reichstag seats. Famine in U.S.S.R. In U.S., Congress sets up Reconstruction Finance Corporation to stimulate economy. Veterans march on Washington—most leave after Senate rejects payment of cash bonuses; others removed by troops under Douglas MacArthur. U.S. protests Japanese aggression in Manchuria. Amelia Earhart is first woman to fly Atlantic solo. Charles A. Lindbergh's baby son kidnapped, killed. (Bruno Richard Hauptmann arrested in **1934**, convicted in **1935**, executed in **1936**.)

1933 Hitler appointed German chancellor, gets dictatorial powers. Reichstag fire in Berlin; Nazi terror begins. *(See* special material on "The Holocaust.") Germany and Japan withdraw from League of Nations. Giuseppe Zangara executed for attempted assassination of President-elect Roosevelt in which Chicago Mayor Cermak is fatally shot. Roosevelt inaugurated ("the only thing we have to fear is fear itself"); launches New Deal. Prohibition repealed. U.S.S.R. recognized by U.S.

Arthur Conan Doyle, *English writer* (1859–1930)
Knut Hamsun, *Norwegian novelist* (1859–1952)
Henri Bergson, *French philosopher* (1859–1941)
John Dewey, *American philosopher* (1859–1952)
Georges Seurat, *French painter* (1859–1891)
Pierre Curie, *French physicist* (1859–1906)
Anton Chekhov, *Russian dramatist* (1860–1904)
Gustav Mahler, *German composer* (1860–1911)
Rabindranath Tagore, *Indian poet* (1861–1941)
Alfred North Whitehead, *British philosopher-mathematician* (1861–1947)
Edith Wharton, *American author* (1862–1937)
Claude Debussy, *French composer* (1862–1918)
David Lloyd George, *British statesman* (1863–1945)
Henry Ford, *American automobile pioneer* (1863–1947)
William Randolph Hearst, *American newspaper magnate* (1863–1951)
Henri Toulouse-Lautrec, *French painter* (1864–1901)
George Washington Carver, *American botanist* (1864–1943)
Richard Strauss, *German composer* (1864–1949)
Rudyard Kipling, *English writer* (1865–1936)
William Butler Yeats, *Irish poet* (1865–1939)
Jean Sibelius, *Finnish composer* (1865–1957)
Sun Yat-sen, *Chinese statesman* (1866–1927)
Benedetto Croce, *Italian philosopher* (1866–1952)

THE HOLOCAUST (1933–1945)

"Holocaust" is the term describing the Nazi annihilation of about 6 million Jews (two thirds of the pre-World War II European Jewish population), including 4,500,000 from Russia, Poland, and the Baltic; 750,000 from Hungary and Romania; 290,000 from Germany and Austria; 105,000 from The Netherlands; 90,000 from France; 54,000 from Greece, etc.

The Holocaust was unique in its being *genocide*—the systematic destruction of a people solely because of religion, race, ethnicity, or nationality—on an unmatched scale. Along with the Jews, another 9 to 10 million people—Gypsies, Slavs (Poles, Ukrainians, and Belorussians)—were exterminated.

The only comparable act of genocide in modern times was launched in April 1915, when 1.5 million Armenians were massacred by the Turks.

1933 Hitler named German Chancellor **(Jan.)**. Dachau, first concentration camp, established **(March)**. Boycotts against Jews begin **(April)**.

1935 Anti-Semitic Nuremberg Laws passed by Reichstag **(Sept.)**.

1937 Buchenwald concentration camp opens **(July)**.

1938 Extension of anti-Semitic laws to Austria after annexation **(March)**. *Kristallnacht* (Night of Broken Glass)—anti-Semitic riots in Germany and Austria **(Nov. 9)**. 26,000 Jews sent to concentration camps; Jewish children expelled from schools **(Nov.)**. Expropriation of Jewish property and businesses **(Dec.)**.

1940 As war continues, Nazi acts against Jews extended to German-conquered areas.

1941 Deportation of German Jews begins; massacres of Jews in Odessa and Kiev—68,000 killed **(Nov.)**; in Riga and Vilna—almost 60,000 killed **(Dec.)**.

1942 Unified Jewish resistance in ghettos begins **(Jan.)**. 300,000 Jews from Warsaw Ghetto deported to Treblinka death camp **(July)**.

1943 Warsaw Ghetto uprisings **(Jan. and April)**; Ghetto exterminated **(May)**.

1944 476,000 Hungarian Jews sent to Auschwitz **(May-June)**. D-day **(June 6)**. Soviet Army liberates Maidanek death camp **(July)**. Nazis try to hide evidence of death camps **(Nov.)**.

1945 Americans liberate Buchenwald, Bergen-Belsen camps **(April)**. Nuremberg War Crimes Trial **(Nov. 1945 to Oct. 1946)**.

1934 Chancellor Dollfuss of Austria assassinated by Nazis. Hitler becomes Führer. U.S.S.R. admitted to League of Nations. Dionne sisters, first quintuplets to survive beyond infancy, born in Canada.

1935 Saar incorporated into Germany after plebiscite. Nazis repudiate Versailles Treaty, introduce compulsory military service. Mussolini invades Ethiopia; League of Nations invokes sanctions. Roosevelt opens second phase of New Deal in U.S., calling for social security, better housing, equitable taxation, and farm assistance. Huey Long assassinated in Louisiana.

1936 Germans occupy Rhineland. Italy annexes Ethiopia. Rome-Berlin Axis proclaimed (Japan to join in **1940**). Trotsky exiled to Mexico. King George V dies; succeeded by son, Edward VIII, who soon abdicates to marry American-born divorcée, and is succeeded by brother, George VI. Spanish civil war begins. (Franco's fascist forces defeat Loyalist forces by **1939**, when Madrid falls.) War between China and Japan begins, to continue through World War II. Japan and Germany sign anti-Commintern pact; joined by Italy in **1937**.

1937 Hitler repudiates war guilt clause of Versailles Treaty; continues to build German power. Italy withdraws from League of Nations. U.S. gunboat *Panay* sunk by Japanese in Yangtze River. Japan invades China, conquers most of coastal area. Amelia Earhart lost somewhere in Pacific on round-the-world flight.

1938 Hitler marches into Austria; political and geographical union of Germany and Austria proclaimed. Munich Pact—Britain, France, and Italy agree to let Germany partition Czechoslovakia. Germany occupies Sudetenland, about one third of Czechoslovakia. Douglas "Wrong-Way" Corrigan flies from New York to Dublin.

1939 Germany occupies Bohemia and Moravia; renounces pacts with Poland and England and concludes 10-year non-aggression pact with U.S.S.R. Russo-Finnish War begins; Finns to lose one tenth of territory in **1940** peace treaty. World War II begins (*see* special material on "World War II"). In U.S., Roosevelt submits $1,319-million defense budget, proclaims U.S. neutrality, and declares limited emergency. Einstein writes FDR about feasibility of atomic bomb. New York World's Fair opens.

1940 Trotsky assassinated in Mexico. Estonia, Latvia, and Lithuania annexed by U.S.S.R. U.S. trades 50 destroyers for leases on British bases in Western Hemisphere. Selective Service Act signed.

1941 Japanese surprise attack on U.S. fleet at Pearl Harbor brings U.S. into World War II. Manhattan Project (atomic bomb research) begins. Roosevelt enunciates "four freedoms," signs lend-lease act, declares national emergency, promises aid to U.S.S.R.

Wilbur Wright, *American aviation pioneer* (1867–1912)
Arturo Toscanini, *Italian conductor* (1867–1957)
Marie (Sklodowska) Curie, *Polish-French scientist* (1867–1937)
Maxim Gorki, *Russian writer* (1868–1936)
Robert A. Millikan, *American physicist* (1869–1953)
Mohandas Gandhi, *Indian leader* (1869–1948)
André Gide, *French author* (1869–1951)
Henri Matisse, *French painter* (1869–1954)
Frank Lloyd Wright, *American architect* (1869–1959)
Nikolai Lenin, *Russian revolutionist* (1870–1924)
Orville Wright, *American aviation pioneer* (1871–1948)
Rasputin, *Russian monk* (1871–1916)
Stephen Crane, *American author* (1871–1900)
Theodore Dreiser, *American novelist* (1871–1945)
Marcel Proust, *French author* (1871–1922)
Bertrand Russell, *English philosopher* (1872–1970)
Enrico Caruso, *Italian tenor* (1873–1921)
Chaim Weizmann, *first president of Israel* (1874–1952)

WORLD WAR II (1939–1945)

Axis powers (Germany, Italy, Japan, Hungary, Romania, Bulgaria) *vs.* Allies (U.S., Britain, France, U.S.S.R., Australia, Belgium, Brazil, Canada, China, Denmark, Greece, Netherlands, New Zealand, Norway, Poland, South Africa, Yugoslavia).

1939 Germany invades Poland and annexes Danzig; Britain and France give Hitler ultimatum (**Sept. 1**), declare war (**Sept. 3**). Disabled German pocket battleship Admiral Graf Spee blown up off Montevideo, Uruguay, on Hitler's orders (**Dec. 17**). Limited activity ("Sitzkrieg") on Western Front.

1940 Nazis invade Netherlands, Belgium, and Luxembourg (**May 10**). Chamberlain resigns as Prime Minister; Churchill takes over (**May 10**). Germans cross French frontier (**May 12**) using air/tank/infantry "Blitzkrieg" tactics. Dunkerque evacuation—about 335,000 out of 400,000 Allied soldiers rescued from Belgium by British civilian and naval craft (**May 26-June 3**). Italy declares war on France and Britain; invades France (**June 10**). Germans enter Paris; city undefended (**June 14**). France and Germany sign armistice at Compiègne (**June 22**). Nazis bomb Coventry, England (**Nov. 14**).

1941 Germans launch attacks in Balkans. Yugoslavia surrenders—General Mihajlovic continues guerrilla warfare; Tito leads left-wing guerrillas (**April 17**). Nazi tanks enter Athens; remnants of British Army quit Greece (**April 27**). Hitler attacks Russia (**June 22**). Atlantic Charter—FDR and Churchill agree on war aims (**Aug. 14**). Japanese attacks on Pearl Harbor, Philippines, Guam force U.S. into war; U.S. Pacific fleet crippled (**Dec. 7**). U.S. and Britain declare war on Japan. Germany and Italy declare war on U.S.; Congress declares war on those countries (**Dec. 11**).

1942 British surrender Singapore to Japanese (**Feb. 15**). U.S. forces on Bataan peninsula in Philippines surrender (**April 9**). U.S. and Filipino troops on Corregidor island in Manila Bay surrender to Japanese (**May 6**). Village of Lidice in Czechoslovakia razed by Nazis (**June 10**). U.S. and Britain land in French North Africa (**Nov. 8**).

1943 Casablanca Conference—Churchill and FDR agree on unconditional surrender goal (**Jan. 14–24**). German 6th Army surrenders at Stalingrad—turning point of war in Russia (**Feb. 1–2**). Remnants of Nazis trapped on Cape Bon, ending war in Africa (**May 12**). Mussolini deposed; Badoglio named premier (**July 25**). Allied troops land on Italian mainland after conquest of Sicily (**Sept. 3**). Italy surrenders (**Sept. 8**). Nazis seize Rome (**Sept. 10**). Cairo Conference: FDR, Churchill, Chiang Kai-shek pledge defeat of Japan, free Korea (**Nov. 22–26**). Teheran Conference: FDR, Churchill, Stalin agree on invasion plans (**Nov. 28-Dec. 1**).

1944 U.S. and British troops land at Anzio on west Italian coast and hold beachhead (**Jan. 22**). U.S. and British troops enter Rome (**June 4**). D-Day—Allies launch Normandy invasion (**June 6**). Hitler wounded in bomb plot (**July 20**). Paris liberated (**Aug. 25**). Athens freed by Allies (**Oct. 13**). Americans invade Philippines (**Oct. 20**). Germans launch counteroffensive in Belgium—Battle of Bulge (**Dec. 16**).

1945 Yalta Agreement signed by FDR, Churchill, Stalin—establishes basis for occupation of Germany, returns to Soviet Union lands taken by Germany and Japan; U.S.S.R. agrees to friendship pact with China (**Feb. 11**). Mussolini killed at Lake Como (**April 28**). Admiral Doenitz takes command in Germany; suicide of Hitler announced (**May 1**). Berlin falls (**May 2**). V-E Day—Germany signs unconditional surrender terms at Rheims (**May 7**). Potsdam Conference—Truman, Churchill, Atlee (after **July 28**), Stalin establish council of foreign ministers to prepare peace treaties; plan German postwar government and reparations (**July 17-Aug. 2**). A-bomb blasts Hiroshima (**Aug. 6**). U.S.S.R. declares war on Japan (**Aug. 8**). Nagasaki hit by A-bomb (**Aug. 9**). Japan surrenders (**Aug. 14**). V-J Day—Japanese sign surrender terms aboard battleship *Missouri* (**Sept. 2**).

1942 Declaration of United Nations signed in Washington. Women's military services established. Enrico Fermi achieves nuclear chain reaction. Japanese and persons of Japanese ancestry moved inland from Pacific Coast. Coconut Grove nightclub fire in Boston kills 491.

1943 President freezes prices, salaries, and wages to prevent inflation. Income tax withholding introduced.

1944 G.I. Bill of Rights enacted. Bretton Woods Conference creates International Monetary Fund and World Bank. Dumbarton Oaks Conference—U.S., British Commonwealth, and U.S.S.R. propose establishment of United Nations.

1945 Yalta Conference (Roosevelt, Churchill, Stalin) plans final defeat of Germany **(Feb.)**. San Francisco Conference establishes U.N. **(April-June)**. FDR dies **(April 12)**. Potsdam Conference (Truman, Churchill, Stalin) establishes basis of German reconstruction **(July-Aug)**.

1946 First meeting of U.N. General Assembly opens in London **(Jan. 10)**. League of Nations dissolved **(April)**. Italy abolishes monarchy **(June)**. Verdict in Nuremberg war trial: 12 Nazi leaders (including 1 tried in absentia) sentenced to hang; 7 imprisoned; 3 acquitted **(Oct. 1)**. Goering commits suicide a few hours before 10 other Nazis are executed **(Oct. 15)**. Winston Churchill's "Iron Curtain" speech warns against Soviet expansion. Xerography invented by Chester Carlson.

1947 Britain nationalizes coal mines **(Jan. 1)**. Peace treaties for Italy, Romania, Bulgaria, Hungary, Finland signed in Paris **(Feb. 10)**. Soviet Union rejects U.S. plan for U.N. atomic-energy control **(March 4)**. Truman Doctrine proposed—the first significant U.S. attempt to "contain" communist expansion **(March 12)**. Marshall Plan for European recovery proposed—a coordinated program to help European nations recover from ravages of war **(June)**. (By **1951**, this "European Recovery Program" had cost $11 billion.) India and Pakistan gain independence from Britain **(Aug. 15)**. Cominform (Communist Information Bureau) founded under Soviet auspices to rebuild contacts among European Communist parties, missing since dissolution of Comintern in **1943 (Sept.)**. (Yugoslav party expelled in **1948** and Cominform disbanded in **1956**.)

1948 Gandhi assassinated in New Delhi by Hindu fanatic **(Jan. 30)**. Communists seize power in Czechoslovakia **(Feb. 23–25)**. Burma and Ceylon granted independence by Britain. Organization of American States (OAS) Charter signed at Bogotá, Colombia **(April 30)**. Nation of Israel proclaimed; British end Mandate at midnight; Arab armies attack **(May 14)**. Berlin airlift begins **(June 21)**; ends **May 12, 1949**. Stalin and Tito break **(June 28)**. Independent Republic of Korea is proclaimed, following election supervised by U.N. **(Aug. 15)**. Verdict in Japanese war trial: Tojo and six others sentenced to hang (hanged **Dec. 23**); 18 imprisoned **(Nov. 12)**. United States of Indonesia established as Dutch and Indonesians settle conflict **(Dec. 27)**. Alger Hiss, former U.S. State Department official, indicted on perjury charges after denying passing secret documents to communist spy ring. Convicted in second trial **(1950)** and sentenced to five-year prison term.

1949 Cease-fire in Palestine **(Jan. 7)**. Truman proposes Point Four Program to help world's backward areas **(Jan. 20)**. Israel signs armistice with Egypt **(Feb. 24)**. Start of North Atlantic Treaty Organization (NATO)—treaty signed by 12 nations **(April 4)**. German Federal Republic (West Germany) established **(Sept. 21)**. Truman discloses Soviet Union has set off atomic explosion **(Sept. 23)**. Communist People's Republic of China formally proclaimed **(Oct. 1)**.

1950 Truman orders development of hydrogen bomb **(Jan. 31)**. Korean War *(see special material on the "Korean War")*. Assassination attempt on President Truman by Puerto Rican nationalists **(Nov. 1)**. Brink's robbery in Boston; almost $3 million stolen **(Jan. 17)**.

1951 Six nations agree to Schuman Plan to pool European coal and steel **(March 19)**—in effect **Feb. 10, 1953**. Julius and Ethel Rosenberg sentenced to death for passing atomic secrets to Russians **(March)**. Japanese peace treaty signed in San Francisco by 49 nations **(Sept. 8)**. Color television introduced in U.S.

1952 George VI dies; his daughter becomes Elizabeth II **(Feb. 6)**. NATO

Winston Churchill, *British statesman* (1874–1965)
Gertrude Stein, *American writer* (1874–1946)
Arnold Schönberg, *Austrian composer* (1874–1951)
Guglielmo Marconi, *Italian physicist* (1874–1935)
Thomas Mann, *German novelist* (1875–1955)
C. G. Jung, *Swiss psychiatrist* (1875–1961)
Carl Sandburg, *American poet* (1878–1967)
Martin Buber, *Jewish philosopher* (1878–1965)
Joseph Stalin, *Russian dictator* (1879–1953)
Leon Trotsky, *Russian revolutionist* (1879–1940)
Paul Klee, *Swiss painter* (1879–1940)
Albert Einstein, *German-American physicist* (1879–1955)
Douglas MacArthur, *American general* (1880–1964)
Pablo Picasso, *Spanish-born French painter* (1881–1973)
Béla Bartók, *Hungarian composer* (1881–1945)
Alexander Fleming, *English scientist* (1881–1955)
Franklin D. Roosevelt, *American President* (1882–1945)
Eamon de Valera, *Irish statesman* (1882–1975)
James Joyce, *Irish author* (1882–1941)
Georges Braque, *French painter* (1882–1963)
Igor Stravinsky, *Russian composer* (1882–1971)
Benito Mussolini, *Italian dictator* (1883–1945)
Franz Kafka, *Czechoslovakian-born Austrian author* (1883–1924)
John Maynard Keynes, *English economist* (1883–1946)
Walter Gropius, *German architect* (1883–1969)
Harry S. Truman, *American President* (1884–1972)
Eduard Benes, *Czechoslovakian statesman* (1884–1948)
D. H. Lawrence, *English writer* (1885–1930)

KOREAN WAR (1950–1953)

1950 North Korean Communist forces invade South Korea **(June 25)**. U.N. calls for cease-fire and asks U.N. members to assist South Korea **(June 27)**. Truman orders U.S. forces into Korea **(June 27)**. North Koreans capture Seoul **(June 28)**. Gen. Douglas MacArthur designated commander of unified U.N. forces **(July 8)**. Pusan Beachhead—U.N. forces counterattack and capture Seoul **(Aug.-Sept.)**, capture Pyongyang, North Korean capital **(Oct.)**. Chinese Communists enter war **(Oct. 26)**, force U.N. retreat toward 39th parallel **(Dec.)**.

1951 Gen. Matthew B. Ridgeway replaces MacArthur after he threatens Chinese with massive retaliation **(April 11)**. Armistice negotiations **(July)** continue with interruptions until **June 1953**.

1953 Armistice signed **(June 26)**. Chinese troops withdraw from North Korea **(Oct. 26, 1958)**, but over 200 violations of armistice noted to **1959**.

conference approves European army **(Feb.)**. AEC announces "satisfactory" experiments in hydrogen-weapons research; eyewitnesses tell of blasts near Eniwetok **(Nov.)**.

1953 Gen. Dwight D. Eisenhower inaugurated President of United States **(Jan. 20)**. Stalin dies **(March 5)**. Malenkov becomes Soviet Premier; Beria, Minister of Interior; Molotov, Foreign Minister **(March 6)**. Dag Hammarskjold begins term as U.N. Secretary-General **(April 10)**. Edmund Hillary, of New Zealand, and Tenzing Norkay, of Nepal, reach top of Mt. Everest **(May 29)**. East Berliners rise against Communist rule; quelled by tanks **(June 17)**. Egypt becomes republic ruled by military junta **(June 18)**. Julius and Ethel Rosenberg executed in Sing Sing prison **(June 19)**. Korean armistice signed **(July 27)**. Moscow announces explosion of hydrogen bomb **(Aug. 20)**.

1954 First atomic submarine *Nautilus*, launched **(Jan. 21)**. Five U.S. Congressmen shot on floor of House as Puerto Rican nationalists fire from spectators' gallery; all five recover **(March 1)**. Army *vs.* McCarthy inquiry—Senate subcommittee report blames both sides **(Apr. 22-June 17)**. Dien Bien Phu, French military outpost in Vietnam, falls to Vietminh army **(May 7)**. *(See* special material on the "Vietnam War.") U.S. Supreme Court (in *Brown* v. *Board of Education of Topeka*) unanimously bans racial segregation in public schools **(May 17)**. Eisenhower launches world atomic pool without Soviet Union **(Sept. 6)**. Eight-nation Southeast Asia defense treaty (SEATO) signed at Manila **(Sept. 8)**. West Germany is granted sovereignty, admitted to NATO and Western European Union **(Oct. 23)**. Dr. Jonas Salk starts innoculating children against polio. Algerian War of Independence against France begins **(Nov.)**; France struggles to maintain colonial rule until 1962 when it agrees to Algeria's independence.

1955 Nikolai A. Bulganin becomes Soviet Premier, replacing Malenkov **(Feb. 8)**. Churchill resigns; Anthony Eden succeeds him **(April 6)**. Federal Republic of West Germany becomes a sovereign state **(May 5)**. Warsaw Pact, east European mutual defense agreement, signed **(May 14)**. Argentina ousts Perón **(Sept. 19)**. President Eisenhower suffers coronary thrombosis in Denver **(Sept. 24)**. Martin Luther King, Jr., leads black boycott of Montgomery, Ala., bus system **(Dec. 1)**; desegregated service begun **(Dec. 21)**. AFL and CIO become one organization—AFL-CIO **(Dec. 5)**.

1956 Nikita Khrushchev, First Secretary of U.S.S.R. Communist Party, denounces Stalin's excesses **(Feb. 24)**. First aerial H-bomb tested over Namu islet, Bikini Atoll—10 million tons TNT equivalent **(May 21)**. Worker's uprising against Communist rule in Poznan, Poland, is crushed **(June 28–30)**. Egypt takes control of Suez Canal **(July 26)**. Israel launches attack

Ezra Pound, *American poet* (1885–1972)
Sinclair Lewis, *American novelist* (1885–1951)
Alban Berg, *Austrian composer* (1885–1935)
Niels Bohr, *Danish physicist* (1885–1962)
David Ben-Gurion, *Israeli statesman* (1886–1973)
Chiang Kai-shek, *Chinese statesman* (1887–1975)
Le Corbusier (C.E. Jeanneret), *Swiss-born French architect* (1887–1965)
T. S. Eliot, *Anglo-American poet* (1888–1965)
Eugene O'Neill, *American dramatist* (1888–1953)
Ludwig Wittgenstein, *Austrian philosopher* (1889–1951)
Adolf Hitler, *German dictator* (1889–1945)
Charles Chaplin, *English screen actor-director* (1889–1977)
Dwight D. Eisenhower, *American President* (1890–1969)
Charles de Gaulle, *French soldier and statesman* (1890–1970)
Sergei Prokofiev, *Russian composer* (1891–1953)
Frederick Banting, *Canadian discoverer of insulin* (1891–1941)

VIETNAM WAR (1950–1975)

U.S., South Vietnam, and Allies versus North Vietnam and National Liberation Front (Viet Cong). Outstanding events:

1950 President Truman sends 35-man military advisory group to aid French fighting to maintain colonial power in Vietnam.

1954 After defeat of French at Dienbienphu, Geneva Agreements **(July)** provide for withdrawal of French and Vietminh to either side of demarcation zone (DMZ) pending reunification elections, which are never held. Presidents Eisenhower and Kennedy (from **1954** onward) send civilian advisors and, later, military personnel to train South Vietnamese.

1960 Communists form National Liberation Front in South.

1963 Ngo Dinh Diem, South Vietnam's premier, slain in coup **(Nov. 1)**.

1961–1963 U.S. military advisors rise from 2,000 to 15,000.

1964 North Vietnamese torpedo boats reportedly attack U.S. destroyers in Gulf of Tonkin **(Aug. 2)**. President Johnson orders retaliatory air strikes. Congress approves Gulf of Tonkin resolution **(Aug. 7)** authorizing President to take necessary steps to "maintain peace."

1965 U.S. planes begin combat missions over South Vietnam. In **June**, 23,000 American advisors committed to combat. By end of year over 184,000 U.S. troops in area.

1966 B-52s bomb DMZ, reportedly used by North Vietnam for entry into South **(July 31)**.

1967 South Vietnam National Assembly approves election of Nguyen Van Thieu as President **(Oct. 21)**.

1968 U.S. has almost 525,000 men in Vietnam. In Tet offensive **(Jan.-Feb.)**, Viet Cong guerrillas attack Saigon, Hue, and some provincial capitals. President Johnson orders halt to U.S. bombardment of North Vietnam **(Oct. 31)**. Saigon and N.L.F. join U.S. and North Vietnam in Paris peace talks.

1969 President Nixon announces Vietnam peace offer **(May 14)**—begins troop withdrawals **(June)**. Viet Cong forms Provisional Revolutionary Government. U.S. Senate calls for curb on commitments **(June 25)**. Ho Chi Minh, 79, North Vietnam president, dies **(Sept. 3)**; collective leadership chosen. Some 6,000 U.S. troops pulled back from Thailand and 1,000 marines from Vietnam (announced **Sept. 30**). Massive demonstrations in U.S. protest or support war policies **(Oct. 15)**.

1970 Nixon announces sending of troops to Cambodia **(April 30)**. Last U.S. troops removed from Cambodia **(June 29)**.

1971 Congress bars use of combat troops, but not air power, in Laos and Cambodia **(Jan. 1)**. South Vietnamese troops, with U.S. air cover, fail in Laos thrust. Many American ground forces withdrawn from Vietnam combat. *New York Times* publishes Pentagon papers, classified material on expansion of war **(June)**.

1972 Nixon responds to North Vietnamese drive across DMZ by ordering mining of North Vietnam ports and heavy bombing of Hanoi-Haiphong area **(April 1)**. Nixon orders "Christmas bombing" of north to get North Vietnamese back to conference table **(Dec.)**.

1973 President orders halt to offensive operations in North Vietnam **(Jan. 15)**. Representatives of North and South Vietnam, U.S., and N.L.F. sign peace pacts in Paris, ending longest war in U.S. history **(Jan. 27)**.

1974 Both sides accuse each other of frequent violations of cease-fire agreement.

1975 Full-scale warfare resumes. Communists victorious **(April 30)**. South Vietnam Premier Nguyen Van Thieu resigns **(April 21)**. American troops evacuated **(April 30)**. More than 140,000 Vietnamese refugees leave by air and sea, many to settle in U.S. Provisional Revolutionary Government takes control **(June 6)**.

1976 Election of National Assembly paves way for reunification of North and South.

on Egypt's Sinai peninsula and drives toward Suez Canal **(Oct. 29)**. British and French invade Egypt at Port Said **(Nov. 5)**. Cease-fire forced by U.S. pressure stops British, French, and Israeli advance **(Nov. 6)**. Revolt starts in Hungary—Soviet troops and tanks crush anti-Communist rebellion **(Nov.)**.

1957 Eisenhower Doctrine calls for aid to Mideast countries which resist armed aggression from Communist-controlled nations **(Jan. 5)**. Eisenhower sends troops to Little Rock, Ark., to quell mob and protect school integration **(Sept. 24)**. Russians launch *Sputnik I*, first earth-orbiting satellite—the Space Age begins **(Oct. 4)**.

1958 Army's Jupiter-C rocket fires first U.S. earth satellite, *Explorer I*, into orbit **(Jan. 31)**. Egypt and Syria merge into United Arab Republic **(Feb. 1)**. European Economic Community (Common Market) established by Rome Treaty becomes effective **Jan. 1, 1958**. Khrushchev becomes Premier of Soviet Union as Bulganin resigns **(Mar. 27)**. Gen. Charles de Gaulle becomes French premier **(June 1)**, remaining in power until **1969**. New French constitution adopted **(Sept. 28)**, de Gaulle elected president of 5th Republic **(Dec. 21)**. Eisenhower orders U.S. Marines into Lebanon at request of President Chamoun, who fears overthrow **(July 15)**.

1959 Cuban President Batista resigns and flees—Castro takes over **(Jan. 1)**. Tibet's Dalai Lama escapes to India **(Mar. 31)**. St. Lawrence Seaway opens, allowing ocean ships to reach Midwest **(April 25)**.

1960 American U-2 spy plane, piloted by Francis Gary Powers, shot down over Russia **(May 5)**. Khrushchev kills Paris summit conference because of U-2 **(May 16)**. Powers sentenced to prison for 10 years **(Aug. 19)**—freed in **February 1962** in exchange for Soviet spy. Top Nazi murderer of Jews, Adolf Eichmann, captured by Israelis in Argentina **(May 23)**—executed in Israel in **1962**. Communist China and Soviet Union split in conflict over Communist ideology. Belgium starts to break up its African colonial empire, gives independence to Belgian Congo (Zaire) on **June 30**. Cuba begins confiscation of $770 million of U.S. property **(Aug. 7)**.

1961 U.S. breaks diplomatic relations with Cuba **(Jan. 3)**. John F. Kennedy inaugurated President of U.S. **(Jan. 20)**. Kennedy proposes Alliance for Progress—10-year plan to raise Latin American living standards **(Mar. 13)**. Moscow announces putting first man in orbit around earth, Maj. Yuri A. Gagarin **(April 12)**. Cuba invaded at Bay of Pigs by an estimated 1,200 anti-Castro exiles aided by U.S.; invasion crushed **(April 17)**. First U.S. spaceman, Navy Cmdr. Alan B. Shepard, Jr., rockets 116.5 miles up in 302-mile trip **(May 5)**. Virgil Grissom becomes second American astronaut, making 118-mile-high, 303-mile-long rocket flight over Atlantic **(July 21)**. Gherman Stepanovich Titov is launched in Soviet spaceship *Vostok II;* makes 17½ orbits in 25 hours, covering 434,960 miles before landing safely **(Aug. 6)**. East Germans erect Berlin Wall between East and West Berlin to halt flood of refugees **(Aug. 13)**. U.S.S.R. fires 50-megaton hydrogen bomb, biggest explosion in history **(Oct. 29)**.

1962 Lt. Col. John H. Glenn, Jr., is first American to orbit earth—three times in 4 hr 55 min **(Feb. 20)**. Adolf Eichmann hanged in Israel for his part in Nazi extermination of six million Jews **(May 31)**. France transfers sovereignty to new republic of Algeria **(July 3)**. Cuban missile crisis—U.S.S.R. to build missile bases in Cuba; Kennedy orders Cuban blockade, lifts blockade after Russians back down **(Aug.-Nov.)**. James H. Meredith, escorted by Federal marshals, registers in University of Mississippi **(Oct. 1)**. Pope John XXIII opens Second Vatican Council **(Oct. 11)**—Council holds four sessions, finally closing Dec. 8, 1965. Cuba releases 1,113 prisoners of 1961 invasion attempt **(Dec. 24)**.

1963 France and West Germany sign treaty of cooperation ending four centuries of conflict **(Jan. 22)**. Pope John XXIII dies **(June 3)**—succeeded June 21 by Cardinal Montini, who becomes Paul VI. U.S. Supreme Court rules no locality may require recitation of Lord's Prayer or Bible verses in public schools **(June 17)**. Civil rights rally held by 200,000 blacks and whites in Washington, D.C. **(Aug. 28)**. Washington-to-Moscow "hot line" communications link opens, designed to reduce risk of accidental war **(Aug. 30)**. President Kennedy shot and killed by sniper in Dallas, Tex. Lyndon B. Johnson becomes President same day **(Nov. 22)**. Lee Harvey Oswald, accused assassin of President Kennedy, is shot and killed by Jack Ruby, Dallas nightclub owner **(Nov. 24)**.

1964 U.S. Supreme Court rules that Congressional districts should be roughly equal in population **(Feb. 17)**. Jack Ruby convicted of murder in slaying of Lee Harvey Oswald; sentenced to death by Dallas jury **(March 14)** —conviction reversed **Oct. 5, 1966**; Ruby dies **Jan. 3, 1967**, before second trial can be held. Three civil rights workers—Schwerner, Goodman, and Cheney—murdered in Mississippi **(June)**. Twenty-one arrests result in trial and conviction of seven by Federal jury. President's Commission on the Assassination of President Kennedy issues Warren Report con-

Tito (Josip Broz), *Yugoslavian President* (1892–1980)
Haile Selassie, *Ethiopian emperor* (1892–1975)
Hermann Goering, *Nazi leader* (1893–1946)
Mao Zedong, *Chinese Communist leader* (1893–1976)
Nikita Khrushchev, *Russian leader* (1894–1971)
Martha Graham, *American dancer* (1894–)
Paul Hindemith, *German-American composer* (1895–1963)
Bertolt Brecht, *German dramatist* (1898–1956)
Ernest Hemingway, *American author* (1898–1961)
Federico García Lorca, *Spanish author* (1899–1936)
Francis Poulenc, *French composer* (1899–1963)
Kurt Weill, *German-American composer* (1900–1950)
Aaron Copland, *American composer* (1900–)
Werner Heisenberg, *German physicist* (1901–)
Walt Disney, *American cartoonist* (1901–1966)
Enrico Fermi, *Italian-American physicist* (1901–1954)
John Steinbeck, *American novelist* (1902–1968)
Dmitri Shostakovich, *Russian composer* (1906–1975)
W. H. Auden, *English poet* (1907–1973)
Albert Camus, *French author* (1913–1960)
John F. Kennedy, *American President* (1917–1963)

cluding that Lee Harvey Oswald acted alone.

1965 Rev. Dr. Martin Luther King, Jr., and more than 2,600 other blacks arrested in Selma, Ala., during three-day demonstrations against voter-registration rules **(Feb. 1)**. Malcolm X, black-nationalist leader, shot to death at Harlem rally in New York City **(Feb. 21)**. U.S. Marines land in Dominican Republic as fighting persists between rebels and Dominican army **(April 28)**. Medicare, senior citizens' government medical assistance program, begins **(July 1)**. Blacks riot for six days in Watts section of Los Angeles: 34 dead, over 1,000 injured, nearly 4,000 arrested, fire damage put at $175 million **(Aug. 11–16)**. Power failure in Ontario plant blacks out parts of eight northeastern states of U.S. and two provinces of southeastern Canada **(Nov. 9)**.

1966 Black teen-agers riot in Watts, Los Angeles; two men killed and at least 25 injured **(March 15)**. Michael E. De Bakey implants artificial heart in human for first time at Houston hospital; plastic device functions and patient lives **(April 21)**.

1967 Three Apollo astronauts—Col. Virgil I. Grissom, Col. Edward White II, and Lt. Cmdr. Roger B. Chaffee—killed in spacecraft fire during simulated launch **(Jan. 27)**. Israeli and Arab forces battle; six-day war ends with Israel occupying Sinai Peninsula, Golan Heights, Gaza Strip, and east bank of Suez Canal **(June 5)**. Red China announces explosion of its first hydrogen bomb **(June 17)**. Racial violence in Detroit; 7,000 National Guardsmen aid police after night of rioting. Similar outbreaks occur in New York City's Spanish Harlem, Rochester, N.Y., Birmingham, Ala., and New Britain, Conn. **(July 23)**. Thurgood Marshall sworn in as first black U.S. Supreme Court justice **(Oct. 2)**. Dr. Christiaan N. Barnard and team of South African surgeons perform world's first successful human heart transplant **(Dec. 3)**—patient dies 18 days later.

1968 North Korea seizes U.S. Navy ship *Pueblo;* holds 83 on board as spies **(Jan. 23)**. President Johnson announces he will not seek or accept presidential renomination **(March 31)**. Martin Luther King, Jr., civil rights leader, is slain in Memphis **(April 4)**—James Earl Ray, indicted in murder, captured in London on **June 8**. In **1969** Ray pleads guilty and is sentenced to 99 years. Sen. Robert F. Kennedy is shot and critically wounded in Los Angeles hotel after winning California primary **(June 5)**—dies **June 6**. Sirhan B. Sirhan convicted **1969**. Czechoslovakia is invaded by Russians and Warsaw Pact forces to crush liberal regime **(Aug. 20)**.

1969 Richard M. Nixon is inaugurated 37th President of the U.S. **(Jan. 20)**. Apollo 11 astronauts—Neil A. Armstrong, Edwin E. Aldrin, Jr., and Michael Collins—take man's first walk on moon **(July 20)**. Sen. Edward M. Kennedy pleads guilty to leaving scene of fatal accident at Chappaquiddick, Mass. **(July 18)** in which Mary Jo Kopechne was drowned—gets two-month suspended sentence **(July 25)**.

1970 Biafra surrenders after 32-month fight for independence from Nigeria **(Jan. 12)**. Rhodesia severs last tie with British Crown and declares itself a racially segregated republic **(March 1)**. Four students at Kent State University in Ohio slain by National Guardsmen at demonstration protesting April 30 incursion into Cambodia **(May 4)**. Senate repeals Gulf of Tonkin resolution **(June 24)**.

1971 Supreme Court rules unanimously that busing of students may be ordered to achieve racial desegregation **(April 20)**. Anti-war militants attempt to disrupt government business in Washington **(May 3)**—police and military units arrest as many as 12,000; most are later released. Twenty-sixth Amendment to U.S. Constitution lowers voting age to 18. U.N. seats Communist China and expels Nationalist China **(Oct. 25)**.

1972 President Nixon makes unprecedented eight-day visit to Communist China **(Feb.)**. Britain takes over direct rule of Northern Ireland in bid for peace **(March 24)**. Okinawa reverts to Japan after 27 years of U.S. rule **(May 14)**. Gov. George C. Wallace of Alabama is shot by Arthur H. Bremer at Laurel, Md., political rally **(May 15)**—Wallace paralyzed for life from the waist down. Bremer is sentenced to 63 years in prison on **Aug. 4**. Five men are apprehended by police in attempt to bug Democratic National Committee headquarters in Washington D.C.'s Watergate complex—start of the Watergate scandal **(June 17)**. Supreme Court rules that death penalty is unconstitutional **(June 29)**. Bobby Fischer becomes first American world chess champion, defeating Boris Spassky of U.S.S.R. **(Sept. 1)**. Eleven Israeli athletes at Olympic Games in Munich are killed after eight members of an Arab terrorist group invade Olympic Village; five guerrillas and one policeman are also killed **(Sept. 5)**.

1973 Great Britain, Ireland, and Denmark enter European Common Market **(Jan. 1)**. Indians hold 10 hostages after seizing settlement of Wounded Knee, S.D., demand Government discuss their grievances **(Feb. 28)**—surrender on **May 9**. Nixon, on national TV, accepts responsibility, but not blame, for Watergate; accepts resignations of advisers H. R. Haldeman and John D. Ehrlichman, fires John W. Dean III as counsel. **(April 30)**. Greek military junta abolishes monarchy and proclaims republic **(June 1)**. U.S. bombing of Cambodia ends, marking official halt to 12 years of combat activity in Southeast Asia **(Aug. 15)**. Violent military coup in Chile deposes President Salvador Allende Gossens, who reportedly commits suicide **(Sept. 11)**. Fourth and biggest Arab-Israeli War begins as Egyptian and Syrian forces attack Israel as Jews mark Yom Kippur, holiest day in their calendar. **(Oct. 6)**. Spiro T. Agnew resigns as Vice President and then, in Federal Court in Baltimore, pleads no contest to charges of evasion of income taxes on $29,500 he received in 1967 while Governor of Maryland. He is fined $10,000 and put on three years' probation **(Oct. 10)**. In the "Saturday Night Massacre," Nixon fires special Watergate prosecutor Archibald Cox and Deputy Attorney General William D. Ruckelshaus; Attorney General Elliot L. Richardson resigns **(Oct. 20)**. Egypt and Israel sign U.S.-sponsored cease-fire accord **(Nov. 11)**.

1974 Patricia Hearst, 19-year-old daughter of publisher Randolph Hearst, kidnapped by Symbionese Liberation Army. **(Feb. 5)**—Bloodless coup restores Portuguese democracy **(April 25)**. House Judiciary Committee adopts three articles of impeachment charging President Nixon with obstruction of justice, failure to uphold laws, and refusal to produce material subpoenaed by the committee **(July 30)**. Richard M. Nixon announces he will resign the next day, the first President to do so **(Aug. 8)**. Vice President Gerald R. Ford of Michigan is sworn in as 38th President of the U.S. **(Aug. 9)**. Ford grants "full, free, and absolute pardon" to ex-President Nixon **(Sept. 8)**.

1975 John N. Mitchell, H. R. Haldeman, John D. Ehrlichman, and Robert C. Mardian found guilty of Watergate cover-up. Mitchell, Haldeman, and Ehrlichman are sentenced on Feb. 21 to 30 months-8 years in jail and Mardian to 10 months-3 years **(Jan. 1)**. American merchant ship *Mayaguez*, seized by Cambodian forces, is rescued in operation by U.S. Navy and Marines, 38 of whom are killed **(May 15)**. Suez Canal reopens after eight years **(June 5)**. *Apollo* and *Soyuz* spacecraft take off for U.S.-Soviet link-up in space **(July 15)**. Federal jury clears Gov. James A. Rhodes of Ohio; Robert J. White, former Kent State University President, and 27 Ohio National Guardsmen in $46-million damage suit brought by 9 wounded students and parents of 4 slain on campus in **1970 (Aug. 27)**. President Ford escapes assassination attempt in Sacramento, Calif., **(Sept. 5)**. Patricia Hearst apprehended by FBI. **(Sept. 18)**. President Ford escapes second assassination attempt in 17 days. **(Sept. 22)**.

1976 Palestine Liberation Organization seated at U.N. **(Jan 13)**. U.S. and Spain sign five-year treaty of friendship and cooperation **(Jan. 25)**. Supreme Court rules that blacks and other minorities are entitled to retroactive job seniority **(March 24)**. Senate Select Intelligence Committee reports that FBI, CIA, Army intelligence, and other agencies illegally investigated citizen groups, makes sweeping recommendations to control intelligence community **(April 28)**. Ford signs Federal Election Campaign Act **(May 11)**. Many killed and wounded when South African police fire on students in Soweto, near Johannesburg, largest black urban center in country **(June 16)**. Francis E. Meloy, Jr., U.S. Ambassador to Lebanon, assassinated in Beirut; all Americans advised to leave country as civil war continues; deaths exceed 30,000 **(June 17)**. Supreme Court rules that death penalty is not inherently cruel or unusual and is a constitutionally acceptable form of punishment **(July 3)**. Nation celebrates Bicentennial **(July 4)**. Israeli airborne commandos attack Uganda's Entebbe Airport and free 103 hostages held by pro-Palestinian hijackers of Air France plane; one Israeli and several Ugandan soldiers killed in raid **(July 4)**. New York disbars ex-President Nixon **(July 8)**. Britain's Ambassador to Ireland and aide are killed when land mine explodes under their car in Dublin **(July 22)**. Mysterious disease that eventually claims 29 lives strikes American Legion convention in Philadelphia **(Aug. 4)**. Prince Bernhard of The Netherlands, caught up in Lockheed Aircraft bribery scandal, resigns all military and business posts **(Aug. 26)**. Supreme Court lifts stay on death penalties **(Oct. 4)**. Jimmy Carter elected U.S. President **(Nov. 2)**. Chinese explode atmospheric nuclear device; fallout over U.S. **(Nov. 17)**.

1977 First woman Episcopal priest ordained **(Jan. 1)**. Scientists identify previously unknown bacterium as cause of mysterious "legionnaire's disease" **(Jan. 18)**. Astronomers discover water outside of Earth's galaxy, indicating possibility of life in outer space **(Jan. 19)**. New Chinese Government allows films, plays, and artists previously banned by Cultural Revolution **(Jan. 21)**. Carter pardons Vietnam draft evaders **(Jan. 21)**. TV adaptation of *Roots* has total of 130 million viewers, breaking all records **(Jan. 30)**. Supreme Court upholds use of racial quotas in state reapportionment plans **(March 1)**. U.S. extends its control of the seas to 200-mile limit **(March**

1). NASA reports planet Uranus has five rings **(March 30)**. Spain legalizes Communist Party after 38-year ban **(April 9)**. Israeli Labor Government defeated in general election by "hawkish" Likud Party **(May 17)**. Scientists report using bacteria in lab to make insulin **(May 23)**. Lockheed under-the-table payments to foreign nationals to win aircraft contracts revealed to reach $38 million **(May 26)**. Tongsun Park identified as Korean agent who allegedly spent millions to influence U.S. officials **(June 4)**. Soviets charge Anatoly Shcharansky, Jewish human-rights activist, with treason **(June 4)**. Laetrile found useless as cancer cure **(June 15)**. Supreme Court rules that states are not required to spend Medicaid funds on elective abortions **(June 20)**. Deng Xiaoping, purged Chinese leader, restored to power as "Gang of Four" is expelled from Communist Party **(July 22)**. First oil from Alaska's Prudhoe Bay fields pours from 799-mile pipeline at ice-free port of Valdez **(July 28)**. U.S. and Cuban Missions open as significant step to restore official relations **(Sept. 1)**. Tongsun Park charged by U.S. Justice Department with influence-buying **(Sept. 8)**. Nuclear-proliferation pact, curbing spread of nuclear weapons, signed by 15 countries, including U.S. and U.S.S.R. **(Sept. 21)**. Thirty-eight persons killed as earthen dam at Toccoa, Ga., collapses during heavy rains **(Nov. 6)**. Vatican and Italy agree on accord replacing 1929 concordat; Roman Catholicism no longer state religion **(Nov. 7)**. Inquiry into prison death of Steven Biko, black leader, absolves South African security police; U.S. State Department expresses shock **(Dec. 2)**. Carter names G. William Miller to replace Arthur F. Burns as Federal Reserve Board Chairman **(Dec. 28)**.

1978 Crown of St. Stephen, symbol of sovereignty, returned to Hungary from U.S. **(Jan. 6)**. President chooses Federal Appeals Court Judge William H. Webster as FBI director **(Jan. 19)**. Soviet spy satellite with atomic reactor breaks up over northwest Canada **(Jan. 24)**; signs of radiation found **(Jan. 28)**. Rhodesia's Prime Minister Ian D. Smith and three black leaders agree on transfer to black majority rule **(Feb. 15)**. Soviet revokes citizenship of expatriate cellist-conductor Mstislav Rostropovich and wife, singer Galina Vishnevskaya **(March 15)**. Former Italian Premier Aldo Moro kidnapped by left-wing terrorists, who kill five bodyguards **(March 16)**; he is found slain **(May 9)**. U.S. Senate approves Panama Canal neutrality treaty **(March 16)**; votes treaty to turn canal over to Panama by year 2000 **(April 18)**. *Holocaust*, four-night TV dramatization of Nazi extermination of Jews, viewed by 120 million in nation **(April 20)**. Supreme Court upholds corporate spending in elections under constitutional right of free speech **(April 26)**. All 51 construction workers killed in collapse of power plant cooling tower under construction at St. Mary's, W. Va. **(April 27)**. David Berkowitz pleads guilty and gets 25 years to life in each of New York's six "Son of Sam" killings **(May 8)**. New 15-cent first-class postage rate takes effect **(May 28)**. Californians in referendum approve Proposition 13 for nearly 60% slash in property tax revenues **(June 6)**. Mormon Church ends ban on blacks **(June 9)**. Supreme Court, in Bakke case, bars quota system in college admissions, but affirms constitutionality of programs giving advantage to minorities **(June 28)**; Justices support affirmative action to remedy past discrimination in employment **(July 3)**. Baby girl born in England from egg fertilized outside womb in what is believed world's first such case **(July 26)**. *New York Times* reporter, M.A. Farber, jailed after losing fight against turning over files in New Jersey murder case; paper fined $5,000 a day **(Aug. 4)**; Farber released after 27 days in jail as Jersey Supreme Court suspends contempt citation against him and the *Times* **(Aug. 30)**. Pope Paul VI, dead at 80, mourned **(Aug. 6)**; new Pope, John Paul I, 65, dies unexpectedly after 34 days in office **(Sept. 28)**; succeeded by Karol Cardinal Wojtyla of Poland as John Paul II **(Oct. 16)**. William and Emily Harris plead guilty in Symbionese Liberation Army kidnapping of Patricia Hearst **(Aug. 31)**. "Framework for Peace" in Middle East signed by Egypt's President Anwar el-Sadat and Israeli Premier Menachem Begin after 13-day conference at Camp David led by President Carter **(Sept. 17)**. Senate extends deadline for equal rights amendment ratification until June 30, 1982 **(Oct. 8)**. Exodus of Vietnam refugees in small boats hits record; thousands perish at sea **(Nov. 7)**. Republicans score gains in Congressional and state elections; Democrats retain political domination **(Nov. 8)**. Carter signs energy act including provision to spur conversion from oil and gas to coal **(Nov. 9)**. 911 in cult die in mass murder-suicide in Guyanan jungle after California Congressman and four others perish in ambush **(Nov. 20)**. Coastal States Gas Corp. reports pact for first oil imports from Communist China **(Nov. 21)**. San Francisco Mayor and a city supervisor slain **(Nov. 27)**. Former supervisor convicted **(May 21, 1979)**. U.S. and China agree to begin diplomatic relations; Carter reassures Taiwan **(Dec. 15)**. Oregon man acquitted of raping wife in nation's first such trial **(Dec. 27)**.

1979 Oil spills pollute ocean waters in Atlantic and Gulf of Mexico (**Jan. 1, June 8, July 21**). Ohio agrees to pay $675,000 to families of dead and injured in Kent State University shootings (**Jan. 4**). Vietnam and Cambodian insurgents it backs announce fall of Phnom Penh, Cambodian capital, and collapse of Pol Pot regime (**Jan. 7**). Shah leaves Iran after year of turmoil (**Jan. 16**); revolutionary forces under Moslem leader, Ayatollah Ruhollah Khomeini, take over (**Feb. 1, et seq.**). Pope John Paul II acclaimed on visit to Latin America (**Jan 25–31**). Senior Deputy Prime Minister of China, Deng Xiaoping, acclaimed on visit to U.S.; confers with President Carter (**Jan. 28-Feb. 5**). Patricia Hearst, convicted in bank robbery, freed from Federal penitentiary under clemency order (**Feb. 2**). Chinese invade Vietnam (**Feb. 18**); withdraw troops (**March 5**); report 20,000 casualties, with probably 5,000 deaths (**May 2**). Total eclipse of sun viewed in U.S. (**Feb. 26**). Six Common Market countries develop monetary system to encourage trade and investment (**March 13**). Boston Symphony plays and teaches in China (**March 13–19**). Conservatives win British election; Margaret Thatcher new Prime Minister (**March 28**). Nuclear power plant accident at Three Mile Island, Pa., releases radioactivity (**March 28**). Jane M. Byrne elected Mayor of Chicago after defeating Democratic machine (**April 3**). Former Prime Minister Zulfikar Ali Bhutto hanged in Pakistan (**April 4**). Government bans interstate shipment of aerosol propellants (**April 15**). Supreme Court backs Federal bugging powers (**April 18**). Los Angeles court orders Lee Marvin to pay $104,000 to singer with whom actor lived out of wedlock for six years (**April 18**). Bishop Abel T. Muzorewa wins interracial Rhodesia election (**April 24**). Gasoline shortage spreads across nation; many states adopt odd-even rationing (**May 10, et seq.**). Harvard toughens graduation standards with new "core curriculum" (**May 15**). Baseball umpires win new contract after strike (**May 18**). Crash of American Airlines DC-10 jetliner kills 275 at Chicago (**May 25**); U.S. Grounds DC-10s indefinitely (**June 6**); FAA lifts ban (**June 19**) and orders stringent inspections (**July 13**). Florida executes John Arthur Spenkelink, 30, for murder after pleas fail, first involuntary execution in nation since 1967 (**May 25**). Millions cheer Pope on triumphal visit to native Poland (**June 2–10**). Carter offers $18.2-billion health plan for poor and elderly (**June 12**). Carter and Brezhnev sign SALT II agreement (**June 14**). Supreme Court upholds Federal ban on controversial cancer drug laetrile (**June 18**). Nationwide truckers' protest halts 40% of major carriers' hauling capacity (**June 21**). Jeremy Thorpe, former British Liberal Party leader, acquitted in London of plotting to murder alleged former homosexual lover (**June 22**). Supreme Court upholds preference for blacks in jobs (**June 27**). China signs three-year trade treaty with U.S. (**July 7**). President's energy address calls for conservation and increases in oil and gas production (**July 15**). Carter shakes up Cabinet and White House staff (**July 17**). House committee finds conspiracy in John Kennedy assassination (**July 17**). Nicaraguan President Gen. Anastasio Somoza Debayle resigns and flees to Miami (**July 17**); Sandinists form government (**July 19**). Congress votes international trade liberalization (**July 23**). Andrew Young resigns as U.N. delegate from U.S. after reprimand for unauthorized talks with P.L.O. (**Aug 15**). Carter lifts controls on price of domestic crude oil (**Aug. 17**). Diana Nyad, 30, swims from Bahamas to Florida (**Aug. 20**). Earl Mountbatten of Burma, 79, British World War II hero, and three others killed by blast on fishing boat off Irish coast (**Aug. 27**); two I.R.A. members accused (**Aug. 30**). Hurricane David takes heavy death toll in Caribbean; thousands injured and homeless (**Aug. 30**). Spacecraft *Pioneer II* gets first close photos of Saturn (**Sept. 1**). Carter decides on mobile missile system, MX (**Sept. 7**). Worst smog in 24 years hits Southern California (**Sept. 14**). U.S. drops moves to suppress article that it says reveals H-bomb secrets (**Sept. 17**). British and French wind up Concorde production (**Sept. 21**). Carter approves controversial Tellico hydroelectric dam on Little Tennessee River (**Sept. 25**). Vietnamese start offensive against Pol Pot regime in Cambodia (**Sept. 25**). Thousands cheer Pope on visit to Ireland and U.S. (**Sept. 29-Oct. 7**). Congress approves Carter proposal for new Department of Education (**Sept. 27**). Carter announces response to Soviet troops in Cuba; reports Russian assurance force has no combat function (**Oct. 1**). Chilean Supreme Court bars extradition of three indicted in U.S. for planning murder of Chilean exile leader (**Oct. 1**). W. A. Boyle, 78, former UMW president, again sentenced to life after new trial in Yablonski killings (**Oct. 11**). Senate votes to denounce Senator Herman E. Talmadge of Georgia on expense account and campaign fund charges (**Oct. 11**).

(For later events, *See* Current Events, 1979–80, in Table of Contents.)

WORLD STATISTICS

Area and Population by Country

Estimated Mid-1980

Country	Area[1]	Population
ghanistan	251,000	15,875,000
bania	11,100	2,730,000
geria	919,951	19,750,000
dorra	175	30,000
gola	481,350	7,100,000
gentina	1,972,067	27,070,000
stralia	2,967,909	14,600,000
stria	32,375	7,500,000
hamas	4,404	225,000
hrain	240	300,000
ngladesh	55,126	87,650,000
rbados	166	250,000
lgium	11,781	9,860,000
nin	43,483	3,560,000
utan	19,305	1,300,000
livia	424,162	5,580,000
tswana	222,000	775,000
azil	3,286,470	122,000,000
lgaria	42,823	9,000,000
rma	261,789	33,620,000
rundi	10,747	4,500,000
mbodia	70,000	8,800,000
meroon	183,569	8,400,000
nada	3,851,809	23,850,000
pe Verde	1,557	320,000
ntral African Republic	241,313	2,500,000
ad	495,752	4,530,000
ile	286,396	11,150,000
ina, People's Republic of[2]	3,691,521	957,000,000
ina, Republic of[3]	13,592	17,750,000
lombia	455,355	27,600,000
moros	692	330,000
ngo	132,046	1,550,000
sta Rica	19,652	2,210,000
ba	44,218	9,950,000
prus	3,572	625,000
echoslovakia	49,374	15,360,000
nmark[4]	16,615	5,140,000
ibouti	8,996	325,000
minica	300	85,000
minican Republic	18,704	5,450,000
uador	105,685	8,350,000
ypt	386,872	42,000,000
Salvador	8,260	4,750,000
uatorial Guinea	10,830	370,000
hiopia	457,142	31,100,000
i	7,055	620,000
nland	130,119	4,770,000
ance	212,973	53,680,000
bon	102,317	550,000
mbia	4,016	595,000
rmany, East[5]	40,646	16,720,000
rmany, West[6]	95,815	61,350,000
ana	92,100	11,680,000
eece	50,547	9,510,000
enada	133	100,000
atemala	42,042	7,250,000
inea	94,925	5,000,000
inea-Bissau	13,948	570,000
yana	83,000	860,000
iti	10,714	5,000,000
nduras	43,277	3,680,000
ngary	35,919	10,720,000
Iceland	39,702	230,000
India[7]	1,229,737	663,600,000
Indonesia[8]	735,268	151,880,000
Iran	636,363	38,000,000
Iraq	172,000	13,230,000
Ireland	26,600	3,400,000
Israel	7,992[9]	3,870,000
Italy	116,304	57,100,000
Ivory Coast	124,502	8,250,000
Jamaica	4,411	2,200,000
Japan	143,574	116,900,000
Jordan	37,297	3,200,000
Kenya	224,960	15,800,000
Kiribati	264	60,000
Korea, North	46,768	17,900,000
Korea, South	38,031	38,200,000
Kuwait	7,780	1,340,000
Laos	91,429	3,700,000
Lebanon	4,015	3,170,000
Lesotho	11,720	1,340,000
Liberia	43,000	1,860,000
Libya	679,536	2,950,000
Liechtenstein	61	25,000
Luxembourg	999	365,000
Madagascar	230,035	8,730,000
Malawi	45,747	5,795,000
Malaysia	128,328	13,650,000
Maldives	115	150,000
Mali	464,873	6,660,000
Malta	122	350,000
Mauritania	419,229	1,640,000
Mauritius	787	920,000
Mexico	761,600	71,900,000
Monaco	([10])	30,000
Mongolia	604,250	1,625,000
Morocco	171,593	20,050,000
Mozambique	303,073	10,460,000
Nauru	8.2	8,000
Nepal	54,362	14,000,000
Netherlands	13,967	14,125,000
New Zealand[11]	103,736	3,199,000
Nicaragua	57,143	2,565,000
Niger	489,206	5,300,000
Nigeria	356,700	77,100,000
Norway	125,182	4,085,000
Oman[12]	82,000	880,000
Pakistan[13]	342,750	82,350,000
Panama	29,306	1,935,000
Papua New Guinea	183,540	3,170,000
Paraguay	157,047	3,055,000
Peru	496,222	17,770,000
Philippines	115,707	49,150,000
Poland	120,359	35,450,000
Portugal	35,340	9,940,000
Qatar	4,000	220,000
Romania	91,700	22,300,000
Rwanda	10,169	4,800,000
St. Lucia	238	115,000
St. Vincent and the Grenadines	250	100,000
San Marino	23.6	20,000
São Tomé and Príncipe	372	85,000
Saudi Arabia	873,000	8,350,000

Country	Area[1]	Population
Senegal	76,124	5,650,000
Seychelles	171	65,000
Sierra Leone	27,925	3,470,000
Singapore	238	2,400,000
Solomon Islands	11,500	215,000
Somalia	246,155	3,650,000
South Africa[14]	438,073	23,500,000
Spain[15]	194,885	37,575,000
Sri Lanka	25,332	15,150,000
Sudan	967,491	18,350,000
Suriname	63,251	380,000
Swaziland	6,704	550,000
Sweden	173,665	8,300,000
Switzerland	15,941	6,340,000
Syria	71,498	8,610,000
Tanzania[16]	362,820	17,600,000
Thailand	198,455	47,160,000
Togo	21,853	2,530,000
Tonga	290	100,000
Trinidad and Tobago	1,980	1,115,000
Tunisia	63,379	6,350,000
Turkey	301,380	45,430,000
Tuvalu	10	6,500
Uganda	91,134	13,675,000
U.S.S.R.	8,649,489	265,750,000
United Arab Emirates	32,000	800,000
United Kingdom	94,249	55,800,000
United States	3,540,939	222,600,000
Upper Volta	105,870	6,900,000
Uruguay	68,548	2,900,000
Vanuatu (New Hebrides)	5,700	110,000
Vatican City State	([17])	1,000
Venezuela	352,143	13,925,000
Vietnam	126,436	52,300,000
Western Samoa	1,133	155,000
Yemen, People's Democratic Republic of[18]	111,000	1,950,000
Yemen Arab Republic	75,290	5,940,000
Yugoslavia	98,766	22,310,000
Zaire	905,063	28,750,000
Zambia	290,724	5,840,000
Zimbabwe	150,333	7,350,000

1. Square miles. 2. Including Manchuria and Tibet. 3. Excluding Quemoy and Matsu. 4. Excluding Faeroe Islands and Greenland. 5. Including East Berlin. 6. Excluding West Berlin. 7. Including Jammu and Kashmir and Sikkim. 8. Including Portuguese East Timor, annexed in 1976, and Irian Jaya (former Netherlands New Guinea and later West Irian). 9. Excluding territory occupied in 1967 war. 10. 0.65 square mile. 11. Excluding dependencies. 12. Excluding Kuria Muria Islands. 13. Excluding Jammu and Kashmir. 14. Excluding South-West Africa (Namibia), Bophuthatswana, Transkei, and Venda. 15. Including Balearic and Canary Islands. 16. Including Zanzibar. 17. 0.17 square mile. 18. Excluding Perim and Kamaran Islands.

Largest Cities of the World

Census figures and population estimates in the following table are based on data reflecting different years. Some cities include metropolitan areas or contiguous suburbs, while others report only those residing within precise geographical or physical boundaries. Therefore, the ratings in this listing must be considered approximate.

City	Population	Year[1]
Shanghai	10,888,000	1975E
Mexico City	8,988,000	1978E
Tokyo	8,514,000	1978E
Peking	8,487,000	1975E
Calcutta	8,297,000	1977E
Moscow	8,011,000	1979C
Seoul, South Korea	7,823,000	1978E
Bombay	7,605,000	1977E
Manila	7,500,000	1977E
São Paulo, Brazil	7,199,000	1977E
London	6,918,000	1978E
New York	6,808,370	1980C
Jakarta, Indonesia	6,179,000	1977E
Cairo	5,423,000	1977E
Bangkok, Thailand	4,875,000	1978E
Rio de Janeiro	4,857,000	1977E
Leningrad	4,588,000	1979C
Teheran, Iran	4,496,000	1976C
Karachi, Pakistan	4,465,000	1975E
Lima, Peru	4,376,000	1978E

Source: United Nations *Demographic Yearbook, 1978,* and official estimates. NOTE: E = estimate; C = census.

Some Other Large Foreign Cities

City	Population	Year[1]
Addis Ababa, Ethiopia	1,179,000	1979E
Ahmedabad, India	1,585,544	1971C
Alexandria, Egypt	2,318,655	1976C
Algiers	2,500,000	1979E
Alma Ata, U.S.S.R.	910,000	1979C
Amsterdam	957,700	1979E
Ankara, Turkey	2,018,000	1978E
Antwerp, Belgium	927,200[2]	1978E
Athens	867,023[2]	1971C
Auckland, New Zealand	750,600[2]	1979E
Baghdad, Iraq	3,205,600	1977E
Baku, U.S.S.R.	1,550,000	1979C
Badung, Indonesia	1,201,730	1971C
Bangalore, India	1,540,741	1971C
Barcelona	1,846,250	1976E
Barranquilla, Colombia	868,000	1979E
Belfast, Northern Ireland	354,000	1978E
Belgrade, Yugoslavia	870,000	1975E
Belo Horizonte, Brazil	3,057,000	1977E
Berlin[3]	3,038,700	1979E
Bern, Switzerland	142,800	1979E
Birmingham, England	1,041,000	1978E
Bogotá, Colombia	4,055,900	1979E
Bonn, West Germany	285,000	1977E

City	Population	Year[1]
Brasilia, Brazil	763,250	1977E
Brisbane, Australia	1,004,500[2]	1978E
Brussels	1,029,000[2]	1978E
Bucharest	1,807,000	1977E
Budapest	2,093,200	1979E
Buenos Aires	2,982,000	1978E
Calgary, Canada	469,917	1976C
Cali, Colombia	1,189,000	1979E
Canton, China	2,300,000	1970E
Cape Town, South Africa	842,600	1976E
Caracas, Venezuela	2,850,000	1979E
Casablanca, Morocco	2,113,000	1978E
Chongqing (Chungking), China	3,500,000	1970E
Cologne, West Germany	976,400	1978E
openhagen	689,300	1977E
Córdoba, Argentina	781,600	1975E
Dacca, Bangladesh	1,679,600	1974E
Damascus, Syria	1,113,000	1978E
Delhi, India	3,287,883	1971C
Dnepropetrovsk, U.S.S.R.	1,066,000	1979C
Donetsk, U.S.S.R.	1,021,000	1979C
Dublin	543,600	1979E
dinburgh, Scotland	456,500	1978E
lorence, Italy	463,300	1978E
rankfurt, West Germany	633,400	1978E
ukuoka, Japan	1,039,300[2]	1977E
eneva	151,000	1979E
enoa, Italy	789,500	1978E
lasgow, Scotland	809,700	1978E
orki, U.S.S.R.	1,344,000	1979C
uadalajara, Mexico	1,813,000	1978E
uyaquil, Ecuador	1,022,000	1978E
The Hague	671,500	1979E
aifa, Israel	227,200	1976E
amburg, West Germany	1,672,200	1978E
arbin, China	2,750,000	1970E
avana	1,981,300	1978E
elsinki, Finland	483,600	1979E
o Chi Minh City (Saigon), Vietnam	3,460,500	1976E
yderabad, India	1,607,396	1971C
yderabad, Pakistan	628,310	1972C
adan, Nigeria	847,000	1975E
tanbul	2,800,000	1978E
erusalem	376,000	1978E
ohannesburg, South Africa	1,416,700	1978E
anpur, India	1,154,388	1971C
harkov, U.S.S.R.	1,444,000	1979C
iev, U.S.S.R.	2,144,000	1979C
inshasa, Zaire	2,008,250	1974E
itakyushu, Japan	1,068,000[2]	1977E
obe, Japan	1,366,500[2]	1977E
uibyshev, U.S.S.R.	1,216,000	1979C
unming, China	1,700,000	1970E
agos, Nigeria	3,500,000	1977E
ahore, Pakistan	2,165,372	1972C
a Paz, Bolivia	654,700	1976E
ausanne, Switzerland	136,300	1979E
ège, Belgium	617,000[2]	1978E
sbon	861,500	1979E
verpool, England	528,000	1978E
ódz, Poland	814,800	1977E
ucknow, India	749,239	1971C
uda, China	4,000,000	1970E
yallpur, Pakistan	822,263	1972C
yons, France	462,841	1975C
adras, India	2,469,449	1971C
adrid	4,120,000	1979E
arseilles, France	914,356	1975C
Medellín, Colombia	1,748,000	1979E
Melbourne	2,717,600[2]	1978E
Milan, Italy	1,696,250	1978E
Minsk, U.S.S.R.	1,276,000	1979C
Monterrey, Mexico	1,054,000	1978E
Montevideo, Uruguay	1,229,700	1975E
Montreal	1,080,546	1976C
Munich, West Germany	1,293,900	1978E
Nagoya, Japan	2,080,000	1976E
Nagpur, India	866,076	1971C
Nanjing (Nanking), China	2,000,000	1970E
Nantes, France	263,689	1975C
Naples, Italy	1,226,100	1978E
Nice, France	346,620	1975C
Novosibirsk, U.S.S.R.	1,312,000	1979C
Odessa, U.S.S.R.	1,046,000	1979C
Osaka, Japan	2,750,500	1976E
Oslo	460,400	1978E
Ottawa	394,462	1976C
Paris	2,299,800	1975C
Poona, India	856,105	1971C
Port-au-Prince, Haiti	703,100	1977E
Porto Alegre, Brazil	869,795[2]	1973E
Prague	1,188,600	1979E
Pusan, South Korea	2,454,051	1975C
Pyongyang, North Korea	1,500,000	1976E
Quebec	177,082	1976C
Quezon City, Philippines	994,700	1975E
Quito, Ecuador	742,900	1978E
Rangoon, Burma	2,276,000[2]	1977E
Recife, Brazil	1,249,800	1977E
Rome	2,914,600	1979E
Rosario, Argentina	750,500	1975E
Rostov-on-Don, U.S.S.R.	934,000	1979C
Rotterdam	1,014,800	1979E
Salvador, Brazil	1,237,400[2]	1975E
Santiago, Chile	3,448,700	1978E
Santo Domingo, Dominican Republic	1,103,400	1979E
Sapporo, Japan	1,307,700[2]	1977E
Seville, Spain	612,900	1976E
Shenyang, China	3,750,000[2]	1970E
Singapore, Singapore	2,308,200	1977E
Sofia, Bulgaria	1,000,000	1978E
Stockholm	654,000	1979E
Surabaja, Indonesia	1,556,255	1971C
Sverdlovsk, U.S.S.R.	1,211,000	1979C
Sydney, Australia	3,155,200[2]	1978E
Taipai, Taiwan	2,161,300	1978E
Tashkent, U.S.S.R.	1,779,000	1979C
Tbilisi, U.S.S.R.	1,066,000	1979C
Tel Aviv-Jaffa, Israel	348,500	1977E
Tianjin (Tientsin), China	4,280,000	1970E
Toronto	633,318	1976C
Tunis, Tunisia	960,000[2]	1976E
Turin, Italy	1,172,900	1978E
Valparaiso, Chile	248,500	1978E
Valencia, Spain	748,730	1976E
Vancouver, Canada	410,188	1976C
Venice	358,400	1978E
Vienna	1,580,600	1978E
Volgograd, U.S.S.R.	929,000	1979C
Warsaw	1,552,000	1979E
Wellington, New Zealand	327,100[2]	1979E
Winnipeg, Canada	560,874	1976C
Wuhan, China	3,000,000	1970E
Yokohama, Japan	2,694,500[2]	1977E
Zurich	376,500	1979E

E = estimated; C = census. 2. Figure is for metropolitan area and may include suburbs or some rural population. 3. West erlin, 1,909,700; East Berlin, 1,129,000. NOTE: The population of many other cities will be found throughout the World story section under individual countries. *See* Table of Contents.

Expectation of Life by Age and Sex for Selected Countries

Country	Period	Average future lifetime in years at stated age											
		Males						Females					
		0	1	10	20	40	60	0	1	10	20	40	60
NORTH AMERICA													
United States	1975	68.7	68.9	60.3	50.8	32.6	16.8	76.5	76.6	67.9	58.1	39.0	21.8
Canada	1970–72	69.3	69.8	61.2	51.7	33.2	17.0	76.4	76.6	67.9	58.2	39.0	21.4
Mexico	1975	62.8	68.0	59.2	49.9	32.7	17.9	66.6	69.3	62.6	53.1	35.3	19.1
Puerto Rico	1976	70.2	70.8	62.1	52.3	34.8	19.0	77.1	77.5	68.7	58.9	39.7	22.0
Trinidad and Tobago	1970	64.1	65.6	57.3	47.8	29.5	13.6	68.1	69.3	60.9	51.3	32.7	16.3
CENTRAL AND SOUTH AMERICA													
Brazil	1960–70	57.6	—	56.2	47.0	30.0	15.0	61.1	—	58.9	49.7	32.5	16.6
Chile	1969–70	60.5	64.9	56.7	47.3	29.9	15.5	66.0	70.0	62.2	52.7	34.5	18.0
Colombia	1950–52	44.2	50.4	48.2	39.6	24.8	11.8	45.9	51.1	49.4	40.9	26.6	12.8
Costa Rica	1972–74	66.3	69.1	61.3	51.8	33.8	17.4	70.5	72.7	64.9	55.2	36.5	19.2
Ecuador	1962–74	54.9	60.5	55.5	47.1	31.3	16.2	58.1	62.8	58.0	49.3	33.0	17.3
Guatemala	1963–65	48.3	52.5	51.3	43.2	28.1	14.8	49.7	53.4	52.8	44.6	29.2	14.7
Panama	1970	64.3	66.4	59.9	50.8	33.4	17.0	67.5	69.4	62.7	53.6	36.1	19.9
Uruguay	1963–64	65.5	68.0	59.5	50.0	31.7	15.9	71.6	73.7	65.2	55.5	36.7	19.5
Venezuela[1]	1961	66.4	68.8	61.8	52.4	34.6	18.9	—	—	—	—	—	—
EUROPE													
Austria	1976	68.1	—	59.9	50.4	32.0	15.7	75.1	—	66.6	56.8	37.6	19.7
Belgium	1968–72	67.8	68.4	59.9	50.3	31.6	15.2	74.2	74.5	65.9	56.1	36.9	19.2
Cyprus	1973	70.0	70.7	62.1	52.3	33.5	16.5	72.9	74.2	65.7	55.8	36.4	18.5
Czechoslovakia	1970	66.2	67.0	58.4	49.9	30.6	14.6	72.9	72.6	64.9	55.2	35.9	18.3
Denmark[2]	1975–76	71.1	70.9	62.3	52.6	33.7	17.1	76.8	76.5	67.7	57.9	38.5	21.1
Finland	1975	67.4	67.1	58.5	48.9	30.6	15.0	75.9	75.6	66.8	57.0	37.7	19.7
France	1976	69.2	69.2	60.5	51.0	32.5	16.7	77.2	77.0	68.3	58.6	39.3	21.5
Germany, East[3]	1976	68.8	69.0	60.4	50.8	32.2	15.9	74.4	74.3	65.6	55.9	36.6	18.8
Germany, West[3]	1975–77	68.6	69.0	60.4	50.9	32.3	15.8	75.2	75.4	66.7	56.9	37.7	19.9
Greece	1970	70.1	72.2	63.8	54.1	35.1	17.5	73.6	75.3	66.9	57.1	37.8	19.3
Hungary	1974	66.5	68.2	59.5	49.9	31.5	15.5	72.4	73.7	65.1	55.3	36.1	18.7
Ireland	1970–72	68.8	69.2	60.6	51.0	32.1	15.6	73.5	73.8	65.1	55.3	40.8	18.7
Italy	1970–72	69.0	70.1	61.6	52.0	33.2	16.7	74.9	75.8	67.1	57.3	38.1	20.2
Netherlands	1977	72.0	71.8	63.2	53.5	34.4	17.4	78.4	78.1	69.4	59.6	40.2	22.1
Norway	1976–77	72.1	71.9	63.2	53.6	34.7	17.7	78.4	78.1	69.4	59.5	40.0	21.8
Poland	1970–72	66.8	68.0	59.4	49.8	31.6	15.5	73.8	74.6	66.0	56.2	37.0	19.3
Portugal	1974	65.3	67.2	59.0	49.6	31.5	15.4	72.0	73.5	65.3	55.6	36.5	18.7
Spain	1970	69.7	—	62.0	52.4	33.7	17.0	75.0	—	66.9	57.1	38.0	20.1
Sweden	1972–76	72.1	71.9	63.1	53.5	34.7	17.6	77.8	77.4	68.6	58.8	39.5	21.4
Switzerland	1968–73	70.3	70.5	62.0	52.4	33.6	16.7	76.2	76.2	67.6	57.8	38.4	20.4
U.S.S.R.	1971–72	64.0	—	—	—	—	—	74.0	—	—	—	—	—
United Kingdom													
England and Wales	1974–76	69.6	—	—	—	—	—	75.8	—	—	—	—	—
Northern Ireland	1975–77	67.5	67.9	59.3	49.7	31.2	14.9	73.8	74.2	65.5	55.7	36.4	19.0
Scotland	1971–73	67.2	67.8	59.2	49.8	31.3	15.0	73.6	74.1	65.4	55.6	36.3	18.9
Yugoslavia	1970–72	65.4	68.0	59.7	50.1	31.8	15.7	70.2	72.8	64.6	54.9	35.8	18.2
ASIA													
Bangladesh	1974	45.8	53.5	50.5	42.5	28.1	14.4	46.6	53.5	50.3	42.2	27.7	14.1
India	1951–60	41.9	48.4	45.2	36.9	22.1	11.8	40.6	46.0	43.8	35.6	22.4	12.9
Iran	1973–76	57.6	63.5	59.1	49.7	31.4	16.1	57.4	64.0	60.9	51.6	33.7	17.9
Israel	1977	71.3	71.7	63.0	53.5	34.6	17.6	74.7	74.9	66.3	56.5	37.1	19.2
Japan[4]	1974	71.2	71.0	62.5	52.8	33.0	17.0	76.3	76.0	67.4	57.5	38.3	20.3
Korea, South	1970	63.0	66.0	58.0	49.0	31.0	16.0	67.0	69.0	61.0	52.0	34.0	17.0
Pakistan	1962	53.7	60.6	57.0	47.8	30.8	15.6	48.8	53.9	51.7	42.9	27.7	15.5
Sri Lanka	1967	64.8	67.4	60.5	51.2	33.2	17.0	66.9	68.9	62.4	53.0	35.0	17.8
Syria	1970	54.5	60.7	56.4	47.4	30.5	15.2	58.7	64.1	59.5	50.5	33.3	17.3
AFRICA													
Egypt	1960	51.6	56.2	56.6	47.7	30.5	15.1	53.8	59.9	62.0	52.9	35.0	18.0
Kenya	1969	46.9	52.6	51.0	43.0	28.3	14.5	51.2	56.6	54.1	45.7	30.3	15.7
South Africa (white population)	1959–61	64.7	65.9	57.5	48.0	30.2	15.0	71.7	72.5	64.1	54.4	35.5	18.6
OCEANIA													
Australia[5]	1965–67	67.6	68.1	59.5	50.0	31.4	15.8	74.2	74.4	65.8	56.0	36.9	19.5
New Zealand	1970–72	68.5	—	—	—	—	—	74.6	—	—	—	—	—

1. Figures for male and female together. 2. Excluding data for Faeroe Islands and Greenland. 3. Includes relevant data relating to Berlin. No separate data have been supplied. 4. Japanese nationals in Japan only. 5. Excludes full-blooded aborigines. *Source*: United Nations *Demographic Yearbook, 1978.*

Estimates of World Population by Regions

	Estimated population in millions							
Year	North America[1]	Latin America[2]	Europe[3]	U.S.S.R.	Asia[4]	Africa	Oceania	World total
1650	1	7	103	[5]	257	100	2	470
1750	1	10	144	[5]	437	100	2	694
1850	26	33	274	[5]	656	100	2	1,091
1900	81	63	423	[5]	857	141	6	1,571
1930	134	108	355[6]	179	1,120[7]	164	10	2,070
1950	166	164	392[6]	180	1,368[7]	219	13	2,501
1960	199	216	425[6]	214	1,644[7]	273	16	2,986
1970	226	283	459[6]	243	2,027[7]	352	19	3,610
1977	240	340	478[6]	259	2,413[7]	430	22	4,182
1978	242	349	480[6]	262	2,461[7]	442	22	4,258

1. U.S. (including Alaska and Hawaii), Bermuda, Canada, Greenland, and St. Pierre and Miquelon. 2. Mexico, Central and South America, and Caribbean Islands. 3. Includes Russia 1650–1900. 4. Excludes Russia (U.S.S.R.). 5. Included in Europe. 6. Excludes European Turkey, which is included in Asia. 7. Includes both Asian and European Turkey. *Sources:* W.F. Willcox, 1650–1900; United Nations, 1930–78.

Crude Birth and Death Rates for Selected Countries

(per 1,000 population)

	Birth rates					Death rates				
Country	1979	1978	1975	1970	1965	1979	1978	1975	1970	1965
Australia	15.5	15.7	16.9	20.6	19.6	7.4	7.6	7.9	9.0	8.8
Austria	11.4	11.3	12.5	15.2	17.9	12.2	12.5	12.8	13.4	13.0
Belgium	12.6	12.4	12.2	14.7	16.4	11.4	11.7	12.2	12.3	12.5
Canada	n.a.	15.3	15.8	17.4	21.4	n.a.	7.3	7.4	7.3	7.5
Czechoslovakia	17.8	18.4	19.6	15.9	16.4	11.5	11.5	11.5	11.6	10.0
Denmark	11.6	11.6	14.2	14.4	18.2	10.7	10.4	10.1	9.8	10.1
El Salvador	n.a.	39.7	38.9	40.0	46.5	n.a.	6.9	7.9	9.9	10.6
Finland	n.a.	13.5	13.9	14.0	17.0	n.a.	9.2	9.3	9.6	7.9
France	14.1	13.8	14.1	16.8	17.7	10.2	10.3	10.6	10.7	11.1
Germany, East	14.0	13.9	10.8	13.9	16.5	13.9	13.9	14.3	14.1	13.3
Germany, West	9.5	9.4	9.7	11.4	17.9	11.6	11.8	12.1	12.1	11.2
Greece	15.9	15.9	15.7	16.5	17.7	8.7	8.8	8.9	8.4	7.9
Hungary	15.0	15.7	18.4	14.7	13.1	12.8	13.1	12.4	11.6	10.7
Ireland	n.a.	21.7	21.5	21.8	22.2	n.a.	10.3	10.6	11.4	11.5
Israel	24.7	25.1	28.2	26.9	25.4	6.7	6.8	7.1	7.1	6.2
Italy	11.8	12.5	14.8	16.8	19.2	9.4	9.4	9.9	9.7	10.0
Japan	14.2	14.9	17.2	18.9	18.6	5.9	6.1	6.4	6.9	7.1
Luxembourg	11.2	11.4	11.2	13.2	15.6	11.1	11.8	12.2	12.3	11.8
Malta	16.6	17.4	18.3	16.3	17.6	8.9	9.9	8.8	9.4	9.4
Mauritius	27.5	27.1	25.1	26.0	35.4	7.3	7.1	8.1	7.8	8.6
Mexico	n.a.	34.0	37.5	42.1	45.3	n.a.	6.0	7.2	9.6	9.5
Netherlands	12.5	12.6	13.0	18.3	19.9	8.0	8.2	8.3	8.4	8.0
New Zealand	16.7	16.3	18.4	22.1	22.8	8.2	7.9	8.1	8.8	8.7
Norway	12.6	12.7	14.1	16.6	17.5	10.1	9.8	9.9	10.0	9.1
Panama	29.4	28.3	32.3	37.2	39.1	n.a.	n.a.	n.a.	8.8[1]	7.3
Poland	19.5	19.0	18.9	16.8	17.3	9.2	9.3	8.7	8.2	7.4
Portugal	n.a.	16.8	19.1	20.0	22.9	n.a.	9.8	10.4	10.8	10.1
Singapore	17.3	16.9	17.8	23.0	31.1	5.3	5.2	5.1	5.2	5.6
Spain	16.1	17.2	19.1	19.5	21.3	7.8	7.9	8.2	8.3	8.7
Sweden	11.6	11.2	12.6	13.7	15.9	11.0	10.8	10.8	9.9	10.1
Switzerland	11.6	11.3	12.3	15.8	18.7	9.0	9.1	8.7	9.1	9.3
Tunisia	n.a.	n.a.	36.6	36.4	44.3	n.a.	n.a.	n.a.	17.6[1]	11.8
United Kingdom	n.a.	12.3	12.5	16.3	18.4	n.a.	11.9	11.9	11.8	11.5
United States	15.8	15.3	14.8	18.3	19.4	8.7	8.8	8.9	9.4	9.4
Yugoslavia	17.1	17.4	18.2	17.8	20.9	8.5	8.7	8.7	8.9	8.7

1. 1969–70 figure. NOTE: n.a. = not available. *Source:* United Nations, *Monthly Bulletin of Statistics,* July 1980.

Suicide Rates for Selected Countries

(per 100,000 population)

Country	Year	Rate	Country	Year	Rate	Country	Year	Rate
Angola	1972	1.0	Guatemala	1972	3.4	Singapore	1977	9.7
Australia	1977	11.1	Hong Kong	1977	12.3	South Africa		
Argentina	1977	7.8	Hungary	1977	40.3	Black	1971	5.6
Austria	1976	22.7	Iceland	1977	10.4	White	1971	14.5
Barbados	1975	1.2	Ireland	1975	4.7	Spain	1975	3.9
Belgium	1976	16.6	Israel	1977	6.5	Sweden	1975	19.4
Bulgaria	1976	14.1	Italy	1972	5.8	Switzerland	1977	23.8
Canada	1976	12.8	Jamaica	1971	1.0	Trinidad and		
Chile	1976	5.7	Japan	1977	17.8	Tobago	1976	8.9
Costa Rica	1977	4.4	Mexico	1975	1.7	Turkey	1971	1.9
Cuba	1971	15.0	Netherlands	1977	9.2	United Kingdom		
Czechoslovakia	1976	20.8	New Zealand	1976	9.2	England and		
Denmark	1976	23.9	Norway	1977	11.4	Wales	1976	7.8
Ecuador	1975	2.7	Panama	1975	2.6	Northern		
El Salvador	1971	8.7	Paraguay	1977	1.8	Ireland	1977	4.6
Finland	1974	25.1	Peru	1972	1.8	Scotland	1977	8.1
France	1970	15.4	Philippines	1974	1.1	United States	1976	12.5
Germany, East	1970	30.5	Poland	1977	12.4	Uruguay	1976	10.8
Germany, West	1976	21.7	Portugal	1975	8.5	Venezuela	1977	4.6
Greece	1976	2.8	Puerto Rico	1977	9.5	Yugoslavia	1975	13.4

Source: United Nations *Demographic Yearbook, 1978.*

Cost of Living of United Nations Personnel in Selected Cities as Reflected by Index of Retail Prices, 1979

(New York City = 100)

City	Index	City	Index	City	Index
Addis Ababa, Ethiopia	90	Dar es Salaam, Tanzania	92	New Delhi, India	83
Algiers, Algeria	118	Geneva	166	Nicosia, Cyprus	83
Amman, Jordan	130	Guatemala City, Guatemala	99	Paris	146
Ankara, Turkey	89	The Hague, the Netherlands	147	Quito, Ecuador	85
Athens	112	Havana	89	Rabat, Morocco	119
Baghdad, Iraq	88	Jakarta, Indonesia	104	Rangoon, Burma	88
Bangkok, Thailand	83	Kabul, Afghanistan	89	Rio de Janeiro	80
Beirut, Lebanon	91	Islamabad, Pakistan	86	Rome	102
Belgrade, Yugoslavia	108	Katmandu, Nepal	83	San José, Costa Rica	99
Bogotá, Colombia	96	Kingston, Jamaica	60	San Salvador, El Salvador	99
Bonn, West Germany	154	Kinshasha, Zaire	141	Santiago, Chile	111
Brazzaville, Congo	138	La Paz, Bolivia	109	Seoul, South Korea	117
Brussels, Belgium	151	Lagos, Nigeria	111	Sofia, Bulgaria	101
Budapest	96	Lima, Peru	80	Sydney, Australia	100
Buenos Aires	143	London	125	Teheran, Iran	110
Cairo	87	Madrid	123	Tokyo	153
Caracas, Venezuela	140	Manila	95	Tripoli, Libya	133
Colombo, Sri Landa	57	Mexico City	86	Tunis, Tunisia	126
Cophenhagen	147	Montevideo, Uruguay	101	Vienna	141
Dacca, Bangladesh	89	Montreal	79	Vientiane, Laos	88
Dakar, Senegal	130	Nairobi, Kenya	101	Warsaw	72
Damascus, Syria	125	Nassau, Bahamas	107	Washington, D.C.	93

Source: United Nations, *Monthly Bulletin of Statistics, March 1980.*

New Hourly Minimum Wage Benefits Millions

Five million workers will gain when the federal minimum wage rises by law to $3.35 an hour on January 1, 1981. The previous minimum wage was $3.10 an hour. In 1977 when the minimum wage was $2.30 an hour, Congress amended the minimum wage law to provide for a series of increases that brought it up to its present level.

Certain employers are exempt from the requirement to pay the minimum wage. They are the retail and service industries with annual sales of less than $325,000. On January 1, 1982, the cutoff will rise to $362,500.

Employers of workers who receive tips are partly exempt from the requirement to pay the minimum wage. The law allows such employers to count 40% of employees' tips toward the minimum wage.

Value of Exports and Imports

(in millions of U.S. dollars)

Country	Exports[1]	Imports[1]
Afghanistan	$ 431	326
Algeria	8,198[2]	8,531[2]
Angola	1,227[3]	625[3]
Argentina	6,400[2]	3,834[2]
Australia	18,427	16,347
Austria	15,483	20,254
Bahamas	1,989[4]	3,053[4]
Bahrain	2,416	4,026[5]
Bangladesh	576[2]	1,294[2]
Barbados	130[2]	312[2]
Belgium–Luxembourg	56,258	60,410
Benin	31[4]	246[4]
Bolivia	725[2]	769[2]
Brazil	15,244	19,804
Bulgaria	8,879	8,447
Burma	363	319
Burundi	92[4]	78[4]
Cameroon	1,129	1,271
Canada	46,065[2]	43,434[2]
Central African Republic	72[2]	57[2]
Chad	59[6]	118[6]
Chile	3,763	4,218
Colombia	3,381	4,437
Congo	139[2]	261[2]
Costa Rica	923	1,409
Cuba	4,456[2]	4,687[2]
Cyprus	456[5]	1,009[5]
Czechoslovakia	13,198	14,262
Denmark	14,506	106,994
Dominican Republic	869	1,055
Ecuador	1,494[2]	1,627[2]
Egypt	1,840	3,837
El Salvador	1,118	1,028[2]
Ethiopia	423	576
Fiji	249	470
Finland	11,175	838
France	98,059	157,747
Gabon	1,307[2]	589[2]
Gambia	58	141
Germany, East	15,063	16,214
Germany, West	171,540	157,747
Ghana	965[4]	1,143[4]
Greece	3,855	753
Guatemala	1,089[2]	1,286[2]
Guyana	289[2]	279[2]
Haiti	155[2]	212[2]
Honduras	596[2]	693[2]
Hungary	1,673	8,674
Iceland	791	838
India	6,398	8,150
Indonesia	15,578	7,225
Iran	19,433[5]	16,019[2 5]
Iraq	21,449[5]	4,213[2 5]
Ireland	7,180	9,837
Israel	4,301	7,398
Italy	72,242	77,970
Ivory Coast	2,516	2,488
Jamaica	744[2]	874[2]
Japan	103,032	110,672
Jordan	402[5]	1,949[5]
Kenya	1,062	1,535
Korea, South	15,055	20,339
Kuwait	17,496[5]	4,605[2 5]
Laos	5[7]	65[7]
Lebanon	497[7]	1,224[7]
Liberia	486[2]	464[4]

Country	Exports[1]	Imports[1]
Libya	9,907[2]	4,602[2]
Madagascar	386[2]	443[2]
Malawi	233	400
Malaysia	5,937[2]	5,265
Mali	107[2]	219
Malta	424	753
Mauritania	148	259
Mauritius	326[2]	501[2]
Mexico	8,768	12,004
Morocco	1,925	3,678
Mozambique	129[4]	278[4]
Netherlands	63,667	67,284
New Zealand	4,694	4,542
Nicaragua	646[2]	594[2]
Niger	134[6]	127[6]
Nigeria	9,483[2]	12,857[2]
Norway	13,271	13,818
Oman	2,284[5]	1,387[5]
Pakistan	2,056	4,061
Panama	288	942[2]
Papua New Guinea	963	810
Paraguay	305	432
Peru	1,433[4]	1,614[4]
Philippines	3,425[2]	5,143[2]
Poland	16,233	17,488
Portugal	3,468	6,085
Qatar	3,598[5]	1,425[5]
Romania	9,731	10,917
Rwanda	70[2]	179[2]
Saudi Arabia	60,106[5]	20,424[2 5]
Senegal	623[4]	762[4]
Sierra Leone	278[2]	146
Singapore	14,233	17,635
Solomon Islands	36[2]	35[2]
Somalia	107[2]	241[2]
Spain	17,903	25,432
Sri Lanka	890	1,441
Sudan	533[2]	1,198[2]
Suriname	308[4]	396[4]
Sweden	27,244	28,488
Switzerland	26,507	29,354
Syria	1,634[5]	3,309[5]
Tanzania	457[2]	1,117[2]
Thailand	5,308	1,441
Togo	159[4]	284[4]
Tonga	8	29
Trinidad and Tobago	2,476	1,946
Tunisia	1,690	2,748
Turkey	2,261	4,597[2]
Uganda	663	187[4]
U.S.S.R.	64,762	57,773
United Arab Emirates	13,170[5]	5,368[2 5]
United Kingdom	91,030	102,969
United States	178,578	217,664
Upper Volta	42[2]	191[2]
Uruguay	795	716[2]
Venezuela	10,614[2]	9,126[2]
Western Samoa	18	66
Yemen, People's Dem. Republic of	221[2]	544[4]
Yemen Arab Republic	7[2]	1,283[2]
Yugoslavia	6,491	12,862
Zaire	925[2]	589[2]
Zambia	853[2]	630[2]
Zimbabwe	1,154	937

1. 1979 unless otherwise indicated. 2. 1978. 3. 1974. 4. 1977. 5. Excluding petroleum. 6. 1976. 7. 1973. *Source:* United Nations, *Monthly Bulletin of Statistics*, August 1980.

Consumer Price Indexes for Selected Countries
(1967—100)

Country	Total Indexes 1978	1977	1975	1970	Average annual percent change, 1970–1978	Indexes for Selected Items, 1978: Food[1]	Clothing	Housing[2]	Transportation
Australia	245.8	227.9	178.7	109.8	10.6	227.4	264.0	277.3	n.a.
Austria	184.4	178.0	157.2	110.6	6.6	173.8	161.2	206.7	192.1
Belgium	202.2	193.6	165.6	110.7	7.8	191.8	n.a.	n.a.	n.a
Canada	202.5	185.9	160.1	112.4	7.6	231.4	160.2	210.0	188.4
Denmark	247.2	224.7	185.5	119.1	9.6	275.6	193.0[3]	n.a.	n.a.
Finland	280.0	260.3	202.0	114.6	11.8	299.4	n.a.	n.a.	n.a.
France	233.9	214.5	178.9	117.1	9.0	246.6	216.2	234.5	257.3
Germany, West	160.6	156.5	144.1	107.0	5.2	150.7	161.9	171.2	167.1
Greece	270.3	240.1	189.0	105.8	12.4	299.4	n.a.	n.a.	n.a.
Iceland	1,200.0[3]	841.8	488.2	159.7	28.7[4]	n.a.	n.a.	n.a.	n.a.
Ireland	327.6	304.2	226.8	121.7	13.2	350.7	n.a.	n.a.	n.a.
Italy	289.8	258.5	186.9	109.2	13.0	292.1	318.1	254.0	334.8
Japan	252.1	241.9	204.5	119.3	9.8	266.2	256.7	204.4	272.8
Luxembourg	188.0	182.4	155.7	109.9	6.9	192.3	n.a.	n.a.	n.a.
Netherlands	212.5	203.8	175.3	115.5	7.9	183.7	231.5	212.0	197.6
New Zealand	284.4	254.0	189.6	116.6	11.8	277.7	n.a.	n.a.	n.a.
Norway	227.2	210.1	176.5	118.0	8.5	230.0	211.7	n.a.	n.a.
Portugal	423.4	371.2	247.6	122.7	16.7	474.6	n.a.	n.a.	n.a.
Spain	350.9	293.2	200.3	113.3	15.2	342.7	n.a.	n.a.	n.a.
Sweden	222.0	201.8	164.3	112.0	8.9	240.2	174.9	236.9	n.a.
Switzerland	164.0	162.3	157.5	108.8	5.3	153.0	156.7	n.a.	n.a.
Turkey	676.8	418.1	282.5	120.1	24.1	n.a.	n.a.	n.a.	n.a.
United Kingdom	316.6	292.4	216.5	117.4	13.2	372.7	255.0	296.2	323.1
United States	195.4	181.5	161.2	116.3	6.7	211.4	159.6	202.8	185.5
Yugoslavia	449.8	391.0	309.2	125.5	17.3	481.5	n.a.	n.a.	n.a.

1. Restaurant meals, alcohol, and tobacco are included for some countries, excluded for others. 2. Includes shelter, utilities, and household furnishings and operations. However, actual coverage and measurement methods vary significantly from country to country. 3. June 1978. 4. 1970 to June 1978. NOTE: n.a. = not available. *Source:* United States Department of Labor, Bureau of Labor Statistics.

Energy, Petroleum, and Coal, by Country

Country	Energy consumed[1] (coal equiv.) Total (mil. metric tons) 1976	1970	Per capita (kilograms) 1976	1970	Electric energy production[2] (bil. kwh) 1977	1970	Crude petroleum production[3] (mil. metric tons) 1977	1970	Coal production[4] (mil. metric tons) 1977	1970
Algeria	12.6	6.6	729	460	4.7	2.0	53.9	49.0	—	—
Argentina	46.4	39.2	1,804	1,691	32.5	21.7	22.2	20.0	.5	.6
Australia	90.8	67.2	6,657	5,375	82.5[6]	53.9[6]	21.0[7]	8.5[7]	71.0	45.2
Austria	30.2	25.3	4,013	3,424	37.7	30.0	1.8	2.8	—	—
Bahrain	3.2	1.0	11,998	4,720	.9[8]	.2[8]	2.9	3.8	n.a.	n.a.
Belgium	59.8	59.3	6,049	5,923	47.1	30.5	n.a.	n.a.	7.1	11.4
Brazil	79.8	44.6	731	478	99.9[5]	45.5[5]	7.8	8.0	3.9	2.4
Bulgaria	41.3	33.4	4,710	3,937	29.7	19.5	.1	.3	.3	.4
Canada	230.3	201.1	9,950	9,393	316.5[5]	204.7[5]	62.0	60.4	23.0	11.6
Chile	10.3	12.5	987	1,287	9.8	7.6	.9	1.5	1.2	1.4
China, People's Republic of	590.1	391.2	706	515	n.a.	n.a.	100.0[9]	23.9	490.0[9] [10]	360.0[9] [10]
China, Republic of[11]	31.7[12]	15.3	1,904[12]	1,055	30.5	14.0	.3	.1	3.0	4.5
Colombia	16.7	12.7	685	601	15.2	8.8	7.1	11.3	3.8	2.3
Cuba	11.6	9.4	1,225	1,109	7.7	4.9	.2	.2	n.a.	n.a.
Czechoslovakia	110.3	93.3	7,397	6,510	66.5	45.2	.1	.2	28.4[13]	28.2
Denmark	27.0	28.8	5,320	5,838	22.4	20.0	.5	—	n.a.	n.a.
Ecuador	3.3.	1.8	455	293	2.1	.9	9.3	.2	n.a.	n.a.
Egypt	18.0	8.8	473	265	13.0	7.6	20.9	16.4	—	—

Country	Energy consumed[1] (coal equiv.) Total (mil. metric tons) 1976	1970	Per capita (kilograms) 1976	1970	Electric energy production[2] (bil. kwh) 1977	1970	Crude petroleum production[3] (mil. metric tons) 1977	1970	Coal production[4] (mil. metric tons) 1977	1970
Finland	24.5[14]	19.2	5,177[14]	4,159	31.7[5]	21.2[5]	n.a.	n.a.	n.a.	n.a.
France	231.9	192.8	4,380	3,794	210.8	147.0	1.0	2.3	23.0[13]	37.8[13]
Germany, East	114.0	102.1	6,789	5,984	92.0	67.7	.1	.1	.3	1.0
Germany, West	364.3	317.8	5,922	5,239	335.3	242.6	5.4	7.5	91.3[15]	116.3[15]
Greece	20.6	11.2	2,250	1,274	19.0	9.8	—	—	n.a.	n.a.
Hong Kong	5.8	4.0	1,313	1,010	9.5[8]	5.1[8]	n.a.	n.a.	n.a.	n.a.
Hungary	37.7	32.9	3,553	3,185	23.4	14.5	2.2	1.9	2.9[13]	4.2[13]
India	132.9	96.8	218	179	99.1[16]	61.2[16]	10.2	6.8	100.1	73.7
Indonesia	30.4	13.3	218	112	4.4[8]	2.1[8]	83.0	42.6	.2	.2
Iran	49.8	27.1	1,490	945	18.0	7.0	282.6	191.3	.9[17]	.5[9 17]
Iraq	8.4	5.8	725	617	5.0[8]	1.9[8]	122.4	76.5	n.a.	n.a.
Ireland	10.0[14]	9.0[14]	3,170[14]	3,064[14]	9.3[16]	6.1[16]	n.a.	n.a.	.1	.2
Israel	9.0	7.4	2,541	2,524	11.1	6.9	—	5.0[18]	n.a.	n.a.
Italy	184.5	144.1	3,284	2,689	166.5	117.4	1.1	1.4	—	.3
Jamaica	4.0	2.6	1,937	1,377	2.0	1.5	n.a.	n.a.	n.a.	n.a.
Japan	414.9	332.4	3,679	3,215	532.6[16]	359.5[16]	.6	.8	18.2[19]	39.7[19]
Korea, North	49.9	28.2	3,072	2,027	n.a.	n.a.	n.a.	n.a.	45.1[9]	21.8[9]
Korea, South	36.6	25.4	1,020	819	28.1	9.6	n.a.	n.a.	17.2	12.4
Kuwait	9.5[20]	10.0	9,198[20]	13,352	6.0[8]	2.2[8]	98.7[20]	150.6	n.a.	n.a.
Libya	4.0	1.1	1,589	577	1.5[8]	.4[8]	99.5	159.8	n.a.	n.a.
Malaysia	6.0[21]	4.3[21]	578[21]	468[21]	6.7[21]	3.3[21]	8.8	.9	n.a.	n.a.
Mexico	76.4	60.7	1,227	1,241	50.6[5]	28.7[5]	49.3	21.5	6.6	3.0
Netherlands	85.7	66.0	6,224	5,066	58.3	40.9	1.4	1.9	—	4.3
New Zealand	11.4	8.0	3,617	2,835	21.3[8 16]	13.7[8 16]	.7	.1[7]	2.1	2.2
Nigeria	6.1	2.5	94	45	3.5	1.6	103.0	54.2	.6	.1
Norway	21.2	18.7	5,263	4,822	72.5	57.6	13.6	—	.5	.5
Pakistan	13.1	12.2[22]	181	93[22]	11.1[6]	8.7[6 22]	.4	.5	1.1[6 10]	1.3[6 10]
Peru	10.3	8.6	642	633	8.6	5.5	4.5	3.6	—	.2
Philippines	14.4	10.8	329	292	15.8	8.7	n.a.	n.a.	.2	—
Poland	180.5	138.9	5,253	4,270	109.4	64.5	.4	.4	186.1	140.1
Portugal	10.1	6.1	1,050	702	13.3	7.5	n.a.	n.a.	.2	.3
Romania	86.6	58.4	4,036	2,883	59.9	35.1	14.7	13.4	7.4[13]	6.4[13]
Saudia Arabia	17.6[20]	6.3	1,901[20]	808	2.5[8]	.7[8]	458.5[20]	188.4[20]	n.a.	n.a.
Singapore	5.2	1.7	2,262	808	5.1[8]	2.2[8]	n.a.	n.a.	n.a.	n.a.
South Africa	87.4[23]	63.2[23]	2,985[23]	2,618[23]	80.2	50.8	n.a.	n.a.	85.6	54.6
Spain	86.3	50.2[24]	2,399	1,485[24]	93.8	56.5	.8	.2	12.1[13]	10.8[13]
Sweden	49.7	49.7	6,046	6,183	90.0	60.6	n.a.	n.a.	z	z
Switzerland	21.3	21.6	3,340	3,475	45.9[5 25]	33.2[5 25]	n.a.	n.a.	n.a.	n.a.
Syria	5.7	2.9	744	457	2.0	.9	10.1	4.2	n.a.	n.a.
Thailand	13.2	8.8	308	256	11.7	4.5	—	—	n.a.	n.a.
Trinidad and Tobago	4.7	4.7	4,272	4,542	1.6	1.2	11.8	7.2	n.a.	n.a.
Tunisia	2.6	1.3	456	257	1.7	.8	4.3	4.2	n.a.	n.a.
Turkey	29.8	16.9	743	480	20.6	8.6	2.7	3.5	4.4	4.6
U.S.S.R.	1,349.9[14]	1,054.7[14]	5,259[14]	4,345[14]	1,150.1	740.9	545.8[7]	353.0[7]	499.8	432.7
United Arab Emirates	3.1	1.4	13,322	7,446	.7[26]	.1[26]	96.7	37.7	n.a.	n.a.
United Kingdom	295.3	300.2	5,268	5,377	283.3	249.0	37.5	.1	122.2[13]	147.1[13]
United States	2,485.5	2,269.5	11,554	11,077	2,211[5]	1,640[5]	402.5	475.3	603.8	550.4
Uruguay	3.1	2.6	1,000	913	3.0	2.2	n.a.	n.a.	n.a.	n.a.
Venezuela	35.1	25.6	2,838	2,457	23.1	12.7	117.0	194.3	.1	z
Vietnam	5.8	5.5[27]	124	302[27]	1.3[27 28]	1.2[27]	n.a.	n.a.	6.0[9 29]	3.0[9 29]
Yugoslavia	43.5	29.3	2,016	1,438	48.5	26.0	4.0	2.9	.5	.6
Zaire	1.6	1.8	62	81	4.1	3.2	1.1	—	.1	.1
Zambia	2.8	2.1	548	494	8.7[5]	.9[5]	n.a.	n.a.	.7	.6
World, total	**8,318.4**	**6,820.1**	**2,069**	**1,892**	**7,210**	**4,923**	**2,986**	**2,277**	**2,476**	**2,143**

1. Based on apparent consumption of coal, lignite, petroleum products, natural gas, and hydro and nuclear electricity. 2. Comprises utilities generating primarily for public use. Relates to production at generating centers, including station use and transmission losses. 3. Includes shale oil, but excludes natural gasoline. 4. Excludes lignite and brown coal, except as noted. 5. Net production, i.e., excluding station use. 6. Year ending June 30. 7. Includes gas condensates. 8. Excludes production by industrial establishments for own use. 9. Data from United States Department of the Interior, Bureau of Mines. 10. Includes lignite and brown coal. 11. *Source:* United States Department of Commerce, Bureau of the Census. Data from Republic of China publications. 12. For 1977. 13. Includes slurries. 14. Includes peat. 15. Includes low-grade coal at its hard-coal equivalent. 16. Year beginning April. 17. Year beginning March 21. 18. Includes estimated production in the occupied Sinai Peninsula (1970, 4.9 million metric tons). 19. Includes brown coal. 20. Includes share of production and consumption in the Neutral Zone. 21. West Malaysia only. 22. Includes Bangladesh. 23. Includes data for Botswana, Lesotho, Namibia, and Swaziland. 24. Includes Canary Islands and Ceuta. 25. Year ending Sept. 30. 26. Abu Dhabi only. 27. Data for former Republic of South Vietnam only. 28. For 1975. 29. Data for former Democratic Republic of Vietnam only. NOTES: metric ton = 1.1023 short tons. n.a. = not available. z = less than 50,000 metric tons. A dash represents zero. *Source:* Except as noted, Statistical Office of the United Nations, New York, N.Y., *Statistical Yearbook*, (Copyright.)

Labor Force, Manufacturing, Steel, Iron Ore, Cement, Cotton Yarn, and Fish, 1977

Country	Economically active population[1] (thousands)	Persons engaged in Manufacturing[2] (thousands)	Steel: Production[3] (mil. metric tons)	Steel: Consumption[4] Total (mil. metric tons)	Steel: Consumption[4] Per capita (kilograms)	Production: Iron ore[5] (iron content) (mil. metric tons)	Production: Cement[6] (mil. metric tons)	Production: Cotton yarn[7] (thousands metric tons)	Production: Fish catches[8] (thousands metric tons)
Algeria	2,565	n.a.	.2	2.0	110	1.7	1.8	9[12]	44
Argentina	9,011	n.a.	2.7	3.6	140	.3	6.0	95[13]	393
Australia	5,330	1,175[14, 15]	7.5[14]	5.1	365	60.2[14]	5.0	20[13, 14]	128[14]
Austria	3,098	677[12, 16, 17]	4.1	2.5	335	1.1	6.0	20	3
Belgium	3,638	n.a.	11.3	4.0[18]	388[18]	z	7.8	41	45
Brazil	29,557	3,638[16, 19, 20]	11.2	12.0	107	56.6[21]	20.5	70[22, 23]	790[24]
Bulgaria	4,268	1,180[25]	2.6	2.4	276	.7	4.7	86	138
Canada	8,162[26]	1,748[22]	13.6	12.8	550	31.8[27]	9.9	63[22]	1,280
Chile	2,607	236[12, 28]	.5[29]	.6	60	4.9	1.1	23[13, 30]	1,285
China, People's Republic of	n.a.	n.a.	27.0[21]	32.5	38	32.5[21]	40.0[21]	1,450[13]	6,880[24]
China, Republic of[31]	5,748	1,735	.6	3.2	192	n.a.	10.3	277[32]	855
Colombia	5,134	457[12, 16, 33]	.2	.8	31	.5	3.3	28[19]	75[24]
Cuba	2,633	n.a.	.3	.5	53	n.a.	2.7	24[13]	185
Czechoslovakia	6,996	2,489[25]	15.1	10.5	700	6	9.8	126	18
Denmark	2,313	380[22, 34]	.7	1.8	356	z	2.3	2	1,807
Dominican Rep.	856	n.a.	n.a.	.1	28	n.a.	.6[21]	z[22, 35]	5
Ecuador	1,443	75[12, 16, 36]	n.a.	.4	46	n.a.	.6[20]	1[22]	476
Egypt	7,782	693[30, 37]	.3[21]	1.0	26	.7	3.2	210[13]	105
El Salvador	1,315	51[12, 16, 38]	n.a.	.1	21	n.a.	.3	6[13]	8
Finland	2,129	498[20]	2.2	1.5	326	.8	1.7	18[22]	117
France	20,439	5,760[39]	22.1	19.5	368	11.1	29.0	238	760
Germany, East	8,214	3,112[40]	6.9	9.9	591	z	12.1	135[41]	209
Germany, West	26,494	6,915[42]	39.0	33.0	538	.9	32.2	178[41]	432
Ghana	3,332	61[43, 44, 45]	n.a.	.1	11	n.a.	.7[22]	n.a.	383
Greece	3,388[46]	573[12]	.5[21]	1.6	176	.9	10.6	87[13, 22]	106[24]
Guatemala	1,364	69[12, 20]	n.a.	.2	26	n.a.	.5	n.a.	3
Hong Kong	1,655	755	n.a.	1.2	262	—	1.0	200	158
Hungary	4,989	1,331[40]	3.7	3.7	343	.1	4.6	60[47]	35
India	180,373	5,662[22, 48, 49]	9.8[29]	10.2	16	26.5	19.2	1,034[50]	2,540
Indonesia	40,100	759[12, 51]	n.a.	1.2	8	n.a.	2.9	54[30]	1,545
Iran	7,584	396[12, 33, 52]	n.a.	4.7	137	.7[21, 53]	6.0[22]	65[22, 35]	2[24]
Iraq	n.a.	134[12, 54]	n.a.	.7	60	n.a.	2.5[21]	1[12, 13]	26
Ireland	1,120	203[30, 55]	z[21]	.5	150	n.a.	1.6	4[56]	96
Israel	956	255[20, 43]	.1[21]	.7	195	n.a.	2.0	26	24
Italy	18,750	3,624[12, 57]	23.3	20.8	368	.2	38.2	212	427
Japan	53,321	11,212[16, 22, 58]	102.4	58.2	512	.5[59]	73.1	441	10,733
Korea, North	n.a.	n.a.	3.1[21]	3.2	190	3.8[21]	7.0[21]	n.a.	1,600[24]
Korea, South	10,378	1,717[20, 22, 44]	2.7[29]	6.8	186	.4	14.2	189	2,419
Lebanon	n.a.	n.a.	n.a.	.2	79	n.a.	1.4[21]	5[13, 30]	3[24]
Liberia	412	n.a.	n.a.	z	19	12.0	.1[21]	n.a.	16[24]
Luxembourg	131	45[12, 57]	4.3	[18]	[18]	.5	.3	n.a.	n.a.
Malaysia	3,430	261[16, 19, 60]	n.a.	.6	50	.2	1.8[61]	18[13, 61]	619
Mexico	12,910	n.a.	5.5	6.5	100	3.6	13.3	158[12, 13]	670
Morocco	3,981	n.a.	z[12, 62]	.8	44	.2	2.6	14[19]	261
Netherlands	4,169	1,022[63, 64]	4.9	4.5	322	n.a.	3.9	28	313
New Zealand	1,026[9]	299[22, 48, 65]	n.a.	.9	280	—	.9	n.a.	111
Nigeria	18,036	186[19, 44, 54]	n.a.	1.8	27	n.a.	1.3	5[12, 13]	506
Norway	1,469	367[20, 22]	.7	1.6	405	2.4	2.3	1	3,562
Pakistan	39,591	n.a.	n.a.	.7	9	n.a.	3.1[14]	283[13, 14, 50]	249
Peru	3,872	258[20, 30]	.4[21]	.6	37	4.0	2.0[21]	n.a.	2,530
Philippines	11,355	532[19, 20]	n.a.	1.4	31	—	4.1	31[13, 47]	1,511
Poland	16,944	4,284[66]	17.3	18.7	.5	.2[67]	21.3	219[41]	665
Portugal	3,424	629[16, 22, 60]	.4	1.5	156	z	4.3	85[13]	310
Rhodesia[79]	110	n.a.	.3[21]	.5	74	.3[21]	.5	n.a.	2[24]
Romania	10,362	1,635[68]	11.5	9.8[12]	464[12]	.6	13.1	171[41, 47]	151
South Africa	7,986	1,315[58, 69]	7.2[29, 70]	4.9[71]	161[71]	16.6	6.6	67	603
Spain	11,865	2,279[16, 22, 72]	10.9	9.1	249	4.2	28.0	66	1,455
Sri Lanka	3,459	n.a.	n.a.	z	2	n.a.	.4	5[13]	139
Sweden	3,413	925	4.0	3.8	463	16.1	2.5	7[22]	192
Switzerland	3,005	675[16, 73]	.7[74]	2.3	356	n.a.	3.6	45	4

Country	Economically active population[1] (thousands)	Persons engaged in Manufacturing[2] (thousands)	Steel: Production[3] (mil. metric tons)	Steel: Consumption[4] Total (mil. metric tons)	Steel: Consumption[4] Per capita (kilograms)	Production: Iron ore[5] (iron content) (mil. metric tons)	Production: Cement[6] (mil. metric tons)	Production: Cotton yarn[7] (thousands metric tons)	Production: Fish catches[8] (thousands metric tons)
Syria	1,525	176	n.a.	.6	76	n.a.	1.4	28[13]	2
Thailand	16,850	n.a.	.3[21]	1.4	31	z	5.1	73[13 22 47]	1,778
Tunisia	1,094	84[16 22 75]	.2[62]	.4	63	z	.6	7[13 22]	38
Turkey	15,829	738[22 33]	1.5	4.7	112	1.4	13.4	167[22 50]	155[24]
U.S.S.R.	115,204	30,562	146.7	145.6[22]	567[22]	131.4	127.1	1,597	9,352
United Kingdom	22,754[76]	7,472[12]	20.4	19.5	349	.9	15.5	126	1,004
United States	82,897[9]	n.a.	113.7[10]	133.9	618	35.0[11]	72.6	1,145	3,102
Uruguay	1,012	239	z	z	16	—	.7[21]	n.a.	48
Venezuela	3,015	324[12]	.8[21]	3.6	285	8.5	3.3	16[43]	152
Vietnam	5,742[77]	n.a.	n.a.	.3	7	n.a.	.7[21]	10[13 30 77]	1,014[24 77]
Yugoslavia	8,890	1,811[22 78]	2.4	5.2	239	1.5	8.2	121	61
World, total	n.a.	n.a.	**667.0**	n.a.	n.a.	**482.8**	**759.0**	n.a.	**73,500**

1. Comprises all persons engaged in or actively seeking productive work in some branch of the economy during a specified period of time. Generally, data are for a specific date in the 1960's and 1970's. 2. Comprises average number of employees, working proprietors, and unpaid family workers engaged in production of manufactured goods, including assembly of component parts and, except in the case of consumer goods, repair services. Except as noted, excludes gas manufacture and electricity. 3. Total production of crude steel, both ingots and steel for castings. Excludes wrought (puddled) iron. 4. Data represent apparent consumption (i.e., production plus imports minus exports) and do not take into account changes in stocks. 5. Refers generally to iron content of marketable ores mined, including manganiferous iron ores but excluding pyrites. Some data are rough estimates obtained by applying a fixed percentage to figures for crude ore production. 6. Covers, as far as possible, all hydraulic cements used for construction (portland, metallurgic, aluminous, natural, etc.). 7. Covers pure and mixed yarn and excludes tire cord yarn, except as noted. 8. Covers both sea and inland fisheries, in terms of live weight. Includes shellfish; excludes whales, dolphins, etc. 9. Excludes Armed Forces abroad. 10. Excludes steel for castings made in foundries operated by companies not producing ingots. 11. Includes iron content of byproduct ore. 12. For 1975. 13. Pure cotton yarn only. 14. Year ending June 30. 15. All establishments except single-establishment enterprises with fewer than 4 employees. 16. For one period of the year indicated. 17. Establishments with 20 or more employees. 18. Luxembourg included with Belgium. 19. For 1974. 20. Establishments with 5 or more engaged. 21. Data from U.S. Bureau of Mines. 22. For 1976. 23. Production in the State of São Paulo only. 24. FAO estimate. 25. All enterprises in socialist sector except publishing. 26. Excludes armed services. 27. Shipments from mines. 28. Establishments with 50 or more engaged. 29. Ingots only. 30. For 1973. 31. *Source:* United States Department of Commerce, Bureau of the Census. Data from Republic of China publications. 32. For 1969. 33. Establishments with 10 or more engaged. 34. Establishments with 6 or more employees. 35. Mixed yarn only. 36. Establishments with 7 or more engaged. 37. Private establishments with 10 or more engaged and all public establishments. 38. Establishments with 5 or more employees. 39. Total mining and manufacturing. 40. All enterprises. 41. Includes tire cord yarn. 42. Establishments with 20 or more engaged. 43. For 1972. 44. Includes homeworkers. 45. Establishments with 30 or more engaged. 46. Includes Armed Forces abroad. 47. Excludes yarn made from waste. 48. Year ending March 31. 49. Establishments with 10 or more engaged using power, or with 20 or more engaged not using power. 50. Mill production only. 51. Establishments with 20 or more workers. 52. Year ending March 20. 53. Year beginning March 21. 54. Establishments with 10 or more employees. 55. Establishments with 3 or more engaged. 56. Data from International Cotton Advisory Committee. 57. Enterprises with 20 or more engaged. 58. All private establishments. 59. Includes iron content of iron sand and pyrites. 60. Establishments in selected industries. 61. West Malaysia only. 62. Crude steel for casting only. 63. Work-years. 64. All kind-of-activity units in mining and manufacturing. 65. Establishments with 2 or more engaged. 66. All establishments in the socialist sector, except publishing. 67. Includes iron content of iron pyrites. 68. State enterprises under direction of central government. 69. For one period of year ending June 30, 1976. 70. Includes concast steel billets. 71. Includes data for Botswana, Lesotho, Namibia, and Swaziland. 72. All establishments, but certain industries not covered. 73. Establishments subject to labor laws. 74. Data from United Nations Economic Commission for Europe. 75. All units with 5 or more employees. 76. For England and Wales only. 77. Data for former Republic of South Vietnam only. 78. All enterprises in the socialist sector, except licensed handicrafts. 79. Now Zimbabwe. NOTES: n.a. = not available. z = less than 50,000 metric tons (metric ton = 1.1023 short tons. *Source:* Except as noted, Statistical Office of the United Nations, New York, N.Y., *Statistical Yearbook* and *Demographic Yearbook*. (Copyright.)

Wheat and Rice—Production by Country

(in thousands of metric tons)[1]

Country	Wheat 1978	Wheat 1977	Wheat 1976	Wheat 1971–75 average	Wheat 1966–70 average	Rice[1] 1978	Rice[1] 1977	Rice[1] 1976	Rice[1] 1971–75 average	Rice[1] 1966–70 average
Afghanistan	2,830	2,652	2,936	2,533	2,240	448[3]	458	448	405	382
Argentina	8,100	5,300	11,000	6,936	6,249	310	320	309	302	283
Australia	18,300	9,370	11,667	10,104	10,697	490	530	417	331	224
Austria	1,195	1,072	1,234	965	949	—	—	—	—	—
Bangladesh	343	259	218	109	70	18,898	19,441	17,628	16,793	16,560
Belgium	1,053[2]	795[2]	939[2]	958[2]	763	—	—	—	—	—
Brazil	2,677	2,066	3,215	1,934	1,064	7,242	8,935	9,560	7,012	6,639
Bulgaria	3,450	3,028	3,152	3,123	2,920	50[3]	68	41	63	54

Country	Wheat					Rice[1]				
	1978	1977	1976	1971–75 average	1966–70 average	1978	1977	1976	1971–75 average	1966–70 average
Burma	94	76	57	39	55	10,500	9,455	9,320	8,386	7,715
Cambodia	—	—	—	—	—	1,750[1]	1,800[1]	1,800[1]	1,569	2,880
Canada	21,146	19,862	23,587	15,092	16,727	—	—	—	—	—
Chile	893	1,219	866	1,050	1,258	105	120	98	64	73
China, People's Republic of[3]	44,003	40,003	45,001	36,601	28,157	131,775	130,472	129,054	121,532	100,769
China, Republic of[4]	n.a.	1	1	2	17	n.a.	2,649[5]	2,713[5]	2,397[5]	2,419
Colombia	38	29	45	58	87	1,715	1,307	1,560	1,231	708
Cuba	—	—	—	—	—	460[3]	459	451	375	165
Czechoslovakia	5,600	5,214	4,807	4,360	2,869	—	—	—	—	—
Denmark	653	606	593	566	445	—	—	—	—	—
Ecuador	38	40	65	57	79	285	328	368	241	171
Egypt	1,933	1,699	1,962	1,821	1,417	2,351	2,275	2,300	2,396	2,343
Ethiopia	423	592	507	648	762	—	—	—	—	—
Finland	241	295	654	516	456	—	—	—	—	—
France	21,057	17,349	16,126	17,022	13,590	45	23	32	56	98
Germany, East	3,200	2,914	2,715	2,797	2,006	—	—	—	—	—
Germany, West	8,118	7,235	6,702	7,132	5,642	—	—	—	—	—
Greece	2,660	1,716	2,450	1,934	1,836	92	92	69	87	91
Hungary	5,669	5,319	5,148	4,299	3,008	51	35	32	64	42
India	31,328	29,010	28,846	24,172	15,414	79,010	79,094	63,052	64,510	57,140
Indonesia	—	—	—	—	—	25,739	23,356	23,301	21,151	16,277
Iran	5,700	5,517	6,044	4,644	4,245	1,650[3]	1,400	1,566	1,265	1,038
Iraq	910	696	1,312	1,318	1,128	172	199	163	172	268
Ireland	247	250	200	264	325	—	—	—	—	—
Israel	175	220	206	252	156	—	—	—	—	—
Italy	8,764	6,329	9,516	9,528	9,585	950	721	907	950	739
Japan	367	236	222	280	853	16,000	17,000	15,292	15,689	17,764
Korea, North	350[3]	310[3]	340[3]	292[3]	96[3]	4,500[3]	4,610[1]	4,150[1]	3,195[1]	2,780[1]
Korea, South	36	45	82	123	256	8,058	8,340	7,249	5,915	5,212
Laos	—	—	—	—	—	796	847	858	865	827
Madagascar	—	—	—	—	—	1,981	2,154	2,043	1,855	1,836
Malaysia	—	—	—	—	—	1,590	1,893	1,995	1,942	1,422
Mexico	2,643	2,454	3,363	2,264	2,009	397	545	463	476	385
Nepal	401	362	387	275	202	2,400[3]	2,282	2,386	2,365	2,170
Netherlands	792	661	710	676	667	—	—	—	—	—
New Zealand	357	369	388	297	365	—	—	—	—	—
Pakistan	8,289	9,144	8,691	7,222	5,716	4,706	4,424	4,106	3,593	2,848
Panama	—	—	—	—	—	211	186	144	157	150
Peru	90	120	127	124	128	400	587	570	516	430
Philippines	—	—	—	—	—	6,907	6,895	6,461	5,386	4,735
Poland	6,000	5,308	5,745	5,605	4,260	—	—	—	—	—
Portugal	252	229	694	624	552	131	102	97	151	164
Romania	6,235	6,463	6,724	5,399	4,688	45	47	37	57	63
South Africa	1,730	1,860	2,239	1,735	1,125	3[3]	3[1]	3	3	n.a.
Spain	4,795	4,064	4,436	4,564	4,921	411	379	406	368	379
Sri Lanka	—	—	—	—	—	1,992	1,677	1,253	1,355	1,298
Sweden	1,306	1,522	1,765	1,352	932	—	—	—	—	—
Switzerland	407	324	400	386	383	—	—	—	—	—
Syria	1,651	1,217	1,790	1,249	767	—	—	1	1	n.a.
Thailand	—	—	—	—	—	17,000	13,910	15,068	13,948	12,774
Turkey	16,500	16,720	16,578	12,372	10,020	280	270	251	248	233
U.S.S.R.	120,800	92,165	96,882	88,935	90,192	2,100	2,217	2,001	1,753	1,011
United Kingdom	6,450	5,274	4,740	5,045	3,690	—	—	—	—	—
United States	48,954	55,420	58,307	47,972	38,992	6,251	4,501	5,246	4,579	4,121
Uruguay	150	173	505	354	356	226	228	213	148	115
Venezuela	1	1	1	1	n.a.	600	508	277	256	227
Vietnam	—	—	—	—	—	9,880	10,885	12,076	10,732	9,130
Yugoslavia	5,355	5,595	5,979	5,177	4,493	30	36	23	33	24
World, total	**441,474**	**385,736**	**419,661**	**358,794**	**314,826**	**376,448**	**370,592**	**350,365**	**329,180**	**288,629**

1. Rice data cover rough and paddy, except as noted. Data for each country pertain to the calendar year in which all or most of the crop was harvested. 2. Includes Luxembourg. 3. FAO estimate. 4. Source: United States Department of Commerce, Bureau of the Census. Data from Republic of China publications. 5. Paddy only. NOTES: metric ton = 1.1023 short tons, n.a. = not available. *Source:* Except as noted, Statistical Office of the United Nations, New York, N.Y. *Statistical Yearbook.* (Copyright.)

Communications

(telephones, mail, newspapers, radio, and television)

Country	Telephones, in use,[1] 1977 (thousands)	Telephones per 100 population, 1977	Pieces of mail sent, domestic,[2] 1977 (millions)	Daily newspapers,[3] 1975: Number	Daily newspapers,[3] 1975: Circulation: Total (thousands)	Daily newspapers,[3] 1975: Circulation: Copies per 1,000 population	Receiving sets, 1976: Radio[4] (thousands)	Receiving sets, 1976: Television[5] (thousands)
Algeria	298	1.6	218	4	285	17	173	30
Argentina	2,342	9.0	620[9]	164	2,773[10]	n.a.	838[7]	180[7]
Australia	5,685[11]	40.4[11]	2,069[12]	70	5,320	394	770[13]	351[13]
Austria	2,443	32.5	1,618	30	2,405	320	291[13]	236[13]
Bangladesh	98	.1	251	30	356[14]	n.a.	n.a.	n.a.
Belgium	3,100	31.5	2,581	30	2,340	239	409[13]	268[13]
Bolivia	49[15]	.9[15]	3	14	199	35	74	n.a.
Brazil	4,836	4.1	2,178	280[15]	4,050[15]	39[15]	158[7]	96
Bulgaria	946	10.7	n.a.	13	2,023	232	314[13]	176[13]
Burma	32	.1	75[7]	7	319	10	22[13]	—
Cambodia	71[7]	11.2[7]	1[15]	16	n.a.	n.a.	14[7]	4
Canada	14,488	61.8	5,638[16 17]	121	4,872[18]	n.a.	1,011	428
Chile	467	4.8	68[8]	47	n.a.	n.a.	172	68
China, People's Republic of	n.a.	n.a.	n.a.	n.a.	n.a.	n.a.	16[19]	1[15]
China, Republic of[20]	1,690	10.1	690	31[9]	n.a.	n.a.	90	55
Colombia	1,396	5.6	119[21]	40	1,248[22]	n.a.	117	70
Costa Rica	151	7.2	9	6	174	88	74	77
Cuba	321	3.3	42[7]	15	53[23]	n.a.	222	69
Cyprus	83	13.5	14	12	78[24]	n.a.	313[13]	89[13]
Czechoslovakia	2,863	19.0	2,216[15 25]	29	4,436	300	263[13]	254[13]
Denmark	2,718[26]	53.4[26]	1,268[16]	49	1,723	341	365[13]	323[13]
Dominican Republic	127[9]	2.6[9]	6[7]	10	197	42	41	33
Ecuador	221	2.9	7	29	331	49	279[19]	41
Egypt	503[21]	1.4[21]	206	14[21]	773[21]	21[21]	138	17[7]
El Salvador	72	1.9	21[27]	12	234[28]	n.a.	340	33
Ethiopia	79	.3	21[15]	8	70	3	7	1
Finland	2,032	42.9	676[8]	60	n.a.	n.a.	461[13]	363[13]
France	17,519	32.9	11,382[9]	98	11,341	214	330[13]	274[13]
Germany, East	2,860	17.1	968	40	7,946	472	367[13]	309[13]
Germany, West	22,932	37.4	12,368	334	19,298	312	329[13]	311[7 13]
Ghana	67	.7	58[16]	4	500	51	105	3
Greece	2,320	25.0	283	106	n.a.	n.a.	300	127
Guatemala	53[15]	1.0[15]	27[9]	11	165[29]	n.a.	42	19
Honduras	19[9]	.7[9]	21	8	99[30]	n.a.	57	17
Hong Kong	1,132[9]	25.5[9]	157[16]	82	n.a.	n.a.	527	191[13]
Hungary	1,104	10.3	1,611[8]	27	2,454	233	241[7 13]	236[13]
Iceland	95	42.9	18[8]	5	94	431	291[13]	241
India	2,096	.3	7,421[16]	835	9,383	16	24[13]	1[13]
Indonesia	347	.3	189	172	2,171[31]	n.a.	37[13]	2
Iran	782[9]	2.3[9]	858[32]	20	484	15	63	51
Iraq	320[9]	2.8[9]	33[9]	7	192[33]	n.a.	113[7]	37
Ireland	519	16.1	320[8 16]	7	693	222	300[13]	207[13]
Israel	993[34]	27.1[34]	316[16]	23	1,337[35]	n.a.	189	137
Italy	16,125	28.5	3,031[9]	78	6,296	113	232[13]	220[13]
Jamaica	109[9]	5.4[9]	77[9]	3	131[23]	n.a.	270	54
Japan	48,646[34]	42.4[34]	12,186[9 16]	108[21]	57,820[21]	526[21]	530	239[7]
Kenya	144	1.0	106	3	134	10	37	4
Korea, South	1,976	5.4	720	36	6,010	173	139	64[13]
Kuwait	155	13.8	5[16]	6[21]	80[21]	86[21]	487	183[7]
Lebanon	192[19]	6.8[19]	26[36]	33	283[37]	n.a.	540	144
Luxembourg	186	52.3	46	7	161[38]	n.a.	575	293
Madagascar	32[9]	.4[9]	22[7]	9[21]	59[21]	9[21]	74	1
Malaysia	375	3.0	330[8 39]	31	1,038	87	118	45
Mexico	3,712	5.9	1,068[9]	256	n.a.	n.a.	301[7]	84[7]
Morocco	210	1.2	101	9	360	21	84	29[13]
Netherlands	5,846	41.8	3,737	95[19]	4,100[19]	315[19]	290[13]	274[13]
New Zealand	1,674[40]	53.3[40]	578[8 16 17]	39	n.a.	n.a.	865	259[13]
Nigeria	121[9]	.2[9]	959	12	613[24]	n.a.	79	2
Norway	1,563	38.6	1,008[12]	80	1,657	412	320[13]	270[13]
Pakistan	259[9]	.3[9]	502[9]	102	358[41]	n.a.	17[13]	5
Panama	155[9]	9.0[9]	7[15]	6	131	79	157	108

Country	Telephones, in use,[1] 1977 (thousands)	Telephones per 100 population, 1977	Pieces of mail sent, domestic,[2] 1977 (millions)	Daily newspapers,[3] 1975			Receiving sets, 1976	
					Circulation			
				Number	Total (thousands)	Copies per 1,000 population	Radio[4] (thousands)	Television[5] (thousands)
Paraguay	40[9]	1.4[9]	n.a.	8	73[30]	n.a.	66	20
Peru	403	2.6	n.a.	35	n.a.	n.a.	129	37
Philippines	567	1.3	630[36]	15	686[42]	n.a.	43	18
Poland	2,925	8.4	1,730[8 9]	44	8,429	248	239[13]	198[13]
Portugal	1,175	12.0	462	30	612	70	161[13]	76[13]
Puerto Rico	515[9]	16.0[9]	n.a.	5[21]	405[21]	132[21]	549	196
Rhodesia[47]	190[9]	2.9[9]	112	3	116	18	39	11
Romania	1,196[7]	5.6[7]	686[7]	20[21]	2,716[21]	129[21]	145[13]	138[13]
Saudi Arabia	160[9]	2.1[9]	52	11[21]	96[21]	11[21]	28	14
Singapore	395[34]	17.1[34]	116	10[21]	n.a.	n.a.	156[13]	129[13]
South Africa	2,191	8.3	1,383	24	1,776	70	96	n.a.
Spain	9,528	26.1	3,578	115	3,491	98	259	185
Sri Lanka	72[7]	.5[7]	580[16]	18	n.a.	n.a.	58	—
Sudan	62	.3	32[8]	4	n.a.	n.a.	77[7 13]	6[7]
Sweden	5,930	71.7	2,551[8]	135	4,678	572	390[13]	363[13]
Switzerland	4,145	65.7	2,929	95	2,573	402	332[13]	285[13]
Syria	193	2.5	23[15]	6	n.a.	n.a.	224[19]	30
Thailand	367	.8	184	56	n.a.	n.a.	131[7]	18
Trinidad and Tobago	70[9]	6.5[9]	21[43]	3	100[23]	n.a.	253	103
Tunisia	144	2.5	70	4	190	33	141	36
Turkey	1,131[9]	2.8[9]	608	437[19]	n.a.	n.a.	105[13]	44
U.S.S.R.	19,600[44]	7.5[44]	5,069	691	100,928	397	481[7]	217[7]
United Kingdom	23,182	41.5	8,840[8 16 17 27]	111	21,700	388	706[13]	317[13]
United States	162,072	74.4	88,970[6 7 8]	1,812	61,222	287	1,882[7]	571[7]
Uruguay	268	9.5	17	30	637[36]	n.a.	516	114
Venezuela	742[9]	6.0[9]	202[21]	49	1,067[45]	n.a.	407	116
Vietnam[46]	47[15]	.3[15]	59[15 27]	n.a.	n.a.	n.a.	24[19]	—
Yugoslavia	1,556	7.1	644	26	1,896	89	210[13]	161[13]
World total	**423,082**	**10.4**	**n.a.**	**n.a.**	**n.a.**	**n.a.**	**n.a.**	**n.a.**

1. Comprises public and private telephones installed which can be connected to a central exchange. 2. Items mailed for distribution within national territories. Comprises letters, postcards, printed matter, merchandise samples, small packets and phonopost packets. Includes mail carried without charge, but excludes ordinary packages, and insured letters and boxes. 3. Publications containing general news and appearing at least 4 times a week; may range in size from a single sheet to 50 or more pages. Circulation data include copies sold outside the country. 4. Data cover estimated number of receivers in use, except as noted, and apply to all types of receivers for radio broadcasts to the public, including receivers connected to a radio "redistribution system" but excluding television sets. 5. Estimated number of sets in use, except as noted. 6. Includes ordinary packages as well as insured letters and boxes. 7. For 1975. 8. Excludes small packets. 9. For 1976. 10. 147 dailies. 11. Year ending June 30. 12. Year beginning July 1. 13. Number of licenses issued. 14. 27 dailies. 15. For 1973. 16. Year beginning April 1. 17. Excludes printed matter. 18. 117 dailies. 19. For 1970. 20. *Source:* United States Department of Commerce Bureau of the Census. Data from Republic of China publications. 21. For 1974. 22. 34 dailies. 23. 2 dailies. 24. 10 or more dailies. 25. Domestic and foreign. 26. Includes Faeroe Islands and Greenland. 27. Excludes postcards. 28. 8 dailies. 29. 7 dailies. 30. 4 dailies. 31. 55 dailies. 32. For 1971. 33. 5 dailies. 34. As of March 31 of the following year. 35. 19 dailies. 36. For 1969. 37. 17 dailies. 38. 6 dailies. 39. Data refer to West Malaysia only. 40. Year ending March 31. 41. 18 dailies. 42. 12 dailies. 43. For 1972. 44. Excludes telephone systems of the military forces. 45. 30 dailies. 46. Data are for former Republic of South Vietnam. 47. Now Zimbabwe. NOTE: n.a. = not available. *Source:* Except as noted, Statistical Office of the United Nations, New York, N.Y., *Statistical Yearbook.* (Copyright.)

Corn, Meat, and Sugar—Production by Country

(in thousands of metric tons)

Country	Corn			Meat[1]			Sugar[2]		
	1978	1977	1971–1976, average	1978	1977	1971–1976, average	1977	1976	1971–1975, average
Argentina	9,700	8,300	8,158	3,540	3,269	2,683	1,666	1,559	1,364
Australia	130	144	156	2,843[3]	2,722	2,268[3]	3,452	3,395	2,810
Austria	1,166	1,159	865	504[4]	492	460	506	426	396
Belgium[5]	32	29	26	921	872	855	757	721	723
Brazil	13,533	19,246	15,610	3,148	3,343	2,909	8,759	7,236	6,323
Bulgaria	2,300	2,649	2,589	466[4]	453	387	240	230	225
Canada	4,215	4,196	3,045	1,635	1,687	1,578	155	156	122

Country	Corn			Meat[1]			Sugar[2]		
	1978	1977	1971–1976, average	1978	1977	1971–1976, average	1977	1976	1971–1975, average
Chile	257	355	296	248	253	247	120	240	152
China, People's Republic of	33,120[4]	30,115[4]	29,895[4]	17,017[4]	16,536[4]	13,899[4]	3,800	4,000	3,480
China, Republic of[6]	n.a.	95	95	n.a.	n.a.	n.a.	n.a.	n.a.	n.a.
Colombia	862	753	794	547[4]	531[4]	518[4]	853	935	849
Cuba	95[4]	95[4]	91	208[4]	202[4]	200[4]	6,953	6,151	5,675
Czechoslovakia	628	792	619	1,214[4]	1,136	1,053	924	620	752
Denmark	n.a.	n.a.	n.a.	1,031	987	962	472	432	372
Dominican Republic	42	35	49	62	59	55	1,258	1,287	1,177
Egypt	3,197	2,725	2,624	292[4]	284[4]	273	657	576	549
El Salvador	540	380	359	48	47	41[7]	364	261	216
Ethiopia	1,079	999	1,006	343[4]	338[4]	337	137	136	131
France	9,473	8,505	8,408	3,507[4]	3,414	3,382	3,908	2,721	2,859
Germany, East	2	2	9	1,616[4]	1,608	1,395	700	609	561
Germany, West	620	579	544	3,999[4]	3,856	3,651	n.a.	2,844	2,435
Ghana	350[4]	309	385	29[4]	27[4]	32[4]	25	12	8
Greece	537	422	532	341	343	306	294	386	187
Guatemala	760	798	717	93	83	77	487	517	299
Hungary	6,700	6,007	5,802	1,031[4]	1,002	894	476	395	307
India	5,500	5,947	6,078	646[4]	642[4]	620[4]	5,019	5,033	4,238
Indonesia	2,750	3,143	2,839	328[4]	326[4]	301	1,100	1,380	907
Iran	60	55	40	366[4]	358[4]	331[4]	752	650	603
Ireland	n.a.	n.a.	n.a.	556	551	469	n.a.	n.a.	176[8]
Italy	6,040	6,456	5,016	2,075[4]	2,000	1,812	n.a.	1,758	1,196
Japan	11	8	17	1,590[4]	1,526	1,288	566	506	600
Kenya	2,350	2,553	2,436[4]	181[4]	164[4]	161[4]	185	182	149
Malaysia	35[4]	34[4]	18	62[9]	63[9]	62[9]	60	50	19
Mexico	9,616	10,024	8,613	1,033	1,028	899	2,790	2,710	2,672
Morocco	390	184	371	135	133	159	260	250	246
Netherlands	n.a.	n.a.	n.a.	1,444	1,369	1,221	n.a.	947	822
Nigeria	1,450[4]	1,400[4]	1,054	339[4]	330[4]	314[4]	40	30	34
Pakistan	800[4]	821	749	570[4]	559	424	764	677	506[10]
Peru	550	749	635	186	182	190	900	930	918[8]
Philippines	3,333	3,037	2,361	535	518	484	2,624	2,984	2,338
Poland	400[4]	232	61	2,601	2,279	2,261	1,810	1,774	1,774
Portugal	443	491	519	252	249	224	10	12	13[11]
Rhodesia[13]	1,400	1,300	1,306	171[4]	189[4]	163[4]	200	220	227
Romania	10,179	10,114	8,888	1,108[4]	1,165	978	590	561	577
South Africa	9,930	9,630	8,333	744[4]	708	683	2,369	2,113	1,944
Spain	1,933	1,892	1,892	1,358	1,310	1,106	1,262	1,162	847
Sweden	n.a.	n.a.	n.a.	459	455	417	339	301	280
Switzerland	108	111	114	417[4]	413	374	85	83	71
Thailand	3,030	1,677	2,341	363[4]	352[4]	365[4]	2,361	1,757	1,101[12]
Turkey	1,300	1,265	1,163	624[4]	616	563	1,158	1,090	810
Uganda	660[4]	515	501	94[4]	93[4]	84	20	20	86
U.S.S.R.	9,000	10,979	10,202	13,085[4]	12,732	12,258	8,885	8,500	8,880
United Kingdom	n.a.	n.a.	n.a.	2,005	2,133	2,186	978	657	930
United States	179,886	163,213	142,642	17,605	18,013	16,936	5,523	6,163	5,409
Uruguay	172	121	188	405	404	393	120	120	82
Venezuela	740	799	569	384	372	313	445	510	523
Vietnam	460[4]	408	301[4]	550[4]	511[4]	470[4]	80	—	—
Yugoslavia	7,555	9,870	8,359	1,057[4]	1,048	850	647	580	448
Zaire	487	515	472	60[4]	59[4]	55[7]	65	65	55
World total	**362,971**	**348,461**	**312,489**	**104,360**	**102,494**	**93,407**	**91,826**	**86,573**	**77,610**

1. Beef and veal (incl. buffalo meat), pork (incl. bacon and ham), and mutton and lamb (incl. goat meat). Refers to meat from animals slaughtered within the national boundaries irrespective of origin of animals, and ralates to commercial and farm slaughter. In terms of carcass weight. Excludes lard, tallow, and edible offals, except as noted. 2. Beet and cane. Data generally in terms of raw sugar. 3. Year ending June 30. 4. FAO estimate. 5. Includes Luxembourg for corn and meat. 6. *Source:* United States Department of Commerce, Bureau of the Census. Data from Republic of China publications. 7. Excludes data for 1971. 8. Excludes data for 1975. 9. West Malaysia only. 10. 1971 data for Bangladesh included with Pakistan. 11. Data for 1975 only. 12. Data for 1974 and 1975. 13. Now Zimbabwe. NOTES: Data for each country pertain to the calendar year in which all of most of the crop was harvested. Metric ton = 1.1023 short tons, n.a. = not available. *Source:* Except as noted, Statistical Office of the United Nations, New York, N.Y., *Statistical Yearbook.* (Copyright.)

Freedom in the World

One of the most important aspects of any country is the state of human freedom within its borders. Freedom is not a concept that lends itself to simple tabulation. As basic as freedom is, its measures are subtle and complex. For this reason, the editors of *Information Please* have once again turned to Freedom House for its annual Comparative Survey of Freedom.

Freedom House is a national organization dedicated to strengthening democratic institutions. "For 35 years," said President Carter, "the vigilance of Freedom House in the pursuit of democratic ideals has nourished those ideals throughout the world."

Readers may obtain Freedom House's bimonthly, *Freedom at Issue*, or its complete annual survey, *Freedom in the World: Political Rights and Civil Liberties*, from Freedom House, 20 W. 40th St., New York, N.Y. 10018.

The Criteria of Freedom

The Freedom House Survey defines freedom in terms of both civil and political freedoms, as traditionally understood in constitutional democratic countries.

Political Rights

In the area of *political rights* the Survey asks whether leaders are chosen, or decisions made, on the basis of an open voting process. If they are, then the question arises whether recent votes suggest that a significant opposition is allowed to compete. This would be demonstrated by the size of the opposition and, particularly, whether a recent change of government had resulted from an election or vote. Are there multiple political parties, or at least candidates not selected by the government? Does the polling and counting of votes appear to be generally without coercion and fraud? What share of the political power is exercised by elected representatives?

Also, how is political power allocated among central, regional, and local authorities? A wide dispersion of power is particularly critical in large states, or in states in which most people are isolated from participation in national life by lack of educational and economic development. Even if elections are not important in a country, one needs to ask if power is divided among a wide variety of persons and groups. In some cases a *de facto* balance of power may offer as much political freedom as an ineffective electoral system. Finally, the Survey asks how free the political system is from foreign or military control or influence.

Civil Liberties

Civil liberties generally imply independent news media, free from censorship. The Survey is interested primarily in censorship that is applied in defense of a ruling party or its policies; it has only marginal interest in censorship applied for social or religious reasons. Perhaps the most important civil liberties for the average person are the right to openly express oneself, the right to discuss public affairs with one's fellows without fear, and the right to belong to an independent private organization free of government supervision. Civil liberties include the right to a fair trial, and thus imply that the judiciary is to a degree independent. There is little detailed information readily available on the behavior of many judicial systems, but there often are indications as to whether an individual in a particular country can win a case against the government in court.

Closely allied to this question is the degree to which the security forces of a state respect individual rights. The number of political prisoners (arrested for opinions rather than violent action) and the existence of torture or brutality are important indicators. Finally, civil liberties are usually more operative when a nation is at peace, for increasing numbers of persons feel cowed into silence as levels of political violence rise. The Freedom House Survey also takes some account of the partial denial of rights implied by illiteracy, except on the local level.

The reader should be aware that judgments of civil and political rights are always on a comparative basis, and that Freedom House bases its conclusions on behavior rather than laws or formal systems. One might realize the imperfections of all systems and that the *pattern* of rights, not a simple list of pluses and minuses, is critical.

Political Terror

Contributing to the level of civil liberties in a country is the degree to which its citizens are subject to political terror, either from its government or from groups within the society. Political terror includes a variety of different aspects. Murder, torture, beating, imprisonment without fair trials or just laws, exile, passport restriction, denial of vocation, ubiquitous police controls, threats against relatives, all contribute to the fear that is labeled political terror.

Included again this year is Freedom House's rating of political terror in countries, included in this section. This table measures the crimes against humanity of greatest interest to organizations such as Amnesty International. In so doing, it fills a gap in the explanation of how the Comparative Survey of Freedom relates to other human rights concerns.

Political and Economic Systems

Freedom House further classifies countries according to their political and economic systems. *These classifications appear under each country in the **Countries, Territories, and Dependencies** section.*

Theoretically, the most democratic countries should be those with *decentralized multi-party systems*. More common are *centralized multi-party systems* (such as in France or Japan) in which the central government organizes lower levels of government primarily for reasons of efficiency.

Dominant party systems allow the forms of democracy, but structure the political process so that opposition groups do not have a realistic chance of achieving power.

The now classical form of one-party rule is that of the *communist one-party states* (such as the U.S.S.R. or Vietnam). The slightly larger number of *socialist one-party states* are ruled by groups that use Marxist-Leninist rhetoric and organize ruling parties much along communist lines, but either do not have the disciplined organization of communist states or have explicitly rejected one or another aspect of communism. A final group of *nationalist one-party states* adopt the political form popularized by the communists (and the fascists in the last generation), but the leaders either reject entirely the revolutionary ideologies of socialist or communist states or show little inclination to develop the totalitarian controls that characterize these states. There are several borderline states that might be switched between socialist and nationalist categories (*e.g.*, Libya or Syria). It should also be noted that "socialist" is used here to designate a political rather than economic system. A socialist "vanguard party" will almost surely develop a socialist economy, but a state with a socialist economy need not be ruled by a quasi-communist vanguard party.

Non-party systems can be relatively democratic, as in the small island of Nauru, but generally they are not. Such systems may be *traditional non-party systems*, ranging from Tonga to Saudi Arabia. Much more important are the many *military non-party systems*, such as that in Argentina.

States with *inclusive capitalist* forms are generally developed states in which the ruling assumption remains reliance on the operation of the market and on private provision for industrial welfare. A larger number of states are classified as *noninclusive capitalist* such as Liberia or Thailand, and they do not have over 50% of the population involved in a capitalist modern economy and the bulk of the population still living in traditional terms. In such states the traditional economy may be individual, communal, or feudal, but the direction of change as development proceeds is capitalistic.

Capitalist-statist nations (such as Brazil, Turkey, or Saudi Arabia) have very large government productive enterprises, either because of an elitist development philosophy or major dependence on a key resource such as oil. Government interferes in the economy in a major way in such states, but not primarily because of egalitarian motives.

Capitalist-socialist systems (such as those in Israel, the Netherlands, or Sweden) provide social services on a large scale through governmental or other nonprofit institutions. These nations still see capitalism as legitimate, but its legitimacy is accepted grudgingly by many in government. Governments of other states grouped here (such as Egypt or Poland) proclaim themselves to be socialist, but in fact allow rather large portions of the economy to remain in the private domain. Both variants also have *noninclusive versions* (such as India or Madagascar).

Socialist economies, on the other hand, strive to place an entire national economy under direct or indirect government control. States such as the U.S.S.R. or Cuba may allow some modest private productive property, but this is only by exception, and right to such property can be revoked at any time. The leaders of *noninclusive socialist states* have the same goals as the leaders of industrial socialist states, but their relatively primitive economies and untrained peoples cannot yet be completely socialized. Such states generally have a small socialized modern economy and a large preindustrial economy in which the organization of production and trade is still largely traditional. It should be understood that the classifications given are impressionistic; along the continuum between capitalist and socialist systems the division into categories must, of course, be judgmental.

Freedom in the World—1980

As the 1980s began, 1,601.3 million persons were living in free countries or territories—the largest number so recorded in the eight years of the Comparative Survey of Freedom. The free comprise 37% of the world's population, an increase of 1.9% or 118.1 million people over 1979. The world's not free also increased last year by 102.7 million or 1.5%. They now comprise 41.7% of the population. The partly free were reduced by 121.5 million to 921.2 million and are 21.3% of the people.

Most of the changes reflect relatively small gains or losses in personal freedom: In 25 countries, changes were entirely *within* the categories of free, partly free, or not free; in five nations, however, improvements or declines moved a country from one category to another.

The most dramatic gains were made in Nigeria and Ecuador. Both went from partly free to free. Chile moved from not free to partly free. The most striking decline was Pakistan. It went from partly free to not free. Grenada declined from free to partly free. By these major changes 93.6 million persons gained and 80 million lost.

Some 1,368.7 people live in the 18 countries in which freedom *advanced* without altering the nation's category. One already free country, Dominica, improved further. Twelve nations advanced within the partly free range: Bangladesh, Bolivia, Brazil, Comoro Islands, El Salvador, Ghana, Kenya, Mexico, Nepal, South Korea, Thailand, and Zimbabwe.

Five still not free countries made some advances: Central African Republic, China, (Mainland), Equatorial Guinea, Haiti, and Uganda.

Another 70.4 million people reside in seven nations where freedom *declined* without changing the country's category. In one free land, the Dominican Republic, a small decline was noted. Freedom was reduced in three partly free nations: China (Taiwan), Guyana, and Transkei. There were further losses in three not free countries: Czechoslovakia, East Germany, and Iraq.

The population of the world this year is estimated at 4,326.08 millions residing in 161 sovereign states and 57 related territories, a total of 218 places. The level of political rights and civil liberties as shown comparatively by the Freedom House survey:

Not free: 1,803.6 million (41.7% of the world's population), of whom 1,801.8 million reside in 55 countries (34.2% of the nations) and 1.8 million live in 4 (7%) of the related territories.

Partly free: 921.2 million (21.3%), of whom 911.8 live in 55 nations (34.2%) and 9.4 million live in 26 (45.6%) of the territories.

Free: 1,601.3 million (37%), of whom 1,595.7 million inhabit 51 nations (31.6%) and 5.6 million live in 27 (47.4%) of the territories.

Eight-Year Record of the Survey

(population in millions)

Survey date	World population	Free		Partly free		Not free	
		Number	Percent	Number	Percent	Number	Percent
Jan. 1973	3,334	1,029	32	720	21	1,583	47
Jan. 1974	3,784	1,351	36	812	22	1,618	42
Jan. 1975	3,867	1,366	35	899	23	1,602	42
Jan. 1976	4,063	804	20	1,436	35	1,823	45
Jan. 1977	4,020	790	20	1,464	36	1,766	44
Jan. 1978	4,083	1,455	36	874	21	1,754	43
Jan. 1979	4,227	1,483	35	1,043	25	1,701	40
Jan. 1980	4,326	1,601	37	921	21	1,804	42

The Comparative Survey of Freedom

Table of Nations

	Political Rights[1]	Civil Liberties[1]	Status of Freedom[2]	Outlook[3]
Afghanistan	7	7	NF	0
Albania	7	7	NF	0
Algeria	6	6	NF	+
Angola	7	7	NF	0
Argentina	6	5	NF	+
Australia	1	1	F	0
Austria	1	1	F	0
Bahamas	1	2	F	0
Bahrain	6	4	PF	0
Bangladesh	3+	3+	PF	0
Barbados	1	1	F	0
Belgium	1	1	F	0
Benin	7	6	NF	0
Bhutan	5	5	PF	0
Bolivia	3+	3	PF	+
Botswana	2	3	F	0
Brazil	4	3+	PF	+
Bulgaria	7	7	NF	0
Burma	7	6	NF	0
Burundi	7	7	NF	0
Cambodia	7	7	NF	0
Cameroon	6	6	NF	0
Canada	1	1	F	0
Cape Verde	6	6	NF	0
Central African Republic	7	6+	NF	0
Chad	7−	6	NF	0
Chile	6	5	PF+	0
China, People's Republic of	6	5+	NF	+
China, Republic of	5	5−	PF	+
Colombia	2	3	F	0
Comoro Islands	4+	4	PF	0
Congo	7	7	NF	0
Costa Rica	1	1	F	0
Cuba	6	6	NF	0
Cyprus	3	4	PF	0
Czechoslovakia	7	7−	NF	0
Denmark	1	1	F	0
Djibouti	3	4	PF	0
Dominica	2	2+	F	0
Dominican Republic	2	3−	F	0
Ecuador	2+	2+	F+	0
Egypt	5	5	PF	0
El Salvador	5−	3+	PF	+
Equatorial Guinea	7	6+	NF	0
Ethiopia	7	7	NF	0
Fiji	2	2	F	0
Finland	2	2	F	0
France	1	2	F	0
Gabon	6	6	NF	0
Gambia	2	2	F	0
Germany, East	7	7−	NF	0
Germany, West	1	2	F	0
Ghana	4+	4	PF	0
Greece	2	2	F	0
Grenada	4−	5−	PF−	−
Guatemala	3	5	PF	0
Guinea	7	7	NF	0
Guinea-Bissau	6	6	NF	0
Guyana	4	4−	PF	0
Haiti	6+	5+	NF	0
Honduras	6	3	PF	0
Hungary	6	5	NF	0
Iceland	1	1	F	0
India	2	2	F	0
Indonesia	5	5	PF	0
Iran	5+	6−	PF	−
Iraq	7	7−	NF	0
Ireland	1	1	F	0
Israel	2	2	F	0
Italy	2	2	F	0
Ivory Coast	6	5	PF+	0
Jamaica	2	3	F	0
Japan	2	1	F	0
Jordan	6	6	NF	0
Kenya	5	4+	PF	0
Kiribati	2	2	F	0
Korea, North	7	7	NF	0
Korea, South	4+	5	PF	+
Kuwait	6	4	PF	0
Laos	7	7	NF	0
Lebanon	4	4	PF	0

	Political Rights[1]	Civil Liberties[1]	Status of Freedom[2]	Outlook[3]
Lesotho	5	5	PF	0
Liberia	6	5–	PF	0
Libya	6	6	NF	0
Luxembourg	1	1	F	0
Madagascar	6–	6–	NF–	0
Malawi	6	7	NF	0
Malaysia	3	4	PF	0
Maldives	5	5	PF	0
Mali	7	6	NF	0
Malta	2	2	F	–
Mauritania	6	6	NF	0
Mauritius	2	4	PF	0
Mexico	3+	3+	PF	0
Mongolia	7	7	NF	0
Morocco	3	4	PF	0
Mozambique	7	7	NF	0
Nauru	2	2	F	0
Nepal	5+	4+	PF	+
Netherlands	1	1	F	0
New Zealand	1	1	F	0
Nicaragua	5	5	PF	+
Niger	7	6	NF	0
Nigeria	2+	3	F+	0
Norway	1	1	F	0
Oman	6	6	NF	0
Pakistan	6	6–	NF–	0
Panama	5	5	PF	0
Papua New Guinea	2	2	F	0
Paraguay	5	5	PF	0
Peru	5	4	PF	+
Philippines	5	5	PF	0
Poland	6	5	PF	–
Portugal	2	2	F	0
Qatar	5	5	PF	0
Romania	7	6	NF	0
Rwanda	6	6	NF	0
St. Lucia	2	3	F	0
St. Vincent	2	3	F	0
São Tomé and Príncipe	6	6	NF	0
Saudi Arabia	6	6	NF	0
Senegal	4	3	PF	0
Seychelles	6	5	PF	0
Sierra Leone	5	5	PF	0
Singapore	5	5	PF	0
Solomon Islands	2	2	F	0
Somalia	7	7	NF	0
South Africa	5	6	PF	+
Spain	2	2+	F	0
Sri Lanka	2	3	F	0
Sudan	5	5	PF	0
Suriname	2	2	F	0
Swaziland	5+	5	PF	0
Sweden	1	1	F	0
Switzerland	1	1	F	0
Syria	5	6	PF	0
Tanzania	6	6	NF	0
Thailand	4+	3+	PF	0
Togo	7	6	NF	0
Tonga	5	3	PF	0
Transkei	5	6–	PF	0
Trinidad and Tobago	2	2	F	0
Tunisia	6	5	PF+	0
Turkey	2	3	F	0
Tuvalu	2	2	F	0
Uganda	6+	6+	NF	+
U.S.S.R.	6	6	NF	0
United Arab Emirates	5	5	PF	0
United Kingdom	1	1	F	0
United States	1	1	F	0
Upper Volta	2	3	F	0
Uruguay	6	6	NF	0
Venezuela	1	2	F	0
Vietnam	7	7	NF	0
Western Samoa	4	2	PF	0
Yemen Arab Republic	6	5	NF	0
Yemen, People's Dem. Republic of	6+	7	NF	0
Yugoslavia	6	5	NF	0
Zaire	6+	6	NF	0
Zambia	5	5	PF	0
Zimbabwe	4+	5	PF	+

1. The scales use the numbers 1–7, with 1 comparatively offering the highest level of political or civil rights, and 7 the lowest. A plus or minus following a rating indicates an improvement or decline in the rating since January 1979. For further information on the scale and survey *see Freedom in the World: Political Rights and Civil Liberties, 1980.* available from Freedom House. 2. A free state is designated by F, a partly free state by PF, and a not free state by NF. 3. A positive outlook for freedom is indicated by a plus sign, a negative outlook, by a minus sign, and relative stability of ratings by a zero. The outlook for freedom is based on the problems the country is facing, the way the government and people are reacting to these problems, and the longer run political traditions of the society. A judgment of outlook may also reflect an imminent change, such as the expected adoption of a meaningful new constitution.

Estimated Levels of Political Terror

	Political terror[1]	Status of freedom[2]
Afghanistan	E	NF
Albania	E	NF
Algeria	C	NF
Angola	D	NF
Argentina	D	NF
Australia	A	F
Austria	A	F
Bahamas	A	F
Bahrain	B	PF
Bangladesh	B	PF
Barbados	A	F
Belgium	A	F
Benin	B	NF
Bhutan	B	PF
Bolivia	C	PF
Botswana	B	PF
Brazil	B	PF
Bulgaria	D	NF
Burma	C	NF
Burundi	C	NF
Cambodia	E	NF
Cameroon	C	NF
Canada	A	F
Cape Verde	(3)	NF
Central African Republic	C	NF
Chad	D	NF
Chile	B	NF
China, People's Republic of,	C	NF

	Political terror[1]	Status of freedom[2]
China, Republic of	C	PF
Colombia	C	F
Comoro Islands	B	PF
Congo	D	NF
Costa Rica	A	F
Cuba	C	NF
Cyprus	C	PF
Czechoslovakia	C	NF
Denmark	A	F
Djibouti	C	PF
Dominica	A	F
Dominican Republic	B	F
Ecuador	B	F
Egypt	C	PF
El Salvador	D	PF
Equatorial Guinea	D	NF
Ethiopia	E	NF
Fiji	A	F
Finland	A	F
France	A	F
Gabon	B	NF
Gambia	A	F
Germany, East	C	NF
Germany, West	A	F
Ghana	C	PF
Greece	A	F
Grenada	C	F
Guatemala	D	PF
Guinea	D	NF
Guinea-Bissau	C	NF
Guyana	B	PF
Haiti	C	NF
Honduras	C	PF
Hungary	B	NF
Iceland	A	F
India	B	F
Indonesia	C	PF
Iran	C	PF
Iraq	D	NF
Ireland	A	F
Israel	A	F
Italy	B	F
Ivory Coast	B	PF
Jamaica	B	F
Japan	A	F
Jordan	B	NF
Kenya	B	PF
Kiribati	(3)	F
Korea, North	D	NF
Korea, South	C	PF
Kuwait	A	PF
Laos	D	NF
Lebanon	D	PF
Lesotho	C	PF
Liberia	C	PF
Libya	C	NF
Luxembourg	A	F
Madagascar	C	NF
Malawi	D	NF
Malaysia	C	PF
Maldives	B	PF
Mali	C	NF
Malta	B	F
Mauritania	C	NF
Mauritius	B	PF
Mexico	B	PF
Mongolia	D	NF
Morocco	C	PF
Mozambique	D	NF
Nauru	A	F
Nepal	B	PF
Netherlands	A	F
New Zealand	A	F
Nicaragua	C	PF
Niger	C	NF
Nigeria	B	F
Norway	A	F
Oman	C	NF
Pakistan	C	PF
Panama	B	PF
Papua New Guinea	A	F
Paraguay	D	PF
Peru	B	PF
Philippines	C	PF
Poland	B	PF
Portugal	A	F
Qatar	B	PF
Romania	C	NF
Rwanda	(3)	NF
São Tomé and Príncipe	(3)	NF
St. Lucia	B	F
St. Vincent	(3)	F
Saudi Arabia	B	NF
Senegal	B	PF
Seychelles	(3)	PF
Sierra Leone	C	PF
Singapore	B	PF
Solomon Islands	B	F
Somalia	D	NF
South Africa	C	PF
Spain	B	F
Sri Lanka	B	F
Sudan	B	PF
Suriname	A	F
Swaziland	C	PF
Sweden	A	F
Switzerland	A	F
Syria	C	PF
Tanzania	C	NF
Thailand	B	PF
Togo	C	NF
Tonga	B	PF
Transkei	C	PF
Trinidad and Tobago	B	F
Tunisia	C	PF
Turkey	C	F
Tuvalu	B	F
Uganda	D	NF
U.S.S.R.	C	NF
United Arab Emirates	B	PF
United Kingdom	A	F
United States	A	F
Upper Volta	B	F
Uruguay	D	NF
Venezuela	B	F
Vietnam	D	NF
Western Samoa	B	PF
Yemen Arab Republic	C	NF
Yemen, People's Dem. Republic of	D	NF
Yugoslavia	C	NF
Zaire	D	NF
Zambia	B	PF
Zimbabwe	D	PF

1. Measured on a scale from A to E, with A representing the lowest level of political terror and E representing the highest. The scale measures terror caused by the government as well as that created by groups within the society. 2. A free state is designated by F, a partly free state by PF, and a not free state by NF. 3. Insufficient information. NOTE: For further information on these scales, see *Freedom in the World: Political Rights and Civil Liberties, 1980;* available from Freedom House.

International Treaties, Agreements, and Organizations

Alliance for Progress Agreement

Embodied in the Declaration of Punta del Este, adopted Aug. 17, 1961, by the U.S. and 19 other American republics, Cuba abstaining. The U.S. agreed to provide most of $20 billion needed over the next 10 years for Latin-American economic development. The other nations pledged themselves to increase their own contributions to economic and social development and to make the reforms necessary for all to share fully in the benefits gained under the Alliance for Progress.

Arab League

Formed at Cairo on March 22, 1945, as a loose confederation of Arab states seeking Arab unity. Founding members were Egypt, Iraq, Jordan, Lebanon, Saudi Arabia, Syria, and the Yemen Arab Republic, joined later by Algeria, Bahrain, Djibouti, Kuwait, Libya, Mauritania, Morocco, Oman, Qatar, Somalia, the Sudan, Tunisia, the United Arab Emirates, the Yemen People's Democratic Republic, and the Palestine Liberation Organization. Military cooperation has been hampered by differences among the members, except in the Suez Canal crisis of 1956. The league has proved more effective in economic and cultural affairs. A permanent secretariat was set up at Cairo.

Association of Southeast Asian Nations

A non-military alliance of Thailand, Malaysia, Singapore, Indonesia, and the Philippines, formed in Bangkok in 1967. Its goal of regional economic integration, along the lines of the European Economic Community has not been achieved. However, cooperation on international, political, and economic issues has been evolving. ASEAN took its first major political stand in January 1979 when it condemned Vietnam's invasion of Cambodia.

Central Treaty Organization (CENTO)

Created in 1955 to provide a defense shield on the northern tier of the Middle East against Soviet penetration. Its original members were Turkey, Iran, U.K., Pakistan, and Iraq (which withdrew in 1959). In 1958, the U.S. signed a declaration of collective security to cooperate with the member states. CENTO was known as the Baghdad Pact until 1958, when its headquarters were moved to Ankara, Turkey. Iran and Pakistan withdrew in 1979.

Commonwealth of Nations

An association of equal and independent nations and subordinate areas formerly part of the old British Empire and united by their symbolic allegiance to the Crown. Member nations gained equal status with the U.K. under the Statute of Westminster of 1931, which formally initiated the Commonwealth. Its members consult and cooperate and share trade and other economic benefits. For a list of members, *see* Countries of the World by Groupings.

The European Community

In 1950, the then French Foreign Minister, Robert Schumann, proposed a "Community" of the French and German coal and steel industries, with membership open to other European countries. The *European Coal and Steel Community (ECSC)* was established in 1952; it eliminated customs duties and reduced currency and trade restrictions on coal, iron ore, and scrap. Original members were France, Germany, Italy, Belgium, the Netherlands, and Luxembourg.

By 1955, discussions began on other ways of increasing European economic integration. The *European Economic Community* (the *Common Market* or *EEC*) was established by a treaty, signed in Rome in 1957, by the original members of the ECSC. In 1970, the U.K., Ireland, Denmark, and Norway were invited to join. All except Norway did so in 1972; the enlarged "Community of the Nine" formally came into existence on January 1, 1973. Greece became the tenth EEC member in 1979.

The purposes of the EEC include the removal of trade barriers, coordination of economic policies, and increased mobility of labor and capital among its members—much of which had been achieved by 1978. Its aim is eventual economic union of the member nations and ultimate political confederation.

A second treaty was signed in Rome in 1957 establishing the *European Atomic Energy Community (Euratom)* to integrate activities of member nations concerned with nuclear power and technology.

The three Communities (ECSC, EEC, and Euratom) make up the *European Community*, with a Council of Ministers and a European Parliament. A European Court of Justice and the European Investment Bank also function within the European Community. (*See* R.C. Mowat, *Creating the European Community*, 1973.)

European Free Trade Association (EFTA)

Formed in 1959 (formally begun 1960) to promote economic growth and fair competition, equalize the supply of raw materials among the member states, and to expand world trade. Members now include Austria, Iceland, Norway, Portugal, Sweden, Switzerland, and Finland (associate). Denmark and the U.K., originally members, withdrew before becoming members of the EEC in 1973: at that time a new trade agreement was made between the EFTA and the Common Market. By 1966, custom duties between members had virtually been eliminated. The EFTA is based in Geneva.

The Helsinki Agreement

Popular name for declaration adopted Aug. 1, 1975, by 35 nations—including the United States and the Soviet Union—participating in the Conference on Security and Cooperation in Europe held at Helsinki, Finland. The declaration particularly stressed "fundamental rights, economic and social progress and well-being for all peoples," as well as the need for joint action to promote world peace and security. The participating states reaffirmed their full support for the United Nations and pledged to respect each other's "sovereign equality and individuality. . . . " They pledged to broaden and deepen détente, and renounced the "threat or use of force" and subversion in settling international disputes.

Outstanding in the declaration was the section on cooperation in humanitarian and cultural fields. The signers pledged themselves to respect "fundamental freedoms, including the freedom of thought, conscience, religion or belief."

Among the stated objectives were: Freer movement among persons, institutions, and organizations; wider exchange of information; increased cultural exchanges and broader dissemination of books, films, other media, and artistic works. The agreement was reviewed in an eight-month conference at Belgrade, Yugoslavia, ending in March 1978, which was attended by representatives of the U.S. and Canada, 32 European countries, and the Vatican. After bitter debate, the conference adopted a summary document that did not mention human rights or other issues dividing East and West.

Marshall Plan (European Recovery Program)

Proposed in June 1947 by Gen. George C. Marshall, U.S. Secretary of State, to meet the need for integrated recovery efforts against "hunger, poverty, desperation, and chaos" in Europe. A July conference of 16 nations (the U.S.S.R. and its satellites refusing to participate) estimated four-year-aid requirements at $22.4 billion. In April 1948, Congress appropriated $5.4 billion. The U.S. established the Economic Cooperation Administration; European nations set up the Organization for European Economic Cooperation (OEEC). Each participating country set aside, in its own currency, sums matching the aid it received. The ERP ended in December 1951, a year ahead of schedule, with a total cost of $11 billion. Emphasis by then had been shifted to rearmament. (*See* S.E. Harris, ed., *Foreign Economic Policy for the U.S.*, 1948, 1968.)

North Atlantic Treaty Organization (NATO)

Set up April 4, 1949, under a regional defense treaty for the North Atlantic area stating that "an armed attack against one . . . shall be considered an attack against . . . all" and that participating nations will take necessary joint counteraction under the United Nations Charter, including the use of armed force. The founding members were the U.S., Canada, Iceland, Norway, Great Britain, the Netherlands, Denmark, Belgium, Luxembourg, Portugal, France, and Italy. Greece, Turkey, and West Germany were added later. NATO marked the first time that the United States pledged to go to war to support allies before the outbreak of hostilities. The member nations are represented on the governing NATO Council. Its organization comprises their top foreign, economic, defense, and financial ministers. Its major military commands are SACEUR for Europe and SACLANT for the Atlantic Ocean area. (*See* James Huntley, *The NATO Story*, 1969.)

Organization for Economic Cooperation and Development (OECD)

Founded in 1961 to encourage world trade and economic progress and aid underdeveloped nations. The OECD supersedes the Organization for European Economic Cooperation, which had been established under the Marshall Plan in 1948. Members are Australia, Austria, Belgium, Canada, Denmark, Finland, France, West Germany, Greece, Iceland, Ireland, Italy, Japan, Luxembourg, the Netherlands, New Zealand, Norway, Portugal, Spain, Sweden, Switzerland, Turkey, the U.K. and the U.S. (Yugoslavia has a special association). Its structure is consultative; its decisions, not binding.

Organization of African Unity (OAU)

Founded in May 1963 by 32 African countries, the OAU has grown to include most independent African countries; Rhodesia and South Africa are specifically excluded. Its charter reflects historical Pan-African concern for the political sovereignty, economic advancement, and cultural cooperation of all African peoples. The charter affirms allegiance to United Nations principles; its key section emphasizes the eradication of colonialism and promotion of international cooperation. The OAU has assisted in the relaxation or settlement of border disputes and helped resolve internal crises. In economic cooperation, it has stressed transportation and telecommunications. It maintains a close relationship with the U.N. OAU headquarters are at Addis Ababa, Ethiopia.

Organization of American States (OAS)

Created in April 1948 as a regional agency working with the UN to promote peace, justice, hemispheric solidarity, and economic development; and to defend the sovereignty of member nations. Original members were Argentina, Bolivia, Brazil, Chile, Colombia, Costa Rica, Cuba, the Dominican Republic, Ecuador, El Salvador, Guatemala, Haiti, Honduras, Mexico, Nicaragua, Panama, Paraguay, Peru, the U.S., Uruguay, and Venezuela. Barbados, Grenada, Jamaica, Surinam, and Trinidad and Tobago were admitted later. In 1962 Cuba was suspended. The permanent body of the OAS is the General Secretariat, formerly the Pan-American Union Headquarters, Washington, D.C.

Organization of Petroleum Exporting Countries (OPEC)

Founded in 1960 at Baghdad, Iraq, to advance its members' interests in trade and development and in relations with other oil-producing nations. Venezuela took the initiative; other founders were Iran, Iraq, Kuwait, and Saudi Arabia. They were joined by Algeria, Ecuador, Gabon, Indonesia, Libya, Nigeria, Qatar, and the United Arab Emirates. Through such practices as the 1973–74 embargo, OPEC has maintained high oil prices and has generally fixed the price of oil in international trade.

Panama Canal Treaties

Approved by the U.S. Senate in March and April of 1978. The basic treaty provides for turning the canal over to Panama by the year 2000. Until noon Dec. 31, 1999, the canal will be operated by a new U.S. agency, the Panama Canal Commission, with five Americans and four Panamanians on the board. Until 2000 the U.S. will have primary responsibility for defending the canal; Panama will assume jurisdiction over the 533-square-mile Canal Zone.

The Neutrality Treaty, also effective Dec. 31, 1999, provides that the U.S. and Panama will each have the right to defend the canal against threats to its neutrality or the peaceful passage of ships. A Senate reservation gave the U.S. the unilateral right to use force if necessary to reopen the canal or restore its operations. The Senate specified that any intervention would be only to keep the canal open, not to interfere in Panama's internal affairs. (See *Panama*.)

Treaty for a Partial Nuclear Test Ban

Agreement, effective Oct. 10, 1963, signed in Moscow Aug. 8, 1963, by the U.S., U.K., and the U.S.S.R. Although over 100 nations have since signed, France and China have not. The treaty banned nuclear testing in the atmosphere, in outer space, or under water. The signatories can withdraw under certain conditions.

The Potsdam Declaration

Issued at Potsdam, Germany, July 26, 1945, after a conference of President Truman, Prime Minister Churchill (later, Clement Attlee), and Prime Minister Stalin. Pending entry of the U.S.S.R. into the war against Japan, it was issued in the names of Truman, Churchill, and Chiang Kai-shek (reached by radio). The declaration, designed to clarify and implement the Yalta Agreement, demanded unconditional surrender of Japan and outlined surrender terms. It called for elimination of "irresponsible militarism" and for Allied occupation until Japan's war-making power was destroyed. Other major points included "stern justice" for war criminals, democratic reforms, and respect for fundamental human rights. Successful U.S. testing of the atom bomb was revealed to Stalin at Potsdam.

Strategic Arms Limitation Talks (SALT I)

Two agreements limiting American and Soviet nuclear weapons were signed in Moscow in 1972 after three years of negotiations. One was a five-year interim pact limiting some offensive strategic weapons and the number of launchers for intercontinental ballistic missiles carrying nuclear warheads. The other, a treaty of indefinite duration, restricted antiballistic or defensive missiles to 200 on each side. (That number was reduced to 100 in a 1974 amendment.) The agreements were signed by President Richard M. Nixon and Leonid I. Brezhnev, the Soviet Communist Party leader. The talks originated with discussions at Glassboro, N.J., in 1967 between President Lyndon B. Johnson and the Soviet Prime Minister, Aleksei N. Kosygin. On Nov. 24, 1974, President Gerald R. Ford reached agreement in principle with Mr. Brezhnev at Vladivostok on limiting the numbers of all offensive strategic weapons and delivery systems until Dec. 31, 1985.

(SALT II)

A treaty resulting from the second round of strategic arms limitation talks was signed in Vienna on June 18, 1979, by President Carter and Soviet leader Brezhnev and went to the U.S. Senate for ratification. The treaty runs to 1985 and limits each side to 2,400 intercontinental ballistic missile launchers and long-range bombers within six months. The U.S. is already under this ceiling, but the Russians will have to destroy 100 of their launchers or bombers. By the end of 1981, a new ceiling of 2,250 is to come into effect. The treaty allows each country to develop one new missile and to modernize its existing weapons within certain restrictions. Each side would verify the other's compliance by its own technical means. The agreement ran into sharp opposition in the Senate. A substantial increase in spending on armaments appeared to be the price many senators would set for their affirmative votes. President Carter delayed ratification efforts indefinitely following the Soviet invasion of Afghanistan in December 1979.

Warsaw Pact

Signed May 14, 1955, by Albania, Czechoslovakia, East Germany, Hungary, Poland, Romania, and the U.S.S.R. Albania, barred from meetings in 1962, withdrew in 1968 after ideological differences. The pact is the Communist equivalent of NATO, providing that an attack on one shall be regarded as an attack on all.

The Yalta Agreement

Signed Feb. 11, 1945, at conference of President Roosevelt and Prime Ministers Churchill and Stalin. The U.S., U.K., and the U.S.S.R. agreed to require Germany's unconditional surrender and on dividing Germany into separate zones for occupation, with France invited to join as the fourth occupying power. The agreement pledged disarmament of Germany, breakup of the arms industry, punishment of war criminals, reparations for destruction by the Germans, and the wiping out of nazism and militarism. The conference also agreed on terms for Russia to enter the war against Japan. (See R.F. Fenno, ed., *The Yalta Conference*, 2nd ed., 1972.)

Countries of the World by Groupings

KEY

1—Member of the Organization of American States (OAS)
2—Member of the Organization of African Unity (OAU)
3—Member of the Organization of Petroleum Exporting Countries (OPEC)
4—Member of the North Atlantic Treaty Organization (NATO)
5—Member of the Association of Southeast Asian Nations
6—Member of the Central Treaty Organization (CENTO)
7—Member of the Arab League
8—Member of the Warsaw Pact
9—Member of the European Economic Community (EEC)
10—Member of the European Free Trade Association (EFTA)
11—Member of the British Commonwealth
12—Member of the Economic Community of West African States (ECOWAS)
13—Member of the Organization for Economic Cooperation and Development (OECD)

NORTH AMERICA

Canada: 4, 11, 13
Mexico: 1
United States: 1, 4, 13

SOUTH AMERICA

Argentina: 1
Bolivia: 1
Brazil: 1
Chile: 1
Colombia: 1
Ecuador:1, 3
Guyana: 11
Paraguay: 1
Peru: 1
Suriname: 1
Uruguay: 1
Venezuela: 1,3

CENTRAL AMERICA

Costa Rica: 1
El Salvador: 1
Guatemala: 1
Honduras: 1
Nicaragua: 1
Panama: 1

CARIBBEAN REGION

Bahamas: 11
Barbados: 1, 11
Cuba
Dominica: 11
Dominican Republic: 1
Grenada: 1, 11
Haiti: 1
Jamaica: 1, 11
St. Lucia: 11
St. Vincent and the Grenadines: 11
Trinidad and Tobago: 1, 11

EUROPE

Albania
Andorra
Austria: 10, 13
Belgium: 4, 9, 13
Bulgaria: 8
Cyprus: 11
Czechoslovakia: 8
Denmark: 4, 9, 13
Finland: 10 (assoc. mem.), 13
France: 4, 9, 13
Germany, East: 8
Germany, West: 4, 9, 13
Greece: 4, 9, 13
Hungary: 8
Iceland: 4, 10, 13
Ireland: 9, 13
Italy: 4, 9, 13
Liechtenstein
Luxembourg: 4, 9, 13
Malta: 11
Monaco
Netherlands: 4, 9, 13
Norway: 4, 10, 13
Poland: 8
Portugal: 4, 10, 13
Romania: 8
San Marino
Spain: 13
Sweden: 10, 13
Switzerland, 10, 13
U.S.S.R.: 8
United Kingdom: 4, 6, 9, 11, 13
Vatican City State
Yugoslavia

MIDDLE EAST

Bahrain: 7
Iran: 3
Iraq: 3, 7
Israel
Jordan: 7
Kuwait: 3, 7
Lebanon: 7
Oman: 7
Qatar: 3, 7
Saudi Arabia: 3, 7
Syria: 7
Turkey: 4, 6, 13
United Arab Emirates: 3, 7
Yemen, People's Democratic Republic of: 7
Yemen Arab Republic: 7

FAR EAST

China, People's Republic of
China, Republic of
Japan: 13
Korea, North
Korea, South
Mongolia
Philippines: 5

SOUTHEAST ASIA

Cambodia
Indonesia: 3, 5
Laos
Malaysia: 5, 11
Singapore: 5, 11
Thailand: 5
Vietnam

SOUTH ASIA

Afghanistan
Bangladesh: 11
Bhutan
Burma
India: 11
Maldives
Nepal
Pakistan
Sri Lanka: 11

OCEANIA

Australia: 11
Fiji: 11
Kiribati: 11
Nauru: 11
New Zealand: 11,13
Papua New Guinea: 11
Solomon Islands: 11
Tonga: 11
Tuvalu: 11
Vanuatu (New Hebrides)
Western Samoa: 11

AFRICA

Algeria: 2, 3, 7
Angola: 2
Benin: 2, 12
Bophuthatswana
Botswana: 2, 11
Burundi: 2
Cameroon: 2, 12
Cape Verde: 2
Central African Republic: 2
Chad: 2, 12
Comoro Islands: 2
Congo: 2
Djibouti: 7
Egypt: 2, 7
Equatorial Guinea: 2
Ethiopia: 2
Gabon: 2, 3
Gambia: 2, 11, 12
Ghana: 2, 11, 12
Guinea: 12
Guinea-Bissau: 2, 12
Ivory Coast: 2, 12
Kenya: 2, 11
Lesotho: 2, 11
Liberia: 2, 12
Libya: 2, 3, 7
Madagascar: 2
Malawi: 2, 11
Mali: 2, 12
Mauritania: 2, 7, 12
Mauritius: 2, 11
Morocco: 2, 7
Mozambique: 2
Niger: 2, 12
Nigeria: 2, 3, 11, 12
Rwanda: 2
São Tomé and Príncipe: 2
Senegal: 2, 12
Seychelles: 11
Sierra Leone: 2, 11, 12
Somalia: 2, 7
South Africa, Rep. of
Sudan: 2, 7
Swaziland, 2, 11
Tanzania: 2, 11
Togo: 2, 12
Transkei
Tunisia: 2, 7
Uganda: 2, 11
Upper Volta: 2, 12
Zaire: 2
Zambia: 2, 11
Zimbabwe

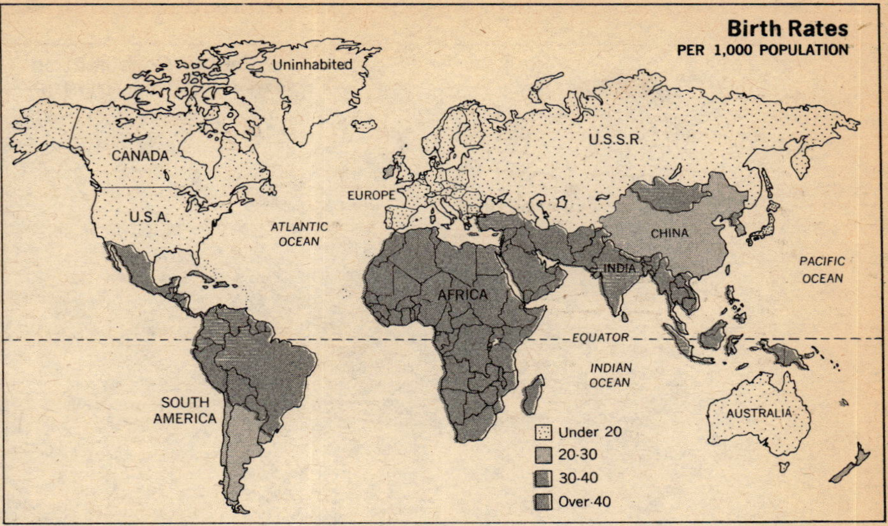

Countries with the lowest birth rate per thousand are West and East Germany (12). United States' rate is 16. There are ten countries with a birth rate of 50 and over, eight of them in Africa.

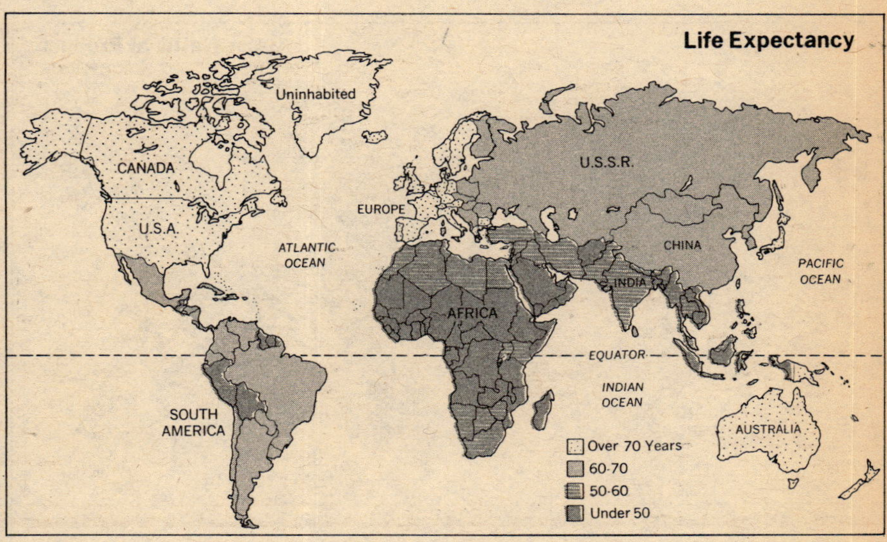

Norway leads with the highest life expectancy (75 years) and Afghanistan has the lowest (35 years). The United States' rate is 71 years. There are seven countries with a life expectancy of under 40 years, all of them in Africa.

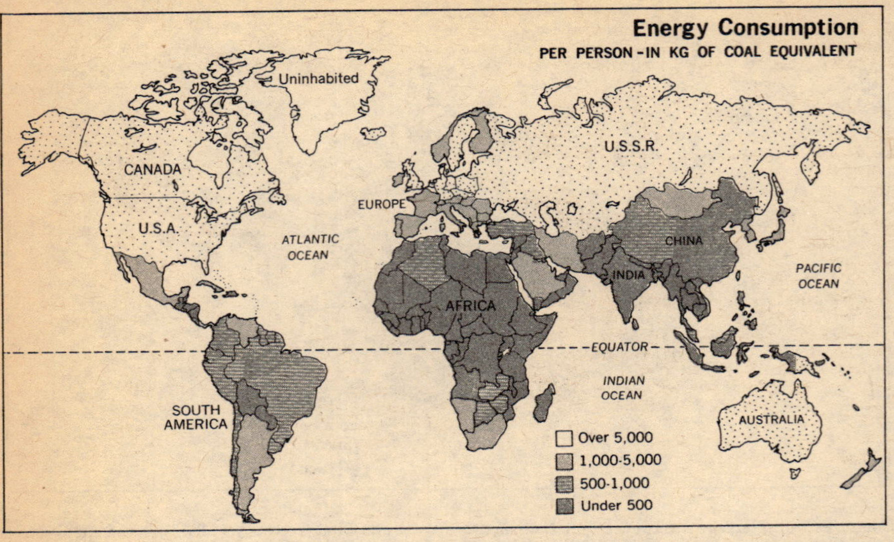

The country with the highest energy consumption per capita is the United States (10,999 kilograms of coal equivalent per person) followed by Canada (9,880 kg coal equivalent per person).

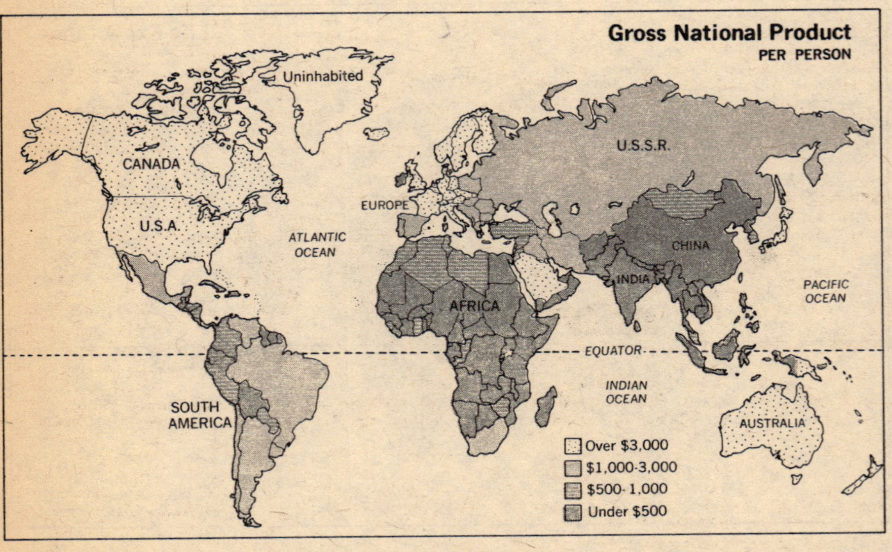

The country with the highest GNP per person is Kuwait ($15,480), about twice as high as the figure for the United States ($7,890). The reason: income from oil production. For the same reason, Saudi Arabia ($4,480) ranks higher than Great Britain ($4,020).

Countries, Territories, and Dependencies

For later developments, ***see*** **Current Events**

Economic data for each country have been drawn from reports of the United States State Department, the Central Intelligence Agency, the Defense Intelligence Agency, and the World Bank.

AFGHANISTAN

Democratic Republic of Afghanistan
President: Babrak Karmal (1979)
Area: 251,000 sq mi. (650,090 sq km)
Population (est. 1980): 15,875,000
Density per square mile: 63.2
Capital: Kabul
Largest cities (est. 1979): Kabul, 891,700; **(est. 1975 by U.N.):** Kandahar, 209,000; Herat, 157,000; **(est. 1973 by U.N.):** Baghlan, 110,900
Monetary unit: Afghani
Languages: Pushtu and Dari Persian (both official)
Religion: Islam (Sunni, 90%; Shiah, 10%)
National name: Jamhouriati Democratici Afghanistan
Freedom House classification: Socialist pre-industrial, one-party communist
Economic summary: Gross national product (1978): $3.5 billion. Average annual growth rate (1970–77): 5.3%. Per capita income: $130. Labor force in agriculture: 80%; principal products: wheat, grains, cotton, fruits, nuts. Labor force in industry: 20%; major products: processed food, textiles, cement, coal. Natural resources: natural gas, oil, coal, copper, sulfur, lead, zinc, iron, salt, precious and semi-precious stones. Exports: fresh and dried fruits, natural gas, karakul skins, carpets, hides, wool, cotton. Imports: non-metallic minerals, sugar, tires, textiles, transportation equipment, wheat. Major trading partners: U.S.S.R., India, U.K., Pakistan, West Germany, Japan.

Geography. Afghanistan, approximately the size of Texas, lies wedged between the U.S.S.R., China, Pakistan, and Iran. The country is split east to west by the Hindu Kush mountain range, rising in the east to heights of 24,000 feet (7,315 m). With the exception of the southwest, most of the country is covered by high snow-capped mountains and is traversed by deep valleys.

Government. A limited monarchy ended July 17, 1973, in a coup that ousted King Mohammad Zahir Shah. Mohammed Daud, a former Prime Minister and brother-in-law of the King, proclaimed a republic, suspended the 1964 Constitution, and abolished the Shura (parliament). On April 27, 1978, Daud himself was overthrown and Noor Mohammad Taraki installed as president of a 35-member Revolutionary Council.

History. Afghanistan occupies the land route to India trod by many conquerors, among them Darius I and Alexander the Great. The Moslems conquered the country from the west, beginning in the 7th century A.D. Genghis Khan in the 13th century and Tamerlane in the 14th century were later conquerors. Tamerlane's descendant, Baber, used the Afghanistan town of Kabul from 1504 to achieve the Mogul conquest of India. The country was torn by tribal and family warfare until Nadir Shah of Persia conquered the area in the 18th century. His commander, Ahmad Shah, established an emirate in 1747 and unified the country.

A later ruler, Dost Mohammed, reigned as the British and Czarist Russia began their struggle for central Asia. The Afghan Wars (1838–42 and 1878–81) that he, his son, and his grandson waged against the British are remembered for the massacre of the British at Kabul in 1842 and for the subsequent assaults on the Khyber Pass.

Afghanistan regained independence, though still under British influence, by the Anglo-Russian agreement of 1907, and full sovereignty by the Treaty of Rawalpindi in 1919. Emir Amanullah founded the kingdom in 1926.

The 1973 coup that ended the monarchy also cut off a 10-year experiment in democracy when Mohammed Daud seized all powers. The April 27, 1978, coup that brought Noor Mohammed Taraki to power resulted not only in the death of Daud but also, according to press reports, in the deaths of thousands of officials and supporters of his government.

Taraki's attempts to create a Marxist state with Soviet aid brought armed resistance from conservative Muslim opposition. Rebels kidnapped U.S. Ambassador Adolph Dubs in an attempt to ransom comrades held by the Taraki government. Dubs was killed on Feb. 14, 1979, when Afghan police attacked his captors and Soviet advisers ignored U.S. appeals for restraint.

Taraki resigned on Sept. 16, 1979, reportedly because of poor health, and was succeeded by Prime Minister Hafizullah Amin. As disorder spread, it was announced on Dec. 28 that Amin had been killed and replaced by Barak Karmal, who had called for Soviet troops under a mutual defense treaty. Pakistan and other Moslem nations called for a U.N. Security Council session and charged that Amin had been executed on Dec. 27 by Soviet troops already present in Kabul. The Council's call for immediate withdrawal of an estimated 40,000 Soviet troops was vetoed by the U.S.S.R. on Jan. 8.

With 85,000 reported in the invasion force by June, the U.S.S.R. and government forces were still unable to quell the rebels. Despite cuts in U.S. exports of high-technology goods and restrictions on food exports, together with a boycott of the Moscow Olympics by Western and Moslem nations, the Soviet Union refused to withdraw its troops.

Although hundreds of thousands of Afghans fled to neighboring Pakistan, resistance continued in mid-September when heavy fighting was reported in the Panjshir valley north of Kabul. Herat, the largest city in western Afghanistan, was reported to be in the hands of the guerrillas, who fought with small arms against Soviet armor and helicopters.

ALBANIA

People's Socialist Republic of Albania
President of Presidium: Haxhi Leshi (1953)
Premier: Mehmet Shehu (1954)
Area: 11,100 sq mi. (28,748 sq km)

Population (est. 1980): 2,730,000
Density per square mile: 245.9
Capital and largest city (est. 1976): Tirana, 192,300
Monetary unit: Lek
Language: Albanian
Religions: Historically Islam 70%; Greek Orthodox, 20%; Roman Catholic, 10%
National name: Republika Popullore Socialiste e Shqipërisë
Freedom House classifications: Socialist industrial, one-party communist
Economic summary: Gross national product (1978): $1.9 billion. Average annual growth rate (1970–77): 4.1%. Per capita income (1972): $520. Land used for agriculture: 43%; labor force: 61%; principal products: wheat, corn, potatoes, sugar beets, cotton, tobacco. Labor force in industry: 18%; major products: textiles, timber, construction materials, fuels, semi-processed minerals. Exports: metal ores, crude petroleum, bitumen, tobacco. Imports: machinery and equipment, rolled steel, wheat. Major trading partners: East European countries.

Geography. Albania is situated on the eastern shore of the Adriatic Sea, with Yugoslavia to the north and east and Greece to the south. Slightly larger than Maryland, it is a mountainous country, mostly over 3,000 feet (914 m) above sea level, with a narrow, marshy coastal plain crossed by several rivers. The centers of population are contained in the interior mountain plateaus and basins.

Government. Under the Constitution that Albania adopted in 1946, supreme power is vested in the popularly elected National Assembly, to which the Cabinet, headed by the Premier, is responsible. The 240 members of the National Assembly all belong to the Labor Party and Democratic Front. The only political party is Labor (Communist), led by First Secretary Enver Hoxha.

History. Albania proclaimed its independence on Nov. 28, 1912, after a history of Roman, Byzantine, and Turkish domination.

A battlefield in World War I, Albania reasserted its independence in 1920. A chief, Ahmet Zogu, proclaimed himself president in 1925 and monarch (King Zog) in 1928. Italy, under Benito Mussolini, drove him into exile in 1939 and annexed the country. The Communists under Enver Hoxha established a government in 1944, issuing a Constitution in 1946 (amended in 1950) declaring the country a people's republic. Close relations with the U.S.S.R. ended in 1961 with the Soviet-Chinese rupture. Thereafter, Albania functioned as a Peking satellite, receiving massive Chinese aid to offset the Soviet boycott.

In 1967, the regime closed all of the nation's 2,169 churches and mosques in a move to make the country "the first atheist state in the world."

Albania's long alliance with China ended with the announcement in 1978, that China was cutting off all aid to its one-time partner. Albanian criticism of Peking following the death of Mao Zedong was cited as the reason, but Tirana called the action "arbitrary." There was no indication from Tirana that Albania was ready to return to the Soviet sphere.

ALGERIA

Democratic and Popular Republic of Algeria
President: Chadli Bendjedid (1979)
Prime Minister: Mohammed Benahmed Abdelghani (1979)
Area: 919,951 sq mi. (2,382,673 sq km)
Population (est. 1980): 19,750,000
Density per square mile: 21.4
Capital: Algiers
Largest cities (est. 1979): Algiers, 2,500,000; Oran, 600,000; Constantine, 500,000; Annaba, 300,000
Monetary unit: Dinar
Languages: Arabic, French, Berber
Religion: Islam
National name: République Algérienne Democratiqe et Populaire—El Djehouria El Djazaïria Demokratia Echaabia
Freedom House classifications: Socialist industrial, one-party socialist
Economic summary: Gross national product (1978): $22.3 billion. Average annual growth rate (1970–77): 2.1%. Per capita income: $1,100. Average rate of inflation (1976): 15%. Land used for agriculture: 19%; labor force: 60%; principal products: wheat, barley, oats, wine, fruits, olives, vegetables, livestock. Labor force in industry: 11%; major products: petroleum, gas, petrochemicals, fertilizers, iron and steel, textiles, transport equipment. Natural resources: petroleum, natural gas, iron ore, phosphates, lead, zinc, mercury. Exports: petroleum products, wine. Imports: food, capital and consumer goods. Major trading partners: U.S., West Germany, France, Italy.

Geography. Nearly four times the size of Texas, Algeria is bordered on the west by Morocco and on the east by Tunisia and Libya. To the south are Mauritania, Mali, and Niger. Low plains cover small areas near the Mediterranean coast, with 68% of the country a plateau between 2,625 and 5,250 feet (800 and 1,600 m) above sea level. The highest point is Mount Tahat in the Sahara, which rises 9,850 feet (3,000 m).

Government. Algeria is governed by the President, whose term runs for 5 years. A new Constitution was approved on Nov. 19, 1976.

A National Popular Assembly of 261 members was elected Feb. 25, 1977, the first since the dismissal of a predecessor body early in 1965. The National Liberation Front, which led the struggle for independence from France, is the only legal party.

History. As ancient Numidia, Algeria became a Roman colony at the close of the Punic Wars (145 B.C.). Conquered by the Vandals about A.D. 440, it fell from a high state of civilization to virtual barbarism, from which it partly recovered after invasion by the Moslems about 650.

In 1492 the Moors and Jews, who had been expelled from Spain, settled in Algeria. Falling under Turkish control in 1518, Algiers served for three centuries as the headquarters of the Barbary pirates. The French took Algeria in 1830 and made it a part of France in 1848.

The fight by Algerian nationalists for independence had widespread political, diplomatic, military, and financial repercussions in France. Politically, it brought Gen. Charles de Gaulle to power when the army and extremist French colonist virtually seceded, set up a "Committee of Public Safety," and demanded that de Gaulle be given power. Ironically, it was de Gaulle who resolved to end the fighting by granting Algeria self-determination and independence, while his former army and French colonial supporters in Algeria joined to create the Secret Army Organization (OAS), a terrorist group that tried to block independence. But metropolitan France, weary of continued warfare, voted by some 15 million to 5 million in January 1961 to approve de Gaulle's proposals.

On July 5, 1962, Algeria was proclaimed independent. In October 1963, Ahmed Ben Bella was elected President. He began to nationalize foreign holdings and aroused opposition. He was overthrown in a military coup on June 19, 1965, by Col. Houari Boumediène, who suspended the Constitution and sought to restore financial stability. While retaining close economic and financial relations with France and the U.S., Algeria entered the Arab bloc and joined the war against Israel in 1967. Thereafter, the U.S.S.R. stepped up development aid.

Friction with Morocco intensified in 1976 as Algeria opposed the annexation of the Spanish Sahara by Morocco and Mauritania following a mass invasion of the former Spanish colony by Moroccan civilians. Algeria formally recognized a Saharan Arab Democratic Republic—composed of Polisario front leaders who fought unsuccessfully for an independent Sahara—on Feb. 27, 1976. The move was accompanied by a break in diplomatic relations with Morocco.

From an agricultural economy closely linked to France even after independence, Algeria became an exporter of energy in the form of petroleum products and then liquefied natural gas. The U.S. replaced France as Algeria's chief trading partner in 1976, buying 40% of Algerian crude oil production. In common with other oil-exporting countries in 1977 and 1978, however, Algeria slowed its general industrial expansion and shifted investment toward increasing oil and gas output and strengthening agriculture. Non-energy industry had proved too costly in relation to income produced and agricultural imports had become a drain on a weakened economy.

Boumediène died in December 1978 after a long illness. Chadli Bendjedid, Secretary-General of the National Liberation Front, took the presidency in a smooth transition of power. On July 4, 1979, he released from house arrest former President Ahmed Ben Bella, who had been treated as an "unperson" in the 14 years since his overthrow.

ANDORRA

Valleys of Andorra
Episcopal Co-Prince: Msgr. Joan Martí Alanis, Bishop of Urgel (1974)
French Co-Prince: Valéry Giscard d'Estaing, President of France (1974)
First Syndic: Estanislau Sangrà Font (1978)
Area: 175 sq mi. (453 sq km)
Population (est. 1980): 30,000
Density per square mile: 171.4
Capital (est. 1975): Andorra la Vella, 10,900
Monetary units: French franc and Spanish peseta
Languages: Catalán (official); French, Spanish
Religion: Roman Catholic
National names: Les Vallées d'Andorre-Valls d'Andorra
Economic summary: Land used for agriculture: 4%; labor force: 20%; principal products: oats, barley, tobacco, cattle, sheep. Labor force in industry: 80%; major products: tobacco products and electric power; tourism. Natural resources: water power, mineral water. Major trading partners: France, Spain, West Germany, Japan.

Geography. Andorra lies high in the Pyrenees Mountains on the French-Spanish border. The country is drained by the Valira River.

Government. A General Council of 24 members, elected for four years, chooses the First Syndic and Second Syndic. In 1976 the Andorran Democratic Association, the principality's first political party, was formed.

History. An autonomous and semi-independent co-principality, Andorra has been under the joint suzerainty of the French state and the Spanish bishops of Urgel since 1278.

ANGOLA

People's Republic of Angola
President: José Eduardo dos Santos (1979)
Area: 481,350 sq mi. (1,246,700 sq km)
Population (est. 1980) 7,100,000
Density per square mile: 14.8
Capital and largest city (est. 1970): Luanda, 475,300
Monetary unit: Kwanza
Languages: Bantu, Portuguese (official)
Religions: Animist, 45%; Roman Catholic, 43%; Protestant, 12%
Freedom House classifications: Socialist pre-industrial, one-party socialist
Economic summary: Gross national product (1978): $2.0 billion. Average annual growth rate (1970–77): −3.4%. Per capita income: $440. Principal agricultural products: coffee, sisal, corn, cotton, sugar, tobacco, bananas. Major industrial products: oil, diamonds, processed fish, tobacco, textiles, cement, processed food and sugar. Natural resources: diamonds, gold, iron, oil. Exports: oil, coffee, diamonds, fish and fish products, iron ore, timber, corn. Imports: machinery and electrical equipment, bulk iron, steel and metals, textiles, clothing. Major trading partners: Cuba, U.S.S.R., Portugal, U.S.

Geography. Angola, more than three times the size of California, extends for more than 1,000 miles (1,609 km) along the South Atlantic in southwestern Africa. Zaire is to the north and east; Zambia to the east, and South-West Africa (Namibia) to the south. A plateau averaging 6,000 feet (1,829 m) above sea level rises abruptly from the coastal lowlands. Nearly all the land is desert or savanna, with hardwood forests in the northeast.

Government. Last of Portugal's African colonies to gain independence, Angola was born amid civil war Nov. 11, 1975. Four months later, the Popular Movement for the Liberation of Angola (MPLA) claimed victory over two rival factions with the aid of Soviet weapons and advisers and Cuban troops. Cuban Premier Fidel Castro's pledge to withdraw all his troops by the end of 1976 was still unredemed two years later, and the situation in Angola remained one of the root causes of U.S.-U.S.S.R. conflict in Africa.

Because of the troop presence, the U.S. vetoed Angolan membership in the U.N. on June 23, 1976. It abstained in a second vote on Nov. 22, 1976, and Angola on December 1 became the 147th member of the world organization.

History. Discovered by the Portuguese navigator Diego Cao in 1482, Angola became a link in trade with India and the Far East. Later it was a major source of slaves for Portugal's New World colony of Brazil. Development of the interior began after the Treaty of Berlin in 1885 fixed the colony's borders, and British and Portuguese investment pushed mining, railways, and agriculture.

Following World War II, independence movements began but were sternly suppressed by military force. The April revolution of 1974 brought about a reversal of Portugal's policy, and the next year President Francisco da Costa Gomes signed an agreement to grant independence to Angola. The plan called for election of a constituent assembly and a settlement of differences by the MPLA and the National Front for the Liberation of Angola (FNLA) and the National Union for the Total Independence of Angola (UNITA).

Despite covert aid to FNLA by the U.S. and open support by neighboring Zaire for the Front's leader, Holden Roberto, the MPLA had the initial advantage of strength in the capital region. Cuban troops were introduced in October and soon routed the poorly trained and equipped FNLA and UNITA forces.

The Organization of African Unity, split over the issue earlier, recognized the MPLA government led by Agostinho Neto on Feb. 11, 1976, and the People's Republic of Angola became the 47th member of the organization.

The new government nationalized 19 major industries on May 19, mostly Portuguese-owned. This, together with Lisbon's objection to the refueling of Cuban troop transports in the Azores, led to a break between the former mother country and Angola.

Although militarily victorious, Neto's regime had yet to consolidate its power in opposition strongholds in the east and south. Less militantly Marxist than their colleagues in the former East African colony of Mozambique, the new leaders sought help from both the Western and Eastern worlds.

In March 1977, Zairean refugees in Angola invaded Zaire's Shaba Province, bringing charges by Zairean President Mobutu Sese Seko that the unsuccessful invasion was Soviet-backed with the collaboration of Angola. The Neto regime, the U.S.S.R., and Cuba all denied complicity. In May 1978, another invasion took place, and this time the U.S. and France joined Mobutu in accusing Angola, the U.S.S.R., and Cuba, all of which again denied guilt.

Neto died in Moscow of cancer on Sept. 10, 1979. The Planning Minister, José Eduardo dos Santos, was named interim President.

ARGENTINA

Argentine Republic
President: Lt. Gen. Jorge Rafaél Videla (1976)
Area: 1,072,067 sq mi. (2,776,654 sq km)
Population (est. 1980): 27,070,000
Density per square mile: 25.3
Capital: Buenos Aires
Largest cities (est. 1978): Buenos Aires, 2,982,000; (est. 1975 by U.N.): Córdoba, 781,600; Rosario, 750,500; La Plata, 391,200; San Miguel de Tucumán, 321,600
Monetary unit: Peso
Language: Spanish
Religion: Predominantly Roman Catholic
National name: República Argentina
Freedom House classifications: Capitalist-statist industrial, non-party military
Economic summary: Gross national product (1978): $50.3 billion. Average annual growth rate (1970–77): 1.8%. Per capita income: $1,840. Land used for agriculture: 57%; labor force: 19%; principal products: grains, oilseeds, livestock products. Labor force in industry: 40%; major products: processed foods, motor vehicles, consumer durables, textiles, chemicals. Natural resources: minerals, lead, zinc, tin, copper, iron, manganese, oil, uranium. Exports: meats, grains, wool. Imports: machinery and electric equipment, wood and lumber, newsprint, crude oil, automotive equipment and parts, iron and steel products, chemicals. Major trading partners: Western European and South American countries, U.S., Japan, U.S.S.R.

Geography. With an area slightly less than one third of the United States and second in South America only to its eastern neighbor, Brazil, in size and population, Argentina is a plain, rising from the Atlantic to the Chilean border and the towering Andes peaks. Aconcagua (23,034 ft.; 7,021 m) is the highest peak in the world outside Asia. It is bordered also by Chile on the west, Bolivia and Paraguay on the north, and by Uruguay on the east.

The northern area is the swampy and partly wooded Gran Chaco, bordering on Bolivia and Paraguay. South of that are the rolling, fertile pampas, rich for agriculture and grazing and supporting most of the population. Next southward is Patagonia, a region of cool, arid steppes with some wooded and fertile sections. The eastern part of Tierra del Fuego, the island southern tip of South America, belongs to Argentina.

Government. Argentina is a federal union of 22 provinces, one national territory, and the Federal District. Under the Constitution of 1853 (restored by a Constituent National Convention in 1957 and amended in 1972), the President and Vice President were elected every four years by direct vote. The President appointed his Cabinet. The Vice President presided over the Senate but had no other powers. The Congress consisted of two houses: a 69-member Senate and a 243-member Chamber of Deputies. All legislators were elected by direct vote for four-year terms.

All political parties have been suspended, along with Congress, since the military coup of March 24, 1976. Meetings or statements by political parties are forbidden.

History. Discovered in 1516 by Juan Díaz de Solís, Argentina developed slowly under Spanish colonial rule. Buenos Aires was settled in 1580; the cattle industry was thriving as early as 1600.

Invading British forces were expelled in 1806–07, and when Napoleon conquered Spain, the Argentinians set up their own government in the name of the Spanish King in 1810. On July 9, 1816, independence was formally declared.

As in World War I, Argentina proclaimed neutrality at the outbreak of World War II, but in the closing phase declared war on the Axis on March 27, 1945, and became a founding member of the United Nations. Juan D. Perón, an army colonel, emerged as the strongman of the postwar era, winning the Presidential elections of 1946 and 1951.

Opposition to Perón's increasing authoritarianism, fanned by worsening relations with the Roman Catholic Church, led to a coup by the armed forces that sent Perón into exile in 1955. The Peronist

Party and Congress dissolved, and Argentina entered a long period of military dictatorships with brief intervals of constitutional government.

In the first free election since 1951, a Perón-endorsed candidate, Hector Campóra, narrowly won the Presidency in 1973. He resigned July 13, seven weeks after his inauguration, in an effort to hand power back to Perón. The former dictator returned from exile and, with his third wife, Maria Estela (Isabel) Martinez de Perón, as Vice-Presidential candidate, swept the election on Sept. 23, 1973, winning 61% of the vote.

Perón launched a three-year plan to double the economic growth rate and boost family incomes by a third; it involved price freezes, wage boosts, and increased government spending. He persuaded subsidiaries of two U.S. auto manufacturers to sell vehicles to Cuba under a $1.2-billion export grant. It was an early break in the hemispheric boycott of Cuba.

Perón died of a heart attack at the age of 78 on July 1, 1974. His widow became the hemisphere's first woman chief of state, but she took over a nation racked by acute economic and political polarization reflected in mounting civil disorders.

Mrs. Perón was re-elected head of the Peronist movement Aug. 24, 1975, at a tumultuous party Congress at which 118 of 238 delegates walked out before the vote. In mid-September she announced she would take a month-long leave of absence to recover from nervous strain and turned the presidential duties over to Italo A. Luder, president of the Senate.

Returning to take up her duties again October 16, Mrs. Perón was greeted with demands for her resignation as both the economic recession and terrorism increased. The inflation rate for 1975 was 334.8%, compared with 40% for 1974, and labor protest mounted despite massive wage boosts.

The long-anticipated military revolt came March 24, 1976, with a junta composed of Army Lt. Gen. Jorge Rafaél Videla, Adm. Eduardo Massera, and Air Force Brig. Gen. Orlando Agosti taking power. Mrs. Perón and her closest advisers were arrested and subsequently charged with misuse of government funds, while thousands of Peronist government officials and labor leaders were placed under detention.

Videla took office as President on March 29 and formed a government of six military officers and two civilians, one of them the industrialist José Martinéz de Hoz, as Minister of the Economy. The new regime suspended the Justicialista (Peronist) Party as well as all others and decreed new security laws and censorship.

Political murders and terrorism under the Videla regime mounted, together with allegations of police torture. Testimony at the United Nations Human Rights Commission in 1977 said 2,300 had died, 10,000 had been jailed for political reasons, and more than 20,000 had disappeared since the new government took power.

The twin plagues of inflation and terrorism continued in 1980, the former somewhat diminished by stringent economic measures. From a 1978 record 169.5% increase in the cost of living, the 1979 increase was held to below 90%, with unemployment at less than 4%.

In 1979, Amnesty International reported that 3 to 10 persons had disappeared every day for the previous three years. The world human rights organization estimated that 4,000 political prisoners were still held in Argentine jails, with only 50 released in 1978.

AUSTRALIA

Commonwealth of Australia
Sovereign: Queen Elizabeth II
Governor-General: Sir Zelman Cowen (1977)
Prime Minister: Malcolm Fraser (1975)
Area: 2,967,909 sq mi. (7,686,843 sq km)
Population (est. 1980): 14,600,000
Density per square mile: 4.9
Capital (est. 1978): Canberra, 214,450
Largest cities (est. 1978 for metropolitan area): Sydney, 3,155,200; Melbourne, 2,717,600; Brisbane, 1,004,500; Adelaide, 930,500; Perth, 864,900; Hobart (on Tasmania), 162,000
Monetary unit: Australian dollar
Language: English
Religions (1971 census): Anglican, 31%; Roman Catholic, 27%; Uniting Church, 17%
Member of Commonwealth of Nations
Freedom House classifications: Capitalist industrial, multi-party decentralized
Economic summary: Gross national product (1978): $113.8 billion. Average annual growth rate (1970–77): 1.6%. Per capita income (1977): $6,830. Land used for agriculture: 63%; labor force: 14%; principal products: cereals, sugar cane, fruits, wine grapes, sheep, cattle, dairy products. Labor force in industry: 47%; major products: motor vehicles, iron and steel, textiles, chemicals. Natural resources: gold, iron ore, bauxite, zinc, lead, tin, coal, oil, uranium, timber. Exports: coal, wool, iron ore, wheat, sugar, beef, veal. Imports: transport equipment, petroleum and petroleum products, machinery, appliances, textiles. Major trading partners: U.S., U.K., Japan, New Zealand.

Geography. The continent of Australia, with the island state of Tasmania, is approximately equal in area to the United States (excluding Alaska and Hawaii), and is more than three fourths the size of Europe.

Mountain ranges run from north to south along the east coast, reaching their highest point in Mount Kosciusko (7,308 ft; 2,228 m). The western half of the continent is occupied by a desert plateau that rises into barren, rolling hills near the west coast. It includes the Great Victoria Desert to the south and the Great Sandy Desert to the north. The Great Barrier Reef lies along the northeast coast.

The island of Tasmania (26,178 sq mi.; 67,800 sq km) is off the southeastern coast.

Government. The Federal Parliament consists of a bicameral legislature. The House of Representatives has 124 members elected for three years by popular vote. The Senate has 64 members elected by popular vote for six years. One half of the Senate is elected every three years. Voting is compulsory at 18. Federal judicial power is vested in a Federal Supreme Court of seven justices, appointed by the Governor-General in Council. Each of the states has its own judicial system.

The major political parties are the Liberal Party (67 seats in the House of Representatives), led by Prime Minister Malcolm Fraser; Australian Labor Party (38 seats), led by William G. Hayden; National Country Party (19 seats), led by J. Douglas Anthony.

History. Dutch, Portuguese, and Spanish ships sighted Australia in the 17th century; the Dutch landed at the Gulf of Carpentaria in 1606. In 1642, Abel Tasman (for whom Tasmania was named) proved that Australia was not part of the Antarctic

Continent. Australia was called New Holland, Botany Bay, and New South Wales until about 1820.

Captain James Cook, in 1770, claimed possession for Great Britain. A British penal colony was set up at what is now Sydney, then Port Jackson, in 1788, and about 161,000 transported English convicts were settled there until the system was suspended in 1839.

Free settlers established six colonies: New South Wales (1786), Tasmania (then Van Diemen's Land) (1825), Western Australia (1829), South Australia (1834), Victoria (1851), and Queensland (1859).

Sheep raising and wheat growing built the economy, and the white population, which had dwindled to 34,000 in 1820, grew to 400,000 by 1850. Discovery of gold in Victoria in 1851 led immigrants to pour in. The six colonies became states and in 1901 federated into the Commonwealth of Australia with a Constitution that incorporated British parliamentary tradition and U.S. federal experience. Australia became known for liberal legislation: free compulsory education, protected trade unionism with industrial conciliation and arbitration, the "Australian" ballot facilitating selection, the secret ballot, women's suffrage, maternity allowances, and sickness and old age pensions.

The Labor Government of Prime Minister Gough Whitlam, elected in 1972, was itself a victim of the twin economic troubles that hit Australia along with most of the rest of the world—inflation and recession. Opposition parties blocked passage of government budget requests to force Whitlam to resign and, in what was called an unconstitutional action, Governor-General Sir John Kerr dissolved both houses of Parliament in November, 1975. Kerr asked Malcolm Fraser, the Liberal Party chief, to form a caretaker government until a new general election in December. Kerr resigned in 1977.

Despite some domestic criticism and warnings from the Soviet Union, Australia in 1980 granted a U.S. request for B-52 bases as part of the buildup of forces in the Indian Ocean.

Australian External Territories

Norfolk Island (14 sq mi.; 36.3 sq km) was placed under Australian administration in 1914. Population in 1978 was about 1,800.

The Ashmore and Cartier Islands (.8 sq mi.) were placed under Australian administration in 1934. In 1938 the islands, which are uninhabited, were annexed to the Northern Territory.

The Australian Antarctic Territory (2,360,000 sq mi.; 6,112,400 sq km), comprising all the islands and territories, other than Adélie Land, situated south of lat. 60° S and lying between long. 160° to 45° E, was placed under Australian administration in 1936.

Heard Island and the McDonald Islands (158 sq mi.; 409.2 sq km), lying in the sub-Antarctic, were placed under Australian administration in 1947. The islands are uninhabited.

The Cocos (Keeling) Islands (5.5 sq mi.; 14.2 sq. km) placed under Australian administration in 1955. Population in 1977 was 447.

Christmas Island (52 sq mi.; 134.7 sq km) was placed under Australian administration in 1958. Population in 1978 was about 1,300.

Coral Sea Islands (400,000 sq mi.; 1,036,000 sq km, but only a few sq mi. of land) became a territory of Australia in 1969. There is no permanent population on the islands.

AUSTRIA

Republic of Austria
President: Rudolf Kirchschläger (1974)
Chancellor: Bruno Kreisky (1970)
Area: 32,375 sq mi. (83,851 sq km)
Population (est. 1980): 7,500,000
Density per square mile: 231.7
Capital: Vienna
Largest cities (est. 1978): Vienna, 1,580,600; **(est. 1976 by U.N.):** Graz, 250,900; Linz, 208,000; Salzburg, 139,000; Innsbruck, 120,400
Monetary unit: Schilling
Language: German
Religion: Roman Catholic, 90%
National name: Republik Österreich
Freedom House classifications: Capitalist-socialist industrial, multi-party centralized
Economic summary: Gross national product (1978): $52.7 billion. Average annual growth rate (1970–77): 3.8%. Per capita income (1977): $6,360. Average rate of inflation (1976–77): 5.5%. Principal agricultural products: livestock, forest products, grains, sugar beets, potatoes. Major industrial products: iron and steel, chemicals, capital equipment, consumer goods. Natural resources: iron ore, petroleum, timber, magnesite, aluminum, coal, lignite, cement, copper. Exports: iron and steel products, timber, paper, textiles, electrotechnical machines, chemical products. Imports: machinery, vehicles, chemicals, iron and steel, metal goods, raw materials, fuels, food stuffs. Major trading partners: U.S., West Germany, Italy, Switzerland, U.K.

Geography. Slightly smaller than Maine, Austria includes much of the mountainous territory of the eastern Alps (about 75% of the area). The country contains many snowfields, glaciers, and snow-capped peaks, the highest being the Grossglockner (12,530 ft; 3,819 m). The Danube is the principal river. Forests and woodlands cover about 40% of the land area.

Almost at the heart of Europe, Austria has as its neighbors Italy, Switzerland, West Germany, Czechoslovakia, Hungary, Yugoslavia, and Liechtenstein.

Government. Austria is a federal republic composed of nine provinces (Bundesländer), including Vienna. The President is elected by the people for a term of six years. The bicameral legislature consists of the Bundesrat, with 58 members chosen by the provincial assemblies, and the Nationalrat, with 183 members popularly elected for four years. Presidency of the Bundesrat revolves every six months, going to the provinces in alphabetical order.

The major political parties are the Social Democratic Party (95 of 183 seats in Nationalrat), led by Chancellor Bruno Kreisky; People's Party (77 seats); Freiheitliche Partei (11 seats).

History. Settled in prehistoric times, the Central

European land that is now Austria was overrun in pre-Roman times by various tribes, including the Celts. Charlemagne conquered the area in 788 and encouraged colonization and Christianity. In 1252, Ottokar, King of Bohemia, gained possession, only to lose the territories to Rudolf of Hapsburg in 1278. Thereafter, until World War I, Austria's history was largely that of its ruling house, the Hapsburgs.

Austria emerged from the Congress of Vienna in 1815 as the Continent's dominant power. The *Ausgleich* of 1867 provided for a dual sovereignty, the empire of Austria and the kingdom of Hungary, under Francis Joseph I, who ruled until his death on Nov. 21, 1916. He was succeeded by his grandnephew, Charles I.

During World War I, Austria-Hungary was one of the Central Powers with Germany, Bulgaria, and Turkey, and the conflict left the country in political chaos and economic ruin. Austria, shorn of Hungary, was proclaimed a republic in 1918, and the monarchy was dissolved in 1919.

A parliamentary democracy was set up by the Constitution of Nov. 10, 1920. To check the power of Nazis advocating union with Germany, Chancellor Engelbert Dollfuss in 1933 established a dictatorship, but was assassinated by the Nazis on July 25, 1934. Kurt von Schuschnigg, his successor, struggled to keep Austria independent, but on March 12, 1938, German troops occupied the country, and Hitler proclaimed its *Anschluss* (union) with Germany, annexing it to the Third Reich.

After World War II, the U.S. and Britain declared the Austrians a "liberated" people. But the Russians prolonged the occupation. Finally Austria concluded a state treaty with the U.S.S.R. and the other occupying powers and regained its independence on May 15, 1955. The second Austrian republic, established Dec. 19, 1945, on the basis of the 1920 Constitution (amended in 1929), was declared by the federal parliament to be permanently neutral. Austria became a member of the Council of Europe in 1956.

Vienna has become a headquarters for international organizations, such as the International Atomic Energy Agency and the Organization of Petroleum Exporting Countries (OPEC). In June 1979, Presidents Jimmy Carter and Leonid Brezhnev met in Vienna to sign the second U.S.-Soviet Strategic Arms Limitation Treaty—SALT II.

BAHAMAS

Commonwealth of the Bahamas
Sovereign: Queen Elizabeth II
Governor-General: Sir Gerald Cash (1979)
Prime Minister: Lynden O. Pindling (1967)
Area: 4,404 sq mi. (11,406 sq km)
Population (est. 1980): 225,000
Density per square mile: 51.1
Capital and largest city (est. 1978 for metropolitan area): Nassau, 133,300
Monetary unit: Bahamian dollar
Language: English
Religions: Baptist, 29%; Anglican, 23%; Roman Catholic, 23%; Methodist, 7%
Member of Commonwealth of Nations
Freedom House classifications: Capitalist industrial, multi-party centralized
Economic summary: Gross national product (1978): $570 million. Average annual growth rate (1970–77): −7.2%. Per capita income: $3,510. Principal agricultural products: fruits, vegetables. Major industrial products: fish, petroleum, pharmaceutical products; tourism. Natural resources: salt, aragonite, timber. Exports: petroleum products, pharmaceuticals, cement, rum. Imports: crude oil, foodstuffs, manufactured goods. Major trading partners: U.S., U.K., Canada, Saudi Arabia, Nigeria, Libya.

Geography. The Bahamas are an archipelago of about 700 islands and 2,400 uninhabited islets and cays lying 50 miles off the east coast of Florida. They extend from northwest to southeast for about 760 miles (1,223 km). Only 22 of the islands are inhabited; the most important is New Providence (80 sq mi.; 207 sq km), on which Nassau is situated. Other islands include Grand Bahama, Abaco, Eleuthera, Andros, Cat Island, San Salvador (or Watling's Island), Exuma, Long Island, Crooked Island, Acklins Island, Mayaguana, and Inagua.

The islands are mainly flat, few rising above 200 feet (61 m). There are a few streams and one large lake (on Inagua).

Government. The Bahamas moved toward greater autonomy in 1968 after the overwhelming victory in general elections of the Progressive Liberal Party, led by Prime Minister Lynden O. Pindling. The black leader's party won 29 seats in the House of Assembly to only 7 for the predominantly white United Bahamians, who had controlled the islands for decades before Pindling became Prime Minister in 1967.

With its new mandate from the 85%-black population, Pindling's government negotiated a new Constitution with Britain under which the colony became the Commonwealth of the Bahama Islands in 1969. On July 10, 1973, The Bahamas became an independent nation as the Commonwealth of the Bahamas.

In the 1977 election, Pindling's Progressive Liberal Party won 30 of 38 seats in Parliament; the Bahamian Democratic Party, 6; the Free National Movement, 2.

History. The islands were reached by Columbus in October 1492, and were a favorite pirate area in the early 18th century. The Bahamas were a crown colony from 1717 until they were granted internal self-government in 1964.

BAHRAIN

State of Bahrain
Amir: Sheik Isa bin-Sulman al-Khalifa (1961)
Prime Minister: Khalifa bin Sulman al-Khalifa (1970)
Area: 240 sq mi. (622 sq km)
Population (est. 1980): 300,000
Density per square mile: 1,250.0
Capital (est. 1976): Manama, 105,400
Monetary unit: Bahrain dinar
Languages: Arabic (official); English
Religion: Islam
Freedom House classifications: Capitalist-statist industrial, non-party non-military
Economic summary: Gross national product (1978): $1.5 billion. Average annual growth rate (1970–77): 0.2%. Per capita income (1977): $2,500. Average rate of inflation

(1975–77): 15%. Land used for agriculture: 10%; labor force: 5%; principal products: eggs, vegetables, fruits. Labor force in industry: 90%; major products: oil, aluminum, fish. Natural resources: oil, fish. Exports: oil, aluminum, fish. Imports: machinery, oil-industry equipment, motor vehicles, foodstuffs. Major trading partners: U.K., U.S., Japan, Saudi Arabia.

Geography. Bahrain is an archipelago in the Persian Gulf off the coast of Saudi Arabia. The islands for the most part are level expanses of sand and rock.

Government. A new Constitution was approved in 1973. It created the first elected parliament in the country's history. Called the National Council, it consisted of 30 members elected by male citizens for four-year terms, plus up to 14 Cabinet ministers as ex-officio members. In August 1975, the Amir dissolved the National Council.

History. A sheikdom that passed from the Persians to the al-Khalifa family from Arabia in 1782, Bahrain became, by treaty, a British protectorate in 1820. It has become a major Middle Eastern oil center and, through use of oil revenues, is one of the most developed of the Persian Gulf sheikdoms. The Amir, Sheik Isa bin-Sulman al-Khalifa, who succeeded to the post in 1961, is a member of the original ruling family. Bahrain announced its independence on Aug. 14, 1971.

BANGLADESH

People's Republic of Bangladesh
President: Gen. Ziaur Rahman (1977)
Prime Minister: Shah Azizur Rahman (1979)
Area: 55,126 sq mi. (142,776 sq km)
Population (est. 1980): 87,650,000
Density per square mile: 1,590.0
Capital and largest city (est. 1974): Dacca, 1,730,250
Monetary unit: Taka
Principal languages: Bengali (official), English
Religions: Islam, 85%; Hindu, 13%
Member of Commonwealth of Nations
Freedom House classifications: Capitalist-statist pre-industrial, multi-party centralized
Economic summary: Gross national product (1978): $7.6 billion. Average annual growth rate (1970–77): –0.2%. Per capita income: $85. Land used for agriculture: 66%; labor force, 75%; principal products: rice, jute, tea, sugar, wheat. Labor force in industry, 7%; major products: jute goods, textiles, leather, sugar, fertilizer, paper, pharmaceuticals. Natural resources: natural gas. Exports: jute goods, jute, tea, leather, seafood. Imports: food grains, fuels, raw cotton, yarn, manufactured goods. Major trading partners: U.S., U.K., Japan.

Geography. Bangladesh, on the northern coast of the Bay of Bengal, is surrounded by India, with a small common border with Burma in the southeast. It is approximately the size of Wisconsin. The country is low-lying riverine land traversed by the many branches and tributaries of the Ganges and Brahmaputra rivers. Elevation averages less than 600 feet (183 m) above sea level. Tropical monsoons and frequent floods and cyclones inflict heavy damage in the delta region.

Government. Bangladesh, formerly East Pakistan, achieved independence in December 1971 when Indian and Bengali troops defeated West Pakistan after a two-week war. The new nation was established as a parliamentary democracy, with the leader of the independence movement, Sheik Mujibur Rahman, as its first Prime Minister. A Constitution approved in December 1972 provided for a National Assembly of 330 seats, with 30 reserved for women.

The Assembly voted unanimously on Jan. 25, 1975, to amend the Constitution to make Mujibur president and to give him full executive powers. Mujibur's assassination on Aug. 15, 1975, ended constitutional government and brought the first of a series of martial-law administrations.

History. Like West Pakistan and India, the former East Pakistan was part of imperial British India until Britain withdrew in 1947. The two Pakistans were united by religion (Islam), but their peoples were separated by culture, physical features, and 1,000 miles of Indian territory. Bangladesh consists primarily of East Bengal (West Bengal is part of India and its people are primarily Hindu) plus the Sylhet district of the Indian state of Assam. For almost 25 years after independence from Britain, its history was as part of Pakistan (*see* Pakistan).

The East Pakistanis unsuccessfully sought greater autonomy from West Pakistan. The first general elections in Pakistani history, in December 1970, saw virtually all 171 seats of the region (out of 300 for both East and West Pakistan) go to Sheik Mujibur Rahman's Awami League, with the rest to other similarly independence-minded minor parties.

Attempts to write an all-Pakistan Constitution to replace the military regime of Gen. Yahya Khan failed. General strikes in East Pakistan followed at Mujibur's direction; he also told his followers to stop paying taxes. Yahya bloodily put down his revolt in March 1971. An estimated one million Bengalis were killed in the fighting or later slaughtered. Ten million more took refuge in India.

In December 1971, India invaded East Pakistan, routed the West Pakistani occupation forces, and created Bangladesh. The U.S. opposed its violent creation, but recognized Bangladesh in April 1972 and provided several hundred million dollars in relief aid.

In February 1974, Pakistan agreed to recognize the independence of Bangladesh. India, Pakistan, and Bangladesh signed an agreement two months later that provided for release of all Pakistani prisoners, improved conditions for the Bihari minority seeking to emigrate from Bangladesh to Pakistan, and negotiations to restore normal communication among the three states.

The charismatic Mujibur had a following of millions and near-dictatorial powers, but he failed to cope with poverty, starvation, sporadic political violence, and widespread government corruption.

Before dawn on Aug. 15, 1975, Mujibur, his wife, and several relatives were assassinated in a coup led by young Army officers. As president, they installed Khondakar Mushtaque Ahmed, a founder of the Awami League who was then Minister of Foreign Trade and Commerce.

A military coup forced Ahmed from power Nov. 6, 1975, and installed former Supreme Court Chief Justice Abu Sadat Mohammed Sayem as president and "chief martial law administrator." On Nov. 30, 1976, Gen Ziaur Rahman, Army Chief of Staff, took over Sayem's powers and blocked the national elections scheduled for early 1977. On April 21,

1977, Ziaur became president following Sayem's resignation. Two years later, Ziaur ended the martial law originally imposed in 1975 and in 1979 permitted parliamentary elections, in which his Bangladesh Nationalist Party won an absolute majority.

BARBADOS

Sovereign: Queen Elizabeth II
Governor-General: Sir Deighton L. Ward (1976)
Prime Minister: J. M. G. Adams (1976)
Area: 166 sq mi. (431 sq km)
Population (est. 1980): 250,000
Density per square mile: 1,506.0
Capital and largest city (1970 census): Bridgetown, 8,900
Monetary unit: Barbados dollar
Language: English
Religions: Anglican, 53%; Methodist, 9%; Roman Catholic, 4%
Member of Commonwealth of Nations
Freedom House classifications: Capitalist industrialist, multi-party centralized
Economic summary: Gross national product (1978): $490 million. Average annual growth rate (1970–77): 2.6%. Per capita income (1977): $1,840. Principal agricultural products: sugar cane, subsistence foods. Major industrial products: light manufactures, sugar milling; tourism. Exports: sugar and sugar cane byproducts, clothing. Imports: foodstuffs, machinery, manufactured goods. Major trading partners: U.S., Caribbean nations, U.K., Canada.

Geography. An island in the Atlantic about 300 miles (483 km) north of Venezuela, Barbados is only 21 miles long (34 km) and 14 miles across (23 km) at its widest point. It is circled by fine beaches and narrow coastal plains. The highest point is Mount Hillaby (1,105 ft; 337 m) in the north central area.

Government. The Barbados legislature dates from 1627. It is bicameral, with a Senate of 21 appointed members and an Assembly of 24 elected members.

The major political parties are the Barbados Labor Party (17 seats in Assembly), led by Prime Minister J. M. G. Adams; Democratic Labor Party (7 seats), led by Errol Barrow.

History. Barbados, with a population 90% black, was settled by the British in 1627. It became a crown colony in 1885. It was a member of the Federation of the West Indies from 1958 to 1962. Britain granted the colony independence on Nov. 30, 1966, and it became a parliamentary democracy.

While retaining membership in the Commonwealth of Nations and economic ties with Britain, Barbados seeks broader economic and political relations with Western Hemisphere countries. Diplomatic ties with Cuba were established in 1972.

BELGIUM

Kingdom of Belgium
Sovereign: King Baudouin I (1951)
Premier: Wilfried Martens (1979)
Area: 11,781 sq mi. (30,513 sq km)
Population (est. 1980): 9,860,000
Density per square mile: 838.7
Capital: Brussels
Largest cities (est. 1978 for metropolitan area): Brussels, 1,029,000; Antwerp, 927,200; Liège, 617,600; Ghent, 486,000
Monetary unit: Belgian franc
Languages: Dutch, 56%; French, 32%; bilingual (Brussels), 11%
Religion: Roman Catholic, 97%
National name: Royaume de Belgique—Koninkrijk België
Freedom House classifications: Capitalist industrial, multi-party decentralized
Economic summary: Gross national product (1978): $89.5 billion. Average annual growth rate (1970–77): 3.5%. Per capita income: $8,040. Land used for agriculture: 47%; labor force: 3.4%; principal products: livestock, poultry, grain, sugar beets, flax, tobacco, potatoes, vegetables, fruits. Labor force in industry: 37%; major products: fabricated metal, iron and steel, coal, textiles, chemicals. Exports: metal products, transport equipment, textiles, glassware, ceramics. Imports: mineral ores, chemicals, machinery and equipment, petroleum products, grains, fruits, natural fibers, processed foods. Major trading partners: West Germany, France, Netherlands, U.K., U.S., Italy.

Geography. A neighbor of France, West Germany, the Netherlands, and Luxembourg, Belgium has about 40 miles of seacoast on the North Sea at the Strait of Dover. In area, it is approximately the size of Maryland. The northern third of the country is a plain extending eastward from the seacoast. North of the Sambre and Meuse Rivers is a low plateau; to the south lies the heavily wooded Ardennes plateau, attaining an elevation of about 2,300 feet (700 m).

The Schelde River, which rises in France and flows through Belgium, emptying into the Schelde estuaries, enables Antwerp to be an ocean port.

Government. Belgium, a parliamentary democracy under a constitutional monarch, consists of nine provinces. Its bicameral legislature has a Senate, with its 181 members elected for four years—106 by general election, 50 by provincial councillors and 25 by the Senate itself. The 212-member Chamber of Representatives is directly elected for four years by proportional representation. There is universal suffrage, and those who do not vote are fined.

Belgium joined the North Atlantic Alliance in 1949 and is a member of the European Community. NATO and the European Community have their headquarters in Brussels. The present Cabinet is a coalition of the Social Christians, Socialists, Flemish nationalists, and Brussels Francophones.

The sovereign, Baudouin I, was born Sept. 7, 1930, the son of King Leopold III and Queen Astrid. He became King on July 17, 1951, after the abdication of his father. He married Doña Fabiola de Mora y Aragón on Dec. 15, 1960. Since he has no children, his brother, Prince Albert, is heir to the throne.

The major political parties are the Flemish-Speaking Social Christian Party (51 Senators, 57 Representatives); French-Speaking Social Christian Party (22 Senators, 25 Representatives); Flemish-Speaking Socialist Party (21 Senators, 26 Representatives); French-Speaking Socialist Party (32 Senators, 32 Representatives); Flemish-Speaking Liberal Party (18 Senators, 22 Representatives); Party for Liberty and Progress of Wallonia (9 Senators, 15 Representatives); Flemish People's Party (11 Senators, 14 Representatives); French-Speaking Brussels Party (9 Senators, 11 Representatives.)

History. Belgium occupies part of the Roman province of Belgica, named after the Belgae, a people of ancient Gaul. The area was conquered by Julius Caesar in 57–50 B.C., then was overrun by the Franks in the 5th century. It was part of Charlemagne's empire in the 8th century, then in the next century was absorbed into Lotharingia and later into the Duchy of Lower Lorraine. In the 12th century it was partitioned into the Duchies of Brabant and Luxembourg, the Bishopric of Liège, and the domain of the Count of Hainaut, which included Flanders.

The rise of the wool industry brought prosperity and power to the country, particularly to the semi-independent cities—Ghent, Bruges, and Ypres. In the 16th century, Belgium, with most of the area of the Low Countries, passed to the Duchy of Burgundy and was the marriage portion of Archduke Maximilian of Hapsburg and the inheritance of his grandson, Charles V, who incorporated it into his empire. Then, in 1555, they were united with Spain.

By the treaty of Utrecht in 1713, the country's sovereignty passed to Austria. During the wars that followed the French Revolution, Belgium was occupied and later annexed to France. But with the downfall of Napoleon, the Congress of Vienna in 1815 gave the country to the Netherlands. The Belgians revolted in 1830 and declared their independence.

Germany's invasion of Belgium in 1914 set off World War I. The Treaty of Versailles (1919) gave the areas of Eupen, Malmédy, and Moresnet to Belgium. Leopold III succeeded Albert, King during World War I, in 1934. In World War II, Belgium was overwhelmed by Nazi Germany, and Leopold III was made prisoner. When he attempted to return in 1950, Socialists and Liberals revolted. He abdicated July 16, 1951, and his son, Baudouin, became King the next day.

The country has long been torn by language disputes between the Dutch-speaking Flemish people and the French-speaking Walloons. The three largest political parties have two leaders, one from each community. Constant compromises must be struck within the government to allow the country to remain unified. In 1972, a major clash occurred over transferring six small hamlets from Flemish to Walloon administrative jurisdiction. When a balancing change was not implemented, the government fell. A new one under Edmond Leburton was formed; this, in turn, was replaced in 1974 by one under Léo Tindemans of the Flemish Social Christian party.

Early in 1978, Tindemans' coalition reached agreement on a plan to begin in January 1979 the transformation of the nation into a federated state by the mid-80's. The plan would divide Belgium into Dutch- and French-speaking areas.

BENIN

People's Republic of Benin
President: Lt. Col. Mathieu Kerekou (1972)
Area: 43,483 sq mi. (112,622 sq km)
Population (est. 1980): 3,560,000
Density per square mile: 81.9
Capital: Porto-Novo
Largest cities (est. 1975 by U.N.): Cotonou, 178,000; Porto-Novo, 104,000
Monetary unit: Franc CFA
Ethnic groups: Fons and Adjas, Baribas, Yorubas, Mahis
Languages: French, African languages
Religions: Animist, Christian, Islam
National name: République Populaire du Benin
Freedom House classifications: Socialist pre-industrial, one-party socialist
Economic summary: Gross national product (1978): $770 million. Average annual growth rate (1970–77): 0.5%. Per capita income (1977): $200. Labor force in agriculture: 85%; principal products: oil palms, peanuts, cotton, coffee, tobacco, corn, rice, livestock, fish. Major industrial products: processed palm oil, palm kernel oil. Natural resources: low-grade iron ore, limestone, some offshore oil. Exports: palm and agricultural products. Imports: clothing, consumer goods, lumber, fuels, foodstuffs, machinery, transportation equipment. Major trading partners: France and Western European countries.

Geography. This West African nation on the Gulf of Guinea, between Togo on the west and Nigeria on the east, is about the size of Tennessee. It is bounded also by Upper Volta and Niger on the north. The land consists of a narrow coastal strip that rises to a swampy, forested plateau and then to highlands in the north. A hot and humid climate blankets the entire country.

Government. The change in name from Dahomey to Benin was announced by President Mathieu Kerekou in November 1975. Benin commemorates an African kingdom that flourished in the 17th century. At the same time, Kerekou announced the formation of a political organization, the Party of the People's Revolution of Benin, to mark the first anniversary of his declaration of a "new society" guided by Marxist-Leninist principles.

History. One of the smallest and most densely populated states in Africa, Benin was annexed by the French in 1893. The area was incorporated into French West Africa in 1904. It became an autonomous republic within the French Community in 1958, and on Aug. 1, 1960, was granted its independence within the Community.

Gen. Christophe Soglo deposed the first president, Hubert Maga, in an army coup in 1963. He dismissed the civilian government in 1965, proclaiming himself chief of state. A group of young army officers seized power in December 1967, deposing Soglo. They promulgated a new Constitution in 1968.

In December 1969, Benin had its fifth coup of the decade, with the army again taking power. In May 1970, a three-man presidential commission was created to take over the government. The commission had a six-year term; each member serves as president for two years. Maga turned over power as scheduled to Justin Ahomadegbe in May 1972, but six months later yet another army coup ousted the triumvirate and installed Lt. Col. Mathieu Kerekou as President.

BHUTAN

Kingdom of Bhutan
Ruler: King Jigme Singye Wangchuk (1972)
Area: 19,305 sq mi. (49,421 sq km)
Population (est. 1980): 1,300,000

Density per square mile: 67.3
Capital (est. 1977 by U.N.): Thimphu, 8,900
Monetary unit: Ngultrum
Language: Dzongkha
Religions: Buddhist, 75%; Hindu, 25%
National name: Druk-yul
Freedom House classifications: Capitalist pre-industrial, non-party non-military
Economic summary: Gross national product (1978): $120 million. Average annual growth rate (1970–77): −0.3%. Per capita income (1976): $70. Labor force in agriculture: 99%; principal products: rice, barley, wheat, potatoes, fruit. Major industrial product: handicrafts. Natural resources: timber, hydroelectric power. Exports: rice, dolomite, handicrafts. Major trading partner: India.

Geography. Mountainous Bhutan, half the size of Indiana, is situated on the southeast slope of the Himalayas, bordered on the north and east by Tibet and on the south and west by India. The landscape consists of a succession of lofty and rugged mountains running generally from north to south and separated by deep valleys. In the north, towering peaks reach a height of 24,000 feet (7,315 m).

Government. Bhutan is a constitutional monarchy. The King rules with a Council of Ministers and a nine-member Advisory Council, of whom five are elected by the people; two represent the monastic order and two are named by the King. There is a National Assembly (Parliament), which meets semiannually, but no political parties.

History. After almost a century of conflict, British troops invaded the country in 1865 and negotiated an agreement under which Britain undertook to pay an annual allowance to Bhutan on condition of good behavior. A treaty with India in 1949 increased this subsidy and placed Bhutan's foreign affairs under Indian control.

In the 1960s, Bhutan undertook modernization, abolishing slavery and the caste system, emancipating women, breaking up estates, and limiting farms to 30 acres.

BOLIVIA

Republic of Bolivia
President: Gen. Luis García Meza Tejada (1980)
Area: 424,162 sq mi. (1,098,581 sq km)
Population (est. 1980): 5,580,000 (Indian, 53%; mestizo, 32%; white, 15%)
Density per square mile: 13.2
Judicial capital (est. 1976): Sucre, 90,000
Administrative capital: La Paz
Largest cities (est. 1976 by U.N.): La Paz, 654,700; Santa Cruz, 237,100; Cochabamba, 194,150; Oruro, 124,100
Monetary unit: Peso boliviano
Languages: Spanish, Quechua, Aymara
Religion: Roman Catholic, 94%
National name: República de Bolivia
Freedom House classifications: Capitalist-statist pre-industrial, multi-party centralized
Economic summary: Gross national product (1978): $2.7 billion. Average annual growth rate (1970–77): 2.9%. Per capita income (1977): $730. Labor force in agriculture: 70%; principal products: potatoes, corn, rice, sugar cane, bananas. Labor force in industry: 10%; major products: refined petroleum, processed foods, tin, textiles, clothing. Natural resources: petroleum, natural gas, tin, lead, zinc, copper, tungsten, bismuth, antimonmy, gold, sulfur, silver, iron ore. Exports: tin, petroleum, lead, zinc, silver, antimony, gold, coffee, sugar, cotton, natural gas. Imports: foodstuffs, chemicals, capital goods, pharmaceuticals, transport equipment. Major trading partners: Western European and Latin American countries, U.S., Japan.

Geography. Landlocked Bolivia, equal in size to California and Texas combined, lies to the west of Brazil. Its other neighbors are Peru and Chile on the west and Argentina and Paraguay on the south.

The country is a low alluvial plain throughout 60% of its area toward the east, drained by the Amazon and Plata river systems. The western part, enclosed by two chains of the Andes, is a great plateau—the Altiplano, with an average altitude of 12,000 feet (3,658 m). More than 80% of the population lives on the plateau, which also contains La Paz. At an altitude of 11,910 feet (3,630 m), it is the highest capital city in the world.

Lake Titicaca, half the size of Lake Ontario, is one of the highest large lakes in the world, at an altitude of 12,507 feet (3,812 m). Islands in the lake hold ruins of the ancient Incas.

Government. Faltering steps toward the restoration of civilian government were abruptly halted on July 17, 1980, when Gen. Luis García Meza Tejada seized power in the 189th coup in Bolivia's 155 years of independence. He chose a 15-member cabinet—only two civilians among them—to replace the interim administration of Bolivia's first woman President, Lydia Gueiler Tejada.

History. Famous since Spanish colonial days for its mineral wealth, modern Bolivia was once a part of the ancient Incan Empire. After the Spaniards defeated the Incas in the 16th century, Bolivia's predominantly Indian population was reduced to slavery. The country won its independence in 1825 and was named after Simón Bolívar, the famed liberator.

Since 1825 Bolivia has had more than 60 revolutions, 70 Presidents, and 11 Constitutions.

Harassed by internal strife, Bolivia lost great slices of territory to three neighbor nations. Several thousand square miles and its outlet to the Pacific were taken by Chile after the War of the Pacific (1879–84). In 1903 a piece of Bolivia's Acre province, rich in rubber, was ceded to Brazil. And in 1938, after a war with Paraguay, Bolivia gave up claim to nearly 100,000 square miles of the Gran Chaco.

Great prosperity came with World War II and its demand for two important Bolivian products, tin and wolframite. But rising prices provoked strikes that were ruthlessly broken and promoted growth of the leftist National Revolutionary Movement. The movement seized power in 1943 but was ousted by a moderate government in 1947.

In 1965 a guerrilla movement mounted from Cuba and headed by Maj. Ernesto (Ché) Guevara began a revolutionary war. With the aid of U.S. military advisers, the Bolivian army, helped by the peasants, smashed the guerrilla movement, wounding and capturing Guevara on Oct. 8, 1967, and shooting him to death the next day.

Bolivia's first elections in 11 years were authorized in July 1977 by Col. Hugo Banzer Suarez, who had seized the presidency seven years before. Gen.

Juan Pereda Asbun, his claimed victory disputed as fraudulent, declared himself the winner with the backing of the armed forces. In August 1978, the U.S. suspended military aid to Bolivia (the combined economic and military-aid program of $56.1 million for fiscal 1979 was the largest in Latin America) as a protest against Pereda's coup. Although he had ruled out elections before 1980, Pereda yielded to external and internal pressure and permitted presidential and congressional elections on July 1, 1979.

Former President Hernan Siles Suazo led in the voting but failed to win a majority, and the Congress chose Walter Guevara Arze as provisional President pending new elections. But in November 1979, Col. Alberto Natusch staged a coup that lasted only 16 days. An interim civilian regime, led by Lydia Gueiler Tejada, was installed and elections rescheduled for June 1980. Again Siles led but fell short of a majority in a three-way race that included two other former Presidents, Gen. Banzer and Victor Paz Estenssoro.

Gen. Luis Garcia Meza, who had become army commander only nine months earlier, seized power on July 17, 1980, in a carefully prepared action that had the support of almost the entire military establishment and the reported aid of Argentina's military regime. U.S. Senator Dennis DeConcina, Arizona Democrat, charged that Garcia Meza and his colleagues were heavily involved in the lucrative cocaine trade. The suspected drug connection was cited as one reason for the withholding of recognition of the new government by the U.S.

BOPHUTHATSWANA

See South Africa

BOTSWANA

Republic of Botswana
President: Quett Masire (1980)
Area: 222,000 sq mi. (576,000 sq km)
Population (est. 1980): 775,000
Density per square mile: 3.5
Capital and largest city (est. 1976): Gaborone, 36,900
Monetary unit: Pula
Languages: English, Setswana
Religions: Christian, 60%; Animist
Member of Commonwealth of Nations
Freedom House classifications: Capitalist pre-industrial, multi-party decentralized
Economic summary: Gross national product (1978): $460 million. Average annual growth rate (1970–77): 16.1%. Per capita income: $480. Land used for agriculture: 5%; labor force: 75%; principal products: livestock, sorghum, corn, millet, cowpeas, beans. Labor force in industry: 56%. Major products: diamonds, copper, nickel, salt, soda ash, potash, coal, frozen beef; tourism. Natural resources: diamonds, copper, nickel, salt, soda ash, potash, coal. Exports: meat products, diamonds, hides and skins. Imports: machinery, transport equipment, manufactured goods, food, chemicals, mineral fuels. Major trading partners: U.K., South Africa.

Geography. Twice the size of Arizona, Botswana is in south central Africa, bounded by South-West Africa, Zambia, Zimbabwe, and South Africa. Most of the country is near-desert, with the Kalahari occupying the western part of the country. The eastern part is hilly, with salt lakes in the north.

Government. The Botswana Constitution provides in addition to the unicameral National Assembly for a House of Chiefs, which has a voice on bills affecting tribal affairs. There is universal suffrage.

The major political parties are the Democratic Party (27 of 32 elective seats in 36-man Legislative Assembly), led by President Quett Masire; People's Party (2 seats), led by Philip Matante; National Front (2 seats), led by Kenneth Koma; Independence Party (1 seat), led by Motsamai Mpho.

History. Botswana is the land of the Batawana tribes, which, when threatened by the Boers in Transvaal, asked Britain in 1885 to establish a protectorate over the country, then known as Bechuanaland. In 1961, Britain granted a Constitution to the country. Self-government began in 1965, and on Sept. 30, 1966, the country became independent. Since 1975, it has been an associate member of the European Common Market.

BRAZIL

Federative Republic of Brazil
President: Gen. João Baptista de Oliveira Figueiredo (1979)
Area: 3,286,470 sq mi. (8,511,957 sq km)
Population (est. 1980): 122,000,000 (approx.: white, 60%; mestizo, 26%; black, 11%)
Density per square mile: 37.1
Capital (est. 1977): Brasília, 763,250
Largest cities (est. 1977): São Paulo, 7,198,600; Rio de Janeiro, 4,857,500; Belo Horizonte, 1,557,500; Recife, 1,249,800
Monetary unit: Cruzeiro
Language: Portuguese
Religion: Roman Catholic, 91%
National name: Brasil
Freedom House classifications: Capitalist-statist industrial, multi-party decentralized
Economic summary: Gross national product (1978): $187 billion. Average annual growth rate (1970–77): 6.7%. Per capita income (1976): $1,191. Land used for agriculture: 17%; labor force: 40%; principal products: coffee, rice, beef, corn, milk, sugar cane, soybeans, cocoa. Labor force in industry: 36%; major products: steel, chemicals, petrochemicals, machinery, motor vehicles, cement, lumber. Natural resources: iron ore, manganese, bauxite, nickel, other industrial metals. Exports: coffee, iron ore, soy meal, soybeans, transport equipment, machinery, cocoa beans, footwear. Imports: capital and consumer goods, petroleum, machinery, chemicals, pharmaceuticals. Major trading partners: U.S., West Germany, Switzerland, U.K., France, Japan.

Geography. Brazil covers about three sevenths of South America, extends 2,965 miles (4,772 km) north-south, 2,691 miles (4,331 km), east-west, and borders every nation on the continent except Chile and Ecuador. It is the fifth largest country in the world, ranking after the U.S.S.R., Canada, China, and the U.S.

More than a third of Brazil is drained by the Amazon and its more than 200 tributaries. The Amazon is navigable for ocean steamers to Iquitos, Peru, 2,300 miles (3,700 km) upstream. Southern Brazil is drained by the Plata system—the Paraguay, Uruguay, and Paraná Rivers. The most important stream entirely within Brazil is the Sao Francisco, navigable for 1,000 miles (1,903 km), but broken near its mouth by the 275-foot (84 m) Paulo Afonso Falls.

Government. Under the Constitution, Brazil is a union of 21 states, 5 territories, and 1 federal district. The President is elected by the vote of an electoral college for a term of five years. The National Congress is composed of two houses—the Senate, whose members serve for eight-year terms, and the Chamber of Deputies, elected for four-year terms. Members of Congress are elected by equal, direct, compulsory, and secret suffrage under proportional representation.

The military took control in 1964, ousting the last elected civilian President and installing a military man (with the Congress ratifying the junta's choice). Gen. Arthur Costa e Silva became President in 1966, but when he died suddenly three years later, the junta (composed of three service ministers) brushed aside the legitimate successor, Vice President Pedro Aleixo, a civilian, and named Gen. Emilio Garrastazu Médici as President. Congress then elected him to the post. In 1970, Médici announced that the military would rule indefinitely (until "economic, social, racial and political democracy" is attained).

The major political parties are the Partido Democrático Social, led by Senator José Sarney (the pro-government party formerly called ARENA, for Aliança Renovadora Nacional); Partido do Movimento Democrático Brasileiro, led by Representative Ulysses Guimarães; Partido Popular, led by Senator Tancredo Neves; and the Partido Trabalhista Brasileiro, led by Yvette Vargas.

History. Brazil is the only Latin American nation deriving its language and culture from Portugal. Adm. Pedro Alvares Cabral claimed the territory for the Portuguese in 1500. He brought to Portugal a cargo of wood, pau-brasil, from which the land received its name. Portugal began colonization in 1532 and made the area a royal colony in 1549.

During the Napoleonic wars, King Joao VI, then Prince Regent, fled the country in 1807 in advance of the French armies and in 1808 set up his court in Rio de Janeiro. Joao was drawn home in 1820 by a revolution, leaving his son as Regent. When Portugal sought to reduce Brazil again to colonial status, the prince declared Brazil's independence on Sept. 7, 1822, and became Pedro I, Emperor of Brazil.

Harassed by his parliament, Pedro I abdicated in 1831 in favor of his five-year-old son, who became Emperor in 1840 as Pedro II. The son was a popular monarch, but discontent built up and, in 1889, following a military revolt, he had to abdicate. Although a republic was proclaimed, Brazil was under two military dictatorships during the next four years. A revolt permitted a gradual return to stability under civilian Presidents. Slavery was abolished in 1888.

The President during World War I, Wenceslau Braz, cooperated with the Allies and declared war on Germany. The President from 1926 to 1930, Washington Luiz Pereira da Souza, was overthrown by a revolutionary group under Getulio Vargas, who took over as provisional President.

Vargas' 1934 Constitution curtailed states' rights and established a nationalistic policy. In 1937, Vargas seized absolute power and adopted another Constitution, extending his term indefinitely. In World War II, Brazil cooperated with the Western Allies, welcoming Allied air bases, patrolling the South Atlantic, and joining the invasion of Italy after declaring war on the Axis.

Vargas was overthrown on Oct. 29, 1945. Succeeding presidents were Gen. Eurico Gaspar Dutra (1945–50); Getulio Vargas (1950–54); João Cafe Filho (1954–55); Juscelino Kubitschek de Oliveira (1955–60); Janio Quadros (1960); João Goulart (1960–63); Gen. Humberto de Alencar Castelo Branco (1963–66); Gen. Arthur Costa e Silva (1966–69); Gen. Emilio Garrastazu Médici (1970–74).

In 1974, Gen. Ernesto Geisel was elected President. The election was the freest in a decade and the least violent in many years. Press censorship was relaxed under a policy of "decompression."

Geisel tightened political controls in 1977, suspending Congress on April 1 when opposition legislators balked at approving election procedures guaranteeing ARENA control over state governments.

Relations with the U.S. remained cool following Geisel's 1977 repudiation of a mutual defense pact after a U.S. State Department report cited the military regime's repression of human rights, and Brazil emphasized that President Carter was coming on his own request when he visited Brazil in March. The U.S. also opposed Brazil's purchase of German nuclear equipment capable of reprocessing spent nuclear fuel into weapons-grade plutonium.

National elections on Nov. 15, 1978, saw the ruling ARENA party lose its majority by a slight margin in popular voting but it retained control of both houses of Congress by a narrow edge. In the 1979 presidential election, Geisel's hand-picked candidate, Gen. João Baptista de Figueiredo, was elected.

BULGARIA

People's Republic of Bulgaria
Chairman of the State Council: Todor Zhivkov (1971)
Prime Minister (Chairman of Council of Ministers): Stanko Todorov (1971)
Area: 42,823 sq mi. (110,912 sq km)
Population (est. 1980): 9,000,000
Density per square mile: 210.2
Capital: Sofia
Largest cities (est. 1978): Sofia, 1,000,000; **(est. 1976 by U.N.):** Plovdiv, 307,400; Varna, 257,700; Ruse, 161,600; Burgas, 146,700; Stara Zagora, 123,900
Monetary unit: Lev
Language: Bulgarian
Religions: Orthodox, 83%; Islam, 13%
National name: Narodna Republika Bulgariya
Freedom House classifications: Socialist industrial, one-party communist
Economic summary: Gross national product (1978): $28.5 billion. Average annual growth rate (1970–77): 5.7%. Labor force in agriculture: 27%; principal products: grains, tobacco, fruits, vegetables. Labor force in industry: 26%; major products: processed agricultural products, machinery. Natural resources: metals, minerals,

lumber. Exports: machinery and transport equipment, fuels, minerals, raw materials, agricultural products. Imports: machinery and transportation equipment, fuels, raw materials, metals, agricultural raw materials. Major trading partners: U.S.S.R., Soviet bloc countries.

Geography. Two mountain ranges and two great valleys mark the topography of Bulgaria, a country the size of Tennessee. Situated on the Black Sea in the eastern part of the Balkan peninsula, it shares borders with Yugoslavia, Romania, Greece, and Turkey. The Balkan belt crosses the center of the country, almost due east-west, rising to a height of 7,800 feet (2,377 m). The Rhodope range breaks off from the Balkans in the west, curves, and then straightens out to run nearly parallel along the southern border. Between the two ranges, is the valley of the Maritsa, Bulgaria's principal river. Between the Balkan range and the Danube, which forms most of the northern boundary with Romania, is the Danubian tableland.

Southern Dobruja, a fertile region of 2,900 square miles (7,511 sq km), below the Danube delta, is an area of low hills, fens, and sandy steppes.

Government. The present Constitution has been in effect since May 18, 1971. The National Assembly, consisting of 400 members elected for five-year terms, is the governing body. It elects the State Council and the Council of Ministers.

The Communist Party is led by the chairman of the State Council, Todor Zhivkov.

History. The first Bulgarians, a tribe of wild horsemen akin to the Huns, crossed the Danube from the north in A.D. 679 and subjugated the Slavic population of Moesia. They adopted a Slav dialect and Slavic customs and twice conquered most of the Balkan peninsula between 893 and 1280. After the Serbs subjected their kingdom in 1330, the Bulgars gradually fell prey to the Turks, and from 1396 to 1878 Bulgaria was a Turkish province. In 1878, Russia forced Turkey to give the country its independence; but the European powers, fearing that Bulgaria might become a Russian dependency, intervened. By the Treaty of Berlin in 1878, Bulgaria became autonomous under Turkish sovereignty.

In 1887, Prince Ferdinand of Saxe-Coburg-Gotha was elected ruler of Bulgaria; on Oct. 5, 1908, he declared the country independent and took the title of Tsar.

Bulgaria joined Germany in World War I and lost. On Oct. 3, 1918, Tsar Ferdinand abdicated in favor of his son, Tsar Boris III. Boris assumed dictatorial powers in 1934–35. When Hitler awarded Bulgaria southern Dobruja, taken from Romania in 1940, the weak but land-hungry Boris joined the Nazis in war the next year and occupied parts of Yugoslavia and Greece. Later the Germans tried to force Boris to send his troops against the Russians. Boris resisted and died under mysterious circumstances on Aug. 28, 1943.

Simeon II, infant son of Boris, became nominal ruler under a regency. Russia declared war on Bulgaria on Sept. 5, 1944. An armistice was agreed to three days later, after Bulgaria had declared war on Germany. Russian troops streamed in the next day, and under an informal armistice a coalition "Fatherland Front" Cabinet was set up under Kimon Georgiev.

A peace treaty negotiated in 1947 permitted Bulgaria to keep southern Dobruja. A Constitution was adopted in 1947 establishing a Soviet-type people's republic.

BURMA

Socialist Republic of the Union of Burma
President: U Ne Win (1974)
Prime Minister: U Maung Maung Kha (1977)
Area: 261,789 sq mi. (678,036 sq km)
Population (est. 1980): 33,620,000
Density per square mile: 128.4
Capital: Rangoon
Largest cities (est. 1977 for metropolitan area by U.N.): Rangoon, 2,276,000; Mandalay, 458,000; Moulmein, 188,000; Bassein, 138,000; Pegu, 135,000
Monetary unit: Kyat
Language: Burmese
Religions: Buddhist, 80%; Christian, Islam, Hindu
National name: Pyidaungsu Socialist Thammada Myanma Naingngandau
Freedom House classifications: Capitalist-socialist pre-industrial, one-party socialist.
Economic summary: Gross national product (1978): $4.9 billion. Average annual growth rate (1970–77): 1.3%. Per capita income (1977): $120. Labor force in agriculture: 70%; principal products: sugar cane, corn, rice, peanuts. Labor force in industry: 15%; major products: textiles, footwear, processed agricultural products, wood and wood products, refined petroleum. Natural resources: timber, nickel, cobalt, copper, gold, rubies, sapphires, jade. Exports: rice, teak. Imports: machinery and transportation equipment, textiles, manufactured goods. Major trading partners: Singapore, Western European countries, China, U.K., Japan.

Geography. Burma occupies the northwest portion of the Indochinese peninsula. India lies to the northwest and China to the northeast. Bangladesh, Laos, and Thailand are also neighbors. The Bay of Bengal touches the southwestern coast.

Slightly smaller than Texas, the country is divided into three natural regions: the Arakan Yoma, a long, narrow mountain range forming the barrier between Burma and India; the Shan Plateau in the east, extending southward into Tenasserim; and the Central Basin, running down to the flat fertile delta of the Irrawaddy in the south. This delta contains a network of intercommunicating canals and nine principal river mouths.

Government. On March 2, 1962, the government of U Nu was overthrown and replaced by a Revolutionary Council, which assumed all power in the state. Gen. U Ne Win, as chairman of the Revolutionary Council, became the chief executive.

A new Constitution was approved in 1973 and took effect Jan. 4, 1974. Under it, Burma is a Socialist Democratic Republic with a 451-seat unicameral legislature called the People's Congress. In 1972, Ne Win and his colleagues resigned their military titles and thereafter ruled as "civilians." In 1974, Ne Win dissolved the Revolutionary Council and became President under the new Constitution; he is also chairman of the Council of State. The Burmese Socialist Program Party, the only legal party, is led by Ne Win.

History. In 1612, the British East India Company sent agents to Burma, but the Burmese long resisted efforts of British traders, and Dutch and Portuguese as well, to establish posts on the Bay of

Bengal. By the Anglo-Burmese War in 1824–26 and two following wars, the British East India Company expanded to the whole of Burma by 1886. Burma was annexed to India. It became a separate colony in 1937.

During World War II, Burma was a key battleground; the 800-mile Burma Road was the Allies' vital supply line to China. The Japanese invaded the country in December 1941, and by May 1942 had occupied most of it, cutting the Burma Road. After one of the most difficult campaigns of the war, Allied forces liberated most of Burma prior to the Japanese surrender in August 1945.

Burma became independent on Jan. 4, 1948. The new government was soon faced by armed uprisings of Communists and of Karen tribesmen. In 1949 the Karen rebels won a large degree of autonomy.

In 1951 and 1952 the Socialists achieved power, and Burma became the first Asian country to introduce social legislation.

In 1968, after the government had made headway against the Communist rebels, the military regime adopted a policy of strict nonalignment and followed "the Burmese Way" to socialism. But the insurgents, reportedly numbering several thousand and armed by China, continued active.

BURUNDI

Republic of Burundi
President: Lt. Col. Jean-Baptiste Bagaza (1976)
Area: 10,747 sq mi. (27,834 sq km)
Population (est. 1980): 4,500,000
Density per square mile: 418.7
Capital and largest city (est. 1977): Bujumbura, 162,600
Monetary unit: Burundi franc
Languages: Kirundi (official), French
Religions: Roman Catholic, 61%; Animist, 35%; Protestant, 4%
National name: Republika Y'Uburundi
Freedom House classifications: Capitalist-socialist pre-industrial, one-party socialist
Economic summary: Gross national product (1978): $610 million. Average annual growth rate (1970–77): 0.6%. Per capita income (1977): $128. Average rate of inflation (1974–78): 15%. Principal agricultural products: coffee, tea, cotton, food crops. Major industrial products: light consumer goods. Natural resources: nickel, uranium, cobalt, unexploited copper and platinum deposits. Exports: coffee, tea. Imports: textiles, food, transport equipment, petroleum products. Major trading partners: Belgium, West Germany, France, U.S.

Geography. Wedged among Tanzania, Zaire, and Rwanda in east central Africa, Burundi occupies a high plateau divided by several deep valleys. It is equal in size to Maryland.

Government. Legislative and executive power is vested in the president.

Burundi's first Constitution, approved July 11, 1974, placed UPRONA (Unity and National Progress), the only political party, in control of national policy and automatically made Lt. Gen. Michel Micombero president.

History. Burundi was once part of German East Africa. An integrated society developed among the Watusi, a tall, warlike people and nomad cattle raisers, and the Bahutu, a Bantu people, who were subject farmers. Belgium won a League of Nations mandate in 1923, and subsequently Burundi, with Rwanda, was transferred to the status of a United Nations trust territory.

In 1962, Burundi gained independence and became a kingdom under Mwami Mwambutsa IV, with his son, Louis Rwangasore, as premier. Shortly after, the son was assassinated. The second man to succeed him, Pierre Ngendandumwe, who took office in 1963, was assassinated in 1965 when an unsuccessful coup against the Watusi led to the massacre of many Bahutus.

Crown Prince Charles, returning from Europe, rallied Watusi extremists, ousted the premier, suspended the Constitution, and renewed relations with Communist China. He deposed his father in 1966, reigned as Ntare V, with Micombero as premier. Three months later, Micombero, in a military coup, overthrew the Mwami and established a republic, installing himself as president.

One of Africa's worst tribal wars, which became genocide, occurred in Burundi in April 1972, following the return of Ntare. He was given a safe-conduct promise in writing by Micombero but was "judged and immediately executed" by the Burundi leader. His return was apparently attended by an invasion of exiles of Burundi's Hutu tribe. Although Hutus make up 85% of the population, they have been dominated for centuries by the minority Tutsi tribe of Micombero. Whether Hutus living in Burundi joined the invasion is unclear, but after it failed, the victorious Tutsis proceeded to massacre some 100,000 persons in six weeks, with possibly 100,000 more slain by summer.

On Nov. 1, 1976, a military coup led by Lt. Col. Jean-Baptiste Bagaza ousted Micombero, who was serving his second term. Bagaza assumed the presidency Nov. 3, suspended the Constitution, and announced that a 30-member Supreme Revolutionary Council would be the governing body.

Early in 1977, the Council gave Bagaza a mandate for a renewable five-year term and proposed its own dissolution, once UPRONA is reorganized.

CAMBODIA

Democratic Kampuchea
President: Heng Samrin (1979)
Prime Minister: Khieu Samphan (1979)
Area: 70,000 sq mi. (181,300 sq km)
Population (est. 1980): 8,800,000
Density per square mile: 125.7
Capital and largest city (est. 1979 for metropolitan area): Phnom Penh, 270,000
Monetary unit: Riel
Ethnic groups: Khmer, 93%; Vietnamese, 4%; Chinese, 3%
Languages: Khmer (official), French, Vietnamese, Chinese
Religion: Theravada Buddhist
Freedom House classifications: Socialist industrial, one-party communist
Economic summary: Gross national product (1971): $500 million. Principal agricultural products: rice, rubber, corn. Major industrial products: fish, wood and wood products, milled rice. Natural resources: timber, gemstones, iron ore, manganese, phosphate. Exports: natural rubber, rice,

pepper, wood. Imports: foodstuffs, fuel, machinery. Major trading partners: China, North Korea.

Geography. Situated on the Indochinese peninsula, Cambodia is bordered by Thailand and Laos on the north and Vietnam on the east and south. The Gulf of Siam is off the western coast. The country, the size of Missouri, consists chiefly of a large alluvial plain ringed in by mountains and on the east by the Mekong River. The plain is centered on Lake Tonle Sap, which is a natural storage basin of the Mekong.

Government. A bloodless coup toppled Prince Sihanouk in 1970. It was led by Lon Nol and Prince Sisowath Sirik Matak, Sihanouk's cousin. Sihanouk moved to Peking to head a government-in-exile. On Oct. 9, 1970, Cambodia became the Khmer Republic, and Lon Nol proclaimed himself President.

The Lon Nol regime was overthrown in April 1975 by Pol Pot, a leader of the Communist Khmers Rouges forces, who instituted a xenophobic reign of terror. Pol Pot was in turn ousted on Jan. 8, 1979, by Heng Samrin, a dissident backed by strong Vietnamese forces.

History. Cambodia came under Khmer rule about A.D. 600. Under the Khmers, magnificent temples were built at Angkor. The Khmer kingdom once ruled over most of Southeast Asia, but attacks by the Thai and the Vietnamese almost annihilated the empire until the French joined Cambodia, Laos, and Vietnam into French Indochina.

Under Norodom Sihanouk, enthroned in 1941, and particularly under Japanese occupation during World War II, nationalism revived. After the ouster of the Japanese, the Cambodians sought independence, but the French returned in 1946, granting the country a Constitution in 1947 and independence within the French Union in 1949. Sihanouk won full military control during the French-Indochinese War in 1953. He abdicated in 1955 in favor of his parents, remaining head of the government, and when his father died in 1960, became chief of state without returning to the throne. In 1963, he sought a guarantee of Cambodia's neutrality from all parties to the Vietnam War.

Sihanouk first favored the Communist-backed Vietcong in Vietnam, but in 1967 he accused the Communists of planning a revolt and veered away from them. In 1968 he announced that under certain conditions he would not oppose "hot pursuit" by American troops of Communist forces across the Cambodian border.

On March 18, 1970, while Sihanouk was abroad trying to get North Vietnamese and the Vietcong out of border sanctuaries near Vietnam, anti-Vietnamese riots occurred, and Sihanouk was overthrown, a move legalized by the legislature. The historically anti-Vietnamese (North and South) Cambodians largely stayed with the government.

North Vietnamese and Vietcong units in border sanctuaries began moving deeper into Cambodia, threatening rapid overthrow of Lon Nol. President Nixon sent South Vietnamese and U.S. troops across the border on April 30. U.S. ground forces, limited to 30-kilometer penetration, withdrew by June 30.

The Vietnam peace agreement of 1973 stipulated withdrawal of foreign forces from Cambodia, but fighting continued between Hanoi-backed insurgents and U.S.-supplied government troops. U.S. air support for the government forces was ended by Congress on Aug. 15, 1973. Lon Nol made overtures for a negotiated settlement, but neither Sihanouk nor leaders of the Khmer Rouge rebels would deal with him.

Fighting continued through 1974, then reached a quick climax early in 1975. In January, the rebels cut off the Mekong River as a supply route to Phnom Penh and fought their way to the outskirts of the capital and began shelling it. In February, the U.S. Congress ignored a request from President Ford for $222 million to supplement Phnom Penh's dwindling arms stores, but a U.S. food airlift to the besieged capital went forward.

As government troops fell back in bitter fighting, there were student protests in Phnom Penh, and foreigners began leaving the country. Lon Nol fled by air April 1, leaving the government under the interim control of Premier Long Boret. On April 16, the government's capitulation ended the five-year war, but not the travails of war-ravaged Cambodia.

The new regime embarked immediately on a sweeping, inward-looking agrarian revolution. Cambodian borders were closed, but 6,000 refugees escaped to Thailand. They reported that all cities had been evacuated, with inhabitants relocated to found new farm settlements in the jungle. They said policy was enforced by Communist troops and teen-aged revolutionaries who summarily shot dissidents and former government soldiers.

The leadership of the new regime was obscure, although Khieu Samphan, wartime leader of the Khmer Rouge and Deputy Premier when the new government was established, appeared to be the strong man of the egalitarian regime. Sihanouk, the nominal chief of state, who had been in exile in Peking, returned to Phnom Penh in September 1975 for the first time since the 1970 coup that overthrew him.

A new Constitution was proclaimed in December, establishing a 250-member People's Assembly, a State Presidium with a President and two Vice Presidents, and a Supreme Judicial Tribunal. The Assembly was elected as of March 20, 1976, and Sihanouk, until then described as Chief of State, resigned on April 7. Samphan replaced him as Head of State.

In 1978, President Carter called the Cambodian government "the worst violator of human rights in the world," and a former Cambodian Information Minister charged that 1 million of his countrymen had died since the Communist takeover. In May, fighting between Cambodia and Vietnam stepped up, with the Vietnamese reported to be using U.S. tanks and other heavy equipment. Saigon offered a truce on June 6, with a demilitarized zone to be established along the disputed border, followed by a peace conference.

By August 1978, Cambodian casualties in the war with Vietnam seemed to be increasing. Vietnamese diplomats in Southeast Asia generated rumors that there was serious internal friction within the Cambodian leadership. The Phnom Penh radio confirmed some changes in the government.

Sihanouk, held under house arrest since 1976, was freed by Pol Pot early in 1979 and sent as a spokesman for the regime to protest the Vietnamese invasion before the U.N. Security Council. Sihanouk eloquently attacked Vietnam while conceding that the Pol Pot regime was inhumane.

His call for Vietnam's withdrawal was barred only by a Soviet veto.

Despite the capture of Phnom Penh on Jan. 8 by Heng Samrin, a dissident Khmer Rouge backed by Vietnamese troops, fighting continued in isolated areas. Retreating Pol Pot forces and refugees totaling 40,000 were driven into Thailand by May. Thai authorities forced 15,000 to return, admitting that "several hundred" may have been killed by waiting Vietnamese troops.

No accurate estimate can be made of the number of Cambodians who died in the holocaust of the Pol Pot years or in the subsequent Vietnamese invasion. In May 1980, a U.N. demographer said the normal increase from the last census, in 1969, would have brought the population to 8.9 million. U.N. relief agencies attempting to feed a starving nation calculated the current population as between 5 million and 5.5 million, making the number of deaths possibly as many as 3.9 million.

CAMEROON

United Republic of Cameroon
President: Ahmadou Ahidjo (1960)
Prime Minister: Paul Biya (1975)
Area: 183,569 sq mi. (475,442 sq km)
Population (est. 1980): 8,400,000
Density per square mile: 45.7
Capital: Yaoundé
Largest cities (est. 1976): Douala, 458,400; Yaoundé, 313,700
Monetary unit: Franc CFA
Languages: French and English (both official); Foulbé, Bamiléke, Ewondo, Donala, Mungaka, Bassa
Religions: Animist, Christian, Islam
National name: République Unie du Cameroun
Freedom House classifications: Capitalist pre-industrial, one-party nationalist
Economic summary: Gross national product (1978): $3.7 billion. Average annual growth rate (1970–77): 1.0%. Per capita income: $328. Land used for agriculture: 35%; labor force: 80%; principal products: coffee, cocoa, tropical agricultural products. Labor force in industry: 10–15%. Major products: small manufacturing, consumer goods, aluminum. Natural resources: timber, some oil, bauxite. Exports: cocoa, coffee, timber, aluminum, cotton. Imports: manufactured consumer goods, capital goods, food, beverages, tobacco, fuel. Major trading partners: France, U.S., neighboring African states, Western European nations.

Geography. Cameroon is a West African nation on the Gulf of Guinea, bordered by Nigeria, Chad, the Central African Empire, the Congo, Equatorial Guinea, and Gabon. It is nearly twice the size of Oregon.

The interior consists of a high plateau, rising to 4,500 feet (1,372 m), with the land descending to a lower, densely wooded plateau and then to swamps and plains along the coast. Mount Cameroon (13,350 ft.; 4,069 m), near the coast, is the highest elevation in the country. The main rivers are the Benue, Nyong, and Sanaga.

Government. After a 1972 plebiscite, a unitary nation was formed out of East and West Cameroon to replace the former Federal Republic. A Constitution was adopted, providing for election of a president every five years and of a 120-seat National Assembly, whose nominal five-year term can be extended or shortened by the president. The Cameroon National Union is the only political party.

History. The United Republic of Cameroon is inhabited by Hamitic and Semitic peoples in the north, where Islam is the principal religion, and by Bantu peoples in the central and southern regions, where native animism prevails. The tribes were conquered by many invaders.

The land escaped colonial rule until 1884, when treaties with tribal chiefs brought the area under German domination. After World War I, the League of Nations gave the French a mandate over 80% of the area, and the British 20% adjacent to Nigeria. After World War II, when the country came under a U.N. trusteeship in 1946, self-government was granted, and the Cameroun People's Union emerged as the dominant party by campaigning for reunification of French and British Cameroon and for independence. Accused of being under Communist control, it waged a campaign of revolutionary terror from 1955 to 1958, when it was crushed. In British Cameroon, unification was pressed also by the leading party, the Kamerun National Democratic Party, led by John Foncha.

France set up Cameroun as an autonomous state in 1957, and the next year its legislative assembly voted for independence by 1960. In 1959 a fully autonomous government of Cameroun was formed under Ahmadou Ahidjo. Cameroun became an independent republic on Jan. 1, 1960, adopted a Constitution in a referendum in February, and chose a National Assembly in April. The Assembly elected Ahidjo president. A federal Constitution was approved in 1961, and the Federal Republic of Cameroon came into being in October, headed by Ahidjo and Foncha.

Ahidjo was re-elected in 1975 for a fourth five-year term. Paul Biya was named prime minister.

CANADA

See separate Canada section

CAPE VERDE

Republic of Cape Verde
President: Aristide Pereira (1975)
Premier: Maj. Pedro Pires (1975)
Area: 1,557 sq mi. (4,033 sq km)
Population: (est. 1980): 320,000
Density per square mile: 205.5
Capital (1970 census): Praia, 21,494
Largest city: Mindelo (est. 1970): 28,800
Monetary unit: Cape Verde escudo
Language: Portuguese
Religions: Mainly Roman Catholic, Protestant, and Christian Racionalist
National name: República de Cabo Verde.
Freedom House classifications: Socialist pre-industrial, one-party socialist
Economic summary: Gross national product (1978): $50 million. Average annual growth rate (1970–77): –2.1%. Per capita income (1978): $180. Principal agricultural products: bananas, corn, sugar cane, coffee. Major

industry: fishing. Natural resources: salt, siliceous rock, minerals. Exports: fish and shellfish, bananas, salt. Imports: machinery, textiles. Major trading partners: Portugal, U.K., Japan, neighboring African states.

Geography: Cape Verde, only slightly larger than Rhode Island, is an archipelago in the Atlantic 385 miles (620 km) west of Dakar, Senegal.

The islands are divided into two groups: Barlavento in the north, comprising Santo Antão (291 sq mi.; 754 sq km), Boa Vista (240 sq mi.; 622 sq km), São Nicolau (132 sq mi.; 342 sq km), São Vicente (88 sq mi.; 246 sq km), Sal (83 sq mi.; 298 sq km), and Santa Luzia (13 sq mi.; 34 sq km); and Sotavento in the south, consisting of São Tiago (383 sq mi.; 992 sq km), Fogo (184 sq mi.; 477 sq km), Maio (103 sq mi.; 267 sq km), and Brava (25 sq mi.; 65 sq km). The islands are mostly mountainous, with the land deeply scarred by erosion. There is an active volcano on Fogo.

Government. The islands became independent on July 5, 1975, under an agreement negotiated with Portugal in 1974. The 56-member National Assembly chose Aristides Pereira as President and Maj. Pedro Pires as Premier. All members of the Assembly belong to the African Party for the Independence of Portuguese Guinea and Cape Verde, then the only party that entered candidates in the election. It is committed to union with Guinea-Bissau, another former Portuguese colony.

History. Uninhabited upon their discovery in 1456, the Cape Verde islands became part of the Portuguese empire in 1495. A majority of their modern inhabitants are of mixed Portuguese and African ancestry. A coaling station developed during the 19th century on the island of Sao Vicente has grown in recent years to an oil and gasoline storage depot for ships and aircraft.

CENTRAL AFRICAN REPUBLIC

President: David Dacko (1979)
Prime Minister: Bernard Christian Ayandho (1979)
Area: 241,313 sq mi. (625,000 sq km)
Population (est. 1980): 2,500,000
Density per square mile: 10.4
Capital and largest city (est. 1979): Bangui, 350,000
Monetary unit: Franc CFA
Ethnic groups: Mandja-Baya, Banda, Mbaka, Azande
Languages: French (official) and Sango
Religions: Animist, 60%; Christian, 35%; Islam, 5%
National name: République Centrafricain
Member of French Community
Freedom House classifications: Capitalist pre-industrial, one-party non-military
Economic summary: Gross national product (1978): $480 million. Average annual growth rate (1970–77): 0.9%. Per capita income: $177. Land used for agriculture: 10%; labor force: 80%; principal products: cotton, coffee, peanuts, food crops, livestock. Major industrial products: timber, textiles, soap, cigarettes, processed food. Natural resources: diamonds, uranium, timber. Exports: diamonds, cotton, timber, coffee. Imports: machinery and equipment, petroleum products, textiles. Major trading partners: France, Algeria, Yugoslavia, Japan, U.S.

Geography. Situated about 500 miles north (805 km) of the equator, the Central African Republic is a landlocked nation bordered by Cameroon, Chad, the Sudan, Zaire, and the Congo. Twice the size of New Mexico, it is covered by tropical forests in the south and semidesert land in the east. The Ubangi and Shari are the largest of many rivers.

Government. On Dec. 4, 1976, the Central African Republic became the Central African Empire. Marshal Jean-Bédel Bokassa, who had ruled the republic since he took power in a military coup Dec. 31, 1965, was declared Emperor Bokassa I. He was overthrown in a coup on Sept. 20, 1979. Former President David Dacko, returned to power and changed the country's name back to the Central African Republic.

History. As the colony of Ubangi-Shari, what is now the Central African Republic was united with Chad in 1905 and joined with Gabon and the Middle Congo in French Equatorial Africa in 1910. After World War II a rebellion in 1946 forced the French to grant self-government. In 1958 the territory voted to become an autonomous republic within the French Community, but on Aug. 13, 1960, President David Dacko proclaimed the republic's independence from France.

Dacko undertook to move the country into Peking's orbit, but was overthrown in a coup on Dec. 31, 1965, by the then Col. Jean-Bédel Bokassa, Army Chief of Staff. In August 1977, the U.S. State Department protested the Emperor's jailing of American and British newsmen.

Bokassa staged an elaborate coronation ceremony on the first anniversary of the Empire, inviting 3,500 guests to see him place a diamond-studded crown on his head and sit on a 2.5-ton gilded bronze throne in the shape of an eagle. The cost of the ceremony was one fourth of the annual foreign-exchange earnings of the country, one of the 25 poorest in the world.

CHAD

Republic of Chad
President: Goukouni Oueddei (1979)
Area: 495,752 sq mi. (1,284,000 sq km)
Population (est. 1980): 4,530,000
Density per square mile: 9.1
Capital and largest city (est. 1978): N'djamena, 281,000
Monetary unit: Franc CFA
Ethnic groups: Baguirmiens, Kanembous, Saras, Massas, Arabs, Toubous, Goranes
Languages: French (official), Sara, Kanembou, Ouddai, Massa, Arabic, Gorane
Religions: Islam, 45%; Animist, 45%; Christian, 10%
National name: République de Tchad
Freedom House classifications: Capitalist pre-industrial, non-party military
Economic summary: Gross national product (1978): $620 million. Average annual growth rate (1970–77): −1.0%. Per capita income: $70. Land used for agriculture: 50%; labor force: 90%; principal products: cotton, cattle, fish, sugar, subsistence crops. Labor force in industry: 4%; major products: livestock and livestock products, beer, bicycle and radio assembly, textiles, cigarettes. Natural resources: petroleum, unexploited uranium, kaolin.

Exports: cotton, livestock and livestock products. Imports: food, motor vehicles and parts, petroleum products, machinery, construction materials. Major trading partners: Western European countries, Nigeria, China.

Geography. A landlocked country in north central Africa, Chad is about 85% the size of Alaska. Its neighbors are Niger, Libya, the Sudan, the Central African Empire, Cameroon, and Nigeria.

Lake Chad, from which the country gets its name, lies on the western border with Niger and Nigeria. In the north is a desert that runs into the Sahara.

Government. After a coup on April 13, 1975, a nine-member military council took over all governmental functions, including those of the 75-member Legislative Assembly. Political parties were banned.

History. Chad was absorbed into the colony of French Equatorial Africa, as part of Ubangi-Shari, in 1910. France began the country's development after 1920, when it became a separate colony. In 1946, French Equatorial Africa was admitted to the French Union. By referendum in 1958 the Chad territory became an autonomous republic within the French Union.

An independence movement led by the first Premier and President, François (later Ngarta) Tombalbaye, achieved complete independence on Aug. 11, 1960. After a coup failed in 1963, Tombalbaye as President and chief of state promulgated a new Constitution and organized a new government.

A six-year sub-Sahara drought caused mass migrations, thousands of deaths, and famine conditions for some 2 million Chadians in 1974. International relief efforts were disrupted October 25, when President Tombalbaye ordered rejection of U.S. grain shipments (45% of the total). He charged that U.S. officials had barred Chadians from policy roles.

Tombalbaye was killed in the 1975 coup and was succeeded by Gen. Félix Malloum, who faced a Libyan-financed rebel movement, the Chadian National Liberation Front (Frolinat), throughout his tenure in office. A ceasefire backed by Libya, Niger, and the Sudan early in 1978 failed to end the fighting, and French military aid, both troops and supplies, was increased.

An agreement betweeen Malloum and Frolinat in March 1979 was followed by the announcement that all 2,500 French troops would be withdrawn. A week later, a provisional government headed by Goukouni Oueddei, a former Frolinat leader, sent Malloum into exile in Nigeria. In August, nine rival groups agreed to form a government of national union, with Oueddei as President.

CHILE

Republic of Chile
President: Gen. Augusto Pinochet Ugarte (1973)
Area: 286,396 sq mi. (741,766 sq km)
Population (est. 1980): 11,150,000
Density per square mile: 38.9
Capital: Santiago
Largest cities (est. 1978 by U.N.): Santiago, 3,448,700; Viña del Mar, 262,100; Valparaiso, 248,200; Talcahuano, 204,100; Concepción, 172,800; Antofagasta, 157,000
Monetary unit: Peso
Language: Spanish
Religion: Roman Catholic
National name: República de Chile
Freedom House classifications: Capitalist industrial, non-party military
Economic summary: Gross national product (1978): $15.2 billion. Average annual growth rate (1970–77): –1.8%. Per capita income: $970. Land used for agriculture: 21%; labor force 30%; principal products: grains, fruits, potatoes, vegetables, wine, livestock. Labor force in industry: 36%; major products: small manufactured goods, refined metal products. Natural resources: copper, timber, iron ore, nitrates. Exports: copper, cellulose, iron ore. Imports: food, petroleum, capital goods. Major trading partners: U.S., West Germany, Japan, Argentina, U.K.

Geography. Situated south of Peru and west of Bolivia and Argentina, Chile fills a narrow 1,800-mile (2,897 km) strip between the Andes and the Pacific. Its area is nearly twice that of Montana.

One third of Chile is covered by the towering ranges of the Andes. In the north is the mineral-rich Atacama Desert, between the coastal mountains and the Andes. In the center is a 700-mile-long (1,127 km) valley, thickly populated, between the Andes and the coastal plateau. In the south, the Andes border on the ocean.

At the southern tip of Chile's mainland is Punta Arenas, the southernmost city in the world, and beyond that lies the Strait of Magellan and Tierra del Fuego, an island divided between Chile and Argentina. The southernmost point of South America is Cape Horn, a 1,390-foot (424-m) rock on Horn Island in the Wollaston group, which belongs to Chile.

The Juan Fernández Islands, in the South Pacific about 400 miles (644 km) west of the mainland, and Easter Island, about 2,000 miles (3,219 km) west, are Chilean possessions.

Government. Under the pre-coup Constitution, the nation elected a President every six years, a Senate of 50 members every eight years (one-half renewable every four years), and a Chamber of Deputies of 150 members every four years.

Leftist parties were abolished immediately after the 1973 military coup that ousted President Salvador Allende Gossens. Other parties were placed "in recess," and on March 12, 1977, the government officially dissolved them.

History. Chile was originally under the control of the Incas in the north and the fierce Araucanian people in the south. In 1541, a Spaniard, Pedro de Valdiva, founded Santiago. Chile won its independence from Spain in 1818 under Bernardo O'Higgins and an Argentinian, José de San Martin. O'Higgins, dictator until 1823, laid the foundations of the modern state with a two-party system and a centralized government.

The dictator from 1830 to 1837, Diego Portales, fought a war with Peru in 1836–39 that expanded Chilean territory. The Conservatives were in power from 1831 to 1861. Then the Liberals, winning a share of power for the next 30 years, disestablished the church and limited presidential power. Chile fought the War of the Pacific with Peru and Bolivia from 1879 to 1883, winning Antofagasta, Bolivia's only outlet to the sea, and extensive areas from Peru. A revolt in 1890 led by Jorge Montt overthrew, in 1891, José Balmaceda and established a parliamentary dictatorship that existed until a new Constitution was adopted in 1925. Industralization began before World War I and led to the formation of Marxist groups.

Juan Antonio Ríos, President during World War II, was originally pro-Nazi but in 1944 led his country into the war on the side of the U.S. After the war, Gabriel González Videla, elected by a coalition including the Communists, turned on them. The Communist Party was outlawed until 1958.

A small abortive army uprising in 1969 raised fear of military intervention to prevent a Marxist, Salvador Allende Gossens, from taking office after his election to the presidency on Sept. 4, 1970, with 36.3% of the vote in a three-way battle. Dr. Allende was the first President in a non-Communist country freely elected on a Marxist-Leninist program.

Allende quickly established relations with Cuba and the People's Republic of China and nationalized several American companies. He promised compensation but imposed retroactive taxes to cancel out most claims, leading to cool but proper relations with the U.S. By 1972, inflation was running over 100% annually.

A middle-class general strike led to a military coup Sept. 11, 1973, then to Allende's overthrow and mysterious death in an army assault on the presidential palace. More than 2,700 deaths were reported in the coup, and many thousands were arrested. The coup ended a 46-year era of constitutional government in Chile, which had boasted the longest such record in Latin America.

The takeover was led by a four-man junta headed by Army Chief of Staff Augusto Pinochet Ugarte, who assumed the office of President and governed under a state of siege that was kept in force by extensions every six months. In March 1978, Pinochet lifted the state of siege because of "support for government" by the public, reported by a Gallup poll to be 75%.

Committed to "exterminate Marxism," the junta embarked on a right-wing dictatorship. It suspended parliament, banned political activity, and broke relations with Cuba.

The Human Rights Commission of the Organization of American States charged the junta with "most grave violations" of basic liberties, but the O.A.S. voted in May 1975 not to hear the report until further evidence was supplied. In July, Chile denied entry to a U.N. investigatory panel. On June 9, 1978, the government reversed that policy to permit the U.N. Human Rights Commission to send an investigative mission to Cuba.

In 1974, it was disclosed that the U.S. Central Intelligence Agency had secretly aided Allende's opponents before his election and had later worked covertly to "destabilize" his government.

In 1977, Pinochet, in a speech marking his fourth year in power, promised elections by 1985 if conditions warranted. Earlier, he had abolished DINA, the secret police, and decreed an amnesty for political prisoners, an action Amnesty International said might affect only 200–400 of some 1,500 political prisoners. In 1978, Pinochet permitted the deportation of Michael V. Townley to the U.S., where he and three Cuban exiles were charged with the murder of Orlando Letellier, a former Chilean foreign minister who had taken refuge in Washington.

Townley, given a reduced sentence in May 1979 because he gave evidence to convict the Cubans, testified that all four had been ordered to act by the secret police. A Chilean court refused to extradite three Chilean officers the U.S. accused of complicity in the assassination.

In September 1980, Pinochet claimed a 2-to-1 victory in a plebiscite that would allow him to remain President until 1997 unless the junta agreed unanimously to choose another leader. Former President Edyardo Frei called the plebiscite "fraudulent" because opponents were muzzled in the election.

CHINA

People's Republic of China
Head of State: Ye Jianying (1978)
Premier: Zhao Ziyang (1980)
Area: 3,691,521 sq mi. (9,561,000 sq km)[1]
Population (est. 1980): 957,000,000
Density per square mile: 259.2
Capital: Peking
Largest cities (est. 1975): Shanghai, 10,888,000; Peking, 8,487,000; **(est. 1970):** Tianjin (Tientsin), 4,280,000; Wuhan, 4,250,000; Luda (Port Arthur and Dairen), 4,000,000; Shenyang (Mukden), 3,750,000; Chongqing (Chungking), 3,500,000; Harbin, 2,750,000; Taiyuan, 2,725,000; Canton, 2,300,000; Nanjing (Nanking), 2,000,000
Monetary unit: Yuan
Language: Chinese, (Mandarin, Cantonese, and local dialects)
Religions: Principally Confucianist, Buddhist, and Taoist
National name: Zhonghua Renmin Gongheguo
Freedom House classifications: Socialist industrial, one-party communist
Economic summary: Gross national product (1978): $425 billion. Average annual growth rate (1970–77): 4.5%. Per capita income: $390. Labor force in agriculture: 80%; principal products: rice, wheat, grains, cotton. Major industrial products: iron and steel, textiles, armaments, petroleum. Natural resources: coal, natural gas, limestone, marble. Exports: agricultural products, oil, minerals, metals, manufactured goods. Imports: grains, chemical fertilizer, steel, industrial raw materials, machinery and equipment. Major trading partners: Japan, Hong Kong, West Germany, Australia, Romania, Canada, U.S.S.R., U.K.

Geography. China, which occupies the eastern part of Asia, is slightly larger in area than the U.S. Its coastline is roughly a semicircle, about 2,150 miles (3,460 km) long. The greater part of the country is mountainous, and only in the lower reaches of the Yellow and Yangtze Rivers are there extensive low plains.

The principal mountain ranges are the Tien Shan, to the northwest; the Kunlun chain, running south of the Taklimakan and Gobi Deserts; and the Trans-Himalaya, connecting the Kunlun with the borders of China and Tibet. Manchuria is largely an undulating plain connected with the north China plain by a narrow lowland corridor. Inner Mongolia contains the relatively fertile southern and eastern portions of the Gobi. The large island of Hainan

(13,500 sq mi.; 34,965 sq km) lies off the southern coast.

Hydrographically, China proper consists of three great river systems. The northern part of the country is drained by the Yellow River (Huang Ho), 2,900 miles long (4,667 km) and mostly unnavigable. The central part is drained by the Chang Jiang (Yangtze Kiang), the fourth longest river in the world 3,602 miles (5,797 km). The Xi Jiang (Si Kiang) in the south is 1,236 miles long (1,989 km) and navigable for a considerable distance. In addition, the Amur (2,704 mi.; 4,352 km) forms part of the northeastern boundary.

Government. With 3,040 deputies, elected for four-year terms by universal suffrage, the National People's Congress is the chief legislative organ. A State Council has the executive authority. The Congress elects the Premier and Deputy Premiers. All ministries are under the State Council, headed by the Premier.

The Communist Party controls the government.

History. By 2000 B.C., the Chinese were living in the Hwang Ho basin, and they had achieved an advanced stage of civilization by 1200 B.C. The great philosophers Lao-tse, Confucius, Mo Ti, and Mencius lived during the Chou dynasty (1122–249 B.C.). The warring feudal states were first united under Emperor Ch'in Shih Huang Ti, during whose reign (246–210 B.C.) work was begun on the Great Wall. Under the Han dynasty (206 B.C.-A.D. 220) China prospered and traded with the West.

In the T'ang dynasty (618–907), often called the golden age of Chinese history, painting, sculpture, and poetry flourished, and printing made its earliest known appearance.

The Mings, last of the native rulers (1368–1644), overthrew the Mongol, or Yuan, dynasty (1280–1368) established by Kublai Khan. The Mings in turn were overthrown in 1644 by invaders from the north, the Manchus.

China closely restricted foreign activities, and by the end of the 18th century only Canton and the Portuguese port of Macao were open to European merchants. Following the Anglo-Chinese War of 1839–42, however, several treaty ports were opened, and Hong Kong was ceded to Britain. Treaties signed after further hostilities (1856–60) weakened Chinese sovereignty and removed foreigners from Chinese jurisdiction. The disastrous Chinese-Japanese War of 1894–95 was followed by a scramble for Chinese concessions by European powers, leading to the Boxer Rebellion (1900), suppressed by an international force.

New Chinese Spelling

Starting in 1978, China has adopted a new system for spelling most Chinese names in the Roman alphabet. The Pinyin ("transcription") system will be used by *Information Please* for current names of people and places, with certain exceptions (e.g., *Tibet* rather than *Xizang* and *Peking* rather than *Beijing*). The new spelling is an attempt to use the Roman alphabet to render more precisely the sounds of Mandarin Chinese. A few letters in Pinyin have unique sounds: x = hs (as in *she*); q = ch (as in *cheek*); zh = ch (as in *jump*).

The death of the Empress Dowager Tzu Hsi in 1908 and the accession of the infant Emperor Hsüan T'ung (Pu-Yi) were followed by a nationwide rebellion led by Dr. Sun Yat-sen, who became first President of the Provisional Chinese Republic in 1911. The Manchus abdicated on Feb. 12, 1912. Dr. Sun resigned in favor of Yuan Shih-k'ai, who suppressed the republicans but was forced by a serious rising in 1915–16 to abandon his intention of declaring himself Emperor. Yuan's death in June 1916 was followed by years of civil war between rival militarists and Dr. Sun's republicans.

Nationalist forces, led by Gen. Chiang Kai-shek and with the advice of Communist experts, soon occupied most of China, setting up a Kuomintang regime in 1928. Internal strife continued, however, and Chiang broke with the Communists.

An alleged explosion on the South Manchurian Railway on Sept. 18, 1931, brought invasion of Manchuria by Japanese forces, who installed the last Manchu Emperor, Henry Pu-Yi, as nominal ruler of the puppet state of "Manchukuo." Japanese efforts to take China's northern provinces in July 1937 were resisted by Chiang, who meanwhile had succeeded in uniting most of China behind him. Within two years, however, Japan seized most of the ports and railways. The Kuomintang government retreated first to Hankow and then to Chungking, while the Japanese set up a puppet government at Nanking headed by Wang Jingwei.

Japan's surrender in 1945 touched off civil war between Nationalist forces under Chiang and Communist forces led by Mao Zedong, the party chairman. Despite U. S. aid, the Chiang forces were overcome by the Maoists, backed by the Soviet bloc, and were expelled from the mainland. The Mao regime, established in Peking as the new capital, proclaimed the People's Republic of China on Oct. 1, 1949, with Zhou Enlai Premier.

The soviet-type government, after prolonged negotiations, signed a 30-year treaty of friendship and mutual aid with the U.S.S.R. on Feb. 14, 1950. Its published terms provided for return of the Changchun railroad to China and the eventual return of Port Arthur and Dairen, occupied by Soviet troops. Later in the year, Chinese troops invaded Tibet and began its subjugation, a campaign that brought China into conflict with India. After the Korean War began in June 1950, China led the Communist bloc in supporting North Korea, and on Nov. 26, 1950, the Mao regime intervened openly.

A deterioration of relations between Peking and Moscow was indicated in 1958 when Peking emerged as an independent center of Communist power, challenging the leadership role of the U.S.S.R. in the Soviet bloc.

In 1958, Mao undertook the "Great Leap Forward" campaign, which combined the establishment of rural communes with a crash program of village industrialization. These efforts also failed, causing Mao to lose influence to Liu Shaoqi, who became President in 1959, to Premier Zhou, and to Party Secretary Deng Xiaoping. Meanwhile China's backing of subversive movements in Asia soured relations with India and Burma, although it very nearly achieved the conquest of Indonesia, and culminated in war on the borders of India late in 1962. By the next year, the break with the U.S.S.R. was complete.

Mao, with the backing of supporters—his wife, Jiang Qing; the Defense Minister, Marshal Lin Biao; his former secretary, Chen Boda; and Premier Zhou—began a struggle to regain power. Zhou

Provinces and Regions of China

Name	Area (sq mi.)	Capital
Provinces		
Anhui (Anhwei)	54,015	Hefei (Hofei)
Fujian (Fukien)	47,529	Fuzhou (Fukien)
Gansu (Kansu)	137,104	Lanzhou (Lanchow)
Guangdong (Kwangtung)	89,344	Canton
Guizhou (Kweichow)	67,181	Guiyang (Kweiyang)
Hebei (Hopei)	81,479	Shijiazhuang (Shitikiachwang)
Heilongjiang (Heilungkiang)[1]	178,996	Harbin
Henan (Honan)	64,479	Zhengzhou (Chengchow)
Hubei (Hupeh)	72,394	Wuhan
Hunan	81,274	Changsha
Jiangsu (Kiangsu)	40,927	Nanjing (Nanking)
Jiangxi (Kiangsi)	63,629	Nanchang
Jilin (Kirin)[1]	72,201	Changchun
Liaoning[1]	53,301	Shenyang
Quinghai (Chinghai)	278,378	Xining (Sining)
Shaanxi (Shensi)	75,598	Xian (Sian)
Shandong (Shantung)	59,189	Jinan (Tsinan)
Shanxi (Shansi)	60,656	Taiyuan
Sichuan (Szechwan)	219,691	Chengdu (Chengtu)
Yunnan	168,417	Kunming
Zhejiang (Chekiang)	39,305	Hangzhou (Hangchow)
Autonomous Region		
Guangxi Zhuang (Kwangsi Chuang)	85,096	Nanning
Nei Monggol (Inner Mongolia)[1]	454,633	Hohhot (Huhehot)
Ningxia Hui	30,039	Yinchuan (Yinchwan)
Xinjiang Uygur (Sinkiang Uighur)[1]	635,829	Urumqi (Urumchi)
Xizang (Tibet)	471,660	Lhasa

1. Together constitute (with Taiwan) what has been traditionally known as Outer China, the remaining territory forming the historical China Proper. NOTE: Names are in Pinyin, with conventional spelling in parentheses.

proposed the movement that became known as the Cultural Revolution at the party congress in 1964, the same year China exploded its first atomic (fission) bomb (it produced a fusion bomb in 1967).

Mao moved to Shanghai, and from that base he and his supporters waged their own Cultural Revolution. President Liu and the party secretary, Deng, took over, and their followers denounced hundreds of party and government officials at rallies and in wall posters. Then, in 1966, Chen became director of the Cultural Revolution; the Army Chief of Staff, Lo Ruiqing, was purged; and Lin replaced Liu as second in the hierarchy. In the spring of 1966 the Mao group formed Red Guard units dominated by youths and students, closing the schools to free the students for agitation. In August 1966, a few days after a Central Committee session at which Liu and Deng retained membership, a rally was held in Peking at which hundreds of thousands of Red Guards took part. During the fall more than 11 million Red Guards went to Peking to take part in rallies, demonstrations, and purges.

The Red Guards campaigned against "old ideas, old culture, old habits, and old customs." Often they were no more than uncontrolled mobs, and brutality was frequent. Early in 1967 efforts were made to restore control. The Red Guards were urged to return home. Schools started opening. But the height of violence was only reached in September 1967 when in Canton the opposing factions used tanks and artillery against each other.

Persistent overtures by the Nixon Administration (relaxed trade and travel restrictions) abruptly climaxed in an invitation to a U.S. table tennis team to visit Peking in April 1971. This was followed by the dramatic announcement in July that Henry Kissinger, Mr. Nixon's national security adviser, had secretly visited Peking and reached agreement on a visit by the President to China.

The movement toward reconciliation, which signaled the end of the U.S. containment policy toward China, provided irresistible momentum for Chinese admission to the U.N. Despite U.S. opposition to expelling Taiwan (Nationalist China), the world body overwhelmingly ousted Chiang in seating Peking.

Mr. Nixon went to Peking for a week early in 1972, meeting Mao as well as Chou. The summit ended with a historic communiqué on February 28, in which both nations promised to work toward improved relations. They differed over Vietnam as well as Taiwan, although the U.S. noted it was withdrawing from Vietnam and said its ultimate goal was withdrawal from Taiwan as well, with interim reductions of those forces as tension in the area diminished.

In 1973, the U.S. and China agreed to set up "liaison offices" in each other's capitals, which constituted de facto diplomatic relations. Full diplomatic relations were barred by China as long as the U.S. continued to recognize Nationalist China.

The National People's Congress held its first meeting in a decade in Peking, Jan. 13–17, 1975. With Mao absent, it re-elected Zhou as Premier. It approved a government realignment that placed

Marshal Ye Jianying in the post of Defense Minister, vacant since Lin's death. It revised the 1954 Constitution to reassert the primacy of the Communist Party and to specify limited rights of citizens to strike and demonstrate, to hold private farm plots, and to work for themselves.

Zhou predicted in a keynote address that "fierce contention" between the U.S. and the U.S.S.R. "is bound to lead to world war some day." He said there is "no détente, let alone lasting peace in the world today."

The same warnings against détente were made during President Ford's visit to China, Dec. 8–12, 1975, by Vice Premier Deng Xiaoping. Deng served as chief host because Zhou was now seriously ill with cancer and Mao, visibly failing, saw the visitor only briefly.

On Jan. 8, 1976, amid a national outpouring of grief, Zhou died. Demonstrations in the capital turned into near riots when mourners suspected the government of trying to suppress the display of emotion. Deng, who had been rehabilitated by Zhou and designated as his successor, was supplanted within a month by Hua Guofeng, former Minister of Public Security. Hua, believed to be a compromise between radicals and the moderates represented by the ousted Deng, became permanent Premier in April. In October he was named successor to Mao as Chairman of the Communist Party.

Mao died September 10, apparently of Parkinson's disease, and China for the second time in a year went into a period of national mourning. Almost immediately afterward, a campaign against his widow, Jiang Qing, and three of her "radical" colleagues began. The "Gang of Four" was denounced for having undermined the party, the government, and the economy.

While the despised four were reviled throughout China, there was evidence by late 1976 that Deng was to be rehabilitated. At the Central Committee meeting of 1977, Deng was reinstated as Deputy Premier, Chief of Staff of the Army, and member of the Central Committee of the Politburo. He was ranked behind Ye Jianying, the Defense Minister, in the third-ranking place in the government.

At the same time, Jiang Qing, Wang Hongwen, Zhang Chunqiao, and Yao Wenyuan—the notorious "Gang of Four"—were removed from all official posts and banished from the party. The final resolution of the committee meeting declared national unity restored and "a new leap forward taking shape in the national economy."

In addition to political reconstruction, China still faced the task of repairing the damage done by the catastrophic earthquake of July 28, 1976, which devastated the northern part of the country. Casualty estimates ranged from 100,000 to 600,000 dead in Tangshan, Tianjin, and Peking.

In August 1977, the 11th national Communist Party Congress and the election of a new Politburo took place as U.S. Secretary of State Cyrus Vance visited China to call for efforts by both China and the U.S. to normalize relations.

The Fifth National People's Congress adopted a new Constitution on March 5, 1978, strengthening civil rights such as free speech and the right to file complaints against the government. The Congress also approved a 10-year plan to increase farm production and add 120 industrial complexes to the nation's industrial base. Hua Guofeng was affirmed as Premier despite rumors that Deputy Premier Deng might take the post.

In May 1978, expulsion of ethnic Chinese by Vietnam produced an open rupture. China withdrew aid technicians and announced a complete cutoff, disclosing for the first time that it had given $10 billion to Vietnam in the past 20 years. Peking sided with Cambodia in the border fighting that flared between Vietnam and Cambodia, charging Hanoi with aggression.

On Aug. 12, 1978, China and Japan signed a treaty of peace and friendship, a treaty attacked by Moscow as hostile to the Soviet Union. Peking and Washington then announced that they would open full diplomatic relations on Jan. 1, 1979. Over Congressional objections, the Carter administration abrogated the Taiwan defense treaty, the last obstacle to full relations. Deputy Premier Deng sealed the agreement with a visit to the United States that coincided with the opening of embassies in both capitals on March 1.

Peking protested Congressional guarantees of Taiwan's defense that were inserted in legislation governing future U.S. relations with the island. The Chinese nevertheless went ahead with the drafting of a trade pact that gave them most-favored-nation status. China agreed to pay $80 million compensation for American property seized after the 1949 Communist take-over of the mainland.

A near proxy war with the Soviet Union erupted on Deng's return from the U.S. as 200,000 to 300,000 Chinese troops invaded Vietnam to avenge alleged violations of Chinese territory. The action was seen as more a reaction to Vietnam's invasion of Cambodia, where China had been the dominant outside influence since 1975. While the Soviet Union stepped up supply airlifts, the Chinese inflicted damage on the northern border, then withdrew.

At home, a political trend that had seen a "freedom wall" in Peking where individuals could publish their opinions without censorship was dampened. But if individual expression was curbed, the leadership encouraged a radical shift from traditional Marxism toward private enterprise in every phase of the national economy.

The first People's Congress in five years marked the culmination of Deng's post-Mao modernization efforts. On Sept. 10, the Congress confirmed Zhao Ziyang, an economic planner, as Premier replacing Hua Guofeng, who had held the post since 1976. Hua retained his chairmanship of the Communist Party. Although Deng retired along with six other Deputy Premiers, the new Premier and his four new Deputies were expected to follow the course set by the 76-year-old Deng.

CHINA (TAIWAN)

Republic of China
President: Chiang Ching-kuo (1978)
Premier: Sun Yun-hsuan (1978)
Area: 13,592 sq mi. (35,203 sq km)[1]
Population (est. 1980): 17,750,000
Density per square mile: 1,305.9
Capital: Taipei

1. Excluding Quemoy and Matsu.

Largest cities (est. 1978): Taipei, 2,161,300; Kaohsiung, 1,063,000; Taichung, 579,000; Tainan, 557,000; Chilung (Keelung), 342,300.
Monetary unit: New Taiwan dollar
Language: Chinese (Mandarin) and various dialects
Religions: Confucianist, Buddhist, Christian, Taoist
Freedom House classifications: Capitalist-statist industrial, dominant party
Economic summary: Gross national product (1978): $23.9 billion. Average annual growth rate (1970–77): 5.5%. Per capita income: $1,170. Labor force in agriculture: 26%; principal products: rice, sweet potatoes, sugar cane, bananas, pineapples, citrus fruits. Labor force in industry: 39%; major products: textiles, clothing, chemicals, processed foods, electronic equipment, cement, ships, plywood. Natural resources: timber, camphor. Exports: textiles, electrical machinery, plywood. Imports: machinery, basic metals, crude oil, chemicals. Major trading partners: U.S., Japan.

Geography. The Republic of China today consists of the former Taiwan Province, including Taiwan, an island 100 miles (161 km) off the Asian mainland in the Pacific; two offshore islands, Quemoy and Matsu; and the nearby islets of the Pescadores chain. It is slightly larger than the combined areas of Massachusetts and Connecticut.

The country is divided by a central mountain range that runs from north to south, rising sharply on the east coast and descending gradually to a broad western plain, where cultivation is concentrated.

Government. The President and the Vice President are elected by the National Assembly for a term of six years. There are five major governing bodies called Yuans: Executive, Legislative, Judicial, Control, and Examination. Taiwan's internal affairs are administered by the Taiwan Provincial Government under the supervision of the Provincial Assembly, which is popularly elected.

The majority and ruling party is the Kuomintang (Nationalist Party) led by President Chiang Ching-kuo. There are also two minority parties: the China Democratic Socialist Party and the Young China Party.

History. Taiwan was inhabited by aborigines of Malayan descent when Chinese from the areas now designated as Fukien and Kwangtung began settling it beginning in the 7th century, becoming the majority.

The Portuguese explored the area in 1590, naming it The Beautiful (Formosa). In 1624 the Dutch set up forts in the south, the Spanish in the North. The Dutch threw out the Spanish in 1641 and controlled the island until 1661, when the Chinese General Koxinga took it over, established an independent kingdom, and expelled the Dutch. The Manchus seized the island in 1683 and held it until 1895, when it passed to Japan after the first Sino-Japanese War. Japan developed and exploited it, and it was heavily bombed by American planes during World War II, after which it was restored to China.

After the defeat of its armies on the mainland, the Nationalist Government of Generalissimo Chiang Kai-shek retreated to Taiwan in December 1949. With only 15% of the population consisting of the 1949 immigrants, Chiang dominated the island, maintaining a 600,000-man army in the hope of eventually recovering the mainland. Japan renounced its claim to the island by the San Francisco Peace Treaty of 1951.

By stationing a fleet in the Strait of Formosa the U.S. prevented a mainland invasion in 1953, and in 1955 the U.S. signed a mutual defense treaty by which it is committed to defend Taiwan and the neighboring islands.

The "China seat" in the U.N., which the Nationalists held with U.S. help for over two decades, was lost in October 1971, when the People's Republic of China was admitted and Taiwan ousted by the world body.

President Nixon's summit meeting with Chinese leaders and the 1972 Sino-American communiqué further eroded Taiwan's position. In it, the U.S. said its eventual goal was complete withdrawal of its forces from Taiwan and progressive cutbacks as tensions in the area eased. With the end of U.S. participation in the war in Vietnam, withdrawal of U.S. air-support forces on the island began in 1973.

Chiang died at 87 of a heart attack on April 5, 1975. His son, Chiang Ching-kuo, continued as Premier and dominant power in the Taipei regime. He assumed the presidency in 1978, and Sun Yun-suan became Premier.

President Carter's announcement that the U.S. would recognize only the People's Republic of China after Jan. 1, 1979, and that the U.S. defense treaty would end aroused protests in Taiwan and in the U.S. Congress. Against Carter's wishes, Congress, in a bill governing future relations with Taiwan, guaranteed U.S. action in the event of an attack on the island. The legislation also provided for the continuation of trade and other relations through an American Institute in Taipei, housed in the former American Embassy.

COLOMBIA

Republic of Colombia
President: Julio César Turbay Ayala (1978)
Area: 455,355 sq mi. (1,179,369 sq km)
Population (est. 1980): 27,600,000 (mestizo, 68%; white, 20%; Indian, 7%; black, 5%)
Density per square mile: 60.6
Capital: Bogotá
Largest cities (est. 1979): Bogotá, 4,055,900; Medellín, 1,748,000; Cali, 1,189,000; Baranquilla, 868,000; Bucaramanga, 443,000; Cartagena, 355,000
Monetary unit: Peso
Language: Spanish
Religion: Roman Catholic
National name: República de Colombia
Freedom House classifications: Capitalist industrial, multi-party centralized
Economic summary: Gross national product (1978): $21.8 billion. Average annual growth rate (1970–77): 3.8%. Per capita income: $830. Land used for agriculture: 30%; labor force: 45%; principal products: coffee, bananas, rice, corn, sugar cane, cotton, tobacco, flowers. Labor force in industry: 14%; major products: textiles, processed food, clothing and footwear, beverages, chemicals, metal products, cement. Natural resources: petroleum, natural gas, coal, iron ore, nickel, gold, copper, emeralds. Exports: coffee, agricultural products, apparel, chemicals, metals. Imports: machinery, electrical equipment, chemical products, metals and metal products, transport equipment. Major trading partners:

U.S., West Germany, Japan, Venezuela, Netherlands.

Geography. Colombia, in the northwestern part of South America, is the only country on that continent that borders on both the Atlantic and Pacific Oceans. It is nearly equal to the combined areas of California and Texas.

Through the western half of the country, three Andean ranges run north and south, merging into one at the Ecuadorean border. The eastern half is a low, jungle-covered plain, drained by spurs of the Amazon and Orinoco, inhabited mostly by isolated, tropical-forest Indian tribes. The fertile plateau and valley of the eastern range are the most densely populated parts of the country.

Government. Colombia's President, who appoints his own Cabinet, serves for a four-year term. The Senate, the upper house of Congress, has 112 members elected for four years by direct vote. The Chamber of Deputies of 199 members is directly elected for four years.

The major political parties are the Liberal Party (62 of 112 seats in Senate, 112 of 199 seats in House), Conservative Party (49 seats in Senate, 83 seats in House), and National Opposition Union, a leftist coalition (1 seat in Senate, 4 seats in House).

History. Spaniards in 1510 founded Darien, the first permanent European settlement on the American mainland. In 1538 the Spaniards established the colony of New Granada, the area's name until 1861. After a 14-year struggle, in which Simón Bolívar's Venezuelan troops won the battle of Boyacá in Colombia on Aug. 7, 1819, independence was attained in 1824. Bolívar united Colombia, Venezuela, Panama, and Ecuador in the Republic of Greater Colombia (1819–30), but lost Venezuela and Ecuador to separatists. Bolívar's Vice President, Francisco de Paula Santander, founded the Liberal Party as the Federalists while Bolívar established the Conservatives as the Centralists.

Santander's presidency (1832–36) re-established order, but later periods of Liberal dominance (1849–57 and 1861–80), when the Liberals sought to disestablish the Roman Catholic Church, were marked by insurrection and even civil war. Rafael Nuñez, in a 15-year-presidency, restored the power of the central government and the church, which led in 1899 to a bloody civil war and the loss in 1903 of Panama over ratification of a lease to the U.S. of the Canal Zone. For 21 years, until 1930, the Conservatives held power as revolutionary pressures built up.

The Liberal administrations of Enrique Olaya Herrera and Alfonso López (1930–38) were marked by social reforms that failed to solve the country's problems, and in 1946, insurrection and banditry broke out, which claimed hundreds of thousands of lives by 1958. Laureano Gómez (1950–53); the Army Chief of Staff, Gen. Gustavo Rojas Pinilla (1953–56), and a military junta (1956–57) sought to curb disorder by repression.

Subsequent Presidents were Alberto Lleras Camargo (1957–62); Guillermo León Valencia (1962–66); Carlos Lleras Restrepo (1966–70); Misael Pastrana Borrero (1970–74); and Alfonso López Michelson (1974–78).

Julio César Turbay Ayala, Liberal Party candidate in 1978, won a narrow victory—approximately 140,000 of a total of nearly 2.5 million votes—over the Conservative Party candidate. The Liberals also retained control of both the Senate and House.

COMOROS

Federal and Islamic Republic of the Comoros
President: Ahmed Abdallah (1978)
Premier: Salim Ben Ali (1978)
Area: 692 sq mi. (1,792 sq km)
Population (est. 1980): 330,000
Density per square mile: 476.9
Capital and largest city (est. 1976): Moroni (on Grande Comoro), 18,300
Monetary unit: Franc CFA
Language: French
Religions: Islam and Christian
National name: État Comorien
Freedom House classifications: Capitalist pre-industrial, non-party non-military
Economic summary: Gross national product (1978): $70 million. Average annual growth rate (1970–77): −5.2%. Per capita income: $153. Principal agricultural products: perfume essences, copra, coconuts, cloves, vanilla, cinnamon, yams; major industrial products: perfume distillations. Exports: perfume essences, vanilla, copra, cloves. Imports: rice, wheat, flour, cotton textiles, cement. Major trading partners: France, Madagascar, U.S., West Germany, Kenya.

Geography. The Comoros Islands—Grande Comoro, Anjouan, Mohéli, and Mayotte (which retains ties to France)—are an archipelago of volcanic origin in the Indian Ocean between Mozambique and Madagascar.

Government. A coup by foreign mercenaries on May 13, 1978, deposed President Ali Soilih, who had held power since 1975. A "political and military directorate" headed by Ahmed Abdallah and Mohammed Ahmed governed until the adoption of a constitution on Oct. 1 ushered in a republic. With the resignation of Ahmed two days later, Abdallah became president.

History. Under French rule since 1886, the Comoros declared themselves independent July 6, 1975. However, Mayotte, with a Christian majority, voted against joining the other, mainly Islamic, islands, in the move to independence and remains French.

A month after independence, Justice Minister Ali Soilih staged a coup with the help of mercenaries, overthrowing the new nation's first president, Ahmed Abdallah. Soilih lowered the voting age to 14, destroyed all records and killed many Comorans. He was overthrown on May 13, 1978, when a small boatload of French mercenaries, some of whom had aided him three years earlier, seized government headquarters.

CONGO

People's Republic of the Congo
President: Col. Denis Sassou-Nguessou (1979)
Prime Minister: Col. Louis-Sylvain Ngoma (1979)
Area: 132,046 sq mi. (342,000 sq km)
Population (est. 1980): 1,550,000
Density per sq mi.: 11.7

Capital and largest city (est. 1974): Brazzaville, 310,500
Monetary unit: Franc CFA
Ethnic groups: Vilis, Bakongo, Batekes, Mbochis
Languages: French, Lingala, Kokongo
Religions: Animist, 60%; Roman Catholic, 38%
National name: République Populaire du Congo
Member of French Community
Freedom House classifications: Capitalist-socialist pre-industrial, one-party socialist.
Economic summary: Gross national product (1978): $780 million. Average annual growth rate (1970–77): 0.8%. Per capita income: $490. Principal agricultural products: sugar cane, wood, coffee, cocoa, peanuts, tobacco. Labor force in industry: 20%; major products: crude oil, cigarettes, soap, beverages, milled sugar. Natural resources: wood, potash, petroleum, natural gas. Exports: oil, lumber, tobacco, veneer and plywood. Imports: machinery, transportation equipment, manufactured consumer goods, iron and steel, foodstuffs. Major trading partners: France and other Western European countries.

Geography. The Congo is situated in west central Africa astride the Equator. It borders on Gabon, Cameroon, the Central African Republic, Zaire, and the Angola exclave of Cabinda, with a short stretch of coast on the South Atlantic. Its area is nearly three times that of Pennsylvania.

Most of the inland is tropical rain forest, drained by tributaries of the Zaire (Congo) River, which flows south along the eastern border with Zaire to Stanley Pool. The narrow coastal plain rises to highlands separated from the inland plateaus by the 200-mile-wide Niari River Valley, which gives passage to the coast.

Government. Since the coup of September 1968 the country has been governed by a National Council of the Revolution. The Congolese Labor Party is the only party.

History. The inhabitants of the former French Congo, mainly Bantu peoples with Pygmies in the north, were subjects of several kingdoms in earlier times.

The Frenchman Pierre Savorgnan de Brazza signed a treaty with Makoko, ruler of the Bateke people, in 1880, which established French control. The area, with Gabon and Ubangi-Shari, was constituted the colony of French Equatorial Africa in 1910. It joined Chad in supporting the Free French cause in World War II. The Congo proclaimed its independence without leaving the French Community in 1960.

Maj. Marien Ngouabi, head of the National Council of the Revolution, took power as president on Jan. 1, 1969. He was sworn in for a second five-year term in 1975. A visit to Moscow by Ngouabi in March ended with the signing of a Soviet-Congolese economic and technical aid pact.

A four-man commando squad assassinated Ngouabi in Brazzaville on March 18, 1977. Five days later the assassination of Émile Cardinal Biayenda, Archbishop of Brazzaville, was announced. Former President Alphonse Massamba-Débat, accused of plotting both deaths, was executed.

Col. Joachim Yhombi-Opango, Army Chief of Staff, assumed the presidency on April 4. In June, the new government agreed to resume diplomatic relations with the U.S., ending a 12-year rift. Yombhi-Opango resigned on Feb. 4, 1979, and was replaced by Col. Denis Sassou-Neguessou.

COSTA RICA

Republic of Costa Rica
President: Rodrigo Carazo Odio (1978)
Area: 19,652 sq mi. (50,898 sq km)
Population (est. 1980): 2,210,000
Density per square mile: 112.5
Capital and largest city (est. 1978 for metropolitan area): San José, 584,700
Monetary unit: Colón
Language: Spanish
Religion: Roman Catholic
National name: República de Costa Rica
Freedom House classifications: Capitalist industrial, multi-party centralized
Economic summary: Gross national product (1978): $3.3 billion. Average annual growth rate (1970–77): 3.2%. Per capita income: $1,370. Labor force in agriculture: 33%; principal products: bananas, coffee, sugar cane, rice, corn, cocoa, livestock. Labor force in industry: 20%; major products: processed foods, textiles and clothing, construction materials, fertilizer. Natural resource: timber. Exports: coffee, bananas, beef, sugar, cacao. Imports: manufactured products, machinery, transportation equipment, chemicals, foodstuffs, fuels, fertilizer. Major trading partners: U.S., Central American countries, West Germany, Japan.

Geography. This Central American country lies between Nicaragua to the north and Panama to the south. Its area slightly exceeds that of Vermont and New Hampshire combined.

Most of Costa Rica is tableland, from 3,000 to 6,000 feet (914 to 1,829 m) above sea level. Cocos Island (10 sq mi.) (26 sq km), about 300 miles (483 km) off the Pacific Coast, is under Costa Rican sovereignty; although it is mostly tropical jungle, it is of potential strategic importance in defense of the Panama Canal.

Government. Under the 1949 Constitution, the president and the one-house Legislative Assembly of 57 members are elected for terms of four years.

The army was abolished in 1949. There is a civil guard of 3,000 and a rural guard of 2,500.

The major political parties are Unity Party (27 of 57 seats in Legislative Assembly), led by Rafael A. Grillo; National Liberation Party (25 seats), led by Armando Arauz; Pueblo Unido Party (3 seats), led by Humberto Vargas Carbonel; Agricola Cartagines Party (1 seat), led by Martin Brenes; Frente Popular Party (1 seat), led by Dr. Rodolfo Cerdas Cruz.

History. Costa Rica was inhabited by 25,000 Indians when Columbus discovered it and probably named it in 1502. Few of the Indians survived the Spanish conquest, which began in 1563. The region was administered as a Spanish province. Costa Rica achieved independence in 1821 but was absorbed for two years by Agustín de Iturbide in his Mexican Empire. It was established as a republic in 1848.

Except for the military dictatorship of Tomás Guardia from 1870 to 1882, Costa Rica has enjoyed one of the most democratic governments in Latin America.

On Feb. 5, 1978, Rodrigo Carazo Odio, leader of a four-party opposition coalition called the Unity Party, defeated the candidate of the ruling National Liberation Party. His victory was attributed partly to the fact that the government had granted protection to Robert L. Vesco, a fugitive U.S. financier. On his inauguration in May, Carazo ordered that Vesco be barred from Costa Rica.

CUBA

Republic of Cuba
President (1976) and Premier (1959): Fidel Castro
Area: 44,218 sq mi. (114,524, sq km)
Population (est. 1980): 9,950,000
Density per square mile: 225.0
Capital: Havana
Largest cities (est. 1978): Havana, 1,981,300; **(est. 1975 by U.N.):** Santiago de Cuba, 315,800; Camagüey, 221,800; Holguín, 151,900; Guantánamo, 148,800; Santa Clara, 146,650
Monetary unit: Peso
Language: Spanish
Religion: Roman Catholic
National name: República de Cuba
Freedom House classifications: Socialist industrial, one-party communist
Economic summary: Gross national product (1978): $7.9 billion. Average annual growth rate (1970–77): –1.2%. Per capita income (constant 1957 prices): $840. Land used for agriculture: 65%; labor force: 34%; principal products: sugar, tobacco, coffee, rice, meat, vegetables, fruits. Labor force in industry: 17%; major products: refined oil products, cement, processed food, metals, light consumer products. Natural resources: metals, primarily nickel. Exports: sugar, nickel oxide and sulfide, tobacco, fish, rum, fruits. Imports: capital equipment, raw materials, petroleum, consumer products. Major trading partners: U.S.S.R., other Communist bloc countries, Spain.

Geography. The largest island of the West Indies group (equal in area to Pennsylvania), Cuba is also the westernmost—just west of Hispaniola (Haiti and the Dominican Republic), and 90 miles (145 km) south of Key West, Fla., at the entrance to the Gulf of Mexico.

The island has mountainous areas in the southeast, central area, and the west (Sierra Maestra). The rest of the country is flat or rolling.

Government. There have been no national elections since 1958. Fidel Castro heads the Council of Ministers, the chief governing body.

The only political party is the Cuban Communist Party, with a 100–member Central Committee; the power rests with a Politbureau of 8 and a Secretariat of 6.

History. Cuba was occupied by the Arawak Indians when Columbus discovered the island in 1492; they died off from diseases brought by sailors and settlers. By 1511, Spaniards under Diego Velásquez were founding settlements that served as bases for Spanish exploration. Cuba soon after served as an assembly point for treasure looted by the conquistadores, attracting French and English pirates.

Black slaves and free laborers were imported to work sugar and tobacco plantations, and waves of chiefly Spanish immigrants maintained a European character in the island's culture. Early slave rebellions and conflicts between colonials and Spanish rulers laid the foundation for an independence movement that turned into open warfare from 1867 to 1878. The poet, José Marti, in 1895 led the struggle that finally ended Spanish rule, thanks largely to U.S. intervention in 1898 after the sinking of the battleship *Maine* in Havana harbor.

An 1899 treaty made Cuba an independent republic under U.S. protection. The U.S. occupation, which ended in 1902, suppressed yellow fever and brought large American investment. From 1906 to 1909, Washington invoked the Platt Amendment to the treaty, which gave it the right to intervene in order to suppress any revolt. U.S. troops came back in 1912 and again in 1917 to restore order.

Gerardo Machado, President during the Depression, planned vast social reforms but abandoned them. The U.S., under President Franklin D. Roosevelt, scrapped the Platt Amendment in 1934. Fulgencio Batista, an army sergeant, led a revolt in 1934 that overthrew the Machado regime and developed into a Batista dictatorship. A succession of constitutionally elected Presidents—Ramón Grau San Martín, Carlos Mendieta, Miguel Mariano Gómez, Carlos Prío Socarrás—pushed through social reforms, hampered by overwhelming corruption manipulated by Batista, who seized power in 1952.

Fidel Castro staged a hopeless revolt in 1953. Captured and paroled, he went to Oriente Province and, aided by an Argentinian adventurer, Ernesto (Ché) Guevara, rebuilt his forces and waged a guerrilla war. The U.S. withdrew support from Batista in 1958. With funds from Soviet sources, Castro bought off the leaders of Batista's army. This and popular support from the intellectual and laboring classes demoralized the army, and Castro's forces grew as he marched on Havana. Batista fled to the Dominican Republic on Jan. 1, 1959.

Executions and torture by the new Castro regime caused a world outcry. Castro antagonized the U.S. in 1959 by confiscating U.S. investments in banks and industries and by seizing large U.S. landholdings, turning them at first into collective farms, then into Soviet-type state farms.

The U.S. broke off relations on Jan. 3, 1961, and Castro disclosed his alliance with the U.S.S.R. and the Soviet bloc. Thousands of Cubans fled to the U.S. From their ranks an invasion force was recruited by an all-party coalition financed and guided by the U.S. Central Intelligence Agency and trained in Florida and Guatemala. It landed in the Bay of Pigs, Cuba, on April 17, 1961, but when President Kennedy refused it air support under Soviet and Latin American pressure, the effort collapsed.

In 1962 the U.S.S.R. built missile sites in Cuba and provided Castro's army with troops, planes, and submarines. Alarmed, Kennedy on Oct. 22, 1962, served notice that the U.S. was willing to risk war to enforce a demand that the Soviet Union remove weapons and troops considered to threaten U.S. security. The U.S. confronted Soviet vessels with U.S. warships. Soviet Premier Nikita Khrushchev agreed to remove the missiles, and the blockade was lifted on November 20. Shortly before Christmas, Castro released 1,113 Bay of Pigs prisoners.

Russia, spending over $1 million a day (about $400 million a year) to keep Cuba afloat, had to increase its contribution by over $100 million in 1971, but gained greater control over Cuba's economy by setting up a joint Soviet-Cuban economic commission on management and efficiency.

Neither nation formally admitted it, but U.S.-Cuban relations began to thaw with negotiation of a 1973 agreement to end air hijacking. Except for political refugees, criminal hijackers will be extradited to their home country or tried for the crime where they land; also, both nations pledged to forbid attacks on the other to be mounted from their territory.

In 1975, both sides signaled readiness to improve relations. U.S. curbs on travel by Cuba'a United Nations delegation were eased and the U.S. joined 15 Latin American republics in voting to scrap economic and diplomatic sanctions the O.A.S. had imposed against Cuba in 1964.

The improving U.S.-Cuban climate cooled in late 1975 with the disclosure that Cuban troops were being used to bolster the Popular Movement for the Liberation of Angola in the former Portuguese African colony. President Ford warned that the Cuban intervention in Angola, as well as continued Cuban support for a Puerto Rican independence faction "erodes any chance for improvement of relations."

The Carter Administration signaled its intention to end the long estrangement when it signed two fishing agreements with Cuba after having removed restrictions on travel to the island by Americans. In May, the Senate Foreign Relations Committee approved a modification of the boycott, which would permit Cuba to buy medicine, food, and agricultural supplies.

In September 1977, Cuban diplomats opened a Cuban interests section in their old embassy in Washington and 10 Americans reopened a similar office in the former U.S. embassy in Havana. The new harmony was shattered early in 1978, however, when Washington charged that Cuban troops were fighting in Ethiopia against Somali and Eritrean rebels. National Security Adviser Zbigniew Brzezinski asserted that 10,000 to 11,000 Cubans were serving in Ethiopia under the command of a Soviet general.

A repetition in May 1978 of the 1977 invasion of Shaba Province in Zaire touched off a world-wide furor as Cuba was accused by the U.S., France, and Zaire of training, arming, and even taking part in the new invasion. Castro denied the charges. He later told U.S. congressmen and newsmen he had tried to halt the invasion. U.S. intelligence sources put Cuban losses in Africa at 1,500 men out of a total of 40,000 sent there.

Late in 1978, Castro announced his willingness to free remaining political prisoners in Cuba, nearly 3,600, if the U.S. would accept them. After meeting with representatives of Cuban exiles in the U.S. and elsewhere, he said he would also let 7,000 former prisoners leave, together with up to 50,000 relatives of Cubans living abroad. Small numbers of these groups began leaving, but both Castro and the exiles complained that U.S. immigration processing was too slow.

Emigration increased dramatically on April 1, 1980, when Castro, irritated at the granting of asylum to would-be refugees by the Peruvian embassy, removed the guards and 10,000 Cubans swarmed into the embassy grounds. An airlift to Costa Rica was organized, but the Castro government insisted that refugees must go directly to the country of their final destination. The government then ordered the port of Mariel opened to Cubans living in the United States to come get relatives.

As a "freedom flotilla" rushed to Mariel, the government ordered the boats to take prisoners, homosexuals, and other undesirables along with relatives of Cuban-Americans. But the eagerness of ordinary citizens to join the exodus created an embarrassment for the regime; nearly 1 million throughout the nation had reportedly signaled their intention to leave. Party militants organized public demonstrations against "traitors" as the total of departures soared past 100,000. The Carter administration, overwhelmed by the flood, moved at the end of May to halt the boatlift, but as late as September an average of 100 Cubans a week were still arriving in Florida.

CYPRUS

Republic of Cyprus
President: Spyros Kyprianou (1977)
Area: 3,572 sq mi (9,251 sq km)
Population (est. 1980): 625,000 (Greek, 82%, Turkish, 18%)
Density per square mile: 175.0
Capital and largest city (est. 1978): Nicosia, 160,000
Monetary unit: Cyprus pound
Languages: Greek, Turkish, English
Religions: Greek Orthodox, 77%; Islam, 18%
National name: Kypriaki Dimokratia—Kibris Cumhuriyeti
Member of Commonwealth of Nations
Freedom House classifications: Capitalist industrial, multi-party decentralized
Economic summary: Gross national product (1978): $1.4 billion. Average annual growth rate (1970–77): 0.3%. Per capita income: $1,580. Land used for agriculture: 57%; labor force: 36%; principal products: vine products, citrus, potatoes, other vegetables. Labor force in industry: 47%; major products: beverages, footwear, clothing, cement, asbestos mining. Natural resources: copper, asbestos, gypsum, building stone, marble, clay, salt. Exports: asbestos, copper, pyrites, citrus, raisins. Imports: manufactured goods, machinery and transportation equipment, petroleum products, foodstuffs. Major trading partners: U.K., Saudi Arabia, Italy, Greece, U.S., Syria, Lebanon.

Geography. The third largest island in the Mediterranean (one and one half times the size of Delaware), Cyprus lies off the southern coast of Turkey and the western shore of Syria. Most of the country consists of a wide plain lying between two mountain ranges that cross the island. The highest peak is Mount Olympus at 6,406 feet (1,953 m).

Government. Under the republic's Constitution, for the protection of the Turkish minority the vice president as well as three of the 10 Cabinet ministers must be from the Turkish community, while the House of Representatives is elected by each community separately, 70% Greek Cypriote and 30% Turkish Cypriote representatives.

The Greek and Turkish communities are self-governing in questions of religion, education, and culture. Other governmental matters are under the jurisdiction of the central government. Each community is entitled to a Communal Chamber.

The Greek Communal Chamber, which had 23 members, was abolished in 1965 and its function was absorbed by the Ministry of Education. The Turkish Communal Chamber, however, has continued to function.

The members of the Parliament were elected in 1976. Thirty-five seats are held by Greeks and 15 by Turks. The following is a breakdown of the 35 seats held by Greeks: Democratic Front of Spyros Kyprianou (19); AKEL Progressive Party of the Working People (9); Socialist Party of Dr. Vassos Lyssarides (4); Independents (3). The 15 Turkish members have not attended sessions of the House since 1964.

History. Cyprus was the site of early Phoenician and Greek colonies. For centuries its rule passed through many hands. It fell to the Turks in 1571, and a large Turkish colony settled on the island.

In World War I, on the outbreak of hostilities with Turkey, Britain annexed the island. It was declared a crown colony in 1925.

For centuries the Greek population, regarding Greece as its mother country, has sought self-determination and reunion with it *(enosis)*. The resulting quarrel with Turkey threatened NATO. Cyprus became an independent nation on Aug. 16, 1960, with Britain, Greece, and Turkey as guarantor powers.

After troubled years, a crisis was averted in 1968 when an American mediator, Cyrus R. Vance, induced Turkey, Greece, and Cyprus to accept a solution proposed by U.N. Secretary General U Thant for withdrawal of the Greek troops and the dismantling of Turkish invasion forces. The ethnic blocs began long direct negotiations for a new Constitution.

Archbishop Makarios, president since 1959, was overthrown July 15, 1974, by a military coup led by the Cypriot National Guard. The new regime named Nikos Giorgiades Sampson as president and Bishop Gennadios as head of the Cypriot Church to replace Makarios. The rebels were led by rightist Greek officers who supported *enosis*.

Diplomacy failed to resolve the crisis. Turkey invaded Cyprus by sea and air July 20, 1974, asserting its right to protect the Turkish Cypriote minority. Greece rejected a Turkish demand for withdrawal of the 650 Greek officers who had engineered the coup. The crisis forced resignation of the military junta that had ruled Greece for seven years.

Geneva talks involving Greece, Turkey, Britain, and the two Cypriote factions failed in mid-August, and the Turks subsequently gained control of 40% of the island. Greece made no armed response to the superior Turkish force, but bitterly suspended military participation in the NATO alliance.

On Cyprus, U.S. Ambassador Rodger P. Davies was shot to death in August during Greek Cypriote riots. The tension continued after Makarios returned to become President on Dec. 7, 1974. He offered self-government to the Turkish minority, but rejected any solution "involving transfer of populations and amounting to partition of Cyprus."

Turkish Cypriots proclaimed a separate state in the northern part of the island and proposed a "bi-regional federation." Some 200,000 Greek Cypriots demanded return to their homes in the Turkish zone and an estimated three fourths of the 45,000 ethnic Turks in the Greek zone crossed into the Turkish area.

Makarios died on Aug. 3, 1977, and Spyros Kiprianou was elected to serve the remaining five months of his term. Kiprianou, running unopposed, won a full five-year term in 1978.

Despite intense pressure from the U.S. and other NATO allies anxious to end the dispute that kept both Greece and Turkey from functioning as defenders of the strategic eastern Mediterranean, intercommunal negotiations were still deadlocked in 1980.

CZECHOSLOVAKIA

Czechoslovak Socialist Republic
President: Gustav Husak (1975)
Premier: Lubomir Strougal (1970)
Area: 49,374 sq mi. (127,877 sq km)
Population (est. 1980): 15,360,000 (Czech, 64%; Slovak, 30%)
Density per square mile: 311.1
Capital: Prague
Largest cities (est. 1979): Prague, 1,188,600; **(est. 1976):** Brno, 359,500; Bratislava, 340,900; Ostrava, 300,900; Košice, 174,400; Plzeň, 156,500
Monetary unit: Koruna
Languages: Czech, Slovak, Hungarian
Religions: Roman Catholic, 70%; Czechoslovak Church, 8%; Protestant, 7%; Greek Orthodox, 5%.
National name: Ceskoslovenská Socialistická Republika
Freedom House classifications: Socialist industrial, one-party communist
Economic summary: Gross national product (1978): $71.3 billion. Average annual growth rate (1970–77): 4.3%. Per capita income (1976): $3,985. Labor force in agriculture: 14%; principal products: wheat, rye, oats, corn, barley, potatoes, sugar beets, hogs, cattle, horses. Labor force in industry: 39%; major products: iron and steel, machinery and equipment, cement, sheet glass, motor vehicles, armaments, chemicals, ceramics. Natural resources: coal/coke, timber, lignite, uranium, magnesite. Exports: machinery, motor vehicles, iron and steel, chemicals. Imports: machinery, equipment, fuels, raw materials, food, consumer goods. Major trading partners: U.S.S.R. and Soviet bloc, Austria, U.K.

Geography. Czechoslovakia lies in central Europe, a neighbor of East and West Germany, Poland, the U.S.S.R., Hungary, and Austria. It is equal in size to New York State. The principal rivers—the Elbe, Danube, Oder, and Moldau—are vital commercially to this landlocked country, for both waterborne commerce and agriculture, which flourishes in fertile valleys irrigated by these rivers and their tributaries.

Government. Since 1969 the supreme organ of the state has been the Federal Assembly, which has two equal chambers: the Chamber of People, with 200 deputies, and the Chamber of Nations, with 150 deputies (75 from the Czech Socialist Republic and 75 from the Slovak Socialist Republic). The chief executive is the President, who is elected by the Federal Assembly for a five-year term. The Premier and his Cabinet are appointed by the President but are responsible to the Federal Assembly.

The major political parties are the Communist Party, led by First Secretary Gustav Husak in both republics; Socialist Party; People's Party in the Czech Socialist Republic; Slovak Freedom Party and Slovak Reconstruction Party in the Slovak Socialist Republic. Together with trade unions, youth organizations, and other organizations, they form the National Front.

History. Probably about the 5th century A.D., Slavic tribes from the Vistula basin settled in the region of modern Czechoslovakia. Slovakia came under Magyar domination. The Czechs founded the kingdom of Bohemia, the Premyslide dynasty, which ruled Bohemia and Moravia from the 10th to the 16th century. One of the Bohemian kings, Charles IV, Holy Roman Emperor, made Prague an imperial capital and a center of Latin scholarship. The Hussite movement founded by Jan Hus (1369?–1415) linked the Slavs to the Reformation and revived Czech nationalism, previously under German domination. A Hapsburg, Ferdinand I, ascended the throne in 1526. The Czechs rebelled in 1618. Defeated in 1620, they were ruled for the next 300 years as part of the Austrian Empire.

In World War I, Czech and Slovak patriots, notably Thomas G. Masaryk and Milan Stefanik, promoted Czech-Slovak independence from abroad while their followers fought against the Central Powers. On Oct. 28, 1918, Czechoslovakia proclaimed itself a republic. Shortly thereafter Masaryk was unanimously elected first President.

Hitler provoked the country's German minority in the Sudetenland, led by Konrad Henlein, to agitate for autonomy. At the Munich Conference on Sept. 30, 1938, France and the U.K., seeking to avoid World War II, agreed that the Nazis could take the Sudetenland. Dr. Eduard Benes, who had succeeded Masaryk, resigned on Oct. 5, 1938, and fled to London. Czechoslovakia became a state within the German orbit and was known as Czecho-Slovakia. In March 1939, the Nazis occupied the country. Beneš organized a government-in-exile in London in 1940.

Soon after Czechoslovakia was liberated in World War II and the government returned in April 1945, it was obliged to cede Ruthenia to the U.S.S.R. In 1946, a Communist, Klement Gottwald, formed a six-party coalition Cabinet. Pressure from Moscow increased until Feb. 23–25, 1948, when the Communists seized complete control in a coup. Following constituent assembly elections in which the Communists and their allies were unopposed, a new Constitution was adopted.

Beneš refused to sign it and resigned; he died mysteriously on Sept. 3, 1948. The Constitution was promulgated June 9. Thereafter, agriculture was collectivized, industry almost completely socialized, and foreign trade conducted chiefly with the Soviet bloc. Industrialization was intensified and concentrated upon heavy industry. The "people's democracy" was converted into a "socialist" state by a new Constitution adopted June 11, 1960.

After the death of Stalin and the relaxing of Soviet controls, Czechoslovakia witnessed a nationalist awakening. In 1968 conservative Stalinists were driven from power and replaced by more liberal, reform-minded Communists.

In more orthodox circles of the U.S.S.R. and its European satellites, fears arose that the trend was undermining Communist rule. Soviet military maneuvers on Czechoslovak soil in May 1968 were followed in July by a meeting of the U.S.S.R. with Poland, Bulgaria, East Germany, and Hungary in Warsaw that demanded an accounting, which Prague refused. Czechoslovak-Soviet talks on Czechoslovak territory, at Cierna, in late July led to an accord. But the Russians charged that the Czechoslovaks had reneged on pledges to modify their policies, and on Aug. 20–21, troops of the five powers, estimated at 600,000, executed a lightning invasion and occupation.

Soviet secret police seized the top Czechoslovak leadership and detained it for several days in Moscow. But Soviet efforts to establish a puppet regime failed. President Ludvik Svoboda negotiated an accord providing for a gradual troop withdrawal in return for "normalization" of political policy.

The purge of liberals was virtually completed in 1970. Only Svoboda remained from 1968. Husak, who became Secretary General of the Communist Party in 1969, promised no show trials, but most liberals were punished. Czechoslovakia signed a new friendship treaty with the U.S.S.R. that codified the "Brezhnev doctrine," under which Russia can invade any Eastern European socialist nation that threatens to leave the satellite camp.

Continuing ferment surfaced early in 1975 with publication in the West of a long letter of protest against repression written by Alexander Dubcek, First Secretary of the Czechoslovak Communist Party during the 1968 "Prague Spring." The letter, addressed to the Presidium of Czechoslovakia's Federal Assembly, charged that the regime had purged thousands of creative workers. Dubcek was later reported transferred to a menial forester's job.

One of the most vigorous of the Eastern European groups formed to support human rights in the wake of the 1975 Helsinki Conference on Security and Cooperation in Europe was the Czech "Charter 77," an association of 240 intellectuals who signed a New Year manifesto protesting the suppression of freedom. Detentions of the signers began immediately, and a second manifesto appeared on January 8 with 300 signatures condemning the official reaction to the first. On Jan. 28, the government offered to let five of the dissidents leave the country, but they refused.

Despite warnings from the U.S., British, and other Western governments, arrests of members of the group continued, and five were sentenced to jail terms in October 1977. Playwright Vaclav Havel, given a suspended sentence, predicted more persecution of the group. Charter 77 adherents marked the first anniversary of their founding by issuing a manifesto Jan. 1, 1978, calling on the government to permit open debate on the observance of human rights in Czechoslovakia.

DENMARK

Kingdom of Denmark
Sovereign: Queen Margrethe II (1972)
Prime Minister: Anker Jørgensen (1975)
Area: 16,615 sq mi. (43,033 sq km)[1]
Population (est. 1980): 5,140,000[1]
Density per square mile: 309.1
Capital: Copenhagen
Largest cities (est. 1977): Copenhagen, 689,300; **(est. 1976 by U.N.):** Arhus, 246,100; Odense, 167,900; Alborg, 154,600
Monetary unit: Krone
Language: Danish

1. Excluding Faeroe Islands and Greenland.

Religion: Lutheran (established)
National name: Kongeriget Danmark
Freedom House classifications: Capitalist-socialist industrial, multi-party centralized
Economic summary: Gross national product (1978): $50.4 billion. Average annual growth rate (1970–77): 2.3%. Per capita income: $9,663; average rate of inflation (1977–78): 10%. Labor force in agriculture: 9%; principal products: meat, dairy products, fish, fur. Labor force in industry: 33%; major products: industrial and construction equipment, electronics, furniture, textiles. Natural resources: oil and gas, zinc, lead, iron ore, coal, molybdenum, cryolite, uranium. Exports: farm products, manufactured goods, fish, furs. Imports: industrial raw materials, fuel, machinery and equipment, transport equipment, consumer goods. Major trading partners: West Germany, Sweden, U.K., U.S., Norway.

Geography. Smallest of the Scandinavian countries (half the size of Maine), Denmark occupies the Jutland peninsula, which extends north from Germany between the tips of Norway and Sweden. To the west is the North Sea and to the east the Baltic.

The country also consists of several Baltic islands; the two largest are Sjaelland, the site of Copenhagen, and Fyn. The narrow waters off the north coast are called the Skagerrak and those off the east, the Kattegat.

Government. Denmark has been a constitutional monarchy since 1849. Legislative power is held jointly by the Sovereign and parliament. The Constitution of 1953 provides for a unicameral parliament called the Folketing, consisting of 179 popularly elected members who serve for four years. The Cabinet is presided over by the Sovereign, who appoints the Prime Minister.

The Sovereign, Queen Margrethe II, was born April 16, 1940, and became Queen—the first in Denmark's history—Jan. 15, 1972, the day after her father, King Frederik IX, died at 72 in the 25th year of his reign. Margrethe was the eldest of his three daughters (by Princess Ingrid of Sweden). The nation's Constitution was amended in 1953 to permit her to succeed her father in the absence of a male heir to the throne. (Denmark was ruled six centuries ago by Margrethe I, but she was never crowned Queen since there was no female right of succession.) Margrethe's sisters are Benedikte (born 1944) and Anne Marie (born 1946), now the former Queen of Greece.

The major political parties are the Social Democratic Party (68 seats in the Folketing), led by Prime Minister Anker Jørgensen; Liberal Democratic Party (22 seats), led by Henning Christophersen; Conservative Party (22 seats), led by Poul Schlüter; Progress Party (20 seats), led by Mogens Glistrup; Socialist People's Party (11 seats), led by Gert Petersen; Radical Liberal Party (10 seats); Center Democratic Party (6 seats); Left Socialist Party (6 seats); Single Tax Party (5 seats). Christian People's Party (5 seats).

History. Denmark emerged with establishment of the Norwegian dynasty of the Ynglinger in Jutland at the end of the 8th century. Danish mariners played a major role in the raids of the Vikings, or Norsemen, on Western Europe and particularly England. The country was Christianized by St. Ansgar and Harald Blaatand (Bluetooth)—the first Christian king—in the 10th century. Harald's son, Sweyn, conquered England in 1013. His son, Canute the Great, who reigned from 1014 to 1035, united Denmark, England, and Norway under his rule; the southern part of Sweden was part of Denmark until the 17th century. On Canute's death, civil war tore the country until Waldemar I (1157–82) re-established Danish hegemony over the north.

In 1282, the nobles won the Great Charter, and Eric V was forced to share power with parliament and a Council of Nobles. Waldemar IV (1340–75) restored Danish power, checked only by the Hanseatic League of north German cities allied with ports from Holland to Poland. His daughter, Margrethe, in 1397 united under her rule Denmark, Norway, and Sweden. But Sweden later achieved autonomy and in 1523, under Gustavus I, independence.

Denmark supported Napoleon, for which it was punished at the Congress of Vienna in 1815 by the loss of Norway to Sweden. In 1864, Bismarck, together with the Austrians, made war on the little country as an initial step in the unification of Germany. Denmark was neutral in World War I.

In 1939, Denmark signed a 10-year pact with Hitler, but less than a year later it was invaded by the Nazis. King Christian X reluctantly cautioned his countrymen to accept the occupation, but there was widespread resistance against the Nazis. In 1944, Iceland declared its independence from Denmark, ending a union that had existed since 1380.

Liberated by British troops in May 1945, the country staged a fast recovery in both agriculture and manufacturing and was a leader in liberalizing trade. It joined the United Nations in 1945 and NATO in 1949.

The Social Democrats largely ran Denmark after the war but were ousted in 1973 when, in an election dominated by protests against high taxes, all established parties lost heavily. The big winner was the new Progress Party. A minority government was formed by the Liberal Democrats, with their leader, Poul Hartling, as Premier. After losing a vote of confidence in January 1975, Hartling resigned and was succeeded by Anker Jørgensen, a Social Democrat who was Premier in 1972–73.

Outlying Territories of Denmark

FAEROE ISLANDS

Status: Autonomous part of Denmark
Commissioner: L. Groth (1972)
Area: 540 sq mi. (1,399 sq km)
Population (est. 1980): 43,000
Density per square mile: 79.9
Capital (1977 census): Thorshavn, 11,600
Monetary unit: Faeroese krone
Economic summary: Gross national product (1978): $350 million. Average annual growth rate (1970–77): 3.9%. Per capita income: $4,340. Principal agricultural products: sheep and cattle. Major industrial product: fish. Exports: fish and fish products. Imports: machinery and transport equipment, foodstuffs, petroleum and petroleum products. Major trading partners: Denmark, Norway, U.K., U.S.

This group of 21 islands, lying in the North Atlantic about 200 miles (322 km) northwest of the Shetland Islands, joined Denmark in 1386 and has since been part of the Danish kingdom. The islands were occupied by British troops during World War II, after the German occupation of Denmark.

The Faeroes have home rule under a bill enacted in 1948; they also have two representatives in the Danish Folketing.

GREENLAND

Status: Integral part of Kingdom of Denmark.
Area: 840,000 sq mi. (incl. 708,069 sq mi. covered by icecap) (2,175,600 sq km).
Population (est. 1980): 50,000
Capital (est. 1978): Godthaab, 8,500
Chief exports: fish, fur skins, cryolite.
Economic summary: Gross national product (1978): $340 million. Average annual growth rate (1970–77): 6.3%. Principal agricultural products: hay, sheep, garden produce. Major industries: mining, slaughtering, fishing, sealing. Natural resource: cryolite. Exports: fish and fish products, metalic ores and concentrates. Imports: petroleum and petroleum products, machinery and transport equipment, foodstuffs. Major trading partners: Denmark, Finland, West Germany, U.K.

Greenland, the world's largest island, was colonized in 985–86 by Eric the Red. Danish sovereignty, which covered only the west coast, was extended over the whole island in 1917. In 1941 the U.S. signed an agreement with the Danish minister in Washington, placing it under U.S. protection during World War II but maintaining Danish sovereignty. A definitive agreement for the joint defense of Greenland within the framework of NATO was signed in 1951. A large U.S. air base at Thule in the far north was completed in 1953.

Under 1953 amendments to the Danish Constitution, Greenland became part of Denmark, with two representatives in the Danish Folketing. On May 1, 1979, Greenland became self-governing, with its own local parliament (Landsting), replacing the Greenland Provincial Council.

Greenland is the world's only source of natural cryolite, important in making aluminum.

DJIBOUTI

Republic of Djibouti
President: Gouled Aptidon Hassan (1977)
Prime Minister: Gourad Hamadou Barkat (1978)
Area: 8,996 sq mi. (23,300 sq km)
Population (est. 1980): 325,000
Density per sq mi.: 36.1
Capital (est. 1978): Djibouti, 160,000
Monetary unit: Djibouti franc
Languages: Arabic, French, Afar, Somali
Religion: Islam
Freedom House classifications: Capitalist industrial, one-party nationalist
Economic summary: Gross national product (1978): $140 million. Average annual growth rate (1970–77): −0.3%. Per capita income: $360. Principal agricultural products: goats, sheep, camels. Industries: port and maritime support, construction. Exports: hides, cattle, coffee (in transit from Ethiopia). Imports: textiles, consumer goods, foodstuffs. Major trading partners: France, Ethiopia, Japan.

Geography. Djibouti lies in northeastern Africa on the Gulf of Aden at the southern entrance to the Red Sea. It borders on Ethiopia and Somalia. The country, the size of Massachusetts, is mainly a stony desert, with scattered plateaus and highlands.

Government. On May 8, 1977, the population of the French Territory of the Afars and Issas voted by more than 98% for independence. Voters also approved a 65-member interim Constituent Assembly. France transferred sovereignty to the new nation of Djibouti on June 27. Later in the year it became a member of the Organization of African Unity and the Arab League. The People's Progress Assembly is the only political party.

History. The territory that is now Djibouti was acquired by France between 1843 and 1886 by treaties with the Somali sultans. Small, arid, and sparsely populated, Djibouti is important chiefly because of the capital city's port, the terminal of the Djibouti-Addis Ababa railway that carries 60% of Ethiopia's foreign trade.

Originally known as French Somaliland, the colony voted in 1958 and 1967 to remain under French rule. It was renamed the Territory of the Afars and Issas in 1967 and took the name of its capital city on attaining independence.

Somali rebels in Ethiopia's Ogaden Province cut the railway to Djibouti in June 1977 and there was fear that the new nation might be absorbed by Somalia. In July 1980, Djibouti granted base rights to United States ships and planes in exchange for undisclosed amounts of aid.

DOMINICA

Commonwealth of Dominica
President: Aurelius Marie (1980)
Prime Minister: Mary Eugenia Charles (1980)
Area: 300 sq mi. (777 sq km)
Population: (est. 1980): 85,000
Density per square mile: 283.3
Capital and largest city (est. 1978): Roseau, 16,800
Monetary unit: East Caribbean dollar
Languages: English and French patois
Religions: Roman Catholic, Anglican, Methodist
Member of Commonwealth of Nations
Freedom House classifications: Capitalist industrial, multi-party centralized
Economy: Gross national product (1978): $30 million. Average annual growth rate (1970–77): −4.1%. Labor force in agriculture: 50%; principal products: bananas, citrus fruits, coconuts, cocoa. Major industries: agricultural processing; tourism. Exports: bananas, lime juice, oil, cocoa. Imports: machinery and equipment, foodstuffs, manufactured goods, cement. Major trading partners: U.K., Commonwealth and Caribbean countries, U.S., Canada.

Geography. Dominica is an island of the Lesser Antilles in the Caribbean south of Guadeloupe and north of Martinique.

Government. Dominica is a republic, with a president elected by the House of Assembly as head of state and a prime minister appointed by the president on the advice of the Assembly. The Freedom Party (17 of 21 seats in the Assembly) is led by Prime Minister Mary Eugenia Charles. The Opposition Democratic Labor Party holds two seats and independents the remaining two.

History. Discovered by Columbus in 1493, Dominica was claimed by Britain and France until 1815, when Britain asserted sovereignty. Dominica, along with other Windward Isles, became a self-governing member of the West Indies Associated States in free association with Britain in 1967.

Full independence was granted on Nov. 3, 1978, in ceremonies at which the first Prime Minister, Patrick R. John, declared a socialist course for the new republic. John aroused strong opposition when he proposed laws curbing the right to strike and freedom of the press. During a demonstration in Roseau in May 1979, police fired at the crowd, killing three. After a general strike, John dissolved the Assembly and set new elections for Dec. 1, but continued disorder forced his resignation and replacement by Oliver Seraphin.

Dissatisfaction over the slow pace of reconstruction after Hurricane David struck the island in September 1979 brought a landslide victory for the opposition Freedom Party in July 1980. The vote gave the prime ministership to Mary Eugenia Charles, a strong advocate of free enterprise.

DOMINICAN REPUBLIC

President: Antonio Guzmán (1978)
Area: 18,704 sq mi. (48,442 sq km)
Population (est. 1980): 5,450,000 (approx.): mestizo and mulatto, 75%; white, 15%; Negro, 10%
Density per square mile: 291.4
Capital: Santo Domingo[1]
Largest cities (est. 1979): Santo Domingo, 1,103,400; **(1970 census):** Santiago de los Caballeros, 155,151
Monetary unit: Peso
Language: Spanish
Religion: Roman Catholic
National name: República Dominicana
Freedom House classifications: Capitalist industrial, multi-party centralized
Economic summary: Gross national product (1978): $4.7 billion. Average annual growth rate (1970–77): 4.6%. Per capital income: $880. Labor force in agriculture: 73%; principal products: sugar cane, coffee, cocoa, tobacco, rice, corn. Labor force in industry: 8%; major products: processed sugar, textiles, cement, nickel, bauxite, and gold mining. Natural resources: nickel, bauxite, gold, silver. Exports: sugar, nickel, coffee, tobacco, cocoa, bauxite. Imports: foodstuffs, petroleum, industrial raw materials, capital equipment. Major trading partner: U.S.

Geography. The Dominican Republic in the West Indies, occupies the eastern two thirds of the island of Hispaniola, which it shares with Haiti. Its area equals that of Vermont and New Hampshire combined.

Crossed from northwest to southeast by a moutain range with elevations exceeding 10,000 feet (3,048 m), the country has fertile, well-watered land in the northeast, where nearly two thirds of the population lives. The southwest part is arid and has poor soil, except around Santo Domingo.

1. Called Cuidad Trujillo from 1936 to 1961.

Government. The president is elected by direct vote every four years. Legislative powers rest with a Senate and a Chamber of Deputies, both elected by direct vote, also for four years. All citizens must vote when they reach 18 years of age, or even earlier if they are married.

The major political parties are the Reformist Party, led by former President Joaquín Balaguer; Dominican Liberation Party, led by Juan Bosch; Partido Quisquellano Demócrata, led by Elías Wessin y Wessin) Movimiento de Integración Democrática Anti-Releccionista, led by Augusto Lora.

History. The Dominican Republic was discovered by Columbus in 1492. He named it La Española, and his son, Diego, was its first viceroy. The capital, Santo Domingo, founded in 1496, is the oldest European settlement in the Western Hemisphere. Spain ceded the colony to France in 1795, and Haitian blacks under Toussaint L'Ouverture conquered it in 1801.

In 1808 the people revolted and the next year captured Santo Domingo, setting up the first republic. Spain regained title to the colony in 1814. In 1821 the people overthrew Spanish rule, but in 1822 they were reconquered by the Haitians. They revolted again in 1844, threw out the Haitians, and established the Dominican Republic, headed by Pedro Santana. Uprisings and Haitian attacks led Santana to make the country a province of Spain from 1861 to 1865. The U.S. Senate refused to ratify a treaty of annexation. Disorder continued until the dictatorship of Ulíses Heureaux, in 1916, when disorder broke out again, the U.S. sent in a contingent of marines, who remained until 1934.

A sergeant in the Dominican army trained by the marines, Rafaél Leonides Trujillo Molina, overthrew Horacio Vásquez in 1930 and established a dictatorship that lasted until his assassination 31 years later. To end border clashes, Trujillo mounted an invasion of Haiti in 1937, killing more than 10,000 Haitians. Trujillo developed the country but ran it for his own benefit and that of his followers; he wound up owning much of the economy.

After Trujillo's assassination on May 30, 1961, disorders forced out the President, Joaquín Balaguer, but a governing council, in spite of an abortive military coup, steered the country to a return to constitutional government.

A new Constitution was adopted in 1962, and the first free elections since 1924 put Juan Bosch, a leftist leader, in office. A planned program of reforms with U.S. support was cut off by a right-wing military coup that replaced Bosch with a civilian triumvirate.

Leftists rebelled April 24, 1965, and President Lyndon Johnson sent in 400 marines to help evacuate U.S. citizens. After an OAS ceasefire request May 6, a compromise installed Hector Garcia-Godoy as provisional president. Balaguer won in free elections in 1966 against Bosch, and an OAS force of 9,000 U.S. troops and 2,000 from other countries withdrew. Balaguer restored political and economic stability and launched a 15-year development program.

Balaguer's longtime support for free elections faltered in May 1978, when the army suspended the counting of ballots as he trailed in a fourth-term bid. After a warning from President Jimmy Carter, however, Balaguer accepted the victory of Antonio Guzmán of the opposition Dominican Revolutionary Party.

ECUADOR

Republic of Ecuador
President: Jaime Roldós Aguilera (1979)
Area: 105,685 sq mi. (273,724 sq km)
Population (est. 1980): 8,350,000
Density per square mile: 79.0
Capital: Quito
Largest cities (est. 1978 by U.N.): Guayaquil, 1,022,000; Quito, 742,900; Cuenca, 128,800
Monetary unit: Sucre
Languages: Spanish, Quéchua, Jibaro
Religion: Roman Catholic
National name: República del Ecuador
Freedom House classifications: Capitalist pre-industrial, multi-party centralized
Economic summary: Gross national product (1978): $6.9 billion. Average annual growth rate (1970–77): 6.1%. Per capita income: $780. Land used for agriculture: 15%; labor force: 56%; principal products: bananas, coffee, cocoa, sugar cane, fruits, corn, potatoes, rice. Labor force in industry: 18%; major products: processed foods, textiles, chemicals, fish, petroleum. Natural resources: petroleum, fish, timber, minerals. Exports: petroleum, bananas, coffee, cocoa, sugar, fish products. Imports: agricultural and industrial machinery, industrial raw materials, building supplies, chemical products, transportation and communication equipment. Major trading partners: U.S., Latin American and Western European countries, Japan.

Geography. Ecuador, equal in area to Nevada, is in the northwest part of South America fronting on the Pacific. To the north is Colombia and to the east and south is Peru. Two high and parallel ranges of the Andes, traversing the country from north to south, are topped by tall volcanic peaks. The highest is Chimborazo at 20,577 feet (6,272 m).

The Galápagos Islands (or Colón Archipelago) (3,029 sq mi.; 7,845 sq km) in the Pacific Ocean about 600 miles (966 km) west of the South American mainland, became part of Ecuador in 1832.

Government. A 1978 Constitution returned Ecuador to civilian government after eight years of military rule. Under its terms, the President is elected by universal suffrage to a term of five years and a House of Representatives of 69 members popularly elected for the same period. A faction of the Concentration of Popular Forces Party led by President Jaime Roldós Aguilera controls a majority of the legislature. An opposing faction of the party, led by Assad Bucaram, holds approximately 20 seats.

History. The tribes in the northern highlands of Ecuador formed the Kingdom of Quito around A.D. 1000 It was absorbed, by conquest and marriage, into the Inca Empire. Pizarro conquered the land in 1532, and through the 17th century a thriving colony was built by exploitation of the Indians. The first revolt against Spain occurred in 1809. Ecuador then joined Venezuela, Colombia, and Panama in a confederacy founded by Simón Bolívar and known as Greater Colombia.

On the collapse of this union in 1830, Ecuador became independent. Subsequent history was one of revolts and dictatorships; it had 48 presidents during the first 131 years of the republic. Conservatives ruled until the Revolution of 1895 ushered in nearly a half century of Radical Liberal rule, during which the church was disestablished and freedom of worship, speech, and press was introduced.

In 1970, following six months of strife between university students and police, President José María Velasco Ibarra, who was elected in 1968 for the fifth time, took supreme powers to "avoid social and economic chaos." He closed universities, jailed some professors and businessmen, and demanded "reform" of the Supreme Court. Opposition political leaders were arrested and a military shake-up ensued.

Velasco was ousted nine months later by a junta, which sharply increased fees charged to foreign oil companies.

A three-man military junta headed by Vice Adm. Alfredo Poveda, which had taken power in a 1976 coup, agreed to a free presidential election on July 16, 1978. Jaime Roldós Aguilera won the runoff on April 29, 1979, backed by a "center leftist" coalition, the Concentration of Popular Forces. Once elected, however, Roldós found himself in conflict with his former mentor, Assad Bucaram, who as president of the House of Representatives blocked administration bills. Roldós threatened a plebiscite on constitutional reform, but on May 19, 1980, he withdrew his proposal after a majority of the House pledged support for his government.

EGYPT

Arab Republic of Egypt
President (1970) and Premier (1980): Anwar el-Sadat
Area: 386,872 sq mi. (1,001,998 sq km)
Population (est. 1980): 42,000,000
Density per square mile: 108.6
Capital: Cairo
Largest cities (est. 1979): Cairo, 5,423,000; **(1976 census):** Alexandria, 2,318,655; Giza, 1,246,713; Shubra el Khema, 393,700; El Mahalla el Kubra, 292,853; Tanta, 284,636; Port Said, 262,620; Mansura, 257,866
Monetary unit: Egyptian pound
Language: Arabic
Religions: Islam, 93%; Christian (mostly Copt), 7%
Freedom House classifications: Capitalist-socialist industrial, dominant party
Economic summary: Gross national product (1978): $15.5 billion. Average annual growth rate (1970–77): 5.2%. Per capita income: $280. Land used for agriculture: 3%; labor force: 50%; principal products: cotton, wheat, rice, corn. Labor force in industry: 12%; major products: textiles, processed foods, tobacco manufactures, chemicals, fertilizer, petroleum and petroleum products. Natural resources: manganese ore, phosphates, petroleum, gold, nickel, tungsten. Exports: cotton, rice, petroleum, manufactured goods. Imports: foodstuffs, capital goods. Major trading partners: U.S.S.R., West Germany, Italy, France, U.K., U.S.

Geography. Egypt, at the northeast corner of Africa on the Mediterranean Sea, is bordered on the west by Libya, on the south by the Sudan, and on the east by the Red Sea and Israel. It is nearly one and one half times the size of Texas.

The historic Nile flows through the eastern third of the country. On either side of the Nile valley are desert plateaus, spotted with oases. In the north, toward the Mediterranean, plateaus are low, while south of Cairo they rise to a maximum of 1,015 feet (309 m) above sea level. At the head of the Red Sea is the Sinai Peninsula, between the Suez Canal and Israel.

Navigable throughout its course in Egypt, the Nile is used largely as a means of cheap transport for heavy goods. The principal port is Alexandria.

The Nile delta starts 100 miles (161 km) south of the Mediterranean and fans out to a sea front of 155 miles between the cities of Alexandria and Port Said. From Cairo north, the Nile branches into many streams, the principal ones being the Damietta and the Rosetta.

Except for a narrow belt along the Mediterranean, Egypt lies in an almost rainless area, in which high daytime temperatures fall quickly at night.

Government. Executive power is held by the President, who is also serving as Premier, and can appoint one or more Vice Presidents.

The major political parties are the National Democratic Party, Free Socialist Party, Nationalist Progressive Party, and Independent Front.

History. Egyptian history dates back to about 4000 B.C., when the kingdoms of upper and lower Egypt, already highly civilized, were united. Egypt's "Golden Age" coincided with the 18th and 19th dynasties (16th to 13th centuries B.C.), during which the empire was established. Persia conquered Egypt in 525 B.C.; Alexander the Great subdued it in 332 B.C.; and then the dynasty of the Ptolemies ruled the land until 30 B.C., when Cleopatra, last of the line, committed suicide and Egypt became a Roman province. From 641 to 1517 the Arab caliphs ruled Egypt, and then the Turks took it for their Ottoman Empire.

Napoleon's armies occupied the country from 1798 to 1801. In 1805, Mohammed Ali, leader of a band of Albanian soldiers, became Pasha of Egypt. After completion of the Suez Canal in 1869, the French and British took increasing interest in Egypt.

British troops occupied Egypt in 1882, and British resident agents became its actual administrators, though it remained under nominal Turkish sovereignty. In 1914, this fiction was ended, and Egypt became a protectorate of Britain.

Pressure by Egyptian nationalists forced Britain to declare Egypt an independent, sovereign state on Feb. 28, 1922, although the British reserved rights for the protection of the Suez Canal and the defense of Egypt. In 1936, by an Anglo-Egyptian treaty of alliance, all British troops and officials were to be withdrawn, except from the Suez Canal Zone. When World War II started, Egypt remained neutral. British imperial troops finally ended the Nazi threat to Suez in 1942 in the battle of El Alamein, which took place west of Alexandria.

In 1951, Egypt abrogated the 1936 treaty and the 1899 Anglo-Egyptian condominium of the Sudan (*See* Sudan.) Rioting and attacks on British troops in the Suez Canal Zone followed, reaching a climax in January 1952. The army, led by Gen. Mohammed Naguib, seized power on July 23, 1952. Three days later, King Farouk abdicated in favor of his infant son. Naguib took over the premiership in September and promised far-reaching reforms. The monarchy was abolished and a republic proclaimed on June 18, 1953, with Naguib holding the posts of Provisional President and Premier. He relinquished the latter in 1954 to Gamal Abdel Nasser, leader of the ruling military junta. Naguib was deposed seven months later. Nasser was confirmed as President in a popular referendum on June 23, 1956.

Nasser's policies embroiled his country in continual conflict. In 1956, the U.S. and Britain withdrew their pledges of financial aid for the building of the Aswan High Dam. In reply, Nasser nationalized the Suez Canal and expelled British oil and embassy officials. Israel, barred from the Canal and exasperated by terrorist raids, invaded the Gaza Strip and the Sinai Peninsula. Britain and France, after demanding Egyptian evacuation of the Canal Zone, attacked Egypt on Oct. 31, 1956. Worldwide pressure forced Britain, France, and Israel to halt the hostilities. A U.N. emergency force occupied the Canal Zone, and all troops were evacuated in the spring of 1957.

On Feb. 1, 1958, Egypt and Syria formed the United Arab Republic, which was joined by Yemen in an association known as the United Arab States. However, Syria withdrew from the United Arab Republic in 1961 and Egypt dissolved its ties with Yemen in the United Arab States. On Sept. 2, 1971, Egypt finally shed the name United Arab Republic.

On June 5, 1967, Israel invaded the Sinai Peninsula, the East Bank of the Jordan River, and the zone around the Gulf of Aqaba. Only a U.N. cease-fire on June 10 saved the Arabs from complete rout. The war left the U.A.R. army, its prestige, and its economy in ruins. The Suez Canal was blocked by wrecks and closed to all traffic. Nasser at first resigned as President, then withdrew the resignation, getting increased power to rebuild the stricken nation. He obtained economic and financial help from the U.S.S.R., China, Kuwait, and former King Saud of Saudi Arabia.

Nasser declared the 1967 cease-fire void along the Canal in April 1969 and began a war of attrition. Egyptian artillery fire across the canal sparked Israeli "deep penetration" raids that attempted to topple Nasser. He went to Moscow in January 1970, and by March, Russians were flying planes with Egyptian markings to defend the Nile delta and were manning some antiaircraft missiles. An estimated 10,000 to 12,000 Russians were in Egypt in 1970. Missiles were moved into the Canal Zone, challenging Israeli air superiority. The U.S. peace plan of June 19, 1970, resulted in Egypt's agreement to reinstate the cease-fire for at least three months, (from August) and to accept Israel's existence within "recognized and secure" frontiers that might emerge from U.N.-mediated talks. In return, Israel accepted the principle of withdrawing from occupied territories.

Then, on Sept. 28, 1970, Nasser died, at 52, of a heart attack in the midst of Jordanian-Palestinian guerrilla hostilities and the hijacking by these guerrillas of four Western jet planes. The new President was Anwar el-Sadat, an associate of Nasser and a former newspaper editor.

With Nasser's death, the pan-Arabism he advocated disintegrated. Sadat seemed more willing to reach a peace settlement with Israel. While receiving more arms from the U.S.S.R. (matched by U.S. sales to Israel), he responded to U.S. peace initiatives by promising to sign a peace agreement if Israel withdrew to its pre-war 1967 borders. The Israelis refused, however.

In 1971, Sadat signed a 15-year treaty of friendship and cooperation with Moscow that legitimized Soviet penetration of Egypt.

The Aswan High Dam, whose financing by the

U.S.S.R. was its first step into Egypt, was completed and dedicated in January 1971.

In July 1972, Sadat ordered the expulsion of Soviet "advisors and experts" from Egypt because the Russians had not provided the sophisticated weapons he felt were needed to retake territory lost to Israel in 1967. Moscow pulled out virtually all of its 18,000 men.

The fourth major Arab-Israeli war broke out Oct. 6, 1973, while Israelis were commemorating Yom Kippur, the Jewish high holy day. Egypt swept deep into the Sinai, while Syria strove to throw Israel off the Golan Heights. Arab oil-producing countries cut off shipments to the U.S. and other Western nations, helping to precipitate a worldwide energy crisis.

A U.N.-sponsored truce was accepted on October 22 after an Israeli thrust across the Suez into Egypt itself cut off Egyptian forces in the Sinai. In January 1974, both sides agreed to a settlement negotiated by U.S. Secretary of State Henry A. Kissinger that gave Egypt a narrow strip along the entire Sinai bank of the Suez Canal. In June, President Nixon made the first visit by a U.S. President to Egypt and full diplomatic relations were established. An Egyptian-American economic commission was established to channel aid to Egypt, including nuclear power reactors. The Suez Canal was cleared and it reopened on June 5, 1975.

Kissinger pursued "shuttle diplomacy" between Cairo and Jerusalem to extend areas of agreement. Israel yielded on three points—the possession of the Mitla and Giddi passes in the Sinai and the Abu Rudeis oil field in the peninsula—and both sides committed themselves to annual renewal of the U.N. peacekeeping force in the Sinai. Although not a peace treaty, the agreement established the U.S. mediating position.

Sadat, defying Arab charges of betrayal in dealing with Israel, gained U.S. aid and the security to turn his attention to an economy beset by 30% inflation and serious unemployment. A 1976 referendum gave Sadat, running unopposed for a second six-year term, a 99.9% vote of approval.

Sadat won promises of major economic help in 1977, when Saudi Arabia and other Arabian Gulf states agreed to lend Egypt $1.5 billion. A consortium of the International Monetary Fund, the European Economic Community, and others recommended loans and credits of $13.1 billion for 1977–80. And the Ford Motor Co. said it would resume manufacture of trucks and diesel engines in an Alexandria plant shut down by the Arab boycott in the 1960s. Goodyear, Union Carbide, and Coca-Cola also began operations in Egypt.

In the most audacious act of his career, Sadat flew to Jerusalem at the invitation of Prime Minister Menachem Begin and pleaded before Israel's Knesset on Nov. 20, 1977, for a permanent peace settlement. The Arab world reacted with fury—only Morocco, Tunisia, Sudan, and Oman voiced approval—and Egyptian Foreign Minister Ismail Fahmy resigned. Hope for progress cooled when political talks in Jerusalem snagged, and Sadat ordered his negotiators home Jan. 17, 1978. The Egyptian was angered by Begin's defense of new settlements on the West Bank and his refusal to discuss the ultimate status of the West Bank and Gaza Strip, which Sadat proposed be placed under Jordanian and Egyptian administration respectively.

Sadat maintained an image of cooperation while Begin reflected intransigence, a perception shared by the U.S. Congress as it voted for Carter's requested package sale of jet fighters to Egypt, Saudi Arabia, and Israel over Israeli protests.

Egyptian and Israeli officials met in the Sinai desert on April 26, 1979, to implement the peace treaty calling for the phased withdrawal of occupation forces from the peninsula. On May 27 ahead of schedule, Israel turned over the gateway town of El Arish to Egyptian administration. By mid-1980, two thirds of the Sinai was transferred, but progress here was not matched in the other area covered by the treaty—the negotiation of Arab autonomy in the Gaza Strip and the West Bank. Stung by continued installation of Jewish settlements in the West Bank and ultimately by Israeli legislation to annex permanently the Arab sector of Jerusalem, Sadat called a halt to further autonomy talks in August 1980.

Suez Canal. The Suez Canal, in Egyptian territory between the Arabian Desert and the Sinai Peninsula, is an artificial waterway about 100 miles (161 km) long between Port Said on the Mediterranean and Suez on the Red Sea. Construction work, directed by the French engineer Ferdinand de Lesseps, was begun April 25, 1859, and the Canal was opened Nov. 17, 1869. The cost was 432,807,882 francs. The concession was held by an Egyptian joint stock company, *Compagnie Universelle du Canal Maritime de Suez*, in which the British government held 353,504 out of a total of 800,000 shares. The concession was to expire Nov. 17, 1968, but the company was nationalized July 26, 1956, by unilateral action of the Egyptian government.

The Canal was closed in June 1967 after the Arab-Israeli conflict. With the help of the U.S. Navy, work was begun on clearing the Canal in 1974, after the cease-fire ending the Arab-Israeli war. It was reopened to traffic June 5, 1975.

EL SALVADOR

Republic of El Salvador
Area: 8,260 sq mi. (21,393 sq km)
Population (est. 1980): 4,750,000
Density per square mile: 575.1
Capital: San Salvador
Largest cities (est. 1976): San Salvador, 500,000; (est. 1969): Santa Ana, 168,000
Monetary unit: Colón
Language: Spanish
Religion: Roman Catholic
National name: República de El Salvador
Freedom House classifications: Capitalist industrial, non-party military
Economic summary: Gross national product (1978): $2.8 billion. Average annual growth rate (1970–77): 2.1%. Per capita income: $610. Land used for agriculture: 67%; labor force: 57%; principal products: coffee, cotton, corn, sugar, rice, beans. Labor force in industry: 14%; major products: processed foods, clothing and textiles, petroleum products. Natural resources: timber, balsam, gold, silver, coal, copper, iron, zinc, mercury, sulfur. Exports: coffee, cotton, sugar. Imports: machinery, automotive vehicles, petroleum, foodstuffs, fertilizer. Major trading partners: U.S., Caribbean countries, Japan.

Geography. Situated on the Pacific coast of Central America, El Salvador has Guatemala to the west and Honduras to the north and east. It is the smallest of the Central American countries, its area equal to that of Massachusetts, and the only one without an Atlantic coastline.

Most of the country is a fertile volcanic plateau about 2,000 feet (607 m) high. There are some active volcanoes and many scenic crater lakes.

Government. The Constitution provides for a President, popularly elected for five years and ineligible to succeed himself, and a unicameral legislature, the National Assembly, consisting of 52 members elected by popular suffrage for two years.

The country is headed by a junta that took power on Oct. 15, 1979.

History. Pedro de Alvarado, a lieutenant of Cortés, conquered El Salvador in 1525. El Salvador, with the other countries of Central America, declared its independence from Spain on Sept. 15, 1821, and was part of a federation of Central American states until that union was dissolved in 1838. Its independent career for several decades thereafter was marked by numerous revolutions and wars against other Central American republics.

In 1931, the first free election in 20 years was held, but Gen. Maximiliano Hernández Martínez took power in December of that year and maintained a dictatorship until he was ousted in 1944. For nearly two decades, politics remained turbulent and unstable, until the 1962 elections.

The new President, Julio Adalberto Rivera, restored free elections. In the next few years, El Salvador assumed a leading role in the Central American Common Market. But in 1968, a drop in exports of coffee and cotton produced a slump. Widespread unemployment in El Salvador and land hunger in Honduras resulted in a conflict between the two nations in 1969. Deportation from Honduras of several thousand Salvadorans led to an invasion by El Salvador. Under threats of economic sanctions and military intervention, El Salvador withdrew its troops. The clash left 1,000 dead and tens of thousands homeless.

Presidential elections in 1972 gave none of four candidates a clear majority; therefore, the National Assembly, in which the National Conciliation Party had an overwhelming majority, proclaimed its candidate, Col. Arturo Armando Molina, as President.

The 1977 presidential elections were marked by at least eight deaths and massive protest demonstrations by the National Opposition Union, which charged extensive voter fraud. Gen. Carlos Humberto Romero, candidate of the governing National Conciliation Party, claimed victory over Lt. Col. Ernesto Claramount, the National Opposition Union candidate, who chose exile rather than prison after the election.

On Oct. 15, 1979, a junta composed of two army officers and three civilians deposed the President, Gen. Carlos Humberto Romero, seeking to halt increasingly violent clashes between leftist and rightist forces. The military officers were Col. Jaime Abdul Gutierrez Avendaño and Col. Adolfo Arnoldo Majano. The civilian members resigned in January and were replaced by two Christian Democrats, José Napoleón Duarte and José Antonio Morales Ehrlich, and a non-party member, José Ramón Avalos Navarrete. The junta strove to halt civil strife but found itself attacked from the left as too conservative and from the right as too liberal, with bloody conflicts continuing.

EQUATORIAL GUINEA

Republic of Equatorial Guinea
Head of junta: Lieut. Col. Theodore Nguema Menzogo (1979)
Area: 10,830 sq mi. (28,051 sq km)
Population (est. 1980): 370,000
Density per square mile: 34.6
Capital and largest city (est. 1970): Malabo (formerly Santa Isabel), 19,300
Monetary unit: Ekuele
Languages: Spanish, Fang, Bubi
Religions: Roman Catholic, Protestant, Animist
National name: Républica de Guinea Ecuatorial
Freedom House classifications: Capitalist-statist pre-industrial, non-party military
Economic summary: Gross national product (1972): $70 million. Per capita income: $240. Land used for agriculture: 85–90%; labor force: 95%; principal products: cocoa, wood, coffee. Natural resource: wood. Exports: cocoa, wood, coffee, bananas, palm oil. Imports: foodstuffs, beverages, tobacco, textiles, machinery. Major trading partner Spain.

Geography. Equatorial Guinea, formerly Spanish Guinea, consists of Rio Muni (10,045 sq mi.; 26,117 sq km), on the western coast of Africa, and several islands in the Gulf of Guinea, the largest of which is Macias Nguema Biyogo (formerly Fernando Po) (785 sq mi.; 2,033 sq km). The other islands are Pagalu (formerly Annobón), Corisco, Elobey Grande, and Elobey Chico. The total area is twice that of Connecticut.

Government. Executive power is vested in a Council of Ministers appointed by and responsible to the president. Legislative power is vested in a 60-member People's National Assembly.

A new Constitution was approved in 1973 and the capital's name was changed from Santa Isabel to Malabo.

The Partido Unico Nacional de Trabajadores, headed by the president, is the only political party.

History. Fernando Po and Annobón came under Spanish control in 1778. From 1827 to 1844, with Spanish consent, Britain administered Fernando Po, but in the latter year Spain reclaimed the island. Río Muni was given to Spain in 1885 by the Treaty of Berlin.

Negotiations with Spain led to independence on Oct. 12, 1968.

In 1969, anti-Spanish incidents in Río Muni, including the tearing down of a Spanish flag by national troops, caused 5,000 Spanish residents to flee for their safety, and diplomatic relations between the two nations became strained. A month later, President Masie Nguema Biyogo Negue Ndong charged that a coup had been attempted against him. He seized dictatorial powers and arrested 80 opposition politicians and even several of his Cabinet ministers and the secretary of the National Assembly.

A coup on Aug. 3, 1979, deposed Masie, and a junta led by Lieut. Col. Theodore Nguema Menzogo took over the government. Menzogo expelled Soviet technicians and reinstated cooperation with Spain.

ETHIOPIA

Head of State: Lt. Col. Mengistu Haile Mariam (1977)
Area: 457,142 sq mi. (1,183,998 sq km)
Population (est. 1980) 31,100,000
Density per square mile: 68.0
Capital: Addis Ababa
Largest cities (est. 1979): Addis Ababa, 1,179,000; (est. 1978 by U.N.): Asmara, 393,800
Monetary unit: Birr
Languages: Amharic (official), Galligna, Tigrigna
Religions: Copt (Christian), Islam
Freedom House classifications: Socialist pre-industrial, non-party military
Economic summary: Gross national product (1978): $3.6 billion. Average annual growth rate (1970–77): 0.2%. Per capita income: $100. Land used for agriculture: 53%; labor force: 90%; principal products: coffee, barley, wheat, corn, sugar cane, cotton, oilseeds, livestock. Labor force in industry: 10%; major products: cement, cotton textiles, refined sugar, processed foods, refined oil. Natural resources: potash, salt, gold, copper, platinum. Exports: coffee, hides and skins, oilseeds. Imports: petroleum. Major trading partners: Saudi Arabia, Japan, Italy, West Germany, Iran, U.K., France.

Geography. Ethiopia is in east central Africa, bordered on the west by the Sudan, the east by Somalia and Djibouti, the south by Kenya, and the north by the Red Sea. It is nearly three times the size of California.

Over its main plateau land, Ethiopia has several high mountains, the highest of which is Ras Dashan at 15,158 feet (4,620 m). The Blue Nile, or Abbai, rises in the northwest and flows in a great semicircle east, south, and northwest before entering the Sudan. Its chief reservoir, Lake Tana, lies in the northwestern part of the plateau.

Government. A provisional military government headed by a 120-member officers' committee (the Dirgue) deposed Ethiopia's traditional monarchy in 1974, suspended parliament, and ruled by decree. It proclaimed Ethiopia a socialist state.

History. Black Africa's oldest state, Ethiopia can trace 2,000 years of recorded history. Its now-deposed royal line claimed descent from King Menelik I, traditionally believed to have been the son of the Queen of Sheba and King Solomon. The present nation is a consolidation of smaller kingdoms that owed feudal allegiance to the Ethiopian Emperor.

Hamitic peoples migrated to Ethiopia from Asia Minor in prehistoric times. Semitic traders from Arabia penetrated the region in the 7th century B.C. Its Red Sea ports were important to the Roman and Byzantine Empires. Coptic Christianity came to the country in A.D. 341, and a variant of that communion became Ethiopia's state religion.

Ancient Ethiopia reached its peak in the 5th century, then was isolated by the rise of Islam and weakened by feudal wars. Modern Ethiopia emerged under Emperor Menelik II, who established its independence by routing an Italian invasion in 1896. He expanded Ethiopia by conquest.

Disorders that followed Menelik's death brought his daughter to the throne in 1917, with his cousin, Tafari Makonnen, as Regent, heir presumptive, and strongman. When the Empress died in 1930, Tafari was crowned Emperor Haile Selassie I.

As Regent, Haile Selassie outlawed slavery. As Emperor, he worked for centralization of his diffuse realm, in which 70 languages are spoken, and for moderate reform. In 1931, he granted a Constitution, revised in 1955, that created a parliament with an appointed Senate and an elected Chamber of Deputies, and a system of courts. But basic power remained with the Emperor.

Bent on colonial empire, fascist Italy invaded Ethiopia on Oct. 3, 1935, forcing Haile Selassie into exile in May 1936. Ethiopia was annexed to Eritrea, then an Italian colony, and Italian Somaliland to form Italian East Africa, losing its independence for the first time in recorded history. In 1941, British troops routed the Italians, and Haile Selassie returned to Addis Ababa.

The Emperor's gradual reforms failed to make headway against key problems. Although 85% of Ethiopians were subsistence farmers, feudal laws vested ownership of 55% of its land in the crown, the church, and the nobility; there was strong pressure for land reform. There was also mounting insurgency in Eritrea, a culturally distinct province where Christians and Moslems have long vied for control, which the United Nations placed under Ethiopian rule in 1952. Violent agitation for Eritrean independence was begun in 1969 by the Moslem-led Eritrean Liberation Front, which used Arab-supplied arms to field a 4,000-man guerrilla force.

Deep discontent erupted in the fall of 1973. A long drought had caused famine that killed 100,000 peasants and drove thousands of others to cities, where food was scarce and inflation was rampant. Charges of mismanagement of drought relief sparked riots in Addis Ababa in 1974, and unpaid troops in Asmara, capital of Eritrea, mutinied to protest conditions. The Cabinet headed by Prime Minister Aklilou Habte-wold resigned.

The Emperor named Endalkachew Makonnen, a moderate, as Prime Minister and agreed to call a constitutional convention. But there was a general strike, students rioted, and mutiny spread to the air force. In mid-April, with disorders growing, army and police units arrested over 200 prominent persons. Late in June the army took virtual control of Addis Ababa and made more arrests.

Endalkachew was ousted on July 24, arrested, and later executed. Under his successor, Michael Imru, a draft Constitution proposing a constitutional monarchy was put forward, but power shifted relentlessly to a new Armed Forces Committee.

In August, the Armed Forces Committee nationalized Haile Selassie's palace and estates and directed him not to leave Addis Ababa. On Sept. 12, 1974, He was peacefully deposed after nearly 58 years as Regent and Emperor. The 82-year-old "Lion of Judah" was placed under guard. Parliament was dissolved and the Constitution suspended.

On December 20, the Armed Forces Committee announced that Ethiopia would become a socialist state directed by one political organization called the Supreme Progressive Council. All financial concerns were nationalized in 1975 and the regime proclaimed nationalization of all rural land, ending 2,000 years of feudal tenure.

On Aug. 27, 1975, Haile Selassie died in a small apartment in his former Addis Ababa palace where he had been treated as a state prisoner. He was 83.

After the coup, revolt in Eritrea escalated from guerrilla conflict to open war. The Eritrean Liberation Front, armed by Libya and other Arab states, demanded full independence. The regime tried and failed to negotiate with the Front and then began vigorous military action. Some 22,000 government troops were in combat in Eritrea by February 1975, and 6,000 deaths, mostly of civilians, were said to have resulted in March.

U.S. military aid, which had been going to Ethiopia since World War II, was suspended after the 1974 coup and only briefly resumed in 1976 as the military government turned increasingly toward the U.S.S.R. In retaliation for the Carter Administration's ruling out further aid to Ethiopia because of human rights violations, the regime in April and May of 1977 shut down the Kagnew communications center in Asmara and other U.S. military and diplomatic offices, ordering some 300 Americans to leave.

Lt. Col. Mengistu Haile Mariam was named head of state Feb. 2, 1977, to replace Brig. Gen. Teferi Benti, who was killed in a factional fight of the Dirgue after having ruled since 1974. The government was losing its fight to hold Eritrea and in the southeastern region of Ogaden, Somali guerrillas backed by Somali regular forces threatened the ancient city of Harar. In October, the U.S.S.R. announced it would end military aid to Somalia and henceforth back its new ally, Ethiopia. This, together with the intervention of Cuban troops in Ogaden, turned the tide for Mengistu. By March 1978, the badly beaten Somalis had retreated to their homeland.

In late July 1978, the Ethiopian government reported that it had gained its first victory over Eritrean rebels in three years in a campaign aimed at cutting them off from their supply lines to the Sudan. In both Eritrea and Ogaden, however, guerrilla resistance was still strong in 1980 and large areas were reported under only sporadic government control.

FIJI

Dominion of Fiji
Sovereign: Queen Elizabeth II
Governor General: Sir George Cakobau (1973)
Prime Minister: Sir Kamisese Mara (1970)
Area: 7,055 sq mi. (18,272 sq km)
Population (est. 1980): 620,000
Density per square mile: 87.9
Capital (1976 census): Suva (on Viti Levu), 63,600
Monetary unit: Fijian dollar
Languages: Fijian, Hindustani, English
Religions: Christian, Hindu, Islam
Member of Commonwealth of Nations
Freedom House classifications: Capitalist pre-industrial, multi-party centralized
Economic summary: Gross national product (1978): $860 million. Average annual growth rate (1970–77): 3.7%. Per capita income (1977): $1,100. Average rate of inflation (1975–77): 9.3%. Labor force in agriculture: 50%; principal products: sugar, copra, bananas, ginger. Major industrial products: refined sugar, gold, lumber. Natural resources: timber, fish, gold, copper. Exports: sugar, copra. Imports: foodstuffs, machinery, manufactured goods, fuels, chemicals. Major trading partners: Australia, Japan, U.K., New Zealand, U.S.

Geography. Fiji consists of more than 500 islands in the southwestern Pacific Ocean about 1,960 miles (3,152 km) from Sydney, Australia. The two largest islands are Viti Levu (4,109 sq mi.; 10,642 sq km) and Vanua Levu (2,242 sq mi.; 5,807 sq km). The island of Rotuma (18 sq mi.; 47 sq km), about 400 miles (644 km) to the north, is a dependency of Fiji. Overall, Fiji is nearly as large as New Jersey.

The largest islands in the group are mountainous and volcanic, with the tallest peak being Mount Victoria (4,341 ft; 1,323 m) on Viti Levu. The islands in the south have dense forests on the windward side and grasslands on the leeward.

Government. Executive authority is vested in the Cabinet and legislative authority in a bicameral 74-member Parliament. The major political parties are the Alliance Party, led by Prime Minister Sir Kamisese Mara; National Federation Party, led by Jai Ram Reddy, and Fijian Nationalist Party, led by Sakeasi Butadroka.

History. In 1874, an offer of cession by the Fijian chiefs was accepted, and Fiji was proclaimed a possession and dependency of the British Crown.

During World War II, the archipelago was an important air and naval station on the route from the U.S. and Hawaii to Australia and New Zealand.

Fiji became independent on Oct. 10, 1970. The next year it joined the five-island South Pacific Forum, which intends to become a permanent regional group to promote collective diplomacy of the newly independent members. The Forum also includes Western Samoa, Tonga, Nauru, and the self-governing segments of the Cook Islands.

FINLAND

Republic of Finland
President: Urho K. Kekkonen (1956)
Premier: Mauno Koivisto (1979)
Area: 130,119 sq mi. (337,009 sq km)
Population (est. 1980): 4,770,000 (Finnish, 93%; Swedish, 6%)
Density per square mile: 36.7
Capital: Helsinki
Largest cities (est. 1979): Helsinki, 483,600; Tampere, 166,000; Turku, 165,000
Monetary unit: Markka
Languages: Finnish, Swedish
Religions: Lutheran, 98%; Orthodox, 1.6%
National name: Suomen Tasavalta—Republiken Finland
Freedom House classifications: Capitalist-socialist industrial, multi-party centralized
Economic summary: Gross national product (1978): $32.4 billion. Average annual growth rate (1970–77): 2.8%. Per capita income (1979): $9,900. Per capita income: $6,110. Land used for agriculture: 8%; labor force: 10%; principal products: dairy products, cereals, sugar beets, potatoes. Labor force in industry: 39%; major products: metal manufactures, forestry and wood products, refined copper, ships. Natural resource: timber. Exports: timber, paper and pulp, ships, machinery, iron and steel, clothing, footwear. Imports: foodstuffs, petroleum and petroleum products, chemicals, transportation equipment, iron and steel, machinery textile yarns. Major trading partners: Western European countries, U.S.S.R., Sweden.

Geography. Finland stretches 700 miles (1,127 km) from the Gulf of Finland on the south to Soviet

Petsamo, north of the Arctic Circle. The U.S.S.R. extends along the entire eastern frontier. In area, Finland is three times the size of Ohio.

Off the southwest coast are the Aland Islands, controlling the entrance to the Gulf of Bothnia. Finland has more than 60,000 lakes. Of the few rivers, only the Oulu (Ulea) is navigable to any important extent.

The Swedish-populated Aland Islands (581 sq mi.; 1,505 sq km) have an autonomous status under a law passed in 1951.

Government. The president, chosen for six years by the popularly elected Electoral College of 300 members, appoints the Cabinet. The one-chamber Diet, the Eduskunta, consists of 200 members elected for four-year terms by proportional representation.

The major political parties are the Social Democratic Party (52 seats in the Eduskanta), led by former Premier Kalevi Sorsa; Conservative Party (46 seats); Center Party (37 seats); People's Democratic League (Communist) (35 seats); Swedish People's Party (10 seats); Christian League (9 seats); Rural Party (7 seats); Liberal Party (4 seats). Premier Mauno Koivisto leads a coalition of Social Democratic, Communist, Center, and Swedish People's Party members totaling 134 seats.

History. At the end of the 7th century, the Finns came to Finland from their Volga settlements, taking the country from the Lapps, who retreated northward. The Finns' repeated raids on the Scandinavian coast impelled Eric IX, the Swedish King, to conquer the country in 1157 and bring it into contact with Western Christendom. By 1809 the whole of Finland was conquered by Alexander I of Russia, who set up Finland as a Grand Duchy.

The first period of Russification (1899–1905) resulted in a lessening of the powers of the Finnish Diet. The Russian language was made official, and the Finnish military system was superseded by the Russian. The pace of Russification was intensified from 1908 to 1914. When Russian control was weakened as a consequence of the March Revolution of 1917, the Diet on July 20, 1917, proclaimed Finland's independence, which became complete on Dec. 6, 1917.

Finland rejected Soviet territorial demands, and the U.S.S.R. attacked on Nov. 30, 1939. The Finns made an amazing stand of three months and finally capitulated, ceding 16,000 square miles (41,440 sq km) to the U.S.S.R. Under German pressure, the Finns joined the Nazis against Russia in 1941, but were defeated again and ceded the Petsamo area to the U.S.S.R. In 1948, a 20-year treaty of friendship and mutual assistance was signed by the two nations and renewed for another 20 years in 1970.

In 1970 Finland entered into a trade agreement with the enlarged European Economic Community (Common Market), which includes Norway and Denmark, and also with Comecom, the Communist East European Economic Group.

The world oil crisis added a practical new reason for maintenance of an unimpaired relationship with Moscow, for Finland imports two thirds of its oil from the U.S.S.R. In 1974, the two nations signed a 10-year energy cooperation pact providing for delivery to Finland of two 440-megawatt nuclear power stations scheduled to go into operation in 1981–82.

Helsinki was the site in 1975 of a summit conference of 35 heads of government convened for the signing of a European security agreement. It was the most inclusive gathering of European leaders since the Congress of Vienna in 1815.

FRANCE

French Republic
President: Valéry Giscard d'Estaing (1974)
Premier: Raymond Barre (1976)
Area: 212,973 sq mi. (551,600 sq km)
Population (est. 1980): 53,680,000
Density per square mile: 252.1
Capital: Paris
Largest cities (est. 1978): Paris, 2,155,200; **(1975 census):** Marseilles, 914,356; Lyons, 462,841; Toulouse, 383,176; Nice, 346,620; Nantes, 263,689; Strasbourg, 257,300; Bordeaux, 226,281
Monetary unit: Franc
Religion (est.): Roman Catholic, 90%; Protestant, Jewish, Islam, and others, 10%
National name: République Française
Freedom House classifications: Capitalist industrial, multi-party centralized
Economic summary: Gross national product (1978): $440 billion. Average annual growth rate (1970–77): 3.1%. Per capita income (1978): $8,759. Rate of inflation (1979): 12.9%. Land used for agriculture: 60%; labor force: 10%; principal products: cereals, feed grains, livestock and dairy products, wine, fruits, vegetables. Labor force in industry: 37%; major products: chemicals, automobiles, processed foods, iron and steel, aircraft, textiles, clothing. Natural resources: coal, iron ore, bauxite, fish, forests. Exports: textiles and clothing, iron and steel products, machinery and transport equipment, agricultural products, wine. Imports: machinery, crude petroleum, iron and steel products, textile fibers, coal and coke, foodstuffs. Major trading partners: West Germany, Italy, U.S., Belgium-Luxembourg, U.K., Netherlands.

Geography. France (80% the size of Texas) is second in size to the U.S.S.R. among Europe's nations. In the Alps near the Italian and Swiss borders is Europe's highest point—Mont Blanc (15,781 ft; 4,810 m). The forest-covered Vosges Mountains are in the northeast, and the Pyrenees are along the Spanish border.

Except for extreme northern France, which is part of the Flanders plain, the country may be described as four river basins and a plateau. Three of the streams flow west—the Seine into the English Channel, the Loire into the Atlantic, and the Garonne into the Bay of Biscay. The Rhône flows south into the Mediterranean. For about 100 miles (161 km), the Rhine is France's eastern border.

West of the Rhône and northeast of the Garonne lies the central plateau, covering about 15% of France's area and rising to a maximum elevation of 6,188 feet (1,886 m). In the Mediterranean, about 115 miles (185 km) east-southeast of Nice, is Corsica (3,367 sq mi.; 8,721 sq km).

Government. The president is elected for seven years by universal suffrage. He appoints the premier, and the Cabinet is responsible to Parliament. The president has the right to dissolve the National Assembly or to ask Parliament for reconsideration of a law. The Parliament consists of two houses: the National Assembly and the Senate.

Rulers of France

Name	Born	Ruled[1]
CAROLINGIAN DYNASTY		
Pepin the Short	c. 714	751–768
Charlemagne[2]	742	768–814
Louis I the Debonair[3]	778	814–840
Charles I the Bald[4]	823	840–877
Louis II the Stammerer	846	877–879
Louis III[5]	c. 863	879–882
Carloman[5]	?	879–884
Charles II the Fat[6]	839	884–887[7]
Eudes (Odo), Count of Paris	?	888–898
Charles III the Simple[8]	879	893–923[9]
Robert I[10]	c. 865	922–923
Rudolf (Raoul), Duke of Burgundy	?	923–936
Louis IV d'Outremer	c. 921	936–954
Lothair	941	954–986
Louis V the Sluggard	c. 967	986–987
CAPETIAN DYNASTY		
Hugh Capet	c. 940	987–996
Robert II the Pious[11]	c. 970	996–1031
Henry I	1008	1031–1060
Philip I	1052	1060–1108
Louis VI the Fat	1081	1108–1137
Louis VII the Young	c.1121	1137–1180
Philip II (Philip Augustus)	1165	1180–1223
Louis VIII the Lion	1187	1223–1226
Louis IX (St. Louis)	1214	1226–1270
Philip III the Bold	1245	1270–1285
Philip IV the Fair	1268	1285–1314
Louis X the Quarreler	1289	1314–1316
John I[12]	1316	1316
Philip V the Tall	1294	1316–1322
Charles IV the Fair	1294	1322–1328
HOUSE OF VALOIS		
Philip VI	1293	1328–1350
John II the Good	1319	1350–1364
Charles V the Wise	1337	1364–1380
Charles VI the Well-Beloved	1368	1380–1422
Charles VII	1403	1422–1461
Louis XI	1423	1461–1483
Charles VIII	1470	1483–1498
Louis XII the Father of the People	1462	1498–1515
Francis I	1494	1515–1547
Henry II	1519	1547–1559
Francis II	1544	1559–1560
Charles IX	1550	1560–1574
Henry III	1551	1574–1589
HOUSE OF BOURBON		
Henry IV of Navarre	1553	1589–1610
Louis XIII	1601	1610–1643
Louis XIV the Great	1638	1643–1715
Louis XV the Well-Beloved	1710	1715–1774
Louis XVI	1754	1774–1792[13]
Louis XVII (Louis Charles de France)[14]	1785	1793–1795
FIRST REPUBLIC		
National Convention	—	1792–1795
Directory (Directoire)	—	1795–1799
CONSULATE		
Napoleon Bonaparte[15]	1769	1799–1804
FIRST EMPIRE		
Napoleon I	1769	1804–1815[16]
RESTORATION OF HOUSE OF BOURBON		
Louis XVIII le Désiré	1755	1814–1824
Charles X	1757	1824–1830[17]
BOURBON-ORLEANS LINE		
Louis Philippe ("Citizen King")	1773	1830–1848[18]
SECOND REPUBLIC		
Louis Napoleon[19]	1808	1848–1852
SECOND EMPIRE		
Napoleon III (Louis Napoleon)	1808	1852–1870[20]
THIRD REPUBLIC (PRESIDENTS)		
Louis Adolphe Thiers	1797	1871–1873
Marie E. P. M. de MacMahon	1808	1873–1879
François P. J. Grévy	1807	1879–1887
Sadi Carnot	1837	1887–1894
Jean Casimir-Périer	1847	1894–1895
François Félix Faure	1841	1895–1899
Émile Loubet	1838	1899–1906
Clement Armand Fallières	1841	1906–1913
Raymond Poincaré	1860	1913–1920
Paul E. L. Deschanel	1856	1920–1920
Alexandre Millerand	1859	1920–1924
Gaston Doumergue	1863	1924–1931
Paul Doumer	1857	1931–1932
Albert Lebrun	1871	1932–1940
VICHY GOVERNMENT (CHIEF OF STATE)		
Henri Philippe Pétain	1856	1940–1944
PROVISIONAL GOVERNMENT (PRESIDENTS)		
Charles de Gaulle	1890	1944–1946
Félix Gouin	1884	1946–1946
Georges Bidault	1899	1946–1947
FOURTH REPUBLIC (PRESIDENTS)		
Vincent Auriol	1884	1947–1954
René Coty	1882	1954–1959
FIFTH REPUBLIC (PRESIDENTS)		
Charles de Gaulle	1890	1959–1969
Georges Pompidou	1911	1969–1974
Valéry Giscard d'Estaing	1926	1974–

1. For Kings and Emperors through the Second Empire, year of end of rule is also that of death, unless otherwise indicated. 2. Crowned Emperor of the West in 800. His brother, Carloman, ruled as King of the Eastern Franks from 768 until his death in 771. 3. Holy Roman Emperor 814–840. 4. Holy Roman Emperor 875–877 as Charles II. 5. Ruled jointly 879–882. 6. Holy Roman Emperor 881–887 as Charles III. 7. Died 888. 8. King 893–898 in opposition to Eudes. 9. Died 929. 10. Not counted in regular line of Kings of France by some authorities. Elected by nobles but killed in Battle of Soissons. 11. Sometimes called Robert I. 12. Posthumous son of Louis X; lived for only five days. 13. Executed 1793. 14. Titular King only. He died in prison according to official reports, but many pretenders appeared during the Bourbon restoration. 15. As First Consul, Napoleon held the power of government. In 1804, he became Emperor. 16. Abdicated first time June 1814. Re-entered Paris March 1815,

after escape from Elba; Louis XVIII fled to Ghent. Abdicated second time June 1815. He named as his successor his son, Napoleon II, who was not acceptable to the Allies. He died 1821. 17. Died 1836. 18. Died 1850. 19. President; became Emperor in 1852. 20. Died 1873.

The major political parties are the Rally for the Republic (154 of 491 seats in the National Assembly), led by Claude Labbé; Union for French Democracy (121 seats), led by Roger Chinaud; Socialists (114 seats), led by Gaston Defferre; Communists (86 seats), led by Robert Ballanger.[1]

History. The history of France, as distinct from ancient Gaul, begins with the Treaty of Verdun (843), dividing the territories corresponding roughly to France, Germany, and Italy among the three grandsons of Charlemagne. Julius Caesar had conquered part of Gaul in 57–52 B.C., and it remained Roman until Franks invaded it in the 5th century.

Charles the Bald, inheritor of *Francia Occidentalis,* founded the Carolingian dynasty, which ruled over a kingdom increasingly feudalized. By 987, the crown passed to Hugh Capet, a princeling who controlled only the Île-de-France, the region surrounding Paris. For 350 years, an unbroken Capetian line added to its domain and consolidated royal authority until the accession in 1328 of Philip VI, first of the Valois line. France was then the most powerful nation in Europe, with a population of 15 million.

The missing pieces in Philip's domain were the French provinces still held by the Plantagenet kings of England, who also claimed the French crown. Beginning in 1338, the Hundred Years' War eventually settled the contest. English longbows defeated French armored knights at Crécy (1346) and the English also won the second landmark battle at Agincourt (1415), but the final victory went to the French peasant girl, Joan of Arc, at Orléans (1429).

Absolute monarchy reached its apogee in the reign of Louis XIV (1643–1715), the Sun King, whose brilliant court was the center of the Western world. Neither Louis XV, nor his grandson, Louis XVI, could sustain the role, however, and the Ancien Régime tottered under the weight of an outmoded society, crushing taxes, and the infiltration of egalitarian philosophy. The monarchy lost French Canada in the Battle of Quebec Sept. 13, 1759, and in its last gasp under Louis XVI aided the American British colonists to gain their freedom.

Revolution plunged France into a blood bath beginning in 1789 and ending with a new authoritarianism under Napoleon Bonaparte, who had successfully defended the infant republic from foreign attack and then made himself First Consul in 1799 and Emperor in 1804. Napoleon set patterns in government, education, and law visible today, and his conquests spread them throughout Europe.

The Congress of Vienna (1815) sought to restore the pre-Napoleonic order in the person of Louis XVIII, but industrialization and the middle class, both fostered under Napoleon, built pressure for change, and a revolution in 1848 drove Louis Philipe, last of the Bourbons, into exile.

A second republic elected as its president Prince Louis Napoleon, a nephew of Napoleon I, who declared the Second Empire in 1852 and took the throne as Napoleon III. His opposition to the rising power of Prussia ignited the Franco-Prussian War (1870–71), ending in his defeat and abdication.

A new France emerged from World War I as the continent's dominant power. But four years of hostile occupation had reduced northeast France to ruins. The postwar Third Republic was plagued by political instability and economic chaos.

From 1919, French foreign policy aimed at keeping Germany weak through a system of alliances, but it failed to halt the rise of Adolf Hitler and the Nazi war machine. On May 10, 1940, mechanized Nazi troops attacked, and, as they approached Paris, Italy joined with Germany. The Germans marched into an undefended Paris and Marshal Henri Philippe Pétain signed an armistice June 22. France was split into an occupied north and an unoccupied south, the latter becoming a totalitarian state with Pétain as its chief.

Allied armies liberated France in August 1944. The French Committee of National Liberation, formed in Algiers in 1943, established a provisional government in Paris headed by Gen. Charles de Gaulle. The Fourth Republic was born Dec. 24, 1946.

The Empire became the French Union; the National Assembly was strengthened and the presidency weakened; and France joined the North Atlantic Treaty Organization. A war against communist insurgents in Indochina was abandoned after the defeat at Dien Bien Phu. A new rebellion in Algeria (*see* Algeria) threatened a military coup, and on June 1, 1958, the Assembly invited de Gaulle to return as premier with extraordinary powers. He drafted a new Constitution for a Fifth Republic, adopted Sept. 28, which strengthened the presidency and reduced legislative power. He was elected president Dec. 21.

The new president negotiated the independence of Algeria on July 5, 1962, nearly all of the other French possessions in Africa having already received their freedom. De Gaulle cultivated the former colonies along with other new nations of what he called the Third World—nations aligned with neither the West nor the Soviet bloc—as a base for French leadership. In 1960, de Gaulle exploded an atomic bomb; in 1963 he negotiated a Franco-German friendship treaty; and the following year he recognized Peking, at the same time improving relations with the U.S.S.R.

De Gaulle took France out of NATO in 1967, expelling all foreign-controlled troops from the country, and in a visit to Canada aroused a storm by speaking out for a "free Quebec." Although he had been re-elected to a seven-year term in 1965, the end of his reign was foreshadowed in 1968 by a rebellion of students. The disorders spread to the workers, who seized plants across the country, resulting in a general strike supported by half the labor force. Obtaining assurances of support from his army commanders, de Gaulle offered, then canceled a referendum and held elections on the promise of reforms, which gave his supporters an overwhelming victory.

In autumn 1968, de Gaulle reformed the universities to give students and faculty a voice in choosing presidents and in controlling most major policy areas. De Gaulle went on to attempt to achieve a long—cherished plan of regional reform. This, however, aroused wide opposition. He decided to stake his fate on a referendum. At the voting in

1. Figures include both members enrolled and members affiliated with party. In addition, there are 16 unaffiliated members in the National Assembly.

April 1969, the electorate defeated the plan. His successor, Georges Pompidou, de Gaulle's premier for six years, reversed the de Gaulle policy of opposing the unification of Europe, which had led de Gaulle to oppose the entrance of the U.K. into the Common Market in 1963.

Pompidou continued the de Gaulle policies of seeking to expand France's influence in the Mideast and Africa, selling arms to South Africa (despite the U.N. embargo), to Libya, and to Greece. He also continued de Gaulle's efforts to improve relations between France and individual members of the Communist bloc, notably the U.S.S.R. and China, and in 1971 he endorsed British entry into the Common Market.

Pompidou died of cancer in April 1974 and was succeeded by Valéry Giscard d'Estaing, the first non-Gaullist president in 15 years. He narrowly defeated the Socialist leader, François Mitterrand, who had Communist backing, by less than 1% of 26 million votes cast.

Giscard was no Gaullist, but depended on Gaullist votes for parliamentary support. He adhered to basic foreign policies set by de Gaulle and Pompidou, but was more cordial and flexible in relations with the U.S. He maintained French aloofness from military participation in NATO, asserting that he did not wish to encourage Soviet fears of military pressure from the West. He cultivated good relations with China. Domestically, he successfully suppported liberalized abortion and divorce laws and lowering of the voting age to 18.

Under Giscard's leadership, the French National Planning Council adopted in 1975 a 10-year program to reduce dependence on foreign fuel to below 60%, from the 76% prevailing in 1973.

Giscard's uneasy alliance with the Gaullists ended Aug. 25, 1976, with the resignation of his premier, Jacques Chirac, who protested that he needed greater powers to tackle rising political and economic problems. The president, saying he could brook no challenge to his own authority, appointed as Chirac's successor a technician without party affiliation, Raymond Barre.

France continued its independent nuclear arms program and emerged as a supplier of nuclear technology to other nations with the sale of five 1,000-megawatt reactors to Iran in 1974 and a $1-billion power plant to South Africa in 1976.

With the establishment of the Republic of Djibouti on June 27, 1977, France released its last possession in mainland Africa. Giscard had made it clear earlier, however, that France would continue to play an active role in Africa when he supplied the airlift for Moroccan troops to help President Mobutu Sese Seko of Zaire fight a rebellion in Shaba Province. The action was hailed by most of the former French African colonies and conservative nations throughout the continent.

France responded even more boldly to a second Shaba invasion in May 1978, moving 1,000 troops to the scene with U.S. aid and repelling the Katangese, again to the applause of most of Africa but to the displeasure of leftists. France was attaining the reputation of a world policeman, with a contingent in the U.N. peacekeeping force in southern Lebanon and a total of 12,000 troops stationed in Djibouti, Chad, and Mauritania—in the last two nations aiding the governments in suppression of guerrilla opposition.

At home, Giscard won a surprise victory in general elections March 19 when pro-government forces won 291 seats and a narrow margin of the popular vote to retain control of the 491-seat National Assembly.

Labor protests against a government program to cut jobs in the steel industry and to reduce subsidies to other industries brought a wave of strikes in 1979. Communist and Socialist motions of no confidence at an emergency session of Parliament in March failed, and the worst rioting in Paris since the student rebellion of 1968 broke out on March 23.

Giscard, the strongest European critic of U.S. energy policies, renewed his attack before the Tokyo summit of industrial nations in June, saying U.S. failure to conserve oil threatened the "cohesion of the West." The French President continued his criticism at the Venice economic summit in July 1980 and further annoyed the Carter administration by meeting Soviet President Leonid I. Brezhnev earlier without having consulted Washington beforehand.

Overseas Departments and Territories of France

FRENCH GUIANA (including ININI)

Status: Overseas Department
Prefect: Désiré Carli (1980)
Area: 35,135 sq mi. (91,000 sq km)
Population (est. 1980): 65,000
Capital (est. 1980): Cayenne, 35,000
Monetary unit: Franc
Language: French
Religion: Roman Catholic
Economic summary: Gross national product (1975): $100 million. Per capita income: $800. Labor force in agriculture: 21%; principal agricultural products: rice, corn, manioc, cocoa, bananas, sugar cane. Labor force in industry: 67%; major industrial products: timber, rum, rosewood essence, gold mining. Natural resources: bauxite, timber, cinnabar, low-grade iron ore. Exports: shrimp, timber, rum, rosewood essence. Imports: food, consumer and producer goods, petroleum. Major trading partners: U.S., France, Martinique.

French Guiana, lying north of Brazil and east of Surinam on the northeast coast of South America, was first settled in 1626. Penal settlements, embracing the area around the mouth of the Maroni River and the Iles du Salut (including Devil's Island), were founded in 1852; they have since been abolished.

During World War II, French Guiana at first adhered to the Vichy government, but the Free French took over in 1943. French Guiana accepted in 1958 the new Constitution of the French Fifth Republic and remained an Overseas Department of the French Republic.

FRENCH POLYNESIA

Status: Overseas Territory
High Commissioner: Paul Cousseran (1977)
Area: 1,544 sq mi. (4,000 sq km)
Population (est. 1980): 140,000
Monetary unit: Colonial franc Pacifique
Religions: Protestant, 55%; Roman Catholic, 32%.
Capital (1977 census): Papeete (on Tahiti), 62,700
Economic summary: Gross domestic product (1970): $259 million. Per capita income: $1,960. Principal agricultural product: coconuts. Major industries: tourism, maintenance of French nuclear test base. Exports: coconut products, mother of pearl. Major trading partners: France, U.S.

The term French Polynesia is applied to the scattered French possessions in the eastern Pacific—Mangareva (Gambier), Makatea, the Marquesas Islands, Rapa, Rurutu, Rimatara, the Society Islands, the Tuamotu Archipelago, Tubuai, Raivavae, and the island of Clipperton—which were organized into a single colony in 1903. There are 120 islands, of which 25 are uninhabited.

The High Commissioner is assisted by a Privy Council and a popularly elected Representative Assembly. The principal and most populous island —Tahiti, in the Society group—was claimed as French in 1768. In 1958, French Polynesia voted in favor of the new Constitution of the French Fifth Republic and remained an Overseas Territory of the French Republic. The natives are mostly Polynesians.

The Pacific Nuclear Test Center on the atoll of Mururoa, 744 miles (1,200 km) from Tahiti, was completed in 1966.

GUADELOUPE

Status: Overseas Department
Prefect: Guy Maillard (1978)
Area: 687 sq mi. (1,779 sq km)
Population (est. 1980): 325,000
Capital (est. 1977): Basse-Terre, 15,800
Largest city (est. 1978): Pointe-à-Pitre, 25,000
Monetary unit: Franc
Languages: French, Creole patois
Religions: Roman Catholic
Economic summary: Gross national product (1978): $910 million. Average annual growth rate (1970–77): 2.9%. Per capita income: $828. Land used for agriculture: 33%; labor force: 25%; principal agricultural products: sugar cane, bananas, rum, pineapples. Major industries: construction, public works. Exports: sugar, bananas, rum. Imports: foodstuffs, clothing, consumer goods, petroleum. Major trading partners: France, West Germany.

Guadeloupe, in the West Indies about 300 miles (483 km) southeast of Puerto Rico, was discovered by Columbus in 1493. It consists of the twin islands of Basse-Terre and Grande-Terre and five dependencies—Marie-Galante, Les Saintes, La Désirade, St. Barthélemy, and the northern half of St. Martin. The volcano Soufrière (4,813 ft; 1,467 m), also called La Grande Soufrière, is the highest point on Guadeloupe. Violent activity in 1976 and 1977 caused thousands to flee their homes.

French colonization began in 1635. In 1958, Guadeloupe voted in favor of the new Constitution of the French Fifth Republic and remained an Overseas Department of the French Republic.

MARTINIQUE

Status: Overseas Department
Prefect: Marcel Julia (1979)
Area: 431 sq mi. (1,116 sq km)
Population (est. 1980): 330,000
Capital (1974 census): Fort-de-France 98,800
Monetary unit: Franc
Languages: French, Creole patois
Religion: Roman Catholic
Economic summary: Gross national product (1978): $1.3 billion. Average annual growth rate (1970–77): 5.7%. Per capita income (1975): $1,366. Land used for agriculture: 47%; labor force: 23%; principal agricultural products: sugar cane, bananas, rum, pineapples. Labor force in industry: 20%; major industries: construction, public works. Natural resource: fish. Exports: iron ore, fish, copper. Imports: foodstuffs, capital goods. Major trading partners: France, Italy, U.S.

Martinique, lying in the Lesser Antilles about 300 miles (483 km) northeast of Venezuela, was probably discovered by Columbus in 1502 and was taken for France in 1635. Following the Franco-German armistice of 1940, it had a semiautonomous status until 1943, when authority was relinquished to the Free French. The area, administered by a Prefect assisted by an elected council, is represented in the French Parliament. In 1958, Martinique voted in favor of the new Constitution of the French Fifth Republic and remained an Overseas Department of the French Republic.

MAYOTTE

Status: Territorial collectivity
Representative of French Government: Philippe Kessler (1980)
Area: 146 sq mi. (378 sq km)
Population (est. 1980): 48,600
Capital: Dzaoudzi (about 3,200)
Principal products: vanilla, essential oils, copra

The most populous of the Comoro Islands in the Indian Ocean, with a Christian majority, Mayotte voted in 1974 and 1976 against joining the other, predominantly Moslem islands, in declaring themselves independent. It continues to retain its ties to France.

NEW CALEDONIA AND DEPENDENCIES

Status: Overseas Territory
High Commissioner: Claude Charbonniaud
Area: 8,548 sq mi. (22,139 sq km)[1]
Population (est. 1980): 140,000
Capital (1976 census): Nouméa, 56,100
Monetary unit: Colonial franc Pacifique
Language: Melanesian and Polynesian dialects
Religion: Christian
Economic summary: Gross national product (1978): $700 million. Average annual growth rate (1970–77): –5.9%. Per capita income (1971): $1,800. Principal agricultural products: coffee, vegetables, beef. Major industrial product: nickel. Natural resources: nickel, chromite, iron ore. Export: nickel. Imports: machinery, transport equipment, foodstuffs. Major trading partners: France, Japan, U.S., Australia.

New Caledonia (6,466 sq mi.; 16,747 sq km), about 1,070 miles (1,722 km) northeast of Sydney, Austrialia, was discovered by Capt. James Cook in 1774 and annexed by France in 1853. The government also administers the Isle of Pines, the Loyalty Islands (Uvéa, Lifu, and Maré), the Belep Islands, the Huon Island group, and the Chesterfield Islands.

New Caledonia chose in 1958 to remain an Overseas Territory of the French Republic. The natives are Melanesians; about one third of the population is white and one fifth Indochinese and Javanese.

1. Including dependencies.

REUNION (BOURBON)

Status: Overseas Department
Prefect: Bernard Landouzy

Area: 970 sq mi. (2,510 sq km)
Population (est. 1980): 500,000
Capital (est. 1980): Saint Denis, 105,000
Monetary unit: Franc
Languages: French, Creole
Religion: Roman Catholic
Economic summary: Gross national product (1978): $1.6 billion. Average annual growth rate (1970–77): –1.0%. Principal agricultural products: sugar cane, vanilla, bananas, perfume plants. Major industrial products: rum, cigarettes, processed sugar. Exports: sugar, perfume essences, rum, molasses. Imports: manufactured goods, foodstuffs, beverages, machinery and transportation equipment, petroleum products. Major trading partners: France, Mauritius.

Discovered by Portuguese navigators in the 16th century, the island of Réunion, then uninhabited, was taken as a French possession in 1643. It is located about 450 miles (724 km) east of Madagascar, in the Indian Ocean. In 1958, Réunion approved the Constitution of the Fifth French Republic and remained an Overseas Department of the French Republic.

ST. PIERRE AND MIQUELON

Status: Overseas Department
Prefect: Clément Bouhin (1979)
Area: 93 sq mi. (242 sq km)
Population (est. 1980): 6,300
Capital (est. 1980): 5,800
Economic summary: Major industries: fishing, canneries. Exports: petroleum products, cattle, fish. Major trading partners: Canada, France, U.S.

The sole remnant of the French colonial empire in North America, these islands were first occupied by the French in 1604. Their only importance arises from proximity to the Grand Banks, located 10 miles south of Newfoundland, making them the center of the French Atlantic cod fisheries. On July 19, 1976, the islands became an Overseas Department of the French Republic.

SOUTHERN AND ANTARCTIC LANDS

Status: Overseas Territory
Administrator: Francis Jacquemont
Area: 169,614 sq mi. (439,300 sq km)
Capital: Port-au-Français

This territory is uninhabited except for the personnel of scientific bases. It consists of Adélie Land (166,752 sq mi.; 431,888 sq km) on the Antarctic mainland and the following islands in the southern Indian Ocean: the Kerguelen and Crozet archipelagos and the islands of Saint-Paul and New Amsterdam.

WALLIS AND FUTUNA ISLANDS

Status: Overseas Territory
Administrator Superior: Pierre Isaac (1979)
Area: 77 sq mi. (200 sq km)
Population (est. 1980): 9,200
Capital (1980): Mata-Utu (on Uvea), 600

The two islands groups in the South Pacific between Fiji and Samoa were settled by French missionaries at the beginning of the 19th century. A protectorate was established in the 1880s. Following a referendum by the Polynesian inhabitants, the status was changed to that of an Overseas Territory in 1961.

GABON

Gabonese Republic
President: Omar Bongo (1967)
Premier: Léon Mébiame (1975)
Area: 102,317 sq mi. (265,001 sq km)
Population (est. 1980): 550,000
Density per square mile: 5.4
Capital and largest city (est. 1978): Libreville, 225,200
Monetary unit: Franc CFA
Ethnic groups: Bateke, Obamba, Bakota, Shake, Pongwés, Adumas, Chiras, Punu, and Lumbu
Languages: French (official) and Bantu dialects
Religions: Animist, Christian, Islam
National name: République Gabonaise
Member of French Community
Freedom House classifications: Capitalist pre-industrial, one-party nationalist
Economic summary: Gross national product (1978): $1.9 billion. Average annual growth rate (1970–77): 6.5%. Per capita income: $250. Labor force in agriculture: 70%; principal products: cocoa, coffee, wood, palm, rice, bananas, peanuts. Labor force in industry: 30%; major products: petroleum, natural gas, processed wood, manganese, uranium, gold, iron. Natural resources: wood, petroleum, iron ore, manganese, uranium. Exports: crude petroleum, wood and wood products, minerals, coffee. Imports: mining and road-building machinery, electrical equipment, foodstuffs, textiles, transport vehicles. Major trading partners: France, U.S., West Germany.

Geography. This West African land with the Atlantic as its western border is also bounded by Equatorial Guinea, Cameroon, and the Congo. Its area is slightly less than Kentucky's.

From mangrove swamps on the coast, the land becomes divided plateaus in the north and east and mountains in the north. Most of the country is covered by a dense tropical forest.

Government. The president is elected for a seven-year term. Legislative powers are exercised by a National Assembly, which is elected for a seven-year term. After his conversion to Islam in 1973, President Bongo changed his given name, Albert Bernard, to Omar. The Parti Démocratique Gabonais (all National Assembly seats) is led by President Bongo. He was re-elected without opposition in 1973.

History. Little is known of Gabon's history, even in oral tradition, but Pygmies are believed to be the original inhabitants. Now there are many tribal groups in the country, the largest being the Fang people who constitute a third of the population.

Gabon was first visited by the Portuguese navigator Diego Cam in the 15th century. In 1839, the French founded their first settlement on the left bank of the Gabon Estuary and gradually occupied the hinterland during the second half of the 19th century. It was organized as a French territory in 1888 and became an autonomous republic within the French Union after World War II and an independent republic on Aug. 17, 1960.

Immense resources in oil, uranium, manganese,

and iron help give Gabon's inhabitants a per capita annual income of $225 to $250, the highest in black Africa. To speed exploitation of a billion-ton iron ore reserve in the Belinga-Mekambo region, the government began work in 1969 on a 350-mile railroad leading from the coast into the area. The project was initiated by President León Mba, who died in 1967, and has been continued by his handpicked successor, Omar Bongo.

In 1974, Bongo negotiated 60% control of an iron-ore venture half-owned by the Bethlehem Steel Corp. In October of that year, he visited Peking and concluded an economic and technical agreement with China.

GAMBIA

Republic of the Gambia
President: Sir Dawda K. Jawara (1970)
Area: 4,016 sq mi. (10,403 sq km)
Population (est. 1980): 595,000
Density per square mile: 148.2
Capital and largest city (est. 1978 by U.N.): Banjul, 45,600
Monetary unit: Dalasi
Languages: Native tongues, English (official)
Religions: Islam, Christian, Animist
Member of Commonwealth of Nations
Freedom House classifications: Capitalist pre-industrial, multi-party centralized
Economic summary: Gross national product (1978): $130 million. Average annual growth rate (1970–77): 5.3%. Per capita income: $210. Land used for agriculture: 55%; labor force: 85%; principal products: peanuts, rice, palm kernels. Major industrial products: processed peanuts. Natural resources: fish. Exports: peanuts and peanut products. Imports: textiles, foodstuffs, tobacco, machinery, petroleum products. Major trading partners: U.K., France, Japan.

Geography. Situated on the Atlantic coast in westernmost Africa and surrounded on three sides by Senegal, Gambia is twice the size of Delaware. The Gambia River flows for 200 miles (322 km) through Gambia on its way to the Atlantic. The country, the smallest on the continent, averages only 20 miles (32 km) in width.

Government. The president's five-year term is linked to the 35-member unicameral House of Representatives, from which he appoints his Cabinet members and the vice president.

The major political party is the People's Progressive Party (29 seats in House of Representatives), led by President Jawara.

History. During the 17th century, Gambia was settled by various companies of English merchants. Slavery was the chief source of revenue until it was abolished in 1807. Gambia became a crown colony in 1843 and an independent nation within the Commonwealth of Nations on Feb. 18, 1965.

A proposal to convert from a monarchy to a republic was approved in a 1970 referendum, and on April 24 of that year Gambia proclaimed itself a republic.

Tourism increased after 1977 because of Alex Haley's book *Roots*. In it, he traced his family's origins back to the Mandinka tribe in Juffure, a Gambian village.

GERMANY, EAST

German Democratic Republic
Chairman of Council of State: Erich Honecker (1976)
Chairman of Council of Ministers: Willi Stoph (1976)
Area: 40,646 sq mi. (195,273 sq km)[1]
Population (est. 1980): 16,720,000
Density per square mile: 41.1
Capital: Berlin (eastern sector)
Largest cities (est. 1979): East Berlin, 1,129,000; (est. 1978 by U.N.): Leipzig, 565,200; Dresden, 511,200; Karl-Marx Stadt, 309,450; Magdeburg, 280,550; Halle, 233,000; Rostock, 219,000; Erfurt, 206,300
Monetary unit: Mark of the Deutsche Demokratische Republik
Language: German
Religions: Protestant, 53%; Roman Catholic, 8%
National name: Deutsche Demokratische Republik
Freedom House classifications: Socialist industrial, one-party communist
Economic summary: Gross national product (1978): $95.5 billion. Average annual growth rate (1970–77): 4.9%. Per capita income: $4,120. Land used for agriculture: 43%; labor force: 9%; principal products: grains, potatoes, sugar beets, meat and dairy products. Labor force in industry: 46%; major products: steel, chemicals, machinery, electrical and precision engineering products, fishing vessels. Natural resources: brown coal, potash, uranium. Exports: machinery and equipment, chemical products, textiles, clothing. Imports: raw materials, fuels, agricultural products, machinery and equipment. Major trading partners: U.S.S.R., Soviet bloc, West Germany.

Geography. East Germany lies on the Baltic Sea with Poland to the east and Czechoslovakia to the south. The border with West Germany is roughly a line running south from Lübeck for about 250 miles. The main river is the Elbe, which flows from Dresden in the southeast to the North Sea in the northwest. The Oder and Neisse Rivers form the border with Poland. Most of the country, which is the size of Tennessee, is situated in the north German plain.

Government. The People's Chamber, composed of 500 deputies elected for five-year terms, chooses the chairman and Council of State and the chairman and Council of Ministers, which carries on executive functions.

The major political party is the Socialist Unity (Communist) Party, led by Secretary General Erich Honecker. Others are Christian Democratic Union, Liberal Democratic Party, Democratic Farmers' Party, National Democratic Party.

History. (For history before 1945, *see* Germany, West.) The area now occupied by East Germany, as well as adjacent areas in Eastern Europe, consists of Mecklenburg, Brandenburg, Lusatia, Saxony, and Thuringia. Soviet armies conquered the five territories by 1945. In the division of 1945 they were allotted to the U.S.S.R. Soviet forces created a State controlled by the secret police with a single party, the Socialist Unity (Communist) Party. The

1. Including East Berlin (156 square miles), which has been incorporated into the German Democratic Republic.

Russians appropriated East German plants to restore their war-ravaged industry.

When the Federal Republic of Germany was established in West Germany, the East German states adopted a more centralized constitution for the Democratic Republic of Germany, and it was put into effect on Oct. 7, 1949. The U.S.S.R. thereupon dissolved its occupation zone, but Soviet troops remained. The Western Allies declared that the East German Republic was a Soviet creation undertaken without self-determination and refused to recognize it. It was recognized only within the Soviet bloc.

In 1953, the U.S.S.R. transferred control of East Germany from the military commander to a civilian commissioner and announced a more liberal policy. Continued austerity and political repression led to workers' riots in East Berlin and other cities, allegedly instigated by the Soviet secret police as part of a power struggle within the Kremlin. Soviet troops ruthlessly reestablished order. But the Soviet authorities made efforts to revive the East German economy.

In 1955, Walter Ulbricht, hard-line dictator, won Soviet recognition of the East German republic and joined the Warsaw Treaty Organization, organizing troops under the guise of police forces. In the middle and late 1960s, East Germany also came to enjoy economic prosperity. Trade, formerly limited largely to the Soviet bloc, expanded to West Germany and developing nations. But trade agreements obliging the East Germans to sell to Russia at low fixed prices and to buy from the U.S.S.R. at prices higher than the world market held per capita income well below that of West Germany.

East German troops took part in the Soviet-bloc occupation of Czechoslovakia in August 1968, but reportedly were withdrawn after the U.S.S.R. questioned whether the 1945 Potsdam agreements permitted German troops on foreign soil.

A constitution adopted in April 1968 reaffirmed one-party rule and narrowed civil rights. Ulbricht continued pressure on West Berlin, opposed liberalization in Czechoslovakia and other parts of the Soviet bloc, impeded Bonn's establishment of ties with East Europe, and pressured Bonn to acknowledge the existence of the two German states.

Talks between the two German states on normalization began in 1970, with the East seeking recognition of its existence and the West wanting easing of pressure on Berlin. West Germany's nonaggression treaty with the U.S.S.R. was cooly received by Ulbricht. In 1971 he resigned and rapprochement between the two Germanys accelerated with agreement on a variety of issues (for details, *see* Germany, West). By 1973, normal relations were established, and the two states entered the United Nations.

A new Constitution unanimously approved by the East German parliament on Sept. 27, 1974, pointedly deleted any reference to eventual reunification of the two Germanys, a principle maintained in the West German constitution.

The 25-year diplomatic hiatus between East Germany and the U.S. ended Sept. 4, 1974, with the establishment of formal relations.

The East German government has repeatedly challenged the Western powers' right of access to Berlin, most recently at the time of President Carter's July 15, 1978, visit to West Berlin. Autobahn traffic between the city and West Germany was deliberately slowed and, as in a similar 1977 case, the U.S., U.K., and France protested to the U.S.S.R. and the East Germans that such action was illegal under the 1971 Four Power Agreement.

Increased Soviet action in Africa in 1978 revealed that East Germany as well as Cuba was actively engaged as a Soviet agent. The East German "Afrika Korps" was reported to number about 4,500 soldiers, with an equal number of civilian technicians. Defense Minister Heinz Hoffmann visited Angola just before the invasion of Zaire's Shaba Province was launched in May. In Angola, 1,000 East German troops were reported serving with the army, and a small number of pilots were flying combat strikes against anti-government guerrillas.

GERMANY, WEST

Federal Republic of Germany
President: Karl Carstens (1979)
Chancellor: Helmut Schmidt (1974)
Area: 95,815 sq mi. (248,161 sq km)[1]
Population (est. 1980): 61,350,000
Density per square mile: 640.3
Capital (est. 1977): Bonn, 285,000
Largest cities (est. 1978): Hamburg, 1,672,200; Munich, 1,293,900; Cologne, 976,400; Essen, 661,500; Frankfurt, 633,400; Dortmund, 614,900; Düsseldorf, 604,100; Stuttgart, 584,100; Bremen, 560,900; Hannover, 540,300
Monetary unit: Deutsche Mark
Language: German
Religions: Protestant, 49%; Roman Catholic, 45%
National name: Bundesrepublik Deutschland
Freedom House classifications: Capitalist industrial, multi-party decentralized
Economic summary: Gross national product (1978): $588 billion. Average annual growth rate (1970–77): 2.2%. Per capita income (1977): $8,400. Labor force in agriculture: 7%; principal products: grains, potatoes, sugar beets. Labor force in industry: 43%; major products: iron, steel, coal, cement, chemicals, machinery, ships, vehicles. Natural resources: timber, coal, potash. Exports: machines and machine tools, chemicals, motor vehicles, iron and steel products. Imports: manufactured and agricultural products, raw materials, fuels. Major trading partners: France, Netherlands, Belgium-Luxembourg, Italy, U.S., U.K.

Geography. The Federal Republic of Germany occupies the western half of the central European area historically regarded as German. This was the part of Germany occupied by the United States, Britain, and France after the German defeat in World War II, when the eastern half of prewar Germany was split roughly between a Soviet-occupied zone, which became the present German Democratic Republic, and an area annexed by Poland.

West Germany's neighbors are France, Belgium, Luxembourg, and the Netherlands on the west, Switzerland and Austria on the south, Czechoslovakia and East Germany on the east, and Denmark on the north.

The northern plain, the central hill country, and the southern mountain district constitute the main physical divisions of West Germany, which is

1. Excluding West Berlin (184 square miles with 1979 population of 1,129,000).

slightly smaller than Oregon. The Bavarian plateau in the southwest averages 1,600 feet (488 m) above sea level, but it reaches 9,721 feet (2,963 m) in the Zugspitze Mountains, the highest point in the country.

Important navigable rivers are the Danube, rising in the Black Forest and flowing east across Bavaria into Austria, and the Rhine, which rises in Switzerland and flows across the Netherlands in two channels to the North Sea and is navigable by smaller vessels as far as Cologne. The Rhine and the Elbe, which also empties into the North Sea, are navigable within Germany for ships of 400 tons. The Weser, flowing into the North Sea, and the Main and Mosel (Moselle), both tributaries of the Rhine, are also important.

Government. Under the Constitution of May 23, 1949, the Federal Republic was established as a parliamentary democracy. The Parliament consists of the Bundesrat, an upper chamber representing and appointed by the 10 Länder, or states (plus West Berlin), and the Bundestag, a lower house elected for four years by universal suffrage. Each house has non-voting representatives from West Berlin. The entire legislature elects the President of the Republic for a five-year term; the Bundestag alone chooses the Chancellor, or Prime Minister. Each of the Länder and West Berlin have an assembly popularly elected for a four-year or five-year term.

The major political parties are the Social Democratic Party (214 of 496 seats in the Bundestag), led by former Chancellor Willy Brandt; Christian Democratic Union-Christian Social Union (243 seats), led by Helmut Kohl; and the Free Democratic Party (39 seats), led by Hans-Dietrich Genscher. Chancellor Helmut Schmidt's government is a coalition with the Free Democrats.

History. Immediately before the Christian era, when the Roman Empire had pushed its frontier to the Rhine, what is now Germany was inhabited by several tribes believed to have migrated from Central Asia between the 6th and 4th centuries B.C. One of these tribes, the Franks, attained supremacy in western Europe under Charlemagne, who was crowned Holy Roman Emperor A.D. 800. By the Treaty of Verdun (843), Charlemagne's lands east of the Rhine were ceded to the German Prince Louis. Additional territory acquired by the Treaty of Mersen (870) gave Germany approximately the area it maintained throughout the Middle Ages. For several centuries after Otto the Great was crowned King in 936, the German rulers were also usually heads of the Holy Roman Empire.

Relations between state and church were changed by the Reformation, which began with Martin Luther's 95 theses, and came to a head in 1547, when Charles V scattered the forces of the Protestant League at Mühlberg. Freedom of worship was guaranteed by the Peace of Augsburg (1555), but a Counter Reformation took place later, and a dispute over the succession to the Bohemian throne brought on the Thirty Years' War (1618–48), which devastated Germany and left the empire divided into hundreds of small principalities virtually independent of the Emperor.

Meanwhile, Prussia was developing into a state of considerable strength. Frederick the Great (1740–86) reorganized the Prussian army and defeated Maria Theresa of Austria in a struggle over Silesia. The conflict with revolutionary France hastened the disintegration of the empire. After the defeat of Napoleon at Waterloo (1815), the struggle between Austria and Prussia for supremacy in Germany continued, reaching its climax in the defeat of Austria in the Seven Weeks' War (1866) and the formation of the Prussian-dominated North German Confederation (1867).

The architect of German unity was Otto von Bismarck, a conservative, monarchist, and militaristic Prussian Junker who had no use for "empty phrase-making and constitutions." From 1862 until his retirement in 1890 he dominated not only the German but also the entire European scene. He unified all Germany in a series of three wars against Denmark (1864), Austria (1866), and France (1870–71), which many historians believe were instigated and promoted by Bismarck in his zeal to build a nation through "blood and iron."

On Jan. 18, 1871, King Wilhelm I of Prussia was proclaimed German Emperor in the Hall of Mirrors at Versailles. The North German Confederation, created in 1867, was abolished, and the Second German Reich, consisting of the North and South German states, was born. With a powerful army, an efficient bureaucracy, and a loyal bourgeoisie, Chancellor Bismarck consolidated a powerful centralized state.

Wilhelm II dismissed Bismarck in 1890 and embarked upon a "New Course," stressing an intensified colonialism and a powerful navy. His chaotic foreign policy culminated in the diplomatic isolation of Germany and the disastrous defeat in World War I (1914–18).

The Second German Empire collapsed following the defeat of the German armies in 1918, the naval mutiny at Kiel, and the flight of the Kaiser to the Netherlands on November 10. The Social Democrats, led by Friedrich Ebert and Philipp Scheidemann, crushed the Communists and established a moderate republic with Ebert as President.

The Weimar Constitution of 1919 provided for a President to be elected for seven years by universal suffrage and a bicameral legislature, consisting of the Reichsrat, representing the states, and the Reichstag, representing the people. It contained a model Bill of Rights. It was weakened, however, by a provision that enables the President to rule by decree.

President Ebert died Feb. 28, 1925, and on April 26, Field Marshal Paul von Hindenburg was elected president.

The mass of Germans regarded the Weimar Republic as a child of defeat, imposed upon a Germany whose legitimate aspirations to world leadership had been thwarted by a world conspiracy. Added to this were a crippling currency debacle, a tremendous burden of reparations, and acute economic distress.

Adolf Hitler, an Austrian war veteran and a fanatical nationalist, fanned discontent by promising a Greater Germany, abrogation of the Treaty of Versailles, restoration of Germany's lost colonies, and destruction of the Jews. When the Social Democrats and the Communists refused to combine against the Nazi threat, President Hindenburg made Hitler chancellor on Jan. 30, 1933.

With the death of Hindenburg on Aug. 2, 1934, Hitler repudiated the Treaty of Versailles and began full-scale rearmament. In 1935 he withdrew Germany from the League of Nations, and the next year he reoccupied the Rhineland and signed the anti-Comintern pact with Japan, at the same time strengthening relations with Italy. Austria was an-

Rulers of Germany and Prussia

Name	Born	Ruled[1]
KINGS OF PRUSSIA		
Frederick I[2]	1657	1701–1713
Frederick William I	1688	1713–1740
Frederick II the Great	1712	1740–1786
Frederick William II	1744	1786–1797
Frederick William III	1770	1797–1840
Frederick William IV	1795	1840–1861
William I	1797	1861–1871[3]
EMPERORS OF GERMANY		
William I	1797	1871–1888
Frederick III	1831	1888–1888
William II	1859	1888–1918[4]
HEADS OF THE REICH		
Friedrich Ebert[5]	1871	1919–1925
Paul von Hindenburg[5]	1847	1925–1934
Adolf Hitler[6 7]	1889	1934–1945
Karl Doenitz[6]	1891	1945–1945
GERMAN FEDERAL REPUBLIC (WEST) (PRESIDENTS)		
Theodor Heuss	1884	1949–1959[9]
Heinrich Luebke	1895	1959–1969[8]
Gustav Heinemann[10]	1899	1969–1974
Walter Scheel	1919	1974–1979
Karl Carstens	1914	1979–
GERMAN DEMOCRATIC REPUBLIC (EAST)		
Wilhelm Pieck[5]	1876	1949–1960
Walter Ulbricht[11]	1893	1960–1973
Willi Stoph[12]	1914	1973–1976
Erich Honecker[12]	1912	1976–

1. Year of end of rule is also that of death, unless otherwise indicated. 2. Was Elector of Brandenburg (1688–1701) as Frederick III. 3. Became Emperor of Germany in 1871. 4. Died 1941. 5. President. 6. Führer. 7. Named Chancellor by President Hindenburg in 1933. 8. Died 1972. 9. Died 1963. 10. Died 1976. 11. Chairman of Council of State. Died 1973. 12. Chairman of Council of State.

nexed in March 1938. By the Munich agreement in September 1938 he gained the Czech Sudetenland, and in violation of this agreement he completed the dismemberment of Czechoslovakia in March 1939. But his invasion of Poland on Sept. 1, 1939, precipitated World War II.

On May 8, 1945, Germany surrendered unconditionally to Allied and Soviet military commanders, and on June 5 the four-nation Allied Control Council became the *de facto* government of Germany.

(For details of World War II, *see* Headline History.)

At the Berlin (or Potsdam) Conference (July 17–Aug. 2, 1945) President Truman, Premier Stalin, and Prime Minister Clement Attlee of Britain set forth the principles by which the Allied Control Council was to be guided. They were Germany's complete disarmament and demilitarization, destruction of its war potential, rigid control of industry, and decentralization of the political and economic structure. Pending final determination of territorial questions at a peace conference, the three victors agreed in principle to the ultimate transfer of the city of Königsberg (now Kaliningrad) and its adjacent area to the U.S.S.R. and to the administration by Poland of former German territories lying generally east of the Oder-Neisse Line.

For purposes of control Germany was divided in 1945 into four national occupation zones, each headed by a Military Governor, assisted by appropriate supervisory and operating staffs.

Efforts to unify Germany were unsuccessful, and the Western powers were unable to agree with the U.S.S.R. on any fundamental issue. Work of the Allied Control Council was hamstrung by repeated Soviet vetoes; and finally, on March 20, 1948, Russia walked out of the Council. Meanwhile, the U.S. and Britain had taken steps to merge their zones economically (Bizone); and on May 31, 1948, the U.S., Britain, France, and the Benelux countries agreed to set up a German state comprising the three Western Zones.

The U.S.S.R. reacted by clamping a blockade on all ground communications between the Western Zones and Berlin, an enclave in the Soviet Zone. The Western Allies countered by organizing a gigantic airlift to fly supplies into the beleaguered city, assigning 60,000 men to it. The U.S.S.R. was finally forced to lift the blockade on May 12, 1949.

The Federal Republic of Germany was proclaimed on May 23, 1949, with its capital at Bonn. In free elections, West German voters gave a majority in the Constituent Assembly to the Christian Democrats, with the Social Democrats largely making up the opposition. Konrad Adenauer became chancellor, and Theodor Heuss of the Free Democrats was elected first president.

With admission into the European Coal and Steel Community and later into the Common Market, West Germany prospered. In 1950 a West Berlin Constitution provided for autonomous municipal government and representation in the Bundestag. A peace contract was given West Germany on May 26, 1952, that created within the North Atlantic Treaty Organization, a European Defense Community, but it was later vetoed by France.

Agreements in Paris in 1954 giving the Federal Republic full independence and complete sovereignty came into force on May 5, 1955. Under it, West Germany and Italy became members of the Brussels treaty organization created in 1948 and renamed the Western European Union. West Germany also became a member of NATO. In 1955 the U.S.S.R. recognized the Federal Republic. The Saar territory, under an agreement between France and West Germany, held a plebiscite and despite economic links to France voted to rejoin West Germany. It became a state of West Germany on Jan. 1, 1957.

In 1963, Chancellor Adenauer concluded a treaty of mutual cooperation and friendship with France and then retired. He was succeeded by his chief inner-party critic, Ludwig Erhard, who was followed in 1966 by Kurt Georg Kiesinger. He, in turn, was succeeded in 1969 by Willy Brandt, former mayor of West Berlin.

The division between West Germany and East Germany was intensified when the Communists erected the Berlin Wall in 1961. In 1968, the East German Communist leader, Walter Ulbricht, imposed restrictions on West German movements into West Berlin. The Soviet-bloc invasion of Czechoslovakia in August 1968 added to the tension.

Willy Brandt's Socialist government pushed through an "Ostpolitik" policy that led to the first official meetings of leaders of East and West Germany, in 1970. A treaty with the U.S.S.R. was signed in Moscow in August 1970 in which force was renounced and respect for the "territorial integrity" of present European states declared.

Three months later, West Germany signed a similar treaty with Poland, renouncing force and setting Poland's western border as the Oder-Neisse Line, thus acknowledging Poland's post-war annexation of 40,000 square miles (103,600 sq km) of former German territory. It subsequently resumed formal relations with Czechoslovakia in a pact that "voided" the Munich treaty that gave Nazi Germany the Sudetenland.

Both German states were admitted to the United Nations in 1973.

Brandt, winner of a Nobel Peace Prize for his foreign policies, was forced to resign in 1974 when an East German spy was discovered to be one of his top staff members. Succeeding him was a moderate Social Democrat, Helmut Schmidt.

Schmidt's government was plagued with terrorism by urban guerrillas known as the Baader-Meinhof gang. Andreas Baader and two of the gang were sentenced to life imprisonment in 1977. Ulrike Meinhof had committed suicide a year earlier. Other members of the gang staged a hijacking to free their imprisoned colleagues, and when the hijackers were captured, Baader killed himself. Some of the gang were known to be still at large but inactive in 1980.

West Germany was host to the fourth annual summit meeting of the seven leading industrial nations July 16–17, 1978. Schmidt, whose economy was Europe's strongest with a trade surplus of $5 billion in 1977, was critical of U.S. failure to curb its oil consumption and inflation. Schmidt had differed with Carter previously, questioning his emphasis on human rights as a threat to détente and refusing to accept U.S. restrictions on the export of nuclear reactors unless all nations accepted such controls.

A 30-year alliance between the Christian Democratic Party and its Bavarian partner, the Christian Social Union, ended in May 1979 with the announcement of candidates from each wing to oppose Chancellor Schmidt's re-election in 1980. Franz Josef Straus, Premier of Bavaria and leader of the Christian Social Union, declared his candidacy just four days before the Christian Democrats nominated Ernst Albrecht, Premier of Saxony.

In preparation for his campaign, Schmidt began to assert German economic power in both the Western Alliance and within the European Community. The Chancellor took an unprecedented step in traveling to Moscow in June to urge Soviet President Leonid I. Brezhnev to pull Soviet troops out of Afghanistan. At the Venice economic summit in July, he lectured President Carter about the vagaries of U.S. foreign policy, and in an interview in August he declared that Germany was no longer a "dependent client" of the U.S. but a "major partner" second only to the U.S. in economic strength.

BERLIN

Status: West Berlin: State of West Germany; East Berlin: capital of East Germany
Governing Mayor, West Berlin: Dietrich Stobbe (1977)
Mayor, East Berlin: Erhard Krack
Area: 340 square miles (West Berlin, 184; East Berlin, 156
Population (est. 1977): 3,057,000 (West Berlin, 1,950,700; East Berlin, 1,106,300)

Berlin, the capital of prewar Germany, lies entirely within the borders of East Germany. After the war, the city was occupied by the forces of the U.S., Britain, France, and the U.S.S.R. The three western sectors, now known as West Berlin, contain 55% of the area and two thirds of the population.

West Berlin is a state of the Federal Republic of Germany, but supreme authority remains in the hands of the three Western powers in accordance with postwar agreements. The government is composed of the governing mayor, the 11-member Senate (his Cabinet), and the House of Representatives, a popularly elected legislative body that elects the governing mayor and the Senate.

East Berlin is governed by a City Assembly elected by Communist Party members, and a Magistrat (City Council) chosen by the Assembly and headed by the mayor. In violation of the Four Power Agreements, the Soviet Sector has been incorporated into the German Democratic Republic and is now the capital of that country.

Major anti-Communist riots broke out in East Berlin in June 1953 and, since Aug. 13, 1961, the Soviet Sector has been virtually sealed off by a Communist-built wall, 26½ miles (43 km) long, running through the city. It was built to stem the flood of refugees seeking freedom in the West, 200,000 having fled in 1961 before the wall was erected.

GHANA

Republic of Ghana
President: Hilla Limann (1979)
Area: 92,100 sq mi. (238,537 sq km)
Population (est. 1980): 11,680,000
Density per square mile: 126.8
Capital: Accra
Largest cities (est. 1975): Accra, 716,600; (est. 1972): Kumasi, 342,982; Sekondi-Takoradi, 161,071
Monetary unit: Cedi
Languages: Native tongues (Twi, Fanti, Ga, Ewe, Dagbani); English
Religions: Christian 43%, Islam, 12%, Animist 38%
Member of Commonwealth of Nations
Freedom House classifications: Capitalist-statist industrial, multi-party centralized
Economic summary: Gross national product (1978): $4.3 billion. Average annual growth rate (1970–77): –2.0%. Per capita income: $790. Land used for agriculture: 70%; labor force: 60%; principal products: cocoa, timber, coconuts, coffee, subsistence crops, rubber. Labor force in industry: 17%; major products: mining products, lumber, light manufactured goods, fish, aluminum.

Natural resources: gold, diamonds, bauxite, manganese, fish. Exports: cocoa beans and products, gold, timber, manganese ore. Imports: petroleum, food, industrial raw materials, machinery, transport equipment. Major trading partners: U.K., U.S., Netherlands, Switzerland, West Germany.

Geography. A West African country bordering on the Gulf of Guinea, Ghana has the Ivory Coast to the west, Upper Volta to the north, and Togo to the east. It compares in size to Oregon.

The coastal belt, extending about 270 miles (435 km), is sandy, marshy, and generally exposed. Behind it is a gradually widening grass strip. The forested plateau region to the north is broken by ridges and hills. The largest river is the Volta.

Government. Ghana, under military rule since 1972, was scheduled to return to civilian government in 1979. In elections held June 18, 1979, the People's National Party won 71 seats in a reconstituted 140-seat Parliament. Hilla Limann, candidate of the People's National Party, won the presidency in a run-off on July 9 against Victor Owusa, leader of the Popular Front Party, which won 42 seats. Splinter parties shared the balance.

History. Created an independent country on March 6, 1957, Ghana is the former British colony of the Gold Coast. The area was first seen by Portuguese traders in 1470. They were followed by the English (1553), the Dutch (1595), and the Swedes (1640). British rule over the Gold Coast began in 1820, but it was not until after quelling the severe resistance of the Ashanti in 1901 that it was firmly established. British Togoland, formerly a colony of Germany, was incorporated into Ghana by referendum in 1956. As the result of a plebiscite, Ghana became a republic on July 1, 1960.

Premier Kwame Nkrumah attempted to take leadership of the Pan-African Movement, holding the All-African People's Congress in his capital, Accra, in 1958 and organizing the Union of African States with Guinea and Mali in 1961. But he oriented his country toward the Soviet Union and China and built an autocratic rule over all aspects of Ghanaian life.

In February 1966, while Nkrumah was visiting Peking and Hanoi, he was deposed by a military coup led by Gen. Emmanuel K. Kotoka. The U.S. recognized the new regime and gave it financial aid. In April 1967, a military junta was crushed, but Kotoka was killed. The military leaders took steps to restore civilian rule and a new Constitution was approved in May 1969.

Another military group took over in January 1972. Its leader, Col. Ignatius Acheampong, proclaimed himself Head of State and chairman of the National Redemption Council, which replaced Parliament. The new regime proposed a union government of military, police, and civilian elements in a referendum approved by the voters in March 1978. Before the plan could be implemented, however, Lt. Gen. Frederick W. K. Akuffo of the military governing council ousted Acheampong on July 5. The shift was apparently related to food shortages and Ghana's raging inflation, running at an annual rate of more than 100%.

A military coup led by Flight Lieutenant Jerry Rawlings, imprisoned after an earlier attempt, overthrew Akuffo on June 4, 1979. Rawlings promised that the election of a civilian president would go ahead as scheduled, and Hilla Limann, candidate of the People's National Party, became President-elect in July.

GREECE

Hellenic Republic
President: Constantine Karamanlis (1980)
Premier: Giorgios Rallis (1980)
Area: 50,547 sq mi. (130,917 sq km)
Population (est. 1980): 9,510,000
Density per square mile: 188.1
Capital: Athens
Largest cities (1971 census): Athens, 867,023; Salonika, 345,799; Piraeus, 187,362; Péristéri, 118,413; Patrai, 111,607
Monetary unit: Drachma
Language: Greek
Religion: Greek Orthodox
National name: Elliniki Dimokratia
Freedom House classifications: Capitalist industrial, multi-party centralized
Economic summary: Gross national product (1978): $30.1 billion. Average annual growth rate (1970–77): 4.0%. Per capita income (1977): $2,885. Average rate of inflation (1975–77): 12.9%. Labor force in agriculture: 38%; principal products: grains, fruits, vegetables, olives, olive oil, tobacco, cotton, livestock, dairy products. Labor force in industry: 27%; major products: textiles, metals, chemicals, electrical equipment, cement, glass, transport equipment, petroleum. Natural resources: bauxite, lignite, forests. Exports: fruits, vegetables, petroleum products, textiles, tobacco, iron and steel. Imports: machinery and automotive equipment, petroleum, consumer goods, chemicals, meat, live animals. Major trading partners: West Germany, Japan, Italy, France, Saudi Arabia, U.S., U.K.

Geography. Greece, on the Mediterranean Sea, is the southernmost country on the Balkan Peninsula in Eastern Europe. It is bordered on the north by Albania, Yugoslavia, and Bulgaria; on the west by the Ionian Sea; and on the east by the Aegean Sea and Turkey. It is slightly smaller than Alabama.

North central Greece, Epirus, and western Macedonia all are mountainous. The main chain of the Pindus Mountains rises to 9,000 feet (2,743 m) in places, separating Epirus from the plains of Thessaly. Mt. Olympus, rising to 9,570 feet (2,909 m) in the north near the Aegean Sea, is the highest point in the country. Greek Thrace is mostly a lowland region separated from European Turkey by the lower Evros River.

Among the many islands are the Ionian group off the west coast; the Cyclades group to the southeast; other islands in the eastern Aegean, including Lesbos, Samos, and Chios; and Crete, the fourth largest Mediterranean island.

The Dodecanese, a group of islands in the Aegean Sea near the coast of Asia Minor, were ceded to Greece by the 1947 Italian peace treaty and were formally transferred on March 7, 1948.

Government. Greece returned to democratic government when the military dictatorship imposed in April 1967, collapsed July 23, 1974. A referendum in December 1974, resulted in 69% support for a republic to replace the monarchy.

The major political parties are the New Democracy Party (175 of 300 seats in the unicameral parliament), led by President Constantine Karamanlis; Panhellenic Socialist Movement (93 seats), led by Andreas Papandreou; Communist Party (11 seats); Union of Democratic Center (5 seats), led by John Zigdis; National Alignment Party (4 seats); Party of Democratic Socialism (3 seats).

History. Greece, with a recorded history going back to 766 B.C., reached the peak of its glory in the 5th century B.C., and by the middle of the 2nd century B.C., it had declined to the status of a Roman province. It remained within the Eastern Roman Empire until Constantinople fell to the Crusaders in 1204.

In 1453, the Turks took Constantinople, and by 1460 Greece was a Turkish province. The insurrection made famous by the poet Lord Byron broke out in 1821, and in 1827 Greece was set up as an independent nation, with sovereignty guaranteed by the U.K., France, and Russia.

The protecting powers chose Prince Otto of Bavaria as the first king of modern Greece in 1832 to reign over an area only slightly larger than the Peloponnese Peninsula. Chiefly under the next king, George I, chosen by the protecting powers in 1863, Greece acquired much of its present territory. During his 57-year reign, a period in which he encouraged parliamentary democracy, Thessaly, Epirus, Macedonia, Crete, and most of the Aegean islands were added from the disintegrating Turkish empire. An unsuccessful war against Turkey after World War I brought down the monarchy, to be replaced by a republic in 1923.

Two military dictatorships and a financial crisis brought George II back from exile, but only until 1941, when Italian and German invaders defeated tough Greek resistance. After British and Greek troops liberated the country in October 1944, Communist guerrillas staged a long campaign in which the government received U.S. aid under the Truman Doctrine, the predecessor of the Marshall Plan.

A military junta seized power in April 1967, sending young King Constantine II into exile December 14. Col. George Papadopoulos, as premier, converted the government to republican form in 1973 and as President ended martial law. He was moving to restore democracy when he was ousted in November of that year by his military colleagues. The regime of the "colonels," which had tortured its opponents and scoffed at human rights, resigned July 23, 1974, after having bungled an attempt to seize Cyprus.

Former Premier Karamanlis returned from exile to become premier of Greece's first civilian government since 1967. The election in November gave him 54% backing, and a new republican Constitution was adopted June 7, 1975.

Greece cut its military ties with the North Atlantic Treaty Organization in mid-August 1974 because of the failure of the U.S. and other members to restrain Turkey, also a member, from invading Cyprus. Efforts to settle the Cyprus problem failed, and in January 1978 opposition leader Andreas Papandreou demanded the closing of U.S. bases remaining in Greece.

A meeting between Karamanlis and Turkish Premier Bülent Ecevit in Switzerland in March was reported to have eased differences over air and sea rights in the Aegean, but Ecevit broke off contact in anger at U.S. Secretary of State Cyrus Vance's statement that the providing of U.S. arms to Turkey would be linked with progress in Cyprus. The Carter Administration in August 1978 obtained a reluctant Congressional reversal of an arms embargo imposed when Turkey intervened in Cyprus. Greece supported a continuing embargo as long as Turkish troops remained on the island.

On May 28, 1979, Greece signed a treaty that will make it the 10th member nation of the European Economic Community, with the date of formal entry set for Jan. 1, 1981. The treaty provides a five-year transition period for the elimination of tariffs and other trade barriers between Greece and the Common Market countries and a seven-year period before Greek workers will be able to move freely within the Community.

GRENADA

State of Grenada
Prime Minister: Maurice Bishop (1979)
Governor General: Paul Scoon (1978)
Area: 133 sq mi. (344 sq km)
Population (est. 1980): 110,000 (black, 53%; mixed, 42%)
Density per square mile: 827.1
Capital and largest city (est. 1974): St. George's, 6,600
Monetary unit: East Caribbean dollar
Ethnic groups: Caribs and Indians
Language: English
Religions: Roman Catholic, Anglican, Methodist
Member of Commonwealth of Nations
Freedom House classifications: Capitalist-socialist industrial, dominant party
Economic summary: Gross national product (1978): $60 million. Average annual growth rate (1970–77): –3.2%. Per capita income: $500. Land used for agriculture: 44%; labor force: 40%; principal products: spices, cocoa, bananas. Exports: nutmeg, cocoa beans, bananas, mace. Imports: foodstuffs, machinery, building materials. Major trading partners: U.K., West Indies countries, West Germany, Netherlands.

Geography. Grenada (the first "a" is pronounced as in "gray") is the most southerly of the Windward Islands, about 100 miles (161 km) from the South American coast. It is a volcanic island traversed by a mountain range, the highest peak of which is Mount St. Catherine (2,756 ft.; 840 m).

History. Grenada was discovered by Columbus in 1498. After more than 200 years of British rule, most recently as part of the West Indies Associated States, it became independent Feb. 7, 1974.

The country began its independence in chaos, as opponents of Prime Minister Eric M. Gairy's curbs on civil liberties—notably the professionals and educated class, as well as some union leaders and businessmen—paralyzed Grenada with a general strike that ended after two weeks when Gairy promised to disband his secret police force.

In 1975, Grenada became a member of the Organization of American States. In June 1977, it was host to the OAS General Assembly.

The United Labor Party, led by Prime Minister Gairy, won only 9 of 15 seats in the House of Assembly, the island's parliament in 1976. Gairy, under increasing attack for his autocratic rule, was ousted on March 13, 1979, by the New Jewel Movement, led by Maurice Bishop.

GUATEMALA

Republic of Guatemala
President: Gen. Romeo Lucas García (1978)
Area: 42,042 sq mi. (108,889 sq km)
Population (est. 1980): 7,250,000
Density per square mile: 172.4
Capital and largest city (est. 1979): Guatemala City, 814,800
Monetary unit: Quetzal
Languages: Spanish, Indian dialects
Religion: Roman Catholic
National name: República de Guatemala
Freedom House classifications: Capitalist pre-industrial, multi-party centralized
Economic summary: Gross national product (1978): $6.0 billion. Average annual growth rate (1970–77): 3.3%. Per capita income: $846; Average rate of inflation (1976–78): 13–17%. Labor force in agriculture: 53%; principal products: corn, beans, coffee, cotton, cattle, sugar, bananas, essential oils, timber. Labor force in industry: 26%; principal products: prepared foods, textiles, construction materials, tires, pharmaceuticals. Natural resources: nickel, timber, shrimp. Exports: coffee, cotton, sugar, meat, bananas. Imports: fuels and lubricants, industrial machinery, motor vehicles, iron and steel. Major trading partners: U.S., Central American nations, West Germany, Japan, Venezuela.

Geography. The northernmost of the Central American nations, Guatemala is the size of Tennessee. Its neighbors are Mexico on the north, west, and east and Belize, Honduras, and El Salvador on the east. The country consists of two main regions—the cool highlands with the heaviest population and the tropical area along the Pacific and Caribbean coasts. The principal mountain range rises to the highest elevation in Central America and contains many volcanic peaks. Volcanic eruptions are frequent.

The Petén region in the north contains important resources and archaeological sites of the Mayan civilization.

Government. Executive power is vested in the president, who is elected for a term of four years, and his Cabinet of 10 members. Legislative power lies with the 61-member National Congress.

The major political parties are National Liberation Movement (20 seats in the National Congress); Democratic Institutional Party (17 seats); Revolutionary Party (14 seats); Christian Democratic Party (7 seats); and the Central Aranista National Party (3 seats).

History. Once the site of the ancient Mayan civilization, Guatemala, conquered by Spain in 1524, set itself up as a republic in 1839. From 1898 to 1920, the dictator Manuel Estrada Cabrera ran the country, and from 1931 to 1944, Gen. Jorge Ubico Castaneda was the strongman. In 1944 the National Assembly elected Gen. Federico Ponce president, but he was overthrown in October. In December, Dr. Juan José Arévalo was elected as the head of a leftist regime that continued to press its reform program. Jacobo Arbenz Guzmán, administration candidate with pro-Communist leanings, won the 1950 elections.

Arbenz expropriated the large estates, including plantations of the United Fruit Company, and exterminated his political enemies. With covert U.S. backing, a revolt was led by Col. Carlos Castillo Armas, and Arbenz took refuge in Havana. Castillo Armas became president but was assassinated in 1957. Constitutional government was restored in 1958, and Gen. Miguel Ydigoras Fuentes was elected president. He was host to the Cuban force that trained for the disastrous landing at the Bay of Pigs in April 1961.

In 1963 the Ydigoras government was overthrown by Enrique Peralta Azurdia, who ruled until 1966, when elections, under a new Constitution, led to Congress's choice of Dr. Julio César Méndez Montenegro.

In 1967, terrorists of the left and right began plaguing the country. The U.S. military and naval attachés were assassinated in Guatemala City in January 1968 and the U.S. Ambassador, John Gordon Mein, was slain in August 1968, when he resisted kidnapping. In a little over two years at least 1,000 people—some estimates make it 4,000—were murdered by extremists.

The left-wing terrorists, abetted by counterterrorists of the right, created widespread fear of anarchy, which led to the election of the coalition's conservative, business-backed Carlos Arana Osorio in 1970. Arana had won fame as an army chief who bloodily put down one rural guerrilla movement (1,500–3,000 peasants killed). On taking office, Arana surprisingly pledged social reform.

Gen. Kjell Laugerud won the 1974 election for president. Political violence attended his inauguration in July and continued after he took office.

A devastating earthquake struck Guatemala on Feb. 4, 1976, killing an estimated 22,000 and injuring 74,000. Despite the heavy casualties, little damage was done to the nation's small, but growing, industrial base.

GUINEA

Revolutionary People's Republic of Guinea
President: Ahmed Sékou Touré (1958)
Premier: Louis Lansana Béavogui (1972)
Area: 94,925 sq mi. (245,857 sq km)
Population (est. 1980): 5,000,000
Density per square mile: 52.7
Capital and largest city (est. 1977): Conakry, 600,000
Monetary unit: Syli
Languages: French (official), native tongues (Malinké, Susu, Fulani)
Religions: Islam and Animist
National name: République Populaire Revolutionnaire de Guinée
Freedom House classifications: Socialist pre-industrial, one-party socialist
Economic summary: Gross national product (1978): $1.1 billion. Average annual growth rate (1970–77): 2.5%. Per capita income: $140. Principal agricultural products: rice, cassava, millet, corn, coffee, bananas, palm products, pineapples. Major industrial products: bauxite, alumina, light manufactured and processed goods. Natural resources: bauxite, iron ore, diamonds, gold, water power. Exports: bauxite, alumina, pineapples, bananas, coffee. Imports: petroleum, machinery, transport equipment, foodstuffs. Major trading partners:

Communist bloc, Western Europe, U.S.

Geography. Guinea, in West Africa on the Atlantic, is also bordered by Guinea-Bissau, Senegal, Mali, the Ivory Coast, Liberia, and Sierra Leone. Slightly smaller than Oregon, the country consists of a coastal plain, a mountainous region, a savanna interior, and a forest area in the Guinea Highlands. The highest peak is Mount Nimba at about 6,000 feet (1,829 m).

Government. The National Assembly has 150 members elected by universal suffrage from a list prepared and presented by the Parti Démocratique de Guinée, the only political party, led by President Ahmed Sékou Touré, Secretary General of the party.

History. Previously part of French West Africa, Guinea achieved independence by rejecting the new French Constitution, and on Oct. 2, 1958, became an independent state with Sékou Touré as president. Touré led the country into being the first avowedly Marxist state in Africa. Diplomatic relations with France were suspended in 1965, with the Soviet Union replacing France as the country's chief source of economic and technical assistance.

In 1966, when a Ghanaian military coup deposed Kwame Nkrumah as President, Touré welcomed him to Guinea and declared him joint president and party leader. The titles proved to be only honorary. Touré accused Ghana of being an American imperialist puppet, and the U.S. Embassy in his capital, Conakry, was sacked. In retaliation the United States ended financial aid. An exchange of letters between the Guinean and U.S. presidents restored relations.

Prosperity came in 1969 after the start of exploitation of bauxite deposits. Touré was re-elected to a seven-year term in 1974.

GUINEA-BISSAU

Republic of Guinea-Bissau
President: Luis Cabral (1974)
Principal Commissioner: João Bernardo Vieira (1978)
Area: 13,948 sq mi. (36,125 sq km)
Population (est. 1980): 570,000
Density per square mile: 40.9
Capital and largest city (est. 1979 for metropolitan area): Bissau, 109,500
Monetary unit: Guinea-Bissau peso
Language: Portugese
Religions: Animist, 66%; Islam, 30%; Roman Catholic, 4%
National name: Guiné Bissau
Freedom House classifications: Socialist pre-industrial, one-party socialist
Economic summary: Gross national product (1978): $160 million. Average annual growth rate (1970–77): −7.7%. Per capita income: $230. Labor force in agriculture: 90%; principal products: palm oil, root crops, rice, coconuts, peanuts. Natural resources: potential bauxite deposits. Exports: peanuts, coconuts, shrimp, fish, wood. Imports: foodstuffs, manufactured goods, fuels, transportation equipment. Major trading partner: Portugal.

Geography. A neighbor of Senegal and Guinea in West Africa, on the Atlantic coast, Guinea-Bissau is about half the size of South Carolina.

The country is a low-lying coastal region of swamps, rain forests, and mangrove-covered wetlands, with about 25 islands off the coast. The Bijagos archipelago extends 30 miles (48 km) out to sea. Internal communications depend mainly on deep estuaries and meandering rivers, since there are no railroads. Bissau, the capital, is the main port.

Government. The president and a 15-member Council of State were elected in 1977 by a National Assembly of 150 members chosen from regional councils elected from lists provided by the sole political party, the African Party for the Independence of Guinea-Bissau and Cape Verde.

History. Guinea-Bissau was discovered in 1446 by the Portuguese Nuno Tristao, and colonists in the Cape Verde Islands obtained trading rights in the territory. In 1879 the connection with the Cape Verde Islands was broken. Early in the 1900s the Portuguese managed to pacify some tribesmen, although resistance to colonial rule remained.

The African Party for the Independence of Guinea-Bissau and Cape Verde was founded in 1956 and several years later began guerrilla warfare that grew increasingly effective. By 1974 the rebels controlled most of the countryside, where they formed a government that was soon recognized by scores of countries. The military coup in Portugal in April 1974 brightened the prospects for freedom, and in August the Lisbon government signed an agreement granting independence to the province as of Sept. 10. The new republic took the name Guinea-Bissau. Its government was immediately recognized by the United States.

On July 7, 1978, Francisco Mendès, who had been premier since 1975, was assassinated.

GUYANA

Cooperative Republic of Guyana
President: Arthur Chung (1970)
Prime Minister: Forbes Burnham (1964)
Area: 83,000 sq mi. (214,969 sq km)
Population (est. 1980): 860,000 (East Indian, 52%; African, 31%; mixed 10%; Amerindian, 5%)
Density per square mile: 10.4
Capital and largest city (est. 1976 by U.N.): Georgetown, 72,000
Monetary unit: Guyana dollar
Languages: English (official), Hindi, Urdu
Religions: Hindu, 37%; Protestant, 32%; Roman Catholic, 13%
Member of Commonwealth of Nations
Freedom House classifications: Capitalist-socialist industrial, multi-party centralized
Economic summary: Gross national product (1978): $460 million. Average annual growth rate (1970–77): 0.4%. Per capita income: $510. Labor force in agriculture: 20%; principal products: sugar, rice. Labor force in industry: 31%; major products: bauxite, alumina. Natural resources: bauxite, gold, diamonds, hardwood timber, shrimp. Exports: sugar, bauxite, alumina, rice, shrimp. Imports: consumer and manufactured goods. Major trading partners: Canada, Caribbean nations, U.K., U.S.

Geography. Guyana is situated on the northern coast of South America east of Venezuela, west of Suriname, and north of Brazil. The country consists of a low coastal area and the Guiana Highlands in the south. There is an extensive north-south network of rivers. Guyana is the size of Idaho.

Government. Guyana, formerly British Guiana, proclaimed itself a republic on Feb. 23, 1970, ending its tie with Britain while remaining in the Commonwealth.

Guyana has a unicameral legislature, the National Assembly, with 53 members elected for four-year terms. A 24-member Cabinet is headed by the Prime Minister.

The major political parties are the People's National Congress (37 of 53 seats in National Assembly), led by Prime Minister Forbes Burnham; People's Progressive Party (14 seats), led by Dr. Cheddi B. Jagan.

History. British Guiana won internal self-government in 1952. The next year the People's Progressive Party, headed by Cheddi B. Jagan, an East Indian dentist, won the elections and Jagan became Prime Minister. British authorities deposed him for alleged Communist connections. A coalition ousted Jagan in 1964, installing a moderate Socialist, Forbes Burnham, a black, as Prime Minister. On May 26, 1966, the country became an independent member of the Commonwealth and resumed its traditional name, Guyana.

The government nationalized mining operations of the U.S.-owned Reynolds Metals Co. in 1975.

In 1978, the International Monetary Fund approved an $18.7-million loan for Guyana, which is trying to overcome a $60-million deficit in balance of payments.

One of the most bizarre incidents in modern history occurred when 911 persons died in a mass murder-suicide on Nov. 19, 1978, at a remote settlement in Guyana founded by a U.S. sect known as the People's Temple. The victims were either shot or forced to drink poisoned Kool-Aid by the Rev. Jim Jones, for whom the site, Jonestown, was named.

Jones ordered his followers to die after his aides had killed U.S. Representative Leo J. Ryan of California and three newsmen who accompanied Ryan on an investigative trip to the colony.

HAITI

Republic of Haiti
Life President: Jean-Claude Duvalier (1971)
Area: 10,714 sq mi. (27,750 sq km)
Population (est. 1980): 5,000,000
Density per square mile: 466.7
Capital and largest city (est. 1978): Port-au-Prince, 703,100
Monetary unit: Gourde
Languages: French, Creole
Religion: Roman Catholic
National name: République d'Haïti
Freedom house classifications: Capitalist pre-industrial, dominant party
Economic summary: Gross national product (1978): $1.2 billion. Average annual growth rate (1970–77): 2.1%. Per capita income: $230. Land used for agriculture: 31%; labor force: 77%; principal products: coffee, sugar cane, rice, corn, sorghum. Labor force in industry: 7%; major products: refined sugar, textiles, flour, cement, bauxite, light assembly products. Natural resource: bauxite. Exports: coffee, light industrial products, bauxite, sugar, essential oils, sisal. Imports: consumer goods, foodstuffs, industrial equipment, petroleum products, construction materials. Major trading partner: U.S.

Geography. Haiti, in the West Indies, occupies the western third of the island of Hispaniola, which it shares with the Dominican Republic. About the size of Maryland, Haiti is two thirds mountainous, with the rest of the country marked by great valleys, extensive plateaus, and small plains. The most densely populated region is the Cul-de-Sac plain near Port-au-Prince.

Government. In 1964, the late President, François Duvalier, known as "Papa Doc," made himself president for life. His son, Jean-Claude, then 19, known as "Baby Doc," inherited the title on his father's death on April 21, 1971. Under a Constitution revised in 1964, the president in periods of crisis may dismiss the National Assembly and Cabinet and govern by decree. The Parti d'Unité Nationale (57 of the 58 seats in the National Assembly), led by President Duvalier, is the only legal party in the country.

History. Discovered by Columbus, who landed at Môle Saint Nicolas on Dec. 6, 1492, Haiti in 1697 became a French possession known as Saint Domingue. An insurrection among a slave population of 500,000 in 1791 ended with a declaration of independence by Pierre-Dominique Toussaint l'Ouverture in 1801. Napoleon Bonaparte suppressed the independence movement, but it eventually triumphed in 1804 under Jean-Jacques Dessalines, who gave the new nation the aboriginal name Haiti.

Its prosperity dissipated in internal strife as well as disputes with neighboring Santo Domingo during a succession of 19th-century dictatorships, a bankrupt Haiti accepted a U.S. customs receivership from 1905 to 1941. Direct U.S. rule from 1915 to 1930 brought a measure of stability and a population growth that made Haiti the most densely populated nation in the hemisphere.

In 1949, after four years of democratic rule by President Dumarsais Estimé, dictatorship returned under Gen. Paul Magloire, who was succeeded by François Duvalier in 1957.

Duvalier established a dictatorship based on secret police, known as the "Ton-ton Macoutes," who gunned down opponents of the regime. Duvalier's son, Jean-Claude, or "Baby Doc," succeeded his father in 1971 as ruler of the poorest nation in the Western Hemisphere.

Limited economic improvement followed an increase in foreign investment under the new regime as 150 foreign companies established Haitian branches to take advantage of low wages. A steady exodus of refugees continued toward the United States, reaching a high of 15,000 in 1980. Previously denied refugee status, Haitian "boat people" were accorded the same temporary entrance rights as Cubans who arrived by boat.

On May 27, 1980, Duvalier married Michelle Bennett in a wedding attended by 5,000 guests and estimated to cost from $3 million to $5 million.

HONDURAS

Republic of Honduras
Provisional President: Gen. Policarpo Paz García (1980)
Area: 43,277 sq mi. (112,088 sq km)
Population (est. 1980): 3,680,000 (60% mestizo)
Density per square mile: 85.0
Capital and largest city (est. 1977): Tegucigalpa, 316,800
Monetary unit: Lempira
Languages: Spanish, some Indian dialects
Religion: Roman Catholic
National name: República de Honduras
Freedom House classifications: Capitalist pre-industrial, non-party military
Economic summary: Gross national product (1978): $1.7 billion. Average annual growth rate (1970–77): 0%. Per capita income: $490. Labor force in agriculture: 66%; principal products: coffee, bananas, corn, beans, cotton, sugar cane, tobacco. Major industrial products: processed agricultural products, textiles and clothing, wood products. Natural resources: timber, gold, silver, lead, zinc, antimony. Exports: bananas, coffee, lumber, meat, petroleum products. Imports: manufactured goods, machinery, transportation equipment, chemicals, petroleum. Major trading partners: U.S., Caribbean countries, West Germany, Venezuela, Japan.

Geography. Honduras, in the north central part of Central America, has a 400-mile (644-km) Caribbean coastline and a 40-mile (64-km) Pacific frontage. Its neighbors are Guatemala to the west, El Salvador to the south, and Nicaragua to the east. Honduras is slightly larger than Tennessee.

Generally mountainous, the country is marked by fertile plateaus, river valleys, and narrow coastal plains.

Government. The military regime in power since 1973 authorized the election of a Constitutional Assembly on April 20, 1980. The Partido Liberal, led by Roberto Suazo Córdova, won 35 of the Assembly seats; the Partido Nacional, led by Ricardo Zuñiga, won 33; the balance were divided between two minor parties. President Policarpo Paz García formally transferred power to the Assembly on July 20, but remained Provisional President until the election of a new leader, scheduled for April 1981.

History. Columbus discovered Honduras on his last voyage in 1502. Honduras, with four other countries of Central America, declared its independence from Spain in 1821 and was part of a federation of Central American states until 1838. In that year it seceded from the federation and became a completely independent country.

It has been troubled by revolution and war ever since. U.S. Marines intervened in 1903 and 1923. In 1931, 1932, and 1937, major revolutions were crushed by force.

In July 1969, El Salvador invaded Honduras after Honduran landowners had deported several thousand Salvadorans. The fighting left 1,000 dead and tens of thousands homeless. By threatening economic sanctions and military intervention, the OAS induced El Salvador to withdraw.

In June 1970, Honduras and El Salvador agreed to a demilitarized zone of 1.8 miles on each side of their ill-defined border and accepted an OAS police force. A year later they agreed, despite two more border flare-ups, to negotiate a peace settlement. Honduras remained largely out of the five-nation Central America Common Market, however, until the Pan-American Highway link with El Salvador was reopened in 1972.

In 1971, Ramon Ernesto Cruz, a lawyer, diplomat, and teacher, became Honduras's first freely elected president since 1949. But strongman Oswaldo López Arellano, citing "chaos and weakness" under the coalition, again seized control (for the third time in two decades). He served until his ouster in 1975.

On Aug. 7, 1978, the military ousted Juan Alberto Melgar Castro as president, naming Gen. Policarpio Paz Garcia as chief of state. This was the second military-originated change of government in three years resulting from charges of corruption.

HUNGARY

Hungarian People's Republic
President: Pál Losonczi (1967)
Premier: Gyorgy Lazar (1975)
Area: 35,919 sq mi. (93,030 sq km)
Population (est. 1980): 10,720,000
Density per square mile: 298.4
Capital: Budapest
Largest cities (est. 1979): Budapest, 2,093,200: **(est. 1977 by U.N.):** Miskolc, 205,600; Debrecen, 194,000; Szeged, 174,600; Pécs, 167,700; Györ, 123,200
Monetary unit: Forint
Language: Magyar
Religions: Roman Catholic, 60%; Protestant, atheist
National name: Magyar Népköztársaság
Freedom House classifications: Socialist industrial, one-party communist
Economic summary: Gross national product (1978): $36.9. Average annual growth rate (1970–77): 5.1%. Per capita income: $2,750. Land used for agriculture: 75%; labor force: 23%; principal products: corn, wheat, potatoes, sugar beets, vegetables, wine grapes, fruits. Labor force in industry: 36%; major products: precision and measuring equipment, pharmaceuticals, textiles, transport equipment. Natural resources: some bauxite and brown coal. Exports: machinery and tools, industrial and consumer goods, raw materials. Imports: machinery, raw materials. Major trading partners: U.S.S.R., West Germany, Warsaw Pact countries.

Geography. This central European country the size of Indiana is bordered by Austria to the west, Czechoslovakia to the north, the U.S.S.R. and Romania to the east, and Yugoslavia to the south.

Most of Hungary is a fertile, rolling plain lying east of the Danube River and drained by the Danube and Tisza rivers. In the extreme northwest is the Little Hungarian Plain. South of that area is Lake Balaton (250 sq mi.; 648 sq km).

Government. Hungary is a People's Republic with legislative power vested in the unicameral National Assembly, whose 352 members are elected directly for four-year terms. The supreme body of state power is the 21-member Presidential Council elected by the National Assembly. The supreme administrative body is the Council of Ministers, headed by the Premier.

The Hungarian Socialist Workers (Communist) Party, led by János Kádár, is the only political party.

History. About 2,000 years ago, Hungary was part of the Roman provinces of Pannonia and Dacia. In A.D. 896 it was invaded by the Magyars, who founded a kingdom. Christianity was accepted during the reign of Stephen I (St. Stephen) (997–1038).

The peak of Hungary's great period of medieval power came during the reign of Louis I the Great (1342–82), whose dominions touched the Baltic, Black, and Mediterranean seas.

War with the Turks broke out in 1389, and for more than 100 years the Turks advanced through the Balkans. When the Turks smashed a Hungarian army in 1526, western and northern Hungary accepted Hapsburg rule to escape Turkish occupation. Transylvania became independent under Hungarian princes. Intermittent war with the Turks was waged until a peace treaty was signed in 1699.

After the suppression of the 1848 revolt against Hapsburg rule, led by Louis Kossuth, the dual monarchy of Austria-Hungary was set up in 1867.

The dual monarchy was defeated with the other Central Powers in World War I. After a short-lived republic in 1918, the chaotic Communist rule of 1919 under Béla Kun ended with the Romanians occupying Budapest on Aug. 4, 1919. When the Romanians left, Adm. Nicholas Horthy entered the capital with a national army. The Treaty of Trianon of June 4, 1920, cost Hungary 68% of its land and 58% of its population. Meanwhile, the National Assembly had restored the legal continuity of the old monarchy; and, on March 1, 1920, Horthy was elected Regent.

Following the German invasion of Russia on June 22, 1941, Hungary joined the attack against the Soviet Union, but the war was not popular and Hungarian troops were almost entirely withdrawn from the eastern front by May 1943. German occupation troops set up a puppet government after Horthy's appeal for an armistice with advancing Soviet troops on Oct. 15, 1944, had resulted in his overthrow. The German regime soon fled the capital, however, and on December 23 a provisional government was formed in Soviet-occupied eastern Hungary. On Jan. 20, 1945, it signed an armistice in Moscow. Early the next year, the National Assembly approved a constitutional law abolishing the thousand-year-old monarchy and establishing a republic.

By the Treaty of Paris (1947), Hungary had to give up all territory it had acquired since 1937 and to pay $300 million reparations to the U.S.S.R., Czechoslovakia, and Yugoslavia. In 1948 the Communist Party, with the support of Soviet troops seized control. Hungary was proclaimed a People's Republic and one-party state in 1949. Industry was nationalized, the land collectivized into state farms, and the opposition terrorized by the secret police.

The terror, modeled after that of the U.S.S.R., reached its height with the trial of Jozsef Cardinal Mindszenty, Roman Catholic primate. He confessed to fantastic charges under duress of drugs or brainwashing and was sentenced to life imprisonment in 1949. Protests were voiced in all parts of the world.

On Oct. 23, 1956, anti-Communist revolution broke out in Budapest. To cope with it, the Communists set up a coalition government and called former Premier Imre Nagy back to head it. But he and most of his ministers were swept by the logic of events into the anti-Communist opposition, and he declared Hungary a neutral power, withdrawing from the Warsaw Treaty and appealing to the United Nations for help.

One of his ministers, János Kádár, established a counter-regime and asked the U.S.S.R. to send in military power. Soviet troops and tanks suppressed the revolution in bloody fighting after 190,000 people had fled the country and Mindszenty, freed from jail, had taken refuge in the U.S. Embassy. By treachery, Nagy and some of his ministers were abducted by the Soviet occupation troops and executed.

Kádár was succeeded as Premier, but not party secretary, by Gyula Kallai in 1965. Continuing his program of national reconciliation, Kádár emptied prisons, reformed the secret police, and eased travel restrictions. But 60,000 Soviet troops remained in Hungary. Further sweeping reforms liberalized the economy in 1968.

Hungary developed the reputation of being the freest East European state, with Kádár's new motto —"If you're not against us, you're with us"—replacing previous police state suspicions. Significant Western capitalist investment was welcomed and some capitalistic methods embraced.

After 15 years' asylum in the U.S. Embassy, Mindszenty, under an agreement between the Vatican and the Hungarian regime, was allowed to travel into exile to Rome in 1971. In a move applauded by Kádár, Pope Paul VI removed Mindszenty from his honorary post as Primate of Hungary in 1974. The Cardinal died in Vienna in 1975.

Relations with the U.S. improved in 1972 when World War II debt claims between the two nations were settled. On Jan. 6, 1978, the U.S. returned to Hungary, over anti-Communist protests, the 977-year-old crown of St. Stephen, held at Fort Knox since World War II.

ICELAND

Republic of Iceland
President: Vigdis Finnbogadottir (1980)
Prime Minister: Gunnar Thoroddsen (1980)
Area: 39,702 sq mi. (102,828 sq km)
Population (est. 1980): 230,000
Density per square mile: 5.8[1]
Capital and largest city (est. 1979): Reykjavik, 83,400
Monetary unit: Króna
Language: Icelandic
Religion: Evangelical Lutheran
National name: Lýdveldid Island
Freedom House classifications: Capitalist industrial, multi-party centralized
Economic summary: Gross national product (1978): $1.9 billion. Average annual growth rate (1970–77): 3.0%. Per capita income (1977): $5,450. Principal agricultural products: livestock, hay, fodder, cheese. Major industrial products: processed aluminum, fish. Natural resources: fish, diatomite, hydroelectric and geothermal power. Exports: fish. Imports: petroleum products, machinery, transport equipment, food, textiles. Major trading partners: U.S., U.S.S.R., Western European countries.

Geography. Iceland, a bleak island about the size of Kentucky, lies in the north Atlantic Ocean east of Greenland and just touches the Arctic Circle. It is

1. Including some offshore islands.

one of the most volcanic regions in the world.

Small fresh-water lakes are to be found throughout the island, and there are many natural phenomena, including hot springs, geysers, sulfur beds, canyons, waterfalls, and swift rivers. More than 13% of the area is covered by snowfields and glaciers, and most of the people live in the 7% of the island comprising fertile coastlands.

Government. The president is elected for four years by popular vote. Executive power resides in the prime minister and his Cabinet. The Althing (Parliament) is composed of 60 members in two houses. They elect 20 of themselves to constitute the Upper House, the remaining 40 representing the Lower House.

The major political parties are the Independence Party (22 of 60 seats in the Althing), led by Geir Hallgrimsson; Progressive Party (17 seats), led by Steingrimur Hermannsson; People's Alliance (11 seats), a Marxist group, led by Ludvik Josefsson; Social Democratic Party (10 seats), led by former Prime Minister Olafur Grøndal. Prime Minister Gunnar Thoroddsen of the Independent Party leads a coalition of the Progressives and the People's Alliance supported by a few of his own party.

History. Iceland was first settled shortly before 900, mainly by Norse. A Constitution drawn up about 930 created a form of democracy and provided for an Althing, or General Assembly.

In 1262–64, Iceland came under Norwegian rule and passed to ultimate Danish control through the formation of the Union of Kalmar in 1483. In 1874, Icelanders obtained their own Constitution. In 1918, Denmark recognized Iceland as a separate state with unlimited sovereignty but still nominally under the Danish king.

On June 17, 1944, after a popular referendum, the Althing proclaimed Iceland an independent republic.

The British occupied Iceland in 1940, immediately after the German invasion of Denmark. In 1942, the U.S. took over the burden of protection. Iceland refused to abandon its neutrality in World War II and thus forfeited charter membership in the United Nations, but it cooperated with the Allies throughout the conflict. Iceland joined the North Atlantic Treaty Organization in 1949.

Iceland unilaterally extended its territorial waters from 12 to 50 nautical miles in 1972, precipitating a running dispute with Britain known as the "cod war." Icelandic warships harassed British trawlers, which then received aid from British gunboats; some trawlers were shelled, and Icelandic and British warships collided in 1973. The World Court ruled in 1974 that the 50-mile limit could not be applied unilaterally, but Iceland rejected the ruling.

An agreement calling for registration of all British trawlers fishing within 200 miles of Iceland and a 24-hour time limit on incursions was finally reached in 1976.

INDIA

Republic of India
President: Neelam Sanjiva Reddy (1977)
Prime Minister: Indira Gandhi (1980)
Area: 1,229,737 sq mi. (3,185,019 sq km)
Population (est. 1980): 663,600,000
Density per square mile: 539.6
Capital (1971 census): New Delhi, 301,801
Largest cities (est. 1977): Calcutta, 8,297,000; Greater Bombay, 7,605,000; **(1971 census):** Delhi, 3,287,883; Madras, 2,469,449; Bangalore, 1,540,741; Ahmedabad, 1,585,544; Kanpur, 1,154,388
Monetary unit: Rupee
Principal languages; Hindi (official), Bengali, Sindhi, Gujarati, Kannarese, Kashmiri, Malayalam, Marathi, Oriya, Punjabi, Tamil, Telugu, Urdu, English
Religions: Hindu, 83%; Islam, 11%; Christian, 3%; Sikh, 2%
National name: Bharat
Member of Commonwealth of Nations
Freedom House classifications: Capitalist-statist, pre-industrial, multi-party decentralized
Economic summary: Gross national product (1978): $113 billion. Average annual growth rate (1970–77): 1.1%. Per capita income: 140. Land used for agriculture: 54%; labor force: 70%; principal products: rice, wheat, oilseeds, cotton, tea. Major industrial products: jute, processed food, steel, machinery, transport machinery, cement. Natural resources: Iron ore, coal, manganese, mica, bauxite, limestone. Exports: engineering goods, cotton apparel and fabrics, handicrafts, tea, iron and steel. Imports: petroleum, food grains, nonelectrical machinery, fertilizer. Major trading partners: U.S., Japan, U.K., U.S.S.R.

Geography. One third the area of the United States, the Republic of India occupies most of the subcontinent of India in south Asia. It borders on China in the northeast. Other neighbors are Pakistan on the west, Nepal and Bhutan on the north, and Burma and Bangladesh on the east.

The country contains a large part of the great Indo-Gangetic plain, which extends from the Bay of Bengal on the east to the Afghan frontier on the Arabian Sea on the west. This plain is the richest and most densely settled part of the subcontinent. Another distinct natural region is the Deccan, a plateau of 2,000 to 3,000 feet (610 to 914 m) in elevation, occupying the southern portion of the subcontinent.

Forming a part of the republic are several groups of islands—the Laccadives (14 islands) in the Arabian Sea and the Andamans (204 islands) and the Nicobars (19 islands) in the Bay of Bengal.

India's three great river systems, all rising in the Himalayas, have extensive deltas. The Ganges flows south and then east for 1,540 miles (2,478 km) across the northern plain to the Bay of Bengal; part of its delta, which begins 220 miles (354 km) from the sea, is within the republic. The Indus, starting in Tibet, flows northwest for several hundred miles in the Kashmir before turning southwest toward the Arabian Sea; it is important for irrigation in Pakistan. The Brahmaputra, also rising in Tibet, flows eastward, first through India and then south into Bangladesh and the Bay of Bengal.

Government. India is a federal republic. It is also a member of the Commonwealth of Nations, a status defined at the 1949 London Conference of Prime Ministers, by which India recognizes the Queen as head of the Commonwealth. Under the Constitution effective Jan. 26, 1950, India has a parliamentary type of government.

The constitutional head of the state is the President, who is elected every five years. He is advised

Political Subdivisions of Republic of India

Subdivisions	Area sq mi.	Population 1971 census
STATES		
Andhra Pradesh	106,052	43,502,708
Assam	30,400[1]	14,625,152[1]
Bihar	67,198	56,353,369
Gujarat	72,154	26,697,475
Haryana	16,670	10,036,808
Himachal Pradesh	10,880	3,460,434
Jammu and Kashmir[2]	85,861	4,616,632
Karnataka[3]	74,122	29,299,014
Kerala	15,003	21,347,375
Madhya Pradesh	171,210	41,654,119
Maharashtra	118,530	50,412,235
Manipur	8,628	1,072,753
Meghalaya	8,700[1]	1,011,699[1]
Nagaland	6,236	516,449
Orissa	60,182	21,944,615
Punjab	21,630	13,551,060
Rajasthan	132,151	25,765,806
Sikkim[4]	2,744	215,000
Tamil Nadu[5]	50,132	41,199,168
Tripura	4,022	1,556,342
Uttar Pradesh	113,452	88,341,144
West Bengal	33,928	44,312,011
UNION TERRITORIES		
Andaman and Nicobar Islands	3,215	115,133
Arunachal Pradesh	31,400	467,511
Chandigarh	44	257,251
Dadra and Nagar-Haveli	189	74,170
Delhi	573	4,065,698
Goa, Daman, and Diu	1,619	857,771
Lakshadweep[6]	11	31,810
Mizoram	8,100	332,390
Pondicherry	196	471,707

1. After reorganization of North East Frontier Agency in December 1971. 2. Status in dispute with Pakistan. 3. Formerly Mysore. 4. Sikkim became an Indian state in May 1975. Population figure is 1974 estimate. 5. Formerly Madras. 6. Formerly Laccadive, Minicoy, and Amindivi Islands.

by the Prime Minister and a Cabinet based on a majority of the bicameral Parliament, which consists of a Council of States (Rajya Sabha), representing the constituent units of the republic and a House of the People (Lok Sabha), elected every five years by universal suffrage.

The major political parties are Congress Party I (351 of 542 seats in the Lok Sabha), led by Prime Minister Indira Gandhi; Lok Dal (secular Janata) Party (41 seats), led by former Prime Minister Charan Singh; Congress II (anti-Gandhi) Party (13 seats); Communist (Marxist independent) Party (35 seats); Communist (pro-Soviet) Party of India (10 seats).

History. The Aryans, or Hindus, who invaded India between 2400 and 1500 B.C. from the northwest found a land already well civilized. Buddhism was founded in the 6th century B.C. and spread through northern India. The earliest exact date in Indian history is 327 B.C., when Alexander the Great invaded India.

In 1526, Mohammedan invaders founded the great Mogul empire, centered on Delhi, which lasted, at least in name, until 1857. Akbar the Great (1542–1605) strengthened this empire and became the ruler of a greater portion of India than had ever before acknowledged the suzerainty of one man. The long reign of his great-grandson, Aurangzeb (1658–1707), represents both the culmination of Mogul power and the beginning of its decay.

Vasco da Gama, the Portuguese explorer, visited India first in 1498, and for the next 100 years the Portuguese had a virtual monopoly on trade with the subcontinent. Meanwhile, the English founded the East India Company, which set up its first factory at Surat in 1612 and began expanding its influence, fighting the Indian rulers and the French, Dutch, and Portuguese traders simultaneously.

Bombay, taken from the Portuguese, became the seat of English rule in 1687. The defeat of French and Islamic armies by Lord Clive in the decade ending in 1760 laid the foundation of the British Empire in India. From then until 1858, when the administration of India was formally transferred to the British Crown following the Sepoy Mutiny of native troops in 1857, the East India Company suppressed native uprisings and extended British rule.

After World War I, in which the Indian states sent more than 6 million troops to fight beside the Allies, Indian nationalist unrest rose to new heights under the leadership of a little Hindu lawyer, Mohandas K. Gandhi, called Mahatma Gandhi. His tactics called for nonviolent revolts against British authority. He soon became the leading spirit of the All-India Congress Party, which was the spearhead of revolt. In 1919 the British gave added responsibility to Indian officials, and in 1935 India was given a federal form of government and a measure of self-rule.

In 1942, with the Japanese pressing hard on the eastern borders of India, the British War Cabinet tried and failed to reach a political settlement with nationalist leaders. The Congress Party took the position that the British must quit India. In 1942, fearing mass civil disobedience, the government of India carried out widespread arrests of Congress leaders, including Gandhi.

Gandhi was released in 1944 and other leaders later. Negotiations for a settlement were resumed, but they proved fruitless. Finally, in February 1947, the Labor government announced its determination to transfer power to "responsible Indian hands" by June 1948 even if a Constitution had not been worked out.

With the appointment at the same time of Lord Mountbatten as Governor-General, events moved swiftly. By June 1947, agreement was reached on the partitioning of India along religious lines (a plan previously opposed by the predominant Hindus and by Britain) and on the splitting of the provinces of Bengal and the Punjab, which the Moslems had claimed.

The Indian Independence Act, passed quickly by the British Parliament, received royal assent on July 18, 1947, and on August 15 the Indian Empire passed into history.

Jawaharlal Nehru, leader of the Congress Party, was made Prime Minister. Before an exchange of populations could be arranged, bloody riots occurred among the communal groups, and armed conflict broke out over rival claims to the princely state of Jammu and Kashmir. Peace was restored only with the greatest difficulty. In 1949 a Constitution, along the lines of the U.S. Constitution, was approved making India a sovereign republic. Under a federal structure the states were organized on linguistic lines.

For a considerable period the dominance of the Congress Party contributed to stability. In 1956 the republic absorbed the former French settlements. Five years later, it forcibly annexed the Portuguese enclaves of Goa, Damao, and Diu.

After a decade of independence, India was once again the target of invasion. Communist China provoked a border dispute in 1957 that proceeded by local skirmishes until Oct. 20, 1962, when the Chinese mounted a massive offensive against Ladakh in the Kashmir and against the North East Frontier Agency. After gaining much territory claimed by India, the Chinese announced a cease-fire on Nov. 20, 1962. An uneasy truce has since prevailed.

Nehru died in 1964. His successor, Lal Bahadur Shastri, died on Jan. 10, 1966, a few hours after having concluded talks with President Ayub Khan of Pakistan arranging for an interim settlement of their differences. Nehru's daughter, Indira Gandhi, became Prime Minister. She continued the policy of nonalignment and made it clear that India's only concern with Communist China was its threat to India's borders.

In 1971 the Pakistani Army moved in to quash the independence movement in East Pakistan that was supported by clandestine aid from India, and some 10 million Bengali refugees poured across the border into India, creating social, economic, and health problems. In August, India signed a friendship treaty with the U.S.S.R. and quantities of Soviet arms began to enter India. After numerous border incidents, India invaded East Pakistan and in two weeks forced the surrender of the Pakistani army and took 93,000 prisoners. East Pakistan was established as an independent state and renamed Bangladesh.

India moved further toward the U.S.S.R. in 1973 with a 15-year economic, technological, and trade cooperation agreement.

India startled the world in 1974 by exploding an atomic device made of plutonium it had surreptitiously removed from a peaceful reactor given by Canada. It became the sixth nation of the world to set off a nuclear blast, and while India disclaimed any intention to make nuclear weapons, there were widespread misgivings about its aims.

In the summer of 1975, the world's largest democracy veered suddenly toward authoritarianism when a judge in Allahabad, Mrs. Gandhi's home constituency, found her landslide victory in the 1971 elections invalid because civil servants had illegally aided her campaign. An appeal to the Supreme Court produced an interim order permitting her to continue as Prime Minister but without a vote in Parliament.

Amid demands for her resignation, Mrs. Gandhi decreed a state of emergency on June 26 and ordered mass arrests of her critics, including all opposition party leaders except the Communists. The government later admitted to 4,400 arrests; opponents put the figure at 54,000. Rigid censorship was clamped on both the national press and foreign correspondents.

Legislation extending the emergency indefinitely passed Parliament July 23. Opposition members walked out after the vote. Their boycott was still in force during the next two weeks, when unhampered Congress Party majorities successively enacted: a bill forbidding courts to invalidate the government's emergency decrees; a constitutional amendment retroactively barring lawsuits challenging the elections of high government officers, including the Prime Minister, and a bill retroactively wiping out Mrs. Gandhi's conviction in the 1971 election case.

In 1976, India and Pakistan formally renewed diplomatic relations, which had been broken off in 1971. Air and land transportation between the two nations was also restored.

Despite strong opposition to her repressive measures and particularly the resentment against compulsory birth control programs, Mrs. Gandhi in 1977 announced parliamentary elections for March. At the same time, she freed most political prisoners, including her former Deputy Prime Minister, Morarji R. Desai, and L. K. Advani, a right-wing Hindu nationalist. Press censorship was relaxed and serious defections from the ruling Congress Party began.

The landslide victory of Desai and his allies unseated Mrs. Gandhi and also defeated a bid for office by her son, Sanjay, himself a focus of much criticism as the recipient of official favors. Taking office, the 81-year-old Desai promised to "drive fear from the society" and restore morality to government.

In state elections in April, Desai's Janata Party toppled the Congress Party in eight of 10 states where the Congress Party had held power, as in the national government, since independence.

In July, Neelam Sanjiva Reddy was elected President, replacing Fakhruddin Ali Ahmed, who died February 11.

Desai moved away from Mrs. Gandhi's pro-Soviet policy, receiving a visit from President Carter Jan. 1–3, 1978, and himself visiting Carter in June. A dispute over the supply of enriched uranium to India, in which the U.S. Nuclear Regulatory Agency sought greater safeguards over its use, was resolved by Carter in India's favor in the hope that India would eventually sign the Non-Proliferation Treaty. Desai's success abroad was not matched at home, however, as economic problems and party squabbles lowered enthusiasm for the new regime.

One of the unifying factors of the Janata Party was the threat of a comeback attempt by former Prime Minister Gandhi, who regrouped a faction of the Congress Party under her leadership. Her announcement in May 1979 that she would not run for a seat in Parliament released the Janata Party's shaky bonds. The party had already been split over the inclusion of a right-wing Hindu element. Deputy Prime Minister Charan Singh's formation of a new "secular" Janata Party brought down the Desai government in mid-July and he became Prime Minister. However, he resigned the next month, but agreed to stay on and head a caretaker government.

Mrs. Gandhi staged a spectacular comeback in elections in January 1980 in which her Congress I Party defeated her rivals so badly that none won the minimum 50 seats required to qualify as an official opposition party. She followed her triumph with victories in eight of nine state legislative elections. Returned to power, Mrs. Gandhi showed a less hostile attitude toward the United States, condemning the Soviet invasion of Afghanistan and obtaining from the Carter administration approval for continued uranium shipments for India's nuclear program. She suffered a personal blow in the death of her son, Sanjay, a close personal aide, in a plane crash on June 23.

Native States. Most of the 560-odd native states and subdivisions of pre-1947 India acceded to the new nation, and the central government pursued a vigorous policy of integration. This took three forms: merger into adjacent provinces, conversion into centrally administered areas, and grouping into unions of states. Finally, under a controversial reorganization plan effective Nov. 1, 1956, the unions of states were abolished and merged into adjacent states, and India became a union of 15 states and 8 centrally administered areas. A 16th state was added in 1962, and in 1966, the Punjab was partitioned into two states.

The status of the large princely state of Jammu and Kashmir on the northwest frontier is in dispute with Pakistan. It is 85% Islamic, but its Hindu ruling prince acceded to India, which took over administration following invasion by Moslem troops in late 1947. The part occupied by India was incorporated into India in 1957.

The controversy over Jammu and Kashmir was waged in the halls of the U.N. until 1965, when India announced that its civil servants would assume administration of the state. Pakistan sent guerrillas into the territory, and India, in response, invaded in August 1965. In September the U.N. sponsored a cease-fire and stationed observers to make sure it was honored, but there were violations.

The U.S.S.R. intervened and arranged a meeting in Tashkent between Prime Minister Shastri of India and President Ayub Khan of Pakistan. With the U.S.S.R. as mediator, they reached an interim settlement, the Declaration of Tashkent, in January 1966. It provided for the withdrawal of troops, observance of the U.N. cease-fire, and continued attempts to resolve their disputes by diplomatic means.

Resolution of the territorial dispute over Kashmir grew out of peace negotiations following the two-week India-Pakistan war of 1971. After sporadic skirmishing, an accord reached July 3, 1972, committed both powers to withdraw troops from a temporary cease-fire line after the border was fixed. Agreement on the border was reached Dec. 7, 1972.

In April 1975, the Indian Parliament voted to make the 300-year-old kingdom of Sikkim a full-fledged Indian state, and the annexation took effect May 16.

Situated in the Himalayas, Sikkim was a virtual dependency of Tibet until the early 19th century. Under an 1890 treaty between China and Great Britain, it became a British protectorate, and was made an Indian protectorate after Britain quit the subcontinent.

INDONESIA

Republic of Indonesia
President and Prime Minister: General Suharto (1969)[1]
Area: 735,268 sq mi. (1,904,344 sq km)[2]
Population (est. 1980): 151,880,000
Density per square mile: 206.6
Capital: Jakarta
Largest cities (est. 1977): Jakarta, 6,178,500; **(1971 census):** Surabaja, 1,556,255; Bandung, 1,201,730; Semarang, 646,590; Medan, 635,562; Palembang, 582,961
Monetary unit: Rupiah
Languages: Bahasa Indonesia (official), Dutch, and more than 60 regional languages
Religions: Islam, 89%; Christian, 7%; Hindu, Buddhist
National name: Republik Indonesia
Freedom House classifications: Capitalist-statist pre-industrial, dominant party
Economic summary: Gross national product (1978): $48.8 billion. Average annual growth rate (1970–77): 5.7%. Per capita income: $310. Land used for agriculture: 11%; labor force: 60%; principal products: rice, cassava, soybeans, copra, rubber, coffee, palm oil, tea. Labor force in industry: 6%; major products: textiles, food and beverages, light manufactures, cement, fertilizer. Natural resources: oil, timber, nickel, natural gas, tin, bauxite, copper. Exports: oil, timber, rubber, tin. Imports: food, chemicals, textiles. Major trading partners: Japan, U.S., West Germany, Singapore.

Geography. Indonesia is part of the Malay archipelago in Southeast Asia with an area nearly three times that of Texas. It consists of the islands of Sumatra, Java, Madura, Borneo (except Sarawak in the north), the Celebes, the Moluccas, and about 30 smaller archipelagos, totaling 13,677 islands, of which about 6,000 are inhabited. Its neighbor to the north is Malaysia and to the east Papua New Guinea.

A backbone of mountain ranges extends throughout the main islands of the archipelago. Earthquakes are frequent, and there are many active volcanoes.

Government. The President is elected by the People's Consultative Assembly, whose 920 members include the functioning legislative arm, the 460-member House of Representatives. Meeting at least once every five years, the Assembly has broad policy functions. The House, 100 of whose members are appointed by the President, meets at least once annually. General Suharto was elected unopposed to a third five-year term in 1978.

The major political parties are Sekber Golkar, 232 of 360 contested seats in the House; Islamic United Development Party, 99 seats; Democratic Party, 29 seats.

History. Indonesia is inhabited by Malayan and Papuan peoples ranging from the more advanced Javanese and Balinese to the more primitive Dyaks of Borneo. Invasions from China and India contributed Chinese and Indian admixtures.

During the first few centuries of the Christian era, most of the islands came under the influence of Hindu priests and traders, who spread their culture and religion. Moslem invasions began in the 13th

1. General Suharto served as Acting President of Indonesia from 1967 to 1969. 2. Includes West Irian (former Netherlands New Guinea), renamed Irian Jaya in March 1973 (159,355 sq mi.; 412,731 sq km), and former Portuguese Timor (5,763 sq mi.; 14,925 sq km), annexed in 1976.

century, and most of the area was Moslem by the 15th. Portuguese traders arrived early in the 16th century but were ousted by the Dutch about 1595. After Napoleon subjugated the Netherlands homeland in 1811, the British seized the islands but returned them to the Dutch in 1816. In 1922 the islands were made an integral part of the Netherlands kingdom.

In World War II, the Japanese military occupation with nominal native self-government continued until August 1945. About the time of the Japanese surrender, a self-styled Indonesian Republic headed by Achmed Sukarno took over effective control of parts of Sumatra and Java. Allied forces, mostly British Indian troops, moved in, and fought the nationalists until November 1946, when Dutch-Indonesian parleys resulted in a draft agreement that contemplated the formation by Jan. 1, 1949, of a Netherlands-Indonesian Union. This would consist on the one hand of the Netherlands, the Netherlands Antilles, and Surinam and on the other of the United States of Indonesia, which was to be a sovereign nation composed of three equal states—the Republic of Indonesia, East Indonesia, and Borneo. Differences of interpretation ensued, and the Dutch resorted to force in July 1947. Both sides issued cease-fire orders the next month in response to a call from the U.N. Security Council.

On Nov. 2, 1949, Dutch and Indonesian leaders agreed upon the terms of union. Sukarno was elected president of the federation and the first all-Indonesian Cabinet was formed with Mohammed Hatta as premier. The transfer of sovereignty took place at Amsterdam on December 27, 1949.

In 1963, Netherlands New Guinea was transferred to Indonesia, and renamed West Irian. In 1973 it became Irian Jaya.

Sukarno, who had himself declared "President for Life," launched a series of guerrilla raids in 1963 to scuttle formation of the new Federation of Malaysia. A treaty between Indonesia and Malaysia in 1966 ended the open conflict. Meanwhile, with Sukarno's encouragement, Communist influence increased.

Early in 1966, Moslem students led an anti-Communist campaign that is believed to have assassinated more than 300,000 Indonesians suspected of Communist ties. Sukarno was forced in March 1966 to yield power to General Suharto, army Chief of Staff. He began a series of trials of Sukarno's associates. The Communist Party was outlawed. Sukarno was forced to give up all power on Feb. 22, 1967, and Suharto became acting President the next month.

He ended hostilities with Malaysia and established close ties with the West. Suharto introduced a "New Order" emphasizing austerity and fiscal responsibility and with Western aid of $200 million—one third provided by the U.S.—began rebuilding the country. In 1968, the Consultative Assembly elected Suharto president for a five-year term.

Suharto also permitted national elections, which moved the nation back toward representative government. The Consultative Assembly elected him unanimously for a second five-year term in 1973.

The economic and political stability achieved by the Suharto regime was tested by external events in 1975. Tightening of world money markets put serious pressures on ambitious industrial development plans underwritten by Pertamina, the state-owned oil company. Communist triumphs in Vietnam and Cambodia encouraged Jakarta toward a policy of non-alignment with any great power and toward closer relationships with other members of the Association of Southeast Asian Nations, a regional grouping of five non-Communist states.

Indonesia annexed the former Portuguese half of the island of Timor in 1976 after the provisional government of the area requested annexation.

Bankruptcy of Pertamina in 1976, and the arrest of Gen. Ibnu Sutowo as an investigation of $10 billion in debts began, dramatically reduced foreign investment. A total of $2 billion in 1975 was cut to $423 million in 1976. The government estimated that debt service for 1977–78 would offset an expected 18% gain in oil revenues.

Indonesia, as one of the countries receiving an influx of "boat people" from Vietnam, was host to a 24-nation conference in May 1979 to consider the problem. Indonesia offered Galang Island, 25 miles south of Singapore, as a refugee processing center, but took none on a permanent basis.

IRAN

Islamic Republic of Iran
President: Abolhassan Bani-Sadr (1980)
Prime Minister: Mohammed Ali Rajai (1980)
Area: 636,363 sq mi. (1,648,180 sq km)
Population (est. 1980): 38,000,000 (Iranian, Kurdish, Azerbaijani)
Density per square mile: 59.7
Capital: Teheran
Largest cities (1976 census): Teheran, 4,496,159; Isfahan, 671,825; Mashed, 670,180; Tabriz, 598,576
Monetary unit: Rial
Languages: Farsi (Persian), Kurdish, Azerbaijani
Religions: Shi'ite Moslem, 93%; Sunni Moslem, 5%
Freedom House classifications: Capitalist-statist pre-industrial, dominant party
Economic summary: Gross national product (1978): $76 billion. Growth rate (1978): 1.1%. Per capita income: $2,170. Land used for agriculture: 14%; labor force: 37%; principal products: wheat, barley, rice, sugar beets, cotton, dates, raisins, sheep, goats. Labor force in industry: 27%; major products: crude and refined oil, textiles, cement, processed foods, steel and copper fabrication. Natural resources: oil, gas, iron, copper. Exports: petroleum, carpets, raw cotton, fruits and nuts, hides and leather. Imports: machinery, iron and steel products, chemicals, pharmaceuticals, electrical equipment, agricultural products. Major trading partners: U.S., Japan, West Germany, U.K., Italy, Netherlands, Spain, France.

Geography. Iran, a Middle Eastern country south of the Caspian Sea and north of the Persian Gulf, is three times the size of Arizona. It shares borders with Iraq, Turkey, the U.S.S.R., Afghanistan, and Pakistan.

In general, the country is a plateau averaging 4,000 feet (1,219 m) in elevation. There are also maritime lowlands along the Persian Gulf and the Caspian Sea. The Elburz Mountains in the north rise to 18,603 feet (5,670 m) at Mt. Damavend. From northwest to southeast, the country is crossed by a desert 800 miles (1,287 km) long.

Government. The Pahlavi dynasty was overthrown

on Feb. 11, 1979, by followers of the Ayatollah Ruhollah Khomeini. After a referendum endorsed the establishment of a republic, Khomeini drafted a Constitution calling for a President to be popularly elected every four years, an appointed Prime Minister, and a unicameral National Consultative Assembly, popularly elected every four years.

Khomeini also instituted a Revolutionary Council to insure the adherence to Islamic principles in all phases of Iranian life. The Council formally handed over its powers to the Assembly after the organization of the legislature in July 1980, but continued to exercise power as a sort of shadow government.

History. Oil-rich Iran was called Persia before 1935. Its key location blocks the lower land gate to Asia and also stands in the way of traditional Russian ambitions for access to the Indian Ocean. After periods of Assyrian, Median, and Achaemenidian rule, Persia became a powerful empire under Cyrus the Great, reaching from the Indus to the Nile at its zenith in 525 B.C. It fell to Alexander in 331–30 B.C. and to the Seleucids in 312–02 B.C., and a native Persian regime arose about 130 B.C. Another Persian regime arose about A.D. 224, but it fell to the Arabs in 637. In the 12th century, the Mongols took their turn ruling Persia, and in the early part of the 18th century, the Turks occupied the country.

An Anglo-Russian convention of 1907 divided Persia into two spheres of influence. British attempts to impose a protectorate over the entire country were defeated in 1919. Two years later, Gen. Reza Pahlavi seized the government and was elected hereditary Shah in 1925. Subsequently he did much to modernize the country and abolished all foreign extraterritorial rights.

Increased pro-Axis activity led to Anglo-Russian occupation of Iran in 1941 and deposition of the Shah in favor of his son, Mohammed Reza Pahlavi.

Ali Razmara became premier in 1950 and pledged to restore efficient and honest government, but he was assassinated after less than nine months in office and Mohammed Mossadegh took over. Mossadegh was ousted in August 1953, by Fazollah Zahedi, whom the Shah had named premier.

Iran established closer relations with the U.S. and the West, and the U.S. began a vast program of economic and military aid. In 1955 the country joined the Central Treaty Organization (then called the Baghdad Pact). At the Shah's insistence, the government undertook a broad program of reform, especially agrarian land reform, distributing crown lands and estates to the landless peasants.

Despite Iran's role as a founding member of the Organization of Petroleum Exporting Countries, Iran did not participate in OPEC's 1973 embargo on oil shipments to the West, and it continued to supply Israel with oil during the 1973 Arab-Israeli war. But it benefited hugely from the fivefold boost in world oil prices forced by OPEC, realizing $18 billion in oil revenues in 1974. The oil profits financed an extraordinary modernization program of education, industrialization, and construction, expected to cost over $400 billion over a 13-year period.

Iran also embarked on an enormous military buildup, contracting for over $2 billion in U.S. military equipment, including modern aircraft, naval vessels, and sophisticated electronic devices.

Iran led nine other members of OPEC in raising oil prices at the end of 1976, and the refusal of Saudi Arabia and the United Arab Emirates to go along resulted in a 38% drop in Iranian oil exports. The loss of revenues forced the government to curtail its aid program. In 1977, a $2.2-billion final contract for the purchase of 160 F-16 fighter planes was signed with the U.S.

Opposition to the Shah spread, despite the imposition of martial law in September 1978, and massive demonstrations demanded the return of the exiled Ayatollah Ruhollah Khomeini. President Carter telephoned his support for the Shah, who instituted a reform program to appease critics. Riots and strikes continued despite the appointment of an opposition leader, Shahpur Bakhtiar, as premier on Dec. 29. The Shah and his family left Iran on Jan. 16, 1979, for a "vacation," leaving power in the hands of a regency council.

Khomeini returned on Feb. 1 to a nation in turmoil as military units loyal to the Shah continued to support Bakhtiar and clashed with revolutionaries. Khomeini appointed Mehdi Bazargan as premier of a provisional government and in two days of fighting, revolutionaries forced the military to capitulate on Feb. 11.

The new government canceled contracts for U.S. military equipment and training and began a program of nationalization of insurance companies, banks and industries both locally and foreign-owned. Oil production fell amid the political confusion, precipitating a fuel crisis in the U.S.

Khomeini, ignoring opposition, proceeded with his plans for revitalizing Islamic traditions. He urged women to return to the veil, or chador; banned alcohol and mixed bathing, and prohibited music from radio and television broadcasting, declaring it to be "no different from opium." More seriously, Khomeini's Revolutionary Council was reported by Amnesty International to have executed from 1,000 to 1,200 persons for having been associated with the monarchy or convicted of violating the Islamic moral code.

Revolutionary militants invaded the U.S. Embassy in Teheran on Nov. 4, 1979, seized staff members as hostages, and precipitated an international crisis. The regime denied responsibility but eventually took the militants' view that the diplomats could legitimately be imprisoned until the Shah and his assets were returned to Iran.

Khomeini refused all appeals, even a unanimous vote by the U.N. Security Council demanding immediate release of the hostages. On a New Year's trip to Teheran, U.N. Secretary-General Kurt Waldheim never saw Khomeini, and a subsequent U.N. commission of inquiry met a similar rebuff.

Election of Abolhassan Bani-Sadr as President on Jan. 25, 1980, raised hopes that his moderate stance might bring a change, but first the Revolutionary Council and then the Assembly—after elections in March dominated by the conservative Islamic Republican Party—maintained a hard line. Iranian hostility toward Washington was reinforced by the Carter administration's ineffective economic boycott and deportation order against Iranian students in the U.S., the break in diplomatic relations and ultimately an aborted U.S. raid in April aimed at rescuing the hostages.

Even the death of the deposed Shah Mohammed Reza Pahlavi on July 17 had no effect. As the first anniversary of the embassy seizure neared, Khomeini and his followers insisted on their original conditions: guarantee by the U.S. not to interfere in Iran's affairs, cancellation of U.S. damage claims against Iran, release of $8 billion in frozen

Iranian assets, an apology, and the return of the assets held by the former imperial family.

IRAQ

Republic of Iraq
President: Saddam Hussein (1979)
Area: 172,000 sq mi. (445,480 sq km)
Population (est. 1980): 13,230,000 (Arab, 75%; Kurdish, 15%; Iranian, 3.8%)
Density per square mile: 76.9
Capital: Baghdad
Largest cities (est. 1977): Baghdad, 3,205,600; **(1965 census):** Basra, 310,950, Mosul, 264,146; Kirkuk, 175,303; An Najaf, 134,027
Monetary unit: Iraqi dinar
Languages: Arabic and Kurdish
Religions: Islam, 96%; Christian, 3%
National name: Al Jumhouriya Al Iraqia
Freedom House classifications: Socialist pre-industrial, one-party socialist
Economic summary: Gross national product (1978): $22.7 billion. Average annual growth rate (1970–77): 7.1%. Per capita income (1977): $1,550. Average rate of inflation (1976–78): 10%. Labor force in agriculture: 70%; principal products: livestock, wheat, barley, cotton, fruits, vegetables. Labor force in industry: 7%; major products: petroleum, cement, textiles. Natural resources: oil, natural gas, phosphates, sulfur. Exports: petroleum, dates. Imports: manufactured goods, food grains, machinery, construction materials, livestock. Major trading partners: France, Italy, U.S.S.R., Japan, West Germany, Turkey, Brazil, U.K.

Geography. Iraq, a triangle of mountains, desert, and fertile river valley, is bounded on the east by Iran, on the north by Turkey, the west by Syria and Jordan, and the south by Saudi Arabia and Kuwait. It is twice the size of Idaho.

The country has arid desertland west of the Euphrates, a broad central valley between the Euphrates and Tigris, and mountains in the northeast. The fertile lower valley is formed by the delta of the two rivers, which join about 120 miles (193 km) from the head of the Persian Gulf. The gulf coastline is 26 miles (42 km) long. The only port for seagoing vessels is Basra, which is on the Shatt-al-Arab River near the head of the Persian Gulf.

Government. Since the coup d'etat of July 1968, Iraq has been governed by the Arab Ba'ath Socialist Party through a Council of Command of the Revolution headed by the President. There is also a Council of Ministers headed by the President.

History. From earliest times Iraq was known as Mesopotamia—the land between the rivers—for it embraces a large part of the alluvial plains of the Tigris and Euphrates.

An advanced civilization existed by 4000 B.C. Sometime after 2000 B.C. the land became the center of the ancient Babylonian and Assyrian empires. It was conquered by Cyrus the Great of Persia in 538 B.C., and by Alexander in 331 B.C. After an Arab conquest in A.D. 637–40, Baghdad became capital of the ruling caliphate. The country was cruelly pillaged by the Mongols in 1258, and during the 16th, 17th, and 18th centuries was the object of repeated Turkish-Persian competition.

Nominal Turkish suzerainty imposed in 1638 was replaced by direct Turkish rule in 1831. In World War I, an Anglo-Indian force occupied most of the country, and Britain was given a mandate over the area in 1920. The British recognized Iraq as a kingdom in 1922 and terminated the mandate in 1932 when Iraq was admitted to the League of Nations. In World War II, Iraq generally adhered to its 1930 treaty of alliance with Britain, but in 1941, British troops were compelled to put down a pro-Axis revolt led by Premier Rashid Ali.

Iraq became a charter member of the Arab League in 1945, and Iraqi troops took part in the Arab invasion of Palestine in 1948. The 1930 treaty of alliance with Britain was terminated in 1955, and replaced by a defense cooperation agreement.

Faisal II, born on May 2, 1935, succeeded his father, Ghazi I, who was killed in an automobile accident on April 4, 1939. Faisal and his uncle, Crown Prince Abdul-Ilah, were assassinated in August 1958 in a swift revolutionary coup that brought to power a military junta headed by Abdul Karem Kassim. The short-lived "Arab Union," formed by the federation of Iraq and Jordan in February 1958, came abruptly to an end with recognition by the United Arab Republic (Egypt) of the rebel government of Iraq. Kassim, in turn, was overthrown and killed in a coup staged March 8, 1963, by the Ba'ath Socialist Party.

President Abdel Salam Arif, a leader in the March coup, staged another coup in November, driving the Ba'ath members of the revolutionary council from power. He adopted a new constitution in 1964. In 1966, he, two Cabinet members, and other supporters died in a helicopter crash. His brother, Gen. Abdel Rahman Arif, assumed the presidency, crushed the opposition, and won an indefinite extension of his term in 1967. His regime was ousted in July 1968 by a junta led by Maj. Gen. Ahmed Hassan al-Bakr.

In 1970, the Baghdad government announced a settlement of the 8½-year sporadic war with the Kurds of northeastern Iraq (who spread over the border into Turkey and Iran), accepting two nationalities in Iraq (Arabs and Kurds) and promising a Kurdish vice president of Iraq and proportional Kurdish representation in a new parliament. The Kurds ultimately refused the government's terms.

The Kurdish rebellion flared anew in 1974, following collapse of an Iraqi plan for Kurdish self-rule. The rebels, armed and reinforced from Iran, withstood Soviet-supplied Iraqi forces for 11 months until Iran ended its aid under an agreement with Iraq. Some 200,000 Kurds fled to Iran and the revolt was liquidated within a month.

In 1972, Iraq signed a 15-year treaty of friendship and cooperation with the U.S.S.R. However, relations with Moscow subsequently cooled. Openly hostile by January 1980, Iraq joined other Arab states in condemning the Soviet invasion of Afghanistan.

IRELAND

President: Patrick J. Hillery (1976)
Taoiseach (Prime Minister): Charles J. Haughey (1979)
Area: 26,600 sq mi. (68,894 sq km)
Population (est. 1980): 3,400,000

Density per square mile: 127.8
Capital: Dublin
Largest cities (est. 1979): Dublin, 543,600; **(1971 census):** Cork, 128,235
Monetary unit: Irish pound (punt)
Languages: Irish, English
Religions: Roman Catholic, 95%; Protestant, 5%
National name: Eire
Freedom House classifications: Capitalist industrial, multi-party centralized
Economic summary: Gross national product (1978): $9.8 billion. Average annual growth rate (1970–77): 2.1%. Per capita income: $3,000. Average rate of inflation (1978): 8%. Labor force in agriculture: 26%; principal products: cattle and dairy products, potatoes, barley, sugar beets, hay, silage, wheat. Labor force in industry: 26%; major products: processed foods, beverages, textiles, chemicals and pharmaceuticals, machinery and construction equipment. Natural resources: zinc, lead, natural gas, barite, copper, gypsum, limestone, dolomite, peat, silver. Exports: livestock, meat, dairy products, machinery, chemicals, textiles. Imports: grains, petroleum products, machinery, transport equipment, chemicals, textile yarn. Major trading partners: U.K., Western European countries, U.S., Canada.

Geography. Ireland is situated in the Atlantic Ocean and separated from Britain by the Irish Sea. Half the size of Arkansas, it occupies the entire island except for the six northern counties of Ulster.

Ireland resembles a basin—a central plain rimmed with mountains, except in the Dublin region. The mountains are low, with the highest peak, Carrantuohill in County Kerry, rising to 3,415 feet (1,041 m).

The principal river is the Shannon, which begins in the north central area, flows south and southwest for about 240 miles (386 km), and empties into the Atlantic.

Government. Ireland is a parliamentary democracy. The National Parliament (Oireachtas) consists of the president and two Houses, the House of Representatives (Dáil Éireann) and the Senate (Seanad Éireann), whose members serve for a maximum term of five years. The House of Representatives has 148 members elected by proportional representation; the Senate has 60 members of whom 11 are nominated by the prime minister, 6 by the universities and the remaining 43 from five vocational panels. The prime minister (Taoiseach), who is the head of government, is appointed by the president on the nomination of the House of Representatives, to which he is responsible.

The major political parties are Fianna Fáil (84 of 148 seats in the Dáil), led by Prime Minister Charles J. Haughey; Fianna Gael (43 seats), led by Garret FitzGerald; Labor Party (17 seats), led by Frank Cluskey.

History. In the Stone and Bronze Ages, Ireland was inhabited by Picts in the north and a people called the Erainn in the south, the same stock, apparently, as in all the isles before the Anglo-Saxon invasion of Britain. About the fourth century B.C., tall, red-haired Celts arrived from Gaul or Galicia. They subdued and assimilated the inhabitants and established a Gaelic civilization.

By the beginning of the Christian Era, Ireland was divided into five kingdoms—Ulster, Connacht, Leinster, Meath, and Munster. St. Patrick introduced Christianity in 432 and the country developed into a center of Gaelic and Latin learning. Irish monasteries, the equivalent of universities, attracted intellectuals as well as the pious and sent out missionaries to many parts of Europe and, some believe, to North America.

Norse depredations along the coasts, starting in 795, ended in 1014 with Norse defeat at the Battle of Clontarf by forces under Brian Borv. In the the 12th century, the Pope gave all Ireland to the English Crown as a papal fief. In 1171, Henry II of England was acknowledged "Lord of Ireland," but local sectional rule continued for centuries, and English control over the whole island was not reasonably absolute until the 17th century. By the Act of Union (1800), England and Ireland became the "United Kingdom of Great Britain and Ireland."

A steady decline in the Irish economy followed in the next decades. The population had reached 8.25 million when the great potato famine of 1846–48 took many lives and drove millions to emigrate to America. By 1921 it was down to 4.3 million.

In the meantime, anti-British agitation continued along with demands for Irish home rule. The advent of World War I delayed the institution of home rule and resulted in the Easter Rebellion in Dublin (April 24–29, 1916), in which Irish nationalists unsuccessfully attempted to throw off British rule. Guerrilla warfare against British forces followed proclamation of a republic by the rebels in 1919.

The Irish Free State was established as a dominion on Dec. 6, 1921, with the six northern counties as part of the United Kingdom. Ireland was neutral in World War II.

In 1948, Eamon de Valera, American-born leader of the Sinn Fein, who had won establishment of the Free State in 1921 in negotiations with Britain's David Lloyd George, was defeated by John A. Costello, who demanded final independence from Britain. The Republic of Ireland was proclaimed on April 18, 1949. It withdrew from the Commonwealth but in 1955 entered the United Nations. Since 1949 the prime concern of successive governments has been economic development.

De Valera, who retired in 1973 after two terms in the largely ceremonial presidency, died Aug. 29, 1975, at the age of 92.

Through the 1960s, two antagonistic currents dominated Irish politics. One sought to bind the wounds of the rebellion and civil war, symbolized in 1967 by the merger of Protestant Trinity College and Catholic University College into the University of Dublin. The other was the effort of the outlawed extremist Irish Republican Army to bring Northern Ireland into the republic. Despite public sympathy for unification of Ireland, the Dublin government dealt rigorously with IRA guerrillas caught inside the republic's borders.

The 1973 election brought to power Liam Cosgrave, at the head of a coalition of the Fianna Gael and the Labor Party, unseating the Fianna Fáil, which had governed for 35 of 41 years of the republic. Cosgrave cooperated with the British government in attempts to control IRA terrorism and, after the assassination of the British Ambassador to Ireland in 1976, pushed through an Emergency Powers Act to strengthen police and court powers in combating terrorists. The unpopularity of the Act became evident after President Cearbhail O Dalaigh resigned when he was criticized by one of Cosgrave's ministers for questioning the law's constitutionality. The Fianna Fáil nominated Patrick J. Hillery to succeed Ó Dalaigh and the government named no candidate to oppose him.

The 1977 election gave the Fianna Fáil a record 84 seats in the Dáil and put John Lynch into the prime minister's post.

Although Lynch drew protests from Britain and Ulster for publicly advocating unification in 1978, he resigned on Dec. 5, 1979, amid intra-party complaints that he was too conciliatory on the issue. Health Minister Charles J. Haughey, the party's choice to suceed Lynch, was under no such handicap. An ardent nationalist, he had been forced to resign as Finance Minister in 1970 because he was accused of smuggling weapons to IRA rebels in the North.

ISRAEL

State of Israel
President: Yitzhak Navon (1978)
Prime Minister: Menachem Begin (1977)
Area: 7,992 sq mi. (20,699 sq km)[1]
Population (est. 1980): 3,870,000
Density per square mile: 484.2
Capital: Jerusalem
Largest cities (est. 1978): Jerusalem, 376,000[2]; Tel Aviv, 343,300; **(est. 1977 by U.N.):** Haifa, 227,800; Ramat Gan, 120,900
Monetary unit: Shekel
Languages: Hebrew, Arabic, English
Religions: Jewish, 85%; Islam, Christian
National name: Medinat Israel
Freedom House classifications: Capitalist-socialist industrial, multi-party centralized
Economic summary: Gross national product (1978): $15.3. Average annual growth rate (1970–77): 2.0%. Per capita income (est. 1979): $3,200. Rate of inflation (1979): 111.4%. Land used for agriculture: 20%; labor force: 48.7%; principal products: citrus and other fruits, vegetables, beef, dairy and poultry products. Labor force in industry: 25%; major products: processed foods, cut diamonds, clothing and textiles, chemicals, metal products, transport and electrical equipment, plastics. Natural resources: sulfur, limestone, rock salt, phosphates, potash, bromine. Exports: polished diamonds, citrus and other fruits, clothing and textiles, processed foods, fertilizer and chemical products. Imports: military equipment, rough diamonds, chemicals, machinery, iron and steel, cereals, textiles, vehicles, ships, aircraft. Major trading partners: Western European countries, U.S., U.K., Switzerland.

Geography. Israel, slightly smaller than Massachusetts, lies at the eastern end of the Mediterranean Sea. It is bordered by Egypt on the west, Syria and Jordan on the east, and Lebanon on the north.

Northern Israel is largely a plateau traversed from north to south by mountains and broken by great depressions, also running from north to south.

The maritime plain of Israel is remarkably fertile. The southern Negev region, which comprises almost half the total area, is largely a wide desert steppe area. The National Water Project irrigation scheme is now transforming it into fertile land. The Jordan, the only important river, flows from the north through Lake Hule (Waters of Merom) and Lake Kinneret (Sea of Galilee or Sea of Tiberias), finally entering the Dead Sea, 1,290 feet (393 m) below sea level. This "sea," which is actually a salt lake (394 sq mi.; 1,020 sq km), has no outlet, its water balance being maintained by evaporation.

Government. Israel, which does not have a written constitution, has a republican form of government headed by a president elected for a five-year term by the Knesset. He may serve no more than two terms. The Knesset has 120 members elected by universal suffrage under proportional representation for four years. The government is administered by the Cabinet, which is headed by the prime minister.

The Knesset decided in June 1950 that Israel would acquire a constitution gradually through the years by the enactment of fundamental laws. Israel grants automatic citizenship to every Jew who desires to settle within its borders, subject to control of the Knesset.

The major political parties are Likud (42 of 120 seats in the Knesset), led by Prime Minister Menachem Begin; Labor Party (33 seats), led by Shimon Peres; National Religious Party (12 seats), led by Yossef Burg; Democratic Movement (6 seats), led by Yigael Yadin.

History. Palestine, cradle of two great religions and homeland of the modern state of Israel, was known to the ancient Hebrews as the "Land of Canaan." Palestine's name derives from the Philistines, a people who occupied the southern coastal part of the country in the 12th century B.C.

A Hebrew kingdom established in 1000 B.C. was later split into the kingdoms of Judah and Israel; they were subsequently invaded by Assyrians, Babylonians, Egyptians, Persians, Macedonians, Romans, and Byzantines. The Arabs took Palestine from the Byzantine Empire A.D. 634–40. With the exception of a Frankish Crusader kingdom from 1099 to 1187, Palestine remained under Moslem rule until the 20th century (Turkish rule from 1516), when British forces under Gen. Sir Edmund Allenby defeated the Turks and captured Jerusalem Dec. 9, 1917. The League of Nations granted Britain a mandate to govern Palestine, effective in 1923.

Jewish colonies—Jews from Russia established one as early as 1882—multiplied after Theodor Herzl's 1897 call for a Jewish state. The Zionist movement received official approval with the publication of a letter Nov. 2, 1917, from Arthur Balfour, British Foreign Secretary, to Lord Rothschild, a British Jewish leader. Balfour promised support for the establishment of a Jewish homeland in Palestine on the understanding that the civil and religious rights of non-Jewish Palestinians would be safeguarded.

A 1937 British proposal called for an Arab and a Jewish state separated by a mandated area incorporating Jerusalem and Nazareth. Arabs opposed this, demanding a single state with minority rights for Jews, and a 1939 British White Paper retreated, offering instead a single state with further Jewish immigration to be limited to 75,000. Although the White Paper satisfied neither side, further discussion ended on the outbreak of World War II, when the Jewish population stood at nearly 500,000, or

1. Excluding 26,473 sq mi. (68,565 sq km) occupied in 1967 war. As of mid-1980, two thirds of the Sinai had been returned to Egypt. 2. Includes East Jerusalem.

30% of the total. Illegal and legal immigration during the war brought the Jewish population to 678,000 in 1946, compared with 1,269,000 Arabs. Unable to reach a compromise, Britain turned the problem over to the United Nations in 1947, which on November 29 voted for partition—despite strong Arab opposition.

Britain did not help implement the U.N. decision and withdrew on expiration of its mandate May 14, 1948. Zionists had already seized control of areas designated as Jewish, and, on the day of British departure, the Jewish National Council proclaimed the State of Israel.

U.S. recognition came within hours. The next day, Jordanian and Egyptian forces invaded the new nation. At the cease-fire Jan. 7, 1949, Israel increased its original territory by 50%, taking western Galilee, a broad corridor through central Palestine to Jerusalem, and part of modern Jerusalem. (In April 1950, Jordan annexed areas of eastern and central Palestine that had been designated for an Arab state, together with the old city of Jerusalem.)

The provisional leaders of the Jewish state, Chaim Weizmann and David Ben-Gurion, became Israel's first president and prime minister. The new government was admitted to the U.N. May 11, 1949.

The next clash with Arab neighbors came when Egypt nationalized the Suez Canal in 1956 and barred Israeli shipping. Coordinating with an Anglo-French force, Israeli troops seized the Gaza Strip and drove through the Sinai to the east bank of the Suez Canal, but withdrew under U.S. and U.N. pressure. In 1967, Israel threatened retaliation against Syrian border raids, and Syria asked Egyptian aid. Egypt demanded the removal of U.N. peace-keeping forces from Suez, staged a national mobilization, closed the Gulf of Aqaba, and moved troops into the Sinai. On June 5, with a simultaneous air attack against Syrian, Jordanian, and Egyptian bases and in a six-day war totally defeated its Arab enemies. Expanding its territory by 200%, Israel at the cease-fire held the Golan Heights, the West Bank of the Jordan River, the Old City, and all of the Sinai and the east bank of the Suez Canal.

Israel demanded as its new terms for peace with its Arab neighbors a guarantee that any occupied territory returned could never be used as a base for aggression. It also insisted that Jerusalem remain a unified city and that peace negotiations be conducted directly, something the Arab states had refused to do because it would constitute a recognition of their Jewish neighbor.

Egypt's President Gamal Abdel Nasser renounced the 1967 cease-fire in 1969 and began a "war of attrition" against Israel, firing Soviet artillery at Israeli forces on the east bank of the canal. Israel used its U.S. Phantom aircraft to stage heavy raids against Egyptian industrial and population centers, prompting Nasser to travel to Moscow twice in 1970 to ask for additional planes, antiaircraft missiles, and Soviet advisers. Nasser died of a heart attack on Sept. 28, 1970, and was succeeded by Anwar el-Sadat.

In the face of Israeli reluctance even to discuss the return of occupied territories, the fourth Mideast war erupted Oct. 6, 1973, with a surprise Egyptian and Syrian assault on the Jewish high holy day of Yom Kippur. Initial Arab gains were reversed when a cease-fire took effect two weeks later, but Israel suffered heavy losses in manpower. The U.S. supplied over $2 billion worth of weapons and, at a point when the U.S.S.R. threatened to intervene, put its nuclear forces on world-wide alert.

U.S. Secretary of State Henry A. Kissinger arranged a disengagement of forces on both the Egyptian and Syrian fronts, which permitted the two Arab nations to recover small amounts of territory they lost in 1967. The disengagement was supervised by U.N. peace-keeping forces, with the U.S.S.R. for the first time sharing the cost. Geneva talks, aimed at a lasting peace, foundered, however, when Israel balked at inclusion of the Palestine Liberation Organization, a guerrilla front increasingly active in terrorism directed against Israel.

At home, criticism of the ruling Labor Party's lack of preparedness cost it five seats in 1973 election, and Prime Minister Golda Meir was forced to head a minority government until her retirement on April 10, 1974. Yitzhak Rabin, a former general formed a successor government, which won narrow approval in the Knesset and, in October assembled a majority coalition.

In the same month, the PLO won recognition as the "representative of the Palestine people" in a resolution passed by the U.N. General Assembly and at an Arab summit meeting in Rabat, Morocco, where the Arab states pledged $2.3 billion in military aid to Israel's neighbors. Amid continuing terrorist attacks and counterattacks by Israeli forces, Rabin refused to negotiate with the PLO on grounds that a Palestinian homeland should be discussed between Israel and Jordan, which opposed PLO claims to the West Bank.

When Kissinger sought a second-stage agreement between Israel and Egypt for disengagement in the Sinai in January 1975, Israel insisted on a formal Egyptian pledge of non-belligerency but eventually signed a three-year agreement in Geneva in September.

The agreement required Israel to give up the strategic Mitla and Gidi passes and to return the captured Abu Rudeis oil fields. Egypt guaranteed passage of Israeli cargoes through the reopened Suez Canal, and both sides renounced force in the settlement of disputes. Two hundred U.S. civilian technicians were stationed in a widened U.N. buffer zone to monitor and warn either side of truce violations.

A U.S. commitment to give Israel $400 million in economic aid and $1 billion in weapons was then disclosed, along with the assurance of a coordinated U.S.-Israeli position in any renewed Geneva negotiations. Nevertheless, an estrangement between Washington and Jerusalem, which began with the 1974 Arab oil boycott, persisted and the solidity of the alliance became increasingly an issue in domestic politics.

For the Israelis, the July 4, 1976, rescue of 103 hostages in a hijacked Air France airliner at Entebbe, Uganda, was a stunning victory against Arab terrorism. The hijacking was the first in a year and a half to be carried out by Palestinians, in this case the Popular Front for the Liberation of Palestine. Rabin contravened government policy in opening negotiations with the terrorists but secretly prepared a commando raid on the airport. When he learned that the hostages faced death in any event, Rabin launched the airborne raid, which killed the terrorists and a score of soldiers, losing only two hostages and one rescuer.

With no progress toward permanent peace and rampant inflation causing severe economic strain, the malaise in the Labor Party deepened in early 1977 when Rabin confessed to maintaining an illegal bank account in the United States. He resigned April 8 and Defense Minister Shimon Peres was named the party's leader for general elections May 17, in which the Labor Party was defeated for the first time since Israel's founding.

Menachem Begin, 63, took office June 21 as the leader of the Likud, a coalition of conservative parties. Begin founded the Irgun Zvai Leumi (National Military Organization) to fight British rule during the Palestine Mandate. His election victory provoked a wave of negative reaction throughout the Arab world and misgivings on the part of Western proponents of a Mideast peace. Attempting to modify his image, the Likud platform on the inauguration of the new government omitted an election claim of permanent sovereignty over the West Bank and agreed to suspend the application of Israeli law to the occupied territories in general while peace negotiations were under way.

A dramatic breakthrough in the tortuous history of Mideast peace efforts occurred Nov. 9, 1977, when Egypt's President Sadat declared his willingness to go anywhere to talk peace Begin on November 15 extended an invitation to the Egyptian leader to address the Knesset. Sadat's arrival in Israel four days later raised worldwide hopes. But optimism ebbed even before Begin was invited to Ismailia by Sadat, December 25–26.

An Israeli peace plan unveiled by Begin on his return, and approved by the Knesset, offered to end military administration in the West Bank and the Gaza Strip, with a degree of Arab self-rule but no relinquishment of sovereignty by Israel. Sadat severed talks on January 18 and, despite U.S. condemnation, Begin approved new West Bank settlements by Israelis. Dissidents within the cabinet, notably Defense Minister Ezer Weizman, kept the door open for negotiations, however, and a foreign ministerial meeting of the two antagonists with U.S. Secretary of State Cyrus Vance took place in England on July 18.

Amid the continuing tension over peace negotiations, a PLO raid on Israel's coast on March 11 killed 30 civilians and provoked a full-scale invasion of southern Lebanon by Israel three days later to attack PLO bases. Israel withdrew three months later, turning over strongpoints to Lebanese Christian militia wherever possible rather than to a U.N. peacekeeping force installed in the area.

Peace talks resumed their painful progress in October as Israeli Foreign Minister Moshe Dayan and Egyptian Defense Minister Kamel Hassan Ali, with the participation of President Carter, agreed on a U.S. draft treaty.

On March 14, 1979, after a visit by Carter, the Knesset approved a final treaty, and 12 days later Begin and Sadat signed the document, together with Carter, in a White House ceremony. Begin said the occasion was the third greatest day in his life, following Israel's independence and the reunification of Jerusalem under Israeli rule. Israel began its withdrawal from the Sinai on May 25 by handing over the coastal town of El Arish and the two countries opened their border on May 29, the same day Israeli navy landing craft transited the Suez Canal for the first time.

On Palestinian automony, there was little progress. On Feb. 10, 1980, Israel inflamed Arab opinion with the Cabinet's approval of Jewish settlements in Hebron, until then an exclusively Arab West Bank city. A right-wing Israeli terrorist campaign that maimed three Arab West Bank mayors and finally, the Knesset's passage of a law annexing East Jerusalem further antagonized the Arabs and stalled the autonomy talks. The Jerusalem action drew a unanimous condemnation—in which the U.S. joined—from the U.N. Security Council and caused the last eight countries still maintaining embassies in Jerusalem to remove them in response to a Council appeal.

ITALY

Italian Republic
President: Sandro Pertini (1978)
Premier: Francesco Cossiga (1979)
Area: 116,304 sq mi. (301,225 sq km)
Population (est. 1980): 57,100,000
Density per square mile: 491.0
Capital: Rome
Largest cities (est. 1979): Rome, 2,914,600; **(est. 1978):** Milan, 1,696,250; Naples, 1,226,100; Turin, 1,172,900; Genoa, 789,500; Palermo, 687,250; Bologna, 476,800; Florence, 463,300; Catania, 399,100; Venice, 358,400.
Monetary unit: Lira
Language: Italian
Religion: Roman Catholic
National name: Repubblica Italiana
Freedom House classifications: Capitalist industrial, multi-party centralized
Economic summary: Gross national product (1978): $218 billion. Average annual growth rate (1970–77): 2.0%. Per capita income: $3,470. Land used for agriculture: 28%; labor force: 15%; principal products: wheat, rice, grapes, olives, citrus fruits. Labor force in industry: 40%; major products: automobiles, machinery, chemicals, textiles, shoes. Natural resources: fish, dwindling natural gas reserves. Exports: machinery and transport equipment, textiles, foodstuffs, chemicals, footwear. Imports: crude oil, machinery and transport equipment, foodstuffs, ferrous and nonferrous metals, wool, cotton. Major trading partners: West Germany, France, Netherlands, U.S., U.K.

Geography. Italy is a long peninsula shaped like a boot bounded on the west by the Tyrrhenian Sea and on the east by the Adriatic. Slightly larger than Arizona, it has for neighbors France, Switzerland, Austria, and Yugoslavia.

Approximately 600 of Italy's 708 miles (1,139 km) of length are in the long peninsula that projects into the Mediterranean from the fertile basin of the Po River. The Apennine Mountains, branching off from the Alps between Nice and Genoa, form the peninsula's backbone, and rise to a maximum height of 9,560 feet (2,912 m) at the Gran Sasso d'Italia (Corno). The Alps form Italy's northern boundary.

Several islands form part of Italy. Sicily (9,926 sq mi.; 25,708 sq km) lies off the toe of the boot, across the Strait of Messina, with a steep and rockbound northern coast and gentler slopes to the sea in the west and south. Mount Etna, an active volcano, rises to 10,741 feet (3,274 m), and most of Sicily is more than 500 feet (3,274 m) in elevation. Sixty-two miles (100 km) southwest of Sicily lies Pantelleria (45 sq mi.; 117 sq km), and south of that are Lampedusa and Linosa. Sardinia (9,301 sq mi.; 24,-

090 sq km), which is just south of Corsica and about 125 miles (200 km) west of the mainland, is mountainous, stony, and unproductive.

Italy has many northern lakes, lying below the snow-covered peaks of the Alps. The largest are Garda (143 sq mi.; 370 sq km), Maggiore (83 sq mi.; 215 sq km), and Como (55 sq mi.; 142 sq km).

The Po, the principal river, flows from the Alps on Italy's western border and crosses the Lombard plain to the Adriatic.

Government. The president is elected for a term of seven years by Parliament in joint session with regional representatives. The president nominates the premier and, upon the premier's recommendations, the members of the Cabinet. Parliament is composed of two houses: a Senate with 315 elective members and a Chamber of Deputies of 630 members elected by the people for a five-year term.

The major political parties are: Christian Democratic Party (262 seats of 630 in Chamber of Deputies), led by Flaminio Piccoli; Communist Party (201 seats), led by Enrico Berlinguer; Socialist Party (62 seats), led by Bettino Craxi; Social Movement Party (30 seats), led by Giorgio Almirante; Social Democratic Party (20 seats), led by Pietro Longo; Radical Party (18 seats), led by Giuseppe Rippa; Republican Party (16 seats), led by Giovanni Spadolini; Liberal Party (9 seats), led by Valerio Zanone; and Proletarian Unity Party (6 seats), led by Lucio Magri.

History. Until A.D. 476, when the German Odoacer became head of the Roman Empire in the west, the history of Italy was largely the history of Rome. From A.D. 800 on, the Holy Roman Emperors, Popes, Normans, and Saracens all vied for control over various segments of the Italian peninsula. Numerous city states, such as Venice and Genoa, and many small principalities flourished in the late Middle Ages.

In 1713, after the War of the Spanish Succession, Milan, Naples, and Sardinia were handed over to Austria, which lost some of its Italian territories in 1735. After 1800, Italy was unified by Napoleon, who crowned himself King of Italy in 1805; but with the Congress of Vienna in 1815, Austria once again became the dominant power in Italy.

Austrian armies crushed Italian uprisings in 1820, 1821, and 1831. In the 1830s Giuseppe Mazzini, brilliant liberal nationalist, organized the Risorgimento (Resurrection), which laid the foundation for Italian unity.

Disappointed Italian patriots looked to the House of Savoy for leadership. Count Camille di Cavour (1810–61), Premier of Sardinia in 1852 and the architect of a united Italy, joined England and France in the Crimean War (1853–56), and in 1859 helped France in a war against Austria, thereby obtaining Lombardy. By plebiscite in 1860, Modena, Parma, Tuscany, and the Romagna voted to join Sardinia. In 1860, Giuseppe Garibaldi conquered Sicily and Naples and turned them over to Sardinia. Victor Emmanuel II, King of Sardinia, was proclaimed King of Italy in 1861.

Allied with Germany and Austria-Hungary in the Triple Alliance of 1882, Italy declared its neutrality upon the outbreak of World War I on the ground that Germany had embarked upon an offensive war. In 1915, Italy entered the war on the side of the Allies.

Benito (Il Duce) Mussolini, a former Socialist, organized discontented Italians in 1919 into the Fascist Party to "rescue Italy from Bolshevism." He led his Black Shirts in a march on Rome and, on Oct. 28, 1922, became premier. He transformed Italy into a dictatorship, embarking on an expansionist foreign policy with the invasion and annexation of Ethiopia in 1935 and allying himself with Adolf Hitler in the Rome-Berlin Axis in 1936. He was executed by Partisans on April 28, 1945 at Dongo on Lake Como.

Following the overthrow of Mussolini's dictatorship and the armistice with the Allies (Sept. 3, 1943), Italy joined the war against Germany as a co-belligerent. King Victor Emmanuel III abdicated May 9, 1946, and left the country after having installed his son as King Humbert II. However, a provisional government held a popular plebiscite three weeks later and the Italians voted to establish a republic. On June 13, King Humbert followed his father into exile.

The peace treaty that took effect Sept. 15, 1947, required Italian renunciation of all claims in Ethiopia and Greece and the cession of the Dodecanese to Greece and of five small Alpine areas to France. In addition, the major part of the Istrian Peninsula, including Fiume and Pola, went to Yugoslavia.

The Trieste area west of the new Yugoslav territory was made a free territory (until 1954, when the city and a 90-square-mile zone were transferred to Italy and the rest to Yugoslavia). Italy was required to pay nearly $400 million in reparations, chiefly to the Soviet Union, Yugoslavia, Greece, Ethiopia, and Albania.

The government of Mario Rumor fell in 1974, following setbacks that included failure by the Christian Democrat to persuade voters to repeal the 1970 divorce law. After a 51-day crisis, a government was formed under Aldo Moro, a left-centrist Christian Democrat who had been Premier three times before.

Withdrawal of the Socialists from Moro's coalition—the 32nd government since World War II—brought his resignation Jan. 7, 1976. In the June elections, the Communists gained but the Christian Democrats still led and, warned by the U.S. and West Germany against a Communist coalition, they chose to govern as a minority under Giulio Andreotti. Petro Ingrao, a Communist, became President of the Chamber of Deputies, however, and Communists won 7 of 26 parliamentary chairmanships.

Andreotti had Communist cooperation in imposing wage limits and taxes to meet International Monetary Fund conditions for a $530-million loan. He also got Communist backing to combat a wave of kidnappings and political terrorism that culminated in the seizure of former Premier Moro in Rome on March 16, 1978, by the ultra-left Red Brigades. The discovery on May 9 of Moro's bullet-ridden body near the site of his kidnapping caused worldwide shock.

A second political shock was the resignation of President Giovanni Leone on June 15, six months before the end of his term, because of his involvement in Lockheed bribery scandals. Moro had been the leading candidate to replace him, but in the wide-open contest that ensued, 81-year-old Sandro Pertini became Italy's first Socialist president.

Tacit Communist support that had enabled Andreotti to govern ended on March 31, 1979, as the Communists insisted on seats in Andreotti's fifth cabinet and joined with the Socialists to defeat the government. Elections in June produced only one surprise—a drop in Communist strength in national voting for the first time since the beginning of the republic. The 4% loss went to splinter parties rather than to the Christian Democrats, however, leaving the political situation stalemated unless Andreotti were to accept Communist ministers.

The long crisis ended on Aug. 5, when Francesco Cossiga, a Christian Democrat, was able to form a minority coalition with the Social Democrats and Liberals. A Christian Democratic decision to bar Communists from Cabinet posts forced his resignation on March 19, 1980, but Cossiga persuaded the Socialists to join a majority coalition despite the ban on Communists. The majority held firm in his support when Communists and neo-Fascists pressed for his impeachment in July on charges that he had warned the son of a colleague to flee Italy to avoid arrest as a terrorist.

Religion. Although Italy is predominantly Roman Catholic, religious freedom is permitted. Catholic religious teaching is given in all elementary and intermediate schools. Relations with the Church were regulated until 1977, by the treaty with the Holy See of Feb. 11, 1929, which established the temporal power of the Pope over Vatican City. In November 1977, a new accord replaced the 1929 Corcordat; Catholicism is no longer to be considered as the state religion and Vatican influence on education and marriage has been reduced.

IVORY COAST

Republic of Ivory Coast
President: Félix Houphouët-Boigny (1960)
Area: 124,502 sq mi. (322,462 sq km)
Population (est. 1980): 8,250,000
Density per square mile: 66.3
Capital and largest city (est. 1975): Abidjan, 685,800
Monetary unit: Franc CFA
Ethnic groups: Agnis, Baoulés, Senoufos, Kroumen, Mandes, Dan-Gouros
Languages: French and African languages
Religions: Animist, 65%; Islam, 23%; Christian, 12%
National name: République de la Côte d'Ivoire
Freedom House classifications: Capitalist pre-industrial, one-party nationalist
Economic summary: Gross national product (1978): $6.6 billion. Average annual growth rate (1970–77): 1.1%. Per capita income: $821. Average rate of inflation (1974–78): 18%. Labor force in agriculture: 80%; principal products: coffee, cocoa, timber, palm oil, sugar, bananas. Major industrial products: food, textiles, shoes, metals. Natural resources: petroleum, iron ore. Exports: coffee, cocoa. Imports: raw materials, consumer goods. Major trading partners: France, U.S., Western European countries.

Geography. The Ivory Coast, in western Africa on the Gulf of Guinea, is a little larger than New Mexico. Its neighbors are Liberia, Guinea, Mali, Upper Volta, and Ghana.

The country consists of a coastal strip in the south, dense forests in the interior, and savannas in the north. Rainfall is heavy, especially along the coast.

Government. The government is headed by a President who is elected every five years by universal direct suffrage, together with a National Assembly of 120 members.

The Parti Démocratique de la Côte d'Ivoire, a member of the Rassemblement Démocratique Africain, is the only political party.

History. The Ivory Coast attracted both French and Portuguese merchants in the 15th century. French traders set up establishments early in the 19th century, and in 1842, the French obtained territorial concessions from local tribes, gradually extending their influence along the coast and inland. The area was organized as a territory in 1893, became an autonomous republic in the French Union after World War II, and achieved independence on Aug. 7, 1960.

The Ivory Coast formed a customs union in 1959 with Dahomey (Benin), Niger, and Upper Volta. The country is one of the most prosperous and stable in West Africa. It succeeded in getting a $10-million loan from European and U.S. private capital in 1960 for low-cost housing and other development work. It also obtained a $30-million U.S. loan to assist in construction of a $96.5-million hydroelectric project.

JAMAICA

Sovereign: Queen Elizabeth II
Governor-General: Florizel Glasspole (1973)
Prime Minister: Michael Manley (1972)
Area: 4,411 sq mi. (11,424 sq km)
Population (est. 1980): 2,200,000
Density per square mile: 498.8
Capital and largest city (est. 1974): Kingston, 169,800
Monetary unit: Jamaican dollar
Language: English
Religions: Anglican, Baptist, Roman Catholic
Member of Commonwealth of Nations
Freedom House classifications: Capitalist-socialist industrial, multi-party centralized
Economic summary: Gross national product (1978): $2.4 billion. Average annual growth rate (1970–77): −2.0%. Per capita income: $1,610. Land used for agriculture: 42%; labor force: 28%; principal products: sugar cane, citrus fruits, bananas, pimentos, coconuts, coffee, cocoa. Labor force in industry: 18%; major products: bauxite, textiles, processed foods, light manufactures. Natural resources: bauxite, gypsum, limestone. Exports: alumina, bauxite, sugar, bananas, citrus fruits, rum, cocoa. Imports: fuels, machinery, transport and electrical equipment, food, fertilizer. Major trading partners: U.S., U.K., Canada, Norway.

Geography. Jamaica is an island in the West Indies, 90 miles (145 km) south of Cuba and 100 miles (161 km) west of Haiti. It is a little smaller than Connecticut.

The island is made up of a plateau and the Blue Mountains, a group of volcanic hills, in the east. Blue Mountain (7,402 ft.; 2,256 m) is the tallest peak.

Government. The legislature is a 60-member House of Representatives elected by universal suffrage and an appointed Senate of 21 members. The Prime Minister is appointed by the Governor-General and must, in the Governor-General's opinion, be the person best able to command the confidence of a majority of the members of the House of Representatives.

The major political parties are the People's National Party (47 seats in the House of Representatives), led by Prime Minister Michael Manley; and Jamaica Labor Party (13 seats), led by Edward P. G. Seaga.

History. Jamaica was inhabited by Arawak Indians when Columbus discovered it in 1494 and named it St. Iago. It remained under Spanish rule until 1655, then became a British possession. The island prospered from wealth brought by buccaneers to their base, Port Royal, the capital, until the city disappeared in the sea in 1692 after an earthquake. The Arawaks died off from disease and exploitation, and slaves, mostly black, were imported to work sugar plantations. Abolition of the slave trade (1807), emancipation of the slaves (1833), and a gradual drop in sugar prices led to depressed economic conditions that resulted in an uprising in 1865.

The following year Jamaica's status was changed to that of a colony, and conditions improved considerably. Introduction of banana cultivation made the island less dependent on the sugar crop for its well-being. Overpopulation and problems inherited from the colonial era, such as illiteracy, produced chronic substantial unemployment, leading to much emigration to the Caribbean countries and to the U.S.

On May 5, 1953, Jamaica attained internal autonomy, and in 1958 it led in organizing the West Indies Federation. This effort at Caribbean unification failed. A nationalist labor leader, Sir Alexander Bustamente, led a campaign for withdrawal from the Federation. As the result of a popular referendum in 1961, Jamaica became independent on Aug. 6, 1962.

Michael Manley became Prime Minister in 1972 and initiated a socialist program, with higher taxes on land and luxuries and on the production of bauxite. In 1977, the government agreed to buy 51% of the Kaiser and Reynolds bauxite operations in Jamaica, ending a dispute with the U.S. companies over heavy taxes imposed earlier.

Although Jamaica's economic problems continued, the restoration of public order brought a revival in 1978 of the tourist industry, hit by civil unrest in the previous two years.

JAPAN

Emperor: Hirohito (1926)
Prime Minister: Zenko Suzuki (1980)
Area: 143,574 sq mi. (371,857 sq km)
Population (est. 1980): 116,900,000
Density per square mile: 814.2
Capital: Tokyo
Largest cities (est. 1978)[1]: Tokyo, 8,514,000; **(est. 1977 by U.N.):** Osaka, 2,723,700; Yokohama, 2,694,500; Nagoya, 2,083,500; Kyoto, 1,465,000; Kobe, 1,366,500; Sapporo, 1,307,700; Kitakyshu, 1,068,000
Monetary unit: Yen
Language: Japanese
Religions: Shintoist, Buddhist, Christian
National name: Nippon
Freedom House classifications: Capitalist industrial, multi-party centralized
Economic summary: Gross national product (1978): $836 billion. Average annual growth rate (1970–77): 3.6%. Per capita income: $6,010. Principal agricultural products: rice, vegetables, fruits, meat, natural silk. Labor force in industry: 34%; major products: machinery and equipment, metals and metal products, textiles, autos, chemicals, electrical and electronic equipment. Natural resource: fish. Exports: machinery and equipment, metals and metal products, textiles. Imports: fossil fuels, metal ore, raw materials, foodstuffs, machinery and equipment. Major trading partners: U.S., Western European countries.

Geography. An archipelago extending more than 1,000 miles from north to south in the Pacific, Japan is separated from the east coast of Asia by the Sea of Japan. It is approximately the size of Montana.

Japan's four main islands are Honshu, Hokkaido, Kyushu, and Shikoku. The Ryukyu chain to the southwest was U.S.-occupied and the Kuriles to the northeast are Russian-occupied. The surface of the main islands consists largely of mountains separated by narrow valleys. There are about 50 more or less active volcanoes, of which the best-known is Mount Fuji.

Government. Japan's Constitution, promulgated on Nov. 3, 1946, replaced the Meiji Constitution of 1889. The 1946 Constitution, sponsored by the U.S. during its occupation of Japan, brought fundamental changes to the Japanese political system, including the abandonment of the Emperor's divine rights. The Diet (Parliament) consists of a House of Representatives of 511 members, elected for four years, and a House of Councilors of 252 members, half of whom are elected every three years for six-year terms. Executive power is vested in the Cabinet, which is headed by a Prime Minister, nominated by the Diet from its members.

Emperor Hirohito, who was born April 29, 1901, succeeded his father, Yoshihito, on Dec. 25, 1926. He was married on Jan. 26, 1924, to Princess Nagako, born in 1903. They have two sons—Crown Prince Akihito (born Dec. 23, 1933) and Prince Hitachi (born Nov. 28, 1935)—and four daughters. Succession to the Japanese throne is in the male line only.

The major political parties are the Liberal Democratic Party (286 of 511 seats in the House of Representatives), led by Prime Minister Zenko Suzuki; Socialist Party (107 seats), led by Kazuo Asukada; Clean Government (Komeito) Party (33 seats), led by Yoshikatsu Takeiri; Communist Party (29 seats), led by Sanzo Nosaka; Democratic Socialist Party (28 seats), led by Ikko Kasuga; New Liberal Club (12 seats).

History. A series of legends attributes creation of Japan to the sun goddess, from whom the later emperors were allegedly descended. The first of them was Jimmu Tenno, supposed to have ascended the throne in 660 B.C.

1. Except for Tokyo, figures refer to *shi*, a minor division that may include some scattered or rural population as well as an urban center.

Recorded Japanese history begins with the first contact with China in the 5th century A.D. Japan was then divided into strong feudal states, all nominally under the Emperor, but with real power often held by a court minister or clan. In 1185, Yoritomo, chief of the Minamoto clan, was designated Shogun (Generalissimo) with the administration of the islands under his control. A dual government system —Shogun and Emperor—continued until 1867.

First contact with the West came about 1542, when a Portuguese ship off course arrived in Japanese waters. Portuguese traders, Jesuit missionaries, and Spanish, Dutch, and English traders followed. Suspicious of Christianity and of Portuguese support of a local Japanese revolt, the shoguns prohibited all trade with foreign countries; only a Dutch trading post at Nagasaki was permitted. Western attempts to renew trading relations failed until 1853, when Commodore Matthew Perry sailed an American fleet into Tokyo Bay.

Japan now quickly made the transition from a medieval to a modern power. Feudalism was abolished and industrialization was speeded. An imperial army was established with conscription. The shogun system was abolished in 1868 by Emperor Meiji, and parliamentary government was established in 1889. After a brief war with China in 1894–95, Japan acquired Formosa (Taiwan), the Pescadores Islands, and part of southern Manchuria. China also recognized the independence of Korea (Chosen), which Japan later annexed (1910).

In 1904–05, Japan defeated Russia in the Russo-Japanese War, gaining the territory of southern Sakhalin (Karafuto) and Russia's port and rail rights in Manchuria. In World War I, Japan, which took a negligible part in military operations, seized Germany's Pacific islands and leased areas in China. The Treaty of Versailles then awarded it a mandate over the islands.

At the Washington Conference of 1921–22, Japan agreed to respect Chinese national integrity. The series of Japanese aggressions that was to lead to the nation's downfall began in 1931 with the invasion of Manchuria. The following year, Japan set up this area as a puppet state, "Manchukuo," under Emperor Henry Pu-Yi, last of China's Manchu dynasty. On Nov. 25, 1936, Japan joined the Axis by signing the anti-Comintern pact. The invasion of China came the next year and the Pearl Harbor attack on the U.S. on Dec. 7, 1941.

(For details of World War II (1939–45), *see* Headline History.)

Japan surrendered formally on Sept. 2, 1945, aboard the battleship *Missouri* in Tokyo Bay after atomic bombs had hit Hiroshima and Nagasaki. Southern Sakhalin and the Kurile Islands reverted to the U.S.S.R., and Formosa (Taiwan) and Manchuria to China. The Pacific islands remained under U.S. occupation. General of the Army Douglas MacArthur was appointed Supreme Commander for the Allied Powers on Aug. 14, 1945.

A new Japanese Constitution went into effect in 1947. In 1949, many of the responsibilities of government were returned to the Japanese. Full sovereignty was granted to Japan by the Japanese Peace Treaty in 1951.

The treaty took effect on April 28, 1952, when Japan returned to full status as a nation. It was admitted into the United Nations in 1958. Japan regained its former economic position in Asia, becoming a leading producer of cotton textiles and ships. Much agitation led the U.S. to withdraw its troops in 1958.

Following the visit of Prime Minister Eisaku Sato to Washington in 1969, the U.S. agreed to return Okinawa and other Ryukyu Islands to Japan in 1972, and both nations renewed the security treaty in 1970.

Events of the 1970s tested Japan's special relationship with the U.S. Trade ties were strained in 1972 by Washington's inconclusive effort to curb textile imports from Japan. The focus of Japanese diplomacy was altered when President Nixon opened a dialogue with Peking in 1972. Prime Minister Kakuei Tanaka, who succeeded Sato in 1972, quickly established diplomatic relations with the mainland Chinese and severed ties with Formosa.

The jump in world oil prices that followed the 1973 Arab boycott squeezed Japan, which imports 85% of its oil from the Middle East. Japan greatly expanded its exports to the oil states and accepted some Arab investments.

Following Communist triumphs in Southeast Asia in the spring of 1975, Japan began moving into the diplomatic and commercial vacuum that followed U.S. withdrawal from the area.

Spending on defense in 1975 was less than 1% of the gross national product, and Japan's all-volunteer Self-Defense Forces numbered only 232,000 —12% below authorized strength.

President Ford visited Japan Nov. 18–24, 1974, the first U.S. President to do so. Substantive results were minimized by Tanaka's domestic political troubles. Tanaka resigned two days after Ford's departure, and was succeeded by Takeo Miki, a compromise choice from the progressive wing of the Liberal Democrats.

While economic recovery continued in 1976, the Lockheed scandal pursued the ruling Liberal Democrats. With the disclosure by the U.S. Senate that $6.3 million in "promotion" money had been paid by the aircraft company to Yoshio Kodama, a rightwing political "fixer," Miki was placed under strong pressure to investigate the ultimate recipients.

Former Prime Minister Tanaka himself was jailed in August, charged with having received $1.7 million of the Lockheed money in violation of exchange controls. The scandal cost the party its control of the House of Representatives in the December election, but nine independents affiliated with the Liberal Democrats to provide a narrow majority. Miki resigned, accepting responsibility for the first defeat since the party took control of the government in 1955, turning over leadership to Takeo Fukuda.

Fukuda, concentrating on economic recovery, achieved a record year in 1977, with exports exceeding imports by $9 billion, nearly twice the previous record of $5.1 billion in 1972. With the U.S. alone, Japan's favorable balance was $7.3 billion, despite a steadily falling dollar in yen terms.

Visiting Washington in May 1978, Fukuda promised "massive efforts" to reduce Japan's surplus, currently running at an annual rate of $14 billion, by cutting automobile, color television, and steel exports and by buying U.S. aircraft. In return, like other U.S. trade partners, he urged Washington to curb inflation at home and support the dollar in foreign markets.

On Aug. 12, 1978, Japan and China signed a treaty of peace and friendship that was viewed by both countries as a foreign-policy landmark. The U.S.S.R. contended that this treaty was anti-Soviet. Japanese diplomats maintained that Japan's policy toward the U.S.S.R. would not change. This pact followed an 8-year, $20-billion economic pact in which Japanese business leaders agreed to provide China with modern technology in return for Chinese natural resources.

Despite pledges to its economic partners at the Bonn summit of industrial powers in July 1978 that it would reduce its trade surplus, Japan reported an all-time high figure of $18.3 billion for the year.

Despite reduced oil consumption, Japan's oil bill of $39.5 billion for the year ended March 31, 1980, produced a record trade deficit of $14.4 billion in contrast to a $13.4 billion surplus the previous year.

A $6-billion favorable balance in trade with the U.S. brought strong pressure from the U.S. auto industry and unions for a reduction in exports of Japanese cars although an earlier voluntary restraint on television exports was dropped.

Masayoshi Ohira, Prime Minister since November 1978, died on June 12, 1980, and in national elections held June 22, the ruling Liberal Democrats reversed an eight-year decline in public support, winning a firm parliamentary majority. The party chose Zenko Suzuki, a little-known 66-year-old follower of Ohira, as the new Prime Minister.

JORDAN

The Hashemite Kingdom of Jordan
Ruler: King Hussein I (1952)
Prime Minister: Mudar Badran (1980)
Area: 37,297 sq mi. (96,599 sq km)[1]
Population (est. 1980): 3,200,000
Density per square mile: 85.8
Capital: Amman
Largest cities (est. 1978): Amman, 775,800; **(est. 1977 by U.N.):** Zarka, 263,500; Irbid, 136,800
Monetary unit: Jordanian dinar
Language: Arabic
Religions: Islam, 94%; Christian, 6%
National name: Al Mamlaka al Urduniya al Hashemiyah
Freedom House classifications: Capitalist industrial, non-party non-military
Economic summary: Gross national product (1978): $2.3 billion. Average annual growth rate (1970–77): 6.5%. Per capita income: $870. Land used for agriculture: 11%; labor force: 23%; principal products: wheat, fruits, vegetables, olive oil. Labor force in industry: 67%; major products: phosphate, refined petroleum products, cement. Natural resources: phosphate, potash. Exports: fruits, vegetables, phosphate. Imports: machinery, transport equipment, cereals, petroleum products. Major trading partners: U.S., U.K., West Germany, Japan, Lebanon, Saudi Arabia.

Geography. The Middle East country of Jordan is bordered on the west by Israel and the Dead Sea, on the north by Syria, on the east by Iraq, and on the south Saudi Arabia. It is comparable in size to Indiana.

Arid hills and mountains make up most of the country. The southern section of the Jordan River flows through the country.

Government. Jordan is a constitutional monarchy with a bicameral parliament. Its Chamber of Deputies of 60 members is elected for four years by the people, and the 30 members of the Senate are appointed by the King.

All political parties were banned in 1957.

History. In biblical times, the country that is now Jordan contained the lands of Edom, Moab, Ammon, and Bashan. In A.D. 106 it became part of the Roman province of Arabia and in 633–36 was conquered by the Arabs.

Taken from the Turks by the British in World War I, Jordan (formerly known as Transjordan) was separated from the Palestine mandate in 1920, and in 1921, placed under the rule of Abdullah ibn Hussein.

In 1923, Britain recognized Jordan's independence, subject to the mandate. In 1946, grateful for Jordan's loyalty in World War II, Britain abolished the mandate. That part of Palestine occupied by Jordanian troops was formally incorporated by action of the Jordanian Parliament in 1950.

King Abdullah was assassinated in 1951. His son Talal was deposed as mentally ill the next year. Talal's son Hussein, born May 2, 1935, succeeded him.

From the beginning of his reign, Hussein had to steer a careful course between his powerful neighbor to the west, Israel, and rising Arab nationalism, frequently a direct threat to his throne. Riots erupted when he joined the Central Treaty Organization (the Baghdad Pact) in 1955, and he incurred further unpopularity when Britain, France, and Israel attacked the Suez Canal in 1956, forcing him to place his army under nominal command of the United Arab Republic of Egypt and Syria.

The 1961 breakup of the UAR eased Arab national pressure on Hussein, who was the first to recognize Syria after it reclaimed its independence. Jordan was swept into the 1967 Arab-Israeli war, however, and lost the old city of Jerusalem and all of its territory west of the Jordan river, the West Bank. Embittered Palestinian guerrilla forces virtually took over sections of Jordan in the aftermath of defeat, and open warfare broke out between the Palestinians and government forces in 1970.

Despite intervention of Syrian tanks, Hussein's Bedouin army defeated the Palestinians, suffering heavy casualties. A U.S. military alert and Israeli armor massed on the Golan Heights contributed psychological weight, but the Jordanians alone drove out the Syrians and invited the departure of 12,000 Iraqui troops who had been in the country since the 1967 war. Ignoring protests from other Arab states, Hussein by mid-1971 crushed Palestinian strength in Jordan and shifted the problem to Lebanon, where many of the guerrillas had fled.

In the Arab-Israeli war of 1973, Jordan remained aloof, whether in deference to $30 million in annual arms aid from the U.S. or in fear of losing more territory. But in October 1974, Hussein concurred in an Arab summit resolution calling for an independent Palestinian state and endorsing the Palestine Liberation Organization as the "sole legitimate representative of the Palestinian people." This apparent reversal of policy changed with the growing disillusion of Arab states with the P.L.O., however, and by 1977 Hussein referred again to the unity of people on both banks of the Jordan.

As Egypt and Israel neared final agreement on a peace treaty early in 1979, Hussein met with Yassir Arafat, the PLO leader, on March 17 and issued a joint statement of opposition. Although the U.S. pressed Jordan to break Arab ranks on the issue, Hussein elected to side with the great majority, cutting ties with Cairo and joining the boycott against Egypt.

1. Includes territory occupied by Israel in 1967 war.

On June 15, 1978, Hussein, who had celebrated his 25th anniversary on the throne, married Elizabeth Halaby, 26, daughter of Najeeb Halaby, former president of Pan American World Airways. In an unexpected gesture, the monarch's fourth wife —his previous wife was killed and the first two divorced—was proclaimed Queen and given the name Noor al-Hussein.

Hussein visited Washington in July, and despite his refusal to soften his opposition to the Camp David agreements, he won the Carter administration's promise to sell Jordan U.S. tanks.

KAMPUCHEA

See Cambodia

KENYA

Republic of Kenya
President: Daniel Arap Moi (1978)
Area: 224,960 sq mi. (582,646 sq km)
Population (est. 1980): 15,800,000
Density per square mile: 70.2
Capital: Nairobi
Largest cities (est. 1978): Nairobi, 820,000; Mombasa, 391,000
Monetary unit: Kenyan shilling
Languages: Swahili (official), Bantu, Kikuyu, English
Religions: Protestant, 36%; Roman Catholic, 22%; Islam, 6%; Animist
Member of Commonwealth of Nations
Freedom House classifications: Capitalist pre-industrial, one-party nationalist
Economic summary: Gross national product (1978): $4.8 billion. Average annual growth rate (1970–77): 0.9%. Per capita income: $270. Land used for agriculture: 10–15%; labor force in agriculture: 23%; principal products: coffee, sisal, tea, pyrethrum, cotton, livestock. Labor force in industry: 14%; major products: plastic goods, furniture, batteries, textiles, soap, cigarettes, refined oil. Natural resources: wildlife. Exports: coffee, tea, livestock products, pyrethrum, tanning extract. Imports: machinery, transport equipment, crude oil, paper and paper products, iron and steel products, textiles. Major trading partners: Western European countries, Japan, Iran, U.S., Zambia.

Geography. Kenya lies on the equator in east central Africa on the coast of the Indian Ocean. It is twice the size of Nevada. Kenya's neighbors are Tanzania, Uganda, the Sudan, Ethiopia, and Somalia.

In the north, the land is arid; the southwestern corner is in the fertile Lake Victoria Basin; and a length of the eastern depression of Great Rift Valley separates western highlands from those that rise from the lowland coastal strip. Large game reserves have been developed.

Government. Under its Constitution of 1963, amended in 1964, Kenya has a one-house National Assembly of 171 members, elected for five years by universal suffrage. Since 1969, the president has been chosen by a general election.

The Kenya African National Union, led by the president, is the only political party.

President Jomo Kenyatta died in his sleep on Aug. 22, 1978. Vice President Daniel Arap Moi was elected to succeed him on Oct. 10.

History. Kenya, formerly a British colony and protectorate, was made a crown colony in 1920. The whites' domination of the rich plateau area, the White Highlands, long regarded by the Kikiyu people as their territory, was a factor leading to native terrorism, called the Mau Mau movement, in 1952. In 1954 the British began preparing the territory for African rule and independence. In 1961 Jomo Kenyatta was freed from banishment to become leader of the Kenya African National Union.

Internal self-government was granted in 1963; Kenya became independent on Dec. 12, 1963, with Kenyatta the first president. Kenya obtained economic and technical assistance from Communist China beginning in 1964 and later a World Bank loan.

In 1967, Kenya, Uganda, and Tanzania agreed to establish an East African trading community and a development bank. Kenya also sought to end dominance of retail trade by the Indian community of 188,000. In 1968 it began a drive against the Asians, and 20,000 left the country. In 1972, Kenyatta ordered all Asians with Kenyan passports to leave, allegedly because of foreign-currency manipulations.

KIRIBATI

Republic of Kiribati
Sovereign: Queen Elizabeth II
Governor General: Reginald J. Wallace (1980)
President: Ieremia Tabai (1979)
Area: 264 sq mi. (683 sq km)
Population (est. 1980): 60,000
Density per square mile: 227.3
Capital (est. 1974): Bairiki (on Tarawa Atoll), 17,100
Monetary unit: Australian dollar
Language: English
Freedom House classifications: Capitalist-statist pre-industrial, non-party non-military
Economic summary: Principal agricultural products: copra, vegetables. Exports: phosphates, copra. Imports: foodstuffs, fuel. Major trading partners: New Zealand, Australia.

Geography. Kiribati, formerly the Gilbert Islands, consists of three widely separated main groups of Southwest Pacific islands, the Gilberts on the equator, the Phoenix Islands to the east, and the Line Islands further east. Ocean Island, producer of phosphates, which constitute 99% of the new nation's annual income of $18 million, is also included in the two million square miles of ocean, which will give Kiribati an important fishery resource.

Government. The president holds executive power. The legislature consists of a House Assembly with 37 members.

History. A British protectorate since 1892, the Gilbert and Ellice Islands became a colony in 1915–16. The two island groups were separated in 1975 and given internal self-government.

Tarawa and others of the Gilbert group were occupied by Japan during World War II. Tarawa was the site of one of the bloodiest battles in U.S. Marine Corps history when Marines landed in November 1943 to dislodge the Japanese defenders.

Princess Anne, representing Queen Elizabeth II,

presented the independence documents to the new government on July 12, 1979.

KOREA, NORTH

Democratic People's Republic of Korea
President: Marshal Kim Il Sung (1972)
Premier: Li Jong-ok (1977)
Area: 46,768 sq mi. (121,129 sq km)
Population (est. 1980): 17,900,000
Density per square mile: 382.7
Capital and largest city (est. 1976): Pyongyang, 1,500,000
Monetary unit: Won
Language: Korean
Religions: None
National name: Chosun Minchu-chui Inmin Konghwa-guk
Freedom House classifications: Socialist industrial, one-party communist
Economic summary: Gross national product (1978): $12.5 billion. Average annual growth rate (1970–77): 5.3%. Per capita income: $590. Labor force in agriculture: 48%; principal products: corn, rice, vegetables. Major industrial products: machines, electric power, chemicals, textiles, processed foods, metallurgical products. Natural resources: coal, iron ore. Exports: minerals, chemical and metallurgical products. Imports: machinery and equipment, petroleum, foodstuffs, coking coal. Major trading partners: U.S.S.R., China, Japan.

Geography. Korea is a 600-mile (966 km) peninsula jutting from Manchuria and China (and a small portion of the U.S.S.R.) into the Sea of Japan and the Yellow Sea off eastern Asia. North Korea occupies an area slightly smaller than Pennsylvania north of the 38th parallel.

The country is almost completely covered by a series of north-south mountain ranges separated by narrow valleys. The Yalu River forms part of the northern border with Manchuria.

Government. The elected Supreme People's Assembly, as the chief organ of government, chooses a Presidium and a Cabinet. The Cabinet, which exercises executive authority, is subject to approval by the Assembly and the Presidium.

The Korean Workers (Communist) Party, led by President Kim Il Sung, is the only political party.

History. According to myth, Korea was founded in 2333 B.C. by Tangun. In the 17th century, it became a vassal of China and was isolated from all but Chinese influence and contact until 1876, when Japan forced Korea to negotiate a commercial treaty, opening the land to the U. S. and Europe. Japan achieved control as the result of its war with China (1894–95) and with Russia (1904–05) and annexed Korea in 1910. Japan developed the country but never won over the Korean nationalists.

After the Japanese surrender in 1945, the country was divided into two occupation zones, the U.S.S.R. north of and the U.S. south of the 38th parallel. When the cold war developed between the U.S. and U.S.S.R., trade between the zones was cut off. In 1948, the division between the zones was made permanent with the establishment of separate regimes in the north and south. By mid-1949, the U.S. and U.S.S.R. withdrew all troops. The Democratic People's Republic of Korea (North Korea) was established on May 1, 1948. The Communist Party, headed by Kim Il Sung, was established in power.

On June 25, 1950, the North Korean army launched a surprise attack on South Korea. On June 26, the U.N. Security Council condemned the invasion as aggression and ordered withdrawal of the invading forces. On June 27, President Harry S. Truman ordered air and naval units into action to enforce the U.N. order. The British government did the same, and soon a multinational U.N. command was set up to aid the South Koreans. The North Korean invaders took Seoul and pushed the South Koreans into the southeast corner of their country.

Gen. Douglas MacArthur, U.N. commander, made an amphibious landing at Inchon on September 15 behind the North Korean lines, which resulted in the complete rout of the North Korean army. The U.N. forces drove north across the 38th parallel, approaching the Yalu River. Then Communist China entered the war, forcing the U.N. forces into headlong retreat. Seoul was lost again, then regained; ultimately the war stabilized near the 38th parallel but dragged on for two years while the belligerents negotiated. An armistice was agreed to on July 27, 1953.

North Korea became embroiled with the U.S. again on Jan. 23, 1968, when it seized the American intelligence ship *Pueblo* and its crew of 83. After more than a year, the crew was released.

When a U.S. helicopter strayed across the 38th parallel July 13, 1977, and was shot down by North Koreans, with the loss of three crewmen, the reaction was much more restrained. President Carter acknowledged U.S. error and, after seven hours of talks at Panmunjom, the North Koreans sent back the three bodies and the lone survivor. The absence of invective was attributed to Northern appreciation of the withdrawal plan for U.S. forces in the South and there were reports that Kim wished to open direct contact with the Carter Administration.

Although Kim appears to be revered, economic troubles have beset his rigidly collectivist country. World bankers say a record of unpaid accounts due the U.S.S.R., as well as non-Communist states, has demolished North Korea's international credit standing. Its armed forces, numbering 467,000, are about three fourths of the South's military establishment, but the North's 600-plane air force holds a 3-to-1 edge over its potential foe, who has relied on U.S. air support in the event of war.

President Carter, visiting Seoul from June 29 to July 1, 1979, proposed that the U.S., North Korea, and South Korea meet "to promote dialogue and reduce tensions in the area," possibly leading to reunification of the two Koreas. Pyongyang's official party newspaper rejected the proposal, saying the North favors reunification talks but without the "alien interference" of the U.S. The paper also denounced Carter's delay of the removal of U.S. troops from the South, an action based on new assessments rating the North's troop strength as greater than the South's.

KOREA, SOUTH

Republic of Korea
President: Chun Doo Hwan (1980)
Premier: Park Choong Hoon (1980)

Area: 38,031 sq mi. (98,500 sq km)
Population (est. 1980): 38,200,000
Density per square mile: 1,000.8
Capital: Seoul
Largest cities (est. 1978): Seoul, 7,823,000; **(1975 census):** Pusan, 2,453,200; Taegu, 1,310,800; Inchon, 800,000; Kwangchu, 607,700; Taejon, 506,700; Chonju, 311,400
Monetary unit: Won
Language: Korean
Religions: Buddhist, Confucianist, Taoist, Christian
National name: Dae Han Min Kook
Freedom House classifications: Capitalist industrial, dominant party
Economic summary: Gross national product (1978): $42.5 billion. Average annual growth rate (1970–77): 7.6%. Per capita income: $880. Land used for agriculture: 23%; labor force: 38%; principal products: rice, barley. Labor force in industry: 23%; major products: clothing and textiles, processed foods, chemical fertilizers, chemicals, plywood, steel, electronics equipment. Natural resources: iron and copper ore, tungsten, graphite, limestone, coal, gold, silver. Exports: clothing and textiles, electric machinery, plywood, footwear, steel, ships. Imports: oil, ships, steel, wood, wheat, organic chemicals, machinery. Major trading partners: U.S., Japan.

Geography. Slightly larger than Indiana, South Korea lies below the 38th parallel on the Korean peninsula. It is mountainous in the east; in the west and south are many harbors on the mainland and offshore islands.

Government. The Constitution, of 1972, as modified, provides for the election of the President by a college of electors chosen by popular vote. The term of office is six years, with no limit of the number of terms. The unicameral National Assembly has 219 members, two-thirds elected by popular vote to six-year terms and the rest appointed by the President for three-year terms.

The major parties are the Democratic Republican Party (83 of 146 elective seats in the National Assembly), led by Prime Minister Park Choong Hoon; New Democratic Party (57 seats), led by Kim Young Sam; Democratic Unification Party (3 seats), and 3 independents. Of the 73 appointed members, most are aligned with the governing party.

Limited martial law was imposed after the assassination of President Park Chung Hee on Oct. 26, 1979. Total military law followed massive protests during April and May of 1980 against the growing assertion of military power by Gen. Chun Doo Hwan.

History. South Korea came into being in the aftermath of World War II as the result of a 1945 agreement making the 38th parallel the boundary between a northern zone occupied by the U.S.S.R. and a southern zone occupied by U.S. forces. (For details, *see* North Korea.)

Elections were held in the U.S. zone in 1948 for a national assembly, which adopted a republican Constitution and elected Syngman Rhee president. The new republic was proclaimed on August 15 and was recognized as the legal government of Korea by the U.N. on Dec. 12, 1948.

On June 25, 1950, South Korea was attacked by North Korean Communist forces. U.S. armed intervention was ordered on June 27 by President Harry S. Truman, and on the same day the U.N. invoked military sanctions against North Korea. Gen. Douglas MacArthur was named commander of the U.N. forces. U.S. and South Korean troops fought a heroic holding action but, by the first week of August, they had been forced back to a 4,000-square-mile beachhead in southeast Korea.

There they stood off superior North Korean forces until September 15, when ia major U.N. amphibious attack was launched far behind the Communist lines at Inchon, port of Seoul. By September 30, U.N. forces were in complete control of South Korea. They then invaded North Korea and were nearing the Manchurian and Siberian borders when several hundred thousand Chinese Communist troops entered the conflict in late October. U.N. forces were then forced to retreat below the 38th parallel.

On May 24, 1951, U.N. forces recrossed the parallel and had made important new inroads into North Korea when truce negotiations began on July 10. An armistice was finally signed at Panmunjom on July 27, 1953, leaving a devastated Korea in need of large-scale rehabilitation. The armistice contemplated an international political conference on the status of Korea, but negotiations for arranging it broke down.

The U.S. and South Korea signed a mutual-defense treaty on Oct. 1, 1953.

Rhee, president since 1948, resigned in 1960 in the face of rising disorders. Posun Yun was elected to succeed him, but political instability continued. In 1961, Gen. Park Chung Hee took power in a coup. He built up the country, maintaining an average growth rate in the economy of 8.5%. The U.S. stepped up military aid, building up South Korea's armed forces to 600,000 men. The South Koreans sent 50,000 troops to Vietnam, most of their cost paid by the U.S.

In mid-1972, following President Nixon's summit meetings in Moscow and Peking, the two Koreas issued a mutual declaration setting a goal of peaceful reunification. (For details, *see* Korea, North).

An announcement by President Carter in March 1977 that he would withdraw U.S. ground troops from South Korea within four to five years brought protests from both the Park government and opposition leaders. A U.S. pledge of $2 billion in arms aid—close to the estimated amount of savings in the troop reduction—together with a commitment that U.S. air and naval forces would stay indefinitely appeared to have reassured Koreans.

Tension between Seoul and Washington also arose over human rights as South Korean dissidents appealed for U.S. support in their demands that Park rescind both the 1972 Constitution and his 1975 emergency powers. Park responded to pressure by releasing 14 political detainees, including several Christian leaders, but not Kim Dae Jung, a former opposition presidential candidate kidnapped from Tokyo in 1973 by the Korean Central Intelligence Agency.

A growing scandal over Korean bribery of U.S. Congressmen accelerated in 1977 with testimony by a defecting ex-Director of the KCIA who named a Washington influence man, Tongsun Park, as a KCIA agent. Two former Democratic Representatives, Richard T. Hanna of California and Otto E. Passman of Louisiana, were indicted in 1978 for accepting bribes, with Hanna sentenced to six months in prison.

A Congressional investigation in 1978 charged four sitting Democratic Representatives, Charles H. Wilson, Edward R. Roybal, and John J. McFall of California, and Edward J. Patten of New Jersey, with having accepted money improperly from Park. The House voted to cut $56 million in food aid for Korea because President Park had refused to permit his former Ambassador to the U.S., Kim Dong Jo, to testify before Congressional committees.

A visit by President Carter to Seoul from June 29 to July 1 ended in a reversal of Carter's earlier decision to withdraw U.S. forces from South Korea. The decision to make no change was based on new estimates of the North's military strength at more than 600,000 troops, an increase of 125,000 from earlier estimates. It was also linked with the North's rejection of three-way talks on reunification suggested by Carter, together with President Park's receptive attitude toward Carter's plea for greater recognition of human rights in the South.

Park's assassination on Oct. 26, 1979, by Kim Jae Kyu, head of the Korean Central Intelligence Agency, at first brought a liberalizing trend as Premier Choi Kyu Hah, the new President, granted amnesty to imprisoned dissidents. The release of Kim Dae Jung, the leading foe of the former regime, on Feb. 29, 1980, aroused emotions that turned into widespread anti-government violence by May. Choi resigned on May 20, to be replaced by a military regime under Gen. Chun Doo Hwan that jailed Kim and harshly repressed opposition. As General Chun took over the Presidency on Sept. 1, however, he promised an early return to constitutional government.

KUWAIT

State of Kuwait
Emir: Sheik Jaber al-Ahmad al-Sabah (1977)
Prime Minister: Sheik Sa'ad Abdullah al-Sabah (1978)
Area: 7,780 sq mi. (20,150 sq km)
Population (est. 1980): 1,340,000
Density per square mile: 172.2
Capital (est. 1975): Kuwait, 78,000
Largest city (est. 1975): Hawalli, 130,300
Monetary unit: Kuwaiti dinar
Languages: Arabic and English
Religions: Islam, 95%; Christian, 5%
National name: Dowlat al Kuwait
Freedom House classifications: Capitalist-statist industrial, non-party non-military
Economic summary: Gross national product (1978): $18.0 billion. Average annual growth rate (1970–77): −0.9%. Land used for agriculture: 1%. Labor force in industry: 22%; major products: crude and refined oil, fertilizer, chemicals, building materials, shrimp. Natural resources: petroleum, fish, shrimp. Exports: crude and refined petroleum, shrimp. Imports: foodstuffs, automobiles, building materials, machinery, textiles. Major trading partners: Japan, U.S., U.K., West Germany.

Geography. Kuwait is situated northeast of Saudi Arabia at the northern end of the Persian Gulf, south of Iraq. It is slightly larger than Hawaii. The low-lying land is mainly sandy and barren.

Government. Sheik Jaber al-Ahmad al-Sabah rules as Emir of Kuwait and appoints the Prime Minister, who appoints his Cabinet (Council of Ministers). The National Assembly, consisting of 50 members elected by adult males, has been suspended. There are no political parties in Kuwait.

History. Kuwait obtained British protection in 1897 when the Sheik feared that the Turks would take over the area. In 1961, Britain ended the protectorate, giving Kuwait independence, but agreed to give military aid on request. Iraq immediately threatened to occupy the area and Sheik Sabah al-Salem al-Sabah called in British troops in 1961. Soon afterward the Arab League sent in troops, replacing the British. The prize was oil.

Oil was discovered in the 1930s. Kuwait proved to have 20% of the world's known oil resources. It has been a major producer since 1946, the world's second largest oil exporter, with the main concession held by a British-American concern. The Sheik, who gets half the profits, devotes most of them to the education, welfare, and modernization of his kingdom. In 1966, Sheik Sabah designated a relative, Jaber al-Ahmad al-Sabah, as his successor. By 1968, the sheikdom had established a model welfare state, and it sought to establish dominance among the sheikdoms and emirates of the Persian Gulf.

Kuwait contributed generously to Egypt and Jordan after the 1967 war with Israel and supported the 1973 war against Israel with funds and by joining the Arab oil boycott of Western nations.

Quadrupling of prices following the embargo sent Kuwait's oil profits rocketing from $2 billion in 1973 to almost $9 billion in 1974, with $7 billion estimated for 1975, when the oil output was reduced somewhat. With per capita income at about $11,000—nearly twice that of the U.S.—little Kuwait became an overnight financial power. It financed domestic improvements on a lavish scale, sponsored a foreign-aid program for favored Arab and African states, and ploughed over $10 billion into profitable corporate investments overseas.

In 1975, the government nationalized Kuwaiti operations of Gulf Oil and British Petroleum. The acquisition, which cost about $180 million, gave Kuwait full control of an estimated 60 billion barrels of petroleum reserves.

LAOS

Lao People's Democratic Republic
President: Souphanouvong (1975)
Premier: Kaysone Phomvihane (1975)
Area: 91,429 sq mi. (236,800 sq km)
Population (est. 1980): 3,700,000
Density per square mile: 40.5
Capital and largest city (est. 1978): Vientiane, 200,000
Monetary unit: Kip
Languages: Lao (official); French, English
Religion: Buddhist
Freedom House classifications: Socialist pre-industrial, one-party communist
Economic summary: Gross national product: (1978): $300 million. Per capita income (1976): $70. Labor force in agriculture: 85%; principal products: rice, corn, vegetables. Major industrial products: tin, timber, tobacco, textiles, electric power. Natural resources: tin, timber, hydroelectric power. Exports: electric power, forest products, tin concentrates, coffee. Imports: rice, foodstuffs, petroleum products, machinery, transport equipment. Major trading partners: Thailand, U.S.S.R., Malaysia, France, China.

Geography. A landlocked nation in Southeast Asia

occupying the northwestern portion of the Indochinese peninsula, Laos is surrounded by China, Vietnam, Cambodia, Thailand, and Burma. It is twice the size of Pennsylvania.

Laos is a mountainous country, especially in the north, where peaks rise above 8,000 feet (2,438 m). Dense forests cover the northern and eastern areas. The Mekong River flows through the country for 300 miles (483 km) of its course.

Government. Laos is a people's democratic republic with executive power in the hands of the premier. The monarchy was abolished Dec. 2, 1975, when the Pathet Lao ousted a coalition government and King Sisavang Vatthana abdicated. The King was appointed "Supreme Adviser" to the President, the former Prince Souphanouvong. Former Prince Souvanna Phouma, Premier since 1962, was made an "adviser" to the government. The Lao People's Revolutionary Party (Pathet Lao), led by President Souphanouvong and Premier Kaysone Phomvihane, is the only political party.

History. Laos became a French protectorate in 1893, and the territory was incorporated into the union of Indochina. A strong nationalist movement developed during World War II, but France re-established control in 1946 and made the King of Luang Prabang constitutional monarch of all Laos. France granted semiautonomy in 1949 and then, spurred by the Viet Minh rebellion in Vietnam, full independence within the French Union in 1950. In 1951, Prince Souphanouvong organized the Pathet Lao, a Communist independence movement, in North Vietnam. The Viet Minh in 1953 established the Pathet Lao in power at Samneua. Viet Minh and Pathet Lao forces invaded central Laos, and civil war resulted.

By the Geneva agreements of 1954 and an armistice of 1955, two northern provinces were given the Pathet Lao, the royal regime the rest. Full sovereignty was given the kingdom by the Paris agreements of Dec. 29, 1954. In 1957, Prince Souvanna Phouma, the royal Premier, and the Pathet Lao leader, Prince Souphanouvong, the Premier's half-brother, agreed to re-establishment of a unified government, with Pathet Lao participation and integration of Pathet Lao forces into the royal army. The agreement broke down in 1959, and armed conflict broke out again.

In 1960, the struggle became three-way as Gen. Phoumi Nosavan, controlling the bulk of the royal army, set up in the south a pro-Western revolutionary government headed by Prince Boun Gum. General Phoumi took Vientiane in December, driving Souvanna Phouma into exile in Cambodia. The Soviet bloc supported Souvanna Phouma. In 1961, a cease-fire was arranged and the three princes agreed to a coalition government headed by Souvanna Phouma.

But North Vietnam, the U.S. (in the form of Central Intelligence Agency personnel), and China remained active in Laos after the settlement. North Vietnam used a supply line (Ho Chi Minh trail) running down the mountain valleys of eastern Laos into Cambodia and South Vietnam, particularly after the U.S.-South Vietnamese incursion into Cambodia in 1970 stopped supplies via Cambodian seaports.

An agreement, reached in 1973 revived coalition government. Royal Laotian rule continued in populous areas, the Pathet Lao controlled the mountainous east, and the two groups exercised joint rule over Vientiane Province. With Souvanna Phouma as premier and Souphanouvong as president of a 42-member National Political Council representing both factions, joint operation of the government began.

Laotian officials confirmed in March 1979 the presence of 30,000 Vietnamese troops in Laos and their use of the country as a staging area for the Vietnamese invasion of Cambodia. They also confirmed that 1,000 Laotian troops were in Cambodia in support of the Heng Samrin regime, which overthrew the Pol Pot government in January.

LEBANON

Republic of Lebanon
President: Elias Sarkis (1976)
Premier: Selim al-Hoss (1976)
Area: 4,015 sq mi. (10,400 sq km)
Population (est. 1980): 3,170,000
Density per square mile: 789.5
Capital: Beirut
Largest cities (est. 1975): Beirut, 1,172,000; (est. 1964): Tripoli, 127,600
Monetary unit: Lebanese pound
Languages: Arabic (official); French, English
Religions: Christian and Islam
National name: Al-Joumhouriya al-Lubnaniya
Freedom House classifications: Capitalist industrial, multi-party decentralized
Economic summary: Gross national product (1973): $3 billion. Annual growth rate: 7–10%. Per capita income: $730. Land used for agriculture: 27%; labor force: 49%; principal products: fruits, wheat, corn, barley, potatoes, tobacco, olives, onions. Labor force in industry: 11%; major products: processed foods, textiles, cement, chemicals, refined oil; tourism. Exports: fruits, vegetables, textiles. Imports: metals, machinery, foodstuffs. Major trading partners: U.S., Western European and Arab countries.

Geography. Lebanon lies at the eastern end of the Mediterranean Sea north of Israel and west of Syria. It is four fifths the size of Connecticut.

The Lebanon Mountains, which parallel the coast on the west, cover most of the country, while on the eastern border is the Anti-Lebanon range. Between the two lies the El Bika Valley, the principal agricultural area.

Government. Lebanon is governed by a President, elected by Parliament for a six-year term, and a Cabinet of Ministers appointed by the President but responsible to Parliament.

Parliament has 99 members elected for a four-year term by universal suffrage and chosen by proportional division of religious groups.

Party breakdown of the Chamber of Deputies is difficult because of the religious groupings required by law and because many deputies join in major parliamentary blocs—Democratic Front, Tri-Partite Coalition, and National Struggle Front. The parties represented in Parliament are: Al-Kataib, led by Pierre Al-Jumayeh; Al-Wataniyin Al-Ahrar, led by Camille Chamoun; Al-Takadumi Al-Ishteraki; Al-Kutla Al-Wataniya, led by Raymond Edde; Al-Dimocrati Al-Eshteraki, led by Kamel El-Assad.

History. In ancient times Lebanon was the mountainous hinterland of the Phoenician coast towns. From the 7th to the 11th century there infiltrated into southern Lebanon the heretics of Islam, who finally coalesced into the Druse community.

In the 19th century the Turkish Sultanate encouraged the Druses to wage civil war against the Christian Maronites. After a massacre of 2,500 Christians in 1860, Lebanon was occupied by the French for a year. From 1864 to 1914, a Christian military government ruled the area under nominal Turkish sovereignty. After World War I, France received a League of Nations mandate over Syria and Lebanon. The French drew a Lebanese border in 1920 to offset predominantly Moslem Syria and proclaimed the area a republic under French control on May 23, 1926. Complete independence came on Nov. 26, 1941. Lebanon joined the Arab League and took part in the invasion of Palestine on May 15, 1948.

In 1958, a civil war broke out, with the Moslems Kamal Jumblatt and Saeb Salam leading the opposition to the Maronite Christian government. Threatened with defeat, President Camille Chamoun obtained the intervention of U.S. military forces. In September, a Maronite Christian military man, Gen. Fouad Chehab, took over the presidency. After a U.N. resolution demanded it, the U.S. forces withdrew.

Palestinian guerrillas using Lebanese territory drew Lebanon into conflict with Israel. Terrorist attacks on Israeli airliners led to an Israeli raid on Arab airlines at Beirut, and terrorist assaults on Israel's northern settlements drew punitive raids against guerrillas in Lebanon by Israeli army and air units. Lebanon appeared powerless.

Intensifying civil war through 1976 led to the ousting of President Suleiman Franjieh by Parliament in May after the virtual destruction of Beirut. Franjieh refused to step down until the end of his six-year term in October when his successor, Elias Sarkis, took office.

At the time of Sarkis' inauguration, Lebanon was divided into a northern sector, controlled by Syrian troops who had entered the country to restore order, and a coastal region under Christian control, with enclaves where leftist Moslems and the Palestine Liberation Organization dominated. With the economy shattered and an estimated 40,000 dead in 18 months of war, many felt that the country might be dismembered.

Notwithstanding flare-ups of civil strife, an Arab League committee of Syria, Egypt, Saudi Arabia, and Kuwait appeared by mid-1977 to have stabilized a reunited Lebanon. Banks had reopened and reconstruction of Beirut began. Although Palestinian guerrilla strength had been reduced, those who remained in Lebanon still constituted a threat to peace, and the Christian Lebanese Front called on the Arab League to resolve the problem of the Palestinians' "illegal presence."

A new crisis began for Lebanon on March 14, 1978, with the invasion of Israeli forces across the entire 60-mile northern border to a depth of from 4 to 10 miles. The invasion was in retaliation for a PLO terrorist raid on Israel and the chief targets were PLO bases in southern Lebanon. On March 19, the U.N. Security Council called for immediate withdrawal and authorized a 4,000-man peacekeeping force to occupy the area, a force later enlarged to 6,000.

Israeli troops withdrew by June but turned over more strongpoints to Lebanese Christian militia than to UNIFIL, the U.N. force. Israel asserted that UNIFIL was allowing PLO guerrillas to infiltrate the border region, threatening Israel as well as the Lebanese Christians in the area. Efforts to establish a Lebanese army "presence" in Southern Lebanon failed, and UNIFIL was supervising a shaky peace a year later, with little prospect of a return to normal.

In Beirut, as Syrian forces withdrew from the city during 1980, the two biggest Christian factions fought a bloody battle, July 7–8, in which more than 300 died. the Phalangist Party claimed total victory over the National Liberal Party of former President Camille Chamoun, and the losers agreed to merge their militia forces into a single force called the National Home Guard.

LESOTHO

Kingdom of Lesotho
Sovereign: King Moshoeshoe II (1966)
Prime Minister: Chief Leabua Jonathan (1966)
Area: 11,720 sq mi. (30,355 sq km)
Population (est. 1980): 1,340,000
Density per square mile: 114.3
Capital and largest city (est. 1976): Maseru, 14,700
Monetary unit: Maloti
Languages: English and Sesotho (official)
Religions: Roman Catholic, 39%; Lesotho Evangelical Church, 24%; Anglican, 10%; non-Christian, 18%
Member of Commonwealth of Nations
Freedom House classifications: Capitalist pre-industrial, dominant party
Economic summary: Gross national product (1978): $360 million. Average annual growth rate (1970–77) 9.9%. Per capita income: $270. Land used for agriculture: 13%; labor force: 50%; principal products: corn, wheat, sorghum, barley, livestock. Labor force in industry: 2%. Natural resources: diamonds. Exports: wool, mohair, wheat, cattle, diamonds, hides and skins. Imports: corn, building materials, clothing, vehicles, machinery. Major trading partner: South Africa.

Geography. Mountainous Lesotho, the size of Maryland, is surrounded by the Republic of South Africa in the east central part of that country except for short borders on the east and south with two discontinuous units of the Republic of Transkei. The Drakensberg Mountains in the east are Lesotho's principal chain. Elsewhere the region consists of rocky tableland.

Government. There is a 93-member interim National Assembly made up of 60 representatives of various political parties, 22 leading chiefs, and 11 appointees.

The major political parties are the Basotho National Party, led by Prime Minister Leabua Jonathan and the Basutoland Congress Party led by G. P. Ramoreboli.

History. Lesotho (formerly Basutoland) was constituted a native state under British protection by a treaty signed with the native chief Moshesh in 1843. It was annexed to Cape Colony in 1871, but in 1884 it was restored to direct control by the Crown.

The colony of Basutoland became the independent nation of Lesotho on Oct. 4, 1966.

In the 1970 elections, Ntsu Mokhehle, head of the Basutoland Congress Party, claimed a victory, but Jonathan declared a state of emergency, suspended the Constitution, and arrested Mokhehle. The major issue in the election was relations with South Africa, with Jonathan for close ties to the surrounding white nation, while Mokhehle was for a more independent policy. Jonathan jailed 45 opposition politicians, declared the King had "technically abdicated" by siding with the opposition party, exiled him to the Netherlands, and named his Queen and her seven-year-old son as Regent.

The King returned after a compromise with Jonathan in which the new Constitution would name him head of state but forbid his participation in politics.

LIBERIA

Republic of Liberia
President: Master Sgt. Samuel K. Doe (1980)
Area: 43,000 sq mi. (111,370 sq km)
Population (est. 1980): 1,860,000
Density per square mile: 43.3
Capital and largest city (est. 1978): Monrovia, 229,300
Monetary unit: Liberian dollar
Languages: English (official) and tribal dialects
Religions: Protestant Christian, Islam, Catholic, Animist
Freedom House classifications: Capitalist pre-industrial, one-party nationalist
Economic summary: Gross national product (1978): $820 million. Average annual growth rate (1970–77): 1.1%. Per capita income: $600. Land used for agriculture: 20%; labor force: 75%; principal products: rubber, rice, palm oil, cassava, coffee, cocoa. Labor force in industry: 25%; major products: iron ore, diamonds, processed rubber, processed food, construction materials. Natural resources: iron ore, rubber, timber, diamonds. Exports: iron ore, rubber, timber, diamonds. Imports: machinery, petroleum products, transport equipment, foodstuffs. Major trading partners: U.S., West Germany, Netherlands, Italy, Belgium.

Geography. Lying on the Atlantic in the southern part of West Africa, Liberia is bordered by Sierra Leone, Guinea, and the Ivory Coast. It is comparable in size to Tennessee.

Most of the country is a plateau covered by dense tropical forests, which thrive under an annual rainfall of about 160 inches a year.

Government. On April 12, 1980, enlisted men of the Liberian army, led by Master Sgt. Samuel K. Doe, overthrew the civilian government and executed President William R. Tolbert, Jr., and 27 others. A Cabinet of five soldiers and 10 civilians, including Gabriel Baccus Matthews, leader of the opposition Progressive People's Party who had been jailed by Tolbert, was briefly installed, but it was soon replaced by the exclusively military People's Redemptive Council. The 17-member Council suspended the Constitution and assumed all executive and legislative powers on April 25.

History. Liberia was founded in 1822 as a result of the efforts of the American Colonization Society to settle freed American slaves in West Africa. In 1847, it became the Free and Independent Republic of Liberia.

The government of Africa's first republic was modeled after that of the United States, and Joseph J. Roberts of Virginia was elected the first president. He laid the foundations of a modern state and initiated efforts, never too successful but pursued for more than a century, to bring the aboriginal inhabitants of the territory to the level of the emigrants. The English-speaking descendants of U.S. blacks, known as Americo-Liberians, are the intellectual and ruling class. The indigenous inhabitants, divided, constitute 99% of the population.

The country's only big enterprises are the million-acre concession granted in 1925 to the Firestone Plantations Co. for rubber cultivation, and a large iron ore concession developed by the Republic Steel Corp., beginning in 1951. After 1920, considerable progress was made toward opening up the interior, a process that was spurred in 1951 by the establishment of a 43-mile (69-km) railroad to the Bomi Hills from Monrovia.

In July 1971, while serving his sixth term as president, William V. S. Tubman died following surgery and was succeeded by his long-time associate, Vice President William R. Tolbert, Jr.

LIBYA

People's Socialist Libyan Arab Public
Head of State: Col. Muammar el-Qaddafi (1969)
Secretary-General of the General People's Congress: 'Abd al-Ati Ubaydi (1979)
Premier: Jadallah Azzuz et Talhi (1979)
Area: 679,536 sq mi. (1,759,998 sq km)
Population (est. 1980): 2,950,000
Density per square mile: 4.3
Capital: Tripoli
Largest cities (est. 1978): Tripoli, 800,000; **(1973 census):** Bengasi, 282,192
Monetary unit: Libyan dinar
Language: Arabic
Religion: Islam
National name: Al-Jumhuria al-Arabia al-Libya
Freedom House classifications: Capitalist-statist industrial, one-party socialist
Economic summary: Gross national product (1978): $19 billion. Average annual growth rate (1970–77): –4.5%. Per capita income: $6,260. Land used for agriculture: 7%; labor force: 20%; principal products: wheat, barley, olives, dates, citrus fruits, peanuts. Labor force in industry: 10%; major products: petroleum, processed foods, textiles, handicrafts. Natural resources: petroleum, natural gas. Export: petroleum. Imports: machinery, foodstuffs, manufactured goods. Major trading partners: Italy, West Germany, U.S., U.K., France.

Geography. Libya stretches along the northeastern coast of Africa between Tunisia and Algeria on the west and Egypt on the east; to the south are the Sudan, Chad, and Niger. It is one sixth larger than Alaska.

A greater part of the country lies within the Sahara. There are many oases along the Mediterranean coast; farther inland is arable plateau land.

Government. In a bloodless coup d'etat on Sept. 1, 1969, the military seized power in Libya. King Idris I, who had ruled since 1951, was deposed and the Libyan Arab Republic proclaimed. The official name was changed in 1977 to People's Socialist Libyan Arab Public. The Revolutionary Council that had governed since the coup was renamed the General Secretariat of the General People's Congress. The Arab Socialist Union Organization is the only political party.

History. Libya was a part of the Turkish dominions from the 16th century until 1911. Following the outbreak of hostilities between Italy and Turkey in that year, Italian troops occupied Tripoli; Italian sovereignty was recognized in 1912.

Libya was the scene of much desert fighting during World War II. After the fall of Tripoli on Jan. 23, 1943, it came under Allied administration. In 1949, the U.N. voted that Libya should become independent by 1952.

Discovery of oil in the Libyan Desert promised financial stability and funds for economic development. Although maintaining cordial relations with the U.S., the government asked for evacuation of the U.S. Wheelus air base by 1971. The first crude oil moved in January 1967 through the 320-mile pipeline from the Sarir oil field to Tobruk, where it was loaded on British tankers. The flow was halted in June, when Libya joined the Arab oil boycott of Britain and the U.S. as a result of the Middle East war but was soon resumed thereafter.

In 1974, President Muammar el-Qaddafi gave up his domestic political powers to Premier Abdul Salam Jallud, but remained the leader in foreign affairs.

In 1975, following a visit by Soviet Premier Alexei N. Kosygin, a major deal for Soviet arms sales to Libya, reported to involve $1 billion to $4 billion in modern military equipment, was concluded. It was followed by a Soviet agreement to supply Libya with a nuclear research reactor in the 2–10 megawatt range.

On July 21, 1977, a four-day war broke out between Libya and Egypt, with Egypt charging that Libyans had attacked a frontier post. Superior Egyptian air power and armor inflicted losses on their opponents and the clash ended after Algerian President Houari Boumediène intervened as peacemaker.

Another military adventure by Qaddafi ended ignominiously in April 1979 with the defeat of a Libyan force of 2,000 sent to the aid of Uganda's President Idi Amin against Ugandan rebels and Tanzanian forces. Qaddafi offered asylum to the ousted Amin and his family.

The United States closed its embassy in Tripoli on Feb. 7 amid growing U.S.-Libyan tension. Four members of the Libyan embassy in Washington were expelled on May 11 for threatening Libyan students in the United States and on July 14 a scandal erupted as Billy Carter, brother of the President, was disclosed to have registered as a Libyan agent. Subsequent information that Billy had received $220,000 from Libyan officials launched a Senate investigation, and the case became an important issue in the presidential election.

In September, Libya and Syria announced that they had agreed on merging the two countries but gave no details on the implementation of the move.

LIECHTENSTEIN

Principality of Liechtenstein
Ruler: Prince Franz Josef II (1938)
Prime Minister: Hans Brunhart (1978)
Area: 61 sq mi. (157 sq km)
Population (est. 1980): 25,000
Density per square mile: 409.8
Capital and largest city (est. 1976: Vaduz, 4,620
Monetary unit: Swiss franc
Language: German (Alemannish dialect)
Religion: Roman Catholic
Economic summary: Per capita income: $16,864. Labor force in agriculture: 4%; principal products: livestock, vegetables, corn, wheat, potatoes, grapes. Labor force in industry: 50%; major products: high-technology products, building equipment, food products, machinery, industrial goods. Natural resources: timber, hydroelectric power, salt. Exports: manufactured metal products, machines and instruments, textiles, chemical products. Imports: raw materials, machinery, processed foods and goods. Major trading partners: Finland, Switzerland and other Western European countries.

Geography. Tiny Liechtenstein, not quite as large as Washington, D.C., lies on the east bank of the Rhine River south of Lake Constance between Austria and Switzerland. It consists of low valley land and Alpine peaks. Falknis (8,401 ft; 2,561 m) and Naatkopf (8,432 ft; 2,570 m) are the tallest.

Government. The Constitution of 1921, amended in 1972, provides for a legislature, the Landtag, of 15 members elected by direct suffrage.

The ruler, Prince Franz Josef II, was born in 1906 and succeeded his great-uncle, Franz I, in 1938. In 1943 he married Countess Gina Wilczek of Austria.

The major political parties are the Homeland Union (8 of 15 seats in the Landtag) and the Progressive Citizens Party (7 seats).

History. Founded in 1719, Liechtenstein was a member of the German Confederation from 1815 to 1866, when it became an independent principality. It abolished its army in 1868 and has managed to stay neutral and undamaged in all European wars since then. It also remained free of ties until after World War I. Since then, it has been oriented toward Switzerland.

LUXEMBOURG

Grand Duchy of Luxembourg
Ruler: Grand Duke Jean (1964)
Premier: Pierre Werner (1979)
Area: 999 sq mi. (2,586 sq km)
Population (est. 1980): 365,000. (Luxembourgian, French, German)
Density per square mile: 365.4
Capital and largest city (est. 1977): Luxembourg, 76,500
Monetary unit: Luxembourg franc
Languages: Letzeburgesch, French, German
Religion: Mainly Roman Catholic
National name: Grand-Duché de Luxembourg
Freedom House classifications: Capitalist industrial, multi-party centralized
Economic summary: Gross national product (1978): $3.7 billion. Average annual growth rate (1970–77): 4.4%. Per capita income: $6,900. Land used for agriculture: 45%; labor force: 6%; principal products: livestock, dairy products, wine. Labor force in industry: 46%; major products: steel, rubber, synthetic fibers. Natural resource: Iron ore. Export: steel. Imports: machinery,

textiles, transport equipment, plastics. Major trading partners: European Common Market countries.

Geography. Luxembourg is a neighbor of Belgium on the west, West Germany on the east, and France on the south. The Ardennes Mountains extend from Belgium into the northern section of Luxembourg.

Government. Luxembourg's unicameral legislature, the Chamber of Deputies, consists of 59 members elected for five years.

The major political parties are the Christian Social Party (24 of 59 seats in Chamber of Deputies), led by Jacques Senter; Socialist-Labor (14 seats), led by Lydie Schmit; Democratic Party (15 seats), led by Premier Pierre Werner; Social Democratic Party (5 seats), led by Henry Cravatte; Communist Party (5 seats), led by René Urbany.

History. Sigefroi, Count of Ardennes, an offspring of Charlemagne, was Luxembourg's first sovereign ruler. In 1060, the country came under the rule of the House of Luxembourg. From the 15th to the 18th century, Spain, France, and Austria held it in turn. The Congress of Vienna in 1815 made it a Grand Duchy and gave it to William I, King of the Netherlands. In 1839 the Treaty of London ceded the western part of Luxembourg to Belgium.

The eastern part, continuing in personal union with the Netherlands and a member of the German Confederation, became autonomous in 1848 and a neutral territory by decision of the London Conference of 1867, governed by its Grand Duke. Germany occupied the duchy in World Wars I and II. Allied troops liberated the enclave in 1944.

In 1961, Prince Jean, son and heir of Grand Duchess Charlotte, was made head of state, acting for his mother. She abdicated in 1964, and Prince Jean became Grand Duke.

By a customs union between Belgium and Luxembourg, which came into force on May 1, 1922, to last for 50 years, customs frontiers between the two countries were abolished. On Jan. 1, 1948, a customs union with Belgium and the Netherlands (Benelux) came into existence. On Feb. 3, 1958, it became an economic union.

MADAGASCAR

Democratic Republic of Madagascar
President and Head of State: Comdr. Didier Ratsiraka (1975)
Prime Minister: Lt. Col. Desiré Rakotoarijaona (1977)
Area: 230,035 sq mi. (595,791 sq km)
Population (est. 1980): 8,730,000
Density per square mile: 38.0
Capital and largest city (est. 1976): Antananarivo, 468,000
Monetary unit: Malagasy franc
Languages: Malagasy, French
Ethnic groups: Merina (or Hova), Betsimisaraka, Betsileo, Tsimihety, Antaisaka, Sakalava, Antandroy
Religions: Animist, 57%; Catholic, 20%; Protestant, 18%; Islam, 5%
National name: Repoblika Demokratika Malagasy
Freedom House classifications: Capitalist-socialist pre-industrial, one-party nationalist
Economic summary: Gross national product (1978): $2.1 billion. Average annual growth rate (1970–77): –2.7%. Per capita income: $250. Average rate of inflation: 9%. Land used for agriculture: 63%; labor force: 26%; principal products: rice, livestock, coffee, vanilla, sugar, cloves, cotton, sisal, peanuts, tobacco. Labor force in industry: 26%; major products: processed food, textiles, refined petroleum products, assembled automobiles, soap, mining products. Natural resources: graphite, chromium, coal, bauxite, ilmenite, tar sands, semiprecious stones. Exports: coffee, cloves, vanilla. Imports: machinery and equipment, chemicals, crude petroleum, rice. Major trading partners: France, U.S.

Geography. Madagascar lies in the Indian Ocean off the southeast coast of Africa opposite Mozambique. The world's fourth-largest island, it is twice the size of Arizona. The country's low-lying coastal area gives way to a central plateau. The once densely wooded interior has largely been cut down.

Government. The Constitution of Dec. 30, 1975, approved by referendum following a military coup, provides for direct election by universal suffrage of a president for a seven-year term, a Supreme Council of the Revolution as a policy-making body, a unicameral People's National Assembly of 137 members (elected for five-year terms), and a military Committee for Development. The new constitution followed a period of martial rule that began with the suspension of the republic's original bicameral legislature in 1972.

History. The present population is of black and Malay stock, with perhaps some Polynesian, called Malagasy. The French took over a protectorate in 1885, and then in 1894–95 ended the monarchy, exiling Queen Rànavàlona III to Algiers. A colonial administration was set up, to which the Comoro Islands were attached in 1908, and other territories later. In World War II, the British occupied Madagascar, which retained ties to Vichy France.

An autonomous republic within the French Community since 1958, Madagascar became an independent member of the Community in 1960. In May 1973, an army coup led by Maj. Gen. Gabriel Ramanantsoa ousted Philibert Tsiranana, president since 1959.

With unemployment and inflation both high, Ramanantsoa resigned Feb. 5, 1975. His leftist-leaning successor, Interior Minister Richard Ratsimandrava, an Army lieutenant colonel, was killed six days later by a machine-gun ambush in Antananarivo, the capital.

On June 15, 1975, Comdr. Didier Ratsiraka was named President. He announced that he would follow a socialist course and, after nationalizing banks and insurance companies, declared all mineral resources nationalized.

MALAWI

Republic of Malawi
Life President: Hastings Kamuzu Banda (1966)
Area: 45,747 sq mi. (118,484 sq km)
Population (est. 1980): 5,975,000
Density per square mile: 130.6
Capital (1977 census): Lilongwe, 102,900
Largest city (1977 census): Blantyre, 222,200
Monetary unit: Kwacha

Languages: English (official), Chichewa
Religion: Animist, 65%; Christian, 33%
Member of Commonwealth of Nations
Freedom House classifications: Capitalist pre-industrial, one-party nationalist
Economic summary: Gross national product (1978): $1.0 billion. Average annual growth rate (1970–77): 3.1%. Per capita income: $154. Average rate of inflation (1974–78): 10%. Land used for agriculture: 30%; labor force: 90%; principal products: tobacco, tea, sugar, corn, peanuts. Labor force in industry: 24%; major products: food, beverages, tobacco, textiles, footwear. Natural resource: limestone. Exports: tobacco, tea, sugar, peanuts. Imports: machinery, transport equipment, manufactured goods, oil. Major trading partners: U.K., U.S., South Africa, Netherlands, Japan, West Germany.

Geography. Malawi is a landlocked country the size of Pennsylvania in southeastern Africa, surrounded by Mozambique, Zambia, and Tanzania. Lake Malawi, formerly Lake Nyasa, occupies most of the country's eastern border. The north-south Rift Valley is flanked by mountain ranges and high plateau areas.

Government. Under a Constitution that came into effect on July 6, 1966, the president is the sole head of state; there is neither a prime minister nor a vice president. The National Assembly has 87 members.

There is only one national party—the Malawi Congress Party (all 87 seats in the National Assembly), led by President Hastings K. Banda.

History. The first European to make extensive explorations in the area was David Livingstone in the 1850s and 1860s. In 1884, Cecil Rhodes's British South African Company received a charter to develop the country. The company came into conflict with the Arab slavers in 1887–89. After Britain annexed the Nyasaland territory in 1891, making it a protectorate in 1892, Sir Harry Johnstone, the first high commissioner, using Royal Navy gunboats, wiped out the slavers.

Nyasaland became the independent nation of Malawi on July 6, 1964. Two years later, it became a republic within the Commonwealth of Nations.

Dr. Hastings K. Banda, Malawi's first Prime Minister, became its first President. He pledged to follow a policy of "discretionary nonalignment." Banda alienated much of Black Africa by maintaining good relations with such white-ruled nations as South Africa and Rhodesia. He argued that his landlocked country had to rely on white-ruled countries for access to the sea and trade.

MALAYSIA

Paramount Ruler: Sultan Haji Ahmad Shah, Sultan of Pahang (1979)
Prime Minister: Hussein bin Onn (1976)
Area: 128,328 sq mi. (332,370 sq km)
Population (est. 1980): 13,650,000
Density per square mile: 106.4
Capital: Kuala Lumpur
Largest cities (est. 1975 by U.N.): Kuala Lumpur, 557,000; **(1970 census):** George Town (Pinang), 269,603; Ipoh, 247,953
Monetary unit: Ringgit
Languages: Malay (official), Chinese, Tamil, English
Religions: Islam, (official), Buddhist, Hindu, Christian, Confucian, Taoist
Member of Commonwealth of Nations
Freedom House classifications: Capitalist-industrial, dominant party
Economic summary: Gross national product (1978): $14.5 billion. Average annual growth rate (1970–77): 4.9%. Per capita income: $990. Land used for agriculture: 59%; labor force: 12%; principal products: natural rubber, palm oil, tin, petroleum, rice, timber. Major industrial products: processed rubber, timber, and palm oil, tin, petroleum, light manufactures, electronics equipment. Natural resources: tin, oil, copper, timber. Exports: natural rubber, palm oil, tin, timber, petroleum. Imports: machinery, transport equipment, chemicals. Major trading partners: Japan, Singapore, U.S., U.K.

Geography. Malaysia is at the southern end of the Malay Peninsula in southeast Asia. The nation also includes Sabah and Sarawak on the island of Borneo to the southeast. Its area slightly exceeds that of New Mexico.

Most of Malaysia is covered by dense jungle and swamps, with a mountain range running the length of the peninsula. Extensive forests provide ebony, sandalwood, teak, and other woods.

Government. Malaysia is a sovereign constitutional monarchy within the Commonwealth of Nations. The Paramount Ruler is elected for a five-year term by the hereditary rulers of the states from among themselves. He is advised by the prime minister and his cabinet. There is a bicameral legislature. The Senate, whose role is comparable more to that of the British House of Lords than to the U.S. Senate, has 68 members, partly appointed by the Paramount Ruler to represent minority and special interests, and partly elected by the legislative assemblies of the various states.

The House of Representatives, or lower house, is made up of 154 members, who are elected for five-year terms.

The major political parties are the National Front, a coalition of 10 parties (131 of 154 seats in the House of Representatives); Democratic Action Party (16 seats); Islamic Party (5 seats).

History. Malaysia came into existence on Sept. 16, 1963, as a federation of Malaya, Singapore, Sabah (North Borneo), and Sarawak. In 1965, Singapore withdrew from the federation. Since 1966, the 11 states of former Malaya have been known as West Malaysia, and Sabah and Sarawak have been known as East Malaysia.

The Union of Malaya was established April 1, 1946, being formed from the Federated Malay States of Negri Sembilan, Pahang, Perak, and Selangor; the Unfederated Malay States of Johore, Kedah, Kelantan, Perlis, and Trengganu; and two of the Straits Settlements—Malacca and Penang. The Malay states had been brought under British administration during the late 19th and early 20th centuries.

It became the Federation of Malaya on Feb. 1, 1948, and the Federation attained full independence within the Commonwealth of Nations in 1957.

Sabah, constituting the extreme northern portion of the island of Borneo, was a British protectorate administered under charter by the British North Borneo Company from 1881 to 1946, when it assumed the status of a colony. It was occupied by Japanese troops from 1942 to 1945.

Sarawak extends along the northwestern coast of Borneo for about 500 miles (805 km). In 1841, part of the present territory was granted by the Sultan of Brunei to Sir James Brooke. Sarawak continued to be ruled by members of the Brooke family until the Japanese occupation.

From 1963, when Malaysia became independent, it was the target of guerrilla infiltration from Indonesia, but beat off invasion attempts. In 1966, when Sukarno fell and the Communist Party was liquidated in Indonesia, hostilities ended.

In the late 1960s, the country was torn by communal rioting directed against Chinese and Indians, who controlled a disproportionate share of the country's wealth. Beginning in 1968, the government moved to achieve greater economic balance through a rural development program.

Malaysia felt the impact of the "boat people" fleeing Vietnam early in 1978. Because the refugees were mostly ethnic Chinese, the government was apprehensive about any increase of a minority that previously had been the source of internal conflict in the country. In November, authorities banned landings and reversed the order only after several hundred refugees drowned when their fragile boats were towed offshore by Malaysian police. Early in 1979, the government reimposed the ban, citing the presence of more than 53,000 "illegal immigrants," and insisted that all camps be emptied before new refugees would be admitted.

MALDIVES

Republic of Maldives
President: Maumoon Abdul Gayoom (1978)
Area: 115 sq mi. (298 sq km)
Population (est. 1980): 150,000
Density per square mile: 1,304.3
Capital and largest city (est. 1978): Malé, 29,600
Monetary unit: Maldivian rupee
Language: Divehi
Religion: Islam
Freedom House classifications: Capitalist pre-industrial, non-party non-military
Economic summary: Gross national product (1978): $20 million. Per capita income: $150. Principal agricultural products: coconuts, millet. Labor force in industry: 50%; major products: fish, processed coconuts. Natural resource: fish. Export: fish. Imports: rice, wheat flour, sugar, drugs, textiles. Major trading partners: Sri Lanka, Japan, India, Singapore.

Geography. The Republic of Maldives is a group of atolls in the Indian Ocean about 500 miles (805 km) southwest of Sri Lanka. Its 1,087 coral islets stretch over an area of 45,000 square miles (116,550 sq km).

Government. The 9-member Cabinet is headed by the president. The Majlis (Parliament) is a unicameral legislature consisting of 48 members. Eight of these are appointed by the president. The others are elected for three-year terms, 2 from the capital island of Malé and 2 from each of the 19 administrative atolls.

There are no political parties in the Maldives.

History. The Maldives (formerly called the Maldive Islands) are inhabited by an Islamic seafaring people. Originally the islands were under the suzerainty of Ceylon. They came under British protection in 1887 and were a dependency of the then colony of Ceylon until 1948. The independence agreement with Britain was signed July 26, 1965.

For centuries a sultanate, the islands adopted a republican form of government in 1952, but the sultanate was restored in 1954. In 1968, however, as the result of a referendum, a republic was again established in the islands.

Ibrahim Nasir, president since 1968, was removed from office by the Majlis in November 1978 and replaced by Maumoon Abdul Gayoom. A national referendum confirmed the new leader.

MALI

Republic of Mali
Chief of State (1968) and Head of Government (1969): Gen. Moussa Traoré
Area: 464,873 sq mi. (1,204,021 sq km)
Population (est. 1980): 6,660,000
Density per square mile: 14.3
Capital and largest city (est. 1976): Bamako, 404,000
Monetary unit: Mali franc
Ethnic groups: Bambara, Peul, Soninke, Malinke, Songhai, Dogon, Senoufo, Minianka, Berbers, and Moors
Languages: French (official), African languages
Religions: Islam, 65%; Animist, 30%; Christian
National name: République de Mali
Freedom House classifications: Capitalist-socialist pre-industrial, one-party nationalist
Economic summary: Gross national product (1978): $760 million. Average annual growth rate (1970–77): 1.9%. Per capita income (1977): $96. Average rate of inflation (1977–78): 13%. Principal agricultural products: millet, sorghum, corn, rice, sugar, cotton, peanuts, livestock. Major industrial products: processed foods, textiles, cigarettes, fish. Natural resources: bauxite, iron ore, maganese, lithium, phosphate, kaolin, salt, limestone, gold. Exports: meat, livestock, cotton, fish, peanuts, tannery products. Imports: food, machinery, vehicles, petroleum products, chemicals and pharmaceuticals, textiles. Major trading partners: France, Ivory Coast, Senegal, U.K., West Germany, U.S.S.R., China.

Geography. Most of Mali, in West Africa, lies in the Sahara. A landlocked country four fifths the size of Alaska, it is bordered by Guinea, Senegal, Mauritania, Algeria, Niger, Upper Volta, and the Ivory Coast.

The only fertile area is in the south, where the Niger and Senegal Rivers provide irrigation.

Government. The army overthrew the government on Nov. 19, 1968, and formed a provisional government. The Military Committee of National Liberation consists of 14 members and forms the decision-making body.

In late 1969 an attempted coup was foiled, and Lt. Moussa Traoré, president of the Military Committee took over as chief of state and later as head of government, ousting Capt. Yoro Diakité as Premier.

The Malian People's Democratic Union, established in 1976, is the only political party.

History. Subjugated by France by the end of the 19th century, this area became a colony in 1904 (named French Sudan in 1920) and in 1946 became part of the French Union. On June 20, 1960, it became independent and, under the name of Sudanese Republic, was federated with the Republic of Senegal in the Mali Federation. However, Senegal seceded from the Federation on Aug. 20, 1960, and the Sudanese Republic then changed its name to the Republic of Mali on September 22.

In the 1960s, Mali concentrated on economic development, continuing to accept aid from both Soviet bloc and Western nations, as well as international agencies. In the late 1960s, it began retreating from close ties with China. But a purge of conservative opponents brought greater power to President Modibo Keita, and in 1968 the influence of the Chinese and their Malian sympathizers increased. By a treaty signed in Peking in 1968, China agreed to help build a railroad from Mali to Guinea, providing Mali with vital access to the sea.

Mali, with Mauritania, the Ivory Coast, Senegal, Dahomey (Benin), Niger, and Upper Volta signed a treaty establishing the Economic Community for West Africa to promote economic development among the seven nations. It came into force on Jan. 1, 1973.

A six-year sub-Sahara drought devastated Mali before disastrously heavy rains began in 1974. Emergency shipments from a dozen nations and international organizations helped alleviate a famine that affected 1.8 million Malians and killed thousands.

MALTA

Republic of Malta
President: Anton Buttigieg (1976)
Prime Minister: Dom Mintoff (1971)
Area: 122 sq mi. (316 sq km)
Population (est. 1980): 350,000
Density per square mile: 2,868.9
Capital (est. 1978): Valetta, 14,000
Largest city (est. 1978): Sliema, 20,100
Monetary unit: Maltese pound
Languages: Maltese and English
Religion: Roman Catholic
National name: Repubblika Ta Malta
Member of Commonwealth of Nations
Freedom House classifications: Capitalist-statist industrial, multi-party centralized
Economic summary: Gross national product (1978): $730 million. Average annual growth rate (1970–77): 11.9%. Per capita income (1977): $1,971. Labor force in agriculture: 6%; principal products: fodder crops, potatoes, onions, fruits and vegetables. Labor force in industry: 29%; major products: textiles, yarn, knitted goods, processed foods, plastics, electronic equipment. Natural resources: limestone, salt. Exports: textiles, yarns, manufactured goods, plants and cut flowers. Imports: manufactured goods, machinery, transport equipment. Major trading partners: West Germany, U.K., Italy.

Geography. The five Maltese islands—with a combined land area smaller than Philadelphia—are in the Mediterranean about 60 miles (97 km) south of the southeastern tip of Sicily.

Government. The government is headed by a Prime Minister, responsible to a 65-member House of Representatives elected by universal suffrage.

The major political parties are Malta Labor Party (34 of 65 seats in House of Representatives), led by Prime Minister Dom Mintoff; Nationalist Party (31 seats), led by Edward Fenech Adami.

History. The strategic importance of Malta was recognized by the Phoenicians, who occupied it, as did in their turn the Greeks, Carthaginians, and Romans. The apostle Paul was shipwrecked there in A.D. 58.

The Knights of St. John (Malta), who obtained the three habitable Maltese islands of Malta, Gozo, and Comino from Charles V in 1530, reached their highest fame when they withstood an attack by superior Turkish forces in 1565.

Napoleon seized Malta in 1798, but the French forces were ousted by British troops the next year, and British rule was confirmed by the Treaty of Paris in 1814.

Malta was heavily attacked by German and Italian aircraft during World War II, but was never invaded by the Axis.

Malta became an independent nation on Sept. 21, 1964, and a republic Dec. 13, 1974, but remained in the British Commonwealth. The Governor-General, Sir Anthony Mamo, was sworn in as first president and Dom Mintoff remained prime minister.

The new government proposed a seven-year plan to end economic dependence on foreign military bases by 1980. It called for a $568-million investment program to create 20,000 new jobs. Britain withdrew its last troops from Malta in 1979, thus ending its annual subsidy of $33 million for use of the island's port facilities.

MAURITANIA

Islamic Republic of Mauritania
Chief of State and Head of Government: Lt. Col. Mohammed Khouna Ould Haydalla (1980)
Area: 419,229 sq mi. (1,085,803 sq km)
Population (est. 1980): 1,640,000
Density per square mile: 3.9
Capital and largest city (est. 1977): Nouakchott, 135,000
Monetary unit: Ouguyia
Ethnic groups: Moors; a black minority (Poulars, Soninkes, and Wolofs)
Languages: Arabic and French
Religion: Islam
National name: République Islamique de Mauritanie
Freedom House classifications: Capitalist-statist pre-industrial, non-party military
Economic summary: Gross national product (1978): $420 million. Average annual growth rate (1970–77): −0.1%. Per capita income: $376. Average rate of inflation (1977–78): 12.5%. Principal agricultural products: livestock, millet, maize, wheat, dates, rice. Major industrial products: iron ore, processed fish. Natural resources: copper, iron ore, gypsum, fish. Exports: iron ore, fish, copper. Imports: foodstuffs, capital goods. Major trading partners: France, Spain, U.S., U.K., Italy, Japan.

Geography. Mauritania, three times the size of

Arizona, is situated in northwest Africa with about 350 miles (592 km) of coastline on the Atlantic Ocean. It is bordered by Morocco on the north, Algeria and Mali on the east, and Senegal on the south.

The country is mostly desert, with the exception of the fertile Senegal River valley in the south and grazing land in the north.

Government. An Army coup on July 10, 1978, deposed Moktar Ould Daddah, who had been President since Mauritania's independence in 1960. Since then, a 13-man Committee for National Recovery has exercised executive and legislative power, having replaced the National Assembly and the single political party that existed before the coup.

History. Mauritania was first explored by the Portuguese. The French organized the area as a territory in 1904.

Mauritania became an independent nation on Nov. 28, 1960, and was admitted to the United Nations in 1961 over the strenuous opposition of Morocco, which claimed the territory. With Moors, Arabs, Berbers, and blacks frequently in conflict, the government in the late 1960s sought to make Arab culture dominant to unify the land.

Mauritania and Morocco planned to divide the territory of the former Spanish Sahara after the departure of the colonial administration. Mauritanian troops moved into the territory but encountered resistance from the Polisario Front, a Saharan independence movement backed by Algeria. Mauritania broke diplomatic relations with Algeria in 1976, after Algerian recognition of the area as an independent state.

The task of pacifying one-third of the former Spanish Sahara (the exact amount of territory acquired by Mauritania in the division with Morocco is unknown) proved a heavy burden. Increased military spending and rising casulaties contributed to the discontent that brought down the civilian government of Ould Daddah in 1978. His military replacement, Lt. Col. Moustapha Saleck, was forced to resign after Premier Ahmed Bouceif and other military leaders were killed in a plane crash on May 27, 1979. Lt. Col. Mohamed Mahmoud Ould Louly held power for only six months and was removed by the junta on Jan. 4, 1980, for unsatisfactory performance. Lt. Col. Mohamed Khouna Ould Haydalla was named new chief of state and government.

MAURITIUS

Governor-General: Sir Dayendranath Burrenchobay (1979)
Prime Minister: Sir Seewoosagur Ramgoolam (1961)
Area: 787 sq mi. (2,040 sq km)
Population (est. 1980): 920,000 (Indian, 51%; Creole, 33%, Pakistani, 16%)
Density per square mile: 1,169.0
Capital and largest city (est. 1979): Port Louis, 144,800
Monetary unit: Mauritian rupee
Languages: English (official), French, Creole.
Religions: Hindu, 51%, Christian (mainly Roman Catholic), 33%; Islam, 16%; Buddhist, 3%
Member of Commonwealth of Nations
Freedom House classifications: Capitalist industrial, multi-party centralized
Economic summary: Gross national product (1978): $760. Average annual growth rate (1970–77): 6.9%. Per capita income: $640. Land used for agriculture: 60%; labor force: 50%; principal products: sugar cane, rice. Labor force in industry: 6%; major products: processed sugar and tea, tobacco, cut diamonds, textiles, electronic equipment. Natural resources: iron ore, gypsum, fish. Exports: sugar, tea, molasses. Imports: foodstuffs, manufactured goods. Major trading partners: Western European countries, U.S., U.K.

Geography. Mauritius is a mountainous island in the Indian Ocean east of Madagascar.

Government. Mauritius is a member of the British Commonwealth, with Queen Elizabeth II as head of state. She is represented by a governor-general, who chooses the prime minister from the unicameral Legislative Assembly. The Legislative Assembly has 70 members, 62 of whom are elected by direct suffrage. The remaining 8 are chosen from among the unsuccessful candidates.

The major parties are a governing coalition of the Labor Party, Parti Mauritien, and the Social Democratic Party (34 of 70 seats in the Legislative Assembly), led by Prime Minister Sir Seewoosagur Ramgoolam, and the opposition Mouvement Militant Mauritien (33 seats). Independents comprise the balance of the Assembly.

History. Mauritius was seized from France by British troops in 1810 and ceded to Britain by the Treaty of Paris in 1814. Until 1903, Mauritius and the Seychelles were administered as a single colony. The colony of Mauritius became an independent nation on March 12, 1968.

The nation has an Indian majority, descendants of laborers imported from India to work the sugar plantations after the abolition of slavery in 1834. The native blacks speak French and are Roman Catholics.

Overpopulation and unemployment continue to be major problems.

MEXICO

United Mexican States
President: José López Portillo (1976)
Area: 761,600 sq mi. (1,972,547 sq km)
Population (est. 1980): 71,900,000 (55% mestizo; 29% Indian)
Density per square mile: 94.4
Capital: Mexico City
Largest cities (est 1978): Mexico City, 8,988,200; (est. **1978 by U.N.):** Guadalajara, 1,813,000; Monterrey, 1,054,000; Puebla de Zaragoza, 678,000
Monetary unit: Peso
Languages: Spanish, Indian languages
Religion: Mainly Roman Catholic
National name: Estados Unidos Mexicanos
Freedom House classifications: Capitalist-statist industrial, dominant party
Economic summary: Gross national product (1978): $84.2 billion. Average annual growth rate (1970–77): 1.2%. Average rate of inflation (1978): 15–20%. Labor force in agriculture: 33%; principal products: corn, cotton, coffee,

sugar cane, vegetables. Labor force in industry: 25%; major products: processed foods, chemicals, basic metals and metal products, petroleum. Natural resources: petroleum, silver, copper, gold, lead, zinc, natural gas, timber. Exports: coffee, cotton, fruits and vegetables, petroleum, sulfur. Imports: machinery, equipment, industrial vehicles, intermediate goods. Major trading partners: U.S., Japan, Western European countries.

Geography. The United States' neighbor to the south, Mexico is about one fifth its size. Baja California in the west, an 800-mile (1,287-km) peninsula, forms the Gulf of California. In the east are the Gulf of Mexico and the Bay of Campeche, which is formed by Mexico's other peninsula, the Yucatán.

Mexico is a great, high plateau, open to the north, with mountain chains on east and west and with ocean-front lowlands lying outside of them.

Government. The President, who is popularly elected for six years and is ineligible to succeed himself, governs with a Cabinet of ministers. Congress has two houses—a 400-member Chamber of Deputies, elected for three years, and a 64-member Senate, elected for six years.

Each of the 31 states has considerable autonomy, with a popularly elected governor, a legislature, and a local judiciary. The President of Mexico appoints the governor of the Federal District.

The major political parties are the Partido Revolucionario Institucional, Authentic Party of the Mexican Revolution; National Action Party; Communist Party; Worker's Party; Democratic Party; and Popular Socialist Party.

History. Mexico's early history is shrouded in mystery. At least two civilized races—the Mayas and later the Toltecs—preceded the wealthy Aztec empire, conquered in 1519–21 by the Spanish under Hernando Cortés. Spain ruled for the next 300 years until 1810 (the date was Sept. 16 and is now celebrated as Independence Day), when the Mexicans first revolted. They continued the struggle and finally won independence in 1821.

Turbulent years followed. From 1821 to 1877, there were two emperors, several dictators, and enough presidents and provisional executives to make a new government on the average of every nine months. Mexico lost Texas (1836), and after defeat in the war with the U.S. (1846–48) it lost the area comprising the present states of California, Nevada, and Utah, most of Arizona and New Mexico, and parts of Wyoming and Colorado.

In 1855, the Indian patriot Benito Juárez began a series of liberal reforms, including the disestablishment of the Catholic Church, which had acquired vast property. A subsequent civil war was interrupted by the French invasion of Mexico (1861), the crowning of Maximilian of Austria as Emperor (1864), and then his overthrow and execution by forces under Juárez, who again became President in 1867.

The years after the fall of the dictator Porfirio Diaz (1877–80 and 1884–1911) were marked by bloody political-military strife and trouble with the U.S., culminating in the punitive expedition into northern Mexico (1916–17) in unsuccessful pursuit of the revolutionary Pancho Villa. There was a continuous succession of various presidents and of internal strife until 1917, when a new Congress was elected and a liberal Constitution adopted. Since a brief period of civil war in 1920, Mexico has enjoyed a period of gradual agricultural, political, and social reforms. Relations with the U.S. were again disturbed in 1938 when all foreign oil wells were expropriated. Agreement on compensation was finally reached in 1941.

Lázaro Çardenas (1934–40), president during the oil seizures, also began a program of distributing land to the peasants and of broad labor reforms. Manual Avila Camacho, president during World War II, followed Cardenas' policy at home but cooperated closely with the United Nations, and established cordial relations with the U.S. His policy was followed by his immediate successors, Miguel Alemán, Adolfo Ruíz Cortines, and Adolfo López Mateos. López Mateos redefined Mexican foreign policy as "independent" rather than neutral or partial, a course followed by Gustavo Díaz Ordaz, who became president in 1964.

Mexico maintained ties with Cuba after the Organization of American States approved a U.S.-sponsored boycott of Fidel Castro's regime in 1962. Mexico opposed the boycott until the OAS repealed it in 1975.

Luis Echeverría Alvarez, who was elected president in 1970, worked vigorously in Latin America and elsewhere in the underdeveloped world to promote more benefits for developing nations from the raw materials they export.

Mexico and Venezuela proposed formation of a Latin American economic system (SELA) to promote regional economic development, and the organization held its first meeting in Caracas in 1976.

Despite a drastic devaluation of the peso in 1976 that quadrupled the price of goods imported from the U.S., the government cut the rate of inflation by mid-1977 to 20%, compared with a rate of 45% for 1976. Recession kept unemployment at 11%, but Mexico's trade deficit with the U.S. was only $91.5 million for the first quarter, compared with $426.3 million a year earlier. A key factor in the improved payments was a 60% increase in tourism from the U.S., hard hit earlier by terrorism and Echevarría's support for Palestine Liberation Organization presence in the United Nations.

Another factor in the improvement of the economy was a 64% increase in export oil sales in 1977, worth nearly $1 billion to the foreign trade balance. The confirmation in June 1978 of new oil reserves in Yucatán, adding 16 billion barrels to the nation's proven reserves, also improved the economic outlook.

Discovery of the Chicontepec basin north of Tampico on the Gulf coast in 1978 raised Mexico's proven reserves to 40 billion barrels. By 1980, Pemex, the government oil monopoly, estimated that Mexican production would continue for 60 years, twice the expectancy for the world's other major producers. In March, President Lopez Portillo said that national production would increase 10% a year for the next two years to meet growing domestic consumption and an export target of 1.17 million barrels a day. Export earnings for 1979 were $3.7 billion, and with price increases were expected to exceed $11 billion for 1980. The first natural-gas exports to the United States began Jan. 15, 1980, with the opening of a transborder pipeline on the Gulf coast.

The worst oil spill in history ended on March 24, 1980, with the capping of Ixtoc I, an offshore well that in nine months had lost 3.1 million barrels of oil. The spill brought about a conflict with the United States when Lopez Portillo refused to discuss compensation for damage to the U.S. Gulf Coast.

Another dispute with Mexico arose when U.S. tuna boats were seized by Mexican naval vessels for fishing within a 200-mile zone unrecognized by the United States. In retaliation, the Carter administration imposed a ban on importation of Mexican tuna products on July 14.

MONACO

Principality of Monaco
Ruler: Prince Rainier III (1949)
Minister of State: André Saint-Mleux (1972)
Area: 0.73 square mile (465 acres)
Population (est. 1980): 30,000, of whom 5,500 are Monégasque citizens
Density per square mile: 41,095.9
Capital: Monaco-Ville
Monetary unit: French franc
Languages: French and Monégasque
Religion: Roman Catholic
National name: Principauté de Monaco

Geography. Monaco is a tiny, hilly wedge driven into the French Mediterranean coast nine miles east of Nice.

Government. Prince Albert of Monaco gave the principality a Constitution in 1911, creating a National Council of 18 members popularly elected for five years. The head of government is the Minister of State.

Prince Rainier III, born May 31, 1923, succeeded his grandfather, Louis II, on the latter's death, May 9, 1949. Rainier was married April 18, 1956, to Grace Kelly, U.S. actress. A daughter, Princess Caroline Louise Marguerite, was born on Jan. 23, 1957 (married to Philippe Junot June 28, 1978); a son, Prince Albert Louis Pierre, on March 14, 1958; and another daughter, Princess Stéphanie Marie Elisabeth, on Feb. 1, 1965.

The special significance attached to the birth of descendants to Prince Rainier stems from a clause in the Treaty of July 17, 1919, between France and Monaco stipulating that in the event of vacancy of the Crown, the Monégasque territory would become an autonomous state under a French protectorate.

The National and Democratic Union (all 18 seats in National Council), led by Auguste Medecin, is the only political party.

History. The Phoenicians, and after them the Greeks, had a temple on the Monacan headland honoring Hercules. From *Monoikos*, the Greek surname for this mythological strong man, the principality took its name. After being independent for 800 years, Monaco was annexed to France in 1793 and was placed under Sardinia's protection in 1815. In 1861, it went under French guardianship but continued to be independent.

By a treaty in 1918, France stipulated that the French government be given a veto over the succession to the throne.

Monaco is a little land of pleasure with a tourist business that runs as high as 1.5 million visitors a year. It had popular gaming tables as early as 1856. Five years later, a 50-year concession to operate the games was granted to François Blanc, of Bad Homburg. This concession passed into the hand of a private company in 1898.

Monaco's practice of providing a tax shelter for French businessmen resulted in a dispute between the countries. When Rainier refused to end the practice, France retaliated with a customs tax. In 1967, Rainier took control of the Société des Bains de Mer, operator of the famous Monte Carlo gambling casino, in a program to increase hotel and convention space. He paid $8 million to Greek shipping magnate Aristotle Onassis for his shares.

MONGOLIA

Mongolian People's Republic
Chairman of Presidium of the Great People's Khural (President): Yumjaagiin Tsedenbal (1974)
Chairman of Council of Ministers (Premier): Jambyn Batmunkh (1974)
Area: 604,250 sq mi. (1,565,000 sq km)
Population (est. 1980): 1,625,000
Density per square mile: 2.7
Capital and largest city (est. 1977): Ulan Bator, 345,000
Monetary unit: Tugrik
Language: Khalkha Mongolian
Religion: Lamaistic Buddhism
National name: Bugd Nairamdakh Mongol Ard Uls
Freedom House classifications: Socialist industrial, one-party communist
Economic summary: Gross national product (1978): $1.5 billion. Average annual growth rate (1970–77): 1.6%. Land used for agriculture: 90%; principal products: livestock, wheat, oats, barley. Major industrial products: animal products, building materials, minerals. Natural resources: coal, copper, molybdenum. Exports: livestock, animal products, nonferrous metals. Imports: machinery and equipment, processed foods, chemicals, sugar, tea. Major trading partners: U.S.S.R. and Soviet bloc countries.

Geography. Mongolia lies in eastern Asia between Soviet Siberia on the north and China on the south. It is slightly larger than Alaska.

The productive regions of Mongolia—a tableland ranging from 3,000 to 5,000 feet (914 to 1,524 m) in elevation—are in the north, which is well drained by numerous rivers, including the Hovd, Onon, Selenga, and Tula.

Much of the Gobi Desert falls within Mongolia. There several mountain ranges, one of which, the Altai Mountains, contains the highest peak in the country—Tabun Bogdo at 15,266 feet (4,653 m).

Government. The Mongolian People's Republic is a socialist state in the form of a people's democracy. The highest organ of state power is the Great People's Khural (Parliament), which is elected for a term of four years and is convened once a year. The Great People's Khural elects the Presidium, which consists of a chairman, two vice chairmen, a secretary, and six members. The Council of Ministers is set up by the Great People's Khural and consists of a chairman, vice chairmen, and ministers.

The Mongolian People's Revolutionary Party, led by President Yumjaagiin Tsedenbal, is the only political party.

History. The Mongolian People's Republic, formerly known as Outer Mongolia, is a Russian satellite. It contains the original homeland of the historic Mongols, whose power reached its zenith during the 13th century under Kublai Khan. The area accepted Manchu rule in 1689, but after the Chinese Revolution of 1911 and the fall of the Manchus in 1912, the northern Mongol princes expelled the Chinese officials and declared independence under the Khutukhtu, or "Living Buddha."

In 1921, Soviet troops entered the country and facilitated the establishment of a republic by Mongolian revolutionaries in 1924 after the death of the last Living Buddha. China, meanwhile, continued to claim Outer Mongolia but was unable to back the claim with any strength. Under the 1945 Chinese-Russian Treaty, China agreed to give up Outer Mongolia, which, after a plebiscite, became a nominally independent country.

The country allied itself with the U.S.S.R. in its dispute with China. It has mobilized troops along its borders since 1968 when the two powers became involved in border clashes on the Kazakh-Sinkiang frontier to the west and on the Amur and Ussuri Rivers. Under a 20-year treaty of friendship and cooperation signed in 1966, it was entitled to call upon the U.S.S.R. for military aid in the event of invasion.

MOROCCO

Kingdom of Morocco
Ruler: King Hassan II (1961)
Premier: Maati Bouabid (1979)
Area: 171,593 sq mi. (444,426 sq km)
Population (est. 1980): 20,050,000
Density per square mile: 116.8
Capital: Rabat
Largest cities (est. 1978): Casablanca, 2,113,000; Rabat, 704,100; **(est. 1975 by U.N.):** Marrakech, 330,400; Fez, 321,450; Meknès, 244,500
Monetary unit: Dirham
Languages: Arabic, French, Spanish
Religions: Chiefly Islam
National name: al-Mamlaka al-Maghrebia
Freedom House classifications: Capitalist pre-industrial, multi-party centralized
Economic summary: Gross national product (1978): $12.6 billion. Average annual growth rate (1970–77): 4.2%. Per capita income (1977): $520. Average rate of inflation (1977): 13%. Labor force in agriculture: 50%; products: barley, wheat, citrus fruits, vegetables, sugar beets, wool. Labor force in industry, 15%; major products: textiles, fish, chemicals. Natural resources: phosphates, iron, manganese, lead, fisheries. Exports: phosphates, citrus fruits, vegetables, canned fruits and vegetables, canned fish, carpets. Imports: industrial capital goods, fuels, foodstuffs, consumer goods. Major trading partners: France, Italy, West Germany.

Geography. Morocco, about one tenth larger than California, is just south of Spain across the Strait of Gibraltar and looks out on the Atlantic from the northwest shoulder of Africa. Algeria is to the east and Mauritania to the south.

On the Atlantic coast there is a fertile plain. The Mediterranean coast is mountainous. The Atlas Mountains, running northeastward from the south to the Algerian frontier, average 11,000 feet (3,353 m) in elevation.

Government. The King, after suspending the 1962 Constitution and dissolving Parliament in 1965, promulgated a new Constitution in 1972. He continued to rule by decree until June 3, 1977, when the first free elections since 1962 took place. The 264-member Chamber of Deputies has 176 elected seats, with the balance chosen by local councils and groups.

A coalition of independents loyal to the King and small right-wing parties has 114 of the 176 elected seats in the Chamber of Deputies; Istiqlal, principal opposition group, 45 seats; Socialist Union of Popular Forces, 16 seats; and the Communist Party of Progress and Socialism, one seat.

History. Morocco was once the home of the Berbers, who helped the Arabs invade Spain in A.D. 711 and then revolted against them and gradually won control of large areas of Spain for a time after 739.

The country was ruled successively by various native dynasties and maintained regular commercial relations with Europe, even during the 17th and 18th centuries when it was the headquarters of the famous Salé pirates. In the 19th century, there were frequent clashes with the French and Spanish. Finally, in 1904, France and Spain divided Morocco into zones of French and Spanish influence, and these were established as protectorates in 1912.

Meanwhile, Morocco had become the object of big-power rivalry, which almost led to a European war in 1905 when Germany attempted to gain a foothold in the rich mineral country. By terms of the Algeciras Conference (1906), Morocco was internationalized economically, and France's privileges were limited.

The Tangier Statute, concluded by Britain, France, and Spain in 1923, created an international zone at the port of Tangier, permanently neutralized and demilitarized. In World War II, Spain occupied the zone, ostensibly to ensure order, but was forced to withdraw in 1945.

Sultan Mohammed V was deposed by the French in 1953 and replaced by his uncle, but nationalist agitation forced his return in 1955. On his death on Feb. 26, 1961, his son, Hassan, became King.

France and Spain recognized the independence and sovereignty of Morocco in 1956. Later the same year, the Tangier international zone was abolished.

In the Middle East war of 1967, Morocco joined the Arab states in their attack on Israel.

In 1975, tens of thousands of Moroccans crossed the border into Spanish Sahara to back their government's contention that the northern part of the territory was historically part of Morocco. At the same time, Mauritania occupied the southern half of the territory in defiance of Spanish threats to resist such a takeover. Abandoning its commitment to self-determination for the territory, Spain withdrew, and only Algeria protested. Algerian recognition of a Saharan republic in 1976 led to a break in relations among the three North African states, and Algerian-backed Polisario Front guerrillas continued to fight Moroccan and Mauritanian forces, preventing exploitation of the region's rich phosphate deposits.

Although Polisario guerrillas were still active in 1977, Hassan dispatched 1,500 troops to Zaire in April to help President Mobuto Sese Seko defeat an invasion from Angola. Radical African states criticized Morocco, but most hailed the successful operation, in which France supplied the airlift.

In the May 1978 invasion of Zaire's Shaba Province, Morocco once again supplied troops, this time only a small number, who were transported to Zaire by the U.S. Air Force. Hassan was one of the few chiefs of government who volunteered to contribute to a permanent pan-African peacekeeping force, discussed but not activated after the second Shaba invasion.

MOZAMBIQUE

People's Republic of Mozambique
President: Samora Moises Machel (1975)
Area: 303,073 sq mi. (784,959 sq km)
Population (est. 1980): 10,460,000
Density per square mile: 34.5
Capital and largest city (est. 1978): Maputo, 500,000
Monetary unit: Mozambique escudo
Languages: Portuguese (official); Bantu languages
Religions: Animist, 66%; Christian, 22%; Islam, 11%
National name: República Popular de Moçambique
Freedom House classifications: Socialist pre-industrial, one-party socialist.
Economic summary: Gross national product (1978): $1.4 billion. Average annual growth rate (1970–77): —4.3%. Per capita income: $220. Labor force in agriculture: 80%; principal products: cotton, cashew nuts, sugar, tea, copra, wheat, peanuts. Labor force in industry: 5%; major products: processed foods, petroleum products, beverages, textiles, tobacco. Natural resources: coal, iron ore, fluorite, tantalite, timber. Exports: cashew nuts, cotton, sugar, mineral and timber products, tea, copra. Imports: machinery and electrical equipment, cotton textiles, vehicles, petroleum products, iron and steel. Major trading partners: Portugal, South Africa, U.S., U.K., West Germany.

Geography. Mozambique stretches for 1,535 miles (2,470 km) along Africa's southeast coast. It is nearly twice the size of California. Tanzania is to the north; Malawi, Zambia, and Zimbabwe to the west; and South Africa and Swaziland to the south.

The country is generally a low-lying plateau broken up by 25 sizable rivers that flow into the Indian Ocean. The largest is the Zambezi, which provides access to central Africa. The principal ports are Maputo and Beira, which is the port for Zimbabwe Rhodesia.

Government. After having been under Portuguese colonial rule for 470 years, Mozambique became independent on June 25, 1975. It is a Marxist state. The first President, Samora Moises Machel, is a militant Maoist and a former nurse who headed the National Front for the Liberation of Mozambique (FRELIMO) in its 10-year guerrilla war for independence.

History. Mozambique was discovered by Vasco da Gama in 1498, although the Arabs had penetrated into the area as early as the 10th century. It was first colonized in 1505, and by 1510, the Portuguese had control of all the former Arab sultanates on the east African coast.

FRELIMO was organized in 1963. Guerrilla activity had become so extensive by 1973 that Portugal was forced to dispatch 40,000 troops to fight the rebels. A cease-fire was signed in September 1974, when Portugal agreed to grant Mozambique independence.

After a brief period of cooperation with neighboring white-ruled Rhodesia, Mozambique closed its border in 1976, cutting off Rhodesia's most direct link to the sea. A series of border clashes between Rhodesian forces and guerrillas based in Mozambique continued until Zimbabwe achieved independence in April 1980, when rail and highway communications between the two countries were reopened.

NAMIBIA

See South Africa

NAURU

Republic of Nauru
President and Premier: Hammer DeRoburt (1978)
Area: 8.2 sq mi. (21 sq km)
Population (est. 1980): 8,000
Density per square mile: 1,000.0
Capital: Yaren
Monetary unit: Australian dollar
Languages: Nauruan, English
Religions: Protestant, 60%; Catholic, 33%
Special relationship within the Commonwealth of Nations
Freedom House classifications: Capitalist-statist industrial, non-party non-military
Economic summary: Gross national product (1975): $120 million. Per capita income: $17,140. Major industrial products: phosphates. Natural resources: phosphates. Exports: phosphates. Imports: foodstuffs, water. Major trading partners: Australia, New Zealand, U.K., Japan.

Geography. Nauru is an island in the Pacific just south of the equator, about 2,500 miles (4,023 km) southwest of Honolulu.

Government. Legislative power is invested in a popularly elected 18-member Parliament, which elects the President from among its members. Executive power rests with the President, who is assisted by a five-member Cabinet.

History. Nauru was annexed by Germany in 1888. It was placed under joint Australian, New Zealand, and British mandate after World War I, and in 1947 it became a U.N. trusteeship administered by the same three powers. On Jan. 31, 1968, Nauru became an independent republic.

NEPAL

Kingdom of Nepal
Ruler: King Birendra Bír Bikram Shah Dev. (1972)
Prime Minister: Surya Bahadur Thapa (1979)
Area: 54,362 sq mi. (140,797 sq km)
Population (est. 1980): 14,000,000
Density per square mile: 257.5
Capital and largest city (est. 1976): Katmandu, 171,400

Monetary unit: Nepalese rupee
Languages: Nepali (official), Newari, Bhutia
Religions: Hindu, 89%; Buddhist, 8%
Freedom House classifications: Capitalist pre-industrial, non-party non-military
Economic summary: Gross national product (1978): $1.6 billion. Average annual growth rate (1970–77): 2.4%. Per capita income: $108. Average rate of inflation (1974–77): 13.2%. Labor force in agriculture: 95%; principal products: rice, maize, wheat, millet, jute, sugar cane, oilseed, potatoes. Labor force in industry: 5%; major products: cigarettes, bricks, sugar, lumber, jute, hydroelectric power, cement. Natural resources: water, timber, hydroelectric potential. Exports: agricultural products and timber. Imports: textiles, manufactured goods. Major trading partner: India.

Geography. A landlocked country the size of Arkansas, lying between India and the Tibetan Autonomous Region of China, Nepal contains Mount Everest (29,028 ft.; 8,848 m), the tallest mountain in the world.Along its southern border, Nepal has a strip of level land that is partly forested, partly cultivated. North of that is the slope of the main section of the Himalayan range, including Everest and many other peaks higher than 20,000 feet (6,096 m).

Government. A new Constitution promulgated by King Mahendra in 1962 provided for a unicameral legislature called the National Panchayat. All political parties were banned in 1960.

History. The Kingdom of Nepal was unified in 1768 by King Prithwi Narayan Shah. A commercial treaty was signed with Britain in 1792, and in 1816, after more than a year's hostilities, the Nepalese agreed to allow British residents to live in Katmandu, the capital. In 1923, Britain recognized the absolute independence of Nepal. Between 1846 and 1951, the country was ruled by the Rana family, which always held the office of prime minister. In 1951, however, the King took over all power and proclaimed a constitutional monarchy.

Mahendra Bir Bikram Shah became King in 1955. Nepal and China settled their differences in 1956, and thereafter Nepal accepted economic aid from the Chinese. The U.S. and the U.S.S.R. also provide aid.

After Mahendra, who had ruled since 1955, died of a heart attack in 1972, Prince Birendra, at 26, succeeded to the throne.

In the first election in 22 years, on May 2, 1980, voters approved the continued autocratic rule by the King with the advice of a partyless Parliament. The King promised, however, that he would eventually permit the election of a new legislature to which the Prime Minister and Cabinet would be responsible.

THE NETHERLANDS

Kingdom of the Netherlands
Sovereign: Queen Beatrix (1980)
Premier: Andries van Agt (1977)
Area: 13,967 sq mi. (36,175 sq km)
Population (est. 1980): 14,125,000
Density per square mile: 1,011.3
Capital: Amsterdam; seat of government: The Hague
Largest cities (est. 1979): Rotterdam, 1,014,800; Amsterdam, 957,700; The Hague, 671,500; Utrecht, 476,400
Monetary unit: Guilder
Language: Dutch
Religions: Roman Catholic, 40%; Dutch Reformed, 24%; unaffiliated, 24%
National name: Koninkrijk der Nederlanden
Freedom House classifications: Capitalist-socialist industrial, multi-party centralized
Economic summary: Gross national product (1978): $117 billion. Average annual growth rate (1970–77): 2.2%. Per capita income: $7,597. Land used for agriculture: 67%; labor force, 10%; principal products: wheat, barley, sugar beets, potatoes, flax, bulbs, meat and dairy products. Labor force in industry: 39%; major products: metal fabrication, textiles, chemicals, electronic equipment. Exports: foodstuffs, machinery, natural gas, chemicals, petroleum products, textiles. Imports: machinery, crude petroleum, chemicals, textiles, mineral ores. Major trading partners: West Germany, Belgium, France, U.K.

Geography. The Netherlands, on the coast of the North Sea, has West Germany to the east and Belgium to the south. It is twice the size of New Jersey.

Part of the great plain of north and west Europe, the Netherlands has maximum dimensions of 190 by 160 miles (360 by 257 km) and is low and flat except in Limburg in the southeast, where some hills rise to 300 feet (92 m). About half the country's area is below sea level, making the famous Dutch dikes a requisite to the use of much land. Reclamation of land from the sea through dikes has continued through recent times.

All drainage reaches the North Sea, and the principal rivers—Rhine, Maas (Meuse), and Schelde—have their sources outside the country. The Rhine is the most heavily used waterway in Europe.

Government. The Netherlands and its former colony of the Netherlands Antilles form the Kingdom of the Netherlands.

The Netherlands is a constitutional monarchy with a bicameral Parliament. The Upper Chamber has 75 members elected for six years by representative bodies of the provinces, half of the members retiring every three years. The Lower Chamber has 150 members elected by universal suffrage for four years. The two Chambers have the right of investigation and interpellation; the Lower Chamber can initiate legislation and amend bills.

The Sovereign, Queen Beatrix Wilhelmina Armgard, born Jan. 31, 1938, was married on March 11, 1966, to Claus von Amsberg, a former West German diplomat. The marriage drew public criticism because of the bridegroom's service in the German army during World War II. In 1967, Beatrix gave birth to a son, Willem-Alexander Claus George Ferdinand, the first male heir to the throne since 1884. She also has two other sons, Johan Friso Bernhard Christian David, born in 1968, and Constantijn Christof Frederik Aschwin, born the next year.

Premier Andries van Agt leads a coalition of center-right parties with 77 seats in the 150 seats in the Lower Chamber. The coalition consists of his Christian Democratic Appeal (49 seats) and the conservative Liberal Party for Freedom and Democracy (28 seats). A dissident bloc of the Christian Democrats objected to the Liberal alliance, but said it would support van Agt in confidence votes, and a half-dozen members of splinter right-wing parties were expected to vote with the government.

History. Julius Caesar found the low-lying Netherlands inhabited by Germanic tribes—the Nervii, Frisii, and Batavi. The Batavi on the Roman frontier did not submit to Rome's rule until 13 B.C., and then only as allies.

A part of Charlemagne's empire in the 8th and 9th centuries A.D., the area later passed into the hands of Burgundy and the Austrian Hapsburgs, and finally in the 16th century came under Spanish rule.

When Philip II of Spain suppressed political liberties and the growing Protestant movement in the Netherlands, a revolt led by William of Orange broke out in 1568. Under the Union of Utrecht (1579), the seven northern provinces became the Republic of the United Netherlands.

The Dutch East India Company was established in 1602, and by the end of the 17th century Holland was one of the great sea and colonial powers of Europe.

The nation's independence was not completely established until after the Thirty Years' War (1618–48), after which the country's rise as a commercial and maritime power began. In 1814, all the provinces of Holland and Belgium were merged into one kingdom, but in 1830 the southern provinces broke away to form the Kingdom of Belgium. A liberal Constitution was adopted by the Netherlands in 1848.

In spite of its neutrality in World War II, the Netherlands was invaded by the Nazis in May 1940, and the East Indies were later taken by the Japanese. The nation was liberated in May 1945. In 1948, after a reign of 50 years, Queen Wilhelmina resigned and was succeeded by her daughter Juliana.

In 1949, after a four-year war, the Netherlands granted independence to the East Indies, which became the Republic of Indonesia. In 1963, it turned over the western half of New Guinea to the new nation, ending 300 years of Dutch presence in Asia. Attainment of independence by Suriname on Nov. 25, 1975, left the Dutch Antilles as the Netherlands' only overseas territory.

A seven-month constitutional crisis during which Prime Minister Joop den Uyl had unsuccessfully sought to form a majority coalition ended in December 1977, when Andries van Agt was able to organize the center-right coalition. Van Agt said that his government would aim chiefly at bringing down both inflation and the 5% unemployment rate.

On Jan. 31, 1980, Queen Juliana announced her intention to abdicate on her 71st birthday, April 31, in favor of the 42-year-old Crown Princess Beatrix. The popular Juliana was reported to have considered earlier retirement but had stayed on to repair the damage to the monarchy caused by charges in 1976 that her husband, Prince Bernhard, had accepted payments from the Lockheed Aircraft Corp. to influence Dutch plane purchases. Beatrix was invested as Queen in a brief ceremony marked by protests of Amsterdam squatters against eviction from their homes.

Netherlands Autonomous Country
NETHERLANDS ANTILLES

Status: Part of the Kingdom of the Netherlands
Governor: Bernardito M. Leito (1970)
Premier: Domenico F. Martina
Area: 817 sq mi. (821 sq km)
Population (est. 1978): 250,000.
The Capital (est. 1978): Willemstad, 152,000
Economic summary: Gross national product (1978): $780 million. Average annual growth rate (1970–77): 0.5%. Per capita income: $1,700. Principal agricultural products: pigs, goats. Major industries: oil refining, tourism. Natural resource: phosphate. Export: petroleum. Import: petroleum. Major trading partners: Venezuela, U.S., Netherlands.

Geography. The Netherlands Antilles comprise two groups of Caribbean islands 500 miles (805 km) apart: one, about 40 miles (64 km) off the Venezuelan coast, consists of Curaçao (173 sq mi.; 448 sq km), Bonaire (95 sq mi.; 246 sq km), and Aruba (69 sq mi.; 179 sq km); the other, lying to the northeast, consists of three small islands with a total area of 34 square miles (88 sq km). The Dutch acquired Curaçao from Spain in 1643.

Government. There is a constitutional government formed by the Governor and Cabinet and an elected Legislative Council. The area has complete autonomy in domestic affairs.

NEW ZEALAND

Dominion of New Zealand
Sovereign: Queen Elizabeth II
Governor-General: Sir Keith Holyoake (1977)
Prime Minister: Robert D. Muldoon (1975)
Area: 103,736 sq mi. (268,676 sq km) (excluding dependencies)
Population (est. 1980): 3,100,000 (European, 90%; Maori and other Polynesian, 10%)
Density per square mile: 29.9
Capital: Wellington
Largest cities (est. 1979 for metropolitan area): Auckland, 750,600; Wellington, 327,100; Christchurch, 296,500; Dunedin, 112,300
Monetary unit: New Zealand dollar
Languages: English, Maori
Religions: Church of England, 35%; Presbyterian, 22%; Roman Catholic, 16%
Member of Commonwealth of Nations
Freedom House classifications: Capitalist industrial, multi-party centralized
Economic summary: Gross national product (1978): $15.3 billion. Average annual growth rate (1970–77): 0.9%. Per capita income (1976): $4,106. Labor force in agriculture: 13%; principal products: wool, meat, dairy products, livestock. Labor force in industry: 30%; major products: processed foods, textiles, machinery, transport equipment, wood and paper products. Natural resources: forests, coal, gold, tungsten, iron ore, asbestos. Exports: agricultural products, some manufactured goods. Imports: petroleum products, machinery and equipment, consumer goods. Major trading partners: Australia, U.K., Japan, U.S.

Geography. New Zealand, about 1,250 miles (2,012 km) east of Australia, consists of two main islands and a number of smaller, outlying islands so scattered that they range from the tropical to the antarctic. The country is the size of Colorado.

New Zealand's two main components are North

Island and South Island, separated by Cook Strait, which varies from 16 to 190 miles (26 to 396 km) in width. North Island (44,281 sq mi.; 114,688 sq km) is 515 miles (829 km) long and volcanic in its south-central part. It contains many hot springs and beautiful geysers. South Island (58,093 sq mi.; 150,461 sq km) has the Southern Alps along its west coast, with Mount Cook (12,349 ft; 3,764 m) the highest point.

The largest of the outlying islands are the Auckland Islands (234 sq mi.; 606 sq km), Campbell Island (44 sq mi.; 114 sq km), the Antipodes Islands (24 sq mi.; 62 sq km), and the Kermadec Islands (13 sq mi.; 34 sq km).

Government. New Zealand was granted self-government in 1852, a full parliamentary system and ministries in 1856, and dominion status in 1907. The Queen is represented by a Governor-General, and the Cabinet is responsible to a unicameral Parliament of 92 members, who are elected by popular vote for three years.

The major political parties are the National Party (52 of 92 seats in the House of Representatives), led by Prime Minister Robert D. Muldoon; Labor Party (49 seats) led by Wallace E. Rowling; and Social Credit Party (1 seat).

History. New Zealand was discovered and named in 1642 by Abel Tasman, a Dutch navigator. Captain James Cook explored the islands in 1769. In 1840, Britain formally annexed them.

From the first, the country has been in the forefront in instituting social welfare legislation. It adopted old age pensions (1898); a national child welfare program (1907); social security for the aged, widows, and orphans, along with family benefit payments; minimum wages; a 40-hour week and unemployment and health insurance (1938); and socialized medicine (1941).

New Zealand supported U.S. policy in Vietnam and supplied military aid to South Vietnam in the orientation of its policy toward the U.S. and Asian neighbors after Britain's entry into the European Common Market. To replace the lost British market —the once prosperous islands had fallen into a local recession since 1972—New Zealand sought to sell more agricultural products to Japan. In 1978, Prime Minister Muldoon announced a pact with Japan enlarging quotas for New Zealand beef, reducing the tariffs on New Zealand fish, and providing for Japanese purchase of butter, skim milk, and other food products.

Cook Islands and Overseas Territories

The Cook Islands (93 sq mi.; 241 sq km) were placed under New Zealand administration in 1901. They achieved self-governing status in association with New Zealand in 1965. Population in 1978 was about 19,600. The seat of government is on Rarotonga Island.

Chief exports in 1978 were citrus juice (37%), clothing (22%), canned fruit (10%), pineapple juice (8%). Leading customer in 1978 was New Zealand (98%). Leading suppliers were New Zealand (83%), Japan (5%).

Niue (100 sq mi.; 259 sq km) was formerly administered as part of the Cook Islands. It was placed under separate New Zealand administration in 1901 and achieved self-governing status in association with New Zealand in 1974. The capital is Alofi. Population in 1976 was 3,800.

Chief exports in 1975 were passion fruit (42%), copra (37%), plaited ware (11%), honey (6%), limes (3%). Leading customer in 1975 was New Zealand (73%). Leading supplier was New Zealand (80%).

The Ross Dependency (160,000 sq mi.; 414,400 sq km), an Antarctic region, was placed under New Zealand administration in 1923.

Tokelau (4 sq mi.; 10 sq km) was formerly administered as part of the Gilbert and Ellice Islands colony. It was placed under New Zealand administration in 1925. Its population in 1976 was 1,575.

NICARAGUA

Republic of Nicaragua
Executive Power is held by a five-member junta, led by Sergio Ramirez Mercada (1979)
Area: 57,143 sq mi. (148,000 sq km)
Population (est. 1980): 2,565,000 (mestizo, 70%; white, 17%; black, 9%; Indian, 4%)
Density per square mile: 44.9
Capital and largest city (est. 1978): Managua, 517,500
Monetary unit: Cordoba
Language: Spanish
Religion: Roman Catholic
National name: República de Nicaragua
Freedom House classifications: Capitalist-socialist industrial, non-party non-military
Economic summary: Gross national product (1978): $2.1 billion. Average annual growth rate (1970–77): 2.5%. Per capita income: $980. Land used for agriculture: 30%; labor force: 43%; principal products: cotton, coffee, sugar cane, rice, corn, beans, cattle. Labor force in industry: 15%; major products: processed foods, chemicals, metal products, clothing and textiles. Natural resources: timber, fisheries. Exports: cotton, coffee, chemical products, meat, sugar. Imports: food and non-food agricultural products, chemicals and pharmaceuticals, transport equipment, clothing, petroleum. Major trading partners: U.S., Caribbean and Western European countries.

Geography. Largest but most sparsely populated of the Central American nations, Nicaragua borders on Honduras to the north and Costa Rica to the south. It is slightly larger than New York State.

Nicaragua is mountainous in the west, with fertile valleys. A plateau slopes eastward toward the Caribbean.

Two big lakes—Nicaragua, about 100 miles long (161 km), and Managua, about 38 miles long (61 km)—are connected by the Tipitapa River. The Pacific coast is bald and rocky. The Caribbean coast, swampy and indented, is aptly called the "Mosquito Coast."

Government. A five-member junta, led by Sergio Ramirez Mercado, took power as a "government of national reconstruction" when troops supporting the junta seized the capital on July 19, 1979. President Anastasio Somoza Debayle, whose family had ruled Nicaragua for 45 years, fled to U.S. exile two days earlier.

History. Nicaragua, which established independence in 1838, was first visited by the Spaniards in 1522. The chief of the country's leading Indian tribe at that time was called Nicaragua, from whom the nation derived its name. A U.S. naval force intervened in 1909 after two American citizens had been executed, and a few U.S. Marines were kept in the country from 1912 to 1925. The Bryan-Chamorro Treaty of 1916 (terminated in 1970) gave the U.S. an option on a canal route through Nicaragua, and naval bases. Disorder after the 1924 elections brought in the marines again.

A guerrilla leader, Gen. César Augusto Sandino, began fighting the occupation force in 1927. He fought the U.S. troops successfully until their withdrawal in 1933. They trained Gen. Anastasio (Tacho) Somoza García to head a National Guard. In 1934, Somoza assassinated Sandino and overthrew the Liberal President Juan Batista Sacassa, establishing a military dictatorship with himself as president. He spurred the economic development of the country, meanwhile enriching his family through estates in the countryside and investments in air and shipping lines. On his assassination in 1956, he was succeeded by his son Luis, who alternated with trusted family friends in the presidency until his death in 1967. Another son, Maj. Gen. Anastasio Somoza Debayle, became President for a five-year term in 1967.

Somoza resigned the presidency in 1972, but remained commander-in-chief and national strongman while the constitution was rewritten to permit him to run for a second term two years later.

One of the worst earthquakes in Nicaragua's history struck Managua on Dec. 23, 1972, destroying an estimated 90% of its commercial establishments and 70% of its housing. Over 6,000 were killed, 20,000 injured, and 300,000 made homeless, and 60,000 were jobless as a result. Rebuilding costs were put at $772 million.

Following his inauguration in December 1974, Somoza obtained loans from the U.S. and international banks totaling $127 million for the reconstruction of Managua. Shortly afterward, he declared martial law after leftist guerrillas had kidnapped 14 prominent officials.

Although the Somoza regime was cited in 1977 by a U.S. State Department report for human-rights violations and Nicaragua's Catholic hierarchy testified to the government's repression and terror, it was not until 1978 that the Carter Administration moved to cut military aid to Somoza.

The situation was aggravated by the murder on January 10 of Pedro Joaquin Chamorro, editor of an opposition newspaper, causing student strikes and wide public protest. In an uncharacteristic response, Somoza made concessions to protesters and announced an inquiry into Chamorro's death. On May 16, the U.S. Congress acted to restore $12 million in military aid to Nicaragua.

Sandinista guerrillas, leftists who took their name from Gen. Sandino, launched a civil war in May 1979, occupying parts of Managua and holding several provincial towns. Somoza ordered bombings to drive the rebels out, an action that embittered Nicaraguans of all classes. He defied appeals by the U.S. and the Organization of American States to step down and permit a peaceful transition to an all-party government. The U.S. sought to win Sandinista agreement to the incorporation of Somoza's National Guard into the armed forces of the new government, but the President flew to exile in the U.S. on July 17 without reaching a settlement.

The five-member junta that took control under the leadership of Sergio Ramirez Mercado also included two other members of the rebel forces and two non-Sandinistas. The resignations of the last two in April 1980 raised fears of a leftist takeover. But the appointment to the junta of Arturo Cruz, former head of Nicaragua's central bank, and Supreme Court Justice Rafael Cordoba Rivas reassured moderate opinion, together with the restoration of civil rights and the cessation of property expropriations.

On the first anniversary of the overthrow of Somoza, the expected announcement of elections for the return of civilian government failed to come, however. Cuba's President Fidel Castro, the chief guest at the celebrations, also attended by a U.S. delegation, urged the United States to increase the $70 million in aid already granted to the revolutionary regime.

NIGER

Republic of Niger
Chief of State: Col. Seyni Kountché (1974)
Area: 489,206 sq mi. (1,267,044 sq km)
Population (est. 1980): 5,300,000
Density per square mile: 10.8
Capital and largest city (est. 1977): Niamey, 225,000
Monetary unit: Franc CFA
Ethnic groups: Hausa, 54%; Djerma and Songhai, 24%; Peul, 11%
Languages: French (official); Hausa, Songhai; Arabic
Religions: Islam, 80%; Animist, Christian, 6%
National name: République du Niger
Freedom House classifications: Capitalist pre-industrial, non-party military
Economic summary: Gross national product (1978): $1.1 billion. Average annual growth rate (1970–77): −1.8%. Per capita income: $100. Land used for agriculture: 3%; labor force: 90%; principal products: peanuts, cotton, livestock, millet, sorghum, vegetables. Major industrial products: uranium, cement, bricks, light industrial products. Natural resources: uranium, coal, iron. Exports: uranium, peanuts, livestock, hides, skins. Imports: fuels, machinery, transport equipment, foodstuffs, consumer goods. Major trading partners: France, other Western European countries, Nigeria.

Geography. Niger, in West Africa's Sahara region, is four fifths the size of Alaska. It is surrounded by Mali, Algeria, Libya, Chad, Nigeria, Benin, and Upper Volta.

The Niger River in the southwest flows through the country's only fertile area. Elsewhere the land is semiarid.

Government. After a military coup on April 15, 1974, Lt. Col. Seyni Kountché suspended the Constitution and instituted rule by decree. Previously, the President was elected by direct universal suffrage for a five-year term and a National House of Assembly of 50 members was elected for the same term.

The Parti Progressiste Nigérien-Rassemblement

Démocratique Africain, the only political party, was dissolved in 1974.

History. Niger was incorporated into French West Africa in 1896. There were frequent rebellions, but when order was restored in 1922, the French made the area a colony. In 1958, the voters approved the French Constitution and voted to make the territory an autonomous republic within the French Community. The republic adopted a Constitution in 1959 and the next year withdrew from the Community, proclaiming its independence.

The 1974 army coup ousted President Hamani Diori, who had held office since 1960. He was charged with having mishandled relief for the terrible drought that had devastated Niger and five neighboring sub-Saharan nations for several years. An estimated 2 million people were starving in Niger, but 200,000 tons of imported food, half U.S.-supplied, substantially ended famine conditions by the year's end. The new President, Lt. Col. Seyni Kountché, Chief of Staff of the army, installed a 12-man military government. A predominantly civilian government was formed by Kountché in 1976.

NIGERIA

Federal Republic of Nigeria
President: Alhaji Shehu Shagari (1979)
Area: 356,700 sq mi. (923,853 sq km)
Population (est. 1980): 77,100,000[1]
Density per square mile: 216.1
Capital: Lagos
Largest cities (est. 1977): Lagos (metropolitan area): 3,500,000; (est. 1975 by U.N.): Ibadan, 847,000; Ogbomosho, 432,000; Kano, 399,000
Monetary unit: Naira
Languages: English (official) and native tongues
Religions: Islam, 47%; Christian, 34%; Animist
Member of Commonwealth of Nations
Freedom House classifications: Capitalist-statist pre-industrial, multi-party decentralized
Economic summary: Gross national product (1978): $45.7 billion. Average annual growth rate (1970–77): 4.4%. Per capita income: $500. Land used for agriculture: 30%; labor force: 70%; principal products: peanuts, cotton, cocoa, rubber, yams, cassava, livestock. Labor force in industry: 10%; major products: crude oil, natural gas, coal, tin, processed rubber, cotton, petroleum, wood, hides, textiles, cement, footwear, chemicals. Natural resources: petroleum, tin, columbite, iron ore, coal, limestone, lead, zinc, timber. Exports: oil, cocoa, palm products, rubber, timber, tin. Imports: machinery and transport equipment, manufactured goods, chemicals. Major trading partners: U.K., Western European countries, U.S.

Geography. Nigeria, one third larger than Texas and black Africa's most populous nation, is situated on the Gulf of Guinea in West Africa. Its neighbors are Benin, Niger, Cameroon, and Chad.

The lower course of the Niger River flows south through the western part of the country into the Gulf of Guinea. Swamps and mangrove forests border the southern coast; inland are hardwood forests.

1. While U.N. and similar sources continue to report figures in this area, interpretations of election data by demographers suggest that, in reality, the population of Nigeria is close to 100 million.

Government. Beginning in 1966, a Supreme Military Council governed the country. In 1977, new local-government councils elected a 203-member national Constituent Assembly, which completed a new draft constitution in 1978. With the election of Alhaji Shehu Shagari, a former finance minister, as President in August 1979, the country returned to civilian rule on Oct. 1 with a United States type of presidential administration.

History. Between 1879 and 1914, private colonial developments by the British, with reorganizations of the Crown's interest in the region, resulted in the formation of Nigeria as it exists today. During World War I, native troops of the West African frontier force joined with French forces to defeat the German garrison in the Cameroons.

Nigeria became independent on Oct. 1, 1960.

Organized as a loose federation of self-governing states, the independent nation faced an overwhelming task of unifying a country with 250 ethnic and linguistic groups. The largest were the Hausa and Fulani in the north and the Ibo and Yoruba in the south, each of which had kingdoms in the late Middle Ages.

Rioting broke out again in 1966, the military commander was seized, and Col. Yakubu Gowon took power. Also in that year, the Moslem Hausas in the north massacred the predominantly Christian Ibos in the east, many of whom had been driven from the north. Thousands of Ibos took refuge in the Eastern Region. The military government there asked Ibos to return to the region and, in May 1967, the assembly voted to secede from the federation and set up the Republic of Biafra. Civil war broke out.

In January 1970, after 31 months of civil war, Biafra surrendered to the federal government. An estimated one million persons, mostly Ibos of the defeated state, were homeless and hungry, but a massive international relief operation kept the death toll down. The overall cost of the civil war was estimated at $840 million.

Gowon's nine-year rule was ended in 1975 by a bloodless coup that made Army Brigadier Muritala Rufai Mohammed the new chief of state. Mohammed was assassinated the next year 1976 by a group of seven young officers, who failed to seize control of the government. The 20-member Supreme Military Council chose Lt. Gen. Olusegun Obasanjo, Chief of Staff of the armed forces, as the new head of the Council and President. The assassins were publicly executed by firing squads.

Although Nigeria ranked seventh in world oil production in 1977 with revenues of $10 billion, a deficit in its balance of payments of $960 million for the year forced the government to impose severe restrictions on imported consumer goods. Nevertheless, Nigeria's prestige as the richest black African nation was emphasized by the visit of President Carter to Lagos on March 31, 1978, the first visit by an American President to black Africa since a brief stopover in Liberia by President Franklin D. Roosevelt during World War II.

NORWAY

Kingdom of Norway
Sovereign: King Olav V (1957)
Prime Minister: Odvar Nordli (1976)

Area: 125,182 sq mi. (324,219 sq km)
Population (est. 1980): 4,085,000
Density per square mile: 32.6
Capital: Oslo
Largest cities (est. 1979): Oslo, 457,300; Bergen, 212,750; Trondheim, 135,550; Stavanger, 88,100
Monetary unit: Krone
Language: Norwegian
Religions: Evangelical Lutheran (state), 94%
National name: Kongeriket Norge
Freedom House classifications: Capitalist-socialist industrial, multi-party centralized
Economic summary: Gross national product (1978): $38.5 billion. Average annual growth rate (1970–77): 3.9%. Per capita income: $8,316. Land used for agriculture: 3%; labor force: 8.7%; principal products: dairy products, livestock, grain, vegetables, fruits, furs, wool. Labor force in industry: 31.6%; major products: oil and gas, fish, pulp and paper, ships, aluminum, iron, steel, nickel, fertilizers, transportation equipment, hydroelectric power, petrochemicals, electronic equipment. Natural resources: fish, timber, hydroelectric power, ores, oil, gas. Exports: minerals, chemicals, crude oil, pulp and paper. Imports: machinery, transport equipment, foodstuffs, iron and steel, textiles and clothing. Major trading partners: Sweden, West Germany, U.K., U.S.

Geography. Norway is situated in the western part of the Scandinavian peninsula. It extends about 1,100 miles (1,770 km) from the North Sea along the Norwegian Sea to more than 300 miles (483 km) above the Arctic Circle, the farthest north of any European country. It is slightly larger than New Mexico. Sweden borders on most of the eastern frontier, with Finland and the U.S.S.R. in the northeast.

Nearly 70% of Norway is uninhabitable and covered by mountains, glaciers, moors, and rivers. The hundreds of deep fiords that cut into the coastline give Norway an overall oceanfront of more than 12,000 miles (19,312 km). Nearly 150,000 islands off the coast form a breakwater and make a safe coastal shipping channel.

Government. Norway is a constitutional hereditary monarchy. Executive power is vested in the King together with a Cabinet, or Council of State, consisting of a Prime Minister and at least seven other members. The Storting, or Parliament, is composed of 155 members elected by the people under proportional representation. The Storting discusses and votes on political and financial questions, but divides itself into two sections (Lagting and Odelsting) to discuss and pass on legislative matters. The King cannot dissolve the Storting before the expiration of its term.

The sovereign is Olav V, born July 2, 1903, only son of Haakon VII and Princess Maud (1869–1938), third daughter of Edward VII of England. He succeeded to the throne on the death of his father Sept. 20, 1957. He married Princess Märtha of Sweden (1901–1954) on March 21, 1929. Their children are Princess Ragnhild Alexandra (born 1930), Princess Astrid (born 1932), and Crown Prince Harald (born 1937). In 1968, the Crown Prince married Sonja Haraldsen, a commoner.

The major political parties are the Labor Party (76 of 155 seats in the Storting), led by Prime Minister Odvar Nordli; Conservative Party (41 seats), led by Käre Willoch. Christian Democrats (22 seats), led by Lars Korvald; Center Party (12 seats), led by Johan J. Jakobsen; Socialist Left Party (2 seats).

History. Norwegians, like the Danes and Swedes, are of Teutonic origin. The Norsemen, also known as Vikings, ravaged the coasts of northwestern Europe from the 8th to the 11th century.

In 1815, Norway fell under the control of Sweden. The union of Norway, inhabited by fishermen, sailors, merchants, and peasants, and Sweden, an aristocratic country of large estates and tenant farmers, was not a happy one, but it lasted for nearly a century. In 1905, the Norwegian Parliament arranged a peaceful separation and invited a Danish prince to the Norwegian throne—King Haakon VII. A treaty with Sweden provided that all disputes be settled by arbitration and that no fortifications be erected on the common frontier.

When World War I broke out, Norway joined with Sweden and Denmark in a decision to remain neutral and to cooperate in the joint interest of the three countries. In World War II, Norway was invaded by the Germans on April 9, 1940. It resisted for two months before the Nazis took over complete control. King Haakon and his government fled to London, where they established a government-in-exile. Maj. Vidkun Quisling, whose name is now synonymous with traitor or fifth columnist, was the most notorious Norwegian collaborator with the Nazis. He was executed by the Norwegians on Oct. 24, 1945.

Despite severe losses in the war, Norway recovered quickly. The country led the world in social experimentation. A neighbor of the U.S.S.R., Norway sought to retain good relations with the Soviet Union without losing its identity with the West. It entered the North Atlantic Treaty Organization in 1949.

Verification of U.S. and Soviet oil strikes in separated areas of Norway's sector of the North Sea bottom led the Storting in 1975 to impose stiff tax and royalty rates on concession holders. Following discovery of a North Sea field expected to produce 900,000 barrels a day by 1984, Parliament in 1976 approved establishment of a national refining and distributing company to market petroleum products at home and abroad.

Dependencies of Norway

Svalbard (23,957 sq mi.; 62,049 sq km), in the Arctic Ocean about 360 miles north of Norway, consists of the Spitsbergen group and several smaller islands, including Bear Island, Hope Island, King Charles Land, and White Island (or Gillis Land). It came under Norwegian administration in 1925. The population in 1979 was 3,640.

Bouvet Island (23 sq mi.; 60 sq km), in the South Atlantic about 1,600 miles south-southwest of the Cape of Good Hope, came under Norwegian administration in 1928.

Jan Mayen Island (144 sq mi.; 273 sq km), in the Arctic Ocean between Norway and Greenland, came under Norwegian administration in 1929. Its population in 1973 was 37.

Peter I Island (96 sq mi.; 249 sq km), lying off Antarctica in the Bellinghausen Sea, came under Norwegian administration in 1931.

Queen Maud Land, a section of Antarctica, came under Norwegian administration in 1939.

OMAN

Sultanate of Oman
Sultan: Qabus Bin Said (1970)
Area: 82,000 sq mi. (212,380 sq km)
Population (est. 1980): 880,000[1]
Density per square mile: 10.7
Capital (est. 1973): Muscat, 15,000
Largest city (est. 1973): Matrah, 18,000
Monetary unit: Omani rial
Language: Arabic
Religion: Islam
National name: Saltanat Oman
Freedom House classifications: Capitalist-statist pre-industrial, non-party non-military
Economic summary: Gross national product (1978): $2.2 billion. Average annual growth rate (1970–77): 4.0%. Per capita income: $4,880. Principal agricultural products: dates, alfalfa, onions, wheat, tobacco, bananas. Major industries: petroleum drilling, fishing, construction. Natural resources: oil, asbestos, marble, copper, limestone, chromium, manganese, iron. Exports: oil. Imports: machinery and transport equipment, food, mineral fuels, tobacco. Major trading partners: U.K., U.S., India, Australia, China, Japan.

Geography. Oman is a 1,000-mile-long (1,609-km) coastal plain at the southeastern tip of the Arabian peninsula lying on the Arabian Sea and the Gulf of Oman. The interior is a plateau. The country is the size of Kansas.

Government. The Sultan of Oman (formerly called Muscat and Oman), an absolute monarch, is assisted by several Personal Advisers, 17 Ministers, and other government officials.

There are no political parties.

History. Although Oman is an independent state under the rule of the Sultan, it has been under British protection since the early 19th century.

Muscat, the capital of the geographical area known as Oman, was occupied by the Portuguese from 1508 to 1648. Then it fell to Persian princes and later was regained by the Sultan.

The Kuria Muria Islands, formerly part of Aden, were given to Oman by the British in 1967.

In a palace coup on July 23, 1970, the Sultan, Sa'id bin Taimur, who had ruled since 1932, was overthrown by his son, who promised to establish a modern government and use new-found wealth to aid the people of this very isolated state.

With the shrinkage of British power, oil-rich Oman moved into the Iranian military orbit.

1. Excluding the Kuria Muria Islands.

PAKISTAN

Islamic Republic of Pakistan
President: Gen. Mohammad Zia ul-Haq (1978)
Area: 342,750 sq mi. (877,723 sq km)[1]
Population (est. 1980): 82,350,000
Density per square mile: 240.3
Capital (1972 census): Islamabad, 77,000
Largest cities (est. 1975 for metropolitan area): Karachi, 4,465,000; **(1972 census):** Lahore, 2,165,372; Lyallpur, 822,263; Hyderabad, 628,310; Rawalpindi, 615,392
Monetary unit: Pakistan rupee
Principal languages: Urdu (national), English (official), Punjabi, Sindhi, Pashtu, and Baluchi
Religions: Islam, 97%; Hindu, Christian
Freedom House classifications: Capitalist-statist pre-industrial, non-party military
Economic summary: Gross national product (1978): $17.5 billion. Average annual growth rate (1970–77): 0.8%. Per capita income: $200. Land used for agriculture: 24%; labor force: 59%; principal products: wheat, rice, cotton. Labor force in industry: 16%; major products: cotton textiles, processed foods, tobacco, chemicals, natural gas. Natural resources: natural gas, limited petroleum, iron ore. Exports: raw and manufactured cotton, rice. Imports: food grains, edible oil, crude oil, machinery, chemicals, transport equipment. Major trading partners: U.S., U.K., Japan, West Germany.

Geography. Pakistan is situated in the western part of the Indian subcontinent, with Afghanistan and Iran on the west, India on the east, and the Arabian Sea on the south.

Nearly twice the size of California, Pakistan consists of towering mountains, including the Hindu Kush in the west, a desert area in the east, the Punjab plains in the north, and an expanse of alluvial plains. The 1,000-mile-long (1,609 km) Indus River flows through the country from the Kashmir to the Arabian Sea.

Government. On July 5, 1977, martial law returned to Pakistan when Gen. Mohammad Zia ul-Haq, Army Chief of Staff, ousted the civilian government of Prime Minister Zulfikar Ali Bhutto. Zia declared himself Chief Administrator of Martial Law as head of a four-man council. The national and state assemblies were dissolved and all political parties banned, while the Chief Justices of the four states replaced the governors.

History. Pakistan was one of the two original successor states to British India. For almost 25 years following independence in 1947, it consisted of two separate regions. East and West Pakistan, but now comprises only the western sector. It consists of Sind, Baluchistan, the former North-West Frontier Province, western Punjab, the princely state of Bahawalpur, and several other smaller native states.

The British became the dominant power in the region in 1797 following Lord Clive's military victory, but rebellious tribes kept the northwest in turmoil. In the northeast, the formation of the Moslem League in 1906 estranged the Moslems from the Hindus. In 1930, the league, led by Mohammed Ali Jinnah, demanded creation of a Moslem state wherever Moslems were in the majority. He supported Britain during the war. Afterward, the league received almost a unanimous Moslem vote in 1946 and Britain agreed to the formation of Pakistan as a separate dominion.

Pakistan was proclaimed a republic March 23, 1956. Iskander Mirza, then Governor General, was elected Provisional President and H. S. Suhrawardy became the first non-Moslem League Prime Minister.

In 1958, Mirza surrendered his power to Gen. Ayub Khan, who purged corrupt and inefficient officeholders, broke up the feudal land system, eliminated much of the black market, tax evasion, and hoarding, and revolutionized education. A vote

1. Excluding Kashmir and Jammu.

of confidence in 1960 extended Ayub's dictatorial rule for five years and gave him power to write a new Constitution, which went into effect in 1962. In 1969, Gen. Yahya Khan ousted Ayub and took over as President.

The election of 1970—the first direct general balloting in Pakistani history—set the stage for bloody civil war. The Awami League, led by Sheik Mujibur Rahman, swept all National Assembly seats allotted the more populous East Pakistan, while the major West Pakistani party, the People's Party, led by Zulfikar Ali Bhutto, won only 82 seats.

Yahya directed the newly elected Assembly to meet March 1, 1971, and in 120 days write a Constitution. The Assembly never convened. Mujibur called general strikes, which turned bloody, and told East Pakistanis to stop paying taxes to the central government. West Pakistan troops moved in and fighting began. The independent state of Bangladesh, or Bengali nation, was proclaimed March 26, 1971.

The intervention of Indian troops permitted the new state to emerge and brought Yahya down. Bhutto took over and accepted Bangladesh as an independent entity. India appeared to have also gained a permanent partition of the Kashmir along cease-fire lines of 1971. The overall effect was to leave Pakistan a much smaller and weaker nation, no longer able to challenge India seriously.

Diplomatically, 1976 saw the resumption of formal relations between India and Pakistan. At the same time, civilian air traffic between the two nations was restored after an 11-year interruption.

Pakistan's first elections under civilian rule took place in March 1977 and provoked bitter opposition protest when Bhutto's party was declared to have won 155 of the 200 elected seats in the 216-member National Assembly. A rising tide of violent protest and political deadlock led to a military takeover on July 5. Gen. Mohammed Zia ul-Haq became Chief Martial Law Administrator.

Bhutto was tried and convicted for the 1974 murder of a political opponent, and despite worldwide protests was executed on April 4, 1979, touching off riots by his supporters. The execution was another step in the consolidation of power by Zia, who had declared himself President on Sept. 16, 1978, when Fazel Elahi Chaudhry resigned in disagreement over Zia's proposal to make Islamic law the law of the land.

The Soviet invasion of Afghanistan in December 1979 made Pakistan a front-line state in the new world crisis. The Moslem League met in Islamabad in January and condemned the invasion. Pakistan became the channel for clandestine aid to the Afghan rebels despite Soviet threats, and by August 1980, 1 million refugees from the conflict were sheltered in the country at an estimated annual cost of $100 million to Pakistan.

PANAMA

Republic of Panama
President: Aristides Royo (1978)
Area: 29,306 sq mi. (75,903 sq km)
Population (est. 1980): 1,935,000 (mestizo, 65%; black, 13%; white, 11%; Indian, 10%)
Density per square mile: 66.0
Capital and largest city (est. 1978): Panama City, 439,900
Monetary unit: Balboa
Language: Spanish (official)
Religion: Roman Catholic, 90%, Protestant
National name: República de Panamá
Freedom House classifications: Capitalist-statist industrial, non-party military
Economic summary: Gross national product (1978): $2.4 billion. Average annual growth rate (1970–77): −0.1%. Per capita income (1977): $1,252. Land used for agriculture: 29%; labor force: 40%; principal products: bananas, corn, sugar, rice, cattle. Labor force in industry: 18%; major industrial products: refined petroleum, sugar. Natural resources: copper (unexploited). Exports: bananas, refined petroleum, sugar, shrimp. Imports: crude oil, capital goods, food. Major trading partners: U.S., West Germany, Venezuela, Saudi Arabia, Ecuador.

Geography. The southernmost of the Central American nations, Panama is south of Costa Rica and north of Colombia. The Panama Canal bisects the isthmus at its narrowest and lowest point, allowing passage from the Caribbean Sea to the Pacific Ocean.

Panama is slightly smaller than South Carolina. It is marked by a chain of volcanic mountains in the west, moderate hills in the interior, and a low range on the east coast. There are extensive forests in the fertile Caribbean area.

Government. Following a military coup in 1968, a two-man junta ruled briefly but was in turn overthrown by Gen. Omar Torrijos, head of the National Guard (army).

In 1972, a new Constitution was approved by a new 505-seat National Assembly of Community Representatives (corregidores), which was created in the first election in five years. The Charter provides for indirect election of the President by the Assembly. The Assembly elected Demetrio Lakas Bahas President but named Torrijos as Head of Government with all civil and military powers for six years. Otherwise the Assembly is more a consultative than legislative body. Torrijos named a legislative committee to assist him in drafting laws.

In the 1978 election, Dr. Aristides Royo was elected president, succeeding Lakas Bahas.

History. Visited by Columbus in 1502 on his fourth voyage and explored by Balboa in 1513, Panama was the principal transshipment point for Spanish treasure and supplies to and from South and Central America in colonial days. In 1821, when Central America revolted against Spain, Panama joined Colombia, which already had declared its independence. For the next 82 years, Panama attempted unsuccessfully to break away from Colombia. After U. S. proposals for canal rights over the narrow isthmus had been rejected by Colombia, Panama proclaimed its independence with U.S. backing in 1903.

For canal rights in perpetuity, the U.S. paid Panama $10 million and agreed to pay $250,000 each year, increased to $430,000 after devaluation of the U.S. dollar in 1933 and was further increased under a revised treaty signed in 1955. In exchange, the U.S. got the Canal Zone—a 10-mile-wide strip across the isthmus—and a considerable degree of influence in Panama's affairs.

In 1968, Dr. Arnulfo Arias was elected President for the third time in three decades. And for the third time, he was thrown out of office by the military. A two-man junta, Col. José M. Pinilla and Col. Bolivar Urrutia, took control. They were ousted by

Gen. Omar Torrijos Herrera, who named a new junta, with Demetrio Lakas Bahas as President.

Panama and the U.S. agreed in 1974 to negotiate the eventual reversion of the canal to Panama, despite strongly expressed opposition in the U.S. Congress. The texts of two treaties—one governing the transfer of the canal and the other guaranteeing its neutrality after transfer—were negotiated by August 1977 and were signed by Torrijos and President Carter in Washington on September 7. A Panamanian referendum approved the treaties by more than two thirds on October 23, but further changes were insisted upon by the U.S. Senate.

The principal change was a reservation sponsored by Senator Dennis De Concini, an Arizona Democrat, specifying that despite the neutrality treaty's specification that only Panama shall maintain forces in its territory after transfer of the canal Dec. 31, 1999, the U.S. should have the right to use military force to keep the canal operating if it should become obstructed. After lengthy debate, the Senate approved the neutrality treaty on March 16, 1978, by 68–32 and by the same vote approved the basic treaty governing the transfer on April 18. On June 16, Carter and Torrijos exchanged instruments of ratification in Panama City.

The basic treaty provides an increase from the present $2.3 million a year in royalties to $10 million a year during the transition period, with an additional annual payment of $10 million if it can be obtained from tolls. It also requires the use of more Panamanians as canal employees in the interim and pledges the U.S. not to pursue the development of another canal without the agreement of Panama.

Panama Canal. First conceived by the Spaniards in 1534, when King Charles V of Spain ordered a survey of a waterway across the Isthmus, a construction concession was granted by the Colombian government in 1878 to St. Lucien N. B. Wyse, representing a French company. Two years later, the French Canal Company, inspired by Ferdinand de Lesseps, began construction of what was to have been a sea-level canal. The effort ended in bankruptcy nine years later and the United States ultimately paid the French $40 million for their rights and assets.

The U.S. project, built on territory controlled by the United States, and calling for the creation of an interior lake connected to both oceans by locks, got under way in 1904. Completed in 1914, the Canal is 40.27 miles long and lifts ships 85 feet above sea level through a series of three locks on the Pacific and Atlantic sides. Enlarged in later years, each lock now measures 1,000 feet in length, 110 feet in width, and 40 feet in depth of water.

PAPUA NEW GUINEA

Sovereign: Queen Elizabeth II
Prime Minister: Sir Julius Chan (1980)
Governor General: Sir Tore Lokoloko (1977)
Area: 183,540 sq mi. (475,369 sq km)
Population (est. 1980): 3,170,000
Density per square mile: 17.3
Capital and largest city (est. 1979): Port Moresby, 120,000
Monetary unit: Kina
Languages: English, Melanesian pidgin, and 717 distinct native languages
Religions: Roman Catholic, 31%; Lutheran, 27%; Anglican, United Church
Member of Commonwealth of Nations
Freedom House classifications: Capitalist pre-industrial, multi-party decentralized
Economic summary: Gross national product (1978): $1.6 billion. Average annual growth rate (1970–77): 2.5%. Labor force in agriculture: 80%; principal products: sweet potatoes, coffee, copra, palm oil, cocoa, tea, rubber, cattle. Major industrial products: soap, concrete products, clothing, light fabricated metal products, paint, furniture. Natural resources: copper, gold, silver, timber, tuna. Exports: copper, gold, and silver concentrates, coffee and cocoa beans, copra, timber. Imports: food, machinery, transport equipment, fuels, chemicals. Major trading partners: Australia, U.K., Japan.

Geography. Papua New Guinea occupies the eastern half of the island of New Guinea, just north of Australia, and many outlying islands. The Indonesian province of Irian Jaya is to the west. To the north and east are the islands of Manus, New Britain, New Ireland, and Bougainville, all part of Papua New Guinea.

Papua New Guinea is about one tenth larger than California. Its mountainous interior has only recently been explored. The high-plateau climate is temperate, in contrast to the tropical climate of the coastal plains. Two major rivers, the Sepik and the Fly, are navigable for shallow-draft vessels.

Government. Papua New Guinea attained independence Sept. 16, 1975, ending a United Nations trusteeship under the administration of Australia. Parliamentary democracy was established by a Constitution that invests power in a single-chamber national legislature.

The Pangu Party, People's Progress Party, and United Party are the largest of half a dozen political parties.

History. The eastern half of New Guinea was first visited by Spanish and Portuguese explorers in the 16th century, but a permanent European presence was not established until 1884, when Germany declared a protectorate over the northern coast and Britain took similar action in the south. Both nations formally annexed their protectorates and, in 1901, Britain transferred its rights to a newly independent Australia. Australian troops invaded German New Guinea in World War I and retained control under a League of Nations mandate that eventually became a United Nations trusteeship, incorporating a territorial government in the southern region, known as Papua.

Australia granted limited home rule in 1951 and, in 1964, organized elections for the first House of Assembly. Autonomy in internal affairs came nine years later.

Just before independence, dissidents on the island of Bougainville, whose copper resources provide the chief foreign earnings for the central government, declared their intention to secede. The central government responded by taking direct control in October 1975, amid warnings from Australia that it would oppose secession. Prime Minister Michael Somare met with pro-secessionists early in 1976 and, after conceding extra powers for a restored provincial government, resolved the dispute.

Somare lost a vote of confidence on March 11, 1980, and was succeeded by Sir Julius Chan, head of the People's Progress Party and former Finance Minister.

PARAGUAY

Republic of Paraguay
President: Gen. Alfredo Stroessner (1954)
Area: 157,047 sq mi. (406,752 sq km)
Population (est. 1980): 3,055,000 (mestizo, 95%; white, 3%; Indian, 2%)
Density per square mile: 19.5
Capital and largest city (est. 1977): Asunción, 460,800
Monetary unit: Guaraní
Languages: Spanish (official), Guaraní
Religion: Roman Catholic (official)
National name: República del Paraguay
Freedom House classifications: Capitalist-statist pre-industrial, dominant party
Economic summary: Gross national product (1978): $2.5 billion. Average annual growth rate (1970–77): 4.3%. Per capita income: $750. Labor force in agriculture: 50%; principal products: oilseeds, cotton, wheat, sweet potatoes, tobacco, corn, rice, sugar cane. Labor force in industry: 19%; major products: packed meats, crushed oilseeds, beverages, textiles, light consumer goods, cement. Natural resource: timber. Exports: cotton, oilseeds, meat products, tobacco, timber, coffee, essential oils. Imports: fuels and lubricants, machinery and motors, motor vehicles, beverages, tobacco, foodstuffs. Major trading partners: Brazil, Argentina, West Germany, U.S., Netherlands, U.K., Japan.

Geography. California-size Paraguay is surrounded by Brazil, Bolivia, and Argentina in south central South America. Eastern Paraguay, between the Paraná and Paraguay Rivers, is upland country with the thickest population settled on the grassy slope that inclines toward the Paraguay River. The greater part of the Chaco region to the west is covered with marshes, lagoons, dense forests, and jungles.

Government. The President is elected by popular vote for five years. The legislature is bicameral, consisting of a Senate of 30 members and a Chamber of Representatives of 60 members. There is also a Council of State, whose members are nominated by the government.

The governing Partido Colorado was further strengthened in 1977 when the Partido Liberal Unido, a merger of the Partido Liberal Radical and Partido Liberal, was declared illegal.

History. In 1526 and again in 1529, Sebastian Cabot explored Paraguay when he sailed up the Paraná and Paraguay Rivers. From 1608 until their expulsion from the Spanish dominions in 1767, the Jesuits maintained an extensive establishment in the south and east of Paraguay. In 1811, Paraguay revolted against Spanish rule and became a nominal republic under two Consuls.

Actually, Paraguay was governed by three dictators during the first 60 years of independence. The third, Francisco López, waged war against Brazil and Argentina in 1864–65, a conflict in which the male population was almost wiped out. A new Constitution in 1870, designed to prevent dictatorships and internal strife, failed to do so, and not until 1912 did a period of comparative economic and political stability begin. The dispute between Paraguay and Bolivia over the Chaco region led to war in 1932 and was finally settled by the 1935 Buenos Aires Peace Conference, which gave most of the Chaco to Paraguay.

After World War II, politics became particularly unstable. Juan Natalicio González was elected President in 1948. Successive revolts on Jan. 30 and Feb. 26, 1949, ousted him and his successor. The leader of the second revolt, Felipe Molas López, was elected President in April but gave way to Federico Chaves. Re-elected in 1953, Chaves was ousted by the army, and Gen. Alfredo Stroessner was elected to complete his term.

Stroessner ruled under a state of siege until 1965, when the dictatorship was relaxed and exiles returned. The Constitution was revised in 1967 to permit Stroessner to be re-elected, and press freedom was briefly restored before the regime again moved to repress opposition.

U.S. companies began exploration for oil in 1974 in the desolate Chaco Boreal section of northwest Paraguay under 40-year contracts that the regime's critics denounced as overgenerous. No oil has been found.

Paraguay was criticized by the U.S. State Department for violation of human rights, but was not one of the countries for which the Carter Administration recommended aid cuts. Amnesty International estimated that about 350 political prisoners were held in Paraguayan jails.

PERU

Republic of Peru
President: Fernando Belaúnde Terry (1980)
Premier: Manuel Ulloa (1980)
Area: 496,222 sq mi. (1,285,216 sq km)
Population (1980): 17,770,000 (white and mestizo, 52%; Indian, 46%)
Density per square mile: 35.8
Capital: Lima
Largest cities (est. 1978 for metropolitan area): Lima, 4,376,100; **(est. 1975 by U.N.):** Arequipa, 304,600; Callao, 296,200; Trujillo, 241,900
Monetary unit: Sol
Languages: Spanish, Quéchua
Religion: Roman Catholic
National name: República del Perú
Freedom House classifications: Capitalist-socialist pre-industrial, non-party military
Economic summary: Gross national product (1978): $12.4 billion. Average annual growth rate (1970–77): 1.8%. Per capita income (1977): $748. Land used for agriculture: 23%; labor force: 43%; principal products: corn, sugar, cotton, coffee, wool. Labor force in industry: 18%; major products: processed minerals, fish meal, refined petroleum, textiles. Natural resources: minerals and metals, fish, petroleum, timber. Exports: copper, fish products, cotton, sugar, coffee, lead, silver, zinc, wool, iron ore. Imports: machinery, cereals, chemicals, pharmaceuticals. Major trading partners: U.S., Japan, Western European, and Latin American countries.

Geography. Peru, in western South America, extends for nearly 1,500 miles (2,414 km) along the Pacific Ocean. Colombia and Ecuador are to the north, Brazil and Bolivia to the east, and Chile to the south.

Five sixths the size of Alaska, Peru is divided by the Andes Mountains into three sharply differentiated zones. To the west is the coastline, much of it arid, extending 50 to 100 miles (80 to 160 km) inland. The mountain area, with peaks over 20,000 feet (6,096 m), lofty plateaus, and deep valleys, lies centrally. Beyond the mountains to the east is the heavily forested slope leading to the Amazonian plains.

Government. The President, elected by universal suffrage for a six-year term, holds executive power. A Senate of 60 members and a Chamber of Deputies of 180 members, both elected for six-year terms, share legislative power.

The major political parties are: Acción Popular (98 of 180 seats in the Chamber and 26 of 60 seats in the Senate), led by President Fernando Belaúnde Terry; Partido Popular Cristiano (10 Chamber seats and 6 Senate seats), led by Luis Bedoya Reyes; and the opposition Partido Aprista Peruano (58 Chamber seats and 18 Senate seats), led by Luis Alberto Sanchez. The Partido Popular Cristiano is allied with Belaúnde.

History. Peru was once part of the great Incan empire and later the major vice-royalty of Spanish South America. It was conquered in 1531–33 by Francisco Pizarro. On July 28, 1821, Peru proclaimed its independence, but the Spanish were not finally defeated until 1824. For a hundred years thereafter, revolutions were frequent, and a new war was fought with Spain in 1864–66.

Peru emerged from 20 years of dictatorship in 1945 with the inauguration of President José Luis Bustamente y Rivero after the first free election in many decades. But he served for only three years and was succeeded in turn by Gen. Manuel A. Odria, Manuel Prado y Ugarteche, and Fernando Belaunde Terry. On Oct. 3, 1968, Belaunde was overthrown by Gen. Juan Velasco Alvarado.

Velasco nationalized the nation's second biggest bank and turned two large newspapers over to Marxists in 1970, but he also allowed a new agreement with a copper-mining consortium of four American firms.

On May 31, 1970, the country suffered the hemisphere's worst natural disaster, an earthquake which, together with a mud slide it caused, took an estimated 50,000 lives.

The World Bank granted Peru $470 million in credits in 1973, which appeared to end a boycott by international financial institutions in which the U.S. has a strong influence. American copper and fishing firms were seized in 1974, but compensation was paid. Peru also became in 1974 the first nation in the Western Hemisphere to receive Soviet military advisers.

On Aug. 29, 1975, Velasco was replaced in a bloodless coup by his Premier, Gen. Francisco Morales Bermúdez. To meet International Monetary Fund requirements for the extension of credit, Morales decreed a severe economic austerity program in 1977, touching off student and leftist demonstrations. Even stiffer measures, ranging from 50% to 100% increases in the prices of essentials, were ordered in 1978.

Fulfilling a pledge to restore civilian government, Morales scheduled elections for May 18, 1980, in which Belaúnde Terry, the last civilian President, won 43% of the vote in a field of 15 candidates. Allied with the small Partido Popular Cristiano, Belaúnde Terry's Acción Popular party was assured of a parliamentary majority. In one of his first moves, the new President returned to private ownership newspapers that had been seized under the Morales regime.

THE PHILIPPINES

Republic of the Philippines
President (1965) and Prime Minister (1973): Ferdinand E. Marcos
Area: 115,707 sq mi. (299,681 sq km)
Population (est. 1980): 49,150,000
Density per square mile: 424.8
Capital: Manila
Largest cities (est. 1977 for metropolitan area): Manila, 7,500,000 (est. 1975 by U.N.): Quezon City, 994,700; Davao, 515,500; Cebu, 418,500
Monetary unit: Peso
Languages: Pilipino, English, Spanish; dialects: Tagalog, Visayan
Religions: Roman Catholic, 85%; Islam, 4%; Aglipayan (Independent Philippine Christian), 4%; Protestant, 3%
National name: Republika ng Pilipinas
Freedom House classifications: Capitalist pre-industrial, one-party dominant-party
Economic summary: Gross national product (1978): $23.3 billion. Average annual growth rate (1970–77): 3.7%. Per capita income: $460. Land used for agriculture: 38%; labor force: 60%; principal products: rice, corn, coconuts, sugar cane, bananas, tobacco. Labor force in industry: 12%; major products: processed agricultural products, textiles, chemicals and chemical products. Natural resources: forests, metallic and non-metallic minerals. Exports: coconut products, sugar, logs and lumber, copper concentrates, bananas, garments, nickel. Imports: petroleum, industrial equipment, wheat. Major trading partners: U.S., Japan.

Geography. The Philippine Islands are an archipelago of over 7,000 islands lying about 500 miles (805 km) off the southeast coast of Asia. The overall land area is comparable to that of Arizona. The northernmost island, Y'Ami, is 65 miles (105 km) from Taiwan, while the southernmost, Saluag, is 40 miles (64 km) east of Borneo.

Only about 7% of the islands are larger than one square mile, and only one third have names. The largest are Luzon in the north (40,420 sq mi.; 04,687 sq km), Mindanao in the south (36,537 sq mi.; 94,631 sq km), Samar (5,124 sq mi.; 13,271 sq km), Negros (4,903 sq mi.; 12,699 sq km), and Palawan (4,550 sq km).

The islands are of volcanic origin, with the larger ones crossed by mountain ranges. The highest peak is Mount Apo (9,690 ft; 2,954 m) on Mindanao.

Government. President Ferdinand E. Marcos proclaimed a new Constitution in 1973, replacing the previous presidential style of government with a parliamentary system. The president became the symbolic head of state and the prime minister the head of government, with Marcos holding both posts. Marcos has ruled by decree since Sept. 21, 1972, and the new Constitution dissolved the previous legislature. A new National Assembly of 186 elected and 31 appointed members was chosen April 7, 1978. Its powers are limited, within the framework of what Marcos has called "constitutional authoritarianism."

History. Fernando Magellan, the Portuguese navigator in the service of Spain, discovered the Philippines in 1521. Twenty-one years later, a Spanish exploration party named the group of islands in honor of Price Philip, later Philip II of Spain. Spain retained possession of the islands for the next 350 years.

The Philippines were ceded to the U.S. in 1899 by the Treaty of Paris after the Spanish-American War. Meanwhile, the Filipinos, led by Emilio Aguinaldo, had declared their independence. They continued guerrilla warfare against U.S. troops until the capture of Aguinaldo in 1901. By 1902, peace was established except among the Moros.

The first U.S. civilian Governor-General was William Howard Taft (1901–04). The Jones Law (1916) provided for the establishment of a Philippine Legislature composed of an elective Senate and House of Representatives. The Tydings-McDuffie Act (1934) provided for a transitional period until 1946, at which time the Philippines would become completely independent.

Under a Constitution approved by the people of the Philippines in 1935, the Commonwealth of the Philippines came into being, with Manuel Quezon y Molina as president.

On Dec. 8, 1941, the Philippines were invaded by Japanese troops. Following the fall of Bataan and Corregidor, Quezon established a government-in-exile, which he headed until his death in 1944. He was succeeded by Vice President Sergio Osmeña.

U.S. forces led by Gen. Douglas MacArthur reinvaded the Philippines in October 1944 and, after the liberation of Manila in February 1945, Osmeña re-established the government.

The Philippines achieved full independence on July 4, 1946. Manuel A. Roxas y Acuña was elected first president. Subsequent presidents have been Elpidio Quirino (1948–53), Ramón Magsaysay (1953–57). Carlos P. García (1957–61), Diosdado Macapagal (1961–65), and Ferdinand E. Marcos (since Dec. 30, 1965).

Marcos became the first president in Philippine history to win re-election in 1969, when he overwhelmingly defeated Sergio Osmeña, Jr., with campaign promises to become less dependent on the U.S. and to establish ties with Communist countries. The campaign violence led to 59 deaths. After his inauguration, the worst peacetime riots in Philippine history occurred when a student-led demonstration tried to storm the presidential palace, with 5 dead and 157 injured, to protest government corruption.

Political, civil, and religious unrest was responsible for the deaths of almost 500 persons in 1971, and disastrous month-long rains that caused enormous flooding added to the toll in 1972. In September 1972, Marcos declared martial law and arrested hundreds of political opponents, journalists, and leftists.

Nearly 8,000 persons died Aug. 17, 1976, when an earthquake measuring 8 on the Richter scale hit Mindanao and other southern islands. The disaster temporarily quelled a rebellion by the Moslem majority in Mindanao, but fighting resumed until a truce was reached in December. Rebel representatives and Manila officials signed an agreement in Tripoli in 1977, providing a degree of autonomy for the Moslem region.

The Philippines was one of six nations criticized by the U.S. State Department for human-rights violations in a report made public in 1977, although the department recommended continuing aid because of the importance of U.S. bases in the Philippines. Marcos at first declared he would reject any aid and threatened to close the bases but later softened, saying they could remain if the U.S. pledged that the bases would be used to defend the Philippines in the event of an attack. He also announced that he would phase out the military tribunals he established in 1972 and in two months freed about 1,000 of 4,774 prisoners being held for military trial.

Political restraints were eased for the legislative elections of 1978. The suppressed Liberal Party and other opposition groups formed the People's Force Party and contested the 21 seats assigned to Manila. Amid charges of fraud, Marcos' New Society Movement won all 21. Marcos freed many political prisoners before his inauguration as prime minister on June 12 and pledged to move toward "making democracy real", although he retained his powers under martial law.

In a surprise move, former Senator Benigno S. Aquino, Jr., was released from seven-and-a-half years of detention on May 8, 1980, and permitted to go to the United States for heart bypass surgery. Although he said he expected to return, Aquino decided to remain in the U.S. after he arrived. He was the last of the national leaders in detention under Marcos' military rule.

POLAND

Polish People's Republic
President of the Council of State: Henryk Jablonski (1972)
Premier: Jozef Pinkowski (1980)
Area: 120,359 sq mi. (311,730 sq km)
Population (est. 1980): 35,450,000
Density per square mile: 294.5
Capital: Warsaw
Largest cities (est. 1979): Warsaw, 1,552,000; **(est. 1977 by U.N.):** Lodz, 814,800; Krakow, 707,000; Wroclaw, 588,700; Poznan, 531,600; Gdansk, 439,000; Szczecin, 380,000; Katowice, 349,800
Monetary unit: Zloty
Language: Polish (more than 90%)
Religions: Roman Catholic, Greek Orthodox, Protestant, Jewish
National name: Polska Rzeczpospolita Ludowa
Freedom House classifications: Capitalist-socialist industrial, one-party communist
Economic summary: Gross national product (1978): $128 billion. Average annual growth rate (1970–77): 6.3%. Per capita income: $2,740. Labor force in agriculture: 32%; principal products: grains, sugar beets, potatoes, hogs and other livestock. Labor force in industry: 26%; major products: iron and steel, chemicals, textiles, processed foods, transport equipment. Natural resources: coal, sulfur, copper, natural gas. Exports: coal, agricultural products. Imports: oil, iron ore, raw materials, grain. Major trading partners: U.S.S.R., East Germany, Czechoslovakia, U.K., Italy, U.S.

Geography. Poland, a country the size of New Mexico in north central Europe, borders on East Germany to the west, Czechoslovakia to the south, and the U.S.S.R. to the east. In the north is the Baltic Sea.

Most of the country is a plain with no natural boundaries except the Carpathian Mountains in the south and the Oder and Neisse Rivers in the east. Other major rivers, which are important to commerce, are the Vistula, Warta, and Bug.

Government. The 1952 Constitution describes Poland as a people's republic. The supreme organ of state authority is the Sejm (Parliament), which is composed of 460 members elected for four years.

The major political parties are the Polish United Workers' (Communist) Party (255 of 460 seats in the Sejm), led by First Secretary Stanislaw Kania; United Peasant Party (117 seats), led by Stanislaw Gucwa; Democratic Party (39 seats), led by Tadeusz W. Mlynczak; non-party members and Catholic organizations (49 seats).

History. Little of certainty is known about Polish history before the 11th century, when King Boleslaus I (the Brave) ruled over Bohemia, Saxony, and Moravia. Mongol invasions in 1241 and 1259 were repelled. Meanwhile, the Teutonic knights were erecting in Prussia a state that included part of Poland and barred the latter's access to the Baltic. The knights were defeated by Wladislaus II at Tannenberg in 1410 and became Polish vassals, and Poland regained a Baltic shoreline. Poland reached the peak of power between the 14th and 16th centuries, scoring military successes against the Russians and Turks. In 1683, John III (John Sobieski) turned back the Turkish tide at Vienna.

These successes did not halt the process of decline that resulted from the lack of strong central authority, and Prussia, Russia, and Austria were able to carry out a first partition of the country in 1772, a second in 1792, and a third in 1795–96. For more than a century thereafter, there was no Polish state, but the Poles never ceased their efforts to regain their independence.

The independence of Poland was formally proclaimed in November 1918, and Marshal Josef Pilsudski was made Chief of State. In 1919, Ignace Paderewski, the famous pianist and patriot, became the first premier. In 1926, Pilsudski seized complete power in a coup and ruled the country dictatorially until his death on May 12, 1935, when he was succeeded by Marshal Edward Smigly-Rydz.

Despite a 10-year nonaggression pact signed with Germany in 1934, Hitler attacked Poland on Sept. 1, 1939. Russian troops invaded from the east on September 17, and on September 28 a German-Russian agreement was signed dividing Poland between Russia and Germany. Wladyslaw Raczkiewicz formed a government-in-exile in France with Gen. Wladyslaw Sikorski as premier. This government moved to London after France's defeat in 1940.

All of Poland was occupied by Germany after the Nazi attack on the U.S.S.R. in June 1941. On July 30, 1941, the government-in-exile signed an agreement with the U.S.S.R. in which the latter voided all German-Soviet agreements effected after Sept. 1, 1939.

The legal Polish government soon fell out with the Russians, however, and, in 1944, a Communist-dominated Polish Committee of National Liberation received Soviet recognition. Moving to Lublin after that city's liberation, it proclaimed itself the Provisional Government of Poland. Some former members of the Polish government in London joined with the Lublin government to form the Polish Government of National Unity, which Britain and the U.S. recognized.

On Aug. 2, 1945, in Berlin, President Harry S. Truman, Joseph Stalin and Prime Minister Clement Attlee of Britain established a new *de facto* western frontier for Poland along the Oder and Neisse Rivers. (The border was finally agreed to by West Germany in a nonaggression pact signed Dec. 7, 1970.) On Aug. 16, 1945, the U.S.S.R. and Poland signed a treaty delimiting the Soviet-Polish frontier. Under these agreements, Poland was shifted westward. In the east it lost 69,860 square miles (180,934 sq km) with 10,772,000 inhabitants; in the west it gained (subject to final peace-conference approval) 38,986 square miles (100,973 sq km) with a prewar population of 8,621,000.

In 1946, a unicameral Parliament was established by referendum. A limited legal opposition was countenanced at first. Then, in 1947, the government bloc won a huge majority in government-controlled elections and after much fighting the underground opposition was suppressed and the Sovietization of Poland begun, with Soviet Marshal Konstantin Rokossovsky as Defense Minister and army commander.

In 1952, a Constitution was promulgated making Poland a "people's democracy" of the Soviet type. In 1955, Poland, which had joined the Council for Economic Mutual Assistance in 1949, became a member of the Warsaw Treaty Organization, and its foreign policy became identical with that of the U.S.S.R. The government undertook persecution of the Roman Catholic Church as one of the remaining source of opposition and in 1953 arrested the primate, Stefan Cardinal Wyszynski. But in June 28–30, 1956, worker and student riots in Poznan forced reconsideration of the repression.

Wladyslaw Gomulka was elected leader of the United Workers (Communist) Party in 1956. He denounced the Stalinist terror, ousted many Stalinists, relieved Rokossovsky, freed Wyszynski, and improved relations with the church. Most collective farms were dissolved, and the press became freer.

Much as the Poznan bread riots of 1956 brought Gomulka to power, so pre-Christmas rioting in 1970 in Gdansk and other Baltic coastal towns caused Gomulka to fall and elevated Edward Gierek to the key post of party boss. Cause of the worker riots, in which at least 45 and probably over 200 died when police and army troops crushed the protest, was steep price rises on meat and other foods. Significantly, no students or intellectuals were involved.

Serious resistance to increased food prices again brought rioting in Polish cities in the summer of 1976 after the government announced a new schedule of prices.

As a result of the riots, the government in 1977 revised its economic goals to put more emphasis on production of consumer goods and reduced foreign borrowing for capital investment, slowing industrial development. Indicative of a growing force to ease government policies, a group of professionals formed the Movement for the Defense of Human and Civil Rights to cooperate with the Workers Defense Committee and to seek freedom of expression for all political groups.

An event of profound importance to Poland's 90% Catholic population was the election in October 1978 of Karol Cardinal Wojtila of Krakow as

Pope John Paul II. His visit to his homeland from June 2 to June 11, 1979, the first papal journey to a Marxist state, met with nervous apprehension from the government and an outpouring of emotion from not only Polish Catholics but also those from neighboring Communist countries who were able to attend events.

Before massive audiences in Warsaw, Czestochowa, Krakow, and Auschwitz, the Pope spoke boldly for religious freedom as a "fundamental right," and he specifically challenged Marxist atheism's view of man as an economic animal. A Polish government spokesman voiced surprise at the Pope's forthright political statements, and a Moscow commentator reacted stiffly to "anti-state purposes" manifested in the visit.

A strike that began in shipyards and spread to other industries in August 1980 produced a stunning victory for workers on Aug. 31 when the economically hard-pressed government accepted for the first time in a Marxist state the right of workers to organize in independent unions. In addition, the strikers won curbs on media censorship and the privileges of Communist Party members over ordinary workers in state enterprises. The strike was supported financially by Western unions and vocally by Pope John Paul II.

The strike also led to major changes in Polish leadership. Edward Babuich, who became Premier early in 1980, was replaced by Jozef Pinkowski, and Edward Gierek, longtime Communist Party boss, was ousted in favor of Stanislaw Kania.

PORTUGAL

Portuguese Republic
President: Gen. António Ramalho Eanes (1976)
Premier: Francisco de Sá Carneiro (1980)
Area: 35,340 sq mi. (91,531 sq km)
Population (est. 1980): 9,940,000
Density per square mile: 281.3
Capital: Lisbon
Largest cities (est. 1979): Lisbon, 861,500; **(est. 1975 by U.N.):** Opporto, 335,700
Monetary unit: Escudo
Language: Portuguese
Religion: Roman Catholic
National name: República Portuguesa
Freedom House classifications: Capitalist-socialist industrial, multi-party centralized
Economic summary: Gross national product (1978): $19.5 billion. Average annual growth rate (1970–77): 3.1%. Land used for agriculture: 48%; labor force: 32%; principal products: grains, potatoes, olives, wine grapes. Labor force in industry: 34%; major products: textiles, footwear, wood pulp, paper, cork, metal products, refined oil, chemicals, canned fish, wine. Natural resources: fish, cork, tungsten ore. Exports: cotton, textiles, cork and cork products, canned fish, wine, timber and timber products, resin. Imports: petroleum, cotton, industrial machinery, iron and steel, chemicals. Major trading partners: U.K., West Germany, U.S., France, Italy.

Geography. Portugal occupies the western part of the Iberian Peninsula, bordering on the Atlantic Ocean to the west and Spain to the north and east. It is slightly smaller than Indiana.

The country is crossed by many small rivers, and also by three large ones that rise in Spain, flow into the Atlantic, and divide the country into three geographic areas. The Minho (Miño in Spain) River, part of the northern boundary, cuts through a mountainous area that extends south to the vicinity of the Douro (Duero) River. South of the Douro, the mountains slope to the plains about the Tagus (Tejo) River. The remaining division is the southern one of Alentejo.

The Azores, stretching over 340 miles (547 km) in the Atlantic, consist of nine islands divided into three groups, with a total area of 924 square miles (2,393 sq km). The nearest continental land is Cape da Roca, Portugal, about 900 miles (1,448 km) to the east. The Azores are an important station on Atlantic air routes, and Britain and the U.S. established air bases there during World War II.

Madeira, consisting of two inhabited islands, Madeira and Porto Santo, and two groups of uninhabited islands, lies in the Atlantic about 535 miles (861 km) southwest of Lisbon.

Government. A new Constitution, adopted in April 1976, provides for popular election of a President for a five-year term and for a legislature, the Assembly of the Republic, for four years.

The major political parties are the Democratic Alliance (128 of 250 seats in the Assembly), led by Premier Francisco de Sá Carneiro; Socialist Party (74 seats), led by former Premier Mário Soares, and Communist Party (47 seats), led by Alvaro Cunhal.

History. Portugal was a part of Spain until it won its independence in the middle of the 12th century. King John I (1385–1433) unified his country at the expense of the Castilians and the Moors of Morocco. The expansion of Portugal was brilliantly coordinated by John's son, Prince Henry the Navigator. In 1488, Bartholomew Diaz reached the Cape of Good Hope, proving that the Far East was accessible by sea. In 1498, Vasco da Gama reached the west coast of India. By the middle of the 16th century, the Portuguese Empire included West and East Africa, Brazil, Persia, Indochina, and Malaya.

In 1581, Philip II of Spain invaded Portugal and held it captive for 60 years. There followed a catastrophic decline of Portuguese commerce. Courageous and shrewd explorers, the Portuguese proved to be inefficient and corrupt colonizers. By the time the Portuguese dynasty was restored in 1640, Dutch, English, and French competitors began to seize the lion's share of the world's colonies and commerce. Portugal retained Angola and Mozambique in Africa, and Brazil (until 1822).

In the first half of the 19th century, Portugal's political history was distinguished by dynasty quarrels and factional strife. The corrupt King Carlos, who ascended the throne in 1889, made João Franco the Premier with dictatorial power in 1906. In 1908, Carlos and his heir were shot dead on the streets of Lisbon. The new King, Manoel II, was driven from the throne in the Revolution of 1910. Portugal was proclaimed a republic with a system modeled upon that of France.

Traditionally friendly to Britain, Portugal fought in World War I on the Allied side in Africa as well as on the Western Front. Weak postwar governments and a revolution in 1926 brought Antonio Oliveira Salazar to power. He kept Portugal neutral in World War II but gave the Allies naval and air bases after 1943.

Portugal lost the tiny remnants of its Indian empire—Goa, Daman, and Diu—to Indian military occupation in 1961, the year an insurrection broke out in Angola. For the next 13 years, Salazar, who died in 1970 after two years in a coma, and his successor, Marcello Caetano, fought independence movements amid growing world criticism. Leftists in the armed forces, weary of a losing battle, launched the "Happy Revolution" of April 25, 1974. They installed Gen. António de Spínola as Provisional President with promises of peace in Africa and reforms at home.

Spínola's moderate left Cabinet failed to satisfy the military leadership, who named Col. Vasco dos Santos Gonçalves as Premier on July 14. After Spínola's resignation on Sept. 30, Gen, Francisco da Costa Gomez, Chief of Staff of the armed forces, became President of an increasingly leftist regime. But conservatism in the country outside Lisbon manifested itself in the 1975 election of delegates to draft a new Constitution, as Socialists led with 38% of the delegates, Popular Democrats captured 28%, and the Communists trailed with only 12.5%.

Anti-Communist violence in rural areas and pressure from non-Communists in the government and military forced Gonçalves out on Aug. 29, 1975, and he was replaced by the more moderate Vice Adm. José Pinheiro. Elections under a new Constitution in 1976 gave Gen. António Ramalho Eanes, Army Chief of Staff, a landslide victory even though he campaigned for a program of economic austerity. With Mário Soares as Premier, tough economic policies slowed inflation but proved unpopular with legislators, who forced Soares out on July 27, 1978.

Pursuit of economic austerity measures brought down Soares' centrist successor, Carlos Alberto Mota Pinto, less than a year later, giving Portugal its first woman Premier, Maria Lurdes Pintassilgo, who acted as caretaker until the victory of Francisco Manoel Lumbrales de Sá Carneiro's Democratic Alliance on Dec. 2, 1979. Sá Carneiro's coalition of his own Social Democratic Party, the Christian Democrats and the small Popular Monarchist Party won a majority of three seats, the first absolute majority for a governing party since the 1974 revolution.

Also, for the first time since 1974, a Portuguese Cabinet contained no military members. When Sá Carneiro's economic proposals for denationalizing businesses and industries were vetoed by the Military Council, he declared his intention to abolish the nine-member council after national elections in October.

Portuguese Overseas Territory

After the April 1974 revolution, the military junta moved to grant independence to the territories, beginning with Portuguese Guinea in September 1974, which became the Republic of Guinea-Bissau.

Mozambique and Angola followed, leaving only Portuguese Timor and Macao of the former Empire. Despite Lisbon's objections, Indonesia annexed Timor.

MACAO

Status: Territory
Governor: Gen. Nuno Viriato Tavares de Melo Egídio (1978)
Area: 6 sq mi. (15.5 sq km)
Population (est. 1980): 280,000
Capital (1970 census): Macao, 241,413
Economic summary: Principal agricultural products: rice and vegetables; major industrial products: textiles, fireworks, fish products. Exports: textiles and clothing, manufactured goods, foodstuffs. Imports: consumer goods, foodstuffs. Major trading partners: West Germany, U.S., France, Hong Kong, Portugal.

Macao comprises the peninsula of Macao and the two small islands of Taipa and Colôane on the South China coast, about 35 miles (53 km) from Hong Kong. Established by the Portuguese in 1557, it is the oldest European outpost in the China trade, but Portugal's sovereign rights to the port were not recognized by China until 1887, and its boundaries are still not delimited. The port has been eclipsed in importance by Hong Kong, but it is still a busy distribution center and also has an important fishing industry. It is notorious for its opium trade and gambling houses. Most of the population is Chinese.

QATAR

State of Qatar
Ruler: Sheik Khalifa bin Hamad al-Thani (1972)
Area: 4,000 sq mi. (19,360 sq km)
Population (est. 1980): 220,000
Density per square mile: 55.0
Capital (est. 1978): Doha, 160,000
Monetary unit: Qatari riyal
Language: Arabic
Religion: Islam
Freedom House classifications: Capitalist-statist industrial, non-party non-military
Economic summary: Gross national product (1978): $2.8 billion. Average annual growth rate (1970–77): –2.4%. Per capita income: $25,320. Major industrial product: oil. Natural resource: oil. Export: oil. Major trading partners: U.K., U.S., France, Japan, West Germany.

Geography. Qatar occupies a small peninsula that extends into the Persian Gulf from the east side of the Arabian Peninsula. Saudi Arabia is to the west and the United Arab Emirates to the south. The country is mainly barren.

Government. Qatar, one of the Persian Gulf sheikdoms, lies between Bahrain and United Arab Emirates. For a long time, it was under Turkish protection, but in 1916, the sultan accepted British protection. After the discovery of oil in the 1940s and its exploitation in the 1950s and 1960s, political unrest spread to the sheikdoms. Qatar declared its independence in 1971. The next year the current Sheik, Khalifa bin Hamad al-Thani, ousted his cousin in a bloodless coup.

ROMANIA

Socialist Republic of Romania
President: Nicolae Ceausescu (1967)
Premier: Ilie Verdet (1979)
Area: 91,700 sq mi. (237,500 sq km)
Population (est. 1980): 22,300,000
Density per square mile: 243.2
Capital: Bucharest
Largest cities (est. 1977 by U.N.): Bucharest, 1,807,000; Timisoara, 268,800; Iasi, 265,000; Cluj-Napoca, 262,400; Brasov, 257,100; Constanta, 256,900; Galati, 239,300; Craiova, 222,400
Monetary unit: Leu
Languages: Romanian, Hungarian, Serbian, German, Turkish
Religions: Romanian Orthodox, 70%; Greek Orthodox, 15%
National name: Republica Socialistă România

Freedom House classifications: Socialist industrial, one-party communist

Economic summary: Gross national product (1978): $38.2 billion. Average annual growth rate (1970–77): 9.9%. Per capita income: $2,360. Land used for agriculture: 63%; labor force: 40%; principal products: corn, wheat, oil seeds, potatoes. Labor force in industry: 25%; major products: power, mining, forestry, metal production and processing, chemicals, food processing, textiles. Natural resources: oil, timber, natural gas, coal. Exports: foodstuffs, lumber, fuel, manufactures. Imports: machinery, rolled steel, iron ore, coke and coking coal, cotton. Major trading partners: U.S.S.R., East Germany, West Germany.

Geography. A country in southeastern Europe slightly smaller than Oregon, Romania is bordered on the west by Hungary and Yugoslavia, on the north and east by the U.S.S.R., on the east by the Black Sea, and on the south by Bulgaria.

The Carpathian Mountains divide Romania's upper half from north to south and connect near the center of the country with the Transylvanian Alps, running east and west.

North and west of these ranges lies the Transylvanian plateau, and to the south and east are the plains of Moldavia and Walachia. In its last 190 miles (306 km), the Danube River flows through Romania only. It enters the Black Sea in northern Dobruja, just south of the border with the Soviet Union.

Government. The supreme body of state power and the sole legislative body is the Grand National Assembly, with 465 members elected for five-year terms. It elects a State Council, which provides for the continuity of state power and settles problems between sessions of the Assembly. The supreme executive and administrative body is the Council of Ministers elected by the Assembly.

The Communist Party, led by Secretary General Nicolae Ceausescu, is the only political party.

History. Most of Romania was the Roman province of Dacia from about A.D. 100 to 275. From the 6th to the 12th century, wave after wave of barbarian conquerors—Vlachs, Bulgars, and others—passed over the area. By the 15th century, the main Romanian principalities of Moldavia and Walachia had become satellites within the Ottoman Empire, although they retained much independence. After the Russo-Turkish War of 1828–29, they became Russian protectorates. In 1848, the Romanians rebelled but were suppressed by the Russians. The nation became a kingdom in 1881 after the Congress of Berlin.

King Ferdinand ascended the throne in 1914. At the start of World War I, Romania proclaimed its neutrality, but later joined the Allied side and in 1916 declared war on the Central Powers. The armistice of Nov. 11, 1918, gave Romania vast territories from Russia and the Austro-Hungarian Empire.

The gains of World War I, making Romania the largest Balkan state, included Bessarabia, Transylvania, and Bukovina. The Banat, a Hungarian area, was divided with Yugoslavia.

In 1925, Crown Prince Carol renounced his rights to the throne, and when King Ferdinand died in 1927, Carol's son, Michael (Mihai) became King under a regency. However, Carol returned from exile in 1930, was crowned King Carol II, and gradually became a powerful political force in the country. In 1938, he abolished the democratic Constitution of 1923.

In 1940, the country was reorganized along Fascist lines, and the Fascist Iron Guard became the nucleus of the new totalitarian party. On June 27, the Soviet Union occupied Bessarabia and northern Bukovina. By the Axis-dictated Vienna Award of 1940, two fifths of Transylvania went to Hungary, after which Carol dissolved Parliament and granted the new premier, Ion Antonescu, full power. He abdicated and again went into exile.

Romania subsequently signed the Axis Pact on Nov. 23, 1940, and the following June joined in Germany's attack on the Soviet Union, reoccupying Bessarabia. Following the invasion of Romania by the Red Army in August 1944, King Michael led a coup that ousted the Antonescu government. An armistice with the Soviet Union was signed in Moscow on Sept. 12, 1944.

A Communist-dominated government bloc won elections in 1946, Michael abdicated on Dec. 30, 1947, and Romania became a "people's republic." In 1955, Romania joined the Warsaw Treaty Organization and the United Nations. A decade later, with the adoption of a new Constitution emphasizing national autonomy, and especially after Nicolae Ceausescu came to power in 1967, Bucharest became an increasingly dissident voice in the Soviet bloc.

Alone of the Warsaw Pact members, Romania maintained ties with China and Albania after the two broke with Moscow. Almost as annoying to the Soviet leadership was Ceausescu's continuing of ties with Israel, a relationship that made possible the secret preparations for the visit to Israel by Egypt's President Anwar el-Sadat in November 1977. Ceausescu also exchanged cultural and scientific accords with Washington in 1974 and visited the United States in 1978. In a New Year's Day speech, 1980, the Romanian leader became the first and only Eastern European voice to protest the Soviet invasion of Afghanistan.

Despite his liberal international record, at home Ceausescu has harshly suppressed dissidents calling for freedom of expression in the wake of the Helsinki agreements.

RWANDA

Republic of Rwanda

President: Maj. Gen. Juvénal Habyarimana (1973)

Area: 10,169 sq mi. (26,338 sq km)

Population (est. 1980): 4,800,000

Density per square mile: 472.0

Capital and largest city (1978 census): Kigali, 118,000

Monetary unit: Rwanda franc

Languages: Kinyarwanda and French

Religions: Roman Catholic, 45%; Protestant, 9%; Animist

Freedom House classifications: Capitalist-socialist pre-industrial, one-party nationalist

Economic summary: Gross national product (1978): $830 million. Average annual growth rate (1970–77): 1.3%. Per capita income: $106. Average rate of inflation (1972–76): 20–25%. Land used for agriculture: 39%; labor force: 95%; principal products: coffee, tea, pyrethrum, beans, potatoes. Labor force in industry: less than 5%; major products: processed foods, light consumer goods, minerals. Natural resources: cassiterite, wolfram. Exports: cassiterite, tea, pyrethrum, wolfram. Imports: textiles, foodstuffs, machinery, petroleum products. Major trading partners: Belgium, West Germany, U.S., Kenya.

Geography. Rwanda, in east central Africa, is surrounded by Zaire, Uganda, Tanzania, and Burundi. It is slightly smaller than Maryland.

Steep mountains and deep valleys cover most of the country. Lake Kivu in the northwest, at an altitude of 4,829 feet (1,472 m) is the highest lake in Africa. Extending south of it are the Virunga Mountains, which include Volcan Karisimbi (14,187 ft.; 4,324 m), Rwanda's highest point.

Government. Grégoire Kayibanda was President from 1962 until he was overthrown in a bloodless coup on July 5, 1973, by the military led by Gen. Juvénal Habyarimana.

In a plebiscite in December 1978, Habyarimana was elected to a five-year term as president and a new constitution adopted that provides for an elected Assembly and a single official party, the National Revolutionary Development Movement.

History. Rwanda, which was part of German East Africa, was first visited by European explorers in 1854. During World War I, it was occupied in 1916 by Belgian troops. After the war, it became a Belgian League of Nations mandate, along with Burundi, under the name of Ruanda-Urundi. The mandate was made a U.N. trust territory in 1946. Until the Belgian Congo achieved independence in 1960, Ruanda-Urundi was administered as part of that colony.

Ruanda became the independent nation of Rwanda on July 1, 1962.

ST. LUCIA

Commonwealth of St. Lucia
Governor-General: Sir Allan Lewis (1978)
Prime Minister: Allan Louisy (1979)
Area: 238 sq mi. (616 sq km)
Population (est 1980): 115,000
Density per square mile: 483.2
Capital (est. 1979): Castries, 45,000
Monetary unit: East Caribbean dollar
Languages: English, patois
Religion: Roman Catholic 86%; Anglican, Methodist
Member of Commonwealth of Nations
Freedom House classifications: Capitalist-socialist industrial, multi-party centralized
Economic summary: Gross national product (1978): $80 million. Average annual growth rate (1970–77): 0.7%. Labor force in agriculture: 50%; principal products: bananas, copra, sugar, cocoa, spices. Major industrial products: processed limes. Exports: sugar, bananas, cocoa. Imports: foodstuffs, machinery and equipment, fertilizers, petroleum products. Major trading partners: U.K., U.S., Canada.

Geography. One of the Windward Isles of the Eastern Caribbean, St. Lucia lies just south of Martinique. It is of volcanic origin. A chain of wooded mountains runs from north to south, and from them flow many streams into fertile valleys.

Government. A governor-general represents the sovereign, Queen Elizabeth II. A prime minister is head of government, chosen by a 17-member House of Assembly elected by universal suffrage for a maximum term of five years.

History. Discovered by Spain in 1503 and ruled by Spain and then France, St. Lucia became a British territory in 1803. With other Windward Isles, St. Lucia was granted home rule in 1967 as one of the West Indies Associated States. On Feb. 22, 1979, St. Lucia achieved full independence in ceremonies boycotted by the opposition St. Lucia Labor Party, which had advocated a referendum before cutting ties with Britain.

Unrest and a strike by civil servants forced Prime Minister John Compton to hold elections in July, in which his United Workers Party lost its majority for the first time in 15 years. The Labor Party, with 12 of 17 seats in the Assembly, elected Allan Louisy as prime minister, and Deputy Prime Minister George Odlum told a victory rally the party will take from the rich to give to the poor—"That's not communism, that's Christianity."

Formerly dependent on a single crop, bananas, St. Lucia has sought to expand tourism and industry to lower its 17% unemployment and a payments deficit of $28 million in 1978. The government provided tax incentives to a U.S. corporation, Amerada Hess, to facilitate location of a $150-million oil refinery and transhipment terminal on the island.

ST. VINCENT

Commonwealth of St. Vincent and the Grenadines
Sovereign: Queen Elizabeth II
Governor-General: Sir Sydney Gunn-Munro (1979)
Prime Minister: Milton Cato (1979)
Area: 150 sq mi. (389 sq km)
Population (est. 1980): 100,000
Density per square mile: 4,000.0
Capital and largest city (est. 1979): Kingstown, 23,650
Monetary unit: East Caribbean dollar
Language: English
Religions: Anglican,Methodist, Roman Catholic
Member of Commonwealth of Nations
Freedom House classifications: Capitalist-socialist industrial, multi-party centralized.
Economic summary: Gross national product (1978): $40 million. Average annual growth rate (1970–77): −2.2%. Principal agricultural products: bananas, arrowroot, coconuts. Major industry: food processing. Exports: bananas, arrowroot, copra. Imports: fertilizers, flour, transportation equipment, lumber, textiles. Major trading partners: U.K., U.S., Canada, Caribbean nations.

Geography. St. Vincent, chief island of the Commonwealth, is 18 miles (29 km) long and 11 miles (18 km) wide. One of the Windward Islands in the Lesser Antilles, it is 100 miles (161 km) west of Barbados. The island is mountainous and well forested. The Grenadines, a chain of nearly 600 islets with a total area of only 17 square miles (27 sq km), extend for 60 miles (96 km) from northeast to southwest between St. Vincent and Grenada, southernmost of the Windwards.

St. Vincent is dominated by the volcano La Soufrière, part of a volcanic range running north and south, which rises to 4,048 feet (1,234 m). The volcano erupted over a 10-day period in April 1979, causing the evacuation of the northern two thirds of the island. (There is also a volcano of the same name on Basse-Terre, Guadeloupe, which became violently active in 1976 and 1977.)

Government. A Governor-General represents the sovereign, Queen Elizabeth II. A Prime Minister, elected by a 13-member unicameral legislature, holds executive power. The Labor Party, led by

Prime Minister Milton Cato, holds 11 of the 13 seats.

History. Discovered by Columbus in 1498, and alternately claimed by Britain and France, St. Vincent became a British colony by the Treaty of Paris in 1783. The islands won home rule in 1969 as part of the West Indies Associated States and achieved full independence Oct. 26, 1979. Prime Minister Milton Cato's government quelled a brief rebellion Dec. 8, 1979, three days after elections had given the ruling Labor Party 11 of 13 seats in the Assembly. The rebellion was attributed to economic problems following the eruption of La Soufrière in April, 1979. Unlike a 1902 eruption which killed 2,000, there was no loss of life but widespread losses to agriculture.

SAN MARINO

Most Serene Republic of San Marino
Co-Regents: Two selected every six months by Grand and General Council
Area: 23.6 sq mi. (62 sq km)
Population (est. 1980): 20,500 (mostly Italian)
Density per square mile: 868.6
Capital and largest city (est. 1978 for metropolitan area): San Marino, 8,300
Monetary unit: Italian lira
Language: Italian
Religion: Roman Catholic
National name: Repubblica di San Marino
Economic summary: Principal agricultural products: wheat and other grains, grapes, fruits, vegetables. Major industrial products: textiles, paper, leather, cement and other building materials. Exports: building stone, lime, chestnuts, wheat, hides, baked goods. Imports: manufactured consumer goods. Major trading partner: Italy.

Geography: One tenth the size of New York City, San Marino is surrounded by Italy. It is situated in the Apennines, a little inland from the Adriatic Sea near Rimini.

Government. The country is governed by two coregents. Executive power is exercised by two secretaries of state—one for foreign and political affairs and one for internal affairs. In 1959, the Grand Council granted women the vote.

The major political parties are the Christian Democratic Party (26 of 60 seats in the Grand and General Council); Communist Party (16 seats), Democratic Socialist Party (11 seats), Socialist Party (7 seats).

History. According to tradition, San Marino was founded about A.D. 350 and had good luck for centuries in staying out of the many wars and feuds on the Italian peninsula. It is the oldest republic in the world.

A person born in San Marino remains a citizen and can vote no matter where he lives.

SÃO TOMÉ AND PRÍNCIPE

Democratic Republic of São Tomé and Príncipe
President: Manuel Pinto da Costa (1975)
Area: 372 sq mi. (964 sq km)
Population (est. 1980): 85,000
Density per square mile: 228.5
Capital and largest city (est. 1977): São Tomé, 20,000
Monetary unit: São Tomé and Príncipe Dobra
Language: Portuguese
Religions: Roman Catholic, Evangelical Protestant, Seventh-Day Adventist
Freedom House classifications: Socialist industrial, one-party socialist
Economic summary: Gross national product (1978): $40 million. Average annual growth rate (1970–77): 8.0%. Per capita income (1974): $160. Average rate of inflation (1972–74): 25%. Principal agricultural products: cacao, coconut palms, coffee, bananas. Major industrial products: beer, palm oil, copra. Exports: cacao, copra, palm kernels. Imports: foodstuffs, textiles, machinery. Major trading partners: Portugal, Netherlands, West Germany.

Geography. The tiny volcanic islands of São Tomé and Príncipe lie in the Gulf of Guinea about 150 miles (241 km) off West Africa. São Tomé (about 330 sq mi.; 855 sq km) is covered by a dense mountainous jungle, out of which have been carved large plantations. Príncipe (about 40 sq mi.; 104 sq km) consists of jagged mountains. Other islands in the republic are Pedras Tinhosas and Rolas.

History. São Tomé and Princípe became independent of Portugal on July 12, 1975. The islands were discovered by the Portuguese in 1471. The majority of the early inhabitants were convicts, Jews from Portugal, and slaves from Brazil and the mainland.

SAUDI ARABIA

Kingdom of Saudi Arabia
Ruler and Prime Minister: King Khalid Bin Abdul-Aziz (1975)
Area: 873,000 sq mi. (2,261,070 sq km)
Population (est. 1980): 8,350,000
Density per square mile: 9.6
Capital: Riyadh
Largest cities (est. 1976): Riyadh, 667,000; **(1974 census):** Jiddah, 561,104; Mecca, 366,801
Monetary unit: Riyal
Language: Arabic
Religion: Islam
National name: Al-Mamlaka al-'Arabiya as-Sa'udiya
Freedom House classifications: Capitalist-statist industrial, non-party non-military
Economic summary: Gross national product (1978): $63 billion. Average annual growth rate (1970–77): 13%. Labor force in agriculture: 28%; principal products: dates, grains, livestock. Labor force in industry: 28%; major products: petroleum, cement, plastic products, furniture. Natural resource: oil. Exports: petroleum and petroleum products. Imports: manufactured goods, transport equipment, construction materials, processed food. Major trading partners: U.S., Western European countries, Japan, West Germany.

Geography. The Middle East oil-producing country of Saudi Arabia occupies most of the Arabian Peninsula, with the Red Sea and the Gulf of Aqaba on the west and the Persian Gulf on the east. Neighbors are Jordan, Iraq, and Kuwait in the north, and, along the perimeter from southwest to east, the two Yemens, Oman, and the United Arab Emirates. The country is more than three times the size of Texas.

Saudi Arabia's oil region lies along the Persian Gulf. The country is mostly desert. The Asir Mountains inland rise to a height of 9,000 feet (2,743 m).

Government. Saudi Arabia is a monarchy whose legitimacy rests on *Shariah* (the Law of Islam) and custom. A Council of Ministers was formed in 1953. It acts as a Cabinet under the leadership of the King and is composed of 21 ministries.

Royal and ministerial decrees account for most of the promulgated legislation, treaties, and conventions.

There are no political parties in Saudi Arabia.

History. Mohammed united the Arabs in the 7th century, and his followers, led by the caliphs, founded a great empire, with its capital at Medina. Later, the caliphate capital was transferred to Damascus and then Baghdad, but Arabia retained its importance because of the holy cities of Mecca and Medina. In the 16th and 17th centuries, the Turks established at least nominal rule over much of Arabia, and in the middle of the 18th century, it was divided into separate principalities.

The Kingdom of Saudi Arabia is almost entirely the creation of King Ibn Saud (1882–1953). A descendant of earlier Wahabi rulers, he seized Riyadh, the capital of Nejd, in 1901 and set himself up as leader of the Arab nationalist movement. By 1906 he had established Wahabi dominance in Nejd. He conquered Hejaz in 1924–25, consolidating it and Nejd into a dual kingdom in 1926. In 1932, Hejaz and Nejd became a single kingdom, which was officially named Saudi Arabia. A year later the region of Asir was incorporated into the kingdom.

Oil was discovered in 1936, and commercial production began during World War II. Saudi Arabia was neutral until nearly the end of the war, but it was permitted to be a charter member of the United Nations. The country joined the Arab League in 1945 and took part in the 1948–49 war against Israel, but followed a less extremist policy as opposed to the line of the 1958–61 United Arab Republic. In 1951, the U.S. was allowed to build an air base at Dhahran.

On Ibn Saud's death in 1953, his eldest son, Saud, began an 11-year reign marked by an increasing hostility toward the radical Arabism of Egypt's Gamal Abdel Nasser. In 1964, the ailing Saud was deposed and replaced by the Premier, Crown Prince Faisal, who gave vocal support but no military help to Egypt in the 1967 Mideast war. He sent a token force of 1,000 to Syria in the 1973 Arab-Israeli war and joined the five-month oil boycott of the West afterward.

Faisal's assassination by a deranged kinsman in 1975 shook the Middle East, but failed to alter his kingdom's course. His successor was his brother, Prince Khalid. Khalid gave influential support to Egypt during negotiations on Israeli withdrawal from the Sinai desert. His government made it clear to the industrial West that Saudi Arabia's relatively moderate oil-pricing policies could change if consumer nations flouted Saudi views.

The growing economic strength of Saudi Arabia was recognized in July 1978 when the riyal, together with Iranian rial, was made one of the 16 world currencies used by the International Monetary Fund to determine the value of the Fund's Special Drawing Rights. Saudi Arabia exercised a moderating influence in the Organization for Petroleum Exporting Countries (OPEC) to restrain prices. In July 1979 President Carter disclosed Crown Prince Fahd's promise to increase Saudi oil production by one million barrels a day for three months to ease the world oil shortage.

Although Carter had hoped that Saudi Arabia would support the Egyptian-Israeli peace treaty—the U.S. sold 60 F-15 fighters to the Saudis in 1978 and sent a fleet to the Arabian Sea when border clashes between the two Yemens alarmed Riyadh—Arab solidarity doomed this hope in 1979. Saudi Arabia joined the majority in condemning Egypt, broke diplomatic relations with Cairo and canceled its commitment to pay for $525 million worth of F-15's for Egypt.

A takeover by an unknown group of the Grand Mosque in Mecca on Nov. 20, 1979, spread fears that the Saudi monarchy might be under internal threat. There were conflicting stories about the uprising's origin, including an Iranian charge of U.S. involvement, which led to anti-American demonstrations in Pakistan and elsewhere in the Moslem world. After the recapture of the mosque by the Army on Dec. 4 at the cost of 130 lives, Saudi officials denied reports of uprisings elsewhere. On Jan. 9, 1980, 63 persons—41 Saudis and the remainder aliens—were beheaded for their participation in the takeover. A tightening of Islamic law and a shakeup in the Army's top command were linked to the incident.

Although the Saudis declined a U.S. request for additional Mideast air bases in the wake of the Iranian and Afghan crisis, a Saudi demand for additional equipment for the F-15 planes was expected to receive Washington's consent. The equipment would more than double the planes' 450-mile range, arousing Israeli concern, but the sale was indirectly linked to an expansion of Saudi oil production capacity and continued supplies to the United States.

SENEGAL

Republic of Senegal
President: Léopold Sédar Senghor (1960)
Premier: Abdou Diouf (1970)
Area: 76,124 sq mi. (197,161 sq km)
Population (est. 1980): 5,650,000
Density per square mile: 74.2
Capital and largest city (est. 1976): Dakar, 798,800
Monetary unit: Franc CFA
Ethnic groups: Wolofs, Sereres, Peuls, Tukulers, and others
Languages: French (official); Wolof, Serer, other tribal dialects
Religion: Islam, 80%; Animist, 15%; Christian, 5%
National name: République du Sénégal
Freedom House classifications: Capitalist-socialist industrial, dominant party.
Economic summary: Gross national product (1978): $1.8 billion. Average annual growth rate (1970–77): 0.4%. Per capita income: $353. Land used for agriculture: 60%; labor force: 80%; principal products: peanuts, millet, cotton, rice, sorghum. Labor force in industry: 8%; major products: peanut oil, fertilizer, cement, processed food and fish, refined petroleum. Natural resources: fish, phosphate. Exports: peanuts, phosphate rock, canned fish. Imports: foodstuffs, consumer goods, machinery, transport equipment. Major trading partners: France, Western European countries.

Geography. The capital of Senegal, Dakar, is the westernmost point in Africa. The country, slightly smaller than South Dakota, surrounds Gambia on three sides and is bordered on the north by Mauritania, on the east by Mali, and on the south by Guinea and Guinea-Bissau.

Senegal is mainly a low-lying country, with a semidesert area in the north and northeast and forests in the southwest. The largest rivers include the Senegal in the north and the Gambia in the central region.

Government. There is a National Assembly of 100 members, elected every five years. There is universal suffrage and a constitutional guarantee of equality before the law.

The major political party is the Socialist Party, led by President Léopold Sédar Senghor. Legal opposition was reconstituted in 1974 with formation of the Senegalese Democratic Party, headed by Abdoulaye Wade, which urged reduction in French and Western influences. The African Independence Party was reorganized in 1976.

History. The Portuguese had some stations on the banks of the Senegal River in the 15th century, and the first French settlement was made at Saint-Louis about 1650. The British took parts of Senegal at various times, but the French gained possession in 1840 and organized the Sudan as a territory in 1904. In 1946, together with other parts of French West Africa, Senegal became part of the French Union. On June 20, 1960, it became an independent republic federated with the Sudanese Republic in the Mali Federation, from which it withdrew two months later.

On Jan. 1, 1973, Senegal joined with six other states to create the West African Economic Community to promote economic development within the region.

SEYCHELLES

Republic of Seychelles
President: Albert René (1977)
Area: 171 sq mi. (443 sq km)
Population (est. 1980): 65,000
Density per square mile: 602
Capital (est. 1977): Victoria, 23,000
Monetary unit: Seychelles rupee
Languages: English, French (both official), Creole patois
Religions: Roman Catholic, 91%; Anglican, 8%
Member of Commonwealth of Nations
Freedom House classifications: Capitalist-socialist industrial, one-party socialist
Economic summary: Gross national product (1978): $70 million. Average annual growth rate (1970–77): 3.8%. Per capita income: $710. Labor force in agriculture: 27%; principal products: vanilla, copra, cinnamon. Labor force in industry: 55%; major products: processed copra and vanilla, coconut oil. Exports: cinnamon, coconut products. Imports: food, tobacco, manufactured goods, machinery, petroleum products, textiles, transport equipment. Major trading partners: U.K., Kenya, India, South Africa.

Geography. Seychelles consists of an archipelago of 89 islands in the Indian Ocean northeast of Madagascar. The principal islands are Mahé (55 sq mi.; 142 sq km), Praslin (15 sq mi.; 38 sq km), and La Digue (4 sq mi.; 10 sq km). The Aldabra, Farquhar, and Desroches groups are included in the territory of the republic.

Government. Seized from France by Britain in 1810, the Seychelles Islands remained a colony until June 28, 1974. The new state is an independent republic within the Commonwealth.

On June 5, 1977, Prime Minister Albert René ousted the islands' first President, James Mancham, suspending the Constitution and the 25-member National Assembly. Mancham, whose "lavish spending" and flamboyance were cited by René in seizing power, charged that Soviet influence was at work. The new president denied this and, while more left than his predecessor, pledged to keep the Seychelles in the Commonwealth.

A new Cabinet was formed with members only from Seychelles People's United Party, none from Mancham's Seychelles Democratic Party.

SIERRA LEONE

Republic of Sierra Leone
President: Dr. Siaka P. Stevens (1971)
First Vice President: Sorie I. Koroma (1978)
Second Vice President: Christian A. Kamara-Taylor (1978)
Area: 27,925 sq mi. (72,326 sq km)
Population (est. 1980): 3,470,000
Density per square mile: 124.3
Capital and largest city (est. 1974): Freetown, 314,340
Monetary unit: Leone
Languages: English (official), Mende, Temne, Creole
Religions: Animist, 66%; Islam, 28%; Christian, 6%
Member of Commonwealth of Nations
Freedom House classifications: Capitalist pre-industrial, one-party socialist
Economic summary: Gross national product (1978): $690 million. Average annual growth rate (1970–77): −1.3%. Per capita income: $176. Average rate of inflation (1972–77): 15%. Land used for agriculture: 2.3%; labor force: 75%; principal products: coffee, cocoa, ginger, rice. Labor force in industry: 15%; major products: diamonds, bauxite, beverages, cigarettes, construction goods. Natural resources: diamonds, bauxite, chromite, iron ore, rutile. Exports: mining and agricultural products. Imports: food, tobacco, crude materials, chemicals, machinery. Major trading partners: U.K., Netherlands, U.S., Japan, China.

Geography. Sierra Leone, on the Atlantic Ocean in West Africa, is half the size of Illinois. Guinea, in the north and east, and Liberia, in the south, are its neighbors.

Mangrove swamps lie along the coast, with wooded hills and a plateau in the interior. The eastern region is mountainous.

Government. Sierra Leone became an independent nation on April 27, 1961, and declared itself a republic, with former Prime Minister Siaka P. Stevens as president for a five-year term, on April 19, 1971.

Sierra Leone became a one party state under the aegis of the All Peoples Congress Party in April 1978.

History. The coastal area of Sierra Leone was ceded to English settlers in 1788 as a home for blacks discharged from the British armed forces and also for runaway slaves who had found asylum in London. The British protectorate over the hinterland was proclaimed in 1896.

After elections in 1967, the British Governor-General replaced Sir Albert Margai, head of SLPP, which had held power since independence, with Dr. Stevens, head of APC, as prime minister. The Army took over the government; then another coup in April 1968 restored civilian rule and put the military leaders in jail.

A coup attempt early in 1971 by the army commander was apparently foiled by loyal army officers, but the then Prime Minister Stevens called in troops of neighboring Guinea's army, under a 1970 mutual defense pact, to guard his residence. After perfunctorily blaming the U.S. for the coup attempt, Stevens switched Governors-General, changed the Constitution, and ended up with a republic, of which he was first president. He was accused of taking "sweeping dictatorial powers," but was re-elected in 1976.

SINGAPORE

Republic of Singapore
President: Benjamin Sheares (1971)
Prime Minister: Lee Kuan Yew (1959)
Area: 238 sq mi. (616 sq km)
Population (est. 1980): 2,400,000 (Chinese, 76%; Malay, 15%; Indian, 7%)
Density per square mile: 10,084.0
Capital (est. 1978): Singapore, 2,335,000
Monetary unit: Singapore dollar
Languages: Malay, Chinese (Mandarin), Tamil, English
Religions: Islam, Christian, Buddhist, Hindu, Confucianist, Taoist
Member of Commonwealth of Nations
Freedom House classifications: Capitalist-statist industrial, dominant party
Economic summary: Gross national product (1978): $7.7 billion. Average annual growth rate (1970–77): 6.6%. Per capita income: $2,800. Average rate of inflation: 2.1%. Labor force in agriculture: 2%; principal products: poultry, hogs, orchids, vegetables, fruits. Labor force in industry: 32%; major industries: petroleum refining, oil exploration, ship repair, rubber processing, electronics and other light industry. Exports: electrical machinery, electronics, textiles. Imports: rice, machinery, petroleum. Major trading partners: U.S., Japan, Malaysia, Saudi Arabia, Australia, Indonesia.

Geography. The Republic of Singapore consists of the main island of Singapore, off the southern tip of the Malay Peninsula between the South China Sea and the Indian Ocean, and 54 nearby islands.

There are extensive mangrove swamps extending inland from the coast, which is broken by many inlets.

Government. The head of state is the President. There is a Cabinet, headed by the Prime Minister, and a Parliament of 69 members elected by universal suffrage.

The People's Action Party, led by Prime Minister Lee Kuan Yew, is the only political party represented in Parliament.

History. Singapore, founded in 1819 by Sir Stamford Raffles, became a separate crown colony of Britain in 1946, when the former colony of the Straits Settlements was dissolved. The other two settlements—Penang and Malacca—were transferred to the Union of Malaya, and the small island of Labuan was transferred to North Borneo. The Cocos (or Keeling) Islands were transferred to Australia in 1955 and Christmas Island in 1958.

Singapore attained full internal self-government in 1959. On Sept. 16, 1963, it joined Malaya, Sabah (North Borneo), and Sarawak in the Federation of Malaysia. It withdrew from the Federation on Aug. 9, 1965, and proclaimed itself a republic the next month.

SOLOMON ISLANDS

Sovereign: Queen Elizabeth II
Governor-General: Baddeley Devesi (1978)
Prime Minister: Peter Kenilorea (1978)
Area: 11,500 sq mi. (29,785 sq km)
Population (est. 1980): 215,000
Density per square mile: 18.7
Capital and largest city (est. 1978): Honiara (on Guadalcanal), 16,500
Monetary unit: Solomon Islands dollar
Languages: Pidgin English, English, Melanesian dialects
Religions: Anglican, 34%; Roman Catholic, 19%; Seventh-Day Adventist, 10%; other Protestant, 31%
Member of British Commonwealth.
Freedom House classifications: Capitalist pre-industrial, non-party non-military
Economic summary: Gross national product (1978): $90 million. Average annual growth rate (1970–77): 1.7%. Principal agricultural products: copra, palm oil, rice, cocoa, cattle, spices. Major industrial products: processed fish, timber, jute, soap, canned meat, handicrafts. Natural resources: fish, timber. Exports: fish, timber, copra, palm oil. Imports: machinery and transport equipment, foodstuffs, fuel, manufactured goods. Major trading partners: Australia, Japan, U.K., U.S.

Geography: Lying east of New Guinea, this island nation consists of the southern islands of the Solomon group: Guadalcanal, Malaita, Santa Isabel, San Cristóbal, Choiseul, New Georgia, and numerous smaller islands.

Government. After 85 years of British rule, the Solomons achieved independence July 7, 1978. The Crown is represented by a Governor-General and legislative power is vested in a unicameral legislature of 38 members, led by the Prime Minister.

History. Discovered in 1567 by Alvaro de Mendana, the Solomons were not visited again for about 200 years. In 1886, Great Britain and Germany divided the islands between them. In 1914, Australian forces took over the German islands and the Solomons became an Australian mandate in 1920. In World War II, most of the islands were occupied by the Japanese. American forces landed on Guadalcanal on Aug. 7, 1942. The islands were the scene of several important U.S. naval and military victories. They are still largely undeveloped, with only 60 miles of paved road and fewer than 1,000 motor vehicles.

SOMALIA

Somali Democratic Republic
President: Maj. Gen. Mohamed Siad Barre (1969)
Area: 246,155 sq mi. (637,541 sq km)
Population (est. 1980): 3,650,000
Density per square mile: 14.8
Capital and largest city (est. 1976 by U.N.): Mogadishu, 286,000
Monetary unit: Somali shilling
Language: Somali
Religion: Islam
National name: Al Jumhouriya As-Somalya Dimocradia
Freedom House classifications: Capitalist-socialist pre-industrial, one-party socialist
Economic summary: Gross national product (1978): $470 million. Average annual growth rate (1970–77): −1.1%. Per capita income: $110. Land used for agriculture: 13%;

labor force: 60%; principal products: livestock, bananas, sorghum, peanuts, sugar cane, cotton, maize. Labor force in industry: 3%; major products: textiles, meat, fish, canned fruit juices. Natural resources: timber, uranium. Exports: livestock, skins and hides, bananas. Imports: machinery, manufactured goods, transport equipment. Major trading partners: Italy, Saudi Arabia.

Geography. Somalia, situated in the Horn of Africa, lies along the Gulf of Aden and the Indian Ocean. It is bounded by Djibouti in the northwest, Ethiopia in the east, and Kenya in the southwest. In area it is slightly smaller than Texas.

Generally arid and barren, Somalia has two chief rivers, the Shebeli and the Juba.

Government. Maj. Gen. Mohamed Siad Barre took power on Oct. 21, 1969, in a bloodless coup that established a Supreme Revolutionary Council as the governing body, replacing a parliamentary government. On July 1, 1976, Barre dissolved the Council, naming its members to the Somali Socialist Party, organized that day as the nation's only legal political party. In December 1979, a 171-member People's Assembly was elected under a new Constitution adopted in August. The Assembly confirmed Barre as President for a six-year term.

History. From the 7th to the 10th century, Arab and Persian trading posts were established along the coast of present-day Somalia. Nomadic tribes occupied the interior, occasionally pushing into Ethiopian territory. In the 16th century, Turkish rule extended to the northern coast and the Sultans of Zanzibar gained control in the south.

After British occupation of Aden in 1839, the Somali coast became its source of food. The French established a coaling station in 1862 at the site of Djibouti and the Italians planted a settlement in Eritrea. Egypt, which for a time claimed Turkish rights in the area, was succeeded by Britain. By 1920, a British protectorate and an Italian protectorate occupied what is now Somalia. The British ruled the entire area after 1941, with Italy returning in 1950 to serve as United Nations trustee for its former territory.

In mid-1960, Britain and Italy granted independence to their respective sectors, enabling the two to join as the Republic of Somalia on July 1. Somalia broke diplomatic relations with Britain in 1963 when the British granted the Somali-populated Northern Frontier District of Kenya to the Republic of Kenya.

On Oct. 15, 1969, President Abdi Rashid Ali Shermarke was assassinated and the army seized power, dissolving the legislature and arresting all government leaders. Maj. Gen. Mohamed Siad Barre, as President of a renamed Somali Democratic Republic, leaned heavily toward the U.S.S.R., which had largely trained and equipped the nation's 9,000-man army. A Soviet naval base was established at Berbera.

In 1977, Somalia openly backed rebels in the westernmost area of Ethiopia, the Ogaden desert, which had been seized by Ethiopia at the turn of the century. The action was an embarrassment to the U.S.S.R., which was heavily involved in Ethiopia's new Marxist government after the ouster of Emperor Haile Selassie in 1974.

After denying Barre's pleas for aid, the U.S.S.R. announced in 1977 the cutoff of military aid to Somalia and the providing of "defensive weapons" to Ethiopia. Somalia then expelled an estimated 1,500 Soviet military and civilian aides and broke diplomatic relations with Cuba, which had furnished military advisers to the Ethiopian troops fighting in the Ogaden.

Somalia acknowledged defeat in an eight-month war against the Ethiopians, having lost many of what had become a 32,000-man army and most of its tanks and planes. In March 1978, the U.S. agreed to supply $7 million in food over six months, in addition to $6 million in emergency food relief provided in December. The U.S. refused to consider weapons sales, however, unless Somalia gave up all claims to northern Kenya, the Ogaden, and the Republic of Djibouti, all once claimed as "Greater Somalia." Barre refused to do this.

A U.S. announcement on Jan. 9, 1980, that bases for U.S. ships and planes in the Indian Ocean would be sought in Somalia, Oman, and Kenya, brought a request from Somalia for $1 billion worth of modern arms and an equal amount of economic aid. In August, an agreement was signed giving the U.S. use of military bases in Somalia in return for $25 million in military aid in 1981 and more in subsequent years.

SOUTH AFRICA

Republic of South Africa
State President: Marais Viljoen (1979)
Prime Minister: Pieter W. Botha (1978)
Area: 438,073 sq mi. (1,133,769 sq km)[1]
Population (est. 1980): 23,500,000[1] (black, 67%; white, 19%; colored (mixed), 11%; Asian, 3%
Density per square mile: 53.6[1]
Administrative capital: Pretoria
Legislative capital: Cape Town
Judicial capital: Bloemfontein
Largest cities (est. 1978): Johannesburg, 1,416,700; Pretoria, 650,600; Bloemfontein, 174,500; (est. 1976): Cape Town, 842,600; (est. 1975): Durban, 837,000; Port Elizabeth, 468,800
Monetary unit: Rand
Languages: English, Afrikaans, Bantu languages
Religions (1970): Dutch Reformed, 16%; Methodist, 10%; Roman Catholic, 9%; Anglican, 8%; other Christian, 55%
National name: Republiek van Suid-Afrika
Freedom House classifications: Capitalist-statist industrial, multi-party centralized
Economic summary: Gross national product (1978): $41 billion. Average annual growth rate (1970–77): 1.1%. Per capita income: $1,450. Labor force in agriculture: 53%; principal products: corn, wool, wheat, sugar cane, tobacco, citrus fruits. Labor force in industry: 15%; major products: assembled automobiles, machinery, textiles, iron and steel, chemicals, fertilizer, fish. Natural resources: gold, diamonds, platinum, uranium, coal, iron ore, asbestos, manganese. Exports: wool, diamonds, corn, uranium, sugar, fruits, hides and skins, asbestos, fish products. Imports: motor vehicles, machinery, metals, petroleum products, chemicals, textiles. Major trading partners: U.S., West Germany, Japan, U.K.

Geography. South Africa, on the continent's southern tip, is washed by the Atlantic Ocean on the west and by the Indian Ocean on the south and east. Its neighbors are South-West Africa (Namibia) in the northwest, Zimbabwe and Botswana in the north, and Mozambique and Swaziland in the northeast. Bophuthatswana, Transkei, and Venda are independent enclaves within South Africa, which occupies an area nearly three times that of California.

The country has a high interior plateau, or veld,

1. Excluding South-West Africa (Namibia), Transkei, Bophuthatswana, and Venda.

nearly half of which averages 4,000 feet (1,219 m) in elevation.

There are no important mountain ranges, although the Great Escarpment, separating the veld from the coastal plain, rises to over 11,000 feet (3,350 m) in the Drakensberg Mountains in the east. The principal river is the Orange, rising in Lesotho and flowing westward for 1,300 miles (2,092 km) to the Atlantic.

The southernmost point of Africa is Cape Agulhas, located in Cape Province about 100 miles (161 km) southeast of the Cape of Good Hope.

Government. The Republic is divided into four provinces (Cape, Transvaal, Orange Free State, and Natal), each with a Provincial Council. A 50-member Senate and 165-member House of Assembly make up the Parliament. Members have five-year terms unless Parliament is dissolved earlier. The President is chosen by Parliament for a seven-year term.

Five "Bantustans," or black homelands, exist within the country. They have unicameral legislatures elected by black voters. (Only whites vote in parliamentary elections.) There are also a Colored (mixed race) Representative Council of 60 members (40 elected) and an Indian Council of 30 members (all elected), which give some representation for these minorities.

The major political parties are the National Party (135 of 165 seats in the House of Assembly), led by Prime Minister Pieter W. Botha; Progressive Federal Party (17 seats), led by Frederick van Zyl Slabbert. New Republic Party (10 seats), led by Vause Raw, and the South Africa Party (3 seats).

History. Dutch settlers arrived in South Africa in 1652 and by the beginning of the 18th century numbered nearly 2,000.

Britain seized the Cape Colony in 1814 and within seven years settled 5,000 Britons there, freeing the slaves on whom the Boer (Dutch) farmers relied for labor. The Boers pushed north of the Orange and Vaal rivers to escape the British, but in 1877 the British annexed the Transvaal territory. Although the Dutch relinquished the territory in 1881, resentment continued to smolder, and the Jameson Raid of 1899 touched off the Boer War, ending in Dutch defeat in 1902.

The four provinces were united in the Union of South Africa in 1910. Louis Botha, the first Prime Minister and a Boer, allied the dominion with Britain in World War I. The Unionist Party, led by Jan Christiaan Smuts, advocated a pro-British line and a more liberal racial policy in the period between wars, while the Nationalist Party urged withdrawal from the Commonwealth and racial separation.

Smuts brought the nation into World War II on the Allied side against Nationalist opposition, and South Africa became a charter member of the United Nations in 1945, but refused to sign the Universal Declaration of Human Rights. Apartheid—racial separation—dominated domestic politics as the Nationalists gained power and imposed greater restrictions on Bantus, Coloreds, and Asians.

Boer hostility to Britain triumphed in 1961 with the declaration on May 31 of the Republic of South Africa and the severing of ties with the Commonwealth. Nationalist Prime Minister H. F. Verwoerd's government in 1963 asserted the power to restrict freedom of those who opposed rigid racial laws. Three years later, amid increasing racial tension and criticism from the outside world, Verwoerd was assassinated. His Nationalist successor, Balthazar J. Vorster, launched a campaign of conciliation toward conservative black African states, offering development loans and trade concessions. He accelerated the program for developing Bantustans, giving independence to the Transkei in 1976 and to Bophuthatswana in 1977.

The late 1960s and early 1970s were economic boom years for South Africa, giving blacks there the highest incomes in Africa, even though two thirds of the national income was going to the white fifth of the population. Vorster continued to wield a harsh hand against domestic opposition and aided white Rhodesians in their fight against black guerrillas, but also sought to improve relations with black Africa.

A critical issue was South-West Africa, the former German territory ruled by South Africa since World War I, a rule challenged by the United Nations when it asserted responsibility for the territory in 1974 under the name Namibia. African demands for immediate freedom for Namibia led to an attempt to expel South Africa from the U.N. in 1974, a move blocked by a U.S., British, and French veto. The General Assembly barred South Africa from its seat anyway, and the seat has remained empty.

In the 1975–76 Angolan civil war, Vorster engaged 4,000 troops on the side of the National Union for the Total Independence of Angola, which lost to the Soviet-backed Popular Movement for the Liberation of Angola. Defeat in Angola was followed by a wave of riots in black townships in South Africa, originating in protests against the use of the Afrikaans language in schools. More than 300 died as the movement widened to ask more freedoms, the strongest challenge to the white regime in a generation.

At the same time, outside pressure forced Vorster to withdraw military aid to Rhodesia in mid-1976. He met with U.S. Secretary of State Henry A. Kissinger in Zurich in September. As a result, Premier Ian Smith of Rhodesia's white government agreed to negotiate with nationalists in Rhodesia for a majority rule.

Unrest in Soweto, the principal black township near Johannesburg, continued through 1978 despite the elimination of compulsory schooling in Afrikaans and relaxation of "petty apartheid." Under white as well as black pressure, the government desegregated theaters and opera houses, although movie theaters in white areas remained segregated. The death of Steven Biko on Sept. 12, 1977, caused widespread protest when the anti-apartheid activist was discovered to have died from a brain injury while jailed. The U.S. expressed shock that an official inquest had held nobody responsible.

Economic restrictions tightened on South Africa following a vote by the Security Council imposing a mandatory embargo on arms in retaliation for South Africa's crackdown on opponents of apartheid. Although the U.S., Britain, and France vetoed mandatory economic sanctions against South Africa, U.S. and European businesses, unions, and church groups acted to cut trade with it.

Reflecting this as well as global economic recession, the 1978–79 South African budget of $11.3 billion projected a deficit of nearly $500 million to stimulate an economy, which grew at only 1.3% in 1977. Unemployment was up and immigration figures for 1977 showed a net loss of 1,178—the first decline since 1960.

Progress toward granting independence to Namibia (South-West Africa) slowed in 1978 as Pretoria rejected a proposal by five Western members of the Security Council for a U.N.-supervised transition to independence. Instead, the government went ahead with elections of its own in December for a constituent assembly. The Democratic Turnhalle Alliance, a conservative multiracial party, won 44 of the 50 Assembly seats.

Events in Namibia were overshadowed by scandal at home, an affair christened "Muldergate" by the press when it was disclosed that former Information Minister Connie Mulder had lost millions of dollars of secret funds earmarked to finance South African propaganda abroad. In the U.S., it was alleged, $11 million destined for the purchase of *The Washington Star* was diverted by publisher John McGoff for the purchase of *The Sacramento* (Calif.) *Union.* When Vorster was linked to the scandal by Mulder's testimony, he resigned as President on June 4, 1979, a post to which he had been elected after leaving the prime ministership in September.

The new Prime Minister, Pieter W. Botha, gave indications of moving toward a more liberal policy in interracial relations. Jobs previously restricted to whites were opened to blacks and black union rights were extended in 1979.

Mounting gold prices brought unexpected benefits to South Africa in March 1980, when the government announced income tax cuts ranging from 23% to 48% and increased subsidies on food. Gold revenues for the fiscal year ending March 31 were $14.5 billion, 20% more than estimated, permitting South Africa to drop taxes on imports and ease currency restrictions.

BOPHUTHATSWANA

Republic of Bophuthatswana
President: Chief Lucas Mangope (1977)
Area: 15,610 sq mi. (40,430 sq km)
Population (est. 1980): 1,250,000 (Tswana, 99.6%)
Density per square mile: 79.8
Capital: Mmabatho
Largest city (est. 1973): Ga-Rankuwa, 64,200
Monetary unit: South African rand
Languages: Central Tswana, English, Afrikaans
Religions: Methodist, Lutheran, Anglican, and Bantu Christian

Geography. Bophuthatswana consists of half a dozen discontinuous areas within the boundaries of South Africa, most of them in the northern sector near Botswana.

Government. The republic has a 99-member Legislative Assembly, approximately half of whom are elected and the others appointed. President Mangope's Democratic Party is the majority party.

History. Bophuthatswana was given independence by South Africa on Dec. 6, 1977, following Transkei as the second "homeland" to be established by Pretoria. The new state and Transkei are recognized only by South Africa and each other.

Mangope, as chief minister in the pre-independence period, sought linkage of the six units into a consolidated area, but was unable to achieve his objective. A second issue, the citizenship of Tswanas in South Africa who wished to remain South African nationals, was settled by enabling them to have citizenship in South African homelands not yet independent.

About two thirds of the population of Bophuthatswana live permanently or as migrants in white areas of South Africa.

Economy. Bophuthatswana is richer than many other South African homelands, as it has more than half of the republic's platinum deposits. All foreign trade is included with South Africa's, and it is economically dependent at present on that country.

SOUTH-WEST AFRICA (NAMIBIA)

Status: Mandate
Area: 318,261 sq mi. (824,296 sq km)
Population (est. 1980): 1,000,000
Density per square mile: 3.1
Administrator: Gerrit Viljoen (1979)
Capital (est. 1975): Windhoek, 77,400
Summer capital: Swakopmund **(est. 1975):** 13,700
Monetary unit: South African rand
National name: Suidwes-Afrika
Economic summary: Gross domestic product (1972): $680 million. Annual growth rate: 10%. Per capita income (1972): white, $5,525; non-white, $325. Land used for agriculture: 30%; labor force: 68%; principal products: corn, millet, sorghum, livestock. Labor force in industry: 4%; major products: canned meat, dairy products, tanned leather, textiles, clothing. Natural resources: diamonds, copper, lead, zinc, uranium, fish. Exports: diamonds, copper, lead, zinc, beef cattle, karakul pelts. Imports: construction materials, fertilizer, grain, foodstuffs. Major trading partner: South Africa.

Geography. The mandate, bounded on the north by Angola and Zambia and on the east by Botswana and South Africa, was discovered by the Portuguese explorer Diaz in the late 15th century. It is for the most part a portion of the high plateau of southern Africa with a general elevation of from 3,000 to 4,000 feet.

History. The territory became a German colony in 1884 but was taken by South African forces in 1915, becoming a South African mandate by the terms of the Treaty of Versailles.

South Africa's application for incorporation of the territory was rejected by the U.N. General Assembly in 1946 and South Africa was invited to prepare a trusteeship agreement instead. By a law passed in 1949, however, the territory was brought into much closer association with South Africa—including representation in its Parliament.

In 1969, South Africa extended its laws to the mandate over the objection of the U.N., particularly its black African members. When South Africa refused to withdraw them, the Security Council condemned it.

Under a 1974 Security Council resolution, South Africa was required to begin the transfer of power to the Namibians by May 30, 1975, or face U.N. action, but 10 days before the deadline Prime Minister Balthazar J. Vorster rejected U.N. supervision. He said, however, that his government was prepared to negotiate Namibian independence, but not with the South-West African People's Organization, the principal black separatist group. Meanwhile, the all-white legislature of South-West Africa eased several laws on apartheid in public places.

Despite international opposition, the Turnhalle Conference in Windhoek drafted a constitution to organize an interim government based on racial divisions, a proposal overwhelmingly endorsed by white voters in the territory in 1977. At the urging of ambassadors of the five Western members of the Security Council—the U.S., Britain, France, West Germany, and Canada—South Africa on June 11 announced rejection of the Turnhalle constitution and acceptance of the Western proposal to include the South-West Africa People's Organization (SWAPO) in negotiations.

With the approval of SWAPO, a militant nationalist group, Justice Marthinus T. Steyn was appointed by South Africa to serve as administrator of the territory during the transition to independence. At the same time, Pretoria announced that it would retain control of Walvis Bay, the territory's only deepwater port.

Apartheid laws were repealed by Steyn, and South-West representation in the South African parliament ended.

TRANSKEI

Republic of Transkei
President: Paramount Chief Kaiser Matanzima (1979)
Prime Minister: Paramount Chief George Matanzima (1979)
Area: 15,831 sq mi. (41,002 sq km)
Population (est. 1979): 2,200,000
Density per square mile: 137.6
Capital (est. 1978): Umtala, 30,000
Monetary unit: South African rand
Languages: English, Xhosa, Southern Sotho
Religions: Christian, 66%; tribal, 24%
Freedom House classifications: Capitalist pre-industrial, dominant party
Economic summary: Gross domestic product: $150 million. Per capita income: $86. Principal agricultural products: tea, corn, sorghum, dry beans. Major industrial products: timber, textiles. Natural resource: timber. Exports: timber, tea, sacks. Imports: foodstuffs, machines, equipment. Major trading partner: South Africa.

Geography. Transkei occupies three discontinuous enclaves within southeast South Africa that add up to twice the size of Massachusetts. It has a 270-mile (435 km) coastline on the Indian Ocean. A port is being developed at Port St. Johns. The capital, Umtata, is connected by rail to the South African port of East London, 100 miles (161 km) to the southwest.

Government. Transkei was granted independence by South Africa as of Oct. 26, 1976. A constitution called for organization of a parliament composed of 75 representative chiefs and 75 elected members, with a ceremonial president and executive power in the hands of a prime minister.

The Organization of African States and the chairman of the United Nations Special Committee Against Apartheid denounced the new state as a sham and urged governments not to recognize it.

History. British rule was established over the Transkei region between 1866 and 1894, and the Transkeian Territories were formed in 1903. Under the Native Land Act of 1913, the Territories were reserved for black occupation. In 1963, Transkei was given internal self-government and a legislature that elected Paramount Chief Kaiser Matanzima as Chief Minister, a post he retained in elections in 1968 and 1973.

Economy. Some 60% of Transkei is cultivated, producing corn, wheat, beans, and sorghum. Grazing is important. Some light industry has been established.

VENDA

Republic of Venda
President: Chief Patrick R. Mphephu (1979).
Area: 2,448 sq mi. (6,340 sq km)
Population (est. 1979): 500,000
Density per square mile: 204.2
Capital: Thohoyandou
Largest town (est. 1976): Makearela, 2,000
Monetary unit: South African rand
Languages: Venda, English, Afrikaans
Religions: Christian, tribal
Economic Summary: Gross domestic product: $156 million. Per capita income: $312. Principal agricultural products: meat, tea, fruit, sisal, corn. Major industrial products: timber, graphite, magnetite.

Geography. Venda is composed of two noncontiguous territories in northeast South Africa with a total area of about half that of Connecticut. It is mountainous but fertile, well-watered land, with a climate ranging from tropical to subtropical.

Government. The third of South Africa's homelands to be granted independence, Venda became a separate republic on Sept. 13, 1979, unrecognized by any government other than South Africa and its sister homelands, Transkei and Bophuthatswana. The President is popularly elected. An 84-seat legislature is half elected, half appointed.

History. The first European reached Venda in 1816, but the isolation of the area prevented its involvement in the wars of the 19th century between blacks and whites and with other tribes. Venda came under South African administration after the Boer War in 1902. Limited home rule was granted in 1962. Chief Patrick R. Mphephu, leader of one of the 27 tribes that historically made up the Venda nation, became Chief Minister of the interim government in 1973 and President upon independence in 1979.

SOVIET UNION

Union of Soviet Socialist Republics
Chairman of Presidium (President): Leonid I. Brezhnev (1977)
Chairman of Council of Ministers (Premier): Aleksei N. Kosygin (1964)
Area: 8,649,489 sq mi. (22,402,200 sq km)
Population (est. 1980): 265,750,000 (Russian, 52%; Ukrainian, 17%; Uzbek, 5%; Byelorussian, 4%; Tatar, 2%; others, 20%)
Density per square mile: 30.7
Capital: Moscow
Largest cities (1979 census): Moscow, 8,011,000; Leningrad, 4,588,000; Kiev, 2,144,000; Tashkent, 1,779,000; Baku, 1,550,000; Kharkov, 1,444,000; Gorki, 1,344,000; Novosibirsk, 1,312,000; Minsk, 1,276,000; Kuibyshev, 1,216,000; Sverdlovsk, 1,211,000; Dnepropetrovsk, 1,066,000; Tbilisi, 1,066,000; Odessa, 1,046,000; Chelyabinsk, 1,031,000; Donetsk, 1,021,000; Yerevan, 1,019,000; Omsk, 1,014,000
Monetary unit: Ruble
Languages: *See* Population, above
Religions: Russian Orthodox (predominant), Islam, Roman Catholic, Jewish, Lutheran
National name: Soyuz Sovyetskikh Sotsialisticheskikh Respublik
Freedom House classifications: Socialist industrial, one-party communist
Economic summary: Gross national product (1978): $966 billion. Average annual growth rate (1970–77): 4.4%. Per capita income: $3,990. Land used for agriculture: 27%; labor force: 23%; principal products: wheat, rye, corn, oats, potatoes, sugar beets, cotton and flax, cattle, pigs, sheep. Labor force in industry: 76%; major products: ferrous and nonferrous metals, fuels and power, building

Republics of the U.S.S.R.

Republic and capital	Area sq mi.	Population est. 1977 (thousands)
Russian S.F.S.R. (Moscow)	6,593,391	135,600
Ukraine (Kiev)	233,089	49,300
Kazakhstan (Alma-Ata)	1,064,092	14,498
Byelorussia (Minsk)	80,154	9,414
Uzbekistan (Tashkent)	158,069	14,474
Georgia (Tbilisi)	26,872	4,999
Azerbaijan (Baku)	33,475	5,776
Lithuania[1] (Vilnius)	25,174	3,342
Moldavia (Kishinev)	13,012	3,885
Latvia[1] (Riga)	24,595	2,512
Kirghizia (Frunze)	76,641	3,443
Tadzhikistan (Duschambe)	55,019	3,591
Armenia (Erevan)	11,506	2,893
Turkmenistan (Ashkhabad)	188,417	2,650
Estonia[1] (Tallinn)	17,413	1,447

1. Soviet jurisdiction not recognized by the United States.

materials, chemicals, machinery. Natural resources: fossil fuels, water power, timber, manganese, lead, zinc, nickel, mercury, potash, phosphate. Exports: fossil fuels, raw materials, machinery and equipment, semifinished products. Imports: machinery and equipment, foodstuffs, raw materials. Major trading partners: Soviet bloc, Cuba, U.S., Japan, Finland, Yugoslavia, Italy, France.

Geography. The U.S.S.R. is the largest unbroken political unit in the world, occupying more than one seventh of the land surface of the globe. The greater part of its territory is a vast plain stretching from eastern Europe to the Pacific Ocean. This plain, relieved only occasionally by low mountain ranges (notably the Urals), consists of three zones running east and west: the frozen marshy tundra of the Arctic; the more temperate forest belt; and the steppes or prairies to the south, which in southern Soviet Asia become sandy deserts.

The topography is more varied in the south, particularly in the Caucasus between the Caspian and Black Seas, and in the Tien-Pamir mountain system bordering Afghanistan, Sinkiang, and Mongolia. Mountains (Stanovoi and Kolyma) and great rivers (Amur, Yenisei, Lena) also break up the sweep of the plain in Siberia.

In the west, the major rivers are the Volga, Dnieper, Don, Kama, and Southern Bug.

Government. Legislative authority is vested in the Supreme Soviet of the U.S.S.R., which consists of two chambers—the Soviet of the Union, with 767 members, and the Soviet of Nationalities, with 750 members. All members of the Supreme Soviet are elected for five years by the people.

A Presidium is elected by the Supreme Soviet to deal with state matters when the latter is not in session. It consists of a chairman, first vice chairman, 15 vice chairmen (one for each union republic), 21 members, and a secretary. The chairman of the Presidium is sometimes referred to as the President.

Executive authority rests with the Council of Ministers. It is appointed by the Supreme Soviet and includes a chairman, a first vice chairman, and various vice chairmen, chairmen of state committees, ministers, etc. The chairman of the Council of Ministers is often referred to as the Premier.

Judicial authority is vested in the Supreme Court of the U.S.S.R. It consists of a chairmen, vice chairman, members, and people's assessors, who are elected by the Supreme Soviet for five years.

Each of the 15 union republics and the 20 autonomous republics has a Supreme Soviet (with a Presidium), a Council of Ministers, and a Supreme Court. Each of the eight autonomous regions has a Soviet of People's Deputies.

The Communist Party of the Soviet Union is the only party. It is the basic power in the country and today has a membership of over 16,800,000.

The supreme organ of the party is the Party Congress, which meets at least once in five years. It elects a Central Committee, consisting of 287 members and 139 candidate members, to carry on party work between sessions of the Congress.

Rulers of Russia Since 1533

Name	Born	Ruled[1]
Ivan IV the Terrible	1530	1533–1584
Theodore I	1557	1584–1598
Boris Godunov	c.1551	1598–1605
Theodore II	1589	1605–1605
Demetrius I[2]	?	1605–1606
Basil IV Shuiski	?	1606–1610[3]
"Time of Troubles"	—	1610–1613
Michael Romanov	1596	1613–1645
Alexis I	1629	1645–1676
Theodore III	1656	1676–1682
Ivan V[4]	1666	1682–1689[5]
Peter I the Great[4]	1672	1682–1725
Catherine I	c.1684	1725–1727
Peter II	1715	1727–1730
Anna	1693	1730–1740
Ivan VI	1740	1740–1741[6]
Elizabeth	1709	1741–1762
Peter III	1728	1762–1762
Catherine II the Great	1729	1762–1796
Paul I	1754	1796–1801
Alexander I	1777	1801–1825
Nicholas I	1796	1825–1855
Alexander II	1818	1855–1881
Alexander III	1845	1881–1894
Nicholas II	1868	1894–1917[7]
PROVISIONAL GOVERNMENT (PREMIERS)		
Prince Georgi Lvov	1861	1917–1917
Alexander Kerensky	1881	1917–1917
U.S.S.R. (PREMIERS)		
N. Lenin	1870	1917–1924
Aleksei Rykov	1881	1924–1930
Vyacheslav Molotov	1890	1930–1941
Joseph Stalin[8]	1879	1941–1953
Georgi M. Malenkov	1902	1953–1955
Nikolai A. Bulganin	1895	1955–1958
Nikita S. Khrushchev	1894	1958–1964
Aleksei N. Kosygin	1904	1964–

1. For Czars through Nicholas II, year of end of rule is also that of death, unless otherwise indicated. 2. Also known as Pseudo-Demetrius. 3. Died 1612. 4. Ruled jointly until 1689, when Ivan was deposed. 5. Died 1696. 6. Died 1764. 7. Killed 1918. 8. General Secretary of Communist Party, 1924–53.

Within the Central Committee is a Political Bureau (Politburo), which was called the Presidium from 1952 to 1966. It functions between sessions of the Central Committee. Also within the Central Committee is the Secretariat. The present General Secretary of the Central Committee, Leonid I. Brezhnev, has served since Oct. 15, 1964. Named President in June 1977 to succeed Nikolai V. Podgorny, he is the first man in Soviet history to hold both posts simultaneously. Earlier First Secretaries were Nikita S. Khrushchev (1953–64), Georgi M. Malenkov (briefly in 1953), and Joseph Stalin (1922–53).

History. Tradition says the Viking Rurik came to Russia in A.D. 862 and founded the first Russian dynasty in Novgorod. The various tribes were united by the spread of Christianity in the 10th and 11th centuries; Vladimir "the Saint" was converted in 988. During the 11th century, the grand dukes of Kiev held such centralizing power as existed. In 1240, Kiev was destroyed by the Mongols, and the Russian territory was split into numerous smaller dukedoms, out of which three large centers emerged—Galicia, Moscow, and Novgorod. The early dukes of Moscow extended their dominions through their office of tribute collector for the Mongols.

In the late 15th century, Duke Ivan III acquired Novgorod and Tver and threw off the Mongol yoke. Ivan IV, the Terrible (1533–84), first Muscovite Tsar, is considered to have founded the Russian state. He crushed the power of rival princes and boyars (great landowners), but Russia remained largely medieval until the reign of Peter the Great (1682–1725), grandson of the first Romanov Tsar, Michael (1613–45). Peter made extensive reforms aimed at westernization and, through his defeat of Charles XII of Sweden at the Battle of Poltava in 1709, he extended Russia's boundaries to the west.

Catherine the Great (1762–96) continued Peter's westernization program and also expanded Russian territory, acquiring the Crimea and part of Poland. During the reign of Alexander I (1801–25), Napoleon's attempt to subdue Russia was defeated (1812–13), and new territory was gained, including Finland (1809) and Bessarabia (1812). Alexander originated the Holy Alliance, which for a time crushed Europe's rising liberal movement.

Alexander II (1855–81) pushed Russia's borders to the Pacific and into central Asia. Serfdom was abolished in 1861, but heavy restrictions were imposed on the emancipated class. Revolutionary strikes following Russia's defeat in the war with Japan forced Nicholas II (1894–1917) to grant a representative national body (Duma), elected by narrowly limited suffrage. It met for the first time in 1906. Nicholas continued in his reactionary course, however, and the overwhelmingly liberal Duma had little or no influence.

World War I demonstrated tsarist corruption and the inefficiency of the tsarist regime, although the call of patriotism held the poorly equipped army together for a time. Disorders broke out in Petrograd (now Leningrad) in March 1917, and defection of the Petrograd garrison launched the revolution. Nicholas II was forced to abdicate on March 15, 1917, and he and his family were killed by revolutionists on July 16, 1918.

A provisional government composed of conservative and radical elements under the successive premierships of Prince Lvov and a moderate, Alexander Kerensky, lost ground to the radical, or Bolshevik, wing of the Socialist Democratic Labor Party. On Nov. 7, 1917, the Bolshevik revolution, engineered by N. Lenin[1] and Leon Trotsky, took place. The Kerensky government was overthrown, and authority was vested in a Council of People's Commissars, with Lenin as Premier.

The humiliating Treaty of Brest-Litovsk (March 3, 1918) concluded the war with Germany, but civil war and foreign intervention delayed Communist control of all Russia until 1920. A brief war with Poland in 1920 resulted in Russian defeat.

The Union of Soviet Socialist Republics was established as a federation on Dec. 30, 1922.

The death of Lenin on Jan. 21, 1924, precipitated an intraparty struggle between Joseph Stalin, General Secretary of the party, and Trotsky, who favored swifter socialization at home and fomentation of revolution abroad. Stalin won. Trotsky was dismissed as Commissar of War in 1925 and banished from the Soviet Union in 1929. He was murdered in Mexico City on Aug. 21, 1940, by a political agent.

Stalin further consolidated his power by a series of purges in the late 1930s, liquidating prominent party leaders and military officers. Stalin assumed the premiership May 6, 1941.

Soviet foreign policy, at first friendly toward Germany and antagonistic toward Britain and France and then, after Hitler's rise to power in 1933, becoming anti-Fascist and pro-League of Nations, took an abrupt turn on Aug. 24, 1939, with the signing of a nonaggression pact with Nazi Germany. The next month, Moscow joined in the German attack on Poland, seizing territory later incorporated into the Ukrainian and Byelorussian S.S.R.'s. The war with Finland, 1939-40, added territory to the Karelian S.S.R. set up March 31, 1940; the annexation of Bessarabia and Bukovina from Romania became part of the new Moldavian S.S.R. on Aug. 2, 1940; and the annexation of the Baltic republics of Estonia, Latvia, and Lithuania in June 1940 (still unrecognized by the U.S.) created the 14th, 15th, and 16th Soviet Republics. (The number of so-called "Union" republics was reduced to 15 in 1956 when the Karelian S.S.R. became one of the 20 Autonomous Soviet Socialist Republics based on ethnic groups.)

The Soviet-German collaboration ended abruptly with a lightning attack by Hitler on June 22, 1941, which seized 500,000 square miles of Russian territory before Soviet defenses, aided by U.S. and British arms, could halt it. The Soviet resurgence at Stalingrad from November 1942 to February 1943 marked the turning point in a long battle, ending in the final offensive of January 1945.

Then, after denouncing a 1941 nonaggression pact with Japan in April 1945, when Allied forces were nearing victory in the Pacific, the Soviet Union declared war on Japan on Aug. 8, 1945, and quickly occupied Manchuria, Karafuto, and the Kurile islands.

Postwar territorial acquisitions include the Carpatho-Ukraine (12,617 sq mi.; 32,678 sq km) obtained from Czechoslovakia June 29, 1945, incorporated into the Ukrainian S.S.R.; the Republic of Tannu Tuva in central Asia (64,000 sq mi.; 165,760 sq km), incorporated early in 1945 into the Russian Soviet Federal Socialist Republic (R.S.F.S.R.); Karafuto or southern Sakhalin (13,935 sq mi.; 36,092 sq km) and the Kurile Islands (3,944 sq mi.; 10,215 sq km), occupied by Soviet troops in August 1945 and incorporated into the R.S.F.S.R.; the northern part of eastern Prussia (about 7,000 sq

1. N. Lenin was the pseudonym taken by Vladimir Ilich Ulyanov. It is sometimes given as Nikolai Lenin or V. I. Lenin.

mi.; 18,130 sq km), placed under *de facto* Soviet administration at the Potsdam Conference and incorporated into the R.S.F.S.R.; the Petsamo district of Finland, obtained *de jure* under the 1947 treaty and incorporated into the R.S.F.S.R.; and Poland east of the Curzon Line (69,860 sq mi.; 180,937 sq km), under terms of the Soviet-Polish treaty of Aug. 16, 1945, incorporated into the Ukrainian and Byelorussian S.S.R.'s.

The U.S.S.R. built a cordon of Communist states running from Poland in the north to Albania and Bulgaria in the south, including East Germany, Czechoslovakia, Hungary, and Romania, composed of the territories Soviet troops occupied at the war's end. With its Eastern front solidified, the Soviet Union launched a political offensive against the non-Communist West, moving first to block the Western access to Berlin. The Western powers countered with an airlift, completed unification of West Germany, and organized the defense of Western Europe in the North Atlantic Treaty Organization.

Stalin died on March 6, 1953, and was succeeded the next day by G. M. Malenkov as Premier. His chief rivals for power—Lavrenti P. Beria (chief of the secret police), Nikolai A. Bulganin, and Lazar M. Kaganovich—were named first deputies. Beria was purged in July and executed on Dec. 23, 1953.

The new power in the Kremlin was Nikita S. Khrushchev, First Secretary of the party. He replaced Malenkov with Bulganin in the premiership and then removed Malenkov, Kaganovich, and Vyacheslav M. Molotov from the Politburo. At the 20th Party Congress in 1956, Khrushchev denounced the "personality cult" of Stalin and in 1958 unseated Bulganin to become head of the government as well as of the party.

Khrushchev formalized the Eastern European system into a Council for Mutual Economic Assistance (Comecon) and a Warsaw Pact Treaty Organization as a counterweight to NATO. Tiny Albania was allowed to break away to join China in contesting Soviet domination of the Communist world, as Yugoslavia had done earlier. However, no mercy was shown to the Hungarians who rebelled in 1956, nor to the Czechs in their political struggle for liberation 12 years later.

In its technological race with the U.S., the Soviet Union exploded a hydrogen bomb in 1953, developed an intercontinental ballistic missile by 1957, sent the first satellite into space (Sputnik I) in 1957, and put Yuri Gagarin in the first orbital flight around the earth in 1961. On July 24, 1975, the 44-hour linkup of a Soviet Soyuz space vehicle (and two crewmen) with a U.S. Apollo spacecraft and its crew of three) demonstrated—for the first time openly—the level of Soviet space capability.

Although he had denounced personality cults, Khrushchev wielded enormous power. His downfall stemmed from his decision to place Soviet nuclear missiles in Cuba and then, when challenged by the U.S., backing down and removing the weapons. He was also blamed for the ideological break with China after 1963.

Khrushchev was forced into retirement on Oct. 15, 1964, and was replaced by Leonid I. Brezhnev as First Secretary of the Party and Aleksei N. Kosygin as Premier.

President Nixon visited the U.S.S.R. for summit talks in May 1972, concluding agreements on strategic-arms limitation and a declaration of principles on future U.S.-Soviet relations. The welcome given Nixon at a time when the U.S. was bombing North Vietnam, a Soviet ally, was regarded as proof that 25 years of cold war had ended.

The 1972 Strategic Arms Limitation Treaty (SALT I) set a ceiling of 200 anti-ballistic missiles (ABM's) for each side and the U.S.S.R. was frozen at 1,618 land-based intercontinental missiles (ICBM's), with the U.S. held to 1,054. Submarine-based missiles were restricted by a complicated formula giving the U.S.S.R. a numerical advantage, balanced by permitting the U.S. more warheads for its more reliable and accurate missiles.

Brezhnev visited the U.S. in 1973 to discuss further arms limitations, but a return visit to Moscow by Nixon the following year failed to produce an expected permanent treaty. The two sides agreed to reduce ABM's to 100 each and to restrict underground nuclear testing (air, sea, and space tests were already prohibited), but there was no agreement to stop the proliferation of multi-warhead missiles (MIRV's).

Presidents Gerald R. Ford and Brezhnev met in Vladivostok in November 1974 and reached tentative agreements to be incorporated into a treaty at the Geneva SALT talks in 1975. They proposed a ceiling of 2,400 ICBM's for each side, of which no more than 1,320 could have MIRV's. There was hard bargaining but no decision on verification methods nor on whether the new U.S. subsonic Cruise missile and the Soviet Backfire bomber should be covered.

Ford and Brezhnev renewed the discussions without progress at the 35-nation Conference on Security and Cooperation in Europe. This 1975 Helsinki conference recognized Europe's post-World War II boundaries, a long-sought goal of Soviet policy. It also pledged participants to recognize basic human rights of their citizens.

President Jimmy Carter, actively pursuing both human rights and disarmament, joined with the Soviet Union in September 1977 to declare that the SALT I accord, which would have expired October 1 without further action, be maintained in effect while the two sides sought a new agreement (SALT II).

Despite recurrent friction, desire for détente appeared to moderate the Kremlin's policies toward the U.S. after the 1972 summit. There was a near-confrontation during the Arab-Israeli war of October 1973, when a Soviet threat to intervene to aid trapped Egyptian forces led Washington to call a world-wide nuclear alert, but the crisis was eased when the United Nations approved a truce plan developed by the U.S. and the U.S.S.R. After the war, Moscow provided arms and encouragement to militant Arab states, but did not actively resist the Israeli-Egyptian interim accord of 1975. The Kremlin made no overt move to capitalize on the fall of U.S.-backed governments in Indochina in the spring of 1975, but hailed the war's end as an incentive to improvement in relations with the U.S.

Brezhnev's 1977 election to the presidency followed publication of a new Constitution supplanting the one adopted in 1936. It specified the dominance of the Communist Party, previously unstated, and in what was taken to be a weapon against dissidents, declared that "rights and freedoms shall be inseparable from the performance by citizens of their duties." This was thought to restrict dissidents when they cited constitutional guarantees of individual freedom.

Although Brezhnev promised an end to the "illegal repressions" of the Stalin era, the issue of human rights remained a major one in both domestic and foreign policy. Dissidents continued to cite the Helsinki Agreement, and Carter's public support for Anatoly Shcharansky drew the angry charge from Brezhnev that Carter was conducting "ideological warfare" against the U.S.S.R. Amid the verbal fireworks, there was serious concern about the extent to which human rights might become an obstacle to SALT negotiations and to Soviet-U.S. relations in general.

Charges of Soviet interference by Carter and particularly by Security Adviser Zbigniew Brezezinski in Africa brought heated comments from Moscow in 1978. The State Department warned, after Brezhnev had complained of SALT delays, that Soviet military aid to Ethiopia threatened all U.S.-Soviet relations. The Soviet news agency, Tass, said on February 26 that Soviet aid to Ethiopia was to counter Somali aggression and would end with a ceasefire. Similar friction occurred following the May invasion by rebels from Soviet-allied Angola, culminating in a speech by Carter to graduates of the U.S. Naval Academy telling the Russians they must "choose either confrontation or cooperation." The speech did not reduce tensions, but increased Soviet uneasiness about American intentions.

A crisis arose July 10 when, despite warnings from the Carter Administration, the government brought two prominent Jewish dissidents to trial, only two days before the opening of a new round of SALT negotiations in Geneva. Amid worldwide protest, a Moscow judge sentenced Anatoly Scharansky to three years in prison and 10 years in a forced labor camp on charges of treason. Scharansky, a leading spokesman for Jews seeking to emigrate to Israel, was accused of passing classified information to U.S. agents.

Aleksandr Ginzburg, manager of a fund established by exiled writer Aleksandr Solzhenytsin to aid political prisoners, was sentenced to eight years in a labor camp. Ginzburg was found guilty of "anti-Soviet agitation."

Carter condemned the action and temporarily halted the export of high technology goods to the Soviet Union. In April 1979, the issue was partly resolved with the exchange of Ginzburg and four other dissidents for two Soviet spies held by the United States. For 1979, the final count of Soviet Jews allowed to emigrate was 51,320, the highest number since emigration was permitted.

Carter and the ailing Brezhnev signed the SALT II treaty in Vienna on June 18, 1979, setting ceilings on each nation's arsenal of intercontinental ballistic missiles. Doubts about Senate ratification grew, and became a certainty on Dec. 27, when Soviet troops invaded Afghanistan. Despite protests from the Moslem and Western worlds, Moscow insisted that Afghan President Hafizullah Amin had asked for aid in quelling a nationalist rebellion.

In the face of evidence that Amin had been liquidated by Soviet advisers before the troops arrived, the Soviet Union vetoed a Security Council resolution on Jan. 7, 1980, that called for a withdrawal. Carter ordered a freeze on grain exports and high-technology equipment and stated that his "opinion of the Russians has changed more drastically in the last week than even in the previous two-and-a-half years."

On Jan. 20, Carter called for a world boycott of the Summer Olympic Games scheduled for Moscow. The boycott, less than complete, nevertheless marred the first Olympics to be held in Moscow as the United States, Canada, Japan, and to a partial extent all the western allies except France and Italy shunned the event. By the Games' end, on Aug. 3, Soviet athletes had captured a record number of 80 gold medals in what Western writers called a "joyless" competition.

As of mid-August, an estimated 100,000 Soviet troops remained in Afghanistan, with guerrilla resistance continuing, and Moscow's motives still unclear. The invasion was regarded by some U.S. theoreticians as having been prompted by the weak response of the Carter administration to the seizure of the U.S. Embassy in Teheran. Others suggested that Soviet leaders were only routinely backing a Marxist regime threatened with overthrow. With Iran racked by internal struggles, there was also the opportunity for Soviet military power to intervene from a flanking position, possibly gaining for Moscow both Iranian oil and the access to the Indian Ocean, coveted since Tsarist days.

SPAIN

Spanish State
Ruler: King Juan Carlos I (1975)
Premier: Adolfo Suárez González (1976)
Area: 194,885 sq mi. (504,750 sq km)[1]
Population (est. 1980): 37,575,000 (Spanish, Basque, Catalan, Galician)
Density per square mile: 192.8
Capital: Madrid
Largest cities (est. 1979): Madrid, 4,120,000; (est. 1976): Barcelona, 1,846,250; Valencia, 748,730; Seville, 612,900; Zaragoza, 589,600; Bilbao, 486,600
Monetary unit: Peseta
Languages: Spanish, Basque, Catalan, Galician
Religion: Roman Catholic
National name: Estado Español
Freedom House classifications: Capitalist industrial, multi-party centralized.
Economic summary: Gross national product (1978): $129 billion. Average annual growth rate (1970–77): 3.6%. Per capita income: $3,190. Land used for agriculture: 39%; labor force: 19%; principal products: cereals, vegetables, citrus fruits, wine, olives and olive oil, livestock. Labor force in industry: 37%; major products: processed foods, textiles, footwear, petro-chemicals, steel, automobiles, ships. Natural resources: coal, lignite, water power, uranium, mercury, pyrites, fluorospar, gypsum, iron ore, zinc, lead, tungsten, copper. Exports: fresh fruits, iron and steel products, textiles, footwear, mercury, ships, canned fruits and vegetables. Imports: machinery and transportation equipment, petroleum and petroleum products, grains, cotton, coal, iron, steel. Major trading partners: France, West Germany, U.S., U.K., and OPEC nations.

Geography. Spain occupies 85% of the Iberian Peninsula in southwestern Europe, which it shares with Portugal; France is to the northeast. It is touched by the Bay of Biscay in the north, the Atlantic Ocean in the west, and the Mediterranean Sea in the south and east.

Spain, less than 10 miles (16 km) from Africa at the Strait of Gibraltar, is separated from France by the Pyrenees. The country is generally a broad plateau sloping to south and east and crossed by a series of mountain ranges and river valleys.

Principal rivers are the Ebro in the northeast, the Tagus in the central region, and the Guadalquivir in the south.

Off Spain's east coast in the Mediterranean are the Balearic Islands (1,936 sq mi.; 5,014 sq km), the largest of which is Majorca. Sixty miles (97 km) west of Africa are the Canary Islands (2,808 sq mi.; 7,273 sq km).

1. Including the Balearic and Canary Islands.

Government. King Juan Carlos I (born Jan. 5, 1938) succeeded Generalissimo Francisco Franco Bahamonde as Chief of State Nov. 22, 1975. The King appoints the Premier from a list of three candidates submitted by the Council of the Realm.

The Cortes, or Parliament, consists of a Chamber of Deputies of 350 members and a Senate of 208, all elected by universal suffrage. The new Cortes, replacing one that was largely appointed or elected by special constituencies, was organized under a constitution adopted by referendum Dec. 6, 1978.

The major political parties are the 12-party coalition of the Union of the Democratic Center (168 of 350 seats in the Chamber of Deputies, 120 of 208 elected Senate seats), led by Premier Adolfo Suárez González; Spanish Socialist Workers Party (121 seats in Chamber, 68 in Senate); Communist Party (23 seats in Chamber, none in Senate), led by Santiago Carrillo; Democratic Coalition (9 seats in Chamber, 3 in Senate); Convergencia i Unión (Catalonian Party) (8 seats in Chamber, 1 in Senate); Basque Party (7 seats in Chamber, 8 in Senate).

History. Spain, originally inhabited by Celts, Iberians, and Basques, became a part of the Roman Empire in 201 B.C., when it was conquered by Scipio Africanus. In A.D. 412, the barbarian Visigothic leader Ataulf crossed the Pyrenees and ruled Spain, first in the name of the Roman emperor and then independently. In 711, the Moslems under Tariq entered Spain from Africa and within a few years completed the subjugation of the country. In 732, the Franks, led by Charles Martel, defeated the Moslems near Poitiers, thus preventing the further expansion of Islam in southern Europe. Internal dissension of Spanish Islam invited a steady Christian conquest from the north.

Aragon and Castile were the most important Spanish states from the 13th to the 15th century, in time absorbing all the other peoples of Spain. Aragon and Castile were consolidated by the marriage of Ferdinand II and Isabella I. The last Moslem stronghold, Granada, was captured in 1492. With Moslem control ended, Roman Catholicism was established as the official state religion. The Jews (1492) and the Moslems (1502) were expelled at the cost of incalculable suffering and loss of life.

In the era of exploration, discovery, and colonization, Spain amassed tremendous wealth and a vast colonial empire. The conquest of Peru by Pizarro (1532–33) and of Mexico by Cortés (1519–21) brought great prosperity to the motherland. The Spanish Hapsburg monarchy, through wars, diplomatic negotiations, and marriages, became for a time one of the most powerful in the world.

In 1588, Philip II sent his Invincible Armada to invade England, but its destruction cost Spain its supremacy on the seas and paved the way for England's colonization of America. Spain then sank rapidly to the status of a second-rate power and never again played a major role in European politics. Its colonial empire in the Americas and the Philippines vanished in wars and revolutions during the 18th and 19th centuries.

In World War I, Spain maintained a position of neutrality. In 1923, Gen. Miguel Primo de Rivera became dictator. In 1930, King Alfonso XIII revoked the dictatorship, but a strong antimonarchist and republican movement led to his leaving Spain in 1931.[2] The new Constitution declared Spain a workers' republic, broke up the large estates, separated church and state, and secularized the schools. The elections held in 1936 returned a strong Popular Front majority, with Manuel Azaña as President.

But political chaos persisted. On July 18, 1936, a conservative army officer in Morocco, Francisco Franco Bahamonde, led a mutiny against the government. The civil war that followed lasted three years and cost the lives of nearly a million people. Franco was aided by Fascist Italy and Nazi Germany, while Soviet Russia helped the Loyalist side. Several hundred leftist Americans served in the Abraham Lincoln Brigade on the side of the republic. The war ended when Franco took Madrid on March 28, 1939.

Franco became head of the state, national chief of the Falange Party (the governing party), and Premier and Caudillo (leader). The country was ruled by Franco's Cabinet, the National Council of the Falange Party, and the Cortes, which formulated laws subject to Franco's veto. At first the jails were filled with Franco opponents. But after the dictator consolidated his power, he undertook a policy of reconciliation.

In a referendum in 1947, the Spanish people approved a Franco-drafted succession law declaring Spain a monarchy again. Franco, however, continued as Chief of State.

In 1969, Franco and the Cortes designated Prince Juan Carlos Alfonso Victor María de Borbón (who married Princess Sophia of Greece on May 14, 1962) to become King of Spain when the provisional government headed by Franco came to an end. He is the grandson of Alfonso XIII and the son of Don Juan, pretender to the throne.

In 1967 Spain concluded its first economic-social development plan, which had raised levels of living dramatically within a decade and, combined with Spanish migration to higher-wage countries in Western Europe, had virtually eradicated unemployment. A new Constitution, adopted in 1966, allowed for the direct election of one fourth of the Cortes.

Franco died of a heart attack on Nov. 20, 1975, after more than a year of ill health, and Juan Carlos was proclaimed King two days later.

Over strong rightist opposition, the government legalized the Communist Party in advance of the 1977 elections and permitted the return of Dolores Ibarruri, "La Pasionaria" of the 1930s, from long exile in Moscow. Premier Adolfo Suaraz Gonzalez's Union of the Democratic Center, a coalition of a dozen centrist and rightist parties, claimed 34.3% of the popular vote in the election.

The Spanish Socialist Workers Party (PSOE) ran the strongest opposition campaign to win 28.5% of the vote, with the Communists following at 9% and the right-wing Popular Alliance trailing with 8.2%.

The strong stand for the "Eurocommunist" philosophy of separation from Moscow's leadership taken by Santiago Carrillo, the Communist Party leader, was a feature of the election and drew a sharp attack from the Soviet Union.

Responding to growing agitation for regional autonomy in Catalonia and the Basque provinces, the Suárez government moved from symbolic measures in 1977 to home-rule referendums in both areas in 1979. Despite the opposition of the extremist Basque nationalist movement, ETA, which called for a boycott of the referendum, the proposal won approval of Basques and Catalonians.

In elections of regional parliaments in March 1980, Basque moderates won the largest bloc of a 60-seat body, followed by front organizations for

2. However, he did not abdicate. In 1941, shortly before his death, he renounced his claim to the throne in favor of his third son, Don Juan.

ETA, while conservatives led in voting for the 135-seat Catalonian assembly. In both elections, centrists backed by Suárez did poorly.

Economic difficulties—Spain's 11% unemployment, the highest in Western Europe, brought a motion of censure against Suárez in the Cortes, which he narrowly survived on May 30. Attacked from all sides because of the faltering economy and by the right for his failure to halt continuing ETA terrorism, Suárez sustained a new blow on June 6 when French President Valéry Giscard d'Estaing called for a delay in Spain's entry into the European Common Market. Spain was tentatively scheduled to join the European Community on Jan. 1, 1983, and the government had made this a precondition for adherence to the North Atlantic Treaty.

SRI LANKA

Democratic Socialist Republic of Sri Lanka
President: J. R. Jayawardene (1978)
Prime Minister: Ranasinghe Premadasa (1978)
Area: 25,332 sq mi. (65,610 sq km)
Population (est. 1980): 15,150,000
Density per square mile: 598.1
Capital: Colombo
Largest cities (est. 1977): Colombo, 616,000; **(est. 1976):** Dehiwela, 166,000; Jaffna, 117,000
Monetary unit: Sri Lanka rupee
Languages: Sinhala, Tamil, English
Religions: Buddhist, 67%; Hindu, 18%; Christian, 8%; Islam, 7%
Member of Commonwealth of Nations
Freedom House classifications: Capitalist-statist industrial, multi-party centralized.
Economic summary: Gross national product (1978): $2.7 billion. Average annual growth rate (1970–77): 1.3%. Per capita income: $220. Land used for agriculture: 39%; labor force: 45%; principal products: tea, coconuts, rubber, rice, spices. Labor force in industry: 10%; major products: consumer goods, textiles, chemicals, paper and paper products. Natural resources: limestone, graphite, gems. Exports: tea, rubber. Imports: foodstuffs, petroleum, fertilizer. Major trading partners: Pakistan, U.K., Saudi Arabia, Iran.

Geography. An island in the Indian Ocean off the southeast tip of India, Sri Lanka is about half the size of Alabama. Most of the land is flat and rolling; mountains in the south central region rise to over 8,000 feet (2,438 m).

Government. After 24 years as a British dominion, Ceylon became an independent republic and reverted to the traditional name Sri Lanka (resplendent island) on May 22, 1972. A new Constitution was adopted, replacing that of 1948. William Gopallawa, the former Governor-General, was named President and Mrs. Sirimavo R. D. Bandaranaike remained Prime Minister.

The new Constitution set up the National State Assembly, which consists of as many elected representatives of the people as a Delimitation Commission may determine. The 168-member Assembly is a unicameral legislature and serves for six years unless dissolved earlier.

The major political parties are the United National Party (141 of 168 seats in the National Assembly), led by President J.R. Jayawardene; Tamil United Liberation Front (17 seats); Sri Lanka Freedom Party (9 seats), led by former Prime Minister Bandaranaike.

History. Following Portuguese and Dutch rule, Ceylon became an English crown colony in 1798. The British developed coffee, tea, and rubber plantations and granted six Constitutions between 1798 and 1924. The Constitution of 1931 gave a large measure of self-government.

Ceylon became a self-governing dominion of the Commonwealth of Nations in 1948. Rioting by the Tamils seeking a separate state within a federal system occurred in 1958 and 1961, resulting in the outlawing of their party. In 1962, the Prime Minister, Mrs. Bandaranaike, a radical, nationalized Western oil and other business facilities and became embroiled with the U.S. and Britain over compensation. She was ousted in the 1965 elections by a multiparty coalition.

Following considerable pre-election violence, Mrs. Bandaranaike was returned to power in a landslide victory in 1970, with her three-party leftist coalition capturing over two thirds of parliament. An important factor was the 800,000 youths 18-to-21 years old given the vote for the first time; they proved largely left-leaning.

Worsening economic conditions and charges of corruption combined to produce a crushing defeat for Mrs. Bandaranaike in general elections of 1977. Junius Richard Jayawardene, 73-year-old leader of the small United National Party, became Prime Minister.

Amid opposition criticism, Jayawardene was sworn in as president on Feb. 3, 1978, in a constitutional change to the presidential system of government. He named his deputy party leader, Ranasingle Premadasa, as prime minister.

SUDAN

Democratic Republic of the Sudan
President: (1971): Maj. Gen. Gaafar Mohamed Nimeiri
Area: 967,491 sq mi. (2,505,802 sq km)
Population (est. 1980): 18,350,000
Density per square mile: 19.0
Capital: Khartoum
Largest cities (est. 1977): Khartoum, 1,089,300; **(est. 1973):** Omdurman, 250,000; Port Sudan, 130,000
Monetary unit: Sudanese pound
Languages: Arabic, English, tribal dialects
Religions: Sunni Moslem, Christian, Animist
National name: Jamhuryat es-Sudan Al Demogratia
Freedom House classifications: Capitalist-socialist pre-industrial, one-party national.
Economic summary: Gross national product (1978): $5.5 billion. Average annual growth rate (1970–77): 2.5%. Per capita income: $165. Land used for agriculture: 3%; labor force: 86%; principal products: cotton, peanuts, sesame seeds, gum arabic, sorghum, wheat sugar cane. Labor force in industry: 6%; major products: cement, textiles, pharmaceuticals, shoes, processed foods. Natural resources: some iron ore, copper, chrome, industrial metals. Exports: cotton, peanuts, gum arabic, livestock. Imports: manufactured goods, machinery and transport equipment, food, livestock. Major trading partners: Japan, China, West Germany, U.S.S.R., Italy, India, U.K., France.

Geography. The Sudan, in northeast Africa, is the largest country on the continent, measuring about one fourth the size of the United States. Its neighbors are Chad and the Central African Empire on the west, Egypt and Libya on the north, Ethiopia on the east, and Kenya, Uganda, and Zaire on the south. The Red Sea washes about 500 miles of the eastern coast.

The country extends from north to south about

1,200 miles (1,931 km) and west to east about 1,000 miles (1,609 km). The northern region is a continuation of the Libyan Desert. The southern region is fertile, abundantly watered, and, in places, heavily forested. It is traversed from north to south by the Nile, all of whose great tributaries are partly or entirely within its borders.

Government. Since the revolution of May 25, 1969, the Sudan has been governed by a 10-member Council for the Revolution. The provisional Constitution was abrogated. All political parties were dissolved by the Council for the Revolution.

History. The early history of the Sudan (known as the Anglo-Egyptian Sudan between 1898 and 1955) is linked with that of Nubia, where a powerful local kingdom was formed in Roman times with its capital at Dongola. After conversion to Christianity in the 6th century, it joined with Ethiopia and resisted Mohammedanization until the 14th century. Thereafter the area was broken up into many small states until 1820–22, when it was conquered by Mohammed Ali, Pasha of Egypt. Egyptian forces were evacuated during the Mahdist revolt (1881–98), but the Sudan was reconquered by the Anglo-Egyptian expeditions of 1896–98, and in 1899 became an Anglo-Egyptian condominium, which was reaffirmed by the Anglo-Egyptian treaty of 1936.

Egypt and Britain agreed in 1953 to grant self-government to the Sudan under an appointed Governor-General. An all-Sudanese Parliament was elected in November-December 1953, and an all-Sudanese government was formed. In December 1955, the Parliament declared the independence of the Sudan, which, with the approval of Britain and Egypt, was proclaimed on Jan. 1, 1956.

In October 1969, Maj. Gen. Gaafar Mohamed Nimeiri, the president of the Council for the Revolution, took over as prime minister. He was elected the nation's first president in 1971 by a reported 98.6% of the vote in a national referendum. His term was for six years.

On March 2, 1973, eight Palestinian terrorists invaded the Saudi Arabian embassy in Khartoum and killed one Belgian and two American diplomats after their demands for the release of Arab terrorist prisoners in different countries were refused. The terrorists surrendered after three days and were captured, but Nimeiri postponed bringing them to trial in the face of Arab calls for their release.

The terrorists were convicted of murder June 24, 1974, but Nimeiri freed them the next day and turned them over to the Palestine Liberation Army, which flew them to Cairo. The U.S. withdrew its Ambassador in protest, but he returned in October 1974 after the men were imprisoned in Egypt.

In 1976, a third attempted coup against Nimeiri left 1,000 rebels and loyal troops dead after a fierce battle in Khartoum. Nimeiri accused President Muammar el Qaddifi of Libya of having instigated the attempt and broke relations with Libya. Firing squads executed 81 convicted rebels.

Nimeiri also charged Soviet involvement in the attempt and in 1977 expelled 90 Soviet advisers. He moved closer to Egypt—he was one of the few Arab leaders who supported Sadat's dramatic visit to Israel in November 1977—and the U.S. Nimeiri publicly backed the Eritrean rebel movement in 1977 in its fight against the pro-Soviet Ethiopian central government, which accused him of giving material aid as well as moral support to the rebels.

SURINAME

Republic of Suriname
President: Dr. Henk R. Chin A Sen (1980)
Area: 63,251 sq mi. (163,820 sq km)
Population (est. 1980): 380,000 (Hindi, 37%; Creole, 31%; Indonesian, 15%; Bush Negro, 10%)
Density per square mile: 6.0
Capital and largest city (est. 1973): Paramaribo, 150,000
Monetary unit: Suriname guilder
Language: Dutch, Surinamese (lingua franca)
Religions: Protestant, Roman Catholic, Hindu, Islam
Freedom House classifications: Capitalist industrial, multi-party centralized.
Economic summary: Gross national product (1978): $820. Average annual growth rate (1970–77): 6.3%. Per capita income: $1,240. Land used for agriculture: 0.3%; labor force: 29%; principal products: rice, citrus fruits, sugar, coffee. Labor force in industry: 15%; major products: aluminum, alumina, processed foods, lumber, bricks, cigarettes. Natural resources: bauxite, iron ore, timber, fish, shrimp. Exports: bauxite, alumina, aluminum, lumber and wood products. Imports: food and beverages, machinery, petroleum, textiles, vehicles. Major trading partners: U.S., Western European countries.

Geography. Suriname lies on the northeast coast of South America, with Guyana to the west, French Guiana to the east, and Brazil to the south. It is about one tenth larger than Michigan. The principal rivers are the Corantijn on the Guyana border, the Marowijne in the east, and the Suriname, on which the capital city of Paramaribo is situated. The Tumuc-Humac Mountains are on the border with Brazil.

Government. Suriname, formerly known as Dutch Guiana, became an independent republic on Nov. 25, 1975. The first prime minister, Henck A. E. Arron, was ousted by a seven-man military junta on Feb. 25, 1980, and replaced by Dr. Henk R. Chin A. Sen.

Chin A Sen was elevated to the office of President by the junta on Aug. 14, 1980, and the 39-member National Assembly was abolished. A military cabinet was designated to conduct the government.

History. England established the first European settlement on the Suriname River in 1650 but transferred sovereignty to the Dutch in 1667 in the Treaty of Breda, by which the British acquired New York. Colonization was confined to a narrow coastal strip, and until the abolition of slavery in 1863, African slaves furnished the labor for the plantation economy. After 1870, laborers were imported from British India and the Dutch East Indies.

In 1948, the colony was integrated into the Kingdom of the Netherlands and two years later was granted full home rule in other than foreign affairs and defense. After race rioting over unemployment and inflation, the Netherlands offered complete independence in 1973. Henck A. E. Arron, leader of a coalition of Creole (Surinamese of African descent) parties, advocated independence, while Jaggernath Lachmon, leader of the Surinamese of East Indian descent, urged delay.

Arron retained power in the first post-independence elections in 1977 but held only a one-seat margin over Lachmon's group early in 1980. He had promised early elections when seven Army sergeants and a lieutenant staged a coup on Feb. 25 and installed a civilian, Dr. Henk R. Chin A Sen, as Prime Minister. A subsequent military intervention made Chin A Sen President, abolishing the legislature and instituting a military government.

SWAZILAND

Kingdom of Swaziland
Ruler: King Sobhuza II (1967)
Prime Minister: Prince Mabandla Dlamini (1979)
Area: 6,704 sq mi. (17,363 sq km)
Population (est. 1980): 550,000
Density per square mile: 82.0
Capital and largest city (est. 1976): Mbabane, 23,000
Monetary unit: Lilangeni
Languages: English and Siswati (official)
Religions: Christian, 60%, and Animist.
Member of Commonwealth of Nations
Freedom House classifications: Capitalist pre-industrial, non-party non-military
Economic summary: Gross national product (1978): $310 million. Average annual growth rate (1970–77): 5.6%. Per capita income: (1975): $440. Land used for agriculture: 8%; labor force: 31%; principal products: corn, livestock, sugar cane, citrus fruits, cotton, rice, pineapples. Labor force in industry: 25%; major products: milled sugar, ginned cotton, processed meat and wood, chemicals, machinery. Natural resources: iron ore, asbestos, coal. Exports: sugar, wood products, iron ore, asbestos, citrus fruits, canned fruits. Imports: motor vehicles, fuels and lubricants, foodstuffs, clothing. Major trading partners: South Africa, U.K., U.S.

Geography. Swaziland, 85% the size of New Jersey, is surrounded by South Africa and Mozambique. The country consists of a high veld in the west and a series of plateaus descending from a maximum of 6,000 feet (1,829 m) to a low veld of 1,500 feet (457 m).

Government. In 1967, a new Constitution established King Sobhuza II as head of state and provided for an Assembly of 24 members elected by universal suffrage, together with a Senate of 12 members—half appointed by the Assembly and half by the King. In 1973, the King renounced the Constitution, suspended political parties, and took total power for himself. In 1977, he replaced the Parliament with an assembly of tribal leaders. The Parliament reconvened in 1979.

History. Bantu peoples migrated southwest to the area of Mozambique in the 16th century. A number of clans broke away from the main body in the 18th century and settled in Swaziland. In the 19th century they organized as a tribe, partly because they were in constant conflict with the Zulu. Their ruler, Mswazi, applied to the British in the 1840s for help against the Zulu. The British and the Transvaal governments guaranteed the independence of Swaziland in 1881. In 1890 a provisional government, representing the Swazi, the British, and the Transvaal, was established.

South Africa held Swaziland as a protectorate from 1894 to 1899, but after the Boer War, in 1902, Swaziland was transferred to British administration. The Paramount Chief was recognized as the native authority in 1941.

In 1963, the territory was constituted a protectorate, and on Sept. 6, 1968, it became the independent nation of Swaziland.

SWEDEN

Kingdom of Sweden
Sovereign: King Carl XVI Gustaf (1973)
Prime Minister: Thorbjörn Fälldin (1980)
Area: 173,665 sq mi. (449,792 sq km)
Population (est. 1980): 8,300,000
Density per square mile: 47.8
Capital: Stockholm
Largest cities (est. 1979): Stockholm, 654,000; (est. 1976): Göteborg, 442,500; Malmö, 240,300
Monetary unit: Krona
Language: Swedish
Religion: Swedish Lutheran, 95%
National name: Konungariket Sverige
Freedom House classifications: Capitalist-socialist industrial, multi-party centralized
Economic summary: Gross national product (1978): $84.8 billion. Average annual growth rate (1970–77): 1.2%. Per capita income: $12,020. Average annual rate of inflation (1975–79): 9.7%. Principal agricultural products: dairy products, grains, sugar beets, potatoes, wood. Labor force in industry: 33%; major products: machinery, instruments, metal products, automobiles. Natural resources: forests, iron ore, hydroelectric power, unmined uranium. Exports: wood products, iron ore, machinery, iron and steel bearings, ships, instruments, automobiles. Imports: machinery, instruments, petroleum, yarns, foodstuffs. Major trading partners: Norway, Denmark, West Germany, U.K., U.S.S.R.

Geography. Sweden occupies the eastern part of the Scandinavian peninsula, with Norway to the west, Finland and the Gulf of Bothnia to the east, and Denmark and the Baltic Sea in the south. It is one tenth larger than California.

The country slopes eastward and southward from the Kjólen Mountains along the Norwegian border, where the peak elevation is Kebnekaise at 6,965 feet (2,123 m) in Lapland. In the north are mountains and many lakes. To the south and east are central lowlands and south of them are fertile areas of forest, valley, and plain.

Along Sweden's rocky coast, chopped up by bays and inlets, are many islands, the largest of which are Gotland and Öland.

Government. Sweden is a constitutional monarchy. Under the 1975 Constitution, the Riksdag is the sole governing body. The prime minister is the political chief executive.

In 1967, agreement was reached on part of a new Constitution after 13 years of work. It provided for a single-house Riksdag of 350 members (later amended to 349 seats) to replace the 104-year old bicameral Riksdag. The members are popularly elected for three years. Eighty present members of the Riksdag are women.

The King, Carl XVI Gustaf, was born April 30, 1946, and became the world's youngest reigning monarch when he succeeded to the throne Sept. 19, 1973, on the death at 90 of his grandfather, Gustaf VI Adolf. Carl Gustaf was married on June 19, 1976, to Silvia Sommerlath, a West German commoner. Their first child, Princess Victoria, was born on July 14, 1977. Their second, Prince Carl Philip, was born on May 13, 1979. Under the new Act of Succession, effective Jan. 1, 1980, the first child of the reigning monarch, regardless of sex, is heir to the throne.

The major political parties are the Social Democratic Party (154 seats in the Riksdag), led by former Prime Minister Olof Palme; Conservative Party (73 seats), led by Gösta Bohman; Center

Party (64 seats), led by Prime Minister Thorbjörn Fälldin; Liberal Party (38 seats), led by former Prime Minister Olla Ullsten; Communist Party (20 seats), led by Lars Werner. The Center, Liberal, and Conservative parties form the coalition government.

History. The earliest historical mention of Sweden is found in Tacitus' *Germania*, where reference is made to the powerful king and strong fleet of the Suiones. Toward the end of the 10th century, Olaf Sköttkonung established a Christian stronghold in Sweden. Around 1400, an attempt was made to unite the northern nations into one kingdom, but this led to bitter strife between the Danes and the Swedes.

In 1520, the Danish King, Christian II, conquered Sweden and in the "Stockholm Bloodbath" put leading Swedish personalities to death. Gustavus Vasa (1523–60) broke away from Denmark and fashioned the modern Swedish state.

Sweden played a leading role in the second phase (1630–35) of the Thirty Years' War (1618–48). By the Treaty of Westphalia (1648), Sweden obtained western Pomerania and some neighboring territory on the Baltic. In 1700, a coalition of Russia, Poland, and Denmark united against Sweden and by the Peace of Nystad (1721) forced it to relinquish Livonia, Ingria, Estonia, and parts of Finland.

Sweden emerged from the Napoleonic Wars with the acquisition of Norway from Denmark and with a new royal dynasty stemming from Marshal Jean Bernadotte of France, who became King Charles XIV (1818–44). The artificial union between Sweden and Norway led to an uneasy relationship, and the union was finally dissolved in 1905.

Sweden maintained a position of neutrality in both World Wars.

An elaborate structure of welfare legislation, imitated by many larger nations, began with the establishment of old-age pensions in 1911. Economic prosperity based on its neutralist policy enabled Sweden, together with Norway, to pioneer in public health, housing, and job security programs.

Forty-four years of Socialist government were ended in 1976 with the election of a conservative coalition headed by Thorbjörn Fälldin, a 50-year-old sheep farmer. The surprise conservative victory was credited to public opposition to a nuclear power program backed by the Socialists and to a program that would have given control of all businesses to labor unions within 20 years.

Nuclear-power policy dominated Swedish policy in the ensuing years. Fälldin resigned on Oct. 5, 1978, when his conservative parties partners demanded less restrictions on nuclear power, and his successor, Ola Ullsten, resigned a year later after failing to achieve a consensus on the issue. Returned to office by his coalition partners, Fälldin said he would follow the course directed by a national referendum. On March 23, 1980, voters backed the development of 12 nuclear plants and use of them for at least 25 years to supply 40% of national energy needs while the search for alternative sources continued.

SWITZERLAND

Swiss Confederation
President: Georges-André Chevallaz (1980)
Vice President: Kurt Furgler (1980)
Area: 15,941 sq mi. (41,288 sq km)
Population (est. 1980): 6,345,000 (Swiss, 85%; Italian, 8%; German, 2%; Spanish, 2%; French, 1%—figures by place of birth)
Density per square mile: 398.0
Capital: Bern
Largest cities (est. 1979): Zurich, 376,500; Basel, 182,800; Geneva, 151,000; Bern, 142,800; Lausanne, 136,300; Winterthur, 85,000
Monetary unit: Swiss franc
Languages: German, 65%; French, 18%; Italian, 12%; Romansch, 1%
Religions: Roman Catholic, 49%; Protestant, 48%
National name: Schweiz/Suisse/Svizzera
Freedom House classifications: Capitalist industrial, multi-party decentralized
Economic summary: Gross national product (1978): $76 billion. Average annual growth rate (1970–77): 0.1%. Per capita income: $11,606. Land used for agriculture: 49%; labor force: 16%; principal products: cheese and other dairy products, livestock, fruits, grains, wine. Labor force in industry: 47%; major products: watches and clocks, precision instruments, machinery, chemicals, pharmaceuticals, textiles, generators, turbines. Natural resources: water power, timber, salt. Exports: electrical machinery and appliances, yarn and textiles, dyestuffs, chemicals. Imports: nonelectrical machinery, transport equipment, electrical machinery and appliances, iron and steel. Major trading partners: West Germany, France, U.S., Netherlands, Italy, U.K.

Geography. Switzerland, in central Europe, is the land of the Alps. Its tallest peak is the Dufourspitze at 15,203 feet (4,634 m) on the Swiss side of the Italian border, one of 10 summits of the Monte Rose massif in the Pennine Alps. The tallest peak in all of the Alps, Mont Blanc (15,771 ft; 4,807 m), is actually in France.

Most of Switzerland comprises a mountainous plateau bordered by the great bulk of the Alps on the south and by the Jura Mountains on the northwest. About one fourth of the total area is covered by mountains and glaciers.

The country's largest lakes—Geneva, Constance (Bodensee), and Maggiore—straddle the French, German-Austrian, and Italian borders, respectively.

The Rhine, navigable from Basel to the North Sea, is the principal inland waterway. Other rivers are the Aare and the Rhône.

Switzerland, twice the size of New Jersey, is surrounded by France, West Germany, Austria, Liechtenstein, and Italy.

Government. The Swiss Confederation consists of 26 sovereign cantons, of which three are divided into half-cantons. Federal authority is vested in a bicameral legislature. The Standerat, or State Council, consists of 46 members, two from each canton. The lower house, the Nationalrat, or National Council, has 200 deputies, elected for four-year terms.

Executive authority rests with the Bundesrat, or Federal Council, consisting of seven members chosen by parliament. The parliament elects the President, who serves for one year and is succeeded by the Vice President. The federal government regulates foreign policy, railroads, postal service, and the national mint. Each canton reserves for itself important local powers.

A constitutional amendment adopted in 1971 by referendum gave women the vote in federal elections and right to hold federal office. Women previously had the rights in some cantons and now have them in all but one.

The major political parties are the Social Democratic Party (51 of 200 seats in National Council), led by Helmut Hubacher; Radical Democratic Party (51 seats), led by Yann Richter; Conservative Christian-Social Party (44 seats), led by Hans Wyer; People's Party (23 seats), led by Fritz Hofmann. These four parties constitute the ruling coalition.

History. Called Helvetia in ancient times, Switzerland in the Middle Ages was a league of cantons of the Holy Roman Empire. Fashioned around the nucleus of three German forest districts of Schwyz, Uri, and Unterwalden, the Swiss Confederation slowly added new cantons. In 1648 the Treaty of Westphalia gave Switzerland its independence from the Holy Roman Empire.

French revolutionary troops occupied the country in 1798 and named it the Helvetic Republic, but Napoleon in 1803 restored its federal government. By 1815, the French- and Italian-speaking peoples of Switzerland had been granted political equality.

In 1815, the Congress of Vienna guaranteed the neutrality and recognized the independence of Switzerland. In the revolutionary period of 1847, the Catholic cantons seceded and organized a separate union called the *Sonderbund.* In 1848 the new Swiss Constitution established a union modeled upon that of the U.S. The Federal Constitution of 1874 established a strong central government while maintaining large powers of control in each canton.

National unity and political conservatism grew as the country prospered from its neutrality. Its banking system became the world's leading repository for international accounts. Strict neutrality was its policy in World Wars I and II. Geneva was the seat of the League of Nations, and Geneva, along with The Hague in the Netherlands, became the headquarters of a number of international organizations.

In 1971, the Swiss Supreme Court ruled that Swiss banks must show U.S. tax officials records of U.S. citizens suspected of tax fraud, thus significantly modifying a 1934 law that had seemed to forbid any bank disclosures.

SYRIA

Syrian Arab Republic
President: Hafez al-Assad (1971)
Premier: Abdel Raouf al-Kasm (1980)
Area: 71,498 sq mi. (185,180 sq km)
Population (est. 1980): 8,610,000
Density per square mile: 120.4
Capital: Damascus
Largest cities (est. 1978 by U.N.): Damascus, 1,113,000; Aleppo, 878,000; Homs, 306,000; Hama, 180,000
Monetary unit: Syrian pound
Languages: Arabic (official), Kurdish, Armenian, Turkish, Circassian
Religions: Islam, 85%; Christian, 14%
National name: Al-Jamhouriya al Arabiya As-Souriya
Freedom House classifications: Capitalist-socialist industrial, dominant party
Economic summary: Gross national product (1978): $7.5 billion. Average annual growth rate (1970–77): 6.1%. Per capita income: $780. Land used for agriculture: 47%; labor force: 32%; principal products: cotton, wheat, sugar beets, sheep, goats. Labor force in industry: 26%; major products: textiles, cement, glass, petroleum, processed food, soap. Natural resources: chrome, manganese, asphalt, iron ore, rock salt, phosphate, oil, natural gas. Exports: petroleum, textiles, tobacco, fruits and vegetables, cotton. Imports: machinery and metal products, textiles, fuels, foodstuffs. Major trading partners: Italy, West Germany, U.S.S.R., Yugoslavia, Saudi Arabia.

Geography. Slightly larger than North Dakota, Syria lies at the eastern end of the Mediterranean Sea. It is bordered by Lebanon and Israel on the west, Turkey on the north, Iraq on the east, and Jordan on the south.

Coastal Syria is a narrow plain, in back of which is a range of coastal mountains, and still farther inland a steppe area. In the east is the Syrian Desert, and in the south is the Jebel Druze Range. The highest point in Syria is Mount Hermon (9,232 ft; 2,814 m) on the Lebanese border.

Government. Syria's first permanent Constitution was approved in 1973, replacing a provisional charter that had been in force for 10 years. It provided for an elected People's Council as the legislature. No national religion is specified, although Islamic law is the basis of the state law.

In the first election in 10 years, in 1973, the Ba'ath Arab Socialist Party of President Hafez al-Assad, running on a unified National Progressive ticket with the Communist and Socialist parties, won 70% of the vote and a commensurate proportion of the seats for a four-year term in the People's Council. In the 1977 Council elections, the ruling Ba'athists won 125 of the now 195 seats; the National Progressive Front coalition, 34 seats; various rightist candidates, 36 seats.

History. Ancient Syria was conquered by Egypt about 1500 B.C., and after that by Hebrews, Phoenicians, Assyrians, Chaldeans, Persians, and Greeks. From 64 B.C. until the Arab conquest in A.D. 636, it was part of the Roman Empire except during brief periods. The Arabs made it a trade center for their extensive empire, but it suffered severely from the Mongol invasion in 1260 and fell to the Ottoman Turks in 1516. Syria remained a Turkish province until World War I.

A secret Anglo-French pact of 1916 put Syria in the French zone of influence. The League of Nations gave France a mandate over Syria after World War I, but the French were forced to put down several nationalist uprisings. In 1930, France recognized Syria as an independent republic, but still subject to the mandate. After nationalist demonstrations in 1939, the French High Commissioner suspended the Syrian Constitution. In 1941, British and Free French forces invaded Syria to eliminate Vichy control. During the rest of World War II, Syria was an Allied base.

Again in 1945, nationalist demonstrations broke into actual fighting, and British troops had to restore order. Syrian forces met a series of reverses while participating in the Arab invasion of Palestine in 1948. In 1958, Egypt and Syria formed the United Arab Republic, with Gamal Abdel Nasser of Egypt as President. However, Syria became independent again on Sept. 29, 1961, following a revolution.

In the war of 1967, Israel quickly vanquished the Syrian army. Before acceding to the U.N. cease-fire, the Israeli forces took over control of the fortified Golan Heights commanding the Sea of Galilee.

Syria joined Egypt in attacking Israel in October 1973 in the fourth Arab-Israeli war, but was pushed back from initial successes on the Golan Heights to end up losing more land. However, in the settlement worked out by U.S. Secretary of State Henry

A. Kissinger in 1974, the Syrians recovered all the territory lost in 1973 and a token amount of territory, including the deserted town of Quneitra, lost in 1967. Syria agreed to negotiate a permanent settlement with Israel, its first de facto recognition of that country.

Resumption of relations with the U.S. in 1974 moderated Syria's tone, but not the goals of its policy toward Israel. Syria initiated a resolution declaring the Palestine Liberation Organization to be the sole representative of the Palestinian people, a measure that was adopted by the U.N. General Assembly in October 1974 and became the vehicle for legitimizing the insurgent organization. As Israeli-Egyptian peace negotiations continued, Syria's hostility toward Egypt increased.

At the Arab League conference in Baghdad in March 1979, Syria demanded even harsher measures against Egypt than the break in diplomatic relations and economic boycott proposed by the conference. Syria asked that the boycott, including oil supplies, be applied to the U.S. as well.

Syrian troops, in Lebanon since they arrived in 1976 to block a partition of the country between the Christian minority and the Moslem majority, remained there in mid-1980 after other Arab contributions to a peace-keeping force had left.

In September 1980, Syria and Libya agreed on a merger of their two countries, but gave no details as to how the move would be effected.

TANZANIA

United Republic of Tanzania
President: Julius K. Nyerere (1964)
Prime Minister: Edward Sokoine (1977)
Area: 362,820 sq mi. (939,704 sq km)[1]
Population (est. 1980): 17,600,000
Density per square mile: 48.5
Capital and largest city (est. 1977): Dar es Salaam, 460,000
Monetary unit: Tanzanian shilling
Languages: Swahili, Bantu, Arabic, English
Religions: Animist, 35%; Christian, 31%; Islam, 31%
Member of Commonwealth of Nations
Freedom House classifications: Socialist pre-industrial, one-party socialist
Economic summary: Gross national product (1978): $3.9 billion. Average annual growth rate (1970–77): 2.1%. Per capita income: $200. Labor force in agriculture: 90%; Principal products: sugar, maize, rice, wheat, cotton, coffee, sisal, cashew nuts, tea, tobacco, pyrethrum, cloves. Major industrial products: textiles, light manufactures, refined oil, processed agricultural products, cement, fertilizer. Natural resources: hydroelectric potential, unexploited iron and coal, natural gas. Exports: coffee, cotton, sisal, diamonds, cloves, cashew nuts. Imports: manufactured goods, textiles, machinery and transport equipment, foodstuffs. Major trading partners: U.K., China, India, Indonesia, Pakistan, Singapore.

Geography. Tanzania is in East Africa on the Indian Ocean. To the north are Uganda and Kenya; to the west, Burundi, Rwanda, and Zaire; and to the south, Mozambique, Zambia, and Malawi. Its area is three times that of New Mexico.

Tanzania contains three of Africa's best-known lakes—Victoria in the north, Tanganyika in the west, and Nyasa in the south. Mount Kilimanjaro in the north, 19,340 feet (5,895 m), is the highest point on the continent.

1. Including Zanzibar.

Government. Under the republican form of government, Tanzania has a President elected by universal suffrage who appoints the Cabinet ministers. The 218-member National Assembly is composed of 96 elected members from the mainland, 10 members appointed by the President (from both Tanganyika and Zanzibar), 35 national members (elected by the National Assembly after nomination by various national institutions), 32 members of the Zanzibar Revolutionary Council, 20 other Zanzibar members appointed by the President in agreement with the President of Zanzibar, and up to 20 other Zanzibar members appointed by the President in agreement with the first Vice President, who represents Zanzibar.

The Tanganyika African National Union, the only authorized party on the mainland, and the Afro-Shirazi Party, the only party in Zanzibar and Pemba, merged in 1977 as the Revolutionary Party (Chama Cha Mapinduzi) and elected Julius K. Nyerere as its head.

History. Arab traders first began to colonize the area in A.D. 700. Portuguese explorers reached the coastal regions in 1500 and held some control until the 17th century, when the Sultan of Oman took power. With what are now Burundi and Rwanda, Tanganyika became the colony of German East Africa in 1885. After World War I, it was administered by Britain under a League of Nations mandate and later as a U.N. trust territory.

Although not mentioned in old histories until the 12th century, Zanzibar was believed always to have had connections with southern Arabia. The Portuguese made it one of their tributaries in 1503 and later established a trading post, but they were driven out by Arabs from Oman in 1698. Zanzibar was declared independent of Oman in 1861 and, in 1890, it became a British protectorate.

Tanganyika became independent on Dec. 9, 1961; Zanzibar, on Dec. 10, 1963. On April 26, 1964, the two nations merged into the United Republic of Tanganyika and Zanzibar. The name was changed to Tanzania six months later.

In 1975, the 1,163-mile (1,872 km) Tanzam railway linking the Tanzanian port of Dar es Salaam with Zambia was officially opened. Built and financed by China, the railway provided a direct route for Zambian copper exports to the sea, replacing a longer route through white-ruled Rhodesia to Mozambique.

In 1977, Tanzania closed its border with Kenya because of a dispute over the operation of East African Airways, an entity of the East African Community. The breakup of the airline left the East African Posts and Telecommunications Corporation as the only community agency still functioning.

An invasion by Ugandan troops in November 1978 was followed by a counterattack in January 1979, in which 5,000 Tanzanian troops were joined by 3,000 Ugandan exiles opposed to President Idi Amin. Within a month, full-scale war developed and the Tanzania/exile force pushed north and captured Kampala on April 11. The cost of the military operation was heavy, and Nyerere sought aid from the Western powers. He dismissed African criticism of his intervention, saying "Should one let a thief get away with his crime?"

THAILAND

Kingdom of Thailand
Ruler: King Bhumibol Adulyadej (1946)
Premier: Gen. Prem Tinsulanonda (1980)
Area: 198,455 sq mi. (514,000 sq km)
Population (est. 1980): 47,160,000 (incl. 2.5 million of Chinese descent born in Thailand)
Density per square mile: 237.6
Capital and largest city (est. 1978): Bangkok, 4,875,000
Monetary unit: Baht
Languages: Thai (Siamese), Chinese, English
Religions: Buddhist, 95%; Islam, 4%
National name: Muang Thai
Freedom House classifications: Capitalist pre-industrial, multi-party centralized
Economic summary: Gross national product (1978): $21.8 billion. Average annual growth rate (1970–77): 4.1%. Per capita income (1977): $426. Land used for agriculture: 71%; labor force: 76%; principal products: rice, rubber, corn, tapioca, sugar, pineapples. Labor force in industry: 7%; major products: processed food, textiles, wood, cement. Natural resources: fish, natural gas, forests, fluorite, tin, tungsten. Exports: rice, tapioca, sugar, rubber, maize, tin, pineapples, textiles. Imports: transport and construction equipment, nonelectrical machinery, crude oil, textile fibers, chemicals. Major trading partners: Japan, U.S., Singapore, West Germany, Netherlands, U.K.

Geography. Thailand occupies the western half of the Indochinese peninsula and the northern two thirds of the Malay peninsula in southeast Asia. Its neighbors are Burma on the north and west, Laos on the east, and Cambodia and Malaysia on the south. Thailand is about three fourths the size of Texas.

Most of the population is supported in the fertile central alluvial plain, which is drained by the Chao Phnaya River and its tributaries.

Government. King Bhumibol Adulyadej, who was born Dec. 5, 1927, second son of Prince Mahidol of Songkhla, succeeded to the throne on June 9, 1946, when his brother, King Ananda Mahidol, died of a gunshot wound. He was married on April 28, 1950, to Queen Sirikit; their son, Vajiralongkorn, born July 28, 1952, is the Crown Prince.

After three years of civilian government ended with a military coup on Oct. 6, 1976, Thailand reverted to military rule. The junta permitted national elections in 1979, however, which confirmed the junta's designated premier, Gen. Kriangsak Chamanan. When Chamanan resigned on March 12, 1980, the National Assembly was allowed to elect his successor. Political parties, banned after the coup, gained limited freedom in 1980.

History. The Thais first began moving down into their present homeland from the Asiatic continent in the 6th century A.D. and by the end of the 13th century ruled most of the western portion. During the next 400 years, the Thais fought sporadically with the Cambodians and the Burmese. The British obtained recognition of paramount interest in Thailand in 1824, and in 1896 an Anglo-French accord guaranteed the independence of Thailand.

A coup in 1932 changed the absolute monarchy into a representative government with universal suffrage. After five hours of token resistance on Dec. 8, 1941, Thailand yielded to Japanese occupation and became one of the springboards in World War II for the Japanese campaign against Malaya.

After the fall of its pro-Japanese puppet government in July 1944, Thailand pursued a policy of passive resistance against the Japanese, and after the Japanese surrender, Thailand repudiated the declaration of war it had been forced to make against Britain and the U.S. in 1942. By a treaty signed with Britain and India in 1946, Thailand renounced all wartime acquisitions of Malayan territory.

Thailand's major problem in the late 1960s was suppressing guerrilla action by Communist invaders in the north. The prospect of a U.S. withdrawal from Southeast Asia alarmed the Thais, who sought and obtained reassurance from the U.S. that they would not be abandoned.

Although Thailand had received $2 billion in U.S. economic and military aid since 1950 and had sent troops (paid by the U.S.) to Vietnam while permitting U.S. bomber bases on its territory, the collapse of South Vietnam and Cambodia in the spring of 1975 brought rapid changes in the country's diplomatic posture.

At the Thai government's insistence, the U.S. agreed to withdraw all 23,000 U.S. military personnel remaining in Thailand by March 1976. Diplomatic relations with China were established in 1975. Meanwhile, overtures toward an accommodation with the new regime in South Vietnam were initiated.

Thailand protested vigorously when 1,100 U.S. Marines were airlifted to Thai bases May 14, 1975, for use in the rescue of the crew of the cargo ship Mayaguez after its seizure by a Cambodian gunboat. The marines were withdrawn the next day, and Thailand later accepted a U.S. apology for unauthorized use of its territory.

In 1973, when Field Marshal Thanom Kittikachorn resigned under the pressure of massive student demonstrations, Thailand returned to a civilian government and in 1975 had its first general elections. Premier Seni Pramoj, was ousted in 1976 by Admiral Sa-Ngad Chaloryu and the National Administrative Reform Council after rioting by leftist students. The junta appointed Thanin Kraivichien, a supreme court justice, as premier and appointed a 340-member National Assembly, 110 of them military officers.

As insurgent activity increased and skirmishes along the Cambodian border continued despite Thai efforts to make peace with the Communist regime in Phnom Penh, the military, in 1977, ousted Thanin as "weak," replacing him with Gen. Kriangsak Chamanan.

Refugees from Laos, Cambodia, and Vietnam flooded into Thailand in 1978 and 1979, and despite efforts by the United States and other Western countries to resettle them, a total of 130,000 Laotian and Vietnamese refugees were living in camps along the Cambodian border in mid-1980. A drive by Vietnamese occupation forces on western Cambodian areas loyal to the Pol Pot government, culminating in invasions of Thai territory in late June, drove an estimated 100,000 Cambodians across the line as refugees, adding to the 200,000 of their countrymen already in Thailand. The total of 430,000 were being fed by United Nations and church relief organizations but the Thai government complained of the burden of their presence.

The Vietnamese incursions, notwithstanding Hanoi's claim that the troops were only seeking guerrillas hidden in the refugee camps, prompted a Thai appeal to Washington for military aid. In July, 35 reconditioned tanks and other weapons were flown to Thailand, and the Carter administration pledged its help in the event of a larger attack.

TOGO

Republic of Togo
President: Gen. Gnassingbé Eyadema (1967)
Area: 21,853 sq mi. (56,599 sq km)
Population (est. 1980): 2,530,000
Density per square mile: 115.8
Capital and largest city (est. 1976): Lomé, 229,400
Monetary unit: Franc CFA
Languages: Ewé, Mina (south), Kabyé, Cotocoli (north), French (official), and many dialects
Religions: Animist, 75%; Christian, 20%; Islam, 5%
National name: République Togolaise
Freedom House classifications: Capitalist-socialist pre-industrial, one-party nationalist
Economic summary: Gross national product (1978): $770 million. Average annual growth rate (1970–77): 5.3%. Per capita income: $300. Land used for agriculture: 96%; labor force: 78%; principal products: yams, manioc, millet, sorghum, cocoa, coffee, rice, cotton. Labor force in industry: 22%; major products: phosphate, textiles. Natural resources: marble, iron, manganese, phosphate, limestone. Exports: phosphate, cocoa, coffee. Imports: consumer goods, fuels, machinery, foodstuffs. Major trading partners: France, U.K., West Germany, Netherlands.

Geography. Togo, twice the size of Maryland, is on the south coast of West Africa bordering on Ghana to the west, Upper Volta to the north and Benin to the east.

The Gulf of Guinea coastline, only 32 miles long (51 km), is low and sandy. The only port is at Lomé. The Togo hills traverse the central section.

Government. The government of Nicolas Grunitzky was overthrown in a bloodless coup on Jan. 13, 1967, led by Lt. Col. Etienne Eyadema (now Gen. Gnassingbé Eyadema). A National Reconciliation Committee was set up to rule the country. In April, however, Eyadema dissolved the Committee and took over as President. In December 1979, a 67-member National Assembly was voted in by national referendum. The Assembly of the Togolese People is the only political party.

History. Brazilians were the first traders to settle in Togo. Established as a German colony (Togoland) in 1884, the area was split between the British and the French as League of Nations mandates after World War I and subsequently administered as U. N. trusteeships. The British portion voted for incorporation with Ghana.

Togo became independent on April 27, 1960. Sylvanus Olympio, its first President, was assassinated in 1963 and succeeded by Nicolas Grunitzky.

TONGA

Kingdom of Tonga
Sovereign: King Taufa'ahau Tupou IV (1965)
Prime Minister: Prince Tu'ipelehake (1965)
Area: 290 sq mi. (751 sq km)
Population (est. 1980): 100,000
Density per square mile: 370.4
Capital (est. 1976): Nuku'alofa, 18,300
Monetary unit: Pa'anga
Languages: Tongan, English
Religion: Christian
Member of Commonwealth of Nations
Freedom House classifications: Capitalist pre-industrial, non-party non-military
Economic summary: Gross national product (1978): $40 million. Average annual growth rate (1970–77): 0.9%. Land used for agriculture: 80%; labor force: 75%; principal products: yams, taro, papaya, pineapples, cassava, tobacco, peanuts, bananas, copra. Major industrial products: copra, desiccated coconut. Natural resources: fish, timber. Exports: copra, bananas. Imports: manufactures, foodstuffs, transport equipment. Major trading partners: New Zealand, Australia, Netherlands, Norway.

Geography. Situated east of the Fiji Islands in the South Pacific, Tonga (also called the Friendly Islands) consists of some 150 islands, of which 36 are inhabited.

Most of the islands contain active volcanic craters; others are coral atolls.

Government. Tonga is a constitutional monarchy. Executive authority is vested in the Sovereign, a Privy Council, and a Cabinet headed by the Prime Minister. Legislative authority is vested in the Legislative Assembly.

History. The present dynasty of Tonga was founded in 1831 by Taufa'ahau Tupou, who took the name George I. He consolidated the kingdom by conquest and in 1875 granted a Constitution.

In 1900, his great-grandson, George II, signed a treaty of friendship with Britain, and the country became a British protected state. The treaty was revised in 1959.

Queen Salote Tupou reigned from 1918 to 1964 and was succeeded by her son, who became King Taufa'ahau Tupou IV.

Tonga became independent on June 4, 1970.

TRANSKEI

See South Africa

TRINIDAD AND TOBAGO

Republic of Trinidad and Tobago
President: Ellis Clarke (1976)
Prime Minister: Dr. Eric E. Williams (1962)
Area: 1,980 sq mi. (5,128 sq km)
Population (est. 1980): 1,115,000 (black, 43%; East Indian, 40%; mixed, 14%)
Density per square mile: 580.8
Capital and largest city (est. 1976): Port-of-Spain, 47,300
Monetary unit: Trinidad and Tobago dollar
Languages: English (official); Hindi, French, Spanish
Religions: Roman Catholic, 31%; Protestant, 27%; Islam, 13%; Hindu, 6%
Member of Commonwealth of Nations
Freedom House classifications: Capitalist industrial, multi-party centralized
Economic summary: Gross national product (1978): $3.3 billion. Average annual growth rate (1970–77): 1.5%. Per capita income: $3,040. Land used for agriculture: 30%; labor force: 13%; principal products: sugar cane, cocoa, coffee, rice, bananas. Labor force in industry: 50%; major products: petroleum, processed food, cement; tourism. Natural resources: petroleum. Exports: petroleum, sugar. Imports: crude oil, foodstuffs, machinery and equipment. Major trading partners: U.S., U.K., Saudi Arabia, Indonesia, Iran, Japan.

Geography. Trinidad and Tobago lies in the Caribbean Sea off the northeast coast of Venezuela. The area of the two islands is slightly less than that of Delaware.

Trinidad, the larger, is mainly flat and rolling, with mountains in the north that reach a height of 3,085 feet (940 m) at Mount Aripo. Tobago is heavily forested with hardwood trees.

Government. The legislature consists of a 24-member Senate and a 36-member House of Representatives.

The major political parties are the People's National Movement, led by Prime Minister Eric E. Williams (24 seats in the House of Representatives); United Labor Front (10 seats), led by Raffique Shah and Basdeo Panday; Democratic Action Congress (2 seats).

History. Trinidad was discovered by Columbus in 1498 and remained in Spanish possession, despite raids by other European nations, until it capitulated to the British in 1797 during a war between Britain and Spain.

Trinidad was ceded to Britain in 1802, and in 1899 it was united with Tobago as a colony. From 1958 to 1962, Trinidad and Tobago was a part of the West Indies Federation, and on Aug. 31, 1962, it became independent.

On Aug. 1, 1976, Trinidad and Tobago cut its ties with Britain and became a republic, remaining within the Commonwealth and recognizing Queen Elizabeth II only as head of that organization.

TUNISIA

Republic of Tunisia
President: Habib Bourguiba (1957)
Premier: Mohammed Mzali (1980)
Area: 63,379 sq mi. (164,152 sq km)
Population (est. 1980): 6,350,000
Density per square mile: 100.2
Capital and largest city (est. 1976 for metropolitan area): Tunis, 960,000
Monetary unit: Tunisian dinar
Languages: Arabic, French
Religions: Predominantly Islam; Roman Catholic, Jewish, Greek Orthodox
National name: Al-Djoumhouria Attunusia
Freedom House classifications: Capitalist-socialist industrial, one-party socialist
Economic summary: Gross national product (1978): $5.8 billion. Average annual growth rate (1970–77): 6.5%. Per capita income: $930. Labor force in agriculture: 45%; principal products; wheat, olives, citrus fruits, grapes, fish. Labor force in industry: 21%; major products: crude oil, phosphates, olive oil, textiles. Natural resources: oil, phosphates, iron ore, lead, zinc. Exports: petroleum, phosphates, olive oil. Imports: machinery and equipment, consumer goods, foodstuffs. Major trading partners: France, West Germany, Italy, U.K., U.S.

Geography. Tunisia, at the northernmost bulge of Africa, thrusts out toward Sicily to mark the division between the eastern and western Mediterranean Sea. Twice the size of South Carolina, it is bordered on the west by Algeria and by Libya on the east.

The country is covered by plains in the east and projects southward to the Sahara. In the north, the Atlas Mountains continue from Algeria but do not reach great height.

Government. Executive power is vested by the Constitution in the president, elected for five years and eligible for re-election to two additional terms. Legislative power is vested in a National Assembly elected by universal suffrage.

In 1975, the National Assembly amended the Constitution to make Habib Bourguiba President for life. At 71, Bourguiba was re-elected to a fourth five-year term when he ran unopposed in 1974. The only party, the Socialist Destourian, is led by Bourguiba.

History. Tunisia was settled by the Phoenicians and Carthaginians in ancient times. Except for an interval of Vandal conquest in A.D. 439–533, it was part of the Roman Empire until the Arab conquest of 648–69. It was ruled by various Arab and Berber dynasties until the Turks took it in 1570–74. French troops occupied the country in 1881, and the Bey signed a treaty acknowledging a French protectorate.

Nationalist agitation forced France to grant internal autonomy to Tunisia in 1955 and to recognize Tunisian independence and sovereignty in 1956. The Constituent Assembly deposed the Bey on July 25, 1957, declared Tunisia a republic, and elected Habib Bourguiba as President.

Bourguiba maintained a pro-Western foreign policy that earned him enemies. Tunisia refused to break relations with the U.S. during the Israeli-Arab war in June 1967, and it cracked down on anti-U.S. demonstrators.

Tunisia ended its traditionally neutral role in the Arab world when it joined with the majority of Arab League members to condemn Egypt for concluding a peace treaty with Israel. The Tunisian capital was offered as the temporary headquarters of the League, following the expulsion of Egypt and the shutting of the Cairo offices. At the League's first session in Tunis on June 28, Tunisian Minister of Information Chedli Klibi was elected Secretary-General to replace Mahmoud Riad of Egypt, who resigned.

TURKEY

Republic of Turkey
President: (acting): I. Sabri Cagliyangil (1979)
Head of National Security Council: Gen. Kenan Evran (1980)
Area: 301,380 sq mi. (incl. 9,121 in Europe) (780,576 sq km)
Population (est. 1980): 45,430,000
Density per square mile: 150.7
Capital: Ankara
Largest cities (est. 1978): Istanbul, 2,800,000; Ankara, 2,018,000; **(1975 census):** Izmir (Smyrna), 640,000; Adana, 470,000; Bursa, 350,000; Gaziantep, 300,000
Monetary unit: Turkish lira
Language: Turkish
Religion: Islam
National name: Türkiye Cumhuriyeti
Freedom House classifications: Capitalist-statist industrial, multi-party centralized
Economic summary: Gross national product (1978): $51.8 billion. Average annual growth rate (1970–77): 4.5%. Per capita income: $1,070. Land used for agriculture: 35%; labor force: 60%; principal products: cotton, tobacco, cereals, sugar beets, fruits, nuts. Labor force in industry: 16%; major products: textiles, processed foods. Natural resources: coal, chromite, copper, boron, oil. Exports: cotton, tobacco, fruits, nuts, livestock products, textiles. Imports: machinery, transport equipment, metals, mineral

fuels, fertilizer, chemicals. Major trading partners: West Germany, U.S., Italy, Switzerland, France.

Geography. Turkey is at the northeastern end of the Mediterranean Sea in southeast Europe and southwest Asia. To the north is the Black Sea and to the west the Aegean Sea. Its neighbors are Greece and Bulgaria to the west, the U.S.S.R. to the north, Iran to the east, and Syria and Iraq to the south. Overall, it is more than twice the size of Montana.

The country is divided into two natural areas by the historic waterway formed by the Dardanelles, the Sea of Marmara, and the Bosporus.

Turkey in Europe comprises an area about equal to the state of Massachusetts. It is hilly country drained by the Maritsa River and its tributaries.

Turkey in Asia, or Anatolia, about the size of Texas, is roughly a rectangle in shape with its short sides on the east and west. Its center is a treeless plateau rimmed by mountains.

Government. The President is elected by the Grand National Assembly for a seven-year term and is not eligible for re-election.

In a military coup on Sept. 11, 1980, led by Gen. Kenan Evran, the Army Chief of Staff, Premier Süleyman Demirel was ousted, the Grand National Assembly dissolved and the Constitution suspended. Demirel, former Premier Bülent Ecevit, and some 100 legislators and political figures were detained. Martial law was declared and all political parties were dissolved.

A six-man National Security Council was set up to run the country. It pledge to end extremist violence, restore political stability, and to recognize Turkey's commitments to NATO.

History. The Ottoman Turks first appeared in the early 13th century in Anatolia, subjugating Turkish and Mongol bands pressing against the eastern borders of Byzantium. They gradually spread through the Near East and Balkans, capturing Contantinople in 1453 and storming the gates of Vienna two centuries later. At its height, the Ottoman Empire stretched from the Persian Gulf to western Algeria.

Defeat of the Turkish navy at Lepanto by the Holy League in 1571 and failure of the siege of Vienna heralded the decline of Turkish power. By the 18th century, Russia was seeking to establish itself as the protector of Christians in Turkey's Balkan territories. Russian ambitions were checked by Britain and France in the Crimean War (1854–56), but the Russo-Turkish War (1877–78) gave Bulgaria virtual independence and Romania and Serbia liberation from their nominal allegiance to the Sultan.

Turkish weakness stimulated a revolt of young liberals known as the Young Turks in 1909. They forced Sultan Abdul Hamid to grant a constitution and install a liberal government. Reforms were no barrier to further defeats, however, in a war with Italy (1911–12) and the Balkan Wars (1912–13). Under the influence of German military advisors, Turkey signed a secret alliance with Germany on Aug. 2, 1914, that led to a declaration of war by the Allied powers and the ultimate humiliation of the occupation of Turkish territory by Greek and other Allied troops.

In 1919, the new Nationalist movement, headed by Mustafa Kemal, was organized to resist the Allied occupation and, in 1920, a National Assembly elected him President of both the Assembly and the government. Under his leadership, the Nationalist government was recognized by foreign powers, the Greeks were driven out of Smyrna, and other Allied forces were withdrawn.

The present Turkish boundaries (with the exception of Alexandretta, ceded to Turkey by France in 1939) were fixed by the Treaty of Lausanne (1923) and later negotiations. The caliphate and sultanate were separated, and the sultanate was abolished in 1922. On Oct. 29, 1923, Turkey formally became a republic, with Mustafa Kemal, who took the name Kemal Atatürk, as its first President. The caliphate was abolished in 1924, and Atatürk proceeded to carry out an extensive program of reform, modernization, and industrialization.

Gen. Ismet Inönü was elected to succeed Atatürk in 1938 and was re-elected in 1939, 1943, and 1946. Defeated in 1950, he was succeeded by Celâl Bayar. In 1939, a mutual assistance pact was concluded with Britain and France. Turkey followed a neutral course during most of World War II. However, on Feb. 23, 1945, it declared war on Germany and Japan, but took no active part in the conflict.

Turkey became a full member of NATO in 1952.

In 1971, the Turkish military demanded the ouster of Ismet Inönü, Premier since 1961, who was replaced by Nihat Erim. He pushed through a law that forbade growing of opium poppies after 1972. The move was taken under strong U.S. requests because about two thirds of the illicit heroin reaching U.S. markets is grown in Turkey.

The poppy-growing ban was shelved after Bülent Ecevit, a liberal, became Premier in 1974. Instead, the government required bulk-harvesting of all poppies and consignment of dried "poppy hay" to legal refineries abroad, maintaining that the method would prevent farmers from diverting raw opium to illicit channels. The system was continued after conservative Premier Süleyman Demirel took over the government in 1975.

Turkey invaded Cyprus by sea and air July 20, 1974, following the failure of diplomatic efforts to resolve the crisis caused by the ouster of Archbishop Makarios. Turkey, asserting its right to protect the minority Turkish Cypriot community, demanded the withdrawal of the 650 Greek officers who had led the coup. Greece refused the demand.

Talks in Geneva involving Greece, Turkey, Britain, and Greek Cypriot and Turkish Cypriot leaders broke down in mid-August. Turkey was apparently determined to achieve through military means what it had failed to achieve in negotiations: the establishment of an autonomous Turkish Cypriot region encompassing the northern third of Cyprus. Turkey unilaterally announced a cease-fire August 16, after having gained control of 40% of the island.

More than a year of diplomatic negotiations failed to produce a settlement on Cyprus, where tensions were compounded after Turkish Cypriots established their own state in the north on Feb. 13, 1975.

U.S.-Turkish relations, excellent for a generation, were seriously damaged when Congress voted to end arms sales to Turkey in 1975 because arms the U.S. had supplied for mutual defense had been used in the invasion of Cyprus. Congress maintained the ban despite warnings from President Ford that it would imperil the future of 20 U.S. air and intelligence bases in Turkey and could affect Turkey's role as NATO's anchor in the Eastern Mediterranean.

In July 1975, after a 30-day warning, Turkey took over control of all the installations except the big joint defense base at Incirlik, which it reserved for "NATO tasks alone." Some 7,000 U.S. military men remained on duty under Turkish orders, but relations between Ankara and Washington hit a 30-year low.

In August 1978, the Carter administration won a reluctant Congressional reversal of the arms embargo, but a year later there was renewed Congressional opposition to granting military aid because Turkey had balked at allowing U.S. U-2 reconnaissance planes to use its air space. The planes were to check on Soviet compliance with SALT II, the strategic arms limitation treaty. Ecevit said the U-2's would be acceptable only if the Soviet Union agreed to their presence.

Economic problems and civil disturbances plagued the government in 1979, and a $1.45-billion aid package organized by the U.S. and Western European nations—conditioned on economic reforms—was advanced to help Turkey finance imports. Meanwhile, the Soviet Union agreed to build an atomic power plant for Turkey and supply fuel for it, the first such agreement with a NATO member. Moscow also increased its oil shipments to Turkey.

After conservative gains in the elections of Oct. 14, 1979, Ecevit resigned and Demirel returned to power at the head of a minority government. Strikes and terrorism, stimulated by continuing inflation and rising unemployment, brought Turkey to the brink of anarchy in 1980. In March, a mission of the Organization for Economic Cooperation and Development abandoned efforts to negotiate Ankara's request for a $3-billion loan to stabilize the economy.

TUVALU

Sovereign: Queen Elizabeth II
Governor-General: Fiatau Penitala Teo (1978)
Prime Minister: Toalipi Lauti (1978)
Area: 10 sq mi. (26 sq km)
Population (est. 1980): 6,500
Density per square mile: 650.0
Capital and largest city (est. 1979): Funafuti, 2,200
Monetary unit: Australian dollar
Languages: Samoan and Gilbertese
Member of the Commonwealth of Nations
Freedom House classifications: Capitalist pre-industrial, non-party non-military
Economic summary: Principal agricultural products: copra and coconuts. Export: copra.

Geography. Formerly the Ellice Islands, Tuvalu consists of nine small islands scattered over 500,000 square miles of the western Pacific, just south of the equator.

Government. Official executive power is vested in a Governor-General, representing the Queen, who is appointed by her on the recommendation of the Tuvalu government. Actual executive power lies with a Prime Minister, who is responsible to a House of Assembly composed of eight elected members.

History. The Ellice Islands became a British protectorate in 1892 and were annexed by Britain in 1915–16 as part of the Gilbert and Ellice Islands Colony. The Ellice Islands were separated in 1975, given home rule, and renamed Tuvalu. Full independence was granted on Sept. 30, 1978.

UGANDA

Republic of Uganda
Chairman of Military Commission: Paulo Muwanga (1980)
Area: 91,134 sq mi. (236,036 sq km)
Population (est. 1980): 13,675,000
Density per square mile: 150.1
Capital and largest city (est. 1979): Kampala, 540,000
Monetary unit: Ugandan shilling
Languages: English (official), Swahili, Luganda, Ateso, Luo
Religions: Christian, Islam
Member of Commonwealth of Nations
Freedom House classifications: Capitalist-socialist pre-industrial, one-party nationalist
Economic summary: Gross national product (1976): $2.8 billion. Annual growth rate: 0%. Per capita income: $240. Average rate of inflation (1972–76): 50%. Land used for agriculture: 35%; labor force: 90%; principal products: coffee, tea, cotton. Labor force in industry: 3%; major products: processed agricultural products, copper, cement, shoes, fertilizer, steel, beverages. Natural resources: copper, miscellaneous minerals. Exports: coffee, cotton, tea, copper. Imports: petroleum products, machinery, transport equipment. Major trading partners: U.S., U.K., Kenya, France, West Germany, Japan.

Geography. Uganda, twice the size of Pennsylvania, is in east central Africa. It is bordered on the west by Zaire, on the north by the Sudan, on the east by Kenya, and on the south by Tanzania and Rwanda.

The country, which lies across the Equator, is divided into three main areas—swampy lowlands, a fertile plateau with wooded hills, and a desert region. Lake Victoria forms part of the southern border.

Government: Paulo Muwanga, a civilian, heads a Military Commission that assumed power on May 12, 1980. An election for president is expected to be held by the end of the year. Four parties are expected to enter candidates: the Uganda People's Congress, the Democratic Party, the Conservative Party, and the Uganda Patriotic Movement.

History. Uganda was first visited by European explorers as well as Arab traders in 1844. An Anglo-German agreement of 1890 declared it to be in the British sphere of influence in Africa, and the Imperial British East Africa Company was chartered to develop the area. The company did not prosper financially, and in 1894 a British protectorate was proclaimed.

Uganda became independent on Oct. 9, 1962.

As its first president, the country chose Mutesa II, King of the ancient kingdom of Buganda. Dr. Milton Obote had been Prime Minister. In 1965, he suspended the Constitution and assumed the powers of the government, later abolishing the offices of President and Vice President.

Obote in 1970 passed laws declaring that 40,000 British Asians—Asian-born persons, mostly Indian, who lived in Uganda but chose British citizenship in 1962 rather than Ugandan—needed a variety of passes and permits to remain in the country. In 1971, Idi Amin, an unpredictable army sergeant, ousted Obote and made himself President. The next year, he began expelling the Asians. He also expelled Israeli advisors rather than pay Israel's military aid bill and applauded Hitler's treatment of Jews.

With his country's potentially rich agricultural economy in turmoil, partly because of large purchases of weapons for its 20,000-man army, Amin nationalized all land in 1975, without compensation to former owners.

In 1976, Amin had himself proclaimed President for Life by the Defense Council, which replaced the Council of Ministers as Uganda's ruling body.

An Israeli commando raid against Entebbe airport on July 4, 1977, freed 103 hostages in a hijacked French airliner that had been held at the airport for a week by Palestinian guerrillas. Hostages, and the government of Israel, charged that Amin had collaborated with the hijackers.

The world condemned Amin's atrocities—Amnesty International reported in 1977 that 300,000 may have died under his rule, including Cabinet ministers and church leaders. Few African leaders denounced him, however, until President Julius K. Nyuerere of Tanzania launched an invasion in November 1978, with the tacit acquiescence of most of Africa. Libya's chief, Muammar el-Qaddafi, came to Amin's defense with troops and arms, but the Libyans only temporarily halted the invaders. Kampala was taken on April 11, 1979, and Amin fled to Libya.

A National Consultative Council formed by exiles picked Yusufu Lule, a former professor, as President, but he was soon replaced by Godfrey Binaisa, Attorney General in the Obote government, who was summoned from exile in New York. On May 12, 1980, a Military Commission headed by Paulo Muwanga, a civilian, ousted Binaisa. The junta lifted the ban on opposition political parties, and on May 27, Obote returned to campaign for the presidency in an election expected to take place before the end of the year.

UNION OF SOVIET SOCIALIST REPUBLICS

See Soviet Union

UNITED ARAB EMIRATES

Head of State: Sheik Zayed Bin Sultan Al-Nahayan (1971)
Prime Minister: Sheik Rashid bin Said al-Maktoum (1979)
Area: 32,000 sq mi. (82,880 sq km)
Population (est. 1980): 800,000
Density per square mile: 25.0
Capital and largest city (est. 1975): Abu Dhabi, 95,000
Monetary unit: Dirham
Language: Arabic
Religion: Islam
Freedom House classifications: Capitalist-statist industrial, non-party non-military
Economic summary: Gross national product (1978): $11 billion. Average annual growth rate (1970–77): −3.6%. Per capita income: $18,500. Land used for agriculture: 8%; labor force: 10%; principal products: vegetables, meats, dates. Labor force in industry: 65%; major products: fish, light manufactures, petroleum, construction materials. Natural resources: oil. Exports: petroleum, pears, fish. Imports: machinery, consumer goods, food. Major trading partners: Western European nations, Japan, U.S., India.

Geography. The United Arab Emirates, in the eastern part of the Arabian Peninsula, extends along part of the Gulf of Oman and the southern coast of the Persian Gulf. The nation is the size of Maine. Its neighbors are Saudi Arabia in the west and south, Qatar in the north, and Oman in the east. Most of the land is barren and sandy.

Government. The United Arab Emirates was formed in 1971 by seven emirates known as the Trucial States—Abu Dhabi (the largest), Dubai, Sharjah, Ajman, Fujairah, Ras al Khaimah and Umm al-Qaiwain.

The loose federation allows joint policies in foreign relations, defense, and development, with each member state keeping its internal local system of government headed by its own ruler. A 40-member legislature consists of eight seats each for Abu Dhabi and Dubai, six seats each for Ras al Khaimah and Sharjah, and four each for the others. It is a member of the Arab League.

History. Originally the area was inhabited by a seafaring people who were converted to Islam in the seventh century. Later, a dissident sect, the Carmathians, established a powerful sheikdom, and its army conquered Mecca. After the sheikdom disintegrated, its people became pirates.

Threatening the sultanate of Muscat and Oman early in the 19th century, the pirates provoked the intervention of the British, who in 1820 enforced a partial truce and in 1853 a permanent truce. Thus what had been called the Pirate Coast was renamed the Trucial Coast.

UNITED KINGDOM

United Kingdom of Great Britain and Northern Ireland
Sovereign: Queen Elizabeth II (1952)
Prime Minister: Margaret Thatcher (1979)
Area: 94,250 sq mi. (244,108 sq km)
Population (est. 1980): 55,800,000 (English, Scottish, Welsh, Northern Irish)
Density per square mile: 592.0
Capital: London, England
Largest cities (est. 1978): London (Greater), 6,918,000; Birmingham, England, 1,041,000; Glasgow, Scotland, 809,700; Leeds, England, 728,500; Bradford, England, 563,100; Sheffield, England, 547,900; Liverpool, England, 528,000; Manchester, England, 489,300; Edinburgh, Scotland, 456,500
Monetary unit: Pound sterling (£)
Languages: English, Welsh, Gaelic
Religions: Church of England (established church); Church of Wales (disestablished); Church of Scotland (established church—Presbyterian); Church of Ireland (disestablished); Roman Catholic; Methodist; Congregational; Baptist; Jewish
Freedom House classifications: Capitalist-socialist industrial, multi-party centralized
Economic summary: Gross national product (1978): $281 billion. Average annual growth rate (1970–77): 1.6%. Per capita income: $4,360. Principal agricultural products: cereals, livestock and livestock products. Major industrial products: steel, heavy engineering and metal manufactures, textiles, motor vehicles and aircraft, electronics, chemicals. Natural resources: coal, oil, gas. Exports: machinery, transport equipment, chemicals, beverages. Imports: foodstuffs, petroleum, machinery, crude materials. Major trading partners: Western European nations, U.S., Canada, France.

Geography. The United Kingdom, consisting of England, Wales, Scotland, and Northern Ireland, is twice the size of New York State. England, in the southeast part of the British Isles, is separated from Scotland on the north by the granite Cheviot Hills; from them the Pennine chain of uplands extends south through the center of England, reaching its highest point in the Lake District in the northwest.

Area and Population of United Kingdom

Subdivision	Area sq mi.	Area sq km	Population (est. 1978)
England and Wales	58,381	151,207	49,117,000
Scotland	30,416	78,777	5,685,000
Northern Ireland	5,452	14,121	1,539,000
Total	**94,249**	**244,105**	**56,341,000**

To the west along the border of Wales—a land of steep hills and valleys—are the Cambrian Mountains, while the Cotswolds, a range of hills in Gloucestershire, extend into the surrounding shires.

The remainder of England is plain land, though not necessarily flat, with the rocky sand-topped moors in the southwest, the rolling downs in the south and southeast, and the reclaimed marshes of the low-lying fens in the east central districts.

Scotland is divided into three physical regions—the Highlands, the Central Lowlands, containing two-thirds of the population, and the Southern Uplands. The western Highland coast is intersected throughout by long, narrow sea-lochs, or fiords. Scotland also includes the Outer and Inner Hebrides and other islands off the west coast and the Orkney and Shetland Islands off the north coast.

Wales is generally hilly; the Snowdon range in the northern part culminates in Mount Snowdon (3,560 ft, 1,085 m), highest in both England and Wales.

Important rivers flowing into the North Sea are the Thames, Humber, Tees, and Tyne. In the west are the Severn and Wye, which empty into the Bristol Channel and are navigable, as are the Mersey and Ribble.

Government. The United Kingdom is a constitutional monarchy, with a Queen and a Parliament that has two houses: the House of Lords with about 830 hereditary peers, 26 spiritual peers, about 270 life peers and peeresses, and 9 law-lords, who are hereditary, or life, peers, and the House of Commons, which since 1974 has had 635 popularly elected members. Supreme legislative power is vested in Parliament, which sits for five years unless sooner dissolved.

The executive power of the Crown is exercised by the Cabinet, headed by the Prime Minister. The latter, normally the head of the party commanding a majority in the House of Commons, is appointed by the Sovereign, with whose consent he or she in turn appoints the rest of the Cabinet. All ministers must be members of one or the other house of Parliament; they are individually and collectively responsible to the Crown and Parliament. The Cabinet proposes bills and arranges the business of Parliament, but it depends entirely on the votes in the House of Commons. The Lords cannot hold up "money" bills, but they can delay other bills for a maximum of one year.

By the Act of Union (1707), the Scottish Parliament was assimilated with that of England, and Scotland is now represented in Commons by 71 members. The Secretary of State for Scotland, a member of the Cabinet, is responsible for the administration of Scottish affairs.

The major political parties are the Conservative Party (337 of the 635 seats in the House of Commons), led by Prime Minister Margaret Thatcher; Labor Party (266 seats), led by former Prime Minister James Callaghan; Liberal Party (11 seats), led by David Steel; Ulster Unionists and other Northern Irish parties (12 seats); Scottish Nationalist Party (2 seats); Welsh Nationalist Party (2 seats).

Ruler: Queen Elizabeth II, born April 21, 1926, elder daughter of King George VI and Queen Elizabeth, succeeded to the throne on the death of her father on Feb. 6, 1952; married Nov. 20, 1947, to Prince Philip, Duke of Edinburgh, born June 10, 1921; their children are Prince Charles[1] (heir presumptive), born Nov. 14, 1948; Princess Anne, born Aug. 15, 1950; Prince Andrew, born Feb. 19, 1960; and Prince Edward, born March 10, 1964. The Queen's sister is Princess Margaret, born Aug. 21, 1930.

History. Roman invasions of the 1st century B.C. brought Britain into contact with the Continent. When the Roman legions withdrew in the 5th century A.D., Britain fell easy prey to the invading hordes of Angles, Saxons, and Jutes from Scandinavia and the Low Countries. Seven large kingdoms were established, and the original Britons were forced into Wales and Scotland. It was not until the 11th century that the country finally became united under the Danish King Canute. Following the death of Edward the Confessor (1066), a dispute about the succession arose, and William, Duke of Normandy, invaded England, defeating the Saxon King, Harold II, at the Battle of Hastings (1066). The Norman conquest introduced Norman law and feudalism.

The reign of Henry II (1154–89), first of the Plantagenets, saw an increasing centralization of royal power at the expense of the nobles, but in 1215 John (1199–1216) was forced to sign the Magna Carta, which awarded the people, especially the nobles, certain basic rights. Edward I (1272–1307) continued the conquest of Ireland, reduced Wales to subjection and made some gains in Scotland. In 1314, however, English forces led by Edward II were ousted from Scotland after the Battle of Bannockburn. The late 13th and early 14th centuries saw the development of a separate House of Commons with tax-raising powers.

Edward III's claim to the throne of France led to the Hundred Years' War (1338–1453) and the loss of almost all the large English territory in France. In England, the great poverty and discontent caused by the war were intensified by the Black Death, a plague that reduced the population by about one third. The Wars of the Roses (1455–85), a struggle for the throne between the House of York and the House of Lancaster, ended in the victory of Henry Tudor (Henry VII) at Bosworth Field (1485).

During the reign of Henry VIII (1509–47), the Church in England asserted its independence from the Roman Catholic Church. Under Edward VI and Mary, the two extremes of religious fanaticism were reached, and it remained for Henry's daughter, Elizabeth I (1558–1603), to set up the Church of England on a moderate basis. In 1588, the Spanish Armada, a fleet sent out by Catholic King Philip II of Spain, was defeated by the English and destroyed during a storm. During Elizabeth's reign, England became a world power.

Elizabeth's heir was a Stuart—James VI of Scotland—who joined the two crowns as James I (1603–

1. The title Prince of Wales, which is not inherited, was conferred on Prince Charles by his mother on July 26, 1958. The investiture ceremony took place on July 1, 1969. The previous Prince of Wales was Prince Edward Albert, who held the title from 1911 to 1936 before he became Edward VIII.

Rulers of England and Great Britain

Name	Born	Ruled[1]
SAXONS[2]		
Egbert[3]	c. 775	828–839
Ethelwulf	?	839–858
Ethelbald	?	858–860
Ethelbert	?	860–866
Ethelred I	?	866–871
Alfred the Great	849	871–899
Edward the Elder	c. 870	899–924
Athelstan	895	924–939
Edmund I the Deed-doer	921	939–946
Edred	c. 925	946–955
Edwy the Fair	c. 943	955–959
Edgar the Peaceful	943	959–975
Edward the Martyr	c. 962	975–979
Ethelred II the Unready	968	979–1016
Edmund II Ironside	c. 993	1016–1016
DANES		
Canute	995	1016–1035
Harold I Harefoot	c.1016	1035–1040
Hardecanute	c.1018	1040–1042
SAXONS		
Edward the Confessor	c.1004	1042–1066
Harold II	c.1020	1066–1066
HOUSE OF NORMANDY		
William I the Conqueror	1027	1066–1087
William II Rufus	c.1056	1087–1100
Henry I Beauclerc	1068	1100–1135
Stephen of Blois	c.1100	1135–1154
HOUSE OF PLANTAGENET		
Henry II	1133	1154–1189
Richard I Coeur de Lion	1157	1189–1199
John Lackland	1167	1199–1216
Henry III	1207	1216–1272
Edward I Longshanks	1239	1272–1307
Edward II	1284	1307–1327
Edward III	1312	1327–1377
Richard II	1367	1377–1399[4]
HOUSE OF LANCASTER		
Henry IV Bolingbroke	1367	1399–1413
Henry V	1387	1413–1422
Henry VI	1421	1422–1461[5]
HOUSE OF YORK		
Edward IV	1442	1461–1483[5]
Edward V	1470	1483–1483
Richard III	1452	1483–1485
HOUSE OF TUDOR		
Henry VII	1457	1485–1509
Henry VIII	1491	1509–1547
Edward VI	1537	1547–1553
Jane (Lady Jane Grey)[6]	1537	1553–1553
Mary I ("Bloody Mary")	1516	1553–1558
Elizabeth I	1533	1558–1603
HOUSE OF STUART		
James I[7]	1566	1603–1625
Charles I	1600	1625–1649
COMMONWEALTH		
Council of State	—	1649–1653
Oliver Cromwell[8]	1599	1653–1658
Richard Cromwell[8]	1626	1658–1659[9]
RESTORATION OF HOUSE OF STUART		
Charles II	1630	1660–1685
James II	1633	1685–1688[10]
William III[11]	1650	1689–1702
Mary II[11]	1662	1689–1694
Anne	1665	1702–1714
HOUSE OF HANOVER		
George I	1660	1714–1727
George II	1683	1727–1760
George III	1738	1760–1820
George IV	1762	1820–1830
William IV	1765	1830–1837
Victoria	1819	1837–1901
HOUSE OF SAXE-COBURG[12]		
Edward VII	1841	1901–1910
HOUSE OF WINDSOR[12]		
George V	1865	1910–1936
Edward VIII	1894	1936–1936[13]
George VI	1895	1936–1952
Elizabeth II	1926	1952–

1. Year of end of rule is also that of death, unless otherwise indicated. 2. Dates for Saxon kings are still subject of controversy. 3. Became King of West Saxons in 802; considered (from 828) first King of all England. 4. Died 1400. 5. Henry VI reigned again briefly 1470–71. 6. Nominal Queen for 9 days; not counted as Queen by some authorities. She was beheaded in 1554. 7. Ruled in Scotland as James VI (1567–1625). 8. Lord Protector. 9. Died 1712. 10. Died 1701. 11. Joint rulers (1689–1694). 12. Name changed from Saxe-Coburg to Windsor in 1917. 13. Was known after his abdication as the Duke of Windsor; died 1972.

25). The Stuart kings incurred large debts and were forced either to depend on Parliament for taxes or to raise money by illegal means. In 1642, war broke out between Charles I and a large segment of the Parliament; Charles was defeated and executed in 1649, and the monarchy was then abolished. After the death in 1658 of Oliver Cromwell, the Lord Protector, the Puritan Commonwealth fell to pieces and Charles II was placed on the throne in 1660. The struggle between the King and Parliament continued, but Charles II knew when to compromise. His brother, James II (1685–88), possessed none of his ability and was ousted by the Revolution of 1688, which confirmed the primacy of Parliament. James's daughter, Mary, and her husband, William of Orange, were now the rulers.

Queen Anne's reign (1702–14) was marked by the Duke of Marlborough's victories over France at Blenheim, Oudenarde, and Malplaquet in the War of the Spanish Succession. England and Scotland meanwhile were joined by the Act of Union (1707). Upon the death of Anne, the distant claims of the elector of Hanover were recognized, and he became King of Great Britain and Ireland as George I.

The unwillingness of the Hanoverian kings to rule resulted in the formation by the royal ministers of a Cabinet, headed by a Prime Minister, which directed all public business. Abroad, the constant wars with France expanded the British Empire all over the globe, particularly in North America and India. This imperial growth was checked by the

British Prime Ministers Since 1770

Name	Term
Lord North (Tory)	1770–1782
Marquis of Rockingham (Whig)	1782–1782
Earl of Shelburne (Whig)	1782–1783
Duke of Portland (Coalition)	1783–1783
William Pitt, the Younger (Tory)	1783–1801
Henry Addington (Tory)	1801–1804
William Pitt, the Younger (Tory)	1804–1806
Baron Grenville (Whig)	1806–1807
Duke of Portland (Tory)	1807–1809
Spencer Perceval (Tory)	1809–1812
Earl of Liverpool (Tory)	1812–1827
George Canning (Tory)	1827–1827
Viscount Goderich (Tory)	1827–1828
Duke of Wellington (Tory)	1828–1830
Earl Grey (Whig)	1830–1834
Viscount Melbourne (Whig)	1834–1834
Sir Robert Peel (Tory)	1834–1835
Viscount Melbourne (Whig)	1835–1841
Sir Robert Peel (Tory)	1841–1846
Earl Russell (Whig)	1846–1852
Earl of Derby (Tory)	1852–1852
Earl of Aberdeen (Coalition)	1852–1855
Viscount Palmerston (Liberal)	1855–1858
Earl of Derby (Conservative)	1858–1859
Viscount Palmerston (Liberal)	1859–1865
Earl Russell (Liberal)	1865–1866
Earl of Derby (Conservative)	1866–1868
Benjamin Disraeli (Conservative)	1868–1868
William E. Gladstone (Liberal)	1868–1874
Benjamin Disraeli (Conservative)	1874–1880
William E. Gladstone (Liberal)	1880–1885
Marquis of Salisbury (Conservative)	1885–1886
William E. Gladstone (Liberal)	1886–1886
Marquis of Salisbury (Conservative)	1886–1892
William E. Gladstone (Liberal)	1892–1894
Earl of Rosebery (Liberal)	1894–1895
Marquis of Salisbury (Conservative)	1895–1902
Earl Balfour (Conservative)	1902–1905
Sir H. Campbell-Bannerman (Liberal)	1905–1908
Herbert H. Asquith (Liberal)	1908–1915
Herbert H. Asquith (Coalition)	1915–1916
David Lloyd George (Coalition)	1916–1922
Andrew Bonar Law (Conservative)	1922–1923
Stanley Baldwin (Conservative)	1923–1924
James Ramsay MacDonald (Labor)	1924–1924
Stanley Baldwin (Conservative)	1924–1929
James Ramsay MacDonald (Labor)	1929–1931
James Ramsay MacDonald (Coalition)	1931–1935
Stanley Baldwin (Coalition)	1935–1937
Neville Chamberlain (Coalition)	1937–1940
Winston Churchill (Coalition)	1940–1945
Clement R. Attlee (Labor)	1945–1951
Sir Winston Churchill (Conservative)	1951–1955
Sir Anthony Eden (Conservative)	1955–1957
Harold Macmillan (Conservative)	1957–1963
Sir Alec Frederick Douglas-Home (Conservative)	1963–1964
Harold Wilson (Labor)	1964–1970
Edward Heath (Conservative)	1970–1974
Harold Wilson (Labor)	1974–1976
James Callaghan (Labor)	1976–1979
Margaret Thatcher (Conservative)	1979–

revolt of the American colonies (1775–81).

Struggles with France broke out again in 1793 and, during the Napoleonic Wars, which ended at Waterloo (1815), Britain was pitted at one time against almost all of Europe.

The Victorian era, named after Queen Victoria (1837–1901), saw the growth of a democratic system of government that had begun with the Reform Bill of 1832. The two important wars in Victoria's reign were the Crimean War against Russia (1853–56) and the Boer War (1899–1902), the latter enormously extending Britain's influence in Africa.

Increasing uneasiness at home and abroad marked the reign of Edward VII (1901–10). Within four years after the accession of George V in 1910, Britain entered World War I when Germany invaded Belgium. The nation was led by coalition Cabinets, headed first by Herbert Asquith and then, starting in 1916, by the Welsh statesman David Lloyd George. Postwar labor unrest culminated in the general strike of 1926.

King Edward VIII succeeded to the throne on Jan. 20, 1936, at his father's death, but abdicated on Dec. 11, 1936 (in order to marry an American divorcee, Wallis Warfield Simpson) in favor of his brother, who became George VI.

The efforts of Prime Minister Neville Chamberlain to stem the rising threat of Nazism in Germany failed with the German invasion of Poland on Sept. 1, 1939, which was followed by Britain's entry into World War II on September 3. Allied reverses in the spring of 1940 led to Chamberlain's resignation and the formation of another coalition war Cabinet by the Conservative leader, Winston Churchill, who led Britain through most of World War II. Churchill resigned shortly after V-E Day, May 7, 1945, but then formed a "caretaker" government that remained in office until after the parliamentary elections in July, which the Labor Party won overwhelmingly. The government formed by Clement R. Attlee began a moderate socialist program.

For details of World War II (1939–45), *see* Headline History.

In 1951, Churchill again became Prime Minister at the head of a Conservative government. George VI died Feb. 6, 1952, and was succeeded by his daughter Elizabeth II.

Churchill stepped down in 1955 in favor of Sir Anthony Eden, who resigned on grounds of ill health in 1957, and was succeeded by Harold Macmillan and Sir Alec Douglas-Home. In 1964, Harold Wilson led the Labor Party to victory.

Wilson, the first Labor Prime Minister in 13 years, was a skilled strategist from the party's center who instituted no great changes domestically. His ambition for success abroad was thwarted by the French veto of Britain's bid for entry into the European Economic Community and by his own inept handling of the unilateral declaration of independence by Southern Rhodesia, the last sizable British colony.

A lagging economy brought the Conservatives back to power in 1970. Prime Minister Edward Heath won Britain's admission to the European Community, a move affirmed by 67.2% in the nation's first referendum. Heath narrowly lost a February 1974 election overshadowed by a coal strike, returning Wilson to the leadership and the first minority government since 1929. A bare three-seat majority resulted from an election nine months later, but an alliance with the Liberal Party assured control.

Party elections after Wilson's announcement of his intention to retire elevated James Callaghan from the Foreign Ministry to the Prime Minister's office in 1976.

Despite economic troubles, unemployment, and continuing conflict in Northern Ireland and Rhodesia, Britons in June 1977 celebrated the Silver Jubilee of Queen Elizabeth II with genuine affection. The Queen's first grandchild, Peter Mark Andrew Phillips, son of Princess Anne, was born November 14. On May 24, 1978, the first divorce in the immediate royal family in more than 150 years took place when Princess Margaret's 18-year marriage to the Earl of Snowdon was legally ended.

Margaret Thatcher became Britain's first woman Prime Minister as the Conservatives won 339 seats for a 43-seat majority in elections on May 3, 1979. The 53-year-old, Oxford-educated daughter of a grocer campaigned for lower taxes, curbs on labor unions, and less government at home coupled with a more decisive foreign policy.

Mrs. Thatcher moved quickly to implement her domestic program but was blocked by African and U.S. resistance from granting early recognition to the Muzorewa government in Zimbabwe (Rhodesia). In September 1979, a bold initiative by her foreign minister, Lord Carrington, brought all parties in the conflict to a conference in London at which she threatened and cajoled the white minority and black factions until all agreed on a new Constitution. The successful conduct of elections in February and the transfer of sovereignty on April 18, 1980, was a political triumph for the Conservatives.

A similar gamble, with Mrs. Thatcher threatening to pull Britain out of the European Economic Community, brought a major reduction in the British contribution to the E.E.C. Although the victory avoided sharp increases in food prices, the dispute strengthened the growing sentiment in Britain for withdrawal from the E.E.C.

Despite rising income from North Sea oil production, the British economy presented a gloomy picture in 1980 of lagging industry, a postwar record of 6.1% unemployment, and inflation again moving above 20%.

NORTHERN IRELAND

Status: Part of United Kingdom
Secretary of State: Humphrey Atkins (1979)
Area: 5,452 sq mi. (14,121 sq km)
Population (est. 1979): 1,525,000
Density per square mile: 279.7
Capital and largest city (est. 1978): Belfast, 354,000
Monetary Unit: British pound sterling
Languages: English, Gaelic
Religions: Roman Catholic, 35%; Presbyterian, 29%; Church of Ireland, 24%; Methodist, 5%

Geography. Northern Ireland comprises the counties of Antrim, Armagh, Down, Fermanagh, Londonderry, and Tyrone, which make up predominantly Protestant Ulster and form the northern part of the island of Ireland, westernmost of the British Isles. It is slightly larger than Connecticut.

Government. Northern Ireland is an integral part of the United Kingdom (it has 12 representatives in the British House of Commons), but under the terms of the Government of Ireland Act in 1920, it had a semiautonomous government. But in 1972, after three years of internal strife which resulted in over 400 dead and thousands injured, Britain suspended the Ulster parliament. The Ulster counties became governed directly from London after an attempt to return certain powers to an elected Assembly in Belfast.

The Northern Ireland Assembly was dissolved in 1975 and a Constitutional Convention was elected to write a Constitution acceptable to Protestants and Catholics. The convention failed to reach agreement and closed down the next year.

The major political parties are the United Ulster Unionist Coalition (Protestant) (46 of 78 delegates to the Constitutional Convention); Social Democratic Labor Party (Catholic) (17 delegates); Alliance Party (8 delegates); New Unionist Party of Northern Ireland (Protestant) (5 delegates).

History. Ulster was part of Catholic Ireland until the reign of Elizabeth I (1558–1603) when, after crushing three Irish rebellions, the crown confiscated lands in Ireland and settled in Ulster the Scot Presbyterians who became rooted there. Another rebellion in 1641–51, crushed as brutally by Oliver Cromwell, resulted in the settlement of Anglican Englishmen in Ulster. Subsequent political policy favoring Protestants and disadvantaging Catholics encouraged further settlement in Northern Ireland.

But the North did not separate from the South until William Gladstone presented in 1886 his proposal for home rule in Ireland as a means of settling the Irish Question. The Protestants in the North, although they had grievances like the Catholics in the South, feared domination by the Catholic majority. Industry, moreover, was concentrated in the north and dependent on the British market.

When World War I began, civil war threatened between the regions. Northern Ireland, however, did not become a political entity until the six counties accepted the Home Rule Bill of 1920. This set up a semiautonomous Parliament in Belfast and a Crown-appointed Governor advised by a Cabinet of the Prime Minister and eight ministers, as well as a 12-member representation in the House of Commons in London.

As the Republic of Ireland gained its sovereignty, relations improved between North and South, although the Irish Republican Army, outlawed in recent years, continued the struggle to end the partition of Ireland. In 1966–69, communal rioting and street fighting between Protestants and Catholics occurred in Londonderry, fomented by extremist nationalist Protestants, who feared the Catholics might attain a local majority, and by Catholics demonstrating for civil rights.

Rioting, terrorism, and sniping killed more than 2,000 persons from 1969 through 1980, and the religious communities, Catholic and Protestant, became hostile armed camps. British troops were brought in to separate them but themselves became a target of Catholics.

In 1973, a new British charter created a 78-member Assembly elected by proportional representation that gave more weight to Catholic strength. It created a Province Executive with committee chairmen of the Assembly heading all government departments except law enforcement, which remained under London's control. Assembly elections in 1973 produced a majority for the new Constitution that included Catholic assemblymen. Dublin urged Ulster Catholics to work with the new system.

Ulster's leaders agreed in 1973 to create an 11-member Executive Body with six seats assigned to Unionists (Protestants) and four to members of Catholic parties. Unionist leader Brian Faulkner headed the Executive. Also agreed to was a Council of Ireland, with 14 seats evenly divided between Dublin and Belfast, which could act only by unanimous vote.

Although the Council lacked real authority, its creation sparked a general strike by Protestant extremists in 1974. The two-week strike caused Faulkner's resignation from the Executive and resumption of direct rule from London.

In April 1974, London instituted a new program that responded to some Catholic grievances, but assigned more British troops to cut off movement of arms and munitions to Ulster's violence-racked cities.

Violence continued unabated, with new heights reached early in 1976 when the British government announced the end of special privileges for political prisoners in Northern Ireland. British Prime Minister James Callaghan visited Belfast in July and pledged that Ulster would remain part of the United Kingdom unless a clear majority wished to separate.

In October 1977, the 1976 Nobel Prize for Peace was awarded to Mairead Corrigan and Betty Williams for their campaign for peace in Northern Ireland. Intermittent violence continued, however, and on Aug. 27, 1979, an I.R.A. bomb killed Earl Mountbatten as he was sailing off southern Ireland. The death of the 79-year-old cousin of the Queen, a World War II hero and the last Viceroy of India, shocked the world. Mrs. Thatcher visited Ulster two days later and denounced terrorism. After Mountbatten's state funeral in Westminster Abbey on Sept. 5, Mrs. Thatcher met with Irish Premier John Lynch to discuss security measures against the I.R.A. Lynch urged an attack on the "root cause," the division of Ireland.

New talks aimed at a restoration of home rule in Northern Ireland began and quickly ended in January 1980. In May, Mrs. Thatcher met with the new Prime Minister of the Irish Republic, Charles Haughey, but she insisted that the future of Ulster must be decided only by its people and the British Parliament. Haughey declared that an internal solution "cannot and will not succeed."

Dependencies of the United Kingdom

ANGUILLA, ANTIGUA

See West Indies Associated States

BELIZE

Status: Self-governing dependency
Governor: James P.I. Hennessy (1979)
Prime Minister: George C. Price (1961)
Area: 8,867 sq mi. (22,965 sq km)
Population (est. 1980): 160,000
Capital: (est. 1980): Belmopan, 4,500
Monetary unit: Belize dollar
Economic summary: Gross national product (1978): $110 million. Average annual growth rate (1970–77): 4.7%. Per capita income: $700. Land used for agriculture: 38%; labor force: 39%; principal products: sugar cane, citrus fruits, corn, molasses, rice, bananas, livestock. Labor force in industry: 20%; major products: timber, processed foods, furniture, rum, soap. Natural resource: timber. Exports: sugar, molasses, clothing, lumber, citrus fruits, fish. Imports: vehicles, building materials, petroleum, foodstuffs, textiles, machinery. Major trading partners: U.S., U.K., Mexico, Canada, Jamaica.

Formerly known as British Honduras, Belize became a British crown colony in 1884. It is situated in Central America south of Mexico and east and north of Guatemala on the Caribbean Sea. Belize was probably overrun by Hernando Cortés in 1524. British buccaneers settled the former capital, Belize, in the 17th century.

In the first popular election, in 1954, the People's United Party, nationalistic and anti-British, came to power. Eventually the nationalists won a Constitution, which, effective in 1964, established self-government under a British-appointed Governor.

BERMUDA

Status: Self-governing dependency
Governor: Sir Peter Ramsbotham (1977)
Prime Minister: J. David Gibbons (1977)
Area: 20 sq mi. (52 sq km)
Population (est. 1980): 65,000
Capital (est. 1978): Hamilton, 2,500
Monetary unit: Bermuda dollar
Economic summary: Gross national product (1978): $500 million. Average annual growth rate (1970–77): 2.4%. Per capita income: $7,540. Land used for agriculture: 12%; labor force: 1.3%; principal products: bananas, vegetables, citrus fruits, dairy products. Labor force in industry: 6.2%; major products: structural concrete, paints, perfumes, furniture. Natural resource: limestone. Exports: semi-tropical produce, light manufactures. Imports: foodstuffs, manufactured goods. Major trading partners: U.S., U.K., Canada.

Bermuda is an archipelago of about 360 small islands, 580 miles (934 km) east of North Carolina. The largest is (Great) Bermuda, or Long Island. Discovered by Juan de Bermúdez, a shipwrecked Spaniard, early in the 16th century, the islands were settled in 1612 by an offshoot of the Virginia Company and became a crown colony in 1684.

In 1940, sites on the islands were leased for 99 years to the U.S. for air and navy bases. Bermuda is also the headquarters of the West Indies and Atlantic squadron of the Royal Navy.

In 1968, Bermuda was granted a new Constitution, its first Prime Minister, and autonomy, except for foreign relations, defense, and internal security. The predominantly white United Bermuda Party has retained power in three elections against the opposition—the black-led Progressive Laborites—although Bermuda's population is 60% black. Serious rioting occurred in December 1977 after two blacks were hanged for a series of murders, including the 1973 assassination of the Governor, Sir Richard Sharples, and British troops were summoned to restore order.

BRITISH ANTARCTIC TERRITORY

Status: Dependency
High Commissioner: Rex Masterson Hunt (1980)
Area: 500,000 sq mi. (1,395,000 sq km)
Population (1976): 55

The British Antarctic Territory consists of the South Shetland Islands, South Orkney Islands, and Nearby Graham Land on the Antarctic continent, largely uninhabited. They were dependencies of the British crown colony of the Falkland Islands but received a separate administration in 1962, being governed by a British-appointed High Commissioner who is Governor of the Falklands.

BRITISH INDIAN OCEAN TERRITORY

Status: Dependency
Commissioner: John Adam Robson (1979)
Administrator: A. G. Munro
Administrative headquarters: Victoria, Seychelles
Area: 85 sq mi, (220 sq km)

This dependency, consisting of the Chagos Archipelago and other small island groups, was formed in 1965 by agreement with Mauritius and the Seychelles. There is no permanent civilian population in the territory.

BRITISH VIRGIN ISLANDS

Status: Dependency
Governor: James A. Davidson (1978)
Area: 59 sq mi. (153 sq km)
Population (est. 1979): 12,000
Capital (est. 1975): Road Town (on Tortola): 3,500
Monetary unit: U.S. dollar

Some 36 islands in the Caribbean Sea northeast of Puerto Rico and west of the Leeward Islands, the British Virgin Islands are economically interdependent with the U.S. Virgin Islands to the south. They were formerly part of the administration of the Leeward Islands. They received a separate administration in 1956 as a crown colony. In 1967 a new Constitution was promulgated that provided for a ministerial system of government headed by the Governor. The principal islands are Tortola, Virgin Gorda, Anegada and Jost Van Dyke.

BRUNEI

Status: Independent state
Sultan: Hassanel Bolkiah (1968)
High Commissioner: (Vacant)
Area: 2,226 sq mi. (5,765 sq km)
Population (est. 1980): 220,000
Capital (est. 1978): Bandar Seri Begawan, 70,000
Monetary unit: Brunei dollar
Economic summary: Gross national product (1978): $1.8 billion. Average annual growth rate (1970–77): 7.7%. Per capita income: $2,970. Land used for agriculture: 3%; labor force: 31%; principal agricultural products: rubber, rice, pepper. Labor force in industry: 33%; major industrial products: crude petroleum, liquefied natural gas. Natural resources: petroleum, natural gas. Exports: crude petroleum, liquefied natural gas. Imports: machinery, transport equipment, manufactured goods, foodstuffs. Major trading partners: Japan, U.S., U.K., Singapore.

A sultanate on the northwest coast of the island of Borneo on the South China Sea, Brunei consists of two prongs into the territory of Sarawak, East Malaysia. It was a powerful state from the 16th to the 19th century, ruling over the northern part of Borneo and adjacent island chains. But it fell into decay and lost Sarawak in 1841, becoming a British protectorate in 1888 and a British dependency in 1905.

The Sultan regained control over internal affairs by a Constitution he instituted in 1959, along with an agreement with the Crown delegating responsibility for defense and foreign affairs. Britain, which is responsible for foreign affairs, is represented by a High Commissioner; government is by a Privy Council and Council of Ministers, both presided over by the Sultan, and a Legislative Council.

Sultan Bolkiah was crowned in 1968 at the age of 22. He succeeded his father, Sir Omar Ali Saifuddin, who had abdicated.

Most of the inhabitants are Malays, Borneans, and Chinese. The majority of the population lives in and around the capital, situated on the Brunei River nine miles from its mouth.

CAYMAN ISLANDS

Status: Dependency
Governor: Thomas Russell (1974)
Area: 118 sq mi. (306 sq km)
Population (est. 1978): 14,000
Capital (1970 census): Georgetown (on Grand Cayman), 3,800
Monetary unit: Cayman Islands dollar

This dependency consists of three islands—Grand Cayman (76 sq mi; 197 sq km), Cayman Brac (22 sq mi; 57 sq km), and Little Cayman (20 sq mi; 52 sq km)—situated about 180 miles (290 km) northwest of Jamaica. They were dependencies of Jamaica until 1959, when they became a unit territory within the Federation of the West Indies. In 1962, upon the dissolution of the Federation, the Cayman Islands became a British dependency.

The islands' chief export is turtle products.

CHANNEL ISLANDS

Status: Crown dependencies
Lieutenant Governor of Jersey: Gen. Sir Desmond Fitzpatrick
Lieutenant Governor of Guernsey: Vice Adm. Sir John Martin (1974)
Area: 75 sq mi. (194 sq km)
Population (est. 1978): 125,000
Capital of Jersey: St. Helier
Capital of Guernsey: St. Peter Port
Monetary units: Guernsey pound; Jersey pound

This group of islands, lying in the English Channel off the northwest coast of France, is the only portion of the Duchy of Normandy belonging to the English Crown, to which it has been attached since the conquest of 1066. It was the only British possession occupied by Germany during World War II.

For purposes of government, the islands are divided into the Bailiwick of Jersey (45 sq mi.; 117 sq km) and the Bailiwick of Guernsey (30 sq mi.; 78 sq km), including Alderney (3 sq mi.; 7.8 sq km); Sark (2 sq mi.; 5.2 sq km), Herm, Jethou, etc. The islands are administered according to their own laws and customs by local governments. Acts of Parliament in London are not binding on the islands unless they are specifically mentioned. The Queen is represented in each Bailiwick by a Lieutenant Governor.

English is now the language in daily use, although the French patois is still spoken by some people. New legislation is drafted in English, but French has been retained for ceremonial purposes in the legislative bodies.

FALKLAND ISLANDS AND DEPENDENCIES

Status: Dependency
Governor: Rex Masterson Hunt (1980)

Area: 4,700 sq mi. (12,173 sq km)
Population: est. (1978): 2,000
Capital (est. 1978): Stanley (on East Falkland), 1,100
Monetary unit: Falkland Island pound

This sparsely inhabited dependency consists of a group of islands in the South Atlantic, about 250 miles (402 km) east of the South American mainland. The largest islands are East Falkland and West Falkland. Dependencies are South Georgia Island (1,450 sq mi.; 3,756 sq km), the South Sandwich Islands, and other islets. Three former dependencies—Graham Land, the South Shetland Islands, and the South Orkney Islands—were established as a new British dependency, the British Antarctic Territory, in 1962.

The chief industry is sheep raising and, apart from the production of wool, hides and skins, and tallow, there are no known resources. The whaling industry is carried on from South Georgia Island.

The chief export is wool.

GIBRALTAR

Status: Self-governing dependency
Governor: Sir William Jackson (1978)
Chief Minister: Sir Joshua Hassan
Area: 2.25 sq mi. (5.8 sq km)
Population (est. 1980): 30,000
Monetary unit: Gibraltar pound
Economic summary: Gross national product (1978): $110 million. Average annual growth rate (1970–77): 4.6%. Exports: re-exports of tobacco, petroleum, wine. Imports: manufactured goods, fuels, foodstuffs. Major trading partners: U.K., Morocco, Portugal, Netherlands.

Gibraltar, at the south end of the Iberian Peninsula, is a rocky promonotory commanding the western entrance to the Mediterranean. Aside from its strategic importance, it is also a free port, naval base, and coaling station. It was captured by the Arabs crossing from Africa into Spain in A.D. 711. In the 15th century, it passed to the Moorish ruler of Granada and later became Spanish. It was captured by an Anglo-Dutch force in 1704 during the War of the Spanish Succession and passed to Great Britain by the Treaty of Utrecht in 1713. Most of the inhabitants of Gibraltar are of Spanish, Italian, and Maltese descent.

Spanish efforts to recover Gibraltar culminated in a referendum in 1967 in which the residents voted overwhelmingly to retain their link with Britain. Spain sealed Gibraltar's land border in 1969 and did not open communications until April 1980, after the two governments had agreed to solve their dispute in keeping with a United Nations resolution calling for restoration of the "Rock" to Spain.

HONG KONG

Status: Dependency
Governor: Sir Crawford Murray MacLehose (1971)
Area: 398 sq mi. (1,031 sq km)
Population (est. 1980): 4,800,000
Capital (1976 census): Victoria (Hong Kong Island), 501,700
Monetary unit: Hong Kong dollar
Economic summary: Gross national product (1978): $14.1 billion. Average annual growth rate (1970–77): 5.8%. Per capita income (1976): $2,176. Labor force in agriculture: 2%; principal products: vegetables, rice, dairy products. Labor force in industry: 51%; major industrial products: textiles, clothing, toys, transistor radios, watches, electronic components. Exports: clothing, textiles, toys, watches, transistor radios, electronic components. Imports: raw materials, consumer goods, food. Major trading partners: U.S., U.K., Japan, West Germany, China.

The crown colony of Hong Kong comprises the island of Hong Kong (32 sq mi.; 83 sq km), Stonecutters' Island, Kowloon Peninsula, and the New Territories on the adjoining mainland. The island of Hong Kong, located at the mouth of the Pearl River about 90 miles (145 km) southeast of Canton, was ceded to the Britain in 1841.

Stonecutters' Island and Kowloon were annexed in 1860, and the New Territories, which are mainly agricultural lands, were leased from China in 1898 for 99 years. Hong Kong was attacked by Japanese troops Dec. 7, 1941, and surrendered the following Christmas. It remained under Japanese occupation until August 1945.

Possessing an excellent natural harbor, the only safe deep-sea anchorage between Shanghai and Southeast Asia, Hong Kong is the transshipment center for trade throughout southern China and the western Pacific.

The cities of Victoria and Kowloon contain the greater part of the population, which is overwhelmingly Chinese. Besides those Chinese engaged in agriculture or industry, many live in sampans or junks either in Victoria harbor or neighboring bays, supporting themselves by fishing or by performing labor on the wharves.

In 1974, Hong Kong rescinded a policy of accepting illegal immigrants from China that had, since 1968, made the crowded city a sanctuary for thousands of Chinese refugees.

ISLE OF MAN

Status: Dependency
Lieutenant Governor: Sir John Paul (1973)
Area: 227 sq mi. (588 sq km)
Population (est. 1978): 60,500
Capital (est. 1976): Douglas, 20,300
Monetary unit: Isle of Man pound

Situated in the Irish Sea, equidistant from Scotland, Ireland, and England, the Isle of Man is administered according to its own laws by a government composed of the Lieutenant Governor, a Legislative Council, and a House of Keys, one of the most ancient legislative assemblies in the world.

The chief exports are beef and lamb, fish, and livestock.

LEEWARD ISLANDS

See British Virgin Islands; Montserrat; West Indies Associated States

MONTSERRAT

Status: Dependency
Governor: G. Wyn Jones (1977)
Area: 40 sq mi. (104 sq km)
Population (est. 1978): 13,500
Capital (est. 1975): Plymouth, 1,260
Monetary unit: East Caribbean dollar

The island of Montserrat is in the Lesser Antilles of the West Indies. Until 1956, it was a division of the Leeward Islands. It did not join the West Indies Associated States established in 1967.

The chief exports are cattle, potatoes, cotton, lint, recapped tires, mangoes, tomatoes.

PITCAIRN ISLAND

Status: Dependency
Governor: Sir Harold Smedley
Island Magistrate: Pervis Young
Area: 1.75 sq mi. (4.5 sq km)
Population (est. 1979): 65
Capital: Adamstown

Pitcairn Island, in the South Pacific about midway between Australia and South America, consists of the island of Pitcairn and the three uninhabited islands of Henderson, Duicie, and Oeno. The island of Pitcairn was settled in 1790 by British mutineers from the ship *Bounty*, commanded by Capt. William Bligh. It was annexed as a British colony in 1838. Overpopulation forced removal of the settlement to Norfolk Island in 1856, but about 40 persons soon returned.

The colony is governed by a 10-member Council presided over by the Island Magistrate, who is elected for a three-year term.

ST. HELENA

Status: Dependency
Governor: G. C. Guy (1976)
Area: 47 sq mi. (122 sq km)
Population (est 1978): 5,200
Capital (est. 1978): Jamestown, 1,500
Monetary unit: Pound sterling

St. Helena is a volcanic island in the South Atlantic about 1,100 miles (1,770 km) from the west coast of Africa. It is famous as the place of exile of Napoleon (1815–21).

It was taken for England in 1659 by the East India Company and was brought under the direct government of the Crown in 1834.

St. Helena has two dependencies: Ascension (34 sq mi.; 88 sq km), an island about 700 miles (1,127 km) northwest of St. Helena; and Tristan da Cunha (40 sq mi.; 104 sq km), a group of six islands about 1,500 miles (2,414 km) south-southwest of St. Helena.

Leading suppliers in 1968 were U.K. (61%), South Africa (28%).

ST. KITTS-NEVIS

See West Indies Associated States

TURKS AND CAICOS ISLANDS

Status: Dependency
Governor: J. C. Strong
Area: 193 sq mi. (500 sq km)
Population (est. 1978): 6,200
Capital (est. 1977): Grand Turk, 2,900
Monetary unit: U.S. dollar

These two groups of islands are situated at the southeast end of the Bahamas. The principal islands in the Turks group are Grand Turk and Salt Cay; the principal ones in the Caicos group are South Caicos, East Caicos, Middle (or Grand) Caicos, North Caicos, Providenciales, and West Caicos.

The Turks and Caicos Islands were dependencies of Jamaica until 1959, when they became a unit territory within the Federation of the West Indies. In 1962, when Jamaica became independent, the Turks and Caicos became a British crown colony. The present Constitution has been in force since 1969.

Chief exports in 1974 were crayfish (73%) and conch (25%).

VIRGIN ISLANDS

See British Virgin Islands

WEST INDIES ASSOCIATED STATES

Status: Self-governing territories in free association with the United Kingdom, which is responsible for defense and external affairs. The British Government conducts its affairs with the West Indies Associated States through an official representative, whose office is in Bridgetown, Barbados.
British Representative: J. S. Arthur (1978)
Area: Antigua, 171 sq mi. (443 sq km); St. Christopher (Kitts)-Nevis-Anguilla, 153 sq mi. (397 sq km)
Population (est. 1980): Antigua, 80,000; St. Christopher (Kitts)-Nevis-Anguilla, 70,000
Capitals: Antigua: St. Johns, 23,500; St. Christopher (Kitts)-Nevis-Anguilla: Basseterre (on St. Kitts), 15,900
Monetary unit: East Caribbean dollar
Economic summary: Antigua: Gross national product (1978): $70 million. Average annual growth rate (1970–77): −3.7%. Per capita income: $720. Principal agricultural product: cotton. Major industries: oil refining, tourism. Exports: petroleum products, cotton. Imports: crude oil, foodstuffs, clothing. Major trading partners: U.K., U.S., Commonwealth Caribbean countries. St. Christopher–Nevis–Anguilla: Gross domestic product (1977): $32 million. Per capita income: $580. Principal agricultural products: sugar, cotton. Major industries: sugar processing, salt extraction. Exports: sugar, molasses, cotton, salt, copra. Imports: foodstuffs, fuel, manufactured goods. Major trading partners: U.S., U.K., Japan.

The West Indies Associated States were established in 1967 and consisted of Antigua and St. Kitts-Nevis-Anguilla of the Leeward Islands, and Dominica, Grenada, St. Lucia, and St. Vincent of the Windward Islands. Statehood for St. Vincent was held up until 1969 because of local political uncertainties. (Grenada became independent in 1974, Dominica in 1978, and St. Lucia and St. Vincent in 1979.)

Two members of the Leeward group—the British Virgin Islands and Montserrat—did not become Associated States.

Each of the Associated States is fully self-governing in its internal affairs.

The association between Britain and each state is to be free and voluntary. As a guarantee of its voluntary nature, association will be terminable by either party. On termination of association, the state would become independent of Britain.

In 1967, Anguilla declared its independence from the St. Kitts-Nevis-Anguilla federation. Britain however, did not recognize this action. In February 1969, Anguilla voted to cut all ties with Britain and become an independent republic. In March, Britain landed troops on the island and, on March 30, a truce was signed. In July 1971, Anguilla became a dependency of Britain and two months later Britain ordered the withdrawal of all its troops.

A new Constitution for Anguilla, effective in February 1976, provides for separate administration and a government of elected representatives. The Associated State of St. Kitts-Nevis-Anguilla remains in being, but Anguilla has a separate relationship with Britain.

WINDWARD ISLANDS

See West Indies Associated States

UPPER VOLTA

Republic of Upper Volta
President: Gen. Sangoulé Lamizana (1966)
Premier: Joseph Conombo (1978)
Area: 105,870 sq mi. (274,200 sq km)
Population (est 1980): 6,900,000
Density per square mile: 65.2
Capital and largest city (est. 1975): Ouagadougou, 168,600
Monetary unit: Franc CFA
Ethnic groups: Mossis, Bobos
Languages: French, African languages
Religion: Animist, 50%; Islam, 17%; Roman Catholic, 8%
National name: République de Haute-Volta
Freedom House classifications: Capitalist pre-industrial, multi-party centralized
Economic summary: Gross national product (1978): $870 million. Average annual growth rate (1970–77): 1.6%. Per capita income (1977): $113. Average rate of inflation: 12%. Labor force in agriculture: 95%; principal products: millet, sorghum, corn, rice, livestock, peanuts, sugar cane, cotton. Major industrial products: processed agricultural products, light industrial items, brick, brewed products. Natural resources: manganese, limestone, marble, gold, uranium, bauxite, copper. Exports: livestock, peanuts, cotton. Imports: textiles, food and consumer goods, transport equipment, machinery, fuels. Major trading partners: Ivory Coast, France, Ghana, Western European nations.

Geography. Slightly larger than Colorado, Upper Volta is a landlocked country in West Africa. Its neighbors are the Ivory Coast, Mali, Niger, Benin, Togo, and Ghana. The country consists of extensive plains, low hills, high savannas, and a desert area in the north.

Government. Under a Constitution adopted by referendum in 1977, executive power is vested in a President elected by popular vote for a four-year term. Legislative power rests with a 57-member National Assembly elected for four years.

History. Upper Volta consists chiefly of the lands of the Mossi Empire, where France established a protectorate over the Kingdom of Ouagadougou in 1897. Upper Volta became a separate colony in 1919, was partitioned among Niger, the Sudan, and the Ivory Coast in 1933 and was reconstituted in 1947. An autonomous republic within the French Community, it became independent on Aug. 5, 1960.

President Maurice Yameogo was deposed on Jan. 3, 1966, by a military coup led by Col. Sangoulé Lamizana, who dissolved the National Assembly and suspended the Constitution. A new Constitution was adopted later that year and a new Assembly was elected. However, dissension within the Volta Democratic Union, the major party, led to renewed military rule. Constitutional rule returned in 1978 with the election of an Assembly and a presidential vote in June in which Gen. Lamizana won by a narrow margin over three other candidates.

In 1973, Upper Volta formed, with six other nations, the Economic Community for West Africa to promote economic development in the region.

After a referendum favoring a return to civilian rule, the first legislative elections in four years took place in 1978. The Volta Democratic Union won 28 of the National Assembly's 57 seats. Lamizana was elected President on May 28, defeating Macaire Ouedraogo.

URUGUAY

Oriental Republic of Uruguay
President: Aparicio Méndez (1976)
Area: 68,548 sq mi. (177,539 sq km)
Population (est. 1980): 2,900,000
Density per square mile: 42.3
Capital and largest city (est. 1975): Montevideo, 1,229,700
Monetary unit: New peso
Language: Spanish
Religion: Roman Catholic
National name: República Oriental del Uruguay
Freedom House classifications: Capitalist-socialist industrial, non-party military
Economic summary: Gross national product (1978): $4.7 billion. Average annual growth rate (1970–77): 1.3%. Per capita income (1976): $1,090. Land used for agriculture: 85%; labor force: 8%; principal products: livestock, grains. Labor force in industry: 34%; major products: processed meats, wool and hides, textiles, shoes, handbags and leather wearing apparel, cement, refined petroleum. Natural resources: hydroelectric power potential. Exports: meat, hides, shoes, leather products, furs, wool, fish. Imports: fuels, chemicals, machinery, metals. Major trading partners: U.S., Brazil, Argentina.

Geography. Uruguay, on the east coast of South America south of Brazil and east of Argentina, is comparable in size to the State of Washington.

The country consists of a low, rolling plain in the south and a low plateau in the north. It has a 120-mile (193 km) Atlantic shore line, a 235-mile (378 km) frontage on the Rio de la Plata, and 270 miles (435 km) on the Uruguay River, its western boundary.

Government. The President serves for a term of five years. He appoints a Council of 11 ministers to assist him. Before it was dissolved, Congress consisted of the Senate and the House of Deputies. Members remained in office for five years.

In June 1973, President Juan María Bordaberry yielded to military pressure and dissolved Congress, thus ending 40 years of constitutional rule. His decree announced creation of a Council of State to perform Congressional functions, oversee presidential activities, and formulate constitutional reforms for a national plebiscite.

Political activity has been banned since 1973.

History. Juan Díaz de Solis, a Spaniard, discovered Uruguay in 1516, but the Portuguese were first to settle it when they founded Colonia in 1680. After a long struggle, Spain wrested the country from Portugal in 1778. Uruguay revolted against Spain in 1811, only to be conquered in 1816–20 by the Portuguese from Brazil. Independence was reasserted with Argentine help in 1825, and the republic was set up in 1830.

Independence, however, did not restore order, and a revolt in 1836 touched off nearly 50 years of factional strife, with occasional armed intervention from Argentina and Brazil.

Alberto Heber, who became President in 1966, vigorously championed reform, and a referendum authorized revision of the Constitution to vest executive powers in a President and a Cabinet of Ministers. Oscar Diego Gestido, elected President later that year, devoted much effort to improving the ailing economy. But he died the next year and was succeeded by Jorge Pacheco Areco.

Siege-state regulations were instituted after the Tupámaros first urban guerrilla organization launched a series of spectacular kidnappings, bank and casino robberies (one gold haul netted over $250,000), and arms raids on military arsenals to embarrass what was then the most democratic government in South America. In 1970, the Tupámaros kidnapped a U.S. aid adviser, Dan Mitrione, and killed him when their ransom demands were not met.

The continuing economic, political, and guerrilla problems precipitated impeachment proceedings against Pacheco in 1971. A bitterly fought election followed, with Juan María Bordaberry, Pacheco's hand-picked choice, the winner.

Disputes between the government and the military, coupled with worsening economic problems (the peso was devalued 32 times during Bordaberry's first three years in office), led to a military revolt in February 1973 that ended in an agreement with Bordaberry in which the military promised to maintain the constitutional system but virtually took over control of the government.

Despite the military takeover, inflation soared at a 100% yearly rate and the Tupámaros continued to be active. Their assassinations and bombings were matched by government repression; an estimated 3,500 persons were arrested on political charges in the year after Congress was dissolved, and the press was kept tightly in line.

Military leaders, citing Bordaberry's opposition to the return of constitutional government, removed him from office in 1976. The National Council of 25 military officers and 21 civilians designated Aparicio Méndez to take over the Presidency for a five-year term.

Although the government in 1977 reported that sentences for political prisoners would be reduced, Amnesty International estimated that 5,000 such prisoners were being held in Uruguay, more than in any other Latin nation. The Carter Administration cut economic aid from $220,000 to $25,000 and eliminated military sales credits of $3 million for Uruguay because of the human-rights situation. The Uruguayan government then declared that it would refuse any U.S. aid. In the summer of 1977, the government announced that the country would return to civil rule through general elections in 1981.

VANUATU

Republic of Vanuatu
President: George Sokomanu (1980)
Prime Minster: Rev. Walter Lini (1980)
Area: 5,700 sq mi. (14,763,sq km)
Population (est. 1980): 110,000
Density per square mile: 19.3
Capital (est. 1976): Vila (metropolitan area): 17,400
Monetary unit: Pound
Religion: Christian
Economic Summary: Gross national product (1978): $60 million. Average annual growth rate (1970–77): 1.8%. Principal agricultural products: copra, cocoa, coffee, livestock. Exports: copra, cocoa, coffee, frozen fish. Major trading partners: France, U.S., Japan.

Geography. Formerly known as the New Hebrides, Vanuatu is an archipelago of some 80 islands lying between New Caledonia and Fiji in the South Pacific. Largest of the islands is Espiritu Santo (875 sq mi.; 2,266 sq km); others are Efate, Malekula, Malo, Pentecost, and Tanna. The population is largely Melanesian of mixed blood.

Government. The constitution by which Vanuatu achieved independence on July 30, 1980, vests executive authority in a President, elected by an electoral college for a five-year term. A unicameral legislature of 39 members exercises legislative power. The Vanuaaku party, led by Prime Minister Walter Lini, holds 26 seats.

History. The islands were discovered by Pedro Fernandes de Queiros of Portugal in 1606 and were charted and named by the British navigator James Cook in 1774. Conflicting British and French interests were resolved by a joint naval commission that administered the islands from 1887. A condominium government was established in 1906.

The islands' plantation economy, based on imported Vietnamese labor, was prosperous until the 1920s, when markets for its products declined. The New Hebrides escaped Japanese occupation in World War II and the French population was among the first to support the Gaullist Free French movement.

A brief rebellion by French settlers and plantation workers on Espiritu Santo led by Jimmy Stevens in May 1980 threatened the scheduled independence of the islands. Britain sent a company of Royal Marines and France a contingent of 50 policemen to quell the revolt, which the new government said was financed by the Phoenix Foundation, a right-wing U.S. group. With the British and French forces replaced by soldiers from Papua New Guinea, independence ceremonies took place on July 30. The next month it was reported that Stevens had been arrested and the revolt quelled.

VATICAN CITY STATE

Ruler: Pope John Paul II (1978)
Area: 0.17 sq mi. (0.44 sq km)
Population (est. 1980): 1,000 (Italian, 85%; Swiss and others, 15%)
Density per square mile: 5,882.4
Monetary unit: Lira
Languages: Latin, Italian
Religion: Roman Catholic
National name: Stato della Città del Vaticano

Geography. The Vatican City State is situated on the Vatican hill, on the right bank of the Tiber River, within the commune of Rome.

Government. The Pope has full legal, executive, and judicial powers. Executive power over the area is in the hands of a Commission of Cardinals appointed by the Pope. The College of Cardinals is the Pope's chief advisory body, and upon his death the cardinals elect his successor for life. The cardinals themselves are created for life by the Pope.

In the Vatican the central administration of the Roman Catholic Church throughout the world is carried on by 11 congregations, three tribunals, three main secretariats, and numerous councils, committees, and commissions. In its diplomatic relations, the Holy See is represented by the Papal Secretary of State.

History. The Vatican City State, sovereign and independent, together with the Lateran palaces, have been intimately associated with the history of the Roman Catholic Church since the martyrdom of St. Peter. From these areas the Pope exercised temporal sway for many centuries over a large part of central Italy; in 1859, the Papal States comprised an area of some 17,000 square miles (44,030 sq km). During the struggle for Italian unification, from 1860 to 1870, most of this area became part of Italy.

By an Italian law of May 13, 1871, the temporal power of the Pope was abrogated, and the territory of the Papacy was confined to the Vatican and Lateran palaces and the villa of Castel Gandolfo. The Popes consistently refused to recognize this arrangement and, by the Lateran Treaty of Feb. 11, 1929, between the Vatican and the Kingdom of Italy, the exclusive dominion and sovereign jurisdiction of the Holy See over the city of the Vatican was again recognized, thus restoring the Pope's temporal authority over the area.

The first session of Ecumenical Council Vatican II was opened by John XXIII on Oct. 11, 1962, to plan and set policies for the modernization of the Roman Catholic Church. Pope Paul VI continued the Council, opening the second session on Sept. 29, 1963.

On Aug. 26, 1978, Cardinal Albino Luciani was chosen by the College of Cardinals to succeed Paul VI, who had died of a heart attack on Aug. 6. The new Pope, who took the name John Paul I, was born on Oct. 17, 1912, at Forno di Canale in Italy.

Pope John Paul I succeeded a pontiff who stood implacably against relaxing the church's traditional stand against birth control, on the Latin rite's insistence upon clerical celibacy, and on conservatism in theological speculation. During his reign, however, he paid much attention to improving ecumenical relations with other denominations.

(For a listing of all the Popes, *see* the Index.)

Only 34 days after his election, John Paul I died of a heart attack, ending the shortest reign in 373 years. On Oct. 16, Cardinal Karol Wojtyla, 58, was chosen Pope and took the name John Paul II. The first Polish Pope was also the first to have been named from a communist nation.

John Paul II visited his homeland in June 1979, exhorting millions to "never lose your spiritual freedom" and telling workers that Christ would not accept that man be considered "merely as a means of production." The trip was a triumph for the warm, outgoing Pontiff despite the Polish government's undisguised efforts to dampen the public impact of his visit.

A visit to the Irish Republic and to the United States in September and October 1979, followed by a 12-nation African tour in May 1980 and a visit in July to Brazil, the most populous Catholic nation, further established John Paul's image as a "people's" Pope. But he also used his travels to preach a more conservative doctrine, cautioning U.S. nuns against seeking priestly functions and sternly opposing abortion and contraception. During his African journey, he reaffirmed long-ignored canon laws against political roles for the clergy, prompting the retirement announcement of the only Catholic priest ever elected to the U.S. Congress, Rep. Robert F. Drinan, a Massachusetts Democrat.

VENEZUELA

Republic of Venezuela
President: Luis Herrera Campíns (1979)
Area: 352,143 sq mi. (912,050 sq km)
Population (est. 1980): 13,925,000 (mestizo, 69%; white, 20%; black, 9%; Indian, 2%)
Density per square mile: 39.5
Capital: Caracas
Largest cities (est. 1979 for metropolitan area): Caracas, 2,850,000; **(est. 1976 by U.N.):** Maracaibo, 792,000; Valencia, 439,000; Maracay, 301,000
Monetary unit: Bolívar
Language: Spanish
Religion: Roman Catholic
National name: República de Venezuela
Freedom House classifications: Capitalist-statist industrial, multi-party centralized
Economic summary: Gross national product (1978): $40.7 billion. Average annual growth rate (1970–77): 3.2%. Per capita income: $2,590. Land used for agriculture: 2%; labor force, 24%; principal products: rice, coffee, corn, sugar, bananas, dairy, meat, and poultry products. Labor force in industry, 23%; principal products: refined petroleum products, iron and steel, paper products, aluminum, textiles, transport equipment. Natural resources: petroleum, natural gas, iron ore, gold, hydroelectric power. Exports: petroleum, iron ore, cocoa, coffee. Imports: machinery and transport equipment, manufactures, chemicals, foodstuffs. Major trading partners: U.S., West Germany, Japan.

Geography. Venezuela, a third larger than Texas, occupies most of the northern coast of South America on the Caribbean Sea. It is bordered by Colombia to the west, Guyana to the east, and Brazil to the south.

Mountain systems break Venezuela into four distinct areas: (1) the Maracaibo lowlands; (2) the mountainous region in the north and northwest; (3) the Orinoco basin, with the llanos (vast grass-covered plains) on its northern border and great forest areas in the south and southeast; (4) the Guiana Highlands, south of the Orinoco, accounting for nearly half the national territory. About 80% of Venezuela is drained by the Orinoco and its tributaries.

Government. Venezuela is a federal republic consisting of 20 states, the Federal District, two territories and 72 islands in the Caribbean. There is a bicameral Congress, the 52 members of the Senate and the 213 members of the Chamber of Deputies being elected by popular vote to five-year terms. The President is also elected for five years. He must be a Venezuelan by birth and over 30 years old. He is not eligible for re-election until 10 years after the end of his term.

The major political parties are the Democratic Action Party, with 23 of 52 Senate seats and 83 of 213 seats in the Chamber of Deputies; Social Christian Party, with 22 Senate seats and 83 Chamber seats, People's Electoral Movement, Democratic Republican Union.

History. Columbus discovered Venezuela on his third voyage in 1498. A subsequent Spanish explorer gave the country its name, meaning "Little Venice." There were no important settlements until Caracas was founded in 1567. Simón Bolívar, who led the liberation of much of the continent from Spain, was born in Caracas in 1783. With Bolívar taking part, Venezuela was one of the first South American colonies to revolt against Spain, in 1810, but it was not until 1821 that independence was won. Federated at first with Colombia and Ecuador, the country set up a republic in 1830 and then sank for many decades into a condition of revolt, dictatorship, and corruption.

From 1908 to 1935, Gen. Juan Vicente Gómez ruled tyrannically, picking satellites to alternate with him in the presidential palace. Thereafter, there was a struggle between democratic forces and those backing a return to strong-man rule. Dr. Rómulo Betancourt and the liberal Acción Democrática Party won a majority of seats in a constituent assembly to draft a new Constitution in 1946. A well-known writer, Rómulo Gallegos, candidate of Betancourt's party, easily won the presidential election of 1947. But, the army ousted Gallegos the next year and instituted a military junta.

Following elections in 1952, the junta presented its resignations to the army, which named Col. Marcos Pérez Jiménez as Provisional President. He re-established strongman rule. But the country overthrew the dictatorship in 1958 and thereafter enjoyed democratic government. Rafael Caldera Rodríguez, President from 1969 to 1974, legalized the Communist Party and established diplomatic relations with Moscow.

Venezuela and neighboring Guyana in 1970 called a 12-year moratorium on their border dispute (Venezuela claims 50,000 square miles of Guyana's 83,000).

As a charter member of the Organization of Petroleum Exporting Countries (OPEC), Venezuela shared the benefits of the tripled oil prices engineered by OPEC, but did not join the 1973 Arab oil boycott. President Carlos Andrés Pérez took office in 1974, committed to give all Venezuelans a stake in the oil bonanza that made his country the richest in South America.

In 1976, Venezuela nationalized 21 oil companies, mostly subsidiaries of U.S. firms, offering compensation of $1.28 billion. Oil income in that year was $9.9 billion, and although production decreased 2.2%, revenue remained at the same level in 1977 because of higher prices, largely financing an ambitious social welfare program.

A continuing decline in oil production as world markets slackened forced the government to impose austerity measures early in 1978.

Despite his difficulties at home, Pérez continued to play an active foreign role in extending economic aid to Latin neighbors, in backing the human—rights policy of President Carter, and in supporting Carter's return of the Panama Canal to Panama.

Opposition Christian Democrats capitalized on Pérez's domestic problems to elect Luis Herrera Campíns President in Venezuela's fifth consecutive free election, on Dec. 3, 1978. At his inauguration in March 1979, Herrera called for "fiscal discipline" to reduce a record foreign debt of $7.4 billion despite soaring oil revenues.

Venezuela was host to the OPEC meeting on Dec. 20, 1979, that abandoned uniform pricing and permitted Venezuela to raise its own price to an avarage of $26 a barrel in January 1980. Despite its position as the largest Latin producer (2.35 million barrels a day in 1979, of which 1.9 million were exported), Venezuela's continuing balance of payments deficit forced the government to seek foreign loans to pay a debt estimated in January at $13.3 billion.

VIETNAM

Socialist Republic of Vietnam
President (acting): Nguyen Huu Tho (1980)
Premier: Pham Van Dong (1976)
Area: 126,436 sq mi. (327,469 sq km)
Population (est. 1980): 52,300,000
Density per square mile: 413.6
Capital Hanoi
Largest cities (est. 1976): Ho Chi Minh City (Saigon),[1] 3,460,500; Hanoi, 1,443,500; (est. 1973): Da Nang, 492,200; Na Trang, 216,200; Qui Non, 213,750; Hue, 209,000; **(1960 census):** Haiphong, 182,490
Monetary unit: Dong
Languages: Vietnamese, French, Chinese
Religions: Buddhist, Roman Catholic, Cao-Dai, Hoa-Hao, Confucian, Animist
National name: Công Hòa Xa Hôi Chú Nghia Viêt Nam
Freedom House classifications: Socialist industrial, one-party communist
Economic summary: Gross national product (1978): $8.9 billion. Per capita income: $140. Labor force in agriculture: 70%; principal products: rice, rubber, fruits and vegetables, corn, sugar cane, fish. Labor force in industry, 8%; major products: processed foods, textiles, cement, chemical fertilizers, glass, tires. Natural resources: forests, coal. Exports: agricultural products, coal, mineral ores. Imports: petroleum, steel products, railroad equipment, chemicals, medicines, raw cotton, fertilizer, grain. Major trading partners: U.S.S.R., Soviet bloc nations, Japan.

Geography. Vietnam occupies the eastern and southern part of the Indochinese peninsula in Southeast Asia, with the South China Sea along its entire coast. China is to the north and Laos and Cambodia to the west. Long and narrow on a north-south axis, Vietnam is about twice the size of Arizona.

The Mekong River delta lies in the south and the Red River delta in the north. Heavily forested mountain and plateau regions make up most of the country.

Government. Less than a year after the capitulation of the former Republic of Vietnam (South Vietnam) on April 30, 1975, a joint National Assembly convened with 249 deputies representing the North and 243 representing the South. The Assembly set July 2, 1976, as the official reunification date. Hanoi became the capital and Ton Duc Thang, President of the Northern regime since 1969, became President of the new republic.

Pham Van Dong, Premier in Hanoi since 1955, took over the new administration, and the Northern flag, anthem, and crest became the symbols of the new Vietnam. The only concession to the former Provisional Revolutionary Government of South Vietnam, which nominally administered the South in the interim period of less than a year after South Vietnam surrendered, was the installation of its President, Nguyen Huu Tho, as one of two Vice Presidents.

Dang Cong san Vietnam (Communist Party), led by First Secretary Le Duan, is the only political party.

History. The Vietnamese are descendants of Mongoloid nomads from China and migrants from Indonesia. They recognized Chinese suzerainty until the 15th century, an era of nationalistic expansion, when Cambodians were pushed out of the southern area of what is now Vietnam.

A century later, the Portuguese were the first Europeans to enter the area. France established its influence early in the 19th century and within 80 years conquered the three regions into which the country was then divided—Cochin-China in the south, Annam in the center, and Tonkin in the north.

France first unified Vietnam in 1887, when a single governor-generalship was created, followed by

1. Includes suburb of Cholon.

the first physical links between north and south—a rail and road system. Even at the beginning of World War II, however, there were internal differences among the three regions.

Japan took over military bases in Vietnam in 1940 and a pro-Vichy French administration remained until 1945. A veteran Communist leader, Ho Chi Minh, organized an independence movement known as the Vietminh to exploit a confused situation. At the end of the war, Ho's followers seized Hanoi and declared a short-lived republic, which ended with the arrival of French forces in 1946.

Paris proposed a unified government within the French Union under the former Annamite emperor, Bao Dai. Cochin-China and Annam accepted the proposal, and Bao Dai was proclaimed emperor of all Vietnam in 1949. Ho and the Vietminh withheld support, and the revolution in China gave them the outside help needed for a war of resistance against French and Vietnamese troops armed largely by the U.S.

A bitter defeat at Dien Bien Phu in northwest Vietnam on May 5, 1954, broke the French military campaign and brought the division of Vietnam at the conference of Geneva that year. More than 1 million North Vietnamese, mainly Christians, fled south across the 17th parallel dividing line.

In the new South, Ngo Dinh Diem, Premier under Bao Dai, deposed the monarch in 1955 and established a republic with himself as President. Diem used strong U.S. backing to create an authoritarian regime that suppressed all opposition but could not eradicate the Northern-supplied Communist Viet Cong.

Skirmishing grew into a full-scale war, with escalating U.S. involvement. A military coup, U.S.-inspired in the view of many, ousted Diem Nov. 1, 1963, and a kaleidoscope of military governments followed. The most savage fighting of the war occurred in early 1968, during the Tet holidays.

Although the Viet Cong failed to overthrow the Saigon government, U.S. public reaction to the apparently endless war forced a limitation of U.S. troops to 550,000 and a new emphasis on shifting the burden of further combat to the South Vietnamese. Ho Chi Minh's death on Sept. 3, 1969, brought a quadrumvirate to replace him but no flagging in Northern will to fight.

U.S. bombing and invasion of Cambodia in the summer of 1970—an effort to destroy Viet Cong bases in the neighboring state—marked the end of major U.S. participation in the fighting. Most American ground troops were withdrawn from combat by mid-1971 as heavy bombing of the Ho Chi Minh trail from North Vietnam appeared to cut the supply of men and matériel to the South.

Secret negotiations for peace by Secretary of State Henry A. Kissinger with North Vietnamese officials during 1972 after heavy bombing of Hanoi and Haiphong brought the two sides near agreement in October. When the Northerners demanded the removal of the South's President Nguyen Van Thieu as their price, President Nixon ordered the "Christmas bombing" of the North. The conference resumed and a peace settlement was signed in Paris on Jan. 27, 1973. It called for release of all U.S. prisoners, withdrawal of U.S. forces, limitation of both sides' forces inside South Vietnam, and a commitment to peaceful reunification.

Despite Chinese and Soviet endorsement, the agreement foundered in a welter of charges and countercharges—the North asserting that the U.S. was violating the limitation on arms supplies, Washington and Saigon accusing Hanoi of infiltrating troops to the south. U.S. bombing of Communist-held areas in Cambodia was halted by Congress in August 1973, and in the following year Communist action in South Vietnam increased.

An armored attack across the 17th parallel in January 1975 panicked the South Vietnamese army and brought the invasion within 40 miles of Saigon by April 9. Thieu resigned on April 21 and fled, to be replaced by Vice President Tran Van Huong, who quit a week later, turning over the office to Gen. Duong Van Minh. "Big Minh" surrendered Saigon on April 30, ending a war that took 1.3 million Vietnamese and 56,000 American lives, at the cost of $141 billion in U.S. aid.

U.S. helicopters evacuated 1,373 Americans and 5,595 Vietnamese from Saigon in the final days, and 135,000 other South Vietnamese escaped in small boats to seek refuge in the U.S. Congress appropriated $405 million to resettle 130,000 refugees—mostly Vietnamese—in the U.S.

Although the new regime in the South at first appeared to be taking a moderate line, "re-education" of former South Vietnamese government and army personnel began immediately. By mid-1976, virtually all foreigners were expelled, even those married to Vietnamese. There were reports of pressure on city residents to return to the countryside, although there was no forced exodus as in Cambodia. There were also reports that Northern carpetbaggers were moving into government posts in the South.

On May 3, 1977, the U.S. and Vietnam opened negotiations in Paris to normalize relations. One of the first results was the withdrawal of U.S. opposition to Vietnamese membership in the United Nations, formalized in the Security Council on July 20 when the Council accepted the application without a vote. Two major issues remained to be settled, however: the return of the bodies of some 2,500 U.S. servicemen missing in the war and the claim by Hanoi that former President Nixon had promised reconstruction aid under the 1973 agreement.

Negotiations failed to resolve these issues, and the question of recognition appeared to have been shelved indefinitely when the U.S. expelled the Vietnamese Ambassador to the United Nations, Dinh Ba Thi, early in 1978. Thi was accused of complicity in an espionage case in which a U.S. citizen and a Vietnamese refugee were later convicted of delivering U.S. intelligence to Hanoi.

The new year also brought an intensification of border clashes between Vietnam and Cambodia and accusations by China that Chinese residents of Vietnam were being subjected to persecution. Peking cut off all aid and withdrew 800 technicians.

By June, 133,000 ethnic Chinese were reported to have fled Vietnam, and a year later as many as 500,000 of the 1.8 million Vietnamese of Chinese ancestry were believed to have escaped. Half of these had gone by land or sea to China, where the government made it clear that no more refugees were welcome and tens of thousands more had survived boat passage to Thailand, Malaysia, Indonesia, or Hong Kong. U.S. officials said 100,000 may have died. Survivors said they had paid up to $5,000 in bribes to leave Vietnam, and U.S. and British officials charged Hanoi with a deliberate extortion policy.

Replying to worldwide criticism, Premier Pham Van Dong said only that he would try to limit the outflow. Other Vietnamese officials dismissed the "boat people" as misfits the government was unwilling and unable to keep in the country.

Hanoi was undoubtedly preoccupied with a continuing war in Cambodia, where 60,000 Vietnamese troops were aiding the Heng Samrin regime in suppressing the last forces of the pro-Chinese Pol Pot regime. In early 1979, Vietnam was conducting a two-front war, defending its northern border against a Chinese invasion and at the same time supporting its army in Cambodia.

Only a Soviet veto prevented Vietnam from being labeled an aggressor by the U.N. Security Council as Prince Shihanouk of Cambodia, released from house arrest by the Pol Pot regime, presented the case against Hanoi after the fall of Phnom Penh. Vietnam's ambassador, backed by the Soviet Union and the Soviet bloc, sought condemnation of Peking's invasion but could find no sympathizers.

Despite Hanoi's claims of total victory, resistance in Cambodia continued in 1980. By June, Vietnamese troops were raiding Thai territory in an attempt to wipe out guerrilla bases across the border, prompting the United States to send emergency arms aid to Thailand in July. Vietnam's second conflict, on its border with China, also flared sporadically following Peking's breakoff of peace talks in March.

(For a Vietnam War chronology, see Headline History.)

WESTERN SAMOA

Independent State of Western Samoa
Head of State: Malietoa Tanumafili II (1962)
Prime Minister: Taisi Tupuola Efi (1976)
Area: 1,133 sq mi. (2,934 sq km)
Population (est. 1980): 155,000
Density per square mile: 136.8
Capital and largest city (1976 census): Apia, 32,100
Monetary unit: Tala
Languages: Samoan and English
Religions: Congregational, 50%; Roman Catholic, 22%; Methodist, 16%
National name: Samoa i Sísifo
Member of Commonwealth of Nations
Freedom House classifications: Capitalist pre-industrial, non-party non-military
Economic summary: Gross national product (1978): $70 million. Per capita income: $290. Average rate of inflation: (1973–77): 12%. Land used for agriculture: 50%; labor force: 50%; principal products: copra, cocoa, bananas, timber. Labor force in industry: 10%; major products: timber, light industrial products. Natural resource: timber. Exports: copra, cocoa, bananas, foodstuffs. Major trading partners: Australia, New Zealand, Netherlands, Japan.

Geography. Western Samoa, the size of Rhode Island, is in the South Pacific Ocean about 2,200 miles (3,540 km) south of Hawaii midway to Sydney, Australia, and about 800 miles (1,287 km) northeast of Fiji. The larger islands in the Samoan chain are mountainous and of volcanic origin. There is little level land except in the coastal areas, where most cultivation takes place.

Government. Western Samoa has a 47-member Legislature, consisting mainly of the titleholders (chiefs) of family or tribal groups, with two members elected by universal suffrage to represent those not belonging to such groups. When the present Chiefs of State die, successors will be elected by the Legislature.

History. The Samoan islands were discovered in the 18th century and visited by Dutch and French traders. Toward the end of the 19th century, conflicting interests of the U.S., Britain, and Germany resulted in a treaty signed in 1899. It recognized the paramount interests of the U.S. in those islands east of 171° west longitude (American Samoa) and Germany's interests in the other islands (Western Samoa); the British withdrew in return for recognition of their rights in Tonga and the Solomons.

New Zealand occupied Western Samoa in 1914, and was granted a League of Nations mandate. In 1947, the islands became a U.N. trust territory administered by New Zealand.

Western Samoa became independent on Jan. 1, 1962.

YEMEN

People's Democratic Republic of Yemen
President: Ali Nasser Mohammed (1980)
Area: 111,000 sq mi. (287,490 sq km)[1]
Population (est. 1980): 1,950,000[1]
Density per square mile: 17.6[1]
National capital and largest city (est. 1977 for metropolitan area by U.N.): Aden, 285,400
Administrative capital: Madinat ash Sha'b
Monetary unit: Yemen dinar
Language: Arabic
Religion: Islam
National name: Jumhurijah al-Yemen al Dimuqratiyah al Sha'abijah
Freedom House classifications: Socialist pre-industrial, one-party socialist
Economic summary: Gross national product (1978): $740 million. Average annual growth rate (1970–77): 11.2%. Per capita income: $290. Land used for agriculture: 0.3%; labor force: 70–80%; principal products: sorghum, millet, wheat, cotton, coffee. Labor force in industry: 2–3%; major products: refined oil products, salt, fish meal, cloth. Natural resource: fish. Exports: petroleum products, textiles, cotton. Imports: crude oil, foodstuffs, manufactured goods. Major trading partners: U.K., Japan, Iran, Kuwait, Yemen Arab Republic.

Geography. Formerly known as Southern Yemen, the People's Democratic Republic of Yemen extends along the southern part of the Arabian Peninsula on the Gulf of Aden and the Indian Ocean. It is comparable in size to Nevada. The Yemen Arab Republic is to the northwest, Saudia Arabia to the north, and Oman to the east.

A 700-mile (1,130-km) narrow coastal plain gives way to a mountainous region and then a plateau area.

Government. On June 23, 1969, President Qahtan Mohammed al Shaabi resigned and was replaced by a five-man Presidential Council.

A Constitution published in 1970 changed the state's name from Southern Yemen and established a 101-seat legislature, the People's Supreme Council. The only legal political party is the Yemeni Socialist Party.

History. The People's Republic of Southern Yemen was established Nov. 30, 1967, when Britain granted independence to the Federation of South

1. Excluding Perim and Kamaran islands.

Arabia. This Federation consisted of the state (once the colony) of Aden and 16 of the 20 states of the Protectorate of South Arabia (once the Aden Protectorate). The four states of the Protectorate that did not join the Federation later became part of Southern Yemen.

Salim Robea Ali, Chairman of the Presidential Council since its establishment in 1969, was ousted and executed June 26, 1978, two days after the assassination of President Ahmed Hussein al-Ghashmi of the Yemen Arab Republic. Premier Ali Nasser Mohammed assumed the added duty of Council head.

Abdul Fattah Ismail, Secretary General of the ruling party who was elected President by the Supreme Council on Dec. 27, 1978, reversed Robea's movement toward reconciliation with the Yemen Arab Republic and an accommodation with Saudi Arabia. Despite Fattah Ismail's acquiescence to the continuing build-up of Soviet military strength in the country in conjunction with the Soviet invasion of Afghanistan, he proved to be an embarrassment to Moscow. His sudden resignation on April 21, 1980, was reported to have stemmed from the new Soviet desire to win friends in the Yemen Arab Republic and Saudi Arabia.

With the opening of reunification talks between the new President, Ali Nasser Mohammed, and the Yemen Arab Republic's Premier, Abdul Aziz Abdulghani, and the shipment of Soviet arms to the North, the prospect for both a unified Yemen and a larger Soviet role in the Arabian Peninsula appeared.

YEMEN ARAB REPUBLIC

Chief of State: Lieut. Col. Ali Abdulla Saleh (1978)
Premier: Abdul Aziz Abdulghani (1975)
Area: 75,290 sq mi. (195,000 sq km)
Population (est. 1980): 5,940,000
Density per square mile: 78.9
Capital and largest city (est. 1975): San'a', 134,600
Monetary unit: Rial
Language: Arabic
Religion: Islam
National name: Al Jamhuriya al Arabiya Yamaniya
Freedom House classifications: Capitalist pre-industrial, non-party military
Economic summary: Gross national product (1978): $3 billion. Per capita income: $180. Land used for agriculture: 42%; labor force: 73%; principal products: wheat, sorghum, cattle, sheep, cotton, fruits. Major industrial products: consumer goods, construction materials. Natural resources: traces of copper, sulfur, coal, quartz. Exports: cotton, coffee, hides and skins. Imports: foodstuffs, manufactures, machinery and transport equipment, chemicals, fuel, lubricants, tobacco. Major trading partners: Japan, Australia, Arab nations, U.S.S.R., U.K.

Geography. The Yemen Arab Republic occupies the southwestern tip of the Arabian Peninsula, with its western coast on the Red Sea opposite Ethiopia. Its neighbors are Saudi Arabia to the north and east and the People's Democratic Republic of Yemen to the south. Its area is slightly less than that of South Dakota.

A north-south coastal plain 20–50 miles wide (32–80 km) lies in the west; eastward, there are the interior highlands, which attain a height of 12,000 feet (3,660 m), and the expanse of the Rub 'al-Khali Desert.

Government. The country's first permanent Constitution was submitted to the National Assembly in 1971. It provided for a 179-member legislature, the Consultative Council, 20 of whose members would be chosen by the President and the rest elected every four years. A five-man executive Presidential Council was to be chosen by the Consultative Council.

A merger agreement between Yemen and the People's Democratic Republic of Yemen (Southern Yemen) was signed by the two states in 1972 after bitter border clashes between them over a five-year period. A new Constitution was to be drafted, but meanwhile the joint government was to be "republican, nationalist, and democratic," ruled by a single, merged Presidential Council and unified legislative, executive, and judicial branches.

In 1974, the army ousted the government in a bloodless coup and suspended the Constitution and its various legislative bodies. No political organizations are permitted.

History. The history of Yemen dates back to the Minaean kingdom (1200–650 B.C.). It accepted Islam in A.D. 628, and in the 10th century came under the control of the Rassite dynasty of the Zaidi sect. The Turks occupied the area from 1538 to 1630 and from 1849 to 1918. The sovereign status of Yemen was confirmed by treaties signed with Saudi Arabia and Britain in 1934.

Yemen joined the Arab League in 1945 established diplomatic relations with the U.S. in 1946.

In 1962, a military revolt of elements favoring President Gamal Abdel Nasser of Egypt broke out. A ruling junta proclaimed a republic, and Yemen became an international battleground, with Egypt and the U.S.S.R. supporting the revolutionaries, and King Saud of Saudi Arabia and King Hussein of Jordan the royalists. The civil war continued until the war between the Arab states and Israel broke out in June 1967. Nasser had to pull out many of his troops and agree to a cease-fire and withdrawal of foreign forces. The war finally ended with the defeat of the royalists in mid-1969.

In 1977, Col. Ibrahim al-Hamidi was assassinated after three years as head of government and was succeeded by Lt. Col. Ahmed Hussein al-Ghashmi as head of the Presidential Council. On June 24, 1978, al-Ghashmi was killed by a bomb as he received the credentials of a new ambassador from the People's Democratic Republic of Yemen. The People's Council elected Col. Ali Abdulla Saleh as President on July 17.

YUGOSLAVIA

Socialist Federal Republic of Yugoslavia
President: Cvijetin Mijatovic (1980)
President of Federal Executive Council (Premier): Veselin Djuranovic (1977)
Area: 98,766 sq mi. (255,804 sq km)
Population (est. 1980): 22,310,000 (Serbian, 42%; Croatian, 24%; Slovene, 9%; Macedonian, 5%; Albanian, 4%)
Density per square mile: 225.9
Capital: Belgrade
Largest cities (est. 1975 by U.N.): Belgrade, 870,000; **(1971 census):** Zagreb, 566,224; Skopje, 312,980; Sarajevo, 243,980; Ljubljana, 173,853; Split, 152,905
Monetary unit: Dinar
Languages: Serbo-Croatian, Slovene, Macedonian (all official)

Religions: Greek Orthodox, 41%; Roman Catholic, 32%; Islam, 12%
National name: Socijalisticka Federativna Republika Jugoslavija
Freedom House classifications: Capitalist-socialist industrial, one-party communist
Economic summary: Gross national product (1978): $52 billion. Average annual growth rate (1970–77): 5.1%. Per capita income: $2,210. Land used for agriculture: 33%; labor force: 48%; principal products: corn, wheat, tobacco, sugar beets. Labor force in industry: 52%; major products: wood, processed food, nonferrous metals, machinery, textiles. Natural resources: bauxite, timber, antimony, chromium, lead, zinc, asbestos, mercury, cadmium. Exports: timber, nonferrous metals, machinery and metal products, textiles, iron and steel. Imports: machinery and metal products, chemicals, textiles, iron, petroleum, steel. Major trading partners: West Germany, Italy, U.S.S.R., Iraq.

Geography. Yugoslavia fronts on the eastern coast of the Adriatic Sea opposite Italy. Its neighbors are Austria, Italy, and Hungary to the north, Romania and Bulgaria to the east, and Greece and Albania to the south. It is slightly larger than Wyoming.

About half of Yugoslavia is mountainous. In the north, the Dinaric Alps rise abruptly from the sea and progress eastward as a barren limestone plateau called the Karst. Montenegro is a jumbled mass of mountains, containing also some grassy slopes and fertile river valleys. Southern Serbia, too, is mountainous. A rich plain in the north and northeast, drained by the Danube, is the most fertile area of the country.

Government. Yugoslavia is a federal republic composed of six socialist republics—Serbia (which includes the provinces of Vojvodina and Kosovo), Croatia, Slovenia, Bosnia-Herzegovina, Macedonia, and Montenegro. Actual administration is carried on by the Federal Executive Council and its secretaries.

The League of Communists and the Socialist Alliance of the Working People are the major political parties.

History. Yugoslavia was formed Dec. 1, 1918, from the patchwork of Balkan states and territories where World War I began with the assassination of Archduke Ferdinand of Austria at Sarajevo on June 28, 1914. The new Kingdom of Serbs, Croats, and Slovenes included the former kingdoms of Serbia and Montenegro; Bosnia-Herzegovina, previously administered jointly by Austria and Hungary; Croatia-Slavonia, a semi-autonomous region of Hungary, and Dalmatia, formerly administered by Austria. King Peter I of Serbia became the first monarch, his son acting as Regent until his accession as Alexander I on Aug. 16, 1921.

Croatian demands for a federal state forced Alexander to assume dictatorial powers in 1929 and to change the country's name to Yugoslavia. Serbian dominance continued despite his efforts, amid the resentment of other regions. A Macedonian associated with Croatian dissidents assassinated Alexander in Marseilles, France, on Oct. 9, 1934, and his cousin, Prince Paul, became Regent for the King's son, Prince Peter.

Paul's pro-Axis policy brought Yugoslavia to sign the Axis Pact on March 25, 1941, and opponents overthrew the government two days later. On April 6 the Nazis occupied the country, and the young King and his government fled. Two guerrilla armies —the Chetniks under Draza Mihajlovic supporting the monarchy and the Partisans under Tito (Josip Broz) leaning toward the U.S.S.R.—fought the Nazis for the duration of the war. In 1943, Tito established an Executive National Committee of Liberation to function as a provisional government.

Tito won the election held in the fall of 1945, as monarchists boycotted the vote. A new Assembly abolished the monarchy and proclaimed the Federal People's Republic of Yugoslavia, with Tito as Prime Minister.

Ruthlessly eliminating opposition, the Tito government executed Mihajlovic in 1946. With Soviet aid, Tito annexed the greater part of Italian Istria under the 1947 peace treaty with Italy but failed in his claim to the key port of Trieste. Zone B of the former free territory of Trieste went to Yugoslavia in 1954.

Tito broke with the Soviet bloc in 1948 and Yugoslavia has since followed a middle road, combining orthodox Communist control of politics and general overall economic policy with a varying degree of freedom in the arts, travel, and individual enterprise. Tito, who became President in 1953 and President for life under a revised Constitution adopted in 1963, has played a major part in the creation of a "non-aligned" group of states, the so-called "third world."

The Marshal supported his one-time Soviet mentors in their quarrel with Communist China, but even though he imprisoned the writer Mihajlo Mihajlov and other dissenters at home, he criticized Soviet repression of Czecholovakia in 1968.

Tito welcomed President Nixon to Yugoslavia in 1970 for the first U.S. Presidential visit, and he went to the U.S. the following year, but the relationship has been touchy.

Tito's death on May 4, 1980, three days before his 88th birthday, removed from the scene the last World War II leader. A rotating presidency designed to avoid internal dissension was put into effect immediately, and the feared clash of Yugoslavia's multiple nationalities and regions appeared to have been averted. On May 15, Cvijetin Mijatovic of the Serbian republic began a one-year term. A collective presidency, rotated annually among the six republics and two autonomous provinces of the federal republic, was to continue to govern according to a constitutional change made in 1974.

In a show of support for Yugoslavia's independent stance between the Soviet bloc and the West, a position that Tito had declared to be the proper place for the nonaligned nations, most of the world's leaders attended the funeral on May 8. President Carter's absence, attributed to the Iranian crisis, was strongly criticized. Despite Tito's split from the Soviet bloc, Soviet President Leonid Brezhnev was among the official mourners.

ZAIRE

Republic of Zaire
President: Mobutu Sese Seko (1965)
Prime Minister: Nguza Karl-i-Bond (1980)
Area: 905,063 sq mi. (2,344,113 sq km)
Population (est. 1980): 28,750,000
Density per square mile: 31.8
Capital: Kinshasa
Largest cities (est. 1977): Kinshasha, 2,710,000; (est. 1974 by U.N.): Kananga, 601,250; Luluabourg, 506,000; Lubumbashi, 403,600

Monetary unit: Zaire
Languages: French; Bantu dialects, mainly Swahili, Lingala, Ishiluba, and Kikongo
Religions: Animist, 50%; Roman Catholic, Protestant, Islam
Ethnic groups: Bantu, Sudanese, Nilotics, Pygmies, Hamites
National name: République du Zaïre
Freedom House classifications: Capitalist-statist pre-industrial, one-party nationalist
Economic summary: Gross national product (1978): $5.5 billion. Average annual growth rate (1970–77): –1.4%. Per capita income (1976): $132. Land used for agriculture: 2%; labor force: 70–80%; principal products: coffee, palm oil, rubber, tea, cotton, cocoa, manioc, bananas, plantains, vegetables, fruits. Major industrial products: processed and unprocessed minerals, consumer products, metal and chemical products, construction materials, steel. Natural resources: copper, cobalt, zinc, industrial diamonds, manganese, tin, gold, rare metals, bauxite, iron, coal, 13% of world hydroelectric potential. Exports: copper, cobalt, diamonds, gold, manganese, coffee, palm oil, wood. Imports: crude petroleum, petroleum products, chemicals, transport equipment, textiles, food. Major trading partners: Belgium, France, West Germany, U.S., U.K.

Geography. Zaire is situated in west central Africa and is bordered by the Congo, the Central African Empire, the Sudan, Uganda, Rwanda, Burundi, Tanzania, Zambia, Angola, and the Atlantic Ocean. It is one quarter the size of the U.S.

The principal rivers are the Ubangi and Bomu in the north and the Zaire (Congo) in the west, which flows into the Atlantic. The entire length of Lake Tanganyika lies along the eastern border with Tanzania and Burundi.

Government. Under the Constitution approved by referendum in 1967 and amended in 1974, the third Constitution since 1960, the president and a unicameral Legislature were to have been elected by universal suffrage for five-year terms.

In 1971, the government proclaimed that the Democratic Republic of the Congo would be known as the Republic of Zaire, since the Congo River's name had been changed to the Zaire. In addition, President Joseph D. Mobutu took the name Mobutu Sese Seko and Katanga Province became Shaba.

There is only one political party: the Popular Movement of the Revolution, led by President Mobutu.

History. Formerly the Belgian Congo, this territory was inhabited by ancient Negrito peoples (Pygmies), who were pushed into the mountains by Bantu and Nilotic invaders. The American correspondent Henry M. Stanley navigated the Congo River in 1877 and opened the interior to exploration. Commissioned by King Leopold II of the Belgians, Stanley made treaties with native chiefs that enabled the King to obtain personal title to the territory at the Berlin Conference of 1885.

Criticism of forced labor under royal exploitation prompted Belgium to take over administration of the Congo, which remained a colony until agitation for independence forced Brussels to grant freedom on June 30, 1960. Moise Tshombe, Premier of the then Katanga Province seceded from the new republic on July 11, and another mining province, South Kasai, followed. Belgium sent paratroopers to quell the civil war, and with President Joseph Kasavubu and Premier Patrice Lumumba of the national government in conflict, the United Nations flew in a peacekeeping force.

Kasavubu staged an army coup in 1960 and handed Lumumba over to the Katangan forces. A U.N. investigating commission found that Lumumba had been killed by a Belgian mercenary in the presence of Tshombe. Dag Hammarskjold, U.N. Secretary-General, died in a plane crash en route to a peace conference with Tshombe on Sept. 17, 1961.

U.N. Secretary-General U Thant submitted a national reconciliation plan in 1962 that Tshombe rejected. Tshombe's troops fired on the U.N. force in December, and in the ensuing conflict Tshombe capitulated on Jan. 14, 1963. The peacekeeping force withdrew, and, in a complete about-face, Kasavubu named Tshombe Premier to fight a spreading rebellion. Tshombe used foreign mercenaries and, with the help of Belgian paratroops airlifted by U.S. planes, defeated the most serious opposition, a Communist-backed regime in the northeast.

Kasavubu abruptly dismissed Tshombe in 1965 and was himself ousted by Gen. Joseph-Desiré Mobutu, Army Chief of Staff. The new President nationalized the Union Minière, the Belgian copper mining enterprise that had been a dominant force in the Congo since colonial days. The plane carrying the exiled Tshombe was hijacked in 1967 and he was held prisoner in Algeria until his death from a heart attack was announced June 29, 1969.

Mobutu eliminated opposition to win election in 1970 to a term of seven years, which was renewed in a 1977 election. He invited U.S., South African, and Japanese investment to replace Belgian interests. In 1975, he nationalized much of the economy, barred religious instruction in schools, and decreed the adoption of African names.

In the Angolan civil war of 1975–76, Mobutu backed the National Front for the Liberation of Angola, whose leader, Holden Roberto, is related to him by marriage. The Zairean government opposed the recognition of the Soviet-backed Popular Movement for the Liberation of Angola and reluctantly accepted its victory.

On March 8, 1977, invaders from Angola calling themselves the Congolese National Liberation Front pushed into Shaba and threatened the important mining center of Kolwezi. France and Belgium responded to Mobutu's pleas for help with weapons, but the U.S. gave only nonmilitary supplies.

In April, France flew 1,500 Moroccan troops to Shaba to defeat the invaders, who were, Mobutu charged, Soviet-inspired, and Cuban-led. U.S. intelligence sources, however, confirmed Soviet and Cuban denials of any participation and identified the rebels as former Katanga gendarmes who had fled to Angola after their 1963 defeat.

On May 15, 1978, a new assult from Angola resulted in the capture of Kolwezi and the death of 100 whites and 300 blacks. In this second invasion, France and Belgium intervened directly as 1,000 Foreign Legion paratroopers repelled the Katangese and 1,750 Belgian soldiers helped evacuate 2,000 Europeans. The U.S. supplied 18 air transports for both the troop movement and the evacuation. This time President Carter himself backed Mobutu's renewed assertions of Soviet-Cuban participation.

France led in organizing Western aid for the restoration of the shattered mining operations at Kolwezi, an important part of the Shaba industry that is the mainstay of Zaire's economy.

ZAMBIA

Republic of Zambia
President: Kenneth D. Kaunda (1964)
Prime Minister: Daniel Lisulo (1978)
Area: 290,724 sq mi. (752,975 sq km)
Population (est. 1980): 5,840,000
Density per square mile: 20.1
Capital: Lusaka
Largest cities (est. 1978 for metropolitan area): Lusaka, 559,000; **(est. 1978 by U.N.):** Kitwe, 310,000; Ndola, 291,000; Chingola, 173,000; Mufulira, 170,000
Monetary unit: Kwacha
Languages: English and local dialects
Religions: Animist, 82%; Christian, 17%
Member of Commonwealth of Nations
Freedom House classifications: Capitalist-socialist pre-industrial, one-party socialist
Economic summary: Gross national product (1978): $2.5 billion. Average annual growth rate (1970–77): –0.2%. Per capita income: $480. Land used for agriculture: 70%; labor force: 85%; principal products: maize, tobacco, cotton, sugar cane. Labor force in industry: 15%; major products: foodstuffs, beverages, chemicals, textiles, fertilizers. Natural resources: copper, zinc, lead, cobalt, coal. Exports: copper, zinc, lead, cobalt, tobacco. Imports: manufactured goods, machinery and transport equipment, foodstuffs. Major trading partners: U.K., Japan, South Africa, U.S., West Germany, China.

Geography. Zambia, a landlocked country in south central Africa, is about one tenth larger than Texas. It is surrounded by Angola, Zaire, Tanzania, Malawi, Mozambique, Zimbabwe, Botswana, and South-West Africa (Namibia). The country is mostly a plateau that rises to 8,000 feet (2,434 m) in the east.

Government. Zambia (formerly Northern Rhodesia) is governed by a president, elected by universal suffrage, and a Legislative Assembly, consisting of 105 members elected by universal suffrage and up to 10 additional members nominated by the president.

In 1972, the Assembly passed a law making the ruling United National Independence Party, led by President Kenneth D. Kaunda, the only legal political party.

History. Empire builder Cecil Rhodes obtained mining concessions in 1889 from King Lewanika of the Barotse and sent settlers to the area soon thereafter. It was ruled by the British South Africa Company, which he established, until 1924, when the British government took over the administration.

From 1953 to 1964, Northern Rhodesia was federated with Southern Rhodesia and Nyasaland in the Federation of Rhodesia and Nyasaland. On Oct. 24, 1964, Northern Rhodesia became the independent nation of Zambia.

Kenneth Kaunda, the first president, kept Zambia within the Commonwealth of Nations. The country's economy, dependent on copper exports, was threatened when Rhodesia declared its independence from British rule in 1965 and defied U.N. sanctions, which Zambia supported, an action that deprived Zambia of its trade route through Rhodesia. The U.S., Britain, and Canada organized an airlift in 1966 to ship gasoline into Zambia. In 1967, Britain agreed to finance new trade routes for Zambia.

Kaunda visited China in 1967, and China later agreed to finance a 1,000-mile railroad from the copper fields to Dar es Salaam in Tanzania. A pipeline was opened in 1968 from Ndola in Zambia's copper belt to the Indian Ocean at Dar es Salaam, ending the three-year oil drought.

In 1969, Kaunda announced the nationalization of the foreign copper-mining industry, with Zambia to take 51% (over $1 billion, estimated), and an agreement was reached with the companies on payment. He then announced a similar takeover of foreign oil producers.

Despite the opening of the Tanzam railroad in 1975, congestion at the port of Dar es-Salaam, eastern terminal of the line, reduced the value of Zambia's new link to the Indian Ocean. Fighting in Angola during the latter part of 1975 and early 1976 brought the Benguela railway to a halt, forcing Zambia to stockpile a third of its copper production.

Falling copper prices in 1978 forced Kaunda to seek further aid from the U.S. and Britain, although he continued to attack their soft policy toward the white regime in Rhodesia. Kaunda favored Joshua Nkomo's faction of the Zimbabwean guerrillas, and the presence of guerrilla bases on Zambian territory brought a devastating series of Rhodesian raids in late 1979 that destroyed nearly all rail and road links from Zambia to the outside. Despite Kaunda's demands and riots directed against British installations in Zambia, Britain refused to pay the costs of reconstruction.

ZIMBABWE

President: Rev. Canaan Banana (1980)
Prime Minister: Robert Mugabe (1980)
Area: 150,333 sq mi. (389,362 sq km)
Population (est. 1980): 7,360,000 (black, 96%; white, 4%)
Density per square mile: 49.0
Capital: Salisbury
Largest cities (est. 1979 for metropolitan area): Salisbury, 641,000; Bulawayo, 375,000
Monetary unit: Zimbabwean dollar
Languages: English (official), Sindebele, Shona
Religions: Christian, 20%; Animist
Freedom House classifications: Capitalist-statist pre-industrial, multi-party centralized
Economic summary: Gross national product (1978): $3.3 billion. Average annual growth rate (1970–77): –0.1%. Per capita income: $520. Principal agricultural products: tobacco, corn, sugar, cotton, livestock. Major industrial products: steel, textiles, chemicals, vehicles, gold, copper. Natural resources: gold, copper. Exports: gold, tobacco, asbestos, copper, meat, chrome, nickel, clothing, sugar. Imports: machinery, petroleum products, wheat, transport equipment. Major trading partner: South Africa.

Geography. Zimbabwe, a landlocked country in south central Africa, is slightly smaller than California. It is bordered by Botswana on the west, Zambia on the north, Mozambique on the east, and South Africa on the south.

A high veld up to 6,000 feet (1,829 m) crosses the country from northeast to southwest. This is flanked by a somewhat lower veld that contains ranching country. Tropical forests that yield hardwoods lie in the southeast.

In the north, on the border with Zambia, is the 175-mile-long (128-m) Kariba Lake, formed by the Kariba Dam across the Zambezi River. It is the site of one of the world's largest hydroelectric projects.

Government. Executive power rests with the 21-member Cabinet, headed by the Prime Minister.

The President, elected by a majority of the House of Assembly, exercises formal executive powers. The legislature is composed of a 100-member House of Assembly, 80 of whom are elected by black voters and 20 by whites, and a 40-member Senate. Black House members elect 14 Senators and whites elect 10. Ten tribal chiefs—five from Mashonaland and five from Matabeleland—are elected by their peers and six appointed by the President complete the Senate membership.

Major political parties are the Zimbabwe African National Union (57 seats in the House of Assembly), led by Prime Minister Robert Mugabe; Zimbabwe African People's Union (20 seats), led by Joshua Nkomo; and the United African National Council (3 seats), led by former Prime Minister Abel Muzorewa. The Rhodesian Front, led by former Prime Minister Ian Smith, holds all 20 seats reserved for whites.

History. Zimbabwe, formerly called Rhodesia, was colonized by Cecil Rhodes's British South Africa Company at the end of the 19th century. In 1923, European settlers voted in a referendum to become the self-governing British colony of Southern Rhodesia rather than merge with what was then the Union of South Africa. After a brief federation with Northern Rhodesia and Nyasaland in the post-World War II period, Southern Rhodesia chose to remain a colony when its two partners voted for independence in 1963.

On Nov. 11, 1965, the white-minority government of Rhodesia unilaterally declared its independence from Britain.

In 1967, Rhodesia became the first country against which the United Nations ever imposed mandatory sanctions. The U.S. stopped virtually all trade with Rhodesia. The country refused to cave in, but began a slow movement toward meeting the demands of the black Africans. The white-minority regime of Prime Minister Ian Smith withstood British pressure, economic sanctions, guerrilla attacks, and a right-wing assault.

On March 1, 1970, Rhodesia formally proclaimed itself a republic, and within the month nine nations, including the U.S., closed their consulates there.

In 1972 the international economic boycott of Rhodesia began to break down. The U.S. was one country that resumed trade by buying Rhodesian chrome ore, but restored the ban a year later.

Black terrorism, which began late in 1972, resulted in the death of several hundred black rebels and several dozen white citizens and soldiers. The army draft size was doubled and other steps were taken to counter the security threat, including uprooting 8,000 black Africans from the area bordering Mozambique in an attempt to create a 200-mile-long (322 km) buffer zone.

Heightened guerrilla war and a withdrawal of South African military aid—particularly helicopters—marked the beginning of the collapse of Smith's 11 years of resistance in the spring of 1976. Under pressure from South Africa's Prime Minister, Johannes Vorster, Smith agreed with U.S. Secretary of State Henry A. Kissinger that majority rule should come within two years.

In the fall, Smith met with black nationalist leaders in Geneva. The meeting broke up six weeks later when the Rhodesian Premier insisted that whites must retain control of the police and armed forces during the transition to majority rule. A British proposal called for Britons to take over these powers.

Divisions between Rhodesian blacks—Bishop Abel Muzorewa of the African National Congress and Ndabaningi Sithole as moderates versus Robert Mugabe and Joshua Nkomo of the Patriotic Front as advocates of guerrilla force—sharpened in 1977 and no agreement was reached. In July, with white residents leaving in increasing numbers and the economy showing the strain of war, Smith rejected outside mediation and called for general elections in order to work out an "internal solution" of the transfer of power.

On March 3, 1978, Smith, Muzorewa, Sithole, and Chief Jeremiah Chirau signed an agreement to transfer power to the black majority by Dec. 31, 1978. They constituted themselves an Executive Council, with chairmanship rotating but Smith retaining the title of Prime Minister. Blacks were named to each cabinet ministry, serving as co-ministers with the whites already holding these posts. African nations and the Patriotic Front leaders immediately denounced the action, but Western governments were more reserved, although none granted recognition to the new regime.

Despite continuing fighting, white voters ratified a new constitution on Jan. 30, 1979, enfranchising all blacks, establishing a black majority Senate and Assembly, and changing the country's name to Zimbabwe Rhodesia. A general election on April 24 gave Muzorewa's party 67.3% of the vote, and although the Patriotic Front urged a boycott, more than 60% of the eligible blacks went to the polls.

As black African states refused recognition and the United Nations sanctions remained in force, Muzorewa agreed to negotiate with Mugabe and Nkomo in British-sponsored talks beginning Sept. 9. By December, all parties accepted a new draft constitution, a cease-fire, and a period of British administration pending a general election. Lord Christopher Soames arrived on Dec. 12 to head the government, followed by British and Commonwealth troops who were to serve as peace-keeping forces as Patriotic Front guerrillas were grouped at 40 assembly points throughout the country.

The United Nations Security Council ended sanctions on Dec. 21, the day the formal agreement was signed by all parties.

In voting completed on Feb. 29, 1980, Mugabe's ZANU-Patriotic Front party won 57 of the 80 Assembly seats reserved for blacks. Nkomo's ZAPU-Patriotic Front party won 20 seats and Muzorewa's United African National Council only three. In an earlier vote on Feb. 14, the Rhodesian Front won all 20 seats reserved for whites in the Assembly.

At a ceremony on April 18, Prince Charles of Britain handed to President-elect Rev. Canaan Banana the symbols of independence. Mugabe, a Marxist, had already pledged his support for continuation of the existing free-market economy. Britain announced a two-year $165-million aid program for the new government, and the United States, opening the first embassy in Salisbury, offered $15 million for rural rehabilitation and $2 million to rebuild rural clinics.

Despite optimistic economic forecasts based on a favorable balance of trade for 1979 and a continuing strong industrial and farm base, reconstruction and the cost of black demands for greater social benefits were expected to generate more aid requirements. White emigration, while down from its peak, was running at 1,500 a month in mid-1980.

(For late reports, see Current Events of 1979–80)

CANADA

Sovereign: Queen Elizabeth II
Governor General: Edward R. Schreyer (1979)
Prime Minister: Pierre E. Trudeau (1980)
Area: 3,851,809 sq mi. (9,976,139 sq km)
Population (est. 1980): 23,850,000 (British, 44.6%; French, 28.7%; other European, 23%)
Density per square mile: 6.2
Capital: Ottawa, Ont.
Largest cities (1979) Winnipeg, Man. 578,000; Calgary, Alta. 530,846; Edmonton, Alta., 491,359; Regina, Sask., 153,848; **(1976 census)** Montreal, Que., 1,080,545; Toronto, Ont., 633,318; Vancouver, B.C., 410,188; Hamilton, Ont., 312,003; Ottawa, Ont., 304,462; London, Ont., 240,392; Windsor, Ont., 196,526; Quebec, Que., 177,082
Monetary Unit: Canadian dollar
Languages: English, French
Religions: Roman Catholic, 46.2%; United Church, 17.5%; Anglican, 11.8%; Presbyterian, 4%; Lutheran, 3.3%; Baptist, 3.1%; others, 14.1%
Gross national product (1978): $216 billion
Average annual growth rate (1970–77): 3.4%
Freedom House classifications: Capitalist industrial, multi-party decentralized

Geography. Covering most of the northern part of the North American continent and with an area larger than that of the United States, Canada has an extremely varied topography. The northeastern region, including most of Quebec, northern Ontario and Manitoba, and the Northwest Territories, with Hudson Bay in the center, is an important source of minerals, wood pulp, and water power. In the east the mountainous maritime provinces have an irregular coast line on the Gulf of St. Lawrence and the Atlantic. The St. Lawrence plain, covering most of southern Quebec and Ontario, and the interior continental plain, covering southern Manitoba and Saskatchewan and most of Alberta, are the principal cultivable areas. They are separated by a forested plateau rising from lakes Superior and Huron.

Westward toward the Pacific, most of British Columbia, Yukon, and part of western Alberta are covered by parallel mountain ranges including the Rockies. The Pacific border of the coast range is ragged with fiords and channels. The highest point in Canada is Mount Logan (19,850 ft; 6,050 m), which is in the Yukon.

Canada has an abundance of large and small lakes. In addition to the Great Lakes on the U.S. border, there are 9 others that are more than 100 miles long (161 km) and 35 that are more than 50 miles long (80 km).

The two principal river systems are the Mackenzie and the St. Lawrence. The St. Lawrence, with its tributaries, is navigable for over 1,900 miles (3,058 km).

Government. Canada, a self-governing member of the Commonwealth of Nations, is a federal union of 10 provinces whose powers are laid down in the British North America Act of 1867. The executive powers nominally rest in the hands of the Governor General, who represents the Queen and is appointed by her upon the recommendation of the Canadian government.

Actually the Governor General acts only with the advice of the Canadian Prime Minister and the members of the Cabinet, who also sit in the federal Parliament. The Parliament has two houses: a Senate of 104 members appointed for life, and a House of Commons of 264 members apportioned according to provincial population. Elections are held at least every five years or whenever the party in power is voted down in the House of Commons or considers it expedient to appeal to the people. The Prime Minister is the leader of the majority party in the House of Commons—or, if no single party holds a majority, the leader of the party able to command the support of a majority of members of the House. Laws must be passed by both houses of Parliament and signed by the Governor General in the Queen's name.

The 10 provincial governments are nominally headed by Lieutenant Governors appointed by the federal government, but the executive power in each actually is vested in a Cabinet headed by a Premier, who is leader of the majority party. The provincial legislatures are composed of one-house assemblies whose members are elected for four-year terms. They are known as Legislative Assemblies, except in Newfoundland, where it is the House of Assembly, and in Quebec, where it is the National Assembly.

The judicial system consists of a Supreme Court in Ottawa (established in 1875), with appellate jurisdiction, and a Supreme Court in each province, as well as county courts with limited jurisdiction in most of the provinces. The Governor General in Council appoints these judges.

The major political parties are the Liberal (147 of 282 seats in House of Commons), led by Prime Minister Pierre Elliott Trudeau; Progressive Conservative Party (103 seats), led by former Prime Minister Charles Joseph Clark; New Democratic Party (32), led by John Edward Broadbent; Social Credit Party (no seats) led by Fabien Roy. No Independents hold a seat and there are no vacancies.

History. The Norse explorer Leif Ericson probably reached the shores of Canada (Labrador or Nova Scotia) in A.D. 1000, but the history of the white man in the country actually began in 1497, when John Cabot, an Italian in the service of Henry VII of England, reached Newfoundland or Nova Scotia. Canada was taken for France in 1534 by Jacques Cartier. The actual settlement of New France, as it was then called, began in 1604 at Port Royal in what is now Nova Scotia; in 1608, Quebec was founded. France's colonization efforts were not very successful, but French explorers by the end of the 17th century had penetrated beyond the Great Lakes to the western prairies and south along the Mississippi to the Gulf of Mexico. Meanwhile, the English Hudson's Bay Company had been established in 1670. Because of the valuable fisheries and fur trade, a conflict developed between the French and English; in 1713, Newfoundland, Hudson Bay, and Nova Scotia (Acadia) were lost to England.

During the Seven Years' War (1756–63), England extended its conquest, and the British Maj. Gen. James Wolfe won his famous victory over Gen. Louis Montcalm outside Quebec on Sept. 13,

Canadian Governors General and Prime Ministers Since 1867

Term of office	Governor General	Term	Prime Minister	Party
1867–1868	Viscount Monck[1]	1867–1873	Sir John A. Macdonald	Conservative
1869–1872	Baron Lisgar	1873–1878	Alexander Mackenzie	Liberal
1872–1878	Earl of Dufferin	1878–1891	Sir John A. Macdonald	Conservative
1878–1883	Marquess of Lorne	1891–1892	Sir John J. C. Abbott	Conservative
1883–1888	Marquess of Lansdowne	1892–1894	Sir John S. D. Thompson	Conservative
1888–1893	Baron Stanley of Preston	1894–1896	Sir Mackenzie Bowell	Conservative
1893–1898	Earl of Aberdeen	1896	Sir Charles Tupper	Conservative
1898–1904	Earl of Minto	1896–1911	Sir Wilfrid Laurier	Liberal
1904–1911	Earl Grey	1911–1917	Sir Robert L. Borden	Conservative
1911–1916	Duke of Connaught	1917–1920	Sir Robert L. Borden	Unionist
1916–1921	Duke of Devonshire	1920–1921	Arthur Meighen	Unionist
1921–1926	Baron Byng of Vimy	1921–1926	W. L. Mackenzie King	Liberal
1926–1931	Viscount Willingdon	1926	Arthur Meighen	Conservative
1931–1935	Earl of Bessborough	1926–1930	W. L. Mackenzie King	Liberal
1935–1940	Baron Tweedsmuir	1930–1935	Richard B. Bennett	Conservative
1940–1946	Earl of Athlone	1935–1948	W. L. Mackenzie King	Liberal
1946–1952	Viscount Alexander	1948–1957	Louis S. St. Laurent	Liberal
1952–1959	Vincent Massey	1957–1963	John G. Diefenbaker	Progressive-Conservative
1959–1967	George P. Vanier			
1967–1973	Roland Michener	1963–1968	Lester B. Pearson	Liberal
1974–1979	Jules Léger	1968–1979	Pierre Elliott Trudeau	Liberal
1979–	Edward R. Schreyer	1979–1980	Charles Joseph Clark	Conservative
		1980–	Pierre Elliott Trudeau	Liberal

1. Became Governor General of British North America in 1861.

1759. The Treaty of Paris in 1763 gave England control.

At that time the population of Canada was almost entirely French, but in the next few decades, thousands of British colonists emigrated to Canada from the British Isles and from the American colonies. In 1849, the right of Canada to self-government was recognized. By the British North America Act of 1867, the Dominion of Canada was created through the confederation of Upper and Lower Canada, Nova Scotia, and New Brunswick. Prince Edward Island joined the Dominion in 1873.

In 1869 Canada purchased from the Hudson's Bay Company the vast middle west (Rupert's Land) from which the provinces of Manitoba (1870), Alberta, and Saskatchewan (1905) were later formed. In 1871, British Columbia joined the Dominion. The country was linked from coast to coast in 1885 by the Canadian Pacific Railway.

During the formative years between 1866 and 1896, the Conservative Party, led by Sir John A. Macdonald, governed the country, except during the years 1873–78. In 1896, the Liberal Party took over and, under Sir Wilfrid Laurier, an eminent French Canadian, ruled until 1911.

In World War I, more than 500,000 Canadian soldiers fought for the Allied cause. After the Treaty of Versailles, Canada, a full-fledged nation, was admitted to the League of Nations and appointed its own representatives in foreign countries. By the Statute of Westminster in 1931 the British Dominions, including Canada, were formally declared to be partner nations with Britian, "equal in status, in no way subordinate to each other," and bound together only by allegiance to a common Crown.

Newfoundland became Canada's 10th province on March 31, 1949, following a plebiscite. Besides the provinces, Canada includes two territories—the Yukon Territory, the area north of British Columbia and east of Alaska, and the Northwest Territories, including all of Canada north of 60° north latitude except Yukon and the northernmost sections of Québec and Newfoundland. This area includes all of the Arctic north of the mainland, Norway having recognized Canadian sovereignty over the Svendrup Islands in the Arctic in 1931.

The Liberal Party, led by William Lyon Mackenzie King, dominated Canadian politics from 1921 until 1957, when it was succeeded by the Progressive Conservatives. The Liberals, under the leadership of Lester B. Pearson, returned to power in 1963. Pearson remained Prime Minister until 1968, when he retired and was replaced by a former law professor, Pierre Elliott Trudeau. Trudeau maintained Canada's defensive alliance with the United States, but began moving toward a more independent policy in world affairs.

Trudeau set about creating what he termed a "just society," stressing domestic reforms. His election was considered in part a response to the most serious problem confronting the country, the division between French- and English-speaking Canadians, which had led to a separatist movement in the predominantly French province of Quebec. Trudeau, himself a French Canadian, supported programs for bilingualism and an increased measure of provincial autonomy, although he would not tolerate the idea of separatism. In 1974, the provincial government voted to make French the official language of Quebec.

Capturing the Quebec provincial government from the long-entrenched local Liberal Party, René Lévesque and his separatist Parti Québécois pledged that they would seek independence for the province. He shocked English-speaking Canadians with a New York speech two months after his election in which he said the question was not when but *how* Quebec would attain independence.

Conflicts over the law establishing French as the dominant language in Quebec, particularly in schooling, kept separatism as a national issue, but by-elections in 1977 produced easy victories for Trudeau's ruling Liberals in four Quebec seats in the national legislature, and polls showed a decline in separatist support both in the province and elsewhere in Canada. Early in 1978, Trudeau declared that he would use force to prevent any illegal declaration of independence by Lévesque.

Economic problems appeared to take precedence over politics in 1978, as the Sun Life Assurance Company of Canada, the nation's largest insurance firm, announced that it would move its headquarters from Montreal to Toronto. Many businesses had left the province earlier, but Sun Life was the first to cite the language law as the reason for its departure.

Despite Trudeau's removal of price and wage controls in 1978, continuing inflation and a high rate of unemployment caused him to delay elections until May 22, 1979, the first time since 1935 that a Canadian government had retained office for the allowable five-year term. The delay gave Trudeau no advantage—the Progressive Conservatives under Charles Joseph Clark defeated the Liberals everywhere except in Quebec, New Brunswick, and Newfoundland. The Liberals actually won the larger share of the popular vote with 40%, but because their strength was concentrated in Quebec they won only 114 seats to the Conservatives' 136 and 36% of the popular vote.

Clark took office as the head of Canada's fifth minority government in the last 20 years, needing the support of 26 New Democratic Party members and six Social Credit members to obtain an absolute majority in the 282-seat House.

Trudeau's defeat after 11 years in power was attributed to the continuing inflation (running at 9.8% for the year preceding the election), to western opposition to his energy policies and, in the opinion of some, public distaste over a "true confessions" autobiography written by the Prime Minister's estranged wife.

Trudeau had also aroused strong provincial opposition when he proposed changes in the Canadian constitution. Even Levesque, the premier of Quebec who had announced a provincial referendum for 1980 on the question of independence for the French-speaking province, opposed constitutional changes until federal-provincial relationships were clarified. Surprisingly, all premiers rejected Trudeau's proposal that the Governor-General be made Head of State rather than Queen Elizabeth when the monarch is not in Canada, saying they opposed giving symbolic power of the crown to an official subject to removal by Parliament. On another matter, the premiers and Trudeau agreed that marriage and divorce should be made a matter of provincial jurisdiction.

Unexpectedly, the first controversy in the new government arose in foreign policy, when Clark moved to implement a campaign pledge to Jewish voters to move Canada's embassy in Israel from Tel Aviv to Jerusalem. Massive Arab pressure on Canadian exporters brought a hasty reconsideration, and Foreign Secretary Flora MacDonald assured Arab diplomats that no deadline had been set for such a move.

Clark's government collapsed after only six months when a motion to defeat the Tory budget carried by 139–133 on Dec. 13, 1979. On the same day, the Quebec law making French the exclusive official language of the province—an issue which had been expected to provide Clark's first major internal test—was voided by the Canadian Supreme Court.

In national elections Feb. 18, 1980, the resurgent Liberals under Trudeau scored an unexpectedly big victory, winning 146 seats (147 when a vacancy was filled a month later), while the Conservatives fell from 136 to 103 and the New Democrats won 32 seats. The House became a three-party legislature for the first time in half a century when the Social Credit party failed to win a single seat.

Trudeau promised to hold down energy costs—the Tory defeat was blamed on a proposed 18 cents a gallon gasoline tax—and to continue his efforts for reform of federal-provincial relations. The Quebec challenge was crushed shortly after the new government took power when a referendum for the negotiation of a separate status for the province went down to a crushing defeat.

Economy. Agriculture, including horticulture, fruit growing, and the raising of stock and poultry, is the largest single industry. Canada is one of the world's greatest wheat-exporting countries; production is concentrated in Manitoba, Saskatchewan, and Alberta.

Population of Canada by Provinces and Territories

Province	1980 (Jan. Estimate)	1979 (Jan. Estimate)	1971 (Census)	1961 (Census)	1951 (Census)
Alberta	2,053,100	1,985,200	1,627,874	1,331,944	939,501
British Columbia	2,611,700	2,555,800	2,184,621	1,629,082	1,165,210
Manitoba	1,026,200	1,029,900	988,247	921,686	776,541
New Brunswick	704,800	699,200	634,557	597,936	515,697
Newfoundland	577,400	572,900	522,104	457,853	361,416
Nova Scotia	851,000	845,400	788,960	737,007	642,584
Ontario	8,543,300	8,479,900	7,703,106	6,236,092	4,597,542
Prince Edward Island	123,900	122,300	111,641	104,629	98,429
Quebec	6,288,300	6,289,600	6,027,764	5,259,211	4,055,681
Saskatchewan	965,300	952,500	926,242	925,181	831,728
Northwest Territories	43,100	43,100	34,807	22,998	16,004
Yukon Territory	21,800	21,800	18,388	14,628	9,096
Total	**23,809,800**	**23,597,600**	**21,568,311**	**18,238,247**	**14,009,429**
Rural	—	—	5,157,525	5,537,857	5,381,176
Urban	—	—	16,410,785	12,700,390	8,628,253

1. *Source:* Statistics Canada.

Stock raising and dairy farming have grown greatly since 1920. Ontario and Quebec are the most important dairying provinces.

Canadian manufactures rely mainly on domestic raw materials; growing industries that depend largely on material imported in a raw or semi-finished state include the manufacture of automobiles, sugar, and rubber goods, as well as the iron and steel industry in Nova Scotia, Quebec, and Ontario. The latter two provinces account for more than 80% of all manufactures. The abundance of cheap water power is one of the chief factors in the growth of Canadian industry.

The most important industries in terms of output are pulp and paper, nonferrous-metals smelting and refining, petroleum products, meatpacking, motor vehicles, and sawmill products.

Canada's mineral resources are both rich and varied. Metals come mainly from two widely separated regions, the mountain ranges of the Pacific coast and the province of Ontario. Copper ore also exists in Quebec, Manitoba, and Newfoundland. Production of petroleum centers in Alberta. There are deposits of uranium in the Northwest Territories.

The total area of land covered by forests is estimated at 1,300,000 square miles (3,367,000 sq km), of which only 435,000 square miles (1,126,650 sq km) are commercially productive and accessible. The manufacture of pulp and paper is one of the leading industries.

Fishing, Canada's oldest industry, is carried on along the Atlantic and Pacific coasts and on the inland lakes.

Chief exports in 1978 were motor vehicles (24%); nonferrous metals (6%); timber (6%); chemicals (6%); newsprint (6%); cereals (5%); metal ores (5%). Leading customers were U.S. (70%); Japan (6%). Leading suppliers were U.S. (71%); Japan (5%).

In 1978, Canada's exports totaled about $49.3 billion, while imports were $47.4 billion. Tourism in 1977 accounted for gross receipts of $1.6 billion from 12.7 visitors.

In 1979, Canada's inflation rate was 9.3% and unemployment reached 7.4%, an improvement over 1978.

Government of Canada

Governor General and Commander-in-Chief: His Excellency The Right Honorable Edward R. Schreyer

GOVERNOR GENERAL'S HOUSEHOLD

Secretary to the Governor General and Secretary General of the Order of Canada, and Secretary General of the Order of Military Merit: Esmond U. Butler, Esq., C.V.O.

Comptroller of the Household: D. C. McKinnon, C.V.O.

Director of Honors: Roger de C. Nantel, Esq. C.D.

Administrative Secretary: Alain C. E. Joly de Lotbiniere

Cultural Advisor to the Governor General: Robert H. Hubbard

Press Secretary: René Chertier

THE CANADIAN MINISTRY

Prime Minister: The Right Hon. Pierre Trudeau

Deputy Prime Minister and Minister of Finance: The Hon. Allan MacEachen

Minister of Transport: The Hon. Jean-Luc Pepin

Minister of Justice and State for Social Development: The Hon. Jean Chrétien

Minister of Indian Affairs and Northern Development: The Hon. John Munro

Minister of State for Economic Development and Senate House Leader: The Hon. H. A. (Bud) Olson

Minister of Industry, Trade and Commerce: The Hon. Herb Gray

Minister of Agriculture: The Hon. Eugene Whelan

Minister of Consumer and Corporate Affairs and Postmaster General: The Hon. André Ouellet

Minister of Veterans Affairs: The Hon. Daniel MacDonald

Minister of Energy, Mines and Resources: The Hon. Marc Lalonde

Leader of the Government in the Senate: The Hon. Ray Perrault

Minister of Fisheries and Oceans: The Hon. Roméo Le Blanc

Minister of State for Science and Technology and Minister of the Environment: The Hon. John Roberts

Minister of National Health and Welfare: The Hon. Monique Bégin

Minister of Supply and Services: The Hon. Jean-Jacques Blais

Secretary of State and Minister of Communications: The Hon. Francis Fox

Minister of National Defense: The Hon. Gilles Lamontagne

Minister of Regional Economic Expansion: The Hon. Pierre De Bané

Minister of State for the Wheat Board: The Hon. Hazen Argue

Minister of Labor and Minister of State for Sports: The Hon. Gerald Regan

Secretary of State for External Affairs: The Hon. Mark MacGuigan

Solicitor General: The Hon. Robert Kaplan

Minister of State for Multiculturalism: The Hon. James Fleming

Minister of National Revenue: The Hon. William Rompkey

Minister of State in the Department of Finance: The Hon. Pierre Bussières

Minister of State for Small Business: The Hon. Charles Lapointe

Minister of State for Trade: The Hon. Ed Lumley

President of the Privy Council and Government House Leader: The Hon. Yvon Pinard

President of the Treasury Board: The Hon. Donald Johnston

Minister of Employment and Immigration and Minister of State for the Status of Women: The Hon. Lloyd Axworthy

Minister of Public Works with Responsibility for C.M.H.C.: The Hon. Paul Cosgrove

Minister of State for Mines: The Hon. Judy Erola

Federal Courts

Federal courts in Canada include the Supreme Court of Canada, the Federal Court of Canada, and various Specialized tribunals such as the Tax Review Board, the Court Martial Appeal Court, and the Immigration Appeal Board. These courts and tribunals are created by Parliament.

Provinces and Territories

ALBERTA

Capital: Edmonton
Lieut. Governor: The Hon. Frank Lynch-Staunton
Premier: The Hon. Peter Lougheed
Provincial Treasurer: Hon. Louis D. Hyndman
Atty. General: Hon. Neil Crawford
Entered Confederation: September 1, 1905
Provincial flower: Wild rose (1930)
Population (1980 est.): 2,063,800
Area: 255,200 sq mi.
Largest cities: (1979) Edmonton (491,359) Calgary (530,816) Lethbridge (51,668) Medicine Hat (36,356) Red Deer (39,370)
Provincial parks: 54 (4,184 sq mi.)
Province revenue: (1979) $5.3 billion
Province expenditure: (1979) $4.6 billion

Alberta was inhabited by various Indian groups for at least 10,000 years. European explorers first appeared in the 1750s to extend the fur trade. By the last quarter of the 18th century The Hudson's Bay Company and the North West Company had established trading posts. From 1821, when the companies merged, until 1870 the Hudson's Bay Company governed the area. In 1870 it was transferred to the Dominion of Canada, and officially became a province in 1905.

Alberta today has become the most dynamic and fastest growing of Canada's ten provinces. Economic progress, spurred on in recent years by developments in the energy resources sector is rapidly transforming the province into a leading North American economic region. Out of a Gross Domestic Product of $28.4 billion in 1978, the net value of production of commodity producing industries was $16.9 billion. The relative shares of this production were: mining (particularly oil and natural gas), 53%; construction, 20%; manufacturing, 16%; agriculture, 9%; logging, fisheries, and trapping, 2%.

Among Alberta's attractions are Elk Island National Park, Banff and Jasper National Parks in the Rocky Mountains, Wood Buffalo National Park which straddles the Alberta-Northwest Territories border, Dinosaur Provincial Park, fur trading post of Rocky Mountain House, Provincial Museum and Archives of Alberta in Edmonton, and Heritage Park in Calgary.

BRITISH COLUMBIA

Capital: Victoria
Lieut. Governor: The Hon. Henry P. Bell-Irving
Premier: The Hon. William R. Bennett
Deputy Premier: The Hon. Grace McCarthy
Minister of Finance: The Hon. Hugh A. Curtis
Atty. General: The Hon. L. Allan Williams
Entered Confederation: July 20, 1871
Provincial flower: Dogwood (1956)
Population (1980 est.): 2,570,400
Area: 366,255 sq mi.
Largest cities: Vancouver (410,188); Burnaby (131,599); Surrey (116,497); Richmond (80,034); Victoria (62,551)
Provincial parks: 352 (17,524.8 sq mi.)
Province revenue (1979-80): $5.5 billion
Province expenditure (1979-80): $4.81 billion

British Columbia was one of the last regions of the North American continent to be explored and settled, with the impetus coming from the fur trade and the gold that lay in its mountains. Spanish ships visited the coast in 1774, followed by Capt. James Cook, whose account of the fur wealth led to the influx of fur traders. The first trading post was established in 1805 at McLeod Lake. The gold strike of 1858 made Fort Victoria into a city, opened up the mainland to settlement, and resulted in its proclamation as the Colony of British Columbia in 1858. With the arrival of the Canadian Pacific Railway at Port Moody in 1885, a new era opened with permanent railroad and lumbering settlements established along the route.

The chief elements of the province's economy are: forest industries, mining, tourism, shipping, and agriculture, with forest industries the leader. The mining sector is also a large contributor to the economy with copper, crude oil, molybdenum, zinc lead, and natural gas the most valuable products.

Among British Columbia's attractions are the recreated gold rush town of Barkerville, Pacific Rim National Park, the fur trading post of Fort St. James, and Fort Langley where the province's salmon export industry began.

MANITOBA

Capital: Winnipeg
Lieut. Governor: Hon. Francis L. Jobin
Premier: Hon. Sterling R. Lyon
Minister of Finance: Hon. Donald W. Craik
Atty. General: Hon. Gerald W.J. Mercier
Entered Confederation: July 15, 1870
Provincial flower: Prairie crocus (1906)
Population (1979 est.): 1,030,500
Area: 251,000 sq mi.
Largest cities: Winnipeg (578,000); Brandon (34,901); Thompson (17,291); Portage la Prairie (12,555); Selkirk (9,862)
Provincial parks: 58 (3,960 sq mi.)
Province revenue (1979–80): $1,689,600,700
Province expenditure (1979–80): $1,812,163,100

Sir Thomas Button, an English explorer, came through Hudson Bay in 1612. After its foundation in 1670, the Hudson's Bay Company began to build forts in the area. Britain's claim to the Hudson Bay region was recognized by the Treaty of Utrecht in 1713, but meanwhile the French entered Manitoba from the east. La Verendrye explored and built several forts in Manitoba between 1733 and 1738. Later, British and French traders from Montreal reopened trade routes in southern and central Manitoba. In 1783, the North West Company based in Montreal began to compete for furs with the Hudson's Bay Company. A fur war ensued which ended in 1821 when the companies merged. The first settlement of Manitoba came in 1812 when Thomas Douglas, 5th earl of Selkirk, received a grant of land on the Red River from the Hudson's Bay Company. The Dominion of Canada acquired all of the Hudson's Bay Company territory in 1869–70 and part of it became the province of Manitoba under the Manitoba Act of 1870.

Its southern farmlands are the backbone of the

province's economy. Wheat is the main crop. Mineral production and forest products are other leading contributors to the economy. The major minerals are nickel, copper, gold, lead, silver, and zinc. Pulpwood for paper manufacture accounts for 60% of the timber cut. Manufacturing accounts for more than one third of the value of goods and services produced in the province every year.

Among Manitoba's attractions are Lower Fort Garry near Selkirk, restored to recreate a 19th century Hudson's Bay Company post, and Riding Mountain National Park.

NEW BRUNSWICK

Capital: Fredericton
Lieut. Governor: The Hon. Hedard Robichaud
Premier: The Hon. Richard B. Hatfield
Minister of Finance: The Hon. Fernand G. Dube
Minister of Justice: The Hon. Rodman E. Logan
Entered Confederation: July 1, 1867
Provincial flower: Purple violet (1936)
Coat of Arms: Assigned by Queen Victoria in 1868
Motto: Spem Reduxit (Hope Restored)
Provincial flag: Adopted 1965
Provincial tartan: Adopted 1959
Geographic center: Boiestown
Number of counties: 15
Language: French is the first language of 36% of the population. New Brunswick is the only officially bilingual province in Canada.
Population (1979 est.): 701,000
Area: 27,985 sq mi.
Largest cities (1977): St. John (metro 114,400); Moncton (79,100); Fredericton (45,900); Bathurst (16,200); Edmundston (12,600); Campbellton (19,100)
Provincial parks: 62 (86.4 sq mi.)
Province revenue (1978–79): $1,313.7 million
Province expenditure (1978–79): $1,441 million

New Brunswick is one of the four original provinces making up the national Confederation in 1867. It was first known to Europeans as a portion of a region called Acadia, settled by the French. By the mid-18th century, British expansion on the neighboring Nova Scotian peninsula led to confrontation with the French. The Acadians were expelled after the British victory of 1755. A British proclamation of 1763 incorporated the area into Nova Scotia but in 1784 it was separated from it and was established as the province of New Brunswick. The first English settlement was established at Maugerville in 1792. During the American Revolution, 14,000 Loyalists settled on the banks of the St. John and St. Croix rivers. Responsible home government was granted by Britain in 1848 and New Brunswick entered the Confederation in 1867.

Since 88% of the province is forested, it is no surprise that New Brunswick's major industries are forest-related, including the manufacture of pulp and paper. Fishing is another economic mainstay on the Bay of Fundy and northeast coasts with herring, lobster, and cod the top catches. New Brunswick is also an important mining center, ranking first in the nation in the production of antimony and bismuth, third in zinc, lead, and silver, and fifth in copper. New Brunswick agriculture and potatoes are synonymous, while the dairy industry ranks second. Food processing is a major employer. Tourism is a growing sector.

Among the province's attractions are King's Landing, a recreated Loyalist village where 60 buildings and a costumed staff portray the 1780–1890 era; Village Historique Acadien which depicts the Acadian way of life between 1780–1880; Fundy and Kouchibouguac National Parks; F.D. Roosevelt's summer home on Campobello Island; the N.B. Museum, one of the oldest in the country; more than 90 covered bridges; beaches; golf courses; numerous crafts festivals.

NEWFOUNDLAND

Capital: St. John's
Lieut. Governor: Hon. Gordon A. Winter
Premier: The Hon. A. Brian Pickford
Minister of Finance: The Hon. Dr. John Collins
Minister of Justice: Hon. G. Ottenheimer
Entered Confederation: March 31, 1949
Provincial flower: Pitcher plant (1954)
Population (1977 est.): 562,500
Area: 156,185 sq mi.
Largest cities: St. John's (86,576); Corner Brook (35,198); Stephenville (10,284); Mount Pearl (10,193); Conception Bay South (9,743)
Provincial parks: 72 (3,099.0 sq mi.)
Province revenue (1979-80): $1,203,560
Province expenditure (1979-80): $1,203,560

John Cabot, sailing under the English flag, reached the island of Newfoundland in 1497 and is its official discoverer. His enthusiastic reports led to international rivalries over the region, with English, French, Basque, and Portuguese fishermen contesting for catches. By 1600 England and France were the chief rivals. Attempts at colonization during the 17th century were met with hostility by the English fishermen and after 1634 by the English crown. In 1699 Parliment prohibited settlement except for maintaining fisheries. French-English rivalries were settled by treaties in 1713 and 1783 recognizing British sovereignty. The island's population increased despite repressive legislation, and in 1729 Britain appointed a naval governor and in 1792 established a judical system. With the appointment of a resident governor and council in 1824, it was acknowledged as a settled colony. A popularly elected assembly was established in 1832 and in 1855 the island was granted full responsible government. Between 1864 and 1869 and again in 1895, the subject of Newfoundland joining the Canadian Confederation was broached but was rejected at the polls. Not until 1948, in the second of two referenda, was there a clear majority for confederation. The administration of Labrador remained unsettled until 1927 when it was awarded to Newfoundland.

Newfoundland's economy is dependent upon mineral production, pulp and paper products, and fish products, with mining playing the major role as a consequence of western Laborador's vast iron reserves. Oil has been discovered at the Hybernia Well, some 200 miles offshore from St. John's on Eastern Grand Banks.

Among Newfoundland's attractions are an ancient Indian burial ground at Port aux Choix and a Norse settlement at L'Anse aux Meadows.

NORTHWEST TERRITORIES

Capital: Yellowknife
Commissioner: John H. Parker
Deputy Commissioner: Robert S. Pilot
Created: July 15, 1870
Reconstituted: Sept. 1, 1905
Flower: Mountain avens (1959)
Population (1979 est.): 46,257
Area: 1,304,903 sq mi.
Largest cities: Yellowknife (10,112), Hay River (3,345), Inuvik (2,892), Frobisher Bay (2,454), Fort Smith (2,234)
Territories revenue (Fiscal 1979): $276,846,000
Territories expenditure (Fiscal 1979): $282,167,000

The Athabascan Indian people have lived in the forested and barrenland regions of what is now the Northwest Territories during the last 2,500 years. The Inuit (Eskimo) have lived in the Arctic regions for about 1,000 years.

Many believe the first Europeans to visit the Northwest Territories were the Norse. According to their history, they sailed by an icy and mountainous land they called Helluland, which was probably what we now call Baffin Island.

In the late 16th century, British trading companies began searching for a shorter more secure shipping route to the Pacific Ocean and the Orient, and Arctic exploration began. In 1576 Martin Frobisher took possession of Baffin Island. In 1668 the ship *Nonsuch* entered Hudson Bay to establish a trade in furs. This led to the establishment of the Hudson's Bay Company in 1670, a company which continues to this day.

In 1818 the British Admiralty began a serious effort to find the Northwest Passage. Ten expeditions were mounted over the next 30 years. But it wasn't until 1903, when *The Gjoa*, commanded by Norwegian Roald Amundsen, sailed from Europe, that the Passage was finally navigated, after three winters in the Arctic.

Meanwhile land expeditions by Sir John Franklin, Thomas Simpson, and others had resulted in exploration and mapping of the Mackenzie District and northern coastline during the 1820s and 1830s.

Commercial ventures followed in the footsteps of the explorers. Many fur trading posts were established in the Mackenzie Valley. Whaling fleets began in Baffin Bay, Hudson Bay and later the western Arctic.

Not far behind were the missionaries, followed by the Royal Canadian Mounted Police, who were made responsible for maintaining law and order.

In 1920 oil was struck north of Fort Norman. There was a dramatic increase in traffic on the Mackenzie River. The introduction of the airplane increased the demand for fuel and the refinery expanded at Norman Wells in 1939.

The first gold brick was poured in 1938 at Yellowknife and two gold mines are still producing. Mining became the principal industry. Today lead and zinc are the main products. Exploration for oil and gas is proceeding at a high pitch with good potential for the future.

There has been an evolution toward more responsible government in the Northwest Territories. In 1967 Yellowknife was named capital of the N.W.T. and the Territorial Government was located there. By 1970 most provincial-type responsibilities had been transferred from the federal government to the Territorial Government. The exception was and still is nonrenewable resources which remain with the federal administration. The Territorial Council has developed from a combination of elected representatives and federal appointees to a fully elected legislative assembly with up to seven of its members responsible for government departments and forming an Executive Committee or cabinet along with the Commissioner and Deputy Commissioner who are public servants.

Among the Northwest Territories' attractions are Wood Buffalo National Park, which straddles the Alberta-Northwest Territories border, home of the largest herd of bison on the continent; Nahanni National Park with its spectacular Virginia Falls; and Auyuittuq, on Baffin Island, Canada's first national park above the Arctic Circle.

NOVA SCOTIA

Capital: Halifax
Lieut. Governor: The Hon. John Elvin Shaffner
Premier: The Hon. John M. Buchanan
Mayor: His Worship Edmund L. Morris
Minister of Finance: The Hon. Joel Matheson
Atty. General: The Hon. Henry W. How
Entered Confederation: July 1, 1867
Provincial flower: Trailing Arbutus (1901) "Mayflower"
Population (1979 est.): 848,500
Area: Land 20,743 sq mi. Water 325 sq mi.
Highest Point: 1,747 ft
Origin of Name: Latin for New Scotland. Derived from the Latin charter by which New Scotland was granted to Sir Wm. Alexander (afterwards Earl of Stirling) in 1621
Slogan: Canada's Ocean Playground
Flag: Consists of the ancient Arms granted in 1625 by King Charles I, with the cross of Saint Andrew extended in a rectangle three-quarters as wide as its length. Colors: Red, yellow, royal blue, and white
Tartan: The Nova Scotia tartan was the first provincial tartan in Canada. Originally designed in 1953, the popular tartan was registered in 1956 in Her Majesty's Register Office in Edinburgh, Scotland. Colors: red, gold, blue, white, and green
No. of counties: 18
Largest cities: Halifax (117,882); Dartmouth (65,341); Sydney (30,645); Glace Bay (21,836); Truro (12,840)
Provincial parks: 100 (28.1 sq mi.)
Province revenue: $1,371,603,600. Recoveries: $135,058,100
Province expenditure: $1,493,629,200

Nova Scotia is one of the four British colonies federated into the Dominion of Canada in 1867. It was the site of the first permanent North American settlement north of Florida, established by the French in 1605. The 17th and 18th centuries were characterized by struggles for power between the British and French. In 1713 the French began construction of Louisbourg fortress and Halifax was founded in 1749 as a counterbalance. In 1848 Nova Scotia became the first British colony to have a government responsible to the people through elected representatives. There was economic and political opposition to the proposed confederation with Ontario, Quebec, and New Brunswick, but the union was carried out in 1867.

The chief components of the province's economy are fisheries, agriculture (livestock, poultry, dairying), the pulp industry, and mining (coal and industrial minerals).

Among Nova Scotia's attractions are Fort Ann,

the first national historic park; the restored fortress of Louisbourg; Champlain's habitation at Port Royal; the Halifax Citadel; Alexander Graham Bell National Historic Park; and Cape Breton Highlands National Park.

ONTARIO

Capital: Toronto
Lieut. Governor: The Hon. Pauline M. McGibbon
Premier: The Hon. William G. Davis
Provincial Treasurer: The Hon. Frank S. Miller
Atty. General: The Hon. Roy McMurtry
Entered Confederation: July 1, 1867
Provincial flower: White trillium (1937)
Population (1977 est.): 8,373,500
Area: 412,582 sq mi.
Largest cities: Toronto (633,318); North York (558,398); Scarborough (387,149); Hamilton (312,003); Ottawa (304,462)
Provincial parks: 127 (20,503.8 sq mi.)
Province revenue (1978-79): $12.3 billion
Province expenditure (1978-79): $14.0 billion

The first known white man in the province was the French explorer Etienne Brûlé on an expedition to the Ottawa River in 1610-11. He was followed by Samuel de Champlain, other French explorers, fur traders, and missionaries. France established Fort Frontenac (present-day Kingston) in 1673 to provide military protection to its fur empire. However, no French colonization had taken place, except for a small farming settlement near Detroit, by the time Canada was ceded to Great Britain in 1763. The Quebec Act of 1774 established Ontario as part of an extended colony ruled from Quebec. The Constitution Act of 1791 divided Quebec colony into Lower Canada (French–Quebec) and Upper Canada (Loyalist–Ontario). John Graves Simcoe, the first lieutenant governor of Upper Canada fixed the capital at York (now Toronto). In 1841 the provinces were united. Responsible cabinet government was achieved in 1848. Canadian federation—in 1867—was brought about in large part by John A. Macdonald and George Brown, Ontario politicians.

Leading elements of the province's economy are agriculture, mining (the province mines 51% of the world's nickel), forest products, and manufacturing (steel, automobiles, industrial machinery).

Among Ontario's attractions are Upper Canada Village near Morrisburg, a recreation of a 19th century Ontario community; Fort Henry at Kingston, and Fort George at Niagara Falls; and Bellevue House National Historic Park in Kingston.

PRINCE EDWARD ISLAND

Capital: Charlottetown
Lieut. Governor: The Hon. J.A. Doiron
Premier: The Hon. J. Angus MacLean
Minister of Finance: The Hon. Lloyd G. MacPhail
Atty. General: The Hon. Horace B. Carver
Entered Confederation: July 1, 1873
Provincial flower: Lady's slipper (1947)
Population (1980 est.): 123,200
Area: 2,184 sq mi.
Largest cities: Charlottetown (17,063); Summerside (8,592); Sherwood (5,602); St. Elanors (2,495); Parkdale (2,172)
Provincial parks: 40 (12.2 sq mi.)
Province revenue: $242,071,900
Province expenditure: $240,930,800

John Cabot may have seen the island in 1497 but Jacques Cartier, the French navigator, is credited with its discovery in June 1534. Samuel de Champlain claimed it for France in 1603 but it was not colonized until 1720. The British occupied the island in 1758 and it was formally ceded to Great Britain in 1763. Representative government reached the island in 1851. A conference in 1864 to discuss the possible union of the three Maritime Provinces was the forerunner of the Quebec Conference of 1864 which resulted in the founding of the Dominion of Canada. Thus Prince Edward Island has been known as the "Cradle of Confederation" although it did not join the union until 1873.

Agriculture is the basic element in the island's economy, followed by the tourist industry and fisheries. Manufacturing and processing are becoming more important, especially electronic equipment and frozen french fries.

Among the province's attractions are Province House in Charlottetown, which is a national historic site; 1,100 miles of pink, sandy beaches; and Fort Amherst National Historic Park, which has a full-sized reproduction of a Micmac Indian village.

QUEBEC

Capital: Quebec City
Lieut. Governor: The Hon. Jean-Pierre Côté
Premier: Rene Levesque
Vice Premier: Jacques-Yvan Morin
Minister of Finance: Jacques Parizeau
Minister of Justice: Marc-André Bédard
Entered Confederation: July 1, 1867
Provincial flower: White garden (Madonna) lily (1963)
Population (1979): 6,301,200
Area: 636,400 sq mi.
Largest cities: Montreal (1,080,546); Laval (246,243); Quebec (177,082); Longueuil (122,429); St. Léonard 78,452)
Provincial parks: 100
Province revenue (1978–79): $12,060,000,000
Province expenditure (1978–79): $13,335,000,000

Jacques Cartier landed at present-day Gaspé in 1534 and took possession of the land in the name of the King of France. New France began with the founding of Quebec City by Samuel de Champlain in 1608, Trois-Rivière in 1616, and Montreal in 1642. Following capitulation of the French army to the British in 1760, the land was ceded to Britain in 1763. The Quebec Act of 1774 created what is now Quebec and tried to fuse British and French institutions in the new political entity. In 1791 Canada was divided into Lower Canada (French) and Upper Canada (English). An attempt to unite them in 1822 failed but in 1841 an Act of Union joined the provinces and in 1867 the British North American Act created the Confederation of Canada.

The economy of the province breaks down as follows: 61% service industries, 30% manufacturing-processing industries, 8% agricultural-extractive. Iron ore, electric power, and forest products (pulp and paper plants) are the chief resources.

Among the province's attractions are Cartier-

Brebeuf Park in Quebec City, which marks Jacques Cartier's first wintering spot in the New World; La Mauricie National Park in the Laurentian Mountains; Forillon National Park, on the Gaspé peninsula; and Laurentide Park, established for the conservation of caribou.

SASKATCHEWAN

Capital: Regina
Lieut. Governor: The Hon. Irwin McIntosh
Premier: The Hon. Allan E. Blakeney
Minister of Finance: The Hon. E.L. (Ed) Tchorzewski
Atty. General: The Hon. Roy J. Romanow
Entered Confederation: September 1, 1905
Provincial flower: Western red lily (1941)
Provincial bird emblem: Prairie sharp-tailed grouse
Population (1979 est.): 960,000
Area: 251,700 sq mi.
Largest cities: Regina (153,848); Saskatoon (144,269); Moose Jaw (33,441); Prince Albert (30,121); Yorkton (15,077)
Provincial and Regional parks: 116 (2,191 sq mi.)
National Park: 1 (1,500 sq mi.)
Province revenue: $2,019,345,400
Province expenditure: $2,018,302,570

The first white man known to see the Saskatchewan River was Henry Kelsey in 1691. The area which became the Province of Saskatchewan was first granted to the Hudson's Bay Company. In 1868 it was surrendered back to the British crown by the Rupert's Land Act to be turned over to the newly formed Dominion of Canada, which was done in 1870. In 1873 Canada created the North West Mounted Police to maintain law and order. The territories were granted an executive council in 1875 and by 1897 had won responsible parliamentary government. Saskatchewan entered the Confederation in 1905 under the Saskatchewan Act.

The chief elements of the province's economy are agriculture, oil, gas, potash, coal and uranium.

Among its attractions are Prince Albert National Park, Cypress Hills Provincial Park, and Fort Walsh, the first headquarters of the North West Mounted police, R.C.M.P. Training Depot, Provincial and Western Development Museums.

YUKON TERRITORY

Capital: Whitehorse
Acting Commissioner: Douglas Bell
Created a separate territory: June 1898
Flower: Fireweed (1957)
Population: 24,865
Area: 207,000 sq mi.
Largest cities: Whitehorse (16,847); Faro (1,687); Watson (1,351)
Territories revenue: $38,000,000
Territories expenditure: $122,001,800

The Yukon was among the last areas of the North American continent to be explored by white men. Two explorers for the Hudson's Bay Company, John Bell and Robert Campbell, first entered the region around 1840. Fort Yukon was established in 1847 on the Yukon River in what was Russian territory. It was relocated in 1867 after the United States purchased Alaska from Russia, and it was relocated again in 1890. It was a center for a small fur trade. Gold discoveries in the 1870s brought some prospectors into the area, but it was the discovery of rich deposits in Bonanza Creek in 1896 that led to the gold rush of 1898. In the same year the Canadian Parliament separated the rapidly growing area from the Northwest Territories and gave it separate territorial status.

The territory's economy is dependent upon mining, with tourism, a rapidly expanding industry, second. Logging is carried out in some southern areas.

Among the Yukon's attractions are Klune National Park, which contains Canada's highest peak, Mount Logan; and Dawson City, the old gold rush boom town, which has been restored.

Party Standings—House of Commons

Thirty-second Parliament—Speaker, Jeanne Sauvé; The Clerk of the House of Commons, C.B. Koester

Province	Lib.[1]	P.C.[2]	N.D.P.[3]	S.Cr.[4]	Ind.	Vacancies	Seats by provinces
Alberta	0	21	—	—	—	—	21
British Columbia	—	16	12	—	—	—	28
Manitoba	2	5	7	—	—	—	14
New Brunswick	7	3	—	—	—	—	10
Newfoundland	5	2	—	—	—	—	7
Nova Scotia	5	6	—	—	—	—	11
Ontario	52	38	5	—	—	—	95
Prince Edward Island	2	2	—	—	—	—	4
Quebec	74	1	—	—	—	—	75
Saskatchewan	—	7	7	—	—	—	14
Yukon/NWT	—	2	1	—	—	—	3
National totals	**147**	**103**	**32**				**282**

1. Liberal Party—Leader, Rt. Hon. Pierre Elliott Trudeau. 2. Progressive Conservative Party—Leader, Joseph Clark. 3. New Democratic Party—Leader, John Edward Broadbent. 4. Social Credit Party—Leader, Fabien Roy. NOTE: Last three General Elections were held on July 8, 1974, May 22, 1979 and Feb. 18, 1980. The legal duration is five years.

Principal Trading Partners in 1979
(in thousands of Canadian dollars)

Selected countries	Imports	Exports
United States	$45,203,044	$43,243,913
Japan	2,152,388	4,081,067
United Kingdom	1,926,015	2,588,580
West Germany	1,538,096	1,367,823
Netherlands	247,925	1,079,635
U.S.S.R.	62,934	762,953
Italy	634,117	729,048
Venezuela	1,556,919	698,264
Belgium/Luxembourg	240,311	667,642
France	775,918	619,090
People's Republic of China	167,533	591,907
Australia	463,661	559,188
Brazil	311,305	416,646
South Korea	461,794	364,300
Argentina	65,072	279,840
Norway	83,982	279,321
Poland	82,556	261,623
Cuba	105,844	257,371
Saudi Arabia	1,228,153	251,891
Mexico	207,304	236,275
Total	**$57,514,871**	**$59,336,377**

National Holidays

	1979	1980	1981
New Year's Day	Jan. 1	Jan. 1	Jan. 1
Good Friday	April 13	April 4	April 17
Easter Monday	April 16	April 7	April 20
Victoria Day	May 21	May 19	May 18
Dominion Day	July 1	July 1	July 1
Labor Day	Sept. 3	Sept. 1	Sept. 7
Thanksgiving	Oct. 8	Oct. 13	Oct. 12
Remembrance Day	Nov. 11	Nov. 11	Nov. 11
Christmas Day	Dec. 25	Dec. 25	Dec. 25

National Flag and Motto

The National Flag of Canada, otherwise known as the Canadian Flag, was approved by Parliament and proclaimed by Her Majesty the Queen on February 15, 1965, and is described as a red flag of the proportions two by length and one by width, containing in its center a white square the width of the flag, bearing a single red maple leaf.

The Flag is flown on land daily from sunrise to sunset at all federal government buildings, airports, and military bases and establishments within and outside Canada, and may appropriately be flown or displayed by individuals and organizations.

The Canada Shipping Act provides that the National Flag is the proper national colors for all Canadian ships and boats; and it is the flag flown on Canadian Naval vessels.

The motto—*A mari usque ad mare* ("From sea to sea")—is from the Latin version of Psalm LXXII: 8: "He shall have dominion also from sea to sea, and from the river unto the ends of the earth."

Canadian Museums and Related Institutions

Region	Art galleries	History museums	Restorations	Science and technology museums	Living science museums[1]	General museums	Community museums	Archives	Other institutions[2]	Total
Atlantic	10	9	65	8	2	3	44	14	5	160
Quebec	11	19	16	4	11	1	27	11	6	106
Ontario	35	22	73	14	12	3	106	19	9	293
Central	19	39	45	10	8	7	113	12	8	261
British Columbia	11	12	14	9	8	2	49	7	6	118
Yukon and Northwest Territories	—	—	2	—	—	1	3	1	—	7
Total	**86**	**101**	**215**	**45**	**41**	**17**	**342**	**64**	**34**	**945**

1. Aquaria, zoos, botanical gardens, arboretums, and conservatories. 2. Including nature park museums or nature centers. *Source:* Statistics Canada, July 1979, based on a 1976 survey.

Percentage Distribution of Canadian Population by Provinces and Territories

Province or territory	1978 (est.)	1971	1961	1951	1941	1931	1911
Alberta	8.31	7.55	7.30	6.71	6.92	7.05	5.19
British Columbia	10.77	10.13	8.93	8.32	7.11	6.69	5.45
Manitoba	4.40	4.58	5.05	5.54	6.34	6.75	6.40
New Brunswick	2.96	2.94	3.28	3.68	3.97	3.94	4.88
Newfoundland	2.42	2.42	2.51	2.58	—	—	—
Nova Scotia	3.58	3.66	4.04	4.59	5.02	4.94	6.83
Ontario	35.96	35.71	34.19	32.82	32.92	33.07	35.07
Prince Edward Island	0.52	0.52	0.58	0.70	0.83	0.85	1.30
Quebec	26.77	27.95	28.84	28.95	28.96	27.70	27.83
Saskatchewan	4.03	4.29	5.07	5.94	7.79	8.88	6.84
Northwest Territories	0.19	0.16	0.13	0.11	0.10	0.09	0.09
Yukon Territory	0.09	0.09	0.08	0.06	0.04	0.04	0.12
Totals	**100.00**	**100.00**	**100.00**	**100.00**	**100.00**	**100.00**	**100.00**

Growth Components of Canada's Population

Period	Total population growth (thousands)	Births (thousands)	Deaths (thousands)	Natural increase (thousands)	Ratio of natural increase to total growth (percent)	Immigration (thousands)	Emigration (thousands)	Net migration (thousands)	Ratio of net migration to total growth (percent)
1851–1861	793	1,281	670	611	77.0	352	170	182	23.0
1861–1871	460	1,370	760	610	132.6	260	410	−150	−32.6
1871–1881	636	1,480	790	690	108.5	350	404	−54	−8.5
1881–1891	508	1,524	870	654	128.7	680	826	−146	−28.7
1891–1901	538	1,548	880	668	124.2	250	380	−130	−24.2
1901–1911	1,835	1,925	900	1,025	55.9	1,550	740	810	44.1
1911–1921	1,581	2,340	1,070	1,270	80.3	1,400	1,089	311	19.7
1921–1931	1,589	2,420	1,060	1,360	85.5	1,200	970	230	14.5
1931–1941	1,130	2,294	1,072	1,222	108.1	149	241	−92	−8.1
1941–1951[1]	2,503	3,212	1,220	1,992	92.3	548	382	166	7.7
1951–1961	4,228	4,468	1,320	3,148	74.5	1,543	463	1,080	25.5
1961–1971	3,330	4,105	1,497	2,608	78.3	1,429	707	722	21.7
1971–1976[2]	1,424	1,756	822	934	65.6	841	351	490	34.4

1. Includes Newfoundland in 1951 but not in 1941. 2. *Source: Canada Year Book 1978–79,* latest information available, Statistics Canada.

Canadian Motor Vehicle Registrations, 1978

Province or territory	Passenger cars[1]	Motor trucks	Motor buses	Motorcycles	Other motor vehicles[2]	Total motor vehicles
Alberta	960,284	405,679	6,566	40,644	(3)	1,413,173
British Columbia	1,176,883	420,724[4]	(5)	36,132[6]	(3)	1,633,739
Manitoba	445,546	166,041	349[7]	15,594[6]	897[8]	628,427
New Brunswick	243,301	76,713	1,414	10,903	8,446	340,777
Newfoundland	132,449	45,362	1,195	3,358[6]	5,993	188,357
Nova Scotia	284,559	108,913	961	13,882	4,345	412,660
Ontario	3,597,371	783,032	19,814	86,377	(3)	4,496,105
Prince Edward Island	46,413	16,887	424	1,677	(3)	65,401
Quebec	2,449,668	372,346	16,994	116,426	40,898	2,996,332
Saskatchewan	395,089	306,712	5,180	14,399	870	722,250
N.W.T.	6,020	7,877	69	1,321[6]	55	15,342
Yukon T.	7,411	7,546	(5)	668[6]	(3)	15,625
Total	**9,744,944**	**2,717,832**	**52,966**	**341,381**	**61,504**	**12,918,677**

1. Includes taxis and for-hire cars. 2. Ambulances, fire trucks, etc. 3. Included with passenger cars or trucks. 4. Includes taxicabs. 5. Included in trucks. 6. Includes mopeds. 7. Excludes school buses which are licensed as passenger cars. 8. Includes only antique vehicles and vehicles for road testing. *Source:* Statistics Canada.

Percent of Homes With Selected Appliances[1]

Item	1974	1975	1976	1977	1978	1979
Air conditioners, room	7.6	9.2	9.7	10.9	10.7	11.5
Central unit	2.6	3.2	3.7	4.4	4.5	5.0
Automatic dishwashers	12.9	15.2	18.6	21.8	23.8	26.3
Clothes dryers	48.3	51.6	54.7	58.7	59.4	60.0
Floor polishers	48.3	n.a.	41.0	n.a.	n.a.	n.a.
Home freezers	39.8	41.8	43.5	47.5	47.2	48.9
Microwave ovens	n.a.	0.8	n.a.	n.a.	n.a.	4.7
Portable humidifiers	n.a.	20.0	n.a.	20.3	n.a.	n.a.
Power lawn mowers, gasoline	34.7	n.a.	35.4	n.a.	37.1	n.a.
Electric	14.6	n.a.	15.8	n.a.	16.1	n.a.
Hand	6.9	n.a.	5.5	n.a.	4.1	n.a.
Radios (except car)	98.2	98.3	98.5	98.0	98.4	98.4
Record–playing equipment	74.5	75.7	75.6	77.4	78.8	77.3
Refrigerators	98.9	98.9	99.2	99.4	99.4	99.4
Sewing machines, electric	n.a.	65.4	n.a.	64.3	n.a.	n.a.
Smoke detectors	n.a.	n.a.	n.a.	n.a.	n.a.	38.5
Snowblowers	6.5	n.a.	7.8	n.a.	9.5	n.a.
Tape records	n.a.	34.7	n.a.	37.3	n.a.	54.9
Television: black and white, one	61.4	58.1	54.1	49.0	45.7	43.8
Two or more	11.9	9.7	8.3	7.3	6.5	5.6
Color, one	42.7	50.7	57.0	62.5	65.7	68.8
Two or more	1.9	2.7	3.7	5.3	6.6	7.9
Vacuum cleaners	n.a.	86.5	n.a.	88.7	n.a.	n.a.
Washing machines, automatic	48.9	52.1	55.9	59.2	59.1	60.5
Other electric	28.6	24.8	20.2	17.2	17.2	15.2
Total households (000's)	**6,493**	**6,703**	**6,918**	**7,119**	**7,320**	**7,558**

1. 1974–75 figures are for April; 1976–79 are for May. NOTE: n.a.=not available. *Source: Household Facilities and Equipment,* Statistics Canada.

Growth Statistics
(in Canadian dollars)

Year	Exports (including re-exports (millions of dollars)	Imports (millions of dollars)	Industry selling price indexes for manufacturing (1971=100)	Railway gross revenues[1] (millions of dollars)	Railway operating expenses[1] (millions of dollars)	Tons of revenue freight carried one mile[1] (millions)	Freight carried on welland canal (thousands of tons)	Vessels other than coastal entered & cleared (thousands of reg net tons)
1891	n.a.	n.a.	n.a.	$ 48	$ 35	n.a.	975	18,803
1901	n.a.	n.a.	n.a.	73	50	n.a.	620	26,030
1911	n.a.	n.a.	n.a.	189	131	16,048	2,538	47,430
1921	$ 814	$ 799	n.a.	458	423	26,622	3,076	54,649
1941	1,640	1,449	n.a.	538	404	49,982	13,230	64,766
1951	3,963	4,085	n.a.	1,089	978	64,300	16,198	100,259
1961	5,896	5,771	82.4	1,156	1,053	65,828	31,404	156,987
1965	8,767	8,633	n.a.	1,369	1,288	87,052	53,437	199,454
1966	10,326	9,866	n.a.	1,476	1,367	94,944	59,137	202,170
1967	11,411	11,075	n.a.	1,514	1,438	92,239	52,850	197,422
1968	13,624	12,358	92.3	1,528	1,433	93,147	58,105	204,777
1969	14,890	14,130	95.8	1,579	1,496	94,688	53,532	197,391
1970	16,819	13,952	98.1	1,672	1,570	108,210	62,963	217,621
1971	17,820	15,618	100.0	1,797	1,693	119,412	63,058	228,561
1972	20,140	18,669	104.4	1,843	1,750	119,135	64,194	243,376
1973	25,301	23,303	116.1	2,029	1,935	125,471	67,195	244,466
1974	32,177	31,639	138.1	2,476	2,394	133,554	52,360	227,175
1975	32,755	34,668	153.7	2,618	2,668	130,997	59,849	231,345
1976	38,028	37,391	161.6	3,058	2,927	132,589	64,340	124,071
1977	44,375	42,156	174.3	3,388	3,186	137,745	71,736	264,425
1978	52,605	49,606	190.4	3,709	3,500	141,747	72,389	n.a.

1. Six major railways, representing about 95% of the industry in terms of operating revenues and other performance indicators. NOTE: n.a. = not available. *Source:* Statistics Canada.

Growth Statistics
(in Canadian dollars)

Year	Motor vehicle registrations (thousands)	Telephones in use (thousands)	Post office and money order revenue (thousands)	Index numbers of weekly earnings[1] 1961 = 100	Strikes and lockouts: Employees affected (thousands)	Strikes and lockouts: Time lost working days (thousands)	Federal finance: Total revenue (millions of dollars)	Federal finance: Total expenditure (millions of dollars)	Federal finance: Net debt (millions of dollars)
1881	n.a.	n.a.	1,345	n.a.	n.a.	n.a.	$ 30	$ 34	$ 155
1891	n.a.	n.a.	2,516	n.a.	n.a.	n.a.	39	41	238
1901	n.a.	n.a.	3,421	n.a.	24	738	53	58	268
1911	22	303	9,147	n.a.	29	1,821	118	123	340
1921	465	902	26,331	n.a.	28	1,049	436	528	2,341
1931	1,201	1,364	30,416	n.a.	11	204	356	442	2,262
1941	1,573	1,562	40,383	34.1	87	434	872	1,250	3,649
1951	2,872	3,114	90,455	64.0	103	902	3,113	2,901	11,645
1961	5,517	6,014	202,004	100.0	98	1,335	5,618	5,958	12,437
1965	6,669	7,445	263,704	116.2	172	2,350	7,180	7,218	15,504
1966	7,035	7,883	275,994	127.8	411	5,178	7,696	7,735	15,543
1967	7,482	8,358	295,529	130.6	252	3,975	8,358	8,780	15,965
1968	7,877	8,818	337,023	140.3	224	5,083	9,029	9,824	16,760
1969	8,254	9,296	374,902	150.8	307	7,752	10,163	11,938	17,336
1970	8,497	9,750	444,069	162.8	262	6,540	12,321	11,928	16,943
1971	9,022	10,269	432,911	176.7	240	2,867	12,803	13,182	17,322
1972	9,481	10,987	504,211	191.4	706	7,754	14,227	14,841	17,937
1973	10,158	11,677	563,159	205.4	348	5,776	16,602	16,121	17,456
1974	11,002	12,454	591,133	227.6	592	9,255	19,383	20,056	18,128
1975	11,443	13,165	617,743	261.7	479	10,859	24,909	26,055	19,275
1976	11,786	13,885	568,190	295.8	1,571[2]	11,685	29,956	33,978	23,296
1977	12,547	14,488	774,860	326.2	218	3,742	32,721	39,011	29,586
1978	n.a.	n.a.	n.a.	350.3	402	7,393	32,846	42,879	39,619

1. In manufacturing. 2. This figure includes 830,000 affected by "day of protest." NOTE: n.a. = not available. *Source:* Statistics Canada

Canadian Consumer Price Index
(1971 = 100)

Year	Food	Housing	Clothing	Transportation	Health and personal care	Recreation and reading	Tobacco and alcohol	All-item index
1962	77.5	74.0	78.4	76.9	71.6	74.3	78.8	75.9
1963	80.0	74.8	80.3	76.9	73.5	75.4	78.9	77.2
1964	81.3	76.0	82.4	77.8	75.8	76.6	80.4	78.6
1965	83.4	77.3	83.8	80.7	79.4	77.9	81.7	80.5
1966	88.7	79.5	87.0	82.6	81.8	80.1	83.7	83.5
1967	89.9	82.9	91.4	86.1	86.0	84.1	85.8	86.5
1968	92.8	86.7	94.1	88.3	89.5	88.3	93.6	90.0
1969	96.7	91.2	96.7	92.4	93.8	93.5	97.2	94.1
1970	98.9	95.7	98.5	96.1	98.0	96.8	98.4	97.2
1971	100.0	100.0	100.0	100.0	100.0	100.0	100.0	100.0
1972	107.6	104.7	102.6	102.6	104.8	102.8	102.7	104.8
1973	123.3	111.4	107.7	105.3	109.8	107.1	106.0	112.7
1974	143.4	121.1	118.0	115.8	119.4	116.4	111.8	125.0
1975	161.9	133.2	125.1	129.4	133.0	128.5	125.3	138.5
1976	166.2	145.7	132.0	143.3	144.3	136.2	134.3	148.9
1977	180.1	161.9	141.0	153.3	155.1	142.7	143.8	160.8
1978	208.0	170.8	146.4	162.2	166.2	148.2	155.5	175.2
1979	235.4	186.2	159.9	178.0	181.2	158.4	166.7	191.2
Feb. 1980	248.4	194.6	171.1	190.9	191.2	167.0	175.9	201.8

Source: Statistics Canada

Estimates of the Civilian Labor Force and Its Main Components, Annual Averages

(in thousands)

Year	Civilian population[1]	Civilian labor force[1]: Employed	Unemployed	Total labor force	Persons not in the labor force[1]	Unemployment rate percent	Participation rate percent
1966	13,475	7,152	267	7,420	6,055	3.6	55.1
1967	13,874	7,379	315	7,694	6,179	4.1	55.5
1968	14,264	7,537	382	7,919	6,344	4.8	55.5
1969	14,638	7,780	382	8,162	6,475	4.7	55.8
1970	15,016	7,879	495	8,374	6,642	5.9	55.8
1971	15,388	8,079	552	8,631	6,757	6.4	56.1
1972	15,747	8,329	562	8,891	6,856	6.3	56.5
1973	16,125	8,759	520	9,279	6,846	5.6	57.5
1974	16,562	9,137	525	9,662	6,900	5.4	58.3
1975	16,470	9,363	697	10,060	6,410	6.9	61.1
1976	16,873	9,572	736	10,308	6,565	7.1	61.1
1977	17,250	9,754	862	10,616	6,634	8.1	61.5
1978[2]	17,381	9,972	911	10,882	6,499	8.4	62.6
1979[2]	17,691	10,369	838	11,207	6,484	7.5	63.3

1. 14 years of age, or over. 2. 15 years of age, or over. *Source:* Statistics Canada.

Average Temperature and Precipitation Data

Station	Temperature °C: Mean Jan.	Mean July	Extreme Max.	Extreme Min.	Average frost date: Last in spring	First in fall	Average total annual precip. (mm)	Aver. ann. snowfall (cm)
St. John's A, Nfld.	−3.8	15.3	30.6	−23.3	June 3	Oct. 12	1511.5	363.7
Charlottetown A, P.E.I.	−6.7	18.4	34.4	−27.8	May 17	Oct. 15	1127.8	305.1
Halifax, N.S.	−3.2	18.3	34.4	−25.0	May 1	Nov. 1	1318.8	210.8
Sydney A, N.S.	−4.4	17.9	35.0	−25.6	May 23	Oct. 16	1340.9	288.0
Yarmouth A, N.S.	−2.7	16.4	30.0	−21.0	May 2	Oct. 24	1283.2	204.5
Chatham A, N.B.	−9.3	19.2	37.8	−35.0	May 22	Sept. 21	1051.2	309.4
Moncton A, N.B.	−7.9	18.6	37.2	−32.2	May 23	Sept. 23	1099.3	313.7
Saint John A, N.B.	−7.1	17.1	34.4	−36.7	May 18	Oct. 2	1400.3	204.7
Fort Chimo A, Que.	−23.4	11.4	32.2	−46.7	June 27	Aug. 30	483.8	236.7
Montreal McGill, Que.	−8.9	21.6	36.1	−33.9	April 22	Oct. 23	999.0	243.1
Quebec A, Que.	−11.6	19.2	35.6	−36.1	May 18	Sept. 28	1088.6	326.6
Schefferville (Knob Lake) A, Que.	−22.7	12.6	31.7	−50.6	June 18	Aug. 31	722.5	335.5
Sherbrooke, Que.	−9.6	20.1	36.7	−41.1	May 12	Sept. 27	972.6	244.6
London A, Ont.	−6.0	20.5	36.7	−31.7	May 9	Oct. 6	924.5	201.2
Ottawa A, Ont.	−10.9	20.7	37.8	−36.1	May 11	Oct. 1	850.9	215.6
Thunder Bay A, Ont.	−14.8	17.5	37.2	−41.1	May 31	Sept. 10	738.5	222.0
Toronto, Ont.	−4.4	21.8	40.6	−32.8	April 20	Oct. 30	789.9	141.0
Churchill A. Man.	−27.6	12.0	33.9	−45.0	June 22	Sept. 12	396.6	183.9
The Pas A, Man.	−22.4	17.9	36.7	−49.4	May 28	Sept. 20	449.7	157.2
Winnipeg A, Man.	−18.3	19.7	40.6	−45.0	May 25	Sept. 21	535.2	131.3
Regina A, Sask.	−17.3	18.9	43.3	−50.0	May 27	Sept. 12	397.9	114.8
Saskatoon A, Sask.	−18.7	18.8	40.0	−47.8	May 27	Sept. 15	352.6	112.5
Beaverlodge CDA, Alta.	−14.9	15.6	36.7	−47.8	May 22	Sept. 7	454.7	183.6
Calgary A, Alta.	−10.9	16.5	36.1	−45.0	May 28	Sept. 12	437.1	153.9
Edmonton Ind. A, Alta.	−14.7	17.5	34.4	−48.3	May 14	Sept. 19	446.5	132.1

STATION (A = Airport)	Elevation (ft)	Temperature °C Mean daily Ann.	Temperature °C Extreme Max.	Temperature °C Extreme Min.	Average frost dates Last in spring	Average frost dates First in fall	Average total annual precip. (mm)	Aver. ann. snowfall (cm)
Kamloops A, B.C.	−6.0	20.9	40.6	−37.2	May 5	Sept. 28	260.6	77.0
Prince George A, B.C.	−11.8	14.9	34.4	−50.0	June 10	Aug. 28	620.7	233.4
Prince Rupert, B.C.	1.8	13.6	32.2	−21.1	April 19	Nov. 5	2414.5	113.0
Vancouver A, B.C.	2.4	17.4	33.3	−17.8	March 31	Oct. 30	1068.1	52.3
Dawson, Y.T.	−28.6	15.5	35.0	−58.3	May 26	Aug. 27	325.5	136.4
Whitehorse A, Y.T.	−18.9	14.1	34.4	−52.2	June 5	Sept. 1	260.3	127.8
Coppermine, N.W.T.	−29.4	9.3	32.2	−50.0	June 27	Aug. 21	216.3	101.9
Fort Simpson A, N.W.T.	−27.6	16.1	35.0	−53.3	May 31	Aug. 29	343.2	137.9
Frobisher Bay A, N.W.T.	−26.2	7.9	24.4	−45.6	June 30	Aug. 29	415.2	246.9
Resolute A, N.W.T.	−32.6	4.3	18.3	−52.2	July 10	July 20	136.4	78.7

A = Airport, Ind. A = Industrial Airport CDA = Canada Department of Agriculture *Source: Canada Year Book 1978–79,* Statistics Canada.

Highest Elevations

Province or territory	Height in feet	Height in meters
Alberta—Mount Columbia	12,294	3,747
British Columbia—Mt. Fairweather	15,300	4,663
Manitoba—Baldy Mountain	2,729	832
New Brunswick—Mount Carleton	2,690	820
Newfoundland—Cirque Mt., Labrador Penin.	5,160	1,573
Nova Scotia—North Barren Mt., Cape Breton Island	1,747	532
Ontario—Ogidaki Mt.	2,183	665
Prince Edward Island—highest point Queens County	465	142
Quebec—Mt. Jacques Cartier, Gaspé Penin.	4,160	1,268
Saskatchewan—Cypress Hills	4,546	1,386
Northwest Territories—Mt. Sir James MacBrien	9,062	2,762
Yukon Territory—Mount Logan	19,850	6,050

Mileage Between Principal Points in Canada

(via rail or water)

Approximate distances by rail or water	Nfld. St. John's	N.S. Halifax	P.E.I. Charlottetown	N.B. Saint John	N.B. Fredericton	Que. Quebec	Que. Montreal	Ont. Ottawa	Ont. Toronto	Ont. Thunder Bay	Man. Winnipeg	Sask. Regina	Sask. Saskatoon	Alta. Calgary	Alta. Edmonton	B.C. Vancouver	B.C. Victoria	B.C. Pr. Rupert
St. John's	0	930	1,041	1,081	1,094	1,466	1,563	1,675	1,897	2,521	2,797	3,153	3,268	3,531	3,646	4,262	4,362	4,543
Halifax	930	0	239	279	292	664	761	873	1,095	1,719	1,995	2,351	2,466	2,729	2,844	3,460	3,560	3,741
Charlottetown	1,041	239	0	215	230	600	684	795	1,018	1,653	1,950	2,305	2,421	2,772	2,751	3,413	3,498	3,707
Saint John	1,081	279	215	0	67	425	482	594	816	1,470	1,894	2,250	2,374	2,726	2,699	3,368	3,324	3,655
Fredericton	1,094	292	230	67	0	403	454	565	788	1,423	1,753	2,108	2,224	2,575	2,554	3,216	3,301	3,510
Quebec City	1,466	664	600	425	403	0	164	276	498	1,152	1,521	1,877	1,992	2,353	2,323	2,995	2,898	3,279
Montreal	1,563	761	684	482	454	164	0	112	334	988	1,357	1,713	1,828	2,244	2,151	2,886	2,900	3,115
Ottawa	1,675	873	795	594	565	276	112	0	247	887	1,301	1,658	1,772	2,133	2,098	2,775	2,789	3,054
Toronto	1,897	1,095	1,018	816	788	498	334	247	0	809	1,233	1,590	1,704	2,065	2,030	2,707	2,755	2,986
Thunder Bay	2,521	1,719	1,653	1,470	1,423	1,152	988	877	809	0	424	781	895	1,256	1,221	1,898	1,967	2,177
Winnipeg	2,797	1,995	1,950	1,894	1,753	1,521	1,357	1,301	1,233	424	0	356	471	832	797	1,474	1,548	1,753
Regina	3,153	2,351	2,305	2,250	2,108	1,877	1,713	1,658	1,590	781	356	0	161	476	487	1,118	1,193	1,443
Saskatoon	3,268	2,466	2,421	2,374	2,224	1,992	1,828	1,772	1,704	895	471	161	0	399	326	1,097	1,131	1,282
Calgary	3,531	2,729	2,772	2,726	2,575	2,353	2,244	2,133	2,065	1,256	832	476	399	0	195	642	727	1,151
Edmonton	3,646	2,844	2,751	2,699	2,554	2,323	2,151	2,098	2,030	1,221	797	487	326	195	0	771	846	956
Vancouver	4,262	3,460	3,413	3,368	3,216	2,995	2,886	2,775	2,707	1,898	1,474	1,118	1,097	642	771	0	85	546
Victoria	4,362	3,560	3,498	3,324	3,301	2,898	2,900	2,789	2,755	1,967	1,548	1,193	1,131	727	846	85	0	631
Prince Rupert	4,543	3,741	3,707	3,655	3,510	3,279	3,115	3,054	2,986	2,177	1,753	1,443	1,282	1,151	956	546	641	0

Air Distances Between Cities
(via Air Canada)

From	To	Miles[1]
Gander	Montreal	1,109
Gander	Toronto	1,494
Halifax	Moncton	120
Halifax	Montreal	571
Halifax	North Bay	1,034
Halifax	Ottawa	665
Halifax	Toronto	897
Halifax	Vancouver	3,015
Halifax	Winnipeg	1,893
Lethbridge	Calgary	124
Lethbridge	Edmonton	301
Montreal	Boston	778
Montreal	Edmonton	2,019
Montreal	Goose Bay	824
Montreal	Moncton	451
Montreal	New York	350
Montreal	Ottawa	94
Montreal	Toronto	326
Montreal	Vancouver	2,444
Montreal	Windsor	521
Ottawa	Winnipeg	1,174
St. John's, Nfld.	Montreal	1,147
Sydney	Halifax	200
Toronto	Chicago	435
Toronto	Cleveland	195
Toronto	Edmonton	1,693
Toronto	New York	375
Toronto	Tampa	1,119
Toronto	Vancouver	2,118
Toronto	Winnipeg	942
Vancouver	Victoria	47
Winnipeg	Calgary	750
Winnipeg	Edmonton	753

1. Statute miles. *Source:* Air Canada.

Land and Fresh Water Areas of Canada

Province, territory, or district	Land sq miles	Fresh water sq miles	Total sq miles	Percent of total area
Alberta	248,800	6,485	255,285	6.6
British Columbia	359,279	6,976	366,255	9.5
Manitoba	211,775	39,225	251,000	6.5
New Brunswick	27,835	519	28,354	0.7
Newfoundland	143,045	13,140	156,185	4.1
Nova Scotia	20,402	1,023	21,425	0.6
Ontario	344,092	68,490	412,582	10.7
Prince Edward Island	2,184	—	2,184	0.1
Quebec	523,860	71,000	594,860	15.4
Saskatchewan	220,182	31,518	251,700	6.5
Northwest Territories	1,253,438	51,465	1,304,903	33.9
Franklin	541,753	7,500	549,253	14.3
Keewatin	218,460	9,700	228,160	5.9
Mackenzie	493,225	34,265	527,490	13.7
Yukon Territory	205,346	1,730	207,076	5.4
Totals	**3,560,238**	**291,571**	**3,851,809**	**100.0**

Institutions, Full-time Teachers, Full-time Enrollment and Expenditures, Canada and Provinces[1]

Level and subgroup	Institutions	Full-time teachers	Full-time enrollment	Total expenditures (millions of dollars)
Alberta				
Elementary-Secondary	1,430	22,375	446,450	1,172.3
Post-secondary				
Non-university	19	1,955	18,290	146.9
University	5	2,780	30,085	379.9
Total all levels	1,456	27,110	494,825	1,699.2

Level and subgroup	Institutions	Full-time teachers	Full-time enrollment	Total expenditures (millions of dollars)
British Columbia				
Elementary-Secondary	1,856	27,330	528,250	1,363.5
Post-secondary				
Non-university	21	1,520	17,410	188.1
University	5	2,935	28,940	372.7
Total all levels	1,882	31,785	574,600	1,924.3
Manitoba				
Elementary-Secondary	804	12,180	220,850	573.2
Post-secondary				
Non-university	8	355	2,890	19.0
University	7	1,650	16,060	181.2
Total all levels	819	14,185	239,800	773.5
New Brunswick				
Elementary-Secondary	480	7,620	153,815	330.6
Post-secondary				
Non-university	8	260	2,175	12.0
University	4	1,035	10,460	101.4
Total all levels	492	8,915	166,450	443.9
Newfoundland				
Elementary-Secondary	687	7,490	147,045	262.1
Post-secondary				
Non-university	6	205	1,990	—
University	1	790	6,050	—
Total all levels	694	8,485	155,085	370.7
Nova Scotia				
Elementary-Secondary	608	10,650	187,540	423.4
Post-secondary				
Non-university	14	340	2,685	30.7
University	10	1,620	17,250	156.8
Total all levels	632	12,610	207,475	610.9
Ontario				
Elementary-Secondary	5,182	97,995	1,903,595	5,208.7
Post-secondary				
Non-university	30	5,650	70,110	396.1
University	21	12,550	147,960	1,490.3
Total all levels	5,233	116,195	2,121,665	7,095.1
Prince Edward Island				
Elementary-Secondary	73	1,368	25,965	57.3
Post-secondary				
Non-university	2	70	790	—
University	1	120	1,360	—
Total all levels	76	1,558	28,115	79.0
Quebec				
Elementary-Secondary	3,006	63,710	1,204,340	3,886.7
Post-secondary				
Non-university	74	9,170	125,600	718.7
University	7	7,530	85,945	1,132.5
Total all levels	3,087	80,410	1,415,885	5,738.0
Saskatchewan				
Elementary-Secondary	1,049	10,845	213,365	527.2
Post-secondary				
Non-university	3	370	2,410	30.0
University	3	1,400	13,765	159.7
Total all levels	1,055	12,615	229,540	717.0
Yukon[2]				
Total Elementary and Secondary Schools	23	278	5,130	—[3]

Level and subgroup	Institutions	Full-time teachers	Full-time enrollment	Total expenditures (millions of dollars)
Northwest Territories[2]				
Total Elementary and Secondary Schools	70	725	13,440	184.7[3]

1. For 1980–81. 2. No post-secondary institutions. 3. Includes both Yukon and Northwest Territories and undistributed. *Source: Advance Statistics of Education 1979–80*, Statistics Canada.

Major Canadian Awards, 1979

Governor General's Literary Awards

Fiction: English: Jack Hodgins for *The Resurrection of Joseph Bourne;* French: Marie-Clair Blais for *Le Sourd dan la Ville*
Poetry: English: Michael Ondaatje for *There's a Trick with a Knife;* French: Robert Melancon for *Painture Aveugle*
Nonfiction: English: Maria Tippett for *Emily Carr;* French: Dominique Clift and Shelia McLeod Arnopolous for *Le Fait Anglais au Quebec*

Juno Award Winners

Female Vocalist: Anne Murray
Male Vocalist: Burton Cummings
Group: Trooper
Country Female Vocalist: Anne Murray
Country Male Vocalist: Murray McLauchlan
Country Group: The Good Brothers
Best New Female Vocalist: France Joli
Best New Male Vocalist: Walter Rossi
Best New Group: Streetheart
Folksinger: Bruce Cockburn
Instrumental Artist: Frank Mills
Composer: Frank Mills
Best Jazz Recording: Ed Bickert and Don Thompson for *Sackville 4005*
Best Classical Recording: Judy Loman for *The Crown of Ariadne*

Actra Awards

The Earle Grey Award for the Best Acting Performance in Television in a Leading Role: Don Francks, *They're Drying Up the Streets*
The Andrew Allan Award for the Best Acting Performance in Radio: Kate Reid, *Grasshopper Hill*
Best Variety Performance in Television: Burton Cummings
Best Supporting Actor in Television: Paul Harding, *A Man Called Intrepid*
Du Maurier Award for Best New Television Performer: Sarah Torgov, *They're Drying Up the Streets*
Best Television Host-Interviewer: Brian Lineham
Best Radio Host-Interviewer: Barbara Frum and Alan Maitland
The Foster Hewitt Award for Excellence in Sportcasting: Dave Hodge
Gordon Sinclair Award for outspoken opinions and integrity in broadcasting: Ricki Katz, Susan Millican
The John Drainie Award for Distinguished Contribution to Broadcasting: Norman Campbell
Best Television Program of the Year: *They're Drying Up the Streets*
Best Radio Program: *Aftermath of Jonestown*
Best Children's Television Show: *Intergalactic Thanksgiving*
Best Dramatic Writer—Television: Ralph Thomas, Roy McGregor, *Every Person is Guilty*
Best Dramatic Writer—Radio: Betty Lambert, *Grasshopper Hill*
Best Documentary Writer—Television: Barbara Young, *Penny Kitchen*
Best Documentary Writer—Radio: Terence McKenna, *Aftermath of Jonestown*
Best Variety Writer—Television: Johnny Wayne, Frank Schuster, Kate Lonsdale and Ted Lonsdale

National Newspaper Awards

Enterprise Reporting: Bill Dampier, *Toronto Star*
Feature Writing: Val Sears, *Toronto Star*
Editorial Writing: Oakland Ross, *Toronto Globe and Mail*
Spot News Reporting: The Toronto Bureau of The Canadian Press
Sports Writing: Allen Abel, *Toronto Globe and Mail*
Critical Writing: John Hofsess, *Calgary Albertan*
Spot News Photography: Bill Sandford, *Toronto Sun*
Feature Photography: Bill Keay, *Vancouver Sun*
Cartooning: Ed Uluschak, *Edmonton Journal*
Citation for Merit in Sports Writing: Alison Gordon, *Toronto Star*
Citation for Merit in Spot News Reporting: *London Free Press* team

The Royal Bank Award

In 1967, as a Canadian centennial project, The Royal Bank of Canada established the Royal Bank Award to honor "a Canadian citizen or person domiciled in Canada whose outstanding achievement is of such importance that it is contributing to human welfare and the common good." The award consists of a gold medal and a cash grant of $50,000.

1967 Dr. Wilder Penfield, neurosurgeon
1968 Dr. C. J. Mackenzie, engineer
1969 His Eminence Paul-Émile Cardinal Léger
1970 Morley Callaghan, novelist
1971 Arthur Erickson, architect
1972 Dr. Gustave Gingras, rehabilitation expert
1973 Dr. J. A. Corry, educationalist
1974 Jean Gascon, actor/director
1975 Dr. R. Keith Downey and Dr. Baldur R. Stefansson, agricultural scientists
1976 Mary Pack, organizer of the Canadian Arthritis and Rheumantism Society
1977 Dr. W. A. Paddon and Dr. Gordon W. Thomas, frontier medical pioneers
1978 Dr. H. Northrop Frye, literary scholar
1979 Dr. Lotta Hitschmanova, founder and executive director, Unitarian Service Committee of Canada
1980 Dr. Jacques Genest, founder and director, Clinical Research Institute of Montreal

Information for Air Travelers

Source: Civil Aeronautics Board.

Refunds

If you paid for your ticket with cash, you can usually get an immediate refund from the issuing airline at any of its ticket offices. If you paid with a personal check or credit card, the refund will generally have to be processed through the airline's accounting department and mailed to you.

When you pay by credit card, your charge account is billed whether you use your tickets or not. You won't receive credit unless the unused tickets are returned to the airline, and you can't get a cash refund for a credit card charge.

If you buy your tickets with a credit card and then change your flights, the ticket agent may want to credit the amount of the old tickets and issue another set with a second charge to your account. Insist that the value of your old tickets be applied to the new ones, with the difference in price charged or credited to your account. While this creates a little extra work for the airline, it prevents double-billing to your charge account.

Lost Tickets

You can usually use an airline ticket for its original flight and date, or change it. The airline will apply the fare printed on the ticket for another flight or a different itinerary. Because of this ease of exchange, you should guard your ticket carefully. If you lose it, anyone who picks it up can bring it to any airline and have it reissued for transportation on a different flight, even to another city. And replacing or refunding a lost ticket can be a time-consuming nuisance. As a precaution, you should jot down the ticket number on a separate sheet of paper and put it in a place where you're likely not to lose it. If the ticket does go astray, the airline can process your refund application more quickly, and perhaps issue an on-the-spot replacement ticket, when you can give them this number.

You should report a lost ticket to the airline immediately, and you must register the loss with the carrier that issued the ticket. (If you bought the ticket from a travel agent, the issuing carrier is the airline whose name was imprinted on the ticket.)

Once the airline establishes that you actually bought the ticket, they will process your refund application. Some airlines will do this right away, while others may wait up to four months. If anyone uses or cashes in your ticket while the refund is pending, the airline may refuse to give you your money back. Finally, there is a handling charge, usually $5 or $10, that the carrier may deduct from the refund.

Overbooking

Most airlines overbook their flights to a certain extent, and passengers are sometimes left behind or "bumped" as a result. The CAB has new rules to encourage people, who aren't in a hurry, to give up their seats voluntarily, in exchange for money and a later flight. And those passengers bumped against their will are, with a few exceptions, entitled to compensation.

Voluntary bumping. CAB rules now require airlines to seek out people who are willing to give up their seats for some compensation before bumping anyone involuntarily.

At the check-in or boarding area, airline employees will look for volunteers when it appears that the flight has been oversold. If you're not in a rush to arrive at your next destination, you can sell back your seat to the airline.

But before you do this, you may want to get answers to these important questions:

1. What is the next flight on which the airline can confirm your seat? The alternate flight may be just as acceptable to you. On the other hand, if they offer to put you on a waiting-list or make you a standby on another flight that is full, you could be stranded.

2. Will the airline provide other amenities such as free meals, hotel rooms, telegrams, or transportation? If not, you might have to spend the money they offer you on food or lodging while you wait for the next flight.

Since the CAB has not said how much the airline has to pay you to volunteer, airlines may negotiate with their passengers for a mutually acceptable sum. Airlines give employees suggested guidelines for passenger payments, and they may select those volunteers offering to sell back their tickets for the lowest price.

Involuntary bumping. The CAB also requires each airline to give every passenger who is bumped involuntarily a written statement explaining how the carrier decides who gets to board an oversold flight and who doesn't. Those travelers who don't get to fly are almost always entitled to an on-the-spot payment of denied boarding compensation. The amount depends on the price of their ticket and the length of the delay.

Under a new policy, airlines, including foreign carriers, have the choice of offering travelers bumped from overbooked flights a voucher for a free flight or a check for cash in addition to honor-

NOTE: The Civil Aeronautics Board has made every effort to supply the latest information for air travelers. However, during this period of deregulation airlines are making many changes in the way they do business. So by the time you read this, a few of the rules explained here may be different. Contact the airline that you plan to use or the nearest CAB office if you have any questions.

ing the ticket the passenger bought, but was unable to use.

The C.A.B. stipulates that the passenger must have the option of a free flight or cash and that the value of the free flight must be at least equal to the monetary compensation, which is based on the mileage of the overbooked flight.

Exceptions. To qualify for compensation, you must have a confirmed reservation and you must meet the airline's deadline for buying your ticket. Most airlines require passengers to arrive at the boarding gate ten minutes (sometimes more) before the scheduled flight. If you don't, you may lose your reservation and your right to compensation.

If the airline substitutes a smaller plane for the one they originally planned to use, the airline isn't required to pay people who are bumped as a result.

If you are bumped to accommodate government travelers on emergency official business, you aren't entitled to denied boarding compensation.

Baggage

The bags you check should be labeled inside and out with your name, address, and phone number. Add the name and address of a person to contact at your destination if it's practical to do so. Almost all of the bags that are misplaced by airlines do turn up sooner or later. With proper labeling, the bag and its owner can usually be reunited within a few hours.

Lock your bags to help prevent pilferage. But if they do arrive with broken locks or torn sides, check inside immediately. If something is missing, report it to the airline right away.

At check-in, the airline will put baggage destination tags on your luggage and give you the stubs to use as a claim check. Each tag has a three-letter code and flight number which show the baggage sorters on which plane and to which airport you luggage is supposed to go. Double-check the tag and flight number before your bag goes down the conveyor belt. (The airline will be glad to tell you the code for your destination when you make reservations or buy your tickets.) Be sure all of the tags from previous trips are removed from your bag, since they may confuse busy baggage handlers. Don't lose your claim checks—they are your only proof that you really did check bags with the airline.

If your bags are delayed, lost or damaged on a domestic flight, the airline may invoke a $750 ceiling on the amount of money they'll pay you. When your luggage and its contents are worth more than that, you may decide to buy "excess valuation" from the airline as you check in. This will increase the carrier's potential liability. Excess valuation costs about 10 cents for each additional $100 worth of coverage so if you want to raise the airline's liability to cover $2,000 worth of baggage, you would pay $1,30. The airline may refuse to sell excess valuation on some items that are especially valuable or breakable, such as antiques, musical instruments, jewelry, manuscripts, negotiable securities and cash.

Damage. If your suitcase arrives smashed or torn, the airline will usually pay for repairs. If it can't be fixed, they will negotiate a settlement to pay you its depreciated value. The same holds true for clothing packed inside.

There are times when airlines won't pay for damage, however, if it is caused by the fragile nature of whatever they have broken or by your carelessness in packing, rather than the airline's rough handling. Airlines may also refuse to give you money for any damaged items inside the bag when there's no evidence of external damage to the suitcase. But airlines may not disclaim liability for fragile merchandise packed in its original factory-sealed carton, a cardboard mailing tube, or other container designed for shipping and packed with protective padding material.

When you check in, the airline must let you know if they think your suitcase or package may not survive the trip intact. Before accepting a questionable item, they will ask you to sign a statement in which you agree to check it in at your own risk. But even if you do sign this form, the airline must pay for damage if it is caused by its own negligence shown by external injury to the suitcase or package.

Delayed bags. If you and your suitcase don't connect at your destination, don't panic. The airlines have very sophisticated systems that can track down about 98% of the bags they misplace and return them to their owners within hours. They will also generally absorb reasonable expenses you incur while they look for your missing belongings. You and the airline may have different ideas of what's reasonable, however, and the amount they will pay you may be subject to negotiation.

If your bags don't come off the conveyor belt, report this to the airline **before you leave the airport.** You must fill out a form describing the bag, listing its contents and providing other information for the baggage-tracing staff. Be sure you keep a copy of this form for your records.

Most carriers set guidelines for their airport employees that allow them to disburse some money at the airport for emergency purchases. The amount depends on whether or not you're away from home and how long it takes to track down your bags and return them to you.

If the airline misplaces sporting equipment, they will pay for the rental of replacements. For replacement clothing, the carrier might offer to absorb only half its purchase cost, arguing that you will be able to use some of the new clothes in the future. If this is not acceptable to you, the airline will probably agree to pay the full replacement costs, but you'll be asked to return the new clothing to the airline.

When you've checked in fresh foods or any other perishable goods and they are ruined because their delivery is delayed, the airline won't reimburse you. Airlines are liable only if they lose or damage perishable items, but they won't accept responsibility for spoilage caused by temporary loss.

Airlines are liable for consequential damages (up to the $750 limit or whatever excess valuation you purchased) in connection with the delay. If you can't resolve the claim with the airline's airport staff, keep a record of the names of the employees with whom you dealt, hold on to all travel documents and receipts for any money you spend in connection with the mishandling, and write to the airline's consumer office when you get home.

Lost luggage. Once your bag is declared officially lost, the claim form you filled out is usually referred to a central office, and the negotiations between you and the airline begin.

Airlines don't automatically pay the full amount of every claim that is filed with them. First, they will use the information on your form to estimate the value of your lost belongings. Like insurance companies, airlines consider the depreciated value of your possessions, not their replacement costs.

If you're tempted to exaggerate your claim, don't. Airlines may completely deny claims they feel are inflated or fraudulent. They often ask for sales receipts and other documentation to back up claims, especially if a large amount of money is involved. If you don't keep extensive records, you can expect to dicker with the airlines over the value of your goods.

Generally, it takes an airline anywhere from six weeks to three months to pay you for your lost luggage. During this waiting period, you should stay in touch with the company both to show your concern and to be sure they're following up on your claim. Even though the airlines lose relatively few bags, when they're yours, you'll want to keep a watchful eye of the airline's treatment of your claim.

Smoking

Present rules require airlines to provide a seat in the no-smoking section for each passenger who asks for one, even if flight attendants must rearrange people after seat assignments are given out. The cabin crew is also supposed to make sure that the rules stick. During the flight, no one may smoke in the restricted area. Smoking is still permitted in non-restricted sections. But even here, special rules limit where people may smoke pipes and cigars, and some airlines don't allow any cigar or pipe smoking on board their planes.

If you are refused a no-smoking seat or if the crew fails to enforce these rules, report the incident to the airline's consumer office and CAB's Bureau of Consumer Protection.

Complaining

When passengers comment on airline service, most carriers do listen. They analyze and keep track of the complaints and compliments they receive and use the information to determine what the public wants and to identify problem areas that need special attention. They also try to resolve individual complaints.

Like other businesses, airlines use a lot of discretion in responding to problems. While you do have some rights as a passenger, your demands for monetary compensation will probably be subject to negotiation, and the kind of action you get depends in large part on the way you go about complaining.

Start with the airline—before you write to the CAB or some other agency for help with an air travel problem, you should give the airline a chance to resolve it.

As a rule, airlines have trouble shooters at the airports (they're usually called Customer Service Representatives) who can take care of most problems on the spot. They can arrange meals and hotel rooms for stranded passengers, write checks for denied boarding compensation, arrange luggage repairs, and settle other routine claims or complaints that involve relatively small amounts of money.

If you can't resolve that problem at the airport and want to file a complaint, it's best to send a letter to the airline's consumer office. Take notes at the time the incident occurs, and jot down the names of the carrier employees with whom you dealt. Keep all of your travel documents (ticket receipts, baggage check stubs, boarding passes, etc.) as well as receipts for any out-of-pocket expenses that were incurred as a result of the mishandling. Here are some tips to help you write your letter:

1. Type the letter and, if at all possible, limit it to one page in length.
2. No matter how angry you might be, keep your letter businesslike in tone and don't exaggerate what happened. If the complaint sounds very vehement or sarcastic, you might wait a day and then consider rewriting.
3. Start by saying what reservations you held, what happened, and at which ticket office, airport, or flight the incident occurred.
4. Send copies, never the originals, of tickets and receipts or other documents that can back up your claims.
5. Include the names of any employees who were rude or made things worse, as well as anyone who might have been especially helpful.
6. Don't clutter up your complaint with petty gripes that can obscure what you're really angry about.
7. Let the airline know if you've suffered any special inconvenience or monetary losses.
8. Say just what you expect the carrier to do to make amends. You might want a written apology from a rude employee or reimbursement for some loss you incurred, but the airline has to know what you want before they can decide what action to take.
9. Be reasonable. If your demands are way out of line, your letter might earn you a polite apology and a place in the airline's crank files.

If you follow these guidelines, the airline will probably treat your complaint seriously. Your letter will help them to determine what caused your problem, as well as to suggest actions the company can take to keep the same thing from happening to other people.

What the CAB can do. If your letter to the airline does not produce the desired results and if you still want to pursue the complaint, you may write to the Civil Aeronautics Board Bureau of Consumer Protection, Washington, D.C. 20428. The CAB will make sure your letter reaches someone at the airline who will review the way your complaint was handled and get back in touch with you. They will provide information on what rights you may or may not have and answer any of your questions about the airline's responsibility to you. One of their consumer specialists will review your complaint and the airline's response. If the airline has not resolved your problem and the CAB thinks it might help, they will ask the carrier to reconsider the way they handled the complaint.

The CAB uses their complaint files to identify possible violations of the Board's consumer protection regulations, and their lawyers and investigators use these records to back up many of their enforcement efforts.

If your complaint is about something you feel is a safety hazard, write to the Federal Aviation Administration:

Community and Consumer Liaison Division
APA-100
Federal Aviation Administration
800 Independence Avenue, S.W.
Washington, D.C. 20591

If the CAB is unable to negotiate a settlement for you, and if your demands appear to be reasonable, the CAB will try to refer you to someone in your community who can give you information about how to sue in small claims court.

The local field offices of the CAB listed below will provide assistance with complaints and answers to many of your questions about air travel.

Illinois
Civil Aeronautics Board
Room 254
2300 East Devon Ave.
Des Plaines, Ill. 60018
(312) 694-2686

Texas
Civil Aeronautics Board
P.O. Box 1689
Fort Worth, Texas 76101
(817) 429-0951

Florida
Civil Aeronautics Board
Box 592616
Miami, Fla. 33159
(305) 526-2535

Alaska
Civil Aeronautics Board
632—6th Avenue
Anchorage, Alaska 99501

New York
Civil Aeronautics Board
90 Church Street
Room 1316
New York, N.Y. 10007
(212) 264-1700

California
Civil Aeronautics Board
P.O. Box 92007
Los Angeles, Calif. 90009
(213) 536-6297

Washington
Civil Aeronautics Board
Airport Plaza Building
19415 Pacific Highway South
Seattle, Wash. 98188
(206) 764-3587

International Tourist Arrivals and Receipts, 1977–78

Area	Arrivals (millions)		Receipts (billions)	
	1978	1979[1]	1978	1979[1]
Africa	4.90	5.30	1.50	1.80
Americas	47.50	49.50	13.50	16.00
East Asia and the Pacific	12.00	13.80	4.00	5.00
Europe	189.00	196.00	44.00	50.00
Middle East	3.80	3.60	1.45	1.40
South Asia	2.10[2]	2.00	0.80[2]	0.66
Total	**259.40**	**270.00**	**65.00**	**75.00**

1. Estimated. 2. Revised figure. *Source:* World Tourism Organization.

U.S. Travel Industry Statistics

Volume, receipts, employment	1977	1976	1975
Domestic travel volume[1] (in millions of passenger-miles)			
Automobile	1,104.4	1,078.1	n.a.
Air	154.8	144.5	131.8
Bus	16.6	15.9	n.a.
Rail	4.2	4.2	3.8
Total (billions)	**1,280.1**	**1,242.9**	**n.a.**
Industry receipts[2] (in billions of dollars)			
Transportation	$ 67.7	$ 63.2	$ 57.7
Lodging	17.1	15.7	13.7
Food service	63.8	57.8	51.4
Amusements	22.8	20.6	18.0
Total (billions)	**$171.4**	**$157.4**	**$140.8**
Employment[3] (in millions of jobs)			
Transportation	1.04	1.04	1.02
Lodging	.86	.86	.82
Food service	3.85	3.62	3.33
Total (billions)	**5.76**	**5.52**	**5.17**

1. Includes: Auto: Main rural road passenger-miles; Air: Domestic certified air carrier revenue passenger-miles; Bus: All intercity bus passenger-miles; Rail: Amtrak passenger-miles. 2. Includes: Transportation: Air and rail transportation companies, gasoline service stations; Lodging: Commercial lodging places; Food Service: Eating and drinking places; Amusements: Amusement and recreation services. 3. Includes: Transportation: Air transportation, intercity highway transportation and gasoline service stations; Lodging: Commercial lodging places; Food Service: Eating and drinking places. NOTE: n.a. = not available. *Source:* U.S. Travel Data Center, Washington, D.C.

Expenditures of U.S. Travelers to Foreign Countries
(in millions of dollars)

Type of expense	1979	1978	1977	1976	1975
Transportation fare payments	$5,161	$4,680	$4,473	$4,012	$3,726
Foreign flag carriers	3,100	2,896	2,748	2,568	2,263
U.S. flag carriers	2,061	1,784	1,725	1,444	1,463
Travel payments in foreign countries	9,413	8,475	7,451	6,856	6,417
Canada	1,599	1,407	1,433	1,371	1,306
Mexico	2,400	2,121	1,918	1,723	1,637
Mexican border zone	1,291	1,128	1,165	1,007	1,047
Total overseas areas	5,354	4,947	4,100	3,762	3,474
Europe and Mediterranean	3,185	2,942	2,398	2,150	1,918
Western Europe	2,842	2,600	2,103	1,885	1,709
United Kingdom	826	771	585	494	404
France	355	287	233	254	226
Italy	300	260	240	207	194
Switzerland	158	153	145	129	121
West Germany	283	220	203	195	174
Austria	84	75	73	70	65
Denmark	54	70	51	38	43
Sweden	38	52	40	37	29
Norway	47	49	37	40	44
Netherlands	71	65	49	58	60
Belgium and Luxembourg	50	37	34	35	39
Spain	200	213	151	117	135
Portugal	58	53	37	14	19
Ireland	115	110	97	83	55
Greece	163	140	102	90	73
Other Western Europe	40	45	26	24	28
Other Europe and Mediterranean	343	342	295	265	209
Israel	157	144	146	118	57
Other[1]	186	198	149	147	152
Caribbean Area and Central America	1,019	888	790	784	787
Bermuda	164	136	123	133	118
Bahamas	224	198	158	168	161
Jamaica	122	118	100	109	118
Other British West Indies	100	153	144	125	103
Netherlands West Indies	138	114	106	102	97
Other West Indies and Central America	181	169	159	147	190
South America	288	306	254	232	242
Other overseas areas	862	811	658	596	527
Japan	142	155	149	145	131
Hong Kong	137	113	87	74	75
Australia and New Zealand	153	123	92	82	54
Other	430	420	330	295	267
Total expenses[2]	**14,574**	**13,155**	**11,924**	**10,868**	**10,143**

1. Includes U.S.S.R. 2. Cruise passenger fare payments included in transportation payments (predominantly foreign flag carriers). Shore expenditures included in regional and country totals. *Source:* Department of Commerce, Bureau of Economic Analysis.

Price Index Figures for Domestic Travel and Selected Components, 1976–1979
(1967 = 100)

	1976	1977	1978	1979
Travel price index	169.9	187.8	203.3	234.3
Gasoline	177.9	188.2	196.3	265.6
Common carrier transportation fares				
Taxicab	176.9	189.9	203.5	221.7
Intercity train	165.3	180.6	194.6	212.4
Air	172.2	182.0	190.6	205.8
Bus	196.9	223.5	240.2	260.0
Lodging	172.9	187.0	212.7	245.8
Food service	186.1	200.3	218.4	242.9
Entertainment services	127.4	166.2	175.4	187.6
Incidentals	—	161.5	168.7	178.0

Source: U.S. Travel Data Center.

Travelers from the U.S. to Foreign Countries[1] by Country and Region Visited

(in thousands)

Country or region visited	1979	1978	1977	1976	1975
Canada[2]	10,561[3]	11,660	11,451	11,658	12,499
Mexico[4]	4,000[4]	3,073	2,735	2,671	2,786
Total Overseas	7,835	7,790	7,390	6,897	6,354
Europe and Mediterranean	4,068	4,105	3,920	3,523	3,185
Western Europe	3,866	3,914	3,663	3,295	2,990
Austria	419	426	359	395	377
Belgium-Luxembourg	257	234	240	290	289
Denmark	206	271	238	214	230
France	943	882	786	902	809
Greece	309	284	257	229	178
Ireland	278	296	303	251	191
Italy	718	718	715	665	650
Netherlands	379	363	317	432	416
Norway	137	165	147	133	135
Portugal	195	195	134	57	95
Spain	443	524	334	309	370
Sweden	136	213	180	154	150
Switzerland	535	572	620	585	567
United Kingdom	1,617	1,725	1,559	1,386	1,199
West Germany	864	765	768	802	733
Other Western Europe	167	219	122	140	142
Israel	258	277	316	264	138
Other Europe and Mediterranean[5]	509	606	489	494	515
Caribbean Areas and Central America	2,533	2,365	2,203	2,201	2,065
South America	434	515	483	436	447
Other Overseas Areas	800	805	784	737	657
Total	**22,396**	**22,523**	**21,576**	**21,226**	**21,639**

1. Excludes travel by military personnel and other government employees stationed abroad. 2. Visitors staying one or more nights. 3. Preliminary figure. 4. Mexican National Tourist Council. Visitors staying one or more nights. 5. Includes the U.S.S.R. *Sources:* Department of Commerce, Bureau of Economic Analysis, and *Statistics Canada.*

Domestic Travel Expenditures

(in billions of dollars)

Trips 200 miles or more away from home	1977
Total Expenditures[1]	**$90.2**
By type of expenditure:	
Transportation	35.9
Food	26.1
Lodging	13.1
Gifts and incidentals	7.5
Entertainment and recreation	7.5
By mode of transportation:	
Auto and truck travelers	50.1
Air travelers	31.8
Bus travelers	1.7
Train travelers	0.8
Mixed mode	4.7
Other	1.1
By purpose of trip:	
Visiting friends and relatives	25.7
Business	23.4
Convention	2.5
Outdoor recreation	11.7
Sightseeing and entertainment	12.9
Personal and family	7.6
Other	6.5
By type of trip:	
Weekend travel	17.3
Vacation trips	45.7

1. Excludes U.S. expenditures by foreign visitors. *Source:* U.S. Travel Data Center, Washington, D.C.

Object of Travel by Passport Recipients[1]

Object	1979	1978	1977	1973
Personal reasons	48.6%	48.5%	32.4%	45.6%
Pleasure	17.4	25.4	35.5	39.5
Business	6.4	5.1	6.1	5.7
Education	2.9	2.3	2.5	3.5
Religious	.4	.3	.3	.3
Scientific	.04	.05	.03	.02
Health	.02	.03	.04	.04
Government	4.6	4.4	5.0	4.6
Not Stated	19.5	13.9	18.2	.8

1. Percentages rounded off. *Source: Summary of Passport Statistics,* Department of State, Bureau of Consular Affairs.

Passport Recipients by Sex and Age Groups, 1979

Age group	Male	Female	Total
Under 5	54,370	51,370	105,740
5–14	106,520	106,230	212,750
15–24	221,590	315,470	537,060
25–44	553,090	516,220	1,069,310
45–59	375,040	366,090	741,130
60–69	159,890	179,510	339,400
70–over	72,990	91,619	164,609
Total	**1,543,490**	**1,626,509**	**3,169,999**

Source: Summary of Passport Statistics Department of State, Bureau of Consular Affairs.

Volume of Domestic Travel by U.S. Residents

(in millions of person-trips)

Domestic Travel	1979
Mode of Transportation:	
Auto, truck, recreational vehicle	910.1
Airplane	155.4
Bus	22.2
Train	11.1
Other	11.1
Purpose of trip:	
Visiting friends and relatives	426.8
Other pleasures	386.1
Business and convention	155.1
Other	141.9
Type of trip:	
Vacation	623.7
Weekend	587.4
Total person–trips	**1,109.9**

Source: U.S. Travel Data Center, Washington, D.C.

U.S. Passport and Customs Information

Source: Department of State, Passport Services and Department of the Treasury, Customs Service

Passports

With a few exceptions, a passport is required for all United States citizens to depart from and enter the United States and to enter most foreign countries. A United States citizen is not required by United States laws or regulations to have a valid passport for travel to or in North, South, or Central America, except Cuba. It is, however, recommended that a passport be obtained for travel to Central and South America since many of the countries require that United States citizens be in possession of a valid passport. United States travelers should carry documentary evidence of their United States citizenship and identity to facilitate re-entry into the United States. Travelers should check passport and visa requirements with consular officials of the countries to be visited well in advance of their departure date.

Applications for passport may be made to any Passport Agent; to a clerk of any Federal court or State court of record, or a judge or clerk or any probate court, accepting applications; or at a Post Office selected to accept passport applications. Passport agencies are located in Boston; Chicago; Detroit; Honolulu; Houston; Los Angeles; Miami; New Orleans; New York; Philadelphia; San Francisco; Seattle; Stamford, Conn.; and Washington, D.C.

A first passport must be applied for in person. Applicants must present evidence of citizenship (e.g., a birth certificate), personal identification (e.g., driver's license), two identical photographs taken within six months (2 x 2 inches, with the image size measured from the bottom of the chin to the top of the head [including hair] not less than 1 inch nor more than 1⅜ inches, signed in the center on the reverse; vending machine photographs not acceptable), plus two identical photographs of any included children and the application. A fee of $10 plus a $4 execution fee is charged.

You may apply by mail if you have been the bearer of a passport issued within eight years prior to the date of a new application; are able to submit your most recent United States passport with your new application; your previous passport was not issued before your 18th birthday; you are not applying for an official, diplomatic, or no-fee passport; you do not wish to include children under 13 years of age. This procedure may be used only in the United States. If you are eligible to apply by mail, include your previous passport, completed and signed Application for Passport by Mail, new signed photographs, and the $10 passport fee. The $4 execution fee is not required when applying by mail.

If you claim citizenship by naturalization, a Certificate of Naturalization is required.

Passports may be amended to show a married name or legal change of name, to correct descriptive data, to include your children or brothers and sisters under 13 years of age, or to exclude a person previously included. You must personally present the amendment form and have it executed by an authorized person if the amendment is an inclusion.

Any alterations by the bearer other than change of address and notification data appearing on the inside cover of the passport are forbidden.

Your passport is valid for five years from date of issue unless specifically limited by the Secretary of State to a shorter period of validity.

The passport is a traveler's principal means of identification abroad, and its loss is very serious. It should be reported immediately to the nearest United States embassy or consular office. Loss of a passport in the United States should be reported in writing to Passport Services, Department of State, Washington, D.C. 20524, or the nearest Passport Agency.

Customs

United States residents must declare all articles acquired abroad and in their possession at the time of their return. In addition, articles acquired in the U.S. Virgin Islands, American Samoa, or Guam and not accompanying you must be declared at the time of your return. The wearing or use of an article acquired abroad does *not* exempt it from duty. Customs declaration forms are distributed on vessels and planes, and should be prepared in advance of arrival for presentation to the immigration and customs inspectors.

If you have not exceeded the duty-free exemption allowed, you may make an oral declaration to the customs inspector. A written declaration is necessary when (1) total fair retail value of articles exceeds $300 (keep your sales slips); (2) over 1 liter of liquor, 200 cigarettes, or 100 cigars are included; (3) items are not intended for your personal or household use, or articles brought home for another person; and (4) when a customs duty or internal revenue tax is collectible on any article in your possession.

An exception to the above are regulations applicable to articles purchased in the Virgin Islands, American Samoa, or Guam where you may receive a customs exemption of $600. Not more than $300 of this exemption may be applied to merchandise obtained elsewhere than in these islands. Articles acquired in and sent from these islands to the United States may be claimed under your duty-free personal exemption if properly declared at the time of your return.

Articles accompanying you, in excess of your personal exemption, up to $600 will be assessed at a flat rate of duty of 10% based on fair retail value in country of acquisition. (If articles were acquired in the insular possessions, the flat rate of duty is 5% and these goods may accompany you or be shipped home.) These articles must be for your personal use or for use as gifts and not for sale. This provision may be used every 30 days, excluding the day of your last arrival. Any items which have a "free" duty rate will be excluded before duty is calculated.

Other exemptions include in part: automobiles, boats, planes, or other vehicles taken abroad for noncommercial use. Foreign-made personal articles (e.g., watches, cameras, etc.) taken abroad should be registered with Customs before departure. Gifts of not more than $25 can be shipped back to the United States tax and duty free ($40 if mailed from the Virgin Islands, American Samoa, or Guam). Household effects and tools of trade which you take out of the United States are duty free at time of return.

Prohibited and restricted articles include in part: absinthe, narcotics and dangerous drugs, obscene articles and publications, seditious and treasonable materials, hazardous articles (e.g., fireworks, dangerous toys, toxic and poisonous substances) and switchblade knives, biological materials of public health or veterinary importance, fruit, vegetables and plants, meats, poultry and products thereof, birds, monkeys, and turtles.

If you understate the value of an article you declare, or if you otherwise misrepresent an article in your declaration, you may have to pay a penalty in addition to payment of duty. Under certain circumstances, the article could be seized and forfeited if the penalty is not paid.

If you fail to declare an article acquired abroad, not only is the article subject to seizure and forfeiture, but you will be liable for a personal penalty in an amount equal to the value of the article in the United States. In addition, you may also be liable to criminal prosecution.

If you carry more than $5,000 into or out of the United States in currency (either United States or foreign money), negotiable instruments in bearer form, or travelers checks, a report must be filed with United States Customs at the time you arrive or depart with such amounts.

As U.S. restrictions on travel to Cuba, North Korea, Vietnam, and Cambodia have been eased, the Office of Foreign Assets Control (FAC) issued a general license, effective March 21, 1977, which allows visitors to those countries to purchase a maximum of $100 worth of goods. This amount is based on foreign market or retail value in the country where acquired. These articles must be for personal use—not for resale—and must accompany the traveler on his entry into the U.S. This allowance may be used only once every 6 months.

Concorde Fuel Consumption Costly

At peak efficiency, the 1,350-miles-per-hour supersonic Concorde uses four times as much fuel on a transoceanic trip as a Boeing 747.

Western-Style Medical Help for Travelers

Source: International Association for Medical Assistance to Travellers.

The aim of the nonprofit International Association for Medical Assistance to Travellers (IAMAT) is to provide help to travelers in need of medical attention when traveling outside of their country of residence, and to advise them of the sanitary and health conditions in different parts of the world. There is no charge for this invaluable service, nor a membership fee.

By writing to IAMAT, 350 Fifth Ave., Suite 5620, New York, N.Y. 10001, you will receive a membership card, a directory listing IAMAT centers in 450 cities in 120 countries, a "Traveler Clinical Record," a "World Immunization Chart," "World Malaria Risk Chart," and "How to Protect Yourself Against Malaria."

All IAMAT-appointed physicians speak English and will give members the type of medical care that they are used to receiving at home. The physicians have pledged to see you immediately in case of an emergency, and have agreed to a fixed price schedule of $15 for an office visit, $20 for a house visit, and $25 should you summon them on a Sunday or a local holiday.

IAMAT also offers the "World Climate Chart," a set of 24 folders covering climatic data and the sanitary conditions of food, water, and milk in 1,440 cities around the world.

Although contributions are not required, they are appreciated since IAMAT subsists wholly on gifts from members. All donations are tax exempt.

American Consuls for the Traveler Abroad

American consuls will advise or help you if you are in serious difficulty or distress. However, they cannot do the work of travel agencies, information bureaus, banks and the police; nor can they help you find work or get residence or driving permits; and it is not a part of their duties to act as travel couriers or interpreters, to search for missing luggage or to settle disputes with hotel managers.

Legal Aid. If you find yourself in a dispute which could lead to legal or police action, it is wise to consult the consul.

If Detained. If you are detained by the police or other authorities in a foreign country, you should ask at once to be allowed to communicate with the consul.

If Destitute. The consul may be able to assist you to make inquiries of your family, friends, bankers and employers, or anyone else you may designate, to see if there is any way of getting you out of your difficulties.

Finances. The American consul is not provided with funds to disburse to American citizens who find themselves in financial difficulties while abroad; nor can he cash or guarantee checks for you.

Average Daily Temperatures (°F) in Tourist Cities

Location	January		April		July		October	
	High	Low	High	Low	High	Low	High	Low
U.S. CITIES (See Weather and Climate Section)								
CANADA (See Canadian Section)								
MEXICO								
Acapulco	85	70	87	71	89	75	88	74
Mexico City	66	42	78	52	74	54	70	50
OVERSEAS								
Australia (Sydney)	78	65	71	58	60	46	71	56
Austria (Vienna)	34	26	57	41	75	59	55	44
Bahamas (Nassau)	77	65	81	69	88	75	85	73
Bermuda (Hamilton)	68	58	71	59	85	73	79	69
Brazil (Rio de Janeiro)	84	73	80	69	75	63	77	66
Denmark (Copenhagen)	36	29	50	37	72	55	53	42
Egypt (Cairo)	65	47	83	57	96	70	86	65
France (Paris)	42	32	60	41	76	55	59	44
Germany (Berlin)	35	26	55	38	74	55	55	41
Greece (Athens)	54	42	67	52	90	72	74	60

Location	January High	January Low	April High	April Low	July High	July Low	October High	October Low
Hong Kong	64	56	75	67	87	78	81	73
India (Calcutta)	80	55	97	76	90	79	89	74
Italy (Rome)	54	39	68	46	88	64	73	53
Israel (Jerusalem)	55	41	73	50	87	63	81	59
Japan (Tokyo)	47	29	63	46	83	70	69	55
Nigeria (Lagos)	88	74	89	77	83	74	85	74
Netherlands (Amsterdam)	40	34	52	43	69	59	56	48
Puerto Rico (San Juan)	81	67	84	69	87	74	87	73
South Africa (Cape Town)	78	60	72	53	63	45	70	52
Spain (Madrid)	47	33	64	44	87	62	66	48
United Kingdom (London)	44	35	56	40	73	55	58	44
United Kingdom (Edinburgh)	43	35	50	39	65	52	53	44
U.S.S.R. (Moscow)	21	9	47	31	76	55	46	34
Venezuela (Caracas)	75	56	81	60	78	61	79	61
Yugoslavia (Belgrade)	37	27	64	45	84	61	65	47

Expenditures of Visitors in U.S.
(in millions of dollars)

Country or region of permanent residence	1979	1978	1977	1976	1975
Transportation—U.S. Flag Carriers	$1,677	$1,238	$1,025	$ 937	$ 767
Expenditures in U.S.	8,335	7,186	6,150	5,742	4,697
Canada	2,092	2,248	2,150	1,983	1,561
Mexico	1,869	1,459	1,316	1,364	1,311
Overseas Visitors	4,374	3,479	2,684	2,395	1,825
Western Europe	1,667	1,323	1,003	852	611
United Kingdom	375	308	205	183	144
Germany	440	333	263	206	145
France	180	140	121	96	68
Italy	84	70	61	59	41
Netherlands	97	84	57	49	36
Belgium	n.a.	34	29	23	14
Sweden	n.a.	54	40	37	23
Switzerland	n.a.	72	51	43	32
Other	n.a.	228	176	156	108
Caribbean and Central America	375	322	276	289	206
South America	793	660	455	360	303
Other Areas	1,539	1,174	950	894	705
Japan	699	539	450	439	410
Total expenditures	**10,012**	**8,424**	**7,175**	**6,679**	**5,464**

Source: Department of Commerce, Bureau of Economic Analysis.

Smithsonian Seeks Public Health Artifacts

The Smithsonian Institution's Museum of History and Technology is conducting a search to identify, locate, and collect important artifacts related to the history of public health in America. A partial listing of objects to be collected includes:

Vaccination and immunization materials, diagnostic kits, water and sewage testing apparatus, quarantine signs, public health uniforms and medals, and public health inspection kits.

Persons who have such objects or know of their whereabouts please contact Dr. Ramunas Kondratas, Room 5000, Medical Sciences Division, National Museum of History and Technology, Washington, D.C. 20560. Do not send artifacts to the museum.

Information Sources for Travel

Many government and private organizations provide tourist information as a public service. Almost all of the 50 states and the various territories of the U.S. have government-financed tourism offices to provide information about their areas. Many states have welcome centers located on major highways near their borders. Nearly every city has a visitor's bureau, convention center, or chamber of commerce—people very willing to inform visitors about their city or region. Travel agencies—which are business organizations financed by commissions from airlines, cruise lines, hotels, and other elements of the travel industry—make available a variety of travel brochures and general information, almost always without charge. International travel organizations, like American Express, also offer travel information.

Libraries and bookstores have many tour guides to the United States on their shelves. Among the best known are:

Fodor's USA (1 volume and 11 regional guides) (David McKay)
Mobil Travel Guides (7 volumes) (Mobil Oil Corp. and Rand McNally)
National Park Guide (Rand McNally)
Vacationland, USA (National Geographic Society)

Some publications covering accommodations are:

AYH Hostel Guide and Handbook (American Youth Hostels)
Country Inns and Back Roads (Berkshire Traveller Press)
Directory (Budget Motels & Hotels of America)
National Directory of Budget Motels (Pilot Industries)
Hotel and Motel Red Book (American Hotel Association)
Where to Stay USA (Council on International Educational Exchange)

For camping—including recreational vehicles and trailers:

Campground and Trailer Park Guide (Rand McNally)
KOA Kampground Directory and RV Buyers Guide (Kampgrounds of America)
Trailering Parks & Campgrounds (Woodall)

Many foreign governments maintain tourist offices in major American cities. International airlines generally have available detailed information about cities and countries along their routes. Travel agencies and international travel organizations like American Express and Thomas Cook also offer travel information, almost always without charge.

Libraries and bookstores have many guides to specific countries. Among the best known are:

Fodor's Europe (David McKay) (plus 19 guides to individual countries)
Fielding's Travel Guide to Europe (Fielding)
Let's Go: Europe (Harvard Student Agencies)
Let's Go: Britain & Ireland (Harvard Student Agencies)
Let's Go: France (Harvard Student Agencies)
Arthur Frommer's Guides (Frommer/Pasmantier) (18 guides to European countries and cities)
Michelin Guides (Michelin Tyre Co.)
Eurail Guide (Saltzman)
Nagel's Guides (Nagel) (76 guides in English)

State and City Tourism Offices

The following is a selected list of state, territorial, and city tourism offices. Where a toll-free telephone number is available, it is given.

ALABAMA
Bureau of Publicity and Information
State Highway Building
Montgomery, Ala. 36130
800–633–5761

ALASKA
Alaska Division of Tourism
Pouch E
Juneau, Alaska 99811

AMERICAN SAMOA
Director of the Office of Tourism
Pago Pago, American Samoa 96799

ARIZONA
Arizona Office of Tourism
1700 W. Washington
Phoenix, Ariz. 85007

Phoenix
Phoenix & Valley of the Sun Convention and Visitor's Bureau
2701 E. Camelback Road
Phoenix, Ariz. 85016

Tucson
Visitor's Bureau
P.O. Box 991
Tucson, Ariz. 85702

ARKANSAS
Arkansas Department of Parks and Tourism
149 State Capitol Building
Little Rock, Ark. 72201

Hot Springs
Hot Springs Chamber of Commerce Convention and Visitors Division
P.O. Box 1500
Hot Springs, Ark. 71901

CALIFORNIA
Office of Visitor Services
Department of Economics and Business Development
1120 N. St.
Sacramento, Calif. 95814

San Francisco
San Francisco Convention and Visitor's Bureau
1390 Market Street, Suite 260
San Francisco, Calif. 94102

COLORADO
Office of Tourism
Colorado Division of Commerce and Development
313 Sherman St., Room 500
Denver, Colo. 80203
800–525–3083

CONNECTICUT
Tourism Promotion Service
Connecticut Department of Commerce
210 Washington St.
Hartford, Conn. 06106

DELAWARE
State Visitors Service
Division of Economic Development
630 State College Rd.
Dover, Del. 19901

DISTRICT OF COLUMBIA
Washington Area Convention and Visitor's Association
1129 20th St., NW
Washington, D.C. 20036

Public Citizen Visitors Center
1200 15th St., NW
Washington, D.C. 20005

FLORIDA
Division of Tourism
107 West Gaines Street
Tallahassee, Fla. 32304

Miami
Miami Metro Department of Publicity & Tourism
499 Biscayne Blvd.
Miami, Fla. 33132

GEORGIA
Tourist Division
P.O. Box 1776
Atlanta, Ga. 30301

GUAM
Guam Visitors Bureau
P.O. Box 3520
Agana, Guam 96910

HAWAII
Hawaii Visitors Bureau
2270 Kalakana Ave. Suite 801
Honolulu, Hawaii 96815

IDAHO
Division of Tourism and Industrial Development
State Capitol Building, Room 108
Boise, Idaho 83720

ILLINOIS
Office of Tourism
222 South College
Springfield, Ill. 62706

Chicago
Convention and Tourism Bureau
332 S. Michigan Avenue, Room 2050
Chicago, Ill. 60604

INDIANA
Tourism Development Division
State House, Room 336
Indianapolis, Ind. 46204

IOWA
Travel Development Division
250 Jewett Building
Des Moines, Iowa 50309

KANSAS
Tourist Division
Department of Economic Development
503 Kansas Ave.
6th Floor
Topeka, Kan. 66603

KENTUCKY
Division of Advertising and Travel Promotion
Capitol Annex
Frankfort, Ky. 40601

LOUISIANA
Louisiana Tourist Development Commission
P.O. Box 44291, Capitol Station
Baton Rouge, La. 70804

New Orleans
Greater New Orleans Tourist & Convention Commission
334 Royal Street
New Orleans, La. 70130

MAINE
State Development Office
193 State St.
Augusta, Maine 04333

MARYLAND
Division of Tourist Development
1748 Forest Drive
Annapolis, Md. 21401

MASSACHUSETTS
Division of Tourism
100 Cambridge Street
Boston, Mass. 02202

Boston
Convention and Tourist Bureau, Inc.
900 Boylston Street
Boston, Mass. 02215

MICHIGAN
Travel Bureau
Department of Commerce
P.O. Box 30226
Law Building
Lansing, Mich. 48909
800–248–5456

MINNESOTA
Tourism Division
480 Cedar St., Hanover Bldg.
St. Paul, Minn. 55101

MISSISSIPPI
Department of Tourism and Development
Mississippi Agricultural and Industrial Board
P.O. Box 849
Jackson, Miss. 39205

MISSOURI
Missouri Division of Tourism
308 E. High St.
P.O. Box 1055
Jefferson City, Mo. 65101

MONTANA
Travel Promotion Unit
Department of Highways
Helena, Mont. 59601

NEBRASKA
Division of Travel and Tourism
P.O. Box 94666, State Capitol
Lincoln, Neb. 68509

NEVADA
Tourism Division
108 W. Second St.
Carson City, Nev. 89710

Las Vegas
Las Vegas Chamber of Commerce
2301 E. Sahara Avenue
Las Vegas, Nev. 89104

NEW HAMPSHIRE
Office of Vacation Travel
P.O. Box 856
Concord, N.H. 03301

NEW JERSEY
Division of Travel and Tourism
P.O. Box 400
Trenton, N.J. 08625

Atlantic City
Greater Atlantic City Chamber of Commerce
10 Central Pier
Atlantic City, N.J. 08401

NEW MEXICO
Commerce and Industry Department
Travel Division
Bataan Memorial Building
Santa Fe, N.M. 87503
800–545–9877

NEW YORK
Travel Bureau
New York State
99 Washington Avenue
Albany, N.Y. 12245

New York City
New York Convention and Visitor's Bureau
2 Columbus Circle
New York, N.Y. 10019

NORTH CAROLINA
Travel and Tourism Division
Department of Commerce
Box 25249
Raleigh, N.C. 27611

NORTH DAKOTA
North Dakota Travel Division
State Highway Department
Capitol Grounds
Bismarck, N.D. 58505

OHIO
Travel Bureau
30 East Broad Street
Columbus, Ohio 43215
800–848–1300

OKLAHOMA
Tourism Promotion Division
505 Will Rogers Building
Oklahoma City, Okla. 73105

OREGON
Travel Information Section
101 Transportation Building
Salem, Oreg. 97310
800–547–4901

PENNSYLVANIA
Bureau of Travel Development
206 South Office Building
Harrisburg, Pa. 17120

Philadelphia
Convention and Visitor's Bureau
1525 John F. Kennedy Blvd.
Philadelphia, Pa. 19102

PUERTO RICO
Puerto Rico Tourism Development Company
P.O. Box 3072
Old San Juan Station
San Juan, Puerto Rico 00913

RHODE ISLAND
Department of Economic Development
Tourist Division
1 Weybosset Hill
Providence, R.I. 02903

SOUTH CAROLINA
Department of Parks, Recreation and Tourism
Division of Tourism
Suite 113, Edgar A. Brown Building
1205 Pendleton St.
Columbia, S.C. 29202

SOUTH DAKOTA
Division of Tourism
Joe Foss Building
Pierre, S.D. 57501
800–843–1930

TENNESSEE
Department of Tourism Development

505 Fesslers Lane
Nashville, Tenn. 37219

TEXAS
Travel and Information Division
Department of Highways and Public Transportation
Austin, Tex. 78711

UTAH
Utah Travel Council
Council Hall, Capitol Hill
Salt Lake City, Utah 84114

VERMONT
Agency of Development and Community Affairs
Travel Division
61 Elm Street
Montpelier, Vt. 05602

VIRGIN ISLANDS
Division of Tourism
P.O. Box 1692
St. Thomas, Virgin Islands 00801

VIRGINIA
Virginia State Travel Service
9th and Grace Sts.
Richmond, Va. 23219

WASHINGTON
Travel Development Division
General Administration Bldg.
Room 101
Olympia, Wash. 98504

WASHINGTON, D.C.
See District of Columbia

WEST VIRGINIA
Travel Development Division
1900 Washington Street, East
Charleston, W.Va. 25305

WISCONSIN
Division of Tourism
Box 7606
Madison, Wis. 53707

WYOMING
Wyoming Travel Commission
I-25 at Etchepare Circle
Cheyenne, Wyo. 82002

Homes of the Presidents and Presidential Libraries–Museums

Source: American Automobile Association *Tour Books* and *Information Please* questionnaires.

GEORGE WASHINGTON
George Washington Birthplace National Monument: Washingtons Birthplace, Va. 22575. Open: daily 9–5 (closed Jan. 1, Dec. 25). Free admission.
Mount Vernon: on George Washington Memorial Parkway, Mount Vernon, Va. 22121 (16 mi. south of Washington, D.C.). Open: March 1–Oct. 31 daily 9–5; Nov. 1–Feb. 28–daily 9–4. Adm. $3 (senior citizens, $2.50; children 6–11, $1.50 under 6, free).
Washington's home.

JOHN ADAMS and JOHN QUINCY ADAMS
John Adams and John Quincy Adams Birthplaces: 141 Franklin St., Quincy, Mass. 02169. Open: April 19–Oct. 15, daily 9–5. Adm. Free. Tour of grounds while houses undergo restoration.
Family home of the Adamses.

Adams National Historic Site: 135 Adams St., Quincy, Mass. 02169. Open: April 19–Nov. 10—daily 9–5. Adm. 50¢ (children under 16 free).
Home of Adams family from 1788 to 1927; built in 1731. Contains furnishings used by four Adams generations.

THOMAS JEFFERSON
Monticello: on Route 53, 3 mi. southeast of Charlottesville, Va. 22902. Open: March 1–Oct. 31—daily 8–5; Nov. 1–Feb. 28—daily. 9–4:30 (closed Dec. 25). Adm. $3 (children 6–11, $1).
Home of Jefferson; begun in 1769; finished in 1809. National shrine contains Jefferson mementos.

JAMES MADISON
Montpelier: Montpelier Station, Va., 22957; on Route 20, 5 mi. west of Orange, Va. Estate not open to public, but graveyard may be visited.
Madison's home.

JAMES MONROE
Ash Lawn: off Route 53, 2½ mi. beyond Monticello, near Charlottesville, Va. 22901. Open: daily, March–Oct. 9–6, Nov.-Feb. 10–5. (closed Jan. 1, Thanksgiving, Dec. 25). Adm. $2.50 (children 6–11, 75¢; under 6, free).
Monroe's home from 1799 to 1823; a working farm planned in 1798 by Jefferson; craft demonstrations; owned by College of William and Mary.

ANDREW JACKSON
The Hermitage: off I–40 east on U.S. 70N, 12 mi. east of Nashville, Tenn. 37076. Open: daily 9–5 (closed Dec. 25). Adm. $3 (children 6–13, $1; under 6, free). Student rates available.
Jackson's home.

MARTIN VAN BUREN
Martin Van Buren National Historic Site (Lindenwald): on Route 9H, 2 mi. south of Kinderhook, N.Y. 12106. Open: daily, May-Sept.
Van Buren's home from 1839 to 1862. Designated a National Historic Site in 1974, the house is now undergoing restoration by the National Park Service; not open to visitors. Daily tours of grounds, Memorial Day weekend to Labor Day.

WILLIAM HENRY HARRISON
Berkeley Plantation (Harrison's Landing): halfway between Richmond and Williamsburg, Va., on Virginia Route 5. Open daily 8–5 (closed Dec. 25). Adm. $3.50 (children 6–12, $1.25). Group rate $2.75.
Birthplace of William Henry Harrison and ancestral home of Benjamin Harrison. Site of first official Thanksgiving in America, in 1619.

JOHN TYLER
Sherwood Forest: on Virginia Route 5, 20 mi. west of Colonial Williamsburg, Charles City, Va. 23030. Open: daily 9–5 (closed Dec. 25). Adm. $3 (students and senior citizens, $2.50, children 6–12, $1.50).
Tyler's home; built circa 1730, it is the longest frame residence in America—300 feet in length. Original furnishings. Still occupied by Tyler family.

FRANKLIN PIERCE
Franklin Pierce Homestead: near junction of Routes 9 and 31, northwest of Hillsboro, N.H. 03244. Open: mid-June-Labor Day, Tues.-Sun. 9–5. Adm. 50¢ (visitors under 18 free).
Pierce's home.

JAMES BUCHANAN
Wheatland: 1120 Marietta Ave., Route 23, Lancaster, Pa. 17603. Open: April 1–Nov. 30—Mon.-Sat. 10–5, Sun. 10–5. Last tour: 4:30. Adm. $2.20 (students, $1.50; children under 12, 55¢). Group rate $1.
Home of the nation's only bachelor President;

built in 1828. It contains 19th-century American furniture and decorative arts.

ABRAHAM LINCOLN
Lincoln Home National Historic Site: 430 South 8th St., Springfield, Ill. 62703. Open: daily, 8–5 (closed Jan. 1, Dec. 25). Adm. Free.
House is only home owned by Lincoln.

ANDREW JOHNSON
Andrew Johnson National Historic Site: Greeneville, Tenn. 37743. Open: daily 9–5 (closed Dec. 25). Adm. to Homestead (June 1–Sept. 15): 50¢ (children under 16 free).
Contains two houses where Johnson lived, tailor shop where he worked, and Andrew Johnson National Cemetery.

ULYSSES S. GRANT
U. S. Grant Home State Historic Site: 510 Bouthillier, Galena, Ill. 61036. Open: daily 9–5 (closed Jan. 1, Thanksgiving, Dec. 25). Free admission.

RUTHERFORD B. HAYES
Rutherford B. Hayes Library and Museum State Memorial: 1337 Hayes Ave., Fremont, Ohio 43420. Museum open: Mon.-Sat 9–5, Sun and hldys. 1:30–5. Adm.: $1.25 (children 6–12, 50¢). Library open: Mon.-Fri. 9–5, Sat. 9–12 (closed Sun.); free. Home open (tours only): Wed.-Sat. 9–5, Sun.-Tues. and hldys. 2–5. Adm.: $1.25 (children 6–12, 50¢; under 6, free). All three sites closed Jan. 1, Thanksgiving, and Dec. 25.
Estate is known as Spiegel Grove. It contains Hayes' home, his tomb, and White House gates.

JAMES A. GARFIELD
Lawnfield: 8095 Mentor Ave., Mentor, Ohio 44060. Open: April 15–Nov. 15, Tues.-Sat. 9–5, Sun and hldys. 1–5. Adm. $1.50 (children 10–16, $1; under 10 with adult, free). Group rates available.
Garfield's home and Lake County Historical Society Museum.

BENJAMIN HARRISON
Benjamin Harrison Memorial Home: 1230 North Delaware St., Indianapolis, Ind. 46202. Open: Mon.-Sat. 10–4, Sun. 12:30–4 (closed Jan. 1, Thanksgiving, Dec. 25). Adm. $1.50 (students, 75¢).
Harrison's home; completed in 1875.

THEODORE ROOSEVELT
Theodore Roosevelt Birthplace National Historic Site: 28 E. 20th St., New York, N.Y. 10003. Open: Wed.-Sun. 9–5 in winter; daily 9–5, Memorial Day-Labor Day (closed Jan. 1, Thanksgiving, Dec. 25). Adm. 50¢. (children under 16 and persons 62 and over, free).
Sagamore Hill National Historic Site: 3 mi. east of Oyster Bay, L.I., N.Y. 11771, via E. Main St. Open: daily 9:30–5; (closed Jan. 1, Thanksgiving, Dec. 25). Adm. 50¢ (children under 16 and persons 62 and over, free).
Roosevelt's home and rural estate.

WOODROW WILSON
Birthplace of Woodrow Wilson: Coalter and Frederick Sts., Staunton, Va. 24401. Open: daily 9–5 (closed Sun., Dec.-Feb.; Jan. 1, Thanksgiving, Dec. 25). Adm. $2 (children 6–16 and students, $1).
Woodrow Wilson House: 2340 S St. N.W., Washington, D.C. 20008. Open: Tues.-Fri. 10–2; Sat., Sun., hldys. 12–4 (closed Jan. 1, Thanksgiving, Dec. 25). Adm.: $1.50 (children and senior citizens, 50¢).
Wilson retired to this house after his second term and died here three years later in 1924.

WARREN G. HARDING
Warren G. Harding Home and Museum: 380 Mt. Vernon Ave., Marion, Ohio 43302. Open: April 1–Nov. 1, Wed.-Sat. 9:30–5; Sun. 1–5 (closed Mon., Tues.). Adm. $1 (children 6–12, 50¢).

CALVIN COOLIDGE
Calvin Coolidge Birthplace and Plymouth Notch Historic District: Route 100A, Plymouth, Vt. 05056. Open: mid-May to mid-Oct.—daily 9:30–5:30. Adm. $1 (children under 14 free).

HERBERT HOOVER
Herbert Hoover National Historic Site: ½ mi. north of I-80, exit 254, West Branch, Iowa 52358. Grounds open daily 8–5. (closed Jan. 1, Thanksgiving, Dec. 25). Free admission.
Restored two-room cottage where Hoover was born; replica of his father's blacksmith shop. Quaker meetinghouse, grave site.
Herbert Hoover Presidential Library–Museum: Interstate 80, West Branch, Iowa 52358. Open: Sept.–May, Mon.-Sat. 9–5, Sun. 12–5; Memorial Day–Labor Day, Mon.-Sat. 9–6, Sun. 10–6. (closed Jan. 1, Thanksgiving, Dec. 25). Adm. 75¢ (children under 16 free).
Exhibits portray Hoover as engineer, public servant, and humanitarian. Located in surrounding park are birthplace cottage. Quaker Meeting House, replica of Jesse Hoover's blacksmith shop, and graves of President and Mrs. Hoover.

FRANKLIN D. ROOSEVELT
Home of Franklin D. Roosevelt National Historic Site: on U.S. 9, south end of Hyde Park, N.Y. 12538. Open: daily 9–5 (closed Jan. 1, Dec. 25). Adm. $1.50 (children under 16 and adults over 62, free). Fee includes admission to Vanderbilt Mansion and the Library–Museum.
Franklin D. Roosevelt Library and Museum: Albany Post Road, Hyde Park, N.Y. 12538. Open: daily 9–5; summer 9–6 (closed Jan. 1, Dec. 25). Adm. $1.50, includes admission to Roosevelt Home and Vanderbilt Mansion (children under 16 and adults over 62, free). Archives open Mon-Fri. 9–5 (closed natl. hldys).
Exhibits feature lives and special interests of Franklin D. and Eleanor Roosevelt. Archives contain historic papers of President and Mrs. Roosevelt and of prominent figures in his Administration. Near the Library are Roosevelt family home, which is open to public, and graves of President and Mrs. Roosevelt.

HARRY S. TRUMAN
Harry S. Truman Birthplace State Historic Site: Truman Ave. & 11th St., Lamar, Mo. 64759. Open: Mon.-Sat. 10–4; Sun. 12–5 (closed Jan. 1, Easter, Thanksgiving, Dec. 25). Free.
Harry S. Truman Library and Museum: U.S. Highway 24 and Delaware St., Independence, Mo. 64050. Open: daily, 9–5 (closed Jan. 1, Thanksgiving, Dec. 25). Adm 75¢ (children under 16 free).
Copy of Truman's White House office, United Nations Charter Table, state gifts and Japanese surrender documents. Film programs. Mural by Thomas Hart Benton decorates entrance hall. Truman gravesite in courtyard is open 9–5 daily.

DWIGHT D. EISENHOWER

Eisenhower Birthplace State Historical Site: 208 E. Day St., Denison, Tex. 75020. Open: June 1–Aug. 31, daily, 8–5; Sept. 1–May 31, daily, 10–12, 1–5 (closed Dec. 25). Adm.: 50¢ (children under 12, 25¢; under 6, free).

Dwight D. Eisenhower Library: Kansas Highway 15, Abilene, Kan. 67410. Open: daily 9–4:45 (closed Jan. 1, Thanksgiving, Dec. 25). Adm. 75¢.

Exhibits of paintings and memorabilia relating to Eisenhower Administration are on display in Library and Museum. Place of Meditation, where Eisenhower is buried, and his boyhood home are nearby and are open to visitors.

JOHN F. KENNEDY

John F. Kennedy National Historic Site: 83 Beals St., Brookline, Mass. 02146. Open: daily 9–4:30 (closed Jan. 1, Thanksgiving, Dec. 25). Adm. 50¢ (children under 16 and senior citizens, free).

Kennedy's birthplace.

John Fitzgerald Kennedy Library: Columbia Point on Douchester Bay, Boston, Mass. 02125. Open: Daily, 9–5 (closed Jan. 1, Thanksgiving, Dec. 25).

Research rooms, exhibits and educational activities relating to Kennedy, his times and Administration.

LYNDON B. JOHNSON

Lyndon B. Johnson National Historic Site: P.O. Box 329, Johnson City, Tex. 78636. Open: daily 9–5 (closed Dec. 25). Free.

Site includes LBJ Ranch, birthplace and family cemetery at Stonewall (15 miles west of Johnson City) and his boyhood home and grandfather's ranch headquarters in Johnson City.

Lyndon Baines Johnson Library: 2313 Red River, Austin, Tex. 78705. Open daily 9–5 (closed Dec. 25). Free.

Documents, photographs, art objects, audio tapes, films, and memorabilia concerning the Presidency are exhibited. Audio tapes and film recreate four decades of U.S. history. Archives house 31 million documents. Replica of Oval Office during Johnson's Presidency is on view.

Malaria Warning for Travelers

Malaria, thought to be on its way to elimination, is rapidly increasing again. Four million U.S. residents travel each year to areas where malaria is prevalent. The areas are South and Southeast Asia, Central Africa, Central America, northern South America, and parts of the Caribbean. Estimates indicate that 800 to 900 travelers brought malaria home with them in 1979. The growing incidence of malaria in the United States is attributed in part to the ignorance of many travelers about the cause and prevention of the disease.

Tourist literature does not always warn about the malaria danger. Therefore, if you plan to go anywhere but in highly developed countries, have your travel agent or physician check the Center for Disease Control's annual booklet "Health Information For International Travel," which is readily available to travel and medical professionals. Or ask your municipal health department for guidance.

Your physician can prescribe pills that you can take on your trip in order to prevent you from getting the disease.

Warning on Taking Catalytic Equipped Vehicles Abroad

Catalytic equipped vehicles (1976 or later model) driven outside the United States, Canada, or Mexico will not, in most cases, meet EPA standards when brought back to the U.S. As unleaded fuel generally is not available in other countries, the catalytic converter will become inoperative and will have to be replaced. Contact Environmental Protection Agency, Public Information Center (PM-215), Washington, D.C. 20460, for details and exceptions.

EPA Fuel Economy

EPA tests automobiles to make sure they meet federal emission standards and compiles information about the gas mileage consumers can expect from their automobiles.

Copies of a booklet on these gas mileage figures can be obtained from: Printing Management, Office (PM-215), Environmental Protection Agency, Washington, D.C. 20460.

Travel Phone U.S.A.

Foreign visitors to the United States who are unfamiliar with English can dial 1–800–255–3050, a toll-free number, in order to obtain travel information in French, German, Japanese, Spanish, and Italian. Operators are on duty from 7 a.m. to 1 a.m. In an emergency, the multilingual operator at that number will also act as an interpreter over the phone.

Foreign Currency Exchange

Visitors to foreign countries can usually change their U.S. dollars into the appropriate currency at their point of departure. Most airports have currency exchange facilities, generally open from 9:00 A.M. to 10:00 P.M. The Deak-Perera Group, the largest private organization specializing in foreign money exchange, has offices in some airports. It is generally advisable for an American traveling to a foreign destination to have a small amount of the foreign currency on hand on arrival. Currency can usually be exchanged at foreign entry points.

Visitors to the United States can usually exchange their currency into U.S. dollars at their port of entry. A large number of banks also exchange foreign currency during normal banking hours.

Road Mileages Between U.S. Cities[1]

Cities	Birming-ham	Boston	Buffalo	Chicago	Cleveland	Dallas	Denver
Birmingham, Ala.	—	1,194	947	657	734	653	1,318
Boston, Mass.	1,194	—	457	983	639	1,815	1,991
Buffalo, N.Y.	947	457	—	536	192	1,387	1,561
Chicago, Ill.	657	983	536	—	344	931	1,050
Cleveland, Ohio	734	639	192	344	—	1,205	1,369
Dallas, Tex.	653	1,815	1,387	931	1,205	—	801
Denver, Colo	1,318	1,991	1,561	1,050	1,369	801	—
Detroit, Mich.	754	702	252	279	175	1,167	1,301
El Paso, Tex.	1,278	2,358	1,928	1,439	1,746	625	652
Houston, Tex.	692	1,886	1,532	1,092	1,358	242	1,032
Indianapolis, Ind.	492	940	510	189	318	877	1,051
Kansas City, Mo.	703	1,427	997	503	815	508	616
Los Angeles, Calif.	2,078	3,036	2,606	2,112	2,424	1,425	1,174
Louisville, Ky.	378	996	571	305	379	865	1,135
Memphis, Tenn.	249	1,345	965	546	773	470	1,069
Miami, Fla.	777	1,539	1,445	1,390	1,325	1,332	2,094
Minneapolis, Minn.	1,067	1,402	955	411	763	969	867
New Orleans, La.	347	1,541	1,294	947	1,102	504	1,305
New York, N.Y.	983	213	436	840	514	1,604	1,780
Omaha, Neb.	907	1,458	1,011	493	819	661	559
Philadelphia, Pa.	894	304	383	758	432	1,515	1,698
Phoenix, Ariz.	1,680	2,664	2,234	1,729	2,052	1,027	836
Pittsburgh, Pa.	792	597	219	457	131	1,237	1,411
St. Louis, Mo.	508	1,179	749	293	567	638	871
Salt Lake City, Utah	1,805	2,425	1,978	1,458	1,786	1,239	512
San Francisco, Calif.	2,385	3,179	2,732	2,212	2,540	1,765	1,266
Seattle, Wash.	2,612	3,043	2,596	2,052	2,404	2,122	1,373
Washington, D.C.	751	440	386	695	369	1,372	1,635

Cities	Detroit	El Paso	Houston	Indian-apolis	Kansas City	Los Angeles	Louisville
Birmingham, Ala.	754	1,278	692	492	703	2,078	378
Boston, Mass.	702	2,358	1,886	940	1,427	3,036	996
Buffalo, N.Y.	252	1,928	1,532	510	997	2,606	571
Chicago, Ill.	279	1,439	1,092	189	503	2,112	305
Cleveland, Ohio	175	1,746	1,358	318	815	2,424	379
Dallas, Tex.	1,167	625	242	877	508	1,425	865
Denver, Colo.	1,310	652	1,032	1,051	616	1,174	1,135
Detroit, Mich.	—	1,696	1,312	290	760	2,369	378
El Paso, Tex.	1,696	—	756	1,418	936	800	1,443
Houston, Tex.	1,312	756	—	1,022	750	1,556	981
Indianapolis, Ind.	290	1,418	1,022	—	487	2,096	114
Kansas City, Mo.	760	936	750	487	—	1,609	519
Los Angeles, Calif.	2,369	800	1,556	2,096	1,609	—	2,128
Louisville, Ky.	378	1,443	981	114	519	2,128	—
Memphis, Tenn.	756	1,095	586	466	454	1,847	396
Miami, Fla.	1,409	1,957	1,237	1,225	1,479	2,757	1,111
Minneapolis, Minn.	698	1,353	1,211	600	466	2,041	716
New Orleans, La.	1,101	1,121	365	839	839	1,921	725
New York, N.Y.	671	2,147	1,675	729	1,216	2,825	785
Omaha, Neb.	754	1,015	903	590	204	1,733	704
Philadelphia, Pa.	589	2,065	1,586	647	1,134	2,743	703
Phoenix, Ariz.	1,986	402	1,158	1,713	1,226	398	1,749
Pittsburgh, Pa.	288	1,778	1,395	360	847	2,456	416
St. Louis, Mo.	529	1,179	799	239	255	1,864	264
Salt Lake City, Utah	1,721	877	1,465	1,545	1,128	728	1,647
San Francisco, Calif.	2,475	1,202	1,958	2,299	1,882	403	2,401
Seattle, Wash.	2,339	1,760	2,348	2,241	1,909	1,150	2,355
Washington, D.C.	526	1,997	1,443	565	1,071	2,680	601

1. These figures represent estimates and are subject to change.

Road Mileages Between U.S. Cities

Cities	Memphis	Miami	Minne-apolis	New Orleans	New York	Omaha	Phila-delphia
Birmingham, Ala.	249	777	1,067	347	983	907	894
Boston, Mass.	1,345	1,539	1,402	1,541	213	1,458	304
Buffalo, N.Y.	965	1,445	955	1,294	436	1,011	383
Chicago, Ill.	546	1,390	411	947	840	493	758
Cleveland, Ohio	773	1,325	763	1,102	514	819	432
Dallas, Tex.	470	1,332	969	504	1,604	661	1,515
Denver, Colo.	1,069	2,094	867	1,305	1,780	559	1,698
Detroit, Mich.	756	1,409	698	1,101	671	754	589
El Paso, Tex.	1,095	1,957	1,353	1,121	2,147	1,015	2,065
Houston, Tex.	586	1,237	1,211	365	1,675	903	1,586
Indianapolis, Ind.	466	1,225	600	839	729	590	647
Kansas City, Mo.	454	1,479	466	839	1,216	204	1,134
Los Angeles, Calif.	1,847	2,757	2,041	1,921	2,825	1,733	2,743
Louisville, Ky.	396	1,111	716	725	785	704	703
Memphis, Tenn.	—	1,025	854	401	1,134	658	1,045
Miami, Fla.	1,025	—	1,801	892	1,328	1,683	1,239
Minneapolis, Minn.	854	1,801	—	1,255	1,259	373	1,177
New Orleans, La.	401	892	1,255	—	1,330	1,043	1,241
New York, N.Y.	1,134	1,328	1,259	1,330	—	1,315	93
Omaha, Neb.	658	1,683	373	1,043	1,315	—	1,233
Philadelphia, Pa.	1,045	1,239	1,177	1,241	93	1,233	—
Phoenix, Ariz.	1,464	2,359	1,644	1,523	2,442	1,305	2,360
Pittsburgh, Pa.	810	1,250	876	1,118	386	932	304
St. Louis, Mo.	295	1,241	559	696	968	459	886
Salt Lake City, Utah	1,556	2,571	1,243	1,743	2,282	967	2,200
San Francisco, Calif.	2,151	3,097	1,997	2,269	3,036	1,721	2,954
Seattle, Wash.	2,363	3,389	1,641	2,606	2,900	1,705	2,818
Washington, D.C.	902	1,101	1,114	1,098	229	1,170	140

Cities	Phoenix	Pitts-burgh	St. Louis	Salt Lake City	San Francisco	Seattle	Wash-ington
Birmingham, Ala.	1,680	792	508	1,805	2,385	2,612	751
Boston, Mass.	2,664	597	1,179	2,425	3,179	3,043	440
Buffalo, N.Y.	2,234	219	749	1,978	2,732	2,596	386
Chicago, Ill.	1,729	457	293	1,458	2,212	2,052	695
Cleveland, Ohio	2,052	131	567	1,786	2,540	2,404	369
Dallas, Tex.	1,027	1,237	638	1,239	1,765	2,122	1,372
Denver, Colo.	836	1,411	871	512	1,266	1,373	1,635
Detroit, Mich.	1,986	288	529	1,721	2,475	2,339	526
El Paso, Tex.	402	1,778	1,179	877	1,202	1,760	1,997
Houston, Tex.	1,158	1,395	799	1,465	1,958	2,348	1,443
Indianapolis, Ind.	1,713	360	239	1,545	2,299	2,241	565
Kansas City, Mo.	1,226	847	255	1,128	1,882	1,909	1,071
Los Angeles, Calif.	398	2,456	1,864	728	403	1,150	2,680
Louisville, Ky.	1,749	416	264	1,647	2,401	2,355	601
Memphis, Tenn.	1,464	810	295	1,556	2,151	2,363	902
Miami, Fla.	2,359	1,250	1,241	2,571	3,097	3,389	1,101
Minneapolis, Minn.	1,644	876	559	1,243	1,997	1,641	1,114
New Orleans, La.	1,523	1,118	696	1,743	2,269	2,626	1,098
New York, N.Y.	2,442	386	968	2,282	3,036	2,900	229
Omaha, Neb.	1,305	932	459	967	1,721	1,705	1,178
Philadelphia, Pa.	2,360	304	886	2,200	2,954	2,818	140
Phoenix, Ariz.	—	2,073	1,485	651	800	1,482	2,278
Pittsburgh, Pa.	2,073	—	599	1,899	2,653	2,517	241
St. Louis, Mo.	1,485	599	—	1,383	2,137	2,164	836
Salt Lake City, Utah	651	1,899	1,383	—	754	883	2,110
San Francisco, Calif.	800	2,653	2,137	754	—	817	2,864
Seattle, Wash.	1,482	2,517	2,164	883	817	—	2,755
Washington, D.C.	2,278	241	836	2,110	2,864	2,755	—

Air Distances Between U.S. Cities in Statute Miles

Cities	Birmingham	Boston	Buffalo	Chicago	Cleveland	Dallas	Denver
Birmingham, Ala.	—	1,052	776	578	618	581	1,095
Boston, Mass.	1,052	—	400	851	551	1,551	1,769
Buffalo, N. Y.	776	400	—	454	173	1,198	1,370
Chicago, Ill.	578	851	454	—	308	803	920
Cleveland, Ohio	618	551	173	308	—	1,025	1,227
Dallas, Tex.	581	1,551	1,198	803	1,025	—	663
Denver, Colo.	1,095	1,769	1,370	920	1,227	663	—
Detroit, Mich.	641	613	216	238	90	999	1,156
El Paso, Tex.	1,152	2,072	1,692	1,252	1,525	572	557
Houston, Tex.	567	1,605	1,286	940	1,114	225	879
Indianapolis, Ind.	433	807	435	165	263	763	1,000
Kansas City, Mo.	579	1,251	861	414	700	451	558
Los Angeles, Calif.	1,802	2,596	2,198	1,745	2,049	1,240	831
Louisville, Ky.	331	826	483	269	311	726	1,038
Memphis, Tenn.	217	1,137	803	482	630	420	879
Miami, Fla.	665	1,255	1,181	1,188	1,087	1,111	1,726
Minneapolis, Minn.	862	1,123	731	355	630	862	700
New Orleans, La.	312	1,359	1,086	833	924	443	1,082
New York, N. Y.	864	188	292	713	405	1,374	1,631
Omaha, Neb.	732	1,282	883	432	739	586	488
Philadelphia, Pa.	783	271	279	666	360	1,299	1,579
Phoenix, Ariz.	1,456	2,300	1,906	1,453	1,749	887	586
Pittsburgh, Pa.	608	483	178	410	115	1,070	1,320
St. Louis, Mo.	400	1,038	662	262	492	547	796
Salt Lake City, Utah	1,466	2,099	1,699	1,260	1,568	999	371
San Francisco, Calif.	2,013	2,699	2,300	1,858	2,166	1,483	949
Seattle, Wash.	2,082	2,493	2,117	1,737	2,026	1,681	1,021
Washington, D.C.	661	393	292	597	306	1,185	1,494

Cities	Detroit	El Paso	Houston	Indianapolis	Kansas City	Los Angeles	Louisville
Birmingham, Ala.	641	1,152	567	433	579	1,802	331
Boston, Mass.	613	2,072	1,605	807	1,251	2,596	826
Buffalo, N. Y.	216	1,692	1,286	435	861	2,198	483
Chicago, Ill.	238	1,252	940	165	414	1,745	269
Cleveland, Ohio	90	1,525	1,114	263	700	2,049	311
Dallas, Tex.	999	572	225	763	451	1,240	726
Denver, Colo.	1,156	557	879	1,000	558	831	1,038
Detroit, Mich.	—	1,479	1,105	240	645	1,983	316
El Paso, Tex.	1,479	—	676	1,264	839	701	1,254
Houston, Tex.	1,105	676	—	865	644	1,374	803
Indianapolis, Ind.	240	1,264	865	—	453	1,809	107
Kansas City, Mo.	645	839	644	453	—	1,356	480
Los Angeles, Calif.	1,983	701	1,374	1,809	1,356	—	1,829
Louisville, Ky.	316	1,254	803	107	480	1,829	—
Memphis, Tenn.	623	976	484	384	369	1,603	320
Miami, Fla.	1,152	1,643	968	1,024	1,241	2,339	919
Minneapolis, Minn.	543	1,157	1,056	511	413	1,524	605
New Orleans, La.	939	983	318	712	680	1,673	623
New York, N. Y.	482	1,905	1,420	646	1,097	2,451	652
Omaha, Neb.	669	878	794	525	166	1,315	580
Philadelphia, Pa.	443	1,836	1,341	585	1,038	2,394	582
Phoenix, Ariz.	1,690	346	1,017	1,499	1,049	357	1,508
Pittsburgh, Pa.	205	1,590	1,137	330	781	2,136	344
St. Louis, Mo.	455	1,034	679	231	238	1,589	242
Salt Lake City, Utah	1,492	689	1,200	1,356	925	579	1,402
San Francisco, Calif.	2,091	995	1,645	1,949	1,506	347	1,986
Seattle, Wash.	1,938	1,376	1,891	1,872	1,506	959	1,943
Washington, D.C.	396	1,728	1,220	494	945	2,300	476

Source: National Geodetic Survey.

Air Distances Between U.S. Cities in Statute Miles

Cities	Memphis	Miami	Minne-apolis	New Orleans	New York	Omaha	Phila-delphia
Birmingham, Ala.	217	665	862	312	864	732	783
Boston, Mass.	1,137	1,255	1,123	1,359	188	1,282	271
Buffalo, N. Y.	803	1,181	731	1,086	292	883	279
Chicago, Ill.	482	1,188	355	833	713	432	666
Cleveland, Ohio	630	1,087	630	924	405	739	360
Dallas, Tex.	420	1,111	862	443	1,374	586	1,299
Denver, Colo.	879	1,726	700	1,082	1,631	488	1,579
Detroit, Mich.	623	1,152	543	939	482	669	443
El Paso, Tex.	976	1,643	1,157	983	1,905	878	1,836
Houston, Tex.	484	968	1,056	318	1,420	794	1,341
Indianapolis, Ind.	384	1,024	511	712	646	525	585
Kansas City, Mo.	369	1,241	413	680	1,097	166	1,038
Los Angeles, Calif.	1,603	2,339	1,524	1,673	2,451	1,315	2,394
Louisville, Ky.	320	919	605	623	652	580	582
Memphis, Tenn.	—	872	699	358	957	529	881
Miami, Fla.	872	—	1,511	669	1,092	1,397	1,019
Minneapolis, Minn.	699	1,511	—	1,051	1,018	290	985
New Orleans, La.	358	669	1,051	—	1,171	847	1,089
New York, N. Y.	957	1,092	1,018	1,171	—	1,144	83
Omaha, Neb.	529	1,397	290	847	1,144	—	1,094
Philadelphia, Pa.	881	1,019	985	1,089	83	1,094	—
Phoenix, Ariz.	1,263	1,982	1,280	1,316	2,145	1,036	2,083
Pittsburgh, Pa.	660	1,010	743	919	317	836	259
St. Louis, Mo.	240	1,061	466	598	875	354	811
Salt Lake City, Utah	1,250	2,089	987	1,434	1,972	833	1,925
San Francisco, Calif.	1,802	2,594	1,584	1,926	2,571	1,429	2,523
Seattle, Wash.	1,867	2,734	1,395	2,101	2,408	1,369	2,380
Washington, D.C.	765	923	934	966	205	1,014	123

Cities	Phoenix	Pitts-burgh	St. Louis	Salt Lake City	San Francisco	Seattle	Wash-ington
Birmingham, Ala.	1,456	608	400	1,466	2,013	2,082	661
Boston, Mass.	2,300	483	1,038	2,099	2,699	2,493	393
Buffalo, N. Y.	1,906	178	662	1,699	2,300	2,117	292
Chicago, Ill.	1,453	410	262	1,260	1,858	1,737	597
Cleveland, Ohio	1,749	115	492	1,568	2,166	2,026	306
Dallas, Tex.	887	1,070	547	999	1,483	1,681	1,185
Denver, Colo.	586	1,320	796	371	949	1,021	1,494
Detroit, Mich.	1,690	205	455	1,492	2,091	1,938	396
El Paso, Tex.	346	1,590	1,034	689	995	1,376	1,728
Houston, Tex.	1,017	1,137	679	1,200	1,645	1,891	1,220
Indianapolis, Ind.	1,499	330	231	1,356	1,949	1,872	494
Kansas City, Mo.	1,049	781	238	925	1,506	1,506	945
Los Angeles, Calif.	357	2,136	1,589	579	347	959	2,300
Louisville, Ky.	1,508	344	242	1,402	1,986	1,943	476
Memphis, Tenn.	1,263	660	240	1,250	1,802	1,867	765
Miami, Fla.	1,982	1,010	1,061	2,089	2,594	2,734	923
Minneapolis, Minn.	1,280	743	466	987	1,584	1,395	934
New Orleans, La.	1,316	919	598	1,434	1,926	2,101	966
New York, N. Y.	2,145	317	875	1,972	2,571	2,408	205
Omaha, Neb.	1,036	836	354	833	1,429	1,369	1,014
Philadelphia, Pa.	2,083	259	811	1,925	2,523	2,380	123
Phoenix, Ariz.	—	1,828	1,272	504	653	1,114	1,983
Pittsburgh, Pa.	1,828	—	559	1,668	2,264	2,138	192
St. Louis, Mo.	1,272	559	—	1,162	1,744	1,724	712
Salt Lake City, Utah	504	1,668	1,162	—	600	701	1,848
San Francisco, Calif.	653	2,264	1,744	600	—	678	2,442
Seattle, Wash.	1,114	2,138	1,724	701	678	—	2,329
Washington, D.C.	1,983	192	712	1,848	2,442	2,329	—

Source: National Geodetic Survey.

Air Distances Between World Cities in Statute Miles

Cities	Berlin	Buenos Aires	Cairo	Calcutta	Cape Town	Caracas	Chicago
Berlin	—	7,402	1,795	4,368	5,981	5,247	4,405
Buenos Aires	7,402	—	7,345	10,265	4,269	3,168	5,598
Cairo	1,795	7,345	—	3,539	4,500	6,338	6,129
Calcutta	4,368	10,265	3,539	—	6,024	9,605	7,980
Cape Town, South Africa	5,981	4,269	4,500	6,024	—	6,365	8,494
Caracas, Venezuela	5,247	3,168	6,338	9,605	6,365	—	2,501
Chicago	4,405	5,598	6,129	7,980	8,494	2,501	—
Hong Kong	5,440	11,472	5,061	1,648	7,375	10,167	7,793
Honolulu, Hawaii	7,309	7,561	8,838	7,047	11,534	6,013	4,250
Istanbul	1,078	7,611	768	3,638	5,154	6,048	5,477
Lisbon	1,436	5,956	2,363	5,638	5,325	4,041	3,990
London	579	6,916	2,181	4,947	6,012	4,660	3,950
Los Angeles	5,724	6,170	7,520	8,090	9,992	3,632	1,745
Manila	6,132	11,051	5,704	2,203	7,486	10,620	8,143
Mexico City	6,047	4,592	7,688	9,492	8,517	2,232	1,691
Montreal	3,729	5,615	5,414	7,607	7,931	2,449	744
Moscow	1,004	8,376	1,803	3,321	6,300	6,173	4,974
New York	3,965	5,297	5,602	7,918	7,764	2,132	713
Paris	545	6,870	1,995	4,883	5,807	4,736	4,134
Rio de Janeiro	6,220	1,200	6,146	9,377	3,773	2,810	5,296
Rome	734	6,929	1,320	4,482	5,249	5,196	4,808
San Francisco	5,661	6,467	7,364	7,814	10,247	3,904	1,858
Shanghai, China	5,218	12,201	5,183	2,117	8,061	9,501	7,061
Stockholm	504	7,808	2,111	4,195	6,444	5,420	4,278
Sydney, Australia	10,006	7,330	8,952	5,685	6,843	9,513	9,272
Tokyo	5,540	11,408	5,935	3,194	9,156	8,799	6,299
Warsaw	320	7,662	1,630	4,048	5,958	5,517	4,667
Washington, D.C.	4,169	5,218	5,800	8,084	7,901	2,059	597

Cities	Hong Kong	Honolulu	Istanbul	Lisbon	London	Los Angeles	Manila
Berlin	5,440	7,309	1,078	1,436	579	5,724	6,132
Buenos Aires	11,472	7,561	7,611	5,956	6,916	6,170	11,051
Cairo	5,061	8,838	768	2,363	2,181	7,520	5,704
Calcutta	1,648	7,047	3,638	5,638	4,947	8,090	2,203
Cape Town, South Africa	7,375	11,534	5,154	5,325	6,012	9,992	7,486
Caracas, Venezuela	10,167	6,013	6,048	4,041	4,660	3,632	10,620
Chicago	7,793	4,250	5,477	3,990	3,950	1,745	8,143
Hong Kong	—	5,549	4,984	6,853	5,982	7,195	693
Honolulu, Hawaii	5,549	—	8,109	7,820	7,228	2,574	5,299
Istanbul	4,984	8,109	—	2,012	1,552	6,783	5,664
Lisbon	6,853	7,820	2,012	—	985	5,621	7,546
London	5,982	7,228	1,552	985	—	5,382	6,672
Los Angeles, Calif.	7,195	2,574	6,783	5,621	5,382	—	7,261
Manila	693	5,299	5,664	7,546	6,672	7,261	—
Mexico City	8,782	3,779	7,110	5,390	5,550	1,589	8,835
Montreal	7,729	4,910	4,789	3,246	3,282	2,427	8,186
Moscow	4,439	7,037	1,091	2,427	1,555	6,003	5,131
New York	8,054	4,964	4,975	3,364	3,458	2,451	8,498
Paris	5,985	7,438	1,400	904	213	5,588	6,677
Rio de Janeiro	11,021	8,285	6,389	4,796	5,766	6,331	11,259
Rome	5,768	8,022	843	1,161	887	6,732	6,457
San Francisco	6,897	2,393	6,703	5,666	5,357	347	6,967
Shanghai, China	764	4,941	4,962	6,654	5,715	6,438	1,150
Stockholm	5,113	6,862	1,348	1,856	890	5,454	5,797
Sydney, Australia	4,584	4,943	9,294	11,302	10,564	7,530	3,944
Tokyo	1,794	3,853	5,560	6,915	5,940	5,433	1,866
Warsaw	5,144	7,355	863	1,715	899	5,922	5,837
Washington, D.C.	8,147	4,519	5,215	3,562	3,663	2,300	8,562

Source: Encyclopaedia Britannica.

Air Distances Between World Cities in Statute Miles

Cities	Mexico City	Montreal	Moscow	New York	Paris	Rio de Janeiro	Rome
Berlin	6,047	3,729	1,004	3,965	545	6,220	734
Buenos Aires	4,592	5,615	8,376	5,297	6,870	1,200	6,929
Cairo	7,688	5,414	1,803	5,602	1,995	6,146	1,320
Calcutta	9,492	7,607	3,321	7,918	4,883	9,377	4,482
Cape Town, South Africa	8,517	7,931	6,300	7,764	5,807	3,773	5,249
Caracas, Venezuela	2,232	2,449	6,173	2,132	4,736	2,810	5,196
Chicago	1,691	744	4,974	713	4,134	5,296	4,808
Hong Kong	8,782	7,729	4,439	8,054	5,985	11,021	5,768
Honolulu	3,779	4,910	7,037	4,964	7,438	8,285	8,022
Istanbul	7,110	4,789	1,091	4,975	1,400	6,389	843
Lisbon	5,390	3,246	2,427	3,364	904	4,796	1,161
London	5,550	3,282	1,555	3,458	213	5,766	887
Los Angeles	1,589	2,427	6,003	2,451	5,588	6,331	6,732
Manila	8,835	8,186	5,131	8,498	6,677	11,259	6,457
Mexico City	—	2,318	6,663	2,094	5,716	4,771	6,366
Montreal	2,318	—	4,386	320	3,422	5,097	4,080
Moscow	6,663	4,386	—	4,665	1,544	7,175	1,474
New York	2,094	320	4,665	—	3,624	4,817	4,281
Paris	5,716	3,422	1,544	3,624	—	5,699	697
Rio de Janeiro	4,771	5,097	7,175	4,817	5,699	—	5,684
Rome	6,366	4,080	1,474	4,281	697	5,684	—
San Francisco	1,887	2,539	5,871	2,571	5,558	6,621	6,240
Shanghai, China	8,022	7,053	4,235	7,371	5,754	11,336	5,677
Stockholm	5,959	3,667	762	3,924	958	6,651	1,234
Sydney, Australia	8,052	9,954	9,012	9,933	10,544	8,306	10,136
Tokyo	7,021	6,383	4,647	6,740	6,034	11,533	6,135
Warsaw	6,365	4,009	715	4,344	849	6,467	817
Washington, D.C.	1,887	488	4,858	205	3,829	4,796	4,434

Cities	San Francisco	Shanghai	Stockholm	Sydney	Tokyo	Warsaw	Washington
Berlin	5,661	5,218	504	10,006	5,540	320	4,169
Buenos Aires	6,467	12,201	7,808	7,330	11,408	7,662	5,218
Cairo	7,364	5,183	2,111	8,952	5,935	1,630	5,800
Calcutta	7,814	2,117	4,195	5,685	3,194	4,048	8,084
Cape Town, South Africa	10,247	8,061	6,444	6,843	9,156	5,958	7,901
Caracas, Venezuela	3,904	9,501	5,420	9,513	8,799	5,517	2,059
Chicago	1,858	7,061	4,278	9,272	6,299	4,667	597
Hong Kong	6,897	764	5,113	4,584	1,794	5,144	8,147
Honolulu	2,393	4,941	6,862	4,943	3,853	7,355	4,519
Istanbul	6,703	4,962	1,348	9,294	5,560	863	5,215
Lisbon	5,666	6,654	1,856	11,302	6,915	1,715	3,562
London	5,357	5,715	890	10,564	5,940	899	3,663
Los Angeles	347	6,438	5,454	7,530	5,433	5,922	2,300
Manila	6,967	1,150	5,797	3,944	1,866	5,837	8,562
Mexico City	1,887	8,022	5,959	8,052	7,021	6,365	1,887
Montreal	2,539	7,053	3,667	9,954	6,383	4,009	488
Moscow	5,871	4,235	762	9,012	4,647	715	4,858
New York	2,571	7,371	3,924	9,933	6,740	4,344	205
Paris	5,558	5,754	958	10,544	6,034	849	3,829
Rio de Janeiro	6,621	11,336	6,651	8,306	11,533	6,467	4,796
Rome	6,240	5,677	1,234	10,136	6,135	817	4,434
San Francisco	—	6,140	5,361	7,416	5,135	5,841	2,442
Shanghai, China	6,140	—	4,825	4,899	1,097	4,951	7,448
Stockholm	5,361	4,825	—	9,696	5,051	501	4,123
Sydney, Australia	7,416	4,899	9,696	—	4,866	9,696	9,758
Tokyo	5,135	1,097	5,051	4,866	—	5,249	6,772
Warsaw	5,841	4,951	501	9,696	5,249	—	4,457
Washington, D.C.	2,442	7,448	4,123	9,758	6,772	4,457	—

Source: Encyclopedia Britannica.

The Seven Wonders of the World

(Not all classical writers list the same items as the Seven Wonders, but most of them agree on the following.)

The Pyramids of Egypt. A group of three pyramids, *Khufu, Khafra,* and *Menkaura* at Giza, outside modern Cairo, is often called the first wonder of the world. The largest pyramid, built by Khufu (Cheops), a king of the fourth Dynasty, had an original estimated height of 482 ft (now approximately 450 ft). The base has sides 755 ft long. It contains 2,300,000 blocks; the average weight of each is 2.5 tons. Estimated date of construction is 2800 B.C. Of all the Seven Wonders, the pyramids alone survive.

Hanging Gardens of Babylon. Often listed as the second wonder, these gardens were supposedly built by Nebuchadnezzar about 600 B.C. to please his queen, Amuhia. They are also associated with the mythical Assyrian Queen, Semiramis. Archeologists surmise that the gardens were laid out atop a vaulted building, with provisions for raising water. The terraces were said to rise from 75 to 300 ft.

The Walls of Babylon, also built by Nebuchadnezzar, are sometimes referred to as the second (or the seventh) wonder instead of the Hanging Gardens.

Statue of Zeus (Jupiter) at Olympia. The work of Phidias (5th century B.C.), this colossal figure in gold and ivory was reputedly 40 ft high. All trace of it is lost, except for reproductions on coins.

Temple of Artemis (Diana) at Ephesus. A beautiful structure, begun about 350 B.C. in honor of a non-Hellenic goddess who later became identified with the Greek goddess of the same name. The temple, with Ionic columns 60 ft high, was destroyed by invading Goths in A.D. 262.

Mausoleum at Halicarnassus. This famous monument was erected by Queen Artemisia in memory of her husband, King Mausolus of Caria in Asia Minor, who died in 353 B.C. Some remains of the structure are in the British Museum. This shrine is the source of the modern word "mausoleum."

Colossus at Rhodes. This bronze statue of Helios (Apollo), about 105 ft high, was the work of the sculptor Chares, who reputedly labored for 12 years before completing it in 280 B.C. It was destroyed during an earthquake in 224 B.C.

Pharos of Alexandria. The seventh wonder was the Pharos (lighthouse) of Alexandria, built by Sostratus of Cnidus during the 3rd century B.C. on the island of Pharos off the coast of Egypt. It was destroyed by an earthquake in the 13th century.

Famous Structures

Ancient

The *Great Sphinx of Egypt,* one of the wonders of ancient Egyptian architecture, adjoins the pyramids of Giza and has a length of 240 ft. It was built in the 4th dynasty.

Other Egyptian buildings of note include the *Temples of Karnak* and *Edfu* and the *Tombs at Beni Hassan.*

The *Parthenon of Greece,* built on the Acropolis in Athens, was the chief temple to the goddess Athena. It was believed to have been completed by 438 B.C. The present temple remained intact until the 5th century A.D. Today, though the Parthenon is in ruins, its majestic proportions are still discernible.

Other great structures of ancient Greece were the *Temples at Paestum* (about 540 and 420 B.C.); the *Temple of Poseidon* (about 460 B.C.); the *Temple of Apollo* at Corinth (about 540 B.C.); the *Temple of Apollo* at Bassae (about 450–420 B.C.); the famous *Erechtheum* atop the Acropolis (about 421–405 B.C.); the *Temple of Athena Niké* at Athens (about 426 B.C.); the *Olympieum* at Athens (174 B.C.–A.D. 131); the *Athenian Treasury* at Delphi (about 515 B.C.); the *Propylaea* of the Acropolis at Athens (437–432 B.C.); the *Theater of Dionysus* at Athens (about 350–325 B.C.); the *House of Cleopatra* at Delos (138 B.C.) and the *Theater* at Epidaurus (about 325 B.C.).

The *Colosseum (Flavian Amphitheater) of Rome,* the largest and most famous of the Roman amphitheaters, was opened for use A.D. 80. Elliptical in shape, it consisted of three stories and an upper gallery, rebuilt in stone in its present form in the third century A.D. Its seats rise in tiers, which in turn are buttressed by concrete vaults and stone piers. It could seat between 40,000 and 50,000 spectators. It was principally used for gladiatorial combat.

The *Pantheon* at Rome, begun by Agrippa in 27 B.C. as a temple, was rebuilt in its present circular form by Hadrian (A.D. 110–25). Literally the Pantheon was intended as a temple of "all the gods." It is remarkable for its perfect preservation today, and it has served continuously for 20 centuries as a place of worship.

Famous Roman arches include the *Arch of Constantine* (about A.D. 315) and the *Arch of Titus* (about A.D. 80).

Later European

St. Mark's Cathedral in Venice (1063–67), one of the great examples of Byzantine architecture, was begun in the 9th century. Partly destroyed by fire in 976, it was later rebuilt as a Byzantine edifice.

Other famous Byzantine examples of architecture are *St. Sophia* in Istanbul (A.D. 532–37); *San Vitale* in Ravenna (542); *St. Paul's Outside the Walls,* Rome (5th century); the *Kremlin* baptism and marriage church, Moscow (begun in 1397); and *St. Lorenzo Outside the Walls,* Rome, begun in 588.

The *Cathedral Group* at Pisa (1067–1173), one of the most celebrated groups of structures built in Romanesque style, consists of the cathedral, the cathedral's baptistery, and the *Leaning Tower.* This trio forms a group by itself in the northwest corner of the city. The cathedral and baptistery are built in varicolored marble. The campanile *(Leaning Tower)* is 179 ft. high and leans more than 16 ft out of the perpendicular. There is little reason to believe that the architects intended to have the tower lean.

Other examples of Romanesque architecture include the *Vézelay Abbey* in France (1130); the *Church of Notre-Dame-du-Port* at Clermont-Ferrand in France (1100); the *Church of San Zeno* (begun in 1138) at Verona, and *Durham Cathedral* in England.

The *Alhambra* (1248–1354), located in Granada, Spain, is universally esteemed as one of the greatest masterpieces of Moslem architecture. Designed as a palace and fortress for the Moorish monarchs of Granada, it is surrounded by a heavily fortified wall more than a mile in perimeter. The location of the Alhambra in the Sierra Nevada provides a magnificent setting for this jewel of Moorish Spain.

The *Tower of London* is a group of buildings and towers covering 13 acres along the north bank of the Thames. The central *White Tower,* begun in 1078 during the reign of William the Conqueror, was originally a fortress and royal residence, but was later used as a prison. The *Bloody Tower* is associated with Anne Boleyn and other notables.

Westminster Abbey, in London, was begun in 1045 and completed in 1065. It was rebuilt and enlarged in 1245–50.

Notre-Dame de Paris (begun in 1163), one of the great examples of Gothic architecture, is a twin-towered church with a steeple over the crossing and immense flying buttresses supporting the masonry at the rear of the church.

Other famous Gothic structures are *Chartres Cathedral* (12th century); *Sainte Chapelle,* Paris (1246–48); *Laon Cathedral,* France (1160–1205); *Reims Cathedral* (about 1210–50; rebuilt after its almost complete destruction in World War I); *Rouen Cathedral* (13th–16th centuries); *Amiens Cathedral* (1218–69); *Beauvais Cathedral* (begun 1247); *Salisbury Cathedral* (1220–60); *York Minster* or the *Cathedral of St. Peter* (begun in the 7th century); *Milan Cathedral* (begun 1386); and *Cologne Cathedral* (13th–19th centuries; badly damaged in World War II.

The Duomo (cathedral) in Florence was founded in 1298, completed by Brunelleschi and consecrated in 1436. The oval-shaped dome dominates the entire structure.

The *Vatican* is a group of buildings in Rome comprising the official residence of the Pope. The *Basilica of St. Peter,* the largest church in the Christian world, was begun in 1450. The *Sistine Chapel,* begun in 1473, is noted for the art masterpieces of Michelangelo, Botticelli, and others. The *Basilica of the Savior* (known as *St. John Lateran*) is the first-ranking Catholic Church in the world, for it is the cathedral of the Pope.

Other examples of Renaissance architecture are the *Palazzo Riccardi,* the *Palazzo Pitti* and the *Palazzo Strozzi* in Florence; the *Farnese Palace* in Rome; *Palazzo Grimani* (completed about 1550) in Venice; the *Escorial* (1563–93) near Madrid; the *Town Hall* of Seville (1527–32); the *Louvre,* Paris; the *Château* at Blois, France; *St. Paul's Cathedral,* London (1675–1710; badly damaged in World War II); the *École Militaire,* Paris (1752); the *Pazzi Chapel,* Florence, designed by Brunelleschi (1429); the Palace of *Fontainebleau* and the *Château de Chambord* in France.

The *Palace of Versailles,* containing the famous Hall of Mirros, was built during the reign of Louis XIV and served as the royal palace until 1793.

Outstanding European buildings of the 18th and 19th centuries are the *Superga* at Turin, the *Hôtel-Dieu* in Lyons, the *Belvedere Palace* at Vienna, the *Royal Palace* of Stockholm, the *Opera House* of Paris (1863–75); the *Bank of England,* the *British Museum,* the *University of London,* and the *Houses of Parliament,* all in London; the *Panthéon,* the *Church of the Madeleine,* the *Bourse,* and the *Palais de Justice* in Paris.

The *Eiffel Tower,* in Paris, was built for the Exposition of 1889 by Alexandre Eiffel. It is 984 ft high.[1]

Asiatic and African

The *Taj Mahal* (1632–50), at Agra, India, built by Shah Jahan as a tomb for his wife, is considered by some as the most perfect example of the Mogul style and by others as the most beautiful building in the world. Four slim white minarets flank the building, which is topped by a white dome; the entire structure is of marble.

Other examples of Indian architecture are the temples at Benares and Tanjore.

Among famed Moslem edifices are the *Dome of the Rock* or *Mosque of Omar,* Jerusalem (A.D. 691); the *Citadel* (1166), and the *Tombs of the Mamelukes* (15th century), in Cairo; the *Tomb of Humayun* in Delhi; the *Blue Mosque* (1468) at Tabriz, and the *Tamerlane Mausoleum* at Samarkand.

Angkor Wat, outside the city of Angkor Thom, Cambodia, is one of the most beautiful examples of Cambodian or Khmer architecture. The sanctuary was built during the 12th century.

Great Wall of China (228 B.C.?), designed specifically as a defense against nomadic tribes, has numerous large watch towers which could be called buildings. It was erected by Emperor Ch'in Shih Huang Ti and is 1,400 miles long. Built mainly of earth and stone, it varies in height between 18 and 30 ft.

Typical of Chinese architecture are the pagodas or temple towers. Among some of the better-known pagodas are the *Great Pagoda of the Wild Geese* at Sian (founded in 652); *Nan t'a* (11th century) at Fang Shan; the *Pagoda of Sung Yueh Ssu* (A.D. 523) at Sung Shan, Honan.

Other well-known Chinese buildings are the *Drum Tower* (1273), the *Three Great Halls* in the Purple Forbidden City (1627), *Buddha's Perfume Tower* (19th century), the *Porcelain Pagoda,* and the *Summer Palace,* all at Peking.

United States

Rockefeller Center, in New York City, extends from 5th Ave. to the Avenue of the Americas between 48th and 52nd Sts. (and halfway to 7th Ave. between 47th and 51st Sts.). It occupies more than 22 acres and has 19 buildings.

The Cathedral of St. John the Divine, at 112th St. and Amsterdam Ave. in New York City, was begun in 1892 and is now in the final stages of completion. When completed, it will be the largest cathedral in the world: 601 ft long, 146 ft wide at the nave, 320 ft wide at the transept. The east end is designed in

1. 1,056 ft, including the television tower.

Romanesque-Byzantine style, and the nave and west end are Gothic.

St. Patrick's Cathedral, at Fifth Ave. and 50th St. in New York City, has a seating capacity of 2,500. The nave was opened in 1877, and the cathedral was dedicated in 1879.

Louisiana Superdome, in New Orleans, is the largest arena in the history of mankind. The main area can accommodate up to 95,000 people. It is the world's largest steel-constructed room. Unobstructed by posts, it covers 13 ac. and reaches 27 stories at its peak.

World Trade Center, in New York City, was dedicated in 1973. Its twin towers are 110 stories high (1,350 ft), and the complex contains over 9 million sq ft of office space. The world's highest observation deck is at the top of the South Tower. A restaurant is on the 107th floor of the No. Tower.

World's Highest Dams

Name	River	Maximum height		Reservoir capacity in acre-feet	Reservoir capacity in millions of cubic meters	Year completed
		feet	meters			
Rogunsky	Vakhsh, U.S.S.R.	1,066	325	9,485,000	11,700	UC
Nurek	Vakhsh, U.S.S.R.	1,040	317	8,424,000	10,400	UC
Grand Dixence	Dixence, Switzerland	935	285	325,000	401	1962
Inguri	Inguri, U.S.S.R.	892	272	801,000	1,100	UC
Vaiont	Vaiont, Italy	869	265	137,000	169	1961
Chicoasen	Grijalva, Mexico	869	265	1,346,000	1,660	UC
Mica	Columbia, Canada	794	242	20,000,000	24,670	1974
Sayanskaya	Yenesei, U.S.S.R.	794	242	25,353,000	31,300	UC
Chivor	Bata, Colombia	778	237	661,000	815	1975
Mauvoisin	Drance de Bagnes, Switzerland	777	237	148,000	182	1957
Oroville	Feather, California	770	235	3,538,000	4,299	1968
Chirkey	Sulak, U.S.S.R.	764	233	2,252,000	2,780	1975
Bhakra	Sutlej, India	742	226	8,000,000	9,868	1963
Hoover	Colorado, Arizona-Nevada	726	221	29,755,000	36,703	1936
Contra	Verzasca, Switzerland	722	220	86,000	106	1965
Piva (Mratinje)	Piva, Yugoslavia	722	220	713,000	880	1975
Dworshak	North Fork, Clearwater, Idaho	717	219	3,453,000	4,259	1974
Glen Canyon	Colorado, Arizona	710	216	27,000,000	33,305	1964
Daniel Johnson	Manicougan, Canada	703	214	115,000,000	141,852	1968
Toktogul	Naryn, U.S.S.R.	699	213	15,800,000	19,500	1978
Auburn	North Fork, California	685	209	2,300,000	2,837	UC
Luzzone	Brenno di Luzzone, Switzerland	682	208	71,000	88	1963
Keban	Firat, Turkey	679	207	25,110,000	31,000	1974
Dez	Dez, Iran	666	203	2,707,000	3,340	1963
Almendra	Turmes-Douro, Spain	662	202	2,148,000	2,649	1970
Karoun	Karoun, Iran	656	200	2,351,000	2,900	1975
Kölnbrein	Malta, Austria	656	200	162,000	200	1977
New Bullard's Bar	North Yuba, California	637	194	960,000	1,184	1970
New Melones	Stanislaus, California	625	191	2,400,000	2,960	1975
Kurobe No. 4	Kurobe, Japan	610	186	162,000	199	1964
Swift	Lewis, Washington	610	186	756,000	932	1958
Mossyrock	Cowlitz, Washington	605	184	1,300,000	1,603	1968
Shasta	Sacramento, California	602	183	4,552,000	5,615	1945
W.A.C. Bennett	Peace, Canada	600	183	57,006,000	70,309	1967
Tignes	Isere, France	591	180	186,000	230	1952
Amir Kabir (Karad)	Karadj, Iran	591	180	166,000	205	1962
Tachien (Techi)	Tachia, Taiwan	591	180	207,000	255	1974
Dartmouth	Mitta-Mitta, Australia	591	180	5,232,000	4,000	1978
Emosson	Barberine, Switzerland	590	180	184,000	227	1974
Don Pedro	Tuolume, California	585	178	2,030,000	2,504	1971
Alpa-Gera	Cormor, Italy	584	178	53,000	65	1965
Kopperston Tailings No. 3	Jones Branch, West Virginia	580	177	—	—	1963
Hungry Horse	South Fork, Flathead, Montana	564	172	3,468,000	4,278	1953
Idikki	Periyar, India	561	171	1,182,000	1,460	1974
Cabora Bassa	Zambezi, Mozambique	561	171	51,900,000	64,000	1974
Charvak	Chirchik, U.S.S.R.	551	168	1,620,000	2,000	1970
Grand Coulee	Columbia, Washington	550	168	9,724,000	11,795	1942
Vidraru	Arges-Danube, Romania	547	167	380,000	465	1966
Kremasta (King Paul)	Acheloos, Greece	541	165	3,850,000	4,750	1965
Ross	Skagit, Washington	540	165	1,435,000	1,770	1949
Trinity	Trinity, California	537	164	2,448,000	3,020	1962
Talbingo	Tumut, Australia	530	162	747,000	921	1971
Yellowtail	Bighorn, Montana	525	160	1,375,000	1,696	1966

Name	River	Maximum height feet	Maximum height meters	Reservoir capacity in acre-feet	Reservoir capacity in millions of cubic meters	Year completed
Gokcekaya	Sakarya, Turkey	525	160	737,000	910	1973
Cougar	South Fork, McKenzie, Oregon	519	158	219,000	270	1964
Curnera	Rein de Curnera, Switzerland	518	158	33,000	41	1966
Okutadami	Tadami, Japan	515	157	487,000	601	1961
Speccheri	Leno di Vallarsa, Italy	514	157	8,000	10	1957
Zeuzier	Lienne, Switzerland	512	156	41,000	51	1957
Sakuma	Tenryu, Japan	510	156	265,000	327	1956
Monteynard	Drac, France	509	155	195,000	240	1962
Nagawado	Azusa, Japan	509	155	99,000	123	1969
Göscheneralp	Göschenerreuss, Switzerland	508	155	62,000	76	1960
Bhumiphol (Yanhee)	Ping-Chao Phaya, Thailand	505	154	10,914,000	13,462	1964
Flaming Gorge	Green, Utah	502	153	3,789,000	4,674	1964
Place Moulin	Buthier, Italy	502	153	81,000	100	1965
Gepatsch	Faggenbach, Austria	500	153	113,000	139	1965
Santa Giustina	Noce-Adige, Italy	500	153	148,000	183	1950
Zervreila	Valserrhein, Switzerland	495	151	81,000	100	1957
Roselend	Doron-de-Beaufort, France	492	150	152,000	187	1961
Canelles	Noguera, Spain	492	150	549,000	678	1960

NOTE: UC = under construction in 1979. *Source:* Department of the Interior, Bureau of Reclamation.

World's Largest Hydroelectric Plants

Name of dam	Location	Rated capacity (Mw) Present	Rated capacity (Mw) Ultimate	Year of initial operation
Itaipu	Brazil–Paraguay	—	12,870	UC
Raul Leoni	Venezuela	2,100	10,100	1968
Grand Coulee	Washington	6,263[1]	10,080	1941
Guri	Venezuela	524	6,500	1967
Sayanskaya	U.S.S.R.	—	6,400	UC
Krasnoyarsk	U.S.S.R.	6,096	6,096	1968
La Grande 2	Canada	—	5,328	UC
Churchill Falls	Canada	5,225	5,225	1971
Bratsk	U.S.S.R.	4,100	4,600	1964
Sukhovo	U.S.S.R.	—	4,500	UC
Ust-Ipimsk	U.S.S.R.	720	4,320	1974
Cabora Bassa	Mozambique	2,075	4,150	1975
Paulo Afonso	Brazil	1,524	3,409	1955
Inga 1	Zaire	360	2,820	1974
John Day	Oregon–Washington	2,160	2,700	1968
Solteira	Brazil	2,650	2,650	1973
Volgograd—22nd Congress	U.S.S.R.	2,560	2,560	1958
Volga—V.I. Lenin (Kuibisher)	U.S.S.R.	2,300	2,300	1955
Iron Gates 1	Romania–Yugoslavia	2,300	2,300	1970
W.A.C. Bennett	Canada	2,116	2,270	1969
High Aswan (Sadd-el-Aali)	Egypt	2,100	2,100	1967
Tarbela	Pakistan	700	2,100	1977
Chief Joseph	Washington	1,879	2,069	1956
Robert Moses-Niagara	New York	1,950	1,950	1961
Salto Grande	Argentina—Uruguay	135	1,890	1979
Ludington	Michigan	1,872	1,872	1973
St. Lawrence Power Dam	United States—Canada	1,824	1,824	1958
The Dalles	Washington	1,807	1,807	1957
Kemano	Canada	813	1,670	1954
Beauharnois	Canada	1,021	1,574	1950
Kariba	Zimbabwe–Zambia	1,266	1,566	1959
Raccoon Mountain	Tennessee	1,530	1,530	1975
Tumut 3	Australia	1,500	1,500	1972
Jupia	Brazil	1,411	1,411	1966
McNary	Oregon	980	1,406	1953

1. Present dam being enlarged. NOTE: UC = under construction in 1980. *Source:* Department of the Interior, Bureau of Reclamation.

America's Tallest Buildings

City	Building	Stories	Height ft	Height m	City	Building	Stories	Height ft	Height m
Chicago	Sears Tower	110	1,454	443	Boston	John Hancock Tower	60	790	241
New York	World Trade Center	110	1,377	419	San Francisco	Bank of America	52	779	237
New York	Empire State	102	1,250	381	Minneapolis	IDS Tower	57	775	236
Chicago	Standard Oil (Indiana)	80	1,136	346	New York	One Liberty Plaza	54	775	236
Chicago	John Hancock Center	100	1,127	343	New York	One Penn Plaza	57	774	236
New York	Chrysler	77	1,046	319	Atlanta	Peachtree Plaza	73	754	230
New York	American International	66	952	290	New York	Exxon	54	750	229
New York	Citicorp Center	59	915	279	Boston	Prudential Tower	52	750	229
New York	40 Wall Tower	71	900	274	Detroit	Detroit Plaza Hotel	73	747	228
Chicago	Water Tower Place	74	859	262	Los Angeles	Security Pacific Plaza	55	743	226
Los Angeles	United California Bank	62	858	261	New York	One Astor Plaza	54	730	222
San Francisco	Transamerica Pyramid	61	853	260	New York	Marine Midland	52	724	221
Chicago	First National Bank	60	851	259	Houston	One Shell Plaza	50	714	218
New York	RCA	70	850	259	Dallas	First International	56	710	216
Pittsburgh	U.S. Steel Headquarters	64	841	256	Cleveland	Terminal Tower	52	708	216
New York	Chase Manhattan	60	813	248	New York	Union Carbide	52	707	215
New York	Pan Am	59	808	246	New York	General Motors	50	705	215
New York	Woolworth	55	792	241	New York	Metropolitan Life	50	700	213

NOTE: Does not include buildings under construction and not completed in 1980. Height does not include TV towers and antennas. *Source: Information Please* questionnaires to buildings.

Notable Tunnels

Railroad, excluding subways

Name	Location	Length mi.	Length km	Year completed
Seikan	Tsugara Strait, Japan	33.1	53.3	UC
Simplon (I and II)	Alps, Switzerland-Italy	12.3	19.8	1906 & 1922
Kammon Straits	Honshu to Kyoshu Islands, Japan	11.6	18.7	UC
Apennine	Genoa, Italy	11.5	18.5	1934
St. Gotthard	Swiss Alps	9.3	14.9	1881
Lötschberg	Swiss Alps	9.1	14.6	1911
Nakayama	Komochi Mountain, Japan	8.8	14.2	UC
Mont Cénis	French Alps	8.5[1]	13.7	1871
New Cascade	Cascade Mountains, Washington	7.8	12.6	1929
Vosges	Vosges, France	7.0	11.3	1940
Arlberg	Austrian Alps	6.3	10.1	1884
Moffat	Rocky Mountains, Colorado	6.2	9.9	1928
Shimuzu	Shimuzu, Japan	6.1	9.8	1931
Rimutaka	Wairarapa, New Zealand	5.5	8.9	1955

Vehicular

Name	Location	Length mi.	Length km	Year completed
St. Gotthard	Alps, Switzerland	10.2	16.4	1980
Mt. Blanc	Alps, France-Italy	7.5	12.1	1965
Mt. Ena	Japan Alps, Japan	5.3	8.5	1976[2]
Great St. Bernard	Alps, Switzerland-Italy	3.4	5.5	1964
Mount Royal	Montreal, Canada	3.2	5.1	1918
Lincoln	Hudson River, New York-New Jersey	2.5	4.0	1937
Queensway Road	Mersey River, Liverpool, England	2.2	3.5	1934
Brooklyn-Battery	East River, New York City	2.1	3.4	1950
Holland	Hudson River, New York-New Jersey	1.7	2.7	1927
Hampton Roads	Norfolk, Virginia	1.4	2.3	1957
Queens-Midtown	East River, New York City	1.3	2.1	1940
Liberty Tubes	Pittsburgh, Pennsylvania	1.2	1.9	1923
Baltimore Harbor	Baltimore, Maryland	1.2	1.9	1957
Allegheny Tunnels	Pennsylvania Turnpike	1.2	1.9	1940[3]

1. Lengthened to its present 8.5 miles in 1881. 2. Parallel tunnel begun in 1976. 3. Parallel tunnel built in 1965, twin tunnel in 1966. NOTE: UC = under construction. *Source:* American Society of Civil Engineers.

Notable Modern Bridges

Suspension

Name	Location	Length of main span, ft	m	Year completed
Humber	Hull, Britain	4,626	1,410	UC
Verrazano-Narrows	Lower New York Bay	4,260	1,298	1964
Golden Gate	San Francisco Bay	4,200	1,280	1937
Mackinac Straits	Michigan	3,800	1,158	1957
Bosporus	Istanbul	3,524	1,074	1973
George Washington	Hudson River at New York City	3,500	1,067	1931
Ponte 25 de Abril	Tagus River at Lisbon	3,323	1,013	1966
Forth Road	Queensferry, Scotland	3,300	1,006	1964
Severn	Severn River at Beachley, England	3,240	988	1966
Tacoma Narrows	Puget Sound at Tacoma, Wash.	2,800	853	1950
Kanmon Strait	Kyushu-Honshu, Japan	2,336	712	1973
Angostura	Orinoco River at Ciudad Bolívar, Venezuela	2,336	712	1967
Transbay (twin spans)	San Francisco Bay	2,310	704	1936
Bronx-Whitestone	East River, New York City	2,300	701	1939
Pierre Laporte	St. Lawrence River at Quebec, Canada	2,190	668	1970
Delaware Memorial (twin bridges)	Delaware River near Wilmington, Del.	2,150	655	1951, 1968
Seaway Skyway	St. Lawrence River at Ogdensburg, N.Y.	2,150	655	1960
Gas Pipe Line	Atchafalaya River, Louisiana	2,000	610	1951
Walt Whitman	Delaware River at Philadelphia	2,000	610	1957
Tancarville	Seine River at Tancarville, France	1,995	608	1959
Lillebaelt	Lillebaelt Strait, Denmark	1,969	600	1970
Ambassador International	Detroit River at Detroit	1,850	564	1929
Throgs Neck	East River, New York City	1,800	549	1961
Benjamin Franklin	Delaware River at Philadelphia	1,750	533	1926
Skjomen	Narvik, Norway	1,722	525	1972
Kvalsund	Hammerfest, Norway	1,722	525	1977
Kleve-Emmerich	Rhine River at Emmerich, West Germany	1,640	500	1965
Bear Mountain	Hudson River at Peekskill, N.Y.	1,632	497	1924
Wm. Preston Lane, Jr., Memorial (twin bridges)	Near Annapolis, Md.	1,600	488	1952, 1973
Williamsburg	East River, New York City	1,600	488	1903
Newport	Narragansett Bay at Newport, R.I.	1,600	488	1969
Brooklyn	East River, New York City	1,595	486	1883

Cantilever

Name	Location	ft	m	Year completed
Quebec Railway	St. Lawrence River at Quebec, Canada	1,800	549	1917
Forth Railway (twin spans)	Queensferry, Scotland	1,710	521	1890
Minato Ohashi	Osaka, Japan	1,673	510	1974
Commodore John Barry	Chester, Pa.	1,644	501	1974
Greater New Orleans	Mississippi River, Louisiana	1,576	480	1958
Howrah	Hooghly River at Calcutta	1,500	457	1943
Transbay Bridge	San Francisco Bay	1,400	427	1936
Baton Rouge	Mississippi River, Louisiana	1,235	376	1968
Tappan Zee	Hudson River at Tarrytown, N.Y.	1,212	369	1955
Longview	Columbia River at Longview, Wash.	1,200	366	1930
Patapsco River	Baltimore Outer Harbor Crossing	1,200	366	1976
Queensboro	East River, New York City	1,182	360	1909

Steel Arch

Name	Location	ft	m	Year completed
New River Gorge	Fayetteville, W. Va.	1,700	518	1977
Bayonne	Kill Van Kull at Bayonne, N.J.	1,675	510	1931
Sydney Harbor	Sydney, Australia	1,670	509	1932
Fremont	Portland, Ore.	1,255	383	1973
Zdákov	Vltava River, Czechoslovakia	1,244	380	1967
Port Mann	Fraser River at Vancouver, British Columbia	1,200	366	1964
Thatcher Ferry	Panama Canal, Panama	1,128	344	1962
Laviolette	St. Lawrence River, Trois Rivieres, Quebec	1,100	335	1967
Runcorn-Widnes	Mersey River, England	1,082	330	1961
Birchenough	Sabi River at Fort Victoria, Rhodesia	1,080	329	1935

Cable-Stayed

Name	Location	Length of main span, ft	m	Year completed
Second Hooghly	Calcutta	1,500	457	UC
St.-Nazaire	Loire River, St.-Nazaire, France	1,325	404	1975
Stretto di Rande	Spain	1,312	400	UC
Luling	Missippi River, Luling, La.	1,235	376	UC
Düsseldorf-Flehe	Rhine River, West Germany	1,205	367	UC
Yamatogawa	Osaka, Japan	1,165	355	UC
Duisburg-Neuenkamp	Duisburg, West Germany	1,148	350	1970
Mesopotamia	Corrientes, Argentina	1,116	340	1972
West Gate	Lower Yarra River at Melbourne, Australia	1,102	336	1970
Zárate	Paraná River, Argentina	1,083	330	1976
Brazo Largo	Paraná River, Argentina	1,083	330	1977
Köhlbrand	Hamburg, West Germany	1,066	325	1974
Kniebrücke	Rhine River at Düsseldorf, West Germany	1,050	320	1969
Brotonne[1]	Seine River, France	1,050	320	1976
Erskine	Clyde River at Glasgow, Scotland	1,000	305	1971

Continuous Truss

Name	Location	ft	m	Year completed
Astoria	Columbia River at Astoria, Oregon	1,232	376	1966
Oshima	Oshima Island, Japan	1,066	325	1976
Croton Reservoir	Croton, N.Y.	1,052	321	1970
Tenmon	Kumamoto, Japan	984	300	1966
Kuronoseto	Nagashima-Kyushu, Japan	984	300	1974
Ravenswood	Ohio River, Ravenswood, W. Va.	902	275	UC
Dubuque	Mississippi River at Dubuque, Iowa	845	258	1943
Braga Memorial	Taunton River at Somerset, Mass.	840	256	1966
Graf Spee	Germany	839	256	1936

Concrete Arch

Name	Location	ft	m	Year completed
KRK	Zagreb, Yugoslavia	1,280	390	1979
Gladesville	Parramatta River at Sydney, Australia	1,000	305	1964
Amizade	Paraná River at Foz do Iguassu, Brazil	951	290	1964
Arrábida	Porto, Portugal	886	270	1963
Sandö	Angerman River at Kramfors, Sweden	866	264	1943
Shibenik	Krka River, Yugoslavia	808	246	1966
Fiumarella	Catanzaro, Italy	758	231	1961
Zaporozhe	Old Dnepr River, U.S.S.R.	748	228	1952
Novi Sad	Danube River, Yugoslavia	692	211	1961

1. Concrete bridge. NOTE: UC = under construction. *Source: Encyclopaedia Britannica* and American Society of Civil Engineers.

Famous Ship Canals

Name	Location	Length (miles)[1]	Width (feet)	Depth (feet)	Locks	Year opened
Albert	Belgium	80.0	53.0	16.5	6	1939
Amsterdam–Rhine	Netherlands	45.0	164.0	41.0	3	1952
Beaumont–Port Arthur	United States	40.0	200.0	34.0	—	1916
Chesapeake and Delaware	United States	19.0	250.0	27.0	—	1927
Houston	United States	43.0	300.0	34.0	—	1914
Kiel (Nord-Ostsee Kanal)	Germany	61.3	144.0	36.0	4	1895
Panama	Canal Zone	50.7	110.0	41.0	12	1914
St. Lawrence Seaway	U.S. and Canada	2,400.0[2]	(3)	—	—	1959
Montreal to Prescott	U.S. and Canada	11.5	80.0	30.0	7	1959
Welland	Canada	27.5	80.0	27.0	8	1931
Sault Ste. Marie	Canada	1.2	60.0	16.8	1	1895
Sault Ste. Marie	United States	1.6	80.0	25.0	4	1915
Suez	Egypt	100.6[4]	197.0	36.0	—	1869

1. Statute miles. 2. From Montreal to Duluth. 3. 442–550 feet; there are 11.5 miles of locks, 80 feet wide and 30 feet deep. 4. From Port Said lighthouse to entrance channel in Suez roads. *Source:* American Society of Civil Engineers.

World's Largest Dams

Dam	Location	Volume (thousands) Cubic meters	Cubic yards	Year completed
New Cornelia Tailings	Arizona	209,500	274,026	1973
Tarbela	Pakistan	121,000	158,268	1975
Fort Peck	Montana	96,034	125,612	1940
Raul Leoni	Venezuela	78,000	102,014	(1)
Ataturk	Turkey	73,700	96,400	UC
Guri	Venezuela	70,762	92,557	UC
Oahe	South Dakota	70,343	92,008	1963
Oosterschelde	Netherlands	70,000	91,560	UC
Yacyreta-Apipe	Argentina–Paraguay	70,000	91,560	UC
Mangla	Pakistan	65,651	85,872	1967
Gardiner	Canada	65,553	85,743	1968
Afsluitdijk	Netherlands	63,400	82,927	1932
Oroville	California	59,639	78,008	1968
San Luis	California	59,378	77,666	1967
Nurek	U.S.S.R.	58,000	75,864	UC
Garrison	North Dakota	50,846	66,506	1956
Cochiti	New Mexico	49,417	64,631	1975
Tabka	Syria	46,000	60,168	1975
Kiev	U.S.S.R.	44,000	57,552	1964
W.A.C. Bennett	Canada	43,733	57,203	1967
High Aswan (Sadd-el-Aali)	Egypt	43,733	57,203	1970
Dantiwada Left Earthen Bank	India	41,040	53,680	1965
Saratov	U.S.S.R.	40,400	52,843	1967
Mission Tailings #2	Arizona	40,088	52,435	1973
Fort Randall	South Dakota	38,383	50,205	1956
Kanev	U.S.S.R.	37,860	49,520	1974
Kakhova	U.S.S.R.	35,640	46,617	1955
Tsimlyanska	U.S.S.R.	33,891	44,323	1952

1. Present dam being enlarged. NOTE: Based on total volume of dam structure. All dams listed are predominantly earth or rockfill and may contain masonry sections. UC = under construction in 1980. *Source:* Department of the Interior, Bureau of Reclamation.

Chinese Calendar

The Chinese lunar year is divided into 12 months of 29 or 30 days. The calendar is adjusted to the length of the solar year by the addition of extra months at regular intervals.

The years are arranged in major cycles of 60 years. Each successive year is named after one of 12 animals. These 12-year cycles are continuously repeated. The Chinese New Year is celebrated at the first new moon after the sun enters Aquarius—sometime between Jan. 21 and Feb. 19.

Rat	Ox	Tiger	Cat (Rabbit)	Dragon	Snake	Horse	Sheep (Goat)	Monkey	Rooster	Dog	Pig
1864	1865	1866	1867	1868	1869	1870	1871	1872	1873	1874	1875
1876	1877	1878	1879	1880	1881	1882	1883	1884	1885	1886	1887
1888	1889	1890	1891	1892	1893	1894	1895	1896	1897	1898	1899
1900	1901	1902	1903	1904	1905	1906	1907	1908	1909	1910	1911
1912	1913	1914	1915	1916	1917	1918	1919	1920	1921	1922	1923
1924	1925	1926	1927	1928	1929	1930	1931	1932	1933	1934	1935
1936	1937	1938	1939	1940	1941	1942	1943	1944	1945	1946	1947
1948	1949	1950	1951	1952	1953	1954	1955	1956	1957	1958	1959
1960	1961	1962	1963	1964	1965	1966	1967	1968	1969	1970	1971
1972	1973	1974	1975	1976	1977	1978	1979	1980	1981	1982	1983
1984	1985	1986	1987	1988	1989	1990	1991	1992	1993	1994	1995

The Stages of Invention

Alexander von Humbolt (1769–1859), the German naturalist, said that an invention goes through three stages: doubt of its existence, denial of its importance, and, finally, credit for its discovery going to someone else.

One example of the truth in this perception is the invention of the "Pullman," the railroad sleeping car. The first sleeper was built by Richard Imlay of Philadelphia. It ran between Chambersburg and Harrisburg, Pa., in 1838. At least eight railroads advertised some kind of sleeping car before 1850. Pullman's first car was not built until 1859. George M. Pullman and his friend Ben Field patented the folding upper berth in 1864. Pullman seems to have been a better businessman and a better promoter.

UNITED NATIONS

The 153 Members of the United Nations

Country	Joined U.N.[1]
Afghanistan	1946
Albania	1955
Algeria	1962
Angola	1976
Argentina	1945
Australia	1945
Austria	1955
Bahamas	1973
Bahrain	1971
Bangladesh	1974
Barbados	1966
Belgium	1945
Benin	1960
Bhutan	1971
Bolivia	1945
Botswana	1966
Brazil	1945
Bulgaria	1955
Burma	1948
Burundi	1962
Byelorussian S.S.R.	1945
Cambodia	1955
Cameroon	1960
Canada	1945
Cape Verde	1975
Central African Republic	1960
Chad	1960
Chile	1945
China[2]	1945
Colombia	1945
Comoro Islands	1975
Congo	1960
Costa Rica	1945
Cuba	1945
Cyprus	1960
Czechoslovakia	1945
Denmark	1945
Djibouti	1977
Dominica	1978
Dominican Republic	1945
Ecuador	1945
Egypt	1945
El Salvador	1945
Equatorial Guinea	1968
Ethiopia	1945
Fiji	1970
Finland	1955
France	1945
Gabon	1960
Gambia	1965
Germany, East	1973
Germany, West	1973
Ghana	1957
Greece	1945
Grenada	1974
Guatemala	1945
Guinea	1958
Guinea-Bissau	1974
Guyana	1966
Haiti	1945
Honduras	1945
Hungary	1955
Iceland	1946
India	1945
Indonesia	1950
Iran	1945
Iraq	1945
Ireland	1955
Israel	1949
Italy	1955
Ivory Coast	1960
Jamaica	1962
Japan	1956
Jordan	1955
Kenya	1963
Kuwait	1963
Laos	1955
Lebanon	1945
Lesotho	1966
Liberia	1945
Libya	1955
Luxembourg	1945
Madagascar	1960
Malawi	1964
Malaysia	1957
Maldives	1965
Mali	1960
Malta	1964
Mauritania	1961
Mauritius	1968
Mexico	1945
Mongolia	1961
Morocco	1956
Mozambique	1975
Nepal	1955
Netherlands	1945
New Zealand	1945
Nicaragua	1945
Niger	1960
Nigeria	1960
Norway	1945
Oman	1971
Pakistan	1947
Panama	1945
Papua New Guinea	1975
Paraguay	1945
Peru	1945
Philippines	1945
Poland	1945
Portugal	1955
Qatar	1971
Romania	1955
Rwanda	1962
St. Lucia	1979
Sao Tomé and Principe	1975
Saudi Arabia	1945
Senegal	1960
Seychelles	1976
Sierra Leone	1961
Singapore	1965
Solomon Islands	1978
Somalia	1960
South Africa	1945
Spain	1955
Sri Lanka	1955
Sudan	1956
Suriname	1975
Swaziland	1968
Sweden	1946
Syria	1945
Tanzania	1961
Thailand	1946
Togo	1960
Trinidad and Tobago	1962
Tunisia	1956
Turkey	1945
Uganda	1962
Ukrainian S.S.R.	1945
U.S.S.R.	1945
United Arab Emirates	1971
United Kingdom	1945
United States	1945
Upper Volta	1960
Uruguay	1945
Venezuela	1945
Vietnam	1977
Western Samoa	1976
Yemen Arab Republic	1947
Yemen, People's Dem. Republic of	1967
Yugoslavia	1945
Zaire	1960
Zambia	1964
Zimbabwe	1980

1. The U.N. officially came into existence on Oct. 24, 1945. 2. On Oct. 25, 1971, the U.N. voted membership to the People's Republic of China, which replaced the Republic of China (Taiwan) in the world body.

United Nations Costs

The current budget for the two-year period 1980–81 is $1,247,793,200.

Member Countries' Assessments to U.N. Budget, 1980

Country	Total	Country	Total	Country	Total
Afghanistan	$ 51,206	Germany, West	$ 42,795,947	Pakistan	$ 358,440
Albania	51,206	Ghana	157,617	Panama	102,411
Algeria	622,469	Greece	1,792,198	Papua New Guinea	51,206
Angola	47,206	Grenada	51,206	Paraguay	51,206
Argentina	3,970,045	Guatemala	102,411	Peru	307,234
Australia	9,486,645	Guinea	51,206	Philippines	512,057
Austria	3,663,604	Guinea-Bissau	51,206	Poland	6,289,508
Bahamas	51,206	Guyana	51,206	Portugal	972,908
Bahrain	51,206	Haiti	51,206	Qatar	157,617
Bangladesh	204,823	Honduras	51,206	Romania	1,063,320
Barbados	51,206	Hungary	1,689,788	Rwanda	51,206
Belgium	6,303,096	Iceland	157,617	Sao Tomé and Príncipe	51,206
Benin	51,206	India	3,040,344	Saudi Arabia	3,109,931
Bhutan	51,206	Indonesia	827,292	Senegal	51,206
Bolivia	51,206	Iran	3,428,371	Seychelles	51,206
Botswana	51,206	Iraq	630,469	Sierra Leone	51,206
Brazil	6,595,126	Ireland	823,292	Singapore	409,646
Bulgaria	827,292	Israel	1,288,143	Solomon Islands	55,206
Burma	51,206	Italy	17,693,970	Somalia	51,206
Burundi	51,206	Ivory Coast	157,617	South Africa	2,150,639
Byelorussian S.S.R.	1,989,021	Jamaica	102,411	Spain	8,772,970
Cambodia	51,206	Japan	49,431,072	Sri Lanka	102,411
Cameroon	51,206	Jordan	51,206	Sudan	51,206
Canada	16,892,711	Kenya	51,206	Suriname	51,206
Cape Verde	51,206	Kuwait	1,044,114	Swaziland	51,206
Central African Republic	51,206	Laos	51,206	Sweden	6,735,948
Chad	51,206	Lebanon	153,617	Syria	157,617
Chile	350,440	Lesotho	51,206	Tanzania	52,334
China	6,743,325	Liberia	51,206	Thailand	512,057
Colombia	563,263	Libya	1,205,732	Togo	51,206
Comoros	51,206	Luxembourg	260,028	Trinidad and Tobago	153,617
Congo	51,206	Madagascar	51,206	Tunisia	157,617
Costa Rica	102,411	Malawi	51,206	Turkey	1,547,841
Cuba	563,263	Malaysia	460,851	Uganda	51,528
Cyprus	51,206	Maldives	51,206	Ukrainian S.S.R.	7,448,034
Czechoslovakia	4,246,073	Mali	51,206	U.S.S.R.	56,638,340
Denmark	3,829,222	Malta	51,206	United Arab Emirates	524,057
Djibouti	51,206	Mauritania	51,206	United Kingdom	22,813,748
Dominica	55,206	Mauritius	51,206	United States	149,735,605
Dominican Republic	157,617	Mexico	3,879,633	Upper Volta	51,206
Ecuador	102,411	Mongolia	51,206	Uruguay	204,823
Egypt	354,440	Morocco	256,028	Venezuela	2,604,285
El Salvador	51,206	Mozambique	47,206	Viet Nam	153,617
Equatorial Guinea	51,206	Nepal	51,206	Western Samoa	51,206
Ethiopia	51,206	Netherlands	8,430,531	Yemen Arab Republic	51,206
Fiji	51,206	New Zealand	1,386,555	Yemen, People's Dem. Republic of	51,206
Finland	2,473,874	Nicaragua	51,206	Yugoslavia	2,162,639
France	32,230,775	Niger	51,206	Zaire	107,202
Gabon	106,411	Nigeria	831,292	Zambia	102,411
Gambia	51,206	Norway	2,580,289		
Germany, East	7,141,594	Oman	51,206		

United Nations Headquarters

The first regular session of the General Assembly held at Central Hall, Westminster, London, voted that interim headquarters of the Organization should be located in New York. From London the U.N. moved to Hunter College in the Bronx. In August 1946, an interim headquarters was set up at Lake Success on Long Island, in a part of the Sperry Gyroscope Co.'s plant. The New York City building at Flushing Meadows, site of the 1939 World's Fair, was converted for the use of the General Assembly. The search for a permanent home ended in December 1946, when the General Assembly accepted an offer from John D. Rockefeller, Jr., of $8,500,000[1] for the purchase of the present Headquarters site—an 18-acre tract in Manhattan, alongside the East River. The U.S. Government lent the U.N. $65,000,000 interest free, which is being repaid in annual installments.

Architectural plans drawn up by an international Board of Design were approved by the Assembly, and construction began in September 1948. By mid-1950, the 39-story Secretariat Building was ready for occupancy, and in the spring of 1951 "United Nations, New York" became the Organization's permanent address. The other main structures are the Conference Building, the General Assembly Hall, and the Dag Hammarskjold Library. All are interconnected.

1. This amount paid for two-thirds of the land; New York City gave one-third.

Preamble of the United Nations Charter

The Charter of the United Nations was adopted at the San Francisco Conference of 1945. The complete text may be obtained by writing to the United Nations Sales Section, United Nations, New York, N.Y. 10017, and enclosing $1.

We the peoples of the United Nations determined to save succeeding generations from the scourge of war, which twice in our lifetime has brought untold sorrow to mankind, and

To reaffirm faith in fundamental human rights, in the dignity and worth of the human person, in the equal rights of men and women and of nations large and small, and

To establish conditions under which justice and respect for the obligations arising from treaties and other sources of international law can be maintained, and

To promote social progress and better standards of life in larger freedom, and for these ends

To practice tolerance and live together in peace with one another as good neighbors, and

To unite our strength to maintain international peace and security, and

To insure, by the acceptance of principles and the institution of methods, that armed force shall not be used, save in the common interest, and

To employ international machinery for the promotion of the economic and social advancement of all peoples, have resolved to combine our efforts to accomplish these aims.

Accordingly, our respective Governments, through representatives assembled in the city of San Francisco, who have exhibited their full powers found to be in good and due form, have agreed to the present Charter of the United Nations and do hereby establish an international organization to be known as the United Nations.

Principal Organs of the United Nations

Secretariat

This is the directorate on U.N. operations, apart from political decisions. All members contribute to its upkeep. Its staff of over 6,000 specialists is recruited from member nations on the basis of as wide a geographical distribution as possible. The staff works under the Secretary-General, whom it assists and advises.

Secretaries-General

Kurt Waldheim, Austria, Jan. 1, 1972.
U Thant, Burma, Nov. 3, 1961, to Dec. 31, 1971.
Dag Hammarskjöld, Sweden, April 11, 1953, to Sept. 17, 1961.
Trygve Lie, Norway, Feb. 1, 1946, to April 10, 1953.

General Assembly

The General Assembly is the world's forum for discussing matters affecting world peace and security, and for making recommendations concerning them. It has no power of its own to enforce decisions.

The Assembly is composed of the 51 original member nations and those admitted since, a total of 153. Each nation has one vote. On major questions involving international peace and security, a two-thirds majority of those present and voting is required. Decisions on other questions are made by a simple majority.

The Assembly's agenda can be as broad as the Charter. It can make recommendations to member nations, the Security Council, or both. Emphasis is given questions relating to international peace and security brought before it by any member, the Security Council, or nonmembers.

The Assembly also maintains a broad program of international cooperation in economic, social, cultural, educational, and health fields, and for assisting in human rights and freedoms.

Among other duties, the Assembly has functions relating to the trusteeship system, and considers and approves the U.N. Budget. Every member contributes to operating expenses according to its means.

The President of the Assembly in 1980–81 is Rüdiger von Wechmar of West Germany.

Security Council

The Security Council is the primary instrument for establishing and maintaining international peace. Its main purpose is to prevent war by settling disputes between nations.

Under the Charter, the Council is permitted to dispatch a U.N. force to stop aggression. All member nations undertake to make available armed forces, assistance, and facilities to maintain international peace and security.

Any member may bring a dispute before the Security Council or the General Assembly. Any nonmember may do so if it accepts the charter obligations of pacific settlement.

The Security Council has 15 members. There are five permanent members: the United States, the Soviet Union, Britain, France, and China and 10 temporary members elected by the General Assembly for two-year terms, with different regions of the world rotating.

Voting on procedural matters requires a nine-vote majority to carry. However, on questions of substance, the vote of each of the five permanent members is required. Thus, any one of the five possess a veto.

Current temporary members are (term expires Dec. 31, 1980): Bangladesh, Jamaica, Norway, Portugal, Zambia; (term expires Dec. 31, 1981): East Germany, Mexico, Niger, Philippines, Tunisia.

Economic and Social Council

This council is composed of 54 members elected by the General Assembly to 3-year terms. It works closely with the General Assembly as a link with groups formed within the U.N. to help peoples in such fields as education, health, and human rights. It insures that there is no overlapping and sets up commissions to deal with economic conditions and collect facts and figures on conditions over the world. It issues studies and reports and may make recommendations to the Assembly and specialized agencies.

Functional Commissions

Statistical Commission; Population Commission; Commission for Social Development; Commission on Human Rights; Commission on the Status of

Women; Commission on Narcotic Drugs.

Regional Economic Commissions

Economic Commission for Europe; Economic and Social Commission for Asia and the Pacific; Economic Commission for Latin America; Economic Commission for Africa; Economic Commission for Western Asia.

Trusteeship Council

This council supervises territories administered by various nations and placed under an international trusteeship system by the United Nations. Each nation is charged with developing the self-government of the territory and preserving and advancing the cultural, political, economic, and other forms of welfare of the people.

The Trusteeship Council is currently composed of 5 members: 1 member—the United States—that administers a trust territory, and 4 members—China, France, the Soviet Union, and the United Kingdom—that are permanent members of the Security Council but do not administer trust territories.

The following countries ceased to be administering members because of the independence of territories they had administered: Italy and France in 1960, Belgium in 1962, New Zealand and the United Kingdom in 1968 and Australia in 1975. France and the U. K. became nonadministering members.

As of December 1980, there was only one trust territory: the Trust Territory of the Pacific Islands (administered by the United States).

International Court of Justice

The International Court of Justice sits at The Hague, the Netherlands. Its 15-judge bench was established to hear disputes among states, who must agree to accept its verdicts. Its judges, charged with administering justice under international law, deal with cases ranging from disputes over territory to those concerning rights of passage.

Following are the members of the Court and the years in which their terms expire:

President: Sir Humphrey Waldock, U.K. (1982)
Vice President: Taslim Owale Elias, Nigeria (1985)
Isaac Forster, Senegal (1982)
André Gros, France (1982)
Nagendra Singh, India (1982)
José María Ruda, Argentina (1982)
Manfred Lachs, Poland (1985)
Hermann Mösler, West Germany (1985)
Shigeru Oda, Japan (1985)
Salah El Dine Tarazi, Syria (1985)
Platon D. Morozov, U.S.S.R. (1988)
Roberto Ago, Italy (1988)
Abdullah Ali El-Erian, Egypt (1988)
José Sette–Câmara, Brazil (1988)
Richard R. Baxter, U.S. (1988)

Agencies of the United Nations

INTERNATIONAL ATOMIC ENERGY AGENCY (IAEA)

Established: Statute for IAEA, approved on Oct. 26, 1956, at a conference held at U.N. Headquarters, New York, came into force on July 29, 1957. The Agency is under the aegis of the U.N., but unlike the following, it is not a specialized agency.

Purpose: To promote the peaceful uses of atomic energy; to ensure that assistance provided by it or at its request or under its supervision or control is not used in such a way as to further any military purpose.

Headquarters: P.O. Box 100 A-1400, Vienna, Austria.

FOOD AND AGRICULTURE ORGANIZATION OF THE UNITED NATIONS (FAO)

Established: October 16, 1945, when constitution became effective.

Purpose: To raise nutrition levels and living standards; to secure improvements in production and distribution of food and agricultural products.

Headquarters: Via delle Terme di Caracalla, 00100, Rome, Italy.

GENERAL AGREEMENT ON TARIFFS AND TRADE (GATT)

Established: Jan. 1, 1948.

Purpose: An International Trade Organization (ITO) was planned when the U.N. Agencies were first set up. Although this agency has not materialized, some of its objectives have been embodied in an international commercial treaty, the General Agreement on Tariffs and Trade. Its purpose is to sponsor trade negotiations.

Headquarters: Centre William Rappard, 154 Rue de Lausanne, 1211, Geneva 21, Switzerland.

INTER-GOVERNMENTAL MARITIME CONSULTATIVE ORGANIZATION (IMCO)

Established: March 17, 1958.

Purpose: To give advisory and consultative help to promote international cooperation in maritime navigation and to encourage the highest standards of safety and navigation. Its aim is to bring about a uniform system of measuring ship tonnage; systems now vary widely in different parts of the world. Other activities include cooperation with other U.N. agencies on matters affecting the maritime field.

Headquarters: 101–104 Piccadilly, London, W1V OAE, England.

INTERNATIONAL BANK FOR RECONSTRUCTION AND DEVELOPMENT (IBRD) (WORLD BANK)

Established: December 27, 1945, when Articles of Agreement drawn up at Bretton Woods Conference in July 1944 came into force. Began operations on June 25, 1946.

Purpose: To assist in reconstruction and development of economies of members by facilitating capital investment and by making loans to governments and furnishing technical advice.

Headquarters: 1818 H St., N.W., Washington, D.C. 20433.

INTERNATIONAL CIVIL AVIATION ORGANIZATION (ICAO)

Established: April 4, 1947, after working as a provisional organization since June 1945.

Purpose: To study problems of international civil aviation; to establish international standards and regulations; to promote safety measures, uniform regulations for operation, simpler procedures at international borders, and the use of new technical methods and equipment. It has evolved standards for meteorological services, traffic control, communications, radio beacons and ranges, search and rescue organization, and other facilities. It has brought about much simplification of customs, immigration, and public health regulations as they apply to international air transport. It drafts international air law conventions, and is concerned with economic aspects of air travel.

Headquarters: International Aviation Square, 1000 Sherbrooke St. West, Montreal, Quebec, Canada H3A 2R2.

INTERNATIONAL DEVELOPMENT ASSOCIATION (IDA)

Established: Sept. 24, 1960. An affiliate of the World Bank, IDA has the same officers and staff as the Bank.

Purpose: To further economic development of its members by providing finance on terms which bear less heavily on balance of payments of members than those of conventional loans.

Headquarters: 1818 H St., N.W., Washington, D.C. 20433.

INTERNATIONAL FINANCE CORPORATION (IFC)

Established: Charter of IFC came into force on July 20, 1956. Although IFC is affiliated with the World Bank, it is a separate legal entity, and its funds are entirely separate from those of the Bank. However, membership in the Corporation is open only to Bank members.

Purpose: To further economic development by encouraging the growth of productive private enterprise in its member countries, particularly in the less developed areas; to invest in productive private enterprises in association with private investors, without government guarantee of repayment where sufficient private capital is not available on reasonable terms; to serve as a clearing house to bring together investment opportunities, private capital (both foreign and domestic), and experienced management.

Headquarters: 1818 H St., N.W., Washington, D.C. 20433.

INTERNATIONAL LABOR ORGANIZATION (ILO)

Established: April 11, 1919, when constitution was adopted as Part XIII of Treaty of Versailles. Became specialized agency of U.N. in 1946.

Purpose: To contribute to establishment of lasting peace by promoting social justice; to improve labor conditions and living standards through international action; to promote economic and social stability. The U.S. withdrew from the ILO in 1977 and resumed membership in 1980.

Headquarters: 4 route des Morillons, CH-1211 Geneva 22, Switzerland.

INTERNATIONAL MONETARY FUND (IMF)

Established: Dec. 27, 1945, when Articles of Agreement drawn up at Bretton Woods Conference in July 1944 came into force. Fund began operations on March 1, 1947.

Purpose: To promote international monetary cooperation and expansion of international trade; to promote exchange stability; to assist in establishment of multilateral system of payments in respect of currency transactions between members.

Headquarters: 700 19th St., N.W., Washington, D.C. 20431.

INTERNATIONAL TELECOMMUNICATION UNION (ITU)

Established: 1865. Became specialized agency of U.N. in 1947.

Purpose: To extend technical assistance to help members keep up with present day telecommunication needs; to standardize communications equipment and procedures; to lower costs. It also works for orderly sharing of radio frequencies and makes studies and recommendations to benefit its members.

Headquarters: Place des Nations, 1211 Geneva 20, Switzerland.

UNITED NATIONS EDUCATIONAL, SCIENTIFIC, AND CULTURAL ORGANIZATION (UNESCO)

Established: Nov. 4, 1946, when twentieth signatory to constitution deposited instrument of acceptance with government of U.K.

Purpose: To promote collaboration among nations through education, science, and culture in order to further justice, rule of law, and human rights and freedoms without distinction of race, sex, language, or religion.

Headquarters: UNESCO House, 7 Place de Fontenoy, F 75700, Paris, France.

UNIVERSAL POSTAL UNION (UPU)

Established: Oct. 9, 1874. Became specialized agency of U.N. in 1947.

Purpose: To facilitate reciprocal exchange of correspondence by uniform procedures by all UPU members; to help governments modernize and speed up mailing procedures.

Headquarters: Weltpostrasse 4, 3000 Berne 15, Switzerland.

WORLD HEALTH ORGANIZATION (WHO)

Established: April 7, 1948, when 26 members of the U.N. had accepted its constitution, adopted July 22, 1946, by the International Health Conference in New York City.

Purpose: To aid attainment by all people of highest possible level of health.

Headquarters: 20 Avenue Appia, 1211 Geneva, Switzerland.

WORLD INTELLECTUAL PROPERTY ORGANIZATION (WIPO)

Established: April 26, 1970, when its Convention came into force. Originated as International Bureau of Paris Union (1883) and Berne Union (1886), later succeeded by United International Bureau for the Protection of Intellectual Property (BIRPI). Became a specialized agency of the U.N. in December 1974.

Purpose: To promote legal protection of intellectual property, including artistic and scientific works, artistic performances, sound recordings, broadcasts, inventions, trademarks, industrial designs, and commercial names.

Headquarters: 32 Chemin des Colombettes, 1211 Geneva 20, Switzerland.

WORLD METEOROLOGICAL ORGANIZATION (WMO)

Established: March 23, 1950, succeeding the International Meteorological Organization, a nongovernmental organization founded in 1878.

Purpose: To promote international exchange of weather reports and maximum standardization of observations; to help developing countries establish weather services for their own economic needs; to fill gaps in observation stations; to promote meteorological investigations affecting jet aircraft, satellites, energy resources, etc.

Headquarters: 41 Avenue Giuseppe Motta, Geneva, Switzerland.

The Year in Energy—1980

Petroleum

If 1979 was the year when the Western World's energy situation seemed darkest, 1980 was certainly the year in which several rays of light began to appear at the end of the tunnel. Gasoline and fuel oil supplies and prices, the most obvious and painful indicators of the energy crunch, both stabilized during the year, and long gas station lines and odd-even rationing became nothing more than unpleasant memories for most Americans. Despite a steady climb in OPEC crude prices to more than $30 per barrel, conservation, especially by motorists, resulted in such an abundant supply of gasoline that automotive fuel prices actually began to decline.

More important, though, was the retreat from panic to a realization of the true nature of the petroleum energy supply situation plus a renewed emphasis on technology to make more efficient use of existing energy supplies and develop those which will be needed in the future. In terms of oil, it is now understood that although sources of cheap, light crude are apparently approaching exhaustion and chances for new large discoveries are unlikely, supplies of so-called heavy crude are enormous and well known. Heavy crudes are more like molasses or tar, and they are often bound in mineral structures like shales or sand. Chemically, they have a higher carbon-to-hydrogen ratio than conventional light crude, and they may contain larger amounts of such objectional impurities as sulfur, nickel, and vanadium. Fortunately, a major portion of North and South American petroleum deposits are in the form of heavy crudes: Alberta has more than 2 trillion barrels worth in the Athabasca tar sands (this is several times the amount of all the oil in the Mideast), the U.S. has at least 500 million barrels in tar sands, oil shale, and conventional wells, but Venezuela leads the hemisphere with a 4-trillion-barrel reservoir. California is already producing one half million barrels per day. Clearly, there is no long-range petroleum raw material shortage; the problem is to refine the heavy crude to useful products at a cost that is competitive with existing light crude-based supplies. One step was taken in this direction when a major U.S. oil company announced a process called atmospheric-reduced crude, which enables refiners to produce 94 octane unleaded gasoline from heavy residual oils now used primarily as industrial boiler fuel. The process could increase the gasoline yield of a barrel of crude by 25%, and as a bonus, remove most sulfur pollutants.

Synfuels

Of even greater significance, however, was the passage, during 1980, of the $25-billion Synfuels Energy Bill. Together with the Windfall Profits Tax and the establishment of the Energy Mobilization Board, the Synfuels Bill completes President Carter's energy package. The Bill creates the Synthetic Fuels Corp., a central source of funding for the development of processes and facilities to produce synthetic oil and natural gas from coal, oil shale, and other non-petroleum raw materials. The goal is to produce one half million barrels a day by 1987 and four times that amount by 1992.

A number of synthetic fuel projects have been under development for years, and some were in widespread commercial use up to 50 years ago. Germany, the Republic of South Africa, and Brazil, with limited or nonexistent petroleum supplies of their own, have been traditional leaders in this field. In the U.S., a major oil company dedicated a plant using the so-called donor solvent process to produce gasoline blending stocks, light oils, and boiler fuels by combining pulverized coal in an oil-based slurry with hydrogen gas at 800 degrees Fahrenheit and pressures up to 2000 pounds per square inch. The new pilot plant produces only 700 barrels of liquid per day from 250 tons of coal, but a commercial-sized plant could produce up to 30,000 barrels a day. Such large plants would cost $1.5 billion each.

Another synthetic fuel, one already in commercial use, is ethanol, the alcohol found in beer, wine, and liquor. By the end of 1980, more than 1000 gas stations were offering "gasohol," a blend of 10% ethanol and 90% gasoline, to the public at prices slightly above high octane premium fuel. Adding 10% ethanol increases the octane rating of gasoline by an average of three points and improves performance in terms of miles per gallon. It is also cleaner burning than the pure petroleum product. Brazil, which already produces large quantities of ethanol for gasohol from surplus sugar cane, plans to go one step further. This year, the Brazilians announced plans to have one million vehicles fueled by ethanol alone by 1985. The Brazilians are also planning to convert their huge forest surplus into methanol for use as an automotive fuel. Methanol, sometimes known as wood alcohol, is actually a better fuel, and is more economical to produce on a tons-per-acre basis than ethanol produced from grains or sugar cane. In a related development, a major U.S. oil company announced a new one-step catalytic process that will produce 93 octane unleaded gasoline from either methanol or ethanol. New Zealand announced plans for a 12,500 barrel-per-day plant using this process, but a U.S. industrial firm, in conjunction with the Department of Energy, will build a giant version in Baskett, Ky. The $3-billion plant will liquefy high sulfur coking coal to 16,000 tons of methanol per day, then use the new process to convert this to up to 50,000 barrels of gasoline daily.

Synfuel production is not without its problems. Exploitation of oil shale reserves by strip mining (the most economical method) will leave tremendous quantities of finely powdered waste rock to be disposed of. Conversion of grains, cane, or sugar beets to alcohol fuels raises cogent moral arguments in a world heavily dependent on U.S. agricultural output. From an environmental standpoint, coal liquefaction and gasification processes are known to produce chemicals that are highly carcinogenic or mutagenic (chromosome-altering).

On the positive side, however, 1980 saw the recognition of these problems in an atmosphere that was, once again, quite optimistic.

Automobiles

About 41% of the world's 300 million automobiles ply American roads, and together with trucks and buses, they account for six million barrels of gasoline daily—or 18% of the nation's energy requirements. While automotive fuel consumption decreased during 1980, efforts continued to improve fuel economy or, alternatively, develop a practical electric car. A significant milestone in the latter program was reached in 1980 with the invention of an aluminum-air fuel cell which could eventually give electric cars a range of 1000 to 3000 miles on a single "charge." Key to the effectiveness of the new cell is its high energy content per unit weight. Cost and acceleration problems remain to be solved, but the first commercial-scale vehicle could be on the road by 1985–86. Meanwhile, work progressed on the use of hydrogen as an automotive fuel. Hydrogen is the cleanest burning of all fuels: its only emissions are water vapor and the nitrogen oxides designated No_X. Hydrogen-fueled engines can be leaned down to the point where No_X emissions are reduced considerably, but a study completed in 1980 showed that this also reduces power and necessitates a larger, less efficient engine. Along more conventional lines, 1980 brought the development of an ionic fuel control system for gasoline-burning autos. The new system improves fuel economy by maintaining the proper lean fuel-to-air mixture under all driving conditions, and is currently under test by several major automakers.

Nuclear Energy

The year 1980 marked the first anniversary of the loss-of-coolant accident at the Three Mile Island nuclear power station near Harrisburg, Pa. Exhaustive tests showed that, thankfully, the major injuries to the population were not at all caused by exposure to radiation. Indeed, the escape of radioactivity from the plant turned out to be minor and, to the extent of present knowledge, harmless. Widespread and sometimes severe psychological effects were detected, however. These included mental stress, depression, distrust of authority, and continued high levels of demoralization. The accident led to the cancellation of several reactor projects and the delay of numerous others. It also resulted in a major top-level restructuring of the Nuclear Regulatory Commission by President Carter and a tightening of nuclear safety standards nationwide. Lessons learned from the TMI disaster were, in fact, applied when a similar incident occurred at the Crystal River Plant of the Florida Power Corp. in March, 1980. By not making the same mistakes that led to the Pennsylvania reactor's loss of cooling water, the Florida reactor operators were able to prevent damage to the reactor core and bring the plant to a safe, orderly shutdown.

Advanced Energy Systems

Behind the highly publicized and politically involved advances in petroleum and synfuel-based energy programs, work continued to progress on energy systems that will provide our power in the next century. One such scheme is fusion power, which seeks to harness the thermonuclear reactions that fire the Sun or hydrogen bombs in the same sense that conventional nuclear reactors tame atomic bombs to produce useful electricity. There are two principal methods by which this can be accomplished, and proponents of both announced significant advances in 1980. One method uses a powerful magnetic field to confine a plasma, or stream, of very hot ionized gas until temperatures reach the millions of degrees necessary to trigger the fusion reaction. The two discoveries related to this technology were the finding that one can produce, or at least enhance, the fusion reaction by injecting a high-energy stream of hydrogen into the plasma and, secondly, that the somewhat cumbersome arrangement of magnetic coils needed for the process—called a tokamak—can be rearranged into a more open structure, dubbed a spheromak, and still produce the needed toroidal, or doughnut-shaped plasma. The second fusion method uses ultrahigh-powered lasers to bombard a tiny deuterium-tritium fuel pellet; again, in order to raise it to fusion temperatures. Researchers operating such a device were encouraged when their trials produced more energy than they expected.

Along more conventional lines, NASA and industrial groups announced plans to develop a 20-kilowatt solar powered electric generator. The unit will use concentrated sunlight to heat air to 1500 degrees Fahrenheit, and the expansion of this superheated air will drive a turbine-generator to produce electricity. For a more detailed discussion of solar energy, see page 358.

Finally, geologists have announced their belief that a body of magma, or semimolten rock, underlies much of the U.S. west of the Rockies. The magma is three to six miles below the surface and is at a temperature of 1800 to 2000 degrees Fahrenheit. Potentially, these hot rocks contain enough energy to supply 5000 times the nation's requirements. Hot stuff, but commercial exploitation is many years in the future.

Konrad J.A. Kundig

Be Wary of Gas Gadgets

With most motorists concerned about getting more miles per gallon of gasoline, the promoters of "miracle" devices and additives are having a field day. But be wary of the claims, warns the Automotive Information Council (AIC), because most of them will do nothing for the car's mileage.

The auto manufacturers have used their best engineering know-how to gain maximum miles per gallon, not only for competitive but for regulatory reasons. If there was a product on the market which would increase the mileage, the car companies would be using it.

A Primer on Solar Energy

Source: Engineer's Guide To Solar Energy, Y. Howell and J. A. Bereny, Solar Energy Information Services (SEIS), San Mateo, Calif., 94401.

Optimistic proponents of solar energy predict that by the year 2000, more than 20% of the United States' needs could be supplied by solar power. The attainment of this goal will depend upon the combined efforts of competent solar practioners and advocates in research, government, industry, commerce, and education.

What is Solar Energy?

The term solar energy means different things to different people. However, a consensus of scientists has defined it as embracing six interrelated but distinct technologies, whose common denominator is the use of solar energy. These technologies are:

Solar heating and cooling, in which the sun's heat is collected and used to heat buildings, provide hot water and heat swimming pools, and in some instances to cool buildings.

Photovoltaics, in which electricity is generated by sunlight falling on the junction of two semiconducting materials in a solar cell. The U.S. space program has been the largest developer and user of photovoltaic technology.

Wind energy conversion, in which mechanical or electrical energy is generated by machines with blades or airfoils that are propelled by the wind.

Solar thermal/electric conversion, in which electricity is generated from the sun's heat through the use of solar concentrating mirrors, absorbers, and a high-temperature thermodynamic cycle.

Ocean thermal energy conversion, in which electricity is generated by using the temperature difference between the warm water at the ocean surface and the colder water at its depth to run a heat engine.

Biomass conversion, in which heat, fuel, electricity, or chemical feedstocks are produced through cultivation and chemical processing of plants, or through processing of waste materials.

Solar Heating and Cooling

Solar heating is the specific technology that is now ready for widespread use around the globe. Solar hardware for most technologies is already being utilized around the world on a modest scale. Combinations of various solar energy conversion systems to simultaneously provide different forms of energy for different purposes offer some exciting possibilities for the future.

There are two approaches to the application of solar energy to date. They are:

Passive solar system. In this approach, the building itself is designed to collect and store the solar heat. This is often the most cost-effective method of space heating and cooling, especially for new buildings.

Active solar systems. In active systems, special equipment is added to the building to collect, store, and distribute the solar energy. The basic new element is the solar collector which is the device that collects and converts the solar radiation into heat.

The simplest use of solar energy is for swimming pool heating. No longer are there any technical barriers to this application. Several good systems are now on the market, some of which are cost-effective even when the competing fuel is natural gas.

The heating of domestic water is another relatively simple application. Solar water heaters have been in use for more than 50 years in many parts of the world. Commonplace are the thermosiphon and tank-type units in which the hot water flows directly from the heater to the household.

The technology for heating buildings with solar systems is well developed, and in some regions, the cost of solar heating is competitive with electric heating. Space heating can be done either with liquid collectors and water storage (for the heat) or with air collectors and rockbed storage.

Solar cooling has the great advantage of having the largest supply of solar energy available when the demand for air conditioning is highest. Considerable research is still needed to produce a solar cooling system that is low in cost and high enough in performance to compete with the conventional air conditioner.

Photovoltaics

Photovoltaic cells are used to convert solar radiation directly into electricity. These cells are made of various semiconductors, which are materials that are only moderately good conductors of electricity. The materials most commonly used are the element silicon (Si) and the compounds cadmium sulfide (CdS), cuprous sulfide (Cu_2S), and gallium arsenide (GaAs).

The most-developed silicon cells have powered many satellites and space missions, and are increasingly being used to provide electricity for rural villages and remote instrument sites.

Clusters of these cells can be assembled in various arrangements to deliver power at any desired voltage. For example, it takes 40 cells connected in series to charge one 12-volt acid-battery. By covering the roof of a single-family home with the present commercial cells, one could obtain considerably more electric power than a family now uses. However, the cost of installation today would be prohibitive, even though the price of silicon cells has dropped considerably over the past few years.

Silicon is an abundant chemical (25% of the earth's crust), and silicon minerals are cheap; but silicon cells must be individually fashioned by a long, complicated process. It is expected that new techniques in fabrication and manufacturing will increase cell production, and will radically lower the price within a few more years.

Wind Energy Conversion

Wind energy used to supply a significant amount of the energy consumed in rural areas of the United States. From about 1850 to about 1935, more than six million small wind machines of less than one horsepower each were used to pump water, generate electricity, and perform milling operations. However, their number declined drastically in the

1930s when the government's Rural Electrification Administration introduced electrical cooperatives. At present, about 150,000 wind machines are still in operation, primarily in the western states for watering livestock on remote power.

Many different wind-energy collectors have been devised. Almost any physical configuration that produces an asymmetric force in the wind can be made to rotate, translate, or oscillate; and power can be extracted. It is sometimes claimed that there are more patents for wind systems than for any other type of device.

Several countries now have major development projects to perfect new and more cost-effective wind machines of varying types and sizes.

The consensus reached in many studies financed by the U.S. Government, and several state governments as well, suggests that wind energy should soon become a viable energy option.

Solar Thermal/Electric Conversion

There are two types of solar thermal/electric systems, both of which require the same basic elements: solar collection, conversion of solar to thermal energy. The collected thermal energy is then transported by a fluid through a network of pipe to a heat engine and generator.

The *distributed collector system* has a large number of individual solar collectors that collect and concentrate solar energy and convert it to thermal energy. The collected thermal energy is transported by a fluid through a network of pipe to a heat engine and generator.

The *central receiver system* has a large number of mirrors that reflect the solar energy to a single receiver mounted on a tall tower. The concentrated solar energy at the receiver is converted to thermal energy, which is transported by a fluid to a heat engine and generator. Given the present state-of-the-art, central receiver systems appear to be more efficient than distributed systems.

Ocean Thermal Energy Conversion

The ocean itself is the largest solar collector and storage system. The surface temperature of oceans between the Tropic of Cancer and the Tropic of Capricorn stays remarkably constant at about 77°F; the warm surface waters are separated by as little as 2000 feet from a practically inexhaustible source of cold water—the 40°F water in the depths.

Ocean thermal energy conversion (OTEC) uses the thermal gradient as a renewable source of energy to produce electric power, utilizing the warm surface water as a heat source and the cold water from the depths as a heat sink.

If a solar sea plant is installed that is large enough to span the temperature differential, heat may be extracted from the water and used to power an engine. The engine would be similar in principle to the standard heat engine (turbine) that is normally used in the production of electricity.

While the major thermal resources of the oceans are available only in tropical latitudes, a relatively large quantity of thermal energy can be harnessed close to populated areas of the United States; for example, the warm Gulf Stream is located only 15 miles off the coast of Miami, Florida.

Other favorable U.S. locations for the generation of electricity include the Gulf of Mexico, Hawaii, Puerto Rico, and the Virgin Islands.

Biomass Conversion

The photosynthesis process and its modification are at the heart of solar bioconversion. Photosynthesis is the name given to the building-block process used by plants to produce organic matter (biomass) with the help of sunlight. This "biomass resource" represents a chemical form of energy which may be used in a variety of ways.

Deriving clean fuel from plant biomass or waste organic materials is the only "renewable" method of fuel production now known. (For example: the alcohol content of Gasohol is made from grain and other argicultural materials.) The variety of possible energy crops, organic wastes, and conversion processes is very large. However, the degree of technological development for the different production and conversion processes varies greatly.

Thus some processes, such as combustion of solid waste, are already being commercially utilized while others are still in the developmental stage.

The final products of these processes may be methane, ethane, hydrogen, alcohol, heat, steam, char or other solid fuels, and synthetic oil, as well as organic chemicals and other potentially useful residues.

Tips on Buying Wood for Home Heating

Wood is usually sold by the cord or fraction thereof. There is a standard cord, face cord, short cord, long cord, a solid cord, and maybe others.

The standard cord should be specified when you order wood. It is a pile of wood measuring four feet high, eight feet wide, and four feet long. A face cord measures four feet high by eight feet wide but the pieces may be any length. So a face cord of stove-length (16 in.) wood would be only one third of a standard cord. The term "short cord" is another way of saying "face cord."

When buying cord, be sure that the pile you measure is tightly stacked with all the wood pieces lying in the same direction. Otherwise, you will pay for the air space instead of wood. Even piled carefully, a cord has only 80 cubic feet of solid wood in it, although its dimensions measure 128 cubic feet.

Pound for pound, most species of wood produce about the same amount of heat if the wood is dry. Some species of wood are lighter than others, so a cord of wood such as aspen will weigh about half as much as a cord of dry white oak and will therefore have about half the heat value.

Ask the seller how long the wood was "air-dried" and whether it was cut to length and split before drying. If the answers are "at least nine months" and "yes," respectively, you can assume that you'll get fair heat value for the weight.

U.S. Energy Supply and Disposition
(in quadrillion Btus)

Activity and fuel	1960	1965	1970	1975	1976	1977	1978	1979[1]
SUPPLY								
Production								
Crude Oil and Lease Condensate	14.93	16.52	20.40	17.73	17.26	17.45	18.43	18.02
Natural Gas Plant Liquids	1.46	1.88	2.51	2.37	2.33	2.33	2.25	2.38
Natural Gas[2]	12.66	15.78	21.67	19.64	19.48	19.57	19.49	19.19
Coal[3]	11.12	13.38	15.05	15.19	15.85	15.83	15.04	17.41
Nuclear Power	0.01	0.04	0.24	1.90	2.11	2.70	2.98	2.75
Hydropower	1.60	2.06	2.63	3.15	2.98	2.34	2.96	2.96
Other[4]	(Z)	0.01	0.02	0.07	0.08	0.08	0.07	0.09
Total Production	**41.78**	**49.67**	**62.51**	**60.06**	**60.09**	**60.30**	**61.21**	**62.80**
Imports								
Crude Oil[5]	2.20	2.65	2.81	8.72	11.24	14.03	13.46	13.53
Refined Petroleum Products[6]	1.80	2.75	4.66	4.23	4.43	4.73	4.36	4.11
Natural Gas	0.16	0.47	0.85	0.98	0.99	1.04	0.99	1.27
Other[7]	0.07	0.04	0.07	0.19	0.18	0.30	0.44	0.38
Total Imports	4.23	5.92	8.39	14.11	16.84	20.09	19.26	19.28
Adjustments[8]	−0.44	−0.74	−1.41	−1.08	−0.21	−1.91	−0.36	−1.18
Total Supply	**45.57**	**54.85**	**69.49**	**73.09**	**76.72**	**78.49**	**80.11**	**80.90**
DISPOSITION								
Consumption								
Refined Petroleum Products[9]	19.92	23.25	29.52	32.73	35.17	37.18	37.97	37.02
Natural Gas[2]	12.39	15.77	21.79	19.95	20.35	19.93	20.00	19.86
Coal[5]	10.12	11.89	12.66	12.82	13.73	14.14	13.85	15.08
Nuclear Power	0.01	0.04	0.24	1.90	2.11	2.70	2.98	2.75
Hydropower[10]	1.65	2.06	2.65	3.22	3.07	2.52	3.17	3.16
Other	(Z)	0.01	0.02	0.07	0.08	0.08	0.07	0.09
Net Imports of Coal Coke	−0.01	−0.02	−0.06	0.01	(Z)	0.02	0.13	0.07
Total Consumption	**44.08**	**52.99**	**66.83**	**70.71**	**74.51**	**76.56**	**78.15**	**78.02**
Exports								
Coal[3]	1.02	1.38	1.94	1.79	1.62	1.47	1.10	1.78
Other[11]	0.46	0.48	0.73	0.60	0.59	0.63	0.85	1.10
Total Exports	**1.48**	**1.86**	**2.66**	**2.39**	**2.21**	**2.10**	**1.95**	**2.88**
Total Disposition	**45.57**	**54.85**	**69.49**	**73.09**	**76.72**	**78.66**	**80.11**	**80.90**

1. Preliminary. 2. Dry marketed gas. 3. Includes bituminous, lignite, and anthracite coal. 4. Geothermal, wood, refuse, and other vegetal fuels used for electricity generation at utilities. 5. Includes imports of crude oil for the Strategic Petroleum Reserve. 6. Also includes imports of unfinished oils and natural gas plant liquids. 7. Includes bituminous, lignite, and anthracite coal, as well as coke made from coal, and hydropower. 8. A balancing item. Includes stock changes, losses, gains, miscellaneous blending compounds, unaccounted for supply, and shipments of anthracite coal to U.S. Armed Forces in Europe. 9. Refined petroleum products supplied includes natural gas plant liquids and crude oil burned as fuel. 10. Includes industrial generation of hydropower and net electricity imports. 11. Includes crude oil, refined petroleum products, natural gas, coke made from coal, and hydropower. (Z) = Less than 0.005 quadrillion Btu. NOTE: The sum of the components may not equal the total due to independent rounding. *Source:* Energy Information Administration, Annual Report to Congress 1979, Volume 2.

Comparing Energy Sources[1]
(converting energy sources into BTU equivalents)

One British Thermal Unit (BTU) = the amount of heat needed to increase the temperature of one pound of water by 1° F. (252 calories).

	BTU (in thousands)
Bituminous Coal and Lignite	
Production, average/short ton	23,500.0
Consumption, average/short ton	22,800.0
Electricity generation/short ton	21,630.0
Anthracite, short ton	25,400.0
Crude petroleum, barrel (42 gallons)	5,800.0
Natural gas, dry, cubic foot	1.021
Nuclear power, kilowatt-hour	10.66
Hydropower[2] kilowatt-hour	10.38

1. For helpful conversion factors, *see* the "Science" section of this *Almanac.* 2. Calculated from national average heat rates for fossil-fueled steam-electric plants.

World's Ten Largest Electric Energy Producers, 1978[1]

(in billion kilowatt hours)

Country	Production Hydro	Nuclear	Thermal	Total
United States	204,750[2]	260,500	1,863,050	2,328,300[3]
U.S.S.R.	159,343	36,200	995,009	1,190,552
Japan	75,815[2]	31,825	457,495	565,135
West Germany	18,950	35,400	297,750	352,100
Canada	229,285	28,775	69,020	327,080[3]
United Kingdom	5,500	37,400	246,000	288,900
China	67,000	—	158,000	225,000
France	73,430	21,120	123,650	218,200
Italy	52,700[2]	3,390	117,310	173,400
Poland	2,514	—	112,318	114,832
Sub-total	889,287	454,610	4,439,602	5,783,499
All others	668,697	76,822	1,087,902	1,833,426
World total	**1,557,984**	**531,432**	**5,527,504**	**7,616,925**

1. U.N. Statistical Office estimate. 2. Production from geothermal sources included. 3. Net production. *Source:* United Nations, *World Energy Supplies, 1973–1978* (Statistical Papers, Series J No. 22).

Per Capita Electric Energy Consumption, 1978

(20 highest per capita consumers)

Country	kwh per capita[1]	Population (thousands)	Production plus net imports[2]
Norway	18,379	4,050	79,600
Panama Canal Zone	14,500	45	1,657
Canada	13,118	23,445	329,275
Iceland	12,108	227	2,700
Luxembourg	11,096	370	4,200
New Caledonia	11,029	140	1,500
U.S. Virgin Islands	10,821	101	725
Christmas Island	10,667	3	32
United States	10,638	218,525	2,343,300
Sweden	10,510	8,300	92,500
Guam	9,907	104	1,060
Qatar	9,109	200	920
Finland	7,113	4,750	34,400
New Zealand	6,950	3,130	21,595
Netherland Antilles	6,809	250	1,750
Australia	6,035	14,220	85,981
West Germany	5,851	61,250	369,600
Kuwait	5,843	1,190	7,000
Switzerland	5,760	6,310	49,500
East Germany	5,753	16,570	98,720
World	**1,803**	**4,258,000**	**7,736,178**

1. Production plus net imports divided by total population. 2. In billion kilowatt hours. NOTE: Date on consumption are derived from the formula "production plus imports minus exports." Accordingly, apparent consumption may occasionally be only an indication of the magnitude of actual gross inland availability. Where relatively small populations are involved, large fluctuations in per capita consumption series may derive from small quantitative variations. *Source:* United Nations, *World Energy Supplies, 1973–78* (Statistical Papers, Series J No. 22).

World Production, Trade, and Consumption of Commercial Energy, 1978

(in million metric tons of coal equivalent)

Activity	World	Developed countries[1]	Developing countries[2]	Centrally planned economic[3]	U.S.[4]	U.S.S.R.	Saudi Arabia
Total primary energy production	9,332	3,271	2,868	3,193	2,021	1,854	617
Imports of commercial energy	3,316	2,497	590	230	626	34	1
Exports of commercial energy	3,281	522	2,356	403	58	313	584
Total energy consumption							
Solid fuel	2,803	1,115	140	1,548	519	502	—
Liquid fuels	3,959	2,560	625	774	1,178	507	12
Natural gas	1,737	1,099	132	506	746	473	9
Hydro/nuclear electricity	256	179	39	39	59	23	—
Total commercial energy in kg per capita	**2,074**	**6,360**	**449**	**2,112**	**11,374**	**5,500**	**1,306**

1. Australia, Canada, Israel, Japan, New Zealand, South Africa, U.S., Western Europe (incl. Yugoslovia). 2. Developing market economies of Africa, Caribbean, Middle East (incl. Turkey), Far East, etc. 3. Albania, Bulgaria, Czechoslovakia, East Germany, Hungary, Poland, Romania, U.S.S.R. 4. Data includes imports of natural gasoline, not shown elsewhere. *Source:* United Nations, *World Energy Supplies, 1973–78* (Statistical Papers, Series J No. 22).

Petroleum Imported Directly[1] from OPEC[2] Countries, 1969–1979
(thousand barrels per day)

Year	Saudi Arabia	Iran	Venezuela	Libya	Indonesia	United Arab Emirates	Algeria	Nigeria	Other OPEC[3]	Total OPEC
1969	64	46	875	134	89	14	2	49	61	1,324
1970	30	39	989	47	70	63	8	50	38	1,334
1971	128	112	1,020	58	112	79	15	102	47	1,673
1972	190	142	960	123	164	73	92	251	68	2,063
1973	486	223	1,135	164	213	71	136	459	106	2,993
1974	461	469	979	4	300	74	190	713	88	3,280
1975	715	280	703	232	390	117	282	762	121	3,601
1976	1,230	299	700	453	539	254	432	1,025	134	5,066
1977	1,380	535	690	723	541	335	559	1,143	287	6,193
1978	1,144	555	645	654	573	385	649	919	226	5,751
1979[4]	1,346	297	676	651	396	281	621	1,059	204	5,531

1. Excludes indirect imports from OPEC countries which refers to U.S. imports of refined petroleum products, primarily from Caribbean and West European areas, which were refined from crude oil produced in OPEC countries. 2. Organization of Petroleum Exporting Countries. 3. Includes Ecuador, Gabon, Iraq, Kuwait, and Qatar. 4. Preliminary. NOTE: Includes data for individual countries prior to their entrance into OPEC. Data include imports for Strategic Petroleum Reserve, which began in 1977. Sum of components may not equal total due to independent rounding. *Source:* 1960 through 1975—U.S. Dept. of the Interior, Bureau of Mines, *Mineral Industry Surveys,* "Petroleum Statement Annual"; 1976 through 1978—U.S. Dept. of Energy, Energy Information Administration, *Energy Data Reports,* "Petroleum Statement, Annual"; 1979—U.S. Dept. of Energy, Energy Information Administration, *Energy Data Reports,* "Petroleum Statement, Monthly."

Production of Crude Petroleum by Countries
(in thousands of 42-gallon barrels)

Area and country	1979	1978	Percent change
Western Hemisphere	5,602,385	5,391,780	3.9
Argentina	170,455	167,170	2.0
Bolivia	10,950	12,045	−9.1
Brazil	58,765	58,400	0.6
Canada	546,040	479,245	13.9
Chile	8,395	6,570	27.8
Colombia	45,260	47,815	−5.3
Ecuador	82,125	73,730	11.4
Mexico	533,265	440,555	21.0
Peru	73,175	55,845	27.5
Trinidad and Tobago	78,475	84,680	−7.3
United States	3,137,540	3,175,865	−1.2
Venezuela	859,940	789,495	8.3
Western Europe	829,645	638,020	3.0
Austria	12,775	12,775	—
Denmark	4,380	3,650	20.0
France	7,300	7,300	—
West Germany	34,310	36,135	−5.1
Italy	10,950	6,205	76.5
Netherlands	9,125	10,950	−16.7
Norway	147,095	129,940	13.2
Spain	5,475	6,570	−16.7
United Kingdom	572,320	394,930	44.9
Yugoslavia	25,550	29,200	−12.5
Middle East	7,847,500	7,738,000	1.4
Abu Dhabi[1]	534,360	528,520	1.1
Bahrain	18,250	19,345	−5.7
Dubai	129,210	132,130	−2.2
Iran	1,134,785	1,921,360	−40.9
Iraq	1,253,410	959,585	30.6
Israel	13,140	4,015	227.3
Kuwait	806,285	680,725	18.4
Neutral Zone[2]	206,955	170,090	21.7
Oman	107,675	114,975	−6.3
Qatar	182,135	177,025	2.9
Saudi Arabia	3,376,615	2,941,535	14.8
Sharjah[1]	4,745	8,030	−40.9
Syria	59,495	62,050	−4.1
Turkey	20,440	18,250	12.0
Asia–Pacific	1,043,535	1,020,905	2.2
Australia	160,965	157,680	2.1
Burma	10,950	9,125	20.0
Brunei–Malaysia	182,135	165,710	9.9
India	89,425	82,490	8.4
Indonesia	582,175	597,505	−2.6
Japan	2,920	3,650	−20.0
Pakistan	3,650	3,650	—
Philippines	9,490	—	—
Taiwan	1,825	1,825	—
Africa	2,390,385	2,234,165	7.0
Algeria	405,880	447,125	−9.2
Angola	16,060	13,140	22.2
Cabinda[3]	37,595	34,675	8.4
Cameroon	12,410	3,650	240.0
Congo	20,805	12,045	72.7
Egypt	184,690	176,660	4.5
Gabon	74,460	82,125	−9.3
Libya	750,440	723,430	3.7
Morocco	365	365	—
Nigeria	843,880	697,150	21.0
Tunisia	36,500	36,500	—
Zaire	7,665	7,300	5.0
Communist bloc	5,196,505	5,080,070	2.3
China	786,575	759,200	3.6
Romania	98,550	109,500	−10.0
U.S.S.R.	4,271,595	4,171,220	2.4
Other	40,150	40,150	—
World total	**22,909,955**	**22,102,575**	**3.7**

1. A state within the United Arab Emirates. 2. Shared by Kuwait and Saudi Arabia. 3. An enclave in West Africa on Atlantic coast between the Congo and Angola. *Source: Oil & Gas Journal,* Feb. 25, 1980.

Largest Nuclear Power Plants in the United States

(over a million kilowatts)

Location	Operating utility	Capacity (kilowatts)	Year operative
Port Gibson, Miss. (Unit 1)	Mississippi Power & Light Co.	1,250,000	1981
Scottsboro, Ala. (Unit 1)	Tennessee Valley Authority	1,213,000	1981
Cowans Ford Dam, N.C. (Unit 1)	Duke Power Co.	1,180,000	1980
Cowans Ford Dam, N.C. (Unit 2)	Duke Power Co.	1,180,000	1981
Spring City, Tenn. (Unit 1)	Tennessee Valley Authority	1,177,000	1980
Spring City, Tenn. (Unit 2)	Tennessee Valley Authority	1,177,000	1981
Daisy, Tenn. (Unit 1)	Tennessee Valley Authority	1,148,000	1980
Daisy, Tenn. (Unit 2)	Tennessee Valley Authority	1,148,000	1980
Lake Wylie, S.C. (Unit 1)	Duke Power Co.	1,145,000	1981
Prescott, Ore. (Unit 1)	Portland General Electric Co.	1,130,000	1976
Salem, N.J. (Unit 2)	Public Service Electric and Gas, N.J.	1,115,000	1980
Taft, La. (Unit 3)	Louisiana Power & Light Co.	1,113,000	1981
Glen Rose, Texas (Unit 1)	Texas Utilities Generating Co.	1,111,000	1981
Diablo Canyon, Calif. (Unit 2)	Pacific Gas & Electric Co.	1,106,000	1979
Bridgman, Mich. (Unit 2)	Indiana & Michigan Electric Co.	1,100,000	1978
Richland, Wash.	Washington Public Power Supply System	1,100,000	1980
San Clemente, Calif. (Unit 2)	So. Calif. Edison Co. & San Diego Gas & Electric Co.	1,100,000	1981
Salem, N.J. (Unit 1)	Public Service Electric and Gas, N.J.	1,090,000	1977
Diablo Canyon, Calif. (Unit 1)	Pacific Gas & Electric Co.	1,084,000	1979
Seneca, Ill. (Unit 1)	Commonwealth Edison Co.	1,078,000	1980
Seneca, Ill. (Unit 2)	Commonwealth Edison Co.	1,078,000	1981
Decatur, Ala. (Unit 1)	Tennessee Valley Authority	1,065,000	1974
Decatur, Ala. (Unit 2)	Tennessee Valley Authority	1,065,000	1975
Decatur, Ala. (Unit 3)	Tennessee Valley Authority	1,065,000	1977
Peach Bottom, Pa. (Unit 2)	Philadelphia Electric Co.	1,065,000	1974
Peach Bottom, Pa. (Unit 3)	Philadelphia Electric Co.	1,065,000	1974
Bridgman, Mich. (Unit 1)	Indiana & Michigan Electric Co.	1,054,000	1975
Berwick, Pa. (Unit 1)	Pennsylvania Power & Light Co.	1,050,000	1981
Zion, Ill. (Unit 1)	Commonwealth Edison Co.	1,040,000	1973
Zion, Ill. (Unit 2)	Commonwealth Edison Co.	1,040,000	1974

Source: Nuclear Regulatory Commission.

U.S. Motor Vehicle Fuel Consumption

(1978 estimate)

Type of vehicle	Total travel (million vehicle miles)	Number of registered vehicles (thousands)	Average miles traveled per vehicle	Fuel consumed (million gallons)	Average fuel consumption per vehicle (gallons)	Average miles per gallon
All passenger vehicles	1,200,307	122,217,318	9,821	84,796,129	694	14.16
Total personal passenger vehicles	1,194,231	121,716,956	9,812	83,774,644	688	14.26
Cars	1,171,092	116,574,999	10,046	83,311,868	715	14.06
Motorcycles	23,139	5,141,957	4,500	462,776	90	50.00
All buses	6,076	500,362	12,143	1,021,485	2,041	5.95
Commercial	3,085	101,558	30,377	614,542	6,051	5.02
School and other nonrevenue	2,991	398,804	7,500	406,943	1,020	7.35
All cargo vehicles	347,906	31,702,604	10,974	40,271,280	1,270	8.64
Single unit trucks	280,570	30,336,022	9,249	27,780,000	916	10.10
Combinations	67,328	1,366,582	49,267	12,491,280	9,141	5.39
All motor vehicles	**1,548,213**	**153,919,922**	**10,059**	**125,067,409**	**813**	**12.38**

Source: Department of Transportation, Federal Highway Administration.

A Profile of Your 1985 Car

Federal regulations require each car company to achieve an average of 27.5 miles per gallon for its cars made in the 1985 model year. Smaller and lighter cars will be the result. And to meet that federal average, companies will be providing some two-passenger commuter cars.

Four-passenger cars will be dominant, with only about 25% of the total capable of carrying five or six people. V-8 engines will decline to perhaps 10% of the total and will be much lower in power than the V-8's of today.

More extensive use of materials such as plastics and aluminum will be used and entire hoods and door panels might be made of plastic by 1985.

Discover Energy Saving Food Preservation Process

A new food preservation process that is substantially more energy-efficient than canning or freezing has been developed by University of Maryland scientists. Named Gaspak, the new process calls for putting a food into a chamber and removing all air. Subsequently, the food is treated with a combination of carbon monoxide, sulfur dioxide, and other gases to inhibit bacterial growth and deterioration. The treated food is then packaged in a germ-free container filled with the gas.

The new method permits food to be kept fresh at room temperature in warehouses, stores, and homes. Tests have indicated that food samples were well preserved and palatable after 30 days and after 250 days.

The research done at the Maryland Agricultural Experiment Station shows that the Gaspak process uses half as much energy as freezing and canning. Gaspak produce uses 7,962 BTU's per pound, as compared with 14,000 BTU's for canned or frozen products.

Work is now being done to perfect the process. The project is financed by the Maryland Agricultural Experiment Station and the Department of Energy.

Radiation Doses

Radiation doses were originally measured in *roentgens,* (r), a unit of exposure to X-ray or gamma-ray radiation in the air. The roentgen drew its name from Wilhelm Conrad Roentgen (1845–1923), who discovered X-rays in 1895 and who received the first Nobel Prize in physics in 1901.

Today, the *rad* (ra) is the unit commonly used for measuring the amount of radiation to which the whole body, as contrasted with a single organ, is exposed.

The *millirad* is one-thousandth of a rad. Most scientists believe that a dose of a few millirads is safe, but there is significant controversy over the threshold at which a dose becomes hazardous.

The *rem* (for "roentgen equivalent, man") is a measure of ionizing radiation of the type that produces the same damage to human beings as one roentgen of approximately 200 kilowatts of X-radiation.

Millirem is the term used to describe the amount of absorption of radiation by humans. The average American is exposed to 100–200 millirems of radiation per year from man-made and natural sources. A normal chest X-ray exposes one to 20–30 millirems.

Mineral Operations on Federal Land Yield Record Income

The U.S. Geological Survey, Dept. of the Interior, has estimated that royalties collected in fiscal year 1979 from production of oil, gas, coal, potash, phosphate, sodium, and other minerals on federal and Indian lands will exceed $1.8 billion, setting a new high. The increases are due, mainly, to continued increases in oil and gas prices.

Royalties accruing for mineral leases supervised by the Survey are ultimately credited to the states, the Indians, the Reclamation Fund, the Land and Water Conservation Fund, and the U.S. Treasury.

Buying Gasoline—Converting Liters to Gallons[1]

(Rounded-off Figures)

Liters	Gallons	Liters	Gallons	Liters	Gallons	Liters	Gallons
1	.3	26	6.9	51	13.5	76	20.1
2	.5	27	7.1	52	13.7	77	20.3
3	.8	28	7.4	53	14.0	78	20.6
4	1.1	29	7.7	54	14.3	79	20.9
5	1.3	30	7.9	55	14.5	80	21.1
6	1.6	31	8.2	56	14.8	81	21.4
7	1.8	32	8.5	57	15.0	82	21.7
8	2.1	33	8.7	58	15.3	83	21.9
9	2.4	34	9.0	59	15.6	84	22.2
10	2.6	35	9.2	60	15.9	85	22.5
11	2.9	36	9.5	61	16.1	86	22.7
12	3.2	37	9.8	62	16.4	87	23.0
13	3.4	38	10.0	63	16.6	88	23.2
14	3.7	39	10.3	64	16.9	89	23.5
15	4.0	40	10.6	65	17.2	90	23.8
16	4.2	41	10.8	66	17.4	91	24.0
17	4.5	42	11.1	67	17.7	92	24.3
18	4.8	43	11.4	68	18.0	93	24.6
19	5.0	44	11.6	69	18.2	94	24.8
20	5.3	45	11.9	70	18.5	95	25.1
21	5.5	46	12.2	71	18.8	96	25.4
22	5.8	47	12.4	72	19.0	97	25.6
23	6.1	48	12.7	73	19.3	98	25.9
24	6.3	49	12.9	74	19.6	99	26.1
25	6.6	50	13.2	75	19.8	100	26.4

1. For precise conversion: 1 liter=.2642 gallons. 1 gallon=3.785 liters. Multiplying prices per liter by 3.785 gives price per gallon.

The Year in Science—1980

Geologists were presented with a rare opportunity to study earth-shaping processes at work when Mt. St. Helens, located in the State of Washington, erupted violently at 8:32 a.m. on May 18. The eruption blasted 1300 feet off the north face of the previously 9,677-foot-high mountain, leaving a giant bowl-shaped amphitheater. Steam, hot ash, gases, and assorted volcanic debris quickly rose 11 to 15 miles into the sky, then spread eastward to drop light fluffy ash to a depth of several inches hundreds of miles away. Very fine ash, which had been propelled into the stratosphere, was bouyant enough to circle the globe several times, producing spectacular red sunsets. Heat, blast effects, mudslides, and floods triggered by the eruption were held responsible for at least 30 deaths, with scores of people still unaccounted for weeks after the event. No actual lava flows were observed, probably because of the thick, viscuous composition of the silicate magma (molten rock) underlying the volcano. Mt. St. Helens is expected to erupt periodically over a period of many years as it slowly rebuilds its former shape.

More on Magma

Scientists meanwhile have come a step closer to understanding the structure of the earth's core by duplicating in the laboratory the extreme-pressure processes that occur underground. By squeezing minerals in a press equipped with special diamond-tipped anvils, researchers have been able to observe the chemical and structural changes brought about when pressures as high as 25 million pounds per square inch are applied. It appears from this research that the earth's core is not a nickel-iron alloy, as had previously been believed, but a mixture of iron and some lighter elements, possibly oxygen and sulfur, which take on metallic properties at these high pressures.

Old Stuff

Paleontologists have unearthed what are believed to be the oldest forms of life on earth. Life, in the form of bacterial cells, apparently existed 3.5 billion years ago, or roughly only 1 billion years after the earth was formed. The fossilized bacteria were discovered by painstakingly examining old sedimentary rocks found in Australia under a powerful microscope. About five different forms of bacteria have been identified that are almost identical to their modern-day cousins. The discovery pushes the origin of life back 1.2 billion years further than had been thought beforehand.

Earliest Human Precursor

Not quite that old, but old enough, are the fossilized remains of a cat-like mammal dubbed *Aegyptopithicus* after the site of their discovery near Cairo. The little creature, which lived in groups, was active in the daytime, ate fruits, and possibly walked semiupright, is believed to be the common primate ancestor of both man and apes. It lived during the Archeozoic Era, about 30 million years ago. Separation into two distinct lineages, man and ape, probably occurred somewhat later, about 20 million years ago. Most of what is known or surmised about *Aegyptopithicus* is derived from detailed studies of the mammal's jaw and skull structure. With a cranial capacity of 30 cubic centimeters, our ancestor was easily the smartest animal around at the time.

A new theory has been offered to explain the sudden extinction of the dinosaurs (along with most other life-forms of the time) at the end of the Cretaceous period, some 65 million years ago. The discovery of a very thin layer between rocks of the Cretaceous and Tertiary periods is the key to the new theory. The boundary layer is unusually rich in the metal iridium. Iridium is quite scarce on earth, but is about 1000 times more abundant in meteorites. So, says the theory, the dinosaurs became extinct when a large (about six miles in diameter) meteorite or asteroid struck the earth, blanketing the atmosphere with thick, opaque dust clouds. The clouds cut off the sunlight and upset the planet's ecological balance. This sudden disruption in the food cycle proved fatal to a large fraction of the earth's plant and animal population, including the dinosaurs. Truly, a monumental environmental impact.

Cloning a Mammoth

It was reported that Soviet scientists plan to attempt to clone a mammoth, a hairy elephant-like creature that roamed the earth until about 10,000 B.C. Thirty-six frozen and reasonably well preserved mammoth carcases have been found in Siberian permafrost over the years. The attempt at cloning will depend on finding a cell in one of these mammoths that has not been damaged by ice crystals. The nucleus will be removed from such a cell and inserted into the ova, or egg cell, of a living elephant. The combined mammoth-elephant egg will then be fertilized and implanted in the elephant's womb. If the experiment is successful, the elephant will give birth to a baby mammoth, the first one to walk the earth in thousands of years.

Early Americans

Archeologists have traced the Maya civilization to the shores of Belize's Caribbean coast, where settlements dating to 9000 B.C. have been discovered. The find marks the earliest known instance of Maya culture. The early inhabitants of the Yucatàn Peninsula were apparently drawn to the area for its plentiful supply of food from the sea. Maya civilization has been broken down into five cultural periods, dating from 9000 B.C. to 2500 B.C., at which time known Maya culture began. The large and highly advanced civilization collapsed inexplicably around A.D. 900.

Cold Computers

Using principles first discovered by Nobel Laureate Brian Josephson in 1962, physicists have assembled a tiny computer switch which promises to increase computing speed by 10 to 100 times. Known as Josephson junction, the switch is made from niobium metal wires only 1/500,000th of an inch wide, or about 100–200 atomic diameters. The junction must be cooled to 455 degrees Fahrenheit below zero in order to operate, since at that temperature the niobium wires become superconducting and lose virtually all electrical resistance. IBM scientists, who developed the switch, hope for the first Josephson effect computer to be operational in 1984.

Physicists have also proposed that the speed of light, which is the fastest velocity anything can achieve according to Einstein's Theory of Relativity, may not be limiting after all. By applying complex mathematics known as group theory to quantum mechanics and relativity, a small group of maverick physicists including Josephson and principally Jack Sarfatti predict that faster-than-light speed is theoretically possible. Further, claim the proponents, the effect may have profound implications to what they believe is the physical mechanism of human consciousness. However, the theory has so far met with considerable scepticism among other researchers in the field.

Chemists have discovered a whole new class of chemical compounds, known as electrides, in which electrons themselves take on properties of metals. The compounds are highly reactive, have no known uses as yet, and have not been stabilized above 140 degrees below zero.

Biological Tinker Toys

Using gene-splicing techniques, more properly referred to as recombinant DNA research, medical researchers have succeeded in producing two substances previously manufactured only in the human body. The chemicals are both hormones: Thymosin alpha 1 is produced by the human thymus gland and is thought to be useful in defending against infection; human proinsulin, the other compound, may eventually find application in the large-scale production of insulin for diabetics. Both hormones were produced by bacteria which had been "instructed" to do so by implanting genetic codes into their cellular DNA.

A new rabies vaccine has been produced which is claimed to be safer, more effective, and easier to use than the current variety. The new vaccine, which is produced by viruses grown in human cell cultures, requires only five injections, as opposed to the 23 needed previously.

DNA, or deoxyribonucleic acid, has long been understood to be the genetic code for all forms of life. Each life-form, indeed, each individual of the higher forms of life, has its own characteristic DNA molecule based on the arrangement of chemical sub-groups within the huge spiral-shaped protein. DNA had always been thought to be right-handed, the spiral turning in one direction only. Now, however, more complex left-handed spiralling DNA has been identified, and its implications may prove important to cancer research. In the left-handed DNA, amino acid groups known as guanines are located in such a way as to make them more susceptible to the action of carcinogenic chemicals. Or, it may be that this particular type of DNA breaks down the known carcinogens into forms which are even more cancer-producing.

In other cancer research, about $10 million has been earmarked for the purchase, production, and testing of interferon. The available monies could buy 150 billion standard units of the substance, about enough to treat 450 patients. The demand for interferon is very high owing to the great deal of publicity it received over the past few years, but some researchers have come to doubt its effectiveness.

Bird Migration Mystery Solved

Zoologists believe they have unraveled the mystery of how birds can navigate for up to thousands of miles during their annual migrations. Pigeons have been found to have minute particles of the magnetic mineral magnetite, or lodestone, in their skulls. The magnetite possibly acts as a built-in compass which, in combination with the birds' senses of hearing and smell, plus an uncanny ability to sense changes in earth's gravity, apparently leads the animals to their destinations. Magnetite has also been discovered in certain species of bacteria. Magnetite-containing bacteria found in the Northern Hemisphere align themselves facing north; those recently discovered in New Zealand and Australia use their internal compasses to follow earth's magnetic flux lines southward and downward (the magnetic flux lines curve down into the earth nearer the poles), leading them to food supplies at the bottom of ponds. Other interesting biological discoveries involve previously unknown species of *square* bacteria. The microbes live in extremely salty pools near the coast of the Sinai Peninsula. They are thought to be square (and other shapes with corners) because they lack the internal osmotic pressures that keep ordinary bacteria confined to more rounded shapes.

More from the Wild Kingdom

A newly discovered beetle, found in Michigan, may be a carrier for ergot fungus, a disease of wheat. The finding is important to livestock growers since the ergot produces a poison which is harmful to cattle. An attempt to communicate with dolphins, the intelligent and playful marine mammals, has met with reasonable success. Dolphins have been taught up to 25 "words" communicated via hand signals. The most startling finding is that the animals are apparently able to grasp the abstract meaning of the signals, correctly interpreting them when they are used in new and unfamiliar commands. Also at sea, scientists have discovered the function of the narwhal's unicorn-like tusk. The long, pointed spear, which protrudes from the front of the whale's head, is used in play, sexual activity, and aggression. Do narwhals *actually* poke fun at each other? Finally, zoologists have found that preying mantises mate only during the 20 minutes immediately before dawn. The limited visibility of the early morning hours allows the male mantis to mate with the female before she can find him and, as she sometimes does, have him for breakfast.

Konrad J.A. Kundig

Table of Geological Periods

It is now generally assumed that planets are formed by the accretion of gas and dust in a cosmic cloud, but there is no way of estimating the length of this process. Our earth acquired its present size, more or less, between 4,000 and 5,000 million years ago. Life on earth originated about 2,000 million years ago, but there are no good fossil remains from periods earlier than the Cambrian, which began about 550 million years ago. The largely unknown past before the Cambrian Period is referred to as the Pre-Cambrian and is subdivided into the Lower (or older) and Upper (or younger) Pre-Cambrian—also called the Archaeozoic and Proterozoic Eras.

The known geological history of the earth since the beginning of the Cambrian Period is subdivided into three "eras," each of which comprises a number of "periods." They, in turn, are subdivided into "subperiods." In a subperiod, a certain section may be especially well known because of rich fossil finds. Such a section is called a "formation," and it is usually identified by a place name.

Paleozoic Era

This era began 550 million years ago and lasted for 355 million years. The name was compounded from Greek *palaios* (old) and *zoön* (animal).

Period	Duration[1]	Subperiods	Events
Cambrian (from *Cambria,* Latin name for Wales)	70	Lower Cambrian Middle Cambrian Upper Cambrian	Invertebrate sea life of many types, proliferating during this and the following period
Ordovician (from Latin *Ordovices,* people of early Britain)	85	Lower Ordovician Upper Ordovician	
Silurian (from Latin *Silures,* people of early Wales)	40	Lower Silurian Upper Silurian	First known fishes; gigantic sea scorpions
Devonian (from Devonshire in England)	50	Lower Devonian Upper Devonian	Proliferation of fishes and other forms of sea life; land still largely lifeless
Carboniferous (from Latin *carbo* = coal + *fero* = to bear)	85	Lower or Mississippian Upper or Pennsylvanian	Period of maximum coal formation in swampy forests; early insects and first known amphibians
Permian (from district of Perm in Russia)	25	Lower Permian Upper Permian	Early reptiles and mammals; earliest form of turtles

Mesozoic Era

This era began 195 million years ago and lasted for 135 million years. The name was compounded from Greek *mesos* (middle) and *zoön* (animal). Popular name: Age of Reptiles.

Period	Duration[1]	Subperiods	Events
Triassic (from *trias* = triad)	35	Lower or Buntsandstein (from German *bunt* = colorful + *Sandstein* = sandstone) Middle or Muschelkalk (from German *Muschel* = clam + *Kalk* = limestone) Upper or Keuper (old miners' term)	Early saurians
Jurassic (from Jura Mountains)	35	Lower or Black Jurassic, or Lias (from French *liais* = hard stone) Middle or Brown Jurassic, or Dogger (old provincial English for ironstone) Upper or White Jurassic, or Malm (Middle English for sand)	Many sea-going reptiles; early large dinosaurs; somewhat later, flying reptiles (pterosaurs), earliest known birds
Cretaceous (from Latin *creta* = chalk)	65	Lower Cretaceous Upper Cretaceous	Maximum development of dinosaurs; birds proliferating; oppossum-like mammals

Cenozoic Era

This era began 60 million years ago and includes the geological present. The name was compounded from Greek *kainos* (new) and *zoön* (animal). Popular name: Age of Mammals.

Period	Duration[1]	Subperiods	Events
Tertiary (originally thought to be the third of only three periods)	c. 60	Paleocene (from Greek *palaios* = old + *kainos* = new)	First mammals other than marsupials
		Eocene (from Greek *eos* = dawn + *kainos* = new)	Formation of amber; rich insect fauna; early bats
		Oligocene (from Greek *oligos* = few + *kainos* = new)	Steady increase of large mammals
		Miocene (from Greek *meios* = less + *kainos* = new)	
		Pliocene (from Greek *pleios* = more + *kainos* = new)	Mammals closely resembling present types; protohumans
Pleistocene (from Greek *pleistos* = most + *kainos* = new) (popular name: Ice Age)	1	Four major glaciations, named Günz, Mindel, Riss, and Würm, originally the names of rivers. Last glaciation ended 10,000 to 15,000 years ago	Various forms of early man
Holocene (from Greek *holos* = entire + *kainos* = new)		The present	The last 3,000 years are called "history"

1. In millions of years.

Chemical Elements

Element	Symbol	Atomic no.	Atomic weight	Specific gravity	Melting point °C	Boiling point °C	Number of isotopes[1]	Discoverer	Year
Actinium	Ac	89	227[2]	10.07[2]	1050	3200±300	11	Debierne	1899
Aluminum	Al	13	26.9815	2.6989	660.37	2467	8	Wöhler	1827
Americium	Am	95	243[6]	13.67	994±4	2607	13[3]	Seaborg et al.	1944
Antimony	Sb	51	121.75	6.691	630.74	1750	29	Early historic times	—
Argon	Ar	18	39.948	1.7837[4]	−189.2	−185.7	8	Rayleigh and Ramsay	1894
Arsenic (gray)	As	33	74.9216	5.73	817 (28 atm.)	613[5]	14	Albertus Magnus	1250?
Astatine	At	85	~210	—	302	337	21	Corson et al.	1940
Barium	Ba	56	137.34	3.5	725	1640	25	Davy	1808
Berkelium	Bk	97	247[6]	14.00[7]	—	—	8[3]	Seaborg et al.	1949
Beryllium	Be	4	9.01218	1.848	1278±5	2970 (5 mm.)	6	Vauquelin	1798
Bismuth	Bi	83	208.9806	9.747	271.3	1560±5	19	Geoffroy	1753
Boron	B	5	10.81	2.37[8]	2300	2550[5]	6	Gay-Lussac and Thénard; Davy	1808
Bromine	Br	35	79.904	3.12[4]	−7.2	58.78	19	Balard	1826
Cadmium	Cd	48	112.40	8.65	320.9	765	22	Stromeyer	1817
Calcium	Ca	20	40.08	1.55	839±2	1484	14	Davy	1808
Californium	Cf	98	251[6]	—	—	—	12[3]	Seaborg et al.	1950
Carbon	C	6	12.011	1.8–3.5[9]	~3550	4827	7	Prehistoric	—
Cerium	Ce	58	140.12	6.771	798±3	3257	19	Berzelius and Hisinger; Klaproth	1803
Cesium	Cs	55	132.9055	1.873	28.40	678.4	22	Bunsen and Kirchhoff	1860
Chlorine	Cl	17	35.453	1.56[4]	−100.98	−34.6	11	Scheele	1774
Chromium	Cr	24	51.996	7.18–7.20	1857±20	2672	9	Vauquelin	1797
Cobalt	Co	27	58.9332	8.9	1495	2870	14	Brandt	c.1735
Copper	Cu	29	63.546	8.96	1083.4±0.2	2567	11	Prehistoric	—
Curium	Cm	96	247[6]	13.51[2]	1340±40	—	13[3]	Seaborg et al.	1944
Dysprosium	Dy	66	162.50	8.540	1409	2335	21	Boisbaudran	1886
Einsteinium	Es	99	254[6]	—	—	—	12[3]	Ghiorso et al	1952
Erbium	Er	68	167.26	9.045	1522	2510	16	Mosander	1843
Europium	Eu	63	151.96	5.283	822±5	1597	21	Demarcay	1896
Fermium	Fm	100	257[6]	—	—	—	10[3]	Ghiorso et al	1953
Fluorine	F	9	18.9984	1.108[4]	−219.62	−188.14	6	Moissan	1886
Francium	Fr	87	223[6]	—	27[2]	677[2]	21	Perey	1939
Gadolinium	Gd	64	157.25	7.898	1311±1	3233	17	Marignac	1880
Gallium	Ga	31	69.72	5.904	29.78	2403	14	Boisbaudran	1875
Germanium	Ge	32	72.59	5.323	937.4	2830	17	Winkler	1886
Gold	Au	79	196.9665	19.32	1064.43	2807	21	Prehistoric	—
Hafnium	Hf	72	178.49	13.31	2227±20	4602	17	Coster and von Hevesy	1923
Helium	He	2	4.00260	0.1785[4]	−272.2 (26 atm.)	−268.934	5	Janssen	1868
Holmium	Ho	67	164.9303	8.781	1470	2720	29	Delafontaine and Soret	1878
Hydrogen	H	1	1.0080	0.070[4]	−259.14	−252.87	3	Cavendish	1766
Indium	In	49	114.82	7.31	156.61	2080	34	Reich and Richter	1863

Element	Symbol	Atomic no.	Atomic weight	Specific gravity	Melting point °C	Boiling point °C	Number of isotopes[1]	Discoverer	Year
Iodine	I	53	126.9045	4.93	113.5	184.35	24	Courtois	1811
Iridium	Ir	77	192.22	22.42	2410	4130	25	Tennant	1803
Iron	Fe	26	55.847	7.894	1535	2750	10	Prehistoric	—
Krypton	Kr	36	83.80	3.733[4]	−156.6	−152.30±0.10	23	Ramsay and Travers	1898
Lanthanum	La	57	138.9055	6.166	920±5	3454	19	Mosander	1839
Lawrencium	Lr	103	257[6]	—	—	—	20[3]	Ghiorso et al.	1961
Lead	Pb	82	207.2	11.35	327.502	1740	29	Prehistoric	—
Lithium	Li	3	6.941	0.534	180.54	1347	5	Arfvedson	1817
Lutetium	Lu	71	174.97	9.835	1656±5	3315	22	Urbain	1907
Magnesium	Mg	12	24.305	1.738	648.8±0.5	1090	8	Black	1755
Manganese	Mn	25	54.9380	7.21–7.44[10]	1244±3	1962	11	Gahn, Scheele, and Bergman	1774
Mendelevium	Md	101	256[6]	—	—	—	3[3]	Ghiorso et al.	1955
Mercury	Hg	80	200.59	13.546	−38.87	356.58	26	Prehistoric	—
Molybdenum	Mo	42	95.94	10.22	2617	4612	20	Scheele	1778
Neodymium	Nd	60	144.24	6.80 & 7.004[10]	1010	3127	16	von Welsbach	1885
Neon	Ne	10	20.179	0.89990 (g/l 0°C/1 atm)	−248.67	−246.048	8	Ramsay and Travers	1898
Neptunium	Np	93	237.0482	20.25	640±1	3902	15[3]	McMillan and Abelson	1940
Nickel	Ni	28	58.71	8.902	1453	2732	11	Cronstedt	1751
Niobium (Columbium)	Nb	41	92.9064	8.57	2468±10	4742	24	Hatchett	1801
Nitrogen	N	7	14.0067	0.808[4]	−209.86	−195.8	8	Rutherford	1772
Nobelium	No	102	254[6]	—	—	—	7[3]	Ghiorso et al.	1957
Osmium	Os	76	190.2	22.57	3045±30	5027±100	19	Tennant	1803
Oxygen	O	8	15.9994	1.14[4]	−218.4	−182.962	8	Priestley	1774
Palladium	Pd	46	106.4	12.02	1552	3140	21	Wollaston	1803
Phosphorus	P	15	30.9738	1.82 (white)	44.1	280	7	Brand	1669
Platinum	Pt	78	195.09	21.45	1772	3827±100	32	Ulloa	1735
Plutonium	Pu	94	244[6]	19.84	641	3232	16[3]	Seaborg et al.	1940
Polonium	Po	84	~210[6]	9.32	254	962	34	Curie	1898
Potassium	K	19	39.102	0.862	63.65	774	10	Davy	1807
Praseodymium	Pr	59	140.9077	6.772	931±4	3212	15	von Welsbach	1885
Promethium	Pm	61	145[6]	—	~1080	2460?	14	Marinsky et al.	1945
Protactinium	Pa	91	231.0359	15.37[2]	<1600	—	14	Hahn and Meitner	1917
Radium	Ra	88	226.0254	5.0?	700	1140	15	P. and M. Curie	1898
Radon	Rn	86	222[6]	4.4[4]	−71	−61.8	20	Dorn	1900
Rhenium	Re	75	186.2	21.02	3180	5627[7]	21	Noddack, Berg, and Tacke	1925
Rhodium	Rh	45	102.9055	12.41	1966±3	3727±100	20	Wollaston	1803
Rubidium	Rb	37	85.4678	1.532	38.89	688	20	Bunsen and Kirchoff	1861
Ruthenium	Ru	44	101.07	12.44	2310	3900	16	Klaus	1844
Samarium	Sm	62	150.4	7.536	1072±5	1778	17	Boisbaudran	1879
Scandium	Sc	21	44.9559	2.989	1539	2832	15	Nilson	1879
Selenium	Se	34	78.96	4.79 (gray)	217	684.9±1	20	Berzelius	1817
Silicon	Si	14	28.086	2.33	1410	2355	8	Berzelius	1824
Silver	Ag	47	107.868	10.50	961.93	2212	27	Prehistoric	—
Sodium	Na	11	22.9898	0.971	97.81±0.03	882.9	7	Davy	1807
Strontium	Sr	38	87.62	2.54	769	1384	18	Davy	1808
Sulfur	S	16	32.06	2.07[11]	112.8	444.674	10	Prehistoric	—
Tantalum	Ta	73	180.9479	16.654	2996	5425±100	19	Ekeberg	1801
Technetium	Tc	43	98.9062	11.50[2]	2172	4877	23	Perrier and Segrè	1937
Tellurium	Te	52	127.60	6.24	449.5±0.3	989.8±3.8	29	von Reichenstein	1782
Terbium	Tb	65	158.9254	8.234	1360±4	3041	24	Mosander	1843
Thallium	Tl	81	204.37	11.85	303.5	1457±10	28	Crookes	1861
Thorium	Th	90	232.0381	11.72	1750	~4790	12	Berzelius	1828
Thulium	Tm	69	168.9342	9.314	1545±15	1727	18	Cleve	1879
Tin	Sn	50	118.69	7.31 (white)	231.9681	2270	28	Prehistoric	—
Titanium	Ti	22	47.90	4.55	1660±10	3287	9	Gregor	1791
Tungsten (Wolfram)	W	74	183.85	19.3	3410±20	5660	22	J. and F. d'Elhuyar	1783
Uranium	U	92	238.029	~18.95	1132.3±0.8	3818	15	Peligot	1841
Vanadium	V	23	50.9414	6.11	1890±10	3380	9	del Rio	1801
Xenon	Xe	54	131.30	3.52[4]	−111.9	−107.1±3	31	Ramsay and Travers	1898
Ytterbium	Yb	70	173.04	6.972	824±5	1193	16	Marignac	1878
Yttrium	Y	39	88.9059	4.457	1523±8	3337	21	Gadolin	1794
Zinc	Zn	30	65.38	7.133	419.58	907	15	Prehistoric	—
Zirconium	Zr	40	91.22	6.506[2]	1852±2	4377	20	Klaproth	1789

1. Isotopes are different forms of the same element having the same atomic number but different atomic weights. 2. Calculated figure. 3. Artificially produced. 4. Liquid. 5. Sublimation point. 6. Mass number of the isotope of longest known life. 7. Estimated. 8. Amorphous. 9. Depending on whether amorphous, graphite or diamond. 10. Depending on allotropic form. 11. Rhombic. ~ Is approximately. < Is less than. NOTE: There is a dispute between groups at the Lawrence Berkeley Laboratory of the University of California and at the Dubna Laboratory in the Soviet Union concerning the discovery of elements 104, 105, and 106. The Lawrence Berkeley Laboratory claims that 104 and 105 were discovered in 1969 and 1970, respectively, by Ghiorso et al. and has suggested the names Rutherfordium and Hahnium. The U.S. laboratory claims also that Ghiorso et al. discovered element 106 in 1974. No name has yet been suggested for this element. Names will not be official until the controversy is resolved and they have been approved by the International Union for Pure and Applied Chemistry.

Atomic Energy

Just as the Space Age is said to have started with the orbiting of Sputnik I, the Atomic Age is said to have started with the explosion of a test bomb on July 16, 1945, near Alamogordo, N.M., at 5:30 A.M. local time. The bomb was placed on top of a steel tower, and observers were stationed in bunkers 10,000 yards away. The explosion vaporized the steel tower, produced a mushroom cloud rising to 40,000 feet, and melted the desert sand into glass for distances up to 800 yards from the tower.

The first operational use of an atom bomb took place only three weeks later, when a uranium bomb was exploded over Hiroshima, Japan, on Aug. 6, 1945. The bomb, cylindrical in shape, 10 feet long with a diameter of 2 feet 4 inches, weighed about 9,000 pounds. Its explosive force was equal to 20,000 tons of TNT, hence the term "20-kiloton bomb." Three days later another atomic bomb, this time of plutonium, was exploded over Nagasaki.

Of course, the Atomic Age did not begin with the explosion of the test bomb at Alamogordo, just as the Space Age did not begin with the orbiting of the first artificial satellite. In both cases these visible feats were just experiments which proved the theory that had been built up patiently over decades.

At the turn of the century, scientists began to wonder whether the atoms of the chemical elements might not be composed of smaller particles. This was actually a contradiction in terms, because the Greek word *atomos,* from which the word *atom* was derived, meant "indivisible." But there were some indications of particles smaller than an atom —the electrons. In 1905, Albert Einstein suggested that matter might just be "condensed energy" and gave the conversion formula $E = mc^2$, in which E represents the energy, m the mass, and c the velocity of light. If this formula was correct, a small piece of matter should represent enormous amounts of energy.

Fission and Fusion

As is now generally known, atomic energy can be released in two ways. One is the *fission* of elements with very heavy atoms, such as uranium and plutonium, which will split when struck by a neutron, a sub-atomic particle. The splitting of the heavy atom releases more neutrons, which are then available to split other atoms—the so-called chain reaction. The other way of obtaining atomic energy is *fusion;* four light atoms (hydrogen) are fused together into the next heavier element (helium). The fusion reaction requires enormous heat and very high pressures. These pressures, coupled with very high temperatures, can most easily be produced by exploding a fission bomb, which is the reason why it is often said that a fission bomb is the trigger for a fusion (hydrogen) bomb.

Interestingly enough, the fusion reaction was discovered first, though only on paper. For the period from, say, 1910 to 1930, most physicists believed that the release of atomic energy, if it could be done, would be of no practical value. They asserted that causing the release would require more energy than could be obtained. Most astronomers, on the other hand, were convinced that atomic energy was released in the sun and the other stars because there was no other way to account for the energy the stars radiated into space. Trying to account for the energy radiated by the stars led to theoretical papers predicting what we now call the fusion reaction. At the time (1930), atomic fission was still unknown; it was discovered first by Enrico Fermi in 1934. But nobody yet knew that the sudden bursts of energy observed in the experiments were due to the fission of the uranium-235 atom. This was established (by way of calculation) by Dr. Lise Meitner. Once it was known what happened, the way to a premeditated release of atomic energy was clear.

But nobody could be quite certain whether the release would take the form of an explosion or whether it would be slow enough to be used to generate power. American scientists proceeded under the assumption that the release would be sudden and violent (and the Alamogordo test proved them right), while Professor Heisenberg in Germany thought the slow release to be more likely, which is the reason why the Germans did not start a large-scale atomic energy project.

Atoms for Peace

The *peaceful* Atomic Age can be said to have been born in 1954, when the original U.S. Atomic Energy Act was amended to release many so-called "secrets" of nuclear energy so that nuclear power plants could be built and radioactive isotopes be used in medicine. The next year, the first International Conference on the Peaceful Uses of the Atom was convened at Geneva, bringing together scientists from all over the world to discuss what hitherto had been considered to be secret.

Actually there was little that was really secret about nuclear energy. When the results of the 1938 experiments were brought to the United States, scientists from different parts of the world openly stated that the possibility of atomic bombs was inherent in the scientific findings.

Once the veil of "secrecy" had been dispelled by revision of the Atomic Energy Act and the Geneva meeting, construction of plants to produce electricity by controlled fission of uranium atoms got under way in the United States and several other industrialized nations. Electric power was first produced as a result of nuclear fission in December 1951 at the National Reactor Testing Station in Idaho. When a reactor was connected to a generator, the nuclear power plant produced enough electricity for about 50 homes.

From that early beginning, the nuclear power industry has grown until in 1979, 71 nuclear power plants were operable in 26 states in the U.S. Construction permits were granted for an additional 91 operations, and another 24 were otherwise planned. A total of 38 states currently contain sites for nuclear power plants either operating, under construction, or planned.

More than 20 other nations have nuclear power plants in operation. Of the non-Communist countries, 18 had operating nuclear power generating stations at the end of 1979.

The United States was by far the largest producer of nuclear power generating stations, producing 270.7 billion gross kilowatt hours of electricity in 1979, down from 297.7 in 1978. The decrease was the result of shutdowns which stemmed from the accident at the Three Mile Island plant in Pennsylvania and the earlier temporary shutdown of five reactors because of potential design deficiencies. Total installed capacity was unchanged in 1979 due to the suspension of licensing new reactors.

Scientific Inventions, Discoveries, and Theories

Most inventions are the results of the discoveries, theories, experiments, and improvements of many people. This list tries to suggest the development of certain particularly important ideas. In some instances, it tries to connect the fundamental theory with the ultimate practical invention.

Abacus: *See* Calculating machine
Adding machine: *See* Calculating machine; Computer
Adrenaline: (isolation of) Jokichi Takamine, U.S., 1901
Air brake: George Westinghouse, U.S., 1868
Air conditioning: Willis Carrier, U.S., 1911
Airplane: (first powered, sustained, controlled flight) Orville and Wilbur Wright, U.S., 1903. *See also* Jet propulsion, aircraft
Airship: (non-rigid) Henri Giffard, France, 1852; (rigid) Ferdinand von Zeppelin, Germany, 1900
Aluminum manufacture: (by electrolytic action) Charles M. Hall, U.S., 1866
Anesthetic: (first use of anesthetic—ether—on man) Crawford W. Long, U.S., 1842
Antibiotics: (first demonstration of antibiotic effect) Louis Pasteur, Jules-François Joubert, France, 1887; (penicillin, first modern antibiotic) Alexander Fleming, England, 1928
Antiseptic: (surgery) Joseph Lister, England, 1867
Antitoxin, diphtheria: Emil von Behring, Germany, 1890
Atomic theory: (ancient) Leucippus, Democritus, Greece, c.500 B.C.; Lucretius, Rome, c.100 B.C.; (modern) John Dalton, England, 1808
Automobile: (first with internal combustion engine, 250 rpm) Karl Benz, Germany, 1885; (first with practical high-speed internal combustion engine, 900 rpm) Gottlieb Daimler, Germany, 1885; (first true automobile, not carriage with motor) René Panhard, Emile Lavassor, France, 1891; (carburetor, spray) Charles E. Duryea, U.S., 1892
Bacteria: Anton van Leeuwenhoek, The Netherlands, 1683
Bakelite: *See* Plastics
Balloon, hot-air: Joseph and Jacques Montgolfier, France, 1783
Ball-point pen: *See* Pen
Barometer: Evangelista Torricelli, Italy, 1643
Bicycle: Karl D. von Sauerbronn, Germany, 1816; (first modern model) James Starley, England, 1884
Bifocal lens: *See* Lens, bifocal
Blood, circulation of: William Harvey, England, 1628
Braille: Louis Braille, France, 1829
Bullet: (conical) Claude Minié, France, 1849
Calculating machine: (Abacus) China, c.190; (logarithms: made multiplying easier and thus calculators practical) John Napier, Scotland, 1614; (slide rule) William Oughtred, England, 1632; (digital calculator) Blaise Pascal, 1642; (multiplication machine) Gottfried Leibnitz, Germany, 1671; (important 19th-century contributors to modern machine) Frank S. Baldwin, Jay R. Monroe, Dorr E. Felt, W. T. Ohdner, William Burroughs, all U.S.; ("analytical engine" design, included concepts of programming, taping) Charles Babbage, England, 1835. *See also* Computer
Camera: (hand-held) George Eastman, U.S., 1888; (Polaroid Land) Edwin Land, U.S., 1948. *See also* Photography
Carburetor: *See* Automobile
Celanese: *See* Fibers, man-made
Celluloid: *See* Plastics
Classification of plants and animals: (by genera and species) Carolus Linnaeus, Sweden, 1737–53
Clock, pendulum: Christian Huygens, The Netherlands, 1656
Combustion: (nature of) Antoine Lavoisier, France, 1777
Computer: (differential analyzer, mechanically operated) Vannevar Bush, U.S., 1928; (Mark I, first information-processing digital computer) Howard Aiken, U.S., 1944; (ENIAC, Electronic Numerical Integrator and Calculator, first all-electronic) J. Presper Eckert, John W. Mauchly, U.S., 1946; (stored-program concept) John von Neumann, U.S., 1947
Conditioned reflex: Ivan Pavlov, Russia, c.1910
Converter, Bessemer: William Kelly, U.S., 1851
Cosmetics: Egypt, c.4000 B.C.
Cotton gin: Eli Whitney, U.S., 1793
Crossbow: China, c.300 B.C.
Cyclotron: Ernest O. Lawrence, U.S., 1931
Deuterium: (heavy hydrogen) Harold Urey, U.S., 1931
DNA: (deoxyribonucleic acid) Friedrich Meischer, Germany, 1869; (determination of double-helical structure) F. H. Crick, England, James D. Watson, U.S., 1953
Dynamite: Alfred Nobel, Sweden, 1867
Electric generator (dynamo): (laboratory model) Michael Faraday, England, 1832; Joseph Henry, U.S., c.1832; (hand-driven model) Hippolyte Pixii, France, 1833; (alternating-current generator) Nikola Tesla, U.S., 1892
Electric lamp: (arc lamp) Sir Humphrey Davy, England, 1801; (fluorescent lamp) A. E. Becquerel, France, 1867; (incandescent lamp) Sir Joseph Swann, England, Thomas A. Edison, U.S., contemporaneously, 1870s; (carbon arc street lamp) Charles F. Brush, U.S., 1879; (first widely marketed incandescent lamp) Thomas A. Edison, U.S., 1879; (mercury vapor lamp) Peter Cooper Hewitt, U.S., 1903; (neon lamp) Georges Claude, France, 1911; (tungsten filament) Irving Langmuir, U.S., 1915
Electric motor: *See* Motor
Electromagnet: William Sturgeon, England, 1823
Electron: Sir Joseph J. Thompson, England, 1897
Elevator, passenger: (safety device permitting use by passengers) Elisha G. Otis, U.S., 1852; (elevator utilizing safety device) 1857
$E = mc^2$: (equivalence of mass and energy) Albert Einstein, Switzerland, 1905
Engine, internal combustion: No single inventor. Fundamental theory established by Sadi Carnot, France, 1824; (two-stroke) Etienne Lenoir, France, 1860; (ideal operating cycle for four-stroke) Alphonse Beau de Rochet, France, 1862; (operating four-stroke) Nikolaus Otto, Germany, 1876; (diesel) Rudolf Diesel, Germany, 1892; (rotary) Felix Wankel, Germany, 1956. *See also* Automobile
Engine, steam: *See* Steam engine
Evolution: (by natural selection) Charles Darwin, England, 1859
Falling bodies, law of: Galileo Galilei, Italy, 1590
Fermentation: (micro-organisms as cause of) Louis Pasteur, France, c.1860
Fibers, man-made: (nitrocellulose fibers treated to change flammable nitrocellulose to harmless cel-

lulose, precursor of rayon) Sir Joseph Swann, England, 1883; (rayon) Count Hilaire de Chardonnet, France, 1889; (Celanese) Henry and Camille Dreyfuss, U.S., England, 1921; (research on polyesters and polyamides, basis for modern man-made fibers) U.S., England, Germany, 1930s; (nylon) Wallace H. Carothers, U.S., 1935

Fountain pen: *See* Pen

Geometry, elements of: Euclid, Alexandria, Egypt, c.300 B.C.

Gravitation, law of: Sir Isaac Newton, England, c.1665 (published 1687)

Gunpowder: China, c.700

Gyrocompass: Elmer A. Sperry, U.S., 1905

Gyroscope: Léon Foucault, France, 1852

Helicopter: Igor Sikorsky, U.S., 1939

Helium first observed on sun: Sir Joseph Lockyer, England, 1868

Heredity, laws of: Gregor Mendel, Austria, 1865

Induction, electric: Joseph Henry, U.S., 1828

Insulin: Sir Frederick G. Banting, J. J. R. MacLeod, Canada, 1922

Intelligence testing: Alfred Binet, Theodore Simon, France, 1905

Isotopes: (concept of) Frederick Soddy, England, 1912; (stable isotopes) J. J. Thompson, England, 1913; (existence demonstrated by mass spectrography) Francis W. Ashton, 1919

Jet propulsion, aircraft: Sir Frank Whittle, England, 1930

Laser: (theoretical work on) Charles H. Townes, Arthur L. Schawlow, U.S., N. Basov, A. Prokhorov, U.S.S.R., 1958; (first working model) T. H. Maiman, U.S., 1960

Lens, bifocal: Benjamin Franklin, U.S., c.1760

Light, nature of: (wave theory) Christian Huygens, Denmark, 1678; (electromagnetic theory) James Clerk Maxwell, England, 1873

Light, speed of: (theory that light has finite velocity) Olaus Roemer, Denmark, 1675

Lightning rod: Benjamin Franklin, U.S., 1752

Linotype: *See* Printing

Lithography: *See* Printing

Locomotive: (steam-powered) Richard Trevithick, England, 1804; (first practical, due to multiple-fire-tube boiler) George Stephenson, England, 1829; (largest steam-powered) Union Pacific's "Big Boy," U.S., 1941

Logarithms: *See* Calculating machine

Loom: (horizontal, two-beamed) Egypt, c.4400 B.C.; (Jacquard drawloom, pattern controlled by punch cards) Jacques de Vaucanson, France, 1745, Joseph-Marie Jacquard, 1801; (flying shuttle) John Kay, England, 1733; (power-driven loom) Edmund Cartwright, England, 1785

Machine gun: James Puckle, England, 1718; Richard J. Gatling, U.S., 1861

Match: (phosphorus) François Derosne, France, 1816; (friction) Charles Sauria, France, 1831; (safety) J. E. Lundstrom, Sweden, 1855

Mendelian law: *See* Heredity

Microscope: (compound) Zacharias Janssen, The Netherlands, 1590; (electron) Vladimir Zworykin et al., U.S., Canada, Germany, 1932–1939

Motion pictures: Thomas A. Edison, U.S., 1893

Motion pictures, sound: Product of various inventions. First picture with synchronized musical score: *Don Juan,* 1926; with spoken dialogue: *The Jazz Singer,* 1927; both Warner Bros.

Motor, electric: Michael Faraday, England, 1822; (alternating-current) Nikola Tesla, U.S., 1892

Motor, gasoline: *See* Engine, internal combustion

Motorcycle: (motor tricycle) Edward Butler, England, 1884; (gasoline-engine motorcycle) Gottieb Daimier, Germany, 1885

Neptunium: (first transuranic element, synthesis of) Edward M. McMillan, Philip H. Abelson, U.S., 1940

Neutron: James Chadwick, England, 1832

Neutron-induced radiation: Enrico Fermi et al., Italy, 1934

Nitroglycerin: Ascanio Sobrero, Italy, 1846

Nuclear fission: Otto Hahn, Fritz Strassmann, Germany, 1938

Nuclear reactor: Enrico Fermi et al., U.S., 1942

Nylon: *See* Fibers, man-made

Ohm's law: (relationship between strength of electric current, electromotive force, and circuit resistance) Georg S. Ohm, Germany, 1827

Ozone: Christian Schönbein, Germany, 1839

Paper: China, c.100 B.C.

Parachute: Louis S. Lenormand, France, 1783

Pen: (fountain) Lewis E. Waterman, U.S., 1884; (ball-point, for marking on rough surfaces) John H. Loud, U.S., 1888; (ball-point, for handwriting) Lazlo Biro, Argentina, 1944

Penicillin: *See* Antibiotics

Periodic law: (that properties of elements are functions of their atomic weights) Dmitri Mendeleev, Russia, 1869

Periodic table: (arrangement of chemical elements based on periodic law) Dmitri Mendeleev, Russia, 1869

Phonograph: Thomas A. Edison, U.S., 1877

Photography: (first paper negative, first photograph, on metal) Joseph Nicéphore Niepce, France, 1816–1827; (discovery of fixative powers of hyposulfite of soda) Sir John Herschel, England, 1819; (first direct positive image on silver plate, the daguerreotype) Louis Daguerre, based on work with Niepce, France, 1839; (first paper negative from which a number of positive prints could be made) William Talbot, England, 1841. Work of these four men, taken together, forms basis for all modern photography. (First color images) Alexandre Becquerel, Claude Niepce de Saint-Victor, France, 1848–60; (commercial color film with three emulsion layers, Kodachrome) U.S., 1935. *See also* Camera

Plastics: (first material, nitrocellulose softened by vegetable oil, camphor, precursor to Celluloid) Alexander Parkes, England, 1855; (Celluloid, involving recognition of vital effect of camphor) John W. Hyatt, U.S., 1869; (Bakelite, first completely synthetic plastic) Leo H. Baekeland, U.S., 1910; (theoretical background of macromolecules and process of polymerization on which modern plastics industry rests) Hermann Staudinger, Germany, 1922. *See also* Fibers, man-made

Plow, forked: Mesopotamia, before 3000 B.C.

Plutonium, synthesis of: Glenn T. Seaborg, Edwin M. McMillan, Arthur C. Wahl, Joseph W. Kennedy, U.S., 1941

Polaroid Land camera: *See* Camera

Polio, vaccine against: (vaccine made from dead virus strains) Jonas E. Salk, U.S., 1955; (vaccine made from live virus strains) Albert Sabin, U.S., 1960

Positron: Carl D. Anderson, U.S., 1932

Pressure cooker: (early version) Denis Papin, France, 1679

Printing: (block) Japan, c.700; (movable type) Korea, c.1400; Johann Gutenberg, Germany, c.1450 (lithography, offset) Aloys Senefelder, Germany, 1796; (rotary press) Richard Hoe, U.S., 1844; (linotype) Ottman Mergenthaler, U.S. 1884

Programming, information: *See* Calculating machine
Propeller, screw: Sir Francis P. Smith, England, 1836; John Ericsson, England, worked independently of and simultaneously with Smith, 1837
Proton: Ernest Rutherford, England, 1919
Psychoanalysis: Sigmund Freud, Austria, c.1904
Quantum theory: Max Planck, Germany, 1901
Rabies immunization: Louis Pasteur, France, 1885
Radar: (limited to one-mile range) Christian Hulsmeyer, Germany, 1904; (pulse modulation, used for measuring height of ionosphere) Gregory Breit, Merle Tuve, U.S., 1925; (first practical radar—radio detection and ranging) Sir Robert Watson-Watt, England, 1934–35
Radio: (electromagnetism, theory of) James Clerk Maxwell, England, 1873; (spark coil, generator of electromagnetic waves) Heinrich Hertz, Germany, 1886; (first practical system of wireless telegraphy) Guglielmo Marconi, Italy, 1895; (vacuum electron tube, basis for radio telephony) Sir John Fleming, England, 1904; (triode amplifying tube) Lee de Forest, U.S., 1906; (regenerative circuit, allowing long-distance sound reception) Edwin H. Armstrong, U.S., 1912; (frequency modulation—FM) Edwin H. Armstrong, U.S., 1933
Radioactivity: (X-rays) William K. Roentgen, Germany, 1895; (radioactivity of uranium) Henri Becquerel, France, 1896; (radioactive elements, radium and polonium in uranium ore) Marie Sklodowska-Curie, Pierre Curie, France, 1898; (classification of alpha and beta particle radiation) Pierre Curie, France, 1900; (gamma radiation) Paul-Ulrich Villard, France, 1900; (carbon dating) Willard F. Libby et al., U.S., 1955
Rayon: *See* Fibers, man-made
Reaper: Cyrus McCormick, U.S., 1834
Relativity: (special and general theories of) Albert Einstein, Switzerland, Germany, U.S., 1905–53
Revolver: Samuel Colt, U.S., 1835
Rifle: (muzzle-loaded) Italy, Germany, c.1475; (breech-loaded) England, France, Germany, U.S., c.1866; (bolt-action) Paul von Mauser, Germany, 1889; (automatic) John Browning, U.S., 1918
Roller bearing: (wooden for cartwheel) Germany or France, c.100 B.C.
Rubber: (vulcanization process) Charles Goodyear, U.S., 1839
Safety match: *See* Match
Solar system, universe: (sun-centered universe) Nicolaus Copernicus, Warsaw, 1543; (establishment of planetary orbits as elliptical) Johannes Kepler, Germany, 1609; (infinity of universe) Giordano Bruno, Italian monk, 1584
Spectrum: (heterogeneity of light) Sir Isaac Newton, England, 1665–66
Spermatozoa: Anton van Leeuwenhoek, The Netherlands, 1683
Spinning: (spinning wheel) India, introduced to Europe in Middle Ages; (Saxony wheel, continuous spinning of wool or cotton yarn) England, c.1500–1600; (spinning jenny) James Hargreaves, England, 1764; (spinning frame) Sir Richard Arkwright, England, 1769; (spinning mule, completed mechanization of spinning, permitting production of yarn to keep up with demands of modern looms) Samuel Crompton, England, 1779
Steam engine: (first commercial version based on principles of French physicist Denis Papin) Thomas Savery, England, 1639; (atmospheric steam engine) Thomas Newcomen, England, 1705; (steam engine for pumping water from collieries) Savery, Newcomen, 1725; (modern condensing, double-acting) James Watt, England, 1782
Steam engine, railroad: *See* Locomotive
Steamship: Claude de Jouffroy d'Abbans, France, 1783; James Rumsey, U.S., 1787; John Fitch, U.S., 1790. All preceded Robert Fulton, U.S., 1807, credited with launching first commercially successful steamship
Sulfa drugs: (parent compound, para-aminobenzenesulfanomide) Paul Gelmo, Austria, 1908; (antibacterial activity) Gerhard Domagk, Germany, 1935
Syphilis, test for: *See* Wassermann test
Tank, military: Sir Ernest Swinton, England, 1914
Telegraph: Samuel F. B. Morse, U.S., 1837
Telephone: Alexander Graham Bell, U.S., 1876
Telescope: Hans Lippershey, The Netherlands, 1608
Television: (mechanical disk-scanning method) successfully demonstrated by J. L. Baird, England, C. F. Jenkins, U.S., 1926; (electronic scanning method) Vladimir K. Zworykin, U.S., 1928; (color, all-electronic) Zworykin, 1925; (color, mechanical disk) Baird, 1928; (color, compatible with black and white) George Valensi, France, 1938; (color, sequential rotating filter) Peter Goldmark, U.S., first introduced, 1951; (color, compatible with black and white) commercially introduced in U.S., National Television Systems Committee, 1953
Thermometer: (open-column) Galileo Galilei, c.1593; (clinical) Santorio Santorio, Padua, c.1615; (mercury, also Fahrenheit scale) Gabriel D. Fahrenheit, Germany, 1714; (centigrade scale) Anders Celsius, Sweden, 1742; (absolute-temperature, or Kelvin, scale) William Thompson, Lord Kelvin, England, 1848
Tire, pneumatic: Robert W. Thompson, England, 1845; (bicycle tire) John B. Dunlop, Northern Ireland, 1888
Toilet, flush: Product of Minoan civilization, Crete, c.2000 B.C. Alleged invention by "Thomas Crapper" is untrue.
Tractor: Benjamin Holt, U.S., 1900
Transformer, electric: William Stanley, U.S., 1885
Transistor: John Bardeen, William Shockley, Walter Brattain, U.S., 1948
Uncertainty principle: (that position and velocity of an object cannot both be measured exactly, at the same time) Werner Heisenberg, Germany, 1927
Vaccination: Edward Jenner, England, 1796
Vacuum tube: *See* Radio
Van Allen (radiation) Belt: (around the earth) James Van Allen, U.S., 1958
Vitamins: (hypothesis of disease deficiency) Sir F. G. Hopkins, Casimir Funk, England, 1912; (vitamin A) Elmer V. McCollum, M. Davis, U.S., 1912–14; (vitamin B) Elmer V. McCollum, U.S., 1915–16; (thiamin, B_1) Casimir Funk, England, 1912; (riboflavin, B_2) D. T. Smith, E. G. Hendrick, U.S., 1926; (niacin) Conrad Elvehjem, U.S., 1937; (B_6) Paul Gyorgy, U.S., 1934; (vitamin C) C. A. Holst, T. Froelich, Norway, 1912; (vitamin D) Elmer V. McCollum, U.S., 1922; (folic acid) Lucy Wills, England, 1933
Wassermann test: (for syphilis) August von Wassermann, Germany, 1906
Weaving, cloth: *See* Loom
Wheel: (cart, solid wood) Mesopotamia, c.3800–3600 B.C.
Windmill: Persia, c.600
X-ray: *See* Radioactivity
Xerography: Chester Carlson, U.S., 1938
Zero: India, c.600; (absolute zero, cessation of all molecular energy) William Thompson, Lord Kelvin, England, 1848

WEIGHTS & MEASURES

Measures and Weights

Source: Department of Commerce, National Bureau of Standards.

The International System (Metric)

The International System of Units is a modernized version of the metric system, established by international agreement, i.e. provides a logical and interconnected framework for all measurements in science, industry, and commerce. The system is built on a foundation of seven basic units, and all other units are derived from them. (Use of metric weights and measures was legalized in the United States in 1866, and our customary units of weights and measures are defined in terms of the meter and kilogram.)

Length. Meter. The meter is defined as 1,650,763.73 wavelengths in vacuum of the orange-red line of the spectrum of krypton-86.

Time. Second. The second is defined as the duration of 9,192,631,770 cycles of the radiation associated with a specified transition of the cesium 133 atom.

Mass. Kilogram. The standard for the kilogram is a cylinder of platinum-iridium alloy kept by the International Bureau of Weights and Measures at Paris. A duplicate at the National Bureau of Standards serves as the mass standard for the United States. The kilogram is the only base unit still defined by a physical object.

Temperature. Kelvin. The kelvin is defined as the fraction 1/273.16 of the thermodynamic temperature of the triple point of water; that is, the point at which water forms an interface of solid, liquid and vapor. This is defined as 0.01°C on the Centigrade or Celsius scale and 32.02°F on the Fahrenheit scale. The temperature 0°K is called "absolute zero."

Electric Current. Ampere. The ampere is defined as that current that, if maintained in each of two long parallel wires separated by one meter in free space, would produce a force between the two wires (due to their magnetic fields) of 2×10^{-7} newton for each meter of length. (A newton is the unit of force which when applied to one kilogram mass would experience an acceleration of one meter per second per second.)

Luminous Intensity. Candela. The candela is defined as the luminous intensity of 1/600,000 of a square meter of a cavity at the temperature of freezing platinum (2,042K).

Amount of Substance. Mole. The mole is the amount of substance of a system that contains as many elementary entities as there are atoms in 0.012 kilograms of carbon-12.

Tables of Metric Weights and Measures

LINEAR MEASURE

10 millimeters (mm) = 1 centimeter (cm)
10 centimeters = 1 decimeter (dm) = 100 millimeters
10 decimeters = 1 meter (m) = 1,000 millimeters
10 meters = 1 dekameter (dam)
10 dekameters = 1 hectometer (hm) = 100 meters
10 hectometers = 1 kilometer (km) = 1,000 meters

AREA MEASURE

100 square millimeters (mm^2) = 1 sq centimeter (cm^2)
10,000 square centimeters = 1 sq meter (m^2) = 1,000,000 sq millimeters
100 square meters = 1 are (a)
100 ares = 1 hectare (ha) = 10,000 sq meters
100 hectares = 1 sq kilometer (km^2) = 1,000,000 sq meters

VOLUME MEASURE

10 milliliters (ml) = 1 centiliter (cl)
10 centiliters = 1 deciliter (dl) = 100 milliliters
10 deciliters = 1 liter (1) = 1,000 milliliters
10 liters = 1 dekaliter (dal)
10 dekaliters = 1 hectoliter (hl) = 100 liters
10 hectoliters = 1 kiloliter (kl) = 1,000 liters

CUBIC MEASURE

1,000 cubic millimeters (mm^3) = 1 cu centimeter (cm^3)
1,000 cubic centimeters = 1 cu decimeter (dm^3) = 1,000,000 cu millimeters
1,000 cubic decimeters = 1 cu meter (m^3) = 1 stere = 1,000,000 cu centimeters = 1,000,000,000 cu millimeters

WEIGHT

10 milligrams (mg) = 1 centigram (cg)
10 centigrams = 1 decigram (dg) = 100 milligrams
10 decigrams = 1 gram (g) = 1,000 milligrams
10 grams = 1 dekagram (dag)
10 dekagrams = 1 hectogram (hg) = 100 grams
10 hectograms = 1 kilogram (kg) = 1,000 grams
1,000 kilograms = 1 metric ton (t)

Tables of Customary U.S. Weights and Measures

LINEAR MEASURE

12 inches (in.) = 1 foot (ft)
3 feet = 1 yard (yd)
5 1/2 yards = 1 rod (rd), pole, or perch (16 1/2 ft)
40 rods = 1 furlong (fur) = 220 yds = 660 ft
8 furlongs = 1 statute mile (mi.) = 1,760 yds = 5,280 ft
3 land miles = 1 league
5,280 feet = 1 statute or land mile
6,076.11549 feet = 1 international nautical mile

AREA MEASURE

144 square inches = 1 sq ft
9 square feet = 1 sq yd = 1,296 sq in.
30 1/4 square yards = 1 sq rd = 272 1/4 sq ft
160 square rods = 1 acre = 4,840 sq yds = 43,560 sq ft
640 acres = 1 sq mi.
1 mile square = 1 section (of land)
6 miles square = 1 township = 36 sections = 36 sq mi.

CUBIC MEASURE

1,728 cubic inches = 1 cu ft
27 cubic feet = 1 cu yd

LIQUID MEASURE

When necessary to distinguish the liquid pint or quart from the dry pint or quart, the word "liquid" or the abbreviation "liq" should be used in combination with the name or abbreviation of the liquid unit.

4 gills (gi) = 1 pint (pt) (= 28.875 cu in.)
2 pints = 1 quart (qt) (= 57.75 cu in.)
4 quarts = 1 gallon (gal) (= 231 cu in.) = 8 pts = 32 gills

APOTHECARIES FLUID MEASURE

60 minims (min.) = 1 fluid dram (fl dr) (= 0.2256 cu in.)
8 fluid drams = 1 fluid ounce (fl oz) (= 1.8047 cu in.)
16 fluid ounces = 1 pt (= 28.875 cu in.) = 128 fl drs
2 pints = 1 qt (= 57.75 cu in.) = 32 fl oz = 256 fl drs
4 quarts = 1 gal (= 231 cu in.) = 128 fl oz = 1,024 fl drs

DRY MEASURE

When necessary to distinguish the dry pint or quart from the liquid pint or quart; the word "dry" should be used in combination with the name or abbreviation of the dry unit.

2 pints = 1 qt (=67.2006 cu in.)
8 quarts = 1 peck (pk) (=537.605 cu in.) = 16 pts
4 pecks = 1 bushel (bu) (= 2,150.42 cu in.) = 32 qts

AVOIRDUPOIS WEIGHT

When necessary to distinguish the avoirdupois dram from the apothecaries dram, or to distinguish the avoirdupois dram or ounce from the fluid dram or ounce, or to distinguish the avoirdupois ounce or pound from the troy or apothecaries ounce or pound, the word "avoirdupois" or the abbreviation "avdp" should be used in combination with the name or abbreviation of the avoirdupois unit.
(The "grain" is the same in avoirdupois, troy, and apothecaries weights.)

27 11/32 grains = 1 dram (dr)
16 drams = 1 oz = 437 1/2 grains
16 ounces = 1 lb = 256 drams = 7,000 grains
100 pounds = 1 hundredweight (cwt)[1]
20 hundredweights = 1 ton (tn) = 2,000 lbs[1]

In "gross" or "long" measure, the following values are recognized:

112 pounds = 1 gross or long cwt[1]
20 gross or long hundredweights = 1 gross or long ton = 2,240 lbs[1]

1. When the terms "hundredweight" and "ton" are used unmodified, they are commonly understood to mean the 100-pound hundredweight and the 2,000-pound ton, respectively; these units may be designated "net" or "short" when necessary to distinguish them from the corresponding units in gross or long measure.

UNITS OF CIRCULAR MEASURE

Second (″) = —
Minute (′) = 60 seconds
Degree (°) = 60 minutes
Right angle = 90 degrees
Straight angle = 180 degrees
Circle = 360 degrees

TROY WEIGHT

24 grains = 1 pennyweight (dwt)
20 pennyweights = 1 ounce troy (oz t) = 480 grains
12 ounces troy = 1 pound troy (lb t) = 240 pennyweights = 5,760 grains

APOTHECARIES WEIGHT

20 grains = 1 scruple (s ap)
3 scruples = 1 dram apothecaries (dr ap) = 60 grains
8 drams apothecaries = 1 ounce apothecaries (oz ap) = 24 scruples = 480 grains
12 ounces apothecaries = 1 pound apothecaries (lb ap) = 96 drams apothecaries = 288 scruples = 5,760 grains

GUNTER'S OR SURVEYOR'S CHAIN MEASURE

7.92 inches = 1 link (li)
100 links = 1 chain (ch) = 4 rods = 66 ft
80 chains = 1 statute mile = 320 rods = 5,280 ft

Metric and U.S. Equivalents

1 angstrom[1] (light wave measurement)	0.1 millimicron 0.000 1 micron 0.000 000 1 millimeter 0.000 000 004 inch
1 cable's length	120 fathoms 720 feet 219.456 meters
1 centimeter	0.3937 inch
1 chain (Gunter's or surveyor's)	66 feet 20.1168 meters
1 decimeter	3.937 inches
1 dekameter	32.808 feet
1 fathom	6 feet 1.8288 meters
1 foot	0.3048 meter
1 furlong	10 chains (surveyor's) 660 feet 220 yards 1/8 statute mile 201.168 meters

1 inch	2.54 centimeters
1 kilometer	0.621 mile
1 league (land)	3 statute miles 4.828 kilometers
1 link (Gunter's or surveyor's)	7.92 inches 0.201 168 meter
1 meter	39.37 inches 1.094 yards
1 micron	0.001 millimeter 0.000 039 37 inch
1 mil	0.001 inch 0.025 4 millimeter
1 mile (statute or land)	5,280 feet 1.609 kilometers
1 mile (nautical international)	1.852 kilometers 1.151 statute miles 0.999 U.S. nautical miles
1 millimeter	0.03937 inch
1 millimicron (mμ)	0.001 micron 0.000 000 039 37 inch
1 nanometer	0.001 micrometer or 0.000 000 039 37 inch
1 point (typography)	0.013 837 inch 1/72 inch (approximately) 0.351 millimeter
1 rod, pole, or perch	16 1/2 feet 5.0292 meters
1 yard	0.9144 meter

AREAS OR SURFACES

1 acre	43,560 square feet 4,840 square yards 0.405 hectare
1 are	119.599 square yards 0.025 acre
1 hectare	2.471 acres
1 square centimeter	0.155 square inch
1 square decimeter	15.5 square inches
1 square foot	929.030 square centimeters
1 square inch	6.4516 square centimeters
1 square kilometer	0.386 square mile 247.105 acres
1 square meter	1.196 square yards 10.764 square feet
1 square mile	258.999 hectares
1 square millimeter	0.002 square inch
1 square rod, square pole or square perch	25.293 square meters
1 square yard	0.836 square meters

CAPACITIES OR VOLUMES

1 barrel, liquid	31 to 42 gallons[2]
1 barrel, standard for fruits, vegetables, and other dry commodities except cranberries	7,056 cubic inches 105 dry quarts 3.281 bushels, struck measure
1 barrel, standard, cranberry	5.286 cubic inches 86 45/64 dry quarts 2.709 bushels, struck measure
1 bushel (U.S.) struck measure	2,150.42 cubic inches 35.238 liters
1 bushel, heaped (U.S.)	2,747.715 cubic inches 1.278 bushels, struck measure[3]
1 cord (firewood)	128 cubic feet
1 cubic centimeter	0.061 cubic inches
1 cubic decimeter	61.024 cubic inches
1 cubic foot	7.481 gallons 28.316 cubic decimeters
1 cubic inch	0.554 fluid ounce 4.433 fluid drams 16.387 cubic centimeters
1 cubic meter	1.308 cubic yards
1 cubic yard	0.765 cubic meter
1 cup, measuring	8 fluid ounces 1/2 liquid pint
1 dram, fluid or liquid (U.S.)	1/8 fluid ounces 0.226 cubic inch 3.697 milliliters 1.041 British fluid drachms
1 dekaliter	2.642 gallons 1.135 pecks
1 gallon (U.S.)	231 cubic inches 3.785 liters 0.833 British gallon 128 U.S. fluid ounces
1 gallon (British Imperial)	277.42 cubic inches 1.201 U.S. gallons 4.546 liters 160 British fluid ounces
1 gill	7.219 cubic inches 4 fluid ounces 0.118 liter
1 hectoliter	26.418 gallons 2.838 bushels
1 liter	1.057 liquid quarts 0.908 dry quart 61.024 cubic inches
1 milliliter	0.271 fluid drams 16.231 minims 0.061 cubic inch
1 ounce, fluid or liquid (U.S.)	1.805 cubic inch 29.574 milliliters 1.041 British fluid ounces

1 peck	8.810 liters
1 pint, dry	33.600 cubic inches 0.551 liter
1 pint, liquid	28.875 cubic inches 0.473 liter
1 quart, dry (U.S.)	67.201 cubic inches 1.101 liters 0.969 British quart
1 quart, liquid (U.S.)	57.75 cubic inches 0.946 liter 0.833 British quart
1 quart (British)	69.354 cubic inches 1.032 U.S. dry quarts 1.201 U.S. liquid quarts
1 tablespoon, measuring	3 teaspoons 4 fluid drams 1/2 fluid ounce
1 teaspoon, measuring	1/3 tablespoon 1 1/3 fluid drams
1 assay ton[4]	29.167 grams
1 carat	200 milligrams 3.086 grains
1 dram, apothecaries	60 grains 3.888 grams
1 dram, avoirdupois	27 11/32 (=27.344) grains 1.772 grams
1 grain	64.798 91 milligrams
1 gram	15.432 grains 0.035 ounce, avoirdupois
1 hundredweight, gross or long[5]	112 pounds 50.802 kilograms
1 hundredweight, net or short	100 pounds 45.359 kilograms
1 kilogram	2.205 pounds
1 microgram [μg (the Greek letter mu in combination with the letter g)]	0.000 001 gram
1 milligram	0.015 grain
1 ounce, avoirdupois	437.5 grains 0.911 troy or apothecaries ounce 28.350 grams
1 ounce, troy or apothecaries	480 grains 1.097 avoirdupois ounces 31.103 grams
1 pennyweight	1.555 grams
1 point	0.01 carat 2 milligrams
1 pound, avoirdupois	7,000 grains 1.215 troy or apothecaries pounds 453.592 37 grams
1 pound, troy or apothecaries	5,760 grains 0.823 avoirdupois pound 373.242 grams
1 ton, gross or long[5]	2,204 pounds 1.12 net tons 1.016 metric tons
1 ton, metric	2,204.623 pounds 0.984 gross ton 1.102 net tons
1 ton, net or short	2,000 pounds 0.893 gross ton 0.907 metric ton

1. The angstrom is basically defined as 10^{-10} meter. 2. There is a variety of "barrels" established by law or usage. For example, federal taxes on fermented liquors are based on a barrel of 31 gallons; many state laws fix the "barrel for liquids" at 31 1/2 gallons; one state fixes a 36-gallon barrel for cistern measurement; federal law recognizes a 40-gallon barrel for "proof spirits"; by custom, 42 gallons comprise a barrel of crude oil or petroleum products for statistical purposes, and this equivalent is recognized "for liquids" by four states. 3. Frequently recognized as 1 1/4 bushels, struck measure. 4. Used in assaying. The assay ton bears the same relation to the milligram that a ton of 2,000 pounds avoirdupois bears to the ounce troy; hence the weight in milligrams of precious metal obtained from one assay ton of ore gives directly the number of troy ounces to the net ton. 5. The gross or long ton and hundredweight are used commercially in the United States to only a limited extent, usually in restricted industrial fields. These units are the same as the British "ton" and "hundredweight."

Miscellaneous Units of Measure

Acre: An area of 43,560 square feet. Originally, the area a yoke of oxen could plow in one day.

Agate: Originally a measurement of type size (5 1/2 points). Now equal to 1/14 inch. Used in printing for measuring column length.

Ampere: Unit of electric current. A potential difference of one volt across a resistance of one ohm produces a current of one ampere.

Astronomical Unit (A.U.): 93,000,000 miles, the average distance of the earth from the sun. Used in astronomy.

Bale: A large bundle of goods. In the U.S., the approximate weight of a bale of cotton is 500 pounds. The weight varies in other countries.

Board Foot (fbm): 144 cubic inches (12 in. x 12 in. x 1 in.). Used for lumber.

Bolt: 40 yards. Used for measuring cloth.

BTU: British thermal unit. Amount of heat needed to increase the temperature of one pound of water by one degree Fahrenheit (252 calories).

Carat (c): 200 milligrams or 3.086 grains troy.

Originally the weight of a seed of the carob tree in the Mediterranean region. Used for weighing precious stones. *See also* Karat.

Chain (ch): a chain 66 feet or one-tenth of a furlong in length, divided into 100 parts called links. One mile is equal to 80 chains. Used in surveying and sometimes called Gunter's or surveyor's chain.

Cubit: 18 inches or 45.72 cm. Derived from distance between elbow and tip of middle finger.

Decibel: Unit of relative loudness. One decibel is the smallest amount of change detectable by the human ear.

Ell, English: 1 1/4 yards or 1/32 bolt. Used for measuring cloth.

Freight Ton (also called Measurement Ton): 40 cubic feet of merchandise. Used for cargo freight.

Great Gross: 12 gross or 1728.

Gross: 12 dozen or 144.

Hand: 4 inches or 10.16 cm. Derived from the width of the hand. Used for measuring the height of horses at withers.

Hertz: Modern unit for measurement of electromagnetic wave frequencies (equivalent to "cycles per second").

Hogshead: (hhd): 2 liquid barrels or 14,653 cubic inches.

Horsepower: The power needed to lift 33,000 pounds a distance of one foot in one minute (about 1 1/2 times the power an average horse can exert). Used for measuring power of steam engines, etc.

Karat (kt): A measure of the purity of gold, indicating how many parts out of 24 are pure. For example, 18 karat gold is 3/4 pure. Sometimes spelled *carat.*

Knot: Not a distance, but the rate of speed of one nautical mile per hour. Used for measuring speed of ships.

League: Rather indefinite and varying measure, but usually estimated at 3 miles in English-speaking countries.

Light-Year: 5,880,000,000,000 miles, the distance light travels in a year at the rate of 186,281.7 miles per second. (If an astronomical unit were represented by one inch, a light-year would be represented by about one mile.) Used for measurements in interstellar space.

Magnum: Two-quart bottle. Used for measuring wine, etc.

Ohm: Unit of electrical resistance. A circuit in which a potential difference of one volt produces a current of one ampere has a resistance of one ohm.

Parsec: Approximately 3.26 light-years of 19.2 trillion miles. Term is combination of first syllables of *par*allax and *sec*ond, and distance is that of imaginary star when lines drawn from it to both earth and sun form a maximum angle or parallax of one second (1/3600 degree). Used for measuring interstellar distances.

Pi (π): 3.14159265+. The ratio of the circumference of a circle to its diameter. For practical purposes, the value is used to four decimal places: 3.1416.

Pica: 1/6 inch or 12 points. Used in printing for measuring column width, etc.

Pipe: 2 hogsheads. Used for measuring wine and other liquids.

Point: .013837 (approximately 1/72) inch or 1/12 pica. Used in printing for measuring type size.

Quintal: 100,000 grams or 220.46 pounds avoirdupois.

Quire: Used for measuring paper. Sometimes 24 sheets but more often 25. There are 20 quires in a ream.

Ream: Used for measuring paper. Sometimes 480 sheets, but more often 500 sheets.

Roentgen: Dosage unit of radiation exposure produced by X-rays.

Score: 20 units.

Sound, Speed of: Usually placed at 1,088 ft per second at 32°F at sea level. It varies at other temperatures and in different media.

Span: 9 inches or 22.86 cm. Derived from the distance between the end of the thumb and the end of the little finger when both are outstretched.

Square: 100 square feet. Used in building.

Stone: Legally 14 pounds avoirdupois in Great Britain.

Therm: 100,000 BTU's.

Township: U. S. land measurement of almost 36 square miles. The south border is 6 miles long. The east and west borders, also 6 miles long, follow the meridians, making the north border slightly less than 6 miles long. Used in surveying.

Tun: 252 gallons, but often larger. Used for measuring wine and other liquids.

Watt: Unit of power. The power used by a current of one ampere across a potential difference of one volt equals one watt.

Kelvin Scale

Absolute zero, −273.16° on the Celsius (Centigrade) scale, is 0° Kelvin. Thus, degrees Kelvin are equivalent to degrees Celsius plus 273.16. The freezing point of water, 0°C. and 32°F., is 273.16°K. The conversion formula is $K^\circ = C^\circ + 273.16$.

Conversion of Miles to Kilometers and Kilometers to Miles

Miles	Kilometers	Miles	Kilometers	Miles	Kilometers	Kilometers	Miles	Kilometers	Miles	Kilometers	Miles
1	1.6	8	12.8	60	96.5	1	0.6	8	4.9	60	37.2
2	3.2	9	14.4	70	112.6	2	1.2	9	5.5	70	43.4
3	4.8	10	16.0	80	128.7	3	1.8	10	6.2	80	49.7
4	6.4	20	32.1	90	144.8	4	2.4	20	12.4	90	55.9
5	8.0	30	48.2	100	160.9	5	3.1	30	18.6	100	62.1
6	9.6	40	64.3	1,000	1609	6	3.7	40	24.8	1,000	621
7	11.2	50	80.4			7	4.3	50	31.0		

Bolts and Screws: Conversion from Fractions of an Inch to Millimeters

Inch	mm	Inch	mm	Inch	mm	Inch	mm
1/64	0.40	17/64	6.75	33/64	13.10	49/64	19.45
1/32	0/79	9/32	7.14	17/32	13.50	25/32	19.84
3/64	1.19	19/64	7.54	35/64	13.90	51/64	20.24
1/16	1.59	5/16	7.94	9/16	14.29	13/16	20.64
5/64	1.98	21/64	8.33	37/64	14.69	53/64	21.03
3/32	2.38	11/32	8.73	19/32	15.08	27/32	21.43
7/64	2.78	23/64	9.13	39/64	15.48	55/64	21.83
1/8	3.18	3/8	9.53	5/8	15.88	7/8	22.23
9/64	3.57	25/64	9.92	41/64	16.27	57/64	22.62
5/32	3.97	13/32	10.32	21/32	16.67	29/32	23.02
11/64	4.37	27/64	10.72	43/64	17.06	59/64	23.42
3/16	4.76	7/16	11.11	11/64	17.46	15/16	23.81
13/64	5.16	29/64	11.51	45/64	17.86	61/64	24.21
7/32	5.56	15/32	11.91	23/32	18.26	31/32	24.61
15/64	5.95	31/64	12.30	47/64	18.65	63/64	25.00
1/4	6.35	1/2	12.70	3/4	19.05	1	25.40

U.S.—Metric Cooking Conversions

U.S. customary system				Metric			
Capacity		Weight		Capacity		Weight	
1/5 teaspoon	1 milliliter	1 fluid oz	30 milliliters	1 milliliter	1/5 teaspoon	1 gram	.035 ounce
1 teaspoon	5 ml		28 grams	5 ml	1 teaspoon	100 grams	3.5 ounces
1 tablespoon	15 ml	1 pound	454 grams	15 ml	1 tablespoon	500 grams	1.10 pounds
1/5 cup	50 ml			34 ml	1 fluid oz	1 kilogram	2.205 pounds
1 cup	240 ml			100 ml	3.4 fluid oz		35 oz
2 cups (1 pint)	470 ml			240 ml	1 cup		
4 cups (1 quart)	.95 liter			1 liter	34 fluid oz		
4 quarts (1 gal.)	3.8 liters				4.2 cups		
					2.1 pints		
					1.06 quarts		
					0.26 gallon		

Cooking Measurement Equivalents

16 tablespoons = 1 cup
12 tablespoons = 3/4 cup
10 tablespoons + 2 teaspoons = 2/3 cup
8 tablespoons = 1/2 cup
6 tablespoons = 3/8 cup
5 tablespoons + 1 teaspoon = 1/3 cup
4 tablespoons = 1/4 cup

2 tablespoons = 1/8 cup
2 tablespoons + 2 teaspoons = 1/6 cup
1 tablespoon = 1/16 cup
2 cups = 1 pint
2 pints = 1 quart
3 teaspoons = 1 tablespoon
48 teaspoons = 1 cup

Conversion Factors

To change	To	Multiply by
acres	hectares	.4047
acres	square feet	43,560
acres	square miles	.001562
atmospheres	cms. of mercury	76
BTU	horsepower-hour	.0003931
BTU	kilowatt-hour	.0002928
BTU/hour	watts	.2931
bushels	cubic inches	2150.4
bushels (U.S.)	hectoliters	.3524
centimeters	inches	.3937
centimeters	feet	.03281
circumference	radians	6.283
cubic feet	cubic meters	.0283
cubic meters	cubic feet	35.3145
cubic meters	cubic yards	1.3079
cubic yards	cubic meters	.7646
degrees	radians	.01745
dynes	grams	.00102
fathoms	feet	6.0
feet	meters	.3048
feet	miles (nautical)	.0001645
feet	miles (statute)	.0001894
feet/second	miles/hour	.6818
furlongs	feet	660.0
furlongs	miles	.125
gallons (U.S.)	liters	3.7853
grains	grams	.0648
grams	grains	15.4324
grams	ounces avdp	.0353
grams	pounds	.002205
hectares	acres	2.4710
hectoliters	bushels (U.S.)	2.8378
horsepower	watts	745.7
hours	days	.04167
inches	millimeters	25.4000
inches	centimeters	2.5400
kilograms	pounds avdp or t	2.2046
kilometers	miles	.6214
kilowatts	horsepower	1.341
knots	nautical miles/hour	1.0
knots	statute miles/hour	1.151
liters	gallons (U.S.)	.2642
liters	pecks	.1135
liters	pints (dry)	1.8162
liters	pints (liquid)	2.1134
liters	quarts (dry)	.9081
liters	quarts (liquid)	1.0567
meters	feet	3.2808
meters	miles	.0006214
meters	yards	1.0936
metric tons	tons (long)	.9842
metric tons	tons (short)	1.1023
miles	kilometers	1.6093
miles	feet	5280
miles (nautical)	miles (statute)	1.1516
miles (statute)	miles (nautical)	.8684
miles/hour	feet/minute	88
millimeters	inches	.0394
ounces avdp.	grams	28.3495
ounces	pounds	.0625
ounces (troy)	ounces (avdp)	1.09714
pecks	liters	8.8096
pints (dry)	liters	.5506
pints (liquid)	liters	.4732
pounds ap or t	kilograms	.3782
pounds avdp	kilograms	.4536
pounds	ounces	16
quarts (dry)	liters	1.1012
quarts (liquid)	liters	.9463
radians	degrees	57.30
rods	meters	5.029
rods	feet	16.5
square feet	square meters	.0929
square kilometers	square miles	.3861
square meters	square feet	10.7639
square meters	square yards	1.1960
square miles	square kilometers	2.5900
square yards	square meters	.8361
tons (long)	metric tons	1.1060
tons (short)	metric tons	.9072
tons (long)	pounds	2240
tons (short)	pounds	2000
watts	BTU/hour	3.4129
watts	horsepower	.001341
yards	meters	.9144
yards	miles	.0005682

Fahrenheit and Celsius (Centigrade) Scales

Zero on the Fahrenheit scale represents the temperature produced by the mixing of equal weights of snow and common salt.

	F	C
Boiling point of water	212°	100°
Freezing point of water	32°	0°
Absolute zero	−459.6°	−273.1°

Absolute zero is theoretically the lowest possible temperature, the point at which all molecular motion would cease.

To convert Fahrenheit to Celsius (Centigrade), subtract 32 and multiply by 5/9.

To convert Celsius (Centigrade) to Fahrenheit, multiply by 9/5 and add 32.

° Centigrade	° Fahrenheit	° Centigrade	° Fahrenheit
−273.1	**−459.6**	30	86
−250	−418	35	95
−200	−328	40	104
−150	−238	45	113
−100	−148	50	122
− 50	− 58	55	131
− 40	− 40	60	140
− 30	− 22	65	149
− 20	− 4	70	158
− 10	14	75	167
0	**32**	80	176
5	41	85	185
10	50	90	194
15	59	95	203
20	68	**100**	**212**
25	77		

Prefixes and Multiples

Prefix	Symbol	Equivalent	Multiple/ submultiple	Prefix	Symbol	Equivalent	Multiple/ submultiple
atto	a	quintillionth part	10^{-18}	deci	d	tenth part	10^{-1}
femto	f	quadrillionth part	10^{-15}	deka	da	tenfold	10
pico	p	trillionth part	10^{-12}	hecto	h	hundredfold	10^{2}
nano	n	billionth part	10^{-9}	kilo	k	thousandfold	10^{3}
micro	μ	millionth part	10^{-6}	mega	M	millionfold	10^{6}
milli	m	thousandth part	10^{-3}	giga	G	billionfold	10^{9}
centi	c	hundredth part	10^{-2}	tera	T	trillionfold	10^{12}

Common Formulas

Circumference

Circle: $C=\pi d$, in which π is 3.1416 and d the diameter.

Area

Triangle: $A=\frac{ab}{2}$, in which a is the base and b the height.

Square: $A=a^2$, in which a is one of the sides.

Rectangle: $A=ab$, in which a is the base and b the height.

Trapezoid: $A=\frac{h(a+b)}{2}$, in which h is the height, a the longer parallel side, and b the shorter.

Regular pentagon: $A=1.720a^2$, in which a is one of the sides.

Regular hexagon: $A=2.598a^2$, in which a is one of the sides.

Regular octagon: $A=4.828a^2$, in which a is one of the sides.

Circle: $A=\pi r^2$, in which π is 3.1416 and r the radius.

Volume

Cube: $V=a^3$, in which a is one of the edges.

Rectangular prism: $V=abc$, in which a is the length, b the width, and c the depth.

Pyramid: $V=\frac{Ah}{3}$, in which A is the area of the base and h the height.

Cylinder: $V=\pi r^2 h$, in which π is 3.1416, r the radius of the base, and h the height.

Cone: $V=\frac{\pi r^2 h}{3}$, in which π is 3.1416, r the radius of the base, and h the height.

Sphere: $V=\frac{4\pi r^3}{3}$, in which π is 3.1416 and r the radius.

Miscellaneous

Speed per second acquired by falling body: $v=32t$, in which t is the time in seconds.

Distance in feet traveled by falling body: $d=16t^2$, in which t is the time in seconds.

Speed of sound in feet per second through any given temperature of air: $V=\frac{1087\sqrt{273+t}}{16.52}$, in which t is the temperature Centigrade.

Cost in cents of operation of electrical device: $C=\frac{Wtc}{1000}$, in which W is the number of watts, t the time in hours, and c the cost in cents per kilowatt-hour.

Conversion of matter into energy (Einstein's Theorem): $E=mc^2$, in which E is the energy in ergs, m the mass of the matter in grams, and c the speed of light in centimeters per second. ($c^2=9\cdot10^{20}$).

Decimal Equivalents of Common Fractions

1/2	.5000	1/10	.1000	2/7	.2857	3/11	.2727	5/9	.5556	7/11	.6364
1/3	.3333	1/11	.0909	2/9	.2222	4/5	.8000	5/11	.4545	7/12	.5833
1/4	.2500	1/12	.0833	2/11	.1818	4/7	.5714	5/12	.4167	8/9	.8889
1/5	.2000	1/16	.0625	3/4	.7500	4/9	.4444	6/7	.8571	8/11	.7273
1/6	.1667	1/32	.0313	3/5	.6000	4/11	.3636	6/11	.5455	9/10	.9000
1/7	.1429	1/64	.0156	3/7	.4286	5/6	.8333	7/8	.8750	9/11	.8182
1/8	.1250	2/3	.6667	3/8	.3750	5/7	.7143	7/9	.7778	10/11	.9091
1/9	.1111	2/5	.4000	3/10	.3000	5/8	.6250	7/10	.7000	11/12	.9167

Roman Numerals

Roman numerals are expressed by letters of the alphabet and are rarely used today except for formality or variety.

There are three basic principles for reading Roman numerals:

1. A letter repeated once or twice repeats its value that many times. (XXX=30, CC=200, etc.).

2. One or more letters placed after another letter of greater value increases the greater value by the amount of the smaller. (VI=6, LXX=70, MCC=1200, etc.).

3. A letter placed before another letter of greater value decreases the greater value by the amount of the smaller. (IV=4, XC=90, CM=900, etc.).

Letter	Value	Letter	Value	Letter	Value	Letter	Value	Letter	Value
I	1	VII	7	XXX	30	LXXX	80	$\overline{V}$	5,000
II	2	VIII	8	XL	40	XC	90	$\overline{X}$	10,000
III	3	IX	9	L	50	C	100	$\overline{L}$	50,000
IV	4	X	10	LX	60	D	500	$\overline{C}$	100,000
V	5	XX	20	LXX	70	M	1,000	$\overline{D}$	500,000
VI	6							$\overline{M}$	1,000,000

Mean and Median

The mean, also called the average, of a series of quantities is obtained by finding the sum of the quantities and dividing it by the number of quantities. In the series 1,3,5,18,19,20,25, the mean or average is 13—i.e., 91 divided by 7.

The median of a series is that point which so divides it that half the quantities are on one side, half on the other. In the above series, the median is 18.

The median often better expresses the common-run, since it is not, as is the mean, affected by an excessively high or low figure. In the series 1,3,4,7,-55, the median of 4 is a truer expression of the common-run than is the mean of 14.

Prime Numbers Between 1 and 1,000

1	2	3	5	7	11	13	17	19	23
29	31	37	41	43	47	53	59	61	67
71	73	79	83	89	97	101	103	107	109
113	127	131	137	139	149	151	157	163	167
173	179	181	191	193	197	199	211	223	227
229	233	239	241	251	257	263	269	271	277
281	283	293	307	311	313	317	331	337	347
349	353	359	367	373	379	383	389	397	401
409	419	421	431	433	439	443	449	457	461
463	467	479	487	491	499	503	509	521	523
541	547	557	563	569	571	577	587	593	599
601	607	613	617	619	631	641	643	647	653
659	661	673	677	683	691	701	709	719	727
733	739	743	751	757	761	769	773	787	797
809	811	821	823	827	829	839	853	857	859
863	877	881	883	887	907	911	919	929	937
941	947	953	967	971	977	983	991	997	(1009)

Definitions of Gold Terminology

The term "fineness" defines a gold content in parts per thousand. For example, a gold nugget containing 885 parts of pure gold, 100 parts of silver, and 15 parts of copper would be considered 885-fine.

The word "karat" indicates the proportion of solid gold in an alloy based on a total of 24 parts. Thus, 14-karat (14K) gold indicates a composition of 14 parts of gold and 10 parts of other metals.

The term "gold-filled" is used to describe articles of jewelry made of base metal which are covered on one or more surfaces with a layer of gold alloy. No article having a gold alloy portion of less than one twentieth by weight may be marked "gold-filled." Articles may be marked "rolled gold plate" provided the proportional fraction and fineness designations are also shown.

Electroplated jewelry items carrying at least 7 millionths of an inch of gold on significant surfaces may be labeled "electroplate." Plate thicknesses less than this may be marked "gold flashed" or "gold washed."

Portraits and Designs of U.S. Paper Currency[1]

Currency	Portrait	Design on back
$1	Washington	ONE between obverse and reverse of Great Seal of U.S.
$2[2]	Jefferson	Monticello
$2[3]	Jefferson	"The Signing of the Declaration of Independence"
$5	Lincoln	Lincoln Memorial
$10	Hamilton	U.S. Treasury Building
$20	Jackson	White House

Currency	Portrait	Design on back
$50	Grant	U.S. Capitol
$100	Franklin	Independence Hall
$500	McKinley	Ornate FIVE HUNDRED
$1,000	Cleveland	Ornate ONE THOUSAND
$5,000	Madison	Ornate FIVE THOUSAND
$10,000	Chase	Ornate TEN THOUSAND
$100,000[4]	Wilson	Ornate ONE HUNDRED THOUSAND

1. Denominations of $500 and higher were discontinued in 1969. 2. Discontinued in 1966. 3. New issue, April 13, 1976. 4. For use only in transactions between Federal Reserve System and Treasury Department.

The Year in Space

A New Beginning?

Studies of the X-rays reaching the Earth from space have led to a new theory regarding the formation of the universe. According to this new thinking, the evolution of galaxies from whatever existed beforehand depended on a sequence of catastrophic explosions such as those associated with supernovas. Earlier theory held that gravity pulled together dust to form stars, then galaxies, etc., even though it has long been known that gravitational forces are quite weak and may not have been strong enough to accomplish the task. However, shock waves from supernova explosions may have provided sufficient force to coalesce primordial dust into stars, as when our sun was formed 4.6 billion years ago. It was proposed that a chain reaction of up to 100 supernovas exploding over the relatively short time of 1 million years could have been sufficient to form the core of galaxies. The theory receives some support from the discovery of a large and extremely hot gas bubble in the constellation Cygnus (the Swan). The bubble, possibly the remnant of between 30 and 100 supernovas that occurred three to five million years ago, contains matter equivalent to the mass of 10,000 suns, and has a temperature measured at 3.5 million degrees Fahrenheit. Alternatively, magnetohydrodynamic (MHD) pinch effects have also been proposed as the means by which a pre-existing plasma of protons and electrons may have been formed into hydrogen atoms, the simplest form of elemental matter. MHD is being studied in laboratories as a possible new energy conversion process for the production of electric power. Another hint at the beginning of the universe is provided by the finding of a slight anomaly in the blackbody radiation thought to be the remnant of the original "big bang." This anomaly may emanate from a supercluster of galaxies in the constellation Virgo. The cluster may contain 30 to 40% more galaxies than should occupy the volume of space, about 2 million light-years across, in which they may exist. (A light-year is the distance that light, traveling at 186,000 miles per second, reaches in one earth year, or about 5.88 trillion miles.) The problem for astronomers is that such a cluster is too large to have formed since the postulated beginning of the universe, so it may have been present in some form at the beginning. This is in direct conflict with the traditional view that the original structure of the universe was homogeneous, not "lumpy." Just how old the universe actually is was also questioned by new measurements of radio emissions from hydrogen gas clouds in distant galaxies. The data indicate an age of only 9 billion years, rather than the traditionally accepted 15–18 billion years.

Largest Object, Other Observations

Using a large radiotelescope in Effelsberg, West Germany, astronomers have identified what may be the largest known object in the observable universe. The object, one of several associated with four well-known quasars including quasar 3C345, is believed to stretch 24 megaparsecs, or about 78 million light years. Our own Milky Way galaxy has also been found to be a bit larger than previously thought: it is surrounded on its perimeter by a gaseous halo extending to about 15 kiloparsecs. The gas is very hot, about 100,000° Kelvin, but contains only three particles per 10,000 cubic meters, about five times as rarified as the best vacuum ever produced on earth. Other galaxies may have similar halos.

The second and third known binary pulsars, designated PSR 0820+02 and PSR 0655+64, were identified in 1980. Pulsars are rarely known to be associated with binary systems, although most stars in the universe are binaries or multiples. PSR 0820+02 has an orbital period of 1700 days; that for PSR 0655+64 is 24 hours, 41 minutes. The latter system has an unusually circular orbit and is only 1000 light-years from earth.

A vibrating neutron star, a supernova remnant in the Large Magellanic Cloud, has been suggested as the plausible source for a recently detected momentary burst of X-rays. This is the first time that such a burst has been identified with an observable stellar object and if true, according to theory, gives further evidence for the existence of gravity waves.

Closer to Home: The Solar System

Major new observations of the bodies in our solar system (including the Earth) continue to be made from the massive data accumulated by the several interplanetary vehicles launched during the past few years. Additional information is forthcoming from 1980-vintage spacecraft sent to examine the Sun, Venus, and our own planet. A few highlights:

The Sun. 1980 saw the periodic maximum in the Sun's 11-year sunspot cycle. Evidence has now been found to explain this well-known phenomenon. It has been determined that certain band-like zones on the Sun's surface move faster, by about three meters per second (seven miles per hour) than neighboring zones. The effect resembles the red and white stripes on a rotating barber pole. Sunspots apparently form along the boundaries between these zones, especially as the zones approach the Sun's equator. Movement of the zones may be driven by oscillations in the Sun's magnetic field originating deep within its interior. Sunspot activity creates magnetic disturbances in the earth's atmosphere which disrupt radio and other communications. Sunspots may also have an effect on our weather.

On Feb. 14, 1980, NASA launched the Solar Maximum Mission (Solar Max, for short) carrying seven instruments to study a wide band of ultraviolet, X-ray, and gamma-ray wavelengths. Solar Max will concentrate on solar flares, extremely large and powerful outbursts of particles and energy from the Sun's surface. The sun-watching satellite, incidentally, is the first Modular Multimission Spacecraft (MMS), consisting of standardized modules fitted to an equally standardized frame. The frame is equipped with grapples, enabling it to be picked up by the Space Shuttle, an event planned for 1982.

The Sun appears to be in a temporary shrinking phase, losing about five feet per hour in the horizontal dimension and half that vertically. Because it is so rapid, the change in the Sun's size is believed to be part of a cyclical variation. Records of ancient solar eclipses, furthermore, indicate that the Sun has shrunk before, only to expand again later on.

Venus. Radar mapping of Venus by the orbiting satellite *Pioneer Venus* has now produced pictures of more than 83% of the planet's surface. Radar mapping is necessary since the dense and multilayered Venusian atmosphere prevents visual observations. Surface features indicate that Venus has little if any of the tectonic, or geologic, plate activity known to cause earthquakes and continental drift on our own planet. In fact, about 84% of Venus seems to be encircled by a "supercontinent" containing very large elevated regions. One such region, Ishtar Terra, is as large as the continental United States, and contains a high plain, the Lakshmi Planum, rising 3300 meters (10,834 feet) above what would be "sea level," if Venus had seas. The largest mountainous massif on Ishtar Terra is Maxwell Montes, which is two kilometers (1.2 miles) taller than Mt. Everest and may be of volcanic origin.

Revised interpretations of gas chromatograph and mass spectrometry (instruments for chemical analysis of gases) data on the atmosphere of Venus shows that the 60 parts per million of oxygen originally thought to be present is actually argon, and what was first thought to be argon is carbon monoxide. In what must be the worst case of "air" pollution on record, scientists are as yet unable to determine how much free oxygen exists in the Venusian atmosphere. Mysterious dark spots in the planet's ultraviolet radiation bands may be due to sulfur, sulfur dioxide or, as one report had it, "something else."

Mars. *Viking 2,* which landed on Mars Sept. 3, 1976, has stopped transmitting data after its batteries finally ran down too much to be useful. The remaining instruments on station include *Lander 1,* which continues to send minimal data and photographs, and *Viking 1,* still in orbit around the planet. *Viking 1,* however, literally ran out of gas (used to control its position) in mid-1980.

There is evidence that the Solis Lacus (Lake of the Sun) area of Mars, located about 25° south of the equator, periodically outgasses unusual amounts of water vapor. There are no open bodies of water on the planet's surface. Rather, the outgassing may originate from subterranean ice, which could be partially melted. Elsewhere on Mars, the huge Tharsis Rise formation may not be a geologic bulge but merely a thickening of the crust. The formation contains several volcanoes, including the enormous Olympus Mons, three times as high as Mt. Everest and as wide as New Mexico. Tharsis Rise is large enough to have caused changes in Mars' axial tilt, which could have produced major changes in the planet's weather.

Mars' two moons, Phobos and Diemos, have not escaped attention. Measurements of light reflected from their surfaces indicate that they are probably both composed of material similar to a type of meteorite known as carbonaceous chondrites. The two satellites look different because of differences in their surface structures but, chemically, they are quite the same.

Jupiter. This colorful giant and its many interesting moons continue to garner most of the astronomical attention in our solar system. The Jovian moon count rises periodically: satellite number 15, designated 1979 S2, was found slightly more than 151,000 kilometers above Jupiter's spectacular atmosphere. It lies between the orbits of Amalthea (107,000 km) and Io (350,000 km) with an orbital period of 16 hours, 16 minutes. The satellite's only observed dimension is a scant 80 km (about 50 miles), but it may very well be elongated, with its long axis permanently pointed toward Jupiter's surface. Little is known about the structure of the new moon, but its surface is dark and similar to that of Amalthea.

The violently volcanic Jovian moon, Io, has been found to emit radiation at the rate of 48 ± 24 microcalories per square centimeter per second, about 30 times that of the Earth and 90 times that of our moon. Still, temperatures on Io average a chilly −148°C. As much as 200 square kilometers (77 square miles) of the satellite's surface may be at 327°C (621°F)—these are the volcanic hot spots—and 40,000 square kilometers (15,376 square miles) may be a balmy 27°C (81°F).

Maps of much of the surfaces of Jupiter's major, or Galilean, moons has been completed.

Saturn. In addition to the finding of additional ring structure and satellites, the length of the Saturnian day has been precisely determined to be 16 hours, 39.9 minutes ± 0.3 minutes. The ringed planet has at least 13 moons and may have as many as 18, according to data gathered from long-ranging satellites and observations from the Earth. A most interesting finding is that at least one, and perhaps two, of Saturns moons apparently share their orbits with additional objects, which oscillate about gravitationally stable positions ahead of, and behind the primary satellite. One or more such objects have been spotted in the orbit of Dione, about 377,00 kilometers (235,000 miles) from the planet. Some 74° ahead of Dione lies an object tentatively named Dione B. It is pulling ahead of Dione at the current rate of 0.026° per day, but is probably oscillating about a point 60° in front of Dione, the so-called L-4 libration point in the Saturn-Dione system. Another object has been found at the L-5 trailing libration point, but data are still sketchy. The same phenomenon may also exist for the Saturnian satellite known as the "Fountain-Larson object" after its discoverers. Voyager 1 passed Saturn in September, 1980; Voyager 2 is scheduled to pass the planet in 1981.

Uranus. A ring system, similar to but much fainter than that of Saturn, is now known to encircle the planet Uranus. The rotational period of Uranus has

(Continued on page 393)

Major U.S. Space Projects

Scientific Satellites

Applications Technology Satellite (ATS). Series of spacecraft designed to test techniques and equipment in space for future communications, weather, and navigational systems. *ATS-1* was launched Dec. 6, 1966. *ATS-6*, the most powerful and versatile communications satellite ever developed, was launched on May 30, 1974. It is transmitting educational TV programs and health services to scores of isolated communities in Appalachia, the Rocky Mountains, and Alaska, as well as to school children and adults in 5,000 isolated villages and cities in India.

Biosatellite. Earth-orbiting biological laboratory, carrying a variety of plants and animals into space to determine effects of weightlessness (zero gravity). *Biosatellite 1*, launched Dec. 14, 1966, was unrecovered. *Biosatellite 2*, launched Sept. 7, 1967, was highly successful. The last in the series, *Biosatellite 3*, launched June 29, 1969, was returned to Earth because of the deteriorating condition of its primate passenger.

Explorer. Largest group of satellites in U.S. space program, used for a variety of scientific purposes in atmosphere, ionosphere and interplanetary space. *Explorer 1*, launched July 1, 1958, was America's first successful satellite. It confirmed the existence of the Van Allen radiation belts which girdle the Earth. First Explorer weighed about 18 lb; current spacecraft average about 100 lb, but some weigh as much as 500 lb. Orbits and design vary.

Geostationary Scientific Satellite (GEOS). A series of satellites designed to study the magnetosphere, that region of near-Earth space where the magnetic field of the Earth still plays a dominating role. *GEOS-2*, launched July 14, 1978, for the European Space Agency (ESA), carried out the mission originally conceived for *GEOS-1*, which did not achieve proper orbit April 20, 1977, due to a premature separation of the Delta second and third stages.

Helios. A joint U.S.-German program to obtain new information on interplanetary space in the region close to the Sun. *Helios 1*, launched Dec. 10, 1974, flew within 28 million miles of the Sun—closer than any previous spacecraft—at times encountering temperatures hot enough to melt lead (700 degrees F). *Helios 2* was launched on Jan. 15, 1976.

High Energy Astronomy Observatory (HEAO). Series of space platforms designed for research in high-energy astrophysics—the domain of peculiar astronomical objects such as quasars, pulsars, and black holes in space. Weighing 2,200 lb, *HEAO-1* was launched into a 225-mile Earth orbit Aug. 12, 1977, to perform a detailed X-ray survey of the celestial sphere. After *HEAO-3*, 1979, HEAO scientific instruments will be carried into space by NASA's Space Shuttle.

Intelsat. Series of communications satellites launched by NASA on a reimbursable basis for the Communications Satellite Corporation (Comsat) to form a commercial, worldwide communications satellite system. Comsat is the U.S. member of the 102-nation consortium that owns the Intelsat network. *Early Bird*, launched April 6, 1965, was the world's first operational commercial communications satellite. The network now is composed of ten satellites, furnishing communications service including telecasts for North America, Europe, and Asia. The satellites are positioned about 22,000 miles above the Equator and, moving at the same speed as Earth, appear to hover permanently over one spot.

Landsat. Series of NASA satellites conducting a variety of earth resources observations (mineralogy, geography, mapping, land use) from space. *ERTS-1* (now called *Landsat* 1) was launched July 23, 1972, into a 570-mile circular polar-orbit around Earth. Weight: 1,800 lb. It was retired in 1978. *Landsat 3* was launched March 3, 1978. Orbiting Earth 14 times a day, Landsats scan a swath 115 miles wide in four bands of the spectrum that reveal much about Earth's natural resources that can be used to help manage them more wisely. The satellites pass over almost the entire globe every 18 days.

Laser Geodynamic Satellite (LAGEOS). Laser-carrying satellite designed to make detailed measurements of plate tectonic (continental drift) motions, regional fault motions, and the rotation and wobble of Earth. Weighing about 900 lb each, LAGEOS is a solid sphere fitted with 600 laser retroreflectors. Laser beams from ground stations are bounced off it and returned to Earth, permitting very accurate positioning of both ground station and satellite. The first *LAGEOS*, launched on May 4, 1976, is in a circular Earth orbit at 3,440 miles.

Large Space Telescope (LST). The LST program calls for the construction of a 10-ton telescope orbiting the Earth at a distance of 380 miles. This national facility, with a 2.4-meter (8-foot) aperture, would make possible astronomical observations 10 times deeper and with more detail than has ever been possible. It would be placed in orbit via the United States' Space Shuttle.

Marisat. Series of three satellites that make up the first Maritime Communications Satellite systems, owned by the Communications Satellite Corp. (Comsat). The first, *Marisat I*, was launched on Feb. 19, 1976, into a geosynchronous (appearing to hover over one spot on Earth) orbit.

Nimbus. Advanced meteorological satellites for detailed global weather and atmosphere soundings. Equipped with advanced television cameras and a high resolution infrared camera system, Nimbus can provide both day and night pictures of Earth's cloud cover. *Nimbus 1* was launched Aug. 28, 1964.

Orbiting Astronomical Observatory (OAO). Earth-orbiting observatory, operating above the obscuring effects of Earth's atmosphere, is able to study entire celestial sphere in electromagnetic wavelengths not easily accessible from the ground. *OAO-3* is one of the heaviest (4900 lb) U.S. unmanned satellites and carries 11 telescopes. It was launched Aug. 21, 1972, into a nearly circular, 740-mile Earth orbit.

Orbiting Geophysical Observatory (OGO). Large (1,000 lb) multipurpose space platforms designed to study Earth, Sun, and the interplanetary space in between. Carrying many scientific instruments, OGO has the advantage over smaller satellites of being able to observe numerous phenomena simultaneously over prolonged periods of time. *OGO 1* was launched Sept. 5, 1964, into a 13,910–92,845-mile orbit around Earth. The last *OGO* in the series was launched June 5, 1969

Orbiting Solar Observatory (OSO). Series of one-ton space platforms designed to study the Sun and phenomena such as solar flares above the obscuring effects of Earth's atmosphere. Most sophisticated version, *OSO-I,* was launched June 20, 1975. Carrying such instruments as X-ray and gamma-ray monitors, the OSO's have provided scientists with invaluable basic details about the functioning of the Sun. They orbit Earth at a distance of about 300 miles.

Pegasus. Among the heaviest (3,000 lb) of U.S. scientific satellites, with a wing-like structure spanning 96 feet. Designed to determine the frequency and depth of punctures by micrometeoroids (tiny particles of matter speeding through space faster than a bullet). Data from Pegasus helped prepare man for the Apollo lunar landing mission. *Pegasus I,* was launched Feb. 16, 1965.

Relay. Communications satellite system designed to demonstrate feasibility of intercontinental and transoceanic transmission of television and radio signals with a medium-altitude (up to 12,000 miles) radio-equipped satellite. *Relay I* was launched Dec. 13, 1962.

Small Astronomy Satellite (SAS). X-ray satellites designed to monitor the intensity of X-ray sources in our Galaxy and beyond. *SAS-1,* weighing about 400 lb, was launched Dec. 12, 1970.

Seasat. Series of satellites which are the first to study ocean data exclusively. *Seasat-A* was launched June 26, 1978. It circled the globe 14 times a day. Its mission was to determine if microwave instruments scanning the oceans from space can provide useful scientific data for oceanographers, meteorologists, and commercial users of the seas. The spacecraft sent back information on surface winds and temperatures, currents, wave heights, ice conditions, ocean topography, and coastal storm activity. On Oct. 9, 1978, it went dead in orbit, apparently from a short circuit.

Solar Maximum Mission (S.M.M.). Designed to study solar flares. The 5,100-lb spacecraft is the first to be built so that it could be repaired or retrieved by astronauts flying the space shuttle. The spacecraft, nicknamed Solar Max, was launched into a 356-mile high orbit on Feb. 14, 1980.

Synchronous Meteorological Satellite (SMS). Series of geostationary (hovering over same spot above Earth) satellites designed to keep continuous watch on fast-changing storms, such as hurricanes and tornadoes, sending back high resolution pictures every 30 minutes. *SMS-1* was launched May 17, 1974. With the launch of a second *SMS,* on Feb. 6, 1975, day-and-night surveillance is provided over the U.S. and adjacent ocean areas.

Syncom. First communications satellite to be placed in a synchronous Earth orbit for global communication. Three Syncom satellites were launched between Feb. 14, 1963, and Aug. 19, 1964.

Telstar. Early experimental communications satellite system operated by American Telephone and Telegraph Co. *Telstar 1* was launched July 1, 1962, by NASA for AT&T on a reimbursable basis.

Tiros. Spectacularly successful early weather satellite system developed by NASA. *Tiros 1,* launched April 1, 1960, took more than 22,000 cloud-cover pictures in 78 days and transmitted them to ground stations. Operational system, called ITOS (Improved Tiros), is now handled by the National Oceanic and Atmospheric Administration (NOAA) of the Department of Commerce. Tiros stands for Television and Infrared Observation Satellite. Contributes significantly to early detection of hurricanes and other destructive storms. Provides weathermen with daily pictures of weather over the entire globe. Weight: Approximately 750 lb. Orbits Earth at distance of about 450 miles. *ITOS-H (NOAA-5)* was launched on July 29, 1976. More satellites are planned in the Tiros series.

Transit. Department of Defense navigational satellite system for military vessels. Consisting of four satellites, system is designed to allow ships to determine their precise position regardless of weather or time of day.

Vanguard. Earth-orbiting geodetic survey satellites. *Vanguard I,* launched March 17, 1958, determined that Earth is slightly pear-shaped.

Westar. Domestic communications system developed by Western Union. Spacecraft are launched into a 200-by-19,500-mile Earth orbit. Program was begun in 1974, with the launch of *Westar 1* on April 13.

Unmanned Planetary and Lunar Programs

Lunar Orbiter. Series of spacecraft designed to orbit the Moon, taking pictures and obtaining data in support of the subsequent manned Apollo landings. The U.S. launched five *Lunar Orbiters* between Aug. 10, 1966 and Aug. 2, 1967.

Mariner. Designation for a series of spacecraft designed to fly past or orbit the planets, particularly Mercury, Venus, and Mars. *Mariners* provided the early information on Venus and Mars. *Mariner 9,* orbiting Mars in 1971, returned the most startling photographs of that planet to date, and helped pave the way for a *Viking* landing in 1976. *Mariner 10* explored Venus and Mercury in 1973 and was the first probe to use a planet's gravity to whip it toward another.

Pioneer. Designation for the United States' first series of sophisticated interplanetary spacecraft. *Pioneers 10* and *11* reached Jupiter in 1973 and 1974 and continued on to explore Saturn and the other outer planets. *Pioneer 11,* renamed *Pioneer Saturn,* examined the Saturn system in September 1979. Significant discoveries were the finding of a small new moon and a narrow new ring. In 1986, *Pioneer 10* will be the first man-made object to escape the solar system. *Pioneer Venus 1* and *2* reached Venus in 1978 and provided detailed information about that planet's surface and atmosphere.

Ranger. NASA's earliest moon exploration program. Spacecraft were designed for a crash landing on the Moon, taking pictures and returning scientific data up to the moment of impact. Provided the first closeup views of the lunar surface. The *Rangers* provided more than 17,000 closeup pictures, giving us more information about the Moon in a few years than in all the time that had gone before.

Surveyor. Series of unmanned spacecraft designed to land gently on the Moon and provide information on the surface in preparation for the manned lunar landings. Their legs were instrumented to return data on the surface hardness of the Moon. *Surveyor* dispelled the fear that Apollo spacecraft might sink several feet or more into the lunar dust.

Viking. Designation for two spacecraft designed to conduct detailed scientific examination of the planet Mars, including a search for life. *Viking 1* landed on July 20, 1976; *Viking 2,* Sept. 3, 1976. More was learned about the Red Planet in a few short months than in all the time that had gone before. But the question of life on Mars remains unresolved.

Voyager. Designation for two spacecraft designed to explore Jupiter and the other outer planets. *Voyager 1* and *Voyager 2* passed Jupiter in 1979 and sent back startling color TV images of that planet and its moons. They took a total of about 33,000 pictures. *Voyager 1* passed Saturn November 1980 and *Voyager 2* is scheduled to pass Saturn in 1981.

Manned Space Flight Projects

Mercury. *Project Mercury,* America's first manned space program, was designed to further knowledge about man's capabilities in space. *Mercury 9,* with astronaut Gordon L. Cooper, was the longest flight. It proved conclusively that man can live and work in space for at least 34 hours, despite the high-gravity forces of launch and re-entry, and weightlessness.

Gemini. *Gemini* was an extension of *Project Mercury,* to determine the effects of prolonged space flight on man—two weeks or longer. "Walks in space" provided invaluable information for astronauts' later walks on the Moon. The *Gemini* spacecraft, twice as large as the *Mercury* capsule, accommodated two astronauts.

Apollo. *Apollo* was the designation for the United States' effort to land a man on the Moon and return him safely to Earth. The goal was successfully accomplished with *Apollo 11* on July 20, 1969, culminating eight years of rehearsal and centuries of dreaming. Astronauts Neil A. Armstrong and Col. Edwin E. Aldrin, Jr., scooped up and brought back the first lunar rocks ever seen on Earth—about 47 pounds. Six *Apollo* flights followed, ending with Apollo 17 in December, 1972. The last three *Apollos* carried mechanized vehicles called lunar rovers for wide-ranging surface exploration of the Moon by astronauts. The rendezvous and docking of an *Apollo* spacecraft with a Russian *Soyuz* craft in Earth orbit on July 18, 1975, closed out the *Apollo* program.

Skylab. America's first Earth-orbiting space station. *Project Skylab* was designed to demonstrate that men can work and live in space for prolonged periods without ill effects. Originally the spent third stage of a Saturn 5 moon rocket, *Skylab* measured 118 feet from stem to stern, and carried the most varied assortment of experimental equipment ever assembled in a single spacecraft. Three three-man crews visited the space stations, spending more than 740 hours observing the Sun and bringing home more than 175,000 solar pictures. These were the first recordings of solar activity above Earth's obscuring atmosphere. *Skylab* also evaluated systems designed to gather information on Earth's resources and environmental conditions. *Skylab* biomedical findings indicated that man adapts well to space for at least a period of three months, provided he has a proper diet and adequately programmed exercise, sleep, work, and recreation periods. *Skylab* orbited Earth at a distance of about 300 miles. Five years after the last *Skylab* mission, the 77-ton space station's orbit began to deteriorate faster than expected, owing to unexpectedly high sunspot activity. On July 11, 1979, the parts of *Skylab* that did not burn up in the atmosphere came crashing down on parts of Australia and the Indian Ocean. No one was hurt.

Space Shuttle. The *Space Shuttle* is a new manned space transportation system being developed by NASA to reduce the cost of using space for commercial, scientific, and defense needs. In effect, the *Shuttle* is a manned rocket which, after depositing its payload in space, can be flown back to Earth like a conventional airplane and be available for re-use. Because of its versatility and large cargo-carrying capacity, the *Space Shuttle* can combine missions. For example, on one trip to space the *Shuttle* might place a weather satellite and a scientific satellite into different orbits, and then retrieve a communications satellite and return it to Earth for servicing. Or, if the repairs required by the communications satellite were relatively simple, the *Shuttle* might carry technicians who would repair it in orbit. Although most of its cargoes will be unmanned, the *Shuttle* can serve as an inhabited Earth-orbiting laboratory for up to 30 days. Since *Shuttle* test flights began in 1977, it has suffered from a number of technical problems which have delayed its becoming operational in 1980.

Gasohol Isn't New

Farmers knew they could make motor fuels long before the current energy crisis. So did Henry Ford. He built his Model T to run on gasoline, alcohol, or any mixture in between.

During the depression, farmers often raised more corn than they could eat, feed to livestock, or haul to markets. By fermenting the grain to get alcohol and feed, they found new ways to use their crops. Some burned the stuff in their "Tin Lizzies," trimming the gas bill at a time when the dollar was hard to come by.

Notable Unmanned Lunar and Interplanetary Probes

Spacecraft	Launch date	Destination	Remarks
Pioneer 1 (U.S.)	Oct. 11, 1958	Moon	Max. alt.: 71,300 mi. Flight duration: 43 h 17.5 min
Pioneer 3 (U.S.)	Dec. 6, 1958	Moon	Max. alt.: 66,654 mi. Discovered outer Van Allen layer.
Lunik 1 (U.S.S.R.)	Sept. 12, 1959	Moon	Landed in area of Mare Serenitatis.
Pioneer 5 (U.S.)	March 11, 1960	Interplanetary	Orbited sun between Earth & Venus. Radio transmission over record distance of 20 million miles.
Ranger 4 (U.S.)	April 23, 1962	Moon	730-lb probe. Impacted on Moon's far side April 26. No transmission.
Mariner 2 (U.S.)	Aug. 27, 1962	Venus	Venus probe. Successful mid-course correction. Passed 21,648 mi. from Venus Dec. 14, 1962. Reported 800°F. surface temp. Contact lost Jan. 3, 1963 at 54 million mi.
Ranger 7 (U.S.)	July 28, 1964	Moon	Impacted near Crater Guericke 68.5 h after launch. Sent 4,316 pictures during last 15 min of flight as close as 1,000 ft above lunar surface.
Mariner 4 (U.S.)	Nov. 28, 1964	Mars	After mid-course correction, passed behind Mars July 14, 1965, taking 22 pictures from about 6,000 mi.
Ranger 8 (U.S.)	Feb. 17, 1965	Moon	809 lb. After 64.9 h, crashed into Mare Tranquilitatis, 2.59° N of lunar equator. Sent 7,137 pictures.
Ranger 9 (U.S.)	March 21, 1965	Moon	After 64.5 h, hit Crater Alphonsus. Sent 5,814 pictures.
Zond 3 (U.S.S.R.)	July 18, 1965	Moon	Sent close-ups of 3 million sq mi. of Moon. Now in solar orbit.
Venera 3 (U.S.S.R.)	Nov. 16, 1965	Venus	2,112 lb. Entered Venus atmosphere (March 1, 1966). No data sent.
Pioneer 6 (U.S.)	Dec. 16, 1965	Interplanetary	Successfully orbiting Sun (every 311 days) to check space conditions between Earth & Venus. Perihelion: 75.6 million mi. Aphelion: 90.7 million mi.
Luna 9 (U.S.S.R.)	Jan. 31, 1966	Moon	3,428 lb. Instrument capsule of 220 lb soft-landed Feb. 3, 1966. Sent back about 30 pictures.
Luna 10 (U.S.S.R.)	March 31, 1966	Moon	540 lb. Orbit achieved April 2, 1966.
Surveyor 1 (U.S.)	May 30, 1966	Moon	Landed June 2, 1966. Sent almost 10,400 pictures, a number after surviving the 14-day lunar night.
Lunar Orbiter 1 (U.S.)	Aug. 10, 1966	Moon	Orbited Moon Aug. 14. 21 pictures sent.
Pioneer 7 (U.S.)	Aug. 17, 1966	Sun Orbit	Orbiting sun (400 days). Perihelion: 92 million mi. Aphelion: 102 million mi.
Luna 11 (U.S.S.R.)	Aug. 24, 1966	Moon	Moon orbit achieved Aug. 27.
Luna 12 (U.S.S.R.)	Oct. 22, 1966	Moon	Moon orbit achieved Oct. 25 for 3.5 h. Transmission difficulties.
Lunar Orbiter 2 (U.S.)	Nov. 7, 1966	Moon	Orbit achieved Nov. 10. Sent hundreds of excellent pictures.
Luna 13 (U.S.S.R.)	Dec. 21, 1966	Moon	Soft-landed 80 h after launch. Good pictures. Drove spike into Moon's surface.
Lunar Orbiter 3 (U.S.)	Feb. 4, 1967	Moon	Orbited Moon Feb. 8. Terminated Oct. 9, 1967. Excellent pictures.
Surveyor 3 (U.S.)	April 17, 1967	Moon	Soft-landed 65 h after launch on Oceanus Procellarum. Scooped and tested lunar soil.
Lunar Orbiter 4 (U.S.)	May 4, 1967	Moon	Achieved orbit May 7. Changed orbit on command.
Venera 4 (U.S.S.R.)	June 12, 1967	Venus	Arrived Oct. 17. Instrument capsule sent temperature and chemical data.
Mariner 5 (U.S.)	June 14, 1967	Venus	Fly-by Oct. 19, confirming Mariner 2 and Venera 4 findings
Surveyor 4 (U.S.)	July 14, 1967	Moon	Contact lost 2.5 min before landing
Explorer 35 (U.S.)	July 19, 1967	Moon	Orbit July 22. Perilune: 500 mi.; apolune: 4000 mi.
Lunar Orbiter 5 (U.S.)	Aug. 2, 1967	Moon	Orbited Aug. 5, Perilune: 125 mi.; apolune: 3,760 mi. Time 3 h 50 min. After filming, was crashed on Moon.
Surveyor 5 (U.S.)	Sept. 8, 1967	Moon	Landed near lunar equator Sept. 10. Radiological analysis of lunar soil. Mechanical claw for digging soil.
Surveyor 6 (U.S.)	Nov. 7, 1967	Moon	Landed in Sinus Medii Nov. 10. Jumped 8 ft to photograph original position. Sent back 11,524 pictures.
Pioneer 8 (U.S.)	Dec. 12, 1967	Sun Orbit	Achieved Solar orbit. Stopped functioning April 28, 1968.
Surveyor 7 (U.S.)	Jan. 6, 1968	Moon	Landed near Crater Tycho Jan. 10. Soil analysis. Sent 3,343 pictures.
Zond 4 (U.S.S.R.)	March 2, 1968	Unknown	Achieved parking orbit but was unable to leave. Re-entered March 3.
Zond 5 (U.S.S.R.)	Sept. 14, 1968	Moon	Circumlunar flight
Pioneer 9 (U.S.)	Nov. 8, 1968	Sun Orbit	Achieved orbit. Six experiments returned solar radiation data.
Zond 6 (U.S.S.R.)	Nov. 10, 1968	Moon	Circumlunar flight
Venera 5 (U.S.S.R.)	Jan. 5, 1969	Venus	Landed May 16, 1969. Returned atmospheric data.
Venera 6 (U.S.S.R.)	Jan. 10, 1969	Venus	Landed May 17, 1969. Sent data as Venera 5.
Mariner 6 (U.S.)	Feb. 24, 1969	Mars	Came within 2000 mi. of Mars July 31, 1969. Sent back data & TV pictures.
Mariner 7 (U.S.)	March 27, 1969	Mars	Came within 2000 mi. of Mars Aug. 5, 1969. Sent back data & TV pictures.

Spacecraft	Launch date	Destination	Remarks
Luna 15 (U.S.S.R.)	July 13, 1969	Moon	Lunar orbiter landed on Moon July 21, 1969 after completing varying orbits.
Zond 7 (U.S.S.R.)	Aug. 8, 1969	Moon	Circumlunar. Recovered Aug. 14, 1969.
Pioneer E (U.S.)	Aug. 27, 1969	Inter-planetary	To obtain data on particles and magnetic fields, but failed to achieve orbit.
Venera 7 (U.S.S.R.)	Aug. 17, 1970	Venus	Reached Venus Dec. 15, 1970. Sent data, apparently from surface, for 58 min.
Luna 16 (U.S.S.R.)	Sept. 12, 1970	Moon	Soft-landed Sept. 20, scooped up rock, returned to earth Sept. 24.
Zond 8 (U.S.S.R.)	Oct. 20, 1970	Moon	Circumlunar. Photographed Moon and Earth. Returned Oct. 27, 1970.
Luna 17 (U.S.S.R.)	Nov. 10, 1970	Moon	Soft-landed on Sea of Rains Nov. 17. Lunokhod 1, self-propelled vehicle, used for first time. Sent TV photos, made soil analysis, etc.
Mars 2 (U.S.S.R.)	May 19, 1971	Mars	Reached Mars Nov. 27. Dropped landing capsule on surface.
Mars 3 (U.S.S.R.)	May 28, 1971	Mars	Like Mars 2. Capsule landed Dec. 2. TV transmission cut short.
Mariner 9 (U.S.)	May 30, 1971	Mars	First craft to orbit Mars, Nov. 13. 7,300 pictures, 1st close-ups of Mars' moon. Transmission ended Oct. 27, 1972.
Luna 19 (U.S.S.R.)	Sept. 28, 1971	Moon	Orbited Moon, making measurements & taking photos. Soft-landed Feb. 21 in Sea of Fertility. Returned Feb. 25 with rock samples.
Pioneer 10 (U.S.)	March 3, 1972	Jupiter	620-million-mile flight path through asteroid belt passed Jupiter Dec. 3, 1973, to give man first close-up of planet. In 1986, will become first man-made object to escape solar system.
Venera 8 (U.S.S.R.)	March 27, 1972	Venus	Landed July 22. Sent signals for 50 min. Capsule burned or crushed because of surface heat and pressure. Sent data on atmosphere and surface.
Luna 21 (U.S.S.R.)	Jan. 8, 1973	Moon	Soft-landed Jan. 16. Lunokhod 2 (moon-car) scooped up soil samples, returned them to Earth Jan. 27.
Pioneer 11 (U.S.)	April 6, 1973	Jupiter	Flew by 25,000 mi. from Jupiter Dec. 3, 1974—3 times closer than Pioneer 10.
Mars 4 (U.S.S.R.)	July 21, 1973	Mars	Arrived Feb. 1974, briefly sending back photos
Mars 5 (U.S.S.R.)	July 25, 1973	Mars	Sister craft of Mars 4
Mariner 10 (U.S.)	Nov. 3, 1973	Venus, Mercury	Passed Venus Feb. 5, 1974. Arrived Mercury March 29, 1974, for man's first close-up look at planet. First time gravity of one planet (Venus) used to whip spacecraft toward another (Mercury).
Luna 22 (U.S.S.R.)	May 29, 1974	Moon	Orbited Moon June 2, 1974
Venera 9 (U.S.S.R.)	June 8, 1975	Venus	Soft-landed Oct. 25, 1976. Photographed surface of planet.
Venera 10 (U.S.S.R.)	June 14, 1975	Venus	(See Venera 9)
Viking 1 (U.S.)	Aug. 20, 1975	Mars	Carrying life-detection labs. Landed July 20, 1976, for detailed scientific research, including pictures.
Viking 2 (U.S.)	Sept. 9, 1975	Mars	Like Viking 1. Landed Sept. 3, 1976.
Luna 24 (U.S.S.R.)	Aug. 9, 1976	Moon	Soft-landed Aug. 18, 1976. Returned soil samples Aug. 22, 1976.
Voyager 1 (U.S.)	Sept. 5, 1977	Jupiter, Saturn, Uranus	Fly-by mission. Reached Jupiter in March 1979; to encounter Saturn 1980, Uranus 1986.
Voyager 2 (U.S.)	Sept. 20, 1977	Jupiter, Saturn, Uranus	Like Voyager 1. Encountered Jupiter in July 1979; to fly by Saturn 1981, then perhaps Uranus and Neptune.
Pioneer Venus 1 (U.S.)	May 20, 1978	Venus	Arrived Dec. 4 and orbited Venus, photographing surface and atmosphere.
Pioneer Venus 2 (U.S.)	Aug. 8, 1978	Venus	Four-part multi-probe, landed Dec. 9.
Venera 11 (U.S.S.R.)	Sept. 9, 1978	Venus	Soft-landed Dec. 25, 1978. Transmitted data for 95 minutes.
Venera 12 (U.S.S.R.)	Sept. 14, 1978	Venus	Like Venera 11. Landed Dec. 21 and transmitted data for 110 minutes.

"Go West, Young Man"

It was not Horace Greeley but John Babsone Lane Soule, editor of the Terre Haute (Indiana) *Express* who gave this advice in 1851. As 100,000 pioneers moved west to Oregon and California in the 1840s, Greeley called their trek "an aspect of insanity."

From 1840 to 1870, about 254,000 emigrants traveled from the Missouri River to the Pacific; 43,000 more stopped in Utah.

In this 30-year period, only 342 emigrants were killed by Indians, while 426 Indians were killed by whites, reports Charles D. Unruh in *The Plains Across* (1979). Nine out of 10 deaths on the trail came from disease; almost as many died from drowning as from Indian action.

Notable Manned Space Flights

Designation and country	Date	Astronauts	Orbit: perigee/apogee (km)	Orbital period (min)	Number of orbits	Flight time (h/min)	Remarks
Vostok 1(U.S.S.R.)	April 12, 1961	Yuri A. Gagarin	181/327	89.1	1	1/48	First manned orbital flight
MR III(U.S.)	May 5, 1961	Alan B. Shepard, Jr.	—	—	(1)	0/15	Range 486 km (302 mi.), peak 187 km (116.5 mi.); capsule recovered
MR IV (U.S.)	July 21, 1961	Virgil I. Grissom	—	—	(1)	0/16	Range 487 km, peak 190 km; capsule lost
Vostok 2 (U.S.S.R.)	Aug. 6–7, 1961	Gherman S. Titov	178/257	88.6	17.5	25/18	First long-duration flight
MA VI (U.S.)	Feb. 20, 1962	John H. Glenn, Jr.	161/261	88.5	3	4/55	First American in orbit
MA VII (U.S.)	May 24, 1962	M. Scott Carpenter	161/268	88.3	3	4/56	Overshot landing area; otherwise fine
Vostok 3 (U.S.S.R.)	Aug. 11–15, 1962	Andrian G. Nikolavev	173/221	88.1	64	94/22	Vostoks 3 and 4 approached within 5 km
MA VIII (U.S.)	Oct. 3, 1962	Walter M. Schirra, Jr.	161/283	88.5	6	9/13	First splashdown close to aiming point
MA IX (U.S.)	May 15–16, 1963	L. Gordon Cooper, Jr.	161/267	88.4	22	34/20	Longest Mercury flight
Vostok 5 (U.S.S.R.)	June 14–19, 1963	Valery F. Bykovsky	180/235	88.4	81	119/6	Longest Russian orbital flight to date
Vostok 6 (U.S.S.R.)	June 16–19, 1963	Valentina V. Tereshkova	183/233	88.3	48	70/50	First orbital flight by female cosmonaut
Voskhod 1 (U.S.S.R.)	Oct. 12, 1964	Vladimir M. Komarov; Konstantin P. Feoktistov; Boris G. Yegorov	177/409	90.1	16	24/17	First 3-man orbital flight; also first flight without space suits
Voskhod 2 (U.S.S.R.)	March 18, 1965	Alexei A. Leonov; Pavel I. Belyayev	174/495	90.9	17	26/2	First "space walk" (by Leonov), 10 min
GT III (U.S.)	March 23, 1965	Virgil I. Grissom; John W. Young	161/224	88.3	3	4/53	First manned test of Gemini spacecraft
GT IV (U.S.)	June 3–7, 1965	James A. McDivitt; Edward H. White 2d	161/282	89.0	62	97/48	First American "space walk" (by White), lasting slightly over 20 min
GT VI (U.S.)	Dec. 15–16, 1965	Walter M. Schirra, Jr.; Thomas P. Stafford	151/258	88.7	16	25/52	Orbit was extended to 298 km to make rendezvous with orbiting GT VII
GT VIII (U.S.)	March 16–17, 1966	Neil A. Armstrong; David R. Scott	160/270	88.8	6.5	10/42	Only Gemini flight cut short by malfunction: one thruster kept firing after rendezvous and docking with an orbiting Agena rocket had been accomplished
GT IX (U.S.)	June 3–6, 1966	Thomas P. Stafford; Eugene A. Cernan	167/169	90.0	44	72/21	Rendezvous (but no docking)
GT X (U.S.)	July 18–21, 1966	John W. Young; Michael Collins	165/274	88.8	43	70/47	Docking with orbiting Agena rocket
GT XI (U.S.)	Sept. 12–15, 1966	Charles Conrad, Jr.; Richard F. Gordon, Jr.	161/281	89.0	44	71/17	Docking with orbiting Agena on first orbit; apogee of orbit then extended to 1,368 km (850 mi.)
GT XII (U.S.)	Nov. 11–15, 1966	James A. Lovell, Jr.; Edwin E. Aldrin, Jr.	161/282	89.0	59	94/33	Docking with Agena visually, without computer; co-pilot outside spacecraft for total of 5½ hours
Soyuz 1 (U.S.S.R.)	April 23, 1967	Vladimir M. Komarov	201/224	88.6	17	26/40	First test of Soyuz spacecraft; crashed after re-entry, killing Komarov
Apollo 7 (U.S.)	Oct. 11–22, 1968	Walter M. Schirra, Jr.; Donn F. Eisele; R. Walter Cunningham	233/285	89.9	163	260/9	First manned test of Apollo command module; first live TV transmissions from orbit

Soyuz 3 (U.S.S.R.)	Oct. 26–30, 1968	Georgi T. Beregovoi	204/224	88.6	64	94/51	First manned rendezvous and possible docking by Soviet cosmonaut
Apollo 8 (U.S.)	Dec. 21–27, 1968	Frank Borman; James A. Lovell, Jr.; William A. Anders	—	—	10^3	147/00	First spacecraft in circumlunar orbit; TV transmissions from this orbit
Soyuz 5 (U.S.S.R.)	Jan. 15–18, 1969	Boris V. Volynov; Alexei S. Yeliseyev; Yevgeny V. Khrunov	208/232	88.8	49	72/46	Rendezvoused and docked with Soyuz 4; Khrunov and Yeliseyev perform EVA and transfer to Soyuz 4
Apollo 9 (U.S.)	Mar. 3–13, 1969	James A. McDivitt; David R. Scott; Russell L. Schweikart	197/508	91.5	151	241/1	First manned flight of Lunar Module
Apollo 10 (U.S.)	May 18–26, 1969	Thomas P. Stafford; Eugene A. Cernan; John W. Young	—	—	—	192/3	First descent to within 9 miles of Moon's surface by manned craft
Apollo 11 (U.S.)	July 16–24, 1969	Neil A. Armstrong; Edwin E. Aldrin, Jr.; Michael Collins	—	—	—	195/18	First manned landing and EVA on Moon; soil and rock samples collected; experiments left on lunar surface
Soyuz 6 (U.S.S.R.)	Oct. 11–16, 1969	Gorgiy Shonin; Valriy Kabasov	186/221	88.4	80	118/42	Three spacecraft and seven men put into earth orbit simultaneously for first time
Apollo 12 (U.S.)	Nov. 14–24, 1969	Charles Conrad, Jr.; Richard F. Gordon, Jr.; Alan Bean	—	—	—	244/36	Manned lunar landing mission; investigated Surveyor 3 spacecraft; collected lunar samples. EVA time: 15 h 30 min
Apollo 13 (U.S.)	April 11–17, 1970	James A. Lovell, Jr.; Fred W. Haise, Jr.; John L. Swigert, Jr.	—	—	—	142/54	Third manned lunar landing attempt; aborted due to pressure loss in liquid oxygen in service module and failure of fuel cells
Soyuz 9 (U.S.S.R.)	June 1–17, 1970	Andreiyan Nikolayez; Vitaly Sevastianov	236/249	89.3	287	424/59	Mission to test man's ability to withstand long periods of weightlessness
Apollo 14 (U.S.)	Jan. 31–Feb. 9, 1971	Alan B. Shepard; Stuart A. Roosa; Edgar D. Mitchell	—	—	—	216/42	Third manned lunar landing: returned largest amount of lunar material
Soyuz 10 (U.S.S.R.)	April 22–24, 1971	Vladimir A. Shatalov; Alexei S. Yeliseyev; Nikolai Rukavishnikov	208/246	88.9	—	47/46	Linked up for 5½ hours with orbiting space station, Salyut 1
Soyuz 11 (U.S.S.R.)	June 6–30, 1971	Georgiy Tomofeyevich Dobrovolskiy; Vladislav Nikolayevich Volkov; Viktor Ivanovich Patsyev	185/217	88.3	—	569/40	Linked up with first space station, Salyut 1. Astronauts died just before re-entry due to loss of pressurization in spacecraft
Apollo 15 (U.S.)	July 26–Aug. 7, 1971	David R. Scott; James B. Irwin; Alfred M. Worden	—	—	—	295/12	Fourth manned lunar landing; first use of Lunar Rover propelled by Scott and Worden; first live pictures of LM lift-off from Moon; exploration time: 18 hours
Apollo 16 (U.S.)	April 16–27, 1972	John W. Young; Thomas K. Mattingly; Charles M. Duke, Jr.	—	—	—	265/51	Fifth manned lunar landing; second use of Lunar Rover Vehicle, propelled by Young and Duke. Total exploration time on the Moon was 20 h 14 min, setting new record. Mattingly's in-flight "walk in space" was 1 h 23 min. Approximately 213 lb of lunar rock returned

Designation and country	Date	Astronauts	Orbit: perigee/apogee (km)	Orbital period (min)	Number of orbits	Flight time (h/min)	Remarks
Apollo 17 (U.S.)	Dec. 7–19, 1972	Eugene A. Cernan; Ronald E. Evans; Harrison H. Schmitt	—	—	—	301/51	Sixth and last manned lunar landing; third to carry lunar rover. Cernan and Schmitt, during three EVA's, completed total of 22 h 05 min 3 sec. USS Ticonderoga recovered crew and about 250 lbs of lunar samples.
Skylab SL-1 (U.S.)	May 14, 1973	—	423/440	93.4	—	—	Unmanned portion of Skylab comprised of Orbital Workshop (OWS), Airlock Module (AM), Multiple Docking Adapter (MDA), Apollo Telescope Mount (ATM), Instrument Unit (IU), and Payload Shroud (PS)
Skylab SL-2 (U.S.)	May 25-June 22, 1973	Charles Conrad, Jr.; Joseph P. Kerwin; Paul J. Weitz	401/424	93.2	—	672/50	First manned Skylab launch. Established Skylab Orbital Assembly and conducted scientific and medical experiments
Skylab SL-3 (U.S.)	July 28-Sept. 25, 1973	Alan L. Bean, Jr.; Jack R. Lousma; Owen K. Garriott	401/424	93.2	—	1427/9	Second manned Skylab launch. New crew remained in space for 59 days, continuing scientific and medical experiments and earth observations from orbit.
Skylab SL-4 (U.S.)	Nov. 16, 1973-Feb. 8, 1974	Gerald Carr; Edward Gibson; William Pogue	401/424	93.2	—	2017/16	Third manned Skylab launch; obtained medical data on crew for use in extending the duration of manned space flight; crews "walked in space" 4 times, totaling 44 h 40 min. Longest space mission yet—84 d 1 h 16 min. Splashdown in Pacific, Feb. 9, 1974.
Soyuz 12 (U.S.S.R.)	Sept. 27–29, 1973	Vasily G. Lazarev; Oleg K. Makarov	202/231	88.7	—	50/12	Two-day test flight. First Soviet manned flight since ill-fated Soyuz 11.
Soyuz 13 (U.S.S.R.)	Dec. 18–26, 1973	Pyotr Klimuk; Valentin Lebedev	188/246	88.9	—	188/55	Modified spacecraft to be used for rendezvous with U.S. spacemen in 1975
Soyuz 14 (U.S.S.R.)	July 3–19, 1974	Pavel Popovich; Yuri Artyukhin	201/338	89.9	—	377/29	Crewmen spent two weeks on board Soviet space station Salyut 3
Soyuz 17 (U.S.S.R.)	Jan. 11–Feb. 9, 1975	Col. Aleksey Gubarev; Georgi Grechko				709/20	Crew spent 30 days in Salyut 4 space station, which was launched Dec. 26, 1974 and placed in Earth orbit
Apollo/Soyuz Test Project (U.S. and U.S.S.R.)	July 15–24, 1975 (U.S.)	U.S.: Brig. Gen. Thomas P. Stafford, Vance D. Brand, Donald K. Slayton	152/166	87.7 89.0 (docked)	138 (docked)	216/05	World's first international manned rendezvous and docking in space; aimed at developing a space rescue capability.
	July 15–21, 1975 (U.S.S.R.)	U.S.S.R.: Col. A. A. Leonov, V. N. Kubasov	191/218	91.0 89.0 (docked)	138 (docked)	223/35	Apollo and Soyuz docked and crewmen exchanged visits on July 17, 1975. Mission duration for Soyuz: 142 h 31

							min. For Apollo: 217 h, 28 min.
Soyuz 21 (U.S.S.R.)	July 6–Aug. 24, 1976	Col. Boris Volynov; Lt. Col. Vitali Zholobov	114/409	89.7	—	1218/24	Crew spent 50 days aboard Salyut 5 space station, which was launched June 22
Soyuz 24 (U.S.S.R.)	Feb. 7–25, 1977	Col. V. Gorbatko; Lt. Col. Yuri Glaszkov	173/323	89.5	—	425/23	Docked and transferred to Salyut 5 on Feb. 8. Returned Feb. 25
Soyuz 31 (U.S.S.R.)	Aug. 26–Nov. 2, 1978	Valery Bykovsky; Sigmund Jaehn	337/353	91.4	—	1632/0[2]	Docked with Salyut 6 and Soyuz 29; crew returned in Soyuz 29 on Sept. 3, 1978
Soyuz 32 (U.S.S.R.)	Feb. 25–Aug. 19, 1979	Lt. Col. V. Lyakhov; Valery Ryumin	—	—	—	4200/36	Docked with Salyut 6; crew set duration record of 175 days in space.
Soyuz 33 (U.S.S.R.)	April 11–12, 1979	N. Rukavishnikov; G. Ivanov	—	—	—	—	Commander veteran of Soyuz 16
Soyuz 35 (U.S.S.R.)	April 9, 1980	Valery Ryumin; Leonid Popov	—	—	—	—	Docked with Salyut 6; still in orbit
Soyuz T2 (U.S.S.R.)	June 5–9, 1980	Lt. Col. Yuri V. Mayyshev; Vladimir V. Aksenov	—	—	—	—	Docked with Salyut 6; tested new model spacecraft, T2

1. Suborbital flight. 2. Approximate time. 3. Number of orbits around moon. NOTE: The letters MR stand for Mercury (capsule) and Redstone (rocket); MA, for Mercury and Atlas (rocket); GT, for Gemini (capsule) and Titan-II (rocket). The first astronaut listed in the Gemini and Apollo flights is the command pilot. The Mercury capsules had names: MR-III was *Freedom 7*, MR-IV was *Liberty Bell 7*, MA-VI was *Friendship 7*, MA-VII was *Aurora 7*, MA-VIII was *Sigma 7*, and MA-IX was *Faith 7*. The figure 7 referred to the fact that the first group of U.S. astronauts numbered seven men. Only one Gemini capsule had a name: GT-III was called *Molly Brown* (after the Broadway musical *The Unsinkable Molly Brown*); thereafter the practice of naming the capsules was discontinued.

THE YEAR IN SPACE

(Continued from page 384)

been calculated to be 12.8 hours ± 1.7 hours.

Neptune. Observations made using a charge-coupled device (CCD) linked to the 1.54 meter telescope at the University of Arizona show large cloudlike formations in Neptune's northern and southern hemispheres. The clouds are separated by a dark band at the planet's equator. The diffuse structures probably represent formations of high-altitude methane ice crystals.

Pluto. There are indications that Pluto may also have a methane atmosphere that contains some argon gas.

Meanwhile, back on Earth . . .

Significant attention is being given to the distribution of tektites, or glassy meteorlike objects scattered over wide areas of the Earth's surface. The pattern of these tektite fields, which often extend for thousands of miles and cover continents as well as the sea floor, suggests that our planet may at one time also have had a debris ring emanating from a large meteor or asteroid impact. If such a ring did exist, its shadow could have been responsible for the major climatic changes that brought about the ice ages. Another new field of meteorites has been found in Antarctica, 200 miles north of the American base at McMurdo Sound. Because of the severe and virtually sterile conditions, these meteorites are almost unchanged from the condition they were in when they landed on Earth.

In late 1979, NASA launched *Magsat*, the first satellite designed exclusively to measure the Earth's magnetic field and thereby be helpful to mineral and petroleum exploration and aid geologic mapping. The satellite has a low orbit, 350 to 500 kilometers (219 to 313 miles) and was originally expected to remain aloft for only 120 days. Soviet cosmonauts Valery Ryumin and Leonid Popov boarded the Russian space station *Salyut 6* on April 10 in a possible attempt to establish a new record for time spent in space. On June 9, the Soviets launched *Soyuz T-2* with cosmonauts Lt. Col. Yuri V. Malyshev and Vladimir V. Aksenov. The T-2 spacecraft is described as an improved version of the old *Soyuz* workhorse used by the Soviets since the mid-1960s. For the first time, the craft contains an on-board computer that enables the cosmonauts to maneuver their ship in space. Earlier versions were controlled exclusively from the ground. In another development, Russia is training Vietnamese and possibly Indian cosmonauts. The move may be designed as a propaganda ploy, since China has announced a bold space program of its own, including the launching of an experimental communications satellite, scheduled for 1981. Key to the Chinese development is a new launch vehicle, the three-stage rocket *Long March 3*. The European Space Agency's *Ariane* rocket, second in a series, failed to enter orbit when all four of its primary stage engines quit after liftoff. The launcher was carrying the (German) Max Planck Institute's *Firewheel* satellite, designed to study the Earth's magnetic field with injections of lithium and barium. *Ariane 2* also carried an amateur radio satellite, *OSCAR 9*. The American Space Shuttle was delayed due to technical and administrative problems.

Konrad J.A. Kundig

Major Soviet Space Projects

Scientific Satellites

Cosmos. A designation that began in 1962 for many different kinds of Soviet satellites. *Cosmos 1* studied cosmic rays and other varieties of radiation. *Cosmos 936,* launched Aug. 3, 1977, performed biomedical experiments in cooperation with the U.S., France, and Communist bloc countries.

Elektron. Satellites launched in pairs to map radiation belts. Apogee: 40,000 miles; perigee: 4,000 miles. Four *Elektron* satellites were launched in 1964.

Intercosmos. Russian scientific satellites carrying experiments from other countries. The announced countries participating are from the Soviet bloc. *Intercosmos I* was launched October 14, 1969. *Intercosmos 17,* measuring charged particles and micrometeorites, was launched Sept. 26, 1977.

Oreol. Scientific satellites designed to study the upper atmosphere. Launched jointly with France. *Oreol I* was launched in 1971; *Oreol 2,* 1973.

Meteor. Designation for a series of about two dozen weather satellites, beginning with *Meteor I* on March 26, 1969. In 1977, four *Meteors* were put in orbit, the last weighing over 3 tons.

Molniya. A communications satellite appearing in a highly elliptical orbit over the same portion of Earth each day on each of its climbs to apogee (the highest point), giving good coverage to the Soviet Union. *Molniya 1* and *2* were launched October 14, 1965. In 1975 and 1976, nine *Molniya* satellites were put in orbit.

Prognoz. A solar irradiation and magnetosphere satellite for the study of the solar wind. The last *Prognoz* was launched Dec. 22, 1975.

Polyot. Earth satellites incorporating on-board propulsion systems which enable them to change their orbits. Only two have been launched to date, in 1963 and 1964.

Sputnik. An early designation for Soviet unmanned spacecraft. *Sputnik 1,* launched October 4, 1957, was the world's first Earth-orbiting satellite, and is considered to have ushered in the Space Age.

Unmanned Planetary and Lunar Programs

Luna. Unmanned spacecraft launched to the Moon. These include lunar orbiters, lunar landers, and lunar lander return missions.

Mars. Unmanned spacecraft launched to explore the planet Mars. Three spacecraft, each weighing about 1,940 lb, were launched in 1962, but failed to reach their target. *Mars 4* was launched July 21, 1973, arriving at Mars in February, 1974, and briefly transmitting photographs of the planet back to Earth. *Mars 5, 6,* and *7* were launched between July 25 and August 9, 1974, but missed the planet.

Venera. Unmanned spacecraft launched to explore the planet Venus. The program was begun in 1961 but, out of 10 known tries, only four can be termed successful. *Venera 11* and *12* were twinned probes, launched Sept. 9 and Sept. 14, 1978, respectively. They soft-landed in late December and transmitted data to earth for 95 minutes and 110 minutes before failing under the intense heat and pressure of the Venusian atmosphere.

Zond. Soviet lunar and planetary probes not otherwise designated. *Zond* spacecraft have been launched to Venus, Mars, and the Moon.

Manned Space Flight Programs

Vostok. The Soviets' first manned capsule, roughly spherical, used to place the first six cosmonauts in Earth orbit (1961–65).

Voskhod. Adaptation of the *Vostok* capsule to accommodate two and three cosmonauts. *Voskhod 1* orbited three persons, and *Voskhod 2* orbited two persons performing the world's first manned extravehicular activity.

Soyuz. Late-model manned spacecraft with provisions for three cosmonauts and a "working compartment" accessible through a hatch. Soyuz is the Russian word for "union". Since 1973, all *Soyuz* spacecraft have carried two cosmonauts. *Soyuz 19,* launched July 15, 1975, docked with the American *Apollo* spacecraft. A new model of the spacecraft, *Soyuz-T2,* was launched in 1980.

Salyut. Earth-orbiting space station intended for prolonged occupancy and re-visitation by cosmonauts. They are usually launched by Soviet Proton rockets. *Salyut 1* was launched April 19, 1971, and was docked with by *Soyuz 10* and *11. Salyut 2,* launched April 3, 1973, malfunctioned in orbit and was never occupied. *Salyut 3,* visited by *Soyuz 14* and *16,* was launched June 25, 1974. *Salyut 4* was launched Dec. 26, 1974, and is still in orbit. It was visited by *Soyuz 17, 18,* and *20* (which was unmanned). *Salyut 5,* launched June 22, 1976, was docked with by *Soyuz 21* and *24. Salyut 6* was launched on Sept. 29, 1977, and was visited by *Soyuz 26, 27, 28, 29, 30, 31,* and *32* (the crew of which spent a record-breaking 175 days in space). *Soyuz-T2* astronauts were 10th crew to visit *Salyut 6,* June 6, 1980.

Space Telescope Eagerly Awaited

There is a heavy anticipated demand for use of the Space Telescope, when the U.S. Space Shuttle brings the 10-ton satellite into a 500-kilometer (310.5-mile) high orbit in late 1983. The 2.4-meter (7-ft-10½-in.) Space Telescope is designed to last past the end of this century and is to be serviced about every two and a half years by Space Shuttle astronauts. It will be taken back to earth occasionally for overhaul and relaunching during its 20-year lifetime.

U.S. Armed Forces Personnel[1]

Year	Army	Air Force[2]	Navy	Marines	Men[3]	Women[3]	Coast Guard[4]
1940	269,023	—	160,997	28,345	456,984	1,381	13,621
1941	1,462,315	—	284,427	54,359	1,794,997	6,104	19,036
1942	3,075,608	—	640,570	142,613	3,844,538	14,253	58,998
1943	6,994,472	—	1,741,750	308,523	8,918,574	126,171	154,976
1944	7,994,750	—	2,981,365	475,604	11,241,173	210,542	169,264
1945	8,267,958	—	3,380,817	474,680	11,858,499	265,006	171,518
1946	1,891,011	—	983,398	155,679	2,972,081	58,007	29,736
1947	991,285	—	498,661	93,053	1,563,241	19,758	18,972
1950	593,167	411,277	381,538	74,279	1,438,192	22,069	23,190
1951	1,531,774	788,381	736,680	192,620	3,209,830	39,625	29,000
1955	1,109,296	959,946	660,695	205,170	2,899,916	35,191	28,500
1957	997,994	919,835	677,108	200,861	2,763,625	32,173	28,322
1959	861,964	840,435	626,340	175,571	2,472,456	31,718	29,984
1962	1,066,404	884,025	666,428	190,962	2,775,606	32,213	31,500
1966	1,199,784	887,353	745,205	261,716	3,061,469	32,589	34,767
1969	1,512,169	862,353	775,869	309,771	3,420,656	39,506	38,331
1970	1,322,548	791,349	692,660	259,737	3,024,815	41,479	38,172
1971	1,123,810	755,300	623,248	212,369	2,671,952	42,775	38,029
1972	810,960	725,838	588,043	198,238	2,278,046	45,033	37,866
1973	800,973	691,182	564,534	196,098	2,197,385	55,402	36,588
1974	783,330	643,970	545,903	188,802	2,087,290	74,715	36,407
1975	784,333	612,751	535,085	195,951	2,031,252	96,868	35,952
1976	782,668	583,281	527,781	189,851	1,971,828	111,753	37,898
1977	782,246	570,695	529,895	191,707	1,955,577	118,966	38,918
1978	771,624	569,712	530,253	190,815	1,928,092	134,312	38,059[5]
1979	758,852	559,455	523,937	185,250	1,876,412	151,082	38,295[6]

1. As of June 30 from 1940–1975. From September 30 as of 1976. 2. Before July 26, 1947, when the National Military Establishment was established, the Air Force was a part of the Army. 3. Not including Coast Guard personnel. 4. In peacetime, Coast Guard operates under Dept. of Transportation; in time of war or at direction of President, it is attached to Navy Dept. 5. Includes 761 women. 6. As of June 30. Includes 1,317 women. *Sources:* Department of Defense and the Coast Guard.

History of the Armed Services

Source: Department of Defense.

U.S. Army

On June 14, 1775, the Continental Congress "adopted" the New England Army—a mixed force of militia and volunteers besieging the British in Boston—by appointing a committee to draft "Rules and regulations for the government of the Army" and voting to raise 10 rifle companies as a reinforcement. The next day, it appointed Washington commander-in-chief of the "Continental forces to be raised for the defense of liberty," and he took command at Boston on July 3, 1775. The Continental Army that fought the Revolution was our first national military organization, and hence the Army is the senior service. After the war, the Continental Army was radically reduced but enough survived to form a small Regular Army of about 700 men under the Constitution in 1789, a nucleus for expansion in the 1790s to successfully meet threats from the Indians and from France. From these humble beginnings, the U.S. Army has developed, normally expanding rapidly by absorbing citizen soldiers in wartime and contracting just as rapidly after each war.

U.S. Navy

The antecedents of the U.S. Navy go back to September 1775, when Gen. Washington commissioned 7 schooners and brigantines to prey on British supply vessels bound for the Colonies or Canada. In Oct. 1775, a motion in the Continental Congress called for the construction of 2 vessels for the purpose of intercepting enemy transports. With its passage a Naval Committee of 7 men was formed, and they rapidly obtained passage of legislation calling for construction of additional vessels. The Continental Navy was supplemented by privateers and ships operated as state navies, but soon after the British surrender it was disestablished.

In 1794, because of dissatisfaction with the payment of tribute to the Barbary pirates, Congress authorized construction of 6 frigates. The first, *United States,* was launched May 10, 1797, but the Navy still remained under the control of the Secretary of War until April 1798, when the Secretary of the Navy was given full Cabinet rank and the U.S. Navy came into its own.

U.S. Air Force

Until creation of the National Military Establishment in September 1947, which united the services under one department, military aviation was a part of the U.S. Army. In the Army, aeronautical operations came under the Signal Corps from 1907 to 1918, when the U.S. Air Service was established. In 1926, the U.S. Air Corps came into being and remained until 1942, when the Army Air Forces succeeded it as the Army's air arm. In 1947, the U.S. Air Force was established as an independent military service under the National Military Establishment. At that time, the name "Army Air Forces" was abolished.

U.S. Coast Guard

Our country's oldest continuous seagoing service, the U.S. Coast Guard, traces its history back to 1790, when the first Congress authorized the construction of ten vessels for the collection of revenue. Known first as the Revenue Marine, and later as the Revenue Cutter Service, the Coast Guard received its present name in 1915 under an act of Congress combining the Revenue Cutter Service with the Life-Saving Service. In 1939, the Lighthouse Service was also consolidated with this unit. The Bureau of Marine Inspection and Navigation was transferred temporarily to the Coast Guard in 1942, permanently in 1946. Through its antecedents, the Coast Guard is one of the oldest organizations under the federal government and, until the Navy Department was established in 1798, served as the only U.S. armed force afloat. In times of peace, it operates under the Department of Transportation, serving as the nation's primary agency for promoting marine safety and enforcing federal maritime laws. In times of war, or on direction of the President, it is attached to the Navy Department.

U.S. Marine Corps

Founded in 1775 and observing its official birthday on Nov. 10, the U.S. Marine Corps was developed to serve on land, on sea, and in the air.

Marines have fought in every U.S. war. From an initial two battalions in the Revolution, the Corps reached a peak strength of six divisions and five aircraft wings in World War II. Its present strength is three active divisions and aircraft wings and a Reserve division/aircraft wing team. In 1947, the National Security Act set Marine Corps strength at not less than three divisions and three aircraft wings.

Service Academies

U.S. Military Academy

Source: U.S. Military Academy.

Established in 1802 by an act of Congress, the U.S. Military Academy is located on the west bank of the Hudson River some 50 miles north of New York City. To gain admission a candidate must first secure a nomination from an authorized source. These sources, and the number of cadetships allocated to each, are:

Congressional

Representatives	5 each
Senators	5 each
Other: Vice Presidential	5
District of Columbia	5
Puerto Rico	6
Am. Samoa, Guam, Virgin Is.	1 each

Military-Service-Connected Nominations (Each Class)

Presidential	100
Enlisted members of Army	85
Enlisted members of Army Reserve/ National Guard	85
Sons and daughters of deceased and disabled veterans (approximately)	10
Honor military, naval schools and ROTC	20
Sons and daughters of persons awarded the Medal of Honor	(unlimited)

Any number of applicants can meet the requirements for a *nomination* in these categories. *Appointments* (offers of admission), however, can only be made to the number of applicants shown above.

Candidates may be nominated for vacancies during the year preceding the day of admission, which occurs in early July. The best time to apply is during the junior year in high school.

Candidates must be citizens of the U.S., be unmarried, be at least 17 but not yet 22 years old on July 1 of the year admitted, have a secondary-school education or its equivalent, and be able to meet the academic, medical, and physical aptitude requirements. Academic qualification is determined by an analysis of entire scholastic record, and performance on either the American College Testing (ACT) Assessment Program Test or the College Entrance Examination Board Scholastic Aptitude Test (SAT). Entrance requirements and procedures for appointment are described in the Admissions Bulletin, available without charge from Admissions, U.S. Military Academy, West Point, N.Y. 10996.

Cadets are members of the Regular Army. As such they receive full scholarships and annual salaries from which they pay for their uniforms, textbooks, and incidental expenses. Upon successful completion of the four-year course, the graduate receives the degree of Bachelor of Science and is commissioned a second lieutenant in the Regular Army with a requirement to serve as an officer for a minimum of five years.

U.S. Naval Academy

Source: U.S. Naval Academy.

The Naval School, established in 1845 at Fort Severn, Annapolis, Md., was renamed the U.S. Naval Academy in 1850. A four-year course was adopted a year later.

The Superintendent is a rear admiral. A civilian academic dean heads the academic program. A captain heads the 4,200-man Brigade of Midshipmen and military, professional, and physical training. The faculty is half military and half civilian.

Graduates are awarded the Bachelor of Science or Bachelor of Science in Engineering and are commissioned as officers in the U.S. Navy or Marine Corps.

The primary avenues to selection for appointment as midshipmen follow. Congressmen, the Vice President, the Mayor of Washington, D. C., and the Resident Commissioner of Puerto Rico may each have 5 midshipmen at the Academy at any one time. Ten candidates may be nominated for each vacancy. Well over half of the more than 1,300 appointments as midshipmen made annually originate from these sources.

The President appoints the 65 best-qualified sons and daughters of deceased or disabled veterans, or sons and daughters of prisoners of war or servicemen missing in action, and the 100 best-qualified sons and daughters of officers and enlisted men in the regular Armed Services. He also appoints sons and daughters of Medal of Honor holders.

The Secretary of the Navy awards 170 (85 + 85) appointments to regular and reserve personnel of the Navy or Marine Corps; 150 to congressional alternate nominees, all on a competitive, best-qualified basis; and 20 outstanding graduates of NROTC or Honor Naval and Military Schools. He may also make additional appointments each year, to bring the Brigade up to authorized strength, from among qualified congressional and competitive nominees, again on a best-qualified basis. Three fourths of these additional appointments must, by law, be congressional nominees.

There are also limited numbers of appointments available from the Philippines, Canal Zone, Virgin Islands, Guam, American Samoa, and the American republics.

To have basic eligibility for admission, candidates must be citizens of the U.S., of good moral character, at least 17 and not more than 22 years of age on July 1 of their entering year, in the top 40% of their high school class, and unmarried.

In order to be considered for admission, a candidate must obtain a nomination from one of the sources of appointments listed above. The Admissions Board at the Naval Academy examines the candidate's school record, College Board or ACT scores, recommendations from school officials, extracurricular activities, and evidence from other sources concerning his or her character, leadership potential, academic preparation, and physical fitness. Qualification for admission is based on all of the above factors.

Tuition, board, lodging, and medical and dental care are provided. Midshipmen receive $317.10 a month for books, uniforms, and personal needs.

For a catalogue or answers to specific questions, write: Superintendent, U.S. Naval Academy, (Attention: Candidate Guidance), Annapolis, Md. 21402.

U.S. Air Force Academy

Source: U.S. Air Force Academy.

The bill establishing the Air Force Academy was signed by President Eisenhower on April 1, 1954. The first class of 306 cadets was sworn in on July 11, 1955, at Lowry Air Force Base, Denver, the Academy's temporary location. The Cadet Wing moved into the Academy's permanent home north of Colorado Springs in 1958.

Cadets receive four years of academic, military, and physical education to prepare them for leadership as officers in the Air Force. The Academy is authorized a total of 4,544 cadets. Each new class averages 1,500. This includes approximately 1,330 men and 170 women. The candidates for the Academy must be at least 17 but less than 22 on July 1 of the year for which they seek admission, must be a United States citizen, be single, and be able to meet the mental and physical requirements. A candidate is required to take the following examinations and tests: (1) the Service Academies' Qualifying Medical Examination; (2) either the American College Testing (ACT) Assessment Program test or the College Entrance Examination Board Scholastic Aptitude Test (SAT), and (3) a Physical Aptitude Examination.

Cadets receive their entire education at government expense and, in addition, are paid $375 monthly. From this sum, they pay for their uniforms, textbooks, tailoring, laundry, entertainment tickets, etc. Upon completion of the four-year course, leading to a Bachelor of Science degree, a cadet who meets the physical qualifications is commissioned a second lieutenant in the regular U.S. Air Force. Many go on to pilot or navigator training. For details on admissions, write: Director of Cadet Admissions, USAF Academy, Colo. 80840.

U.S. Coast Guard Academy

Source: U.S. Coast Guard Academy.

The U.S. Coast Guard Academy, New London, Conn., was founded on July 31, 1876, to serve as the "School of Instruction" for the Revenue Cutter Service, predecessor to the Coast Guard.

The J.C. Dobbin, a converted schooner, housed the first Coast Guard Academy, and was succeeded in 1878 by the barque Chase, a ship built for cadet training. First winter quarters were in a sail loft at New Bedford, Mass. The school was moved in 1900 to Curtis Bay, Md., to provide a more technical education, and in 1910 was moved back to New England to Fort Trumbull, New London, Conn. In 1932 the Academy moved to its present location in New London.

The Academy today offers a four-year curriculum for the professional and academic training of cadets, which leads to a Bachelor of Science degree and a commission as ensign in the Coast Guard.

Cadets receive appointment through nationwide competition, which includes either the December administration of the College Entrance Examination Board tests, or the American College Testing (ACT) Program tests. Applications must be submitted to the Coast Guard not later than December 15 and to the College Entrance Examination Board, 30 days prior to the tests.

Women were admitted to the Coast Guard Academy for the first time during 1976 as members of the Class of 1980. Candidates must be between 17 and 22 years of age, physically sound, and unmarried. They must agree to remain unmarried until graduation and to serve at least five years on active duty. Cadets receive $4,140 per year to cover their uniform and incidental expenses and are furnished their rations and quarters. Applications may be made to Director of Admissions, U.S. Coast Guard Academy, New London, Conn. 06320.

U.S. Merchant Marine Academy

Source: U.S. Merchant Marine Academy.

The U.S. Merchant Marine Academy, situated at Kings Point, N.Y., on the north shore of Long Island, was dedicated Sept. 30, 1943. It is maintained by the Department of Commerce under direction of the Maritime Administration.

The Academy has a complement of approximately 1,000 men and women representing every state, D.C., the Canal Zone, Puerto Rico, Guam, American Samoa, and the Virgin Islands. It is also authorized to admit up to 12 candidates from Central and South America.

Candidates are nominated by Senators and members of the House of Representatives. Nominations to the Academy are governed by a state and territory quota system based on population and the results of the College Entrance Examination Board tests.

A candidate must be a citizen not less than 17 and not yet 22 years of age by July 1 of the year in which admission is sought. Fifteen high school credits, including 3 units in mathematics (from algebra, geometry and/or trigonometry), 1 unit in science (physics or chemistry) and 3 in English are required.

The course is four years and includes one year of practical training aboard a merchant ship. Study includes marine engineering including nuclear studies, navigation, satellite navigation and communications, electricity, ship construction, naval science and tactics, economics, business, languages, history, etc.

Upon completion of the course of study, a graduate receives a Bachelor of Science degree, a license as a merchant marine deck or engineering officer, and a commission as an ensign in the Naval Reserve.

The National Guard

Source: Departments of the Army and the Air Force, National Guard Bureau.

The National Guard of the U.S. originated with the Old North and East Regiments of the Colonial Militia in Massachusetts in 1636. It is the oldest military force in the country. Guardsmen have served overseas in every major conflict in which the U.S. has participated.

As of March 31, 1980, the Army and Air National Guard totaled about 449,096 men and women serving in 4,500 Army and Air Guard units in all 50 states, Puerto Rico, the Virgin Islands, and the District of Columbia. ANG units 322 (current Mar. 31, 1980), ARNG units 4,178.

In peacetime, the National Guard is commanded by the governors of the respective states/territories and may be called to state active duty by the governor to assist in state emergencies, disasters, and civil disturbances. During a war or national emergency, the National Guard may be called to active duty by the President or Congress. The National Guard serves as the primary source of augmentation for the Army and the Air Force.

Budget requests for fiscal 1980 are $1.9 billion for the Army National Guard and $1.6 billion for the Air National Guard. Additional money is appropriated directly for the National Guard by the states. Substantial support is also provided by state, county, and municipal governments in land, police and fire protection, maintenance of roads, and the provision of direct county and municipal fiscal support to local units.

The Army National Guard provides 30% of the Army's entire organized structure and about 46% of its combat elements. That support consists of 8 combat divisions, 21 separate combat brigades, 4 armored cavalry units, 2 special forces groups, 1 infantry group arctic recon, 18 major command headquarters, and 1,164 other separate battalions, companies, headquarters, and detachments.

Army National Guard forces are an integral part of the nation's first-line defenses. For example, the 29th Infantry Brigade in the Hawaii National Guard is a round-out brigade for the active Army's 25th Infantry Division. Under the round-out concept, National Guard units work and train with the active Army unit to which they would be assigned upon mobilization. Under the total force policy, the program for increasing readiness is continually being improved. In 1980, 73 Army National Guard units will deploy overseas to participate in realistic contingency mission-oriented training. Three of these units will participate in an exchange with units from England and Norway, and selected individuals from other units with a NATO contingency mission will participate in orientation training in Germany. In order to improve readiness of the individual soldier, the Skill Qualification Training (Test) Program has been implemented in all states, and over 150,000 Guard members will participate in it during CY 1980. National Guard units take part in Joint Chiefs of Staff and Army exercises with the active forces to further develop the readiness of both units and individuals.

The Air National Guard has 91 flying units and 231 specialized ground support units which, upon mobilization, would be gained by one of five major commands of the USAF. The gaining major commands are Tactical Air Command (TAC), Strategic Air Command (SAC), Military Airlift Command (MAC), Air Force Communications Service (AFCS), and Pacific Air Forces (PACAF).

Air National Guard flying units support four mission areas; strategic with aerial refuelers in the offensive role and in the defensive role with interceptors and defense system evaluation; general purpose with tactical fighters, reconnaissance, electronic warfare and air support; mobility with tactical airlift; and defense wide with rescue and recovery. These are supported by communications, flight facilities, tactical air control, electronics installation, civil engineering, medical, and weather units.

The National Guard is administered by the National Guard Bureau, a joint Army and Air Force office in the Pentagon. Chief of the Bureau is Maj. Gen. LaVern E. Weber of Oklahoma.

The Army National Guard offers its young men and women a broad spectrum of educational opportunities. These not only include skill training associated with their military assignment, but in many instances embrace civilian occupations as well. The list of skills is not limited to those that are equipment oriented but includes management, medical, and other career fields. Some of these educational opportunities may even be pursued in civilian institutions, specifically that of the Clinical Specialist, which is compatible with a Licensed Practical Nurse or Licensed Vocational Nurse.

Participation in the military education system by Army National Guard personnel is not limited to initial entry-skill-level training. There are opportunities available to become a qualified aviator, improve managerial and leadership abilities through attendance at courses designed for the functioning middle managers, and, finally, there are the courses offered at the prestigious Senior Service Colleges that address the needs of personnel at the executive level and positions of greater responsibilities.

If openings exist, young men and women between the ages of 17 and 35 may enlist for a period of six years. In certain circumstances the period of active participation may be less than six years. Upon enlistment, they serve a minimum of 12 weeks on active duty, training with the U.S. Army or the U.S. Air Force, depending upon which branch of the National Guard they choose. The remainder of their six weeks is spent in part-time training with their Guard unit.

A woman between the ages of 17 and 35 who has no previous military experience may also enlist in the National Guard for a period of six years. Women in the Army National Guard will receive basic training at either Fort McClellan, Ala., Fort Leonard Wood, Mo., or Fort Jackson, S.C.; women in the Air National Guard train at Lackland Air Force Base, Tex. Advanced individual training will be received at an appropriate training center.

A Guard member receives a full day's pay of his/her military rank for each unit assembly he attends. Additionally, he receives a day's pay of his military rank for each day of his 15 days of annual training, plus any other days on active duty for training at military schools or special assignments. All such training counts toward retirement eligibility at age 60 with 20 or more years of service.

Pay Grades of Enlisted Personnel

Army ranks[1]	Air Force ranks	Marine ranks	Navy and Coast Guard ranks	Pay grades
Command Sergeant Major and Staff Sergeant Major	Chief Master Sergeant	Sergeant Major and Master Gunnery Sergeant	Master Chief Petty Officer	E-9
1st Sergeant and Master Sergeant	Senior Master Sergeant	1st Sergeant and Master Sergeant	Senior Chief Petty Officer	E-8
Sergeant 1st Class	Master Sergeant	Gunnery Sergeant	Chief Petty Officer	E-7
Staff Sergeant	Technical Sergeant	Staff Sergeant	Petty Officer 1st Class	E-6
Sergeant	Staff Sergeant	Sergeant	Petty Officer 2nd Class	E-5
Corporal	Sergeant	Corporal	Petty Officer 3rd Class	E-4
Private 1st Class	Airman 1st Class	Lance Corporal	Seaman	E-3
Private	Airman	Private 1st Class	Seaman Apprentice	E-2
Private	Airman/Basic	Private	Seaman Recruit	E-1

1. Army specialist pay grades correspond to numbers: Specialist 4 (E-4), etc. *Source:* Department of Defense

Pay Grades of Commissioned Officers and Warrant Officers

Rank			
Army, Air Force, and Marine Corps	Navy, Coast Guard, and National Oceanic and Atmospheric Adm. (NOAA)	Public Health Service	Pay grade
General	Admiral[1]	—	0–10
Lieutenant General	Vice Admiral	—	0–9
Major General	Rear Admiral (upper half)	Surgeon General; Deputy Surgeon General; Assistant Surgeon General	0–8
Brigadier General	Rear Admiral (lower half) and Commodore	Assistant Surgeon General	0–7
Colonel	Captain	Director Grade	0–6
Lieutenant Colonel	Commander	Senior Grade	0–5
Major	Lieutenant Commander	Full Grade	0–4
Captain	Lieutenant	Senior Assistant Grade	0–3
First Lieutenant	Lieutenant (junior grade)	Assistant Grade	0–2
Second Lieutenant	Ensign	Junior Assistant Grade	0–1
Chief Warrant Officer	Chief Warrant Officer[1]	—	W–4
Chief Warrant Officer	Warrant Officer[1]	—	W–3
Chief Warrant Officer	Warrant Officer[1]	—	W–2
Warrant Officer	Warrant Officer[1]	—	W–1

1. Not applicable to National Oceanic and Atmospheric Administration (NOAA). *Source:* Department of Defense.

Monthly Basic Pay and Allowance for Quarters Rates by Pay Grades, 1980

Pay Grade	Pay rates: Years of service: 2 or less	Over 2	Over 3	Over 4	Over 6	Over 8	Over 10	Over 12	Over 14	Over 16	Over 18	Over 20	Over 22	Over 26	Over 30	Allowance for quarters: Without dependents: Full rate[1]	Partial rate[2]	With dependents
COMMISSIONED OFFICERS																		
O-10[3]	$3529.80	$3654.00	$3654.00	$3654.00	$3654.00	$3794.10	$3794.10	$4084.80	$4084.80	$4377.00[4]	$4377.00[4]	$4669.80[4]	$4669.80[4]	$4961.10[4]	$4961.10[4]	$383.10	$50.70	$479.10
O-9	3128.40	3210.60	3278.70	3278.70	3278.70	3362.40	3362.40	3501.90	3501.90	3794.10	3794.10	4084.80	4084.80	4377.00[4]	4377.00[4]	383.10	50.70	479.10
O-8	2833.50	2918.40	2987.70	2987.70	2987.70	3210.60	3210.60	3362.40	3362.40	3501.90	3654.00	3794.10	3946.20	3946.20	3946.20	383.10	50.70	479.10
O-7	2354.40	2514.60	2514.60	2514.60	2627.10	2627.10	2779.80	2779.80	2918.40	3210.60	3431.10	3431.10	3431.10	3431.10	3431.10	383.10	50.70	479.10
O-6	1745.10	1917.60	2042.70	2042.70	2042.70	2042.70	2042.70	2042.70	2112.00	2446.50	2571.60	2627.10	2779.80	3014.70	3014.70	343.80	39.60	419.40
O-5	1395.90	1639.20	1752.30	1752.30	1752.30	1752.30	1805.70	1902.30	2029.50	2181.60	2307.00	2376.60	2459.70	2459.70	2459.70	316.80	33.00	381.60
O-4	1176.60	1432.20	1528.20	1528.20	1556.10	1625.40	1736.10	1833.90	1917.60	2001.30	2057.10	2057.10	2057.10	2057.10	2057.10	282.30	26.70	340.50
O-3[2]	1093.50	1222.20	1306.50	1445.70	1514.70	1569.60	1653.90	1736.10	1778.70	1778.70	1778.70	1778.70	1778.70	1778.70	1778.70	248.10	22.20	306.30
O-2[2]	953.10	1041.30	1250.70	1293.00	1319.70	1319.70	1319.70	1319.70	1319.70	1319.70	1319.70	1319.70	1319.70	1319.70	1319.70	215.40	17.70	272.70
O-1[2]	827.40	861.30	1041.30	1041.30	1041.30	1041.30	1041.30	1041.30	1041.30	1041.30	1041.30	1041.30	1041.30	1041.30	1041.30	168.00	13.20	219.00
COMMISSIONED OFFICERS WITH OVER 4 YEARS ACTIVE SERVICE AS ENLISTED MEMBERS																		
O-3	0.	0.	0.	1445.70	1514.70	1569.60	1653.90	1736.10	1805.70	1805.70	1805.70	1805.70	1805.70	1805.70	1805.70	—	—	—
O-2	0.	0.	0.	1293.00	1319.70	1361.70	1432.20	1487.40	1528.20	1528.20	1528.20	1528.20	1528.20	1528.20	1528.20	—	—	—
O-1	0.	0.	0.	1041.30	1112.10	1153.20	1194.90	1236.60	1293.00	1293.00	1293.00	1293.00	1293.00	1293.00	1293.00	—	—	—
WARRANT OFFICERS																		
W-4	1113.90	1194.90	1194.90	1222.20	1278.00	1334.40	1390.20	1487.40	1556.10	1611.30	1653.90	1707.90	1765.20	1902.30	1902.30	271.80	25.20	328.20
W-3	1012.50	1098.30	1098.30	1112.10	1125.30	1207.50	1278.00	1319.70	1361.70	1402.50	1445.70	1501.50	1556.10	1611.30	1611.30	242.40	20.70	298.80
W-2	886.30	959.10	959.10	987.00	1041.30	1098.30	1139.70	1181.40	1222.20	1265.10	1306.50	1347.90	1402.50	1402.50	1402.50	210.90	15.90	268.20
W-1	738.90	847.20	847.20	917.70	959.10	1000.50	1041.30	1084.20	1125.30	1166.70	1207.50	1250.70	1250.70	1250.70	1250.70	190.50	13.80	246.60
ENLISTED MEMBERS																		
E-9[5]	0.	0.	0.	0.	0.	0.	1265.40	1294.20	1323.60	1354.20	1384.20	1411.20	1485.60	1629.60	1629.60	205.20	18.60	288.60
E-8	0.	0.	0.	0.	0.	1061.70	1091.40	1120.50	1149.90	1179.90	1207.20	1236.90	1309.50	1455.60	1455.60	189.00	15.30	266.70
E-7	741.30	800.10	829.80	858.60	888.30	916.20	945.60	975.00	1019.10	1047.90	1077.60	1091.40	1164.90	1309.50	1309.50	160.80	12.00	248.10
E-6	640.20	698.10	727.20	757.80	786.00	814.80	844.90	888.30	916.30	945.60	960.00	960.00	960.00	960.00	960.00	146.10	9.90	228.30
E-5	562.20	611.70	641.40	669.30	713.10	742.20	771.90	800.10	814.80	814.80	814.80	814.80	814.80	814.80	814.80	140.40	8.70	209.70
E-4	540.30	570.60	603.90	651.00	676.80	676.80	676.80	676.80	676.80	676.80	676.80	676.80	676.80	676.80	676.80	123.90	8.10	184.50
E-3	519.60	548.10	570.30	592.80	592.80	592.80	592.80	592.80	592.80	592.80	592.80	592.80	592.80	592.80	592.80	110.70	7.80	160.80
E-2	500.10	500.10	500.10	500.10	500.10	500.10	500.10	500.10	500.10	500.10	500.10	500.10	500.10	500.10	500.10	97.80	7.20	160.80
E-1	448.80	448.80	448.80	448.80	448.80	448.80	448.80	448.80	448.80	448.80	448.80	448.80	448.80	448.80	448.80	92.40	6.90	160.80

1. Payment of the full rate of basic allowance for quarters at these rates for members of the uniformed services to personnel without dependents is authorized by 37 U.S. Code 403 and Part IV of Executive Order 11157, as amended. 2. Payment of the partial rate of basic allowance for quarters at these rates to members of the uniformed services without dependents who, under 37 U.S. Code 403(b) or 403(c), are not entitled to the full rate of basic allowance for quarters, is authorized by 37 U.S. Code 1009(d) and Part IV of Executive Order 11157, as amended. 3. For duration of service as Chairman of the Joint Chiefs of Staff, Chief of Staff of the Army, Chief of Naval Operations, Chief of Staff of the Air Force, or Commandant of the Marine Corps, basic pay for this grade is $5,473.80 regardless of cumulative years of service. 4. Basic pay is limited to $4,466.40 by Section 5308 of Title 5 of the Level V of the Executive Schedule. 5. Highest Enlisted Rank. For duration of service as Sergeant Major of the Army, Master Chief Petty Officer of the Navy, Chief Master Sergeant of the Air Force, or Sergeant Major of the Marine Corps, basic pay for this grade is $1,980.90 regardless of cumulative years of service. *Source:* Department of Defense.

Extra Pay for Service During Hostilities

Act of March 3, 1847, during the Mexican War, provided for $2 a month extra pay for "distinguished service." This continued beyond the war and applied in the Civil War.

In the Spanish-American War, there was a 20% increase in enlisted men's pay for war service.

In World War I, additional incentive pay was offered for all types of services. Among these items was pay for certificate of merit of $2 a month. By the law passed in 1920, the reasons for additional pay had expanded. Recipients of the Medal of Honor, Distinguished Service Cross, and Distinguished Service Medal received $2 a month extra, while each bar in lieu of these medals also added another $2 a month. Added to this was a foreign service bonus of 20%.

Act of June 30, 1944, authorized $5 a month to enlisted men qualified as expert infantrymen and $10 to those qualified as combat infantrymen. Amounts were payable for the duration of war and 6 months thereafter.

By the Act of July 6, 1945, for the duration of war and for 6 months thereafter, enlisted men entitled to wear Medical Badges received additional pay of $10 a month.

Act of July 10, 1952, authorized $45 a month for each month beginning after May 31, 1950, for which the member was entitled to receive basic pay and during which he was a member of a combat unit in Korea.

The Combat Duty Pay Act of 1952 was repealed by the Uniformed Services Pay Act of 1963, which authorized special pay for duty subject to hostile fire under certain conditions at the rate of $55 (now $65) a month.

Family Separation Allowance

Military members with dependents in grades E-4 (over 4 years of service) and above are entitled to an allowance of $30 a month in addition to allowances or per diem when on a permanent change of station, with movement of dependents not authorized and dependents not residing near his station; or be on board ship or temporary duty for more than 30 days, with dependents not residing near the temporary duty station.

A second type of family separation allowance at the rate equal to the quarters allowance for a member in the same grade without dependents is payable to a member with dependents when assigned to permanent duty outside the United States or in Alaska when government quarters, or quarters under the jurisdiction of a uniformed service, are not available to the member. Further, the member's dependents must not be residing at or near his permanent duty station and are not authorized to movement to or near the permanent duty station at Government expense.

Allowances for Subsistence

Officers receive $62.80 per month. Enlisted personnel receive allowances for subsistence under the following provisions: (1) when rations in kind are not available, $3.38 per day; (2) when on leave or authorized to mess separately, $3.00 per day; (3) when assigned to duty under emergency conditions where no messing facilities of the U.S. are available, $4.48 per day.

Special Pay

Medical, Dental, Optometry, and Veterinary Officers

Monthly special pay for medical officers is based on cumulative service: 0–2 years, $100; 2 or more years, $350. For dental officers: 0–2 years, $100; 2–6 years, $150; 6–10 years, $250; 10 or more years, $350.

Monthly special pay for optometry and veterinary officers who entered on active duty before July 1, 1975, is $100 regardless of years of service. Those who entered after July 1, 1975, are not eligible for the special pay.

Variable Incentive Pay for Physicians

Selected physicians who are serving in critical specialties and have completed at least 4 years of an initial active-duty obligation may, if otherwise qualified and approved, agree in writing to remain on active duty for a specified number of years for which they may be paid not more than $13,500 for each year of the agreement. This is in addition to other pays and allowances.

Diving Duty

The monthly pay is not more than $110 for periods during which diving duty is actually performed. It may not be paid in addition to incentive pay.

Career Sea Pay

An enlisted member of uniformed services who is in pay grade E-4 or above is entitled to a special "Career Sea Pay," which was enacted to be effective October 1, 1979. The level of sea pay is as follows:

Over 3 years of sea duty: $25 per month; over 5: $35; over 7: $45; over 12: $55. However, this is an interim scale and new rates will be effective October 1, 1981. The level at which sea pay has been set is as follows:

Over 3 years of sea duty: $25 per month; over 5: $35; over 7: $45; over 9: $55; over 10: $65; over 11: $75; over 12: $100.

Proficiency Pay for Enlisted Members

1. A qualified career member serving in a designated specialty may receive shortage specialty pay. This type of proficiency pay is paid to personnel in high training cost specialties in which there is a critical shortage of career members. Monthly rates authorized for FY 79 are $50, $100, or $150.

2. A qualified member serving in a designated duty assignment may receive special duty assignment pay. This is paid to individuals on special duty assignments for which the number of volunteers is inadequate. Monthly rates authorized for FY 79 are $30, $50, $75, $100, or $150.

3. When employed, eligible members serving in a specialty not designated for receipt of another type of proficiency pay may compete for superior performance pay. Monthly rates authorized were $30 and $50. (Not currently being used.)

Duty Subject to Hostile Fire

Except in time of war declared by Congress and under regulations prescribed by the Secretary of Defense, special pay at the rate of $65 a month will be paid to a member of the uniformed services for any month during which he was subject to hostile fire.

Incentive Pay for Hazardous Duty

Members of the uniformed services are entitled to incentive pay for special kinds of hazardous duty. For the following kinds, an officer is entitled to $110 a month, and an enlisted man to $55 a month:

1. Frequent and regular participation in aerial flights *not* as a crew member.
2. Frequent and regular participation in glider flights.
3. Parachute jumping as an essential part of military duty.
4. Duty involving contact with lepers.
5. Demolition of explosives as primary duty (including training).
6. Duty inside a high- or low-pressure chamber.
7. Duty as a human acceleration or deceleration experimental subject.
8. Duty as a human test subject in thermal stress experiments.
9. Frequent and regular participation in flight operations on the flight deck of an aircraft carrier.

For duty as an enlisted crew member of an aircraft or a crew member of a submarine, the rates for incentive pay are as follows:

O–10—$165 regardless of yrs of service.
O–9—$165 regardless of yrs of service.
O–8—Under 3 yrs service, $155; over 3 yrs, $165.
O–7—Under 3 yrs service, $150; over 3 yrs, $160.
O–6—Under 3 yrs service, $200; 3–16 yrs, $215; 16–18 yrs, $220; over 18 yrs, $245.
O–5—Under 3 yrs service, $190; 3–12 yrs, $205; 12–14 yrs, $210; 14–16 yrs, $225; 16–18 yrs, $230; over 18 yrs, $245.
O–4—Under 3 yrs service, $170; 3–8 yrs, $185; 8–10 yrs, $195; 10–12 yrs, $210; 12–14 yrs. $215; 14–16 yrs, $220; 16–18 yrs, $230; over 18 yrs, $240.
O–3—Under 3 yrs service, $145; 3–4 yrs, $155; 4–6 yrs, $165; 6–8 yrs, $180; 8–10 yrs, $185; 10–12 yrs, $190; 12–14 yrs, $200; over 14 yrs, $205.
O–2—Under 2 yrs service, $115; 2–3 yrs, $125; 3–6 yrs, $150; 6–8 yrs, $160; 8–10 yrs, $165; 10–12 yrs, $170; 12–14 yrs, $180; over 14 yrs, $185.
O–1—Under 2 yrs service, $100; 2–3 yrs, $105; 3–6 yrs, $135; 6–8 yrs, $140; 8–10 yrs, $145; 10–12 yrs, $155; 12–14 yrs, $160; over 14 yrs, $170.
W–4—Under 6 yrs service, $115; 6–8 yrs, $120; 8–10 yrs, $125; 10–12 yrs, $135; 12–14 yrs, $145; 14–16 yrs, $155; 16–18 yrs, $160; over 18 yrs, $165.
W–3—Under 2 yrs service, $110; 2–6 yrs, $115; 6–10 yrs, $120; 10–12 yrs, $125; 12–14 yrs, $135; over 14 yrs, $140.
W–2—Under 2 yrs service, $105; 2–6 yrs, $110; 6–8 yrs, $115; 8–10 yrs, $120; 10–12 yrs, $125; 12–14 yrs, $130; over 14 yrs, $135.
W–1—Under 2 yrs service, $100; 2–6 yrs, $105; 6–8 yrs, $110; 8–10 yrs, $120; 10–12 yrs, $125; over 12 yrs, $130.
E–9—$105 regardless of yrs of service.
E–8—$105 regardless of yrs of service.
E–7—Under 2 yrs service, $80; 2–6 yrs, $85; 6–8 yrs, $90; 8–10 yrs, $95; 10–12 yrs, $100; over 12 yrs, $105.
E–6—Under 2 yrs service, $70; 2–4 yrs, $75; 4–6 yrs, $80; 6–8 yrs, $85; 8–10 yrs, $90; 10–14 yrs, $95; over 14 yrs, $100.
E–5—Under 2 yrs service, $60; 2–4 yrs, $70; 4–8 yrs, $80; 8–10 yrs, $85; 10–12 yrs, $90; over 12 years, $95.
E–4—Under 2 yrs service, $55; 2–4 yrs, $65; 4–6 yrs, $70; 6–8 yrs, $75; over 8 yrs, $80.
E–3—Under 2 yrs service, $55; over 2 yrs, $60.
E–2—Under 2 yrs service, $50; over 2 yrs, $60.
E–1—Under 2 yrs service, $50; over 2 yrs, $55.

NOTE: The information on military pay was correct at presstime (summer 1980). However, pay rates may be changed in 1981.

Veterans' Benefits

Although benefits of various kinds date back to Colonial days, veterans of World War I were the first to receive disability compensation, allotments for dependents, life insurance, medical care, and vocational rehabilitation. In 1940, these benefits were slowly broadened.

The following benefits available to veterans require certain minimum periods of active duty during qualifying periods of service and, except for service personnel, are applicable only to those whose discharges are not dishonorable.

Unemployment allowances. Every effort is being made to secure employment for Vietnam veterans. Unemployment benefits are administered by the U.S. Department of Labor.

Loans. GI loans are made for a variety of purposes, such as: to buy or build a home; to purchase a mobile home with or without a lot; and to refinance a home presently owned and occupied by the veteran. The VA will guarantee the lender against loss up to 60% of a home loan with a maximum of $25,000. On mobile home loans, the amount of the guaranty is 50% of the loan with a maximum of $17,500. The interest rate may not exceed the maximum rate set by the VA and in effect when the loan is made.

Compensation and rehabilitation benefits. These are available to those having some service-connected illness or disability.

Disability compensation. The VA pays from $44 to $809 per month, and for specific conditions up to $2,308 per month, plus allowances for dependents, where the disability is rated 50% or more.

Vocational rehabilitation. Necessary training expenses, special equipment, etc., toward a definite job objective are paid for, plus a monthly allowance of up to $241, with increased amounts for dependents, in addition to compensation.

Medical and dental care. This includes care in VA and, in certain instances, in non-VA, or other federal hospitals. It also covers outpatient treatment at a VA field facility or, in some cases, by an approved private physician or dentist. Full domiciliary care is also provided where necessary. Nursing home care may be provided at certain VA medical facilities or in approved community nursing homes. Hospital and other medical care may also be provided for the spouse and child dependents of a veteran who is permanently and totally disabled due to a service-connected disability; or for survivors of a veteran who dies from a service-connected disability; or for survivors of a veteran who at the time of death had a total disability, permanent in nature, resulting from a service-connected disability. These latter benefits are usually provided in nonfederal facilities. Eligibility criteria for these benefits vary, and veterans and/or their dependents or survivors should always apply in advance. Contact the nearest VA medical facility.

Dependents' Educational Assistance. The VA pays $311 a month for up to 45 months of schooling to sons and daughters of veterans who died of service-connected causes or who were permanently and totally disabled from service-connected causes or while permanently and totally disabled or who are missing in action, captured in the line of duty, or forcibly detained or interned in line of duty by a foreign power for more than 90 days. Students must usually be between 18 and 26.

Spouses of veterans whose deaths are adjudged to be service-connected, and spouses of veterans who are permanently and totally disabled due to service-connected causes or who are prisoners of war or are missing in action are also eligible for this educational benefit.

Veterans readjustment education. Veterans who served on active duty for at least 181 days after Jan. 31, 1955, but before Jan. 1, 1977, may receive monthly educational assistance under the new GI Bill for post-Korean conflict veterans, varying from $311 for single full-time students to $422 for veterans with two dependents, plus $26 for each additional dependent. Veterans and servicepersons who initially entered the military on or after Jan. 1, 1977, may receive educational assistance under a contributory plan. Individuals contribute $50 to $75 from military pay, up to a maximum of $2,700. Participants receive monthly payments for the number of months they contributed, or for 36 months, whichever is less.

Pensions. The Veterans Pension Act of 1959, effective July 1, 1960, provides a sliding-scale formula for pension benefits for wartime veterans totally disabled from non-service-connected causes. These benefits are based on need. Surviving spouses and orphans of Mexican Border service, World War II, Korea, and Vietnam veterans have the same eligibility status.

Insurance. The VA life insurance programs have approximately 7.4 million policyholders with total coverage of about $86.1 billion. Detailed information on NSLI (National Service Life Insurance), USGLI (United States Government Life Insurance), and VMLI (Veterans Mortgage Life Insurance) may be obtained at any VA Office. Information regarding SGLI (Servicemen's Group Life Insurance) and VGLI (Veterans Group Life Insurance) may be obtained from the VA Center, P.O. Box 8079, Philadelphia, Pa. 19101, or the Office of Servicemen's Group Life Insurance, 212 Washington St., Newark, N.J. 07102

Highest Ranking Officers in the Armed Forces

ARMY[1]

General of the Army: Omar N. Bradley

Generals: Edward C. Meyer, Chief of Staff; Bernard W. Rogers, Supreme Allied Commander, Europe; John J. Hennessey; Frederick J. Kroesen; John W. Vessey, Jr.; John R. Guthrie; Donn A. Starry; Robert M. Shoemaker; Volney F. Warner; John A. Wickham.

AIR FORCE

Generals: David C. Jones, Chairman, Joint Chiefs of Staff; Lew Allen, Jr.; Richard H. Ellis; Robert E. Huyser; William G. Moore, Jr.; James R. Allen; James E. Hill.

NAVY

Admirals: Thomas B. Hayward, Chief of Naval Operations; Hyman G. Rickover; Harold E. Shear; Robert L. J. Long; Donald C. Davis; Alfred J. Whittle, Jr.; Harry D. Train II; James D. Watkins; William J. Crowe, Jr.

MARINE CORPS

Generals: Robert H. Barrow, Commandant of the Marine Corps; Kenneth McLennan, Assistant Commandant and Chief of Staff.

Lieutenant Generals: Andrew W. O'Donnell; Edward J. Miller; Philip D. Shutler; Adolph G. Schwenk; John H. Miller; William J. White; Edward J. Bronars; Paul X. Kelley.

COAST GUARD

Admiral: John B. Hayes, Commandant.

Vice Admirals: Robert H. Scarborough, Jr., Vice Commandant; Robert I. Price, Commander, Atlantic Area; James S. Gracey, Commander, Pacific Area.

1. On March 15, 1978, George Washington, the commander of the Continental Army in the American Revolution and our first President, was promoted to the newly-created rank of General of the Armies of the United States. Congress authorized this title two years ago to make it clear that Washington is the Army's senior general. *Source:* Department of Defense.

Women in the Armed Services

(In thousands except percent. As of June 30 except, beginning 1977, as of Sept. 30)

Item	1960	1965	1970	1972	1974	1975	1976	1977	1978
TOTAL MILITARY	2,476	2,655	3,066	2,323	2,162	2,128	2,082	2,074	2,062
Women	32	31	42	45	75	97	109	119	134
Percent	1.3	1.2	1.4	1.9	3.5	4.6	5.2	5.7	6.5
Officers, total	317	339	402	336	303	292	281	276	274
Women	11	11	13	13	13	14	14	15	17
Percent	3.4	3.1	3.3	3.8	4.3	4.6	5.0	5.4	6.2
Enlisted personnel	2,160	2,317	2,664	1,987	1,860	1,836	1,801	1,798	1,788
Women	21	20	.28	32	62	83	95	104	117
Percent	1.0	.9	1.1	1.6	3.3	4.5	5.3	5.8	6.5

Source: U.S. Department of Defense.

Department of Defense Personnel and Payroll

Year	Personnel (in thousands): Total	Active duty military	Direct hire civilian	Military retirees	Payroll (in billions of dollars): Total	Active duty military[1]	Direct hire civilian[2]	Military pensions payments[3]
1950	2,213	1,460	753	132	8.2	5.3	2.9	n.a.
1955	4,122	2,935	1,187	180	13.8	9.1	4.7	n.a.
1960	3,523	2,476	1,047	256	15.1	9.3	5.8	n.a.
1965	3,689	2,655	1,034	481	18.5	11.4	7.1	n.a.
1968	4,865	3,548	1,317	651	25.8	16.4	9.4	2.0
1969	4,802	3,460	1,342	714	28.2	17.9	10.3	2.2
1970	4,260	3,066	1,194	773	30.7	19.4	11.3	2.5
1971	3,842	2,715	1,127	831	30.8	19.2	11.6	3.1
1972	3,406	2,323	1,083	890	32.0	19.8	12.2	3.6
1973	3,284	2,253	1,031	948	32.6	20.3	12.3	4.1
1974	3,233	2,162	1,071	1,012	32.7	19.9	12.8	4.9
1975	3,170	2,128	1,042	1,073	34.0	20.2	13.8	6.1
1976	3,092	2,082	1,010	1,132	35.0	20.4	14.6	7.3
1977[4]	3,057	2,057	982	1,200	36.8	21.0	15.8	8.2
1978[4]	3,043	2,062	980	1,243[5]	38.6	21.0	17.6	9.0

1. Excludes troop subsistence, transportation, movement of personnel, etc. 2. Excludes benefits, etc. 3. For U.S. only. 4. Personnel as of Sept. 30; payroll for year ending Sept. 30. 5. Estimated. n.a. = not available. *Source:* Department of Defense.

Federal Budget Outlays for National Defense and Veterans Benefits and Services

(in billions of dollars, except percent)

Year	Total federal outlays, all functions	Total national defense and veterans outlays	National defense: Total: Current dollars	Total: Annual percent change	Current dollars as percent of—: Total federal outlays	Current dollars as percent of—: GNP[1]	Southeast Asia: Full costs[2]	Southeast Asia: Incremental costs[3]	Veterans benefits and services: Total	Veterans: Percent of total federal outlays
1950	42.6	21.2	12.4	−31.4[5]	29.1	4.7	—	—	8.8	20.7
1955	68.5	44.6	39.9	26.3	58.2	10.5	—	—	4.7	6.9
1960	92.2	50.6	45.2	2.6	49.0	9.1	—	—	5.4	5.9
1962	106.8	54.6	49.0	4.1	45.8	9.0	—	—	5.6	5.3
1963	111.3	55.6	50.1	2.2	45.0	8.7	—	—	5.5	5.0
1964	118.6	57.2	51.5	2.8	43.4	8.4	—	—	5.7	4.8
1965	118.4	53.2	47.5	−7.8	40.1	7.2	.1	.1	5.7	4.8
1966	134.7	60.8	54.9	15.6	40.8	7.6	5.8	5.8	5.9	4.4
1967	158.3	75.1	68.2	24.2	43.1	8.8	20.1	18.4	6.9	4.4
1968	178.8	85.7	78.8	15.5	44.1	9.5	26.5	20.5	6.9	3.8
1969	184.5	87.0	79.4	.8	43.0	8.8	28.8	21.5	7.6	4.1
1970	196.6	87.3	78.6	1.0	40.0	8.2	23.1	17.4	8.7	4.4
1971	211.4	85.6	75.8	−3.6	35.9	7.4	14.7	11.5	9.8	4.6
1972	232.0	87.3	76.6	1.1	33.0	6.9	9.4	7.2	10.7	4.6
1973	247.1	86.5	74.5	−2.7	30.1	6.0	6.3	5.3	12.0	4.9
1974	269.6	91.2	77.8	4.4	28.9	5.7	3.1	2.7	13.4	5.0
1975	326.1	102.2	85.6	10.0	26.2	5.9	1.4	1.1	16.6	5.1
1976	365.6	107.8	89.4	4.4	24.5	5.5	.3	.3	18.4	5.0
1976, TQ[4]	94.7	26.3	22.3	n.a.	23.5	n.a.	.3	.1	4.0	4.2
1977	401.9	115.5	97.5	9.1	24.2	5.3	—	—	18.0	4.5
1978	450.8	124.2	105.2	7.9	23.3	4.8	—	—	19.0	4.2
1979, est.	493.4	134.8	114.5	8.8	23.2	5.0	—	—	20.3	4.1
1980, est.	531.6	146.3	125.8	9.9	23.7	5.0	—	—	20.5	3.8

1. Gross national product. 2. Included in national defense total. 3. Incremental war cost figures reflect the estimated costs being incurred over and above the normal peacetime operating costs of the base line force. 4. Transition quarter, July-Sept. 1976. 5. Change from prior year shown; for 1950, change from 1945. NOTE: Through 1976, for years ending June 30, except as noted; 1977, year ending Sept. 30. Includes outlays of Department of Defense, Veterans Administration, and other agencies for activities primarily related to national defense and veterans programs. n.a. = not available. *Source:* Office of Management and Budget and the Department of Defense.

Budget Outlays for National Defense Functions

(in billions of dollars, except as indicated[6])

item	1979	1978	1977	1976	1975	1974	1972	1970
Defense Dept., military	111.9	105.3	95.7	88.0	85.0	77.6	75.2	77.2
Military personnel	28.2	26.8	25.7	25.1	25.0	23.7	23.0	23.0
Percent of military	25.2	25.5	26.9	28.5	29.4	30.6	30.7	29.9
Active forces	26.1	24.9	23.9	23.3	23.2	22.1	21.6	22.0
Reserve forces	2.1	2.0	1.9	1.8	1.7	1.6	1.4	1.1
Military retirees	10.3	9.2	8.2	7.3	6.2	5.1	3.9	2.8
Operation, maintenance	35.9	33.5	30.6	27.9	26.3	22.5	21.7	21.6
Procurement[2]	22.5	21.6	18.2	16.0	16.0	15.2	17.1	21.6
Army	3.4	3.6	2.6	1.4	2.5	2.6	3.9	5.2
Navy[3]	10.5	9.3	8.5	8.0	8.1	7.3	7.1	7.9
Air Force	8.3	8.5	6.9	6.5	5.3	5.4	6.0	8.4
Research and develop	11.7	10.7	9.8	8.9	8.9	8.6	7.9	7.2
Military construction	1.9	1.9	1.9	2.0	1.5	1.4	1.1	1.2
Family housing	1.4	1.5	1.4	1.2	1.1	.9	.7	.6
Civil defense	.1	.1	.1	.1	.1	.1	.1	.1
Other[4]	(1)	(1)	−.2	−.4	−.1	−.2	−.3	−1.0
Atomic energy activities[5]	2.5	2.3	1.9	1.6	1.5	1.5	1.4	1.4
Defense-related activities	.1	(1)	−.1	−.1	−.9	−1.3	—	—
Total	**114.5**	**107.6**	**97.5**	**89.4**	**85.5**	**77.8**	**76.6**	**78.6**

1. Less than $50 million. 2. Includes other defense agencies not shown separately. 3. Includes Marine Corps. 4. Revolving and management funds, trust funds, special foreign currency program, allowances, and offsetting receipts. 5. Defense activities only. 6. For years ending June 30 except, beginning 1979, ending Sept. 30, 1979 data are estimates. *Source:* Office of Management and Budget.

Department of Defense Outlays by Branch of Service

Year	Outlays (in millions of dollars)					Percent distribution			
	Total	Army	Navy	Air Force	Other	Army	Navy	Air Force	Other
1965	47,098	11,552	13,339	18,146	4,061	24.5	28.3	38.5	8.6
1968	78,027	25,223	22,071	25,734	4,999	32.3	28.3	33.0	6.4
1970	78,349	25,147	22,656	25,233	5,313	32.1	28.9	32.2	6.8
1971	76,005	23,909	22,374	24,749	4,973	31.5	29.4	32.6	6.5
1972	76,674	23,473	22,736	24,845	5,620	30.6	29.7	32.4	7.3
1973	74,473	21,140	22,985	24,538	5,811	28.4	30.9	32.9	7.8
1974	77,651	22,371	24,616	25,736	4,927	28.8	31.7	33.1	6.4
1975	84,988	23,678	28,299	26,709	6,303	27.9	33.3	31.4	7.4
1976	87,950	25,025	30,404	28,248	4,272	28.5	34.6	32.1	4.9
1977	94,810	24,231	31,287	28,356	10,936	25.6	33.0	29.9	11.5
1978	102,682	26,250	33,573	29,344	13,515	25.6	32.7	28.6	13.2

Source: Department of the Treasury.

U.S. Navy Combatant Vessels, 1980

Type	Number	Type	Number
Carriers	13	Mine warfare	3
Destroyers	78	Patrol ships	3
Cruisers	26	Amphibious warfare	63
Frigates	68	Auxiliaries	80
Submarines[1]	121	Total	455

1. 79 attack submarines, 41 missile submarines, and 1 other. NOTE: As of May 1980, exact figures are classified information *Source:* Department of Navy.

World's First Atomic Sub Decommissioned

The pioneer nuclear-powered attack submarine USS *Nautilus* was decommissioned on March 3, 1980, because it had become too expensive to overhaul. The submarine was launched January 17, 1955.

The Nautilus was the first ship to reach the geographic North Pole and the first ship to complete a voyage across the top of the world, by cruising under the Arctic ice cap from the Bering Strait to the Greenland Sea.

U.S. Military Actions Other Than Declared Wars

Hawaii (1893): U.S. Marines, ordered to land by U.S. Minister John L. Stevens, aided the revolutionary Committee of Safety in overthrowing the native government. Stevens then proclaimed Hawaii a U.S. protectorate. Annexation, resisted by the Democratic administration in Washington, was not formally accomplished until 1898.

China (1900): Boxers (a group of Chinese revolutionists) occupied Peking and laid siege to foreign legations. U.S. troops joined an international expedition which relieved the city.

Panama (1903): After Colombia had rejected a proposed agreement for relinquishing sovereignty over the Panama Canal Zone, revolution broke out, aided by promoters of the Panama Canal Co. Two U.S. warships were standing by to protect American privileges. The U.S. recognized the Republic of Panama on November 6.

Dominican Republic (1904): When the Dominican Republic failed to meet debts owed to the U.S. and foreign creditors, President Theodore Roosevelt declared the U.S. intention of exercising "international police power" in the Western Hemisphere whenever necessary. The U.S. accordingly administered customs and managed debt payments of the Dominican Republic from 1905 to 1907.

Nicaragua (1911): The possibility of foreign control over Nicaragua's canal route led to U.S. intervention and agreement. The U.S. landed Marines in Nicaragua (Aug. 14, 1912) to protect American interests there. A small detachment remained until 1933.

Mexico (1914): Mexican dictator Victoriano Huerta, opposed by President Woodrow Wilson, had the support of European governments. An incident involving unarmed U.S. sailors in Tampico led to the landing of U.S. forces on Mexican soil. Veracruz was bombarded by the Navy to prevent the landing of munitions from a German vessel. At the point of war, both powers agreed to mediation by Argentina, Brazil, and Chile. Huerta abdicated, and Venustiano Carranza succeeded to the presidency.

Haiti (1915): U.S. Marines imposed a military occupation. Haiti signed a treaty making it a virtual protectorate of the U.S. until troops were withdrawn in 1934.

Mexico (1916): Raids by Pancho Villa cost American lives on both sides of the border. President Carranza consented to a punitive expedition led by Gen. John J. Pershing, but antagonism grew in Mexico. Wilson withdrew the U.S. force when war with Germany became imminent.

Dominican Republic (1916): Renewed intervention in the Dominican Republic with internal administration by U.S. naval officers lasted until 1924.

Korea (1950): In this undeclared war, which terminated with the July 27, 1953, truce at Panmunjom and the establishment of a neutral nations' supervisory commission, the U.S. and 15 member-nations of the U.N. came to the aid of the Republic of South Korea, whose 38th-parallel border was crossed by the invading Russian Communist-controlled North Koreans, who were later joined by the Chinese Communists.

Lebanon (1958): Fearful of the newly formed U.A.R. abetting the rebels of his politically and economically torn country, President Camille Chamoun appealed to the U.S. for military assistance. U.S. troops landed in Beirut in mid-July and left before the end of the year, after internal and external quiet were restored.

Dominican Republic (1965): On April 28, when a political coup-turned-civil war endangered the lives of American nationals, President Lyndon B. Johnson rushed 400 marines into Santo Domingo, the beginning of an eventual U.S. peak-commitment of 30,000 troops, constituting the preponderant military strength of the OAS-created Inter-American Peace Force, and 6,500 troops, including 5,000 Americans, remained until after the peaceful inauguration of President Joaquín Balaguer on July 1, 1966, and the entire force left the country on September 20.

Vietnam: This longest war in U.S. history began with economic and technical assistance after 1954 Geneva accords ending the Indochinese War. By 1964 it had escalated into a major conflict.

This involvement spanning the administrations of five Presidents led to domestic discontent in the late 1960s. By April 1969, U.S. troop strength reached a peak of 543,400. Peace negotiations began in Paris in 1968 but proved fruitless. Finally, on Jan. 27, 1973, a peace accord was signed in Paris by the U.S., North and South Vietnam, and the Vietcong. Within 60 days, U.S. POWs were returned, and the U.S. withdrew all military forces from South Vietnam.

Casualties in World War I

Country	Total mobilized forces	Killed or died[1]	Wounded	Prisoners or missing	Total casualties
Austria-Hungary	7,800,000	1,200,000	3,620,000	2,200,000	7,020,000
Belgium	267,000	13,716	44,686	34,659	93,061
British Empire[2]	8,904,467	908,371	2,090,212	191,652	3,190,235
Bulgaria	1,200,000	87,500	152,390	27,029	266,919
France[2]	8,410,000	1,357,800	4,266,000	537,000	6,160,800
Germany	11,000,000	1,773,700	4,216,058	1,152,800	7,142,558
Greece	230,000	5,000	21,000	1,000	27,000

Country	Total mobilized forces	Killed or died[1]	Wounded	Prisoners or missing	Total casualties
Italy	5,615,000	650,000	947,000	600,000	2,197,000
Japan	800,000	300	907	3	1,210
Montenegro	50,000	3,000	10,000	7,000	20,000
Portugal	100,000	7,222	13,751	12,318	33,291
Romania	750,000	335,706	120,000	80,000	535,706
Russia	12,000,000	1,700,000	4,950,000	2,500,000	9,150,000
Serbia	707,343	45,000	133,148	152,958	331,106
Turkey	2,850,000	325,000	400,000	250,000	975,000
United States	4,734,991	116,516	204,002	—	320,518

1. Includes deaths from all causes. 2. Official figures. NOTE: For additional U.S. figures, *see* the table on U.S. Casualties in Major Wars in this section.

Casualties in World War II

Country	Men in war	Battle deaths	Wounded
Australia	1,000,000	26,976	180,864
Austria	800,000	280,000	350,117
Belgium	625,000	8,460	55,513[1]
Brazil[2]	40,334	943	4,222
Bulgaria	339,760	6,671	21,878
Canada	1,041,080	32,412	53,145
China[3]	17,250,521	1,324,516	1,762,006
Czechoslovakia	—	6,683[4]	8,017
Denmark	—	4,339	—
Finland	500,000	79,047	50,000
France	—	201,568	400,000
Germany	20,000,000	3,250,000[4]	7,250,000
Greece	—	17,024	47,290
Hungary	—	147,435	89,313
India	2,393,891	32,121	64,354
Italy	3,100,000	149,496[4]	66,716
Japan	9,700,000	1,270,000	140,000
Netherlands	280,000	6,500	2,860
New Zealand	194,000	11,625[4]	17,000
Norway	75,000	2,000	—
Poland	—	664,000	530,000
Romania	650,000[5]	350,000[6]	—
South Africa	410,056	2,473	—
U.S.S.R.	—	6,115,000[4]	14,012,000
United Kingdom	5,896,000	357,116[4]	369,267
United States	16,112,566	291,557	670,846
Yugoslavia	3,741,000	305,000	425,000

1. Civilians only. 2. Army and navy figures. 3. Figures cover period July 7, 1937–Sept. 2, 1945, and concern only Chinese regular troops. They do not include casualties suffered by guerrillas and local military corps. 4. Deaths from all causes. 5. Against Soviet Russia; 385,847 against Nazi Germany. 6. Against Soviet Russia; 169,822 against Nazi Germany. NOTE: The figures in this table are unofficial estimates obtained from various sources. For additional U.S. Figures, *see* the tables on U.S. Casualties in Major Wars in this section.

U.S. Casualties in Major Wars

War	Branch of service	Numbers engaged	Battle deaths	Other deaths	Total deaths	Wounds not mortal	Total casualties[1]
Revolutionary War 1775 to 1783	Army	n.a.	4,044	n.a.	n.a.	6,004	n.a.
	Navy	n.a.	342	n.a.	n.a.	114	n.a.
	Marines	n.a.	49	n.a.	n.a.	70	n.a.
	Total	**n.a.**	**4,435**	**n.a.**	**n.a.**	**6,188**	**n.a.**
War of 1812 1812 to 1815	Army	n.a.	1,950	n.a.	n.a.	4,000	n.a.
	Navy	n.a.	265	n.a.	n.a.	439	n.a.
	Marines	n.a.	45	n.a.	n.a.	66	n.a.
	Total	**286,730**	**2,260**	**n.a.**	**n.a.**	**4,505**	**n.a.**

War	Branch of service	Numbers engaged	Battle deaths	Other deaths	Total deaths	Wounds not mortal	Total casualties[1]
Mexican War 1846 to 1848	Army	n.a.	1,721	11,550	13,271	4,102	17,373
	Navy	n.a.	1	n.a.	n.a.	3	n.a.
	Marines	n.a.	11	n.a.	n.a.	47	n.a.
	Total	**78,718**	**1,733**	**n.a.**	**n.a.**	**4,152**	**n.a.**
Civil War[2] 1861 to 1865	Army	2,128,948	138,154	221,374	359,528	280,040	639,568
	Navy	84,415	2,112	2,411	4,523	1,710	6,233
	Marines		148	312	460	131	591
	Total	**2,213,363**	**140,414**	**224,097**	**364,511**	**281,881**	**646,392**
Spanish-American War 1898	Army	280,564	369	2,061	2,430	1,594	4,024
	Navy	22,875	10	0	10	47	57
	Marines	3,321	6	0	6	21	27
	Total	**306,760**	**385**	**2,061**	**2,446**	**1,662**	**4,108**
World War I 1917 to 1918	Army	4,057,101	50,510	55,868	106,378	193,663	300,041
	Navy	599,051	431	6,856	7,287	819	8,106
	Marines	78,839	2,461	390	2,851	9,520	12,371
	Total	**4,734,991**	**53,402**	**63,114**	**116,516**	**204,002**	**320,518**
World War II 1941 to 1946	Army[3]	11,260,000	234,874	83,400	318,274	565,861	884,135
	Navy	4,183,466	36,950	25,664	62,614	37,778	100,392
	Marines	669,100	19,733	4,778	24,511	67,207	91,718
	Total	**16,112,566**	**291,557**	**113,842**	**405,399**	**670,846**	**1,076,245**
Korean War 1950 to 1953	Army	2,834,000	27,704	9,429	37,133	77,596	114,729
	Navy	1,177,000	458	4,043	4,501	1,576	6,077
	Marines	424,000	4,267	1,261	5,528	23,744	29,272
	Air Force	1,285,000	1,200	5,884	7,084	368	7,452
	Total	**5,720,000**	**33,629**	**20,617**	**54,246**	**103,284**	**157,530**
War in Southeast Asia[4]	Army	4,386,000	30,717	7,194	37,911	201,536	239,447
	Navy[5]	1,842,000	1,535	909	2,444	10,078	12,522
	Marines	794,000	13,025	1,680	14,705	88,633	103,338
	Air Force	1,740,000	1,339	603	1,942	3,457	5,399
	Total	**8,744,000**	**46,616**	**10,386**	**57,002**	**303,704**	**360,706**

1. Excludes captured or interned and missing in action who were subsequently returned to military control. 2. Union forces only. Totals should probably be somewhat larger as data or disposition of prisoners are far from complete. Final Confederate deaths, based on incomplete returns, were 133,821, to which should be added 26,000–31,000 personnel who died in Union prisons. 3. Army data include Air Force. 4. As of Sept. 30, 1977. 5. Includes a small number of Coast Guard. NOTE: All data are subject to revision. For wars before World War I, information represents best data from available records. However, due to incomplete records and possible difference in usage of terminology, reporting systems, etc., figures should be considered estimates. n.a. = not available. *Source:* Department of Defense.

Defense Budget by Major Programs

(Current millions of dollars)

Military programs	1977	1978	1979	1980[2]	1981[2]
Strategic forces	$ 9,359	$ 9,182	$ 8,419	$ 10,880	$ 12,031
General purpose forces	38,107	42,414	47,392	51,948	58,009
Intelligence and communications	7,412	7,898	8,057	9,117	10,668
Airlift and sealift	1,519	1,619	1,743	2,008	2,288
Guard and reserve forces	5,928	6,950	6,961	7,322	8,331
Research and development	9,866	10,106	10,813	11,772	14,025
Central supply and maintenance	11,060	11,955	12,830	14,476	16,731
Training, medical, other general personnel activities	22,449	23,923	25,736	28,700	32,704
Administration and associated activities	2,057	2,188	2,347	2,569	2,975
Support of other nations[1]	219	259	461	550	977
Total	**107,975**	**116,494**	**124,759**	**139,343**	**158,739**

1. Excluding Military Assistance Program. 2. Figures are latest available and are subject to change. NOTE: Figures represent Total Obligational Authority (TOA), that is, the value of the direct Defense program for each fiscal year regardless of the method of financing (which could include balances available from prior years of resources available from sale of items from inventory). *Source:* Department of Defense.

U.S. Military Sales Deliveries to Foreign Governments

(in millions of dollars)

Country	1970–1978[1]	1978	1977	1975	1960–1969
Argentina	88.0	11.0	6.1	8.0	57.7
Australia	668.4	151.8	28.9	19.9	487.5
Austria	51.9	2.0	28.6	2.0	42.1
Belgium	84.7	28.0	6.5	5.6	76.4
Bolivia	1.0	.1	(3)	.4	.5
Brazil	176.2	8.4	9.9	38.8	61.9
Canada	537.9	82.3	66.8	77.2	243.3
Chile	143.8	12.0	57.4	12.3	18.6
China (Taiwan)	794.0	131.1	142.4	115.0	29.1
Colombia	13.3	2.0	1.0	.8	2.6
Denmark	117.0	12.2	22.0	20.6	52.0
Dominican Republic	.6	.1	(3)	(3)	.9
Ecuador	22.7	7.8	9.1	1.4	2.7
Egypt	61.3	50.8	10.5	—	1.6
Ethiopia	89.6	—	59.2	9.8	.2
France	79.8	6.3	3.4	3.7	258.9
Germany	2,985.3	238.5	342.6	394.1	2,471.1
Greece	1,049.7	128.1	242.9	131.8	22.7
Guatemala	22.0	2.4	2.3	3.4	2.0
Honduras	7.2	.5	.4	.6	.2
India	11.5	1.2	1.6	2.4	19.3
Indonesia	51.5	6.3	19.4	8.0	.6
Iran	8,478.1	1,792.9	2,245.9	913.3	237.8
Israel	5,188.7	951.4	875.3	656.5	156.2
Italy	360.8	28.9	41.1	52.2	322.8
Japan	257.4	42.4	24.2	24.8	179.6
Jordan	415.4	110.8	116.4	16.5	74.7
Kampuchea	—	—	—	—	—
Korea[2]	843.8	414.3	184.8	57.5	2.2
Kuwait	373.1	190.8	88.5	7.6	—
Laos	—	—	—	—	—
Lebanon	19.4	8.7	1.0	.9	1.7
Liberia	2.5	.1	.5	.4	.4
Libya	12.3	n.a.	—	(3)	17.3
Malaysia	53.1	3.4	2.3	29.0	3.9
Mexico	7.9	n.a.	4.2	.2	7.9
Morocco	165.3	89.1	31.9	2.4	9.8
Netherlands	192.9	54.4	24.6	24.6	74.3
New Zealand	67.6	4.3	3.3	2.9	53.0
Nicaragua	3.0	.9	.4	.2	.6
Nigeria	17.2	5.9	2.0	3.3	.4
Norway	214.3	28.8	33.2	21.5	101.9
Pakistan	158.9	48.3	38.6	13.0	40.3
Panama	4.5	.2	.3	1.6	(3)
Paraguay	.3	.1	(3)	(3)	(3)
Peru	92.6	13.9	26.0	8.2	16.4
Philippines[2]	100.6	37.8	33.9	5.1	3.5
Portugal	6.8	1.2	.3	.8	5.9
Saudia Arabia	5,985.3	2,317.9	1,617.4	342.2	126.6
Singapore	49.7	9.8	15.2	4.2	.8
South Vietnam	1.2	—	—	(3)	(3)
Spain	539.1	69.1	165.8	47.6	60.0
Sweden	37.0	4.7	19.3	1.5	29.7
Switzerland	184.3	48.8	51.9	7.3	50.5
Thailand[2]	184.2	95.1	17.7	9.7	.5
Tunisia	6.0	1.6	3.3	.2	1.6
Turkey	420.9	159.9	38.2	89.3	1.5
U.K.	987.1	91.7	108.8	56.3	948.4
Uruguay	14.1	1.2	5.6	2.0	1.5
Venezuela	125.6	4.5	27.4	34.5	71.9
Yemen	54.7	27.8	24.9	1.8	—
Yugoslavia	2.4	.2	1.5	(3)	8.9
Zaire	41.6	12.1	8.2	.8	1.4
Other countries	111.7	102.3	1.8	2.8	19.7
International Organizations	273.2	40.8	51.7	30.2	166.5

1. For years ending June 30 except, beginning 1977, ending Sept. 30. Includes transactions for the transition quarter, July-Sept. 1976. 2. Includes Military Assistance Program and Military Assistance Service Funded Program for military assistance deliveries. 3. Less than $50,000. *Source:* Defense Security Assistance Agency.

Projected Nuclear Arsenal in Europe, Mid-1980s

NATO Countries	Number	Warsaw Pact Countries	Number
Cruise missiles	464		
Intermediate-range ballistic missiles[1]	108	Intermediate-range ballistic missiles	710
Short-ranged ballistic missiles	180	Short-range ballistic missiles[2]	416
Submarine-based ballistic missiles	128	Submarine-based ballistic missiles	87
Bombers[3]	237	Bombers[4]	503

1. Pershing-2 missiles having 1,000-mile-plus range and a single warhead. 2. Includes 120 SS-20 missiles having 3,000 to 4,000-mile range and three warheads. 3. 1,500-mile range. 4. Includes 50 plus advanced Backfire bombers. *Source:* International Institute for Strategic Studies, London.

New Battle Tank Honors Gen. Abrams

The XM-1 is the Army's first new main battle tank designed in 20 years. It has been named the Abrams tank in honor of the late Gen. Creighton W. Abrams, Army Chief of Staff.

The Abrams tank has a crew of four, a turbine engine, weighs 60 tons, and can travel at 45 miles per hour on a road and can go 30 miles per hour cross country. The top speed of the former main battle tank, the M-60, is 30 miles per hour.

At present, the XM-1 has a 105-millimeter gun. There are plans to replace this in 1984 with a new West German 120-millimeter gun now being developed. 7,058 of the new tanks are scheduled to be built in the next ten years.

Arms Exports and Imports, Supplier and Recipient Countries
(in millions of constant 1976 dollars)

Country	1968-70	1971-74	1975	1976	1977
SUPPLIERS					
Canada	$ 764	$ 847	$ 84	$ 120	$ 66
China, Mainland	733	1,544	169	100	85
Czechoslovakia	459	1,063	485	440	445
France	921	3,059	711	925	1,232
Germany, West	593	1,030	442	650	758
Poland	692	1,140	242	350	294
U.S.S.R.	6,466	17,740	4,003	4,700	4,929
United Kingdom	682	2,271	527	675	782
United States	14,270	21,705	4,951	5,900	6,540
Other	680	2,771	1,386	1,740	1,569
RECIPIENTS—Developed countries	8,646	14,514	3,740	4,280	3,720
Australia	429	470	32	80	95
Canada	201	409	169	190	161
Czechoslovakia	369	1,379	379	300	237
Germany, East	600	1,739	464	575	445
Germany, West	775	2,613	606	500	455
Hungary	184	729	190	200	152
Italy	324	644	74	170	142
Japan	259	346	63	180	123
Poland	553	1,498	327	390	313
Romania	184	525	179	130	133
U.S.S.R.	890	1,098	411	490	521
United Kingdom	1,208	368	95	240	142
United States	907	777	147	100	114
Other	1,763	1,919	604	735	687
RECIPIENTS—Developing countries	17,906	38,650	9,192	11,355	12,967
Algeria	91	143	95	270	265
Brazil	171	371	105	180	114
Cambodia	112	702	316	—	—
China: Taiwan	942	878	169	160	171
Cuba	76	274	105	140	76
Egypt	1,313	2,469	379	160	190
Greece	546	808	274	525	445
India	635	1,048	179	310	436
Indonesia	52	126	32	80	57
Iran	798	2,935	1,159	2,000	2,275
Iraq	391	1,783	606	825	1,043
Israel	679	2,059	711	1,000	1,043
Jordan	229	269	84	140	123
Korea, North	216	1,063	137	70	104
Korea, South	1,397	1,281	200	320	265
Laos	307	640	21	20	28
Libya	127	842	506	800	900
Nigeria	85	82	84	50	9
Pakistan	324	512	95	140	190
Peru	123	356	105	200	408
Saudi Arabia	296	681	263	470	877
Spain	196	553	169	180	275
Syria	230	3,323	337	460	545
Turkey	1,073	1,068	242	310	133
Vietnam, Socialist Rep.	1,632	2,061	137	50	9
Vietnam, South	3,944	7,211	895	—	—
Other	1,921	5,112	1,787	2,495	2,986
World, total	**26,260**	**53,170**	**13,000**	**15,600**	**16,700**

Source: U.S. Arms Control and disarmament Agency, World Military Expenditures and Arms Transfers, annual.

Department of Defense Hotline for Preventing Waste and Fraud

The Department of Defense operates a toll-free "Defense Hotline" for citizens to report suspected cases of fraud and waste involving the Department of Defense. The nationwide, toll-free number is 800–424–9098. It is operated in Washington, D.C., between 8 a.m. and 4:30 p.m. The Defense Investigative Service operates the hotline with assurance that the anonymity of any caller will be respected.

U.S. Military Strength

(As of June 30 except, beginning 1977, as of Sept. 30)

Description	1960	1965	1970	1973	1974	1975	1976	1977	1978
Department of the Army									
Divisions	14	16	16	13	13	14	16	16	16
Maneuver battalions	n.a.	176	191	138	140	148	160	163	166
Air defense battalions/batteries	288	227	195	182	184	147	156	150	159
Special forces groups	—	7	6	4	4	3	3	3	4
Total aircraft	**5,564**	**7,142**	**12,166**	**9,923**	**9,708**	**9,517**	**9,298**	**8,789**	**8,625**
Department of the Navy									
Ship operating force	900	1,020	847	649	587	577	555	543	531
Active fleet	812	936	769	584	512	496	476	464	453
Naval fleet auxilary force[1]	—	2	5	6	13	18	19	20	21
Naval reserve force	88	82	73	59	62	63	60	59	57
Tactical air squadrons[2]	104	113	88	79	79	79	74	69	65
Antisubmarine air squadrons[3]	29	31	20	18	15	18	19	22	22
Marine divisions	3	3	3	3	3	3	3	3	3
Marine aircraft combat squad									
Fixed-wing squadrons	37	36	32	31	32	31	30	30	30
Rotary-wing squadrons	12	16	21	19	19	19	19	19	19
Total aircraft	**11,272**	**9,725**	**8,646**	**7,448**	**7,423**	**7,035**	**6,839**	**6,593**	**6,359**
Department of the Air Force									
Intercontinental ballistic missile launchers	5	854	1,054	1,054	1,054	1,054	1,054	1,054	1,054
Selected aircraft squadrons	280	219	181	137	132	126	124	125	130
Strategic	142	65	33	31	29	28	27	26	26
Air defense	65	39	17	9	8	7	6	6	6
Tactical (excluding air-lift)	73	115	131	97	95	91	91	93	98
Total aircraft	**21,283**	**16,487**	**14,983**	**12,044**	**11,376**	**10,736**	**10,276**	**10,140**	**10,022**
Active	18,351	14,668	13,545	10,801	10,156	9,336	9,286	9,256	9,138

1. Civilian manned. 2. Includes Special Mission. 3. Does not include patrol squadrons. NOTE: n.a. = not available. *Source.* U.S. Department of Defense, Office of the Secretary, releases and unpublished data.

Insignia and Ranks of the Armed Forces

Army, Air Force, and Marines: Insignia	Rank	Navy and Coast Guard: Insignia	Rank	Stripes[1]
Five silver stars	General of the Army, AF	Five silver stars	Fleet Admiral	1—4—0
Four silver stars	General	Four silver stars	Admiral	1—3—0
Three silver stars	Lieutenant General	Three silver stars	Vice Admiral	1—2—0
Two silver stars	Major General	Two silver stars	Rear Admiral	1—1—0
One silver star	Brigadier General	One silver star	Commodore	1—0—0[2]
Silver eagle	Colonel	Silver eagle	Captain	0—4—0
Silver oak leaf	Lieutenant Colonel	Silver oak leaf	Commander	0—3—0
Gold oak leaf	Major	Gold oak leaf	Lt. Commander	0—2—1
Two silver bars	Captain	Two silver bars	Lieutenant	0—2—0
One silver bar	First Lieutenant	One silver bar	Lieutenant (jg)	0—1—1
One gold bar	Second Lieutenant	One gold bar	Ensign	0—1—0
Silver bar with 4 enamel bands[3]	Chief Warrant Officer (W-4)	Silver bar with 3 enamel bands[3]	Chief Warrant Officer (W-4)	0—1—0[4]
Silver bar with 3 enamel bands[3]	Chief Warrant Officer (W-3)	Silver bar with 2 enamel bands[3]	Chief Warrant Officer (W-3)	0—1—0[5]
Silver bar with 2 enamel bands[3]	Chief Warrant Officer (W-2)	Gold bar with 3 enamel bands[3]	Chief Warrant Officer (W-2)	0—1—0[6]
Silver bar with 1 enamel band[3]	Warrant Officer (W-1)	Gold bar with 2 enamel bands[3]	Warrant Officer (W-1)	0—0—1[6]

1. Of gold embroidery; first figure is number of 2-in. stripes, second is number of 1/2-inch strips, third is number of 1/4-in. stripes. 2. Wartime only. 3. Navy and Marine Corps use same size insignia as Army when worn on shoulder straps, but miniature size on shirt collars. Enamel bands are black for Army, scarlet for Marines, medium blue for Air Force, and blue for Navy and Coast Guard. 4. One break. 5. Two breaks. 6. Three breaks.

WEATHER & CLIMATE

World and U.S. Extremes of Climate

Highest recorded temperature

	Place	Date	Degree Fahrenheit	Degree Centigrade
World (Africa)	El Azizia, Libya	Sept. 13, 1922	136	58
North America (U.S.)	Death Valley, Calif.	July 10, 1913	134	57
Asia	Tirat Tsvi, Israel	June 21, 1942	129	54
Australia	Cloncurry, Queensland	Jan. 16, 1889	128	53
Europe	Seville, Spain	Aug. 4, 1881	122	50
South America	Rivadavia, Argentina	Dec. 11, 1905	120	49
Antarctica	Esperanza, Palmer Peninsula	Oct. 20, 1956	58	14

Lowest recorded temperature

	Place	Date	Degree Fahrenheit	Degree Centigrade
World (Antarctica)	Vostok	Aug. 24, 1960	−127	−88
Asia	Verkhoyansk/Oimekon	Feb. 6, 1933	−90	−68
Greenland	Northice	Jan. 9, 1954	−87	−66
North America (excl. Greenland)	Snag, Yukon, Canada	Feb. 3, 1947	−81	−63
Europe	Ust 'Shchugor, U.S.S.R.	n.a.	−67	−55
South America	Sarmiento, Argentina	Jan. 1, 1907	−27	−33
Africa	Ifrane, Morocco	Feb. 11, 1935	−11	−24
Australia	Charlotte Pass, N.S.W.	July 22, 1947	−8	−22
United States	Prospect Creek, Alaska	Jan. 23, 1971	−80	−62

Greatest rainfalls

	Place	Date	Inches	Centimeters
1 minute (U.S.)	Unionville, Md.	—	1.23	3.1
20 minutes (Romania)	Curtea-de-Arges	—	8.1	20.6
42 minutes (U.S.)	Holt, Mo.	—	12	30
12 hours (Indian Ocean)	Belouve, La Réunion	—	53	135
24 hours (Indian Ocean)	Cilaos, La Réunion	—	74	188
5 days (Indian Ocean)	Cilaos, La Réunion	—	152	386
1 month (India)	Cherrapunji	—	366	930
1 month (U.S.)	Kukui, Maui, Hawaii	—	460	1,168
12 months (India)	Cherrapunji	—	1,042	2,647

Greatest snowfalls

	Place	Date	Inches	Centimeters
1 month (U.S.)	Tamarack, Calif.	Jan. 1911	390	991
24 hours (U.S.)	Silver Lake, Colo.	April 14–15, 1921	76	193
19 hours (France)	Bessans	—	68	173
1 storm (U.S.)	Mt. Shasta Ski Bowl, Calif.	—	189	480
1 season (U.S.)	Paradise Ranger Sta., Wash.	—	1,122	2,850

NOTE: n.a. = not available. *Source:* National Oceanic and Atmospheric Administration, Environmental Data Service.

Tropical Storms and Hurricanes, 1886–1979

	Jan.–April	May	June	July	Aug.	Sept.	Oct.	Nov.	Dec.	Total
Number of tropical storms (incl. hurricanes)	3	13	50	61	183	262	172	33	5	782
Number of tropical storms that reached hurricane intensity	1	3	21	32	132	168	84	15	2	458

Climate of Selected U.S. Cities, 1979

(T = trace)

	Temperature, °F				Precipitation				
Month	Average maximum	Average minimum	Record high	Record low	Rainfall, inches	Snowfall, inches	Days with precipitation	Percentage possible sunshine	Percentage relative humidity at noon
Bakersfield, California (Kern County Air Terminal): lat. 35° 25′ N, long. 119° 03′ W; elevation: 475 ft									
January	60.4	42.7	71	26	1.80	T	14	—	69
April	76.1	50.2	88	42	T	0.0	0	—	51
July	98.1	71.1	110	61	0.00	0.0	0	—	36
October	81.5	59.7	93	42	0.28	0.0	2	—	51
Annual	79.8	55.7	112	26	6.19	T	45	—	52
Caribou, Maine (Municipal Airport): lat. 46° 52′ N, long. 68° 01′ W; elevation: 624 ft									
January	23.5	7.2	45	−27	4.49	32.1	19	—	62
April	48.4	33.9	74	18	3.08	14.9	16	—	60
July	80.4	56.8	91	44	3.36	0.0	17	—	56
October	52.8	37.6	77	25	1.68	0.7	17	—	62
Annual	50.5	33.1	92	17	41.80	95.4	179	—	61
Charleston, South Carolina (Municipal Airport): lat. 32° 54′ N, long. 80° 02′ W; elevation: 40 ft									
January	57.6	33.1	76	20	3.43	0.0	13	67	50
April	76.5	53.2	82	40	3.81	0.0	7	79	48
July	90.8	73.1	97	65	8.35	0.0	13	69	58
October	78.0	53.9	86	38	3.87	0.0	5	81	50
Annual	75.2	54.1	98	20	57.98	1.8	117	72	55
Chicago, Illinois (Midway Airport): lat. 41° 47′ N, long. 87° 45′ W; elevation: 607 ft									
January	21.2	3.8	36	−17	2.81	34.3	15	—	68
April	54.5	36.4	77	19	4.92	0.1	15	—	61
July	84.4	59.5	94	43	2.19	0.0	8	—	55
October	62.7	43.9	84	27	1.49	0.0	9	—	54
Annual	57.5	38.4	94	−17	37.10	48.1	127	—	60
Dallas-Fort Worth, Texas (Regional Airport): lat. 32° 54′ N, long. 97° 02′ W; elevation: 551 ft									
January	42.5	28.2	68	13	3.35	1.8	12	35	73
April	74.6	54.2	90	38	2.03	0.0	8	55	59
July	96.0	73.0	102	67	1.94	0.0	7	75	53
October	84.3	57.2	102	45	3.38	0.0	3	75	43
Annual	74.8	52.9	103	13	32.42	2.5	85	62	57
Denver, Colorado (Stapleton International Airport): lat. 39° 45′ N, long. 104° 52′ W; elevation: 5,283 ft									
January	30.6	5.4	54	−11	0.34	9.1	8	77	52
April	62.1	36.1	78	14	1.41	8.1	7	82	35
July	89.5	57.8	96	51	0.81	0.0	5	82	28
October	67.7	39.9	86	23	1.28	2.7	6	73	43
Annual	62.6	36.3	99	−11	20.36	90.9	94	77	42
Duluth, Minnesota (International Airport): lat. 46° 50′ N, long. 92° 11′ W; elevation: 1,428 ft									
January	9.4	−8.3	26	−32	0.76	11.9	13	63	59
April	42.9	26.0	60	2	1.15	4.2	10	53	59
July	76.5	55.7	88	43	5.45	0.0	12	56	58
October	50.7	35.3	68	25	3.01	0.8	13	33	62
Annual	46.2	28.7	88	−32	30.92	66.6	147	49	61

Month	Temperature, °F				Precipitation			Percentage possible sunshine	Percentage relative humidity at noon
	Average maximum	Average minimum	Record high	Record low	Rainfall, inches	Snowfall, inches	Days with precipi-tation		
Great Falls, Montana (International Airport): lat. 47° 29′ N, long. 111° 22′ W; elevation: 3,662 ft									
January	15.3	−2.3	42	−20	0.71	12.0	12	58	63
April	51.4	29.9	72	16	2.05	8.6	13	42	50
July	84.4	53.6	98	42	0.27	0.0	5	76	37
October	62.3	36.5	86	21	0.84	0.7	5	42	44
Annual	56.8	31.9	100	−28	9.91	52.9	94	58	46
Kansas City, Missouri (International Airport): lat. 39° 17′ N, long. 94° 43′ W; elevation: 1,014 ft									
January	20.8	4.1	40	−11	2.35	13.3	13	74	67
April	61.1	42.0	79	25	2.35	2.0	12	74	64
July	84.1	67.6	93	56	4.68	0.0	13	44	71
October	69.2	46.2	87	27	3.56	0.0	7	63	44
Annual	61.1	41.7	94	−12	31.75	21.5	103	66	59
Los Angeles, California (International Airport): lat. 33° 56′ N, long. 118° 24′ W; elevation: 97 ft									
January	61.7	47.4	70	34	5.26	0.0	10	—	63
April	67.3	53.1	74	49	0.00	0.0	0	—	65
July	74.7	62.0	81	58	0.00	0.0	0	—	67
October	72.9	59.2	79	49	0.31	0.0	3	—	62
Annual	71.0	55.7	103	34	13.52	0.0	39	—	61
Miami, Florida (International Airport): lat. 25° 48′ N, long. 80° 16′ W; elevation: 7 ft									
January	72.5	57.4	81	40	1.28	0.0	10	52	61
April	83.8	71.7	90	66	17.29	0.0	4	76	65
July	88.9	77.4	91	72	5.06	0.0	10	83	58
October	83.7	72.0	88	65	3.63	0.0	13	75	63
Annual	81.9	69.5	94	40	60.11	0.0	123	70	60
New Orleans, Louisiana (International Airport): lat. 29° 59′ N, long. 90° 15′ W; elevation: 4 ft									
January	54.2	37.5	74	23	5.55	T	12	57	65
April	79.5	62.7	85	46	4.90	0.0	10	46	64
July	91.2	75.9	97	70	11.43	0.0	20	48	70
October	82.8	59.1	90	46	1.49	0.0	2	80	56
Annual	77.2	58.7	97	23	60.24	T	111	57	63
New York, New York (Central Park): lat. 40° 47′ N, long. 73° 58′ W; elevation: 132 ft									
January	40.2	26.9	63	8	10.52	6.6	13	—	62
April	60.0	45.1	81	32	4.04	T	13	—	52
July	84.9	68.8	95	53	1.76	0.0	7	—	54
October	64.0	50.6	88	36	3.87	T	8	—	58
Annual	62.8	48.5	95	0	52.13	30.2	129	—	55
Phoenix, Arizona (Sky Harbor International Airport): lat. 33° 26′ N, long. 112° 01′ W; elevation: 1,112 ft									
January	59.2	40.9	70	29	2.16	0.0	8	55	61
April	86.3	53.8	97	39	0.02	0.0	2	96	21
July	108.1	79.5	114	73	0.34	0.0	3	93	25
October	91.3	63.1	104	45	0.09	0.0	1	90	23
Annual	86.0	58.8	117	29	6.80	0.0	36	86	31
Salt Lake City, Utah (International Airport): lat. 40° 46′ N, long. 111° 58′ W; elevation: 4,220 ft									
January	29.8	14.3	46	−8	0.72	13.8	13	38	72
April	62.7	39.4	78	29	1.04	7.7	8	68	45
July	94.3	63.5	101	55	0.40	0.0	3	89	21

Month	Temperature, °F: Average maximum	Average minimum	Record high	Record low	Precipitation: Rainfall, inches	Snowfall, inches	Days with precipitation	Percentage possible sunshine	Percentage relative humidity at noon
October	70.8	42.6	88	28	1.29	0.0	5	71	40
Annual	65.0	40.2	104	−8	8.70	50.6	80	70	46
San Francisco, California (International Airport): lat. 37° 37′ N, long. 122° 23′ W; elevation: 8 ft									
January	54.1	40.8	61	31	6.61	T	13	—	81
April	62.7	48.2	69	42	0.69	0.0	8	—	68
July	73.1	54.5	82	51	0.09	0.0	1	—	65
October	70.2	54.9	79	47	2.20	0.0	5	—	68
Annual	65.8	49.4	100	31	24.57	T	67	—	70
Seattle, Washington (Seattle-Tacoma Airport): lat. 47° 27′ N, long. 122° 18′ W; elevation: 400 ft									
January	43.4	32.2	53	20	2.25	0.5	10	45	60
April	58.7	42.9	76	36	0.81	0.0	10	52	71
July	78.7	56.1	98	47	0.73	0.0	4	84	58
October	60.7	47.6	77	41	3.38	0.0	13	43	74
Annual	60.8	45.2	98	20	32.26	2.1	129	52	68
Washington, D.C. (National Airport): lat. 38° 51′ N, long. 77° 02′ W; elevation: 10 ft									
January	41.9	28.3	63	10	6.64	4.0	14	35	57
April	64.2	47.8	79	35	1.88	0.0	11	48	57
July	86.0	71.1	93	57	3.43	0.0	11	60	63
October	67.0	50.1	84	36	5.54	0.3	12	54	65
Annual	66.2	49.9	97	6	47.33	34.9	126	56	59

Source: Department of Commerce, National Oceanic and Atmospheric Administration, Environmental Data Service.

Other Recorded Extremes

Highest average annual temperature (World): Dallol, Ethiopia (1960–66), 94°F (34.4°C). **(U.S.):** Key West, Fla. (30-year normal), 78.2°F (25.7°C).

Lowest average annual temperature (Antarctica): Plateau Station −70°F (−56.7°C). **(U.S.):** Barrow, Alaska (30-year normal), 9.3°F (−12.6°C).

Greatest average yearly rainfall (U.S.): Mt. Waialeale, Kauai, Hawaii (1912–58), 460 in. (1,168 cm). **(India):** Cherrapunji (74-year avg), 450 in. (1,143 cm).

Minimum average yearly rainfall (Chile): Arica (59-year avg), 0.03 in. (0.08 cm) (no rainfall for 14 consecutive years). **(U.S.):** Death Valley, Calif. (49-year avg), 1.63 in. (4.14 cm). (Bagdad, Calif., holds the U.S. record for the longest period with no measurable rain, 767 days, from Oct. 3, 1912 to Nov. 8, 1914).

Hottest summer avg in Western Hemisphere (U.S.): Death Valley, Calif., 98°F (36.7°C).

Longest hot spell (W. Australia): Marble Bar, 100°F (37.8°C) (or above) for 162 consecutive days.

Largest hailstone (U.S.): Potter, Neb., 1½ lb (.68 kg).

Wind Chill Factors

Wind speed (mph)	Thermometer reading (degrees Fahrenheit): 35	30	25	20	15	10	5	0	−5	−10	−15	−20	−25	−30	−35	−40	−45
5	33	27	21	19	12	7	0	−5	−10	−15	−21	−26	−31	−36	−42	−47	−52
10	22	16	10	3	−3	−9	−15	−22	−27	−34	−40	−46	−52	−58	−64	−71	−77
15	16	9	2	−5	−11	−18	−25	−31	−38	−45	−51	−58	−65	−72	−78	−85	−92
20	12	4	−3	−10	−17	−24	−31	−39	−46	−53	−60	−67	−74	−81	−88	−95	−103
25	8	1	−7	−15	−22	−29	−36	−44	−51	−59	−66	−74	−81	−88	−96	−103	−110
30	6	−2	−10	−18	−25	−33	−41	−49	−56	−64	−71	−79	−86	−93	−101	−109	−116
35	4	−4	−12	−20	−27	−35	−43	−52	−58	−67	−74	−82	−89	−97	−105	−113	−120
40	3	−5	−13	−21	−29	−37	−45	−53	−60	−69	−76	−84	−92	−100	−107	−115	−123
45	2	−6	−14	−22	−30	−38	−46	−54	−62	−70	−78	−85	−93	−102	−109	−117	−125

NOTES: This chart gives equivalent temperatures for combinations of wind speed and temperatures. For example, the combination of a temperature of 10° Fahrenheit and a wind blowing at 10 mph has a cooling power equal to −9° F. Wind speeds of higher than 45 mph have little additional cooling effect.

Weather Glossary

blizzard: storm characterized by strong winds, low temperatures, and large amounts of snow.

cyclone: circulation of winds rotating counterclockwise in the northern hemisphere and clockwise in the southern hemisphere. Hurricanes and tornadoes are both examples of cyclones.

drizzle: uniform close precipitation of tiny drops with diameter of less than .02 inch.

flash flood: dangerous rapid rise of water levels in streams, rivers, or over land area.

gale warning: winds in the 33–48 knot (38–55 mph) range forecast.

heavy snow warnings: issued when 4 inches or more of snow are expected to fall in a 12-hour period or when 6 inches or more are anticipated in a 24-hour period.

hurricane: devastating cyclonic storm; winds over 74 mph near storm center; usually tropical in origin; called cyclone in Indian Ocean, typhoon in the Pacific.

hurricane warning: winds in excess of 64 knots (74 mph) in connection with hurricane.

snow flurries: snow falling for a short time at intermittent periods; accumulations are usually small.

snow squall: brief, intense falls of snow, usually accompanied by gusty winds.

storm warnings: winds greater than 48 knots (55 mph) are forecast.

temperature-humidity index (THI): measure of personal discomfort based on the combined effects of temperature and humidity. Most people are uncomfortable when the THI is 75. A THI of 80 produces acute discomfort for almost everyone.

tidal waves: series of ocean waves caused by earthquakes; can reach speeds of 600 mph; they grow in height as they reach shore and can crest as high as 100 feet.

thunder: the sound produced by the rapid expansion of air heated by lightning.

tornado: dangerous whirlwind associated with the cumulonimbus clouds of severe thunderstorms; winds up to 300 mph.

tornado warning: tornado has actually been detected by radar or sighted in designated area.

tornado watch: potential exists in the watch area for storms that could contain tornadoes.

tsunami: *see* tidal waves.

warning: the designated condition is imminent.

wind-chill factor: combined effect of temperature and wind speed as compared to equivalent temperature in calm air.

Tornadoes That Caused Outstanding Damage

Date	Number of tornadoes	Deaths	Property losses	States in which storms occurred
1884, Feb. 19	60	800	(1)	Mississippi, Alabama, North and South Carolina, Tennessee, Kentucky, Indiana
1917, May 26–27	(1)	249	$ 5,555,000	Illinois, Indiana, Arkansas, Kentucky, Tennessee, Alabama, Mississippi
1920, April 20	6	220	3,525,000	Mississippi, Alabama, Tennessee
1924, April 29–30	22	115	4,372,300	Oklahoma, Arkansas, Alabama, Georgia, Louisiana, North and South Carolina, Virginia
1924, June 28	4	96	13,050,000	Ohio and Pennsylvania
1925, March 18	8	792	17,872,000	Missouri, Illinois, Indiana, Kentucky, Tennessee, Alabama
1927, May 8–9	36	227	7,877,000	Texas, Louisiana, Missouri, Nebraska, Indiana, Michigan
1932, March 21	27	321	5,514,000	Alabama, Mississippi, Georgia, Tennessee
1936, April 5–6	22	498	21,800,000	Arkansas, Alabama, Tennessee, Georgia, South Carolina
1944, June 23	4	153	5,160,000	Pennsylvania, West Virginia, Maryland
1947, April 9–10	8	167	10,030,750	Texas, Oklahoma, Kansas
1952, March 21–22	31	343	15,327,100	Arkansas, Tennessee, Missouri, Mississippi, Alabama, Kentucky
1953, June 7–9	12	234	93,230,840	Michigan, Ohio, and New England states
1953, May 11	1	114	39,500,000	Texas
1955, May 25	13	102	11,747,500	Oklahoma and Kansas
1965, April 11–12	47	257	200,000,000	Iowa, Illinois, Wisconsin, Michigan, Indiana, Ohio
1968, May 15	7	63	65,000,000	Arkansas, Iowa, Illinois
1970, May 11	1	26	135,000,000	Texas
1971, Feb. 21	(1)	117	17,000,000	Louisiana, Mississippi
1973, March 31	2	9	115,000,000	Georgia, South Carolina
1973, May 26–28	96	22	(1)	Hawaii and 18 states in South, Southwest, Midwest, and East
1974, April 3–4	144	307	500,000,000+	13 states in East, South, and Midwest
1975, May 6	3	3	400,000,000+	Nebraska
1977, April 4	7	22	15,000,000	Alabama
1978, Dec. 3	13	4	100,000,000+	Louisiana and Arkansas
1979, April 10	10	54	(1)	Texas and Oklahoma
1979, Oct. 3	1	3	200,000,000	Connecticut

1. Not definitely known; believed to be large. NOTE: Additional storms may be listed in the *Current Events* section. *Source:* Data for 1884–1953, reprinted from *Tornadoes of the United States*, by S. D. Flora, copyright 1954, by University of Oklahoma Press. Used by permission. Also, Department of Commerce, National Oceanic and Atmospheric Administration.

Devastating North Atlantic Hurricanes of the 20th Century

The following is a selected list of North Atlantic hurricanes based on casualties, damage, and general public interest. Facts about each storm are taken from Weather records, although in some cases only estimates of wind speed are available. Data given in this list pertain only to U.S. land areas except where indicated otherwise.

Date	Areas hardest hit	Land stations with highest wind speed	Deaths (U.S. only)	Est. damage (millions)	Remarks
1900, Aug. 27-Sept. 15	Galveston, Tex.	Galveston, Tex. (120[1] mph)	6,000	$30	Damage due to both winds and storm wave. Galveston Is. inundated.
1909, Sept. 10–21	Louisiana and Mississippi	New Orleans, La. (53 mph)	350	5	Winds 50–75 mi. W of New Orleans, where deaths occurred, were stronger than 68 mph.
1915, Aug. 5–23	East Texas and Louisiana	Galveston, Tex. (120 mph)	275	50	Water 5–6 ft deep in Galveston business district. 90% of homes demolished. Warnings issued well ahead of time.
1915, Sept. 22-Oct. 1	Mid-Gulf Coast	Burrwood, La. (140 mph)	275	13	Many casualties due to persons insisting on staying in low-lying areas despite warnings.
1919, Sept. 2–15	Florida, Louisiana, and Texas	Sand Key, Fla. (84[1] mph)	287	22	488 persons drowned at sea.
1926, Sept. 11–22	Florida and Alabama	Miami, Fla. (138 mph)	243	112	Most deaths were in Miami area. Said to have been one of most destructive storms of century.
1928, Sept. 6–20	Southern Florida	Lake Okeechobee, Fla. (75[1] mph)	1,836	25	1,870 injured. Nearly all deaths were in Lake Okeechobee area. Winds estimated as high as 160 mph caused Lake to overflow into populated areas.
1935, Aug. 29-Sept. 10	Southern Florida	Tampa, Fla. (86 mph)	408	6	Sustained winds over Florida Keys est. 150–200 mph. Remembered as "Labor Day Storm."
1938, Sept. 10–22	Long Island and Southern New England	Blue Hills Obs., Mass. (183 mph)	600	306	Unusually destructive. Storm center moved as fast as 56 mph at times. 1,754 injured.
1944, Sept. 9–16	North Carolina to New England	Cape Henry, Va. (150[1] mph)	46	100	344 deaths at sea. Shipping lanes were crowded with war-time activity.
1944, Oct. 12–23	Florida	Dry Tortugas Is. (120 mph)	18	100	About 300 were killed in Cuba area before storm reached U.S. Evacuation of thousands from threatened areas in Fla. prevented higher toll.
1947, Sept. 4–21	Florida and Mid-Gulf Coast	Hillsboro Light, Fla. (155 mph)	51	110	Wind damage especially heavy Along Gulf Coast and Florida east coast.
1954, Aug. 25–31	North Carolina to New England	Block Island, R.I. (135 mph)	60	461	"CAROL"—more damage than any other single storm to this date. Water and high waves flooded low-lying areas; 1,000 injuries in Long Island–New England area.
1954, Sept. 2–14	New Jersey to New England	Block Island, R.I. (87 mph)	21	40	"EDNA"—New England again heavily hit. Gusts of 120 mph at Martha's Vineyard, Mass.
1954, Oct. 5–18	South Carolina to New York	New York, N.Y. (113 mph) (See Remarks)	95	252	"HAZEL"—several N.C. localities had winds of 130–150 mph with unusually heavy wave damage resulting. Est. 400–1,000 casualties in Haiti. In Canada there were 78 deaths, mostly due to flooding.
1955, Aug. 7–21	North Carolina to New England	Wilmington, N.C. (83 mph)	184	832	"DIANE"—worst floods in history in Southern New England. 16 in. of rain in Hartford area.
1957, June 25–28	Texas to Alabama	Sabine Pass, Tex. (100 mph)	390	150	"AUDREY"—gave an early start to the hurricane season and wiped out Cameron, La. Two

Date	Areas hardest hit	Land stations with highest wind speed	Deaths (U.S. only)	Est. damage (millions)	Remarks
					weeks later "BERTHA" struck same area.
1960, Aug. 29-Sept. 13	Florida to New England	Ft. Myers, Fla. (92 mph) Block Island, R.I. (130 mph) (See Remarks)	50	500	"DONNA"—hurricane winds from a single storm swept the entire Atlantic seaboard from Florida to New England for the first time in a 75-year record. Winds estimated near 140 mph with gusts 175–180 mph on Central Keys and lower southwest Florida coast. 115 deaths in Antilles, most from flash floods in Puerto Rico.
1961, Sept. 3–15	Texas coast	Port Lavaca, Tex. (145 mph)	46	408	"CARLA"—devastated Texas Gulf Coast Cities with 15-foot tides and 15-inch rains. Gusts to 175 mph at Port Lavaca.
1964, Aug. 20-Sept. 5	Southern Florida, Eastern Virginia	Miami, Fla. (110 mph)	3	129	"CLEO"—first hurricane in Miami area since 1950. Killed 214 in Caribbean Islands.
1964, Aug. 28-Sept. 16	Northeastern Florida, Southern Georgia	St. Augustine, Fla. (125 mph)	5	250	"DORA"—first storm of full hurricane force on record to move inland from east over northeastern Florida.
1965, Aug. 27-Sept. 12	Southern Florida and Louisiana	Port Sulphur, La. (136 mph)	75	1,420	"BETSY"—Damage in Louisiana, $1.2 billion. 27,000 homes destroyed, 17,500 injured or ill, 300,000 evacuated. Gusts of 165 mph at Pine Key, Fla.
1967, Sept. 5–22	Southern Texas	Brownsville, Texas (109 mph gust)	15	200	"BEULAH"—main damage was caused by torrential rains.
1969, Aug. 14–22	Mississippi, Louisiana, Alabama, Virginia, W. Virginia	Oil drilling rig east of Boothville, La. (172 mph)	256	1,420	"CAMILLE"—68 additional persons missing. One of most destructive killer storms ever to hit U.S.
1970, July 23-Aug. 5	Texas coast	Corpus Christi, Tex. (130 mph)	11	453.8	"CELIA"—Costliest storm in history to hit Texas coast. Gusts of 161 mph recorded.
1972, June 14–23	Florida to New York	Key West, Fla. (43 mph)	117	3,097	"AGNES"—Devastating floods with many record-breaking river crests. Pa. hardest hit, with 50 deaths.
1975, Sept. 13–24	Florida and Southern Alabama	Ozark, Ala. (104 mph)	21	490	"ELOISE"—Structures destroyed from Panama City Beach, Fla., to Ft. Walton Beach, Fla. Major flooding from rainfall.
1976, Aug. 6–10	New York, New Jersey, and Southern New England	Bridgeport, Conn. (77 mph gust)	5	100	"BELLE"—Crop damage in the Northeast. Considerable Inland stream and road flooding.
1979, Aug. 25-Sept. 7	Florida to New England	Fort Pierce, Fla. (95 mph gust)	5	320	"DAVID"—1200 deaths in the Dominican Republic. Homes 80 percent destroyed in Dominica.
1979, Aug. 29-Sept. 14	Alabama and Mississippi	Dauphin Island, Alabama (145 mph gust)	5	2300	"FREDERIC"— highest dollar dammage ever in the United States.
1980, Aug. 3–10	Caribbean Islands to Texas Gulf Coast	Yucatan Channel (185 mph)	18	50+	"ALLEN"—Highest tides in 61 years. 88 people killed in Caribbean Islands. Extensive crop damage in Caribbean.

1. Wind-measuring equipment disabled at speed indicated. NOTE: Additional hurricanes may be listed in *News Chronology*. *Source:* Department of Commerce, National Oceanic and Atmospheric Administration.

Tornado Fatalities

In the 1970s, there were 8,573 tornadoes in the United States resulting in the deaths of 986 people. If the previous decades are any indication of the future, the National Oceanic and Atmospheric Administration forsees that there will be at least 7,000 tornadoes during the 1980s in which up to 1,000 Americans will be killed.

ASTRONOMY

Astronomical Terms

Planet is the term used for a body in orbit around the Sun. Its origin is Greek; even in antiquity it was known that a number of "stars" did not stay in the same relative positions to the others. There were five such restless "stars" known—Mercury, Venus, Mars, Jupiter, and Saturn—and the Greeks referred to them as *planetes,* a word which means "wanderers." That the earth is one of the planets was realized later. The additional planets were discovered after the invention of the telescope.

Satellite (or *moon*) is the term for a body in orbit around a planet. As long as our own Moon was the only moon known, there was no need for a general term for the moons of planets. But when Galileo Galilei discovered the four main moons of the planet Jupiter, Johannes Kepler (in a letter to Galileo) suggested "satellite" (from the Latin *satelles,* which means attendant) as a general term for such bodies. The word is used interchangeably with "moons": astronomers speak and write about the moons of Neptune, Saturn, etc. A satellite may be any size.

Orbit is the term for the path traveled by a body in space. It comes from the Latin *orbis,* which means circle, circuit, etc., and *orbita,* which means a rut or a wheel track. Theoretically, four mathematical figures are possible orbits: two are open (hyperbola and parabola) and two are closed (ellipse and circle), but in reality all closed orbits are ellipses. These ellipses can be nearly circular, as are the orbits of most planets, or very elongated, as are the orbits of most comets. In these orbits, the Sun is in one focal point of the ellipse, and the other focal point is empty. In the orbits of satellites, the planet stands in one focal point of the orbit. The *primary* of an orbit is the body in the focal point. For planets, the point of the orbit closest to the Sun is the *perihelion,* and the point farthest from the Sun is the *aphelion.* For orbits around the Earth, the corresponding terms are *perigee* and *apogee;* for orbits around other planets, corresponding terms are coined when necessary.

Two heavenly bodies are in *inferior* or *superior conjunction* when they have the same Right Ascension, or are in the same meridian; that is, when one is due north or south of the other. If the bodies appear near each other as seen from the Earth, they will rise and set at the same time. They are in *opposition* when they are opposite each other in the heavens: when one rises as the other is setting. *Greatest elongation* is the greatest apparent angular distance from the Sun, when a planet is most favorably suited for observation. Mercury can be seen with the naked eye only at about this time. An *occultation* of a planet or star is an eclipse of it by some other body, usually the Moon.

Stars are the basic units of population in the universe. Our Sun is the nearest star. Stars are very large (our Sun has a diameter of 865,400 miles—a comparatively small star). Stars are composed of intensely hot gasses, deriving their energy from nuclear reactions going on in their interiors.

Galaxies are immense systems containing billions of stars. All that you can see in the sky (with a very few exceptions) belongs to our galaxy—a system of roughly 100 billion stars. The few exceptions are other galaxies. Our own galaxy, the rim of which we see as the "Milky Way," is about 100,000 light-years in diameter and about 10,000 light-years in thickness. Its shape is roughly that of a thick lens; more precisely it is a "spiral nebula," a term first used for other galaxies when they were discovered and before it was realized that these were separate and distant galaxies. The spiral galaxy nearest to ours is in the constellation An-

Astronomical Constants

Light-year (distance traveled by light in one year)	5,880,000,000,000 mi.
Parsec (parallax of one second, for stellar distances)	3.259 light-yrs.
Velocity of light	186,281.7 mi./sec.
Astronomical unit (A.U.), or mean distance earth-to-sun	ca. 93,000,000 mi.[1]
Mean distance, earth to moon	238,860 mi.
General precession	50″.26
Obliquity of the ecliptic	23° 27′ 8″.26–0″.4684(t – 1900)[2]
Equatorial radius of the earth	3963.34 statute mi.
Polar radius of the earth	3949.99 statute mi.
Earth's mean radius	3958.89 statute mi.
Oblateness of the earth	1/297
Equatorial horizontal parallax of the moon	57′ 2″.70
Earth's mean velocity in orbit	18.5 mi./sec.
Sidereal year	365d.2564
Tropical year	365d.2422
Sidereal month	27d.3217
Synodic month	29d.5306
Mean sidereal day	23h56m4s.091 of mean solar time
Mean solar day	24h3m56s.555 of sidereal time

1. Actual mean distance derived from radar bounces: 92,935,700 mi. The value of 92,897,400 mi. (based on parallax of 8″.80) is used in calculations. 2. *t* refers to the year in question, for example, 1980.

dromeda. It is somewhat larger than our own galaxy and is visible to the naked eye.

Recent developments in radio astronomy have revealed additional celestial objects that are still incompletely understood.

Quasars ("quasi-stellar" objects), originally thought to be peculiar stars in our own galaxy, are now believed to be the most remote objects in the Universe. Spectral studies of quasars indicate that some are 9 billion light years away and moving away from us at the incredible rate of 150,000 miles per second. Quasars emit tremendous amounts of light and microwave radiation. Although they appear to be far smaller than ordinary galaxies, some quasars emit as much as 100 times more energy. Some astronomers believe that quasars are the cores of violently exploding galaxies.

Pulsars are believed to be rapidly spinning neutron stars, so crushed by their own gravity that a million tons of their matter would hardly fill a thimble. Pulsars are so named because they emit bursts of radio energy at regular intervals. Some have pulse rates as rapid as 10 per second.

A *black hole* is the theoretical end-product of the total gravitational collapse of a massive star or group of stars. Crushed even smaller than an incredibly dense neutron star, such a body may become so dense that not even light can escape its gravitational field. It has been suggested that black holes may be detectable in proximity to normal stars when they draw matter away from their visible neighbors. Strong sources of X-rays in our galaxy and beyond may also indicate the presence of black holes. One possible black hole now being studied is the invisible companion to a supergiant star in the constellation Cygnus.

Origin of the Universe

Evidence uncovered in recent years tends to confirm that the universe began its existence about 15 billion years ago as a dense, hot globule of gas expanding rapidly outward. At that time, the universe contained nothing but hydrogen and a small amount of helium. There were no stars and no planets. The first stars probably began to condense out of the primordial hydrogen when the universe was about 100 million years old and continued to form as the universe aged. The Sun arose in this way 4.6 billion years ago. Many stars came into being before the Sun was formed; many others formed after the Sun appeared. This process continues, and through telescopes we can now see stars forming out of compressed pockets of hydrogen in outer space.

Birth and Death of a Star

When a star begins to form as a dense cloud of gas, the individual hydrogen atoms fall toward the center of the cloud under the force of the star's gravity. As they fall, they pick up speed, and their energy increases. The increase in energy heats the gas. When this process has continued for some millions of years, the temperature reaches about 20 million degrees Fahrenheit. At this temperature,

The Brightest Stars

Star	Constellation	Mag.	Dist. (l.-y.)
Sirius	Canis Major	−1.6	8
Canopus	Carina	−0.9	650
Alpha Centauri	Centaurus	+0.1	4
Vega	Lyra	0.1	23
Capella	Auriga	0.2	42
Arcturus	Boötes	0.2	32
Rigel	Orion	0.3	545
Procyon	Canis Minor	0.5	10
Achernar	Eridanus	0.6	70
Beta Centari	Centaurus	0.9	130
Altair	Aquila	0.9	18
Betelgeuse	Orion	0.9	300
Aldebaran	Taurus	1.1	54
Spica	Virgo	1.2	190
Pollux	Gemini	1.2	31
Antares	Scorpius	1.2	170
Fomalhaut	Piscis Austrinus	1.3	27
Deneb	Cygnus	1.3	465
Regulus	Leo	1.3	70
Beta Crucis	Crux	1.5	465
Eta Carinae	Carina	1–7	—
Alpha-one Crucis	Crux	1.6	150
Castor	Gemini	1.6	44
Gamma Crucis	Crux	1.6	—
Epsilon Canis Majoris	Canis Major	1.6	325
Epsilon Ursae Majoris	Ursa Major	1.7	50
Bellatrix	Orion	1.7	215
Lambda Scorpii	Scorpius	1.7	205
Epsilon Carinae	Carina	1.7	325
Mira	Cetus	2–10	250

Mars Atlas Available

A new hard-bound atlas of Mars containing over 120 maps of the planet may be purchased from the Superintendent of Documents, Government Printing Office, Washington, D.C. 20402, at $7.00 per copy, prepaid. Send checks or money orders payable to Superintendent of Documents.

Additional information on planetary map projects may be obtained from the U.S. Geological Survey, Branch of Astrogeological Studies, 2255 North Gemini Drive, Flagstaff, Ariz. 86001, telephone (602) 779–3311, ext. 1352.

U.S. Share of World Science Declines

The estimated U.S. share of all world science and technology has fallen from about 33% in 1967 to less than 25% in 1980.

Between 1968 and 1978, the number of scientists and engineers in the U.S. workforce declined 13%. During this same time, the Soviet Union is estimated to have more than doubled its number of scientists and engineers. And Japan, with less than half the U.S. population, now has about the same number of scientists and engineers as the U.S. engaged in nonmilitary research and development.

Data for Sun, Moon, and Planets

	Mean distance from Sun in millions of miles	Period of revolution around the Sun	Eccentricity of orbit	Inclination to ecliptic ° ′	Diameter (miles)	Period of rotation on axis	Inclination of equator to orbit plane °	Surface gravity (earth = 1)	Density H_2O = 1	Number of satellites	Mean velocity in orbit (mi./sec.)	Max. stellar mag.
Sun	—	—	—	—	865,400	24d.64[2]	7.2	28	1.4	0	—	−26.7
Moon	—	(27d.322)[1]	0.05	5 8	2,160	27d.322	6.7	0.16	3.3	0	0.63	−12.6
Mercury	36.00	87d.969	0.21	7 0	3,100	58.66d	7	0.28	3.8	0	30	−1.2
Venus	67.27	224d.701	0.01	3 24	7,700	243.2d	—	0.85	5.1	0	22	−4.4
Earth	93.00	365d.256	0.02	0 0	7,927[3]	23h56m	23.4	1.00	5.5	1	18.5	—
Mars	141.71	1y.881	0.09	1 51	4,200	24h37m	25.2	0.38	4.0	2	15	−2.8
Jupiter	483.88	11y.862	0.05	1 18	88,700[3]	9h50m [2]	3.1	2.6	1.3	16[4]	8	−2.5
Saturn	887.14	29y.458	0.06	2 29	75,100[3]	16h39m [2]	26.8	1.2	0.7	+13	6	−0.4
Uranus	1783.98	84y.013	0.05	0 46	32,000	12.8h	98	1.1	1.3	5	4	+5.7
Neptune	2795.46	164y.794	0.01	1 46	27,700	15h.8	29	1.4	2.2	2	3	+7.8
Pluto	3675.27	248y.430	0.25	17 9	1,500(?)	6d8h(?)	—	—	>1.0	1	<3	+14

1. Period of revolution around the earth. 2. Voyager 1 and 2 data. 3. The equatorial diameters of the earth, Jupiter, and Saturn are given; polar diameters are: earth, 7,900.0 mi., Jupiter 82,789 mi., Saturn 67,170 mi. 4. Recent analysis indicates the presence of a fifteenth satellite. OTHER DATA ON THE EARTH: Equatorial circumference, 24,902.4 mi.; total area, 196,949,-970 sq mi.; mass, 6.6 sextillion tons; mean diameter, 7,917.8 mi.

the hydrogen within the star ignites and burns in a continuing series of nuclear reactions in which all the elements in the universe are manufactured from hydrogen and helium. The onset of these reactions marks the birth of a star. When a star begins to exhaust its hydrogen supply, its life nears an end. The first sign of old age is a swelling and reddening of its outer regions. Such an aging, swollen star is called a red giant. The Sun, a middle-aged star, will probably swell to a red giant in 5 billion years, vaporizing the earth and any creatures that may be left on its surface. When all its fuel has been exhausted, a star cannot generate sufficient pressure at its center to balance the crushing force of gravity. The star collapses under the force of its own weight; if it is a small star, it collapses gently and remains collapsed. Such a collapsed star, at its life's end, is called a white dwarf. The Sun will probably end its life in this way. A different fate awaits a large star. Its final collapse generates a violent explosion, blowing the innards of the star out into space. There, the materials of the exploded star mix with the primeval hydrogen of the universe. Later in the history of the galaxy, other stars are formed out of this mixture. The Sun is one of these stars. It contains the debris of countless other stars that exploded before the Sun was born.

Formation of the Solar System

The Sun, like other stars, seems to have been formed 4.6 billion years ago from a cloud of hydrogen mixed with small amounts of other substances that had been manufactured in the bodies of other stars before the Sun was born. This was the parent cloud of the solar system. The dense hot gas at the center of the cloud gave rise to the Sun; the outer regions of the cloud—cooler and less dense—gave birth to the planets.

Our solar system consists of one star (the Sun), nine planets and all their moons, several thousand minor planets called asteroids or planetoids, and an equally large number of comets.

The Sun

All the stars, including our Sun, are gigantic balls of superheated gas, kept hot by atomic reactions in their centers. In our Sun, this atomic reaction is hydrogen fusion: four hydrogen atoms are combined to form one helium atom. The temperature at the core of our Sun must be 20 million degrees centigrade, the surface temperature is around 6,-000 degrees centigrade, or about 11,000 degrees Fahrenheit. The diameter of the sun is 865,400 miles, and its surface area is approximately 12,000 times that of the Earth. Compared with other stars, our Sun is just a bit below average in size and temperature. Its fuel supply (hydrogen) is estimated to last for another 5 billion years.

Our Sun is not motionless in space; in fact it has two proper motions. One is a seemingly straight-line motion in the direction of the constellation Hercules at the rate of about 12 miles per second. But since the Sun is a part of the Milky Way system and since the whole system rotates slowly around its own center, the Sun also moves at the rate of 175 miles per second as part of the rotating Milky Way system.

In addition to this motion, the Sun rotates on its axis. Observing the motion of sun spots (darkish areas which look like enormous whirling storms) and solar flares, which are usually associated with sun spots, has shown that the rotational period of our Sun is just short of 25 days. But this figure is valid for the Sun's equator only; the sections near the Sun's poles seem to have a rotational period of 34 days. Naturally, since the Sun generates its own heat and light, there is no temperature difference between poles and equator.

What we call the Sun's "surface" is technically known as the photosphere. Since the whole Sun is a ball of very hot gas, there is really no such thing as a surface; it is a question of visual impression. The next layer outside the photosphere is known as the chromosphere, which extends several thousand miles beyond the photosphere. It is in steady motion, and often enormous prominences can be seen to burst from it, extending as much as 100,000 miles into space. Outside the chromosphere is the corona. The corona consists of very tenuous gases (essentially hydrogen) and makes a magnificent sight when the Sun is eclipsed.

The Moon

Mercury and Venus do not have any moons. Therefore, the Earth is the planet nearest the Sun to be orbited by a moon.

The next planet farther out, Mars, has two very small moons. Jupiter has four major moons and nine or ten minor ones. Saturn, the ringed planet, has ten known moons, of which one (Titan) is larger than the planet Mercury. Uranus has five known moons (four of them large) as well as rings, while Neptune has one large and one small moon. Pluto has one moon, discovered in 1978. Some astronomers still consider Pluto to be a "runaway moon" of Neptune.

Our own Moon, with a diameter of 2,160 miles, is one of the larger moons in our solar system and is especially large when compared with the planet that it orbits. In fact, the common center of gravity of the Earth-Moon system is only about 1,000 miles below the Earth's surface. The closest our Moon can come to us (its perigee) is 221,463 miles; the farthest it can go away (its apogee) is 252,710 miles. The period of rotation of our Moon is equal to its period of revolution around the Earth. Hence from Earth we can see only one hemisphere of the Moon. Both periods are 27 days, 7 hours, 43 minutes and 11.47 seconds. But while the rotation of the Moon is constant, its velocity in its orbit is not, since it moves more slowly in apogee than in perigee. Consequently, some portions near the rim which are not normally visible will appear briefly. This phenomenon is called "libration," and by taking advantage of the librations, astronomers have succeeded in mapping approximately 59% of the lunar surface. The other 41% can never be seen from the earth but has been mapped by American and Russian Moon-orbiting spacecraft.

Though the Moon goes around the Earth in the time mentioned, the interval from new Moon to new Moon is 29 days, 12 hours, 44 minutes and 2.78 seconds. This delay of nearly two days is due to the fact that the Earth is moving around the Sun, so that the Moon needs two extra days to reach a spot in its orbit where no part is illuminated by the Sun, as seen from Earth.

If the plane of the Earth's orbit around the Sun (the ecliptic) and the plane of the Moon's orbit around the Earth were the same, the Moon would be eclipsed by the Earth every time it is full, and the Sun would be eclipsed by the Moon every time the Moon is "new" (it would be better to call it the "black Moon" when it is in this position). But because the two orbits do not coincide, the Moon's shadow normally misses the Earth and the Earth's shadow misses the Moon. The inclination of the two orbital planes to each other is 5 degrees. The tides are, of course, caused by the Moon with the help of the Sun, but in the open ocean they are surprisingly low, amounting to about one yard. The very high tides which can be observed near the shore in some places are due to funnelling effects of the shorelines. At new Moon and at full Moon the tides raised by the Moon are reinforced by the Sun; these are the "spring tides." If the Sun's tidal power acts at right angles to that of the Moon (quarter moons) we get the low "neap tides."

Our Planet Earth

The Earth, circling the Sun at an average distance of 93 million miles, is the fifth largest planet and the third from the Sun. It orbits the Sun at a speed of 67,000 miles per hour, making one revolution in 365 days, 5 hours, 48 minutes, and 45.51 seconds. The Earth completes one rotation on its axis every 23 hours, 56 minutes, and 4.09 seconds. Actually a bit pear-shaped rather than a true sphere, the Earth has a diameter of 7,927 miles at the Equator and a few miles less at the poles. It has an estimated mass of about 6.6 sextillion tons, with an average density of 5.52 grams per cubic centimeter. The Earth's surface area encompasses 196,949,970 square miles, of which about three-fourths is water.

Origin of the Earth. The Earth, along with the other planets, is believed to have been born 4.5 billion years ago as a solidified cloud of dust and gases left over from the creation of the Sun. For perhaps 500 million years, the interior of the Earth stayed solid and relatively cool, perhaps 2000° F. The main ingredients, according to the best available evidence, were iron and silicates, with small amounts of other elements, some of them radioactive. As millions of years passed, energy released by radioactive decay —mostly of uranium, thorium, and potassium—gradually heated the Earth, melting some of its constituents. The iron melted before the silicates, and, being heavier, sank toward the center. This forced upward the silicates that it found there. After many years, the iron reached the center, almost 4,000 miles deep, and began to accumulate. No eyes were around at that time to view the turmoil which must have taken place on the face of the Earth—gigantic heaves and bubbling of the surface, exploding volcanoes, and flowing lava covering everything in sight. Finally, the iron in the center accumulated as the core. Around it, a thin but fairly stable crust of solid rock formed as the Earth cooled. Depressions in the crust were natural basins in which water, rising from the interior of the planet through volcanoes and fissures, collected to form the oceans. Slowly the Earth acquired its present appearance.

The Earth Today. As a result of radioactive heating over millions of years, the Earth's molten *core* is probably fairly hot today, around 11,000° F. By comparison, lead melts at around 800° F. Most of the Earth's 2,100-mile-thick core is liquid, but there is evidence that the center of the core is solid. The liquid outer portion, about 95% of the core, is constantly in motion, causing the Earth to have a magnetic field that makes compass needles point north and south. The details are not known, but the latest evidence suggests that planets which have a magnetic field probably have a solid core or a partially liquid one.

Outside the core is the Earth's *mantle*, 1,800 miles thick, and extending nearly to the surface. The mantle is composed of heavy silicate rock, similar to that brought up by volcanic eruptions. It is somewhere between liquid and solid, slightly yielding, and therefore contributing to an active, moving Earth. Most of the Earth's radioactive material is in the thin *crust* which covers the mantle, but some is in the mantle and continues to give off heat. The crust's thickness ranges from 5 to 25 miles.

Continental Drift. A great deal of recent evidence confirms the long-disputed theory that the continents of the Earth, made mostly of relatively light granite, float in the slightly yielding mantle, like logs in a pond. For many years it had been noticed that if North and South America could be pushed toward western and southern Europe and western Africa, they would fit like pieces in a jigsaw puzzle. Today, there is little question—the continents have drifted widely and continue to do so.

In 10 million years, the world as we know it may be unrecognizable, with California drifting out to sea, Florida joining South America, and Africa moving farther away from Europe and Asia.

The Earth's Atmosphere. The thin blanket of atmosphere that envelops the Earth extends several hundred miles into space. From sea level—the very bottom of the ocean of air—to a height of about 60 miles, the air in the atmosphere is made up of the same gases in the same ratio: about 78% nitrogen, 21% oxygen, and the remaining 1% being a mixture of argon, carbon dioxide, and tiny amounts of neon, helium, krypton, xenon, and other gases. The atmosphere becomes less dense with increasing altitude: more than three-fourths of the Earth's huge envelope is concentrated in the first 5 to 10 miles above the surface. At sea level, a cubic foot of the atmosphere weighs about an ounce and a quarter. The entire atmosphere weighs 5,700,000,000,000,000 tons, and the force with which gravity holds it in place causes it to exert a pressure of nearly 15 pounds per square inch. Going out from the Earth's surface, the atmosphere is divided into five regions. The regions, and the heights to which they extend, are: *Troposphere*, 0 to 7 miles (at middle latitudes); *stratosphere*, 7 to 30 miles; *mesosphere*, 30 to 50 miles; *thermosphere*, 50 to 400 miles; and *exosphere*, above 400 miles. The boundaries between each of the regions are known respectively as the *tropopause*, *stratopause*, *mesopause*, and *thermopause*. Alternate terms often used for the layers above the troposhere are *ozonosphere* (for stratosphere) and *ionosphere* for the remaining upper layers.

The Seasons. Seasons are caused by the 23.4 degree tilt of the Earth's axis, which alternately turns the North and South Poles toward the Sun. Times when the Sun's apparent path crosses the Equator are known as *equinoxes*. Times when the Sun's apparent path is at the greatest distance from the Equator are known as *solstices*. The lengths of the days are most extreme at each solstice. If the Earth's axis were perpendicular to the plane of the Earth's orbit around the Sun, there would be no seasons, and the days always would be equal in length. Since the Earth's axis is at an angle, the Sun strikes the Earth directly at the Equator only twice a year: in March (vernal equinox) and September (autumnal equinox). In the Northern Hemisphere, spring begins at the vernal equinox, summer at the summer solstice, fall at the autumnal equinox, and winter at the winter solstice. The situation is reversed in the Southern Hemisphere.

Mercury

Mercury is the planet nearest the Sun. Appropriately named for the wing-footed Roman messenger of the gods, Mercury whizzes around the Sun at a speed of 30 miles per second, completing one circuit in 88 days. The planet rotates on its axis over a period of nearly 59 days. Daytime on cratered Mercury is hot, about 800 degrees F., although at night the temperature may fall to room temperature. Mercury has no moons, but it does have a trace of atmosphere and a weak magnetic field, according to findings of Mariner 10. Until this spacecraft flew by Mercury in 1974 and 1975, very little was known about the planet, primarily because of its short angular distance from the Sun as seen from Earth, which puts it too close to the Sun to be easily observed.

- Mercury is a naked eye object at morning or evening twilight when it is at greatest elongation.

Venus

Although Venus is Earth's nearest neighbor, little is known about this planet because it is permanently covered by thick clouds. In 1962, Soviet and American space probes, coupled with Earth-based radar and infrared spectroscopy, began slowly unraveling some of the mystery surrounding Venus. According to the latest results, Venus' atmosphere is about 96% carbon dioxide, exerting a pressure at the surface 90.5 times greater than Earth's. Walking on Venus would be as difficult as walking a half-mile beneath the ocean. Because of the thick blanket of carbon dioxide, a "greenhouse effect" exists on Venus: Venus intercepts twice as much of the Sun's light as does the Earth. The light enters freely through carbon dioxide gas and is changed to heat radiation in molecular collisions. But carbon dioxide prevents the heat from escaping. Consequently, the temperature of the surface of Venus is over 800 degrees F., hot enough to melt lead. The atmosphere appears to have five distinct layers and to flash almost continuously with lightning. Radar bounced off the planet recently revealed what appear to be large craters and an immense, 900-mile-long canyon. Venus rotates in retrograde motion for a reason not yet known.

- Venus is the brightest of all the planets and is often visible in the morning or evening, when it is frequently referred to as the Morning Star or Evening Star. At its brightest, it can sometimes be seen with the naked eye in full daylight, if one knows where to look.

Mars

Mars, on the other side of the Earth from Venus, is Venus' direct opposite in terms of physical properties. Its atmosphere is cold, thin, and transparent, and readily permits observation of the planet's features. We know more about Mars than any other planet except Earth. Mars is a forbidding, rugged planet with huge volcanoes and deep chasms. The largest volcano, Olympus Mons rises 78,000 feet above the surface, higher than Mount Everest. The plains of Mars are pockmarked by the hits of thousands of meteors over the years. Most of our information about Mars comes from the Mariner 9 spacecraft, which orbited the planet in 1971. Mariner 9, photographing 100% of the planet, uncovered spectacular geological formations, including a Martian Grand Canyon that dwarfs the one on Earth. The spacecraft's cameras also recorded what appeared to be dried riverbeds, suggesting the onetime presence of water on the planet. The latter idea gives encouragement to scientists looking for life on Mars, for where there is water, there may be life. However, by 1979, no evidence of life has been found. Temperatures near the equator range from −17 degrees F. in the daytime to −130 degrees F. at night. Mars rotates upon its axis in nearly the same period as Earth—24 hours, 37 minutes—so that a Mars day is almost identical to an Earth day. Mars takes 687 days to make one trip around the Sun. Because of its eccentric orbit Mars' distance from the Sun can vary by about 36 million miles. Its distance from Earth can vary by as much as 200 million miles. The atmosphere of Mars is much thinner than Earth's; atmospheric pressure is about 1% that of our planet. Its gravity is one-third of Earth's. Major constituents are carbon dioxide and nitrogen. Water vapor and oxygen are minor constituents. Mars' polar caps, composed mostly of carbon dioxide, recede and advance according to the Martian seasons. Mars was named for the Roman god of war, because when seen from Earth its distinct red color reminded the ancient people of blood. We know now that the reddish hue reflects the oxidized (rusted) iron in the surface material. The landing of two robot Viking spacecraft on the surface of Mars in 1976 provided more information about Mars in a few months than in all the time that has gone before.

Jupiter

Jupiter, with an equatorial diameter of 88,000 miles, is the largest of a group of planets which differ markedly from the terrestrial planets. The others in the group are Saturn, Uranus, and Neptune. All are large, with very dense atmospheres, and indeed may be giant balls of gas without any perceptible surfaces. They all whirl rapidly around their axes, but more slowly around the Sun, resulting in short days and long years. They have many moons. Majestic Jupiter, named for the king of the Roman gods, rotates so fast that it is greatly flattened at the poles. According to Pioneers 10 and 11, which flew past Jupiter in 1974 and 1975, this planet is a whirling ball of liquid hydrogen with perhaps an Earth-sized iron core. Other atmospheric constituents are helium, methane, and ammonia. Its clouds are probably ammonia ice crystals, becoming ammonia droplets deeper towards the "surface." Temperatures range from perhaps minus 300 degrees F. at the tops of the cloud decks to 100,000 degrees F. or more deep down at the center. The pressure at the center of the planet is estimated to be a crushing 10 million pounds per square inch. The Great Red Spot, a 13,000-mile-wide storm that may have been raging for thousands of years, was found by Voyagers 1 and 2 in 1979 to be cooler at the top than the surrounding clouds, indicating that the Red Spot may tower high above them. Jupiter has possibly 16 satellites, more than any other planet. The four largest moons, called Galilean moons, are Europa, Ganymede, Io, and Callisto. Voyagers 1 and 2 found them to be very different from each other in terms of surface relief, volcanic activity, and other characteristics.

• Even when nearest the Earth, Jupiter is still almost 400 million miles away. But because of its size, it may rival Venus in brilliance when near. Jupiter's four large moons may be seen through field glasses, moving rapidly around Jupiter and changing their position from night to night.

Saturn

Saturn, the second largest planet in the solar system, is the least dense. It would float in an ocean if there were one big enough to hold it. Aside from its rings, Saturn is very similar to Jupiter except that it is probably colder, being twice as far from the Sun. Recent radar observations of Saturn's rings indicate that they are no more than 10 miles thick, and probably composed of chunks of rock and ice averaging a meter in size. There are five rings. The system begins about 7000 miles from the planet's disk, and extends out to about 35,000 miles. Recent observations have shown Saturn to have between 13 and 18 moons. The two Voyager probes that examined Jupiter in 1979 are scheduled to encounter Saturn in 1980 and 1981 and then possibly Uranus in 1986.

• Saturn is the last of the planets visible to the naked eye. Saturn is never an object of overwhelming brilliance, but it looks like a bright star. The rings can be seen with a small telescope.

Uranus and Neptune

Little is known about the distant giant planets Uranus and Neptune, but they are believed to be similar to Saturn and Jupiter. Being twice as far from the Sun as Saturn, Uranus must be a grim frozen world, and Neptune, 11 A.U. beyond Uranus, must be even colder and darker. The axis of Uranus is tilted at 98 degrees, so it goes around the Sun nearly lying on its side. In 1977, American astronomers made the startling discovery that Uranus has rings, like Saturn. The first Voyager to Uranus may take pictures of the rings in 1986. Uranus has five known moons; Neptune, two. Neptune's Triton, Jupiter's Ganymede and Callisto, and Saturn's Titan are the four largest moons in the solar system.

• Uranus and Neptune can—on rare occasion—become bright enough to be seen with the naked eye, if one knows exactly where to look; normally, they are objects for good field glasses or small portable telescopes.

Pluto

Pluto, the outermost and smallest planet in the solar system, looks more like a terrestrial planet than a gaseous planet. But so little is known about it, that it is difficult to classify. Appropriately named for the Roman god of the underworld, it must be frozen, dark, and dead.

In 1978, light curve studies gave evidence of a moon revolving around Pluto with the same period as Pluto's rotation. Therefore, it stays over the same point on Pluto's surface. In addition, it keeps the same face toward the planet. The discovery of this moon of 500–600 miles in diameter reduces the previously estimated diameter of Pluto to little more than 1,500 miles, making the pair more like a double planet than any other in the solar system. Previously, the Earth-Moon system held this distinction. The density of Pluto is slightly greater than that of water.

Pluto was predicted by calculation when Percival Lowell noticed irregularities in the orbits of Uranus and Neptune. Clyde Tombaugh discovered the planet in 1930, precisely where Lowell predicted it would be. The name Pluto was chosen because the first two letters represent the initials of Percival Lowell.

• Pluto has the most eccentric orbit in the solar system, bringing it at times closer to the Sun than Neptune. Pluto is now approaching the perihelion of its orbit, and for the rest of this century will be closer to the Sun than Neptune. Even then, it can be seen only with a large telescope.

The First Ten Minor Planets (Asteroids)

Name	Year of discovery	Mean distance from sun (millions of miles)	Orbital period (years)	Diameter (miles)	Magnitude
1. Ceres	1801	257.0	4.60	485	7.4
2. Pallas	1802	257.4	4.61	304	8.0
3. Juno	1804	247.8	4.36	118	8.7
4. Vesta	1807	219.3	3.63	243	6.5
5. Astraea	1845	239.3	4.14	50	9.9
6. Hebe	1847	225.2	3.78	121	8.5
7. Iris	1847	221.4	3.68	121	8.4
8. Flora	1847	204.4	3.27	56	8.9
9. Metis	1848	221.7	3.69	78	8.9
10. Hygeia	1849	292.6	5.59	40(?)	9.5

The Asteroids

Between the orbits of Mars and Jupiter are an estimated 30,000 pieces of rocky debris, known collectively as the asteroids, or planetoids. The first and, incidentally, the largest was discovered during the New Year's night of 1801 by the Italian astronomer Father Piazzi, and its orbit was calculated by the German mathematician Karl Friedrich Gauss. (Gauss invented a new method of calculating orbits on that occasion.) A German amateur astronomer, the physician Olbers, discovered the second asteroid. The number now known, catalogued, and named is around 1,600; the estimated total is about 20 times that figure. A few asteroids do not move in orbits beyond the orbit of Mars, but in orbits which cross the orbit of Mars. The first of them was named Eros because of this peculiar orbit. It had become the rule to bestow female names on the asteroids, but when it was found that Eros crossed the orbit of a major planet, it received a male name. Since then around two dozen orbit-crossers have been discovered, and they are often referred to as the "male asteroids." A few of them—Albert, Adonis, Apollo, Amor, and Icarus—cross the orbit of the Earth, and two of them may come closer than our Moon; but the crossing is like a bridge crossing a highway, not like two highways intersecting. Hence there is very little danger of collision from these bodies. They are all small, three to five miles in diameter, and therefore very difficult objects to identify, even when quite close. Some scientists believe the asteroids represent the remains of an exploded planet.

Comets

Comets, according to the noted astronomer, Fred L. Whipple, are enormous "snowballs" of frozen gases (mostly carbon dioxide, methane, and water vapor) and contain very little solid material. The whole behavior of comets can then be explained as the behavior of frozen gas being heated by the Sun. When the comet Kohoutek made its first appearance to man in 1973, its behavior seemed to confirm this Whipple theory of the make-up of comets.

Kohoutek will probably not appear in view for another 75,000 years. The next comet large and brilliant enough to be very easily seen is predicted for 1986, when Halley's comet will approach perihelion (the point of its orbit closest to the Sun) again.

But a large and brilliant comet is possible at any time. More than 1,000 comets are on the lists now, with several new ones being discovered every year. But while there is a comet visible to the unaided eye almost every year, none of them since the last appearance of Halley's comet in 1910–11 has been conspicuous to a casual watcher.

Since comets appear in the sky without any warning, people in classical times and especially during the Middle Ages believed that they had a special meaning, which, of course, was bad. Since a natural catastrophe of some sort or a military conflict occurs every year, it was quite simple to blame the comet that happened to be visible. But even in the past, there were some people who used logical reasoning. When, in Roman times, a comet was blamed for the loss of a battle and hence was called a "bad omen," a Roman writer observed that the victors in the battle probably did not think so.

Up until the middle of the sixteenth century, comets were believed to be phenomena of the upper atmosphere; they were usually "explained" as "burning vapors" which had risen from "distant

21 Famous Comets

Year and no.	Name of comet	Period (years)
1744	De Chéseaux's Comet	—
1806	Biela's Comet	6.7
1811 I	Great Comet of 1811	3000
1812	Di Vico's Comet	70.7
1815	Olbers' Comet	74.0
1819 I	Encke's Comet	3.3
1819	Pons-Winnecke Comet	6.0
1835 III	Halley's Comet	76.3
1843 I	Great Comet of 1843	512.4
1844 II	Great Comet of 1844	102,050
1858 VI	Donati's Comet	2,040(?)
1864 II	Great Comet of 1864	2,800,000
1871 III	Tuttle's Comet	13.8
1874 III	Coggia's Comet	6,000(?)
1879	Brorsen's Comet	5.6
1881 II	Tebbutt's Comet	—
1889 VI	Swift's 2nd Comet	7.0
1892 III	Holmes' Comet	6.9
1923	d'Arrest's Comet	6.6
1925 II	Comet Schwassmann-Wachmann	16.2
1973 I	Comet Kohoutek	75,000(?)

swamps." That nobody had ever actually seen burning vapors rise from a swamp did not matter.

But a large comet which appeared in 1577 was carefully observed by Tycho Brahe, a Danish astronomer who is often, and with the best of reasons, called "eccentric" but who insisted on precise measurements for everything. It was Tycho Brahe's accumulation of literally thousands of precise measurements which later enable his younger collaborator, Johannes Kepler, to discover the laws of planetary motion. Measuring the motion of the comet of 1577, Tycho Brahe could show that it had been far beyond the atmosphere, even though he could not give figures for the distance. Tycho Brahe's work proved that comets were astronomical and not meteorological phenomena.

In 1682, the second Astronomer Royal of Great Britain, Dr. Edmond Halley, checked the orbit of a bright comet that was in the sky then and compared it with earlier comet orbits which were known in part. Halley found that the comet of 1682 was the third to move through what appeared to be the same orbit. And the three appearances were roughly 76 years apart. Halley concluded that this was the same comet, moving around the Sun in a closed orbit, like the planets. He predicted that it would reappear in 1758 or 1759. Halley himself died in 1742, but a large comet appeared sixteen years after his death as predicted and was immediately referred to as "Halley's comet."

In the Spring of 1973, the discovery of comet Kohoutek, apparently headed for a close-Christmastime rendezvous with the Sun, created worldwide excitement. The comet was a visual disappointment, but turned out to be a treasure trove of information on these little-understood celestial objects. Given an unprecedented advance notice of nine months on the advent of the fiery object, scientists were able to study the comet in visible, ultraviolet and infrared light; with optical telescopes, radio telescopes, and radar. They observed it from the ground, from high-flying aircraft, with instruments aboard unmanned satellites, with sounding rockets, and telescopes and cameras on the Earth-orbiting Skylab space station.

Astronomers refer to comets as "periodic" or as "non-periodic" comets, but the latter term does not mean that these comets have no period; it merely means that their period is not known. The actual periods of comets run from 3.3 years (the shortest known) to many thousands of years. Their orbits are elliptical, like those of the planets, but they are very eccentric, long and narrow ellipses. Only comet Schwassmann-Wachmann has an orbit which has such a low eccentricity (for a cometary orbit) that it could be the orbit of a minor planet.

When a comet, coming from deep space, approaches the Sun, it is at first indistinguishable from a minor planet. Somewhere between the orbits of Mars and Jupiter its outline becomes fuzzy; it is said to develop a "coma" (the word used here is the Latin word *coma*, which means "hair," not the phonetically identical Greek word which means "deep sleep"). Then, near the orbit of Mars, the comet develops its tail, which at first trails behind. This grows steadily as the comet comes closer and closer to the Sun. As it rounds the Sun (as first noticed by Girolamo Fracastoro) the tail always points away from the Sun so that the comet, when moving away from the Sun, points its tail ahead like the landing lights of an airplane.

The reason for this behavior is that the tail is pushed in these directions by the radiation pressure of the Sun. It sometimes happens that a comet loses its tail at perihelion; it then grows another one. Although the tail is clearly visible against the black of the sky, it is very tenuous. It has been said that if the tail of Halley's comet could be compressed to the density of iron, it would fit into a small suitcase.

Although very low in mass, comets are among the largest members of the solar system. The nucleus of a comet may be up to 10,000 miles in diameter; its coma between 10,000 and 50,000 miles in diameter; and its tail as long as 28 million miles.

Important Meteor Showers

Approx. date	Name of meteor stream	Radiant in constellation
Jan. 1–4	Quadrantids	Boötes
Feb. 5–10	Alpha Aurigids	Auriga
March 10–12	Zeta Boötids	Boötes
April 19–23	Lyrids	Hercules
May 1–6	May Aquarids	Aquarius
May 30	Eta Pegasids	Pegasus
June 27–30	Pons-Winnecke meteors	Draco
July 14	Alpha Cygnids	Cygnus
July 26–31	Delta Aquarids	Aquarius
Aug. 10–14	Perseids	Cassiopeia
Aug. 10–20	Kappa Cygnids	Cygnus
Aug. 21–31	Zeta Draconids	Draco
Sept. 22	Alpha Aurigids	Auriga
Oct. 2	Quadrantids	Boötes
Oct. 9	Giacobinids	Draco
Oct. 18–23	Orionids	Orion
Nov. 14–18	Leonids	Leo
Dec. 10–13	Geminids	Gemini

Meteors and Meteorites

The term "meteor" for what is usually called a "shooting star" bears an unfortunate resemblance to the term "meteorology," the science of weather and weather forecasting. This resemblance is due to an ancient misunderstanding which wrongly considered meteors an atmospheric phenomenon. Actually, the streak of light in the sky that scientists call a meteor is essentially an astronomical phenomenon: the entry of a small piece of cosmic matter into our atmosphere.

The distinction between "meteors" and "fireballs" (formerly also called "bolides") is merely one of convenience; a fireball is an unusually bright meteor. Incidentally, it also means that a fireball is larger than a faint meteor.

Bodies which enter our atmosphere become visible when they are about 60 miles above the ground. The fact that they grow hot enough to emit light is not due to the "friction" of the atmosphere, as one can often read. The phenomenon responsible for the heating is one of compression. Unconfined air cannot move faster than the speed of sound. Since the entering meteorite moves with 30 to 60 times the speed of sound, the air simply cannot get out of the way. Therefore, it is compressed like the air in the cylinder of a Diesel engine and is heated by compression. This heat—or part of it—is transferred to the moving body. The details of this process are now fairly well understood as a result of re-entry tests with ballistic-missile nose cones.

The average weight of a body producing a faint "shooting star" is only a small fraction of an ounce. Even a bright fireball may not weigh more than 2 or 3 pounds. Naturally, the smaller bodies are worn

The 88 Recognized Constellations

In astronomical works, the Latin names of the constellations are used. The letter N or S following the Latin name indicates whether the constellation is located to the north or south of the Zodiac. The letter Z indicates that the constellation is within the Zodiac.

Latin name	Letter	English version	Latin name	Letter	English version	Latin name	Letter	English version
Andromeda	N	Andromeda	Delphinus	N	Dolphin	Pavo	S	Peacock
Antlia	S	Airpump	Dorado	S	Swordfish	Pegasus	N	Pegasus
Apus	S	Bird of Paradise			(Goldfish)	Perseus	N	Perseus
Aquarius	Z	Water Bearer	Draco	N	Dragon	Phoenix	S	Phoenix
Aquila	N	Eagle	Equuleus	N	Filly	Pictor	S	Painter (or his
Ara	S	Altar	Eridanus	S	Eridanus (river)			Easel)
Aries	Z	Ram	Fornax	S	Furnace	Pisces	Z	Fishes
Auriga	N	Charioteer	Gemini	Z	Twins	Piscis		
Boötes	N	Herdsmen	Grus	S	Crane	Austrinus	S	Southern Fish
Caelum	S	Sculptor's Tool	Hercules	N	Hercules	Puppis	S	Poop (of Argo)[1]
Camelopardalis	N	Giraffe	Horologium	S	Clock	Pyxis	S	Mariner's
Cancer	Z	Crab	Hydra	N	Sea Serpent			Compass
Canes Venatici	N	Hunting Dogs	Hydrus	S	Water Snake	Reticulum	S	Net
Canis Major	S	Great Dog	Indus	S	Indian	Sagitta	N	Arrow
Canis Minor	S	Little Dog	Lacerta	N	Lizard	Sagittarius	Z	Archer
Capricornus	Z	Goat (or Sea-	Leo	Z	Lion	Scorpius	Z	Scorpion
		Goat)	Leo Minor	N	Little Lion	Sculptor	S	Sculptor
Carina	S	Keel (of Argo)[1]	Lepus	S	Hare	Scutum	N	Shield
Cassiopeia	N	Cassiopeia	Libra	Z	Scales	Serpens	N	Serpent
Centaurus	S	Centaur	Lupus	S	Wolf	Sextans	S	Sextant
Cepheus	N	Cepheus	Lynx	N	Lynx	Taurus	Z	Bull
Cetus	S	Whale	Lyra	N	Lyre (Harp)	Telescopium	S	Telescope
Chamaeleon	S	Chameleon	Mensa	S	Table	Triangulum	N	Triangle
Circinus	S	Compasses			(mountain)	Triangulum		Southern
Columba	S	Dove	Microscopium	S	Microscope	Australe	S	Triangle
Coma Berenices	N	Berenice's Hair	Monoceros	S	Unicorn	Tucana	S	Toucan
Corona Australis	S	Southern Crown	Musca	S	Southern Fly	Ursa Major	N	Big Dipper
Corona Borealis	N	Northern Crown	Norma	S	Rule	Ursa Minor	N	Little Dipper
Corvus	S	Crow (Raven)			(straightedge)	Vela	S	Sail (of Argo)[1]
Crater	S	Cup	Octans	S	Octant	Virgo	Z	Virgin
Crux	S	Southern Cross	Ophiuchus	N	Serpent-Bearer	Volans	S	Flying Fish
Cygnus	N	Swan	Orion	S	Orion	Vulpecula	N	Fox

1. The original constellation Argo Navis (the Ship Argo) has been divided into Carina, Puppis, and Vela. Normally the brightest star in each constellation is designated by alpha, the first letter of the Greek alphabet, the second brightest by beta, the second letter of the Greek alphabet, and so forth. But the Greek letters run through Carina, Puppis, and Vela as if it were still one constellation.

to dust by the passage through the atmosphere; only rather large ones reach the ground. Those that are found are called meteorites. (The "meteor," to repeat, is the term for the light streak in the sky.)

The largest meteorite known is still imbedded in the ground near Grootfontein in SW Africa and is estimated to weight 70 tons. The second largest known is the 34-ton Anighito (on exhibit in the Hayden Planetarium, New York), which was found by Admiral Peary at Cape York in Greenland. The largest meteorite found in the United States is the Willamette meteorite (found in Oregon, weight ca. 15 tons), but large portions of this meteorite weathered away before it was found. Its weight as it struck the ground may have been 20 tons.

All these are iron meteorites (an iron meteorite normally contains about 7% nickel), which form one class of meteorites. The other class consists of the stony meteorites, and between them there are the so-called "stony irons." The so-called "tektites" consist of glass similar to our volcanic glass obsidian, and because of the similarity, there is doubt in a number of cases whether the glass is of terrestrial or of extra-terrestrial origin.

Though no meteorite larger than the Grootfontein is actually known, we do know that the Earth has, on occasion, been struck by much larger bodies. Evidence for such hits are the meteorite craters, of which an especially good example is located near the Cañon Diablo in Arizona. Another meteor crater in the United States is a rather old crater near Odessa, Texas. A large number of others are known, especially in eastern Canada; and for many "probables," meteoric origin has now been proved.

The meteor showers are caused by multitudes of very small bodies travelling in swarms. The Earth travels in its orbit through these swarms like a car driving through falling snow. The point from which the meteors seem to emanate is called the *radiant* and is named for the constellation in that area. The Perseid meteor shower in August is the most spectacular of the year, boasting at peak roughly 60 meteors per hour under good atmospheric conditions. The presence of a bright moon diminishes the number of visible meteors.

The Constellations

Constellations are groupings of stars which form patterns that can be easily recognized and remembered, for example, Orion and the Big Dipper. Actually, the stars of the majority of all constellations do not "belong together." Usually they are at greatly varying distances from the Earth and just happen to lie more or less in the same line of sight as seen from our solar system. But in a few cases the stars of a constellation are actually associated; most of the bright stars of the Big Dipper travel together and form what astronomers call an open cluster.

If you observe a planet, say Mars, for one complete revolution, you will see that it passes successively through twelve constellations. All planets (except Pluto at certain times) can be observed only in these twelve constellations, which form the so-called Zodiac, and the Sun also moves through the signs of the Zodiac, though the Sun's apparent movement is actually caused by the movement of the Earth.

Although the constellations are due mainly to the optical accident of line of sight and have no real significance, astronomers have retained them as reference areas. It is much easier to speak of a star in Orion than to give its geometrical position in the sky. During the Astronomical Congress of 1928, it was decided to recognize 88 constellations. A description of their agreed-upon boundaries was published at Cambridge, England, in 1930, under the title *Atlas Céleste*.

The Auroras

The "northern lights" *(Aurora borealis)* as well as the "southern lights" *(Aurora australis)* are upper-atmosphere phenoma of astronomical origin. The auroras center around the magnetic (not the geographical) poles of the Earth, which explains why, in the Western Hemisphere, they have been seen as far to the south as New Orleans and Florida while the equivalent latitude in the Eastern Hemisphere never sees an aurora. The northern magnetic pole happens to be in the Western Hemisphere.

The lower limit of an aurora is at about 50 miles. Upper limits have been estimated to be as high as 400 miles. Since about 1880, a connection between the auroras on Earth and the sun spots has been suspected and has gradually come to be accepted. It was said that the sun spots probably eject "particles" (later the word *electrons* was substituted) which on striking the Earth's atmosphere, cause the auroras. But this explanation suffered from certain difficulties. Sometimes a very large sun spot group on the Sun, with individual spots bigger than the Earth itself, would not cause an aurora. Moreover, even if a sun spot caused an aurora, the time that passed between the appearance of the one and the occurrence of the other was highly unpredictable.

This problem of the time lag is, in all probability, solved by the discovery of the Van Allen layer by artificial satellite *Explorer I.* The Van Allen layer is a double layer of charged sub-atomic particles around the Earth. The inner layer, with its center some 1,500 miles from the ground, reaches from about 40°N. to about 40°S. and does not touch the atmosphere. The outer layer, much larger and with its center several thousand miles from the ground, does touch the atmosphere in the vicinity of the magnetic poles.

It seems probable that the "leakage" of electrons from the outer Van Allen layer causes the auroras. A new burst of electrons from the Sun seems to be caught in the outer layer first. Under the assumption that all electrons are first caught in the outer layer, the time lag can be understood. There has to be an "overflow" from the outer layer to produce an aurora.

The Atmosphere

Astronomically speaking, the presence of our atmosphere is deplorable. Though reasonably transparent to visible light, the atmosphere may absorb as much as 60% of the visible and near-visible light. It is opaque to most other wave-lengths, except certain fairly short radio waves. In addition to absorbing much light, our atmosphere bends light rays entering at a slant (for a given observer) so that the true position of a star close to the horizon is not what it seems to be. One effect is that we see the Sun above the horizon before it actually is. And the unsteady movement of the atmosphere causes the "twinkling" of the stars, which may be romantic but is a nuisance when it comes to observing.

The composition of our atmosphere near the ground is 78% nitrogen and 21% oxygen, the remaining 1% consisting of other gases, most of it argon. The composition stays the same to an altitude of at least 70 miles (except that higher up two impurities, carbon dioxide and water vapor, are missing), but the pressure drops very fast. At 18,000 feet, half of the total mass of the atmosphere is below, and at 100,000 feet, 99% of the mass of the atmosphere is below. The upper limit of the atmosphere is usually given as 120 miles; no definitive figure is possible, since there is no boundary line between the incredibly attenuated gases 120 miles up and space.

Astronomical Telescopes

Optical telescopes used in astronomy are of two basic kinds: refracting and reflecting. In the *refractor telescope,* a lens is used to collect light from a distant object and bring it to a focus. A second lens, the eyepiece, then magnifies the image which may be examined visually or photographed directly. The *reflector telescope* uses a concave mirror instead of a lens, which reflects the light rays back toward the upper end of the telescope where they are magnified and observed or photographed. Most large optical telescopes now being built are reflectors.

Radio telescopes are used to study radio waves coming from outside the Earth's atmosphere. The waves are gathered by an antenna or "dish," which is a parabolic reflecting surface made of metal or finely meshed wire. Radio signals have been received from the Sun, Moon, and planets, and from the center of our galaxy and other galaxies. Radio signals are the means by which the distant and mysterious quasars and pulsars were recently discovered.

Symbols

☉ the sun	♀ Venus	♃ Jupiter	♆ Neptune	✔ occultation	☽ first quarter
☾ the moon	⊕ the earth	♄ Saturn	♇ Pluto	☍ opposition	○ full moon
☿ Mercury	♂ Mars	♅ Uranus	☌ conjunction	● new moon	☾ last quarter

Notable Reflector Telescopes

Diameter in inches	Observatory	Location
236	Academy of Sciences	Zelenchukskaya, U.S.S.R.
200	Hale	Mount Palomar, Calif.
176[1]	Smithsonian Astrophysical Observatory	Mt. Hopkins, Ariz.
158	Kitt Peak National	Tucson, Ariz.
158	Inter-American	Cerro Tololo, Chile
150	Anglo Australian	Siding Spring Mt., Australia
142	European Southern	Cerro La Silla, Chile
140[2]	French, Canadian, Hawaiian	Mauna Loa, Hawaii
120	Lick	Mount Hamilton, Calif.
107	McDonald	Mount Locke, Tex.
102	Crimean Astrophysical	Nauchny, U.S.S.R.
101	Carnegie Southern	Cerro Las Campanas, Chile
100	Hale	Mount Wilson, Calif.
98	Royal Greenwich	Herstmonceux, England
90	Steward	Tucson, Ariz.

1. Six 72-in. mirrors whose outer edges form a 264-in. circle. 2. Under construction. *Source:* L. W. Fredrick

Notable Radio Telescopes

Diameter in feet	Observatory	Location
(1)	National Radio Astronomy Observatory	Socorro, New Mexico
9842[2]	Solar Physics	Culgoora, Australia
5249[3]	Westerbork Radio	Hooghalen, Netherlands
1900[4]	U.S.S.R. Academy of Sciences	Caucasus, U.S.S.R.
1001	Arecibo	Arecibo, Puerto Rico
3000/397	Mullard Radio Astronomy	Cambridge, England
328	Effelsberg Radiotelescope	Bonn, West Germany
300	National Radio Astronomy	Green Bank, W. Va.
656/131	Paris-Meudon	Nancy, France
249	Nuffield Radio Astronomy	Jodrell Bank, Macclesfield, England
210	Australian National Radio Astronomy	New South Wales, Australia
210	NASA/JPL Goldstone Deep Space Communications Complex	Goldstone, Calif.
341/70	Ohio State–Ohio Wesleyan Radio	Delaware, Ohio
150	Stanford Center for Radar Astronomy	Stanford, Calif.
150	Sagamore Hill Radio	Hamilton, Mass.
150	Algonquin Radio	Lake Traverse, Canada
140	National Radio Astronomy	Green Bank, W. Va.
130	Owens Valley Radio	Big Pine, Calif.
118	Haystack	Tyngsboro, Mass.

1. Symmetrical Y, each arm 13 miles long and consisting of nine 25-meter telescopes. 2. Diameter of 96-telescope circular array. 3. Length of 12-telescope array. 4. Under construction. *Source:* L. W. Fredrick

Phenomena, 1981

Configurations of Sun, Moon, and Planets

JANUARY

d	h	
2	02	Earth at perihelion
2	11	Uranus 5° S of Moon
4	09	Venus 3° S of Moon
4	12	Neptune 3° S of Moon
5	22	Venus 0°.6 S of Neptune
6	07	NEW MOON
7	21	Mars 1°.6 S of Moon
10	22	Ceres at opposition
12	00	Vesta stationary
13	10	FIRST QUARTER
14	08	Jupiter 1°.1 S of Saturn
15	04	Moon at perigee
16	17	Aldebaran 0°.9 S of Moon
19	20	Saturn stationary
20	08	FULL MOON (Penumbral Eclipse)
23	22	Mercury 0°.3 S of Mars
25	10	Jupiter stationary
25	17	Saturn 2° S of Moon
25	18	Jupiter 3° S of Moon
27	20	Moon at apogee
28	04	LAST QUARTER
29	21	Uranus 5° S of Moon
31	23	Neptune 3° S of Moon

FEBRUARY

d	h	
2	01	Mercury greatest elong. E (18°)
2	01	Pluto stationary
3	17	Venus 1°.6 S of Moon
4	22	NEW MOON (Eclipse)
5	20	Mars 0°.6 S of Moon
6	04	Mercury 4° N of Moon
7	22	Mercury stationary
8	23	Moon at perigee
10	18	Mercury 4° N of Mars
11	18	FIRST QUARTER
12	22	Aldebaran 0°.9 S of Moon
17	11	Mercury in inferior conjunction
18	23	FULL MOON
19	07	Jupiter 1°.1 S of Saturn
21	23	Vesta at opposition
22	00	Jupiter 3° S of Moon
22	00	Saturn 2° S of Moon
22	01	Mercury 5° N of Venus
24	17	Moon at apogee
26	07	Uranus 5° S of Moon
27	01	LAST QUARTER
27	07	Ceres stationary
28	05	Juno stationary
28	09	Neptune 2° S of Moon

MARCH

1	15	Mercury stationary
4	14	Mercury 2° N of Moon
5	02	Uranus stationary
6	11	NEW MOON
8	12	Moon at perigee
12	04	Aldebaran 1°.0 S of Moon
13	02	FIRST QUARTER
16	01	Mercury greatest elong. W (28°)
20	15	FULL MOON
20	17	Equinox
21	01	Jupiter 3° S of Moon
21	04	Saturn 1°.7 S of Moon
24	09	Moon at apogee
25	14	Uranus 5° S of Moon
26	06	Jupiter at oppostion
27	05	Saturn at opposition
27	07	Neptune stationary
27	18	Neptune 2° S of Moon
28	20	LAST QUARTER

APRIL

2	14	Mars in conjunction with Sun
3	06	Mercury 1°.1 N of Moon
4	20	NEW MOON
5	19	Moon at perigee
7	09	Venus in superior conjunction
11	11	FIRST QUARTER
11	14	Vesta stationary
13	00	Pluto at opposition
17	01	Jupiter 3° S of Moon
17	06	Saturn 1°.7 S of Moon
19	08	FULL MOON
20	01	Juno at opposition
20	16	Moon at apogee
21	19	Uranus 5° S of Moon
24	00	Neptune 2° S of Moon
27	10	LAST QUARTER
27	16	Mercury in superior conjunction

MAY

4	04	NEW MOON
4	05	Moon at perigee
10	22	FIRST QUARTER
14	01	Mercury 8° N of Aldebaran
14	03	Jupiter 3° S of Moon
14	09	Saturn 1°.8 S of Moon
17	18	Moon at apogee
18	22	Uranus 5° S of Moon
19	00	FULL MOON
19	04	Uranus at opposition
20	06	Venus 6° N of Aldebaran
21	04	Neptune 1°.9 S of Moon
26	21	LAST QUARTER
27	04	Mercury greatest elong. E (23°)
28	09	Jupiter stationary

JUNE

1	14	Moon at perigee
2	12	NEW MOON
3	13	Venus 4° N of Moon
3	23	Mercury 3° N of Moon
6	02	Saturn stationary
9	08	Mercury stationary
9	11	Mercury 1°.7 S of Venus
9	12	FIRST QUARTER
10	09	Jupiter 3° S of Moon
10	14	Saturn 2° S of Moon
14	03	Moon at apogee
14	16	Neptune at opposition
15	02	Uranus 5° S of Moon
17	09	Neptune 1°.9 S of Moon
17	13	Juno stationary
17	15	FULL MOON
19	20	Mars 6° N of Aldebaran
21	12	Solstice
22	01	Mercury in inferior conjunction
24	20	Venus 5° S of Pollux
25	04	LAST QUARTER
29	19	Moon at perigee
30	06	Mars 4° N of Moon

JULY

1	19	NEW MOON
3	13	Venus 1°.3 N of Moon
3	14	Mercury stationary
3	23	Earth at aphelion
7	20	Jupiter 4° S of Moon
7	23	Saturn 2° S of Moon
8	21	Pluto stationary
9	03	FIRST QUARTER
11	18	Moon at apogee
12	08	Uranus 5° S of Moon
14	14	Mercury greatest elong. W (21°)
14	15	Neptune 2° S of Moon
17	05	FULL MOON (Eclipse)
21	14	Pallas in conjunction with Sun
23	21	Venus 1°.2 N of Regulus
24	10	LAST QUARTER
27	09	Moon at perigee
29	00	Mars 3° N of Moon
29	19	Mercury 6° S of Pollux
30	22	Jupiter 1°.2 S of Saturn
31	04	NEW MOON (Eclipse)

AUGUST

2	13	Venus 2° S of Moon
4	12	Jupiter 4° S of Moon
4	12	Saturn 3° S of Moon
4	13	Uranus stationary
7	19	FIRST QUARTER
8	12	Moon at apogee
8	15	Uranus 5° S of Moon
10	06	Mercury in superior conjunction
10	22	Neptune 2° S of Moon
15	17	FULL MOON
21	21	Moon at perigee
22	14	LAST QUARTER
23	17	Mars 6° S of Pollux
25	22	Venus 2° S of Saturn
26	15	Mars 1°.4 N of Moon
28	01	Venus 0°.9 S of Jupiter
29	15	NEW MOON
30	23	Mercury 4° S of Moon

SEPTEMBER

1	01	Saturn 3° S of Moon
1	06	Jupiter 4° S of Moon
1	13	Vesta 0°.2 N of Moon
1	15	Venus 5° S of Moon
3	13	Neptune stationary
5	00	Uranus 5° S of Moon
5	07	Moon at apogee
6	13	FIRST QUARTER
6	21	Venus 1°.9 N of Spica
7	06	Neptune 1°.9 S of Moon
10	15	Mercury 4° S of Saturn
13	19	Mercury 3° S of Jupiter
14	03	FULL MOON
15	12	Ceres in conjunction with Sun
17	04	Moon at perigee
20	19	Mercury 0°.4 S of Spica
20	20	LAST QUARTER
23	03	Equinox
23	16	Mercury greatest elong. E (26°)
24	05	Mars 0°.04 S of Moon
28	04	NEW MOON
30	01	Vesta 0°.4 S of Moon
30	02	Mercury 9° S of Moon

OCTOBER

1	21	Venus 7° S of Moon
2	10	Uranus 4° S of Moon
3	01	Moon at apogee
4	14	Neptune 1°.7 S of Moon
6	04	Saturn in conjunction with Sun
6	08	FIRST QUARTER
6	11	Mercury stationary
7	11	Venus 2° S of Uranus
13	13	FULL MOON
14	05	Jupiter in conjunction with Sun
15	02	Moon at perigee
17	06	Venus 1°.9 N of Antares
17	18	Pluto in conjunction with Sun
18	11	Mercury in inferior conjunction
19	17	Mars 1°.1 N of Regulus
20	04	LAST QUARTER
22	17	Mars 1°.4 S of Moon
26	04	Saturn 3° S of Moon
26	21	Mercury stationary
27	20	NEW MOON
29	20	Uranus 4° S of Moon
30	01	Venus 5° S of Neptune
30	16	Moon at apogee
31	22	Neptune 1°.4 S of Moon

NOVEMBER

1	03	Venus 6° S of Moon
3	01	Mercury 5° N of Spica
3	04	Mercury greatest elong. W (19°)
5	01	FIRST QUARTER
6	00	Mercury 1°.2 N of Jupiter
11	02	Venus greatest elong. E (47°)
11	22	FULL MOON
12	11	Moon at perigee
15	00	Vesta in conjunction with Sun
18	15	LAST QUARTER
20	04	Mars 2° S of Moon
22	16	Saturn 3° S of Moon
22	19	Uranus in conjunction with Sun
23	04	Juno in conjunction with Sun
23	13	Jupiter 4° S of Moon
26	15	NEW MOON
26	21	Moon at apogee
28	06	Neptune 1°.3 S of Moon
30	20	Venus 3° S of Moon

DECEMBER

4	16	FIRST QUARTER
10	15	Mercury in superior conjunction
11	00	Moon at perigee
11	09	FULL MOON
16	15	Neptune in conjunction with Sun
16	19	Venus greatest brilliancy
18	06	LAST QUARTER
18	13	Mars 3° S of Moon
20	03	Saturn 3° S of Moon
21	06	Jupiter 4° S of Moon
21	23	Solstice
23	15	Uranus 4° S of Moon
23	23	Moon at apogee
24	16	Vesta 0°.1 S of Moon
26	10	NEW MOON
29	05	Venus 2° N of Moon
30	08	Venus stationary

NOTE: The hour listings are in Universal Time. For conversion to United States time zones, see conversion table in this section.

Phases of the Moon, 1981

	Date	U.T.
JANUARY		
New Moon	6	07:24
First Quarter	13	10:10
Full Moon	20	07:39
Last Quarter	28	04:19
FEBRUARY		
New Moon	4	22:14
First Quarter	11	17:49
Full Moon	18	22:58
Last Quarter	27	01:14
MARCH		
New Moon	6	10:31
First Quarter	13	01:50
Full Moon	20	15:22
Last Quarter	28	19:34
APRIL		
New Moon	4	20:19
First Quarter	11	11:11
Full Moon	19	07:59
Last Quarter	27	10:14
MAY		
New Moon	4	04:19
First Quarter	10	22:22
Full Moon	19	00:04
Last Quarter	26	21:00
JUNE		
New Moon	2	11:32
First Quarter	9	11:33
Full Moon	17	15:04
Last Quarter	25	04:25

	Date	U.T.
JULY		
New Moon	1	19:03
First Quarter	9	02:39
Full Moon	17	04:39
Last Quarter	24	09:40
New Moon	31	03:52
AUGUST		
First Quarter	7	19:26
Full Moon	15	16:37
Last Quarter	22	14:16
New Moon	29	14:43
SEPTEMBER		
First Quarter	6	13:26
Full Moon	14	03:09
Last Quarter	20	19:47
New Moon	28	04:07
OCTOBER		
First Quarter	6	07:45
Full Moon	13	12:49
Last Quarter	20	03:40
New Moon	27	20:13
NOVEMBER		
First Quarter	5	01:09
Full Moon	11	22:26
Last Quarter	18	14:54
New Moon	26	14:38
DECEMBER		
First Quarter	4	16:22
Full Moon	11	08:41
Last Quarter	18	05:47
New Moon	26	10:10

NOTE: For conversion to United States time zones, *see* conversion table in this section.

A Salute to Galileo

Nearly four centuries ago, Galileo became the first man in history to sight the moons of Jupiter using his newly developed spyglass. Now, under the joint sponsorship of the United States and West German governments, over 100 scientists are cooperating on the most ambitious space project of this decade: to orbit a spacecraft around Jupiter and send a detachable probe into its atmosphere in order to seek clues about the evolution and origin of the solar system.

If financial and technical obstacles can be overcome in time, project Galileo will be launched in January 1982, when planetary conditions will permit aiming the spacecraft toward Mars using that planet's gravitational pull to help the spacecraft gain velocity and bend its trajectory toward Jupiter.

This would be the first mission to use the new Space Shuttle as an interplanetary launch vehicle. The journey would take 3½ years. Galileo would then orbit Jupiter for 20 months, providing more detailed observations than have been obtained on previous rapid fly-by missions. Scientific instruments would transmit data to Earth concerning the atmosphere of Jupiter, the surfaces of its moons, and its magnetic field.

Eclipses of the Sun and the Moon, 1981

January 20: Penumbral eclipse of the Moon. Beginning phase visible in North America, South America, northwestern Africa, western Europe, Arctic Regions; end visible in northwestern South America, North America, Arctic regions, eastern Australia, New Zealand, eastern Africa.

February 4–5: Annular eclipse of the Sun. Visible in Australia except the western part, New Zealand, Antarctica, west of South America.

July 17: Partial eclipse of the Moon. Beginning of umbral phase visible in South America, North America except the northwestern part, Africa except the northeastern part, southwestern Europe, Antarctica; end visible in New Zealand, extreme northwestern Africa, North America except the northern part, South America, Antarctica.

July 31: Total eclipse of the Sun: Visible in eastern Europe, Asia except extreme south, Hawaiian Islands, northwest of North America, arctic regions.

Conversion of Universal Time (U. T.) to Civil Time

U.T.	E.D.T.[1]	E.S.T.[2]	C.S.T.[3]	M.S.T.[4]	P.S.T.[5]	U.T.	E.D.T.[1]	E.S.T.[2]	C.S.T.[3]	M.S.T.[4]	P.S.T.[5]
00	*8P	*7P	*6P	*5P	*4P	12	8A	7A	6A	5A	4A
01	*9P	*8P	*7P	*6P	*5P	13	9A	8A	7A	6A	5A
02	*10P	*9P	*8P	*7P	*6P	14	10A	9A	8A	7A	6A
03	*11P	*10P	*9P	*8P	*7P	15	11A	10A	9A	8A	7A
04	M	*11P	*10P	*9P	*8P	16	N	11A	10A	9A	8A
05	1A	M	*11P	*10P	*9P	17	1P	N	11A	10A	9A
06	2A	1A	M	*11P	*10P	18	2P	1P	N	11A	10A
07	3A	2A	1A	M	*11P	19	3P	2P	1P	N	11A
08	4A	3A	2A	1A	M	20	4P	3P	2P	1P	N
09	5A	4A	3A	2A	1A	21	5P	4P	3P	2P	1P
10	6A	5A	4A	3A	2A	22	6P	5P	4P	3P	2P
11	7A	6A	5A	4A	3A	23	7P	6P	5P	4P	3P

1. Eastern Daylight Time. 2. Eastern Standard Time, same as Central Daylight Time. 3. Central Standard Time, same as Mountain Daylight Time. 4. Mountain Standard Time, same as Pacific Daylight Time. 5. Pacific Standard Time. NOTES: *denotes previous day. N = noon. M = midnight.

Moon at Perigee and Apogee, 1981

Perigee	U.T.	Apogee	U.T.
Jan. 15	04	Dec. 30, 1979	23
Feb. 8	23	Jan. 27	20
March 8	12	Feb. 24	17
April 5	19	March 24	09
May 4	05	April 20	16
June 1	14	May 17	18
June 29	19	June 14	03
July 27	09	July 11	18
Aug. 21	21	Aug. 8	12
Sept. 17	04	Sept. 5	07
Oct. 15	02	Oct. 3	01
Nov. 12	11	Oct. 30	16
Dec. 11	00	Nov. 26	21
Jan. 8, 1982	12	Dec. 23	23

NOTE: For conversion to United States time zones, *see* conversion table in this section.

Planets at Perihelion and Aphelion, 1981

Planet	Perihelion	Aphelion
Mercury	Feb. 5	March 21
	May 4	June 17
	July 31	Sept. 13
	Oct. 27	Dec. 10
Venus	—	Feb. 24
	June 17	Oct. 7
Earth	Jan. 2	July 3
Mars	Feb. 2	—

NOTE: Saturn, Uranus, Neptune, and Pluto do not attain perihelion or aphelion positions in 1981. Jupiter attains Aphelion, July 28.

Morning and Evening Stars, 1981

Planet	Morning	Evening
Mercury	Feb. 23—April 20	Jan. 15—Feb. 12
	June 30—Aug. 2	May 5—June 14
	Oct. 25—Nov. 24	Aug. 19—Oct. 13
		Dec. 26—Dec. 31
Venus	Jan. 1—Feb. 25	May 16—Dec. 31
Mars	June 8—Dec. 31	Jan. 1—Jan. 26
Jupiter	Jan. 1—March 26	March 26—Oct. 1
	Oct. 27—Dec. 31	
Saturn	Jan. 1—March 27	March 27—Sept. 19
	Oct. 23—Dec. 31	
Uranus	Jan. 1—May 19	May 19—Nov. 22
	Nov. 22—Dec. 31	
Neptune	Jan. 1—June 14	June 14—Dec. 16
Pluto	Jan. 1—April 13	April 13—Oct. 17
	Oct. 17—Dec. 31	

NOTE: A *morning star* is any planet that is above the horizon at sunrise; an *evening star* is any planet that is above the horizon at sunset. Dates given are approximate.

Conjunctions of Mercury, 1981

Inferior conjunction	U.T.	Superior conjunction	U.T.
Feb. 17	11	April 27	16
June 22	01	Aug. 10	06
Oct. 18	11	Dec. 10	15

NOTE: For conversion to United States time zones, *see* conversion table in this section.

Soviets Solve Tunguska Explosion Mystery

The Soviet Union has announced that a colossal midair explosion of a meteorite occurred over the Stony Tunguska River basin in Siberia on June 30, 1908. Soviet scientists used a special furnace to burn peat presumed to have come from layers formed in 1908. Analysis of the ashes indicated carbon 14. The presence of carbon 14 has been interpreted as evidence that the material was of celestial origin.

The percentage level of carbon 14 in the peat ashes enabled the scientists to calculate that the amount of celestial matter that fell to earth from the explosion was at least 4,000 tons.

CALENDAR & HOLIDAYS

1981

JANUARY

S	M	T	W	T	F	S
–	–	–	–	1	2	3
4	5	6	7	8	9	10
11	12	13	14	15	16	17
18	19	20	21	22	23	24
25	26	27	28	29	30	31

1– New Year's Day
6– Epiphany

FEBRUARY

S	M	T	W	T	F	S
1	2	3	4	5	6	7
8	9	10	11	12	13	14
15	16	17	18	19	20	21
22	23	24	25	26	27	28

2–Groundhog Day
12–Lincoln s Birthday
14–St. Valentine's Day
16–Washington's Birthday

MARCH

S	M	T	W	T	F	S
1	2	3	4	5	6	7
8	9	10	11	12	13	14
15	16	17	18	19	20	21
22	23	24	25	26	27	28
29	30	31				

4– Ash Wednesday
17– St. Patrick s Day
20– Purim

APRIL

S	M	T	W	T	F	S
–	–	–	1	2	3	4
5	6	7	8	9	10	11
12	13	14	15	16	17	18
19	20	21	22	23	24	25
26	27	28	29	30		

12–Palm Sunday
17–Good Friday
19–Easter
19–1st Day of Passover
26–Daylight Savings Time begins

MAY

S	M	T	W	T	F	S
–	–	–	–	–	1	2
3	4	5	6	7	8	9
10	11	12	13	14	15	16
17	18	19	20	21	22	23
24	25	26	27	28	29	30
31						

10–Mother's Day
25–Memorial Day
28–Ascension Day

JUNE

S	M	T	W	T	F	S
–	1	2	3	4	5	6
7	8	9	10	11	12	13
14	15	16	17	18	19	20
21	22	23	24	25	26	27
28	29	30				

7–Pentecost
8–1st Day of Shabuoth
14–Trinity Sunday
14–Flag Day
21–Father's Day

JULY

S	M	T	W	T	F	S
–	–	–	1	2	3	4
5	6	7	8	9	10	11
12	13	14	15	16	17	18
19	20	21	22	23	24	25
26	27	28	29	30	31	

4– Independence Day

AUGUST

S	M	T	W	T	F	S
–	–	–	–	–	–	1
2	3	4	5	6	7	8
9	10	11	12	13	14	15
16	17	18	19	20	21	22
23	24	25	26	27	28	29
30	31					

SEPTEMBER

S	M	T	W	T	F	S
–	–	1	2	3	4	5
6	7	8	9	10	11	12
13	14	15	16	17	18	19
20	21	22	23	24	25	26
27	28	29	30			

7–Labor Day
29–1st Day of Rosh Hashana

OCTOBER

S	M	T	W	T	F	S
–	–	–	–	1	2	3
4	5	6	7	8	9	10
11	12	13	14	15	16	17
18	19	20	21	22	23	24
25	26	27	28	29	30	31

8– Yom Kippur
12– Columbus Day
13– 1st Day of Sukkoth
25– Daylight Savings Time ends
31–Halloween

NOVEMBER

S	M	T	W	T	F	S
1	2	3	4	5	6	7
8	9	10	11	12	13	14
15	16	17	18	19	20	21
22	23	24	25	26	27	28
29	30					

1–All Saints' Day
3–Election Day
11–Veterans Day
26–Thanksgiving Day
29– 1st Sunday of Advent

DECEMBER

S	M	T	W	T	F	S
–	–	1	2	3	4	5
6	7	8	9	10	11	12
13	14	15	16	17	18	19
20	21	22	23	24	25	26
27	28	29	30	31		

21–1st Day of Hanukkah
25– Christmas

Seasons for the Northern Hemisphere, 1981

Eastern Standard Time

March 20, 12:03 p.m., sun enters sign of Aries; spring begins

June 21, 6:45 a.m., sun enters sign of Cancer; summer begins

Sept. 22, 10:05 p.m., sun enters sign of Libra; fall begins

Dec. 21, 5:51 p.m., sun enters sign of Capricorn; winter begins

1980

JANUARY

S	M	T	W	T	F	S
–	–	1	2	3	4	5
6	7	8	9	10	11	12
13	14	15	16	17	18	19
20	21	22	23	24	25	26
27	28	29	30	31		

FEBRUARY

S	M	T	W	T	F	S
–	–	–	–	–	1	2
3	4	5	6	7	8	9
10	11	12	13	14	15	16
17	18	19	20	21	22	23
24	25	26	27	28	29	

MARCH

S	M	T	W	T	F	S
–	–	–	–	–	–	1
2	3	4	5	6	7	8
9	10	11	12	13	14	15
16	17	18	19	20	21	22
23	24	25	26	27	28	29
30	31					

APRIL

S	M	T	W	T	F	S
–	–	1	2	3	4	5
6	7	8	9	10	11	12
13	14	15	16	17	18	19
20	21	22	23	24	25	26
27	28	29	30			

MAY

S	M	T	W	T	F	S
–	–	–	–	1	2	3
4	5	6	7	8	9	10
11	12	13	14	15	16	17
18	19	20	21	22	23	24
25	26	27	28	29	30	31

JUNE

S	M	T	W	T	F	S
1	2	3	4	5	6	7
8	9	10	11	12	13	14
15	16	17	18	19	20	21
22	23	24	25	26	27	28
29	30					

JULY

S	M	T	W	T	F	S
–	–	1	2	3	4	5
6	7	8	9	10	11	12
13	14	15	16	17	18	19
20	21	22	23	24	25	26
27	28	29	30	31		

AUGUST

S	M	T	W	T	F	S
–	–	–	–	–	1	2
3	4	5	6	7	8	9
10	11	12	13	14	15	16
17	18	19	20	21	22	23
24	25	26	27	28	29	30
31						

SEPTEMBER

S	M	T	W	T	F	S
–	1	2	3	4	5	6
7	8	9	10	11	12	13
14	15	16	17	18	19	20
21	22	23	24	25	26	27
28	29	30				

OCTOBER

S	M	T	W	T	F	S
–	–	–	1	2	3	4
5	6	7	8	9	10	11
12	13	14	15	16	17	18
19	20	21	22	23	24	25
26	27	28	29	30	31	

NOVEMBER

S	M	T	W	T	F	S
–	–	–	–	–	–	1
2	3	4	5	6	7	8
9	10	11	12	13	14	15
16	17	18	19	20	21	22
23	24	25	26	27	28	29
30						

DECEMBER

S	M	T	W	T	F	S
–	1	2	3	4	5	6
7	8	9	10	11	12	13
14	15	16	17	18	19	20
21	22	23	24	25	26	27
28	29	30	31			

1982

JANUARY

S	M	T	W	T	F	S
–	–	–	–	–	1	2
3	4	5	6	7	8	9
10	11	12	13	14	15	16
17	18	19	20	21	22	23
24	25	26	27	28	29	30
31						

FEBRUARY

S	M	T	W	T	F	S
–	1	2	3	4	5	6
7	8	9	10	11	12	13
14	15	16	17	18	19	20
21	22	23	24	25	26	27
28						

MARCH

S	M	T	W	T	F	S
–	1	2	3	4	5	6
7	8	9	10	11	12	13
14	15	16	17	18	19	20
21	22	23	24	25	26	27
28	29	30	31			

APRIL

S	M	T	W	T	F	S
–	–	–	–	1	2	3
4	5	6	7	8	9	10
11	12	13	14	15	16	17
18	19	20	21	22	23	24
25	26	27	28	29	30	

MAY

S	M	T	W	T	F	S
–	–	–	–	–	–	1
2	3	4	5	6	7	8
9	10	11	12	13	14	15
16	17	18	19	20	21	22
23	24	25	26	27	28	29
30	31					

JUNE

S	M	T	W	T	F	S
–	–	1	2	3	4	5
6	7	8	9	10	11	12
13	14	15	16	17	18	19
20	21	22	23	24	25	26
27	28	29	30			

JULY

S	M	T	W	T	F	S
–	–	–	–	1	2	3
4	5	6	7	8	9	10
11	12	13	14	15	16	17
18	19	20	21	22	23	24
25	26	27	28	29	30	31

AUGUST

S	M	T	W	T	F	S
1	2	3	4	5	6	7
8	9	10	11	12	13	14
15	16	17	18	19	20	21
22	23	24	25	26	27	28
29	30	31				

SEPTEMBER

S	M	T	W	T	F	S
–	–	–	1	2	3	4
5	6	7	8	9	10	11
12	13	14	15	16	17	18
19	20	21	22	23	24	25
26	27	28	29	30		

OCTOBER

S	M	T	W	T	F	S
–	–	–	–	–	1	2
3	4	5	6	7	8	9
10	11	12	13	14	15	16
17	18	19	20	21	22	23
24	25	26	27	28	29	30
31						

NOVEMBER

S	M	T	W	T	F	S
–	1	2	3	4	5	6
7	8	9	10	11	12	13
14	15	16	17	18	19	20
21	22	23	24	25	26	27
28	29	30				

DECEMBER

S	M	T	W	T	F	S
–	–	–	1	2	3	4
5	6	7	8	9	10	11
12	13	14	15	16	17	18
19	20	21	22	23	24	25
26	27	28	29	30	31	

PERPETUAL CALENDAR

1800	4	1844	9	1888	8	1932	13	1976	12	2020	11
1801	5	1845	4	1889	3	1933	1	1977	7	2021	6
1802	6	1846	5	1890	4	1934	2	1978	1	2022	7
1803	7	1847	6	1891	5	1935	3	1979	2	2023	1
1804	8	1848	14	1892	13	1936	11	1980	10	2024	9
1805	3	1849	2	1893	1	1937	6	1981	5	2025	4
1806	4	1850	3	1894	2	1938	7	1982	6	2026	5
1807	5	1851	4	1895	3	1939	1	1983	7	2027	6
1808	13	1852	12	1896	11	1940	9	1984	8	2028	14
1809	1	1853	7	1897	6	1941	4	1985	3	2029	2
1810	2	1854	1	1898	7	1942	5	1986	4	2030	3
1811	3	1855	2	1899	1	1943	6	1987	5	2031	4
1812	11	1856	10	1900	2	1944	14	1988	13	2032	12
1813	6	1857	5	1901	3	1945	2	1989	1	2033	7
1814	7	1858	6	1902	4	1946	3	1990	2	2034	1
1815	1	1859	7	1903	5	1947	4	1991	3	2035	2
1816	9	1860	8	1904	13	1948	12	1992	11	2036	10
1817	4	1861	3	1905	1	1949	7	1993	6	2037	5
1818	5	1862	4	1906	2	1950	1	1994	7	2038	6
1819	6	1863	5	1907	3	1951	2	1995	1	2039	7
1820	14	1864	13	1908	11	1952	10	1996	9	2040	8
1821	2	1865	1	1909	6	1953	5	1997	4	2041	3
1822	3	1866	2	1910	7	1954	6	1998	5	2042	4
1823	4	1867	3	1911	1	1955	7	1999	6	2043	5
1824	12	1868	11	1912	9	1956	8	2000	14	2044	13
1825	7	1869	6	1913	4	1957	3	2001	2	2045	1
1826	1	1870	7	1914	5	1958	4	2002	3	2046	2
1827	2	1871	1	1915	6	1959	5	2003	4	2047	3
1828	10	1872	9	1916	14	1960	13	2004	12	2048	11
1829	5	1873	4	1917	2	1961	1	2005	7	2049	6
1830	6	1874	5	1918	3	1962	2	2006	1	2050	7
1831	7	1875	6	1919	4	1963	3	2007	2	2051	1
1832	8	1876	14	1920	12	1964	11	2008	10	2052	9
1833	3	1877	2	1921	7	1965	6	2009	5	2053	4
1834	4	1878	3	1922	1	1966	7	2010	6	2054	5
1835	5	1879	4	1923	2	1967	1	2011	7	2055	6
1836	13	1880	12	1924	10	1968	9	2012	8	2056	14
1837	1	1881	7	1925	5	1969	4	2013	3	2057	2
1838	2	1882	1	1926	6	1970	5	2014	4	2058	3
1839	3	1883	2	1927	7	1971	6	2015	5	2059	4
1840	11	1884	10	1928	8	1972	14	2016	13	2060	12
1841	6	1885	5	1929	3	1973	2	2017	1	2061	7
1842	7	1886	6	1930	4	1974	3	2018	2	2062	1
1843	1	1887	7	1931	5	1975	4	2019	3	2063	2

DIRECTIONS: The number given with each year in the key above is number of calendar to use for that year

1

JANUARY

S	M	T	W	T	F	S
1	2	3	4	5	6	7
8	9	10	11	12	13	14
15	16	17	18	19	20	21
22	23	24	25	26	27	28
29	30	31				

FEBRUARY

S	M	T	W	T	F	S
			1	2	3	4
5	6	7	8	9	10	11
12	13	14	15	16	17	18
19	20	21	22	23	24	25
26	27	28				

MARCH

S	M	T	W	T	F	S
			1	2	3	4
5	6	7	8	9	10	11
12	13	14	15	16	17	18
19	20	21	22	23	24	25
26	27	28	29	30	31	

APRIL

S	M	T	W	T	F	S
						1
2	3	4	5	6	7	8
9	10	11	12	13	14	15
16	17	18	19	20	21	22
23	24	25	26	27	28	29
30						

MAY

S	M	T	W	T	F	S
	1	2	3	4	5	6
7	8	9	10	11	12	13
14	15	16	17	18	19	20
21	22	23	24	25	26	27
28	29	30	31			

JUNE

S	M	T	W	T	F	S
				1	2	3
4	5	6	7	8	9	10
11	12	13	14	15	16	17
18	19	20	21	22	23	24
25	26	27	28	29	30	

JULY

S	M	T	W	T	F	S
						1
2	3	4	5	6	7	8
9	10	11	12	13	14	15
16	17	18	19	20	21	22
23	24	25	26	27	28	29
30	31					

AUGUST

S	M	T	W	T	F	S
		1	2	3	4	5
6	7	8	9	10	11	12
13	14	15	16	17	18	19
20	21	22	23	24	25	26
27	28	29	30	31		

SEPTEMBER

S	M	T	W	T	F	S
					1	2
3	4	5	6	7	8	9
10	11	12	13	14	15	16
17	18	19	20	21	22	23
24	25	26	27	28	29	30

OCTOBER

S	M	T	W	T	F	S
1	2	3	4	5	6	7
8	9	10	11	12	13	14
15	16	17	18	19	20	21
22	23	24	25	26	27	28
29	30	31				

NOVEMBER

S	M	T	W	T	F	S
			1	2	3	4
5	6	7	8	9	10	11
12	13	14	15	16	17	18
19	20	21	22	23	24	25
26	27	28	29	30		

DECEMBER

S	M	T	W	T	F	S
					1	2
3	4	5	6	7	8	9
10	11	12	13	14	15	16
17	18	19	20	21	22	23
24	25	26	27	28	29	30
31						

2

JANUARY

S	M	T	W	T	F	S
	1	2	3	4	5	6
7	8	9	10	11	12	13
14	15	16	17	18	19	20
21	22	23	24	25	26	27
28	29	30	31			

FEBRUARY

S	M	T	W	T	F	S
				1	2	3
4	5	6	7	8	9	10
11	12	13	14	15	16	17
18	19	20	21	22	23	24
25	26	27	28			

MARCH

S	M	T	W	T	F	S
				1	2	3
4	5	6	7	8	9	10
11	12	13	14	15	16	17
18	19	20	21	22	23	24
25	26	27	28	29	30	31

APRIL

S	M	T	W	T	F	S
1	2	3	4	5	6	7
8	9	10	11	12	13	14
15	16	17	18	19	20	21
22	23	24	25	26	27	28
29	30					

MAY

S	M	T	W	T	F	S
		1	2	3	4	5
6	7	8	9	10	11	12
13	14	15	16	17	18	19
20	21	22	23	24	25	26
27	28	29	30	31		

JUNE

S	M	T	W	T	F	S
					1	2
3	4	5	6	7	8	9
10	11	12	13	14	15	16
17	18	19	20	21	22	23
24	25	26	27	28	29	30

JULY

S	M	T	W	T	F	S
1	2	3	4	5	6	7
8	9	10	11	12	13	14
15	16	17	18	19	20	21
22	23	24	25	26	27	28
29	30	31				

AUGUST

S	M	T	W	T	F	S
			1	2	3	4
5	6	7	8	9	10	11
12	13	14	15	16	17	18
19	20	21	22	23	24	25
26	27	28	29	30	31	

SEPTEMBER

S	M	T	W	T	F	S
						1
2	3	4	5	6	7	8
9	10	11	12	13	14	15
16	17	18	19	20	21	22
23	24	25	26	27	28	29
30						

OCTOBER

S	M	T	W	T	F	S
	1	2	3	4	5	6
7	8	9	10	11	12	13
14	15	16	17	18	19	20
21	22	23	24	25	26	27
28	29	30	31			

NOVEMBER

S	M	T	W	T	F	S
				1	2	3
4	5	6	7	8	9	10
11	12	13	14	15	16	17
18	19	20	21	22	23	24
25	26	27	28	29	30	

DECEMBER

S	M	T	W	T	F	S
						1
2	3	4	5	6	7	8
9	10	11	12	13	14	15
16	17	18	19	20	21	22
23	24	25	26	27	28	29
30	31					

3

JANUARY

S	M	T	W	T	F	S
		1	2	3	4	5
6	7	8	9	10	11	12
13	14	15	16	17	18	19
20	21	22	23	24	25	26
27	28	29	30	31		

FEBRUARY

S	M	T	W	T	F	S
					1	2
3	4	5	6	7	8	9
10	11	12	13	14	15	16
17	18	19	20	21	22	23
24	25	26	27	28		

MARCH

S	M	T	W	T	F	S
					1	2
3	4	5	6	7	8	9
10	11	12	13	14	15	16
17	18	19	20	21	22	23
24	25	26	27	28	29	30
31						

APRIL

S	M	T	W	T	F	S
	1	2	3	4	5	6
7	8	9	10	11	12	13
14	15	16	17	18	19	20
21	22	23	24	25	26	27
28	29	30				

MAY

S	M	T	W	T	F	S
			1	2	3	4
5	6	7	8	9	10	11
12	13	14	15	16	17	18
19	20	21	22	23	24	25
26	27	28	29	30	31	

JUNE

S	M	T	W	T	F	S
						1
2	3	4	5	6	7	8
9	10	11	12	13	14	15
16	17	18	19	20	21	22
23	24	25	26	27	28	29
30						

JULY

S	M	T	W	T	F	S
	1	2	3	4	5	6
7	8	9	10	11	12	13
14	15	16	17	18	19	20
21	22	23	24	25	26	27
28	29	30	31			

AUGUST

S	M	T	W	T	F	S
				1	2	3
4	5	6	7	8	9	10
11	12	13	14	15	16	17
18	19	20	21	22	23	24
25	26	27	28	29	30	31

SEPTEMBER

S	M	T	W	T	F	S
1	2	3	4	5	6	7
8	9	10	11	12	13	14
15	16	17	18	19	20	21
22	23	24	25	26	27	28
29	30					

OCTOBER

S	M	T	W	T	F	S
		1	2	3	4	5
6	7	8	9	10	11	12
13	14	15	16	17	18	19
20	21	22	23	24	25	26
27	28	29	30	31		

NOVEMBER

S	M	T	W	T	F	S
					1	2
3	4	5	6	7	8	9
10	11	12	13	14	15	16
17	18	19	20	21	22	23
24	25	26	27	28	29	30

DECEMBER

S	M	T	W	T	F	S
1	2	3	4	5	6	7
8	9	10	11	12	13	14
15	16	17	18	19	20	21
22	23	24	25	26	27	28
29	30	31				

4

JANUARY

S	M	T	W	T	F	S
			1	2	3	4
5	6	7	8	9	10	11
12	13	14	15	16	17	18
19	20	21	22	23	24	25
26	27	28	29	30	31	

FEBRUARY

S	M	T	W	T	F	S
						1
2	3	4	5	6	7	8
9	10	11	12	13	14	15
16	17	18	19	20	21	22
23	24	25	26	27	28	

MARCH

S	M	T	W	T	F	S
						1
2	3	4	5	6	7	8
9	10	11	12	13	14	15
16	17	18	19	20	21	22
23	24	25	26	27	28	29
30	31					

APRIL

S	M	T	W	T	F	S
		1	2	3	4	5
6	7	8	9	10	11	12
13	14	15	16	17	18	19
20	21	22	23	24	25	26
27	28	29	30			

MAY

S	M	T	W	T	F	S
				1	2	3
4	5	6	7	8	9	10
11	12	13	14	15	16	17
18	19	20	21	22	23	24
25	26	27	28	29	30	31

JUNE

S	M	T	W	T	F	S
1	2	3	4	5	6	7
8	9	10	11	12	13	14
15	16	17	18	19	20	21
22	23	24	25	26	27	28
29	30					

JULY

S	M	T	W	T	F	S
		1	2	3	4	5
6	7	8	9	10	11	12
13	14	15	16	17	18	19
20	21	22	23	24	25	26
27	28	29	30	31		

AUGUST

S	M	T	W	T	F	S
					1	2
3	4	5	6	7	8	9
10	11	12	13	14	15	16
17	18	19	20	21	22	23
24	25	26	27	28	29	30
31						

SEPTEMBER

S	M	T	W	T	F	S
	1	2	3	4	5	6
7	8	9	10	11	12	13
14	15	16	17	18	19	20
21	22	23	24	25	26	27
28	29	30				

OCTOBER

S	M	T	W	T	F	S
			1	2	3	4
5	6	7	8	9	10	11
12	13	14	15	16	17	18
19	20	21	22	23	24	25
26	27	28	29	30	31	

NOVEMBER

S	M	T	W	T	F	S
						1
2	3	4	5	6	7	8
9	10	11	12	13	14	15
16	17	18	19	20	21	22
23	24	25	26	27	28	29
30						

DECEMBER

S	M	T	W	T	F	S
	1	2	3	4	5	6
7	8	9	10	11	12	13
14	15	16	17	18	19	20
21	22	23	24	25	26	27
28	29	30	31			

5

JANUARY

S	M	T	W	T	F	S
				1	2	3
4	5	6	7	8	9	10
11	12	13	14	15	16	17
18	19	20	21	22	23	24
25	26	27	28	29	30	31

FEBRUARY

S	M	T	W	T	F	S
1	2	3	4	5	6	7
8	9	10	11	12	13	14
15	16	17	18	19	20	21
22	23	24	25	26	27	28

MARCH

S	M	T	W	T	F	S
1	2	3	4	5	6	7
8	9	10	11	12	13	14
15	16	17	18	19	20	21
22	23	24	25	26	27	28
29	30	31				

APRIL

S	M	T	W	T	F	S
			1	2	3	4
5	6	7	8	9	10	11
12	13	14	15	16	17	18
19	20	21	22	23	24	25
26	27	28	29	30		

MAY

S	M	T	W	T	F	S
					1	2
3	4	5	6	7	8	9
10	11	12	13	14	15	16
17	18	19	20	21	22	23
24	25	26	27	28	29	30
31						

JUNE

S	M	T	W	T	F	S
	1	2	3	4	5	6
7	8	9	10	11	12	13
14	15	16	17	18	19	20
21	22	23	24	25	26	27
28	29	30				

JULY

S	M	T	W	T	F	S
			1	2	3	4
5	6	7	8	9	10	11
12	13	14	15	16	17	18
19	20	21	22	23	24	25
26	27	28	29	30	31	

AUGUST

S	M	T	W	T	F	S
						1
2	3	4	5	6	7	8
9	10	11	12	13	14	15
16	17	18	19	20	21	22
23	24	25	26	27	28	29
30	31					

SEPTEMBER

S	M	T	W	T	F	S
		1	2	3	4	5
6	7	8	9	10	11	12
13	14	15	16	17	18	19
20	21	22	23	24	25	26
27	28	29	30			

OCTOBER

S	M	T	W	T	F	S
				1	2	3
4	5	6	7	8	9	10
11	12	13	14	15	16	17
18	19	20	21	22	23	24
25	26	27	28	29	30	31

NOVEMBER

S	M	T	W	T	F	S
1	2	3	4	5	6	7
8	9	10	11	12	13	14
15	16	17	18	19	20	21
22	23	24	25	26	27	28
29	30					

DECEMBER

S	M	T	W	T	F	S
		1	2	3	4	5
6	7	8	9	10	11	12
13	14	15	16	17	18	19
20	21	22	23	24	25	26
27	28	29	30	31		

6

JANUARY

S	M	T	W	T	F	S
					1	2
3	4	5	6	7	8	9
10	11	12	13	14	15	16
17	18	19	20	21	22	23
24	25	26	27	28	29	30
31						

FEBRUARY

S	M	T	W	T	F	S
	1	2	3	4	5	6
7	8	9	10	11	12	13
14	15	16	17	18	19	20
21	22	23	24	25	26	27
28						

MARCH

S	M	T	W	T	F	S
	1	2	3	4	5	6
7	8	9	10	11	12	13
14	15	16	17	18	19	20
21	22	23	24	25	26	27
28	29	30	31			

APRIL

S	M	T	W	T	F	S
				1	2	3
4	5	6	7	8	9	10
11	12	13	14	15	16	17
18	19	20	21	22	23	24
25	26	27	28	29	30	

MAY

S	M	T	W	T	F	S
						1
2	3	4	5	6	7	8
9	10	11	12	13	14	15
16	17	18	19	20	21	22
23	24	25	26	27	28	29
30	31					

JUNE

S	M	T	W	T	F	S
		1	2	3	4	5
6	7	8	9	10	11	12
13	14	15	16	17	18	19
20	21	22	23	24	25	26
27	28	29	30			

JULY

S	M	T	W	T	F	S
				1	2	3
4	5	6	7	8	9	10
11	12	13	14	15	16	17
18	19	20	21	22	23	24
25	26	27	28	29	30	31

AUGUST

S	M	T	W	T	F	S
1	2	3	4	5	6	7
8	9	10	11	12	13	14
15	16	17	18	19	20	21
22	23	24	25	26	27	28
29	30	31				

SEPTEMBER

S	M	T	W	T	F	S
			1	2	3	4
5	6	7	8	9	10	11
12	13	14	15	16	17	18
19	20	21	22	23	24	25
26	27	28	29	30		

OCTOBER

S	M	T	W	T	F	S
					1	2
3	4	5	6	7	8	9
10	11	12	13	14	15	16
17	18	19	20	21	22	23
24	25	26	27	28	29	30
31						

NOVEMBER

S	M	T	W	T	F	S
	1	2	3	4	5	6
7	8	9	10	11	12	13
14	15	16	17	18	19	20
21	22	23	24	25	26	27
28	29	30				

DECEMBER

S	M	T	W	T	F	S
			1	2	3	4
5	6	7	8	9	10	11
12	13	14	15	16	17	18
19	20	21	22	23	24	25
26	27	28	29	30	31	

7

JANUARY

S	M	T	W	T	F	S
						1
2	3	4	5	6	7	8
9	10	11	12	13	14	15
16	17	18	19	20	21	22
23	24	25	26	27	28	29
30	31					

FEBRUARY

S	M	T	W	T	F	S
		1	2	3	4	5
6	7	8	9	10	11	12
13	14	15	16	17	18	19
20	21	22	23	24	25	26
27	28					

MARCH

S	M	T	W	T	F	S
		1	2	3	4	5
6	7	8	9	10	11	12
13	14	15	16	17	18	19
20	21	22	23	24	25	26
27	28	29	30	31		

APRIL

S	M	T	W	T	F	S
					1	2
3	4	5	6	7	8	9
10	11	12	13	14	15	16
17	18	19	20	21	22	23
24	25	26	27	28	29	30

MAY

S	M	T	W	T	F	S
1	2	3	4	5	6	7
8	9	10	11	12	13	14
15	16	17	18	19	20	21
22	23	24	25	26	27	28
29	30	31				

JUNE

S	M	T	W	T	F	S
			1	2	3	4
5	6	7	8	9	10	11
12	13	14	15	16	17	18
19	20	21	22	23	24	25
26	27	28	29	30		

JULY

S	M	T	W	T	F	S
					1	2
3	4	5	6	7	8	9
10	11	12	13	14	15	16
17	18	19	20	21	22	23
24	25	26	27	28	29	30
31						

AUGUST

S	M	T	W	T	F	S
	1	2	3	4	5	6
7	8	9	10	11	12	13
14	15	16	17	18	19	20
21	22	23	24	25	26	27
28	29	30	31			

SEPTEMBER

S	M	T	W	T	F	S
				1	2	3
4	5	6	7	8	9	10
11	12	13	14	15	16	17
18	19	20	21	22	23	24
25	26	27	28	29	30	

OCTOBER

S	M	T	W	T	F	S
						1
2	3	4	5	6	7	8
9	10	11	12	13	14	15
16	17	18	19	20	21	22
23	24	25	26	27	28	29
30	31					

NOVEMBER

S	M	T	W	T	F	S
		1	2	3	4	5
6	7	8	9	10	11	12
13	14	15	16	17	18	19
20	21	22	23	24	25	26
27	28	29	30			

DECEMBER

S	M	T	W	T	F	S
				1	2	3
4	5	6	7	8	9	10
11	12	13	14	15	16	17
18	19	20	21	22	23	24
25	26	27	28	29	30	31

8

JANUARY

S	M	T	W	T	F	S
1	2	3	4	5	6	7
8	9	10	11	12	13	14
15	16	17	18	19	20	21
22	23	24	25	26	27	28
29	30	31				

FEBRUARY

S	M	T	W	T	F	S
			1	2	3	4
5	6	7	8	9	10	11
12	13	14	15	16	17	18
19	20	21	22	23	24	25
26	27	28	29			

MARCH

S	M	T	W	T	F	S
				1	2	3
4	5	6	7	8	9	10
11	12	13	14	15	16	17
18	19	20	21	22	23	24
25	26	27	28	29	30	31

APRIL

S	M	T	W	T	F	S
1	2	3	4	5	6	7
8	9	10	11	12	13	14
15	16	17	18	19	20	21
22	23	24	25	26	27	28
29	30					

MAY

S	M	T	W	T	F	S
		1	2	3	4	5
6	7	8	9	10	11	12
13	14	15	16	17	18	19
20	21	22	23	24	25	26
27	28	29	30	31		

JUNE

S	M	T	W	T	F	S
					1	2
3	4	5	6	7	8	9
10	11	12	13	14	15	16
17	18	19	20	21	22	23
24	25	26	27	28	29	30

JULY

S	M	T	W	T	F	S
1	2	3	4	5	6	7
8	9	10	11	12	13	14
15	16	17	18	19	20	21
22	23	24	25	26	27	28
29	30	31				

AUGUST

S	M	T	W	T	F	S
			1	2	3	4
5	6	7	8	9	10	11
12	13	14	15	16	17	18
19	20	21	22	23	24	25
26	27	28	29	30	31	

SEPTEMBER

S	M	T	W	T	F	S
						1
2	3	4	5	6	7	8
9	10	11	12	13	14	15
16	17	18	19	20	21	22
23	24	25	26	27	28	29
30						

OCTOBER

S	M	T	W	T	F	S
	1	2	3	4	5	6
7	8	9	10	11	12	13
14	15	16	17	18	19	20
21	22	23	24	25	26	27
28	29	30	31			

NOVEMBER

S	M	T	W	T	F	S
				1	2	3
4	5	6	7	8	9	10
11	12	13	14	15	16	17
18	19	20	21	22	23	24
25	26	27	28	29	30	

DECEMBER

S	M	T	W	T	F	S
						1
2	3	4	5	6	7	8
9	10	11	12	13	14	15
16	17	18	19	20	21	22
23	24	25	26	27	28	29
30	31					

9

JANUARY

S	M	T	W	T	F	S
	1	2	3	4	5	6
7	8	9	10	11	12	13
14	15	16	17	18	19	20
21	22	23	24	25	26	27
28	29	30	31			

FEBRUARY

S	M	T	W	T	F	S
				1	2	3
4	5	6	7	8	9	10
11	12	13	14	15	16	17
18	19	20	21	22	23	24
25	26	27	28	29		

MARCH

S	M	T	W	T	F	S
					1	2
3	4	5	6	7	8	9
10	11	12	13	14	15	16
17	18	19	20	21	22	23
24	25	26	27	28	29	30
31						

APRIL

S	M	T	W	T	F	S
	1	2	3	4	5	6
7	8	9	10	11	12	13
14	15	16	17	18	19	20
21	22	23	24	25	26	27
28	29	30				

MAY

S	M	T	W	T	F	S
			1	2	3	4
5	6	7	8	9	10	11
12	13	14	15	16	17	18
19	20	21	22	23	24	25
26	27	28	29	30	31	

JUNE

S	M	T	W	T	F	S
						1
2	3	4	5	6	7	8
9	10	11	12	13	14	15
16	17	18	19	20	21	22
23	24	25	26	27	28	29
30						

JULY

S	M	T	W	T	F	S
	1	2	3	4	5	6
7	8	9	10	11	12	13
14	15	16	17	18	19	20
21	22	23	24	25	26	27
28	29	30	31			

AUGUST

S	M	T	W	T	F	S
				1	2	3
4	5	6	7	8	9	10
11	12	13	14	15	16	17
18	19	20	21	22	23	24
25	26	27	28	29	30	31

SEPTEMBER

S	M	T	W	T	F	S
1	2	3	4	5	6	7
8	9	10	11	12	13	14
15	16	17	18	19	20	21
22	23	24	25	26	27	28
29	30					

OCTOBER

S	M	T	W	T	F	S
		1	2	3	4	5
6	7	8	9	10	11	12
13	14	15	16	17	18	19
20	21	22	23	24	25	26
27	28	29	30	31		

NOVEMBER

S	M	T	W	T	F	S
					1	2
3	4	5	6	7	8	9
10	11	12	13	14	15	16
17	18	19	20	21	22	23
24	25	26	27	28	29	30

DECEMBER

S	M	T	W	T	F	S
1	2	3	4	5	6	7
8	9	10	11	12	13	14
15	16	17	18	19	20	21
22	23	24	25	26	27	28
29	30	31				

10

JANUARY

S	M	T	W	T	F	S
		1	2	3	4	5
6	7	8	9	10	11	12
13	14	15	16	17	18	19
20	21	22	23	24	25	26
27	28	29	30	31		

FEBRUARY

S	M	T	W	T	F	S
					1	2
3	4	5	6	7	8	9
10	11	12	13	14	15	16
17	18	19	20	21	22	23
24	25	26	27	28	29	

MARCH

S	M	T	W	T	F	S
						1
2	3	4	5	6	7	8
9	10	11	12	13	14	15
16	17	18	19	20	21	22
23	24	25	26	27	28	29
30	31					

APRIL

S	M	T	W	T	F	S
		1	2	3	4	5
6	7	8	9	10	11	12
13	14	15	16	17	18	19
20	21	22	23	24	25	26
27	28	29	30			

MAY

S	M	T	W	T	F	S
				1	2	3
4	5	6	7	8	9	10
11	12	13	14	15	16	17
18	19	20	21	22	23	24
25	26	27	28	29	30	31

JUNE

S	M	T	W	T	F	S
1	2	3	4	5	6	7
8	9	10	11	12	13	14
15	16	17	18	19	20	21
22	23	24	25	26	27	28
29	30					

JULY

S	M	T	W	T	F	S
		1	2	3	4	5
6	7	8	9	10	11	12
13	14	15	16	17	18	19
20	21	22	23	24	25	26
27	28	29	30	31		

AUGUST

S	M	T	W	T	F	S
					1	2
3	4	5	6	7	8	9
10	11	12	13	14	15	16
17	18	19	20	21	22	23
24	25	26	27	28	29	30
31						

SEPTEMBER

S	M	T	W	T	F	S
	1	2	3	4	5	6
7	8	9	10	11	12	13
14	15	16	17	18	19	20
21	22	23	24	25	26	27
28	29	30				

OCTOBER

S	M	T	W	T	F	S
			1	2	3	4
5	6	7	8	9	10	11
12	13	14	15	16	17	18
19	20	21	22	23	24	25
26	27	28	29	30	31	

NOVEMBER

S	M	T	W	T	F	S
						1
2	3	4	5	6	7	8
9	10	11	12	13	14	15
16	17	18	19	20	21	22
23	24	25	26	27	28	29
30						

DECEMBER

S	M	T	W	T	F	S
	1	2	3	4	5	6
7	8	9	10	11	12	13
14	15	16	17	18	19	20
21	22	23	24	25	26	27
28	29	30	31			

11

JANUARY

S	M	T	W	T	F	S
			1	2	3	4
5	6	7	8	9	10	11
12	13	14	15	16	17	18
19	20	21	22	23	24	25
26	27	28	29	30	31	

FEBRUARY

S	M	T	W	T	F	S
						1
2	3	4	5	6	7	8
9	10	11	12	13	14	15
16	17	18	19	20	21	22
23	24	25	26	27	28	29

MARCH

S	M	T	W	T	F	S
1	2	3	4	5	6	7
8	9	10	11	12	13	14
15	16	17	18	19	20	21
22	23	24	25	26	27	28
29	30	31				

APRIL

S	M	T	W	T	F	S
			1	2	3	4
5	6	7	8	9	10	11
12	13	14	15	16	17	18
19	20	21	22	23	24	25
26	27	28	29	30		

MAY

S	M	T	W	T	F	S
					1	2
3	4	5	6	7	8	9
10	11	12	13	14	15	16
17	18	19	20	21	22	23
24	25	26	27	28	29	30
31						

JUNE

S	M	T	W	T	F	S
	1	2	3	4	5	6
7	8	9	10	11	12	13
14	15	16	17	18	19	20
21	22	23	24	25	26	27
28	29	30				

JULY

S	M	T	W	T	F	S
			1	2	3	4
5	6	7	8	9	10	11
12	13	14	15	16	17	18
19	20	21	22	23	24	25
26	27	28	29	30	31	

AUGUST

S	M	T	W	T	F	S
						1
2	3	4	5	6	7	8
9	10	11	12	13	14	15
16	17	18	19	20	21	22
23	24	25	26	27	28	29
30	31					

SEPTEMBER

S	M	T	W	T	F	S
		1	2	3	4	5
6	7	8	9	10	11	12
13	14	15	16	17	18	19
20	21	22	23	24	25	26
27	28	29	30			

OCTOBER

S	M	T	W	T	F	S
				1	2	3
4	5	6	7	8	9	10
11	12	13	14	15	16	17
18	19	20	21	22	23	24
25	26	27	28	29	30	31

NOVEMBER

S	M	T	W	T	F	S
1	2	3	4	5	6	7
8	9	10	11	12	13	14
15	16	17	18	19	20	21
22	23	24	25	26	27	28
29	30					

DECEMBER

S	M	T	W	T	F	S
		1	2	3	4	5
6	7	8	9	10	11	12
13	14	15	16	17	18	19
20	21	22	23	24	25	26
27	28	29	30	31		

12

JANUARY

S	M	T	W	T	F	S
				1	2	3
4	5	6	7	8	9	10
11	12	13	14	15	16	17
18	19	20	21	22	23	24
25	26	27	28	29	30	31

FEBRUARY

S	M	T	W	T	F	S
1	2	3	4	5	6	7
8	9	10	11	12	13	14
15	16	17	18	19	20	21
22	23	24	25	26	27	28
29						

MARCH

S	M	T	W	T	F	S
	1	2	3	4	5	6
7	8	9	10	11	12	13
14	15	16	17	18	19	20
21	22	23	24	25	26	27
28	29	30	31			

APRIL

S	M	T	W	T	F	S
				1	2	3
4	5	6	7	8	9	10
11	12	13	14	15	16	17
18	19	20	21	22	23	24
25	26	27	28	29	30	

MAY

S	M	T	W	T	F	S
						1
2	3	4	5	6	7	8
9	10	11	12	13	14	15
16	17	18	19	20	21	22
23	24	25	26	27	28	29
30	31					

JUNE

S	M	T	W	T	F	S
		1	2	3	4	5
6	7	8	9	10	11	12
13	14	15	16	17	18	19
20	21	22	23	24	25	26
27	28	29	30			

JULY

S	M	T	W	T	F	S
				1	2	3
4	5	6	7	8	9	10
11	12	13	14	15	16	17
18	19	20	21	22	23	24
25	26	27	28	29	30	31

AUGUST

S	M	T	W	T	F	S
1	2	3	4	5	6	7
8	9	10	11	12	13	14
15	16	17	18	19	20	21
22	23	24	25	26	27	28
29	30	31				

SEPTEMBER

S	M	T	W	T	F	S
			1	2	3	4
5	6	7	8	9	10	11
12	13	14	15	16	17	18
19	20	21	22	23	24	25
26	27	28	29	30		

OCTOBER

S	M	T	W	T	F	S
					1	2
3	4	5	6	7	8	9
10	11	12	13	14	15	16
17	18	19	20	21	22	23
24	25	26	27	28	29	30
31						

NOVEMBER

S	M	T	W	T	F	S
	1	2	3	4	5	6
7	8	9	10	11	12	13
14	15	16	17	18	19	20
21	22	23	24	25	26	27
28	29	30				

DECEMBER

S	M	T	W	T	F	S
			1	2	3	4
5	6	7	8	9	10	11
12	13	14	15	16	17	18
19	20	21	22	23	24	25
26	27	28	29	30	31	

13

JANUARY

S	M	T	W	T	F	S
					1	2
3	4	5	6	7	8	9
10	11	12	13	14	15	16
17	18	19	20	21	22	23
24	25	26	27	28	29	30
31						

FEBRUARY

S	M	T	W	T	F	S
	1	2	3	4	5	6
7	8	9	10	11	12	13
14	15	16	17	18	19	20
21	22	23	24	25	26	27
28	29					

MARCH

S	M	T	W	T	F	S
		1	2	3	4	5
6	7	8	9	10	11	12
13	14	15	16	17	18	19
20	21	22	23	24	25	26
27	28	29	30	31		

APRIL

S	M	T	W	T	F	S
					1	2
3	4	5	6	7	8	9
10	11	12	13	14	15	16
17	18	19	20	21	22	23
24	25	26	27	28	29	30

MAY

S	M	T	W	T	F	S
1	2	3	4	5	6	7
8	9	10	11	12	13	14
15	16	17	18	19	20	21
22	23	24	25	26	27	28
29	30	31				

JUNE

S	M	T	W	T	F	S
			1	2	3	4
5	6	7	8	9	10	11
12	13	14	15	16	17	18
19	20	21	22	23	24	25
26	27	28	29	30		

JULY

S	M	T	W	T	F	S
					1	2
3	4	5	6	7	8	9
10	11	12	13	14	15	16
17	18	19	20	21	22	23
24	25	26	27	28	29	30
31						

AUGUST

S	M	T	W	T	F	S
	1	2	3	4	5	6
7	8	9	10	11	12	13
14	15	16	17	18	19	20
21	22	23	24	25	26	27
28	29	30	31			

SEPTEMBER

S	M	T	W	T	F	S
				1	2	3
4	5	6	7	8	9	10
11	12	13	14	15	16	17
18	19	20	21	22	23	24
25	26	27	28	29	30	

OCTOBER

S	M	T	W	T	F	S
						1
2	3	4	5	6	7	8
9	10	11	12	13	14	15
16	17	18	19	20	21	22
23	24	25	26	27	28	29
30	31					

NOVEMBER

S	M	T	W	T	F	S
		1	2	3	4	5
6	7	8	9	10	11	12
13	14	15	16	17	18	19
20	21	22	23	24	25	26
27	28	29	30			

DECEMBER

S	M	T	W	T	F	S
				1	2	3
4	5	6	7	8	9	10
11	12	13	14	15	16	17
18	19	20	21	22	23	24
25	26	27	28	29	30	31

14

JANUARY

S	M	T	W	T	F	S
						1
2	3	4	5	6	7	8
9	10	11	12	13	14	15
16	17	18	19	20	21	22
23	24	25	26	27	28	29
30	31					

FEBRUARY

S	M	T	W	T	F	S
		1	2	3	4	5
6	7	8	9	10	11	12
13	14	15	16	17	18	19
20	21	22	23	24	25	26
27	28	29				

MARCH

S	M	T	W	T	F	S
			1	2	3	4
5	6	7	8	9	10	11
12	13	14	15	16	17	18
19	20	21	22	23	24	25
26	27	28	29	30	31	

APRIL

S	M	T	W	T	F	S
						1
2	3	4	5	6	7	8
9	10	11	12	13	14	15
16	17	18	19	20	21	22
23	24	25	26	27	28	29
30						

MAY

S	M	T	W	T	F	S
	1	2	3	4	5	6
7	8	9	10	11	12	13
14	15	16	17	18	19	20
21	22	23	24	25	26	27
28	29	30	31			

JUNE

S	M	T	W	T	F	S
				1	2	3
4	5	6	7	8	9	10
11	12	13	14	15	16	17
18	19	20	21	22	23	24
25	26	27	28	29	30	

JULY

S	M	T	W	T	F	S
						1
2	3	4	5	6	7	8
9	10	11	12	13	14	15
16	17	18	19	20	21	22
23	24	25	26	27	28	29
30	31					

AUGUST

S	M	T	W	T	F	S
		1	2	3	4	5
6	7	8	9	10	11	12
13	14	15	16	17	18	19
20	21	22	23	24	25	26
27	28	29	30	31		

SEPTEMBER

S	M	T	W	T	F	S
					1	2
3	4	5	6	7	8	9
10	11	12	13	14	15	16
17	18	19	20	21	22	23
24	25	26	27	28	29	30

OCTOBER

S	M	T	W	T	F	S
1	2	3	4	5	6	7
8	9	10	11	12	13	14
15	16	17	18	19	20	21
22	23	24	25	26	27	28
29	30	31				

NOVEMBER

S	M	T	W	T	F	S
			1	2	3	4
5	6	7	8	9	10	11
12	13	14	15	16	17	18
19	20	21	22	23	24	25
26	27	28	29	30		

DECEMBER

S	M	T	W	T	F	S
					1	2
3	4	5	6	7	8	9
10	11	12	13	14	15	16
17	18	19	20	21	22	23
24	25	26	27	28	29	30
31						

The Calendar

History of the Calendar

The purpose of a calendar is to reckon time in advance, to show how many days have to elapse until a certain event takes place—the harvest, a religious festival, or whatever. The earliest calendars, naturally, were crude, and they must have been strongly influenced by the geographical location of the people who made them. In the Scandinavian countries, for example, where the seasons are pronounced, the concept of the year was determined by the seasons, specifically by the end of winter. The Norsemen, before becoming Christians, are said to have had a calendar consisting of ten months of 30 days each.

But in warmer countries, where the seasons are less pronounced, the Moon became the basic unit for time reckoning; an old Jewish book actually makes the statement that "the Moon was created for the counting of the days." All the oldest calendars of which we have reliable information were lunar calendars, based on the time interval from one new moon to the next—a so-called "lunation." But even in a warm climate there are annual events that pay no attention to the phases of the Moon. In some areas it was a rainy season; in Egypt it was the annual flooding of the Nile. It was, therefore, necessary to regulate daily life and religious festivals by lunations, but to take care of the annual event in some other manner.

The calendar of the Assyrians was based on the phases of the Moon. The month began with the first appearance of the lunar crescent, and since this can best be observed in the evening, the day began with sunset. They knew that a lunation was 29½ days long, so their lunar year had a duration of 354 days, falling eleven days short of the solar year.[1] After three years such a lunar calendar would be off by 33 days, or more than one lunation. We know that the Assyrians added an extra month from time to time, but we do not know whether they had developed a special rule for doing so or whether the priests proclaimed the necessity for an extra month from observation. If they made every third year a year of 13 lunations, their three-year period would cover 1,091½ days (using their value of 29½ days for one lunation), or just about four days too short. In one century this mistake would add up to 133 days by their reckoning (in reality closer to 134 days), requiring four extra lunations per century.

We now know that an eight-year period, consisting of five years with 12 months and three years with 13 months would lead to a difference of only 20 days per century, but we do not know whether such a calendar was actually used.

The best approximation that was possible in antiquity was a 19-year period, with seven of these 19 years having 13 months. This means that the period contained 235 months. This, still using the old value for a lunation, made a total of 6,932½ days, while 19 solar years added up to 6,939.7 days, a difference of just one week per period and about five weeks per century. Even the 19-year period required constant adjustment, but it was the period that became the basis of the religious calendar of the Jews. The Arabs used the same calendar at first, but Mohammed forbade shifting from 12 months to 13 months, so that the Islamic religious calendar, even today, has a lunar year of 354 days. As a result the Islamic religious festivals run through all the seasons of the year three times per century.

The Egyptians had a traditional calendar with 12 months of 30 days each. At one time they added five extra days at the end of every year. These turned into a five-day festival because it was thought to be unlucky to work during that time.

When Rome emerged as a world power, the difficulties of making a calendar were well known, but the Romans complicated their lives because of their superstition that even numbers were unlucky. Hence their months were 29 or 31 days long, with the exception of February, which had 28 days. However, four months of 31 days, seven months of 29 days, and one month of 28 days added up to only 355 days. Therefore, the Romans invented an extra month called Mercedonius of 22 or 23 days. It was added every second year.

Even with Mercedonius, the Roman calendar was so far off that Caesar, advised by the astronomer Sosigenes, ordered a sweeping reform in 45 B.C. One year, made 445 days long by imperial decree, brought the calendar back in step with the seasons. Then the solar year (with the value of 365 days and 6 hours) was made the basis of the calendar. The months were 30 or 31 days in length, and to take care of the six hours, every fourth year was made a 366-day year. Moreover, Caesar decreed, the year began with the first of January, not with the vernal equinox in late March.

This was the Julian calendar, named after Julius Caesar. It is still the calendar of the Eastern Orthodox churches.

However, the year is 11½ minutes shorter than the figure written into Caesar's calendar by Sosigenes, and after a number of centuries, even 11½ minutes add up, as the table below shows.

While Caesar could decree that the vernal equinox should not be used as the first day of the new year, the vernal equinox is still a fact of Nature that could not be disregarded. One of the first (as far as we know) to become alarmed about this was Roger Bacon. He sent a memorandum to Pope Clement IV, who apparently was not impressed. But Pope Sixtus IV (reigned 1471 to 1484) decided that another reform was needed and called the German astronomer Regiomontanus to Rome to advise him. Regiomontanus arrived in 1475, but one year later he died in an epidemic, one of the recurrent outbreaks of the plague. The Pope himself survived, but his reform plans died with Regiomontanus.

Less than a hundred years later, in 1545, the Council of Trent authorized the then Pope, Gregory XIII, to reform the calendar once more. Most of the mathematical and astronomical work was done by Father Christopher Clavius, S.J. The immediate correction, advised by Father Clavius and ordered by Pope Gregory XIII, was that Thursday, Oct. 4, 1582, was to be the last day of the Julian calendar. The next day was Friday, with the date of October 15. For long-range accuracy, a formula suggested by the Vatican librarian Aloysius Giglio (latinized into Lilius) was adopted: every fourth year is a leap year *unless* it is a century year like 1700 or 1800. Century years can be leap years *only* when they are divisible by 400 (e.g., 1600).

1. The correct figures are: lunation: 29 d, 12 h, 44 min, 2.8 sec (29.530585 d); solar year: 365 d, 5 h, 48 min, 46 sec (365.242216 d); 12 lunations: 354 d, 8 h, 48 min, 34 sec (354.3671 d).

Drift of the Vernal Equinox in the Julian Calendar

Date	Julian year	Date	Julian year	Date	Julian year
March 21	325 A.D.	March 17	837 A.D.	March 13	1349 A.D.
March 20	453 A.D.	March 16	965 A.D.	March 12	1477 A.D.
March 19	581 A.D.	March 15	1093 A.D.	March 11	1605 A.D.
March 18	709 A.D.	March 14	1221 A.D.		

This rule eliminates three leap years in four centuries, making the calendar sufficiently correct for all ordinary purposes.

Unfortunately, all the Protestant princes in 1582 chose to ignore the papal bull; they continued with the Julian calendar. It was not until 1698 that the German professor Erhard Weigel persuaded the Protestant rulers of Germany and of the Netherlands to change to the new calendar. In England the shift took place in 1752, and in Russia it needed the revolution to introduce the Gregorian calendar in 1918.

The average year of the Gregorian calendar, in spite of the leap year rule, is about 26 seconds longer than the earth's orbital period. But this discrepancy will need 3,323 years to build up to a single day.

Modern proposals for calendar reform do not aim at a "better" calendar, but at one that is more convenient to use, especially for commercial purposes. A 365-day year cannot be divided into equal halves or quarters; the number of days per month is haphazard; the months begin or end in the middle of a week; a holiday fixed by date (e.g., the Fourth of July) will wander through a week; a holiday fixed in another manner (e.g., Easter) can fall on thirty-five possible dates. The Gregorian calendar, admittedly, keeps the calendar dates in reasonable unison with astronomical events, but it still is full of minor annoyances. Moreover, you need a calendar every year to look up dates; an ideal calendar should be one that you can memorize for one year and that is valid for all other years, too.

In 1834 an Italian priest, Marco Mastrofini, suggested taking one day out of every year. It would be made a holiday and *not* be given the name of a weekday. That would make every year begin with January 1 as a Sunday. The leap-year day would be treated the same way, so that in leap years there would be two unnamed holidays at the end of the year.

About a decade later the philosopher Auguste Comte also suggested a 364-day calendar with an extra day, which he called Year Day.

Since then there have been other unsuccessful attempts at calendar reform.

Time and Calendar

The two natural cycles on which time measurements are based are the year and the day. The year is defined as the time required for the Earth to complete one revolution around the Sun, while the day is the time required for the Earth to complete one turn upon its axis. Unfortunately the Earth needs 365 days plus about six hours to go around the Sun once, so that the year does not consist of so and so many days; the fractional day has to be taken care of by an extra day every fourth year.

But because the Earth, while turning upon its axis, also moves around the Sun there are two kinds of days. A day may be defined as the interval between the highest point of the Sun in the sky on two successive days. This, averaged out over the year, produces the customary 24-hour day. But one might also define a day as the time interval between the moments when a certain point in the sky, say a conveniently located star, is directly overhead. This is called:

Sidereal time. Astronomers use a point which they call the "vernal equinox" for the actual determination. Such a sidereal day is somewhat shorter than the "solar day," namely by about 3 minutes and 56 seconds of so-called "mean solar time."

Apparent solar time is the time based directly on the Sun's position in the sky. In ordinary life the day runs from midnight to midnight. It begins when the Sun is invisible by being 12 hours from its zenith. Astronomers use the so-called "Julian Day," which runs from noon to noon; the concept was invented by the astronomer Joseph Scaliger, who named it after his father Julius. To avoid the problems caused by leap-year days and so forth, Scaliger picked a conveniently remote date in the past and suggested just counting days without regard to weeks, months, and years. The Julian Day 2,440,-225.5 is Jan. 1, 1969. The reason for having the Julian Day run from noon to noon is the practical one that astronomical observations usually extend across the midnight hour, which would require a change in date (or in the Julian Day number) if the astronomical day, like the civil day, ran from midnight to midnight.

Mean solar time, rather than apparent solar time, is what is actually used most of the time. The mean solar time is based on the position of a fictitious "mean sun." The reason why this fictitious sun has to be introduced is the following: the Earth turns on its axis regularly; it needs the same number of seconds regardless of the season. But the movement of the Earth around the Sun is not regular because the Earth's orbit is an ellipse. This has the result (as explained in the section The Seasons) that the Earth moves faster in January and slower in July. Though it is the Earth that changes velocity, it looks to us as if the Sun did. In January, when the Earth moves faster, the *apparent* movement of the Sun looks faster. The "mean sun" of time measurements, then, is a sun that moves regularly all year round; the real Sun will be either ahead of or behind the "mean sun." The difference between the real Sun and the fictitious mean sun is called the *equation of time.*

When the real Sun is west of the mean sun we have the "sun fast" condition, with the real Sun crossing the meridian ahead of the mean sun. The opposite is the "sun slow" situation when the real Sun crosses the meridian after the mean sun. Of course, what is observed is the real Sun. The equation of time is needed to establish mean solar time, kept by the reference clocks.

But if all clocks were actually set by mean solar time we would be plagued by a welter of time differences that would be "correct" but a major nuisance. A clock on Long Island, correctly showing mean solar time for its location (this would be *local*

The Names of the Days

Latin	Saxon	English	French	Italian	Spanish	German
Dies Solis	Sun's Day	Sunday	Dimanche	domenica	domingo	Sonntag
Dies Lunae	Moon's Day	Monday	Lundi	lunedì	lunes	Montag
Dies Martis	Tiw's Day	Tuesday	Mardi	martedì	martes	Dienstag
Dies Mercurii	Woden's Day	Wednesday	Mercredi	mercoledì	miércoles	Mittwoch
Dies Jovis	Thor's Day	Thursday	Jeudi	giovedì	jueves	Donnerstag
Dies Veneris	Frigg's Day	Friday	Vendredi	venedrì	viernes	Freitag
Dies Saturni	Seterne's Day	Saturday	Samedi	sabato	sábado	Sonnabend

NOTE: The Romans gave one day of the week to each planet known, the Sun and Moon being considered planets in this connection. The Saxon names are a kind of translation of the Roman names: Tiw was substituted for Mars, Woden (Wotan) for Mercury, Thor for Jupiter (Jove), Frigg for Venus, and Seterne for Saturn. The English names are adapted Saxon. The Spanish and Italian names, which are normally not capitalized, and the French are derived from the Latin. The German names follow the Saxon pattern with two exceptions: Wednesday is Mittwoch (Middle of the Week), and Saturday is Sonnabend (Sunday's Eve).

civil time), would be slightly ahead of a clock in Newark, N.J. The Newark clock would be slightly ahead of a clock in Trenton, N.J., which, in turn, would be ahead of a clock in Philadelphia. This condition actually prevailed in the past until 1883, when *standard time* was introduced. Standard time is the correct mean solar time for a designated meridian, and this time is used for a certain area to the east and west of this meridian. In the U.S. four meridians have been designated to supply standard times; they are 75°, 90°, 105°, and 120° west of Greenwich. The 75° meridian determines Eastern Standard Time. It happens to run through Camden, N.J., where standard time, therefore, is also mean solar time and local civil time. The 90° meridian (which happens to pass through the western part of Memphis, Tenn.) determines Central Standard Time, the 105° meridian (passing through Denver) determines Mountain Standard Time, and the 120° meridian (which runs through Lake Tahoe) determines Pacific Standard Time.

Canada, extending over more territory from west to east, adds one time zone on either side: Atlantic Standard Time (based on 60° west of Greenwich) for New Brunswick, Nova Scotia, and Quebec, and Yukon Standard Time (determined by the 135° meridian) for its extreme West. Alaska, extending still farther to the west, adds two more time zones, Alaska Standard Time (determined by the 150° meridian that passes through Anchorage) and Nome Standard Time, based on the 165° meridian just east of Nome.

In general the Earth is divided into 24 such time zones, which run one hour apart. For practical purposes the time zones sometimes show indentations, and there are a few "subzones" that differ from the neighboring zone by only half an hour, e.g., Newfoundland.

The date line. While the time zones are based on the natural event of the Sun crossing the meridian, the date must be an arbitrary decision. The meridians are traditionally counted from the meridian of the observatory of Greenwich in England, which is called the zero meridian. The logical place for changing the date is 12 hours, or 180° from Greenwich. Fortunately, the 180th meridian runs mostly through the open Pacific. The date line makes a zigzag in the north to incorporate the eastern tip of Siberia into the Siberian time system and then another one to incorporate a number of islands into the Alaska time system. In the south there is a similar zigzag for the purpose of tying a number of British-owned islands to the New Zealand time system. Otherwise the date line is the same as 180° from Greenwich. At points to the east of the date line the calendar is one day earlier than at points to the west of it. A traveller going eastward across the date line from one island to another would not have to re-set his watch because he would stay inside the time zone (provided he does so where the date line does *not* coincide with the 180° meridian), but it would be the same time of the previous day.

The Seasons

The seasons are caused by the tilt of the Earth's axis (23.4°) and not by the fact that the Earth's orbit around the Sun is an ellipse. The average distance of the Earth from the Sun is 93 million miles; the difference between aphelion (farthest away) and perihelion (closest to the Sun) is 3 million miles, so that perihelion is about 91.4 million miles from the Sun. The Earth goes through the perihelion point a few days after New Year, just when the northern hemisphere has winter. Aphelion is

The Names of the Months

January: named after Janus, protector of the gateway to heaven
February: named after Februalia, a time period when sacrifices were made to atone for sins
March: named after Mars, the god of war, presumably signifying that the campaigns interrupted by the winter could be resumed
April: from *aperire*, Latin for "to open" (buds)
May: named after Maia, the goddess of growth of plants
June: from *juvenis*, Latin for "youth"
July: named after Julius Caesar
August: named after Augustus, the first Roman Emperor
September: from *septem*, Latin for "seven"
October: from *octo*, Latin for "eight"
November: from *novem*, Latin for "nine"
December: from *decem*, Latin for "ten"

NOTE: The earliest Latin calendar was a 10-month one; thus September was the seventh month, October, the eighth, etc. July was originally called Quintilis, as the fifth month; August was originally called Sextilis, as the sixth month.

passed during the first days in July. This by itself shows that the distance from the Sun is not important within these limits. What is important is that when the Earth passes through perihelion, the northern end of the Earth's axis happens to tilt away from the Sun, so that the areas beyond the Tropic of Cancer receive only slanting rays from a Sun low in the sky.

The tilt of the Earth's axis is responsible for four lines you find on every globe. When, say, the North Pole is tilted away from the Sun as much as possible, the farthest points in the North which can still be reached by the Sun's rays are 23½° from the pole. This is the Arctic Circle. The Antarctic Circle is the corresponding limit 23.4° from the South Pole; the Sun's rays cannot reach beyond this point when we have mid-summer in the North.

When the Sun is vertically above the equator, the day is of equal length all over the Earth. This happens twice a year, and these are the "equinoxes" in March and in September. After having been over the equator in March, the Sun will seem to move northward. The northernmost point where the Sun can be straight overhead is 23.4° north of the equator. This is the Tropic of Cancer; the Sun can never be vertically overhead to the north of this line. Similarly the Sun cannot be vertically overhead to the south of a line 23.4° south of the equator—the Tropic of Capricorn.

This explains the climatic zones. In the belt (the Greek word *zone* means "belt") between the Tropic of Cancer and the Tropic of Capricorn, the Sun can be straight overhead; this is the tropical zone. The two zones where the Sun cannot be overhead but will be above the horizon every day of the year are the two temperate zones; the two areas where the Sun will not rise at all for varying lengths of time are the two polar areas, Arctic and Antarctic.

Holidays

Religious and Secular, 1981

Since 1971, by federal law, Washington's Birthday, Memorial Day, Columbus Day, and Veterans' Day have been celebrated on Mondays to create three-day weekends for federal employees. Many states now observe these holidays on the same Mondays. (*See* page 443.) The dates given for the holidays listed below are the traditional ones.

New Year's Day, Thursday, Jan. 1. A legal holiday in all states and the District of Columbia, New Year's Day has its origin in Roman times, when sacrifices were offered to Janus, the two-faced Roman deity who looked back on the past and forward to the future.

Epiphany, Tuesday, Jan. 6. Falls the twelfth day after Christmas and commemorates the manifestation of Jesus as the Son of God, as represented by the adoration of the Magi, the baptism of Jesus, and the miracle of the wine at the marriage feast at Cana. Epiphany originally marked the beginning of the carnival season preceding Lent, and the evening (sometimes the eve) is known as Twelfth Night.

Lincoln's Birthday, Thursday, Feb. 12. A legal holiday in many states, this day was first formally observed in Washington, D.C., in 1866, when both houses of Congress gathered for a memorial address in tribute to the assassinated President.

St. Valentine's Day, Saturday, Feb. 14. This day is the festival of two third-century martyrs, both named St. Valentine. It is not known why this day is associated with lovers. It may derive from an old pagan festival about this time of year, or it may have been inspired by the belief that birds mate on this day.

Shrove Tuesday, March 3. Falls the day before Ash Wednesday and marks the end of the carnival season, which once began on Epiphany but is now usually celebrated the last three days before Lent. In France, the day is known as Mardi Gras (Fat Tuesday), and Mardi Gras celebrations are also held in several American cities, particularly in New Orleans. The day is sometimes called Pancake Tuesday by the English because fats, which were prohibited during Lent, had to be used up.

Ash Wednesday, March 4. The first day of the Lenten season, which lasts 40 days. Having its origin sometime before A.D. 1000, it is a day of public penance and is marked in the Roman Catholic Church by the burning of the palms blessed on the previous year's Palm Sunday. With his thumb, the priest then marks a cross upon the forehead of each worshipper. The Anglican Church and a few Protestant groups in the United States also observe the day, but generally without the use of ashes.

Washington's Birthday, Sunday, Feb. 22. The birthday of George Washington is celebrated as a legal holiday in every state of the Union, the District of Columbia, and all territories. The observance began in 1796.

Purim (Feast of Lots), Friday, March 20 (14 Adar). A day of joy and feasting celebrating deliverance of the Jews from a massacre planned by the Persian Minister Haman. The Jewish Queen Esther interceded with her husband, King Ahasuerus, to spare the life of her uncle, Mordecai, and Haman was hanged on the same gallows he had built for Mordecai. The holiday is marked by the reading of the Book of Esther (megillah), and by the exchange of gifts, donations to the poor, and the presentation of Purim plays.

St. Patrick's Day, Tuesday, March 17. St. Patrick, patron saint of Ireland, has been honored in America since the first days of the nation. There are many dinners and meetings but perhaps the most notable part of the observance is the annual St. Patrick's Day parade on Fifth Avenue in New York City.

Palm Sunday, April 12. Is observed the Sunday before Easter to commemorate the entry of Jesus into Jerusalem. The procession and the ceremonies introducing the benediction of palms probably had their origin in Jerusalem.

First Day of Passover (Pesach), Sunday, April 19 (15 Nisan). The Feast of the Passover, also called the Feast of Unleavened Bread, commemorates the escape of the Jews from Egypt. As the Jews fled they ate unleavened bread, and from that time the Jews have allowed no leavening in the houses during Passover, bread being replaced by matzoth.

Good Friday, April 17. This day commemorates the Crucifixion, which is retold during services from the Gospel according to St. John. A feature in Roman Catholic churches is the Liturgy of the Passion; there is no Consecration, the Host having been consecrated the previous day. The eating of hot cross buns on this day is said to have started in England.

Easter Sunday, April 19. Observed in all Christian churches, Easter commemorates the Resurrection of Jesus. It is celebrated on the first Sunday after the full moon which occurs on or next after March 21 and is therefore celebrated between March 22 and April 25 inclusive. This date was fixed by the Council of Nicaea in A.D. 325. The Orthodox Church celebrates Easter on April 6, 1980.

Ascension Day, Thursday, May 28. Took place in the presence of His apostles 40 days after the Resurrection of Jesus. It is traditionally held to have occurred on Mount Olivet in Bethany.

First Day of Shavuot (Hebrew Pentecost), Monday, June 8 (6 Sivan). This festival, sometimes called the Feast of Weeks, or of Harvest, or of the First Fruits, falls 50 days after Passover and originally celebrated the end of the seven-week grain harvesting season. In later tradition, it also celebrated the giving of the Law to Moses on Mount Sinai.

Pentecost (Whitsunday), June 7. This day commemorates the descent of the Holy Ghost upon the apostles 50 days after the Resurrection. The sermon by the Apostle Peter, which led to the baptism of 3,000 who professed belief, originated the ceremonies that have since been followed. "Whitsunday" is believed to have come from "white Sunday" when, among the English, white robes were worn by those baptized on the day.

Memorial Day, Saturday, May 30. Also known as Decoration Day, Memorial Day is a legal holiday in most of the states and in the territories, and is also observed by the armed forces. In 1868, Gen. John A. Logan, Commander in Chief of the Grand Army of the Republic, issued an order designating the day as one in which the graves of soldiers would be decorated. The holiday was originally devoted to honoring the memory of those who fell in the Civil War, but is now also dedicated to the memory of all war dead.

Flag Day, Sunday, June 14. This day commemorates the adoption by the Continental Congress on June 14, 1777, of the Stars and Stripes as the U.S. flag. Although it is a legal holiday only in Pennsylvania, President Truman, on Aug. 3, 1949, signed a bill requesting the President to call for its observance each year by proclamation.

Independence Day, Saturday, July 4. The day of the adoption of the Declaration of Independence in 1776, celebrated in all states and territories. The observance began the next year in Philadelphia.

Labor Day, Monday, Sept. 7. Observed the first Monday in September in all states and territories, Labor Day was first celebrated in New York in 1882 under the sponsorship of the Central Labor Union, following the suggestion of Peter J. McGuire, of the Knights of Labor, that the day be set aside in honor of labor.

First Day of Rosh Hashana (Jewish New Year), Tuesday, Sept. 29 (1 Tishri). This day marks the beginning of the Jewish year 5742 and opens the Ten Days of Penitence closing with Yom Kippur.

Yom Kippur (Day of Atonement), Thursday, Oct. 8 (10 Tishri). This day marks the end of the Ten Days of Penitence that began with Rosh Hashana. It is described in *Leviticus* as a "Sabbath of rest," and synagogue services begin the preceding sundown, resume the following morning, and continue to sundown.

First Day of Sukkot (Feast of Tabernacles), Tuesday, Oct. 13 (15 Tishri). This festival, also known as the Feast of the Ingathering, originally celebrated the fruit harvest, and the name comes from the booths or tabernacles in which the Jews lived during the harvest, although one tradition traces it to the shelters used by the Jews in their wandering through the wilderness. During the festival many Jews build small huts in their back yards or on the roofs of their houses.

Simhat Torah (Rejoicing of the Law), Wednesday, Oct. 21 (23 Tishri). This joyous holiday falls on the eighth day of Sukkot. It marks the end of the year's reading of the Torah (Five Books of Moses) in the synagogue every Saturday and the beginning of the new cycle of reading.

Columbus Day, Monday, Oct. 12. A legal holiday in many states, commemorating the discovery of America by Columbus in 1492. Quite likely the first celebration of Columbus Day was that organized in 1792 by the Society of St. Tammany, or Columbian Order, more widely known as Tammany Hall.

Halloween, Saturday, Oct. 31. Eve of All Saints' Day, formerly called All Hallows and Hallowmass. Halloween is traditionally associated in some countries with old customs such as bonfires, masquerading, and the telling of ghost stories. These are old Celtic practices that marked the beginning of winter.

All Saints' Day, Sunday, Nov. 1. A Roman Catholic and Anglican holiday celebrating all saints, known and unknown.

Election Day, (legal holiday in certain states), Tuesday, Nov. 3. Since 1845, by Act of Congress, the first Tuesday after the first Monday in November is the date for choosing Presidential electors. State elections are also generally held on this day.

Veterans Day, Wednesday, Nov. 11. Armistice Day was established in 1926 to commemorate the signing in 1918 of the Armistice ending World War I. On June 1, 1954, the name was changed to Veterans Day to honor all men and women who have served America in its armed forces.

Thanksgiving, Thursday, Nov. 26. Observed nationally on the fourth Thursday in November by Act of Congress (1941), the first such national proclamation having been issued by President Lincoln in 1863, on the urging of Mrs. Sarah J. Hale, editor of *Godey's Lady's Book*. Most Americans believe that the holiday dates back to the day of thanks ordered by Governor Bradford of Plymouth Colony in New England in 1621, but scholars point out that days of thanks stem from ancient times.

First Sunday of Advent, Nov. 29. Advent is the season in which the faithful must prepare themselves for the advent of the Saviour on Christmas. The four Sundays before Christmas are marked by special church services.

First Day of Hanukkah (Festival of Lights), Monday, Dec. 21 (25 Kislev). This festival was instituted by Judas Maccabaeus in 165 B.C. to celebrate the purification of the Temple of Jerusalem, which had been desecrated three years earlier by Antiochus Epiphanes, who set up a pagan altar and offered sacrifices to Zeus Olympius. In Jewish homes, a light is lighted on each night of the eight-day festival.

Christmas (Feast of the Nativity), Friday, Dec. 25. The most widely celebrated holiday of the Christian year, Christmas is observed as the anniversary of the birth of Jesus. Christmas customs are centuries old. The mistletoe, for example, comes from the Druids, who, in hanging the mistletoe, hoped for peace and good fortune. Use of such plants as holly comes from the ancient belief that such plants blossomed at Christmas. Comparatively recent is the Christmas tree, first set up in Germany in the 17th century, and the use of candles on trees developed from the belief that candles appeared by miracle on the trees at Christmas. Colonial Manhattan Islanders introduced the name Santa Claus, a corruption of the Dutch name for the 4th-century Asia Minor St. Nicholas.

National Holidays Around the World, 1981

Afghanistan	Aug. 19	Grenada	Feb. 7	Papua New Guinea	Sept. 16
Albania	Nov. 29	Guatemala	Sept. 15	Paraguay	May 14
Algeria	Nov. 1	Guinea	Oct. 2	Peru	July 28
Angola	Nov. 11	Guinea-Bissau	Sept. 12	Philippines	June 12
Argentina	May 25	Guyana	Feb. 23	Poland	July 22
Australia	Jan. 26	Haiti	Jan. 1	Portugal	June 10
Austria	Oct. 26	Honduras	Sept. 15	Qatar	Sept. 3
Bahamas	July 10	Hungary	April 4	Romania	Aug. 23
Bahrain	Dec. 16	Iceland	June 17	Rwanda	July 1
Bangladesh	March 26	India	Jan. 26	St. Lucia	Dec. 13
Barbados	Nov. 30	Indonesia	Aug. 17	St. Vincent and the Grenadines	Oct. 27
Belgium	July 21	Iran	April 1	São Tomé and Príncipe	July 12
Benin	Nov. 30	Iraq	July 14	Saudi Arabia	Sept. 23
Bhutan	Dec. 17	Ireland	March 17	Senegal	April 4
Bolivia	Aug. 6	Israel	May 7[1]	Seychelles	June 5
Botswana	Sept. 30	Italy	June 2	Sierra Leone	April 19
Brazil	Sept. 7	Ivory Coast	Dec. 7	Singapore	Aug. 9
Bulgaria	Sept. 9	Jamaica	Aug. 3[2]	Somalia	Oct. 21
Burma	Jan. 4	Japan	April 29	South Africa	May 31
Burundi	July 1	Jordan	May 25	Spain	Oct. 12
Cambodia	April 17	Kenya	Dec. 12	Sri Lanka	Feb. 4
Cameroon	May 20	Kuwait	Feb. 25	Sudan	Jan. 1
Canada	July 1	Laos	Dec. 2	Suriname	Nov. 25
Cape Verde	Sept. 12	Lebanon	Nov. 22	Swaziland	Sept. 6
Central African Republic	Dec. 1	Lesotho	Oct. 4	Sweden	April 30
Chad	April 13	Liberia	July 26	Syria	April 17
Chile	Sept. 18	Libya	Sept. 1	Tanzania	April 26
China	Oct. 1	Luxembourg	June 23	Thailand	Dec. 5
Colombia	July 20	Madagascar	June 26	Togo	April 27
Congo	Aug. 15	Malawi	July 6	Trinidad and Tobago	Aug. 31
Costa Rica	Sept. 15	Malaysia	Aug. 31	Tunisia	June 1
Cuba	Jan. 1	Maldives	July 26	Turkey	Oct. 29
Cyprus	Oct. 1	Mali	Sept. 22	Uganda	Oct. 9
Czechoslovakia	May 9	Malta	March 31	U.S.S.R.	Nov. 7
Denmark	April 16	Mauritania	Nov. 28	United Arab Emirates	Dec. 2
Djibouti	June 27	Mauritius	March 12	United States	July 4
Dominican Republic	Feb. 27	Mexico	Sept. 16	Upper Volta	Dec. 11
Ecuador	Aug. 10	Mongolia	July 11	Uruguay	Aug. 25
Egypt	July 23	Morocco	March 3	Venezuela	July 5
El Salvador	Sept. 15	Mozambique	June 25	Vietnam	Sept. 2
Equatorial Guinea	March 5	Nepal	Dec. 28	Western Samoa	June 1
Ethiopia	Sept. 12	Netherlands	April 30	Yemen, People's Dem. Republic of	Oct. 14
Fiji	Oct. 10	New Zealand	Feb. 6	Yemen Arab Republic	Sept. 26
Finland	Dec. 6	Nicaragua	Sept. 15	Yugoslavia	Nov. 29
France	July 14	Niger	Dec. 18	Zaire	June 30
Gabon	Aug. 17	Nigeria	Oct. 1	Zambia	Oct. 24
Gambia	Feb. 18	Norway	May 17	Zimbabwe	April 18
Germany, East	Oct. 7	Oman	Nov. 18		
Ghana	March 6	Pakistan	March 23		
Greece	March 25	Panama	Nov. 3		

1. Changes yearly according to Hebrew calendar. 2. Celebrated on first Monday in August. *Source:* United Nations.

Legal Holidays in the 50 States, D.C., and Puerto Rico

HOLIDAYS WIDELY OBSERVED

January 1, New Year's Day: All states, D.C., Puerto Rico.

February 12, Lincoln's Birthday: Alaska, California, Colorado, Connecticut, Illinois, Indiana, Iowa, Kansas, Kentucky, Maryland, Missouri, Montana, Nebraska, New Jersey, New Mexico, New York, Utah, Vermont, Washington, West Virginia.

February (first Monday), Lincoln's Birthday: Delaware, Oregon.

February (second Monday), Lincoln Day: Arizona.

February (third Monday), Washington's Birthday: All states, D.C., Puerto Rico. Called **Washington Day** in Arizona. Called **President's Day** in Hawaii, Nebraska, Pennsylvania, South Dakota. Called **Founders Day** in Minnesota; **Washington-Lincoln Day** in Ohio, Wisconsin, Wyoming.

May 28, Memorial Day: Puerto Rico.

May 30, Memorial Day: Delaware, Illinois, Maryland, New Hampshire, New Mexico, Vermont.

May (4th Monday), Memorial Day: West Virginia

May (last Monday), Memorial Day: All states, D.C., except those listed above, and Alabama, Mississippi, South Carolina.

July 4, Independence Day: All states, D.C., Puerto Rico.

September (1st Monday), Labor Day: All states, D.C., Puerto Rico.

October 12, Columbus Day: Maryland, Puerto Rico.

October (2nd Monday), Columbus Day: All states, D.C., except Alaska, Iowa, Maryland, Michigan, Mississippi, Nevada, North Carolina, North Dakota, Oregon, South Carolina, Washington, Puerto Rico. Also called **Fraternal Day** in Alabama. Called **Discovers' Day** in Hawaii, **Farmers' Day** in Florida, **Pioneers' Day** in South Dakota.

November (4th Thursday), Thanksgiving Day: All states, D.C., Puerto Rico.

November, Day after Thanksgiving: Nebraska.

November (first Tuesday after the first Monday), Election Day: Arkansas, California, Colorado, D.C., Delaware, Florida, Hawaii, Idaho, Illinois, Indiana, Kentucky, Louisiana, Maryland, Missouri, Montana, New Hampshire, New Jersey, New York, Oklahoma, Pennsylvania, Rhode Island, South Carolina, Tennessee, Texas, Virginia, West Virginia, Wisconsin, Wyoming, Puerto Rico.

November 11, Veterans' Day: All states, D.C., Puerto Rico. Called **Armistice Day** and **Veterans' Day** in New Mexico.

December 25, Christmas: All states, D.C., Puerto Rico.

OTHER HOLIDAYS

January 6, Three Kings' Day: Puerto Rico.

January 8, Battle of New Orleans Day: Louisiana.

January 11, De Hostos' Birthday: Puerto Rico.

January 15, Martin Luther King Day: Connecticut, D.C., Illinois, Kentucky, Maryland, Massachusetts, New Jersey, Pennsylvania, South Carolina.[1]

January 19, Robert E. Lee's Birthday: Arkansas, Georgia, Kentucky, Louisiana, South Carolina.[1] Called **Confederate Heroes Day** in Texas, also in honor of Jefferson Davis and other Confederate heroes.

January (third Sunday), Martin Luther King Day: New York.

January (third Monday), Martin Luther King Day: Ohio.

January (third Monday), Robert E. Lee's Birthday: Alabama, Mississippi. **Lee-Jackson Day** in Virginia.

January 30, F. D. Roosevelt's Birthday: Kentucky.

February or March (1 day before Ash Wednesday), Mardi Gras (Shrove Tuesday): Alabama, Louisiana (in some parishes).

February 19, Robert E. Lee Day: Kentucky.

March (first Tuesday), Town Meeting Day: Vermont.

March 2, Texas Independence Day: Texas.

March 17, Evacuation Day: Massachusetts (in Suffolk Co. only).

March or April (2 days before Easter), Good Friday: Connecticut, Delaware, Florida, Hawaii, Indiana, Louisiana, Maryland, New Jersey, North Dakota, Pennsylvania, Tennessee, Wisconsin (11 a.m.-3 p.m.).

March or April (1 day after Easter), Easter Monday: North Carolina.

March 21, Youth Day: Oklahoma.

March 22, Abolition Day: Puerto Rico.

March 25, Maryland Day: Maryland.

March 26, Prince Jonah Kuhio Kalanianaole Day: Hawaii.

March (last Monday), Seward's Day: Alaska.

April 13, Thomas Jefferson's Birthday: Alabama, Oklahoma.

April 16, De Diego's Birthday: Puerto Rico.

April (third Monday), Patriot's Day: Maine, Mass.

April 21, San Jacinto Day: Texas.

April 22, Arbor Day: Nebraska.

April 22, Oklahoma Day: Oklahoma.

April 26, Confederate Memorial Day: Florida, Georgia.

April (4th Monday), Fast Day: New Hampshire.

April (last Monday), Confederate Memorial Day: Alabama, Mississippi.

April (last Friday), Arbor Day: Utah.

May (1st Tuesday, after first Monday), Primary Election Day: Indiana.

May (2nd Sunday), Mother's Day: Arizona, Okla.

May 4, Rhode Island Independence Day: Rhode Island.

May 8, Truman Day: Missouri.

May 10, Confederate Memorial Day: South Carolina.[1]

May 20, Mecklenburg Independence Day: North Carolina.

June (first Monday), Jefferson Davis' Birthday: Alabama, Mississippi.

June (second Sunday), Flag Day: New York.

June (third Sunday), Fathers' Day: Arizona.

June 3, Jefferson Davis' Birthday: Florida, Georgia, South Carolina, also called **Confederate Memorial Day** in Kentucky and Louisiana.

June 9, Senior Citizens Day: Oklahoma.

June 11, King Kamehameha I Day: Hawaii.

June 14, Flag Day: Pennsylvania.

June 15, Separation Day: Delaware.

June 17, Bunker Hill Day: Massachusetts (in Suffolk Co. only).

June 19, Emancipation Day: Texas.

June 20, West Virginia Day: West Virginia.

July 17, Muñoz Rivera's Birthday: Puerto Rico.

July 24, Pioneer Day: Utah.

July 25, Constitution Day: Puerto Rico.

July 27, Barbosa's Birthday: Puerto Rico.

August (first Sunday), American Family Day: Arizona.

1. Optional, two of three allowed.

August (first Monday), Colorado Day: Colo.
August (second Monday), Victory Day: Rhode Island.
August 16, Bennington Battle Day: Vermont.
August (third Friday), Admission Day: Hawaii.
August 27, Lyndon B. Johnson's Birthday: Texas.
August 30, Huey P. Long Day: Louisiana.
September (first Tuesday), Primary Election Day: Wisconsin.
September 9, Admission Day: California.
September 12, Defenders' Day: Maryland.
September 16, Cherokee Strip Day: Oklahoma.
September (1st Saturday after full moon), Indian Day: Oklahoma.
October 10, Oklahoma Historical Day: Oklahoma.
October 18, Alaska Day: Alaska.
October 31, Nevada Day: Nevada.
November 1, All Saints' Day: Louisiana.
November 4, Will Rogers Day: Oklahoma.
November 19, Discovery Day: Puerto Rico.
December 7, Delaware Day: Delaware.

Movable Holidays, 1981–1989

CHRISTIAN AND SECULAR

Year	Ash Wednesday	Easter	Pentecost	Labor Day	Election Day	Thanksgiving	1st Sun. Advent
1981	March 4	April 19	June 7	Sept. 7	Nov. 3	Nov. 26	Nov. 29
1982	Feb. 24	April 11	May 30	Sept. 6	Nov. 2	Nov. 25	Nov. 28
1983	Feb. 16	April 3	May 22	Sept. 5	Nov. 8	Nov. 24	Nov. 27
1984	March 7	April 22	June 10	Sept. 3	Nov. 6	Nov. 22	Dec. 2
1985	Feb. 20	April 7	May 26	Sept. 2	Nov. 5	Nov. 28	Dec. 1
1986	Feb. 12	March 30	May 18	Sept. 1	Nov. 4	Nov. 27	Nov. 30
1987	March 4	April 19	June 7	Sept. 7	Nov. 3	Nov. 26	Nov. 29
1988	Feb. 17	April 3	May 22	Sept. 5	Nov. 8	Nov. 24	Nov. 27
1989	Feb. 8	March 26	May 14	Sept. 4	Nov. 7	Nov. 23	Dec. 3

Shrove Tuesday: 1 day before Ash Wednesday
Palm Sunday: 7 days before Easter
Maundy Thursday: 3 days before Easter
Good Friday: 2 days before Easter
Holy Saturday: 1 day before Easter
Ascension Day: 10 days before Pentecost
Trinity Sunday: 7 days after Pentecost
Corpus Christi: 11 days after Pentecost

NOTE: Easter is celebrated on April 26, 1981, by the Orthodox Church.

JEWISH

Year	Purim[1]	1st day Passover[2]	1st day Shavuot[3]	1st day Rosh Hashana[4]	Yom Kippur[5]	1st day Sukkot[6]	Simhat Torah[7]	1st day Hanukkah[8]
1981	March 20	April 19	June 8	Sept. 29	Oct. 8	Oct. 13	Oct. 21	Dec. 21
1982	March 9	April 8	May 28	Sept. 18	Sept. 27	Oct. 2	Oct. 10	Dec. 11
1983	Feb. 27	March 29	May 18	Sept. 8	Sept. 17	Sept. 22	Sept. 30	Dec. 1
1984	March 18	April 17	June 6	Sept. 27	Oct. 6	Oct. 11	Oct. 19	Dec. 19
1985	March 7	April 6	May 26	Sept. 16	Sept. 25	Sept. 30	Oct. 8	Dec. 8
1986	March 25	April 24	June 13	Oct. 4	Oct. 13	Oct. 18	Oct. 26	Dec. 27
1987	March 15	April 14	June 3	Sept. 24	Oct. 3	Oct. 8	Oct. 16	Dec. 16
1988	March 3	April 2	May 22	Sept. 12	Sept. 21	Sept. 26	Oct. 4	Dec. 4
1989	March 21	April 20	June 9	Sept. 30	Oct. 9	Oct. 14	Oct. 22	Dec. 23

1. Feast of Lots. 2. Feast of Unleavened Bread. 3. Hebrew Pentecost; or Feast of Weeks, or of Harvest, or of First Fruits. 4. Jewish New Year. 5. Day of Atonement. 6. Feast of Tabernacles, or of the Ingathering. 7. Rejoicing of the Law. 8. Festival of Lights.

Length of Jewish holidays (O=Orthodox, C=Conservative, R=Reform):

Passover: O & C, 8 days (holy days: first 2 and last 2); R, 7 days (holy days: first and last)
Shavuot: O & C, 2 days; R, 1 day
Rosh Hashana: O & C, 2 days; R, 1 day.
Yom Kippur: All groups, 1 day
Sukkot: All groups, 7 days (holy days: O & C, first 2; R, first only) O & C observe two additional days: Shemini Atseret (Eighth Day of the Feast) and Simhat Torah R observes Shemini Atseret but not Simhat Torah
Hanukkah: All groups, 8 days

NOTE: All holidays begin at sundown on the evening before the date given.

Labors of Hercules

Hercules, hero and strong man, was the son of Zeus and Alcmene. He performed twelve labors or deeds to be free from bondage under Eurystheus. After his death, he became immortal. His twelve mythological labors were: (1) killing the Nemean lion; (2) killing the Lernaean Hydra; (3) capturing the Erymanthian boar; (4) capturing the Cerynean hind; (5) killing the man-eating Stymphalian birds; (6) procuring the girdle of Hippolyte; (7) cleaning the Augean stables; (8) capturing the Cretan bull; (9) capturing the man-eating horses of Diomedes; (10) capturing the cattle of Geryon; (11) procuring the golden apples of Hesperides; (12) bringing Cerberus up from Hades.

Major Religions of the World

Judaism

The determining factors of Judaism are: descendance from Israel, the *Torah*, and Tradition.

The name Israel (Jacob, a patriarch) also signifies his descendants as a people. During the 15th–13th centuries B.C., Israelite tribes, coming from South and East, gradually settled in Palestine, then inhabited by Canaanites. They were held together by Moses, who gave them religious unity in the worship of *Jahweh*, the God who had chosen Israel to be his people.

Under Judges, the 12 tribes at first formed an amphictyonic covenant. Saul established kingship (circa 1050 B.C.), and under David, his successor (1000–960 B.C.), the State of Israel comprised all of Palestine with Jerusalem as religio-political center. A golden era followed under Solomon (965–926 B.C.), who built *Jahweh* a temple.

After Solomon's death, the kingdom separated into Israel in the North and Judah in the South. A period of conflicts ensued, which ended with the conquest of Israel by Assyria in 722 B.C. The Babylonians defeated Judah in 586 B.C., destroying Jerusalem and its temple, and deporting many to Babylon.

The era of the kings is significant also in that the great prophets worked in that time, emphasizing faith in *Jahweh* as both God of Israel and God of the universe, and stressing social justice.

When the Persians permitted the Jews to return from exile (539 B.C.), temple and cult were restored in Jerusalem. The Persian rulers were succeeded by the Seleucides. The Maccabaean revolt against these Hellenistic kings gave independence to the Jews in 128 B.C., which lasted till the Romans occupied the country.

Important groups that exerted influence during these times were the Sadducees, priests in the temple in Jerusalem; the Pharisees, teachers of the Law in the synagogues; Essenes, a religious order (from whom Dead Sea Scrolls, discovered in 1947, came); Apocalyptists, who were expecting the heavenly Messiah; and Zealots, who were prepared to fight for national independence.

When the latter turned against Rome in A.D. 66, Roman armies under Titus suppressed the revolt, destroying Jerusalem and its temple in A.D. 70. The Jews were scattered in the *diaspora* (Dispersion), subject to oppressions until the Age of the Enlightenment (18th century) brought their emancipation, although persecutions did not end entirely.

The fall of the Jerusalem temple was an important event in the religious life of the Jews, which now developed around *Torah* (Law) and synagogue. Around A.D. 100 the Sacred Scriptures were codified. Synagogue worship became central, with readings from *Torah* and prophets. Most important prayers are the *Shema* (Hear) and the Prayer of the 18 Benedictions.

Religious life is guided by the commandments contained in the *Torah:* circumcision and *Sabbath*, as well as other ethical and ceremonial commandments.

The *Talmud*, based on the *Mishnah* and its interpretations, took shape over many centuries in the Babylonian and Palestinian Schools. It was a strong binding force of Judaism in the Dispersion.

In the 12th century, Maimonides formulated his "13 Articles of Faith," which carried great authority. Fundamental in this creed are: belief in God and his oneness *(Shema)*, belief in the changeless

Estimated Membership of the Principal Religions of the World

Statistics of the world's religions are only very rough approximations. Aside from Christianity, few religions, if any, attempt to keep statistical records; and even Protestants and Catholics employ different methods of counting members. All persons of whatever age who have received baptism in the Catholic Church are counted as members, while in most Protestant Churches only those who "join" the church are numbered. The compiling of statistics is further complicated by the fact that in China one may be at the same time a Confucian, a Taoist, and a Buddhist. In Japan, one may be both a Buddhist and a Shintoist.

Religion	North America[1]	South America	Europe	Asia	Africa	Oceania[2]	World
Total Christian	235,109,500	177,266,000	342,630,400	95,987,240	129,717,000	18,063,500	998,773,640
Roman Catholic	132,489,000	165,640,000	176,087,300	55,077,000	47,224,500	4,395,500	580,913,300
Eastern Orthodox	4,763,000	517,000	57,035,600	2,428,000	14,306,000	414,000	79,463,600
Protestant	97,857,500	11,109,000	109,507,500	38,482,240	68,186,500	13,254,000	338,396,740
Jewish[3]	6,155,340	635,800	4,061,620	3,212,860	176,400	76,000	14,318,020
Moslem	371,200	251,500	14,145,000	427,266,000	145,214,700	87,000	587,335,400
Zoroastrian	250	2,100	7,000	254,000	650	—	264,000
Shinto	60,000	92,000	—	57,003,000	200	—	57,155,200
Taoist	16,000	10,000	—	31,261,000	—	—	31,287,000
Confucian	97,100	70,150	—	157,887,500	1,500	80,300	158,136,550
Buddhist	171,250	192,300	192,000	254,241,000	14,000	30,000	254,840,550
Hindu	88,500	849,300	350,000	473,073,000	1,079,800	499,000	475,939,600
Total	**242,069,140**	**179,369,150**	**361,386,020**	**1,500,185,600**	**276,204,250**	**18,835,800**	**2,578,049,960**

1. Includes Central America and West Indies. 2. Includes Australia and New Zealand, as well as islands of the South Pacific. 3. Includes total Jewish population, whether or not related to the synagogue. *Source: Britannica Book of the Year, 1980.*

Torah, in the words of Moses and the prophets, belief in reward and punishment, the coming of the Messiah, and the resurrection of the dead.

Judaism is divided into theological schools, the main divisions of which are Orthodox, Conservative, and Reform.

Christianity

Christianity is founded upon Jesus Christ, to whose life the New Testament writings testify. Jesus, a Jew, was born in about 7 B.C. and assumed his public life, after his 30th year, in Galilee. The Gospels tell of many extraordinary deeds that accompanied his ministry. He proclaimed the Kingdom of God, a future reality that is at the same time already present. Nationalistic-Jewish expectations of the Messiah he rejected. Rather, he referred to himself as the "Son of Man," the Christ, who has power to forgive sins now and who shall also come as Judge at the end of time. Jesus set forth the religio-ethical demands for participation in the Kingdom of God as change of heart and love of God and neighbor.

At the Last Supper he signified his death as a sacrifice, which would inaugurate the New Covenant, by which many would be saved. Circa A.D. 30 he died on a cross in Jerusalem. The early Church carried on Jesus' proclamation, the apostle Paul emphasizing his death and resurrection.

The person of Jesus is fundamental to the Christian faith since it is believed that in his life, death, and resurrection, God's revelation became historically tangible. He is seen as the turning point in history, and man's relationship to God as determined by his attitude to Jesus.

Historically Christianity thus arose out of Judaism, claiming fulfillment of the promises of the Old Testament in Jesus. The early Church designated itself as "the true Israel," which expected the speedy return of Jesus. The mother church was at Jerusalem, but churches were soon founded in many other places. The apostle Paul was instrumental in founding and extending a Gentile Christianity that was free from Jewish legalism.

The new religion spread rapidly throughout the eastern and western parts of the Roman Empire. In coming to terms with other religious movements within the Empire, Christianity began to take definite shape as an organization in its doctrine, liturgy, and ministry circa A.D. 200. In the 4th century the Catholic Church had taken root in countries stretching from Spain in the West to Persia and India in the East. Christians had been repeatedly subject to persecution by the Roman state, but finally gained tolerance under Constantine the Great (A.D. 313). Since that time, the Church became favored under his successors and in 380 the Emperor Theodosius proclaimed Christianity the State religion. Paganism was suppressed and public life was gradually molded in accordance with Christian ethical demands.

It was in these years also that the Church was able to achieve a certain unity of doctrine. Due to differences of interpretation of basic doctrines concerning Christ, which threatened to divide the Catholic Church, a standard Christian Creed was formulated by bishops at successive Ecumenical Councils, the first of which was held in A.D. 325 (Nicaea). The chief doctrines formulated concerned the doctrine of the Trinity, i.e., that there is one God in three persons: Father, Son, and Holy Spirit (Constantinople, A.D. 381); and the nature of Christ as both divine and human (Chalcedon, A.D. 541).

Through differences and rivalry between East and West the unity of the Church was broken by schism in 1054. In 1517 a separation occurred in the Western Church with the Reformation. From the major Protestant denominations [Lutheran, Presbyterian, Anglican (Episcopalian)], many Free Churches separated themselves in an age of individualism.

In the 20th century, however, the direction is toward unity. The Ecumenical Movement led to the formation of the World Council of Churches in 1948 (Amsterdam), which has since been joined by many Protestant and Orthodox Churches.

Through its missionary activity Christianity has spread to most parts of the globe.

Eastern Orthodoxy

Eastern Orthodoxy comprises the faith and practice of Churches stemming from ancient Churches in the Eastern part of the Roman Empire. The term covers Orthodox Churches in communion with the See of Constantinople, Uniate Churches in communion with Rome, and Nestorian and Monophysite Churches.

The Orthodox, Catholic, Apostolic Church is the direct descendant of the Byzantine State Church and consists of a series of independent national churches that are united by Doctrine, Liturgy, and Hierarchical organization (deacons and priests, who may either be married or be monks before ordination, and bishops, who must be celebates). The heads of these Churches are patriarchs or metropolitans; the Patriarch of Constantinople is only "first among equals." Rivalry between the Pope of Rome and the Patriarch of Constantinople, aided by differences and misunderstandings that existed for centuries between the Eastern and Western parts of the Empire, led to a schism in 1054. Repeated attempts at reunion have failed in past centuries. The mutual excommunication pronounced in that year was lifted in 1965, however, and because of greater interaction in theology between Orthodox Churches and those in the West, a climate of better understanding has been created in the 20th century. First contacts were with Anglicans and Old Catholics. Orthodox Churches belong to the World Council of Churches.

The Eastern Orthodox Churches recognize only the canons of the seven Ecumenical Councils (325–787) as binding for faith and they reject doctrines that have been added in the West.

The central worship service is called the Liturgy, which is understood as representation of God's acts of salvation. Its center is the celebration of the Eucharist, or Lord's Supper.

In their worship *icons* (sacred pictures) are used that have a sacramental meaning as representation. The Mother of Christ, angels, and saints are highly venerated.

The number of sacraments in the Orthodox Church is the same as in the Western Catholic Church.

Orthodox Churches are found in the Balkans and the Soviet Union also, since the 20th century, in Western Europe and other parts of the world, particularly in America.

Eastern Orthodoxy also includes the Uniate Churches that recognize the authority of the Pope but keep their own traditional liturgies and those Churches dating back to the 5th century that emancipated themselves from the Byzantine State

Church: the Nestorian Church in the Near East and India with approximately half a million members and the Monophysite Churches with some 17 million members (Coptic, Ethiopian, Syrian, Armenian, and the Mar Thoma Church in India).

Roman Catholicism

Roman Catholicism comprises the belief and practice of the Roman Catholic Church. The Church stands under the authority of the Bishop of Rome, the Pope, and is ruled by him and bishops who are held to be, through ordination, successors of Peter and the Apostles, respectively. Fundamental to the structure of the Church is the juridical aspect: doctrine and sacraments are bound to the power of jurisdiction and consecration of the hierarchy. The Pope, as the head of the hierarchy of archbishops, bishops, priests, and deacons, has full ecclesiastical power, granted him by Christ, through Peter. As successor to Peter, he is the Vicar of Christ. The powers that others in the hierarchy possess are delegated.

Roman Catholics believe their Church to be the one, holy, catholic, and apostolic Church, possessing all the properties of the one, true Church of Christ.

The faith of the Church is understood to be identical with that taught by Christ and his Apostles and contained in Bible and Tradition, i.e. the original deposit of faith, to which nothing new may be added. New definitions of doctrines, such as the Immaculate Conception of Mary (1854) and the bodily Assumption of Mary (1950), have been declared by Popes, however, in accordance with the principle of development (implicit-explicit doctrine).

At Vatican Council I (1870) the Pope was proclaimed "endowed with infallibility, *ex cathedra*, i.e., when exercising the office of Pastor and Teacher of all Christians."

The center of Roman Catholic worship is the celebration of the Mass, the Eucharist, which is the commemoration of Christ's sacrificial death and of his resurrection. Other sacraments are Baptism, Confirmation, Confession, Matrimony, Ordination, and Extreme Unction, seven in all. The Virgin Mary and saints, and their relics, are highly venerated and prayers are made to them to intercede with God, in whose presence they are believed to dwell.

The Roman Catholic Church is the largest Christian organization in the world, found in most countries. Some 8 million belong to the Uniate rites, the vast majority to the Latin rite.

Since Vatican Council II (1962–65), and the effort to "update" the Church, many interesting changes and developments have been taking place.

Protestantism

Protestantism comprises the Christian churches that separated from Rome during the Reformation in the 16th century, initiated by an Augustinian monk, Martin Luther. "Protestant" was originally applied to followers of Luther, who protested at the Diet of Spires (1529) against the decree which prohibited all further ecclesiastical reforms. Subsequently, Protestantism came to mean rejection of attempts to tie God's revelation to earthly institutions, and a return to the Gospel and the Word of God as sole authority in matters of faith and practice. Central in the biblical message is the justification of the sinner by faith alone. The Church is understood as a fellowship and the priesthood of all believers stressed.

The Augsburg Confession (1530) was the principal statement of Lutheran faith and practice. It became a model for other Confessions of Faith, which in their turn had decisive influence on Church polity. Major Protestant denominations are the Lutheran, Reformed (Calvinist), Presbyterian, and Anglican (Episcopal). Smaller ones are the Mennonite. Schwenkfeldians, and Unitarians. In Great Britain and America there are the Congregationalists, Baptists, Quakers, Methodists, and other free church types of communities. (In regarding themselves as being faithful to original biblical Christianity, these Churches differ from such religious bodies as Unitarians, Mormons, Jehovah's Witnesses, and Christian Scientists, who either teach new doctrines or reject old ones.)

Since the latter part of the 19th century, national councils of churches have been established in many countries, e.g. the Federal Council of Churches of Christ in America in 1908. Denominations across countries joined in federations and world alliances, beginning with the Anglican Lambeth Conference in 1867.

Protestant missionary activity, particularly strong in the last century, resulted in the founding of many younger churches in Asia and Africa. The Ecumenical Movement, which originated with Protestant missions, aims at unity among Christians and churches.

Islam

Islam is the religion founded in Arabia by Mohammed between 610 and 632. Its 400 million adherents are found in countries stretching from Morocco in the West to Indonesia in the East.

Mohammed was born in A.D. 570 at Mecca and belonged to the Quraysh tribe, which was active in caravan trade. At the age of 25 he joined the caravan trade from Mecca to Syria in the employment of a rich widow, Khadiji, whom he married. Critical of the idolatry of the inhabitants of Mecca, he began to lead a contemplative life in the deserts. There he received a series of revelations. Encouraged by Khadiji, he gradually became convinced that he was given a God-appointed task to devote himself to the reform of religion and society. Idolatry was to be abandoned.

The *Hegira (Hijra)* (migration) of Mohammed from Mecca, where he was not honored, to Medina, where he was well received, occurred in 622 and marks the beginning of the Muslim era. In 630 he marched on Mecca and conquered it. He died at Medina in 632. His grave there has since been a place of pilgrimage.

Mohammed's followers, called Moslems, revered him as the prophet of *Allah* (God), beside whom there is no other God. Although he had no close knowledge of Judaism and Christianity, he considered himself succeeding and completing them as the seal of the Prophets. Sources of the Islamic faith are the *Qur'an*, regarded as the uncreated, eternal Word of God, and Tradition *(hadith)* regarding sayings and deeds of the prophet.

Islam means surrender to the will of *Allah*. He is the all-powerful, whose will is supreme and determines man's fate. Good deeds will be rewarded at the Last Judgment in paradise and evil deeds will be punished in hell.

The Five Pillars, primary duties, of Islam are: witness; confessing the oneness of God and of Mohammed, his prophet; prayer, to be performed five times a day; almsgiving to the poor and the mosque (house of worship); fasting during daylight hours in the month of Ramadan; and pilgrimage to Mecca at least once in the Moslem's lifetime.

The practice of Holy War *(jihad)*, at first responsible for the rapid growth of the new religion, could not be maintained. Mohammed curtailed the practice of polygamy by limiting it to four wives. In modern times the position of women has improved, due to Western influence. The eating of pork and drinking of intoxicants is forbidden.

Islam, upholding the law of brotherhood, succeeded in uniting an Arab world that had disintegrated into tribes and castes. Disagreements concerning the succession of the prophet caused a great division in Islam between *Sunnis* and *Shias*. Among these, other sects arose *(Wahhabi)*. Doctrinal issues also led to the rise of different schools of thought in theology. Nevertheless, since Arab armies turned against Syria and Palestine in 635, Islam has expanded successfully under Mohammed's successors. Its rapid conquests in Asia and Africa are unsurpassed in history. Turning against Europe, Moslems conquered Spain in 713. In 1453 Constantinople fell into their hands and in 1529 Moslem armies besieged Vienna. Since then, Islam has lost its foothold in Europe.

In modern times it has made great gains in Africa.

Hinduism

In India alone there are more than 300 million adherents of Hinduism. In contrast to other religions, it has no founder. Considered the oldest religion in the world, it dates back, perhaps, to prehistoric times.

Hinduism is hard to define, there being no common creed, no one doctrine to bind Hindus together. Intellectually there is complete freedom of belief, and one can be monotheist, polytheist, or atheist. What matters is the social system: a Hindu is one born into a caste.

As a religion, Hinduism is founded on the sacred scriptures, written in Sanskrit and called the *Vedas* (*Veda*-knowledge). There are four Vedic books, among which the *Rig Veda* is the most important. It speaks of many gods and also deals with questions concerning the universe and creation. The dates of these works are unknown (1000 B.C.?).

The *Upanishads* (dated 1000–300 B.C.), commentaries on the Vedic texts, have philosophical speculations on the origin of the universe, the nature of deity, of *atman* (the human soul), and its relationship to *Brahman* (the universal soul).

Brahman is the principle and source of the universe who can be indicated only by negatives. As the divine intelligence, he is the ground of the visible world, a presence that pervades all beings. Thus the many Hindu deities came to be understood as manifestations of the one *Brahman* from whom everything proceeds and to whom everything ultimately returns. The religio-social system of Hinduism is based on the concept of reincarnation and transmigration in which all living beings, from plants below to gods above, are caught in a cosmic system that is an everlasting cycle of becoming and perishing.

Life is determined by the law of *karma*, according to which rebirth is dependent on moral behavior in a previous phase of existence. The doctrine of transmigration thus provides a rationale for the caste system. In this view, life on earth is regarded as transient *(maya)* and a burden. The goal of existence is liberation from the cycle of rebirth and redeath and entrance into the indescribable state of what in Buddhism is called *nirvana* (extinction of passion).

Further important sacred writings are the Epics *(puranas)*, which contain legendary stories about gods and men. They are the *Mahabharata* (composed between 200 B.C. and A.D. 200) and the *Ramayana*. The former includes the *Bhagavad-Gita* (Song of the Lord), its most famous part, that tells of devotion to *Krishna* (Lord), who appears as an *avatar* (incarnation) of the god *Vishnu*, and of the duty of obeying caste rules. The work begins with a praise of the *yoga* (discipline) system.

The practice of Hinduism consists of rites and ceremonies, performed within the framework of the caste system and centering on the main socio-religious occasions of birth, marriage, and death. There are many Hindu temples, which are dwelling places of the deities and to which people bring offerings. There are also places of pilgrimages, the chief one being Benares on the Ganges, most sacred among the rivers in India.

In modern times work has been done to reform and revive Hinduism. One of the outstanding reformers was Ramakrishna (1836-86), who inspired many followers, one of whom founded the Ramakrishna mission, which seeks to convert others to its religion. The mission is active both in India and in other countries.

Buddhism

Founded in the 6th century B.C. in northern India by Gautama Buddha, who was born in southern Nepal as son to a king. His birth is surrounded by many legends, but Western scholars agree that he lived from 563 to 483 B.C. Warned by a sage that his son would become an ascetic or a universal monarch, the king confined him to his home. He was able to escape and began the life of a homeless wanderer in search of peace, passing through many disappointments until he finally came to the Tree of Enlightenment, under which he lived in meditation till enlightenment came to him and he became a Buddha (enlightened one).

Now he understood the origin of suffering, summarized in the *Four Noble Truths*, which constitutes the foundation of Buddhism. The Four are the truth of suffering, which all living beings must endure; of the origin of suffering, which is craving and which leads to rebirth; that it can be destroyed; and of the way that leads to cessation of pain, i.e., the *Noble Eightfold Way*, which is the rule of practical Buddhism: right views, right intention, right speech, right action, right livelihood, right effort, right concentration, and right ecstasy.

Nirvana is the goal of all existence, the state of complete redemption, into which the redeemed enters. Buddha's insight can free every man from the law of reincarnation through complete emptying of the self.

The nucleus of Buddha's church or association was originally formed by monks and lay-brothers, whose houses gradually became monasteries used as places for religious instruction. The worship service consisted of a sermon, expounding of Scripture, meditation, and confession. At a later stage pilgrimages to the holy places associated with the Buddha came into being, as well as veneration of relics.

In the 3rd century B.C., King Ashoka made Buddhism the State religion of India but, as centuries passed, it gradually fell into decay through splits, persecutions, and the hostile Brahmans. Buddhism spread to countries outside India, however.

At the beginning of the Christian era, there occurred a split that gave rise to two main types: *Hinayana* (Little Vehicle), or southern Buddhism, and *Mahayana* (Great Vehicle), or northern Buddhism. The former type, more individualistic, survived in Ceylon and southern Asia. *Hinayana* retained more closely the original teachings of the Buddha, which did not know of a personal god or soul. *Mahayana*, more social, polytheistic, and developing a pluralistic pompous cult, was strong in the Himalayas, Tibet, Mongolia, China, Korea, and Japan.

In the present century, Buddhism has found believers also in the West and Buddhist associations have been established in Europe and the U. S.

Confucianism

Confucius (K'ung Fu-tzu), born in the state of Lu (northern China), lived from 551 to 479 B.C. Tradition, exaggerating the importance of Confucius in life, has depicted him as a great statesman but, in fact, he seems to have been a private teacher. Anthologies of ancient Chinese classics, along with his own Analects *(Lun Yu)*, became the basis of Confucianism. These Analects were transmitted as a collection of his sayings as recorded by his students, with whom he discussed ethical and social problems. They developed into men of high moral standing, who served the State as administrators.

In his teachings, Confucius emphasized the importance of an old Chinese concept *(li)*, which has the connotation of proper conduct. There is some disagreement as to the religious ideas of Confucius, but he held high the concepts handed down from centuries before him. Thus he believed in Heaven *(T'ien)* and sacrificed to his ancestors. Ancestor worship he indeed encouraged as an expression of filial piety, which he considered the loftiest of virtues.

Piety to Confucius was the foundation of the family as well as the State. The family is the nucleus of the State, and the "five relations," between king and subject, father and son, man and wife, older and younger brother, and friend and friend, are determined by the virtues of love of fellow men, righteousness, and respect.

An extension of ancestor worship may be seen in the worship of Confucius, which became official in the 2nd century B.C. when the emperor, in recognition of Confucius' teachings as supporting the imperial rule, offered sacrifices at his tomb.

Mencius (Meng Tse), who lived around 400 B.C., did much to propagate and elaborate Confucianism in its concern with ordering society. Thus, for two millennia, Confucius' doctrine of State, with its emphasis on ethics and social morality, rooted in ancient Chinese tradition and developed and continued by his disciples, has been standard in China and the Far East.

With the revolution of 1911 in China, however, students, burning Confucius in effigy, called for the removel of "the old curiosity shop."

Shintoism

Shinto, the Chinese term for the Japanese *Kami no Michi*, i.e., the Way of the Gods, comprises the religious ideas and cult indigenous to Japan. *Kami*, or gods, considered divine forces of nature that are worshipped, may reside in rivers, trees, rocks, mountains, certain animals, or, particularly, in the sun and moon. The worship of ancestors, heroes, and deceased emperors was incorporated later.

After Buddhism had come from Korea, Japan's native religion at first resisted it. Then there followed a period of compromise and amalgamation with Buddhist beliefs and ceremonies, resulting, since the 9th century A.D., in a syncretistic religion, a Twofold Shinto. Buddhist deities came to be regarded as manifestations of Japanese deities and Buddhist priests took over most of the Shinto shrines.

In modern times Shinto regained independence from Buddhism. Under the reign of the Emperor Meiji (1868–1912) it became the official State religion, in which loyalty to the emperor was emphasized. The line of succession of emperors is traced back to the first Emperor Jimmu (660 B.C.) and beyond him to the Sun-goddess *Amaterasuomikami.*

The centers of worship are the shrines and temples in which the deities are believed to dwell and believers approach them through *torii* (gateways). Most important among the shrines is the imperial shrine of the Sun-goddess at Ise, where state ceremonies were once held in June and December. The *Yasukuni* shrine of the war dead in Tokyo is also well known.

Acts of worship consist of prayers, clapping of hands, acts of purification, and offerings. On feast days processions and performances of music and dancing take place and priests read prayers before the gods in the shrines, asking for good harvest, the well-being of people and emperor, etc. In Japanese homes there is a god-shelf, a small wooden shrine that contains the tablets bearing the names of ancestors. Offerings are made and candles lit before it.

After World War II the Allied Command ordered the disestablishment of State Shinto. To be distinguished from State Shinto is Sect Shinto, consisting of 13 recognized sects. These have arisen in modern times, gaining large followings. Most important among them is *Tenrikyo* in Tenri City (Nara), in which healing by faith plays a central role.

Taoism

Taoism, a religion of China, was, according to tradition, founded by Lao Tse, a Chinese philosopher, long considered one of the prominent religious leaders from the 6th century B.C.

Data about him are for the most part legendary, however, and the *Tao Te Ching* (the classic of the Way and of its Power), traditionally ascribed to him, is now believed by many scholars to have originated in the 3rd century B.C. The book is composed in short chapters, written in aphoristic rhymes. Central are the word *Tao*, which means way or path and, in a deeper sense, signifies the principle that underlies the reality of this world and manifests itself in nature and in the lives of men, and the word *Te* (power).

The virtuous man draws power from being absorbed in *Tao*, the ultimate reality within an ever-changing world. By non-action and keeping away from human striving it is possible for man to live in harmony with the principles that underlie and govern the universe. *Tao* cannot be comprehended by reason and knowledge, but only by inward quiet.

Besides the *Tao Te Ching*, dating from approximately the same period, there are two Taoist works, written by Chuang Tse and Lieh Tse.

Theoretical Taoism of this classical philosophical movement of the 4th and 3rd centuries B.C. in China differed from popular Taoism, into which it gradually degenerated. The standard of theoretical Taoism was maintained in the classics, of course, and among the upper classes it continued to be alive until modern times.

Religious Taoism is a form of religion dealing with deities and spirits, magic and soothsaying. In the 2nd century A.D. it was organized with temples, cult, priests, and monasteries and was able to hold its own in the competition with Buddhism that came up at the same time.

After the 7th century A.D., however, Taoist religion further declined. Split into numerous sects, which often operate like secret societies, it has become a syncretistic folk religion in which some of the old deities and saints live on.

History of Leading Religious Groups in the United States

(50,000 members or over)

Source: Yearbook of American and Canadian Churches, 1980.

BAPTIST

American Baptist Association: A group of independent Missionary Baptist Churches, mainly in the South, Southeast, and Southwest, organized in 1905. Members (1979): 1,500,000. Headquarters: 4605 N. State Line Ave., Texarkana, Tex. 75501.

American Baptist Churches in the U.S.A.: Formerly known as the Northern Baptist Convention and the American Baptist Convention, this body changed its name in 1973. Although national missionary organizational developments began in 1814 with the establishment of the American Baptist Foreign Mission Society, the Convention was not formed until 1907. Members (1977): 1,316,760. Headquarters: Valley Forge, Pa. 19481.

Baptist General Conference: Formerly known as the Swedish Baptist General Conference of America. It has operated as a general conference since 1879. Members (1978): 131,000. Headquarters: 1233 Central St., Evanston, Ill. 60201.

Baptist Missionary Association of America: Formerly called the North American Baptist Association. It was organized in 1950 in Little Rock, Ark. Members (1978): 219,697. Office of president: 6901 S. Shartel, Oklahoma City, Okla. 73139.

Conservative Baptist Association of America: Organized in 1947. Adherents regard the Bible as infallible. Local churches are independent, autonomous, and free from ecclesiastical or political authority. Members (1977): 300,000. Headquarters: Geneva Rd., Box 66, Wheaton, Ill. 60187.

Free Will Baptists: A body of evangelical Baptists, organized in 1727 in the South and 1780 in the North. Members (1978): 216,831. Headquarters: 1134 Murfreesboro Rd., Nashville, Tenn. 37217.

General Association of Regular Baptist Churches: Founded in 1932 in Chicago by a group of churches which had withdrawn from the Northern Baptist Convention (now the American Baptist Convention) because of doctrinal differences. Members (1979): 240,000. Headquarters: 1300 N. Meacham Rd., Schaumburg, Ill. 60185.

General Baptists (General Association of): An Arminian group of Baptists, organized in England in 1607 and transplanted to the colonies in 1714. It died out along the Seaboard, but revived in the Midwest in 1823. Members (1977): 72,000. Office of moderator: 113 South 10th, Poplar Bluff, Mo. 63901.

National Baptist Convention, U.S.A.: The older and parent convention of Black Baptists. This body is to be distinguished from the National Baptist Convention of America, usually referred to as the "unincorporated" body. Members (1958): 5,500,000. Office of president: 405 E. 31st St., Chicago, Ill. 60616.

National Baptist Convention of America: This is a body usually referred to as the "unincorporated" convention, not to be confused with the "incorporated" National Baptist Convention, U.S.A., Inc., from which this body withdrew. Organized in 1880. Members (1956): 2,668,799. Office of president: 954 Kings Rd., Jacksonville, Fla. 32204.

National Primitive Baptist Convention: A group of Baptists having local associations and a National Convention. Organized in 1907. Members (1975): 250,000. Headquarters: Box 2355, Tallahassee, Fla.

North American Baptist Association: *See* Baptist Missionary Association of America.

Primitive Baptists: A large group of Baptists, largely through the South, who are opposed to all centralization and to modern missionary societies. Members (1960): 72,000. Headquarters: Cayce Publishing Co., S. Second St., Thornton, Ariz., 71766.

Progressive National Baptist Convention, Inc.: A body that held its organizational meeting in Cincinnati in 1961 and its first annual session in Philadelphia in 1962. Members (1967): 521,692. Office of president: Bethany Baptist Church, 460 Sumner Ave., Brooklyn, N.Y. 11216.

U. S. Church Membership

Religious group	Members
Protestant bodies and others	73,704,162
Roman Catholics	49,602,035
Jewish congregations[1]	5,781,000
Eastern churches	3,632,555
Old Catholic, Polish National Catholic, Armenian churches	808,684
Buddhist Churches of America	60,000
Miscellaneous	160,340
Total[2]	**133,748,776**

1. Includes Orthodox, Conservative, and Reform. 2. As reported in the *1980 Yearbook* from statistics furnished by 222 religious bodies in the United States.

Southern Baptist Convention: In 1845, Southern Baptists withdrew from the General Missionary Convention over the question of slavery and other matters and formed the Southern Baptist Convention. Members (1978): 13,191,394. Office of president: 515 McCullough, San Antonio, Tex. 78215.

United Free Will Baptist Church: A body which set up its organization in 1870. Members (1952): 100,000. Headquarters: Kinston College, 1000 University St., Kinston, N.C. 28501.

CATHOLIC AND ORTHODOX

American Carpatho-Russian Orthodox Greek Catholic Church: This church is a self-governing diocese in communion with the Ecumenical Patriarchate of Constantinople. On Sept. 19, 1938, the late Patriarch Benjamin I canonized the diocese in the name of the Orthodox Church of Christ. Members (1976): 100,000. Headquarters: Johnstown, Pa. 15906.

Antiochian Orthodox Christian Archdiocese of North America: Formed in 1975 by merger of the Antiochian Orthodox Christian Archdiocese of New York and All North America (formerly the Syrian Antiochian Orthodox Archdiocese of New York and North America) and the Antiochian Orthodox Archdiocese of Toledo, Ohio, and Dependencies in North America. The new Archdiocese is under the jurisdiction of the Patriarch of Antioch. Members (1977): 152,000. Headquarters: 358 Mountain Rd., Englewood, N.J. 07631.

Armenian Apostolic Church of America: The Armenian Church divided into two separate dioceses in 1933 because of a dispute regarding the political activities of the prelate at that time, and because of the status of the church in Soviet Armenia. Since 1956, this diocese has been under the jurisdiction of the Holy See of Cilicia, Beirut, Lebanon. Members (1972): 125,000. Headquarters: 138 E. 39th St., New York, N.Y. 10016.

Armenian Church of America, Diocese of the (including Diocese of California): The American branch of the Ancient Church of Armenia. Established in the U. S. in 1889. Diocesan organization is under the jurisdiction of the Holy See of Etchmiadzin, Armenia, U.S.S.R. Members (1978): 326,500. Headquarters: St. Vartan Cathedral, 630 Second Ave., New York, N.Y. 10016.

Bulgarian Eastern Orthodox Church (Diocese of North and South America and Australia): A Synod of the Bulgarian Eastern Orthodox Church, established as the Bulgarian Orthodox Mission in 1909. Became a canonical metropolitan archdiocese in 1947. Members (1971): 86,000. Headquarters: 312 W. 101st St., New York, N.Y. 10025; 1953 Stockbridge Rd., Akron, Ohio, 44313.

Greek Orthodox Archdiocese of North and South America: Greek-speaking Orthodox Christians have parishes in the U. S., Canada, and South America. These are under the Ecumenical Patriarchate of Constantinople. Members (1977): 1,950,000. Headquarters: 8–10 E. 79th St., New York, N.Y. 10021.

North American Old Roman Catholic Church: A body with the doctrine of the Old Catholics; identical with the Roman Catholic Church in most worship and discipline. It is not under Papal jurisdiction. Members (1978): 67,314. Office of presiding bishop: 4200 N. Kedvale Ave., Chicago, Ill. 60641.

Orthodox Church in America (The Russian Orthodox Greek Catholic Church of America): This body entered Alaska in 1792. In 1872, its headquarters were moved from Sitka to San Francisco and, in 1905, to New York. Members (1978): 1,000,000. Office of primate: Box 675, Syosset, N.Y. 11791.

Polish National Catholic Church of America: After long dissatisfaction with Roman Catholic administration and ideology, this group was organized in 1897. Members (1960): 282,411. Headquarters: 529 E. Locust St., Scranton, Pa. 18505.

Roman Catholic Church: The largest single group of Christians in the U. S., the Roman Catholic Church is under the spiritual leadership of the Pope. This group dates back to the priests who accompanied Columbus on his second voyage to the New World. A settlement, later discontinued, was made at St. Augustine, Fla. The continuous history of this Church in the colonies began at St. Mary's in 1634, in Maryland. Members (1978): 49,602,035. National Conference of Catholic Bishops, 1312 Massachusetts Ave., N.W., Washington, D.C. 20005.

Russian Orthodox Church in the U.S.A., Patriarchial Parishes of the: This autonomous body is the direct canonical successor of the Orthodox Catholic mission established in Alaska by the Russian Orthodox Church in 1793. It is under the spiritual jurisdiction of the Patriarch of Moscow and all Russia, His Holiness Pimen. In 1962 an administration was established for the Orthodox Mission in Puerto Rico and the Spanish-speaking people in the United States. Members (1975): 51,500. Headquarters: St. Nicholas Patriarchal Cathedral, 15 E. 97th St., New York, N.Y. 10029.

Russian Orthodox Church Outside Russia: The governing body was set up in Constantinople. In 1950, it came to the U. S. Members (1955): 55,000. Headquarters: 75 E. 93rd St., New York, N.Y. 10028.

Serbian Eastern Orthodox Church for the U.S.A. and Canada: This body of the Eastern Orthodox Church is autonomous. Members (1967): 65,000. Chancery: St. Sava Monastery, Box 519, Libertyville, Ill. 60048.

Syrian Antiochian Orthodox Archdiocese of New York and North America: *See* Antiochian Orthodox Christian Archdiocese of New York and All North America.

Ukrainian Orthodox Church in the U.S.A.: This church was organized in the U.S. in 1919. Members (1966): 87,745. Headquarters: South Bound Brook, N.J. 08880.

JEWISH

Jews arrived in the colonies before 1650. The first congregation is recorded in 1654, in New York City, the Shearith Israel (Remnant of Israel). Members (1978): 5,781,000.

Following are the major Jewish organizations:

Central Conference of American Rabbis: 790 Madison Ave., New York, N.Y. 10021

Rabbinical Alliance of America: 156 Fifth Ave., New York, N.Y. 10011
Rabbinical Assembly: 3080 Broadway, New York, N.Y. 10027
Rabbinical Council of America: 1250 Broadway, New York, N.Y. 10001
Synagogue Council of America: 432 Park Ave. South, New York, N.Y. 10016
Union of American Hebrew Congregations: 838 Fifth Ave., New York, N.Y. 10021
Union of Orthodox Jewish Congregations of America: 116 E. 27th St., New York, N.Y. 10016
United Synagogue of America: 155 Fifth Ave., New York, N.Y. 10010

LUTHERAN

American Lutheran Church: This church is the result of the merger in 1960 of the American Lutheran Church, the Evangelical Lutheran Church, and the United Evangelical Lutheran Church. In 1963, the Lutheran Free Church merged with The American Lutheran Church. Members (1978): 2,377,235. Headquarters: 422 S. Fifth St., Minneapolis, Minn. 55415.

Evangelical Lutheran Churches, Association of: Formed in 1976, this group is made up mainly of former affiliates of the Lutheran Church-Missouri Synod, plus some new and some formerly independent congregations. Its members have joined together to be in mission and ministry. Members (1978): 106,684. Headquarters: 12015 Manchester Rd., St. Louis, Mo. 63131.

Lutheran Church—Missouri Synod: This body, the largest constituent part of the Evangelical Lutheran Synodical Conference of North America, was organized in 1847. It is the leader in the conservative group among the Lutherans. Members (1978): 2,631,374. Headquarters: 500 N. Broadway, St. Louis, Mo. 63102.

Lutheran Church in America: This body was organized in 1962 by the consolidation of the American Evangelical Lutheran Church (1874), the Augustana Evangelical Lutheran Church (1860), the Finnish Evangelical Lutheran Church (1890), and the United Lutheran Church in America (1918). Members (1978): 2,942,002. Headquarters: 231 Madison Ave., New York, N.Y. 10016.

Wisconsin Evangelical Lutheran Synod: This body was organized in Wisconsin in 1850. Members (1978): 402,972. Office of president: 3512 W. North Ave., Milwaukee, Wis. 53208.

METHODIST

African Methodist Episcopal Church: This church began in 1787 in Philadelphia when persons in a Methodist Episcopal Church withdrew. In 1816, the denomination was started. Members (1979): 1,970,000. Office of senior bishop: 1002 Kirkwood Ave., Nashville, Tenn. 37203.

African Methodist Episcopal Zion Church: This group was organized in 1796, having withdrawn from the John Street Methodist Church, New York. Members (1978): 1,093,001. Office of president: 3753 Springhill Ave., Mobile, Ala. 36608.

Christian Methodist Episcopal Church: In 1870, the General Conference of the M.E. Church, South, approved the request of its black membership for the formation of their conferences into a separate body. Members (1965): 466,718. Office of secretary: Box 74, Memphis, Tenn. 38101.

Free Methodist Church of North America: This body, organized in 1860, grew out of a movement in the Genesee Conference of the Methodist Episcopal Church about 1850 towards a more original Methodism. Members (1978): 73,294. Headquarters: 901 College Ave., Winona Lake, Ind. 46590.

United Methodist Church: The United Methodist Church was formed in April, 1968, by the union of the Methodist Church and the Evangelical United Brethren Church. The two churches shared a common historical and spiritual heritage. The Methodist Church resulted in 1939 from the unification of three branches of Methodism—the Methodist Episcopal Church; the Methodist Episcopal Church South; and the Methodist Protestant Church. The Methodist movement began in 18th-century England under the preaching of John Wesley, but the so-called Christmas Conference of 1784 in Baltimore is regarded as the date on which the organized Methodist Church was founded as an ecclesiastical organization. The Evangelical United Brethren Church was formed in 1946 with the merger of the Evangelical Church and the Church of the United Brethren in Christ, both of which had their beginnings in Pennsylvania in the evangelistic movement of the 18th and early 19th centuries. Members (1978): 9,731,779. Office of Secretary of General Conference, Perkins School of Theology, Southern Methodist University, Dallas, Tex. 75222.

PRESBYTERIAN

Cumberland Presbyterian Church: An outgrowth of the Great Revival of 1800, the Cumberland Presbytery was organized in 1810 in Tennessee. A union with the Presbyterian Church, U.S.A., in 1906, was only partially successful, and the Cumberland Presbyterian Church continued as a separate denomination. Members (1978): 93,268. Office of moderator: P.O. Drawer G, Denton, Tex. 76201.

Presbyterian Church in America: Formed in Birmingham, Ala., in 1973 after separating from the Presbyterian Church in the United States, this body believes the Bible is the only infallible rule of faith and practice. It is committed to the Reformed Faith as set forth in the Westminster Confession and Catechisms. Members (1978): 82,095. Office of stated clerk: Box 312, Brevard, N.C. 28712.

Presbyterian Church in the United States: This body is a branch of the Presbyterian Church established in separate existence in 1861. Members (1978): 862,416. Headquarters: 341 Ponce de Leon Ave., NE, Atlanta, Ga. 30308.

United Presbyterian Church in the United States of America: This group was formed in 1958 by a merger of the Presbyterian Church in the U.S.A. (dating from 1706) and the United Presbyterian Church of North America (established in 1858). Members (1978): 2,520,367. Headquarters: 475 Riverside Dr., New York, N.Y. 10027.

OTHER RELIGIOUS BODIES

Apostolic Overcoming Holy Church of God: A black body incorporated in Alabama in 1919. It is evangelistic in purpose and emphasizes sanctification, holiness, and divine healing. Members (1956):

75,000. Office of secretary, 909 Jasper Rd. W., Birmingham, Ala. 35204.

Assemblies of God: A pentecostal, evangelical, missionary denomination which grew out of the spiritual revivals of the early 1900's. The organization is composed of self-governing churches. Founded in Arkansas in 1914. Members (1978): 1,293,394. Headquarters: 1445 Boonville Ave., Springfield, Mo. 65802.

Bahá'í Faith: Baháís are followers of Bahá'u'lláh (1817–1892), whose religion upholds the basic principle of progressive revelation, religious unity and a new world order. There is a spiritual and administrative world center in Haifa, Israel. Headquarters, 536 Sheridan Rd., Wilmette, Ill. 60091.

Buddhist Churches of America: Organized in 1914 as the Buddhist Mission of North America, this body was incorporated in 1942 under the present name and represents the Jodo Shinshu Sect of Buddhism in this country. Members (1975): 60,000. Headquarters: 1710 Octavia St., San Francisco, Calif. 94109.

Christian and Missionary Alliance: An evangelical, evangelistic, and missionary movement organized in 1887. It stresses "the deeper Christian life and consecration to the Lord's service." Members (1978): 158,218. Headquarters: 350 N. Highland Ave., Nyack, N.Y. 10960.

Christian Congregation, The: Incorporated in 1887, denomination provides ministerial affiliation for independent clergymen. Members (1978): 81,604. Office of general superintendent: 804 W. Hemlock St., LaFollette, Tenn. 37766.

Christian Church (Disciples of Christ): In the revival period of the early nineteenth century, a movement resulted in the establishment of a fellowship called "Christians" or "Disciples." This movement calls for the reunion of the church on the basis of a return to New Testament faith and order. It is congregational in government. Members (1978): 1,231,817. Headquarters: 222 S. Downey Ave., Box 1986, Indianapolis, Ind. 46206.

Christian Churches and Churches of Christ: This fellowship, congregational in polity, has its origin in the movement to "restore the New Testament church in doctrine, ordinances and life." Members (1979): 1,054,266. North American Christian Convention, Box 39456, Cincinnati, Ohio 45231.

Christian Reformed Church in North America: A group of Dutch Calvinists which dissented from the Reformed Church in America in 1857 and which was strengthened by later accessions from the same source and by immigration. Members (1978): 211,302. Office of stated clerk: William P. Brink, 2850 Kalamazoo Ave., S.E., Grand Rapids, Mich. 49508.

Church of Christ, Scientist: Founded by Mary Baker Eddy in 1879 to reinstate the healing power of original Christianity. As defined by Mrs. Eddy, her religion is the scientific system of divine healing.[1] Headquarters: Christian Science Church, Boston, Mass. 02115.

Church of God: Inaugurated by Bishop A. J. Tomlinson, who served as General Overseer 1903–43. Episcopal in administration. Members (1978): 75,890. Headquarters: 2504 Arrow Wood Dr., S.E., Huntsville, Ala. 35803.

Church of God (Anderson, Ind.): This group is one of the largest of the groups which have taken the name "Church of God." It originated about 1880 and emphasizes Christian unity. Members (1978): 173,753. Headquarters: Box 2420, Anderson, Ind. 46011.

Church of God (Cleveland, Tenn.): This church is one of the large groups which use the name "Church of God." Organized in 1886 in Tennessee as the Christian Union, it was reorganized in 1902 as the Holiness Church, and in 1907 under its present name. Members (1978): 392,551. Headquarters: Keith St. at 25th., N.W., Cleveland, Tenn. 37311.

Church of God in Christ: Organized in Arkansas in 1895, by C. P. Jones and C. H. Mason, who believed there was no salvation without holiness; incorporated 1897. Members (1965): 425,000. Headquarters: 938 Mason St., Memphis, Tenn. 38126.

Church of God in Christ, International: Organized in 1969 in Kansas City, Mo., by 14 bishops of the Church of God in Christ of Memphis, Tenn., after disagreement over polity and governmental authority. Church is Wesleyan in theology. Members (1971): 501,000. Headquarters: 170 Adelphi St., Brooklyn, N.Y. 11025.

Church of God of Prophecy: Organized in 1903 at Murphy, N. C. Doctrine stresses justification by faith and the second coming of Christ. Members (1975): 65,801. Headquarters: Bible Place, Cleveland, Tenn. 37311.

Church of the Brethren: German pietists from Krefeld, Germany, under the leadership of Peter Becker, entered the colonies in 1719, and settled at Germantown, Philadelphia, Pa. They hold to the principles of nonviolence, temperance, and the expression of religion through the good life. Members (1978): 175,335. Headquarters: 1451 Dundee Ave., Elgin, Ill. 60120.

Church of the Nazarene: One of the larger holiness bodies, organized in Pilot Point, Tex., in 1908. It is in general accord with the early doctrines of Methodism and emphasizes entire sanctification. Members (1978): 462,724. Headquarters: 6401 The Paseo, Kansas City, Mo. 64131.

Churches of Christ: This body is made up of a large group of churches, formerly reported with the Disciples of Christ but, since the religious census of 1906, reported separately. They are strictly congregational and have no organization larger than the local congregation. Members (1978): 3,000,000.

Community Churches, National Council of: This body was formed in 1946 by the merger of the Biennial Council of Community Churches, a black group, with white churches which had the name of

1. Membership figure not available. The manual of the church forbids "the numbering of people and the reporting of such statistics for publication."

the present Council. Its members are ecumenically minded, congregationally governed, non-creedal Protestant churches. Members (1979): 190,000. Headquarters: 89 E. Wilson Bridge Rd., Worthington, Ohio, 43085.

Congregational Christian Churches: *See* United Church of Christ.

Congregational Christian Churches, National Association of: Organized in Detroit, Mich., in 1955 to continue the Congregational way of faith and order in church life. It has no doctrinal requirements, and participation by member churches is voluntary. Members (1978): 95,000. Headquarters: Box 1620, Oak Creek, Wis. 53154.

Disciples of Christ: *See* Christian Church.

Episcopal Church: *See* Protestant Episcopal Church.

Evangelical and Reformed Church: *See* United Church of Christ.

Evangelical Covenant Church of America: This church has its roots in historical Christianity as it emerged in the Protestant Reformation in the biblical instruction of the Lutheran State Church of Sweden. Organized in 1885 in Chicago. Prior to 1957, it was known as the Evangelical Mission Covenant Church of America. Members (1978): 74,678. Headquarters: 5101 N. Francisco Ave., Chicago, Ill. 60625.

Evangelical Free Church of America: Organized in the 1880's in Boone, Iowa, as the Swedish Evangelical Free Mission. Later the name was changed to the Evangelical Free Church of America. In 1950, the Evangelical Free Church Association merged with this group. Members (1977): 100,000. Headquarters: 1515 E. 66th St., Minneapolis, Minn. 55423.

Evangelical United Brethren Church: *See* United Methodist Church under Methodist Churches.

Friends United Meeting: The Five Years Meeting of Friends was formed in 1902 by 11 Yearly Meetings entering into a loose confederation. Since then, two of the original Yearly Meetings have withdrawn (Kansas and Oregon) and two American and three Yearly Meetings outside the U. S. have joined. In 1965, the name was changed to Friends United Meeting. Members (1978): 62,080. Office of presiding clerk: 101 Quaker Hill Dr., Richmond, Ind. 47374.

Independent Fundamental Churches of America: Organized in 1930 by representatives of various independent churches. Members (1978): 87,582. Headquarters: 1860 Mannheim Rd., Westchester, Ill. 60153.

International Church of the Foursquare Gospel: An evangelistic missionary body organized by Aimee Semple McPherson in 1927. The parent church is Angelus Temple, 1100 Glendale Blvd., Los Angeles, Calif. 90026. Members (1963): 89,215.

Jehovah's Witnesses: A group calling themselves primitive Christians. They believe that the Kingdom under Christ will replace all earthly governments. Members (1978): 519,218. Headquarters: 124 Columbia Heights, Brooklyn, N.Y. 11201.

Latter-day Saints, Church of Jesus Christ of: Organized in 1830. A group in which the Bible, the Book of Mormon, the Doctrine and Covenants, and the Pearl of Great Price are regarded as the word of God. Their belief is summed up in 13 Articles of Faith written by Joseph Smith. Members (1978): 2,952,000. Headquarters: 50 E. North Temple St., Salt Lake City, Utah, 84111.

Latter-day Saints, Reorganized Church of Jesus Christ of: A division among the Latter-day Saints (non-Mormon) occurred on the death of Joseph Smith in 1844. His son, Joseph Smith, became presiding officer of this group, which has headquarters at Independence, Mo. Members (1978): 185,636. Headquarters: the Auditorium, Box 1059, Auditorium, Independence, Mo. 64051.

Mennonite Church: The largest group of the Mennonites who began arriving in the U. S. in 1683, settling in Germantown, Pa. They derive their name from Menno Simons, born 1496. Members (1978): 97,142. Headquarters: 528 E. Madison St., Lombard, Ill. 60148.

Moravian Church in America (Unitas Fratrum): In 1735, Moravian missionaries of the pre-Reformation faith of John Hus came to Georgia, in 1740 to Pennsylvania, and in 1753 to North Carolina. Members (Northern Province, 1978): 32,519; (Southern Province, 1978): 21,002. Headquarters: 69 W. Church St., Box 1245, Bethlehem, Pa. 18018.

Open Bible Standard Churches: An evangelical, full gospel denomination emphasizing evangelism, missions, and the message of the Open Bible. Members (1979): 60,000. Headquarters: 2020 Bell Ave., Des Moines, Iowa 50315.

Pentecostal Church of God: Organized in 1919 at Chicago, Ill. The first convention was held in October, 1933. Members (1977): 110,870. Headquarters: Messenger Plaza, 221 Main St., Joplin, Mo. 64801.

Pentecostal Holiness Church, Inc.: This body grew out of the holiness movement in the South and Middle West from 1895 to 1900. Members (1977): 86,103. Headquarters: Box 12609, Oklahoma City, Okla. 73112.

Plymouth Brethren: This orthodox and evangelical movement began in Britain in the 1820s and has since become worldwide. It is made of up two groups—the smaller "exclusive" branch, which stresses the interdependency of congregations, and the "open" branch, in which each assembly is guided by local elders. Members (1978): 74,000.

Protestant Episcopal Church: This group entered the colonies with the earliest settlers as the Church of England. It became autonomous, adopted its present name in 1789. It is an integral part of the Anglican Communion. In 1967, the General Convention adopted "The Episcopal Church" as an alternate name. Members (1978): 2,815,359. Headquarters: 815 Second Ave., New York, N.Y. 10017.

Reformed Church in America: This group was established by the earliest Dutch settlers of New York as the Reformed Protestant Dutch Church in 1628. Members (1978): 348,080. Headquarters: 475 Riverside Dr., New York, N.Y. 10115.

Salvation Army: An evangelistic organization, with a military government, first set up by General William Booth in England in 1865 and introduced into the U.S. in 1880. Members (1978): 414,035. Headquarters: 120–30 W. 14th St., New York, N.Y. 10011.

Seventh-day Adventists: This body developed out of an interdenominational movement in the early decades of the 19th century, but was not formally organized until 1863. Their two cardinal points of faith are belief in the personal, imminent, premillennial return of Christ and observance of the seventh day as the Sabbath. Members (1978): 535,705. Headquarters: 6840 Eastern Ave., N.W., Washington, D.C. 20012.

Triumph the Church and Kingdom of God in Christ (International): Organized by Elder E. D. Smith in Georgia in 1902. This group emphasizes the sanctification and the Second Coming of Christ. Members (1972): 54,307. Headquarters: 213 Farrington Ave., Atlanta, Ga. 30318.

Unitarian Universalist Association: This association is the result of a merger in 1961 of the American Unitarian Association, formed in 1825, and the Universalist Church in America, organized in the 1770's. Members (1978): 136,207. Headquarters, 25 Beacon St., Boston, Mass. 02108.

United Church of Christ: A merger in 1961 of the Evangelical and Reformed Church and the Congregational Christian Churches. Members (1978): 1,769,104. Headquarters: 105 Madison Ave., New York, N.Y. 10016.

United Pentecostal Church, International: Pentecostal Church, Inc., and Pentecostal Assemblies of Jesus Christ merged in 1945 at St. Louis. Members (1979): 450,000. Headquarters: 8855 Dunn Rd., Hazlewood, Mo. 63042.

Wesleyan Church: Originated through the uniting of the Pilgrim Holiness Church (1897) and the Wesleyan Methodist Church of America (1843) in 1968. Members (1978): 99,016. Headquarters: Box 2000, Marion, Ind. 46952.

Other Religious Groups

(1,000–50,000 members)

Advent Christian Church (1978: 31,324)
African Orthodox Church (1957: 6,000)
Albanian Orthodox Archdiocese in America (1978: 40,000)
Albanian Orthodox Diocese of America (1979: 5,250)
American Rescue Workers (1978: 2,140)
Anglican Orthodox Church (1972: 2,630)
Apostolic Christian Church (Nazarean) (1977: 4,804)
Apostolic Christian Churches of America (1977: 17,888)
Apostolic Faith (1978: 4,100)
Apostolic Lutheran Church of America (1974: 9,384)
Associate Reformed Presbyterian Church (General Synod) (1978: 32,139)
Beachy Amish Mennonite Church (1978: 4,762)
Berean Fundamental Church (1976: 4,269)
Bethel Ministerial Association (1971: 5,000)
Bible Church of Christ, (1979: 2,300)
Bible Protestant Church (1978: 2,077)
Bible Way Church of Our Lord Jesus Christ World Wide (1970: 30,000)
Brethren Church (Ashland, Ohio) (1978: 15,802)
Brethren in Christ Church (1977: 11,384)
Christ Catholic Church (1978: 1,365)
Christadelphians (1964: 15,800)
Christian Catholic Church (Evangelical-Protestant) (1979: 2,500)
Christian Church of North America, General Council (1979: 12,000)
Christian Nation Church U.S.A. (1976: 2,000)
Christian Union (1976: 4,590)
Church of Christ (1972: 2,400)
Church of Christ (Holiness) U.S.A. (1972: 9,289)
Church of God General Conference (Oregon, Ill.) (1978: 7,550)
Church of God (Seventh Day) (1960: 2,000)
Church of God (Seventh Day), Denver (1976: 8,000)
Church of God by Faith (1973: 4,500)
Church of God in Christ (Mennonite) (1978: 7,400)
Church of God of the Mountain Assembly (1977: 3,125)
Church of Illumination (1963: 9,000)
Church of Jesus Christ (Bickertonites) (1978: 2,551)
Church of Our Lord Jesus Christ of the Apostolic Faith (1954: 45,000)
Church of the Living God (1964: 45,320)
Church of the Lutheran Brethren of America (1978: 9,192)
Church of the Lutheran Confession (1978: 9,316)
Churches of Christ in Christian Union (1979: 10,300)
Churches of God, General Conference (1975: 36,016)
Congregational Holiness Church (1966: 4,859)
Conservative Congregational Christian Conference (1978: 22,750)
Coptic Orthodox Church (1976: 40,000)
Duck River (and Kindred) Association of Baptists (1975: 8,632)
Elim Fellowship (1973: 5,000)
Estonian Evangelical Lutheran Church (1978: 8,548)
Ethical Culture Movement (1978: 5,000)
Evangelical Church of North America (1978: 12,210)
Evangelical Congregational Church (1978: 28,459)
Evangelical Friends Alliance (1975: 25,531)
Evangelical Lutheran Church in America (Eielsen Synod) (1957: 2,500)
Evangelical Lutheran Synod (1977: 19,634)
Evangelical Mennonite Brethren Conference (1977: 2,023)
Evangelical Mennonite Church (1978: 3,634)
Evangelical Methodist Church (1974: 10,502)
Free Christian Zion Church of Christ (1956: 22,260)
Free Lutheran Congregations, Association of (1979: 14,738)
Friends General Conference (1974: 26,184)
Full Gospel Assemblies, International (1978: 2,800)
General Church of the New Jerusalem (1971: 2,143)
General Conference of Mennonite Brethren Churches (1978: 16,042)
General Convention, The Swedenborgian Church (1977: 2,640)
General Conference of the Evangelical Baptist Church (1952: 2,200)
Grace Brethren Churches, Fellowship of (1978: 39,605)
Grace Gospel Fellowship (1978: 3,500)
Holy Ukrainian Autocephalic Orthodox Church in Exile (1965: 4,800)
House of God, Which Is the Church of the Living God, the Pillar and Ground of the Truth (1956: 2,350)
Hungarian Reformed Church in America (1978: 10,500)
Hutterian Bretheren (1976: 3,500)
International Pentecostal Church of Christ (1977: 11,659)
Latvian Evangelical Lutheran Church in America (1978: 12,308)
Liberal Catholic Church—Province of the United States of America (1973: 2,393)
Mennonite Church, The General Conference (1976: 36,397)
Metropolitan Community Churches, Universal Fellowship of (1978: 25,520)

Missionary Church, The (1972: 20,078)
National Spiritual Alliance of the U.S.A., The (1971: 3,230)
National Spiritualist Association of Churches (1976: 5,168)
Netherlands Reformed Congregations (1978: 4,904)
New Apostolic Church of North America (1978: 26,384)
North American Baptist Conference (1978: 42,499)
North American Old Roman Catholic Church (Archdiocese of New York) (1978: 2,500)
Old German Baptist Brethren (1978: 4,898)
Old Order Amish Church (1978: 33,000)
Old Order (Wisler) Mennonite (1972: 8,000)
(Original) Church of God, The (1971: 20,000)
Orthodox Presbyterian Church, The (1978: 15,806)
Pentecostal Assemblies of the World (1960: 4,500)
Pillar of Fire (1949: 5,100)
Primitive Methodist Church, U.S.A. (1978: 10,222)
Protestant Conference (Lutheran), The (1977: 2,635)
Protestant Reformed Churches in America (1978: 4,040)
Reformed Baptists (1979: 5,000)
Reformed Church in the United States (1977: 3,790)
Reformed Episcopal Church (1977: 6,211)
Reformed Methodist Union Episcopal Church (1976: 3,800)
Reformed Presbyterian Church, Evangelical Synod (1977: 25,448)
Reformed Presbyterian Church of North America (1977: 4,878)
Reformed Zion Union Apostolic Church (1965: 16,000)
Religious Society of Friends (Conservative) (1976: 1,728)
Religious Society of Friends (Unaffiliated Meetings) (1975: 5,696)
Romanian Orthodox Episcopate of America, The (1977: 40,000)
Schwenkfelder Church, The (1977: 2,748)
Second Cumberland Presbyterian Church in U.S. (1959: 30,000)
Separate Baptists in Christ (1962: 7,496)
Seventh-Day Baptist General Conference (1978: 5,181)
Social Brethren (1975: 1,784)
Southern Methodist Church (1977: 11,000)
Syrian Orthodox Church of Antioch (Archdiocese of the U.S.A. and Canada) (1978: 30,000)
Ukrainian Orthodox Church in America (Ecumenical Patriarchate) (1977: 25,000)
United Brethren in Christ (1976: 28,035)
United Holy Church of America (1960: 28,980)
Unity of the Brethren (1964: 6,142)
Vedanta Society of New York (1978: 1,000)
Volunteers of America (1978: 36,634)

Roman Catholic Pontiffs

St. Peter, of Bethsaida in Galilee, Prince of the Apostles, was the first Pope. He lived first in Antioch and then in Rome for 25 years. In AD 64 or 67, he was martyred. St. Linus became the second Pope.

Name	Birthplace	Reigned From	To
St. Linus	Tuscia	67	76
St. Anacletus (Cletus)	Rome	76	88
St. Clement	Rome	88	97
St. Evaristus	Greece	97	105
St. Alexander I	Rome	105	115
St. Sixtus I	Rome	115	125
St. Telesphorus	Greece	125	136
St. Hyginus	Greece	136	140
St. Pius I	Aquileia	140	155
St. Anicetus	Syria	155	166
St. Soter	Campania	166	175
St. Eleutherius	Epirus	175	189
St. Victor I	Africa	189	199
St. Zephyrinus	Rome	199	217
St. Callistus I	Rome	217	222
St. Urban I	Rome	222	230
St. Pontian	Rome	230	235
St. Anterus	Greece	235	236
St. Fabian	Rome	236	250
St. Cornelius	Rome	251	253
St. Lucius I	Rome	253	254
St. Stephen I	Rome	254	257
St. Sixtus II	Greece	257	258
St. Dionysius	Unknown	259	268
St. Felix I	Rome	269	274
St. Eutychian	Luni	275	283
St. Caius	Dalmatia	283	296
St. Marcellinus	Rome	296	304
St. Marcellus I	Rome	308	309
St. Eusebius	Greece	309[1]	309[1]
St. Meltiades	Africa	311	314
St. Sylvester I	Rome	314	335
St. Marcus	Rome	336	336
St. Julius I	Rome	337	352
Liberius	Rome	352	366
St. Damasus I	Spain	366	384
St. Siricius	Rome	384	399
St. Anastasius I	Rome	399	401
St. Innocent I	Albano	401	417
St. Zozimus	Greece	417	418
St. Boniface I	Rome	418	422
St. Celestine I	Campania	422	432
St. Sixtus III	Rome	432	440
St. Leo I (the Great)	Tuscany	440	461
St. Hilary	Sardinia	461	468
St. Simplicius	Tivoli	468	483
St. Felix III (II)[2]	Rome	483	492
St. Gelasius I	Africa	492	496
Anastasius II	Rome	496	498
St. Symmachus	Sardinia	498	514
St. Hormisdas	Frosinone	514	523
St. John I	Tuscany	523	526
St. Felix IV (III)	Samnium	526	530
Boniface II	Rome	530	532
John II	Rome	533	535
St. Agapitus I	Rome	535	536
St. Silverius	Campania	536	537
Vigilius	Rome	537	555
Pelagius I	Rome	556	561
John III	Rome	561	574
Benedict I	Rome	575	579
Pelagius II	Rome	579	590
St. Gregory I (the Great)	Rome	590	604
Sabinianus	Tuscany	604	606
Boniface III	Rome	607	607
St. Boniface IV	Marsi	608	615
St. Deusdedit (Adeodatus I)	Rome	615	618
Boniface V	Naples	619	625
Honorius I	Campania	625	638
Severinus	Rome	640	640
John IV	Dalmatia	640	642
Theodore I	Greece	642	649
St. Martin I	Todi	649	655
St. Eugene I[3]	Rome	654	657
St. Vitalian	Segni	657	672
Adeodatus II	Rome	672	676

Name	Birthplace	Reigned From	To
Donus	Rome	676	678
St. Agatho	Sicily	678	681
St. Leo II	Sicily	682	683
St. Benedict II	Rome	684	685
John V	Syria	685	686
Conon	Unknown	686	687
St. Sergius I	Syria	687	701
John VI	Greece	701	705
John VII	Greece	705	707
Sisinnius	Syria	708	708
Constantine	Syria	708	715
St. Gregory II	Rome	715	731
St. Gregory III	Syria	731	741
St. Zachary	Greece	741	752
Stephen II (III)[4]	Rome	752	757
St. Paul I	Rome	757	767
Stephen III (IV)	Sicily	768	772
Adrian I	Rome	772	795
St. Leo III	Rome	795	816
Stephen IV (V)	Rome	816	817
St. Paschal I	Rome	817	824
Eugene II	Rome	824	827
Valentine	Rome	827	827
Gregory IV	Rome	827	844
Sergius II	Rome	844	847
St. Leo IV	Rome	847	855
Benedict III	Rome	855	858
St. Nicholas I (the Great)	Rome	858	867
Adrian II	Rome	867	872
John VIII	Rome	872	882
Marinus I	Gallese	882	884
St. Adrian III	Rome	884	885
Stephen V (VI)	Rome	885	891
Formosus	Portus	891	896
Boniface VI	Rome	896	896
Stephen VI (VII)	Rome	896	897
Romanus	Gallese	897	897
Theodore II	Rome	897	897
John IX	Tivoli	898	900
Benedict IV	Rome	900	903
Leo V	Ardea	903	903
Sergius III	Rome	904	911
Anastasius III	Rome	911	913
Landus	Sabina	913	914
John X	Tossignano	914	928
Leo VI	Rome	928	928
Stephen VII (VIII)	Rome	928	931
John XI	Rome	931	935
Leo VII	Rome	936	939
Stephen VIII (IX)	Rome	939	942
Marinus II	Rome	942	946
Agapitus II	Rome	946	955
John XII	Tusculum	955	964
Leo VIII[5]	Rome	963	965
Benedict V[5]	Rome	964	966
John XIII	Rome	965	972
Benedict VI	Rome	973	974
Benedict VII	Rome	974	983
John XIV	Pavia	983	984
John XV	Rome	985	996
Gregory V	Saxony	996	999
Sylvester II	Auvergne	999	1003
John XVII	Rome	1003	1003
John XVIII	Rome	1004	1009
Sergius IV	Rome	1009	1012
Benedict VIII	Tusculum	1012	1024
John XIX	Tusculum	1024	1032
Benedict IX[6]	Tusculum	1032	1044
Sylvester III	Rome	1045	1045

Name	Birthplace	Reigned From	To
Benedict IX (2nd time)	—	1045	1045
Gregory VI	Rome	1045	1046
Clement II	Saxony	1046	1047
Benedict IX (3rd time)	—	1047	1048
Damasus II	Bavaria	1048	1048
St. Leo IX	Alsace	1049	1054
Victor II	Germany	1055	1057
Stephen IX (X)	Lorraine	1057	1058
Nicholas II	Burgundy	1059	1061
Alexander II	Milan	1061	1073
St. Gregory VII	Tuscany	1073	1085
Bl. Victor III	Benevento	1086	1087
Bl. Urban II	France	1088	1099
Paschal II	Ravenna	1099	1118
Gelasius II	Gaeta	1118	1119
Callistus II	Burgundy	1119	1124
Honorius II	Fiagnano	1124	1130
Innocent II	Rome	1130	1143
Celestine II	Città di Castello	1143	1144
Lucius II	Bologna	1144	1145
Bl. Eugene III	Pisa	1145	1153
Anastasius IV	Rome	1153	1154
Adrian IV	England	1154	1159
Alexander III	Siena	1159	1181
Lucius III	Lucca	1181	1185
Urban III	Milan	1185	1187
Gregory VIII	Benevento	1187	1187
Clement III	Rome	1187	1191
Celestine III	Rome	1191	1198
Innocent III	Anagni	1198	1216
Honorius III	Rome	1216	1227
Gregory IX	Anagni	1227	1241
Celestine IV	Milan	1241	1241
Innocent IV	Genoa	1243	1254
Alexander IV	Anagni	1254	1261
Urban IV	Troyes	1261	1264
Clement IV	France	1265	1268
Bl. Gregory X	Piacenza	1271	1276
Bl. Innocent V	Savoy	1276	1276
Adrian V	Genoa	1276	1276
John XXI[7]	Portugal	1276	1277
Nicholas III	Rome	1277	1280
Martin IV[8]	France	1281	1285
Honorius IV	Rome	1285	1287
Nicholas IV	Ascoli	1288	1292
St. Celestine V	Isernia	1294	1294
Boniface VIII	Anagni	1294	1303
Bl. Benedict XI	Treviso	1303	1304
Clement V	France	1305	1314
John XXII	Cahors	1316	1334
Benedict XII	France	1334	1342
Clement VI	France	1342	1352
Innocent VI	France	1352	1362
Bl. Urban V	France	1362	1370
Gregory XI	France	1370	1378
Urban VI	Naples	1378	1389
Boniface IX	Naples	1389	1404
Innocent VII	Sulmona	1404	1406
Gregory XII	Venice	1406	1415
Martin V	Rome	1417	1431
Eugene IV	Venice	1431	1447
Nicholas V	Sarzana	1447	1455
Callistus III	Jativa	1455	1458
Pius II	Siena	1458	1464
Paul II	Venice	1464	1471
Sixtus IV	Savona	1471	1484
Innocent VIII	Genoa	1484	1492

Name	Birthplace	Reigned From	To
Alexander VI	Jativa	1492	1503
Pius III	Siena	1503	1503
Julius II	Savona	1503	1513
Leo X	Florence	1513	1521
Adrian VI	Utrecht	1522	1523
Clement VII	Florence	1523	1534
Paul III	Rome	1534	1549
Julius III	Rome	1550	1555
Marcellus II	Montepulciano	1555	1555
Paul IV	Naples	1555	1559
Pius IV	Milan	1559	1565
St. Pius V	Bosco	1566	1572
Gregory XIII	Bologna	1572	1585
Sixtus V	Grottammare	1585	1590
Urban VII	Rome	1590	1590
Gregory XIV	Cremona	1590	1591
Innocent IX	Bologna	1591	1591
Clement VIII	Florence	1592	1605
Leo XI	Florence	1605	1605
Paul V	Rome	1605	1621
Gregory XV	Bologna	1621	1623
Urban VIII	Florence	1623	1644
Innocent X	Rome	1644	1655
Alexander VII	Siena	1655	1667
Clement IX	Pistoia	1667	1669
Clement X	Rome	1670	1676
Bl. Innocent XI	Como	1676	1689
Alexander VIII	Venice	1689	1691
Innocent XII	Spinazzola	1691	1700
Clement XI	Urbino	1700	1721
Innocent XIII	Rome	1721	1724
Benedict XIII	Gravina	1724	1730
Clement XII	Florence	1730	1740
Benedict XIV	Bologna	1740	1758
Clement XIII	Venice	1758	1769
Clement XIV	Rimini	1769	1774
Pius VI	Cesena	1775	1799
Pius VII	Cesena	1800	1823
Leo XII	Genga	1823	1829
Pius VIII	Cingoli	1829	1830
Gregory XVI	Belluno	1831	1846
Pius IX	Senegallia	1846	1878
Leo XIII	Carpineto	1878	1903
St. Pius X	Riese	1903	1914
Benedict XV	Genoa	1914	1922
Pius XI	Desio	1922	1939
Pius XII	Rome	1939	1958
John XXIII	Sotto il Monte	1958	1963
Paul VI	Concesio	1963	1978
John Paul I	Forno di Canale	1978	1978
John Paul II	Wadowice, Poland	1978	

1. Or 310. 2. He should be called Felix II, and his successors of the same name should be numbered accordingly. The discrepancy was caused by the erroneous insertion in some lists of the name of St. Felix of Rome, Martyr. 3. He was elected during the exile of St. Martin I, who endorsed him as Pope. 4. After St. Zachary died, a Roman priest named Stephen was elected but died before his consecration as Bishop of Rome. His name is not included in all lists for this reason. In view of this historical confusion, the *National Catholic Almanac* lists the true Stephen II as Stephen II (III), the true Stephen III as Stephen III (IV), etc. 5. Confusion exists concerning the legitimacy of claims. If the deposition of John was invalid, Leo was an antipope until after the end of Benedict's reign. If the deposition of John was valid, Leo was the legitimate Pope and Benedict an antipope. 6. If the triple removal of Benedict IX was not valid, Sylvester III, Gregory VI, and Clement II were antipopes. 7. Elimination was made of the name of John XX in an effort to rectify the numerical designation of Popes named John. The error dates back to the time of John XV. 8. The names of Marinus I and Marinus II were construed as Martin. In view of these two pontificates and the earlier reign of St. Martin I, this pontiff was called Martin IV. *Source: National Catholic Almanac,* from *Annuarto Pontificio.*

Antipopes

Antipopes were those who falsely claimed Papal Sovereignty. The dates and, in some cases, Roman numerals after the names account for occasional discrepancies in the succession of the Popes.

Name	Alleged reign
St. Hippolytus	217–235
Novatian	251
Felix II	355–365
Ursinus	366–367
Eulalius	418–419
Lawrence	498; 501–505
Dioscorus	530
Theodore	ended 687
Paschal	ended 687
Constantine	767–769
Philip	768
John	ended 844
Anastasius	855
Christopher	903–904
Boniface VII	974; 984–985
John XVI	997–998
Gregory	ended 1012
Benedict X	1058–1059
Honorius II	1061–1072
Clement III	1080–1100
Theodoric	ended 1100
Albert	ended 1102
Sylvester IV	1105–1111
Gregory VIII	1118–1121
Celestine II	ended 1124
Anacletus II	1130–1138
Victor IV	1138
Victor IV[1]	1159–1164
Paschal III	1164–1168
Callistus III	1168–1178
Innocent III	1179–1180
Nicholas V	1328–1330
Clement VII	1378–1394
Benedict XIII	1394–1423
Alexander V	1409–1410
John XXIII	1410–1415
Felix V	1439–1449

1. Did not recognize his predecessor of 1138, who, only two months after claiming the Papacy, submitted to the rightful Pope, Innocent II.

U.S. SOCIETIES & ASSOCIATIONS

Source: Information Please questionnaires to organizations.

Names are listed alphabetically according to key word in title; figure in parentheses is year of founding; other figure is membership.

Abortion Federation, National (1976): 110 E. 59th St., New York, N.Y. 10022. Uta Landy, Executive Director.

Abortion Rights Action League, National (1969): 825 15th St., N.W., Washington, D.C. 20005. 85,000; Karen Mulhauser, Executive Director.

Accountants, American Institute of Certified Public (1887): 1211 Avenue of the Americas, New York, N.Y. 10036. 160,000; Philip B. Chenok, President.

Accountants, National Association of (1919): 919 Third Ave., New York, N.Y. 10022. 94,000; W. M. Young, Jr., Executive Director.

Actors' Equity Association (1913): 165 W. 46th St., New York, N.Y. 10036. 30,000; Donald Grody, Executive Secretary.

Aeronautic Association, National (1922): 821 15th St., N.W., Washington, D.C. 20005. 160,000; Ev Langworthy, Acting Executive Director.

Aeronautics and Astronautics, American Institute of (1932): 1290 Avenue of the Americas, New York, N.Y. 10019. 29,500; James J. Harford, Executive Secretary.

African-American Institute, The (1953): 833 United Nations Plaza, New York, N.Y. 10017. Wilbur Jones, Director of Administration.

AFS International/Intercultural Programs (1947): 313 E. 43rd St., New York, N.Y. 10017. 164,000; Stephen H. Rhinesmith, President.

Air Force Association (1946): 1750 Pennsylvania Ave., N.W., Washington, D.C. 20006. 150,000; James H. Straubel, Executive Director.

Air Line Pilots Association (1931): 1625 Massachusetts Ave., N.W., Washington, D.C. 20036. 33,000; John J. O'Donnell, President.

Air Pollution Control Association (1907): P.O. Box 2861, Pittsburgh, Pa. 15230. 7,310; William G. Hamlin, Executive Vice President.

Alcohol Problems, American Council on (1900): 119 Constitution Ave., N.E., Washington, D.C. 20002. 2,000; William N. Plymat, Executive Director.

Alcoholics Anonymous (1935): P.O. Box 459, Grand Central Station, New York, N.Y. 10017. 1,000,000. Address communications to General Service Office.

America-Mideast Educational and Training Services (1951): 1717 Massachusetts Ave., N.W., Washington, D.C. 20036. 350; Orin D. Parker, President.

American Federation of Labor and Congress of Industrial Organizations (AFL-CIO) (1955): 815 16th St., N.W., Washington, D.C. 20006. 13,600,000; Saul I. Miller, Director of Information.

American Friends Service Committee (1917): 1501 Cherry St., Philadelphia, Pa. 19102. Paul E. Brink, Director of Information.

American Indian Affairs, National Association on (1923): 432 Park Ave. S., New York, N.Y. 10016. 50,000; Steven Unger, Executive Director.

American Legion (1919): P.O. Box 1055, Indianapolis, Ind. 46206. 2,500,000; Frank C. Momsen, National Adjutant.

American Legion Auxiliary (1919): 777 N. Meridian St., Indianapolis, Ind. 46204. 940,000; Miriam Junge, National Secretary.

Americans for Democratic Action (1947): 1411 K St., N.W., Washington, D.C. 20005. 75,000; Leon Shull, National Director.

AMVETS (American Veterans of World War II, Korea, and Vietnam) (1944): 4647 Forbes Blvd., Lanham, Md. 20801. 200,000; Leon Sanchez, National Executive Director.

AMVETS National Auxiliary (1946): Saco Rd., Old Orchard Beach, Me. 04064. 60,000. Rita J. Potvin, Executive Secretary.

Animals, American Society for the Prevention of Cruelty to (1866): 441 E. 92nd St., New York, N.Y. 10028. 18,000; John F. Kullberg, Executive Director.

Animals, Fund For (1967): 140 W. 57th St., New York, N.Y. 10019. 175,000; Cleveland Amory, President.

Anti-Vivisection Society, The American (1883): Suite 204, Noble Plaza, 801 Old York Rd., Jenkintown, Pa. 19046. 15,000; William A. Cave, President.

Arbitration Association, American (1926): 140 W. 51st St., New York, N.Y. 10020. 4,441; E. W. Dippold, Corporate Secretary.

Architects, American Institute of (1857): 1735 New York Ave., N.W., Washington, D.C. 20006. 34,000; David O. Meeker, Jr., Executive Vice President.

Army, Association of the United States (1950): 2425 Wilson Blvd., Arlington, Va. 22201. 103,000; Robert F. Cocklin, Executive Vice President.

Arthritis Foundation (1948): 3400 Peachtree Rd., N.E., Atlanta, Ga. 30326. 71 local chapters; Clifford M. Clarke, President.

Arts and Letters, American Academy and Institute of (1904): 633 W. 155th St., New York, N.Y. 10032. 250; Margaret M. Mills, Executive Director.

Astronomical Society, American (1899): Department of Physics and Astronomy, Louisiana State University, Baton Rouge, La. 70803. 3,700; Arlo U. Landolt, Secretary.

Audubon Society, National (1905): 950 Third Ave., New York, N.Y. 10022. 400,000; Andrew Bihun, Conservation Information.

Authors League of America (1912): 234 W. 44th St., New York, N.Y. 10036. 8,200; Shirley S. Beck, Administrator.

Automobile Association, American (1902): 8111 Gatehouse Rd., Falls Church, Va. 22047. 21,000,000; J. B. Creal, President.

Automobile Club, National (1924): One Market Plaza, San Francisco, Calif. 94105. 427,780; Gene Halliburton, President.

Bar Association, American (1898): 1155 E. 60th St., Chicago, Ill. 60637. 263,000; Bert H. Early, Executive Director.

Barbershop Quartet Singing in America, Society for the Preservation and Encouragement of (1938): Box 575, Kenosha, Wis. 53141. 36,000; Hugh

Ingraham, Executive Director.

Bible Society, American (1816): 1865 Broadway, New York, N.Y. 10023. 328,000; Charles W. Baas, John D. Erickson, Alice E. Ball, General Officers.

Big Brothers/Big Sisters of America (1977): 117 S. 17th St., Suite 1200, Philadelphia, Pa. 19103. Betty Larkin, Coordinator, Information and Liaison.

Blind, National Federation of the (1940): 1800 Johnson St., Baltimore, Md. 21230. 50,000; Kenneth Jernigan, President.

Blindness, National Society to Prevent (1908): 79 Madison Ave., New York, N.Y. 10016. 349 chapters; Virginia Boyce, Executive Director.

Blue Shield Association (1946): 676 St. Clair, Chicago, Ill. 60611. 70 affiliates; Tom K. Mura, Vice President, Advertising.

B'nai B'rith (1843): 1640 Rhode Island Ave., N.W., Washington, D.C. 20036. 500,000; Hank Siegel, Press Officer.

B'nai B'rith, Anti-Defamation League of (1913): 823 United Nations Plaza, New York, N.Y. 10017. Nathan Perlmutter, National Director.

Boy Scouts of America (1910): P.O. Box 61030, Dallas-Fort Worth Airport, Tex. 75261. 4,493,491.

Boys' Clubs of America (1906): 771 First Ave., New York, N.Y. 10017. 1,000,000; Joan R. Licursi, Director of Communications Services.

Brookings Institution, The (1927): 1775 Massachusetts Ave., N.W., Washington, D.C. 20036. James D. Farrell, Information Editor.

Camp Fire, Inc. (1910): 4601 Madison Ave., Kansas City, Mo. 64112. 750,000; Roberta van der Voort, National Executive Director.

Campers & Hikers Association, National (1949): 7172 Transit Rd., Buffalo, N.Y. 14221. 57,000 families. Fran Opela, National Office Manager.

Camping Association, The American (1910): Bradford Woods, Martinsville, Ind. 46151. 6,000; Armand Ball, Executive Vice President.

Cancer Society, American (1913): 777 Third Ave., New York, N.Y. 10017. 2,300,000 volunteers; Lane W. Adams, Executive Vice President.

CARE (Cooperative for American Relief Everywhere) (1945): 660 First Ave., New York, N.Y. 10016. 26 agencies; Louis Samia, Executive Director.

Catholic Bishops, National Conference of (1966): 1312 Massachusetts Ave., N.W., Washington, D.C. 20005. 340; Most Rev. John R. Quinn, President.

Catholic Charities, National Conference of (1910): 1346 Connecticut Ave., N.W., Washington, D.C. 20036. 3,000; Rev. Msgr. Lawrence Corcoran, Executive Director.

Catholic Conference, United States (1966): 1312 Massachusetts Ave., N.W., Washington, D.C. 20005. Bishop Thomas C. Kelly, O.P., General Secretary.

Catholic Daughters of the Americas (1903): 10 W. 71st St., New York, N.Y. 10023. 175,000; Lorraine McMahon, Executive Secretary.

Catholic War Veterans of the U.S.A. (1935): 2 Massachusetts Ave., N.W., Washington, D.C. 20001. 75,000; Francis F. Fox, National Commander.

Cerebral Palsy Associations United (1949): 66 E. 34th St., New York, N.Y. 10016. 250 affiliates; Earl H. Cunerd, Executive Director.

Chamber of Commerce of the U.S. (1912): 1615 H St., N.W., Washington, D.C. 20062. 83,100; Richard L. Lesher, President.

Chartered Life Underwriters, American Society of (1929): 270 Bryn Mawr Ave., Bryn Mawr, Pa. 19010. 27,000; John R. Driskill, Executive Vice President.

Chemical Engineers, American Institute of (1908): 345 E. 47th St., New York, N.Y. 20017. 50,000; J. Charles Forman, Executive Director and Secretary.

Chemical Society, American (1876): 1155 16th St., N.W., Washington, D.C. 20036. 116,000; Raymond P. Mariella, Executive Director.

Chess Federation, United States (1939): 186 Rt. 9W, New Windsor, N.Y. 12550. 50,000; Gerard J. Dullea, Executive Director.

Child Welfare League of America (1920): 67 Irving Pl., New York, N.Y. 10003. Edwin F. Watson, Executive Director.

Chiropractic Association, American (1963): 2200 Grand Ave., Des Moines, Iowa 50312. 15,000; Louis O. Gearhart, Executive Director.

Christians and Jews, National Conference of (1928): 43 W. 57th St., New York, N.Y. 10019. 200,000; David Hyatt, President.

Churches, National Council of (1950): 475 Riverside Drive, New York, N.Y. 10115. 32 Protestant and Orthodox communions; Claire Randall, General Secretary.

Civil Engineers, American Society of (1852): 345 E. 47th St., New York, N.Y. 10017. 78,000; Eugene Zwoyer, Executive Director.

Civil Liberties Union, American (1920): 132 W. 43rd St., New York, N.Y. 10036. 200,000; Alan Reitman, Associate Director.

Colleges, Association of American (1915): 1818 R St., N.W., Washington, D.C. 20009. 620 institutions; Mark H. Curtis, President.

Colored Women's Clubs, National Association of (1896): 5808 16th St., N.W., Washington, D.C. 20011. 40,000; Mrs. Inez W. Tinsley, National President.

Common Cause (1970): 2030 M St., N.W., Washington, D.C. 20036. 225,000; Archibald Cox, Chairman.

Composers, Authors, and Publishers, American Society of (ASCAP) (1914): One Lincoln Plaza, New York, N.Y. 10023. 23,400; Hal David, President.

Congress of Racial Equality (CORE) (1942): 1916–38 Park Ave., New York, N.Y. 10037. Nationwide network of chapters; Roy Innis, National Director.

Conscientious Objectors, Central Committee for (1948): 2208 South St., Philadelphia, Pa. 19146.

Consumer Federation of America (1967): 1012 14th St., N.W., Suite 901, Washington, D.C. 20005. 220 member organizations; Stephen Brobeck, Executive Director.

Consumers Union (1936): 256 Washington St., Mt. Vernon, N.Y. 10550. 2,500,000 subscribers to *Consumer Reports;* Rhoda H. Karpatkin, Executive Director.

Contract Bridge League, American (1927): 2200 Democrat Rd., Memphis, Tenn. 38116. 200,000; Richard L. Goldberg, Executive Secretary.

Cooperative League of the U.S.A. (1916): 1828 L St., N.W., Washington, D.C. 20036. 30,000,000 families; Glenn M. Anderson, President.

Country Music Association (1958): Box 22299, Nashville, Tenn. 37202. 5,500; Jo Walker, Executive Director.

Crime and Delinquency, National Council on (1907): Continental Plaza, Hackensack, N.J. 07601. Nationwide membership; Milton G. Rector, President.

Daughters of the American Revolution, National Society (1890): 1776 D St., N.W., Washington, D.C.

20006. 208,000; Mrs. Richard Denny Shelby, President General.

Daughters of the Confederacy, United (1894): 328 N. Boulevard, Richmond, Va. 23220. 26,000; Mrs. Charlotte P. Crippen, Executive Secretary.

Deaf, National Association of the (1880): 814 Thayer Ave., Silver Spring, Md. 20005. Albert T. Pimentel, Executive Director.

Defense Preparedness Association, American (1919): 1700 N. Moore St., Arlington, Va. 22209. 34,000; H.A. Miley, Jr., President.

Democratic Club, National (1834): Chemists Club, 52 E. 41st St., New York, N.Y. 10017. 500; John G. Treacy, Secretary.

Dental Association, American (1859): 211 E. Chicago Ave., Chicago, Ill. 60611. 135,000; John M. Coady, Executive Director.

Diabetes Association, American (1940): 600 Fifth Ave., New York, N.Y. 10020. John L. Dugan, Jr., Executive Vice President.

Dignity (1969): 1500 Massachusetts Ave., N.W., Washington, D.C. 20005. 5,000; Frank Scheuren, President.

Disabled American Veterans (1922): P.O. Box 14301, Cincinnati, Ohio 45214. 670,000; Richard M. Wilson, Assistant National Adjutant for Public Relations.

Ducks Unlimited (1937): Box 66300, Chicago, Ill. 60666. 350,000; Kenneth V. McCreary, Executive Secretary.

Eagles, Fraternal Order of (1898): 2401 W. Wisconsin Ave., Milwaukee, Wis. 53233. 850,000; Art Ehrmann, Publications Editor.

Easter Seal Society, The National (1921): 2023 W. Ogden Ave., Chicago, Ill. 60612. 50 affiliated state societies; John R. Garrison, Executive Director.

Eastern Star, Order of the, General Grand Chapter (1876): 1618 New Hampshire Ave., N.W., Washington, D.C. 20009. 3,000,000; Thelma R. Bailey, Most Worthy Grand Matron.

Education Association, National (1857): 1201 16th St., N.W., Washington, D.C. 20036. 1,600,000; Terry Herndon, Executive Director.

Electrochemical Society, The (1902): P.O. Box 2071, Princeton, N.J. 08540. 4,476; Donna N. Kimberlin, Administrative Assistant.

Elks of the U.S.A., Benevolent and Protective Order of the (1868): 2750 Lake View Ave., Chicago, Ill. 60614. 1,650,000; Stanley F. Kocur, Grand Secretary.

English-Speaking Union of the United States (1920): 16 E. 69th St., New York, N.Y. 10021. 32,000; John D. Walker, Executive Director.

Euthanasia Foundation, American (1972): 95 N. Birch Rd., Fort Lauderdale, Fla. 33304. Vincent F. Sullivan, Executive Director.

Exploration Geophysicists, Society of (1930): P.O. Box 3098, Tulsa, Okla. 74101. 13,300; John Hyden, Executive Director.

Family Service Association of America (1911): 44 E. 23rd St., New York, N.Y. 10010. 275 member agencies; W. Keith Daugherty, General Director.

Farm Bureau Federation, American (1919): 225 Touhy Ave., Park Ridge, Ill. 60068. 3,198,631 member families; J. Patrick Batts, Director of Information.

Fleet Reserve Association (1924): 1303 New Hampshire Ave., N.W., Washington, D.C. 20036. 149,000; Robert W. Nolan, National Executive Secretary.

Foreign Policy Association (1918): 205 Lexington Ave., New York, N.Y. 10016. Thetis Reavis, Vice President for Public Affairs.

Foreign Relations, Council on (1921): 58 E. 68th St., New York, N.Y. 10021. 1,946; Winston Lord, President.

Foreign Study, American Institute for (1965): 102 Greenwich Ave., Greenwich, Conn. 06830. 250,000; Henry C. Kahn, President.

Foreign Trade Council, Inc., National (1914): 10 Rockefeller Plaza, New York, N.Y. 10020. Over 600 companies; Richard W. Roberts, President.

Foster Parents Plan International (1937): Box 400, Warwick, R.I. 02887. 160,000; George W. Ross, International Executive Director.

4-H Program (early 1900s): SEA-Extension, U.S. Department of Agriculture, Washington, D.C. 20250. 5,200,00; Hope S. Daugherty, Acting Deputy Administrator.

Future Farmers of America (1928): 5632 Mt. Vernon Hgwy, Alexandria, Va. 22309. 494,394; Byron F. Rawls, National Advisor.

Future Homemakers of America (1945): 2010 Massachusetts Ave., N.W., Washington, D.C. 20036. 450,000; Mildred Reel, Executive Director.

Gamblers Anonymous Fellowship: Box 17173, Los Angeles, Calif. 90017. 7,000; Jim Z., National Executive Secretary.

Geographic Society, National (1888): 17th and M Sts., N.W., Washington, D.C. 20036. 10,000,000; Gilbert M. Grosvenor, President.

Geriatrics Society, American (1942): 10 Columbus Circle, New York, N.Y. 10019. 9,000; Kathryn S. Henderson, Executive Director.

Gideons International, The (1889): 2900 Lebanon Rd., Nashville, Tenn. 37214. 66,000; M.A. Henderson, Executive Director.

Girl Scouts of the U.S.A. (1912): 830 Third Ave., New York, N.Y. 10022. 2,971,000; Richard G. Knox, Director of Public Relations.

Girls Clubs of America (1945): 205 Lexington Ave., New York, N.Y. 10016. 220,000; Edith B. Phelps, National Executive Director.

Hadassah, The Women's Zionist Organization of America (1912): 50 W. 58th St., New York, N.Y. 10019. 360,000; Aline Kaplan, Executive Director.

Health, Physical Education, Recreation, and Dance, American Alliance for (1885): 1201 16th St., N.W., Washington, D.C. 20036. 50,000; George F. Anderson, Executive Director.

Hearing and Speech Action, National Association for (1919): 6110 Executive Blvd., Rockville, Md. 20852. 153 agencies.

Heart Association, American (1924): 7320 Greenville Ave., Dallas, Tex. 75231. 115,000; William W. Moore, Executive Vice President.

Hemispheric Affairs, Council on (1975): 1201 16th St., N.W., Washington, D.C. 20036. Laurence R. Birns, Director.

Historical Association, American (1884): 400 A St., S.E., Washington, D.C. 20003. 15,000; Mack Thompson, Executive Director.

Home Economics Association, American (1909): 2010 Massachusetts Ave., N.W., Washington, D.C. 20036. 40,000; Kinsey Green, Executive Director.

Horticultural Society, American (1922): Mt. Vernon, Va. 22121. 35,000; Thomas W. Richards, Executive Vice President.

Hospital Association, American (1898): 840 N. Lake Shore Dr., Chicago, Ill. 60611. 6,165 institutions; J. Alexander McMahon, President.

Humane Association, American (1877): 5351 S. Roslyn St., Englewood, Colo. 80111.

Humane Society of the United States (1954): 2100 L St., N.W., Washington, D.C. 20037. 130,500; Patrick B. Parkes, Vice President for Administration.

Indian Rights Association (1882): 1505 Race St., Philadelphia, Pa. 19102. 2,400; Sandra L. Cadwalader, Executive Director.

Interfraternity Conference, National (1909): 3901 W. 86th St., Indianapolis, Ind. 46268. 51; Jack L. Anson, Executive Director.

Jaycees, The United States (1920): 4 W. 21st St., Tulsa, Okla. 74121. 370,000; Don Varnadore, Executive Vice President.

Jewish Appeal, United (1939): 1290 Avenue of the Americas, New York, N.Y. 10019. Irving Bernstein, Executive Vice Chairman.

Jewish Committee, American (1906): 165 E. 56th St., New York, N.Y. 10022. 40,000; Morton Yarmon, Director of Public Relations.

Jewish Community Centers, World Confederation of (1946): 15 E. 26th St., New York, N.Y. 10010. Herbert Millman, Executive Director.

Jewish War Veterans of the U.S.A. (1896): 1712 New Hampshire Ave., N.W., Washington, D.C. 20009.

JWB (National Jewish Welfare Board) (1917): 15 E. 26th St., New York, N.Y. 10010. 275 affiliated community centers and YM–YWHAs; Arthur Rotman, Executive Vice President.

Jewish Women, National Council of (1893): 15 E. 26th St., New York, N.Y. 10010. Shirley I. Leviton, National President.

John Birch Society (1958): 395 Concord Ave., Belmont, Mass. 02178. 100,000; Ellen Sproul, Clerk of Corporation.

Journalists, Society of Professional, Sigma Delta Chi (1909): 35 E. Wacker Dr., Chicago, Ill. 60601. 35,000; Russell E. Hurst, Executive Officer.

Judaism, American Council for (1943): 307 Fifth Ave., New York, N.Y. 10016. 10,000; Clarence L. Coleman, Jr., President.

Junior Achievement (1919): 550 Summer St., Stamford, Conn. 06901. 3,400,000; "graduates"; Glenn V. Gardinier, National Public Relations Director.

Junior Leagues, Association of (1921): 825 Third Ave., New York, N.Y. 10022. 130,000.

Kennel Club, American (1884): 51 Madison Ave., New York, N.Y. 10010. 412 member clubs; Mark T. Mooty, Secretary.

Kiwanis International (1915): 101 E. Erie, Chicago, Ill. 60611. 300,000; R. P. Merridew, International Secretary.

Knights of Columbus (1882): One Columbus Plaza, New Haven, Conn. 06507. 1,327,209; Virgil Dechant, Supreme Knight.

Knights of Pythias, Supreme Lodge (1864): 47 N. Grant St., Stockton, Calif. 95202. 130,645; Jule O. Pritchard, Supreme Secretary.

Knights Templar, Grand Encampment of (1816): 14 E. Jackson Blvd., Suite 1700, Chicago, Ill. 60604. 360,000; Paul C. Rodenhauser, Grand Recorder.

La Leche League International (1956): 9616 Minneapolis Ave., Franklin Park, Ill. 60131. 53,543; Betty Wagner, Chief Executive Officer.

Library Association, American (1876): 50 E. Huron St., Chicago, Ill. 60611. 35,524; Robert Wedgeworth, Executive Director.

Life Underwriters, National Association of (1890): 1922 F St., N.W., Washington, D.C. 20006. Jack E. Bobo, Executive Vice President.

Lions Clubs, The International Association of (1917): 300 22nd St., Oak Brook, Ill. 60570. 1,280,000; Roy Schaetzel, Executive Administrator.

Management Associations, American (1923): 135 W. 50th St., New York, N.Y. 10020. 75,000; Joseph P. Keyes, Vice President Public Relations.

Manufacturers, National Association of (1895): 1776 F St., N.W., Washington, D.C. 20006. 13,000; Edmund W. Haskins, Secretary.

March of Dimes Birth Defects Foundation (1938): 1275 Mamaroneck Ave., White Plains, N.Y. 10605. 850 chapters; Charles L. Massey, President.

Marine Corps League (1923): 933 N. Kenmore St., Arlington, Va. 22201. 20,000; F. B. Starr, National Adjutant Paymaster.

Masons, Ancient and Accepted Scottish Rite, Northern Masonic Jurisdiction, Supreme Council 33° (1867): 33 Marrett Rd., Lexington, Mass. 02173. 505,539; Laurence E. Eaton, Grand Secretary General.

Masons, Ancient and Accepted Scottish Rite, Southern Jurisdiction, Supreme Council (1801): 1733 16th St., N.W., Washington, D.C. 20009. 658,600; C. Fred Kleinknecht, Grand Secretary General.

Masons, Royal Arch, International General Grand Chapter (1797): Box 5320, Lexington, Ky. 40505. 460,000; Charles K.A. McGaughey, General Grand Secretary.

Mathematical Society, American (1888): 201 Charles St., Providence, R.I. 02940. 19,468; William J. LeVeque, Executive Director.

Mayflower Descendants, General Society of (1897): 4 Winslow St., P.O. Box 297, Plymouth, Mass. 02360. 17,500; Mrs. Lester A. Hall, Historian General.

Mechanical Engineers, American Society of (1880): 345 E. 47th St., New York, N.Y. 10017. 101,162; Rogers Finch, Executive Director.

Medical Association, American (1847): 535 N. Dearborn St., Chicago, Ill. 60610.

Mental Health Association, National (1909): 1800 N. Kent St., Arlington, Va. 22209. 1,000,000; Lynn Schultz-Writsel, Acting Director, Public Information and Education.

Mining, Metallurgical and Petroleum Engineers, American Institute of (1871): 345 E. 47th St., New York, N.Y. 10017. 73,001; Joe B. Alford, Executive Director.

Modern Language Association of America (1883): 62 Fifth Avenue., New York, N.Y. 10011. 30,000.

Modern Woodmen of America (1883): Mississippi River at 17th St., Rock Island, Ill. 61201. 500,000; W.B. Foster, President.

Moose, Loyal Order of (1888): Mooseheart, Ill. 60539. 1,719,273; Carl A. Weis, Supreme Secretary.

Motion Picture Arts & Sciences, Academy of (1927): 8949 Wilshire Blvd., Beverly Hills, Calif. 90211. James M. Roberts, Executive Director.

Multiple Sclerosis Society, National (1946): 205 E. 42nd St., New York, N.Y. 10017. Sylvia Lawry, Executive Director.

Muscular Dystrophy Association (1950): 810 Seventh Ave., New York, N.Y. 10019. 1,800,000 volunteers. Jerry Lewis, National Chairman.

Museums, American Association of (1906): 1055 Thomas Jefferson St., N.W., Washington, D.C. 20007. 7,100; Lawrence Reger, Director.

Musicians, American Federation of (1896): 1500 Broadway, New York, N.Y. 10036. 300,000; Victor W. Fuentealba, President.

National Association for the Advancement of Colored People (1909): 1790 Broadway, New York, N.Y. 10019. 450,000; Benjamin L. Hooks, Executive Director.

National Grange, The (1867): 1616 H St., N.W., Washington, D.C. 20006. 460,000; Edward Andersen, Master.

National PTA (National Congress of Parents and Teachers) (1897): 700 N. Rush St., Chicago, Ill. 60611. 6,170,027; Becky Schergens, Executive Director.

Negro College Fund, Inc., United (1944): 500 E. 62nd St., New York, N.Y. 10021. 41 colleges; Christopher F. Edley, Executive Director.

Newspaper Publishers Association, American (1887): The Newspaper Center, P.O. Box 17407, Dulles International Airport, Washington, D.C. 20041. 1,375; Jerry W. Friedheim, Executive Vice President and General Manager.

Nurses' Association, American (1896): 2420 Pershing Rd., Kansas City, Mo. 64108. 180,000.

Odd Fellows, Independent Order of (1819): 16 W. Chase St., Baltimore, Md. 21201. 1,200,000; Edward T. Rogers, Sovereign Grand Secretary.

Olympic Committee, United States (1921): 1750 Boulder St., Colorado Springs, Colo. 80909. Bob Paul, Director of Communications.

Organization of American States, General Secretariat (1890): 17th Street and Constitution Avenue, N.W., Washington, D.C. 20006. 28 member nations.

ORT Federation, American (1922): 817 Broadway, New York, N.Y. 10003. 154,000; Paul Bernick, Executive Director.

Overeaters Anonymous (1960): 2190 190th St., Torrance, Calif. 90504. 85,000.

Parents Without Partners, Inc. (1957): 7910 Woodmont Ave., N.W., Washington, D.C. 20852. 190,000; Virginia L. Martin, Executive Director.

Parks and Conservation Association, National (1919): 1701 18th St., N.W., Washington, D.C. 20009. 35,000; Gilbert F. Stucker, Chairman.

Philatelic Society, American (1886): P.O. Box 800, State College, Pa. 16801. 50,000; James DeVoss, Executive Director.

Philosophical Society, American (1743): 104 S. 5th St., Philadelphia, Pa. 19106. 600; W. J. Bell, Jr., Executive Officer.

Photographic Society of America (1933): 2005 Walnut St., Philadelphia, Pa. 19103. 18,600; Harold J. Vermes, Executive Director.

Physical Society, American (1899): 335 E. 45th St., New York, N.Y. 10017. 30,000; W. W. Havens, Jr., Executive Secretary.

Physics, American Institute of (1931): 335 E. 45th St., New York, N.Y. 10017. 65,000; H. William Koch, Director.

Planned Parenthood Federation of America (1916): 810 Seventh Ave., New York, N.Y. 10019. 188 affiliates.

Political Science, Academy of (1880): 619 W. 114th St., Suite 500, New York, N.Y. 10025. 10,500; Robert H. Connery, President.

Professional Engineers, National Society of (1934): 2029 K St., N.W., Washington, D.C. 20006. 80,000; Donald G. Weinert, Executive Director.

Psychiatric Association (1844): 1700 18th St., N.W., Washington, D.C. 20009. 25,000; Donald Langsley, M.D., President.

Psychological Association, American (1892): 1200 17th St., N.W., Washington, D.C. 20036. 50,000; Michael S. Pallak, Executive Officer.

Public Health Association, American (1872): 1015 15th St., N.W., Washington, D.C. 20005. 29,648; William H. McBeath, M.D., Executive Director.

Puppeteers of America (1937): 2311 Connecticut Ave., Washington, D.C. 20008. 2,500; Nancy L. Staub, Executive Director.

Red Cross, American (1881): 17th and D Sts., N.W., Washington, D.C. 20006. George M. Elsey, President.

Rehabilitation Association, National (1925): 1522 K St., N.W., Washington, D.C. 20005. 23,000; David L. Mills, Executive Director.

Reserve Officers Association of the United States (1922): 1 Constitution Ave., N.E., Washington, D.C. 20002. 118,000; J. Milnor Roberts, Executive Director.

Retarded Citizens, Association for (1950): 2501 Avenue J, Arlington, Tex. 76011. 1,900 units; Philip Roos, Executive Director.

Retired Federal Employees, National Association of (1921): 1533 New Hampshire Ave., N.W., Washington, D.C. 20036. 313,000; Michael C. Nave, President.

Retired Persons, American Association of (1958): 1909 K St., N.W., Washington, D.C. 20049. 12,000,000; Cyril F. Brickfield, Executive Director.

Retired Teachers Association, National (1947): 1909 K St., N.W., Washington, D.C. 20049. 534,000; Cyril F. Brickfield, Executive Director.

Rifle Association of America, National (1871): 1600 Rhode Island Ave., N.W., Washington, D.C. 20036. 1,750,000; Harlon B. Carter, Executive Vice President.

Right to Life, National Committee (1973): 529 14th St., N.W., Washington, D.C. 20045. Iris Ruegg, Office Manager.

Rotary International (1905): 1600 Ridge Ave., Evanston, Ill. 60201. 853,000; Herbert A. Pigman, General Secretary.

Safety Council, National (1913): 444 N. Michigan Ave., Chicago, Ill. 60611. Charles C. Vance, Director of Public Relations.

Salvation Army, The (1865): 120 W. 14th St., New York, N.Y. 10011. 414,035; Col. G.E. Murray, National Chief Secretary.

Save-the-Redwoods League (1918): 114 Sansome St., San Francisco, Calif. 94104. 55,000; John B. Dewitt, Executive Director.

Science, American Association for the Advancement of (1848): 1515 Massachusetts Ave., N.W., Washington, D.C. 20005. 130,000; Carol L. Rogers, Public Information.

Screen Actors Guild (1933): 7750 Sunset Blvd., Hollywood, Calif. 90046. 42,000; Kim Fellner, Information Director.

Seeing Eye (1929): Morristown, N.J. 07960. 25,000; Stuart Grout, Executive Vice President.

Shrine of North America (Shriners Hospitals) (1872): Box 25356, Tampa, Fla. 33623. 938,404; Charles G. Cumpstone, Jr., Executive Secretary of Fraternal Affairs.

Sierra Club (1892): 530 Bush St., San Francisco, Calif. 94108. 180,000; Michael McCloskey, Executive Director.

Small Business Association, National (1937): 1604 K St., N.W., Washington, D.C. 20006. 40,000; Herbert Liebenson, President.

Social Welfare, National Conference on (1873): 1730 M St., N.W., Washington, D.C. 20036. 8,500; John E. Hansan, Executive Director.

Social Workers, National Association of (1955):

1425 H St., N.W., Washington, D.C. 20005. 85,000; Chauncey A. Alexander, Executive Director.

Sons of Italy in America, Order (1905): 1520 Locust St., Philadelphia, Pa. 19102. 2,300 lodges; Frank J. Montemuro, National President.

Sons of the American Revolution, National Society of the (1889): 1000 S. 4th St., Louisville, Ky. 40203. 23,000; Col. Ralph H. Goodell, Jr., Executive Secretary.

Soroptimist International of the Americas (1921): 1616 Walnut St., Philadelphia, Pa. 19103. 34,000; Mary Helen Madden, Executive Director.

Southern Christian Leadership Conference (1957): 334 Auburn Ave., N.E., Atlanta, Ga. 30303. 1,000,000; 350 chapters, 260 affiliated organizations; Dr. Joseph E. Lowery, President.

Speech•Language•Hearing Association, American (1925): 10801 Rockville Pike, Rockville, Md. 20852. 35,000; Frederick T. Spahr, Executive Secretary.

Sports Car Club of America (1944): 6750 S. Emporia, Englewood, Colo. 80112. 23,000; Mac DeMere, National Press Officer.

Student Association, United States (1947): 1220 G St., S.E., Washington, D.C. 20003. Frank X. Viggiano, Executive Director.

Surgeons, American College of (1913): 55 E. Erie, St., Chicago, Ill. 60611. 42,000; C. Rollins Hanlon, Director.

Teachers, American Federation of (1916): 11 Dupont Circle, N.W., Washington, D.C. 20036. 550,000; Albert Shanker, President.

Travel Agents, American Society of (ASTA) (1931): 711 Fifth Ave., New York, N.Y. 10022. 16,000; Curtis L. Nabors, Executive Vice President.

Travelers Aid Society of New York (1905): 204 E. 39th St., New York, N.Y. 10016. Elizabeth P. Anderson, General Director.

University Women, American Association of (1882): 2401 Virginia Ave., N.W., Washington, D.C. 20037. 190,000; Quincalee Brown, Executive Director.

Urban League, National (1910): 500 E. 62nd St., New York, N.Y. 10021. 116; James D. Williams, Director of Communications.

Veterans Committee, American (AVC) (1944): 1346 Connecticut Ave., N.W., Suite 930, Washington, D.C. 20036. 25,000; June A. Willenz, Executive Director.

Veterans of Foreign Wars of the U.S. (1899): V.F.W. Bldg., 34th and Broadway, Kansas City, Mo. 64111. V.F.W. and Auxiliary, 2,590,000; Julian Dickenson, Adjutant General.

Veterinary Medical Association, American (1863): 930 N. Meacham Rd., Schaumburg, Ill. 60196. 32,000; Dr. D. A. Price, Executive Vice President.

Wildlife Federation, National (1936): 1412 16th St., N.W., Washington, D.C. 20036. 4,600,000; Thomas L. Kimball, Executive Vice President.

Woman's Christian Temperance Union, National (1874): 1730 Chicago Ave., Evanston, Ill. 60201. 250,000; Edith K. Stanley, President.

Women Voters of the U.S., League of (1920): 1730 M St., N.W., Washington, D.C. 20036. 117,000; Harriet Hentges, Executive Director.

Women's American ORT (1927): 1250 Broadway, New York, N.Y. 10001. 140,000; Nathan Gould, National Executive Director.

Women's Clubs, General Federation of (1890): 1734 N St., N.W., Washington, D.C. 20036. 600,000; Mildred Baptista, Executive Director.

Young Men's Christian Associations, National Council of (1844): 291 Broadway, New York, N.Y. 10007. 10,000,000; Solon B. Cousins, Executive Director.

Young Women's Christian Association of the U.S.A. (1858 in U.S.A., 1855 in England): 600 Lexington Ave., New York, N.Y. 10022. 2,471,000; Jane Pinkerton, Director of Communications.

Youth Hostels, American (1934): National Campus, Delaplane, Va. 22025. 90,000.

Zionist Organization of America (1897): ZOA House, 4 E. 34th St., New York, N.Y. 10016. 120,000; Paul I. Flacks, National Executive Director.

Getting Uncle Sam to Enforce your Civil Rights

Do you know what to do if you believe you have been discriminated against on the basis of race, color, religion, sex, national origin, age, or handicap? One option available to you is to file a complaint with the federal government.

Single copies of the 44-page booklet, "Getting Uncle Sam to Enforce your Civil Rights," are available free from the Publications Division, U.S. Commission on Civil Rights, Washington, D.C. 20425.

This handy booklet can help you to decide whether to file your complaint at the federal level, or whether to seek help from your state or local government.

Selected CB 10-Codes

10–1	Receiving poorly	10–21	Call by phone	10–51	Wrecker needed at . . .
10–2	Receiving well	10–23	Stand by	10–52	Ambulance needed at . . .
10–3	Stop transmitting	10–25	Can you contact?	10–53	Road blocked
10–4	OK, message received	10–26	Disregard last information	10–59	Convoy or escort
10–5	Relay message	10–27	I am moving to channel . . .	10–62	Unable to copy, use phone
10–6	Stand by	10–28	Identify your station	10–66	Message cancellation
10–7	Out of service	10–29	I am leaving this location	10–70	Fire at . . .
10–8	In service	10–30	Does not conform to FCC rules	10–73	Speed Trap at . . .
10–9	Repeat message	10–32	Radio check	10–75	You are causing interference
10–10	Transmission completed,	10–33	Emergency traffic at this station	10–77	ETA (estimated time of arrival
	standing by	10–34	Trouble here, help needed	10–82	Reserve lodging
10–11	Speak more slowly	10–36	Correct time is . . .	10–91	Talk closer to mike
10–12	Visitors present	10–39	Your message delivered	10–92	Have your transmitter checked
10–13	Report road conditions, weather	10–44	I have a message for . . .	10–93	Check my frequency
10–17	Urgent business	10–45	All units please report	10–94	Give me a long count
10–20	Location . . .	10–46	Assist motorist	10–200	Police needed at . . .
		10–50	Accident at . . .		

Domestic Mail Service

First Class

First-class mail consists of letters and written and sealed matter. The rate is 15¢ for the first oz; 13¢ for each additional oz, or fraction of an oz, up to 12 oz. Pieces over 12 oz are subject to priority-mail (heavy pieces) rates. Single postcards, 10¢; double postcards, 20¢ (10¢ for each half). The post office sells prestamped single and double postal cards. Consult your postmaster for information on business-reply mail and presort rates.

The weight limit for first-class mail is 70 lb, and the maximum size is 100 in. in combined length and girth.

Weight	Rates
First oz	$ .15
Over 1 oz, but not over 2	.28
Over 2 oz, but not over 3	.41
Over 3 oz, but not over 4	.54
Over 4 oz, but not over 5	.67
Over 5 oz, but not over 6	.80
Over 6 oz, but not over 7	.93
Over 7 oz, but not over 8	1.06
Over 8 oz, but not over 9	1.19
Over 9 oz, but not over 10	1.32
Over 10 oz, but not over 11	1.45
Over 11 oz, but not over 12	1.58
Over 12 oz, *see* Priority Mail	

Priority Mail (over 12 oz to 70 lb)

The zone rate applies to mailable matter over 12 oz of any class carried by air. Such matter shall not exceed 100 in. in length and girth combined. Your local post office will supply free official zone tables appropriate to your location.

Airmail

First-class and priority mail receive airmail service.

Second Class

Second-class mail is used primarily by newspapers, magazines, and other periodicals with second-class mail privileges. Copies mailed by the public are 10¢ for the first 2 oz, 6¢ for each additional oz or fraction, or the applicable fourth-class rate, whichever is lower.

Third Class (under 16 oz)

Third-class mail is used for circulars, books, printed matter, and all other mailable matter not in first or second class. There are two rate structures for this class, a single-piece and a bulk rate.

Many community organizations, as well as businesses, find it economical to use this service. Because of the number of categories of third-class mail, you should consult your postmaster for the one best suited to your needs.

Third-Class, Single-Piece Rates

Weight	Rates	Weight	Rates
0 to 2 oz	20¢	Over 8 oz to 10 oz	$ .79
Over 2 oz to 4 oz	40¢	Over 10 oz to 12 oz	.92
Over 4 oz to 6 oz	53¢	Over 12 oz to 14 oz[1]	1.05
Over 6 oz to 8 oz	66¢	Over 14 oz to 15.99 oz	1.18

1. Fourth-class zone rate is charged if it is lower.

Fourth Class (Parcel Post—16 oz and over)

Fourth-class mail is used for merchandise, books, printed matter, and all other mailable matter not in first, second, or third class. Special fourth-class rates apply to books, library books, publications or records for the blind, and certain controlled-circulation publications.

Packages should be taken to your local post office, where the postage will be determined according to the weight of the package and the distance it is being sent. Information on weight and size limits for fourth-class mail may be obtained there.

Special Fourth-Class Rate

The special fourth-class rate is restricted specifically to books; 16-mm or narrower width films and catalogs of such films (except when mailed to or from commercial theaters); printed music, printed objective-test materials, sound recordings, and playscripts and manuscripts for books, periodicals, and music; printed educational reference charts permanently processed for preservation; looseleaf pages, and binders therefor, consisting of medical information for distribution to doctors, hospitals, medical schools, and medical students. The rate is 59¢ for the first lb or fraction, plus 22¢ for each additional lb or fraction through 7 lb, 13¢ for each additional lb or fraction over 7 lb.

Consult your postmaster for information on the Library Rate which allows certain restricted educational materials to be sent at a lower rate if mailed by or to certain educational institutions.

Special Services

Registered Mail. When you use registered mail service, you are buying security—the safest way to send valuables. The full value of your mailing must be declared when mailed. You receive a receipt and the movement of your mail is controlled throughout the postal system. For an additional fee, a return receipt showing to whom, when, and where delivered may be obtained.

Value	Fees (in addition to postage)	
	For articles not covered by commercial or other insurance	For articles also covered by commercial or other insurance
0.00 to $ 100	$ 3.00	$ 3.00
100.01 to 200	3.30	3.30
200.01 to 400	3.70	3.70
400.01 to 600	4.10	4.10
600.01 to 800	4.50	4.50
800.01 to 1,000	4.90	4.90
1,000.01 to 2,000	5.30	$4.90 plus handling charge of 35¢ per $1,000 or fraction over first $1,000
2,000.01 to 3,000	5.70	
3,000.01 to 4,000	6.10	
4,000.01 to 5,000	6.50	
5,000.01 to 6,000	6.90	
6,000.01 to 7,000	7.30	
7,000.01 to 8,000	7.70	
8,000.01 to 9,000	8.10	
9,000.01 to 10,000[1]	8.50	

1. Consult your postmaster for registry fees for values over $10,000.

Certified Mail. Certified mail service provides for a receipt to the sender and a record of delivery at the post office of address. No record is kept at the post office where mailed. It is handled in the ordinary mails and no insurance coverage is provided.

Any mail prepaid at the first-class rate having no intrinsic value will be accepted as certified mail. Return-receipt service, requested at the time of mailing only, and special-delivery service are available.

Fee in addition to postage, 80¢; restricted delivery (additional fee), 80¢.

Return Receipts. Requested at time of mailing:

Showing to whom and date delivered	$ .45
Showing to whom, date, and address where delivered	.55
Requested after mailing:	
Showing to whom and date delivered	2.10

C.O.D. Mail. Consult your postmaster for fees and conditions of mailing.

Insured Mail. Fees, in addition to postage, for coverage against loss or damage:

Liability	Fees
$ .01 to $15	$ .50
$ 15.01 to $50	.85
$ 50.01 to $100	1.10
$100.01 to $150	1.40
$150.01 to $200	1.75
$200.01 to $300	2.25
$300.01 to $400[1]	2.75

1. Liability for insured mail is limited to $400.

Special Delivery. The payment of the special-delivery fee entitles mail to the most expeditious transportation and delivery. The fee is in addition to the regular postage.

Class of mail	Weight/Fees		
	Not more than 2 lb	More than 2 lb but not more than 10 lb	More than 10 lb
First-class and priority mail	$2.00	$2.25	$2.85
All other classes	2.25	2.85	3.25

Special Handling. Payment of the special-handling fee entitles third- and fourth-class matter to the most expeditious handling and transportation, but not special delivery. The fee is in addition to the regular postage.

Weight	Fees
Not more than 10 lb	$ .70
More than 10 lb	1.25

Money Orders. Money orders are used for the safe transmission of money.

Amount of money order	Fees
$ .01 to $10	$ .55
$10.01 to $50	.80
$50.01 to $400	1.10

Minimum Mail Sizes

All mail must be at least 0.007 in. thick and mail that is 1/4 in. or less in thickness must be at least 3 1/2 in. in height, at least 5 in. long, and rectangular in shape.

As of July 15, 1979, there is a surcharge of 7¢ applied to first-class mail weighing one ounce or less and single-piece third-class mail weighing two ounces or less that is more than 6 1/8 inches high or 11 1/2 inches long or 1/4 inch thick. Also subject to the surcharge are pieces with a length less than 1.3 times the height or more than 2.5 times the height.

Adhesive Stamps Available

Purpose	Form	Denomination and prices
Ordinary postage	Single or sheet	1, 2, 3, 4, 5, 9, 10, 11, 12, 13, 14, 15, 16, 18, 20, 21, 24, 25, 29, 30, 40, and 50¢; $1 and $5.
	Book	8–15¢ = $1.20; 24–15¢ = $3.60
	Coils of 100[1]	13 and 15¢
	Coils of 500	1, 2, 3, 5, 9, 10, 13, 15, and 16¢ and $1
	Coils of 3,000	1, 2, 3, 5, 9, 10, 13, 15, 16, and 25¢
International airmail postage	Single or sheet	21, 25, 26, and 31¢

1. Dispenser to hold coil of 100 stamps may be purchased for 5¢.

International Mail Service

Canada and Mexico—Surface Rates

Weight	Letter mail	Printed matter and small packets
1 oz	$ .15	—
2 oz	.28	$ .20
3 oz	.41	—
4 oz	.54	.40
5 oz	.67	—
6 oz	.80	.53
7 oz	.93	—
8 oz	1.06	.66
9 oz	1.19	—
10 oz	1.32	.79
11 oz	1.45	—
12 oz	1.58	.92
14 oz	—	1.05
16 oz	2.25	1.18
Postcards	.10	—

Consult your postmaster for rates for heavier items.

International Airmail

Destination	Letters and letter packages[1]	Post-cards	Air letter sheets[2]
Central America Colombia, Venezuela, Caribbean Islands, Bahamas, Bermuda, St. Pierre and Miquelon	25¢ per half oz through 2 oz 21¢ each additional half oz or fraction	21¢	22¢
All other countries	31¢ per half oz through 2 oz 26¢ each additional half oz or fraction	21¢	22¢

1. Weight limit, 4 lb. 2. No enclosures permitted.

For Canada and Mexico, *see* Surface Rates.

International Money Order Fees

Amount of money order	Fees
$ .01 to $10	$ .90
$10.01 to $50	1.10
$50.01 to $300	1.40

Countries Other Than Canada and Mexico—Surface Rates

Ounces	Letter mail	Printed matter	Small packets
1	$ .20	$ .20	$ .20
2	.36	.20	.20
4	.48	.40	.40
8	.96	.66	.66
16	1.84	1.05	1.05
32	3.20	1.26	1.26
64	5.20	1.68	—
Each additional 32 oz	—	0.84	—

International Surface Parcel Post

Weight through lb	Canada, Mexico, Central America, Caribbean Islands, Bahamas, Bermuda, St. Pierre and Miquelon	All other countries
2	$2.19	$2.34
3	2.71	2.93
4	3.23	3.52
5	3.75	4.11
6	4.27	4.70
7	4.79	5.29
8	5.31	5.88
9	5.83	6.47
10	6.35	7.06
	52¢ each additional lb or fraction	59¢ each additional lb or fraction

Consult your postmaster for weight and size limits.

For other international services and rates consult your local postmaster.

United Nations Stamps

United Nations stamps are issued in three different currencies, namely, U.S. dollars, Swiss francs, and Austrian schillings. Stamps in all three currencies are available at face value at each of the U.N. Postal Administration offices in New York, Geneva, and Vienna. They may be purchased over the counter, by mail, or by opening a Customer Deposit Account.

Mail orders for mint (unused) stamps and postal stationery may be sent to the U.N. Postal Administration in New York, Geneva, and Vienna. A special order form, listing all available mint issues, is available on request. Write to: United Nations Postal Administration, P.O. Box 5900, Grand Central Station, New York, N.Y. 10017. All mint stamps and postal stationery are sold by the U.N. Postal Administration at face value.

Customers who purchase their stamps by mail always receive advance information about U.N. stamps with their returned orders.

Authorized 2-Letter State Abbreviations

When the Post Office instituted the ZIP Code for mail in 1963, it also drew up a list of two-letter abbreviations for the states which would gradually replace the traditional ones in use. Following is the official list, including the District of Columbia, Guam, Puerto Rico, and the Virgin Islands (note that only capital letters are used):

Alabama	AL	Kentucky	KY	Ohio	OH
Alaska	AK	Louisiana	LA	Oklahoma	OK
Arizona	AZ	Maine	ME	Oregon	OR
Arkansas	AR	Maryland	MD	Pennsylvania	PA
California	CA	Massachusetts	MA	Puerto Rico	PR
Colorado	CO	Michigan	MI	Rhode Island	RI
Connecticut	CT	Minnesota	MN	South Carolina	SC
Delaware	DE	Mississippi	MS	South Dakota	SD
Dist. of Columbia	DC	Missouri	MO	Tennessee	TN
Florida	FL	Montana	MT	Texas	TX
Georgia	GA	Nebraska	NE	Utah	UT
Guam	GU	Nevada	NV	Vermont	VT
Hawaii	HI	New Hampshire	NH	Virginia	VA
Idaho	ID	New Jersey	NJ	Virgin Islands	VI
Illinois	IL	New Mexico	NM	Washington	WA
Indiana	IN	New York	NY	West Virginia	WV
Iowa	IA	North Carolina	NC	Wisconsin	WI
Kansas	KS	North Dakota	ND	Wyoming	WY

The Mail Order Merchandise Rule

The mail order rule adopted by the Federal Trade Commission in October 1975 provides that when you order by mail:

You must receive the merchandise when the seller says you will.

If you are not promised delivery within a certain time period, the seller must ship the merchandise to you no later than 30 days after your order comes in.

If you don't receive it shortly after that 30-day period, you can cancel your order and get your money back.

How the Rule Works

The seller must notify you if the promised delivery date (or the 30-day limit) cannot be met. The seller must also tell you what the new shipping date will be and give you the option to cancel the order and receive a full refund or agree to the new shipping date. The seller must also give you a free way to send back your answer, such as a stamped envelope or a postage-paid postcard. *If you don't answer, it means that you agree to the shipping delay.*

The seller must tell you if the shipping delay is going to be more than 30 days. You then can agree to the delay or, if you do not agree, the seller must return your money by the end of the first 30 days of the delay.

If you cancel a prepaid order, the seller must mail you the refund within seven business days. Where there is a credit sale, the seller must adjust your account within one billing cycle.

It would be impossible, however, for one rule to apply uniformly to such a varied field as mail order merchandising. For example, the rule does not apply to mail order photo finishing, magazine subscriptions, and other serial deliveries (except for the initial shipment); to mail order seeds and growing plants; to COD orders; or to credit orders where the buyer's account is not charged prior to shipment of the merchandise.

Consider Unordered Mail Merchandise a Gift

Have you ever received something in the mail you did not order? If so, you may consider it a gift and keep it without paying for it.

Only two kinds of merchandise can be sent legally through the mails without a consumer's prior consent: (1) free samples, clearly marked as such, and (2) merchandise mailed by a charitable organization for contributions. Even though unordered merchandise from charitable organizations can legally be sent to your house, the same rule applies: you don't have to pay for it.

It's illegal for the sender to pressure you to return unordered merchandise or to send you a bill for it.

The Pony Express

Established in April 1860, the Pony Express provided fast mail service between St. Joseph, Mo., the westernmost extent of the U.S. telegraph line, and Sacramento, Calif. The freighting and stagecoach firm of Russell, Majors & Waddell hired expert riders to ride fleet horses in relays over the 1,838-mile distance. Along the route, there were 157 stations, spaced about 12 miles apart, at which the riders changed horses. Each man changed horses about six times before being replaced by another. The route, which was covered in about ten days, passed through hostile Indian territory, and, during the Paiute War in the summer of 1860, Indians burned a number of stations and killed the occupants. October 24, 1861, the day the first telegram to San Francisco was transmitted, marked the downfall of the Pony Express. No longer the crucial link to the West, the Pony Express was discontinued. Though a financial failure, it remains one of the most colorful episodes of American history.

Famous Firsts in Aviation

1782 **First balloon flight.** Jacques and Joseph Montgolfier of Annonay, France, sent up a small smoke-filled balloon about mid-November.

1783 **First hydrogen-filled balloon flight.** Jacques A. C. Charles, Paris physicist, supervised construction by A. J. and M. N. Robert of a 13-ft diameter balloon that was filled with hydrogen. It got up to about 3,000 ft and traveled about 16 mi. in a 45-min flight (Aug. 27).

First human balloon flights. A Frenchman, Jean Pilâtre de Rozier, made the first captive-balloon ascension (Oct. 15). With the Marquis d'Arlandes, Pilâtre de Rozier made the first free flight, reaching a peak altitude of about 500 ft, and traveling about 5½ mi. in 20 min (Nov. 21).

1784 **First powered balloon.** Gen. Jean Baptiste Marie Meusnier developed the first propeller-driven and elliptically-shaped balloon—the crew cranking three propellers on a common shaft to give the craft a speed of about 3 mph.

First woman to fly. Mme. Thible, a French opera singer (June 4).

1793 **First balloon flight in America.** Jean Pierre Blanchard, a French pilot, made it from Philadelphia to near Woodbury, Gloucester County, N.J., in a little over 45 min (Jan. 9).

1794 **First military use of the balloon.** Jean Marie Coutelle, using a balloon built for the French Army, made two 4-hr observation ascents. The military purpose of the ascents seems to have been to damage the enemy's morale.

1797 **First parachute jump.** André-Jacques Garnerin dropped from about 6,500 ft over Monceau Park in Paris in a 23-ft diameter parachute made of white canvas with a basket attached (Oct. 22).

1843 **First air transport company.** In London, William S. Henson and John Stringfellow filed articles of incorporation for the Aerial Transit Company (March 24). It failed

1852 **First dirigible.** Henri Giffard, a French engineer, flew in a controllable (more or less) steam-engine powered balloon, 144 ft long and 39 ft in diameter, inflated with 88,000 cu ft of coal gas. It reached 6.7 mph on a flight from Paris to Trappe (Sept. 24).

1860 **First aerial photographers.** Samuel Archer King and William Black made two photos of Boston, still in existence.

1872 **First gas-engine powered dirigible.** Paul Haenlein, a German engineer, flew in a semi-rigid-frame dirigible, powered by a 4-cylinder internal-combustion engine running on coal gas drawn from the supporting bag.

1873 **First transatlantic attempt.** *The New York Daily Graphic* sponsored the attempt with a 400,000 cu ft balloon carrying a lifeboat. A rip in the bag during inflation brought collapse of the balloon and the project.

1897 **First successful metal dirigible.** An all-metal dirigible, designed by David Schwarz, a Hungarian, took off from Berlin's Tempelhof Field and, powered by a 16-hp Daimler engine, got several miles before leaking gas caused it to crash (Nov. 13).

1900 **First Zeppelin flight.** Germany's Count Ferdinand von Zeppelin flew the first of his long series of rigid-frame airships. It attained a speed of 18 mi. per h and got 3½ mi. before its steering gear failed (July 2).

1903 **First successful heavier-than-air machine flight.** Aviation was really born on the sand dunes at Kitty Hawk, N.C., when Orville Wright crawled to his prone position between the wings of the biplane he and his brother Wilbur had built, opened the throttle of their homemade 12-hp engine and took to the air. He covered 120 ft in 12 sec. Later that day, in one of four flights, Wilbur stayed up 59 sec and covered 852 ft (Dec. 17).

1904 **First airplane maneuvers.** Orville Wright made the first turn with an airplane (Sept. 15); 5 days later his brother Wilbur made the first complete circle.

1905 **First airplane flight over half an hour.** Orville Wright kept his craft up 33 min 17 sec (Oct. 4).

1906 **First European airplane flight.** Alberto Santos-Dumont, a Brazilian, flew a heavier-than-air machine at Bagatelle Field, Paris (Sept. 13).

1908 **First airplane fatality.** Lt. Thomas E. Selfridge, U.S. Army Signal Corps, was in a group of officers evaluating the Wright plane at Fort Myer, Va. He was up about 75 ft with Orville Wright when the propeller hit a bracing wire and was broken, throwing the plane out of control, killing Selfridge and seriously injuring Wright (Sept. 17).

1910 **First licensed woman pilot.** Baroness Raymonde de la Roche of France, who learned to fly in 1909, received ticket No. 36 on March 8.

First flight from shipboard. Lt. Eugene Ely, USN, took a Curtiss plane off from the deck of cruiser *Birmingham* at Hampton Roads, Va., and flew to Norfolk (Nov. 14). The following January, he reversed the process, flying from Camp Selfridge to the deck of the armored cruiser *Pennsylvania* in San Francisco Bay (Jan. 18).

1911 **First U.S. woman pilot.** Harriet Quimby, a magazine writer, who got ticket No. 37.

1913 **First multi-engined aircraft.** Built and flown by Igor Ivan Sikorsky while still in his native Russia.

1914 **First aerial combat.** In August, Allied and German pilots and observers started shooting at each other with pistols and rifles—with negligible results.

1915 **First air raids on England.** German Zeppelins started dropping bombs on four English communities (Jan. 19).

1918 **First U.S. air squadron.** The U.S. Army Air Corps made its first independent raids over enemy lines, in DH-4 planes (British-designed) powered with 400-hp American-designed Liberty engines (April 8).

First regular airmail service. Operated for the Post Office Department by the Army, the first regular service was inaugurated with one round trip a day (except Sunday) between Washington, D.C., and New York City (May 15).

1919 **First transatlantic flight.** The NC-4, one of four Curtiss flying boats commanded by Lt. Comdr. Albert C. Read, reached Lisbon, Portugal, (May 27) after hops from Trepassy Bay, Newfoundland, to Horta, Azores (May 16–17), to Ponta Delgada (May 20). The Liberty-powered craft was piloted by Walter Hinton.

First nonstop transatlantic flight. Capt. John Alcock and Lt. Arthur Whitten Brown, British World War I flyers, made the 1,900 mi. from St. John's, Newfoundland, to Clifden, Ireland, in 16 h 12 min in a Vickers-Vimy bomber with two 350-hp Rolls-Royce engines (June 15–16).

First lighter-than-air transatlantic flight. The British dirigible R-34, commanded by Maj. George H. Scott, left Firth of Forth, Scotland, (July 2) and touched down at Mineola, L.I., 108 h later. The eastbound trip was made in 75 h (completed July 13).

First scheduled passenger service (using airplanes). Aircraft Travel and Transport inaugurated London-Paris service (Aug. 25). Later the company started the first trans-channel mail service on the same route (Nov. 10).

1921 **First naval vessel sunk by aircraft.** Two battleships being scrapped by treaty were sunk by bombs dropped from Army planes in demonstration put on by Brig. Gen. William S. Mitchell (July 21).

First helium balloon. The C-7, non-rigid Navy dirigible was first to use non-inflammable helium as lifting gas, making a flight from Hampton Roads, Va., to Washington, D.C. (Dec. 1).

1922 **First member of Caterpillar Club.** Lt. (later Maj. Gen.) Harold Harris bailed out of a crippled plane he was testing at McCook Field, Dayton, Ohio (Oct. 20), and became the first man to join the Caterpillar Club—those whose lives have been saved by parachute.

1923 **First nonstop transcontinental flight.** Lts. John A. Macready and Oakley Kelly flew a single-engine Fokker T-2 nonstop from New York to San Diego, a distance of just over 2,500 mi. in 26 h 50 min (May 2–3).

First autogyro flight. Juan de la Cierva, a brilliant Spanish mathematician, made the first successful flight in a rotary wing aircraft in Madrid (June 9).

1924 **First round-the-world flight.** Four Douglas Cruiser biplanes of the U.S. Army Air Corps took off from Seattle under command of Maj. Frederick Martin (April 6). 175 days later, two of the planes (Lt. Lowell Smith's and Lt. Erik Nelson's) landed in Seattle after a circuitous route—one source saying 26,345 mi., another saying 27,553 mi.

1926 **First polar flight.** Then-Lt. Cmdr. Richard E. Byrd, acting as navigator, and Floyd Bennett as pilot, flew a trimotor Fokker from Kings Bay, Spitsbergen, over the North Pole and back in 15½ h (May 8–9).

1927 **First solo transatlantic flight.** Charles Augustus Lindbergh lifted his Wright-powered Ryan monoplane, *Spirit of St. Louis,* from Roosevelt Field, L.I., to stay aloft 33 h 39 min and travel 3,600 mi. to Le Bourget Field outside Paris (May 20–21).

First transatlantic passenger. Charles A. Levine was piloted by Clarence D. Chamberlin from Roosevelt Field, L.I., to Eisleben, Germany, in a Wright-powered Bellanca (June 4–5).

1928 **First east-west transatlantic crossing.** Baron Guenther von Huenefeld, piloted by German Capt. Hermann Koehl and Irish Capt. James Fitzmaurice, left Dublin for New York City (April 12) in a single-engine all-metal Junkers monoplane. Some 37 h later, they crashed on Greely Island, Labrador. Rescued.

First U.S.-Australia flight. Sir Charles Kingsford-Smith and Capt. Charles T. P. Ulm, Australians, and two American navigators, Harry W. Lyon and James Warner, crossed the Pacific from Oakland to Brisbane. They went via Hawaii and the Fiji Islands in a trimotor Fokker (May 31–June 8).

First transarctic flight. Sir Hubert Wilkins, an Australian explorer and Carl Ben Eielson, who served as pilot, flew from Point Barrow, Alaska, to Spitsbergen (mid-April).

1929 **First of the endurance records.** With Air Corps Maj. Carl Spaatz in command and Capt. Ira Eaker as chief pilot, an Army Fokker, aided by refueling in the air, remained aloft 150 h 40 min at Los Angeles (Jan. 1–7).

First blind flight. James H. Doolittle proved the feasibility of instrument-guided flying when he took off and landed entirely on instruments (Sept. 24).

First rocket-engine flight. Fritz von Opel, a German auto maker, stayed aloft in his small rocket-powered craft for 75 sec, covering nearly 2 mi. (Sept. 30).

First South Pole flight. Comdr. Richard E. Byrd, with Bernt Balchen as pilot, Harold I. June, radio operator, and Capt. A. C. McKinley, photographer, flew a trimotor Fokker from the Bay of Whales, Little America, over the South Pole and back (Nov. 28–29).

1930 **First Paris–New York nonstop flight.** Dieudonné Coste and Maurice Bellonte, French pilots, flew a Hispano-powered Breguet biplane from Le Bourget Field to Valley Stream, L.I., in 37 h 18 min. (Sept. 2–3).

1931 **First flight into the stratosphere.** Auguste Piccard, a Swiss physicist, and Charles Knipfer, ascended in a balloon from Augsburg, Germany, and reached a height of 51,793 ft in a 17-h flight that terminated on a glacier near Innsbruck, Austria (May 27).

First nonstop transpacific flight. Hugh Herndon and Clyde Pangborn took off from Sabishiro Beach, Japan, dropped their landing gear, and flew 4,860 mi. to near Wenatchee, Wash., in 41 h 13 min. (Oct. 4–5).

1932 **First woman's transatlantic solo.** Amelia Earhart, flying a Pratt & Whitney Wasp-powered Lockheed Vega, flew alone from Harbor Grace, Newfoundland, to Ireland in approximately 15 h (May 20–21).

First westbound transatlantic solo. James A. Mollison, a British pilot, took a de Havilland Puss Moth from Portmarnock, Ireland, to Pennfield, N.B. (Aug. 18).

First woman airline pilot. Ruth Rowland Nichols, first woman to hold three international records at the same time—speed, distance, altitude—was employed by N.Y.-New England Airways.

1933 **First round-the-world solo.** Wiley Post took a Lockheed Vega, *Winnie Mae,* 15,596 mi. around the world in 7 d 18 h 49½ min (July 15–22).

1937 **First successful helicopter.** Hanna Reitsch, a German pilot, flew Dr. Heinrich Focke's FW-61 in free, fully-controlled flight at Bremen (July 4).

1939 **First turbojet flight.** Just before their invasion of Poland, the Germans flew a Heinkel He-178 plane powered by a Heinkel S3B turbojet (Aug. 27).

1942 **First American jet plane flight.** Robert Stanley, chief pilot for Bell Aircraft Corp., flew the Bell XP-59 *Airacomet* at Muroc Army Base, Calif. (Oct. 1).

1947 **First piloted supersonic flight in an airplane.** Capt. Charles E. Yeager, U.S. Air Force, flew the X-1 rocket-powered research plane built by Bell Aircraft Corp., faster than the speed of sound at Muroc Air Force Base, California (Oct. 14).

1949 **First round-the-world nonstop flight.** Capt. James Gallagher and USAF crew of 13 flew a Boeing B-50A Superfortress around the world nonstop from Ft. Worth, returning to same point: 23,452 mi. in 94 h 1 min, with 4 aerial refuelings enroute (Feb. 27–March 2).

1950 **First nonstop transatlantic jet flight.** Col. David C. Schilling (USAF) flew 3,300 mi. from England to Limestone, Maine, in 10 h 1 min (Sept. 22).

1951 **First solo across North Pole.** Charles F. Blair, Jr., flew a converted P-51 (May 29).

1952 **First jetliner service.** De Havilland Comet flight inaugurated by BOAC between London and Johannesburg, South Africa (May 2). Flight, including stops, took 23 h 38 min.

First transatlantic helicopter flight. Capt. Vincent H. McGovern and 1st Lt. Harold W. Moore piloted 2 Sikorsky H-19s from Westover, Mass., to Prestwick, Scotland (3,410 mi.). Trip was made in 5 steps, with flying time of 42 h 25 min (July 15–31).

First transatlantic round trip in same day. British Canberra twin-jet bomber flew from Aldergrove, Northern Ireland, to Gander, Newfoundland, and back in 7 h 59 min flying time (Aug. 26).

1955 **First transcontinental round trip in same day.** Lt. John M. Conroy piloted F-86 Sabrejet across U.S. (Los Angeles–New York) and back—5,085 mi.—in 11 h 33 min 27 sec (May 21).

1957 **First round-the-world, nonstop jet plane flight.** Maj. Gen. Archie J. Old, Jr., USAF, led a flight of 3 Boeing B-52 bombers, powered with 8 10,000-lb. thrust Pratt & Whitney Aircraft J57 engines around the world in 45 h 19 min; distance 24,325 mi.; average speed 525 mph. (Completed Jan. 18.)

1958 **First transatlantic jet passenger service.** BOAC, New York to London (Oct. 4). Pan American started daily service, N.Y. to Paris (Oct. 26).

First domestic jet passenger service. National Airlines inaugurated service between New York and Miami (Dec. 10).

1976 **First regularly-scheduled commercial supersonic transport (SST) flights begin.** Air France and British Airways inaugurate service (January 21). Air France flies the Paris-Rio de Janeiro route; B.A., the London-Bahraine. Both airlines begin SST service to Washington, D.C. (May 24).

1977 **First successful man-powered aircraft.** Paul MacCready, an aeronautical engineer from Pasadena, Calif., was awarded the Kremer Prize for creating the world's first successful man-powered aircraft. The *Gossamer Condor* was flown by Bryan Allen over the required 3-mile course on Aug. 23.

1978 **First successful transatlantic balloon flight.** Three Albuquerque, N.M., men, Ben Abruzzo, Larry Newman, and Maxie Anderson, completed the crossing (Aug. 16. Landed, Aug. 17) in their hot air balloon, *Double Eagle II.*

1979 **First man-powered aircraft to fly across the English Channel.** The Kremer Prize for the Channel crossing was won by Bryan Allen who flew the *Gossamer Albatross* from Folkestone, England to Cape Gris-Nez, France, in 2 h 55 min (June 12).

1980 **First nonstop transcontinental balloon flight,** and also record for longest overland voyage in a balloon. Maxie Anderson and his son, Kris, completed four-day flight from Fort Baker, Calif., to successful landing outside Matane, Quebec, on May 12 in their helium-filled balloon, *Kitty Hawk.*

Official World Airplane Records

Source: National Aeronautic Association.

Speed Over Measured Straightaway Course

Speed (mph)	Date	Type plane	Pilot	Place
314.32	Dec. 25, 1934	Caudron	Raymond Delmotte (France)	Istres, France
352.39	Sept. 13, 1935	Hughes Special	Howard Hughes (U.S.)	Santa Ana, Calif.
379.63	Nov. 11, 1937	BF-113R	Herman Wurster (Germany)	Augsburg, Germany
469.22	April 26, 1939	ME-109R	Fritz Wendel (Germany)	Augsburg, Germany
606.25	Nov. 7, 1945	Gloster Meteor IV	Group Capt. H. Wilson (U.K.)	Herne Bay, England
615.78	Sept. 7, 1946	Gloster Meteor	Group Capt. E. M. Donalson (U.K.)	Littlehampton, England
650.80	Aug. 25, 1947	Douglas D-558	Maj. Marion Carl, USMC	Muroc AFB, Calif.
670.98	Sept. 15, 1948	North American F-86A	Maj. R. L. Johnson (USAF)	Muroc AFB, Calif.
698.51	Nov. 19, 1952	North American F-86D	Capt. James S. Nash (USAF)	Salton Sea, Calif.
755.14	Oct. 29, 1953	North American YF	Lt. Col. F. K. Everest, Jr. (USAF)	Salton Sea, Calif.
822.27	Aug. 20, 1955	North American F-100C	Col. Horace A. Hanes (U.S.)	Palmdale, Calif.
1,132.14	March 10, 1956	Fairey Delta 2	L. Peter Twiss, D.S.C. (U.K.)	Ford-Chichester, England
1,207.60	Dec. 12, 1957	McDonnell F-101A	Maj. Adrian E. Drew (USAF)	Edwards AFB, Calif.
1,404.09	May 16, 1958	Lockheed F104	Capt. Walter W. Irwin (USAF)	Edwards AFB, Calif.
1,483.85	Oct. 31, 1959	Sukhoi S-66	G. Mossolov (U.S.S.R.)	U.S.S.R.
1,525.96	Dec. 15, 1959	F-106A Delta Wing Monoplane	Maj. Joseph W. Rogers (USAF)	Edwards AFB, Calif.
1,606.32	Nov. 22, 1961	McDonnell F4H	Lt. Col. R. B. Robinson (USMC)	Edwards AFB, Calif.
1,665.89	July 7, 1962	E-166 Jet	G. Mossolov (U.S.S.R.)	U.S.S.R.
2,070.101	May 1, 1965	Lockheed YF-12A Jet	Col. R. L. Stephens (USAF)	Edwards AFB, Calif.
2,196.17	July 28, 1976	Lockheed SR-71	Capt. Eldon W. Joersz (USAF)	Beale AFB, Calif.

Fastest U.S. continental: Capt. Robert G. Sowers (USAF)—Convair B-58 "Hustler"—from Long Beach, Calif., to Kennedy International Airport, N.Y.—2,458.58 statute miles—2 h 0 min 58.71 sec—average speed, 1,214.65 mph—March 5, 1962.

Distance, Straight Line

Distance (mi.)	Date	Crew	From	To
4,911.93	Sept. 27–29, 1929	Costes & Bellonte (France)	Le Bourget, France	Manchuria
5,011.35	July 28–30, 1931	Russel N. Boardman, John Polando (U.S.)	New York	Istanbul
5,656.93	Aug. 5–7, 1933	Maurice Rossi, Paul Codos (France)	New York	Ryack, Syria
6,305.66	July 12–14, 1937	Gromov, Youmachev, Daniline (U.S.S.R.)	Moscow	San Jacinto, Calif.
7,158.44	Nov. 5–7, 1938	Sqd. Ldr. R. Kellett (U.K.)	Ismailia, Egypt	Darwin, Australia
7,916.00	Nov. 19–20, 1945	Col. C. S. Irvine & Lt. Col. G. R. Stanley (U.S.)	Guam	Washington, D. C.
11,235.60	Sept. 29–Oct. 1, 1946	Comdr. Thomas D. Davies, Comdrs. Eugene P. Rankin, Walter S. Reid, Lt. Comdr. Ray A. Tabeling (USN)	Perth, Australia	Columbus, Ohio
12,532.28	Jan. 10–11, 1962	Maj. Clyde P. Evely (USAF)	Kadena, Okinawa	Madrid

Longest light airplane (3,858–6,614 lb) distance: Maximillian A. Conrad—U. S. Piper Comanche 250, Lycoming 0-540-AIAS (250 hp), from Casablanca, Morocco, to Los Angeles, 7,668.48 mi.—June 2–4, 1959.

Distance, Closed Course

Distance (mi.)	Date	Crew	Place
6,587.441	March 23–26, 1932	Bossoutrot & Rossi (France)	Oran
7,239.588	May 13–15, 1938	Comdr. Fujita & Sgt. Maj. Takahashi (Japan)	Kisarasu, Japan
8,037.899	July 30–Aug. 1, 1939	Angelo Tondi, Roberto Dagasso, Ferrucio Vignoli (Italy)	Rome
8,854.308	Aug. 1–2, 1947	Lt. Col. O. F. Lassiter (U.S.) Capt. W. J. Valentine (U.S.)	Tampa, Fla.
10,078.84	Dec. 13–14, 1960	Lt. Col. J. R. Grissom (USAF)	Edwards AFB, Calif.
11,336.92	June 6–7, 1962	Capt. William Stevenson (USAF)	Seymour-Johnson, N.C.

Altitude

Height (ft)	Date	Crew	Place
44,819	Sept. 28, 1933	G. Lemoine (France)	Villacoublay, France
47,352	April 11, 1934	Comdr. Renato Donati (Italy)	Rome
49,944	Sept. 28, 1936	Sqd. Ldr. F. R. D. Swain (U.K.)	South Farnborough, England
53,937	June 30, 1937	Fl. Lt. M. J. Adam (U.K.)	Farnborough, England
56,046	Oct. 22, 1938	Col. Mario Pezzi (Italy)	Montecelio

Altitude

Height (ft)	Date	Crew	Place
59,445[1]	March 23, 1948	John Cunningham (U.K.)	Hatfield, England
63,668[1]	May 4, 1953	Walter F. Gibb (U.K.)	Bristol, England
65,889[1]	Aug. 29, 1955	Walter F. Gibb (U.K.)	Bristol, England
70,308[1]	Aug. 28, 1957	Michael Randrup (U.K.)	Luton, England
91,243[1]	May 7, 1958	Maj. H. C. Johnson (USAF)	Palmdale, Calif.
103,389[1]	Nov. 14, 1959	Capt. Joe B. Jordan (USAF)	Edwards AFB, Calif.
314,750[2]	July 17, 1962	Maj. Robert M. White (USAF)	Edwards AFB, Calif.
118,898	July 25, 1973	Alexander Fedotov (U.S.S.R.)	U.S.S.R.
123,524	Aug. 31, 1977	Alexander Fedotov (U.S.S.R.)	U.S.S.R.

1. Jet-propelled aircraft. 2. X–15–1–rocket plane.

World's 50 Busiest Airports in 1979

Airport	Passengers[1]
O'Hare; Chicago	47,842,510
Hartsfield International; Atlanta	41,665,488
International; Los Angeles	34,923,205
Heathrow; London	27,979,196
Kennedy; New York	26,976,675
International; San Francisco	24,159,924
Dallas–Ft. Worth	22,579,117
Stapleton International; Denver	20,542,684
International; Miami	19,627,851
La Guardia; New York	18,391,035
Osaka	16,824,124
Frankfurt	16,627,795
Logan; Boston	15,195,948
Orly; Paris	14,780,667
International; Honolulu	14,534,717
National; Washington, D.C.	14,277,825
Fiumicino; Rome	11,405,843
Metro Wayne; Detroit	11,164,576
Pittsburgh	11,139,164
Intercontinental; Houston	10,901,067
Las Vegas; Nevada	10,574,127
International; Philadelphia	10,449,357
Mexico City	10,412,022
Charles de Gaulle; Paris	9,992,605
Seattle–Tacoma; Seattle, Wash.	9,820,490
Amsterdam	9,703,173
Copenhagen	9,346,647
Minneapolis–St. Paul	9,309,370
International; Newark	9,296,942
International; St. Louis	9,098,512
Gatwick; London	8,701,013
International; Tampa, Fla.	8,198,579
Hopkins; Cleveland	7,688,940
Zurich	7,519,518
Narita; Tokyo	7,262,000
Sky Harbor International; Phoenix	7,021,985
Dusseldorf	6,851,151
Sydney	6,755,016
International; New Orleans	6,562,291
International; San Diego, Calif.	6,541,820
Memphis, Tennessee	6,261,172
International; Orlando, Fla.	6,260,235
Hong Kong	6,230,163
Munich	6,084,917
P.R. International; San Juan, P.R.	6,081,310
Ft. Lauderdale, Fla.	5,984,807
International; Kansas City, Mo.	5,979,343
Linate; Milan	5,210,958
San Paulo	5,191,943
Melbourne	4,698,187

1. Enplaned, deplaned, and transfer, in millions. *Source:* Airport Operators Council International.

World Airplane Hijackings and Attempts

	Place of flight origin		
Years	U.S.	Foreign	Total
1930–67	12	67	79
1968	22	13	35
1969	40	47	87
1970	27	56	83
1971	27	31	58
1972	31	31	62
1973	2	20	22
1974	7	19	26
1975	12	13	25
1976	4	14	18
1977	6	26	32
1978	13	18	31
1979	13	14	27
Total	**216**	**369**	**585**

Source: Department of Transportation, Federal Aviation Administration.

Disposition of Hijackers of Aircraft in U.S. Commerce, 1930–79[1]

Disposition of case	Number
Convictions	122
United States	109
Foreign	13
Acquittals	4
Committed to mental institution	24
Cases dismissed	9
No prosecution	7
Killed or Suicide	22
Cases pending	14
Fugitives[2]	88
Total	**290**

1. Through December 31, 1979. 2. Includes a number of passive companions indicted along with active hijackers. *Source:* Department of Transportation, Federal Aviation Administration.

U. S. Airlines Transport Planes

Manufacturer	Type	Number of passengers	Maximum speed, mph	Typical gross weight, lbs	Wingspan, ft	Maximum length, ft
4-ENGINE						
Boeing	707–120B	100–181	600	258,000	142.4	145.1
Boeing	707–320, –402/Intercontinental	108–189	600	316,000	142.4	152.9
Boeing	707–320B, C/Intercontinental	145	600	336,000	145.8	152.9
Boeing	747–100B/Superjet	442	640	733,000[1]	195.7	231.9
Boeing	747–200B, C/Superjet	442	640	785,000[1]	195.7	231.9
Boeing	747SR/Superjet	512	640	600,000[1]	195.7	231.9
Boeing	747SP/Superjet	321	640	696,000[1]	195.7	184.7
Douglas	DC–6B	90–100	300	100,000	117.5	106.8
McDonnell Douglas	DC–8/Series 30,40	116–176	600+	315,000	142.3	150.5
McDonnell Douglas	DC–8/Series 50	116–189	600	325,000	142.3	150.5
McDonnell Douglas	DC–8/Super 61	259	600	325,000	142.3	187.4
McDonnell Douglas	DC–8/Super 62	189	600	325,000	148.4	157.4
McDonnell Douglas	DC–8/Super 63	259	600	350,000	148.4	187.4
DeHavilland	DHC–7	50	270	26,700	93.0	80.6
Lockheed	L–188	94	373	113,000	99.0	104.5
3-ENGINE						
Airbus Industries	A–300	269–345	600	347,100	147.1	175.1
Boeing	727–100	70–131	600+	170,000	108.0	133.1
Boeing	727–200/Advanced	145	600+	191,500	108.0	153.1
McDonnell Douglas	DC–10/Series 10	250–380	600+	455,000	155.3	182.3
McDonnell Douglas	DC–10/Series 30	250–380	600+	572,000	165.3	181.6
McDonnell Douglas	DC–10/Series 40	250–350	600+	572,000	165.3	182.3
Lockheed	L–1011–1/TriStar	240–400	620+	430,000	155.3	177.7
Lockheed	L–1011–100, –200/TriStar	250–400	620+	466,000	155.3	177.7
Lockheed	L–1011–500/TriStar	230–330	620+	496,000	155.3	164.2
2-ENGINE						
Beech	B–99	15	285	10,900	45.8	44.6
Boeing	737–100	112	586	111,000	93.0	94.0
Boeing	737–200/Advanced	115	586	116,000	93.0	100.2
Boeing	737–200/Advanced[2]	115	586	125,000	93.0	100.2
Cessna	402	6–10	242	6,885	44.1	36.4
Conveir	580	50	270	52,000	105.4	81.5
DeHavilland	DHC–6	20	210	12,500	65.0	51.7
Douglas	DC–3	21–30	200	24,800	95.0	64.5
McDonnell Douglas	DC–9/Series 10	90	576	90,700	89.4	104.4
McDonnell Douglas	DC–9/Series 20	90	576	98,000	93.4	104.4
McDonnell Douglas	DC–9 Series 30	115	576	121,000	93.4	119.3
McDonnell Douglas	DC–9/Series 40	125	576	121,000	93.4	125.6
McDonnell Douglas	DC–9/Series 50	139	576	122,000	93.4	133.6
McDonnell Douglas	DC–9/Series 80	167	576	140,000	107.8	149.9
Marcel Dassault	Falcon–10	4–7	600+	10,760	42.9	45.5
Piper	PA–23	6	247	5,200	37.3	31.2
Piper	PA–31	6	247	6,500	40.7	32.6
Short Brothers Harland	SH–330	30	228	22,600	74.7	58.0
Swearingen	SA–226TC	20	300	12,500	46.4	59.4

1. All Cargo config. (644 cu-ft cargo space). 2. High gross weight structure. NOTE: Data show the most-used manufacturers' type and model aircraft used by air carriers and commercial operators as of April 1980. *Source:* Federal Aviation Administration.

Active Pilot Certificates Held
(as of January 1)

Year	Total[1]	Airline transport	Commercial	Private
1970	720,028	31,442	176,585	299,491
1975	733,728	41,002	192,425	305,848
1980	814,667	63,652	182,097	343,276

1. Includes other pilot categories—helicopter, glider and lighter-than-air (1979: 14,591); and students (1979: 204,874). *Source:* Department of Transportation, Federal Aviation Administration.

Important American Aircraft Types (U.S. Air Force)

Abbreviations: GA—Garrett AiResearch; All—Detroit Diesel Allison Div. of General Motors; Con—Continental; GD—General Dynamics; GE—General Electric; Lyc—Lycoming; RI—Rockwell International; P&W—Pratt & Whitney; PWC—Pratt & Whitney Aircraft of Canada, Ltd; Wr—Curtiss Wright; kt—knots.

Type	Manufacturer	Popular name	Power plant	Crew	Wing-span, ft/in.	Length, ft/in.	Height, ft/in.	Gross weight, lb	Speed, mph
ATTACK									
A-7D	LTV Aerospace	Corsair II	1 All TF41-A-1	1	38/7	46/1	16/0	42,000	620
A-10A	Fairchild Hiller	Thunderbolt II	2 GE TF34-GE-100	1	57/5	53/3	14/6	46,038	400 kt
A-37B	Cessna	Dragonfly	2 GE J85-GE-17A	1	35/8	29/3	8/9	14,000	425 kt
BOMBERS									
B-52D	Boeing	Stratofortress	8 P&W J57-P-29W	6	185/0	156/6	48/4	450,000	650
B-52G	Boeing	Stratofortress	8 P&W J57-P-43W	6	185/0	161/11	40/8	488,000	650
B-52H	Boeing	Stratofortress	8 P&W TF33-P-3	6	185/0	159/3	40/8	488,000	650
FB-111A	GD/Ft. Worth	—	2 P&W TF30-P-7	2	70/0[3]	73/6	17/0	114,000	Mach 2+
FIGHTERS									
F-4D/E	McDonnell Douglas	Phantom II	2GEJ79-GE-15/17(E)	2	38/6	63/0	16/5	58,000	Mach 2.2
F-15A/C	McDonnell Douglas	Eagle	2 P&W F100-PW-100	1	42/8	63/8	18/6	41,000	Mach 2.5
F-5A	Northrop	Freedom Fighter	2J85-GE-13	1	25/3	47/2	13/2	20,500	Mach 1.4
F-16A	GD/Ft. Worth	—	1 P&W F100-PW-100	1	31/0	47/6	16/4	22,000	Mach 2
F-106A	GD/Convair	Delta Dart	1 P&W J75-P-17	1	38/3	70/8	20/3	36,000	Mach 2
F-111	GD/Ft. Worth	—	2 P&W TF30-P-3/100(F)	2	63/0[4]	73/6	17/0	100,000	Mach 2.5
RECONNAISSANCE									
RF-4C	McDonnell Douglas	Phantom II	2 GE J79-GE-15	2	38/4	62/9	16/5	58,000	Mach 2.2
SR-71	Lockheed/Calif.	—	2 P&W J58	2	55/6	107/4	18/5	—	Mach 3
U/WU-2	Lockheed/Calif.	—	1 P &W J75	1	80/0	49/6	13/0	17,000	400 kt
OBSERVATION									
0-2A	Cessna		2 Con 10-360-D	1	38/0	29/2	9/5	4,850	192 kt
OV-10A[1]	RI/Columbus	Bronco	2 T76-G-10/12	2	40/0	39/7	15/1	14,466	350 kt
EARLY WARNING COMMAND, CONTROL AND COMMUNICATIONS									
E-3A	Boeing		4 P&W TF33-P-100A	17	145/9	152/1	42/0	325,000	473
E-4A/B	Boeing	—	4 GE CF6-50E	5	195/7	231/3	63/5	803,000	—
CARGO/TRANSPORT									
C-5A	Lockhead/Georgia	Galaxy	4 GE TF39	7	222/8	245/9	65/1	764,500	550
C-9A	McDonnell Douglas	Nightingale	2 P&W JT8D-9	2–7	93/3	119/3	27/5	108,000	570
C-12A[2]	Beech		2 PWC PT6A-38	2	54/5	43/6	14/6	12,500	260 kt
C-130E/H	Lockheed/Georgia	Hercules	4 All T56-A-7/-15(H)	5	132/6	99/5	38/4	155,000	360
C-140A	Lockheed/Georgia	Jetstar	4 P&W J60-P-5	5	54/4	60/4	20/4	40,921	525
C-141A	Lockheed/Georgia	Starlifter	4 P&W TF33-P-7	4–9	160/7	145/0	39/3	325,000	505
KC-135A	Boeing	Stratotanker	4 P&W J57-P-59W	4	130/9	136/3	38/4	297,000	530
C-137C	Boeing	Stratoliner	4 P&W JT3D-3B	4	145/9	152/9	42/5	328,000	Mach 0.84
CT-39	RI/General Aviation	Sabreliner	2 P&W J60-P-3	2	44/5	43/8	15/9	18,650	Mach 0.75
TRAINERS									
T-33A	Lockheed/Calif.	Shooting Star	1 All J33-A-35	2	38/9	37/7	11/7	15,100	505
T-37B	Cessna		2 CAE J69-T-25	2	33/8	29/3	9/2	6,575	425
T-38A	Northrop	Talon	2 GE J85-5	2	25/3	46/4	12/1	12,500	Mach 1.2
T-41B/C	Cessna	Mescalero	1 CON 10-360-D	2	36/2	26/5	8/9	2,550	142
T-43A	Boeing	—	2 P&W JT8D-9	2	93/0	100/0	37/0	115,500	—

1. Air Force/Marines. 2. Air Force/Army. 3. Wing extended; 34 ft fully swept. 4. Wing extended; 31.11 ft fully swept. *Source:* Department of the Air Force.

First Land Vehicle to Break Sound Barrier

Stan Barrett, a movie stunt man, drove the three-wheeled "Budweiser Rocket" up to 739.66 miles an hour on December 18, 1979, at Edwards Air Force Base, Calif. According to Air Force measurements, the speed of his vehicle reached Mach 1.0106.

His dart-shaped vehicle was powered by a 48,000-horsepower main engine that received an extra 6,000 pounds thrust from the engine of a Sidewinder missile.

In regard to its figures, the Air Force stated that while its best engineering practices had checked the radar information, the data were "not calibrated or certified" and in its judgment "these data would not be sanctioned."

Helicopter Records

Source: National Aeronautic Association.

Distance in Straight Line
International: 2,213.04 mi., 3,561.55 km.
Robert G. Ferry (U.S.) in Hughes YOH-6A helicopter powered by Allison T-63-A-5 engine; from Culver City, Calif., to Daytona Beach, Fla., April 6–7, 1966.

Distance, Closed Circuit
International: 1,739.96 mi; 2,800.20 km.
Jack Schweibold (U.S.) in Hughes YOH-6A helicopter powered by Allison T-62-A-5 engine; Edwards Air Force Base, Calif., March 26, 1966.

Altitude
International: 40,820 ft; 12,442 m.
Jean Boulet (France) in Alouette SA 315-001 "Lama" powered by Artouste IIIB 735 KW engine; Istres, France, June 21, 1972.

Maximum Speed
International: 228.91 mph; 368.4 kph.
Gourguen Karapetyan (U.S.S.R.) in A-10 helicopter powered by 2 TB-3-117 engines; Podmoskovnoye, U.S.S.R., Sept. 21, 1978.

Speed for 100 Km (Closed Circuit)
International: 211.35 mph; 340.15 kph.
Boris Galitsky (U.S.S.R.) in MI-6 helicopter powered by 2 TB-2BM turbine engines; Podmoskovnoye, U.S.S.R., Aug. 26, 1964.

Speed for 500 Km (Closed Circuit)
International: 205.688 mph; 331.023 kph.
Galina Rastorgoueva (U.S.S.R.) in A-10 helicopter powered by 2 TV2 117A engines; Ramenskoye, U.S.S.R., Aug. 1, 1975.

Speed for 1,000 Km (Closed Circuit)
International: 200.48 mph; 322.646 kph.
Galina Rastorgoueva (U.S.S.R.) in A-10 helicopter powered by 2 TV2 117A engines; Aug. 13, 1975.

Speed for 2,000 Km (Closed Circuit)
International: 146.09 mph; 235.119 kph.
Inna Kopets (U.S.S.R.) in MI-8 helicopter; Sept. 14, 1967.

Average Hours and Earnings in Aircraft Industries

Hours and earnings	1978	1977	1976	1975	1970	1965	1960	1955
Average weekly hours								
Aircraft industries	42.1	42.7	41.6	40.4	41.0	41.2	40.6	41.4
Engines and parts industries	41.7	42.0	41.0	41.4	40.5	42.1	41.1	40.6
Average weekly earnings								
Aircraft industries	$324.17	$310	$283	$250	$171	$130	$110	$90
Engines and parts industries	$325.26	$315	$281	$249	$166	$133	$112	$86
Average hourly earnings								
Aircraft industries	$7.70	$7.27	$6.81	$6.20	$4.17	$3.16	$2.71	$2.17
Engines and parts industries	$7.80	$7.50	$6.86	$6.03	$4.10	$3.17	$2.73	$2.13

NOTE: Figures are latest available. *Source:* Department of Transportation, Federal Aviation Administration.

Traditional Wedding Anniversary Gift List

Anniversary	Gift	Anniversary	Gift	Anniversary	Gift
1st	Paper	9th	Pottery, willow	25th	Silver
2nd	Cotton	10th	Tin, aluminum	30th	Pearl
3rd	Leather	11th	Steel	35th	Coral
4th	Fruit, flowers	12th	Silk, linen	40th	Ruby
5th	Wood	13th	Lace	50th	Gold
6th	Candy, iron	14th	Ivory	55th	Emerald
7th	Wool, copper	15th	Crystal	60th	Diamond
8th	Bronze, pottery	20th	China	75th	Diamond

Source: Jewelry Industry Council.

Modern Wedding Anniversary Gift List

Anniversary	Gift	Anniversary	Gift	Anniversary	Gift
1st	Clock	10th	Diamond jewelry	19th	Bronze
2nd	China	11th	Fashion jewelry and accessories	20th	Platinum
3rd	Crystal, glass			25th	Sterling Silver Jubilee
4th	Electrical Appliances	12th	Pearls or colored gems	30th	Diamond
5th	Silverware	13th	Textiles, furs	35th	Jade
6th	Wood	14th	Gold jewelry	40th	Ruby
7th	Desk sets, pen and pencil sets	15th	Watches	45th	Sapphire
		16th	Silver hollow ware	50th	Golden Jubilee
8th	Linens, laces	17th	Furniture	55th	Emerald
9th	Leather	18th	Porcelain	60th	Diamond Jubilee

Source: Jewelry Industry Council

WHERE TO FIND OUT MORE

Reference Books And Other Sources

This cannot be a complete record of all the thousands of available sources of information. Nevertheless, these selected references will enable the reader to locate additional facts about many subjects covered in the *Information Please Almanac*. The editors have chosen sources that they believe will be most helpful to the general reader.

General References

Encyclopedias are a unique category, since they attempt to cover most subjects quite thoroughly. Two most valuable multivolume encyclopedias are the **Encyclopaedia Britannica** and the **Encyclopedia Americana.** Useful one-volume encyclopedias are the **New Columbia Encyclopedia** and the **Random House Encyclopedia.**

Dictionaries and similar "word books" are also unique: **Webster's New International Dictionary** (third edition, unabridged). **Random House Dictionary. Merriam Webster's Collegiate Dictionary** (eighth edition, abridged). **Oxford English Dictionary. Bartlett's Familiar Quotations. Roget's Thesaurus. Modern American Usage.**

There are a number of useful **atlases: New York Times Atlas of the World,** a number of historical atlases (Penguin Books), **Oxford Economic Atlas of the World, Atlas of the Universe** (Rand McNally), **Atlas of the Historical Geography of the U.S.** (Carnegie Institution of Washington and the American Geographical Society), and contemporary road atlases of the U.S. (Rand McNally).

A source of information on virtually all subjects is the United States Government Printing Office. For information write: Superintendent of Documents, Washington, D.C. 20402.

For help on any subject, consult: **Subject Guide to Books in Print, The New York Times Index,** and the **Reader's Guide to Periodical Literature** in your library.

Specific References

America Votes (Congressional Quarterly, Inc.)
American Indian, Reference Encyclopedia of the (Todd Publications)
Amphibians of the World, Living (Doubleday)
Animal Life Encyclopedia (Van Nostrand Reinhold)
Antiques, Collectors Encyclopedia of (Crown)
Architecture, World (McGraw-Hill)
Art, Encyclopedia of World (McGraw-Hill)
Art, History of (Prentice-Hall)
Art, Oxford Companion to (Oxford University Press)
Art, Who's Who in American (R.R. Bowker)
Art Directory, American (R.R. Bowker)
Authors, 1000–1900, European (H.W. Wilson)
Authors, 1600–1900, American (H.W. Wilson)
Authors, Twentieth Century (H.W. Wilson)
Authors Before 1800 (H.W. Wilson)
Authors of the Nineteenth Century, British (H.W. Wilson)
Auto Racing, The New York Times Complete Guide to (Quadrangle)
Banking and Finance, Encyclopedia of (Bankers Publishing Co.)
Baseball Encyclopedia (Information Concepts/Macmillan)
(Baseball) **World Series Records** (The Sporting News)
Basketball, Modern Encyclopedia of (Four Winds Press)
Biographical Dictionary, Chambers (St. Martin's Press)
Biographical Dictionary, Webster's (G. & C. Merriam)
Biography Yearbook, Current (H.W. Wilson)
Birds of America (Audubon)
Book Review Digest, 1905— (H.W. Wilson)
Business Almanac, Dow Jones-Irwin (Dow Jones-Irwin)
Catholic Encyclopedia, New (Publishers Guild/McGraw-Hill)
CB: Citizens Band Radio Service Rules (Government Printing Office)
Chemistry, Encyclopedia of (Van Nostrand Reinhold)
Chemistry and Physics, Handbook of (Chemical Rubber Co.)
Christian Church, Oxford Dictionary of the (Oxford University Press)
Church Annual, Episcopal (Morehouse-Barlow)
Churches, Yearbook of American and Canadian (Abingdon Press)
Climate and Man (U.S. Department of Agriculture)
Communist Affairs, Yearbook on International (Hoover Institution Press)
Composers, Great, 1300–1900; A Biographical and Critical Guide (H.W. Wilson)
Composers Since 1900; A Biographical and Critical Guide (H.W. Wilson)
Congressional Quarterly Directory (Congressional Quarterly, Inc.)
(Consumer) **Agriculture, Yearbook of: Gardening for Food and Fun** (Government Printing Office)
(Consumer) **HELP: The Indispensable Almanac of Consumer Information 1980** (Everest House)
Consumer Sourcebook (Gale Research Co.)
Consumer Reports (Consumers Union)
Dance Encyclopedia (Simon & Schuster)
Drama, Crowell's Handbook of Classical (Crowell)
Ecology Information and Organizations, Guide to (H.W. Wilson)
Energy, Encyclopedia of (McGraw-Hill)
Environment, Living With Our (Government Printing Office)
Environmental Quality Report (Council on Environmental Quality)
Environmental Science, Encyclopedia of (McGraw-Hill)
Europa Year Book (Europa Publications)
Facts, Famous First (H.W. Wilson)
Facts on File (Facts on File, Inc.)
Film, Oxford Companion to (Oxford University Press)
Filmgoer's Companion (Hill & Wang)
Fishing Encyclopedia, New Standard (Holt, Rinehart & Winston)

Football, Encyclopedia of (A.S. Barnes & Co.)
Foreign Terms, Dictionary of (Crowell)
Foundation Directory (Columbia University Press, dist.)
Game, Rules of the (Bantam Books)
Geographical Dictionary, Webster's New (G. & C. Merriam)
Geography, Dictionary of (Penguin Books)
Government Manual, U.S. (U.S. Office of the Federal Register)
History, Album of American (Charles Scribner's)
History, Atlas of American (Oxford University Press)
History, Dictionary of American (Charles Scribner's)
History, Documents of American (Appleton-Century-Crofts)
History, Encyclopedia of Latin American (Bobbs-Merrill)
History, Encyclopedia of World (Houghton-Mifflin)
History, Timetables of (Simon & Schuster)
History and Literature, Oxford Companion to Canadian (Oxford University Press)
Ice Hockey, Complete Encyclopedia of (Prentice-Hall)
Investments, American and Foreign, Manual of (Moody's Investors Service)
Jazz in the Seventies, Encyclopedia of (Horizon)
Job Outlook in Brief, The (Government Printing Office)
Judaica, Encyclopaedia (Macmillan)
Libraries, World Guide to (R.R. Bowker)
Library Directory, American (R.R. Bowker)
Literary History of the United States (Macmillan)
Literature, Oxford Companion to American (Oxford University Press)
Literature, Oxford Companion to Classical (Oxford University Press)
Literature, Oxford Companion to English (Oxford University Press)
Literature, Reader's Adviser to the Best in (R.R. Bowker)
Literature, Reader's Encyclopedia of American (Crowell)
Medical Adviser, Modern Home (Doubleday)
Museums, Directory of World (Columbia University Press)
Music, Handbook of American (Free Press, Div. of Macmillan)
(Music) ASCAP. Biographical Dictionary (American Society of Authors, Composers, and Publishers)
Music, Concise Oxford Dictionary of (Oxford University Press)
Music, Harvard Dictionary of (Harvard University Press)
Music and Musicians, Grove's Dictionary of (St. Martin's Press)
Musical Terms, Dictionary of (Gordon Press)
Mythology, (Larousse) World (G.P. Putnam's Sons)
Nations, Handbook of New (Crowell)
Nations, Worldmark Encyclopedia of the (Harper & Row)
Negro Reference Book, American (Prentice-Hall)
Newspapers and Periodicals, Ayer Directory of (Ayer Press)
Opera Book, Kobbe's Complete (G.P. Putnam's)
Pain, Coping With Chronic (Crown Publishers)
Periodicals Directory, International (Ulrich's)
Physics and Electronics, International Dictionary of (Van Nostrand Reinhold)
Pocket Data Book, U.S.A. (Bureau of Census)
Poetry, Granger's Index to (Columbia University Press)
Politics, Almanac of American (Gambit, Inc.)
Politics, Who's Who in American (R.R. Bowker)
Private Schools, Handbook of (Porter Sargent)
Robert's Rules of Order (Morrow & Co.)
Science, American Men and Women of (R.R. Bowker)
Science and Technology, Asimov's Biographical Encyclopedia of (Doubleday)
Scientific Encyclopedia, Van Nostrand's (Van Nostrand Reinhold)
Scientific Terms, McGraw-Hill Dictionary of (McGraw-Hill)
Space, Encyclopedia of (McGraw-Hill)
Sports Dictionary, Webster's (G. & C. Merriam Co.)
Sports, Encyclopedia of (A.S. Barnes & Co.)
States, Book of (Council of State Governments)
Statesman's Yearbook (Burke's Peerage, Ltd.)
TV Guide® Almanac, The (Ballantine)
Tennis, Encyclopedia of (Viking Press)
Theater, Oxford Companion to the (Oxford University Press)
Theater, Who's Who in the (Gale Research Co.)
Trotting and Pacing Guide (U.S. Trotting Association)
United Nations, Demographic Yearbook (U.N. Publishing Service)
United States, Historical Statistics of the (U.S. Department of Commerce)
United States, Statistical Abstract of the (Government Printing Office)
United Nations, Statistical Yearbook of the (U.N. Publishing Service)
Washington Information Directory (Congressional Quarterly, Inc.)
Way Things Work (Simon & Schuster)
Weather Almanac (Gale Research Co.)
Wildlife, Atlas of World (Rand McNally)
Women, Notable American, 1607–1950 (Belknap Press)
Women's Movement, Practical Guide to the (Women's Action Alliance, Inc.)
Who's Who (British), (St. Martin's Press)
Who's Who in America (Marquis)
World, Harper Encyclopedia of the Modern (Harper & Row)
Zip Code and Post Office Directory, National (Government Printing Office)

See the full range of publications of Dun & Bradstreet and Standard & Poor's for corporate financial and stockholder information.

For detailed information on American colleges and universities, see the many publications of the **American Council on Education.**

Also see the many specialized **Who's Who** volumes issued by Marquis for biographies of famous contemporaries in many fields.

Flowing Diamonds

The highest steady pressure ever produced in the laboratory is 25.2 million pounds per square inch—700 times the pressure produced by Mount Everest on the earth's crust. This pressure, generated at Carnegie's Geographical Laboratory in 1978, was enough to cause a diamond to flow like plastic.

Rules for Correct Punctuation, Capitalization, Abbreviation

Blanche Ormont

Punctuation

Period (.) Use a period: (1) After a statement or command: *Panama is roughly the size of South Carolina. Go to the head of the line.*

(2) After most abbreviations: C.O.D., Ms., U.S. (In familiar abbreviations, where the letters themselves are usually spoken, the period is often omitted: *CIO, NBC, SPCA.*)

(3) With decimals and in dollars and cents: *.05, 22.5, $12.95.* Do not use a period after *percent,* as in *twenty percent;* if cents is written out or the cents sign is used, as in *27 cents, 27¢;* or after Roman numerals, *XXIII, Act III,* except when numbering or listing.

Question Mark (?) Use the question mark after a direct question: *Do you know why the world's climate is changing?* Do not use the question mark after an indirect question or request: *The teacher asked him if he knew the capital of South Dakota. Will you please return this book as soon as possible.*

Exclamation Point (!) Use an exclamation point after an emphatic statement or after a sentence, phrase, or word expressing strong feeling: *You're absolutely wrong! Ouch! That hurts!*

Comma (,) The comma is the most commonly used (and misused) punctuation mark. It indicates a slight separation between words or groups of words and should serve primarily to make the writer's meaning clear. Too many commas may cause the reader to separate words that should be grouped together, or they may unnecessarily slow the movement of a sentence. Too few commas, or misplaced commas, may seriously distort the writer's meaning. Although one should always use good judgment in deciding when and where to use commas, the following rules are generally applicable. Use a comma:

(1) To separate words, phrases, or clauses (a clause is a group of words that has a subject and a predicate) in a series of three or more items: *Tuition, board, lodging, and medical and dental care are provided.* (Note that the comma before the second *and* has been omitted because *medical and dental care* is considered a single unit. However, in some cases it is necessary to insert the comma before *and* to avoid misreading: *The course includes navigation, electricity, ship construction, marine biology, and engineering.*)

Commas are used between two or more adjectives preceding a noun if each separately could modify the noun and if switching the order of the adjectives does not alter the sense: *It was a cold, bleak, rainy day.* Do not use commas if the first adjective qualifies the entire expression following it: *Their constitution established a strong central government.*

Use a comma after *etc.* (abbreviation of *et cetera*) when it is the last of a series within a sentence: *Books, papers, cartons, etc., lay scattered about the room.*

(2) Between independent clauses (clauses that could stand alone as complete sentences) joined by *and, but, for, or, nor: Pluto has the most eccentric orbit in the solar system, and at times it comes closer to the sun than Neptune. A huge fireball appeared in the sky, but the natives were not afraid.* In a short compound sentence—a sentence made up of two or more independent clauses—the comma is often omitted: *The canoe turned over and everyone fell into the water*

(3) To set off introductory words, phrases, or clauses: *Outraged, he slammed the door behind him. During the wars that followed the French Revolution, Belgium was occupied and later annexed to France. Because Bolivia has no access to the sea, foreign trade must pass through free ports in Chile and river ports on the Amazon.*

If the introductory phrase or clause is very short, or if it is the subject of the sentence, do not use a comma: *Because of its beaches the state is a popular resort area. To cross the sea in ancient times was an extraordinary feat.*

Such introductory transitional words as *yes, no, still, nevertheless, moreover, however, therefore, besides, furthermore,* and weak exclamations like *well, oh,* and *why* should be followed by a comma: *No, I cannot go with you. Well, that's a long story. Why, how nice!*

(4) To set off nonessential elements—words, phrases, or clauses that are not closely related to the rest of the sentence and could be left out without drastically changing its meaning: *Hinduism dates back, perhaps, to prehistoric times. The emperor, in recognition of Confucius' teachings, offered sacrifices at his tomb. Gold, which was responsible for California's settlement boom, is still found in that state.*

To determine whether a modifying expression is restrictive or nonrestrictive (essential or nonessential), see if it can be omitted without significantly changing the meaning. If it is essential to the meaning of the sentence, commas are not used: *Delhi residents who would not limit their families were denied government assistance.* The clause "who would not limit their families" is clearly restrictive; if it were removed, the sentence would indicate that *all* Delhi residents were denied government assistance.

Use the comma before *for, although, though, as, since,* and *because* when these words introduce nonrestrictive clauses or phrases: *The Age of Enlightenment brought about the Jews' emancipation, although persecutions did not end entirely.* But: *The famous Dutch dikes are requisite to the use of much land because half of the country's area is below sea level.* (No comma before *because,* which introduces a restrictive clause.)

Appositives are words or phrases that directly follow a noun or pronoun and identify or explain it. If an appositive is nonrestrictive, it is set off by commas: *The fur-bearing chinchilla, a native of the colder plateau regions, is also raised.* If it is restrictive, no commas are used: *The phrase "hot line" refers to the emergency communications link between Washington and Moscow.*

Contrasting expressions introduced by such words and phrases as *not, but not,* and *though not* are usually nonrestrictive and are therefore set off by commas: *Venus, not Mars, is Earth's nearest neighbor.*

When nonrestrictive words, phrases, or clauses occur within a sentence, they must be set off by *two* commas—one before the expression and one after.

(5) In certain conventional places: (a) To separate items in addresses and dates: *He wrote to his aunt at 94 Birch Road, Omaha, Nebraska, on June 12, 1924.* (b) With numbers greater than three figures: *1,422, 12,498,620.* (c) In letters, after salutations (in informal letters) and after the complimentary close: *Dear Aunt Mary, Sincerely yours,*. (d) To set off the name of a person addressed: *John, please close the door. Listen carefully, Sarah, because this is important.* (e) To separate degrees and titles from names: *Margaret Harrison, M.D., Ph.D. Frank Simmons, Treasurer.* (f) To set off direct quotations: *"Happiness," someone said, "is a warm puppy."* With exclamations or very short quotations, no comma is necessary: *"Hi there!" she called. He constantly said "like" and "you know."*

(6) Whenever necessary to avoid misunderstanding: *Several months after, he saw his father.* (Without the comma the sentence changes meaning, turning into the clause *Several months after he saw his father.)*

Semicolon (;) The semicolon is a mark of separation that functions like a weak period or a strong comma. Use a semicolon:

(1) Between two independent clauses which are not joined by a conjunction: *The soil is generally poor; high crop yields are dependent upon large-scale use of fertilizers.*

(2) Between two independent clauses containing one or more commas even if a conjunction is used: *After members of the committee have debated the bill, a vote is taken; and if the vote is favorable, the bill is sent back to the floor of the house.*

(3) Between two main clauses linked by such connecting words as *therefore, however, finally, thus, otherwise, nevertheless,* and by such phrases as *for example, in fact, on the contrary: The first game of lawn tennis in the United States was played in 1874; however, it was not until 1880 that standard measurements for the court were established.*

(4) Between items in a series if one or more are subdivided by commas: *Among the great libraries of the world are the British Museum, with more than 6,000,000 printed volumes; the National Diet Library in Tokyo, containing more than 4,100,000 volumes; and, of course, the United States Library of Congress, whose extensive collections total over 72,466,000 volumes.*

Colon (:) The colon is a mark of anticipation introducing material that follows it. Use a colon:

(1) To introduce a long quotation, explanatory statement, or question: *The Declaration of Independence states: "We hold these truths to be self-evident, that all men are created equal, that they are endowed by their Creator with certain unalienable Rights, that among these are Life, Liberty, and the Pursuit of Happiness." In 1976, the World Health Organization accomplished a major goal: It virtually eliminated one of mankind's most ancient enemies—smallpox. The question we discussed was: What are the real differences between Socialism and Communism?*

(2) To introduce a list of items. The colon here is frequently, though not always, preceded by such phrases as *the following* or *as follows: Among the great Gothic structures of Europe are the following: Chartres Cathedral, Notre Dame de Paris, Milan Cathedral, and Cologne Cathedral.*

(3) In these customary places: (Note preceding use of colon.) After a formal salutation in a letter: *Dear Sir:;* between hours and minutes: *10:15 a.m.;* between volume and page in formal footnotes and bibliography: *The Dictionary of Dates 2:120–142;* between chapter and verse in the Bible: *Genesis 1:10;* between numerical elements in ratios: *4:2;* after the name of a speaker in a play: *Lady Macbeth: Out, damned spot!*

Quotation Marks (" ") Use quotation marks:

(1) To enclose a direct quotation: *"Life," said Julia Ward Howe, who lived to be ninety-one, "is like a cup of tea; the sugar is all at the bottom."*

Quotation marks are always used in *pairs,* before the quoted material and after it. However, if you quote two or more paragraphs, place quotation marks at the beginning of each paragraph and at the end of the entire quotation.

Single marks are used to enclose a quotation within a quotation. *"His constant use of such words as 'cool' and 'far out' has become very tiresome," the teacher remarked.*

(2) To enclose the title of a short literary work—a chapter, article, essay, poem, or short story—and titles of paintings, short musical compositions, and radio and television programs. The titles of longer works should be italicized. (Joyce's collection of short stories *Dubliners* includes the famous story "The Dead.")

(3) To enclose all words or phrases that are borrowed, that the writer does not wish to claim as his own, or that he uses ironically: *The term "the chain of being" was for centuries a descriptive name for the universe. For many of the world's poor, "home" is a tarpaper shack or a large oil pipe.*

(4) To enclose words or phrases which themselves are being discussed: *Many women now prefer the term "feminism" to the earlier phrase "women's lib."*

(5) When quotation marks are used with other punctuation, they appear as follows:

Outside a comma or period. *"I'm tired," she said. "It's been a long day."*

Inside the semicolon or colon: *A foreign phrase commonly misused to describe aristocracy is "hoi polloi"; actually, it means "the common people."*

Outside a question mark or exclamation point if either is part of the quotation—otherwise, inside. *"Get out of here!" she shrieked. Who wrote "The Unfinished Symphony"?*

Apostrophe (') Use an apostrophe:

(1) In contractions to indicate the omission of a letter: *haven't.*

(2) Before an *s* to form the plural of figures and

letters: *Two size 12's. Cross your t's and dot your i's.*

(3) To form possessives: *Mary's house, men's clothing.* If a plural ends in *s*, add only the apostrophe: *girls' sports, hostesses' duties.* If a singular ends in *s*, add the apostrophe and *s: James's car.* However, the second *s* may be omitted, especially if the word would become more difficult to pronounce: *Socrates' teachings.* Be sure never to use the apostrophe with the possessive pronouns *his, hers, its, yours, ours, theirs.*

Hyphen (-) Use a hyphen:

(1) To link many compound words—two or more words considered as a single unit: *secretary-treasurer, bull's-eye, heavy-hearted, cease-fire.* Do not use a hyphen if a compound modifier follows the noun: *This scientist is well known.* (But note use of hyphen in *a well-known scientist.*) Do not use a hyphen in a compound modifier that includes an adverb ending in *-ly* even if it precedes the noun: *richly deserved praise.*

(2) With certain prefixes and suffixes: *self-support, ex-wife, anti-American, co-worker, president-elect, husband-to-be.* When the parts have become merged in general use, the hyphen may be unnecessary: *midsummer, prehistoric, nonaligned.* (Since usage here is often inconsistent, it is wise, when in doubt, to consult a dictionary.)

(3) In compound numbers from twenty-one to ninety-nine and in fractions: *twenty-five, one-third.*

(4) To divide a word *between syllables* at the end of a line.

(5) Wherever misreading might occur, as in *a navy-blue uniform,* or if a prefix ends with a vowel and the root word begins with the same vowel: *re-elected, anti-inflationary, semi-independent.*

Dash (—) The dash indicates greater separation than a comma but lesser separation than parentheses. Use the dash:

(1) To indicate a sudden change in thought or sentence structure: *We rescheduled the picnic for the following Sunday—we hoped it would be a nice day—but it rained again.*

(2) To emphasize parenthetic, appositive, or explanatory matter. *Imagine a device that is only a cubic foot in size—the size of a hat box—containing 40,000 electronic parts!*

(3) To set off a parenthetic or appositive expression that is itself broken by commas: *She was beset by fears—of heights, open spaces, animals, traffic, strangers—and, as a result, she never left her home.*

Parentheses (()) Generally speaking, dashes add emphasis to the material they enclose, while parentheses tend to subordinate it. Use parentheses:

(1) To enclose incidental or explanatory material that may be relevant but is not strictly necessary: *The rivers, lakes, and surrounding seas (except the Black Sea) are rich in fish. During the reign of Henry VIII (1509–47), the Church of England asserted its independence from the Roman Catholic Church.*

(2) Around figures or letters to enumerate items in a series: *Three qualities of good writing are (1) clarity, (2) consistency, and (3) coherence.*

Parenthetical statements within a sentence begin with a small letter and have no end punctuation, except a question mark or exclamation point if needed. If a comma, semicolon, or colon are necessary after the parenthetical material within a sentence, they are placed outside the closing curve. A complete parenthetic sentence within a paragraph but not within another sentence has an initial capital and end punctuation placed within the closing curve: *Although Nigeria was the world's sixth largest oil producer (its 1974 oil revenues totaled $8 billion), the country's per capita income was only $120 per year. (Even so, it remained black Africa's wealthiest nation.) This problem contributed to continuing government instability.*

Brackets ([]) Use brackets to enclose parenthetic comments inserted in a quotation by the person using the quotation: *In his Nobel Lecture, Martin Luther King said, "In a dark, confused world [where war, poverty, and racism exist] the kingdom of God may yet reign in the hearts of men."*

Capitalization

The use of capital letters is quite standardized in general English. Avoid unnecessary capitals, and when in doubt consult a dictionary. As a rule, capitalize the following:

(1) The first word of a complete sentence: *The modern museum originated during the Renaissance.;* of a quoted sentence: *Freud said, "What does a woman want?";* of each line of poetry:

Had we but world enough, and time,
This coyness, lady, were no crime.—Andrew Marvell

(2) Proper names. A proper name is the name of a *particular* person, place, or thing. Capitalize all proper names including adjectives and abbreviations derived from proper names. Among the proper names to be capitalized are the names of specific persons or places: *John F. Kennedy, Vermont, China, Central Park;* organizations, institutions, buildings, and monuments: *the Republican Party, the Bank of America, Harvard University, the Museum of Modern Art, the Lincoln Memorial;* peoples, languages, religions, and political groups: *Africans, Indians, French, Caucasian, Methodist, Communist;* days of the week, months, holidays: *Tuesday, August, New Year's Day, Easter;* historical periods, events, or documents: *the Dark Ages, the Renaissance, the Holocaust, the Civil War, the Magna Carta, the Social Security Act;* geographical names and regions: *Yellowstone National Park, Lake Huron, the South Pole, the Northeast* (when words like *south* and *north* refer to directions rather than regions, they are not capitalized); names of departments of government and of institutions: *Department of Commerce, Police Department, the City Council, the English Department, the Graduate School;* stars, planets, constellations, satellites, except the sun, earth, and moon: *Sirius, Venus, Orion, Viking I, Halley's Comet;* words referring to the Deity, the Bible, and other sacred writings: *Jehovah, the Messiah, the Virgin, Genesis, Lamentations, the Koran.*

(3) Titles preceding proper names and titles of high rank used without the name: *Professor Cohen, Mayor Daley, Sergeant Jones, Aunt Ellen, the Pope, the President, the Secretary of State, the Queen Mother.*

(4) First and last words and all other words, except the articles *a, an, the,* conjunctions, and prepositions in titles of books, plays, poems, articles, movies, etc.: *Wild Animals of the World, Ode to the West Wind, All in the Family, Porgy and Bess.*

(5) The pronoun *I* and the exclamation *O: If I forget thee, O Jerusalem, let my right hand forget her cunning.*—Psalms

Abbreviations

Abbreviations are useful and appropriate in notetaking, in reference works, in statistical tables, and in certain other situations where speed and space-saving are important. In general writing, however, abbreviations should be avoided. A few standard abbreviations that are correct in all writing are the following:

(1) Titles and names: *Mr., Messrs., Mrs., Dr., Esq., Sr., Jr., Ph.D., M.D., LL.D.* Do not use a title both before and after a name: *Mr. James T. Smith* or *James T. Smith, Ph.D.*, not *Mr. James T. Smith, Ph.D.*

Do not abbreviate civil, professional (except *Dr.*), military, or political titles, except when the person's first name or initials are used: *Professor Downey* or *Prof. Charles Downey, General Marshall* or *Gen. G. C. Marshall*, never *Prof. Downey* or *Gen. Marshall.*

First names should, as a rule, be spelled out: *William Shakespeare*, not *Wm. Shakespeare.*

(2) Certain units of measurements: *a.m., p.m., A.D., B.C., mph,* when used with figures, as in *50 mph; No.* with numbers expressed in figures, as in *No. 8.* Write out other expressions for time, weight, and size, as in *three ounces, two miles, four hours,* unless such expressions appear in directions, recipes, or technical writing: *½ tsp salt, 10 ft 2 in.*

(3) Names of organizations, governmental agencies, scientific words, trade names, and other expressions that are familiar to most people and are frequently referred to by their initials: *YMCA, AFL-CIO, FCC, CIA, FBI, NASA, DDT, DNA, CBS, MGM.* Generally no period is used. (Exceptions: *C.O.D., F.O.B.*) Abbreviations like *Co., Inc., Ltd.,* or *Corp.* are correct when they are part of the company name: *Jones Publishing, Inc.*

(4) Certain literary abbreviations: *i.e.* (that is); *e.g.* (for example); *ibid.* (in the same place); *etc.* (and so forth).

In ordinary usage, write out: names of states, countries, months, days of the week; words like *street, road, square* when they are used as part of a proper name: *Maple Street;* and numbers that can be expressed in not more than one or two words: *twenty books, four hundred miles* (but *$3,560.23, 60,211 miles*).

> These are "general" rules of punctuation, capitalization, and abbreviation designed to make writing as clear and "correct" as possible. There are no absolutes. Many publications have modifications of these basic rules that reflect their own special needs.

Forms of Address[1]

Abbot. *Address:* The Right Reverend ______, O.S.B. (or other initials of the order), Abbot of ______. *Begin:* Right Reverend and Dear Father.

Ambassador (U.S.). *Address:* The Honorable ______ ______, American Ambassador; **(to the U.S.):** His Excellency ______ ______, Ambassador of ______. *Begin:* Sir; *or* Dear Mr. Ambassador.

Archbishop. *Address:* The Most Reverend Archbishop of ______; *or* The Most Reverend ______ ______, Archbishop of ______. *Begin:* Your Excellency; *or* Dear Archbishop ______.

Archdeacon. *Address:* The Venerable the Archdeacon of ______. *Begin:* Venerable Sir.

Armed Forces (U.S.). See *Military and Naval Officers.*

Assemblyman. *Address:* The Honorable ______ ______, The Assembly, State Capitol. *Begin:* Dear Mr. ______.

Associate Justice (Supreme Court). *Address:* Mr. Justice ______, The Supreme Court of the United States. *Begin:* Dear Mr. Justice.

Attorney. *Address:* Mr. ______ ______, Attorney-at-Law; *or* ______ ______, Esq. *Begin:* Dear Mr. ______.

Bishop (Episcopal). *Address:* The Right Reverend ______ ______, Bishop of ______. *Begin:* Right Reverend Sir; *or* Dear Bishop ______.

Bishop (Roman Catholic). *Address:* The Most Reverend ______ ______, Bishop of ______. *Begin:* Your Excellency; *or* Dear Bishop ______.

Bishop (other denominations). *Address:* The Reverend ______ ______. *Begin:* Reverend Sir; *or* Dear Bishop ______.

Brother (Roman Catholic). *Address:* Brother ______ (first name followed by initials of the order). *Begin:* Dear Brother ______.

Cabinet Officer (U.S.). *Address:* The Honorable ______ ______, Secretary of State (or other department); *or* The Honorable ______ ______, Attorney General of the United States. *Begin:* Dear Sir.

Cardinal. *Address:* His Eminence John Cardinal Smith. *Begin:* Your Eminence; *or* Dear Cardinal ______.

Chargé d'Affaires (U.S.). *Address:* ______ ______, Esq., American Chargé d'Affaires. *Begin:* Dear Sir.

Chief Justice (Supreme Court). *Address:* The Chief Justice of the United States. *Begin:* Dear Mr. Chief Justice.

Clergyman (Protestant). *Address:* The Reverend ______ ______; *or* (if a Doctor of Divinity) The Reverend Dr. ______ ______; *Begin:* Dear Sir; *or* Dear Mr. ______; *or* Dear Dr. ______.

Commissioner (of a Department or Bureau). *Address:* The Honorable ______ ______. *Begin:* Dear Mr. ______.

Consul. *Address:* ______ ______, Esq., American Consul. *Begin:* Dear Sir.

Dean (of a Cathedral). *Address:* The Very Reverend ______ ______; *or* Dean ______ ______. *Begin:*

1. Since the relationship between correspondents affects the form of address used in letters, no rigid guidelines can be set down for all occasions. When two salutations are shown, it is to be understood that the formal styling precedes the informal. In salutations where the addressee is a woman, it is to be understood that in formal address Madam may be substituted for Sir, and in informal address Mrs. or Miss or Ms. may be substituted for Mr. 2. From Webster's Eighth New Collegiate Dictionary. NOTE: Forms of Address for foreign dignitaries may be obtained from their United Nations missions in New York City.

Very Reverend Sir; *or* Dear Dean ______.

Dean (of a College or University). *Address:* Dean ______ ______. *Begin:* Dear Dean ______.

Dentist. *Address:* ______ ______, D.D.S. (office address); *or* Dr. ______ ______ (home address). *Begin:* Dear Dr. ______.

Divorced Woman. *Address:* Ordinarily use *Mrs.* with her maiden name as a prename. Some divorced women prefer to resume the *Miss.*[2]

Doctor of Divinity. See *Clergyman.*

Doctor of Philosophy, Laws, etc. *Address:* ______ ______, Ph.D. (LL.D.) (or other degree). *Begin:* Dear Sir; *or* Dear Dr. ______.

Governor. *Address:* The Honorable ______ ______, Governor of ______. *Begin:* Dear Governor ______.

Governor-General of Canada. *Address:* His Excellency The Right Honourable ______ ______ (plus personal rank or title, if any). *Begin:* My Lord; *or* Sir (according to rank).[2]

Governor-General's Wife. *Address:* Her Excellency ______ ______ (plus personal rank or title, if any). *Begin:* Madam.[2]

Judge (Federal). *Address:* The Honorable ______ ______, United States District Judge. *Begin:* Dear Judge ______.

Judge (State or Local). *Address:* The Honorable ______ ______, Judge of the Court of Appeals (or other court). *Begin:* Dear Judge ______.

King. *Address:* The King's Most Excellent Majesty; *or* His Most Gracious Majesty, King ______. *Begin:* Sir; *or* May It Please Your Majesty.[2]

Lieutenant Governor. *Address:* The Honorable ______ ______, Lieutenant Governor of ______. *Begin:* Dear Mr. ______.

Mayor (in Canadian Cities and Towns, and English Boroughs and Cities). *Address:* The Right Worshipful the Mayor of ______ (English cities only); His Worship, The Mayor of ______ (other). *Begin:* Sir.[2]

Mayor (U.S.). *Address:* The Honorable ______ ______, Mayor of ______. *Begin:* Dear Mayor ______.

Member of Parliament (or of a Legislative Council). The ordinary form of address followed by M.P. (or M.L.C.).[2]

Military and Naval Officers (U.S.): *Address:* (full rank) ______ ______, U.S.N. (or U.S.A., U.S.A.F., U.S.M.C., U.S.C.G.). *Begin:* Sir (admirals and generals only); *or* Dear (full rank) ______ (other officers, including admirals and generals); *or* Dear Mr. ______ (lieutenant commander, lieutenant, ensign only).

Minister (to U.S.). *Address:* The Honorable ______ ______, Minister of ______. *Begin:* Sir; *or* Dear Mr. Minister.

Minister of Religion. See *Clergyman, Priest, Rabbi.*

Monsignor. *Address:* The Right Reverend Monsignor ______. *Begin:* Dear Monsignor ______.

Mother Superior of a Sisterhood. *Address:* The Reverend Mother Superior, O.S.F. (or other initials of the order); *Begin:* Reverend Mother; or Dear Reverend Mother.

Nun. See *Sister of a Religious Order.*

Papal Nuncio or Internuncio or Apostolic Delegate. *Address:* His Excellency, The Papal Nuncio (*or* Internuncio *or* Apostolic Delegate) to ______. *Begin:* Your Excellency.[2]

Patriarch (Eastern Church). *Address:* His Beatitude the Patriarch of ______. *Begin:* Most Reverend Lord.

Physician. *Address:* ______ ______, M.D. (office address); *or* Dr. ______ ______ (home address). *Begin:* Dear Dr. ______.

Pope. *Address:* His Holiness Pope ______; *or* His Holiness the Pope. *Begin:* Your Holiness; *or* Most Holy Father.

President of a College or University. *Address:* President ______ ______. *Begin:* Dear President ______.

President of a State Senate. *Address:* The Honorable ______ ______, President of the Senate of ______. *Begin:* Dear Senator ______.[2]

President of the U.S. *Address:* The President. *Begin:* Dear Mr. President.

President of the U.S. (Former). *Address:* The Honorable ______ ______. *Begin:* Dear Mr. ______.

Priest (Roman Catholic). *Address:* The Reverend Father ______; *or* The Reverend ______ ______. *Begin:* Dear Father ______; *or* Dear Father.

Prime Minister of Canada. *Address:* The Right Honourable ______ ______, P.C., Prime Minister of Canada. *Begin:* Sir.[2]

Privy Councillor (of Canada). *Address:* The Honourable ______ ______. *Begin:* Sir.[2]

Professor at a College or University. *Address:* Professor ______ ______. *Begin:* Dear Professor ______.

Queen. *Address:* The Queen's Most Excellent Majesty; *or* Her Gracious Majesty, The Queen. *Begin:* Madam; *or* May It Please Your Majesty.[2]

Rabbi. *Address:* Rabbi ______ ______; *or* Rabbi ______ ______, D.D. (if a Doctor of Divinity). *Begin:* Dear Rabbi ______; *or* Dear Dr. ______.

Representative (State). *Address:* The Honorable ______ ______, House of Representatives, State Capitol. *Begin:* Dear Mr. ______.

Representative (U.S.). *Address:* The Honorable ______ ______, The United States House of Representatives. *Begin:* Dear Mr. ______.

Secretary-General of the U.N. *Address:* His Excellency ______ ______, Secretary-General of the United Nations. *Begin:* Excellency; *or* Dear Mr. Secretary-General; *or* Dear Mr. ______.

Senator (State). *Address:* The Honorable ______ ______, The State Senate, State Capitol. *Begin:* Dear Senator ______.

Senator (U.S.). *Address:* The Honorable ______ ______, United States Senate. *Begin:* Dear Senator ______.

Sister of a Religious Order. *Address:* Sister ______ ______, S.C. (or other initials of the order). *Begin:* Dear Sister ______ ______; *or* Dear Sister.

Speaker of the House of Commons (Canada). *Address:* The Honourable ______ ______, The Speaker of the House of Commons. *Begin:* Dear Mr. Speaker.[2]

Speaker of the House of Representatives (U.S.). *Address:* The Honorable ______ ______, Speaker of the House of Representatives. *Begin:* Dear Mr. Speaker.

Superior of a Brotherhood. *Address:* Brother ______ (first name followed by initials of the order), Superior. *Begin:* Dear Brother ______.

United Nations Representative (Foreign). *Address:* His Excellency ______ ______, Representative of ______ to the United Nations. *Begin:* Excellency; *or* Dear Mr. Ambassador.[2]

United Nations Representative (U.S.). *Address:* The Honorable ______ ______, United States Representative to the United Nations. *Begin:* Sir; *or* Dear Mr. Ambassador.[2]

Veterinarian. *Address:* ______ ______, D.V.M. (office address); or Dr. ______ ______ (home address). *Begin:* Dear Dr. ______.

Vice President of the U.S. *Address:* The Vice President, United States Senate. *Begin:* Dear Mr. Vice President.

Widow. Ordinarily addressed by her former title: as, Mrs. John Doe, not Mrs. Jane Doe, unless the latter form is preferred by the person herself.[2]

Foreign Words and Phrases

(The English meanings given are not necessarily literal translations.)

ab ovo: from the beginning
à bon marché: good bargain; cheap
à deux: for two; between two
a priori: from something previous
à votre santé: to your health
ad infinitum: to infinity; with no end
ad valorem: according to its value
al fresco: outdoors
alma mater: one's college or school
alter ego: other self
amicus curiae: friend of the court
ancien regime: the old order
anno Domini: year of our Lord
ante bellum: before the war
au contraire: on the contrary
au courant: current; up-to-date
auf Wiedersehen: goodbye
bête noire: particular nemesis
bienvenue: welcome
bon mot: a funny or witty saying
bon vivant: a gourmet, an epicure
bona fide: in good faith; genuine; honest
carpe diem: enjoy today; seize the day
carte blanche: unlimited authority
cause célèbre: a cause that generates wide interest
caveat emptor: buy at your own risk; let the buyer beware
circa: about; approximately
chacun à son goût: each to his own taste
combien: how much?
corpus delicti: fundamental fact or facts about the commission of a crime
coup de grâce: finishing blow
cum grano salis: with a grain of salt
d'accord: in accord; agreement
de facto: as a matter of fact; actual
de profundis: out of the depths
Deo gratias: thanks be to God
Deo volente: God willing
dernier cri: the last word
deus ex machina: artificially produced to bring a solution to some extreme difficulty
dramatis personae: characters in a play
ecce homo: this is the man
en masse: all together
en passant: in passing
fait accompli: an accomplished fact
faux pas: a false step; a mistake
flagrante delicto: caught in the act
Gesundheit: good health (God bless you)
habeas corpus: common-law writ to bring a person before a court or judge
hoi polloi: the common people
honi soit qui mal y pense: evil to him who thinks evil of it
hors d'oeuvre: appetizer
idée fixe: fixed idea; obsession
in loco parentis: in place of a parent
ipso facto: by the very fact
je ne sais quoi: I don't know what; an elusive quality
jeunesse dorée: gilded youth
laissez faire: noninterference
l'chaim: to life
maven: an expert; connoisseur
mea culpa: I am to blame
mirabile dictu: wonderful to relate
modus operandi: method of operation; way of working
nom de plume: pen name
non compos mentis: not of sound mind
non sequitur: it does not follow
O tempora! O mores!: What sad times and customs
omnia vincit amor: love conquers all
per annum: by the year
per capita: by the head; individually
per diem: by the day; daily
persona non grata: an unwelcome or unacceptable person
plus ça change, plus c'est le même chose: the more things change, the more they remain the same
post mortem: after death
pro bono publico: for the public good
pro tempore (pro tem): for the time being; temporary
quid pro quo: something done or given in exchange for something else
repondez s'il vous plait: please reply; please answer (abbr. R.S.V.P.)
requiescat in pace: rest in peace
sans souci: without worry or care
savoir faire: know-how; manners for all occasions
semper fidelis: always faithful
shalom: peace
sic transit gloria mundi: so passes the glory of the world
s'il vous plait: if you please; please
sine die: with no day set for the next meeting
sine qua non: indispensable
status (in) quo: state in which anything is
sui generis: in a class by itself
tempus fugit: time flies
tout de suite: immediately
veni, vidi, vici: I came, I saw, I conquered
vis-à-vis: face-to-face

Improved Technique for Carbon 14 Dating

The normal method for determining the age of a fossil by carbon 14 dating usually requires samples so large that the fossil being analyzed is often destroyed. A new technique developed by the University of Rochester uses a special high-voltage generator to directly measure the carbon 14 remaining in the sample. The advantage of the new technique is that it requires only a one-milligram sample for testing.

Copyrights

Source: Library of Congress, Copyright Office.

The copyright law (Title 17 of the United States Code) has been amended by the enactment of a statute for its general revision, Public Law 94-553 (90 Stat. 2541), which was signed by the President on October 19, 1976. The new law superseded the copyright act of 1909, as amended, which remained effective until the new enactment took effect on January 1, 1978.

Under the new law, all copyrightable works, whether published or unpublished, are subject to a single system of statutory protection which gives a copyright owner the exclusive right to reproduce the copyrighted work in copies or phonorecords and distribute them to the public by sale, rental, lease, or lending. Among the other rights given to the owner of a copyright are the exclusive rights to prepare derivative works based upon the copyrighted work, to perform the work publicly if it be literary, musical, dramatic, choreographic, a pantomime, motion picture, or other audiovisual work, and in the case of literary, musical, dramatic, and choreographic works, pantomimes, and pictorial, graphic, or sculptural works, including the individual images of a motion picture or other audiovisual work, to display the copyrighted work publicly. All of these rights are subject to certain exceptions, including the principle of "fair use" which the new statute specifically recognizes.

Special provisions are included which permit compulsory licensing for the recording of musical compositions, noncommercial transmissions by public broadcasters of published musical and graphic works, performances of copyrighted music by jukeboxes, and the secondary transmission of copyrighted works on cable television systems.

Copyright protection under the new law extends to original works of authorship fixed in any tangible medium of expression, now known or later developed, from which they can be perceived, reproduced, or otherwise communicated, either directly or with the aid of a machine or device. Works of authorship include books, periodicals and other literary works, musical compositions with accompanying lyrics, dramas and dramatico-musical compositions, pantomimes and choreographic works, motion pictures and other audiovisual works, and sound recordings.

As a mandatory condition of copyright protection under the law in effect before 1978, all published copies of a work were required to bear a copyright notice. The 1976 Act provides for a notice on published copies, but omission or errors will not immediately result in forfeiture of the copyright, and can be corrected within certain time limits. Innocent infringers misled by the omission or error will be shielded from liability.

Registration in the Copyright Office is not a condition of copyright protection but will be a prerequisite to bringing an action in a court of law for infringement. With certain exceptions, the remedies of statutory damages and attorney's fees will not be available for infringements occurring before registration. Copies or phonorecords published in the United States with notice of copyright are required to be deposited for the collections of the Library of Congress, not as a condition of copyright protection, but under provisions of the law subjecting the copyright owner to certain penalties for failure to deposit after a demand by the Register of Copyrights. Registration is permissive, but may be made either at the time the depository requirements are satisfied or at any other time during the subsistence of the copyright.

For works already under statutory protection, the new law retains the present term of copyright of 28 years from first publication (or from registration in some cases), renewable by certain persons for a second period of protection, but it increases the length of the second period to 47 years. Copyrights in their first term on January 1, 1978, must still be renewed during the last (28th) year of the original copyright term to receive the maximum statutory term of 75 years (a first term of 28 years plus a renewal term of 47 years).

Copyrights in their second term on January 1, 1978, are automatically extended up to a maximum of 75 years, without the need for further renewal. Unpublished works that are already in existence on January 1, 1978, but are not protected by statutory copyright and have not yet gone into the public domain, will generally obtain automatic Federal copyright protection for the author's life, plus an additional 50 years after the author's death, but in any event, for a minimal term of 25 years (that is, until December 31, 2002), and if the work is published before that date, then for an additional term of 25 years, through the end of 2027.

For works created on or after January 1, 1978, the new law provides a term lasting for the author's life, plus an additional 50 years after the author's death. For works made for hire, and for anonymous and pseudonymous works (unless the author's identity is revealed in Copyright Office records), the new term will be 75 years from publication or 100 years from creation, whichever is shorter. The new law provides that all terms of copyright will run through the end of the calendar year in which they would otherwise expire. This will not only affect the duration of copyrights, but also the time-limits for renewal registrations.

Works already in the public domain cannot be protected under the new law. The 1976 Act provides no procedure for restoring protection to works in which copyright has been lost for any reason. In general, works published before September 19, 1906, are not under copyright protection in the United States, at least insofar as any version published before that date is concerned.

The new law requires that all visually perceptible copies published in the United States or elsewhere bear a notice of copyright affixed in such manner and location as to give reasonable notice of the claim of copyright. The notice consists of the symbol © (the letter C in a circle), the word "Copyright," or the abbreviation "Copr.," and the year of first publication of the work, and the name of the owner of copyright in the work. EXAMPLE: © *1978 John Doe.*

The notice of copyright prescribed for sound recordings consists of the symbol ℗ (the letter P in a circle), the year of first publication of the sound recording, and the name of the owner of copyright in the sound recording, placed on the surface of the phonorecord, or on the phonorecord label or container, in such manner and location as to give reasonable notice of the claim of copyright. EXAMPLE: ℗ *1978 Doe Records, Inc.*

A work by a U.S. citizen may obtain copyright protection in all countries that are members of the Universal Copyright Convention (UCC), provided the copyright notice appearing on all copies from the date of first publication includes the symbol ©, together with the name of the copyright owner and the year date of publication. EXAMPLE: © *John Doe 1978.*

Further information and application forms may be obtained free of charge upon request from the Copyright Office, Library of Congress, Washington, D.C. 20559.

Patents

Source: Department of Commerce, Patent and Trademark Office.

A patent, in the most general sense, is a document issued by a government, conferring some special right or privilege. The term is now restricted mainly to patents for inventions; occasionally, land patents.

The grant of a patent for an invention gives the inventor the privilege, for a limited period of time, of excluding others from making, using, or selling a certain article. However, it does not give him the right to make, use, or sell his own invention if it is an improvement on some unexpired patent whose claims are infringed thereby.

In the U.S., the law provides that a patent may be granted, for a term of 17 years, to any person who has invented or discovered any new and useful art, machine, manufacture, or composition of matter, as well as any new and useful improvements thereof. A patent may also be granted to a person who has invented or discovered and asexually reproduced a new and distinct variety of plant (other than a tuber-propagated one) or has invented a new, original and ornamental design for an article of manufacture.

A patent is granted only upon a regularly filed application, complete in all respects; upon payment of the fees; and upon determination that the disclosure is complete and that the invention is new, useful, and, in view of the prior art, unobvious to one skilled in the art. The disclosure must be of such nature as to enable others to reproduce the invention.

A complete application, which must be addressed to the Commissioner of Patents and Trademarks, Washington, D.C. 20231, consists of a specification with one or more claims; oath or declaration; drawing (whenever the nature of the case admits of it); and a basic filing fee of $65, plus certain additional charges for claims. The filing fee is not returned to the applicant if the patent is refused. If the patent is allowed, another fee of $100, plus additional printing charges, is required before the patent is issued. The fees for design patents vary.

Applications are ordinarily considered in the order in which they are received. Patents are not granted for printed matter, for methods of doing business, or for devices for which claims contrary to natural laws are made. Applications for a perpetual-motion machine have been made from time to time, but until a working model is presented that actually fulfills the claim, no patent will be issued.

Trademarks

Source: Department of Commerce, Patent and Trademark Office.

A trademark may be defined as a word, letter, device, or symbol, as well as some combination of these, which is used in connection with merchandise and which points distinctly to the origin of the goods.

Certificates of registration of trademarks are issued under the seal of the Patent and Trademark Office and may be registered by the owner if he is engaged in interstate or foreign commerce, since any Federal jurisdiction over trademarks arises under the commerce clause of the Constitution. Trademarks may be registered by foreign owners who comply with our law, as well as by citizens of foreign countries with which the U.S. has treaties relating to trademarks. American citizens may register trademarks in foreign countries by complying with the laws of those countries. The right to registration and protection of trademarks in many foreign countries is guaranteed by treaties.

General jurisdiction in trademark cases involving Federal Registrations is given to Federal courts. Adverse decisions of examiners on applications for registration are appealable to the Trademark Trial and Appeal Board, whose affirmances, and decisions in *inter partes* proceedings, are subject to court review. Before adopting a trademark, a person should make a search of prior marks to avoid infringing unwittingly upon them.

The duration of a trademark registration is 20 years, but it may be renewed indefinitely for 20-year periods, provided the trademark is still in use at the time of expiration.

Birthstones

Month	Stone	Month	Stone
January	Garnet	July	Ruby or Star Ruby
February	Amethyst	August	Peridot or Sardonyx
March	Aquamarine or Bloodstone	September	Sapphire or Star Sapphire
April	Diamond	October	Opal or Tourmaline
May	Emerald	November	Topaz
June	Pearl, Alexandrite, or Moonstone	December	Turquoise or Zircon

Source: Jewelry Industry Council.

GREAT DISASTERS

(For later disasters, see Current Events of 1980).

Earthquakes and Volcanic Eruptions

A.D. 79 **Aug. 24, Italy:** eruption of Mt. Vesuvius buried cities of Pompeii and Herculaneum, killing thousands.

1556 **Jan. 24, Shaanxi (Shensi) Province, China:** most deadly earthquake in history; 830,000 killed.

1755 **Nov. 1, Portugal:** one of the most severe of recorded earthquakes leveled Lisbon and was felt as far away as southern France and North Africa; 10,000–20,000 killed in Lisbon.

1883 **Aug. 26–28, Netherlands Indies:** eruption of Krakatoa; violent explosions destroyed two thirds of island. Sea waves occurred as far away as Cape Horn, and possibly England. Estimated 36,000 dead.

1902 **May 8, Martinique, West Indies:** Mt. Pelée erupted and wiped out city of St. Pierre; 40,000 dead.

1906 **April 18, San Francisco:** earthquake accompanied by fire razed more than 4 sq mi.; more than 500 dead or missing; property damage about $250–300 million.

1908 **Dec. 28, Messina, Sicily:** about 85,000 killed and city totally destroyed.

1920 **Dec. 16, Gansu (Kansu) Province, China:** earthquake killed 200,000.

1923 **Sept. 1, Japan:** earthquake destroyed third of Tokyo and most of Yokohama; more than 140,000 killed.

1933 **March 10, Long Beach, Calif.:** 117 left dead by earthquake.

1935 **May 31, India:** earthquake at Quetta killed an estimated 50,000.

1939 **Jan. 24, Chile:** earthquake razed 50,000 sq mi.; about 30,000 killed.

Dec. 27, Northern Turkey: severe quakes destroyed city of Erzingan; about 100,000 casualties.

1946 **April 1, Alaska, Hawaii, West Coast:** earthquake and tsunami (tidal wave) left 173 dead in Hawaii.

1950 **Aug. 15, India:** earthquake affected 30,000 sq mi. in Assam; 20,000–30,000 believed killed.

1963 **July 26, Skoplje, Yugoslavia:** four fifths of city destroyed; 1,011 dead, 3,350 injured.

1964 **March 27, Alaska:** strongest earthquake ever to strike North America hits 80 miles east of Anchorage; followed by seismic wave 50 feet high that traveled 8,445 miles at 450 miles per hour; 117 killed and damage in Alaska and West Coast $500–750 million.

1970 **May 31, Peru:** earthquake left 50,000 dead, 17,000 missing.

1971 **Feb. 9, Los Angeles:** earthquake rocked San Fernando Valley. Death toll 64. damage $1 billion.

1972 **April 10, Iran:** 5,000 killed in earthquake 600 miles south of Teheran.

Dec. 22, Managua, Nicaragua: earthquake devastated city, leaving up to 6,000 dead.

1976 **Feb. 4, Guatemala:** earthquake left over 23,000 dead.

June 26, Irian-Jaya, Indonesia: earthquake and landslides killed over 3,000, with another 3,000 missing.

July 28, Tangshan, China: earthquake devastated 20-sq-mi. area of city leaving estimated 242,000 dead.

Aug. 17, Mindanao, Philippines: earthquake and tidal wave left up to 8,000 dead or missing.

1977 **March 4, Bucharest:** earthquake razed most of downtown Bucharest; 1,541 reported dead, over 11,000 injured.

1978 **Sept. 16, Tabas, Iran:** earthquake destroyed city in eastern Iran, leaving 25,000 dead.

Floods, Avalanches, and Tidal Waves

1228 **Holland:** 100,000 persons reputedly drowned by sea flood in Friesland.

1642 **China:** rebels destroyed Kaifeng seawall; 300,-000 drowned.

1889 **May 31, Johnstown, Pa.:** more than 2,200 died in flood.

1896 **June 15, Sanriku, Japan:** earthquake and tidal wave killed 27,000.

1928 **March 12, Santa Paula, Calif.:** collapse of St. Francis Dam left 450 dead.

1953 **Northwest Europe:** storm followed by floods devastated North Sea coastal areas. Netherlands was hardest hit with 1,794 dead.

1959 **Dec. 2, Frejus, France:** flood caused by collapse of Malpasset Dam left 412 dead.

1960 **Agadir, Morocco:** 10,000–12,000 dead as earthquake set off tidal wave and fire, destroying most of city.

1962 **Jan. 10, Peru:** avalanche down Huascaran, extinct Andean volcano, killed more than 3,000 persons.

1963 **Oct. 9, Italy:** landslide collapsed Vaiont Dam; flood killed about 2,000.

1966 **Oct. 21, Aberfan, Wales:** avalanche of coal, waste, mud, and rocks killed 144 persons, including 116 children in school.

1969 **Jan. 18–26, Southern California:** floods and mudslides from heavy rains caused widespread property damage; at least 100 dead. Another downpour (Feb. 23–26) caused further floods and mudslides; at least 18 dead.

1970 **Nov. 13, East Pakistan:** 200,000 killed by cyclone-driven tidal wave from Bay of Bengal. Over 100,000 missing.

1971 **Sept. 29, Orissa State, India:** cyclone and tidal wave off Bay of Bengal killed as many as 10,000.

1972 **Feb. 26, Man, W. Va.:** more than 118 died when slag-pile dam collapsed under pressure of torrential rains and flooded 17-mile valley.

June 9–10, Rapid City, S.D.: flash flood caused 237 deaths and $160 million in damage.

June 20, Eastern Seaboard: tropical storm Agnes, in 10-day rampage, caused widespread flash floods. Death toll was 129, 115,000 were left homeless, and damage estimated at $3.5 billion.

1976 **Aug. 1, Loveland, Colo.:** Flash flood along Route 34 in Big Thompson Canyon left 139 dead.

1977 **Nov. 6, Toccoa, Ga.:** rupture of Kelly Barnes Dam left 39 dead.

Nov. 19, Andhra Pradesh State, India: cyclone and flood from Bay of Bengal left 7,000–10,000 dead.

Storms and Weather

(For U.S. tornadoes and hurricanes, see Index)

1864 **Oct. 5, India:** most of Calcutta denuded by cyclone; 70,000 killed.
1930 **Sept. 3. Santo Domingo:** hurricane killed about 2,000 and injured 6,000.
1934 **Sept. 21, Japan:** hurricane killed more than 4,000 on Honshu.
1942 **Oct. 16, India:** cyclone devastated Bengal; about 40,000 lives lost.
1963 **May 28–29, East Pakistan:** cyclone killed about 22,000 along coast.
Oct. 2–7, Caribbean: Hurricane Flora killed up to 7,000 in Haiti and Cuba.
1965 **May 11–12 and June 1–2, East Pakistan:** cyclones killed about 47,000.
Dec. 15, Karachi, Pakistan: cyclone killed about 10,000.
1974 **Sept. 20, Honduras:** Hurricane Fifi strikes northern section of country, leaving 8,000 dead, 100,000 homeless.
Dec. 25, Darwin, Australia: cyclone destroys nearly the entire city, causing mass evacuation.
1977 **Nov. 19, India:** cyclone strikes state of Andhra Pradesh, killing 10,000.

Fires and Explosions

1666 **Sept. 2, England:** "Great Fire of London" destroyed St. Paul's Church, etc. Damage £10 million.
1812 **Sept. 14, Russia:** fire started by Russians in Moscow after French occupation destroyed 30,800 houses.
1835 **Dec. 16, New York City:** 530 buildings destroyed by fire.
1871 **Oct. 8, Chicago:** the "Chicago Fire" burned 17,450 buildings, killed 250 persons; $196 million damage.
Oct. 8. Peshtigo, Wis.: 1,152 lives lost; 2 billion trees burned.
1872 **Nov. 9, Boston:** fire destroyed 800 buildings; $75-million damage.
1876 **Dec. 5, New York City:** fire in Brooklyn Theater killed more than 300.
1881 **Dec. 8, Vienna:** at least 620 died in fire at Ring Theatre.
1900 **May 1, Scofield, Utah:** explosion of blasting powder in coal mine killed 200.
June 30, Hoboken, N.J.: piers of North German Lloyd Steamship line burned; 326 dead.
1903 **Dec. 30, Chicago:** Iroquois Theatre fire killed 602.
1904 **Feb. 7, Baltimore:** business section burned; estimated $125-million damage.
1906 **March 10, France:** explosion in coal mine in Courrières killed 1,060.
1907 **Dec. 6, Monongha, W. Va.:** coal mine explosion killed 361.
Dec. 19, Jacobs Creek, Pa.: explosion in coal mine left 239 dead.
1909 **Nov. 13, Cherry, Ill.:** explosion in coal mine killed 259.
1911 **March 25, New York City:** fire in Triangle Shirtwaist Factory fatal to 145.
1913 **Oct. 22, Dawson, N.M.:** coal mine explosion left 263 dead.
1917 **April 10, Eddystone, Pa.:** explosion in munitions plant killed 133.
Dec. 6, Canada: explosion and fire at Halifax when ammunition ship collided with a vessel; 1,500 dead.
1930 **April 21, Columbus, Ohio:** fire in Ohio State Penitentiary killed 320 convicts.
1937 **March 18, New London, Tex.:** explosion destroyed schoolhouse; 294 killed.
1942 **April 26, Manchuria:** explosion in Honkeiko Colliery killed 1,549.
Nov. 28, Boston: Cocoanut Grove nightclub fire killed 491.
1944 **July 6, Hartford, Conn.:** fire and ensuing stampede in main tent of Ringling Brothers Circus killed 168, injured 487.
July 17, Port Chicago, Calif.: 322 killed as ammunition ships explode.
Oct. 20, Cleveland: liquid-gas tanks exploded, killing 130.
1946 **Dec. 7, Atlanta:** fire in Winecoff Hotel killed 119.
1947 **April 16–18, Texas City, Tex.:** most of city destroyed, 561 dead following explosion on ship.
1949 **Sept. 2, China:** fire on Chongqing (Chungking) waterfront killed 1,700.
1953 **Oct. 16, Boston:** explosion and fire aboard U.S.S. *Leyte* killed 37.
1954 **May 26, off Quonset Point, R.I.:** explosion and fire aboard aircraft *Bennington* killed 103 crewmen.
1955 **June 11, France:** crash and explosion of racing car into crowd during Grand Prix race, Le Mans, killed 82.
1956 **Aug. 7, Colombia:** about 1,100 reported killed when seven army ammunition trucks exploded at Cali.
Aug. 8, Belgium: 262 died in coal mine fire at Marcinelle.
1958 **Dec. 1, Chicago:** fire at Our Lady of the Angels school killed 95.
1960 **Jan. 21, Coalbrook, South Africa:** coal mine explosion killed 437.
Nov. 13, Syria: 152 children killed in moviehouse fire.
Dec. 19. Brooklyn, N.Y.: blaze on aircraft carrier *Constellation* killed 49 workmen.
1961 **Dec. 17, Niteroi, Brazil:** circus fire fatal to 323.
1962 **Feb. 7, Saarland, West Germany:** coal mine gas explosion killed 298.
1963 **Nov. 9, Japan:** explosion in coal mine at Omuta killed 447.
1965 **May 28, India:** coal mine fire in state of Bihar killed 375.
June 1, near Fukuoka, Japan: coal mine explosion killed 236.
1966 **Oct. 17, New York City:** 12 firemen were killed in sudden collapse of burning building.
Oct. 26, off South Vietnam: fire on U.S. carrier *Oriskany* killed 43.
1967 **May 22, Brussels:** fire in L'Innovation, major department store, left 322 dead.
July 29, off North Vietnam: fire on U.S. carrier *Forrestal* killed 134.
1969 **Jan. 14, Pearl Harbor, Hawaii:** nuclear aircraft carrier *Enterprise* ripped by explosions; 27 dead, 82 injured.
April 6, New Orleans: Taiwanese freighter and string of oil-loaded barges collided in fiery explosion on Mississippi River; 25 dead.
1970 **Nov. 1, Saint-Laurent-du-Pont, France:** fire in dance hall killed 146 young people.
Dec. 30, Wooten, Ky.: coal-dust explosion in coal mine killed 38.
1972 **May 2, Kellogg, Idaho:** fire in Sunshine silver mine killed 91 miners; two men survived.

May 13, Osaka, Japan: 118 people died in fire in nightclub on top floor of Sennichi department store.

June 6, Wankie, Rhodesia: explosion in coal mine killed 427.

1973 **Nov. 29, Kumamoto, Japan:** fire in Taiyo department store killed 101.

1974 **Feb. 1, Sao Paulo, Brazil:** fire in upper stories of bank building killed 189 persons, many of whom leaped to death.

1975 **Dec. 27, Dhanbad, India:** explosion in coal mine followed by flooding from nearby reservoir left 372 dead.

1977 **Feb. 25, Moscow:** fire in 6,000-bed Hotel Rossiya fatal to at least 45 guests.

May 28, Southgate, Ky.: fire in Beverly Hills Supper Club; 167 dead.

June 26, Columbia, Tenn.: fire believed set by inmate is fatal to 42 prisoners and visitors at Maury County Jail.

Dec. 22, Westwego, La.: explosion destroyed Continental Grain Company plant, killing 36.

1978 **July 11, Tarragona, Spain:** 140 killed at coastal campsite when tank truck carrying liquid gas overturns and explodes.

Aug. 20, Abadan, Iran: nearly 400 killed when arsonists set fire to crowded theater.

1979 **July 12, Saragossa, Spain:** fire in 10-story Hotel Corona de Aragon killed more than 72 guests when a pastry machine exploded.

Dec. 31, Chapais, Quebec, Canada: fire at Opemiska Club fatal to 45 New Year's Eve partygoers.

Shipwrecks

1833 **May 11, *Lady of the Lake:*** bound from England to Quebec, struck iceberg; 215 perished.

1853 **Sept. 29 *Annie Jane:*** emigrant vessel off coast of Scotland; 348 died.

1865 **April 27, *Sultana:*** boiler explosion on Mississippi River steamboat near Memphis, 1,547 killed.

1898 **Nov. 26, *City of Portland:*** Loss of 157 off Cape Cod.

1904 **June 15, *General Slocum:*** excursion steamer burned in East River, New York; 1,021 perished.

1912 **March 5, *Principe de Asturias:*** Spanish steamer struck rock off Sebastien Point; 500 drowned.

April 15, *Titanic:* sank after colliding with iceberg; 1,513 died.

1914 **May 29, *Empress of Ireland:*** sank after collision in St. Lawrence River; 1,024 perished.

1915 **July 24, *Eastland:*** Great Lakes excursion steamer overturned in Chicago River; 812 died.

1928 **Nov. 12, *Vestris:*** British steamer sank in gale off Virginia; 110 died.

1931 **June 14:** French excursion steamer overturned in gale off St. Nazaire; approximately 450 died.

1934 **Sept. 8, *Morro Castle:*** 134 killed in fire off Asbury Park, N.J.

1939 **May 23, *Squalus:*** submarine with 59 men sank off Hampton Beach, N.H.; 33 saved.

June 1, Submarine *Thetis:* sank in Liverpool Bay, England; 99 perished.

1942 **Oct. 2, *Queen Mary:*** rammed and sank a British cruiser; 338 aboard the cruiser died.

1945 **April 9:** U.S. ship, loaded with aerial bombs, exploded at Bari, Italy; at least 360 killed.

1948 **Dec. 3, *Kiangya:*** Chinese refugee ship wrecked in explosion; about 1,000 believed dead.

1949 **Sept. 17, *Noronic:*** Canadian Great Lakes cruise ship burned at Toronto dock; about 130 died.

1951 **April 16, *Affray:*** British submarine sank in English Channel; 75 dead.

1952 **April 26, *Hobson:*** minesweeper collided with aircraft carrier *Wasp* and sank during night maneuvers in mid-Atlantic; 176 persons lost.

1953 **Jan. 9, *Chang Tyong-Ho:*** South Korean ferry foundered off Pusan; 249 reported dead.

Jan. 31, *Princess Victoria:* British ferry sank in Irish Sea; 133 lost.

1956 **July 25, *Andrea Doria:*** Italian liner collided with Swedish liner *Stockholm* off Nantucket Island, Mass., sinking next day; 52, mostly passengers on Italian ship, dead or unaccounted for; over 1,600 rescued.

1962 **April 8, *Dara,*** British liner, exploded and sank in Persian Gulf; 236 persons dead. Caused by time bomb.

1963 **April 10, *Thresher:*** atomic-powered submarine sank in North Atlantic; 129 dead.

May 4: U.A.R. ferry capsized and sank in upper Nile; over 200 died.

1964 **Nov. 26, *Shalom:*** Israeli liner collided with Norwegian tanker *Stolt Dagali* off New Jersey coast; 19 of tanker's crew dead.

1965 **Nov. 13, *Yarmouth Castle:*** cruise ship burned and sank 60 miles northeast of Nassau en route from Miami to Bahamas; 90 dead.

1968 **Late May, *Scorpion:*** nuclear submarine sank in Atlantic 400 miles S.W. of Azores; 99 dead. (Located Oct. 31.)

1970 **Aug. 1:** ferry between Basseterre, St. Kitts, and Charlestown, Nevis, capsized in Caribbean; 125 believed lost.

Dec. 15: ferry in Korean Strait capsized; 261 lost.

1976 **Oct. 20, Luling, La.: *George Prince,*** Mississippi River ferry, rammed by Norwegian tanker *Frosta;* 77 dead.

1980 **Jan. 28, *Blackthorn:*** Coast Guard cutter and Tanker *Capricorn* collided under Sunshine Skyway near Tampa, Fla. 23 members of cutter's crew lost.

Aircraft Accidents

1921 **Aug. 24, England:** *ZR-2* British dirigible, broke in two on trial trip near Hull; 62 died.

1925 **Sept. 3, Caldwell, Ohio:** U.S. dirigible *Shenandoah* broke apart; 14 dead.

1933 **April 4, New Jersey Coast:** U.S. dirigible *Akron* crashed; 73 died.

1937 **May 6, Lakehurst, N.J.:** German zeppelin *Hindenburg* destroyed by fire at tower mooring; 36 killed.

1945 **July 28, New York City:** U.S. Army bomber crashed into Empire State Building; 13 dead.

1946 **May 20, New York City:** U.S. Army plane crashed into Manhattan Company building; five dead.

1949 **Nov. 1, Washington, D.C.:** fighter plane rammed airliner, killing 55.

1951 **Dec. 16, Elizabeth, N.J.:** nonscheduled airliner crash killed 56.

1952 **Jan. 22, Elizabeth, N.J.:** 29 killed, including former Secretary of War Robert P. Patterson, when airliner hit apartments; seven of dead were on ground.

Feb. 11, Elizabeth, N.J.: third major air disaster in Elizabeth within two months fatally injured 33.

1953 **June 18, near Tokyo:** crash of U.S. Air Force "Globemaster" killed 129 servicemen.

1955 **Nov. 1, near Longmont, Colo.:** time bomb hidden in luggage destroyed airliner in flight, killing 44.

1956 **June 30, Grand Canyon, Ariz.:** 128 died in collision of TWA Super Constellation and United Airlines DC-7.

1957 **March 17, near Cebu City, Philippines:** President Ramón Magsaysay and 24 others killed in crash.

1959 **Feb. 3, New York City:** American Airlines Lockheed Electra turboprop plane crashed in East River; 65 dead.

1960 **Feb. 25, Rio de Janeiro:** U.S. Navy plane, flying Navy musicians to perform at dinner given by visiting President Eisenhower, collided with Brazilian airliner, killing 61.

Sept. 19, near Guam: crash shortly after take-off of World Airways plane took 78 lives.

Oct. 4, Boston Harbor: Eastern Airlines plane sank; 61 dead.

Dec. 16, New York City: United and Trans World planes collided in fog, crashed in two boroughs, killing 134 in air and on ground.

1961 **Feb. 15, near Brussels:** 72 on board and farmer on ground killed in crash of Sabena plane; U.S. figure skating team wiped out.

1962 **March 1, New York City:** American Airlines jetliner crashed into Jamaica Bay, near Idlewild Airport, killing all 95 on board.

June 3, Paris: chartered Air France Boeing Jet 707 crashed at Orly Airport; 130 dead.

June 22, Grande-Teree Island, Guadeloupe: Air France Boeing 707 crashed, killing all 113 aboard.

1965 **Feb. 8, New York City:** Eastern Airlines DC-7B went down in Atlantic shortly after take-off from Kennedy International Airport; 84 dead.

1966 **Jan. 24, Mont Blanc:** Indian airliner crashed into mountain in fog; 117 dead.

March 5, Japan: British airliner caught fire and crashed into Mt. Fuji; 124 dead.

Dec. 24, Binh Thai, South Vietnam: crash of military-chartered plane into village killed 129.

1967 **April 20, Nicosia, Cyprus:** crash of chartered Swiss Turboprop killed 126.

July 19, near Hendersonville, N.C.: Piedmont Airlines Boeing 727 collided with private plane; 82 dead.

1968 **May 3, near Dawson, Tex.:** Braniff airliner crashed; 85 dead.

1969 **March 16, Maracaibo, Venezuela:** Venezuelan jetliner crashed and exploded; 84 crew members and passengers died and 71 were killed on ground.

Sept. 9, Shelbyville, Ind.: Allegheny Airlines jetliner and single-engine plane flown by student pilot collided in air and crashed; 83 dead.

Dec. 8, Keratea, Greece: rain and hurricane winds caused Greek airliner to crash into 2,000-foot mountain while approaching Athens; 90 dead.

1970 **Feb. 15, Santo Domingo, Dominican Republic:** Dominican Republic jetliner plunged into Caribbean on takeoff; 102 dead.

July 4, Arbucias, Spain: British Comet crashed into mountains while coming in for landing at Barcelona; 112 dead.

July 5, Toronto: Canadian jetliner crashed on landing approach; 109 dead.

Aug. 9, Cuzco, Peru: Peruvian turboprop, with 51 teen-age U.S. students among passengers, crashed shortly after takeoff; 99 dead.

Nov. 14, Huntington, W. Va.: chartered plane carrying 43 players and coaches of Marshall University football team crashed; 75 dead.

1971 **June 6, near Los Angeles:** Air West DC-9 and Navy F-4 fighter collided over San Gabriel Canyon; 49 killed; one Navy crewman parachuted to safety.

July 30, Morioka, Japan: Japanese Boeing 727 and F-86 fighter collided in mid-air; toll was 162.

Sept. 4, near Juneau, Alaska: Alaska Airlines Boeing 727 crashed into Chilkoot Mountains; 111 killed.

1972 **May 5, Palermo, Sicily:** Alitalia DC-8 hit mountain, killing 115.

June 18, London: B.E.A. Trident jetliner plunged into field minutes after take-off from Heathrow Airport; all 118 aboard dead.

Aug. 14, East Berlin, East Germany: Soviet-built East German Ilyushin plane crashed, killing 156.

Oct. 13, Moscow: 176 died when Soviet Ilyushin airliner crashed.

Dec. 3, Santa Cruz de Tenerife, Canary Islands: Spanish charter jet carrying West German tourists crashed on take-off; all 155 aboard killed.

Dec. 30, Miami, Fla.: Eastern Airlines Lockheed 1011 TriStar Jumbo jet crashed into Everglades; 101 killed, 75 survived.

1973 **Jan. 22, Kano, Nigeria:** 171 Nigerian Moslems returning from Mecca and five crewmen died in crash.

April 10, Hochwald, Switzerland: British airliner carrying tourists to Swiss fair crashed in blizzard; 106 dead.

July 11, Paris: Boeing 707 of Varig Airlines, en route to Rio de Janeiro, crashed near airport, killing 122 of 134 passengers.

July 31, Boston: Delta Airlines jet crashed in heavy fog in landing at Logan International Airport killing 88 of 89 aboard.

1974 **Jan. 31, Pago Pago, Samoa:** Pan American 707 crashed while landing; 97 of 101 persons aboard killed.

March 3, Paris: Turkish DC-10 jumbo jet crashed in forest shortly after take-off; all 346 passengers and crew killed in worst single-plane disaster to date.

Dec. 1, Berryville, Va.: all 92 aboard killed in crash of TWA 727 into wooded area.

Dec. 4, Colombo, Sri Lanka: Dutch DC-8 carrying Moslems to Mecca crashed on landing approach, killing all 191 persons aboard.

1975 **April 4, near Saigon, Vietnam:** Air Force Galaxy C-5A crashed after take-off, killing 172, mostly Vietnamese children.

June 24, New York City: Eastern Airlines Boeing 727, arriving from New Orleans, crashed at Kennedy International Airport, killing 113.

Aug. 3, Agadir, Morocco: Chartered Boeing 707, returning Moroccan workers home after vacation in France, plunged into mountainside; all 188 aboard killed.

Aug. 20, Damascus, Syria: Czech airliner crashed while landing, killing 126 of 128 persons aboard.

1976 **Sept. 10, Zagreb, Yugoslavia:** midair collision between British Airways Trident and Yugoslav charter DC-9 fatal to all 176 persons aboard; worst mid-air collision on record.

1977 **March 27, Santa Cruz de Tenerife, Canary Islands:** Pan American and KLM Boeing 747s collided on runway. All 249 on KLM plane and 333 of 394 aboard Pan Am jet killed. Total of 582 is highest for any type of aviation disaster.

1978 **Jan. 1, Bombay:** Air India 747 with 213 aboard explodes and plunges into sea minutes after takeoff.
Sept. 25, San Diego, Calif.: Pacific Southwest plane collided in midair with Cessna. All 135 on airliner, 2 in Cessna, and 7 on ground killed for total of 144.
Nov. 15, Colombo, Sri Lanka: Chartered Icelandic Airlines DC-8, carrying 249 Moslem pilgrims from Mecca, crashed in thunderstorm during landing approach; 183 killed.

1979 **May 26, Chicago:** American Airlines DC-10 lost left engine upon take-off and crashed seconds later, killing all 272 persons aboard and three on the ground, in worst U.S. air disaster.
Aug. 15, Ukraine, U.S.S.R.: Two planes collided in mid-air; 150 killed.
Oct. 15, Mexico City: Western Airlines DC-10 crashed on landing, killing 73.
Nov. 26, Jidda, Saudi Arabia: Pakistan International Airlines 707 carrying pilgrims returning from Mecca crashed on take-off; all 156 aboard killed.
Nov. 28, Mt. Erebus, Antarctica: Air New Zealand DC-10 crashed on sightseeing flight; 257 killed.

1980 **Jan. 21, near Laskgarak, Iran:** Iran Air Boeing 727 crashed into mountains, killing all 128 aboard.
March 14, Warsaw: LOT Polish Airlines Ilyushin 62 crashed while attempting landing; 22 boxers and officials of a U.S. amateur boxing team killed along with 65 others.
April 25, Santa Cruz de Tenerife, Canary Islands: Chartered Boeing 727 carrying 138 British vacationers and crew of 8 crashed into mountain while approaching for landing; all killed.

Railroad Accidents

1904 **Aug. 7, Eden, Colo.:** Two-train collision killed 96.

1910 **March 1, Wellington, Wash.:** two trains swept into canyon by avalanche; 96 dead.

1915 **May 22, Gretna, Scotland:** two passenger trains and troop train collided; 227 killed.

1917 **Dec. 12, Modane, France:** nearly 550 killed in derailment of troop train near mouth of Mt. Cenis tunnel.

1918 **Nov. 1, New York City:** derailment of subway train in Malbone St. tunnel in Brooklyn left 92 dead.

1939 **Dec. 22, near Magdeburg, Germany:** more than 125 killed in collision; 99 killed in another wreck near Friedrichshafen.

1943 **Dec. 16, near Rennert, N.C.:** 72 killed in derailment and collision of two Atlantic Coast Line trains.

1944 **March 2, near Salerno, Italy:** 521 suffocated when Italian train stalled in tunnel.
Dec. 31, near Ogden, Utah: 48 killed in collision of two sections of Southern Pacific's Pacific Limited.

1946 **April 25, Naperville, Ill.:** at least 47 killed in collision of two trains of Burlington Railroad.

1949 **Oct. 22, near Nowy Dwor, Poland:** more than 200 reported killed in derailment of Danzig-Warsaw express.

1950 **Feb. 17, Rockville Centre, N.Y.:** head-on crash of two Long Island Rail Road commuter trains killed 30.
Nov. 22, Richmond Hill, N.Y.: 79 died when one Long Island Rail Road commuter train crashed into rear of another.

1951 **Feb. 6, Woodbridge, N.J.:** 85 died when Pennsylvania Railroad commuter train plunged through temporary overpass.

1952 **Oct. 8, Harrow-Wealdstone, England:** two express trains crashed into commuter train; 112 dead.

1953 **Dec. 24, near Sakvice, Czechoslovakia:** two trains crashed; over 100 dead.

1956 **Sept. 2, near Mahbubnagar, India:** at least 120 killed when bridge collapsed under train.

1957 **Sept. 1, near Kendal, Jamaica:** about 175 killed when train plunged into ravine.
Sept. 29, near Montgomery, West Pakistan: express train crashed into standing oil train; nearly 300 killed.
Dec. 4, St. John's, England: 92 killed, 187 injured as one commuter train crashed into another in fog.

1958 **Sept. 15, near Bayonne, N.J.:** over 40 killed when Central Railroad of New Jersey train went through open drawbridge.

1960 **Nov. 14, Pardubice, Czechoslovakia:** two trains collided; 110 dead, 106 injured.

1962 **May 3, near Tokyo:** 163 killed and 400 injured when train crashed into wreckage of collision between inbound freight train and outbound commuter train.

1963 **Nov. 9, near Yokohama, Japan:** two passenger trains crashed into derailed freight, killing 162.

1964 **July 26, Custoias, Portugal:** passenger train derailed; 94 dead.

1970 **Feb. 4, near Buenos Aires:** 236 killed when express train crashed into standing commuter train.

1972 **July 21, Seville, Spain:** head-on crash of two passenger trains killed 76.
Oct. 6, near Saltillo, Mexico: train carrying religious pilgrims derailed and caught fire, killing 204 and injuring over 1,000.
Oct. 30, Chicago: two Illinois Central commuter trains collided during morning rush hour; 45 dead and over 200 injured.

1974 **Aug. 30, Zagreb, Yugoslavia:** train entering station derailed, killing 153 and injuring over 60.

1977 **Feb. 4, Chicago:** 11 killed and over 180 injured when elevated train hit rear of another, sending two cars to street.

Miscellaneous

1955 **June 11, Le Mans, France:** Racing car in Grand Prix hurtled into grandstand, killing 82 spectators.

1967 **Aug. 27, Huron, Ohio:** Sky divers jumping through overcast from off-course plane landed in Lake Erie; 16 killed.

1978 **April 27, St. Mary's, W. Va.:** Scaffolding in power-plant cooling tower under construction collapsed; killing 57 workmen.
Aug. 4, Lac d'Argent, Quebec: Bus carrying handicapped theatergoers plunged into lake, killing 40.

1980 **Jan. 20, Sincelejo, Colombia:** Bleachers at a bullring collapsed, leaving 222 dead.
March 30, Stavanger, Norway: Floating hotel in North Sea collapsed, killing 123 oil workers.
May 9, St. Petersburg, Fla.: *Summit Venture,* 606-foot phosphate carrier, struck Sunshine Skyway Bridge in blinding rain squall; 1,300-foot section of roadway fell into Tampa Bay, taking with it several passenger cars and a Greyhound bus; 35 killed.

World Geography

Explorations and Discoveries

(All years are A.D. unless B.C. is specified.)

Country or place	Event	Explorer or discoverer	Date
AFRICA			
Sierra Leone	Visited	Hanno, Carthaginian seaman	c. 520 B.C.
Congo River	Mouth discovered	Diogo Cão, Portuguese	c. 1484
Cape of Good Hope	Rounded	Bartholomeu Diaz, Portuguese	1488
Gambia River	Explored	Mungo Park, Scottish explorer	1795
Sahara	Crossed	Dixon Denham and Hugh Clapperton, English explorers	1822–23
Zambezi River	Discovered	Davis Livingstone, Scottish explorer	1851
Sudan	Explored	Heinrich Barth, German explorer	1852–55
Victoria Falls	Discovered	Livingstone	1855
Lake Tanganyika	Discovered	Richard Burton and John Speke, British explorers	1858
Congo River	Traced	Sir Henry M. Stanley, British explorer	1877
ASIA			
Punjab (India)	Visited	Alexander the Great	327 B.C.
China	Visited	Marco Polo, Italian traveler	c. 1272
Tibet	Visited	Odoric of Pordenone, Italian monk	c. 1325
Southern China	Explored	Niccolò dei Conti, Venetian traveler	c. 1440
India	Visited (Cape route)	Vasco da Gama, Portuguese navigator	1498
Japan	Visited	St. Francis Xavier of Spain	1549
Arabia	Explored	Carsten Niebuhr, German explorer	1762
China	Explored	Ferdinand Richthofen, German scientist	1868
Mongolia	Explored	Nikolai M. Przhevalsky, Russian explorer	1870–73
Central Asia	Explored	Sven Hedin, Swedish scientist	1890–1908
EUROPE			
Shetland Islands	Visited	Pytheas of Massilia (Marseille)	c. 325 B.C.
North Cape	Rounded	Ottar, Norwegian explorer	c. 870
Iceland	Colonized	Norwegian noblemen	c. 890–900
NORTH AMERICA			
Greenland	Colonized	Eric the Red, Norwegian	c. 985
Labrador; Nova Scotia (?)	Discovered	Leif Ericson, Norse explorer	1000
West Indies	Discovered	Christopher Columbus, Italian	1492
North America	Coast discovered	Giovanni Caboto (John Cabot), for British	1497
Pacific Ocean	Discovered	Vasco Núñez de Balboa, Spanish explorer	1513
Florida	Explored	Ponce de León, Spanish explorer	1513
Mexico	Conquered	Hernando Cortés, Spanish adventurer	1519–21
St. Lawrence River	Discovered	Jacques Cartier, French navigator	1534
Southwest U. S.	Explored	Francisco Coronado, Spanish explorer	1540–42
Colorado River	Discovered	Hernando de Alarcón, Spanish explorer	1540
Mississippi River	Discovered	Hernando de Soto, Spanish explorer	1541
Frobisher Bay	Discovered	Martin Frobisher, English seaman	1576

Country or place	Event	Explorer or discoverer	Date
Maine Coast	Explored	Samuel de Champlain, French explorer	1604
Jamestown, Va.	Settled	John Smith, English colonist	1607
Hudson River	Explored	Henry Hudson, English navigator	1609
Hudson Bay (Canada)	Discovered	Henry Hudson	1610
Baffin Bay	Discovered	William Baffin, English navigator	1616
Lake Michigan	Navigated	Jean Nicolet, French explorer	1634
Arkansas River	Discovered	Jacques Marquette and Louis Jolliet, French explorers	1673
Mississippi River	Explored	Sieur de La Salle, French explorer	1682
Bering Strait	Discovered	Vitus Bering, Danish explorer	1728
Alaska	Discovered	Vitus Bering	1741
Mackenzie River (Canada)	Discovered	Sir Alexander Mackenzie, Scottish-Canadian explorer	1789
Northwest U. S.	Explored	Meriwether Lewis and William Clark	1804–06
Northeast Passage (Arctic Ocean)	Navigated	Nils Nordenskjöld, Swedish explorer	1879
Greenland	Explored	Robert Peary, American explorer	1892
Northwest Passage	Navigated	Roald Amundsen, Norwegian explorer	1906
SOUTH AMERICA			
Continent	Visited	Columbus, Italian	1498
Brazil	Discovered	Pedro Alvarez Cabral, Portuguese	1500
Peru	Conquered	Francisco Pizarro, Spanish explorer	1532–33
Amazon River	Explored	Francisco Orellana, Spanish explorer	1541
Cape Horn	Discovered	Willem C. Schouten, Dutch navigator	1615
OCEANIA			
New Guinea	Visited	Jorge de Menezes, Portuguese explorer	1526
Australia	Visited }	Abel Janszoon Tasman, Dutch navigator	1642
Tasmania	Discovered }		
Australia	Explored	John McDouall Stuart, English explorer	1828
Australia	Explored	Robert Burke and William Wills, Australian explorers	1861
New Zealand	Sighted (and named)	Abel Janszoon Tasman	1642
New Zealand	Visited	James Cook, English navigator	1769
ARCTIC, ANTARCTIC, AND MISCELLANEOUS			
Ocean exploration	Expedition	Magellan's ships circled globe	1519–22
Galápagos Islands	Visited	Diego de Rivadeneira, Spanish captain	1535
Spitsbergen	Visited	Willem Barents, Dutch navigator	1596
Antarctic Circle	Crossed	James Cook, English navigator	1773
Antarctica	Discovered	Nathaniel Palmer, U. S. whaler (archipelago) and Fabian Gottlieb von Bellingshausen, Russian admiral (mainland)	1820–21
Antarctica	Explored	Charles Wilkes, American explorer	1840
North Pole	Reached	Robert E. Peary, American explorer	1909
South Pole	Reached	Roald Amundsen, Norwegian explorer	1911

The Continents

A continent is defined as a large unbroken land mass completely surrounded by water, although in some cases continents are (or were in part) connected by land bridges.

The hypothesis first suggested late in the 19th century was that the continents consist of lighter rocks that rest on heavier crustal material in about the same manner that icebergs float on water. That the rocks forming the continents are lighter than the material below them and under the ocean bottoms is now established. As a consequence of this fact, Alfred Wegener (for the first time in 1912) suggested that the continents are slowly moving, at a rate of about one yard per century, so that their relative positions are not rigidly fixed. Many geologists that were originally skeptical have come to accept this theory of Continental Drift.

When describing a continent, it is important to remember that there is a fundamental difference between a deep ocean, like the Atlantic, and shallow seas, like the Baltic and most of the North Sea, which are merely flooded portions of a continent. Another and entirely different point to remember is that political considerations have often overridden geographical facts when it came to naming continents.

Geographically speaking, Europe, including the British Isles, is a large western peninsula of the continent of Asia; and many geographers, when referring to Europe and Asia, speak of the Eurasian Continent. But traditionally, Europe is counted as a separate continent, with the Ural and the Caucasus mountains forming the line of demarcation between Europe and Asia.

To the south of Europe, Asia has an odd-shaped peninsula jutting westward, which has a large number of political subdivisions. The northern section is taken up by Turkey; to the south of Turkey there are Syria, Iraq, Israel, Jordan, Saudi Arabia, and a number of smaller Arab countries. All this is part of Asia. Traditionally, the island of Cyprus in the Mediterranean is also considered to be part of Asia, while the island of Crete is counted as European.

The large islands of Java, Borneo, and Sumatra and the smaller islands near them are counted as part of "tropical Asia," while New Guinea is counted as related to Australia. In the case of the Americas, the problem arises as to whether they should be considered one or two continents. There are good arguments on both sides, but since there is now a land bridge between North and South America (in the past it was often flooded) and since no part of the sea east of the land bridge is deep ocean, it is more logical to consider the Americas as one continent.

Politically, based mainly on history, the Americas are divided into North America (from the Arctic to the Mexican border), Central America (from Mexico to Panama, with the Caribbean islands), and South America. Greenland is considered a section of North America, while Iceland is traditionally counted as a European island because of its political ties with the Scandinavian countries.

The island groups in the Pacific are often called "Oceania," but this name does *not* imply that scientists consider them the remains of a continent.

Volcanoes of the World

About 500 volcanoes have had recorded eruptions within historical times. Almost two thirds of these are in the Northern Hemisphere. Most volcanoes occur at the boundaries of the earth's crustal plates, such as the famous "Ring of Fire" that surrounds the Pacific Ocean plate. Of the world's active volcanoes, about 60% are along the perimeter of the Pacific, about 17% on mid-oceanic islands, about 14% in an arc along the south of the Indonesian islands, and about 9% in the Mediterranean area, Africa, and Asia Minor. Many of the world's volcanoes are submarine and have unrecorded eruptions.

Pacific "Ring of Fire"

NORTHWEST

Japan: At least 33 active vents.

Aso (5,223 ft; 1,592 m), on Kyushu, has one of the largest craters in the world.

Asama (over 8,300 ft; 2,530 m), on Honshu, is continuously active; violent eruption in 1783.

Azuma (nearly 7,700 ft; 2,347 m), on Honshu, erupted in 1900.

Chokai (7,300 ft; 2,225 m), on Honshu, erupted in 1974 after having been quiescent since 1861.

Fujiyama (Fujisan) (12,385 ft; 3,775 m), on Honshu, southwest of Tokyo. Symmetrical in outline, snow-covered. Regarded as a sacred mountain.

On-take (3,668 ft; 1,118 m), on peninsula of Kyushu. Strong smoke emissions and explosions began November 1973 and continued through 1974.

U.S.S.R.: Kamchatka peninsula, 14–18 active volcanoes. Klyuchevskaya (Kluchev) (15,500 ft; 4,724 m) reported active in 1974.

Kuril Islands: At least 13 active volcanoes and several submarine outbreaks.

SOUTHWEST

New Zealand: Mount Tarawera (3,645 ft; 1,112 m), on North Island, had a severe eruption in 1886 that destroyed the famous Pink and White sinter terraces of Rotomahana, a hot lake.

Ngauruhoe (7,515 ft; 2,291 m), on North Island, emits steam and vapor constantly. Erupted 1974.

Papua New Guinea: Karkar Island (4,920 ft; 1,500 m). Mild eruptions 1974.

Philippine Islands: About 100 eruptive centers; Hibok Hibok, on Camiguin, erupted September 1950 and again in December 1951, when about 750 were reported killed or missing; eruptions continued during 1952–53.

Taal (4,752 ft; 1,448 m), on Luzon. Major eruption in 1965 killed 190; erupted again, 1968.

Volcano Islands: Mount Suribachi (546 ft; 166 m), on Iwo Jima. A sulfurous steaming volcano. Raising of U.S. flag over Mount Suribachi was one of the dramatic episodes of World War II.

NORTHEAST

Alaska: Mount Wrangell (14,163 ft; 4,317 m) and Mount Katmai (about 6,700 ft; 2,042 m). On June 6, 1912, a violent eruption (Nova Rupta) of Mount Katmai occurred, during which the "Valley of Ten Thousand Smokes" was formed.

Aleutian Islands: There are 32 active vents known and numerous inactive cones. Akutan Island (over 4,000 ft; 1,220 m) erupted in 1974, with ash and debris rising over 300 ft.

Great Sitkin (5,741 ft; 1,750 m). Explosive activity February-September 1974, accompanied by earthquake originating at volcano that registered 2.3 on Richter scale.

California, Oregon, Washington: Lassen Peak (10,453 ft; 3,186 m) in California is one of two observed active volcanoes in the U.S. outside Alaska and Hawaii. The last period of activity was 1914–17. Mt. St. Helens (9,677 ft; 2,950 m) in the Cascade Range of southwest Washington became active on March 27, 1980. It last erupted in 1857. Other mountains of volcanic origin include Mount Shasta (California), Mount Hood (Oregon), Mount Mazama (Oregon)—the mountain continaing Crater Lake, Mount Rainier (Washington), and Mount Bakêr (Washington), which has been steaming since October 1975, but gives no sign of an impending eruption.

SOUTHEAST
Chile and Argentina: About 25 active or potentially active.
Colombia: Huila (nearly 18,900 ft; 5,760 m), a vapor-emitting volcano, and Tolima (nearly 18,500 ft; 5,640 m). Eruption of Puracé (15,600 ft; 4,755 m) in 1949 killed 17 people.
Ecuador: Cayambe (nearly 19,000 ft; 5,791 m). Almost on the equator.
Cotopaxi (19,344 ft; 5,896 m). Perhaps highest active volcano in the world. Possesses a beautifully formed cone.
Reventador (11,434 ft; 3,485 m). Observed in active state in late 1973.
El Salvador: Izalco ("beacon of Central America") (7,830 ft; 2,387 m) first appeared in 1770 and is still growing (erupted in 1950, 1956; last erupted in October-November 1966). San Salvador (6,187 ft; 1,886 m) had a violent eruption in 1923. Conchagua (about 4100 ft; 1250 m) erupted with considerable damage early in 1947.
Guatemala: Santa Maria Quezaltenango (12,361 ft; 3,768 m). Frequent activity between 1902–08 and 1922–28 after centuries of quiescence. Most dangerously active vent of Central America. Other volcanoes include Tajumulco (13,814 ft; 4,211 m) and Atitlán (11,633 ft; 3,546 m).
Mexico: Boquerón ("Big Mouth"), on San Benedicto, about 250 mi. south of Lower California. Newest volcano in Western Hemisphere, discovered September 1952.
Colima (about 14,000 ft; 4,270 m), in group that has had frequent eruptions.
Orizaba (Citlaltépetl) (18,701 ft; 5,700 m).
Parícutin (7,450 ft; 2,270 m). First appeared in February 1943. In less than a week, a cone over 140 ft high developed with a crater one quarter mile in circumference. Cone grew more than 1,500 ft (457 m) in 1943. Erupted 1952.
Popocatépetl (17,887 ft; 5,452 m). Large, deep, bell-shaped crater. Not entirely extinct; steam still escapes.
Nicaragua: Volcanoes include Telica, Coseguina, and Momotombo. Between Momotombo on the west shore of Lake Managua and Coseguina overlooking the Gulf of Fonseca, there is a string of more than 20 cones, many still active. One of these, Cerro Negro, erupted in July 1947, with considerable damage and loss of life, and again in 1971.
Concepción (5,100 ft; 1,555 m). Ash eruptions 1973–74.

Mid-oceanic Islands

Canary Islands: Pico de Teide (12,192 ft; 3,716 m), on Tenerife.
Cape Verde Islands: Fogo (nearly 9,300 ft; 2,835 m). Severe eruption in 1857; quiescent until 1951.
Caribbean: La Soufrière (4,813 ft; 1,467 m), on Basse-Terre, Guadeloupe. Also called La Grande Soufrière. Violent activity in July-August 1976 caused evacuation of 73,000 people; renewed activity in April 1977 again caused thousands to flee their homes.
La Soufrière (4,048 ft; 1,234 m), on St. Vincent. Major eruption in 1902 killed over 1,000 people.
Comoro Islands: One volcano, Karthala (nearly 8,000 ft; 2,440 m), is visible for over 100 miles. Last erupted in 1904.
Hawaii: Mauna Loa ("Long Mountain") (13,680 ft; 4,170 m), on Hawaii, discharges from its high side vents more lava than any other volcano. Largest volcanic mountain in the world in cubic content. Area of crater is 3.7 sq mi. Violent eruption in June 1950, with lava pouring 25 miles into the ocean. Last major eruption in July 1975.
Mauna Kea (13,796 ft; 4,205 m), on Hawaii. Highest mountain in state.
Kilauea (4,090 ft; 1,247 m) is a vent in the side of Mauna Loa, but its eruptions are apparently independent. One of the most spectacular and active craters. Crater has an area of 4.14 sq mi. Earthquake in July 1975 caused major eruption. Eruptions began in September 1977 and reached a height of 980 ft (300 m). Activity ended Oct. 1.
Iceland: At least 25 volcanoes active in historical times. Very similar to Hawaiian volcanoes. Askja (over 4,700 ft; 1,433 m) is the largest.
Lesser Antilles (West Indian Islands): Mount Pelée (over 4,500 ft; 1,370 m), northwestern Martinique. Eruption in 1902 destroyed town of St. Pierre and killed approximately 40,000 people.
Réunion Island (east of Madagascar): Piton de la Fournaise (Le Volcan) (8,610 ft; 2,624 m). Large lava flows. Last erupted in 1972.
Samoan archipelago: Savai'i Island had an eruption in 1905 that caused considerable damage. Niuafoo (Tin Can), in the Tonga Islands, has a crater that extends 6,000 feet below and 600 feet above water.

Indonesia

Sumatra: Ninety volcanoes have been discovered; 12 are now active. The most famous, Krakatau, is a small volcanic island in the Sunda Strait. Numerous volcanic discharges occurred in 1883. One extremely violent explosion caused the disappearance of the highest peak and the northern part of the island. Fine dust was carried around the world in the upper atmosphere. Over 36,000 persons lost their lives in resultant tidal waves that were felt as far away as Cape Horn. Active in 1972.

Mediterranian Area

Italy: Mount Etna (10,902 ft; 3,323 m), eastern Sicily. Two new craters formed in eruptions of February-March 1947. Worst eruption in 50 years occurred November 1950-Jaunary 1951. Erupted again in 1974, 1975, 1977, and 1978.
Stromboli (about 3,000 ft; 914 m), Lipari Islands (north of Sicily). Called "Lighthouse of the Mediterranean." Reported active in 1971.
Mount Vesuvius (4,200 ft; 1,280 m), southeast of Naples. Only active volcano on European mainland. Pompeii buried by an eruption, A.D. 79.

Measuring Earthquakes

Earthquakes are generally measured on the scale developed by Charles F. Richter in 1935. The scale is logarithmic—the release of energy increases about 10 times with each whole number of the scale. A quake whose magnitude is less than 2 will not be noticed by humans; there are thousands of such tremors per year. Earthquakes whose magnitude is more than 4.5 can cause damage; 6.5 indicates a serious and hazardous quake. At a magnitude of about 8, great damage can occur. The San Francisco earthquake of 1906 has been variously estimated at 7.8 to 8.3. The April 1979 quake in Yugoslavia was measured at magnitude 7.2; it caused heavy casualties because it occurred in a densely populated area.

Interesting Caves and Caverns of the World

Aggtelek. In village of same name, northern Hungary. Large stalactitic cavern about 5 miles long.

Altamira Cave. Near Santander, Spain. Contains animal paintings (Old Stone Age art) on roof and walls.

Antiparos. On island of same name in the Grecian Archipelago. Some stalactites are 20 ft long. Brilliant colors and fantastic shapes.

Blue Grotto. On island of Capri, Italy. Cavern hollowed out in limestone by constant wave action. Now half filled with water because of sinking coast. Name derived from unusual blue light permeating the cave. Source of light is a submerged opening, light passing through the water.

Carlsbad Caverns. Southeast New Mexico. Largest underground labyrinth yet discovered. Three levels: 754,900, and 1,320 ft below the surface.

Fingal's Cave. On island of Staffa off coast of western Scotland. Penetrates about 200 ft inland. Contains basaltic columns almost 40 ft high.

Ice Cave. Near Dobsina, Czechoslovakia. Noted for its beautiful crystal effects.

Jenolan Caves. In Blue Mountain plateau, New South Wales, Australia. Beautiful stalactitic formations.

Kent's Cavern. Near Torquay, England. Source of much information on Paleolithic man.

Luray Cavern. Near Luray, Va. Has large stalactitic and stalagmitic columns of many colors.

Mammoth Cave. Limestone cavern in central Kentucky. Cave area is about 10 miles in diameter but has at least 150 miles of irregular subterranean passageways at various levels. Temperature remains fairly constant at 54°F.

Peak Cavern or **Devil's Hole.** Derbyshire, England. About 2,250 ft into a mountain. Lowest part is about 600 ft below the surface.

Postojna (Postumia) Grotto. Near Postumia in Julian Alps, about 25 miles northeast of Trieste. Stalactitic cavern, largest in Europe. Piuca (Pivka) River flows through part of it. Caves have numerous beautiful stalactites.

Singing Cave. Iceland. A lava cave; name derived from echoes of people singing in it.

Wind Cave. In Black Hills of South Dakota. Limestone caverns with stalactites and stalagmites almost entirely missing. Variety of crystal formations called "boxwork."

Wyandotte Cave. In Crawford County, southern Indiana. A limestone cavern with five levels of passages; one of the largest in North America. "Monumental Mountain," approximately 135 ft high, is believed to be one of the world's largest underground "mountains."

MAPS

Prepared by Vaughn Gray and Dyno Lowenstein
"Quick Maps" by Dyno Lowenstein

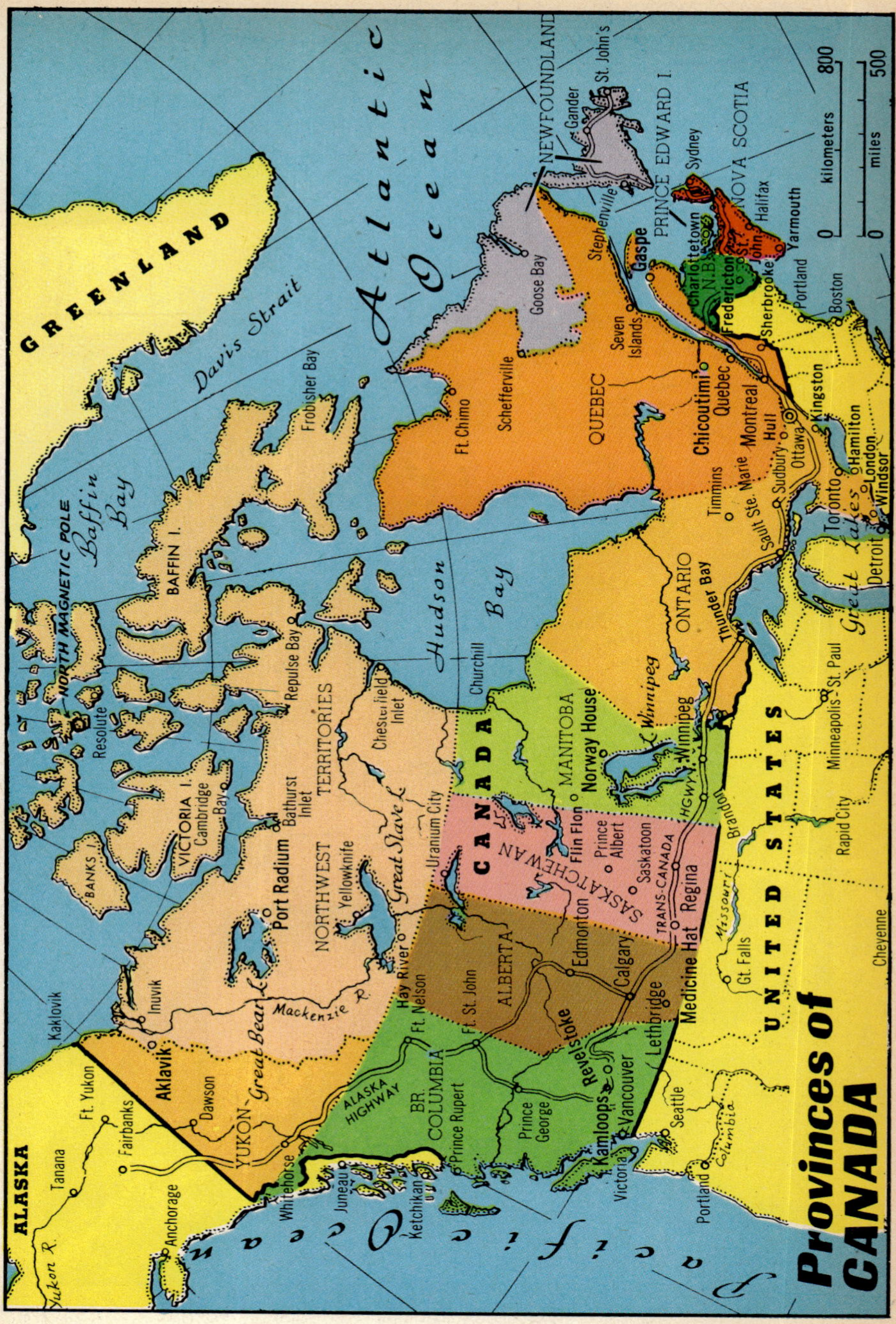
Provinces of CANADA
GREENLAND
Davis Strait
Baffin Bay
NORTH MAGNETIC POLE
BAFFIN I.
Frobisher Bay
Atlantic Ocean
Hudson Bay
Pacific Ocean
ALASKA
Kaklovik
Tanana
Ft. Yukon
Fairbanks
Anchorage
Yukon R.
Aklavik
Inuvik
Dawson
YUKON
Whitehorse
Juneau
Ketchikan
Great Bear L.
Mackenzie R.
NORTHWEST TERRITORIES
Port Radium
Yellowknife
Great Slave L.
Hay River
Ft. Nelson
ALASKA HIGHWAY
BR. COLUMBIA
Prince Rupert
Prince George
Ft. St. John
Revelstoke
Kamloops
Vancouver
Victoria
BANKS I.
VICTORIA I.
Cambridge Bay
Resolute
Bathurst Inlet
Repulse Bay
Chesterfield Inlet
Uranium City
Churchill
ALBERTA
Edmonton
Calgary
Lethbridge
Medicine Hat
SASKATCHEWAN
Prince Albert
Saskatoon
Regina
TRANS-CANADA HGWY.
Flin Flon
MANITOBA
Norway House
L. Winnipeg
Winnipeg
Brandon
CANADA
ONTARIO
Thunder Bay
Timmins
Sault Ste. Marie
Sudbury
Toronto
Hamilton
London
Windsor
Detroit
Great Lakes
Ottawa
Hull
Kingston
Montreal
Quebec
Chicoutimi
QUEBEC
Ft. Chimo
Schefferville
Seven Islands
Goose Bay
Gaspe
Stephenville
NEWFOUNDLAND
Gander
St. John's
PRINCE EDWARD I.
Charlottetown
N.B.
Fredericton
St. John
NOVA SCOTIA
Sydney
Halifax
Yarmouth
Sherbrooke
Portland
Boston
UNITED STATES
Minneapolis-St. Paul
Rapid City
Missouri
Cheyenne
Gt. Falls
Seattle
Portland
Columbia
0 kilometers 800
0 miles 500

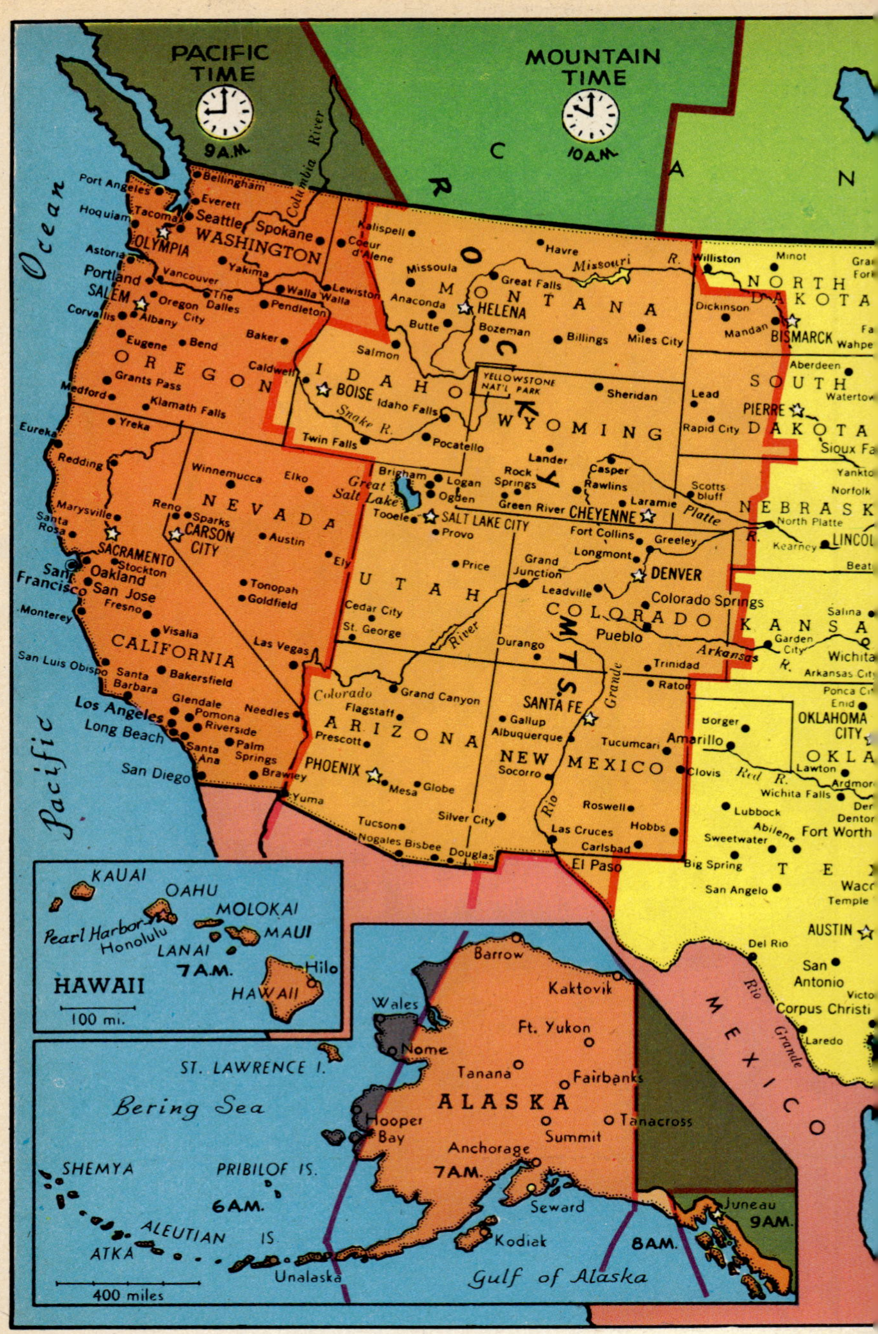
PACIFIC TIME
9 A.M.
MOUNTAIN TIME
10 A.M.
CANADA
Pacific Ocean
WASHINGTON
OREGON
CALIFORNIA
NEVADA
IDAHO
MONTANA
WYOMING
UTAH
COLORADO
ARIZONA
NEW MEXICO
NORTH DAKOTA
SOUTH DAKOTA
NEBRASKA
KANSAS
OKLAHOMA
TEXAS
MEXICO
ROCKY MTS.
OLYMPIA
SALEM
SACRAMENTO
CARSON CITY
BOISE
HELENA
SALT LAKE CITY
CHEYENNE
DENVER
PHOENIX
SANTA FE
BISMARCK
PIERRE
LINCOLN
OKLAHOMA CITY
AUSTIN
Seattle
Spokane
Portland
San Francisco
Los Angeles
San Diego
Las Vegas
Albuquerque
El Paso
HAWAII
KAUAI
OAHU
MOLOKAI
MAUI
LANAI
HAWAII
Pearl Harbor
Honolulu
Hilo
7 A.M.
100 mi.
ALASKA
Bering Sea
ST. LAWRENCE I.
PRIBILOF IS.
ALEUTIAN IS.
SHEMYA
ATKA
Barrow
Kaktovik
Wales
Nome
Ft. Yukon
Tanana
Fairbanks
Hooper Bay
Tanacross
Summit
Anchorage
Seward
Kodiak
Juneau
Unalaska
Gulf of Alaska
6 A.M.
7 A.M.
8 A.M.
9 A.M.
400 miles

ENTRAL TIME
11 A.M.
EASTERN TIME
12 N.
A
D
A
ST. LAWRENCE SEAWAY
Quebec
Montreal
Ottawa
St. Lawrence R.
Presque Isle
MAINE
Bangor
AUGUSTA
MONTPELIER
VT.
N.H.
CONCORD
Portland
Portsmouth
BOSTON
C. Cod
MASS
New Bedford
PROVIDENCE
R. I.
HARTFORD
CONN.
Lake Champlain
NEW YORK
ALBANY
Toronto
L. Ontario
Niagara Falls
Buffalo
Jamestown
L. Erie
Erie
Scranton
PA.
HARRISBURG
Newark
New York
TRENTON
Philadelphia
NEW JERSEY
DOVER, DEL.
Pittsburgh
Baltimore
ANNAPOLIS
MD.
WASHINGTON, D.C.
Chesapeake Bay
Norfolk
Portsmouth
Cleveland
Youngstown
Akron
Canton
Toledo
Lima
OHIO
Wheeling
COLUMBUS
Dayton
Cincinnati
WEST VIRGINIA
CHARLESTON
Alexandria
RICHMOND
Roanoke
VIRGINIA
Bluefield
Durham
RALEIGH
Goldsboro
Cape Hatteras
NORTH CAROLINA
Winston Salem
Charlotte
Bristol
Wilmington
Rock Hill
Florence
SOUTH CAROLINA
COLUMBIA
Savannah R.
Charleston
Savannah
Brunswick
ATLANTA
Augusta
Rome
Macon
Columbus
GEORGIA
Waycross
Thomasville
Jacksonville
St. Augustine
Daytona Beach
Gainesville
TALLAHASSEE
Cape Canaveral
Orlando
Tampa
St. Petersburg
FLORIDA
L. Okeechobee
Fort Myers
West Palm Beach
Miami Beach
Miami
Key West
Atlantic Ocean
L. Superior
Houghton
Calumet
Marquette
Sault Ste. Marie
MICH.
Cheboygan
L. Huron
Traverse City
MICHIGAN
Saginaw
Flint
Grand Rapids
LANSING
Detroit
L. Michigan
Sheboygan
Milwaukee
Racine
Oshkosh
Green Bay
Eau Claire
WISCONSIN
Superior
Duluth
NNESOTA
ternational Falls
rainerd
St. Cloud
ST. PAUL
neapolis
Rochester
Mankato
Austin
La Crosse
MADISON
Beloit
Rockford
Mason City
Waterloo
Cedar Rapids
ioux City
IOWA
S MOINES
Council Bluffs
maha
Fort Madison
Rock Island
Chicago
Joliet
Gary
South Bend
Fort Wayne
Peoria
Muncie
INDIANAPOLIS
INDIANA
Decatur
SPRINGFIELD
ILLINOIS
Keokuk
St. Joseph
Missouri
Kansas City
TOPEKA
E. St. Louis
Belleville
St. Louis
Evansville
Ohio
Louisville
FRANKFORT
Lexington
KENTUCKY
Middlesboro
JEFFERSON CITY
MISSOURI
Springfield
Joplin
Cairo
Paducah
Bowling Green
NASHVILLE
Knoxville
TENNESSEE
Chattanooga
Jackson
Memphis
ulsa
kmulgee
Muskogee
Jonesboro
ARKANSAS
LITTLE ROCK
Pine Bluff
Texarkana
Mississippi R.
Clarksdale
Greenville
Columbus
Tennessee
Huntsville
Birmingham
Anniston
MISSISSIPPI
MONTGOMERY
Meridian
Vicksburg
JACKSON
ALABAMA
Natchez
Laurel
Dothan
Hattiesburg
Mobile
Pensacola
Marshall
Monroe
Shreveport
Alexandria
Sabine R.
LOUISIANA
BATON ROUGE
Biloxi
Gulfport
New Orleans
Port Arthur
Galveston
aumont
ston
UNITED STATES
Gulf of Mexico
CUBA
Miles
0
500
Kilometers
0
800

EUROPE
Capitals
30
20
10
West
0
East
10
Norwegian Sea
Reykjavik
Keflavik
ICELAND
Atlantic Ocean
FAEROE IS. (Den.)
60
SHETLAND IS.
Trondheim
Bergen
NORWAY
SWEDE
Oslo
Stockh
Skagerrak
Göteborg
UNITED KINGDOM
Inverness
SCOTLAND
N. IRELAND
Edinburgh
North Sea
Belfast
IRELAND
Dublin
Limerick
DENMARK
Copenhag
Liverpool
WALES
ENGLAND
London
NETHERLANDS
Hamburg
Bremen
Southampton
50
The Hague
Amsterdam
Berlin
GERMANY (WEST)
(EAST) U.S.S.R.
Bonn
Cherbourg
CHANNEL IS. (Br.)
Brussels
BELGIUM
Brest
Paris
LUX.
SAAR
Frankfurt
Prague
CZECHOS
Nantes
Loire R.
Seine R.
Rhine R.
Danube R.
Elbe R.
Munich
Bay of Biscay
FRANCE
Vienna
AUSTRIA
Bern
SWITZ.
Geneva
Lyon
Bordeaux
Garonne R.
Rhone R.
Turin
Venice
Trieste
Po R.
Genoa
Oporto
40
Ebro R.
ANDORRA
Nice
Marseilles
RIVIERA
Florence
Adriatic
PORTUGAL
Lisbon
Madrid
SPAIN
Tagus R.
ITALY
CORSICA (Fr.)
Barcelona
Rome
Valencia
BALEARIC IS.
SARDINIA
Naples
Guadalquivir R.
Cadiz
Granada
TANGIER
Gibraltar (Br.)
Palermo
SICILY
MT. ETNA
Mediterranean
Casablanca
Rabat
Oran
Algiers
Tunis
MOROCCO
ALGERIA
TUNISIA
MALTA
Tripoli
LIBYA

Kilometers
0
800
Miles
0
500
Kirkenes
40
50
Murmansk
White Sea
Archangel
N. Dvina R.
URAL MTS.
FINLAND
L. Onega
L. Ladoga
Sverdlovsk
Leningrad
Tallinn
ESTONIA
Kama R.
UNION OF SOVIET SOCIALIST REPUBLICS
Magnitogorsk
Volga R.
Moscow
Riga
LATVIA
LITHUANIA
Dvina R.
Smolensk
Oka R.
Kuibyshev
Ural R.
Saratov
1938 BORDER
Bug R.
Don R.
Volgograd
Kiev
Dnieper R.
Kharkov
Volga R.
UKRAINE
Donetsk
Astrakhan
Dnepropetrovsk
Rostov
Dniester R.
Pruth R.
Odessa
Sea of Azov
Caspian Sea
RUMANIA
CRIMEA
Sevastopol
Yalta
CAUCASUS
Bucharest
Tbilisi
Baku
Danube R.
Black Sea
BULGARIA
Batum
Sofia
Istanbul
Bosporus
Erivan
THRACE
AZERBAIJAN
Tabriz
L. Van
L. Urmia
Ankara
Teheran
Dardanelles
TURKEY
Mosul
Salonika
Izmir
Aegean Sea
IRAN
GREECE
Tigris R.
Adana
Athens
Aleppo
SYRIA
Baghdad
RHODES
LEBANON
CYPRUS
IRAQ
Beirut
Damascus
CRETE
Euphrates R.
Basra
ISRAEL
Tel Aviv
Amman
KUWAIT
Jerusalem
Dead Sea
Persian Gulf
Alexandria
JORDAN
SAUDI ARABIA
SUEZ CANAL
EGYPT
Cairo
HELD BY ISRAEL

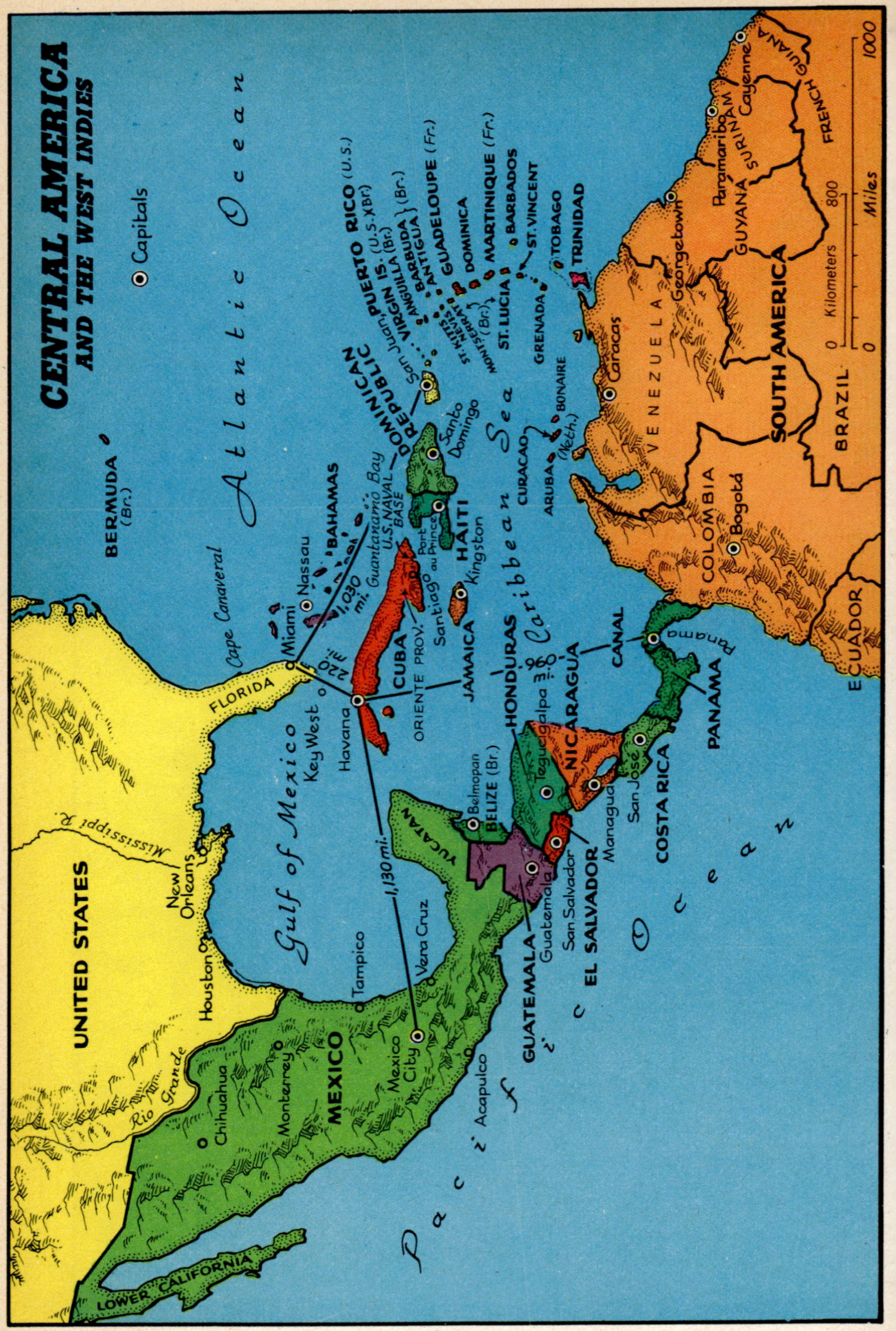

CENTRAL AMERICA
AND THE WEST INDIES
Capitals
BERMUDA (Br.)
Atlantic Ocean
UNITED STATES
Mississippi R.
New Orleans
Houston
Rio Grande
Chihuahua
Monterrey
MEXICO
Mexico City
Tampico
Vera Cruz
Acapulco
LOWER CALIFORNIA
FLORIDA
Cape Canaveral
Miami
Key West
Gulf of Mexico
220 mi.
1,130 mi.
1,030 mi.
960 mi.
Nassau
BAHAMAS
Havana
CUBA
ORIENTE PROV.
Santiago
Guantanamo Bay
U.S. NAVAL BASE
JAMAICA
Kingston
HAITI
Port au Prince
DOMINICAN REPUBLIC
Santo Domingo
San Juan
PUERTO RICO (U.S.)
VIRGIN IS. (U.S.)(Br.)
ANGUILLA (Br.)
BARBUDA
ANTIGUA
ST. KITTS
NEVIS
MONTSERRAT (Br.)
GUADELOUPE (Fr.)
DOMINICA
MARTINIQUE (Fr.)
ST. LUCIA
BARBADOS
ST. VINCENT
GRENADA
TOBAGO
TRINIDAD
ARUBA
CURACAO
BONAIRE
(Neth.)
Caribbean Sea
YUCATAN
Belmopan
BELIZE (Br.)
GUATEMALA
Guatemala
EL SALVADOR
San Salvador
HONDURAS
Tegucigalpa
NICARAGUA
Managua
COSTA RICA
San Jose
PANAMA
Panama
CANAL
Pacific Ocean
COLOMBIA
Bogotá
ECUADOR
VENEZUELA
Caracas
GUYANA
Georgetown
SURINAM
Paramaribo
FRENCH GUIANA
Cayenne
BRAZIL
SOUTH AMERICA
0 Kilometers 800 1000
0 Miles

SOUTH AMERICA
Miles 0 1000
Kilometers 0 1,600
VENEZUELA
COLOMBIA
ECUADOR
PERU
BOLIVIA
CHILE
ARGENTINA
PARAGUAY
URUGUAY
BRAZIL
GUYANA
SURINAM
FR. GUIANA
TRINIDAD & TOBAGO
CURAÇAO
WEST INDIES
PANAMA CANAL
Maracaibo
Caracas
Ciudad Bolivar
ANGEL FALLS
Georgetown
Paramaribo
Cayenne
Bogotá
Quito
Guayaquil
Iquitos
Lima
Callao
Arequipa
La Paz
Sucre
Manaus
Belém
Fortaleza
Natal
Recife
Salvador
MATO GROSSO
Brasília
FEDERAL DISTRICT
Corumbá
Belo Horizonte
Campinas
São Paulo
Rio de Janeiro
Asunción
Antofagasta
Tucumán
Pôrto Alegre
Rio Grande
Cordoba
Rosario
Montevideo
Buenos Aires
Río de la Plata
Valparaiso
Santiago
MT. ACONCAGUA 22,835 Ft.
Bahia Blanca
PAMPAS
PATAGONIA
ANDES
Punta Arenas
TIERRA DEL FUEGO
Strait of Magellan
Cape Horn
Orinoco
Magdalena
Negro
Branco
Amazon R.
Juruá
Madeira
Tapajos
Xingu
Araguaia
Parnaiba
São Francisco
Paraná
Marañon
Ucayali
Uruguay
Paraguay
Salado
Colorado
Negro
Pacific Ocean
Atlantic Ocean
OIL
IRON
STEEL
TUNGSTEN
MANGANESE
TIN
COPPER
NITRATES
BAUXITE
COAL
DIAMONDS
RUBBER
COFFEE
COCOA
CATTLE
SHEEP
CLIMATE
Tropical Rainforest
Savanna
Highland
Subtropical
Marine
Desert and Steppe

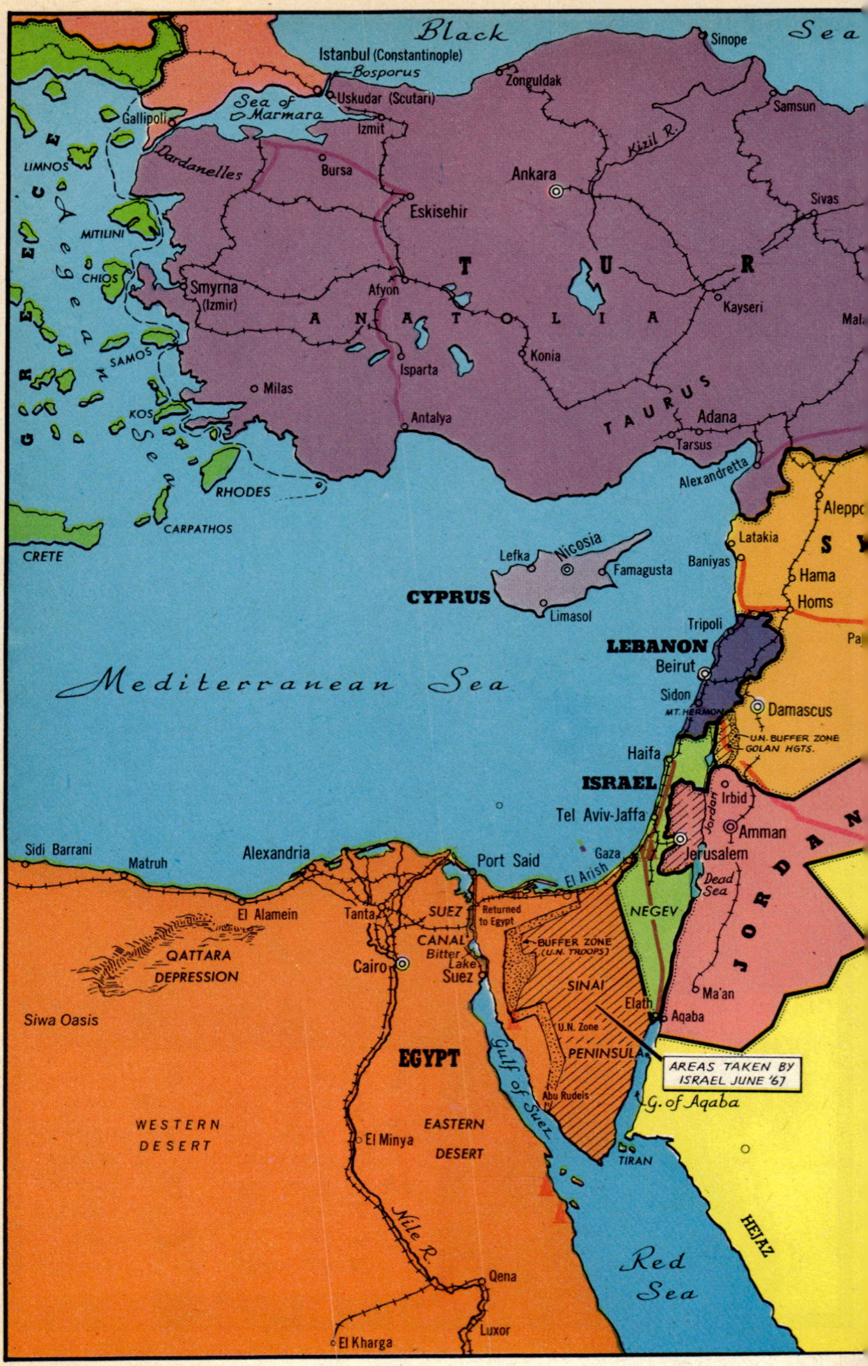
Black Sea
Istanbul (Constantinople)
Bosporus
Sinope
Zonguldak
Samsun
Sea of Marmara
Uskudar (Scutari)
Izmit
Gallipoli
Dardanelles
Bursa
Ankara
Kizil R.
Sivas
LIMNOS
Eskisehir
MITILINI
GREECE
Aegean Sea
CHIOS
T U R
Smyrna (Izmir)
Afyon
Kayseri
ANATOLIA
SAMOS
Isparta
Konia
Milas
KOS
TAURUS
Antalya
Adana
Tarsus
RHODES
Alexandretta
CARPATHOS
Aleppo
CRETE
Latakia
Lefka
Nicosia
Famagusta
Baniyas
Hama
CYPRUS
Limasol
Homs
Tripoli
LEBANON
Beirut
Mediterranean Sea
Sidon
Damascus
MT. HERMON
U.N. BUFFER ZONE GOLAN HGTS.
Haifa
ISRAEL
Irbid
Tel Aviv-Jaffa
Jordan
Amman
Sidi Barrani
Matruh
Alexandria
Port Said
Gaza
Jerusalem
El Arish
Dead Sea
El Alamein
Tanta
SUEZ CANAL
Returned to Egypt
NEGEV
JORDAN
QATTARA DEPRESSION
BUFFER ZONE (U.N. TROOPS)
Bitter Lake
Cairo
Suez
SINAI
Ma'an
Siwa Oasis
Elath
Aqaba
U.N. Zone
PENINSULA
AREAS TAKEN BY ISRAEL JUNE '67
EGYPT
Gulf of Suez
Abu Rudeis
G. of Aqaba
WESTERN DESERT
El Minya
EASTERN DESERT
TIRAN
HEJAZ
Nile R.
Red Sea
Qena
Luxor
El Kharga

MIDDLE EAST
Oil fields
Pipelines and pumping stations
Principal railways
0 kilometers 320
0 miles 200
Batum
GEORGIAN S.S.R.
Tbilisi (Tiflis)
U.S.S.R.
AZERBAIJAN S.S.R.
APSHERON PENINSULA
Baku
Trabzon (Trebizond)
Kars
Leninakan
ARMENIAN S.S.R.
Kirovabad
Kura R.
Erivan
Erzurum
Aras R.
MT. ARARAT
Firat R.
Nakhichevan
Caspian Sea
Maku
Aras R.
Astara
Murat R.
L. Van
Bitlis
Siirt
Diyarbakir
Mardin
Tabriz
L. Urmia
Urmia
Ardabil
AZERBAIJAN
Rasht
ELBURZ MTS.
Qazvin
Zanjan
Teheran
KURDISTAN
NINEVEH
Mosul
Irbil
Tigris R.
Kirkuk
Euphrates R.
MESOPOTAMIA
ZAGROS MTS.
Hamadan
Khanaqin
Kermanshah
IRAN
(PERSIA)
Samarra
Haditha
SYRIAN DESERT
Baghdad
Isfahan
Ramadi
IRAQ
Karabala
BABYLON
Tigris R.
LALI
Shushtar
Karun R.
Amarah
Ahwaz
ERECH
Euphrates R.
AGHA JARI
UR
Basra
Abadan
GACH SARAN
Jalamid
RUMAILA
Fao
KUWAIT
Kuwait
BURGAN
Rafha
NEUTRAL ZONE
SAUDI ARABIA
WAFRA
Persian Gulf
SAFANIYA
Wariah
Dhahran
ABQAIQ
BAHRAIN
GHAWAR
Hofuf

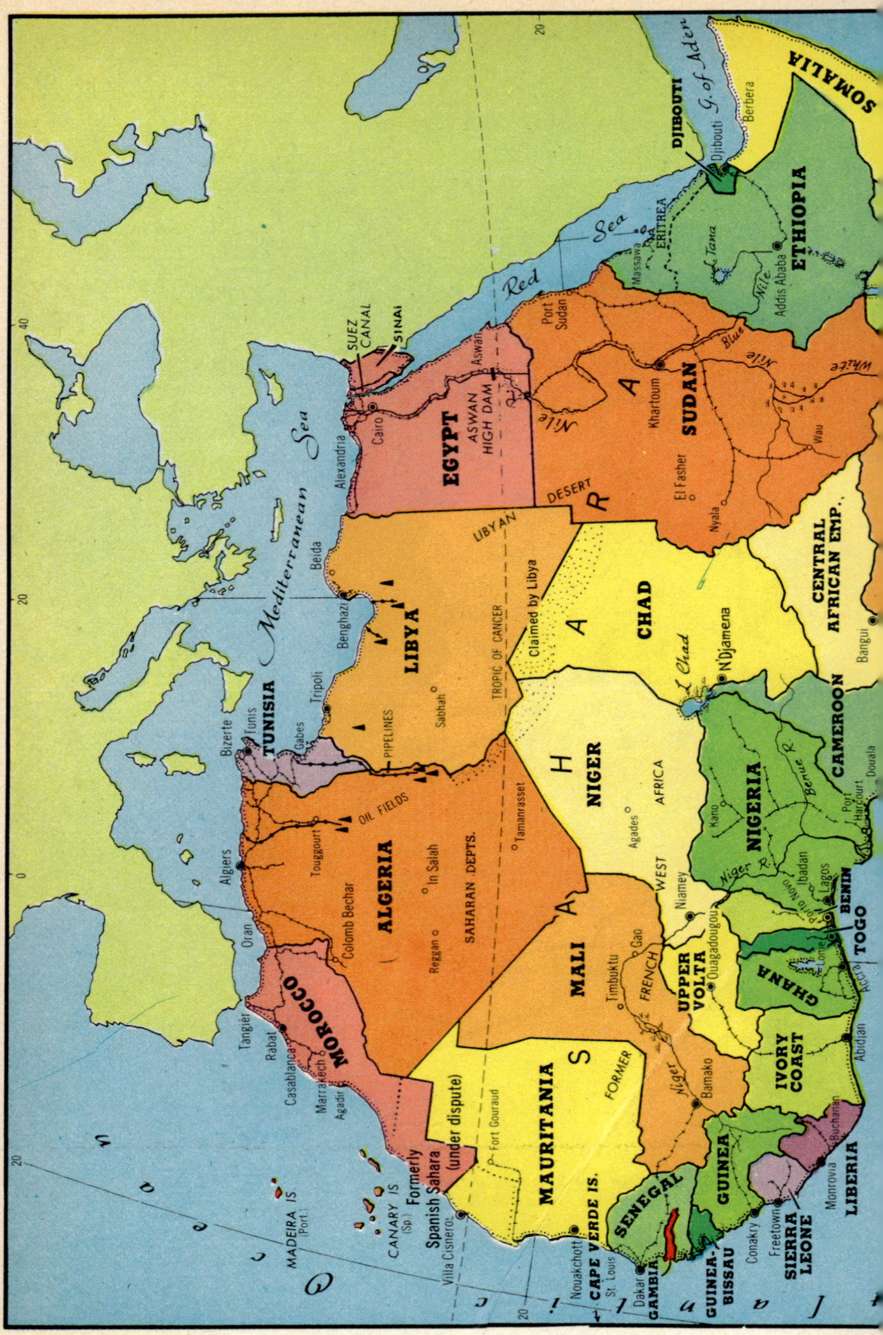

MOROCCO
ALGERIA
TUNISIA
LIBYA
EGYPT
SUDAN
ETHIOPIA
SOMALIA
DJIBOUTI
ERITREA
CHAD
NIGER
MALI
MAURITANIA
SENEGAL
GAMBIA
GUINEA-BISSAU
GUINEA
SIERRA LEONE
LIBERIA
IVORY COAST
GHANA
TOGO
BENIN
UPPER VOLTA
NIGERIA
CAMEROON
CENTRAL AFRICAN EMP.
Formerly Spanish Sahara (under dispute)
CAPE VERDE IS.
CANARY IS. (Sp.)
MADEIRA IS. (Port.)
Mediterranean Sea
Red Sea
G. of Aden
SUEZ CANAL
SINAI
ASWAN HIGH DAM
LIBYAN DESERT
SAHARAN DEPTS.
OIL FIELDS
PIPELINES
TROPIC OF CANCER
Claimed by Libya
FORMER FRENCH WEST AFRICA
S A H A R A
Tangier
Rabat
Casablanca
Marrakech
Agadir
Oran
Algiers
Colomb Bechar
Reggan
In Salah
Touggourt
Tamanrasset
Bizerte
Tunis
Gabes
Tripoli
Sabhah
Benghazi
Beida
Alexandria
Cairo
Aswan
Port Sudan
Khartoum
El Fasher
Nyala
Wau
Massawa
Addis Ababa
Djibouti
Berbera
L. Tana
Blue Nile
White Nile
Nile
N'Djamena
L. Chad
Bangui
Douala
Port Harcourt
Benue R.
Niger R.
Kano
Ibadan
Lagos
Porto Novo
Lomé
Accra
Abidjan
Niamey
Agades
Ouagadougou
Gao
Timbuktu
Bamako
Niger
Fort Gouraud
Villa Cisneros
Nouakchott
St. Louis
Dakar
Conakry
Freetown
Monrovia
Buchanan

AFRICA
Principal railways
EQUATOR
Guinea
PRINCIPE
GABON
Libreville
CONGO REP.
Brazzaville
Pointe Noire
CABINDA
Matadi
Kinshasa
(Leopoldville)
ZAIRE
Kasai R.
Zaire (Congo)
Port Francqui
Luluabourg
Kamina
SHABA
Lubumbashi
(Elisabethville)
Albertville
Kindu-Pt.Empain
Bukava
RWANDA
BURUNDI
L. Victoria
Nairobi
MT. KILIMANJARO 19,565
Mombasa
PEMBA
ZANZIBAR
Dar es Salaam
TANZANIA
L. Tanganyika
L. Malawi
(L. Nyasa)
MALAWI
Mtwara
ZAMBIA
Lusaka
Livingstone
ANGOLA
Luanda
Lobito
Moçâmedes
Malange
Nova Lisboa
Villa Serpa Pinto
KARIBA DAM
ZIMBABWE
Salisbury
Bulawayo
Zambezi R.
MOZAMBIQUE
Beira
Mozambique Channel
Moçambique
COMORO IS.
Majunga
Tamatave
Tananarive
MADAGASCAR
(MALAGASY REP.)
Fianarantsoa
Tuléar
TROPIC OF CAPRICORN
Indian Ocean
BOTSWANA
Gaborone
Johannesburg
Pretoria
Mafeking
Maputo
SWAZILAND
Durban
LESOTHO
(Basutoland)
TRANSKEI
East London
Port Elizabeth
SOUTH AFRICA
Kimberley
Orange R.
Cape of Good Hope
Cape Town
SOUTH WEST AFRICA
(NAMIBIA)
(S.A.)
Windhoek
Walvis Bay
(S.A.)
Luderitz
miles
kilometers
0
500
1,000
0
800
1600
20
0

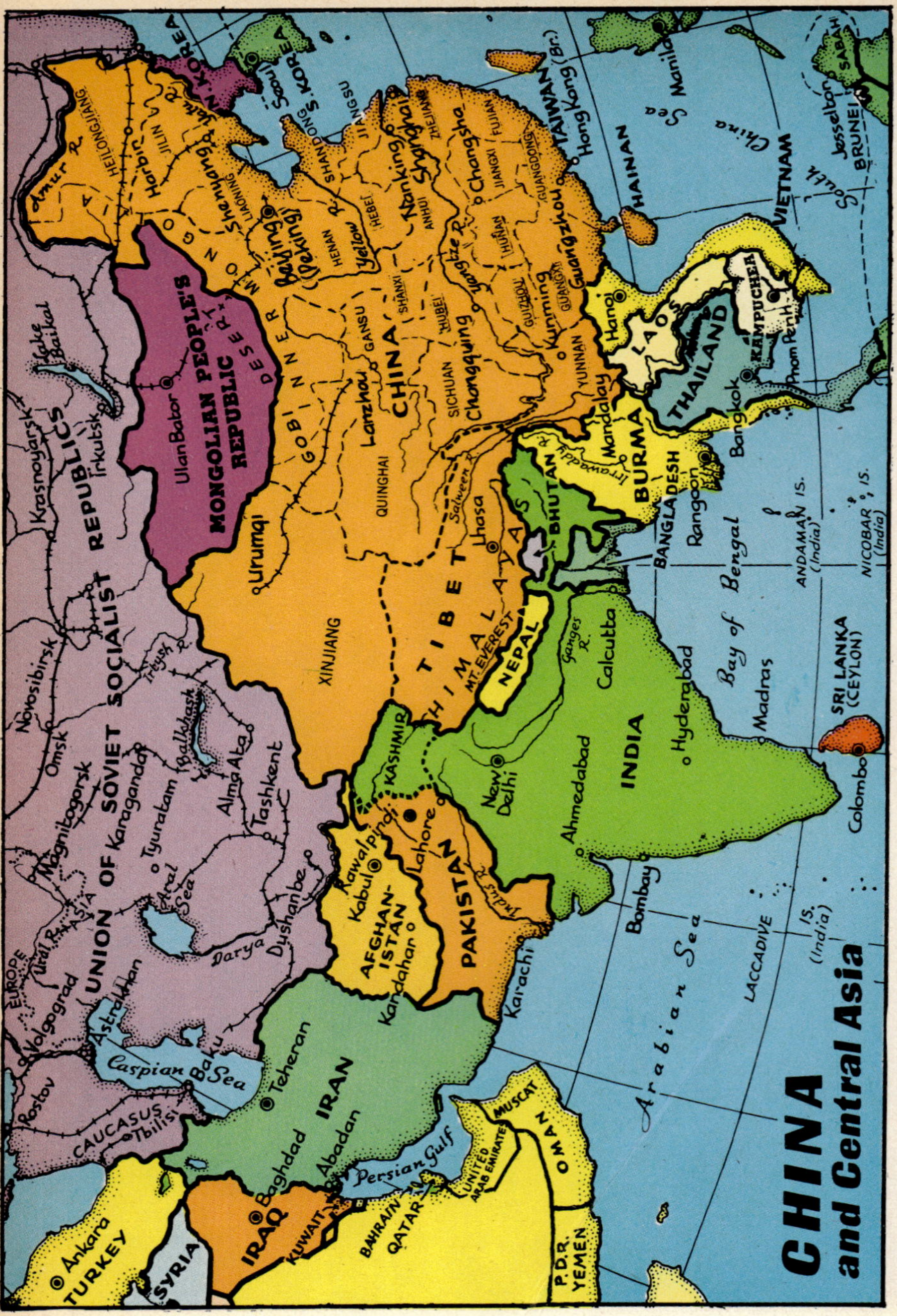
CHINA
and Central Asia
UNION OF SOVIET SOCIALIST REPUBLICS
MONGOLIAN PEOPLE'S REPUBLIC
CHINA
TIBET
XINJIANG
INDIA
PAKISTAN
AFGHAN-ISTAN
IRAN
IRAQ
TURKEY
SYRIA
KUWAIT
BAHRAIN
QATAR
UNITED ARAB EMIRATES
MUSCAT
OMAN
P.D.R. YEMEN
NEPAL
BHUTAN
BANGLADESH
BURMA
THAILAND
LAOS
KAMPUCHEA
VIETNAM
HAINAN
TAIWAN
N. KOREA
S. KOREA
BRUNEI
SABAH
KASHMIR
SRI LANKA (CEYLON)
HIMALAYAS
MT. EVEREST
GOBI DESERT
INNER MONGOLIA
HEILONGJIANG
JILIN
LIAONING
HEBEI
SHANDONG
JIANGSU
HENAN
SHANXI
SHAANXI
ANHUI
ZHEJIANG
JIANGXI
FUJIAN
HUNAN
HUBEI
GUIZHOU
GUANGXI
GUANGDONG
SICHUAN
YUNNAN
GANSU
QUINGHAI
Beijing (Peking)
Shenyang
Harbin
Nanking
Shanghai
Changsha
Guangzhou
Hong Kong (Br.)
Kunming
Chongquing
Lanzhou
Lhasa
Urumqi
Ulan Bator
Irkutsk
Krasnoyarsk
Novosibirsk
Omsk
Magnitogorsk
Karaganda
Tyuratam
Alma Ata
Tashkent
Dushanbe
Volgograd
Astrakhan
Rostov
Baku
Tbilisi
Ankara
Baghdad
Abadan
Teheran
Kabul
Kandahar
Rawalpindi
Lahore
Karachi
New Delhi
Ahmedabad
Bombay
Hyderabad
Madras
Calcutta
Colombo
Rangoon
Mandalay
Bangkok
Phnom Penh
Hanoi
Manila
Jesselton
Seoul
Amur R.
Yalu R.
Yellow R.
Yangtze R.
Salween R.
Irrawaddy R.
Ganges R.
Indus R.
Irtysh R.
Ural R.
Lake Baikal
Balkhash
Aral Sea
Darya
Caspian Sea
Persian Gulf
Arabian Sea
Bay of Bengal
South China Sea
CAUCASUS
EUROPE
ASIA
ANDAMAN IS. (India)
NICOBAR IS. (India)
LACCADIVE IS. (India)

WESTERN PACIFIC
U.S.S.R.
MONGOLIAN PEOPLE'S REPUBLIC
Ulan Bator
Kamchatka Peninsula
Sakhalin I.
Amur R.
Khabarovsk
KURIL IS.
Attu
ALEUTIAN ISLANDS (U.S.)
International Date Line
Harbin
Vladivostok
Sapporo
Hokkaido
Shenyang
Beijing
Tianjin
Yellow R.
Pyongyang
N. KOREA
Seoul
S. KOREA
Tsintao
Honshu
Kyoto
Kobe
Osaka
Tokyo
JAPAN
Nagasaki
Kyushu
Pacific Ocean
Nanjing
Wuhan
Yangtze R.
Shanghai
CHINA
EAST CHINA SEA
Okinawa
RYUKYU IS.
Bonin
Fuzhou
Taipei
Taiwan
Marcus I.
Tropic of Cancer
BURMA
Guangzhou
Macao (Port.)
Hong Kong (Br.)
LAOS
Hanoi
Hainan
Vientiane
THAIL.
Bangkok
VIETNAM
KAMPUCHEA
Ho Chi Minh City
SOUTH CHINA SEA
Luzon
Manila
PHILIPPINE SEA
PHILIPPINES
Samar
MARIANA ISLANDS
Saipan
Guam (U.S.)
Wake I. (U.S.)
MARSHALL ISLANDS
Kwajalein
CAROLINE ISLANDS
Truk
KIRIBATI
Tarawa
NAURU
TUVALU
Mindanao
Davao
Palau Is.
Kuala Lumpur
BRUNEI (Br.)
MALAYSIA
Kuching
Menado
Halmahera
SINGAPORE
BORNEO
Padang
Palembang
Bandjermasin
SUMATRA
Makassar
CELEBES
INDONESIA
EQUATOR
Kotabaru
IRIAN JAYA
PAPUA NEW GUINEA
Rabaul
NEW IRELAND
NEW BRITAIN
Bougainville
SOLOMON IS. (Br.)
Jakarta
Jogjakarta
JAVA
Surabaja
Flores
Sumba
TIMOR
ARAFURA SEA
Port Moresby
Santa Cruz Is.
Melville Is.
Indian Ocean
ARNHEM LAND
Wyndham
Great Barrier Reef
CORAL SEA
REP. OF VANUATU (NEW HEBRIDES)
Vanua Levu
FIJI
NORTHERN TERRITORIES
Great Dividing Range
Townsville
Great Sandy Desert
Alice Springs
QUEENSLAND
NEW CALEDONIA (Fr.)
Noumea
Tropic of Capricorn
Carnarvon
WESTERN AUSTRALIA
AUSTRALIA
Brisbane
NORFOLK I. (Aust.)
Victoria Desert
SOUTH AUSTRALIA
Broken Hill
NEW SOUTH WALES
Port Pirie
TASMAN SEA
Perth
Freemantle
Sydney
Canberra
AUSTRALIAN CAPITAL TERR.
Great Australian Bight
Adelaide
Auckland
Melbourne
VICTORIA
NORTH I.
NEW ZEALAND
Wellington
TASMANIA
Hobart
SOUTH I.
Christchurch
Dunedin
Stewart I.
Auckland Is.

CENTRAL ASIA

MAJOR OIL PRODUCING COUNTRIES

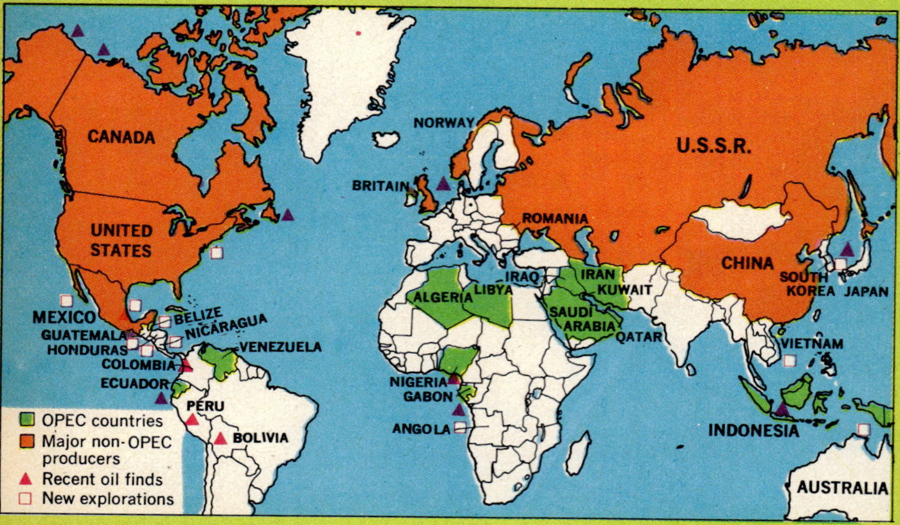

ANCIENT EMPIRES

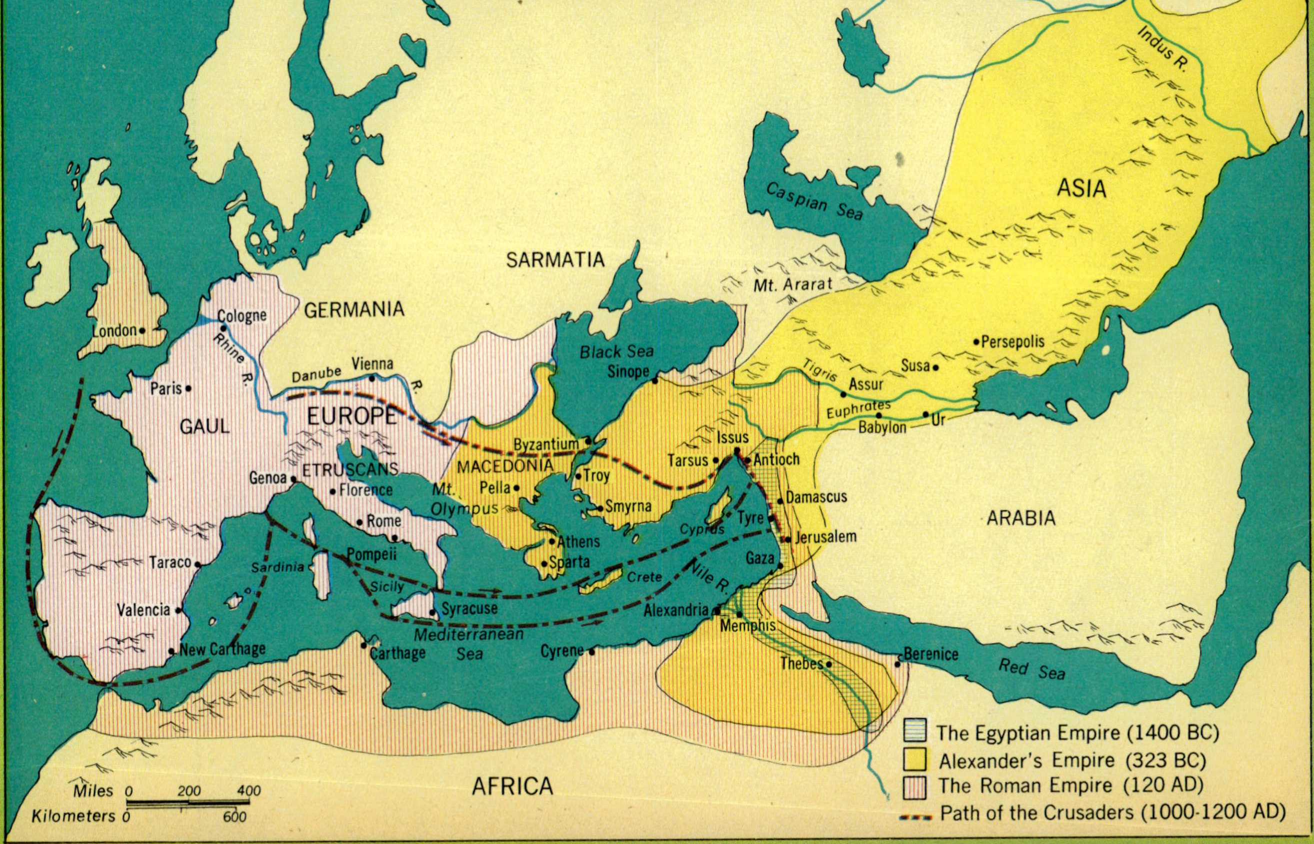

THE MOON
SEEN FROM THE EARTH

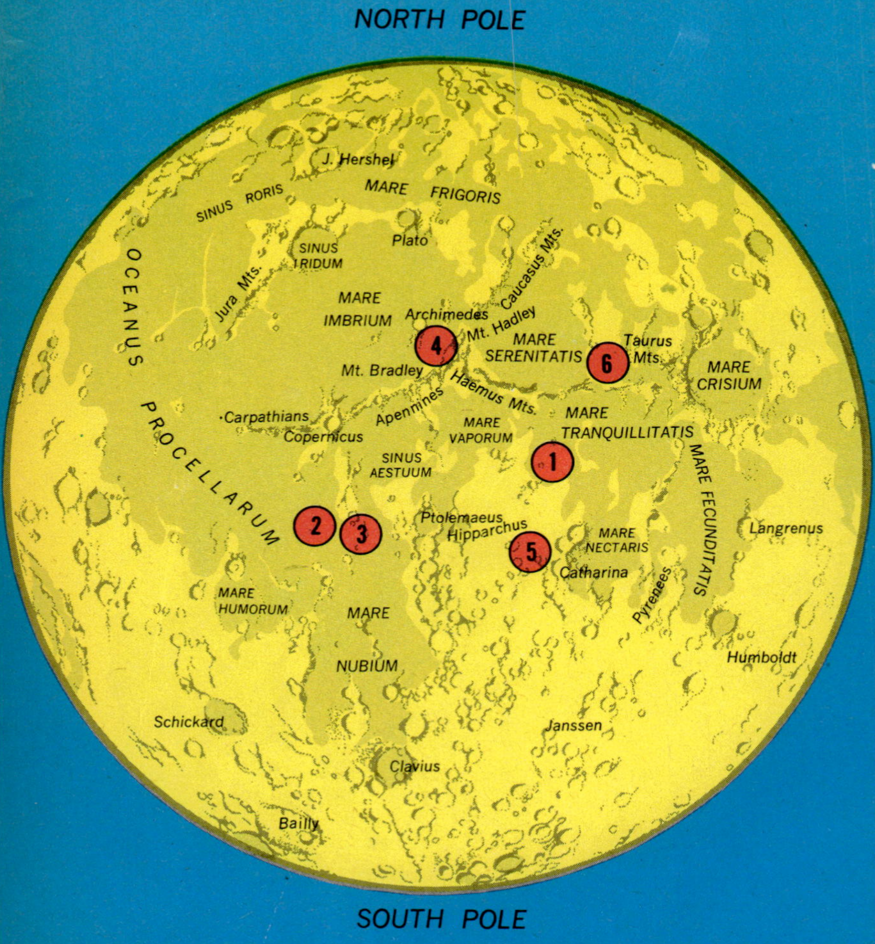

AMERICAN MANNED LANDINGS

1. Apollo 11: July 16-24, 1969
2. Apollo 12: Nov. 14-24, 1969
3. Apollo 14: Jan. 31-Feb. 9, 1971
4. Apollo 15: July 26-Aug. 7, 1971
5. Apollo 16: April 16-27, 1972
6. Apollo 17: Dec. 7-19, 1972

World Population, Land Areas, and Elevations

Area	Estimated population, 1978	Approximate Land area sq mi.	Percent of total land area	Population density per sq mi.	Elevation, feet: Higest	Elevation, feet: Lowest	Dimensions, miles: East-West	Dimensions, miles: North-South
WORLD	4,258,000,000	58,451,000	100.0	81.2[1]	Mt. Everest, Asia, 29,028	Dead Sea, Asia, 1,290 below sea level	24,902	24,860
ASIA, incl. Phillippines, Indonesia, and European and Asiatic Turkey; excl. Asiatic U.S.S.R.	2,461,000,000	10,678,000	18.2	230.5	Mt. Everest, Tibet-Nepal, 29,028	Dead Sea, Israel-Jordan, 1,290 below sea level	5,400[2]	5,300[2]
AFRICA	442,000,000	11,714,000	20.0	37.7	Mt. Kilimanjaro, Tanzania, 19,340	Qattara Depression, Egypt, 440 below sea level	4,600	5,000
NORTH AMERICA, including Hawaii, Central America, and Caribbean region	359,000,000	9,363,000	16.0	38.3	Mt. McKinley; Alaska, 20,320	Death Valley, Calif., 282 below sea level	3,200[5]	4,000[5]
SOUTH AMERICA	233,000,000	6,885,000	11.8	33.8	Mt. Aconcagua, Arg.-Chile, 23,034	Sea level	3,200	4,600
ANTARCTICA	—	6,000,000	10.3	—	Vinson Massif, Sentinel Range, 16,863	Sea level	—	—
EUROPE, incl. Iceland; excl. European U.S.S.R. and European Turkey	480,000,000	1,906,000	3.3	251.8	Mont Blanc, France, 15,781	Sea level	3,300[3]	2,400[3]
OCEANIA, incl. Australia, New Zealand, Melanesia, Micronesia, and Polynesia[4]	22,100,000	3,286,000	5.6	6.7	Mauna Kea, Hawaii, 13,796	Lake Eyre, Australia, 38 below sea level	—	—
U.S.S.R., both European and Asiatic	262,000,000	8,649,000	14.8	30.3	Communism Peak, Pamir, 24,547	Caspian Sea, 96 below sea level	5,000	2,500

1. In computing density per square mile, the area of Antarctica is omitted. 2. Including Asiatic U.S.S.R. 3. Including European U.S.S.R. 4. Although Hawaii is geographically part of Oceania, its population is included in the population figure for North America. 5. Excludes Hawaii. *Source:* United Nations *Demographic Yearbook, 1977.*

Some Countries With High Population Densities (per square mile)

Monaco	41,095.9	Netherlands	1,011.3	Lebanon	789.5	India	539.6
Singapore	10,084.0	South Korea	1,000.8	West Germany	640.3	Jamaica	498.8
Bangladesh	1,590.0	Belgium	838.7	Sri Lanka	598.1	Italy	491.0
China, Rep. of	1,305.9	Japan	814.2	United Kingdom	592.0	Israel	484.2

Longitude and Latitude of Foreign Cities

(and time corresponding to 12:00 noon, eastern standard time)

City	Long. ° ′	Lat. ° ′	Time
Aberdeen, Scotland	2 9 w	57 9 n	5:00 p.m.
Adelaide, Australia	138 36 e	34 55 s	2:30 a.m.[1]
Algiers	3 0 e	36 50 n	6:00 p.m.
Amsterdam	4 53 e	52 22 n	6:00 p.m.
Ankara, Turkey	32 55 e	39 55 n	7:00 p.m.
Asunción, Paraguay	57 40 w	25 15 s	1:00 p.m.
Athens	23 43 e	37 58 n	7:00 p.m.
Auckland, New Zealand	174 45 e	36 52 s	5:00 a.m.[1]
Bangkok, Thailand	100 30 e	13 45 n	midnight[1]
Barcelona	2 9 e	41 23 n	6:00 p.m.
Belém, Brazil	48 29 w	1 28 s	2:00 p.m.
Belfast, Northern Ireland	5 56 w	54 37 n	5:00 p.m.
Belgrade, Yugoslavia	20 32 e	44 52 n	6:00 p.m.
Berlin	13 25 e	52 30 n	6:00 p.m.
Birmingham, England	1 55 w	52 25 n	5:00 p.m.
Bogotá, Colombia	74 15 w	4 32 n	12:00 noon
Bombay	72 48 e	19 0 n	10:30 p.m.
Bordeaux, France	0 31 w	44 50 n	6:00 p.m.
Bremen, West Germany	8 49 e	53 5 n	6:00 p.m.
Brisbane, Australia	153 8 e	27 29 s	3:00 a.m.[1]
Bristol, England	2 35 w	51 28 n	5:00 p.m.
Brussels	4 22 e	50 52 n	6:00 p.m.
Bucharest	26 7 e	44 25 n	7:00 p.m.
Budapest	19 5 e	47 30 n	6:00 p.m.
Buenos Aires	58 22 w	34 35 s	2:00 p.m.
Cairo	31 21 e	30 2 n	7:00 p.m.
Calcutta	88 24 e	22 34 n	10:30 p.m.
Canton, China	113 15 e	23 7 n	1:00 a.m.[1]
Cape Town, South Africa	18 22 e	33 55 s	7:00 p.m.
Caracas, Venezuela	67 2 w	10 28 n	12:30 p.m.
Cayenne, French Guiana	52 18 w	4 49 n	1:00 p.m.
Chihuahua, Mexico	106 5 w	28 37 n	11:00 a.m.
Chungking, China	106 34 e	29 46 n	1:00 a.m.[1]
Copenhagen	12 34 e	55 40 n	6:00 p.m.
Córdoba, Argentina	64 10 w	31 28 s	2:00 p.m.
Dakar, Senegal	17 28 w	14 40 n	5:00 p.m.
Darwin, Australia	130 51 e	12 28 s	2:30 a.m.[1]
Djibouti	43 3 e	11 30 n	8:00 p.m.
Dublin	6 15 w	53 20 n	5:00 p.m.
Durban, South Africa	30 53 e	29 53 s	7:00 p.m.
Edinburgh, Scotland	3 10 w	55 55 n	5:00 p.m.
Frankfurt	8 41 e	50 7 n	6:00 p.m.
Georgetown, Guyana	58 15 w	6 45 n	1:15 p.m.
Glasgow, Scotland	4 15 w	55 50 n	5:00 p.m.
Guatemala City, Guatemala	90 31 w	14 37 n	11:00 a.m.
Guayaquil, Ecuador	79 56 w	2 10 s	12:00 noon
Hamburg	10 2 e	53 33 n	6:00 p.m.
Hammerfest, Norway	23 38 e	70 38 n	6:00 p.m.
Havana	82 23 w	23 8 n	12:00 noon
Helsinki, Finland	25 0 e	60 10 n	7:00 p.m.
Hobart, Tasmania	147 19 e	42 52 s	3:00 a.m.[1]
Iquique, Chile	70 7 w	20 10 s	1:00 p.m.
Irkutsk, U.S.S.R.	104 20 e	52 30 n	1:00 a.m.[1]
Jakarta, Indonesia	106 48 e	6 16 s	0:30 a.m.[1]
Johannesburg, South Africa	28 4 e	26 12 s	7:00 p.m.
Kingston, Jamaica	76 49 w	17 59 n	12:00 noon
Kinshasa, Zaire	15 17 e	4 18 s	6:00 p.m.
La Paz, Bolivia	68 22 w	16 27 s	1:00 p.m.
Leeds, England	1 30 w	53 45 n	5:00 p.m.
Leningrad	30 18 e	59 56 n	8:00 p.m.
Lima, Peru	77 2 w	12 0 s	12:00 noon
Lisbon	9 9 w	38 44 n	5:00 p.m.
Liverpool, England	3 0 w	53 25 n	5:00 p.m.
London	0 5 w	51 32 n	5:00 p.m.
Lyons, France	4 50 e	45 45 n	6:00 p.m.
Madrid	3 42 w	40 26 n	6:00 p.m.
Manchester, England	2 15 w	53 30 n	5:00 p.m.
Manila	120 57 e	14 35 n	1:00 a.m.[1]
Marseilles, France	5 20 e	43 20 n	6:00 p.m.
Mazatlán, Mexico	106 25 w	23 12 n	10:00 a.m.
Mecca, Saudi Arabia	39 45 e	21 29 n	8:00 p.m.
Melbourne	144 58 e	37 47 s	3:00 a.m.[1]
Mexico City	99 7 w	19 26 n	11:00 a.m.
Milan, Italy	9 10 e	45 27 n	6:00 p.m.
Montevideo, Uruguay	56 10 w	34 53 s	2:00 p.m.
Moscow	37 36 e	55 45 n	8:00 p.m.
Munich, Germany	11 35 e	48 8 n	6:00 p.m.
Nagasaki, Japan	129 57 e	32 48 n	2:00 a.m.[1]
Nagoya, Japan	136 56 e	35 7 n	2:00 a.m.[1]
Nairobi, Kenya	36 55 s	1 25 s	8:00 p.m.
Nanking, China	118 53 e	32 3 n	1:00 a.m.[1]
Naples, Italy	14 15 e	40 50 n	6:00 p.m.
Newcastle-on-Tyne, Eng.	1 37 w	54 58 n	5:00 p.m.
Odessa, U.S.S.R.	30 48 e	46 27 n	8:00 p.m.
Osaka, Japan	135 30 e	34 32 n	2:00 a.m.[1]
Oslo	10 42 e	59 57 n	6:00 p.m.
Panama City, Panama	79 32 w	8 58 n	12:00 noon
Paramaribo, Suriname	55 15 w	5 45 n	1:30 p.m.
Paris	2 20 e	48 48 n	6:00 p.m.
Peking	116 25 e	39 55 n	1:00 a.m.[1]
Perth, Australia	115 52 e	31 57 s	1:00 a.m.[1]
Plymouth, England	4 5 w	50 25 n	5:00 p.m.
Port Moresby, Papua New Guinea	147 8 e	9 25 s	3:00 a.m.[1]
Prague	14 26 e	50 5 n	6:00 p.m.
Rangoon, Burma	96 0 e	16 50 n	11:30 p.m.
Reykjavik, Iceland	21 58 w	64 4 n	4:00 p.m.
Rio de Janeiro	43 12 w	22 57 s	2:00 p.m.
Rome	12 27 e	41 54 n	6:00 p.m.
Salvador, Brazil	38 27 w	12 56 s	2:00 p.m.
Santiago, Chile	70 45 w	33 28 s	1:00 p.m.
São Paulo, Brazil	46 31 w	23 31 s	2:00 p.m.
Shanghai, China	121 28 e	31 10 n	1:00 a.m.[1]
Singapore	103 55 e	1 14 n	0:30 a.m.[1]
Sofia, Bulgaria	23 20 e	42 40 n	7:00 p.m.
Stockholm	18 3 e	59 17 n	6:00 p.m.
Sydney, Australia	151 0 e	34 0 s	3:00 a.m.[1]
Tananarive, Madagascar	47 33 e	18 50 s	8:00 p.m.
Teheran, Iran	51 45 e	35 45 n	8:30 p.m.
Tokyo	139 45 e	35 40 n	2:00 a.m.[1]
Tripoli, Libya	13 12 e	32 57 n	7:00 p.m.
Venice	12 20 e	45 26 n	6:00 p.m.
Veracruz, Mexico	96 10 w	19 10 n	11:00 a.m.
Vienna	16 20 e	48 14 n	6:00 p.m.
Vladivostok, U.S.S.R.	132 0 e	43 10 n	3:00 a.m.[1]
Warsaw	21 0 e	52 14 n	6:00 p.m.
Wellington, New Zealand	174 47 e	41 17 s	5:00 a.m.[1]
Zürich	8 31 e	47 21 n	6:00 p.m.

1. On the following day.

WORLD TIME ZONES

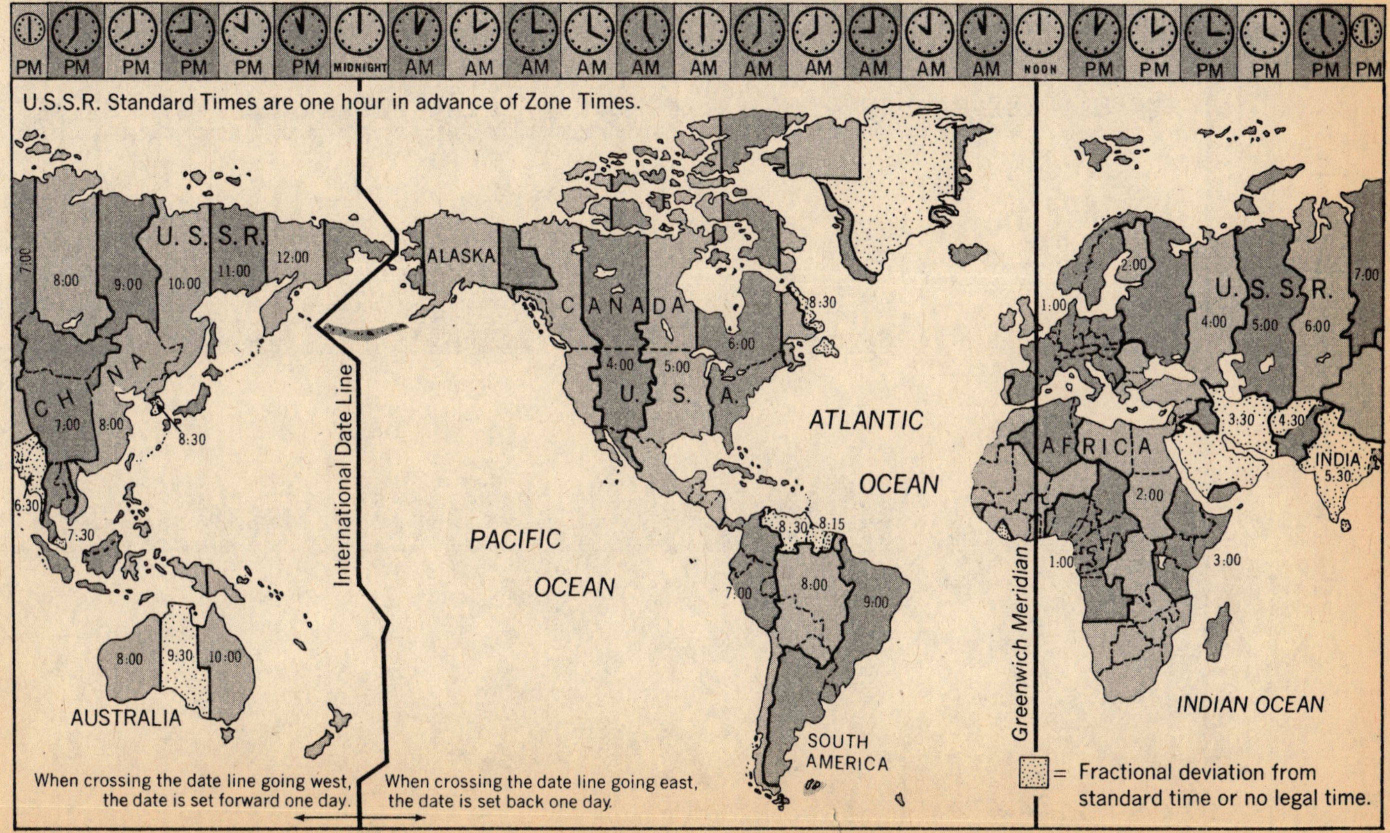

Highest Mountain Peaks of the World

(For U.S. peaks, see Index)

Mountain peak	Range	Location	Height feet	Height meters
Everest[1]	Himalayas	Nepal-Tibet	29,028	8,848
Godwin Austen (K-2)	Karakoram	India	28,741	8,750
Kanchenjunga	Himalayas	Nepal-Sikkim	28,208	8,598
Lhotse	Himalayas	Nepal-Tibet	27,890	8,501
Makalu	Himalayas	Tibet-Nepal	27,790	8,470
Dhaulagiri I	Himalayas	Nepal	26,810	8,172
Manaslu	Himalayas	Nepal	26,760	8,156
Cho Oyu	Himalayas	Nepal	26,750	8,153
Nanga Parbat	Himalayas	India	26,660	8,126
Annapurna I	Himalayas	Nepal	26,504	8,078
Gasherbrum I	Karakoram	India	26,470	8,068
Broad Peak	Karakoram	India	26,400	8,047
Gasherbrum II	Karakoram	India	26,360	8,033
Gosainthan	Himalayas	Tibet	26,291	8,013
Gasherbrum III	Karakoram	India	26,090	7,952
Annapurna II	Himalayas	Nepal	26,041	7,937
Gasherbrum IV	Karakoram	India	26,000	7,925
Kangbachen	Himalayas	Nepal	25,925	7,902
Gyachung Kang	Himalayas	Nepal	25,910	7,897
Himal Chuli	Himalayas	Nepal	25,895	7,893
Disteghil Sar	Karakoram	India	25,868	7,885
Nuptse	Himalayas	Nepal	25,850	7,829
Kunyang Kish	Karakoram	India	25,760	7,852
Dakum (Peak 29)	Himalayas	Nepal	25,760	7,852
Masherbrum	Karakoram	India	25,660	7,821
Nanda Devi	Himalayas	India	25,645	7,817
Chomolonzo	Himalayas	Nepal-Tibet	25,640	7,815
Rakaposhi	Karakoram	India	25,550	7,788
Batura	Karakoram	India	25,540	7,785
Kanjut Sar	Karakoram	India	25,460	7,760
Kamet	Himalayas	India-Tibet	25,447	7,756
Namche Barwa	Himalayas	Tibet	25,445	7,756
Dhaulagiri II	Himalayas	Nepal	25,427	7,750
Saltoro Kangri	Karakoram	India	25,400	7,742
Gurla Mandhata	Himalayas	Tibet	25,355	7,728
Ulugh Muztagh	Kunlun	Tibet	25,341	7,724
Trivor	Karakoram	India	25,330	7,721
Jannu	Himalayas	Nepal	25,294	7,710
Saser Kangri	Karakoram	India	25,170	7,672
Makalu II	Himalayas	Nepal	25,130	7,660
Chogolisa	Karakoram	India	25,110	7,654
Dhaulagiri IV	Himalayas	Nepal	25,064	7,639
Fang	Himalayas	Nepal	25,013	7,624
Kula Gangri	Himalayas	Tibet	24,783	7,554
Changtse	Himalayas	Tibet	24,780	7,553
Muztagh Ata	Muztagh Ata	China	24,757	7,546
Skyang Kangri	Himalayas	Kashmir	24,750	7,544
Communism Peak	Pamir	U.S.S.R.	24,547	7,482
Victory Peak	Pamir	U.S.S.R.	24,406	7,439
Sia Kangri	Himalayas	Kashmir	24,340	7,419
Chamlang	Himalayas	Nepal	24,012	7,319
Alung Gangri	Himalayas	Tibet	23,999	7,315
Chomo Lhari	Himalayas	Tibet-Bhutan	23,996	7,314
Muztagh (K-5)	Kunlun	China	23,891	7,282
Amne Machin	Kunlun	China	23,490	7,160
Gaurisankar	Himalayas	Nepal-Tibet	23,440	7,145
Lenin Peak	Pamir	U.S.S.R.	23,405	7,134
Korzhenevski Peak	Pamir	U.S.S.R.	23,310	7,105
Kangto	Himalayas	Tibet	23,260	7,090
Dunagiri	Himalayas	India	23,184	7,066
Pauhunri	Himalayas	India-Tibet	23,180	7,065
Aconcagua	Andes	Argentina-Chile	23,034	7,021
Revolution Peak	Pamir	U.S.S.R.	22,880	6,974
Kangchenjhan	Himalayas	India	22,700	6,919
Siniolchu	Himalayas	India	22,620	6,895
Ojos des Salado	Andes	Argentina-Chile	22,588	6,885

Mountain peak	Range	Location	Height feet	Height meters
Bonete	Andes	Argentina-Chile	22,546	6,872
Simvuo	Himalayas	India	22,346	6,811
Tup	Andes	Argentina	22,309	6,800
Kungpu	Himalayas	Bhutan	22,300	6,797
Falso-Azufre	Andes	Argentina-Chile	22,277	6,790
Moscow Peak	Pamir	U.S.S.R.	22,260	6,785
Veladero	Andes	Argentina	22,244	6,780
Pissis	Andes	Argentina	22,241	6,779
Mercedario	Andes	Argentina-Chile	22,211	6,770
Huascarán	Andes	Peru	22,198	6,766
Tocorpuri	Andes	Bolivia-Chile	22,162	6,755
Karl Marx Peak	Pamir	U.S.S.R.	22,067	6,726
Llullaillaco	Andes	Argentina-Chile	22,057	6,723
Libertador	Andes	Argentina	22,047	6,720
Kailas	Himalayas	Tibet	22,027	6,714
Lingtren	Himalayas	Nepal-Tibet	21,972	6,697
Incahuasi	Andes	Argentina-Chile	21,719	6,620
Carnicero	Andes	Peru	21,689	6,611
Kurumda	Pamir	U.S.S.R.	21,686	6,610
Garmo Peak	Pamir	U.S.S.R.	21,637	6,595
Sajama	Andes	Bolivia	21,555	6,570
Ancohuma	Andes	Bolivia	21,490	6,550
El Muerto	Andes	Argentina-Chile	21,456	6,540
Nacimiento	Andes	Argentina	21,302	6,493
Illimani	Andes	Bolivia	21,184	6,457
Antofalla	Andes	Argentina-Chile	21,129	6,440
Coropuña	Andes	Peru	21,079	6,425
Cuzco (Ausangate)	Andes	Peru	20,995	6,399
Toro	Andes	Argentina-Chile	20,932	6,380
Parinacota	Andes	Bolivia-Chile	20,768	6,330
Chimboraso	Andes	Ecuador	20,702	6,310
Salcantay	Andes	Peru	20,575	6,271
General Manuel Belgrano	Andes	Argentina	20,505	6,250
Chañi	Andes	Argentina	20,341	6,200
Caca Aca	Andes	Bolivia	20,328	6,196
McKinley	Alaska	Alaska	20,320	6,194
Vudor Peak	Pamir	U.S.S.R.	20,118	6,132
Condoriri	Andes	Bolivia	20,095	6,125
Solimana	Andes	Peru	20,069	6,117
Nevada	Andes	Argentina	20,023	6,103

1. The U. S. Air Force Planning Charts list the height of Mt. Everest as 29,141 ft.

Oceans and Seas

Name	Area sq mi.	Area sq km	Average depth feet	Average depth meters	Greatest known depth feet	Greatest known depth meters	Place greatest known depth
Pacific Ocean	64,000,000	165,760,000	13,215	4,028	37,782	11,516	Mindanao Deep
Atlantic Ocean	31,815,000	82,400,000	12,880	3,926	30,246	9,219	Puerto Rico Trough
Indian Ocean	25,300,000	65,526,700	13,002	3,963	24,460	7,455	Sunda Trench
Arctic Ocean	5,440,200	14,090,000	3,953	1,205	18,456	5,625	77° 45′ N; 175° W
Mediterranean Sea[1]	1,145,100	2,965,800	4,688	1,429	15,197	4,632	Off Cape Matapan, Greece
Caribbean Sea	1,049,500	2,718,200	8,685	2,647	22,788	6,946	Off Cayman Islands
South China Sea	895,400	2,319,000	5,419	1,652	16,456	5,016	West of Luzon
Bering Sea	884,900	2,291,900	5,075	1,547	15,659	4,773	Off Buldir Island
Gulf of Mexico	615,000	1,592,800	4,874	1,486	12,425	3,787	Sigsbee Deep
Okhotsk Sea	613,800	1,589,700	2,749	838	12,001	3,658	146° 10′ E; 46° 50′ N
East China Sea	482,300	1,249,200	617	188	9,126	2,782	25° 16′ N; 125° E
Hudson Bay	475,800	1,232,300	420	128	600	183	Near entrance
Japan Sea	389,100	1,007,800	4,429	1,350	12,276	3,742	Central Basin
Andaman Sea	308,100	797,700	2,854	870	12,392	3,777	Off Car Nicobar Island
North Sea	222,100	575,200	308	94	2,165	660	Skagerrak
Red Sea	169,100	438,000	1,611	491	7,254	2,211	Off Port Sudan
Baltic Sea	163,000	422,200	180	55	1,380	421	Off Gotland

1. Includes Black Sea and Sea of Azov. NOTE: For Caspian Sea, *see* Large Lakes of World elsewhere in this section.

World's Greatest Man-Made Lakes[1]

Name of dam	Location	Millions of cubic meters	Thousands of acre-feet	Year completed
Owen Falls	Uganda	204,800	166,000	1954
Bratsk	U.S.S.R.	169,270	137,220	1964
High Aswān	Egypt	169,000	137,000	1970
Kariba	Zambia–Zimbabwe	160,368	130,000	1958
Akosombo	Ghana	148,000	120,000	1965
Daniel Johnson	Canada	141,852	115,000	1968
Raul Leoni	Venezuela	136,000	110,257	UC
Krasnoyarsk	U.S.S.R.	73,300	59,425	1972
W. A. C. Bennett	Canada	70,309	57,006	1967
Zeya	U.S.S.R.	68,400	55,452	1975
Cabora Bassa	Mozambique	64,000	51,900	1974
LaGrande	Canada	62,260	50,475	UC
Ust–Ilimsk	U.S.S.R.	59,300	48,100	UC
Volga-V. I. Lenin	U.S.S.R.	58,000	47,020	1955
Bukhtarma	U.S.S.R.	53,000	42,970	1960
Ataturk	Turkey	48,700	39,481	UC
Irkutsk	U.S.S.R.	46,000	37,290	1956
Hoover	Nevada-Arizona	36,703	29,755	1936
Vilyui	U.S.S.R.	35,900	29,104	1967
Sobradinho	Brazil	34,200	27,700	UC
Tucurui	Brazil	34,000	27,564	UC
Volgograd-22nd Congress	U.S.S.R.	33,500	27,160	1958
Glen Canyon	Arizona	33,305	27,000	1964
Keban	Turkey	31,000	25,110	1974
Garrison	North Dakota	30,000	24,321	1956
Iroquois	U.S.-Canada	29,960	24,288	1958
Oahe	South Dakota	29,100	23,591	1963

1. Formed by construction of dams. NOTE: UC means under construction in 1980. *Source:* Department of the Interior, Bureau of Reclamation.

Large Lakes of the World

Name and location	Area		Length		Maximum depth	
	sq mi.	sq km	mi.	km	feet	meters
Caspian Sea, U.S.S.R.-Iran[1]	152,239	394,299	745	1,199	3,104	946
Superior, U.S.-Canada	31,820	82,414	383	616	1,333	406
Victoria, Tanzania–Uganda	26,828	69,485	200	322	270	82
Aral, U.S.S.R.	25,659	66,457	266	428	223	68
Huron, U.S.-Canada	23,010	59,596	247	397	750	229
Michigan, U.S.	22,400	58,016	321	517	923	281
Tanganyika, Tanzania-Zaire	12,700	32,893	420	676	4,708	1,435
Baikal, U.S.S.R.	12,162	31,500	395	636	5,712	1,741
Great Bear, Canada	12,000	31,080	232	373	270	82
Nyasa, Malawi-Mozambique-Tanzania	11,600	30,044	360	579	2,316	706
Great Slave, Canada	11,170	28,930	298	480	2,015	614
Chad,[2] Chad-Niger-Nigeria	9,946	25,760	—	—	23	7
Erie, U.S.-Canada	9,930	25,719	241	388	210	64
Winnipeg, Canada	9,094	23,553	264	425	204	62
Ontario, U.S.-Canada	7,520	19,477	193	311	778	237
Balkash, U.S.S.R.	7,115	18,428	376	605	87	27
Ladoga, U.S.S.R.	7,000	18,130	124	200	738	225
Onega, U.S.S.R.	3,819	9,891	154	248	361	110
Titicaca, Bolivia-Peru	3,141	8,135	110	177	1,214	370
Nicaragua, Nicaragua	3,089	8,001	110	177	230	70
Athabaska, Canada	3,058	7,920	208	335	407	124
Rudolf, Kenya	2,473	6,405	154	248	—	—
Reindeer, Canada	2,444	6,330	152	245	—	—
Eyre, South Australia	2,400[3]	6,216	130	209	varies	varies
Issyk-Kul, U.S.S.R.	2,394	6,200	113	182	2,297	700
Urmia,[2] Iran	2,317	6,001	81	130	49	15
Torrens, South Australia	2,200	5,698	130	209	—	—
Vänern, Sweden	2,141	5,545	87	140	322	98

Name and location	Area		Length		Maximum depth	
	sq mi.	sq km	mi.	km	feet	meters
Winnipegosis, Canada	2,086	5,403	152	245	59	18
Mobutu Sese Seko, Uganda	2,046	5,299	100	161	180	55
Nettilling, Baffin Island, Canada	1,950	5,051	70	113	—	—
Nipigon, Canada	1,870	4,843	72	116	—	—
Manitoba, Canada	1,817	4,706	140	225	22	7
Great Salt, U.S.	1,800	4,662	75	121	15/25	5/8
Kioga, Uganda	1,700	4,403	50	80	about 30	9
Koko-Nor, China	1,630	4,222	66	106	—	—

1. The Caspian Sea is called "sea" because the Romans, finding it salty, named it *Mare Caspium.* Many geographers, however, consider it a lake because it is land-locked. 2. Figures represent high-water data. 3. Varies with the rainfall of the wet season. It has been reported to dry up almost completely on occasion.

Principal Rivers of the World

(For other U.S. rivers, see Index)

River	Source	Outflow	Approx. length	
			miles	km
Nile	Tributaries of Lake Victoria, Africa	Mediterranean Sea	4,180	6,690
Amazon	Glacier-fed lakes, Peru	Atlantic Ocean	3,912	6,296
Mississippi-Missouri-Red Rock	Source of Red Rock, Montana	Gulf of Mexico	3,741	6,020
Yangtze Kiang	Tibetan plateau, China	China Sea	3,602	5,797
Ob	Altai Mts., U.S.S.R.	Gulf of Ob	3,459	5,567
Yellow (Huang Ho)	Eastern part of Kunlan Mts., west China	Gulf of Chihli	2,900	4,667
Yenisei	Tannu-Ola Mts., western Tuva, U.S.S.R.	Arctic Ocean	2,800	4,506
Paraná	Confluence of Paranaiba and Grande rivers	Río de la Plata	2,795	4,498
Irtish	Altai Mts., U.S.S.R.	Ob River	2,758	4,438
Congo	Confluence of Lualaba and Luapula rivers, Zaire	Atlantic Ocean	2,716	4,371
Amur	Confluence of Shilka (U.S.S.R.) and Argun (Manchuria) rivers	Tatar Strait	2,704	4,352
Lena	Baikal Mts., U.S.S.R.	Arctic Ocean	2,652	4,268
Mackenzie	Head of Finlay River, British Columbia, Canada	Beaufort Sea (Arctic Ocean)	2,635	4,241
Niger	Guinea	Gulf of Guinea	2,600	4,184
Mekong	Tibetan highlands	South China Sea	2,500	4,023
Mississippi	Lake Itasca, Minnesota	Gulf of Mexico	2,348	3,779
Missouri	Confluence of Jefferson, Gallatin, and Madison rivers, Montana	Mississippi River	2,315	3,726
Volga	Valdai plateau, U.S.S.R.	Caspian Sea	2,291	3,687
Madeira	Confluence of Beni and Maumoré rivers, Bolivia-Brazil boundary	Amazon River	2,012	3,238
Purus	Peruvian Andes	Amazon River	1,993	3,207
São Francisco	Southwest Minas Gerais, Brazil	Atlantic Ocean	1,987	3,198
St. Lawrence	Lake Ontario	Gulf of St. Lawrence	1,900	3,058
Yukon	Junction of Lewes and Pelly rivers, Yukon Territory, Canada	Bering Sea	1,900	3,058
Rio Grande	San Juan Mts., Colorado	Gulf of Mexico	1,885	3,034
Brahmaputra	Himalayas	Ganges River	1,800	2,897
Indus	Himalayas	Arabian Sea	1,800	2,897
Danube	Black Forest, W. Germany	Black Sea	1,766	2,842

River	Source	Outflow	Approx. length miles	km
Euphrates	Confluence of Murat Nehri and Kara Su rivers, Turkey	Shatt-al-Arab	1,739	2,799
Darling	Central part of Eastern Highlands, Australia	Murray River	1,702	2,739
Zambezi	11°21′S, 24°22′E, Zambia	Mozambique Channel	1,700	2,736
Tocantins	Goiás, Brazil	Pará River	1,677	2,699
Murray	Australian Alps, New South Wales	Indian Ocean	1,609	2,589
Nelson	Head of Bow River, western Alberta, Canada	Hudson Bay	1,600	2,575
Paraguay	Mato Grosso, Brazil	Paraná River	1,584	2,549
Ural	Southern Ural Mts., U.S.S.R.	Caspian Sea	1,574	2,533
Ganges	Himalayas	Bay of Bengal	1,557	2,506
Amu Darya (Oxus)	Nicholas Range, Pamir Mts., U.S.S.R.	Aral Sea	1,500	2,414
Japurá	Andes, Colombia	Amazon River	1,500	2,414
Salween	Tibet, south of Kunlun Mts.	Gulf of Martaban	1,500	2,414
Arkansas	Central Colorado	Mississippi River	1,450	2,333
Colorado	Grand County, Colorado	Gulf of California	1,450	2,333
Dnieper	Valdai Hills, U.S.S.R.	Black Sea	1,419	2,284
Ohio-Allegheny	Potter County, Pennsylvania	Mississippi River	1,306	2,102
Irrawaddy	Confluence of Nmai and Mali rivers, northeast Burma	Bay of Bengal	1,300	2,092
Orange	Lesotho	Atlantic Ocean	1,300	2,092
Orinoco	Serra Parima Mts., Venezuela	Atlantic Ocean	1,281	2,062
Pilcomayo	Andes Mts., Bolivia	Paraguay River	1,242	1,999
Xi Jiang (Si Kiang)	Eastern Yunnan Province, China	China Sea	1,236	1,989
Columbia	Columbia Lake, British Columbia, Canada	Pacific Ocean	1,232	1,983
Don	Tula, R.S.F.S.R., U.S.S.R.	Sea of Azov	1,223	1,968
Sungari	China-North Korea boundary	Amur River	1,215	1,955
Saskatchewan	Canadian Rocky Mts.	Lake Winnipeg	1,205	1,939
Peace	Stikine Mts., British Columbia, Canada	Great Slave River	1,195	1,923
Tigris	Taurus Mts., Turkey	Shatt-al-Arab	1,180	1,899

Highest Waterfalls of the World

Waterfall	Location	River	Height feet	meters
Angel	Venezuela	Tributary of Caroní	3,281	1,000
Tugela	Natal, South Africa	Tugela	3,000	914
Cuquenán	Venezuela	Cuquenán	2,000	610
Sutnerland	South Island, N.Z.	Arthur	1,904	580
Takkakaw	British Columbia	Tributary of Yoho	1,650	503
Ribbon (Yosemite)	California	Creek flowing into Yosemite	1,612	491
Upper Yosemite	California	Yosemite Creek, tributary of Merced	1,430	436
Gavarnie	Southwest France	Gave de Pau	1,384	422
Vettisfoss	Norway	Mörkedola	1,200	366
Widows' Tears (Yosemite)	California	Tributary of Merced	1,170	357
Staubbach	Switzerland	Staubbach (Lauterbrunnen Valley)	984	300

Waterfall	Location	River	Height feet	Height meters
Middle Cascade (Yosemite)	California	Yosemite Creek, tributary of Merced	909	277
King Edward VIII	Guyana	Courantyne	850	259
Gersoppa	India	Sharavati	829	253
Kaieteur	Guyana	Potaro	822	251
Skykje	Norway	In Skykjedal (valley of Inner Hardinger Fjord)	820	250
Kalambo	Tanzania-Zambia	—	720	219
Fairy (Mount Rainier Park)	Washington	Stevens Creek	700	213
Trummelbach	Switzerland	Trummelbach (Lauterbrunnen Valley)	700	213
Aniene (Teverone)	Italy	Tiber	680	207
Cascata delle Marmore	Italy	Velino, tributary of Nera	650	198
Maradalsfos	Norway	Stream flowing into Ejkisdalsvand (lake)	643	196
Feather	California	Fall River	640	195
Maletsunyane	Lesotho	Maletsunyane	630	192
Bridalveil (Yosemite)	California	Yosemite Creek	620	189
Multnomah	Oregon	Multnomah Creek, tributary of Columbia	620	189
Voringsfos	Norway	Bjoreia	597	182
Nevada (Yosemite)	California	Merced	594	181
Skjeggedal	Norway	Tysso	525	160
Marina	Guyana	Tributary of Kuribrong, tributary of Potaro	500	152
Tequendama	Colombia	Funza, tributary of Magdalena	425	130
King George's	Cape of Good Hope, South Africa	Orange	400	122
Illilouette (Yosemite)	California	Illilouette Creek, tributary of Merced	370	113
Victoria	Rhodesia-Zambia boundary	Zambezi	355	108
Handöl	Sweden	Handöl Creek	345	105
Lower Yosemite	California	Yosemite	320	98
Comet (Mount Rainier Park)	Washington	Van Trump Creek	320	98
Vernal (Yosemite)	California	Merced	317	97
Virginia	Northwest Territories, Canada	South Nahanni, tributary of Mackenzie	315	96
Lower Yellowstone	Wyoming	Yellowstone	310	94

NOTE: Niagara Falls (New York-Ontario), though of great volume, has parallel drops of only 158 and 167 feet.

Large Islands of the World

Island	Location and status	Area sq mi.	Area sq km
Greenland	North Atlantic (Danish)	839,999	2,175,597
New Guinea	Southwest Pacific (Irian Jaya, Indonesian, west part; Papua New Guinea, east part)	316,615	820,033
Borneo	West mid-Pacific (Indonesian, south part; British protectorate, and Malaysian, north part)	286,914	743,107
Madagascar	Indian Ocean (Malagasy Republic)	226,657	587,042
Baffin	North Atlantic (Canadian)	183,810	476,068
Sumatra	Northeast Indian Ocean (Indonesian)	182,859	473,605
Honshu	Sea of Japan-Pacific (Japanese)	88,925	230,316
Great Britain	Off coast of NW Europe (England, Scotland, and Wales)	88,758	229,883
Ellesmere	Arctic Ocean (Canadian)	82,119	212,688
Victoria	Arctic Ocean (Canadian)	81,930	212,199
Celebes	West mid-Pacific (Indonesian)	72,986	189,034
South Island	South Pacific (New Zealand)	58,093	150,461
Java	Indian Ocean (Indonesian)	48,990	126,884
North Island	South Pacific (New Zealand)	44,281	114,688

Island	Location and status	Area	
		sq mi.	sq km
Cuba	Caribbean Sea (republic)	44,218	114,525
Newfoundland	North Atlantic (Canadian)	42,734	110,681
Luzon	West mid-Pacific (Philippines)	40,420	104,688
Iceland	North Atlantic (republic)	39,768	102,999
Mindanao	West mid-Pacific (Philippines)	36,537	94,631
Ireland	West of Great Britain (republic, south part; United Kingdom, north part)	32,597	84,426
Hokkaido	Sea of Japan—Pacific (Japanese)	30,372	78,663
Hispaniola	Caribbean Sea (Dominican Republic, east part; Haiti, west part)	29,355	76,029
Tasmania	South of Australia (Australian)	26,215	67,897
Sri Lanka (Ceylon)	Indian Ocean (republic)	25,332	65,610
Sakhalin (Karafuto)	North of Japan (U.S.S.R.)	24,560	63,610
Banks	Arctic Ocean (Canadian)	23,230	60,166
Devon	Arctic Ocean (Canadian)	20,861	54,030
Tierra del Fuego	Southern tip of South America (Argentinian, east part; Chilean, west part)	18,605	48,187
Kyushu	Sea of Japan—Pacific (Japanese)	16,223	42,018
Melville	Arctic Ocean (Canadian)	16,141	41,805
Axel Heiberg	Arctic Ocean (Canadian)	15,779	40,868
Southampton	Hudson Bay (Canadian)	15,700	40,663

Principal Deserts of the World

Desert	Location	Approximate size	Approx. elevation, ft
Atacama	North Chile	400 mi. long	7,000–13,500
Black Rock	Northwest Nevada	About 1,000 sq mi.	2,000–8,500
Colorado	Southeast California from San Gorgonio Pass to Gulf of California	200 mi. long and a maximum width of 50 mi.	Few feet above to 250 below sea level
Dasht-e-Kavír	Southeast of Caspian Sea, Iran	—	2,000
Dasht-e-Lūt	Northeast of Kerman, Iran	—	1,000
Gobi (Shamo)	Covers most of Mongolia	500,000 sq mi.	3,000–5,000
Great Arabian	Most of Arabia	1,500 mi. long	—
An Nafud (Red Desert)	South of Jauf	400 mi. by avg of 140 mi.	3,000
Dahna	Northeast of Nejd	400 mi. by 30 mi.	—
Rub' al-Khali	South portion of Nejd	Over 200,000 sq mi.	—
Syrian (Al-Hamad)	North of lat. 30°N	—	1,850
Great Australian	Western portion of Australia	About one half the continent	600–1,000
Great Salt Lake	West of Great Salt Lake to Nevada–Utah boundary	About 110 mi. by 50 mi.	4,500
Kalahari	South Africa—South-West Africa	About 120,000 sq mi.	Over 3,000
Kara Kum (Desert of Kiva)	Southwest Turkmen, U.S.S.R.	115,000 sq mi.	—
Kyzyl Kum	Uzbek and Kazakh, U.S.S.R.	Over 100,000 sq mi.	160 near Lake Aral to 2,000 in southeast
Libyan	Libya, Egypt, Sudan	Over 500,000 sq mi.	—
Mojave	North of Colorado Desert and south of Death Valley, southeast California	15,000 sq mi.	2,000
Nubian	From Red Sea to great west bend of the Nile, Sudan	—	2,500
Painted Desert	Northeast Arizona	Over 7,000 sq mi.	High plateau, 5,000
Sahara	North Africa to about lat. 15°N and from Red Sea to Atlantic Ocean	3,200 mi. greatest length along lat. 20°N; area over 3,500,000 sq mi.	440 below sea level to 11,000 above; avg elevation, 1,400–1,600
Takla Makan	South central Sinkiang, China	Over 100,000 sq mi.	—
Thar (Indian)	Pakistan-India	Nearly 100,000 sq mi.	Over 1,000

U.S. Geography

Miscellaneous Data for the United States

Source: Department of the Interior, U.S. Geological Survey.

Highest point: Mount McKinley, Alaska	20,320 ft (6,193 m)
Lowest point: Death Valley, Calif.	282 ft (86 m) below sea level
Approximate mean altitude	2,500 ft (762 m)
Points farthest apart (50 states):	
Log Point, Elliot Key, Fla., and Kure Island, Hawaii	5,852 mi. (9,418 km)
Geographic center (50 states):	
In Butte County, S.D. (west of Castle Rock)	44° 58′ N. lat. 103° 46′ W. long.
Geographic center (48 conterminous states):	
In Smith County, Kan. (near Lebanon)	39° 50′ N. lat. 98° 35′ W. long.
Boundaries:	
Between Alaska and Canada	1,538 mi. (2,475 km)
Between the 48 conterminous states and Canada (incl. Great Lakes)	3,987 mi. (6,416 km)
Between the United States and Mexico	1,933 mi. (3,111 km)

Coastline of the United States

Fourth (April 1, 1961) Edition

State	Lengths, statute miles: General coastline[1]	Lengths, statute miles: Tidal shoreline[2]
Atlantic Coast:		
Maine	228	3,478
New Hampshire	13	131
Massachusetts	192	1,519
Rhode Island	40	384
Connecticut	—	618
New York	127	1,850
New Jersey	130	1,792
Pennsylvania	—	89
Delaware	28	381
Maryland	31	3,190
Virginia	112	3,315
North Carolina	301	3,375
South Carolina	187	2,876
Georgia	100	2,344
Florida (Atlantic)	580	3,331
Total Atlantic coast	2,069	28,673
Gulf Coast:		
Florida (Gulf)	770	5,095
Alabama	53	607
Mississippi	44	359
Louisiana	397	7,721
Texas	367	3,359
Total Gulf coast	1,631	17,141
Pacific Coast:		
California	840	3,427
Oregon	296	1,410
Washington	157	3,026
Hawaii	750	1,052
Alaska (Pacific)	5,580	31,383
Total Pacific coast	7,623	40,298
Arctic Coast:		
Alaska (Arctic)	1,060	2,521
Total Arctic coast	1,060	2,521
States Total	**12,383**	**88,633**

1. Figures are lengths of general outline of seacoast. Measurements made with unit measure of 30 minutes of latitude on charts as near scale of 1:1,200,000 as possible. Coastline of bays and sounds is included to point where they narrow to width of unit measure, and distance across at such point is included. 2. Figures obtained in 1939–40 with recording instrument on largest-scale maps and charts then available. Shoreline of outer coast, offshore islands, sounds, bays, rivers, and creeks is included to head of tidewater, or to point where tidal waters narrow to width of 100 feet. *Source:* Department of Commerce, National Oceanic and Atmospheric Administration, National Ocean Survey.

The Continental Divide

The Continental Divide is a ridge of high ground which runs irregularly north and south through the Rocky Mountains and separates eastward-flowing from westward-flowing streams. The waters which flow eastward empty into the Atlantic Ocean, chiefly by way of the Gulf of Mexico; those which flow westward empty into the Pacific.

Highest, Lowest, and Mean Altitudes in the United States

State	Altitude, ft[1]	Highest point	Altitude, ft	Lowest point	Altitude, ft
Alabama	500	Cheaha Mountain	2,407	Gulf of Mexico	Sea level
Alaska	1,900	Mount McKinley	20,320	Pacific Ocean	Sea level
Arizona	4,100	Humphreys Peak	12,633	Colorado River	70
Arkansas	650	Magazine Mountain	2,753	Ouachita River	55
California	2,900	Mount Whitney	14,494	Death Valley	282[2]
Colorado	6,800	Mount Elbert	14,433	Arkansas River	3,350
Connecticut	500	Mount Frissell, on south slope	2,380	Long Island Sound	Sea level
Delaware	60	On Ebright Road	442	Atlantic Ocean	Sea level
D. C.	150	Tenleytown, northwest part	410	Potomac River	1
Florida	100	Sec. 30, T6N, R20W[3]	345	Atlantic Ocean	Sea level
Georgia	600	Brasstown Bald	4,784	Atlantic Ocean	Sea level
Hawaii	3,030	Mauna Kea	13,796	Pacific Ocean	Sea level
Idaho	5,000	Borah Peak	12,662	Snake River	710
Illinois	600	Charles Mound	1,235	Mississippi River	279
Indiana	700	Franklin Township, Wayne County	1,257	Ohio River	320
Iowa	1,100	Sec. 29, T100N, R41W[4]	1,670	Mississippi River	480
Kansas	2,000	Mount Sunflower	4,039	Verdigris River	680
Kentucky	750	Black Mountain	4,145	Mississippi River	257
Louisiana	100	Driskill Mountain	535	New Orleans	5[2]
Maine	600	Mount Katahdin	5,268	Atlantic Ocean	Sea level
Maryland	350	Backbone Mountain	3,360	Atlantic Ocean	Sea level
Massachusetts	500	Mount Greylock	3,491	Atlantic Ocean	Sea level
Michigan	900	Mount Curwood	1,980	Lake Erie	572
Minnesota	1,200	Eagle Mountain	2,301	Lake Superior	602
Mississippi	300	Woodall Mountain	806	Gulf of Mexico	Sea level
Missouri	800	Taum Sauk Mountain	1,772	St. Francis River	230
Montana	3,400	Granite Peak	12,799	Kootenai River	1,800
Nebraska	2,600	Johnson Township, Kimball County	5,426	Southeast corner of state	840
Nevada	5,500	Boundary Peak	13,143	Colorado River	470
New Hampshire	1,000	Mount Washington	6,288	Atlantic Ocean	Sea level
New Jersey	250	High Point	1,803	Atlantic Ocean	Sea level
New Mexico	5,700	Wheeler Peak	13,161	Red Bluff Reservoir	2,817
New York	1,000	Mount Marcy	5,344	Atlantic Ocean	Sea level
North Carolina	700	Mount Mitchell	6,684	Atlantic Ocean	Sea level
North Dakota	1,900	White Butte	3,506	Red River	750
Ohio	850	Campbell Hill	1,550	Ohio River	433
Oklahoma	1,300	Black Mesa	4,973	Little River	287
Oregon	3,300	Mount Hood	11,239	Pacific Ocean	Sea level
Pennsylvania	1,100	Mount Davis	3,213	Delaware River	Sea level
Rhode Island	200	Jerimoth Hill	812	Atlantic Ocean	Sea level
South Carolina	350	Sassafras Mountain	3,560	Atlantic Ocean	Sea level
South Dakota	2,200	Harney Peak	7,242	Big Stone Lake	962
Tennessee	900	Clingmans Dome	6,643	Mississippi River	182
Texas	1,700	Guadalupe Peak	8,749	Gulf of Mexico	Sea level
Utah	6,100	Kings Peak	13,528	Beaverdam Creek	2,000
Vermont	1,000	Mount Mansfield	4,393	Lake Champlain	95
Virginia	950	Mount Rogers	5,729	Atlantic Ocean	Sea level
Washington	1,700	Mount Rainier	14,410	Pacific Ocean	Sea level
West Virginia	1,500	Spruce Knob	4,863	Potomac River	240
Wisconsin	1,050	Timms Hill	1,952	Lake Michigan	581
Wyoming	6,700	Gannett Peak	13,804	Belle Fourche River	3,100
United States	2,500	Mount McKinley (Alaska)	20,320	Death Valley (California)	282[2]

1. Approximate mean altitude. 2. Below sea level. 3. Walton County. 4. Osceola County. *Source:* Department of the Interior, U.S. Geological Survey.

Mason and Dixon's Line

Mason and Dixon's Line (often called the Mason-Dixon Line) is the boundary between Pennsylvania and Maryland, running at a north latitude of 39°43'19.11". The greater part of it was surveyed from 1763–67 by Charles Mason and Jeremiah Dixon, English astronomers who had been appointed to settle a dispute between the colonies. As the line was partly the boundary between the free and the slave states, it has come to signify the division between the North and the South.

Named Summits in the U. S. Over 14,000 Feet Above Sea Level

Name	State	Height	Name	State	Height	Name	State	Height
Mt. McKinley	Alaska	20,320	Mt. Antero	Colo.	14,269	Windom Peak	Colo.	14,087
Mt. St. Elias	Alaska	18,008	Torreys Peak	Colo.	14,267	Mt. Russell	Calif.	14,086
Mt. Foraker	Alaska	17,400	Castle Peak	Colo.	14,265	Mt. Eolus	Colo.	14,084
Mt. Bona	Alaska	16,421	Quandary Peak	Colo.	14,265	Mt. Columbia	Colo.	14,073
Mt. Blackburn	Alaska	16,390	Mt. Evans	Colo.	14,264	Mt. Augusta	Alaska	14,070
Mt. Sanford	Alaska	16,237	Longs Peak	Colo.	14,255	Missouri Mtn.	Colo.	14,067
South Buttress	Alaska	15,885	Mt. Wilson	Colo.	14,246	Humboldt Peak	Colo.	14,064
Mt. Vancouver	Alaska	15,700	White Mtn.	Calif.	14,246	Mt. Bierstadt	Colo.	14,060
Mt. Churchill	Alaska	15,638	North Palisade	Calif.	14,242	Sunlight Peak	Colo.	14,059
Mt. Fairweather	Alaska	15,300	Shavano Peak	Colo.	14,229	Split Mtn.	Calif.	14,058
Mt. Hubbard	Alaska	15,015	Crestone Needle	Colo.	14,197	Handies Peak	Colo.	14,048
Mt. Bear	Alaska	14,831	Mt. Belford	Colo.	14,197	Culebra Peak	Colo.	14,047
East Buttress	Alaska	14,730	Mt. Princeton	Colo.	14,197	Mt. Lindsey	Colo.	14,042
Mt. Hunter	Alaska	14,573	Mt. Yale	Colo.	14,196	Middle Palisade	Calif.	14,040
Mt. Alverstone	Alaska	14,565	Mt. Bross	Colo.	14,172	Little Bear Peak	Colo.	14,037
Browne Tower	Alaska	14,530	Kit Carson Mtn.	Colo.	14,165	Mt. Sherman	Colo.	14,036
Mt. Whitney	Calif.	14,494	Mt. Wrangell	Alaska	14,163	Redcloud Peak	Colo.	14,034
Mt. Elbert	Colo.	14,433	Mt. Shasta	Calif.	14,162	Mt. Langley	Calif.	14,028
Mt. Massive	Colo.	14,421	Mt. Sill	Calif.	14,162	Mt. Tyndall	Calif.	14,018
Mt. Harvard	Colo.	14,420	El Diente Peak	Colo.	14,159	Pyramid Peak	Colo.	14,018
Mt. Rainier	Wash.	14,410	Maroon Peak	Colo.	14,156	Wilson Peak	Colo.	14,017
Mt. Williamson	Calif.	14,375	Tabeguache Mtn.	Colo.	14,155	Mt. Muir	Calif.	14,015
Blanca Peak	Colo.	14,345	Mt. Oxford	Colo.	14,153	Wetterhorn Peak	Colo.	14,015
La Plata Peak	Colo.	14,336	Mt. Sneffels	Colo.	14,150	No. Maroon Pk.	Colo.	14,014
Uncompahgre Pk.	Colo.	14,309	Mt. Democrat	Colo.	14,148	San Luis Peak	Colo.	14,014
Crestone Peak	Colo.	14,294	Capitol Peak	Colo.	14,130	Huron Peak	Colo.	14,005
Mt. Lincoln	Colo.	14,286	Pikes Peak	Colo.	14,110	Mt. of the Holy Cross	Colo.	14,005
Grays Peak	Colo.	14,270	Snowmass Mtn.	Colo.	14,092	Sunshine Peak	Colo.	14,001

Source: Department of the Interior, U.S. Geological Survey.

Extreme Points of the United States (50 States)

Extreme point	Latitude	Longitude	Distance[1]	
			mi.	km
Northernmost point: Point Barrow, Alaska	71°23′ N	156°29′ W	2,502	4,027
Easternmost point: West Quoddy Head, Me.	44°49′ N	66°57′ W	1,785	2,873
Southernmost point: Ka Lae (South Cape), Hawaii	18°56′ N	155°41′ W	3,456	5,562
Westernmost point: Cape Wrangell, Alaska (Attu Island)	52°55′ N	172°27′ E	3,620	5,826

1. From geographic center of United States (incl. Alaska and Hawaii), west of Castle Rock, S.D., 44°58′ N. lat., 103°46′ W long.

Rivers of the United States

(350 or more miles long)

Alabama (735 mi.; 1,183 km): From junction of Tallapoosa R. and Coosa R. in Alabama to Mobile R.

Altamaha-Ocmulgee (392 mi.; 631 km): From junction of Yellow R. and South R., Newton Co. in Georgia to Atlantic Ocean.

Apalachicola-Chattahoochee (524 mi.; 843 km): From Towns Co. in Georgia to Gulf of Mexico in Florida.

Arkansas (1,459 mi.; 2,348 km): From Lake Co. in Colorado to Mississippi R. in Arkansas.

Brazos (870 mi.; 1,400 km): From junction of Salt Fork and Double Mountain Fork in Texas to Gulf of Mexico.

Canadian (906 mi.; 1,458 km): From Las Animas Co. in Colorado to Arkansas R. in Oklahoma.

Cimarron (600 mi.; 966 km): From Colfax Co. in New Mexico to Arkansas R. in Oklahoma.

Clark Fork-Pend Oreille (505 mi.; 813 km): From Silver Bow Co. in Montana to Columbia R. in British Columbia.

Colorado (1,450 mi.; 2,333 km): From Rocky Mountain National Park in Colorado to Gulf of California in Mexico.

Colorado (840 mi.; 1,352 km): From Borden Co. in Texas to Matagorda Bay.

Columbia (1,243 mi.; 2,000 km): From Columbia Lake in British Columbia to Pacific Ocean (entering between Oregon and Washington).

Colville (350 mi.; 563 km): From Brooks Range in Alaska to Beaufort Sea.

Connecticut (407 mi.; 655 km): From Third Connecticut Lake in New Hampshire to Long Island Sound in Connecticut.

Cumberland (720 mi.; 1,159 km): From junction of Poor and Clover Forks in Harlan Co. in Kentucky to Ohio R.

Delaware (390 mi.; 628 km): From Schoharie County in New York to Liston Point, Delaware Bay.
Gila (630 mi.; 1,014 km): From Catron Co. in New Mexico to Colorado R. in Arizona.
Green (360 mi.; 579 km): From Lincoln Co. in Kentucky to Ohio R. in Kentucky.
Green (730 mi.; 1,175 km): From Sublette Co. in Wyoming to Colorado R. in Utah.
Illinois (420 mi.; 676 km): From St. Joseph Co. in Indiana to Mississippi R. at Grafton in Illinois.
James (sometimes called *Dakota*) (710 mi.; 1,143 km): From Wells Co. in North Dakota to Missouri R. in South Dakota.
Kanawha-New (352 mi.; 566 km): From junction of North and South Forks of New R. in North Carolina to Ohio R.
Koyukuk (470 mi.; 756 km): From Brooks Range in Alaska to Yukon R.
Kuskokwim (680 mi.; 1,094 km): From Alaska Range in Alaska to Kuskokwim Bay.
Licking (350 mi.; 563 km): From Magoffin Co. in Kentucky to Ohio R. at Cincinnati in Ohio.
Little Missouri (560 mi.; 901 km): From Crook Co. in Wyoming to Missouri R. in North Dakota.
Milk (625 mi.; 1,006 km): From junction of forks in Alberta Province to Missouri R.
Mississippi (2,348 mi.; 3,779 km): From Lake Itasca in Minnesota to mouth of Southwest Pass.
Mississippi-Missouri-Red Rock (3,710 mi.; 5,971 km): From source of Red Rock R. in Montana to mouth of Southwest Pass in Louisiana.
Missouri (2,315 mi.; 3,726 km): From junction of Jefferson R., Gallatin R., and Madison R. in Montana to Mississippi R. near St. Louis.
Missouri-Red Rock (2,533 mi.; 4,076 km): From source of Red Rock R. in Montana to Mississippi R. near St. Louis.
Mobile-Alabama-Coosa (780 mi.; 1,255 km): From junction of Etowah R. and Oostanaula R. in Georgia to Mobile Bay.
Neosho (460 mi.; 740 km): From Morris Co. in Kansas to Arkansas R. in Oklahoma.
Niobrara (431 mi.; 694 km): From Niobrara Co. in Wyoming to Missouri R. in Nebraska.
Noatak (350 mi.; 563 km): From Brooks Range in Alaska to Kotzebue Sound.
North Canadian (760 mi.; 1,223 km): From Union Co. in New Mexico to Canadian R. in Oklahoma.
North Platte (618 mi.; 995 km): From Jackson Co. in Colorado to junction with So. Platte R. in Nebraska to form Platte R.
Ohio (981 mi.; 1,579 km): From junction of Allegheny R. and Monongahela R. at Pittsburgh to Mississippi R. between Illinois and Kentucky.
Ohio-Allegheny (1,306 mi.; 2,102 km): From Potter Co. in Pennsylvania to Mississippi R. at Cairo in Illinois.
Osage (500 mi.; 805 km): From east-central Kansas to Missouri R. near Jefferson City in Missouri.
Ouachita (605 mi.; 974 km): From Polk Co. in Arkansas to Red R. in Louisiana.
Pearl (411 mi.; 661 km): From Neshoba County in Mississippi to Gulf of Mexico (Mississippi-Louisiana).
Pecos (735 mi.; 1,183 km): From Mora Co. in New Mexico to Rio Grande in Texas.
Pee Dee-Yadkin (435 mi.; 700 km): From Watauga Co. in North Carolina to Winyah Bay in South Carolina.
Pend Oreille (490 mi.; 789 km): Near Butte in Montana to Columbia R. on Washington-Canada border.
Porcupine (460 mi.; 740 km): From Yukon Territory, Canada, to Yukon R. in Alaska.
Potomac (383 mi.; 616 km): From Garrett Co. in Maryland to Chesapeake Bay at Point Lookout in Maryland.
Powder (375 mi.; 603 km): From junction of forks in Johnson Co. in Wyoming to Yellowstone R. in Montana.
Red (1,270 mi.; 2,044 km): From junction of forks in Harmon Co. in Oklahoma to Mississippi R. in Louisiana.
Red (officially called *Red River of the North*) (545 mi.; 877 km): From junction of Otter Tail R. and Bois de Sioux R. in Minnesota to Lake Winnipeg in Manitoba.
Republican (445 mi.; 716 km): From junction of North Fork and Arikaree R. in Nebraska to junction with Smoky Hill R. in Kansas to form Kansas R.
Rio Grande (1,885 mi.; 3,034 km): From San Juan Co. in Colorado to Gulf of Mexico.
Roanoke (380 mi.; 612 km): From junction of forks in Montgomery Co. in Virginia to Albemarle Sound in North Carolina.
Sabine (380 mi.; 612 km): From junction of forks in Hunt Co. in Texas to Sabine Lake between Texas and Louisiana.
Sacramento (377 mi.; 607 km): From Siskiyou Co. in California to Suisun Bay.
Saint Francis (425 mi.; 684 km): From Iron Co. in Missouri to Mississippi R. in Arkansas.
Salmon (420 mi.; 676 km): From Custer Co. in Idaho to Snake R.
San Joaquin (350 mi.; 563 km): From junction of forks in Madera Co. in California to Suisun Bay.
San Juan (360 mi.; 579 km): From Archuleta Co. in Colorado to Colorado R. in Utah.
Santee-Wateree-Catawba (538 mi.; 866 km): From McDowell Co. in North Carolina to Atlantic Ocean in South Carolina.
Smoky Hill (540 mi.; 869 km): From Cheyenne Co. in Colorado to junction with Republican R. in Kansas to form Kansas R.
Snake (1,038 mi.; 1,670 km): From Ocean Plateau in Wyoming to Columbia R. in Washington.
South Platte (424 mi.; 682 km): From Park Co. in Colorado to junction with North Platte R. in Nebraska to form Platte R.
Susquehanna (444 mi.; 715 km): From Otsego Lake in New York to Chesapeake Bay in Maryland.
Tanana (620 mi.; 998 km): From Wrangell Mts. in Yukon Territory, Canada, to Yukon R. in Alaska.
Tennessee (652 mi.; 1,049 km): From junction of Holston R. and French Broad R. in Tennessee to Ohio R. in Kentucky.
Tennessee-French Broad (900 mi.; 1,448 km): From Bland Co. in Virginia to Ohio R. at Paducah in Kentucky.
Tombigbee (525 mi.; 845 km): From junction of forks in Itawamba Co. in Mississippi to Mobile R. in Alabama.
Trinity (360 mi.; 579 km): From junction of forks in Dallas Co. in Texas to Galveston Bay.
Wabash (529 mi.; 851 km): From Darke Co. in Ohio to Ohio R. between Illinois and Indiana.
Washita (500 mi.; 805 km): From Hemphill Co. in Texas to Red R. in Oklahoma.
White (720 mi.; 1,159 km): From Madison Co. in Arkansas to Mississippi R.
Wisconsin (430 mi.; 692 km): From Vilas Co. in Wisconsin to Mississippi R.
Yellowstone (671 mi.; 1,080 km): From Park Co. in Wyoming to Missouri R. in North Dakota.
Yukon (1,770 mi.; 2,848 km): From junction of Lewes R. and Pelly R. in Yukon Territory, Canada, to Bering Sea in Alaska.

Longitude and Latitude of U.S. and Canadian Cities
(and time corresponding to 12:00 noon, eastern standard time)

City	Long. w °	Long. w ′	Lat. n °	Lat. n ′	Time
Albany, N.Y.	73	45	42	40	12:00 noon
Amarillo, Tex.	101	50	35	11	11:00 a.m.
Anchorage, Alaska	149	54	61	13	7:00 a.m.
Atlanta	84	23	33	45	12:00 noon
Atlantic City, N.J.	74	25	39	22	12:00 noon
Austin, Nev.	117	4	39	29	9:00 a.m.
Baker, Ore.	117	50	44	47	9:00 a.m.
Baltimore	76	38	39	18	12:00 noon
Bangor, Me.	68	47	44	48	12:00 noon
Birmingham, Ala.	86	50	33	30	11:00 a.m.
Bismarck, N.D.	100	47	46	48	11:00 a.m.
Boise, Idaho	116	13	43	36	10:00 a.m.
Boston	71	5	42	21	12:00 noon
Buffalo, N.Y.	78	50	42	55	12:00 noon
Calgary, Alberta	114	1	51	1	10:00 a.m.
Carlsbad, N.M.	104	15	32	26	10:00 a.m.
Charleston, S.C.	79	56	32	47	12:00 noon
Charleston, W.Va.	81	38	38	21	12:00 noon
Charlotte, N.C.	80	50	35	14	12:00 noon
Cheyenne, Wyo.	104	52	41	9	10:00 a.m.
Chicago	87	37	41	50	11:00 a.m.
Cincinnati	84	30	39	8	12:00 noon
Cleveland	81	37	41	28	12:00 noon
Columbia, S.C.	81	2	34	0	12:00 noon
Columbus, Ohio	83	1	40	0	12:00 noon
Dallas	96	46	32	46	11:00 a.m.
Denver	105	0	39	45	10:00 a.m.
Des Moines, Iowa	93	37	41	35	11:00 a.m.
Detroit	83	3	42	20	12:00 noon
Dubuque, Iowa	90	40	42	31	11:00 a.m.
Duluth, Minn.	92	5	46	49	11:00 a.m.
Eastport, Me.	67	0	44	54	12:00 noon
El Centro, Calif.	115	33	32	38	9:00 a.m.
El Paso	106	29	31	46	10:00 a.m.
Eugene, Ore.	123	5	44	3	9:00 a.m.
Fargo, N.D.	96	48	46	52	11:00 a.m.
Flagstaff, Ariz.	111	41	35	13	10:00 a.m.
Fresno, Calif.	119	48	36	44	9:00 a.m.
Garden City, Kan.	100	53	37	58	10:00 a.m.
Grand Junction, Colo.	108	33	39	5	10:00 a.m.
Grand Rapids, Mich.	85	40	42	58	12:00 noon
Havre, Mont.	109	43	48	33	10:00 a.m.
Helena, Mont.	112	2	46	35	10:00 a.m.
Honolulu	157	50	21	18	7:00 a.m.
Hoquiam, Wash.	123	54	46	59	9:00 a.m.
Hot Springs, Ark.	93	3	34	31	11:00 a.m.
Idaho Falls, Idaho	112	1	43	30	10:00 a.m.
Indianapolis	86	10	39	46	12:00 noon
Jackson, Miss.	90	12	32	20	11:00 a.m.
Jacksonville, Fla.	81	40	30	22	12:00 noon
Juneau, Alaska	134	24	58	18	9:00 a.m.
Kansas City, Mo.	94	35	39	6	11:00 a.m.
Key West, Fla.	81	48	24	33	12:00 noon
Kingston, Ont.	76	30	44	15	12:00 noon
Klamath Falls, Ore.	121	44	42	10	9:00 a.m.
Knoxville, Tenn.	83	56	35	57	12:00 noon
Lander, Wyo.	108	40	42	50	10:00 a.m.
Las Vegas, Nev.	115	12	36	10	9:00 a.m.
Lewiston, Idaho	117	2	46	24	9:00 a.m.
Lincoln, Neb.	96	40	40	50	11:00 a.m.
London, Ont.	81	34	43	2	12:00 noon
Los Angeles	118	15	34	3	9:00 a.m.
Louisville, Ky.	85	46	38	15	12:00 noon
Manchester, N.H.	71	30	43	0	12:00 noon
Memphis, Tenn	90	3	35	9	11:00 a.m.
Miami, Fla.	80	12	25	46	12:00 noon
Milwaukee	87	55	43	2	11:00 a.m.
Minneapolis	93	14	44	59	11:00 a.m.
Mobile, Ala.	88	3	30	42	11:00 a.m.
Montgomery, Ala.	86	18	32	21	11:00 a.m.
Montpelier, Vt.	72	32	44	15	12:00 noon
Montreal, Que.	73	35	45	30	12:00 noon
Moose Jaw, Sask.	105	31	50	37	10:00 a.m.
Nashville, Tenn.	86	47	36	10	11:00 a.m.
Needles, Calif.	114	36	34	50	9:00 a.m.
Nelson, B.C.	117	17	49	30	9:00 a.m.
New Haven, Conn.	72	55	41	19	12:00 noon
New Orleans	90	4	29	57	11:00 a.m.
New York	73	58	40	47	12:00 noon
Nogales, Ariz.	110	56	31	21	10:00 a.m.
Nome, Alaska	165	30	64	25	6:00 a.m.
North Platte, Neb.	100	46	41	8	11:00 a.m.
Oklahoma City	97	28	35	26	11:00 a.m.
Ottawa, Ont.	75	43	45	24	12:00 noon
Philadelphia	75	10	39	57	12:00 noon
Phoenix, Ariz.	112	4	33	29	10:00 a.m.
Pierre, S.D.	100	21	44	22	11:00 a.m.
Pittsburgh	79	57	40	27	12:00 noon
Port Arthur, Ont.	89	17	48	30	12:00 noon
Portland, Me.	70	15	43	40	12:00 noon
Portland, Ore.	122	41	45	31	9:00 a.m.
Providence, R.I.	71	24	41	50	12:00 noon
Quebec, Que.	71	11	46	49	12:00 noon
Raleigh, N.C.	78	39	35	46	12:00 noon
Reno, Nev.	119	49	39	30	9:00 a.m.
Richfield, Utah	112	5	38	46	10:00 a.m.
Richmond, Va.	77	29	37	33	12:00 noon
Roanoke, Va.	79	57	37	17	12:00 noon
Sacramento, Calif.	121	30	38	35	9:00 a.m.
St. John, N.B.	66	10	45	18	1:00 p.m.
St. Louis	90	12	38	35	11:00 a.m.
Salmon, Idaho	113	54	45	11	10:00 a.m.
Salt Lake City, Utah	111	54	40	46	10:00 a.m.
San Antonio	98	33	29	23	11:00 a.m.
San Diego, Calif.	117	10	32	42	9:00 a.m.
San Francisco	122	26	37	47	9:00 a.m.
San Juan, P.R.	66	10	18	30	1:00 p.m.
Santa Fe, N.M.	105	57	35	41	10:00 a.m.
Sault Ste. Marie, Mich.	84	21	46	30	11:00 a.m.
Savannah, Ga.	81	5	32	5	12:00 noon
Scranton, Pa.	75	39	41	24	12:00 noon
Seattle	122	20	47	37	9:00 a.m.
Shreveport, La.	93	42	32	28	11:00 a.m.
Sioux Falls, S.D.	96	44	43	33	11:00 a.m.
Sitka, Alaska	135	15	57	10	9:00 a.m.
Spokane, Wash.	117	26	47	40	9:00 a.m.
Springfield, Ill.	89	38	39	48	11:00 a.m.
Springfield, Mass.	72	34	42	6	12:00 noon
Springfield, Mo.	93	17	37	13	11:00 a.m.
Syracuse, N.Y.	76	8	43	2	12:00 noon
Tampa, Fla.	82	27	27	57	12:00 noon
Toronto, Ont.	79	24	43	40	12:00 noon
Trinidad, Colo.	104	30	37	10	10:00 a.m.
Victoria, B.C.	123	21	48	25	9:00 a.m.
Watertown, N.Y.	75	55	43	58	12:00 noon
Wichita, Kan.	97	17	37	43	11:00 a.m.
Wilmington, N.C.	77	57	34	14	12:00 noon
Winnipeg, Man.	97	7	49	54	11:00 a.m.

AWARDS

Nobel Prizes

The Nobel prizes are awarded under the will of Alfred Bernhard Nobel, Swedish chemist and engineer, who died in 1896. The interest of the fund is divided annually among the persons who have made the most outstanding contributions in the fields of physics, chemistry, and physiology of medicine, who have produced the most distinguished literary work of an idealist tendency, and who have contributed most toward world peace.

In 1968, a Nobel Prize of economic sciences was established by Riksbank, the Swedish bank, in celebration of its 300th anniversary. The prize was awarded for the first time in 1969.

The prizes for physics and chemistry are awarded by the Swedish Academy of Science in Stockholm, the one for physiology or medicine by the Caroline Medical Institute in Stockholm, that for literature by the academy in Stockholm, and that for peace by a committee of five elected by the Norwegian Storting. The distribution of prizes was begun on December 10, 1901, the anniversary of Nobel's death. The amount of each prize varies with the income from the fund and currently is about $190,000. No Nobel prizes were awarded for 1940, 1941, and 1942; prizes for Literature were not awarded for 1914, 1918, and 1943.

PEACE

1901 Henri Dunant (Switzerland); Frederick Passy (France)
1902 Elie Ducommun and Albert Gobat (Switzerland)
1903 Sir William R. Cremer (England)
1904 Institut de Droit International (Belgium)
1905 Bertha von Suttner (Austria)
1906 Theodore Roosevelt (U.S.)
1907 Ernesto T. Moneta (Italy) and Louis Renault (France)
1908 Klas P. Arnoldson (Sweden) and Frederik Bajer (Denmark)
1909 Auguste M. F. Beernaert (Belgium) and Baron Paul H. B. B. d'Estournelles de Constant de Rebecque (France)
1910 Bureau International Permanent de la Paix (Switzerland)
1911 Tobias M. C. Asser (Holland) and Alfred H. Fried (Austria)
1912 Elihu Root (U.S.)
1913 Henri La Fontaine (Belgium)
1915 No award
1916 No award
1917 International Red Cross
1919 Woodrow Wilson (U.S.)
1920 Léon Bourgeois (France)
1921 Karl H. Branting (Sweden) and Christian L. Lange (Norway)
1922 Fridtjof Nansen (Norway)
1923 No award
1924 No award
1925 Sir Austen Chamberlain (England) and Charles G. Dawes (U.S.)
1926 Aristide Briand (France) and Gustav Stresemann (Germany)
1927 Ferdinand Buisson (France) and Ludwig Quidde (Germany)
1928 No award
1929 Frank B. Kellogg (U.S.)
1930 Lars O. J. Söderblom (Sweden)
1931 Jane Addams and Nicholas M. Butler (U.S.)
1932 No award
1933 Sir Norman Angell (England)
1934 Arthur Henderson (England)
1935 Karl von Ossietzky (Germany)
1936 Carlos de S. Lamas (Argentina)
1937 Lord Cecil of Chelwood (England)
1938 Office International Nansen pour les Réfugiés (Switzerland)
1939 No award
1944 International Red Cross
1945 Cordell Hull (U.S.)
1946 Emily G. Balch and John R. Mott (U.S.)
1947 American Friends Service Committee (U.S.) and British Society of Friends' Service Council (England)
1948 No award
1949 Lord John Boyd Orr (Scotland)
1950 Ralph J. Bunche (U.S.)
1951 Léon Jouhaux (France)
1952 Albert Schweitzer (French Equatorial Africa)
1953 George C. Marshall (U.S.)
1954 Office of U.N. High Commissioner for Refugees
1955 No award
1956 No award
1957 Lester B. Pearson (Canada)
1958 Rev. Dominique Georges Henri Pire (Belgium)
1959 Philip John Noel-Baker (England)
1960 Albert John Luthuli (South Africa)
1961 Dag Hammarskjöld (Sweden)
1962 Linus Pauling (U.S.)
1963 Intl. Comm. of Red Cross; League of Red Cross Societies (both Geneva)
1964 Rev. Dr. Martin Luther King, Jr. (U.S.)
1965 UNICEF (United Nations Children's Fund)
1966 No award
1967 No award
1968 René Cassin (France)
1969 International Labour Organization
1970 Norman E. Borlaug (U.S.)
1971 Willy Brandt (West Germany)
1972 No award
1973 Henry A. Kissinger (U.S.); Le Duc Tho (North Vietnam)[1]
1974 Eisaku Sato (Japan); Sean MacBride (Ireland)
1975 Andrei D. Sakharov (U.S.S.R.)
1976 Mairead Corrigan and Betty Williams (both Northern Ireland)
1977 Amnesty International
1978 Menachem Begin (Israel) and Anwar el-Sadat (Egypt)
1979 Mother Teresa of Calcutta (Albania)

1. Le Duc Tho refused prize, charging that peace had not yet been really established in South Vietnam.

LITERATURE

1901 René F. A. Sully Prudhomme (France)
1902 Theodor Mommsen (Germany)
1903 Björnstjerne Björnson (Norway)
1904 Frédéric Mistral (France) and José Echegaray (Spain)
1905 Henryk Sienkiewicz (Poland)
1906 Giosuè Carducci (Italy)

1907 Rudyard Kipling (England)
1908 Rudolf Eucken (Germany)
1909 Selma Lagerlöf (Sweden)
1910 Paul von Heyse (Germany)
1911 Maurice Maeterlinck (Belgium)
1912 Gerhart Hauptmann (Germany)
1913 Rabindranath Tagore (India)
1915 Romain Rolland (France)
1916 Verner von Heidenstam (Sweden)
1917 Karl Gjellerup (Denmark) and Henrik Pontoppidan (Denmark)
1919 Carl Spitteler (Switzerland)
1920 Knut Hamsun (Norway)
1921 Anatole France (France)
1922 Jacinto Benavente (Spain)
1923 William B. Yeats (Ireland)
1924 Wladyslaw Reymont (Poland)
1925 George Bernard Shaw (England)
1926 Grazia Deledda (Italy)
1927 Henri Bergson (France)
1928 Sigrid Undset (Norway)
1929 Thomas Mann (Germany)
1930 Sinclair Lewis (U.S.)
1931 Erik A. Karlfeldt (Sweden)
1932 John Galsworthy (England)
1933 Ivan G. Bunin (Russia)
1934 Luigi Pirandello (Italy)
1935 No award
1936 Eugene O'Neill (U.S.)
1937 Roger Martin du Gard (France)
1938 Pearl S. Buck (U.S.)
1939 Frans Eemil Sillanpää (Finland)
1944 Johannes V. Jensen (Denmark)
1945 Gabriela Mistral (Chile)
1946 Hermann Hesse (Switzerland)
1947 André Gide (France)
1948 Thomas Stearns Eliot (England)
1949 William Faulkner (U.S.)
1950 Bertrand Russell (England)
1951 Pär Lagerkvist (Sweden)
1952 François Mauriac (France)
1953 Sir Winston Churchill (England)
1954 Ernest Hemingway (U.S.)
1955 Halldór Kiljan Laxness (Iceland)
1956 Juan Ramón Jiménez (Spain)
1957 Albert Camus (France)
1958 Boris Pasternak (U.S.S.R.) (declined)
1959 Salvatore Quasimodo (Italy)
1960 St.-John Perse (Alexis St.-Léger Léger) (France)
1961 Ivo Andric (Yugoslavia)
1962 John Steinbeck (U.S.)
1963 Giorgios Seferis (Seferiades) (Greece)
1964 Jean-Paul Sartre (France) (declined)
1965 Mikhail Sholokhov (U.S.S.R.)
1966 Shmuel Yosef Agnon (Israel) and Nelly Sachs (Sweden)
1967 Miguel Angel Asturias (Guatemala)
1968 Yasunari Kawabata (Japan)
1969 Samuel Beckett (France)
1970 Aleksandr Solzhenitsyn (U.S.S.R.)
1971 Pablo Neruda (Chile)
1972 Heinrich Böll (Germany)
1973 Patrick White (Australia)
1974 Eyvind Johnson and Harry Martinson (both Sweden)
1975 Eugenio Montale (Italy)
1976 Saul Bellow (U.S.)
1977 Vicente Aleixandre (Spain)
1978 Isaac Bashevis Singer (U.S.)
1979 Odysseus Elytis (Greece)

PHYSICS

1901 Wilhelm K. Roentgen (Germany), for discovery of Roentgen rays
1902 Hendrik A. Lorentz and Pieter Zeeman (Netherlands), for work on influence of magnetism upon radiation
1903 A. Henri Becquerel (France), for work on spontaneous radioactivity; and Pierre and Marie Curie (France), for study of radiation
1904 John Strutt (Lord Rayleigh) (England), for discovery of argon in investigating gas density
1905 Philipp Lenard (Germany), for work with cathode rays
1906 Sir Joseph Thomson (England), for investigations on passage of electricity through gases
1907 Albert A. Michelson (U.S.), for spectroscopic and metrologic investigations
1908 Gabriel Lippmann (France), for method of reproducing colors by photography
1909 Guglielmo Marconi (Italy) and Ferdinand Braun (Germany), for development of wireless
1910 Johannes D. van der Waals (Netherlands), for work with the equation of state for gases and liquids
1911 Wilhelm Wien (Germany), for his laws governing the radiation of heat
1912 Gustaf Dalén (Sweden), for discovery of automatic regulators used in lighting lighthouses and light buoys
1913 Heike Kamerlingh-Onnes (Netherlands), for work leading to production of liquid helium
1914 Max von Laue (Germany), for discovery of diffraction of Roentgen rays passing through crystals
1915 Sir William Bragg and William L. Bragg (England), for analysis of crystal structure by X rays
1916 No award
1917 Charles G. Barkla (England), for discovery of Roentgen radiation of the elements
1918 Max Planck (Germany), discoveries in connection with quantum theory
1919 Johannes Stark (Germany), discovery of Doppler effect in Canal rays and decomposition of spectrum lines by electric fields
1920 Charles E. Guillaume (Switzerland), for discoveries of anomalies in nickel steel alloys
1921 Albert Einstein (Germany), for discovery of the law of the photoelectric effect
1922 Niels Bohr (Denmark), for investigation of structure of atoms and radiations emanating from them
1923 Robert A. Millikan (U.S.), for work on elementary charge of electricity and photoelectric phenomena
1924 Karl M. G. Siegbahn (Sweden), for investigations in X-ray spectroscopy
1925 James Franck and Gustav Hertz (Germany), for discovery of laws governing impact of electrons upon atoms
1926 Jean B. Perrin (France), for work on discontinous structure of matter and discovery of the equilibrium of sedimentation
1927 Arthur H. Compton (U.S.), for discovery of Compton phenomenon; and Charles T. R. Wilson (England), for method of perceiving paths taken by electrically charged particles
1928 In 1929, the 1928 prize was awarded to Sir Owen Richardson (England), for work on the phenomenon of thermionics and discovery of the Richardson Law
1929 Prince Louis Victor de Broglie (France), for discovery of the wave character of electrons
1930 Sir Chandrasekhara Raman (India), for work on diffusion of light and discovery of the Raman effect

1931 No award
1932 In 1933, the prize for 1932 was awarded to Werner Heisenberg (Germany), for creation of the quantum mechanics
1933 Erwin Schrödinger (Austria) and Paul A. M. Dirac (England), for discovery of new fertile forms of the atomic theory
1934 No award
1935 James Chadwick (England), for discovery of the neutron
1936 Victor F. Hess (Austria), for discovery of cosmic radiation; and Carl D. Anderson (U.S.), for discovery of the positron
1937 Clinton J. Davisson (U.S.) and George P. Thomson (England), for discovery of diffraction of electrons by crystals
1938 Enrico Fermi (Italy), for identification of new radioactivity elements and discovery of nuclear reactions effected by slow neutrons
1939 Ernest Orlando Lawrence (U.S.), for development of the cyclotron
1943 Otto Stern (U.S.), for detection of magnetic momentum of protons
1944 Isidor Isaac Rabi (U.S.), for work on magnetic movements of atomic particles
1945 Wolfgang Pauli (Austria), for work on atomic fissions
1946 Percy Williams Bridgman (U.S.), for studies and inventions in high-pressure physics
1947 Sir Edward Appleton (England), for discovery of layer which reflects radio short waves in the ionosphere
1948 Patrick M. S. Blackett (England), for improvement on Wilson chamber and discoveries in cosmic radiation
1949 Hideki Yukawa (Japan), for mathematical prediction, in 1935, of the meson
1950 Cecil Frank Powell (England), for method of photographic study of atom nucleus, and for discoveries about mesons
1951 Sir John Douglas Cockcroft (England) and Ernest T. S. Walton (Ireland), for work in 1932 on transmutation of atomic nuclei
1952 Edward Mills Purcell and Felix Bloch (U.S.), for work in measurement of magnetic fields in atomic nuclei
1953 Fritz Zernike (Netherlands), for development of "phase contrast" microscope
1954 Max Born (England), for work in quantum mechanics; and Walther Bothe (Germany), for work in cosmic radiation
1955 Polykarp Kusch and Willis E. Lamb, Jr. (U.S.), for atomic measurements
1956 William Shockley, Walter H. Brattain, and John Bardeen (U.S.), for developing electronic transistor
1957 Tsung Dao Lee and Chen Ning Yang (China), for disproving principle of conservation of parity
1958 Pavel A. Cherenkov, Ilya M. Frank, and Igor E. Tamm (U.S.S.R.), for work resulting in development of cosmic-ray counter
1959 Emilio Segre and Owen Chamberlain (U.S.), for demonstrating the existence of the anti-proton
1960 Donald A. Glaser (U.S.), for invention of "bubble chamber" to study subatomic particles
1961 Robert Hofstadter (U.S.), for determination of shape and size of atomic nucleus; Rudolf Mössbauer (Germany), for method of producing and measuring recoil-free gamma rays
1962 Lev D. Landau (U.S.S.R.), for his theories about condensed matter
1963 Eugene Paul Wigner, Maria Goeppert Mayer (both U.S.), and J. Hans D. Jensen (Germany), for research on structure of atom and its nucleus
1964 Charles Hard Townes (U.S.), Nikolai G. Basov, and Aleksandr M. Prochorov (both U.S.S.R.), for developing maser and laser principle of producing high-intensity radiation
1965 Richard P. Feynman, Julian S. Schwinger (both U.S.), and Shinichero Tomonaga (Japan), for research in quantum electrodynamics
1966 Alfred Kastler (France), for work on energy levels inside atom
1967 Hans A. Bethe (U.S.), for work on energy production of stars
1968 Luis Walter Alvarez (U.S.), for study of subatomic particles
1969 Murray Gell-Mann (U.S.), for study of subatomic particles
1970 Hannes Alfvén (Sweden), for theories in plasma physics; and Louis Néel (France), for discoveries in antiferromagnetism and ferrimagnetism
1971 Dennis Gabor (England), for invention of holographic method of three-dimensional imagery
1972 John Bardeen, Leon N. Cooper, and John Robert Schrieffer (all U.S.), for theory of superconductivity, where electrical resistance in certain metals vanishes above absolute zero temperature
1973 Ivar Giaever (U.S.), Leo Esaki (Japan), and Brian D. Josephson (U.K.), for theories that have advanced and expanded the field of miniature electronics
1974 Antony Hewish (England), for discovery of pulsars; Martin Ryle (England), for using radiotelescopes to probe outer space with high degree of precision
1975 James Rainwater (U.S.) and Ben Mottelson and Aage N. Bohr (both Denmark), for showing that the atomic nucleus is asymmetrical
1976 Burton Richter and Samuel C. C. Ting (U.S.), for discovery of subatomic particles known as J and psi
1977 Philip W. Anderson and John H. Van Vleck (both U.S.), and Nevill F. Mott (U.K.), for work underlying computer memories and electronic devices
1978 Arno A. Penzias and Robert W. Wilson (both (U.S.), for work in cosmic microwave radiation; Piotr L. Kapitsa (U.S.S.R.), for basic inventions and discoveries in low-temperature physics
1979 Steven Weinberg and Sheldon L. Glashow (both U.S.) and Abdus Salam (Pakistan), for developing theory that electromagnetism and the "weak" force, which causes radioactive decay in some atomic nuclei, are facets of the same phenomenon

CHEMISTRY

1901 Jacobus H. van't Hoff (Netherlands), for laws of chemical dynamics and osmotic pressure in solutions
1902 Emil Fischer (Germany), for experiments in sugar and purin groups of substances
1903 Svante A. Arrhenius (Sweden), for his electrolytic theory of dissociation
1904 Sir William Ramsay (England), for discovery and determination of place of inert gaseous elements in air
1905 Adolf von Baeyer (Germany), for work on organic dyes and hydroaromatic combinations
1906 Henri Moissan (France), for isolation of fluorine, and introduction of electric furnace

1907 Eduard Buchner (Germany), discovery of cell-less fermentation and investigations in biological chemistry
1908 Sir Ernest Rutherford (England), for investigations into disintegration of elements
1909 Wilhelm Ostwald (Germany), for work on catalysis and investigations into chemical equilibrium and reaction rates
1910 Otto Wallach (Germany), for work in the field of alicyclic compounds
1911 Marie Curie (France), for discovery of elements radium and polonium
1912 Victor Grignard (France), for reagent discovered by him; and Paul Sabatier (France), for methods of hydrogenating organic compounds
1913 Alfred Werner (Switzerland), for linking up atoms within the molecule
1914 Theodore W. Richards (U.S.), for determining atomic weight of many chemical elements
1915 Richard Willstätter (Germany), for research into coloring matter of plants, especially chlorophyll
1916 No award
1917 No award
1918 Fritz Haber (Germany), for synthetic production of ammonia
1919 No award
1920 Walther Nernst (Germany), for work in thermochemistry
1921 Frederick Soddy (England), for investigations into origin and nature of isotopes
1922 Francis W. Aston (England), for discovery of isotopes in nonradioactive elements and for discovery of the whole number rule
1923 Fritz Pregl (Austria), for method of microanalysis of organic substances discovered by him
1924 No award
1925 In 1926, the 1925 prize was awarded to Richard Zsigmondy (Germany), for work on the heterogeneous nature of colloid solutions
1926 Theodor Svedberg (Sweden), for work on disperse systems
1927 In 1928 the 1927 prize was awarded to Heinrich Wieland (Germany), for investigations of bile acids and kindred substances
1928 Adolf Windaus (Germany), for investigations on constitution of the sterols and their connection with vitamins
1929 Sir Arthur Harden (England) and Hans K. A. S. von Euler-Chelpin (Sweden), for research of fermentation of sugars
1930 Hans Fischer (Germany), for work on coloring matter of blood and leaves and for his synthesis of hemin
1931 Karl Bosch and Friedrich Bergius (Germany), for invention and development of chemical high-pressure methods
1932 Irving Langmuir (U.S.), for work in realm of surface chemistry
1933 No award
1934 Harold C. Urey (U.S.), for discovery of heavy hydrogen
1935 Frédéric and Irène Joliot-Curie (France), for synthesis of new radioactive elements
1936 Peter J. W. Debye (Netherlands), for investigations on dipole moments and diffraction of X rays and electrons in gases
1937 Walter N. Haworth (England), for research on carbohydrates and Vitamin C; and Paul Karrer (Switzerland), for work on carotenoids, flavins, and Vitamins A and B
1938 Richard Kuhn (Germany), for carotinoid study and vitamin research (declined the prize)
1939 Adolf Butenandt (Germany), for work on sexual hormones (declined the prize); and Leopold Ruzicka (Switzerland), for work with polymethylenes
1943 Georg Hevesy De Heves (Hungary), for work on use of isotopes as indicators
1944 Otto Hahn (Germany), for work on atomic fission
1945 Artturi Ilmari Virtanen (Finland), for research in the field of conservation of fodder
1946 James B. Sumner (U.S.), for crystallizing enzymes; John H. Northrop and Wendell M. Stanley (U.S.), for preparing enzymes and virus proteins in pure form
1947 Sir Robert Robinson (England), for research in plant substances
1948 Arne Tiselius (Sweden), for biochemical discoveries and isolation of mouse paralysis virus
1949 William Francis Giauque (U.S.), for research in thermodynamics, especially effects of low temperature
1950 Otto Diels and Kurt Alder (Germany), for discovery of diene synthesis enabling scientists to study structure of organic matter
1951 Glenn T. Seaborg and Edwin H. McMillan (U.S.), for discovery of plutonium
1952 Archer John Porter Martin and Richard Laurence Millington Synge (England), for development of partition chromatography
1953 Hermann Staudinger (Germany), for research in giant molecules
1954 Linus C. Pauling (U.S.), for study of forces holding together protein and other molecules
1955 Vincent du Vigneaud (U.S.), for work on pituitary hormones
1956 Sir Cyril Hinshelwood (England) and Nikolai N. Semenov (U.S.S.R.), for parallel research on chemical reaction kinetics
1957 Sir Alexander Todd (England), for research with chemical compounds that are factors in heredity
1958 Frederick Sanger (England), for determining molecular structure of insulin
1959 Jaroslav Heyrovsky (Czechoslovakia), for development of polarography, an electrochemical method of analysis
1960 Willard F. Libby (U.S.), for "atomic time clock" to measure age of objects by measuring their radioactivity
1961 Melvin Calvin (U.S.), for establishing chemical steps during photosynthesis
1962 Max F. Perutz and John C. Kendrew (England), for mapping protein molecules with X rays
1963 Carl Ziegler (Germany) and Giulio Natta (Italy), for work in uniting simple hydrocarbons into large molecule substances
1964 Dorothy Mary Crowfoot Hodgkin (England), for determining structure of compounds needed in combating pernicious anemia
1965 Robert B. Woodward (U.S.), for work in synthesizing complicated organic compounds
1966 Robert Sanderson Mulliken (U.S.), for research on bond holding atoms together in molecule
1967 Manfred Eigen (Germany), Ronald G. W. Norrish, and George Porter (both England), for work in high-speed chemical reactions
1968 Lars Onsager (U.S.), for development of system of equations in thermodynamics
1969 Derek H. R. Barton (England) and Odd Hassel (Norway), for study of organic molecules
1970 Luis F. Leloir (Argentina), for discovery of sugar nucleotides and their role in biosynthesis of carbohydrates

1971 Gerhard Herzberg (Canada), for contributions to knowledge of electronic structure and geometry of molecules, particularly free radicals

1972 Christian Boehmer Anfinsen, Stanford Moore, and William Howard Stein (all U.S.), for pioneering studies in enzymes

1973 Ernst Otto Fischer (W. Germany) and Geoffrey Wilkinson (U.K.), for work that could solve problem of automobile exhaust pollution

1974 Paul J. Flory (U.S.), for developing analytic methods to study properties and molecular structure of long-chain molecules

1975 John W. Cornforth (Australia) and Vladimir Prelog (Switzerland), for research on structure of biological molecules such as antibiotics and cholesterol

1976 William N. Lipscomb, Jr. (U.S.), for work on the structure and bonding mechanisms of boranes

1977 Ilya Prigogine (Belgium), for contributions to nonequilibrium thermodynamics, particularly the theory of dissipative structures

1978 Peter Mitchell (U.K.), for contributions to the understanding of biological energy transfer

1979 Herbert C. Brown (U.S.) and Georg Wittig (West Germany), for developing a group of substances that facilitate very difficult chemical reactions

PHYSIOLOGY OR MEDICINE

1901 Emil A. von Behring (Germany), for work on serum therapy against diphtheria

1902 Sir Ronald Ross (England), for work on malaria

1903 Niels R. Finsen (Denmark), for his treatment of lupus vulgaris with concentrated light rays

1904 Ivan P. Pavlov (U.S.S.R.), for work on the physiology of digestion

1905 Robert Koch (Germany), for work on tuberculosis

1906 Camillo Golgi (Italy) and Santiago Ramón y Cajal (Spain), for work on structure of the nervous system

1907 Charles L. A. Laveran (France), for work with protozoa in the generation of disease

1908 Paul Ehrlich (Germany), and Elie Metchnikoff (U.S.S.R.), for work on immunity

1909 Theodor Kocher (Switzerland), for work on the thyroid gland

1910 Albrecht Kossel (Germany), for achievements in the chemistry of the cell

1911 Allvar Gullstrand (Sweden), for work on the dioptrics of the eye

1912 Alexis Carrel (France), for work on vascular ligature and grafting of blood vessels and organs

1913 Charles Richet (France), for work on anaphylaxy

1914 Robert Bárány (Austria), for work on physiology and pathology of the vestibular system

1915 No award

1916 No award

1917 No award

1918 No award

1919 Jules Bordet (Belgium), for discoveries in connection with immunity

1920 August Krogh (Denmark), for discovery of regulation of capillaries' motor mechanism

1921 No award

1922 In 1923, the 1922 prize was shared by Archibald V. Hill (England), for discovery relating to heat-production in muscles; and Otto Meyerhof (Germany), for correlation between consumption of oxygen and production of lactic acid in muscles

1923 Sir Frederick Banting (Canada) and John J. R. Macleod (Scotland), for discovery of insulin

1924 Willem Einthoven (Netherlands), for discovery of the mechanism of the electrocardiogram

1925 No award

1926 Johannes Fibiger (Denmark), for discovery of the Spiroptera carcinoma

1927 Julius Wagner-Jauregg (Austria), for use of malaria inoculation in treatment of dementia paralytica

1928 Charles Nicolle (France), for work on typhus exanthematicus

1929 Christiaan Eijkman (Netherlands), for discovery of the antineuritic vitamins; and Sir Frederick Hopkins (England), for discovery of growth-promoting vitamins

1930 Karl Landsteiner (U.S.), for discovery of human blood groups

1931 Otto H. Warburg (Germany), for discovery of the character and mode of action of the respiratory ferment

1932 Sir Charles Sherrington (England) and Edgar D. Adrian (U.S.), for discoveries of the function of the neuron

1933 Thomas H. Morgan (U.S.), for discoveries on hereditary function of the chromosomes

1934 George H. Whipple, George R. Minot, and William P. Murphy (U.S.), for discovery of liver therapy against anemias

1935 Hans Spemann (Germany), for discovery of the organizer-effect in embryonic development

1936 Sir Henry Dale (England) and Otto Loewi (Germany), for discoveries on chemical transmission of nerve impulses

1937 Albert Szent-Györgyi von Nagyrapolt (Hungary), for discoveries on biological combustion

1938 Corneille Heymans (Belgium), for determining importance of sinus and aorta mechanisms in the regulation of respiration

1939 Gerhard Domagk (Germany), for antibacterial effect of prontocilate

1943 Henrik Dam (Denmark) and Edward A. Doisy (U.S.), for analysis of Vitamin K

1944 Joseph Erlanger and Herbert Spencer Gasser (U.S.), for work on functions of the nerve threads

1945 Sir Alexander Fleming, Ernst Boris Chain, and Sir Howard Florey (England), for discovery of penicillin

1946 Herman J. Muller (U.S.), for hereditary effects of X rays on genes

1947 Carl F. and Gerty T. Cori (U.S.), for work on animal starch metabolism; Bernardo A. Houssay (Argentina), for study of pituitary

1948 Paul Mueller (Switzerland), for discovery of insect-killing properties of DDT

1949 Walter Rudolf Hess (Switzerland), for research on brain control of body; and Antonio Caetano de Abreu Freire Egas Moniz (Portugal), for development of brain operation

1950 Philip S. Hench, Edward C. Kendall (both U.S.), and Tadeus Reichstein (Switzerland), for discoveries about hormones of adrenal cortex

1951 Max Theiler (South Africa), for development of anti-yellow-fever vaccine

1952 Selman A. Waksman (U.S.), for co-discovery of streptomycin

1953 Fritz A. Lipmann (Germany-U.S.) and Hans Adolph Krebs (Germany-England), for studies of living cells

1954 John F. Enders, Thomas H. Weller, and Frederick C. Robbins (U.S.), for work with cultivation of polio virus

1955 Hugo Theorell (Sweden), for work on oxidation enzymes

1956 Dickinson W. Richards, Jr., André F. Cournand (both U.S.), and Werner Forssmann (Germany), for new techniques in treating heart disease

1957 Daniel Bovet (Italy), for development of drugs to relieve allergies and relax muscles during surgery

1958 Joshua Lederberg (U.S.), for work with genetic mechanisms; George W. Beadle and Edward L. Tatum (U.S.), for discovering how genes transmit hereditary characteristics

1959 Severo Ochoa and Arthur Kornberg (U.S.), for discoveries related to compounds within chromosomes, which play a vital role in heredity

1960 Sir Macfarlane Burnet (Australia) and Peter Brian Medawar (England), for discovery of acquired immunological tolerance

1961 Georg von Bekesy (U.S.), for discoveries about physical mechanisms of stimulation within cochlea

1962 James D. Watson (U.S.), Maurice H. F. Wilkins, and Francis H. C. Crick (England), for determining structure of deoxyribonucleic acid (DNA)

1963 Alan Lloyd Hodgkin, Andrew Fielding Huxley (both England), and Sir John Carew Eccles (Australia), for research on nerve cells

1964 Konrad E. Bloch (U.S.) and Feodor Lynen (Germany), for research on mechanism and regulation of cholesterol and fatty acid metabolism

1965 François Jacob, André Lwolff, and Jacques Monod (France), for study of regulatory activities in body cells

1966 Charles Brenton Huggins (U.S.), for studies in hormone treatment of cancer of prostate; Francis Peyton Rous (U.S.), for discovery of tumor-producing viruses

1967 Haldan K. Hartline, George Wald, and Ragnar Granit (U.S.), for work on human eye

1968 Robert W. Holley, Har Gobind Khorana, and Marshall W. Nirenberg (U.S.), for studies of genetic code

1969 Max Delbruck, Alfred D. Hershey, and Salvador E. Luria (U.S.), for study of mechanism of virus infection in living cells

1970 Julius Axelrod (U.S.), Ulf S. von Euler (Sweden), and Sir Bernard Katz (England), for studies of how nerve impulses are transmitted within the body

1971 Earl W. Sutherland, Jr., (U.S.), for research on how hormones work

1972 Gerald M. Edelman (U.S.), and Rodney R. Porter (U.K.), for research on the chemical structure and nature of antibodies

1973 Karl von Frisch and Konrad Lorenz (Austria), and Nikolaas Tinbergen (Netherlands), for their studies of individual and social behavior patterns

1974 George E. Palade and Christian de Duve (both U.S.) and Albert Claude (Belgium), for contributions to understanding inner workings of living cells

1975 David Baltimore, Howard M. Temin and Renato Dulbecco (all U.S.), for work in interaction between tumor viruses and genetic material of the cell

1976 Baruch S. Blumberg and D. Carleton Gajdusek (U.S.), for discoveries concerning new mechanisms for the origin and dissemination of infectious diseases

1977 Rosalyn S. Yalow, Roger C. L. Guillemin, and Andrew V. Schally (all U.S.), for research in role of hormones in chemistry of the body

1978 Daniel Nathans and Hamilton Smith (both U.S.) and Werner Arber (Switzerland), for discovery of restriction enzymes and their application to problems of molecular genetics

1979 Allan McLeod Cormack (U.S.) and Godfrey Newbold Hounsfield (England), for developing computed axial tomography (CAT scan) X-ray technique

ECONOMIC SCIENCE

1969 Ragnar Frisch (Norway) and Jan Tinbergen (Netherlands), for work in econometrics (application of mathematics and statistical methods to economic theories and problems)

1970 Paul A. Samuelson (U.S.), for efforts to raise the level of scientific analysis in economic theory

1971 Simon Kuznets (U.S.), for developing concept of using a country's gross national product to determine its economic growth

1972 Kenneth J. Arrow (U.S.) and Sir John R. Hicks (U.K.), for theories that help to assess business risk and government economic and welfare policies

1973 Wassily Leontief (U.S.), for devising the input-output technique to determine how different sectors of an economy interact

1974 Gunnar Myrdal (Sweden) and Friedrich A. von Hayek (Austria), for pioneering analysis of the interdependence of economic, social and institutional phenomena

1975 Leonid V. Kantorovich (U.S.S.R.) and Tjalling C. Koopmans (U.S.), for work on the theory of optimum allocation of resources

1976 Milton Friedman (U.S.), for work in consumption analysis and monetary history and theory, and for demonstration of complexity of stabilization policy

1977 Bertil Ohlin (Sweden) and James E. Meade (U.K.), for contributions to theory of international trade and international capital movements

1978 Herbert A. Simon (U.S.), for research into the decision-making process within economic organizations

1979 Sir Arthur Lewis (England) and Theodore Schultz (U.S.), for work on economic problems of developing nations

National Book Critics Circle Awards, 1980

Fiction: *The Year of the French*, by Thomas Flanagan (Holt, Rinehart, and Winston)

General nonfiction: *Munich: The Price of Peace*, by Telford Taylor (Doubleday)

Poetry: *Ashes* and *7 Years From Somewhere*, by Philip Levine (Atheneum)

Criticism: *The Gnostic Gospels*, by Elaine Pagels (Random House)

Motion Picture Academy Awards (Oscars)

	Picture	Director	Actress
1928	*Wings,* Paramount	Frank Borzage, *Seventh Heaven;* Lewis Milestone, *Two Arabian Nights*	Janet Gaynor, *Seventh Heaven, Street Angel, Sunrise*
1929	*The Broadway Melody,* M-G-M	Frank Lloyd, *The Divine Lady*	Mary Pickford, *Coquette*
1930	*All Quiet on the Western Front,* Universal	Lewis Milestone, *All Quiet on the Western Front*	Norma Shearer, *The Divorcee*
1931	*Cimarron,* RKO Radio	Norman Taurog, *Skippy*	Marie Dressler, *Min and Bill*
1932	*Grand Hotel,* M-G-M	Frank Borzage, *Bad Girl*	Helen Hayes, *The Sin of Madelon Claudet*
1933	*Cavalcade,* Fox	Frånk Lloyd, *Cavalcade*	Katharine Hepburn, *Morning Glory*
1934	*It Happened One Night,* Columbia	Frank Capra, *It Happened One Night*	Claudette Colbert *It Happened One Night*
1935	*Mutiny on the Bounty,* M-G-M	John Ford, *The Informer*	Bette Davis, *Dangerous*
1936	*The Great Ziegfeld,* M-G-M	Frank Capra, *Mr. Deeds Goes to Town*	Luise Rainer, *The Great Ziegfeld*
1937	*The Life of Emile Zola,* Warner Bros.	Leo McCarey, *The Awful Truth*	Luise Rainer, *The Good Earth*
1938	*You Can't Take It with You,* Columbia	Frank Capra, *You Can't Take It with You*	Bette Davis, *Jezebel*
1939	*Gone with the Wind,* Selznick-M-G-M	Victor Fleming, *Gone with the Wind*	Vivien Leigh, *Gone with the Wind*
1940	*Rebecca,* Selznick-UA	John Ford, *The Grapes of Wrath*	Ginger Rogers, *Kitty Foyle*
1941	*How Green Was My Valley,* 20th Century-Fox	John Ford, *How Green Was My Valley*	Joan Fontaine, *Suspicion*
1942	*Mrs. Miniver,* M-G-M	William Wyler, *Mrs. Miniver*	Greer Garson, *Mrs. Miniver*
1943	*Casablanca,* Warner Bros.	Michael Curtiz, *Casablanca*	Jennifer Jones, *The Song of Bernadette*
1944	*Going My Way,* Paramount	Leo McCarey, *Going My Way*	Ingrid Bergman, *Gaslight*
1945	*The Lost Weekend,* Paramount	Billy Wilder, *The Lost Weekend*	Joan Crawford, *Mildred Pierce*
1946	*The Best Years of Our Lives,* Goldwyn-RKO Radio	William Wyler, *The Best Years of Our Lives*	Olivia de Havilland, *To Each His Own*
1947	*Gentleman's Agreement,* 20th Century-Fox	Elia Kazan, *Gentleman's Agreement*	Loretta Young, *The Farmer's Daughter*
1948	*Hamlet,* Rank-Two Cities-U-I	John Houston, *Treasure of Sierra Madre*	Jane Wyman, *Johnny Belinda*
1949	*All the King's Men,* Rossen-Columbia	Joseph L. Mankiewicz, *A Letter to Three Wives*	Olivia de Havilland, *The Heiress*
1950	*All About Eve,* 20th Century-Fox	Joseph L. Mankiewicz, *All About Eve*	Judy Holliday, *Born Yesterday*
1951	*An American in Paris,* M-G-M	George Stevens, *A Place in the Sun*	Vivien Leigh, *A Streetcar Named Desire*
1952	*The Greatest Show on Earth,* DeMille-Paramount	John Ford, *The Quiet Man*	Shirley Booth, *Come Back, Little Sheba*
1953	*From Here to Eternity,* Columbia	Fred Zinnemann, *From Here to Eternity*	Audrey Hepburn, *Roman Holiday*
1954	*On the Waterfront,* Horizon-American Corp., Columbia	Elia Kazan, *On the Waterfront*	Grace Kelley, *The Country Girl*
1955	*Marty,* Hecht and Lancaster, United Artists	Delbert Mann, *Marty*	Anna Magnani, *The Rose Tattoo*
1956	*Around the World in 80 Days,* Michael Todd Co., Inc.-UA	George Stevens, *Giant*	Ingrid Bergman, *Anastasia*
1957	*The Bridge on the River Kwai,* Horizon Picture, Columbia	David Lean, *The Bridge on the River Kwai*	Joanne Woodward, *The Three Faces of Eve*
1958	*Gigi,* Arthur Freed Productions, Inc., M-G-M	Vincente Minnelli, *Gigi*	Susan Hayward, *I Want to Live!*
1959	*Ben-Hur,* M-G-M	William Wyler, *Ben-Hur*	Simone Signoret, *Room at the Top*
1960	*The Apartment,* Mirisch Co., Inc., United Artists	Billy Wilder, *The Apartment*	Elizabeth Taylor, *Butterfield 8*
1961	*West Side Story,* Mirisch Pictures, Inc., and B and P Enterprises, Inc., United Artists	Robert Wise and Jerome Robbins, *West Side Story*	Sophia Loren, *Two Women*

Actor	Supporting Actress	Supporting Actor	
Emil Jannings, *The Way of All Flesh, The Last Command*	—	—	1928
Warner Baxter, *In Old Arizona*	—	—	1929
George Arliss, *Disraeli*	—	—	1930
Lionel Barrymore, *A Free Soul*	—	—	1931
Frederic March, *Dr. Jekyll and Mr. Hyde,* and Wallace Beery, *The Champ*	—	—	1932
Charles Laughton, *The Private Life of Henry VIII*	—	—	1933
Clark Gable, *It Happened One Night*	—	—	1934
Victor McLaglen, *The Informer*	—	—	1935
Paul Muni, *The Story of Louis Pasteur*	Gale Sondergaard, *Anthony Adverse*	Walter Brennan, *Come and Get It*	1936
Spencer Tracy, *Captains Courageous*	Alice Brady, *In Old Chicago*	Joseph Schildkraut, *The Life of Emile Zola*	1937
Spencer Tracy, *Boys Town*	Fay Bainter, *Jezebel*	Walter Brennan, *Kentucky*	1938
Robert Donat, *Goodbye, Mr. Chips*	Hattie McDaniel, *Gone with the Wind*	Thomas Mitchell, *Stagecoach*	1939
James Stewart, *The Philadelphia Story*	Jane Darwell, *The Grapes of Wrath*	Walter Brennan, *The Westerner*	1940
Gary Cooper, *Sergeant York*	Mary Astor, *The Great Lie*	Donald Crisp, *How Green Was My Valley*	1941
James Cagney, *Yankee Doodle Dandy*	Teresa Wright, *Mrs. Miniver*	Van Heflin, *Johnny Eager*	1942
Paul Lukas, *Watch on the Rhine*	Katina Paxinou, *For Whom the Bell Tolls*	Charles Coburn, *The More the Merrier*	1943
Bing Crosby, *Going My Way*	Ethel Barrymore, *None But the Lonely Heart*	Barry Fitzgerald, *Going My Way*	1944
Ray Milland, *The Lost Weekend*	Anne Revere, *National Velvet*	James Dunn, *A Tree Grows in Brooklyn*	1945
Fredric March, *The Best Years of Our Lives*	Anne Baxter, *The Razor's Edge*	Harold Russell, *The Best Years of Our Lives*	1946
Ronald Colman, *A Double Life*	Celeste Holm, *Gentleman's Agreement*	Edmund Gwenn, *Miracle on 34th Street*	1947
Laurence Olivier, *Hamlet*	Claire Trevor, *Key Largo*	Walter Huston, *Treasure of Sierra Madre*	1948
Broderick Crawford, *All the King's Men*	Mercedes McCambridge, *All the King's Men*	Dean Jagger, *Twelve O'Clock High*	1949
José Ferrer, *Cyrano de Bergerac*	Josephine Hull, *Harvey*	George Sanders, *All About Eve*	1950
Humphrey Bogart, *The African Queen*	Kim Hunter, *A Streetcar Named Desire*	Karl Malden, *A Streetcar Named Desire*	1951
Gary Cooper, *High Noon*	Gloria Grahame, *The Bad and the Beautiful*	Anthony Quinn, *Viva Zapata!*	1952
William Holden, *Stalag 17*	Donna Reed, *From Here to Eternity*	Frank Sinatra, *From Here to Eternity*	1953
Marlon Brando, *On the Waterfront*	Eva Marie Saint, *On the Waterfront*	Edmond O'Brien, *The Barefoot Contessa*	1954
Ernest Borgnine, *Marty*	Jo Van Fleet, *East of Eden*	Jack Lemmon, *Mister Roberts*	1955
Yul Brynner, *The King and I*	Dorothy Malone, *Written on the Wind*	Anthony Quinn, *Lust for Life*	1956
Alec Guinness, *The Bridge on the River Kwai*	Miyoshi Umeki, *Sayonara*	Red Buttons, *Sayonara*	1957
David Niven, *Separate Tables*	Wendy Hiller, *Separate Tables*	Burl Ives, *The Big Country*	1958
Charlton Heston, *Ben-Hur*	Shelley Winters, *The Diary of Anne Frank*	Hugh Griffith, *Ben-Hur*	1959
Burt Lancaster, *Elmer Gantry*	Shirley Jones, *Elmer Gantry*	Peter Ustinov, *Spartacus*	1960
Maximilian Schell, *Judgment at Nuremberg*	Rita Moreno, *West Side Story*	George Chakiris, *West Side Story*	1961

	Picture	Director	Actress
1962	*Lawrence of Arabia,* Horizon Pictures, Ltd.-Columbia	David Lean, *Lawrence of Arabia*	Anne Bancroft, *The Miracle Worker*
1963	*Tom Jones,* A Woodfall Production, UA-Lopert Pictures	Tony Richardson, *Tom Jones*	Patricia Neal, *Hud*
1964	*My Fair Lady,* Warner Bros.	George Cukor, *My Fair Lady*	Julie Andrews, *Mary Poppins*
1965	*The Sound of Music,* Argyle Enterprises Production, 20th Century-Fox	Robert Wise, *The Sound of Music*	Julie Christie, *Darling*
1966	*A Man for All Seasons,* Highland Films, Ltd., Production, Columbia	Fred Zinnemann, *A Man for All Seasons*	Elizabeth Taylor, *Who's Afraid of Virginia Woolf?*
1967	*In the Heat of the Night,* Mirisch Corp. Production, United Artists	Mike Nichols, *The Graduate*	Katharine Hepburn, *Guess Who's Coming to Dinner*
1968	*Oliver!,* Columbia Pictures	Sir Carol Reed, *Oliver!*	Katharine Hepburn, *The Lion in Winter, and Barbara Streisand, Funny Girl*
1969	*Midnight Cowboy,* Jerome Hellman-John Schlesinger Production, United Artists	John Schlesinger, *Midnight Cowboy*	Maggie Smith, *The Prime of Miss Jean Brodie*
1970	*Patton,* Frank McCarthy-Franklin J. Schaffner Production, 20th Century-Fox	Franklin J. Schaffner, *Patton*	Glenda Jackson, *Women in Love*
1971	*The French Connection,* D'Antoni Productions, 20th Century-Fox	William Friedkin, *The French Connection*	Jane Fonda, *Klute*
1972	*The Godfather,* Albert S. Ruddy Production, Paramount	Bob Fosse, *Cabaret*	Liza Minnelli, *Cabaret*
1973	*The Sting,* Universal-Bill-Phillips-George Roy Hill Production, Universal	George Roy Hill, *The Sting*	Glenda Jackson, *A Touch of Class*
1974	*The Godfather, Part II,* Coppola Co. Production, Paramount	Francis Ford Coppola, *The Godfather, Part II*	Ellen Burstyn, *Alice Doesn't Live Here Anymore*
1975	*One Flew Over the Cuckoo's Nest,* Fantasy Films Production, United Artists	Milos Forman, *One Flew Over the Cuckoo's Nest*	Louise Fletcher, *One Flew Over the Cuckoo's Nest*
1976	*Rocky,* Robert Chartoff-Irwin Winkler Production, United Artists	John G. Avildsen, *Rocky*	Faye Dunaway *Network*
1977	*Annie Hall,* Jack Rollins-Charles H. Joffe Production, United Artists	Woody Allen, *Annie Hall*	Diane Keaton, *Annie Hall*
1978	*The Deer Hunter,* Michael Cimino Film Production, Universal	Michael Cimino, *The Deer Hunter*	Jane Fonda, *Coming Home*
1979	*Kramer vs. Kramer,* Stanley Jaffe Production, Columbia Pictures	Robert Benton, *Kramer vs. Kramer*	Sally Field, *Norma Rae*

Other Academy Awards for 1979

Art direction: Philip Rosenberg and Tony Walton; **set decoration,** Edward Stewart and Gary Brink, *All That Jazz*
Cinematography: Vittorio Storaro, *Apocalypse Now*
Costume design: Albert Wolsky, *All That Jazz*
Documentary (feature): *Best Boy;* **short subject:** *Paul Robeson: Tribute to an Artist*
Editing: Alan Heim, *All That Jazz*
Foreign-language film: *The Tin Drum*
Music (original score): Georges Delerue, *A Little Romance*
Scoring (adaptation): Ralph Burns, *All That Jazz*
Screenplay (original): Steve Tesich, *Breaking Away;* **adaptation:** Robert Benton, *Kramer vs. Kramer*
Short subject (animated): *Every Child;* **live,** *Board and Care*
Song: "It Goes Like It Goes," by David Shire and Norman Gimbel, from *Norma Rae*
Sound: Walter Murch, Mark Berger, Richard Beggs and Nat Boxer, *Apocalypse Now*
Visual effects: H.R. Giger, Carlo Rambaldi, Brian Johnson, Nick Allder, and Denny Aling, *Alien*

SPECIAL AWARDS
Jean Hersholt Humanitarian Award: Robert Benjamin
Irving G. Thalberg Memorial Award: Ray Stark
Lifetime Achievement Award: Alec Guinness

"Oscar"

In 1928, the Academy of Motion Picture Arts and Sciences began the annual presentation of its awards for motion picture excellence. The "Oscar" was originally sketched by Cedric Gibbons. The statue is 10 inches tall, weighs 7 pounds, and is made of gold plate over bronze. When Margaret Harrick, the Academy's first executive director, saw the statue, she remarked that it looked like her Uncle Oscar. The nickname stuck, and today the "Oscar" is the most important and sought after of film awards.

Actor	Supporting Actress	Supporting Actor	
Gregory Peck, *To Kill a Mockingbird*	Patty Duke, *The Miracle Worker*	Ed Begley, *Sweet Bird of Youth*	1962
Sidney Poitier, *Lilies of the Field*	Margaret Rutherford, *The V.I.P.s*	Melvyn Douglas, *Hud*	1963
Rex Harrison, *My Fair Lady*	Lila Kedrova, *Zorba the Greek*	Peter Ustinov, *Topkapi*	1964
Lee Marvin, *Cat Ballou*	Shelley Winters, *A Patch of Blue*	Martin Balsam, *A Thousand Clowns*	1965
Paul Scofield, *A Man for All Seasons*	Sandy Dennis, *Who's Afraid of Virginia Woolf?*	Walter Matthau, *The Fortune Cookie*	1966
Rod Steiger, *In the Heat of the Night*	Estelle Parsons, *Bonnie and Clyde*	George Kennedy, *Cool Hand Luke*	1967
Cliff Robertson, *Charly*	Ruth Gordon, *Rosemary's Baby*	Jack Albertson, *The Subject Was Roses*	1968
John Wayne, *True Grit*	Goldie Hawn, *Cactus Flower*	Gig Young, *They Shoot Horses, Don't They?*	1969
George C. Scott, *Patton*	Helen Hayes, *Airport*	John Mills, *Ryan's Daughter*	1970
Gene Hackman, *The French Connection*	Cloris Leachman, *The Last Picture Show*	Ben Johnson, *The Last Picture Show*	1971
Marlon Brando, *The Godfather*	Eileen Heckart, *Butterflies Are Free*	Joel Grey, *Cabaret*	1972
Jack Lemmon, *Save the Tiger*	Tatum O'Neal, *Paper Moon*	John Houseman, *The Paper Chase*	1973
Art Carney, *Harry and Tonto*	Ingrid Bergman, *Murder on the Orient Express*	Robert De Niro, *The Godfather, Part II*	1974
Jack Nicholson, *One Flew Over the Cuckoo's Nest*	Lee Grant, *Shampoo*	George Burns, *The Sunshine Boys*	1975
Peter Finch, *Network*	Beatrice Straight, *Network*	Jason Robards, *All the President's Men*	1976
Richard Dreyfuss, *The Goodbye Girl*	Vanessa Redgrave, *Julia*	Jason Robards, *Julia*	1977
Jon Voight, *Coming Home*	Maggie Smith, *California Suite*	Christopher Walken, *The Deer Hunter*	1978
Dustin Hoffman, *Kramer vs. Kramer*	Meryl Streep, *Kramer vs. Kramer*	Melvyn Douglas, *Being There*	1979

George Foster Peabody Awards for Broadcasting, 1979

Radio

WCBS, New York: *Follow That Cab: The Great Taxi Rip-Off*

WGBH, Boston: *Currer Bell, Esquire,* with Julie Harris as Charlotte Bronte

KSJN, St. Paul, Minn.: *The Way to 8—A,* study of process of commitment to mental institutions

Children's Radio Theatre, Washington: *Henny Penny Playwriting Contest,* series of plays written by children 5–13

Canadian Broadcasting Corporation: *The Longest Journey,* documentary on a baby's nine months before birth

Television

KTVI, St. Louis: *The Adventures of Whistling Sam,* cartoon comments on current issues

WMAQ, Chicago: *Strip and Search,* exposé of strip-searching of women brought in on minor charges by Chicago police

CBS: *CBS News Sunday Morning,* Charles Kuralt, host; *The Boston Goes to China,* coverage of Boston Symphony Orchestra's trip; *Dummy,* story of illiterate black deaf youth charged with murder

ABC: *Valentine,* love story of two people in their declining years; *Friendly Fire,* a family's involvement in Vietnam War; *A Special Gift,* about a boy who reconciles his talents in basketball and ballet

NBC: *When Hell Was in Session,* story of a prisoner of war in Vietnam

NBC and British Broadcasting Corporation: *Treasures of the British Crown*

KRON, San Francisco: *Politics of Poison,* exposé of health problems by herbicide sprayings

KOOL, Phoenix, Ariz.: *The Long Eyes of Kitt Peak,* a look at complex astronomical research facility

WTTW, Chicago: *Miles to Go Before We Sleep,* about age discrimination as a result of mandatory retirement; *Little Rock Central High School,* the years since school's desegregation

KNXT, Hollywood: *Down at the Dunbar,* about jazz musicians who made Dunbar Hotel famous

WGBH, Boston: *World,* international documentaries on a variety of subjects

Roger Mudd, CBS News: *Teddy,* interview with Senator Edward M. Kennedy of Massachusetts

Robert Trout, ABC News: For his 50 years as a commentator

Sylvia Fine Kaye: *Musical Comedy Tonight,* four eras of stage musicals

Pulitzer Prize Awards

(For years not listed, no award was made.)

Source: Columbia University.

Pulitzer Prizes in Journalism

MERITORIOUS PUBLIC SERVICE

1918 *New York Times;* also special award to Minna Lewinson and Henry Beetle Hough
1919 *Milwaukee Journal*
1921 *Boston Post*
1922 *New York World*
1923 *Memphis Commercial Appeal*
1924 *New York World*
1926 *Columbus* (Ga.) *Enquirer Sun*
1927 *Canton* (Ohio) *Daily News*
1928 *Indianapolis Times*
1929 *New York Evening World*
1931 *Atlanta Constitution*
1932 *Indianapolis News*
1933 *New York World-Telegram*
1934 *Medford* (Ore.) *Mail Tribune*
1935 *Sacramento Bee*
1936 *Cedar Rapids* (Iowa) *Gazette*
1937 *St. Louis Post-Dispatch*
1938 *Bismarck* (N.D.) *Tribune*
1939 *Miami Daily News*
1940 *Waterbury* (Conn.) *Republican* and *American*
1941 *St. Louis Post-Dispatch*
1942 *Los Angeles Times*
1943 *Omaha World-Herald*
1944 *New York Times*
1945 *Detroit Free Press*
1946 *Scranton* (Pa.) *Times*
1947 *Baltimore Sun*
1948 *St. Louis Post-Dispatch*
1949 (Lincoln) *Nebraska State Journal*
1950 *Chicago Daily News;* and *St. Louis Post-Dispatch*
1951 *Miami Herald;* and *Brooklyn Eagle*
1952 *St. Louis Post-Dispatch*
1953 *Whiteville* (N.C.) *News Reporter;* and *Tabor City* (N.C.) *Tribune*
1954 *Newsday* (Garden City, L.I.)
1955 *Columbus* (Ga.) *Ledger* and *Sunday Ledger-Enquirer*
1956 *Watsonville* (Calif.) *Register-Pajaronian*
1957 *Chicago Daily News*
1958 (Little Rock) *Arkansas Gazette*
1959 *Utica* (N.Y.) *Observer Dispatch* and *Utica Daily Press*
1960 *Los Angeles Times*
1961 *Amarillo* (Tex.) *Globe-Times*
1962 *Panama City* (Fla.) *News-Herald*
1963 *Chicago Daily News*
1964 *St. Petersburg* (Fla.) *Times*
1965 *Hutchinson* (Kan.) *News*
1966 *Boston Globe*
1967 *Louisville Courier-Journal* and *Milwaukee Journal*
1968 *Riverside* (Calif.) *Press-Enterprise*
1969 *Los Angeles Times*
1970 *Newsday* (Garden City, L.I.)
1971 *Winston-Salem* (N.C.) *Journal and Sentinel*
1972 *New York Times*
1973 *Washington Post*
1974 *Newsday* (Garden City, L.I.)
1975 *Boston Globe*
1976 *Anchorage* (Alaska) *Daily News*
1977 *Lufkin* (Tex.) *News*
1978 *Philadelphia Inquirer*
1979 *Point Reyes* (Calif.) *Light*
1980 *Boston Globe*

EDITORIAL

1917 *New York Tribune*
1918 *Louisville Courier-Journal*
1920 Harvey E. Newbranch *(Omaha Evening World-Herald)*
1922 Frank M. O'Brien *(New York Herald)*
1923 William Allen White *(Emporia* [Kan.] *Gazette)*
1924 *Boston Herald* (Frank Buxton); special prize: Frank I. Cobb *(New York World)*
1925 *Charleston* (S.C.) *News and Courier*
1926 *New York Times* (Edward M. Kingsbury)
1927 *Boston Herald* (F. Lauriston Bullard)
1928 Grover Cleveland Hall *(Montgomery* [Ala.] *Advertiser)*
1929 Louis Isaac Jaffe *(Norfolk Virginian-Pilot)*
1931 Charles S. Ryckman *(Fremont* [Neb.] *Tribune)*
1933 *Kansas City* (Mo.) *Star*
1934 E. P. Chase *(Atlantic* [Iowa] *News Telegraph)*
1936 Felix Morley *(Washington Post);* George B. Parker (Scripps-Howard Newspapers)
1937 John W. Owens *(Baltimore Sun)*
1938 W. W. Waymack *(Des Moines Register and Tribune)*
1939 Ronald G. Callvert *(Portland Oregonian)*
1940 Bart Howard *(St. Louis Post-Dispatch)*
1941 Reuben Maury *(New York Daily News)*
1942 Geoffrey Parsons *(New York Herald Tribune)*
1943 Forrest W. Seymour *(Des Moines Register and Tribune)*
1944 *Kansas City* (Mo.) *Star* (Henry J. Haskell)
1945 George W. Potter *(Providence* [R.I.] *Journal-Bulletin)*
1946 Hodding Carter ([Greenville, Miss.] *Delta Democrat-Times*)
1947 William H. Grimes *(Wall Street Journal)*
1948 Virginius Dabney *(Richmond Times-Dispatch)*
1949 John H. Crider *(Boston Herald);* Herbert Elliston *(Washington Post)*
1950 Carl M. Saunders *(Jackson* [Mich.] *Citizen Patriot)*
1951 William H. Fitzpatrick *(New Orleans States)*
1952 Louis LaCoss *(St. Louis Globe-Democrat)*
1953 Vermont C. Royster *(Wall Street Journal)*
1954 *Boston Herald* (Don Murray)
1955 *Detroit Free Press* (Royce Howes)
1956 Lauren K. Soth *(Des Moines Register and Tribune)*
1957 Buford Boone *Tuscaloosa* ([Ala.] *News)*
1958 Harry S. Ashmore *(Arkansas Gazette)*
1959 Ralph McGill *(Atlanta Constitution)*
1960 Lenoir Chambers *(Virginian-Pilot)*
1961 William J. Dorvillier *(San Juan* [P.R.] *Star)*
1962 Thomas M. Storke *(Santa Barbara* [Calif.] *News-Press)*
1963 Ira B. Harkey, Jr. *(Pascagoula* [Miss.] *Chronicle)*
1964 Hazel Brannon Smith *(Lexington* [Miss.] *Advertiser)*
1965 John R. Harrison *(Gainesville* [Fla.] *Daily Sun)*

1966 Robert Lasch *(St. Louis Post-Dispatch)*
1967 Eugene Patterson *(Atlanta Constitution)*
1968 John S. Knight (Knight Newspapers)
1969 Paul Greenberg *(Pine Bluff* [Ark.] *Commercial)*
1970 Philip L. Geyelin *(Washington Post)*
1971 Horance G. Davis, Jr. *(Gainesville* [Fla.] *Sun)*
1972 John Strohmeyer *(Bethlehem* [Pa.] *Globe Times)*
1973 Roger Bourne Linscott *(Berkshire Eagle* [Pittsfield, Mass.])
1974 F. Gilman Spencer *(Trenton* [N.J.] *Trentonian)*
1975 John Daniell Maurice *(Charleston* [W. Va] *Daily Mail)*
1976 Philip P. Kerby *(Los Angeles Times)*
1977 Warren L. Lerude, Foster Church and Norman F. Cardoza *(Reno* [Nev.] *Gazette* and *Nevada State Journal)*
1978 Meg Greenfield *(Washington Post)*
1979 Edwin M. Yoder, Jr. *(Washington Star)*
1980 Robert L. Bartley *(Wall Street Journal)*

CORRESPONDENCE

1929 Paul Scott Mowrer *(Chicago Daily News)*
1930 Leland Stowe *(New York Herald Tribune)*
1931 H. R. Knickerbocker *(Philadelphia Public Ledger* and *New York Evening Post)*
1932 Walter Duranty *(New York Times)*; Charles G. Ross *(St. Louis Post-Dispatch)*
1933 Edgar Ansel Mowrer *(Chicago Daily News)*
1934 Frederick T. Birchall *(New York Times)*
1935 Arthur Krock *(New York Times)*
1936 Wilfred C. Barber *(Chicago Tribune)*
1937 Anne O'Hare McCormick *(New York Times)*
1938 Arthur Krock *(New York Times)*
1939 Louis P. Lochner (Associated Press)
1940 Otto D. Tolischus *(New York Times)*
1941 Group award[1]
1942 Carlos P. Romulo *(Philippines Herald)*
1943 Hanson W. Baldwin *(New York Times)*
1944 Ernie Pyle (Scripps-Howard Newspaper Alliance)
1945 Harold V. (Hal) Boyle (Associated Press)
1946 Arnaldo Cortesi *(New York Times)*
1947 Brooks Atkinson *(New York Times)*
1948 Discontinued

CARTOON

1922 Rollin Kirby *(New York World)*
1924 Jay Norwood Darling *(New York Tribune)*
1925 Rollin Kirby *(New York World)*
1926 D. R. Fitzpatrick *(St. Louis Post-Dispatch)*
1927 Nelson Harding *(Brooklyn Eagle)*
1928 Nelson Harding *(Brooklyn Eagle)*
1929 Rollin Kirby *(New York World)*
1930 Charles R. Macauley *(Brooklyn Eagle)*
1931 Edmund Duffy *(Baltimore Sun)*
1932 John T. McCutcheon *(Chicago Tribune)*
1933 H. M. Talburt *(Washington Daily News)*
1934 Edmund Duffy *(Baltimore Sun)*
1935 Ross A. Lewis *(Milwaukee Journal)*
1937 C. D. Batchelor *(New York Daily News)*
1938 Vaughn Shoemaker *(Chicago Daily News)*
1939 Charles G. Werner (*Daily Oklahoman* [Oklahoma City])
1940 Edmund Duffy *(Baltimore Sun)*
1941 Jacob Burck *(Chicago Times)*
1942 Herbert L. Block (NEA Service)
1943 Jay Norwood Darling *(New York Herald Tribune)*

1. For the public services and the individual achievements of American news reporters in the war zones.

1944 Clifford K. Berryman *(Washington Evening Star)*
1945 Bill Mauldin (United Features Syndicate)
1946 Bruce Alexander Russell *(Los Angeles Times)*
1947 Vaughn Shoemaker *(Chicago Daily News)*
1948 Reuben L. Goldberg *(New York Sun)*
1949 Lute Pease *(Newark Evening News)*
1950 James T. Berryman *(Washington Evening Star)*
1951 Reg (Reginald W.) Manning (*Arizona Republic* [Phoenix])
1952 Fred L. Packer *(New York Mirror)*
1953 Edward D. Kuekes *(Cleveland Plain Dealer)*
1954 Herbert L. Block *(Washington Post* and *Times-Herald)*
1955 Daniel R. Fitzpatrick *(St. Louis Post-Dispatch)*
1956 Robert York *(Louisville Times)*
1957 Tom Little *(Nashville Tennessean)*
1958 Bruce M. Shanks *(Buffalo Evening News)*
1959 Bill Mauldin *(St. Louis Post-Dispatch)*
1961 Carey Orr *(Chicago Tribune)*
1962 Edmund S. Valtman *(Hartford Times)*
1963 Frank Miller *(Des Moines Register)*
1964 Paul Conrad (formerly of *Denver Post*, later on *Los Angeles Times*)
1966 Don Wright *(Miami News)*
1967 Patrick B. Oliphant *(Denver Post)*
1968 Eugene Gray Payne *(Charlotte* [N.C.] *Observer)*
1969 John Fischetti *(Chicago Daily News)*
1970 Thomas F. Darcy (*Newsday* [Garden City, L.I.])
1971 Paul Conrad *(Los Angeles Times)*
1972 Jeffrey K. MacNelly *(Richmond* [Va.] *News Leader)*
1974 Paul Szep *(Boston Globe)*
1975 Garry Trudeau (Universal Press Syndicate)
1976 Tony Auth *(Philadelphia Inquirer)*
1977 Paul Szep *(Boston Globe)*
1978 Jeffrey K. MacNelly *(Richmond [Va.] News Leader)*
1979 Herbert L. Block *(Washington Post)*
1980 Don Wright *(Miami News)*

NEWS PHOTOGRAPHY

1942 Milton Brooks *(Detroit News)*
1943 Frank Noel (Associated Press)
1944 Frank Filan (Associated Press); Earle L. Bunker *(Omaha World-Herald)*
1945 Joe Rosenthal (Associated Press)
1947 Arnold Hardy
1948 Frank Cushing *(Boston Traveler)*
1949 Nat Fein *(New York Herald Tribune)*
1950 Bill Crouch *(Oakland Tribune)*
1951 Max Desfor (Associated Press)
1952 John Robinson and Don Ultang *(Des Moines Register & Tribune)*
1953 William M. Gallagher *(Flint* [Mich.] *Journal)*
1954 Mrs. Walter M. Schau
1955 John L. Gaunt, Jr. *(Los Angeles Times)*
1956 *New York Daily News*
1957 Harry A. Trask *(Boston Traveler)*
1958 William C. Beall *(Washington Daily News)*
1959 William Seaman *(Minneapolis Star)*
1960 Andrew Lopez (United Press International)
1961 Yasushi Nagao (Mainichi Newspapers, Tokyo)
1962 Paul Vathis (Harrisburg [Pa.] bureau of Associated Press)
1963 Hector Rondon (*La Republica*, Caracas, Venezuela)
1964 Robert H. Jackson *(Dallas Times Herald)*
1965 Horst Faas (Associated Press)

1966 Kyoichi Sawada (United Press International)
1967 Jack R. Thornell (Associated Press)
1968 News: Rocco Morabito *(Jacksonville* [Fla.] *Journal);* features: Toshio Sakai (United Press International)
1969 Spot news: Edward T. Adams (Associated Press); features: Moneta Sleet, Jr.
1970 Spot news: Steve Starr (Associated Press); features: Dallas Kinney *(Palm Beach Post)*
1971 Spot news: John Paul Filo (*Valley Daily News and Daily Dispatch* [Tarentum and New Kensington, Pa.]); features: Jack Dykinga *(Chicago Sun-Times)*
1972 Spot news: Horst Faas and Michel Laurent (Associated Press); features: Dave Kennerly (United Press International)
1973 Spot News: Huynh Cong Ut *(Associated Press);* features: Brian Lanker *(Topeka Capital-Journal)*
1974 Spot news: Anthony K. Roberts (Associated Press); features: Slava Veder (Associated Press)
1975 Spot news: Gerald H. Gay *(Seattle Times);* features: Matthew Lewis *(Washington Post)*
1976 Spot news: Stanley J. Forman *(Boston Herald-American);* features: photographic staff of *Louisville Courier-Journal* and *Times)*
1977 Spot news: Neal Ulevich (Associated Press) and Stanley J. Forman *(Boston Herald-American);* features: Robin Hood *(Chattanooga News-Free Press)*
1978 Spot news: John Blair, freelance, Evansville, Ind.; features: J. Ross Baughman (Associated Press)
1979 Spot news: Thomas J. Kelly, 3rd *(Pottstown* [Pa.] *Mercury);* features: photographic staff of *Boston Herald American*
1980 Feature: Erwin H. Hagler *(Dallas Times Herald)*

NATIONAL TELEGRAPHIC REPORTING

1942 Louis Stark *(New York Times)*
1944 Dewey L. Fleming *(Baltimore Sun)*
1945 James Reston *(New York Times)*
1946 Edward A. Harris *(St. Louis Post-Dispatch)*
1947 Edward T. Folliard *(Washington Post)*

NATIONAL REPORTING

1948 Bert Andrews *(New York Herald Tribune);* Nat S. Finney *(Minneapolis Tribune)*
1949 C. P. Trussel *(New York Times)*
1950 Edwin O. Guthman *(Seattle Times)*
1952 Anthony Leviero *(New York Times)*
1953 Don Whitehead (Associated Press)
1954 Richard Wilson (Cowles Newspapers)
1955 Anthony Lewis *(Washington Daily News)*
1956 Charles L. Bartlett *(Chattanooga Times)*
1957 James Reston *(New York Times)*
1958 Relman Morin (Associated Press) and Clark Mollenhoff *(Des Moines Register & Tribune)*
1959 Howard Van Smith *(Miami News)*
1960 Vance Trimble (Scripps-Howard Newspaper Alliance)
1961 Edward R. Cony *(Wall Street Journal)*
1962 Nathan G. Caldwell and Gene S. Graham *(Nashville Tennessean)*
1963 Anthony Lewis *(New York Times)*
1964 Merriman Smith (United Press International)
1965 Louis M. Kohlmeier *(Wall Street Journal)*
1966 Haynes Johnson *(Washington Evening Star)*
1967 Stanley Penn and Monroe Karmin *(Wall Street Journal)*
1968 Howard James *(Christian Science Monitor);* Nathan K. (Nick) Kotz *(Des Moines Register* and *Minneapolis Tribune)*
1969 Robert Cahn *(Christian Science Monitor)*
1970 William J. Eaton *(Chicago Daily News)*
1971 Lucinda Franks and Thomas Powers (United Press International)
1972 Jack Anderson *(United Feature Syndicate)*
1973 Robert Boyd and Clark Hoyt *(Knight Newspapers)*
1974 Jack White *(Providence* [R.I.] *Journal-Bulletin);* and James R. Polk *(Washington Star-News)*
1975 Donald L. Barlett and James B. Steele *(Philadelphia Inquirer)*
1976 James Risser *(Des Moines Register)*
1977 Walter Mears (Associated Press)
1978 Gaylord D. Shaw *(Los Angeles Times)*
1979 James Risser *(Des Moines Register)*
1980 Bette Swenson Orsini and Charles Stafford *(St. Petersburg Times)*

INTERNATIONAL TELEGRAPHIC REPORTING

1942 Laurence Edmund Allen (Associated Press)
1943 Ira Wolfert (North American Newspaper Alliance, Inc.)
1944 Daniel De Luce (Associated Press)
1945 Mark S. Watson *(Baltimore Sun)*
1946 Homer W. Bigart *(New York Herald Tribune)*
1947 Eddy Gilmore (Associated Press)

INTERNATIONAL REPORTING

1948 Paul W. Ward *(Baltimore Sun)*
1949 Price Day *(Baltimore Sun)*
1950 Edmund Stevens *(Christian Science Monitor)*
1951 Keyes Beech and Fred Sparks *(Chicago Daily News);* Homer Bigart and Marguerite Higgins *(New York Herald Tribune);* Relman Morin and Don Whitehead (Associated Press)
1952 John M. Hightower (Associated Press)
1953 Austin C. Wehrwein *(Milwaukee Journal)*
1954 Jim G. Lucas (Scripps-Howard Newspapers)
1955 Harrison E. Salisbury *(New York Times)*
1956 William Randolph Hearst, Jr., and Frank Conniff (Hearst newspapers) and Kingsbury Smith (INS)
1957 Russell Jones (United Press)
1958 *New York Times*
1959 Joseph Martin and Philip Santora *(New York Daily News)*
1960 A. M. Rosenthal *(New York Times)*
1961 Lynn Heinzerling (Associated Press)
1962 Walter Lippmann (New York Herald Tribune Syndicate)
1963 Hal Hendrix *(Miami News)*
1964 Malcolm W. Browne (Associated Press) and David Halberstam *(New York Times)*
1965 J. A. Livingston *(Philadelphia Bulletin)*
1966 Peter Arnett (Associated Press)
1967 R. John Hughes *(Christian Science Monitor)*
1968 Alfred Friendly *(Washington Post)*
1969 William Tuohy *(Los Angeles Times)*
1970 Seymour M. Hersh (Dispatch News Service)
1971 Jimmie Lee Hoagland *(Washington Post)*
1972 Peter R. Kann *(Wall Street Journal)*
1973 Max Frankel *(New York Times)*
1974 Hedrick Smith *(New York Times)*
1975 William Mullen and Ovie Carter *(Chicago Tribune)*
1976 Sydney H. Schanberg *(New York Times)*
1978 Henry Kamm *(New York Times)*
1979 Richard Ben Cramer *(Philadelphia Inquirer)*

1980 Joel Brinkley and Jay Mather *(Louisville Courier-Journal)*

REPORTING

1917 Herbert B. Swope *(New York World)*
1918 Harold A. Littledale *(New York Evening Post)*
1920 John J. Leary, Jr. *(New York World)*
1921 Louis Seibold *(New York World)*
1922 Kirke L. Simpson (Associated Press)
1923 Alva Johnston *(New York Times)*
1924 Magner White *(San Diego Sun)*
1925 James W. Mulroy and Alvin H. Goldstein *(Chicago Daily News)*
1926 William Burke Miller *(Louisville Courier-Journal)*
1927 John T. Rogers *(St. Louis Post-Dispatch)*
1929 Paul Y. Anderson *(St. Louis Post-Dispatch)*
1930 Russell D. Owen *(New York Times);* special award: W. O. Dapping *(Auburn* [N.Y.] *Citizen)*
1931 A. B. MacDonald *(Kansas City* [Mo.] *Star)*
1932 W. C. Richards, D. D. Martin, J. S. Pooler, F. D. Webb, J. N. W. Sloan (all of *Detroit Free Press)*
1933 Francis A. Jamieson (Associated Press)
1934 Royce Brier *(San Francisco Chronicle)*
1935 William H. Taylor *(New York Herald Tribune)*
1936 Lauren D. Lyman *(New York Times)*
1937 John J. O'Neill *(New York Herald Tribune)*, William Leonard Laurence *(New York Times)*, Howard W. Blakeslee (Associated Press), Gobind Behari Lal (Universal Service), David Dietz (Scripps-Howard Newspapers)
1938 Raymond Sprigle *(Pittsburg Post-Gazette)*
1939 Thomas L. Stokes *(New York World-Telegram)*
1940 S. Burton Heath *(New York World-Telegram)*
1941 Westbrook Pegler *(New York World-Telegram)*
1942 Stanton Delaplane *(San Francisco Chronicle)*
1943 George Weller *(Chicago Daily News)*
1944 Paul Schoenstein and associates *(New York Journal-American)*
1945 Jack S. McDowell *(San Francisco Call-Bulletin)*
1946 William Leonard Laurence *(New York Times)*
1947 Frederick Woltman *(New York World-Telegram)*
1948 George E. Goodwin *(Atlanta Journal)*
1949 Malcolm Johnson *(New York Sun)*
1950 Meyer Berger *(New York Times)*
1951 Edward S. Montgomery *(San Francisco Examiner)*
1952 George de Carvalho *(San Francisco Chronicle)*
1953 Editorial staff *(Providence Journal and Evening Bulletin);*[1] Edward J. Mowery *(New York World-Telegram and Sun)*[2]
1954 *Vicksburg* (Miss.) *Sunday Post-Herald;*[1] Alvin Scott McCoy *(Kansas City* [Mo.] *Star)*[2]
1955 Mrs. Caro Brown *(Alice* [Tex.] *Daily Echo);*[1] Roland Kenneth Towery *(Cuero* [Tex.] *Record)*[2]
1956 Lee Hills *(Detroit Free Press);*[1] Arthur Daley *(New York Times)*[2]
1957 *Salt Lake Tribune;*[1] Wallace Turner and William Lambert *(Portland Oregonian)*[2]
1958 *Fargo* [N.D.] *Forum;*[1] George Beveridge *(Washington* [D.C.] *Evening Star)*[2]
1959 Mary Lou Werner *(Washington* [D.C.] *Evening Star);*[1] John Harold Brislin *(Scranton* [Pa.] *Tribune & Scrantonian)*[2]

1. Reporting under pressure of edition deadlines. 2. Reporting not under pressure of edition deadlines.

1960 Jack Nelson *(Atlanta Constitution);*[1] Miriam Ottenberg *(Washington Evening Star)*[2]
1961 Sanche de Gramont *(New York Herald Tribune);*[1] Edgar May *(Buffalo Evening News)*[2]
1962 Robert D. Mullins (*Deseret News,* Salt Lake City); [1] George Bliss *(Chicago Tribune)*[2]
1963 Sylvan Fox, Anthony Shannon, and William Longgood *(New York World-Telegram and Sun);*[1] Oscar Griffin, Jr. (former editor of *Pecos* [Tex.] *Independent and Enterprise,* now on staff of *Houston Chronicle)*[2]

GENERAL LOCAL REPORTING

1964 Norman C. Miller *(Wall Street Journal)*
1965 Melvin H. Ruder (*Hungry Horse News,* Columbia Falls, Mont.)
1966 Staff of *Los Angeles Times*
1967 Robert V. Cox *(Chambersburg* [Pa.] *Public Opinion)*
1968 Staff of *Detroit Free Press*
1969 John Fetterman *(Louisville Times* and *Courier-Journal)*
1970 Thomas Fitzpatrick *(Chicago Sun-Times)*
1971 Staff of *Akron* (Ohio) *Beacon*
1972 Richard Cooper and John Machacek *(Rochester* [N.Y.] *Times-Union)*
1973 *Chicago Tribune*
1974 Arthur M. Petacque and Hugh F. Hough *(Chicago Sun-Times)*
1975 *Xenia* (Ohio) *Daily Gazette*
1976 Gene Miller *(Miami Herald)*
1977 Margo Huston *(Milwaukee Journal)*
1978 Richard Whitt *(Louisville Courier-Journal)*
1979 Staff of *San Diego* (Calif.) *Evening Tribune*
1980 Staff of *Philadelphia Inquirer*

SPECIAL LOCAL REPORTING

1964 James V. Magee, Albert V. Gaudiosi, and Frederick A. Meyer *(Philadelphia Bulletin)*
1965 Gene Goltz *(Houston Post)*
1966 John A. Frasca *(Tampa Tribune)*
1967 Gene Miller *(Miami Herald)*
1968 J. Anthony Lukas *(New York Times)*
1969 Albert L. Delugach and Denny Walsh *(St. Louis Globe-Democrat)*
1970 Harold Eugene Martin *(Montgomery Advertiser)*
1971 William Hugh Jones *(Chicago Tribune)*
1972 Timothy Leland, Gerard N. O'Neill, Stephen A. Kurkjian, and Ann DeSantis *(Boston Globe)*
1973 Sun Newspapers of Omaha, Neb.
1974 William Sherman *(New York Daily News)*
1975 *Indianapolis Star*
1976 *Chicago Tribune*
1977 Acel Moore and Wendell Rawls, Jr. *(Philadelphia Inquirer)*
1978 Anthony R. Dolan *(Stamford* [Conn.] *Advocate)*
1979 Gilbert M. Gaul and Elliot G. Jaspin *(Pottsville Pa. Republican)*
1980 Nils J. Bruzelius, Alexander B. Hawes, Jr., Stephen A. Kurkjian, and Joan Vennochi *(Boston Globe)*

FEATURE WRITING

1979 Jon D. Franklin *(Baltimore Evening Sun)*
1980 Madeleine Blais *(Miami Herald)*

COMMENTARY

1970 Marquis W. Childs *(St. Louis Post-Dispatch)*

1971 William A. Caldwell (*Record* [Hackensack, N.J.])
1972 Mike Royko *(Chicago Daily News)*
1973 David S. Broder *(Washington Post)*
1974 Edwin A. Roberts, Jr. *(National Observer)*
1975 Mary McGrory *(Washington Star)*
1976 Walter W. (Red) Smith *(New York Times)*
1977 George F. Will (*Washington Post* Writers Group)
1978 William Safire *(New York Times)*
1979 Russell Baker *(New York Times)*
1980 Ellen H. Goodman *(Boston Globe)*

CRITICISM

1970 Ada Louise Huxtable *(New York Times)*
1971 Harold C. Schonberg *(New York Times)*
1972 Frank Peters, Jr. *(St. Louis Post-Dispatch)*
1973 Ronald Powers *(Chicago Sun-Times)*
1974 Emily Genauer (Newsday Syndicate)
1975 Roger Ebert *(Chicago Sun-Times)*
1976 Alan M. Kriegsman *(Washington Post)*
1977 William McPherson *(Washington Post)*
1978 Walter Kerr *(New York Times)*
1979 Paul Gapp *(Chicago Tribune)*
1980 William A. Henry 3rd *(Boston Globe)*

SPECIAL CITATIONS

1938 *Edmonton* (Alberta) *Journal*, special bronze plaque for editorial leadership in defense of freedom of press in Province of Alberta.
1941 *New York Times* for the public educational value of its foreign news report.
1944 Byron Price, Director of the Office of Censorship, for the creation and administration of the newspaper and radio codes. Mrs. William Allen White, for her husband's interest and services during the past seven years as a member of the Advisory Board of the Graduate School of Journalism, Columbia University. Richard Rodgers and Oscar Hammerstein II for their musical *Oklahoma!*
1945 The cartographers of the American press for their war maps.
1947 (Pulitzer centennial year.) Columbia University and the Graduate School of Journalism, for their efforts to maintain and advance the high standards governing the Pulitzer Prize awards. The *St. Louis Post-Dispatch*, for its unswerving adherence to the public and professional ideals of its founder and its leadership in American journalism.
1948 Dr. Frank D. Fackenthal, for his interest and service.
1951 Cyrus L. Sulzberger *(New York Times)* for his exclusive interview with Archbishop Stepinac in a Yugoslav prison.
1952 *Kansas City Star* for coverage of 1951 floods; Max Kase *(New York Journal-American)* for exposures of bribery in college basketball.
1953 *New York Times* for its 17-year publication of "News of the Week in Review"; and Lester Markel, its founder.
1957 Kenneth Roberts for his historical novels.
1958 Walter Lippmann *(New York Herald Tribune)* for his "wisdom, perception and high sense of responsibility" in his commentary on national and international affairs.
1960 Garrett Mattingly, for *The Armada.*
1961 *American Heritage Picture History of the Civil War,* as distinguished example of American book publishing.
1964 Gannett Newspapers, Rochester, N.Y.
1973 James Thomas Flexner for his biography *George Washington.*
1974 Roger Sessions, for his "life's work in music."
1976 John Hohenberg for "services for 22 years as administrator of the Pulitzer Prizes." Scott Joplin for his contributions to American music.
1977 Alex Haley for his novel, *Roots*
1978 E.B.White of *New Yorker* magazine and Richard L. Strout of *Christian Science Monitor*

Pulitzer Prizes in Letters

FICTION[1]

1918 *His Family.* Ernest Poole
1919 *The Magnificent Ambersons.* Booth Tarkington
1921 *The Age of Innocence.* Edith Wharton
1922 *Alice Adams.* Booth Tarkington
1923 *One of Ours.* Willa Cather
1924 *The Able McLaughlins.* Margaret Wilson
1925 *So Big.* Edna Ferber
1926 *Arrowsmith.* Sinclair Lewis
1927 *Early Autumn.* Louis Bromfield
1928 *The Bridge of San Luis Rey.* Thornton Wilder
1929 *Scarlet Sister Mary.* Julia Peterkin
1930 *Laughing Boy.* Oliver La Farge
1931 *Years of Grace.* Margaret Ayer Barnes
1932 *The Good Earth.* Pearl S. Buck
1933 *The Store.* T. S. Stribling
1934 *Lamb in His Bosom.* Caroline Miller
1935 *Now in November.* Josephine Winslow Johnson
1936 *Honey in the Horn.* Harold L. Davis
1937 *Gone with the Wind.* Margaret Mitchell
1938 *The Late George Apley.* John Phillips Marquand
1939 *The Yearling.* Marjorie Kinnan Rawlings
1940 *The Grapes of Wrath.* John Steinbeck
1942 *In This Our Life.* Ellen Glasgow
1943 *Dragon's Teeth.* Upton Sinclair
1944 *Journey in the Dark.* Martin Flavin
1945 *A Bell for Adano.* John Hersey
1947 *All the King's Men.* Robert Penn Warren
1948 *Tales of the South Pacific.* James A. Michener
1949 *Guard of Honor.* James Gould Cozzens
1950 *The Way West.* A. B. Guthrie, Jr.
1951 *The Town.* Conrad Richter
1952 *The Caine Mutiny.* Herman Wouk
1953 *The Old Man and the Sea.* Ernest Hemingway
1955 *A Fable.* William Faulkner
1956 *Andersonville.* MacKinlay Kantor
1958 *A Death in the Family.* James Agee
1959 *The Travels of Jaimie McPheeters.* Robert Lewis Taylor
1960 *Advise and Consent.* Allen Drury

1. Before 1948, award was for novels only.

1961 *To Kill a Mockingbird.* Harper Lee
1962 *The Edge of Sadness.* Edwin O'Connor
1963 *The Reivers.* William Faulkner
1965 *The Keepers of the House.* Shirley Ann Grau
1966 *Collected Stories of Katherine Anne Porter.* Katherine Anne Porter
1967 *The Fixer.* Bernard Malamud
1968 *The Confessions of Nat Turner.* William Styron
1969 *House Made of Dawn.* N. Scott Momaday
1970 *Collected Stories.* Jean Stafford
1972 *Angle of Repose.* Wallace Stegner
1973 *The Optimist's Daughter.* Eudora Welty
1975 *The Killer Angels.* Michael Shaara
1976 *Humboldt's Gift.* Saul Bellow
1978 *Elbow Room.* James Alan McPherson
1979 *The Stories of John Cheever.* John Cheever
1980 *The Executioner's Song.* Norman Mailer

DRAMA

1918 *Why Marry?* Jesse Lynch Williams
1920 *Beyond the Horizon.* Eugene O'Neill
1921 *Miss Lulu Bett.* Zona Gale
1922 *Anna Christie.* Eugene O'Neill
1923 *Icebound.* Owen Davis
1924 *Hell-Bent Fer Heaven.* Hatcher Hughes
1925 *They Knew What They Wanted.* Sidney Howard
1926 *Craig's Wife.* George Kelly
1927 *In Abraham's Bosom.* Paul Green
1928 *Strange Interlude.* Eugene O'Neill
1929 *Street Scene.* Elmer L. Rice
1930 *The Green Pastures.* Marc Connelly
1931 *Alison's House.* Susan Glaspell
1932 *Of Thee I Sing.* George S. Kaufman, Morrie Ryskind, and Ira Gershwin
1933 *Both Your Houses.* Maxwell Anderson
1934 *Men in White.* Sidney Kingsley
1935 *The Old Maid.* Zöe Akins
1936 *Idiot's Delight.* Robert E. Sherwood
1937 *You Can't Take It with You.* Moss Hart and George S. Kaufman
1938 *Our Town.* Thornton Wilder
1939 *Abe Lincoln in Illinois.* Robert E. Sherwood
1940 *The Time of Your Life.* William Saroyan
1941 *There Shall Be No Night.* Robert E. Sherwood
1943 *The Skin of Our Teeth.* Thornton Wilder
1945 *Harvey.* Mary Chase
1946 *State of the Union.* Russel Crouse and Howard Lindsay
1948 *A Streetcar Named Desire.* Tennessee Williams
1949 *Death of a Salesman.* Arthur Miller
1950 *South Pacific.* Richard Rodgers, Oscar Hammerstein II, and Joshua Logan
1952 *The Shrike.* Joseph Kramm
1953 *Picnic.* By William Inge
1954 *The Teahouse of the August Moon.* John Patrick
1955 *Cat on a Hot Tin Roof.* Tennessee Williams
1956 *The Diary of Anne Frank.* Frances Goodrich and Albert Hackett
1957 *Long Day's Journey Into Night.* Eugene O'Neill
1958 *Look Homeward, Angel.* Ketti Frings
1959 *J.B.* Archibald MacLeish
1960 *Fiorello!* George Abbott, Jerome Weidman, Jerry Bock, and Sheldon Harnick
1961 *All the Way Home.* Tad Mosel
1962 *How to Succeed in Business Without Really Trying.* Frank Loesser and Abe Burrows
1965 *The Subject Was Roses.* Frank D. Gilroy
1967 *A Delicate Balance.* Edward Albee
1969 *The Great White Hope.* Howard Sackler
1970 *No Place to Be Somebody.* Charles Gordone
1971 *The Effect of Gamma Rays on Man-in-the-Moon Marigolds.* Paul Zindel
1973 *That Championship Season.* Jason Miller
1975 *Seascape.* Edward Albee
1976 *A Chorus Line.* Conceived by Michael Bennett
1977 *The Shadow Box.* Michael Cristofer
1978 *The Gin Game.* Donald L. Coburn
1979 *Buried Child.* Sam Shepard
1980 *Talley's Folly.* Lanford Wilson

HISTORY OF UNITED STATES

1917 *With Americans of Past and Present Days.* J. J. Jusserand, Ambassador of France to United States
1918 *A History of the Civil War, 1861–1865.* James Ford Rhodes
1920 *The War with Mexico.* Justin H. Smith
1921 *The Victory at Sea.* William Sowden Sims in collaboration with Burton J. Hendrick
1922 *The Founding of New England.* James Truslow Adams
1923 *The Supreme Court in United States History.* Charles Warren
1924 *The American Revolution—A Constitutional Interpretation.* Charles Howard McIlwain
1925 *A History of the American Frontier.* Frederic L. Paxson
1926 *The History of the United States.* Edward Channing
1927 *Pinckney's Treaty.* Samuel Flagg Bemis
1928 *Main Currents in American Thought.* Vernon Louis Parrington
1929 *The Organization and Administration of the Union Army, 1861–1865.* Fred Albert Shannon
1930 *The War of Independence.* Claude H. Van Tyne
1931 *The Coming of the War: 1914.* Bernadotte E. Schmitt
1932 *My Experiences in the World War.* John J. Pershing
1933 *The Significance of Sections in American History.* Frederick J. Turner
1934 *The People's Choice.* Herbert Agar
1935 *The Colonial Period of American History.* Charles McLean Andrews
1936 *The Constitutional History of the United States.* Andrew C. McLaughlin
1937 *The Flowering of New England.* Van Wyck Brooks
1938 *The Road to Reunion, 1865–1900.* Paul Herman Buck
1939 *A History of American Magazines.* Frank Luther Mott
1940 *Abraham Lincoln: The War Years.* Carl Sandburg
1941 *The Atlantic Migration, 1607–1860.* Marcus Lee Hansen
1942 *Reveille in Washington.* Margaret Leech
1943 *Paul Revere and the World He Lived In.* Esther Forbes
1944 *The Growth of American Thought.* Merle Curti
1945 *Unfinished Business.* Stephen Bonsal
1946 *The Age of Jackson.* Arthur M. Schlesinger, Jr.
1947 *Scientists Against Time.* James Phinney Baxter, 3rd
1948 *Across the Wide Missouri.* Bernard DeVoto

1949 *The Disruption of American Democracy.* Roy Franklin Nichols
1950 *Art and Life in America.* Oliver W. Larkin
1951 *The Old Northwest, Pioneer Period 1815–1840.* R. Carlyle Buley
1952 *The Uprooted.* Oscar Handlin
1953 *The Era of Good Feelings.* George Dangerfield
1954 *A Stillness at Appomattox.* Bruce Catton
1955 *Great River: The Rio Grande in North American History.* Paul Horgan
1956 *The Age of Reform.* Richard Hofstadter
1957 *Russia Leaves the War: Soviet-American Relations, 1917–1920.* George F. Kennan
1958 *Banks and Politics in America: From the Revolution to the Civil War.* Bray Hammond
1959 *The Republican Era: 1869–1901.* Leonard D. White, assisted by Jean Schneider
1960 *In the Days of McKinley.* Margaret Leech
1961 *Between War and Peace: The Potsdam Conference.* Herbert Feis
1962 *The Triumphant Empire, Thunder-Clouds Gather in the West.* Lawrence H. Gipson
1963 *Washington, Village and Capital, 1800–1878.* Constance McLaughlin Green
1964 *Puritan Village: The Formation of a New England Town.* Sumner Chilton Powell
1965 *The Greenback Era.* Irwin Unger
1966 *Life of the Mind in America.* Perry Miller
1967 *Exploration and Empire: The Explorer and Scientist in the Winning of the American West.* William H. Goetzmann
1968 *The Ideological Origins of the American Revolution.* Bernard Bailyn
1969 *Origins of the Fifth Amendment.* Leonard W. Levy
1970 *Present at the Creation: My Years in the State Department.* Dean Acheson
1971 *Roosevelt: The Soldier of Freedom.* James McGregor Burns
1972 *Neither Black Nor White. Slavery and Race Relations in Brazil and the United States.* Carl N. Degler
1973 *People of Paradox: An Inquiry Concerning the Origin of American Civilization.* Michael Kammen
1974 *The Americans: The Democratic Experience, Vol. 3.* Daniel J. Boorstin
1975 *Jefferson and His Time.* Dumas Malone
1976 *Lamy of Santa Fe.* Paul Horgan
1977 *The Impending Crisis: 1841–1861.* David M. Potter (posth)
1978 *The Invisible Hand: The Managerial Revolution in American Business.* Alfred D. Chandler Jr.
1979 *The Dred Scott Case: Its Significance in Law and Politics.* Don E. Fehrenbacher
1980 *Been in the Storm So Long.* Leon F. Litwack

BIOGRAPHY OR AUTOBIOGRAPHY

1917 *Julia Ward Howe.* Laura E. Richards and Maude Howe Elliott, assisted by Florence Howe Hall
1918 *Benjamin Franklin, Self-Revealed.* William Cabell Bruce
1919 *The Education of Henry Adams.* Henry Adams
1920 *The Life of John Marshall.* Albert J. Beveridge
1921 *The Americanization of Edward Bok.* Edward Bok
1922 *A Daughter of the Middle Border.* Hamlin Garland
1923 *The Life and Letters of Walter H. Page.* Burton J. Hendrick
1924 *From Immigrant to Inventor.* Michael Idvorsky Pupin
1925 *Barrett Wendell and His Letters.* M. A. DeWolfe Howe
1926 *The Life of Sir William Osler.* Harvey Cushing
1927 *Whitman.* Emory Holloway
1928 *The American Orchestra and Theodore Thomas. Charles Edward Russell*
1929 *The Training of an American. The Earlier Life and Letters of Walter H. Page.* Burton J. Hendrick
1930 *The Raven.* Marquis James
1931 *Charles W. Eliot.* Henry James
1932 *Theodore Roosevelt.* Henry F. Pringle
1933 *Grover Cleveland.* Allan Nevins
1934 *John Hay.* Tyler Dennett
1935 *R. E. Lee.* Douglas S. Freeman
1936 *The Thought and Character of William James.* Ralph Barton Perry
1937 *Hamilton Fish.* Allan Nevins
1938 *Pedlar's Progress.* Odell Shepard. *Andrew Jackson.* Marquis James
1939 *Benjamin Franklin.* Carl Van Doren
1940 *Woodrow Wilson. Life and Letters,* Vols. VII and VIII. Ray Stannard Baker
1941 *Jonathan Edwards.* Ola E. Winslow
1942 *Crusader in Crinoline.* Forrest Wilson
1943 *Admiral of the Ocean Sea.* Samuel Eliot Morison
1944 *The American Leonardo: The Life of Samuel F. B. Morse.* Carleton Mabee
1945 *George Bancroft: Brahmin Rebel.* Russel Blaine Nye
1946 *Son of the Wilderness.* Linnie Marsh Wolfe
1947 *The Autobiography of William Allen White*
1948 *Forgotten First Citizen: John Bigelow.* Margaret Clapp
1949 *Roosevelt and Hopkins.* Robert E. Sherwood
1950 *John Quincy Adams and the Foundations of American Foreign Policy.* Samuel Flagg Bemis
1951 *John C. Calhoun: American Portrait.* Margaret Louise Coit
1952 *Charles Evans Hughes.* Merlo J. Pusey
1953 *Edmund Pendleton 1721–1803.* David J. Mays
1954 *The Spirit of St. Louis.* Charles A. Lindbergh
1955 *The Taft Story.* William S. White
1956 *Benjamin Henry Latrobe.* Talbot F. Hamlin
1957 *Profiles in Courage.* John F. Kennedy
1958 *George Washington.* Douglas Southall Freeman (Vols. 1–6) and John Alexander Carroll and Mary Wells Ashworth (Vol. 7)
1959 *Woodrow Wilson, American Prophet.* Arthur Walworth
1960 *John Paul Jones.* Samuel Eliot Morison
1961 *Charles Sumner and the Coming of the Civil War.* David Donald
1963 *Henry James: Vol. II, The Conquest of London, 1870–1881; Vol. III, The Middle Years, 1881–1895.* Leon Edel
1964 *John Keats.* Walter Jackson Bate
1965 *Henry Adams* (3 vols.). Ernest Samuels
1966 *A Thousand Days.* Arthur M. Schlesinger, Jr.
1967 *Mr. Clemens and Mark Twain.* Justin Kaplan
1968 *Memoirs, 1925–1950.* George F. Kennan
1969 *The Man from New York.* B. L. Reid
1970 *Huey Long.* T. Harry Williams
1971 *Robert Frost: The Years of Triumph, 1915–1938.* Lawrance Thompson
1972 *Eleanor and Franklin: The Story of Their*

Relationship Based on Eleanor Roosevelt's Private Papers. Joseph P. Lash
1973 *Luce and His Empire.* W. A. Swanberg
1974 *O'Neill, Son and Artist.* Louis Sheaffer
1975 *The Power Broker: Robert Moses and the Fall of New York.* Robert A. Caro
1976 *Edith Wharton: A Biography.* Richard W. B. Lewis
1977 *A Prince of Our Disorder.* John E. Mack
1978 *Samuel Johnson.* Walter Jackson Bate
1979 *Days of Sorrow and Pain: Leo Baeck and the Berlin Jews.* Leonard Baker
1980 *The Rise of Theodore Roosevelt.* Edmund Morris

POETRY[1]

1918 *Love Songs.* Sara Teasdale
1919 *Old Road to Paradise.* Margaret Widdemer; *Corn Huskers.* Carl Sandburg
1922 *Collected Poems.* Edwin Arlington Robinson
1923 *The Ballad of the Harp-Weaver; A Few Figs from Thistles;* eight sonnets in *American Poetry, 1922, A Miscellany.* Edna St. Vincent Millay
1924 *New Hampshire: A Poem with Notes and Grace Notes.* Robert Frost
1925 *The Man Who Died Twice.* Edwin Arlington Robinson
1926 *What's O'Clock.* Amy Lowell
1927 *Fiddler's Farewell.* Leonora Speyer
1928 *Tristram.* Edwin Arlington Robinson
1929 *John Brown's Body.* Stephen Vincent Benét
1930 *Selected Poems.* Conrad Aiken
1931 *Collected Poems.* Robert Frost
1932 *The Flowering Stone.* George Dillon
1933 *Conquistador.* Archibald MacLeish
1934 *Collected Verse.* Robert Hillyer
1935 *Bright Ambush.* Audrey Wurdemann
1936 *Strange Holiness.* Robert P. T. Coffin
1937 *A Further Range.* Robert Frost
1938 *Cold Morning Sky.* Marya Zaturenska
1939 *Selected Poems.* John Gould Fletcher
1940 *Collected Poems.* Mark Van Doren
1941 *Sunderland Capture.* Leonard Bacon
1942 *The Dust Which Is God.* William Rose Benét
1943 *A Witness Tree.* Robert Frost
1944 *Western Star.* Stephen Vincent Benét
1945 *V-Letter and Other Poems.* Karl Shapiro
1947 *Lord Weary's Castle.* Robert Lowell
1948 *The Age of Anxiety.* W. H. Auden
1949 *Terror and Decorum.* Peter Viereck
1950 *Annie Allen.* Gwendolyn Brooks
1951 *Complete Poems.* Carl Sandburg
1952 *Collected Poems.* Marianne Moore
1953 *Collected Poems 1917–1952.* Archibald MacLeish
1954 *The Waking.* Theodore Roethke
1955 *Collected Poems.* Wallace Stevens
1956 *Poems—North & South.* Elizabeth Bishop
1957 *Things of This World.* Richard Wilbur
1958 *Promises: Poems 1954–1956.* Robert Penn Warren
1959 *Selected Poems, 1928–1958.* Stanley Kunitz
1960 *Heart's Needle.* William Snodgrass
1961 *Times Three: Selected Verse from Three Decades.* Phyllis McGinley
1962 *Poems.* Alan Dugan
1963 *Pictures from Breughel.* William Carlos Williams
1964 *At the End of the Open Road.* Louis Simpson
1965 *77 Dream Songs.* John Berryman
1966 *Selected Poems.* Richard Eberhart
1967 *Live or Die.* Anne Sexton
1968 *The Hard Hours.* Anthony Hecht
1969 *Of Being Numerous.* George Oppen
1970 *Untitled Subjects.* Richard Howard
1971 *The Carrier of Ladders.* William S. Merwin
1972 *Collected Poems.* James Wright
1973 *Up Country.* Maxine Winokur Kumin
1974 *The Dolphin.* Robert Lowell
1975 *Turtle Island.* Gary Snyder
1976 *Self-Portrait in a Convex Mirror.* John Ashbery
1977 *Divine Comedies.* James Merrill
1978 *Collected Poems.* Howard Nemerov: *Poems 1976–1978.*
1979 *Now and Then* Robert Penn Warren.
1980 *Selected Poems.* Donald Rodney Justice

GENERAL NONFICTION

1962 *The Making of the President 1960.* Theodore H. White
1963 *The Guns of August.* Barbara W. Tuchman
1964 *Anti-intellectualism in American Life.* Richard Hofstadter
1965 *O Strange New World.* Howard Mumford Jones
1966 *Wandering Through Winter.* Edwin Way Teale
1967 *The Problem of Slavery in Western Culture.* David Brion Davis
1968 *Rousseau and Revolution.* Will and Ariel Durant
1969 *So Human an Animal.* Rene Jules Dubos *The Armies of the Night.* Norman Mailer
1970 *Gandhi's Truth.* Erik H. Erikson
1971 *The Rising Sun.* John Toland
1972 *Stilwell and the American Experience in China, 1911–1945.* Barbara W. Tuchman
1973 *Fire in the Lake: The Vietnamese and the Americans in Vietnam.* Frances FitzGerald; and *Children of Crisis* (Vols. 1 and 2). Robert M. Coles
1974 *The Denial of Death.* Ernest Becker
1975 *Pilgrim at Tinker Creek.* Annie Dillard
1976 *Why Survive? Being Old in America.* Robert N. Butler
1977 *Beautiful Swimmers: Watermen, Crabs and the Chesapeake Bay.* William W. Warner
1978 *The Dragons of Eden.* Carl Sagan
1979 *On Human Nature.* Edward O. Wilson
1980 *Gödel, Escher, Bach: An Eternal Golden Braid.* Douglas R. Hofstadter

Pulitzer Prizes in Music

1943 *Secular Cantata No. 2, A Free Song.* William Schuman
1944 *Symphony No. 4* (Op. 34). Howard Hanson
1945 *Appalachian Spring.* Aaron Copland
1946 *The Canticle of the Sun.* Leo Sowerby
1947 *Symphony No. 3.* Charles Ives
1948 *Symphony No. 3.* Walter Piston
1949 *Louisiana Story* music. Virgil Thomson
1950 *The Consul.* Gian Carlo Menotti
1951 Music for opera *Giants in the Earth.* Douglas Stuart Moore

1. This prize was established in 1922. The 1918 and 1919 awards were made from gifts provided by the Poetry Society.

1952 *Symphony Concertante.* Gail Kubik
1954 *Concerto for Two Pianos and Orchestra.* Quincy Porter
1955 *The Saint of Bleecker Street.* Gian Carlo Menotti
1956 *Symphony No. 3.* Ernst Toch
1957 *Meditations on Ecclesiastes.* Norman Dello Joio
1958 *Vanessa.* Samuel Barber
1959 *Concerto for Piano and Orchestra.* John La Montaine
1960 *Second String Quartet.* Elliott Carter
1961 *Symphony No. 7.* Walter Piston
1962 *The Crucible.* Robert Ward
1963 *Piano Concerto No. 1.* Samuel Barber
1966 *Variations for Orchestra.* Leslie Bassett
1967 *Quartet No. 3.* Leon Kirchner
1968 *Echoes of Time and the River.* George Crumb
1969 *String Quartet No. 3.* Karel Husa
1970 *Time's Encomium.* Charles Wuorinen
1971 *Synchronisms No. 6 for Piano and Electronic Sound.* Mario Davidowsky
1972 *Windows.* Jacob Druckman
1973 *String Quartet No. 3.* Elliott Carter
1974 *Notturno.* Donald Martino
1975 *From the Diary of Virginia Woolf.* Dominick Argento
1976 *Air Music.* Ned Rorem
1977 *Visions of Terror and Wonder.* Richard Wernick
1978 *Déjà Vu for Percussion Quartet and Orchestra.* Michael Colgrass
1979 *Aftertones of Infinity.* Joseph Schwantner
1980 *In Memory of a Summer Day.* David Del Tredici

Antoinette Perry (Tony) Awards, 1980

Dramatic play: *Children of a Lesser God,* by Mark Medoff
Musical: *Evita,* by Tim Rice and Andrew Lloyd Webber
Revival: *Morning's at Seven,* by Paul Osborn
Actor (play): John Rubinstein, *Children of a Lesser God*
Actress (play): Phyllis Frelich, *Children of a Lesser God*
Actor (musical): Jim Dale, *Barnum*
Actress (musical): Patti LuPone, *Evita*
Actor, featured (play): David Rounds, *Morning's at Seven*
Actress, featured (play): Dinah Manoff, *I Ought to Be in Pictures*
Actor, featured (musical): Mandy Patinkin, *Evita*
Actress, featured (musical): Priscilla Lopez, *A Day in Hollywood/A Night in the Ukraine*
Director (play): Vivian Matalon, *Morning's at Seven*
Director (musical): Harold Prince, *Evita*
Score: Andrew Lloyd Webber, music; Tim Rice, lyrics, *Evita*
Musical Book: Tim Rice, *Evita*
Choreography: Tommy Tune and Thommie Walsh, *A Day in Hollywood/A Night in the Ukraine*
Scenic design: John Lee Beatty, *Talley's Folly,* and David Mitchell, *Barnum*
Costumes: Theoni V. Aldredge, *Barnum*
Lighting: David Hersey, *Evita*
Lawrence Langner Award for distinguished achievement: Helen Hayes
Special awards: Actors Theater of Louisville, Goodspeed Opera House, Mary Tyler Moore
Theater Award '80: Richard Fitzgerald, of Sound Associates, for developing an amplification device to aid hearing-impaired theatergoers; Hobe Morrison, drama critic of *Variety*

Sigma Delta Chi Journalism Awards, 1979

General reporting: Gene Miller, Carl Hiaasen, Patrick Malone and William D. Montalbano, *Miami Herald*
Editorial writing: Rick Sinding, *Hackensack (N.J.) Record*
Washington correspondence: Gordon Eliot White, *Salt Lake City Deseret News*
Foreign correspondence: Karen DeYoung, *Washington Post*
News photography: Eddie Adams, Associated Press
Editorial cartoon: John P. Trever, *Albuquerque (N.M.) Journal*
Public service in newspaper journalism: *Miami Herald*
Magazine reporting: Michael W. Vargo, *Pennsylvania Illustrated*
Public service in magazine journalism: *National Geographic*
Radio reporting: ABC; News
Editorializing on radio, WTLC, Indianapolis
Television reporting: ABC News and Bob Dyk
Public service in television journalism: KXAS, Fort Worth–Dallas
Editorializing on television: KPIX, San Francisco
Research about journalism: Lloyd Wendt, Sarasota, Fla.

Enrico Fermi Award

Named in honor of Enrico Fermi, the atomic pioneer, the $25,000 award is given in recognition of "exceptional and altogether outstanding" scientific and technical achievement in atomic energy.

1954 Enrico Fermi
1956 John von Neumann
1957 Ernest O. Lawrence
1958 Eugene P. Wigner
1959 Glenn T. Seaborg
1961 Hans A. Bethe
1962 Edward Teller
1963 J. Robert Oppenheimer
1964 Hyman G. Rickover
1966 Otto Hahn, Lise Meitner, and Fritz Strassman
1968 John A. Wheeler
1969 Walter H. Zinn
1970 Norris E. Bradbury
1971 Shields Warren and Stafford L. Warren
1972 Manson Benedict
1976 William L. Russell

NOTE: No award has been given since 1976.

New York Drama Critics' Circle Awards

1935–36
Winterset, Maxwell Anderson
1936–37
High Tor, Maxwell Anderson
1937–38
Of Mice and Men, John Steinbeck
Shadow and Substance, Paul Vincent Carroll[1]
1938–39
(No award) *The White Steed,* Paul Vincent Carroll[1]
1939–40
The Time of Your Life, William Saroyan
1940–41
Watch on the Rhine, Lillian Hellman
The Corn Is Green, Emlyn Williams[1]
1941–42
(No award) *Blithe Spirit,* Noel Coward[1]
1942–43
The Patriots, Sidney Kingsley
1943–44
(No award) *Jacobowsky and the Colonel.* Franz Werfel and S. N. Behrman[1]
1944–45
The Glass Menagerie, Tennessee Williams
1945–46
(No award) *Carousel,* Richard Rodgers and Oscar Hammerstein II[2]
1946–47
All My Sons, Arthur Miller
No Exit, Jean-Paul Sartre[1]
Brigadoon, Alan Jay Lerner and Frederick Loewe[2]
1947–48
A Streetcar Named Desire, Tennessee Williams
The Winslow Boy, Terence Rattigan[1]
1948–49
Death of a Salesman, Arthur Miller
The Madwoman of Chaillot, Jean Giraudoux and Maurice Valency[1]
South Pacific, Richard Rodgers, Oscar Hammerstein II, and Joshua Logan[2]
1949–50
The Member of the Wedding, Carson McCullers
The Cocktail Party, T. S. Eliot[1]
The Consul, Gian Carlo Menotti[2]
1950–51
Darkness at Noon, Sidney Kingsley[3]
The Lady's Not for Burning, Christopher Fry[1]
Guys and Dolls, Abe Burrows, Jo Swerling and Frank Loesser[2]
1951–52
I Am a Camera, John Van Druten[4]
Venus Observed, Christopher Fry[1]
Pal Joey, Richard Rodgers, Lorenz Hart, and John O'Hara[2]
Don Juan in Hell, George B. Shaw[5]
1952–53
Picnic, William Inge
The Love of Four Colonels, by Peter Ustinov[1]
Wonderful Town, Joseph Fields, Jerome Chodorov, Betty Comden, Adolph Green, and Leonard Bernstein[2]
1953–54
The Teahouse of the August Moon, John Patrick
Ondine, Jean Giraudoux[1]
The Golden Apple, John Latouche and Jerome Moross[2]
1954–55
Cat on a Hot Tin Roof, Tennessee Williams
Witness for the Prosecution, Agatha Christie[1]
The Saint of Bleecker Street, Gian Carlo Menotti[2]
1955-56
The Diary of Anne Frank, Frances Goodrich and Albert Hackett
Tiger at the Gates, Jean Giraudoux and Christopher Fry[1]
My Fair Lady, Frederick Loewe and Alan Jay Lerner[2]
1956–57
Long Day's Journey Into Night, Eugene O'Neill
Waltz of the Toreadors, Jean Anouilh[1]
The Most Happy Fella, Frank Loesser[2] [6]
1957–58
Look Homeward, Angel, Ketti Frings[7]
Look Back in Anger, John Osborne[1]
The Music Man, Meredith Willson[2]
1958–59
A Raisin in the Sun, Lorraine Hansberry
The Visit, Friedrich Duerrenmatt–Maurice Valency[1]
La Plume de ma Tante, Robert Dhery and Gerard Calvi[2]
1959–60
Toys in the Attic, Lillian Hellman
Five Finger Exercise, Peter Shaffer[1]
Fiorello!, Jerome Weidman, George Abbott, Jerry Bock, and Sheldon Harnick[2]
1960–61
All the Way Home, Tad Mosel[8]
A Taste of Honey, Shelagh Delaney[1]
Carnival, Michael Stewart[2]
1961–62
The Night of the Iguana, Tennessee Williams
A Man for All Seasons, Robert Bolt[1]
How to Succeed in Business Without Really Trying, Abe Burrows, Jack Weinstock, Willie Gilbert, and Frank Loesser[2] [9]
1962–63
Who's Afraid of Virginia Woolf?, Edward Albee
Beyond the Fringe, Alan Bennett, Peter Cook, Jonathan Miller, and Dudley Moore[10]
1963–64
Luther, John Osborne
Hello, Dolly!, Michael Stewart and Jerry Herman[2] [11]
The Trojan Women, Euripides[10] [12]
1964–65
The Subject Was Roses, Frank D. Gilroy
Fiddler on the Roof, Joseph Stein, Jerry Bock, and Sheldon Harnick[2] [13]
1965–66
The Persecution and Assassination of Marat as Performed by the Inmates of the Asylum of Charenton under the Direction of the Marquis de Sade, Peter Weiss
The Man of La Mancha, Dale Wasserman, Mitch Leigh, and Joe Darion
1966–67
The Homecoming, Harold Pinter
Cabaret, Joe Masteroff, John Kander, and Fred Ebb[2] [14]
1967–68
Rosencrantz and Guilderstern Are Dead, Tom Stoppard
Your Own Thing, Donald Driver, Hal Hester, and Danny Apolinar[2]
1968–69
The Great White Hope, Howard Sackler
1776, Sherman Edwards and Peter Stone[2]
1969–70
Borstal Boy, Frank McMahon[15]
The Effect of Gamma Rays on Man-in-the-Moon Marigolds, Paul Zindel[16]

Company, George Furth and Stephen Sondheim[2]
1970–71
Home, David Storey
The House of Blue Leaves, John Guare[16]
Follies, James Goldman and Stephen Sondheim[2]
1971–72
That Championship Season, Jason Miller
Two Gentlemen of Verona, adapted by John Guare and Mel Shapiro[2]
The Screens, Jean Genet[1]
1972–73
The Changing Room, David Storey
The Hot l Baltimore, by Lanford Wilson[16]
A Little Night Music, Hugh Wheeler and Stephen Sondheim[2]
1973–74
The Contractors, David Storey
Short Eyes, Miguel Piñero[16]
Candide, Leonard Bernstein, Hugh Wheeler, and Richard Wilbur[2]
1974–75
Equus, Peter Shaffer
The Taking of Miss Janie, Ed Bullins[16]
A Chorus Line, James Kirkwood and Nicholas Dante[2]
1975–76
Travesties, Tom Stoppard
Streamers, David Rabe[16]
Pacific Overtures, Stephen Sondheim, John Weidman, and Hugh Wheeler[2]
1976–77
Otherwise Engaged, Simon Gray
American Buffalo, David Mamet[6]
Annie, Thomas Meehan, Charles Strouse, and Martin Charnin[2]
1977–78
Da, Hugh Leonard
Ain't Misbehavin', conceived by Richard Maltby, Jr.[2]
1978–79
The Elephant Man, Bernard Pomerance
Sweeney Todd, Hugh Wheeler and Stephen Sondheim[2]
1979–80
Talley's Folly, Lanford Wilson
Evita,[2] Andrew Lloyd Webber and Tim Rice
Betrayal, Harold Pinter[1]

1. Citation for best foreign play. 2. Citation for best musical. 3. Based on a novel by Arthur Koestler. 4. Based on Christopher Isherwood's *Berlin Stories.* 5. For "distinguished and original contribution to the theater." 6. Based on Sidney Howard's *They Knew What They Wanted.* 7. Based on a novel by Thomas Wolfe. 8. Based on James Agee's *A Death in the Family.* 9. Based on a book by Shepherd Mead. 10. Special citation. 11. Based on Thornton Wilder's *The Matchmaker.* 12. Translated by Edith Hamilton. 13. Based on Sholem Aleichem's Tevye stories, translated by Arnold Perl. 14. Based on John Van Druten's *I Am a Camera,* which won the award for the best play in 1951–52. 15. Based on Brendan Behan's autobiography. 16. Citation for best American play.

Major American Book Awards, 1980

Fiction: *Sophie's Choice,* by William Styron.
First novel: *Birdy,* by William Wharton.
General nonfiction: *The Right Stuff,* by Tom Wolfe.
History: *White House Years,* by Henry A. Kissinger.
Biography: *The Rise of Theodore Roosevelt,* by Edmund Morris.
Autobiography: *By Myself,* by Lauren Bacall.
Religion: *The Gnostic Gospels,* by Elaine Pagels.
Science: *Godel, Escher, Bach,* by Douglas Hofstadter.
Science Fiction: *Jem,* by Frederik Pohl.
Current interest: *Julia Child and More Company,* by Julia Child.
Mystery: *The Green Ripper,* by John D. MacDonald.
Poetry: *Ashes,* by Philip Levine.
General reference: *Congressional Quarterly's Guide to the U.S. Supreme Court,* edited by Elder Witt.
Children's books: *A Gathering of Days,* by Joan W. Blos.
Translation: Jane Gary Harris and Constance Link for *The Complete Critical Prose and Letters* of Osip E. Mandelstam.
Western: *Bendigo Shafter,* by Louis L'Armour.

American Library Association Awards for Children's Books, 1980

John Newbery Medal for best book: *A Gathering of Days: A New England Girl's Journal 1830–32,* by Joan W. Blos (Charles Scribner's)
Newbery Honor Book: *The Road From Home: The Story of an Armenian Girl,* by David Kherdian (Greenwillow Books)
Randolph Caldecott Medal for best picture book: *Ox-Cart Man,* by Barbara Cooney (Viking Press)
Caldecott Honor Books: *Ben's Trumpet,* by Rachel Isadora (Greenwillow); *The Treasure,* illustrated by Uri Shulevitz (Farrar, Straus & Giroux); *The Garden of Abdul Gasazi,* by Chris Van Allsburgh (Houghton Mifflin)
Laura Ingalls Wilder Award for contribution to children's literature: Theodore Geisel (Dr. Seuss)

Poets Laureate of England

Edmund Spenser	1591–1599	Nicholas Rowe	1715–1718	William Wordsworth	1843–1850
Samuel Daniel	1599–1619	Laurence Eusden	1718–1730	Alfred Lord Tennyson	1850–1892
Ben Jonson	1619–1637	Colley Cibber	1730–1757	Alfred Austin	1896–1913
William Davenant	1638–1668	William Whitehead	1757–1785	Robert Bridges	1913–1930
John Dryden[1]	1670–1689	Thomas Warton	1785–1790	John Masefield	1930–1967
Thomas Shadwell	1689–1692	Henry James Pye	1790–1813	C. Day Lewis	1967–1972
Nahum Tate	1692–1715	Robert Southey	1813–1843	Sir John Betjeman	1972–

1. First to bear the title officially. *Source: Encyclopaedia Britannica.*

Presidential Medal of Freedom

The nation's highest civilian award, the Presidential Medal of Freedom, was established in 1963 by President John F. Kennedy to continue and expand Presidential recognition of meritorious service which, since 1945, had been granted as the Medal of Freedom. NOTE: An asterisk following a year denotes a posthumous award.

AWARDED BY PRESIDENT KENNEDY

Marian Anderson (contralto)	1963
Ralph J. Bunche (statesman)	1963
Ellsworth Bunker (diplomat)	1963
Pablo Casals (cellist)	1963
Genevieve Caulfield (educator)	1963
James B. Conant (educator)	1963
John F. Enders (bacteriologist)	1963
Felix Frankfurter (jurist)	1963
Karl Horton (youth authority)	1963
John XXIII (Pope)	1963*
Robert J. Kiphuth (athletic director)	1963
Edwin H. Land (inventor)	1963
Herbert H. Lehman (statesman)	1963*
Robert A. Lovett (statesman)	1963
J. Clifford MacDonald (educator)	1963*
John J. McCloy (banker and statesman)	1963
George Meany (labor leader)	1963
Alexander Meiklejohn (philosopher)	1963
Ludwig Mies van der Rohe (architect)	1963
Jean Monnet (European statesman)	1963
Luis Muñoz-Marín (Governor of Puerto Rico)	1963
Clarence B. Randall (industrialist)	1963
Rudolf Serkin (pianist)	1963
Edward Steichen (photographer)	1963
George W. Taylor (educator)	1963
Alan T. Waterman (scientist)	1963
Mark S. Watson (journalist)	1963
Annie D. Wauneka (public health worker)	1963
E. B. White (author)	1963
Thornton N. Wilder (author)	1963
Edmund Wilson (author and critic)	1963
Andrew Wyeth (artist)	1963

AWARDED BY PRESIDENT JOHNSON

Dean G. Acheson (statesman)	1964
Eugene R. Black (banker)	1969
Detlev W. Bronk (neurophysiologist)	1964
McGeorge Bundy (government service)	1969
Ellsworth Bunker (diplomat)	1968
Clark Clifford (statesman)	1969
Aaron Copland (composer)	1964
Michael E. DeBakey (surgeon)	1969
Willem de Kooning (artist)	1964
Walt Disney (cartoon film producer)	1964
J. Frank Dobie (author)	1964
David Dubinsky (labor leader)	1969
Lena F. Edwards (physician and humanitarian)	1964
Thomas Stearns Eliot (poet)	1964
Ralph Ellison (author)	1969
Lynn Fontanne (actress)	1964
Henry Ford II (industrialist)	1969
John W. Gardner (educator)	1964
W. Averell Harriman (statesman)	1969
Rev. Theodore M. Hesburgh (educator)	1964
Bob Hope (comedian)	1969
Clarence L. Johnson (aircraft engineer)	1964
Edgar F. Kaiser (industrialist)	1969
Frederick R. Kappel (telecommunications executive)	1964
Helen A. Keller (educator)	1964
John Fitzgerald Kennedy (U.S. President)	1963*
Robert W. Komer (government service)	1968
Mary Lasker (philanthropist)	1969
John L. Lewis (labor leader)	1964
Walter Lippmann (journalist)	1964
Eugene M. Locke (diplomat)	1968
Alfred Lunt (actor)	1964
John W. Macy, Jr. (government service)	1969
Ralph McGill (journalist)	1964
Robert S. McNamara (government service)	1968
Samuel Eliot Morison (historian)	1964
Lewis Mumford (urban planner and critic)	1964
Edward R. Murrow (radio-TV commentator)	1964
Reinhold Niebuhr (theologian)	1964
Gregory Peck (actor)	1969
Leontyne Price (soprano)	1964
A. Philip Randolph (labor leader)	1964
Laurance S. Rockefeller (conservationist)	1969
Walt Whitman Rostow (government service)	1969
Deak Rusk (statesman)	1969
Carl Sandburg (poet and biographer)	1964
Merriman Smith (journalist)	1969
John Steinbeck (author)	1964
Helen B. Taussig (pediatrician)	1964
Cyrus R. Vance (government service)	1969
Carl Vinson (legislator)	1964
Thomas J. Watson, Jr. (industrialist)	1964
James E. Webb (NASA administrator)	1968
Paul Dudley White (physician)	1964
William S. White (journalist)	1969
Roy Wilkins (social welfare executive)	1969
Whitney M. Young, Jr. (social welfare executive)	1969

AWARDED BY PRESIDENT NIXON

Edwin E. Aldrin (astronaut)	1969
Apollo 13 Mission Operations Team	1970
Neil A. Armstrong (astronaut)	1969
Earl Charles Behrens (journalist)	1970
Manlio Brosio (NATO secretary general)	1971
Michael Collins (astronaut)	1969
Edward K. "Duke" Ellington (musician)	1969
Edward T. Folliard (journalist)	1970
John Ford (film director)	1973
Samuel Goldwyn (film producer)	1971
Fred Wallace Haise, Jr. (astronaut)	1970
William M. Henry (journalist)	1970*
Paul G. Hoffman (statesman)	1974
William J. Hopkins (White House service)	1971
Arthur Krock (journalist)	1970
Melvin R. Laird (government service)	1974
David Lawrence (journalist)	1970
George Gould Lincoln (journalist)	1970
James A. Lovell, Jr. (astronaut)	1970
Dr. Charles L. Lowman (orthopedist)	1974
Raymond Moley (journalist)	1970
Eugene Ormandy (conductor)	1970
William P. Rogers (diplomat)	1973
Adela Rogers St. Johns (journalist)	1970
John Leonard Swigert, Jr. (astronaut)	1970
John Paul Vann (adviser, Vietnam war)	1972*
DeWitt and Lila Wallace (founders, *Reader's Digest*)	1972

AWARDED BY PRESIDENT FORD

I. W. Abel (labor leader)	1977
John Bardeen (physicist)	1977
Irving Berlin (composer)	1977
Norman Borlaug (agricultural scientist)	1977
Omar N. Bradley (national security)	1977
David K. E. Bruce (diplomat)	1976
Arleigh Burke (national security)	1977
Alexander Calder (sculptor)	1977*
Bruce Catton (historian)	1977
Joseph P. DiMaggio (baseball star)	1977

Ariel Durant (author)	1977
Will Durant (author)	1977
Arthur Fiedler (conductor)	1977
Henry J. Friendly (jurist)	1977
Martha Graham (dancer-choreographer)	1976
Claudia "Lady Bird" Johnson (service to U.S. scenic beauty)	1977
Henry A. Kissinger (statesman)	1977
Archibald MacLeish (poet)	1977
James A. Michener (author)	1977
Georgia O'Keeffe (artist)	1977
Jesse Owens (track champion)	1976
Nelson A. Rockefeller (government service)	1977
Norman Rockwell (illustrator)	1977
Artur Rubinstein (pianist)	1976
Donald H. Rumsfeld (government service)	1977
Katherine Filene Shouse (service to the performing arts)	1977
Lowell Thomas (radio-TV commentator)	1977
James D. Watson (biochemist)	1977

AWARDED BY PRESIDENT CARTER

Ansel Adams (photographer)	1980
Rachel Carson (author)	1980*
Lucia Chase (ballet director)	1980
Arthur J. Goldberg (government service)	1978
Hubert H. Humphrey (government service)	1980*
Archbishop Iakovos (churchman)	1980
Lyndon B. Johnson (U.S. President)	1980*
Rev. Dr. Martin Luther King, Jr. (civil rights leader)	1977*
Margaret Mead (anthropologist)	1979*
Clarence Mitchell, Jr. (civil rights leader)	1980
Roger Tory Peterson (ornithologist)	1980
Adm. Hyman Rickover (national security)	1980
Jonas Salk (medical research)	1977
Beverly Sills (opera singer)	1980
Robert Penn Warren (author and poet)	1980
John Wayne (actor)	1980*
Eudora Welty (author)	1980
Tennessee Williams (playwright)	1980
Horace M. Albright (government service)	1980

Major Grammy Awards for Recording in 1979

Record: "What a Fool Believes," Doobie Brothers (Warner Bros.)
Album: "52d Street," Billy Joel (Columbia)
Song: "What a Fool Believes," Kenny Loggins and Michael McDonald
New Artist: Rickie Lee Jones (Warner Bros.)
Pop Vocalists: Dionne Warwick, "I'll Never Love This Way Again" (Arista); Billy Joel, "52d Street" (Columbia)
Pop Group: Doobie Brothers, "Minute by Minute" (Warner Bros.)
Pop Instrumentalist: Herb Alpert, "Rise" (A. & M.)
Rock Vocalists: Donna Summer, "Hot Stuff" (Casablanca); Bob Dylan, "Gotta Serve Somebody" (Columbia)
Rock Group: Eagles, "Heartache Tonight" (Asylum)
Rock Instrumentalists: Wings, "Rockestra Theme" (Columbia)
Country Vocalists: Emmylou Harris, "Blue Kentucky Girl" (Warner Bros.); Kenny Rogers, "The Gambler" (United Artists)
Country Group: Charlie Daniels Band, "The Devil Went Down to Georgia" (Epic)
Country Instrumentalists: Doc and Merle Watson, "Big Sandy/Leather Britches" (United Artists)
Country Song: "You Decorated My Life," Bob Morrison and Debbie Hupp
Rhythm and Blues Vocalists: Dionne Warwick, "Déjà Vu" (Arista); Michael Jackson, "Don't Stop 'Til You Get Enough" (Epic)
Rhythm and Blues Group: Earth, Wind, & Fire, "After the Love Has Gone" (ARC/Columbia)
Rhythm and Blues Instrumentalists: Earth, Wind, & Fire, "Boogie Wonderland" (ARC/Columbia)
Rhythm and Blues Song: "After the Love Has Gone," David Foster, Jay Graydon, and Bill Champlin
Jazz Vocalist: Ella Fitzgerald, "Fine and Mellow" (Pablo)
Jazz Instrumentalist: Oscar Peterson, "Jousts" (Pablo)
Jazz Instrumentalists, Group: Gary Burton and Chick Corea, "Duet" (Warner Bros.)
Jazz, Big Band: Duke Ellington, "At Fargo, 1940 Live" (Book-of-the-Month Club)
Jazz Fusion: Weather Report, "8:30" (ARC/Columbia)
Gospel, Contemporary: Imperials, "Heed the Call" (Dayspring)
Gospel, Traditional: Blackwood Brothers, "Lift Up the Name of Jesus" (Skylite)
Soul Gospel, Contemporary: Andrae Crouch, "I'll Be Thinking of You" (Light)
Soul Gospel, Traditional: Mighty Clouds of Joy, "Changing Times" (Epic)
Inspirational: B.J. Thomas, "You Gave Me Love (When Nobody Gave Me a Prayer)" (Myrrh)
Ethnic or Traditional: Muddy Waters, "Muddy (Mississippi) Waters Live" (Blue Sky/CBS)
Latin: Irakere, "Irakere" (Columbia)
For Children: "The Muppet Movie," the Muppets (Atlantic)
Comedy: "Reality ... What a Concept," Robin Williams (Casablanca)
Spoken Word: "Ages of Man (Readings From Shakespeare)," Sir John Gielgud (Caedmon)
Instrumental Composition: "Main Title Theme From 'Superman'," John Williams
Motion Picture Score: "Superman," John Williams (Warner Bros.)
Cast Show Album: "Sweeney Todd," Stephen Sondheim (Thomas Z. Shepard)
Classical Album: Brahms: The Four Symphonies, Sir Georg Solti conducting Chicago Symphony Orchestra (London)
Classical, Orchestral Recording: Brahms: The Four Symphonies, Sir Georg Solti conducting Chicago Symphony Orchestra (London)
Opera: "Peter Grimes," by Benjamin Britten, Colin Davis conducting Orchestra and Chorus of Royal Opera House, Covent Garden (Philips)
Classical, Choral: "A German Requiem," by Brahms, Sir Georg Solti conducting Chicago Symphony Orchestra and Chorus, Margaret Hillis, choral director (London)
Chamber Music: "Appalachian Spring," by Aaron Copland, Colin Davis conducting St. Paul Chamber Orchestra (Sound 80)
Classical, Soloist With Orchestra: Maurizio Pollini, Concertos for Piano Nos. 1 and 2 by Bela Bartok, with Claudio Abbado conducting Chicago Symphony Orchestra (Deutsche Grammophon)
Classical, Soloist Without Orchestra: Vladimir Horowitz, "The Horowitz Concerts, 1978—79" (RCA)
Classical, vocalist: Luciano Pavarotti, "O Sole Mio (Favorite Neapolitan Songs)" (London)

Winners of Bollingen Prize in Poetry

($5,000 award is currently given biennially)

1949 Ezra Pound
1950 Wallace Stevens
1951 John Crowe Ransom
1952 Marianne Moore
1953 Archibald MacLeish and William Carlos Williams
1954 W. H. Auden
1955 Léonie Adams and Louise Bogan
1956 Conrad Aiken
1957 Allen Tate
1958 E.E. Cummings
1959 Theodore Roethke
1960 Delmore Schwartz
1961 Yvor Winters
1962 John Hall Wheelock and Richard Eberhart
1963 Robert Frost
1965 Horace Gregory
1967 Robert Penn Warren
1969 John Berryman and Karl Shapiro
1971 Richard Wilbur and Mona Van Duyn
1973 James Merrill
1975 Archie Randolph Ammons
1977 David Ignatow
1979 W. S. Merwin

Templeton Foundation Prize for Progress in Religion

Dr. Ralph Wendell Burhoe, a Chicago scientist and theologian, became the first American to receive the Templeton Prize since its inception. Presentation of the prize, £90,000 ($206,000) was made by Prince Philip in London on May 13, 1980. The award was given for Dr. Burhoe's work in evolutionary theory.

The prize, which was inaugurated in 1972 and first presented in 1973, was founded by John M. Templeton, a financial analyst and Presbyterian layman, to honor a person whose work is of pioneering nature and is likely to result in a new and better understanding of God. Recipients to date are:

1973 Mother Teresa of Calcutta, founder of the Missionaries of Charity
1974 Brother Roger, Founder and Prior of the Taize Community in France
1975 Dr. Sarvepalli Radhakrishnan, former President of India and Oxford Professor of Eastern Religions and Ethics
1976 H.E. Leon Joseph Cardinal Suenes, Archbishop of Malines-Brussels
1977 Chiara Lubich, Founder of the Focolare Movement, Italy
1978 Prof. Thomas F. Torrence, Edinburgh University
1979 Nikkyo Niwano, The Rissho Kosei-Kai Movement, Japan

Major U.S. Fairs and Expositions

1853 Crystal Palace Exposition, New York City: modeled on similar fair held in London.
1876 Centennial Exposition, Philadelphia: celebrating 100th year of independence.
1893 World's Columbian Exposition, Chicago: commemorating 400th anniversary of Columbus' voyage to America.
1894 Midwinter International Exposition, San Francisco: promoting business revival after Depression of 1893.
1898 Trans-Mississippi and International Exposition, Omaha, Neb.: exhibiting products, resources, industries, and civilization of states and territories west of the Mississippi River.
1901 Pan-American Exposition, Buffalo, N.Y.: promoting social and commercial interest of Western Hemisphere nations.
1904 Louisiana Purchase Exposition, St. Louis: marking 100th anniversary of major land acquisition from France and opening up of the West.
1905 Lewis and Clark Centennial Exposition, Portland, Ore.: commemorating 100th anniversary of exploration of a land route to the Pacific.
1907 Jamestown Ter Centennial Exposition, Hampton Roads, Va.: marking 300th anniversary of first permanent English settlement in America.
1909 Alaska-Yukon-Pacific Exposition, Seattle: celebrating growth of the Puget Sound area.
1915–16 Panama-Pacific International Exposition, San Francisco: celebrating opening of the Panama Canal.
1915–16 Panama-California Exposition, San Diego: promoting resources and opportunities for development and commerce of the Western states.
1926 Sesquicentennial Exposition, Philadelphia: marking 150th year of independence.
1933–34 Century of Progress International Exposition, Chicago: celebrating 100th anniversary of incorporation of Chicago as a city.
1935 California Pacific International Exposition, San Diego: marking 400 years of progress since the first Spaniard landed on the West Coast.
1939–40 New York World's Fair, New York City: "The World of Tomorrow," symbolized by Trylon and Perisphere. Officially commemorating 150th anniversary of inauguration of George Washington as President in New York.
1939–40 Golden Gate International Exposition, Treasure Island, San Francisco: celebrating new Golden Gate Bridge and Oakland Bay Bridge.
1962 The Century 21 Exposition, Seattle: "Man in the Space Age," symbolized by 600-foot steel space needle.
1964–65 New York World's Fair, New York City: "Peace Through Understanding."
1974 Expo '74, Seattle: "Tomorrow's Fresh, New Environment."

PEOPLE

Many public figures not listed here may be found elsewhere in the *Information Please Almanac.*

A name in parentheses is the original name or form of name. Localities are places of birth. Dates of birth appear as month/day/year. **Boldface** years in parentheses are dates of **(birth-death).**
Information has been gathered from many sources, including the individuals themselves. However, the *Information Please Almanac* cannot guarantee the accuracy of every individual item.

A

Aalto, Alvar (architect); Kuortane, Finland **(1898–1976)**
Abbott, Bud (William) (comedian); Asbury Park, N.J. **(1898–1974)**
Abbott, George (stage producer); Forestville, N.Y., 6/25/1889
Abel, Walter (actor); St. Paul, 6/6/1898
Abernathy, Ralph (civil rights leader); Linden, Ala., 3/11/1926
Acheson, Dean (statesman); Middletown, Conn. **(1893–1971)**
Acuff, Roy Claxton (musician); nr. Maynardsville, Tenn. 9/15/1903
Adams, Charles Francis (diplomat); Boston **(1807–1886)**
Adams, Don (actor); New York City, 4/19/1927
Adams, Edie (actress); Kingston, Pa., 4/16/1929
Adams, Franklin Pierce (columnist and author); Chicago **(1881–1960)**
Adams, Henry Brooks (historian); Boston **(1838–1918)**
Adams, Joey (comedian); New York City, 1/6/1911
Adams, Maude (Maude Kiskadden) (actress); Salt Lake City, **(1872–1953)**
Adams, Samuel (American Revolutionary patriot); Boston **(1722–1803)**
Adamson, Joy (naturalist); Troppau, Silesia **(1910–1980)**
Addams, Charles (cartoonist); Westfield, N.J., 1/7/1912
Addams, Jane (social worker); Cedarville, Ill. **(1860–1935)**
Adderley, Julian "Cannonball" (jazz saxophonist); Tampa, Fla. **(1928–1975)**
Ade, George (humorist); Kentland, Ind. **(1866–1944)**
Adenauer, Konrad (statesman); Cologne, Germany **(1876–1967)**
Adler, Alfred (psychoanalyst); Vienna **(1870–1937)**
Adler, Larry (musician); Baltimore, 2/10/1914
Adler, Richard (songwriter); New York City, 8/3/1921
Adoree, Renée (Renée La Fonte) (actress); Lille, France **(1898–1933)**
Aeschylus (dramatist); Eleusis (Greece) **(525–456 B.C.)**
Aesop (fabulist); birthplace unknown **(lived c. 600 B.C.)**
Aherne, Brian (actor); King's Norton, England, 5/2/1902
Aiken, Conrad (poet); Savannah, Ga. **(1889–1973)**
Ailey, Alvin (choreographer); Rogers, Tex., 1/5/1931
Aimee, Anouk (actress); Paris, 4/27/1934
Albanese, Licia (operatic soprano); Bari, Italy, 7/22/1913
Albee, Edward (playwright); Washington, D.C., 3/12/1928
Albers, Josef (painter); Bottrop, Germany **(1888–1976)**
Albert, Eddie (Edward Albert Heimberger) (actor); Rock Island, Ill., 4/22/1908
Albertson, Jack (actor); Malden, Mass., 6/16/1910(?)
Albright, Lola (actress); Akron, Ohio, 7/20/1925
Alcott, Louisa May (novelist); Germantown, Pa. **(1832–1888)**
Alda, Alan (actor); New York City, 1/28/1936
Alda, Robert (Alphonso d'Abruzzo) (actor); New York City, 2/26/1914
Alden, John (American Pilgrim); England **(1599?–1687)**
Alexander the Great (monarch and conqueror); Pella (Greece) **(356–323 B.C.)**
Alger, Horatio (author); Revere, Mass. **(1834–1899)**
Algren, Nelson (novelist); Detroit, 3/28/1909
Allen, Ethan (American Revolutionary soldier); Litchfield, Conn. **(1738–1789)**
Allen, Fred (John Florence Sullivan) (comedian); Cambridge, Mass. **(1894–1956)**
Allen, Gracie (Grace Ethel Cecile Rosalie Allen) (comedienne); San Francisco **(1906–1964)**
Allen, Mel (Melvin Israel) (sportscaster); Birmingham, Ala., 2/14/1913
Allen, Steve (TV entertainer); New York City, 12/26/1921
Allen, Woody (Allen Stewart Konigsberg) (actor, writer, and director); Brooklyn, N.Y., 12/1/1935
Allison, Fran (actress); LaPorte City, Iowa, 1924(?)
Allman, Gregg (singer); Nashville, Tenn., 12/8/1947
Allyson, June (Jan Allyson) (actress); New York City, 10/7/1923
Alonso, Alicia (ballerina); Havana, 12/21/1921(?)
Alpert, Herb (band leader); Los Angeles, 3/31/1935(?)
Alsop, Joseph W., Jr. (journalist); Avon, Conn., 10/11/1910
Alsop, Stewart (journalist); Avon, Conn. **(1914–1974)**
Altman, Robert (film director); Kansas City, Mo., 2/20/1925
Ambler, Eric (suspense writer); London, 6/28/1909
Ameche, Don (Dominic Amici) (actor); Kenosha, Wis., 5/31/1908
Amis, Kingsley (novelist); London, 4/16/1922
Amory, Cleveland (writer and conservationist); Nahant, Mass., 9/2/1917
Amos (Freeman F. Gosden) (radio comedian); Richmond, Va., 5/5/1899
Amsterdam, Morey (actor); Chicago, 12/14/1914
Andersen, Hans Christian (author of fairy-tales); Odense, Denmark **(1805–1875)**
Anderson, Eddie. *See* Rochester
Anderson, Jack (journalist); Long Beach, Calif., 10/19/1922
Anderson, Dame Judith (actress); Adelaide, Australia, 2/10/1898
Anderson, Lindsay (Gordon) (director); Bangalore, India, 4/17/1923
Anderson, Lynn (singer); Grand Forks, N.D., 9/26/1947
Anderson, Marian (contralto); Philadelphia, 2/17/1902
Anderson, Maxwell (dramatist); Atlantic, Pa. **(1888–1959)**
Anderson, Robert (playwright); New York City, 4/28/1917
Andersson, Bibi (actress); Stockholm, 11/11/1935
Andress, Ursula (actress); Switzerland, 3/19/1938
Andrews, Dana (actor); Collins, Miss., 1/1/1909
Andrews, Julie (Julia Wells) (actress and singer); Walton-on-Thames, England, 10/1/1935
Andrews, La Verne (singer); Minneapolis **(1916–1967)**
Andrews, Maxene (singer); Minneapolis, 1/3/1918
Andrews, Patti (singer); Minneapolis, 2/16/1920
Andy (Charles J. Correll) (radio comedian); Peoria, Ill. **(1890–1972)**
Angeles, Victoria de los (Victoria Gamez Cima) (operatic soprano); Barcelona, 11/1/1924
Anka, Paul (singer and composer); Ottawa, 7/30/1941
Ann-Margret (Ann-Margret Olsson) (actress); Valsjobyn, Sweden, 4/28/1941
Annabella (actress); Paris, 1912
Anouilh, Jean (playwright); Bordeaux, France, 6/23/1910
Anthony, Susan Brownell (woman suffragist); Adams, Mass. **(1820–1906)**
Antonioni, Michelangelo (director); Ferrara, Italy, 9/29/1912
Antony, Mark (Marcus Antonius) (statesman); Rome **(83?–30 B.C.)**
Anuszkiewicz, Richard (painter); Erie, Pa., 5/23/1930
Aquinas, St. Thomas (philosopher); nr. Aquino (Italy) **(1225? –1274)**
Arbuckle, Roscoe "Fatty" (actor and director); San Jose, Calif. **(1887–1933)**
Archimedes (physicist and mathematician); Syracuse (Italy) **(287?–212 B.C.)**
Archipenko, Alexandre (sculptor); Kiev, Russia **(1887–1964)**
Arden, Elizabeth (Florence Nightingale Graham) (cosmetics executive); Woodbridge, Canada **(1891–1966)**
Arden, Eve (Eunice Quedens) (actress); Mill Valley, Calif., 4/30/1912
Arendt, Hannah (historian); Hannover, Germany **(1906–1975)**
Aristophanes (dramatist); Athens **448?–380 B.C.)**
Aristotle (philosopher); Stagira (Greece) **(384–322 B.C.)**
Arkin, Alan (actor and director); New York City, 3/26/1934
Arledge, Roone (TV executive); Forest Hills, N.Y., 7/8/1931
Arlen, Harold (Hyman Arluck) (composer); Buffalo, N.Y., 2/15/1905
Arlen, Richard (actor); Charlottesville, Va. **(1900–1976)**
Arliss, George (actor); London **(1868–1946)**
Armstrong, Louis ("Satchmo") (musician); New Orleans **(1900–1971)**
Armstrong-Jones, Anthony. *See* Snowden, Earl of
Arnaz, Desi (Desiderio) (actor and producer); Santiago, Cuba, 3/2/1917
Arnaz, Desi, Jr. (actor); Los Angeles, 1953
Arnaz, Lucie (actress); Hollywood, Calif., 1951

Arness, James (James Aurness) (TV actor); Minneapolis, 5/26/1923
Arno, Peter (cartoonist); New York City **(1904–1968)**
Arnold, Benedict (American Revolutionary War General, convicted of treason); Norwich, Conn. **(1741–1801)**
Arnold, Eddy (singer); Henderson, Tenn., 5/15/1918
Arnold, Edward (actor); New York City **(1890–1956)**
Arnold, Matthew (poet and critic); Laleham, England **(1822–1888)**
Arp, Jean (sculptor and painter); Strasbourg (France) **(1887–1966)**
Arquette, Cliff ("Charley Weaver") (actor); Toledo, Ohio **(1905–1974)**
Arrau, Claudio (pianist); Chillán, Chile, 2/6/1903
Arthur, Bea (Bernice Frankel) (actress); New York City, 5/13/1926(?)
Arthur, Jean (Gladys Greene) (actress); New York City, 10/17/1905
Asch, Sholem (novelist); Kutno, Poland **(1880–1957)**
Ashkenazy, Vladimir (concert pianist); Gorki, U.S.S.R., 7/6/1937
Ashley, Elizabeth (actress); Ocala, Fla., 8/30/1939
Asimov, Isaac (author); Petrovichi, Russia, 1/2/1920
Asner, Edward (actor); Kansas City, Mo., 11/15/1929
Astaire, Fred (Frederick Austerlitz) (dancer and actor); Omaha, Neb., 5/10/1899
Astor, John Jacob (financier); Waldorf (Germany) **(1763–1848)**
Astor, Mary (Lucile Langhanke) (actress); Quincy, Ill., 5/3/1906
Atkins, Chet (guitarist); nr. Luttrell, Tenn., 6/20/1924
Atkinson, Brooks (drama critic); Melrose, Mass., 11/28/1894
Attenborough, Richard (actor); Cambridge, England, 8/29/1923
Attila (King of Huns, called "Scourge of God") **(406?–453)**
Attlee, Clement Richard (statesman); London **(1883–1967)**
Auchincloss, Louis (author); Lawrence, N.Y., 9/27/1917
Auden, W(ystan) H(ugh); York, England **(1907–1973)**
Audubon, John James (naturalist and painter); Haiti **(1785–1851)**
Auer, Leopold (violinist and teacher); Veszprém, Hungary **(1845–1930)**
Auer, Mischa (actor); St. Petersburg, Russia **(1905–1967)**
Augustine, Saint (Aurelius Augustinus) (philosopher); Numidia (Algeria) **(354–430)**
Augustus (Gaius Octavius) (Roman emperor); Rome **(63 B.C.–A.D. 14)**
Aumont, Jean-Pierre (actor); Paris, 1/5/1913
Austen, Jane (novelist); Steventon, England **(1775–1817)**
Autry, Gene (singer and actor); Tioga, Tex., 9/29/1907
Avalon, Frankie (singer); Philadelphia, 9/18/1940
Avedon, Richard (photographer); New York City, 5/15/1923
Avery, Milton (painter); Altmar, N.Y. **(1893–1965)**
Axelrod, George (playwright); New York City, 6/9/1922
Ayckbourn Alan (playwright); London, 4/12/1939
Ayres, Lew (actor); Minneapolis, 12/28/1908

B

Bacall, Lauren (Betty Joan Perske) (actress); New York City, 9/16/1924
Bach, Johann Sebastian (composer); Eisenach (Germany) **(1685–1750)**
Bacharach, Burt (songwriter); Kansas City, Mo., 5/12/1929
Backus, Jim (actor); Cleveland, 2/25/1913
Bacon, Francis (painter); Dublin, 1910
Bacon, Francis (philosopher and essayist); London **(1561–1626)**
Bacon, Roger (philosopher and scientist); Ilchester, England **(1214?–1294)**
Baedeker, Karl (travel-guidebook publisher); Essen (Germany) **1801–1859)**
Baez, Joan (folk singer); Staten Island, N.Y., 1/9/1941
Bagnold, Enid (novelist); Rochester, England, 12/27/1889
Bailey, F. Lee (lawyer); Waltham, Mass., 6/10/1933
Bailey, Pearl (singer); Newport News, Va., 3/29/1918
Bainter, Fay (actress); Los Angeles **(1891–1968)**
Baird, Bil (William B.) (puppeteer); Grand Island, Neb., 8/15/1904
Baker, Carroll (actress); Johnstown, Pa., 5/28/1935
Baker, Josephine (singer and dancer); St. Louis **(1906–1975)**
Baker, Kenny (singer and actor); Monrovia, Calif., 9/30/1912
Baker, Russell (columnist); Loudoun County, Va., 8/14/1925
Balanchine, George (choreographer); St. Petersburg, Russia, 1/9/1904
Balboa, Vasco Nuñez de (explorer); Jerez de los Caballeros (Spain) **(1475–1517)**
Baldwin, Faith (novelist); New Rochelle, N.Y. **(1893–1978)**
Baldwin, James (novelist); New York City, 8/2/1924
Balenciaga, Cristóbal (fashion designer); Guetaria, Spain **(1895–1972)**
Ball, Lucille (Dianne Belmont) (actress and producer); Celoran, N.Y., 8/6/1911
Ballard, Kaye (Catherine Gloria Balotta) (actress); Cleveland, 11/20/1926
Balmain, Pierre (fashion designer); St.-Jean-de-Maurienne, France, 5/18/1914
Balsam, Martin (actor); New York City, 11/4/1919
Balzac, Honoré de (novelist); Tours, France **(1799–1850)**
Bancroft, Anne (Annemarie Italiano) (actress); New York City, 9/17/1931
Bancroft, George (actor); Philadelphia **(1882–1956)**
Bankhead, Tallulah (actress); Huntsville, Ala. **(1903–1968)**
Banneker, Benjamin (almanacker and mathematician-astronomer on District of Columbia site survey), Ellicott, Md. **(1731–1806)**
Bara, Theda (Theodosia Goodman) (actress); Cincinnati **(1890–1955)**
Barber, Red (Walter Lanier) (sportscaster); Columbus, Miss., 2/17/1908
Barber, Samuel (composer); West Chester, Pa., 3/9/1910
Bardot, Brigitte (actress); Paris, 1935
Barenboim, Daniel (concert pianist and conductor); Buenos Aires, 11/15/1942
Barnard, Christiaan N. (heart surgeon); Beauford West, South Africa, 1923
Barnum, Phineas Taylor (showman); Bethel, Conn. **(1810–1891)**
Barrie, Sir James Matthew (author); Kirriemuir, Scotland **(1860–1937)**
Barrie, Wendy (actress); Hong Kong **(1913–1978)**
Barry, Gene (Eugene Klass) (actor); New York City, 6/4/1922
Barry, John (naval officer); County Wexford, Ireland **(1745–1803)**
Barrymore, Diana (actress); New York City **(1921–1960)**
Barrymore, Ethel (Ethel Blythe) (actress); Philadelphia **(1879–1959)**
Barrymore, Georgiana Drew (actress); Philadelphia **(1856–1893)**
Barrymore, John (John Blythe) (actor); Philadelphia **(1882–1942)**
Barrymore, John, Jr. (John Drew Barrymore) (actor); Beverly Hills, Calif., 1932
Barrymore, Lionel (Lionel Blythe) (actor); Philadelphia **(1878–1954)**
Barrymore, Maurice (Herbert Blythe) (actor and playwright); Agra, India **(1847–1905)**
Barthelme, Donald (novelist); Philadelphia, 4/7/1931
Barthelmess, Richard (actor); New York City **(1897–1963)**
Bartholomew, Freddie (actor); London, 3/28/1924
Bartok, Béla (composer); Nagyszentmiklos (Romania) **(1881–1945)**
Barton, Clara (founder of American Red Cross); Oxford, Mass. **(1821–1912)**
Baruch, Bernard Mannes (statesman); Camden, S.C. **(1870–1965)**
Baryshnikov, Mikhail Nikolayevich (ballet dancer); Riga, Latvia, 1/27/1948
Basehart, Richard (actor); Zanesville, Ohio, 8/31/1919
Basie, Count (William) (band leader); Red Bank, N.J., 8/21/1904
Bassey, Shirley (singer); Cardiff, Wales, 1/8/1937
Batchelor, Clarence Daniel (political cartoonist); Osage City, Kan., 4/1/1888
Bates, Alan (actor); Allestree, England, 2/17/1934
Baudelaire, Charles Pierre (poet); Paris **(1821–1867)**
Baudouin (King); Palace of Laeken, Belgium, 9/7/1930
Baxter, Anne (actress); Michigan City, Ind., 5/7/1923
Baxter, Warner (actor); Columbus, Ohio **(1891–1951)**
Bean, Orson (Dallas Frederick Burrows) (actor); Burlington, Vt., 7/22/1928
Beardsley, Aubrey Vincent (illustrator); Brighton, England **(1872–1898)**
Beaton, Cecil (photographer and designer); London **(1904–1980)**
Beatty, Warren (actor and producer); Richmond, Va., 3/30/1937
Becket, Thomas à (Archbishop of Canterbury); London **(1118?–1170)**
Beckett, Samuel (playwright); Dublin, 4/13/1906
Beckmann, Max (painter); Leipzig, Germany **(1884–1950)**
Bede, Saint ("The Venerable Bede") (scholar); Monkwearmouth, England **(673–735)**
Beecham, Sir Thomas (conductor); St. Helens, England **(1879–1961)**
Beecher, Henry Ward (clergyman); Litchfield, Conn. **(1813–1887)**
Beerbohm, Sir Max (author); London **(1872–1956)**
Beery, Noah, Jr. (actor); New York City, 8/10/1916
Beery, Wallace (actor); Kansas City, Mo. **(1886–1949)**
Beethoven, Ludwig van (composer); Bonn (Germany) **(1770–1827)**
Begley, Ed (actor); Hartford, Conn. **(1901–1970)**
Belafonte, Harry (singer and actor); New York City, 3/1/1927
Belasco, David (dramatist and producer); San Francisco **(1854–1931)**
Bell, Alexander Graham (inventor); Edinburgh, Scotland **(1847–1922)**
Bellamy, Edward (author); Chicopee Falls, Mass. **(1850–1898)**
Bellamy, Ralph (actor); Chicago, 6/17/1904
Bellini, Giovanni (painter); Venice **(c.1430–1516)**
Bellow, Saul (novelist); Lachine, Quebec, Canada, 7/10/1915
Bellows, George Wesley (painter and lithographer); Columbus, Ohio **(1882–1925)**
Belmondo, Jean-Paul (actor); Neuilly-sur-Seine, France, 4/9/1933
Belushi, John (comedian, actor); Chicago, 1/24/1949
Benchley, Peter Bradford (novelist); New York City, 5/8/1940
Benchley, Robert Charles (humorist); Worcester, Mass. **(1889–1945)**
Bendix, William (actor); New York City **(1906–1964)**
Benes, Eduard (statesman); Kozlany (Czechoslovakia) **(1884–1948)**
Benét, Stephen Vincent (poet and story writer); Bethlehem, Pa. **(1898–1943)**
Benét, William Rose (poet and novelist); Ft. Hamilton, Brooklyn, N.Y. **(1886–1950)**
Ben-Gurion, David (David Green) (statesman); Plónsk (Poland) **(1886–1973)**
Benjamin, Richard (actor); New York City, 5/22/1938
Bennett, Constance (actress); New York City **(1905–1965)**
Bennett, Enoch Arnold (novelist and dramatist); Hanley, England **(1867–1931)**
Bennett, James Gordon (editor); Keith, Scotland **(1795–1872)**
Bennett, Joan (actress); Palisades, N.J., 2/27/1910
Bennett, Robert Russell (composer); Kansas City, Mo., 6/15/1894

Bennett, Tony (Anthony Benedetto) (singer); Astoria, Queens, N.Y., 8/3/1926
Benny, Jack (Benjamin Kubelsky) (comedian); Chicago **(1894–1974)**
Benton, Thomas Hart (painter); Neosho, Mo. **(1889–1975)**
Berg, Gertrude (writer and actress); New York City **(1899–1966)**
Bergen, Candice (actress); Beverly Hills, Calif., 5/9/1946
Bergen, Edgar (ventriloquist); Chicago, **(1903–1978)**
Bergen, Polly (actress and singer); Knoxville, Tenn., 7/14/1930
Bergman, Ingmar (film director); Uppsala, Sweden, 7/14/1918
Bergman, Ingrid (actress); Stockholm, 8/29/1917
Berle, Milton (Milton Berlinger) (comedian); New York City, 7/12/1908
Berlin, Irving (Israel Baline) (songwriter); Temum, Russia, 5/11/1888
Berlioz, Louis Hector (composer); La Côte-Saint-André, France **(1803–1869)**
Berman, Lazar (concert pianist); Leningrad, 1930.
Berman, Shelley (Sheldon) (comedian); Chicago, 2/3/1926
Bernardi, Herschel (actor); New York City, 1923
Bernhardt, Sarah (Rosine Bernard) (actress); Paris **(1844–1923)**
Bernini, Gian Lorenzo (sculptor and painter); Naples (Italy) **(1598–1680)**
Bernstein, Leonard (conductor); Lawrence, Mass., 8/25/1918
Berry, Chuck (Charles Edward Berry) (singer); San Jose, Calif., 1/15/1926
Betjeman, Sir John (Poet Laureate); London, 8/28/1906
Bickford, Charles (actor); Cambridge, Mass. **(1889–1967)**
Bierce, Ambrose Gwinnett (journalist); Meigs County, Ohio **(1842–1914?)**
Bikel, Theodore (actor and folk singer); Vienna, 5/2/1924
Bing, Sir Rudolf (opera manager); Vienna, 1/9/1902
Bingham, George Caleb (painter); Augusta Co., Va. **(1811–1879)**
Bishop, Joey (Joseph Gottlieb) (comedian); New York City, 2/3/1919
Bismarck-Schonhausen, Prince Otto Eduard Leopold von (statesman); Schönhausen (Germany) **(1815–1898)**
Bisset, Jacqueline (actress); Weybridge, England, 9/13/1944
Bixby, Bill (actor); San Francisco 1/22/1934
Bizet, Georges (Alexandre César Léopold Bizet) (composer); Paris **(1838–1875)**
Black, Cilla (singer and actress); Liverpool, England, 5/27/1943
Black, Karen (actress); Park Ridge, Ill., 7/1/1942
Black, Shirley Temple (former actress); Santa Monica, Calif., 4/23/1927
Blackman, Honor (actress); London, 8/22/1929
Blackmer, Sidney (actor); Salisbury, N.C. **(1898–1973)**
Blackstone, Sir William (jurist); London **(1723–1780)**
Blaine, Vivian (actress and singer); Newark, N.J., 11/21/1924
Blair, Janet (actress); Altoona, Pa., 4/23/1921
Blake, Amanda (Beverly Louise Neill) (actress); Buffalo, N.Y., 1931
Blake, Eubie (James Hubert) (pianist); Baltimore, 2/7/1883
Blake, Robert (Michael Gubitosi) (actor); Nutley, N.J., 9/18/1933
Blake, William (poet and artist); London **(1757–1827)**
Blanc, Mel(vin Jerome) (actor and voice specialist); San Francisco, 5/30/1908
Blass, Bill (fashion designer); Fort Wayne, Ind., 6/22/1922
Bloch, Ernest (composer); Geneva **(1880–1959)**
Blondell, Joan (actress); New York City **(1909–1979)**
Bloom, Claire (actress); London, 2/15/1931
Bloomgarden, Kermit (producer); Brooklyn, N.Y. **(1904–1976)**
Blue, Monte (actor); Indianapolis **(1890–1963)**
Blyth, Ann (actress); New York City, 8/16/1928
Boccaccio, Giovanni (author); Paris **(1313–1375)**
Boccioni, Umberto (painter and sculptor); Reggio di Calabria, Italy **(1882–1916)**
Bock, Jerry (composer); New Haven, Conn., 11/23/1928
Bogarde, Dirk (Derek Van den Bogaerde) (film actor and director); London, 3/28/1921
Bogart, Humphrey DeForest (actor); New York City **(1899–1957)**
Bogdanovich, Peter (producer and director); Kingston, N.Y., 7/30/1939
Bohlen, Charles E. (diplomat); Clayton, N.Y. **(1904–1974)**
Bohr, Niels (atomic physicist); Copenhagen **(1885–1962)**
Bolger, Ray (dancer and actor); Dorchester, Mass., 1/10/1904
Bolivar, Simón (South American liberator); Caracas, Venezuela **(1783–1830)**
Bologna, Giovanni da (sculptor); Douai (France) **(1529–1608)**
Bombeck, Erma (author, columnist); Dayton, Ohio 2/21/1927
Bond, Julian (Georgia legislator); Nashville, Tenn., 1/14/1940
Bondi, Beulah (actress); Chicago, 1892
Bonnard, Pierre (painter); Fontenayaux-Roses, France **(1867–1947)**
Bono, Sonny (Salvatore) (singer); Detroit, 2/16/1935
Boone, Daniel (frontiersman); nr. Reading, Pa. **(1734–1820)**
Boone, Pat (Charles) (singer); Jacksonville, Fla., 6/1/1934
Boone, Richard (actor); Los Angeles, 6/18/1917
Booth, Edwin Thomas (actor); Bel Air, Md. **(1833–1893)**
Booth, Evangeline Cory (religious leader); London **(1865–1950)**
Booth, John Wilkes (actor; assassin of Lincoln); Harford County, Md. **(1838–1865)**
Booth, Shirley (Thelma Booth Ford) (actress); New York City, 8/30/1909
Bordoni, Irene (actress); Ajaccio (France) **(1895–1953)**
Borge, Victor (pianist and comedian); Copenhagen, 1/3/1909
Borgia, Cesare (nobleman and soldier); Rome **(1475?–1507)**
Borgia, Lucrezia (Duchess of Ferrara); Rome **(1480–1519)**
Borgnine, Ernest (actor); Hamden, Conn., 1/24/1917
Borromini, Francesco (architect); Bissone (Italy) **(1599–1667)**
Bosch, Hieronymus (Hieronymus van Aeken) (painter); Hertogenbosch (Netherlands) **(c.1450–1516)**
Bosley, Tom (actor); Chicago, 10/1/1927
Boswell, Connee (singer); New Orleans **(1907–1976)**
Boswell, James (diarist and biographer); Edinburgh, Scotland **(1740–1795)**
Botticelli, Sandro (Alessandro di Mariano dei Filipepi) (painter); Florence (Italy) **(1444?–1510)**
Boulez, Pierre (conductor); Montbrison, France, 3/26/1925
Bouton, Jim (James Alan) (sportscaster); Newark, N.J., 3/8/1939
Bow, Clara (actress); Brooklyn, N.Y. **(1905–1965)**
Bowen, Catherine Drinker (biographer); Haverford, Pa. **(1897–1973)**
Bowie, David (David Jones) (actor and musician); London, 1/8/1947(?)
Bowie, James (soldier); Burke County, Ga. **(1799–1836)**
Bowles, Chester (diplomat); Springfield, Mass., 4/5/1901
Bowman, Lee (actor); Cincinnati, 12/28/1914
Boyd, Bill (William) ("Hopalong Cassidy") (actor); Cambridge, Ohio **(1898–1972)**
Boyd, Stephen (actor); Belfast, Northern Ireland **(1928–1977)**
Boyer, Charles (actor); Figeac, France **(1899–1978)**
Bracken, Eddie (actor); Astoria, Queens, N.Y., 2/7/1920
Bradbury, Ray Douglas (science-fiction writer); Waukegan, Ill., 8/22/1920
Bradlee, Benjamin C. (editor); Boston, 8/26/1921
Bradley, Omar N. (5-star general); Clark, Mo., 2/12/1893
Bradley, Thomas (Mayor of Los Angeles); Calvert, Tex., 12/29/1917
Brady, Scott (actor); Brooklyn, N.Y., 9/13/1924
Brahms, Johannes (composer); Hamburg **(1833–1897)**
Braille, Louis (teacher of blind); Coupvray, France **(1809–1862)**
Brailowsky, Alexander (pianist); Kiev, Russia **(1896–1976)**
Bramante, Donato D'Agnolo (architect); Monte Asdrualdo (now Fermignano) (Italy) **(1444–1514)**
Brancusi, Constantin (sculptor); Pestisansi, Romania **(1876–1957)**
Brando, Marlon (actor); Omaha, Neb., 4/3/1924
Brandt, Willy (Herbert Frahm) (ex-Chancellor); Lübeck, Germany, 12/18/1913
Braque, Georges (painter); Argenteuil, France **(1882–1963)**
Brasselle, Keefe (actor); Elyria, Ohio, 2/7/1923
Braun, Wernher von (rocket scientist); Wirsitz, Germany **(1912–1977)**
Brazzi, Rossano (actor); Bologna, Italy, 9/18/1916
Brecht, Bertolt (dramatist and poet); Augsburg (Germany) **(1898–1956)**
Brel, Jacques (singer and composer); Brussels, **(1929–1978)**
Brennan, Walter (actor); Lynn, Mass. **(1894–1974)**
Brent, George (actor); Dublin **(1904–1979)**
Breslin, Jimmy (journalist); Jamaica, Queens, N.Y., 10/17/1930
Breuer, Marcel (architect and designer); Pécs (Hungary), 5/21/1902
Brewer, Teresa (singer); Toledo, Ohio, 5/7/1931
Brewster, Kingman, Jr. (ex-president of Yale); Longmeadow, Mass., 6/17/1919
Brezhnev, Leonid I. (Communist Party Secretary); Dneprodzerzhinsk, Ukraine, 12/19/1906
Brice, Fanny (Fannie Borach) (comedienne); New York City **(1892–1951)**
Bridges, Beau (actor); Los Angeles, 12/9/1941
Bridges, Lloyd (actor); San Leandro, Calif. 1/15/1913
Brinkley, David (TV newscaster); Wilmington, N.C., 7/10/1920
Britt, May (Maybritt Wilkins) (actress); Sweden, 3/22/1936
Britten, Benjamin (composer); Lowestoft, England **(1913–1976)**
Britton, Barbara (actress); Long Beach, Calif. **(1920–1980)**
Bromfield, Louis (novelist); Mansfield, Ohio **(1896–1956)**
Bronson, Charles (Charles Buchinsky) (actor); Ehrenfield, Pa., 11/3/1922(?)
Brontë, Charlotte (novelist); Thornton, England **(1816–1855)**
Brontë, Emily Jane (novelist); Thornton, England **(1818–1848)**
Bronzino, Agnolo (painter); Monticelli (Italy) **(1503–1572)**
Brook, Peter (director); London, 3/21/1925
Brooke, Rupert (poet); Rugby, England **(1887–1915)**
Brooks, Geraldine (Geraldine Stroock) (actress); New York City **(1925–1977)**
Brooks, Gwendolyn (poet); Topeka, Kan., 6/7/1917
Brooks, Mel (Melvin Kaminsky) (writer and film director); Brooklyn, N.Y., 1926(?)
Broun, Matthew Heywood Campbell (journalist); Brooklyn, N.Y. **(1888–1939)**
Brown, Helen Gurley (author); Green Forest, Ark., 2/18/1922
Brown, James (singer); Augusta, Ga., 5/3/1934
Brown, Joe E. (comedian); Holgate, Ohio **(1892–1973)**
Brown, John (abolitionist); Torrington, Conn. **(1800–1859)**
Brown, John Mason (critic); Louisville, Ky. **(1900–1969)**
Brown, Les (band leader); Reinerton, Pa., 1912
Brown, Pamela (actress); London **(1918–1975)**
Brown, Vanessa (Smylla Brind) (actress); Vienna, 3/24/1928
Browne, Jackson (singer and guitarist); Heidelberg, Germany, 10/9/late 1940's

Browning, Elizabeth Barrett (poet); Durham, England **(1806–1861)**
Browning, Robert (poet); London **(1812–1889)**
Brubeck, Dave (musician); Concord, Calif., 12/6/1920
Bruce, Lenny (comedian); Long Island, N.Y. **(1926–1966)**
Brueghel, Pieter (painter); nr. Breda (Netherlands) **(1520?–1569)**
Bruhn, Erik (Belton Evers) (ballet dancer); Copenhagen, 10/3/1928
Brunelleschi, Filippo (architect); Florence (Italy) **(1377–1446)**
Brutus, Marcus Junius (Roman politician); **(85?–42 B.C.)**
Bryan, William Jennings (orator and politician); Salem, Ill. **(1860–1925)**
Bryant, Anita (singer); Barnsdall, Okla., 3/25/1940
Bryant, William Cullen (poet and editor); Cummington, Mass. **(1794–1878)**
Brynner, Yul (Taidje Khan) (actor); Sakhalin Island, Russia, 7/11/1920
Brzezinski, Zbigniew (presidential adviser); Warsaw, 3/28/1928
Buber, Martin (philosopher and theologian); Vienna **(1878–1965)**
Buchanan, Edgar (actor); Humansville, Mo., **(1903–1979)**
Buchholz, Horst (actor); Berlin, 12/4/1933
Buchwald, Art (Arthur) (columnist); Mount Vernon, N.Y., 10/20/1925
Buck, Pearl S(ydenstricker) (author); Hillsboro, W. Va. **(1892–1973)**
Buckley, William F., Jr. (journalist); New York City, 11/24/1925
Buddha. *See* Gautama Buddha
Buffalo Bill (William Frederick Cody) (scout); Scott County, Iowa **(1846–1917)**
Bujold, Genevieve (actress); Montreal, 7/1/1942
Bujones, Fernando (ballet dancer); Miami, Fla., 3/9/1955
Bullins, Ed (playwright); Philadelphia, 7/2/1935
Bumbry, Grace (mezzo-soprano); St. Louis, 1/4/1937
Bunche, Ralph J. (statesman); Detroit **(1904–1971)**
Bundy, McGeorge (Ford Foundation president); Boston, 3/30/1919
Bundy, William Putnam (editor); Washington, D.C., 9/24/1917
Buñuel, Luis (film director); Calanda, Spain, 2/22/1900
Bunyan, John (preacher and author); Elstow, England **(1628–1688)**
Burbank, Luther (horticulturist); Lancaster, Mass. **(1849–1926)**
Burke, Adm. Arleigh A. (ex-Chief of Naval Operations); Boulder, Colo., 10/19/1901
Burke, Billie (comedienne); Washington, D.C. **(1885–1970)**
Burke, Edmund (statesman); Dublin **(1729–1797)**
Burne-Jones, Edward Coley (painter); Birmingham, England **(1833–1898)**
Burnett, Carol (comedienne); San Antonio, 4/26/1936
Burns, George (Nathan Birnbaum) (comedian); New York City, 1/20/1896
Burns, Robert (poet); Alloway, Scotland **(1759–1796)**
Burr, Aaron (political leader); Newark, N.J. **(1756–1836)**
Burr, Raymond (William Stacey Burr) (actor); New Westminster, British Columbia, Canada, 5/21/1917
Burroughs, Edgar Rice (novelist); Chicago **(1875–1950)**
Burrows, Abe (playwright and director); New York City, 12/18/1910
Burstyn, Ellen (Edna Rae Gillooly) (actress); Detroit, 12/7/1932
Burton, Richard (Richard Jenkins) (actor); Pontrhydfen, Wales, 11/10/1925
Busch, Mae (actress); Melbourne **(1891–1946)**
Bush, Vannevar (scientist); Everett, Mass. **(1890–1974)**
Bushman, Francis X. (actor); Baltimore **(1883–1966)**
Butler, Samuel (author); Langar, England **(1835–1902)**
Buttons, Red (Aaron Chwatt) (actor); New York City, 2/5/1919
Buzzi, Ruth (comedienne); Wequetequock, Conn., 7/24/1936
Byrd, Richard Evelyn (polar explorer); Winchester, Va. **(1888–1957)**
Byrne, Jane (Mayor of Chicago); Chicago, 5/24/1934
Byron, George Gordon (6th Baron Byron) (poet); London **(1788–1824)**

C

Caan, James (actor); The Bronx, N.Y., 3/26/1939
Cabot, John (Giovanni Caboto) (navigator); Genoa **(1450–1498)**
Cabot, Sebastian (navigator); Venice **(1476?–1557)**
Cadmus, Paul (painter and etcher); New York City, 12/17/1904
Caesar, Gaius Julius (statesman); Rome **(100?–44 B.C.)**
Caesar, Sid (comedian); Yonkers, N.Y., 9/8/1922
Cagney, James (actor); New York City, 7/17/1899
Cahn, Sammy (songwriter); New York City, 6/18/1913
Caine, Michael (Maurice J. Micklewhite) (actor); London, 3/14/1933
Calder, Alexander (sculptor); Lawnton, Pa. **(1898–1976)**
Caldwell, Erskine (novelist); White Oak, Ga., 12/17/1903
Caldwell, Sarah (opera director and conductor); Maryville, Mo., 1928
Caldwell, Taylor (novelist); Manchester, England, 9/7/1900
Caldwell, Zoe (actress); Hawthorn, Australia, 9/14/1933
Calhern, Louis (Carl Henry Vogt) (actor); Brooklyn, N.Y. **(1895–1956)**
Calhoun, John Caldwell (statesman); nr. Calhoun Mills, S.C. **(1782–1850)**
Calhoun, Rory (actor); Los Angeles, Calif., 1922
Calisher, Hortense (novelist); New York City, 12/20/1911
Callas, Maria (Maria Calogeropoulos) (dramatic soprano); New York City **(1923–1977)**
Calloway, Cab (Cabell) (band leader); Rochester, N.Y., 12/25/1907
Calvet, Corinne (actress); Paris, 4/30/1926
Calvin, John (Jean Chauvin) (religious reformer); Noyon (France) **(1509–1564)**
Cambridge, Godfrey (comedian); New York City **(1933–1976)**
Cameron, Rod (Rod Cox) (actor); Calgary, Alberta, Canada, 12/7/1912
Campbell, Glen (singer); nr. Delight, Ark., 4/22/1938
Camus, Albert (author); Mondovi, Algeria **(1913–1960)**
Caniff, Milton (cartoonist); Hillsboro, Ohio, 2/28/1907
Cannon, Dyan (actress); Tacoma, Wash., 1/4/1937
Canova, Judy (comedienne); Jacksonville, Fla., 11/20/1916
Cantinflas (Mario Moreno) (comedian); Mexico City, 8/12/1911
Cantor, Eddie (Edward Iskowitz) (actor); New York City **(1892–1964)**
Cantrell, Lana (singer); Sydney, Australia, 1944
Capote, Truman (novelist); New Orleans, 9/30/1924
Capp, Al (Alfred Gerald Caplin) (cartoonist); New Haven, Conn. **(1909–1979)**
Capra, Frank (film producer, director); Palermo, Italy, 5/18/1897
Caravaggio, Michelangelo Merisi da (painter); Caravaggio (Italy) **(1573–1610)**
Cardin, Pierre (fashion designer); nr. Venice, 7/7/1922
Cardinale, Claudia (actress); Tunis, Tunisia, 1939
Carey, Harry (actor); New York City **(1878–1947)**
Carey, Macdonald (actor); Sioux City, Iowa, 3/15/1913
Carlisle, Kitty (singer and actress); New Orleans, 9/3/1915
Carlson, Richard (actor); Albert Lea, Minn., **(1912–1977)**
Carlyle, Thomas (essayist and historian); Ecclefechan, Scotland **(1795–1881)**
Carmichael, Hoagy (Hoagland Howard) (songwriter); Bloomington, Ind., 11/22/1899
Carne, Judy (Joyce Botterill) (singer): Northampton, England, 1939
Carnegie, Andrew (industrialist); Dunfermline, Scotland **(1835–1919)**
Carney, Art (actor); Mt. Vernon, N.Y., 11/4/1918
Carnovsky, Morris (actor); St. Louis, 9/5/1897
Caron, Leslie (actress); Paris, 7/1/1931
Carr, Vikki (singer); El Paso, 7/19/1942
Carracci, Annibale (painter); Bologna (Italy) **(1560–1609)**
Carracci, Lodovico (painter); Bologna (Italy) **(1555–1619)**
Carradine, David (actor); Hollywood, Calif., 12/8/1936
Carradine, John (actor); New York City, 2/5/1906
Carrillo, Leo (actor); Los Angeles **(1881–1961)**
Carroll, Diahann (Carol Diahann Johnson) (singer and actress); Bronx, N.Y., 7/17/1935
Carroll, Leo G. (actor); Weedon, England **(1892–1972)**
Carroll, Lewis (Charles Lutwidge Dodgson) (author and mathematician); Daresbury, England **(1832–1898)**
Carroll, Madeleine (actress); West Bromwich, England, 2/26/1909
Carroll, Pat (comedienne); Shreveport, La., 5/5/1927
Carson, Johnny (TV entertainer); Corning, Iowa, 10/23/1925
Carson, Kit (Christopher) (scout); Madison County, Ky. **(1809–1868)**
Carson, Rachel (biologist and author); Springdale, Pa. **(1907–1964)**
Carter, (Bessie) Lillian (President's mother); Richland, Ga., 8/15/1898
Carter, Jack (comedian); New York City, 1923
Cartier-Brisson, Henri (photographer); Chanteloup, France, 8/22/1908
Cartland, Barbara (author); England, 7/9/1901
Caruso, Enrico (Errico) (tenor); Naples, Italy **(1873–1921)**
Carver, George Washington (botanist); Missouri **(1864–1943)**
Cary, Arthur Joyce Lunel (novelist); Londonderry, Ireland **(1888–1957)**
Casals, Pablo (cellist); Vendrell, Spain **(1876–1973)**
Casanova de Seingalt, Giovanni Jacopo (adventurer); Venice **(1725–1798)**
Cash, Johnny (singer); nr. Kingsland, Ark., 2/26/1932
Cass, Peggy (comedienne); Boston, 5/21/1926
Cassatt, Mary (painter); Allegheny, Pa. **(1844–1926)**
Cassavetes, John (actor and director); New York City, 12/9/1929
Cassidy, David (singer); New York City, 4/12/1950
Cassidy, Jack (actor); Richmond Hill, Queens, N.Y. **(1927–1976)**
Cassini, Oleg (Oleg Lolewski-Cassini) (fashion designer); Paris, 4/11/1913
Castagno, Andrea del (painter); San Martino a Corella (Italy) **(c.1421–1457)**
Castellano, Richard (actor); New York City, 9/2/1934
Castle, Irene (Irene Foote) (actress and dancer); New Rochelle, N.Y. **(1893–1969)**
Castle, Vernon Blythe (dancer and aviator); Norwich, England **(1887–1918)**
Castro Ruz, Fidel (Premier); Mayari, Oriente, Cuba, 8/13/1926
Cather, Willa Sibert (novelist); Winchester, Va. **(1876–1947)**
Cato, Marcus Porcius (called Cato the Elder) (statesman); Tusculum (Italy) **(234–149 B.C.)**
Catt, Carrie Chapman Lane (woman suffragist); Ripon, Wis. **(1859–1947)**
Catton, Bruce (historian); Petoskey, Mich., 10/9/1899
Cavallaro, Carmen (band leader); New York City, 1913
Cavett, Dick (Richard) (TV entertainer); Gibbon, Neb., 11/19/1936
Cellini, Benvenuto (goldsmith and sculptor); Florence (Italy) **(1500–1571)**
Cervantes Saavedra, Miguel de (novelist); Alcalá de Henares, Spain **(1547–1616)**
Cézanne, Paul (painter); Aix-en-Provence, France **(1839–1906)**
Chagall, Marc (painter); Vitebsk, Russia, 7/7/1887
Chaliapin, Feodor Ivanovitch (operatic basso); Kazan, Russia **(1873–1938)**

Chamberlain, Arthur Neville (statesman) Edgbaston, England **(1869–1940)**
Chamberlain, Richard (actor); Los Angeles, 3/31/1935(?)
Champion, Gower (choreographer); Geneva, Ill. **(1921–1980)**
Champion, Marge (actress and dancer); Los Angeles, 9/2/1923
Champlain, Samuel de (explorer); nr. Rochefort, France **(1567?–1635)**
Chancellor, John (TV commentator); Chicago, 7/14/1927
Chandler, Raymond (writer); Chicago **(1888–1959)**
Chanel, "Coco" (Gabriel Bonheur) (fashion designer); Issoire, France **(1883–1971)**
Chaney, Lon (actor); Colorado Springs, Colo. **(1883–1930)**
Channing, Carol (actress); Seattle, 1/31/1923
Chaplin, Geraldine (actress); Santa Monica, Calif., 7/31/1944
Chaplin, Sir Charles (actor); London **(1889–1977)**
Chaplin, Sydney (actor); Los Angeles, 3/31/1926
Charisse, Cyd (Tula Finklea) (dancer and actress); Amarillo, Tex., 3/8/1923
Charlemagne (Holy Roman Emperor); birthplace unknown **(742–814)**
Charles, Ray (Ray Charles Robinson) (pianist, singer, and songwriter); Albany Ga., 9/23/1932
Chase, Chevy (comedian); New York City, 1944
Chase, Ilka (author and actress); New York City **(1905–1978)**
Chase, Lucia (ballet company manager); Waterbury, Conn., 3/24/1907
Chatterton, Ruth (actress); New York City **(1893–1961)**
Chaucer, Geoffrey (poet); London **(1340?–1400)**
Chavez, Carlos (composer); nr. Mexico City, **(1899–1978)**
Chávez, Cesar (labor leader); nr. Yuma, Ariz., 3/31/1927
Chayefsky, Paddy (Sidney) (playwright); New York City, 1/29/1923
Checker, Chubby (Ernest Evans) (performer); Philadelphia, 10/3/1941
Cheever, John (novelist); Quincy, Mass., 5/27/1912
Chekhov, Anton Pavlovich (dramatist and short-story writer); Taganrog, Russia **(1860–1904)**
Cher (Cherilyn LaPiere) (singer); El Centro, Calif., 5/20/1946
Chesterton, Gilbert Keith (author); Kensington, England **(1874–1936)**
Chevalier, Maurice (entertainer); Paris **(1888–1972)**
Chiang Ch'ing (political leader); Chucheng, China, 1913(?)
Chiang Kai-shek (Chief of State); Feng-hwa, China **(1887–1975)**
Child, Julia (food expert); Pasadena, Calif., 8/15/1912
Chippendale, Thomas (cabinet-maker); Otley, England **(1718?–1779)**
Chirico, Giorgio de (painter); Vólos, Greece, **(1888–1978)**
Chisholm, Shirley (ex-Representative); Brooklyn, N.Y., 11/30/1924
Chopin, Frédéric François (composer); nr. Warsaw **(1810–1849)**
Chou En-lai. *See* Zhou Enlai
Christian, Linda (Blanca Rosa Welter) (actress); Tampico, Mexico, 11/13/1924
Christie, Agatha (mystery writer); Torquay, England, **(1890–1976)**
Christie, Julie (actress); Chukua, India, 4/14/1941
Christopher, Jordon (actor and musician); Youngstown, Ohio, 1941
Christy, June (singer); Springfield, Ill., 1925
Churchill, Sarah (actress); London, 10/7/1914
Churchill, Sir Winston Leonard Spencer (statesman); Blenheim Palace, Oxfordshire, England **(1874–1965)**
Cicero, Marcus Tullius (orator and statesman); Arpinum (Italy) **(106–43 B.C.)**
Cilento, Diane (actress); Queensland, Australia, 10/5/1933
Cimabue, Giovanni (painter); Florence (Italy) **(c.1240–c.1302)**
Clair, René (René Chomette (film director); Paris, 11/11/1898
Claire, Ina (Ina Fagan) (actress); Washington, D.C., 10/15/1895
Clapton, Eric (singer and guitarist); Ripley, England, 3/30/1945
Clark, Dane (Barney Zanville) (actor); New York City, 2/18/1915
Clark, Dick (TV personality); Mt. Vernon, N.Y., 11/30/1929
Clark, Mark W. (general); Madison Barracks, N.Y., 5/1/1896
Clark, Petula (singer); Epsom, England, 11/15/1934
Clark, Roy (country music artist); Meherrin, Va., 4/15/1933
Clark, William (explorer); Caroline County, Va. **(1770–1838)**
Claude Lorrain (Claude Gellée) (painter); Champagne, France **(1600–1682)**
Clay, Henry (statesman); Hanover County, Va. **(1777–1852)**
Clay, Lucius D. (banker, ex-general); Marietta, Ga. **(1897–1978)**
Clayburgh, Jill (actress); New York City, 4/30/1944
Clemenceau, Georges (statesman); Mouilleron-en-Pareds, Vendée, France **(1841–1929)**
Clemens, Samuel L. *See* Mark Twain
Cleopatra (Queen of Egypt); Alexandria, Egypt **(69–30 B.C.)**
Cliburn, Van (Harvey Lavan Cliburn, Jr.) (concert pianist); Shreveport, La., 7/12/1934
Clifford, Clark M. (ex-Secretary of Defense); Ft. Scott, Kan., 12/25/1906
Clift, Montgomery (actor); Omaha, Neb. **(1920–1966)**
Clooney, Rosemary (singer); Maysville, Ky., 5/23/1928
Clurman, Harold (stage producer); New York City **(1901–1980)**
Cobb, Irvin Shrewsbury (humorist); Paducah, Ky. **(1876–1944)**
Cobb, Lee J. (Leo Jacob) (actor); New York City **(1911–1976)**
Coburn, Charles Douville (actor); Savannah, Ga. **(1877–1961)**
Coburn, James (actor): Laurel, Neb., 8/31/1928
Coca, Imogene (comedienne); Philadelphia, 1914(?)
Cocker, Joe (John Robert Cocker) (singer); Sheffield, England 5/20/1944
Coco, James (actor); New York City, 3/21/1929
Cocteau, Jean (author); Maison-Lafitte, France **(1891–1963)**
Cody, W. F. *See* Buffalo Bill
Cohan, George Michael (actor and dramatist); Providence, R.I. **(1878–1942)**
Cohen, Leonard (singer and songwriter); Montreal, 1935
Colbert, Claudette (Lily Chauchoin) (actress); Paris, 9/13/1905
Colby, William E. (ex-Director of CIA); St. Paul, 1/4/1920
Cole, Nat "King" (singer); Montgomery, Ala. **(1919–1965)**
Cole, Natalie (singer); Los Angeles, 2/6/1950
Cole, Thomas (painter); Lancashire, England **(1801–1848)**
Coleridge, Samuel Taylor (poet); Ottery St. Mary, England **(1772–1834)**
Colette (Sidonie-Gabrielle Colette) (novelist); St.-Sauveur, France **c.1873–1954)**
Collingwood, Charles (TV commentator); Three Rivers, Mich., 6/4/1917
Collins, Dorothy (Marjorie Chandler) (singer); Windsor, Ontario, Canada, 11/18/1926
Collins, Joan (actress); London, 1933
Collins, Judy (singer); Seattle, 5/1/1939
Colman, Ronald (actor); Richmond, England **(1891–1958)**
Colonna, Jerry (comedian); Boston, 1905
Columbus, Christopher (Cristoforo Colombo) (discoverer of America); Genoa (Italy) **(1451–1506)**
Comden, Betty (writer); New York City, 5/3/1919
Commager, Henry Steele (historian); Pittsburgh, 10/25/1902
Como, Perry (Pierino) (singer); Canonsburg, Pa., 5/18/1913
Compton, Karl Taylor (physicist); Wooster, Ohio **(1887–1954)**
Conant, James B. (educator and statesman); Dorchester, Mass. **(1893–1978)**
Condon, Eddie (jazz musician); Goodland, Ind. **(1905–1973)**
Confucius (K'ung Fu-tzu) (philosopher); Shantung province, China **(c.551–479 B.C.)**
Congreve, William (dramatist); nr. Leeds, England **(1670–1729)**
Connelly, Marc (playwright); McKeesport, Pa., 12/13/1890
Connery, Sean (actor); Edinburgh, Scotland, 8/25/1930
Conniff, Ray (band leader); Attleboro, Mass., 1916
Connors, Chuck (actor); Brooklyn, N.Y., 4/10/1921
Connors, Mike (Krekor Ohanian) (actor); Fresno, Calif., 8/15/1925
Conrad, Joseph (Teodor Jozef Konrad Korzeniowski) (novelist); Berdichev, Ukraine **(1857–1924)**
Conrad, Robert (actor); Chicago, 1935
Conrad, William (actor); Louisville, Ky., 9/27/1920
Conried, Hans (Frank Foster) (actor); Baltimore, 1917
Constable, John (painter); East Bergholt, Suffolk, England **(1776–1837)**
Constantine II (ex-king); Athens, 6/2/1940
Conte, Richard (actor); New York City **(1916–1975)**
Converse, Frank (actor); St. Louis, 1938
Conway, Tim (actor); Chagrin Falls, Ohio, 1933
Coogan, Jackie (actor); Los Angeles, 10/26/1914
Cooke, Alistair (Alfred Alistair); (TV narrator and journalist); Manchester, England, 11/20/1908
Cooley, Denton A(rthur) (heart surgeon); Houston, Tex., 8/22/1920
Coolidge, Rita (singer); Nashville, Tenn., 1944
Cooper, Alice (Vincent Furnier) (rock musician); Detroit, 2/4/1948
Cooper, Gary (Frank James Cooper) (actor); Helena, Mont. **(1901–1961)**
Cooper, Jackie (actor and director); Los Angeles, 9/15/1922
Cooper, James Fenimore (novelist); Burlington, N.J. **(1789–1851)**
Cooper, Peter (industrialist and philanthropist); New York City **(1791–1883)**
Copernicus, Nicolaus (Mikolaj Kopernik) (astronomer); Thorn, Poland **(1473–1543)**
Copland, Aaron (composer); Brooklyn, N.Y., 11/14/1900
Copley, John Singleton (painter); Boston, Mass. **(1738–1815)**
Coppola, Francis Ford (film director); Detroit, 4/7/1939
Corelli, Franco (operatic tenor); Ancona, Italy, 4/8/1923
Corneille, Pierre (dramatist); Rouen, France **(1606–1684)**
Cornell, Katharine (actress); Berlin **(1893–1974)**
Corot, Jean Baptiste Camille (painter); Paris **(1796–1875)**
Correggio, Antonio Allegri da (painter); Correggio (Italy) **(1494–1534)**
Corsaro, Frank (opera director); New York harbor, 12/22/1924
Cortés (or Cortez), Hernando (explorer); Medellín, Spain **(1485–1547)**
Cosby, Bill (actor); Philadelphia, 7/12/1937
Cosell, Howard (Howard Cohen) (sportscaster); Winston-Salem, N.C., 3/25/1920
Costa-Gavras, Henri (Kostantinos Gavras) (film director); Athens, 1933
Costello, Lou (comedian); Paterson, N.J. **(1908–1959)**
Cotten, Joseph (actor); Petersburg, Va., 5/15/1905
Courbet, Gustave (painter); Ornans, France **(1819–1877)**
Courrèges, André (fashion designer); Pau, France, 3/9/1923
Courtenay, Tom (actor); Hull, England, 2/25/1937
Cousins, Norman (publisher); Union Hill, N.J., 6/24/1915
Cousteau, Jacques-Yves (marine explorer); St. André-de-Cubzac, France, 6/11/1910
Coward, Sir Noel (playwright and actor); Teddington, England **(1899–1973)**
Cowles, Gardner (newspaper publisher); Algona, Iowa, 1/31/1903

Cowper, William (poet); Great Berkhamstead, England **(1731–1800)**
Cozzens, James Gould (novelist); Chicago, 8/19/1903
Crabbe, Buster (Clarence) (actor); Oakland, Calif., 2/7/1908
Crain, Jeanne (actress); Barstow, Calif., 5/25/1925
Cranach, Lucas, the elder (painter); Kronach (Germany) **(1472–1553)**
Crane, Hart (poet); Garrettsville, Ohio **(1899–1922)**
Crane, Stephen (novelist and poet); Newark, N.J. **(1871–1900)**
Crawford, Broderick (actor); Philadelphia, 12/9/1911
Crawford, Cheryl (stage producer); Akron, Ohio, 9/24/1902
Crawford, Joan (Lucille LeSueur) (actress and business executive); San Antonio **(1908–1977)**
Crenna, Richard (actor); Los Angeles, 11/30/1927
Crespin, Régine (operatic soprano); Marseilles, France, 2/23/1929
Crichton, (John) Michael (novelist); Chicago, 10/23/1942
Crisp, Donald (actor); London **(1880–1974)**
Croce, Benedetto (philosopher); Pescasseroli, Aquila, Italy **(1866–1952)**
Croce, Jim (singer); Philadelphia **(1942–1973)**
Crockett, Davy (David) (frontiersman); Greene County, Tenn. **(1786–1836)**
Cromwell, Oliver (statesman); Huntingdon, England **(1599–1658)**
Cronin, A. J. (Archibald J. Cronin) (novelist); Cardross, Scotland, 7/19/1896
Cronkite, Walter (TV newscaster); St. Joseph, Mo., 11/4/1916
Cronyn, Hume (actor); London, Ontario, Canada, 7/18/1911
Crosby, Bing (Harry Lillis) (singer, actor); Tacoma, Wash. **(1904–1977)**
Crosby, Bob (musician); Spokane, Wash., 8/23/1913
Crosby, David (singer); Los Angeles, 8/14/1941
Cross, Milton (opera commentator); New York City **(1897–1975)**
Crouse, Russel (playwright); Findlay, Ohio **(1893–1966)**
Cugat, Xavier (band leader); Barcelona, Spain, 1/1/1900
Cukor, George (film director); New York City, 7/7/1899
Cullen, Bill (William Lawrence Cullen) (radio and TV entertainer); Pittsburgh, 2/18/1920
Culp, Robert (actor); Berkeley, Calif., 8/16/1931
Cummings, E. E. (Edward Estlin Cummings) (poet); Cambridge, Mass. **(1894–1962)**
Cummings, Robert (actor); Joplin, Mo., 6/9/1910
Curie, Marie (Marja Sklodowska) (physical chemist); Warsaw **(1867–1934)**
Curtin, Phyllis (soprano); Clarksburg, W.Va., 12/3/1927
Curtis, Tony (Bernard Schwartz) (actor); Bronx, N.Y., 6/3/1925
Curzon, Clifford (concert pianist); London, 5/18/1907
Custer, George Armstrong (army officer); New Rumley, Ohio **(1839–1876)**

D

Dache, Lilly (fashion designer); Bègles, France
Dahl, Arlene (actress); Minneapolis, 8/11/1928
Dailey, Dan (actor and dancer); New York City, **(1917–1978)**
Daley, Richard J. (Mayor of Chicago); Chicago **(1902–1976)**
Dali, Salvador (painter); Figueras, Spain, 5/11/1904
Daly, James (actor); Wisconsin Rapids, Wis., 10/23/1918
Daly, John (radio and TV news analyst); Johannesburg, South Africa **(1918–1978)**
d'Amboise, Jacques (ballet dancer); Dedham, Mass., 7/28/1934
Damone, Vic (Vito Farinola) (singer); Brooklyn, N.Y., 6/12/1928
Damrosch, Walter Johannes (orchestra conductor); Breslau (Poland) **(1862–1950)**
Dana, Charles Anderson (editor); Hinsdale, N.H. **(1819–1897)**
Dandridge, Dorothy (actress); Cleveland **(1923–1965)**
Dangerfield, Rodney (comedian); Babylon, L.I., N.Y., 1921
Daniels, Bebe (Virginia Daniels) (actress); Dallas **(1901–1971)**
Danilova, Alexandra (ballerina); Peterhof, Russia, 1/20/1904
D'Annunzio, Gabriele (soldier and author); Francaville al Mare, Pescara, Italy **(1863–1938)**
Dante (or **Durante**) **Alighieri** (poet); Florence (Italy) **(1265–1321)**
Danton, Georges Jacques (French Revolutionary leader); Arcis-sur-Aube, France **(1759–1794)**
Darnell, Linda (actress); Dallas **(1921–1965)**
Darren, James (actor); Philadelphia, 6/8/1936
Darrieux, Danielle (actress); Bordeaux, France, 5/1/1917
Darrow, Clarence Seward (lawyer); Kinsman, Ohio **(1857–1938)**
Darwin, Charles Robert (naturalist); Shrewsbury, England **(1809–1882)**
daSilva, Howard (actor); Cleveland, 5/4/1909
Dassin, Jules (film director); Middletown, Conn., 12/18/1911
Daumier, Honoré (caricaturist); Marseilles, France **(1808–1879)**
Dauphin, Claude (actor); Corbeil, France, 8/19/1903
David, Jacques-Louis (painter); Paris **(1748–1825)**
David (King of Israel and Judah) **(died c. 973 B.C.)**
Davidson, John (singer and actor); Pittsburgh, 12/13/1941
Davies, Marion (Marion Douras) (actress); New York City **(1898?–1961)**
da Vinci, Leonardo (painter and scientist); Vinci, Tuscany (Italy) **(1452–1519)**
Davis, Bette (actress); Lowell, Mass., 4/5/1908
Davis, Elmer Holmes (radio commentator); Aurora, Ind. **(1890–1958)**
Davis, Jefferson (President of the Confederacy); Christian (now Todd) County, Ky. **(1808–1889)**
Davis, Mac (singer); Lubbock, Tex.
Davis, Miles (jazz trumpeter); Alton, Ill., 5/25/1926
Davis, Ossie (actor and writer); Cogdell, Ga., 12/18/1917
Davis, Sammy, Jr. (actor and singer); New York City, 12/8/1925
Davis, Skeeter (Mary Francis Penick) (singer); Dry Ridge, Ky., 12/30/1931
Davis, Stuart (painter); Philadelphia **(1894–1964)**
Day, Dennis (singer); New York City, 5/21/1917
Day, Doris (Doris von Kappelhoff) (singer and actress); Cincinnati, 4/3/1924
Day, Laraine (La Raine Johnson) (actress); Roosevelt, Utah, 10/13/1920
Dayan, Moshe (ex-Defense Minister of Israel); Dagania, Palestine (Jordan), 5/20/1915
Dean, James (actor); Marion, Ind. **(1931–1955)**
Dean, Jimmy (singer); Seth Ward, nr. Plainview, Tex., 8/10/1928
De Bakey, Michael E. (heart surgeon); Lake Charles, La., 9/7/1908
de Beauvoir, Simone (novelist and philosopher); Paris, 1/9/1908
Debs, Eugene Victor (Socialist leader); Terre Haute, Ind. **(1855–1926)**
Debussy, Claude Achille (composer); St. Germain-en-Laye, France **(1862–1918)**
De Carlo, Yvonne (Peggy Yvonne Middleton) (actress); Vancouver, B.C., Canada, 9/1/1924
de Chirico, Giorgio (painter); Volos, Greece, **(1888–1978)**
Dee, Ruby (Ruby Ann Wallace) (actress); Cleveland, 10/27/1924(?)
Dee, Sandra (Alexandra Zuck) (actress); Bayonne, N.J., 4/23/1942
Defoe, Daniel (novelist); London **(1659?–1731)**
Degas, Hilaire Germain Edgar (painter); Paris **(1834–1917)**
De Gaulle, Charles André Joseph Marie (soldier and statesman); Lille, France **(1890–1970)**
DeHaven, Gloria (actress); Los Angeles, 7/23/1925
De Havilland, Olivia (actress); Tokyo, 7/1/1916
Dekker, Albert (actor); Brooklyn, N.Y. **(1904–1968)**
De Kooning, Willem (painter); Rotterdam, 4/24/1904
Delacroix, Eugène (painter); Charenton-St. Maurice, France **(1798–1863)**
de la Renta, Oscar (fashion designer); Santo Domingo, Dominican Republic, 7/22/1932
Delaunay, Robert (painter); Paris **(1885–1941)**
De Laurentiis, Dino (film producer); Torre Annunziata, Bay of Naples, Italy, 8/8/1919
Delon, Alain (actor); Sceaux, France, 11/8/1935
Del Rio, Dolores (actress); Durango, Mexico, 8/3/1905
DeLuise, Dom (comedian); Brooklyn, N.Y., 1933
Demarest, William (actor); St. Paul, 2/27/1892
de Mille, Agnes (choreographer); New York City
De Mille, Cecil Blount (film director); Ashfield, Mass. **(1881–1959)**
Demosthenes (orator); Athens **(385?–322 B.C.)**
Deneuve, Catherine (actress); Paris, 10/22/1943
De Niro, Robert (actor); New York City, 8/17/1943
Dennis, Sandy (actress); Hastings, Neb., 4/27/1937
Denver, John (Henry John Deutschendorf, Jr.) (singer); Roswell, N.M., 12/31/1943
Derain, André (painter); Chatou, Seine-et-Oise, France **(1880–1954)**
Dern, Bruce (actor); Chicago, 6/4/1936
Descartes, René (philosopher and mathematician); La Haye, France **(1596–1650)**
De Seversky, Alexander P. (aviator); Tiflis, Russia **(1894–1974)**
De Sica, Vittorio (film director); Sora, Italy **(1901–1974)**
Desmond, Johnny (composer); Detroit, 11/14/1921
Desmond, William (actor); Dublin **(1878–1949)**
De Soto, Hernando (explorer); Barcarrota, Spain **(1500?–1542)**
De Valera, Eamon (ex-President of Ireland); New York City **(1882–1975)**
Devine, Andy (actor); Flagstaff, Ariz. **(1905–1977)**
De Vries, Peter (novelist); Chicago, 2/27/1910
Dewey, George (admiral); Montpelier, Vt. **(1837–1917)**
Dewey, John (philosopher and educator); Burlington, Vt. **(1859–1952)**
Dewey, Thomas E. (politician); Owosso, Mich. **(1902–1971)**
Dewhurst, Colleen (actress); Montreal, 1926(?)
Diamond, Neil (singer); Brooklyn, N.Y., 1/24/1941
Dickens, Charles John Huffam (novelist); Portsea, England **(1812–1870)**
Dickey, James (poet); Atlanta, 2/2/1923
Dickinson, Angie (Angeline Brown) (actress); Kulm, N.D., 9/30/1931
Dickinson, Emily Elizabeth (poet); Amherst, Mass. **(1830–1886)**
Diddley, Bo (Elias McDaniel) (guitarist); McComb, Miss., 12/30/1928
Diefenbaker, John G. (ex-Prime Minister); Grey County, Ontario, Canada **(1895–1979)**
Dietrich, Marlene (Maria Magdalena von Losch) (actress); Berlin, 12/27/1901
Diggs, Dudley (actor); Dublin **(1879–1947)**
Diller, Phyllis (Phyllis Driver) (comedienne); Lima, Ohio, 7/17/1917
Dillinger, John (American bank robber); prob. Indianapolis **(1902–1934)**
Dillman, Bradford (actor); San Francisco, 4/14/1930
Dine, Jim (painter); Cincinnati, 6/16/1935
Diogenes (philosopher); Sinope (Turkey) **(412?–323 B.C.)**
Dion (Dion DiMucci) (singer); Bronx, N.Y., 7/18/1939
Dior, Christian (fashion designer); Granville, France **(1905–1957)**

Disney, Walt(er) Elias (film animator and producer); Chicago **(1901–1966)**
Disraeli, Benjamin (Earl of Beaconsfield) (statesman); London **(1804–1881)**
Dix, Dorothea (civil rights reformer); Hampden, Me. **(1802–1887)**
Dix, Richard (Ernest Carlton Brimmer) (actor); St. Paul **(1894–1949)**
Dixon, Jeane (Jeane Pinckert) (seer); Medford, Wis., 1918
Doctorow, E.L. (Edgar Laurence) (novelist); New York City, 1/6/1931
Dodgson, C. L. *See* Carroll, Lewis.
Dolin, Anton (dancer); Slinfold, England, 7/27/1904
Domingo, Placido (tenor); Madrid, 1/21/1941
Domino, Fats (Antoine) (musician); New Orleans, 2/26/1928
Donahue, Phil (television personality); Cleveland, 12/21/1935
Donahue, Troy (Merle Johnson) (actor); New York City, 1/27/1938
Donat, Robert (actor); Withington, England **(1905–1958)**
Donatello (Donato Niccolò di Betto Bardi) (sculptor); Florence (Italy) **(c.1386–1466)**
Donne, John (poet); London **(1573–1631)**
Donovan (Donovan Leitch) (singer and songwriter); Glasgow, Scotland, 2/10/1946
Doolittle, James H. (ex-Air Force general); Alameda, Calif., 12/14/1896
Dorati, Antal (orchestra conductor); Budapest, 4/9/1906
Dors, Diana (Diana Fluck) (actress); Swondon, England, 10/23/1931
Dos Passos, John (author); Chicago **(1896–1970)**
Dostoevski, Fyodor Mikhailovich (novelist); Moscow **(1821–1881)**
Douglas, Helen Gahagan (ex-Representative); Boonton, N.J. **(1900–1980)**
Douglas, Kirk (Issur Danielovitch) (actor); Amsterdam, N.Y., 12/9/1916
Douglas, Melvyn (Melvyn Hesselberg) (actor); Macon, Ga., 4/5/1901
Douglas, Mike (Michael D. Dowd, Jr.) (TV personality); Chicago, 8/11/1920
Douglas, Paul (actor); Philadelphia **(1907–1959)**
Douglas, Stephen Arnold (politician); Brandon, Vt. **(1813–1861)**
Dowling, Eddie (Edward Goucher) (actor and stage producer); Woonsocket, R.I., **(1894–1976)**
Downs, Hugh (TV entertainer); Akron, Ohio, 2/14/1921
Doyle, Sir Arthur Conan (novelist and spiritualist); Edinburgh, Scotland **(1859–1930)**
Drake, Alfred (singer and actor); New York City, 10/7/1914
Drake, Sir Francis (navigator); Tavistock, England **(1545–1596)**
Dreiser, Theodore (writer); Terre Haute, Ind. **(1871–1945)**
Dressler, Marie (Leila Koeber) (actress); Cobourg, Ontario, Canada **(1869–1934)**
Dreyfus, Alfred (French army officer); Mulhouse (France) **(1859–1935)**
Dreyfuss, Richard (actor); Brooklyn, N.Y., 10/29/1947
Drury, Allen (novelist); Houston, 9/2/1918
Dryden, John (poet); Northamptonshire, England **(1631–1700)**
Dubcek, Alexander (ex-President of Czechoslovakia); Uhroved (Czechoslovakia), 11/27/1921
Dubinsky, David (David Dobnievski) (labor leader); Brest-Litovsk (U.S.S.R.), 2/22/1892
Duchamp, Marcel (painter); Blainville, France **(1887–1968)**
Duchin, Peter (pianist and band leader); New York City, 7/28/1937
Duff, Howard (actor); Bremerton, Wash., 1917
Dufy, Raoul (painter); Le Havre, France **(1877–1953)**
Duke, James B. (industrialist); nr. Durham, N.C. **(1856–1925)**
Duke, Patty (Anna Marie Duke) (actress); New York City, 12/14/1946
Dullea, Keir (actor); Cleveland, 5/30/1936(?)
Dulles, Allen Welsh (ex-Director of CIA); Watertown, N.Y. **(1893-1969)**
Dulles, John Foster (statesman); Washington, D.C. **(1888–1959)**
Dumas, Alexandre (called Dumas fils) (novelist); Paris **(1824–1895)**
Dumas, Alexandre (called Dumas père) (novelist); Villers-Cotterets, France **(1802–1870)**
Du Maurier, Daphne (novelist); London, 5/13/1907
Du Maurier, George Louis Palmella Busson (novelist); Paris **(1834–1896)**
Dumont, Margaret (actress); **(1889–1965)**
Dunaway, Faye (actress); Bascom, Fla., 1/14/1941
Duncan, Isadora (dancer); San Francisco **(1878–1927)**
Duncan, Sandy (actress); Henderson, Tex., 2/20/1946
Dunn, James (actor); Santa Monica, Calif. **(1905–1967)**
Dunne, Irene (actress); Louisville, Ky., 12/20/1904
Dunnock, Mildred (actress); Baltimore, 1/25/(?)
Du Pont, Pierre S. (economist); Paris **(1739–1817)**
Durante, Jimmy (comedian); New York City **(1893–1980)**
Durbin, Deanna (Edna Mae) (actress); Winnipeg, Canada, 12/4/1922
Durer, Albrecht (painter and engraver); Nürnberg (Germany) **(1471–1528)**
Durrell, Lawrence George (novelist); Julundur, India, 2/27/1912
Duse, Eleonora (actress); Chioggia, Italy **(1859–1924)**
Duvalier, Jean-Claude (President; son of "Papa Doc"); Port-au-Prince, Haiti, 7/3/1951
Duvall, Robert (actor); San Diego, Calif., 1931.
Dvorak, Antonín (composer); Nelahozeves (Czechoslovakia) **(1841–1904)**
Dylan, Bob (Robert Zimmerman) (folk singer and composer); Duluth, Minn., 5/24/1941

E

Eagels, Jeanne (actress); Kansas City, Mo. **(1894–1929)**
Eakins, Thomas (painter and sculptor); Philadelphia, **(1844–1916)**
Earhart, Amelia (aviator); Atchison, Kan. **(1898–1937)**
Eastman, George (inventor); Waterville, N.Y. **(1854–1932)**
Eastwood, Clint (actor); San Francisco, 5/31/1931(?)
Ebsen, Buddy (Christian Ebsen, Jr.) (actor); Belleville, Ill., 4/2/1908
Eckstine, Billy (singer); Pittsburgh, 7/8/1914
Eddy, Duane (band leader); Corning, N.Y., 4/26/1938
Eddy, Mary Baker (founder of Christian Science Church); Bow, N.H. **(1821–1910)**
Eddy, Nelson (baritone and actor); Providence, R.I. **(1901–1967)**
Eden, Sir Anthony (Earl of Avon) (ex-Prime Minister); Durham, England **(1897–1977)**
Eden, Barbara (Barbara Huffman) (actress); Tucson, Ariz., 1934
Edison, Thomas Alva (inventor); Milan, Ohio **(1847–1931)**
Edwards, Ralph (TV and radio producer); Merino, Colo., 1913
Edwards, Vincent (actor); Brooklyn, N.Y., 7/7/1928
Egan, Richard (actor); San Francisco, 7/29/1923
Eggar, Samantha (actress); London, 5/3/1939
Eglevsky, André (ballet dancer); Moscow **(1917–1977)**
Ehrlich, Paul (bacteriologist); Strzelin (Poland) **(1854–1915)**
Einstein, Albert (physicist); Ulm, Germany **(1879–1955)**
Eisenhower, Milton S. (educator); Abilene, Kan., 9/15/1899
Eisenstaedt, Alfred (photographer and photojournalist); Dirschau (Poland), 12/6/1898
Ekberg, Anita (actress); Malmö, Sweden, 9/29/1931
Eldridge, Florence (Florence McKechnie) (actress); Brooklyn, N.Y., 9/5/1901
Elgar, Sir Edward (composer); Worcester, England **(1857–1934)**
Elgart, Larry (band leader); New London, Conn., 3/20/1922
El Greco (Domenicos Theotocopoulos) (painter); Candia (Greece) **(c.1541–1614)**
Eliot, George (Mary Ann Evans) (novelist); Chilvers Coton, England **(1819–1880)**
Eliot, Thomas Stearns (poet); St. Louis **(1888–1965)**
Ellington, Duke (Edward Kennedy) (jazz musician); Washington, D.C. **(1899–1974)**
Elliot, "Mama" Cass (Ellen Naomi Cohen) (singer); Baltimore **(1941–1974)**
Elman, Mischa (violinist); Stalnoye, Ukraine **(1891–1967)**
Emerson, Ralph Waldo (philosopher and poet); Boston **(1803–1882)**
Enesco, Georges (composer); Dorohoi, Romania **(1881–1955)**
Engels, Friedrich (Socialist writer); Barmen (Germany) **(1820–1895)**
Entremont, Philippe (concert pianist); Rheims, France, 6/7/1934
Epicurus (philosopher); Samos (Greece) **(341–270 B.C.)**
Epstein, Sir Jacob (sculptor); New York City **(1880–1959)**
Erasmus, Desiderius (Gerhard Gerhards) (scholar); Rotterdam **(1466?–1536)**
Erhard, Ludwig (ex-Chancellor); Furth, Germany **(1897–1977)**
Erickson, Leif (actor); Alameda, Calif., 10/27/1911
Ericson, Leif (navigator); **(c. 10th century A.D.)**
Erikson, Erik H. (psychoanalyst); Frankfurt, Germany, 6/15/1902
Ernst, Max (painter); Bruhl, Germany **(1891–1976)**
Euclid (mathematician); Megara (Greece) **(c. 300 B.C.)**
Euripides (dramatist); Salamis (Greece) **(c.484–407 B.C.)**
Evans, Dale (Frances Butts) (actress and singer); Uvalde, Tex., 10/31/1912
Evans, Dame Edith (actress); London **(1888–1976)**
Evans, Maurice (actor); Dorchester, England, 6/3/1901
Everett, Chad (actor); South Bend, Ind., 1937
Evers, Charles (civil rights leader); Decatur, Miss., 9/14/1923(?)
Evers, Medgar (civil rights leader); Decatur, Miss. **(1925–1963)**
Ewell, Tom (Yewell Tompkins) (actor); Owensboro, Ky., 4/29/1909

F

Fabian (Fabian Anthony Forte) (singer); Philadelphia, 2/6/1943
Fabray, Nanette (Nanette Fabares) (actress); San Diego, Calif., 10/27/1922
Fadiman, Clifton (literary critic); Brooklyn, N.Y., 5/15/1904
Fairbanks, Douglas (Julius Ullman) (actor); Denver **(1883–1939)**
Fairbanks, Douglas, Jr. (actor); New York City, 12/9/1909
Faith, Percy (conductor); Toronto **(1908–1976)**
Falk, Peter (actor); New York City, 9/16/1927
Falla, Manuel de (composer); Cadiz, Spain **(1876–1946)**
Faraday, Michael (physicist); Newington, England **(1791–1867)**
Farber, Barry (radio broadcaster); Baltimore, Md., 1930
Farentino, James (actor); Brooklyn, N.Y., 2/24/1938
Farmer, James (civil rights leader); Marshall, Tex., 1/12/1920
Farnum, William (actor); Boston **(1876–1953)**

Farrell, Charles (actor); Onset Bay, Mass., 1901
Farrell, Eileen (soprano); Willimantic, Conn., 2/13/1920
Farrell, Glenda (actress); Enid, Okla. **(1904–1971)**
Farrell, James T. (novelist); Chicago **(1904–1979)**
Farrell, Suzanne (ballerina); Cincinnati, 8/16/1945
Farrow, Mia (actress); Los Angeles, 2/9/1946
Fasanella, Ralph (painter); New York City, 9/2/1914
Fassbinder, Rainer Werner (film and stage director); Bad Worishofen, West Germany, 5/31/1946
Fast, Howard (novelist); New York City, 11/11/1914
Faulkner, William (novelist); New Albany, Miss. **(1897–1962)**
Fawcett-Majors, Farrah (actress); Corpus Christi, Tex., 2/2/1947(?)
Faye, Alice (Ann Leppert) (actress); New York City, 5/5/1915
Feiffer, Jules (cartoonist); New York City, 1/26/1929
Feininger, Lyonel (painter); New York City **(1871–1956)**
Feldon, Barbara (actress); Pittsburgh, 3/12/1941
Feliciano, José (singer); Larez, Puerto Rico, 9/10/1945
Felker, Clay S. (editor and publisher); St. Louis, 10/2/1925(?)
Fellini, Federico (film director); Rimini, Italy, 1/20/1920
Fender, Freddie (Baldemar Huerta) (singer); San Benito, Tex., 1937
Ferber, Edna (novelist); Kalamazoo, Mich. **(1885–1968)**
Ferguson, Maynard (jazz trumpeter); Verdun, Quebec, Canada, 5/4/1928
Fermi, Enrico (atomic physicist); Rome **(1901–1954)**
Fernandel (Fernand Joseph Desire Contandin) (actor); Marseilles, France **(1903–1971)**
Ferrer, José (actor and director); Santurce, Puerto Rico, 1/8/1912
Ferrer, Mel (actor); Elberon, N.J., 8/25/1917
Fetchit, Stepin (comedian); Key West, Fla., 1902
Fiedler, Arthur (conductor); Boston **(1894–1979)**
Field, Eugene (poet); St. Louis **(1850–1895)**
Field, Marshall (merchant); nr. Conway, Mass. **(1834–1906)**
Field, Sally (actress); Pasadena, Calif., 11/6/1946
Fielding, Henry (novelist); nr. Glastonbury, England **(1707–1754)**
Fields, Gracie (comedienne); Rochdale, England **(1898–1979)**
Fields, Totie (comedienne); Hartford, Conn. **(1931–1978)**
Fields, W. C. (William Claude Dukenfield) (comedian); Philadelphia **(1880–1946)**
Filene, Edward A. (merchant); **(1860–1937)**
Finch, Peter (actor); Kensington, England **(1916–1977)**
Finney, Albert (actor); Salford, England, 5/9/1936
Firkusny, Rudolf (pianist); Napajedla (Czechoslovakia), 2/11/1912
Fischer-Dieskau, Dietrich (baritone); Berlin, 5/28/1925
Fisher, Eddie (Edwin) (singer); Philadelphia, 8/10/1928
Fitzgerald, Barry (William Joseph Shields) (actor); Dublin **(1888–1961)**
Fitzgerald, Edward (radio broadcaster); Troy, N.Y., 1898(?)
Fitzgerald, Ella (singer); Newport News, Va., 4/25/1918
Fitzgerald, F. Scott (Francis Scott Key) (novelist); St. Paul, Minn. **(1896–1940)**
Fitzgerald, Geraldine (actress); Dublin, 11/24/1914
Fitzgerald, Pegeen (radio broadcaster); Norcatur, Kan., 1910
Flack, Roberta (singer); Black Mountain, N.C., 2/10/1940
Flagstad, Kirsten (Wagnerian soprano); Hamar, Norway **(1895–1962)**
Flatt, Lester Raymond (bluegrass musician); Overton County, Tenn. **(1914–1979)**
Flaubert, Gustave (novelist); Rouen, France **(1821–1880)**
Fleming, Sir Alexander (bacteriologist); Lochfield, Scotland **(1881–1955)**
Fleming, Rhonda (Marilyn Louis) (actress); Los Angeles, 8/10/1923
Flynn, Errol (actor); Hobart, Tasmania **(1909–1959)**
Foch, Nina (actress); Leyden, Netherlands, 4/20/1924
Fodor, Eugene (violinist); Turkey Creek, Colo., 3/5/1950
Fonda, Henry (actor); Grand Island, Neb., 5/16/1905
Fonda, Jane (actress); New York City, 12/21/1937
Fonda, Peter (actor); New York City, 2/23/1939
Fontaine, Frank (singer and comedian); Cambridge, Mass. **(1920–1979)**
Fontaine, Joan (Joan de Havilland) (actress); Tokyo, 10/22/1917
Fontanne, Lynn (actress); London, 12/6/1887(?)
Fonteyn, Dame Margot (Margaret Hookham) (ballerina); Reigate, England, 5/18/1919
Forbes, Malcolm S(tevenson) (publisher and sportsman); Brooklyn, N.Y., 8/19/1919
Ford, Glenn (Gwyllyn Ford) (actor); Quebec, 5/1/1916
Ford, Henry (industrialist); Greenfield, Mich. **(1863–1947)**
Ford, Henry, II (auto maker); Detroit, 9/4/1917
Ford, John (film director); Cape Elizabeth, Me. **(1895–1973)**
Ford, Paul (actor); Baltimore **(1901–1976)**
Ford, Tennessee Ernie (Ernie Jennings Ford) (singer); Bristol, Tenn., 2/13/1919
Forsythe, John (actor); Carney's Point, N.J., 1/29/1918
Fosdick, Harry Emerson (clergyman); Buffalo, N.Y. **(1878–1968)**
Fosse, Bob (Robert Louis) (choreographer and director); Chicago, 6/23/1927
Foster, Jodie (actress); Los Angeles, 1962
Foster, Stephen Collins (composer); nr. Pittsburgh **(1826–1864)**
Foxx, Redd (John Elroy Sanford) (actor and comedian); St. Louis, 12/9/1922
Foy, Eddie, Jr. (dancer and actor); New Rochelle, N.Y., 2/4/1905
Fra Angelico (Giovanni da Fiesole) (painter); Vicchio in the Mugello, Tuscany (Italy) **(c.1387–1455)**
Fracci, Carla (ballerina); Milan, Italy, 8/20/1936
Fragonard, Jean Honoré (painter); Grasse, France **(1732–1806)**
Frampton, Peter (rock musician); Beckenham, England, 4/20/1950
France, Anatole (Jacques Anatole François Thibault) (author); Paris **(1844–1924)**
Francescatti, Zino (violinist); Marseilles, France, 8/9/1905
Franciosa, Anthony (Anthony Papaleo) (actor); New York City, 10/25/1928
Francis, Arlene (Arlene Francis Kazanjian) (actress); Boston, 10/20/1908
Francis, Connie (Concetta Franconero) (singer); Newark, N.J., 12/12/1938
Francis, Kay (Katherine Edwina Gibbs) (actress); Oklahoma City **(1903–1968)**
Franciscus, James (actor); Clayton, Mo., 1/31/1934
Franck, César Auguste (composer); Liège (Belgium) **(1822–1890)**
Franco Bahamonde, Francisco (Chief of State); El Ferrol, Spain **(1892–1975)**
Franklin, Aretha (singer); Memphis, Tenn., 3/25/1942
Franklin, Benjamin (statesman and scientist); Boston **(1706–1790)**
Frazer, Sir James George (anthropologist); Glasgow, Scotland **(1854–1941)**
Freud, Sigmund (psychoanalyst); Moravia (Czechoslovakia) **(1856–1939)**
Friedan, Betty (Betty Noami Goldstein) (feminist); Peoria, Ill., 2/4/1921
Fromm, Erich (psychoanalyst); Frankfurt-am-Main, Germany **(1900–1980)**
Frost, David (TV entertainer); Tenterden, England, 4/7/1939
Frost, Robert Lee (poet); San Francisco **(1874–1963)**
Fry, Christopher (playwright); Bristol, England, 12/18/1907
Frye, David (impressionist); Brooklyn, N.Y., 1934
Fuller, R(ichard) Buckminster (Jr.) (architect and educator); Milton, Mass., 7/12/1895
Fulton, Robert (inventor); Lancaster County, Pa. **(1765–1815)**
Funt, Allen (TV producer); Brooklyn, N.Y., 9/16/1914
Furness, Betty (Elizabeth) (ex-actress and consumer advocate); New York City, 1/3/1916

G

Gabel, Martin (actor and producer); Philadelphia, 1912
Gabin, Jean (actor); Paris **(1904–1976)**
Gable, (William) Clark (actor); Cadiz, Ohio **(1901–1960)**
Gabo, Naum (sculptor); Briansk, Russia **(1890–1977)**
Gabor, Eva (actress); Budapest, 2/11/1926(?)
Gabor, Zsa Zsa (Sari) (actress); Budapest, 2/6/1923
Gainsborough, Thomas (painter); Sudbury, Suffolk, England **(1727–1788)**
Galbraith, John Kenneth (economist); Iona Station, Ontario, Canada, 10/15/1908
Galilei, Galileo (astronomer and physicist); Pisa (Italy) **(1564–1642)**
Gallico, Paul (novelist); New York City **(1897–1976)**
Gallup, George H. (poll taker); Jefferson, Iowa, 11/18/1901
Galsworthy, John (novelist and dramatist); Coombe, England **(1867–1933)**
Galway, James (flutist); Belfast, Northern Ireland, 12/8/1939
Gambling, John A. (radio broadcaster); New York City, 1930
Gandhi, Indira (Indira Nehru) (ex-Prime Minister); Allahabad, India, 11/19/1917
Gandhi, Mohandas Karamchand (called Mahatma Gandhi) (Hindu leader); Porbandar, India **(1869–1948)**
Gannett, Frank E. (editor and publisher); **(1876–1957)**
Garagiola, Joe (Joseph Henry) (sportscaster); St. Louis, 2/12/1926
Garbo, Greta (Greta Gustafsson) (actress); Stockholm, 9/18/1905
Gardner, Ava (Lucy Johnson) (actress); Smithfield, N.C., 12/24/1922
Gardner, Erle Stanley (novelist); Malden, Mass. **(1889–1970)**
Garfield, John (Jules Garfinkle) (actor); New York City **(1913–1952)**
Garfunkel, Art (Arthur) (singer); Newark, N.J., 11/5/1941
Gargan, William (actor); Brooklyn, N.Y., **(1905–1979)**
Garibaldi, Giuseppe (Italian nationalist leader); Nice, France **(1807–1882)**
Garland, Judy (Frances Gumm) (actress and singer); Grand Rapids, Minn. **(1922–1969)**
Garner, Erroll (jazz pianist); Pittsburgh **(1921–1977)**
Garner, James (James Bumgarner) (actor); Norman, Okla., 4/7/1928
Garner, Peggy Ann (actress); Canton, Ohio, 2/3/1932
Garrett, Betty (actress); St. Joseph, Mo., 5/23/1919
Garrick, David (actor); Hereford, England **(1717–1779)**
Garrison, William Lloyd (abolitionist); Newburyport, Mass. **(1805–1879)**
Garroway, Dave (TV host); Schenectady, N.Y., 7/13/1913
Garson, Greer (actress); County Down, Northern Ireland, 9/29/1912(?)
Gary, John (singer); Watertown, N.Y., 11/29/1932
Gassman, Vittorio (film actor and director); Genoa, Italy, 9/1/1922
Gaudí, Antonio (architect); Reus, Spain **(1852–1926)**
Gauguin, Eugène Henri Paul (painter); Paris **(1848–1903)**
Gautama Buddha (Prince Siddhartha) (philosopher); Kapilavastu (India) **(563?–?483 B.C.)**

Gavin, John (actor); Los Angeles, 4/8/1935
Gayle, Crystal (Brenda Gayle Webb) (singer); Paintsville, Ky., 1951
Gaynor, Janet (actress); Philadelphia, 10/6/1906
Gaynor, Mitzi (Francesca Mitzi Marlene de Czanyi von Gerber) (actress); Chicago, 9/4/1931
Gazzara, Ben (Biago Anthony Gazzara) (actor); New York City, 8/28/1930
Gebel-Williams, Gunther (animal trainer); Schweidnitz (Poland), 1934
Geddes, Barbara Bel (actress); New York City, 10/31/1922
Genghis Khan (Temujin) (conqueror); nr. Lake Baikal (U.S.S.R.) **(1162–1227)**
Genn, Leo (actor); London **(1905–1978)**
Gentry, Bobbie (Roberta Streeter) (singer); Chickasaw Co., Miss., 7/27/1944
Gericault, Jean Louis (painter); Rouen, France **(1791–1824)**
Gernreich, Rudi (fashion designer); Vienna, 8/8/1922
Geronimo (Goyathlay) (Apache chieftain); Arizona **(1829–1909)**
Gershwin, George (composer); Brooklyn, N.Y. **(1898–1937)**
Gershwin, Ira (lyricist); New York City, 12/6/1896
Getty, J. Paul (oil executive); Minneapolis **(1892–1976)**
Getz, Stan (saxophonist); Philadelphia, 2/2/1927
Ghiberti, Lorenzo (goldsmith and sculptor); Florence **(1378–1455)**
Giacometti, Alberto (sculptor); Switzerland **(1901–1966)**
Giannini, Giancarlo (actor); La Spezia, Italy, 8/1/1942
Gibbon, Edward (historian); Putney, England **(1737–1794)**
Gibson, Charles Dana (illustrator); Roxbury, Mass. **(1867–1944)**
Gibson, Hoot (Edward) (actor); Tememah, Neb. **(1892–1962)**
Gide, André (author); Paris **(1869–1951)**
Gielgud, Sir John (actor); London, 4/14/1904
Gilbert, John (movie actor); Logan, Utah **(1897–1936)**
Gilbert, Sir William Schwenck (librettist); London **(1836–1911)**
Gilels, Emil (concert pianist); Odessa, Ukraine, 1916
Gillespie, Dizzy (John Birks Gillespie) (jazz trumpeter); Cheraw, S.C., 10/21/1917
Gimbel, Bernard F. (merchant); Vincennes, Ind. **(1885–1966)**
Gingold, Hermione (actress and comedienne); London, 12/9/1897
Ginsberg, Allen (poet); Newark, N.J., 6/3/1926
Giorgione (painter); Castelfranco, (Italy) **(c.1477–1510)**
Giotto di Bondone (painter); Vespignamo (Italy) **(c.1266–1337)**
Giovanni, Nikki (poet); Knoxville, Tenn., 6/7/1943
Giroud, Françoise (French government official); Geneva, 9/21/1916
Gish, Dorothy (actress); Massillon, Ohio **(1898–1968)**
Gish, Lillian (Lillian de Guiche) (actress); Springfield, Ohio, 10/14/1896(?)
Givenchy, Hubert (fashion designer); Beauvais, France, 2/21/1927
Gladstone, William Ewart (statesman); Liverpool, England **(1809–1898)**
Gleason, Jackie (comedian); Brooklyn, N.Y., 2/26/1916
Gleason, James (actor); New York City **(1886–1959)**
Gluck, Christoph Willibald (composer); Erasbach (Germany) **(1714–1787)**
Gobel, George (comedian); Chicago, 5/20/1920
Godard, Jean Luc (film director); Paris, 12/3/1930
Goddard, Paulette (Marion Levy) (actress); Great Neck, N.Y., 6/3/1911
Godfrey, Arthur (entertainer); New York City, 8/31/1903
Goebbels, Joseph Paul (Nazi leader); Rheydt, Germany **(1897–1945)**
Goering, Hermann (Nazi leader); Rosenheim, Germany **(1893–1946)**
Goethals, George Washington (engineer); Brooklyn, N.Y. **(1858–1928)**
Goethe, Johann Wolfgang von (poet); Frankfurt am Main, Germany **(1749–1832)**
Gogol, Nikolai Vasilievich (novelist); nr. Mirgorod, Ukraine **(1809–1852)**
Goldberg, Rube (cartoonist); San Francisco **(1883–1970)**
Golden, Harry (Harry Goldhurst) (author); New York City, 5/6/1902
Goldsmith, Oliver (dramatist and poet); County Longford, Ireland **(1728–1774)**
Goldwyn, Samuel (Samuel Goldfish) (film producer); Warsaw **(1882–1974)**
Golenpaul, Dan (creator of Information Please radio show and editor of almanac of same name); New York City **(1900–1974)**
Gompers, Samuel (labor leader); London **(1850–1924)**
Goodall, Jane (Baroness van Lawick-Goodall) (ethologist); London, 4/3/1934
Goodman, Benny (clarinetist); Chicago, 5/30/1909
Goodyear, Charles (inventor); New Haven, Conn. **(1800–1860)**
Gordimer, Nadine (novelist and short-story writer); Springs, South Africa, 12/20/1923
Gordon, Max (stage producer); New York City; **(1892–1978)**
Gordon, Ruth (actress); Wollaston, Mass., 10/30/1896
Gordy, Berry, Jr. (record company executive); Detroit, 11/28/1929
Gore, Lesley (singer); Tenafly, N.J., 1946
Goren, Charles H. (bridge expert); Philadelphia, 3/4/1901
Gorki, Maxim (Alexei Maximovich Peshkov) (author); Nizhni Novgorod, Russia **(1868–1936)**
Gorky, Arshile (painter); Armenia **(1904–1948)**
Gormé, Eydie (singer); Bronx, N.Y., 8/16/1932
Gorshin, Frank (actor); Pittsburgh, 4/5/1934
Gosden, Freeman F. *See* Amos
Gould, Chester (cartoonist); Pawnee, Okla., 11/20/1900
Gould, Elliott (Elliott Goldstein) (actor); Brooklyn, N.Y., 8/29/1938
Gould, Glenn (concert pianist); Toronto, 9/25/1932
Gould, Morton (composer); Richmond Hill, Queens, N.Y., 12/10/1913
Goulet, Robert (singer); Lawrence, Mass., 11/26/1933
Gounod, Charles François (composer); Paris **(1818–1893)**
Goya y Lucientes, Francisco José de (painter); Fuendetodos, Spain **(1746–1828)**
Grable, Betty (actress); St. Louis **(1916–1973)**
Graham, Bill (Wolfgang Grajonca) (rock impresario); Berlin, 1931
Graham, Billy (William F.) (evangelist); Charlotte, N.C., 11/7/1918
Graham, Katharine Meyer (newspaper publisher); New York City, 6/16/1917
Graham, Martha (choreographer); Pittsburgh, 5/11/1894(?)
Grahame, Gloria (Gloria Hallwood) (actress); Los Angeles, 11/28/1929
Gramm, Donald (bass-baritone); Milwaukee, 2/26/1927
Granger, Farley (actor); San Jose, Calif., 7/1/1925
Granger, Stewart (James Stewart) (actor); London, 5/6/1913
Grant, Cary (Alexander Archibald Leach) (actor); Bristol, England, 1/18/1904
Grant, Kathryn (actress); Houston, Tex., 1933
Grant, Lee (Lyova Haskell Rosenthal) (actress); New York City, 10/31/1930
Granville, Bonita (actress and producer); New York City, 1923
Grass, Günter (novelist); Danzig (Poland), 10/16/1927
Grauer, Ben (radio and TV announcer); New York City **(1908–1977)**
Graves, Peter (Peter Arness) (actor); Minneapolis, 3/18/1926
Graves, Robert (poet); London, 7/26/1895
Gray, Barry (Bernard Yaroslaw) (radio interviewer); Atlantic City, N.J., 7/2/1916
Gray, Dolores (singer and actress); Chicago, 6/7/1930
Gray, Thomas (poet); London **(1716–1771)**
Grayson, Kathryn (Zelma Hednick) (singer and actress); Winston-Salem, N.C., 2/9/1923
Greco, Buddy (singer); Philadelphia, 8/14/1926
Greco, José (dancer); Montorio nei Frentani, Italy, 12/23/1918
Greeley, Horace (journalist and politician); Amherst, N.H. **(1811–1872)**
Green, Adolph (actor and lyricist); New York City, 12/2/1915
Green, Al (singer); Forrest City, Ark., 4/13/1946
Greene, Graham (novelist); Berkhamsted, England, 10/2/1904
Greene, Lorne (actor); Ottowa, 2/12/1915
Greene, Martyn (actor); London **(1899–1975)**
Greenstreet, Sydney (actor); Sandwich, England **(1879–1954)**
Greenwood, Joan (actress and director); London, 3/4/1921
Greer, Germaine (feminist); Melbourne, 1/29/1939
Gregory, Cynthia (ballerina); Los Angeles, 7/8/1946
Gregory, Dick (comedian); St. Louis, 1932
Greuze, Jean-Baptiste (painter); Tournus, France **(1725–1805)**
Grey, Joel (Joel Katz) (actor); Cleveland, 4/11/1932
Grey, Zane (author); Zanesville, Ohio **(1875–1939)**
Grieg, Edvard Hagerup (composer); Bergen, Norway **(1843–1907)**
Grier, Roosevelt (entertainer and former athlete); Cuthbert, Ga., 7/14/1932
Griffin, Merv (TV entertainer); San Mateo, Calif., 7/6/1925
Griffith, Andy (actor); Mount Airy, N.C., 6/1/1926
Griffith, David Lewelyn Wark (film producer); La Grange, Ky. **(1875–1948)**
Grigorovich, Yuri (choreographer); Leningrad, 1/1/1927
Grimes, Tammy (actress); Lynn, Mass., 1/30/1934
Grimm, Jacob (author of fairy tales); Hanau (Germany) **(1785–1863)**
Grimm, Wilhelm (author of fairy tales); Hanau (Germany) **(1786–1859)**
Gris, Juan (José Victoriano González) (painter); Madrid **(1887–1927)**
Grizzard, George (actor); Roanoke Rapids, N.C., 4/1/1928
Gromyko, Andrei A. (diplomat); Starye Gromyki, Russia, 7/5/1909
Gropius, Walter (architect); Berlin **(1883–1969)**
Gropper, William (painter, illustrator); New York City **(1897–1977)**
Grosz, George (painter); Germany **(1893–1959)**
Guardino, Harry (actor); New York City, 12/23/1925
Guggenheim, Meyer (capitalist); Langnau, Switzerland **(1828–1905)**
Guinness, Sir Alec (actor); London, 4/2/1914
Guitry, Sacha (Alexandre) (actor and film director); St. Petersburg, Russia **(1885–1957)**
Gunther, John (author); Chicago **(1901–1970)**
Gutenberg, Johann (printer); Mainz (Germany) **(1400?–?1468)**
Guthrie, Arlo (singer); New York City, 7/10/1947
Guthrie, Woody (folk singer and composer); Okemah, Okla. **(1912–1967)**
Gwenn, Edmund (actor); London **(1875–1959)**

H

Hackett, Bobby (trumpeter); Providence, R.I. **(1915–1976)**
Hackett, Buddy (Leonard Hacker) (comedian and actor); Brooklyn, N.Y., 8/31/1924
Hackman, Gene (actor); San Bernardino, Calif., 1/30/1931
Hagen, Uta (actress); Göttingen, Germany, 6/12/1919
Haggard, Merle (songwriter); Bakersfield, Calif., 4/6/1937

Haig, Alexander Meigs, Jr. (ex-general); Bala-Cynwyd, Pa., 12/2/1924
Haile Selassie (Ras Tafari Makonnen) (ex-Emperor); Ethiopia **(1892–1975)**
Hailey, Arthur (novelist); Luton, England, 4/5/1920
Halberstam, David (journalist); New York City, 4/10/1934
Hale, Edward Everett (clergyman and author); Boston **(1822–1909)**
Hale, Nathan (American Revolutionary officer); Coventry, Conn. **(1755–1776)**
Haley, Alex (writer); Ithaca, N.Y., 8/11/1921
Hall, Monty (TV personality); Winnipeg, Canada, 1923
Hals, Frans (painter); Antwerp (Netherlands) **(1580?–1666)**
Halsey, William Frederick, Jr. (naval officer); Elizabeth, N.J. **(1882–1959)**
Hamill, Pete (journalist); Brooklyn, N.Y., 6/24/1935
Hamilton, Alexander (statesman); Nevis I. (West Indies Associated States) **(1757?–1804)**
Hamilton, George (actor); Memphis, Tenn., 8/12/1939
Hamilton, Margaret (actress); Cleveland, 9/12/1902
Hamlisch, Marvin (composer and pianist); New York City, 6/2/1944
Hammarskjøld, Dag (U.N. Secretary-General); Jönköping, Sweden **(1905–1961)**
Hammerstein, Oscar, II (librettist and stage producer); New York City **(1895–1960)**
Hampden, Walter (Walter Hampden Dougherty) (actor); Brooklyn, N.Y. **(1879–1955)**
Hampton, James (actor); Oklahoma City, 7/9/1936
Hampton, Lionel (vibraharpist and band leader); Birmingham, Ala., 4/20/1914
Hancock, John (statesman); Braintree, Mass. **(1737–1793)**
Hand, Learned (jurist); Albany, N.Y. **(1872–1961)**
Handel, George Frederick (Georg Friedrich Händel) (composer); Halle (Germany) **(1685–1759)**
Handy, William Christopher (blues composer); Florence, Ala. **(1873–1958)**
Hannibal (Carthaginian general) **(247–183 B.C.)**
Hanson, Howard (conductor); Wahoo, Neb., 10/28/1896
Harburg, E. Y. "Yip" (songwriter); New York City, 4/8/1896
Harding, Ann (actress); San Antonio, Tex., 8/7/1902
Hardwicke, Sir Cedric (actor); Stourbridge, England **(1893–1964)**
Hardy, Oliver (comedian); Atlanta **(1892–1957)**
Hardy, Thomas (novelist); Dorsetshire, England **(1840–1928)**
Harkness, Edward S. (capitalist); Cleveland **(1874–1940)**
Harlow, Jean (Harlean Carpentier) (actress); Kansas City, Mo. **(1911–1937)**
Harnick, Sheldon (lyricist); Chicago, 4/30/1924
Harper, Valerie (actress); Suffern, N.Y., 8/22/1940(?)
Harriman, W. (William) Averell (ex-Governor of New York); New York City, 11/15/1891
Harris, Barbara (actress); Evanston, Ill., 1935
Harris, Emmylou (singer); Birmingham, Ala., 1949
Harris, Julie (actress); Grosse Pointe Park, Mich., 12/2/1925
Harris, Phil (actor and band leader); Linton, Ind., 6/24/1906
Harris, Richard (actor); Limerick, Ireland, 10/1/1933
Harris, Rosemary (actress); Ashby, England, 9/19/1930
Harris, Roy (composer); Lincoln County, Olka. **(1898–1979)**
Harrison, George (singer and songwriter); Liverpool, England, 2/25/1943
Harrison, Noel (singer and actor); London, 1/29/1936
Harrison, Rex (Reginald Carey) (actor); Huyton, England, 3/5/1908
Hart, Lorenz (lyricist); New York **(1895–1943)**
Hart, Moss (playwright); New York City **(1904–1961)**
Hart, William S. (actor); Newburgh, N.Y. **(1862–1946)**
Harte, Bret (Francis Brett Harte) (author); Albany, N.Y. **(1836–1902)**
Hartford, Huntington (George Huntington Hartford II) (A.&P. heir); New York City, 4/18/1911
Hartford, John (singer and banjoist); New York City, 12/30/1937
Hartman, Elizabeth (actress); Youngstown, Ohio, 12/23/1941
Harvey, Laurence (Larushka Skikne) (actor); Joniskis, Lithuania **(1928–1973)**
Harvey, William (physician); Folkestone, England **(1578–1657)**
Hasso, Signe (actress); Stockholm, 8/15/1915
Haver, June (actress); Rock Island, Ill., 6/10/1926
Havoc, June (June Hovick) (actress); Seattle, 1916
Hawkins, Jack (actor); London **(1910–1973)**
Hawn, Goldie (actress); Washington, D.C., 11/21/1945
Haworth, Jill (actress); Sussex, England, 1945
Hawthorne, Nathaniel (novelist); Salem, Mass. **(1804–1864)**
Hay, John Milton (statesman); Salem, Ind. **(1838–1905)**
Hayakawa, S(amuel) I(chiye) (semanticist and Senator); Vancouver, B.C., Canada, 7/18/1906
Hayakawa, Sessue (actor); Honshu, Japan **(1890–1973)**
Hayden, Melissa (ballerina); Toronto, 4/25/1928
Hayden, Sterling (Sterling Relyea Walter) (actor and writer); Montclair, N.J., 3/26/1916
Haydn, Franz Joseph (composer); Rohrau (Austria) **(1732–1809)**
Hayes, Helen (Helen Hayes Brown) (actress); Washington, D.C., 10/10/1900
Hayes, Isaac (composer); Covington, Tenn., 8/20/1942
Hayward, Louis (actor); Johannesburg, South Africa, 1909
Hayward, Susan (Edythe Marrener) (actress). Brooklyn, N.Y. **(1919?–1975)**
Hayworth, Rita (Margarita Cansino) (actress); New York City, 10/17/1918
Head, Edith (costume designer); Los Angeles, 10/28/1907
Hearst, William Randolph (publisher); San Francisco **(1863–1951)**
Hearst, William Randolph, Jr. (publisher); New York City, 1/27/1908
Heath, Edward (ex-Prime Minister); Broadstairs, England, 7/9/1916
Heatherton, Joey (actress); Rockville Centre, N.Y., 9/14/1944
Hecht, Ben (author); New York City **(1894–1964)**
Heckart, Eileen (actress); Columbus, Ohio, 3/29/1919
Heflin, Van (Emmet Evan Heflin) (actor); Walters, Okla. **(1910–1971)**
Hefner, Hugh (publisher); Chicago, 4/9/1926
Hegel, Georg Wilhelm Friedrich (philosopher); Stuttgart (Germany) **(1770–1831)**
Heifetz, Jascha (concert violinist); Vilna, Russia, 2/2/1901
Heine, Heinrich (Harry) (poet); Düsseldorf (Germany) **(1797–1856)**
Heinemann, Gustav (ex-President of Germany); Schweim, Germany **(1899–1976)**
Heller, Joseph (novelist); Brooklyn, N.Y., 5/1/1923
Hellman, Lillian (playwright); New Orleans, 6/20/1905
Hemingway, Ernest Miller (novelist); Oak Park, Ill. **(1899–1961)**
Hemmings, David (actor); Guilford, England, 1941
Henderson, Florence (actress); Dale, Ind., 2/14/1934
Henderson, Skitch (Lyle Russell Cedric) (conductor and pianist); Birmingham, England(?), 1/27/1918
Hendrix, Jimi (James Marshall Hendrix) (guitarist); Seattle **(1942–1970)**
Henning, Doug (magician and actor); Winnipeg, Canada, 1947(?)
Henreid, Paul (actor); Trieste, 1/10/1908
Henri, Robert (painter); Cincinnati **(1865–1926)**
Henry, O. (William Sydney Porter) (story writer); Greensboro, N.C. **(1862–1910)**
Henry, Patrick (statesman); Hanover County, Va. **(1736–1799)**
Henson, Jim (puppeteer); Greenville, Miss., 9/24/1936
Hepburn, Audrey (actress); Brussels, Belgium, 5/4/1929
Hepburn, Katharine (actress); Hartford, Conn., 11/8/1909
Hepplewhite, George (furniture designer); England **(?–1786)**
Hepworth, Barbara (sculptor); Wakefield, England **(1903–1975)**
Herbert, Victor (composer); Dublin **(1859–1924)**
Herblock (Herbert L. Block) (political cartoonist); Chicago, 10/13/1909
Herman, Woody (Woodrow Charles) (band leader); Milwaukee, 5/16/1913
Herod (Herodes) (called Herod the Great) (King of Judea) **(73?–4 B.C.)**
Herodotus (historian); Halicarnassus (Turkey) **(c. 484–425 B.C.)**
Hershfield, Harry (humorist and raconteur); Cedar Rapids, Iowa **(1885–1974)**
Hersholt, Jean (actor); Copenhagen **(1886–1956)**
Heston, Charlton (actor); Evanston, Ill., 10/4/1924
Heyerdahl, Thor (ethnologist and explorer); Larvik, Norway, 10/6/1914
Hildegarde (Hildegarde Loretta Sell) (singer); Adell, Wis., 2/1/1906
Hill, Arthur (actor); Melfort, Canada, 8/1/1922
Hillary, Sir Edmund (mountain climber); New Zealand, 7/20/1919
Hiller, Wendy (actress); Bramhall, England, 8/15/1912
Hilliard, Harriet. *See* Nelson, Harriet
Hindemith, Paul (composer); Hanau, Germany **(1895–1963)**
Hindenburg, Paul von (statesman); Posen (Poland) **(1847–1934)**
Hines, Earl "Fatha" (jazz pianist); Duquesne, Pa., 12/28/1905
Hines, Jerome (Jerome Heinz) (basso); Los Angeles, 11/8/1921
Hingle, Pat (actor); Denver, 7/19/1924
Hippocrates (physician); Kos (Turkey) **(460?–?377 B.C.)**
Hirohito (Emperor); Tokyo, 4/29/1901
Hirschfeld, Al (Albert) (cartoonist); St. Louis, 6/21/1903
Hirschhorn, Joseph Herman (financier, speculator, and art collector); Mitau, Latvia, 8/11/1899
Hirt, Al (trumpeter); New Orleans, 11/7/1922
Hitchcock, Alfred J. (film director); London **(1899–1980)**
Hitler, Adolf (Adolf Schicklgruber) (German dictator); Braunau, Austria **(1889–1945)**
Hitzig, William Maxwell (physician); Austria, 12/15/1904
Hobson, Laura Z. (Laura K. Zametkin) (novelist); New York City, 1900(?)
Hodges, Eddie (actor); Hattiesburg, Miss., 3/5/1947
Hoffa James R(iddle) (labor leader); Brazil, Ind., 2/14/1913 (presumed dead, **1977)**
Hoffman, Dustin (film actor and director); Los Angeles, 8/8/1937
Hofmann, Hans (painter); Germany **(1880–1966)**
Hogarth, William (painter and engraver); London **(1697–1764)**
Holbein, Hans (the Elder) (painter); Augsburg (Germany) **(1465?–1524)**
Holbein, Hans (the Younger) (painter); Augsburg (Germany) **(1497?–1543)**
Holbrook, Hal (actor); Cleveland, 2/17/1925
Holden, William (William Franklin Beedle, Jr.) (actor); O'Fallon, Ill., 4/17/1918
Holder, Geoffrey (dancer); Port-of-Spain, Trinidad, 8/1/1930
Holiday, Billie (Eleanora Fagan) (jazz–blues singer); Baltimore **(1915–1959)**
Holliday, Judy (Judith Tuvim) (comedienne); New York City **(1922–1965)**

Holloway, Stanley (actor); London, 10/1/1890
Holloway, Sterling (actor); Cedartown, Ga., 1905
Holm, Celeste (actress); New York City, 4/29/1919
Holmes, Oliver Wendell (author); Cambridge, Mass. **(1809–1894)**
Holmes, Oliver Wendell (jurist); Boston **(1841–1935)**
Holt, Jack (actor); Winchester, Va. **(1888–1951)**
Holtz, Lou (comedian); San Francisco, 4/11/1898
Home, Lord (Alexander Frederick Douglas-Home) (diplomat); London, 7/2/1903
Homeier, Skip (actor); Chicago, 1930
Homer, Winslow (painter); Boston, Mass. **(1836–1910)**
Homer (Greek poet) **(c.850 B.C.?)**
Homolka, Oscar (actor); Vienna **(1898–1978)**
Honegger, Arthur (composer); Le Havre, France **(1892–1955)**
Hook, Sidney (philosopher); New York City, 12/20/1902
Hoover, J. Edgar (FBI director); Washington, D.C. **(1895–1972)**
Hope, Bob (Leslie Townes Hope) (comedian); London, 5/29/1903
Hopkins, Anthony (actor); Port Talbot, Wales, 12/31/1937
Hopkins, Johns (financier); Anne Arundel County, Md. **(1795–1873)**
Hopkins, Miriam (actress); Bainbridge, Ga. **(1902–1973)**
Hopper, Dennis (actor); Dodge City, Kan., 5/17/1936
Hopper, Edward (painter); Nyack, N.Y. **(1882–1967)**
Horace (Quintus Horatius Flaccus) (poet); Venosa (Italy) **(65–8 B.C.)**
Horne, Lena (singer); Brooklyn, N.Y., 6/30/1917
Horne, Marilyn (mezzo-soprano); Bradford, Pa., 1/16/1934
Horowitz, Vladimir (pianist); Kiev, Russia, 10/1/1904
Horton, Edward Everett (comedian); Brooklyn, N.Y. **(1887–1970)**
Houdini, Harry (Ehrich Weiss) (magician); Appleton, Wis. **(1874–1926)**
Houseman, John (John Haussmann) (producer, director, and actor); Bucharest, 9/22/1902
Housman, Alfred Edward (poet); Fockburg, England **(1859–1936)**
Houston, Samuel (political leader); Rockbridge County, Va. **(1793–1863)**
Howard, Leslie (Leslie Stainer) (actor); London **(1893–1943)**
Howard, Trevor (actor); Kent, England, 9/29/1916
Howe, Elias (inventor); Spencer, Mass. **(1819–1867)**
Howe, Irving (literary critic); New York City, 6/11/1920
Howe, Julia Ward (poet and reformer); New York City **(1819–1910)**
Howes, Sally Ann (actress); London, 7/20/1934
Hudson, Henry (English navigator) **(?–1611)**
Hudson, Rock (born Roy Scherer, Jr.; took Roy Fitzgerald as legal name) (actor); Winnetka, Ill., 11/17/1925
Hughes, Charles Evans (jurist); Glens Falls, N.Y. **(1862–1948)**
Hughes, Howard (industrialist and film producer); Houston **(1905–1976)**
Hugo, Victor Marie (author); Besançon, France **(1802–1885)**
Hume, David (philosopher); Edinburgh, Scotland **(1711–1776)**
Humperdinck, Engelbert (Arnold Dorsey) (singer); Madras, India, 5/2/1936
Humperdinck, Engelbert (composer); Siegburg (Germany) **(1854–1921)**
Hunt, H. L. (industrialist); nr. Vandalia, Ill. **(1889–1974)**
Hunt, Marsha (actress); Chicago, 10/17/1917
Hunter, Kim (Janet Cole) (actress); Detroit, 11/12/1922
Hunter, Tab (Arthur Andrew Gelien) (actor); New York City, 7/11/1931
Huntley, Chet (TV newscaster); Cardwell, Mont. **(1911–1974)**
Hurok, Sol (Solomon) (impresario); Pogar, Russia **(1884–1974)**
Hurst, Fannie (novelist); Hamilton, Ohio **(1889–1968)**
Hussein I (King); Jordan, 5/2/1935
Huston, John (film director and writer); Nevada, Mo., 8/5/1906
Huston, Walter (Walter Houghston) (actor); Toronto **(1884–1950)**
Hutchins, Robert M. (educator); Brooklyn, N.Y. **(1899–1977)**
Hutton, Barbara (Woolworth heiress); New York City **(1912–1979)**
Hutton, Betty (Betty Thornburg) (actress); Battle Creek, Mich., 2/26/1921
Hutton, Lauren (model and actress); Charleston, S.C., 1944
Huxley, Aldous (author); Godalming, England **(1894–1963)**
Huxley, Sir Julian S. (biologist and author); London **(1887–1975)**
Huxley, Thomas Henry (biologist); Ealing, England **(1825–1895)**

I

Ian, Janis (singer); New York City, 5/7/1951
Ibsen, Henrik (dramatist); Skien, Norway **(1828–1906)**
Inge, William (playwright); Independence, Kan. **(1913–1973)**
Ingres, Jean Auguste Dominique (painter); Montauban, France **(1780–1867)**
Inness, George (painter); nr. Newburgh, N.Y. **(1825–1894)**
Ionesco, Eugène (playwright); Slatina, Romania, 11/26/1912
Ireland, John (actor); Vancouver, B.C., Canada, 1/30/1915
Irving, Washington (author); New York City **(1783–1859)**
Isherwood, Christopher (novelist and playwright); nr. Dilsey and High Lane, England, 8/26/1904
Iturbi, José (concert pianist); Valencia, Spain **(1895–1980)**
Ives, Burl (Icle Ivanhoe) (singer); Hunt, Ill., 6/14/1909
Ives, Charles E(dward) (composer); Danbury, Conn. **(1874–1954)**

J

Jackson, Anne (actress); Millvale, Pa., 9/3/1926
Jackson, Glenda (actress); Hoylake, England, 1937(?)
Jackson, Rev. Jesse (civil rights leader); Greenville, N.C., 10/8/1941
Jackson, Kate (actress); Alabama, 1949
Jackson, Mahalia (gospel singer); New Orleans **(1912–1972)**
Jackson, Thomas Jonathan ("Stonewall") (general); Clarksburg, Va. (now W. Va.) **(1824–1863)**
Jacobi, Lou (actor); Toronto, 12/28/1913
Jacobs, Jane (urbanologist); Scranton, Pa., 5/1/1916.
Jaffe, Sam (actor); New York City, 3/8/1898
Jagger, Dean (actor); Lima, Ohio, 11/7/1903
Jagger, Mick (Michael Philip) (singer); Dartford, England, 7/26/1944
James, Harry (trumpeter); Albany, Ga., 3/15/1916
James, Henry (novelist); New York City **(1843–1916)**
James, Jesse Woodson (outlaw); Clay County, Mo. **(1847–1882)**
James, William (psychologist); New York City **(1842–1910)**
Jameson, (Margaret) Storm (novelist); Whitby, England, 1897
Janis, Byron (pianist); McKeesport, Pa., 3/24/1928
Jannings, Emil (actor); Brooklyn, N.Y. **(1886–1950)**
Janssen, David (David Meyer) (actor); Naponee, Neb. **(1930–1980)**
Jay, John (statesman and jurist); New York City **(1745–1829)**
Jeanmaire, Renée (dancer); Paris, 4/29/1924
Jenner, Edward (physician); Berkeley, England **(1749–1823)**
Jennings, Waylon (singer); Littlefield, Tex., 1937
Jessel, George (entertainer); New York City, 4/3/1898
Jessup, Philip C. (jurist); New York City, 1/5/1897
Joan of Arc (Jeanne d'Arc) (saint and patriot); Domremy-la-Pucelle, France **(1412–1431)**
Joffrey, Robert (Abdullah Jaffa Bey Khan) (choreographer); Seattle, 12/24/1930
John, Elton (Reginald Kenneth Dwight) (singer and pianist); Pinner, England, 3/25/1947
Johns, Glynis (actress); Pretoria, South Africa, 10/5/1923
Johns, Jasper (painter and sculptor); Augusta, Ga., 5/15/1930
Johnson, James Weldon (author and educator); Jacksonville, Fla. **(1871–1938)**
Johnson, Philip Cortelyou (architect); Cleveland, Ohio, 7/8/1906
Johnson, Samuel (lexicographer and author); Lichfield, England **(1709–1784)**
Johnson, Van (actor); Newport, R.I., 8/20/1916
Joliot-Curie, Frédéric (physicist); Paris **(1900–1958)**
Joliot-Curie, Irène (Irène Curie) (physicist); France **(1897–1956)**
Jolliet (or **Joliet**), Louis (explorer); Beaupré, Canada **(1645–1700)**
Jolson, Al (Asa Yoelson) (actor and singer); St. Petersburg, Russia **(1886–1950)**
Jones, Carolyn (singer and actress); Amarillo, Tex., 4/28/1933
Jones, Dean (actor); Morgan County, Ala., 1/25/1935
Jones, George (singer); Saratoga, Tex., 9/12/1931
Jones, Inigo (architect); London **(1573–1652)**
Jones, James (novelist); Robinson, Ill. **(1921–1977)**
Jones, James Earl (actor); Arkabutla, Miss., 1/17/1931
Jones, Jennifer (Phyllis Isley) (actress); Tulsa, Okla., 3/2/1919
Jones, John Paul (John Paul) (naval officer); Scotland **(1747–1792)**
Jones, Quincy (composer); Chicago, 3/14/1933
Jones, Shirley (singer and actress); Smithtown, Pa., 3/31/1934
Jones, Tom (Thomas Jones Woodward) (singer); Pontypridd, Wales, 6/7/1940
Jong, Erica (writer); New York City, 3/26/1942
Jonson, Ben (Benjamin) (poet and dramatist); Westminster, England **(1572–1637)**
Joplin, Janis (singer); Port Arthur, Tex. **(1943–1970)**
Jordan, Barbara (ex-congresswoman); Houston, 2/21/1936
Jory, Victor (actor); Dawson City, Yukon, Canada, 11/23/1903
Jourdan, Louis (Louis Gendre) (actor); Marseilles, France, 6/19/1920
Joyce, James (novelist); Dublin **(1882–1941)**
Juárez, Benito Pablo (statesman); Guelatao, Mexico **(1806–1872)**
Juliana (Queen); The Hague, Netherlands, 4/30/1909
Jung, Carl Gustav (psychoanalyst); Basel, Switzerland **(1875–1961)**
Jurado, Katy (actress); Guadalajara, Mexico, 1927

K

Kabalevsky, Dmitri (composer); St. Petersburg, Russia, 12/30/1904
Kádár, János (Communist Party leader); Hungary, 1912
Kahn, Louis I. (architect); Oesel Island, Estonia **(1901–1974)**
Kahn, Madeline (actress); Boston, 9/29/1942
Kaminska, Ida (actress); Odessa, Russia, 9/4/1899
Kandinsky, Wassily (painter); Moscow **(1866–1944)**
Kanin, Garson (playwright); Rochester, N.Y., 11/24/1912
Kant, Immanuel (philosopher); Königsberg (Germany) **(1724–1804)**
Kantor, MacKinlay (novelist); Webster City, Iowa **(1904–1977)**

Kaplan, Gabe (actor); Brooklyn, N.Y., 1945
Karloff, Boris (William Henry Pratt) (actor); London **(1887–1969)**
Kaufman, George S. (playwright); Pittsburgh **(1889–1961)**
Kaye, Danny (David Daniel Kominski) (comedian); Brooklyn, N.Y., 1/18/1913
Kaye, Sammy (band leader); Cleveland, 3/13/1910
Kazan, Elia (director); Constantinople, Turkey, 9/7/1909
Kazan, Lainie (singer); New York City, 1940
Keach, Stacy (actor); Savannah, Ga., 6/2/1941
Keaton, Buster (Joseph Frank Keaton) (comedian); Piqua, Kan. **(1896–1966)**
Keaton, Diane (actress); Santa Ana, Calif., 1946
Keats, John (poet); London **(1795–1821)**
Keel, Howard (singer and actor); Gillespie, Ill., 4/13/1919
Keeler, Ruby (Lehy Keeler) (actress and dancer); Halifax, Nova Scotia, Canada, 8/25/1910
Kefauver, Estes (legislator); Madisonville, Tenn. **(1903–1963)**
Keith, Brian (actor); Bayonne, N.J., 11/14/1921
Keller, Helen Adams (author and educator); Tuscumbia, Ala. **(1880–1968)**
Kellerman, Sally (actress); Long Beach, Calif., 6/2/1938
Kelly, Emmett (clown); Sedan, Kan., **(1898–1979)**
Kelly, Gene (dancer and actor); Pittsburgh, 8/23/1912
Kelly, Grace (Princess Grace of Monaco) (former actress); Philadelphia, 11/12/1929
Kelly, Patsy (actress and comedienne); Brooklyn, N.Y., 1/12/1910
Kelly, Walt (cartoonist); Philadelphia **(1913–1973)**
Kemal Ataturk (Mustafa Kemal) (Turkish soldier and statesman); Salonika (Greece) **(1881–1938)**
Kennan, George F. (diplomat); Milwaukee, 2/16/1904
Kennedy, Arthur (actor); Worcester, Mass., 2/17/1914
Kennedy, George (actor); New York City, 2/18/1925
Kennedy, Jacqueline. *See* Onassis, Jacqueline
Kennedy, Joseph P. (financier); Boston **(1888–1969)**
Kennedy, Robert Francis (legislator); Brookline, Mass. **(1925–1968)**
Kennedy, Rose Fitzgerald (President's mother); Boston, 7/22/1890
Kent, Rockwell (painter); Tarrytown Heights, N.Y. **(1882–1971)**
Kenton, Stan (Stanley Newcomb) (jazz musician); Wichita, Kan. **(1912–1979)**
Kepler, Johannes (astronomer); Weil (Germany) **(1571–1630)**
Kerensky, Alexander Fedorovich (statesman); Simbirks, Russia **(1881–1970)**
Kern, Jerome David (composer); New York City **(1885–1945)**
Kerr, Deborah (actress); Helensburgh, Scotland, 9/30/1921
Kesey, Ken (novelist); La Junta, Colo., 9/17/1935
Kettering, Charles F. (engineer and inventor); nr. Loudonville, Ohio **(1876–1958)**
Key, Francis Scott (lawyer and author of national anthem); Frederick (now Carroll) County, Md. **(1779–1843)**
Keyes, Frances Parkinson (novelist); Charlottesville, Va., 7/21/1885
Keynes (1st Baron of Tilton) (John Maynard Keynes) (economist); Cambridge, England **(1883–1946)**
Khachaturian, Aram (composer); Tiflis, Russia **(1903–1978)**
Khrushchev, Nikita S. (Soviet leader); Kalinovka, nr. Kursk, Ukraine **(1894–1971)**
Kibbee, Guy (actor); El Paso **(1886–1956)**
Kidd, Michael (choreographer); Brooklyn, N.Y., 1917
Kidd, William (called Captain Kidd) (pirate); Greenock, Scotland **(1645?–1701)**
Kieran, John (writer); New York City, 8/2/1892
Kiesinger, Kurt Georg (diplomat); Ebingen, Germany, 4/6/1904
Kiley, Richard (actor and singer); Chicago, 3/31/1922
Kilmer, Alfred Joyce (poet); New Brunswick, N.J. **(1886–1918)**
King, Alan (Irwin Alan Kniberg) (entertainer); Brooklyn, N.Y., 12/26/1927
King, B.B. (Riley King) (guitarist); Itta Bena, Miss., 9/16/1925
King, Carole (singer and songwriter); Brooklyn, N.Y., 2/9/1941
King, Coretta Scott (civil rights leader); Marion, Ala., 4/27/1927
King, Martin Luther, Jr. (civil rights leader); Atlanta **(1929–1968)**
King, Pee Wee (Frank) (singer); Abrams, Wis., 2/18/1914
Kingsley, Sidney (Sidney Kirschner) (playwright); New York City, 10/18/1906
Kipling, Rudyard (author); Bombay **(1865–1936)**
Kipnis, Alexander (basso); Ukraine, **(1891–1978)**
Kirby, George (comedian); Chicago, 1923(?)
Kirk, Grayson (educator); Jeffersonville, Ohio, 10/12/1903
Kirk, Lisa (actress and singer); Charleroi, Pa., 1925
Kirk, Phyllis (actress); Plainfield, N.J., 9/18/1930
Kirkland, Gelsey (ballerina); Bethelhem, Pa., 12/29/1952
Kirkpatrick, Ralph (harpsichordist); Leominster, Mass., 6/10/1911
Kirkwood, James (actor); Grand Rapids, Mich. **(1883–1963)**
Kirsten, Dorothy (soprano); Montclair, N.J., 7/6/1919
Kissinger, Henry (Heinz Alfred Kissinger) (ex-Secretary of State); Furth, Germany, 5/27/1923
Kitt, Eartha (singer); North, S.C., 1/26/1928
Klee, Paul (painter); Münchenbuchsee, nr. Bern, Switzerland **(1879–1940)**
Klein, Calvin (fashion designer); Bronx, N.Y., 11/19/1942
Klein, Robert (comedian); Bronx, N.Y., 2/8/1942
Klemperer, Otto (conductor); Breslau (Poland) **(1885–1973)**
Klemperer, Werner (actor); Cologne, Germany, 3/22/1920
Klugman, Jack (actor); Philadelphia, 1922
Knievel, Evel (Robert Craig) (daredevil motorcyclist); Butte, Mont., 10/17/1938
Knight, Gladys (singer); Atlanta, 5/28/1944
Knight, John S. (publisher); Bluefield, W. Va. 10/26/1894
Knopf, Alfred A. (publisher); New York City, 9/12/1892
Knotts, Don (actor); Morgantown, W.Va., 7/21/1924
Knox, John (religious reformer); Haddington, East Lothian, Scotland **(1505–1572)**
Koch, Robert (physician); Klausthal (Germany) **(1843–1910)**
Koestler, Arthur (novelist); Budapest, 9/5/1905
Kokoschka, Oskar (painter); Póchlarn Austria **(1886–1980)**
Kooper, Al (singer and pianist); Brooklyn, N.Y., 2/5/1944
Korman, Harvey (actor); Chicago, 2/15/1927
Kosciusko, Thaddeus (Tadeusz Andrzej Bonawentura Kosciuszko) (military officer); Grand Duchy of Lithuania **(1746–1817)**
Kostelanetz, André (orchestra conductor); St. Petersburg, Russia **(1901–1980)**
Kosygin, Aleksei N. (Premier); St. Petersburg, Russia, 2/20/1904
Koussevitzky, Serge (Sergei) Alexandrovitch (orchestra conductor); Vishni Volochek, Tver, Russia **(1874–1951)**
Kovacs, Ernie (comedian); Trenton, N.J. **(1919–1962)**
Kramer, Stanley E. (film producer and director); New York City, 9/29/1913
Kraus, Lili (pianist); Budapest, 3/4/1905(?)
Kreisler, Fritz (violinist and composer); Vienna **(1875–1962)**
Kresge, S. S. (merchant); Bald Mount, Pa. **(1867–1966)**
Krips, Josef (orchestra conductor); Vienna **(1902–1974)**
Kristofferson, Kris (singer); Brownsville, Tex., 6/22/1936
Kruger, Otto (actor); Toledo, Ohio **(1885–1974)**
Krupa, Gene (drummer); Chicago **(1909–1973)**
Kubelik, Rafael (conductor); Bychory (Czechoslovakia), 6/29/1914
Kublai Khan (Mongol conqueror) **(1216–1294)**
Kubrick, Stanley (producer and director); New York City, 7/26/1928
Kuralt, Charles (TV journalist); North Carolina, 1934
Kurosawa, Akira (film director); Tokyo, 3/23/1910
Kurtz, Efrem (conductor); St. Petersburg, Russia, 11/7/1900
Ky, Nguyen Cao (ex-Vice President of South Vietnam); Son Tay (Vietnam), 9/8/1930

L

Ladd, Alan (actor); Hot Springs, Ark. **(1913–1964)**
Ladd, Cheryl (actress); Huron, S.D., 4/2/(?)
Lafayette, Marquis de (Marie Joseph Paul Yves Roch Gilbert du Motier) (military officer); Auvergne, France **(1757–1834)**
La Follette, Robert Marin (politician); Primrose, Wis. **(1855–1925)**
La Guardia, Fiorello Henry (Mayor of New York); New York City **(1882–1947)**
Lahr, Bert (Irving Lahrheim) (comedian); New York City **(1895–1967)**
Laine, Frankie (Frank Paul LoVecchio) (singer); Chicago, 3/30/1913
Laird, Melvin (ex-Secretary of Defense); Omaha, Neb., 9/1/1922
Lamarck, Chevalier de (Jean Baptiste Pierre Antoine de Monet) (naturalist); Bazantin, France **(1744–1829)**
Lamarr, Hedy (Hedwig Kiesler) (actress); Vienna, 1915
Lamas, Fernando (actor); Buenos Aires, 1/9/1915
Lamb, Charles (Elia) (essayist); London **(1775–1834)**
Lamour, Dorothy (Dorothy Kaumeyer) (actress); New Orleans, 10/10/1914
Lancaster, Burt (actor); New York City, 11/2/1913
Lanchester, Elsa (Elsa Sullivan) (actress); London, 10/28/1902
Landau, Martin (actor); Brooklyn, N.Y. 1925(?)
Landers, Ann (columnist); Sioux City, Iowa, 7/14/1918
Landon, Michael (Michael Orowitz) (actor); Forest Hills, Queens, N.Y., 10/31/1936(?)
Lane, Abbe (singer); New York City, 1933
Lang, Fritz (film director); Vienna **(1890–1976)**
Lang, Paul Henry (music critic); Budapest, 8/28/1901
Lange, Hope (actress); Redding Ridge, Conn., 11/28/1933
Langella, Frank (actor); Bayonne, N.J., 1940
Langford, Frances (singer); Lakeland, Fla., 4/4/1913
Langmuir, Irving (chemist); Brooklyn, N.Y. **(1881–1957)**
Langtry, Lily (Emily Le Breton) (actress); Island of Jersey **(1852–1929)**
Lansbury, Angela (actress); London, 10/16/1925
Lansing, Robert (actor); San Diego, Calif., 6/5/1929
Lanza, Mario (Alfred Arnold Cocozza) (singer and actor); Philadelphia **(1925–1959)**
Lao-Tzu (or **Lao-Tse**) (Li Erh) (philosopher); Honan Province, China **(c. 604–531 B.C.)**
Lardner, Ring (Ringgold Wilmer Lardner) (story writer); Niles, Mich. **(1885–1933)**
La Salle, Sieur de (Robert Cavelier) (explorer); Rouen, France **(1643–1687)**

Lasser, Louise (actress); New York City, 1940(?)
Lauder, Sir Harry (Harry MacLennan) (singer); Portobello, Scotland **(1870–1950)**
Laughton, Charles (actor); Scarborough, England **(1899–1962)**
Laurel, Stan (Arthur Jefferson) (comedian); Ulverston, England **(1890–1965)**
Laurents, Arthur (playwright); New York City, 7/14/1918
Laurie, Piper (actress); Detroit, 1/22/1932
Lavoisier, Antoine-Laurent (chemist); Paris **(1743–1794)**
Lawford, Peter (actor); London, 9/7/1923
Lawrence, Carol (Carol Maria Laraia) (dancer and actress); Melrose Park, Ill., 9/5/1932
Lawrence, David Herbert (novelist); Nottingham, England **(1885–1930)**
Lawrence, Gertrude (Gertrud Klasen) (actress); London **(1900–1952)**
Lawrence, Marjorie (singer); Deans Marsh, Australia **(1908–1979)**
Lawrence, Steve (Sidney Leibowitz) (singer); Brooklyn, N.Y., 7/8/1935
Lawrence, Vicki (actress); Inglewood, Calif., 1949
Lawrence of Arabia (Thomas Edward Lawrence, later changed to Shaw) (author and soldier); Tremadoc, Wales **(1888–1935)**
Leachman, Cloris (actress); Des Moines, Iowa, 4/30/1926(?)
Lean, David (film director); Croydon, England, 3/25/1908
Lear, Edward (nonsense poet); London **(1812–1888)**
le Carré, John (David John Moore Cornwell) (novelist); Poole, England, 10/19/1931
Le Corbusier (Charles Edouard Jeanneret) (architect); La Chaux-de-Fonds, Switzerland **(1887–1965)**
Lederer, Francis (actor); Prague, 11/6/1906
Lee, Christopher (actor); London, 5/27/1922
Lee, Gypsy Rose (Rose Louise Hovick) (entertainer); Seattle **(1919–1970)**
Lee, Peggy (Norma Engstrom) (singer); Jamestown, N.D., 5/26/1920
Lee, Robert Edward (Confederate general); Stratford Estate, Va. **(1807–1870)**
Leek, Sybil (Sybil Falk) (astrologer); Staffordshire, England, 1923
Le Gallienne, Eva (actress); London, 1/11/1899
Lehár, Franz (composer); Komárom (Czechoslovakia) **(1870–1948)**
Lehman, Herbert H. (Governor and Senator); New York City **(1878–1963)**
Lehmann, Lotte (soprano); Perleberg (Germany) **(1888–1976)**
Leigh, Janet (Jeanette Morrison) (actress); Merced, Calif., 7/6/1927
Leigh, Vivien (Vivien Mary Hartley) (actress); Darjeeling, India **(1913–1967)**
Leighton, Margaret (actress); nr. Birmingham, England **(1922–1976)**
Leinsdorf, Erich (conductor); Vienna, 2/4/1912
Lemmon, Jack (actor); Boston, 2/8/1925
Lenin, Nicolai (Vladimir Ilich Ulyanov) (Soviet leader); Simbirsk, Russia **(1870–1924)**
Lennon, John (singer and songwriter); Liverpool, England, 10/9/1940
Lenya, Lotte (Karoline Balmauer) (singer and actress); Hitzing, Austria, 1905
Leonard, Sheldon (actor and director); New York City, 2/22/1907
Lerner, Alan Jay (lyricist); New York City, 8/31/1918
Lerner, Max (columnist); Minsk, Russia, 12/20/1902
Le Roy, Mervyn (film producer); San Francisco, 10/15/1900
Leslie, Joan (actress); Detroit, 1/26/1925
Lessing, Doris (novelist); Kermanshah, Iran, 10/22/1919
Lester, Mark (actor); Richmond, England, 1958
Levant, Oscar (pianist); Pittsburgh **(1906–1972)**
Levene, Sam (actor); New York City, 8/28/1905
Levenson, Sam (humorist); New York City **(1911–1980)**
Levi, Carlo (novelist); Turin, Italy **(1902–1975)**
Levine, James (music director, Metropolitan Opera); Cincinnati, 6/23/1943
Levine, Joseph E. (film producer); Boston, 9/9/1905
Lewis, Jerry (Joseph Levitch) (comedian and film director); Newark, N.J., 3/16/1926
Lewis, Jerry Lee (singer); Ferriday, La., 9/29/1935
Lewis, John Llewellyn (labor leader); Lucas, Iowa **(1880–1969)**
Lewis, Meriwether (explorer); Albemarle Co., Va. **(1774–1809)**
Lewis, Shari (Shari Hurwitz) (puppeteer); New York City, 1/17/1934
Lewis, Sinclair (novelist); Sauk Centre, Minn. **(1885–1951)**
Lewis, Ted (entertainer); Circleville, Ohio **(1891–1971)**
Ley, Willy (science writer); Berlin **(1906–1969)**
Liberace (Wladziu Liberace) (pianist); West Allis, Wis., 5/16/1919
Lichtenstein, Roy (painter); New York City, 10/27/1923
Lie, Trygve Halvdan (first U.N. Secretary-General); Oslo **(1896–1968)**
Lightfoot, Gordon (singer and songwriter); Orillia, Ontario, Canada, c.1939
Lillie, Beatrice (Lady Peel) (actress and comedienne); Toronto, 5/29/1898
Lin Yutang (author); Changchow, China **(1895–1976)**
Lind, Jenny (Johanna Maria Lind) (soprano); Stockholm **(1820–1887)**
Lindbergh, Anne Morrow (author); Englewood, N.J., 6/22/1906
Lindbergh, Charles A. (aviator); Detroit **(1902–1974)**
Linden, Hal (actor); New York City, 3/20/1931
Lindfors, Viveca (actress); Uppsala, Sweden, 12/29/1920
Lindsay, Howard (dramatist); Waterford, N.Y. **(1889–1968)**
Lindsay, John Vliet (ex-Mayor of New York City); New York City, 11/24/1921
Lindstrom, Pia (TV newscaster); Stockholm, 11/?/1938
Linkletter, Art (radio-TV personality); Moose Jaw, Saskatchewan, Canada, 7/17/1912
Lipchitz, Jacques (sculptor); Druskieniki, Latvia **(1891–1973)**
Lippmann, Walter (columnist, author, and political analyst); New York City **(1889–1974)**
Lister, (1st Baron of Lyme Regis) (Joseph Lister) (surgeon); Upton, England **(1827–1912)**
Liszt, Franz (composer and pianist); Raiding (Hungary) **(1811–1886)**
Little, Cleavon (actor and comedian); Chickasha, Okla., 6/1/1939
Little, Rich (impressionist); Ottawa, 11/26/1938
Livesey, Roger (actor); Barry, Wales **(1906–1976)**
Livingstone, David (missionary and explorer); Lanarkshire, Scotland **(1813–1873)**
Livingstone, Mary (Sadye Marks) (comedienne); Seattle, 1909
Llewellyn, Richard (novelist); St. David's, Wales
Lloyd, Harold (comedian); Burchard, Neb. **(1894–1971)**
Lloyd George, David (Earl of Dwyfor) (statesman); Manchester, England **(1863–1945)**
Locke, John (philosopher); Somersetshire, England **(1632–1704)**
Lockhart, Gene (actor); London, Ontario, Canada **(1891–1957)**
Lockhart, June (actress); New York City, 6/25/1925
Lockwood, Margaret (actress); Karachi (Pakistan), 9/15/1916
Lodge, Henry Cabot (legislator); Boston **(1850–1924)**
Lodge, Henry Cabot, Jr. (diplomat); Nahant, Mass., 7/5/1902
Loesser, Frank (composer); New York City **(1910–1969)**
Loewe, Frederick (composer); Vienna, 6/10/1904
Logan, Joshua (director and producer); Texarkana, Tex., 10/5/1908
Lollobrigida, Gina (actress); Subiaco, Italy, 1928
Lombard, Carole (Carol Jane Peters) (actress); Ft. Wayne, Ind. **(1908–1942)**
Lombardo, Guy (band leader); London, Ontario, Canada **(1902–1977)**
London, George (baritone); Montreal, 5/30/1920
London, Jack (John Griffith London) (novelist); San Francisco **(1876–1916)**
London, Julie (Julie Peck) (singer and actress); Santa Rosa, Calif., 9/26/1926
Long, Huey Pierce (politician); Winnfield, La. **(1893–1935)**
Longfellow, Henry Wadsworth (poet); Portland, Me. **(1807–1882)**
Longworth, Alice Roosevelt (social figure); New York City **(1884–1980)**
Loos, Anita (novelist); Sissons, Calif., 4/26/1893
Lopez, Trini (Trinidad Lopez III) (singer); Dallas, 5/15/1937
Lopez, Vincent (band leader); Brooklyn, N.Y. **(1895–1975)**
Lord, Jack (actor); New York City, 12/30/1930
Loren, Sophia (Sofia Scicolone) (actress); Rome, 9/20/1934
Lorre, Peter (Laszlo Löewenstein) (actor); Rosenberg (Czechoslovakia) **(1904–1964)**
Louise, Tina (actress); New York City, 2/11/1937
Lowell, Amy (poet); Brookline, Mass. **(1874–1925)**
Lowell, James Russell (poet); Cambridge, Mass. **(1819–1891)**
Lowell, Robert (poet); Boston **(1917–1977)**
Loy, Myrna (Myrna Williams) (actress); nr. Helena, Mont., 8/2/1905
Loyola, St. Ignatius of (Iñigo de Oñez y Loyola) (founder of Jesuits); Gúipuzcoa Province, Spain **(1491–1556)**
Lubitsch, Ernst (film director); Berlin **(1892–1947)**
Luce, Clare Boothe (playwright and former Ambassador); New York City, 4/10/1903
Luce, Henry Robinson (editor and publisher); Tengchow, China **(1898–1967)**
Lugosi, Bela (Bela Lugosi Blasko) (actor); Logos, Hungary **(1888–1956)**
Lukas, Paul (actor); Budapest **(1895–1971)**
Lumet, Sidney (film and TV director); Philadelphia, 6/25/1924
Lunt, Alfred (actor); Milwaukee **(1892–1977)**
Lupino, Ida (actress and director); London, 2/4/1918
Luther, Martin (religious reformer); Eisleben (Germany) **(1483–1546)**
Lynde, Paul (comedian); Mt. Vernon, Ohio, 6/13/1926
Lynley, Carol (actress); New York City, 2/13/1942
Lynn, Jeffrey (actor); Auburn, Mass., 1909
Lynn, Loretta (singer); Butcher's Hollow, Ky., 4/14/1935

M

Maazel, Lorin (conductor); Neuilly, France, 3/5/1930
MacArthur, Charles (playwright); Scranton, Pa. **(1895–1956)**
MacArthur, Douglas (five-star general); Little Rock Barracks, Ark. **(1880–1964)**
MacArthur, James (actor); Los Angeles, 12/8/1937
Macaulay, Thomas Babington (author); Rothley Temple, England **(1800–1859)**
MacDermot, Galt (composer); Montreal, 12/19/1928
MacDonald, James Ramsay (statesman); Lossiemouth, Scotland **(1866–1937)**
MacDonald, Jeanette (actress and soprano); Philadelphia **(1907–1965)**

Macdonald, Ross (Kenneth Millar) (mystery writer); Los Gatos, Calif., 12/13/1915
MacDowell, Edward Alexander (composer); New York City **(1861–1908)**
Macfadden, Bernarr (physical culturist); nr. Mill Spring, Mo. **(1868–1955)**
MacGraw, Ali (actress); New York City, 4/1/1939
Machiavelli, Niccolò (political philosopher); Florence (Italy) **(1469–1527)**
Mack, Ted (TV personality); Greeley, Colo. **(1904–1976)**
MacKenzie, Gisele (Marie Marguerite Louise Gisele LaFleche) (singer and actress); Winnipeg, Manitoba, Canada, 1/10/1927
MacLaine, Shirley (Shirley MacLean Beaty) (actress); Richmond, Va., 4/24/1934
MacLeish, Archibald (poet); Glencoe, Ill., 5/7/1892
Macmillan, Harold (ex-Prime Minister); London, 2/10/1894
MacMurray, Fred (actor); Kankakee, Ill., 8/30/1908
MacNeil, Cornell (baritone); Minneapolis, 1925
MacRae, Gordon (singer); East Orange, N.J., 3/12/1921
MacRae, Sheila (comedienne); London, 9/24/1924
Madison, Guy (Robert Moseley) (actor); Bakersfield, Calif., 1/19/1922
Maeterlinck, Count Maurice (author); Ghent, Belgium **(1862–1949)**
Magellan, Ferdinand (Fernando de Magalhaes) (navigator); Sabrosa, Portugal **(1480?–1521)**
Magnani, Anna (actress); Rome **(1908–1973)**
Magritte, René (painter); Belgium **(1898–1967)**
Magsaysay, Ramón (statesman); Iba, Luzon, Philippines **(1907–1957)**
Mahan, Alfred Thayer (naval historian); West Point, N.Y. **(1840–1914)**
Mahler, Gustav (composer and conductor); Kalischt (Czechoslovakia) **(1860–1911)**
Mailer, Norman (novelist); Long Branch, N.J., 1/31/1923
Maillol, Aristide (sculptor); Banyuls-sur-Mer, Rousillon, France **(1861–1944)**
Main, Marjorie (Mary Tomlinson Krebs) (actress); Acton, Ind. **(1890–1975)**
Mainbocher (Main Rousseau Bocher) (fashion designer); Chicago **(1891–1976)**
Majors, Lee (actor); Wyandotte, Mich., 1942
Makarova, Natalia (ballerina); Leningrad, 11/21/1940
Makeba, Miriam (singer); Johannesburg, South Africa, 3/4/1932
Malamud, Bernard (novelist); New York City, 4/26/1914
Malden, Karl (Mladen Sekulovich) (actor); Chicago, 3/22/1914
Malone, Dorothy (actress); Chicago, 1/30/1925
Malraux, André (author); Paris **(1901–1976)**
Manchester, Melissa (singer); Bronx, N.Y., 2/15/1951
Manchester, William (writer); Attleboro, Mass., 4/1/1922
Mancini, Henry (composer and conductor); Cleveland, 4/16/1924
Manet, Edouard (painter); Paris **(1832–1883)**
Mangano, Silvana (actress); Rome, 4/21/1930
Mangione, Chuck (hornist, pianist, composer); Rochester, N.Y., 11/29/1940
Manilow, Barry (singer); Brooklyn, N.Y., 6/17/1946
Mankiewicz, Frank F. (columnist); New York City, 5/16/1924
Mankiewicz, Joseph L. (film writer and director); Wilkes-Barre, Pa., 2/11/1909
Mann, Horace (educator); Franklin, Mass. **(1796–1859)**
Mann, Thomas (novelist); Lübeck, Germany **(1875–1955)**
Mannes, Marya (writer); New York City, 11/14/1904
Mansfield, Jayne (Jayne Palmer) (actress); Bryn Mawr, Pa. **(1932–1967)**
Mansfield, Katherine (story writer); Wellington, New Zealand **(1888–1923)**
Mantovani, Annunzio (conductor); Venice **(1905–1980)**
Mao Zedong (Tse-tung) (Chinese leader); Shao Shan, China **(1893–1976)**
Marat, Jean Paul (French revolutionist); Boudry, Neuchâtel, Switzerland **(1743–1793)**
Marceau, Marcel (mime); Strasbourg, France, 3/22/1923
March, Fredric (Frederick Bickel) (actor); Racine, Wis. **(1897–1975)**
Marconi, Guglielmo (inventor); Bologna, Italy **(1874–1937)**
Marcus Aurelius (Marcus Annius Verus) (Roman emperor); Rome **(121–180)**
Marcuse, Herbert (philosopher); Berlin, **(1898–1979)**
Margaret Rose (Princess); Glamis Castle, Angus, Scotland, 8/21/1930
Margrethe II (Queen); Copenhagen, 4/16/1940
Marie Antoinette (Josèphe Jeanne Marie Antoinette) (Queen of France); Vienna **(1755–1793)**
Marisol (sculptor); Venezuela, 1930
Markham, Edwin (poet); Oregon City, Ore. **(1852–1940)**
Markova, Dame Alicia (ballerina); London, 12/1/1910
Marley, Bob (reggae singer and songwriter); Kingston, Jamaica, c.1946
Marlowe, Christopher (dramatist); Canterbury, England **(1564–1593)**
Marlowe, Julia (Sarah Frances Frost) (actress); Cumberlandshire, England **(1866–1950)**
Marquand, John Phillips (novelist); Wilmington, Del. **(1893–1960)**
Marquette, Jacques (missionary and explorer); Laon, France **(1637–1675)**
Marriner, Neville (conductor); Lincoln, England, 4/15/1924
Marsh, Jean (actress); Stoke Newington, England, 7/1/1934
Marshall, E.G. (actor); Owatonna, Minn., 6/18/1910
Marshall, George Catlett (general); Uniontown, Pa. **(1880–1959)**
Marshall, Herbert (actor); London **(1890–1968)**
Marshall, John (jurist); nr. Germantown, Va. **(1755–1835)**
Marshall, Penny (actress); New York City, 10/15/1942
Martin, Dean (Dino Crocetti) (singer and actor); Steubenville, Ohio, 6/17/1917
Martin, Dick (actor and comedian); Battle Creek, Mich., 1/30/1922
Martin, Mary (singer and actress); Weatherford, Tex., 12/1/1914
Martin, Steve (comedian); prob. Waco, Tex., 1945(?)
Martin, Tony (Alvin Morris) (singer); San Francisco, 12/25/1914
Martin, William McChesney, Jr. (ex-chairman of Federal Reserve Board); St. Louis, 12/17/1906
Martinelli, Giovanni (tenor); Montagnana, Italy **(1885–1969)**
Marvin, Lee (actor); New York City, 2/19/1924
Marx, Chico (Leonard) (comedian); New York City **(1891–1961)**
Marx, Groucho (Julius) (comedian); New York City **(1890–1977)**
Marx, Harpo (Arthur) (comedian); New York City **(1893–1964)**
Marx, Karl (Socialist writer); Treves (Germany) **(1818–1883)**
Marx, Zeppo (Herbert) (comedian); New York City, 2/25/1901
Mary Stuart (Queen of Scotland); Linlithgow, Scotland **(1542–1587)**
Masaryk, Jan Garrigue (statesman); Prague (Czechoslovakia) **(1886–1948)**
Masaryk, Thomas Garrigue (statesman); Hodonin (Czechoslovakia) **(1850–1937)**
Masefield, John (poet); Ledbury, England **(1878–1967)**
Masekela, Hugh (trumpeter); Wilbank, South Africa, 4/4/1939
Mason, James (actor); Huddersfield, England, 5/15/1909
Massenet, Jules Emile Frédéric (composer); Montaud, France **(1842–1912)**
Massey, Raymond (actor); Toronto, 8/30/1896
Massine, Léonide (choreographer); Moscow, **(1895–1979)**
Masters, Edgar Lee (poet); Garnett, Kan. **(1869–1950)**
Mastroianni, Marcello (actor); Fontana Liri, Italy, 9/28/1924
Mathis, Johnny (singer); San Francisco, 9/30/1935
Matisse, Henri (painter); Le Cateau, France **(1869–1954)**
Matthau, Walter (Walter Matuschanskayasky) (actor); New York City, 10/1/1920
Mature, Victor (actor); Louisville, Ky., 1/19/1916
Maugham, (William) Somerset (author); Paris **(1874–1965)**
Mauldin, Bill (political cartoonist); Mountain Park, N.M., 10/29/1921
Maupassant, Henri René Albert Guy de (story writer); Normandy, France **(1850–1893)**
Maurois, André (Emile Herzog) (author); Elbeuf, France **(1885–1967)**
Maximilian (Ferdinand Maximilian Joseph) (Emperor of Mexico); Vienna **(1832–1867)**
Maxwell, James Clerk (physicist); Edinburgh, Scotland **(1831–1879)**
May, Elaine (entertainer); Philadelphia, 1932
May, Rollo (psychologist); Ada, Ohio, 4/21/1909
Mayall, John (singer and songwriter); Manchester, England, 11/29/1933
Mayo, Charles H. (surgeon); Rochester, Minn. **(1865–1939)**
Mayo, Charles W. (surgeon); Rochester, Minn. **(1898–1968)**
Mayo, Virginia (actress); St. Louis, 1920
Mayo, William J. (surgeon); Le Sueur, Minn. **(1861–1939)**
McBride, Mary Margaret (radio personality); Paris, Mo. **(1899–1976)**
McBride, Patricia (ballerina); Teaneck, N.J., 8/23/1942
McCallum, David (actor); Glasgow, Scotland, 9/19/1933
McCambridge, Mercedes (actress); Joliet, Ill., 3/17/1918
McCarthy, Eugene J. (ex-Senator); Watkins, Minn., 3/29/1916
McCarthy, Joseph Raymond (Senator); Grand Chute, Wis. **(1908–1957)**
McCarthy, Kevin (actor); Seattle, 1915
McCarthy, Mary (novelist); Seattle, 6/21/1912
McCartney, Paul (singer and songwriter); Liverpool, England, 6/18/1942
McClellan, George Brinton (general); Philadelphia **(1826–1885)**
McCloy, John J. (lawyer and banker); Philadelphia, 3/31/1895
McClure, Doug (actor); Glendale, Calif., 5/11/1938
McCormack, John (tenor); Athlone, Ireland **(1884–1945)**
McCormack, John W. (ex-Speaker of House); Boston, 12/21/1891
McCormack, Patty (actress); New York City, 8/21/1945
McCormick, Cyrus Hall (inventor); Rockbridge County, Va. **(1809–1884)**
McCoy, Col. Tim (actor); Saginaw, Mich. **(1891–1978)**
McCracken, James (dramatic tenor); Gary, Ind., 12/16/1926
McCrea, Joel (actor); Los Angeles, 11/5/1906
McCullers, Carson (novelist); Columbus, Ga. **(1917–1967)**
McDowall, Roddy (actor); London, 9/17/1928
McDowell, Malcolm (actor); Leeds, England, 6/19/1943
McGavin, Darren (actor); San Joaquin, Calif., 5/7/1922
McGinley, Phyllis (poet and writer); Ontario, Ore. **(1905–1978)**
McGoohan, Patrick (actor); Astoria, Queens, N.Y., 1928
McGuire, Dorothy (actress); Omaha, Neb., 6/14/1919
McKenna, Siobhan (actress); Belfast, Northern Ireland, 5/24/1923
McKuen, Rod (singer and composer); Oakland, Calif., 4/29/1933
McLaglen, Victor (actor); Tunbridge Wells, Kent, England **(1886–1959)**
McLaughlin, John (guitarist); Yorkshire, England, 1942
McLean, Don (singer and songwriter); New Rochelle, N.Y., 10/2/1945
McLuhan, Marshall (Herbert Marshall) (communications writer); Edmonton, Canada, 7/21/1911
McMahon, Ed (TV personality); Detroit, 3/6/1923
McNamara, Robert S. (president of World Bank); San Francisco, 6/9/1916

McQueen, Steve (Terence Stephen McQueen) (actor); Indianapolis, 3/24/1930(?)
Mead, Margaret (anthropologist); Philadelphia, **(1901–1978)**
Meadows, Audrey (actress); Wu Chang, China, 1922(?)
Meadows, Jayne (actress); Wu Chang, China 9/27/1926
Meany, George (labor leader); New York City **(1894–1980)**
Meara, Anne (actress); New York City, 1929
Medici, Lorenzo de' (called Lorenzo the Magnificent) (Florentine ruler); Florence (Italy) **(1449–1492)**
Meeker, Ralph (Ralph Rathgeber) (actor); Minneapolis, 11/21/1920
Mehta, Zubin (conductor); Bombay, 4/29/1936
Meir, Golda (Golda Myerson, nee Mabovitz) (ex-Premier of Israel); Kiev, Russia, **(1898–1978)**
Melanie (Melanie Safka) (singer and songwriter); New York City, 2/3/1947
Melba, Dame Nellie (Helen Porter Mitchell) (soprano); nr. Melbourne **(1861–1931)**
Melchior, Lauritz (Lebrecht Hommel) (heroic tenor); Copenhagen **(1890–1973)**
Mellon, Andrew William (financier); Pittsburgh **(1855–1937)**
Melville, Herman (novelist); New York City **(1819–1891)**
Mencken, Henry Louis (writer); Baltimore **(1880–1956)**
Mendel, Gregor Johann (geneticist); Heinzendorf, Austrian Silesia **(1822–1884)**
Mendeleyev, Dmitri Ivanovich (chemist); Tobolsk, Russia **(1834–1907)**
Mendelssohn-Bartholdy, Jakob Ludwig Felix (composer); Hamburg **(1809–1847)**
Mendès-France, Pierre (ex-Premier); Paris, 1/11/1905
Menjou, Adolphe (actor); Pittsburgh **(1890–1963)**
Mennin, Peter (Peter Mennini) (composer); Erie, Pa., 5/17/1923
Menninger, William C. (psychiatrist); Topeka, Kan. **(1899–1966)**
Menotti, Gian Carlo (composer); Cadegliano, Italy, 7/7/1911
Menuhin, Yehudi (violinist and conductor); New York City, 4/22/1916
Menzies, Robert Gordon (ex-Prime Minister); Jeparit, Australia **(1894–1978)**
Mercer, Johnny (songwriter); Savannah, Ga. **(1909–1976)**
Mercer, Mabel (singer); Burton-on-Trent, England, 1/?/1900
Mercouri, Melina (actress); Athens, 10/18/1925
Meredith, Burgess (actor); Cleveland, 11/16/1908
Merkel, Una (actress); Covington, Ky., 12/10/1903
Merman, Ethel (Ethel Zimmerman) (singer and actress); Astoria, Queens, N.Y., 1/16/1909
Merrick, David (David Margulois) (stage producer); St. Louis, 11/27/1912
Merrill, Dina (actress); New York City, 12/9/1925
Merrill, Gary (actor); Hartford, Conn., 8/2/1914
Merrill, Robert (baritone); Brooklyn, N.Y., 6/4/1919
Merton, Thomas (clergyman and writer); France **(1915–1968)**
Mesmer, Franz Anton (physician); Itzmang, nr. Constance (Germany) **(1733–1815)**
Mesta, Perle (social figure); Sturgis, Mich. **(1889–1975)**
Metternich, Prince Klemens Wenzel Nepomuk Lothar von (statesman); Coblenz (Germany) **(1773–1859)**
Michelangelo Buonarroti (painter, sculptor, and architect); Caprese (Italy) **(1475–1564)**
Michener, James A. (novelist); New York City, 2/3/1907
Midler, Bette (singer); Honolulu, 1945
Mielziner, Jo (stage designer); Paris **(1901–1976)**
Mies van der Rohe, Ludwig (architect and designer); Aachen, Germany **(1886–1969)**
Mikoyan, Anastas I. (diplomat); Sanain, Armenia, **(1895–1978)**
Miles, Sarah (actress); Essex, England, 12/31/1943
Miles, Sylvia (actress); New York City, 9/9/1932
Miles, Vera (Vera Ralston) (actress); nr. Boise City, Okla., 8/23/1929
Milhaud, Darius (composer); Aix-en-Provence, France **(1892–1974)**
Mill, John Stuart (philosopher); London, **(1806–1873)**
Milland, Ray (Reginald Truscott-Jones) (actor); Neath, Wales, 1/3/1907
Millay, Edna St. Vincent (poet); Rockland, Me. **(1892–1950)**
Miller, Ann (Lucille Ann Collier) (dancer and actress); Cherino, Tex., 4/12/1919
Miller, Arthur (playwright); New York City, 10/17/1915
Miller, Glenn (band leader); Clarinda, Iowa **(1909?–1944)**
Miller, Henry (novelist); New York City **(1891–1980)**
Miller, Jason (John Miller) (playwright); New York City, 1939(?)
Miller, Mitch (Mitchell) (musician); Rochester, N.Y., 7/4/1911
Miller, Roger (singer); Fort Worth, 1/2/1936
Millet, Jean François (painter); Gruchy, France **(1814–1875)**
Millett, Kate (feminist); St. Paul, 9/14/1934
Mills, Hayley (actress); London, 4/18/1946
Mills, John (actor); Felixstowe, England, 2/22/1908
Milne, A(lan) A(lexander) (author); London **(1882–1956)**
Milstein, Nathan (concert violinist); Odessa, Russia, 12/31/1904
Milton, John (poet); London **(1608–1674)**
Mimieux, Yvette (actress); Hollywood, Calif., 1/8/1941
Mineo, Sal (actor); New York City **(1939–1976)**
Minnelli, Liza (singer and actress); Hollywood, Calif., 3/12/1946
Minnelli, Vincente (film director); Chicago, 2/28/1913
Minuit, Peter (Governor of New Amsterdam); Wesel (Germany) **(1580–1638)**
Miranda, Carmen (Maria do Carmo da Cunha) (singer and dancer); Lisbon **(1913–1955)**
Miro, Joan (painter); Barcelona, 4/20/1893
Mitchell, Cameron (actor); Dallastown, Pa., 4/11/1918
Mitchell, Guy (actor); Detroit, 2/27/1927
Mitchell, John N. (former Attorney General); Detroit, 9/15/1913
Mitchell, Joni (Roberta Joan Anderson) (singer and songwriter); Ft. MacCleod, Canada, 11/7/1943
Mitchell, Margaret (novelist); Atlanta **(1900–1949)**
Mitchum, Robert (actor); Bridgeport, Conn., 8/6/1917
Mitropoulos, Dimitri (orchestra conductor); Athens **(1896–1960)**
Mix, Tom (actor); Mix Run, Pa. **(1880–1940)**
Modigliani, Amedeo (painter); Leghorn, Italy **(1884–1920)**
Moffo, Anna (soprano); Wayne, Pa., 6/27/1934
Mohammed (prophet); Mecca (Saudi Arabia) **(570–632)**
Molière (Jean Baptiste Poquelin) (dramatist); Paris **(1622–1673)**
Molnar, Ferenc (dramatist); Budapest **(1878–1952)**
Molotov, Vyacheslav M. (V. M. Skryabin) (diplomat); Kukarka, Russia, 3/9/1890
Mondrian, Piet (painter); Amersfoort, Netherlands **(1872–1944)**
Monet, Claude (painter); Paris **(1840–1926)**
Monk, Thelonious (pianist); Rocky Mount, N.C., 10/10/1918
Monroe, Marilyn (Norma Jean Mortenson or Baker) (actress); Los Angeles **(1926–1962)**
Monroe, Vaughn (Wilton) (band leader); Akron, Ohio **(1912–1973)**
Monsarrat, Nicholas (novelist); Liverpool, England, **(1910–1979)**
Montaigne, Michel Eyquem de (essayist); nr. Bordeaux, France **(1533–1592)**
Montalban, Ricardo (actor); Mexico City, 11/25/1920
Montand, Yves (Yves Montand Livi) (actor and singer); Mansummano, Italy, 10/13/1921
Montez, Maria (actress); Dominican Republic **(1918–1951)**
Montezuma II (Aztec emperor); Mexico **(1480?–1520)**
Montgomery, Elizabeth (actress); Hollywood, Calif., 4/15/1933
Montgomery, George (George Letz) (actor); Brady, Mont., 1929
Montgomery, Robert (Henry, Jr.) (actor); Beacon, N.Y., 5/21/1904
Montgomery of Alamein, 1st Viscount of Hindhead (Sir Bernard Law Montgomery) (military leader); London **(1887–1976)**
Montoya, Carlos (guitarist); Madrid, 12/13/1903
Moore, Clement Clarke (author); New York City **(1779–1863)**
Moore, Garry (Thomas Garrison Morfit) (TV personality); Baltimore, 1/31/1915
Moore, Grace (soprano); Jellico, Tenn. **(1901–1947)**
Moore, Henry (sculptor); Castleford, England, 7/30/1898
Moore, Marianne (poet); Kirkwood, Mo. **(1887–1972)**
Moore, Mary Tyler (actress); Brooklyn, N.Y., 12/29/1937
Moore, Melba (Beatrice) (singer and actress); New York City, 10/27/1945
Moore, Roger (actor); London, 10/14/1927(?)
Moore, Thomas (poet); Dublin **(1779–1852)**
Moore, Victor (actor); Hammonton, N.J. **(1876–1962)**
Moorehead, Agnes (actress); Clinton, Mass. **(1906–1974)**
More, Sir Thomas (statesman and author); London **(1478–1535)**
Moreau, Jeanne (actress); Paris, 1/23/1928
Moreno, Rita (Rosita Dolores Alverio) (actress); Humacao, Puerto Rico, 12/11/1931
Morgan, Dennis (actor); Prentice, Wis., 12/10/1920
Morgan, Helen (singer); Danville, Ohio **(1900?–1941)**
Morgan, Henry (comedian); New York City, 3/31/1915
Morgan, Jane (Florence Currier) (singer); Boston, 1920
Morgan, John Pierpont (financier); Hartford, Conn. **(1837–1913)**
Moriarty, Michael (actor); Detroit, 4/5/1941
Morini, Erica (concert violinist); Vienna, 1/5/1910
Morison, Samuel Eliot (historian); Boston **(1887–1976)**
Morley, Christopher Darlington (novelist); Haverford, Pa. **(1890–1957)**
Morley, Robert (actor); Semley, England, 5/26/1908
Morrison, Jim (James Douglas Morrison) (singer and songwriter); Melbourne, Fla. **(1943–1971)**
Morse, Marston (mathematician); Waterville, Me. **(1892–1977)**
Morse, Robert (actor); Newton, Mass., 5/18/1931
Morse, Samuel Finley Breese (painter and inventor); Charlestown, Mass. **(1791–1872)**
Moses, Grandma (Mrs. Anna Mary Robertson Moses) (painter); Greenwich, N.Y. **(1860–1961)**
Moses, Robert (urban planner); New Haven, Conn., 12/18/1888
Mostel, Zero (Samuel Joel Mostel) (actor); Brooklyn, N.Y. **(1915–1977)**
Moussorgsky, Modest Petrovich (composer); Karev, Russia **(1839–1881)**
Moyers, Bill D. (Billy Don) (journalist); Hugo, Okla., 6/5/1934
Moynihan, Daniel Patrick (New York Senator); Tulsa, Okla., 3/16/1927
Mozart, Wolfgang Amadeus (Johannes Chrysostomus Wolfgangus Theophilus Mozart) (composer); Salzburg (Austria) **(1756–1791)**
Mudd, Roger (TV newscaster); Washington, D.C., 2/9/1928
Muggeridge, Malcolm (Thomas) (writer); Croydon, England, 3/24/1903

Muhammad, Elijah (Elijah Poole) (religious leader); Sandersville, Ga. **(1897–1975)**
Mulhare, Edward (actor); Ireland, 1923
Mumford, Lewis (cultural historian and city planner); Flushing, Queens, N.Y., 10/19/1895
Munch, Edvard (painter); Löten, Norway **(1863–1944)**
Muni, Paul (Muni Weisenfreund) (actor); Lemburg (Ukraine) **(1895–1967)**
Munsel, Patrice (soprano); Spokane, Wash., 5/14/1925
Murdoch, Rupert (publisher); Melbourne, 3/11/1931
Murillo, Bartolomé Esteban (painter); Seville, Spain **(1617–1682)**
Murphy, Audie (actor and war hero); Kingston, Tex. **(1924–1971)**
Murphy, George (actor, dancer, and ex-Senator); New Haven, Conn., 7/4/1902
Murray, Arthur (dance teacher); New York City, 4/4/1895
Murray, Kathryn (dance teacher); Jersey City, N.J., 1906
Murray, Ken (Don Court) (producer); New York City, 7/14/1903
Murray, Mae (Marie Adrienne Koenig) (actress); Portsmouth, Va. **(1890–1965)**
Murrow, Edward R. (commentator and government official); Greensboro, N.C. **(1908–1965)**
Mussolini, Benito (Italian dictator); Dovia, Forli, Italy **(1883–1945)**
Myerson, Bess (consumer advocate); Bronx, N.Y., 1924
Myrdal, Gunnar (sociologist and economist); Gustaf Parish, Sweden, 12/6/1898

N

Nabokov, Vladimir (novelist); St. Petersburg, Russia **(1899–1977)**
Nabors, Jim (actor and singer); Sylacauga, Ala., 6/12/1932
Nader, Ralph (consumer advocate); Winsted, Conn., 2/27/1934
Nagel, Conrad (actor); Keokuk, Iowa **(1897–1970)**
Naish, J. Carrol (actor); New York City **(1900–1973)**
Naldi, Nita (Anita Donna Dooley) (actress); New York City **(1899–1961)**
Napoleon Bonaparte (Emperor of the French); Ajaccio, Corsica (France) **(1769–1821)**
Nash, Graham (singer); Blackpool, England, 1942
Nash, Ogden (poet); Rye, N.Y. **(1902–1971)**
Nasser, Gamal Abdel (statesman); Beni Mor, Egypt **(1918–1970)**
Nast, Thomas (cartoonist); Landau (Germany) **(1840–1902)**
Nation, Carry Amelia (temperance leader); Garrard County, Ky. **(1846–1911)**
Natwick, Mildred (actress); Baltimore, 6/19/1908
Nazimova, Alla (actress); Yalta, Crimea, Russia **(1879–1945)**
Neagle, Anna (Marjorie Robertson) (actress); London, 10/20/1908
Neal, Patricia (actress); Packard, Ky., 1/20/1926
Neff, Hildegarde (actress); Ulm, Germany, 12/28/1925
Negri, Pola (Appolina Chapulez) (actress); Bromberg (Poland), c. 1897
Nehru, Jawaharlal (First Prime Minister of India); Allahabad, India **(1889–1964)**
Nelson, Barry (actor); San Francisco, 1920
Nelson, David (actor); New York City, 10/24/1936
Nelson, Harriet Hilliard (Peggy Lou Snyder) (actress); Des Moines, Iowa, 1914
Nelson, Ozzie (Oswald) (actor); Jersey City, N.J. **(1907–1975)**
Nelson, Ricky (Eric) (singer and actor); Teaneck, N.J., 5/8/1940
Nelson, Viscount Horatio (naval officer); Burnham Thorpe, England **(1758–1805)**
Nenni, Pietro (Socialist leader); Faenza, Italy, 2/9/1891
Nero (Nero Claudius Caesàr Drusus Germanicus) (Roman emperor); Antium (Italy) **(37–68)**
Nero, Peter (pianist); New York City, 5/22/1934
Nesbit, Cathleen (actress); Cheshire, England, 1889
Nevelson, Louise (sculptor); Kiev, Russia, 9/23/1900
Newhart, Bob (entertainer); Chicago, 9/5/1929
Newhouse, Samuel I. (publisher); New York City **(1895–1979)**
Newley, Anthony (actor and song writer); London, 9/24/1931
Newman, Edwin (news commentator); New York City, 1/25/1919
Newman, Paul (actor and director); Cleveland, 1/26/1925
Newman, Randy (singer); Los Angeles, 11/28/1943
Newton, Huey (black activist); New Orleans, 2/17/1942
Newton, Sir Isaac (mathematician and scientist); nr. Grantham, England **(1642–1727)**
Newton, Wayne (singer); Norfolk, Va., 4/3/1942
Newton-John, Olivia (singer); Cambridge, England, 9/26/1948
Nichols, Mike (Michael Peschkowsky) (stage and film director); Berlin, 11/6/1931
Nicholson, Jack (actor); Neptune, N.J., 4/22/1937
Nietzsche, Friedrich Wilhelm (philosopher); nr. Lützen (Germany) **(1844–1900)**
Nightingale, Florence (nurse); Florence (Italy) **(1820–1910)**
Nijinsky, Waslaw (ballet dancer); Warsaw **(1890–1950)**
Nilsson, Harry (singer and songwriter); Brooklyn, N.Y., 6/15/1941
Nilsson, Birgit (soprano); West Karup, Sweden, 5/17/1923
Nimitz, Chester W. (naval officer); Fredericksburg, Tex. **(1885–1966)**
Nimoy, Leonard (actor); Boston, 3/26/1931
Nin, Anaïs (author and diarist); Neuilly, France **(1903–1977)**
Niven, David (actor); Kirriemuir, Scotland, 3/1/1910
Nizer, Louis (lawyer and author); London, 2/6/1902
Nobel, Alfred Bernhard (industrialist); Stockholm **(1833–1896)**
Noguchi, Isamu (sculptor); Los Angeles, 11/7/1904
Nolan, Lloyd (actor); San Francisco, 8/11/1902
Nolte, Nick (actor); Omaha, Neb., 1940
Norell, Norman (Norman Levinson) (fashion designer); Noblesville, Ind. **(1900–1972)**
Norstad, Gen. Lauris (ex-commander of NATO forces); Minneapolis, 3/24/1907
North, John Ringling (circus director); Baraboo, Wis., 8/14/1903
North, Sheree (actress); Los Angeles, 1/17/1933
Norton, Eleanor Holmes (New York City government official, lawyer); Washington, D.C., 6/13/1937
Nostradamus (Michel de Notredame) (astrologer); St. Rémy, France **(1503–1566)**
Novaes, Guiomar (pianist); São João de Boa Vista, Brazil **(1895–1979)**
Novak, Kim (Marilyn Novak) (actress); Chicago, 2/13/1933
Novarro, Ramon (Ramon Samaniegoes) (actor); Durango, Mexico **(1899–1968)**
Nugent, Elliott (actor and director); Dover, Ohio, **(1899–1980)**
Nureyev, Rudolf (ballet dancer); U.S.S.R., 3/17/1938
Nuyen, France (actress); Marseilles, France, 7/31/1939
Nyro, Laura (singer and songwriter); Bronx, N.Y., 1947

O

Oakie, Jack (actor); Sedalia, Mo. **(1903–1978)**
Oates, Joyce Carol (novelist); Lockport, N.Y., 6/16/1938
Oberon, Merle (Estelle Merle O'Brien Thompson) (actress); Tasmania **(1911–1979)**
O'Brian, Hugh (Hugh J. Krampe) (actor); Rochester, N.Y., 4/19/1930
O'Brien, Edmond (actor); New York City, 9/10/1915
O'Brien, Lawrence F. (commissioner of National Basketball Association); Springfield, Mass., 7/7/1917
O'Brien, Margaret (Angela Maxine O'Brien) (actress); San Diego, Calif., 1/15/1937
O'Brien, Pat (William Joseph O'Brien, Jr.) (actor); Milwaukee, 11/11/1899
O'Casey, Sean (playwright); Dublin **(1881–1964)**
Ochs, Adolph Simon (publisher); Cincinnati **(1858–1935)**
O'Connor, Carroll (actor); New York City, 8/2/1924
O'Connor, Donald (actor); Chicago, 8/28/1925
Odets, Clifford (playwright); Philadelphia **(1906–1963)**
Odetta (Odetta Holmes) (folk singer and actress); Brimingham, Ala., 12/31/1930
Offenbach, Jacques (composer); Cologne, Germany **(1819–1880)**
O'Hara, John (novelist); Pottsville, Pa. **(1905–1970)**
O'Hara, Maureen (Maureen FitzSimons) (actress); Dublin, 8/17/1921
Oistrakh, David (concert violinist); Odessa, Russia **(1908–1974)**
O'Keeffe, Georgia (painter); Sun Prairie, Wis., 11/15/1887
Oland, Warner (actor); Umea, Sweden **(1880–1938)**
Olav V (King of Norway); Sandringham, England, 7/2/1903
Oldenburg, Claes (painter); Stockholm, Sweden, 1/28/1929
Olivier, Lord (Laurence) (actor); Dorking, England, 5/22/1907
Olmsted, Frederick Law (landscape architect); Hartford, Conn. **(1822–1903)**
Olsen, Ole (John Sigvard Olsen) (comedian); Peru, Ind. **(1892–1963)**
Omar Khayyam (poet and astronomer); Nishapur (Iran) **(died c. 1123)**
Onassis, Aristotle (shipping executive); Smyrna, Turkey **(1906–1975)**
Onassis, Christina (shipping executive); New York City, 12/11/1950
Onassis, Jacqueline Kennedy (Jacqueline Bouvier) (President's widow); Southampton, N.Y., 7/28/1929
O'Neal, Ryan (Patrick) (actor); Los Angeles, 4/20/1941
O'Neal, Tatum (actress); Los Angeles, Calif., 1963
O'Neill, Eugene Gladstone (playwright); New York City **(1888–1953)**
O'Neill, Jennifer (actress); Rio de Janeiro, 2/20/1949
Oppenheimer, J. Robert (nuclear physicist); New York City **(1904–1967)**
Orff, Carl (composer); Munich, Germany, 7/10/1895
Orlando, Tony (singer); New York City, 1944
Ormandy, Eugene (conductor); Budapest, 11/18/1899
Orozco, José Clemente (painter); Zapotlán, Jalisco, Mexico **(1883–1949)**
Orwell, George (Eric Arthur Blair) (British author); Motihari, India **(1903–1950)**
Osborn, Paul (playwright); Evansville, Ind., 9/4/1901
Osborne, John (playwright); London, 12/12/1929
Osler, Sir William (physician); Bondhead, Ontario, Canada **(1849–1919)**
Osmond, Donny (singer); Ogden, Utah, 12/9/1957
Osmond, Marie (singer); Ogden, Utah, 1959
O'Sullivan, Maureen (actress); County Roscommon, Ireland, 5/17/1911
Otis, Elisha (inventor); Halifax, Vt. **(1811–1861)**
O'Toole, Peter (actor); Connemara, Ireland, 8/2/1933
Ovid (Publius Ovidius Naso) (poet); Sulmona (Italy) **(43 B.C.–? A.D. 17)**

Owens, Buck (Alvis Edgar Owens) (singer); Sherman, Tex., 8/12/1929

P

Paar, Jack (TV personality); Canton, Ohio, 5/1/1918
Pacino, Al (Alfred) (actor); New York City, 4/25/1940
Packard, Vance (author); Granville Summit, Pa., 5/22/1914
Paderewski, Ignace Jan (pianist and statesman); Kurylowka, Russian Podolia **(1860–1941)**
Paganini, Nicolò (violinist); Genoa (Italy) **(1782–1840)**
Page, Geraldine (actress); Kirksville, Mo., 11/22/1924
Page, Patti (Clara Ann Fowler) (singer and entertainer); Claremore, Okla., 11/8/1927
Paige, Janis (actress); Tacoma, Wash., 9/16/1922
Paine, Thomas (political philosopher); Thetford, England **(1737–1809)**
Palance, Jack (Walter Palanuik) (actor); Lattimer, Pa., 2/18/1920
Paley, William S. (broadcasting executive); Chicago, 9/28/1901
Palladio, Andrea (architect); Padua or Vicenza (Italy) **(1508–1580)**
Palmer, Betsy (actress); East Chicago, Ind., 1929
Palmer, Lilli (actress); Posen (Poland), 5/24/1914
Palmerston, Henry John Templeton (3rd Viscount) (statesman); Broadlands, England **(1784–1865)**
Papanicolaou, George N. (physician); Coumi, Greece **(1883–1962)**
Papas, Irene (actress); Chiliomodion, Greece, 1929
Papp, Joseph (Joseph Papirofsky) (stage producer and director); Brooklyn, N.Y., 6/22/1921
Park, Chung Hee (President of South Korea); Sangmo-ri, Korea **(1917–1979)**
Parker, Dorothy (Dorothy Rothschild) (author); West End, N.J. **(1893–1967)**
Parker, Eleanor (actress); Cedarville, Ohio, 6/26/1922
Parker, Fess (actor); Fort Worth, Tex., 1925
Parker, Suzy (model and actress); San Antonio, 10/28/1933
Parkinson, C. (Cyril) Northcote (historian); Durham, England, 7/30/1909
Parks, Bert (Bert Jacobson) (entertainer); Atlanta, 12/30/1914
Parks, Gordon (film director); Ft. Scott, Kan., 11/30/1912
Parnell, Charles Stewart (statesman); Avondale, Ireland **(1846–1891)**
Parnis, Mollie (Mollie Parnis Livingston) (fashion designer); New York City, 3/18/1905
Parsons, Estelle (actress); Marblehead, Mass., 11/20/1927
Parton, Dolly (singer); Locust Ridge, Tenn. 1/19/1946
Pascal, Blaise (philosopher); Clermont, France **(1623–1662)**
Pasternak, Boris Leonidovich (author); Moscow **(1890–1960)**
Pasternak, Joseph (film producer); Silagy-Somlyo, Romania, 9/19/1901
Pasteur, Louis (chemist); Dôle, France **(1822–1895)**
Patton, George Smith, Jr. (general); San Gabriel, Calif., **(1885–1945)**
Paul, Les (Lester William Polfus) (guitarist); Waukesha, Wis., 6/9/1915
Paul VI (Giovanni Battista Montini) (Pope); Concesio, nr. Brescia, Italy **(1897–1978)**
Pauling, Linus Carl (chemist); Portland, Ore., 2/28/1901
Pavarotti, Luciano (tenor); Modena, Italy, 10/12/1935
Pavlov, Ivan Petrovich (physiologist); Ryazan district, Russia **(1849–1936)**
Pavlova, Anna (ballerina); St. Petersburg, Russia **(1885–1931)**
Payne, John (actor); Roanoke, Va., 1912
Peale, Norman Vincent (clergyman); Bowersville, Ohio, 5/31/1898
Pearl, Minnie (Sarah Ophelia Colley Cannon) (comedienne and singer); Centerville, Tenn., 10/25/1912
Pears, Peter (tenor); Farnham, England, 6/22/1910
Pearson, Drew (Andrew Russel Pearson) (columnist); Evanston, Ill. **(1897–1969)**
Pearson, Lester B. (statesman); Toronto **(1897–1972)**
Peary, Robert Edwin (explorer); Cresson, Pa. **(1856–1920)**
Peck, Gregory (actor); La Jolla, Calif., 4/5/1916
Peckinpah, Sam (film director); Fresno, Calif., 2/21/1925
Peerce, Jan (tenor); New York City, 1904
Pegler, (James) Westbrook (columnist); Minneapolis, **(1894–1969)**
Pei, I. M. (architect); Canton, China, 4/26/1917
Penn, Arthur (stage and film director); Philadelphia, 9/27/1922
Penn, William (American colonist); London **(1644–1718)**
Penney, James C. (merchant); Hamilton, Mo. **(1875–1971)**
Peppard, George (actor); Detroit, 10/1/1933
Pepys, Samuel (diarist); Bampton, England **(1633–1703)**
Perelman, S. J. (Sidney J.) (humorist); Brooklyn, N.Y. **(1904–1979)**
Pericles (statesman); Athens **(died 429 B.C.)**
Perkins, Osgood (actor); West Newton, Mass. **(1892–1937)**
Perkins, Tony (Anthony) (actor); New York City, 4/14/1932
Perlman, Itzhak (violinist); Tel Aviv (Israel), 8/31/1945
Perón, Isabel (María Estela Martínez Cartas) (former chief of state); La Rioja, Argentina, 2/4/1931
Perón, Juan D. (statesman); nr. Lobos, Argentina **(1895–1974)**
Perón, Maria Eva Duarte de (political leader); Los Toldos, Argentina **(1919–1952)**
Perrine, Valerie (actress and dancer); Galveston, Tex., 9/3/1943
Pershing, John Joseph (general); Linn County, Mo. **(1860–1948)**
Peters, Bernadette (actress); New York City, 1944
Peters, Jean (actress); Canton, Ohio, 10/15/1926
Peters, Roberta (Roberta Peterman) (soprano); New York City, 5/4/1930
Petrarch (Francesco Petrarca) (poet); Arezzo (Italy) **(1304–1374)**
Philip (Philip Mountbatten) (Duke of Edinburgh); Corfu, Greece, 6/10/1921
Piaf, Edith (Edith Gassion) (chanteuse); Paris **(1916–1963)**
Piatigorsky, Gregor (cellist); Ekaterinoslav, Russia **(1903–1976)**
Piazza, Ben (actor); Little Rock, Ark., 7/30/1934
Piazza, Marguerite (soprano); New Orleans, 5/6/1926
Picasso, Pablo (painter and sculptor); Málaga, Spain **(1881–1973)**
Pickford, Jack (Jack Smith) (actor); Toronto **(1896–1933)**
Pickford, Mary (Gladys Mary Smith) (actress); Toronto, 4/8/1893
Picon, Molly (actress); New York City, 6/1/1898
Pidgeon, Walter (actor); East St. John, New Brunswick, Canada, 9/23/1898
Pinter, Harold (playwright); London, 10/10/1930
Pinza, Ezio (basso); Rome **(1892–1957)**
Pirandello, Luigi (dramatist and novelist); nr. Girgenti, Italy **(1867–1936)**
Pissaro, Camille Jacob (painter); St. Thomas (U.S. Virgin Islands) **(1830–1903)**
Piston, Walter (composer); Rockland, Me. **(1894–1976)**
Pitman, Sir (Isaac) James (educator and publisher); Bath, England, 8/14/1901
Pitt, William ("Younger Pitt") (statesman); nr. Bromley, England **(1759–1806)**
Pitts, ZaSu (actress); Parsons, Kan. **(1898–1963)**
Pius XII (Eugenio Pacelli) (Pope); Rome **(1876–1958)**
Pizarro, Francisco (explorer); Trujillo, Spain **(1470?–1541)**
Plato (Aristocles) (philosopher); Athens (?) **(427?–347 B.C.)**
Pleasence, Donald (actor); Worksop, England, 10/5/1919
Pleshette, Suzanne (actress); New York City, 1/31/1937
Plimpton, George (author); New York City, 3/18/1927
Plisetskaya, Maya (ballerina); Moscow, 11/20/1925
Plowright, Joan (actress); Brigg, England, 10/28/1929
Plummer, Christopher (actor); Toronto, 12/13/1929
Plutarch (biographer); Chaeronea (Greece) **(46?–?120)**
Pocahontas (Matoaka) (American Indian princess); Virginia (?) **(1595?–1617)**
Podhoretz, Norman (author); Brooklyn, N.Y., 1/16/1930
Poe, Edgar Allan (poet and story writer); Boston, Mass. **(1809–1849)**
Poitier, Sidney (film actor and director); Miami, Fla., 2/20/1924
Polanski, Roman (film director); Paris, 8/18/1933
Pollard, Michael J. (actor); Passaic, N.J., 5/30/1939
Pollock, Jackson (painter); Cody, Wyo. **(1912–1956)**
Polo, Marco (traveler); Venice **(1254?–?1324)**
Pompey (Gnaeus Pompeius Magnus) (general); Rome (?) **(106–48 B.C.)**
Ponce de Leon, Juan (explorer); Servas, Spain **(1460?–1521)**
Pons, Lily (coloratura soprano); Cannes, France **(1904–1976)**
Ponti, Carlo (director); Milan, Italy, 1913
Pope, Alexander (poet); London **(1688–1744)**
Porter, Cole (songwriter); Peru, Ind. **(1892–1964)**
Porter, Katherine Anne (novelist); Indian Creek, Tex. **(1890–1980)**
Post, Wiley (aviator); Grand Plain, Tex. **(1900–1935)**
Poston, Tom (actor); Columbus, Ohio, 10/17/1927
Potok, Chaim (author); New York City, 2/17/1929
Pound, Ezra (poet); Hailey, Idaho **(1885–1972)**
Powell, Adam Clayton, Jr. (Congressman); New Haven, Conn. **(1908–1972)**
Powell, Dick (actor); Mt. View, Ark. **(1904–1963)**
Powell, Eleanor (actress); Springfield, Mass., 11/21/1912
Powell, Jane (Suzanne Burce) (actress and singer); Portland, Ore., 4/1/1929
Powell, William (actor); Pittsburgh, 7/29/1892
Power, Tyrone (actor); Cincinnati, Ohio **(1914–1958)**
Powers, Stephanie (Taffy Paul) (actress); Hollywood, Calif., 11/12/1942
Praxiteles (sculptor); Athens **(c.370–c.330 B.C.)**
Preminger, Otto (film director and producer); Vienna, 12/5/1906
Prentiss, Paula (Paula Ragusa) (actress); San Antonio, 1939
Presley, Elvis (singer and actor); Tupelo, Miss. **(1935–1977)**
Preston, Robert (Robert Preston Meservey) (actor); Newton Highlands, Mass., 6/8/1918
Previn, André (conductor); Berlin, 4/6/1929
Previn, Dory (singer); Rahway, N.J., 10/22/1929(?)
Price, Leontyne (Mary) (soprano); Laurel, Miss., 2/10/1927
Price, Ray (country music artist); Perryville, Tex., 1/12/1926
Price, Vincent (actor); St. Louis, 5/27/1911
Pride, Charley (singer); Sledge, Miss., 3/18/1938(?)
Priestley, J. B. (John B.) (author); Bradford, England, 9/13/1894
Priestley, Joseph (chemist); nr. Leeds, England **(1733–1804)**
Primrose, William (violist); Glasgow, Scotland, 8/23/1904
Prince, Harold (stage producer); New York City, 1/30/1928
Prinze, Freddie (actor); New York City **(1954–1977)**
Pritchett, V(ictor) S(awdon) (literary critic); Ipswich, England, 12/16/1900
Procter, William (scientist); Cincinnati **(1872–1951)**
Prokofieff, Sergei Sergeevich (composer); St. Petersburg, Russia **(1891–1953)**

Proust, Marcel (novelist); Paris **(1871–1922)**
Provine, Dorothy (actress); Deadwood, S. Dak., 1/20/1937
Prowse, Juliet (actress); Bombay, 9/25/1936
Pryor, Richard (comedian); Peoria, Ill., 12/1/1940
Ptolemy (Claudius Ptolemaeus) (astronomer and geographer); Ptolemais Hermii (Egypt) **(2nd century** A.D.**)**
Pucci, Emilio (Marchese di Barsento) (fashion designer); Naples, Italy, 11/20/1914
Puccini, Giacomo (composer); Lucca, Italy **(1858–1924)**
Puente, Tito (band leader); New York City, 4/20/1923
Pulaski, Casimir (military officer); Podolia, Poland **(1748–1779)**
Pulitzer, Joseph (publisher); Makó (Hungary) **(1847–1911)**
Pullman, George (inventor); Brockton, N.Y. **(1831–1897)**
Pusey, Nathan M. (educator); Council Bluffs, Iowa, 4/4/1907
Pushkin, Alexander Sergeevich (poet and dramatist); Moscow **(1799–1837)**
Puzo, Mario (novelist); New York City, 10/15/1921
Pyle, Ernest Taylor (journalist); Dana, Ind. **(1900–1945)**
Pythagoras (mathematician and philosopher); Samos (Greece) **(6th century** B.C.**)**

Q

Quayle, Anthony (actor); Ainsdale, England, 9/7/1913
Queen, Ellery: pen name of Frederic Dannay and the late Manfred B. Lee.
Quinn, Anthony (actor); Chihuahua, Mexico, 4/21/1916

R

Rabe, David (playwright); Dubuque, Iowa, 3/10/1940
Rabelais, François (satirist); nr. Chinon, France **(1494?–1553)**
Rabi, I. I. (Isidor Isaac) (physicist); Rymanow (Poland), 7/29/1898
Rachmaninoff, Sergei Wassilievitch (pianist and composer); Oneg Estate, Novgorod, Russia **(1873–1943)**
Racine, Jean Baptiste (dramatist); La Ferté-Milon, France **(1639–1699)**
Radner, Gilda (comedienne); Detroit, 6/28/1946
Raft, George (actor); New York City, 9/27/1896
Rainer, Luise (actress); Vienna, 1912
Raines, Ella (actress); Snoqualmie Falls, Wash., 1921
Rainier III (Prince); Monaco, 5/31/1923
Rains, Claude (actor); London **(1889–1967)**
Raitt, Bonnie (singer); Los Angeles, 1950
Raleigh, Sir Walter (courtier and navigator); London **(1552?–1618)**
Randall, Tony (Leonard Rosenberg) (actor); Tulsa, Okla., 2/26/1924
Randolph, Asa Philip (labor leader); Crescent City, Fla., 4/15/1889
Raphael (Raffaello Santi) (painter and architect); Urbino (Italy) **(1483–1520)**
Rasputin, Grigori Efimovich (monk); Tobolsk Province, Russia **(1871?–1916)**
Rathbone, Basil (actor); Johannesburg, South Africa **(1892–1967)**
Rather, Dan (TV newscaster); Wharton, Tex., 10/31/1931
Ratoff, Gregory (film director); St. Petersburg, Russia **(1897–1960)**
Rattigan, Terence (playwright); London, **(1911–1978)**
Rauschenberg, Robert (painter); Port Arthur, Tex., 1925
Ravel, Maurice Joseph (composer); Ciboure, France **(1875–1937)**
Rawls, Lou (singer); Chicago, 12/1/1936
Ray, Man (painter); Philadelphia **(1890–1976)**
Ray, Satyajat (film director); Calcutta, 5/2/1922
Rayburn, Gene (TV personality); Christopher, Ill., 12/22/1917
Raye, Martha (Margie Yvonne Reed) (comedienne and actress); Butte, Mont., 8/27/1916
Raymond, Gene (actor); New York City, 8/13/1908
Reagan, Ronald (actor, ex-Gov. California); Tampico, Ill., 2/6/1911
Reasoner, Harry (TV commentator); Dakota City, Iowa, 4/17/1923
Redding, Otis (singer); Dawson, Ga. **(1941–1967)**
Reddy, Helen (singer); Melbourne, 10/25/1941
Redford, Robert (Charles Robert Redford, Jr.) (actor); Santa Monica, Calif., 8/18/1937
Redgrave, Lynn (actress); London, 3/8/1943
Redgrave, Sir Michael (actor); Bristol, England, 3/20/1908
Redgrave, Vanessa (actress); London, 1/30/1937
Reed, Donna (actress); Denison, Iowa, 1/27/1921
Reed, Rex (critic); Ft. Worth, 10/2/1940
Reed, Walter (army surgeon); Belroi, Va. **(1851–1902)**
Reese, Della (Deloreese Patricia Early) (singer); Detroit, 7/6/1932
Reeves, Jim (singer); Panola County, Tex. **(1923–1964)**
Reid, Wallace (actor); St. Louis **(1891–1923)**
Reiner, Carl (actor); New York City, 3/20/1922
Reiner, Fritz (conductor); Budapest **(1888–1963)**
Reiner, Robert (actor); Bronx, N.Y., 1945
Reinhardt, Max (Max Goldmann) (theater producer); nr. Vienna **(1873–1943)**
Remarque, Erich Maria (novelist); Osnabruk, Germany **(1898–1970)**
Rembrandt (Rembrandt Harmensz van Rijn) (painter); Leyden (Netherlands) **(1606–1669)**
Remick, Lee (Ann) (actress); Boston, 12/14/1935
Rennert, Günther (opera director and producer); Essen, Germany, 4/1/1911
Rennie, Michael (actor); Bradford, England **(1909–1971)**
Renoir, Jean (film director and writer); Paris, **(1894–1979)**
Renoir, Pierre Auguste (painter); Limoges, France **(1841–1919)**
Resnais, Alain (film director); Vannes, France, 6/3/1922
Resnik, Regina (mezzo-soprano); New York City, 8/30/1922
Respighi, Ottorino (composer); Bologna, Italy **(1879–1936)**
Reston, James (journalist); Clydebank, Scotland, 11/3/1909
Reuther, Walter (labor leader); Wheeling, W. Va. **(1907–1970)**
Revere, Paul (silversmith and hero of famous ride); Boston **(1735–1818)**
Revson, Charles (business executive); Boston **(1906–1975)**
Reynolds, Burt (actor); Waycross, Ga., 2/11/1936
Renolds, Debbie (Marie Frances Reynolds) (actress); El Paso, 4/1/1932
Reynolds, Sir Joshua (painter); nr. Plymouth, England **(1723–1792)**
Rhodes, Cecil John (South African statesman); Bishop Stortford, England **(1853–1902)**
Rice, Elmer (playwright); New York City **(1892–1967)**
Rice, Grantland (sports writer); Murfreesboro, Tenn. **(1880–1954)**
Rich, Buddy (Bernard) (drummer); Brooklyn, N.Y., 6/30/1917
Rich, Charlie (singer); Colt, Ark., 12/14/1934
Richardson, Elliot L. (ex-Cabinet member); Boston, 7/20/1920
Richardson, Sir Ralph (actor); Cheltenham, England, 12/19/1902
Richardson, Tony (director); Shipley, England, 6/5/1928
Richelieu, Duc de (Armand Jean du Plessis) (cardinal); Paris **(1585–1642)**
Richter, Charles Francis (seismologist); Hamilton, Canada, 4/26/1900
Richter, Sviatoslav (pianist); Zhitomir, Ukraine, 3/20/1914
Rickenbacker, Edward V. (aviator); Columbus, Ohio **(1890–1973)**
Rickles, Don (comedian); New York City, 5/8/1926
Rickover, Vice Admiral Hyman G. (atomic energy expert); Russia, 1/27/1900
Riddle, Nelson (composer); Hackensack, N.J., 6/1/1921
Ridgway, General Matthew B. (ex-Army Chief of Staff); Ft. Monroe, Va., 3/3/1895
Rigg, Diana (actress); Doncaster, England, 7/20/1938
Riley, James Whitcomb (poet); Greenfield, Ind. **(1849–1916)**
Rimsky-Korsakov, Nikolai Andreevich (composer); Tikhvin, Russia **(1844–1908)**
Rinehart, Mary (née Roberts) (novelist); Pittsburgh **(1876–1958)**
Ritchard, Cyril (actor and director); Sydney, Australia **(1898–1977)**
Ritter, John (Jonathan) (actor); Burbank, Calif., 9/17/1948
Ritter, Tex (Woodward Maurice Ritter) (singer) Panola County, Tex., **(1905–1973)**
Ritz, Al (Al Joachim) (comedian); Newark, N.J. **(1901–1965)**
Rivera, Diego (painter); Guanajuato, Mexico **(1886–1957)**
Rivera, Geraldo (Miguel) (TV newscaster); New York City, 7/3/1943
Rivers, Joan (comedienne); Brooklyn, N.Y., 1935(?)
Rivers, Larry (Yitzroch Loiza Grossberg) (painter); New York City, 8/17/1923
Robards, Jason, Jr. (actor); Chicago, 7/26/1922
Robards, Jason, Sr. (actor); Hillsdale, Mich. **(1892–1963)**
Robbins, Harold (Harold Rubin) (novelist); New York City, 5/21/1916
Robbins, Jerome (Jerome Rabinowitz) (choreographer); New York City, 10/11/1918
Robbins, Marty (singer); Glendale, Ariz., 12/26/1925
Roberts, (Granville) Oral (evangelist and publisher); nr. Ada, Okla., 1/24/1918
Robertson, Cliff (actor); La Jolla, Calif., 9/9/1925
Robertson, Dale (actor); Oklahoma City, 1923
Robeson, Paul (singer and actor); Princeton, N.J., **(1898–1976)**
Robespierre, Maximilien François Marie Isidore de (French Revolutionist); Arras, France **(1758–1794)**
Robinson, Bill "Bojangles" (Luther) (dancer); Richmond, Va. **(1878–1949)**
Robinson, Edward G. (Emanuel Goldenberg) (actor); Bucharest **(1893–1973)**
Robinson, Edwin Arlington (poet); Head Tide, Me. **(1869–1935)**
Robson, Dame Flora (actress); South Shields, England, 3/28/1902
Rochester (Eddie Anderson) (actor); Oakland, Calif. **(1905–1977)**
Rockefeller, David (banker); New York City, 6/12/1915
Rockefeller, John Davison (capitalist); Richford, N.Y. **(1839–1937)**
Rockefeller, John Davison, Jr. (industrialist); Cleveland **(1874–1960)**
Rockefeller, John D., 3rd (philanthropist); New York City **(1906–1978)**
Rockefeller, Laurance S. (conservationist); New York City, 5/26/1910
Rockwell, Norman (painter and illustrator); New York City, **(1894–1978)**
Rodgers, Jimmie (singer); Meridian, Miss. **(1897–1933)**
Rodgers, Richard (composer); New York City **(1902–1979)**
Rodin, François Auguste René (sculptor); Paris **(1840–1917)**
Roentgen, Wilhelm Konrad (physicist); Lennep, Prussia **(1845–1923)**
Rogers, Buddy (Charles) (actor); Olathe, Kan., 8/13/1904
Rogers, Ginger (Virginia McMath) (dancer and actress); Independence, Mo., 7/16/1911

Rogers, Roy (Leonard Slye) (actor); Cincinnati, 11/5/1912
Rogers, Will (William Penn Adair Rogers) (humorist); Oologah, Okla. **(1879–1935)**
Rogers, Will, Jr. (actor); New York City, 10/20/1911
Rogers, William P. (ex-Secretary of State); Norfolk, N.Y., 6/23/1913
Roland, Gilbert (actor); Juarez, Mexico, 12/11/1905
Rolland, Romain (author); Clamecy, France **(1866–1944)**
Rollins, Sonny (saxophonist); New York City, 9/7/1930
Romberg, Sigmund (composer); Szeged (Hungary) **(1887–1951)**
Rome, Harold (composer); Hartford, Conn., 5/27/1908
Romero, Cesar (actor); New York City, 2/15/1907
Romney, George W. (ex-Secretary of HUD); Chihuahua, Mexico, 7/8/1907
Romulo, Carlos P. (diplomat and educator); Manila, 1/14/1899
Ronstadt, Linda (singer); Tucson, Ariz., 7/30/1946
Rooney, Mickey (Joe Yule, Jr.) (actor); Brooklyn, N.Y., 9/23/1920
Roosevelt, Anna Eleanor (reformer and humanitarian); New York City **(1884–1962)**
Rose, Billy (showman); New York City **(1899–1966)**
Rose, Leonard, (concert cellist); Washington, D.C., 7/27/1918
Ross, Diana (singer); Detroit, 3/26/1944
Ross, Katharine (actress); Hollywood, Calif., 1/29/1943
Rossellini, Roberto (film director); Rome **(1906–1977)**
Rossetti, Dante Gabriel (painter and poet); London, **(1828–1882)**
Rossini, Gioacchino Antonio (composer); Pesaro (Italy) **(1792–1868)**
Rostand, Edmond (dramatist); Marseilles, France **(1868–1918)**
Rostow, Walt Whitman (economist); New York City, 10/7/1916
Rostropovich, Mstislav (cellist and conductor); Baku, U.S.S.R., 8/12/1927
Roth, Lillian (singer); Boston **(1910–1980)**
Roth, Philip (novelist); Newark, N.J., 3/19/1933
Rothko, Mark (Marcus Rothkovich) (painter); Russia **(1903–1970)**
Rouault, Georges (painter); Paris, France **(1871–1958)**
Roundtree, Richard (actor); New Rochelle, N.Y., 9/7/1942
Rousseau, Henri (painter); Laval, France **(1844–1910)**
Rousseau, Jean Jacques (philosopher); Geneva **(1712–1778)**
Rovere, Richard H. (journalist); Jersey City, N.J., 5/5/1915
Rowan, Dan (comedian); Beggs, Okla., 7/2/1922
Rowlands, Gena (actress); Cambria, Wis., 6/19/1936(?)
Rubens, Sir Peter Paul (painter); Siegen (Germany) **(1577–1640)**
Rubenstein, Artur (concert pianist); Lódz (Poland), 1/28/1887
Rubinstein, Helena (cosmetics executive); Kraków (Poland) **(1882?–1965)**
Rudel, Julius (conductor); Vienna, 3/6/1921
Ruggles, Charles (actor); Los Angeles **(1892–1970)**
Rule, Janice (actress); Norwood, Ohio, 8/15/1931
Runyon, (Alfred) Damon (journalist); Manhattan, Kan. **(1884–1946)**
Rusk, Dean (ex-Sec. of State); Cherokee County, Ga., 2/9/1909
Ruskin, John (art critic); London **(1819–1900)**
Russell, Lord Bertrand (Arthur William) (mathematician and philosopher); Trelleck, Wales **(1872–1970)**
Russell, Jane (actress); Bemidji, Minn., 6/21/1921
Russell, Leon (pianist and singer); Lawton, Okla., 4/2/1941
Russell, Lillian (Helen Louise Leonard) (soprano); Clinton, Iowa **(1861–1922)**
Russell, Nipsy (comedian); Atlanta, 1924(?)
Russell, Rosalind (actress); Waterbury, Conn. **(1912–1976)**
Rustin, Bayard (civil rights leader); West Chester, Pa., 1910
Rutherford, Dame Margaret (actress); London, England **(1892–1972)**
Ryan, Robert (actor); Chicago **(1909–1973)**
Rydell, Bobby (singer); Philadelphia, 1942
Rysanek, Leonie (dramatic soprano); Vienna, 11/14/1928

S

Saarinen, Eero (architect); Finland **(1910–1961)**
Sabin, Albert B. (polio researcher); Bialystok (Poland), 8/26/1906
Sadat, Anwar el- (President); Egypt, 12/25/1918
Sagan, Françoise (novelist); Cajarc, France, 6/21/1935
Sahl, Mort (Morton Lyon Sahl) (comedian); Montreal, 5/11/1927
Saint, Eva Marie (actress); Newark, N.J., 7/4/1924
Saint-Gaudens, Augustus (sculptor); Dublin **(1848–1907)**
St. James, Susan (actress); Los Angeles, 1946
St. John, Jill (actress); Los Angeles, 8/19/1940
St. Johns, Adela Rogers (journalist and author); Los Angeles, 5/20/1894
Saint-Laurent, Yves (Henri Donat Mathieu) (fashion designer); Oran, Algeria, 8/1/1936
Saint-Saëns, Charles Camille (composer); Paris **(1835–1921)**
Sainte-Marie, Buffy (Beverly) (folk singer); Craven, Saskatchewan, Canada, 2/20/1942(?)
Salinger, J. D. (Jerome David) (novelist); New York City, 1/1/1919
Salisbury, Harrison E. (journalist); Minneapolis, 11/14/1908
Salk, Jonas (polio researcher); New York City, 10/28/1914
Salk, Lee (psychologist); New York City, 1926
Salomon, Haym (American Revolution financier); Leszno, Poland **(1740–1785)**
Sand, George (Amandine Lucille Aurore Dudevant, née Dupin) (novelist); Paris **(1804–1876)**
Sandburg, Carl (poet and biographer); Galesburg, Ill. **(1878–1967)**
Sanders, George (actor); St. Petersburg, Russia **(1906–1972)**
Sands, Tommy (singer); Chicago, 8/27/1937
Sanger, Margaret (birth control leader); Corning, N.Y. **(1883–1966)**
Santayana, George (philosopher); Madrid **(1863–1952)**
Sappho (poet); Lesbos (Greece) **(lived c. 600 B.C.)**
Sargent, John Singer (painter); Florence, Italy **(1856–1925)**
Sarnoff, David (radio executive); Minsk, Russia **(1891–1971)**
Saroyan, William (novelist); Fresno, Calif., 8/31/1908
Sarrazin, Michael (actor); Quebec, 5/22/1940
Sarto, Andrea del (Andrea Domenico d'Agnolo di Francesco) (painter); Florence (Italy) **(1486–1531)**
Sartre, Jean-Paul (existentialist writer); Paris **(1905–1980)**
Sassoon, Vidal (hair stylist); London, 1/(?)/1928
Saul (King of Israel) **(11th century B.C.)**
Savalas, Telly (Aristoteles) (actor); Garden City, N.Y., 1/21/1924(?)
Sayao, Bidú (soprano); Rio de Janeiro, 5/11/1906
Scaasi, Arnold (Arnold Isaacs) (fashion designer); Montreal
Schary, Dore (producer and writer); Newark, N.J. **(1905–1980)**
Schell, Maria (actress); Vienna, 1/15/1926
Schell, Maximilian (actor); Vienna, 12/8/1930
Schiaparelli, Elsa (fashion designer); Rome **(1890?–1973)**
Schiff, Dorothy (newspaper publisher); New York City, 3/11/1903
Schildkraut, Joseph (actor); Vienna **(1896–1964)**
Schiller, Johann Christoph Friedrich von (dramatist and poet); Marbach (Germany) **(1759–1805)**
Schippers, Thomas (conductor); Kalamazoo, Mich. **(1930–1977)**
Schlesinger, Arthur M., Jr. (historian); Columbus, Ohio, 10/15/1917
Schneider, Romy (Rose-Marie Albach) (actress); Vienna, 9/23/1938
Schoenberg, Arnold (composer); Vienna **(1874–1951)**
Schopenhauer, Arthur (philosopher); Danzig (Poland) **(1788–1860)**
Schubert, Franz Peter (composer); Vienna **(1797–1828)**
Schulberg, Budd (novelist); New York City, 3/27/1914
Schulz, Charles M. (cartoonist); Minneapolis, 11/26/1922
Schuman, Robert (statesman); Luxembourg **(1886–1963)**
Schuman, William (composer); New York City, 8/4/1910
Schumann, Robert Alexander (composer); Zwickau (Germany) **(1810–1856)**
Schwartz, Arthur (song writer); Brooklyn, N.Y., 11/25/1900
Schwartz, Maurice (actor); Russia **(1891–1960)**
Schwarzkopf, Elisabeth (soprano); Jarotschin, Poznán (Poland), 12/9/1915
Schweitzer, Albert (humanitarian); Kaysersburg, Upper Alsace **(1875–1965)**
Scofield, Paul (actor); Hurstpierpoint, England, 1/21/1922
Scorsese, Martin (film director); Flushing, N.Y., 11/17/1942
Scott, George C. (actor); Wise, Va., 10/18/1927
Scott, Lizabeth (Emma Matso) (actress); Scranton, Pa., 1923
Scott, Martha (actress); Jamesport, Mo., 9/22/1914
Scott, Randolph (Randolph Crane) (actor); Orange County, Va., 1/23/1903
Scott, Robert Falcon (explorer); Devonport, England **(1868–1912)**
Scott, Sir Walter (novelist); Edinburgh, Scotland **(1771–1832)**
Scott, Zachary (actor); Austin, Tex. **(1914–1965)**
Scotto, Renata (operatic soprano); Savona, Italy, 2/?/1936?
Scruggs, Earl Eugene (bluegrass musician); Cleveland County, N.C., 1/6/1924
Sebastian, John (composer); New York City, 3/17/1944
Seberg, Jean (actress); Marshalltown, Iowa **(1938–1979)**
Sedaka, Neil (singer); Brooklyn, N.Y., 3/13/1939
Seeger, Pete (folk singer); New York City, 5/3/1919
Segal, Erich (novelist); Brooklyn, N.Y., 6/16/1937
Segal, George (actor); New York City, 2/13/1936
Segovia, Andrés (guitarist); Linares, Spain, 2/21/1893
Sellers, Peter (actor); Southsea, England **(1925–1980)**
Selye, Hans (physician); Vienna, 1/26/1907
Selznick, David O. (film producer); Pittsburgh **(1902–1965)**
Sendak, Maurice (Bernard) (children's book author and illustrator); Brooklyn, N.Y., 6/10/1928
Sennett, Mack (Michael Sinnott) (film producer); Richmond, Quebec, Canada **(1880–1960)**
Serkin, Rudolf (pianist); Eger (Hungary), 3/28/1903
Serling, Rod (story writer); Syracuse, N.Y. **(1924–1975)**
Sessions, Roger (composer); Brooklyn, N.Y., 12/28/1896
Seurat, Georges (painter); Paris **(1859–1891)**
Seuss, Dr. (Theodor Seuss Geisel) (author and illustrator); Springfield, Mass., 3/2/1904
Sevareid, Eric (TV commentator); Velva, N.D., 11/26/1912
Severinsen, Doc (band leader); Arlington, Ore., 1927
Sexton, Anne (poet); Newton, Mass. **(1928–1974)**
Shahn, Ben(jamin) (painter); Kaunas, Lithuania **(1898–1969)**
Shakespeare, William (dramatist); Stratford on Avon, England **(1564–1616)**
Shankar, Ravi (sitar player); Benares, India, 4/7/1920

Shanker, Albert (labor leader); New York City, 9/14/1928
Sharif, Omar (Michael Shalhoub) (actor); Alexandria, Egypt, 4/10/1932
Shatner, William (actor); Montreal, 3/22/1931
Shaw, Artie (Arthur Arshawsky) (band leader); New York City, 5/23/1910
Shaw, George Bernard (dramatist); Dublin, **(1856–1950)**
Shaw, Irwin (novelist); Brooklyn, N.Y., 2/27/1913
Shaw, Robert (actor); Lancashire, England, 8/9/1927
Shaw, Robert (chorale conductor); Red Bluff, Calif., 4/30/1916
Shearer, Moira (ballerina); Dunfermline, Scotland, 1/17/1926
Shearer, Norma (actress); Montreal, 1904
Shearing, George (pianist); London, 8/13/1920
Sheen, Fulton J. (Peter Sheen) (Roman Catholic bishop); El Paso, Ill. **(1895–1979)**
Sheen, Martin (Ramon Estevez) (actor); Dayton, Ohio, 8/3/1940
Shelley, Percy Bysshe (poet); nr. Horsham, England **(1792–1822)**
Shepard, Sam (playwright); Ft. Sheridan, Ill. 11/5/1943
Sheraton, Thomas (furniture designer); Stockton-on-Tees, England **(1751–1806)**
Sheridan, Ann (actress); Denton, Tex. **(1915–1967)**
Sheridan, Philip (army officer); Albany, N.Y. **(1831–1888)**
Sheridan, Richard Brinsley (dramatist); Dublin, **(1751–1816)**
Sherman, William Tecumseh (army officer); Lancaster, Ohio **(1820–1891)**
Sherwood, Robert Emmet (playwright); New Rochelle, N.Y. **(1896–1955)**
Shirer, William L. (journalist and historian); Chicago, 2/23/1904
Sholokhov, Mikhail (novelist); Veshenskaya, Russia, 5/24/1905
Shore, Dinah (Frances Rose Shore) (singer); Winchester, Tenn., 3/1/1917(?)
Short, Bobby (Robert Waltrip Short) (singer and pianist); Danville, Ill., 9/15/1924
Shostakovich, Dmitri (composer); St. Petersburg, Russia **(1906–1975)**
Shriver, Sargent (Robert Sargent Shriver, Jr.) (business executive); Westminster, Md., 11/9/1915
Shulman, Max (novelist); St. Paul, 3/14/1919
Sibelius, Jean (Johann Julius Christian Sibelius) (composer); Tavastehus (Finland) **(1865–1957)**
Sidney, Sylvia (actress); New York City, 8/8/1910
Siepi, Cesare (basso); Milan, Italy, 2/14/1923
Signoret, Simone (Simone Kaminker) (actress); Wiesbaden, Germany, 3/25/1921
Sikorsky, Igor I. (inventor); Kiev, Russia **(1889–1972)**
Sills, Beverly (Belle Silverman) (soprano); Brooklyn, N.Y., 5/25/1929
Silone, Ignazio (Secondo Tranquilli) (novelist); Pescina del Marsi, Italy, 5/1/1900
Silverman, Fred (broadcasting executive); New York City, 9/13/1937
Silvers, Phil (Philip Silversmith) (comedian); Brooklyn, N.Y., 5/11/1912
Sim, Alastair (actor); Edinburgh, Scotland **(1900–1976)**
Simenon, Georges (Georges Sim) (mystery writer); Liège, Belgium, 2/13/1903
Simmons, Jean (actress); Crouch Hill, London, 1/31/1929
Simon, Carly (singer and songwriter); New York City, 6/25/1945
Simon, Neil (playwright); Bronx, N.Y., 7/4/1927
Simon, Norton (business executive); Portland, Ore., 2/5/1907
Simon, Paul (singer and songwriter); Newark, N.J., 11/5/1942
Simon, Simone (actress); Marseilles, France, 4/23/1914
Simone, Nina (Eunice Kathleen Waymon) (singer and pianist); Tryon, N.C., 2/21/1933
Simpson, Adele (Adele Smithline) (fashion designer); New York City, 12/8/1903
Sinatra, Frank (singer and actor); Hoboken, N.J., 12/12/1915
Sinatra, Frank, Jr. (singer); Jersey City, N.J., 1944
Sinatra, Nancy (singer); Jersey City, N.J., 6/8/1940
Sinclair, Upton Beall (novelist); Baltimore **(1878–1968)**
Singer, Isaac Bashevis (novelist); Radzymin (Poland), 7/14/1904
Siqueiros, David (painter); Chihuahua, Mexico **(1896–1974)**
Sisley, Alfred (painter); Paris **(1839–1899)**
Sitting Bull (Prairie Sioux Indian Chief); on Grand River, S.D. **(c. 1835–1890)**
Skelton, Red (Richard) (comedian); Vincennes, Ind., 7/18/1913
Skinner, B. F. (Burrhus Frederic) (psychologist); Susquehanna, Pa., 3/20/1904
Skinner, Cornelia Otis (writer and actress); Chicago, **(1901–1979)**
Skinner, Otis (actor); Cambridge, Mass. **(1858–1942)**
Slezak, Walter (actor); Vienna, 5/3/1902
Sloan, Alfred P., Jr. (industrialist); New Haven, Conn. **(1875–1966)**
Sloan, John (painter); Lock Haven, Pa. **(1871–1951)**
Smetana, Bedrich (composer); Litomysl (Czechoslovakia) (1824–1884)
Smith, Adam (economist); Kirkaldy, Scotland **(1723–1790)**
Smith, Alexis (actress); Penticon, Canada, 6/8/1921
Smith, Alfred Emanuel (politician); New York City **(1873–1944)**
Smith, David (sculptor); Decatur, Ind. **(1906–1965)**
Smith, H. Allen (humorist); McLeansboro, Ill. **(1907–1976)**
Smith, Howard K. (TV commentator); Ferriday, La., 5/12/1914
Smith, Jaclyn (actress); Houston, 10/26/(?)
Smith, John (American colonist); Willoughby, Lincolnshire, England **(1580–1631)**
Smith, Joseph (religious leader); Sharon, Vt. **(1805–1844)**
Smith, Kate (Kathryn) (singer); Greenville, Va., 5/1/1909
Smith, Maggie (actress); Ilford, England, 12/28/1934
Smith, Red (Walter) (sports columnist); Green Bay, Wis., 9/25/1905
Smothers, Dick (Richard) (comedian); Governors Island, New York City, 11/20/1939
Smothers, Tom (Thomas) (comedian); Governors Island, New York City, 2/2/1937
Snow, Lord (Charles Percy) (author); Leicester, England **(1905–1980)**
Snowden, Earl of (Anthony Armstrong-Jones) (photographer); London, 3/7/1930
Snyder, Tom (TV personality); Milwaukee, 5/12/1936
Socrates (philosopher); Athens **(469–399 B.C.)**
Solomon (King of Israel); Jerusalem (?) **(died c. 933 B.C.)**
Solon (lawgiver); Salamis (Greece) **(638?–?559 B.C.)**
Solti, Sir Georg (conductor); Budapest, 10/21/1912
Solzhenitsyn, Aleksandr (novelist); Kislovodsk, Russia, 12/11/1918
Sommer, Elke (Elke Schletz) (actress); Berlin, 11/5/1942
Sondheim, Stephen (composer); New York City, 3/22/1930
Sontag, Susan (author and film director); New York City, 1/28/1933
Sophocles (dramatist); nr. Athens **(496?–406 B.C.)**
Sothern, Ann (Harriette Lake) (actress); Valley City, N.D., 1/22/1911
Soul, David (David Solberg) (actor); Chicago, 8/28/(?)
Sousa, John Philip (composer); Washington, D.C. **(1854–1932)**
Soyer, Raphael (painter); Borisoglebsk, Russia, 12/25/1899
Spaak, Paul-Henri (statesman); Brussels **(1899–1972)**
Spacek, Sissy (Mary Elizabeth) (actress); Quitman, Tex., 12/25/1949
Spark, Muriel (novelist); Edinburgh, Scotland, 2/1/1918
Spector, Phil (rock producer); Bronx, N.Y., 12/25/1940
Spencer, Herbert (philosopher); Derby, England **(1820–1903)**
Spender, Stephen (poet); nr. London, 2/28/1909
Spengler, Oswald (philosopher); Blankenburg, Germany **(1880–1936)**
Spenser, Edmund (poet); London **(1552?–1599)**
Spewack, Bella (playwright); Hungary, 1899
Spiegel, Sam (producer); Jaroslaw (Poland), 11/11/1901
Spielberg, Steven (film director); Cincinnati, 12/18/1947
Spillane, Mickey (Frank Spillane) (mystery writer); Brooklyn, N.Y., 3/9/1918
Spinoza, Baruch (philosopher); Amsterdam (Netherlands) **(1632–1677)**
Spivak, Lawrence (TV producer); Brooklyn, N.Y., 1900
Spock, Benjamin (pediatrician); New Haven, Conn., 5/2/1903
Springsteen, Bruce (singer and songwriter); Freehold, N.J., 9/23/1949
Sproul, Robert G. (educator); San Francisco **(1891–1975)**
Stack, Robert (actor); Los Angeles, 1/13/1919
Stafford, Jo (singer); Coalinga, Calif., 1918
Stalin, Joseph Vissarionovich (Iosif V. Dzhugashvili) (Soviet leader); nr. Tiflis, Russia **(1879–1953)**
Stalina, Svetlana Alliluyeva (Stalin's daughter); Moscow, 2/28/1926
Stallone, Sylvester (actor and writer); New York City, 7/6/1946
Stamp, Terrence (actor); London, 1940
Stang, Arnold (comedian); Chelsea, Mass., 1925
Stanislavski (Konstantin Sergeevich Alekseev) (stage producer); Moscow **(1863–1938)**
Stanley, Sir Henry Morton (John Rowlands) (explorer); Denbigh, Wales **(1841–1904)**
Stanley, Kim (Patricia Reid) (actress); Tularosa, N.M., 2/11/1925
Stans, Maurice H. (ex-Secretary of Commerce); Shakope, Minn., 3/22/1908
Stanton, Frank (broadcasting executive); Muskegon, Mich., 3/20/1908
Stanwyck, Barbara (Ruby Stevens) (actress); Brooklyn, N.Y., 7/16/1907
Stapleton, Jean (Jeanne Murray) (actress); New York City, 1/19/1923
Stapleton, Maureen (actress); Troy, N.Y., 6/21/1925
Starker, Janós (cellist); Budapest 7/5/1926
Starr, Kay (Starks) (singer); Dougherty, Okla., 7/21/1922
Starr, Ringo (Richard Starkey) (singer and songwriter); Liverpool, England, 7/7/1940
Stassen, Harold E. (ex-government official); West St. Paul, Minn., 4/13/1907
Steegmuller, Francis (biographer); New Haven, Conn., 7/3/1906
Steele, Tommy (singer); London, 12/17/1936
Stegner, Wallace (Earle) (novelist and critic); Lake Mills, Iowa, 2/18/1909
Steiger, Rod (Rodney) (actor); Westhampton, N.Y., 4/14/1925
Stein, Gertrude (author); Allegheny, Pa. **(1874–1946)**
Steinbeck, John Ernst (novelist); Salinas, Calif. **(1902–1968)**
Steinberg, William (conductor); Cologne, Germany **(1899–1978)**
Steinem, Gloria (feminist); Toledo, Ohio, 3/25/1935(?)
Steinmetz, Charles (electrical engineer); Breslau (Poland) **(1865–1923)**
Stendhal (Marie Henri Beyle) (novelist); Grenoble, France **(1783–1842)**
Sterling, Jan (actress); New York City, 1923
Stern, Isaac (concert violinist); Kreminiecz, Russia, 7/21/1920
Sterne, Laurence (novelist); Clonmel, Ireland **(1713–1768)**
Stevens, Cat (Steven Georgiou) (singer and songwriter); London, 7/?/1947
Stevens, Connie (Concetta Ingolia) (singer); Brooklyn, N.Y., 8/8/1938
Stevens, George (film director); Oakland, Calif. **(1905–1975)**

Stevens, Risë (mezzo-soprano); New York City, 6/11/1913
Stevens, Stella (actress); Yazoo City, Miss., 10/1/1936
Stevenson, Adlai Ewing (statesman); Los Angeles **(1900–1965)**
Stevenson, McLean (actor); Bloomington or Normal, Ind., 11/14/1929(?)
Stevenson, Robert Louis Balfour (novelist and poet); Edinburgh, Scotland **(1850–1894)**
Stewart, James (actor); Indiana, Pa., 5/20/1908
Stewart, Rod (Roderick David) (singer); London, 1/10/1945
Stickney, Dorothy (actress); Dickinson, N.D. 6/21/1903
Stills, Stephen (singer and songwriter); Dallas, 1/3/1945
Stokes, Carl (TV newscaster); Cleveland, 6/21/1927
Stokowski, Leopold (conductor); London **(1882–1977)**
Stone, Edward Durell (architect); Fayetteville, Ark. **(1902–1978)**
Stone, Ezra (actor and producer); New Bedford, Mass., 12/2/1917
Stone, I. F. (Isidor Feinstein Stone) (journalist); Philadelphia, 12/24/1907
Stone, Irving (Irving Tennenbaum) (novelist); San Francisco, 7/14/1903
Stone, Lewis (actor); Worcester, Mass. **(1879–1953)**
Stone, Lucy (woman suffragist); nr. West Brookfield, Mass. **(1818–1893)**
Stone, Sly (Sylvester) (rock musician); 1944
Storm, Gale (actress); Bloomington, Tex., 1922
Stout, Rex (mystery writer); Noblesville, Ind. **(1886–1975)**
Stowe, Harriet Elizabeth Beecher (novelist); Litchfield, Conn. **(1811–1896)**
Stradivari, Antonio (violinmaker); Cremona (Italy) **(1644–1737)**
Strasberg, Lee (stage director); Budanov, Austria, 11/17/1901
Strasberg, Susan (actress); New York City, 5/22/1938
Straus, Oskar (composer); Vienna **(1870–1954)**
Strauss, Johann (composer); Vienna **(1825–1899)**
Strauss, Lewis L. (naval officer and scientist); Charleston, W. Va. **(1896–1974)**
Strauss, Richard (composer); Munich, Germany **(1864–1949)**
Stravinsky, Igor (composer); Orienbaum, Russia **(1882–1971)**
Streep, Meryl (Mary Louise) (actress); Summit, N.J., 6/22/1949
Streisand, Barbra (singer and actress); Brooklyn, N.Y., 4/24/1942
Stritch, Elaine (actress); Detroit, 2/2/1928
Struthers, Sally Ann (actress); Portland, Ore., 7/28/1948
Stuart, Gilbert Charles (painter); Rhode Island **(1755–1828)**
Stuart, James Ewell Brown (known as Jeb) (Confederate army officer); Patrick County, Va. **(1833–1864)**
Stuyvesant, Peter (Governor of New Amsterdam); West Friesland (Netherlands) **(1592–1672)**
Styron, William (William Clark Styron, Jr.) (novelist); Newport News, Va., 6/11/1925
Sullavan, Margaret Brooke (actress); Norfolk, Va. **(1911–1960)**
Sullivan, Sir Arthur Seymour (composer); London **(1842–1900)**
Sullivan, Barry (Patrick Barry) (actor); New York City, 8/29/1912
Sullivan, Ed (columnist and TV personality); New York City **(1901–1974)**
Sullivan, Francis Loftus (actor); London **(1903–1956)**
Sullivan, Frank (Francis John) (humorist); Saratoga Springs, N.Y. **(1892–1976)**
Sullivan, Louis Henry (architect); Boston, Mass. **(1856–1924)**
Sulzberger, Arthur Ochs (newspaper publisher); New York City, 2/5/1926
Sumac, Yma (singer); Ichocan, Peru, 9/10/1927
Summer, Donna (singer); Boston, 12/31/1948
Sun Yat-sen (statesman); nr. Macao **(1866–1925)**
Susann, Jacqueline (novelist); Philadelphia **(1926?–1974)**
Susskind, David (TV producer); New York City, 12/19/1920
Sutherland, Joan (soprano); Sydney, Australia, 11/7/1926
Suzuki, Pat (actress); Cressey, Calif., 1931
Swados, Elizabeth (composer, playwright); Buffalo, N.Y., 2/5/1951
Swanson, Gloria (Josephine Swenson) (actress); Chicago, 3/27/1899
Swarthout, Gladys (soprano); Deepwater, Mo. **(1904–1969)**
Swayze, John Cameron (news commentator); Wichita, Kan., 4/4/1906
Swift, Jonathan (satirist); Dublin **(1667–1745)**
Swinburne, Algernon Charles (poet); London **(1837–1909)**
Swope, Herbert Bayard (journalist); St. Louis **(1882–1958)**
Sydow, von, Max (Carl Adolf von Sydow) (actor); Lund, Sweden, 4/10/1929
Synge, John Millington (dramatist); nr. Dublin **(1871–1909)**
Szilard, Leo (physicist); Budapest **(1898–1964)**

T

Taft, Robert Alphonso (legislator); Cincinnati **(1889–1953)**
Tagore, Sir Rabindranath (poet); Calcutta **(1861–1941)**
Tallchief, Maria (ballerina); Fairfax, Okla., 1/24/1925
Talleyrand-Perigord, Charles Maurice de (statesman); Paris **(1754–1838)**
Talmadge, Norma (actress); Niagara Falls, N.Y. **(1897–1957)**
Tamerlane (Timur) (Mongol conqueror); nr. Samarkand (U.S.S.R.) **(1336?–1405)**
Tandy, Jessica (actress); London, 6/7/1909
Tarkington, (Newton) Booth (novelist); Indianapolis **(1869–1946)**
Tate, Allen (John Orley) (poet and critic); Winchester, Ky., **(1899–1979)**
Tate, Sharon (actress); Dallas **(1943–1969)**
Tati, Jacques (Jacques Tatischeff) (actor); Pecq, France, 10/9/1908
Taylor, Elizabeth (actress); London, 2/27/1932
Taylor, Estelle (actress); Wilmington, Del. **(1899–1958)**
Taylor, Harold (educator); Toronto, 9/28/1914
Taylor, James (singer and songwriter); Boston, 3/12/1948
Taylor, (Joseph) Deems (composer); New York City **(1885–1966)**
Taylor, Laurette (Laurette Cooney) (actress); New York City **(1884–1946)**
Taylor, Gen. Maxwell D. (former Army Chief of Staff); Keytesville, Mo., 8/26/1901
Taylor, Robert (Spangler Arlington Brugh) (actor); Filley, Neb. **(1911–1969)**
Taylor, Rod (actor); Sydney, Australia, 1/11/1930
Tchaikovsky, Peter (Pëtr) Ilich (composer); Votkinsk, Russia **(1840–1893)**
Teasdale, Sara (poet); St. Louis **(1884–1933)**
Tebaldi, Renata (lyric soprano); Pesaro, Italy, 1/2/1922
Tecumseh (Shawnee Indian chief); nr. Springfield, Ohio **(1768?–1813)**
Teller, Edward (atomic physicist); Budapest, 1/15/1908
Temple, Shirley. *See* Black, Shirley Temple
Tennyson, Alfred (1st Baron Tennyson) (poet); Somersby, England **(1809–1892)**
Terhune, Albert Payson (novelist and journalist); Newark, N.J. **(1872–1942)**
Terry, Ellen Alicia (actress); Coventry, England **(1848–1928)**
Terry-Thomas (Thomas Terry Hoar Stevens) (actor); London, 7/14/1911
Tesla, Nikola (electrician and inventor); Smiljan (Yugoslavia) **(1856–1943)**
Thackeray, William Makepeace (novelist); Calcutta **(1811–1863)**
Thant, U (U.N. statesman); Pantanaw (Burma) **(1909–1974)**
Tharp, Twyla (dancer and choreographer); Portland, Ind., 7/1/1941(?)
Thatcher, Margaret (political leader); Grantham, England, 10/13/1925
Thaxter, Phyllis (actress); Portland, Me., 1921
Thebom, Blanche (mezzo-soprano); Monessen, Pa., 9/19/1919
Theodorakis, Mikis (composer); Chios, Greece, 7/29/1925
Thieu, Nguyen Van (ex-President of South Vietnam); Trithuy (Vietnam) 4/5/1923
Thomas, Danny (Amos Jacobs) (entertainer and TV producer); Deerfield, Mich., 1/6/1914
Thomas, Dylan Marlais (poet); Carmarthenshire, Wales **(1914–1953)**
Thomas, Lowell (explorer, commentator); Woodington, Ohio, 4/6/1892
Thomas, Marlo (actress); Detroit, 11/21/1943
Thomas, Michael Tilson (conductor); Hollywood, Calif., 12/21/1944
Thomas, Norman Mattoon (Socialist leader); Marion, Ohio **(1884–1968)**
Thomas, Richard (actor); New York City, 6/13/1951
Thompson, Dorothy (writer); Lancaster, N.Y. **(1894–1961)**
Thompson, Sada (actress); Des Moines, Iowa, 9/27/1929
Thoreau, Henry David (naturalist and author); Concord, Mass. **(1817–1862)**
Thorndike, Dame Sybil (actress); Gainsborough, England **(1882–1976)**
Thurber, James Grover (author and cartoonist); Columbus, Ohio **(1894–1961)**
Tibbett, Lawrence (baritone); Bakersfield, Calif. **(1896–1960)**
Tierney, Gene (actress); Brooklyn, N.Y., 11/20/1920
Tiffin, Pamela (actress); Oklahoma City, 10/13/1942
Tillstrom, Burr (puppeteer); Chicago, 10/13/1917
Tintoretto, Il (Jacopo Robusti) (painter); Venice **(1518–1594)**
Tiny Tim (Herbert Khaury) (entertainer); New York City, 1923(?)
Tiomkin, Dmitri (composer); St. Petersburg, Russia **(1894–1979)**
Titian (Tiziano Vecelli) (painter); Pieve di Cadore (Italy) **(1477–1576)**
Tito (Josip Broz or Brozovich) (President of Yugoslavia); Croatia (Yugoslavia) **(1892–1980)**
Tocqueville, Alexis de (writer); Verneuil, France **(1805–1859)**
Todd, Thelma (actress); Lawrence, Mass. **(1905–1935)**
Tolstoi, Count Leo (Lev) Nikolaevich (novelist); Tula Province, Russia **(1828–1910)**
Tomlin, Lily (comedienne); Detroit, 1939(?)
Tone, Franchot (actor); Niagara Falls, N.Y. **(1905–1968)**
Torme, Mel (Melvin) (singer); Chicago, 9/13/1925
Torn, Rip (Elmore Torn, Jr.) (actor and director); Temple, Tex., 2/6/1931
Toscanini, Arturo (orchestra conductor); Parma, Italy **(1867–1957)**
Toulouse-Lautrec (Henri Marie Raymond de Toulouse-Lautrec Monfa) (painter); Albi, France **(1864–1901)**
Toynbee, Arnold J. (historian); London **(1889–1975)**
Tracy, Spencer (actor); Milwaukee **(1900–1967)**
Traubel, Helen (Wagnerian soprano); St. Louis **(1903–1972)**
Travolta, John (actor); Englewood, N.J., 2/18/1954
Treacher, Arthur (actor); Brighton, England **(1894–1975)**
Trevor, Claire (actress); New York City, 1909
Trigère, Pauline (fashion designer); Paris, 11/4/1912
Trilling, Lionel (author and educator); New York City **(1905–1975)**
Trotsky, Leon (Lev Davidovich Bronstein) (statesman); Elisavetgrad, Russia **(1879–1940)**
Trudeau, Pierre Elliott (Prime Minister); Montreal, 10/18/1919
Truffaut, François (film director); Paris, 2/6/1932
Trujillo y Molina, Rafael Leonidas (Dominican Republic dictator); San Cristóbal, Dominican Republic **(1891–1961)**
Truman, Margaret (author); Independence, Mo., 2/17/1924

Tryon, Thomas (actor and novelist); Hartford, Conn., 1/14/1926
Tucker, Forrest (actor); Plainfield, Ind., 2/12/1919
Tucker, Richard (tenor); New York City **(1914–1975)**
Tucker, Sophie (Sophie Abuza) (singer); Boston **(1884?–1966)**
Tudor, Antony (choreographer); London, 4/4/1909
Turgenev, Ivan Sergeevich (novelist); Orel, Russia **(1818–1883)**
Turner, Ike (singer); Clarksdale, Miss., 11/?/1931
Turner, Joseph M.W. (painter); London **(1775–1851)**
Turner, Lana (Julia Jean Mildred Frances Turner) (actress); Wallace, Idaho, 2/8/1920
Turner, Nat (civil rights leader); Southampton County, Va. **(1800–1831)**
Turner, Tina (Annie Mae Bullock) (singer); Brownsville, Tex., 1939
Turpin, Ben (comedian); New Orleans **(1874–1940)**
Tushingham, Rita (actress); Liverpool, England, 3/14/1942
Twain, Mark (Samuel Langhorne Clemens) (author); Florida, Mo. **(1835–1910)**
Tweed, William Marcy (politician); New York City **(1823–1878)**
Twiggy (Leslie Hornby) (model); London, 9/19/1949
Twining, Gen. Nathan F. (former Air Force Chief of Staff); Monroe, Wis., 10/11/1897
Twitty, Conway (Harold Lloyd Jenkins) (singer and guitarist); Friars Point, Miss., 9/1/1933
Tyson, Cicely (actress); New York City, 12/19/1939(?)

U

Udall, Stewart L. (ex-Secretary of the Interior); St. Johns, Ariz., 1/31/1920
Uggams, Leslie (singer and actress); New York City, 5/25/1943
Ulanova, Galina (ballerina); St. Petersburg, Russia, 1/10/1910
Ullmann, Liv (actress); Tokyo, 12/16/1939
Ulric, Lenore (actress); New Ulm, Minn. **(1894–1970)**
Untermeyer, Louis (anthologist and poet); New York City **(1885–1977)**
Updike, John (novelist); Shillington, Pa., 3/18/1932
Urey, Harold C. (physicist); Walkerton, Ind., 4/29/1893
Uris, Leon (novelist); Baltimore, 8/3/1924
Ustinov, Peter (actor and producer); London, 4/16/1921
Utrillo, Maurice (painter); Paris **(1883–1955)**

V

Vaccaro, Brenda (actress); Brooklyn, N.Y., 11/18/1939
Valentine, Karen (actress); Santa Rosa, Calif., 1947
Valentino, Rudolph (Rodolpho d'Antonguolla) (actor); Castellaneta, Italy **(1895–1926)**
Valentino (Valentino Garavani) (fashion designer); nr. Milan, Italy, 5/11/1932
Vallee, Rudy (Hubert Vallée) (band leader and singer); Island Pond, Vt., 7/28/1901
Van Allen, James Alfred (space physicist); Mt. Pleasant, Iowa, 9/7/1914
Van Buren, Abigail (Mrs. Morton Phillips) (columnist); Sioux City, Iowa, 7/14/1918
Vance, Vivian (actress); Cherryvale, Kan. **(1912–1979)**
Vanderbilt, Alfred G. (sportsman); London, 9/22/1912
Vanderbilt, Cornelius (financier); Port Richmond, N.Y. **(1794–1877)**
Vanderbilt, Gloria (artist and heiress); New York City, 2/20/1924
Van Doren, Carl (writer and educator); Hope, Ill. **(1885–1950)**
Van Doren, Mamie (actress); Rowena, S.D., 1933
Van Dyke, Dick (actor); West Plains, Mo., 12/13/1925
Vandyke (or Van Dyck), Sir Anthony (painter); Antwerp (Belgium) **(1599–1641)**
Van Eyck, Jan (painter); Maeseyck (Belgium) **(c.1390–1441)**
van Gogh, Vincent (painter); Groot Zundert, Brabant **(1853–1890)**
van Hamel, Martine (ballerina); Brussels, 11/16/1945
Van Heusen, Jimmy (Edward Chester Babcock) (songwriter); Syracuse, N.Y., 1/26/1913
Van Peebles, Melvin (playwright); Chicago, 9/21/1932
Vaughan, Sarah (singer); Newark, N.J., 3/27/1924
Vaughan Williams, Ralph (composer); Down Ampney, England **(1872–1958)**
Vaughn, Robert (actor); New York City, 11/22/1932
Velazquez, Diego Rodriguez de Silva y (painter); Seville, Spain **(1599–1660)**
Velez, Lupe (Guadelupe Velez de Villalobos) (actress); San Luis Potosi, Mexico **(1908–1944)**
Venturi, Robert (Charles) (architect); Philadelphia, 6/25/1925
Verdi, Giuseppe (composer); Roncole (Italy) **(1813–1901)**
Verdon, Gwen (actress); Culver City, Calif., 1/13/1926
Vereen, Ben (actor and singer); Miami, Fla., 10/10/1946
Vermeer, Jan (or Jan van der Meer van Delft) (painter); Delft (Netherlands) **(1632–1675)**
Verne, Jules (author); Nantes, France **(1828–1905)**
Verrazano, Giovanni da (navigator); Florence (Italy) **(1485?–1528)**
Verrett, Shirley (mezzo-soprano); New Orleans, 5/31/1933
Vespucci, Amerigo (navigator); Florence (Italy) **(1454–1512)**
Vickers, Jon (tenor); Prince Albert, Sask., Canada, 10/29/1926
Vidal, Gore (novelist); West Point, N.Y., 10/3/1925
Vidor, King (film director and producer); Galveston, Tex., 2/8/1895
Villa, Pancho (Doroteo Arango) (bandit); Rio Grande, Mexico **(1877–1923)**
Villella, Edward (ballet dancer); Bayside, Queens, N.Y., 10/1/1936
Villon, François (François de Montcorbier) (poet); Paris **(1431–1463)**
Vinton, Bobby (singer); Canonsburg, Pa., 4/16/1935(?)
Virgil (or Vergil) (Publius Vergilius Maro) (poet); nr. Mantua (Italy) **(70–19 B.C.)**
Vishnevskaya, Galina (soprano); Leningrad, 10/25/1926
Vlaminck, Maurice de (painter); Paris **(1876–1958)**
Voight, Jon (actor); Yonkers, N.Y., 12/29/1938
Voltaire (François Marie Arouet) (author); Paris **(1694–1778)**
Von Braun. *See* Braun
von Furstenberg, Betsy (actress); Neiheim-Heusen, Germany, 8/16/1935
von Furstenberg, Diane (Diane Simone Michelle Halfin) (fashion designer); Brussels, 12/31/1946
von Karajan, Herbert (conductor); Salzburg (Austria), 4/5/1908
Vonnegut, Kurt, Jr. (novelist); Indianapolis, 11/11/1922
Von Stroheim, Erich Oswald Hans Carl Maria von Nordenwall (film actor and director); Vienna **(1885–1957)**
Vorster, Balthazar Johannes (Prime Minister); Jamestown, Cape Province, South Africa, 12/13/1915
Vreeland, Diana (Dalziel) (fashion journalist and museum consultant); Paris, 1903(?)

W

Wagner, Lindsay (actress); Los Angeles, 1949
Wagner, Robert (actor); Detroit, 2/10/1930
Wagner, Robert F. (ex-Mayor of New York City); New York City, 4/20/1910
Wagner, Wilhelm Richard (composer); Leipzig (Germany) **(1813–1883)**
Waldheim, Kurt (U.N. Secretary-General); St. Andrae-Wörden, Austria, 12/21/1918
Walker, Clint (actor); Hartford, Ill., 5/30/1927
Walker, Nancy (Ann Myrtle Swoyer); (actress and comedienne); Philadelphia, 5/10/1922
Wallace, DeWitt (publisher); St. Paul, 11/12/1889
Wallace, George C. (Governor); Clio, Ala., 8/25/1919
Wallace, Irving (novelist); Chicago, 3/19/1916
Wallace, Mike (Myron Wallace) (TV interviewer and commentator); Brookline, Mass., 5/9/1918
Wallach, Eli (actor); Brooklyn, N.Y., 12/7/1915
Waller, Thomas "Fats" (pianist); New York City **(1904–1943)**
Wallis, Hal (film producer); Chicago, 9/14/1899
Waltari, Mika (novelist); Helsinki, Finland, **(1908–1979)**
Walter, Bruno (Bruno Walter Schlesinger) (orchestra conductor); Berlin **(1876–1962)**
Walters, Barbara (TV commentator); Boston, 9/25/1931
Walton, Izaak (author); Stafford, England **(1593–1683)**
Wambaugh, Joseph (author and screenwriter); East Pittsburgh, Pa., 1/22/1937
Wanamaker, John (merchant); Philadelphia **(1838–1922)**
Ward, Barbara (economist); York, England, 5/23/1914
Warhol, Andy (artist and producer); Cleveland, 8/8/1930(?)
Waring, Fred (band leader); Tyrone, Pa., 6/9/1900
Warner, H. B. (Henry Bryan Warner Lickford) (actor); London **(1876–1958)**
Warren, Earl (Chief Justice of the U.S.); Los Angeles **(1891–1974)**
Warren, Robert Penn (novelist); Guthrie, Ky., 4/24/1905
Warwicke, Dionne (singer); East Orange, N.J., 1941
Washington, Booker Taliaferro (educator); Franklin County, Va. **(1856–1915)**
Waters, Ethel (actress and singer); Chester, Pa. **(1896–1977)**
Waters, Muddy (McKinley Morganfield) (singer and guitarist); Rolling Fork, Miss., 4/4/1915
Watson, Thomas John (industrialist); Campbell, N.Y. **(1874–1956)**
Watt, James (inventor); Greenock, Scotland **(1736–1819)**
Watteau, Jean-Antoine (painter); Valenciennes, France **(1684–1721)**
Watts, André (concert pianist); Nuremberg, Germany, 6/20/1946
Waugh, Alec (Alexander Raban Waugh) (novelist); London, 7/8/1898
Waugh, Evelyn (satirist); London **(1903–1966)**
Wayne, Anthony (military officer); Waynesboro (family farm), nr. Paoli, Pa. **(1745–1796)**
Wayne, David (David McMeakan) (actor); Traverse City, Mich., 1/30/1914
Wayne, John (Marion Michael Morrison) (actor); Winterset, Iowa, **(1907–1979)**
Weaver, Dennis (actor); Joplin, Mo., 6/4/1925
Weaver, Fritz (actor); Pittsburgh, 1/19/1926
Webb, Clifton (Webb Parmelee Hollenbeck) (actor); Indianapolis **(1893–1966)**
Webb, Jack (film actor and producer); Santa Monica, Calif., 4/2/1920

Weber, Karl Maria Friedrich Ernst von (composer); nr. Lübeck (Germany) **(1786–1826)**
Webster, Daniel (statesman); Salisbury, N.H. **(1782–1852)**
Webster, Noah (lexicographer); West Hartford, Conn. **(1758–1843)**
Weill, Kurt (composer); Dessau, Germany **(1900–1950)**
Weizmann, Chaim (statesman); Grodno Province, Russia **(1874–1952)**
Welch, Raquel (Raquel Tejada) (actress); Chicago, 9/5/1942
Weld, Tuesday (Susan) (actress); New York City, 8/27/1943
Welk, Lawrence (band leader); Strasburg, N.D., 3/11/1903
Welles, Orson (actor and producer); Kenosha, Wis., 5/6/1915
Wellington, Duke of (Arthur Wellesley) (statesman); Ireland **(1769–1852)**
Wells, H(erbert) G(eorge) (author); Bromley, England **(1866–1946)**
Welty, Eudora (novelist); Jackson, Miss., 4/13/1909
Werfel, Franz (novelist); Prague **(1890–1945)**
Werner, Oskar (Josef Schliessmayer) (film actor and director); Vienna, 11/13/1922
Wertmuller, Lina (film director); Rome, 1926(?)
Wesley, John (religious leader); Epworth Rectory, Lincolnshire, England **(1703–1791)**
West, Jessamyn (novelist); nr. North Vernon, Ind., 7/18/1902
West, Mae (actress); Brooklyn, N.Y., 8/17/1893
West, Nathanael (Nathan Weinstein) (novelist); New York City **(1902–1940)**
West, Dame Rebecca (Cicily Fairchild) (novelist); County Kerry, Ireland, 12/25/1892
Westinghouse, George (inventor); Central Bridge, N.Y. **(1846–1914)**
Westmoreland, William Childs (ex-Army Chief of Staff); Saxon, S.C., 3/26/1914
Wharton, Edith Newbold (née Jones) (novelist); New York City **(1862–1937)**
Wheeler, Bert (Albert Jerome Wheeler) (comedian); Paterson, N.J. **(1895–1968)**
Whistler, James Abbott McNeill (painter and etcher); Lowell, Mass. **(1834–1903)**
White, E. B. (Elwyn Brooks White) (author); Mt. Vernon, N.Y., 7/11/1899
White, Stanford (architect); New York City **(1853–1906)**
White, Theodore H. (historian); Boston, 5/6/1915
White, William Allen (journalist); Emporia, Kan. **(1868–1944)**
Whitehead, Alfred North (mathematician and philosopher); Isle of Thanet, England **(1861–1947)**
Whiteman, Paul (band leader); Denver **(1891–1967)**
Whitman, Walt (Walter) (poet); West Hills, N.Y. **(1819–1892)**
Whitmore, James (actor); White Plains, N.Y., 10/1/1921
Whitney, Cornelius Vanderbilt (sportsman); New York City, 2/20/1899
Whitney, Eli (inventor); Westboro, Mass. **(1765–1825)**
Whitney, John Hay (publisher); Ellsworth, Me., 8/17/1904
Whittier, John Greenleaf (poet); Haverhill, Mass. **(1807–1892)**
Widmark, Richard (actor); Sunrise, Minn., 12/26/1914
Wiesel, Elie (Eliezer) (author); Sighet, Romania, 9/30/1928
Wilbur, Richard (poet); New York City, 3/1/1921
Wilde, Cornel (film actor and producer); New York City, 10/13/1918
Wilde, Oscar Fingal O'Flahertie Wills (author); Dublin **(1854–1900)**
Wilder, Billy (film producer and director); Vienna, 6/22/1906
Wilder, Gene (Jerome Silberman) (actor); Milwaukee, 6/11/1935(?)
Wilder, Thornton (author); Madison, Wis. **(1897–1975)**
Wilding, Michael (actor); Westcliff, England **(1912–1979)**
Wilkins, Roy (civil rights leader); St. Louis, 8/30/1901
Williams, Andy (singer); Wall Lake, Iowa, 12/3/1930
Williams, Cindy (actress); Van Nuys, Calif., 8/22/(?)
Williams, Edward Bennett (lawyer); Hartford, Conn., 5/31/1920
Williams, Emlyn (actor and playwright); Mostyn, Wales, 11/26/1905
Williams, Esther (actress); Los Angeles, 8/8/1923
Williams, Gluyas (cartoonist); San Francisco, 7/23/1888
Williams, Hank, Sr. (Hiram King Williams) (singer); Georgiana, Ala. **(1923–1953)**
Williams, Robin (comedian); Chicago, 7/?/1952
Williams, Roger (clergyman); London **(1603?–1683)**
Williams, Tennessee (Thomas L. Williams) (playwright); Columbus, Miss., 3/26/1911
Willkie, Wendell Lewis (lawyer); Elwood, Ind. **(1892–1944)**
Willson, Meredith (composer); Mason City, Iowa, 5/18/1902
Wilson, Don (radio and TV announcer); Lincoln, Neb., 1924
Wilson, Flip (Clerow) (comedian); Jersey City, N.J., 12/8/1933
Wilson, Harold (ex-Prime Minister); Huddersfield, England, 3/11/1916
Wilson, Nancy (singer); Chillicothe, Ohio, 2/20/1937
Wilson, Sloan (novelist); Norwalk, Conn., 5/8/1920
Winchell, Walter (columnist); New York City **(1897–1972)**
Windsor, Duchess of (Bessie Wallis Warfield); Blue Ridge Summit, Pa., 6/19/1896
Windsor, Duke of (formerly King Edward VIII of England); Richmond Park, England **(1894–1972)**
Winkler, Henry (actor); New York City, 10/30/1945
Winter, Johnny (guitarist); Leland, Miss., 2/23/1944
Winters, Jonathan (comedian); Dayton, Ohio, 11/11/1925
Winters, Shelley (Shirley Schrift) (actress); East St. Louis, Ill., 8/18/1922
Winthrop, John (first Governor, Massachusetts Bay Colony); Suffolk, England **(1588–1649)**
Wise, Stephen Samuel (rabbi); Budapest **(1874–1949)**
Withers, Jane (actress); Atlanta, 1927
Wittgenstein, Ludwig (Josef Johann) (philosopher); Vienna **(1889–1951)**
Wodehouse, P(elham) G(renville) (novelist); Guildford, England **(1881–1975)**
Wolfe, Thomas Clayton (novelist); Asheville, N.C. **(1900–1938)**
Wolfe, Tom (journalist); Richmond, Va., 3/2/1931
Wolsey, Thomas (prelate and statesman); Ipswich, England **(1475?–1530)**
Wonder, Stevie (Steveland Judkins, later Steveland Morris) (singer and songwriter); Saginaw, Mich., 5/13/1950
Wong, Anna May (Lu Tsong Wong) (actress); Los Angeles **(1907–1961)**
Wood, Grant (painter); Anamosa, Iowa **(1892–1942)**
Wood, Natalie (Natasha Gurdin) (film actress); San Francisco, 7/20/1938
Woodward, Joanne (film actress); Thomasville, Ga., 2/27/1930
Woolf, Adeline Virginia (née Stephens) (novelist); London **(1882–1941)**
Woollcott, Alexander (author); Phalanx, N.J. **(1887–1943)**
Woolley, Monty (Edgar Montillion Woolley) (actor); New York City **(1888–1963)**
Woolworth, Frank (merchant); Rodman, N.Y. **(1852–1919)**
Wordsworth, William (poet); Cockermouth, England **(1770–1850)**
Worley, Jo Anne (actress and singer); Lowell, Ind., 9/6/1937
Wouk, Herman (novelist); New York City, 5/27/1915
Wray, Fay (actress); Alberta, Canada, 1907
Wren, Sir Christopher (architect); East Knoyle, England **(1632–1723)**
Wright, Frank Lloyd (architect); Richland Center, Wis. **(1869–1959)**
Wright, Orville (inventor); Dayton, Ohio **(1871–1948)**
Wright, Richard (novelist); nr. Natchez, Miss. **(1908–1960)**
Wright, Teresa (actress); New York City, 10/27/1918
Wright, Wilbur (inventor); Millville, Ind. **(1867–1912)**
Wyatt, Jane (film actress); Campgaw, N.J., 8/12/1912
Wyeth, Andrew (painter); Chadds Ford, Pa., 7/12/1917
Wyler, William (film director); Mulhouse (France), 7/1/1902
Wyman, Jane (Sarah Jane Fulks) (actress); St. Joseph, Mo., 1/4/1914
Wynette, Tammy (Wynette Pugh) (singer); Tupelo, Miss. 5/5/1942
Wynn, Ed (Isaiah Edwin Leopold) (comedian); Philadelphia **(1886–1966)**
Wynn, Keenan (actor); New York City, 7/27/1916
Wynter, Dana (actress); London, 6/8/1930

Y

Yeats, William Butler (poet); nr. Dublin **(1865–1939)**
Yevtushenko, Yevgeny (poet); Zima, U.S.S.R., 7/18/1933
York, Michael (actor); Fulmer, England, 3/27/1942
York, Susannah (Fletcher) (actress); London, 1/9/1942
Yorty, Samuel W. (ex-Mayor of Los Angeles); Lincoln, Neb., 10/1/1909
Young, Alan (actor); North Shield, England, 11/19/1919
Young, Brigham (religious leader); Whitingham, Vt. **(1801–1877)**
Young, Gig (Byron Barr) (actor); St. Cloud, Minn., **(1917–1978)**
Young, Loretta (Gretchen Young) (actress); Salt Lake City, Utah, 1/6/1913
Young, Neil (singer and songwriter); Toronto, 11/12/1945
Young, Robert (actor); Chicago, 2/22/1907
Youngman, Henny (comedian); England, 1906

Z

Zanuck, Darryl F. (film producer); Wahoo, Neb. **(1902–1979)**
Zappa, Frank (Francis Vincent Zappa, Jr.) (singer and songwriter); Baltimore, 12/21/1940
Zeffirelli, Franco (director); Florence, Italy, 2/12/1923
Zhou Enlai (Premier); Hualyin, China **(1898–1976)**
Ziegfeld, Florenz (theatrical producer); Chicago **(1869–1932)**
Zimbalist, Efrem (concert violinist); Rostov-on-Don, Russia, 4/9/1889
Zimbalist, Efrem, Jr. (actor); New York City, 11/30/1923
Zola, Emile (novelist); Paris **(1840–1902)**
Zoroaster (religious leader); Persian Empire **(c. 6th century B.C.)**
Zukerman, Pinchas (violinist); Tel Aviv, Israel 7/16/1948
Zweig, Stefan (author); Vienna **(1881–1942)**

Vitamin Use

In 23.5 million households in the U.S., vitamins are taken regularly. In 1980, the average bill was $55.32 per household.

THE DECLARATION OF INDEPENDENCE

In Congress, July 4, 1776

The unanimous Declaration of the thirteen united States of America.

When in the Course of human events it becomes necessary for one people to dissolve the political bands which have connected them with another, and to assume among the powers of the earth, the separate and equal station to which the Laws of Nature and of Nature's God entitle them, a decent respect to the opinions of mankind requires that they should declare the causes which impel them to the separation.

We hold these truths to be self-evident, that all men are created equal, that they are endowed by their Creator with certain unalienable Rights, that among these are Life, Liberty and the pursuit of Happiness.—That to secure these rights, Governments are instituted among Men, deriving their just powers from the consent of the governed,—That whenever any Form of Government becomes destructive of these ends, it is the Right of the People to alter or to abolish it, and to institute new Government, laying its foundation on such principles and organizing its powers in such form, as to them shall seem most likely to effect their Safety and Happiness. Prudence, indeed, will dictate that Governments long established should not be changed for light and transient causes; and accordingly all experience hath shewn that mankind are more disposed to suffer, while evils are sufferable, than to right themselves by abolishing the forms to which they are accustomed. But when a long train of abuses and usurpations, pursuing invariably the same Object evinces a design to reduce them under absolute Despotism, it is their right, it is their duty, to throw off such Government, and to provide new Guards for their future security.—Such has been the patient sufferance of these Colonies; and such is now the necessity which constrains them to alter their former Systems of Government. The history of the present King of Great Britain is a history of repeated injuries and usurpations, all having in direct object the establishment of an absolute Tyranny over these States. To prove this, let Facts be submitted to a candid world.

He has refused his Assent to Laws, the most wholesome and necessary for the public good.

He has forbidden his Governors to pass Laws of immediate and pressing importance, unless suspended in their operation till his Assent should be obtained; and when so suspended, he has utterly neglected to attend to them.

He has refused to pass other Laws for the accommodation of large districts of people, unless those people would relinquish the right of Representation in the Legislature, a right inestimable to them and formidable to tyrants only.

He has called together legislative bodies at places unusual, uncomfortable, and distant from the depository of their Public Records, for the sole purpose of fatiguing them into compliance with his measures.

He has dissolved Representative Houses repeatedly, for opposing with manly firmness his invasions on the rights of the people.

He has refused for a long time, after such dissolutions, to cause others to be elected; whereby the Legislative Powers, incapable of Annihilation, have returned to the People at large for their exercise; the State remaining in the mean time exposed to all the dangers of invasion from without, and convulsions within.

He has endeavoured to prevent the population of these States; for that purpose obstructing the Laws for Naturalization of Foreigners; refusing to pass others to encourage their migrations hither, and raising the conditions of new Appropriations of Lands.

He has obstructed the Administration of Justice, by refusing his Assent to Laws for establishing Judiciary Powers.

He has made Judges dependent on his Will alone, for the tenure of their offices, and the amount and payment of their salaries.

He has erected a multitude of New Offices, and sent hither swarms of Officers to harass our people, and eat out their substance.

He has kept among us, in times of peace, Standing Armies without the Consent of our legislatures.

He has affected to render the Military independent of and superior to the Civil Power.

He has combined with others to subject us to a jurisdiction foreign to our constitution, and unacknowledged by our laws; giving his Assent to their Acts of pretended Legislation:

For quartering large bodies of armed troops among us:

For protecting them, by a mock Trial, from punishment for any Murders which they should commit on the Inhabitants of these States:

For cutting off our Trade with all parts of the

NOTE: On April 12, 1776, the legislature of North Carolina authorized its delegates to the Continental Congress to join with others in a declaration of separation from Great Britain; the first colony to instruct its delegates to take the actual initiative was Virginia on May 15. On June 7, 1776, Richard Henry Lee of Virginia offered a resolution to the Congress to the effect "that these United Colonies are, and of right ought to be, free and independent States. . . ." A committee, consisting of Thomas Jefferson, John Adams, Benjamin Franklin, Robert R. Livingston, and Roger Sherman was organized to "prepare a declaration to the effect of the said first resolution." The Declaration of Independence was adopted on July 4, 1776.

Most delegates signed the Declaration August 2, but George Wythe (Va.) signed August 27; Richard Henry Lee (Va.), Elbridge Gerry (Mass.), and Oliver Wolcott (Conn.) in September; Matthew Thornton (N. H.), not a delegate until September, in November; and Thomas McKean (Del.), although present on July 4, not until 1781 by special permission, having served in the army in the interim.

world:

For imposing Taxes on us without our Consent:

For depriving us in many cases, of the benefits of Trial by Jury:

For transporting us beyond Seas to be tried for pretended offences:

For abolishing the free System of English Laws in a neighbouring Province, establishing therein an Arbitrary government, and enlarging its Boundaries so as to render it at once an example and fit instrument for introducing the same absolute rule into these Colonies:

For taking away our Charters, abolishing our most valuable Laws and altering fundamentally the Forms of our Governments:

For suspending our own Legislatures, and declaring themselves invested with power to legislate for us in all cases whatsoever.

He has abdicated Government here, by declaring us out of his Protection and waging War against us.

He has plundered our seas, ravaged our Coasts, burnt our towns, and destroyed the lives of our people.

He is at this time transporting large Armies of foreign Mercenaries to compleat the works of death, desolation, and tyranny, already begun with circumstances of Cruelty & Perfidy scarcely paralleled in the most barbarous ages, and totally unworthy the Head of a civilized nation.

He has constrained our fellow Citizens taken Captive on the high Seas to bear Arms against their Country, to become the executioners of their friends and Brethren, or to fall themselves by their Hands.

He has excited domestic insurrections amongst us, and has endeavoured to bring on the inhabitants of our frontiers, the merciless Indian Savages, whose known rule of warfare, is an undistinguished destruction of all ages, sexes and conditions.

In every stage of these Oppressions We have Petitioned for Redress in the most humble terms: Our repeated Petitions have been answered only by repeated injury. A Prince, whose character is thus marked by every act which may define a Tyrant, is unfit to be the ruler of a free people.

Nor have We been wanting in attentions to our Brittish brethren. We have warned them from time to time of attempts by their legislature to extend an unwarrantable jurisdiction over us. We have reminded them of the circumstances of our emigration and settlement here. We have appealed to their native justice and magnanimity, and we have conjured them by the ties of our common kindred to disavow these usurpations, which would inevitably interrupt our connections and correspondence. They too have been deaf to the voice of justice and of consanguinity. We must, therefore, acquiesce in the necessity, which denounces our Separation, and hold them, as we hold the rest of mankind, Enemies in War, in Peace Friends.

We, therefore, the Representatives of the United States of America, in General Congress, Assembled, appealing to the Supreme Judge of the world for the rectitude of our intentions, do, in the Name, and by Authority of the good People of these Colonies, solemnly publish and declare, That these United Colonies are, and of Right ought to be Free and Independent States; that they are Absolved from all Allegiance to the British Crown, and that all political connection between them and the State of Great Britain, is and ought to be totally dissolved; and that as Free and Independent States, they have full Power to levy War, conclude Peace, contract Alliances, establish Commerce, and to do all other Acts and Things which Independent States may of right do.—And for the support of this Declaration, with a firm reliance on the protection of Divine Providence, we mutually pledge to each other our Lives, our Fortunes and our sacred Honor.

John Hancock

New Hampshire
Josiah Bartlett
Wm. Whipple
Matthew Thornton

Rhode Island
Step. Hopkins
William Ellery

Connecticut
Roger Sherman
Sam'el Huntington
Wm. Williams
Oliver Wolcott

New York
Wm. Floyd
Phil. Livingston
Frans. Lewis
Lewis Morris

New Jersey
Richd. Stockton
Jno. Witherspoon
Fras. Hopkinson
John Hart
Abra. Clark

Pennsylvania
Robt. Morris
Benjamin Rush
Benj. Franklin
John Morton
Geo. Clymer
Jas. Smith
Geo. Taylor
James Wilson
Geo. Ross

Massachusetts-Bay
Saml. Adams
John Adams
Robt. Treat Paine
Elbridge Gerry

Delaware
Caesar Rodney
Geo. Read
Tho. M'Kean

Maryland
Samuel Chase
Wm. Paca
Thos. Stone
Charles Carroll of Carrollton

Virginia
George Wythe
Richard Henry Lee
Th. Jefferson
Benj. Harrison
Ths. Nelson, Jr.
Francis Lightfoot Lee
Carter Braxton

North Carolina
Wm. Hooper
Joseph Hewes
John Penn

South Carolina
Edward Rutledge
Thos. Heyward, Junr.
Thomas Lynch, Junr.
Arthur Middleton

Georgia
Button Gwinnett
Lyman Hall
Geo. Walton

Constitution of the United States of America

(Historical text has been edited to conform to contemporary American usage. The bracketed words are designations for your convenience; they are not part of the Constitution.)

The oldest federal constitution in existence was framed by a convention of delegates from twelve of the thirteen original states in Philadelphia in May, 1787, Rhode Island failing to send a delegate. George Washington presided over the session, which lasted until September 17, 1787. The draft (originally a preamble and seven Articles) was submitted to all thirteen states and was to become effective when ratified by nine states. It went into effect on the first Wednesday in March, 1789, having been ratified by New Hampshire, the ninth state to approve, on June 21, 1788. The states ratified the Constitution in the following order:

Delaware	December 7, 1787
Pennsylvania	December 12, 1787
New Jersey	December 18, 1787
Georgia	January 2, 1788
Connecticut	January 9, 1788
Massachusetts	February 6, 1788
Maryland	April 28, 1788
South Carolina	May 23, 1788
New Hampshire	June 21, 1788
Virginia	June 25, 1788
New York	July 26, 1788
North Carolina	November 21, 1789
Rhode Island	May 29, 1790

[Preamble]

We the people of the United States, in order to form a more perfect Union, establish justice, insure domestic tranquility, provide for the common defence, promote the general welfare, and secure the blessings of liberty to ourselves and our posterity, do ordain and establish this Constitution for the United States of America.

Article I

Section 1

[Legislative powers vested in Congress.] All legislative powers herein granted shall be vested in a Congress of the United States, which shall consist of a Senate and House of Representatives.

Section 2

[Composition of the House of Representatives.—1.] The House of Representatives shall be composed of members chosen every second year by the people of the several States, and the electors in each State shall have the qualifications requisite for electors of the most numerous branch of the State Legislature.

[Qualifications of Representatives.—2.] No Person shall be a Representative who shall not have attained to the age of twenty-five years, and been seven years a citizen of the United States, and who shall not, when elected, be an inhabitant of that State in which he shall be chosen.

[Apportionment of Representatives and direct taxes—census.[1]—3.] (Representatives and direct taxes shall be apportioned among the several States which may be included within this Union, according to their respective numbers, which shall be determined by adding to the whole number of free persons, including those bound to service for a term of years, and excluding Indians not taxed, three fifths of all other persons.) The actual enumeration shall be made within three years after the first meeting of the Congress of the United States, and within every subsequent term of ten years, in such manner as they shall by law direct. The number of Representatives shall not exceed one for every thirty thousand, but each State shall have at least one Representative; and until such enumeration shall be made, the State of New Hampshire shall be entitled to choose three, Massachusetts eight, Rhode-Island and Providence Plantations one, Connecticut five, New York six, New Jersey four, Pennsylvania eight, Delaware one, Maryland six, Virginia ten, North Carolina five, South Carolina five, and Georgia three.

[Filling of vacancies in representation.—4.] When vacancies happen in the representation from any State, the Executive Authority thereof shall issue writs of election to fill such vacancies.

[Selection of officers; power of impeachment.—5.] The House of Representatives shall choose their Speaker and other officers; and shall have the sole power of impeachment.

Section 3[2]

[The Senate.—1.] The Senate of the United States shall be composed of two Senators from each State, chosen by the Legislature thereof, for six years; and each Senator shall have one vote.

[Classification of Senators; filling of vacancies.—2.] Immediately after they shall be assembled in consequence of the first election, they shall be divided as equally as may be into three classes. The seats of the Senators of the first class shall be vacated at the expiration of the second year, of the second class at the expiration of the fourth year, and of the third class at the expiration of the sixth year, so that one-third may be chosen every second year; and if vacancies happen by resignation, or otherwise, during the recess of the Legislature of any State, the Executive thereof may make temporary appointments (until the next meeting of the Legislature, which shall then fill such vacancies).

[Qualification of Senators.—3.] No person shall be a Senator who shall not have attained to the age of thirty years, and been nine years a citizen of the United States, and who shall not, when elected, be an inhabitant of that State for which he shall be chosen.

[Vice President to be President of Senate.—4.] The Vice President of the United States shall be President of the Senate, but shall have no vote, unless they be equally divided.

[Selection of Senate officers; President pro tempore.—5.] The Senate shall choose their other officers, and also a President pro tempore, in the absence of the Vice President, or when he shall exercise the office of President of the United States.

[Senate to try impeachments.—6.] The Senate

shall have the sole power to try all impeachments. When sitting for that purpose, they shall be on oath or affirmation. When the President of the United States is tried, the Chief Justice shall preside: and no person shall be convicted without the concurrence of two thirds of the members present.

[Judgment in cases of Impeachment.—7.] Judgment in cases of impeachment shall not extend further than to removal from office, and disqualification to hold and enjoy any office of honor, trust, or profit under the United States: but the party convicted shall nevertheless be liable and subject to indictment, trial, judgment and punishment, according to Law.

Section 4

[Control of congressional elections.—1.] The times, places, and manner of holding elections for Senators and Representatives, shall be prescribed in each State by the Legislature thereof; but the Congress may at any time by law make or alter such regulations, except as to the places of choosing Senators.

[Time for assembling of Congress.[3]—2.] The Congress shall assemble at least once in every year, and such meeting shall be on the first Monday in December, unless they shall by law appoint a different day.

Section 5

[Each house to be the judge of the election and qualifications of its members; regulations as to quorum.—1.] Each House shall be the judge of the elections, returns, and qualifications of its own members, and a majority of each shall constitute a quorum to do business; but a smaller number may adjourn from day to day, and may be authorized to compel the attendance of absent members, in such manner, and under such penalties as each House may provide.

[Each house to determine its own rules.—2.] Each House may determine the rules of its proceedings, punish its members for disorderly behavior, and, with the concurrence of two thirds, expel a member.

[Journals and yeas and nays.—3.] Each House shall keep a journal of its proceedings, and from time to time publish the same, excepting such parts as may in their judgment require secrecy; and the yeas and nays of the members of either House on any question shall, at the desire of one fifth of those present, be entered on the journal.

[Adjournment.—4.] Neither House, during the session of Congress, shall, without the consent of the other, adjourn for more than three days, nor to any other place than that in which the two Houses shall be sitting.

Section 6

[Compensation and privileges of members of Congress.—1.] The Senators and Representatives shall receive a compensation for their services, to be ascertained by law, and paid out of the Treasury of the United States. They shall in all cases, except treason, felony, and breach of the peace, be privileged from arrest during their attendance at the session of their respective Houses, and in going to and returning from the same; and for any speech or debate in either House, they shall not be questioned in any other place.

[Incompatible offices; exclusions.—2.] No Senator or Representative shall, during the time for which he was elected, be appointed to any civil office under the authority of the United States, which shall have been created, or the emoluments whereof shall have been increased during such time; and no person holding any office under the United States shall be a member of either House during his continuance in office.

Section 7

[Revenue bills to originate in House.—1.] All bills for raising revenue shall originate in the House of Representatives; but the Senate may propose or concur with amendments as on other bills.

[Manner of passing bills; veto power of President.—2.] Every bill which shall have passed the House of Representatives and the Senate, shall, before it becomes a law, be presented to the President of the United States; if he approve he shall sign it, but if not he shall return it, with his objections to that House in which it shall have originated, who shall enter the objections at large on their journal, and proceed to reconsider it. If after such reconsideration two thirds of that House shall agree to pass the bill, it shall be sent, together with the objections, to the other House, by which it shall likewise be reconsidered, and if approved by two thirds of that House, it shall become a law. But in all such cases the votes of both Houses shall be determined by yeas and nays, and the names of the persons voting for and against the bill shall be entered on the journal of each house, respectively. If any bill shall not be returned by the President within ten days (Sundays excepted) after it shall have been presented to him, the same shall be a law, in like manner as if he had signed it, unless the Congress by their adjournment prevent its return, in which case it shall not be a law.

[Concurrent orders or resolutions, to be passed by President.—3.] Every order, resolution, or vote to which the concurrence of the Senate and House of Representatives may be necessary (except on a question of adjournment) shall be presented to the President of the United States; and before the same shall take effect, shall be approved by him, or being disapproved by him, shall be repassed by two thirds of the Senate and House of Representatives, according to the rules and limitations prescribed in the case of a bill.

Section 8

[General powers of Congress.[4]]

[Taxes, duties, imposts, and excises.—1.] The Congress shall have power to lay and collect taxes, duties, imposts and excises, to pay the debts and provide for the common defense and general welfare of the United States; but all duties, imposts and excises shall be uniform throughout the United States;

[Borrowing of money.—2.] To borrow money on the credit of the United States;

[Regulation of commerce.—3.] To regulate commerce with foreign nations, and among the several States, and with the Indian tribes;

[Naturalization and bankruptcy.—4.] To establish a uniform rule of naturalization, and uniform laws on the subject of bankruptcies throughout the United States;

[Money, weights and measures.—5.] To coin money, regulate the value thereof, and of foreign coin, and fix the standard of weights and measures;

[Counterfeiting.—6.] To provide for the punishment of counterfeiting the securities and current coin of the United States;

[Post offices.—7.] To establish post offices and post roads;

[Patents and copyrights.—8.] To promote the

progress of science and useful arts, by securing for limited times to authors and inventors the exclusive right to their respective writings and discoveries;

[**Inferior courts.—9.**] To constitute tribunals inferior to the Supreme Court;

[**Piracies and felonies.—10.**] To define and punish piracies and felonies commited on the high seas, and offences against the law of nations;

[**War; marque and reprisal.—11.**] To declare war, grant letters of marque and reprisal, and make rules concerning captures on land and water;

[**Armies.—12.**] To raise and support armies, but no appropriation of money to that use shall be for a longer term than two years;

[**Navy.—13.**] To provide and maintain a navy;

[**Land and naval forces.—14.**] To make rules for the government and regulation of the land and naval forces;

[**Calling out militia.—15.**] To provide for calling forth the militia to execute the laws of the Union, suppress insurrections, and repel invasions.

[**Organizing, arming, and disciplining militia.—16.**] To provide for organizing, arming, and disciplining, the militia, and for governing such part of them as may be employed in the service of the United States, reserving to the States, respectively, the appointment of the officers, and the authority of training the militia according to the discipline prescribed by Congress;

[**Exclusive legislation over District of Columbia.—17.**] To exercise exclusive legislation in all cases whatsoever, over such district (not exceeding ten miles square) as may, by cession of particular States, and the acceptance of Congress,become the seat of the Government of the United States, and to exercise like authority over all places purchased by the consent of the Legislature of the State in which the same shall be, for the erection of forts, magazines, arsenals, dock-yards, and other needful buildings;—And

[**To enact laws necessary to enforce Constitution.—18.**] To make all laws which shall be necessary and proper for carrying into execution the foregoing powers, and all other powers vested by this Constitution in the Government of the United States, or in any department or officer thereof.

Section 9

[**Migration or importation of certain persons not to be prohibited before 1808.—1.**] The migration or importation of such persons as any of the States now existing shall think proper to admit, shall not be prohibited by the Congress prior to the year one thousand eight hundred and eight, but a tax or duty may be imposed on such importation, not exceeding ten dollars for each person.

[**Writ of habeas corpus not to be suspended; exception.—2.**] The privilege of the writ of habeas corpus shall not be suspended, unless when in cases of rebellion or invasion the public safety may require it.

[**Bills of attainder and ex post facto laws prohibited.—3.**] No bill of attainder or ex post facto law shall be passed.

[**Capitation and other direct taxes.—4.**] No capitation, or other direct, tax shall be laid, unless in proportion to the census or enumeration herein before directed to be taken.[5]

[**Exports not to be taxed.—5.**] No tax or duty shall be laid on articles exported from any State.

[**No preference to be given to ports of any State; interstate shipping.—6.**] No preference shall be given by any regulation of commerce or revenue to the ports of one State over those of another: nor shall vessels bound to, or from, one State, be obliged to enter, clear, or pay duties in another.

[**Money, how drawn from treasury; financial statements to be published.—7.**] No money shall be drawn from the Treasury, but in consequence of appropriations made by law; and a regular statement and account of the receipts and expenditures of all public money shall be published from time to time.

[**Titles of nobility not to be granted; acceptance by government officers of favors from foreign powers.—8.**] No title of nobility shall be granted by the United States: and no person holding any office of profit or trust under them, shall, without the consent of the Congress, accept of any present, emolument, office, or title, of any kind whatever, from any king, prince, or foreign state.

Section 10

[**Limitations of the powers of the several States.—1.**] No State shall enter into any treaty, alliance, or confederation; grant letters of marque and reprisal; coin money; emit bills of credit; make any thing but gold and silver coin a tender in payment of debts; pass any bill of attainder, ex post facto law, or law impairing the obligation of contracts, or grant any title of nobility.

[**State imposts and duties.—2.**] No State shall, without the consent of the Congress, lay any imposts or duties on imports or exports, except what may be absolutely necessary for executing its inspection laws: and the net produce of all duties and imposts, laid by any State on imports or exports, shall be for the use of the Treasury of the United States; and all such laws shall be subject to the revision and control of the Congress.

[**Further restrictions on powers of States.—3.**] No State shall, without the consent of Congress, lay any duty of tonnage, keep troops, or ships of war in time of peace, enter into any agreement or compact with another state, or with a foreign power, or engage in war, unless actually invaded, or in such imminent danger as will not admit of delay.

Article II

Section 1

[**The President; the executive power.—1.**] The executive power shall be vested in a President of the United States of America. He shall hold his office during the term of four years, and, together with the Vice President, chosen for the same term, be elected, as follows

[**Appointment and qualifications of presidential electors.—2.**] Each State shall appoint, in such manner as the Legislature thereof may direct, a number of electors, equal to the whole number of Senators and Representatives to which the State may be entitled in the Congress: but no Senator or Representative, or person holding an office of trust or profit under the United States, shall be appointed an elector.

[**Original method of electing the President and Vice President.[6]**] (The electors shall meet in their respective States, and vote by ballot for two persons, of whom one at least shall not be an inhabitant of the same State with themselves. And they shall make a list of all the persons voted for, and of the number of votes for each; which list they shall sign and certify, and transmit sealed to the seat of the Government of the United States, directed to the President of the Senate. The President of the Senate shall, in the presence of the Senate and House of Representatives, open all the certificates, and the votes shall then be counted. The person having the greatest number of votes shall be the President, if such number be a majority of the whole number of electors appointed; and if there be more than one who have such majority, and have an equal number of votes, then the House of Representatives shall immediately choose by ballot one of them for President; and if no person have a majority, then from the five highest on the list the said House shall in like manner choose the President. But in choosing the President, the votes shall be taken by States, the representation from each State having one vote; A quorum for this purpose shall consist of a member or members from two thirds of the States, and a majority of all the states shall be necessary to a choice. In every case, after the choice of the President, the person having the greatest number of votes of the electors shall be the Vice President. But if there should remain two or more who have equal votes, the Senate should choose from them by ballot the Vice President.)

[Congress may determine time of choosing electors and day for casting their votes.—3.] The Congress may determine the time of choosing the electors, and the day on which they shall give their votes; which day shall be the same throughout the United States.

[Qualifications for the office of President.[7]—4.] No person except a natural born citizen, or a citizen of the United States, at the time of the adoption of this Constitution, shall be eligible to the office of President; neither shall any person be eligible to that office who shall not have attained to the age of thirty-five years, and been fourteen years a resident within the United States.

[Filling vacancy in the office of President.[8]—5.] In case of the removal of the President from office, or of his death, resignation, or inability to discharge the powers and duties of the said office, the same shall devolve on the Vice President, and the Congress may by law provide for the case of removal, death, resignation or inability, both of the President and Vice President, declaring what officer shall then act as President, and such officer shall act accordingly, until the disability be removed, or a President shall be elected.

[Compensation of the President.—6.] The President shall, at stated times, receive for his services, a compensation, which shall neither be increased nor diminished during the period for which he shall have been elected, and he shall not receive within that period any other emolument from the United States, or any of them.

[Oath to be taken by the President.—7.] Before he enter on the execution of his office, he shall take the following oath or affirmation:—"I do solemnly swear (or affirm) that I will faithfully excute the office of President of the United States, and will to the best of my ability, preserve, protect, and defend the Constitution of the United States."

Section 2

[The President to be commander in chief of army and navy and head of executive departments; may grant reprieves and pardons.—1.] The President shall be Commander in Chief of the Army and Navy of the United States, and of the militia of the several States, when called into the actual service of the United States; he may require the opinion, in writing, of the principal officer in each of the executive departments, upon any subject relating to the duties of their respective offices, and he shall have power to grant reprieves and pardons for offences against the United States, except in cases of impeachment.

[President may, with concurrence of Senate, make treaties, appoint ambassadors, etc.; appointment of inferior officers, authority of Congress over.—2.] He shall have power, by and with the advice and consent of the Senate, to make treaties, provided two thirds of the Senators present concur; and he shall nominate, and by and with the advice and consent of the Senate, shall appoint ambassadors, other public ministers and consuls, judges of the Supreme Court, and all other officers of the United States, whose appointments are not herein otherwise provided for, and which shall be established by law: but the Congress may by law vest the appointment of such inferior officers, as they think proper, in the President alone, in the courts of law, or in the heads of departments.

[President may fill vacancies in office during recess of Senate.—3.] The President shall have power to fill up all vacancies that may happen during the recess of the Senate, by granting commissions which shall expire at the end of their session.

Section 3

[President to give advice to Congress; may convene or adjourn it on certain occasions; to receive ambassadors, etc.; have laws executed and commission all officers.] He shall from time to time give to the Congress information of the state of the Union, and recommend to their consideration such measures as he shall judge necessary and expedient; he may, on extraordinary occasions, convene both Houses, or either of them, and in case of disagreement between them, with respect to the time of adjournment, he may adjourn them to such time as he shall think proper; he shall receive ambassadors and other public ministers: he shall take care that the laws be faithfully executed, and shall commission all the officers of the United States.

Section 4

[All civil officers removable by impeachment.] The President, Vice President, and all civil officers of the United States shall be removed from office on impeachment for, and conviction of, treason, bribery, or other high crimes and misdemeanors.

Article III

Section 1

[Judicial powers; how vested; term of office and compensation of judges.] The judicial Power of the United States, shall be vested in one Supreme Court, and in such inferior courts as the Congress may from time to time ordain and establish. The judges, both of the supreme and inferior courts, shall hold their offices during good behavior, and shall, at stated times, receive for their services, a compensation, which shall not be diminished during their continuance in office.

Section 2

[Jurisdiction of Federal courts.[9]—1.] The judicial power shall extend to all cases, in law and equity, arising under this Constitution, the laws of the United States, and treaties made, or which shall be made, under their authority; to all cases affecting ambassadors, other public ministers and consuls; to all cases of admiralty and maritime jurisdiction; to controversies to which the United States, shall be a party; to controversies between two or more States; between a State and citizens of another State; between citizens of different States, between citizens of the same State claiming lands under grants of different states, and between a State, or the citizens thereof, and foreign states, citizens, or subjects.

[Original and appellate jurisdiction of Supreme Court.—2.] In all cases affecting ambassadors, other public ministers and consuls, and those in which a State shall be party, the Supreme Court shall have original jurisdiction. In all the other cases before mentioned, the Supreme Court shall have appellate jurisdiction, both as to law and fact, with such exceptions, and under such regulations, as the Congress shall make.

[Trial of all crimes, except impeachment, to be by jury.—3.] The trial of all crimes, except in cases of impeachment, shall be by jury; and such trial shall be held in the State where the said crimes shall have been committed; but when not committed within any State, the trial shall be at such place or places as the Congress may by law have directed.

Section 3

[Treason defined; conviction of.—1.] Treason against the United States, shall consist only in levying war against them, or, in adhering to their enemies, giving them aid and comfort. No person shall be convicted of treason unless on the testimony of two witnesses to the same overt act, or on confession in open court.

[Congress to declare punishment for treason; proviso.—2.] The Congress shall have power to declare the punishment of treason, but no attainder of treason shall work corruption of blood, or forfeiture except during the life of the person attainted.

Article IV

Section 1

[Each State to give full faith and credit to the public acts and records of other States.] Full faith and credit shall be given in each State to the public acts, records, and judicial proceedings of every other State. And the Congress may by general laws prescribe the manner in which such acts, records, and proceedings shall be proved, and the effect thereof.

Section 2

[Privileges of citizens.—1.] The citizens of each State shall be entitled to all privileges and immunities of citizens in the several States.

[Extradition between the several States.—2.] A person charged in any State with treason, felony, or other crime, who shall flee from justice, and be found in another State, shall on demand of the Executive authority of the State from which he fled, be delivered up, to be removed to the State having jurisdiction of the crime.

[Persons held to labor or service in one State, fleeing to another, to be returned.—3.] No person held to service or labor in one State, under the laws thereof, escaping into another, shall, in consequence of any law or regulation therein, be discharged from such service or labor, but shall be delivered up on claim of the party to whom such service or labor may be due.

Section 3

[New States.—1.] New States may be admitted by the Congress into this Union; but no new State shall be formed or erected within the jurisdiction of any other State; nor any State be formed by the junction of two or more States, or parts of States, without the consent of the Legislatures of the States concerned as well as of the Congress.

[Regulations concerning territory.—2.] The Congress shall have power to dispose of and make all needful rules and regulations respecting the territory or other property belonging to the United States; and nothing in this Constitution shall be so construed as to prejudice any claims of the United States, or of any particular State.

Section 4

[Republican form of government and protection guaranteed the several States.] The United States shall guarantee to every State in this Union a Republican form of government, and shall protect each of them against invasion; and on application of the Legislature, or of the Executive (when the Legislature cannot be convened) against domestic violence.

Article V

[Ways in which the Constitution can be amended.] The Congress, whenever two thirds of both Houses shall deem it necessary, shall propose amendments to this Constitution, or, on the application of the Legislatures of two thirds of the several States shall call a convention for proposing amendments, which, in either case, shall be valid to all intents and purposes, as part of this Constitution, when ratified by the Legislatures of three fourths of the several States, or by conventions in three fourths thereof, as the one or the other mode of ratification may be proposed by the Congress; provided that no amendment which may be made prior to the year one thousand eight hundred and eight shall in any manner affect the first and fourth clauses in the ninth Section of the first Article; and that no State, without its consent, shall be deprived of its equal suffrage in the Senate.

Article VI

[Debts contracted under the confederation secured.—1.] All debts contracted and engagements entered into, before the adoption of this Constitution, shall be as valid against the United States under this Constitution, as under the Confederation.

[Constitution, laws, and treaties of the United States to be supreme.—2.] This Constituion, and the laws of the United States which shall be made in pursuance thereof; and all treaties made, or which shall be made, under the authority of the United States, shall be the supreme law of the land; and the judges in every State shall be bound thereby, any thing in the Constitution or laws of any State to the contrary notwithstanding.

[Who shall take constitutional oath; no religious test as to official qualification.—3.] The Senators and Representatives before mentioned, and the

1. The clause included in parentheses is amended by the 14th Amendment, Section 2. 2. The first paragraph of this section and the part of the second paragraph included in parentheses are amended by the 17th Amendment. 3. Amended by the 20th Amendment, Section 2. 4. By the 16th Amendment, Congress is given the power to lay and collect taxes on income. 5. See the 16th Amendment. 6. This clause has been superseded by the 12th Amendment. 7. For qualifications of the Vice President, see 12th Amendment. 8. Amended by the 20th Amendment, Sections 3 and 4. 9. This section is abridged by the 11th Amendment. 10. See the 13th Amendment.

members of the several State Legislatures, and all executive and judicial officers, both of the United States and of the several States, shall be bound by oath or affirmation, to support this Constitution; but no religious test shall ever be required as a qualification to any office or public trust under the United States.

Article VII

[Constitution to be considered adopted when ratified by nine States.] The ratification of the conventions of nine States shall be sufficient for the establishment of this Constitution between the States so ratifying the same.

Done in convention by the unanimous consent of the States present the seventeenth day of September in the year of our Lord one thousand seven hundred and eighty seven and of the independence of the United States of America the Twelfth. In witness whereof we have hereunto subscribed our names.

GEORGE WASHINGTON
President and Deputy from Virginia

NEW HAMPSHIRE
John Langdon — Nicholas Gilman

MASSACHUSETTS
Nathaniel Gorham — Rufus King

CONNECTICUT
Wm. Saml. Johnson — Roger Sherman

NEW YORK
Alexander Hamilton

NEW JERSEY
Wil. Livingston — Wm. Paterson
David Brearley — Jona. Dayton

PENNSYLVANIA
B. Franklin — Thomas Mifflin
Robt. Morris — Geo. Clymer
Thos. FitzSimons — Jared Ingersoll
James Wilson — Gouv. Morris

DELAWARE
Geo. Read — Gunning Bedford Jun.
John Dickinson — Richard Bassett
Jaco. Broom

MARYLAND
James McHenry — Dan. of St. Thos. Jenifer
Danl. Carroll

VIRGINIA
John Blair — James Madison, Jr.

NORTH CAROLINA
Wm. Blount — Richd Dobbs Spaight
Hu. Williamson

SOUTH CAROLINA
J. Rutledge — Charles Cotesworth Pinckney
Charles Pinckney — Pierce Butler

GEORGIA
William Few — Abr. Baldwin

Attest: William Jackson, Secretary

Amendments to the Constitution of the United States

(Amendments I to X inclusive, popularly known as the Bill of Rights, were proposed and sent to the states by the first session of the First Congress. They were ratified Dec. 15, 1791.)

Article I

[Freedom of religion, speech, of the press, and right of petition.] Congress shall make no law respecting an establishment of religion, or prohibiting the free exercise thereof; or abridging the freedom of speech, or of the press; or the right of the people peaceably to assemble, and to petition the Government for a redress of grievances.

Article II

[Right of people to bear arms not to be infringed.] A well regulated militia, being necessary to the security of a free State, the right of the people to keep and bear arms, shall not be infringed.

Article III

[Quartering of troops.] No soldier shall, in time of peace be quartered in any house, without the consent of the owner, nor in time of war, but in a manner to be prescribed by law.

Article IV

[Persons and houses to be secure from unreasonable searches and seizures.] The right of the people to be secure in their persons, houses, papers, and effects, against unreasonable searches and seizures, shall not be violated, and no warrants shall issue, but upon probable cause, supported by oath or affirmation, and particularly describing the place to be searched, and the persons or things to be seized.

Article V

[Trials for crimes; just compensation for private property taken for public use.] No person shall be held to answer for a capital, or otherwise infamous crime, unless on a presentment or indictment of a Grand Jury, except in cases arising in the land or naval forces, or in the militia, when in actual service in time of war or public danger; nor shall any person be subject for the same offence to be twice put in jeopardy of life or limb; nor shall be compelled in any criminal case to be a witness, against himself, nor be deprived of life, liberty, or property, without due process of law; nor shall private property be taken for public use, without just compensation.

Article VI

[Civil rights in trials for crimes enumerated.] In all criminal prosecutions, the accused shall enjoy the right to a speedy and public trial, by an impartial jury of the State and district wherein the crime shall have been committed, which district shall have been previously ascertained by law, and to be informed of the nature and cause of the accusation;

to be confronted with the witnesses against him; to have compulsory process for obtaining witnesses in his favor, and to have the assistance of counsel for his defense.

Article VII

[Civil rights in civil suits.] In suits at common law, where the value in controversy shall exceed twenty dollars, the right of trial by jury shall be preserved, and no fact tried by a jury, shall be otherwise re-examined in any court of the United States, than according to the rules of the common law.

Article VIII

[Excessive bail, fines, and punishments prohibited.] Excessive bail shall not be required, nor excessive fines imposed, nor cruel and unusual punishments inflicted.

Article IX

[Reserved rights of people.] The enumeration in the Constitution, of certain rights, shall not be construed to deny or disparage others retained by the people.

Article X

[Powers not delegated, reserved to states and people respectively.] The powers not delegated to the United States by the Constitution, nor prohibited by it to the States, are reserved to the States, respectively, or to the people.

Article XI

(The proposed amendment was sent to the states Mar. 5, 1794, by the Third Congress. It was ratified Feb. 7, 1795.)

[Judicial power of United States not to extend to suits against a State.] The judicial power of the United States shall not be construed to extend to any suit in law or equity, commenced or prosecuted against one of the United States by citizens of another State, or by citizens or subjects of any foreign state.

Article XII

(The proposed amendment was sent to the states Dec. 12, 1803, by the Eighth Congress. It was ratified July 27, 1804.)

[Present mode of electing President and Vice-President by electors.[1]] The electors shall meet in their respective states, and vote by ballot for President and Vice President, one of whom, at least, shall not be an inhabitant of the same state with themselves; they shall name in their ballots the person voted for as President, and in distinct ballots the person voted for as Vice President, and they shall make distinct lists of all persons voted for as President, and of all persons voted for as Vice President, and of the number of votes for each, which lists they shall sign and certify, and transmit sealed to the seat of the government of the United States, directed to the President of the Senate; the President of the Senate shall, in the presence of the Senate and House of Representatives, open all the certificates and the votes shall then be counted; the person having the greatest number of votes for President, shall be the President, if such number be a majority of the whole number of electors appointed; and if no person have such majority, then from the persons having the highest numbers not exceeding three on the list of those voted for as President, the House of Representatives shall choose immediately, by ballot, the President. But in choosing the President, the votes shall be taken by states, the representation from each State having one vote; a quorum for this purpose shall consist of a member or members from two thirds of the states, and a majority of all the states shall be necessary to a choice. And if the House of Representatives shall not choose a President whenever the right of choice shall devolve upon them, before the fourth day of March next following, then the Vice President shall act as President, as in the case of the death or other constitutional disability of the President. The person having the greatest number of votes as Vice President, shall be the Vice President, if such number be a majority of the whole number of electors appointed, and if no person have a majority, then from the two highest numbers on the list, the Senate shall choose the Vice President; a quorum for the purpose shall consist of two thirds of the whole number of Senators, and a majority of the whole number shall be necessary to a choice. But no person constitutionally ineligible to the office of President shall be eligible to that of Vice President of the United States.

Article XIII

(The proposed amendment was sent to the states Feb. 1, 1865, by the Thirty-eighth Congress. It was ratified Dec. 6, 1865.)

Section 1

[Slavery prohibited.] Neither slavery nor involuntary servitude, except as a punishment for crime whereof the party shall have been duly convicted, shall exist within the United States, or any place subject to their jurisdiction.

Section 2

[Congress given power to enforce this article.] Congress shall have power to enforce this article by appropriate legislation.

Article XIV

(The proposed amendment was sent to the states June 16, 1866, by the Thirty-ninth Congress. It was ratified July 9, 1868.)

Section 1

[Citizenship defined; privileges of citizens.] All persons born or naturalized in the United States, and subject to the jurisdiction thereof, are citizens of the United States and of the State wherein they reside. No State shall make or enforce any law which shall abridge the privileges or immunities of citizens of the United States; nor shall any State deprive any person of life, liberty, or property, without due process of law; nor deny to any person within its jurisdiction the equal protection of the laws.

Section 2

[Apportionment of Representatives.] Representatives shall be apportioned among the several States according to their respective numbers, counting the whole number of persons in each State, excluding Indians not taxed. But when the right to vote at any election for the choice of electors for President and Vice President of the United

States, Representatives in Congress, the executive and judicial officers of a State, or the members of the Legislature thereof, is denied to any of the male inhabitants of such State, being twenty-one years of age, and citizens of the United States, or in any way abridged, except for participation in rebellion, or other crime, the basis of representation therein shall be reduced in the proportion which the number of such male citizens shall bear to the whole number of male citizens twenty-one years of age in such State.

Section 3

[Disqualification for office; removal of disability.] No person shall be a Senator or Representative in Congress, or elector of President and Vice President, or hold any office, civil or military, under the United States, or under any State, who, having previously taken an oath, as a member of Congress, or as an officer of the United States, or as a member of any State Legislature, or as an executive or judicial officer of any State, to support the Constitution of the United States, shall have engaged in insurrection or rebellion against the same, or given aid or comfort to the enemies thereof. But Congress may by a vote of two thirds of each House, remove such disability.

Section 4

[Public debt not to be questioned; payment of debts and claims incurred in aid of rebellion forbidden.] The validity of the public debt of the United States, authorized by law, including debts incurred for payment of pensions and bounties for services in suppressing insurrection or rebellion, shall not be questioned. But neither the United States nor any State shall assume or pay any debt or obligation incurred in aid of insurrection or rebellion against the United States, or any claim for the loss or emancipation of any slave; but all such debts, obligations, and claims shall be held illegal and void.

Section 5

[Congress given power to enforce this article.] The Congress shall have power to enforce, by appropriate legislation, the provisions of this article.

Article XV

(The proposed amendment was sent to the states Feb. 27, 1869, by the Fortieth Congress. It was ratified Feb. 3, 1870.)

Section 1

[Right of certain citizens to vote established.] The right of citizens of the United States to vote shall not be denied or abridged by the United States or by any State on account of race, color, or previous condition of servitude.

Section 2

[Congress given power to enforce this article.] The Congress shall have power to enforce this article by appropriate legislation.

Article XVI

(The proposed amendment was sent to the states July 12, 1909, by the Sixty-first Congress. It was ratified Feb. 3, 1913.)

[Taxes on income; Congress given power to lay and collect.] The Congress shall have power to lay and collect taxes on incomes, from whatever source derived, without apportionment among the several States, and without regard to any census or enumeration.

Article XVII

(The proposed amendment was sent to the states May 16, 1912, by the Sixty-second Congress. It was ratified April 8, 1913.)

[Election of United States Senators; filling of vacancies; qualifications of electors.]
The Senate of the United States shall be composed of two Senators from each State, elected by the people thereof, for six years; and each Senator shall have one vote. The electors in each State shall have the qualifications requisite for electors of the most numerous branch of the State Legislatures.

When vacancies happen in the representation of any State in the Senate, the executive authority of such State shall issue writs of election to fill such vacancies: Provided, that the legislature of any State may empower the executive thereof to make temporary appointment until the people fill the vacancies by election as the legislature may direct.

This amendment shall not be so construed as to affect the election or term of any Senator chosen before it becomes valid as part of the Constitution.

Article XVIII[2]

(The proposed amendment was sent to the states Dec. 18, 1917, by the Sixty-fifth Congress. It was ratified by three quarters of the states by Jan. 16, 1919, and became effective Jan. 16, 1920.)

Section 1

[Manufacture, sale, or transportation of intoxicating liquors, for beverage purposes, prohibited.] After one year from the ratification of this article the manufacture, sale, or transportation of intoxicating liquors within, the importation thereof into, or the exportation thereof from the United States and all territory subject to the jurisdiction thereof for beverage purposes is hereby prohibited.

Section 2

[Congress and the several States given concurrent power to pass appropriate legislation to enforce this article.] The Congress and the several States shall have concurrent power to enforce this article by appropriate legislation.

Section 3

[Provisions of article to become operative, when adopted by three fourths of the States.] This article shall be inoperative unless it shall have been ratified as an amendment to the Constitution by the legislatures of the several States, as provided in the Constitution, within seven years from the date of the submission hereof to the States by Congress.

Article XIX

(The proposed amendment was sent to the states June 4, 1919, by the Sixty-sixth Congress. It was ratified Aug. 18, 1920.)

[The right of citizens to vote shall not be denied because of sex.] The right of citizens of the United States to vote shall not be denied or abridged by the United States or by any State on account of sex.

[Congress given power to enforce this article.] Congress shall have power to enforce this article by appropriate legislation.

Article XX

(The proposed amendment, sometimes called the "Lame Duck Amendment," was sent to the states Mar. 3, 1932, by the Seventy-second Congress. It was ratified Jan. 23, 1933; but, in accordance with Section 5, Sections 1 and 2 did not go into effect until Oct. 15, 1933.)

Section 1

[Terms of President, Vice President, Senators, and Representatives.] The terms of the President and Vice President shall end at noon on the twentieth day of January, and the terms of Senators and Representatives at noon on the third day of January, of the years in which such terms would have ended if this article had not been ratified; and the terms of their successors shall then begin.

Section 2

[Time of assembling Congress.] The Congress shall assemble at least once in every year, and such meeting shall begin at noon on the third day of January, unless they shall by law appoint a different day.

Section 3

[Filling vacancy in office of President.] If, at the time fixed for the beginning of the term of the President, the President-elect shall have died, the Vice President-elect shall become President. If a President shall not have been chosen before the time fixed for the beginning of his term, or if the President-elect shall have failed to qualify, then the Vice President shall have qualified; and the Congress may by law provide for the case wherein neither a President-elect nor a Vice President-elect shall have qualified, declaring who shall then act as President, or the manner in which one who is to act shall be selected, and such person shall act accordingly until a President or Vice President shall have qualified.

Section 4

[Power of Congress in Presidential succession.] The Congress may by law provide for the case of the death of any of the persons from whom the House of Representatives may choose a President whenever the right of choice shall have devolved upon them, and for the case of the death of any of the persons from whom the Senate may choose a Vice President whenever the right of choice shall have devolved upon them.

Section 5

[Time of taking effect.] Sections 1 and 2 shall take effect on the 15th day of October following the ratification of this article.

Section 6

[Ratification.] This article shall be inoperative unless it shall have been ratified as an amendment to the Constitution by the legislatures of three fourths of the several States within seven years from the date of its submission.

Article XXI

(The proposed amendment was sent to the states Feb. 20, 1933, by the Seventy-second Congress. It was ratified Dec. 5, 1933.)

Section 1

[Repeal of Prohibition Amendment.] The eighteenth article of amendment to the Constitution of the United States is hereby repealed.

Section 2

[Transportation of intoxicating liquors.] The transportation or importation into any State, territory, or possession of the United States for delivery or use therein of intoxicating liquors, in violation of the laws thereof, is hereby prohibited.

Section 3

[Ratification.] This article shall be inoperative unless it shall have been ratified as an amendment to the Constitution by convention in the several States, as provided in the Constitution, within seven years from the date of the submission thereof to the States by the Congress.

Article XXII

(The proposed amendment was sent to the states Mar. 21, 1947, by the Eightieth Congress. It was ratified Feb. 27, 1951.)

Section 1

[Limit to number of terms a President may serve.] No person shall be elected to the office of the President more than twice, and no person who has held the office of President, or acted as President, for more than two years of a term to which some other person was elected President shall be elected to the office of the President more than once. But this article shall not apply to any person holding the office of President when this article was proposed by the Congress, and shall not prevent any person who may be holding the office of President, or acting as President, during the term within which this article becomes operative from holding the office of President or acting as President during the remainder of such term.

Section 2

[Ratification.] This article shall be inoperative unless it shall have been ratified as an amendment to the Constitution by the legislatures of three fourths of the several States within seven years from the date of its submission to the States by the Congress.

Article XXIII

(The proposed amendment was sent to the states June 16, 1960, by the Eighty-sixth Congress. It was ratified March 29, 1961.)

Section 1

[Electors for the District of Columbia.] The District constituting the seat of Government of the United States shall appoint in such manner as the Congress may direct:

A number of electors of President and Vice President equal to the whole number of Senators and Representatives in Congress to which the District would be entitled if it were a State, but in no event more than the least populous State; they shall be in addition to those appointed by the States, but they shall be considered, for the purposes of the election of President and Vice President, to be electors appointed by a State; and they shall meet in the District and perform such duties as provided by the twelfth article of amendment.

Section 2

[Congress given power to enforce this article.] The Congress shall have the power to enforce this article by appropriate legislation.

Article XXIV

(The proposed amendment was sent to the states Aug. 27, 1962, by the Eighty-seventh Congress. It was ratified Jan. 23, 1964.)

Section 1

[Payment of poll tax or other taxes not to be prerequisite for voting in federal elections.] The right of citizens of the United States to vote in any primary or other election for President or Vice President, for electors for President or Vice President, or for Senator or Representative in Congress, shall not be denied or abridged by the United States or any State by reasons of failure to pay any poll tax or other tax.

Section 2

[Congress given power to enforce this article.] The Congress shall have the power to enforce this article by appropriate legislation.

Article XXV

(The proposed amendment was sent to the states July 6, 1965, by the Eighty-ninth Congress. It was ratified Feb. 10, 1967.)

Section 1

[Succession of Vice President to Presidency.] In case of the removal of the President from office or of his death or resignation, the Vice President shall become President.

Section 2

[Vacancy in office of Vice President.] Whenever there is a vacancy in the office of the Vice President, the President shall nominate a Vice President who shall take office upon confirmation by a majority vote of both Houses of Congress.

Section 3

[Vice President as Acting President.] Whenever the President transmits to the President pro tempore of the Senate and the Speaker of the House of Representatives his written declaration that he is unable to discharge the powers and duties of his office, and until he transmits to them a written declaration to the contrary, such powers and duties shall be discharged by the Vice President as Acting President.

Section 4

[Vice President as Acting President.] Whenever the Vice President and a majority of either the principal officers of the executive departments or of such other body as Congress may by law provide, transmit to the President pro tempore of the Senate and the Speaker of the House of Representatives their written declaration that the President is unable to discharge the powers and duties of his office, the Vice President shall immediately assume the powers and duties of the office as Acting President.

Thereafter, when the President transmits to the President pro tempore of the Senate and the Speaker of the House of Representatives his written declaration that no inability exists, he shall resume the powers and duties of his office unless the Vice President and a majority of either the principal officers of the executive department or of such other body as Congress may by law provide, transmit within four days to the President pro tempore of the Senate and the Speaker of the House of Representatives their written declaration that the President is unable to discharge the powers and duties of his office. Thereupon Congress shall decide the issue, asssembling within forty-eight hours for that purpose if not in session. If the Congress, within twenty-one days after receipt of the latter written declaration, or, if Congress is not in session, within twenty-one days after Congress is required to assemble, determines by two thirds vote of both Houses that the President is unable to discharge the powers and duties of his office, the Vice President shall continue to discharge the same as Acting President; otherwise, the President shall resume the powers and duties of his office.

Article XXVI

(The proposed amendment was sent to the states Mar. 23, 1971, by the Ninety-second Congress. It was ratified July 1, 1971.)

Section 1

[Voting for 18-year-olds.] The right of citizens of the United States, who are 18 years of age or older, to vote shall not be denied or abridged by the United States or by any state on account of age.

Section 2

[Congress given power to enforce this article.] The Congress shall have power to enforce this article by appropriate legislation.

1. Amended by the 20th Amendment, Sections 3 and 4. 2. Repealed by the 21st Amendment.

The White House

Source: Department of the Interior, U.S. National Park Service.

The White House, the official residence of the President, is at 1600 Pennsylvania Avenue in Washington, D.C. The site, covering about 18 acres, was selected by President Washington and Pierre Charles L'Enfant, and the architect was James Hoban. The design of the residence is said to have been suggested by the Duke of Leinster's house in Ireland. The cornerstone was laid Oct. 13, 1792, and the first residents were President and Mrs. John Adams in November 1800. The building was fired by the British in 1814. The sandstone exterior was painted white during the course of the reconstruction.

From December 1948 to March 1952, the interior of the White House was rebuilt, and the outer walls were strengthened.

The rooms for public functions are on the first floor; on the second and third are the President's apartments. The most celebrated public room is the East Room, where formal receptions take place. Other public rooms are the Red Room, the Green Room, and the Blue Room. The State Dining Room is used for formal dinners. There are 132 rooms.

The Mayflower Compact

On Sept. 6, 1620, the *Mayflower*, a sailing vessel of about 180 tons, started her memorable voyage from Plymouth, England, with about 100[1] pilgrims aboard, bound for Virginia to establish a private permanent colony in North America. Arriving at what is now Provincetown, Mass., on Nov. 11 (Nov. 21, new style calendar), 41 of the passengers signed the famous "Mayflower Compact" as the boat lay at anchor in that Cape Cod harbor. A small detail of the pilgrims, led by William Bradford, assigned to select a place for permanent settlement landed at what is now Plymouth, Mass., on Dec. 21 (n.s.).

The text of the compact follows:

> In the name of God, Amen. We, whose names are underwritten, the Loyal Subjects of our dread Sovereign Lord, King *James*, by the Grace of God, of *Great Britain, France* and *Ireland*, King, *Defender of the Faith*, &,
>
> Having undertaken for the Glory of God, and Advancement of the Christian Faith, and the Honour of our King and Country, a voyage to plant the first colony in the northern Parts of Virginia; do by these Presents, solemnly and mutually in the Presence of God and one of another, covenant and combine ourselves together into a civil Body Politick, for our better Ordering and Preservation, and Furtherance of the Ends aforesaid; And by Virtue hereof to enact, constitute, and frame, such just and equal Laws, Ordinances, Acts, Constitutions and Offices, from time to time, as shall be thought most meet and convenient for the General good of the Colony; unto which we promise all due Submission and Obedience.
>
> In Witness whereof we have hereunto subscribed our names at *Cape Cod* the eleventh of *November*, in the Reign of our Sovereign Lord, King *James* of *England, France* and *Ireland*, the eighteenth, and of *Scotland* the fifty-fourth. *Anno Domini*, 1620

John Carver
Digery Priest
William Brewster
Edmund Margesson
John Alden
George Soule
James Chilton
Francis Cooke
Moses Fletcher
John Ridgate
Christopher Martin
William Mullins
Thomas English
John Howland
Stephen Hopkins
Edward Winslow
Gilbert Winslow
Miles Standish
Richard Bitteridge
Francis Eaton
John Tilly
John Billington
Thomas Tinker
Samuel Fuller
Richard Clark
John Allerton
Richard Warren
Edward Liester
William Bradford
Thomas Williams
Isaac Allerton
Peter Brown
John Turner
Edward Tilly
John Craxton
Thomas Rogers
John Goodman
Edward Fuller
Richard Gardiner
William White
Edward Doten

1. Historians differ as to whether 100, 101, or 102 passengers were aboard.

The Monroe Doctrine

The Monroe Doctrine was announced in President James Monroe's message to Congress, during his second term on Dec. 2, 1823, in part as follows:

"In the discussions to which this interest has given rise, and in the arrangements by which they may terminate, the occasion has been deemed proper for asserting as a principle in which rights and interests of the United States are involved, that the American continents, by the free and independent condition which they have assumed and maintain, are henceforth not to be considered as subjects for future colonization by any European power. . . . We owe it, therefore, to candor and to the amicable relations existing between the United States and those powers to declare that we should consider any attempt on their part to extend their system to any portion of this hemisphere as dangerous to our peace and safety. With the existing colonies or dependencies of any European power we have not interfered and shall not interfere. But with the governments who have declared their independence and maintain it, and whose independence we have, on great consideration and on just principles, acknowledged, we could not view any interposition for the purpose of oppressing them or controlling in any other manner their destiny by any European power in any other light than as the manifestation of an unfriendly disposition toward the United States."

Order of Presidential Succession

1. The Vice President
2. Speaker of the House
3. President pro tempore of the Senate
4. Secretary of State
5. Secretary of the Treasury
6. Secretary of Defense
7. Attorney General
8. Secretary of the Interior
9. Secretary of Agriculture
10. Secretary of Commerce
11. Secretary of Labor
12. Secretary of Health, Education, and Welfare
13. Secretary of Housing and Urban Development
14. Secretary of Transportation
15. Secretary of Energy

NOTE: An official cannot succeed to the Presidency unless he meets the Constitutional requirements.

The Star-Spangled Banner

Francis Scott Key, 1814

O say, can you see, by the dawn's early light,
What so proudly we hail'd at the twilight's last gleaming?
Whose broad stripes and bright stars, thro' the perilous fight,
O'er the ramparts we watch'd, were so gallantly streaming?
And the rockets' red glare, the bombs bursting in air,
Gave proof thro' the night that our flag was still there.
O say, does that star-spangled banner yet wave
O'er the land of the free and the home of the brave?

On the shore dimly seen thro' the mists of the deep,
Where the foe's haughty host in dread silence reposes,
What is that which the breeze, o'er the towering steep,
As it fitfully blows, half conceals, half discloses?
Now it catches the gleam of the morning's first beam,
In full glory reflected, now shines on the stream:
'T is the star-spangled banner: O, long may it wave
O'er the land of the free and the home of the brave!

And where is that band who so vauntingly swore
That the havoc of war and the battle's confusion,
A home and a country should leave us no more?
Their blood has wash'd out their foul footsteps' pollution.
No refuge could save the hireling and slave
From the terror of flight or the gloom of the grave:
And the star-spangled banner in triumph doth wave
O'er the land of the free and the home of the brave.

O thus be it ever when free-men shall stand
Between their lov'd home and the war's desolation;
Blest with vict'ry and peace, may the heav'n-rescued land
Praise the Pow'r that hath made and preserv'd us a nation!
Then conquer we must, when our cause it is just,
And this be our motto: "In God is our trust!"
And the star-spangled banner in triumph shall wave
O'er the land of the free and the home of the brave!

On Sept. 13, 1814, Francis Scott Key visited the British fleet in Chesapeake Bay to secure the release of Dr. William Beanes, who had been captured after the burning of Washington, D.C. The release was secured, but Key was detained on ship overnight during the shelling of Fort McHenry, one of the forts defending Baltimore. In the morning, he was so delighted to see the American flag still flying over the fort that he began a poem to commemorate the occasion. First published under the title "Defense of Fort M'Henry," and later as "The Star-Spangled Banner," the poem soon attained wide popularity as sung to the tune "To Anacreon in Heaven." The origin of this tune is obscure, but it may have been written by John Stafford Smith, a British composer born in 1750. "The Star-Spangled Banner" was officially made the National Anthem by Congress in 1931, although it had been already adopted as such by the Army and the Navy.

The Emancipation Proclamation

January 1, 1863

By the President of the United States of America:

A Proclamation.

Whereas on the 22d day of September, A.D. 1862, a proclamation was issued by the President of the United States, containing, among other things, the following, to wit:

"That on the 1st day of January, A.D. 1863, all persons held as slaves within any State or designated part of a State the people whereof shall then be in rebellion against the United States shall be then, thenceforward, and forever free; and the executive government of the United States, including the military and naval authority thereof, will recognize and maintain the freedom of such persons and will do no act or acts to repress such persons, or any of them, in any efforts they may make for their actual freedom.

"That the executive will on the 1st day of January aforesaid, by proclamation, designate the States and parts of States, if any, in which the people thereof, respectively, shall then be in rebellion against the United States; and the fact that any State or the people thereof shall on that day be in good faith represented in the Congress of the United States by members chosen thereto at elections wherein a majority of the qualified voters of such States shall have participated shall, in the absence of strong countervailing testimony, be deemed conclusive evidence that such State and the people thereof are not then in rebellion against the United States."

Now, therefore, I, Abraham Lincoln, President

of the United States, by virtue of the power in me vested as Commander-in-Chief of the Army and Navy of the United States in time of actual armed rebellion against the authority and government of the United States, and as a fit and necessary war measure for suppressing said rebellion, do, on this 1st day of January, A.D. 1863, and in accordance with my purpose so to do, publicly proclaimed for the full period of one hundred days from the first day above mentioned, order and designate as the States and parts of States wherein the people thereof, respectively, are this day in rebellion against the United States the following, to wit:

Arkansas, Texas, Louisiana (except the parishes of St. Bernard, Plaquemines, Jefferson, St. John, St. Charles, St. James, Ascension, Assumption, Terrebonne, Lafourche, St. Mary, St. Martin, and Orleans, including the city of New Orleans), Mississippi, Alabama, Florida, Georgia, South Carolina, North Carolina, and Virginia (except the forty-eight counties designated as West Virginia, and also the counties of Berkeley, Accomac, Northhampton, Elizabeth City, York, Princess Anne, and Norfolk, including the cities of Norfolk and Portsmouth), and which excepted parts are for the present left precisely as if this proclamation were not issued.

And by virtue of the power and for the purpose aforesaid, I do order and declare that all persons held as slaves within said designated States and parts of States are, and henceforward shall be, free; and that the Executive Government of the United States, including the military and naval authorities thereof, will recognize and maintain the freedom of said persons.

And I hereby enjoin upon the people so declared to be free to abstain from all violence, unless in necessary self-defense; and I recommend to them that, in all cases when allowed, they labor faithfully for reasonable wages.

And I further declare and make known that such persons of suitable condition will be received into the armed service of the United States to garrison forts, positions, stations, and other places, and to man vessels of all sorts in said service.

And upon this act, sincerely believed to be an act of justice, warranted by the Constitution upon military necessity, I invoke the considerate judgment of mankind and the gracious favor of Almighty God.

The Confederate States of America

State	Seceded from Union	Readmitted to Union[1]
1. South Carolina	Dec. 20, 1860	July 9, 1868
2. Mississippi	Jan. 9, 1861	Feb. 23, 1870
3. Florida	Jan. 10, 1861	June 25, 1868
4. Alabama	Jan. 11, 1861	July 13, 1868
5. Georgia	Jan. 19, 1861	July 15, 1870[2]
6. Louisiana	Jan. 26, 1861	July 9, 1868
7. Texas	March 2, 1861	March 30, 1870
8. Virginia	April 17, 1861	Jan. 26, 1870
9. Arkansas	May 6, 1861	June 22, 1868
10. North Carolina	May 20, 1861	July 4, 1868
11. Tennessee	June 8, 1861	July 24, 1866

1. Date of readmission to representation in U.S. House of Representatives. 2. Second readmission date. First date was July 21, 1868, but the representatives were unseated March 5, 1869. NOTE: Four other slave states—Delaware, Kentucky, Maryland, and Missouri—remained in the Union.

Lincoln's Gettysburg Address

The Battle of Gettysburg, one of the most noted battles of the Civil War, was fought on July 1, 2, and 3, 1863. On Nov. 19, 1863, the field was dedicated as a national cemetery by President Lincoln in a two-minute speech that was to become immortal. At the time of its delivery the speech was relegated to the inside pages of the papers, while a two-hour address by Edward Everett, the leading orator of the time, caught the headlines.

The following is the text of the address revised by President Lincoln from his own notes:

Fourscore and seven years ago our fathers brought forth on this continent a new nation conceived in liberty and dedicated to the proposition that all men are created equal. Now we are engaged in a great civil war testing whether that nation, or any nation so conceived and so dedicated, can long endure. We are met on a great battlefield of that war. We have come to dedicate a portion of that field as a final resting-place for those who here gave their lives that that nation might live. It is altogether fitting and proper that we should do this. But, in a larger sense, we cannot dedicate, we cannot consecrate, we cannot hallow this ground. The brave men, living and dead, who struggled here have consecrated it far above our poor power to add or detract. The world will little note nor long remember what we say here, but it can never forget what they did here. It is for us the living rather to be dedicated here to the unfinished work which they who fought here have thus far so nobly advanced. It is rather for us to be here dedicated to the great task remaining before us—that from these honored dead we take increased devotion to that cause for which they gave the last full measure of devotion—that we here highly resolve that these dead shall not have died in vain, that this nation under God shall have a new birth of freedom, and that government of the people, by the people, for the people shall not perish from the earth.

The Early Congresses

At the urging of Massachusetts and Virginia, the First Continental Congress met in Philadelphia on Sept. 5, 1774, and was attended by representatives of all the colonies except Georgia. Patrick Henry of Virginia declared: "The distinctions between Pennsylvanians, New Yorkers and New Englanders are no more. I am not a Virginian but an American." This Congress, which adjourned Oct. 26, 1774, passed intercolonial resolutions calling for extensive boycott by the colonies against British trade.

The following year, most of the delegates from the colonies were chosen by popular election to attend the Second Continental Congress, which assembled in Philadelphia on May 10. As war had already begun between the colonies and England, the chief problems before the Congress were the procuring of military supplies, the establishment of an army and proper defenses, the issuing of continental bills of credit, etc. On June 15, 1775, George Washington was elected to command the Continental army. Congress adjourned Dec. 12, 1776.

Other Continental Congresses were held in Baltimore (1776–77), Philadelphia (1777), Lancaster, Pa. (1777), York, Pa. (1777–78), and Philadelphia (1778–81).

In 1781, the Articles of Confederation, although establishing a league of the thirteen states rather than a strong central government, provided for the continuance of Congress. Known thereafter as the Congress of the Confederation, it held sessions in Philadelphia (1781–83), Princeton, N.J. (1783), Annapolis, Md. (1783–84), and Trenton, N.J. (1784). Five sessions were held in New York City between the years 1785 and 1789.

The Congress of the United States, established by the ratification of the Constitution, held its first meeting on March 4, 1789, in New York City. Several sessions of Congress were held in Philadelphia, and the first meeting in Washington, D.C., was on Nov. 17, 1800.

Presidents of the Continental Congresses

Name	Elected	Born	Died
Peyton Randolph, Va.	Sept. 5, 1774	c.1721	1775
Henry Middleton, S.C.	Oct. 22, 1774	1717	1784
Peyton Randolph, Va.	May 10, 1775	c.1721	1775
John Hancock, Mass.	May 24, 1775	1737	1793
Henry Laurens, S.C.	Nov. 1, 1777	1724	1792
John Jay, N.Y.	Dec. 10, 1778	1745	1829
Samuel Huntington, Conn.	Sept. 28, 1779	1731	1796
Thomas McKean, Del.	July 10, 1781	1734	1817
John Hanson, Md.	Nov. 5, 1781	1715	1783
Elias Boudinot, N.J.	Nov. 4, 1782	1740	1821
Thomas Mifflin, Pa.	Nov. 3, 1783	1744	1800
Richard Henry Lee, Va.	Nov. 30, 1784	1732	1794
John Hancock, Mass.[1]	Nov. 23, 1785	1737	1793
Nathaniel Gorham, Mass.	June 6, 1786	1738	1796
Arthur St. Clair, Pa.	Feb. 2, 1787	1734	1818
Cyrus Griffin, Va.	Jan. 22, 1788	1748	1810

1. Resigned May 29, 1786, never having served, because of continued illness.

The Great Seal of the U.S.

On July 4, 1776, the Continental Congress appointed a committee consisting of Benjamin Franklin, John Adams, and Thomas Jefferson "to bring in a device for a seal of the United States of America." After many delays, a verbal description of a design by William Barton was finally approved by Congress on June 20, 1782. The seal shows an American bald eagle with a ribbon in its mouth bearing the device *E pluribus unum* (One out of many). In its talons are the arrows of war and an olive branch of peace.

The Liberty Bell

The Liberty Bell was cast in England in 1752 for the Pennsylvania Statehouse (now named Independence Hall) in Philadelphia. It was recast in Philadelphia in 1753. It is inscribed with the words, "Proclaim liberty throughout all the land unto all the inhabitants thereof" (Lev. 25:10). The bell was rung on July 8, 1776, for the first public reading of the Declaration of Independence. Hidden in Allentown during the British occupation of Philadelphia, it was replaced in Independence Hall in 1778. The bell cracked on July 8, 1835, while tolling the death of Chief Justice John Marshall. In 1976 the Liberty Bell was moved to a special exhibition building near Independence Hall.

History of the Flag

Source: Encyclopaedia Britannica.

The first official American flag, the Continental or Grand Union flag, was displayed on Prospect Hill, Jan. 1, 1776, in the American lines besieging Boston. It had 13 alternate red and white stripes, with the British Union Jack in the upper left corner.

On June 14, 1777, the Continental Congress adopted the design for a new flag, which actually was the Continental flag with the red cross of St. George and the white cross of St. Andrew replaced on the blue field by 13 stars, one for each state. No rule was made as to the arrangement of the stars, and while they were usually shown in a circle, there were various other designs. It is uncertain when the new flag was first flown, but its first official announcement is believed to have been on Sept. 3, 1777.

The first public assertion that Betsy Ross made the first Stars and Stripes appeared in a paper read before the Historical Society of Pennsylvania on March 14, 1870, by William J. Canby, a grandson. However, Mr. Canby on later investigation found no official documents of any action by Congress on the flag before June 14, 1777. Betsy Ross's own story, according to her daughter, was that Washington, Robert Morris, and George Ross, as representatives of Congress, visited her in Philadelphia in June 1776, showing her a rough draft of the flag and asking her if she could make one. However, the only actual record of the manufacture of flags by Betsy Ross is a voucher in Harrisburg, Pa., for 14 pounds and some shillings for flags for the Pennsylvania navy.

On Jan. 13, 1794, Congress voted to add two stars and two stripes to the flag in recognition of the admission of Vermont and Kentucky to the Union. By 1818, there were 20 states in the Union, and as it was obvious that the flag would soon become unwieldly, Congress voted April 18 to return to the original 13 stripes and to indicate the admission of a new state simply by the addition of a star the following July 4. The 49th star, for Alaska, was added July 4, 1959; and the 50th star, for Hawaii, was added July 4, 1960.

The first Confederate flag, adopted in 1861 by the Confederate convention in Montgomery, Ala., was called the Stars and Bars; but because of its similarity in colors to the American flag, there was much confusion in the Battle of Bull Run. To remedy this situation, Gen. G. T. Beauregard suggested a battle flag, which was used by the Southern armies throughout the war. The flag consisted of a red field on which was placed a blue cross of St. Andrew separated from the field by a white fillet and adorned with 13[1] white stars for the Confederate states. In May 1863, at Richmond, an official flag was adopted by the Confederate Congress. This flag was white and twice as long as wide; the union, two-thirds the width of the flag, contained the battle flag designed for Gen. Beauregard. A broad transverse stripe of red was added Feb. 4, 1865, so that the flag might not be mistaken for a signal of truce.

1. 11 states formally seceded, and unofficial groups in Kentucky and Missouri adopted ordinances of secession. On this basis, these two states were admitted to the Confederacy, although the official state governments remained in the Union.

The Pledge of Allegiance[1] to the Flag

"I pledge allegiance to the Flag of the United States of America, and to the Republic for which it stands, one Nation under God,[2] indivisible, with liberty and justice for all."

1. The original pledge was published in the Sept. 8, 1892, issue of *The Youth's Companion* in Boston. For years, the authorship was in dispute between James B. Upham and Francis Bellamy of the magazine's staff. In 1939, after a study of the controversy, the United States Flag Association decided that authorship be credited to Bellamy. 2. The phrase "under God" was added to the pledge on June 14, 1954.

Statistical History of The United States

There are many ways of looking at American history—at the growth of the United States, its people, and its economy. One of the most interesting is to examine certain aspects of American life "by the numbers." This "Statistical History" makes such an examination possible. The data below—stripped of the men and women, events, and technological changes that have shaped American society—reveal much that is often hidden in the complex folds of the fabric of history.

This section includes over 1,100 entries in over 100 categories, from population to the price of steak. Teachers, writers, and editors will find these data particularly useful as they seek to make events of a particular era more understandable.

History buffs should discover that this material can add significantly to their knowledge of the past. And browsers in *Information Please* will find that this "Statistical History" is a counterpoint to the "Headline History" that appears elsewhere in this book.

Item	Unit	1975	1970	1960	1950	1940
1. Population estimates[1]	thousands	213,540	204,879	180,671[2]	151, 684	132,122
2. Land area	sq miles	3,536,855	3,536,855	3,540,911[2]	2,974,726	2,977,128
3. Population per sq mile[3]		60.2	57.5	50.6[2]	50.7	44.2
4. Median age of population	years	28.8	28.1	29.5[2]	30.2	29.0
5. Number of households	thousands	71,120	63,401	52,799[2]	43,554	34,949
6. Average household size		2.94	3.14	3.33[2]	3.37	3.67
7. Homicides		21,310	16,848	8,464[2]	7,942	8,329
8. Rate per 100,000 population		10.0	8.3	4.7[2]	5.3	6.3
9. Suicides		27,063	23,480	19,041[2]	17,145	18,907
10. Rate per 100,000 population		12.7	11.6	10.6[2]	11.4	14.4
11. Number of immigrants		386,200	373,326	265,398	249,187	70,756
Immigrants by selected occupations						
12. Professional[4]		38,500	46,151	21,940	20,502	6,802
13. Farmers[4,5]		900	3,839	3,050	17,642	847
14. Skilled[4,6]		38,500	46,622	34,135	41,450	5,710
15. Laborers[4,7]		13,000	14,148	12,838	5,693	2,120
16. Total Gross National Product—Current prices	billion dollars	1,516.3	977.1	503.7[2]	284.8	99.7
17. Per capita Gross National Product—Current prices	dollars	7,016	4,808	2,788[2]	1,877	754
Retail prices of selected foods in U.S. cities						
18. Flour—5 lb	¢/unit shown	99.5	58.9	55.4	49.1	21.5
19. Bread—1 lb	¢/unit shown	36.0	24.3	20.3	14.3	8.0
20. Round steak—1 lb	¢/unit shown	188.5	130.2	105.5	93.6	36.4
21. Butter—1 lb	¢/unit shown	102.5	86.6	74.9	72.9	36.0
22. Potatoes—10 lb	¢/unit shown	134.0	89.7	71.8	46.1	23.9
23. Sugar—5 lb	¢/unit shown	186.0	64.8	58.2	48.7	26.0
24. Total labor force[10]	thousands 16 years and over	94,793	82,049	69,877[2,11]	59,643[11]	53,011[11]
25. Percent of population		61.8	59.0	56.1[2,11]	54.1[11]	52.9[11]
26. Percent of civilian labor force unemployed[13]	10 years and over	8.5	4.9	5.5[2]	5.3	14.6
Physical output of selected manufactured commodities						
27. Wheat flour	mil. bbl	—	129.1	130.4	115.4	110.9
28. Beer	thou. bbl	158,000	134,654	94,548	88,807	54,892
29. Cigarettes	millions	627,000	562,154	506,127	391,956	189,373
30. Total raw steel	thou. short tons	116,642	131,514	99,282	96,836	66,983
31. Total value of new construction put in place	mil. dollars	132,043	94,855	54,738	33,575	8,682
32. Total concerns in business	thousands	2,679	2,442	2,708	2,687	2,156
33. Business failure rate	per 10,000 listed enterprises	43	44	57	34	63
34. Average annual earnings of employees	dollars	10,434[17]	7,564	4,743	2,992	1,299
Average annual earnings per full time employee in selected industries						
35. Services[19]	current $	8,141[20]	5,946	3,513	2,183	953
36. Agriculture, Forestry, and Fisheries	current $	5,756[20]	3,063	1,658	1,282	407
37. Manufacturing	current $	10,834[20]	8,150	5,352	3,302	1,432
38. Mining[21]	current $	12,935[20]	9,262	5,676	3,460	1,388
39. Construction	current $	12,206[20]	9,293	5,443	3,333	1,330
40. Transportation	current $	12,616[20]	9,928	6,185	3,714	1,756
41. Communications and public utilities	current $	12,353[20]	8,897	5,681	3,346	1,717
42. Wholesale and retail trade	current $	8,749[20]	6,886	4,597	3,045	1,382
43. Finance, insurance, and real estate	current $	9,854[20]	8,026	5,030	3,223	1,725
44. Government	current $	10,632[20]	7,965	4,676	3,014	1,344
45. Total farm population	thousands	8,864	9,712	15,635	23,048	30,547
46. Number of farms	thousands	2,808	2,954	3,962	5,388	6,102
47. Total land in farms	mil. acres	1,086.0	1,102.8	1,176.9	1,161.4	1,065.1
48. Total value of all farm property	mil. dollars	—	265,744	167,564	101,117[22]	41,829
49. Average value per farm of land and buildings	dollars	—	70,485	32,854	14,005	5,532
50. Farm wages, per day, with room and board	dollars	16.13[17]	10.70	6.50	4.45	1.30

1930	1920	1910	1900	1890	1880	1870	1860	1850	1840	
123,188	106,461	92,407	76,094	63,056	50,262	39,905	31,513	23,261	17,120	1.
2,977,128	2,969,451	2,969,565	2,969,834	2,969,640	2,969,640	2,969,640	2,969,640	2,940,042	1,749,462	2.
41.2	35.6	31.0	25.6	21.2	16.9	13.4	10.6	7.9	9.8	3.
26.5	25.3	24.1	22.9	22.0	20.9	20.2	19.4	18.9	17.8	4.
29,905	24,352	20,256	15,964	12,690	9,946	7,579	5,211	3,598	—	5.
4.11	4.34	4.54	4.76	4.93	5.04	5.09	5.28	5.55	—	6.
10,331	5,815	2,161	230	—	—	—	—	—	—	7.
8.8	6.8	4.6	1.2	—	—	—	—	—	—	8.
18,323	8,790	7,283	2,036	—	—	—	—	—	—	9.
15.6	10.2	15.3	10.2	—	—	—	—	—	—	10.
241,700	430,001	1,041,570	448,572	455,302	457,257	387,203	179,691	315,337	92,207	11.
8,585	10,540	9,689	2,392	3,236	1,773	1,831	792	918	481	12.
8,375	12,192	11,793	5,433	29,296	47,204	35,656	21,742	42,873	18,476	13.
32,474	55,991	121,847	54,793	44,540	49,929	35,698	19,342	26,369	10,811	14.
18,080	83,496	216,909	164,261	139,365	105,012	84,577	31,268	46,640	9,640	15.
90.4	91.5	35.3	18.7	13.1	11.2[8]	7.4[9]	—	—	—	16.
734	860	382	246	208	205[8]	170[9]	—	—	—	17.
23.0	40.5	18.0	12.5	14.5	—	—	—	—	—	18.
8.6	11.5	—	—	—	—	—	—	—	—	19.
42.6	39.5	17.4	13.2	12.3	—	—	—	—	—	20.
46.4	70.1	35.9	26.1	25.5	—	—	—	—	—	21.
36.0	63.0	17.0	14.0	16.0	—	—	—	—	—	22.
30.5	97.0	30.0	30.5	34.5	—	—	—	—	—	23.
48,830[12]	41,614[12]	38,167[12]	29,073[12]	23,318[12]	17,392[12]	12,506[12]	—	—	—	24.
49.5[12]	50.3[12]	53.3[12]	50.2[12]	49.2[12]	47.3[12]	44.3[12]	—	—	—	25.
8.7	5.2	5.9	5.0	4.0	—	—	—	—	—	26.
123.6[14]	130.4	107.2	105.8	83.3	64.3	47.9	39.8	—	—	27.
3,681	9,200	59,500	39,500	27,600	13,300	6,600	—	—	—	28.
124,193	48,091	9,782	3,870	2,505	533	16	—	—	—	29.
44,591	46,183	28,330	11,227	—	—	—	—	—	—	30.
8,741	6,749	3,262	—	—	—	—	—	—	—	31.
2,183	1,821	1,515	1,174	1,111	747	427	230[15]	—	—	32.
122[16]	48	84	92	99	63	83	170[15]	—	—	33.
1,368	1,236[18]	517[18]	375[18]	—	—	—	—	—	—	34.
1,066	912	447	340	—	—	—	—	—	—	35.
388	528	223	178	—	—	—	—	—	—	36.
1,488	1,532	651	487	—	—	—	—	—	—	37.
1,424	1,684	668	479	—	—	—	—	—	—	38.
1,526	1,710	804	593	—	—	—	—	—	—	39.
1,610	1,645	607	505	—	—	—	—	—	—	40.
1,499	1,238	516	470	—	—	—	—	—	—	41.
1,569	1,270	630	508	—	—	—	—	—	—	42.
1,973	1,758	1,301	1,040	—	—	—	—	—	—	43.
1,553	1,245	725	584	—	—	—	—	—	—	44.
30,529	31,974	32,077	29,875	24,771	21,973	—	—	—	—	45.
6,295	6,454	6,366	5,740	4,565	4,009	2,660	2,044	1,449	—	46.
990.1	958.7	881.4	841.2	623.2	536.1	407.7	407.2	293.6	—	47.
57,689	78,386	40,959	20,365	16,439	12,404	9,412	7,980	3,967	—	48.
7,624	10,295	5,480	2,895	2,909	2,544	2,799	3,251	2,258	—	49.
1.80	2.80	1.05	.75[23]	.70	.65	.65[24]	—	—	—	50.

(continued)

Item	Unit	1830	1820	1810	1800	1790
1. Population estimates[1]	thousands	12,901	9,618	7,224	5,297	3,929
2. Land area	sq miles	1,749,462	1,749,462	1,681,828	864,746	864,746
3. Population per sq mile[3]		7.4	5.5	4.3	6.1	4.5
4. Median age of population	years	17.2	16.7	—	—	—
5. Number of households	thousands	—	—	—	—	—
6. Average household size		—	—	—	—	5.79
7. Homicides		—	—	—	—	—
8. Rate per 100,000 population		—	—	—	—	—
9. Suicides		—	—	—	—	—
10. Rate per 100,000 population		—	—	—	—	—
11. Number of immigrants		24,837	10,311	—	—	—
Immigrants by selected occupations						
12. Professional[4]		136	105	—	—	—
13. Farmers[4 5]		1,424	874	—	—	—
14. Skilled[4 6]		1,745	1,090	—	—	—
15. Laborers[4 7]		720	334	—	—	—
16. Total Gross National Product—Current prices	billion dollars	—	—	—	—	—
17. Per capita Gross National Product—Current prices	dollars	—	—	—	—	—
Retail prices of selected foods in U.S. cities						
18. Flour—5 lb	¢/unit shown	—	—	—	—	—
19. Bread—1 lb	¢/unit shown	—	—	—	—	—
20. Round steak—1 lb	¢/unit shown	—	—	—	—	—
21. Butter—1 lb	¢/unit shown	—	—	—	—	—
22. Potatoes—10 lb	¢/unit shown	—	—	—	—	—
23. Sugar—5 lb	¢/unit shown	—	—	—	—	—
24. Total labor force[10]	thousands 16 years and over	—	—	—	—	—
25. Percent of population		—	—	—	—	—
26. Percent of civilian labor force unemployed[13]	10 years and over	—	—	—	—	—
Physical output of selected manufactured commodities						
27. Wheat flour	mil. bbl	—	—	—	—	—
28. Beer	thou. bbl	—	—	—	—	—
29. Cigarettes	millions	—	—	—	—	—
30. Total raw steel	thou. short tons	—	—	—	—	—
31. Total value of new construction put in place	mil. dollars	—	—	—	—	—
32. Total concerns in business	thousands	—	—	—	—	—
33. Business failure rate	per 10,000 listed enterprises	—	—	—	—	—
34. Average annual earnings of employees	dollars	—	—	—	—	—
Average annual earnings per full time employee in selected industries						
35. Services[19]	current $	—	—	—	—	—
36. Agriculture, Forestry, and Fisheries	current $	—	—	—	—	—
37. Manufacturing	current $	—	—	—	—	—
38. Mining[21]	current $	—	—	—	—	—
39. Construction	current $	—	—	—	—	
40. Transportation	current $	—	—	—	—	—
41. Communications and public utilities	current $	—	—	—	—	—
42. Wholesale and retail trade	current $	—	—	—	—	—
43. Finance, insurance, and real estate	current $	—	—	—	—	—
44. Government	current $	—	—	—	—	—
45. Total farm population	thousands	—	—	—	—	—
46. Number of farms	thousands	—	—	—	—	—
47. Total land in farms	mil. acres	—	—	—	—	—
48. Total value of all farm property	mil. dollars	—	—	—	—	—
49. Average value per farm of land and buildings	dollars	—	—	—	—	—
50. Farm wages, per day, with room and board	dollars	—	—	—	—	—

Item	Unit	1975	1970	1960	1950	1940
Farm Productivity						
51. Wheat—yield per acre	bushels	31.0	31.0	25.2[25]	17.3[26]	17.1[27]
52. Wheat—man-hours	100 bushels	9	9	12[25]	27[26]	44[27]
53. Cotton—yield per acre	pounds	473	438	475[25]	296[26]	260[27]
54. Cotton—man-hours	bale	23	26	47[25]	107[26]	182[27]
55. Potatoes—yield per acre	cwt	239.0	229.0	194.9[25]	151.2[26]	82.1[27]
56. Potatoes—man-hours	ton	4	4	5[25]	8[26]	17[27]
57. Tobacco—yield per acre	pounds	2,000	2,121	1,879[25]	1,292[26]	1,026[27]
58. Tobacco—man-hours	100 pounds	14	23	26[25]	36[26]	43[27]
59. Milk cows—milk per cow	pounds	10,200.0	9,385.0	7,507.0[25]	5,440.0[26]	4,653.0[27]
60. Milk cows—man-hours	cwt of milk	0.6	0.7	1.2[25]	2.2[26]	3.1[27]
61. Total use of electrical energy	mil. kwh	—	1,641,731	848,723[2]	396,346	181,706
62. Residential	mil. kwh	—	453,015	196,296[2]	72,200	24,068
63. Commercial	mil. kwh	—	295,057	121,437[2]	52,091	22,373
64. Industrial	mil. kwh	—	685,693	415,699[2]	194,835	92,390
65. Value of exports	mil. dollars	107,591	43,265	20,603	10,816	4,030
66. Value of imports	mil. dollars	96,940	40,189	15,046	9,125	7,433
67. Passenger car factory sales	thousands	6,713.0	6,546.8	6,674.7	6,665.8	3,717.3
68. Total motor vehicle registrations	millions	133.7	108.4	73.9	49.2	32.4
69. Miles of travel by motor vehicles	mil. miles	1,300,100	1,120,705	718,845	458,246	302,188
70. Number of operating railroads		341[20]	351	407[2]	471	574
71. Railroad passengers	thousands	275,000[20]	289,469	327,172[2]	488,019	456,088
Air transportation						
72. Number of operators		30	33	42	52	19
73. Aircraft in service		2,267	2,437	1,594	960	369
74. Revenue passengers carried	thousands	189,000[34]	153,408[34]	56,352[34]	17,345[34]	2,523[34]
75. Total school enrollments—elementary and secondary	thousands	50,562[20]	51,319	41,762[2]	28,492	28,045
76. High school graduates	thousands	3,139[17]	2,906	1,864	1,200	1,221
77. Percent of persons 17 years old	percent	74.3[17]	75.6	63.4	57.4	49.0
78. Total institutions of higher education		2,747	2,525	1,959[2]	1,863	1,708
79. Bachelor's or first professional degrees conferred		944,000[17]	827,234	389,183	432,058	186,500
Radio and television						
80. Radio sets produced	thousands	—	16,406	17,127	13,468	11,831
81. Households with radio sets	thousands	—	62,000	50,193	40,700	28,500
82. Television sets produced	thousands	—	4,852	5,708	7,464	—
83. Households with television sets	thousands	—	59,550	45,750	3,875	—
84. Books published		39,372	36,071	15,012	11,022	11,328
85. Daily newspapers—number		1,756	1,748	1,763	1,772	1,878
86. Daily newspapers—circulation	thousands	60,655	62,108	58,882	53,829	41,132
87. Telephones per 1,000 population		695.0	583.4	407.8	280.9	165.1
88. Average number of daily telephone conversations	thousands	633,000	485,200	285,386	170,623	98,783
89. Patents issued for inventions		71,994	64,427	47,170	43,040	42,238
90. Currency in circulation	mil. dollars	92,095.0	54,351.0	32,064.6	27,156.3	7,847.5
91. Total social welfare expenditures under public programs	mil. dollars	286,547[38]	145,893	52,293	23,508	8,795
92. Percent of GNP	percent	19.9[38]	15.3	10.6	8.9	9.2
93. Percent of all government expenditures	percent	58.4[38]	47.8	38.0	37.6	49.0
94. Per capita (actual prices)	dollars	1,319[38]	701	286	153	66
95. Per capita health expenditure	dollars	484.73[20]	343.44	146.30	81.86	29.62
96. Number of physicians		394,000[20]	348,328	274,833[2]	191,947	165,989
97. Rate per 100,000 population		186	166	148[2]	128	126
Summary of federal government finances						
98. Receipts	mil. dollars	281,000.0	193,700.0	92,500.0	40,900.0	6,900.0
99. Outlays	mil. dollars	324,600.0	196,600.0	92,200.0	43,100.0	9,600.0
100. Total public debt	mil. dollars	533,200.0	370,918.7	286,300.8	257,357.4	42,967.5
101. Per capita public debt	dollars	2,496	1,811	1,585	1,697	325
102. Paid civilian employees of the federal government		2,896,944	2,981,574	2,398,704	1,960,708	1,042,420
103. Military personnel on active duty[54]		2,127,000[55]	3,066,294[55]	2,476,435	1,460,261	458,365[56]

(continued)

	Item	Unit	1930	1920	1910	1900
	Farm Productivity					
51.	Wheat—yield per acre	bushels	13.5[28]	13.8[29]	14.4[30]	13.9
52.	Wheat—man-hours	100 bushels	70[28]	90[29]	106[30]	108
53.	Cotton—yield per acre	pounds	184[28]	155[29]	201[30]	189
54.	Cotton—man-hours	bale	252[28]	296[29]	276[30]	284
55.	Potatoes—yield per acre	cwt	64.6[28]	64.6[29]	59.8[30]	—
56.	Potatoes—man-hours	ton	21[28]	23[29]	25[30]	—
57.	Tobacco—yield per acre	pounds	784[28]	773[29]	816[30]	—
58.	Tobacco—man-hours	100 pounds	47[28]	46[29]	44[30]	—
59.	Milk cows—milk per cow	pounds	4,289.0[28]	4,000.0[29]	3,842.0[30]	—
60.	Milk cows—man-hours	cwt of milk	3.4[28]	3.6[29]	3.8[30]	—
61.	Total use of electrical energy	mil. kwh	115,783	57,125	14,262[31]	6,029[32]
62.	Residential	mil. kwh	11,018	3,190	—	—
63.	Commercial	mil. kwh	13,944	6,150	—	—
64.	Industrial	mil. kwh	61,023	31,500	—	—
65.	Value of exports	mil. dollars	4,013	8,664	1,919	1,499
66.	Value of imports	mil. dollars	3,500	5,784	1,646	930
67.	Passenger car factory sales	thousands	2,787.4	1,905.5	181.0	4.1
68.	Total motor vehicle registrations	millions	26.7	9.2	.5	.008
69.	Miles of travel by motor vehicles	mil. miles	206,320	55,027[33]	—	—
70.	Number of operating railroads		775	1,085	1,306	1,224
71.	Railroad passengers	thousands	707,987	1,269,913	971,683	576,831
	Air transportation					
72.	Number of operators		43	—	—	—
73.	Aircraft in service		497	—	—	—
74.	Revenue passengers carried	thousands	385[35]	—	—	—
75.	Total school enrollments—elementary and secondary	thousands	28,329	23,278	19,372	16,885
76.	High school graduates	thousands	667	311	156	95
77.	Percent of persons 17 years old	percent	28.8	16.3	8.6	6.3
78.	Total institutions of higher education		1,409	1,041	951	977
79.	Bachelor's or first professional degrees conferred		122,484	48,622	37,199	27,410
	Radio and television					
80.	Radio sets produced	thousands	3,789	100[37]	—	—
81.	Households with radio sets	thousands	13,750	60[37]	—	—
82.	Television sets produced	thousands	—	—	—	—
83.	Households with television sets	thousands	—	—	—	—
84.	Books published		10,027	8,422	13,470	6,356
85.	Daily newspapers—number		1,942	2,042	—	—
86.	Daily newspapers—circulation	thousands	39,589	27,791	—	—
87.	Telephones per 1,000 population		162.6	123.4	82.0	17.6
88.	Average number of daily telephone conversations	thousands	83,520	51,814	36,161	7,882
89.	Patents issued for inventions		45,226	37,060	35,141	24,644
90.	Currency in circulation	mil. dollars	4,521.0	5,467.6	3,148.7	2,081.2
91.	Total social welfare expenditures under public programs	mil. dollars	4,085	—	1,000[39]	—
92.	Percent of GNP	percent	4.2	—	2.5[39]	—
93.	Percent of all government expenditures	percent	—	—	34.0[39]	—
94.	Per capita (actual prices)	dollars	33	—	—	—
95.	Per capita health expenditure	dollars	29.49[14]	—	—	—
96.	Number of physicians		153,803	144,977	151,132	132,002
97.	Rate per 100,000 population		125	137	164	173
	Summary of federal government finances					
98.	Receipts	mil. dollars	4,057.9	6,648.9	675.5	567.2
99.	Outlays	mil. dollars	3,320.2	6,357.7	693.6	520.9
100.	Total public debt	mil. dollars	16,185.3	24,299.3	1,146.9	1,263.4
101.	Per capita public debt	dollars	132	228	12	17
102.	Paid civilian employees of the federal government		601,319	655,265	388,708	239,476[44]
103.	Military personnel on active duty[54]		255,648	343,302	139,344[57]	125,923

1890	1880	1870	1860	1850	1840	1830	1820	1810	1800	1790	
—	13.2	—	—	—	15.0	—	—	—	15.0	—	51.
—	152	—	—	—	233	—	—	—	373	—	52.
—	188	—	—	—	147	—	—	—	147	—	53.
—	303	—	—	—	438	—	—	—	601	—	54.
—	—	—	—	—	—	—	—	—	—	—	55.
—	—	—	—	—	—	—	—	—	—	—	56.
—	—	—	—	—	—	—	—	—	—	—	57.
—	—	—	—	—	—	—	—	—	—	—	58.
—	—	—	—	—	—	—	—	—	—	—	59.
—	—	—	—	—	—	—	—	—	—	—	60.
—	—	—	—	—	—	—	—	—	—	—	61.
—	—	—	—	—	—	—	—	—	—	—	62.
—	—	—	—	—	—	—	—	—	—	—	63.
—	—	—	—	—	—	—	—	—	—	—	64.
910	853	451	400	152	132	74	70	67	71	20	65.
823	761	462	362	178	107	71	74	85	91	23	66.
—	—	—	—	—	—	—	—	—	—	—	67.
—	—	—	—	—	—	—	—	—	—	—	68.
—	—	—	—	—	—	—	—	—	—	—	69.
1,013	—	—	—	—	—	—	—	—	—	—	70.
492,431	—	—	—	—	—	—	—	—	—	—	71.
—	—	—	—	—	—	—	—	—	—	—	72.
—	—	—	—	—	—	—	—	—	—	—	73.
—	—	—	—	—	—	—	—	—	—	—	74.
14,479	9,868[36]	6,872[36]	—	—	—	—	—	—	—	—	75.
44	24	16	—	—	—	—	—	—	—	—	76.
3.5	2.5	2.0	—	—	—	—	—	—	—	—	77.
998	811	563	—	—	—	—	—	—	—	—	78.
15,539	12,896	—	—	—	—	—	—	—	—	—	79.
—	—	—	—	—	—	—	—	—	—	—	80.
—	—	—	—	—	—	—	—	—	—	—	81.
—	—	—	—	—	—	—	—	—	—	—	82.
—	—	—	—	—	—	—	—	—	—	—	83.
4,559	2,076	—	—	—	—	—	—	—	—	—	84.
—	—	—	—	—	—	—	—	—	—	—	85.
—	—	—	—	—	—	—	—	—	—	—	86.
3.6	0.9	—	—	—	—	—	—	—	—	—	87.
1,448	239	—	—	—	—	—	—	—	—	—	88.
25,313	12,903	12,137	4,357	883	458	544	155	223	41	3	89.
1,429.3	973.4	775.0	435.4	278.8	186.3	87.3	67.1	55.0	26.5	—	90.
318	—	—	—	—	—	—	—	—	—	—	91.
2.4	—	—	—	—	—	—	—	—	—	—	92.
38.0	—	—	—	—	—	—	—	—	—	—	93.
—	—	—	—	—	—	—	—	—	—	—	94.
—	—	—	—	—	—	—	—	—	—	—	95.
104,805	85,671	64,414	55,055	40,755	—	—	—	—	—	—	96.
166	171	162	175	176	—	—	—	—	—	—	97.
403.1	333.5	411.3	56.1	43.6	19.5	24.8	17.9	9.4	10.8	4.4[41]	98.
318.0	267.6	309.7	63.1	39.5	24.3	15.1	18.3	8.2	10.8	4.3[41]	99.
1,222.4	2,090.9	2,436.5	64.8	63.5	3.6	48.6	91.0	53.2	83.0	75.5[42]	100.
18	42	61	2	3[43]	—	—	—	—	—	—	101.
157,442[45]	100,020[46]	51,020[47]	36,672[48]	26,274[49]	18,038[50]	11,491[51]	6,914[52]	4,837[53]	—	—	102.
38,666	37,894	50,348	27,958[58]	20,824	21,616	11,942	15,113	11,554	7,108[59]	718[60]	103.

Statistical History Table—Footnotes

1. Total, including Armed Forces overseas, as of July 1. For population during Colonial years (1610–1780), *see* table of Colonial Population Estimates. 2. Beginning with 1960, figures include Alaska and Hawaii. 3. Based on resident population figures, excluding Armed Forces overseas. 4. Like occupations have been grouped as closely as possible to allow for changing definitions over the years. *See* source for definitions and further explanation. 5. For 1900–75, includes "Farmers and Farm Managers." 6. For 1900–75, includes craftsmen, foremen, operatives, and kindred workers; for 1820–90, includes those occupations requiring special training of a manual rather than mental nature. 7. For 1900–75, excludes farm and mine laborers. 8. Decade average; 1879–88. 9. Decade average; 1869–78. 10. 1940–75, includes Armed Forces. 11. Data for persons 14 years old and over. 12. Data for persons 10 years old and over reporting a gainful occupation. 13. Prior to 1950, figures are for persons 14 years old and over. Annual averages. Unemployment percentages for the Depression years are as follows: 1931, 15.9%; 1932, 23.6%; 1933, 24.9%; 1934, 21.7%; 1935, 20.1%; 1936, 16.9%; 1937, 14.3%; 1938, 19.0%; 1939, 17.2%. 14. Figure is for 1929. 15. Figure is for 1859. 16. In 1932, the rate reached a high of 154. 17. Estimate. 18. After deduction for unemployment. 19. Includes workers in personal, medical, and other health services, domestic, nonprofit, educational service industries. 20. Figure is for 1974. 21. Includes workers in anthracite coal, bituminous coal, and metal mining. 22. Figure is for 1949. 23. Figure is for 1899. 24. Figure is for 1869. 25. Figures are annual averages for 1960–64. 26. Figures are annual averages for 1950–54. 27. Figures are annual averages for 1940–44. 28. Figures are annual averages 1930–34. 29. Figures are annual averages for 1920–24. 30. Figures are annual averages for 1910–14. 31. Figure is for 1907. 32. Figure is for 1902. 33. Figure is for 1921. 34. Duplication has been eliminated where the same passengers were carried on more than one route of an air carrier, but still exists where the same passengers were carried by more than one air carrier. 35. Includes nonrevenue passengers. 36. Figure for public day schools only. 37. Figure is for 1922. 38. Preliminary figures. 39. Figure is for 1913. 40. Includes hospital care, professional services, drugs and sundries, eyeglasses and appliances, nursing home care, expenses for prepayment and administration, government public health activities, other health services, and research and medical facilities construction. 41. Figure is for 1789–91, 42. Figure is for 1791. 43. Figure is for 1851. 44. Figure is for 1901. 45. Figure is for 1891. 46. Figure is for 1881. 47. Figure is for 1871. 48. Figure is for 1861. 49. Figure is for 1851. 50. Figure is for 1841. 51. Figure is for 1831. 52. Figure is for 1821. 53. Figure is for 1816. 54. Excludes Coast Guard. 55. Estimated. 56. In 1945, 12,123,455 people were on active military duty. 57. In 1918, 2,897,167 people were on active military duty. 58. In 1865, 1,062,848 people were on active military duty. 59. Figure is for 1801. 60. Figure is for 1789.
Source: Historical Statistics of the U.S., Department of Commerce, Bureau of the Census.

Washington Monument

Construction of this magnificent Washington, D.C., monument, which draws some two million visitors a year, took nearly a century of planning, building, and controversy. Provision for a large equestrian statue of George Washington was made in the original city plan, but the project was soon dropped. After Washington's death it was taken up again, and a number of false starts and changes of design were made. Finally, in 1848, work was begun on the monument that stands today. The design, by architect Robert Mills, then featured an ornate base. In 1854, however, political squabbling and a lack of money brought construction to a halt. Work was resumed in 1880, and the monument was completed in 1884 and opened to the public in 1888. The tapered shaft, faced with white marble and rising from walls 15 feet thick (4.6 m) at the base was modeled after the obelisks of ancient Egypt. The monument, one of the tallest masonry constructions in the world, stands just over 555 feet (169 m). Memorial stones from the 50 States, foreign countries, and organizations line the interior walls. The top, reached only by elevator, commands a panoramic view of the city.

U.S. Capitol

When the French architect and engineer Maj. Pierre L'Enfant first began to lay out the plans for a new Federal city (now Washington, D.C.), he noted that Jenkins' Hill, overlooking the area, seemed to be "a pedestal waiting for a monument." It was here that the U.S. Capitol would be built. The basic structure as we know it today evolved over a period of more than 150 years. In 1792 a competition was held for the design of a capitol building. Dr. William Thornton, a physician and amateur architect, submitted the winning plan, a simple, low-lying structure of classical proportions with a shallow dome. Later, internal modifications were made by Benjamin Henry Latrobe. After the building was burned by the British in 1814, Latrobe and architect Charles Bulfinch were responsible for its reconstruction. Finally, under Thomas Walter, who was Architect of the Capitol from 1851 to 1865, the House and Senate wings and the imposing cast iron dome topped with the Statue of Freedom were added, and the Capitol assumed the form we see today. It was in the old Senate chamber that Daniel Webster cried out, "Liberty and Union, now and forever, one and inseparable!" In Statuary Hall, which used to be the old House chamber, a small disk on the floor marks the spot where John Quincy Adams was fatally stricken after more than 50 years of service to his country. A whisper from one side of this room can be heard across the vast space of the hall. Visitors can see the original Supreme Court chamber a floor below the Rotunda.

In addition to its historical association, the Capitol Building is also a vast artistic treasure house. The works of such famous artists as Gilbert Stuart, Rembrandt Peale, and John Trumbull are displayed on the walls. The Great Rotunda, with its 180-foot- (54.9-m-) high dome, is decorated with a massive fresco by Constantino Brumidi, which extends some 300 feet (90 m) in circumference. Throughout the building are many paintings of events in U.S. history and sculptures of outstanding Americans. The Capitol itself is situated on a 68-acre (27.5-ha) park designed by the 19th-century landscape architect Frederick Law Olmsted. There are free guided tours of the Capitol, which include admission to the House and Senate galleries. Those who wish to visit the visitors' gallery in either wing without taking the tour may obtain passes from their Senators or Congressmen. Visitors may ride on the monorail subway that joins the House and Senate wings of the Capitol with the Congressional office buildings.

Biographies of the Presidents

GEORGE WASHINGTON was born on Feb. 22, 1732 (Feb. 11, 1731/2, old style) in Westmoreland County, Va. While in his teens, he trained as a surveyor, and at the age of 20 he was appointed adjutant in the Virginia militia. For the next three years, he fought in the wars against the French and Indians, serving as Gen. Edward Braddock's aide in the disastrous campaign against Fort Duquesne. In 1759, he resigned from the militia, married Martha Dandridge Custis, a widow, and settled down as a gentleman farmer at Mount Vernon, Va.

As a militiaman, Washington had been exposed to the arrogance of the British officers, and his experience as a planter with British commercial restrictions increased his anti-British sentiment. He opposed the Stamp Act of 1765 and after 1770 became increasingly prominent in organizing resistance. A delegate to the Continental Congress, Washington was selected as commander in chief of the Continental Army and took command at Cambridge, Mass., on July 3, 1775.

Inadequately supported and sometimes covertly sabotaged by the Congress, in charge of troops who were inexperienced, badly equipped, and impatient of discipline, Washington conducted the war on the policy of avoiding major engagements with the British and wearing them down by harassing tactics. His able generalship, along with the French alliance and the growing weariness within Britain, brought the war to a conclusion with the surrender of Cornwallis at Yorktown, Va., on Oct. 19, 1781.

The chaotic years under the Articles of Confederation led Washington to return to public life in the hope of promoting the formation of a strong central government. He presided over the Constitutional Convention and yielded to the universal demand that he serve as first President. He was inaugurated on April 30, 1789, in New York, the first national capital. In office, he sought to unite the nation and establish the authority of the new government at home and abroad. Greatly distressed by the emergence of the Hamilton-Jefferson rivalry, Washington worked to maintain neutrality but actually sympathized more with Hamilton. Following his unanimous re-election in 1792, his second term was dominated by the Federalists. His Farewell Address on Sept. 17, 1796 (published but never delivered) rebuked party spirit and warned against "permanent alliances" with foreign powers.

He died at Mount Vernon on Dec. 14, 1799.

JOHN ADAMS was born on Oct. 30 (Oct. 19, old style), 1735, at Braintree (now Quincy), Mass. A Harvard graduate, he considered teaching and the ministry but finally turned to law and was admitted to the bar in 1758. Six years later, he married Abigail Smith. He opposed the Stamp Act, served as lawyer for patriots indicted by the British, and by the time of the Continental Congresses, was in the vanguard of the movement for independence. In 1778, he went to France as commissioner. Subsequently he helped negotiate the peace treaty with Britain, and in 1785 became envoy to London. Resigning in 1788, he was elected Vice President under Washington and was re-elected in 1792.

Though a Federalist, Adams did not get along with Hamilton, who sought to prevent his election to the presidency in 1796 and thereafter intrigued against his administration. In 1798, Adams's independent policy averted a war with France but completed the break with Hamilton and the right-wing Federalists; at the same time, the enactment of the Alien and Sedition Acts, directed against foreigners and against critics of the government, exasperated the Jeffersonian opposition. The split between Adams and Hamilton resulted in Jefferson's becoming the next President. Adams retired to his home in Quincy. He and Jefferson died on the same day, July 4, 1826, the 50th anniversary of the signing of the Declaration of Independence.

His *Defence of the Constitutions of Government of the United States* (1787) contains original and striking, if conservative, political ideas.

THOMAS JEFFERSON was born on April 13 (April 2, old style), 1743, at Shadwell in Goochland (now Albemarle) County, Va. A William and Mary graduate, he studied law, but from the start showed an interest in science and philosophy. His literary skill and political clarity brought him to the forefront of the revolutionary movement in Virginia. As delegate to the Continental Congress, he drafted the Declaration of Independence. In 1776, he entered the Virginia House of Delegates and initiated a comprehensive reform program for the abolition of feudal survivals in land tenure and the separation of church and state.

In 1779, he became governor, but constitutional limitations on his power, combined with his own lack of executive energy, caused an unsatisfactory administration, culminating in Jefferson's virtual abdication when the British invaded Virginia in 1781. He retired to his beautiful home at Monticello, Va., to his family. His wife, Martha Wayles Skelton, whom he married in 1772, died in 1782.

Jefferson's *Notes on Virginia* (1784–85) illustrate his many-faceted interests, his limitless intellectual curiosity, his deep faith in agrarian democracy. Sent to Congress in 1783, he helped lay down the decimal system and drafted basic reports on the organization of the western lands. In 1785 he was appointed minister to France, where the Anglo-Saxon liberalism he had drawn from John Locke, the British philosopher, was stimulated by contact with the thought that would soon ferment in the French Revolution. In 1789, Washington appointed him Secretary of State. While favoring the Constitution and a strengthened central government, Jefferson came to believe that Hamilton contemplated the establishment of a monarchy. Growing differences resulted in Jefferson's resignation on Dec. 31, 1793.

Elected vice president in 1796, Jefferson continued to serve as spiritual leader of the opposition to Federalism, particularly to the repressive Alien and Sedition Acts. He was elected President in 1801 by the House of Representatives as a result of Hamilton's decision to throw the Federalist votes to him rather than to Aaron Burr, who had tied him in electoral votes. He was the first President to be inaugurated in Washington, which he had helped to design.

The purchase of Louisiana from France in 1803, though in violation of Jefferson's earlier constitutional scruples, was the most notable act of his administration. Re-elected in 1804, with the Federalist Charles C. Pinckney opposing him, Jefferson tried desperately to keep the United States out of the Napoleonic Wars in Europe, employing to this end the unpopular embargo policy.

After his retirement to Monticello in 1809, he developed his interest in education, founding the University of Virginia and watching its development with never-flagging interest. He died at Monticello on July 4, 1826. Jefferson had an enormous variety of interests and skills, ranging from education and science to architecture and music.

JAMES MADISON was born in Port Conway, Va., on March 16, 1751 (March 5, 1750/1, old style). A Princeton graduate, he joined the struggle for independence on his return to Virginia in 1771. In the 1770s and 1780s he was active in state politics, where he championed the Jefferson reform program, and in the Continental Congress. Madison was influential in the Constitutional Convention as leader of the group favoring a strong central government and as recorder of the debates; and he subsequently wrote, in collaboration with Alexander Hamilton and John Jay, the *Federalist* papers to aid the campaign for the adoption of the Constitution.

Serving in the new Congress, Madison soon emerged as the leader in the House of the men who opposed Hamilton's financial program and his pro-British leanings in foreign policy. Retiring from Congress in 1797, he continued to be active in Virginia and drafted the Virginia Resolution protesting the Alien and Sedition Acts. His intimacy with Jefferson made him the natural choice for Secretary of State in 1801.

In 1809, Madison succeeded Jefferson as President, defeating Charles C. Pinckney. His attractive wife, Dolley Payne Todd, whom he married in 1794, brought a new social sparkle to the executive mansion. In the meantime, increasing tension with Britain culminated in the War of 1812—a war for which the United States was unprepared and for which Madison lacked the executive talent to clear out incompetence and mobilize the nation's energies. Madison was re-elected in 1812, running against the Federalist De Witt Clinton. In 1814, the British actually captured Washington and forced Madison to flee to Virginia.

Madison's domestic program capitulated to the Hamiltonian policies that he had resisted 20 years before and he now signed bills to establish a United States Bank and a higher tariff.

After his presidency, he remained in retirement in Virginia until his death on June 28, 1836.

JAMES MONROE was born on April 28, 1758, in Westmoreland County, Va. A William and Mary graduate, he served in the army during the first years of the Revolution and was wounded at Trenton. He then entered Virginia politics and later national politics under the sponsorship of Jefferson. In 1786, he married Elizabeth (Eliza) Kortright.

Fearing centralization, Monroe opposed the adoption of the Constitution and, as senator from Virginia, was highly critical of the Hamiltonian program. In 1794, he was appointed minister to France, where his ardent sympathies with the Revolution exceeded the wishes of the State Department. His troubled diplomatic career ended with his recall in 1796. From 1799 to 1802, he was governor of Virginia. In 1803, Jefferson sent him to France to help negotiate the Louisiana Purchase and for the next few years he was active in various negotiations on the Continent.

In 1808, Monroe flirted with the radical wing of the Republican Party, which opposed Madison's candidacy; but the presidential boom came to naught and, after a brief term as governor of Virginia in 1811, Monroe accepted Madison's offer to become Secretary of State. During the War of 1812, he vainly sought a field command and instead served as Secretary of War from September 1814 to March 1815.

Elected President in 1816 over the Federalist Rufus King, and re-elected without opposition in 1820, Monroe, the last of the Virginia dynasty, pursued the course of systematic tranquilization that won for his administrations the name "the era of good feeling." He continued Madison's surrender to the Hamiltonian domestic program, signed the Missouri Compromise, acquired Florida, and with the able assistance of his Secretary of State, John Quincy Adams, promulgated the Monroe Doctrine in 1823, declaring against foreign colonization or intervention in the Americas. He died in New York City on July 4, 1831, the third president to die on the anniversary of Independence.

JOHN QUINCY ADAMS was born on July 11, 1767, at Braintree (now Quincy), Mass., the son of John Adams. He spent his early years in Europe with his father, graduated from Harvard, and entered law practice. His anti-Jeffersonian newspaper articles won him political attention. In 1794, he became minister to the Netherlands, the first of several diplomatic posts that occupied him until his return to Boston in 1801. In 1797, he married Louisa Catherine Johnson.

In 1803, Adams was elected to the Senate, nominally as a Federalist, but his repeated displays of independence on such issues as the Louisiana Purchase and the embargo caused his party to demand his resignation and ostracize him socially. In 1809, Madison rewarded him for his support of Jefferson by appointing him minister to St. Petersburg. He helped negotiate the Treaty of Ghent in 1814, and in 1815 became minister to London. In 1817 Monroe appointed him Secretary of State where he served with great distinction, gaining Florida from Spain without hostilities and playing an equal part with Monroe in formulating the Monroe Doctrine.

When no presidential candidate received a majority of electoral votes in 1824, Adams, with the support of Henry Clay, was elected by the House in 1825 over Andrew Jackson, who had the original plurality. Adams had ambitious plans of government activity to foster internal improvements and promote the arts and sciences, but congressional obstructionism, combined with his own unwillingness or inability to play the role of a politician, resulted in little being accomplished. After being defeated for re-elected by Jackson in 1828, he successfully ran for the House of Representatives in 1830. There though nominally a Whig, he pursued as ever an independent course. He led the fight to force Congress to receive antislavery petitions and fathered the Smithsonian Institution.

Stricken on the floor of the House, he died on Feb. 23, 1848. His long and detailed *Diary* gives a unique picture of the personalities and politics of the times.

ANDREW JACKSON was born on March 15, 1767, in what is now generally agreed to be Waxhaw, S.C. After a turbulent boyhood as an orphan and a British prisoner, he moved west to Tennessee, where he soon qualified for law practice but found time for such frontier pleasures as horse racing, cockfighting, and dueling. His marriage to Rachel Donelson Robards in 1791 was complicated by subsequent legal uncertainties about the status of her divorce. During the 1790s, Jackson served in the Tennessee Constitutional Convention, the United States House of Representatives and Senate, and on the Tennessee Supreme Court.

After some years as a country gentleman, living at the Hermitage near Nashville, Jackson in 1812 was given command of Tennessee troops sent against the Creeks. He defeated the Indians at Horseshoe Bend in 1814; subsequently he became a major general and won the Battle of New Orleans over veteran British troops, though after the treaty of peace had been signed at Ghent. In 1818, Jackson invaded Florida, captured Pensacola, and hanged two Englishmen named Arbuthnot and Ambrister, creating an international incident. A presidential boom began for him in 1821, and to foster it, he returned to the Senate (1823–25). Though he won a plurality of electoral votes in 1824, he lost in the House when Clay threw his strength to Adams. Four years later, he easily defeated Adams.

As President, Jackson greatly expanded the power and prestige of the presidential office and carried through an unprecedented program of domestic reform, vetoing the bill to extend the United States Bank, moving toward a hard-money currency policy, and checking the program of federal internal improvements. He also vindicated federal authority against South Carolina with its doctrine of nullification and against France on the question of debts. The support given his policies by the workingmen of the East as well as by the farmers of the East, West, and South resulted in his triumphant re-election in 1832 over Clay.

After watching the inauguration of his handpicked successor, Martin Van Buren, Jackson retired to the Hermitage, where he maintained a lively interest in national affairs until his death on June 8, 1845.

MARTIN VAN BUREN was born on Dec. 5, 1782, at Kinderhook, N.Y. After graduating from the village school, he became a law clerk, entered practice in 1803, and soon became active in state politics as state senator and attorney general. In 1820, he was elected to the United States Senate. He threw the support of his efficient political organization, known as the Albany Regency, to William H. Crawford in 1824 and to Jackson in 1828. After leading the opposition to Adams's administration in the Senate, he served briefly as governor of New York (1828–29) and resigned to become Jackson's Secretary of State. He was soon on close personal terms with Jackson and played an important part in the Jacksonian program.

In 1832, Van Buren became vice president; in 1836, President. The Panic of 1837 overshadowed his term. He attributed it to the overexpansion of the credit and favored the establishment of an independent treasury as repository for the federal funds. In 1840, he established a 10-hour day on public works. Defeated by Harrison in 1840, he was the leading contender for the Democratic nomination in 1844 until he publicly opposed immediate annexation of Texas, and was subsequently beaten by the Southern delegations at the Baltimore convention. This incident increased his growing misgivings about the slave power.

After working behind the scenes among the antislavery Democrats, Van Buren joined in the movement that led to the Free-Soil Party and became its candidate for President in 1848. He subsequently returned to the Democratic Party while continuing to object to its pro-Southern policy. He died in Kinderhook on July 24, 1862. His *Autobiography* throws valuable sidelights on the political history of the times.

His wife, Hannah Hoes, whom he married in 1807, died in 1819.

WILLIAM HENRY HARRISON was born in Charles City County, Va., on Feb. 9, 1773. Joining the army in 1791, he was active in Indian fighting in the Northwest, became secretary of the Northwest Territory in 1798 and governor of Indiana in 1800. He married Anna Symmes in 1795. Growing discontent over white encroachments on Indian lands led to the formation of an Indian alliance under Tecumseh to resist further aggressions. In 1811, Harrison won a nominal victory over the Indians at Tippecanoe and in 1813 a more decisive one at the Battle of the Thames, where Tecumseh was killed.

After resigning from the army in 1814, Harrison had an obscure career in politics and diplomacy, ending up 20 years later as a county recorder in Ohio. Nominated for President in 1835 as a military hero whom the conservative politicians hoped to be able to control, he ran surprisingly well against Van Buren in 1836. Four years later, he defeated Van Buren but caught pneumonia and died in Washington on April 4, 1841, a month after his inauguration. Harrison was the first president to die in office.

JOHN TYLER was born in Charles City County, Va., on March 29, 1790. A William and Mary graduate, he entered law practice and politics, serving in the House of Representatives (1817–21), as governor of Virginia (1825–27), and as senator (1827–36). A strict constructionist, he supported Crawford in 1824 and Jackson in 1828, but broke with Jackson over his United States Bank policy and became a member of the Southern state-rights group that cooperated with the Whigs. In 1836, he resigned from the Senate rather than follow instructions from the Virginia legislature to vote for a resolution expunging censure of Jackson from the Senate record.

Elected vice president on the Whig ticket in 1840, Tyler succeeded to the presidency on Harrison's death. His strict-constructionist views soon caused a split with the Henry Clay wing of the Whig party and a stalemate on domestic questions. Tyler's more considerable achievements were his support of the Webster-Ashburton Treaty with Britain and his success in bringing about the annexation of Texas.

After his presidency he lived in retirement in Virginia until the outbreak of the Civil War, when he emerged briefly as chairman of a peace convention and then as delegate to the provisional Congress of the Confederacy. He died on Jan. 18, 1862. He married Letitia Christian in 1813 and, two years after her death in 1842, Julia Gardiner.

JAMES KNOX POLK was born in Mecklenburg County, N.C., on Nov. 2, 1795. A graduate of the University of North Carolina, he moved west to Tennessee, was admitted to the bar, and soon became prominent in state politics. In 1825, he was elected to the House of Representatives, where he opposed Adams and, after 1829, became Jackson's floor leader in the fight against the Bank. In 1835, he became Speaker of the House. Four years later, he was elected governor of Tennessee, but was beaten in tries for re-election in 1841 and 1843.

The supporters of Van Buren for the Democratic nomination in 1844 counted on Polk as his running mate; but, when Van Buren's stand on Texas alienated Southern support, the convention swung to Polk on the ninth ballot. He was elected over Henry Clay, the Whig candidate. Rapidly disillusioning those who thought that he would not run his own administration, Polk proceeded steadily and precisely to achieve four major objectives—the acquisition of California, the settlement of the Oregon question, the reduction of the tariff, and the establishment of the independent treasury. He also enlarged the Monroe Doctrine to exclude all non-American intervention in American affairs, whether forcible or not, and he forced Mexico into a war that he waged to a successful conclusion.

His wife, Sarah Childress, whom he married in 1824, was a woman of charm and ability. Polk died in Nashville, Tenn., on June 15, 1849.

ZACHARY TAYLOR was born at Montebello, Orange County, Va., on Nov. 24, 1784. Embarking on a military career in 1808, Taylor fought in the War of 1812, the Black Hawk War, and the Seminole War, meanwhile holding garrison jobs on the frontier or desk jobs in Washington. A brigadier general as a result of his victory over the Seminoles at Lake Okeechobee (1837), Taylor held a succession of Southwestern commands and in 1846 established a base on the Rio Grande, where his forces engaged in hostilities that precipitated the war with Mexico. He captured Monterrey in September 1846 and, disregarding Polk's orders to stay on the defensive, defeated Santa Anna at Buena Vista in February 1847, ending the war in the northern provinces.

Though Taylor had never cast a vote for president, his party affiliations were Whiggish and his availability was increased by his difficulties with Polk. He was elected president over the Democrat Lewis Cass. During the revival of the slavery controversy, which was to result in the Compromise of 1850, Taylor began to take an increasingly firm stand against appeasing the South; but he died in Washington on July 9, 1850, during the fight over the Compromise. He married Margaret Mackall Smith in 1810. His bluff and simple soldierly qualities won him the name Old Rough and Ready.

MILLARD FILLMORE was born at Locke, Cayuga County, N.Y., on Jan. 7, 1800. A lawyer, he entered politics with the Anti-Masonic Party under the sponsorship of Thurlow Weed, editor and party boss, and subsequently followed Weed into the Whig Party. He served in the House of Representatives (1833–35 and 1837–43) and played a leading role in writing the tariff of 1842. Defeated for governor of New York in 1844, he became State comptroller in 1848, was put on the Whig ticket with Taylor as a concession to the Clay wing of the party, and became president upon Taylor's death in 1850.

As president, Fillmore broke with Weed and William H. Seward and associated himself with the pro-Southern Whigs, supporting the Compromise of 1850. Defeated for the Whig nomination in 1852, he ran for president in 1856 as candidate of the American, or Know-Nothing Party, which sought to unite the country against foreigners in the alleged hope of diverting it from the explosive slavery issue. Fillmore opposed Lincoln during the Civil War. He died in Buffalo on March 8, 1874.

He was married in 1826 to Abigail Powers, who died in 1853, and in 1858 to Caroline Carmichael McIntosh.

FRANKLIN PIERCE was born at Hillsboro, N.H., on Nov. 23, 1804. A Bowdoin graduate, lawyer, and Jacksonian Democrat, he won rapid political advancement in the party, in part because of the prestige of his father, Gov. Benjamin Pierce. By 1831 he was Speaker of the New Hampshire House of Representatives; from 1833 to 1837, he served in the federal House and from 1837 to 1842 in the Senate. His wife, Jane Means Appleton, whom he married in 1834, disliked Washington and the somewhat dissipated life led by Pierce; in 1842 Pierce resigned from the Senate and began a successful law practice in Concord, N.H. During the Mexican War, he was a brigadier general.

Thereafter Pierce continued to oppose antislavery tendencies within the Democratic Party. As a result, he was the Southern choice to break the deadlock at the Democratic convention of 1852 and was nominated on the 49th ballot. In the election, Pierce overwhelmed Gen. Winfield Scott, the Whig candidate.

As president, Pierce followed a course of appeasing the South at home and of playing with schemes of territorial expansion abroad. The failure of his foreign and domestic policies prevented his renomination; and he died in Concord on Oct. 8, 1869, in relative obscurity.

JAMES BUCHANAN was born near Mercersburg, Pa., on April 23, 1791. A Dickinson graduate and a lawyer, he entered Pennsylvania politics as a Federalist. With the disappearance of the Federalist Party, he became a Jacksonian Democrat. He served with ability in the House (1821–31), as minister to St. Petersburg (1832–33), and in the Senate (1834–45), and in 1845 became Polk's Secretary of State. In 1853, Pierce appointed Buchanan minister to Britain, where he participated with other American diplomats in Europe in drafting the expansionist Ostend Manifesto.

He was elected president in 1856, defeating John C. Frémont, the Republican candidate, and former President Millard Fillmore of the American Party. The growing crisis over slavery presented Buchanan with problems he lacked the will to tackle. His appeasement of the South alienated the Stephen Douglas wing of the Democratic Party without reducing Southern militancy on slavery issues. While denying the right of secession, Buchanan also denied that the federal government could do anything about it. He supported the administration during the Civil War and died in Lancaster, Pa., on June 1, 1868.

The only president to remain a bachelor throughout his term, Buchanan used his charming niece, Harriet Lane, as White House hostess.

ABRAHAM LINCOLN was born in Hardin (now Larue) County, Ky., on Feb. 12, 1809. His family moved to Indiana and then to Illinois, and Lincoln gained what education he could along the way. While reading law, he worked in a store, managed a mill, surveyed, and split rails. In 1834, he went to the Illinois legislature as a Whig and became the party's floor leader. For the next 20 years he practiced law in Springfield, except for a single term (1847–49) in Congress, where he denounced the Mexican War. In 1855, he was a candidate for senator and the next year he joined the new Republican Party.

A leading but unsuccessful candidate for the vice-presidential nomination with Frémont, Lincoln gained national attention in 1858 when, as Republican candidate for senator from Illinois, he engaged in a series of debates with Stephen A. Douglas, the Democratic candidate. He lost the election, but continued to prepare the way for the 1860 Republican convention and was rewarded with the presidential nomination on the third ballot. He won the election over three opponents.

From the start, Lincoln made clear that, unlike Buchanan, he believed the national government had the power to crush the rebellion. Not an abolitionist, he held the slavery issue subordinate to that of preserving the Union, but soon perceived that the war could not be brought to a successful conclusion without freeing the slaves. His administration was hampered by the incompetence of many Union generals, the inexperience of the troops, and the harassing political tactics both of the Republican Radicals, who favored a hard policy toward the South, and the Democratic Copperheads, who desired a negotiated peace. The Gettysburg Address of Nov. 19, 1863, marks the high point in the record of American eloquence. Lincoln's long search for a winning combination finally brought Generals Ulysses S. Grant and William T. Sherman to the top; and their series of victories in 1864 dispelled the mutterings from both Radicals and Peace Democrats that at one time seemed to threaten Lincoln's re-election. He was re-elected in 1864, defeating Gen. George B. McClellan, the Democratic candidate. His inaugural address urged leniency toward the South: "With malice toward none, with charity for all . . . let us strive on to finish the work we are in; to bind up the nation's wounds . . . " This policy aroused growing opposition on the part of the Republican Radicals, but before the matter could be put to the test, Lincoln was shot by the actor John Wilkes Booth at Ford's Theater, Washington, on April 14, 1865. He died the next morning.

Lincoln's marriage to Mary Todd in 1842 was often unhappy and turbulent, in part because of his wife's pronounced instability.

ANDREW JOHNSON was born at Raleigh, N.C., on Dec. 29, 1808. Self-educated, he became a tailor in Greeneville, Tenn., but soon went into politics, where he rose steadily. He served in the House of Representatives (1843–54), as governor of Tennessee (1853–57), and as a senator (1857–62). Politically he was a Jacksonian Democrat and his specialty was the fight for a more equitable land policy. Alone among the Southern Senators, he stood by the Union during the Civil War. In 1862, he became war governor of Tennessee and carried out a thankless and difficult job with great courage. Johnson became Lincoln's running mate in 1864 as a result of an attempt to give the ticket a nonpartisan and nonsectional character. Succeeding to the presidency on Lincoln's death, Johnson sought to carry out Lincoln's policy, but without his political skill. The result was a hopeless conflict with the Radical Republicans who dominated Congress, passed measures over Johnson's vetoes, and attempted to limit the power of the executive concerning appointments and removals. The conflict culminated with Johnson's impeachment for attempting to remove his disloyal Secretary of War in defiance of the Tenure of Office Act which required senatorial concurrence for such dismissals. The opposition failed by one vote to get the two thirds necessary for conviction.

After his presidency, Johnson maintained an interest in politics and in 1875 was again elected to the Senate. He died near Carter Station, Tenn., on July 31, 1875. He married Eliza McCardle in 1827.

ULYSSES SIMPSON GRANT was born (as Hiram Ulysses Grant) at Point Pleasant, Ohio, on April 27, 1822. He graduated from West Point in 1843 and served without particular distinction in the Mexican War. In 1848 he married Julia Dent. He resigned from the army in 1854, after warnings from his commanding officer about his drinking habits, and for the next six years held a wide variety of jobs in the Middle West. With the outbreak of the Civil War, he sought a command and soon, to his surprise, was made a brigadier general. His continuing successes in the western theaters, culminating in the capture of Vicksburg, Miss., in 1863, brought him national fame and soon the command of all the Union armies. Grant's dogged, implacable policy of concentrating on dividing and destroying the Confederate armies brought the war to an end in 1865. The next year, he was made full general.

In 1868, as Republican candidate for president, Grant was elected over the Democrat, Horatio Seymour. From the start, Grant showed his unfitness for the office. His Cabinet was weak, his domestic policy was confused, many of his intimate associates were corrupt. The notable achievement in foreign affairs was the settlement of controversies with Great Britain in the Treaty of London (1871), negotiated by his able Secretary of State, Hamilton Fish.

Running for re-election in 1872, he defeated Horace Greeley, the Democratic and Liberal Republican candidate. The Panic of 1873 graft scandals close to the presidency created difficulties for his second term.

After retiring from office, Grant toured Europe for two years and returned in time to accede to a third-term boom, but was beaten in the convention of 1880. Illness and bad business judgment darkened his last years, but he worked steadily at the *Personal Memoirs,* which were to be so successful when published after his death at Mount McGregor, near Saratoga, N.Y., on July 23, 1885.

RUTHERFORD BIRCHARD HAYES was born in Delaware, Ohio, on Oct. 4, 1822. A graduate of Kenyon College and the Harvard Law School, he practiced law in Lower Sandusky (now Fremont) and then in Cincinnati. In 1852 he married Lucy Webb. A Whig, he joined the Republican party in 1855. During the Civil War he rose to major general. He served in the House of Representatives from 1865 to 1867 and then confirmed a reputation for honesty and efficiency in two terms as Governor of Ohio (1868–72). His election to a third term in 1875 made him the logical candidate for those Republicans who wished to stop James G. Blaine in 1876, and he was nominated.

The result of the election was in doubt for some time and hinged upon disputed returns from South Carolina, Louisiana, Florida, and Oregon. Samuel J. Tilden, the Democrat, had the larger popular vote but was adjudged by the strictly partisan decisions of the Electoral Commission to have one fewer electoral vote, 185 to 184. The national acceptance of this result was due in part to the general understanding that Hayes would pursue a conciliatory policy toward the South. He withdrew the troops from the South, took a conservative position on financial and labor issues, and urged civil service reform.

Hayes served only one term by his own wish and spent the rest of his life in various humanitarian endeavors. He died in Fremont on Jan. 17, 1893.

JAMES ABRAM GARFIELD, the last president to be born in a log cabin, was born in Cuyahoga County, Ohio, on Nov. 19, 1831. A Williams graduate, he taught school for a time and entered Republican politics in Ohio. In 1858, he married Lucretia Rudolph. During the Civil War, he had a promising career, rising to major general of volunteers; but he resigned in 1863, having been elected to the House of Representatives, where he served until 1880. His oratorical and parliamentary abilities soon made him the leading Republican in the House, though his record was marred by his unorthodox acceptance of a fee in the DeGolyer paving contract case and by suspicions of his complicity in the Crédit Mobilier scandal.

In 1880, Garfield was elected to the Senate, but instead became the presidential candidate on the 36th ballot as a result of a deadlock in the Republican convention. In the election, he defeated Gen. Winfield Scott Hancock, the Democratic candidate. Garfield's administration was barely under way when he was shot by Charles J. Guiteau, a disappointed office seeker, in Washington on July 2, 1881. He died in Elberon, N.J., on Sept. 19.

CHESTER ALAN ARTHUR was born at Fairfield, Vt., on Oct. 5, 1830. A graduate of Union College, he became a successful New York lawyer. In 1859, he married Ellen Herndon. During the Civil War, he held administrative jobs in the Republican state administration and in 1871 was appointed collector of the Port of New York by Grant. This post gave him control over considerable patronage. Though not personally corrupt, Arthur managed his power in the interests of the New York machine so openly that President Hayes in 1877 called for an investigation and the next year Arthur was suspended.

In 1880 Arthur was nominated for vice president in the hope of conciliating the followers of Grant and the powerful New York machine. As president upon Garfield's death, Arthur, stepping out of his familiar role as spoilsman, backed civil service reform, reorganized the Cabinet, and prosecuted political associates accused of post office graft. Losing machine support and failing to gain the reformers, he was not nominated for a full term in 1884. He died in New York City on Nov. 18, 1886.

STEPHEN GROVER CLEVELAND was born at Caldwell, N.J., on March 18, 1837. He was admitted to the bar in Buffalo, N.Y., in 1859 and lived there as a lawyer, with occasional incursions into Democratic politics, for more than 20 years. He did not participate in the Civil War. As mayor of Buffalo in 1881, he carried through a reform program so ably that the Democrats ran him successfully for governor in 1882. In 1884 he won the Democratic nomination for President. The campaign contrasted Cleveland's spotless public career with the uncertain record of James G. Blaine, the Republican candidate, and Cleveland received enough Mugwump (independent Republican) support to win.

As president, Cleveland pushed civil service reform, opposed the pension grab and attacked the high tariff rates. While in the White House, he married Frances Folsom in 1886. Renominated in 1888, Cleveland was defeated by Benjamin Harrison, polling more popular but fewer electoral votes. In 1892, he was elected over Harrison.When the Panic of 1893 burst upon the country, Cleveland's attempts to solve it by sound-money measures alienated the free-silver wing of the party, while his tariff policy alienated the protectionists. In 1894, he sent troops to break the Pullman strike. In foreign affairs, his firmness caused Great Britain to back down in the Venezuela border dispute.

In his last years Cleveland was an active and much-respected public figure. He died in Princeton, N.J., on June 24, 1908.

BENJAMIN HARRISON was born in North Bend, Ohio, on Aug. 20, 1833, the grandson of William Henry Harrison, the ninth president. A graduate of Miami University in Ohio, he took up the law in Indiana and became active in Republican politics. In 1853, he married Caroline Lavinia Scott. During the Civil War, he rose to brigadier general. A sound-money Republican, he was elected senator from Indiana in 1880. In 1888, he received the Republican nomination for President on the eighth ballot. Though behind on the popular vote, he won over Grover Cleveland in the electoral college by 233 to 168.

As President, Harrison failed to please either the bosses or the reform element in the party. In foreign affairs he backed Secretary of State Blaine, whose policy foreshadowed later American imperialism. Harrison was renominated in 1892 but lost to Cleveland. His wife died in the White House in 1892 and Harrison married her niece, Mary Scott (Lord) Dimmick, in 1896. After his presidency, he resumed law practice. He died in Indianapolis on March 13, 1901.

WILLIAM McKINLEY was born in Niles, Ohio, on Jan. 29, 1843. He taught school, then served in the Civil War, rising from the ranks to become a major. Subsequently he opened a law office in Canton, Ohio, and in 1871 married Ida Saxton. Elected to Congress in 1876, he served there until 1891, except for 1883–85. His faithful advocacy of business interests culminated in the passage of the highly protective McKinley Tariff of 1890. With the support of Mark Hanna, a shrewd Cleveland businessman interested in safeguarding tariff protection, McKinley became governor of Ohio in 1892 and Republican presidential candidate in 1896. The business community, alarmed by the progressivism of William Jennings Bryan, the Democratic candidate, spent considerable money to assure McKinley's victory.

The chief event of McKinley's administration was the war with Spain, which resulted in our acquisition of the Philippines and other islands. With imperialism an issue, McKinley defeated Bryan again in 1900. On Sept. 6, 1901, he was shot at Buffalo, N.Y., by Leon F. Czolgosz, an anarchist, and he died there eight days later.

THEODORE ROOSEVELT was born in New York City on Oct. 27, 1858. A Harvard graduate, he was early interested in ranching, in politics, and in writing picturesque historical narratives. He was a Republican member of the New York Assembly in 1882–84, an unsuccessful candidate for mayor of New York in 1886, a U.S. Civil Service Commissioner under Benjamin Harrison, Police Commissioner of New York City in 1895, and Assistant Secretary of the Navy under McKinley in 1897. He resigned in 1898 to help organize a volunteer regiment, the Rough Riders, and take a more direct part in the war with Spain. He was elected governor of New York in 1898 and vice president in 1900, in spite of lack of enthusiasm on the part of the bosses.

Assuming the presidency of the assassinated McKinley in 1901, Roosevelt embarked on a wide-ranging program of government reform and conservation of natural resources. He ordered antitrust suits against several large corporations, threatened to intervene in the anthracite coal strike of 1902, which prompted the operators to accept arbitration, and, in general, championed the rights of the "little man" and fought the "malefactors of great wealth." He was also responsible for such progressive legislation as the Elkins Act of 1901, which outlawed freight rebates by railroads; the bill establishing the Department of Commerce and Labor; the Hepburn Act, which gave the I.C.C. greater control over the railroads; the Meat Inspection Act; and the Pure Food and Drug Act.

In foreign affairs, Roosevelt pursued a strong policy, permitting the instigation of a revolt in Panama to dispose of Colombian objections to the Panama Canal and helping to maintain the balance of power in the East by bringing the Russo-Japanese War to an end, for which he won the Nobel Peace Prize, the first American to achieve a Nobel prize in any category. In 1904, he decisively defeated Alton B. Parker, his conservative Democratic opponent.

Roosevelt's increasing coldness toward his successor, William Howard Taft, led him to overlook his earlier disclaimer of third-term ambitions and to re-enter politics. Defeated by the machine in the Republican convention of 1912, he organized the Progressive Party (Bull Moose) and polled more votes than Taft, though the split brought about the election of Woodrow Wilson. From 1915 on, Roosevelt strongly favored intervention in the European war. He became deeply embittered at Wilson's refusal to allow him to raise a volunteer division. He died in Oyster Bay, N.Y., on Jan. 6, 1919. He was married twice: in 1880 to Alice Hathaway Lee, who died in 1884, and in 1886 to Edith Kermit Carow.

WILLIAM HOWARD TAFT was born in Cincinnati on Sept. 15, 1857. A Yale graduate, he entered Ohio Republican politics in the 1880s. In 1886 he married Helen Herron. From 1887 to 1890, he served on the Ohio Superior Court; 1890–92, as solicitor general of the United States; 1892–1900, on the federal circuit court. In 1900 McKinley appointed him president of the Philippine Commission and in 1901 governor general. Taft had great success in pacifying the Filipinos, solving the problem of the church lands, improving economic conditions, and establishing limited self-government. His period as Secretary of War (1904–08) further demonstrated his capacity as administrator and conciliator, and he was Roosevelt's hand-picked successor in 1908. In the election, he polled 321 electoral votes to 162 for William Jennings Bryan, who was running for the presidency for the third time.

Though he carried on many of Roosevelt's policies, Taft got into increasing trouble with the progressive wing of the party and displayed mounting irritability and indecision. After his defeat in 1912, he became professor of constitutional law at Yale. In 1921 he was appointed Chief Justice of the United States. He died in Washington on March 8, 1930.

THOMAS WOODROW WILSON was born in Staunton, Va., on Dec. 28, 1856. A Princeton graduate, he turned from law practice to post-graduate work in political science at Johns Hopkins University, receiving his Ph.D. in 1886. He taught at Bryn Mawr, Wesleyan, and Princeton, and in 1902 was made president of Princeton. After an unsuccessful attempt to democratize the social life of the university, he welcomed an invitation in 1910 to be the Democratic gubernatorial candidate in New Jersey, and was elected. His success in fighting the machine and putting through a reform program attracted national attention.

In 1912, at the Democratic convention in Baltimore, Wilson won the nomination on the 46th ballot and went on to defeat Roosevelt and Taft in the election. Wilson proceeded under the standard of the New Freedom to enact a program of domestic reform, including the Federal Reserve Act, the Clayton Antitrust Act, the establishment of the Federal Trade Commission, and other measures designed to restore competition in the face of the great monopolies. In foreign affairs, while privately sympathetic with the Allies, he strove to maintain neutrality in the European war and warned both sides against encroachments on American interests.

Re-elected in 1916 as a peace candidate, he tried to mediate between the warring nations; but when the Germans resumed unrestricted submarine warfare in 1917, Wilson brought the United States into what he now believed was a war to make the world safe for democracy. He supplied the classic formulations of Allied war aims and the armistice of Nov. 11, 1918 was negotiated on the basis of Wilson's Fourteen Points. In 1919 he strove at Versailles to lay the foundations for enduring peace. He accepted the imperfections of the Versailles Treaty in the expectation that they could be remedied by action within the League of Nations. He probably could have secured ratification of the treaty by the Senate if he had adopted a more conciliatory attitude toward the mild reservationists; but his insistence on all or nothing eventually caused the diehard isolationists and diehard Wilsonites to unite in rejecting a compromise.

In September 1919 Wilson suffered a paralytic stroke that limited his activity. After leaving the presidency he lived on in retirement in Washington, dying on Feb. 3, 1924. He was married twice—in 1885 to Ellen Louise Axson, who died in 1914, and in 1915 to Edith Bolling Galt.

WARREN GAMALIEL HARDING was born in Morrow County, Ohio, on Nov. 2, 1865. After attending Ohio Central College, Harding became interested in journalism and in 1884 bought the *Marion* (Ohio) *Star*. In 1891 he married a wealthy widow, Florence Kling De Wolfe. As his paper prospered, he entered Republican politics, serving as state senator (1899–1903) and as lieutenant governor (1904–06). In 1910, he was defeated for governor, but in 1914 was elected to the Senate. His reputation as an orator made him the keynoter at the 1916 Republican convention.

When the 1920 convention was deadlocked between Leonard Wood and Frank O. Lowden, Harding became the dark-horse nominee on his solemn affirmation that there was no reason in his past that he should not be. Straddling the League question, Harding was easily elected over James M. Cox, his Democratic opponent. His Cabinet contained some able men, but also some manifestly unfit for public office. Harding's own intimates were mediocre when they were not corrupt. The impending disclosure of the Teapot Dome scandal in the Interior Department and illegal practices in the Justice Department and Veterans' Bureau, as well as political setbacks, profoundly worried him. On his return from Alaska in 1923, he died unexpectedly in San Francisco on Aug. 2.

JOHN CALVIN COOLIDGE was born in Plymouth, Vt., on July 4, 1872. An Amherst graduate, he went into law practice at Northampton, Mass., in 1897. He married Grace Anna Goodhue in 1905. He entered Republican state politics, becoming successively mayor of Northampton, state senator, lieutenant governor and, in 1919, governor. His use of the state militia to end the Boston police strike in 1919 won him a somewhat undeserved reputation for decisive action and brought him the Republican vice-presidential nomination in 1920. After Harding's death Coolidge handled the Washington scandals with care and finally managed to save the Republican Party from public blame for the widespread corruption.

In 1924, Coolidge was elected without difficulty, defeating the Democrat, John W. Davis, and Robert M. La Follette running on the Progressive ticket. His second term, like his first, was characterized by a general satisfaction with the existing economic order. He stated that he did not choose to run in 1928.

After his presidency, Coolidge lived quietly in Northampton, writing an unilluminating *Autobiography* and conducting a syndicated column. He died there on Jan. 5, 1933.

HERBERT CLARK HOOVER was born at West Branch, Iowa, on Aug. 10, 1874, the first president to be born west of the Mississippi. A Stanford graduate, he worked from 1895 to 1913 as a mining engineer and consultant throughout the world. In 1899, he married Lou Henry. During World War I, he served with distinction as chairman of the American Relief Committee in London, as chairman of the Commission for Relief in Belgium, and as U.S. Food Administrator. His political affiliations were still too indeterminate for him to be mentioned as a possibility for either the Republican or Democratic nomination in 1920, but after the election he served Harding and Coolidge as Secretary of Commerce.

In the election of 1928, Hoover overwhelmed Gov. Alfred E. Smith of New York, the Democratic candidate and the first Roman Catholic to run for the presidency. He soon faced the worst depression in the nation's history, but his attacks upon it were hampered by his devotion to the theory that the forces that brought the crisis would soon bring the revival and then by his belief that there were too many areas in which the federal government had no power to act. In a succession of vetoes, he struck down measures proposing a national employment system or national relief, he reduced income tax rates, and only at the end of his term did he yield to popular pressure and set up agencies such as the Reconstruction Finance Corporation to make emergency loans to assist business.

After his 1932 defeat, Hoover returned to private business. In 1946, President Truman charged him with various world food missions; and from 1947 to 1949 and 1953 to 1955, he was head of the Commission on Organization of the Executive Branch of the Government. He died in New York City on Oct. 20, 1964.

FRANKLIN DELANO ROOSEVELT was born in Hyde Park, N.Y., on Jan. 30, 1882. A Harvard graduate, he attended Columbia Law School and was admitted to the New York bar. In 1910, he was elected to the New York State Senate as a Democrat. Re-elected in 1912, he was appointed Assistant Secretary of the Navy by Woodrow Wilson the next year. In 1920, his radiant personality and his war service resulted in his nomination for vice president as James M. Cox's running mate. After his defeat, he returned to law practice in New York. In August 1921, Roosevelt was stricken with infantile paralysis while on vacation at Campobello, New Brunswick. After a long and gallant fight, he recovered partial use of his legs. In 1924 and 1928, he led the fight at the Democratic national conventions for the nomination of Gov. Alfred E. Smith of New York, and in 1928 Roosevelt was himself induced to run for governor of New York. He was elected, and was re-elected in 1930.

In 1932, Roosevelt received the Democratic nomination for president and immediately launched a campaign that brought new spirit to a weary and discouraged nation. He defeated Hoover by a wide margin. His first term was characterized by an unfolding of the New Deal program, with greater benefits for labor, the farmers, and the unemployed, and the progressive estrangement of most of the business community.

At an early stage, Roosevelt became aware of the menace to world peace posed by totalitarian fascism, and from 1937 on he tried to focus public attention on the trend of events in Europe and Asia. As a result, he was widely denounced as a warmonger. He was re-elected in 1936 over Gov. Alfred M. Landon of Kansas by the overwhelming electoral margin of 523 to 8, and the gathering international crisis prompted him to run for an unprecedented third term in 1940. He defeated Wendell L. Willkie.

Roosevelt's program to bring maximum aid to Britain and, after June 1941, to Russia was opposed, until the Japanese attack on Pearl Harbor restored national unity. During the war, Roosevelt shelved the New Deal in the interests of conciliating the business community, both in order to get full production during the war and to prepare the way for a united acceptance of the peace settlements after the war. A series of conferences with Winston Churchill and Joseph Stalin laid down the bases for the postwar world. In 1944 he was elected to a fourth term, running against Gov. Thomas E. Dewey of New York.

On April 12, 1945, Roosevelt died of a cerebral hemorrhage at Warm Springs, Ga., shortly after his return from the Yalta Conference. His wife, Anna Eleanor Roosevelt, whom he married in 1905, was a woman of great ability who made significant contributions to her husband's policies.

HARRY S. TRUMAN was born on a farm near Lamar, Mo., on May 8, 1884. During World War I, he served in France as a captain with the 129th Field Artillery. He married Bess Wallace in 1919. After engaging briefly and unsuccessfully in the haberdashery business in Kansas City, Mo., Truman entered local politics. Under the sponsorship of Thomas Pendergast, Democratic boss of Missouri, he held a number of local offices, preserving his personal honesty in the midst of a notoriously corrupt political machine. In 1934, he was elected to the Senate and was re-elected in 1940. During his first term he was a loyal but quiet supporter of the New Deal, but in his second term, an appointment as head of a Senate committee to investigate war production brought out his special qualities of honesty, common sense, and hard work, and he won widespread respect.

Elected vice president in 1944, Truman became president upon Roosevelt's sudden death in April 1945 and was immediately faced with the problems of winding down the war against the Axis and preparing the nation for postwar adjustment.

The years 1947–48 were distinguished by civil-rights proposals, the Truman Doctrine to contain the spread of Communism, and the Marshall Plan to aid in the economic reconstruction of war-ravaged nations. Truman's general record, highlighted by a vigorous Fair Deal campaign, brought about his unexpected election in 1948 over the heavily favored Thomas E. Dewey.

Truman's second term was primarily concerned with the Cold War with the Soviet Union, the implementing of the North Atlantic Pact, the United Nations police action in Korea, and the vast rearmament program with its accompanying problems of economic stabilization.

On March 29, 1952, Truman announced that he would not run again for the presidency. After leaving the White House, he returned to his home in Independence, Mo., to write his memoirs. He further busied himself with the Harry S. Truman Library there. He died in Kansas City, Mo., on Dec. 26, 1972.

DWIGHT DAVID EISENHOWER was born in Denison, Tex., on Oct. 14, 1890. His ancestors lived in Germany and emigrated to America, settling in Pennsylvania, early in the 18th century. His father, David, had a general store in Hope, Kan., which failed. After a brief time in Texas, the family moved to Abilene, Kan.

After graduating from Abilene High School in 1909, Eisenhower did odd jobs for almost two years. He won an appointment to the Naval Academy at Annapolis, but was too old for admittance. Then he received an appointment in 1910 to West Point, from which he graduated as a second lieutenant in 1915.

He did not see service in World War I, having been stationed at Fort Sam Houston, Tex. There he met Mamie Geneva Doud, whom he married in Denver on July 1, 1916, and by whom he had two sons: Doud Dwight (died in infancy) and John Sheldon Doud.

Eisenhower served in the Philippines from 1935 to 1939 with Gen. Douglas MacArthur. Afterward, Gen. George C. Marshall, the Army Chief of Staff, brought him into the War Department's General Staff and in 1942 placed him in command of the invasion of North Africa. In 1944, he was made Supreme Allied Commander for the invasion of Europe.

After the war, Eisenhower served as Army Chief of Staff from November 1945 until February 1948, when he was appointed president of Columbia University.

In December 1950, President Truman recalled Eisenhower to active duty to command the North Atlantic Treaty Organization forces in Europe. He held this post until the end of May 1952.

At the Republican convention of 1952 in Chicago, Eisenhower won the presidential nomination on the first ballot in a close race with Senator Robert A. Taft of Ohio. In the election, he defeated Gov. Adlai E. Stevenson of Illinois.

Through two terms, Eisenhower hewed to moderate domestic policies. He sought peace through Free World strength in an era of new nationalisms, nuclear missiles, and space exploration. He fostered alliances pledging the United States to resist Red aggression in Europe, Asia, and Latin America. The Eisenhower Doctrine of 1957 extended commitments to the Middle East.

At home, the popular president lacked Republican Congressional majorities after 1954, but he was re-elected in 1956 by 457 electoral votes to 73 for Stevenson.

While retaining most Fair Deal programs, he stressed "fiscal responsibility" in domestic affairs. A moderate in civil rights, he sent troops to Little Rock, Ark., to enforce court-ordered school integration.

With his wartime rank restored by Congress, Eisenhower returned to private life and the role of elder statesman, with his vigor hardly impaired by a heart attack, an ileitis operation, and a mild stroke suffered while in office. He died in Washington on March 28, 1969.

JOHN FITZGERALD KENNEDY was born in Brookline, Mass., on May 29, 1917. His father, Joseph P. Kennedy, was Ambassador to Great Britain from 1937 to 1940.

Kennedy was graduated from Harvard University in 1940 and joined the Navy the next year. He became skipper of a PT boat that was sunk in the Pacific by a Japanese destroyer. Although given up for lost, he swam to a safe island, towing an injured enlisted man.

After recovering from a war-aggravated spinal injury, Kennedy entered politics in 1946 and was elected to Congress. In 1952, he ran against Senator Henry Cabot Lodge, Jr., of Massachusetts, and won.

Kennedy was married on Sept. 12, 1953, to Jacqueline Lee Bouvier, by whom he had three children: Caroline, John Fitzgerald, Jr., and Patrick Bouvier (died in infancy).

In 1957 Kennedy won the Pulitzer Prize for a book he had written earlier, *Profiles in Courage*.

After strenuous primary battles, Kennedy won the Democratic presidential nomination on the first ballot at the 1960 Los Angeles convention. With a plurality of only 118,574 votes, he carried the election over Vice President Richard M. Nixon and became the first Roman Catholic president.

Kennedy brought to the White House the dynamic idea of a "New Frontier" approach in dealing with problems at home, abroad, and in the dimensions of space. Out of his leadership in his first few months in office came the 10-year Alliance for Progress to aid Latin America, the Peace Corps, and accelerated programs that brought the first Americans into orbit in the race in space.

Failure of the U.S.-supported Cuban invasion in April 1961 led to the entrenchment of the Communist-backed Castro regime, only 90 miles from United States soil. When it became known that Soviet offensive missiles were being installed in Cuba in 1962, Kennedy ordered a naval "quarantine" of the island and moved troops into position to eliminate this threat to U.S. security. The world seemed on the brink of a nuclear war until Soviet Premier Khrushchev ordered the removal of the missiles.

A sudden "thaw," or the appearance of one, in the cold war came with the agreement with the Soviet Union on a limited test-ban treaty signed in Moscow on Aug. 6, 1963.

In his domestic policies, Kennedy's proposals for medical care for the aged, expanded area redevelopment, and aid to education were defeated, but on minimum wage, trade legislation, and other measures he won important victories.

Widespread racial disorders and demonstrations led to Kennedy's proposing sweeping civil rights legislation. As his third year in office drew to a close, he also recommended an $11-billion tax cut to bolster the economy. Both measures were pending in Congress when Kennedy, looking forward to a second term, journeyed to Texas for a series of speeches.

While riding in a procession in Dallas on Nov. 22, 1963, he was shot to death by an assassin firing from an upper floor of a building. The alleged assassin, Lee Harvey Oswald, was killed two days later in the Dallas city jail by Jack Ruby, owner of a strip-tease place.

At 46 years of age, Kennedy became the fourth president to be assassinated and the eighth to die in office.

LYNDON BAINES JOHNSON was born in Stonewall, Tex., on Aug. 27, 1908. On both sides of his family he had a political heritage mingled with a Baptist background of preachers and teachers. Both his father and his paternal grandfather served in the Texas House of Representatives.

After his graduation from Southwest Texas State Teachers College, Johnson taught school for two years. He went to Washington in 1932 as secretary to Rep. Richard M. Kleberg. During this time, he married Claudia Alta Taylor, known as "Lady Bird." They had two children: Lynda Bird (Robb) and Luci Baines (Nugent).

In 1935, Johnson became Texas administrator for the National Youth Administration. Two years later, he was elected to Congress as an all-out supporter of Franklin D. Roosevelt, and served until 1949. He was the first member of Congress to enlist in the armed forces after the attack on Pearl Harbor. He served in the Navy in the Pacific and won a Silver Star.

Johnson was elected to the Senate in 1948 after he had captured the Democratic nomination by only 87 votes. He was 40 years old. He became the Senate Democratic leader in 1953. A heart attack in 1955 threatened to end his political career, but he recovered fully and resumed his duties.

At the height of his power as Senate leader, Johnson sought the Democratic nomination for president in 1960. When he lost to John F. Kennedy, he surprised even some of his closest associates by accepting second place on the ticket.

Johnson was riding in another car in the motorcade when Kennedy was assassinated in Dallas on Nov. 22, 1963. He took the oath of office in the presidential jet on the Dallas airfield.

With Johnson's insistent backing, Congress finally adopted a far-reaching civil-rights bill, a voting-rights bill, a Medicare program for the aged, and measures to improve education and conservation. Congress also began what Johnson described as "an all-out war" on poverty.

Amassing a record-breaking majority of nearly 16 million votes, Johnson was elected president in his own right in 1964, defeating Senator Barry Goldwater of Arizona.

The double tragedy of a war in Southeast Asia and urban riots at home marked Johnson's last two years in office. Faced with disunity in the nation and challenges within his own party, Johnson surprised the country on March 31, 1968, with the announcement that he would not be a candidate for re-election. He died of a heart attack suffered at his LBJ Ranch on Jan. 22, 1973.

RICHARD MILHOUS NIXON was born in Yorba Linda, Calif., on Jan. 9, 1913, to Midwestern-bred parents, Francis A. and Hannah Milhous Nixon, who raised their five sons as Quakers.

Nixon was a high school debater and was undergraduate president at Whittier College in California, where he was graduated in 1934. As a scholarship student at Duke University Law School in North Carolina, he graduated third in his class in 1937.

After five years as a lawyer, Nixon joined the Navy in August 1942. He was an air transport officer in the South Pacific and a legal officer stateside before his discharge in 1946 as a lieutenant commander.

Running for Congress in California as a Republican in 1946, Nixon defeated Rep. Jerry Voorhis. As a member of the House Un-American Activities Committee, he made a name as an investigator of Alger Hiss, a former high State Department official, who was later jailed for perjury. In 1950, Nixon defeated Rep. Helen Gahagan Douglas, a Democrat, for the Senate. He was criticized for portraying her as a Communist dupe.

Nixon's anti-Communism, his Western base, and his youth figured in his selection in 1952 to run for vice president on the ticket headed by Dwight D. Eisenhower. Demands for Nixon's withdrawal followed disclosure that California businessmen had paid some of his Senate office expenses. He televised rebuttal, known as "the Checkers speech" (named for a cocker spaniel given to the Nixons), brought him support from the public and from Eisenhower. The ticket won easily in 1952 and again in 1956.

Eisenhower gave Nixon substantive assignments, including missions to 56 countries. In Moscow in 1959, Nixon won acclaim for his defense of U.S. interests in an impromptu "kitchen debate" with Soviet Premier Nikita S. Khrushchev.

Nixon lost the 1960 race for the presidency to John F. Kennedy.

In 1962, Nixon failed in a bid for California's

governorship and seemed to be finished as a national candidate. He became a Wall Street lawyer, but kept his old party ties and developed new ones through constant travels to speak for Republicans.

Nixon won the 1968 Republican presidential nomination after a shrewd primary campaign, then made Gov. Spiro T. Agnew of Maryland his surprise choice for vice president. In the election, they edged out the Democratic ticket headed by Vice President Hubert H. Humphrey by 510,314 votes out of 73,212,065 cast.

Committed to wind down the U.S. role in the Vietnamese War, Nixon pursued "Vietnamization" —training and equipping South Vietnamese to do their own fighting. American ground combat forces in Vietnam fell steadily from 540,000 when Nixon took office to none in 1973 when the military draft was ended. But there was heavy continuing use of U.S. air power.

Nixon improved relations with Moscow and reopened the long-closed door to mainland China with a good-will trip there in February 1972. In May of that year, he visited Moscow and signed agreements on arms limitation and trade expansion and approved plans for a joint U.S.-Soviet space mission in 1975.

Inflation was a campaign issue for Nixon, but he failed to master it as president. On Aug. 15, 1971, with unemployment edging up, Nixon abruptly announced a new economic policy: a 90-day wage-price freeze, stimulative tax cuts, a temporary 10% tariff, and spending cuts. A second phase, imposing guidelines on wage, price and rent boosts, was announced October 7.

The economy responded in time for the 1972 campaign, in which Nixon played up his foreign-policy achievements. Played down was the burglary on June 17, 1972, of Democratic national headquarters in the Watergate apartment complex in Washington. The Nixon-Agnew re-election campaign cost a record $60 million and swamped the Democratic ticket headed by Senator George McGovern of South Dakota with a plurality of 17,-999,528 out of 77,718,554 votes. Only Massachusetts, with 14 electoral votes, and the District of Columbia, with 3, went for McGovern.

In January 1973, hints of a cover-up emerged at the trial of six men found guilty of the Watergate burglary. With a Senate investigation under way, Nixon announced on April 30 the resignations of his top aides, H. R. Haldeman and John D. Ehrlichman, and the dismissal of White House counsel John Dean III. Dean was the star witness at televised Senate hearings that exposed both a White House cover-up of Watergate and massive illegalities in Republican fund-raising in 1972.

The hearings also disclosed that Nixon had routinely tape-recorded his office meetings and telephone conversations.

On Oct. 10, 1973, Agnew resigned as vice president, then pleaded no-contest to a negotiated federal charge of evading income taxes on alleged bribes. Two days later, Nixon nominated the House minority leader, Rep. Gerald R. Ford of Michigan, as the new vice president. Congress confirmed Ford on Dec. 6, 1973.

In June 1974, Nixon visited Israel and four Arab nations. Then he met in Moscow with Soviet leader Leonid I. Brezhnev and reached preliminary nuclear arms limitation agreements.

But, in the month after his return, Watergate ended the Nixon regime. On July 24 the Supreme Court ordered Nixon to surrender subpoenaed tapes. On July 30, the Judiciary Committee referred three impeachment articles to the full membership. On August 5, Nixon bowed to the Supreme Court and released tapes showing he halted an FBI probe of the Watergate burglary six days after it occurred. It was in effect an admission of obstruction of justice, and impeachment appeared inevitable.

Nixon resigned on Aug. 9, 1974, the first president ever to do so. A month later, President Ford issued an unconditional pardon for any offenses Nixon might have committed as president, thus forestalling possible prosecution.

In 1940, Nixon married Thelma Catherine (Pat) Ryan. They had two daughters, Patricia (Tricia) Cox and Julie, who married Dwight David Eisenhower II, grandson of the former president.

GERALD RUDOLPH FORD was born in Omaha, Neb., on July 14, 1913, the only child of Leslie and Dorothy Gardner King. His parents were divorced in 1915. His mother moved to Grand Rapids, Mich., and married Gerald R. Ford. The boy was renamed for his stepfather.

Ford captained his high school football team in Grand Rapids, and a football scholarship took him to the University of Michigan, where he starred as varsity center before his graduation in 1935. A job as assistant football coach at Yale gave him an opportunity to attend Yale Law School, from which he graduated in the top third of his class in 1941.

He returned to Grand Rapids to practice law, but entered the Navy in April 1942. He saw wartime service in the Pacific on the light aircraft carrier *Monterey* and was a lieutenant commander when he returned to Grand Rapids early in 1946 to resume law practice and dabble in politics.

Ford was elected to Congress in 1948 for the first of his 13 terms in the House. He was soon assigned to the influential Appropriations Committee and rose to become the ranking Republican on the subcommittee on Defense Department appropriations and an expert in the field.

As a legislator, Ford described himself as "a moderate on domestic issues, a conservative in fiscal affairs, and a dyed-in-the-wool internationalist." He carried the ball for Pentagon appropriations, was a hawk on the war in Vietnam, and kept a low profile on civil-rights issues.

He was also dependable and hard-working and popular with his colleagues. In 1963, he was elected chairman of the House Republican Conference. He served in 1963–64 as a member of the Warren Commission that investigated the assassination of John F. Kennedy. A revolt by dissatisfied younger Republicans in 1965 made him minority leader.

Ford shelved his hopes for the Speakership on Oct. 12, 1973, when Nixon nominated him to fill the vice presidency left vacant by Agnew's resignation under fire. It was the first use of the procedures for filling vacancies in the vice presidency laid down in the 25th Amendment to the Constitution, which Ford had helped enact.

Congress confirmed Ford as vice president on Dec. 6, 1973. Once in office, he said he did not believe Nixon had been involved in the Watergate scandals, but criticized his stubborn court battle against releasing tape recordings of Watergate-related conversations for use as evidence.

The scandals led to Nixon's unprecedented resignation on Aug. 9, 1974, and Ford was sworn in immediately as the 38th president, the first to enter the White House without winning a national election.

Ford assured the nation when he took office that "our long national nightmare is over" and pledged "openness and candor" in all his actions. He won a warm response from the Democratic 93rd Congress when he said he wanted "a good marriage" rather than a honeymoon with his former colleagues. In December 1974 Congressional majorities backed his choice of former New York Gov. Nelson A. Rockefeller as his successor in the again-vacant vice presidency.

The cordiality was chilled by Ford's announcement on Sept. 8, 1974, that he had granted an unconditional pardon to Nixon for any crimes he might have committed as president. Although no formal charges were pending, Ford said he feared "ugly passions" would be aroused if Nixon were brought to trial. The pardon was widely criticized.

To fight inflation, the new president first proposed fiscal restraints and spending curbs and a 5% tax surcharge that got nowhere in the Senate and House. Congress again rebuffed Ford in the spring of 1975 when he appealed for emergency military aid to help the governments of South Vietnam and Cambodia resist massive Communist offensives.

In November 1974, Ford visited Japan, South Korea, and the Soviet Union, where he and Soviet leader Leonid I. Brezhnev conferred in Vladivostok and reached a tentative agreement to limit the number of strategic offensive nuclear weapons. It was Ford's first meeting as president with Brezhnev, who planned a return visit to Washington in the fall of 1975.

Politically, Ford's fortunes improved steadily in the first half of 1975. Badly divided Democrats in Congress were unable to muster votes to override his vetoes of spending bills that exceeded his budget. He faced some right-wing opposition in his own party, but moved to pre-empt it with an early announcement—on July 8, 1975—of his intention to be a candidate in 1976.

Early state primaries in 1976 suggested an easy victory for Ford despite Ronald Reagan's bitter attacks on administration foreign policy and defense programs. But later Reagan primary successes threatened the President's lead. At the Kansas City convention, Ford was nominated by the narrow margin of 1,187 to 1,070. But Reagan had moved the party to the right, and Ford himself was regarded as a caretaker president lacking in strength and vision. He was defeated in November by Jimmy Carter.

In 1948, Ford married Elizabeth Anne (Betty) Bloomer. They had four children, Michael Gerald, John Gardner, Steven Meigs, and Susan Elizabeth.

(For Carter's biography see Election of 1980, page 21.)

Presidents

Name and (party)[1]	Term	State of birth	Born	Died	Religion	Age at inaug.	Age at death
1. Washington (F)[2]	1789–1797	Va.	2/22/1732	12/14/1799	Episcopalian	57	67
2. J. Adams (F)	1797–1801	Mass.	10/30/1735	7/4/1826	Unitarian	61	90
3. Jefferson (DR)	1801–1809	Va.	4/13/1743	7/4/1826	Deist	57	83
4. Madison (DR)	1809–1817	Va.	3/16/1751	6/28/1836	Episcopalian	57	85
5. Monroe (DR)	1817–1825	Va.	4/28/1758	7/4/1831	Episcopalian	58	73
6. J. Q. Adams (DR)	1825–1829	Mass.	7/11/1767	2/23/1848	Unitarian	57	80
7. Jackson (D)	1829–1837	S.C.	3/15/1767	6/8/1845	Presbyterian	61	78
8. Van Buren (D)	1837–1841	N.Y.	12/5/1782	7/24/1862	Reformed Dutch	54	79
9. W. H. Harrison (W)[3]	1841	Va.	2/9/1773	4/4/1841	Episcopalian	68	68
10. Tyler (W)	1841–1845	Va.	3/29/1790	1/18/1862	Episcopalian	51	71
11. Polk (D)	1845–1849	N.C.	11/2/1795	6/15/1849	Methodist	49	53
12. Taylor (W)[3]	1849–1850	Va.	11/24/1784	7/9/1850	Episcopalian	64	65
13. Fillmore (W)	1850–1853	N.Y.	1/7/1800	3/8/1874	Unitarian	50	74
14. Pierce (D)	1853–1857	N.H.	11/23/1804	10/8/1869	Episcopalian	48	64
15. Buchanan (D)	1857–1861	Pa.	4/23/1791	6/1/1868	Presbyterian	65	77
16. Lincoln (R)[4]	1861–1865	Ky.	2/12/1809	4/15/1865	Liberal	52	56
17. A. Johnson (U)[5]	1865–1869	N.C.	12/29/1808	7/31/1875	(6)	56	66
18. Grant (R)	1869–1877	Ohio	4/27/1822	7/23/1885	Methodist	46	63
19. Hayes (R)	1877–1881	Ohio	10/4/1822	1/17/1893	Methodist	54	70
20. Garfield (R)[4]	1881	Ohio	11/19/1831	9/19/1881	Disciples of Christ	49	49
21. Arthur (R)	1881–1885	Vt.	10/5/1830	11/18/1886	Episcopalian	50	56
22. Cleveland (D)	1885–1889	N.J.	3/18/1837	6/24/1908	Presbyterian	47	71
23. B. Harrison (R)	1889–1893	Ohio	8/20/1833	3/13/1901	Presbyterian	55	67
24. Cleveland (D)[7]	1893–1897	—	—	—	—	55	—
25. McKinley (R)[4]	1897–1901	Ohio	1/29/1843	9/14/1901	Methodist	54	58
26. T. Roosevelt (R)	1901–1909	N.Y.	10/27/1858	1/6/1919	Reformed Dutch	42	60
27. Taft (R)	1909–1913	Ohio	9/15/1857	3/8/1930	Unitarian	51	72
28. Wilson (D)	1913–1921	Va.	12/28/1856	2/3/1924	Presbyterian	56	67
29. Harding (R)[3]	1921–1923	Ohio	11/2/1865	8/2/1923	Baptist	55	57
30. Coolidge (R)	1923–1929	Vt.	7/4/1872	1/5/1933	Congregationalist	51	60
31. Hoover (R)	1929–1933	Iowa	8/10/1874	10/20/1964	Quaker	54	90
32. F. D. Roosevelt (D)[3]	1933–1945	N.Y.	1/30/1882	4/12/1945	Episcopalian	51	63
33. Truman (D)	1945–1953	Mo.	5/8/1884	12/26/1972	Baptist	60	88
34. Eisenhower (R)	1953–1961	Tex.	10/14/1890	3/28/1969	Presbyterian	62	78
35. Kennedy (D)[4]	1961–1963	Mass.	5/29/1917	11/22/1963	Roman Catholic	43	46

Name and (party)[1]	Term	State of birth	Born	Died	Religion	Age at inaug.	Age at death
36. L. B. Johnson (D)	1963–1969	Tex.	8/27/1908	1/22/1973	Disciples of Christ	55	64
37. Nixon (R)[8]	1969–1974	Calif.	1/9/1913	—	Quaker	56	—
38. Ford (R)	1974–1977	Neb.	7/14/1913	—	Episcopalian	61	—
39. Carter (D)	1977–	Ga.	10/1/1924	—	Southern Baptist	52	—

1. F—Federalist; DR—Democratic-Republican; D—Democratic; W—Whig; R—Republican; U—Union. 2. No party for first election. The party system in the U.S. made its appearance during Washington's first term. 3. Died in office. 4. Assassinated in office. 5. The Republican National Convention of 1864 adopted the name Union Party. It renominated Lincoln for President; for Vice President it nominated Johnson, a War Democrat. Although frequently listed as a Republican Vice President and President, Johnson undoubtedly considered himself strictly a member of the Union Party. When that party broke apart after 1868, he returned to the Democratic Party. 6. Johnson was not a professed church member; however, he admired the Baptist principles of church government. 7. Second nonconsecutive term. 8. Resigned Aug. 9, 1974.

Vice Presidents

Name and (party)[1]	Term	State of birth	Birth and death dates	President served under
1. John Adams (F)[2]	1789–1797	Massachusetts	1735–1826	Washington
2. Thomas Jefferson (DR)	1797–1801	Virginia	1743–1826	J. Adams
3. Aaron Burr (DR)	1801–1805	New Jersey	1756–1836	Jefferson
4. George Clinton (DR)[3]	1805–1812	New York	1739–1812	Jefferson and Madison
5. Elbridge Gerry (DR)[3]	1813–1814	Massachusetts	1744–1814	Madison
6. Daniel D. Tompkins (DR)	1817–1825	New York	1774–1825	Monroe
7. John C. Calhoun[4]	1825–1832	South Carolina	1782–1850	J. Q. Adams and Jackson
8. Martin Van Buren (D)	1833–1837	New York	1782–1862	Jackson
9. Richard M. Johnson (D)	1837–1841	Kentucky	1780–1850	Van Buren
10. John Tyler (W)[5]	1841	Virginia	1790–1862	W. H. Harrison
11. George M. Dallas (D)	1845–1849	Pennsylvania	1792–1864	Polk
12. Millard Fillmore (W)[5]	1849–1850	New York	1800–1874	Taylor
13. William R. King (D)[3]	1853	North Carolina	1786–1853	Pierce
14. John C. Breckinridge (D)	1857–1861	Kentucky	1821–1875	Buchanan
15. Hannibal Hamlin (R)	1861–1865	Maine	1809–1891	Lincoln
16. Andrew Johnson (U)[5]	1865	North Carolina	1808–1875	Lincoln
17. Schuyler Colfax (R)	1869–1873	New York	1823–1885	Grant
18. Henry Wilson (R)[3]	1873–1875	New Hampshire	1812–1875	Grant
19. William A. Wheeler (R)	1877–1881	New York	1819–1887	Hayes
20. Chester A. Arthur(R)[5]	1881	Vermont	1830–1886	Garfield
21. Thomas A. Hendricks (D)[3]	1885	Ohio	1819–1885	Cleveland
22. Levi P. Morton (R)	1889–1893	Vermont	1824–1920	B. Harrison
23. Adlai E. Stevenson (D)	1893–1897	Kentucky	1835–1914	Cleveland
24. Garrett A. Hobart (R)[3]	1897–1899	New Jersey	1844–1899	McKinley
25. Theodore Roosevelt (R)[5]	1901	New York	1858–1919	McKinley
26. Charles W. Fairbanks (R)	1905–1909	Ohio	1852–1918	T. Roosevelt
27. James S. Sherman (R)[3]	1909–1912	New York	1855–1912	Taft
28. Thomas R. Marshall (D)	1913–1921	Indiana	1854–1925	Wilson
29. Calvin Coolidge (R)[5]	1921–1923	Vermont	1872–1933	Harding
30. Charles G. Dawes (R)	1925–1929	Ohio	1865–1951	Coolidge
31. Charles Curtis (R)	1929–1933	Kansas	1860–1936	Hoover
32. John N. Garner (D)	1933–1941	Texas	1868–1967	F. D. Roosevelt
33. Henry A. Wallace (D)	1941–1945	Iowa	1888–1965	F. D. Roosevelt
34. Harry S. Truman (D)[5]	1945	Missouri	1884–1972	F. D. Roosevelt
35. Alben W. Barkley (D)	1949–1953	Kentucky	1877–1956	Truman
36. Richard M. Nixon (R)	1953–1961	California	1913–	Eisenhower
37. Lyndon B. Johnson (D)[5]	1961–1963	Texas	1908–1973	Kennedy
38. Hubert H. Humphrey (D)	1965–1969	South Dakota	1911–1978	Johnson
39. Spiro T. Agnew (R)[6]	1969–1973	Maryland	1918–	Nixon
40. Gerald R. Ford (R)[7]	1973–1974	Nebraska	1913–	Nixon
41. Nelson A. Rockefeller (R)[8]	1974–1977	Maine	1908–1979	Ford
42. Walter F. Mondale (D)	1977–	Minnesota	1928–	Carter

1. F—Federalist; DR—Democratic-Republican; D—Democratic; W—Whig; R—Republican; U—Union. 2. No party for first election. The party system in the U.S. made its appearance during Washington's first term as President. 3. Died in office. 4. Democratic-Republican with J. Q. Adams; Democratic with Jackson. Calhoun resigned in 1832 to become a U.S. Senator. 5. Succeeded to presidency on death of President. 6. Resigned Oct. 10, 1973, after pleading no contest to Federal income tax evasion charges. 7. Nominated by Nixon on Oct. 12, 1973, under provisions of 25th Amendment. Confirmed by Congress on Dec. 6, 1973, and was sworn in same day. He became President Aug. 9, 1974, upon Nixon's resignation. 8. Nominated by Ford Aug. 20, 1974; confirmed by Congress on Dec. 19, 1974, and was sworn in same day.

Burial Places of the Presidents

President	Burial place	President	Burial place
Washington	Mt. Vernon, Va.	Grant	New York City
J. Adams	Quincy, Mass.	Hayes	Fremont, Ohio
Jefferson	Charlottesville, Va.	Garfield	Cleveland, Ohio
Madison	Montpelier Station, Va.	Arthur	Albany, N.Y.
Monroe	Richmond, Va.	Cleveland	Princeton, N.J.
J. Q. Adams	Quincy, Mass.	B. Harrison	Indianapolis
Jackson	The Hermitage, nr. Nashville, Tenn.	McKinley	Canton, Ohio
		T. Roosevelt	Oyster Bay, N.Y.
Van Buren	Kinderhook, N.Y.	Taft	Arlington National Cemetery
W. H. Harrison	North Bend, Ohio	Wilson	Washington National Cathedral
Tyler	Richmond, Va.	Harding	Marion, Ohio
Polk	Nashville, Tenn.	Coolidge	Plymouth, Vt.
Taylor	Louisville, Ky.	Hoover	West Branch, Iowa
Fillmore	Buffalo, N.Y.	F. D. Roosevelt	Hyde Park, N.Y.
Pierce	Concord, N.H.	Truman	Independence, Mo.
Buchanan	Lancaster, Pa.	Eisenhower	Abilene, Kan.
Lincoln	Springfield, Ill.	Kennedy	Arlington National Cemetery
A. Johnson	Greeneville, Tenn.	L. B. Johnson	Stonewall, Tex.

Wives and Children of the Presidents

President	Wife's name	Year and place of wife's birth	Married	Wife died	Children of President[1]	
					Sons	Daughters
Washington	Mrs. Martha Dandridge Custis	1732, Va.	1759	1802	—	—
John Adams	Abigail Smith	1744, Mass.	1764	1818	3	2
Jefferson	Mrs. Martha Wayles Skelton	1748, Va.	1772	1782	1	5
Madison	Mrs. Dorothy "Dolley" Payne Todd	1768, N.C.	1794	1849	—	—
Monroe	Elizabeth "Eliza" Kortright	1768, N.Y.	1786	1830	—	2
J. Q. Adams	Louisa Catherine Johnson	1775, England	1797	1852	3	1
Jackson	Mrs. Rachel Donelson Robards	1767, Va.	1791	1828	—	—
Van Buren	Hannah Hoes	1788, N.Y.	1807	1819	4	—
W. H. Harrison	Anna Symmes	1775, N.J.	1795	1864	6	4
Tyler	Letitia Christian	1790, Va.	1813	1842	3	4
	Julia Gardiner	1820, N.Y.	1844	1889	5	2
Polk	Sarah Childress	1803, Tenn.	1824	1891	—	—
Taylor	Margaret Smith	1788, Md.	1810	1852	1	5
Fillmore	Abigail Powers	1798, N.Y.	1826	1853	1	1
	Mrs. Caroline Carmichael McIntosh	1813, N.J.	1858	1881	—	—
Pierce	Jane Means Appleton	1806, N.H.	1834	1863	3	—
Buchanan	(Unmarried)	—	—	—	—	—
Lincoln	Mary Todd	1818, Ky.	1842	1882	4	—
A. Johnson	Eliza McCardle	1810, Tenn.	1827	1876	3	2
Grant	Julia Dent	1826, Mo.	1848	1902	3	1
Hayes	Lucy Ware Webb	1831, Ohio	1852	1889	7	1
Garfield	Lucretia Rudolph	1832, Ohio	1858	1918	5	2
Arthur	Ellen Lewis Herndon	1837, Va.	1859	1880	2	1
Cleveland	Frances Folsom	1864, N.Y.	1886	1947	2	3
B. Harrison	Caroline Lavinia Scott	1832, Ohio	1853	1892	1	1
	Mrs. Mary Scott Lord Dimmick	1858, Pa.	1896	1948	—	1
McKinley	Ida Saxton	1847, Ohio	1871	1907	—	2
T. Roosevelt	Alice Hathaway Lee	1861, Mass.	1880	1884	—	1
	Edith Kermit Carow	1861, Conn.	1886	1948	4	1
Taft	Helen Herron	1861, Ohio	1886	1943	2	1
Wilson	Ellen Louise Axson	1860, Ga.	1885	1914	—	3
	Mrs. Edith Bolling Galt	1872, Va.	1915	1961	—	—
Harding	Mrs. Florence Kling DeWolfe	1860, Ohio	1891	1924	—	—
Coolidge	Grace Anna Goodhue	1879, Vt.	1905	1957	2	—
Hoover	Lou Henry	1875, Iowa	1899	1944	2	—
F. D. Roosevelt	Anna Eleanor Roosevelt	1884, N.Y.	1905	1962	5	1
Truman	Bess Wallace	1885, Mo.	1919	—	—	1
Eisenhower	Mamie Geneva Doud	1896, Iowa	1916	1979	2	—
Kennedy	Jacqueline Lee Bouvier	1929, N.Y.	1953	—	2	1

President	Wife's name	Year and place of wife's birth	Married	Wife died	Children of President[1]	
					Sons	Daughters
L. B. Johnson	Claudia Alta "Lady Bird" Taylor	1912, Tex.	1934	—	—	2
Nixon	Thelma Catherine "Pat" Ryan	1912, Nev.	1940	—	—	2
Ford	Mrs. Elizabeth "Betty" Bloomer Warren	1918, Ill.	1948	—	3	1
Carter	Rosalynn Smith	1928, Ga.	1946	—	3	1

1. Includes children who died in infancy.

Elections

How a President is Nominated and Elected

The National Conventions of both major parties are held during the summer of a presidential-election year. Earlier, each party selects delegates by primaries, conventions, committees, etc.

For their 1980 National Convention, the Republicans allowed each state a base of 6 delegates at large; the District of Columbia, 14; Puerto Rico, 14; Guam and the Virgin Islands, 4 each. In addition, each state received 3 district delegates for each of its Representatives in the House. This did not apply to the District of Columbia, Puerto Rico, Guam and the Virgin Islands.

Each state was awarded additional delegates at large on the basis of having supported the Republican candidate for President in 1976 and electing Republican candidates for Senator, Governor, and U.S. Representative in the 1976 and 1978 elections.

The number of delegates at the 1980 convention, held in Detroit starting July 14, was 1,997.

Following is the apportionment of delegates:

Ala.	27	Fla.	51	Ky.	27	Mont.	20	Ohio	77	Tex.	80
Alaska	19	Ga.	36	La.	31	Neb.	25	Okla	34	Utah	21
Ariz.	28	Guam	4	Me.	21	Nev.	17	Ore.	29	Vt.	19
Ark.	19	Hawaii	14	Md.	30	N.H.	22	Pa.	83	Va.	51
Calif.	168	Idaho	21	Mass.	42	N.J.	66	P.R.	14	V.I.	4
Colo.	31	Ill.	102	Mich.	82	N.M.	22	R.I.	13	Wash.	37
Conn.	35	Ind.	54	Minn.	34	N.Y.	123	S.C.	25	W. Va.	18
Del.	12	Iowa	37	Miss.	22	N.C.	40	S.D.	22	Wis.	34
D.C.	14	Kan.	32	Mo.	37	N.D.	17	Tenn.	32	Wyo.	19

The Democrats also based the number of delegates on a state's showing in the 1976 and 1978 elections. At the 1980 convention, held in New York City starting Aug. 11, there were 3,331[1] delegates casting votes. Following is the apportionment:

Ala.	45	D.C.	19	Kan.	37	Mo.	77	N.D.	14	Tenn.	55
Alaska	11	Fla.	100	Ky.	50	Mont.	19	Ohio	161	Tex.	152
Ariz.	29	Ga.	63	La.	51	Neb.	24	Okla.	42	Utah	20
Ark.	33	Guam	4	Me.	22	Nev.	12	Ore.	39	Vt.	12
Calif.	306	Hawaii	19	Md.	59	N.H.	19	Pa.	185	V.I.	4
Canal Zone	4	Idaho	17	Mass.	111	N.J.	113	P.R.	41	Va.	64
Colo.	40	Ill.	179	Mich.	141	N.M.	20	R.I.	23	Wash.	58
Conn.	54	Ind.	80	Minn.	75	N.Y.	282	S.C.	37	W.Va.	35
Del.	14	Iowa	50	Miss.	32	N.C.	69	S.D.	19	Wis.	75
										Wyo.	11

1. Includes three votes for Democrats abroad.

The Conventions

At each convention, a temporary chairman is chosen. After a credentials committee seats the delegates, a permanent chairman is elected. The convention then votes on a platform, drawn up by the platform committee.

By the third or fourth day, presidential nominations begin. The chairman calls the roll of states alphabetically. A state may place a candidate in nomination or yield to another state.

Voting, again alphabetically by roll call of states, begins after all nominations have been made and seconded. A simple majority is required in each party, although this may require many ballots.

Finally, the vice-presidential candidate is selected. Although there is no law saying that the candidates *must* come from different states, it is, practically, necessary for this to be the case. Otherwise, according to the Constitution (*see* Amendment XII), electors from that state could vote for only one of the candidates and would have to cast their other vote for some person of another state. This could result in a presidential candidate's receiving a majority electoral vote and his running mate's failing to.

The Electoral College

The next step in the process is the nomination of electors in each state, according to its laws. These electors must not be Federal office holders. In the November election, the voters cast their votes for electors, not for President. In some states, the ballots include only the names of the presidential and vice-presidential candidates; in others, they include only names of the electors. Nowadays, it is rare for electors to be split between parties. The last such occurrence was in North Carolina in 1968[1]; the last before that, in Tennessee in 1948. On three occasions (1824, 1876, and 1888), the presidential candidate with the largest popular vote failed to obtain an electoral-vote majority.

Each state has as many electors as it has Senators and Representatives. For the 1976 election, the total electors were 538, based on 100 Senators, 435 Representatives, plus 3 electoral votes from the District of Columbia as a result of the 23rd Amendment to the Constitution.

On the first Monday after the second Wednesday in December, the electors cast their votes in their respective state capitols. Constitutionally they may vote for someone other than the party candidate but usually they do not since they are pledged to one party and its candidate on the ballot. Should the presidential or vice-presidential candidate die between the November election and the December meetings, the electors pledged to vote for him could vote for whomever they pleased. However, it seems certain that the national committee would attempt to get an agreement among the state party leaders for a replacement candidate.

The votes of the electors, certified by the states, are sent to Congress, where the president of the Senate opens the certificates and has them counted in the presence of both Houses on January 6. The new President is inaugurated at noon on January 20.

Should no candidate receive a majority of the electoral vote for President, the House of Representatives chooses a President from among the three highest candidates, voting, not as individuals, but as states, with a majority (now 26) needed to elect. Should no vice-presidential candidate obtain the majority, the Senate, voting as individuals, chooses from the highest two.

1. In 1956, 1 of Alabama's 11 electoral votes was cast for Walter B. Jones. In 1960, 6 of Alabama's 11 electoral votes and 1 of Oklahoma's 8 electoral votes were cast for Harry Flood Byrd. (Byrd also received all 8 of Mississippi's electoral votes.)

National Committee Chairmen Since 1932

Chairman and (state)	Term
REPUBLICAN	
Everett Sanders (Ind.)	1932–34
Henry P. Fletcher (Pa.)	1934–36
John Hamilton (Kan.)	1936–40
Joseph W. Martin, Jr. (Mass.)	1940–42
Harrison E. Spangler (Iowa)	1942–44
Herbert Brownell, Jr. (N.Y.)	1944–46
Carroll Reece (Tenn.)	1946–48
Hugh D. Scott, Jr. (Pa.)	1948–49
Guy G. Gabrielson (N.J.)	1949–52
Arthur E. Summerfield (Mich.)	1952–53
Wesley Roberts (Kan.)	1953
Leonard W. Hall (N.Y.)	1953–57
Meade Alcorn (Conn.)	1957–59
Thruston B. Morton (Ky.)	1959–61
William E. Miller (N.Y.)	1961–64
Dean Burch (Ariz.)	1964–65
Ray C. Bliss (Ohio)	1965–69
Rogers C. B. Morton (Md.)	1969–71
Robert Dole (Kan.)	1971–73
George H. Bush (Tex.)	1973–74
Mary Louise Smith (Iowa)	1974–77
William E. Brock III (Tenn.)	1977–

Chairman and (state)	Term
DEMOCRATIC	
James A. Farley (N.Y.)	1932–40
Edward J. Flynn (N.Y.)	1940–43
Frank C. Walker (Mont.)	1943–44
Robert E. Hannegan (Mo.)	1944–47
J. Howard McGrath (R.I.)	1947–49
William M. Boyle, Jr. (Mo.)	1949–51
Frank E. McKinney (Ind.)	1951–52
Stephen A. Mitchell (Ill.)	1952–54
Paul M. Butler (Ind.)	1955–60
Henry M. Jackson (Wash.)	1960–61
John M. Bailey (Conn.)	1961–68
Lawrence F. O'Brien (Mass.)	1968–69
Fred R. Harris (Okla.)	1969–70
Lawrence F. O'Brien (Mass.)	1970–72
Jean Westwood (Utah)	1972
Robert S. Strauss (Tex.)	1972–77
Kenneth M. Curtis (Me.)	1977
John C. White (Tex.)	1977–

Republican National Committee: 310 First St., S.E., Washington, D. C. 20003.
Democratic National Committee: 1625 Massachusetts Ave., N.W., Washington, D. C. 20036.

Facts About Elections

Candidate with highest popular vote: Nixon (1972), 47,169,911.
Candidate with highest electoral vote: F. D. Roosevelt (1936), 523.
Candidate carrying most states: Nixon (1972), 49.
Candidate running most times: Norman Thomas, 6 (1928, 1932, 1936, 1940, 1944, 1948).
Candidate elected, defeated, then reelected: Cleveland (1884, 1888, 1892).

Presidential Elections, 1789 to 1976

For the original method of electing the President and the Vice President (elections of 1789, 1792, 1796, and 1800), see Article II, Section 1, of the Constitution. The election of 1804 was the first one in which the electors voted for President and Vice President on separate ballots. (See Amendment XII to the Constitution.)

Year	Presidential candidates	Party	Electoral vote
1789[1]	George Washington	(no party)	69
	John Adams	(no party)	34
	Scattering	(no party)	35
	Votes not cast		8
1792	George Washington	Federalist	132
	John Adams	Federalist	77
	George Clinton	Anti-Federalist	50
	Thomas Jefferson	Anti-Federalist	4
	Aaron Burr	Anti-Federalist	1
	Votes not cast		6
1796	John Adams	Federalist	71
	Thomas Jefferson	Dem.-Rep.	68
	Thomas Pinckney	Federalist	59
	Aaron Burr	Dem.-Rep.	30
	Scattering		48
1800[2]	Thomas Jefferson	Dem.-Rep.	73
	Aaron Burr	Dem.-Rep.	73
	John Adams	Federalist	65
	Charles C. Pinckney	Federalist	64
	John Jay	Federalist	1

Year	Presidential candidates	Party	Electoral vote	Vice-presidential candidates	Party	Electoral vote
1804	Thomas Jefferson	Dem.-Rep.	162	George Clinton	Dem.-Rep.	162
	Charles C. Pinckney	Federalist	14	Rufus King	Federalist	14
1808	James Madison	Dem.-Rep.	122	George Clinton	Dem.-Rep.	113
	Charles C. Pinckney	Federalist	47	Rufus King	Federalist	47
	George Clinton	Dem.-Rep.	6	John Langdon	Ind. (no party)	9
	Votes not cast		1	James Madison	Dem.-Rep.	3
				James Monroe	Dem.-Rep.	3
				Votes not cast		1
1812	James Madison	Dem.-Rep.	128	Elbridge Gerry	Dem.-Rep.	131
	De Witt Clinton	Federalist	89	Jared Ingersoll	Federalist	86
	Votes not cast		1	Votes not cast		1
1816	James Monroe	Dem.-Rep.	183	Daniel D. Tompkins	Dem.-Rep.	183
	Rufus King	Federalist	34	John E. Howard	Federalist	22
	Votes not cast		4	James Ross	Ind. (no party)	5
				John Marshall	Federalist	4
				Robert G. Harper	Ind. (no party)	3
				Votes not cast		4
1820	James Monroe	Dem-Rep	231	Daniel D. Tompkins	Dem.-Rep.	218
	John Quincy Adams	Ind. (no party)	1	Richard Stockton	Ind. (no party)	8
	Votes not cast		3	Daniel Rodney	Ind. (no party)	4
				Richard Rush	Ind. (no party)	1
				Robert G. Harper	Ind. (no party)	1
				Votes not cast		3
1824[3]	John Quincy Adams	(no party)	84	John C. Calhoun	(no party)	182
	Andrew Jackson	(no party)	99	Nathan Sanford	(no party)	30
	William H. Crawford	(no party)	41	Nathaniel Macon	(no party)	24
	Henry Clay	(no party)	37	Andrew Jackson	(no party)	13
				Martin Van Buren	(no party)	9
				Henry Clay	(no party)	2
				Votes not cast		1
1828	Andrew Jackson	Democratic	178	John C. Calhoun	Democratic	171
	John Quincy Adams	Natl. Rep.	83	Richard Rush	Natl. Rep.	83
				William Smith	Democratic	7
1832	Andrew Jackson	Democratic	219	Martin Van Buren	Democratic	189
	Henry Clay	Natl. Rep.	49	John Sergeant	Natl. Rep.	49
	John Floyd	Ind. (no party)	11	Henry Lee	Ind. (no party)	11
	William Wirt	Antimasonic[4]	7	Amos Ellmaker	Antimasonic	7
	Votes not cast		2	William Wilkins	Ind. (no party)	30
				Votes not cast		2

Year	Presidential candidates	Party	Electoral vote	Vice-presidential candidates	Party	Electoral vote
1836	Martin Van Buren	Democratic	170	Richard M. Johnson[5]	Democratic	147
	William H. Harrison	Whig	73	Francis Granger	Whig	77
	Hugh L. White	Whig	26	John Tyler	Whig	47
	Daniel Webster	Whig	14	William Smith	Ind. (no party)	23
	W. P. Mangum	Ind. (no party)	11			
1840	William H. Harrison[6]	Whig	234	John Tyler	Whig	234
	Martin Van Buren	Democratic	60	Richard M. Johnson	Democratic	48
				L. W. Tazewell	Ind. (no party)	11
				James K. Polk	Democratic	1
1844	James K. Polk	Democratic	170	George M. Dallas	Democratic	170
	Henry Clay	Whig	105	Theo. Frelinghuysen	Whig	105
1848	Zachary Taylor[7]	Whig	163	Millard Fillmore	Whig	163
	Lewis Cass	Democratic	127	William O. Butler	Democratic	127
1852	Franklin Pierce	Democratic	254	William R. King	Democratic	254
	Winfield Scott	Whig	42	William A. Graham	Whig	42
1856	James Buchanan	Democratic	174	John C. Breckinridge	Democratic	174
	John C. Frémont	Republican	114	William L. Dayton	Republican	114
	Millard Fillmore	American[8]	8	A. J. Donelson	American[8]	8
1860	Abraham Lincoln	Republican	180	Hannibal Hamlin	Republican	180
	John C. Breckinridge	Democratic	72	Joseph Lane	Democratic	72
	John Bell	Const. Union	39	Edward Everett	Const. Union	39
	Stephen A. Douglas	Democratic	12	H. V. Johnson	Democratic	12
1864	Abraham Lincoln[9]	Union[10]	212	Andrew Johnson	Union[15]	212
	George B. McClellan	Democratic	21	G. H. Pendleton	Democratic	21
1868	Ulysses S. Grant	Republican	214	Schuyler Colfax	Republican	214
	Horatio Seymour	Democratic	80	Francis P. Blair, Jr.	Democratic	80
	Votes not counted[11]		23	Votes not counted[11]		23

Year	Presidential candidates	Party	Electoral vote	Popular vote	Vice-presidential candidates and party
1872	Ulysses S. Grant	Republican	286	3,597,132	Henry Wilson—R
	Horace Greeley	Dem., Liberal Rep.	([12])	2,834,125	B. Gratz Brown—D, LR—(47)
	Thomas A. Hendricks	Democratic	42		Scattering—(19)
	B. Gratz Brown	Dem., Liberal Rep.	18		Votes not counted—(14)
	Charles J. Jenkins	Democratic	2		
	David Davis	Democratic	1		
	Votes not counted		17		
1876[13]	Rutherford B. Hayes	Republican	185	4,033,768	William A. Wheeler—R
	Samuel J. Tilden	Democratic	184	4,285,992	Thomas A. Hendricks—D
	Peter Cooper	Greenback	0	81,737	Samuel F. Cary—G
1880	James A. Garfield[14]	Republican	214	4,449,053	Chester A. Arthur—R
	Winfield S. Hancock	Democratic	155	4,442,035	William H. English—D
	James B. Weaver	Greenback	0	308,578	B. J. Chambers—G
1884	Grover Cleveland	Democratic	219	4,911,017	Thomas A. Hendricks—D
	James G. Blaine	Republican	182	4,848,334	John A. Logan—R
	Benjamin F. Butler	Greenback	0	175,370	A. M. West—G
	John P. St. John	Prohibition	0	150,369	William Daniel—P
1888	Benjamin Harrison	Republican	233	5,440,216	Levi P. Morton—R
	Grover Cleveland	Democratic	168	5,538,233	A. G. Thurman—D
	Clinton B. Fisk	Prohibition	0	249,506	John A. Brooks—P
	Alson J. Streeter	Union Labor	0	146,935	Charles E. Cunningham—UL
1892	Grover Cleveland	Democratic	277	5,556,918	Adlai E. Stevenson—D
	Benjamin Harrison	Republican	145	5,176,108	Whitelaw Reid—R
	James B. Weaver	People's[15]	22	1,041,028	James G. Field—Peo
	John Bidwell	Prohibition	0	264,133	James B. Cranfill—P

Year	Presidential candidates	Party	Electoral vote	Popular vote	Vice-presidential candidates and party
1896	William McKinley	Republican	271	7,035,638	Garret A. Hobart—R
	William J. Bryan	Dem., People's[15]	176	6,467,946	Arthur Sewall—D—(149)
					Thomas E. Watson—Peo—(27)
	John M. Palmer	Natl. Dem.	0	133,148	Simon B. Buckner—ND
	Joshua Levering	Prohibition	0	132,007	Hale Johnson—P
1900	William McKinley[16]	Republican	292	7,219,530	Theodore Roosevelt—R
	William J. Bryan	Dem., People's[15]	155	6,358,071	Adlai E. Stevenson—D, Peo
	Eugene V. Debs	Social Democratic	0	94,768	Job Harriman—SD
1904	Theodore Roosevelt	Republican	336	7,628,834	Charles W. Fairbanks—R
	Alton B. Parker	Democratic	140	5,084,491	Henry G. Davis—D
	Eugene V. Debs	Socialist	0	402,400	Benjamin Hanford—S
1908	William H. Taft	Republican	321	7,679,006	James S. Sherman—R
	William J. Bryan	Democratic	162	6,409,106	John W. Kern—D
	Eugene V. Debs	Socialist	0	402,820	Benjamin Hanford—S
1912	Woodrow Wilson	Democratic	435	6,286,214	Thomas R. Marshall—D
	Theodore Roosevelt	Progressive	88	4,126,020	Hiram Johnson—Prog
	William H. Taft	Republican	8	3,483,922	Nicholas M. Butler—R[17]
	Eugene V. Debs	Socialist	0	897,011	Emil Seidel—S
1916	Woodrow Wilson	Democratic	277	9,129,606	Thomas R. Marshall—D
	Charles E. Hughes	Republican	254	8,538,221	Charles W. Fairbanks—R
	A. L. Benson	Socialist	0	585,113	G. R. Kirkpatrick—S
1920	Warren G. Harding[18]	Republican	404	16,152,200	Calvin Coolidge—R
	James M. Cox	Democratic	127	9,147,353	Franklin D. Roosevelt—D
	Eugene V. Debs	Socialist	0	917,799	Seymour Stedman—S
1924	Calvin Coolidge	Republican	382	15,725,016	Charles G. Dawes—R
	John W. Davis	Democratic	136	8,385,586	Charles W. Bryan—D
	Robert M. LaFollette	Progressive, Socialist	13	4,822,856	Burton K. Wheeler—Prog S
1928	Herbert Hoover	Republican	444	21,392,190	Charles Curtis—R
	Alfred E. Smith	Democratic	87	15,016,443	Joseph T. Robinson—D
	Norman Thomas	Socialist	0	267,420	James H. Maurer—S
1932	Franklin D. Roosevelt	Democratic	472	22,821,857	John N. Garner—D
	Herbert Hoover	Republican	59	15,761,841	Charles Curtis—R
	Norman Thomas	Socialist	0	884,781	James H. Maurer—S
1936	Franklin D. Roosevelt	Democratic	523	27,751,597	John N. Garner—D
	Alfred M. Landon	Republican	8	16,679,583	Frank Knox—R
	Norman Thomas	Socialist	0	187,720	George Nelson—S
1940	Franklin D. Roosevelt	Democratic	449	27,244,160	Henry A. Wallace—D
	Wendell L. Willkie	Republican	82	22,305,198	Charles L. McNary—R
	Norman Thomas	Socialist	0	99,557	Maynard C. Krueger—S
1944	Franklin D. Roosevelt[19]	Democratic	432	25,602,504	Harry S. Truman—D
	Thomas E. Dewey	Republican	99	22,006,285	John W. Bricker—R
	Norman Thomas	Socialist	0	80,518	Darlington Hoopes—S
1948	Harry S. Truman	Democratic	303	24,179,345	Alben W. Barkley—D
	Thomas E. Dewey	Republican	189	21,991,291	Earl Warren—R
	J. Strom Thurmond	States' Rights Dem.	39	1,176,125	Fielding L. Wright—SR
	Henry A. Wallace	Progressive	0	1,157,326	Glen Taylor—Prog
	Norman Thomas	Socialist	0	139,572	Tucker P. Smith—S
1952	Dwight D. Eisenhower	Republican	442	33,936,234	Richard M. Nixon—R
	Adlai E. Stevenson	Democratic	89	27,314,992	John J. Sparkman—D
1956[20]	Dwight D. Eisenhower	Republican	457	35,590,472	Richard M. Nixon—R
	Adlai E. Stevenson	Democratic	73	26,022,752	Estes Kefauver—D
1960	John F. Kennedy[22]	Democratic	303	34,226,731	Lyndon B. Johnson—D
	Richard M. Nixon	Republican	219	34,108,157	Henry Cabot Lodge—R

Year	Presidential candidates	Party	Electoral vote	Popular vote	Vice-presidential candidates and party
1964	Lyndon B. Johnson	Democratic	486	43,129,484	Hubert H. Humphrey—D
	Barry M. Goldwater	Republican	52	27,178,188	William E. Miller—R
1968	Richard M. Nixon	Republican	301	31,785,480	Spiro T. Agnew—R
	Hubert H. Humphrey	Democratic	191	31,275,166	Edmund S. Muskie—D
	George C. Wallace	American Independent	46	9,906,473	Curtis F. LeMay—AI
1972	Richard M. Nixon[23]	Republican	520[24]	47,169,911	Spiro T. Agnew—R
	George McGovern	Democratic	17	29,170,383	Sargent Shriver—D
	John G. Schmitz	American	0	1,099,482	Thomas J. Anderson—A
1976	Jimmy Carter	Democratic	297	40,830,763	Walter F. Mondale—D
	Gerald R. Ford	Republican	240[25]	39,147,973	Robert J. Dole—R
	Eugene J. McCarthy	Independent	0	756,631	None

1. Only 10 states participated in the election. The New York legislature chose no electors, and North Carolina and Rhode Island had not yet ratified the Constitution. 2. As Jefferson and Burr were tied, the House of Representatives chose the President. In a vote by states, 10 votes were cast for Jefferson, 4 for Burr; 2 votes were not cast. 3. As no candidate had an electoral-vote majority, the House of Representatives chose the President from the first three. In a vote by states, 13 votes were cast for Adams, 7 for Jackson, and 4 for Crawford. 4. The Antimasonic Party on Sept. 26, 1831, was the first party to hold a nominating convention to choose candidates for President and Vice-President. 5. As Johnson did not have an electoral-vote majority, the Senate chose him 33–14 over Granger, the others being legally out of the race. 6. Harrison died April 4, 1841, and Tyler succeeded him April 6. 7. Taylor died July 9, 1850, and Fillmore succeeded him July 10. 8. Also known as the Know-Nothing Party. 9. Lincoln died April 15, 1865, and Johnson succeeded him the same day. 10. Name adopted by the Republican National Convention of 1864. Johnson was a War Democrat. 11. 23 Southern electoral votes were excluded. 12. See Election of 1872 in *Unusual Voting Results* under Elections, Presidential, in Index. 13. See Election of 1876 in *Unusual Voting Results* under Elections, Presidential, in Index. 14. Garfield died Sept. 19, 1881, and Arthur succeeded him Sept. 20. 15. Members of People's Party were called Populists. 16. McKinley died Sept. 14, 1901, and Roosevelt succeeded him the same day. 17. James S. Sherman, Republican candidate for Vice President, died Oct. 30, 1912, and the Republican electoral votes were cast for Butler. 18. Harding died Aug. 2, 1923, and Coolidge succeeded him Aug. 3. 19. Roosevelt died April 12, 1945, and Truman succeeded him the same day. 20. One electoral vote from Alabama was cast for Walter B. Jones. 21. Sen. Harry F. Byrd received 15 electoral votes. 22. Kennedy died Nov. 22, 1963, and Johnson succeeded him the same day. 23. Nixon resigned Aug. 9, 1974, and Gerald R. Ford succeeded him the same day. 24. One electoral vote from Virginia was cast for John Hospers, Libertarian Party. 25. One electoral vote from Washington was cast for Ronald Reagan.

Estimated Population of Voting Age, 1976

(in thousands)

	18–24 years	25–44 years	45–64 years	65 years and over	Total
Alabama	470	922	720	390	2,501
Alaska	65	104	52	9	231
Arizona	301	575	441	238	1,555
Arkansas	257	534	434	278	1,503
Calif.	2,918	5,856	4,400	2,119	15,294
Colorado	380	711	467	215	1,773
Conn.	388	814	682	328	2,211
Delaware	84	153	115	52	403
D.C.	102	202	139	71	514
Florida	1,020	2,008	1,861	1,436	6,326
Georgia	672	1,343	914	445	3,375
Hawaii	142	230	168	61	600
Idaho	110	210	165	82	567
Illinois	1,427	2,845	2,282	1,163	7,718
Indiana	695	1,368	1,038	538	3,640
Iowa	355	707	582	366	2,010
Kansas	307	561	455	287	1,610
Kentucky	445	875	679	375	2,374
Louisiana	522	958	697	355	2,532
Maine	132	263	218	128	741
Maryland	563	1,121	831	348	2,863
Mass.	771	1,498	1,225	679	4,173
Michigan	1,260	2,385	1,795	828	6,268
Minnesota	534	1,011	730	446	2,721
Miss.	308	557	420	260	1,544
Missouri	607	1,190	943	608	3,348
Montana	98	188	156	76	518
Nebraska	204	380	300	196	1,080
Nevada	78	169	130	48	424
N.H.	101	223	161	89	574
N.J.	853	1,862	1,657	783	5,154
N.M.	166	294	216	95	771
New York	2,175	4,709	3,982	2,043	12,910
N.C.	764	1,480	1,091	512	3,847
N.D.	86	147	125	74	432
Ohio	1,417	2,769	2,195	1,078	7,459
Oklahoma	348	697	553	340	1,937
Oregon	295	613	478	266	1,653
Pa.	1,430	2,897	2,714	1,400	8,441
R.I.	112	220	201	115	648
S.C.	411	750	533	239	1,933
S.D.	91	154	138	86	469
Tenn.	532	1,122	850	455	2,958
Texas	1,702	3,257	2,349	1,195	8,503
Utah	190	299	200	94	783
Vermont	61	127	86	53	327
Virginia	738	1,356	998	436	3,528
Wash.	485	975	700	375	2,536
W.Va.	209	452	406	214	1,281
Wis.	617	1,163	911	519	3,211
Wyoming	53	99	80	34	266
Total	**28,055**	**55,403**	**43,664**	**22,918**	**150,041**

NOTE: Resident population; includes aliens. *Source:* Department of Commerce, Bureau of the Census.

Percent Popular Vote Cast for President and Congress by Party

(Dem.=Democratic Party, Rep.=Republican Party. Excludes minor parties and independents.)

	Percent vote cast for—						Party Composition (seats held)[1]			
	President		House of Representatives		Senate		House of Representatives		Senate	
Year and region	Dem.	Rep.	Dem.	Rep.	Dem.	Rep.	Dem.	Rep.	Dem.	Rep.
1960, U.S	49.7	49.5	54.8	44.8	54.6	44.8	263	174	65	35
Northeast	52.7	47.1	52.3	46.8	44.5	54.9	56	59	7	11
North Central	47.6	52.2	49.5	50.4	52.1	47.6	51	78	12	12
South	49.9	47.6	71.0	28.2	64.9	33.7	123	11	26	6
West	48.5	51.1	52.2	47.8	51.5	48.2	33	26	20	6
1964, U.S	61.1	38.5	57.2	42.3	56.3	42.9	295	140	68	32
Northeast	68.3	31.5	57.7	41.5	55.7	42.8	70	38	10	8
North Central	61.3	38.5	53.8	46.1	56.8	43.0	66	59	15	9
South	53.3	45.3	64.8	34.0	60.6	37.7	112	21	26	6
West	59.4	40.4	53.6	46.4	52.3	47.7	47	22	17	9
1968, U.S	42.7	43.4	50.0	48.2	49.2	47.5	243	192	57	43
Northeast	50.2	43.0	48.4	46.7	39.2	50.9	64	44	8	10
North Central	43.7	46.8	45.8	54.1	49.5	50.2	46	79	13	11
South	33.5	36.5	60.9	37.9	57.2	40.4	97	36	22	10
West	43.7	48.7	45.7	53.2	52.5	46.4	36	33	14	12
1972, U.S	37.5	60.7	51.7	46.5	45.4	52.5	239	192	56	42
Northeast	41.5	57.6	48.8	47.0	37.1	60.7	57	46	8	9
North Central	39.4	59.1	48.2	50.9	44.0	55.0	50	70	15	9
South	30.4	68.2	58.5	40.4	49.5	47.4	91	42	18	13
West	39.1	57.2	53.0	45.8	46.1	52.9	41	34	15	11
1976, U.S	50.1	48.0	56.2	42.1	54.4	43.8	292	143	61	38
Northeast	50.9	47.5	56.3	41.8	54.2	44.7	73	31	10	8
North Central	48.3	49.7	52.3	46.7	53.3	44.5	68	53	16	8
South	54.0	44.8	61.9	36.2	59.0	39.5	100	34	22	9
West	45.7	51.0	54.7	43.0	51.2	45.9	51	25	13	13

1. For beginning of the first session of Congress following the year shown. Excludes vacant seats. *Source:* Compiled by U.S. Bureau of the Census from Elections Research Center, Washington, D.C., *America Votes,* biennial (copyright); and U.S. Congress, Joint Committee on Printing, *Congressional Directory,* annual.

Qualifications for Voting

The Supreme Court decision of March 21, 1972, declared lengthy requirements for voting in state and local elections unconstitutional and suggested that 30 days was an ample period. Most of the states have changed or eliminated their durational residency requirements to comply with the ruling, as shown.

NO DURATIONAL RESIDENCY REQUIREMENT

Alabama, Arkansas, California, Connecticut,[14] Delaware,[13] District of Columbia,[2] Georgia,[2] Hawaii, Idaho, Iowa,[6] Louisiana,[2] Maine, Maryland, Massachusetts,[8] Nebraska,[9] New Hampshire, New Mexico,[7] North Carolina, Oklahoma, South Carolina,[2] South Dakota,[10] Tennessee,[12] Texas, Virginia, West Virginia,[2] Wyoming[2]

30-DAY RESIDENCY REQUIREMENT

Alaska, Arizona,[11] Florida,[5] Illinois, Indiana, Kentucky,[2] Michigan, Mississippi, Montana, Nevada, New Jersey, New York, North Dakota,[3] Ohio, Pennsylvania, Rhode Island, Utah, Washington

OTHER

Colorado,[1] Kansas, Minnesota, Oregon, 20 days; Missouri,[4] 6 months; Vermont, 17 days;[15] Wisconsin, 10 days

1. 29-day for Presidential elections, 32 for all other. 2. 30-day registration requirement. 3. 10-day for Presidential elections. 4. 28 days in St. Louis County, 4th Wednesday prior to elections in rest of state. 5. For Presidential elections, 45-day for all other. 6. 10-day registration requirement. 7. 42-day registration requirement. 8. Registration deadline 28 days prior to primary or state elections. 9. Registration requirement, 2nd Friday prior to elections. 10. 15-day registration requirement. 11. 50-day for state. 12. 20-day registration requirement. 13. Must reside in Delaware and register by the last day that the books are open for registration. 14. 21-day registration requirement for elections; 14-day for primaries. 15. Administrative cut-off date for processing applications. *Source: Information Please* questionnaires to the states.

Plurality and Majority

In order to win a plurality, a candidate must receive a greater number of votes than anyone running against him. If he receives 50 votes, for example, and two other candidates receive 49 and 2, he will have a plurality of one vote over his closest opponent.

However, a candidate does not have a majority unless he receives more than 50% of the total votes cast. In the example above, the candidate does not have a majority, because his 50 votes are less than 50% of the 101 votes cast.

Presidential Election of 1968

Principal Candidates for President and Vice President
Republican: Richard M. Nixon; Spiro T. Agnew
Democratic: Hubert H. Humphrey; Edmund S. Muskie
American Independent Party: George C. Wallace; Curtis E. LeMay

		Nixon	Humphrey	Wallace		Electoral Vote			Votes at Natl. Convs.	
State	**Total**	**Rep.**	**Dem.**	**Am. Ind.**	**Plurality**	**R**	**D**	**A**	**Dem.**	**Rep.**
Alabama	1,049,922	146,923	196,579[1]	691,425[2]	494,846 A	—	—	10	32	26
Alaska	83,035	37,600	35,411	10,024	2,189 R	3	—	—	22	12
Arizona	486,936	266,721	170,514	46,573	96,207 R	5	—	—	19	16
Arkansas	619,969	190,759	188,228	240,982	50,223 A	—	—	6	33	18
California	7,251,587	3,467,664	3,244,318	487,270	223,346 R	40	—	—	174	86
Colorado	811,199	409,345	335,174	60,813	74,171 R	6	—	—	35	18
Connecticut	1,256,232	556,721	621,561	76,650	64,840 D	—	8	—	44	16
Delaware	214,367	96,714	89,194	28,459	7,520 R	3	—	—	22	12
D.C.	170,578	31,012	139,566	—	108,554 D	—	3	—	23	9
Florida	2,187,805	886,804	676,794	624,207	210,010 R	14	—	—	63	34
Georgia	1,250,266	380,111	334,440	535,550	155,439 A	—	—	12	43	30
Hawaii	236,218	91,425	141,324	3,469	49,899 D	—	4	—	26	14
Idaho	291,183	165,369	89,273	36,541	76,096 R	4	—	—	25	14
Illinois	4,619,749	2,174,774	2,039,814	390,958	134,960 R	26	—	—	118	58
Indiana	2,123,597	1,067,885	806,659	243,108	261,226 R	13	—	—	63	26
Iowa	1,167,931	619,106	476,699	66,422	142,407 R	9	—	—	46	24
Kansas	872,783	478,674	302,996	88,921	175,678 R	7	—	—	38	20
Kentucky	1,055,893	462,411	397,541	193,098	64,870 R	9	—	—	46	24
Louisiana	1,097,450	257,535	309,615	530,300	220,685 A	—	—	10	36	26
Maine	392,936	169,254	217,312	6,370	48,058 D	—	4	—	27	14
Maryland	1,235,039	517,995	538,310	178,734	20,315 D	—	10	—	49	26
Massachusetts	2,331,752	766,844	1,469,218	87,088	702,374 D	—	14	—	72	34
Michigan	3,306,250	1,370,665	1,593,082	331,968	222,417 D	—	21	—	96	48
Minnesota	1,588,506	658,643	857,738	68,931	199,095 D	—	10	—	52	26
Mississippi	654,509	88,516	150,644	415,349	264,705 A	—	—	7	24	20
Missouri	1,809,502	811,932	791,444	206,126	20,488 R	12	—	—	60	24
Montana	274,404	138,835	114,117	20,015	24,718 R	4	—	—	26	14
Nebraska	536,851	321,163	170,784	44,904	150,379 R	5	—	—	30	16
Nevada	154,218	73,188	60,598	20,432	12,590 R	3	—	—	22	12
New Hampshire	297,298	154,903	130,589	11,173	24,314 R	4	—	—	26	8
New Jersey	2,875,395	1,325,467	1,264,206	262,187	61,261 R	17	—	—	82	40
New Mexico	327,350	169,692	130,081	25,737	39,611 R	4	—	—	26	14
New York	6,791,688	3,007,932	3,378,470[3]	358,864	370,538 D	—	43	—	190	92
North Carolina	1,587,493	627,192	464,113	496,188	131,004 R	12	—	1	59	26
North Dakota	247,882	138,669	94,769	14,244	43,900 R	4	—	—	25	8
Ohio	3,959,698	1,791,014	1,700,586	467,495	90,428 R	26	—	—	115	58
Oklahoma	943,086	449,697	301,658	191,731	148,039 R	8	—	—	41	22
Oregon	819,622	408,433	358,866	49,683	49,567 R	6	—	—	35	18
Pennsylvania	4,747,928	2,090,017	2,259,405	378,582	169,388 D	—	29	—	130	64
Rhode Island	385,000	122,359	246,518	15,678	124,159 D	—	4	—	27	14
South Carolina	666,978	254,062	197,486	215,430	38,632 R	8	—	—	28	22
South Dakota	281,264	149,841	118,023	13,400	31,818 R	4	—	—	26	14
Tennessee	1,248,617	472,592	351,233	424,792	47,800 R	11	—	—	51	28
Texas	3,079,406	1,227,844	1,266,804	584,269	38,960 D	—	25	—	104	56
Utah	422,568	238,728	156,665	26,906	82,063 R	4	—	—	26	8
Vermont	161,404	85,142	70,255	5,104	14,887 R	3	—	—	22	12
Virginia	1,361,491	590,319	442,387	321,833	147,932 R	12	—	—	54	24
Washington	1,304,281	588,510	616,037	96,990	27,527 D	—	9	—	47	24
West Virginia	754,206	307,555	374,091	72,560	66,536 D	—	7	—	38	14
Wisconsin	1,691,538	809,997	748,804	127,835	61,193 R	12	—	—	59	30
Wyoming	127,205	70,927	45,173	11,105	25,754 R	3	—	—	22	12
Total	**73,212,065**	**31,785,480**	**31,275,166**	**9,906,473**	**510,314 R**	**301**	**191**	**46**	**2,622[4]**	**1,333[5]**

1. This vote, cast for Humphrey, is a combination of National Democratic (54,144) and Independent Democratic (142,435). 2. This vote for Wallace was cast as Democratic in Alabama. 3. Contains 3,066,848 Democratic and 311,622 Liberal votes. 4. Includes 23 votes allocated to U.S. territories. 5. Includes 8 votes allocated to U.S. territories.
OTHER CANDIDATES FOR PRESIDENT: New Party, Dick Gregory; Peace and Freedom Party, Eldridge Cleaver; Prohibition Party, E. Harold Munn; Socialist Labor Party, Hennings Blomen; Socialist Workers Party, Fred Halstead.
NATIONAL TOTAL OF OTHER VOTES: 244,946, from 30 states.
Source: America Votes, compiled and edited by Richard M. Scammon.

Presidential Election of 1972

Principal Candidates for President and Vice President
Republican: Richard M. Nixon; Spiro T. Agnew
Democratic: George McGovern; Sargent Shriver
American Party[1]: John G. Schmitz; Thomas J. Anderson

		Nixon	McGovern	Schmitz		Electoral vote			Votes at Natl. Convs.	
State	Total	Republican	Democratic	American	Plurality	R	D	A	Dem.	Rep.
Alabama	1,006,111	728,701	256,923	11,928	471,778 R	9	—	—	37	17
Alaska	95,219	55,349	32,967	6,903	22,382 R	3	—	—	10	12
Arizona	622,926	402,812	198,540	21,208	204,272 R	6	—	—	25	18
Arkansas	651,320	448,541	199,892	2,887	248,649 R	6	—	—	27	18
California	8,367,862	4,602,096	3,475,847	232,554	1,126,249 R	45	—	—	271	96
Colorado	953,884	597,189	329,980	17,269	267,209 R	7	—	—	36	20
Connecticut	1,384,277	810,763	555,498	17,239	255,265 R	8	—	—	51	22
Delaware	235,516	140,357	92,283	2,638	48,074 R	3	—	—	13	12
D.C.	163,421	35,226	127,627	—	92,401 D	—	3	—	15	9
Florida	2,583,283	1,857,759	718,117	—	1,139,642 R	17	—	—	81	40
Georgia	1,174,772	881,496	289,529	812	591,967 R	12	—	—	53	24
Hawaii	270,274	168,865	101,409	—	67,456 R	4	—	—	17	14
Idaho	310,379	199,384	80,826	28,869	118,558 R	4	—	—	17	14
Illinois	4,723,236	2,788,179	1,913,472	2,471	874,707 R	26	—	—	170	58
Indiana	2,125,529	1,405,154	708,568	—	696,586 R	13	—	—	76	32
Iowa	1,225,944	706,207	496,206	22,056	210,001 R	8	—	—	46	20
Kansas	916,095	619,812	270,287	21,808	349,525 R	7	—	—	35	24
Kentucky	1,067,499	676,446	371,159	17,627	305,287 R	9	—	—	47	20
Louisiana	1,051,491	686,852	298,142	52,099	388,710 R	10	—	—	44	8
Maine	417,042	256,458	160,584	—	95,874 R	4	—	—	20	26
Maryland	1,353,812	829,305	505,781	18,726	323,524 R	10	—	—	53	34
Massachusetts	2,458,756	1,112,078	1,332,540	2,877	220,462 D	—	14	—	102	48
Michigan	3,489,727	1,961,721	1,459,435	63,321	502,286 R	21	—	—	132	26
Minnesota	1,741,652	898,269	802,346	31,407	95,923 R	10	—	—	64	26
Mississippi	645,963	505,125	126,782	11,598	378,343 R	7	—	—	25	13
Missouri	1,855,803	1,153,852	697,147	—	456,705 R	12	—	—	73	30
Montana	317,603	183,976	120,197	13,430	63,779 R	4	—	—	17	14
Nebraska	576,289	406,298	169,991	—	236,307 R	5	—	—	24	16
Nevada	181,766	115,750	66,016	—	49,734 R	3	—	—	11	12
New Hampshire	334,055	213,724	116,435	3,386	97,289 R	4	—	—	18	14
New Jersey	2,997,229	1,845,502	1,102,211	34,378	743,291 R	17	—	—	109	40
New Mexico	386,241	235,606	141,084	8,767	94,522 R	4	—	—	18	14
New York	7,165,919	4,192,778	2,951,084	—	1,241,694 R	41	—	—	278	88
North Carolina	1,518,612	1,054,889	438,705	25,018	616,184 R	13	—	—	64	32
North Dakota	280,514	174,109	100,384	5,646	73,725 R	3	—	—	14	12
Ohio	4,094,787	2,441,827	1,558,889	80,067	882,938 R	25	—	—	153	56
Oklahoma	1,029,900	759,025	247,147	23,728	511,878 R	8	—	—	39	22
Oregon	927,946	486,686	392,760	46,211	93,926 R	6	—	—	34	18
Pennsylvania	4,592,106	2,714,521	1,796,951	70,593	917,570 R	27	—	—	182	60
Rhode Island	415,808	220,383	194,645	25	25,738 R	4	—	—	22	8
South Carolina	673,960	477,044	186,824	10,075	290,220 R	8	—	—	32	22
South Dakota	307,415	166,476	139,945	—	26,531 R	4	—	—	17	14
Tennessee	1,201,182	813,147	357,293	30,373	455,854 R	10	—	—	49	26
Texas	3,471,281	2,298,896	1,154,289	6,039	1,144,607 R	26	—	—	130	52
Utah	478,476	323,643	126,284	28,549	197,359 R	4	—	—	19	14
Vermont	186,947	117,149	68,174	—	48,975 R	3	—	—	12	12
Virginia	1,457,019	988,493	438,887	19,721	549,606 R	11[2]	—	—	53	30
Washington	1,470,847	837,135	568,334	58,906	268,801 R	9	—	—	52	24
West Virginia	762,399	484,964	277,435	—	207,529 R	6	—	—	35	18
Wisconsin	1,852,890	989,430	810,174	47,525	179,256 R	11	—	—	67	18
Wyoming	145,570	100,464	44,358	748	56,106 R	3	—	—	11	12
Total	**77,718,554**	**47,169,911**	**29,170,383**	**1,099,482**	**17,999,528 R**	**520**	**17**	**0**	**3,016[3]**	**1,346[4]**

1. Known as American Independent Party and by other names in some states. 2. One Virginia elector cast vote for Libertarian Party. 3. Includes 16 votes allocated to U.S. territories. 4. Includes 11 votes allocated to U.S. territories.
OTHER CANDIDATES FOR PRESIDENT: Communist, Gus Hall, Libertarian Party, John Hospers; People's Party, Benjamin Spock; Prohibition Party, Earle H. Munn; Socialist Labor Party, Louis Fisher; Socialist Workers Party, Linda Jenness.
NATIONAL TOTALS OF OTHER VOTES: People's, 78,756; Social Workers, 66,677; Socialist Labor, 53,814; Communist, 25,595; Prohibition, 13,505; others and scattered, 40,431.
Source: America Votes 10, compiled and edited by Richard M. Scammon.

Presidential Election of 1976

Principal Candidates for President and Vice President
Democratic: Jimmy Carter; Walter F. Mondale
Republican: Gerald R. Ford; Robert J. Dole
Independent: Eugene J. McCarthy

		Carter	Ford	McCarthy		Electoral vote		Votes at Natl. Convs.	
State	**Total**	**Dem.**	**Rep.**	**Ind.**	**Plurality**	**D**	**R**	**Dem.**	**Rep.**
Alabama	1,182,850	659,170	504,070	99	155,100 D	9	—	35	37
Alaska	123,574	44,058	71,555	—	27,497 R	—	3	10	19
Arizona	742,719	295,602	418,642	19,229	123,040 R	—	6	25	29
Arkansas	767,535	498,604	267,903	639	230,701 D	6	—	26	27
California	7,867,117	3,742,284	3,882,244	58,412	139,960 R	—	45	280	167
Colorado	1,081,554	460,801	584,278	26,047	123,477 R	—	7	35	31
Connecticut	1,381,526	647,895	719,261	3,759	71,366 R	—	8	51	35
Delaware	235,834	122,596	109,831	2,437	12,765 D	3	—	12	17
D.C.	168,830	137,818	27,873	—	109,945 D	3	—	17	14
Florida	3,150,631	1,636,000	1,469,531	23,643	166,469 D	17	—	81	66
Georgia	1,467,458	979,409	483,743	991	495,666 D	12	—	50	48
Hawaii	291,301	147,375	140,003	—	7,372 D	4	—	17	19
Idaho	344,071	126,549	204,151	1,194	77,602 R	—	4	16	21
Illinois	4,718,914	2,271,295	2,364,269	55,939	92,974 R	—	26	169	101
Indiana	2,220,362	1,014,714	1,183,958	—	169,244 R	—	13	75	54
Iowa	1,279,306	619,931	632,863	20,051	12,932 R	—	8	47	36
Kansas	957,845	430,421	502,752	13,185	72,331 R	—	7	34	34
Kentucky	1,167,142	615,717	531,852	6,837	83,865 D	9	—	46	37
Louisiana	1,278,439	661,365	587,446	6,588	73,919 D	10	—	41	41
Maine	483,216	232,279	236,320	10,874	4,041 R	—	4	20	20
Maryland	1,439,897	759,612	672,661	4,541	86,951 D	10	—	53	43
Massachusetts	2,547,558	1,429,475	1,030,276	65,637	399,199 D	14	—	104	43
Michigan	3,653,749	1,696,714	1,893,742	47,905	197,028 R	—	21	133	84
Minnesota	1,949,931	1,070,440	819,395	35,490	251,045 D	10	—	65	42
Mississippi	769,361	381,309	366,846	4,074	14,463 D	7	—	24	30
Missouri	1,953,600	998,387	927,443	24,029	70,944 D	12	—	71	49
Montana	328,734	149,259	173,703	—	24,444 R	—	4	17	20
Nebraska	607,668	233,293	359,219	9,409	125,926 R	—	5	23	25
Nevada	201,876	92,479	101,273	—	8,794 R	—	3	11	18
New Hampshire	339,618	147,645	185,935	4,095	38,290 R	—	4	17	21
New Jersey	3,014,472	1,444,653	1,509,688	32,717	65,035 R	—	17	108	67
New Mexico	418,409	201,148	211,419	1,161	10,271 R	—	4	18	21
New York	6,534,170	3,389,558	3,100,791	4,303	288,767 D	41	—	274	154
North Carolina	1,678,914	927,365	741,960	780	185,405 D	13	—	61	54
North Dakota	297,188	136,078	153,470	2,952	17,392 R	—	3	13	18
Ohio	4,111,873	2,011,621	2,000,505	58,258	11,116 D	25	—	152	97
Oklahoma	1,092,251	532,442	545,708	14,101	13,266 R	—	8	37	36
Oregon	1,029,876	490,407	492,120	40,207	1,713 R	—	6	34	30
Pennsylvania	4,620,787	2,328,677	2,205,604	50,584	123,073 D	27	—	178	103
Rhode Island	411,170	227,636	181,249	479	46,387 D	4	—	22	19
South Carolina	802,583	450,807	346,149	289	104,658 D	8	—	31	36
South Dakota	300,678	147,068	151,505	—	4,437 R	—	4	17	20
Tennessee	1,476,345	825,879	633,969	5,004	191,910 D	10	—	46	43
Texas	4,071,884	2,082,319	1,953,300	20,118	129,019 D	26	—	130	100
Utah	541,198	182,110	337,908	3,907	155,798 R	—	4	18	20
Vermont	187,765	78,789	100,387	4,001	21,598 R	—	3	12	18
Virginia	1,697,094	813,896	836,554	—	22,658 R	—	12	54	51
Washington	1,555,534	717,323	777,732	36,986	60,409 R	—	8[1]	53	38
West Virginia	750,964	435,914	314,760	113	121,154 D	6	—	33	28
Wisconsin	2,104,175	1,040,232	1,004,987	34,943	35,245 D	11	—	68	45
Wyoming	156,343	62,239	92,717	624	30,478 R	—	3	10	17
Total	**81,555,889**	**40,830,763**	**39,147,793**	**756,631**	**1,682,970D**	**297**	**240**	**3,008[2]**	**2,259[3]**

1. Ninth Washington elector cast vote for Ronald Reagan. 2. Includes 34 votes allocated to U.S. territories and Democrats abroad. 3. Includes 16 votes allocated to U.S. territories.

OTHER CANDIDATES FOR PRESIDENT: Roger L. MacBride, Libertarian; Lester G. Maddox, American Independent; Thomas J. Anderson, American; Peter Camejo, Socialist Workers; Gus Hall, Communist; Margaret Wright, People's; Lyndon LaRouche, United States Labor; Benjamin C. Bubar, Prohibition; Julius Levin, Socialist Labor; Frank P. Zeidler, Socialist.

NATIONAL TOTALS OF OTHER VOTES: Libertarian, 173,011; American Independent, 170,531; American, 160,773; Socialist Workers, 91,314; Communist, 58,992; People's, 49,024; United States Labor, 40,043; Prohibition, 15,934; Socialist Labor, 9,616; Socialist, 6,038; others and scattered, 45,366.

Source: America Votes 12, compiled and edited by Richard M. Scammon and Alice V. McGillivray.

Electoral Vote for President

(For electoral votes by state from 1968 to 1976, see pages 620–22)

States	1964 Johnson, Dem.	1964 Goldwater, Rep.	1960 Kennedy, Dem.	1960 Nixon, Rep.	1956 Eisenhower, Rep.	1956 Stevenson, Dem.	1952 Eisenhower, Rep.	1952 Stevenson, Dem.	1948 Truman, Dem.	1948 Dewey, Rep.	1948 Thurmond, Sts. Rgts.	1944 Roosevelt, Dem.	1944 Dewey, Rep.	1940 Roosevelt, Dem.	1940 Wilkie, Rep.	1936 Roosevelt, Dem.	1936 Landon, Rep.	1932 Roosevelt, Dem.	1932 Hoover, Rep.	1928 Hoover, Rep.	1928 Smith, Dem.
Alabama	—	10	5	—	—	10	—	11	—	—	11	11	—	11	—	11	—	11	—	—	12
Alaska	3	—	—	3	—	—	—	—	—	—	—	—	—	—	—	—	—	—	—	—	—
Arizona	—	5	—	4	4	—	4	—	4	—	—	4	—	3	—	3	—	3	—	3	—
Arkansas	6	—	8	—	—	8	—	8	9	—	—	9	—	9	—	9	—	9	—	—	9
California	40	—	—	32	32	—	32	—	25	—	—	25	—	22	—	22	—	22	—	13	—
Colorado	6	—	—	6	6	—	6	—	6	—	—	—	6	—	6	6	—	6	—	6	—
Connecticut	8	—	8	—	8	—	8	—	—	8	—	8	—	8	—	8	—	—	8	7	—
Delaware	3	—	3	—	3	—	3	—	—	3	—	3	—	3	—	3	—	—	3	3	—
Florida	14	—	—	10	10	—	10	—	8	—	8	—	—	7	—	7	—	7	—	6	—
Georgia	—	12	12	—	—	12	—	12	12	—	—	12	—	12	—	12	—	12	—	—	14
Hawaii	4	—	3	—	—	—	—	—	—	—	—	—	—	—	—	—	—	—	—	—	—
Idaho	4	—	—	4	4	—	4	—	4	—	—	4	—	4	—	4	—	4	—	4	—
Illinois	26	—	27	—	27	—	27	—	28	—	—	28	—	29	—	29	—	29	—	29	—
Indiana	13	—	—	13	13	—	13	—	—	13	—	—	13	—	14	14	—	14	—	15	—
Iowa	9	—	—	10	10	—	10	—	10	—	—	—	10	—	11	11	—	11	—	13	—
Kansas	7	—	—	8	8	—	8	—	—	8	—	—	8	—	9	9	—	9	—	10	—
Kentucky	9	—	—	10	10	—	—	10	11	—	—	11	—	11	—	11	—	11	—	13	—
Louisiana	—	10	10	—	10	—	—	10	—	—	10	10	—	10	—	10	—	10	—	—	10
Maine	4	—	—	5	5	—	5	—	—	5	—	—	5	—	5	—	5	—	5	6	—
Maryland	10	—	9	—	9	—	9	—	—	8	—	8	—	8	—	8	—	8	—	8	—
Massachusetts	14	—	16	—	16	—	16	—	16	—	—	16	—	17	—	17	—	17	—	—	18
Michigan	21	—	20	—	20	—	20	—	—	19	—	19	—	—	19	19	—	19	—	15	—
Minnesota	10	—	11	—	11	—	11	—	11	—	—	11	—	11	—	11	—	11	—	12	—
Mississippi	—	7	—	—	—	8	—	8	—	—	9	9	—	9	—	9	—	9	—	—	10
Missouri	12	—	13	—	—	13	13	—	15	—	—	15	—	15	—	15	—	15	—	18	—
Montana	4	—	—	4	4	—	4	—	4	—	—	4	—	4	—	4	—	4	—	4	—
Nebraska	5	—	—	6	6	—	6	—	—	6	—	—	6	—	7	7	—	7	—	8	—
Nevada	3	—	3	—	3	—	3	—	3	—	—	3	—	3	—	3	—	3	—	3	—
New Hampshire	4	—	—	4	4	—	4	—	—	4	—	4	—	4	—	4	—	—	4	4	—
New Jersey	17	—	16	—	16	—	16	—	—	16	—	16	—	16	—	16	—	16	—	14	—
New Mexico	4	—	4	—	4	—	4	—	4	—	—	4	—	3	—	3	—	3	—	3	—
New York	43	—	45	—	45	—	45	—	—	47	—	47	—	47	—	47	—	47	—	45	—
North Carolina	13	—	14	—	—	14	—	14	14	—	—	14	—	13	—	13	—	13	—	12	—
North Dakota	4	—	—	4	4	—	4	—	—	4	—	—	4	—	4	4	—	4	—	5	—
Ohio	26	—	—	25	25	—	25	—	25	—	—	—	25	26	—	26	—	26	—	24	—
Oklahoma	8	—	—	7	8	—	8	—	10	—	—	10	—	11	—	11	—	11	—	10	—
Oregon	6	—	—	6	6	—	6	—	—	6	—	6	—	5	—	5	—	5	—	5	—
Pennsylvania	29	—	32	—	32	—	32	—	—	35	—	35	—	36	—	36	—	—	36	38	—
Rhode Island	4	—	4	—	4	—	4	—	4	—	—	4	—	4	—	4	—	4	—	—	5
South Carolina	—	8	8	—	—	8	—	8	—	—	8	8	—	8	—	8	—	8	—	—	9
South Dakota	4	—	—	4	4	—	4	—	—	4	—	—	4	—	4	4	—	4	—	5	—
Tennessee	11	—	—	11	11	—	11	—	11	—	1	12	—	11	—	11	—	11	—	12	—
Texas	25	—	24	—	24	—	24	—	23	—	—	23	—	23	—	23	—	23	—	20	—
Utah	4	—	—	4	4	—	4	—	4	—	—	4	—	4	—	4	—	4	—	4	—
Vermont	3	—	—	3	3	—	3	—	—	3	—	—	3	—	3	—	3	—	3	4	—
Virginia	12	—	—	12	12	—	12	—	11	—	—	11	—	11	—	11	—	11	—	12	—
Washington	9	—	—	9	9	—	9	—	8	—	—	8	—	8	—	8	—	8	—	7	—
West Virginia	7	—	8	—	8	—	—	8	8	—	—	8	—	8	—	8	—	8	—	8	—
Wisconsin	12	—	—	12	12	—	12	—	12	—	—	—	12	12	—	12	—	12	—	13	—
Wyoming	3	—	—	3	3	—	3	—	3	—	—	—	3	3	—	3	—	3	—	3	—
Total	486	52	303	219	457	73	442	89	303	189	39	432	99	449	82	523	8	472	59	444	87

Characteristics of Voters in 1976 Presidential Election
(in millions)

Characteristic	Persons of voting age	Persons reporting they voted: Total	Persons reporting they voted: Percent	Persons reporting they did not vote
Male	69.0	41.1	59.6	40.4
Female	77.6	45.6	58.8	41.2
White	129.3	78.8	60.9	39.1
Black	14.9	7.3	48.7	51.3
Spanish origin[1]	6.6	2.1	31.8	68.2
Age: 18–20	12.1	4.6	38.0	62.0
21–24	14.8	6.8	45.6	54.4
25–34	31.5	17.5	55.4	44.6
35–44	22.8	14.4	63.3	36.7
45–64	43.3	29.8	68.7	31.3
65 and over	22.0	13.7	62.2	37.8
Median age	41.5	45.1	—	—
Residence:				
Metropolitan	99.6	58.9	59.2	40.8
Nonmetropolitan	47.0	27.8	59.1	40.9
North and West	99.4	60.8	61.2	38.8
South	47.1	25.9	54.9	45.1
Education:				
8 years or less	24.9	11.0	44.1	55.9
9–11 years	22.2	10.5	47.2	52.8
12 years	55.7	33.1	59.4	40.6
More than 12	43.7	32.2	73.5	26.5
Employed	86.0	53.3	62.0	38.0
Unemployed	6.4	2.8	43.7	56.3
Not in labor force	54.1	30.6	56.5	43.5
Total	**146.5**	**86.7**	**59.2**	**40.8**

1. Persons of Spanish origin may be of any race. *Source:* Department of Commerce, Bureau of the Census.

Unusual Voting Results

Election of 1872

The presidential and vice-presidential candidates of the Liberal Republicans and the northern Democrats in 1872 were Horace Greeley and B. Gratz Brown. Greeley died Nov. 29, 1872, before his 66 electors voted. In the electoral balloting for President, 63 of Greeley's votes were scattered among four other men, including Brown.

Election of 1876

In the election of 1876 Samuel J. Tilden, the Democratic candidate, received a popular majority but lacked one undisputed electoral vote to carry a clear majority of the electoral college. The crux of the problem was in the 22 electoral votes which were in dispute because Florida, Louisiana, South Carolina, and Oregon each sent in two sets of election returns. In the three southern states, Republican election boards threw out enough Democratic votes to certify the Republican candidate, Hayes. In Oregon, the Democratic governor disqualified a Republican elector, replacing him with a Democrat. Since the Senate was Republican and the House of Representatives Democratic, it seemed useless to refer the disputed returns to the two houses for solution. Instead Congress appointed an Electoral Commission with five representatives each from the Senate, the House, and the Supreme Court. All but one Justice was named, giving the Commission seven Republican and seven Democratic members. The naming of the fifth Justice was left to the other four. He was a Republican who first favored Tilden but, under pressure from his party, switched to Hayes, ensuring his election by the Commission voting 8 to 7 on party lines.

Minority Presidents

Fifteen candidates have become President of the United States with a popular vote less than 50% of the total cast. It should be noted, however, that in elections before 1872, presidential electors were not chosen by popular vote in all states. Adams' election in 1824 was by the House of Representatives, which chose him over Jackson, who had a plurality of both electoral and popular votes, but not a majority in the electoral college.

Besides Jackson in 1824, only two other candidates receiving the largest popular vote have failed to gain a majority in the electoral college—Samuel J. Tilden (D) in 1876 and Grover Cleveland (D) in 1888.

The "minority" Presidents follow:

Vote Received by Minority Presidents

Year	President	Electoral Percent	Popular vote Percent
1824	John Q. Adams	31.8	29.8
1844	James K. Polk (D)	61.8	49.3
1848	Zachary Taylor (W)	56.2	47.3
1856	James Buchanan (D)	58.7	45.3
1860	Abraham Lincoln (R)	59.4	39.9
1876	Rutherford B. Hayes (R)	50.1	47.9
1880	James A. Garfield (R)	57.9	48.3
1884	Grover Cleveland (D)	54.6	48.8
1888	Benjamin Harrison (R)	58.1	47.8
1892	Grover Cleveland (D)	62.4	46.0
1912	Woodrow Wilson (D)	81.9	41.8
1916	Woodrow Wilson (D)	52.1	49.3
1948	Harry S. Truman (D)	57.1	49.5
1960	John F. Kennedy (D)	56.4	49.7
1968	Richard M. Nixon (R)	56.1	43.4

Government Officials

Cabinet Members With Dates of Appointment

Although the Constitution made no provision for a President's advisory group, the heads of the three executive departments (State, Treasury, and War) and the Attorney General were organized by Washington into such a group; and by about 1793, the name "Cabinet" was applied to it. With the exception of the Attorney General up to 1870 and the Postmaster General from 1829 to 1872, Cabinet members have been heads of executive departments.

A Cabinet member is appointed by the President, subject to the confirmation of the Senate; and as his term is not fixed, he may be replaced at any time by the President. At a change in Administration, it is customary for him to tender his resignation, but he remains in office until a successor is appointed.

The table of Cabinet members lists only those members who actually served after being duly commissioned.

The dates shown are those of appointment. "Cont." indicates that the term continued from the previous Administration for a substantial amount of time.

With the creation of the Department of Transportation in 1966, the Cabinet consisted of 12 members. This figure was reduced to 11 when the Post Office Department became an independent agency in 1970 but, with the establishment in 1977 of a Department of Energy, became 12 again.

WASHINGTON

Secretary of State	Thomas Jefferson 1789
	Edmund Randolph 1794
	Timothy Pickering 1795
Secretary of the Treasury	Alexander Hamilton 1789
	Oliver Wolcott, Jr. 1795
Secretary of War	Henry Knox 1789
	Timothy Pickering 1795
	James McHenry 1796
Attorney General	Edmund Randolph 1789
	William Bradford 1794
	Charles Lee 1795

J. ADAMS

Secretary of State	Timothy Pickering (Cont.)
	John Marshall 1800
Secretary of the Treasury	Oliver Wolcott, Jr. (Cont.)
	Samuel Dexter 1801
Secretary of War	James McHenry (Cont.)
	Samuel Dexter 1800
Attorney General	Charles Lee (Cont.)
Secretary of the Navy	Benjamin Stoddert 1798

JEFFERSON

Secretary of State	James Madison 1801
Secretary of the Treasury	Samuel Dexter (Cont.)
	Albert Gallatin 1801
Secretary of War	Henry Dearborn 1801
Attorney General	Levi Lincoln 1801
	Robert Smith 1805
	John Breckinridge 1805
	Caesar A. Rodney 1807
Secretary of the Navy	Benjamin Stoddert (Cont.)
	Robert Smith 1801

MADISON

Secretary of State	Robert Smith 1809
	James Monroe 1811
Secretary of the Treasury	Albert Gallatin (Cont.)
	George W. Campbell 1814
	Alexander J. Dallas 1814
	William H. Crawford 1816
Secretary of War	William Eustis 1809
	John Armstrong 1813
	James Monroe 1814
	William H. Crawford 1815
Attorney General	Caesar A. Rodney (Cont.)
	William Pinckney 1811
	Richard Rush 1814
Secretary of the Navy	Paul Hamilton 1809
	William Jones 1813
	B. W. Crowninshield 1814

MONROE

Secretary of State	John Quincy Adams 1817
Secretary of the Treasury	William H. Crawford (Cont.)
Secretary of War	John C. Calhoun 1817
Attorney General	Richard Rush (Cont.)
	William Wirt 1817
Secretary of the Navy	B. W. Crowninshield (Cont.)
	Smith Thompson 1818
	Samuel L. Southard 1823

J. Q. ADAMS

Secretary of State	Henry Clay 1825
Secretary of the Treasury	Richard Rush 1825
Secretary of War	James Barbour 1825
	Peter B. Porter 1828
Attorney General	William Wirt (Cont.)
Secretary of the Navy	Samuel L. Southard (Cont.)

JACKSON

Secretary of State	Martin Van Buren 1829
	Edward Livingston 1831
	Louis McLane 1833
	John Forsyth 1834
Secretary of the Treasury	Samuel D. Ingham 1829
	Louis McLane 1831
	William J. Duane 1833
	Roger B. Taney[3] 1833
	Levi Woodbury 1834
Secretary of War	John H. Eaton 1829
	Lewis Cass 1831
Attorney General	John M. Berrien 1829
	Roger B. Taney 1831
	Benjamin F. Butler 1833
Postmaster General[1]	William T. Barry 1829
	Amos Kendall 1835
Secretary of the Navy	John Branch 1829
	Levi Woodbury 1831
	Mahlon Dickerson 1834

VAN BUREN

Secretary of State	John Forsyth (Cont.)
Secretary of the Treasury	Levi Woodbury (Cont.)
Secretary of War	Joel R. Poinsett 1837
Attorney General	Benjamin F. Butler (Cont.)
	Felix Grundy 1838
	Henry D. Gilpin 1840
Postmaster General	Amos Kendall (Cont.)
	John M. Niles 1840
Secretary of the Navy	Mahlon Dickerson (Cont.)
	James K. Paulding 1838

W. H. HARRISON

Secretary of State	Daniel Webster 1841
Secretary of the Treasury	Thomas Ewing 1841
Secretary of War	John Bell 1841
Attorney General	John J. Crittenden 1841
Postmaster General	Francis Granger 1841
Secretary of the Navy	George E. Badger 1841

TYLER

Secretary of State	Daniel Webster (Cont.)
	Abel P. Upshur 1843
	John C. Calhoun 1844
Secretary of the Treasury	Thomas Ewing (Cont.)
	Walter Forward 1841
	John C. Spencer[3] 1843
	George M. Bibb 1844
Secretary of War	John Bell (Cont.)
	John C. Spencer 1841
	James M. Porter[3] 1843
	William Wilkins 1844
Attorney General	John J. Crittenden (Cont.)
	Hugh S. Legaré 1841
	John Nelson 1843
Postmaster General	Francis Granger (Cont.)
	Charles A. Wickliffe 1841
Secretary of the Navy	George E. Badger (Cont.)
	Abel P. Upshur 1841
	David Henshaw[3] 1843
	Thomas W. Gilmer 1844
	John Y. Mason 1844

POLK

Secretary of State	James Buchanan 1845
Secretary of the Treasury	Robert J. Walker 1845
Secretary of War	William L. Marcy 1845
Attorney General	John Y. Mason 1845
	Nathan Clifford 1846
	Isaac Toucey 1848
Postmaster General	Cave Johnson 1845
Secretary of the Navy	George Bancroft 1845
	John Y. Mason 1846

TAYLOR

Secretary of State	John M. Clayton 1849
Secretary of the Treasury	William M. Meredith 1849
Secretary of War	George W. Crawford 1849
Attorney General	Reverdy Johnson 1849
Postmaster General	Jacob Collamer 1849
Secretary of the Navy	William B. Preston 1849
Secretary of the Interior	Thomas Ewing 1849

FILLMORE

Secretary of State	Daniel Webster 1850
	Edward Everett 1852
Secretary of the Treasury	Thomas Corwin 1850
Secretary of War	Charles M. Conrad 1850
Attorney General	John J. Crittenden 1850
Postmaster General	Nathan K. Hall 1850
	Samuel D. Hubbard 1852
Secretary of the Navy	William A. Graham 1850
	John P. Kennedy 1852
Secretary of the Interior	Thos. M. T. McKennan 1850
	Alex. H. H. Stuart 1850

PIERCE

Secretary of State	William L. Marcy 1853
Secretary of the Treasury	James Guthrie 1853
Secretary of War	Jefferson Davis 1853
Attorney General	Caleb Cushing 1853
Postmaster General	James Campbell 1853
Secretary of the Navy	James C. Dobbin 1853
Secretary of the Interior	Robert McClelland 1853

BUCHANAN

Secretary of State	Lewis Cass 1857
	Jeremiah S. Black 1860
Secretary of the Treasury	Howell Cobb 1857
	Philip F. Thomas 1860
	John A. Dix 1861
Secretary of War	John B. Floyd 1857
	Joseph Holt 1861
Attorney General	Jeremiah S. Black 1857
	Edwin M. Stanton 1860
Postmaster General	Aaron V. Brown 1857
	Joseph Holt 1859
	Horatio King 1861
Secretary of the Navy	Isaac Toucey 1857
Secretary of the Interior	Jacob Thompson 1857

LINCOLN

Secretary of State	William H. Seward 1861
Secretary of the Treasury	Salmon P. Chase 1861
	William P. Fessenden 1864
	Hugh McCulloch 1865
Secretary of War	Simon Cameron 1861
	Edwin M. Stanton 1862
Attorney General	Edward Bates 1861
	James Speed 1864
Postmaster General	Montgomery Blair 1861
	William Dennison 1864
Secretary of the Navy	Gideon Welles 1861
Secretary of the Interior	Caleb B. Smith 1861
	John P. Usher 1863

A. JOHNSON

Secretary of State	William H. Seward (Cont.)
Secretary of the Treasury	Hugh McCulloch (Cont.)
Secretary of War	Edwin M. Stanton (Cont.)
	John M. Schofield 1868
Attorney General	James Speed (Cont.)
	Henry Stanbery 1866
	William M. Evarts 1868
Postmaster General	William Dennison (Cont.)
	Alexander W. Randall 1866
Secretary of the Navy	Gideon Welles (Cont.)
Secretary of the Interior	John P. Usher (Cont.)
	James Harlan 1865
	Orville H. Browning 1866

GRANT

Secretary of State	Elihu B. Washburne 1869
	Hamilton Fish 1869
Secretary of the Treasury	George S. Boutwell 1869
	William A. Richardson 1873
	Benjamin H. Bristow 1874
	Lot M. Morrill 1876
Secretary of War	John A. Rawlins 1869
	William W. Belknap 1869
	Alphonso Taft 1876
	James D. Cameron 1876
Attorney General	Ebenezer R. Hoar 1869
	Amos T. Akerman 1870
	George H. Williams 1871
	Edwards Pierrepont 1875
	Alphonso Taft 1876
Postmaster General	John A. J. Creswell 1869
	Marshall Jewell 1874
	James N. Tyner 1876
Secretary of the Navy	Adolph E. Borie 1869
	George M. Robeson 1869
Secretary of the Interior	Jacob D. Cox 1869
	Columbus Delano 1870
	Zachariah Chandler 1875

HAYES

Secretary of State	William M. Evarts 1877
Secretary of the Treasury	John Sherman 1877
Secretary of War	George W. McCrary 1877
	Alexander Ramsey 1879
Attorney General	Charles Devens 1877
Postmaster General	David M. Key 1877
	Horace Maynard 1880
Secretary of the Navy	Richard W. Thompson 1877
	Nathan Goff, Jr. 1881
Secretary of the Interior	Carl Schurz 1877

GARFIELD

Secretary of State	James G. Blaine 1881
Secretary of the Treasury	William Windom 1881
Secretary of War	Robert T. Lincoln 1881
Attorney General	Wayne MacVeagh 1881
Postmaster General	Thomas L. James 1881
Secretary of the Navy	William H. Hunt 1881
Secretary of the Interior	Samuel J. Kirkwood 1881

ARTHUR

Secretary of State	James G. Blaine (Cont.)
	F. T. Frelinghuysen 1881
Secretary of the Treasury	William Windom (Cont.)
	Charles J. Folger 1881
	Walter Q. Gresham 1884

	Hugh McCulloch 1884
Secretary of War	Robert T. Lincoln (Cont.)
Attorney General	Wayne MacVeagh (Cont.)
	Benjamin H. Brewster 1881
Postmaster General	Thomas L. James (Cont.)
	Timothy O. Howe 1881
	Walter Q. Gresham 1883
	Frank Hatton 1884
Secretary of the Navy	William H. Hunt (Cont.)
	William E. Chandler 1882
Secretary of the Interior	Samuel J. Kirkwood (Cont.)
	Henry M. Teller 1882

CLEVELAND

Secretary of State	Thomas F. Bayard 1885
Secretary of the Treasury	Daniel Manning 1885
	Charles S. Fairchild 1887
Secretary of War	William C. Endicott 1885
Attorney General	Augustus H. Garland 1885
Postmaster General	William F. Vilas 1885
	Don M. Dickinson 1888
Secretary of the Navy	William C. Whitney 1885
Secretary of the Interior	Lucius Q. C. Lamar 1885
	William F. Vilas 1888
Secretary of Agriculture	Norman J. Colman 1889

B. HARRISON

Secretary of State	James G. Blaine 1889
	John W. Foster 1892
Secretary of the Treasury	William Windom 1889
	Charles Foster 1891
Secretary of War	Redfield Proctor 1889
	Stephen B. Elkins 1891
Attorney General	William H. H. Miller 1889
Postmaster General	John Wanamaker 1889
Secretary of the Navy	Benjamin F. Tracy 1889
Secretary of the Interior	John W. Noble 1889
Secretary of Agriculture	Jeremiah M. Rusk 1889

CLEVELAND

Secretary of State	Walter Q. Gresham 1893
	Richard Olney 1895
Secretary of the Treasury	John G. Carlisle 1893
Secretary of War	Daniel S. Lamont 1893
Attorney General	Richard Olney 1893
	Judson Harmon 1895
Postmaster General	Wilson S. Bissell 1893
	William L. Wilson 1895
Secretary of the Navy	Hilary A. Herbert 1893
Secretary of the Interior	Hoke Smith 1893
	David R. Francis 1896
Secretary of Agriculture	Julius Sterling Morton 1893

McKINLEY

Secretary of State	John Sherman 1897
	William R. Day 1898
	John Hay 1898
Secretary of the Treasury	Lyman J. Gage 1897
Secretary of War	Russell A. Alger 1897
	Elihu Root 1899
Attorney General	Joseph McKenna 1897
	John W. Griggs 1898
	Philander C. Knox 1901
Postmaster General	James A. Gary 1897
	Charles E. Smith 1898
Secretary of the Navy	John D. Long 1897
Secretary of the Interior	Cornelius N. Bliss 1897
	Ethan A. Hitchcock 1898
Secretary of Agriculture	James Wilson 1897

T. ROOSEVELT

Secretary of State	John Hay (Cont.)
	Elihu Root 1905
	Robert Bacon 1909
Secretary of the Treasury	Lyman J. Gage (Cont.)
	Leslie M. Shaw 1902
	George B. Cortelyou 1907
Secretary of War	Elihu Root (Cont.)
	William H. Taft 1904
	Luke E. Wright 1908
Attorney General	Philander C. Knox (Cont.)
	William H. Moody 1904
	Charles J. Bonaparte 1906
Postmaster General	Charles E. Smith (Cont.)
	Henry C. Payne 1902
	Robert J. Wynne 1904
	George B. Cortelyou 1905
	George von L. Meyer 1907
Secretary of the Navy	John D. Long (Cont.)
	William H. Moody 1902
	Paul Morton 1904
	Charles J. Bonaparte 1905
	Victor H. Metcalf 1906
	Truman H. Newberry 1908
Secretary of the Interior	Ethan A. Hitchcock (Cont.)
	James R. Garfield 1907
Secretary of Agriculture	James Wilson (Cont.)
Secretary of Commerce and Labor	George B. Cortelyou 1903
	Victor H. Metcalf 1904
	Oscar S. Straus 1906

TAFT

Secretary of State	Philander C. Knox 1909
Secretary of the Treasury	Franklin MacVeagh 1909
Secretary of War	Jacob M. Dickinson 1909
	Henry L. Stimson 1911
Attorney General	George W. Wickersham 1909
Postmaster General	Frank H. Hitchcock 1909
Secretary of the Navy	George von L. Meyer 1909
Secretary of the Interior	Richard A. Ballinger 1909
	Walter L. Fisher 1911
Secretary of Agriculture	James Wilson (Cont.)
Secretary of Commerce and Labor	Charles Nagel 1909

WILSON

Secretary of State	William J. Bryan 1913
	Robert Lansing 1915
	Bainbridge Colby 1920
Secretary of the Treasury	William G. McAdoo 1913
	Carter Glass 1918
	David F. Houston 1920
Secretary of War	Lindley M. Garrison 1913
	Newton D. Baker 1916
Attorney General	James C. McReynolds 1913
	Thomas W. Gregory 1914
	A. Mitchell Palmer 1919
Postmaster General	Albert S. Burleson 1913
Secretary of the Navy	Josephus Daniels 1913
Secretary of the Interior	Franklin K. Lane 1913
	John B. Payne 1920
Secretary of Agriculture	David F. Houston 1913
	Edwin T. Meredith 1920
Secretary of Commerce	William C. Redfield 1913
	Joshua W. Alexander 1919
Secretary of Labor	William B. Wilson 1913

HARDING

Secretary of State	Charles E. Hughes 1921
Secretary of the Treasury	Andrew W. Mellon 1921
Secretary of War	John W. Weeks 1921
Attorney General	Harry M. Daugherty 1921
Postmaster General	Will H. Hays 1921
	Hubert Work 1922
	Harry S. New 1923
Secretary of the Navy	Edwin Denby 1921
Secretary of the Interior	Albert B. Fall 1921
	Hubert Work 1923
Secretary of Agriculture	Henry C. Wallace 1921
Secretary of Commerce	Herbert Hoover 1921
Secretary of Labor	James J. Davis 1921

COOLIDGE

Secretary of State	Charles E. Hughes (Cont.)
	Frank B. Kellogg 1925
Secretary of the Treasury	Andrew W. Mellon (Cont.)
Secretary of War	John W. Weeks (Cont.)
	Dwight F. Davis 1925
Attorney General	Harry M. Daugherty (Cont.)
	Harlan F. Stone 1924
	John G. Sargent 1925
Postmaster General	Harry S. New (Cont.)
Secretary of the Navy	Edwin Denby (Cont.)
	Curtis D. Wilbur 1924
Secretary of the Interior	Hubert Work (Cont.)
	Roy O. West 1928

Secretary of Agriculture	Henry C. Wallace (Cont.) Howard M. Gore 1924 William M. Jardine 1925
Secretary of Commerce	Herbert Hoover (Cont.) William F. Whiting 1928
Secretary of Labor	James J. Davis (Cont.)

HOOVER

Secretary of State	Frank B. Kellogg (Cont.) Henry L. Stimson 1929
Secretary of the Treasury	Andrew W. Mellon (Cont.) Ogden L. Mills 1932
Secretary of War	James W. Good 1929 Patrick J. Hurley 1929
Attorney General	William D. Mitchell 1929
Postmaster General	Walter F. Brown 1929
Secretary of the Navy	Charles F. Adams 1929
Secretary of the Interior	Ray Lyman Wilbur 1929
Secretary of Agriculture	Arthur M. Hyde 1929
Secretary of Commerce	Robert P. Lamont 1929 Roy D. Chapin 1932
Secretary of Labor	James J. Davis (Cont.) William N. Doak 1930

F. D. ROOSEVELT

Secretary of State	Cordell Hull 1933 E. R. Stettinius, Jr. 1944
Secretary of the Treasury	William H. Woodin 1933 Henry Morgenthau, Jr. 1934
Secretary of War	George H. Dern 1933 Harry H. Woodring 1936 Henry L. Stimson 1940
Attorney General	Homer S. Cummings 1933 Frank Murphy 1939 Robert H. Jackson 1940 Francis Biddle 1941
Postmaster General	James A. Farley 1933 Frank C. Walker 1940
Secretary of the Navy	Claude A. Swanson 1933 Charles Edison 1940 Frank Knox 1940 James Forrestal 1944
Secretary of the Interior	Harold L. Ickes 1933
Secretary of Agriculture	Henry A. Wallace 1933 Claude R. Wickard 1940
Secretary of Commerce	Daniel C. Roper 1933 Harry L. Hopkins 1938 Jesse H. Jones 1940 Henry A. Wallace 1945
Secretary of Labor	Frances Perkins 1933

TRUMAN

Secretary of State	E. R. Stettinius, Jr. (Cont.) James F. Byrnes 1945 George C. Marshall 1947 Dean Acheson 1949
Secretary of the Treasury	Henry Morgenthau, Jr. (Cont.) Frederick M. Vinson 1945 John W. Snyder 1946
Secretary of Defense	James Forrestal 1947 Louis A. Johnson 1949 George C. Marshall 1950 Robert A. Lovett 1951
Attorney General	Francis Biddle (Cont.) Tom C. Clark 1945 J. Howard McGrath 1949 James P. McGranery 1952
Postmaster General	Frank C. Walker (Cont.) Robert E. Hannegan 1945 Jesse M. Donaldson 1947
Secretary of the Interior	Harold L. Ickes (Cont.) Julius A. Krug 1946 Oscar L. Chapman 1949
Secretary of Agriculture	Claude R. Wickard (Cont.) Clinton P. Anderson 1945 Charles F. Brannan 1948
Secretary of Commerce	Henry A. Wallace (Cont.) W. Averell Harriman 1946 Charles Sawyer 1948
Secretary of Labor	Frances Perkins (Cont.) Lewis B. Schwellenbach 1945 Maurice J. Tobin 1948
Secretary of War[2]	Henry L. Stimson (Cont.) Robert P. Patterson 1945 Kenneth C. Royall 1947
Secretary of the Navy[2]	James Forrestal (Cont.)

EISENHOWER

Secretary of State	John Foster Dulles 1953 Christian A. Herter 1959
Secretary of the Treasury	George M. Humphrey 1953 Robert B. Anderson 1957
Secretary of Defense	Charles E. Wilson 1953 Neil H. McElroy 1957 Thomas S. Gates, Jr. 1959
Attorney General	Herbert Brownell, Jr. 1953 William P. Rogers 1958
Postmaster General	Arthur E. Summerfield 1953
Secretary of the Interior	Douglas McKay 1953 Frederick A. Seaton 1956
Secretary of Agriculture	Ezra Taft Benson 1953
Secretary of Commerce	Sinclair Weeks 1953 Lewis L. Strauss[3] 1958 Frederick H. Mueller 1959
Secretary of Labor	Martin P. Durkin 1953 James P. Mitchell 1953
Secretary of Health, Education, and Welfare	Oveta Culp Hobby 1953 Marion B. Folsom 1955 Arthur S. Flemming 1958

KENNEDY

Secretary of State	Dean Rusk 1961
Secretary of the Treasury	C. Douglas Dillon 1961
Secretary of Defense	Robert S. McNamara 1961
Attorney General	Robert F. Kennedy 1961
Postmaster General	J. Edward Day 1961 John A. Gronouski 1963
Secretary of the Interior	Stewart L. Udall 1961
Secretary of Agriculture	Orville L. Freeman 1961
Secretary of Commerce	Luther H. Hodges 1961
Secretary of Labor	Arthur J. Goldberg 1961 W. Willard Wirtz 1962
Secretary of Health, Education, and Welfare	Abraham A. Ribicoff 1961 Anthony J. Celebrezze 1962

L. B. JOHNSON

Secretary of State	Dean Rusk (Cont.)
Secretary of the Treasury	C. Douglas Dillon (Cont.) Henry H. Fowler 1965 Joseph W. Barr[4] 1968
Secretary of Defense	Robert S. McNamara (Cont.) Clark M. Clifford 1968
Attorney General	Robert F. Kennedy (Cont.) N. de B. Katzenbach 1965 Ramsey Clark 1967
Postmaster General	John A. Gronouski (Cont.) Lawrence F. O'Brien 1965 W. Marvin Watson 1968
Secretary of the Interior	Stewart L. Udall (Cont.)
Secretary of Agriculture	Orville L. Freeman (Cont.)
Secretary of Commerce	Luther H. Hodges (Cont.) John T. Connor 1964 A. B. Trowbridge 1967 C. R. Smith 1968
Secretary of Labor	W. Willard Wirtz (Cont.)
Secretary of Health, Education, and Welfare	Anthony J. Celebrezze (Cont.) John W. Gardner 1965 Wilbur J. Cohen 1968
Secretary of Housing and Urban Development	Robert C. Weaver 1966 Robert C. Wood[4] 1969
Secretary of Transportation	Alan S. Boyd 1966

NIXON

Secretary of State	William P. Rogers 1969 Henry A. Kissinger 1973
Secretary of the Treasury	David M. Kennedy 1969 John B. Connally 1970 George P. Shultz 1972 William E. Simon 1974

Secretary of Defense	Melvin R. Laird 1969
	Elliot L. Richardson 1973
	James R. Schlesinger 1973
Attorney General	John N. Mitchell 1969
	Richard G. Kleindienst 1972
	Elliot L. Richardson 1973
	William B. Saxbe 1974
Postmaster General[5]	William M. Blount 1969
Secretary of the Interior	Walter J. Hickel 1969
	Rogers C. B. Morton 1971
Secretary of Agriculture	Clifford M. Hardin 1969
	Earl L. Butz 1971
Secretary of Commerce	Maurice H. Stans 1969
	Peter G. Peterson 1972
	Frederick B. Dent 1973
Secretary of Labor	George P. Shultz 1969
	James D. Hodgson 1970
	Peter J. Brennan 1973
Secretary of Health, Education, and Welfare	Robert H. Finch 1969
	Elliot L. Richardson 1970
	Caspar W. Weinberger 1973
Secretary of Housing and Urban Development	George Romney 1969
	James T. Lynn 1973
Secretary of Transportation	John A. Volpe 1969
	Claude S. Brinegar 1973

FORD

Secretary of State	Henry A. Kissinger (Cont.)
Secretary of the Treasury	William E. Simon (Cont.)
Secretary of Defense	James R. Schlesinger (Cont.)
	Donald H. Rumsfeld 1975
Attorney General	William B. Saxbe (Cont.)
	Edward H. Levi 1975
Secretary of the Interior	Rogers C. B. Morton (Cont.)
	Stanley K. Hathaway 1975
	Thomas S. Kleppe 1975
Secretary of Agriculture	Earl L. Butz (Cont.)
Secretary of Commerce	Frederick B. Dent (Cont.)
	Rogers C. B. Morton 1975
	Elliot L. Richardson 1976
Secretary of Labor	Peter J. Brennan (Cont.)
	John T. Dunlop 1975
	William J. Usery, Jr. 1976
Secretary of Health, Education and Welfare	Caspar W. Weinberger (Cont.)
	F. David Mathews 1975
Secretary of Housing and Urban Development	James T. Lynn (Cont.)
	Carla A. Hills 1975
Secretary of Transportation	Claude S. Brinegar (Cont.)
	William T. Coleman, Jr. 1975

CARTER

Secretary of State	Cyrus R. Vance 1977
	Edmund S. Muskie 1980
Secretary of the Treasury	W. Michael Blumenthal 1977
	G. William Miller 1979
Secretary of Defense	Harold Brown 1977
Attorney General	Griffin B. Bell 1977
	Benjamin R. Civiletti 1979
Secretary of the Interior	Cecil D. Andrus 1977
Secretary of Agriculture	Bob S. Bergland 1977
Secretary of Commerce	Juanita M. Kreps 1977
	Philip M. Klutznick 1979
Secretary of Labor	F. Ray Marshall 1977
Secretary of Health and Human Services[6]	Joseph A. Califano, Jr. 1977
	Patricia Roberts Harris 1979
Secretary of Housing and Urban Development	Patricia Roberts Harris 1977
	Moon Landrieu 1979
Secretary of Transportation	Brock Adams 1977
	Neil E. Goldschmidt 1979
Secretary of Energy	James R. Schlesinger 1977
	Charles W. Duncan, Jr. 1979
Secretary of Education	Shirley Mount Hufstedler 1979

1. The Postmaster General did not become a Cabinet member until 1829. Earlier Postmasters General were: Samuel Osgood (1789), Timothy Pickering (1791), Joseph Habersham (1795), Gideon Granger (1801), Return J. Meigs, Jr. (1814), and John McLean (1823). 2. On July 26, 1947, the Departments of War and of the Navy were incorporated into the Department of Defense. 3. Not confirmed by the Senate. 4. Recess appointment. 5. The Postmaster General is no longer a Cabinet member. 6. Known as Department of Health, Education, and Welfare until May 1980.

How a Bill Becomes a Law

When a Senator or a Representative introduces a bill, he sends it to the clerk of his house, who gives it a number and title. This is the *first reading*, and the bill is referred to the proper committee.

The committee may decide the bill is unwise or unnecessary and *table* it, thus killing it at once. Or it may decide the bill is worthwhile and hold hearings to listen to facts and opinions presented by experts and other interested persons. After members of the committee have debated the bill and perhaps offered amendments, a vote is taken; and if the vote is favorable, the bill is sent back to the floor of the house.

The clerk reads the bill sentence by sentence to the house, and this is known as the *second reading*. Members may then debate the bill and offer amendments. In the House of Representatives, the time for debate is limited by a *cloture rule*, but there is no such restriction in the Senate for cloture, where 60 votes are required. This makes possible a *filibuster*, in which one or more opponents hold the floor to defeat the bill.

The *third reading* is by title only, and the bill is put to a vote, which may be by voice or roll call, depending on the circumstances and parliamentary rules. Members who must be absent at the time but who wish to record their vote may be paired if each negative vote has a balancing affirmative one.

The bill then goes to the other house of Congress, where it may be defeated, or passed with or without amendments. If the bill is defeated, it dies. If it is passed with amendments, a joint Congressional committee must be appointed by both houses to iron out the differences.

After its final passage by both houses, the bill is sent to the President. If he approves, he signs it, and the bill becomes a law. However, if he disapproves, he *vetoes* the bill by refusing to sign it and sending it back to the house of origin with his reasons for the veto. The objections are read and debated, and a roll-call vote is taken. If the bill receives less than a two-thirds vote, it is defeated and goes no farther. But if it receives a two-thirds vote or greater, it is sent to the other house for a vote. If that house also passes it by a two-thirds vote, the President's veto is *overridden*, and the bill becomes a law.

Should the President desire neither to sign nor to veto the bill, he may retain it for ten days, Sundays excepted, after which time it automatically becomes a law without signature. However, if Congress has adjourned within those ten days, the bill is automatically killed, that process of indirect rejection being known as a *pocket veto*.

Federal Judiciary

Source: United States Court Directory, 1980

SUPREME COURT OF THE U.S.

(Washington, D.C. 20543)

Chief Justice: Warren E. Burger

Associate Justices:
William J. Brennan, Jr.
Potter Stewart
Byron R. White
Thurgood Marshall
Harry A. Blackmun
Lewis F. Powell, Jr.
William H. Rehnquist
John Paul Stevens

U.S. COURTS OF APPEALS

(CJ indicates Chief Judge)

District of Columbia: J. Skelly Wright, CJ, Carl McGowan, Edward Allen Tamm, Patricia M. Wald, Abner J. Mikva, Spottswood W. Robinson III, Roger Robb, George E. MacKinnon, Malcolm R. Wilkey, all Washington.

First Circuit (Me., Mass., N.H., R.I., Puerto Rico): Frank M. Coffin, CJ, Portland, Me.; Levin H. Campbell, Boston; Hugh H. Bownes, Concord, N.H.

Second Circuit (Conn., N.Y., Vt.): Irving R. Kaufman, CJ, Wilfred Feinberg, Walter R. Mansfield, William H. Mulligan, Amalya Lyle Kearse, all New York City; Ellsworth A. Van Graafeiland, Rochester, N.Y.; James L. Oakes, Brattleboro, Vt.; William H. Timbers, Bridgeport, Conn.; Thomas J. Meskill, New Britain, Conn.

Third Circuit (Del., N.J., Pa., Virgin Is.): Collins J. Seitz, CJ, Wilmington, Del.; Arlin M. Adams, Dolores K. Sloviter, Philadelphia; Ruggero J. Aldisert, Joseph F. Weis, Jr., both Pittsburgh; John J. Gibbons, Leonard I. Garth, both Newark, N.J.; Max Rosenn, Wilkes-Barre, Pa.; James Hunger, III, Camden, N.J.; A. Leon Higginbotham, Jr., Philadelphia.

Fourth Circuit (Md., N.C., S.C., Va., W. Va.): Clement F. Haynsworth, Jr., CJ, Greenville, S.C.; Harrison L. Winter, Francis D. Murnaghan, Jr., both Baltimore, Md.; John D. Butzner, Jr., Richmond, Va.; Donald Stuart Russell, Spartanburg, S.C.; H. Emory Widener, Jr., Abingdon, Va.; Kenneth K. Hall, James M. Sprouse, both Charleston, W. Va.; James Dickson Phillips, Jr., Durham, N.C.

Fifth Circuit (Ala., Fla., Ga., La., Miss., Tex., Canal Zone): James P. Coleman, CJ, Ackerman, Miss.; John R. Brown, Carolyn D. Randall, both Houston; Robert A. Ainsworth, Albert Tate, Jr., both New Orleans; Alvin B. Rubin, Baton Rouge, La.; Thomas G. Gee, Thomas M. Reavley, Samuel D. Johnson, all Austin, Tex.; Irving L. Goldberg, Dallas; John C. Godbold, Frank M. Johnson, both Montgomery, Ala.; Charles Clark, Jackson, Miss.; Paul H. Roney, St. Petersburg, Fla.; Gerald B. Tjoflat, Jacksonville, Fla.; James C. Hill, Atlanta; Peter T. Fay, Miami, Fla.; Robert S. Vance, Birmingham, Ala.; Phyllis A. Kravitch, Albert J. Henderson, Jr., both Atlanta; Reynaldo G. Garza, Brownsville, Tex.; Joseph W. Hatchett, Tallahassee, Fla.; Henry A. Politz, Shreveport, La.; R. Lanier Anderson, Macon, Ga.; Thomas A. Clark, Tampa, Fla.

Sixth Circuit (Ky., Mich., Ohio, Tenn.): Anthony J. Celebrezze, CJ, Nathaniel R. Jones, both Cleveland, Ohio; Gilbert S. Merritt, Nashville, Tenn.; Paul C. Weick, Akron, Ohio; Albert J. Engel, Grand Rapids, Mich.; Pierce Lively, Danville, Ky.; Damon J. Keith, Cornelia G. Kennedy, both Detroit, Mich.; Bailey Brown, Memphis, Tenn.; Boyce F. Martin, Jr., Louisville, Ky.

Seventh Circuit (Ill., Ind., Wis.): Thomas E. Fairchild, CJ, Luther M. Swygert, Walter J. Cummings, Wilbur F. Pell, Jr., Robert A. Sprecher, Philip W. Tone, William J. Bauer, Harlington Wood, Jr., Richard D. Cudahy, all Chicago.

Eighth Circuit (Ark., Iowa, Minn., Mo., Neb., N.D., S.D.): Floyd R. Gibson, CJ, Kansas City, Mo.; Donald P. Lay, Donald R. Ross, both Omaha, Neb.; Gerald W. Heaney, Duluth, Minn.; Myron H. Bright, Fargo, N.D.; Roy L. Stephenson, Des Moines, Iowa; J. Smith Henley, Harrison, Ark.; Theodore McMillian, St. Louis.

Ninth Circuit (Ariz., Calif., Idaho, Mont., Nev., Ore., Wash., Alaska, Hawaii, Guam): James R. Browning, CJ, Joseph T. Sneed, both San Francisco; Shirley M. Hufstedler, Harry Pregerson, Arthur L. Alarcon, all Los Angeles; J. Clifford Wallace, San Diego, Calif.; Eugene A. Wright, Jerome Farris, Betty B. Fletcher, all Seattle; Thomas Tang, Mary M. Schroeder, both Phoenix, Ariz.; Herbert Y. C. Choy, Honolulu; Alfred T. Goodwin, Otto R. Skopil, Jr., both Portland, Ore.; Anthony M. Kennedy, Sacramento, Calif.; J. Blaine Anderson, Boise, Idaho; Procter Hug, Jr., Reno, Nev.

Tenth Circuit (Colo., Kan., N.M., Okla., Utah, Wyo.): Oliver Seth, CJ, Santa Fe, N.M.; William J. Holloway, Jr., Oklahoma City; Robert H. McWilliams, William E. Doyle, both Denver; James E. Barrett, Cheyenne, Wyo.; James K. Logan, Olathe, Kan.; Monroe G. McKay, Salt Lake City, Utah; Stephanie K. Seymour.

U.S. COURT OF CLAIMS

(Washington, D.C. 20005)

Chief Judge: Daniel M. Friedman.

Associate Judges: Oscar H. Davis, Philip Nichols, Jr., Shiro Kashiwa, Robert L. Kunzig, Marion T. Bennett, Edward S. Smith.

U.S. COURT OF CUSTOMS AND PATENT APPEALS

(Washington, D.C. 20439)

Chief Judge: Howard T. Markey.

Associate Judges: Giles S. Rich, Phillip B. Baldwin, Jack R. Miller.

U.S. CUSTOMS COURT

(One Federal Plaza, New York, N.Y. 10007)

Chief Judge: Edward D. Re.

Judges: Paul P. Rao, Morgan Ford, Scovel Richardson, Frederick Landis, James L. Watson, Herbert N. Maletz, Bernard Newman, Nils A. Boe.

U.S. TAX COURT

(Washington, D.C. 20217)

Chief Judge: C. Moxley Featherston

Judges: William M. Drennen, Irene F. Scott, William M. Fay, Howard A. Dawson, Jr., Theodore Tannenwald, Jr., Charles R. Simpson, Leo H. Irwin, Samuel B. Sterrett, William A. Goffe, Cynthia H. Hall, Darrell D. Wiles, Richard C. Wilbur, Herbert L. Chabot, Arthur L. Nims, III, Edna G. Parker, J. Gregory Bruce, Norman O. Tietjens, Bruce M. Forrester, Arnold Raum, William M. Drennen.

NOTE: To keep abreast of changes see *United States Court Directory 1981*

The Growth of Social Security Taxes

A worker who entered the Social Security system in 1937 and paid the maximum tax each year would have contributed only $2,673.60 if he retired 30 years later in 1967. A worker who joined the system in 1968 and continues to pay the maximum rate will pay $27,512.25 after only 20 years assuming that the scheduled tax rate and wage base are not changed.

The initial Social Security tax rate which went into effect in 1937 was 1%. By 1990, this will have risen to 7.65%.

Members of the Supreme Court of the United States

Name	Birth		Religious affiliation (*Source:* Library of Congress)	Appointment		Oath taken		Service terminated				Death	
	Place	Date		From	President	Date	Age	Date	Cause	Years served	Age	Date	Age
CHIEF JUSTICES													
John Jay	N.Y.	1745	Episcopal	N.Y.	Washington	1789	44	1795	resigned	5	49	1829	83
John Rutledge	S.C.	1739	Church of England	S.C.	Washington	1795	55	1795	rejected	0	56	1800	60
Oliver Ellsworth	Conn.	1745	Congregational	Conn.	Washington	1796	50	1800	resigned	4	55	1807	62
John Marshall	Va.	1755	Episcopal	Va.	J. Adams	1801	45	1835	death	34	79	1835	79
Roger B. Taney	Md.	1777	Roman Catholic	Md.	Jackson	1836	59	1864	death	28	87	1864	87
Salmon P. Chase	N.H.	1808	Episcopal	Ohio	Lincoln	1864	56	1873	death	8	65	1873	65
Morrison R. Waite	Conn	1816	Episcopal	Ohio	Grant	1874	57	1888	death	14	71	1888	71
Melville W. Fuller	Me.	1833	Episcopal	Ill.	Cleveland	1888	55	1910	death	21	77	1910	77
Edward D. White	La.	1845	Roman Catholic	La.	Taft	1910	65	1921	death	10	75	1921	75
William H. Taft	Ohio	1857	Unitarian	Conn.	Harding	1921	63	1930	retired	8	72	1930	72
Charles E. Hughes	N.Y.	1862	Baptist	N.Y.	Hoover	1930	67	1941	retired	11	79	1948	86
Harlan F. Stone	N.H.	1872	Episcopal	N.Y.	F. Roosevelt	1941	68	1946	death	4	73	1946	73
Frederick M. Vinson	Ky.	1890	Methodist	Ky.	Truman	1946	56	1953	death	7	63	1953	63
Earl Warren	Calif.	1891	Protestant	Calif.	Eisenhower	1953	62	1969	retired	15	78	1974	83
Warren E. Burger	Minn.	1907	Presbyterian	Va.	Nixon	1969	61	—	—	—	—	—	—
ASSOCIATE JUSTICES													
James Wilson	Scotland	1742	Episcopal	Pa.	Washington	1789	47	1798	death	8	55	1798	55
John Rutledge	S.C.	1739	Church of England	S.C.	Washington	1790	50	1791	resigned	1	51	1800	60
William Cushing	Mass.	1732	Unitarian	Mass.	Washington	1790	57	1810	death	20	78	1810	78
John Blair	Va.	1732	Presbyterian	Va.	Washington	1790	58	1796	resigned	5	64	1800	68
James Iredell	England	1751	Episcopal	N.C.	Washington	1790	38	1799	death	9	48	1799	48
Thomas Johnson	Md.	1732	Episcopal	Md.	Washington	1792	59	1793	resigned	0	60	1819	86
William Paterson	Ireland	1745	Protestant	N.J.	Washington	1793	47	1806	death	13	60	1806	60
Samuel Chase	Md.	1741	Episcopal	Md.	Washington	1796	54	1811	death	15	70	1811	70
Bushrod Washington	Va.	1762	Episcopal	Va.	J. Adams	1799	36	1829	death	30	67	1829	67
Alfred Moore	N.C.	1755	Episcopal	N.C.	J. Adams	1800	45	1804	resigned	3	48	1810	55
William Johnson	S.C.	1771	Presbyterian	S.C.	Jefferson	1804	32	1834	death	30	62	1834	62
Brockholst Livingston	N.Y.	1757	Presbyterian	N.Y.	Jefferson	1807	49	1823	death	16	65	1823	65
Thomas Todd	Va.	1765	Presbyterian	Ky.	Jefferson	1807	42	1826	death	18	61	1826	61
Gabriel Duval	Md.	1752	French Protestant	Md.	Madison	1811	58	1835	resigned	23	82	1844	91
Joseph Story	Mass.	1779	Unitarian	Mass.	Madison	1812	32	1845	death	33	65	1845	65
Smith Thompson	N.Y.	1768	Presbyterian	N.Y.	Monroe	1823	55	1843	death	20	75	1843	75
Robert Trimble	Va.	1777	Protestant	Ky.	J. Q. Adams	1826	49	1828	death	2	51	1828	51
John McLean	N.J.	1785	Methodist-Epis.	Ohio	Jackson	1830	44	1861	death	31	76	1861	76
Henry Baldwin	Conn.	1780	Trinity Church	Pa.	Jackson	1830	50	1844	death	14	64	1844	64
James M. Wayne	Ga.	1790	Protestant	Ga.	Jackson	1835	45	1867	death	32	77	1867	77
Philip P. Barbour	Va.	1783	Episcopal	Va.	Jackson	1836	52	1841	death	4	57	1841	57
John Catron	Pa.	1786	Presbyterian	Tenn.	Jackson	1837	51	1865	death	28	79	1865	79

Name	Birth: Place	Birth: Date	Religious affiliation (Source: Library of Congress)	Appointment: From	Appointment: President	Oath taken: Date	Oath taken: Age	Service terminated: Date	Service terminated: Cause	Service terminated: Years served	Service terminated: Age	Death: Date	Death: Age
John McKinley	Va	1780	Protestant	Ala.	Van Buren	1837	57	1852	death	14	72	1852	72
Peter V. Daniel	Va.	1784	Episcopal	Va.	Van Buren	1841	57	1860	death	18	76	1860	76
Samuel Nelson	N.Y.	1792	Protestant	N.Y.	Tyler	1845	52	1872	retired	27	80	1873	81
Levi Woodbury	N.H.	1789	Protestant	N.H.	Polk	1845	55	1851	death	5	61	1851	61
Robert C. Grier	Pa.	1794	Presbyterian	Pa.	Polk	1846	52	1870	retired	23	75	1870	76
Benjamin R. Curtis	Mass.	1809	(2)	Mass.	Fillmore	1851	41	1857	resigned	5	47	1874	64
John A. Campbell	Ga.	1811	Episcopal	Ala.	Pierce	1853	41	1861	resigned	8	49	1889	77
Nathan Clifford	N.H.	1803	(1)	Maine	Buchanan	1858	54	1881	death	23	77	1881	77
Noah H. Swayne	Va.	1804	Quaker	Ohio	Lincoln	1862	57	1881	retired	18	76	1884	79
Samuel F. Miller	Ky.	1816	Unitarian	Iowa	Lincoln	1862	46	1890	death	28	74	1890	74
David Davis	Md.	1815	(4)	Ill.	Lincoln	1862	47	1877	resigned	14	61	1886	71
Stephen J. Field	Conn.	1816	Episcopal	Calif.	Lincoln	1863	46	1897	retired	34	81	1899	82
William Strong	Conn.	1808	Presbyterian	Pa.	Grant	1870	61	1880	retired	10	72	1895	87
Joseph P. Bradley	N.Y.	1813	Presbyterian	N.J.	Grant	1870	57	1892	death	21	78	1892	78
Ward Hunt	N.Y.	1810	Episcopal	N.Y.	Grant	1872	62	1882	disabled	9	71	1886	75
John M. Harlan	Ky.	1833	Presbyterian	Ky.	Hayes	1877	44	1911	death	33	78	1911	78
William B. Woods	Ohio	1824	Protestant	Ga.	Hayes	1880	56	1887	death	6	62	1887	62
Stanley Matthews	Ohio	1824	Presbyterian	Ohio	Garfield	1881	56	1889	death	7	64	1889	64
Horace Gray	Mass.	1828	(3)	Mass.	Arthur	1882	53	1902	death	20	74	1902	74
Samuel Blatchford	N.Y.	1820	Presbyterian	N.Y.	Arthur	1882	62	1893	death	11	73	1893	73
Lucius Q. C. Lamar	Ga.	1825	Methodist	Miss.	Cleveland	1888	62	1893	death	5	67	1893	67
David J. Brewer	Asia Minor	1837	Protestant	Kan.	Harrison	1889	52	1910	death	20	72	1910	72
Henry B. Brown	Mass.	1836	Protestant	Mich.	Harrison	1890	54	1906	retired	15	70	1913	77
George Shiras, Jr.	Pa.	1832	Presbyterian	Pa.	Harrison	1892	60	1903	retired	10	71	1924	92
Howell E. Jackson	Tenn.	1832	Baptist	Tenn.	Harrison	1893	60	1895	death	2	63	1895	63
Edward D. White	La.	1845	Roman Catholic	La.	Cleveland	1894	48	1910	promoted	16	65	1921	75
Rufus W. Peckham	N.Y.	1838	Episcopal	N.Y.	Cleveland	1895	57	1909	death	13	70	1909	70
Joseph McKenna	Pa.	1843	Roman Catholic	Calif.	McKinley	1898	54	1925	retired	26	81	1926	83
Oliver W. Holmes	Mass.	1841	Unitarian	Mass.	T. Roosevelt	1902	61	1932	retired	29	90	1935	93
William R. Day	Ohio	1849	Protestant	Ohio	T. Roosevelt	1903	53	1922	retired	19	73	1923	74
William H. Moody	Mass.	1853	Episcopal	Mass.	T. Roosevelt	1906	52	1910	disabled	3	56	1917	63
Horace H. Lurton	Ky.	1844	Episcopal	Tenn.	Taft	1909	65	1914	death	4	70	1914	70
Charles E. Hughes	N.Y.	1862	Baptist	N.Y.	Taft	1910	48	1916	resigned	5	54	1948	86
Willis Van Devanter	Ind.	1859	Episcopal	Wyo.	Taft	1910	51	1937	retired	26	78	1941	81
Joseph R. Lamar	Ga.	1857	Ch. of Disciples	Ga.	Taft	1910	53	1916	death	4	58	1916	58
Mahlon Pitney	N.J.	1858	Presbyterian	N.J.	Taft	1912	54	1922	disabled	10	64	1924	66
James C. McReynolds	Ky.	1862	Disciples of Christ	Tenn.	Wilson	1914	52	1941	retired	26	78	1946	84
Louis D. Brandeis	Ky.	1856	Jewish	Mass.	Wilson	1916	59	1939	retired	22	82	1941	84
John H. Clarke	Ohio	1857	Protestant	Ohio	Wilson	1916	59	1922	resigned	5	65	1945	87
George Sutherland	England	1862	Episcopal	Utah	Harding	1922	60	1938	retired	15	75	1942	80
Pierce Butler	Minn.	1866	Roman Catholic	Minn.	Harding	1923	56	1939	death	16	73	1939	73
Edward T. Sanford	Tenn.	1865	Episcopal	Tenn.	Harding	1923	57	1930	death	7	64	1930	64

Harlan F. Stone	N.H.	1872	Episcopal	N.Y.	Coolidge	1925	52	1941	promoted	16	68	1946	73
Owen J. Roberts	Pa.	1875	Episcopal	Pa.	Hoover	1930	55	1945	resigned	15	70	1955	80
Benjamin N. Cardozo	N.Y.	1870	Jewish	N.Y.	Hoover	1932	61	1938	death	6	68	1938	68
Hugo L. Black	Ala.	1886	Baptist	Ala.	F. Roosevelt	1937	51	1971	retired	34	85	1971	85
Stanley F. Reed	Ky.	1884	Protestant	Ky.	F. Roosevelt	1938	53	1957	retired	19	72	1980	95
Felix Frankfurter	Austria	1882	Jewish	Mass.	F. Roosevelt	1939	56	1962	retired	23	79	1965	82
William O. Douglas	Minn.	1898	Presbyterian	Conn.	F. Roosevelt	1939	40	1975	retired	36	77	1980	81
Frank Murphy	Mich.	1890	Roman Catholic	Mich.	F. Roosevelt	1940	49	1949	death	9	59	1949	59
James F. Byrnes	S.C.	1879	Episcopal	S.C.	F. Roosevelt	1941	62	1942	resigned	1	63	1972	92
Robert H. Jackson	N.Y.	1892	Episcopal	Pa.	F. Roosevelt	1941	49	1954	death	13	62	1954	62
Wiley B. Rutledge	Ky.	1894	Unitarian	Iowa	F. Roosevelt	1943	48	1949	death	6	55	1949	55
Harold H. Burton	Mass.	1888	Unitarian	Ohio	Truman	1945	57	1958	retired	13	70	1964	76
Tom C. Clark	Tex.	1899	Presbyterian	Tex.	Truman	1949	49	1967	retired	17	67	1977	78
Sherman Minton	Ind.	1890	Roman Catholic	Ind.	Truman	1949	58	1956	retired	7	65	1965	74
John M. Harlan	Ill.	1899	Presbyterian	N.Y.	Eisenhower	1955	55	1971	retired	16	72	1971	72
William J. Brennan, Jr.	N.J.	1906	Roman Catholic	N.J.	Eisenhower	1956	50	—	—	—	—	—	—
Charles E. Whittaker	Kan.	1901	Methodist	Mo.	Eisenhower	1957	56	1962	disabled	5	61	1973	73
Potter Stewart	Mich.	1915	Episcopal	Ohio	Eisenhower	1958	43	—	—	—	—	—	—
Byron R. White	Colo.	1917	Episcopal	Colo.	Kennedy	1962	44	—	—	—	—	—	—
Arthur J. Goldberg	Ill.	1908	Jewish	Ill.	Kennedy	1962	54	1965	resigned	2	56	—	—
Abe Fortas	Tenn.	1910	Jewish	Tenn.	Johnson	1965	55	1969	resigned	3	58	—	—
Thurgood Marshall	Md.	1908	Episcopalian	N.Y.	Johnson	1967	59	—	—	—	—	—	—
Harry A. Blackmun	Ill.	1908	Methodist	Minn.	Nixon	1970	61	—	—	—	—	—	—
Lewis F. Powell, Jr.	Va.	1907	Presbyterian	Va.	Nixon	1972	64	—	—	—	—	—	—
William H. Rehnquist	Minn.	1924	Lutheran	Wis.	Nixon	1972	47	—	—	—	—	—	—
John Paul Stevens	Ill.	1920	Protestant	Ill.	Ford	1975	55	—	—	—	—	—	—

1. Congregationalist; later Unitarian. 2. Unitarian; then Episcopal. 3. Unitarian or Congregational. 4. Not a member of any church.

Impeachments of Federal Officials

Source: Congressional Directory

The procedure for the impeachment of Federal officials is detailed in Article I, Section 3, of the Constitution. See Index.

The Senate has sat as a court of impeachment in the following cases:

William Blount, Senator from Tennessee; charges dismissed for want of jurisdiction, January 14, 1799.

John Pickering, Judge of the U.S. District Court for New Hampshire; removed from office March 12, 1804.

Samuel Chase, Associate Justice of the Supreme Court; acquitted March 1, 1805.

James H. Peck, Judge of the U.S. District Court for Missouri; acquitted Jan. 31, 1831.

West H. Humphreys, Judge of the U.S. District Court for the middle, eastern, and western districts of Tennessee; removed from office June 26, 1862.

Andrew Johnson, President of the United States; acquitted May 26, 1868.

William W. Belknap, Secretary of War; acquitted Aug. 1, 1876.

Charles Swayne, Judge of the U.S. District Court for the northern district of Florida; acquitted Feb. 27, 1905.

Robert W. Archbald, Associate Judge, U.S. Commerce Court; removed Jan. 13, 1913.

George W. English, Judge of the U.S. District Court for eastern district of Illinois; resigned Nov. 4, 1926; proceedings dismissed.

Harold Louderback, Judge of the U.S. District Court for the northern district of California; acquitted May 24, 1933.

Halsted L. Ritter, Judge of the U.S. District Court for the southern district of Florida; removed from office April 17, 1936.

Congressional Standing Committees, 96th Congress

Committees of the Senate

Agriculture, Nutrition, and Forestry (18 members)
Chairman: Herman E. Talmadge (Ga.)
Ranking Repub.: Jesse A. Helms (N.C.)
Appropriations (28 members)
Chairman: Warren G. Magnuson (Wash.)
Ranking Repub.: Milton R. Young (N.D.)
Armed Services (17 members)
Chairman: John C. Stennis (Miss.)
Ranking Repub.: John G. Tower (Tex.)
Banking, Housing, and Urban Affairs (15 members)
Chairman: William Proxmire (Wis.)
Ranking Repub.: E.J. (Jake) Garn, (Utah)
Budget (20 members)
Chairman: Ernest F. Hollings (S.C.)
Ranking Repub.: Henry Bellmon (Okla.)
Commerce, Science, and Transportation (17 members)
Chairman: Howard W. Cannon (Nev.)
Ranking Repub.: Bob Packwood (Ore.)
Energy and Natural Resources (18 members)
Chairman: Henry M. Jackson (Wash.)
Ranking Repub.: Mark O. Hatfield (Ore.)
Environment and Public Works (14 members)
Chairman: Jennings Randolph (W.Va.)
Ranking Repub.: Robert T. Stafford (Vt.)
Finance (20 members)
Chairman: Russell B. Long (La.)
Ranking Repub.: Robert J. Dole (Kan.)
Foreign Relations (15 members)
Chairman: Frank Church (Idaho)
Ranking Repub.: Jacob K. Javits (N.Y.)
Governmental Affairs (17 members)
Chairman: Abraham A. Ribicoff (Conn.)
Ranking Repub.: Charles H. Percy (Ill.)
Judiciary (17 members)
Chairman: Edward M. Kennedy (Mass.)
Ranking Repub.: Strom Thurmond (S.C.)
Labor and Human Resources (15 members)
Chairman: Harrison A. Williams (N.J.)
Ranking Repub.: Richard S. Schweiker (Pa.)
Rules and Administration (10 members)
Chairman: Claiborne Pell (R.I.)
Ranking Repub.: Mark O. Hatfield (Ore.)
Veterans' Affairs (10 members)
Chairman: Alan Cranston (Calif.)
Ranking Repub.: Alan K. Simpson (Wyo.)

Committees of the House

Agriculture (42 members)
Chairman: Thomas S. Foley (Wash.)
Ranking Repub.: William C. Wampler (Va.)
Appropriations (54 members)
Chairman: Jamie L. Whitten (Miss.)
Ranking Repub.: Silvio O. Conte (Mass.)
Armed Services (45 members)
Chairman: Melvin Price (Ill.)
Ranking Repub.: Bob Wilson (Calif.)
Banking, Finance, and Urban Affairs (43 members)
Chairman: Henry S. Reuss (Wis.)
Ranking Repub.: J. William Stanton (Ohio)
Budget (25 members)
Chairman: Robert N. Giaimo (Conn.)
Ranking Repub.: Delbert L. Latta (Ohio)
District of Columbia (14 members)
Chairman: Ronald V. Dellums (Calif.)
Ranking Repub.: Stewart B. McKinney (Conn.)
Education and Labor (36 members)
Chairman: Carl D. Perkins (Ky.)
Ranking Repub.: John M. Ashbrook (Ohio)
Foreign Affairs (34 members)
Chairman: Clement J. Zablocki (Wis.)
Ranking Repub.: William S. Broomfield (Mich.)
Government Operations (39 members)
Chairman: Jack Brooks (Tex.)
Ranking Repub.: Frank Horton (N.Y.)
House Administration (25 members)
Chairman: Frank Thompson, Jr. (N.J.)
Ranking Repub.: William L. Dickinson (Ala.)
Interior and Insular Affairs (43 members)
Chairman: Morris K. Udall (Ariz.)
Ranking Repub.: Don H. Clausen (Calif.)
Interstate and Foreign Commerce (42 members)
Chairman: Harley O. Staggers (W. Va.)
Ranking Repub.: Samuel L. Devine (Ohio)
Judiciary (31 members)
Chairman: Peter W. Rodino, Jr. (N.J.)
Ranking Repub.: Robert McClory (Ill.)
Merchant Marine and Fisheries (40 members)
Chairman: John M. Murphy (N.Y.)
Ranking Repub.: Paul N. McCloskey, Jr. (Calif.)
Post Office and Civil Service (22 members)
Chairman: James M. Hanley (N.Y.)
Ranking Repub.: Edward J. Derwinski (Ill.)
Public Works and Transportation (46 members)
Chairman: Harold T. Johnson (Calif.)
Ranking Repub.: William H. Harsha (Ohio)
Rules (16 members)
Chairman: Richard Bolling (Mo.)
Ranking Repub.: James H. Quillen (Tenn.)
Science and Technology (41 members)
Chairman: Don Fuqua (Fla.)
Ranking Repub.: John W. Wydler (N.Y.)
Small Business (39 members)
Chairman: Neal Smith (Iowa)
Ranking Repub.: Joseph M. McDade (Pa.)
Standards of Official Conduct (12 members)
Chairman: Charles E. Bennett (Fla.)
Ranking Repub.: Floyd D. Spence (S.C.)
Veterans' Affairs (30 members)
Chairman: Ray Roberts (Tex.)
Ranking Repub.: John P. Hammerschmidt (Ark.)
Ways and Means (36 members)
Chairman: Al Ullman (Ore.)
Ranking Repub.: Barber B. Conable, Jr. (N.Y.)

Select and Special Committees

Aging (10 members)
Chairman: Lawton Chiles (Fla.)
Ranking Repub.: Pete V. Domenici (N.M.)
Ethics (6 members)
Chairman: Adlai E. Stevenson III (Ill.)
Ranking Repub.: Harrison Schmitt (N.M.)
Indian Affairs (5 members)
Chairman: John Melcher (Mont.)
Ranking Repub.: William S. Cohen (Me.)
Intelligence (13 members)
Chairman: Birch Bayh (Ind.)
Ranking Repub.: Barry Goldwater (Ariz.)
Small Business (17 members)
Chairman: Gaylord Nelson (Wis.)
Ranking Repub.: Lowell P. Weicker, Jr. (Conn.)

Speakers of the House of Representatives

Dates served	Congress	Name and state	Dates served	Congress	Name and state
1789–1791	1	Frederick A. C. Muhlenberg (Pa.)	1863–1869	38–40	Schuyler Colfax (Ind.)
1791–1793	2	Jonathan Trumbull (Conn.)	1869–1869	40	Theodore M. Pomeroy (N.Y.)[5]
1793–1795	3	Frederick A. C. Muhlenberg (Pa.)	1869–1875	41–43	James G. Blaine (Me.)
1795–1799	4–5	Jonathan Dayton (N.J.)[1]	1875–1876	44	Michael C. Kerr (Ind.)[6]
1799–1801	6	Theodore Sedgwick (Mass.)	1876–1881	44–46	Samuel J. Randall (Pa.)
1801–1807	7–9	Nathaniel Macon (N.C.)	1881–1883	47	J. Warren Keifer (Ohio)
1807–1811	10–11	Joseph B. Varnum (Mass.)	1883–1889	48–50	John G. Carlisle (Ky.)
1811–1814	12–13	Henry Clay (Ky.)[2]	1889–1891	51	Thomas B. Reed (Me.)
1814–1815	13	Langdon Cheves (S.C.)	1891–1895	52–53	Charles F. Crisp (Ga.)
1815–1820	14–16	Henry Clay (Ky.)[3]	1895–1899	54–55	Thomas B. Reed (Me.)
1820–1821	16	John W. Taylor (N.Y.)	1899–1903	56–57	David B. Henderson (Iowa)
1821–1823	17	Philip P. Barbour (Va.)	1903–1911	58–61	Joseph G. Cannon (Ill.)
1823–1825	18	Henry Clay (Ky.)	1911–1919	62–65	Champ Clark (Mo.)
1825–1827	19	John W. Taylor (N.Y.)	1919–1925	66–68	Frederick H. Gillett (Mass.)
1827–1834	20–23	Andrew Stevenson (Va.)[4]	1925–1931	69–71	Nicholas Longworth (Ohio)
1834–1835	23	John Bell (Tenn.)	1931–1933	72	John N. Garner (Tex.)
1835–1839	24–25	James K. Polk (Tenn.)	1933–1934	73	Henry T. Rainey (Ill.)[7]
1839–1841	26	Robert M. T. Hunter (Va.)	1935–1936	74	Joseph W. Byrns (Tenn.)[8]
1841–1843	27	John White (Ky.)	1936–1940	74–76	William B. Bankhead (Ala.)[9]
1843–1845	28	John W. Jones (Va.)	1940–1947	76–79	Sam Rayburn (Tex.)
1845–1847	29	John W. Davis (Ind.)	1947–1949	80	Joseph W. Martin, Jr. (Mass.)
1847–1849	30	Robert C. Winthrop (Mass.)	1949–1953	81–82	Sam Rayburn (Tex.)
1849–1851	31	Howell Cobb (Ga.)	1953–1955	83	Joseph W. Martin, Jr. (Mass.)
1851–1855	32–33	Linn Boyd (Ky.)	1955–1961	84–87	Sam Rayburn (Tex.)[10]
1855–1857	34	Nathaniel P. Banks (Mass.)	1962–1971	87–91	John W. McCormack (Mass.)[11]
1857–1859	35	James L. Orr (S.C.)	1971–1977	92–94	Carl Albert (Okla.)[12]
1859–1861	36	Wm. Pennington (N.J.)	1977–	95–	Thomas P. O'Neill, Jr. (Mass.)
1861–1863	37	Galusha A. Grow (Pa.)			

1. George Dent (Md.) was elected Speaker pro tempore for April 20 and May 28, 1798. 2. Resigned during second session of 13th Congress. 3. Resigned between first and second sessions of 16th Congress. 4. Resigned during first session of 23rd Congress. 5. Elected Speaker and served the day of adjournment. 6. Died between first and second sessions of 44th Congress. During first session, there were two Speakers pro tempore: Samuel S. Cox (N.Y.), appointed for Feb. 17, May 12, and June 19, 1876, and Milton Sayler (Ohio), appointed for June 4, 1876. 7. Died in 1934 after adjournment of second session of 73rd Congress. 8. Died during second session of 74th Congress. 9. Died during third session of 76th Congress. 10. Died between first and second sessions of 87th Congress. 11. Not a candidate in 1970 election. 12. Not a candidate in 1976 election. *Source:* Congressional Directory.

Floor Leaders of the Senate

Democratic	Republican
Gilbert M. Hitchcock, Neb. (Min. 1919–20)	Charles Curtis, Kan. (Maj. 1925–29)
Oscar W. Underwood, Ala. (Min. 1920–23)	James E. Watson, Ind. (Maj. 1929–33)
Joseph T. Robinson, Ark. (Min. 1923–33, Maj. 1933–37)	Charles L. McNary, Ore. (Min. 1933–44)
Alben W. Barkley, Ky. (Maj. 1937–46, Min. 1947–48)	Wallace H. White, Jr., Me. (Min. 1944–47, Maj. 1947–48)
Scott W. Lucas, Ill. (Maj. 1949–50)	Kenneth S. Wherry, Neb. (Min. 1949–51)
Ernest W. McFarland, Ariz. (Maj. 1951–52)	Styles Bridges, N. H. (Min. 1951–52)
Lyndon B. Johnson, Tex. (Min. 1953–54, Maj. 1955–60)	Robert A. Taft, Ohio (Maj. 1953)
Mike Mansfield, Mont. (Maj. 1961–1977)	William F. Knowland, Calif. (Maj. 1953–54, Min. 1955–58)
Robert C. Byrd, W. Va. (Maj. 1977-)	Everett M. Dirksen, Ill. (Min. 1959–69)
	Hugh Scott, Pa. (Min. 1969–1977)
	Howard H. Baker, Jr., Tenn. (Min. 1977–)

NOTE: Min. = Minority Leader; Maj. = Majority Leader. *Source:* United States Senate, Secretary for the Majority.

Annual Salaries of Federal Officials

President of the U.S.	$200,000[1]	Secretaries of the Army, Navy, Air Force	$60,662
Vice President of the U.S.	79,125[2]	Senators and Representatives	60,622
Cabinet members	69,630	President Pro Tempore of Senate	68,575
Under secretaries of executive departments	55,387	Speaker of the House	79,125
Deputy Secretaries of State, Defense, Treasury	60,662	Majority and Minority Leader of the Senate	68,575
Deputy Attorney General	60,662	Majority and Minority Leader of the House	68,575
Under Secretary of Transportation	60,662	Chief Justice of the United States	75,000
		Associate Justices of the Supreme Court	72,000

1. Plus taxable $50,000 for expenses and a nontaxable sum (not to exceed $100,000 a year) for travel expenses. 2. Plus taxable $10,000 for expenses. NOTE: All salaries shown above are taxable.

Executive Departments and Agencies

Source: U.S. Government Organization Manual.

Unless otherwise indicated, addresses shown are in Washington, D.C.

CENTRAL INTELLIGENCE AGENCY (CIA)
Washington, D.C. (20505)
Established: 1947.
Director: Adm. Stansfield Turner.
Activities: Coordinates intelligence activities of certain government departments and agencies by making recommendations to the National Security Council; correlates and evaluates intelligence and disseminates the results; performs certain additional services for existing intelligence agencies when the National Security Council determines that these can be more efficiently accomplished centrally.

COUNCIL OF ECONOMIC ADVISERS (CEA)
Executive Office Bldg. (20506).
Members: 3.
Established: Feb. 20, 1946.
Chairman: Charles L. Schultze.
Activities: Assists President in preparation of economic reports to Congress; studies economic trends; appraises government activities on nation's economy; recommends economic policies.

COUNCIL ON ENVIRONMENTAL QUALITY
722 Jackson Pl., N.W. (20006).
Members: 3.
Established: 1969.
Chairman: Gus Speth.
Activities: Develops and recommends to President national policies that promote environmental quality.

COUNCIL ON WAGE AND PRICE STABILITY
Wynder Bldg., 600 17th Street, N.W. (20506).
Members: 8.
Established: Aug. 24, 1974.
Chairman: Alfred E. Kahn.
Director: R. Robert Russell.
Activities: Monitors wages and prices and provides guidance on broad terms to labor and management.

DOMESTIC POLICY STAFF
1600 Pennsylvania Ave., N.W. (20500).
Members: 30.
Established: July 1, 1970.
Executive Director: Stuart E. Eizenstat.
Activities: Formulates and coordinates domestic policy recommendations to President. Endeavors to resolve federal-state-local problems.

NATIONAL SECURITY COUNCIL (NSC)
Executive Office Bldg. (20506).
Members: 4.
Established: July 26, 1947.
Chairman: President of U.S.
Other members: Vice President; Secretary of State; Secretary of Defense.
Activities: Assesses and appraises objectives, commitments and risks of United States in relation to our actual and potential military power.

OFFICE OF ADMINISTRATION
Old Executive Office Building (20500).
Established: Dec. 12, 1977.
Director: Richard M. Harden.
Activities: Provides the common services for the Executive Office of the President such as mail, payroll, dataprocessing and messengers.

OFFICE OF MANAGEMENT AND BUDGET
Executive Office Bldg. (20503).
Established: July 1, 1970.
Director: James T. McIntyre, Jr.
Activities: Assists President in preparing budget and formulating fiscal program; supervises administration of budget; coordinates advice on proposed legislation; plans improvements in statistical services; keeps President informed of progress of activities by government agencies so that Congressional appropriations are spent most economically.

OFFICE OF SCIENCE AND TECHNOLOGY POLICY
Executive Office Building (20500).
Established: June 8, 1962.
Director: Frank Press.
Activities: Advises the President on scientific, engineering, and technological aspects of issues requiring his attention.

OFFICE OF THE UNITED STATES TRADE REPRESENTATIVE
1800 G St., N.W. (20506).
Established: Jan. 15, 1963.
Special Representative: Reubin O'D. Askew.
Activities: Advises the President on the administration and carrying out of the trade agreements program and on non-tariff barriers to international trade and international commodity agreements; chairs the Trade Expansion Act Advisory Committee.

Executive Departments

DEPARTMENT OF STATE
2201 C St., N.W. (20520).
Established: 1781 as Department of Foreign Affairs; reconstituted, 1789, following adoption of Constitution; name changed to Department of State Sept. 15, 1789.
Secretary: Edmund S. Muskie
Deputy Secretary: Warren M. Christopher.
Activities: Determines government policy in relation to international problems; formulates measures for promoting friendship with other countries; develops policies and programs for U.S. participation in U.N. and other international organizations; conducts correspondence with our representatives abroad and accredited foreign representatives here; administers Foreign Service, Agency for International Development.

DEPARTMENT OF THE TREASURY
15th St. & Pennsylvania Ave., N.W. (20220).
Established: Sept. 2, 1789.
Secretary: G. William Miller.
Deputy Secretary: Robert Carswell.
Treasurer of the U.S.: Mrs. Azie T. Morton.
Comptroller of the Currency: John G. Heimann.
Activities: Manages national finances; grants war-

rants for money drawn from Treasury pursuant to legal appropriations; handles collection of revenue; keeps and renders public accounts; prepares plans for improvement of revenue and for support of public credit; controls coinage and printing of money; administers Secret Service, Customs Service, Internal Revenue Service, Bureau of Engraving and Printing, Bureau of the Mint, Bureau of Alcohol, Tobacco and Firearms, Federal Law Enforcement Training Center.

DEPARTMENT OF DEFENSE

The Pentagon (20301).

Established: July 26, 1947, as National Department Establishment; name changed to Department of Defense on Aug. 10, 1949. Subordinate to Secretary of Defense are Secretaries of Army, Navy, Air Force.

Secretary: Harold Brown.

Deputy Secretary: W. Graham Claytor, Jr.

Secretary of Army: Clifford L. Alexander, Jr.

Secretary of Navy: Edward Hidalgo.

Secretary of Air Force: Hans Mark.

Commandant of Marine Corps: Gen. Robert H. Barrow.

Joint Chiefs of Staff:[1] Gen. David C. Jones, Chairman; Adm. Thomas B. Hayward, Jr., Navy; Gen. Lew Allen, Jr., Air Force: Gen. Edward C. Meyer, Army; Gen. Robert H. Barrow, Marine Corps.

Activities: Provides for security of U.S. by establishing integrated policies and procedures; co-ordinates and directs the activities of three separately administered military departments (Army, Navy, and Air Force).

1. Consisting of chairman and chiefs of each service.

DEPARTMENT OF JUSTICE

Constitution Ave. between 9th & 10th Sts., N.W. (20530).

Established: Office of Attorney General was created Sept. 24, 1789. Although he was one of original Cabinet members, he was not executive department head until June 22, 1870, when Department of Justice was established.

Attorney General: Benjamin R. Civiletti.

Deputy Attorney General: Charles B. Renfrew.

Solicitor General: Wade H. McCree, Jr.

Director of FBI: William H. Webster.

Activities: Provides means for enforcing federal laws; investigates and detects violations; represents U.S. in legal matters generally and gives advice and opinions when requested by President or heads of executive departments; directs FBI, Bureau of Prisons, Immigration and Naturalization Service, Drug Enforcement Administration, Law Enforcement Assistance Administration, Marshals Service, U.S. Parole Commission, Board of Immigration Appeals.

DEPARTMENT OF THE INTERIOR

C St. between 18th & 19th Sts., N.W. (20240).

Established: March 3, 1849.

Secretary: Cecil D. Andrus.

Under Secretary: James A. Joseph.

Activities: Develops and conserves natural resources of U.S. and territories; supervises public business relating to such offices as Bureau of Land Management, Geological Survey, Bureau of Indian Affairs, National Park Service, Bureau of Mines, Fish and Wildlife Service, Bureau of Reclamation, Heritage Conservation and Recreation Service, Office of Water Research and Technology, Office of Minerals Policy and Research Analysis, Ocean Mining Administration.

DEPARTMENT OF AGRICULTURE

Independence Ave. between 12th & 14th Sts., S.W. (20250).

Established: May 15, 1862. Administered by Commissioner of Agriculture until 1889, when it was made executive department.

Secretary: Bob Bergland.

Deputy Secretary: Jim Williams.

Activities: Conducts comprehensive research and educational program relating to agriculture; provides crop reports, commodity standards, meat inspection and other marketing services; administers national forests; aids in flood control; administers price-support and production-adjustment programs; makes loans to farmers; supervises Farmers Home Administration, Agricultural Marketing Service, Rural Electrification Administration, Federal Grain Inspection Service, Animal and Plant Inspection Service, Food and Nutrition Service, Food Safety and Quality Service, Commodity Credit Corporation, Federal Crop Insurance Corporation, Science and Education Administration.

DEPARTMENT OF COMMERCE

14th St. between Constitution Ave. & E St., N.W. (20230).

Established: Department of Commerce and Labor was created Feb. 14, 1903. On March 4, 1913, all labor activities were transferred out of Department of Commerce and Labor and it was renamed Department of Commerce.

Secretary: Philip M. Klutznick.

Under Secretary: Luther H. Hodges, Jr.

Activities: Fosters and develops foreign and domestic commerce of U.S.; maintains Bureau of the Census, Industry and Trade Administration, Economic Development Administration, Bureau of Economic Analysis, Office of Minority Business Enterprise, Patent and Trademark Office, National Oceanic and Atmospheric Administration (including National Weather Service), National Technical Information Service, Office of Telecommunications, Travel Service, Maritime Administration, National Bureau of Standards, National Fire Prevention and Control Administration.

DEPARTMENT OF LABOR

200 Constitution Ave., N.W. (20210).

Established: Bureau of Labor was created in 1884 under Department of the Interior; later became independent department without executive rank. Returned to bureau status in Department of Commerce and Labor, but on March 4, 1913, became independent executive department under its present name.

Secretary: Ray Marshall.

Under Secretary: John N. Gentry.

Activities: Promotes welfare of wage earners of U.S., improving working conditions and advancing opportunities for profitable employment; directs collection and collation of statistics concerning labor conditions; promulgates and enforces certain maximum-hour, minimum-wage, child-labor, safety and health standards. Maintains Employment and Training Administration, Labor-Management Services Administration, Employment Standards Administration, Occupational Safety and Health

Administration, Bureau of Labor Statistics, Mine Safety and Health Administration.

DEPARTMENT OF HEALTH AND HUMAN SERVICES
330 Independence Ave., S.W. (20201).
Established: April 11, 1953, replacing Federal Security Agency created in 1939.[1]
Secretary: Patricia Roberts Harris.
Under Secretary: Nathan Stark.
Activities: Supervises and coordinates various organizations within the department. Organizations are: Food and Drug Administration, Office of Human Development Services, Public Health Service, Social Security Administration, Alcohol, Drug Abuse and Mental Health Administration, National Institutes of Health, Center for Disease Control, Health Care Financing Administration, Office of Child Support Enforcement, Health Resources Administration.

DEPARTMENT OF HOUSING AND URBAN DEVELOPMENT
451 7th St., S.W. (20410).
Established: 1965, replacing Housing and Home Finance Agency created in 1947.
Secretary: Moon Landrieu.
Under Secretary: Victor Marrero.
Activities: Supervises and coordinates New Community Development Corporation, Federal Disaster Assistance Administration, Federal Insurance Administration, Government National Mortgage Association.

DEPARTMENT OF TRANSPORTATION
400 7th St., S.W. (20590).
Established: Oct. 15, 1966, as result of Department of Transportation Act, which became effective April 1, 1967.
Secretary: Neil E. Goldschmidt.
Deputy Secretary: William J. Beckman, Jr.
Activities: Supervises and coordinates activities of Coast Guard, Federal Aviation Administration, Federal Highway Administration, Federal Railroad Administration, St. Lawrence Seaway Development Corporation, National Highway Traffic Safety Administration, Urban Mass Transportation Administration, Materials Transportation Bureau.

DEPARTMENT OF ENERGY
1000 Independence Ave., S.W. (20585).
Established: August 1977.
Secretary: Charles W. Duncan, Jr.
Deputy Secretary: John C. Sawhill.
Activities: Takes over the Federal Energy Administration, the Federal Power Commission, the Energy Research and Development Administration, and functions of other government agencies concerned with energy. Has management responsibility for such projects as Bonneville Dam, the Energy Information Administration to develop reliable energy statistics, and the Energy Regulatory Administration to audit and police energy companies.

DEPARTMENT OF EDUCATION
400 Maryland Avenue, S.W. (20202)
Established: May 4, 1980

1. Originally Department of Health, Education and Welfare. Name changed in May 1980 when Department of Education was activated.

Secretary: Shirley M. Hufstedler
Under Secretary: Steven A. Minter
Activities: Administers federally mandated education programs that pertain to elementary and secondary education, post-secondary, vocational and adult education, and special education and rehabilitative services. Supervises National Institute of Education, Fund for the Improvement of Postsecondary Education, Institute of Museum Services, and National Center for Educational Statistics.

Independent Agencies

(Titles and addresses of independent agencies not described below follow on pages 640-41)

ACTION
806 Connecticut Ave., N.W. (20525).
Established: July 1, 1971.
Director: Sam W. Brown, Jr.
Activities: Coordinates a system of volunteer services to people in need at home and abroad; administers Peace Corps and VISTA (Volunteers in Service to America).

CIVIL AERONAUTICS BOARD (CAB)
1825 Connecticut Ave., N.W. (20428)
Members: 5.
Established: June 30, 1940.
Chairman: Marvin S. Cohen.
Activities: Regulates economic aspects of U.S. air carrier operation; assists in development of international air transportation; promotes safety in civil aviation.

COMMUNITY SERVICES ADMINISTRATION
1200 19th St., N.W. (20506).
Established: 1974.
Director: Richard J. Rios.
Activities: Assists low-income individuals and persons of limited English-speaking ability to attain the skills, knowledge, and opportunities to become self-sufficient.

CONSUMER PRODUCT SAFETY COMMISSION
1111 18th St., N.W. (20207).
Members: 5.
Established: May 14, 1973.
Chairman: Susan B. King.
Activities. Protects the public against unreasonable risks of injury associated with consumer products; assists consumers to evaluate the comparative safety of products; develops uniform safety standards for products; promotes research into causes and prevention of product-related deaths, illnesses, and injuries.

ENVIRONMENTAL PROTECTION AGENCY (EPA)
401 M St., S.W. (20460).
Established: Dec. 2, 1970.
Administrator: Douglas M. Costle.
Activities: Coordinates governmental action to assure protection of the environment by abating and controlling pollution.

EQUAL EMPLOYMENT OPPORTUNITY COMMISSION (EEOC)
2401 E St., N.W. (20506).
Members: 5.
Established: July 2, 1965.
Chairman: Eleanor Holmes Norton.

Activities: Prohibits employment discrimination based on race, color, religion, sex, or national origin.

FARM CREDIT ADMINISTRATION (FCA)
490 L'Enfant Plaza East, S.W. (20578).
Members: 13.
Established: July 17, 1916.
Chairman of Federal Farm Credit Board: Ralph N. Austin.
Activities: Supervises and coordinates cooperative credit system for agriculture; provides long- and short-term credit to farmers and their cooperative marketing, purchasing, and business service organizations.

FEDERAL COMMUNICATIONS COMMISSION (FCC)
1919 M St., N.W. (20554).
Members: 7.
Established: 1934.
Chairman: Charles D. Ferris.
Activities: Regulates interstate and foreign communications by wire and radio, including amateur radio and TV; regulates operator's licenses; classifies radio stations and prescribes their services.

FEDERAL ELECTION COMMISSION (FEC)
1325 K St., N.W. (20463).
Members: 6.
Established: 1974.
Chairman: Robert O. Tiernan.
Activities: Certifies distribution of public funding of federal elections; regulates compliance with Federal Election Campaign Act; makes available to the public copies of reports filed with the commission.

FEDERAL MARITIME COMMISSION
1100 L St., N.W. (20573).
Members: 5.
Established: Aug. 12, 1961.
Chairman: Richard J. Daschbach.
Activities: Regulates waterborne shipping in foreign and domestic offshore commerce of U.S.

FEDERAL MEDIATION AND CONCILIATION SERVICE (FMCS)
2100 K St., N.W. (20427).
Established: 1947.
Director: Wayne L. Horvitz.
Activities: Assists in labor-management disputes in industries affecting interstate commerce to reach settlements by mediation or conciliation.

FEDERAL RESERVE SYSTEM (FRS), BOARD OF GOVERNORS OF
20th St. & Constitution Ave., N.W. (20551).
Members: 7.
Established: Dec. 23, 1913.
Chairman: Paul A. Volcker.
Activities: Supervises the 12 Federal Reserve banks, 24 branches and member commercial banks; determines country's monetary policy, including setting maximum interest paid by member banks, amount of credit extended for purchase of securities and discount rates charged by members; handles Government deposits and debt issue; regulates open-market operations; issues Federal Reserve notes.

FEDERAL TRADE COMMISSION (FTC)
Pennsylvania Ave. at 6th St., N.W. (20580).
Members: 5.
Established: Sept. 26, 1914.
Chairman: Michael Pertschuk.
Activities: Prevents unfair competition, deceptive practices, false advertising, price discrimination, monopolies.

GENERAL SERVICES ADMINISTRATION (GSA)
18th and F Sts., N.W. (20405).
Established: July 1, 1949.
Administrator: Rear Adm. Rowland G. Freeman III.
Activities: Establishes policy and provides efficient system for management of the government's property and records, including construction and operation of buildings, procurement and distribution of supplies, stockpiling of strategic materials and utilization and disposal of property. Directs National Archives and Records Service, Federal Supply Service, Public Buildings Service, Federal Preparedness Agency, Automated Data and Telecommunications Service.

INTERNATIONAL COMMUNICATION AGENCY
1750 Pennsylvania Ave., N.W. (20547).
Established: April 1, 1978.
Director: John E. Reinhardt.
Activities: Conducts international communication, educational, cultural, and exchange programs with other peoples of the world.

INTERSTATE COMMERCE COMMISSION (ICC)
12th St. & Constitution Ave., N.W. (20423).
Members: 11.
Established: Feb. 4, 1887.
Chairman: Darius W. Gaskins, Jr.
Activities: Regulates railroads, motor carriers, water carriers, and freight forwarders as to rates, through-routes, services, and bills of lading; authorizes mergers or consolidations; authorizes issue of securities by carriers.

NATIONAL AERONAUTICS AND SPACE ADMINISTRATION (NASA)
400 Maryland Ave., S.W. (20546).
Established: 1958.
Administrator: Robert A. Frosch.
Activities: Conducts research into problems of flight within and outside earth's atmosphere.

NATIONAL FOUNDATION ON THE ARTS AND THE HUMANITIES
2401 E St., N.W. (20506).
Established: 1965.
Chairman: National Endowment for the Arts, Livingston L. Biddle, Jr.; National Endowment for the Humanities, Joseph D. Duffey.
Activities: Encourages and supports national progress in the humanities and the arts. Also includes National Councils on the Arts and the Humanities, which coordinates activities of the two endowments and related programs of other agencies.

NATIONAL LABOR RELATIONS BOARD (NLRB)
1717 Pennsylvania Ave., N.W. (20570).
Members: 5.
Established: July 5, 1935.
Chairman: John H. Fanning.
Activities: Prevents unfair labor practices by employers or labor organizations; conducts secret ballots among employees to determine bargaining representatives.

NATIONAL SCIENCE FOUNDATION (NSF)
1800 G St., N.W. (20550).
Established: 1950.
Director: Richard C. Atkinson.
Activities: Awards grants and contracts to support research in the sciences. Encourages research in areas that can lead to improvements in economic growth, productivity, and environmental quality. Administered by 25-member National Science Board.

NATIONAL TRANSPORTATION SAFETY BOARD
800 Independence Ave., S.W. (20594).
Members: 5.
Established: April 1, 1975.
Chairman: James B. King.
Activities: Conducts investigations into accidents, assesses techniques of accident investigation and recommends safety-improvement measures.

NUCLEAR REGULATORY COMMISSION (NRC)
1717 H St., N.W. (20555) and Bethesda, Md. (20014).
Members: 5.
Established: Jan. 19, 1975.
Chairman: John F. Ahearne (acting).
Activities: Regulates civilian nuclear facilities to assure protection of public health and safety and the environment, and safeguarding of nuclear materials and facilities.

SECURITIES AND EXCHANGE COMMISSION (SEC)
500 N. Capitol St., N.W. (20549).
Members: 5.
Established: June 6, 1934.
Chairman: Harold M. Williams.
Activities: Registers and issues regulations for securities and exchanges; registers securities offered for public sale; penalizes violators of regulations subject to appeal to U.S. Court of Appeals.

SMALL BUSINESS ADMINISTRATION (SBA)
1441 L St., N.W. (20416).
Established: July 30, 1953.
Administrator: A. Vernon Weaver, Jr.
Activities: Aids and assists the interests of small business firms to insure a fair share of total government contracts; makes loans to small firms and victims of flood and disaster.

TENNESSEE VALLEY AUTHORITY (TVA)
400 Commerce Ave., Knoxville, Tenn. (37902). Washington office: Woodward Bldg., 15th & H Sts., N.W. (20444).
Members of Board of Directors: 3.
Established: May 18, 1933.
Chairman: S. David Freeman.
Activities: Provides navigable channel and flood control of Tennessee River and some of its larger tributaries; disposes of surplus electric power, improves, increases, and cheapens fertilizer production.

U.S. ARMS CONTROL AND DISARMAMENT AGENCY
Department of State Building (20451).
Established: Sept. 26, 1961.
Director: Ralph Earle II.
Activities: Conducts studies and provides advice relating to arms control and disarmament policy fomulation; prepares for and manages U.S. participation in international negotiations in arms control and disarmament; prepares for, operates, or as needed, directs U.S. participation in international control systems.

COMMISSION ON CIVIL RIGHTS
1121 Vermont Avenue, N.W. (20425).
Members: 6.
Established: 1957.
Chairman: Arthur S. Flemming.
Activities: Collects and studies information concerning discrimination or denial of equal protection of the nation's laws because of race, color, religion, sex, age, handicap, or national origin. Complaints about denials of rights are usually referred to the appropriate Federal agencies for action.

U.S. INTERNATIONAL TRADE COMMISSION
701 E St., N.W. (20436).
Members: 6.
Established: Sept. 8, 1916.
Chairman: Bill Alberger.
Activities: Investigates customs laws, unfair competition, and foreign and domestic manufacturing costs; advises the President on duty rates.

OFFICE OF PERSONNEL MANAGEMENT (OPM)
1900 E St., N.W. (20415).
Members: 3.
Established: Jan. 16, 1883.
Chairman: Alan K. Campbell.
Activities: Provides examinations to test fitness of applicants for positions in competitive service; provides personnel in response to requests from appointing officers; investigates applicants for national security purposes; classifies positions; provides leadership to Federal agencies in personnel matters.

U.S. POSTAL SERVICE
475 L'Enfant Plaza West, S.W. (20260).
Established: Office of Postmaster General and temporary post office system created in 1789. Act of Feb. 20, 1792, made detailed provisions for Post Office Department. Postmaster General became Cabinet member in 1829, and Department received executive status in 1872. In 1970 became independent agency headed by 11-member board of governors. Postmaster General, no longer Cabinet member, is chosen by nine governors, who, with Postmaster General, choose Deputy Postmaster General.
Postmaster General: William F. Bolger.
Deputy Postmaster General: James V.P. Conway.
Activities: Maintains postal system of U.S.

VETERANS ADMINISTRATION (VA)
810 Vermont Ave., N.W. (20420).
Established: July 21, 1930.
Administrator: Max Cleland.
Activities: Administers laws authorizing benefits for veterans and dependents or beneficiaries. Included are hospitals, pensions, insurance, loans, education, etc.

Other Independent Agencies

Executive Department

Administrative Conference of the United States—2120 L St., N.W. (20037).

American Battle Monuments Commission—1000 Independence Ave., S.W. (20314).

Appalachian Regional Commission—1666 Connecticut Ave., N.W. (20235).
Board for International Broadcasting—1030 15th St., N.W. (20005).
Canal Zone Government—425 13th St., N.W. (20004).
Commission of Fine Arts—708 Jackson Place, N.W. (20006).
Commission on Civil Rights—1121 Vermont Ave., N.W. (20425).
Commodity Futures Trading Commission—2033 K St., N.W. (20581).
Export-Import Bank of the United States—811 Vermont Ave., N.W. (20571).
Federal Deposit Insurance Corporation—550 17th St., N.W. (20429).
Federal Home Loan Bank Board—1700 G St., N.W. (20552).
Federal Labor Relations Authority—1900 E St., N.W. (20424).
Foreign Claims Settlement Commission of the U.S.—1111 20th St., N.W. (20579).
Inter-American Foundation—1515 Wilson Blvd., Rosslyn, Va. (22209).
Merit Systems Protection Board—1717 H St., N.W. (20419).
National Center for the Prevention and Control of Rape—5600 Fishers Lane, Rockville, Md. (20857).
National Center for Productivity and Quality of Working Life—2000 M St. (20036).
National Commission on Libraries and Information Science—1717 K St. (20036).
National Credit Union Administration—2025 M St., N.W. (20456).
National Mediation Board—1425 K St., N.W. (20572).
National Science Foundation—1800 G Street, N.W. (20550).
Occupational Safety and Health Review Commission—1825 K St., N.W. (20006).
Overseas Private Investment Corporation—1129 20th St., N.W. (20527).
Panama Canal Company—425 13th St., N.W. (20004).
Pension Benefit Guaranty Corporation—2020 K St., N.W. (20006).
Postal Rate Commission—2000 L St., N.W. (20268).
President's Committee on Employment of the Handicapped—1111 20th St., N.W. (20210).
President's Council on Physical Fitness and Sports—400 6th St., S.W. (20201).
Railroad Retirement Board (RRB)—844 Rush St., Chicago, Ill. (60611). Washington Liaison Office: Room 444, 425 13th St., N.W. (20004).
Selective Service System—National Headquarters, 600 E Street, N.W. (20435).
U.S. Metric Board—1815 N. Lynn St., Arlington, Va. (22209).
U.S. Parole Commission—320 1st St., N.W. (20537).

Legislative Department

ARCHITECT OF THE CAPITOL
U.S. Capitol Building (20515).
Established: First Architect of the Capitol was appointed in 1793; office has been continuous since 1851.
Architect of Capitol: George M. White.
Activities: Architect of the Capitol has charge of structural and mechanical care of Capitol Building and various other government buildings in Washington.

COST ACCOUNTING STANDARDS BOARD
441 G St., N.W. (20548).
Established: Aug. 15, 1970.
Chairman: Elmer B. Staats.
Activities: Promulgates cost-accounting standards to be followed by defense contractors under federal contracts.

GENERAL ACCOUNTING OFFICE
441 G Street, N.W. (20548).
Established: 1921.
Comptroller General: Elmer B. Staats.
Deputy Comptroller General: Robert F. Keller.
Activities: Assists Congress in providing legislative control over receipt, disbursement, and application of public funds.

GOVERNMENT PRINTING OFFICE (GPO)
North Capitol & H Sts., N.W. (20401).
Established: June 23, 1860.
Public Printer: Samuel L. Saylor (acting).
Superintendent of Documents: Carl A. LaBarre.
Activities: Executes printing and binding orders for Congress and federal agencies; distributes government publications.

LIBRARY OF CONGRESS
10 First St., S.E. (20540).
Established: April 24, 1800.
Librarian of Congress: Daniel J. Boorstin.
Activities: Extends services to members of government and offers facilities for persons engaged in scholarly research.

OFFICE OF TECHNOLOGY ASSESSMENT
600 Pennsylvania Ave., S.E. (20510).
Established: 1972.
Director: John H. Gibbons.
Activities: Helps Congress anticipate and plan for the consequences of the uses of technology.

UNITED STATES BOTANIC GARDEN
Office of Director, 245 First St., S.W. (20024).
Established: 1820.
Director: George M. White (acting).
Activities: Collects, cultivates, and grows various vegetable products for exhibition and study.

Quasi-Official Agencies

American National Red Cross—17th & D Sts., N.W. (20006).
Legal Services Corporation—733 15th St., N.W. (20005).
National Academy of Sciences, National Academy of Engineering, National Research Council, Institute of Medicine—2101 Constitution Ave., N.W. (20418).
National Railroad Passenger Corporation (Amtrak)—400 N. Capitol St., N.W. (20001).
Smithsonian Institution—1000 Jefferson Dr., S.W. (20560).
U.S. Railway Association—955 L'Enfant Plaza North, S.W. (20595).

"In God We Trust"

"In God We Trust" first appeared on U.S. coins after April 22, 1864, when Congress passed an act authorizing the coinage of a 2-cent piece bearing this motto. Thereafter, Congress extended its use to other coins. On July 30, 1956, it became the national motto.

Major U.S. Daily Newspapers[1]

City and newspaper	Net paid circulation: Morning[2]	Evening[2]	Sunday
Akron, Ohio: *Beacon Journal*	—	161,835	218,969
Albany, N.Y.: *Times–Union* (M & S); *Knickerbocker News* (E)	82,207[4]	51,780[3,4]	149,516[4]
Albuquerque, N.M.: *Journal* (M & S); *Tribune* (E)	84,364[4]	43,769[4]	129,343[4]
Allentown, Pa.: *Call* (M); *Chronicle* (E); *Call–Chronicle* (S)	103,258[3]	23,707[3]	154,805
Asbury Park, N.J.: *Press*	—	105,368	139,787
Atlanta: *Constitution* (M); *Journal* (E); *Journal and Constitution* (S)	218,807	211,081	501,867
Augusta, Ga.: *Chronicle* (M); *Herald* (E); *Chronicle–Herald* (S)	56,635	18,692	81,861
Austin, Tex.: *American–Statesman*	92,013[3]	35,065[3]	142,428
Bakersfield, Calif.: *Californian*	70,121[4]	—	78,418[4]
Baltimore: *Sun*	177,980[3]	172,868[3]	374,989
News–American	—	150,502[3]	229,777
Baton Rouge, La.: *Advocate* (M & S); *State Times* (E)	76,684	43,192	116,792
Bergen County (Hackensack), N.J.: *Record* (E); *Sunday Record*	—	150,378[3,4]	213,799[4]
Beaumont, Tex.: *Enterprise* (M & S); *Journal* (E)	65,281	14,037	79,266
Binghamton, N.Y.: *Sun–Bulletin* (M); *Press* (E & S)	27,561[3]	67,342[3]	83,259
Birmingham, Ala.: *Post–Herald* (M); *News* (E & S)	68,349[3]	178,074[3]	217,352
Boston: *Globe*	491,682[3,5]		710,731
Herald American			
Christian Science Monitor	172,470[3]	—	—
Bridgeport, Conn.: *Telegram* (M); *Post* (E); *Sunday Post*	16,890[4]	73,711[4]	92,444[4]
Buffalo, N.Y.: *Courier–Express*	126,197	—	254,482
Evening News	—	269,474[3]	170,410
Camden, N.J.: *Courier–Post*	—	126,498[4]	96,030[4]
Canton, Ohio: *Repository*	—	65,048[4]	80,142[4]
Cedar Rapids, Iowa: *Gazette*	—	68,800	76,504
Charleston, W.Va.: *Gazette* (M); *Daily Mail* (E); *Gazette–Mail* (S)	55,940	56,229	106,664
Charlotte, N.C.: *Observer* (M & S); *News* (E)	169,400	51,809	241,194
Chattanooga, Tenn.: *News–Free Press*	—	62,451[3]	78,162
Times	50,346[3]	—	52,019[10]
Chicago: *Tribune*	789,767[3,5]		1,146,474
Sun–Times	657,275[3]	—	700,315
Wall Street Journal (Midwest edition)	523,072[3]	—	—
Cincinnati: *Enquirer* (M & S); *Post* (E)	186,732	168,227	293,826
Cleveland: *Plain Dealer* (M & S); *Press* (E)	392,688	300,889	454,922
Cocoa, Fla.: *Today*	69,017	—	81,637
Colorado Springs, Colo.: *Gazette Telegraph*	25,237	52,063	81,347
Sun	28,674[3]	—	29,239
Columbia, S.C.: *State* (M & S); *Record* (E)	106,180	32,882	126,300
Columbus, Ohio: *Dispatch* (E & S); *Citizen–Journal* (M)	112,195	202,949	341,568
Corpus Christi, Tex.: *Caller* (M); *Times* (E); *Caller–Times* (S)	61,918[3,4]	24,074[3,4]	86,761[4]
Dallas: *Morning News*	286,955	—	353,677
Times Herald	249,890[5]		345,736
Wall Street Journal (Southwest edition)	194,534[3]	—	—
Davenport, Iowa: *Quad City Times*	64,328[5]		83,011
Dayton, Ohio: *Daily News* (E & S); *Journal Herald* (M)	100,886	140,674	217,220
Denver: *Post*	—	260,331[3]	351,149
Rocky Mountain News	271,153	—	293,004
Des Moines, Iowa: *Register* (M & S); *Tribune* (E)	210,577	82,201	390,537
Detroit: *News*	—	630,573[3]	827,168
Free Press	601,721[3]	—	710,018
Duluth, Minn.: *News–Tribune* (M & S); *Herald)* (E)	51,434	20,066[3]	82,049
Erie, Pa.: *News* (M); *Daily Times* (E); *Times–News* (S)	24,264[3]	51,257[3]	93,103
El Paso, Tex.: *Times* (M & S); *Herald–Post* (E)	56,932[4]	34,926[3,4]	90,100[4]

City and newspaper	Net paid circulation Morning[2]	Evening[2]	Sunday
Evansville, Ind.: *Courier* (M); *Press* (E); *Courier & Press* (S)	62,747	43,768	116,302
Flint, Mich.: *Journal*	—	106,777[4]	106,045[4]
Fort Lauderdale, Fla.: *Sun–Sentinel* (M); *News* (E); *News & Sun–Sentinel* (S)	72,911[3]	102,065[3]	201,543
Fort Myers, Fla.: *News–Press*	74,387	—	88,201
Fort Wayne, Ind.: *Journal–Gazette* (M & S); *News–Sentinel* (E)	60,093[4]	71,705[4]	103,903[4]
Fort Worth: *Star–Telegram*	98,439[3]	142,140[3]	256,664
Fresno, Calif.: *Bee*	130,279	—	151,766
Gary, Ind.: *Post–Tribune*	—	83,721	88,848
Grand Rapids, Mich.: *Press*	—	125,222[4]	147,360[4]
Greensboro, N.C.: *Daily News* (M & S); *Record* (E)	83,604	31,823	116,852
Greenville, S.C.: *News* (M); *Piedmont* (E); *News–Piedmont* (S)	85,663[3]	24,069[3]	109,939
Harrisburg, Pa.: *Patriot* (M); *Evening News; Sunday Patriot–News*	48,617[3]	63,433[3]	152,298
Hartford, Conn.: *Courant*	212,244	—	289,124
Honolulu: *Advertiser* (M); *Star–Bulletin* (E); *Star–Bulletin & Advertiser* (S)	85,640	118,952	203,938
Houston: *Chronicle*	—	348,601[3]	436,940
Post	330,203[3]	—	394,853
Indianapolis: *Star* (M & S); *News* (E)	215,858[4]	143,449[4]	357,694[4]
Jackson, Miss.: *Clarion–Ledger* (M); *Daily News* (E); *Clarion–Ledger–Daily News* (S)	66,514[3]	41,011[3]	119,503
Jacksonville, Fla.: *Florida Times–Union* (M & S); *Journal* (E)	153,508	47,177[3]	199,315
Kansas City, Mo.: *Times* (M); *Star* (E & S)	314,007	273,758[3]	406,467
Knoxville, Tenn.: *Journal* (M); *News–Sentinel* (E & S)	56,908	102,488	158,987
Lancaster, Pa.: *Intelligencer–Journal* (M); *New Era* (E); *News* (S)	40,287[4]	59,621[4]	132,520[4]
Lansing, Mich.: *State Journal*	—	73,814	80,755
Las Vegas, Nev.: *Review–Journal*	—	79,292[3]	87,956
Lexington, Ky.: *Herald* (M); *Leader* (E); *Herald–Leader* (S)	70,790[3]	34,105[3]	112,189
Little Rock, Ark.: *Arkansas Gazette*	129,274[3]	—	154,569
Arkansas Democrat	—	66,275[3]	119,052
Long Beach, Calif.: *Independent* (M); *Press–Telegram* (E); *Independent Press–Telegram* (S)	64,709[3]	70,704[3]	135,811
Long Island (Garden City, N.Y.): *Newsday*	—	492,580	557,933
Los Angeles: *Times*	1,024,322[3]	—	1,276,195
Herald Examiner	—	283,710[3]	302,525
Louisville, Ky.: *Courier–Journal* (M); *Times* (E); *Courier–Journal & Times* (S)	190,942	151,977	331,103
Lubbock, Tex.: *Avalanche–Journal*	57,371[3]	14,531[3]	78,750
Macon, Ga.: *Telegraph* (M); *News* (E); *Telegraph & News* (S)	52,904[3]	21,313[3]	85,751
Madison, Wis.: *State Journal* (M & S); *Capital Times* (E)	76,348	33,630	126,330
Memphis, Tenn.: *Commercial Appeal* (M & S); *Press Scimitar* (E)	203,847	98,602	282,484
Miami, Fla.: *Herald* (M & S); *News* (E)	444,058	61,910	576,261
Milwaukee: *Sentinel* (M); *Journal* (E & S)	163,224	323,932	515,108
Minneapolis: *Tribune* (M & S); *Star* (E)	230,815[3]	206,700[3]	597,180
Mobile, Ala.: *Register* (M); *Press* (E); *Press–Register* (S)	50,174[3 4]	53,616[3 4]	97,945[4]
Nashville, Tenn.: *Tennesseean* (M & S); *Banner* (E)	135,688	84,134	246,031
New Haven, Conn.; *Journal–Courier* (M); *Register* (E & S)	37,264[3]	100,093	140,979
New Orleans: *Times–Picayune* (M & S); *States–Item* (E)[6]	213,283[4]	111,043[3 4]	323,302[4]
New York City: *News*	1,554,604[3]	—	2,202,601
Times	914,938[3]	—	1,477,499
Post	—	654,314[3]	421,350[7]
Wall Street Journal (Eastern edition)	714,902[3]	—	—
National edition	1,798,416[3]	—	—
Staten Island Advance	—	73,164[3]	80,409
Newark, N.J.: *Star–Ledger*	407,844[3 4]	—	574,966[4]
Newport News–Hampton, Va.: *Daily Press* (M & S); *Times Herald* (E)	56,669[3 4]	41,004[3 4]	99,303[4]

City and newspaper	Net paid circulation Morning[2]	Evening[2]	Sunday
Norfolk–Portsmouth–Virginia Beach–Chesapeake, Va.: *Virginian–Pilot* (M); *Ledger–Star* (E); *Virginian–Pilot/Ledger Star* (S)	125,787[4]	94,332[4]	200,680[4]
Oakland, Calif.: *Tribune*	—	143,431[3,8]	180,628
Oklahoma City: *Daily Oklahoman* (M); *Times* (E); *Sunday Oklahoman*	181,994[3]	84,657[3]	287,371
Omaha, Neb.: *World–Herald*	125,533[3]	109,780[3]	278,520
Orange County (Santa Ana), Calif.: *Register*	230,533[5]		259,783
Orlando, Fla.: *Sentinel Star*	201,383[3,5]		243,704
Palo Alto, Calif.: *Wall Street Journal* (Western edition)(M); *Peninsula Times–Tribune* (E)	365,908[3]	61,035	—
Peoria, Ill.: *Journal Star*	102,556[5]		120,003
Philadelphia: *Inquirer*	425,075[3]	—	837,209
Bulletin	—	458,849[3]	529,706
Daily News	—	231,310[3]	—
Phoenix, Ariz.: *Arizona Republic* (M & S); *Gazette* (E)	260,090[4]	112,781[4]	399,819[4]
Pittsburgh: *Post–Gazette* (M); *Press* (E & S)	185,215[3]	271,502[3]	659,998
Portland, Me.: *Press–Herald* (M); *Express* (E); *Maine Sunday Telegram*	53,616	29,813	115,519
Portland, Ore.: *Oregonian* (M & S); *Oregon Journal* (S)	248,229	105,485[3]	420,938
Providence, R.I.: *Journal* (M & S); *Bulletin* (E)	75,435[3]	141,759[3]	228,306
Quincy, Mass.: *Patriot–Ledger*	—	82,435[3,4]	80,598[4,7]
Raleigh, N.C.: *News & Observer* (M & S); *Times* (E)	131,921[4]	35,194[4]	165,289[4]
Reading, Pa.: *Times* (M); *Eagle* (E & S)	42,667	43,447	101,216
Richmond, Va.: *Times–Dispatch* (M & S); *News Leader* (E)	135,360	114,295	216,047
Riverside, Calif.: *Enterprise* (M); *Press* (E); *Press–Enterprise* (S)	67,514[3]	33,603[3]	107,322
Roanoke, Va.: *Times & World News*	67,806[3]	49,016[3]	118,273
Rochester, N.Y.: *Democrat & Chronicle* (M & S); *Times–Union* (E)	125,316	121,897	232,367
Rockford, Ill.: *Register Star*	70,633[3,5]		78,363
Sacramento, Calif.: *Bee*	203,779	—	233,034
Union	103,859	—	105,303
St. Louis: *Post–Dispatch*	—	247,237[3]	436,419
Globe–Democrat	264,609[3]	—	264,603[9]
St. Paul: *Pioneer Press* (M & S); *Dispatch* (E)	100,672[3]	114,858[3]	241,904
St. Petersburg, Fla.: *Times* (M & S); *Independent* (E)	230,143	43,593	288,775
Salt Lake City, Utah: *Tribune* (M & S); *Deseret News* (E)	113,956	75,865	189,310
San Antonio: *Express* (M); *News* (E); *Express–News* (S)	82,371[3]	76,594[3]	185,413
Light	—	122,600[3]	187,857
San Bernadino, Calif.: *Sun*	82,833	—	89,663
San Diego, Calif.: *Union* (M & S); *Tribune* (E)	201,798[4]	125,756[4]	321,792[4]
San Francisco: *Chronicle* (M); *Examiner* (E); *Examiner & Chronicle* (S)	506,600[3]	159,325[3]	669,665
San Jose, Calif.: *Mercury* (M); *News* (E); *Mercury–News* (S)	154,983[3]	68,000[3]	269,821
Sarasota, Fla.: *Herald–Tribune* (M & S); *Journal* (E)	87,707	7,102[3]	99,006
Seattle *Times*	—	260,762[3]	348,678
Post–Intelligencer	197,123[3]	—	222,998
Shreveport, La.: *Times* (M & S); *Journal* (E)	87,822[4]	33,988[4]	126,255[4]
South Bend–Mishawaka, Inc.: *Tribune*	—	106,370	125,754
Spokane, Wash.: *Spokesman–Review* (M & S); *Chronicle* (E)	76,648	61,580	124,185
Springfield, Mass.: *Union* (M); *News* (E); *Republican* (S)	72,195	75,729	142,380
Syracuse, N.Y.: *Post–Standard* (M); *Herald–Journal* (E); *Herald–American* (S)	82,181	113,678	231,470
Tacoma, Wash.: *News–Tribune* (E); *News–Tribune & Sunday Ledger*	—	107,860	111,071
Tampa, Fla.: *Tribune* (M); *Times* (E & S)	197,174	25,740	239,399
Toledo, Ohio: *Blade*	—	167,590	209,154
Topeka, Kan.: *Capital* (M); *State Journal* (E); *Capital Journal* (S)	60,390[3]	26,010[3]	75,030
Trenton, N.J.: *Times* (E); *Times–Advertiser* (S)	—	73,520[3]	84,963
Trentonian	65,355	—	56,181
Tucson, Ariz.: *Arizona Daily Star* (M & S); *Citizen* (E)	74,284[4]	67,337[4]	138,266[4]
Tulsa, Okla.: *World* (M & S); *Tribune* (E)	122,385[4]	76,314[4]	211,152[4]
Washington, D.C.: *Post*	601,417[3]	—	827,938
Star	—	345,641[3]	326,512

City and newspaper	Net paid circulation		
	Morning[2]	Evening[2]	Sunday
West Palm Beach, Fla.: *Post* (M); *Times* (E); *Post–Times* (S)	93,117[3]	31,019[3]	141,097
Wichita, Kan.: *Eagle* (M); *Beacon* (E); *Eagle and Beacon* (S)	120,043[3]	37,221[3]	174,832
Wilmington, Del.: *News* (M); *Journal* (E); *Sunday News Journal*	48,603[3 4]	82,983[3 4]	106,572[4]
Winston–Salem, N.C.: *Journal* (M & S); *Sentinel* (E)	71,696	37,731	95,143
Worcester, Mass.: *Telegram* (M & S); *Gazette* (E)	54,212[4]	89,241[4]	109,760[4]
Youngstown, Ohio: *Vindicator*	—	103,298[4]	153,036[4]

1. Listing is of cities in which any one edition of a newspaper exceeds an average net paid circulation of 75,000; newspapers of smaller circulation in those cities are also included. 2. Unless otherwise indicated, figures are average Monday-through-Saturday circulation for six-month period ending March 31, 1980. 3. Average Monday-through-Friday circulation. 4. Three-month average for period ending March 31, 1980. 5. All-day newspaper. 6. Effective May 1980, both newspapers were combined as *The Times–Picayune and The States–Item* to become an all-day paper. 7. Published on Saturday. 8. For period from Nov. 5, 1979, to March 30, 1980. 9. Week-end edition. 10. *The Times* discontinued Sunday edition in May 1980. *Source:* Audit Bureau of Circulations.

Leading Magazines: United States and Canada

Magazine	Circulation[1]
A.D.	270,994[3]
American Journal of Nursing	340,962
American Legion Magazine, The	2,584,517
Apartment Life	830,377
Architectural Digest	441,205
Atlantic Monthly	341,560
Bassmaster	301,809[2]
Better Homes and Gardens	8,007,202
Bon Appetit	1,144,718[2]
Book Digest	991,632
Boys' Life	1,516,405[2]
Bride's	324,963
Business Week	793,519[2]
Business Week/Industrial	321,711
Camping Journal	284,886
Capper's Weekly	421,162
Car and Driver	727,633
Car Craft	376,172
Catholic Digest	540,650
Chatelaine	1,002,785
Chatelaine (French Language Edition)	276,331
Chic	267,327
Co-ed	802,396[2]
Cosmopolitan	2,766,627
Cuisine	772,797
Cycle	477,333
Cycle World	336,752
Decorating and Craft Ideas	802,128
Discovery	1,019,631
Eagle	697,369
Early American Life	327,375
Easyriders	426,476
Ebony	1,271,517
Elks Magazine, The	1,641,689
Esquire	651,960
Essence	601,243
Exploring	357,455[2]
Family Circle	7,611,578
Family Handyman	920,219
Family Health	801,667
Farm Journal	1,335,050
Farmer-Stockman, The	287,681
Field and Stream	2,064,622
Flower and Garden Magazine	509,839
Flying	391,216
Forbes	676,846
Fortune	676,117
Forum	802,276
Gallery	672,694
Games	510,939
Genesis	413,111
Gentlemen's Quarterly	374,378
Girl Scout Leader	532,252[2]
Glamour	1,861,818
Golf Digest	970,118
Golf (incl. Golfing)	709,358
Good Housekeeping	5,178,296
Gourmet	667,726
Grit	899,515[2]
Guns and Ammo (incl. Guns and Hunting)	448,240
Harper's Bazaar	622,298
Harper's Magazine	300,103
High Fidelity	365,702
High Times	301,100[2]
Homeowners "How-To"	306,866
Hot Rod Magazine (incl. Rod and Custom)	876,193
House and Garden	1,035,363
House Beautiful	863,892
Hustler	1,583,638
Jet	705,113
Junior Scholastic	902,939
Kiwanis Magazine, The	278,438
Ladies' Home Journal	5,633,128
Legion Magazine	475,776
Lutheran, The	576,389
McCall's	6,502,880
Maclean's-Canada's News Magazine	644,073
Mademoiselle	930,184
Marvel Comics Group	11,638,028
Mechanix Illustrated	1,751,641
Midnight Globe	1,579,113
Modern Bride	309,359
Modern Photography	610,118
Money	845,048
Mother Earth News	645,713
Motor Trend (incl. Car Life, Sports Car Graphic, and Wheels Afield)	758,394
Ms. Magazine	518,612
National Enquirer	5,011,577
National Future Farmer, The	487,519

Magazine	Circulation[1]
National Geographic Magazine, The	10,249,748
National Lampoon	614,708
Nation's Business	1,238,268
Natural History	461,096
Newsweek	2,934,083
New West	300,903
New Woman	1,068,854
New Yorker, The	498,636
New York Magazine	405,019
Nursing '79	521,261
Omni	829,909[2]
1,001 Decorating Ideas	778,677
Oui	868,810
Outdoor Life	1,731,895
Parents	1,441,393
Penthouse	4,711,849[2]
People Weekly	2,312,444
Photoplay	335,349
Playboy	5,538,559
Playgirl	712,360
Popular Electronics	409,404
Popular Hot Rodding	306,571
Popular Mechanics	1,636,363
Popular Photography	831,209
Popular Science	1,801,605
Progressive Farmer, The	973,047
Psychology Today	1,175,323
Quest/79	302,232
Reader's Digest	18,094,192
Reader's Digest (Canadian English Edition)	1,279,494
Redbook Magazine	4,450,806
Road and Track	592,650
Rolling Stone	624,158
Rotarian, The	456,568
Saturday Evening Post, The	655,514
Saturday Review	519,214[2]
Scholastic Magazines	3,461,063[2]
Scientific American	685,521
Scouting	962,791
Selection du Reader's Digest	323,523
Self	815,467[2]
Senior Scholastic Unit	2,649,291[2]
Seventeen	1,372,994
Signature	606,313
Ski (incl. Ski Life)	417,230
Skiing Magazine	464,184
Smithsonian	1,185,237
Soap Opera Digest	590,426
Southern Living	1,739,307
Sport	1,220,392
Sporting News, The	354,161
Sports Afield	528,793
Sports Illustrated	2,287,159
Star, The	3,160,415
Stereo Review	527,321
Successful Farming	725,063
Sunset, The Magazine of Western Living	1,384,140
'Teen	985,132
Teen Beat	237,927
Tennis Magazine	443,995
Tiger Beat	299,072[2]
Time Atlantic	513,243
Time in Canada	332,590
Time Pacific	351,050
Time, The Weekly Magazine	4,314,279
Today's Education	1,701,125
Trailer Life	320,034
True Confessions	255,010
True Story	1,631,253
TV Guide	19,547,763
TV Guide, Inc. (Canada)	1,098,325
TV Hebdo	275,801
United Church Observer, The	314,879[3]
U.S. News and World Report	2,067,321
Us	848,343
V.F.W. Magazine	1,704,442
Vogue (incl. Vanity Fair)	970,084
Vogue Patterns	477,048
Weight Watchers Magazine	822,480
Westways	481,175
Woman's Day	7,535,855
Woodall's Trailer & RV Travel	296,995
Workbasket, The	1,711,706
Workbench	650,083
Working Woman	265,029
World Tennis	447,063[2]
Yankee	799,518

1. Average total paid circulation for the six-month period ending June 30, 1979. The table lists magazines of over 260,000 circulation. 2. Circulation averages for period ended December 31, 1979. 3. Religious publication using congregation-wide subscription plan. *Source:* Audit Bureau of Circulations. Publishers' Statements for six-month period ending June 30, 1979.

English Language Daily and Sunday U.S. Newspapers

(number of newspapers as of March 30, 1980; circulation as reported for Sept. 30, 1979)

State	Morning papers and circulation		Evening papers and circulation		Total M and E and circulation		Sunday papers and circulation	
Alabama	8	206,372	19	540,734	27	747,106	20	685,845
Alaska	2	29,298	6	73,338	8	102,636	1	53,595
Arizona	2	298,891	17	302,568	19	601,459	6	543,378
Arkansas[1]	5	183,983	29	297,641	33	481,624	15	466,611
California	29	3,336,807	95	2,598,279	122	5,935,086	48	5,550,896
Colorado	4	349,234	24	530,796	28	880,030	9	888,409
Connecticut	6	371,756	19	551,285	25	923,041	7	677,676
Delaware	1	49,546	2	108,967	3	158,513	2	135,127
District of Columbia	1	578,831	1	342,760	2	921,591	2	1,123,263
Florida	21	1,807,472	32	743,930	52	2,551,402	34	2,639,588
Georgia	8	453,596	28	592,211	36	1,045,807	17	1,024,750
Hawaii	1	81,317	4	157,423	5	238,740	2	218,076
Idaho	5	110,093	10	97,559	15	207,652	6	172,037
Illinois[1]	21	1,397,651	70	1,487,471	86	2,885,122	22	2,822,534
Indiana	7	441,365	71	1,198,688	78	1,640,053	18	1,188,280

State	Morning papers and circulation		Evening papers and circulation		Total M and E and circulation		Sunday papers and circulation	
Iowa[1]	4	304,623	38	589,868	41	894,491	9	749,424
Kansas[1]	6	229,602	45	402,992	50	632,594	17	477,099
Kentucky	6	315,593	21	451,550	27	767,143	11	607,320
Louisiana	6	454,041	21	398,371	27	852,412	15	807,217
Maine	5	215,315	4	71,979	9	287,294	1	116,702
Maryland	5	241,157	8	445,567	13	686,724	4	662,919
Massachusetts[1]	7	843,800	42	1,192,362	48	2,036,162	9	1,514,037
Michigan	2	615,377	50	1,842,441	52	2,457,818	17	2,363,198
Minnesota	6	411,076	24	630,720	30	1,041,796	11	1,025,501
Mississippi	5	127,525	20	275,619	25	403,144	13	325,231
Missouri	9	726,573	43	912,613	52	1,639,186	18	1,159,595
Montana	4	148,636	7	47,659	11	196,295	8	197,102
Nebraska	4	190,813	15	301,497	19	492,310	5	391,249
Nevada	3	87,981	6	116,451	9	204,432	5	201,833
New Hampshire[1]	1	32,064	9	162,005	9	194,069	2	75,179
New Jersey	7	661,242	21	1,068,009	28	1,729,251	15	1,486,748
New Mexico	1	81,512	19	185,692	20	267,204	13	246,226
New York	22	5,007,923	58	2,680,197	79	7,688,120	35	6,118,838
North Carolina	10	613,185	43	749,618	53	1,362,803	23	1,112,327
North Dakota[1]	2	37,622	9	159,163	10	196,785	3	106,534
Ohio[1]	12	891,866	85	2,445,154	96	3,337,020	28	2,543,701
Oklahoma	9	424,441	46	454,088	55	878,529	46	886,110
Oregon	3	293,573	19	391,542	22	685,115	5	586,845
Pennsylvania[1]	33	1,639,877	76	2,272,317	104	3,912,194	16	3,045,517
Rhode Island	1	74,088	6	240,501	7	314,589	2	235,931
South Carolina	8	398,224	12	199,700	20	597,924	8	483,970
South Dakota	2	48,698	11	124,030	13	172,728	4	123,542
Tennesse	8	468,152	24	641,283	32	1,109,435	16	1,025,412
Texas[1]	28	1,671,575	91	1,727,654	118	3,399,229	94	3,838,428
Utah	1	106,132	5	166,852	6	272,984	5	277,468
Vermont	2	69,867	6	45,553	8	115,420	3	72,716
Virginia	11	513,636	22	573,258	33	1,086,894	13	838,786
Washington[1]	8	363,436	19	816,465	26	1,179,901	16	1,113,438
West Virginia[1]	9	234,436	17	240,813	25	475,249	9	402,487
Wisconsin	5	272,122	32	970,999	37	1,243,121	9	910,770
Wyoming	6	62,884	4	29,929	10	92,813	3	60,458
Total	**382**	**28,574,879**	**1,405**	**33,648,161**	**1,763**	**62,223,040**	**720**	**54,379,923**
Total U.S., Sept. 30, 1978	355	27,656,739	1,419	34,333,258	1,756	61,989,997	696	53,990,033
Total U.S., Sept. 30, 1977	352	26,742,318	1,435	34,752,822	1,753	61,495,140	668	52,429,234
Total U.S., Sept. 30, 1976	346	25,858,386	1,435	35,118,625	1,762	60,977,011	650	51,565,334
Total U.S., Sept. 30, 1975	339	25,490,186	1,436	35,165,245	1,756	60,655,431	639	51,096,323
Total U.S., Sept. 30, 1974	340	26,144,966	1,449	35,732,231	1,768	61,877,197	641	51,678,726
Total U.S., Sept. 30, 1973	343	26,524,140	1,451	36,623,140	1,774	63,147,280	634	51,717,465
Total U.S., Sept. 30, 1972	337	26,078,386	1,441	36,431,856	1,761	62,510,242	605	50,000,669
Total U.S., Sept. 30, 1970	334	25,933,783	1,429	36,173,744	1,748	62,107,527	586	49,216,602

1. "All-day" newspapers are listed in morning and evening columns but only once in the total, and their circulations are divided between morning and evening figures. Adjustments have been made in state and U.S. total figures. *Source: Editor and Publisher Yearbook, 1980.*

See **the Entertainment and Culture section for additional Media information.**

Consumer Information Catalog

For a copy of the free *Consumer Information Catalog,* a listing of more than 200 selected federal consumer publications on such topics as child care, automobiles, health, employment, housing, energy, etc., send a postcard to the Consumer Information Center, Pueblo, Colo. 81009.

Federal Government Hotlines

Toll-free phone information is available to the public from selected government agencies. These are "live," not recorded.

Cancer: For information on all aspects of cancer, call 800–638–6694.

Consumer product safety: Call 800–638–2666.

Federal Taxes: Call 800–555–1212 for the toll-free IRS number in your areas.

Auto Safety: Call 800–424–9393 for information on auto safety problems, recalls, and complaints about specific makes and models.

Flood insurance: Call 800–424–8872 for information on federally subsidized flood insurance in hazardous areas.

History of the Income Tax in the United States

Source: Touche Ross & Co.

The nation had few taxes in its early history. From 1791 to 1802, the United States Government was supported by internal taxes on distilled spirits, carriages, refined sugar, tobacco and snuff, property sold at auction, corporate bonds, and slaves. The high cost of the War of 1812 brought about the nation's first sales taxes on gold, silverware, jewelry, and watches. In 1817, however, Congress did away with all internal taxes, relying on tariffs on imported goods to provide sufficient funds for running the Government.

In 1862, in order to support the Civil War effort, Congress enacted the nation's first income tax law. It was a forerunner of our modern income tax in that it was based on the principles of graduated, or progressive, taxation and of withholding income at the source. During the Civil War, a person earning from $600 to $10,000 per year paid tax at the rate of 3%. Those with incomes of more than $10,000 paid taxes at a higher rate. Additional sales and excise taxes were added, and an "inheritance" tax also made its debut. In 1866, internal revenue collections reached their highest point in the nation's 90-year history—more than $310 million, an amount not reached again until 1911.

The Act of 1862 established the office of Commissioner of Internal Revenue. The Commissioner was given the power to assess, levy, and collect taxes, and the right to enforce the tax laws through seizure of property and income and through prosecution. His powers and authority remain very much the same today.

In 1868, Congress again focused its taxation efforts on tobacco and distilled spirits and eliminated the income tax in 1872. It had a short-lived revival in 1894 and 1895. In the latter year, the U.S. Supreme Court decided that the income tax was unconstitutional because it was not apportioned among the states in conformity with the Constitution.

By 1913, with the 16th Amendment to the Constitution, the income tax had become a permanent fixture of the U.S. tax system. The amendment gave Congress legal authority to tax income and resulted in a revenue law that taxed incomes of both individuals and corporations. In fiscal year 1918, annual internal revenue collections for the first time passed the billion-dollar mark, rising to $5.4 billion by 1920. With the advent of World War II, employment increased, as did tax collections—to $7.3 billion. The withholding tax on wages was introduced in 1943 and was instrumental in increasing the number of taxpayers to 60 million and tax collections to $43 billion by 1945.

Internal Revenue Service

The Internal Revenue Service (IRS), a bureau of the U.S. Treasury Department, is the federal agency charged with the administration of the tax laws passed by Congress. The IRS functions through a national office in Washington, 7 regional offices, 58 district offices, and 10 service centers.

Operations involving most taxpayers are carried out in the district offices and service centers. District offices are organized into Administration, Audit, Collection, Taxpayer Service, and Intelligence Divisions. All tax returns are filed with the service centers, where the IRS computer operations are located.

Auditing Tax Returns

Most taxpayers' contacts with IRS arise through the auditing of their tax returns. The service has been empowered by Congress to inquire about all persons who may be liable for any tax and to obtain for review the books and/or records pertinent to those taxpayers' returns. A wide-ranging audit operation is carried out in the 58 district offices by some 14,000 field agents and 5,000 office auditors.

Selecting Returns for Audit

The primary method used by the IRS in selecting returns for audits is a computer program that measures the probability of tax error in each return. The data base (established by an in-depth audit of randomly selected returns in various income categories) consists of approximately 200–250 individual items of information taken from each return. These 200–250 variables individually or in combination are weighted as relative indicators of potential tax change. Returns are then scored according to the weights given the combinations of variables as they appear on each return. The higher the score, the greater the tax change potential. Other returns are selected for examination on the basis of claims for refund, multi-year audits, related return audits, and other audits initiated by the IRS as a result of informants' information, special compliance programs, and the information document matching program.

The Appeals Process

The IRS attempts to resolve tax disputes through an administrative appeals system. Taxpayers who, after audit of their tax returns, disagree with a proposed change in their tax liabilities are entitled to an independent review of their cases. A recent change in IRS procedures has reduced the administrative levels of appeals from two to one—the appellate division of the regional office. Proceedings are informal at this level of appeal. A written

Internal Revenue Service

	1979	1978	1977	1970	1960	1950
U.S. population (in thousands)	220,999	219,033	217,329	204,878	180,671	152,271
Number of IRS employees	86,630	85,329	84,414	68,098	50,199	55,551
Cost to govt. of collecting $100 in taxes	$0.46	$0.49	$0.51	$0.45	$0.40	$0.59
Tax per capita	$2,083.32	$1,827.00	$1,648	$955.31	$507.96	$255.84
Collections by principal sources (in thousands of dollars)						
Total IRS collections	$460,412,185	$399,776,389	$358,139,416	$195,722,096	$91,744,803	$38,957,132
Income and profits taxes						
Individual	$251,545,857	$213,058,144	186,755,263	103,651,585	44,945,711	17,153,308
Corporation	71,447,876	65,380,145	60,049,804	35,036,983	22,179,414	10,854,351
Employment taxes	112,849,874	97,291,653	86,076,316	37,449,188	11,158,589	2,644,575
Estate and gift taxes	5,519,074	5,381,499	7,425,325	3,680,076	1,626,348	706,227
Alcohol taxes	5,647,924	5,612,715	5,406,633	4,746,382	3,193,714	2,219,202
Tobacco taxes	2,495,517	2,450,913	2,398,501	2,094,212	1,931,504	1,328,464
Manufacturers' excise taxes	7,057,612	6,555,681	6,068,682	6,683,061	4,735,129	1,836,053
All other taxes	3,848,450	4,045,639	3,958,893	2,380,609	2,004,394	2,214,951

protest to the examining officer's findings does not have to be submitted unless the amount of tax involved in the dispute is more than $2,500. Taxpayers may represent themselves or be represented by an attorney, accountant, or any other advisor authorized to practice before the IRS. In 97% of the cases, the administrative appeal results in a mutually acceptable basis for resolving the dispute. However, the taxpayer at any point may bypass the administrative appeals procedure and appeal directly to the Tax Court. Claims for refunds may be appealed to the U.S. District Court or the Court of Claims. In 1978, 54,715 cases were disposed of by agreement through the administrative process. The Tax Court tried 1,742 cases, and the U.S. District Courts and the Court of Claims tried 447 cases.

Federal Individual Income Tax

The Federal individual income tax is levied on the taxable incomes of both citizens and non-citizens who earn income from U.S. sources. A new term, "tax table income," was introduced by the Tax Reduction and Simplification Act of 1977. For a non-itemizer, "tax table income" is adjusted gross income (*see* below) since the tax tables have been simplified to account for both the standard and itemized deductions and exemptions. Because the standard deduction is built into the tax tables, an individual whose itemized deductions exceed his standard deduction deducts his itemized deductions only to the extent they exceed the standard deduction. Commencing with 1977 returns, the vast majority of taxpayers will use the tax tables to compute tax liability. Taxpayers whose incomes exceed those in the tax tables will be required to compute their tax liabilities in the traditional manner. For this purpose, tax rates are graduated from a minimum of 14% on the first $2,100 of taxable income above $3,400 (for joint returns) to a maximum of 70% of taxable income above $215,400. The maximum rate on earned income, however, is 50%.

Who Must File a Return

You must file a return if you are:	and your gross income is at least:
Single (legally separated, divorced, or married living apart from spouse with dependent child) and are under 65	$3,300
Single (legally separated, divorced, or married living apart from spouse with dependent child) and are 65 or older	$4,300
A person who can be claimed as a dependent on your parent's return, and who has taxable dividends, interest, or other unearned income	$1,000
A qualifying widow(er) with a dependent child and are 65 or older	$5,400
Married, filing jointly, living together at end of year (or at date of death of spouse), and both are under 65	$5,400
Married, filing jointly, living together at end of year (or at date of death of spouse), and one is 65 or older	$6,400
Married, filing jointly, living together at end of year (or at date of death of spouse), and both are 65 or older	$7,400
Married, filing separate return, or married but not living together at end of year	$1,000
A person with income from sources within U.S. possessions	$1,000
Self-employed and your net earnings from self-employment were at least $400	

Adjusted Gross Income

Gross income consists of wages and salaries, tips and gratuities, interest, dividends, annuities, rents and royalties, and certain other types of income. Among the items excluded from gross income, and thus not subject to tax, are social security payments, federal and state unemployment compensation (phased out above a base amount), public assistance benefits, interest on exempt securities (mostly state and local bonds), the first $200 of dividends and interest received ($400 if married and filing jointly), and 60 percent of net long-term capital gains. *Adjusted gross income* is determined by subtracting from gross income those business-type expenses considered necessary in earning income. Job-related moving expenses and alimony may also be deducted in arriving at adjusted gross income.

Deductions

Taxpayers may itemize deductions or use one of two forms of the standard deduction. In itemizing deductions, the following are the major items that may be deducted (with limits, in some instances); interest payments; state and local general sales, income, property, and gasoline taxes; medical expenses; charitable contributions; and casualty losses. The Tax Reduction and Simplification Act of 1977 simplified the use of the standard deduction by eliminating the minimum percentage and maximum standard deduction and replaces them with what is, in effect, a standard deduction of $2,300 for single persons, $3,400 for married individuals filing joint returns, and $1,700 for married individuals filing separate returns.

Personal Exemptions

Personal exemptions are available to the taxpayer, his spouse, and his dependents. The amount is $1,000 for each individual. Additional exemptions of $1,000 each are granted for persons 65 and over and for the blind.

Credits

For tax years beginning after 1978, the earned income credit became permanent. The Revenue Act of 1978 grants a refundable credit for certain lower-income households with dependent children, with a maximum credit of $500 on $5,000 of earned income. This maximum credit will be reduced if earned income or adjusted gross income exceeds $6,000 and the credit will be zero for families with incomes over $10,000.

The Tax Reform Act of 1976 provided for a credit for child or dependent care expense of 20% of employment-related expenses up to $2,000 for one qualifying individual in the taxpayer's household and up to $4,000 if there are two or more qualifying individuals.

The Revenue Act of 1978 extended the child care credit to include payments to grandparents for care of their grandchildren, provided that the parents are not also entitled to a dependency deduction for the grandparents.

The Tax Reform Act of 1976 also provided for a new expanded and simplified credit for the elderly. A credit (a reduction of tax owed) of as much as $375 (if single) or $562.50 (if married and filing jointly) may be claimed by persons 65 or older (or persons under age 65 and retired under a public retirement system) who have retirement income. This credit, however, phases out for married couples with adjusted gross income over $10,000 and single persons with adjusted gross income over $7,500.

Recent Legislation

The Tax Reduction and Simplification Act of 1977. The principal purpose of this law was to simplify the preparation of individual income tax returns.

Another feature of this new law provides impetus for employers to create new jobs. It provides for a jobs credit against tax due for the years 1977 and 1978. The credit applies to individual-, partnership-, and corporation-owned businesses. The maximum credit is $2,100 (50% of the first $4,200 paid to net new employees). The credit is based on the first $4,200 of an employee's wages paid by an employer during a year in excess of 102% of Federal Unemployment Tax Act wages paid during the preceding year. The law also provides for certain limitations and safeguards against abuse.

The tables that will be used by most taxpayers to compute their tax liabilities for 1979 will be based on "tax table" income and the number of exemptions. For taxpayers using the standard deduction, tax table income is adjusted gross income. The personal exemptions, the standard deduction, and the general tax credit are built into the tables.

The Revenue Act of 1978. The Revenue Act of 1978 provided tax reductions to stimulate spending and economic growth. The Act contains three major individual tax cuts: (1) the personal exemption increases from $750 to $1,000; (2) the zero bracket amount and floor under itemized deductions is larger; and (3) the 25 bracket tax rate schedule now has 15 wider brackets. In addition, the earned income tax credit has been increased and simplified.

The top corporate income tax rate is reduced from 48% to 46% and a system of graduated tax rates is established. Also, the investment tax credit is liberalized and expanded.

A major change is to increase the percentage of long-term capital gains deductible from gross income from 50 to 60 percent. Capital gain and excess itemized deduction preferences no longer fall under the regular, or add-on, minimum tax, but under a new alternative minimum tax. "At-risk" concepts, introduced in the 1976 Tax Reform Act, are extended to all activities except equipment leasing actively engaged in by closely held companies and real estate. Other provisions of the Act affect retirement plans, small businesses, carry-over basis of inherited property, and the subchapter S election.

The Technical Corrections Act of 1979. The Technical Corrections Act of 1979 was enacted in 1980 to provide clarification for various provisions of the Revenue Act of 1978. The Act contains technical, clerical, conforming, and clarifying amendments to provisions enacted in 1978.

Some areas covered include: investment credit, cafeteria plans, simplified pension plans, club dues, medical expense reimbursement plans, and tax shelters.

Crude Oil Windfall Profit Tax of 1980. The Crude Oil Windfall Profit Tax of 1980 covers primarily the excise tax provisions affecting domestic oil producers. A temporary excise or severance tax on domestically produced crude oil, it is based on windfall profits, which equals the selling price of the oil less an adjusted base price and less a limited deduction for state severance taxes on removal of crude oil from the ground. The tax is deductible in arriving at federal taxable income for the taxable year in which the tax is paid or accrued.

Federal Individual Income Tax Rates Effective January 1, 1980

MARRIED INDIVIDUALS FILING JOINT RETURNS AND SURVIVING SPOUSES:

If the taxable income is:	*The tax is:*
Not over $3,400	No tax
Over $3,400 but not over $5,500	14% of the excess over $3,400
Over $5,500 but not over $7,600	$294, plus 16% of the excess over $5,500
Over $7,600 but not over $11,900	$630, plus 18% of the excess over $7,600
Over $11,900 but not over $16,000	$1,404, plus 21% of the excess over $11,900
Over $16,000 but not over $20,200	$2,265, plus 24% of the excess over $16,000
Over $20,200 but not over $24,600	$3,273, plus 28% of the excess over $20,200
Over $24,600 but not over $29,900	$4,505, plus 32% of the excess over $24,600
Over $29,900 but not over $35,200	$6,201, plus 37% of the excess over $29,900
Over $35,200 but not over $45,800	$8,162, plus 43% of the excess over $35,200
Over $45,800 but not over $60,000	$12,720, plus 49% of the excess over $45,800
Over $60,000 but not over $85,600	$19,678, plus 54% of the excess over $60,000
Over $85,600 but not over $109,400	$33,502, plus 59% of the excess over $85,600
Over $109,400 but not over $162,400	$47,544, plus 64% of the excess over $109,400
Over $162,400 but not over $215,400	$81,464, plus 68% of the excess over $162,400
Over $215,400	$117,504, plus 70% of the excess over $215,400

HEADS OF HOUSEHOLDS:

If the taxable income is:	*The tax is:*
Not over $2,300	No tax
Over $2,300 but not over $4,400	14% of the excess over $2,300
Over $4,400 but not over $6,500	$294, plus 16% of the excess over $4,400
Over $6,500 but not over $8,700	$630, plus 18% of the excess over $6,500
Over $8,700 but not over $11,800	$1,026, plus 22% of the excess over $8,700
Over $11,800 but not over $15,000	$1,708, plus 24% of the excess over $11,800
Over $15,000 but not over $18,200	$2,476, plus 26% of the excess over $15,000
Over $18,200 but not over $23,500	$3,308, plus 31% of the excess over $18,200
Over $23,500 but not over $28,800	$4,951, plus 36% of the excess over $23,500
Over $28,800 but not over $34,100	$6,859, plus 42% of the excess over $28,800
Over $34,100 but not over $44,700	$9,085, plus 46% of the excess over $34,100
Over $44,700 but not over $60,600	$13,961, plus 54% of the excess over $44,700
Over $60,600 but not over $81,800	$22,547, plus 59% of the excess over $60,600
Over $81,800 but not over $108,300	$35,055, plus 63% of the excess over $81,800
Over $108,300 but not over $161,300	$51,750, plus 68% of the excess over $108,300
Over $161,300	$87,790, plus 70% of the excess over $161,300

The Act places a 70% tax rate on prices above $13 per barrel on oil already discovered and put into production by 1978 ("old" oil). Oil put into production after 1978 ("new" oil) will be taxed at a 30% rate on prices above a base averaging $16.55 per barrel. For stripper oil (oil from properties that average 10 barrels a day or less per well) the rate is 60% on prices above a base price averaging $15.30. All the base prices are to be adjusted for inflation. For independent oil producers, the tax rates for up to 1,000 barrels per day are 50% on already discovered oil and 30% on stripper oil. Those independents producing more than 1,000 barrels per day would apply the above higher rates to the excess. For new oil, the same 30% rate applies.

The taxable windfall profit is limited to 90% of net income on a property. A 33-month phaseout is scheduled to begin in January 1988 or when net revenues reach $227.3 billion, whichever is later.

Also included in the Act are certain residential energy tax credits, business energy investment credits, an increase from $100 to $200 in the dividend exclusion which is now broadened to include an interest exclusion, and certain other business income tax provisions. Of special significance is the repeal of carryover basis for inherited property so that property acquired from a decedent gets a "stepped up" basis to date of death (or alternate valuation date—6 months after death).

Tax Errors

In 1979, 54.6 million taxpayers filed a form 1040, a 2.5% increase over 1978. In 1979, 36.1 million taxpayers filed a form 1040A—6.1% more than in 1978. 40% of all individual taxpayers used the short form 1040A.

Error rates rose from 1978 to 1979:

1978	Form 1040	6.5%
1978	Form 1040A	5.1%
1979	Form 1040	7.3%
1979	Form 1040A	5.5%

Federal Individual Income Tax Rates Effective January 1, 1980

UNMARRIED INDIVIDUALS:

If the taxable income is:	*The tax is:*
Not over $2,300	No tax
Over $2,300 but not over $3,400	14% of the excess over $2,300
Over $3,400 but not over $4,400	$154, plus 16% of the excess over $3,400
Over $4,400 but not over $6,500	$314, plus 18% of the excess over $4,400
Over $6,500 but not over $8,500	$692, plus 19% of the excess over $6,500
Over $8,500 but not over $10,800	$1,072, plus 21% of the excess over $8,500
Over $10,800 but not over $12,900	$1,555, plus 24% of the excess over $10,800
Over $12,900 but not over $15,000	$2,059, plus 26% of the excess over $12,900
Over $15,000 but not over $18,200	$2,605, plus 30% of the excess over $15,000
Over $18,200 but not over $23,500	$3,565, plus 34% of the excess over $18,200
Over $23,500 but not over $28,800	$5,367, plus 39% of the excess over $23,500
Over $28,800 but not over $34,100	$7,434, plus 44% of the excess over $28,800
Over $34,100 but not over $41,500	$9,766, plus 49% of the excess over $34,100
Over $41,500 but not over $55,300	$13,392, plus 55% of the excess over $41,500
Over $55,300 but not over $81,800	$20,982, plus 63% of the excess over $55,300
Over $81,800 but not over $108,300	$37,677, plus 68% of the excess over $81,800
Over $108,300	$55,697, plus 70% of the excess over $108,300

MARRIED INDIVIDUALS FILING SEPARATE RETURNS:

If the taxable income is:	*The tax is:*
Not over $1,700	No tax
Over $1,700 but not over $2,750	14% of the excess over $1,700
Over $2,750 but not over $3,800	$147, plus 16% of the excess over $2,750
Over $3,800 but not over $5,950	$315, plus 18% of the excess over $3,800
Over $5,950 but not over $8,000	$702, plus 21% of the excess over $5,950
Over $8,000 but not over $10,100	$1,132.50, plus 24% of the excess over $8,000
Over $10,100 but not over $12,300	$1,636.50, plus 28% of the excess over $10,100
Over $12,300 but not over $14,950	$2,252.50, plus 32% of the excess over $12,300
Over $14,950 but not over $17,600	$3,100.50, plus 37% of the excess over $14,950
Over $17,600 but not over $22,900	$4,081, plus 43% of the excess over $17,600
Over $22,900 but not over $30,000	$6,360, plus 49% of the excess over $22,900
Over $30,000 but not over $42,800	$9,839, plus 54% of the excess over $30,000
Over $42,800 but not over $54,700	$16,751, plus 59% of the excess over $42,800
Over $54,700 but not over $81,200	$23,772, plus 64% of the excess over $54,700
Over $81,200 but not over $107,700	$40,732, plus 68% of the excess over $81,200
Over $107,700	$58,752, plus 70% of the excess over $107,700

Tax Burden Highest in Large Cities

According to the Census Bureau, the tax burden in large cities is four times the rate in small cities. New York has the highest tax burden, $841.79 per person, and Houston has the lowest at $175.03. The national average is $201 per person in taxes collected by all communities and a per-capita burden of $108 in cities of less than 50,000 residents.

According to the study, which is based on fiscal year 1977–78, the predominant tax source was property which provided $16.3 billion in revenues.

Contributions to Charitable Organizations Double

Americans donated $39.6 billion to charitable causes in 1978 (the latest year for which official data are available), more than double the amount given a decade ago.

Individuals contributed $32.8 billion, or about 83% of all philanthropic donations. Corporations gave $2 billion, and foundations and bequests contributed the remaining $4.8 billion.

Religious organizations received $18.5 billion. Education and health recipients received about $5.5 billion. Contributions to the arts, which more than doubled in the last five years, amounted to $2.5 billion, making it the fastest growing category.

Federal Income Tax Comparisons

Taxes at Selected Brackets After Standard Deductions

Adjusted gross income	Single return listing no dependents				Joint return listing 2 dependents			
	1979	1978[1]	1972[2]	1967	1979	1978[1]	1972[2]	1967
$ 3,000	$ 0	$ 0	$ 141	$ 333	$ −300	$ −300[3]	$ 0	$ 4
5,000	238	274	495	667	−500	−300[3]	102	286
10,000	1,177	1,216	1,545	1,742	374	442	901	1,114
15,000	2,345	2,457	2,703	3,334	1,242	1,375	1,820	2,172
20,000	3,837	3,999	4,255	5,350	2,265	2,524	3,010	3,428
25,000	5,562	5,830	6,090	7,730	3,497	3,857	4,380	4,892

1. Includes $35 general tax credit per exemption or 2% of taxable income up to $180, whichever is greater. 2. A 2.5% surcharge was in effect. 3. Refund based on Earned Income Credit for families with dependent children ($400 maximum), earning up to $8,000 adjusted gross income.

Returns Filed and Examined

Internal Revenue Service

Category	Returns filed for calendar year 1978	Returns examined 1979	Percent coverage
Individual, total	87,338,611	1,844,986	2.11
Form 1040—Standard	28,749,451	191,986	.67
Under $10,000 (non-business)	10,147,045	253,586	2.50
Total	38,896,496	445,572	1.15
$10,000–$15,000 (non-business)	12,627,936	284,585	2.25
$15,000–$50,000 (non-business)	24,227,838	704,024	2.91
$50,000 and over (non-business)	966,659	101,989	10.55
Under $10,000 (business)	4,043,915	132,617	3.28
$10,000–$30,000 (business)	5,132,040	92,933	1.81
$30,000 and over (business)	1,443,728	83,266	5.77
Fiduciary	1,744,478	10,170	.58
Partnership	1,195,186	30,474	2.55
Corporation, total	1,920,371	142,937	7.44
Assets not reported	123,526	8,280	6.70
Under $100,000	959,614	40,178	4.19
$100,000–$1 million	674,357	53,520	7.94
$1 million–$10 million	133,719	28,629	21.41
$10 million–$100 million	24,421	8,373	34.29
$100 million and over	4,734	3,957	83.59
Form 1120S	444,860	11,523	2.59
Form 1120 DISC	7,776	1,435	18.45
Estate, total	158,045	29,232	18.50
Gross estate under $300,000	122,330	12,741	10.42
Gross estate $300,000 and over	35,715	16,491	46.17
Gift	194,848	11,723	6.02
Income, Estate, and Gift, Total	**93,004,175**	**2,082,480**	**2.24[1]**
Excise	881,554	82,104	9.31
Employment	25,592,993	109,019	.43

1. Does not add due to rounding.

Results of Criminal Action in Tax Fraud Cases

Internal Revenue Service

Action	Number of Defendants					
	1979	1978	1977	1976	1975	1974
Plea of guilty nolo contendere	1,270	1,189	1,229	977	1,046	1,062
Convicted after trial	342	225	247	216	173	191
Acquitted	86	70	55	77	83	97
Nol-prossed or dismissed	183	119	110	71	168	115
Total disposals	1,881	1,603	1,641	1,341	1,470	1,465
Indictments and Informations	1,820	1,724	1,636	1,331	1,495	1,441

Federal Corporation Taxes

For tax years beginning after 1978, the old corporate system of normal tax, surtax, and surtax exemption is replaced by a graduated tax rate structure that provides for tax reductions to stimulate the economy. The new rates are graduated over the first four $25,000 amounts of taxable income as follows:

Taxable income	Tax	Percent over excess
$0 to $25,000	$ 0	17% over $0
$25,000–50,000	$ 4,250	20% over $25,000
$50,000–75,000	$ 9,250	30% over $50,000
$75,000–100,000	$16,750	40% over $75,000
$100,000 and over	$26,750	46% over $100,000

The Tax Reform Act of 1976 made certain changes affecting the taxation of corporations. Foreign tax breaks are denied to companies that participate in international boycotts. The foreign tax credit, deferral of earnings of foreign subsidiaries, and benefits derived through Domestic International Sales Corporations (DISC) are denied in proportion to income attributable to boycott activity. The amount of any illegal payments to a foreign official may not be deducted.

DISC is exempt from all federal taxes, but DISC shareholders were deemed to have received as a dividend 50% of the corporation's net income every taxable year. Thus, use of a DISC permitted deferral of tax on one-half of DISC income. The 1976 Tax Reform Act reduced this deferral and permits DISC benefits only to the extent that gross export receipts exceed 67% of the average for a four-year base. Full DISC benefits are retained for those having taxable income of $100,000 or less for a taxable year, but phase out at $150,000.

The tax law provides for a credit for investments in depreciable personal property. The 10% credit as well as the $100,000 limitation on used property eligible for the credit has been made permanent by the Revenue Act of 1978. There is an additional 1% credit if the employer established an Employee Stock Ownership Plan (ESOP) meeting specified criteria. An additional half percent credit is available if employee contributions to an ESOP match the half percent. The tax liability credit limitation is increased over a transitional period. The 1978 Energy Tax Act provides for certain additional investment credits.

The targeted jobs credit replaced the new jobs credit. The credit may be elected by employers who hire individuals from certain target groups. The credit is equal to 50% of the first $6,000 of qualified first-year wages and 25% of the first $6,000 of qualified second-year wages paid to each such individual. However, the qualified first-year wages for all such employees may not exceed 30% of the total unemployment insurance wages (FUTA) paid by the employer during the current year.

State Corporation Income and Franchise Taxes

All states but Nevada, South Dakota, Texas, Washington, and Wyoming impose a tax on corporation net income. The majority of states impose the tax at flat rates ranging from 3% to 12%. Several states have adopted a graduated basis of rates for corporations.

Nearly all states follow the federal law in defining net income. However, many states provide for varying exclusions and adjustments.

A state is empowered to tax all of the net income of its domestic corporations. With regard to nonresident corporations, however, it may only tax the net income on business carried on within its boundaries. Corporations are, therefore, required to apportion their incomes among the states where they do business and pay a tax to each of these states. Nearly all states provide an apportionment to their domestic corporations, too, in order that they not be unduly burdened.

Several states tax unincorporated businesses separately.

Federal Estate and Gift Taxes

A Federal Estate Tax Return must be filed for the estate of every U.S. citizen or resident whose gross estate, if the decedent died in 1980, exceeds $161,563. The size of the estate required for filing increases each year until 1981. The phased-in filing requirements are $134,000 for persons dying in 1978, $147,333 in 1979, $161,563 in 1980, and $175,625 in 1981 and later years. An estate tax return must also be filed for the estate of a nonresident, not a citizen, if the value of his gross estate in the U.S. is more than $30,000 at the date of death. The estate tax return is due nine months after the date of death of the decedent, but reasonable extension of time to file may be obtained for good reason. Tax due is to be paid when the return is filed. The executor of an estate with an interest in closely held business may pay estate tax attributable to the business in from two to ten equal annual installments. To be eligible for this treatment, the interest in the closely held business (or businesses) must represent at least 35% of the gross estate or 50% of the taxable estate. A 15-year extension for the payment of estate taxes may be exercised for that portion of the estate tax attributable to a business whose value constitutes more than 65% of the decedent's adjusted gross estate.

Under the unified federal estate and gift tax structure, a gift tax return is required to be filed on a quarterly basis only when the sum of (1) the taxable gifts made during the calendar quarter plus (2) all other gifts made during the calendar year exceeds $25,000. If a return is required, it should be filed no later than one and one half months after the end of a calendar quarter. The gift tax is due at the same time the return is required to be filed. Effective for returns reporting gifts made in calendar year 1979 and thereafter, the filing of the fourth quarter gift tax return can be made on April 15 rather than February 15.

The Tax Reform Act of 1976 replaced the old $30,000 gift tax exemption and $60,000 estate tax exemption with a unified credit. This credit is used for both estate and gift taxes. Any part of the credit used to offset gift taxes is not available to offset estate taxes. As a result, although they are still taxable as gifts, lifetime transfers no longer cushion the impact of progressive estate tax rates. Lifetime transfers and transfers made at death are cumulated for estate tax rate purposes. Gift taxes are computed by applying the uniform rate schedule to lifetime taxable transfers (after deducting the unified credit) and subtracting the taxes payable for prior taxable periods. In general, estate taxes are computed by applying the uniform rate schedule to cumulated transfers and subtracting the gift taxes paid. An appropriate adjustment is made for taxes on lifetime transfers—such as gifts within three years of death—in a decedent's estate.

Among the deductions allowed in computing the amount of the estate subject to tax are funeral expenditures, administrative costs, claims and bequests to religious, charitable, and fraternal organizations or government welfare agencies, and state inheritance taxes. A marital deduction is also allowable for both estates and gifts. The Tax Reform Act of 1976 provides a maximum estate marital deduction of the greater of $250,000 or one-half of the decedent's adjusted gross estate. As a result, a decedent utilizing the maximum marital deduction will have no estate tax in 1978 if his estate is less than $384,000. The amount phases up to $425,625 for death occurring in 1981 and thereafter. The Tax Reform Act of 1976 provides for a gift marital deduction of $100,000 for the first $100,000 of lifetime gifts made to a spouse, no deduction for the next $100,000 of such gifts, and thereafter a deduction for one half of the aggregate lifetime gifts made to a spouse in excess of $200,000. An annual gift tax exclusion is provided that permits tax-free gifts to each donee of $3,000 for each year.

Unified Credit—Estate & Gift Taxes

Year	Credit
1977	$30,000
1978	34,000
1979	38,000
1980	42,500
1981 & after	47,000

Federal Estate and Gift Taxes

Unified Rate Schedule[1]

If the net amount is: From	To	Tentative tax is: Tax	+ %	On excess over
$ 0	$ 10,000	$ 0	18	$ 0
10,000	20,000	1,800	20	10,000
20,000	40,000	3,800	22	20,000
40,000	60,000	8,200	24	40,000
60,000	80,000	13,000	26	60,000
80,000	100,000	18,200	28	80,000
100,000	150,000	23,800	30	100,000
150,000	250,000	38,800	32	150,000
250,000	500,000	70,800	34	250,000
500,000	750,000	155,800	37	500,000
750,000	1,000,000	248,300	39	750,000
1,000,000	1,250,000	345,800	41	1,000,000
1,250,000	1,500,000	448,300	43	1,250,000
1,500,000	2,000,000	555,800	45	1,500,000
2,000,000	2,500,000	780,800	49	2,000,000
2,500,000	3,000,000	1,025,800	53	2,500,000
3,000,000	3,500,000	1,290,800	57	3,000,000
3,500,000	4,000,000	1,575,800	61	3,500,000
4,000,000	4,500,000	1,880,800	65	4,000,000
4,500,000	5,000,000	2,205,800	69	4,500,000
5,000,000	—	2,550,800	70	5,000,000

1. The estate and gift tax rates are combined in the single rate schedule effective for the estates of decedents dying, and for gifts made, after Dec. 31, 1976.

State General Sales and Use Taxes[1]

(as of August 1, 1980)

State	Percent rate	State	Percent rate	State	Percent rate
Alabama	4	Kentucky	5	Ohio	4
Arizona	4	Louisiana	3	Oklahoma	2
Arkansas	3	Maine	5	Pennsylvania	6
California	4.75	Maryland	5	Rhode Island	6
Colorado	3	Massachusetts	5	South Carolina	4
Connecticut	7.5	Michigan	4	South Dakota	4
D.C.	5	Minnesota	4	Tennessee[3]	4.5
Florida	4	Mississippi	5	Texas	4
Georgia	3	Missouri	3.125	Utah	4
Hawaii	4	Nebraska	3	Vermont	3
Idaho	3	Nevada	3	Virginia	3
Illinois[2]	5	New Jersey	5	Washington	4.5
Indiana	4	New Mexico	3.75	West Virginia[4]	3
Iowa	3	New York	4	Wisconsin	4
Kansas	3	North Carolina	3	Wyoming	3
		North Dakota	3		

1. Local and county taxes, if any, are additional. 2. 4% on food and drugs. 3. Continues temporary State Retail Sales Tax for one year at 4.5%. 4. 1% on food purchased in grocery stores July 1, 1980-June 30, 1981, then no tax. NOTE: Alaska, Delaware, Montana, New Hampshire and Oregon have no statewide sales and use taxes.

Income Tax Rates in Selected Cities

(Population exceeding 50,000)

City	Percent rate	Year begun	City	Percent rate	Year begun
Akron, Ohio	1.5	1962	Kettering, Ohio	1	1968
Allentown, Pa.	1	1958	Lakewood, Ohio	1	1968
Altoona, Pa.	1	1948	Lancaster, Pa.	0.5	1959
Baltimore	(1)	1966	Lansing, Mich.	1	1968
Bethlehem, Pa.	1	1957	Lexington, Ky.	2	1952
Birmingham, Ala.	1	1970	Lima, Ohio	1	1959
Canton, Ohio	1.5	1954	Lorain, Ohio	1	1967
Chester, Pa.	1	1956	Louisville, Ky.	2.2	1948
Cincinnati	2	1954	Mansfield, Ohio	1	1966
Cleveland	1.5	1967	New York	0.9–4.3	1966
Cleveland Heights, Ohio	2	1968	Owensboro, Ky.	1	1960
Columbus, Ohio	1.5	1947	Parma, Ohio	1	1967
Covington, Ky.	2.5	1956	Philadelphia	4.3125	1939
Dayton, Ohio	1.75	1949	Pontiac, Mich.	1	1968
Detroit	2	1965	Reading, Pa.	1	1969
District of Columbia	2–11	1947	Saginaw, Mich.	1	1965
Elyria, Ohio	1.5	1969	St. Louis	1	1948
Erie, Pa.	1	1948	Scranton, Pa.	1.6	1948
Euclid, Ohio	1	1967	Springfield, Ohio	2	1948
Flint, Mich.	1	1965	Toledo, Ohio	1.5	1946
Gadsden, Ala.	2	1956	Warren, Ohio	1	1952
Grand Rapids, Mich.	1	1967	Wilkes-Barre, Pa.	1	1966
Hamilton, Ohio	1.5	1960	Wilmington, Del.	1	1970
Harrisburg, Pa.	1	1966	York, Pa.	1	1965
Kansas City, Mo.	1	1964	Youngstown, Ohio	1.5	1948

1. Tax is 50% of state income tax. NOTE: Rates are for residents only, except in Kentucky, Ohio, and Pennsylvania cities, where non-resident rate is the same. *Source:* Tax Foundation, Inc.

Foreign Study

Young people who want to study in Western Europe will find useful information in a guidebook published by the European Common Market. It lists school fees, entrance requirements, etc., mainly for Common Market countries. *The Handbook for Students* costs $6.15 and it can be obtained from the European Community Information Service, 2100 M Street, N.W., Suite 707, Washington, D.C. 20037.

Sales Tax Rates in Selected Cities[1]

City	Percent rate	City	Percent rate	City	Percent rate
Amarillo, Tex.	1	Ithaca, N.Y.[2]	3	Richmond, Va.	1
Anaheim, Calif.[2]	1.25	Jefferson City, Mo.	1	Roanoke, Va.	1
Austin, Tex.	1	Lincoln, Neb.	1	Sacramento, Calif.[2]	1.25
Baton Rouge, La.[3]	3	Los Angeles[2]	1.25	St. Louis	1
Berkeley, Calif.[2,4]	1.75	Lynchburg, Va.	1	San Antonio, Tex.	1
Birmingham, Ala.	1	Mobile, Ala.	2	San Diego, Calif.[2]	1.25
Boulder, Colo.	2	Montgomery, Ala.	2	San Francisco[2,4]	1.75
Chicago[2]	2	New Orleans[3]	3	Seattle[2]	0.925
Dallas	1	New York	4	Shreveport, La.[3]	2
Denver	3	Nome, Alaska	3	Spokane, Wash.[2]	0.925
Duluth, Minn.	1	Norfolk, Va.	1	Springfield, Ill.[2]	2
El Paso	1	Oakland, Calif.[2,4]	1.75	Topeka, Kan.	0.5
Fort Worth	1	Oklahoma City	2	Troy, N.Y.[2]	3
Fresno, Calif.[2]	1.25	Omaha, Neb.	1.5	Tucson, Ariz.	2
Glendale, Calif.[2]	1.25	Pasadena, Calif.[2]	1.25	Tulsa, Okla.	2
Houston	1	Phoenix, Ariz.	1	Washington, D.C.	5
Huntsville, Ala.	2	Rapid City, S.D.	1.5	Yonkers, N.Y.[2]	4

1. Excludes state and county sales taxes unless otherwise indicated. 2. Combined city and county rate. 3. Includes Parish School Board tax. 4. Includes 0.5% imposed by San Francisco Bay Area Rapid Transit District.

The Erosion of Purchasing Power

In 1970, a $10,000-a-year family had $8,640 to spend after Federal income and Social Security taxes. In 1980, the same family needed a gross income of $20,187 to match its 1970 after-tax spending power. Taxes siphoned off $3,408 of income, while an additional $8,139 was needed to cover the rise in prices over the ten-year period.

Estimates indicate that the median family income for 1980 was $21,350, up from $9,867 in 1970. Despite this 116% rise in income, real purchasing power after taxes was only 7% greater than in 1970.

Books of the Bible

OLD TESTAMENT — STANDARD VERSIONS

Genesis
Exodus
Leviticus
Numbers
Deuteronomy
Joshua
Judges
Ruth
I Samuel
II Samuel
I Kings
II Kings
I Chronicles
II Chronicles
Ezra
Nehemiah
Esther
Job
Psalms
Proverbs
Ecclesiastes
Song of Solomon
Isaiah
Jeremiah
Lamentations
Ezekiel
Daniel
Hosea
Joel
Amos
Obadiah
Jonah
Micah
Nahum
Habakkuk
Zephaniah
Haggai
Zechariah
Malachi

NEW TESTAMENT — STANDARD VERSIONS

Matthew
Mark
Luke
John
Acts
Romans
Corinthians
Galatians
Ephesians
Philippians
Colossians
Thessalonians
Timothy
Titus
Philemon
Hebrews
James
Peter
John
Jude
Revelation

OLD TESTAMENT — DOUAY VERSION[1]

Genesis
Exodus
Leviticus
Numbers
Deuteronomy
Josue
Judges
Ruth
I Kings
II Kings
III Kings
IV Kings
II Esdras
Tobias
Judith
Esther
Job
Psalms
Proverbs
Ecclesiastes
Canticle of Canticles
Wisdom
Ecclesiasticus
Isaias
Jeremias
Lamentations
Baruch
Ezechiel
Daniel
Osee
Joel
Amos
Abdias
Jonas
Micheas
Nahum
Habacuc
Sophonias
Aggeus
Zacharias
Malachias
I Machabees
II Machabees

1. In the Douay Version of the Bible, the books of the New Testament are the same as those of the Authorized (King James) Version, except that the Revelation of St. John is called the Apocalypse of St. John in the Douay Version.

1980 Environmental Quality Index

Source: Copyright 1980 by the National Wildlife Federation.
Reprinted from the February-March issue of *National Wildlife* Magazine.

National Wildlife's annual Environmental Quality (EQ) Index is a subjective analysis of the state of the nation's natural resources. The judgments on resource trends represent the collective thinking of the editors and the National Wildlife Federation staff, based on extensive consultation with government experts, private specialists, and academic researchers.

Wildlife: Same. Through widespread habitat loss continues, important new laws and conservation programs have been established. For the first time in more than a decade, the EQ trendline stopped going down in 1979. The continuing loss of wetlands was slowed somewhat because of a federal crackdown on dredging and draining for urban and agricultural development. Canada and the U.S. tentatively agreed jointly to protect the habitat of the Porcupine caribou herd that migrates between Alaska and the Yukon; The International Whaling Commission tightened regulations on the killing of sperm whales; and there was a dramatic reduction in the accidental killing of porpoises by tuna fisherman. On the negative side, a fierce backlash against virtually all environmental constraint on development emerged in Congress in 1979. As energy pressures increase, it will be difficult to protect wildlife's hard-won gains.

Air: Up. Prodded by tough federal standards, air polluters have slowly cleaned up their act. Although millions of Americans are breathing air that is cleaner than it had been in a decade, the clean air effort has become a scapegoat for the nation's economic woes, as U.S. policy- and auto-makers contend that antipollution costs are "inflationary." In 1979 there was relentless pressure on EPA to lower its air standards and the agency did budge a bit. In spite of gains in 25 major cities, air quality is worsening in some cities. We are still struggling against a tide of increased automobile use and to date carmakers have not met the antipollution goals of the 1970 Clean Air Act. Another cause for concern is President Carter's request to utilities to cut their oil consumption in half, mainly by switching to coal. Such a switch could lead to an increase in sulfur pollution that would exacerbate a relatively new but already serious threat: acid rain.

Minerals: Down. As the U.S. plodded toward a national energy and conservation policy, the days of cheap fuel and abundant minerals vanished forever. Of the seven resources analyzed in the EQ Index, minerals are perhaps the easiest to squander, the hardest to retrieve. Oil, gas, and coal when burned are gone forever, and conservation is the only way to prolong what is left. In 1979, the U.S. moved one year closer to the end of the petroleum era without a comprehensive energy conservation program. However, the news was not all bad. Energy efficiency in homes and apartments increased and industrial energy use decreased without hurting production. Over all the energy consumption rate has slowed down. The most heartening energy news was the revised fix on future U.S. needs. Given the present trend, it will be far less than formerly assumed. This means we can concentrate on the development of environmental benign alternative fuels and it reinforces the idea that conservation, not production, is the safest, most economical way to reduce reliance on overseas energy.

Water: Same. As cleanup efforts began to pay off, the complexities of the country's water pollution problems became more apparent. After a decade of frustration, there were signs of real progress in 1979. Statistics showed several of the worst pollutants have not increased since 1975. Industry is responsible for much of the cleanup progress. About 85 percent of the nation's major industrial polluters are complying with the law. However, if all industrial and municipal water pollution stopped overnight, there would still be a monumental water pollution problem. Every day, vast amounts of urban and agricultural poisons enter the nation's water supplies from "nonpoint" sources. The National Wild Life Federation surveyed all 50 states in 1979 and concluded that a toxic-waste disaster similar to New York's Love Canal could happen "almost anywhere."

Forests: Same. A battery of tough forestry laws ushered in a new era of timber management, offering hope that the U.S. can avoid wood shortages. The U.S. grew more timber than it cut (except in the West) and there was progress toward resolving some old conflicts over how national forests should be run. The federal government is moving on a couple of fronts to increase output: by beefing up its efforts to encourage small private woodlot owners to produce more commercial timber; and, in Congress, there is growing interest in reducing losses to wasteful logging and diseases. There are several new developments that will have to be dealt with in the 1980s, including a sharp decline in housing starts; an expected gobal timber famine; and the growing impact of the energy crisis on forests. American woodlands are suddenly being described as a vast storehouse of untapped energy.

Soil: Same. In the face of rampant soil erosion and urban sprawl, prime farmland has declined while the nation's food needs have grown. Thanks mainly to two new developments, the outlook for America's hard used soil may be better. Erosion in many areas apparently isn't as bad as the experts once feared and there is a good chance the application of harmful pesticides can be drastically curtailed. On the negative side, the massive runoff of fertilizer and pesticide into streams and rivers remains one of the nation's most stubborn pollution problems. Also the conversion of cropland to suburbs continues unabated.

Living Space: Down. Without effective land-use planning, vast stretches of America's land have remained vulnerable to topsy-turvy development. Even with a lower birthrate the U.S. population is expanding rapidly and the strain on living space is relentless. With the coming of age of the "Baby Boom" generation in the 1970s, there was a threefold increase in new households. Upshot: the 35-year-old migration to the suburbs continues, accompanied by blitzkreig developments in scores of agricultural areas. Higher gasoline prices and uncertainty over supply, however, may slow the exurban tide. Although there has been no federal land-use legislation in the works for nearly five years, some states have enacted their own laws. But benefits from programs to improve human and natural environments will be limited as long as the primary cause of the living space crunch—population growth—continues.

Some Endangered Species of the World

Common name	Scientific name	Range
MAMMALS		
Anteater, scaly	*Manis temmincki*	Africa
Bear, brown	*Ursus arctos pruinosus*	China (Tibet)
Bear, brown or grizzly	*Ursus arctos horribilis*	U.S.
Cat, leopard	*Felis bengalensis bengalensis*	Eastern Asia
Cat, tiger	*Felis tigrina*	Costa Rica to northern South America
Cheetah	*Acinonyx jubatus*	Africa to India
Chimpanzee	*Pan troglodytes*	Western and central Africa
Chinchilla	*Chinchilla brevicaudata boliviana*	Bolivia
Deer, Columbian white-tailed	*Odocoileus virginianus leucurus*	U.S. (Ore., Wash.)
Deer, marsh	*Blastocerus dichotomus*	Argentina, Uruguay, Paraguay, Brazil
Deer, musk	*Moschus moschiferus moschiferus*	Southcentral Asia
Elephant, Asian	*Elephas maximus*	India, Burma, Thailand, Cambodia, Laos, Malaysia, Sri Lanka, Vietnam
Gazelle, Clark's (Dibatag)	*Ammordorcas clarki*	Somalia, Ethiopia
Gazelle, slender-horned (Rhim)	*Gazella leptoceros*	Sudan, Algeria, Egypt, Libya
Gorilla	*Gorilla gorilla*	Central and western Africa
Ibex, Walia	*Capra walie*	Ethiopia
Jaguar	*Panthera onca*	Central and South America
Kangaroo, red	*Megaleia rufa*	Australia
Leopard	*Panthera pardus*	Africa, Asia
Leopard, snow	*Panthera uncia*	Central Asia
Lion, Asiatic	*Panthera leo persica*	India
Mandrill	*Papio sphinx*	Central west Africa
Monkey, black howler	*Alouatta pigra*	Mexico, Guatemala, Belize
Ocelot	*Felis pardalis*	Central and South America
Orangutan	*Pongo pygmaeus*	Indonesia, Malaysia, Brunei
Otter, Southern Sea	*Enhydra lutris nereis*	U.S. (Calif.)
Panther, Florida	*Felis concolor coryi*	U.S. (Fla.)
Prairie Dog, Utah	*Synomys parvidens*	U.S. (Utah)
Pronghorn, Sonoran	*Antilocapra americana sonoriensis*	U.S. (Ariz.), Mexico
Rat, Morro Bay kangaroo	*Dipodomys heermanni morroensis*	U.S. (Calif.)
Rhinoceros, great Indian	*Rhinoceros unicornis*	India, Nepal
Sloth, Brazilian three-toed	*Bradypus torquatus*	Brazil
Tiger	*Panthera tigris*	Temperate and tropical Asia
Whale, humpback	*Megaptera novaeangliae*	Oceanic
Wolf, gray	*Canis lupus*	U.S., Mexico
Zebra, mountain	*Equus zebra zebra*	Southern Africa
BIRDS		
Albatross, short-tailed	*Diomedea albatrus*	North Pacific Ocean
Condor, Andean	*Vultur gryphus*	Colombia to Chile and Argentina
Eagle, bald	*Haliaeetus leucocephalus*	U.S.
Falcon, peregrine	*Falco peregrinus peregrinus*	Europe, U.S.S.R.
Parakeet, paradise	*Psephotus pulcherrimus*	Australia
Pelican, brown	*Pelecanus occidentalis*	U.S., West Indies, Central and South America
Penguin, Galápagos	*Spheniscus mendiculus*	Ecuador (Galápagos Islands)
Stork, white oriental	*Ciconia ciconia boyciana*	China, Japan, Korea, U.S.S.R.

Common name	Scientific name	Range
REPTILES		
Alligator, American	*Alligator mississippiensis*	U.S. (Fla., Ga., La., Tex., S.C.)
Crocodile, American	*Crocodylus acutus*	U.S. (Fla.), Central and South America
Iguana, Anegada ground	*Cyclura pinquis*	Virgin Islands
Python, Indian	*Python molurus molurus*	Sri Lanka, India
Snake, Atlantic salt-marsh	*Nerodia fasciata taeniata*	U.S. (Fla.)
Tortoise, Indian flap-shell	*Lissemys punctata punctata*	India, Pakistan, Bangladesh
AMPHIBIANS		
Frog, Israel painted	*Discoglossus nigriventer*	Israel
Toads, African viviparous	*Nectophrynoides* sps.	Tanzania, Guinea
Treefrog, Pine Barrens	*Hyla andersonii*	U.S. (Fla.)
FISH		
Catfish, giant	*Pangasianodon gigas*	Thailand
Pike, blue	*Stizostedion vitreum glaucum*	U.S. (Lakes Erie and Ontario)
Trout, greenback cutthroat	*Salmo clarki stomias*	U.S. (Colo.)

Source: Department of the Interior, Fish and Wildlife Service.

Sources of Information

Source: Brooklyn Botanic Garden, *Handbook on The Environment and The Home Gardener.*

Advice on various aspects of conservation programs and problems is available from national, state, and local organizations. Dr. Richard H. Pough, President of the Natural Area Council, has compiled a list of membership organizations that are happy to help smaller groups get started on worthwhile projects in conservation.

America the Beautiful Fund, Inc., 145 East 52nd St., Rm. 601, New York, N.Y. 10022

American Forestry Association, 1319 18th St., N.W., Washington, D.C. 20036

Defenders of Wildlife, 1244 19th St., N.W., Washington, D.C. 20036

Environmental Defense Fund, Inc., 475 Park Ave. South, New York, N.Y. 10016

Friends of the Earth, 72 Jane St., New York, N.Y. 10014

Izaak Walton League of America, 1800 N. Kent St., Suite 806, Arlington, Va. 22209

National Audubon Society, 950 Third Ave., New York, N.Y. 10022

National Park and Conservation Association, 1701 18th St., N.W., Washington, D.C. 20009

National Trust for Historic Preservation, 748 Jackson Place, N.W., Washington, D.C. 20006

National Wildlife Federation, 1412 16th St., N.W., Washington, D.C. 20036

Natural Science for Youth Foundation, 763 Silvermine Rd., New Canaan, Conn. 06840

The Nature Conservancy, 1800 N. Kent St., Suite 800, Arlington, Va. 22209

Open Space Institute, Inc., 45 Rockefeller Plaza, Room 2350, New York, N.Y. 10020

Sierra Club, 530 Bush St., San Francisco, Calif. 94108

The Wilderness Society, 1901 Pennsylvania Ave., N.W., Washington, D.C. 20006

World Wildlife Fund, 1319 18th St., N.W., Washington, D.C. 20036

Nonpoint Sources of Pollution

(Percent of basins affected,[1] by type of nonpoint source)

Region (number of basins)	Urban runoff	Construction	Hydrologic modification	Silviculture	mining	Agriculture	Solid waste disposal	Individual disposal
Northeast (40)	70	15	20	10	20	55	35	63
Southeast (47)	57	2	21	30	15	62	9	40
Great Lakes (41)	54	7	2	15	41	59	15	39
North Central (35)	54	6	3	6	40	89	9	29
South Central (30)	50	0	23	13	53	87	13	40
Southwest (22)	23	0	18	5	36	73	0	35
Northwest (22)	23	23	23	27	23	55	9	32
Islands (9)	67	67	22	0	0	78	22	89
All basins (246)	52	9	15	15	30	68	14	43

1. In whole or part. *Source:* U.S. Environmental Protection Agency, *National Water Quality Inventory, 1977 Report To Congress.* Environmental Quality—1979, Council on Environmental Quality.

Air Pollutant Emissions, by Source
(estimates)

Year and pollutant	Total emissions[1]	Controllable emissions[1]: Transportation: Total	Transportation: Road vehicles	Fuel combustion[2]: Total	Fuel combustion[2]: Electric utilities	Industrial processes	Solid waste disposal	Misc. uncontrollable[1]
1970								
Carbon monoxide	112.7	88.7	78.2	1.4	.2	8.8	6.8	6.8
Sulfur oxides	32.8	.8	.3	24.9	17.5	6.9	.1	.1
Hydrocarbons	32.5	13.4	11.7	1.7	.1	9.5	1.9	6.1
Particulates[3]	24.5	1.3	.8	7.8	4.5	13.1	1.2	1.0
Nitrogen oxides	21.6	8.2	5.8	12.2	5.7	.7	.3	.2
1975								
Carbon monoxide	106.8	90.4	81.3	1.2	.3	8.0	3.2	4.0
Sulfur oxides	28.8	.8	.3	22.9	18.5	5.1	—	—
Hydrocarbons	29.7	12.5	10.8	1.5	.1	10.1	.9	4.6
Particulates[3]	15.1	1.2	.9	5.5	4.1	7.2	.6	.7
Nitrogen oxides	23.1	9.5	7.1	12.7	6.8	.8	.1	.1
1977								
Carbon monoxide	113.2	94.5	85.1	1.3	.3	9.1	2.9	5.4
Sulfur oxides	30.2	.9	.4	24.7	19.4	4.6	—	—
Hydrocarbons	31.2	12.7	10.9	1.7	.1	11.1	.8	5.0
Particulates[3]	13.7	1.2	.9	5.3	3.7	6.0	.4	.8
Nitrogen oxides	25.5	10.1	7.4	14.3	7.8	.8	.1	.1

1. In millions of tons. 2. Stationary. 3. Suspended particulate matter (particles of smoke or dust, fumes, and droplets of viscous liquid remaining in the air for varying periods of time and ranging from less than 1 micron [1/25,000 in.] to 100 microns). *Source:* Environmental Protection Agency.

Estimated Total Pollution Abatement and Environmental Quality Expenditures, 1978–87
(billions of 1978 dollars)

	1978: Operation and maintenance	1978: Annual capital costs	1978: Total annual costs	1987: Operation and maintenance	1987: Annual capital costs	1987: Total annual costs	Cumulative (1978–87): Capital investment	Cumulative: Operation and maintenance	Cumulative: Capital costs	Cumulative: Total costs
Air Pollution										
Public	1.3	0.4	1.7	2.8	1.2	4.0	6.5	19.6	7.8	27.4
Private										
Mobile	4.3	3.3	7.6	5.1	9.3	14.4	59.6	45.0	66.4	111.4
Industrial	2.8	3.4	6.2	4.8	6.5	11.3	29.9	36.0	51.4	87.4
Utilities	2.2	1.6	3.8	7.5	5.5	13.0	32.4	45.5	34.0	79.5
Subtotal	10.6	8.7	19.3	20.2	22.5	42.7	128.0	146.1	159.6	305.7
Water Pollution										
Public	2.8	10.3	13.1	3.8	16.1	19.9	41.5	32.8	131.7	164.5
Private										
Industrial	2.7	2.0	4.7	6.8	5.2	12.0	34.7	48.5	36.8	85.3
Utilities	1.5	.9	2.4	2.4	1.5	3.9	6.3	19.9	12.2	32.1
Subtotal	7.0	13.2	20.2	13.0	22.8	35.8	82.5	101.2	180.7	281.9
Solid Waste										
Public	1.6	.3	1.9	2.5	.7	3.2	3.2	21.5	5.5	27.0
Private	3.9	.6	4.5	6.5	1.4	7.9	4.2	54.6	11.7	66.3
Subtotal	5.5	.9	6.4	9.0	2.1	11.1	7.4	76.1	17.2	93.3
Toxic Substances	0.1	n.a.	0.1	0.3	n.a.	0.3	n.a.	2.2	n.a.	2.2
Drinking Water	0.3	0.3	0.6	0.8	0.8	1.6	n.a.	6.4	6.1	12.5
Noise	<.05	<.05	<.05	0.6	1.0	1.6	4.8	2.5	4.1	6.6
Pesticides	<.05	<.05	<.05	0.1	<.05	0.1	n.a.	0.5	<.05	0.5
Land Reclamation	0.1	n.a.	0.1	1.0	n.a.	1.0	n.a.	8.0	n.a.	8.0
Total	**23.6**	**23.1**	**46.7**	**45.0**	**49.2**	**94.2**	**249.5**	**343.0**	**367.7**	**710.7**

n.a. = not available. *Source: Environmental Quality—1979,* Council on Environmental Quality.

Water Supply of the World[1]

The Antarctic Icecap is the largest supply of fresh water, nearly 2 percent of the world's total of fresh and salt water. As can be seen from the table below, the amount of water in our atmosphere is over ten times as large as the water in all the rivers taken together. The fresh water actually available for human use in lakes and rivers and the accessible ground water amounts to only about one third of one percent of the world's total water supply.

	Surface area (square miles)	Volume (cubic miles)	Percentage of total
Salt Water			
The oceans	139,500,000	317,000,000	97.2
Inland seas and saline lakes	270,000	25,000	0.008
Fresh Water			
Freshwater lakes	330,000	30,000	0.009
All rivers (average level)	—	300	0.0001
Antarctic Icecap	6,000,000	6,300,000	1.9
Arctic Icecap and glaciers	900,000	680,000	0.21
Water in the atmosphere	197,000,000	3,100	0.001
Ground water within half a mile from surface	—	1,000,000	0.31
Deep-lying ground water	—	1,000,000	0.31
Total (rounded)	—	**326,000,000**	**100.00**

1. All figures are estimated. *Source:* Department of the Interior, Geological Survey.

Speed of Animals

Most of the following measurements are for maximum speeds over approximate quarter-mile distances. Exceptions—which are included to give a wide range of animals—are the lion and elephant, whose speeds were clocked in the act of charging; the whippet, which was timed over a 200-yard course; the cheetah over a 100-yard distance; man for a 15-yard segment of a 100-yard run; and the black mamba, six-lined race runner, spider, giant tortoise, three-toed sloth, and garden snail, which were measured over various small distances.

Animal	Speed mph	Animal	Speed mph	Animal	Speed mph
Cheetah	70	Mongolian wild ass	40	Man	27.89
Pronghorn antelope	61	Greyhound	39.35	Elephant	25
Wildebeest	50	Whippet	35.5	Black mamba snake	20
Lion	50	Rabbit (domestic)	35	Six-line race runner	18
Thomson's gazelle	50	Mule deer	35	Squirrel	12
Quarter horse	47.5	Jackal	35	Pig (domestic)	11
Elk	45	Reindeer	32	Chicken	9
Cape hunting dog	45	Giraffe	32	Spider (Tegeneария atrica)	1.17
Coyote	43	White-tailed deer	30	Giant tortoise	0.17
Gray fox	42	Wart hog	30	Three-toed sloth	0.15
Hyena	40	Grizzly bear	30	Garden snail	0.03
Zebra	40	Cat (domestic)	30		

Source: Natural History Magazine, March 1974, copyright 1974, The American Museum of Natural History; and James Doherty, Curator of Mammals, N.Y. Zoological Society.

Animal Names: Male, Female, and Young

Animal	Male	Female	Young	Animal	Male	Female	Young	Animal	Male	Female	Young
Ass	Jack	Jenny	Foal	Duck	Drake	Duck	Duckling	Sheep	Ram	Ewe	Lamb
Bear	He-bear	She-bear	Cub	Elephant	Bull	Cow	Calf	Swan	Cob	Pen	Cygnet
Cat	Tom	Queen	Kitten	Fox	Dog	Vixen	Cub	Swine	Boar	Sow	Piglet
Cattle	Bull	Cow	Calf	Goose	Gander	Goose	Gosling	Tiger	Tiger	Tigress	Cub
Chicken	Rooster	Hen	Chick	Horse	Stallion	Mare	Foal	Whale	Bull	Cow	Calf
Deer	Buck	Doe	Fawn	Lion	Lion	Lioness	Cub	Wolf	Dog	Bitch	Pup
Dog	Dog	Bitch	Pup	Rabbit	Buck	Doe	Bunny				

Source: James Doherty, Curator of Mammals, N.Y. Zoological Society.

Animal Group Terminology

Source: James Doherty, Curator of Mammals, N.Y. Zoological Society, and *Information Please* data.

ants: colony
bears: sleuth, sloth
bees: grist, hive, swarm
birds: flight, volery
cattle: drove
cats: clutter, clowder
chicks: brood, clutch
clams: bed
cranes: sedge, seige
crows: murder
doves: dule
ducks: brace, team
elephants: herd
elks: gang
finches: charm
fish: school, shoal, draught
foxes: leash, skulk
geese: flock, gaggle, skein
gnats: cloud, horde
goats: trip
gorillas: band
hares: down, husk
hawks: cast
hens: brood
hogs: drift
horses: pair, team
hounds: cry, mute, pack
kangaroos: troop
kittens: kindle, litter
larks: exaltation
lions: pride
locusts: plague
magpies: tidings
mules: span
nightingales: watch
oxen: yoke
oysters: bed
parrots: company
partridges: covey
peacocks: muster, ostentation
pheasants: nest, bouquet
pigs: litter
ponies: string
quail: bevy, covey
rabbits: nest
seals: pod
sheep: drove, flock
sparrows: host
storks: mustering
swans: bevy, wedge
swine: sounder
toads: knot
turkeys: rafter
turtles: bale
vipers: nest
whales: gam, pod
wolves: pack, route
woodcocks: fall

Gestation, Incubation, and Longevity of Certain Animals

Animal	Gestation or incubation, in days & (average)	Longevity, in years & (record exceptions)	Animal	Gestation or incubation, in days & (average)	Longevity, in years & (record exceptions)
Ass	365	18–20 (63)	Horse	329–345 (336)	20–25 (50+)
Bear	180–240[1]	15–30 (47)	Kangaroo	32–39[1]	4–6 (23)
Cat	52–69 (63)	10–12 (26+)	Lion	105–113 (108)	10 (29)
Chicken	22	7–8 (14)	Man	253–303	(2)
Cow	c. 280	9–12 (39)	Monkey	139–270[1]	12–15[1](29)
Deer	197–300[1]	10–15 (26)	Mouse	19–31[1]	1–3 (4)
Dog	53–71 (63)	10–12 (24)	Parakeet (Budgerigar)	17–20 (18)	8 (12+)
Duck	21–35[1](28)	10 (15)	Pig	101–130 (115)	10 (22)
Elephant	510–730 (624)[1]	30–40 (71)	Pigeon	11–19	10–12 (39)
Fox	51–63[1]	8–10 (14)	Rabbit	30–35 (31)	6–8 (15)
Goat	136–160 (151)	12 (17)	Rat	21	3 (5)
Groundhog	31–32	4–9	Sheep	144–152 (151)[1]	12 (16)
Guinea pig	58–75 (68)	3 (6)	Squirrel	44	8–9 (15)
Hamster, golden	15–17	2 (8)	Whale	365–547[1]	—
Hippopotamus	220–255 (240)	30 (49+)	Wolf	60–63	10–12 (16)

1. Depending on kind. 2. For life expectancy charts, *see* Index. *Source:* James Doherty, Curator of Mammals, N.Y. Zoological Society.

Zoological Gardens

North America has more than 30 major zoos, in the United States, Canada, and Mexico. The *Quebec Zoological Society*'s collection is made up of Canadian species; Toronto has many exotic species.

The first zoological garden in the United States was established in Philadelphia in 1874. Since that time nearly every large city in the country has acquired a zoo. Among the largest are San Diego's on the West Coast; Chicago's Brookfield Zoo and those of St. Louis and Kansas City in the Middle West; and, in the East, the New York Zoological Society's park in the Bronx. The *National Zoological Park* in Washington, D.C., in a beautiful setting of hills, woods, and streams, was established in 1890 by an act of Congress. The major U.S. zoos now have created large natural-habitat areas for their collections.

In Europe, zoological gardens have long been popular public institutions. The *Jardin d'Acclimatation*, in the Bois de Boulogne, Paris, is the oldest and largest. Others are located at Clères, Ermenonville, Lyons, Marseilles, Maubeuge, Mulhouse, and Nancy.

Germany had about 20 zoological gardens, many of which were developed in the peacetime years between World Wars I and II. Large zoos were located in Berlin and Frankfurt am Main. In Munich, the animals were grouped according to the continent of their origin. At Stellingen near Hamburg, the *Hagenback Garden* became an outstanding show place and distributing center for animals.

The *Schönbrunn* at Vienna is one of the oldest zoos in Europe. The Budapest zoological gardens house a fine collection of European birds. At Antwerp, the *Royal Zoological Society* founded a large menagerie in 1843. It was seriously damaged by German bombs during World War II.

In the British Isles, a popular zoo is in the garden of the *London Zoological Society* in Regent's Park. Although this zoo received a number of direct bomb hits in 1940–41 and again in 1944, it remained open throughout World War II; visitors during this period numbered 6,500,000. Manchester and Clifton have smaller gardens, and the one at Edinburgh is famous for its collection of penguins. The *Dublin Zoo* is noted for its lions, many of which were born there.

The Amsterdam zoo, with its East Indian collection and its aquarium, and the Rotterdam gardens are the two best known in the Netherlands. Built on a high elevation, the *Skansen Zoo* in Stockholm exhibits north European specimens. The most important gardens in the U.S.S.R. are found in Moscow, where northern as well as exotic species are collected. The zoo at Rome has part of its collection confined in barless pits. At Lisbon there is a small zoological garden, and in Madrid a part of the original royal menagerie.

Notable American Zoos

Source: Information Please questionnaires to the zoos.

Atlanta Zoological Park: 800 Cherokee Ave., S.E., Atlanta, Ga. 30315

Audubon Park and Zoological Garden and Odenheimer Aquarium: St. Charles Ave. between Walnut and Exposition Blvd., New Orleans, La. 70118

Baltimore Zoo: Druid Hill Park, Baltimore, Md. 21217

Belle Isle Aquarium and Zoo: Detroit, Mich. Mailing address: Box 39, Royal Oak, Mich. 48068

Boston Zoo in Franklin Park, Boston, Mass. 02121

Bronx Zoo. *See* New York Zoological Park

Buffalo Zoological Gardens: Delaware Park, Buffalo, N.Y. 14214

Burnet Park Zoo: Coleridge and Wilbur Ave., Syracuse, N.Y. 13204

Central Park Zoo: 830 Fifth Ave. at 64th St., New York, N.Y. 10021

Cheyenne Mountain Zoological Park: Cheyenne Mountain Hwy., P.O. Box 158, Colorado Springs, Colo. 80901

Chicago Zoological Park (Brookfield Zoo): First Ave. and 31st St., Brookfield, Ill. 60513

Cincinnati, Zoological Society of: 3400 Vine St., Cincinnati, Ohio 45220

Cleveland Metroparks Zoo: Brookside Park, Cleveland, Ohio 44109

Columbus Zoo: 9990 Riverside Drive, Powell, Ohio 43065

Dallas Zoo: 621 East Clarendon Drive, Dallas, Tex. 75203

Denver Zoological Gardens: City Park, Denver, Colo. 80205

Detroit Zoological Park: Woodward and Ten Mile Road, Royal Oak, Mich. 48068

El Paso Zoological Park: Evergreen and Paisano, El Paso, Tex. 79905

Fort Worth Zoological Park: 2727 Zoological Park Drive, Fort Worth, Tex. 76110

Hogle Zoological Gardens: 2600 East Sunnyside Ave., Salt Lake City, Utah 84108

Houston Zoological Gardens: Hermann Park, P.O. Box 1562, Houston, Tex. 77001

Jacksonville Zoological Park: 8605 Zoo Road, Jacksonville, Fla. 32218

Kansas City Zoo: Swope Park, Kansas City, Mo. 64132

Lincoln Municipal Zoo: 1300 South 27th St., Lincoln, Neb. 68502

Lincoln Park Zoological Gardens: 2200 N. Cannon Drive, Chicago, Ill. 60614

Los Angeles Zoo: 5333 Zoo Drive, Los Angeles, Calif. 90027

Memphis Zoo and Aquarium: Overton Park, Memphis, Tenn. 38112

Mesker Park Zoo: Bement Ave., Evansville, Ind. 47712

Milwaukee County Zoo: 10001 West Bluemound Road, Milwaukee, Wis. 53226

National Zoological Park: 3000 block of Connecticut Ave. N.W., Washington, D.C. 20008

New York Zoological Park (Bronx Zoo): Fordham Rd., Southern Blvd., Bronx, N.Y. 10460

Oakland Zoo: Golf Links Road, off Freeway 580, Oakland, Calif. 94605

Oklahoma City Zoo: 2101 N.E. 50th St., Oklahoma City, Okla. 73111

Philadelphia Zoo: 34th St. and Girard Ave., Philadelphia, Pa. 19104

Pittsburgh Zoo: Highland Park, P.O. Box 5250, Pittsburgh, Pa. 15206

Rio Grande Zoological Park: 903 Tenth St., S.W., Albuquerque, N.M. 87102

St. Louis Zoological Park: Forest Park, St. Louis, Mo. 63110

St. Paul's Como Zoo: Midway Pkwy. and Kaufman Drive, St. Paul, Minn. 55103

San Diego Zoo: Park Blvd. and Zoo Place, P.O. Box 551, San Diego, Calif. 92112

San Francisco Zoological Gardens: Zoo Road and Skyline Blvd., San Francisco, Calif., 94132

Seneca Park Zoo: 2222 St. Paul St., Rochester, N.Y. 14621

Staten Island Zoo: Barrett Park, W. Brighton, Staten Island, New York 10310

Toledo Zoological Gardens: 2700 Broadway, Toledo, Ohio 43609

Washington Park Zoo: 4001 S.W. Canyon Road, Portland, Ore. 97221

Woodland Park Zoological Gardens: 5500 Phinney Ave. N., Seattle, Wash. 98103

The National Park System

Source: Department of the Interior, National Park Service.

The National Park System of the United States is administered by the National Park Service, a bureau of the Department of the Interior. Started with the establishment of Yellowstone National Park in 1872, the system includes not only the most extraordinary and spectacular scenic exhibits in the United States but also a large number of sites distinguished either for their historic or prehistoric importance or scientific interest, or for their superior recreational assets. The number and extent of the various types of areas that make up the system follow.

Type of area	Number	Total acreage[1]
National Parks	40	16,164,444.71
National Monuments	91	54,596,931.54
National Preserves	2	654,550.00
National Lakeshores	4	196,406.30
National Rivers[4]	10	525,443.33
National Seashores	10	598,089.29
National Historic Sites	60	17,960.72
National Memorials	22	8,245.66
National Military Parks	11	34,730.12
National Battlefield Parks	3	6,685.18
National Battlefields	9	10,514.40
National Battlefield Site	1	12.36
National Historical Parks	22	104,588.04
National Recreation Areas	17	3,661,664.79
National Parkways	4	160,854.45
National Trail[5]	1	52,034.25
Other Parks[2]	10	32,019.48
National Capital Parks[3]	1	6,468.82
White House	1	18.07
National Mall	1	146.35
National Visitor Center	1	0.00
Total	**321**	**76,850,196.86**

1. Acreage as of January 1, 1980, for most areas. New areas reflect data available at time of authorization. Ten national cemeteries administered by the National Park Service are administered in conjunction with associated historical units and are not listed separately. 2. Parks without national designation. 3. Comprises 346 units within the District of Columbia, Maryland, and Virginia. 4. Includes Wild and Scenic Rivers and Riverways. 5. Includes scenic and historic trails.

National Parks

Name, location, and year authorized	Acreage	Outstanding characteristics
Acadia (Maine), 1919	38,631.86	Rugged seashore on Mt. Desert Island and adjacent mainland
Arches (Utah), 1971	73,378.98	Unusual stone arches, windows, pedestals caused by erosion
Badlands (S.D.), 1978	243,302.33	Arid land of fossils, prairie, bison, deer, bighorn, antelope
Big Bend (Tex.), 1935	708,118.40	Mountains and desert bordering the Rio Grande
Bryce Canyon (Utah), 1924	38,835.08	Area of grotesque eroded rocks brilliantly colored
Canyonlands (Utah), 1964	377,570.43	Colorful wilderness with impressive red-rock canyons, spires, arches
Capitol Reef (Utah), 1971	241,904.26	Highly colored sedimentary rock formations in high, narrow gorges
Carlsbad Caverns (N.M.), 1930	46,755.33	The world's largest known caves
Channel Islands (Calif.) 1980	124,740	Area is rich in marine mammals, sea birds, endangered species and archeology.
Crater Lake (Ore.), 1902	160,290.33	Deep blue lake in heart of inactive volcano
Everglades (Fla.), 1934	1,398,800.00	Subtropical area with abundant bird and animal life
Glacier (Mont.), 1910	1,013,594.67	Rocky Mountain scenery with many glaciers and lakes
Grand Canyon (Ariz.), 1919	1,218,375.24	Mile-deep gorge, 4 to 18 miles wide, 217 miles long
Grand Teton (Wyo.), 1929	310,515.89	Picturesque range of high mountain peaks
Great Smoky Mts. (N.C.-Tenn), 1926	517,368.61	Highest mountain range east of Black Hills; luxuriant plant life
Guadalupe Mountains (Tex.), 1966	76,293,06	Contains highest point in Texas: Guadalupe Peak (8,751 ft)
Haleakala (Hawaii), 1960	28,655.25	World-famous 10,023-ft Haleakala volcano (dormant)
Hawaii Volcanoes (Hawaii), 1916	229,177.03	Spectacular volcanic area; luxuriant vegetation at lower levels
Hot Springs (Ark.), 1921	5,826.26	47 mineral hot springs said to have therapeutic value
Isle Royale (Mich.), 1931	571,796.18	Largest wilderness island in Lake Superior; moose, wolves, lakes
Kings Canyon (Calif.), 1940	460,136.20	Huge canyons; high mountains; giant sequoias
Lassen Volcanic (Calif.), 1916	106,372.36	Exhibits of impressive volcanic phenomena
Mammoth Cave (Ky.), 1926	52,452.22	Vast limestone labyrinth with underground river
Mesa Verde (Colo.), 1906	52,085.14	Best-preserved prehistoric cliff dwellings in United States
Mount McKinley (Alaska), 1917	1,939,492.80	Highest mountain in North America; spectacular wildlife
Mount Rainier (Wash.), 1899	235,404,00	Single-peak glacial system; dense forests, flowered meadows
North Cascades (Wash.), 1968	504,780.94	Roadless Alpine landscape; jagged peaks; mountain lakes; glaciers
Olympic (Wash.), 1938	908,781.42	Finest Pacific Northwest rain forest; scenic mountain park
Petrified Forest (Ariz.), 1962	93,492.57	Extensive natural exhibit of petrified wood
Redwood (Calif.), 1968	109,027.04	Coastal redwood forests; contains world's tallest known tree (369.2 ft)
Rocky Mountain (Colo.), 1915	263,808.71	Section of the Rocky Mountains; 107 named peaks over 10,000 ft
Sequoia (Calif.), 1890	403,023.00	Giant sequoias; magnificent High Sierra scenery, including Mt. Whitney
Shenandoah (Va.), 1926	194,826.30	Tree-covered mountains; scenic Skyline Drive
Theodore Roosevelt (N.D.), 1978	70,416.39	Scenic valley of Little Missouri River; T.R. Ranch; Wildlife
Virgin Islands (U.S. V.I.), 1956	14,695.37	Beaches; lush hills; prehistoric Carib Indian relics
Voyageurs (Minn.), 1971	219,128.00	Wildlife, canoeing, fishing, and hiking

Name, location, and year authorized	Acreage	Outstanding characteristics
Wind Cave (S.D.), 1903	28,292.08	Limestone caverns in Black Hills; buffalo herd
Yellowstone (Wyo.-Mont.-Idaho), 1872	2,219,822.70	World's greatest geyser area; abundant falls, wildlife, and canyons
Yosemite (Calif.), 1890	760,917.18	Mountains; inspiring gorges and waterfalls; giant sequoias
Zion (Utah), 1919	146,551.10	Multicolored gorge in heart of southern Utah desert

NATIONAL HISTORICAL PARKS

Name and location	*Total acreage*
Appomattox Court House (Va.)	1,318.70
Boston (Mass.)	40.17
Chesapeake and Ohio Canal (Md.-W.Va.-D.C.)	20,781.00
Colonial (Va.)	9,462.37
Cumberland Gap (Ky.-Tenn.-Va.)	20,350.90
George Rogers Clark (Ind.)	24.30
Harpers Ferry (W.Va.-Md.)	1,909.47
Independence (Pa.)	37.10
Jean Lafitte (La.)	20,000
Klondike Goldrush (Alaska)	13,270.49
Koloko-Honokohau (Hawaii)	1,250.24
Lowell (Mass.)	134.00
Minute Man (Mass.)	752.35
Morristown (N.J.)	1,677.65
Nez Perce (Idaho)	2,109.06
Puuhonua o Honaunau (Hawaii)	181,80
San Antonio Missions (Tex.)	2,500
San Juan Island (Wash.)	1,751.99
Saratoga (N.Y.)	2,455.11
Sitka (Alaska)	107.71
Valley Forge (Pa.)	2,551.04
War in the Pacific (Guam)	1,919.68

NATIONAL MONUMENTS

Name and location	*Total acreage*
Agate Fossil Beds (Neb.)	3,055.22
Alibates Flint Quarries (Tex.)	1,332.56
Aniakchak (Alaska)	364,000
Aztec Ruins (N.M.)	27.14
Bandelier (N.M.)	36,971.20
Bering Land Bridge (Alaska)	2,848,000
Biscayne (Fla.)	103,642.65
Black Canyon (Colo.)	13,672.13
Booker T. Washington (Va.)	223.92
Buck Island Reef (U.S. V.I.)	880.00
Cabrillo (Calif.)	143.94
Cape Krusenstern (Alaska)	677,000
Canyon de Chelly (Ariz.)	83,840.00
Capulin Mountain (N.M.)	775.38
Casa Grande Ruins (Ariz.)	472.50
Castillo de San Marcos (Fla.)	20.49
Castle Clinton (N.Y.)	1.00
Cedar Breaks (Utah)	6,154.60
Chaco Canyon (N.M.)	21,509.40
Chiricahua (Ariz.)	11,088.25
Colorado (Colo.)	20,457.25
Congaree Swamp (S.C.)	15,200.00
Craters of the Moon (Idaho)	53,545.05
Custer Battlefield (Mont.)	765.34
Death Valley (Calif.-Nev.)	2,067,795.06
Denali (Alaska)	3,993,000
Devils Postpile (Calif.)	798.46
Devils Tower (Wyo.)	1,346.91
Dinosaur (Utah-Colo.)	211,058.37
Effigy Mounds (Iowa)	1,474.63
El Morro (N.M.)	1,278.72
Florissant Fossil Beds (Colo.)	5,998.09
Fort Frederica (Ga.)	213.72
Fort Jefferson (Fla.)	47,125.00
Fort Matanzas (Fla.)	298.51
Fort McHenry (Md.)	43.26
Fort Pulaski (Ga.)	5,615.50
Fort Stanwix (N.Y.)	15.52
Fort Sumter (S.C.)	64.27
Fort Union (N.M.)	720.60
Fossil Butte (Wyo.)	8,198.00
Gates of the Arctic (Alaska)	9,432,000
George Washington Birthplace (Va.)	538.23
George Washington Carver (Mo.)	210.00
Gila Cliff Dwellings (N.M.)	533.13
Glacier Bay (Alaska)	3,355,269.49
Gran Quivira (N.M.)	610.94
Grand Portage (Minn.)	709.97
Great Sand Dunes (Colo.)	38,951.50
Hohokam Pima (Ariz.)	1,690.00
Homestead (Neb.)	194.57
Hovenweep (Utah-Colo.)	785.43
Jewel Cave (S.D.)	1,274.56
John Day Fossil Beds (Ore.)	14,044.28
Joshua Tree (Calif.)	559,959.50
Kanai Fjords (Alaska)	672,000
Katmai (Alaska)	4,293,125.74
Kobuk Valley (Alaska)	1,764,000
Lake Clark (Alaska)	2,930,000
Lava Beds (Calif.)	46,821.33
Lehman Caves (Nev.)	640.00
Montezuma Castle (Ariz.)	857.69
Mound City Group (Ohio)	67.50
Muir Woods (Calif.)	553.55
Natural Bridges (Utah)	7,779.14
Navajo (Ariz.)	360.00
Noatak (Alaska)	5,800,000
Ocmulgee (Ga.)	683.48
Oregon Caves (Ore.)	473.80
Organ Pipe Cactus (Ariz.)	330,688.86
Pecos (N.M.)	364.80
Pinnacles (Calif.)	16,221.77
Pipe Spring (Ariz.)	40.00
Pipestone (Minn.)	281.78
Rainbow Bridge (Utah)	160.00
Russell Cave (Ala.)	310.45
Saguaro (Ariz.)	83,576.07
St. Croix Island (Me.)	35.39
Scotts Bluff (Neb.)	2,987.97
Statue of Liberty (N.Y.-N.J.)	58.38
Sunset Crater (Ariz.)	3,040.00
Timpanogos Cave (Utah)	250.00
Tonto (Ariz.)	1,120.00
Tumacacori (Ariz.)	16.65
Tuzigoot (Ariz.)	848.78
Walnut Canyon (Ariz.)	2,249.46
White Sands (N.M.)	144,458.24
Wrangell-St. Elias (Alaska)	11,923,000
Wupatki (Ariz.)	35,253.24
Yucca House (Colo.)	10.00
Yukon-Charley (Alaska)	2,520,000

NATIONAL PRESERVES

Big Cypress (Fla.)	570,000.00
Big Thicket (Tex.)	84,550.00

NATIONAL MILITARY PARKS

Chickamauga and Chattanooga (Ga.-Tenn.)	8,098.21
Fort Donelson (Tenn.)	536.09
Fredericksburg and Spotsylvania (Va.)	5,888.56
Gettysburg (Pa.)	3,862.06
Guilford Courthouse (N.C.)	220.25
Horseshoe Bend (Ala.)	2,040.00
Kings Mountain (S.C.)	3,945.29
Moores Creek (N.C.)	86.78
Pea Ridge (Ark.)	4,300.35
Shiloh (Tenn.)	3,837.50
Vicksburg (Miss.)	1,740.78

NATIONAL BATTLEFIELDS

Big Hole (Mont.)	655.61
Cowpens (S.C.)	841.04
Fort Necessity (Pa.)	900.97
Monocacy (Md.)	1,220.31
Petersburg (Va.)	1,536.26
Stones River (Tenn.)	330.86
Tupelo (Miss.)	1.00
Wilson's Creek (Mo.)	1,749.91

NATIONAL BATTLEFIELD PARKS

Antietam (Md)	3,249.63
Kennesaw Mountain (Ga.)	2,884.38
Manassas (Va.)	3,031.67
Richmond (Va.)	769.13

NATIONAL BATTLEFIELD SITE

Brices Crossroads (Miss.)	1.00

NATIONAL HISTORIC SITES

Name and location	Total acreage
Abraham Lincoln Birthplace (Ky.)	116.50
Adams (Mass.)	9.17
Allegheny Portage Railroad (Pa.)	1,476.00
Andersonville (Ga.)	475.70
Andrew Johnson (Tenn.)	16.68
Bent's Old Fort (Colo.)	800.00
Carl Sandburg Home (N.C.)	247.37
Christiansted (V.I.)	27.15
Clara Barton (Md.)	8.59
Edgar Allan Poe (Pa.)	0.51
Edison (N.J.)	21.25
Eisenhower (Pa.)	690.46
Eleanor Roosevelt (N.Y.)	180.50
Ford's Theatre (Lincoln Museum) (D.C.)	0.29
Fort Bowie (Ariz.)	1,000.00
Fort Davis (Tex.)	460.00
Fort Laramie (Wyo.)	840.52
Fort Larned (Kan.)	718.39
Fort Point (Calif.)	29.00
Fort Raleigh (N.C.)	157.40
Fort Scott (Kan.)	16.86
Fort Smith (Ark.-Okla.)	63.04
Fort Union Trading Post (N.D.-Mont.)	436.45
Fort Vancouver (Wash.)	208.89
Frederick Law Olmsted (Mass.)	1.75
Friendship Hill (Pa.)	675.00
Golden Spike (Utah)	2,203.20
Grant-Kohrs Ranch (Mont.)	1,527.69
Hampton (Md.)	59.44
Herbert Hoover (Iowa)	186.80
Home of F. D. Roosevelt (N.Y.)	263.89
Hopewell Village (Pa.)	848.06
Hubbell Trading Post (Ariz.)	160.09
Jefferson National Expansion Memorial (Mo.)	90.96
John F. Kennedy (Mass.)	0.09
John Muir (Calif.)	8.90
Knife River Indian Villages (N.D.)	1,293.35
Lincoln Home (Ill.)	12.28
Longfellow (Mass.)	1.98
Lyndon B. Johnson (Tex.)	255.94
Maggie L. Walker (Va.)	1.29
Mar-a-Lago (Fla.)	17.17
Martin Van Buren (N.Y.)	39.59
Ninety Six (S.C.)	1,115.08
Palo Alto Battlefield (Tex.)	50.00
Puukohola Heiau (Hawaii)	76.57
Sagamore Hill (N.Y.)	78.00
Saint-Gaudens (N.H.)	149.31
Salem Maritime (Mass.)	9.10
San Juan (P.R.)	53.20
Saugus Iron Works (Mass.)	8.51
Sewall-Belmont House (D.C.)	0.35
Springfield Armory (Mass.)	54.98
Theodore Roosevelt Birthplace (N.Y.)	0.11
Theodore Roosevelt Inaugural (N.Y.)	1.03
Thomas Stone (Md.)	328.25
Tuskegee Institute (Ala.)	74.39
Vanderbilt Mansion (N.Y.)	211.65
Whitman Mission (Wash.)	98.15
William Howard Taft (Ohio)	3.83

NATIONAL MEMORIALS

Arkansas Post (Ark.)	389.18
Chamizal (Tex.)	54.90
Coronado (Ariz.)	4,976.77
Desoto (Fla.)	30.00
Federal Hall (N.Y.)	0.45
Fort Caroline (Fla.)	138.88
Fort Clatsop (Ore.)	130.00
General Grant (N.Y.)	0.76
Hamilton Grange (N.Y.)	0.71
John F. Kennedy Center for Performing Arts (D.C.)	17.50
Johnstown Flood (Pa.)	175.60
Lincoln Boyhood (Ind.)	197.60
Lincoln Memorial (D.C.)	163.63
Lyndon Baines Johnson Memorial Grove on the Potomac (D.C.)	17.00
Mount Rushmore (S.D.)	1,278.45
Perry's Victory and International Peace Memorial (Ohio)	25.38
Roger Williams (R.I.)	4.56
Thaddeus Kosciuszko (Pa.)	0.02
Theodore Roosevelt Island (D.C.)	88.50
Thomas Jefferson Memorial (D.C.)	18.36
Washington Monument (D.C.)	106.01
Wright Brothers (N.C.)	431.40

NATIONAL CEMETERIES[1]

Antietam (Md.)	11.36
Battleground (D.C.)	1.03
Fort Donelson (Tenn.)	15.34
Fredericksburg (Va.)	12.00
Gettysburg (Pa.)	20.58
Poplar Grove (Va.)	8.72
Shiloh (Tenn.)	10.05
Stones River (Tenn.)	20.09
Vicksburg (Miss.)	116.28
Yorktown (Va.)	2.91

NATIONAL SEASHORES

Assateague Island (Md.-Va.)	39,630.93
Canaveral (Fla.)	57,627.07
Cape Cod (Mass.)	44,596.43

1. The National Cemeteries are not independent areas of the National Park System; each is part of the military park, battlefield, etc., with which it is related. Their acreage is kept separately. Arlington National Cemetery is under the Department of the Army. *See* Index.

Name and location	*Total acreage*
Cape Hatteras (N.C.)	30,318.63
Cape Lookout (N.C.)	28,400.00
Cumberland Island (Ga.)	36,978.28
Fire Island (N.Y.)	19,578.55
Gulf Islands (Fla.-Miss.)	139,775.46
Padre Island (Tex.)	133,918.72
Point Reyes (Calif.)	67,265.22

NATIONAL PARKWAYS

Blue Ridge (Va.-N.C.-Ga.)	81,561.56
George Washington Memorial (Va.-Md.)	7,141.63
John D. Rockefeller, Jr., Memorial (Wyo.)	23,777.22
Natchez Trace (Miss.-Tenn.-Ala.)	48,374.04

NATIONAL LAKESHORES

Apostle Islands (Wis.)	42,009.20
Indiana Dunes (Ind.)	12,534.82
Pictured Rocks (Mich.)	70,757.28
Sleeping Bear Dunes (Mich.)	71,105.00

NATIONAL SCENIC RIVERS AND RIVERWAYS

Big South Fork National River & Recreation Area (Ky.-Tenn.)	122,960.00
Buffalo (Ark.)	94,146.00
Lower St. Croix (Minn.-Wis.)	8,716.13
Middle Delaware (N.J.-Pa.)	2,750.00
New River Gorge (W. Va.)	62,024.00
Obed Wild & Scenic River (Tenn.)	5,250.00
Ozark (Mo.)	82,301.29
Rio Grande Wild & Scenic (Tex.)	9,600.00
St. Croix (Minn.-Wis.)	62,695.91
Upper Delaware (N.Y., N.J.-Pa.)	75,000.00

NATIONAL CAPITAL PARKS

National Capital Parks (D.C.-Va.-Md.)	6,467.79

WHITE HOUSE

White House (D.C.)	18.07

OTHER PARKS

Arlington House, the Robert E. Lee Memorial (Va.)	27.91
Catoctin Mountain (Md.)	5,768.90
Fort Benton (Mont.)	0.0
Fort Washington Park (Md.)	341.00
Frederick Douglass Home (D.C.)	8.08
Greenbelt Park (Md.)	1,166.56
Piscataway (Md.)	4,250.85
Prince William Forest (Va.)	18,571.55
Rock Creek Park (D.C.)	1,754.37
Wolf Trap Farm Park for the Performing Arts (Va.)	130.28

NATIONAL RECREATION AREAS

Name and location	*Total acreage*
Amistad (Tex.)	62,451.74
Bighorn Canyon (Wyo.-Mont.)	120,279.97
Chattahoochee River (Ga.)	8,514.57
Chickasaw (Okla.)	9,500.06
Coulee Dam (Wash.)	100,059.00
Curecanti (Colo.)	42,114.47
Cuyahoga Valley (Ohio)	32,460.19
Delaware Water Gap (Pa.-N.J.)	71,000.00
Gateway (N.Y.-N.J.)	26,172.00
Glen Canyon (Ariz.-Utah)	1,236,880.00
Golden Gate (Calif.)	38,676.59
Lake Chelan (Wash.)	61,889.84
Lake Mead (Ariz.-Nev.)	1,496,600.52
Lake Meredith (Tex.)	44,994.30
Ross Lake (Wash.)	117,574.09
Santa Monica Mountains (Calif.)	150,000.00
Whiskeytown-Shasta-Trinity (Calif.)	42,497.45

NATIONAL SCENIC TRAIL

Appalachian (Maine, N.H. Vt., Mass., Conn., N.Y., N.J., Pa., Md., W.Va., Va., N.C., Tenn., Ga.)	52,034.25

NATIONAL MALL

National Mall (D.C.)	146.35

NATIONAL VISITOR CENTER

National Visitor Center (D.C.)	0.00

AFFILIATED AREAS

(National Historic Sites unless otherwise noted.)

American Memorial Park (N. Mariana Is.)	0.00
Benjamin Franklin (Pa.)[1]	0.00
Cherokee Strip Living Museum (Kan.)	6.00
Chicago Portage (Ill.)	91.20
Chimney Rock (Neb.)	83.36
David Burger (Ohio)[1]	—
Ebey's Landing (Wash.)	8,000.00
Eugene O'Neill (Calif.)	14.00
Father Marquette (Mich.)	52.00
Gloria Dei Church (Pa.)	3.71
Ice Age (Wis.)[2]	32,500.00
International Peace Garden (N.D.)	2,330.30
Jamestown (Va.)	20.63
Lewis & Clark Natl. Historic Trail (Ill., Mo., Kan., Neb., Iowa, Idaho, S.D., N.D., Mont., Ore., Wash.)	—
McLoughlin House (OOre.)	0.63
Mormon Pioneer Natl. Historic Trail (Ill., Iowa, Neb., Wyo., Utah)	—
North Country Nat'l Scenic Trail (N.Y., Pa., Ohio, Mich., Wis., Minn., N.D.)	—
Oregon Natl. Historic Trail (Mo., Kan., Neb., Wyo., Idaho, Ore., Wash.)	—
Pennsylvania Avenue (D.C.)	0.00
Pinelands Natl. Reserve (N.J.)	1,000,000.00
Roosevelt-Campobello International Park (Canada)	2,721.50
St. Paul's Church (N.Y.)	6.09
Touro Synagogue (R.I.)	0.23
U.S.S. Arizona Memorial (Hawaii)	—

1. National Memorial. 2. National Scientific Reserve.

Department of Agriculture Sprouts Wings

The U.S. Department of Agriculture has awarded a contract for the construction of an experimental aircraft called the "Heli-Stat." The new aerial device is composed of a large, dirigible-like balloon with four helicopters attached. It could be used for unloading ships where no harbors exist, for transporting large loads that could not be moved over roads, or for fighting fire in or removing logs from environmentally sensitive areas where roads should not be built.

The Heli-Stat is to be completed in two years at a cost of $10 million. If construction is successful, the Heli-Stat will be tested for three years removing logs from what is now considered inaccessible terrain.

The following material was compiled from information provided by the American Red Cross, the American Heart Association, and Edumed, Inc.

First aid is the rendering of prompt and knowledgeable treatment to a person who has been injured or suddenly taken ill and for whom no immediate medical attention is available. Depending on circumstances, effective first aid can mean the difference between life and death or between temporary and permanent disability. Most accidents occur in and about the home and usually involve burns, choking, cuts or serious bleeding, poisons, and heart attacks. Artificial respiration and treatment for shock that sets in after a serious accident are also important factors in the success of first aid. The best course of action to follow after taking emergency measures is to summon assistance from the local police or fire department or from the nearest available doctor.

Burns

Burns are classified according to first degree (reddened skin), second degree (blisters develop), and third degree (deep tissue damage). Face, feet, and hands are critical areas. For first-degree and small second-degree burns, submerge affected area in cold water until pain subsides. Or else apply a thick, dry sterile dressing and bandage firmly to keep air out. *Do not break blisters.* Note: Cold water may be used for any classification of burns, but not if tissue has been exposed, because of the possibility of infection. For third-degree burns, bandage as above, elevate the extremities, and obtain medical help immediately.

Eye burns: For burns of the eye, wash thoroughly with water for 15 minutes—hold the eyelid open and pour the water from the inside corner out. Put a clean pad over both closed eyelids (not only injured eye), bandage, and get medical help.

Poisoning

Speed and a clear head are vital in first aid for poison intake. If the victim loses consciousness, call for an emergency squad and give artificial respiration or cardiopulmonary resuscitation (CPR) if needed to keep the airway open. If the victim is conscious and not in convulsions, dilute the swallowed poison with a glass of water or milk, but stop at signs of nausea. The victim should also be treated for shock.

Next, call your physician or local poison-control center. Be ready to supply information on what poison, and how much of it, was taken and the weight and age of the victim, and to take down instructions for treatment and antidotes. (Antidotes suggested on a poison-container label should not be given without approval by your physician or poison-control center.)

If vomiting occurs, save a vomit specimen along with the container label for the attending physician.

Shock

Shock is caused by many types of severe injuries and severe illnesses—poisoning, damage to the respiratory system, and loss of body fluids resulting from vomiting, dysentery, or burns. It is prudent to give shock care to all seriously injured individuals.

The symptoms are: pale or bluish skin that is cold to the touch (in the case of dark-skinned persons, examine the color of the mucous membranes inside the mouth or under the eyelids, or of the nail beds); moist or clammy skin; weakness of the injured person; rapid pulse; increased rate of breathing, which may be shallow, possibly deep, and irregular; severe thirst; vomiting or retching from nausea.

With possible neck or back injury, a victim should not be moved. Otherwise, a person in shock should be kept lying down and covered only enough to keep him from losing body heat. (*Do not* add extra heat, because raising the body's surface temperature is harmful.)

A patient with severe injuries of the lower face and jaw or who is unconscious should be placed on the side, with care taken to prevent suffocation from vomit and blood. When in doubt about the proper position, keep the person lying flat, making sure the head is not lower than the rest of the body. Fluids may be given by mouth if the victim has no head or abdominal injury, if the victim would probably not need surgery, or if medical help is not immediately available. But fluids *should not* be given to persons who are unconscious, are vomiting, or are having convulsions.

Cardiac Pulmonary Resuscitation (CPR) for Cardiac Arrest[1]

The most common signal of a heart attack is uncomfortable pressure, squeezing, fullness, or pain in the center of the chest behind the breastbone; others may be sweating, nausea, shortness of breath or a feeling of weakness. These signals may subside and return. If these signals persist, activate the emergency medical services system or take the victim to the nearest hospital with 24-hour emergency cardiac care.

Airway: Determine if the collapsed person is conscious by shaking his shoulder and shouting "Are you all right?". If there is no response, you must open his airway. Be sure he is lying flat on his back. If you have to roll him over, move his entire body as a total unit.

To open the airway, lift up his neck (or chin) gently with one hand while pushing down on the forehead with the other to tilt the head back. Place your ear close to the victim's mouth. Look at his chest and stomach for movement. Listen for sounds of breathing. Feel for breath on your cheek.

If none of these signs is present, the victim is not breathing.

Breathing: Use the mouth-to-mouth technique. Turn the hand on the victim's forehead and pinch his nose shut while maintaining the head tilt with the heel of the hand. The other hand should remain under the victim's neck (or chin), lifting up.

Immediately give four quick, full breaths in rapid succession.

Check Pulse: After giving four quick breaths, locate the victim's carotid pulse to see if his heart is beating. Take the hand that is under the victim's neck and locate the voice box. Slide the tips of your index and middle fingers into the groove beside the voice box. Feel for the pulse.

If you cannot find the pulse, you must provide artificial circulation in addition to rescue breathing.

Cardiac Compression: To perform external cardiac compression, kneel at the victim's side near his chest. Locate the notch at the lowest portion of the sternum (breastbone). Place the heel of one hand about 1 to 1 ½ inches from that tip and the other on top of the first. Be sure to keep the fingers off the chest wall. You may find it easier to do by interlocking the fingers.

Bring your shoulders directly over the victim's sternum as you compress downward, keeping your arms straight. Depress the sternum about 1 ½ to 2 inches for an adult victim. Relaxation must follow compression immediately and be of equal time. Do *not* remove your hands from the sternum.

If you are the only rescuer, you must provide both rescue breathing and cardiac compression at the ratio of 15 chest compressions to 2 quick breaths. You must compress at the rate of 80 times per minute, since you will lose compressions when you take time to interpose these breaths.

If there is another rescuer, position yourselves on opposite sides of the victim. One should interpose a breath after every fifth compression; the other should compress the chest at a rate of 60 compressions per minute.

For Infants and Small Children: Do not exaggerate the backward position of the head tilt because it might block breathing passages.

Do not try to pinch off the nose. Cover both the mouth and nose if the victim is not breathing. Use small breaths with less volume to inflate the lungs. Give one small breath every 3 seconds.

Only one hand is used for compression. The other is slipped under the child to provide a firm support for his back.

For infants, use only the *tips* of the index and middle fingers to compress the chest at mid-sternum, depressing between ½ to ¾ inch at a rate of 80 to 100 times per minute.

For small children, use only the *heel* of one hand to compress the chest at midsternum, depressing between ¾ and 1 ½ inches, depending on the size of the child. The rate should be 80 to 100 times per minute.

For both infants and small children, breaths should be interposed after every fifth chest compression.

Neck Fracture: If the victim is injured in a diving or automobile accident, the possibility of a neck fracture should be considered. The airway should be opened by using a modified jaw thrust, keeping the victim's head in a fixed, neutral position.

The Heimlich Maneuver[2]

Food-choking is caused by a piece of food lodging in the throat creating a blockage of the airway, making it impossible for the victim to breathe or speak. The victim will die of strangulation in four minutes if you do not act to save him.

Using the Heimlich Maneuver, you exert pressure that forces the diaphragm upward, compresses the air in the lungs, and expels the object blocking the breathing passage.

The victim should see a physician immediately after the rescue. Performing the Maneuver could result in injury to the victim. However, he will survive only if his airway is quickly cleared.

If no help is at hand, victims should attempt to perform the Heimlich Maneuver on themselves by pressing their own fists upward into the abdomen as described.

What to Look for: The victim of food-choking: (1) Cannot speak or breathe, (2) turns blue, (3) collapses.

Performing the Heimlich Maneuver with the rescuer standing and the victim standing or sitting: Stand behind the victim and wrap your arms around his waist.

Place your fist thumb side against the victim's abdomen, slightly above the navel and below the rib cage.

Grasp your fist with your other hand and press into the victim's abdomen with a **quick upward thrust.**

(When the victim is sitting, the rescuer stands behind the victim's chair and performs the Maneuver in the same manner.)

With the rescuer kneeling and the victim lying face up: Facing the victim, kneel astride his hips.

With one of your hands on top of the other, place the heel of your bottom hand on the abdomen slightly above the navel and below the rib cage.

Press into the victim's abdomen with a **quick upward thrust.**

Repeat several times if necessary.

1. © 1977 American Heart Association. 2. © 1976 Edumed, Inc. Teaching slides, posters, wallet cards, and other instructional materials on the Heimlich Maneuver are now available. To obtain these send a self-addressed, stamped envelope to: Edumed, Inc., Box 52, Cincinnati, Ohio 45201.

New Rabies Vaccine Approved

The Food and Drug Administration has approved a safer, more effective, and less painful vaccine against rabies. Under the old method of treatment, the vaccine was injected into the patient's abdomen and 23 injections were required. The new vaccine is injected into the patient's arm and requires only five injections.

Virus for the new vaccine is grown in cultures of human fetal lung cells and is inactivated before use. The improved vaccine can also be used to protect people who are likely to be exposed to the virus or rabid animals. The vaccine is being made by the Institut Merieux in Lyon, France.

States and Territories

State flower, bird, etc., are official unless otherwise indicated; dates in parentheses are those of adoption. Largest cities include incorporated places only. Land areas for 1970 are revised figures. For secession and readmission dates of the former Confederate states, *see* Index. For lists of Governors, Senators, and Representatives showing the results of the 1980 election, *see* Index. For additional state information, *see* the sections on "Business and the Economy," "Taxes," and "U.S. Statistics."

ALABAMA

Capital: Montgomery
Governor: Forrest H. James, Jr., D (to Jan. 1983)
Lieut. Governor: George McMillan, D (to Jan. 1983)
Secy. of State: Don Seigleman, D (to Jan. 1983)
Controller: George C. Dean, Jr., D
Atty. General: Charles A. Graddick, D (to Jan. 1983)
Organized as territory: March 3, 1817
Entered Union & (rank): Dec. 14, 1819 (22)
Present constitution adopted: 1901
Motto: *Audemus jura nostra defendere* (We dare defend our rights)
State flower: Camellia (1959)
State bird: Yellowhammer (1927)
State song: "Alabama" (1931)
State tree: Southern pine (longleaf) (1949)
Nickname: Yellowhammer State
Origin of name: May come from Choctaw meaning "thicket-clearers" or "vegetation-gatherers"
1970 population & (rank): 3,444,165 (21)
1979 prov. population & (rank): 3,769,000 (22)
1970 land area & (rank): 50,708 sq mi. (131,334 sq km) (28)
Geographic center: In Chilton Co., 12 mi. SW of Clanton
Number of counties: 67
Largest cities (1977 est.): Birmingham, 282,358; Mobile, 205,174; Montgomery, 156,333; Huntsville, 143,906; Tuscaloosa, 69,482; Gadsden, 49,013
State forests: 8 (14,248.58 ac.)
State parks: 21 (45,414 ac.)
Gross receipts (1978–79): $6,457,215,948
Net receipts (1978–79): $4,858,585,835
Net disbursements (1978–79): $4,820,342,128

Spanish explorers are believed to have arrived at Mobile Bay in 1519, and the territory was visited in 1540 by the explorer Hernando de Soto. The first permanent European settlement in Alabama was founded by the French at Fort Louis in 1702. The British gained control of the area in 1763 by the Treaty of Paris, but had to cede almost all the Alabama region to the U.S. after the American Revolution. The Confederacy was founded at Montgomery in February 1861 and, for a time, the city was the Confederate capital.

During the last part of the 19th century, the economy of the state slowly improved. At Tuskegee Institute, founded in 1881 by Booker T. Washington, Dr. George Washington Carver carried out his famous agricultural research.

In the 1950s and '60s, Alabama was the site of such landmark civil-rights actions as the bus boycott in Montgomery (1955–56) and the "Freedom March" from Selma to Birmingham (1965).

Today, Alabama is the leading heavy-industry state in the South. Textiles, iron, and steel lead its manufacturing, which centers around Birmingham, the "Pittsburgh of the South." Industry is growing rapidly in other areas, including the Tennessee River Valley, with its great Muscle Shoals power plant. Manufacturing also includes cement, feed, fertilizer, chemical, rubber, and aluminum products. The state ranks high in the output of poultry, cotton, cattle, hogs, corn, potatoes, peanuts, and fruit.

Points of interest include the George C. Marshall Space Flight Center at Huntsville, Russell Cave National Monument near Bridgeport, and the White House of the Confederacy in Montgomery.

ALASKA

Capital: Juneau
Governor: Jay S. Hammond, R (to Dec. 1982)
Lieut. Governor: Terry Miller, R (to Dec. 1982)
Commissioner of Administration: W. R. Hudson, R (to Dec. 1982)
Atty. General: Avrum M. Gross, D (apptd. by Governor)
Organized as territory: 1912
Entered Union & (rank): Jan. 3, 1959 (49)
Constitution ratified: April 24, 1956
Motto: North to the Future
State flower: Forget-me-not
State tree: Sitka spruce
State bird: Willow ptarmigan
State fish: King salmon
State song: "Alaska's Flag"
Nickname: The state is commonly called "The Last Frontier" or "Land of the Midnight Sun"
Origin of name: Corruption of Aleut word meaning "great land" or "that which the sea breaks against"
1970 population & (rank): 302,173 (50)
1979 prov. population & (rank): 406,000 (50)
1970 land area & (rank): 566,432 sq mi. (1,467,059 sq km) (1)
Geographic center: 60 mi. NW of Mt. McKinley
Number of boroughs: 10
Largest cities (1977 est.): Anchorage, city and borough, 181,754; Fairbanks, 32,900; Juneau, city and borough, 19,093; Ketchikan, 7,804; Sitka, city and borough, 7,315; Kodiak, 4,858; Valdez, 4,267
State forests: None
State parks: 5; 59 waysides and areas (3.3 million ac.)
General revenue (1978–79): $1,117,479,665
General expenditures (1978–79): $982,880,399

Vitus Bering, a Dane working for the Russians, and Alexei Chirikov discovered the Alaskan mainland and the Aleutian Islands in 1741. The tremendous land mass of Alaska—equal to one fifth of the continental U.S.—was unexplored in 1867 when Secretary of State William Seward arranged for its purchase from the Russians for $7,200,000. The transfer of the territory took place on Oct. 18,

1867. Despite a price of about two cents an acre, the purchase was widely ridiculed as "Seward's Folly." The first official census (1880) reported a total of 33,426 Alaskans, all but 430 being of aboriginal stock. The Gold Rush of 1898 resulted in a mass influx of more than 30,000 people. Since then, Alaska has returned billions of dollars' worth of products to the U.S.

In 1968, a large oil and gas reservoir near Prudhoe Bay on the Arctic Coast was found. The Prudhoe Bay reservoir, with an estimated recoverable 10 billion barrels of oil and 27 trillion cubic feet of gas, is twice as large as any other oil field in North America. The Trans-Alaska pipeline was completed in 1977 at a cost of $7.7 billion. On June 20, oil started flowing through the 800-mile-long pipeline from Prudhoe Bay to the port of Valdez.

Other industries important to Alaska's economy are fisheries, wood and wood products, and furs.

Mount McKinley National Park and Mendenhall Glacier in North Tongass National Forest are of interest, as is the large totem pole collection at Sitka National Historical Park. The Katmai National Monument includes the "Valley of Ten Thousand Smokes," an area of active volcanoes.

ARIZONA

Capital: Phoenix
Governor: Bruce Babbitt, D (to Jan. 1981)
Secy. of State: Rose Mofford, D (to Jan. 1981)
Atty. General: Bob Corbin, R (to Jan. 1981)
State Treasurer: Clark Dierks, R (to Jan. 1981)
Organized as territory: Feb. 24, 1863
Entered Union & (rank): Feb. 14, 1912 (48)
Present constitution adopted: 1911
Motto: *Ditat Deus* (God enriches)
State flower: Flower of saguaro cactus (1931)
State bird: Cactus wren (1931)
State colors: Blue and old gold (1915)
State song: "Arizona," a march song (1919)
State tree: Paloverde (1957)
Nickname: Grand Canyon State
Origin of name: From the Indian "Arizonac," meaning "little spring"
1970 population & (rank): 1,772,482 (33)
1979 prov. population & (rank): 2,450,000 (30)
1970 land area & (rank): 113,417 sq mi. (293,750 sq km) (6)
Geographic center: In Yavapai Co., 55 mi. ESE of Prescott
Number of counties: 14
Largest cities (1977 est.): Phoenix, 684,516; Tucson, 301,152; Mesa, 110,079; Tempe, 98,146; Scottsdale, 81,458; Glendale, 73,730; Flagstaff, 32,731
State forests: None
State parks: 10
State revenue (1978): $1,734,733,000
State expenditure (1978): $1,696,911,000

Marcos de Niza, a Spanish Franciscan friar, was the first European to explore Arizona. He entered the area in 1539 in search of the mythical Seven Cities of Gold. Although he was followed a year later by another gold seeker, Francisco Vásquez de Coronado, most of the early settlement was for missionary purposes. In 1776 the Spanish established Fort Tucson. In 1848, after the Mexican War, most of the Arizona territory became part of the U.S., and the southern portion of the territory was added by the Gadsden Purchase in 1853.

In 1973 the world's biggest dam, the New Cornelia Tailings, was completed near Ajo.

Arizona history is rich in legends of America's Old West. It was here that the great Indian chiefs Geronimo and Cochise led their people against the frontiersmen. Tombstone, Ariz., was the site of the West's most famous shoot-out—the gunfight at the O.K. Corral. Today, Arizona has the largest U.S. Indian population; more than 14 tribes are represented on 19 reservations.

Manufacturing has become Arizona's most important industry. Principal products include electrical, communications, and aeronautical items. The state produces over half the country's copper. Agriculture is also important to the state's economy.

State attractions include such famous scenery as the Grand Canyon, the Petrified Forest, and the Painted Desert. Hoover Dam, Lake Mead, Fort Apache, and the reconstructed London Bridge at Lake Havasu City are of particular interest.

ARKANSAS

Capital: Little Rock
Governor: Bill Clinton, D (to Jan. 1981)
Lieut. Governor: Joe Purcell, D (to Jan. 1981)
Secy. of State: Paul Reviere, D (to Jan. 1981)
Atty. General: Steve Clark (to Jan. 1981)
Auditor of State: Jimmie Lou Fisher (to Jan. 1981)
Treasurer of State: Mrs. Nancy Hall, D (to Jan. 1979)
Land Commissioner: Sam Jones, D (to Jan. 1979)
Organized as territory: March 2, 1819
Entered Union & (rank): June 15, 1836 (25)
Present constitution adopted: 1874
Motto: *Regnat populus* (The people rule)
State flower: Apple Blossom (1901)
State tree: Pine (1939)
State bird: Mockingbird (1929)
State insect: Honeybee
State song: "Arkansas" (1963)
Nickname: Land of Opportunity
Origin of name: From the Quapaw Indians
1970 population & (rank): 1,923,295 (32)
1979 prov. population & (rank): 2,180,000 (33)
1970 land area & (rank): 51,945 sq mi. (134,538 sq km) (27)
Geographic center: In Pulaski Co., 12 mi. NW of Little Rock
Number of counties: 75
Largest cities (1977 est.): Little Rock, 153,494; Fort Smith, 68,180; North Little Rock, 62,875; Pine Bluff, 55,817; Hot Springs, 40,569; Fayetteville, 34,488
State forests: None
State parks: 39
State tax receipts (1979): $1,046,652,832
Taxes from all sources (1979): $1,913,121,014
State general expenditure (1979): $1,882,881,533

Hernando de Soto, in 1541, was among the early European explorers to visit the territory. It was a Frenchman, Henri de Tonty, who in 1686 founded the first permanent white settlement—the Arkansas Post. In 1803 the area was acquired by the U.S. as part of the Louisiana Purchase.

Food products are the state's largest employing sector, with lumber and wood products a close second. Arkansas is also a leader in the production of cotton, rice, and soybeans. The state produces 97% of the nation's high-grade domestic bauxite ore—the source of aluminum. It also has the country's only active diamond mine; located near Murfreesboro, it is operated as a tourist attraction.

Hot Springs National Park is a major state attraction. Its 47 curative springs flow at an average temperature of 147°F year round. Blanchard Springs Caverns, the Arkansas Territorial Capitol Restoration at Little Rock, and Dogpatch U.S.A. near Harrison are of interest. There are two large national forests in Arkansas—the Ouachita and the Ozark—and one of the nation's smallest—the St. Francis.

CALIFORNIA

Capital: Sacramento
Governor: Edmund G. Brown, Jr., D (to Jan. 1983)
Lieut. Governor: Mike Curb, R (to Jan. 1983)
Secy. of State: March Fong Eu, D (to Jan. 1983)
Controller: Ken Cory, D (to Jan. 1983)
Atty. General: George Deukmejian, R (to Jan. 1983)
Treasurer: Jesse M. Unruh, D (to Jan. 1983)
Entered Union & (rank): Sept. 9, 1850 (31)
Present constitution adopted: 1879
Motto: *Eureka* (I have found it)
State flower: Golden poppy (1903)
State tree: California redwoods *(Sequoia sempervirens & Sequoia gigantea)* (1937 & 1953)
State bird: California valley quail (1931)
State animal: California grizzly bear (1953)
State fish: California golden trout (1947)
State insect: California dog-face butterfly (unofficial)
State colors: Blue and gold (1951)
State song: "I Love You, California" (1951)
Nickname: Golden State
Origin of name: From a book, *Las Sergas de Esplandián,* by Garcia Ordóñez de Montalvo, c. 1500
1970 population & (rank): 19,953,134 (1)
1979 est. population & (rank): 22,696,000 (1)
1970 land area & (rank): 156,361 sq mi. (404,975 sq km) (3)
Geographic center: In Madera Co., 35 mi. NE of Madera
Number of counties: 58
Largest cities (1977 est.): Los Angeles, 2,761,222; San Diego, 799,725; San Francisco, 655,072; San Jose, 583,402; Long Beach, 336,697; Oakland, 332,385
State forests: 8 (70,283 ac.)
State parks and beaches: 180 (723,000 ac.)
State general revenue (1978–79): $15,211,577,786
State general expenditure (1978–79): $17,159,034,024

Although California was sighted by Spanish navigator Juan Rodríguez Cabrillo in 1542, its first Spanish mission (at San Diego) was not established until 1769. California became a U.S. Territory in 1847 when Mexico surrendered it to John C. Frémont. On Jan. 24, 1848, James W. Marshall discovered gold at Sutter's Mill, starting the California Gold Rush and bringing settlers to the state in large numbers.

In 1964, the U.S. Census Bureau estimated that California had become the most populous state, surpassing New York. California also leads the country in personal income and consumer expenditures.

Leading industries include manufacturing (transportation equipment, machinery, and electronic equipment), agriculture, and fishing. Principal natural resources include petroleum, cement, and natural gas.

The Bank of America National Trust and Savings Association, founded by the Giannini family, ranks first or second in the world.

Death Valley, in the southeast, is 282 feet below sea level, the lowest point in the nation; and Mt. Whitney (14,495 ft) is the highest point in the contiguous 48 states. Lassen Peak is one of two active U.S. volcanos outside of Alaska and Hawaii; its last eruptions were recorded in 1917. The General Sherman Tree in Sequoia National Park is estimated to be about 3,500 years old and a stand of bristlecone pine trees in the White Mountains may be over 4,000 years old.

Other points of interest include Yosemite National Park, Disneyland, Hollywood, the Golden Gate bridge, San Simeon State Park, and Point Reyes National Seashore.

COLORADO

Capital: Denver
Governor: Richard D. Lamm, D (to Jan. 1983)
Lieut. Governor: Nancy E. Dick, D (to Jan. 1983)
Secy. of State: Mary Estill Buchanan, R (to Jan. 1983)
Treasurer: Roy Romer, D (to Jan. 1983)
Controller: Dan S. Whittemore
Atty. General: J. D. MacFarlane, D (to Jan. 1983)
Organized as territory: Feb. 28, 1861
Entered Union & (rank): Aug. 1, 1876 (38)
Present constitution adopted: 1876
Motto: *Nil sine Numine* (Nothing without Providence)
State flower: Rocky Mountain columbine (1899)
State tree: Colorado blue spruce (1939)
State bird: Lark bunting (1931)
State animal: Rocky Mountain bighorn sheep
State colors: Blue and white (1911)
State gemstone: Aquamarine (1971)
State song: "Where the Columbines Grow" (1915)
Nickname: Centennial State
Origin of name: From the Spanish, meaning "ruddy" or "red"
1970 population & (rank): 2,207,259 (30)
1979 prov. population & (rank): 2,772,000 (28)
1970 land area & (rank): 103,766 sq mi. (268,754 sq km) (8)
Geographic center: In Park Co., 30 mi. NW of Pikes Peak
Number of counties: 63
Largest cities (1977 est.): Denver, 475,098; Colorado Springs, 183,534; Aurora, 127,121; Lakewood, 124,350; Pueblo, 102,547; Arvada, 79,958; Boulder, 76,795
State forests: 1 (71,000 ac.)
Total state revenue (1978–79): $2,566,053,000
Total state expenditure (1978–79): $2,362,452,000

First visited by Spanish explorers in the 1500s, the territory was claimed for Spain by Juan de Ulibarri in 1706. The U.S. obtained eastern Colorado as part of the Louisiana Purchase in 1803, the central portion in 1845 with the admission of Texas as a state, and the western part in 1848 as a result of the Mexican War.

Colorado has the highest mean elevation of any state, with more than 1,000 Rocky Mountain peaks over 10,000 feet high and 54 towering above 14,000 feet. Pikes Peak, the most famous of these mountains, was discovered by U.S. Army Lieut. Zebulon M. Pike in 1806.

Gold was first discovered near present-day Denver in 1858 and at Cripple Creek in 1891. Rich silver deposits were also found in 1875.

Once primarily a mining and agricultural state, today Colorado draws the largest segment of its income from manufacturing. Denver is a leader in electronics and space-age industry. Pueblo, the "Pittsburgh of the West," makes iron, steel, brick, tile, and foundry products.

Rich in natural resources, Colorado now produces most of the world's molybdenum. Uranium, vanadium, gold, silver, lead, tin, zinc, and other minerals are also mined. Colorado's highly developed irrigation system promotes farming of wheat, hay, beans, sugar beets, corn, potatoes, barley, and truck vegetables. Cattle and sheep raising is also important.

Tourism has developed into a major industry largely because of Colorado's magnificent scenery. Among the major attractions are Rocky Mountain National Park, Garden of the Gods, Great Sand Dunes and Dinosaur National Monuments, Pikes Peak and Mt. Evans Highways, and Mesa Verde National Park (prehistoric cliff dwellings).

Colorado Springs, with the nearby U.S. Air Force Academy, is probably the most popular tourist center in the Rocky Mountains, while Aspen and Vail have become leading ski resorts.

CONNECTICUT

Capital: Hartford
Governor: Ella T. Grasso, D (to Jan. 1983)
Lieut. Governor: William A. O'Neill, D (to Jan. 1983)
Secy. of State: Barbara B. Kennelly, D (to Jan. 1983)
Comptroller: J. Edward Caldwell, D (to Jan. 1983)
Treasurer: Henry E. Parker, D (to Jan. 1983)
Atty. General: Carl R. Ajello, D (to Jan. 1983)
Entered Union & (rank): Jan. 9, 1788 (5)
Present constitution adopted: Dec. 30, 1965
Motto: *Qui transtulit sustinet* (He who transplanted still sustains)
State flower: Mountain laurel (1907)
State tree: White Oak (1947)
State animal: Sperm whale (1975)
State bird: American robin (1943)
State insect: Praying mantis (1977)
State mineral: Garnet (1977)
State song: "Yankee Doodle" (1978)
Official designation: *Constitution State* (1959)
Nickname: Nutmeg State
Origin of name: From an Indian word (Quinnehtukqut) meaning "beside the long tidal river"
1970 population & (rank): 3,032,217 (24)
1979 prov. population & (rank): 3,115,000 (24)
1970 land area & (rank): 4,862 sq mi. (12,593 sq km) (48)
Geographic center: In Hartford Co., at East Berlin
Number of counties: 8
Largest cities (1977 est.): Bridgeport, 137,116; Hartford, 130,015; New Haven, 122,085; Stamford, 105,136; Waterbury, 104,890; Norwalk, 77,159
State forests: 30 (134,461 ac.)
State parks: 88 (30,316 ac.)
State and local general revenue (1978–79): $3,820,000,000
State and local general expenditure (1978–79): $3,930,000,000

The Dutch navigator, Adriaen Block, was the first European of record to explore the area, sailing up the Connecticut River in 1614. In 1633, Dutch colonists built a fort and trading post near present-day Hartford, but soon lost control to English Puritans migrating south from the Massachusetts Bay Colony.

English settlements, established in the 1630s at Windsor, Wethersfield, and Hartford, united in 1639 to form the Connecticut Colony and adopted the *Fundamental Orders*, considered the world's first written constitution.

The colony's royal charter of 1682 was exceptionally liberal. When Gov. Edmund Andros tried to seize it in 1687, it was hidden in the Hartford Oak, commemorated in Charter Oak Place.

Connecticut played a prominent role in the Revolutionary War, serving as the Continental Army's major supplier. Sometimes called the "Arsenal of the Nation," the state became one of the most industrialized in the nation. Its early business and industrial pioneers included Eli Whitney, Samuel Colt, and Charles Goodyear.

Today, Connecticut factories produce weapons, sewing machines, jet engines, helicopters, motors, hardware and tools, cutlery, clocks, locks, ball bearings, silverware, and submarines. Hartford, which has the oldest U.S. newspaper still being published —the *Courant*, established 1764— is the insurance capital of the nation.

Poultry, fruit, and dairy products account for the largest portion of farm income, and Connecticut shade-grown tobacco is acknowledged to be the nation's most valuable crop, per acre.

Connecticut is a popular resort area with its 250-mile Long Island Sound shoreline and many inland lakes. Among the major points of interest are the American Shakespeare Theatre in Stratford, Yale University's Gallery of Fine Arts and Peabody Museum. Other famous museums include the P.T. Barnum, Winchester Gun, and American Clock and Watch. The town of Mystic features a recreated 19th-century New England seaport and the Mystic Marinelife Aquarium.

DELAWARE

Capital: Dover
Governor: Pierre S. du Pont IV, R (to Jan. 1981)
Lieut. Governor: James D. McGinnis, D (to Jan. 1981)
Secy. of State: Glenn C. Kenton, R (Pleasure of Governor)
State Treasurer: Thomas R. Carper, D (to Jan. 1983)
Atty. General: Richard S. Gebelein (to Jan. 1983)
Entered Union & (rank): Dec. 7, 1787 (1)
Present constitution adopted: 1897
Motto: Liberty and independence
State colors: Colonial blue and buff
State flower: Peach blossom
State tree: American holly
State bird: Blue Hen chicken
State insect: Ladybug
State song: "Our Delaware"
Nicknames: Diamond State; First State
Origin of name: From Delaware River and Bay; named in turn for Sir Thomas West, Lord De La Warr
1970 population & (rank): 548,104 (46)
1979 prov. population & (rank): 582,000 (47)
1970 land area & (rank): 1,982 sq mi. (5,133 sq km) (49)
Geographic center: In Kent Co., 11 mi. S of Dover
Number of counties: 3
Largest cities (1977 est.): Wilmington, 72,943; Newark, 27,737; Dover, 23,021; Elsmere, 8,835; Milford, 5,669; Seaford, 5,515; New Castle, 4,916; Smyrna, 4,474
State forests: 2 (6,200 ac.)
State parks: 9
State receipts (1979): $568,793,926
State disbursements (1979): $524,686,709

Henry Hudson, sailing under the Dutch flag, is credited with Delaware's discovery in 1609. The following year, Capt. Samuel Argall of Virginia named Delaware for his colony's governor, Thomas West, Baron De La Warr. An attempted Dutch settlement failed in 1631. Swedish colonization began at Fort Christina (now Wilmington) in 1638, but New Sweden fell to Dutch forces led by New Netherlands' Gov. Peter Stuyvesant in 1655.

England took over the area in 1664 and it was

transferred to William Penn as the southern Three Counties in 1682. Semiautonomous after 1704, Delaware fought as a separate state in the American Revolution and became the first state to ratify the constitution in 1787.

During the Civil War, although a slave state, Delaware did not secede from the Union.

In 1802, Eleuthère Irénée du Pont established a gunpowder mill near Wilmington that laid the foundation for Delaware's huge chemical industry. Delaware's manufactured products now also include vulcanized fiber, glazed kid and morocco leathers, textiles, paper, dental supplies, metal products, machinery, machine tools, and automobiles.

Delaware also grows a great variety of fruits and vegetables and is a U.S. pioneer in the food-canning industry. Corn, soybeans, potatoes, and hay are important crops. Delaware's broiler chicken farms supply the big Eastern markets, and fishing is another major industry.

Points of interest include the Fort Christina Monument, Hagley Museum, Holy Trinity Church (erected in 1698, the oldest Protestant church in the United States still in use), and Winterthur Museum, in and near Wilmington; central New Castle, an almost unchanged late 18th-century capital; and the Delaware Museum of Natural History.

Popular recreation areas include Cape Henlopen, Delaware Seashore, Trapp Pond State Park, and Rehoboth Beach.

DISTRICT OF COLUMBIA

See listing at end of *50 Largest Cities of the United States.*

FLORIDA

Capital: Tallahassee
Governor: Bob Graham, D (to Jan. 1983)
Lieut. Governor: Wayne Mixson, D (to Jan. 1983)
Secy. of State: George Firestone, D (to Jan. 1983)
Comptroller: Gerald Lewis, D (to Jan. 1983)
Commissioner of Agriculture: Doyle Connor, D (to Jan. 1983)
Atty. General: Jim Smith, D (to Jan. 1983)
Organized as territory: March 30, 1822
Entered Union & (rank): March 3, 1845 (27)
Present constitution adopted: 1969
Motto: In God we trust (1868)
State flower: Orange blossom (1909)
State bird: Mockingbird (1927)
State song: "Suwannee River" (1935)
Nickname: Sunshine State (1970)
Origin of name: From the Spanish, meaning "feast of flowers" (Easter)
1970 population & (rank): 6,789,443 (9)
1979 prov. population & (rank): 8,860,000 (8)
1970 land area & (rank): 54,090 sq mi. (140,093 sq km) (26)
Geographic center: In Hernando Co., 12 mi. NNW of Brooksville
Number of counties: 67
Largest cities (1977 est.): Jacksonville, 527,777; Miami, 346,716; Tampa, 264,884; St. Petersburg, 237,134; Fort Lauderdale, 151,502; Hialeah, 122,793
State forests: 4 (306,881 ac.)
State parks: 68 (187,763 ac.)
State tax receipts (1978–79): $4,372,381,395
Other state revenue (1978–79): $8,177,007,175
State expenditures (1978–79): $12,338,980,083

In 1513, Ponce de Leon, seeking the mythical "Fountain of Youth," named Florida and claimed it for Spain. Later, Florida would be held at different times by Spain, France, and England until Spain finally sold it to the United States in 1819.

Florida's early 19th-century history as a U.S. territory was scarred by savage wars with the Seminole Indians that did not end until 1842.

One of the nation's fastest-growing states, Florida's population has gone from 2.8 million in 1950 to more than 9 million today.

Florida's economy rests on a solid base of tourism, manufacturing, and agriculture. The state entertained more than 27 million visitors, who spent about $9 billion, in 1975.

Oranges and grapefruit lead Florida's crop list, followed by sugarcane, tomatoes, beans, celery, potatoes, field corn, honey, watermelons, limes, and mangoes. Forestry, truck gardening, commercial fishing, and cattle raising are leading industries. Deep-sea fishing for sport is a leading tourist industry.

Florida is expanding in all industrial areas with the greatest development taking place in the research-oriented Space Age manufacturing. The state produces 80% of the nation's phosphate.

Major tourist attractions are Miami Beach, Palm Beach, St. Augustine (founded in 1565 and the oldest city in the U.S.), Daytona Beach, and Fort Lauderdale)—all on the East Coast. West Coast resorts include Sarasota, Tampa, Key West, and St. Petersburg. Disney World, located on a 27,000-acre site near Orlando, is the state's newest attraction.

The John F. Kennedy Space Center at Cape Canaveral, and Everglades National Park, a 5,000-square-mile preserve, also draw many visitors.

GEORGIA

Capital: Atlanta
Governor: George Busbee, D (to Jan. 1983)
Lieut. Governor: Zell Miller, D (to Jan. 1983)
Secy. of State: David Poythress, D (to Jan. 1983)
Comptroller General: Johnnie Caldwell, D (to Jan. 1983)
Atty. General: Arthur K. Bolton, D (to Jan. 1983)
Entered Union & (rank): Jan. 2, 1788 (4)
Present constitution adopted: 1977
Motto: Wisdom, justice, and moderation
State flower: Cherokee rose (1916)
State tree: Live oak (1937)
State bird: Brown thrasher (1935)
State song: "Georgia on my Mind" (1922)
Nicknames: Peach State, Empire State of the South
Origin of name: In honor of George II of England
1970 population & (rank): 4,589,575 (15)
1979 prov. population & (rank): 5,118,000 (14)
1970 land area & (rank): 58,073 sq mi. (150,409 sq km) (21)
Geographic center: In Twiggs Co., 18 mi. SE of Macon
Number of counties: 159
Largest cities (1977 est.): Atlanta, 416,715; Columbus, 165,511; Macon, 121,282; Savannah, 113,020; Augusta, 52,861; Athens, 48,761
State forests: 25,258,000 ac. (67% of total state area)
State parks: 53 (42,600 ac.)
State revenue receipts (1979): $2,585,266,526
State revenue distribution (1979): $2,585,266,526

Hernando de Soto, the Spanish explorer, first traveled parts of Georgia in 1540. British claims later conflicted with those of Spain. After obtaining a royal charter, Gen. James Oglethorpe established the first permanent settlement in Georgia in 1733 as a refuge for English debtors. In 1742, Oglethorpe defeated Spanish invaders in the Battle of Bloody Marsh.

A Confederate stronghold, Georgia was the scene of extensive military action during the Civil War. Union General William T. Sherman burned Atlanta and destroyed a 60-mile wide path to the coast where he captured Savannah in 1864.

The largest state east of the Mississippi, Georgia is typical of the changing South with an ever-increasing industrial development. Atlanta, largest city in the state, is the communications and transportation center for the Southeast and the area's chief distributor of goods.

Georgia leads the nation in the production of paper and board, tufted textile products, and processed chicken. Other major manufactured products are transportation equipment, food products, apparel, and chemicals.

Important agricultural products are corn, cotton, tobacco, soybeans, eggs, and peaches. Georgia produces twice as many peanuts as the next leading state. From its vast stands of pine come more than half the world's resins and turpentine and 74.4% of the U.S. supply. Georgia is also a leader in the production of marble, kaolin, barite, and bauxite.

Principal tourist attractions in Georgia include the Okefenokee National Wildlife Refuge, Andersonville Prison Park and National Cemetery, Chickamauga and Chattanooga National Military Park, the Little White House at Warm Springs where Pres. Franklin D. Roosevelt died in 1945, Sea Island, the enormous Confederate Memorial at Stone Mountain, Kennesaw Mountain National Battlefield Park, and Cumberland Island National Seashore.

HAWAII

Capital: Honolulu (on Oahu)
Governor: George R. Ariyoshi, D (to Dec. 1982)
Lieut. Governor: Jean King, D (to Dec. 1982)
Comptroller: Hideo Murakami, D (to Dec. 1982)
Atty. General: Wayne Minami, D (to Dec. 1982)
Organized as territory: 1900
Entered Union & (rank): Aug. 21, 1959 (50)
Motto: *Ua Mau Ke Ea O Ka Aina I Ka Pono* (The life of the land is perpetuated in righteousness)
State flower: Hibiscus
State song: "Hawaii Ponoi"
State bird: Nene (Hawaiian goose)
Nickname: Aloha State
Origin of name: Uncertain. The islands may have been named by Hawaii Loa, their traditional discoverer. Or they may have been named after Hawaii or Hawaiki, the traditional home of the Polynesians.
1970 population & (rank): 769,913 (40)
1979 prov. population & (rank): 915,000 (40)
1970 land area & (rank): 6,425 sq mi. (16,641 sq km) (47)
Geographic center: In Hawaii Co., off Maui Island
Number of counties: 4
Largest cities (1977 est.): Honolulu, 717,852[1]
State parks and historic sites: 47
Total state government revenues (1978–79): $1,626,907,000
Total state government expenditures (1978–79): $1,607,291,000

1. There are no political boundaries to Honolulu or any other place, but statistical boundaries are assigned under state law.

First settled by Polynesians sailing from other Pacific islands in the 6th century, Hawaii was visited in 1778 by British Captain James Cook who called the group the Sandwich Islands.

Hawaii was a native kingdom throughout most of the 19th century when the expansion of vital sugar and pineapple industries meant increasing U.S. business and political involvement. In 1893, Queen Liliuokalani was deposed and a year later the Republic of Hawaii was established with Sanford B. Dole as president. Then, following its annexation in 1898, Hawaii became a U.S. Territory in 1900.

The Japanese attack on the naval base at Pearl Harbor on Dec. 7, 1941, was directly responsible for U.S. entry into World War II.

Hawaii, 2,100 miles west-southwest of San Francisco, is a 1,600-mile chain of islets and eight main islands—Hawaii, Kahoolawe, Maui, Lanai, Molokai, Oahu, Kauai, and Niihau. Kure (Ocean) Atoll, an uninhabited islet in the Leeward Islands, is administratively part of Hawaii.

The temperature is mild and Hawaii's soil is fertile for tropical fruits and vegetables. Cane sugar and pineapple are the chief products. Hawaii also grows coffee, bananas and nuts. The tourist business is one of Hawaii's largest sources of income.

Hawaii's highest peak is Mauna Kea (13,796 ft.). Mauna Loa (13,680 ft.) is the largest volcanic mountain in the world in cubic content.

Among the major points of interest are Hawaii Volcanoes National Park (Hawaii), Haleakala National Park (Maui), Puuhonua o Honaunau National Historical Park (Hawaii), Polynesian Cultural Center (Oahu), the U.S.S. *Arizona* Memorial at Pearl Harbor, and Iolani Palace (the only royal palace in the U.S.), Bishop Museum, and Waikiki Beach (all in Honolulu).

IDAHO

Capital: Boise
Governor: John V. Evans, D (to Jan. 1981)
Lieut. Governor: Phil Batt, R (to Jan. 1981)
Secy. of State: Pete T. Cenarrusa, R (to Jan. 1981)
State Auditor: Joe R. Williams, D (to Jan. 1981)
Atty. General: David Leroy, R (to Jan. 1981)
Organized as territory: March 3, 1863
Entered Union & (rank): July 3, 1890 (43)
Present constitution adopted: 1890
Motto: *Esto perpetua* (May you last forever)
State flower: Syringa (1931)
State tree: White pine (1935)
State bird: Mountain bluebird (1931)
State horse: Appaloosa (1975)
State gem: Star garnet (1967)
State song: "Here We Have Idaho"
Nicknames: Gem State; Spud State; Panhandle State
Origin of name: Means "Gem of the Mountains"
1970 population & (rank): 713,008 (42)
1979 prov. population & (rank): 905,000 (41)
1970 land area & (rank): 82,677 sq mi. (214,133 sq km) (11)
Geographic center: In Custer Co., at Custer, SW of Challis
Number of counties: 44, plus small part of Yellowstone National Park
Largest cities (1977 est.): Boise, 107,687; Pocatello, 46,736; Idaho Falls, 38,457; Nampa, 26,841; Lewiston, 25,788; Twin Falls, 24,157; Coeur d'Alene, 18,983
State forests: 981,200 ac.
State parks: 18 (21,838 ac.)
State revenue (1978–79): $475,910,308
State expenditure (1978–79): $301,815,606

After its acquisition by the U.S. as part of the Louisiana Purchase in 1803, the region was explored by Meriwether Lewis and William Clark in 1805–06. Northwest boundary disputes with Great Britain were settled by the Oregon Treaty in 1846 and the first permanent U.S. settlement in Idaho was established by the Mormons at Franklin in 1860.

After gold was discovered on Orofino Creek in 1860, prospectors swarmed into the territory, but left little more than a number of ghost towns.

In the 1870s, growing white occupation of Indian lands led to a series of battles between U.S. forces and the Nez Percé, Bannock, and Sheepeater tribes.

Mining, lumbering, and irrigation farming have been important for years. Idaho produces more than one third of all the silver mined in the U.S. It also ranks high among the states in antimony, lead, cobalt, garnet, phosphate rock, vanadium, zinc, and mercury.

Idaho's most impressive growth began when World War II military needs made processing agricultural products a big industry, particularly the dehydrating and freezing of potatoes. The state produces about one fourth of the nation's potato crop, as well as wheat, apples, corn, barley, sugar beets, and hops. More money is made from livestock in the state than from all agricultural products.

With the growth of winter sports, tourism now outranks mining in dollar revenue. Idaho's many streams and lakes provide fishing, camping, and boating sites. The nation's largest elk herds draw hunters from all over the world and the famed Sun Valley resort attracts thousands of visitors to its swimming and skiing facilities.

Other points of interest are the Craters of the Moon National Monument; Nez Percé National Historic Park, which includes many sites visited by Lewis and Clark; and the State Historical Museum in Boise.

ILLINOIS

Capital: Springfield
Governor: James R. Thompson, R (to Jan. 1983)
Lieut. Governor: Dave O'Neal, R (to Jan. 1983)
Secy. of State: Alan J. Dixon, D (to Jan. 1983)
Comptroller: Roland J. Burris, D (to Jan. 1983)
Atty. General: William J. Scott, R (to Jan. 1983)
Treasurer: Jerry Cosentino, D (to Jan. 1983)
Organized as territory: Feb. 3, 1809
Entered Union & (rank): Dec. 3, 1818 (21)
Present constitution adopted: 1970
Motto: State sovereignty, national union
State flower: Violet (1908)
State tree: White oak (1973)
State bird: Cardinal (1929)
State insect: Monarch butterfly
State song: "Illinois" (1925)
State slogan: Land of Lincoln
State mineral: Fluorite (1965)
Nickname: Prairie State
Origin of name: From an Indian word and French suffix meaning "tribe of superior men"
1950 population & (rank): 8,712,176 (4)
1979 prov. population & (rank): 11,230,000 (5)
1970 land area & (rank): 56,400 sq mi. (146,076 sq km) (23)
Geographic center: In St. Clair County near Mascoutah
Number of counties: 102
Largest cities (1977 est.): Chicago, 3,062,881; Rockford, 140,667; Peoria, 125,724; Decatur, 89,690; Springfield, 87,520; Aurora, 78,753; Joliet, 72,102
Public use areas: 187 (275,000 ac.), incl. state parks, memorials, forests and conservation areas
Total state revenue, all sources (fiscal 1978): $8,893,000,000
State expenditure (fiscal 1978): $8,815,000,000

French explorers Marquette and Joliet, in 1673, were the first Europeans of record to visit the region. In 1699 French settlers established the first permanent settlement at Cahokia, near present-day East St. Louis.

Great Britain obtained the region at the end of the French and Indian War in 1763. The area figured prominently in frontier struggles during the Revolutionary War and in Indian wars during the early 19th century.

Significant episodes in the state's early history include the growing migration of Eastern settlers following the opening of the Erie Canal in 1825; the Black Hawk War, which virtually ended the Indian troubles in the area; and the rise of Abraham Lincoln from farm laborer to President-elect.

Today, Illinois stands high in manufacturing, coal mining, agriculture, and oil production. The sprawling Chicago district (including a slice of Indiana) is a great iron and steel producer, meat packer, grain exchange, and railroad center. Chicago is also famous as a busy long-flight airport city and Great Lakes port.

Illinois ranks first in the nation in export of agricultural products and second in hog production. An important dairying state, Illinois is also a leader in corn, oats, wheat, barley, rye, truck vegetables, and nursery products.

The state manufactures a great variety of industrial and consumer products: railroad cars, clothing, furniture, tractors, liquor, watches, and farm implements are just some of the items made in its factories and plants.

Central Illinois is noted for shrines and memorials associated with the life of Abraham Lincoln. In Springfield are the Lincoln Home, the Lincoln Tomb, and the restored Old State Capitol. Other points of interest are the home of Mormon leader Joseph Smith in Nauvoo and, in Chicago: the Art Institute, Field Museum, Museum of Science and Industry, Shedd Aquarium, Adler Planetarium, Merchandise Mart, and Chicago Portage National Historic Site.

INDIANA

Capital: Indianapolis
Governor: Dr. Otis R. Bowen, R (to Jan. 1981)
Lieut. Governor: Robert D. Orr, R (to Jan. 1981)
Secy. of State: Edwin J. Simcox, R (to Dec. 1982)
Treasurer: Julian L. Ridlen, R (to Feb. 1983)
Atty. General: Theodore L. Sendak, R (to Jan. 1981)
Auditor: Charles D. Loos, R (to Dec. 1982)
Organized as territory: May 7, 1800
Entered Union & (rank): Dec. 11, 1816 (19)
Present constitution adopted: 1851
Motto: The Crossroads of America
State flower: Peony (1957)
State tree: Tulip tree (1931)
State bird: Cardinal (1933)
State song: "On the Banks of the Wabash, Far Away" (1913)
Nickname: Hoosier State

Origin of name: Meaning "land of Indians"
1970 population & (rank): 5,193,669 (11)
1979 prov. population & (rank): 5,400,000 (12)
1970 land area & (rank): 36,097 sq mi. (93,491 sq km) (38)
Geographic center: In Boone Co., 14 mi. NNW of Indianapolis
Number of Counties: 92
Largest cities (1977 est.): Indianapolis, 704,556; Fort Wayne, 182,213; Gary, 159,412; Evansville, 133,975; South Bend, 114,011; Hammond, 102,027; Muncie, 82,152
State parks: 22 (66,186 ac.)
State memorials: 19 (931 ac.)
State general revenue (1977–78): $3,887,800,000
State general expenditure (1977–78): $3,474,910,000

First explored for France by La Salle in 1679–80, the region figured importantly in the Franco-British struggle for North America that culminated with British victory in 1763.

George Rogers Clark led American forces against the British in the area during the Revolutionary War and, prior to becoming a state, Indiana was the scene of frequent Indian uprisings until the victory of Gen. William Henry Harrison at Tippecanoe in 1811.

Indiana's 41-mile Lake Michigan waterfront—one of the world's great industrial centers—turns out iron, steel, and oil products. Products include automobile parts and accessories, mobile homes and recreational vehicles, truck and bus bodies, aircraft engines, farm machinery, and fabricated structural steel. Phonograph records, wood office furniture, and pharmaceuticals are also manufactured.

The state is a leader in agriculture with corn the principal crop. Hogs, soybeans, wheat, oats, rye, tomatoes, onions, and poultry also contribute heavily to Indiana's agricultural output. Much of the building limestone used in the U.S. is quarried in Indiana which is also a large producer of coal.

Wyandotte Cave, one of the largest in the U.S., is located in Crawford County in southern Indiana and West Baden and French Lick are well known for their mineral springs. Other attractions include Indiana Dunes National Lakeshore, Indianapolis Motor Speedway, Lincoln Boyhood National Memorial, and the George Rogers Clark National Historical Park.

IOWA

Capital: Des Moines
Governor: Robert D. Ray, R (to Jan. 1983)
Lieut. Governor: Terry Branstad, R (to Jan. 1983)
Secy. of State: Melvin D. Synhorst, R (to Jan. 1983)
Treasurer: Maurice E. Baringer, R (to Jan. 1983)
Atty. General: Tom Miller, D (to Jan. 1983)
Organized as territory: June 12, 1838
Entered Union & (rank): Dec. 28, 1846 (29)
Present constitution adopted: 1857
Motto: Our liberties we prize and our rights we will maintain
State flower: Wild rose (1897)
State bird: Eastern goldfinch (1933)
State colors: Red, white, and blue (in state flag)
State song: "Song of Iowa"
Nickname: Hawkeye State
Origin of name: Probably from an Indian word meaning "I-o-w-a, this is the place," or "The Beautiful Land"
1970 population & (rank): 2,825,041 (25)
1979 prov. population & (rank): 2,903,000 (26)
1970 land area & (rank): 55,491 sq mi. (144,887 sq km) (24)
Geographic center: In Story Co., 5 mi. NE of Ames
Number of counties: 99
Largest cities (1977 est.): Des Moines, 193,772; Cedar Rapids, 107,996; Davenport, 101,410; Sioux City, 85,115; Waterloo, 78,915; Dubuque, 62,349; Council Bluffs, 58,668; Iowa City, 49,154; Ames, 44,020
State forests: 5 (28,000 ac.)
State parks: 95 (49,237)
Total revenue (1979): $1,536,500,000
Total expenditures (1979): $1,575,238,227

The first Europeans to visit the area were the French explorers, Father Jacques Marquette and Louis Jolliet in 1673. The U.S. obtained control of the area in 1803 as part of the Louisiana Purchase.

During the first half of the 19th century, there was heavy fighting between white settlers and Indians. Lands were taken from the Indians after the Black Hawk War in 1832 and again in 1836 and 1837.

When Iowa became a state in 1846, its capital was Iowa City; the more centrally located Des Moines became the new capital in 1857. At that time, the state's present boundaries were also drawn.

Although Iowa produces a tenth of the nation's food supply, the value of Iowa's manufactured products is almost 2½ times that of its agriculture. Major industries are food and associated products, non-electrical machinery, electrical equipment, printing and publishing, and fabricated products.

Iowa stands in a class by itself as an agricultural state. Its farms sell over $7 billion worth of crops and livestock annually. Iowa leads the nation in all livestock and hog marketings, with about 22% of the pork supply and 13% of the grain-fed cattle. Iowa's forests produce hardwood lumber, particularly walnut, and its mineral products include cement, limestone, sand, gravel, gypsum, and coal.

Tourist attractions include the Herbert Hoover birthplace and library near West Branch; the Amana Colonies; Fort Dodge Historical Museum, Fort, and Stockade; the Iowa State Fair at Des Moines in August; and the Effigy Mounds National Monument at Marquette, a prehistoric Indian burial site.

KANSAS

Capital: Topeka
Governor: John W. Carlin, D (to Jan. 1983)
Lieut. Governor: Paul V. Dugan, D (to Jan. 1983)
Secy. of State: Jack H. Brier, R (to Jan. 1983)
Treasurer: Joan Finney, D (to Jan. 1983)
Atty. General: Robert T. Stephan, R (to Jan. 1983)
Organized as territory: May 30, 1854
Entered Union & (rank): Jan. 29, 1861 (34)
Present constitution adopted: 1859
Motto: *Ad astra per aspera* (To the stars through difficulties)
State flower: Sunflower (1903)
State tree: Cottonwood (1937)
State bird: Western meadow lark (1937)
State animal: Buffalo (1955)
State song: "Home on the Range" (1947)
State march: "The Kansas March" (1935)
Nicknames: Sunflower State; Jayhawk State
Origin of name: From a Siouan word meaning "people of the south wind"

1970 population & (rank): 2,249,071 (28)
1979 prov. population & (rank): 2,369,000 (32)
1970 land area & (rank): 81,787 sq mi. (211,828 sq km) (13)
Geographic center: In Barton Co., 15 mi. NE of Great Bend
Number of counties: 105
Largest cities (1977 est.): Wichita, 268,012; Kansas City, 167,064; Topeka, 122,065; Overland Park, 82,372; Lawrence, 51,459; Salina, 39,218
State parks: 22 (14,394 ac.)
State operating revenue (1978–79): $2,145,583,000
State operating expenditure (1978–79): $2,004,634,000

Spanish explorer Francisco de Coronado, in 1541, is considered the first European to have traveled this region. La Salle's extensive land claims for France (1682) included present-day Kansas. Ceded to Spain by France in 1763, the territory reverted back to France in 1800 and was sold to the U.S. as part of the Louisiana Purchase in 1803.

Lewis and Clark, Zebulon Pike, and Stephen H. Long explored the region between 1803 and 1819. The first permanent settlements in Kansas were outposts—Fort Leavenworth (1827), Fort Scott (1842), and Fort Riley (1853)—established to protect travelers along the Santa Fe and Oregon Trails.

Just before the Civil War, the conflict between the pro- and anti-slavery forces earned the region the grim title "Bleeding Kansas."

Today, wheat fields, oil well derricks, herds of cattle, and grain storage elevators are chief features of the Kansas landscape. A leading wheat-growing state, Kansas also raises corn, sorghums, oats, barley, soy beans, and potatoes. Kansas stands high in petroleum production and mines zinc, coal, salt, and lead. It is also the nation's leading producer of helium.

Wichita is one of the nation's leading aircraft manufacturing centers, ranking first in production of private aircraft. Kansas City is an important transportation, milling, and meat-packing center.

Points of interest include the Kansas State Historical Society Museum at Topeka, the Eisenhower boyhood home and the new Eisenhower Memorial Museum and Presidential Library at Abilene, John Brown's cabin at Osawatomie, recreated Front Street in Dodge City, Fort Larned (once the most important military post on the Santa Fe Trail), and Fort Leavenworth and Fort Riley, still active military posts.

KENTUCKY

Capital: Frankfort
Governor: John Y. Brown, Jr., D (to Dec. 1983)
Lieut. Governor: Martha Layne Collins, D (to Dec. 1983)
Secy. of State: Francis Jones Mills, D (to Jan. 1984)
State Treasurer: Drexell Davis, D (to Jan. 1984)
State Auditor: James B. Graham, D (to Jan. 1984)
Atty. General: Steven L. Beshear, D (to Jan. 1984)
Entered Union & (rank): June 1, 1792 (15)
Present constitution adopted: 1891
Motto: United we stand, divided we fall
State tree: Coffeetree
State flower: Goldenrod
State bird: Kentucky cardinal
State song: "My Old Kentucky Home"
Nickname: Bluegrass State
Origin of name: From an Iroquoian word "Ken-tah-ten" meaning "land of tomorrow"
1970 population & (rank): 3,219,311 (23)
1979 prov. population & (rank): 3,527,000 (23)
1970 land area & (rank): 39,650 sq mi. (102,694 sq km) (37)
Geographic center: In Marion Co., 3 mi. NNW of Lebanon
Number of counties: 120
Largest cities (1977 est.): Louisville, 322,870; Lexington, 190,142; Owensboro, 50,490; Covington, 46,925; Bowling Green, 38,466; Paducah, 33,026; Ashland, 26,867
State forests: 9 (44,173 ac.)
State parks: 43 (40,574 ac.)
Total state revenue (1978–79): $3,889,221,084[2]
Total state expenditure (1978–79): $3,422,616,129[1]

Kentucky was the first region west of the Allegheny Mountains settled by American pioneers. James Harrod established the first permanent settlement at Harrodsburg in 1774; the following year Daniel Boone, who had explored the area in 1767, blazed the Wilderness Trail and founded Boonesboro.

Politically, the Kentucky region was originally part of Virginia, but early statehood was gained in 1792.

During the Civil War, as a slaveholding state with a considerable abolitionist population, Kentucky was caught in the middle of the conflict, supplying both Union and Confederate forces with thousands of troops.

In recent years, manufacturing has shown important gains, but agriculture and mining are still vital to Kentucky's economy. Kentucky prides itself on producing some of the nation's best tobacco, horses, and whiskey. Corn, soybeans, wheat, fruit, hogs, cattle, and dairy farming are also important.

Among the manufactured items produced in the state are furniture, aluminum ware, brooms, shoes, lumber products, machinery, textiles, and iron and steel products. Kentucky also produces significant amounts of petroleum, natural gas, fluorspar, clay, and stone. However, coal accounts for 90% of the total mineral income.

Louisville, the largest city, famed for the Kentucky Derby at Churchill Downs, is also the location of a large state university, whiskey distilleries, and cigarette factories. The Bluegrass country around Lexington is the home of some of the world's finest race horses. Other attractions are Mammoth Cave, the George S. Patton, Jr., Military Museum at Fort Knox, and Old Fort Harrod State Park.

LOUISIANA

Capital: Baton Rouge
Governor: David C. Treen, R (to March 1984)
Lieut. Governor: Robert L. Freeman, D (to March 1984)
Secy. of State: James H. Brown, Jr., D (to March 1984)
Atty. General: William J. Guste, Jr., D (to March 1984)
Organized as territory: March 26, 1804
Entered Union & (rank): April 30, 1812 (18)
Present constitution adopted: 1974
Motto: Union, justice, and confidence
State flower: Magnolia (1900)
State tree: Bald cypress
State bird: Pelican
State song: "Give Me Louisiana," and "You Are My Sunshine"
Nicknames: Pelican State; Sportsman's Paradise; Creole State; Sugar State

1. Figures taken from Kentucky's Financial Report for fiscal year ending June 30, 1979. 2. Five operating funds only.

Origin of name: In honor of Louis XIV of France
1970 population & (rank): 3,643,180 (20)
1979 prov. population & (rank): 4,026,000 (20)
1970 land area & (rank): 44,930 sq mi. (116,369 sq km) (33)
Geographic center: In Avoyelles Parish, 3 mi. SE of Marksville
Number of parishes (counties): 64
Largest cities (1977 est.): New Orleans, 561,266; Metropolitan Baton Rouge, 308,178; Shreveport, 188,652; Lake Charles, 78,464; Lafayette, 79,732; Alexandria, 49,918; Monroe, 63,633; Bossier City, 47,737
State forests: 1 (8,000 ac.)
State parks: 30 (13,932 ac.)
State general revenue (1979–80 est.): $3,261,773,987
Federal Grants: $1,283,763,509
State general expenditure (1979–80 est.): $4,676,383,509

Louisiana has a rich, colorful historical background. Early Spanish explorers were Piñeda, 1519; Cabeza de Vaca, 1528; and de Soto in 1541. La Salle reached the mouth of the Mississippi and claimed all the land drained by it and its tributaries for Louis XIV of France in 1682.

Louisiana became a French crown colony in 1731, was ceded to Spain in 1763, returned to France in 1800, and sold by Napoleon to the U.S. as part of the Louisiana Purchase (with large territories to the north and northwest) in 1803.

In 1815, Gen. Andrew Jackson's troops defeated a larger British army in the Battle of New Orleans, neither side aware that the treaty ending the War of 1812 had been signed.

As to total value of its mineral output, Louisiana is a leader in natural gas, salt, petroleum, and sulfur production. Much of the oil and sulfur comes from offshore deposits. The state also produces large crops of sweet potatoes, rice, sugarcane, pecans, soybeans, corn, and cotton.

Leading manufactures include chemicals, processed food, petroleum and coal products, paper, lumber and wood products, transportation equipment, and apparel.

Louisiana marshes supply most of the nation's muskrat fur as well as that of opossum, raccoon, mink, and otter, and large numbers of game birds.

Major points of interest include New Orleans with its French Quarter and Superdome, plantation homes near Natchitoches and New Iberia, Cajun country in the Mississippi delta region, Chalmette National Historical Park, and the state capital at Baton Rouge.

MAINE

Capital: Augusta
Governor: Joseph E. Brennan, D (to Jan. 1983)
Secy. of State: Rodney F. Quinn, D (to Jan. 1983)
Controller: Richard A. Dieffenbach (term indefinite)
Atty. General: Richard S. Cohen, D (to Jan. 1983)
Entered Union & (rank): March 15, 1820 (23)
Present constitution adopted: 1820
Motto: *Dirigo* (I direct)
State flower: White pine cone and tassel (1895)
State tree: White pine tree (1945)
State bird: Chickadee (1927)
State fish: Landlocked salmon (1969)
State mineral: Tourmaline (1971)
State song: "State of Maine Song" (1937)
Nickname: Pine Tree State
Origin of name: First used to distinguish the mainland from the offshore islands. It has been considered a compliment to Henrietta Maria, Queen of Charles I of England. She was said to have owned the province of Mayne in France.
1970 population & (rank): 993,663 (38)
1979 prov. population & (rank): 1,097,000 (38)
1970 land area & (rank): 30,920 sq mi. (80,083 sq km) (39)
Geographic center: In Piscataquis Co., 18 mi. N of Dover-Foxcroft
Number of counties: 16
Largest cities (1977 est.): Portland, 62,127; Lewiston, 40,657; Bangor, 31,628; Auburn, 22,984; South Portland, 21,797; Augusta, 21,164; Biddeford, 19,211
State forests: 1 (21,000 ac.)
State parks: 26 (247,627 ac.)
State historic sites: 18 (403 ac.)
State total revenue (1979): $1,007,792,000
State total expenditure (1979): $1,021,663,000

John Cabot and his son, Sebastian, are believed to have visited the Maine coast in 1498. However, the first permanent English settlements were not established until more than a century later, in 1623.

The first naval action of the Revolutionary War occurred in 1775 when colonials captured the British sloop *Margaretta* off Machias on the Maine coast. In that same year, the British burned Falmouth (now Portland).

Long governed by Massachusetts, Maine became the 23rd state as part of the Missouri Compromise in 1820.

Maine produces one out of every nine potatoes raised in the U.S. and 95% of the nation's low-bush blueberries. Farm income is also derived from apples, sweet corn, peas, and beans, with poultry and eggs the largest items.

The state is one of the world's largest pulp-paper producers. It ranks fifth in boot-and-shoe manufacturing. With more than 80% of its area forested, Maine turns out wood products from boats to toothpicks.

Maine leads the world in the production of the familiar flat tins of sardines, producing more than 100 million of them annually. Lobstermen normally catch 80–90% of the nation's true total of lobsters.

A scenic seacoast, beaches, lakes, mountains, and resorts make Maine a popular vacationland. There are more than 2,500 lakes and 5,000 streams, plus 26 state parks, to attract hunters, fishermen, skiers, and campers.

Major points of interest are: Bar Harbor, Allagash National Wilderness Waterway, the Wadsworth-Longfellow House in Portland, Roosevelt Campobello International Park, and the St. Croix Island National Monument.

MARYLAND

Capital: Annapolis
Governor: Harry Hughes, D (to Jan. 1983)
Lieut. Gov.: Samuel W. Bogley, D (to Jan. 1983)
Secy. of State: Fred L. Wineland, D (appointed by governor)
Comptroller of the Treasury: Louis L. Goldstein, D (to Jan. 1983)
Treasurer: William S. James, D (to Jan. 1983)
Atty. General: Stephen H. Sachs, D (to Jan. 1983)
Entered Union & (rank): April 28, 1788 (7)
Present constitution adopted: 1867
Motto: *Fatti maschii, parole femine* (Manly deeds, womanly words)

State flower: Black-eyed susan (1918)
State tree: White oak (1941)
State bird: Baltimore oriole (1947)
State dog: Chesapeake Bay retriever (1964)
State fish: Rockfish (1965)
State insect: Baltimore checkerspot butterfly (1973)
State sport: Jousting (1962)
State song: "Maryland! My Maryland!" (1939)
Nicknames: Free State; Old Line State
Origin of name: In honor of Henrietta Maria (Queen of Charles I of England)
1970 population & (rank): 3,922,399 (18)
1979 prov. population & (rank): 4,149,000 (18)
1970 land area & (rank): 9,891 sq mi. (25,618 sq km) (42)
Geographic center: In Prince Georges Co., 4½ mi. NW of Davidsonville
Number of counties: 23, and 1 independent city
Largest cities (1977 est.): Baltimore, 804,304; Rockville, 43,441; Bowie, 37,182; Hagerstown, 36,998; Annapolis, 33,124; College Park, 27,121; Gaithersburg, 26,946
State forests: 9 (116,213 ac.)
State parks: 42 (65,559 ac.)
State general revenue (1980 est.): $2,584,429,000
State general expenditure (1980 est.): $2,652,915,593

In 1608, Chesapeake Bay was explored by Capt. John Smith. Charles I granted a royal charter to Cecil Calvert, Lord Baltimore, in 1632 and English Roman Catholics landed on St. Clement's (now Blakistone Island) in 1634. Religious freedom, granted all Christians in the Toleration act passed by the Maryland assembly in 1649, was ended by a Puritan revolt, 1654–58.

In 1814, when the British unsuccessfully tried to capture Baltimore, the bombardment of Fort McHenry inspired Francis Scott Key to write *The Star Spangled Banner.*

Maryland is almost cut in two by the Chesapeake Bay, and the many estuaries and rivers create one of the longest waterfronts of any state. The Bay produces more seafood—oysters, crabs, clams, fin fish—than any comparable body of water. Important agricultural products, in order of cash value, are chickens, dairy products, corn, cattle, tobacco, and vegetables. Maryland is a leader in vegetable canning. Sand, gravel, lime and cement, stone, coal, and clay are the chief mineral products.

Manufacturing industries produce missiles, airplanes, steel, clothing, and chemicals. Baltimore, home of The Johns Hopkins University and Hospital, ranks as the nation's second port in foreign tonnage. Annapolis, site of the U.S. Naval Academy, has one of the earliest state houses (1772–79) still in regular use by a State government.

Among the popular attractions in Maryland are the Fort McHenry National Monument, Harpers Ferry and Chesapeake and Ohio Canal National Historical Parks, St. Marys City restoration near Leonardtown, USS *Constellation* at Baltimore, U.S. Naval Academy in Annapolis, Assateague Island National Seashore, and Catoctin Mountain and Piscataway parks.

MASSACHUSETTS

Capital: Boston
Governor: Edward King, D (to Jan. 1983)
Lieut. Governor: Thomas P. O'Neill III, D (to Jan. 1983)
Secy. of the Commonwealth: Michael Joseph Connolly, D (to Jan. 1983)
Treasurer & Receiver-General: Robert Q. Crane, D (to Jan. 1983)
Auditor of the Commonwealth: Thaddeus Buczko, D (to Jan. 1983)
Atty. General: Francis X. Bellotti (to Jan. 1979)
Entered Union & (rank): Feb. 6, 1788 (6)
Motto: *Ense petit placidam sub libertate quietem* (By the sword we seek peace, but peace only under liberty)
State flower: Mayflower (1918)
State tree: American elm (1941)
State bird: Chickadee (1941)
State colors: Blue and gold
State song: "All Hail to Massachusetts" (1966)
State beverage: Cranberry juice (1970)
State horse: Morgan horse (1970)
State insect: Ladybug (1974)
Nicknames: Bay State; Old Colony State
Origin of name: From two Indian words meaning "Great mountain place"
1970 population & (rank): 5,689,170 (10)
1979 prov. population & (rank): 5,769,000 (10)
1970 land area & (rank): 7,826 sq mi. (20,269 sq km) (45)
Geographic center: In Worcester Co., in S part of city of Worcester
Number of counties: 14
Largest cities (1977 est.): Boston, 618,493; Worcester, 165,229; Springfield, 164,895; Cambridge, 99,296; Fall River, 98,898; New Bedford, 98,845; Quincy, 90,571
State forests and parks: 129 (236,000 ac.)[1]
State general revenue (1978–79): $6,679,793,567
State general expenditure (1978–79): $6,679,479,740

Massachusetts has played a significant role in American history since the Pilgrims, seeking religious freedom, founded Plymouth Colony in 1620.

As one of the most important of the 13 colonies, Massachusetts became a leader in resisting British oppression. In 1773, the Boston Tea Party protested unjust taxation. The Minutemen started the American Revolution by battling British troops at Lexington and Concord on April 19, 1775.

During the 19th century, Massachusetts was famous for the vigorous intellectual activity of famous writers and educators and for its expanding commercial fishing, shipping, and manufacturing interests.

Massachusetts pioneered in the manufacture of textiles and shoes. Today, these industries have been replaced in importance by activity in the electronics and communications equipment fields.

The state's cranberry crop is the nation's largest. Also important are dairy and poultry products, nursery and greenhouse produce, vegetables, and fruit.

Tourism has become an important factor in the economy of the state because of its numerous recreational areas and historical landmarks.

Cape Cod has summer theaters, water sports, and an artists' colony at Provincetown. Tanglewood, in the Berkshires, features the summer concerts of the Boston Symphony.

Among the many other points of interest are Old Sturbridge Village, Minute Man National Historical Park between Lexington and Concord, and, in Boston: Old North Church, Old State House, Faneuil Hall, and the USS *Constitution.*

1. The Metropolitan District Commission, an agency of the Commonwealth serving municipalities in the Boston area, has about 14,000 acres of parkways and reservations under its jurisdiction.

MICHIGAN

Capital: Lansing
Governor: William C. Milliken, R (to Jan. 1983)
Lieut. Governor: James H. Brickley, R (to Jan. 1983)
Secy. of State: Richard H. Austin, D (to Jan. 1983)
Atty. General: Frank J. Kelley, D (to Jan. 1983)
Organized as territory: Jan. 11, 1805
Entered Union & (rank): Jan. 26, 1837 (26)
Present constitution adopted: April 1, 1963, (effective Jan. 1, 1964)
Motto: *Si quaeris peninsulam amoenam circumspice* (If you seek a pleasant peninsula, look around you)
State flower: Apple blossom (1897)
State bird: Robin
State fish: Brook trout (1965)
State gem: Isle Royal Greenstone (Chlorastrolite) (1972)
State stone: Petoskey stone (1965)
Nickname: Wolverine State
Origin of name: From two Indian words meaning "great lake"
1970 population & (rank): 8,875,083 (7)
1979 prov. population & (rank): 9,208,000 (7)
1970 land area & (rank): 56,817 sq mi. (147,156 sq km) (22)
Geographic center: In Wexford Co., 5 mi. NNW of Cadillac
Number of counties: 83
Largest cities (1977 est.): Detroit, 1,289,910: Grand Rapids, 184,954; Warren, 170,084; Flint, 163,594; Lansing, 127,128; Livonia, 108,337; Ann Arbor, 105,602
State forests: 33 (3,762,184 ac.)
State parks and recreation areas: 92 (216,857 ac.)
State general revenue (1978): $8,155,678,000
State general expenditure (1978): $7,918,016,000

Indian tribes were living in the Michigan region when the first European, Étienne Brulé of France, arrived in 1618. Other French explorers, including Marquette, Jolliet, and La Salle, followed, and the first permanent settlement was established in 1668 at Sault Ste. Marie. France was ousted from the territory by Great Britain in 1763, following the French and Indian War.

After the Revolutionary War, the U.S. acquired most of the region, which remained the scene of constant conflict between the British and U.S. forces and their respective Indian allies through the War of 1812.

Bordering on four of the five Great Lakes, Michigan is divided into Upper and Lower Peninsulas by the Straits of Mackinac, which link Lakes Michigan and Huron. The two parts of the state are connected by the Mackinac Bridge, one of the world's longest suspension bridges. To the north, connecting Lakes Superior and Huron are the busy Sault Ste. Marie Canals.

While Michigan ranks first among the states in production of motor vehicles and parts, it is also a leader in many other manufacturing and processing lines including prepared cereals, machine tools, airplane parts, refrigerators, hardware, steel springs, and furniture.

The state produces important amounts of iron, copper, iodine, gypsum, bromine, salt, lime, gravel, and cement. Michigan's farms grow apples, cherries, pears, grapes, potatoes, and sugar beets and the annual value of its forest products is estimated at $2 billion. With over 36,000 miles of streams, some 11,000 lakes, and a 2,000 mile shoreline, Michigan is a prime area for both commercial and sport fishing.

Points of interest are the automobile plants in Dearborn, Detroit, Flint, Lansing, and Pontiac; Mackinac Island; Pictured Rocks and Sleeping Bear Dunes National Lakeshores, Greenfield Village near Dearborn; and the many summer resorts along both the inland and Great Lakes.

MINNESOTA

Capital: St. Paul
Governor: Albert H. Quie, R (to Jan. 1983)
Lieut. Governor: Lou Wangberg, R (to Jan. 1983)
Secy. of State: Joan Grow (to Jan. 1983)
State Auditor: Arne Carlson, R (to Jan. 1983)
Atty. General: Warren Spannus, D (to Jan. 1983)
State Treasurer: Jim Lord (to Jan. 1983)
Organized as territory: March 3, 1849
Entered Union & (rank): May 11, 1858 (32)
Present constitution adopted: 1858
Motto: L'Etoile du Nord (The North Star)
State flower: Showy lady slipper (1902)
State tree: Red (or Norway) pine
State bird: Common loon (also called Great Northern Diver)
State song: "Hail Minnesota"
Nicknames: North Star State; Gopher State; Land of 10,000 Lakes
Origin of name: From a Dakota Indian word meaning "sky-tinted water"
1970 population & (rank): 3,805,069 (19)
1979 prov. population & (rank): 4,060,000 (19)
1970 land area & (rank): 79,289 sq mi. (205,359 sq km) (14)
Geographic center: In Crow Wing Co., 10 mi. SW of Brainerd
Number of counties: 87
Largest cities (1977 est.): Minneapolis, 360,269; St. Paul, 265,971; Duluth, 95,248; Bloomington, 78,052; Rochester, 56,865; Edina, 48,687; St. Cloud, 41,949
State forests: 55 (2,984,000 ac.)
State parks: 92 (202,205 ac.)
Total revenue (Fiscal 1979): $4,514,521,000
Total expenditures (Fiscal 1979): $4,246,730,000

Following the visits of several French explorers, fur traders, and missionaries, including Marquette and Jolliet and La Salle, the region was claimed for Louis XIV by Daniel Greysolon, Sieur Duluth, in 1679.

The U.S. acquired eastern Minnesota from Great Britain after the Revolutionary War and 20 years later bought the western part from France in the Louisiana Purchase of 1803. Much of the region was explored by U.S. Army Lt. Zebulon M. Pike before cession of the northern strip of Minnesota bordering Canada by Britain in 1818.

The state is rich in natural resources. A few square miles of land in the north in the Mesabi, Cuyuna, and Vermillion ranges, produce more than 60% of the nation's iron ore. The state's farms rank high in yields of corn, wheat, rye, alfalfa, and sugar beets. Other leading farm products include butter, eggs, milk, potatoes, green peas, barley, and livestock.

Minnesota's factory production includes non-electrical machinery, fabricated metals, flour-mill products, plastics, electronic computers, scientific instruments, and processed foods.

Minneapolis is the trade center of the Northwest; St. Paul is the nation's biggest publisher of calendars and law books. These "twin cities" are the nation's third largest trucking center. Duluth has the nation's largest inland harbor and now handles a significant amount of foreign trade. Rochester is the home of the Mayo Clinic, an internationally famous medical center.

Today, tourism is a major revenue producer in Minnesota, with fishing, hunting, water sports, and winter sports bringing in millions of visitors each year.

Among the most popular attractions are the St. Paul Winter Carnival; the Tyrone Guthrie Theatre, the Institute of Arts, Walker Art Center, and Minnehaha Park, in Minneapolis; Voyageurs National Park; and North Shore Drive.

MISSISSIPPI

Capital: Jackson
Governor: William F. Winter, D (to Jan. 1984)
Lieut. Governor: Brad Dye, D (to Jan. 1984)
Secy. of State: Edwin Lloyd Pittman, D (to Jan. 1984)
Treasurer: John L. Dale, D (to Jan. 1984)
Atty. General: William A. (Bill) Allain (to Jan. 1984)
Organized as Territory: April 7, 1798
Entered Union & (rank): Dec. 10, 1817 (20)
Present constitution adopted: 1890
Motto: *Virtute es armis* (By valor and arms)
State flower: Flower or bloom of the magnolia or evergreen magnolia (1952)
State tree: Magnolia (1938)
State bird: Mockingbird (1944)
State song: "Go, Mississippi" (1962)
Nickname: Magnolia State
Origin of name: From an Indian word meaning "Father of Waters"
1970 population & (rank): 2,216,912 (29)
1979 prov. population & (rank): 2,406,000 (31)
1970 land area & (rank): 47,296 sq mi. (122,497 sq km) (31)
Geographic center: In Leake Co., 9 mi. WNW of Carthage
Number of counties: 82
Largest cities (1977 est.): Jackson, 190,542; Meridian, 45,215; Biloxi, 44,439; Gulfport, 44,375; Greenville, 43,068; Hattiesburg, 41,131; Pascagoula, 31,506
State forests: 1 (1,760 ac.)
State parks: 27 (16,763 ac.)
State general and special revenue (1980): $919,558,778
State general and special expenditure (1980): $976,989,649

First explored for Spain by Hernando de Soto who discovered the Mississippi River in 1540, the region was later claimed by France. In 1699, a French group under Sieur d'Iberville established the first permanent settlement near present-day Biloxi.

Great Britain took over the area in 1763 after the French and Indian War, ceding it to the U.S. in 1783 after the Revolution. Spain did not relinquish its claims until 1798, and in 1810 the U.S. annexed West Florida from Spain, including what is now southern Mississippi.

Mississippi, the stronghold of the Old South, has until the past decade been one of the least industrialized states, with more than half its population making a living from the soil. However, a recent industrialization program has attracted manufacturing industries such as lumber, furniture, paper, food processing, apparel, chemicals, transportation equipment, and machinery.

Cotton, nevertheless, is still king with the state ranking second to Texas in cotton production, though soybeans have become Mississippi's largest crop. Other important farm products are corn, peanuts, pecans, rice, sugarcane, sweet potatoes, and hay. Poultry and eggs are also important.

The state abounds in historical landmarks and is the home of the Vicksburg National Military Park where visitors may see the remains of forts, trenches, and other military relics used in the 1863 Union-army siege of the city. Other National Park Service areas are Brices Cross Roads National Battlefield Site, Tupelo National Battlefield, and part of Natchez Trace National Parkway. Pre-Civil War mansions are the special pride of Natchez, Oxford, Hattiesburg, and Jackson.

MISSOURI

Capital: Jefferson City
Governor: Joseph P. Teasdale, D (to Jan. 1981)
Lieut. Governor: William C. Phelps, R (to Jan. 1981)
Secy. of State: James C. Kirkpatrick, D (to Jan. 1981)
Auditor: James F. Antonio, R (to Jan. 1983)
Treasurer: James I. Spainhower, D (to Jan. 1981)
Atty. General: John D. Ashcroft, R (to Jan. 1981)
Organized as territory: June 4, 1812
Entered Union & (rank): Aug. 10, 1821 (24)
Present constitution adopted: 1945
Motto: *Salus populi suprema lex esto* (The welfare of the people shall be the supreme law)
State flower: Hawthorn (1923)
State bird: Bluebird (1927)
State colors: Red, white, and blue (1913)
State song: "Missouri Waltz" (1949)
State rock: Mozarkite (1967)
State mineral: Galena (1967)
Nickname: Show-me State
Origin of name: Named after a tribe called Missouri Indians. "Missouri" means "town of the large canoes."
1970 population & (rank): 4,677,399 (13)
1979 prov. population & (rank): 4,868,000 (15)
1970 land area & (rank): 68,995 sq mi. (178,697 sq km) (18)
Geographic center: In Miller Co., 20 mi. SW of Jefferson City
Number of counties: 114, plus 1 independent city
Largest cities (1977 est.): St. Louis, 517,671; Kansas City, 458,573; Springfield, 134,974; Independence, 111,575; St. Joseph, 77,804; Florissant, 70,639; Columbia, 64,612
State forests and Tower sites: 131 (230,000 ac.)
State parks: 65 (96,012 ac.)[1]
State cash receipts (1979): $3,147,311,154
State general expenditure (1979): $3,020,312,747

De Soto visited the Missouri area in 1541. France's claim to the entire region was based on La Salle's travels in 1682. French fur traders established Ste. Genevieve in 1735 and St. Louis was first settled in 1764.

The U.S. gained Missouri from France as part of the Louisiana Purchase in 1803, and the territory was admitted as a state following the Missouri Compromise of 1820. Throughout the pre-Civil War period and during the war, Missourians were sharply divided in their opinions about slavery and in their allegiances, supplying both Union and Confederate forces with troops. However, the state itself remained in the Union.

Historically, Missouri played a leading role as a gateway to the West, St. Joseph being the eastern starting point of the Pony Express, while the much-traveled Santa Fe and Oregon Trails began in Independence. Now a popular vacationland, Missouri has 11 major lakes and numerous fishing streams, springs, and caves. Bagnell Dam, across the Osage

1. Includes 19 historic sites and 1 archaeological site.

River in the Ozarks, completed in 1931, created one of the largest man-made lakes in the world, covering 65,000 acres of surface area.

Manufacturing, paced by the aerospace industry, provides more income and jobs than any other segment of the economy. Missouri is also a leading producer of transportation equipment, shoes, lead, and beer. Among the major crops are corn, soybeans, wheat, oats, barley, potatoes, tobacco, and cotton.

Points of interest include Mark Twain's boyhood home and Mark Twain Cave (Hannibal), the Harry S. Truman Library and Museum (Independence), the house where Jesse James was killed in St. Joseph, Jefferson National Expansion Memorial (St. Louis), and the Ozark National Scenic Riverway.

MONTANA

Capital: Helena
Governor: Thomas L. Judge, D (to Jan. 1981)
Lieut. Governor: Theodore Schwinden, D (to Jan. 1981)
Secy. of State: Frank Murray, D (to Jan. 1981)
Auditor: E. V. "Sonny" Omholt, R (to Jan. 1981)
Atty. General: Michael Greely, D (to Jan. 1981)
Organized as territory: May 26, 1864
Entered Union & (rank): Nov. 8, 1889 (41)
Present constitution adopted: 1972
Motto: *Oro y plata* (Gold and silver)
State flower: Bitterroot (1895)
State tree: Ponderosa pine (1949)
State stones: Sapphire and agate (1969)
State bird: Western meadow lark (1931)
State song: "Montana" (1945)
Nickname: Treasure State
Origin of name: Chosen from Latin dictionary by J. M. Ashley. It is a Latinized Spanish word.
1970 population & (rank): 694,409 (43)
1979 prov. population & (rank): 786,000 (43)
1970 land area & (rank): 145,587 sq mi. (377,070 sq km) (4)
Geographic center: In Fergus Co., 12 mi. W of Lewistown
Number of counties: 56, plus small part of Yellowstone National Park
Largest cities (1977 est.): Billings, 73,303; Great Falls, 60,334; Butte–Silver Bow, 39,704; Missoula, 29,221; Helena, 28,142; Bozeman, 20,309; Kalispell, 15,652
State forests: 7 (214,000 ac.)
State parks and recreation areas: 68 (18,273 ac.)
State general revenue (1978–79): $211,365,216
State general expenditure (1978–79): $192,979,702

First explored for France by François and Louis-Joseph Verendrye in the early 1740s, much of the region was acquired by the U.S. from France as part of the Louisiana Purchase in 1803. Before western Montana was obtained from Great Britain in the Oregon Treaty of 1846, American trading posts and forts had been established in the territory.

The major Indian wars (1867–1877) included the famous 1876 Battle of the Little Big Horn, better known as "Custer's Last Stand," in which Cheyennes and Sioux killed George A. Custer and more than 200 of his men in southeastern Montana.

Much of Montana's early history was concerned with mining with copper, lead, zinc, silver, coal, and oil as principal products.

Butte, sitting on the "richest hill in the world," is the center of the area that once supplied half of the U.S. copper.

Fields of grain cover much of Montana's plains; it ranks high among the states in wheat and barley, with rye, oats, flaxseed, sugar beets, and potatoes other important crops. Sheep and cattle raising make significant contributions to the state's economy.

Tourist attractions include hunting, fishing, skiing, and dude ranching. Glacier National Park, on the Continental Divide, is a scenic and vacation wonderland with 60 glaciers, 200 lakes, and many streams with good trout fishing.

Other major points of interest include the Custer Battlefield National Monument, Virginia City, Yellowstone National Park, Museum of the Plains Indians at Browning, and the Fort Union Trading Post and Grant-Kohr's Ranch National Historic Sites.

NEBRASKA

Capital: Lincoln
Governor: Charles Thone, R (to Jan. 1983)
Lieut. Governor: Roland Luedtke, R (to Jan. 1983)
Secy. of State: Allen J. Beermann, R (to Jan. 1983)
Atty. General: Paul L. Douglas, R (to Jan. 1983)
Auditor: Ray A. C. Johnson, R (to Jan. 1983)
Treasurer: Frank Marsh, R (to Jan. 1983)
Organized as territory: May 30, 1854
Entered Union & (rank): March 1, 1867 (37)
Present constitution adopted: Nov. 1, 1875 (extensively amended 1919–20)
Motto: Equality before the law
State flower: Goldenrod (1895)
State tree: Cottonwood (1972)
State bird: Western meadow lark (1929)
State insect: Honeybee
State gem stone: Blue agate (1967)
State rock: Prairie agate (1967)
State fossil: Mammoth (1967)
State song: "Beautiful Nebraska" (1967)
Nicknames: Cornhusker State; Beef State; Tree Planters State
Origin of name: From an Oto Indian word meaning "flat water"
1970 population & (rank): 1,483,791 (35)
1979 prov. population & (rank): 1,574,000 (35)
1970 land area & (rank): 76,483 sq mi. (198,091 sq km) (15)
Geographic center: In Custer Co., 10 mi. NW of Broken Bow
Number of counties: 93
Largest cities (1977 est.): Omaha, 365,7H; Lincoln, 163,937; Grand Island, 34,161; North Platte, 24,238; Fremont, 23,595; Bellevue, 23,453; Hastings, 22,440
State forests: None
State parks: 93 areas, 4 categories, 5 major areas
State general revenue (1978–79): $631,253,927
State general expenditure (1978–79): $598,762,302

French fur traders first visited Nebraska in the early 1700s. Part of the Louisiana Purchase in 1803, Nebraska was explored by Lewis and Clark in 1804–06.

Robert Stuart pioneered the Oregon Trail across Nebraska in 1812–13 and the first permanent settlement was established at Bellevue in 1823. Western Nebraska was acquired by treaty following the Mexican War in 1848. The Union Pacific began its transcontinental railroad at Omaha in 1865. In 1937, Nebraska became the only state in the Union to have a unicameral (one-house) legislature. Members are elected to it without party designation.

Nebraska is a leading grain-producer with bumper crops of rye, corn, and wheat. More varieties of grass, valuable for forage, grow in this state than in any other in the nation.

The state's sizable cattle and hog industries make Omaha with its surrounding area the nation's largest meat-packing center and the second-largest cattle market in the world.

Manufacturing has become diversified in Nebraska, strengthening the state's economic base. Firms making electronic components, auto accessories, pharmaceuticals, and mobile homes have joined such older industries as clothing, farm machinery, chemicals, and transportation equipment. Oil was discovered in 1939 and natural gas in 1949.

Among the principal attractions are Agate Fossil Beds, Homestead, and Scotts Bluff National Monuments; Chimney Rock National Historic Site; a recreated pioneer village at Minden; the Union stockyards in Omaha; the Stuhr Museum of the Prairie Pioneer with 57 original 19th-century buildings near Grand Island; and the Sheldon Memorial Art Gallery at the University of Nebraska in Lincoln.

NEVADA

Capital: Carson City
Governor: Robert F. List, R (to Jan. 1983)
Lieut. Governor: Myron E. Leavitt, D (to Jan. 1983)
Secy. of State: Wm. D. Swackhamer, D (to Jan. 1983)
State Treasurer: Stan Colton, D (to Jan. 1983)
Controller: Wilson McGowan, R (to Jan. 1983)
Atty. General: Richard H. Bryan, D (to Jan. 1983)
Organized as territory: March 2, 1861
Entered Union & (rank): Oct. 31, 1864 (36)
Present constitution adopted: 1864
Motto: All for Our Country
State flower: Sagebrush (1967)
State tree: Single-leaf pinon (1953)
State bird: Mountain bluebird (1967)
State animal: Desert bighorn sheep (1973)
State colors: Silver and blue (unofficial)
State song: "Home Means Nevada" (1933)
Nicknames: Sagebrush State; Silver State; Battle-born State
Origin of name: Spanish: "snowcapped"
1970 population & (rank): 488,738 (47)
1979 prov. population & (rank): 702,000 (44)
1970 land area & (rank): 109,889 sq mi. (284,613 sq km) (7)
Geographic center: In Lander Co., 26 mi. SE of Austin
Number of counties: 16, plus 1 independent city
Largest cities (1977 est.): Las Vegas, 161,086; Reno, 82,541; North Las Vegas, 40,217; Sparks, 33,785; Carson City, 27,674; Henderson, 20,054; Elko, 8,944
State forests: None
State parks: 13 (104,255 ac., including leased lands)
General fund revenue (1978–79): $295,818,109
General fund expenditure (1978–79): $241,121,445

Trappers and traders, including Jedediah Smith and Peter Skene Ogden, entered the Nevada area in the 1820s. In 1843–45, John C. Fremont and Kit Carson explored the Great Basin and Sierra Nevada.

In 1848 following the Mexican War, the U.S. obtained the region and the first permanent settlement was a Mormon trading post near present-day Genoa.

The driest state in the nation with an average annual rainfall of only 3.73 inches, much of Nevada is uninhabited, sagebrush-covered desert.

Nevada was made famous by the discovery of the fabulous Comstock Lode in 1859 and its mines have produced large quantities of gold, silver, copper, lead, zinc, mercury, barite, and tungsten. Oil was discovered in 1954. Copper now far exceeds all other minerals in value of production.

In 1931, the state created two industries, divorce and gambling. For many years, Reno and Las Vegas were the "divorce capitals of the nation." More liberal divorce laws in many states have ended this distinction, but Nevada is the gambling and entertainment capital of the U.S. State gambling taxes account for 45% of tax revenues. Although Nevada leads the nation in per capita gambling revenue, it ranks only fourth in total gambling revenue.

Near Las Vegas, on the Colorado River, stands Hoover Dam, which impounds the waters of Lake Mead, one of the world's largest artificial lakes.

The state's agricultural crop consists mainly of hay, alfalfa seed, barley, and wheat.

Nevada manufactures gaming devices, chemicals, forest products, suntan lotion, and stone-clay-glass products.

Major resort areas flourish in Lake Tahoe, Reno, and Las Vegas. Recreation areas include those at Pyramid Lake, Lake Tahoe, and Lake Mead and Lake Mohave, both in Lake Mead National Recreation Area. Among the other attractions are Hoover Dam, Virginia City, and Lehman Caves National Monument.

NEW HAMPSHIRE

Capital: Concord
Governor: Hugh Gallen, D (to Jan. 1981)
Secy. of State: William M. Gardner, D (to Jan. 1981)
Comptroller: Arthur H. Fowler
Atty. General: Thomas Rath
Entered Union & (rank): June 21, 1788 (9)
Present constitution adopted: 1784
Motto: Live free or die
State flower: Purple lilac (1919)
State tree: White birch (1947)
State bird: Purple finch (1957)
State songs: "Old New Hampshire" (1949) and "New Hampshire, My New Hampshire" (1963)
Nickname: Granite State
Origin of name: From the English county of Hampshire
1970 population & (rank): 737,681 (41)
1979 prov. population & (rank): 887,000 (42)
1970 land area & (rank): 9,027 sq mi. (23,380 sq km) (44)
Geographic center: In Belknap Co., 3 mi. E of Ashland
Number of counties: 10
Largest cities (1977 est.): Manchester, 85,119; Nashua, 64,273; Concord, 28,980; Portsmouth, 26,417; Dover, 21,685; Keene, 21,167; Rochester, 20,210
State forests & parks: 175 (96,975 ac.)
State revenue (1979): $555,085,804
State expenditure (1979): $552,020,068

Under an English land grant, Capt. John Smith sent settlers to establish a fishing colony at the mouth of the Piscataqua River, near present-day Rye and Dover, in 1623. Capt. John Mason, who participated in the founding of Portsmouth in 1630, gave New Hampshire its name.

After a 38-year period of union with Massachusetts, New Hampshire was made a separate royal colony in 1679. As leaders in the revolutionary cause, New Hampshire delegates received the honor of being the first to vote for the Declaration of Independence on July 4, 1776. New Hampshire is the only state that ever played host at the formal conclusion of a foreign war when, in 1905, Portsmouth was the scene of the treaty ending the Russo-Japanese War.

Abundant water power early turned New Hampshire into an industrial state and manufacturing is the principal source of income in the state. The most important industrial products are leather goods, electrical and other machinery, textiles, and pulp and paper products.

Dairy and poultry farming and growing fruit, truck vegetables, corn, potatoes, and hay are the major agricultural pursuits.

Tourism, because of New Hampshire's scenic and recreational resources, now brings over $400 million into the state annually.

Vacation attractions include Lake Winnipesaukee, largest of 1,300 lakes and ponds; the 724,000-acre White Mountain National Forest; Daniel Webster's birthplace near Franklin; Strawberry Banke, restored building of the original settlement at Portsmouth; and the famous "Old Man of the Mountain" granite head profile, the state's official emblem, at Franconia.

NEW JERSEY

Capital: Trenton
Governor: Brendan T. Byrne, D (to Jan. 1982)
Secy. of State: Donald Lan (to Jan. 1982) (apptd. by Governor)
Treasurer: Clifford A. Goldman, D (to Jan. 1982) (apptd. by Governor)
Atty. General: John J. Degnan, D. (to Jan. 1982)
Entered Union & (rank): Dec. 18, 1787 (3)
Present constitution adopted: 1947
Motto: Liberty and prosperity
State flower: Purple violet (1913)
State bird: Eastern goldfinch (1935)
State insect: Honeybee
State tree: Red oak (1950)
State animal: Horse (1977)
State colors: Buff and blue (1965)
State song: None
Nickname: Garden State
Origin of name: From the Channel Isle of Jersey
1970 population & (rank): 7,168,164 (8)
1979 prov. population & (rank): 7,332,000 (9)
1970 land area & (rank): 7,521 sq mi. (19,479 sq km) (46)
Geographic center: In Mercer Co., 5 mi. SE of Trenton
Number of counties: 21
Largest cities (1977 est.): Newark, 324,138; Jersey City, 232,137; Paterson, 152,414; Elizabeth, 103,479; Trenton, 96,951; Camden, 88,785; Clifton, 76,838
State forests: 11
State parks: 40 (73,483 ac.)
State general revenue (1978–79): $7,495,787,214
State appropriations (1978–79): $7,500,171,146

New Jersey's early colonial history was involved with that of New York (New Netherlands), of which it was a part. One year after the Dutch surrender to England in 1664, New Jersey was organized as an English colony under Gov. Philip Carteret.

In the late 1600s the colony was divided between Carteret and William Penn; later it would be administered by the royal governor of New York. Finally, in 1738, New Jersey was separated from New York under its own royal governor, Lewis Morris.

Because of its key location between New York City and Philadelphia, New Jersey saw much fighting during the American Revolution.

Today, New Jersey, an area of wide industrial diversification, is known as the Crossroads of the East. Products from over 15,000 factories can be delivered overnight to almost 60 million people, representing 12 states and the District of Columbia. The greatest single industry is chemicals and New Jersey is one of the foremost research centers in the world. Many large oil refineries are located in northern New Jersey and other important manufactures are pharmaceuticals, instruments, machinery, electrical goods, and apparel.

Of the total land area, 43% is forested and about 24% is devoted to agriculture. The state ranks high in production of almost all garden vegetables. Tomatoes, asparagus, corn, and blueberries are important crops, and poultry farming and dairying make significant contributions to the state's economy.

Tourism is the second largest industry in New Jersey. The state has numerous resort areas on 127 miles of Atlantic coastline. In 1977, New Jersey voters approved legislation allowing legalized casino gambling in Atlantic City. Points of interest include the Walt Whitman House in Camden, the Delaware Water Gap, the Edison National Historic Site in West Orange, and Princeton University.

NEW MEXICO

Capital: Santa Fe
Governor: Bruce King, D (to Jan. 1983)
Lieut. Governor: Roberto A. Mondeagon, D (to Jan. 1983)
Secy. of State: Shirley Hooper, D (to Jan. 1983)
Atty. General: Jeff Bingaman, D (to Jan. 1983)
State Auditor: Alvino E. Castillo, D (to Jan. 1983)
State Treasurer: Jan Alan Hartke, D (to Jan. 1983)
Commissioner of Public Lands: Alex J. Armijo, D (to Jan. 1983)
Organized as territory: Sept. 9, 1850
Entered Union & (rank): Jan. 6, 1912 (47)
Present constitution adopted: 1911
Motto: *Crescit eundo* (It grows as it goes)
State flower: Yucca (1927)
State tree: Pinon (1949)
State animal: Black bear (1963)
State bird: Roadrunner (1949)
State fish: Cutthroat trout (1955)
State vegetables: Chile and frijol (1965)
State gem: Turquoise (1967)
State colors: Red and yellow of old Spain (1925)
State song: "O Fair New Mexico" (1917)
Spanish language state song: "Asi Es Nuevo Mejico" (1971)
Nicknames: Land of Enchantment; Sunshine State
Origin of name: From the country of Mexico
1970 population & (rank): 1,016,000 (37)
1979 prov. population & (rank): 1,241,000 (37)
1970 land area & (rank): 121,412 sq mi. (314,457 sq km) (5)
Geographic center: In Torrance Co., 12 mi. SSW of Willard
Number of counties: 32
Largest cities (1977 est.): Albuquerque, 291,187; Santa Fe, 46,855; Las Cruces, 41,172; Roswell, 39,130; Farmington, 30,876; Clovis, 30,257; Hobbs, 28,648
State-owned forested land: 933,000 ac.
State parks: 29 (105,012 ac.)
State general revenue (1979 est.): $1,865,000,000
State general expenditure (1979 est.): $1,316,000,000

Francisco Vásquez de Coronado, Spanish explorer searching for gold, traveled the region that became New Mexico in 1540–42. In 1598 the first Spanish settlement was established on the Rio Grande River by Juan de Onate and in 1610 Santa Fe was founded and made the capital of New Mexico.

The U.S. acquired most of New Mexico in 1848, as a result of the Mexican War, and the remainder in the 1853 Gadsden Purchase. Union troops captured the territory from the Confederates during the Civil War. With the surrender of Geronimo in 1886, the Apache Wars and most of the Indian troubles in the area were ended.

Since 1945, New Mexico has been a leader in energy research and development with extensive experiments conducted at Los Alamos Scientific Laboratory and Sandia Laboratories in the nuclear, solar, and geothermal areas.

Minerals are the state's richest natural resource and New Mexico leads the U.S. in output of uranium and potassium salts. Petroleum, natural gas, copper, gold, silver, zinc, lead, and molybdenum also contribute heavily to the state's income.

The principal manufacturing industries include food products, chemicals, transportation equipment, lumber, electrical machinery, and stone-clay-glass products. More than two thirds of New Mexico's farm income comes from livestock products, especially sheep. Cotton, pecans, and sorghum are the most important field crops. Corn, peanuts, beans, onions, and lettuce are also grown.

Tourist attractions in New Mexico include the Carlsbad Caverns National Park, Inscription Rock at El Morro National Monument, the ruins at Fort Union, Billy the Kid mementos at Lincoln, and the White Sands and Gila Cliff Dwellings National Monuments.

NEW YORK

Capital: Albany
Governor: Hugh L. Carey, D (to Jan. 1983)
Lieut. Governor: Mario M. Cuomo, D (to Jan. 1983)
Secy. of State: Basil A. Paterson, D (to Jan. 1983)
Comptroller: Edward V. Regan, R (to Jan. 1983)
Atty. General: Robert Abrams, D (to Jan. 1983)
Entered Union & (rank): July 26, 1788 (11)
Present constitution adopted: 1777 (last revised 1938)
Motto: *Excelsior* (Ever upward)
State animal: Beaver (1975)
State fish: Brook trout (1975)
State gem: Garnet (1969)
State flower: Rose (1955)
State tree: Sugar maple (1956)
State bird: Bluebird
State song: None
Nickname: Empire State
Origin of name: In honor of the English Duke of York
1970 population & (rank): 18,241,266 (2)
1979 prov. population & (rank): 17,649,000 (2)
1970 land area & (rank): 47,831 sq mi. (123,882 sq km) (30)
Geographic center: In Madison Co., 12 mi. S of Oneida and 26 mi. SW of Utica
Number of counties: 62
Largest cities (1977 est.): New York, 7,297,787; Buffalo, 390,065; Rochester, 256,285; Yonkers, 189,139; Syracuse, 177,564; Albany, 107,798; Utica, 80,103
State forest preserves: Adirondacks, 2,500,000 ac., Catskills, 250,000 ac.
State parks: 145 (more than 220,000 ac.)
State general fund income (1980–81): $14,965,000,000
State general fund outgo (1980–81): $14,965,000,000

Giovanni da Verrazano, Italian-born navigator sailing for France, discovered New York Bay in 1524. Henry Hudson, an Englishman employed by the Dutch, reached the bay and sailed up the river now bearing his name in 1609, the same year that northern New York was explored and claimed for France by Samuel de Champlain.

In 1624 the first permanent Dutch settlement was established at Fort Orange (now Albany); one year later Peter Minuit is said to have purchased Manhattan Island from the Indians for trinkets worth about $24 and founded the Dutch colony of New Amsterdam (now New York City), which was surrendered to the English in 1664.

For a short time, New York City was the U.S. capital and George Washington was inaugurated there as first President on April 30, 1789.

New York's extremely rapid commercial growth may be partly attributed to Governor De Witt Clinton, who pushed through the construction of the Erie Canal (Buffalo to Albany), which was opened in 1825. Today, the 559-mile Governor Thomas E. Dewey Thruway connects New York City with Buffalo and with Connecticut, Massachusetts, and Pennsylvania express highways. Two toll-free superhighways, the Adirondack Northway (linking Albany with the Canadian border) and the North-South-Expressway (crossing central New York from the Pennsylvania border to the Thousand Islands) have been opened.

New York, with the great metropolis of New York City, is the spectacular nerve center of the nation. It leads in manufacturing, foreign trade, commercial and financial transactions, book and magazine publishing, and theatrical production.

New York City is not only a national but an international leader. A leading seaport, its John F. Kennedy International Airport is one of the busiest airports in the world. The largest manufacturing center in the country, it had, in 1972, over 24,000 manufacturing establishments employing 757,300 persons and reported $11.6 billion of value added by manufacture. The apparel industry is the city's largest manufacturing employer, with printing and publishing second.

Nearly all the rest of the state's manufacturing is done on Long Island, along the Hudson River north to Albany and through the Mohawk Valley, Central New York, and Southern Tier regions to Buffalo. The St. Lawrence seaway and power projects have opened the North Country to industrial expansion and have given the state a second seacoast. In 1962, the Niagara power development was completed, giving the state the largest hydroelectric installation in the free world.

The state is the nation's manufacturing leader, with 1,711,500 employees and second with $33.6 billion in value added by manufacture in 1973. The principal industries are machinery, printing and publishing, instruments, apparel, and food.

The convention and tourist business is one of the state's most important sources of income.

New York farms are famous for dairying, truck gardening, and the raising of potatoes, onions, cabbage, fruits, and poultry. The state is a leading wine producer.

Among the major points of interest are Castle Clinton, Fort Stanwix, and Statue of Liberty National Monuments; Niagara Falls; U.S. Military Academy at West Point; National Historic Sites that include homes of Franklin D. Roosevelt at Hyde Park and Theodore Roosevelt in Oyster Bay and New York City; National Memorials, including

Grant's Tomb and Federal Hall in New York City; Fort Ticonderoga; the Baseball Hall of Fame in Cooperstown; and the United Nations, skyscrapers, museums, theaters, and parks in New York City.

NORTH CAROLINA

Capital: Raleigh
Governor: James B. Hunt, Jr., D (to Jan. 1981)
Lieut. Governor: James C. Greene (to Jan. 1981)
Secy. of State: Thad Eure, D (to Jan. 1981)
Treasurer: Harlan E. Boyles (to Jan. 1981)
Auditor: Henry L. Bridges, D (to Jan. 1981)
Atty. General: Rufus Edmisten, D (to Jan. 1981)
Entered Union & (rank): Nov. 21, 1789 (12)
Present constitution adopted: 1971
Motto: *Esse quam videri* (To be rather than to seem)
State flower: Dogwood (1941)
State tree: Pine (1963)
State bird: Cardinal (1943)
State mammal: Gray Squirrel (1969)
State insect: Honeybee (1973)
State Reptile: Turtle (1979)
State gem stone: Emerald (1973)
State shell: Scotch bonnet (1965)
State song: "The Old North State" (1927)
State colors: Red and blue (1945)
Nickname: Tar Heel State
Origin of name: In honor of Charles I of England
1970 population & (rank): 5,082,059 (12)
1979 prov. population & (rank): 5,606,000 (11)
1970 land area & (rank): 48,798 sq mi. (126,387 sq km) (29)
Geographic center: In Chatham Co., 10 mi. NW of Sanford
Number of counties: 100
Largest cities (1977 est.): Charlotte, 295,685; Greensboro, 160,562; Winston–Salem, 139,688; Raleigh, 138,005; Durham, 103,686; High Point, 68,343
State forests: 1
State parks: 26 (115,051 ac.)
State revenues (1978–79): $2,901,652,741[1]
State expenditure (1978–79): $3,040,856,479[2]

English colonists, sent by Sir Walter Raleigh, unsuccessfully attempted to settle Roanoke Island in 1585 and 1587. Virginia Dare, born there in 1587, was the first child of English parentage born in America.

In 1653 the first permanent settlements were established by English colonists from Virginia near the Roanoke and Chowan Rivers.

The region was established as an English proprietary colony in 1663–65 and its early history was the scene of Culpepper's Rebellion (1677), the Quaker-led Cary Rebellion of 1708, the Tuscarora Indian War in 1711–13, and many pirate raids.

During the American Revolution, there was relatively little fighting within the state, but many North Carolinians saw action elsewhere. Despite considerable pro-Union, anti-slavery sentiment, North Carolina joined the Confederacy.

North Carolina is the nation's largest furniture, tobacco, brick, and textile producer. It holds second place in the Southeast in population and first place in the value of its industrial and agricultural production. This production is highly diversified, with metalworking, chemicals, and paper constituting enormous industries. Tobacco, corn, cotton, hay, peanuts, and truck and vegetable crops are of major importance. It is the country's leading producer of mica and lithium.

Tourism is also important, with travelers and vacationers spending more than $1 billion annually in North Carolina. Sports include year-round golfing, skiing at mountain resorts, both fresh and salt water fishing, and hunting.

Among the major attractions are the Great Smoky Mountains, the Blue Ridge National Parkway, the Cape Hatteras and Cape Lookout National Seashores, the Wright Brothers National Memorial at Kitty Hawk, Guilford Courthouse and Moores Creek National Military Parks, Carl Sandburg's home near Hendersonville, and the Old Salem Restoration in Winston–Salem.

1. Excludes all Federal revenues and expenditures. 2. All expenditures: operating, and capital improvements.

NORTH DAKOTA

Capital: Bismarck
Governor: Arthur A. Link, D (to Jan. 1981)
Lieut. Governor: Wayne Sanstead, D (to Jan. 1981)
Secy. of State: Ben Meier, R (to Jan. 1981)
Auditor: Robert W. Peterson, R (to Jan. 1981)
Atty. General: Allen I. Olson, R (to Jan. 1981)
Organized as territory: March 2, 1861
Entered Union & (rank): Nov. 2, 1889 (39)
Present constitution adopted: 1889
Motto: Liberty and union, now and forever: one and inseparable
State tree: American Elm (1947)
State bird: Western meadow lark (1947)
State song: "North Dakota Hymn" (1947)
Nickname: Sioux State; Flickertail State
Origin of name: From the Dakotah tribe, meaning "allies"
1970 population & (rank): 617,761 (45)
1979 prov. population & (rank): 657,000 (46)
1970 land area & (rank): 69,273 sq mi (179,417 sq km) (17)
Geographic center: In Sheridan Co., 5 mi. SW of McClusky
Number of counties: 53
Largest cities (1977 est.): Fargo, 57,394; Grand Forks, 42,959; Bismarck, 40,911; Minot, 32,713; Jamestown, 15,288; Mandan, 13,979; Dickinson, 12,603
State forests: None
State parks: 14 (14,922.6 ac.)
Total state collections (1979): $671,634,204
Total state disbursements (1979): $535,197,729

North Dakota was explored in 1738–40 by French Canadians led by Vérendrye. In 1803, the U.S. acquired most of North Dakota from France in the Louisiana Purchase. Lewis and Clark explored the region in 1804–06 and the first settlements were made at Pembina in 1812 by Scottish and Irish families while this area was still in dispute between the U.S. and Great Britian.

In 1818, the U.S. obtained the northeastern part of North Dakota by treaty with Great Britain and took possession of Pembina in 1823.

North Dakota is the most rural of all the states, with farms covering more than 90% of the land. Only Kansas produces more wheat and the state's coal and oil reserves are plentiful.

Other agricultural products include barley, rye, oats and flaxseed, sugar beets, and hay; beef cattle, sheep, and hogs are also important to the state's economy.

Recently, manufacturing industries have grown, especially food processing and farm equipment. The state also produces natural gas, lignite, salt, clay, sand, and gravel.

The Garrison Dam on the Missouri River provides extensive irrigation and produces 400,000 kilowatts of electricity for the Missouri Basin areas.

Known for its waterfowl, grouse, and deer hunting and bass, trout, and northern pike fishing, North Dakota has 20 state parks and recreation areas. Points of interest include the International Peace Garden near Dunseith, Fort Union Trading Post National Historic Site, the State Capitol at Bismarck, the Badlands, and Fort Lincoln, now a state park, from which Gen. George Custer set out on his last campaign in 1876.

OHIO

Capital: Columbus
Governor: James A. Rhodes, R (to Jan. 1983)
Lieut. Governor: (Vacant)
Secy. of State: Anthony J. Celebrezze, Jr., R (to Jan. 1983)
Auditor: Thomas E. Ferguson (to Jan. 1983)
Treasurer: Gertrude W. Donahey, D (to Jan. 1983)
Atty. General: William J. Brown, D (to Jan. 1983)
Entered Union & (rank): March 1, 1803 (17)
Present constitution adopted: 1851
Motto: With God, all things are possible
State flower: Scarlet carnation (1904)
State tree: Buckeye (1953)
State bird: Cardinal (1933)
State insect: Ladybug (1975)
State gem stone: Flint (1965)
State song: "Beautiful Ohio"
State drink: Tomato juice (1965)
Nickname: Buckeye State
Origin of name: From an Iroquoian word meaning "great river"
1970 population & (rank): 10,652,017 (6)
1979 prov. population & (rank): 10,731,000 (6)
1970 land area & (rank): 40,975 sq mi. (106,125 sq km) (35)
Geographic center: In Delaware Co., 25 mi. NNE of Columbus
Number of counties: 88
Largest cities (1977 est.): Cleveland, 609,187; Columbus, 532,339; Cincinnati, 403,363; Toledo, 358,677; Akron, 244,265; Dayton, 197,744; Youngstown, 129,875
State forests: 20 (172,744 ac.)
State parks: 70 (179,794 ac.)
State actual revenue (1978–79): $7,671,113,436
State actual expenditure (1978–79): $7,637,606,421

First explored for France by La Salle in 1669, the Ohio region became British property after the French and Indian War. Ohio was acquired by the U.S. after the Revolutionary War in 1783 and, in 1788, the first permanent settlement was established at Marietta, capital of the Northwest Territory.

The 1790s saw severe fighting with the Indians in Ohio; a major battle was won by Maj. Gen. Anthony Wayne at Fallen Timbers in 1794. In the War of 1812, Commodore Oliver H. Perry defeated the British in the Battle of Lake Erie on Sept. 10, 1813.

Ohio is one of the nation's industrial leaders, ranking third in the value of manufactured products. Important manufacturing centers are located in or near Ohio's major cities. Akron is known for rubber; Canton for roller bearings; Cincinnati for jet engines and machine tools; Cleveland for auto assembly and parts, refining, and steel; Dayton for office machines, refrigeration, and heating and auto equipment; Youngstown and Steubenville for steel; and Toledo for glass and auto parts.

The state's thousands of factories almost overshadow its importance in agriculture and mining. Its fertile soil produces soybeans, corn, oats, grapes, and clover. More than half of Ohio's farm receipts come from dairying and sheep and hog raising. Ohio is the top state in lime production and among the leaders in coal, clay, salt, sand, and gravel. Petroleum, gypsum, cement, and natural gas are also important.

Tourism is a valuable revenue producer, bringing in over $3 billion annually. Attractions include the Indian burial grounds at Mound City Group National Monument, Perry's Victory International Peace Memorial, the Pro Football Hall of Fame at Canton, and the homes of Presidents Grant, Taft, Hayes, Harding, and Garfield.

OKLAHOMA

Capital: Oklahoma City
Governor: George P. Nigh, D (to Jan. 1983)
Lieut. Governor: Spencer Bernard, D (to Jan. 1983)
Secy. of State: Jeannette Edmondson, D (to Jan. 1983)
Treasurer: Leo Winters, D (to Jan. 1983)
Atty. General: Jan Eric Cartwright, D (to Jan. 1983)
Organized as territory: May 2, 1890
Entered Union & (rank): Nov. 16, 1907 (46)
Present constitution adopted: 1907
Motto: *Labor omnia vincit* (Labor conquers all things)
State flower: Mistletoe (1893)
State tree: Redbud (1937)
State bird: Scissor-tailed flycatcher (1951)
State animal: Bison (1972)
State reptile: Mountain boomer lizard (1969)
State stone: Rose Rock (barite rose) (1968)
State colors: Green and white (1915)
State song: "Oklahoma" (1953)
Nickname: Sooner State
Origin of name: From two Choctaw Indian words meaning "red people"
1970 population & (rank): 2,559,253 (27)
1979 prov. population & (rank): 2,892,000 (27)
1970 land area & (rank): 68,782 sq mi. (178,145 sq km) (19)
Geographic center: In Oklahoma Co., 8 mi. N of Oklahoma City
Number of counties: 77
Largest cities (1977 est.): Oklahoma City, 371,802; Tulsa, 334,365; Lawton, 83,785; Norman, 62,521; Midwest City, 50,341; Enid, 50,250; Muskogee, 41,300
State forests: None
State parks: 28 (88,959 ac.)
Total state revenue (1979): $2,797,476,841
Total state expenditure (1979): $2,723,712,003

Francisco Vásquez de Coronado first explored the region for Spain in 1541. The U.S. acquired most of Oklahoma in 1803 in the Louisiana Purchase from France; the Western Panhandle region became U.S. territory with the annexation of Texas in 1845.

In 1834, Oklahoma was set aside as Indian Territory. It remained so until April 22, 1889, when it was opened to homestead settlement. On that one day 50,000 people swarmed in and the term "Sooners" was applied to those who tried to beat the noon starting gun. Other Oklahoma "Land Rushes" took place through 1901.

Oil has made Oklahoma a rich state and Tulsa one of the world's wealthiest cities per capita. Oil refining, meat packing, food processing, and machinery manufacturing (especially construction and oil equipment) are important industries.

Other minerals produced in Oklahoma include natural gas, helium, gypsum, zinc, cement, coal, copper, and silver.

Oklahoma's rich plains produce bumper yields of wheat, as well as large crops of sorghum, corn, cotton, and peanuts. Its beef cattle herd is among the largest in the nation; more than half of Oklahoma's annual farm receipts are contributed by livestock products.

Tourist attractions include the National Cowboy Hall of Fame in Oklahoma City, the Will Rogers Memorial in Claremore, the Cherokee Cultural Center with a restored Cherokee village, the restored Fort Gibson Stockade near Muskogee, and the Lake Texoma recreation area.

OREGON

Capital: Salem
Governor: Victor G. Atiyeh, R (to Jan. 1983)
Secy. of State: Norma Paulus, R (to Jan. 1981)
Treasurer: Clay Myers, R (to Jan. 1981)
Atty. General: James A. Redden, D (to Jan. 1981)
Organized as territory: Aug. 14, 1848
Entered Union & (rank): Feb. 14, 1859 (33)
Present constitution adopted: 1859
Motto: The Union (1957)
State flower: Oregon grape (1899)
State tree: Douglas fir (1939)
State animal: Beaver (1969)
State bird: Western meadow lark (1927)
State fish: Chinook salmon (1961)
State rock: Thunderegg (1965)
State colors: Navy blue and gold (1959)
State song: "Oregon, My Oregon" (1927)
Nickname: Beaver State
Origin of name: Unknown. However, it is generally accepted that the name, first used by Jonathan Carver in 1778, was taken from the writings of Maj. Robert Rogers, an English army officer.
1970 population & (rank): 2,091,385 (31)
1979 prov. population & (rank): 2,527,000 (29)
1970 land area & (rank): 96,184 sq mi. (249,117 sq km) (10)
Geographic center: In Crook Co., 25 mi. SSE of Prineville
Number of counties: 36
Largest cities (1977 est.): Portland, 383,904; Eugene, 99,220; Salem, 83,738; Corvallis, 38,367; Springfield, 37,105; Medford, 35,769; Gresham, 26,898
State forests: 785,062 ac.
State parks: 237 (95,800 ac.)
State general revenue (1979–81 est.): $3,044,437,964
State general expenditure (1979–81 est.): $3,040,631,328

Spanish and English sailors are believed to have sighted the Oregon coast in the 1500s and 1600s. Capt. James Cook, seeking the Northwest Passage, charted some of the coastline in 1778. In 1792, Capt. Robert Gray, in the *Columbia*, discovered the river named after his ship and claimed the area for the U.S.

In 1805 the Lewis and Clark expedition explored the area and John Jacob Astor's fur depot, Astoria, was founded in 1811. Disputes for control of Oregon between American settlers and the Hudson Bay Company were finally resolved in the 1846 Oregon Treaty in which Great Britain gave up claims to the region.

Oregon, with the greatest U.S. reserve of standing timber, has a billion-dollar wood processing industry. Its salmon-fishing industry, centered at Astoria at the mouth of the Columbia, is one of the world's largest.

In agriculture, the state leads in growing peppermint, holly, lily bulbs, cranberries, filberts, Blue Lake beans, and cover seed crops, and also raises strawberries, hops, wheat and other grains, sugar beets, potatoes, green peas, fiber flax, dairy products, livestock and poultry, apples, pears, and cherries. Oregon is the source of all the nickel produced in the U.S.

With the low-cost electric power provided by Bonneville Dam, McNary Dam, and other dams in the Pacific Northwest, Oregon has developed steadily as a manufacturing state. Leading manufactures are lumber and plywood, metalwork, machinery, aluminum, chemicals, paper, food packing, and electronic equipment.

Crater Lake National Park, Mount Hood, and Bonneville Dam on the Columbia are major tourist attractions. Oregon Dunes National Recreation Area has been established near Florence. Other points of interest include the Oregon Caves National Monument, Cape Perpetua in Siuslaw National Forest, Columbia River Gorge between The Dalles and Troutdale, and Hells Canyon.

PENNSYLVANIA

Capital: Harrisburg
Governor: Richard L. Thornburgh, R (to Jan. 1983)
Lieut. Governor: William Scranton, Jr., R (to Jan. 1983)
Secy. of the Commonwealth: William R. Davis (to Jan. 1983)
Auditor General: Al Benedict, D (to Jan. 1983)
Atty. General: Edward Beister, Jr. (to Jan. 1983)
Entered Union & (rank): Dec. 12, 1787 (2)
Present constitution adopted: 1874
Motto: Virtue, liberty, and independence
State flower: Mountain laurel (1933)
State tree: Hemlock (1931)
State bird: Ruffed grouse (1931)
State insect: Firefly
State dog: Great Dane (1965)
State colors: Blue and gold
State song: None
Nickname: Keystone State
Origin of name: In honor of Adm. Sir. William Penn, father of William Penn. It means "Penn's Woodland."
1970 population & (rank): 11,793,909 (3)
1979 prov. population & (rank): 11,731,000 (4)
1970 land area & (rank): 44,966 sq mi. (116,462 sq km) (32)
Geographic center: In Centre Co., 2½ mi. SW of Bellefonte
Number of counties: 67
Largest cities (1977 est.): Philadelphia, 1,778,335; Pittsburgh, 442,139; Erie, 124,469; Allentown, 103,204; Scranton, 91,503; Reading, 78,457; Bethlehem, 72,987
State forests: 1,930,108 ac.
State parks: 120 (297,438 ac.)
Total estimated revenue subject to general appropriations (1980–81): $6,790,625,000
Total approved appropriations (1980–81): $6,785,444,000

Rich in historic lore, Pennsylvania territory was disputed in the early 1600s among the Dutch, the Swedes, and the English. England acquired the region in 1664 with the capture of New York and in 1681 Pennsylvania was granted to William Penn, a Quaker, by King Charles II.

Philadelphia was the seat of the federal government almost continuously from 1776 to 1800; there the Declaration of Independence was signed in

1776 and the U.S. Constitution drawn up in 1787. Valley Forge, of Revolutionary War fame, and Gettysburg, the turning-point of the Civil War, are both in Pennsylvania. The Liberty Bell is located in Independence Hall in Philadelphia.

Approximately 23% of all American pig iron steel is made in Pennsylvania, which ranks first among the states in steel wire and structural metal production. Other manufactures include machinery, chemicals, storage batteries, motor vehicles and trailers, computers, textiles and apparel, shoes, plastics, and explosives. Pennsylvania produces almost all the nation's anthracite coal. Also important are bituminous coal, cement, stone, petroleum, natural gas, lime, clays, zinc, and iron.

Prosperous farms brought in total receipts of more than $1.3 billion in 1973. The state ranked high in milk cows, chickens, and turkeys. Agricultural products include apples, peaches, potatoes, corn, wheat, barley, buckwheat, and mushrooms.

Tourists now spend approximately $6 billion in Pennsylvania annually. Among the chief attractions: the Gettysburg National Military Park, Valley Forge National Historical Park, Independence National Historical Park in Philadelphia, the Pennsylvania Dutch region, the Eisenhower farm near Gettysburg, and the Delaware Water Gap National Recreation Area.

RHODE ISLAND

Capital: Providence
Governor: J. Joseph Garrahy, D (to Jan. 1981)
Lieut. Governor: Thomas R. Di Luglio, D (to Jan. 1981)
Secy. of State: Robert F. Burns, D (to Jan. 1981)
Controller: James A. Carter (civil service)
Atty. General: Dennis J. Roberts II, D (to Jan. 1981)
Entered Union & (rank): May 29, 1790 (13)
Present constitution adopted: 1843
Motto: Hope
State flower: Violet (unofficial)
State tree: Red maple (official)
State bird: Rhode Island Red (official)
State colors: Blue, white, and gold (in state flag)
State song: "Rhode Island" (1946)
Nickname: The Ocean State
Origin of name: From the Greek island of Rhodes
1970 population & (rank): 949,723 (39)
1979 prov. population & (rank): 929,000 (39)
1970 land area & (rank): 1,049 sq mi. (2,717 sq km) (50)
Geographic center: In Kent Co., 1 mi. SSW of Crompton
Number of counties: 5
Largest cities (1977 est.): Providence, 160,982; Warwick, 86,284; Cranston, 73,523; Pawtucket, 69,911; East Providence, 48,917; Woonsocket, 46,464
State forests: 11 (20,900 ac.)
State parks: 17 (8,200 ac.)
State general revenue (1978–79): $881,447,251
State general expenditure (1978–79): $864,740,074

From its beginnings, Rhode Island has been distinguished by its support for freedom of conscience and action, started by Roger Williams, exiled by the Massachusetts Bay Colony Puritans in 1636, and the founder of the present state capital, Providence. Williams was followed by other religious exiles who founded Pocasset, now Portsmouth, in 1638 and Newport in 1639.

The first Baptist church in the U.S. was established in Providence in 1638 and Rhode Island provided a haven for Quakers in 1657 and for Jews from Holland in 1659.

Rhode Island's rebellious, authority-defying nature was further demonstrated by the burnings of the British revenue cutters *Liberty* and *Gaspee* prior to the Revolution, by its early declaration of independence from Great Britain in May 1776, its refusal to participate actively in the War of 1812, and by Dorr's Rebellion of 1842, which protested property requirements for voting.

Rhode Island, smallest of the 50 states, is densely populated and highly industrialized. The state pioneered in the manufacture of jewelry and silverware and still retains first place in the U.S. Other leading industries are primary metal processing, metal products, machinery, rubber and plastics, food processing, chemicals, and apparel.

With more than eight tenths of the population living in urban areas, adjacent areas of the state are involved in dairying and poultry and truck farming. Nursery and greenhouse products, potatoes, corn, apples, oats, and hay lead the crop list.

Newport became famous as the summer capital of society in the mid-19th century. Touro Synagogue (1763) is the oldest in the U.S. Other points of interest include the Roger Williams National Memorial in Providence, Samuel Slater's Mill in Pawtucket, the General Nathaniel Greene Homestead in Coventry, Block Island, and Narragansett Pier.

SOUTH CAROLINA

Capital: Columbia
Governor: Richard W. Riley, D (to Jan. 1983)
Lieut. Governor: Nancy Stevenson, D (to Jan. 1983)
Secy. of State: John T. Campbell, D (to Jan. 1983)
Comptroller General: Earl E. Morris, Jr. (to Jan. 1983)
Atty. General: Daniel R. McLeod, D (to Jan. 1983)
Entered Union & (rank): May 23, 1788 (8)
Present constitution adopted: 1895
Mottoes: *Animis opibusque parati* (Prepared in mind and resources) and *Dum spiro spero* (While I breathe, I hope)
State flower: Carolina yellow jessamine (1924)
State tree: Palmetto tree (1939)
State bird: Carolina wren (1948)
State song: "Carolina" (1911)
Nickname: Palmetto State
Origin of name: In honor of Charles I of England
1979 prov. population & (rank): 2,932,000 (25)
1970 land area & (rank): 30,225 sq mi. (78,283 sq km) (40)
Geographic center: In Richland Co., 13 mi. SE of Columbia
Number of counties: 46
Largest cities (1977 est.): Columbia, 110,851; Charleston, 59,911; North Charleston, 58,658; Greenville, 57,406; Spartanburg, 47,141; Rock Hill, 36,540
State forests: 4 (124,052 ac.)
State parks: 50 (61,726 ac.)
State general fund revenue (1979–80 est.): $1,562,123,828[1]
State general expenditures (1979–80 est.): $1,556,722,589[1]

Following exploration of the coast in 1521 by De Gordillo, the Spanish tried unsuccessfully to establish a colony near present-day Georgetown in 1526 and the French also failed to colonize Parris Island near Fort Royal in 1562.

The first English settlement was made in 1670 at Albemarle Point on the Ashley River, but poor conditions drove the settlers to the site of Charleston (originally called Charles Town). South Carolina,

1. Highway Department has separate funding and expenditures.

officially separated from North Carolina in 1729, was the scene of extensive military action during the Revolution and again during the Civil War. The Civil War began in 1861 as South Carolina troops fired on federal Fort Sumter in Charleston Harbor and the state was the first to secede from the Union.

Once primarily agricultural, South Carolina has built so many large textile and other mills that today its factories produce eight times the output of its farms in cash value. Charleston makes asbestos, wood, pulp, and steel products; chemicals, machinery, and apparel are also important.

Farms have become fewer but larger in recent years. South Carolina grows more peaches than any other state except California; it ranks fourth in tobacco. Other farm products include cotton, peanuts, sweet potatoes, soybeans, corn, and oats. Poultry and dairy products are also important revenue producers.

Points of interest include Fort Sumter National Monument, Fort Moultrie, Fort Johnson, and aircraft carrier USS *Yorktown* in Charleston Harbor; the Middleton, Magnolia, and Cypress Gardens in Charleston; Cowpens National Battlefield; and the Hilton Head resorts.

SOUTH DAKOTA

Capital: Pierre
Governor: William J. Janklow, R (to Jan. 1983)
Lieut. Governor: Lowell C. Hansen II, R (to Jan. 1983)
Atty. General: Mark Meirhenry, R (to Jan. 1983)
Secy. of State: Alice Kundert, R (to Jan. 1983)
State Auditor: Vern Larson, R (to Jan. 1983)
State Treasurer: David L. Volk, R (to Jan. 1983)
Organized as territory: March 2, 1861
Entered Union & (rank): Nov. 2, 1889 (40)
Present constitution adopted: 1889
Motto: Under God the people rule
State flower: American pasqueflower (1903)
State grass: Western wheat grass (1970)
State tree: Black Hills spruce (1947)
State bird: Ring-necked pheasant (1943)
State insect: Honeybee (1978)
State animal: Coyote (1949)
State mineral stone: Rose quartz (1966)
State gem stone: Fairburn agate (1966)
State colors: Blue and gold (in state flag)
State song: "Hail! South Dakota" (1943)
Nicknames: Sunshine State; Coyote State
Origin of name: Same as for North Dakota
1970 population & (rank): 666,257 (44)
1979 prov. population & (rank): 689,000 (45)
1970 land area & (rank): 75,955 sq mi. (196,723 sq km) (16)
Geographic center: In Hughes Co., 8 mi. NE of Pierre
Number of counties: 67 (64 county governments)
Largest cities (1977 est.): Sioux Falls, 74,927; Rapid City, 51,805; Aberdeen, 26,302; Watertown, 14,616; Brookings, 13,952; Mitchell, 13,554; Huron, 13,279
State forests: None[1]
State parks: 13 plus 39 recreational areas (87,269 ac.)[2]
State general revenue (1979 unadj.): $780,854,740[3]
State general expenditure (1979 unadj.): $744,635,990[3]

Exploration of this area began in 1743 when Louis-Joseph and François Verendrye came from France in search of a route to the Pacific.

1. No designated state forests; about 13,000 ac. of state land is forestland. 2. Acreage includes 39 recreation areas and 80 roadside parks, in addition to 12 state parks. 3. Includes Federal funds.

The U.S. acquired the region as part of the Louisiana Purchase in 1803 and it was explored by Lewis and Clark in 1804–06. Fort Pierre, the first permanent settlement, was established in 1817 and, in 1831, the first Missouri River steamboat reached the fort.

Settlement of South Dakota did not begin in earnest until the arrival of the railroad in 1873 and the discovery of gold in the Black Hills the following year.

Agriculture is South Dakota's basic industry today. It normally ranks first in the U.S. in the size of its rye crop and high in spring wheat, flaxseed, oats, and barley. In 1974 South Dakota had 5 million cattle, almost a million sheep, and 2 million hogs.

South Dakota is the nation's second leading producer of gold (Nevada ranks first) and the Homestake Mine is the richest in the U.S. Other minerals produced include berylium, bentonite, granite, silver, petroleum, and uranium.

Processing of foods produced by farms and ranches is the largest South Dakota manufacturing industry, followed by lumber, wood products, and machinery, including farm equipment.

The Black Hills, a great tourist attraction, are the highest mountains east of the Rockies. Mt. Rushmore, in this group, is famous for the likenesses of Washington, Jefferson, Lincoln, and Theodore Roosevelt, which were carved in granite by Gutzon Borglum. The Badlands offer scenic masses of bare rock and clay unrelieved by any vegetation. Other points of interest are Deadwood, where Wild Bill Hickok was killed in 1876; the Crazy Horse Memorial near Custer; and the Corn Palace in Mitchell.

TENNESSEE

Capital: Nashville
Governor: Lamar Alexander, R (to Jan. 1983)
Lieut. Governor: John S. Wilder, D (to Jan. 1981)
Secy. of State: Gentry Crowell, D (to Jan. 1981)
Atty. General: Brooks McLemore, D (to Sept. 1982)
State Treasurer: Harlan Matthews, D (to Jan. 1983)
Entered Union & (rank): June 1, 1796 (16)
Present constitution adopted: 1870; amended 1953, 1960, 1965 and 1973
Motto: "Tennessee—America at its best" (1965)
State flower: Iris (1933)
State tree: Tulip poplar (1947)
State bird: Mockingbird (1933)
State horse: Tennessee walking horse
State animal: Raccoon
State wild flower: Passion flower
State song: "Tennessee Waltz" (1965)
Nickname: Volunteer State
Origin of name: Of Cherokee origin; the exact meaning is unknown
1970 population & (rank): 3,924,164 (17)
1979 prov. population & (rank): 4,380,000 (17)
1970 land area & (rank): 41,328 sq mi. (107,040 sq km) (34)
Geographic center: In Rutherford Co., 5 mi. NE of Murfreesboro
Number of counties: 95
Largest cities (1977 est.): Memphis, 668,443; Nashville–Davidson, 428,957; Knoxville, 184,942; Chattanooga, 165,280; Clarksville, 57,299; Jackson, 46,486; Johnson City, 41,005; Kingsport, 33,277
State forests: 14 (155,752 ac.)
State parks: 21 (130,000 ac.)

State general revenue (1978): $3,275,928
State general expenditure (1978): $3,091,556

First visited by the Spanish explorer de Soto in 1541, the Tennessee area would later be claimed by both France and England as a result of the 1670s and 1680s explorations of Marquette and Jolliet, La Salle, and the Englishmen James Needham and Gabriel Arthur.

Great Britain obtained the region following the French and Indian War in 1763 and it was rapidly occupied by settlers moving in from Virginia and the Carolinas.

During 1784–87, the settlers formed the "state" of Franklin, which was disbanded when the region was allowed to send representatives to the North Carolina legislature. In 1790 Congress organized the territory south of the Ohio River and Tennessee joined the Union in 1796.

Although Tennessee joined the Confederacy during the Civil War, there was much pro-Union sentiment in the state, which was the scene of extensive military action.

The state is now predominantly industrial; in 1970, 58.8% of its population lived in urban areas. Among the most important products are chemicals, textiles, apparel, electrical machinery, furniture, and leather goods. Other lines include food processing, lumber, primary metals, and metal products. The state is known as the U.S. hardwood-flooring center and ranks first in the production of marble, zinc, pyrite, and ball clay.

Tennessee is one of the leading tobacco-producing states in the nation and its farming income is also derived from livestock and dairy products as well as corn, cotton, and soybeans.

With six other states, Tennessee shares the extensive federal reservoir developments on the Tennessee and Cumberland River systems. The Tennessee Valley Authority operates a number of dams and reservoirs in the state.

Among the major points of interest: the Andrew Johnson National Historic Site at Greenville, American Museum of Atomic Energy at Oak Ridge, Great Smoky Mountains National Park, The Hermitage (home of Andrew Jackson near Nashville), Rock City Gardens near Chattanooga, and three National Military Parks.

TEXAS

Capital: Austin
Governor: Bill Clements, R (to Jan. 1983)
Lieut. Governor: William P. Hobby, D (to Jan. 1981)
Secy. of State: George Strake, Jr., R (to Jan. 1983)
Comptroller: Bob Bullock (to Jan. 1983)
Atty. General: Mark White, D (to Jan. 1983)
Entered Union & (rank): Dec. 29, 1845 (28)
Present constitution adopted: 1876
Motto: Friendship
State flower: Bluebonnet (1901)
State tree: Pecan (1919)
State bird: Mockingbird (1927)
State song: "Texas, Our Texas" (1930)
Nickname: Lone Star State
Origin of name: From an Indian word meaning "friends"
1970 population & (rank): 11,196,730 (4)
1979 prov. population & (rank): 13,385,000 (3)
1970 land area & (rank): 262,134 sq mi. (678,927 sq km) (2)
Geographic center: In McCulloch Co., 15 mi. NE of Brady
Number of counties: 254
Largest cities (1977 est.): Houston, 1,554,960; Dallas, 844,528; San Antonio, 793,374; El Paso, 395,419; Fort Worth, 367,993; Austin, 323,250
State forests: 4 (6,306 ac.)
State parks: 83 (64 developed)
State revenue receipts (1978–79): $10,884,709,348
State government cost (1978–79): $10,807,466,326

Spanish explorers, including Cabeza de Vaca and Coronado, were the first to visit the region in the 16th and 17th centuries, settling at Ysleta near present-day El Paso in 1682. In 1685, La Salle established a short-lived French colony at Matagorda Bay.

Americans, led by Stephen F. Austin, began to settle along the Brazos River in 1821 when Texas was controlled by Mexico, recently independent from Spain. In 1836, following a brief war between the American settlers in Texas and the Mexican government, and famous for the battles of the Alamo and San Jacinto, the Independent Republic of Texas was proclaimed with Sam Houston as president.

After Texas became the 28th U.S. state in 1845, border disputes led to the Mexican War of 1846–48.

Today, Texas, second only to Alaska in land area, leads all other states in such categories as oil, cattle, sheep, and cotton. Possessing enormous natural resources, Texas is a major agricultural state and an industrial giant.

Sulfur, salt, helium asphalt, graphite, bromine, natural gas, cement, and clays give Texas first place in mineral production—nearly $8 billion in 1973. Chemicals, oil refining, food processing, machinery, and transportation equipment are among the major Texas manfacturing industries.

Texas ranches and farms produce beef cattle, poultry, rice, pecans, peanuts, sorghum, and an extensive variety of fruits and vegetables.

Millions of tourists spend well over $2 billion annually visiting more than 70 state parks, recreations areas, and points of interest such as the Gulf Coast resort area, the Lyndon B. Johnson Space Center in Houston, the Alamo in San Antonio, the state capital in Austin, and the Big Bend and Guadalupe Mountains National Parks.

UTAH

Capital: Salt Lake City
Governor: Scott M. Matheson, D (to Jan. 1981)
Lieut. Governor/Secretary of State: David S. Monson, R (to Jan. 1981)
Atty. General: Robert B. Hansen, R (to Jan. 1981)
Organized as territory: Sept. 9, 1850
Entered Union & (rank): Jan. 4, 1896 (45)
Present constitution adopted: 1896
Motto: Industry
State flower: Sego lily (1911)
State tree: Blue spruce (1933)
State bird: Seagull (1955)
State emblem: Beehive
State song: "Utah, We Love Thee"
Nickname: Beehive State
Origin of name: From the Ute tribe, meaning "people of the mountains"
1970 population & (rank): 1,059,273 (36)
1979 prov. population & (rank): 1,367,000 (36)
1970 land area & (rank): 82,096 sq mi. (212,629 sq km) (12)
Geographic center: In Sanpete Co., 3 mi. N. of Manti

Number of counties: 29
Largest cities (1977 est.): Salt Lake City, 167,404; Ogden, 68,512; Provo, 55,577; Orem, 42,377; Sandy City, 35,269; Bountiful, 31,830; Murray, 27,178
State forests: None
State parks: 35 (64,097 ac.)
Total state receipt (1979): $1,239,127,495
Total state disbursements (1979): $1,239,613,030
Cash balance—Unappropriated general fund balance (1979): $15,356,766

The region was first explored for Spain by Franciscan friars, Escalante and Dominguez in 1776. In 1824 the famous American frontiersman Jim Bridger discovered the Great Salt Lake.

Fleeing the religious persecution encountered in eastern and middle-western states, the Mormons reached the Great Salt Lake in 1847 and began to build Salt Lake City. The U.S. acquired the Utah region in the treaty ending the Mexican War in 1848 and the first transcontinental railroad was completed with the driving of a golden spike at Promontory Point in 1869.

Mormon difficulties with the federal government about polygamy did not end until the Mormon Church renounced the practice in 1890, six years before Utah became a state.

In recent years, manufacturing has become Utah's most important industry, ahead of mining, agriculture, and tourism. The state's factories produce transportation equipment, food products, machinery, metal products, and electrical equipment. Utah has also become an important aerospace research and production center and is a leading warehousing and distribution point for much of the western U.S.

Rich in natural resources, Utah has long been a leading producer of copper, gold, silver, lead, zinc, and molybdenum. Oil has also become a major product; with Colorado and Wyoming, Utah shares what have been called the world's richest oil shale deposits.

Ranked eighth among the states in number of sheep in 1973, Utah also produces large crops of apricots and cherries as well as sugar beets, potatoes, onions, alfalfa, winter wheat, and beans. Utah's farmlands and crops require extensive irrigation.

Utah is a great vacationland with 11,000 miles of fishing streams and 147,000 acres of lakes and reservoirs. Among the many tourist attractions are Arches, Bryce Canyon, Canyonlands, Capitol Reef, and Zion National Parks; Dinosaur, Natural Bridges, and Rainbow Bridge National Monuments; the Mormon Tabernacle in Salt Lake City; and Monument Valley.

VERMONT

Capital: Montpelier
Governor: Richard A. Snelling, R (to Jan. 1981)
Lieut. Governor: Madeleine M. Kunin (to Jan. 1981)
Secy. of State: James A. Guest, D (to Jan. 1981)
Treasurer: Emory A. Hebard, R (to Jan. 1981)
Auditor of Accounts: Alexander V. Acebo (to Jan. 1981)
Atty. General: M. Jerome Diamond (to Jan. 1981)
Entered Union & (rank): March 4, 1791 (14)
Present constitution adopted: 1793
Motto: Vermont, Freedom, and Unity
State flower: Red clover (1894)
State tree: Sugar maple (1949)
State bird: Hermit thrush (1941)
State animal: Morgan horse (1961)
State insect: Honeybee (1978)
State song: "Hail, Vermont!" (1938)
Nickname: Green Mountain State
Origin of name: From the French "vert mont," meaning "green mountain"
1970 population & (rank): 444,732 (48)
1979 prov. population & (rank): 493,000 (48)
1970 land area & (rank): 9,276 sq mi. (24,025 sq km) (43)
Geographic center: In Washington Co., 3 mi. E of Roxbury
Number of counties: 14
Largest cities (1977 est.): Burlington, 38,517; Rutland, 18,559; South Burlington, 10,307; Barre, 9,934; Montpelier, 7,953; St. Albans, 7,499
State forests: 34 (113,953 ac.)
State parks: 45 (31,325 ac.)
State receipts (1978): $474,935,831
State disbursements (1978): $484,931,873

The Vermont region was explored and claimed for France by Samuel de Champlain in 1609 and the first French settlement was established at Fort Ste. Anne in 1666. The first English settlers moved into the area in 1724 and built Fort Drummer on the site of present-day Brattleboro. England gained control of the area in 1763 after the French and Indian War.

First organized to drive settlers from New York out of Vermont, the Green Mountain Boys, led by Ethan Allen, won fame by capturing Fort Ticonderoga from the British on May 10, 1775, in the early days of the Revolution.

In 1777 Vermont adopted its first constitution abolishing slavery and providing for universal male suffrage without property qualifications. In 1791 Vermont became the first state after the original 13 to join the Union.

Vermont leads the nation in the production of monument granite, marble, and maple syrup. It is also a leader in the production of asbestos and talc.

In ratio to population, Vermont keeps more dairy cows than any other state. Vermont's soil is devoted to dairying, truck farming, and fruit growing because the rugged, rocky terrain discourages extensive farming.

Principal manufactured goods are machine tools, computer components, stone and clay products, lumber, furniture, and paper.

Tourism is a major industry in Vermont. Vermont's many famous ski areas include Stowe, Killington, Mt. Snow, Bromley, Jay Peak, and Sugarbush. Hunting and fishing also attract many visitors to Vermont each year. Among the many points of interest are the Green Mountain National Forest, Bennington Battle Monument, the Calvin Coolidge Homestead at Plymouth, and the Marble Exhibit in Proctor.

VIRGINIA

Capital: Richmond
Governor: John N. Dalton, R (to Jan. 1982)
Lieut. Governor: Charles S. Robb, D (to Jan. 1982)
Secy. of the Commonwealth: Frederick T. Gray, D (apptd. by Governor)
Acting Comptroller: Vincent Pross, Jr. (apptd. by Governor)
Atty. General: J. Marshall Coleman, R (to Jan. 1982)
Entered Union & (rank): June 25, 1788 (10)
Present constitution adopted: 1970
Motto: *Sic semper tyrannis* (Thus always to tyrants)
State flower: American dogwood (1918)
State bird: Cardinal (1950)

State dog: American foxhound (1966)
State shell: Oyster shell
State song: "Carry Me Back to Old Virginia" (1940)
Nicknames: The Old Dominion; Mother of Presidents
Origin of name: In honor of Elizabeth "Virgin Queen" of England
1970 population & (rank): 4,648,494 (14)
1979 prov. population & (rank): 5,197,000 (13)
1970 land area & (rank): 39,780 sq mi. (103,030 sq km) (36)
Geographic center: In Buckingham Co., 5 mi. SW of Buckingham
Number of counties: 95, plus 41 independent cities
Largest cities (1977 est.): Norfolk, 281,962; Virginia Beach, 235,840; Richmond, 223,212; Newport News, 142,262; Hampton, 126,761
State forests: 8 (49,566 ac.)
State parks and recreational parks: 22, plus 3 in process of acquisition and/or development (42,722 ac.)[1]
State revenue (1978–79): $4,719,621,941
State expenditure (1978–79): $4,770,472,368

The history of America is closely tied to that of Virginia, particularly in the Colonial period. Jamestown, founded in 1607, was the first permanent English settlement in North America and slavery was introduced there in 1619. The surrenders ending both the American Revolution (Yorktown) and the Civil War (Appomattox) occurred in Virginia. The state is called the "Mother of Presidents" because eight chief executives of the United States were born there.

Today, Virginia has a large number of diversified manufacturing industries including chemicals, textiles, food products, and clothing. Other important lines are lumber, paper, furniture, cigarettes, electrical machinery, transportation equipment, and stone-glass-clay products.

Agriculture remains an important sector in the Virginia economy and the state ranks among the leaders in the U.S. in tobacco, peanuts, apples, and sweet potatoes. Other crops include corn, vegetables, barley, and peaches. Famous for its turkeys and Smithfield hams, Virginia also has a large dairy industry.

Coal mining accounts for roughly 70% of Virginia's mineral output, and lime, zinc, and stone are also mined.

Points of interest include Mt. Vernon and other places associated with George Washington; Monticello, home of Thomas Jefferson; Stratford, home of the Lees; Richmond, capital of the Confederacy and of Virginia; and Williamsburg, the restored Colonial capital.

The Chesapeake Bay Bridge-Tunnel spans the mouth of Chesapeake Bay, connecting Cape Charles with Norfolk. Consisting of a series of low trestles, two bridges and two mile-long tunnels, the complex is 18 miles (29 km) long. It was opened in 1964.

Other attractions are the Shenandoah National Park, Fredericksburg and Spotsylvania National Military Park, the Booker T. Washington birthplace near Roanoke, Arlington House (the Robert E. Lee Memorial), the Skyline Drive, and the Blue Ridge National Parkway.

1. Does not include portion of Breaks Interstate Park (Va.-Ky., 1,200 ac.) which lies in Virginia.

WASHINGTON

Capital: Olympia
Governor: Dixy Lee Ray, D (to Jan. 1981)
Lieut. Governor: John A. Cherberg, D (to Jan. 1981)
Secy. of State: Bruce K. Chapman, R (to Jan. 1981)
State Treasurer: Robert S. O'Brien, D (to Jan. 1981)
Atty. General: Slade Gorton, R (to Jan. 1981)
Organized as territory: March 2, 1853
Entered Union & (rank): Nov. 11, 1889 (42)
Present constitution adopted: 1889
Motto: *Al-Ki* (Indian word meaning "by and by")
State flower: Rhododendron (1949)
State tree: Western hemlock (1947)
State bird: Willow goldfinch (1951)
State fish: Steelhead trout (1969)
State gem: Petrified wood (1975)
State colors: Green and gold (1925)
State song: "Washington, My Home" (1959)
State dance: Square dance (1979)
Nicknames: Evergreen State; Chinook State
Origin of name: In honor of George Washington
1970 population & (rank): 3,409,169 (22)
1979 prov. population & (rank): 3,926,000 (21)
1970 land area & (rank): 66,570 sq mi (172,416 sq km) (20)
Geographic center: In Chelan Co., 10 mi. WSW of Wenatchee
Number of counties: 39
Largest cities (1977 est.): Seattle, 488,928; Spokane, 175,327; Tacoma, 154,340; Bellevue, 68,679; Yakima, 53,002; Everett, 50,505; Vancouver, 47,402
State forest lands: 1,843,020 ac.
State parks: 175 (170,545 ac.)[1]
State revenue (1979–81 projected): $10,571,900,000
State expenditure (1979–81 projected): $11,034,512,499

As part of the vast Oregon Country, Washington territory was visited by Spanish, American, and British explorers—Bruno Heceta for Spain in 1775, the American Capt. Robert Gray in 1792, and Capt. George Vancouver for Britain in 1792–94. Lewis and Clark explored the Columbia River region and coastal areas for the U.S. in 1805–06.

Rival American and British settlers and conflicting territorial claims threatened war in the early 1840s. However, in 1846 the Oregon Treaty set the boundary at the 49th parallel and war was averted.

Washington is a leading lumber producer. Its rugged surface is rich in stands of Douglas fir, hemlock, ponderosa and white pine, spruce, larch, and cedar. The state holds first place in apples, blueberries, hops, and red raspberries and it ranks high in potatoes, winter wheat, pears, grapes, apricots, and strawberries. Livestock and livestock products make important contributions to total farm revenue and the commercial fishing catch of salmon, halibut, and bottomfish makes a significant contribution to the state's economy.

Manufacturing industries in Washington include aircraft and missiles, shipbuilding and other transportation equipment, lumber, food processing, metals and metal products, chemicals, and machinery.

The Columbia River contains one third of the potential water power in the U.S., harnessed by such dams as the Grand Coulee, one of the greatest power producers in the world. Washington has 90

1. Parks and undeveloped areas administered by Parks and Recreation Dept. Game Dept. administers wildlife and recreation areas totaling 762,895 acres.

dams throughout the state built for irrigation, power, flood control, and water storage. Its abundance of electrical power makes Washington the nation's largest producer of refined aluminum.

Among the major points of interest: Mt. Rainier, Olympic, and North Cascades. In 1980, Mount St. Helens, a peak in the Cascade Range in Southwestern Washington erupted on May 18th. Also of interest are National Parks; Whitman Mission and Fort Vancouver National Historic Sites; and the Pacific Science Center and Space Needle in Seattle.

WEST VIRGINIA

Capital: Charleston
Governor: John D. Rockefeller IV, D (to Jan. 1981)
Secy. of State: James A. Manchin, D (to Jan. 1981)
State Auditor: Glen Gainer (to Jan. 1981)
Atty. General: Chauncey H. Browning, Jr., D (to Jan. 1981)
Entered Union & (rank): June 20, 1863 (35)
Present constitution adopted: 1872
Motto: *Montani semper liberi* (Mountaineers are always free)
State flower: Rhododendron (1903)
State tree: Sugar maple (1949)
State bird: Cardinal (1949)
State animal: Black bear
State colors: Blue and gold (unofficial)
State songs: "West Virginia, My Home Sweet Home," "The West Virginia Hills," and "This Is My West Virginia" (adopted by Legislature in 1947, 1961 and 1963 as official state songs)
Nickname: Mountain State
Origin of name: Same as for Virginia
1970 population & (rank): 1,744,237 (34)
1979 prov. population & (rank): 1,878,000 (34)
1970 land area & (rank): 24,070 sq mi. (62,341 sq km) (41)
Geographic center: In Braxton Co., 4 mi. E of Sutton
Number of counties: 55
Largest cities (1977 est.): Huntington, 69,592; Charleston, 66,965; Wheeling, 43,189; Parkersburg, 38,784; Morgantown, 32,079; Fairmont, 26,170
State forests: 9 (77,000 ac.)
State parks: 34 (65,861 ac.)
Total state revenue (1978–79): $2,157,431,332
Total state expenditure (1978–79): $2,088,568,054

West Virginia's early history from 1609 until 1863 is largely shared with Virginia, of which it was a part until Virginia seceded from the Union in 1861. Then the delegates of 40 western counties formed their own government, which was granted statehood in 1863.

First permanent settlement dates from 1731 when Morgan Morgan founded Mill Creek. In 1742 coal was discovered on the Coal River, an event that would be of great significance in determining West Virginia's future.

The state usually ranks first in bituminous coal production with about 20% of the U.S. total. It also is a leader in steel, glass, aluminum, and chemical manufactures; natural gas, oil, quarry products, and hardwood lumber.

Poultry, dairy products, cattle, and sheep account for the major portion of farm receipts. Apples, peaches, wheat, corn, and hay are profitable crops. More than 75% of West Virginia is covered with forests.

Tourism is increasingly popular in mountainous West Virginia and visitors spend over $750 million annually. More than a million acres have been set aside in 34 state parks and recreation areas and in 9 state forests.

Major points of interest include Harpers Ferry and Chesapeake and Ohio Canal National Historical Parks, White Sulphur Springs and Berkeley Springs resorts, the scenic railroad at Cass, and the historic homes at Charles Town.

WISCONSIN

Capital: Madison
Governor: Lee Sherman Dreyfus, R (to Jan. 1983)
Lieut. Governor: Russell A. Olson, R (to Jan. 1983)
Secy. of State: Vel R. Phillips, D (to Jan. 1983)
State Treasurer: Charles P. Smith, D (to Jan. 1983)
Atty. General: Bronson C. La Follette, D (to Jan. 1983)
Organized as territory: July 4, 1836
Entered Union & (rank): May 29, 1848 (30)
Present constitution adopted: 1848
Motto: Forward
State flower: Wood violet
State tree: Sugar maple
State bird: Robin
State animal: Badger; "wild life" animal: white-tailed deer; "domestic" animal; dairy cow
State insect: Honeybee (1977)
State fish: Musky (Muskellunge)
State song: "On Wisconsin"
State mineral: Galena (1971)
State rock: Red Granite (1971)
Nickname: Badger State
Origin of name: French corruption of an Indian word whose meaning is disputed
1970 population & (rank): 4,417,933 (16)
1979 prov. population & (rank): 4,720,000 (16)
1970 land area & (rank): 54,464 sq mi. (141,062 sq km) (25)
Geographic center: In Wood Co., 9 mi. SE of Marshfield
Number of counties: 72
Largest cities (1977 est.): Milwaukee, 653,417; Madison, 168,932; Racine, 93,497; Green Bay, 90,368; Kenosha, 80,385; West Allis, 69,346; Appleton, 60,311
State forests: 8 (449,486 ac.)
State parks & scenic trails: 55 parks, 8 trails (61,340 ac.)
State revenue (1978–79): $6,317,162,015
State expenditure (1978–79): $6,822,975,820

The Wisconsin region was first explored for France by Jean Nicolet who landed at Green Bay in 1634. In 1660 a French trading post and Roman Catholic mission were established near present-day Ashland.

Great Britain obtained the region in settlement of the French and Indian War in 1763; the U.S. acquired it in 1783 after the Revolutionary War. However, Great Britain retained actual control until after the War of 1812. The region was successively governed as part of the territories of Indiana, Illinois, and Michigan between 1800 and 1836, when it became a separate territory.

Wisconsin leads the nation in milk and cheese production. In 1975, the state ranked first in the number of milk cows (1,812,000), and produced 16% of the nation's total output of milk. Other important farm products are peas, beets, corn, potatoes, cabbage, maple sugar, and cranberries.

The chief industrial products of the state are automobiles, machinery, furniture, paper, beer, and processed foods. Wisconsin ranks second among the 47 paper-producing states. Tourism also ranks among the major industries.

Wisconsin pioneered in social legislation, providing pensions for the blind (1907), aid to dependent children (1913), and old-age assistance (1925). In 1932 it was the first state to enact an unemployment compensation law. In labor legislation, the state has also pioneered in important laws, among them the first workmen's compensation law actually to take effect. Wisconsin had the first state-wide primary-election law and the first successful income-tax law.

The state has over 8,500 lakes, of which Winnebago is the largest. Water sports, ice-boating, and fishing are popular, as are skiing and hunting. Public parks and forests take up one seventh of the land, with 49 state parks, 9 state forests, and 2 national forests.

Among the many points of interest are the Apostle Islands National Lakeshore; Ice Age National Scientific Reserve; the Circus World Museum at Baraboo; the Wolf, St. Croix, and Lower St. Croix national scenic riverways; and the Wisconsin Dells.

WYOMING

Capital: Cheyenne
Governor: Ed Herschler, D (to Jan. 1983)
Secy. of State: Thyra G. Thomson, R (to Jan. 1983)
Auditor: James B. Griffith, Jr., R (to Jan. 1983)
Treasurer: Shirley Wittler, D (to Jan. 1983)
Atty. General: John Troughton, D (apptd. by Governor)
Organized as territory: May 19, 1869
Entered Union & (rank): July 10, 1890 (44)
Present constitution adopted: 1890
Motto: Equal rights (1955)
State flower: Indian paintbrush (1917)
State tree: Cottonwood (1947)
State bird: Meadow lark (1927)
State gemstone: Jade (1967)
State insignia: Bucking horse (unofficial)
State song: "Wyoming" (1955)
Nickname: Equality State
Origin of name: From the Indian, meaning "mountains and valleys alternating"; named after the Wyoming Valley in Pennsylvania
1970 population & (rank): 332,416 (49)
1979 prov. population & (rank): 450,000 (49)
1970 land area & (rank): 97,203 sq mi. (251,756 sq km) (9)
Geographic center: In Fremont Co., 58 mi. ENE of Lander
Number of counties: 23, plus Yellowstone National Park
Largest cities (1977 est.): Cheyenne, 48,274; Casper, 44,012; Laramie, 24,962; Rock Springs, 18,999; Sheridan, 12,270; Gillette, 10,686; Rawlins, 10,218
State forests: None
State parks: 9 (44,732 ac.)
Estimated income (1980–82): $816,225,862
Estimated expenditure (1980–82): $533,345,366

The U.S. acquired the territory from France as part of the Louisiana Purchase in 1803. John Colter, a fur-trapper, is the first white man known to have entered present Wyoming. In 1807 he explored the Yellowstone area and brought back news of its geysers and hot springs.

Robert Stuart pioneered the Oregon Trail across Wyoming in 1812–13 and, in 1834, Fort Laramie, the first permanent trading post in Wyoming, was built. Western Wyoming was obtained by the U.S. in the 1846 Oregon Treaty with Great Britain and as a result of the treaty ending the Mexican War in 1848.

When the Wyoming Territory was organized in 1869 Wyoming women became the first in the nation to obtain the right to vote. In 1925 Mrs. Nellie Taylor Ross was elected first woman governor in the United States.

Wyoming's towering mountains and vast plains provide spectacular scenery, grazing lands for sheep and cattle, and rich mineral deposits.

Mining, particularly oil and natural gas, is the most important industry. In 1973, Wyoming led the nation in sodium carbonate production and was second in uranium.

Wyoming ranks second among the states in wool production. In 1974 its sheep numbered 1.5 million, exceeded only by Texas; it also had 1.6 million cattle. Principal crops include wheat, oats, sugar beets, corn, potatoes, barley, and alfalfa.

Second in mean elevation to Colorado, Wyoming has many attractions for the tourist trade, notably Yellowstone National Park. Cheyenne is famous for its annual "Frontier Days" celebration. Flaming Gorge, the Fort Laramie National Historic Site, and Devils Tower and Fossil Butte National Monuments are other points of interest.

Self-Governing Areas

PUERTO RICO

Capital: San Juan
Governor: Carlos Romero Barceló, New Progressive Party (to Jan. 1981)
Song: "La Borinqueña"
1970 population: 2,712,033
1976 est. population: 3,196,000
1970 land area: 3,421 sq mi. (8,860 sq km)
Largest cities (1970): San Juan (452,749); Ponce (128,233); Bayamón (147,552); Carolina (94,271); Mayagüez (68,872)

Puerto Rico is an island about 100 miles long and 35 miles wide at the northeastern end of the Caribbean Sea. It is a self-governing Commonwealth freely and voluntarily associated with the U.S. Under its Constitution, a Governor and a Legislative Assembly are elected by direct vote for a four-year period. The judiciary is vested in a Supreme Court and lower courts established by law. The people elect a Resident Commissioner to the U.S. House of Representatives, where he has a voice but no vote. The island was formerly an unincorporated territory of the U.S. after being ceded by Spain as a result of the Spanish-American War.

The Commonwealth, established in 1952, has one of the highest standards of living in Latin America. Featuring Puerto Rican economic development is Operation Bootstrap. This program has established over 2,300 new factories and has greatly increased agricultural production, transportation and communications facilities, electric power, housing, and other industries.

The island's chief exports are chemicals, textiles, fish products and petroleum products.

Columbus discovered the island on his second voyage to America in 1493.

GUAM

Capital: Agaña
Governor: Paul M. Calvo
1950 population: 59,498
1960 population: 67,044
1970 population: 84,996
1970 land area: 212 sq mi. (549 sq km)

Guam, the largest of the Mariana Islands, is independent of the trusteeship assigned to the U.S. in 1947. It was acquired by the U.S. from Spain in 1898 (occupied 1899) and was placed under the Navy Department.

In World War II, Guam was seized by the Japanese on Dec. 11, 1941; but on July 21, 1944, it was once more in U. S. hands.

On Aug. 1, 1950, President Truman signed a bill which granted U.S. citizenship to the people of Guam and established self-government. However, the people do not vote in national elections. In 1972 Guam elected its first delegate to the U.S. Congress. The Executive Branch of the Guam government is under the general supervision of the U.S. Secretary of the Interior. In November 1970, Guam elected its first Governor.

Military installations and tourism are important factors in Guam's economy.

Non-Self-Governing Territories

AMERICAN SAMOA

Capital: Fagatogo (on Tutuila Island)
Governor: Peter Tali Coleman
Lieut. Governor: Tufele Liá
1950 population: 18,937
1960 population: 20,051
1980 est. population: 33,506
1970 land area: 76 sq mi. (197 sq km)

American Samoa, a group of five volcanic islands and two coral atolls located some 2,600 miles south of Hawaii in the South Pacific Ocean, is an unincorporated, unorganized territory of the U.S., administered by the Department of the Interior.

By the Treaty of Berlin, signed Dec. 2, 1899, and ratified Feb. 16, 1900, the U.S. was internationally acknowledged to have rights extending over all the islands of the Samoa group east of longitude 171° west of Greenwich. On April 17, 1900, the chiefs of Tutuila and Aunu'u ceded those islands to the U.S. In 1904, the King and chiefs of Manu'a ceded the islands of Ofu, Olosega and Tau (composing the Manu'a group) to the U.S. Swains Island, some 214 miles north of Samoa, was included as part of the territory by Act of Congress March 4, 1925; and on Feb. 20, 1929, Congress formally accepted sovereignty over the entire group and placed the responsibility for administration in the hands of the President. From 1900 to 1951, by Presidential direction, the Department of the Navy governed the territory. On July 1, 1951, administration was transferred to the Department of the Interior. The first Constitution for the territory was signed on April 27, 1960, and became effective on Oct. 17, 1960. It was revised in 1967.

Congress has provided for a non-voting delegate to sit in the House of Representatives in 1980.

The principal products are canned tuna, pet food, fish meal, mats, and handicrafts.

BAKER, HOWLAND, AND JARVIS ISLANDS

These Pacific islands were not to play a role in the extraterritorial plans of the U.S. until May 13, 1936. President F. D. Roosevelt, at that time, placed them under the control and jurisdiction of the Secretary of the Interior for administration purposes.

Baker Island is a saucer-shaped atoll with an area of approximately one square mile. It is about 1,650 miles from Hawaii.

Howland Island, 36 miles to the northeast, is approximately one and a half miles long and half a mile wide.

Jarvis Island is several hundred miles to the east and is approximately two miles long by one and an eighth miles wide.

Baker, Howland, and Jarvis have been uninhabited since 1942. In 1974, these islands became part of the National Wildlife Refuge System, administered by the U.S. Fish & Wildlife Service, Department of The Interior.

CANTON AND ENDERBURY ISLANDS

Canton and Enderbury islands, the largest of the Phoenix group, are jointly administered by the U.S. and Great Britain after an agreement signed April 6, 1939. The status of Canton and Enderbury was the subject of negotiations between the U.S., U.K., and Gilbert Islands Governments in 1979. The negotiations resulted in the signing on September 20, 1979, of a Treaty of Friendship between the U.S. and the Republic of Kiribati, which, once ratified by the U.S. Senate, will formally renounce the U.S. claim to Canton and Enderbury. The Republic of Kiribati declared its independence on July 12, 1979.

Canton is triangular in shape and the largest of the eight islands of this group. It lies about 1,600 miles southwest of Hawaii and was discovered at the turn of the 18th century by U.S. whalers. After World War II it served as an aviation support facility, and later as a missile tracking station. Since 1967, the island has been utilized by the U.S. Air Force Space and Missile Test Center.

Enderbury is rectangular in shape and is 3.5 miles long by 1.5 miles wide. It is unpopulated and lies about 32 miles southeast of Canton.

JOHNSTON ATOLL

Johnston is a coral atoll about 700 miles southwest of Hawaii. It consists of four small islands—Johnston Island, Sand Island, Hikina Island, and Akau Island—which lie on a reef about 9 miles long in a northeast-southwest direction.

The atoll was discovered by Capt. Charles James Johnston of *H.M.S. Cornwallis* in 1807. In 1858 it was claimed by Hawaii, and later became a U.S. possession.

Johnston Atoll is under the administrative control of the Air Force.

KINGMAN REEF

Kingman Reef, located about 1,000 miles south of Hawaii, was discovered by Capt. E. Fanning in

1798, but named for Capt. W. E. Kingman, who rediscovered it in 1853. The reef, drying only on its northeast, east and southeast edges, is of atoll character. A small islet, 3 feet high, lies on its east side. The reef is triangular in shape, with its apex northward; it is about 9.5 miles long, east and west, and 5 miles wide, north and south, within the 100-fathom curve.

MIDWAY ISLANDS

Midway Islands, lying about 1,200 miles west-northwest of Hawaii, were discovered by Captain N. C. Brooks of the Hawaiian bark *Gambia* on July 5, 1859, in the name of the United States. The atoll was formally declared a U.S. possession in 1867, and in 1903 Theodore Roosevelt made it a naval reservation.

Midway Islands consist of a circular atoll, 6 miles in diameter, and enclosing two islands. Eastern Island, on its southeast side, is triangular in shape, and about 1.2 miles long. Sand Island on its south side, is about 2 miles long in a northeast-southwest direction.

The Midway Islands are within a naval defensive sea area. The Navy Department maintains an installation and has jurisdiction over the atoll.

SWAN ISLANDS

The Swan Islands are two small islands, Great Swan and Little Swan, in the Caribbean Sea, 98 miles north of Honduras. They were claimed by the U.S. in 1863, but Honduras also claimed them on the basis of their discovery by the Spanish. After years of dispute, the U.S. in 1971 signed a treaty recognizing Honduran sovereignty over the islands. The treaty ratifications were exchanged on Sept. 1, 1972.

U.S. VIRGIN ISLANDS

Capital: Charlotte Amalie (on St. Thomas)
Governor: Juan Luis
1950 population: 26,665
1960 population: 32,099
1970 population: 62,468 (St. Thomas, 28,960; St. Croix, 31,779; St. John, 1,729)
1979 est. population: 120,000 (St. Thomas, 56,270; St. Croix, 61,260; St. John, 2,470)
1970 land area: 132 sq mi. (342 sq km) (St. Croix, 82 [212 sq km]; St. Thomas, 32 [83 sq km]; St. John, 20 [52 sq km])

The Virgin Islands, consisting of nine main islands and some 75 islets, were discovered by Columbus in 1493. Since 1666, England has held six of the main islands; the other three (St. Croix, St. Thomas, and St. John), as well as about 50 of the islets, were eventually acquired by Denmark, which named them the Danish West Indies. In 1917, these islands were purchased by the U.S. from Denmark for $25 million.

Congress granted U.S. citizenship to Virgin Islanders in 1927; and, in 1931, administration was transferred from the Navy to the Department of the Interior. Universal suffrage was given in 1936 to all persons who could read and write the English language. The Governor was elected by popular vote for the first time in 1970; previously he had been appointed by the President of the U.S. A unicameral 15-man legislature serves the Virgin Islands, and recent Congressional legislation gave the islands a non-voting Representative in Congress.

About 80% of the population is black, and there is limited farming, fishing, and cattle raising. Industrial products include rum, watches, costume jewelry, clothing, alumina, pharmaceuticals, and petroleum products. Tourism is the principal industry.

WAKE ISLAND

Wake Island, about halfway between Midway and Guam, is an atoll comprising the three islets of Wilkes, Peale, and Wake. They were discovered by the British in 1796 and annexed by the U.S. in 1898. The entire area comprises 3 square miles and has no native population. In 1938, Pan American Airways established a seaplane base and Wake Island has been used as a commercial base since then. On Dec. 8, 1941, it was attacked by the Japanese, who finally took possession on Dec. 23. It was surrendered by the Japanese on Sept. 4, 1945.

The Federal Aviation Administration maintained a station on Wake Island until June 1972, when civil administration of the island was taken over by the U.S. Air Force. In 1962, the area was placed under the jurisdiction of the Department of the Interior.

Trust Territory of the Pacific Islands (Micronesia)

In 1885, Germany assumed a protectorate over the Marshall Islands; and, in 1899, she purchased the Northern Mariana and Caroline Islands from Spain. These islands were occupied by the Japanese in 1914 and were mandated to Japan by the League of Nations in 1919. On April 2, 1947, the U. N. Security Council approved a trusteeship agreement proposed by the U.S. under which the Northern Mariana, Caroline, and Marshall Islands became a Strategic Trust Territory under the administration of the U.S. The measure was approved by the President, with the agreement of Congress, on July 18, 1947. Administration was transferred from the Navy to the Department of the Interior on July 1, 1951. However, during 1953, administration of the islands of the Northern Marianas, except Rota, was transferred back to the Navy. The Department of the Interior again took over administration of these islands in July, 1962.

In February 1975 a covenant was signed by the U.S. and the Marianas Political Status Commission that would make the 17 islands in the Northern Marianas a commonwealth under American sovereignty. The covenant was overwhelmingly ratified by the people of the islands and was approved by President Ford on March 24, 1976.

On April 9, 1978, in Hilo, Hawaii, the heads of the three Micronesian political status commissions and the U.S. negotiator signed a statement of agreed principles which is intended to form the basis of a free association relationship between the U.S. and Micronesia. Negotiations now continue on these aspects. It is the U.S.'s objective to end the trusteeship in 1981.

The entire group comprises more than 2,000 islands, but the total land area is only 717 square miles, many of the islands being only tiny coral reefs. The Micronesians are the main ethnic group; however, the inhabitants of two outlying islands, Kapingamarangi and Nukuoro, are Polynesian. The population of the Trust Territory in 1977 was estimated to be 126,440.

MARIANA ISLANDS

The Mariana Islands, east of the Philippines and south of Japan, include the islands of Guam, Rota, Saipan, Tinian, Pagan, Guguan, Agrihan, and Aguijan. Guam, the largest, is independent of the trusteeship, having been acquired by the U.S. from Spain in 1898. (For more information, *see* the entry on Guam in this section.)

Chief crops are copra and fresh fruits and vegetables.

CAROLINE ISLANDS

The Caroline Islands, east of the Philippines and south of the Marianas, include the Yap, Truk, and the Palau groups and the islands of Ponape and Kosrae, as well as many coral atolls.

The islands are composed chiefly of volcanic rock, and their peaks rise 2,000 to 3,000 feet above sea level. Chief exports of the islands are copra, fish products, and handicrafts.

MARSHALL ISLANDS

The Marshall Islands, east of the Carolines, are divided into two chains: the western or Ralik group, including the atolls Jaluit, Kwajalein, Wotho, Bikini, and Enewetak; and the eastern or Ratak group, including the atolls Mili, Majuro, Maloelap, Wotje, and Likiep.

The islands are of the coral-reef type and rise only a few feet above sea level. The chief crop is coconuts; exports include copra, tortoise shell, mother-of-pearl, etc.

Bikini and Enewetak were the scene of several atom-bomb tests after World War II. Enewetak was returned to Trust Territory administration in August 1976. In April 1977, some 55 original inhabitants, the forerunner of 450 returnees, were resettled after an absence of 30 years.

The Statue of Liberty

The Statue of Liberty ("Liberty Enlightening the World") is a 225-ton, steel-reinforced copper female figure, 152 ft in height, facing the ocean from Liberty[1] Island in New York Harbor. The right hand holds aloft a torch, and the left hand carries a tablet upon which is inscribed: "July IV MDCCLXXVI."

The statue was designed by Frederic Auguste Bartholdi of Alsace as a gift to the United States from the people of France to memorialize the alliance of the two countries in the American Revolution and their abiding friendship. The French people contributed the $250,000 cost.

The 150-foot pedestal was designed by Richard M. Hunt and built by Gen. Charles P. Stone, both Americans. It contains steel underpinnings designed by Alexander Eiffel of France to support the statue. The $270,000 cost was borne by popular subscription in this country. President Grover Cleveland accepted the statue for the United States on Oct. 28, 1886.

On Sept. 26, 1972, President Richard M. Nixon dedicated the American Museum of Immigration, housed in structural additions to the base of the statue. Some 200 exhibits memorialize the flow of immigrants into the United States, including as many as 5,000 a day on nearby Ellis Island.

On a tablet inside the pedestal is engraved the following sonnet, written by Emma Lazarus (1849–1887):

1. Called Bedloe's Island prior to 1956.

The New Colossus

Not like the brazen giant of Greek fame,
With conquering limbs astride from land to land;
Here at our sea-washed, sunset gates shall stand
A mighty woman with a torch, whose flame
Is the imprisoned lightning, and her name
Mother of Exiles. From her beacon-hand
Glows world-wide welcome; her mild eyes command
The air-bridged harbor that twin cities frame.
"Keep, ancient lands, your storied pomp!" cries she
With silent lips. "Give me your tired, your poor,
Your huddled masses yearning to breathe free,
The wretched refuse of your teeming shore.
Send these, the homeless, tempest-tost to me,
I lift my lamp beside the golden door!"

Arlington National Cemetery

Arlington National Cemetery occupies 612 acres in Virginia on the Potomac River, directly opposite Washington. This land was part of the estate of John Parke Custis, Martha Washington's son, who built the mansion which later became the home of Robert E. Lee. In 1864, Arlington became a military cemetery. Over 170,000 persons, including many thousands of soldiers as well as hundreds of distinguished Americans, are buried there. Expansion of the cemetery began in fiscal year 1965, using a 180-acre tract of land directly east of the present site.

In 1921, an Unknown American Soldier of World War I was buried in a temporary crypt in the cemetery; the completed Tomb was opened to the public without ceremony in 1932. Two additional Unknowns, one from World War II and one from the Korean War, were buried May 30, 1958. The inscription carved on the side of the Tomb of the Unknown Soldier reads:

HERE RESTS IN
HONORED GLORY
AN AMERICAN
SOLDIER
KNOWN BUT TO GOD

Tabulated Data on State Governments

State	Governor: Term, years	Governor: Annual salary	Legislature[1]: Membership U[3]	Membership L[4]	Term, yrs. U[3]	Term, yrs. L[4]	Salaries of members[5]	Highest Court[2]: Members	Term, years	Annual salary[6]
Alabama	4[10]	$50,000[16]	35	105	4	4	$6,800 per annum[16]	9	6	$39,500
Alaska	4	70,068	20	40	4	2	17,280 per annum	5	(8)	70,068
Arizona	4	50,000	30	60	2	2	6,000 per annum	5	6	47,500
Arkansas	2	35,000	35	100	4	2	7,500 per annum[26]	7	8	41,243
California	4	49,100	40	80	4	2	25,555 per annum	7	12	62,935[26]
Colorado	4	50,000	35	65	4	2	12,000 per annum	7	10	45,600
Connecticut	4	42,000	36	151	2	2	17,000 per biennium	6	8	42,400
Delaware	4[9]	35,000	21	41	4	2	9,600 per annum	3	12	42,000
Florida	4[10]	50,000	40	120	4	2	12,000 per annum	7	6	49,380
Georgia	4[9]	61,050	56	180	2	2	7,200 per annum	7	6	48,530
Hawaii	4	50,000	25	51	4	2	12,000 per session	5	10	45,000
Idaho	4	33,000	35	70	2	2	4,200 per annum	5	6	38,000
Illinois	4	58,000	59	177	4–2	2	28,000 per annum	7	10	58,000
Indiana	4[10]	48,000	50	100	4	2	9,600 per annum	5	(25)	42,000
Iowa	4	60,000	50	100	4	2	12,000 per annum	9	8	49,000
Kansas	4	45,000	40	125	4	2	35 per diem[22]	7	6	47,500
Kentucky	4[7]	45,000	38	100	4	2	50 per diem[22]	7	8	49,000
Louisiana	4	52,400	39	105	4	4	50 per diem[23]	7	10	56,200
Maine	4	35,000	33	151	2	2	7,000 per biennium[16]	6	7	26,000
Maryland	4[10]	60,000	47	141	4	4	17,600 per annum	7	10	56,200
Massachusetts	4	60,000	40	160	2	2	20,335 per annum	7	Life	50,000
Michigan	4	61,500	38	110	4	2	25,500 per annum	7	8	56,500
Minnesota	4	58,000	67	134	4	2	16,500 per annum	9	6	49,000
Mississippi	4[7]	53,000	52	122	4	4	8,100 per session	9	8	46,000
Missouri	4[10]	55,000	34	163	4	2	15,000 per annum[5]	7	12	50,000
Montana	4	37,500	50	100	4	2	40 per diem	7	8	38,000
Nebraska	4[10]	40,000	49[11]	—	4[11]	—	4,800 per annum	7	6	43,000
Nevada	4	50,000	20	40	4	2	4,800 per biennium	5	6	47,250
New Hampshire	2	44,520	24	(12)	2	2	200 per biennium	5	(13)	42,400
New Jersey	4[10]	65,000	40	80	4[14]	2	18,000 per annum	7	7[15]	56,000
New Mexico	4[7]	50,000	42	70	4	2	40 per diem	5	8	44,000
New York	4	85,000	60	150	2	2	23,500 per annum	7	14	69,352
North Carolina	4[7]	50,085	50	120	2	2	6,400 per annum	7	8	50,400
North Dakota	4	42,000	50	100	4	2	5 per diem[16 24]	5	10	41,700
Ohio	4	50,000	33	99	4	2	22,500 per annum	7	6	51,000
Oklahoma	4	48,000	48	101	4	2	12,948 per annum	(19)	6	40,700
Oregon	4[10]	53,394	30	60	4	2	8,400 per annum	7	6	51,356
Pennsylvania	4	66,000	50	203	4	2	25,000 per annum	7	10	64,500
Rhode Island	2	42,500	50	100	2	2	5 per diem[17]	5	(18)	42,198
South Carolina	4[7]	39,500	46	124	4	2	10,000 per annum	5	10	47,000
South Dakota	4[10]	45,000	35	70	2	2	6,000 per biennium	5	8	43,000
Tennessee	4	68,226	33	99	4	2	8,308 per annum	5	8	62,616
Texas	4	71,400	31	150	4	2	7,200 per annum	(20)	6	59,600
Utah	4	40,000	29	75	4	2	25 per diem	5	10	36,000
Vermont	2	44,850	30	150	2	2	225 per week[21]	5	6	35,500
Virginia	4[7]	60,000	40	100	4	2	8,000 per annum	7	12	54,000
Washington	4	63,000	49	98	4	2	11,200 per annum	9	6	51,500
West Virginia	4	50,000	34	100	4	2	5,136 per annum	5	12	40,000
Wisconsin	4	65,801	33	99	4	2	22,632 per annum	7	10	56,016
Wyoming	4	55,000	30	62	4	2	74 per diem	5	8	48,500

1. General Assembly in Ark., Colo., Conn., Del., Ga., Ind., Ky., Md., Mo., N.C., Ohio, Pa., R.I., S.C., Tenn., Vt., Va., Legislative Assembly in N.D., Ore.; General Court in Mass., N.H.; Legislature in other states. Meets biennially in Calif., Ky., Me., Mont., Nev., N.H., N.J., N.C., N.D., Ore., Pa., Texas, Wash. and Wyo.; meets annually in other states. 2. Court of Appeals in Md., N.Y., Supreme Court of Virginia in Va., Supreme Judicial Court in Me., Mass.; Supreme Court in other states. 3. Upper house: Senate in all states. 4. Lower house: Assembly in Calif., Nev., N.Y., Wis.; House of Delegates in Md., Va., W.Va.; General Assembly in N.J.; House of Representatives in other states. 5. Does not include additional payments for expenses, mileage, special sessions, etc., or additional per diem payments beyond salary shown. 6. In some states, Chief Justice receives a higher salary. 7. Cannot succeed himself. 8. Appointed for 3 years; thereafter subject to approval or rejection on a nonpartisan ballot for 10-year term. 9. May serve only 2 terms, consecutive or otherwise. 10. May not serve 3rd consecutive term. 11. Unicameral legislature. 12. Constitutional number: 375–400. 13. Until 70 years old. 14. When term begins in Jan. of 2nd year following U.S. census, term shall be 2 years. 15. 2nd term receive tenure, mandatory retirement at 70. 16. Plus additional expenses. 17. For 60 days only. 18. Term of good behavior. 19. 9 members in Supreme Court, highest in civil cases; 3 in Court of Criminal Appeals. 20. 9 members in Supreme Court, highest in civil cases; 9 in Court of Criminal Appeals. 21. To limit of $6,750 per biennium; $1,800 for special session. 22. When in session. 23. $1,000 per month when not in session. 24. Plus $150 per month. 25. Appointed for 2 years; thereafter elected popularly for 10-year term. 26. To receive cost of living increase not to exceed 10% in the two year period. *Source: Information Please* questionnaires to the states.

Largest Cities of the United States

Source of population and land area: Bureau of the Census. Television households apply to county or counties in which a city is located, except for independent cities; source: the Arbitron Company. Telephones; source: American Telephone & Telegraph Co. Other data were supplied by the cities in response to *Information Please* questionnaires.

ALBUQUERQUE, N.M.

Incorporated as city: 1891
Mayor: David Rusk (to Dec. 1981)
1970 population & (rank): 243,751 (60)
1977 est. population & (rank): 291,187 (50)
1970–77 population change: 19.5%
1976 land area: 95.2 sq mi.
Altitude: 4,958 ft.
Location: Central part of state on Rio Grande River
County: Bernalillo
Churches: 211
City-owned parks: 135
Telephones (Jan. 1, 1978): 213,000
Television households (Jan. 1, 1980): 141,600 (98%)
Radio stations: 14
Television stations: 5
Assessed valuation (1979): $1,086,473,721
City tax rate (1979): $22.22 per $1,000
Bonded debt (1979): $98,515,666
Revenue (1978): $67,756,972
Expenditures (1978): $65,770,824
Chamber of Commerce: Albuquerque Chamber of Commerce, 401 2nd St., N.W., Albuquerque, N.M. 87102. Hispanic Chamber of Commerce 407 Rio Grande Blvd., N.W. Albuquerque, N.M. 87104

ATLANTA, GA.

Incorporated as city: 1847
Mayor: Maynard Jackson (to Jan. 1982)
1970 population & (rank): 495,039 (27)
1977 est. population & (rank): 416,715 (30)
1970–77 population change: –13%
1980 city land area: 136 sq mi.
Altitude: Highest, 1,050 ft; lowest, 940
Location: In northwest central part of state, near Chattahoochee River
Counties: Fulton and De Kalb
Churches (5-county area): 1,500
City-owned parks and parkways: 164 (2,802 ac.)
Telephones (Jan. 1, 1978): 887,476
Television households (Jan. 1980): 366,900 (98%)
Radio stations (15-county area): AM, 22; FM, 9; educational, 5
Television stations (15-county area): 6 commercial; 2 educational
Gross assessed valuation (city, 1979): $3,434,606,314
City tax rate (1979): $43.15 per $1,000
Total bonded debt (1979): $180,974,615
Revenue (1979, incl. General Fund, Airport Revenue, Water/Sewer Fund): $222,912,346
Expenditures (1979): $192,271,513
Chamber of Commerce: Atlanta Chamber of Commerce, 1300 N Omni International, Atlanta, Ga. 30303

Information is gathered on 3 geographic areas: City of Atlanta, 5-county metro area, 15-county SMSA

AUSTIN, TEX.

Incorporated as city: 1839
Mayor: Carole McClellan (to May, 1981)
1970 population & (rank): 251,808 (57)
1977 est. population & (rank): 323,250 (45)[1]
1970–77 population change: +28.3%
1976 city land area: 101.0 sq mi.
Altitude: Highest, 425 ft
Location: In south central part of state, on the Colorado River
County: Seat of Travis Co.
Churches: Protestant, 230; Roman Catholic, 19; Jewish, 2
City-owned parks and playgrounds: 137
Telephones (Jan. 1, 1978): 276,984
Television households (Jan. 1980): 133,300 (98%)
Radio stations: AM, 4; FM, 9
Television stations: 3 commercial; 1 educational
Assessed valuation (1979): $3,664,710,150
Tax rate (1979–80): $18.45 per $1,000
Bonded debt (Sept. 1979): $107,360,000
Revenue (1979–80): $96,540,573
Expenditures (1979–80): $96,868,564
Chamber of Commerce: Austin Chamber of Commerce, 901 W Riverside Dr., Austin, Tex. 78701

1. Includes annexations since 1970.

BALTIMORE, MD.

Incorporated as city: 1797
Mayor: William D. Schaefer (to Dec. 1983)
1970 population & (rank): 905,787 (7)
1977 est. population & (rank): 804,304 (8)
1970–77 population change: –11.2%
1976 land area: 78.3 sq mi.
Altitude: Highest, 490 ft; lowest, sea level
Location: On Patapsco River, about 12 mi. from Chesapeake Bay
County: Independent city
Churches: Roman Catholic, 72; Jewish, 50; Protestant and others, 344
City-owned parks: 347 park areas and tracts (6,314 ac.)
Telephones (Jan. 1, 1978): 1,353,051
Television households (Jan. 1980): 508,200 (99%)
Radio stations: AM, 11; FM, 9
Television stations: 5
Assessed valuation (1980): $2,933,326,000
City tax rate (1979–80): $5.95 per $100
Net bonded debt (March 1980): $426,905,000
Revenue (1980): $1,731,154,967
Expenditures (1980): $1,731,154,967
Chamber of Commerce: Greater Baltimore Committee, 2 Hopkins Plaza, Baltimore, Md. 21201

BOSTON, MASS.

Incorporated as city: 1822
Mayor: Kevin H. White (to Jan. 1984)
1970 population & (rank): 641,071 (16)
1977 est. population & (rank): 618,493 (18)
1970–77 population change: –3.5%
1976 land area: 46.0 sq mi.
Altitude: Highest, 330 ft; lowest, sea level
Location: On Massachusetts Bay, at mouths of Charles and Mystic Rivers
County: Seat of Suffolk Co.
Churches: Protestant, 187; Roman Catholic, 73; Jewish, 28; others, 100
City-owned parks, playgrounds, etc.: 2,276.36 ac.

Telephones (Jan. 1, 1978): 509,534
Television households (Jan. 1980): 256,700 (96%)
Radio stations: AM, 9; FM, 8
Television stations: 7
Assessed valuation (1978–79): $1,738,000,000
City tax rate (1978–79): $252.90 per $1,000
Net bonded debt (June 30, 1979): $516,585,000
Revenue (1978–79): $759,297,234
Expenditures (1978–79): $735,216,414
Chamber of Commerce: Boston Chamber of Commerce, 125 High St., Boston, Mass. 02110

BUFFALO, N.Y.

Incorporated as city: 1832
Mayor: James Griffin (to Dec. 1981)
1970 population & (rank): 462,768 (28)
1977 est. population & (rank): 390,065 (33)
1970–77 population change: −15.7%
1976 land area: 41.3 sq mi.
Altitude: Highest, 698 ft; lowest, 571
Location: At east end of Lake Erie, on Niagara River
County: Seat of Erie Co.
Churches: 60 denominations, with over 1,100 churches
City-owned parks: 10 public parks (3,000 ac.)
Telephones (Jan. 1, 1978): 424,880
Television households (Jan. 1980): 375,000 (98%)
Radio stations: AM, 13; FM, 14
Television stations: 5 (plus reception from 4 Canadian stations)
Assessed valuation (1979–80): $1,014,912,000
City tax rate (1980): $109.40 per $1,000
Total funded debt (long-term, June 30, 1979): $119,086,000
Revenue (general fund, 1978–79): $182,490,933
Expenditures (1978–79): $188,999,515
Chamber of Commerce: Buffalo Area Chamber of Commerce, 107 Delaware Ave., Buffalo, N.Y. 14202

CHARLOTTE, N.C.

Incorporated as city: 1768
Mayor: H. Edward Knox (to Nov. 1981)
1970 population & (rank): 274,784 (53)
1977 est. population & (rank): 295,685 (49)
1970–77 population change: +7.6%
1976 city land area: 108.4 sq mi.
Altitude: 765 ft
Location: In the southern part of state near the border of South Carolina
County: Seat of Mecklenburg Co.
Churches: Protestant, over 400; Roman Catholic, 8; Jewish, 3; Greek Orthodox, 1
City-owned parks and parkways: 87
Telephones (Jan. 1, 1978): 351,982
Television households (Jan. 1980): 131,900 (98%)
Radio stations: AM, 9; FM, 4
Television stations: 4 commercial; 2 educational
Assessed valuation (1979–80): $5,414,828,657
City tax rate (includes county, 1979–80): $16.40 per $1,000
Bonded debt (June 30, 1979): $139,874,000
Revenue (1979–80): $201,000,000
Expenditures (1979–80): $201,000,000
Chamber of Commerce: Greater Charlotte Chamber of Commerce, P.O. Box 32785, Charlotte, N.C., 28232

CHICAGO, ILL.

Incorporated as city: 1837
Mayor: Jane M. Byrne (to April 1983)
1970 population & (rank): 3,369,357 (2)
1977 est. population & (rank): 3,062,881 (2)
1970–77 population change: −9.1%
1976 land area: 222.8 sq mi.
Altitude: Highest, 672 ft; lowest, 578.5
Location: On lower west shore of Lake Michigan
County: Seat of Cook Co.
Churches: Protestant, 850; Roman Catholic, 263; Jewish, 65
City-owned parks: 580
Telephones (Jan. 1, 1978): 2,610,000
Television households (Jan. 1980): 1,882,300 (98%)
Radio stations: AM, 15; FM, 17
Television stations: 8
Assessed valuation (1979): $13,501,395,156
Total Chicago tax rate (1978): $90.16 per $1,000
Total gross bonded debt (1978): $1,374,850
Revenue (1980): $1,420,490,786
Expenditures (1980): $1,408,353,442
Chamber of Commerce: Chicago Association of Commerce & Industry, 130 S Michigan Ave., Chicago, Ill. 60603

CINCINNATI, OHIO

Incorporated as city: 1819
Mayor: J. Kenneth Blackwell (to Dec. 1981)
City Manager: Sylvester Murray
1970 population & (rank): 453,514 (30)
1977 est. population & (rank): 403,363 (31)
1970–77 population change: −11.1%
1976 land area: 78.1 sq mi.
Altitude: Highest, 960 ft; lowest, 441
Location: In southwestern corner of state on Ohio River
County: Seat of Hamilton Co.
Churches: 850
City-owned parks: 96 (4,345 ac.)
Telephones (Jan. 1, 1978): 740,074
Television households (Jan. 1980): 312,300 (98%)
Radio stations: AM, 9; FM, 12 (Greater Cincinnati)
Television stations: 6
Assessed valuation (1979): $2,319,248,470
City tax rate (1979): $11.12 per $1,000
Bonded debt (1979): $184,225,312
Revenue (general fund, 1979): $110,281,151
Expenditures (general fund, 1979): $106,727,063
Chamber of Commerce: Cincinnati Chamber of Commerce, 120 W Fifth St., Cincinnati, Ohio 45202

CLEVELAND, OHIO

Incorporated as city: 1836
Mayor: George V. Voinovich (to Dec. 1981)
1970 population & (rank): 750,879 (10)
1977 est. population & (rank): 609,187 (19)
1970–77 population change: −18.9%
1976 land area: 75.9 sq mi.
Altitude: Highest, 865 ft.; lowest, 573
Location: On Lake Erie at mouth of Cuyahoga River
County: Seat of Cuyahoga Co.
Churches: [1] Protestant, 717; Roman Catholic, 162; Jewish, 23; Eastern Orthodox, 18
City-owned parks: 41 (1,930 ac.)
Telephones (Jan. 1, 1978): 911,182
Television households (Jan. 1980): 548,500 (98%)
Radio stations: AM, 13; FM, 14
Television stations: 7
Assessed valuation (1980): $3,422,279,623
City tax rate (1980): $69.80 per $1,000
Bonded debt (March 31, 1980): $429,622,000
Revenue (est. 1980): $420,291,089
Expenditures (est. 1980): $420,291,089
Chamber of Commerce: Greater Cleveland Growth Association, 690 Union Commerce Building, Cleveland, Ohio 44115

1. 100-mile area.

COLUMBUS, OHIO

Incorporated as city: 1834
Mayor: Tom Moody (to Jan. 1984)
1970 population & (rank): 540,025 (21)
1977 est. population & (rank): 532,339 (22)
1970–77 population change: −1.4%
1977 land area: 172.6 sq. mi.
Altitude: Highest, 902 ft; lowest, 702
Location: In central part of state, on Scioto River
County: Seat of Franklin Co.
Churches: Protestant, 412; Roman Catholic, 43; Jewish, 5
City-owned parks: 135 (10,931 ac.)
Telephones (Jan. 1, 1978): 473,954
Television households (Jan. 1980): 313,800 (98%)
Radio stations: AM, 8; FM, 6
Television stations: 3 commercial, 2 educational
Assessed valuation (1978): $3,153,937,894
City tax rate (1978): $41.70 per $1,000
Bonded debt (Dec. 31, 1978): $293,454,747
Revenue (1978): $835,084,145
Expenditures (1978): $794,753,893
Chamber of Commerce: Columbus Area Chamber of Commerce, P.O. Box 1527, Columbus, Ohio 43216

DALLAS, TEX.

Incorporated as city: 1856
Mayor: Bob Folsom (to April 1981)
City Manager: George Schrader (apptd. Dec. 1972)
1970 population & (rank): 844,401 (8)
1977 est. population & (rank): 844,528 (7)[1]
1970–77 population change: +0.05%
1976 land area: 309.3 sq mi.
Altitude: Highest, 750 ft; lowest, 375
Location: In northeastern part of state, on Trinity River
County: Seat of Dallas Co.
Churches: 1,200 (in Dallas Co.)
City-owned parks: 272 (23,434 ac.)
Telephones (Jan. 1, 1978): 809,921
Television households (Jan. 1980): 524,900 (98%)
Radio stations: AM, 14; FM, 15
Television stations: 7
Assessed valuation (1979–80): $9,685,000,000
City tax rate (1978–79): $13.30 per $1,000
Net revenue bond debt (Sept. 30, 1979): $232,911,000
Net tax supported debt (Sept. 30, 1979): $349,049,000
Revenue (est. 1979–80): $223,138,000
Expenditures (est. 1979–80): $410,785,514
Chamber of Commerce: Dallas Chamber of Commerce. 1507 Pacific, Dallas, Tex. 75201

1. Includes annexations since 1970.

DENVER, COLO.

Incorporated as city: 1861
Mayor: William H. McNichols, Jr. (to July 1, 1983)
1970 population & (rank): 514,678 (25)
1977 est. population & (rank): 475,098 (26)
1970–77 population change: −7.7%
1976 land area: 113.6 sq mi.
Altitude: Highest, 5,470 ft; lowest, 5,130
Location: In northeast central part of state, on South Platte River
County: Coextensive with Denver Co.
Churches: Protestant, 815; Roman Catholic, 63; Jewish, 13[1]
City-owned parks: 155 (3,600 ac.)
City-owned mountain parks: 40 (13,448 ac.)
Telephones (Jan. 1, 1978): 1,186,519
Television households (Jan. 1980): 204,200 (97%)
Radio stations: AM, 18; FM, 13[1]
Television stations: 5
Assessed valuation (1978): $2,099,000,000
City tax rate (1978): $28.08 per $1,000[2]
Bonded debt (1978): $337,210,000[2]
Revenue (1978): $513,786,661[2]
Expenditures (1978): $452,345,417[2]
Chamber of Commerce: Denver Chamber of Commerce, 1301 Welton, Denver, Colo. 80204

1. Metropolitan area. 2. Excluding school district.

DETROIT, MICH.

Incorporated as city: 1815
Mayor: Coleman A. Young (to Jan. 1982)
1970 population & (rank): 1,514,063 (5)
1977 est. population & (rank): 1,289,910 (6)
1970–77 population change: −14.8%
1976 land area: 138.0 sq mi.
Altitude: Highest, 685 ft; lowest, 574
Location: In southeastern part of state, on Detroit River
County: Seat of Wayne Co.
Churches: [1] Protestant, 2,204; Roman Catholic, 333; Jewish, 40
City-owned parks: 60 parks (3,843 ac.); 388 sites (5,838 ac.)
Telephones (Jan. 1, 1978): 1,510,543
Television households (Jan. 1980): 817,600 (98%)
Radio stations: AM, 17; FM, 37 (7-county area)
Television stations: 8 (incl. Windsor, Ontario, Canada)[1]
Assessed valuation (1980): $5,051,552,870
City tax rate (1980–81): $33.91 per $1,000[2]
Net bonded debt (March 1980): General obligations, (net): $422,724,143; revenue and self-supported debt (gross): $261,645,000
Revenue (1979–80): $1,490,367,517[3]
Expenditures (1979–80): $1,490,367,517[3]
Chamber of Commerce: Greater Detroit Chamber of Commerce, 150 Michigan Ave., Detroit, Mich. 48226

1. Six-county metropolitan area. 2. Excludes school system. 3. Includes utilities.

EL PASO, TEX.

Incorporated as city: 1873
Mayor: Tom Westfall (April 1981)
1970 population & (rank): 322,261 (45)
1977 est. population & (rank): 395,419 (32)
1970–77 population change: +22.7%
1976 land area: 161.1 sq mi.
Altitude: 4,000 ft
Location: In far western part of state, on Rio Grande
County: Seat of El Paso Co.
Churches: Protestant, 212; Roman Catholic, 36; Jewish, 2; others, 13
City-owned parks: 83 (4,694 ac.)
Telephones (Jan. 1, 1978): 262,710
Television households (Jan. 1980): 132,600 (98%)
Radio stations: AM, 9; FM, 5
Television stations: 5
Assessed valuation (1979): $2,393,587,285
City tax rate (1978): $13.20 per $1,000, city; $14.90, El Paso Independent School District: $14.90, Ysleta Independent School District.
Bonded debt (1979): $50,144,000
Revenue (1979): $57,307,920
Expenditures (1979): $57,307,920
Chamber of Commerce: El Paso Chamber of Commerce, 10 Civic Center Plaza, El Paso, Tex. 79944

FORT WORTH, TEX.

Incorporated as city: 1873
Mayor: Woodie Woods (to April 1981)

City Manager: Robert L. Herchert
1970 population & (rank): 393,455 (33)
1977 est. population & (rank): 367,993 (36)
1970–77 population change: −6.5%
1976 land area: 230.1 sq mi.
Altitude: Highest, 780 ft; lowest, 520
Location: In north central part of state, on Trinity River
County: Seat of Tarrant Co.
Churches: Protestant, 392; Roman Catholic, 16; Jewish, 2
City-owned parks: 126 (7,817 ac.; 3,500 ac. in Nature Center)
Telephones (Jan. 1, 1978): 347,138
Television households (Jan. 1980): 276,800 (98%)
Radio stations: AM, 6; FM, 8
Television stations: 6 (2 local)
Assessed valuation (1979–80): $2,552,863,770
City tax rate (1979–80): $15.39 per $1,000
Bonded debt (Sept. 30, 1979): $215,798,000
Revenue (1979–80 tax-supported funds): $97,393,604
Expenditures (1979–80 tax-supported funds): $97,393,604
Chamber of Commerce: Fort Worth Chamber of Commerce, 700 Throckmorton, Fort Worth, Tex. 76102

HONOLULU, HAWAII

Incorporated as city and county: 1907
Mayor: Frank F. Fasi (to Jan. 1981)
1970 population & (rank): 324,871 (44)
1977 est. population & (rank): 717,852[1] (11)
1970–77 population change: 13.8%[2]
1974 land area of city and county: 604 sq mi.
Altitude: Highest, 4,025 ft; lowest, sea level
Location: The city and county government's jurisdiction includes the entire island of Oahu
Churches: Roman Catholic, 33; Buddhist, 32; Jewish, 2; Protestant and others, 325
City-owned parks: 4,556 ac.
Telephones (Jan. 1, 1978): 361,901
Television households (Sept. 1976): 204,200 (97%)
Radio stations: AM, 19; FM, 7
Television stations: 5
Assessed valuation (1979): $8,744,000,000 (60% of market value.)
City and county tax rate (1979): $15.23 per $1,000
Bonded debt (June 1979): $256,000,000
Net revenue (1978–79): $285,500,000
Net expenditures (1978–79): $293,800,000; capital improvement budget, $44,000,000
Chamber of Commerce: Chamber of Commerce of Hawaii, 735 Bishop St., Honolulu, Hawaii 96813

1. City and county area. 2. Based on city and county population of 630,528 in 1970.

HOUSTON, TEX.

Incorporated as city: 1837
Mayor: Jim McConn (to Dec. 1981)
1970 population & (rank): 1,233,535 (6)
1977 est. population & (rank): 1,554,960 (5)[1]
1970–77 population change: +26.1%
1976 land area: 489.2 sq mi.
Altitude: Highest, 120 ft; lowest, sea level
Location: In southeastern part of state, near Gulf of Mexico
County: Seat of Harris Co.
Churches: 1,750[2]
City-owned parks: 259 (5,742 ac., not including parkways)
Telephones (Jan. 1, 1978): 1,359,494
Television households (Jan. 1980): 816,400 (98%)
Radio stations: AM, 14; FM, 16[1]
Television stations: 6
Assessed valuation (1978): $12,000,803,000
City tax rate (1978): $15.80 per $1,000
Bonded debt (1978): $1,549,034,000
Revenue (1978): $353,500,000
Expenditures (1978): $364,349,000
Chamber of Commerce: Houston Chamber of Commerce, 1100 Milam Building, Houston, Tex. 77002

1. Includes annexations since 1970. 2. Metropolitan area (Harris County).

INDIANAPOLIS, IND.

Incorporated as city: 1832 (reincorporated 1838)
Mayor: William H. Hudnut III (to Jan. 1984)
1970 population & (rank): 742,925 (11)
1977 est. population & (rank): 704,556 (12)
1970–77 population change: −5.2%
1976 land area: 375.2 sq mi.
Altitude: Highest, 840 ft; lowest, 700
Location: In central part of the state, on West Fork of White River
County: Seat of Marion Co.
Churches: 1,200[1]
City-owned parks: 188 (8,992 ac.)
Telephones (Jan. 1, 1978): 670,039
Television households (Jan. 1980): 267,600 (98%)
Radio stations: AM, 9; FM, 13[1]
Television stations: 6[1]
Assessed valuation (1979): (consolidated city), $2,310,999,010; (Marion County) $2,474,695,580
City tax rate (Center Township, 1980): $125.60 per $1,000
Gross debt (consolidated city, Dec. 31, 1979): $212,344,000
Revenue (1979): $319,228,517
Expenditures (1979): $262,024,320
Chamber of Commerce: Indianapolis Chamber of Commerce, 320 N Meridian St., Indianapolis, Ind. 46202

1. Marion County.

JACKSONVILLE, FLA.

Incorporated as city: 1822
Mayor: Jake M. Godbold (to July 1, 1983)
1970 population & (rank): 528,865 (23)
1977 est. population & (rank): 527,777 (23)
1970–77 population change: +0.02%
1976 land area: 765.7 sq mi.
Altitude: Highest, 71 ft; lowest, sea level
Location: On St. Johns River, 20 miles from Atlantic Ocean
County: Duval
Churches: Protestant, 688; Roman Catholic, 24; Jewish, 4; others, 7
City-owned parks and playgrounds: 138 (1,522 ac.)
Telephones (Jan. 1, 1978): 418,919
Television households (Jan. 1980): 198,700 (98%)
Radio stations: AM, 15; FM, 10
Television stations: 4 commercial, 1 educational
Assessed valuation (1978): $6,192,936,985
City tax rate (1979–80): $17.89 per $1,000 (old city area); $16.80 (old county area)
Bonded debt (1979): $56,668,606
Revenue (1979–80): $915,147,758
Expenditures (1979–80): $915,147,758
Chamber of Commerce: Jacksonville Area Chamber of Commerce, Jacksonville, Fla. 32202

KANSAS CITY, MO.

Incorporated as city: 1850
Mayor: Richard L. Berkley (to April 1983)
City Manager: Robert A. Kipp (apptd. Jan. 1974)
1970 population & (rank): 507,330 (26)
1977 est. population & (rank): 458,573 (27)
1970–77 population change: −9.6%

1976 land area: 316.3 sq mi.
Altitude: Highest, 1,014 ft; lowest, 722
Location: In western part of state, at juncture of Missouri and Kansas Rivers
County: Located in Jackson, Clay, and Platte Co.
Churches: 1,100 churches of all denominations
City-owned parks and playgrounds: 157 (7,320 ac.)
Telephones (Jan. 1, 1978): 342,558
Television households (Jan. 1980): 303,300 (98%)
Radio stations: AM, 14; FM, 13[1]
Television stations: 6[1]
Assessed valuation (1978–79): $1,646,306,046
City tax rate (1978–79): $15.20 per $1,000
Bonded debt (1978–79): $82,361,000
Revenue (1978–79): $253,451,227
Expenditures (1978–79): $247,123,711
Budget (gross total, 1979–80): $294,151,075
Chamber of Commerce: Chamber of Commerce of Greater Kansas City, 920 Main St., Kansas City, Mo. 64105

1. Metropolitan area. 2. Operating and debt.

LONG BEACH, CALIF.

Founded: 1881
Mayor: Dr. Thomas J. Clark (to July 1981)
City Manager: John E. Dever (Jan. 1, 1977)
1970 population & (rank): 358,879 (40)
1977 est. population & (rank): 336,697 (41)
1970–77 population change: −6.2%
1976 land area: 50.1 sq mi.
Altitude: Highest, 170 ft; lowest, sea level
Location: On San Pedro Bay, south of Los Angeles
County: In Los Angeles Co.
Churches: 236
City-owned parks: 43 (1,620 ac.)
Telephones: (included in Los Angeles area)
Television households: (included in Los Angeles area)
Radio stations: AM, 2; FM, 6
Television stations: 1 (cable)
Assessed valuation (1978–79): $1,760,863,000
City tax rate (1978–79): none; county, $40 per $1,000
Bonded debt (June 1979): $6,197,718
Revenue (1978–79): $394,716,336
Expenditures (1978–79): $373,353,678
Chamber of Commerce: Long Beach Chamber of Commerce, 50 Oceangate Plaza, Long Beach, Calif. 90802

LOS ANGELES, CALIF.

Incorporated as city: 1850
Mayor: Tom Bradley (to June 1981)
1970 population & (rank): 2,811,801 (3)
1977 est. population & (rank): 2,761,222 (3)
1970–77 population change: −1.8%
1976 land area: 463.9 sq mi.
Altitude: Highest, 5,081 ft; lowest, sea level
Location: In southwestern part of state, on Pacific Ocean
County: Seat of Los Angeles Co.
Churches: 1,963 of all denominations
City-owned parks: 296 (14,489 ac.)
Telephones (extended area, Jan. 1, 1978): 5,861,543[1]
Television households (Jan. 1980): 2,701,700 (96%)[1]
Radio stations: AM, 32; FM, 40
Television stations: 18
Assessed valuation (1979–80): $15,009,367,784
City tax rate (1979–80): $1.38 per $1,000 (25% ratio)[2]
Gross debt (June 30, 1979): general obligation bonds, $108,275,000; revenue bonds, $109,998,000
Revenue (est. 1979–80): $2,909,074,972
Expenditures (est. 1979–80): $2,909,074,972
Chamber of Commerce: Los Angeles Chamber of Commerce, 404 S Bixel St., Los Angeles, Calif. 90017

1. Includes Long Beach, Calif. 2. City rate for indebtedness. City also receives 33.5% of revenues collected within the county at rate of $40 per $1,000 of assessed value.

LOUISVILLE, KY.

Incorporated as city: 1828
Mayor: William B. Stansbury (to Dec. 1981)
1970 population & (rank): 361,706 (38)
1977 est. population & (rank): 322,870 (46)
1970–77 population change: −10.7%
1976 land area: 60.0 sq mi.
Altitude: Highest, 565 ft; lowest, 477
Location: In north central part of state, on Ohio River
County: Seat of Jefferson Co.
Churches: 678[1]
City-owned parks and playgrounds: 166 (over 7,000 ac.)
Telephones (Jan. 1, 1978): 563,858
Television households (Jan. 1980): 236,100 (99%)
Radio stations: 16
Television stations: 5
Assessed valuation (1979): $3,211,429,843
City tax rate (1979–80): $5.66 per $1,000 (city purposes only; exclusive of schools)
Net bonded debt (Jan. 1, 1980): $42,209,000
Revenue (1978–79): $90,647,841
Expenditures (1978–79): $98,832,491
Chamber of Commerce: Louisville Area Chamber of Commerce, 300 W Liberty St., Louisville, Ky. 40202

MEMPHIS, TENN.

Incorporated as city: 1826
Mayor: Wyeth Chandler (to Dec. 1984)
1970 population & (rank): 623,530 (17)
1977 est. population & (rank): 668,443 (15)
1970–77 population change: +7.2%
1976 land area: 280.1 sq mi.
Altitude: Highest, 331 ft
Location: In southwestern corner of state, on Mississippi River
County: Seat of Shelby Co
Churches: 1,000
Parks and playgrounds: 155 (5,300 ac.)
Telephones (Jan. 1979): 247,000 (98%)
Television households (Jan. 1, 1980): 256,000 (98%)
Radio stations: AM, 13; FM, 8
Television stations: 5
Assessed valuation (1978): $1,875,240,000
City tax rate (1978–79): $37.40 per $1,000
Bonded debt (March 1979): $453,120,000
Revenue (1978–79): $249,997,789
Expenditures (1978–79): $249,997,789
Chamber of Commerce: Memphis Area Chamber of Commerce, P.O. Box 224, Memphis, Tenn. 38103

MIAMI, FLA.

Incorporated as city: 1896
Mayor: Maurice A. Ferre (to Nov. 1981)
City manager: Joseph R. Grassie (apptd. May 1976)
1970 population & (rank): 334,859 (42)
1977 est. population & (rank): 346,716 (40)
1970–77 population change: +3.6%
1976 land area: 34.3 sq mi.
Altitude: Average, 12 ft
Location: In southeastern part of state, on Biscayne Bay
County: Seat of Dade Co.
Churches: Protestant, 592; Roman Catholic, 53; Jewish, 48
City-owned parks: 94

Telephones (Jan. 1, 1978): 1,019,014
Television households (Jan. 1980): 555,600 (98%)
Radio stations: AM, 18; FM, 20; educational, 1
Television stations: 5 commercial, 2 educational
Assessed valuation (1979–80): $4,439,976,680
City tax rate (1979–80): $13.96 per $1,000
Bonded debt (Sept. 1980): $134,655,000
Revenue (1979–80): $164,271,222
Expenditures (1979–80): $164,271,222
Chamber of Commerce: Greater Miami Chamber of Commerce, 391 N.E. 15th St., Miami, Fla. 33132

MILWAUKEE, WIS.

Incorporated as city: 1846
Mayor: Henry W. Maier (to April 1984)
1970 population & (rank): 717,372 (12)
1977 est. population & (rank): 653,417 (17)
1970–77 population change: −8.9%
1976 land area: 95.0 sq mi.
Altitude: 580.60 ft
Location: In southeastern part of state, on Lake Michigan
County: Seat of Milwaukee Co.
Churches: 411
County-owned parks: 14,061 ac.
Telephones (Jan. 1, 1978): 848,381
Television households (Jan. 1980): 353,200 (98%)
Radio stations: AM, 9; FM, 12
Television stations: 7
Assessed valuation (1980): $7,789,445,760
City tax rate (1980): $28.62 per $1,000
Gross debt (1979): $162,228,825
Revenue (1979): $391,755,421
Expenditures (1979): $382,627,764
Chamber of Commerce: Metropolitan Milwaukee Association of Commerce, 828 N. Broadway, Milwaukee, Wis. 53202

MINNEAPOLIS, MINN.

Incorporated as city: 1867
Mayor: Donald M. Fraser (to Jan. 1982)
1970 population & (rank): 434,400 (32)
1977 est. population & (rank): 360,269 (38)
1970–77 population change: −17.1%
1976 land area: 55.5 sq mi.
Altitude: Highest, 945 ft; lowest, 695
Location: In southeast central part of state, on Mississippi River
County: Seat of Hennepin Co.
Churches: 419
City-owned parks: 153
Telephones (incl. St. Paul, Jan. 1, 1978): 1,580,900
Television households (Jan. 1980): 331,700 (98%)
Radio stations: AM, 17; FM, 15 (metro area)
Television stations: 6 (metro area)
Assessed valuation (1978): $1,536,765,690[1]
City tax rate (1979): $125.36 per $1,000
Net debt (Dec. 1978): $254,451,000
Revenue (1977): $181,800,858
Expenditures (1977): $181,800,858
Chamber of Commerce: Greater Minneapolis Chamber of Commerce, 15 S Fifth Street, Minneapolis, Minn. 55402

1. Assessed valuations on majority of properties now range from 25% (homesteads) to 43% (commercial, industrial) of actual market value.

NASHVILLE, TENN.

Incorporated as city: 1806
Mayor: Richard H. Fulton (to Sept. 1983)
1970 population & (rank): 447,877 (31)
1977 est. population & (rank): 428,957 (29)
1970–77 population change: −4.2%
1976 land area: 507.7 sq mi.
Altitude: Highest, 1,100 ft; lowest, approx. 400 ft
Location: In north central part of state, on Cumberland River
County: Davidson
Churches: Protestant, 722; Roman Catholic, 15; Jewish, 3
City-owned parks: 67 (6,612 ac.)
Telephones (Jan. 1, 1978): 405,791
Television households (Jan. 1980): 167,300 (99%)
Radio stations: AM, 11; FM, 8
Television stations: 5
Assessed valuation (1979): $1,858,097,042
City tax rate (1979): $60.00 per $1,000
Bonded debt (June 1979): $202,121,000
Revenue (1979): $274,876,333
Expenditures (1979): $268,494,651
Chamber of Commerce: Nashville Area Chamber of Commerce, 161 Fourth Ave. North, Nashville, Tenn. 37219

NEW ORLEANS, LA.

Incorporated as city: 1805
Mayor: Ernest N. Morial (to May 1982)
1970 population & (rank): 593,471 (19)
1977 est. population & (rank): 561,266 (21)
1970–77 population change: −5.4%
1976 land area: 197.1 sq mi.
Altitude: Highest, 15 ft; lowest, −4
Location: In southeastern part of state, between Mississippi River and Lake Ponchartrain
Parish: Seat of Orleans Parish
Churches: 644
City-owned parks: 69 (21,000 ac.)
Telephones (Jan. 1, 1980): 790,308
Television households (Jan. 1980): 203,800 (98%)
Radio stations: AM, 12; FM, 5
Television stations: 5
Assessed valuation (1980): $1,125,161,891
City tax rate (1979): $94.08 per $1,000
Bonded debt (1980): $160,213,000
Revenue (1980): $253,213,000
Expenditures (1980): $253,213,000
Chamber of Commerce: New Orleans and the River Region Chamber of Commerce, 301 Camp Street, New Orleans, La. 70130.

NEW YORK, N.Y.

Chartered as "Greater New York": 1898
Mayor: Edward Koch (to Dec. 31, 1981)
Borough Presidents: Bronx, Stanley Simon; Brooklyn, Howard Golden; Manhattan, Andrew Stein; Queens, Donald R. Manes; Staten Island, Anthony Gaeta
1970 population & (rank): 7,895,563 (1)[1]
1978 est. population & (rank): 7,149,300 (1)[1]
1970–78 population change: −9.5%
1976 land area: 303.7 sq mi. (Queens, 109.6; Brooklyn, 72.8; Staten Island, 55.8; Bronx, 42.5; Manhattan, 23.0)
Altitude: Highest, 410 ft; lowest, sea level
Location: In south of state, at mouth of Hudson River (also known as the North River as it passes Manhattan)
Counties: Consists of 5 counties: Bronx, Kings (Brooklyn), New York (Manhattan), Queens, Richmond (Staten Island)
Churches: Protestant, 1,766; Jewish, 1,256; Roman Catholic 437; Orthodox, 66
City-owned parks: 1,588 (37,372 ac.)
Telephones (Jan. 1, 1978): 5,936,829
Television households (Jan. 1980): 2,836,000 (97%)
Radio stations: AM and FM, 7; AM only, 10; FM only, 12

Television stations: 6 commercial
Assessed valuation (1979–80): $38,055,969,696[2]
City tax rate: (1979–80): $108.75 per $1,000
Total funded debt (June 30, 1979): $6,968,192,000
Revenue (1980): $13,210,849,029
Expenditures (1980): $13,210,849,029
Chamber of Commerce: New York Chamber of Commerce and Industry, 65 Liberty St., New York, N.Y. 10005

1. For population of boroughs, *see* Index. 2. Taxable property only.

NEWARK, N.J.

Incorporated as city: 1836
Mayor: Kenneth A. Gibson (to July 1982)
1970 population & (rank): 381,930 (35)
1977 est. population & (rank): 324,138 (44)
1970–77 population change: −15.1%
1976 land area: 23.5 sq mi.
Altitude: Highest, 273.4 ft; lowest, sea level
Location: In northeastern part of state, on Passaic River and Newark Bay
County: Seat of Essex Co.
Churches: Roman Catholic, 32; Jewish, 4; Protestant and others, 250
City-owned parks: 40 (and 20 mini parks); (39.3 ac.)
County-governed parks in city: 7 (743.97 ac.)
Telephones (Jan. 1, 1978): 322,523
Television households (Jan. 1980): 290,400 (98%)
Radio stations: AM, 2; FM, 4
Television stations: UHF, 1; VHF, 1
Assessed valuation (1980): $1,064,472,900
City tax rate (1980): $93.10 per $1,000
Net bonded debt (1980): $50,052,055
Revenue (1980): $275,309,938
Expenditures (1980): $275,309,938
Chamber of Commerce: Greater Newark Chamber of Commerce, 50 Park Place, Newark, N.J. 07102

OAKLAND, CALIF.

Incorporated as city: 1854
Mayor: Lionel J. Wilson (to June 30, 1981)
City Manager: David A. Self (appt. April 1978)
1970 population & (rank): 361,561 (39)
1977 est. population & (rank): 332,385 (43)
1970–77 population change: −8.1%
1976 land area: 53.4 sq mi.
Altitude: Highest, 1,700 ft; lowest, sea level
Location: In west central part of state, on east side of San Francisco Bay
County: Seat of Alameda Co.
Churches: 374, representing over 78 denominations in the City; over 500 churches in Alameda County
City-owned parks: 2,196 ac.
Telephones (Jan. 1, 1977): 571,508[1]
Television households: (included in San Francisco area)
Radio stations: AM, 3; FM, 2
Television stations: 9 commercial; 3 educational
Assessed valuation (1978–79): $1,515,972,202 (25% of appraised value)
City tax rate (1978–79): $48.70 per $1,000
Bonded debt (est. June 1979): $5,265,000
Revenue (1978–79): $151,187,000
Expenditures (1978–79): $159,221,000
Chamber of Commerce: Oakland Chamber of Commerce, 1939 Harrison St., Suite 400, Oakland, Calif. 94612

1. Included in East Bay Exchange.

OKLAHOMA CITY, OKLA.

Incorporated as city: 1890
Mayor: Mrs. Patience Latting (to April 1983)
City Manager: James J. Cook (apptd. April 3, 1976)
1970 population & (rank): 368,164 (37)
1977 est. population & (rank): 371,802 (35)
1970–77 population change: +1%
1976 land area: 635.7 sq mi.
Altitude: Highest, 1,320 ft; lowest, 1,140
Location: In central part of state, on North Canadian River
County: Seat of Oklahoma Co.
Churches: Roman Catholic, 15; Jewish, 2; Protestant and others, 741
City-owned parks: 132 (3,934 ac.)
Telephones (Jan. 1, 1978): 616,070
Television households (Jan. 1980): 207,100 (98%)
Television stations: 6
Radio stations: AM, 10; FM, 14
Assessed valuation (1979–80): $874,180,415
City tax rate (1979–80): $27.61 per $1,000
Bonded debt (1979–80): $230,828,670
Revenue (general fund, 1979–80): $114,409,000
Expenditures (general fund, 1979–80): $114,409,000
Chamber of Commerce: Oklahoma City Chamber of Commerce, 1 Santa Fe Plaza, Oklahoma City, Okla. 73102

OMAHA, NEB.

Incorporated as city: 1857
Mayor: Al Veys (to June, 1981)
1970 population & (rank): 358,452 (41)
1977 est. population & (rank): 365,711 (37)
1970–77 population change: +2%
1976 land area: 81.7 sq mi.
Altitude: Highest, 1,270 ft
Location: In eastern part of state, on Missouri River
County: Seat of Douglas Co.
Churches: Protestant, 246; Roman Catholic, 44; Jewish, 4
City-owned parks: 99 (3,671.6 ac.)
Telephones (Jan. 1, 1978): 454,800
Television households (Jan. 1980): 143,400 (98%)
Radio stations: AM, 7; FM, 6
Television stations: 4
Assessed valuation (1980): $1,234,204,832
City tax rate (1980): $18.94 per $1,000
Bonded debt (1980): $70,927,410
Revenue (1979): $133,353,026
Expenditures (1979): $132,914,635
Chamber of Commerce: Omaha Chamber of Commerce, 1620 Dodge St., Omaha, Neb. 68102

PHILADELPHIA, PA.

First charter as city: 1701
Mayor: William J. Green (to Jan. 1984)
1970 population & (rank): 1,949,996 (4)
1977 est. population & (rank): 1,778,345 (4)
1970–77 population change: −8.8%
1976 land area: 128.5 sq mi.
Altitude: Highest, 440 ft; lowest, sea level
Location: In southeastern part of state, at junction of Schuylkill and Delaware Rivers
County: Seat of Philadelphia Co. (coterminous)
Churches: Roman Catholic, 139; Jewish, 70; Protestant and others, 830
City-owned parks: 219 (9,160 ac.)
Telephones (Jan. 1, 1978): 1,683,341
Television households (Jan. 1980): 633,400 (97%)
Radio stations: AM, 20; FM, 22
Television stations: 8
Assessed valuation (1980): $5,705,000,000
City and school district tax rate (1979): $61.75 per $1,000
Net bonded debt (June 30, 1979): $1,637,626,000 (incl. revenue bonds of $338,200,000 for water and sewer;

$167,500,000 for gas works; $72,700,000 for airport)
Revenue (1979): $997,278,173
Expenditures (1979): $983,821,319
Chamber of Commerce: Greater Philadelphia Chamber of Commerce, 1617 John F. Kennedy Blvd., Philadelphia, Pa. 19103

PHOENIX, ARIZ.

Incorporated as city: 1881
Mayor: Margaret T. Hance (to Jan. 1982)
City Manager: Marvin A. Andrews (appt. Oct. 1976)
1970 population & (rank): 589,016 (20)
1977 est. population & (rank): 684,516 (14)
1970–77 population change: +16.2%
1976 land area: 273.4 sq mi.
Altitude: Highest, 2,740 ft.; lowest, 1,017
Location: In center of state, on Salt River
County: Seat of Maricopa Co.
City-owned parks: 130 (25,841 ac.)
Telephones (Jan. 1, 1978): 942,847
Television households (Jan. 1980): 474,200 (97%)
Radio stations: AM, 19; FM, 15
Television stations: 8 commercial; 1 educational
Assessed valuation (est. 1980–81): $1,867,000,000
City tax rate (1979–80): $18.10 per $1,000
Bonded debt (Dec. 1979): $434,232,000
Resources (est. 1980–81): $412,000,000
Expenditures (est. 1980–81): $392,450,000
Chamber of Commerce: Phoenix Chamber of Commerce, 805 N Second St., Phoenix, Ariz. 85004

PITTSBURGH, PA.

Incorporated as city: 1816
Mayor: Richard S. Caliguiri (to Jan. 1982)
1970 population & (rank): 520,089 (24)
1977 est. population & (rank): 442,139 (28)
1970–77 population change: −15%
1976 land area: 55.2 sq mi.
Altitude: Highest, 1,240 ft; lowest, 715
Location: In southwestern part of state, at beginning of Ohio River
County: Seat of Allegheny Co.
Churches: Protestant, 348; Roman Catholic, 86; Jewish, 28; Orthodox, 26
City-owned parks and playgrounds: 88 (2,471 ac.)
Telephones (Jan. 1, 1979): 810,193
Television households (Jan. 1980): 518,600 (98%)
Radio stations: AM, 18; FM, 9
Television stations: 4
Assessed valuation (1980): land, $381,157,486; buildings, $1,107,779,406
City tax rate (1980): $125.50 per $1,000; buildings, $24.75 per $1,000
Net bonded debt (March 1980): $119,642,321
Revenue (1979): $154,591,842
Expenditures (1979): $153,511,606
Chamber of Commerce: The Chamber of Commerce of Greater Pittsburgh, 411 Seventh Ave., Pittsburgh, Pa. 15222

PORTLAND, ORE.

Incorporated as city: 1851
Mayor: Francis Ivancie (to Jan. 1984)
1970 population & (rank): 382,352 (36)
1977 est. population & (rank): 383,904 (34)
1970–77 population change: +0.4%
1976 land area: 94.3 sq mi.
Altitude: Highest, 1,073 ft; lowest, sea level
Location: In northwestern part of state, on Willamette River
County: Seat of Multnomah Co.
Churches: Protestant, 332; Roman Catholic, 27; Jewish, 4; Buddhist, 4; Vedanta Society, 1
City-owned parks: 228 (8,718 ac.)
Telephones (Jan. 1, 1978): 493,172
Television households (Jan. 1980): 211,900 (95%)
Radio stations: AM, 12; FM, 12
Television stations: 5
Assessed valuation (1979–80): $8,713,348,000 (at 100% of cash value)
City tax rate (1979–80): $63.90 per $1,000
Bonded debt (est. July 1, 1981): $155,582,948
Revenue (est. 1980–81): $286,380,885
Expenditures (est. 1980–81): $284,608,896
Chamber of Commerce: Portland Chamber of Commerce, 824 SW Fifth Ave., Portland, Ore. 97204

ST. LOUIS, MO.

Incorporated as city: 1822
Mayor: James F. Conway (to April 1981)
1970 population & (rank): 622,236 (18)
1977 est. population & (rank): 517,671 (24)
1970–77 population change: −16.8%
1976 land area: 61.2 sq mi.
Altitude: Highest, 616 ft; lowest, 413
Location: In east central part of state, on Mississippi River
County: Independent city
Churches: 900[1]
City-owned parks: 89 (2,639 ac.)
Telephones (Jan. 1, 1978): 573,529
Television households (Jan. 1980): 498,100 (98%)
Radio stations: AM, 18; FM, 20[1]
Television stations: 5 commercial; 1 educational
Assessed valuation (1977): $1,370,506,818
City tax rate (1977): $64.20 per $1,000
Bonded debt (general obligation, 1977–78): $82,414,766
Revenue (1977–78): $190,452,564
Expenditures (1977–78): $209,082,414
Chamber of Commerce: St. Louis Regional Commerce and Growth Association, 10 Broadway, St. Louis, Mo. 63102.

1. Metropolitan area.

SAN ANTONIO, TEX.

Incorporated as city: 1837
Mayor: Mrs. Lila Cockrell (to May 1981)
City Manager: Thomas E. Huebner (apptd. Jan. 1977)
1970 population & (rank): 708,582 (14)
1977 est. population & (rank): 793,374 (10)[1]
1970–77 population change: +12%
1976 land area: 263.5 sq mi.
Altitude: 700 ft
Location: In south central part of state, on San Antonio River
County: Seat of Bexar Co.
City-owned parks: Approximately 5,881 ac.
Telephones (Jan. 1, 1977): 413,492
Television households, (Jan. 1980): 295,600 (98%)
Radio stations: AM, 13; FM, 12
Television stations: 5
Assessed valuation (1979): $2,875,195,960
City tax rate (1979): $16.50 per $1,000
Net funded debt (1979): $106,925,851
Revenue (est. 1979–80): $201,785,043
Expenditures (est. 1979–80): $201,486,876
Chamber of Commerce: Greater San Antonio Chamber of Commerce, P.O. Box 1628, 602 E Commerce, San Antonio, Tex. 78296

1. Includes annexations since 1970.

SAN DIEGO, CALIF.

Incorporated as city: 1850
Mayor: Pete Wilson (to Dec. 1984)
City Manager: Ray T. Blair, Jr. (apptd. May 1978)
1970 population & (rank): 697,471 (15)
1977 est. population & (rank): 799,725 (9)
1970–77 population change: +14.7%
1976 land area: 322.9 sq mi.
Altitude: Highest, 1,591 ft; lowest, sea level
Location: In southwesternmost part of state, on San Diego Bay
County: Seat of San Diego Co.
Churches: Roman Catholic, 80; Jewish, 8; Protestant 334; Eastern Orthodox, 7; other, 6
City park and recreation facilities: 200 (15,865 ac.)
Telephones (Jan. 1, 1978): 1,043,695[1]
Television households (Jan. 1980): 675,100 (96%)
Radio stations: AM, 10; FM, 19
Television stations: 4
Assessed valuation (1980): $4,359,553,712
City tax rate (1980): $8.80 per $1,000
Bonded debt (1980): $36,338,000
Revenue (est. 1981): $324,946,275
Expenditures (est. 1981): $324,946,275
Chamber of Commerce: San Diego Chamber of Commerce, 110 W. C St., Suite 1600, San Diego, Calif. 92101

1. Metropolitan area.

SAN FRANCISCO, CALIF.

Incorporated as city: 1850
Mayor: Dianne Feinstein (to Jan. 1984)
1970 population & (rank): 715,674 (13)
1977 est. population & (rank): 655,072 (16)
1970–77 population change: −8.5%
1976 land area: 45.4 sq mi.
Altitude: Highest, 925 ft; lowest, sea level
Location: In northern part of state between Pacific Ocean and San Francisco Bay
County: Coextensive with San Francisco Co.
Churches: 540 of all denominations
City-owned parks and squares: 120
Telephones (Jan. 1, 1978): 815,520
Television households (Jan. 1980): 722,500 (94%)[1]
Radio stations: 22
Television stations: 7
Assessed valuation (1979–80): $4,530,179,104
City and county tax rate (1979–80): $49.70 per $1,000
Bonded debt (June 30, 1977): $586,476,000
Revenue (1976–77): $910,456,871
Expenditures (1976–77): $767,393,645
Chamber of Commerce: Greater San Francisco Chamber of Commerce, 465 California St., San Francisco, Calif. 94104

1. Includes Oakland, Calif.

SAN JOSE, CALIF.

Incorporated as city: 1897
Mayor: Janet Gray Hayes (to Dec. 31, 1982)
1970 population & (rank): 461,212 (29)
1977 est. population & (rank): 583,402 (20)
1970–77 population change: +26.5%
1976 land area: 149.3 sq mi.
Altitude: 80 ft
Location: In northern part of state, on south San Francisco Bay, 50 miles from San Francisco
County: Santa Clara
Churches: Protestant, 195; Roman Catholic, 29; Jewish, 4; others, 24
City-owned parks and playgrounds: 143 (2,882 ac.)[2]
Telephones (Jan. 1, 1978): 601,580
Television households (Jan. 1980): 496,700 (95%)[1]
Radio stations: AM, 5; FM, 6
Television stations: 2 commercial; 1 educational
Assessed valuation (1979–80): $2,747,533,831
City tax rate (1979–80): $6.11 per $1,000
Bonded debt (June 1980): $40,019,000
Revenue (1979–80): $322,281,399
Expenditures (1979–80): $322,281,399
Chamber of Commerce: San Jose Chamber of Commerce, One Paseo de San Antonio, San Jose, Calif. 95113

1. County total. 2. Includes undeveloped sites.

SEATTLE, WASH.

Incorporated as city: 1869
Mayor: Charles Royer (to Nov. 1980)
1970 population & (rank): 530,831 (22)
1977 est. population & (rank): 488,928 (25)
1970–77 population change: −7.9%
1976 land area: 83.6 sq mi.
Altitude: Highest, 540 ft; lowest, sea level
Location: In west central part of state, on Puget Sound
County: Seat of King Co.
Churches: Roman Catholic, 36; Jewish, 13; Protestant and others, 535
City-owned parks, playgrounds, etc.: 278 (4,773.4 ac.)
Telephones (Jan. 1, 1978): 633,972
Television households (Jan. 1980): 439,900 (95%)
Radio stations: AM, 22; FM, 26
Television stations: 3 commercial; 1 educational
Assessed valuation (1977): $7,734,784,281
City tax rate (1979): $16.49 per $1,000
Bonded debt (1978): $303,763,796
Revenue (1979): $480,707,786
Expenditures (1979): $513,936,558
Chamber of Commerce: Seattle Chamber of Commerce, 215 Columbia Street, Seattle, Wash. 98104

TOLEDO, OHIO

Incorporated as city: 1837
Mayor: Doug DeGood (to Dec. 1981)
City Manager: J. Michael Porter (apptd. Feb. 1979)
1970 population & (rank): 383,062 (30)
1977 est. population & (rank): 358,677 (39)
1970–77 population change: −6.4%
1976 land area: 81.2 sq mi.
Altitude: 630 ft
Location: In northwestern part of state, on Maumee River at Lake Erie
County: Seat of Lucas Co.
Churches: Protestant, 301; Roman Catholic, 55; Jewish, 4; others, 98
City-owned parks and playgrounds: 134 (2,650.90 ac.)
Telephones (Jan. 1, 1978): 306,704
Television households (Jan. 1980): 175,400 (98%)
Radio stations: AM, 8; FM, 8
Television stations: 4
Assessed valuation (1980): $2,334,804,145
City tax rate (1979): $51.40 per $1,000
Bonded debt (1980): $148,885,800
Revenue (1979): $152,277,991
Expenditures (1979): $145,220,960
Chamber of Commerce: Toledo Area Chamber of Commerce, 218 Huron St., Toledo, Ohio 43604

TUCSON, ARIZ.

Incorporated as city: 1877
Mayor: Lewis C. Murphy (to Dec. 1983)
1970 population & (rank): 267,464 (54)

1977 est. population & (rank): 301,152 (48)
1970–77 population change: +12.6%
1977 city land area: 91.7 sq mi.
Altitude: 2,500 ft
Location: In southeastern part of state, on the Santa Cruz River
County: Seat of Pima Co.
Churches: Protestant, 181; Roman Catholic, 24; other, 136
City-owned parks and parkways: (2,001.75 ac.)
Telephones (Jan. 1, 1978): 309,266
Television households (Jan. 1980): 167,300 (97%)
Radio stations: AM, 12; FM, 6
Television stations: 3 commercial; 1 educational; 1 other
Assessed valuation (1978): $653,798,524
City tax rate (1979): $14.00 per $1,000
Net bonded debt (1978): $134,357,676
Revenue (1978): $236,995,824
Expenditures (1978): $236,995,242
Chamber of Commerce: Tucson Chamber of Commerce, P.O. Box 991, Tucson, Ariz., 85702

TULSA, OKLA.

Incorporated as city: 1898
Mayor: James Inhofe (to May 1982)
1970 population & (rank): 330,350 (43)
1977 est. population & (rank): 334,365 (42)
1970–77 population change: +1.2%
1976 land area: 177.3 sq mi.
Altitude: 674 ft
Location: In northeastern part of state, on Arkansas River
County: Seat of Tulsa Co.
Churches: Protestant, 593; Roman Catholic, 32; Jewish, 2; others, 4
City parks and playgrounds: 107 (4,811 ac.)
Telephones (Jan. 1, 1978): 401,445
Television households (Jan. 1980): 163,600 (98%)
Radio stations: AM, 9; FM, 6
Television stations: 3 commercial; 1 educational
Assessed valuation (1979–80): $1,034,528,367
City tax rate (1979–80): $77.78 per $1,000
Bonded debt (June 1979): $112,735,333
Revenue (1978–79): $146,879,171
Expenditures (1978–79): $124,592,236[1]
Chamber of Commerce: Metropolitan Tulsa Chamber of Commerce, 616 S Boston, Tulsa, Okla. 74119

1. Does not include sinking fund.

WASHINGTON, D.C.

Land ceded to Congress: 1788 by Maryland; 1789 by Virginia (retroceded to Virginia Sept. 7, 1846)
Seat of government transferred to D. C.: Dec. 1, 1800
Created municipal corporation: Feb. 21, 1871
Mayor: Marion S. Barry, Jr. (to Jan. 1983)
Motto: *Justitia omnibus* (Justice to all)
Flower: American beauty rose
Tree: Scarlet oak
Origin of name: In honor of Columbus
1970 population & (rank): 756,668 (9)
1977 est. population & (rank): 684,891 (13)
1970–77 population change: −9.5%
1976 land area: 61.4 sq mi.
Geographic center: Near corner of Fourth and L Sts., NW
Altitude: Highest, 420 ft; lowest, sea level
Location: Between Virginia and Maryland, on Potomac River
Churches: Protestant, 446; Roman Catholic, 23; Jewish, 10; others, 23
City parks: 753 (7,725 ac.)
Telephones (Jan. 1, 1978): 1,038,376
Television households (Jan. 1980): 273,600 (97%)
Radio stations: AM, 15; FM, 16
Television stations: 6 (including 2 UHF stations)
Assessed valuation (1979): $10,685,484,447[1]
City tax rate (1978–79): $18.30 per $1,000
Bonded debt: None
Revenue (est. 1979): $1,663,843,000
Expenditures (est. 1979): $1,949,764,000
Chamber of Commerce: D.C. Chamber of Commerce, 1319 F St., NW, Washington, D.C. 20004

The District of Columbia—identical with the City of Washington—is the capital of the United States and the first carefully planned capital in the world.

D.C. history began in 1790 when Congress directed selection of a new capital site, 10 miles square, along the Potomac. When the site was determined, it included 30.75 square miles on the Virginia side of the river. In 1846, however, Congress returned that area to Virginia.

The city was planned and partly laid out by Major Pierre Charles L'Enfant, a French engineer. This work was perfected and completed by Major Andrew Ellicott. In 1814, during the War of 1812, a British force fired the capital, and it was from the white paint applied to cover fire damage that the President's home was called the White House.

Until Nov. 3, 1967, the District of Columbia was administered by three commissioners appointed by the President. On that day, a government consisting of a mayor-commissioner and a 9-member Council, all appointed by the President with the approval of the Senate, took office. On May 7, 1974, the citizens of the District of Columbia approved the Home Rule Charter, giving them their first form of elected government in over 100 years. The District also has one non-voting member in the House of Representatives.

On Aug. 22, 1978, the Senate passed a proposed constitutional amendment to give Washington, D.C., voting representation in the Congress. The House had approved the legislation in the spring. The amendment must be ratified by at least 38 state legislatures within the next seven years to become effective.

1. On taxable property only. More than 50% of all land in District of Columbia is owned by the Federal government and tax-exempt organizations, and therefore is nontaxable.

The American's Creed

William Tyler Page

"I believe in the United States of America as a government of the people, by the people, for the people; whose just powers are derived from the consent of the governed; a democracy in a republic; a sovereign Nation of many sovereign States; a perfect union, one and inseparable; established upon those principles of freedom, equality, justice, and humanity for which American patriots sacrificed their lives and fortunes.

"I therefore believe it is my duty to my country to love it, to support its Constitution, to obey its laws, to respect its flag, and to defend it against all enemies."

NOTE: William Tyler Page, Clerk of the U.S. House of Representatives, wrote "The American's Creed" in 1917. It was accepted by the House on behalf of the American people on April 3, 1918.

Tabulated Data on City Governments

City	Mayor		City manager's salary[2]	Council or Commission			
	Term, years	Salary[1]		Name	Members	Term, years	Salary[3]
Albuquerque, N.M.	4	$39,000	$38,500[4]	Council	9	4	$3,900
Atlanta	4	50,000	—	Council	19	4	8,800
Austin, Tex.	2	18,000	64,000	Council	6	2	16,000
Baltimore	4	47,000	—	Council	19	4	19,500
Boston	4	40,000	—	Council	9	2	20,000
Buffalo, N.Y.	4	40,500	—	Council	15	2[5]	20,000
Charlotte, N.C.	2	11,000	51,900	Council	11	2	5,700
Chicago	4	60,000	—	Council	50	4	24,075
Cincinnati	2	27,875	55,295	Council	9	2	24,375
Cleveland	2	50,000	—	Council	33	2	18,000
Columbus, Ohio	4	40,000	—	Council	7	4	10,000
Dallas	2	50[6]	82,000	Council	11	2	50[6]
Denver	4	50,000	—	Council	13	4	18,675
Detroit	4	69,927	—	Council	9	4	37,926
El Paso	2	9,600	—	Council	7[7]	2	4,800
Fort Worth	2	10[8]	54,500	Council	9	2	10[8]
Honolulu	4	55,908	50,820	Council	9	4	17,500[9]
Houston	2	72,000	—	Council	8	2	19,120
Indianapolis	4	40,664	—	Council	29	4	3,700[10]
Jacksonville, Fla.	4	40,000	29,000[11]	Council	19	4	10,000
Kansas City, Mo.	4	35,000	62,440	Council	13[7]	4	9,600
Long Beach, Calif.	2	638[12]	61,636	Council	9[13]	4	638[12]
Los Angeles	4	63,525	72,432[4]	Council	15	4	38,115
Louisville, Ky.	4	31,699	—	Board of Aldermen	12	2	12,417
Memphis, Tenn.	4	40,000[14]	37,500	Council	13	4	6,000
Miami, Fla.	2	6,000[15]	62,920	Commission	8	4	6,000
Milwaukee	4	58,802	—	Council	16	4	24,880
Minneapolis	2	36,250	52,000	Council	13	2	27,985
Nashville, Tenn.	4	50,000	—	Council	41	4	5,400
New Orleans	4	59,868	—	Council	7	4	15,000
New York	4	80,000	66,000	Council	43	4	35,000
Newark, N.J.	4	52,600	38,588[17]	Council	9	4	24,500
Oakland, Calif.	4	15,000	59,500	Council	9[7]	4	([18])
Oklahoma City	4	2,000	55,000	Council	8	4	20[19]
Omaha, Neb.	4	36,000	—	Council	7	4	9,600
Philadelphia	4	55,000	50,000[20]	Council	17	4	25,000
Phoenix, Ariz.	2	25,000	64,000	Council	7[7]	2	15,000
Pittsburgh	4	45,000	—	Council	9	4	([21])
Portland, Ore.	4	49,214	—	Commission	4	4	39,463
St. Louis	4	25,000	—	Board of Aldermen	29	4	12,500
San Antonio	2	3,000[22]	65,000	Council	11[7]	2	20,000[23]
San Diego, Calif.	4	31,250	60,187	Council	8	4	21,500
San Francisco	4	62,710	54,131[24]	Board of Supervisors	11	4	9,600
San Jose, Calif.	4	7,200	55,212	Council	7	4	4,800
Seattle	4	67,176	—	Council	9	4	44,324
Toledo, Ohio	2	23,350	48,000	Council	9[13]	2	7,800
Tucson, Ariz.	4	14,000	45,000	Council	7	4	7,200
Tulsa, Okla.	2	40,000	—	Commission	4	2	30,000
Washington, D.C.	4	60,000	50,000	Council	13	4	35,000[25]

1. Annual salary unless otherwise indicated. 2. Annual salary. City Manager's term is indefinite and at will of Council. 3. Annual salary unless otherwise indicated. In some cities, President of Council receives a higher salary. 4. City Administrative Officer appointed by Mayor, approved by Council. 5. For 9 District Councilmen; 4 years for 5 Councilmen-at-Large. 6. Per Council meeting; not over $2,600 per year. 7. Including Mayor. 8. Per week and per Council meeting. 9. Managing Director appointed by Mayor; no Council approval required. 10. Plus $30 per meeting for three meetings a month. 11. Chief Administrative Officer appointed by Mayor; not subject to Council confirmation. 12. Per month. 13. Including Mayor and Vice-Mayor. 14. Plus $5,000 expense account. 15. Plus $2,500 expense account. 16. No City Manager; salary is for Deputy Mayor. 17. Business Administrator, appointed by Mayor and confirmed by Council. 18. Flat $500 per month, or $6,000 annually. 19. Per Council meeting; not to exceed 5 meetings a month. 20. Appointed by Mayor, with title of Managing Director. 21. 4 members at $22,500; 5 members at $27,500. 22. Plus Council pay. 23. Per Council meeting; not over $1,040 per year. 24. Chief Administrative Officer; appointed by Mayor for 10-year term. 25. $10,000 additional for Chairman. *Source: Information Please* questionnaires to the cities.

Firsts in America

This selection is based on our editorial judgment. Other sources may list different firsts.

Admiral in U.S. Navy: David Glasgow Farragut, 1866.

Air-mail route, first transcontinental: Between New York City and San Francisco, 1920.

Assembly, representative: House of Burgesses, founded in Virginia, 1619.

Bank established: Bank of North America, Philadelphia, 1781.

Birth in America to English parents: Virginia Dare, born Roanoke Island, N.C., 1587.

Botanic garden: Established by John Bartram in Philadelphia, 1728. (Oldest still existing was established in Cambridge, Mass., in 1807.)

Cartoon, colored: "The Yellow Kid," by Richard Outcault, in *New York World,* 1895.

College: Harvard, founded 1636.

College to confer degrees on women: Oberlin (Ohio) College, 1841.

College to establish coeducation: Oberlin (Ohio) College, 1833.

Electrocution of a criminal: William Kemmler in Auburn Prison, Auburn, N.Y., Aug. 6, 1890.

Five and Ten Cents Store: Founded by Frank Woolworth, Utica, N.Y., 1879 (moved to Lancaster, Pa., same year).

Fraternity: Phi Beta Kappa; founded Dec. 5, 1776, at College of William and Mary.

Law to be declared unconstitutional by U.S. Supreme Court: Judiciary Act of 1789. Case: *Marbury* v. *Madison,* 1803.

Library, circulating: Philadelphia, 1731.

Newspaper, illustrated daily: *New York Daily Graphic,* 1873.

Newspaper published daily: *Pennsylvania Packet and General Advertiser,* Philadelphia, Sept., 1784.

Newspaper published over a continuous period: *The Boston News-Letter,* April, 1704.

Newsreel: Pathé Frères of Paris, in 1910, circulated a weekly issue of their *Pathé Journal.*

Oil well, commercial: Titusville, Pa., 1859.

Panel quiz show on radio: *Information Please,* May 17, 1938.

Postage stamps issued: 1847.

Railroad, transcontinental: Central Pacific and Union Pacific railroads, joined at Promontory, Utah, May 10, 1869.

Savings bank: The Provident Institute for Savings, Boston, 1816.

Science museum: Founded by Charleston (S.C.) Library Society, 1773.

Skyscraper: Home Insurance Co., Chicago, 1885 (10 floors, 2 added later).

Slaves brought into America: At Jamestown, Va., 1619, from a Dutch ship.

Sorority: Kappa Alpha Theta, at De Pauw University, 1870.

State to abolish capital punishment: Michigan, 1847.

State to enter Union after original 13: Vermont, 1791.

Steam-heated building: Eastern Hotel, Boston, 1845.

Steam railroad (carried passengers and freight): Baltimore & Ohio, 1830.

Strike on record by union: Journeymen Printers, New York City, 1776.

Subway: Opened in Boston, 1897.

"Tabloid" picture newspaper: *The Illustrated Daily News* (now *The Daily News*), New York City, 1919.

Vaudeville theater: Gaiety Museum, Boston, 1883.

Woman cabinet member: Frances Perkins, Secretary of Labor, 1933.

Woman candidate for President: Victoria Claflin Woodhull, nominated by National Woman's Suffrage Assn. on ticket of Nation Radical Reformers, 1872.

Woman doctor of medicine: Elizabeth Blackwell; M.D. from Geneva Medical College of Western New York, 1849.

Woman elected governor of a state: Mrs. Nellie Tayloe Ross, Wyoming, 1925.

Woman elected to U.S. Senate: Mrs. Hattie Caraway, Arkansas; elected Nov., 1932.

Woman graduate of law school: Mrs. Ada H. Kepley, Union College of Law, Chicago, 1870.

Woman member of U.S. House of Representatives: Jeannette Rankin; elected Nov., 1916.

Woman member of U.S. Senate: Mrs. Rebecca Latimer Felton of Georgia; appointed Oct. 3, 1922.

Woman suffrage granted: Wyoming Territory, 1869.

Written constitution: *Fundamental Orders of Connecticut,* 1639.

Figures and Legends in American Folklore

Appleseed, Johnny (John Chapman, 1774–1847): Massachusetts-born nurseryman; reputed to have spread seeds and seedlings from which rose orchards of the Midwest.

Billy the Kid (William H. Bonney, 1859–1881): New York-born desperado; killed his first man before he reached his teens; after short life of crime in Wild West, was gunned down by Sheriff Pat Garrett; symbol of lawless West.

Boone, Daniel (1734–1820): Frontiersman and Indian fighter, about whom legends of early America have been built; figured in Byron's *Don Juan*.

Brodie, Steve (1863–1901): Reputed to have dived off Brooklyn Bridge on July 23, 1886. (Whether he actually did so has never been proved.)

Buffalo Bill (William F. Cody, 1846–1917): Buffalo hunter and Indian scout; much of legend about him and Wild West stems from his own Wild West show, which he operated in late 19th century.

Bunyan, Paul: Mythical lumberjack; subject of tall tales throughout timber country (that he dug Grand Canyon, for example).

Crockett, David (1786–1836): Frontiersman and member of U.S. Congress, about whom legends have been built of heroic feats; died in defense of Alamo.

Fritchie (or Frietchie), Barbara: Symbol of patriotism; in ballad by John Greenleaf Whittier, 90-year-old Barbara Fritchie defiantly waves Stars and Stripes as "Stonewall" Jackson's Confederate troops march through Frederick, Md.

James, Jesse (1847–1882): Bank and train robber; folklore has given him quality of American Robin Hood.

Jones, Casey (John Luther Jones, 1863–1900): Example of heroic locomotive engineer given to feats of prowess; died in wreck with his hand on brake lever when his Illinois Central "Cannonball" express hit freight train at Vaughan, Miss.

Ross, Betsy (1752–1836): Member of Philadelphia flag-making family; reported to have designed and sewn first American flag. (Report is without confirmation.)

Uncle Sam: Personification of United States and its people; origin uncertain; may be based on inspector of government supplies in Revolutionary War and War of 1812.

Assassinations and Attempts in U. S. Since 1865

Cermak, Anton J. (Mayor of Chicago): Shot Feb. 15, 1933, in Miami by Giuseppe Zangara, who attempted to assassinate Franklin D. Roosevelt; Cermak died March 6.

Ford, Gerald R. (President of U.S.): Escaped assassination attempt Sept. 5, 1975, in Sacramento, Calif., by Lynette Alice (Squeaky) Fromm, who pointed but did not fire .45-caliber pistol.

Ford, Gerald R. (President of U.S.): Escaped assassination attempt in San Francisco, Calif., Sept. 22, 1975, by Sara Jane Moore, who fired one shot from a .38-caliber pistol that was deflected.

Garfield, James A. (President of U.S.): Shot July 2, 1881, in Washington, D.C., by Charles J. Guiteau; died Sept. 19.

Jordan, Vernon E., Jr. (civil rights leader): Shot and critically wounded in assassination attempt May 29, 1980, in Fort Wayne, Ind.

Kennedy, John F. (President of U.S.): Shot Nov. 22, 1963, in Dallas, Tex., allegedly by Lee Harvey Oswald; died same day. Injured was Gov. John B. Connally of Texas. Oswald was shot and killed two days later by Jack Ruby.

Kennedy, Robert F. (U.S. Senator from New York): Shot June 5, 1968, in Los Angeles by Sirhan Bishara Sirhan; died June 6.

King, Martin Luther, Jr. (civil rights leader): Shot April 4, 1968, in Memphis by James Earl Ray; died same day.

Lincoln, Abraham (President of U.S.): Shot April 14, 1865, in Washington, D.C., by John Wilkes Booth; died April 15.

Long, Huey P. (U.S. Senator from Louisiana): Shot Sept. 8, 1935, in Baton Rouge by Dr. Carl A. Weiss; died Sept. 10.

McKinley, William (President of U.S.): Shot Sept. 6, 1901, in Buffalo by Leon Czolgosz; died Sept. 14.

Roosevelt, Franklin D. (President-elect of U.S.): Escaped assassination unhurt Feb. 15, 1933, in Miami. *See* Cermak.

Roosevelt, Theodore (ex-President of U.S.): Escaped assassination (though shot) Oct. 14, 1912, in Milwaukee while campaigning for President.

Seward, William H. (Secretary of State): Escaped assassination (though injured) April 14, 1865, in Washington, D.C., by Lewis Powell (or Paine), accomplice of John Wilkes Booth.

Truman, Harry S. (President of U.S.): Escaped assassination unhurt Nov. 1, 1950, in Washington, D.C., as 2 Puerto Rican nationalists attempted to shoot their way into Blair House.

Wallace, George C. (Governor of Alabama): Shot and critically wounded in assassination attempt May 15, 1972, at Laurel, Md., by Arthur Herman Bremer.

A Preview of the 1981 White House Conference on Aging

Barry Robinson
American Association of Retired Persons

Between Thanksgiving and Christmas 1981, an event of immense importance to all older Americans and to those who will eventually follow in their footsteps will take place in Washington: the White House Conference on Aging.

Why a White House Conference?

White House conferences are always called by the President for one of three basic reasons: because of a Congressional mandate, at the request of a government agency, or in response to growing public demand or concern about a particular issue.

Yet, no matter how influential and authoritative a White House conference may appear to be, its deliberations do not have the force of the law. It can recommend, but it cannot legislate, and this may be the most significant strength of the White House conference process. White House conferences are thus free to espouse the needs of the special populations they represent without having to compromise their recommendations against the hard realities by which legislators have to measure every move they mandate.

They serve to sensitize the American public to the needs and aspirations of the special populations in its midst, acting as a launching pad for ideas which may eventually bloom into fruition years after the conference adjourns. Nowhere has this process proven to be more valid than in the field of American aging.

Putting the Process to Work

Eight hundred people attended the first national conference on aging held at the specific request of President Harry S. Truman in 1950 when there were 12.4 million Americans over 65. Technically not a White House conference, since it was convened and sponsored by the Federal Security Administration, it was the first nationally coordinated effort at focusing on elders.

By 1961, there were over 2,500 delegates at the White House Conference on Aging, and some 947 fairly specific recommendations made. The delegates to the 1961 conference compiled a veritable grocery list of recommendations which, despite being more specific than those of the 1950 conference, gave little indication of a sense of priority. Still, the 1961 conference was not without its triumphs, the greatest of which was the passage of Medicare in 1965.

And within months of the conference's adjournment, the Senate established a Special Committee on Aging; the Social Security law was amended to increase minimum benefits, authorize early retirement at age 62, and declare an additional 160,000 older Americans eligible for coverage; legislation providing for housing and health care facility construction was amended to include special provisions for the elderly; and the Older Americans Act was enacted, creating the Administration on Aging as the chief provider and administrator of service programs for older people.

A Watershed of Sorts

The 1970s will eventually be recognized as the period in which aging finally came of age with the graying of America. More than any other single factor, the 1971 White House Conference on Aging—and the events surrounding it—brought this recognition of reality to the fore of the national consciousness.

The conference served as a catalytic crucible for making the rest of the nation's population aware of the presence in its midst of a growing community of elders. It is most likely pure coincidence, but in the years immediately following the White House Conference, AARP—which then had less than two million members and now has approximately twelve million—achieved its greatest membership growth rate.

One indication of the 1971 conference's impact on America's collective consciousness was the attention paid to the subject of aging in the press and on TV during the years following it.

The portrayal of the elderly in the press and on TV has begun to project a more balanced image, reflective of a broader understanding of the diversity of aging in America today. Even as the number of people who are old is growing, the number of middle-aged people who will soon be old is also growing, leading to an increased desire to obtain at least some notion of what their future lives will be like. It is doubtful, however, if this interest would exist today if it had not been piqued by the 1971 White House Conference on Aging and the attention it attracted.

Barry Robinson is communication counsel for the American Association of Retired Persons and its sister organization, the National Retired Teachers Associations, which—with a combined membership of nearly thirteen million—comprise the largest association of older people in the world today. He is the author of *Options for Older Americans,* published for the 1971 White House Conference on Aging; *On the Beat: Policemen at Work,* and the forthcoming *Geriatric Medicine: Tomorrow's Practice Today.*

Founded in 1947 and 1958, respectively, NRTA and AARP are nonprofit, nonpartisan organizations providing older Americans with a wide range of membership programs and services, including legislative representation at both federal and state levels.

The Great Debate Begins

The 4,000 participants of the 1971 conference produced 663 recommendations. Unlike the 1961 conference's 947 recommendations, the 1971 recommendations indicated a sense of priorities.

As a result, the conference was followed by the enactment of the Supplemental Security Income (SSI) program in 1972, the Employee Retirement Income Security Act (ERISA) in 1974, and amendments to the Equal Credit Opportunity Act in 1975 prohibiting age discrimination in the granting of credit. And, in 1974, the House of Representatives joined the Senate in establishing its own Select Committee on Aging, adding yet another forum for consideration of the aged's concerns.

Perhaps the most significant success of the 1971 conference was the role played in bringing about the beginning of the end of mandatory retirement. For years, the issue had simmered on a back burner despite mounting evidence that many of the socioeconomic, medical, and psychological problems afflicting the elderly stem from the trauma of being driven from the workplace and into exile amidst one of the world's most work-oriented cultures. Yet, the issue did not begin to attract the American public's attention until it exploded practically full-blown at the 1971 conference.

"In the Employment Section and again in the section on Mandatory Retirement, AARP tried to get its position adopted that a mandatory age for retirement is unconstitutional," recalls political scientist Henry J. Pratt in *The Gray Lobby*, his authoritative book on aging advocacy.

"The issue finally went to the conference floor where a bruising debate ensued. Many of the delegates were genuinely confused by the complexity of the points raised and (were) unable to arrive at an independent judgment on such short notice."

As a result, the delegates settled on a compromise resolution calling for greater flexibility while declaring that chronological age should not be the sole criterion for retirement. It was hardly a victory, but at least the question was finally being aired in public so the great dialogue essential for change could get under way.

By late 1977, opposition to mandatory retirement had coalesced to such a degree that legislation amending and strengthening the Age Discrimination in Employment Act of 1967 was able to pass both houses of Congress almost unanimously, and to be signed into law by President Carter in April 1978.

While not abolishing mandatory retirement outright, the ADEA amendments have dealt it a severe blow by making it illegal to force most workers into retirement before age 70, and abolishing mandatory retirement altogether for almost all federal government employees. It is entirely conceivable that this might have happened without the national exposure of the conference, but it would most likely have taken far longer.

On to the 1981 Conference

By the time the 1981 White House Conference on Aging convenes on Nov. 30, 1981, it will have been preceded by more than a year of local, state, and regional meetings designed to convey grassroot concerns and sentiments to the national convocation.

State White House Conferences will take place during the nine months between September 1980 and June 1981. These will be preceded by mini-conferences and community forums which will serve to establish the state-level agenda, and followed by local and regional hearings chaired by conference delegates. Out of this process will come reports on issues which will hopefully influence the shape and substance of the national conference in November.

If you are interested in attending or participating in any of these hearings or conferences, the best way to determine where and when they are being held is to contact the Area Agency on Aging for your state or region (see *Aging* in the "Keys to Finding Help" on page 720). One thing that many people don't understand about White House Conferences is the diversity of the delegates. For the aging conference, for instance, there will be many old people plus social workers and other practitioners who work with—or on behalf of—the elderly. There will be representatives from organizations of older people, such as AARP and the National Council of Senior Citizens, and from professional associations such as the Gerontological Society, American Geriatrics Society, and the National Council on Aging. In addition, within each of these groupings, there will undoubtedly be representation reflective of the varied ethnic make-up of older America.

Not so surprisingly, many of the delegates will be middle-aged and even younger. As professions go, the field of aging and/or the discipline of gerontology are relatively new; thus, the majority of people involved in them—or preparing to enter them—tend to quite young. Then, too, aging is an area of concern about which the young have been exhibiting constantly increasing interest since the early 1970s. To some extent, this may stem from self-interest since the actions taken to affect the condition of older people today will surely influence what it will be like to grow old tomorrow.

U.S. Population by Age
(in millions)

Age		2000[1]	Percent	1980	Percent	1900	Percent
Under 19		100.9	35	70.5	32	33.7	44
20–34		55.6	19	57.1	26	19.4	26
35–44	Middle age	41.3	14	25.7	11	9.2	12
45–54	Middle age	35.8	12	22.6	10	6.4	8
55–64	Young-old	22.9	8	21.1	10	4.0	5
65–74	Young-old	17.1	6	15.4	7	2.2	3
75 & over	Old-old	13.5	5	9.4	4	.9[2]	1

1. Projected. 2. 899,000. NOTE: Percentages are approximate and because of rounding may not add to 100%.

Guide to the Issues

Economic conditions have always constituted the central concern of White House Conferences on Aging, and there is no reason to believe that this year will be any different. Keep in mind, however, that due to the mechanical demands of the publishing process, this preview is being written approximately 18 months before the conference's opening. While circumstances may necessitate a change of emphasis in the way some subjects are approached, it is nonetheless safe to assume that if the topics discussed here do not receive as much attention as anticipated at the conference itself, they will still do so sometime during this decade.

Unless the persistent inflationary spiral subsides by the time of the conference, it is highly likely that restraining inflation—and developing better means for protecting older Americans against its ravages—will be given the highest priority. There will probably be calls for mandatory wage and price controls, and possibly even demands that private pension benefits be indexed to the rising cost of living in the same way that Social Security is. How far the conference will go in supporting such proposals is debatable.

A report issued by AARP and NRTA in June 1980 predicted that the coming decade will be a time of increasing financial hardship for older people. The study, entitled *Inflation and the Elderly*, was conducted for the two associations by Data Resources Inc., the respected economic research firm. DRI projected that inflation will wipe out many of the financial gains made by older Americans during the past decade or so.

One reason for this is that the greatest price increases are—and will most likely continue to be—taking place in the cost of those items upon which older people tend to spend the largest share of their income. Because the cost of food, medical care, heating fuel, and related utilities is increasing faster than the cost of other items included in the Consumer Price Index, the rate of inflation experienced by older consumers usually tends to be greater than that reflected in the CPI. AARP and others have urged that Social Security and other benefit increases be based in the future on an index which would be more indicative of the actual economics of aging.

Social Security itself will continue to be a focus of concern for the conferees. At about the same time as the DRI study was being released, the Social Security system's trustees warned that, unless prompt action is taken to shore-up its funding, the basic old age and survivor's insurance (OASI) portion of the program could run out of funds within two years. This could be prevented, said Social Security Commissioner William J. Driver, by transferring surplus revenues from disability insurance and hospital insurance (which covers in-hospital and related medical expenses under Medicare) funds to the OASI fund.

Even if the short-term problem is resolved by the time the conference convenes, there will undoubtedly be discussion of how similar problems can be prevented in the future. Such discussions could lead to a consideration of restructuring the entire Social Security system and of establishing a mandatory universal private pension system for all workers. This latter proposal was contained in the interim report of the President's Commission on Pension Policy, which was made public in May 1980. These issues are of interest to—and would ultimately affect—middle-aged and younger working people more than they would the elderly.

Of more immediate concern to older Americans and their adult children are the problems engendered by extended illness, an issue also known as

Characteristics of Persons 65 Years Old and Over

(in percentages)

Characteristic	1978 Male	1978 Female	1975 Male	1975 Female	1970 Male	1970 Female	1965 Male	1965 Female
Marital status:[1]								
Single	5.4	6.2	4.7	5.8	7.5	7.7	6.6	7.7
Married	77.5	38.6	79.3	39.1	73.1	35.6	71.3	36.0
Spouse present	74.8	36.7	77.3	37.6	69.9	33.9	67.9	34.1
Spouse absent	2.7	1.8	2.0	1.5	3.2	1.7	3.4	1.9
Widowed	14.2	52.0	13.6	52.5	17.1	54.4	19.5	54.4
Divorced	2.9	3.2	2.5	2.6	2.3	2.3	2.6	1.9
Family status:[1]								
In families	82.1	57.3	83.3	59.3	79.2	58.5	80.3	62.9
Primary individuals	16.3	41.6	15.4	39.4	14.9	35.2	13.9	30.6
Secondary individuals	1.6	1.1	1.2	1.3	2.4	1.9	2.3	2.2
Inmates of institutions[1]	n.a.	n.a.	n.a.	n.a.	3.6	4.4	3.5	4.3
Labor force participation:								
Employed	18.1	8.1	21.1	7.8	26.2	10.0	26.8	10.2
Unemployed	1.1	.3	1.2	.4	1.0	.3	1.3	.4
Not in labor force	80.1	91.6	77.7	91.8	72.8	89.7	71.9	89.5
Living arrangements:[1]								
Living in household	99.7	99.7	99.8	99.8	95.5	95.0	96.2	95.3
Living alone	15.7	40.3	14.8	38.0	14.1	33.8	13.1	28.6
Spouse present	74.8	36.7	77.3	37.6	69.9	33.9	67.9	34.1
Living with someone else	9.3	22.6	7.7	24.2	11.5	27.4	15.2	32.6
Not in household[2]	.3	.3	.2	.2	4.5	5.0	3.8	4.7

1. Resident population as of March of year indicated. 2. In institutions and other group quarters. NOTE: n.a. = not available.
Source: Department of Commerce, Bureau of the Census.

long-term care. It is thus quite probable that there will be much discussion of increased funding for—and greater emphasis upon—home health care which could save many people from having to be hospitalized or placed in a nursing home at great expense to themselves and society.

Medicare reform is also expected to attract considerable attention, especially if enactment of national health insurance legislation is not seen as being particularly imminent. The conference will probably reaffirm its support of NHI. Should NHI be passed, it would probably eliminate the need to reform Medicare by expanding its coverage of out-of-hospital expenses that are currently ignored. The lack of such coverage often forces patients into unnecessary hospital and nursing home stays when they could be treated at home, an option which would cost considerably less than the present institutional approach.

While attention will undoubtedly be paid to the traditional areas of concern—housing, transportation, lifestyles, etc.—two emerging issues may work their way to the fore. If the subjects of geriatric medicine and nutrition policy are not raised extensively at the conference, much will be heard about them in the years to come.

Geriatric medicine is, quite simply, the practice of medicine as it applies to older patients. It is both a body of specific knowledge and an attitude whose adherents insist that sickness and mental deterioration are not necessarily natural concomitants of aging. At the same time, geriatric medicine is an awareness of the untypical symptoms which common ailments sometimes display in some older persons, and of the different ways in which some older patients may react to various medications.

Unfortunately, physicians possessing this knowledge and attitude are still too few and far between although progress is slowly beginning to be made as the medical profession becomes increasingly aware of its own inadequacies and attempts to remedy them. While almost all of the nation's 120 medical schools are now either offering or preparing to offer introductory courses about aging, it will be at least between five and ten years before the first doctors with a solid background in geriatrics begin to graduate.

In the meantime, there are already hundreds of thousands of practicing physicians in the United States whose knowledge of how to treat elderly patients is, by their own admission, inadequate—and these are the doctors with whom most older people come into contact daily. The greatest challenge may very well lie in upgrading their geriatric skills and attitudes—and it is this challenge about which you'll be hearing at the White House Conference and in the years to come.

Like geriatrics, nutrition has only recently become a matter of serious interest to the medical community which had generally abandoned the field to health food and megavitamin enthusiasts. During the last quarter century or so, medical researchers began uncovering firm links between certain illnesses and certain foods—or, in some cases, the absence of certain foods. Thus, the stage was set for the government to take an official stand on the diet consumed by most Americans, but it did not do so until this past year—and the shock waves are still being felt.

First, the head of the National Cancer Institute advised Americans to eat less fat (both saturated and unsaturated) and more foods with a high fiber content. Next came the seven-point dietary guidelines issued by the Department of Agriculture and of Health, Education, and Welfare (now known as Health and Human Services) which reiterated the same basic advice. Several months later, the National Research Council, a wing of the National Academy of Sciences, issued a report questioning the validity of the recommendations about avoiding fatty foods. And, of course, there were more than a few challenges to the validity of the NRC allegations.

What all of this adds up to is considerable confusion in the United States about the relationship, if any, between the nation's health care goals and its nutritional policy—or, as seems to be the case, its lack of one. For instance, even as we are being encouraged by one division of the government department in charge of health to lower the amount of cholesterol or fat in our daily diets, another division of that same department is enforcing regulations requiring any product labeled "noodles" to contain eggs, a prime source of cholesterol.

Because nutrition has been shown to play such a vital role in the maintenance of health and well-being, especially among older persons, contradictions such as the one just mentioned need to be resolved. The need to resolve them—and the demands that need to be met—will probably be a prime topic for discussion at the White House Conference and definitely during the decade to follow it.

Echoes of the 1981 White House Conference on Aging are sure to be heard a year later when the World Assembly on the Elderly convenes in Vienna (the tentative site) under the sponsorship of the Economic and Social Council of the United Nations. Once again, we will be reminded that the problems and potentials of aging are not limited to the United States, and that we are not alone in our concern for our elders.

The Facts of Later Life

Income

Most economists estimate that for retirees to maintain their pre-retirement lifestyle within reasonable limits, they need a retirement income equal to 60–70% of their earnings immediately preceding retirement, plus occasional adjustments for inflation.

Even with recent improvements in Social Security benefits, this is a goal beyond the reach of most older Americans who, on average, have half the income of their younger counterparts.

One-seventh of the over-65 population now lives below the poverty level—an improvement over 1970 when a full quarter of all older Americans did. Poverty most often afflicts women and minority aged. While there are, of course, many well-off older persons, most tend to fall economically somewhere between poverty and affluence.

Most of the aged poor did not become poor until they retired, and their income dropped by 50–66%. These are essentially middle-class working people, and it is probably harder for them to cope with their newfound poverty than it is for people who have been poor all their lives.

The economic situation of almost all older Americans, however, is complicated by years of continually escalating inflation, which steadily saps the purchasing power of people living on fixed incomes. Since the elderly do not generally possess the ability to increase their income in response to inflationary pressures, they are perenially attempting to cut back and catch up with little hope of ever breaking even again.

Even with annual Social Security increments, which are supposed to offset inflation, retirees continue to fall farther and farther behind. This is due to the increments coming at least a year after the fact of a cost-of-living increase and thus never compensating fully for inflation's inroads.

Health

Although generally healthier than previous generations of elders, today's older people are still more subject to chronic illness and disability than younger persons. On average, they visit physicians 50% more often, and have health care and medication costs nearly four times those of younger individuals.

Comprising only 11% of the nation's population, older people account for 29% of total personal health care expenditures ($49.4 billion out of $167.9 billion). Yet, most older Americans regard themselves as being comparatively healthy and capable of caring for themselves well enough to continue living independently.

In a 1975 survey, 69% of the older persons questioned described their health as good or excellent in comparison with others of their own age, and 22% said their health was fair. Those describing their health as being chronically poor reported suffering from arthritis (38%), hearing loss (29%), and vision impairment, hypertension, and heart disease (20% each). Many suffered from several of these conditions simultaneously.

A 1973–74 study found that 83% of the older persons polled had not been hospitalized during the previous year. And most persons entering nursing homes returned later to their own residences.

Employment

In 1900, 67% of men and 8% of women over 65 were actively working. By 1979, only 20% of older men remained employed, while the percentage of women in the workforce had slipped back to eight after rising to ten in 1974. In general, they are working today at part-time jobs, agricultural labor, or self-employment.

Once unemployed, however, older workers usually experience greater difficulty finding new jobs and have longer average periods of unemployment than younger workers. This tendency begins in the mid-to-late 40s and increases with the worker's age.

Marital Status

In 1977, 77% of all older men were married. Among older women, 52% were widows, a figure which rises to 70% after age 75. It is almost predictable: If the husband is five years younger than his wife, the chances of widowhood are 50%; if the husband and wife are the same age, the chances are two out of three; if the husband is five years older than his wife, the chances are three out of four.

Widows outnumber widowers by 5.5 to 1. Men, however, experience greater difficulty adjusting to the loss of a mate—most likely because they don't expect their wives to die before they do.

In 1977, there were 16,760 brides and 30,721 grooms over 65. For approximately 904 of these older brides and 1,438 older grooms, it was a first marriage. For the rest, remarriage came mostly after widowhood rather than divorce. Interestingly, the actual number of marriages involving people over 65 has decreased in the last few years.

Marriage rates for older men in 1977 were seven times those for older women. The number of older men entering into first marriages was 2.5 times that of older women, while the number of older men remarrying was 8.6 times greater than that of older women.

Living Arrangements

While most older persons live in a family setting —with a husband, wife or other relatives—this frequently decreases with advancing age.

More than a third of older Americans—52% of all older women, but only 23% of all older men—live alone or with non-relatives. One reason for this disparity is that women live longer than men, and thus eventually outnumber them in later life.

The majority of older women are widows or divorcees (or, in some cases, both) without adequate means of support and little, if any, preparation for living alone—a circumstance which may in time give rise to new forms of communal living.

Pensions

The newer the retiree, the greater the chances of participation in a company or union pension—and the greater the likelihood of collecting on that pension, thanks to the Employee Retirement Income Security Act (ERISA) of 1974 which regulates pension plans and insures the worker's stake in them.

Prior to that, many workers participated in plans but were unable to collect pensions upon retirement. Thus, most older retirees do not receive private pension payments, but live instead solely on Social Security and whatever savings they have managed to accumulate; some must also depend upon Supplemental Security Income (SSI) payments to assist them in making ends meet.

Of today's active workers, however, it is estimated that nearly half are covered by pension plans.

Transportation

Most public transportation systems are designed primarily to satisfy the needs of the commuting worker. Older people (whose needs are usually quite different) are thus forced either to rely upon automobiles—which are becoming increasingly expensive to own and maintain—or to surrender their mobility and settle for whatever is within walking distance, no matter how inferior it may be.

Some communities have attempted to provide special transportation services at reduced rates for their older residents, but many of these subsidized systems have fallen victim to their own success. The more they are utilized, the more they cost to operate, and the growing cost often exceeds a community's ability to sustain them. In this age of energy scarcity, this looms large as a major problem.

Crime

While violent crimes against the elderly have been increasing lately and have thus received the most news coverage, they are not nearly as prevalent as "bunco" offenses, in which the victim is defrauded of whatever savings he or she may have managed to accumulate over the course of a lifetime.

Older victims tend to suffer more intensely. A younger victim can recoup a monetary loss by accumulating future earnings, but older victims no longer have that opportunity. Similarly, older victims wounded in crimes of violence require longer to heal, leading to prolonged loss of mobility and the increased possibility of medical complications.

Coping

When You Need Help or Information

Whether your concern is for your own later years or for someone you know with problems, the basic approaches to seeking help or information are essentially the same. In general, your primary sources of information are your local telephone directory, your community's public library, and *Your Retirement Information Guide,* a helpful booklet published by the American Association of Retired Persons and its affiliate, the National Retired Teachers Association. Single copies are available free from AARP-NRTA, P.O. Box 2400, Long Beach, Calif. 90801.

A good way to begin is to take stock of your resources relating to the problem. This doesn't necessarily mean financial resources, although they can be undeniably important. There are, however, other resources which you may have built up over a lifetime of activity without really being aware of them.

Did you, for instance, serve in the nation's military services? If so, check with the Veterans Administration (listed in the phonebook under "U.S. Government") to see if it can help.

Are you a union member? Then, contact your nearest local and find out if the union has any programs to help retirees with your particular problem. This also applies to any civic or fraternal organizations to which you may belong.

Don't forget the many local and national organizations for older people; being a member of one or more of them can prove helpful. These are the major national ones:

American Association of Retired Persons/National Retired Teachers Association (AARP/NRTA), 1909 K Street N.W., Washington, D.C. 20049

National Council of Senior Citizens (NCSC), 1511 K Street N.W., Washington, D.C. 20005

National Association of Retired Federal Employees (NARFE), 1533 New Hampshire Avenue N.W., Washington, D.C. 20036

Gray Panthers, 3700 Chestnut Street, Philadelphia, Pa. 19104

Older Women's League Educational Fund, 3800 Harrison Street, Oakland, Calif. 94611

For ages 50–64:

Action for Independent Maturity (AIM), 1909 K Street N.W., Washington, D.C. 20049

There are also organizations of professionals who work with and on behalf of the elderly: National Council on the Aging (NCOA), 1828 L Street N.W., Washington, D.C. 20036; The Gerontological Society, 1835 K Street N.W., Washington, D.C. 20006; American Geriatric Society, 10 Columbus Circle, New York, N.Y. 10019.

When You Have a Problem . . .

For just about every problem today, there is a private public service organization or government program trying to solve it. The trick is for you to get in touch with the right one.

In this *Almanac (see* Index), there is a listing of U.S. Societies and Associations in which you might find the name of an organization dealing with your particular problem. Look in your telephone directory to see if there is a branch office in your area; if not, contact the organization's national headquarters at the address given.

To find government agencies that might be able to help, start with your local government (city, town, or village) and move on to county, state, and federal levels only as necessary. Often, the agency nearest home will be the most help. Again, your telephone directory can be your best source of information; if you can't find exactly what you're looking for there, try phoning the municipal or country clerk's office for more specific guidance.

Keys to Finding Help

A few of the sources of assistance or information to which you might turn when dealing with a specific problem are given below. (Unless an address is given, look in your phonebook for the key-word indicated.)

Aging. Administration on Aging, U.S. Department of Health and Human Services, Washington, D.C. 20201. Locally, try state **Offices, Commissions, Departments,** or **Bureaus** on **Aging** or **Senior Citizens Affairs;** look for county or municipal agencies with similar titles, and for regional **Area Agencies on Aging.**

Career Considerations: If you're unhappy in your present work situation, and are trying to decide whether to stick with it until you can retire gracefully or to attempt to start anew in middle age, these books might provide some helpful insights. *Overcoming Executive Mid-Life Crisis* by Homer R. Figler; *Second Chance: Blueprints for Change* by Herbert B. Livesey; *What Color Is Your Parachute?* by Richard N. Bolles; *The Three Boxes of Life and How to Get Out of Them* by Richard N. Bolles; *The Women's Guide to Re-Entry Employment* by Mary Zimmeth; *What To Do With the Rest of Your Life* by the Catalyst staff.

Federal Government. Your tie-line and guide to the federal bureaucracy is the **Federal Information**

Center, listed in the phonebook under "U.S. Government." If nothing else works, try phoning your Congressional representative's local office; his or her staff can sometimes cut through a lot of red tape.

Food. The key words here are **Food Stamps, Meals on Wheels, National Nutrition Program for the Elderly.** If none of these is listed in your phonebook, check with the agencies listed under Aging.

Health Care. Don't overlook your local **health department.** If your problem involves a hospital, there is probably a staff social worker to whom you can turn. Also, try local medical and dental societies and schools—the latter frequently provide quality care at relatively low cost. For information about health care at home, contact the National Council for Homemaker-Home Health Aide Service, 67 Irving Place, New York, N.Y. 10003.

Housing. The key agency here is the U.S. Department of Housing and Urban Development; check your phonebook for a local office, or write to HUD, Washington, D.C. 20410. If you live in a rural area, contact your agricultural extension agent or write directly to Farmers Home Administration, U.S. Department of Agriculture, 14th Street and Independence Avenue S.W., Washington, D.C. 20250. Your local **housing authority** can also prove helpful.

Legal Problems. Many communities have special legal counseling programs for older residents. Try your local **Aging** agency, or write to National Senior Citizens Law Center, 1709 West 8th Street, Los Angeles, Calif. 90017. Information is also available from the National Resource Center for Consumers of Legal Services, 1302 18th Street N.W., Washington, D.C. 20036.

Middle Age. The processes, problems, and potentials of adult development in the middle years are explored in authoritative depth in two new books, *The Seasons of a Man's Life* by Daniel Levinson and *Transformations* by Roger Gould. The original research and theories of both of these psychiatrists served as a basis for Gail Sheehy's best-selling *Passages*.

Money. Information about **Social Security** and **Supplemental Security Income** may be found in this *Almanac* or from the **Social Security Administration** office nearest you. Also helpful in special circumstances are the U.S. Office of Personnel Management, Compensation Group, Bureau of Retirement, 1900 E Street N.W., Washington, D.C. 20415; and the U.S. Railroad Retirement Board, Headquarters office, 844 Rush Street, Chicago, Ill. 60611.

Nursing Homes. Check with your local **health department,** hospital social worker, or the nearest branches of the American Nursing Home Association and the American Association of Homes for the Aging. Some state **Aging** agencies have a **Nursing Home Ombudsman.** Write for the free pamphlet *Thinking About a Nursing Home* to the American Health Care Association, 1200 15th Street N.W., Washington, D.C. 20005.

Parents. Two excellent books for middle-aged-and-over people with elderly parents are: *You and Your Aging Parent* by Barbara Silverstone and Helen Kandel Hyman and *When Your Parents Grow Old* by Jane Otten and Florence D. Shelley.

Research. If you want to read more about growing older, look in your local library catalog under **aging, gerontology, geriatrics, retirement.**

Volunteering. If you're interested in working as a volunteer, check with your local **hospitals, nonprofit nursing homes, social service agencies,** and **civic organizations.** Or write to: National Center for Citizen Involvement, 1214 16th Street, N.W., Washington, D.C. 20036, ACTION, Older Americans Volunteer Programs, Washington, D.C. 20525; Service Corps of Retired Executives (SCORE), Small Business Administration, 1441 L Street N.W., Washington, D.C. 20416.

Aging: Myths and Truths

Myth: You can't teach an old dog new tricks.
Truth: A smart dog can learn new tricks at any age, and so can most people. Research has shown that older people do not necessarily lose their ability to learn, but sometimes learn differently than when younger. Their speed of comprehension, for instance, may decrease somewhat, but their retention and interpretation of new information may improve. Contrary to common belief, senility is not a state of mind that invariably accompanies old age. Rather, it is a serious and complex illness which, in many cases, can be alleviated through proper medical diagnosis and treatment.

Myth: Sex doesn't exist after age 60, and anyone who thinks it does is a "dirty old man" (or woman).
Truth: Normal sexual activity continues well into later life—sometimes even into the 90s—although frequency may decrease somewhat over the years.

Myth: When you grow old, you end up in a nursing home or some other institution.
Truth: Less than 5% of people 65 and over are institutionalized; the rest maintain their independence in a variety of residential situations. The majority of people who enter nursing homes usually do so following a period of hospitalization and eventually return to their homes.

Myth: Like birds in winter, people head south as soon as they retire.
Truth: While some do move south, most don't. Approximately 86% of the 65-plus population still live in the same house in which they lived before retiring. Of those who have moved, most moved a relatively short distance—frequently to a smaller residence more suited to their needs—while only 2.3% moved to different states, such as Florida, Arizona, and Nevada.

Social Security

The original Social Security Act was passed in 1935 and amended in 1939, 1946, 1950, 1952, 1954, 1956, 1958, 1960, 1961, 1965, 1967, 1969, 1972, 1974, 1977, and 1980.

The act is administered by the Social Security Administration and the Health Care Financing Administration, and other agencies within the Department of Health and Human Services.

For purposes of clarity, the explanations given below will describe the provisions of the act as amended.

Old Age, Disability, and Survivors Insurance

Practically everyone who works fairly regularly is covered by social security. Many state and local government employees are covered under voluntary agreements between states and the Secretary of Health and Human Services. Workers not covered include most federal civilian employees, career railroad workers, and a few other exceptions.

Cash tips count for social security if they amount to $20 or more in a month from employment with a single employer.

To qualify for benefits or make payments possible for your survivors, you must be in work covered by the law for a certain number of "quarters of coverage." Before 1978, a quarter of coverage was earned if a worker was paid $50 or more wages in a 3-month calendar quarter. A self-employed person got 4 "quarters of coverage" for a year in which his net earnings were $400 or more.

In 1978, a worker, whether employed or self-employed, received one quarter of coverage for each $250 of covered annual earnings up to a maximum of four for a year. The quarter of coverage measure was increased to $260 in 1979 and $290 in 1980 and will increase automatically in future years to keep pace with increases in average wages. The number of quarters needed differs for different persons and depends on the date of your birth; in general, it is related to the number of years after 1950, or after the year you reach 21, if later, and up to the year you reach 62, become disabled, or die. One "quarter of coverage" is required for each such year in order for you or your family to get benefits. No one will need more than 40 quarters. Your local social security office can tell you how long you need to work.

Who Pays for the Insurance?

Both workers and their employers pay for the workers' insurance. Self-employed persons pay their own social security contributions annually along with their income tax. The rates include the cost of Medicare hospital insurance. The contribution and benefit base is $29,700 for 1981, and will increase automatically in future years as earnings levels rise. The contribution rate schedules under present law are shown in a table in this section.

The separate payroll contribution to finance hospital insurance is placed in a separate trust fund in the U.S. Treasury. In addition, the medical insurance premiums, currently $9.60 a month, and the government's shares go into another separate trust fund.

Social Security Contribution and Rate Schedule
(percent of covered earnings)

Year	Retirement, survivors, and disability insurance	Hospital insurance	Total
EMPLOYERS AND EMPLOYEES			
1978	4.95%	1.10%	6.05%
1979–80	5.08	1.05	6.13
1981	5.35	1.30	6.65
1982–84	5.40	1.30	6.70
1985	5.70	1.35	7.05
1986–89	5.70	1.45	7.15
1990 & later	6.20	1.45	7.65
SELF-EMPLOYED			
1978	7.00%	1.10%	8.10%
1979–80	7.05	1.05	8.10
1981	8.00	1.30	9.30
1982–84	8.05	1.30	9.35
1985	8.55	1.35	9.90
1986–89	8.55	1.45	10.00
1990 & later	9.30	1.45	10.75

How to Apply for Benefits

You apply for benefits by filing a claim either in person, by mail, or by telephone at any social security office. You can get the address either from the post office or from the phone book under the listing, United States Government—Department of Health and Human Services—Social Security Administration. You will need certain kinds of proof, depending upon the type of benefit you are claiming. If it is a retirement benefit, you should provide a birth or baptismal certificate. If you are unable to get these documents, other old documents showing your age or date of birth—such as census records, school records, early naturalization certificate, etc. —may be acceptable. A widow 60 or older who is claiming widow's benefits based on her husband's earnings should have both proof of age and a copy of the marriage certificate. If formal proof is not available, the social security office will tell you what kinds of information will be acceptable.

What Does Social Security Offer?

The social security contribution you pay gives you four different kinds of protection: (1) retirement benefits, (2) survivors' benefits, (3) disability benefits, and (4) Medicare hospital insurance benefits.

Retirement benefits A worker becomes eligible for the full amount of his retirement benefit at age 65, if he has retired under the definition in the law. A worker may retire at 62 and get 80% of his full benefit. The closer he is to age 65 when he starts collecting his benefit, the larger is the fraction of his full benefit that he will get.

The amount of the retirement benefit you are entitled to at 65 is the key to all other benefits under the program. The retirement benefit is based on covered earnings, generally those after 1950. Your covered earnings will be updated (indexed) to the second year before you reach age 62, become disabled, or die, and will reflect the increases in average wages that have occurred since the earnings were paid.

A worker who delays his retirement past age 65, or who does not receive a benefit for some months after age 65 because of high earnings will get a special credit that can mean a larger benefit. The credit adds to a worker's benefits 1% (3% for workers age 62 after 1978) for each year (1/12 of 1% for each month) from age 65 to age 72 for which he did not get benefits.

The law provides a special minimum benefit at retirement for people who worked under social security for many years. This provision will help people who had low incomes, but above a specific level, in their working years. The amount of the special minimum depends on the number of years of coverage. For a worker retiring at 65 in January 1981 with 30 or more years of coverage, the special minimum benefit would be $289.00 (effective June 1980). These benefits are reduced if a worker is under 65 and are increased automatically for increases in the cost of living.

If you retired at age 65 in January 1981 with average earnings, you would get a benefit of $532.80.

If your wife is also 65, then she will get a wife's benefit that is equal to half your benefit. So if your benefit is $532.80, your wife gets $266.40.

If your wife is between ages 62 and 65, she can draw a reduced benefit; the amount depends on the number of months before 65 that she starts getting checks. If she draws her benefit when she is 62, she will get about ⅜ of your basic benefit, or $199.80. (She will get this amount for the rest of her life, unless you should die first; then she can start getting widow's benefit, described below.)

If your wife is entitled to a worker's retirement benefit on her own earnings, she can draw whichever—the worker's or the wife's—is larger.

If you have children under 18 or a child in school aged 18 up to 22 or a son or daughter who became totally disabled prior to reaching age 22, when you retire they will get a benefit equal to half your full retirement benefits (subject to maximum payments that can be made to a family). If your wife is caring for a child who is under 18 or who became disabled before 22 (and getting benefits too), she is eligible for benefits, even if she is under 62.

In general, the highest retirement check that can be paid to a worker who retired at 65 in January 1981 is about $677.00 a month. Maximum payment to the family of this retired worker is about $1,184.70 in January 1981. When your children reach age 18, their benefits will stop except for children in school aged 18 up to 22, and except for a benefit that is going to a son or daughter who became totally disabled before attaining age 22. Such a person can continue to get his benefits as long as his disability meets the definition in the law.

If you are a woman worker entitled to a retirement benefit and you have a husband aged 62 or over, he may draw a benefit similar to a wife's benefit at 62. If you are divorced, you can get social security benefits (the same as a wife or widow) based on your exhusband's earnings record if you were married at least 10 years and if your exhusband has retired, become disabled, or died.

Survivor benefits. This feature of the social security program gives your family valuable life insurance protection—in some cases benefits to a family could amount to $100,000 or more over a period of years. The amount of protection is again geared to what the worker would be entitled to if he had been age 65 when he died. Your survivors could get:

1. A cash payment to help cover your burial expenses. This "lump-sum death payment" is $255.

2. A benefit for each child until he reaches 18, or 22 if the child is in school, or at any age if disabled before 22. Each eligible child receives 75% of the basic benefit (subject to reduction for the family maximum). (A disabled child can continue to collect benefits after age 22.) If certain conditions are met, dependent grandchildren of insured workers can receive survivor or dependent benefits.

3. A benefit for your widow, or widower, if she has children under 18 or disabled in her care. Her benefit is also 75% of the basic benefit. She can collect this as long as she has a child under 18 or disabled in her care. Payments stop then (they will start again upon application when she is 60 at a slightly lower amount).

Total family survivor benefits are estimated to be as high as $1,125.20 a month, in 1981.

4. If there are no children either under 18 or disabled, your wife can get a widow's benefit starting at age 60. This would come to 71½% of the basic amount at age 60. A widow who first becomes entitled at 65 or later may get 100% of her deceased husband's basic amount (provided neither he nor she ever drew reduced benefits).

5. Dependent parents can sometimes collect survivors' benefits. They are usually eligible if: (a) they were getting at least half their support from the deceased worker when he died, (b) they have reached 62, and (c) they are not eligible for a greater retirement benefit based on their own earnings. A single surviving parent can then get 82½% of the basic benefit. If two parents are eligible, each would get 75%.

A woman worker can provide survivors' benefits for any of these dependents: (1) her children under age 18, or for children in school up to age 22, (2) her disabled child after 18, if the child is unmarried and was disabled before 22, (3) her widowed husband at age 60, if he hasn't remarried, or (4) her parents if they meet the tests in paragraph 5 above. Also, a widowed father can get benefits on the same basis as a widowed mother.

Here is an example of survivors' benefits in one family situation: John Jones died at age 29 in June 1980 leaving a wife and two children aged one and three. He had average covered earnings under social security. Family survivors' benefits would include: (1) a cash lump-sum death payment of $255.00, and (2) a total monthly benefit of $804.40 for the family. When the children reach 18, their benefits stop unless they are attending school full-time, in which case payments continue up to age 22. When the older child no longer collects benefits, the widow and younger child continue to get benefits until that child is 18. If he continues in school, he will still get a benefit, but Mrs. Jones' checks will stop. When Mrs. Jones becomes 60 (assuming she has not remarried), she will be able to get a reduced widow's benefit if she so chooses, or she can wait until age 65 to get a full benefit.

If in addition to your social security benefit as a wife, husband, widow, or widower you receive a pension based on your work in public employment not covered by social security, your benefit as a dependent or survivor will be reduced by the amount of that pension. Under an exception in the law, your government pension will not affect your dependent's or survivor's benefit if you became eligible for that pension before December 1982 and if, at the time you apply or become entitled to your social security benefit as a dependent or survivor, you could have qualified for that benefit if the law in effect in January 1977 had remained in effect. (At that time, men had to prove they were dependent upon their wives for support to be eligible for benefits as a dependent or survivor.) Your government pension, however, will not affect any social security benefit based on your own work covered by social security.

Disability benefits. Disability benefits are paid to three groups of people:

1. An insured worker under age 65 with a severe disability can collect the same amount as if he were 65. Eligible dependents of disabled workers will receive the usual benefits. To be eligible for disability benefits, a person must: (a) have worked in employment (or self-employment) covered by social security long enough and recently enough (any social security office can tell you exactly); (b) be suffering from a physical or mental disability that is expected to last for at least 12 months or result in death; and (c) be so disabled that he can't work, or at least "engage in any substantial gainful activity." If he meets those tests, his benefits will start after a 5-month waiting period.

The applicant is referred to the state vocational rehabilitation agency and, if rehabilitation services are offered and the applicant refuses them without good cause, his disability benefit will be withheld.

2. The permanently disabled son or daughter of a worker who is receiving retirement or disability benefits or who has died can collect benefits after age 18 (when children's benefits are ordinarily cut off). If the child is eligible, his mother can also get a benefit if the child is in her care. The child must be unmarried and have been disabled before age 22 (but he need not have been drawing benefits before 22). The child's benefit would be 50% of a retired or disabled parent's or 75% of a deceased parent's basic benefit, and his mother would get the same amount.

The benefit for an adult disabled since childhood can actually be paid to adults if the above tests are met. For example, an unmarried person, aged 40, who was born blind and is dependent on his father for support, can collect a benefit as soon as his father starts drawing a retirement or disability benefit or dies.

3. The disabled widow, widower, or (under certain conditions) the surviving divorced wife of a worker who worked long enough under social security, may be able to get benefits as early as age 50 if he or she is disabled. The benefit is reduced (50% of the worker's basic benefit if the widow starts getting checks at 50). A widow (or widower or surviving divorced wife) needs no work credits of her own. She is considered disabled only if she has an impairment that is so severe that it would ordinarily prevent a person from working and that is expected to last at least 12 months or result in death. Vocational factors cannot be considered. In general, a widow cannot get these benefits unless her disability starts before her spouse's death or within seven years after his death. However, a widow who received benefits as a mother can be eligible if she becomes disabled before those payments end or within seven years after they end. There is a 5-month waiting period before benefits can start.

You Can Earn Income Without Losing Benefits

If you are 72 or over, you can earn any amount and still get all your benefits if your earnings do not exceed the annual exempt amount. The annual amount for 1980 is $5,000 for people 65 or over and $3,720 for people under 65.

If your earnings go over the annual amount, $1 in benefits is withheld for each $2 of earnings above the limit.

The monthly measure used for 1977 and earlier years to determine whether benefits could be paid for any month during which they earned 1/12 or less of the annual exempt amount and did no substantial work in their business has been eliminated. A person can now use the monthly test only in the first year that he or she has a month in which earnings do not exceed 1/12 of the annual exempt amount or does not perform substantial services in self-employment. If such a month occurs in 1980, a benefit can be paid for any month in which you earn $417 or less (if 65 or older) or $310 (if under 65) and don't perform substantial services in self-employment even though your total yearly earnings exceed the annual amount.

For people 65 or over, the annual exempt amount will increase to $5,500 for 1981, and to $6,000 for 1982. After that, the limit will increase automatically as the level of average wages rises. The limit for people under 65 will also continue to increase.

If a worker's earnings exceed the exempt amount, social security benefits to his dependents may be reduced. However, a dependent's benefits will not be reduced if another dependent has excess earnings.

Anyone earning over the annual exempt amount a year while receiving benefits (and under age 72) must report these earnings to the Social Security Administration. If you continue to work after you have applied for social security, your additional earnings may increase the amount of your monthly payment. This will be done automatically by the Social Security Administration. You need not ask for it.

Medicare

The Medicare program is administered by the Health Care Financing Administration.

Most people 65 and over and many under 65 who have been entitled to disability checks for at least 2 years have Medicare protection. So do insured people and their dependents who need a kidney transplant or dialysis treatment because of permanent kidney failure.

The hospital insurance part of Medicare helps pay the cost of inpatient hospital care and certain kinds of follow-up care. The medical insurance part helps pay for the cost of doctors' services, outpatient hospital services, and for certain other medical items and services.

A person who is eligible for monthly benefits at 65 gets hospital insurance automatically and does not have to pay a premium. He does pay a monthly premium for medical insurance.

Supplemental Security Income

The supplemental security income program started January 1974. These federal payments assure a minimum level of income for aged, blind, and disabled people who have limited income and resources.

This program is administered by the Social Security Administration, but it is financed from general revenues, not from social security contributions. Before 1974, payments to these people were made by state and local public assistance agencies.

Payments of up to $238.00 a month for an individual and up to $357.00 for a couple can be made and States may supplement the federal payments. Further information is available from any social security office.

How to Protect Your Social Security Record

Always show your social security card when you start a new job. In that way you will be sure that your earnings will be credited to *your* social security record and not someone else's. If you lose your social security card, apply for a new one at any social security office. When a woman marries, she should apply for a new card showing her married name (and the same number).

Public Assistance

The Federal government makes grants to the states to help them provide financial assistance, medical care, and social services to certain persons in need, including children dependent because of the death, absence from home, incapacity, or (in some states) unemployment of a parent. In addition, some help is provided from only state and/or local funds to some other needy persons.

Federal sharing in state cash assistance expenditures made in accordance with the Social Security Act is based on formulas which are set forth in the Act. The Social Security Act gives the states the option of using one of two formulas, whichever is to its benefit. One formula limits the amount of assistance payment in which there is federal sharing. The other formula permits federal sharing without a limit on the amount of assistance payment. Administrative costs in all the programs are shared equally by the federal and state governments.

Within these and other general patterns set by the requirements of the Social Security Act and their administrative interpretations, each state initiates and administers its own public assistance programs, including the determination of who is eligible to receive assistance, and how much can be granted and under what conditions. Assistance is in the form of cash payments made to recipients, except for payments for medical care. Other social services are provided, in some instances, to help assistance recipients increase their capacity for self-care and self-support or to strengthen family life.

In the medical assistance Medicaid program, federal funds pay 50% to 83% of the costs for medical care. If it is to a state's benefit, it may use the Medicaid formula for federal sharing for its money payment programs, ignoring the maximum on dollar amounts per recipient.

Unemployment Insurance

Unemployment insurance is managed jointly by the states and the federal government. Most states began paying benefits in 1938 and 1939.

Under What Conditions Can the Worker Collect?

The laws vary from state to state. In general, a waiting period of one week is required after a claim is filed before collecting unemployment insurance; the worker must be able to work, must not have quit without good cause or have been discharged for misconduct; he must not be involved in a labor dispute; above all, he must be ready and willing to work. He may be disqualified if he refuses, without good cause, to accept a job which is suitable for him in terms of his qualifications and experience, unless the wages, hours and working conditions offered are substantially less favorable than those prevailing for similar jobs in the community.

The unemployed worker must go to the local state employment security office and register for work. If that office has a suitable opening available, he must accept it or lose his unemployment payments, unless he has good cause for the refusal. If a worker moves out of his own state, he can still collect at his new residence; the state in which he is now located will act as agent for the other state, which will pay his benefits.

Benefits are paid only to unemployed workers who have had at least a certain amount of recent past employment or earnings in a job covered by the state law. The amount of employment or earnings, and the period used to measure them, vary from state to state, but the intent of the various laws is to limit benefits to workers whose recent records indicate that they are members of the labor force. The amount of benefits an unemployed worker may receive for any week is also determined by application to his past wages of a formula specified in the law. The general objective is to provide a weekly benefit which is about half the worker's customary weekly wages, up to a maximum set by the law (see table). In a majority of states, the total benefits a worker may receive in a 12-month period is limited to a fraction of his total wages in a prior 12-month period, as well as to a stated number of weeks. Thus, not all workers in a state are entitled to benefits for the number of weeks shown in the table.

Who Pays for the Insurance?

The total cost is borne by the employer in all but three states. Each state has a sliding scale of rates. The standard rate is set at 2.7% of taxable payroll in most states. But employers with records of less unemployment (that is, with fewer unemployment benefits paid to their former workers) are rewarded with rates lower than the standard 2.7%. The estimated average rate for employers in 1978 was 2.9% of taxable wages or 1.4% of total wages. As of Jan. 1, 1980, taxes are payable on the first $6,000 of a worker's pay, except that the limit for 1980 is $6,500 in Ill., $6,900 in N.J., $7,200 in N.M. and R.I., $7,400 in Iowa, $7,600 in Mont. and N.D., $7,900 in Nev., $8,000 in Minn., $9,600 in Wash., $10,000 in Alaska and Oreg., $10,800 in Idaho,

$11,000 in Utah, and $11,200 in Hawaii. Employees as well as employers pay a tax in Alaska ranging from 0.3% to 0.8% in accordance with their employer's tax; in N.J., employees pay 0.5% for unemployment insurance. In Ala., employees pay contributions of 0.5% only when the fund is below a specified amount.

Employers pay an additional unemployment tax to the federal government—0.7% of the first $6,000 paid to each employee. This money is used for the federal and state costs of administering the employment security program, including both unemployment insurance and the employment service. Any amount over these costs, up to the greater of $550 million or 0.125% of total wages subject to contributions under the state unemployment compensation laws for the calendar year, is put in a special fund on which the states draw when the benefit payment funds are low. Any remaining excess is distributed to the states in proportion to their taxable payrolls. These excess funds may be used for benefit payments, or may be used for administrative expenses if so appropriated by the state legislature.

Requirements vary from state to state, but all states cover firms having at least one employee for 20 weeks or a quarterly payroll of $1,500 in the current or preceding calendar year. In some states, firms with one employee at any time are covered. Certain classes of workers are specifically excluded under some or all state laws—members of the employer's family, insurance agents on commission, student nurses, internes, casual labor, and the self-employed.

During periods of high unemployment on either a state or national level, federal-state extended benefits are available to workers who have exhausted their regular benefits. An unemployed worker may receive benefits equal to the weekly benefit he received under the state program for one half the weeks of his basic entitlement to benefits up to a maximum (including regular benefits) of 39 weeks.

Federal Unemployment Insurance Programs

Amendments to the Social Security Act provided unemployment insurance for Federal civilian employees (1954) and for ex-servicemen (1958). Benefits under these programs are paid by state employment security agencies as agents of the federal government under agreements with the Secretary of Labor. Eligibility for benefits and the amount of benefits paid are determined according to the terms and conditions of the applicable state unemployment insurance law. Thus, federal civilian employees and ex-servicemen are subject to the same eligibility, disqualification, and benefit payment provisions as are claimants for benefits under the state unemployment insurance system.

Railroad Workers

These are covered by the federal Railroad Retirement Act which provides retirement and survivor annuities and lump-sum death benefits for aged or disabled employees and their families.

State Unemployment Compensation Maximums, 1980

State	Weekly benefit[1]	Maximum duration, weeks
Alabama	$90	26
Alaska	90–120	28
Arizona	95	26
Arkansas	136	26
California	120	26
Colorado	142	26
Connecticut	134–201	26
Delaware	150	26
D. C.	181	34
Florida	95	26
Georgia	90	26
Hawaii	144	26
Idaho	132	26
Illinois	135–180	26
Indiana	84–141	26
Iowa	134–162	26
Kansas	136	26
Kentucky	120	26
Louisiana	149	28
Maine	104–156	26
Maryland	106	26
Massachusetts	131–197	30
Michigan	97–136	26
Minnesota	150	26
Mississippi	90	26
Missouri	105	26
Montana	$119	26
Nebraska	106	26
Nevada	115	26
New Hampshire	114	26
New Jersey	123	26
New Mexico	106	26
New York	125	26
North Carolina	130	26
North Dakota	143	26
Ohio	128–202	26
Oklahoma	132	26
Oregon	127	26
Pennsylvania	162–170	30
Puerto Rico	72	20
Rhode Island	130–150	26
South Carolina	111	26
South Dakota	109	26
Tennessee	110	26
Texas	105	26
Utah	137	36
Vermont	115	26
Virginia	122	26
Washington	137	30
West Virginia	184	28
Wisconsin	160	34
Wyoming	131	26

1. Maximum amounts. When two amounts are shown, higher includes dependents' allowances. *Source:* Department of Labor, Employment and Training Administration.

Railroad workers are also covered by the Railroad Unemployment Insurance Act, which provides unemployment and sickness benefits as well as a placement service. Both acts are administered by the U.S. Railroad Retirement Board. Those covered by the railroad retirement system also participate in the health insurance program (Medicare) provided by the Social Security Act.

Medicare Program

The Medicare program is a federal health-insurance program for persons 65 and over, disabled people under 65 who have been entitled to social security disability benefits at least 24 consecutive months, and insured workers and their dependents who need dialysis treatment or a kidney transplant because of permanent kidney failure.

Enacted under the Social Security Amendments of 1965, Medicare's official name is Title XVIII of the Social Security Act. These amendments also carried Title XIX, providing federal assistance to state medical-aid programs, which has come to be known as Medicaid.

Medicare

It will be helpful to your understanding of the Medicare program if you keep the following points in mind:

- The federal health-insurance program does not of itself offer medical services. It helps pay hospital, doctor, and other medical bills. You choose your own doctor, who prescribes your treatment and place of treatment. But, you should always make sure that health care facilities or persons who provide you with treatment or services are participating in Medicare. Usually, Medicare cannot pay for care from non-participating health care organizations.
- There are two parts of the program:
  (1) The hospital insurance part for the payment of most of the cost of covered care provided by participating hospitals, skilled nursing facilities, and home health agencies.
  (2) The medical insurance part which helps pay doctors' bills and certain other expenses.
- Another important point to remember: While Medicare pays the major share of the costs of many illnesses requiring hospitalization, it does not offer adequate protection for long-term illness or mental illness.
- Therefore, it may be advisable not to cancel any private health insurance you now carry. You may wish to cancel a policy whose benefits are duplicated by the federal program, and consider a new policy that will provide for the payment of costs not covered by the federal program. Private insurance companies offer policies supplementing the protection offered by the federal program.

If you want help in deciding whether to buy private supplemental insurance, ask at any social security office for the pamphlet, *Guide to health insurance for people with Medicare.* This free pamphlet describes the various types of supplemental insurance available.

Do You Qualify for Hospital Insurance?

If you're entitled to monthly social security or railroad retirement checks (as a worker, dependent, or survivor), you have hospital insurance protection automatically when you're 65. Disabled people will have hospital insurance automatically after they have been entitled to social security disability benefits for 24 consecutive months. (Disabled people who get railroad annuities must meet special requirements.) People 65 or older who are not entitled to monthly benefits need credit for some work under social security to get hospital insurance without paying a monthly premium. If they do not have enough work, they can buy hospital insurance. The premium is $78 a month for the 12-month period starting July 1, 1980.

To be sure your protection will start the month you reach 65, apply for Medicare insurance 3 months before reaching 65, even if you don't plan to retire.

Do You Qualify for Voluntary Medical Insurance?

The voluntary medical insurance plan is a vital supplement to the hospital plan. It helps pay for doctors' and other medical services. Many people have not been able to obtain such insurance from private companies because they could not afford it or because of their medical histories.

One difference between the hospital insurance plan and the medical insurance plan is that you do not have to be under the social security or railroad retirement systems to enroll in the medical plan. Anyone who is 65 or older or who is eligible for hospital insurance can enroll in medical insurance.

People who get social security benefits or retirement benefits under the railroad retirement system will be enrolled automatically for medical insurance—unless they say they don't want it—when they become entitled to hospital insurance. Automatic enrollment does not apply to people who are

Is Cancer Insurance Necessary?

The House of Representatives Select Committee on Aging reported that cancer insurance policies are of extremely limited value. Only a minority of people get cancer and most people are covered by general health insurance and those policies will take care of most costs if cancer is diagnosed.

The committee also found that a disproportionate number of cancer policies are sold to the elderly, even though they may be covered by Medicare and often by Medicare supplemental insurance. The committee emphasized that in most instances consumers would be better off to increase their general health insurance rather than buy cancer insurance.

There are at present 20 million cancer insurance policies in effect in the United States, with Americans spending about $1.5 billion on them in 1979.

Medicaid Services by State

(as of December 1, 1979[1])

Basic required Medicaid services: Every Medicaid program must cover at least these services for at least everyone receiving federally supported financial assistance: inpatient hospital care; outpatient hospital services; other laboratory and X-ray services; skilled nursing facility services and home health services for individuals 21 and older; early and periodic screening, diagnosis, and treatment for individuals under 21; family planning; and physician services. Federal financial participation is also available to states electing to expand their Medicaid programs by covering additional services and/or by including people eligible for medical but not for financial assistance. For the latter group, states may offer the services required for financial assistance recipients or may substitute a combination of seven services. Services provided only under the Medicare buy-in or the screening and treatment program for individuals under 21 are not shown on this chart. Definitions and limitations on eligibility and services vary from state to state. Details are available from local welfare offices and state Medicaid agencies.

NOTE: O = Offered for people receiving federally supported financial assistance. X = Offered also for people in public assistance[2] and SSI[3] categories who are financially eligible for medical but not for financial assistance.

States	Basic required Medicaid services	Additional services for which federal financial participation is available to states under Medicaid																
		Clinic services	Prescribed drugs	Dental services	Prosthetic devices	Eyeglasses	Private-duty nursing	Physical therapy and related services[4]	Other diagnostic, screening, preventive, and rehabilitative services	Emergency hospital services	Skilled nursing facility services for patients under 22	Optometrists' services	Podiatrists' services	Chiropractors' services	Care for patients 65 or older in institutions for mental diseases[5]	Care for patients 65 or older in institutions for tuberculosis[5]	Care for patients under 22 in psychiatric hospitals	Institutional services in intermediate care facilities
Alabama	0	—	0	—	0	0	—	—	—	0	0	0	—	—	0	0	0	0[6]
Alaska	0	0	—	—	—	0	—	0	—	0	0	0	—	—	0	0	0	0[6]
Arizona		—	—	—	—	—	—	—	—	—	—	—	—	—	—	—	—	—
Arkansas	X	X	X	X	X	X	—	—	—	X	0	X	—	X	0	0	X	0[6]
California	X	X	X	X	X	X	—	X	X	X	X	X	X	X	X	X	X	X[6]
Colorado	0	0	0	—	0	—	—	—	—	0	0	—	0	—	0	—	0	0[6]
Connecticut	X	X	X	X	X	X	X	X	X	—	X	X	X	X	X	0	X	X[6]
Delaware	0	0	0	—	—	—	—	—	—	0	0	—	0	—	0	—	—	0[6]
D.C.	X	X	X	—	X	X	—	X	X	X	X	X	X	0	X	X	X	X[6]
Florida	0	—	0	—	—	—	—	—	—	0	—	—	—	—	0	0	0	0[6]
Georgia	0	0	0	—	0	—	—	—	—	—	0	—	0	—	0	0	—	0[6]
Guam	X	X	X	X	X	X	—	X	—	X	—	X	—	—	—	—	—	—
Hawaii	X	X	X	X	X	X	—	X	X	X	X	X	X	—	—	—	—	X
Idaho	0	0	0	—	—	—	—	0	0	0	0	0	0	0	0	—	—	0[6]
Illinois	X	X	X	X	X	X	X	X	X	X	X	X	X	X	X	X	X	X[6]
Indiana	0	0	0	0	0	0	0	0	0	0	0	0	0	0	0	—	0	0[6]
Iowa	0	—	0	0	0	0	—	0	0	0	0	0	0	0	0	—	0	0[6]
Kansas	X	X	X	X	X	X	X	X	X	X	X	X	X	X	X	X	X	X[6]
Kentucky	X	X	X	—	X	—	—	X	—	X	X	—	—	—	X	X	X	X[6]
Louisiana	X	X	X	—	X	—	—	—	—	X	0	—	—	X	0	0	0	0[6]
Maine	X	0	X	—	X	—	—	X	X	0	X	—	X	X	X	—	X	X[6]
Maryland	X	X	X	X	X	X	—	X	X	X	X	X	X	—	X	X	—	0[6]
Massachusetts	X	X	X	X	X	X	X	X	—	X	X	X	X	—	X	X	—	X[6]
Michigan	X	X	X	X	X	X	—	X	X	X	X	X	X	X	X	—	X	X[6]
Minnesota	X	X	X	X	X	X	—	X	—	X	X	X	X	X	X	X	X	X[6]
Mississippi	0	—	0	0	—	—	—	—	X	—	0	—	—	—	0	0	—	0[6]
Missouri	0	—	0	0	—	—	—	—	0	0	—	0	—	—	0	0	—	0[6]
Montana	X	X	X	X	X	X	X	X	X	X	X	X	X	—	X	—	X	X[6]
Nebraska	X	X	X	X	X	X	X	X	X	X	X	X	X	X	X	—	X	X[6]
Nevada	0	0	0	—	0	0	0	0	X	0	0	0	0	0	0	—	—	0[6]
New Hampshire	X	X	X	—	X	X	X	X	0	X	X	X	X	X	0	—	—	0[6]
New Jersey	0	0	0	0	0	0	—	0	0	0	0	0	0	0	0	0	0	0[6]
New Mexico	0	0	0	0	0	0	0	0	—	0	0	0	0	—	—	—	—	0[6]
New York	X	X	X	X	X	X	X	X	X	X	X	X	X	—	X	X	X	X[6]
North Carolina	X	X	X	X	—	X	—	—	X	—	X	X	X	X	X	X	X	X[6]
North Dakota	X	X	X	X	X	X	X	X	X	X	X	X	X	X	X	—	X	X
N. Mariana Islands	X	X	X	X	X	X	—	X	—	X	X	X	—	—	X	X	X	—
Ohio	0	0	0	0	0	0	0	0	—	0	0	0	0	0	0	—	0	0[6]
Oklahoma	X	—	X	X	X	—	—	—	X	—	—	—	X	—	X	—	X	X[6]
Oregon	0	0	0	0	0	0	0	0	0	0	0	0	0	0	0	—	0	0[6]
Pennsylvania	X	X	0	—	0	—	—	—	—	X	X	—	0	X	X	—	X	X[6]

States	Basic required Medicaid services	Clinic services	Prescribed drugs	Dental services	Prosthetic devices	Eyeglasses	Private-duty nursing	Physical therapy and related services[4]	Other diagnostic, screening, preventive, and rehabilitative services	Emergency hospital services	Skilled nursing facility services for patients under 22	Optometrists' services	Podiatrists' services	Chiropractors' services	Care for patients 65 or older in institutions for mental diseases[5]	Care for patients 65 or older in institutions for tuberculosis[5]	Care for patients under 22 in psychiatric hospitals	Institutional services in intermediate care facilities
		Additional services for which federal financial participation is available to states under Medicaid																
Puerto Rico	X	X	X	X	—	X	X	X	X	X	—	—	—	—	—	X	—	—
Rhode Island	X	—	X	X	X	X	—	—	—	—	X	X	X	—	X	—	—	0[6]
South Carolina	0	0	0	—	0	—	—	—	—	0	0	—	0	0	0	0	0	0[6]
South Dakota	0	0	0	0	0	—	—	0	0	0	0	—	—	0	0	—	—	0[6]
Tennessee	X	X	X	—	X	—	—	—	—	X	—	—	—	—	X	X	X	X[6]
Texas	0	—	0	—	0	0	—	—	0	0	—	0	0	0	—	0	—	0[6]
Utah	X	X	X	X	X	X	X	X	—	X	X	X	X	X	—	—	X	X[6]
Vermont	X	X	X	—	X	—	—	—	—	X	X	—	X	—	X	—	X	X[6]
Virgin Islands	X	X	X	X	X	X	—	X	—	—	—	—	—	—	—	—	—	—
Virginia	X	X	X	—	—	X	—	X	—	X	X	X	X	—	X	X	—	X[6]
Washington	X	X	X	X	X	X	X	X	X	X	X	X	X	X	X	X	0	X[6]
West Virginia	X	X	X	—	X	X	X	X	—	X	X	X	X	X	X	X	—	X
Wisconsin	X	X	X	X	X	X	X	X	X	X	X	X	X	X	X	X	X	X[6]
Wyoming	0	—	—	—	0	—	—	—	0	—	0	0	—	—	—	—	—	0

1. Data from Regional Office reports of characteristics of state programs and state plan amendments. 2. People qualifying as members of families with dependent children (usually families with at least one parent absent or incapacitated). 3. People qualifying as aged, blind, or disabled under the Supplemental Security Income program. 4. Includes therapy in speech, hearing, and language disorder. 5. In some states, services for age 65 and older may include inpatient hospital services, and/or skilled nursing facilities services, and/or intermediate care facilities services. 6. Including intermediate care facilities services in institutions for the mentally retarded. *Source:* Department of Health, Education, and Welfare, Health Care Financing Administration.

65 but have not worked long enough to be eligible for hospital insurance, who have permanent kidney failure, or who live in Puerto Rico or foreign countries. These people have to apply for medical insurance if they want it. People who have medical insurance pay a monthly premium covering part of the cost of this protection. The other part is paid from general federal revenues. The basic premium for enrollees is $9.60 a month for the 12-month period starting July 1, 1980.

Is Other Insurance Necessary?

As already indicated, Medicare provides only partial reimbursement. Therefore, you should know how much medical cost you can bear and perhaps arrange for other insurance.

In 1980, for the first 60 days of inpatient hospital care in each benefit period, hospital insurance pays for all covered services except for the first $180. For the 61st through 90th day of a covered inpatient hospital stay, hospital insurance pays for all covered services except for $45 a day. People who need to be in a hospital for more than 90 days in a benefit period can use their 60 inpatient hospital reserve days. Hospital insurance pays for all covered services except for $90 a day for each reserve day used. Hospital insurance also does not pay the full cost of an inpatient stay in a skilled nursing facility.

Under medical insurance, the patient must meet an annual deductible of $60. After the patient has $60 in reasonable charges for covered services each year, medical insurance generally pays 80% of the reasonable charges for any additional covered services the patient receives during the rest of the year.

How You Obtain Coverage

If you are receiving social security or railroad retirement monthly benefits, you will receive from the government information concerning Medicare about 3 months before you become entitled to hospital insurance.

If you are not receiving benefits or are not covered under social security, contact any social security office to find out how you can get Medicare. People who have permanent kidney failure also should contact a social security office to apply for Medicare.

U.S. Nursing Homes House 1.3 Million

A recent survey on 1977 nursing home statistics revealed that there are about 1.3 million residents in this country's 18,900 nursing homes. It cost the average resident $689 per month and the primary source of payment for 48% of the residents was Medicaid. The primary payment for about one third came from their own or their families' income.

About 35% of the residents were 85 or older. The median age was 85. It was found that 70% of the residents were female.

The Year in Education

William W. Turnbull
President, Educational Testing Service

Providing quality education during a time of decreasing enrollments may well be the single, greatest problem confronting educators in the '80s. Quality education was difficult enough to achieve before. As overcrowded schools now begin to give way to empty classrooms, many school boards and legislators are inclined to view declining enrollments as a chance to cut budgets rather than as an opportunity to enhance the quality of education through more individualized curricula. Educators, meanwhile, are resisting this recent trend and are attempting to prevent classrooms from remaining overcrowded and understaffed.

Decreasing Enrollments—Increasing Costs

Due to the declining national birth rate, elementary school enrollments will continue to drop until 1984, when the growing number of women of childbearing age is expected to reverse the decrease. Secondary school enrollments will decrease through the late 1980s.

Colleges and universities will also be affected by this trend, but experts disagree as to the extent of the impact. Some researchers project that the declining number of Americans aged 18 to 24 could cut college enrollments by as much as nine percent by 1990. Others argue that increased attendance by minority group members, women, students from overseas, and men over 35 could counteract the effect of this decline and, perhaps, even increase college enrollments by as much as 3.5% by the end of the decade.

Overall, however, educators are not optimistic about the enrollment outlook, particularly in view of the fact that the impact of declining enrollments has been intensified by the rising cost of education. According to the National Center for Education Statistics, school expenditures, from kindergarten to graduate school, will increase $11 billion this year, despite a 1.2% decline in enrollment. At all levels of education, institutional budgets are being squeezed by the increased cost of basic items such as fuel, electricity, security, and salaries. Inflated costs combined with decreasing enrollments have caused the per-pupil cost of education to skyrocket just at a time when taxpayers are rebelling against higher taxes.

In education, this budding tax revolt is fueled by the increased number of adults who have no school-age children, so that voters are rejecting school budgets at the polls more frequently than ever. Even where school budgets have not been rejected outright, pressure to cut services, lay off faculty, and close schools has been growing.

School boards are particularly responsive to budget pressures because they are often composed of businessmen who subscribe to the "factory" model of education. They insist that educators must increase productivity at a lower unit cost per pupil and are alarmed by the fact that current trends are running in the opposite direction.

Accountability

In response to such criticism, educators are likely to question how, and by what standards, educational productivity can be defined. But the more forcefully professionals resist the imposition of community oversight measures, the more persistently the public suspects that the educational community has something to hide.

This is particularly true when the new community standards encompass demands for teacher accountability. Distressed by declining student scores on standardized achievement tests, parents are demanding a renewed emphasis upon academic excellence and are seriously questioning the ability of some teachers to teach. Many parents and school board members are demanding that job candidates pass basic competency tests before they are hired.

Despite all the adverse publicity, however, there are also signs that general public attitudes toward public school education are becoming more positive. A 1980 Gallup Poll revealed that, for the first time in the last seven years, the proportion of adults who think the public schools are doing a better-than-average job has increased. Thirty-five percent of respondents gave public schools an "A" or "B," on a scale from "A" to "F."

Demand is also continuing for emphasis on basic skills and evaluation of students' skills from the earliest grades onward. In many states, minimum graduation standards have been defined and "enforced" through testing, so that students without basic reading, writing, and mathematics skills cannot receive diplomas. National basic-skills-assessment tests are available for states that have not developed their own instruments, but each state sets its own minimum competency requirements. Over the past year, a rift has developed between community representatives who believe that competency exams should test survival skills, such as the ability to read bus schedules, want ads, and the like, and educators who argue that the exams should relate more closely to the curriculum. At the very least, community spokesmen maintain that schools should teach students to relate academic skills to real-life situations. If competency exams are to be at all meaningful, the two groups will have to reconcile the two positions.

In addition, there are those who oppose basic skills assessment and who argue that, in fact, schools should eliminate *all* standardized testing.

The National Education Association has been one of the most active groups in calling for the abolition of standardized testing. These critics contend that if competency tests come to be regarded as indexes of relative quality between schools, then schools will teach only those skills necessary to pass the tests. Most observers agree that tests can be overemphasized and that the curriculum should cover many subjects besides the basics. Although tests of basic skills do not provide a sufficient basis on which to compare schools, many people have suggested that it would be more fruitful to develop better indicators of those qualities not measured by basic skills tests than to dismiss them altogether.

Coping with Scarcity

Colleges and universities have already begun to cope with the prospect of declining enrollments by recruiting students from previously underrepresented segments of the populations. In addition to recruiting minority and foreign students and developing special facilities for the handicapped, colleges are attempting to entice adults who skipped college when young.

In 1980, such strategies have already produced dramatic increases in the enrollment of part-timers (usually older students) on the nation's campuses. Some experts even predict that increased recruitment from previously ignored student populations will enable colleges to more than make up for the decrease in traditional students, but most forecasters don't share their optimism. During the past decade, 141 private institutions have been forced to close, and projections suggest that 200 to 300 small, private colleges will close their doors in the next few years.

The prospect of declining enrollments has already generated considerable competition for students by colleges. In 1980, large numbers of colleges began to recruit students aggressively through direct-mail, newspaper, and television advertising compaigns, prompting charges of hucksterism from critics. Colleges have also been accused of lowering entrance requirements and inflating grades in order to attract students.

At most colleges and universities today, students are subject to few required courses, and there are indications that some are learning little about the world. A recent ETS study that tested over 1,000 college seniors throughout the country on their understanding of world affairs revealed a notable lack of knowledge of fields such as international relations, world economics, and religion. The study suggests the need for a curriculum that would provide them with a basic understanding of the complex world in which we live.

For teachers at all levels, declining enrollments and the deteriorating economy have meant layoffs or inadequate salary increments. College students have turned away from education as a career, and enrollments in teacher-training programs have plummeted. In general, college students, highly conscious of the tightening economy, are less interested in liberal arts programs and are majoring in business programs in greater numbers than ever before.

Planning for the Future

At the elementary and secondary level, some thoughtful planners are beginning to develop ways to insure quality education in the face of enrollment shifts and rising costs. When society is in a position to enjoy an abundance of both schools and teachers, students should benefit, not suffer, from this availability.

At the college and university level, institutions may be expected to expand the base of their enrollments to encompass all segments of the population beyond the teenage years. The historic tendency to cram higher education into the four years after graduation from high school stemmed from an educational perspective that no longer fits the pace of change. Learning is a lifelong process, as society is increasingly aware.

At every level, there is increasing sentiment for redesigning and trimming curricula to meet budgets while improving the quality of education, a neat trick. As teachers prepare students for an increasingly more complicated world, new technological devices, particularly television and computers, are becoming available that enable them to communicate knowledge in an exciting and efficient manner. The 1980s will be a witness to the success of their efforts.

What Do Those Scores Mean?

How scores on standardized tests are interpreted and used is critically important. Although testing can provide much valuable information about student achievement and ability, administrators and teachers need to make responsible judgments about how the test results are used. For instance, scores should not be the sole basis for determining college or graduate school admissions, nor should tests be used alone in any final determinations about grade placement or instructional needs. Rather, they give the most accurate picture when combined with other information, such as grades and personal observations.

Among the types of tests young people are most likely to encounter are college admissions tests, such as the Scholastic Aptitude Test (SAT) and the American College Testing (ACT) Program, and achievement tests administered by their schools. Recently, tests determining minimum competency in the basic skills—reading, writing, and math—have attracted a great deal of national attention.

Test-makers distinguish between types of achievement tests by dividing them into two tongue-twisting categories—*criterion-referenced* tests and *norm-referenced* tests. In simple terms, criterion-referenced tests measure a student's mastery of a certain skill, or knowledge of a field of subject matter, but no attempt is made to compare the student's proficiency with that of other students. Either the skill is mastered or it is not. Minimum compentency tests and most teacher-made tests are examples of criterion-referenced tests.

Norm-referenced tests not only measure student achievement or aptitude—how much the student has learned—but also compare his/her performance on the test with others who have taken the test or others in the same grade across the country. Of the millions of achievement tests administered in elementary and secondary schools each year, most are norm-referenced tests.

For parents and students alike, interpreting test scores can be a chore. Perhaps a brief glossary of terms will help:

Score Scale. The range of scores given on any test. For instance, the College Board Admissions Testing Program, the Law School Admission Test, and the Graduate Management Admission Test use score scales ranging from a low of 200 to a high of 800.

Raw Score. A score based on the number of correct answers or, in some tests, the number of correct responses minus a fraction of the incorrect ones.

Percentile Rank. A number indicating where the student placed in relation to others. A percentile rank of 75 means that the student did as well or better than 75% of some other specified group of students and not as well as 25% of it. The comparisons may be made with others taking the same test or with others in the same age group or grade across the country.

Standard Error of Measurement. An estimate of the range of scores that might be expected if one individual took the test several times. Test-makers give the standard error for each test as a reminder to the public that tests are not perfect and should not be regarded as perfect or unchangeable. The smaller the standard error of measurement, the more confidence a test-taker can have in an actual score.

Grade-Equivalent Score. A numerical designation used to describe a student's achievement level in terms of grade and month. For instance, a sixth-grade student may be scored as reading on an 8.2 level, meaning on the level expected of an eighth grader in the second month of school. Although widely used in elementary and secondary school tests, grade-equivalent scores can be misleading if they are used to describe achievement above or below the student's actual grade.

A Testing Dictionary

In recent years, increasing attention has been paid to *testing*—for admission to schools, for employment, and for increased self-awareness. This listing of established, frequently used achievement, intelligence, and psychological tests from a broad range of test publishers was compiled by the Educational Testing Service. It briefly describes what these tests measure, and how they are used.

Advanced Placement Program. These tests are designed to measure advanced student achievement in a variety of subject areas. They are generally taken by the student in grades 10–12 who is entering college and who wishes to receive credit for college-level work completed during high school. Most colleges in the United States give credit or advanced-placement standing or both for college-level courses taken in the student's own high school.

American College Testing Program (ACT). A series of measures in English, mathematics, social sciences, and natural sciences, which is designed to measure the academic development of the college-bound student who takes these tests in grades 11–13. Scores are reported to the individual student, as well as to the secondary school and designated colleges. Results provide information helpful in formulating educational plans.

Basic Skills Assessment Program. This program for students in grades 8–12 measures student mastery of basic skills in reading, writing, and mathematics. By determining the competency of each student, this program assists the teacher in identifying the need for additional educational assistance.

California Achievement Tests. The tests of this series may be administered by the classroom teacher to measure the achievement growth of pupils at various levels, from kindergarten through high school. The subject areas include: pre-reading, reading, spelling, language, mathematics, and reference skills. Scores indicate both achievement level and mastery of curriculum goals. Score reports are furnished for the individual student and for the teacher as class lists.

California Psychological Inventory. The purpose of this test is to measure specific personality characteristics considered important for social living. Essentially self-administered, the test may be used in schools, colleges, businesses, or counseling agencies. Test results are reported as profiles representing the degree to which individuals exhibit each trait.

CIRCUS. CIRCUS assesses the skills of young children (pre-school to second grade) in language, mathematics, perception, information processing, attitudes and interests, and divergent production. Results aid in determining the child's readiness for academic instruction and in identifying particular needs. Scores are reported to the teacher numerically and in sentence format.

College Board Achievement Tests. A series of achievement tests that measure knowledge in each of fifteen subject areas. They are designed for the college-bound student and are administered in group sessions. The number of tests taken is decided by the student, and scores are reported to designated colleges.

College-Level Examination Program (CLEP). CLEP enables people of all ages to earn college credit by successful achievement on examinations. Two types of tests are offered—General Examinations and Subject Examinations. The General Examinations are based on materials covered in the first two years of college and focus on achievement in five basic areas of the liberal arts: English composition, humanities, mathematics, natural sciences, and social sciences-history. The 47 Subject Examinations measure achievement in specific college courses and are essentially end-of-course tests.

Comprehensive Tests of Basic Skills (CTBS). CTBS measures basic academic skills as well as the ability to apply knowledge to everyday living from kindergarten through high school. The general areas of assessment include reading, language, arithmetic, and study skills. Test results may prove useful to school administrators for educational planning and guidance and for determining minimum competency in necessary life-skills.

Differential Aptitude Tests. The purpose of this test battery is to measure student potential in each of eight areas. Test results may be used as a basis for educational or vocational planning. It is administered in group sessions, and scores, reported separately for each area, yield a profile of relative strengths and weaknesses for each student.

Edwards Personal Preference Schedule. Administered primarily for personal counseling or guidance, this test is used to measure the basic motivations and needs of the individual. The responses may be hand- or machine-scored, and are plotted on an individual profile depicting which of fifteen possible needs are most characteristic of that individual.

Flanagan Aptitude Classification Tests. A series of separate tests for senior high school students and adults that may be used in various combinations to evaluate the potential for success in specific careers. Each test measures a different job-related skill and may be self-scored. Tests are generally administered in the course of vocational counseling or to job applicants.

General Aptitude Test Battery. This battery of tests is available only for use by State Employment Service offices or approved organizations. Each test measures a specific ability associated with a number of occupations. Test scores provide a basis upon which vocational plans may be made.

Graduate Management Admission Test. This test is specifically intended for students who are interested in attending graduate business schools. Verbal, quantitative, and total scores are reported for each student and may be used by the school in screening applicants. Test questions are designed to measure the general abilities associated with success in business and management studies.

Graduate Record Examinations (GRE). The purpose of these tests is to determine the scholastic ability of college seniors who wish to continue their education beyond the college level. The scores are typically used by graduate schools to screen applicants. There is a test of general aptitude, which covers verbal, quantitative, and analytical skills. There are also advanced tests available to measure ability in each of twenty specific subject areas. Some of these tests offer subscores that may be used for guidance and placement by the graduate school.

Henmon-Nelson Tests of Mental Ability. This series is designed for students from kindergarten through high school to provide an evaluation of the abilities considered important for academic success. Appropriate for classroom testing, the scores are reported as group lists. Individual student scores may prove helpful to parents and teachers as indications of future progress.

Kuder Preference Record. To assist high school students and adults in choosing a suitable profession, this test measures the individual's preference for the types of social situations that may influence vocational choice. It is scored by hand, and test results are reported as profiles depicting relative preference for group activities, familiar situations, working with ideas, avoiding conflict, and directing others.

Kuhlmann-Anderson Intelligence Test, Seventh Edition. Designed to measure the mental capacities of the student in grades K–12 as an indication of academic potential. Verbal and quantitative abilities are measured in tests for grade 7 and above. All tests may be administered and scored by the school teacher. Student score-reports depict an intelligence quotient, as well as the student's standing in relation to others of the same age.

Law School Admission Test. This examination is given to college seniors who are considering application to law school. A general measure of the academic skills related to success in the study of law, score reports are made available to the student and to the schools under consideration. They may be used by law schools in the selection and counseling of applicants for admission.

Medical College Admission Test. College seniors wishing to study medicine take this examination to fulfill admissions requirements. Scores are reported to the schools in biology, chemistry, physics, science problems, and skills analysis—reading and quantitative skills.

Metropolitan Achievement Tests. This battery of tests is intended to measure academic achievement from kindergarten through junior high. Areas of assessment include: reading, mathematics, word knowledge, language, spelling, science, and social studies. The test may be administered by the teacher to student groups. Score reports are made to each pupil, and group lists are provided to assist teachers and school administrators.

Minnesota Multiphasic Personality Inventory. This test is designed for ages 16 through adult to evaluate the personality characteristics that affect social and personal adjustment. It may be used, in conjunction with other measures, in personnel selection or in clinical therapy. It is required, however, that the test administrator have training and experience in testing. A tape-recorded version of the test is available for use with semiliterate and disabled persons.

National Teachers Examination. Designed for college students who have completed degree programs in teaching, the tests measure general knowledge within the field of education and readiness for the profession of teaching. Some 26 subject area tests are also available to measure knowledge within specialized fields. Scores are used by school boards in the selection of teaching staff and by states for certification.

Otis-Lennon Mental Ability Tests. A test of general mental ability or scholastic aptitude that may be administered to groups by the classroom teacher. There are various levels appropriate for use from kindergarten through high school. The score for each student is reported within a group list, which indicates an intelligence quotient, as well as the student's relative status by age and grade.

Preliminary Scholastic Aptitude Test (PSAT)/National Merit Scholarship Qualifying Tests. As an abbreviated version of the *Scholastic Aptitude Test*, this examination is designed to provide sophomores, juniors, or seniors in high school with an indication of their ability to handle college work. Consisting of general verbal and mathematical measures, a third score is also reported that is considered for National Merit Scholarship Programs. Scores are reported to the student, the school principal, and/or the school system.

Rorschach Technique. This well-known test is primarily used in clinical therapy for ages 3-up, and may be interpreted only by an experienced examiner. It is designed to identify aspects of the individual's personality through responses to each of a series of inkblots.

Scholastic Aptitude Test (SAT). Designed to measure scholastic ability, the SAT is generally required for admission to college. As an indication of the student's readiness for college curricula, verbal and mathematical reasoning skills are assessed. Scores are reported to each student and to designated college admissions offices, where they are used for selecting applicants.

Stanford Achievement Tests. This achievement battery is useful for assessing the academic performance of students within the classroom (grades 1–9) or within the entire school system. Skills are measured in the areas of reading comprehension, language, science, social science, and auditory proficiency. The scoring system allows for both individual and group reporting.

Stanford-Binet Intelligence Scale. An individually administered test of intelligence that consists of different performance tasks for ages 2-up. Responses may only be recorded and interpreted by an experienced examiner. The test results are reported as an intelligence quotient, which takes into consideration both the age and the performance of the individual being tested.

STEP III. The Sequential Tests of Educational Progress are achievement tests for grades 3–12 that measure the extent of student learning in reading, mathematics computation and concepts, writing skills, listening, study skills, science, and social studies. The tests are designed for out-of-level testing within a single classroom.

The Strong-Campbell Interest Inventory. A test used to determine the occupational interests of students 16 years and older and adults. Feelings about specific occupations, occupational activities, hobbies, amusements, school subjects, and types of people are analyzed to produce an individual profile. Scores are reported on each os 23 basic Interest Scales, as well as each of 125 Occupational Scales to demonstrate the over-all orientation of the individual.

Tests of General Educational Development (GED). These tests measure the educational competency of adults who have not graduated from high school. They provide a means of demonstrating abilities comparable to those of a high school graduate. Measures of language, usage, mathematics, and reading interpretation are available in English, Spanish, and French.

Wechsler Intelligence Scale for Children. This test measures general intelligence. The subtests focus on performance tasks and verbal responses. Appropriate for both children and adolescents, the test is administered individually by persons with extensive training in psychological measurement. Analysis of responses yields an intelligence quotient for the individual tested.

Wonderlic Personnel Test. In the process of gathering information, a business or industrial personnel office may use this brief test to determine the general mental ability of job applicants. It may be administered either on an individual basis or in groups, and the final score is determined by the number of questions answered correctly. Actual score interpretation is limited to those persons who are experienced in psychological testing procedures.

Selected Degree Abbreviations

Source: This material has been taken from *American Universities and Colleges*, 10th and 11th editions, published by the American Council on Education.

A.B. Bachelor of Arts
Ae.E. Aeronautical Engineer
A.M. Master of Arts
A.M.T. Master of Arts in Teaching
B.A. Bachelor of Arts
B.A.E. Bachelor of Arts in Education, or Bachelor of Art Education, Aeronautical Engineering, Agricultural Engineering, or Architectural Engineering
B.Ag. Bachelor of Agriculture
B.Arch. Bachelor of Architecture
B.B.A. Bachelor of Business Administration
B.C.E. Bachelor of Civil Engineering or Bachelor of Christian Education
B.Ch.E. Bachelor of Chemical Engineering
B.D. Bachelor of Divinity
B.E. Bachelor of Education or Bachelor of Engineering
B.E.E. Bachelor of Electrical Engineering
B.F. Bachelor of Forestry
B.F.A. Bachelor of Fine Arts
B.J. Bachelor of Journalism
B.L.S. Bachelor of Liberal Studies or Bachelor of Library Science
B.Litt. Bachelor of Literature
B.M. Bachelor of Medicine or Bachelor of Music
B.Mus. Bachelor of Music
B.N. Bachelor of Nursing
B.Pharm. Bachelor of Pharmacy
B.R.E. Bachelor of Religious Education
B.S. Bachelor of Science
B.S.Ed. Bachelor of Science in Education
C.E. Civil Engineer
Chem.E. Chemical Engineer
D.B.A. Doctor of Business Administration

D.D. Doctor of Divinity[1]
D.D.S. Doctor of Dental Surgery or Doctor of Dental Science
D.L.S. Doctor of Library Science
D.M.D. Doctor of Dental Medicine
D.O. Doctor of Osteopathy
D.M.S. Doctor of Medical Science
D.P.A. Doctor of Public Administration[2]
D.P.H. Doctor of Public Health
D.R.E. Doctor of Religious Education
D.S.W. Doctor of Social Welfare or Doctor of Social Work
D.Sc. Doctor of Science[3]
D.V.M. Doctor of Veterinary Medicine
Ed.D. Doctor of Education[2]
Ed.S. Education Specialist
E.E. Electrical Engineer
E.M. Engineer of Mines or Mining Engineer
E.Met. Engineer of Metallurgy
I.E. Industrial Engineer
J.D. Doctor of Jurisprudence[2]
J.S.D. Doctor of the Science of Law
L.H.D. Doctor of Humane Letters[3]
Litt.M. Master of Letters[4]
LL.B. Bachelor of Laws
LL.D. Doctor of Laws[3]
LL.M. Master of Laws
M.A. Master of Arts
M.Aero.E. Master of Aeronautical Engineering
M.B.A. Master of Business Administration
M.C.E. Master of Christian Education or Master of Civil Engineering
M.C.S. Master of Commercial Science or Master of Computer Science
M.D. Doctor of Medicine
M.Div. Master of Divinity
M.E. Master of Engineering
M.Ed. Master of Education
M.Eng. Master of Engineering
M.F. Master of Forestry
M.F.A. Master of Fine Arts
M.L.S. Master of Library Science
M.M. Master of Music
M.M.E. Master of Mechanical Engineering or Master of Music Education
M.Mus. Master of Music
M.Nurs. Master of Nursing
M.R.E. Master of Religious Education
M.S. Master of Science
M.S.W. Master of Social Work
M.Th. Master of Theology
Nuc.E. Nuclear Engineer
O.D. Doctor of Optometry
Pharm.D. Doctor of Pharmacy[2]
Ph.B. Bachelor of Philosophy
Ph.D. Doctor of Philosophy
S.B. Bachelor of Science
Sc.D. Doctor of Science[3]
S.J.D. Doctor of Juridical Science or Doctor of the Science of Law
S.Sc.D. Doctor of Social Science
S.T.B. Bachelor of Sacred Theology
S.T.D. Doctor of Sacred Theology[2]
S.T.M. Master of Sacred Theology
Th.B. Bachelor of Theology
Th.D. Doctor of Theology
Th.M. Master of Theology

1. Honorary. 2. Earned and honorary. 3. Usually honorary. 4. Sometimes honorary.

Academic Costume: Colors Associated With Fields

Field	Color	Field	Color
Agriculture	Maize	Medicine	Green
Arts, Letters, Humanities	White	Music	Pink
Commerce, Accountancy, Business	Drab	Nursing	Apricot
		Oratory (Speech)	Silver gray
Dentistry	Lilac	Pharmacy	Olive green
Economics	Copper	Philosophy	Dark blue
Education	Light Blue	Physical Education	Sage green
Engineering	Orange	Public Admin. including Foreign Service	Peacock blue
Fine Arts, Architecture	Brown	Public Health	Salmon pink
Forestry	Russet	Science	Golden yellow
Journalism	Crimson	Social Work	Citron
Law	Purple	Theology	Scarlet
Library Science	Lemon	Veterinary Science	Gray

National Earthquake Council Established

The National Earthquake Prediction Evaluation Council has been established to aid the director of the U.S. Geological Survey in issuing any formal predictions of earthquakes.

The Council is expected to focus its efforts on potentially destructive earthquakes, which generally are those of a magnitude of 5.5 or greater on the Richter Scale. Data for smaller earthquakes will also be reviewed to establish a "track record" for prediction techniques.

Under terms of the charter, a prediction is defined to mean a statement on the time of occurrence, location, and magnitude of a future significant earthquake based on qualification or evaluation of the uncertainty of those factors.

If the USGS director decides to issue a prediction, or an advisory or negative evaluation of a prediction, the first people to be notified are the director of the Federal Emergency Management Agency, the Secretary of the Department of the Interior, and the governors of states affected by the predicted earthquake.

Universities—Medieval and Modern

Universities, in the modern sense of the term, sprang up in the 12th and 13th centuries in response to the resurgence of learning that preceded the Renaissance in Europe. Procedure at the early universities was informal, with students gathering at some place in a city to listen to a preeminent teacher. There were no campuses, buildings, or endowments. Actually, the term "university" once meant a guild or corporation; there were, in the medieval period, "universities" of bootmakers, weavers, etc. Thus the university of learning was similar in organization to the guilds. The students filled the role of apprentices, and the teachers were the masters.

The first European university was that of *Salerno* in the 9th century, when it was known as a school of medicine. By the 11th century, it had become one of the most famous medical schools of Europe.

University of Bologna. Originated in the 12th century as student guilds for protection against the merchants and citizens of Bologna who had raised prices of food and lodging, it was famous for its legal scholars. The students were organized into two guilds and exercised a great deal of authority over the administration.

Other Italian universities famed in the Middle Ages included those at *Arezzo, Ferrara, Florence, Modena, Naples, Padua, Pavia, Perugia, Siena,* and *Vicenza.*

University of Paris. Originated between 1150 and 1170 in a cathedral school on the Île de la Cité, it was later moved to the left (south) bank of the Seine, although it remained under the authority of the chancellor of Notre Dame. It developed into the most famous continental center of learning of its day. Its four principal schools were theology, medicine, law, and arts. By the 14th century, the university had some 40 colleges, of which the *Sorbonne* became the most celebrated.

The universities of Paris and Bologna had a marked influence in the subsequent creation of other university centers. About 1167–68 there was a migration of students from Paris to *Oxford* (founded in the 12th century) and about 1210, from Oxford to *Cambridge* (also founded in the 12th century).

Other famous universities of the Middle Ages include the *University of Toulouse* (1233), *Salamanca* (1243), *Seville* (1254), *Orléans* (1305), *Valladolid* (1346), *Prague* (1347), *Kraków* (1364), *Vienna* (1364), *Erfurt* (1379), *Heidelberg* (1385), *Cologne* (1388), *Leipziq* (1409), *Rostock* (1419), and *Louvain* (1426).

The Renaissance

The Renaissance gave fresh impetus to the universities of Europe. In France three of importance arose in the 15th century—the *University of Aix* (1409, Provence), the *University of Poitiers* (1431), and the *University of Caen* (1437).

Other French institutions of note that arose in this era were at *Bordeaux* (1441), *Valence* (1452), *Nantes* (1463), and *Bourges* (1465). New European universities were also founded at *Trier* (1450), *Freiburg* (1455), *Ingolstadt* (1469), *Basel* (1460), *Budapest* (1475), *Mainz* (1476), *Uppsala* (1477), *Tübingen* (1477), *Copenhagen* (1479), *Wittenberg* (1502), *Frankfurt an der Oder* (1506), and *Coimbra* (1537).

St. Andrews, founded in 1411, was the first university in Scotland. Others were the *University of Glasgow* (1453) and the *University of Aberdeen* (1494). The *University of Edinburgh* was established as a college in the post-Reformation period (1582). In Ireland, *Trinity College* was founded in Dublin in 1591. The earliest Dutch university, *Leyden,* was founded in 1575.

Reformation and Post-Reformation

Until the Reformation, most of the institutions of higher learning in Europe were under the tutelage of the Catholic Church. After 1520, however, many established universities declared their independence of the Church. Cromwell's rule brought about new scholastic methods at both Oxford and Cambridge and the establishment of new colleges thoroughly imbued with Protestantism.

But the first Protestant university was that of *Marburg,* Germany, founded in 1527. Other Protestant universities were *Königsberg* (1544), *Jena* (1558), *Helmstedt* (1575), *Altdorf* (1575), *Giessen* (1607), *Strasbourg* (1621), and *Halle* (1693).

18th, 19th, and 20th Centuries

Among the more famous institutions in this era was *Göttingen* (1736), whose school of history became celebrated throughout Europe. Others were *Erlangen* (1743), *Berlin* (1809), *Lemberg* (Lwów) (1816), *Bonn* (1818), *Helsingfors* (1828), the *National University* at Athens (1837), *Bucharest* (1864), *Tokyo* (1877), *Sofia* (1888), and *Kyoto* (1897).

Among the more famous British universities established in the 19th and 20th centuries were the *University of London* (1828), *Manchester* (1851), the *Mason University College* in Birmingham, later *Birmingham University* (1900), *Liverpool* (1903), *Leeds* (1904), and the *University of Sheffield* (1905). The *University of Wales* (1893) is composed of the colleges of Aberystwyth, Bangor, Cardiff, and Swansea.

There are many large and important universities in the British Commonwealth. In Canada, the famous *McGill University* in Montreal was founded in 1821. Others are the *University of Toronto* (1827), *Queens University* at Kingston, Ont. (1841), *Laval University,* Quebec (1852), *Dalhousie,* Halifax (1818), and *Montreal University* (1878).

The early universities in India were patterned after London University, rather than on the Oxford-Cambridge style, and were purely examining institutions. *Calcutta, Bombay,* and *Madras* universities were founded in 1857 as examining bodies.

In Australia, the state plays an important role in the development of universities. The *University of Melbourne* (1853) has the largest enrollment. Among the others are *Adelaide* (1874), *Tasmania* (1890), *Queensland* (1909), *Sydney* (1850), and *Western Australia* (1911).

There are also many well-endowed universities in New Zealand and other parts of the Commonwealth.

By 1800, Russia had only three universities—*Vilna* (1578), *Dorpat* (1632), and *Moscow* (1755). Other institutions developed later were the *University of Kharkov* (1804), *Kazan* (1804), *Warsaw,* now Polish (originally established 1816, but closed 1832–69), *St. Petersburg* (1819), *St. Vladimir* in Kiev (1835), *Odessa* (1865), and *Tomsk,* in Siberia (1888). The building of universities after the Revolution of 1917 was spurred by the Soviet government.

In China, the growth of universities was hampered by the chaotic state of the government in the 1900s, the recurring civil wars, and the conflict with Japan.

The United States

Universities in the United States marched in step with the progress of the nation. The early settlers brought a heritage of European culture, which they planted in New England soil. The first university in the country was started as *Harvard College* in 1636, with an endowment totaling 800 pounds. Harvard was to become probably the most famous of the American universities.

The *College of William and Mary* (1693) was the second institution of higher learning established in the colonies. Others started during the colonial period (current names only) are *Yale* (1701, *University of Pennsylvania* (1740), *Princeton* (1746), *Washington and Lee* (1749), *Columbia* (1754), *Brown* (1764), *Rutgers* (1766), and *Dartmouth* (1769).

After the Revolution of 1776, the state tax-supported university was established. The *University of Virginia* (1819) was a notable early example of this type.

Colleges that until the 1970s were designed only for women grew up in the second quarter of the 19th century. Among these are *Mt. Holyoke* (1837), *Elmira* (1855), *Vassar* (1861), *Wells* (1868), *Hunter* (1870), *Wellesley* (1870), *Smith* (1871), and *Bryn Mawr (1885).*

After the middle of the 19th century, under the Morrill acts, Congress began making appropriations for support of agricultural and mechanical-arts colleges on land granted to individual states by the federal government. These now greatly expanded land-grant universities today offer the full range of curricula, but still also confer 99% of the advanced degrees in agriculture and two fifths of all the engineering degrees in the U.S.

In the latter part of the 19th century, universities established by private endowments arose. Typical of these are *Cornell* (1865), which is also a land-grant institution; *Johns Hopkins* (1876); *Stanford* (1885); and the *University of Chicago* (1891).

School Enrollment, October 1979

(in thousands)

Age	White		Black		Spanish origin[1]		All races	
	Enrolled	Percent	Enrolled	Percent	Enrolled	Percent	Enrolled	Percent
3 and 4 years	1,694	33.9	385	40.8	111	22.5	2,138	35.1
5 and 6 years	4,773	95.8	916	96.0	445	92.5	5,846	95.8
7 to 9 years	8,404	99.2	1,538	99.4	728	98.7	10,179	99.2
10 to 13 years	11,603	99.2	2,072	98.7	875	99.0	13,966	99.1
14 and 15 years	6,419	98.2	1,122	97.4	507	96.3	7,691	98.1
16 and 17 years	6,092	89.0	1,051	90.8	402	82.3	7,279	89.2
18 and 19 years	3,106	44.5	500	46.6	202	39.9	3,693	45.0
20 and 21 years	2,151	31.1	242	23.7	114	22.6	2,446	30.2
22 to 24 years	1,572	15.7	213	15.0	74	10.0	1,844	15.8
25 to 29 years	1,510	9.7	160	7.9	83	7.8	1,728	9.6
30 to 34 years	901	6.3	118	6.8	66	6.7	1,045	6.4
Total	**48,225**	**49.6**	**8,317**	**55.0**	**3,608**	**48.6**	**57,854**	**50.3**

1. Persons of Spanish origin may be of any race. NOTE: Figures include persons enrolled in nursery school, kindergarten, elementary school, high school, and college. *Source:* Department of Commerce, Bureau of the Census.

Statistics of State School Systems

Years	Enrollment[1]			High school graduates[2]			Total expenditures (in thousands)	Current expenditure per pupil in average daily attendance
	Total	Kindergarten through Grade 8	Grades 9 through 12 and postgraduate	Total	Boys	Girls		
1963–64	41,025,000	29,907,000	11,118,000	2,290,000	1,121,000	1,169,000	$21,324,993	$ 460
1965–66	42,835,000	31,177,000	11,658,000	2,632,000	1,308,000	1,324,000	26,248,026	537
1967–68	45,076,000	32,495,000	12,581,000	2,702,000	1,341,000	1,361,000	32,977,182	658
1969–70	46,531,000	33,249,000	13,282,000	2,896,000	1,433,000	1,463,000	40,683,429	816
1971–72	47,002,000	32,910,000	14,092,000	3,008,000	1,490,000	1,518,000	48,050,283	990
1973–74	46,317,000	31,960,000	14,357,000	3,080,000	1,515,000	1,565,000	56,970,355	1,207
1975–76	45,735,000	31,156,000	14,580,000	3,154,000	1,554,000	1,600,000	70,829,345	1,509
1976–77	45,222,000	30,612,000	14,610,000	3,154,000[3]	1,548,000[3]	1,606,000[3]	75,014,155	1,638
1977–78	43,731,000	29,431,000	14,300,000	n.a.	n.a.	n.a.	81,097,000	1,739[4]
1978–79	42,900,000[4]	28,800,000[4]	14,100,000[4]	n.a.	n.a.	n.a.	n.a.	n.a.

1. Estimated from fall date. 2. Includes graduates from public and nonpublic schools. 3. Preliminary data. 4. Estimated. NOTE: n.a. = not available. Most recent data available. *Source:* Department of Education, National Center for Educational Statistics.

School Enrollment by Grade, Control, and Race
(in thousands)

Grade level and type of control	White Oct. 1979	White Oct. 1978	White Oct. 1970	Black Oct. 1979	Black Oct. 1978	Black Oct. 1970	All races[1] Oct. 1979	All races[1] Oct. 1978	All races[1] Oct. 1970
Nursery school: Public	428	351	198	185	210	129	636	587	333
Private	1,110	1,105	695	93	102	49	1,233	1,237	763
Kindergarten: Public	2,069	2,009	2,233	443	414	374	2,593	2,493	2,674
Private	368	444	473	54	38	53	432	496	536
Grades 1–8: Public	20,174	20,551	24,923	4,053	4,154	4,668	24,756	25,252	30,001
Private	2,785	2,973	3,715	243	202	200	3,109	3,238	3,949
Grades 9–12: Public	11,549	11,741	11,599	2,171	2,211	1,794	13,994	14,231	13,545
Private	1,033	1,156	1,124	74	65	41	1,122	1,244	1,170
College: Public	6,672	6,368	5,168	814	822	422	7,699	7,427	5,699
Private	2,037	2,145	1,591	188	199	100	2,280	2,410	1,714
Total: Public	40,892	41,020	44,121	7,666	7,811	7,387	49,679	49,990	52,225
Private	7,333	7,823	7,598	651	606	443	8,176	8,625	8,132
Grand total	**48,225**	**48,843**	**51,719**	**8,317**	**8,416**	**7,830**	**57,854**	**58,616**	**60,357**

1. Includes persons of Spanish origin. *Source:* Department of Commerce, Bureau of the Census.

Federal Grants and Loans for Education, Fiscal Year 1979

Type of support, level, and program area	Amount in millions[1]
Grants, total	$21,919
Elementary-secondary education	6,485
School assistance in federally affected areas	781
Economic opportunity programs	3,892[2]
Supporting services	368
Teacher corps	12
Vocational education	371
Dependents' schools abroad	372
Public lands revenue for schools	282
Assistance in special areas	89
Veterans' education	66
Emergency school assistance	225
Higher education	9,085
Basic research	2,070
Research facilities	452
Training grants, fellowships and traineeships	$1,101
Facilities and equipment	102
Other institutional support	573
Other student assistance	4,787
Vocational-technical and continuing education	6,348
Vocational-technical & work training	5,687
Veterans' education	391
General continuing education	212
Training state and local personnel	58
Loans, total (higher education)	1,100
Student loan program, National Defense Education Act	1,019
College facilities loans	81
Total grants and loans	**23,018**

1. Estimated outlay for fiscal year 1979. 2. Includes assistance for educationally deprived. NOTE: The table lists the federal funds that support education in educational institutions. Excluded are certain other federal funds for education and related activities. *Source:* Department of Education, National Center for Educational Statistics.

Persons Not Enrolled in School, October 1979
(in thousands)

Age	Population	Total not enrolled Number	Total not enrolled Percent	High school graduate Number	High school graduate Percent	Not high school graduate (dropouts)[1] Number	Not high school graduate (dropouts)[1] Percent
14 and 15 years	7,839	148	1.9	4	0.1	144	1.8
16 and 17 years	8,157	878	10.8	175	2.1	704	8.6
18 and 19 years	8,214	4,521	55.0	3,139	38.2	1,382	16.8
20 and 21 years	8,100	5,654	69.8	4,297	53.1	1,356	16.7
22 to 24 years	11,660	9,816	84.2	7,994	68.6	1,822	15.6

1. Persons who are not enrolled in school and who are not high school graduates are considered dropouts. *Source:* Department of Commerce, Bureau of the Census.

State Compulsory School Attendance Laws

State	Enactment[1]	Age limits	State	Enactment[1]	Age limits
Alabama	1915	7–16	Montana	1883	7–16
Alaska	1929	7–16	Nebraska	1887	7–16
Arizona	1899	8–16	Nevada	1873	7–17
Arkansas	1909	7–15	New Hampshire	1871	6–16
California	1874	6–16	New Jersey	1875	6–16
Colorado	1889	7–16	New Mexico	1891	6–17
Connecticut	1872	7–16	New York	1874	6–16
Delaware	1907	6–16	North Carolina	1907	7–16
D. C.	1864	7–16	North Dakota	1883	7–16
Florida	1915	7–16	Ohio	1877	6–18
Georgia	1916	7–16	Oklahoma	1907	8–16
Hawaii	1896	6–18	Oregon	1889	7–18
Idaho	1887	7–16	Pennsylvania	1895	8–17
Illinois	1883	7–16	Rhode Island	1883	7–16
Indiana	1897	7–16	South Carolina	1915	7–16
Iowa	1902	7–16	South Dakota	1883	7–16
Kansas	1874	7–16	Tennessee	1905	7–16
Kentucky	1896	7–16	Texas	1915[2]	7–17
Louisiana	1910	7–15	Utah	1890	6–18
Maine	1875	7–15	Vermont	1867	7–16
Maryland	1902	6–16	Virginia	1908	6–17
Massachusetts	1852	6–16	Washington	1871	8–15
Michigan	1871	6–16	West Virginia	1897	7–16
Minnesota	1885	7–16	Wisconsin	1879	6–16
Mississippi	1918	7–13	Wyoming	1876	7–16
Missouri	1905	7–16			

1. Date of enactment of first compulsory attendance law. 2. A compulsory school attendance law was contained in a law of 1873 establishing free public schools. However, the provision was omitted in superseding legislation passed in 1876. *Source:* Department of Education, National Center for Educational Statistics.

High School and College Graduates

Year of graduation	High School			College[1]		
	Men	Women	Total	Men	Women	Total
1900	38,075	56,808	94,883	22,173	5,237	27,410
1910	63,676	92,753	156,429	28,762	8,437	37,199
1920	123,684	187,582	311,266	31,980	16,642	48,622
1929–30	300,376	366,528	666,904	73,615	48,869	122,484
1939–40	578,718	642,757	1,221,475	109,546	76,954	186,500
1949–50	570,700	629,000	1,199,700	328,841	103,217	432,058
1957–58	727,500	780,400	1,505,900	241,560	121,942	363,502
1959–60	898,000	966,000	1,864,000	254,063	138,377	392,440
1960–61	958,000	1,013,000	1,971,000	254,215	144,495	398,710
1961–62	941,000	984,000	1,925,000	260,531	157,315	417,846
1962–63	959,000	991,000	1,950,000	273,169	174,453	447,622
1963–64	1,121,000	1,169,000	2,290,000	296,676	197,477	494,153
1964–65	1,314,000	1,351,000	2,665,000	316,286	213,717	530,003
1965–66	1,308,000	1,324,000	2,632,000	328,853	222,194	551,047
1966–67	1,332,000	1,348,000	2,679,000	353,349	237,198	590,547
1967–68	1,341,000	1,361,000	2,702,000	390,507	276,203	666,710
1968–69	1,402,000	1,427,000	2,829,000	444,380	319,805	764,185
1969–70	1,433,000	1,463,000	2,896,000	484,174	343,060	827,234
1970–71	1,456,000	1,487,000	2,943,000	511,138	366,538	877,676
1971–72	1,490,000	1,516,000	3,006,000	541,313	389,371	930,684
1972–73	1,501,000	1,536,000	3,037,000	564,680	407,700	972,380
1973–74	1,515,000	1,565,000	3,080,000	575,843	423,749	999,592
1974–75	1,541,000	1,599,000	3,140,000	533,797	425,052	978,849
1975–76	1,554,000	1,600,000	3,154,000	557,817	430,578	988,395
1976–77	1,548,000[2]	1,606,000[2]	3,154,000[2]	547,919	435,989	983,908

1. Includes bachelor's and first-professional degrees. 2. Preliminary data. NOTE: Includes graduates from public and private schools. Beginning in 1959–60, figures include Alaska and Hawaii. Because of rounding, details may not add to totals. Most recent data available. *Source:* Department of Education, National Center for Education Statistics.

Elementary and Secondary Public School Statistics, 1978–79

State	Number of elementary and secondary schools[1]	Pupils enrolled[2]		Classroom teachers	Pupil/ teacher ratio	Annual expenditure[3] (thousands)	Annual expen- diture per pupil[1]	Average annual salary of classroom teachers[3,4]
		Elementary: Kindergarten through grade 8	Secondary: Grades 9–12 and postgraduate					
Alabama	1,328	514,000	233,000	37,600	19.9	$1,016,152	$1,327	$12,109
Alaska	390	62,000	27,000	4,900	18.2	338,525	3,890	23,262
Arizona	858	351,000	153,000	24,000	21.0	780,874	1,944	16,860
Arkansas	1,186	310,000	140,000	22,200	20.3	591,983	1,218	10,404
California	7,040	2,801,000	1,404,000	205,700	20.4	8,478,454	1,802	17,890
Colorado	1,253	367,000	184,000	28,700	19.2	1,186,681	1,950	14,616
Connecticut	1,098	408,000	197,000	36,100	16.8	1,650,000	1,851	15,191
Delaware	188	75,000	41,000	6,000	19.3	247,000	2,108	14,403
D.C.	184	84,000	34,000	6,000	19.7	292,884	2,467	n.a.
Florida	1,962	1,014,000	492,000	69,900	21.5	2,677,901	1,572	11,770
Georgia	1,766	744,000	325,000	52,400	20.4	1,336,190	1,467	12,766
Hawaii	222	113,000	56,000	7,800	21.7	358,964	2,079	18,056
Idaho	908	134,000	64,000	9,500	20.8	260,146	1,348	12,142
Illinois	4,439	1,419,000	720,000	106,000	20.2	4,909,637	2,075	16,000
Indiana	2,083	750,000	372,000	52,100	21.5	1,846,570	1,552	14,034
Iowa	1,864	377,000	201,000	32,000	18.1	1,245,125	1,820	13,205
Kansas	1,639	293,000	145,000	25,400	17.2	823,946	1,731	12,607
Kentucky	1,408	470,000	214,000	32,500	21.0	900,000	1,233	12,465
Louisiana	1,456	565,000	259,000	40,400	20.3	1,242,251	1,433	14,161
Maine	753	163,000	78,000	13,300	18.1	355,000	1,467	12,000
Maryland	1,326	550,000	271,000	42,200	19.5	1,764,992	2,181	16,580
Massachusetts	2,357	777,000	365,000	65,600	17.4	2,467,658	2,230	16,100
Michigan	3,943	1,357,000	640,000	86,600	23.1	4,263,166	2,035	18,144
Minnesota	1,723	522,000	299,000	44,200	19.5	1,898,393	2,012	15,584
Mississippi	1,074	339,000	153,000	24,600	20.0	618,299	1,225	10,800
Missouri	2,249	602,000	312,000	49,100	18.6	1,323,088	1,484	12,476
Montana	802	109,000	57,000	9,600	17.3	331,600	1,950	13,293
Nebraska	1,775	197,000	103,000	17,800	16.9	456,935	1,685	12,328
Nevada	254	93,000	48,000	6,300	22.4	229,200	1,707	14,970
New Hampshire	476	117,000	54,000	9,500	18.0	236,872	1,562	11,600
New Jersey	2,421	940,000	454,000	77,900	17.9	3,102,000	2,285	16,175
New Mexico	602	185,000	92,000	13,700	20.3	463,743	1,634	15,525
New York	4,269	2,062,000	1,106,000	162,700	19.5	8,018,000	2,645	18,470
North Carolina	2,006	799,000	360,000	53,300	21.7	1,849,080	1,389	13,334
North Dakota	773	78,000	45,000	7,300	16.8	201,500	1,632	11,667
Ohio	4,135	1,424,000	717,000	104,300	20.5	3,446,200	1,554	13,925
Oklahoma	1,854	395,000	188,000	30,900	18.9	900,500	1,463	11,700
Oregon	1,284	310,000	154,000	24,100	19.3	948,200	2,195	14,031
Pennsylvania	4,077	1,360,000	729,000	112,000	18.7	4,858,800	2,074	14,950
Rhode Island	335	110,000	53,000	9,000	18.1	320,245	1,860	14,963
South Carolina	1,136	413,000	196,000	29,400	20.7	906,100	1,375	11,905
South Dakota	783	92,000	49,000	8,000	17.6	221,260	1,499	11,546
Tennessee	1,620	595,000	267,000	39,600	21.8	1,149,539	1,334	12,122
Texas	5,350	1,941,000	848,000	146,100	19.1	4,038,834	1,606	13,300
Utah	549	215,000	96,000	12,800	24.3	530,135	1,632	13,588
Vermont	399	70,000	31,000	6,100	16.6	169,586	1,631	11,799
Virginia	1,750	719,000	343,000	59,500	17.8	1,812,509	1,635	13,400
Washington	1,637	507,000	255,000	33,400	22.8	1,527,425	1,835	17,029
West Virginia	1,235	276,000	118,000	20,500	19.2	593,460	1,528	12,517
Wisconsin	2,248	570,000	330,000	52,400	17.2	1,708,898	1,917	14,400
Wyoming	385	62,000	29,000	5,000	18.2	202,500	2,220	14,502
Total	**86,501**	**28,800,000**	**14,100,000**	**2,176,000**	**19.7**	**81,097,000**	**1,816**	**14,836**

1. 1976–77. 2. Estimated from all data. 3. 1977–78. 4. Includes supervisors, principals, and other instructional staff. NOTE: n.a. = not available. Most recent data available. *Source:* Department of Education, National Center for Education Statistics.

U.S. College Enrollment Peaking

According to the Education Department's annual report on the condition of education, it forecasts that enrollment in U.S. colleges and universities will peak at 11.7 million students in 1981. In addition, it is expected that enrollment will drop to about 11 million students by 1988.

Affected most by the decline may be small, private, four-year liberal-arts schools. In the 1970s, 144 institutions closed, mosty small, private, four-year liberal-arts schools.

The report predicted an expansion in adult and occupational education. The number of schools offering adult and continuing-education courses doubled between 1967 and 1977.

Enrollment in Educational Institutions
(in thousands)

Type of School	1960	1966	1970	1972	1973	1974	1975	1976	1977
Kindergarten[1]									
Public	1,923	2,262	2,601	2,483	2,502	2,639	2,784	2,945	2,919
Nonpublic	354[2]	212	200[3]	180[3]	190[3]	180[3]	200[3]	200[3]	200[3]
Total kindergarten	2,293	2,493	2,821	2,683	2,710	2,838	3,002	3,164	3,138
Grades 1–8[4]									
Public	25,679	28,315	29,996	29,782	29,342	28,694	28,137	27,542	27,087
Nonpublic	4,286[3]	4,763	4,000[3]	3,720[3]	3,510[3]	3,420[3]	3,700[3]	3,400[3]	3,400[3]
Residential schools for exceptional children[5]	59[7]	85[3]	87[3]	87[3]		85[3]	85[3]	83[3]	83[3]
Federal schools:					182[3 4]				
For Indians	25	32	34	34		33	31	29	29
On Federal installations	19	29	33[3]	33[3]		25[3]	25	23	24
Total grades 1–8	30,119	33,266	34,190	33,697	33,034	32,297	32,019	31,118	30,664
Grades 9–12[4]									
Public high schools	8,485	11,597	13,022	13,816	13,909	14,076	14,132	14,304	14,310
Nonpublic high schools	1,035[3]	1,329	1,300[3]	1,300[3]	1,300[3]	1,250[3]	1,400[3]	1,400[3]	1,400[3]
Residential schools for exceptional children[5]	24[6]	35[3]	37[3]	39[3]		41[3]	41[3]	41[3]	41[3]
Federal schools:					100[3 4]				
For Indians	12	14	12	12[3]		11	11	11	11
On Federal installations	1	3[3]	3[3]	3[3]		4	4	3	3
Total grades 9–12	9,600	13,021	14,418	15,214	15,309	15,427	15,633	15,804	15,810
Higher education[7]									
Publicly controlled	1,832	3,624	5,112	5,745	6,159	6,389	6,838	7,426	7,275[3]
Privately controlled	1,384	1,902	2,024	2,055	2,106	2,130	2,185	2,306	2,314[3]
Total higher education	3,216	5,526	7,136	7,800	8,265	8,518	9,023	9,731	9,589[3]
Total all levels	**45,228**	**54,306**	**58,566**	**59,394**	**59,318**	**59,080**	**59,677**	**59,817**	**59,201**

1. Includes subcollegiate departments of institutions of higher education, residential schools for exceptional children, and Federal schools, not shown separately. 2. Data from U.S. Bureau of the Census. 3. Estimated. 4. Includes subcollegiate departments of institutions of higher education, not shown separately. 5. Schools for blind, deaf, mentally deficient, epileptic, and delinquent. 6. Estimate based on 1958 survey. 7. Excludes subcollegiate departments of institutions of higher education. Degree-credit enrollment only. *Source:* Department of Education, National Center for Education Statistics.

Major U.S. College and University Libraries
(over 1.75 million volumes)

Institution	Volumes	Microforms[1]
Harvard	9,913,992	1,937,315
Yale	7,246,195	1,190,170
U of Illinois	5,959,666	1,377,970
U of California, Berkeley	5,597,154	1,440,011
U of Michigan	5,135,952	1,621,909
Indiana	5,029,534	1,569,211
Columbia	4,924,469	1,981,532
Stanford	4,577,827	1,981,748
U of Texas	4,406,193	1,990,097
Cornell	4,207,146	1,977,023
U of Chicago	4,182,938	692,540
U of California, Los Angeles	4,109,146	1,790,737
U of Washington	3,788,788	2,665,263
U of Minnesota	3,702,599	1,126,011
U of Wisconsin	3,475,184	1,720,218
Ohio State	3,446,729	1,530,596
Princeton	3,172,238	1,210,189
Duke	3,022,839	318,222
U of Pennsylvania	2,889,788	1,372,445
U of Virginia	2,351,842	2,206,241

Institution	Volumes	Microforms[1]
Johns Hopkins	2,287,058	1,082,320
U of Iowa	2,216,970	1,383,829
U of Arizona	2,184,023	1,192,006
Rutgers	2,166,200	1,334,430
Pennsylvania State	2,092,139	2,108,836
U of Kansas	2,079,434	887,798
U of Florida	2,079,344	1,200,148
U of Missouri	1,984,632	2,040,615
U of Southern California	1,957,853	1,172,760
U of Utah	1,921,278	1,347,371
U of Georgia	1,893,897	1,709,004
SUNY, Buffalo	1,884,943	1,556,476
Syracuse	1,822,027	1,715,889
U of Colorado	1,811,881	1,923,106
Wayne State	1,804,932	803,505
Louisiana State	1,760,696	940,322
Massachusetts Inst. of Tech.	1,759,971	852,957
U of Washington, St. Louis	1,755,180	71,765
U of Kentucky	1,753,044	1,863,084
U of South Carolina	1,752,407	1,580,440

1. Includes reels of microfilm and number of microcards, microprint sheets, and microfiches. *Source:* Association of Research Libraries.

College and University Endowments, 1978–79

(in millions)

Institution	Endowment (market value)	Voluntary support[1]	Expenditures[2]
Harvard U	$1,457.7	$70.0	n.a.
Texas U	1,102.9	53.0	$ 771.7
Stanford U	586.8	64.5	274.9
Yale U	585.4	57.4	213.0
Massachusetts Inst. of Tech.	507.6	37.7	234.1
Columbia U	504.0	37.7	260.1
Princeton U	474.3	24.1	88.5
U of Rochester	328.7	16.2	120.0
U of Chicago	311.2	30.3	477.8
U of California	304.2	68.1	1,850.3
Northwestern U	300.6	24.7	166.9
Rice U	292.9	12.8	36.1
Cornell U	288.1	38.4	282.6
New York U	271.7	24.5	337.2
Washington U (St. Louis)	226.4	16.5	153.9
Johns Hopkins U	202.8	28.4	178.8
Rockefeller U	201.7	13.9	37.0
Dartmouth C	189.5	36.9	66.0
U of Pennsylvania	181.6	35.7	333.2
California Inst. of Tech.	174.7	16.8	63.3
Emory U	168.2	11.0	80.5
U of Notre Dame	137.5	15.5	54.6
Vanderbilt U	137.5	16.4	79.7
Wellesley C	133.7	8.6	18.9
U of So. California	130.2	38.0	226.6
Duke U	129.8	30.8	128.7
U of Michigan	123.6	37.6	360.5
Claremont Colleges	122.9	27.0	38.6
Case-Western Reserve U	118.2	33.2	96.0
Carnegie-Mellon U	112.8	6.8	56.6
Delaware U	109.3	6.6	81.2
Wesleyan U	$107.2	$ 2.6	$ 23.2
Brown U	106.5	12.0	60.0
U of Kansas	98.9	8.1	185.1
Smith C	97.7	11.0	23.0
U of Minnesota	95.3	37.8	395.2
U of Pittsburgh	92.1	10.0	188.9
Oberlin C	89.3	2.8	20.4
U of Cincinnati	88.0	5.9	152.0
Rensselaer Poly. Inst.	87.6	5.9	47.0
Williams C	84.7	7.3	15.3
Amherst C	76.6	3.0	n.a.
Berea C	76.6	4.5	8.3
Swathmore C	75.3	4.5	11.0
Vassar C	74.9	4.7	16.4
Trinity U	73.3	2.6	16.9
Ohio State U	72.6	11.7	292.7
U of Richmond	71.2	4.5	13.8
Princeton Theol. Sem.	68.7	3.6	5.3
Baylor U	62.8	12.8	26.0
U of Wisconsin (Madison)	60.8	29.3	319.8
Brandeis U	59.6	12.0	40.8
Syracuse U	58.9	6.1	100.9
U of Washington	58.1	15.7	284.0
Wake Forest U	57.0	6.6	60.6
Rochester Inst. of Tech.	56.0	3.5	52.5
Lehigh U	55.7	6.1	35.3
Lafayette C	54.3	2.0	12.4
Texas Christian U	53.6	9.8	29.1
Mount Holyoke C	52.5	5.1	13.3
Tulane U	50.5	11.5	73.9
Middlebury C	50.0	2.5	12.6

1. Gifts from business, alumni, religious denominations, and others. 2. Figure represents about 80% of typical operating budget. Does not include auxiliary enterprises and capital outlays. NOTE: C=College; U=University; n.a.=not available. *Source:* Council for Financial Aid to Education.

Degrees Conferred by Institutions of Higher Education, 1977

Field of study	Bachelor's[1]	Master's	Doctorate
Agriculture and natural resources	21.5	3,724	803
Architecture and environmental design	9.2	3,213	73
Area studies	3.0	989	153
Biological sciences	53.6	7,114	3,397
Business and management	152.1	46,545	869
Communications	23.2	3,091	171
Computer and information sciences	6.4	2,798	216
Education	143.7	126,375	7,955
Engineering	49.3	16,245	2,586
Fine and applied arts	41.8	8,636	662
Foreign languages	13.9	3,147	752
Health professions	57.3	12,951	538
Home economics	17.4	2,334	160
Law	.6	1,574	60
Letters	47.1	10,451	2,199
Library sciences	.8	7,572	75
Mathematics	14.2	3,695	823
Military sciences	.9	43	—
Physical sciences	22.5	5,331	3,341
Psychology	47.4	8,301	2,761
Public affairs and services	36.3	19,454	335
Social sciences	117.4	15,458	3,784
Theology	6.1	3,625	1,125
Interdisciplinary studies	33.9	4,498	304
Total	**919.5**	**317,164**	**33,232**
First-professional degrees:			
Dentistry (D.D.S. or D.M.D.)	5,138	—	—
Law (LL.B. or J.D.)	34,104	—	—
Medicine (M.D.)	13,461	—	—
Theological professions (B.D., M. Div., Rabbi)	6,779	—	—
Total first-professional	**59,482**	—	—

1. In thousands. *Source:* Department of Education, National Center for Educational Statistics.

Institutions of Higher Education—Faculty and Enrollment Characteristics and Projections to 1985

(in thousands except for institutions)

Item	1985	1980	1975	1974	1973	1972	1971	1970	1965	1960
Institutions	n.a.	n.a.	2,765	2,747	2,720	2,665	2,606	2,556	2,230	1,968
4-year	n.a.	n.a.	1,767	1,744	1,717	1,701	1,675	1,665	1,551	1,447
2-year	n.a.	n.a.	998	1,003	1,003	964	931	891	679	521
Resident instructional staff	696	730	670	622	599	590	590	573	412	276
ENROLLMENT										
Degree credit	11,000	11,142	9,731	9,023	8,518	8,265	8,116	7,920	5,526	3,583
Male	5,621	5,876	5,321	4,969	4,771	4,701	4,717	4,637	3,375	2,257
Female	5,379	5,266	4,410	4,055	3,747	3,564	3,399	3,284	2,152	1,326
4-year institutions	7,530	7,896	7,223	6,825	6,597	6,473	6,391	6,290	4,685	3,131
2-year institutions	3,470	3,246	2,508	2,198	1,921	1,792	1,725	1,630	841	451
Full-time	6,139	6,585	6,147	5,817	5,683	5,647	5,676	5,489	3,910	2,466
Part-time	4,861	4,557	3,584	3,206	2,835	2,618	2,440	2,431	1,616	1,117
Public	8,756	8,721	7,426	6,838	6,389	6,159	6,014	5,800	3,624	2,116
Private	2,244	2,421	2,306	2,185	2,130	2,106	2,102	2,120	1,902	1,467
Graduate	1,456	1,468	1,263	1,190	1,123	1,066	1,012	1,031	697	356[2]
Undergraduate[1]	9,544	9,674	8,468	7,833	7,395	7,199	7,104	6,889	4,829	3,227
percent of persons 18-21 years	62.4	56.7	51.2	48.4	46.6	46.4	47.0	46.6	39.0	33.2
Male	4,915	5,114	4,621	4,306	4,124	4,074	4,102	4,005	2,910	2,004
Female	4,629	4,560	3,847	3,527	3,271	3,125	3,002	2,884	1,919	1,223
4-year institutions	6,074	6,428	5,960	5,635	5,474	5,407	5,379	5,259	3,988	2,776
Full-time	4,421	4,830	4,619	4,429	4,350	4,350	4,358	4,234	3,159	2,077
Part-time	1,653	1,598	1,341	1,206	1,124	1,057	1,021	1,025	829	699
2-year institutions	3,470	3,246	2,508	2,198	1,921	1,792	1,725	1,630	841	451
Public	7,704	7,663	6,520	5,986	5,589	5,401	5,302	5,076	3,184	1,929
Private	1,840	2,011	1,948	1,847	1,806	1,799	1,802	1,813	1,645	1,298
1st time enrolled	1,709	1,936	1,910	1,854	1,757	1,740	1,766	1,780	1,442	923
Nondegree credit	2,360	2,072	1,453	1,200	1,084	950	833	661	395	206
Total	**13,360**	**13,214**	**11,184**	**10,223**	**9,602**	**9,215**	**8,949**	**7,951**	**5,921**	**3,789**

1. Includes first-professional enrollment. 2. Includes resident only. NOTE: As of fall. Covers universities, colleges, professional schools, junior and teachers colleges, and normal schools, both publicly and privately controlled, regular session. n.a. = not available. *Source:* Department of Education, National Center for Educational Statistics.

Earned Degrees by Sex of Student

Degree level	1976–77	1975–76	1974–75	1973–74	1972–73	1971–72	1970–71
Bachelor's	919,549	925,746	922,933	945,776	922,362	887,273	839,730
Men	495,545	504,925	504,841	527,313	518,191	500,590	475,594
Women	424,004	420,821	418,092	418,463	404,171	386,683	364,136
First professional[1]	64,359	62,649	55,916	53,816	50,018	43,411	37,946
Men	52,374	52,892	48,956	48,530	46,489	40,723	35,544
Women	11,985	9,757	6,960	5,286	3,529	2,688	2,402
Master's	317,164	311,771	292,450	277,033	263,371	251,633	230,509
Men	167,783	167,248	161,570	157,842	154,468	149,550	138,146
Women	149,381	144,523	130,880	119,191	108,903	102,083	92,363
Doctorate	33,232	34,064	34,083	33,816	34,777	33,363	32,107
Men	25,142	26,267	26,817	27,365	28,571	28,090	27,530
Women	8,090	7,797	7,266	6,451	6,206	5,273	4,577

1. Includes degrees in medicine, dentistry, law, theology, veterinary medicine, chiropody or podiatry, optometry, osteopathy, and pharmacy. NOTE: Most recent data available. *Source:* Department of Education, National Center for Education Statistics.

The Uncontrollable Cost of Student Loans

The demand for fully guaranteed student loans was up 40% in 1980 and is expected to rise to 52% in 1981. The Congressional Budget Office estimated that it cost the Treasury $1.9 billion in 1980 to subsidize three million student loans under the Guaranteed Student Loan and National Direct Student Loan programs.

The Government pays the full interest while students are in school, including a special allowance that is pegged 3.5% below the three-month Treasury bill rate. Students pay no interest on these loans while in college, but repay them at 7%, and the National District Student Loan programs at 3%.

The program costs are considered uncontrollable because the government automatically subsidizes any student loan made by a bank or state.

The default rate for guaranteed student loans is 8% and 18% for the direct student loan program.

Community, Junior, and Technical Colleges

An asterisk indicates tuition and required fees of $600 or less for the full academic year 1979–80; where applicable, the costs are for students living within the state and within the institutional district.

ALABAMA

Publicly controlled

Alabama Aviation and Tech. College*	Ozark
Alabama Technical College*	East Gadsden
Alexander City State Junior College*	Alexander City
Bessemer State Technical College*	Bessemer
Brewer State Junior College*	Fayette
Carver State Tech. College*	Mobile
Chattahoochee Valley State Comm. Coll.*	Phenix City
Community College of the Air Force	Maxwell AFB
Enterprise State Junior College*	Enterprise
Gadsden State Junior College*	East Gadsden
George C. Wallace State Comm. College*	Dothan
George C. Wallace State Comm. College*	Hanceville
George Corley Wallace St. Comm. Coll.*	Selma
Harry M. Ayers State Tech. College*	Anniston
Hobson State Technical College*	Thomasville
J. F. Drake State Technical College*	Huntsville
James H. Faulkner State Junior College*	Bay Minette
Jefferson Davis State Junior College*	Brewton
Jefferson State Junior College*	Birmingham
John C. Calhoun State Comm. College*	Decatur
John M. Patterson State Tech. College*	Montgomery
Lawson State Community College*	Birmingham
Lurleen B. Wallace State Junior College*	Andalusia
Northeast Alabama State Junior College*	Rainsville
Northwest Alabama State Junior College*	Phil Campbell
Northwest Alabama State Tech. College*	Hamilton
Patrick Henry State Junior College*	Monroeville
Reid State Technical College*	Evergreen
S. D. Bishop State Junior College*	Mobile
Shelton State Technical College*	Tuscaloosa
Snead State Junior College*	Boaz
Southern Union State Junior College*	Wadley
Southwest State Technical College*	Mobile
Trenholm State Technical College	Montgomery

Privately controlled

Alabama Christian College	Montgomery
Alabama Lutheran College—Academy	Selma
Marion Military Institute	Marion
Selma University	Selma
Walker College	Jasper

ALASKA

Publicly controlled

Univ. of Alaska Community Colleges	College
Anchorage Community College*	Anchorage
Juneau-Douglas Community College*	Juneau
Kenai Peninsula Community College*	Soldotna
Ketchikan Community College*	Ketchikan
Kodiak Community College*	Kodiak
Kuskokwim Community College*	Bethel
Matanuska Susitna Community College	Palmer
Northwest Community College*	Nome
Sitka Community College*	Sitka
Tanana Valley Community College*	Fairbanks

Privately controlled

Sheldon Jackson College	Sitka

ARIZONA

Publicly controlled

Arizona Western College*	Yuma
Central Arizona Coll. District*	Coolidge
Aravaipa Campus*	Winkleman
Signal Peak Campus*	Coolidge
Cochise College*	Douglas
Eastern Arizona College*	Thatcher
Maricopa County Comm. Coll. District	Phoenix
Glendale Community College*	Glendale
Maricopa Technical Community Coll.*	Phoenix
Mesa Community College*	Mesa
Phoenix College*	Phoenix
Rio Salado Community College*	Phoenix
Scottsdale Community College*	Scottsdale
Mohave Community College*	Kingman
Navajo Community College	Tsaile
Northland Pioneer College*	Holbrook
Pima Community College*	Tucson
Community Campus*	Tucson
Downtown Campus*	Tucson
East Education Center*	Tucson
West Campus*	Tucson
Yavapai College	Prescott

Privately controlled

Ganado, College of	Ganado

ARKANSAS

Publicly controlled

Arkansas State Univ.—Beebe Branch*	Beebe
East Arkansas Community College*	Forrest City
Garland County Community College*	Hot Springs
Mississippi County Community College*	Blytheville
North Arkansas Community College*	Harrison
Phillips County Community College*	Helena
Southern Arkansas University	Magnolia
El Dorado Branch*	El Dorado
Technical Branch*	East Camden
Westark Community College*	Fort Smith

Privately controlled

Central Baptist College*	Conway
Crowley's Ridge College	Paragould
Shorter College	North Little Rock
Southern Baptist College	Walnut Ridge

CALIFORNIA

Publicly controlled

Allan Hancock College	Santa Maria
Antelope Valley College*	Lancaster
Barstow Community College	Barstow
Butte College*	Oroville
Cabrillo College*	Aptos
Canyons, College of the*	Valencia
Cerritos College	Norwalk
Chabot College	Hayward
Chaffey College*	Alta Loma
Citrus College*	Azusa
Coast Community College District	Costa Mesa
Coastline Community College	Fountain Valley
Golden West College*	Huntington Beach
Orange Coast College*	Costa Mesa
Compton Community College*	Compton
Contra Costa Community Coll. District	Martinez
Contra Costa College	San Pablo
Diablo Valley College	Pleasant Hill
Los Medanos College*	Pittsburg
Cuesta College*	San Luis Obispo
Desert, College of the*	Palm Desert
El Camino College	Via Torrance

Foothill-Deanza Comm. Coll. District	Los Altos Hills
De Anza College*	Cupertino
Foothill College*	Los Altos Hills
Gavilan College*	Gilroy
Glendale Community College	Glendale
Grossmont Community College District	El Cajon
Cuyamaca College*	El Cajon
Grossmont College*	El Cajon
Hartnell College	Salinas
Imperial Valley College*	Imperial
Kern Community College District	Bakersfield
Bakersfield College	Bakersfield
Cerro Coso Community College	Ridgecrest
Porterville College*	Porterville
Lake Tahoe Community College*	South Lake Tahoe
Lassen College*	Susanville
Long Beach City College	Long Beach
Los Angeles Community College District	Los Angeles
East Los Angeles College	Monterey Park
Los Angeles City College	Los Angeles
Los Angeles Harbor College	Wilmington
Los Angeles Mission College	San Fernando
Los Angeles Pierce College	Woodland Hills
Los Angeles Southwest College	Los Angeles
Los Angeles Trade-Technical College	Los Angeles
Los Angeles Valley College	Van Nuys
West Los Angeles College	Culver City
Los Rios Community College District	Sacramento
American River College	Sacramento
Cosumnes River College	Sacramento
Sacramento City College	Sacramento
Marin County Community Coll. District	Kentfield
Indian Valley Colleges	Novato
Marin, College of	Kentfield
Mendocino College*	Ukiah
Merced College*	Merced
Mira Costa College*	Oceanside
Monterey Peninsula College*	Monterey
Mt. San Antonio College*	Walnut
Mt. San Jacinto College*	San Jacinto
Napa College	Napa
North Orange County Comm. Coll. District	Fullerton
Cypress College	Cypress
Fullerton College*	Fullerton
Ohlone College	Fremont
Palo Verde College*	Blythe
Palomar College*	San Marcos
Pasadena City College*	Pasadena
Peralta Community College District	Oakland
Alameda, College of*	Alameda
Feather River College*	Quincy
Laney College*	Oakland
Merritt College*	Oakland
Vista College	Berkeley
Redwoods, College of the	Eureka
Rio Hondo College	Whittier
Riverside City College*	Riverside
Saddleback College*	Mission Viejo
San Bernardino Community Coll. District	San Bernardino
Crafton Hills College*	Yucaipa
San Bernardino Valley College*	San Bernardino
San Diego Community College District	San Diego
San Diego City College*	San Diego
San Diego Evening College	San Diego
San Diego Mesa College*	San Diego
San Diego Miramar College	San Diego
San Francisco Community Coll. District	San Francisco
San Francisco, City College of	San Francisco
Community College Centers	San Francisco
San Joaquin Delta College*	Stockton
San Jose Community College District	San Jose
Evergreen Valley College	San Jose
San Jose City College*	San Jose
San Mateo County Comm. Coll. District	San Mateo
Canada College*	Redwood City
San Mateo, College of	San Mateo
Skyline College*	San Bruno
Santa Ana College*	Santa Ana
Santa Barbara City College*	Santa Barbara
Santa Monica College*	Santa Monica
Santa Rosa Junior College*	Santa Rosa
Shasta College*	Redding
Sequoias, College of the*	Visalia
Sierra College*	Rocklin
Siskiyous, College of the*	Weed
Solano Community College*	Suisun City
Southwestern College*	Chula Vista
State Center Community College District	Fresno
Fresno City College*	Fresno
Reedley College*	Reedley
Taft College	Taft
Ventura County Community Coll. District	Ventura
Moorpark College*	Moorpark
Oxnard College*	Oxnard
Ventura College*	Ventura
Victor Valley College*	Victorville
West Hills Community College*	Coalinga
West Valley Joint Comm. Coll. District*	Saratoga
Mission College*	Santa Clara
West Valley College*	Saratoga
Yosemite Community College District	Modesto
Columbia College*	Columbia
Modesto Junior College*	Modesto
Yuba College*	Marysville
Privately controlled	
Brooks College	Long Beach
Deep Springs College	Via Dyer, Nevada
Don Bosco Technical Institute	Rosemead
Fashion Inst. of Design/Merch.	Los Angeles
Heald Inst. of Technology	Santa Clara
Humphreys College	Stockton
Marymount Palos Verdes College	Rancho Palos Verdes
Nairobi College	East Palo Alto
Queen of the Holy Rosary College	Mission San

COLORADO

Publicly controlled	
Aims Community College*	Greeley
Arapahoe Community College*	Littleton
Colorado Mountain College	Glenwood Springs
Community Education Unit*	Glenwood Springs
East Campus*	Leadville
West Campus*	Glenwood Springs
Colorado Northwestern Comm. College*	Rangely
Community College of Denver	Denver
Auraria Campus*	Denver
North Campus*	Westminster
Red Rocks Campus*	Golden
Lamar Community College*	Lamar
Morgan Community College*	Fort Morgan
Northeastern Junior College*	Sterling
Otero Junior College*	La Junta
Pikes Peak Community Coll.	Colorado Springs
Pueblo Vocational Community College*	Pueblo
Trinidad State Junior College*	Trinidad

CONNECTICUT

Publicly controlled	
Asnuntuck Community College*	Enfield
Greater Hartford Community College*	Hartford
Greater New Haven State Tech. Coll.*	Hamden
Hartford State Technical College*	Hartford

Housatonic Community College*	Bridgeport
Manchester Community College*	Manchester
Mattatuck Community College*	Waterbury
Middlesex Community College*	Middletown
Mohegan Community College*	Norwich
Northwestern Connecticut Comm. College*	Winsted
Norwalk Community College*	Norwalk
Norwalk State Technical College*	Norwalk
Quinebaug Valley Community College*	Danielson
South Central Community College*	New Haven
Thames Valley State Technical College*	Norwich
Tunxis Community College*	Farmington
Waterbury State Technical College*	Waterbury
Privately controlled	
Hartford College for Women	Hartford
Mitchell College	New London
Mount Sacred Heart College	Hamden
St. Thomas Seminary Junior College	Bloomfield

DELAWARE

Publicly controlled	
Delaware Technical and Comm. College	Dover
Southern Campus*	Georgetown
Stanton Campus*	Newark
Terry Campus*	Dover
Wilmington Campus*	Wilmington
Privately controlled	
Brandywine College	Wilmington

FLORIDA

Publicly controlled	
Brevard Community College*	Cocoa
Broward Community College*	Ft. Lauderdale
Central Florida Community College*	Ocala
Chipola Junior College*	Marianna
Daytona Beach Community College*	Daytona Beach
Edison Community College*	Ft. Myers
Florida Junior Coll. at Jacksonville*	Jacksonville
Downtown Campus*	Jacksonville
Fred H. Kent Campus*	Jacksonville
North Campus*	Jacksonville
South Campus*	Jacksonville
Florida Keys Community College*	Key West
Gulf Coast Community College*	Panama City
Hillsborough Community College*	Tampa
Indian River Community College*	Ft. Pierce
Lake City Community College*	Lake City
Lake-Sumter Community College*	Leesburg
Manatee Junior College*	Bradenton
Miami-Dade Community College*	Miami
Medical Center Campus*	Miami
New World Center Campus*	Miami
North Campus*	Miami
South Campus*	Miami
North Florida Junior College*	Madison
Okaloosa-Walton Junior College*	Niceville
Palm Beach Junior College*	Lake Worth
Pasco-Hernando Community College*	Dade City
Pensacola Junior College	Pensacola
Polk Community College*	Winter Haven
St. Johns River Community College*	Palatka
St. Petersburg Junior College*	St. Petersburg
Santa Fe Community College*	Gainesville
Seminole Community College*	Sanford
South Florida Junior College*	Avon Park
Tallahassee Community College*	Tallahassee
Valencia Community College*	Orlando
Privately controlled	
Florida College	Temple Terrace
International Fine Arts College	Miami
St. John Vianney College Seminary	Miami
Webber College	Babson Park

GEORGIA

Publicly controlled	
Abraham Baldwin Agriculture College*	Tifton
Albany Junior College*	Albany
Atlanta Junior College*	Atlanta
Bainbridge Junior College*	Bainbridge
Brunswick Junior College*	Brunswick
Clayton Junior College*	Morrow
Dalton Junior College*	Dalton
DeKalb Community College*	Clarkston
Emanuel County Junior College*	Swainsboro
Floyd Junior College*	Rome
Gainesville Junior College*	Gainesville
Gordon Junior College*	Barnesville
Macon Junior College*	Macon
Middle Georgia College*	Cochran
South Georgia College*	Douglas
Waycross Junior College*	Waycross
Privately controlled	
Andrew College	Cuthbert
Brewton-Parker College	Mt. Vernon
Emmanuel College	Franklin Springs
Georgia Military College	Milledgeville
Oxford College of Emory University	Oxford
Reinhardt College	Waleska
Truett-McConnell College	Cleveland
Young Harris College	Young Harris

HAWAII

Publicly controlled	
Univ. of Hawaii Community Coll. System*	Honolulu
Hawaii Community College*	Hilo
Honolulu Community College*	Honolulu
Kapiolani Community College*	Honolulu
Kauai Community College*	Lihue Kauai
Leeward Community College*	Pearl City
Maui Community College*	Kahului
Windward Community College*	Kaneohe

IDAHO

Publicly controlled	
North Idaho College*	Coeur d'Alene
Southern Idaho, College of*	Twin Falls
Privately controlled	
Ricks College	Rexburg

ILLINOIS

Publicly controlled	
Belleville Area College*	Belleville
Black Hawk College	Moline
East Campus	Kewanee
Quad Cities Campus	Moline
Carl Sandburg College*	Galesburg
Chicago, City Colleges of	Chicago
Chicago City-Wide College*	Chicago
Chicago Urban Skills Institute	Chicago
Kennedy-King College*	Chicago
Loop College, The*	Chicago
Malcolm X College*	Chicago
Olive Harvey College*	Chicago
Richard J. Daley College*	Chicago
Truman College*	Chicago
Wilbur Wright College*	Chicago
Danville Area Community College*	Danville
DuPage, College of*	Glen Ellyn
Elgin Community College*	Elgin
Highland Community College*	Freeport
Illinois Central College*	East Peoria
Illinois Eastern Community Colleges	Olney
Frontier Community College*	Fairfield
Lincoln Trail College*	Robinson

Olney Central College*	Olney
Wabash Valley College*	Mt. Carmel
Illinois Valley Community College*	Oglesby
John A. Logan College*	Carterville
John Wood Community College*	Quincy
Joliet Junior College*	Joliet
Kankakee Community College	Kankakee
Kaskaskia College*	Centralia
Kishwaukee College*	Malta
Lake County, College of*	Grayslake
Lake Land College*	Mattoon
Lewis and Clark Community College*	Godfrey
Lincoln Land Community College*	Springfield
McHenry County College*	Crystal Lake
Moraine Valley Community College*	Palos Hills
Morton College*	Cicero
Oakton Community College*	Morton Grove
Parkland College*	Champaign
Prairie State College	Chicago Heights
Rend Lake College*	Ina
Richland Community College*	Decatur
Rock Valley College*	Rockford
Sauk Valley College	Dixon
Shawnee Community College*	Ullin
Southeastern Illinois College*	Harrisburg
Spoon River College*	Canton
State Comm. College of East St. Louis*	East St. Louis
Thornton Community College	South Holland
Triton College*	River Grove
Waubonsee Community College*	Sugar Grove
William Rainey Harper College*	Palatine
Privately controlled	
Central YMCA Community College	Chicago
Felician College	Chicago
Lincoln College	Lincoln
MacCormac College	Chicago
Mallinckrodt College	Wilmette
Springfield College in Illinois	Springfield

INDIANA

Publicly controlled	
Indiana Vocational Technical College	Indianapolis
Central Indiana Region	Indianapolis
Columbus Region	Columbus
East Central Region	Muncie
Kokomo Region	Kokomo
Lafayette Region	Lafayette
North Central Region	South Bend
Northeast Region	Fort Wayne
Northwest Region	Gary
South Central Region	Sellersburg
Southeast Region	Madison
Southwest Region	Evansville
Wabash Valley Region	Terre Haute
Whitewater Region	Richmond
Vincennes University	Vincennes
Privately controlled	
Ancilla College	Donaldson
Holy Cross Junior College	Notre Dame

IOWA

Publicly controlled	
Des Moines Area Community College	Ankeny
Ankeny Campus*	Ankeny
Boone Campus*	Boone
Eastern Iowa Community Coll. District	Davenport
Clinton Community College*	Clinton
Muscatine Community College*	Muscatine
Scott Community College	Bettendorf
Hawkeye Institute of Technology*	Waterloo
Indian Hills Community College*	Ottumwa
Centerville Campus	Centerville
Ottumwa Campus	Ottumwa
Iowa Central Community College*	Fort Dodge
Iowa Lakes Community College*	Estherville
North Attendance Center	Estherville
South Attendance Center	Emmetsburg
Iowa Valley Community Coll. District	Marshalltown
Ellsworth Community College*	Iowa Falls
Marshalltown Community College*	Marshalltown
Iowa Western Community College	Council Bluffs
Kirkwood Community College*	Cedar Rapids
North Iowa Area Community College*	Mason City
Northeast Iowa Technical Institute*	Calmar
Northwest Iowa Technical College	Sheldon
Southeastern Community College*	West Burlington
North Campus*	West Burlington
South Campus*	Keokuk
Southwestern Community College*	Creston
Western Iowa Tech. Community College	Sioux City
Privately controlled	
Sioux Empire College	Hawarden
Waldorf College	Forest City

KANSAS

Publicly controlled	
Allen County Community Junior College*	Iola
Barton County Community Junior Coll.*	Great Bend
Butler County Community Junior Coll.*	El Dorado
Cloud County Community Junior College*	Concordia
Coffeyville Community Junior College*	Coffeyville
Colby Community Junior College*	Colby
Cowley County Community Junior Coll.*	Arkansas City
Dodge City Community Junior College*	Dodge City
Fort Scott Community Junior College*	Fort Scott
Garden City Community Junior College*	Garden City
Haskell Indian Junior College	Lawrence
Highland Community Junior College*	Highland
Hutchinson Community Junior College*	Hutchinson
Independence Community Junior Coll.*	Independence
Johnson County Community Junior Coll.*	Overland Park
Kansas City, Kan., Community Jr. Coll.*	Kansas City
Kansas Technical Institute*	Salina
Labette Community Junior College*	Parsons
Neosho County Community Junior Coll.*	Chanute
Pratt Community Junior College*	Pratt
Seward County Community Junior Coll.*	Liberal
Privately controlled	
Brown Mackie College, The	Salina
Central College	McPherson
Donnelly College	Kansas City
Hesston College	Hesston
St. John's College	Winfield

KENTUCKY

Publicly controlled	
Eastern Kentucky Univ.—Office of Community College Programs*	Richmond
Kentucky, Univ. of, Comm. Coll. System	Lexington
Ashland Community College*	Ashland
Elizabethtown Community College*	Elizabethtown
Hazard Community College*	Hazard
Henderson Community College*	Henderson
Hopkinsville Community College*	Hopkinsville
Jefferson Community College*	Louisville
Lexington Technical Institute*	Lexington
Madisonville Community College*	Madisonville
Maysville Community College*	Maysville
Paducah Community College*	Paducah
Prestonsburg Community College*	Prestonsburg
Somerset Community College*	Somerset
Southeast Community College*	Cumberland
Western Kentucky University	Bowling Green
Bowling Green Community Coll.*	Bowling Green

Privately controlled	
Alice Lloyd College	Pippa Passes
Lees Junior College	Jackson
Lindsey Wilson College	Columbia
Midway College	Midway
St. Catharine College	St. Catharine
Sue Bennett College	London

LOUISIANA

Publicly controlled	
Bossier Parish Community College*	Bossier City
Delgado College*	New Orleans
Louisiana State University	Baton Rouge
Alexandria Campus*	Alexandria
Eunice Campus	Eunice
Southern University at Shreveport*	Shreveport

MAINE

Publicly controlled	
Central Maine Vocational Tech. Inst.*	Auburn
Eastern Maine Vocational Tech. Inst.*	Bangor
Kennebec Valley Vocational Tech. Inst.*	Waterville
Maine, University of	Bangor
Augusta Branch	Augusta
Bangor Community College	Bangor
Northern Maine Vocational Tech. Inst.*	Presque Isle
Southern Maine Vocational Tech. Inst.*	South Portland
Washington County Voc. Tech. Inst.*	Calais

MARYLAND

Publicly controlled	
Allegany Community College*	Cumberland
Anne Arundel Community College*	Arnold
Catonsville Community College*	Baltimore
Cecil Community College*	North East
Charles County Community College*	La Plata
Chesapeake College*	Wye Mills
Community College of Baltimore*	Baltimore
Dundalk Community College*	Dundalk
Essex Community College*	Baltimore Co.
Frederick Community College*	Frederick
Garrett Community College*	McHenry
Hagerstown Junior College*	Hagerstown
Harford Community College*	Bel Air
Howard Community College*	Columbia
Montgomery College	Rockville
Germantown Campus	Germantown
Rockville Campus	Rockville
Takoma Park Campus	Takoma Park
Prince George's Community College*	Largo
Wor-Wic. Tech. Community College*	Salisbury
Privately controlled	
Villa Julie College	Stevenson

MASSACHUSETTS

Publicly controlled	
Berkshire Community College*	Pittsfield
Blue Hills Regional Tech. Institute*	Canton
Bristol Community College*	Fall River
Bunker Hill Community College*	Charlestown
Cape Cod Community College*	W. Barnstable
Franklin Institute of Boston	Boston
Greenfield Community College*	Greenfield
Holyoke Community College*	Holyoke
Massachusetts Bay Community College*	Wellesley
Massasoit Community College*	Brockton
Middlesex Community College*	Bedford
Mount Wachusett Community College*	Gardner
North Shore Community College*	Beverly
Northern Essex Community College*	Haverhill
Quincy Junior College	Quincy
Quinsigamond Community College*	Worcester
Roxbury Community College*	Roxbury
Springfield Technical Community Coll.*	Springfield
Privately controlled	
Aquinas Junior College	Milton
Bay Path Junior College	Longmeadow
Becker Junior College	Worcester
Leicester Campus	Leicester
Chamberlayne Junior College	Boston
Dean Junior College	Franklin
Endicott College	Beverly
Fisher Junior College	Boston
Grahm Junior College	Boston
Laboure Junior College	Boston
Lasell Junior College	Newton
Mount Ida Junior College	Newton Centre
Newbury Junior College	Boston
Worcester Junior College	Worcester

MICHIGAN

Publicly controlled	
Alpena Community College*	Alpena
Bay de Noc Community College*	Escanaba
Charles Stewart Mott Community Coll.*	Flint
Delta College	University Center
Glen Oaks Community College*	Centreville
Gogebic Community College*	Ironwood
Grand Rapids Junior College*	Grand Rapids
Henry Ford Community College*	Dearborn
Highland Park Community College	Highland Park
Jackson Community College	Jackson
Kalamazoo Valley Community College*	Kalamazoo
Kellogg Community College*	Battle Creek
Kirtland Community College*	Roscommon
Lake Michigan College*	Benton Harbor
Lansing Community College*	Lansing
Macomb County Community College	Warren
Center Campus*	Mt. Clemens
South Campus*	Warren
Mid Michigan Community College*	Harrison
Monroe County Community College*	Monroe
Montcalm Community College*	Sidney
Muskegon Community College*	Muskegon
North Central Michigan College*	Petoskey
Northwestern Michigan College*	Traverse City
Oakland Community College*	Bloomfield Hills
Auburn Hills Campus	Auburn Heights
Highland Lakes Campus	Union Lake
Orchard Ridge Campus	Farmington
Southeast Campus	Oak Park
St. Clair County Community College*	Port Huron
Schoolcraft College*	Livonia
Southwestern Michigan College*	Dowagiac
Washtenaw Community College*	Ann Arbor
Wayne County Community College*	Detroit
West Shore Community College	Scottville
Privately controlled	
Davenport College of Business	Grand Rapids
Suomi College	Hancock

MINNESOTA

Publicly controlled	
Anoka-Ramsey Community College*	Coon Rapids
Austin Community College*	Austin
Brainerd Community College*	Brainerd
Fergus Falls Community College	Fergus Falls
Hibbing Community College*	Hibbing
Inver Hills Community College*	Inver Grove Heights
Itasca Community College*	Grand Rapids
Lakewood Community College*	White Bear Lake
Mesabi Community College*	Virginia
Minneapolis Community Coll.*	Minneapolis

Minnesota, Univ. of, Technical Coll.	Minneapolis
Crookston Campus	Crookston
Waseca Campus	Waseca
Normandale Community College*	Bloomington
North Hennepin Community College*	Brooklyn Park
Northland Community College*	Thief River Falls
Rainy River Community College	International Falls
Rochester Community College*	Rochester
Vermilion Community College*	Ely
Willmar Area Technical Institute*	Willmar
Willmar Community College*	Willmar
Worthington Community College*	Worthington
Privately controlled	
Bethany Lutheran College	Mankato
Crosier Seminary Junior College	Onamia
Golden Valley Lutheran College	Minneapolis
St. Mary's Junior College	Minneapolis

MISSISSIPPI

Publicly controlled	
Coahoma Junior College*	Clarksdale
Copiah-Lincoln Junior College*	Wesson
East Central Junior College*	Decatur
East Mississippi Junior College*	Scooba
Hinds Junior College*	Raymond
Holmes Junior College*	Goodman
Itawamba Junior College*	Fulton
Jones County Junior College*	Ellisville
Meridian Junior College*	Meridian
Mississippi Delta Junior College*	Moorhead
Mississippi Gulf Coast Junior College	Perkinston
Jackson County Campus*	Gautier
Jefferson Davis Campus*	Gulfport
Perkinston Campus*	Perkinston
Northeast Mississippi Junior College*	Booneville
Northwest Mississippi Junior College*	Senatobia
Pearl River Junior College*	Poplarville
Southwest Mississippi Junior College*	Summit
Utica Junior College*	Utica
Privately controlled	
Clarke College	Newton
Mary Holmes College	West Point
Wood Junior College	Mathiston

MISSOURI

Publicly controlled	
Crowder College*	Neosho
East Central Junior College*	Union
Jefferson College*	Hillsboro
Metropolitan Community Colleges, The	Kansas City
Longview Community College*	Lee's Summit
Maple Woods Community College*	Kansas City
Penn Valley Community College*	Kansas City
Pioneer Community College*	Kansas City
Mineral Area College*	Flat River
Moberly Junior College	Moberly
St. Louis Community College	St. Louis
St. Louis C.C.—Florissant Valley*	St. Louis
St. Louis C.C. at Forest Park*	St. Louis
St. Louis C.C.—Meramec*	St. Louis
State Fair Community College*	Sedalia
Three Rivers Community College*	Poplar Bluff
Trenton Junior College*	Trenton
Privately controlled	
Cottey College	Nevada
Kemper Military School and College	Boonville
St. Mary's College of O'Fallon	O'Fallon
St. Paul's College	Concordia
Wentworth Military Academy	Lexington

MONTANA

Publicly controlled	
Dawson College*	Glendive
Flathead Valley Community College*	Kalispell
Miles Community College*	Miles City

NEBRASKA

Publicly controlled	
Central Technical Comm. Coll. Area	Grand Island
Central Technical Community Coll.*	Hastings
Grand Island Education Center*	Grand Island
Platte Technical Community Coll.*	Columbus
Metropolitan Technical Community Coll.*	Omaha
Mid-Plains Technical Comm. Coll. Area	North Platte
McCook Community College*	McCook
Mid-Plains Community College*	North Platte
Nebraska, Univ. of, Sch. of Tech. Agri.	Curtis
Northeast Technical Community College*	Norfolk
Southeast Community College*	Lincoln
Fairbury/Beatrice Campus*	Fairbury
Lincoln Campus*	Lincoln
Milford Campus*	Milford
Western Technical Comm. Coll. Area	Scottsbluff
Nebraska Western College*	Scottsbluff
Western Nebraska Technical Coll.*	Sidney
Privately controlled	
York College	York

NEVADA

Publicly controlled	
Nevada, Univ. of, Comm. Coll. System	Reno
Clark County Community College	North Las Vegas
Northern Nevada Community College*	Elko
Truckee Meadows Community College*	Sparks
Western Nevada Community College*	Carson City

NEW HAMPSHIRE

Publicly controlled	
New Hampshire Technical Institute	Concord
New Hampshire Vocational Technical Coll.	
Berlin Campus	Berlin
Claremont Campus	Claremont
Laconia Campus	Laconia
Manchester Campus	Manchester
Nashua Campus	Nashua
Portsmouth Campus	Portsmouth
Privately controlled	
Daniel Webster College	Nashua
White Pines College	Chester

NEW JERSEY

Publicly controlled	
Atlantic Community College*	Mays Landing
Bergen Community College*	Paramus
Brookdale Community College*	Lincroft
Burlington County College*	Pemberton
Camden County College*	Blackwood
County College of Morris	Dover
Cumberland County College*	Vineland
Essex County College*	Newark
Gloucester County College*	Sewell
Hudson County Comm. Coll. Commission*	North Bergen
Mercer County Community College*	Trenton
Middlesex County College*	Edison
Ocean County College*	Toms River
Passaic County Community College	Paterson
Salem Community College*	Penns Grove
Somerset County College*	Somerville
Privately controlled	
Edward Williams College	Hackensack
Union College*	Cranford

NEW MEXICO

Publicly controlled

Albuquerque Tech. Voc. Inst.*	Albuquerque
Eastern New Mexico University	Portales
Clovis Campus*	Clovis
Roswell Campus*	Roswell
Luna Vocational Technical Institute*	Las Vegas
New Mexico, University of	Albuquerque
Gallup Campus*	Gallup
New Mexico Junior College*	Hobbs
New Mexico Military Institute	Roswell
New Mexico State University	Las Cruces
Alamogordo Campus	Alamogordo
Carlsbad Campus*	Carlsbad
Dona Ana Branch	Las Cruces
Grants Campus*	Grants
San Juan Campus*	Farmington
Northern New Mexico Community Coll.*	El Rito

Privately controlled

Inst. of American Indian Arts	Santa Fe

NEW YORK

Publicly controlled

Adirondack Community College	Glens Falls
Borough of Manhattan Community Coll.	New York
Bronx Community College	Bronx
Broome Community College	Binghamton
Cayuga County Community College	Auburn
Clinton Community College	Plattsburgh
Columbia-Greene Community College	Hudson
Comm. Coll. of the Finger Lakes	Canandaigua
Corning Community College	Corning
Dutchess Community College	Poughkeepsie
Erie Community College	Buffalo
City Campus	Buffalo
North Campus	Williamsville
South Campus	Orchard Park
Fashion Institute of Technology	New York
Fulton-Montgomery Community College	Johnstown
Genesee Community College	Batavia
Herkimer County Community College	Herkimer
Hostos Community College	Bronx
Hudson Valley Community College	Troy
Jamestown Community College	Jamestown
Jefferson Community College	Watertown
Kingsborough Community College	Brooklyn
Laguardia Community College	Long Island City
Mohawk Valley Community College	Utica
Monroe Community College	Rochester
Nassau Community College	Garden City
New York City Community College	Brooklyn
Niagara County Community College	Sanborn
North Country Community College	Saranac Lake
Onondaga Community College	Syracuse
Orange County Community College	Middletown
Queensborough Community College	Bayside
Rockland Community College	Suffern
Schenectady County Community College	Schenectady
SUNY Agricultural & Technical Colleges	
Alfred Campus	Alfred
Canton Campus	Canton
Cobleskill Campus	Cobleskill
Delhi Campus	Delhi
Farmingdale Campus	Farmingdale
Morrisville Campus	Morrisville
Suffolk County Community College	Selden
Sullivan County Community College	Loch Sheldrake
Tompkins-Cortland Community College	Dryden
Ulster County Community College	Stoneridge
Westchester Community College	Valhalla

Privately controlled

Aeronautics, Academy of	Flushing
Albany, Junior College of	Albany
Cazenovia College	Cazenovia
Elizabeth Seton College	Yonkers
Harriman College	Harriman
Hilbert College	Hamburg
Human Services, College for	New York
Lab Inst. of Merchandising	New York City
Maria College	Albany
Maria Regina College	Syracuse
Mater Dei College	Ogdensburg
Paul Smith's Coll. of Arts & Science	Paul Smiths
Trocaire College	Buffalo
Villa Maria College of Buffalo	Buffalo
Wood School, The	New York City

NORTH CAROLINA

Publicly controlled

Albemarle, College of the*	Elizabeth City
Anson Technical Institute*	Ansonville
Asheville-Buncombe Technical Institute*	Asheville
Beaufort County Technical Institute*	Washington
Bladen Technical Institute*	Dublin
Blue Ridge Technical Institute*	Flat Rock
Caldwell Comm. Coll. and Tech. Inst.*	Hudson
Cape Fear Technical Institute*	Wilmington
Carteret Technical Institute*	Morehead City
Catawba Valley Technical Institute*	Hickory
Central Carolina Technical Institute*	Sanford
Central Piedmont Community College*	Charlotte
Cleveland County Technical Institute*	Shelby
Coastal Carolina Community College*	Jacksonville
Craven Community College*	New Bern
Davidson County Community College*	Lexington
Durham Technical Institute*	Durham
Edgecombe Technical Institute*	Tarboro
Fayetteville Technical Institute*	Fayetteville
Forsyth Technical Institute*	Winston Salem
Gaston College*	Dallas
Guilford Technical Institute*	Jamestown
Halifax Community College*	Weldon
Haywood Technical Institute*	Clyde
Isothermal Community College*	Spindale
James Sprunt Institute*	Kenansville
Johnston Technical Institute*	Smithfield
Lenoir Community College*	Kinston
Martin Community College*	Williamston
Mayland Technical Institute*	Spruce Pine
McDowell Technical Institute*	Marion
Mitchell Community College*	Statesville
Montgomery Technical Institute*	Troy
Nash Technical Institute*	Rocky Mount
Pamlico Technical Institute*	Grantsboro
Piedmont Technical Institute*	Roxboro
Pitt Technical Institute*	Greenville
Randolph Technical Institute*	Asheboro
Richmond Technical Institute*	Hamlet
Roanoke-Chowan Technical Institute*	Ahoskie
Robeson Technical Institute*	Lumberton
Rockingham Community College*	Wentworth
Rowan Technical Institute*	Salisbury
Sampson Technical College*	Clinton
Sandhills Community College*	Carthage
Southeastern Community College*	Whiteville
Southwestern Technical College*	Sylva
Stanly Technical Institute*	Albemarle
Surry Community College*	Dobson
Technical College of Alamance*	Haw River
Tri-County Community College*	Murphy
Vance-Granville Community College*	Henderson
Wake Technical Institute*	Raleigh
Wayne Community College*	Goldsboro
Western Piedmont Community College*	Morganton
Wilkes Community College*	Wilkesboro
Wilson County Technical Institute*	Wilson

Privately controlled

Brevard College	Brevard
Chowan College	Murfreesboro
Durham College	Durham
Lees-McRae College	Banner Elk
Louisburg College	Louisburg
Montreat-Anderson College	Montreat
Mount Olive College	Mount Olive
Peace College	Raleigh
St. Mary's College	Raleigh

NORTH DAKOTA

Publicly controlled

Bismarck Junior College*	Bismarck
Lake Region Junior College	Devils Lake
North Dakota, Univ. of—Williston	Williston
North Dakota State School of Science*	Wahpeton
North Dakota State Univ.—Bottineau*	Bottineau
Turtle Mountain Comm. Coll.	Belcourt

Privately controlled

Standing Rock Comm. Coll.*	Fort Yates

OHIO

Publicly controlled

Akron, Univ. of, Comm. and Tech. Coll.	Akron
Wayne General & Technical Coll.	Orrville
Belmont Technical College	St. Clairsville
Bowling Green Univ.–Firelands Campus	Huron
Central Ohio Technical College	Newark
Cincinnati, University of	Cincinnati
Clermont General & Technical Coll.	Batavia
Ohio College of Applied Science	Cincinnati
Raymond Walters Gen. & Tech. Coll.	Cincinnati
University College	Cincinnati
Cincinnati Technical College	Cincinnati
Clark Technical College	Springfield
Columbus Technical Institute	Columbus
Cuyahoga Community College District*	Cleveland
Eastern Campus*	Warrensville Twnsp.
Metropolitan Campus*	Cleveland
Western Campus	Parma
Edison State Community College	Piqua
Hocking Technical College	Nelsonville
Jefferson Technical College*	Steubenville
Kent State University	Kent
Ashtabula Campus	Ashtabula
East Liverpool Regional Campus	East Liverpool
Geauga Campus	Burton
Salem Campus	Salem
Stark Regional Campus*	Canton
Trumbull Campus	Warren
Tuscarawas Campus	New Philadelphia
Lakeland Community College*	Mentor
Lima Technical College	Lima
Lorain County Community College*	Elyria
Marion Technical College	Marion
Miami University	Oxford
Hamilton Campus	Hamilton
Middletown Campus	Middletown
Michael J. Owens Technical College	Toledo
Muskingum Area Technical College*	Zanesville
North Central Technical College	Mansfield
Northwest Technical College	Archbold
Ohio State University	Columbus
Agricultural Technical Institute	Wooster
Lima Campus	Lima
Mansfield Campus	Mansfield
Marion Campus	Marion
Newark Campus	Newark
Ohio University	Athens
Belmont County Campus*	St. Clairsville
Ironton Campus	Ironton
Chillicothe Campus	Chillicothe
Lancaster Campus	Lancaster
Zanesville Campus	Zanesville
Rio Grande Community College*	Rio Grande
Shawnee State Community College	Portsmouth
Sinclair Community College*	Dayton
Southern State Community College	Wilmington
Stark Technical College	Canton
Terra Technical College*	Fremont
Toledo, Univ. of, Comm. & Tech. Coll.	Toledo
Washington Technical College*	Marietta
Wright State Univ.—Western Branch	Celina
Youngstown State U.—Coll. of Applied Sci.	Youngstown

Privately controlled

Chatfield College	St. Martin
Kettering College of Medical Arts	Kettering
Lourdes College	Sylvania

OKLAHOMA

Publicly controlled

Carl Albert Junior College*	Poteau
Claremore Junior College*	Claremore
Connors State College*	Warner
Eastern Oklahoma State College	Wilburton
El Reno Junior College*	El Reno
Murray State College*	Tishomingo
Northeastern Oklahoma A&M College*	Miami
Northern Oklahoma College*	Tonkawa
Oklahoma State U. Technical Institute	Oklahoma City
Oscar Rose Junior College*	Midwest City
Sayre Junior College*	Sayre
Seminole Junior College*	Seminole
South Oklahoma City Junior College*	Oklahoma City
Tulsa Junior College*	Tulsa
Western Oklahoma State College*	Altus

Privately controlled

Bacone College	Muskogee
Hillsdale Free Will Baptist	Moore
St. Gregory's College	Shawnee

OREGON

Publicly controlled

Blue Mountain Community College*	Pendleton
Central Oregon Community College*	Bend
Chemeketa Community College*	Salem
Clackamas Community College*	Oregon City
Clatsop Community College*	Astoria
Lane Community College*	Eugene
Linn-Benton Community College*	Albany
Mt. Hood Community College*	Gresham
Portland Community College*	Portland
Rogue Community College*	Grants Pass
Southwestern Oregon Community Coll.*	Coos Bay
Treasure Valley Community College*	Ontario
Umpqua Community College*	Roseburg

Privately controlled

Bassist Institute	Portland
Judson Baptist College	Portland

PENNSYLVANIA

Publicly controlled

Bucks County Community College	Newtown
Butler County Community College	Butler
Community Coll. of Allegheny County	Pittsburgh
Allegheny Campus	Pittsburgh
Boyce Campus	Monroeville
College Center—North*	Pittsburgh
South Campus	West Mifflin
Community College of Beaver County*	Monaca
Comm. Coll. of Philadelphia	Philadelphia
Delaware County Community College	Media
Harrisburg Area Community College*	Harrisburg
Lehigh County Community College	Schnecksville

Luzerne County Community College*	Nanticoke
Montgomery County Community College	Blue Bell
Northhampton County Area Comm. Coll.	Bethlehem
Reading Area Community College*	Reading
Westmoreland County Community Coll.	Youngwood
Williamsport Area Community College	Williamsport
Privately controlled	
Center for Degree Studies	Scranton
Central Penn. Business School	Summerdale
Harcum Junior College	Bryn Mawr
Keystone Junior College	La Plume
Lackawanna Junior College	Scranton
Manor Junior College	Jenkintown
Mount Aloysius Junior College	Cresson
Northeastern Christian Junior College	Villanova
Peirce Junior College	Philadelphia
Pennsylvania Junior Coll. of Medical Arts	Harrisburg
Pinebrook Junior College	Coopersburg
Valley Forge Military Junior College	Wayne
Wheeler School	Pittsburgh

PUERTO RICO

Publicly controlled	
Puerto Rico, Univ. of, Regional Colleges	Rio Piedras
Aguadilla Regional College*	Aguadilla
Arecibo Regional College*	Arecibo
Bayamon Regional College*	Bayamon
Carolina Regional College*	Carolina
Ponce Regional College*	Ponce
Privately controlled	
Catholic University of Puerto Rico	Ponce
Aguadilla Center	Aguadilla
Arecibo Center	Arecibo
Guayama Center	Guayama
Ponce Center	Ponce
College of the Sacred Heart Junior Coll.	Santurce
ICPR Junior College	Hato Rey
Interamerican University of Puerto Rico	San Juan
Aguadilla Regional College	Aguadilla
Arecibo Regional College	Arecibo
Barranquitas Regional College	Barranquitas
Bayamon Regional College	Bayamon
Fajardo Regional Campus	Fajardo
Guayama Regional College	Guayama
Ponce Regional College	Ponce
Puerto Rico Junior College	Rio Piedras
Ramirez Coll. of Business Tech.	Santurce

RHODE ISLAND

Publicly controlled	
Rhode Island Junior College*	Warwick

SOUTH CAROLINA

Publicly controlled	
State System of Technical Colleges:	Columbia
Aiken Technical College*	Aiken
Beaufort Technical College*	Beaufort
Chesterfield-Marlboro Technical Coll.*	Cheraw
Denmark Technical College*	Denmark
Florence-Darlington Technical Coll.*	Florence
Greenville Technical College*	Greenville
Horry-Georgetown Technical College*	Conway
Midlands Technical College*	Columbia
Airport Campus	West Columbia
Beltline Campus	Columbia
Orangeburg-Calhoun Technical College*	Orangeburg
Piedmont Technical College*	Greenwood
South Carolina, University of	Columbia
Beaufort Regional Campus	Beaufort
Lancaster Regional Campus	Lancaster
Salkehatchie Regional Campus	Allendale
Sumter Regional Campus	Sumter
Union Campus*	Union
Spartanburg Technical College*	Spartanburg
Sumter Area Technical College*	Sumter
Tri-County Technical College*	Pendleton
Trident Technical College*	No. Charleston
North Campus*	No. Charleston
Palmer Campus*	Charleston
Williamsburg Technical College*	Kingstree
York Technical College*	Rock Hill
Privately controlled	
Anderson College	Anderson
Clinton Junior College	Rock Hill
Friendship College	Rock Hill
North Greenville College	Tigerville
Spartanburg Methodist College	Spartanburg

SOUTH DAKOTA

Publicly controlled	
Black Hills State College—Junior College Division	Spearfish
Oglala Sioux Community College*	Pine Ridge
Privately controlled	
Freeman Junior College	Freeman
Presentation College	Aberdeen
Sinte Gleska College Center*	Rosebud

TENNESSEE

Publicly controlled	
Chattanooga State Tech. Comm. Coll.*	Chattanooga
Cleveland State Community College*	Cleveland
Columbia State Community College*	Columbia
Dyersburg State Community College*	Dyersburg
Jackson State Community College*	Jackson
Motlow State Community College*	Tullahoma
Nashville State Technical Institute*	Nashville
Roane State Community College*	Harriman
Shelby State Community College*	Memphis
State Technical Inst. at Memphis*	Memphis
Volunteer State Community College*	Gallatin
Walters State Community College*	Morristown
Privately controlled	
Aquinas Junior College	Nashville
Cumberland College of Tennessee	Lebanon
Hiwassee College	Madisonville
John A. Gupton College	Nashville
Martin College	Pulaski
Morristown College	Morristown
State Technical Inst. at Knoxville*	Knoxville
Tomlinson College	Cleveland

TEXAS

Publicly controlled	
Alvin Community College*	Alvin
Amarillo College*	Amarillo
Angelina College*	Lufkin
Austin Community College*	Austin
Bee County College*	Beeville
Blinn College*	Brenham
Brazosport College*	Lake Jackson
Central Texas College*	Killeen
Cisco Junior College*	Cisco
Clarendon College*	Clarendon
Cooke County College*	Gainesville
Dallas County Community Coll. District	Dallas
Brookhaven College*	Farmers Branch
Cedar Valley College*	Lancaster
Eastfield College*	Mesquite
El Centro College*	Dallas
Mountain View College*	Dallas
North Lake College*	Irving
Richland College*	Dallas
Del Mar College*	Corpus Christi
El Paso Community College District*	El Paso
Rio Grande Campus*	El Paso
Transmountain Campus*	El Paso
Valle Verde Campus*	El Paso

Frank Phillips College*	Borger
Galveston College*	Galveston
Grayson County Junior College*	Denison
Henderson County Junior College*	Athens
Hill Junior College*	Hillsboro
Houston Community College*	Houston
Howard College at Big Spring*	Big Spring
Kilgore College*	Kilgore
Lamar University*	Beaumont
Orange County Center*	Orange
Port Arthur Branch*	Port Arthur
Laredo Junior College*	Laredo
Lee College*	Baytown
Mainland, College of the*	Texas City
McLennan Community College*	Waco
Midland College*	Midland
Navarro College*	Corsicana
North Harris County College*	Houston
Odessa College*	Odessa
Panola Junior College*	Carthage
Paris Junior College*	Paris
Ranger Junior College*	Ranger
San Antonio Community Coll. District	San Antonio
St. Philip's College*	San Antonio
San Antonio College*	San Antonio
San Jacinto College*	Pasadena
Central Campus*	Pasadena
North Campus*	Houston
South Campus*	Houston
South Plains College*	Levelland
Southwest Texas Junior College*	Uvalde
Tarrant County Junior Coll. District	Fort Worth
Northeast Campus*	Hurst
Northwest Campus*	Fort Worth
South Campus*	Fort Worth
Temple Junior College*	Temple
Texarkana Community College*	Texarkana
Texas Southmost College*	Brownsville
Texas State Technical Institute*	Waco
Harlingen Campus*	Harlingen
Mid-Continent Campus*	Amarillo
Sweetwater Campus*	Sweetwater
Waco Campus*	Waco
Tyler Junior College*	Tyler
Vernon Regional Junior College*	Vernon
Victoria College*	Victoria
Weatherford College*	Weatherford
Western Texas College*	Snyder
Wharton County Junior College*	Wharton
Privately controlled	
Concordia Lutheran College	Austin
Jacksonville College	Jacksonville
Lon Morris College	Jacksonville
Schreiner College	Kerrville
Southwestern Christian College	Terrell
Southwestern Junior College	Waxahachie

UTAH

Publicly controlled	
Dixie College*	St. George
Eastern Utah, College of*	Price
Snow College*	Ephraim
Utah Technical College at Provo*	Provo
Utah Technical College at Salt Lake*	Salt Lake City

VERMONT

Publicly controlled	
Community College of Vermont	Montpelier
Vermont Technical College	Randolph Center
Privately controlled	
Burlington College	Burlington
Champlain College	Burlington
Ethan Allen Community College	Manchester Center
Green Mountain College	Poultney
Vermont College of Norwich University	Montpelier

VIRGINIA

Publicly controlled	
Blue Ridge Community College*	Weyers Cave
Central Virginia Community College*	Lynchburg
Dabney S. Lancaster Community Coll.*	Clifton Forge
Danville Community College*	Danville
Eastern Shore Community College*	Melfa
Germanna Community College*	Locust Grove
J. Sargeant Reynolds Community Coll.*	Richmond
Downtown Campus	Richmond
Parham Road Campus	Richmond
Western Campus	Richmond
John Tyler Community College	Chester
Lord Fairfax Community College*	Middletown
Mountain Empire Community College*	Big Stone Gap
New River Community College*	Dublin
Northern Virginia Community College*	Annandale
Alexandria Campus	Alexandria
Annandale Campus	Annandale
Loudoun Campus	Sterling
Manassas Campus	Manassas
Woodbridge Campus	Woodbridge
Patrick Henry Community College*	Martinsville
Paul D. Camp Community College*	Franklin
Piedmont Virginia Community College*	Charlottesville
Rappahannock Community College	Glenns
North Campus	Warsaw
South Campus	Glenns
Richard Bland College*	Petersburg
Southside Virginia Community College*	Alberta
Christanna Campus*	Alberta
John H. Daniel Campus*	Keysville
Southwest Virginia Community College*	Richlands
Thomas Nelson Community College*	Hampton
Tidewater Community College	Portsmouth
Chesapeake Campus*	Chesapeake
Frederick Campus*	Portsmouth
Norfolk Skills Center*	Norfolk
Virginia Beach Campus*	Virginia Beach
Virginia Highlands Community College*	Abingdon
Virginia Western Community College*	Roanoke
Wytheville Community College*	Wytheville
Privately controlled	
Southern Seminary Junior College	Buena Vista

WASHINGTON

Publicly controlled	
Bellevue Community College*	Bellevue
Big Bend Community College*	Moses Lake
Centralia College*	Centralia
Clark College	Vancouver
Columbia Basin College*	Pasco
Community College District V	Everett
Edmonds Community College*	Lynnwood
Everett Community College*	Everett
Community College District VI	Seattle
North Seattle Community College*	Seattle
Seattle Central Community College*	Seattle
South Seattle Community College*	Seattle
Community College District XVII	Spokane
Spokane Community College*	Spokane
Spokane Falls Community College*	Spokane
Fort Steilacoom Community College*	Tacoma
Grays Harbor College*	Aberdeen
Green River Community College*	Auburn
Highline Community College*	Midway
Lower Columbia College*	Longview
Olympia Technical Community College*	Olympia
Olympic College*	Bremerton

Peninsula College*	Port Angeles
Shoreline Community College*	Seattle
Skagit Valley College*	Mount Vernon
Tacoma Community College*	Tacoma
Walla Walla Community College	Walla Walla
Wenatchee Valley College*	Wenatchee
Whatcom Community College*	Bellingham
Yakima Valley College*	Yakima

WEST VIRGINIA

Publicly controlled

Fairmont Community College*	Fairmont
Marshall Univ.—Community College*	Huntington
Parkersburg Community College*	Parkersburg
Shepherd College—Community College Component*	Shepherdstown
Southern West Virginia Comm. College	Logan
Logan Campus	Logan
Williamson Campus	Williamson
West Virginia Institute of Technology—Community and Technical College*	Montgomery
West Virginia Northern Comm. College*	Wheeling
West Virginia State Comm. College	Institute
West Virginia University—Potomac State College*	Keyser

Privately controlled

Beckley College	Beckley
Ohio Valley College	Parkersburg

WISCONSIN

Publicly controlled

University Center System	Madison
Baraboo-Sauk County Campus	Baraboo
Barron County Campus	Rice Lake
Fond du Lac Campus	Fond du Lac
Fox Valley Campus	Menasha
Manitowoc County Campus	Manitowoc
Marathon County Campus	Wausau
Marinette County Campus	Marinette
Marshfield-Wood County Campus	Marshfield
Medford Campus	Medford
Richland Campus	Richland Center
Rock County Campus	Janesville
Sheboygan Campus	Sheboygan
Washington County Campus	West Bend
Waukesha County Campus	Waukesha
Vocational Tech. & Adult Education Sys.	Madison
Blackhawk Technical Institute*	Janesville
District One Technical Institute*	Eau Claire
Fox Valley Technical Institute*	Appleton
Appleton Campus	Appleton
Oshkosh Campus	Oshkosh
Gateway Technical Institute*	Kenosha
Elkhorn Campus	Elkhorn
Kenosha Campus	Kenosha
Racine Campus	Racine
Lakeshore Technical Institute*	Cleveland
Madison Area Technical Coll.*	Madison
Mid-State Technical Institute*	Wisconsin Rapids
Marshfield Campus*	Marshfield
Stevens Point Campus*	Stevens Point
Wisconsin Rapids Campus*	Wisconsin Rapids
Milwaukee Area Technical College*	Milwaukee
Central Campus*	Milwaukee
North Campus*	Mequon
South Campus*	Oak Creek
West Campus*	West Allis
Moraine Park Technical Institute*	Fond du Lac
Beaver Dam Campus	Beaver Dam
Fond du Lac Campus	Fond du Lac
West Bend Campus	West Bend
Nicolet College and Tech. Institute*	Rhinelander
North Central Technical Institute	Wausau
Antigo Campus	Antigo
Wausau Campus	Wausau
Northeast Wisconsin Technical Inst.*	Green Bay
Green Bay Campus	Green Bay
Marinette Campus	Marinette
Sturgeon Bay Campus	Sturgeon Bay
Southwest Wisconsin Technical Inst.*	Fennimore
Waukesha County Technical Institute*	Pewaukee
Western Wisconsin Technical Institute*	La Crosse
Wisconsin Indianhead VTAE District	Shell Lake
Ashland Campus*	Ashland
New Richmond Campus*	New Richmond
Rice Lake Campus*	Rice Lake
Superior Campus*	Superior

Privately controlled

Milwaukee School of Engineering	Milwaukee

WYOMING

Publicly controlled

Casper College*	Casper
Central Wyoming College*	Riverton
Eastern Wyoming College*	Torrington
Laramie County Community College*	Cheyenne
Northern Wyoming Community College*	Sheridan
Northwest Community College*	Powell
Western Wyoming Community College*	Rock Springs

AMERICAN SAMOA

Publicly controlled

American Samoa Community College*	Pago Pago

CANADA

Publicly controlled

Fraser Valley College*	Chilliwack, B.C.
Grant McEwan Community College*	Edmonton, Alberta
Lambton College*	Sarnia, Ont.
Lethbridge Community College*	Lethbridge, Alberta
Medicine Hat College*	Medicine Hat, Alberta
Mount Royal College*	Calgary, Albta.

GUAM

Publicly controlled

Guam Community College	Guam

MICRONESIA

Publicly controlled

Community Coll. of Micronesia	East Caroline Isl.

PANAMA

Publicly controlled

Panama Canal College*	APO Miami

OTHER COUNTRIES

Privately controlled

American College of Switzerland	Leysin, Switz.
Schiller College—Europe	Heidelberg, W. Ger.
St. Johns College*	British Honduras

Life Expectancy

The average length of a person's life in the United States has increased by more than 50% during this century, with most of the improvement taking place during the first half of the century.

Accredited U.S. Senior Colleges and Universities, Spring 1980

Source: Information Please questionnaires to Colleges and Universities.

Schools listed are those that offer at least a Bachelor's degree, and are fully accredited by one of the institutional and professional accrediting associations recognized by the Council on Postsecondary Accreditation. The number of students is for matriculated undergraduate and graduate students who are working for a degree.

Tuition, room, and board listed are average annual figures, subject to fluctuation, covering two semesters, two out of three trimesters, or three out of four quarters, depending on school calendar.

For further information, write to the Registrar of the school concerned.

Abbreviations used for controls:

AB	American Baptist
AC	Advent Christian
AG	Assembly of God
AL	American Lutheran
AME	African Methodist Episcopal
B	Baptist
BC	Brethren in Christ
CB	Church of Brethren
CC	Church of Christ
CG	Church of God
ChC	Christian Church
CMA	Christian & Missionary Alliance
CME	Christian Methodist Episcopal
CP	Cumberland Presbyterian
CR	Christian Reformed
DC	Disciples of Christ
E	Episcopalian
EC	Evangelical Covenant
ECh	Evangelical Christian
Fed	Federal
FGB	Fellowship of Grace Brethren Churches
FM	Free Methodist
FWB	Free Will Baptist
GGF	Grace Gospel Fellowship
GO	Greek Orthodox
ID	Interdenominational
Ind	Independent
L	Lutheran
LCA	Lutheran Church of America
LDS	Latter Day Saints
M	Methodist
MB	Mennonite Brethren
MC	Missionary Church
Men	Mennonite
Mor	Moravian
Mun	Municipal
Naz	Nazarene
ND	Non-denominational
OBS	Open Bible Standard
P	Private
PH	Pentecostal Holiness
Pres	Presbyterian
PUS	Presbyterian, U.S.
RC	Roman Catholic
RCA	Reformed Church in America
RP	Reformed Presbyterian
S	State
SB	Southern Baptist
SDA	Seventh Day Adventist
SOF	Society of Friends
Sw	Swedenborgian
UCC	United Church of Christ
UM	United Methodist
UP	United Presbyterian
W	Wesleyan

Institution and location	Enrollment		Faculty	Control	Tuition		Rm/Bd
	Male	Female			Res.	Nonres.	
Abilene Christian University; Abilene, Tex. 79699	1,831	1,782	175	P/CC	$2,080	$2,080	$1,290
Academy of Art College; San Francisco, Calif. 94102	941	559	80	P	(1)	(1)	—
Adams State College; Alamosa, Colo. 81102	898[2]	1,026[2]	110	S	680	2,692	1,500
Adelphi University; Garden City, N.Y. 11530	3,978[3]	7,796[3]	302	P	3,510	3,510	2,000
Adrian College; Adrian, Mich. 49221	481[3]	464[3]	58	P/UM	3,360	3,360	1,610
Agnes Scott College; Decatur, Ga. 30030	—	562	67	P	3,900	3,900	1,600
Akron, The University of; Akron, Ohio 44325	11,766[3]	11,598[3]	820	S	990	2,040	1,860
Alabama, The University of; University, Ala. 35486	8,672[3]	8,135[3]	818	S	764	1,629	1,250
Alabama, The University of, in Birmingham; Birmingham, Ala. 35294	14,214[3]		346	S	756	1,512	1,600
Alabama, The University of, in Huntsville; Huntsville, Ala. 35807	1,225[3]	1,251[3]	181	S	768	768	1,980
Alabama A&M University; Normal, Ala. 35762	2,425	2,175	265	S	530	810	1,156
Alabama State University; Montgomery, Ala. 36101	1,645[3]	2,451[3]	202	S	525	870	1,005
Alaska, University of, Anchorage; Anchorage, Alaska 99504	1,350[3]	2,275[3]	118	S	571	1,527	—
Alaska, University of, Fairbanks; Fairbanks, Alaska 99701	1,108[3]	895[3]	395	S	410	1,190	1,980
Albany College of Pharmacy; Albany, N.Y. 12208	270	304	30	P	2,100	2,100	1,700
Albany Law School; Albany, N.Y. 12208	500	213	28	P	4,000	4,000	2,300
Albany Medical College; Albany, N.Y. 12208	380[3]	132[3]	300	P	12,000	12,000	920[4]
Albany State College; Albany, Ga. 31705	575	946	125	S	699	1,653	270
Albertus Magnus College; New Haven, Conn. 06511	2[3]	388[3]	27	P/RC	3,600	3,600	2,260
Albion College; Albion, Mich. 49224	916	790	116	P	3,728	3,728	1,800
Albright College; Reading, Pa. 19603	616[2]	693[2]	83	P/UM	3,740	3,740	1,570
Albuquerque, University of; Albuquerque, N.M. 87140	912	1,085	75	P	936	936	n.a.
Alcorn State University; Lorman, Miss. 39096	911[3]	1,239[3]	143	S	768	1,618	1,232
Alderson–Broaddus College; Philippi, W. Va. 26416	293[3]	567[3]	63	P/B	2,835	2,835	1,367

	Enrollment				Tuition		
Institution and location	Male	Female	Faculty	Control	Res.	Nonres.	Rm/Bd
Alfred Adler Institute of Chicago; Chicago, Ill. 60601	50	98	18	P	[5]	[5]	—
Alfred University[6]; Alfred, N.Y. 14802	1,014[3]	831[3]	142	P/S	4,465	4,465	1,879
Allegheny College; Meadville, Pa. 16335	919	936	120	P	1,785	1,785	490
Allentown College of St. Francis de Sales; Center Valley, Pa. 18034	274	307	40	P/RC	3,300	3,300	1,950
Alliance College; Cambridge Springs, Pa. 16403	114	65	20	P	2,200	2,200	1,828
Alma College; Alma, Mich. 48801	565	566	73	P	4,144	4,144	2,138
Alvernia College; Reading, Pa. 19607	139	179	44	P/RC	1,850	1,850	1,500
Alverno College; Milwaukee, Wis. 53215	—	1,043[3]	75	P/RC	2,950	2,950	1,350
American Baptist College; Nashville, Tenn. 37207	134	13	8	P/B	920	920	880
American College in Paris; Paris, France 75007	200	400	17[7]	P	3,100	3,100	3,500
American Conservatory of Music; Chicago, Ill. 60603	99	96	15	P/S	3,000	3,000	—
American Grad. School of Intl. Mgt.; Glendale, Ariz. 85306	675	276	65	P	3,900	3,900	1,860
American International College; Springfield, Mass. 01109	800[3]	585[3]	84[8]	P	3,060	3,060	1,352
American Technological University; Killeen, Tex. 76541	646	204	11	P	4,060	4,060	2,000
American University, The; Washington, D.C. 20016	3,291[3]	3,272[3]	363	P/M	4,134	4,134	2,126
Americas, University of the; Puebla, Mexico	1,650[8]		55[8]	P	1,377	1,733	n.a.
Amherst College; Amherst, Mass. 01002	1,000[8]	461[8]	145	P	5,150	5,150	2,000
Anderson College; Anderson, Ind. 46011	767[3]	930[3]	93	P/CG	3,200	3,200	1,310
Andrews University; Berrien Springs, Mich. 49104	1,676[3]	1,307[3]	232	P/SDA	3,975	3,975	2,100
Angelo State University; San Angelo, Tex. 76909	2,148[3]	2,002[3]	187	S	120	1,280	1,664
Anna Maria College; Paxton, Mass. 01612	54	325	30	P/RC	2,680	2,680	1,800
Antillian College; Mayaguez, P.R. 00708	340[3]	375[3]	45	P/SDA	1,400	1,400	1,580
Antioch University; Yellow Springs, Ohio 45387	1,586[3]	2,553[3]	200	P	n.a.	n.a.	n.a.
Appalachian Bible College; Bradley, W. Va. 25818	112	83	12	P/Ind	1,825	1,825	1,475
Appalachian State University. *See* North Carolina, University System of							
Arizona, University of; Tucson, Ariz. 85721	16,944[3]	15,026[3]	1,689	S	600	2,500	1,775
Arizona State University; Tempe, Ariz. 85281	18,802	17,318	1,303	S	550	2,100	1,300
Arkansas, Univ. of, at Fayetteville; Fayetteville, Ark. 72701	6,390[9]	4,440[9]	669	S	460	1,090	1,395
Arkansas, Univ. of, at Little Rock; Little Rock, Ark. 72204	4,429[3]	5,609[3]	301	S	600	1,230	—
Arkansas, Univ. of, at Monticello; Monticello, Ark. 71655	740	653	96	S	600	1,230	1,220
Arkansas, Univ. of, at Pine Bluff; Pine Bluff, Ark. 71601	1,160	1,688	168	S	600	1,230	1,164
Arkansas College; Batesville, Ark. 72501	175	279	28	P/PUS	2,150	2,150	1,372
Arkansas State University; State University, Ark. 72467	2,664[3]	2,759[3]	317	S	600	950	1,380
Arkansas Tech. University; Russellville, Ark. 72801	1,395[3]	1,075[3]	125	S	600	1,040	1,240
Armstrong College; Berkeley, Calif. 94704	148[3]	110[3]	25	P	2,178	2,178	n.a.
Armstrong State College; Savannah, Ga. 31406	1,118	1,632	175	S	540	1,332	—
Art Academy of Cincinnati; Cincinnati, Ohio 45202	58[3]	68[3]	12	P	2,340	2,340	—
Art Center College of Design; Pasadena, Calif. 91103	634[3]	375[3]	28[10]	P	3,250	3,250	4,000
Art Institute of Chicago, School of the; Chicago, Ill. 60603	446	528	70	P	3,420	3,420	2,500
Asbury College; Wilmore, Ky. 40390	560	588	91	P/ND	815	815	495
Ashland College; Ashland, Ohio 44805	1,161	779	104	P/BC	3,722	3,722	1,630
Associated Arts, School of the; St. Paul, Minn. 55102	52[3]	48[3]	4	P	2,700	2,700	2,500
Assumption College; Worcester, Mass. 01609	702[3]	769[3]	75	P/RC	3,750[11]	3,750[11]	2,075[11]
Athens State College; Athens, Ala. 35611	281	265	37	S	750	750	1,450
Atlanta Christian College; East Point, Ga. 30344	103	66	12	P/ChC	1,184	1,184	1,220
Atlanta College of Art; Atlanta, Ga. 30309	132[3]	140[3]	30	P	2,600	2,600	3,100
Atlanta University; Atlanta, Ga. 30314	440	485	132	P	[12]	[12]	910
Atlantic, College of the; Bar Harbor, Maine 04609	66	97	21	P	3,800	3,800	—
Atlantic Christian College; Wilson, N.C. 27893	541[3]	962[3]	89	DC	2,200	2,200	1,300
Atlantic Union College; South Lancaster, Mass. 01561	250	340	55	P/SDA	4,048	4,048	2,000
Auburn University; Auburn, Ala. 36849	9,226[3]	6,669[3]	1,076	S	720	1,440	1,475
Augsburg College; Minneapolis, Minn. 55454	661	801	94	P/AL	3,660	3,660	1,837
Augusta College; Augusta, Ga. 30910	1,619[3]	2,083[3]	157	S	609	1,563	—
Augustana College; Rock Island, Ill. 61201	1078[3]	1,156[3]	112	P/LCA	3,540	3,540	1,722
Augustana College; Sioux Falls, S.D. 57197	803	1,342	140	P/AL	3,650	3,650	1,389
Aurora College; Aurora, Ill. 60507	274[3]	295[3]	43	P/AC	3,300	3,300	1,899
Austin College; Sherman, Tex. 75090	633[3]	497[3]	82	P/PUS	3,300[11]	3,300[11]	1,600
Austin Peay State University; Clarksville, Tenn. 37040	2,724[3]	2,746[3]	195	S	495	1,497	900
Averett College; Danville, Va. 24541	349	605	47	P/B	1.980[13]	3,900[14]	—
Avila College; Kansas City, Mo. 64145	192	693	73	P/RC	2,400	2,400	1,450
Azusa Pacific College; Azusa, Calif. 91702	544	662	97	P/ID	3,564	3,564	1,890
Babson College; Babson Park, Mass. 02157	917	362	n.a.	P	4,670	4,670	2,400
Baker University; Baldwin City, Kan. 66006	423[3]	449[3]	57	P	2,600	2,600	1,490
Baldwin–Wallace College; Berea, Ohio 44017	1,000[3]	958[3]	140	P/M	4,131	4,131	2,100
Ball State University; Muncie, Ind. 47306	7,813[3]	9,744[3]	883	S	900	1,935	1,350

Institution and location	Enrollment: Male	Enrollment: Female	Faculty	Control	Tuition: Res.	Tuition: Nonres.	Rm/Bd
Baltimore, University of; Baltimore, Md. 21201	3,510[3]	1,884[3]	127	S	800	1,700	—
Baltimore Hebrew College; Baltimore, Md. 21215	84[8]	125[8]	16	P	850	850	—
Bank Street College of Education; New York, N.Y. 10025	30	200	61	P	4,300	4,300	5,350
Baptist Bible College; Springfield, Mo. 65802	995	774	59	P/B	416	416	1,200
Baptist College at Charleston; Charleston, S.C. 29411	741[3]	810[3]	78	P/B	2,994	2,994	1,910
Barat College; Lake Forest, Ill. 60045	—	497	38	P	1,825	1,825	965
Barber–Scotia College; Concord, N.C. 28025	133	169	24	Pres	1,829	1,829	1,329
Bard College; Annandale-on-Hudson, N.Y. 12504	326	379	53	P	6,430	6,430	2,180
Barnard College. *See* Columbia University							
Barrington College; Barrington, R.I. 02806	160	219	26	P/ECh	3,550	3,550	2,000
Barry College; Miami, Fla. 33161	231	763	76	P/RC	3,500	3,500	1,600
Bartlesville Wesleyan College; Bartlesville, Okla. 74003	195	203	33	W	2,100	2,100	1,650
Bates College; Lewiston, Maine 04240	764	668	114	P	5,720	5,720	1,780
Bayamón Central University; Bayamón, P.R. 00619	1,313[3]	1,391[3]	56	P/RC	2,050	2,050	1,000
Baylor College of Dentistry; Dallas, Tex. 75246	395	125	110	P	510	3,000	—
Baylor University; Waco, Tex. 76703	4,012	4,266	471	P/SB	1,920	1,920	1,470
Beaver College; Glenside, Pa. 19038	119[3]	571[3]	58	P	4,300	4,300	2,050
Behrend College. *See* Pennsylvania State University							
Belhaven College; Jackson, Miss. 39202	203	274	30	Pres	2,140	2,140	1,260
Bellarmine College; Louisville, Ky. 40205	508[3]	523[3]	67	P/RC	2,450	2,450	1,500
Bellevue College; Bellevue, Neb. 68005	379[3]	266[3]	28	P	925	925	—
Belmont Abbey College; Belmont, N.C. 28012	429	286	34	P/RC	1,872	3,322	1,450
Belmont College; Nashville, Tenn. 37203	703	723	76	P/SB	2,050	2,050	1,460
Beloit College; Beloit, Wis. 53511	506[3]	452[3]	75	P	4,500	4,500	1,660
Bemidji State Univ. *See* Minnesota State College System							
Benedict College; Columbia, S.C. 29204	544[3]	1,040[3]	92	P/B	2,200	2,200	1,600
Benedictine College; Atchison, Kan. 66002	507[3]	457[3]	63	P	2,800[11]	2,800[11]	1,701[11]
Bennett College; Greensboro, N.C. 27420	—	600	44	P/UM	2,150	2,150	1,180
Bennington College; Bennington, Vt. 05201	183	350	57	P	7,380	7,380	2,050
Bentley College; Waltham, Mass. 02154	2,249[3]	1,191[3]	137	P	3,970	3,970	2,320
Berea College; Berea, Ky. 40404	609[3]	825[3]	113	P	—	—	1,375
Berklee College of Music; Boston, Mass. 02215	2,224[3]	359[3]	131	P	2,880	2,880	995
Berkshire Christian College; Lenox, Mass. 01240	58	47	12	P/AC	2,200	2,200	2,000
Bernard M. Baruch Coll. *See* New York, City Univ. of							
Berry College; Mount Berry, Ga. 30149	504	743	104	P	1,800	2,400	1,500
Bethany Bible College; Santa Cruz, Calif. 95066	278[3]	247[3]	27	P/AG	1,900	1,900	1,660
Bethany College; Bethany, W. Va. 26032	460	368	63	P/DC	4,485	4,485	1,525
Bethany College; Lindsborg, Kan. 67456	434	408	50	P/LCA	2,434	2,434	1,800
Bethany Nazarene College; Bethany, Okla. 73008	526	592	60	P/Naz	1,860	1,860	1,410
Bethel College; McKenzie, Tenn. 38201	168	129	21	P/CP	1,800	1,800	1,440
Bethel College; Mishawaka, Ind. 46544	225	239	26	P/MC	2,500[2]	2,500[2]	1,450
Bethel College; North Newton, Kan. 67117	343[3]	242[3]	39	P	2,685	2,685	1,639
Bethel College; St. Paul, Minn. 55112	891[3]	1,098[3]	88	P/B	2,990	2,990	1,400
Bethune–Cookman College; Daytona Beach, Fla. 32015	690[3]	1,046[3]	114	P/M	2,728	2,728	1,806
Biola College; La Mirada, Calif. 90639	851[3]	1,184[3]	102	P/ND	3,216	3,216	1,926
Birmingham–Southern College; Birmingham, Ala. 35204	701[3]	701[3]	73	P/M	2,550	2,550	1,400
Biscayne College; Miami, Fla. 33054	872	609	70	P/RC	2,850	2,850	2,160
Bishop College; Dallas, Tex. 75241	581	270	46	P/B	1,000	1,000	1,500
Blackburn College; Carlinville, Ill. 62626	250	300	37	P/Pres	2,550	2,550	n.a.
Black Hills State College; Spearfish, S.D. 57783	812	1,069	95	S	686	1,424	1,255
Bloomfield College; Bloomfield, N.J. 07003	696[3]	756[3]	52	P	3,450	3,450	1,990
Bloomsburg State College; Bloomsburg, Pa. 17815	2,599[3]	3,933[3]	321	S	1,100	2,060	1,202
Bluefield College; Bluefield, Va. 24605	194[3]	174[3]	22	P	1,450	1,450	1,400
Bluefield State College; Bluefield, W. Va. 24701	700	1,700	75	S	380	1,320	—
Blue Mountain College; Blue Mountain, Miss. 38610	67	221	26	P/SB	1,260	1,260	1,170
Bluffton College; Bluffton, Ohio 45817	264[3]	291[3]	44	P/Men	3,211	3,211	1,358
Boise State University; Boise, Idaho 83725	3,606[3]	2,246[3]	450	S	578	1,978	1,690
Borromeo College of Ohio; Wickliffe, Ohio 44092	72[3]	10[3]	13	P/RC	2,375	2,900	1,200
Boston College; Chestnut Hill, Mass. 02167	6,257[3]	7,720[3]	540	P/RC	4,530	4,530	2,500
Boston Conservatory of Music; Boston, Mass. 02215	142[3]	296[3]	30	P	3,100	3,100	1,800
Boston State College; Boston, Mass. 02115	2,497	2,297	286	S	600	2,100	—
Boston University; Boston, Mass. 02215	8,689[3]	9,367[3]	n.a.	P	5,515	5,515	2,605
Bowdoin College; Brunswick, Maine 04011	776	553	99	P	5,100	5,100	1,930
Bowie State College; Bowie, Md. 20715	1,243[3]	1,636[3]	109	S	870	1,825	1,590
Bowling Green State University; Bowling Green, Ohio 43403	7,459[3]	9,448[3]	723	S	1,086	2,448	1,611
Bradford College; Bradford, Mass. 01830	89[3]	160[3]	23	P	4,500	4,500	2,475
Bradley University; Peoria, Ill. 61625	3,035[3]	2,249[3]	297	P	3,626	3,626	1,710
Brandeis University; Waltham, Mass. 02254	1,779	1,692	354	P	5,835	5,835	2,600
Brenau College; Gainesville, Ga. 30501	286[3]	944[3]	60	P	2,160[15]	2,160	2,090

Institution and location	Enrollment		Faculty	Control	Tuition		Rm/Bd
	Male	Female			Res.	Nonres.	
Brescia College; Owensboro, Ky. 42301	195	281	55	P/RC	2,100	2,100	1,510
Briar Cliff College; Sioux City, Iowa 51104	298	479	55	P/RC	2,400	2,400	1,200
Bridgeport, University of; Bridgeport, Conn. 06602	3,436[3]	3,520[3]	288	P	4,500	4,500	2,410
Bridgeport Engineering Institute; Bridgeport, Conn. 06606	609[3]	30[3]	75	P	1,480	1,480	—
Bridgewater College; Bridgewater, Va. 22812	439[3]	459[3]	58	P	2,675	2,675	1,715
Bridgewater State College; Bridgewater, Mass. 02324	1,534	2,785	215	S	600	2,100	1,600
Brigham Young University; Provo, Utah 84601	12,323	9,910	1,144	P/LDS	970[16]	1,454[17]	1,120
Hawaii Campus; Laie, Hawaii 96762	704	958	71	P/LDS	820[16]	1,300[17]	1,500
Brooklyn College. *See* New York, City University of							
Brooklyn College of Pharmacy. *See* Long Island University, Arnold and Marie Schwartz College of Pharmacy and Health Sciences							
Brooklyn Law School; Brooklyn, N.Y. 11201	584	364	31	P	3,200	3,200	—
Brooks Institute; Santa Barbara, Calif. 93108	791	—	41	P	3,750	3,750	—
Brown University; Providence, R.I. 02912	3,589[3]	2,968[3]	479	P	6,140	6,140	2,575
Bryan College; Dayton, Tenn. 37321	276[3]	311[3]	33	P	2,250	2,250	1,950
Bryant College; Smithfield, R.I. 02876	1,782[3]	1,210[3]	90	P	3,000	3,000	1,825
Bryn Mawr College; Bryn Mawr, Pa. 19010	95[3]	1,275[3]	124	P	5,325	5,325	2,300
Bucknell University; Lewisburg, Pa. 17837	1,672[3]	1,474[3]	230	P	4,950	4,950	1,550
Buena Vista College; Storm Lake, Iowa 50588	588[3]	516[3]	55	P/Pres	3,225	3,225	1,280
Butler University; Indianapolis, Ind. 46208	961[3]	1,221[3]	169	P	3,100	3,100	1,450
Cabrini College; Radnor, Pa. 19087	77	351	29	P/RC	2,780	2,780	1,890
Caldwell College; Caldwell, N.J. 07006	—	400	40	P/RC	2,700	2,700	1,850
California, New College of; San Francisco, Calif. 94110	110	130	12	P	2,700	2,700	3,600
California, University of; Berkeley, Calif. 94720	66,941[9]	52,510[9]	7,248	S	720	2,610	2,500
UC, Berkeley; Berkeley, Calif. 94720	18,008[3]	12,454[3]	1,494	S	255	1,055	2,745
UC, Davis; Davis, Calif. 95616	9,479	8,142	n.a.	S	720	3,120	1,800
UC, Irvine; Irvine, Calif. 92717	5,653[3]	4,385[3]	731	S	768	3,168	2,434
UC, Los Angeles; Los Angeles, Calif. 90024	17,280	14,340	2,200	S	759	3,159	1,797
UC, Riverside; Riverside, Calif. 92521	2,521[3]	2,096[3]	417	S	738	3,138	1,600
UC, San Diego; La Jolla, Calif. 92093	6,470	4,362	850	S	741	3,141	2,400
UC, Santa Barbara; Santa Barbara, Calif. 93106	7,248	6,983	1,051	S	—	2,400	1,835
UC, Santa Cruz; Santa Cruz, Calif. 95064	3,018[3]	3,075[3]	346	S	831	3,321	2,500
California Baptist College; Riverside, Calif. 92504	286	279	32	P/SB	2,862	2,862	1,470
California College of Arts and Crafts; Oakland, Calif. 94618	291	501	67	P	3,790	3,790	925[4]
California College of Podiatric Medicine; San Francisco, Calif. 94115	339[3]	57[3]	18	P	6,840	6,840	n.a.
California Institute of Technology; Pasadena, Calif. 91125	1,438	193	258	P	5,229	5,229	1,826
California Institute of the Arts; Valencia, Calif. 91355	433[3]	304[3]	70	P	4,500	4,500	835
California Lutheran College; Thousand Oaks, Calif. 91360	585	655	72	P/L	3,600	3,600	1,860
California Maritime Academy; Vallejo, Calif. 94590	470[8]	15[8]	30	S	645	1,290	2,100
California Polytechnic State University; San Luis Obispo, Calif. 93407[18]	7,807	5,309	746	S	290	290[19]	1,304
California School of Professional Psychology—Berkeley; Berkeley, Calif. 94704	97	133	17	P	5,500	5,500	3,750[20]
California School of Professional Psychology—Fresno; Fresno, Calif. 93721	107	46	3	P	5,445	5,445	3,600
California School of Professional Psychology—Los Angeles; Los Angeles, Calif. 90004	103	161	22	P	4,950	4,950	3,900
California School of Professional Psychology—San Diego; San Diego, Calif. 92121	141	92	20	P	5,445	5,445	—
California State College; California, Pa. 15419	2,187[3]	2,185[3]	303	S	1,100	1,930	1,350
California State College, Bakersfield; Bakersfield, Calif. 93309[18]	1,074	1,102	130	S	180	2,040	1,836
California State College, San Bernardino; San Bernardino, Calif. 92407[18]	1,730	2,286	120	S	201	1,800	1,775
California State Coll., Sonoma. *See* Sonoma State Coll.							
California State Coll., Stanislaus; Turlock, Calif. 95380[18]	1,595[3]	1,963[3]	174	S	212	2,372	1,600
California State Polytechnic University, Pomona; Pomona, Calif. 91768[18]	9,230[3]	5,666[3]	906	S	—	2,160	1,800
California State University and Colleges, Consortium of the; Long Beach, Calif. 90802	170[3]		80	S	495	495	—
California State Univ., Chico; Chico, Calif. 95926[18]	6,639	6,604	n.a.	S	225	2,400	n.a.
California St. Univ., Dominguez Hills; Carson, Calif. 90747[18]	1,540	1,850	275	S	200	2,000	2,700
California State Univ., Fresno; Fresno, Calif. 93740[18]	7,368	7,539	749	S	240	2,400	2,000
California State Univ., Fullerton; Fullerton, Calif. 92634[18]	8,789	12,711	801	S	—	2,388	—
California State Univ., Hayward; Hayward, Calif. 94542[18]	2,634	3,154	498	S	207	2,007	2,000
California State University, Long Beach; Long Beach, Calif. 90840[18]	14,137	15,444	1,600	S	206	1,000	1,550
California State University, Los Angeles; Los Angeles, Calif. 90032[18]	10,202[3]	12,272[3]	743	S	210	2,010	—

Institution and location	Enrollment Male	Enrollment Female	Faculty	Control	Tuition Res.	Tuition Nonres.	Rm/Bd
California State University, Northridge; Northridge, Calif. 91330[18]	7,484[3]	7,923[3]	900	S	200	2,000	2,600
California State University, Sacramento; Sacramento, Calif. 95819[18]	6,431	6,336	680	S	200	2,450	1,700
California Western School of Law; San Diego, Calif. 92101	527	140	21	P	3,980	3,980	n.a.
Calumet College; Whiting, Ind. 46394	234[3]	216[3]	25	P/RC	1,313	1,313	n.a.
Calvary Bible College; Kansas City, Mo. 64111	197	174	19	ND	1,600	1,600	1,250
Calvin College; Grand Rapids, Mich. 49506	1,792[3]	1,888[3]	201	P/CR	2,410	2,410	1,380
Cameron University; Lawton, Okla. 73505	1,269	1,235	175	S	400	1,000	1,286
Campbellsville College; Campbellsville, Ky. 42718	282	299	45	P/B	2,280	2,280	1,600
Campbell University; Buie's Creek, N.C. 27506	1,127[3]	766[3]	125	SB	2,744	2,744	1,439
Canisius College; Buffalo, N.Y. 14208	1,587[3]	1,010[3]	152	P	3,300[11]	3,300[11]	1,850
Capital University; Columbus, Ohio 43209	958[3]	975[3]	148	P/AL	4,280	4,280	1,830
Capitol Institute of Technology; Kensington, Md. 20795	566	34	13	P	2,160	2,160	—
Cardinal Stritch College; Milwaukee, Wis. 53217	98	370	41	P/RC	2,500	2,500	1,400
Caribbean Center for Advanced Studies, Santurce, P.R. 00940	71	108	9	P	2.775	2,775	—
Caribbean University College; Bayamón, P.R. 00619	490	878	32	P	1,410	1,410	—
Carleton College; Northfield, Minn. 55057	934	874	132	P	4,327	4,327	1,800
Carlow College; Pittsburgh, Pa. 15213	19[3]	702[3]	45	P/RC	3,630	3,630	2,000
Carnegie–Mellon University; Pittsburgh, Pa. 15213	2,717[3]	1,367[3]	431	P	4,700	4,700	2,500
Carroll College; Helena, Mont. 59601	484[3]	608[3]	85	P/RC	3,160	3,160	1,574
Carroll College; Waukesha, Wis. 53186	519[3]	556[3]	76	P/PUS	4,366	4,366	1,460
Carson–Newman College; Jefferson City, Tenn. 37760	791[2]	799[2]	91	P/B	2,200	2,300	1,500
Carthage College, Kenosha, Wis. 53141	553[3]	549[3]	81	P/LCA	3,210	3,210	1,400
Case Western Reserve University; Cleveland, Ohio 44106	3,721	2,083	n.a.	P	4,800	4,800	2,150
Castleton State College; Castleton, Vt. 05701	560	703	88	S	1,120	2,760	2,100
Catawba College; Salisbury, N.C. 28144	489	425	68	P/UCC	2,850	2,850	1,360
Cathedral College of the Immaculate Conception; Douglaston, N.Y. 11362	—	135	31	RC	2,600	2,600	2,000
Catholic University of America, The; Washington, D.C. 20064	2,277[3]	2,306[3]	385	P/RC	3,750	3,750	2,000
Cayey University College. *See* Puerto Rico, University of							
Cedar Crest College; Allentown, Pa. 18104	1[3]	702[3]	58	P	4,000	4,000	1,900
Cedarville College; Cedarville, Ohio 45314	615[3]	735[3]	67	P/B	2,600[11]	2,600[11]	1,800
Centenary College; Hackettstown, N.J. 07840	—	681[3]	46	P	5,650[21]	5,650[21]	—
Centenary College of Louisiana; Shreveport, La. 71104	396	387	55	P/UM	2,200	2,200	290
Central Arkansas, University of; Conway, Ark. 72157	1,998	2,975	148	S	600	1,200	1,360
Central Baptist College; Conway, Ark. 72032	98	70	12	B	720	720	1,040
Central Bible College; Springfield, Mo. 65802	673	462	35	AG	1,408	1,408	1,490
Central College, Iowa. *See* Central University of Iowa							
Central Connecticut State College; New Britain, Conn. 06050	3,200	2,802	416	S	726	1,530	1,460
Central Florida, University of; Orlando, Fla. 32816	7,500[3]	5,000[3]	400	S	780	1,740	3,000
Central Methodist College; Fayette, Mo. 65248	305	310	65	M	3,235	3,235	1,500
Central Michigan University; Mt. Pleasant, Mich. 48859	5,773	7,206	673	S	985	2,440	1,800
Central Missouri State University; Warrensburg, Mo. 64093	4,044[3]	4,297[3]	446	S	465	1,125	1,560
Central New England College of Technology; Worcester, Mass. 01610	895	310	22	P	2,400	2,400	1,600
Central State University; Edmond, Okla. 73034	4,866	5,467	333	S	430	1,030	1,280
Central State University; Wilberforce, Ohio 45384	1,212	1,160	112	S	882	1,107	1,182
Central University of Iowa; Pella, Iowa 50219	668[2]	802[2]	77	P/RCA	3,329	3,329	1,296
Central Washington University; Ellensburg, Wash. 98926	2,605	2,539	319	S	618	1,983	1,800
Central Wesleyan College; Central, S.C. 29630	185	199	26	W	2,920	2,920	1,560
Centre College of Kentucky; Danville, Ky. 40422	398	324	70	P	4,100	4,100	1,875
Chadron State College; Chadron, Neb. 69337	650	700	90	S	540	960	1,200
Chaminade University of Honolulu, Hawaii 96816	1,457	786	52	P/RC	1,040	1,040	985
Chapman College; Orange, Calif. 92666	597[3]	587[3]	92	P/DC	4,280[11]	4,280[11]	2,125[11]
Charleston, The College of; Charleston, S.C. 29401	1,314	1,955	190	S	750	1,650	1,500
Charleston, The University of; Charleston, W. Va. 25304	353[3]	528[3]	n.a.	P	930	930	1,500
Chatham College; Pittsburgh, Pa. 15232	—	518	50	P	3,975	3,975	1,965
Chestnut Hill College; Philadelphia, Pa. 19118	—	633	52	P/RC	2,500	2,500	1,750
Cheyney State College; Cheyney, Pa. 19319	1,100	1,257	178	S	1,210	2,040	1,250
Chicago, The University of; Chicago, Ill. 60637	1,800	900	1,020	P	5,100	5,100	3,000
Chicago Coll. of Osteopathic Medicine; Chicago, Ill. 60615	350	38	125	P	6,120	6,120	5,000
Chicago Conservatory College; Chicago, Ill. 60605	23[8]	25[8]	19	P	2,380	2,380	—
Chicago State University; Chicago, Ill. 60628	2,220[3]	3,410[3]	300	S	638	1,754	—
Christian Brothers College; Memphis, Tenn. 38104	722	376	62	P/RC	2,390	2,390	1,620
Christopher Newport College; Newport News, Va. 23606	1,612	2,015	107	S	960	1,260	—
Cincinnati, University of; Cincinnati, Ohio 45221	12,079	9,409	1,884	S	1,005	2,430	1,941

Institution and location	Enrollment: Male	Enrollment: Female	Faculty	Control	Tuition: Res.	Tuition: Nonres.	Rm/Bd
Cincinnati Bible College; Cincinnati, Ohio 45204	258	190	23	P/ChC	1,300	1,300	1,539
Circleville Bible College; Circleville, Ohio 43113	93	77	12	P/CC	1,600	1,600	1,100
Citadel, The; Charleston, S.C. 29409	2,568	817	200	S	125	385	1,420
City College; Seattle, Wash. 98104	816[3]	363[3]	n.a.	P	1,650	1,650	—
City College (NYC). *See* New York, City University of							
Claflin College; Orangeburg, S.C. 29115	286[3]	580[3]	62	P/UM	1,850	1,850	1,125
Claremont Colleges:							
Claremont Graduate School; Claremont, Calif. 91711	433	186	58	P	4,050	4,050	—
Claremont Men's College; Claremont, Calif. 91711	631	186	75	P	4,850	4,850	1,970
Harvey Mudd College; Claremont, Calif. 91711	411	66	61	P	5,350	5,350	2,350
Pitzer College; Claremont, Calif. 91711	302	441	55	P	4,640	4,640	1,884
Pomona College; Claremont, Calif. 91711	695[3]	647[3]	150	P	5,470	5,470	n.a.
Scripps College; Claremont, Calif. 91711	—	541	48	P	4,540	4,540	2,226
Clarion State College; Clarion, Pa. 16214	2,263	2,674	305	S	1,140	2,080	1,250
Clark College; Atlanta, Ga. 30314	669[3]	1,362[3]	124	P/UM	2,080	2,080	1,600
Clarke College; Dubuque, Iowa 52001	81	597	65	P/RC	3,100	3,100	1,550
Clarkson College of Technology; Potsdam, N.Y. 13676	2,890	591	204	P	4,505	4,505	2,140
Clark University; Worcester, Mass. 01610	1,021[22]	934[22]	128	P	3,875	3,875	1,655
Cleary College; Ypsilanti, Mich. 48197	64[3]	230[3]	12	P	1,630	1,630	—
Clemson University; Clemson, S.C. 29631	5,951[3]	3,618[3]	598	S	984	2,088	1,390
Cleveland Institute of Art, The; Cleveland, Ohio 44106	245	284	65	P	2,840	2,840	2,110
Cleveland State University; Cleveland, Ohio 44115	5,233	3,789	523	S	984	1,968	1,785
Clinch Valley College. *See* Virginia, University of							
Coe College; Cedar Rapids, Iowa 52402	595[3]	602[3]	135	P	3,595	3,595	1,400
Cogswell College; San Francisco, Calif. 94108	327	34	24	P	2,400	2,400	—
Coker College; Hartsville, S.C. 29550	97[3]	204[3]	37	P	3,030	3,030	1,530
Colby College; Waterville, Me. 04901	855	754	111	P	5,390[11]	5,390[11]	2,200
Colby–Sawyer College; New London, N.H. 03257	2	598	48	P	3,800	3,800	1,943
Colgate University; Hamilton, N.Y. 13346	1,369[3]	980[3]	201	P	5,400	5,400	2,100
College Misericordia; Dallas, Pa. 18612	109[3]	726[3]	73	P/RC	2,630	2,630	1,650
Colorado, University of; Boulder, Colo. 80302							
U. of Colorado at Boulder; Boulder, Colo. 80309	11,213	8,954	950	S	892	3,250	1,544
U. of Colorado at Colorado Springs; Colorado Springs, Colo. 80907	1,189	1,227	121	S	526	2,314	—
U. of Colorado at Denver; Denver, Colo. 80202	4,515[3]	4,229[3]	310	S	600	2,800	—
Colorado College, The; Colorado Springs, Colo. 80903	973[3]	965[3]	132	P	4,700	4,700	1,700
Colorado School of Mines; Golden, Colo. 80401	2,254	428	178	S	1,282	4,564	1,750
Colorado State University; Fort Collins, Colo. 80523	8,795	7,681	986	S	397	1,424	850
Colorado Women's College; Denver, Colo. 80220	—	450	45	P	([23])	([23])	2,150
Columbia Christian College; Portland, Ore. 97220	125	126	13	CC	2,025	2,025	1,425
Columbia College; Chicago, Ill. 60605	912[3]	932[3]	42	P	2,369	2,369	—
Columbia College; Columbia, Mo. 65216[24]	328[3]	459[3]	49	P	2,900	2,900	1,700
Columbia College; Columbia, S.C. 29203	—	908[3]	62	P/M	2,800	2,800	1,800
Columbia College—Hollywood; Hollywood, Calif. 90038	237	63	41	P	2,400	2,400	—
Columbia Union College; Takoma Park, Md. 20012	382[3]	574[3]	62	P/SDA	3,614	3,614	1,990
Columbia University; New York, N.Y. 10027	9,379	4,706	1,530	P	6010	6,010	2,920
Barnard College; New York, N.Y. 10027	—	2,441[3]	149	P	5,120	5,120	2,320
Teachers College; New York, N.Y. 10027	162[3]	1,118[3]	150	P	([25])	([25])	—
Columbus College; Columbus, Ga. 31907	1,070	1,241	229	S	459	1,245	n.a.
Columbus College of Art and Design, The; Columbus, Ohio 43215	335[3]	359[3]	41	P	2,600	2,600	2,798
Concord College; Athens, W. Va. 24712	760[3]	890[3]	87	S	368	1,308	1,618
Concordia College; Ann Arbor, Mich. 48105	293	221	48	L	2,278	2,278	1,649
Concordia College; Bronxville, N.Y. 10708	151	220	44	P/L	2,145	2,145	1,660
Concordia College; Moorhead, Minn. 56560	1,119[3]	1,488[3]	225	AL	3,635	3,635	1,325
Concordia College; River Forest, Ill. 60305	390[3]	749[3]	88	P/L	2,400	2,400	1,614
Concordia College; St. Paul, Minn. 55104	306[3]	318[3]	56	P/L	2,340	2,340	1,320
Concordia Teachers College, Seward, Neb. 68434	439	530	98	L	2,500	2,500	1,410
Connecticut, University of; Storrs, Conn. 06268	8,642[3]	7,857[3]	1,544	S	540	1,230	1,930
Connecticut College; New London, Conn. 06320	644	1,058	140	P	5,900	5,900	2,180
Converse College; Spartanburg, S.C. 29301	—	732	81	P	5,750[21]	5,750[21]	—
Cooper Union; New York, N.Y. 10003	645	237	50	P	—	—	—
Coppin State College; Baltimore, Md. 21216	528	1,587	122	S	815	1,770	—
Cornell College; Mt. Vernon, Iowa 52314	467[3]	426[3]	67	P	4,220	4,220	1,600
Cornell University[26]; Ithaca, N.Y. 14853	11,059	7,646	1,848	P	5,860	5,860	2,500
Cornish Institute of Allied Arts; Seattle, Wash. 98102	128[3]	162[3]	30	P	2,520	2,520	—
Covenant College; Lookout Mountain, Tenn./Ga. 37350	249	245	30	P/RP	3,380	3,380	1,770
Cranbrook Academy of Art; Bloomfield Hills, Mich. 48013	89	68	9	P	3,000	3,000	2,000
Creative Studies, Center for; Detroit, Mich. 48202	294[3]	252[3]	41	P	2,900	2,900	—

Institution and location	Enrollment		Faculty	Control	Tuition		Rm/Bd
	Male	Female			Res.	Nonres.	
Creighton University; Omaha, Neb. 68178	2,936[3]	1,845[3]	428	P	3,300	3,300	1,638
Culver-Stockton College; Canton, Mo. 63435	173	182	34	P	2,980	2,980	1,700
Cumberland College; Williamsburg, Ky. 40769	861[3]	1,028[3]	102	P	1,600	1,600	1,400
Curry College; Milton, Mass. 02186	389	390	57[8]	P	3,900	3,900	2,200
Daemen College; Buffalo, N.Y. 14226	393	742	81	P	3,430	3,430	1,750
Dakota State College; Madison, S.D. 57042	354[3]	427[3]	47	S	686	1,424	1,300
Dakota Wesleyan University; Mitchell, S.D. 57301	201[3]	295[3]	35	UM	2,065	2,065	1,405
Dallas, University of; Irving, Tex. 75061	879	495	86	P/RC	2,730	2,730	1,870
Dallas Baptist College; Dallas, Tex. 75211	288	293	46	P/B	2,100	2,100	1,380
Dallas Bible College; Dallas, Tex. 75228	145	78	9	P/ID	1,600	1,600	1,675
Dallas Christian College; Dallas, Tex. 75234	75	50	10	P/CC	1,344	1,344	1,200
Dana College; Blair, Neb. 68008	242[3]	261[3]	34	P/AL	2,700	2,700	1,300
Daniel Webster College; Nashua, N.H. 03060	565[3]	155[3]	18	P	3,980	3,980	2,000
Dartmouth College; Hanover, N.H. 03755	2,858	1,257	300	P	5,370	5,370	2,315
David Lipscomb College; Nashville, Tenn. 37203	1,101[3]	1,192[3]	103	CC	1,680	1,680	1,350
Davidson College; Davidson, N.C. 28036	923	456	105	P/Pres	5,540	5,540	n.a.
Davis and Elkins College; Elkins, W. Va. 26241	591	507	67	P/Pres	4,030	4,030	1,920
Dayton, University of; Dayton, Ohio 45469	4,206	2,785	347	P/RC	2,874	2,874	1,540
Defiance College, The; Defiance, Ohio 43512	319[3]	297[3]	50	P/UCC	3,080	3,080	1,385
Delaware, University of; Newark, Del. 19711	6,504[3]	7,345[3]	798	P	940	2,350	1,833
Delaware Law School of Widener University; Wilmington, Del. 19803	581[3]	176[3]	22	P	3,175	3,175	—
Delaware State College; Dover, Del. 19901	987	1,118	141	S	515	1,315	1,480
Delaware Valley College of Science and Agriculture; Doylestown, Pa. 18901	1,023	583	69	P	2,840	2,840	1,358
Delta State University; Cleveland, Miss. 38733	1,011[22]	1,183[22]	157	S	554	1,329	912
Denison University; Granville, Ohio 43023	1,021	990	150	P	4,880	4,880	1,895
Denver, University of; Denver, Colo. 80208	4,072	3,786	463	P	4,530	4,530	1,875
DePaul University; Chicago, Ill. 60604	4,153[3]	3,223[3]	367	P	3,100	3,100	2,250
Goodman School of Drama; Chicago, Ill. 60614	100[3]	100[3]	20	P	3,600	3,600	2,000
DePauw University; Greencastle, Ind. 46135	1,062	1,231	132	P/M	4,808	4,808	2,000
Detroit, University of; Detroit, Mich. 48221	2,300[3]	1,300[3]	245	P/RC	3,840	3,840	1,750
Detroit Bible College; Detroit, Mich. 48018	64	43	13	P/ID	1,970	1,970	800
Detroit College of Business; Dearborn, Mich. 48126	394[3]	898[3]	17	P	2,244	2,244	—
Detroit College of Law; Detroit, Mich. 48201	602	219	29	P	2,600	2,600	—
Detroit Institute of Technology, The; Detroit, Mich. 48201	331[3]	136[3]	27	P	2,100	2,100	—
DeVry Institute of Technology; Chicago, Ill. 60618	2,313[3]	184[3]	44	P	2,425	2,425	—
DeVry Institute of Technology; Dallas, Tex. 75235	774[3]	37[3]	15	P	2,425	2,425	—
DeVry Institute of Technology; Phoenix, Ariz. 85016	2,386[3]	181[3]	36	P	2,425	2,425	—
Dickinson College; Carlisle, Pa. 17013	831	896	110	P	4,500	4,500	1,785
Dickinson School of Law; Carlisle, Pa. 17013	326	149	18	P	2,740	2,740	285[4]
Dickinson State College; Dickinson, N.D. 58601	449[3]	613[3]	74	S	471	1,032	1,200
Dillard University; New Orleans, La. 70122	319	930	90	P[28]	2,400	2,400	1,700
District of Columbia, University of the; Washington, D.C. 20004	2,073[3]	2,091[3]	668	S	165	1,415	2,925
Divine Word College; Epworth, Iowa 52045	90[3]	—	23	P/RC	2,600	2,600	1,100
Doane College; Crete, Neb. 68333	345[3]	345[3]	47	P/UCC	2,995	2,995	1,350
Dominican College of Blauvelt; Orangeburg, N.Y. 10962	164[3]	379[3]	45	P	([29])	([29])	—
Dominican College of San Rafael; San Rafael, Calif. 94901	145[3]	500[3]	39	P/RC	3,300	3,300	2,100
Dordt College; Sioux Center, Iowa 51250	544[3]	674[3]	75	CR	3,050	3,050	1,310
Dowling College; Oakdale, N.Y. 11769	1,500	2,159	66	P	([30])	([30])	1,100[4]
Drake University; Des Moines, Iowa 50311	2,415[3]	2,076[3]	348	P	4,060	4,060	1,930
Drew University; Madison, N.J. 07940	779[3]	853[3]	130	P/UM	4,700[11]	4,700[11]	1,820[11]
Drexel University; Philadelphia, Pa. 19104	5,255	2,128	283	P	3,320	3,320	1,960
Dropsie University, The; Philadelphia, Pa. 19132	42	2	n.a.	P	3,500	3,500	—
Drury College; Springfield, Mo. 65802	528	536	62	P	2,855	2,855	1,580
Dubuque, University of; Dubuque, Iowa 52001	379[3]	248[3]	50	P	3,100	3,100	1,350
Duke University; Durham, N.C. 27706	5,226[3]	3,728[3]	1,407	P	4,740	4,740	2,400
Duquesne University; Pittsburgh, Pa. 15219	2,111[3]	2,323[3]	282	P/RC	3,510	3,510	1,830
D'Youville College; Buffalo, N.Y. 14201	106[3]	1,020[3]	80	P	2,780	2,780	1,550
Earlham College; Richmond, Ind. 47374	435	492	76	P/SOF	4,329	4,329	1,610
East Carolina Univ. *See* North Carolina, Univ. System of							
East Central Oklahoma State University; Ada, Okla. 74820	1,104	1,347	158	S	400	850	1,025
Eastern College; St. Davids, Pa. 19087	243[3]	467[3]	37	B	3,550	3,550	1,550
Eastern Connecticut State College; Willimantic, Conn. 06226	980[3]	1,221[3]	115	S	390	1,030	1,706
Eastern Illinois University; Charleston, Ill. 61920	3,963[3]	4,837[3]	429	S	865	2,077	1,575
Eastern Kentucky University; Richmond, Ky. 40475	6,024	7,644	761	S	580	1,690	3,000

Institution and location	Enrollment		Faculty	Control	Tuition		Rm/Bd
	Male	Female			Res.	Nonres.	
Eastern Mennonite College; Harrisonburg, Va. 22801	360	591	73	P/Men	2,994	2,994	1,401
Eastern Michigan University; Ypsilanti, Mich. 48197	4,261[3]	5,431[3]	622	S	875	2,080	1,646
Eastern Montana College; Billings, Mont. 59101	1,112[3]	2,001[3]	147	S	173	509	1,644
Eastern Nazarene College; Wollaston, Mass. 02170	288[3]	417[3]	50	P/Naz	2,300	2,300	1,650
Eastern New Mexico University; Portales, N.M. 88130	1,286	1,344	143	S	717	1,596	1,250
Eastern Oregan State College; La Grande, Ore. 97850	776[3]	815[3]	100	S	930	930	1,800
Eastern Virginia Medical School; Norfolk, Va. 23501	175	67	104	P	5,500	7,000	3,800
Eastern Washington University; Cheney, Wash. 99004	3,057	3,274	468	S	618	1,983	1,537
East Stroudsburg State College; East Stroudsburg, Pa. 18301	1,706[3]	2,184[3]	218	S	1,208	2,038	1,346
East Tennessee State University; Johnson City, Tenn. 37601	3,830	4,494	525	S	492	1,494	1,410
East Texas Baptist College; Marshall, Tex. 75670	369[3]	352[3]	44	P/B	1,500	1,500	1,435
East Texas State University; Commerce, Tex. 75428	4,028	4,216	341	S	436	1,516	1,464
Eckerd College; St. Petersburg, Fla. 33733	558[3]	456[3]	63	P/PUS	3,995	3,995	1,625
Edgecliff College; Cincinnati, Ohio 45206	88	347	41	P	2,400	2,400	1,600
Edgewood College; Madison, Wis. 53711	95	270	34	P/RC	2,600	2,600	1,375
Edinboro State College; Edinboro, Pa. 16444	2,337[3]	3,259[3]	390	S	1,100	1,930	1,170
Eisenhower College of the Rochester Institute of Technology; Seneca Falls, N.Y. 13148	275	222	48	P	3,879	3,879	2,302
Elizabeth City State University. *See* North Carolina, University System of							
Elizabethtown College; Elizabethtown, Pa. 17022	583[3]	883[3]	100	P/CB	3,825	3,825	1,875
Elmhurst College; Elmhurst, Ill. 60126	1,590[3]		99	P/UCC	3,534[11]	3,534[11]	1,860[11]
Elmira College; Elmira, N.Y. 14901	487[3]	672[3]	65	P	4,100	4,100	1,875
Elon College; Elon College, N.C. 27244	1,223[3]	922[3]	97	P	1,985	1,985	1,091
Embry–Riddle Aeronautical University; Daytona Beach, Fla. 32104	3,900	200	600	P	2,400	2,400	1,800
Emerson College; Boston, Mass. 02116	670	794	78	P	4,360	4,360	2,825
Emmanuel College; Boston, Mass. 02115	3[3]	657[3]	56	RC	3,920	3,920	2,300
Emory and Henry College; Emory, Va. 24327	438[3]	387[3]	55	UM	2,535	2,535	1,455
Emory University; Atlanta, Ga. 30322	4,347	3,157	1,188	P/UM	4,605	4,605	1,695
Emporia State University; Emporia, Kan. 66801	2,411	3,339	228	S	548	1,148	1,450
Erskine College; Due West, S.C. 29639	319[3]	302[3]	43	P/RP	2,950	2,950	1,480
Eureka College; Eureka, Ill. 61530	246[9]	167[9]	26	P/DC	3,050	3,050	1,620
Evangel College; Springfield, Mo. 65802	682	889	67	P/AG	1,940	1,940	1,590
Evansville, University of; Evansville, Ind. 47702	1,344	1,649	193	P/UM	3,249	3,249	1,758
Evergreen State College, The; Olympia, Wash. 98505	941[3]	973[3]	125	S	618	1,983	1,850
Fairfield University; Fairfield, Conn. 06430	1,350[3]	1,350[3]	171	P/RC	3,900	3,900	2,200
Fairleigh Dickinson University; Rutherford, N.J. 07070	3,949[3]	3,248[3]	517	P	3,552	3,552	2,100
Fairmont State College; Fairmont, W. Va. 26554	1,473[3]	1,616[3]	168	S	342	1,282	1,550
Faith Baptist Bible College; Ankeny, Iowa 50021	216	212	24	P/B	1,560	1,560	1,560
Fashion Institute of Technology[31]; New York, N.Y. 10001	506[3]	2,962[3]	166	S	900	1,800	2,180
Fayetteville State U. *See* North Carolina, U. System of							
Federal City College, D.C. *See* District of Columbia, University of the							
Felician College; Lodi, N.J. 07644	—	762[3]	52	P/RC	2,255	2,255	—
Ferris State College; Big Rapids, Mich. 49307	6,312[3]	4,284[3]	500	S	1,011	2,373	1,905
Ferrum College; Ferrum, Va. 24088	885	555	65	P/UM	1,880	1,880	1,110
Findlay College; Findlay, Ohio 45840	497[3]	544[3]	55	P/CG	3,240	3,240	1,478
Fisk University; Nashville, Tenn. 37203	373	668	95	P	3,750	3,750	1,935
Fitchburg State College; Fitchburg, Mass. 01420	1,200	2,400	250	S	600	2,100	n.a.
Flagler College; St. Augustine, Fla. 32084	308	437	35	P	2,200	2,200	900
Florida, University of; Gainesville, Fla. 32611	16,494[3]	11,379[3]	2,759	S	639	2,163	2,200
Florida A&M University; Tallassee, Fla. 32307	2,204[8]	2,211[8]	290	S	675	1,710	1,506
Florida Atlantic University; Boca Raton, Fla. 33431	1,619	1,620	307	S	800	2,307	2,145
Florida Institute of Technology; Melbourne, Fla. 32901	3,315	840	117	P	3,213	3,213	1,860
Florida International University; Miami, Fla. 33199	1,739[3]	1,594[3]	343	S	([32])	([33])	n.a.
Florida Memorial College; Miami, Fla. 33054	400[8]	432[8]	44	P/B	1,440	1,440	1,320
Florida Southern College; Lakeland, Fla. 33802	762	916	84	P/UM	2,430	2,430	1,850
Florida State University; Tallahassee, Fla. 32306	8,130[3]	8,967[3]	1,098	S	735	2,235	2,300
Florida Technical University. *See* Central Florida, University of							
Florida Technological University. *See* Central Florida, University of							
Fontbonne College; St. Louis, Mo. 63105	69	474	61	P/RC	3,200	3,200	1,800
Fordham University; Bronx, N.Y. 10458	4,308[3]	3,943[3]	475	P	3,400	3,400	1,950
Fort Hays State University; Hays, Kan. 67601	2,424[3]	3,220[3]	268	S	637	1,237	1,350
Fort Lauderdale College; Fort Lauderdale, Fla. 33301	770	310	5	P	1,620	1,620	2,300[8]
Fort Lewis College; Durango, Colo. 81301	1,573	1,301	137	S	445	1,959	1,089

Institution and location	Enrollment		Faculty	Control	Tuition		Rm/Bd
	Male	Female			Res.	Nonres.	
Fort Valley State College, The; Fort Valley, Ga. 31030	730[3]	843[3]	152	S	624	1,410	1,215
Fort Wayne Bible College; Fort Wayne, Ind. 46807	179	161	18	P/MC	2,400	2,400	1,600
Fort Wright College; Spokane, Wash. 99204[34]	142	228	32	P/RC	3,240	3,240	2,002
Framingham State College; Framingham, Mass. 01701	946	1,968	160	S	600	2,100	1,466
Francis Marion College; Florence, S.C. 29501	892[3]	827[3]	104	S	590	1,140	950[4]
Franklin and Marshall College; Lancaster, Pa. 17604	1,128[3]	862[3]	132	P	4,950	4,950	1,800
Franklin College of Indiana; Franklin, Ind. 46131	295	272	49	P/B	3,880	3,880	1,675
Franklin Pierce College; Rindge, N.H. 03461	471	329	56	P	3,600	3,600	3,400
Franklin University; Columbus, Ohio 43215	774	606	44	P	(35)	(35)	—
Freed–Hardeman College; Henderson, Tenn. 38340	681	770	70	P/CC	2,030	2,030	n.a.
Free Will Baptist Bible College; Nashville, Tenn. 37205	212[3]	227[3]	30	P/FWB	1,440	1,440	1,540
Fresno Pacific College; Fresno, Calif. 93702	700		35	P/MB	3,000	3,000	2,000
Friends Bible College; Haviland, Kan. 67059	76[3]	60[3]	10	P/SOF	2,600	2,600	1,400
Friends University; Wichita, Kan. 67213	331	297	50	P/SOF	3,000	3,000	1,300
Frostburg State College; Frostburg, Md. 21532	1,401[3]	1,485[3]	188	S	620	1,520	1,492
Furman University; Greenville, S.C. 29613	1,096	976	150	P/B	5,600	5,600	2,192
Gallaudet College; Washington, D.C. 20002	510	706	175	P	684	684	1,725
Gannon College; Erie, Pa. 16541	1,381[3]	935[3]	125	P/RC	2,720	2,720	1,530
Gardner–Webb College; Boiling Springs, N.C. 28017	655[3]	632[3]	73	SB	2,390	2,390	1,386
General Motors Institute; Flint, Mich. 48502	1,542[3]	699[3]	148	P	1,200	1,200	1,080
Geneva College; Beaver Falls, Pa. 15010	792[3]	566[3]	62	P/RP	3,230	3,230	1,740
George Fox College; Newberg, Ore. 97132	314[3]	420[3]	44	P/SOF	2,976	2,976	1,575
George Mason University; Fairfax, Va. 22030	2,700[3]	3,050[3]	404	S	888	1,656	1,320
George Peabody College for Teachers of Vanderbilt University; Nashville, Tenn. 37205	435	770	98	P	4,700	4,700	2,285
Georgetown College; Georgetown, Ky. 40324	520	516	65	P	2,640	2,740	1,740
Georgetown University; Washington, D.C. 20057	6,628[3]	5,153[3]	1,434	P/RC	4,970	4,970	2,000
George Washington University, The; Washington, D.C. 20052	4,902[3]	3,761[3]	1,060	P	3,400	3,400	2,660
George Williams College; Downers Grove, Ill. 60515	237	445	64	P	3,183	3,183	1,590
Georgia, University of; Athens, Ga. 30602	11,993[3]	10,959[3]	2,326	S	753	1,803	1,425
Georgia College; Milledgeville, Ga. 31061	1,461[3]	1,905[3]	172	S	639	1,593	1,146
Georgia Institute of Technology; Atlanta, Ga. 30332	8,078	1,937	657	S	875	2,525	1,980
Southern Technical Institute; Marietta, Ga. 30067	2,200	200	200	S	532	1,318	600[4]
Georgian Court College; Lakewood, N.J. 08701	—	558	79	P/RC	2,300	2,300	1,500
Georgia Southern College; Statesboro, Ga. 30458	2,105	2,505	358	S	597	1,383	1,245
Georgia Southwestern College; Americus, Ga. 31709	764[3]	1,333[3]	124	S	752	1,704	1,556
Georgia State University; Atlanta, Ga. 30303	9,127	11,211	856	S	747	1,647	—
Gettysburg College; Gettysburg, Pa. 17325	978	939	132	P/L	4,720	4,720	1,680
Glassboro State College; Glassboro, N.J. 08028	4,305	5,911	405	S	954	1,658	765
Glenville State College; Glenville, W. Va. 26351	571	643	84	S	364	1,304	1,800
Goddard College; Plainfield, Vt. 05667	656	1,158	49	P	2,460	2,460	2,340
Golden Gate University; San Francisco, Calif. 94105	898	442	66	P	(36)	(36)	—
Goldey Beacom College; Wilmington, Del. 19808	190[3]	617[3]	24	P	1,960	1,960	1,150
Gonzaga University; Spokane, Wash. 99258	1,640[3]	950[3]	167	P/RC	3,490	3,490	1,840
Goodman School of Drama. *See* DePaul University							
Gordon College; Wenham, Mass. 01984	417	522	54	P	3,255	3,255	1,608
Goshen College; Goshen, Ind. 46526	469	635	72	P/Men	2,945	2,945	1,360
Goucher College; Towson, Baltimore, Md. 21204	—	852	78	P	4,650	4,650	2,500
Governors State University; Park Forest South, Ill. 60466	327[3]	414[3]	145	S	558	1,674	—
Grace Bible College; Grand Rapids, Mich. 49509	80[3]	67[3]	8	P/GGF	1,220	1,220	1,710
Grace College; Winona Lake, Ind. 46590	300	355	33	P/FGB	2,432	2,432	1,555
Grace College of the Bible; Omaha, Neb. 68108	210	197	27	P/ID	1,950	1,950	1,480
Graceland College; Lamoni, Iowa 50140	536	576	77	P	2,965	2,965	1,335
Graduate School and University Center (NYC). *See* New York, City University of							
Grambling State University; Grambling, La. 71245	1,571[3]	1,714[3]	192	S	544	1,174	1,260
Grand Canyon College; Phoenix, Ariz. 85017	553[3]	590[3]	34	P/SB	1,952	1,952	1,680
Grand Rapids Baptist College; Grand Rapids, Mich. 49505	408	483	39	P/B	2,290	2,290	1,640
Grand Valley State Colleges; Allendale, Mich. 49401	3,982[3]	2,092[3]	n.a.	S	906	2,002	1,713
Grand View College; Des Moines, Iowa 50316	379[3]	474[3]	70	P/LCA	2,570	2,570	1,650
Gratz College; Philadelphia, Pa. 19141	42[3]	103[3]	18[8]	P	300	300	—
Great Falls, College of; Great Falls, Mont. 59405	300	245	41	P/RC	2,300	2,300	1,240
Great Lakes Bible College; Lansing, Mich. 48901	100	70	10	CC	1,470	1,470	1,430
Green Mountain College; Poultney, Vt. 05764	74	367	35	P	3,700	3,700	2,200
Greensboro College; Greensboro, N.C. 27420	221	417	33	P/M	2,250	2,250	1,390
Greenville College; Greenville, Ill. 62246	366[3]	430[3]	46	P/FM	3,267	3,267	1,700
Grinnell College; Grinnell, Iowa 50112	657	535	100	P	5,140	5,140	1,480

Institution and location	Enrollment		Faculty	Control	Tuition		Rm/Bd
	Male	Female			Res.	Nonres.	
Grove City College; Grove City, Pa. 16127	1,132	1,036	91	P	2,230	2,230	1,420
Guam, University of; Agana, Guam 96910	643	761	183	S	([37])	([38])	2,100
Guilford College; Greensboro, N.C. 27410	700	512	83	P/SOF	2,675	3,225	1,600
Gustavus Adolphus College; St. Peter, Minn. 56082	964[2]	1,258[2]	145	LCA	3,800	3,800	1,300
Gwynedd–Mercy College; Gwynedd Valley, Pa. 19437	62	717	83	P/RC	2,400	2,400	1,650
Hahnemann Medical College; Philadelphia, Pa. 19102	775[3]	897[3]	485	P	10,185	10,185	n.a.
Hamilton College; Clinton, N.Y. 13323	1,005	558	138	P	5,175	5,175	1,850
Hamline University; St. Paul, Minn. 55104	954[3]	641[3]	103	P/UM	3,700	3,700	1,650
Hampden–Sydney College; Hampden–Sydney, Va. 23943	745	—	50	P	4,325	4,325	1,325
Hampshire College; Amherst, Mass. 01002	536	631	72	P	5,625	5,625	2,048
Hampton Institute; Hampton, Va. 23668	1,080	1,609	201	P	2,290	2,290	1,240
Hannibal–LaGrange College; Hannibal, Mo. 63401	170[3]	169[3]	20	P/SB	2,000	2,000	1,200
Hanover College; Hanover, Ind. 47243	491[3]	493[3]	68	P/UP	2,740	2,740	1,540
Harding University; Searcy, Ark. 72143	1,733[3]	1,517[3]	160	P/CC	2,000	2,000	1,400
Hardin–Simmons University; Abilene, Tex. 79698	602	605	87	P/B	2,200	2,200	1,400
Harris–Stowe State College; St. Louis, Mo. 63103	298	763	33	S	225	427	—
Hartford, University of; West Hartford, Conn. 06117	2,576	1,964	293	P	4,060	4,060	2,000
Hartford Graduate Center, The; Hartford, Conn. 06120	1,108	264	18	P	([39])	([39])	—
Hartwick College; Oneonta, N.Y. 13820	605[3]	813[3]	103	P	4,900	4,900	2,000
Harvard University; Cambridge, Mass. 02138	10,498[3]	5,540[3]	n.a.	P	5,300[11]	5,300[11]	2,840[11]
Radcliffe College; Cambridge, Mass. 02138	—	2,246	n.a.	P	5,300	5,300	2,840
Harvey Mudd College. *See* Claremont Colleges							
Hastings College; Hastings, Neb. 68901	342[3]	438[3]	55	P/Pres	2,600	2,600	1,480
Haverford College; Haverford, Pa. 19041	905	32	56	P	5,480	5,480	1,950
Hawaii, University of, at Hilo; Hilo, Hawaii 96720[40]	1,286[3]	1,147[3]	162	S	300	900	1,627
Hawaii, University of, at Manoa; Honolulu, Hawaii 96822[40]	10,204[3]	10,628[3]	1,154	S	450	1,124	1,661
Hawaii Loa College; Kaneohe, Hawaii 96744	118	134	19	P[41]	2,000	2,000	2,000
Hawaii Pacific College; Honolulu, Hawaii 96813[42]	198	133	17	P	1,800	1,800	—
Hebrew College; Brookline, Mass. 02146	16	13	6	P	700	700	—
Heidelberg College; Tiffin, Ohio 44883	392	358	68	P	3,925	3,925	1,580
Hellenic College; Brookline, Mass. 02146	139	37	21	P/GO	2,200	2,200	1,500
Henderson State University; Arkadelphia, Ark. 71923	1,300[3]	1,700[3]	180	S	600	1,200	1,400
Hendrix College; Conway, Ark. 72032	523[3]	461[3]	57	P/M	2,130	2,130	1,130
Herbert H. Lehman College. *See* New York, City University of							
High Point College; High Point, N.C. 27262	562	666	65	P/M	2,300	2,300	1,270
Hillsdale College; Hillsdale, Mich. 49242	558[3]	477[3]	65	P	3,940	3,940	2,000
Hiram College; Hiram, Ohio 44234	478	434	71	P	4,037	4,037	1,375
Hobart and William Smith Colleges; Geneva, N.Y. 14456	1,066[3]	630[3]	119	P	5,500[11]	5,500[11]	2,050[11]
Hofstra University; Hempstead, N.Y. 11550	3,764	2,952	393	P	3,400	3,400	1,922
Hollins College; Hollins College, Va. 24020	9	820	69	P	4,400	4,400	1,850
Holy Cross, College of the; Worcester, Mass. 01610	1,407	1,109	164	P/RC	4,600	4,600	6,850
Holy Family College; Philadelphia, Pa. 19114	68	454	48	P/RC	2,150	2,150	—
Holy Name College; Oakland, Calif. 94619	172	214	48	P	3,370	3,370	2,050
Holy Redeemer College; Waterford, Wis. 53185	49	—	13	RC	1,680	1,680	1,470
Hood College; Frederick, Md. 21701	21	839	95	P	4,060[11]	4,060[11]	2,125
Hope College; Holland, Mich. 49423	1,043[3]	1,024[3]	140	P/RCA	3,920	3,920	1,130
Houghton College; Houghton, N.Y. 14744	508[3]	697[3]	80	P/W	2,790	2,790	1,490
Houston, University of, Central Campus; Houston, Tex. 77004	15,637[3]	12,777[3]	955	S	400	1,260	2,025
Houston, University of, at Clear Lake City; Houston, Tex. 77058	2,347	2,777	190	S	350	1,200	—
Houston, University of, at Victoria; Victoria, Tex. 77901	150	400	27	S	252	1,332	—
Houston Baptist University; Houston, Tex. 77074	709	820	106	P/SB	2,500	2,500	1,800
Howard Payne University; Brownwood, Tex. 76801	560	566	74	P/B	([43])	([43])	1,472
Howard University; Washington, D.C. 20059	4,370	4,402	1,101	P	1,750	1,750	2,392
Humacao College. *See* Puerto Rico, University of							
Humboldt State University; Arcata, Calif. 95521[18]	4,208	3,383	450[8]	S	208	2,368	2,250
Hunter College. *See* New York, City University of							
Huntingdon College; Montgomery, Ala. 36106	248[3]	271[3]	38	P/UM	2,000	2,000	1,650
Huntington College; Huntington, Ind. 46750	250	255	35	BC	3,180	3,180	1,652
Huron College; Huron, S.D. 57350	120	135	26	P/Pres	1,350[11]	1,350[11]	1,650
Husson College; Bangor, Me. 04401	376	324	36	P	3,350	3,350	2,050
Huston–Tillotson College; Austin, Tex. 78702	407	283	36	P	1,400	1,400	1,670
Idaho, The College of; Caldwell, Idaho 83605	248	203	45	P/Pres	3,465	3,465	1,700
Idaho, University of; Moscow, Idaho 83843	4,368[3]	2,455[3]	430	S	490	1,500	1,572
Idaho State University; Pocatello, Idaho 83209	2,703[3]	2,174[3]	313	S	460	1,760	1,365

Institution and location	Enrollment		Faculty	Control	Tuition		Rm/Bd
	Male	Female			Res.	Nonres.	
Illinois, University of; Urbana, Ill. 61801							
Univ. of Illinois at Chicago Circle; Chicago, Ill. 60680	8,993[3]	11,292[3]	1,500	S	885	2,151	—
Univ. of Illinois at the Medical Center; Chicago, Ill. 60612	2,640[3]	2,283[3]	1,079	S	1,137	2,499	—
Univ. of Illinois at Urbana–Champaign, Urbana, Ill. 61801	20,437[3]	13,939[3]	6,785	S	634	902	1,898
Illinois Benedictine College; Lisle, Ill. 60532	646	422	65	P	3,238	3,238	1,900
Illinois College; Jacksonville, Ill. 62650	414	312	45	P	2,550	2,550	1,550
Illinois College of Optometry; Chicago, Ill. 60616	508[3]	88[3]	27	P	1,450	1,450	2,079
Illinois College of Podiatric Medicine; Chicago, Ill. 60610	571	68	26	P	5,200	5,200	—
Illinois State University; Normal, Ill. 61761	6,801	8,549	964	S	863	2,055	1,849
Illinois Wesleyan University; Bloomington, Ill. 61701	731	916	125	P	4,380	4,380	1,915
Immaculata College; Immaculata, Pa. 19345	—	500	52	P/RC	2,500	2,500	1,650
Incarnate Word College; San Antonio, Tex. 78209	189	769	78	P/RC	2,400	2,400	1,511
Indiana Central University; Indianapolis, Ind. 46227	415	643	87	P/UM	3,200	3,200	1,640
Indiana Institute of Technology; Fort Wayne, Ind. 46803	422	80	26	P	2,565	2,565	1,680
Indiana State University; Terre Haute, Ind. 47809	5,901[3]	6,155[3]	661	S	930	2,015	1,275
Indiana University; Bloomington, Ind. 47405	13,776[3]	12,635[3]	1,500	S	744	1,824	1,398
Indiana Univ. at Kokomo; Kokomo, Ind. 46901	500	554	64	Mun	780	1,770	—
Indiana Univ. at South Bend; South Bend, Ind. 46615	2,473	3,327	147	S	847	1,920	—
Indiana University Northwest; Gary, Ind. 46408	501	904	115	S	780	1,020	—
Indiana University Southeast; New Albany, Ind. 47150	704	814	90	S	702	1,536	—
I.U.–Purdue U. at Fort Wayne; Fort Wayne, Ind. 46805	1,641	1,505	280	S	630	1,404	—
I.U.–Purdue U. at Indianapolis; Indianapolis, Ind. 46202	10,984[3]	10,532[3]	1,274	S	780	1,770	720
Indiana University of Pennsylvania; Indiana, Pa. 15701	4,418[3]	6,045[3]	600	S	950	1,780	1,210
Instituto Tecnológico; Monterrey, Mexico	1,879[3]	6,521[3]	223	P	2,000	2,000	2,000
Insurance, The College of; New York, N.Y. 10038	233[3]	86[3]	30	P	3,300	3,300	1,500
Inter American University of Puerto Rico; San Juan, P.R. 00936							
Metropolitan Campus; Hato Rey, P.R. 00919	3,183[3]	4,632[3]	206	P	(44)	(44)	—
San Germán Campus; San Germán, P.R. 00753	2,531	3,011	145	P	1,340	1,340	1,050
San Juan Campus; San Juan, P.R. 00919	3,979[8]	4,865[8]	191	P	(45)	(45)	—
School of Law; Santurce, P.R. 00910	586	256	25	P	3,000	3,000	—
International Training, The School for; Brattleboro, Vt. 05301	298[22]		43	P	4,000	4,000	(46)
Iona College; New Rochelle, N.Y. 10801	3,285	2,297	170[8]	P	3,280	3,280	2,100
Iowa, University of; Iowa City, Iowa 52240	11,780	10,443	1,502	S	830	1,890	1,513
Iowa State University; Ames, Iowa 50011	14,305[3]	9,181[3]	1,816	S	816	1,881	1,467
Iowa Wesleyan College; Mount Pleasant, Iowa 52641	280	428	48	P	3,175	3,175	1,266
Ithaca College; Ithaca, N.Y. 14850	1,926	2,298	292	P	4,584	4,584	2,074
Jackson College for Women. *See* Tufts University							
Jackson State University; Jackson, Miss. 39217	3,007	3,920	383	S	700	825	1,237
Jacksonville State University; Jacksonville, Ala. 36265	2,391[3]	2,625[3]	340	S	600	600	1,200
Jacksonville University; Jacksonville, Fla. 32211	1,173	924	103	P	2,700	2,700	1,830
James Madison University; Harrisonburg, Va. 22801	3,857[3]	4,530[3]	419	S	1,026	1,666	1,800
Jamestown College; Jamestown, N.D. 58401	260[3]	284[3]	40	P/Pres	2,730	2,730	1,375
Jarvis Christian College; Hawkins, Tex. 75765	285	284	31	P/DC	n.a.	n.a.	1,434
Jersey City State College; Jersey City, N.J. 07305	2,179[3]	2,289[3]	300	S	900	1,600	1,300
John Brown University; Siloam Springs, Ark. 72761	350[3]	352[3]	47	P/ID	2,100	2,100	1,500
John Carroll University; University Heights, Ohio 44118	1,496[3]	1,082[3]	172	P/RC	3,200	3,200	1,700
John F. Kennedy University; Orinda, Calif. 94598	202[9]	234[9]	4	P	2,343	2,343	—
John Jay College of Criminal Justice. *See* New York, City University of							
John Marshall Law School, The; Chicago, Ill. 60604	751[2]	227[2]	45	P	3,360	3,360	—
Johns Hopkins University, The; Baltimore, Md. 21218	3,225	1,698	1,339	P	5,075	5,075	2,400
Johnson and Wales College; Providence, R.I. 02903	1,650[3]	1,350[3]	110	P	2,985	2,985	1,695
Johnson C. Smith University; Charlotte, N.C. 28216	621	687	82	P	1,700	1,700	1,276
Johnston College, Calif. *See* Redlands, University of							
Jones College; Jacksonville, Fla. 32211	959		15	P	1,450	1,450	—
Jones College; Orlando, Fla. 32803	1,288		9	P	1,093	1,093	—
Judson College; Elgin, Ill. 60120	227	226	22	P/B	2,640	2,640	1,720
Judson College; Marion, Ala. 36756	—	418	28	P/B	1,760	1,760	3,560
Juilliard School, The; New York, N.Y. 10023	506	386	119	P	3,600	3,600	n.a.
Juniata College; Huntingdon, Pa. 16652	707[3]	567[3]	69	P	4,065[11]	4,065[11]	1,845[11]
Kalamazoo College; Kalamazoo, Mich. 49007	749	691	88	P	4,794	4,794	1,953
Kansas, University of; Lawrence, Kan. 66045	12,627[3]	11,498[3]	1,296	S	770	1,850	1,500
Kansas City Art Institute; Kansas City, Mo. 64111	286	240	47	P	4,200	4,200	935[4]

Institution and location	Enrollment Male	Enrollment Female	Faculty	Control	Tuition Res.	Tuition Nonres.	Rm/Bd
Kansas City College of Osteopathic Medicine; Kansas City, Mo. 64124	542[3]	75[3]	57	P	8,250	8,250	—
Kansas Newman College; Wichita, Kan. 67213	219[3]	239[3]	26	P/RC	2,340	2,340	1,490
Kansas State Coll. of Pittsburg. *See* Pittsburgh State Univ.							
Kansas State University, Manhattan, Kan. 66506	10,476[3]	8,143[3]	837	S	696	1,200	1,500
Kansas Wesleyan University; Salina, Kan. 67401	212	160	33	P/UM	2,455	2,455	870
Kean College of New Jersey; Union, N.J. 07208	2,510	3,403	360	S	690	1,350	1,775
Kearney State College; Kearney, Neb. 68847	1,914	2,370	227	S	570	1,020	1,136
Keene State College; Keene, N.H. 03431	860	1,305	244	S	800	2,500	1,485
Keller Graduate School of Management; Chicago, Ill. 60606	745	235	70	P	4,800	4,800	—
Kendall College; Evanston, Ill. 60201	131	187	25	P	3,234	3,234	1,783
Kendall School of Design; Grand Rapids, Mich. 49503	148	212	14	P	2,520	2,520	—
Kent State University; Kent, Ohio 44242	5,953	6,069	723	S	1,082	2,282	1,614
Kentucky, University of; Lexington, Ky. 40506	9,893	7,890	1,431	S	682	2,032	1,700
Kentucky Christian College; Grayson, Ky. 41143	198	210	17	P/CC	(47)	(47)	1,450
Kentucky State University; Frankfort, Ky. 40601	1,083	1,097	125	S	560	1,470	1,354
Kentucky Wesleyan College; Owensboro, Ky. 42301	267	354	50	P/UM	2,560	2,560	1,460
Kenyon College; Gambier, Ohio 43022	816	618	100	P	5,190	5,190	2,075
Keuka College; Keuka Park, N.Y. 14478	4	545	42	P	4,500	4,500	1,600
King College; Bristol, Tenn. 37620	123	83	25	P/PUS	2,660	2,660	1,420
King of Prussia Graduate Center. *See* Pennsylvania State University							
King's College; Wilkes–Barre, Pa. 18711	955	618	99	P	2,800	2,800	1,600
King's College, The; Briarcliff Manor, N.Y. 10510	339[3]	490[3]	46	P	3,410	3,410	1,540
Kirksville College of Osteopathic Medicine; Kirksville, Mo. 63501	433	67	90	P	10,000	10,000	3,330
Knox College; Galesburg, Ill. 61401	517[3]	412[3]	90	P	4,310	4,310	1,640
Knoxville College; Knoxville, Tenn. 37921	335	265	38	P/UP	2,400	2,400	1,635
Kutztown State College; Kutztown, Pa. 19530	1,477	2,055	343	S	1,100	1,930	1,374
Ladycliff College; Highland Falls, N.Y. 10928	19	356	49	P	2,950	2,950	1,850
Lafayette College; Easton, Pa. 18042	1,224	786	157	P	5,225	5,225	1,975
LaGrange College; LaGrange, Ga. 30240	261	327	40	P/M	1,890	1,890	1,350
Lake Erie College; Painesville, Ohio 44077	129	454	50	P	5,980[21]	5,980[21]	—
Lake Forest College; Lake Forest, Ill. 60045	478	471	87	P	4,615	4,615	1,630
Lake Forest School of Management; Lake Forest, Ill. 60045	252	77	25	P	1,700	1,700	—
Lakeland College; Sheboygan, Wis. 53081	213	194	29	P/UCC	3,220	3,220	2,125
Lake Superior State College; Sault Ste. Marie, Mich. 49783	1,251[3]	1,058[3]	106	S	870	1,788	1,740
Lamar University; Beaumont, Tex. 77710	5,683	6,027	441	S	400	1,200	1,250
Lambuth College; Jackson, Tenn. 38301	311[3]	453[3]	51	P/UM	2,300	2,300	1,350
Lander College; Greenwood, S.C. 29646	501[3]	864[3]	85	S	700	1,300	1,420
Lane College; Jackson, Tenn. 38301	343	314	36	P/CME	1,934	1,934	1,360
Langston University; Langston, Okla. 73050	613	433	60	S	482	1,146	1,200
La Roche College, Pittsburgh, Pa. 15237	486	817	37	P/RC	1,225	1,225	900
La Salle College; Philadelphia, Pa. 19141	2,383[3]	1,581[3]	195	P/RC	3,320	3,320	2,130
La Verne, University of; La Verne, Calif. 91750	863		84	P/CB	4,159	4,159	2,300
Lawrence Institute of Technology; Southfield, Mich. 48075	4,249[8]	612[8]	56	P	460	460	—
Lawrence University; Appleton, Wis. 54912	557	549	115	P	4,740	4,740	1,440
Lebanon Valley College; Annville, Pa. 17003	454	444	75	P/UM	3,720	3,720	1,740
Lee College; Cleveland, Tenn. 37311	746	696	70	P/CG	1,800	1,800	1,250
Lehigh University; Bethlehem, Pa. 18015	3,676[3]	1,232[3]	347	P	5,130	5,130	2,070
LeMoyne-Owen College; Memphis, Tenn. 38126	343[9]	618	47	P	(48)	(48)	—
Lenoir–Rhyne College; Hickory, N.C. 28601	487[3]	693[3]	85	P/LCA	2,775	2,775	1,400
Lesley College; Cambridge, Mass. 02138	30[9]	979[9]	56	P	3,700	3,700	2,230
LeTourneau College; Longview, Tex. 75607	745	82	64	P	2,650	2,650	1,630
Lewis and Clark College; Portland, Ore. 97219	852[3]	1,035[3]	124	P/Pres	4,306	4,306	1,694
Lewis–Clark State College; Lewiston, Idaho 83501	663[3]	821[3]	85	S	380	1,430	1,850
Lewis University; Romeoville, Ill. 60441	1,075	737	109	P/RC	3,360	3,360	1,650
Limestone College; Gaffney, S.C. 29340	142[3]	247[3]	33	P	2,670	2,670	1,580
Lincoln Christian College; Lincoln, Ill. 62656	402	223	33	P/CC	1,838	1,838	1,194
Lincoln Memorial University; Harrogate, Tenn. 37752	501[3]	584[3]	42	P	1,920	1,920	1,380
Lincoln University; Jefferson City, Mo. 65101	1,077	998	157	S	400	800	1,170
Lincoln University; Lincoln University, Pa. 19352	480	462	71	P	1,430	1,930	1,650
Lindenwood Colleges, The; St. Charles, Mo. 63301	952		60	P	2,975	2,975	2,225
Linfield College; McMinnville, Ore. 97128	472	405	65	P	3,370	3,370	1,500
Livingstone College; Salisbury, N.C. 28144	495	407	49	P/AME	2,065	2,065	1,530
Livingston University; Livingston, Ala. 35470	556	638	74	S	525	525	1,200
Lock Haven State College; Lock Haven, Pa. 17745	1,115[3]	1,301[3]	170	S	1,100	1,930	1,208

Institution and location	Enrollment Male	Enrollment Female	Faculty	Control	Tuition Res.	Tuition Nonres.	Rm/Bd
Logan College of Chiropractic; Chesterfield, Mo. 63017	483	104	n.a.	P	3,660	3,660	6,740
Loma Linda University; Loma Linda, Calif. 92350	2,602[3]	2,681[3]	665	P/SDA	3,615	3,615	2,200
La Sierra Campus; Riverside, Calif. 92515	900[3]	991[3]	141	P/SDA	4,125	4,125	1,950
Long Island University Center; Greenvale, N.Y. 11548							
Brooklyn Center; Brooklyn, N.Y. 11201	2,245	2,310	300[8]	P	4,000	4,000	—
C.W. Post Center; Greenvale, N.Y. 11548	3,300	3,200	369	P	3,566	3,566	2,200
Southampton College; Southampton, N.Y. 11968	598	512	68	P	3,880	3,880	2,400
Longwood College; Farmville, Va. 23901	506	1,720	175	S	2,596	3,096	1,838
Loras College; Dubuque, Iowa 52001	1,045[3]	726[3]	149	P/RC	3,190	3,190	1,625
Loretto Heights College; Denver, Colo. 80236	161	652	75	P	3,900	3,900	2,170
Los Angeles Baptist College; Newhall, Calif. 91322	167[3]	192[3]	34	P	2,340	2,340	1,514
Los Angeles College of Chiropractic; Glendale, Calif. 91205	458	87	33	P	4,333	4,333	3,700
Louisianna College; Pineville, La. 71360	511	617	52	P/SB	1,020	1,020	1,270
Louisiana State University; Baton Rouge, La. 70803	12,651	11,157	1,069	S	281	746	670
LSU in Shreveport; Shreveport, La. 71115	1,485	1,716	137	S	480	1,410	—
LSU Medical Center at New Orleans; New Orleans, La. 70112	1,349	1,045	800	S	([49])	([50])	1,500[4]
Louisiana Tech University; Ruston, La. 71272	4,238[3]	3,093[3]	384	S	600	1,200	1,600
Louisville, University of; Louisville, Ky. 40292	6,233[3]	4,570[3]	923	S	570	2,000	1,275
Lowell, University of; Lowell, Mass. 01854	4,398	2,585	415	S	700	2,300	2,000
Loyola College; Baltimore, Md. 21210	1,438[3]	1,084[3]	119	P/RC	2,775	2,775	1,750
Loyola Marymount University; Los Angeles, Calif. 90045	2,478	2,346	221	P	3,558	3,558	1,784
Loyola University, New Orleans; New Orleans, La. 70118	2,250[3]	2,285[3]	187	P/RC	2,725	2,725	1,850
Loyola University of Chicago; Chicago, Ill. 60611	4,263[3]	4,208[3]	660	P/RC	3,380	3,380	1,700
Lubbock Christian College; Lubbock, Tex. 79407	562	547	59	P/CC	1,950	1,950	1,216
Lutheran Bible Institute of Seattle; Issaquah, Wash. 98027	128[3]	154[3]	15	P/L	1,443	1,443	1,526
Luther College; Decorah, Iowa 52101	866	1,148	126	P/AL	4,250	4,250	1,300
Lycoming College; Williamsport, Pa. 17701	649	429	65	P/UM	3,300	3,300	1,600
Lynchburg College; Lynchburg, Va. 24501	690[3]	948[3]	113	P	3,450[11]	3,450[11]	1,850[11]
Lyndon State College; Lyndonville, Vt. 05851	486	386	65	S	1,120	2,700	2,100
Macalester College; St. Paul, Minn. 55105	887[3]	896[3]	120	P	4,725[11]	4,725[11]	1,800[11]
MacMurray College; Jacksonville, Ill. 62650	225	431	53	P/UM	3,710	3,710	1,550
Madison College, Va. *See* James Madison University							
Madonna College; Livonia, Mich. 48150	253[3]	881[3]	79	P	1,508	1,508	1,690
Maine, Univ. of, at Farmington; Farmington, Me. 04938	427[3]	1,136[3]	85	S	930	2,900	1,864
Maine, Univ. of, at Fort Kent; Fort Kent, Me. 04743	198	133	21	S	770	2,625	1,650
Maine, Univ. of, at Machias; Machias, Me. 04654	201[3]	242[3]	35	S	930	2,900	1,950
Maine, Univ. of, at Orono; Orono, Me. 04469	5,712[3]	4,494[3]	800	S	895	2,688	1,855
Maine, Univ. of, at Presque Isle; Presque Isle, Maine 04769	391	494	55	S	800	2,622	1,650
Maine Maritime Academy; Castine, Me. 04421	627[3]	16[3]	43	S	1,621	2,920	n.a.
Malone College; Canton, Ohio 44709	219[3]	244[3]	40	P/SOF	3,193	3,193	1,675
Manchester College; North Manchester, Ind. 46962	587[3]	605[3]	71	P/CB	2,690	2,690	1,400
Manhattan Christian College; Manhattan, Kan. 66502	101[3]	72[3]	15	P/CC	1,420	1,420	1,780
Manhattan College; Riverdale, Bronx, N.Y. 10471	2,743[3]	952[3]	227	P	3,150	3,150	n.a.
Manhattan School of Music; New York, N.Y. 10027	283	266	19	P	3,350	3,350	—
Manhattanville College; Purchase, N.Y. 10577	259[3]	593[3]	82	P	4,880[11]	4,880[11]	2,500[11]
Mankato State University. *See* Minnesota State College System							
Mannes College of Music; New York, N.Y. 10021	116	81	100[51]	P	3,200	3,200	—
Mansfield State College; Mansfield, Pa. 16933	940	1,034	200	S	1,100	1,930	1,460
Marian College; Indianapolis, Ind. 46222	165	335	52	P/RC	2,640	2,640	1,500
Marian College of Fond du Lac; Fond du Lac, Wis. 54935	50	392	45	P/RC	2,650	2,650	1,380
Marietta College; Marietta, Ohio 45750	860[3]	486[3]	105	P	4,500	4,500	1,650
Marion College; Marion, Ind. 46952	395	708	25[8]	P/W	2,880	2,880	1,642
Marist College; Poughkeepsie, N.Y. 12601	938	775	88	P	3,120	3,120	2,000
Marlboro College; Marlboro, Vt. 05344	97	126	21	P	4,970	4,970	2,290
Marquette University; Milwaukee, Wis. 53233	4,957	3,599	535	P	3,620	3,620	1,400
Marshall University; Huntington, W. Va. 25701	5,168[3]	6,362[3]	373	S	375	1,365	1,905
Mars Hill College; Mars Hill, N.C. 28754	705[3]	905[3]	104	P	2,710	2,710	1,235
Mary Baldwin College; Staunton, Va. 24401	—	839	50	P/Pres	3,900	3,900	2,465
Mary College; Bismarck, N.D. 58501	211[3]	491[3]	76	P/RC	2,090	2,090	1,292
Marycrest College; Davenport, Iowa 52804	99[3]	526[3]	60	P	2,925	2,925	1,520
Marygrove College; Detroit, Mich. 48221	168[3]	790[3]	46	P/RC	3,040	3,040	1,980
Mary Hardin–Baylor, University of; Belton, Tex. 76513	318	689	62	P/B	2,016	2,016	1,330
Maryland, University of (System); College Park, Md. 20742							
UM, Baltimore County (UMBC); Catonsville, Md. 21228	2,550[3]	2,650[3]	330	S	860	2,536	2,000

Institution and location	Enrollment		Faculty	Control	Tuition		Rm/Bd
	Male	Female			Res.	Nonres.	
UM, University College (UMUC); College Park, Md. 20742	379	266	n.a.	S	([52])	([52])	—
UM at Baltimore (UMAB); Baltimore, Md. 21201	1,820[3]	2,007[3]	721	S	705	2,550	855
UM at College Park (UMCP); College Park, Md. 20742	14,780[3]	12,893[3]	2,065	S	842	2,562	2,090
UM Eastern Shore (UMES); Princess Anne, Md. 21853	574[3]	543[3]	75	S	570	1,855	1,570
Maryland Institute, College of Art; Baltimore, Md. 21217	325[3]	495[3]	45	P	3,750	3,750	2,800
Marylhurst Educational Center; Marylhurst, Ore. 97036	28[3]	72[3]	35	P	2,100	2,100	—
Marymount College of Kansas; Salina, Kan. 67401	277	509	46	P/RC	2,140	2,140	1,360
Marymount College; Tarrytown, N.Y. 10591	—	770	64	P	3,975	3,975	2,700
Marymount College of Virginia; Arlington, Va. 22207	27	993	54	P/RC	3,100	3,100	1,900
Marymount Manhattan College; New York, N.Y. 10021	23[3]	875[3]	44	P	3,150	3,150	—
Maryville College; Maryville, Tenn. 37801	344[3]	300[3]	47	P/UP	2,800	2,800	1,600
Maryville College; St. Louis, Mo. 63141	160	467	59	P	3,230	3,230	1,750
Mary Washington College; Fredericksburg, Va. 22401	325[3]	1,673[3]	125	S	870	1,715	1,712
Marywood College; Scranton, Pa. 18509	421[3]	1,802[3]	157	P/RC	1,950	1,950	1,500
Massachusetts at Amherst, Univ. of; Amherst, Mass. 01003	12,500[3]	11,500[3]	2,000	S	525	2,750	1,697
Massachusetts at Boston, Univ. of; Boston, Mass. 02125	3,429	3,430	359	S	625	2,150	—
Massachusetts College of Art; Boston, Mass. 02215	391[3]	720[3]	64	S	600	2,100	—
Massachusetts College of Optometry. *See* New England College of Optometry							
Massachusetts Institute of Technology; Cambridge, Mass. 02139	7,057	1,447	994	P	6,200	6,200	2,900
Massachusetts Maritime Academy; Buzzards Bay, Mass. 02532	835	19	48	S	600	600	2,100
Mayo Medical School; Rochester, Minn. 55901[53]	126	39	25	P	4,150	6,000	4,300
Mayville State College; Mayville, N.D. 58257	275[3]	388[3]	42	S	589	1,150	1,071
McKendree College; Lebanon, Ill. 62254	397[3]	403[3]	37	P/M	2,700	2,700	1,500
McMurry College; Abilene, Tex. 79697	791	623	59	P/M	2,145	2,145	1,270
McNeese State University; Lake Charles, La. 70609	1,730[3]	1,943[3]	258	S	452	1,082	1,360
McPherson College; McPherson, Kan. 67460	265[3]	215[3]	32	P/CB	2,660[11]	2,660[11]	1,590[11]
Medaille College; Buffalo, N.Y. 14214	224	343	30	P	2,425	2,425	n.a.
Medical College of Georgia; Augusta, Ga. 30912	1,284[3]	1,022[3]	600	S	708	2,052	3,555
Medical College of Ohio at Toledo; Toledo, Ohio 43699	288[3]	126[3]	283	S	2,660	3,260	—
Medical College of Wisconsin, The; Milwaukee, Wis. 53226	517[3]	164[3]	514	P	5,750	9,500[54]	3,696
Medical Univ. of South Carolina; Charleston, S.C. 29403	1,330	1,160	713	S	1,022	2,270	2,250
Medicine and Dentistry, College of, of New Jersey; Newark, N.J. 07103	1,188[3]	474[3]	589	S	4,500	5,625	—
New Jersey Dental School; Newark, N.J. 07103	211	43	35	S	4,500	5,625	—
New Jersey Medical School; Newark, N.J. 07103	441[3]	150[3]	301	S	4,500	5,625	—
New Jersey School of Osteopathic Medicine; Camden, N.J. 08103	67	14	46	S	4,500	5,625	3,300
Meharry Medical College; Nashville, Tenn. 37208	584	485	239	P	5,000	5,000	2,500
Memphis Academy of Arts, The; Memphis, Tenn. 38112	111[3]	76[3]	17	P	1,900	1,900	1,600
Memphis State University; Memphis, Tenn. 38152	5,861[3]	5,724[3]	757	S	516	1,600	1,765
Menlo College; Menlo Park, Calif. 94025	452[3]	221[3]	50	P	4,530	4,530	2,490
Mercer University; Macon, Ga. 31207	2,500[3]	2,000[3]	200	P/SB	2,406	3,006	1,497
Mercer University in Atlanta, Ga. 30319	779	664	56	P/B	2,394	2,394	—
Southern School of Pharmacy; Atlanta, Ga. 30312	237	115	29	P/B	3,300	3,300	—
Mercy College; Dobbs Ferry, N.Y. 10522	2,359	2,587	130	P	([55])	([55])	—
Mercy College of Detroit; Detroit, Mich. 48219	244	1,094	85	P/RC	2,140	2,640	1,300
Mercyhurst College; Erie, Pa. 16546	437[3]	639[3]	69	P/RC	3,280	3,280	1,650
Meredith College; Raleigh, N.C. 27611	—	1,356	88	P/B	2,350	2,350	1,150
Meredith Manor School of Horsemanship; Waverly, W. Va. 26184	21	152	25	P	8,052[21]	8,052[21]	—
Merrimack College; North Andover, Mass. 01845	1,187[3]	855[3]	118	P/RC	3,200	3,200	2,050
Mesa College; Grand Junction, Colo. 81501	1,345[3]	1,104[3]	120	S	494	2,062	1,550
Messiah College; Grantham, Pa. 17027	454[3]	705[3]	60	P/BC	3,200	3,200	1,740
Methodist College; Fayetteville, N.C. 28301	344	358	60	P/M	1,800	1,800	1,490
Metropolitan State College; Denver, Colo. 80204	3,970	4,335	425	S	627	2,299	—
Metropolitan State University, Minn. *See* Minnesota State University System							
Miami, University of; Coral Gables, Fla. 33124	10,606[3]	7,883[3]	1,215	P	4,530	4,530	2,017
Miami Christian College; Miami, Fla. 33167	86[3]	82[3]	10	P/ID	1,900	1,900	1,600
Miami University; Oxford, Ohio 45056	7,135[3]	7,623[3]	n.a.	S	1,210	1,210	1,590
Michigan, The University of; Ann Arbor, Mich. 48109	17,872	12,511	n.a.	S	1,288	3,788	2,077
Univ. of Michigan—Dearborn; Dearborn, Mich. 48128	3,584[3]	2,816[3]	160	S	964	2,960	—
Univ. of Michigan—Flint; Flint, Mich. 48503	966	1,124	122	S	882	2,862	—
Michigan State University; East Lansing, Mich. 48824	21,085[3]	19,787[3]	3,514	S	1,327[11]	2,880[11]	1,860
Michigan Technological University; Houghton, Mich. 49931	5,594[3]	1,567[3]	361	S	1,059	2,313	1,895

Institution and location	Enrollment		Faculty	Control	Tuition		
	Male	Female			Res.	Nonres.	Rm/Bd
Mid-America Nazarene College; Olathe, Kan. 66061	499[3]	562[3]	50	P/Naz	1,862	1,862	1,450
Middlebury College; Middlebury, Vt. 05753	1,002	920	145	P	7,800[21]	7,800[21]	—
Middle Tennessee State Univ.; Murfreesboro, Tenn. 37132	3,619	3,611	400	S	472	1,474	1,012
Midland Lutheran College; Fremont, Neb. 68025	370[3]	460[3]	61	P	3,200	3,200	1,460
Mid-South Bible College; Memphis, Tenn. 38112	77	30	8	P	1,824	1,824	1,570
Midwestern State University; Wichita Falls, Tex. 76308	1,240[3]	1,245[3]	143	S	120	1,200	1,020
Miles College; Birmingham, Ala. 35208	371	515	74	P/CME	1,700	1,700	1,310
Millersville State College; Millersville, Pa. 17551	2,457[3]	3,563[3]	267	S	950	1,780	1,253
Milligan College; Milligan College, Tenn. 37682	361[3]	411[3]	43	P/CC	2,072	2,072	1,800
Millikin University; Decatur, Ill. 62522	678[3]	680[3]	97	P	3,925	3,925	1,655
Millsaps College; Jackson, Miss. 39210	515	447	63	P/M	3,000	3,000	1,240
Mills College; Oakland, Calif. 94613	23[3]	865[3]	67[8]	P	4,150	4,150	2,350
Milton College; Milton, Wis. 53563	269[3]	222[3]	28	P	3,300	3,300	1,750
Milton S. Hershey Medical Center. *See* Pennsylvania State University							
Milwaukee School of Engineering; Milwaukee, Wis. 53201	1,330	70	108	P	3,600	3,600	1,500
Minneapolis College of Art and Design; Minneapolis, Minn. 55404	256	284	65	P	3,400	3,400	950[4]
Minnesota, The University of; Minneapolis, Minn. 55455	27,476	22,784	4,596	S	927	2,550	2,030
Univ. of Minnesota, Duluth; Duluth, Minn. 55812	3,627[3]	3,228[3]	370	S	864	2,376	1,750
Univ. of Minnesota, Morris; Morris, Minn. 56267	769[2]	681[2]	103	S	870	2,394	1,500
Minnesota Bible College; Rochester, Minn. 55901	60	55	10	CC	1,425	1,425	1,300
Minnesota State University System; St. Paul, Minn. 55101							
Bemidji State University; Bemidji, Minn. 56601	2,078[2]	1,837[2]	200	S	550	1,130	1,250
Mankato State University; Mankato, Minn. 56001	3,798	3,913	533	S	547	1,087	1,148
Metropolitan State University; St. Paul, Minn. 55101	897[2]	1,096[2]	22	S	750	1,305	—
Moorhead State University; Moorhead, Minn. 56560	2,451[3]	2,890[3]	279	S	547	1,087	1,156
St. Cloud State University; St. Cloud, Minn. 56301	3,996	4,121	564	S	547	1,087	1,176
Southwest State University; Marshall, Minn. 56258	939[3]	727[3]	104	S	550	1,090	1,200
Winona State University; Winona, Minn. 55987	2,029	2,877	201	S	585	1,164	1,236
Minot State College; Minot, N.D. 58701	750	1,332	n.a.	S	570	1,128	1,200
Mississippi, The University of; University, Miss. 38677	4,835[3]	3,718[3]	500	S	954	1,804	1,702
Medical Center; Jackson, Miss. 39216	941[3]	571[3]	414	S	730	1,550	—
Mississippi College; Clinton, Miss. 39058	1,483	1,534	n.a.	P/B	1,800	1,800	1,270
Mississippi State University; Starkville, Miss. 39759	5,381	3,434	651	S	870	1,720	1,700
Mississippi University for Women; Columbus, Miss. 39701	—	1,700[3]	161	S	674	1,499	1,564
Mississippi Valley State University; Itta Bena, Miss. 38941	1,521	1,707	151	S	710	1,535	1,133
Missouri, University of; Columbia, Mo. 65201							
Univ. of Missouri—Columbia; Columbia, Mo. 65211	12,642[3]	10,604[3]	n.a.	S	774	2,322	1,450
Univ. of Missouri—Kansas City; Kansas City, Mo. 64110	3,177[3]	2,610[3]	490	S	856	2,404	1,600
Univ. of Missouri—Rolla; Rolla, Mo. 65401	3,868[3]	849[3]	328	S	899	2,598	1,699
Univ. of Missouri—St. Louis; St. Louis, Mo. 63121	3,223[3]	2,732[3]	333	S	645	1,605	—
Missouri Baptist College; St. Louis, Mo. 63141	204[3]	230[3]	20	SB	2,000	2,000	1,600
Missouri Institute of Technology; Kansas City, Mo. 64114	915[3]	37[3]	18	P	2,425	2,425	—
Missouri Southern State College; Joplin, Mo. 64801	1,297	1,271	158	S	440	880	1,130
Missouri Valley College; Marshall, Mo. 65340	223[3]	111[3]	32	P/Pres	2,644	2,644	1,660
Missouri Western State College; St. Joseph, Mo. 64507	1,411	1,415	138	S	510	960	1,200
Mobile College; Mobile, Ala. 36613	293[3]	552[3]	52	P/SB	1,790	1,790	1,480
Molloy College; Rockville Centre, N.Y. 11570	47	1,416	110	P/RC	2,800	2,800	—
Monmouth College; Monmouth, Ill. 61462	340	305	65	P/Pres	3,930	3,930	1,820
Monmouth College; West Long Branch, N.J. 07764	952[3]	964[3]	165	P	3,830	3,830	920
Montana, University of; Missoula, Mont. 59812	3,745[2]	3,257[2]	400	S	625	1,993	1,629
Montana College of Mineral Science and Technology; Butte, Mont. 59701	719	249	65	S	460	1,480	1,613
Montana State University; Bozeman, Mont. 59715	5,702[3]	4,407[3]	537	S	572	1,940	1,923
Montclair State College; Upper Montclair, N.J. 07043	2,994	4,489	582	S	736	1,440	1,600
Monterey Institute of Foreign Studies, Calif. *See* Monterey Institute of International Studies							
Monterey Institute of International Studies; Monterey, Calif. 93933	225[3]	280[3]	29	P	4,659	4,659	3,300
Montevallo, University of; Montevallo, Ala. 35115	800[3]	1,463[3]	148	S	694	994	1,264
Moody Bible Institute; Chicago, Ill. 60610	751	586	86	ID	—	—	2,000
Moody College. *See* Texas A&M University							
Moore College of Art; Philadelphia, Pa. 19103	—	572	45	P	4,000	4,000	1,900
Moorhead State University. *See* Minnesota State University System							
Moravian College; Bethlehem, Pa. 18018	647	634	85	P/Mor	3,900	3,900	1,700
Morehead State University; Morehead, Ky. 40351	3,061	3,968	300	S	480	820	1,610

Institution and location	Enrollment: Male	Enrollment: Female	Faculty	Control	Tuition: Res.	Tuition: Nonres.	Rm/Bd
Morehouse College; Atlanta, Ga. 30314	1,756[3]	—	98	P	2,602	2,602	1,746
Morgan State University; Baltimore, Md. 21239	1,861	2,405	381	S	906	1,806	1,831
Morningside College; Sioux City, Iowa 51106	508	574	74	P/M	3,090	3,090	1,180
Morris Brown College; Atlanta, Ga. 30314	700	1,050	102	P/AME	2,350	2,350	1,845
Morris College; Sumter, S.C. 29150	323[3]	404[3]	41	P/B	1,792	1,792	1,171
Mount Holyoke College; South Hadley, Mass. 01075	—	1,850	168	P	5,430	5,430	2,570
Mount Marty College; Yankton, S.D. 57078	126	315	49	P/RC	2,310	2,310	1,305
Mount Mary College; Milwaukee, Wis. 53222	—	807	80	P/RC	2,550	2,550	1,500
Mount Mercy College; Cedar Rapids, Iowa 52402	168[3]	552[3]	52	P/RC	2,830	2,830	1,470
Mount Saint Clare College; Clinton, Iowa 52732	111[3]	211[3]	7	P/RC	1,500	1,500	1,435
Mount St. Joseph on the Ohio, College of; Mount St. Joseph, Ohio 45051	39[3]	756[3]	53	P/RC	2,624	2,624	1,720
Mount Saint Mary College; Newburgh, N.Y. 12550	77	626	57	P	2,700	2,700	1,690
Mount Saint Mary's College; Emmitsburg, Md. 21727	762	649	63	P	3,200	3,200	1,675
Mount St. Mary's College; Los Angeles, Calif. 90049	7	886	92	P/RC	3,000	3,000	1,770
Mount Saint Vincent, College of; Riverdale, N.Y. 10471	56[3]	860[3]	72	P	3,200[11]	3,200[11]	2,100
Mount Senario College; Ladysmith, Wis. 54848	168	149	30	P	3,260	3,260	1,789
Mount Sinai School of Medicine. *See* New York, City University of							
Mount Union College; Alliance, Ohio 44601	538	456	74	P/UM	3,690	3,690	1,440
Mount Vernon College; Washington, D.C. 20007	—	480	22	P	3,700	3,700	2,600
Mount Vernon Nazarene College; Mount Vernon, Ohio 43050	416[3]	473[3]	50	P/Naz	2,200	2,200	1,460
Muhlenberg College; Allentown, Pa. 18104	848[3]	663[3]	97	P	3,725	3,725	1,465
Multnomah School of the Bible; Portland, Ore. 97220	369	274	40	P	2,410	2,410	1,400
Mundelein College; Chicago, Ill. 60660	1,545		91	P/RC	2,940	2,940	1,850
Murray State University; Murray, Ky. 42071	2,559[3]	2,863[3]	360	S	580	1,490	1,330
Museum Art School; Portland, Ore. 97205	64	126	16	P	2,650	2,650	—
Museum of Fine Arts, School of the; Boston, Mass. 02115	196[3]	364[3]	50	P	3,300	3,300	—
Music, Conservatory of, of Puerto Rico; Hato Rey, P.R. 00918	172	67	27	S	210	210	1,200
Muskingum College; New Concord, Ohio 43762	457	399	68	P/UP	3,850	3,850	1,345
Nasson College; Springvale, Me. 04083	346	240	40	P	4,000	4,000	1,900
Nathaniel Hawthorne College; Antrim, N.H. 03440	428	100	21	P	4,400	4,400	1,650
National College; Rapid City, S.D. 57701	420[3]	706[3]	32	P	2,925	2,925	3,150
National College of Chiropractic; Lombard, Ill. 60148	855[3]	153[3]	70	P	2,700	2,700	—
National College of Education; Evanston, Ill. 60201	51[9]	557[9]	52	P	3,675	3,675	2,025
National University; San Diego, Calif. 92108	2,305[3]	757[3]	40	P	3,480	3,480	—
Naval Postgraduate School; Monterey, Calif. 93940	1,060	40	160	Fed	—	—	—
Nazareth College at Kalamazoo; Nazareth, Mich. 49074	100[3]	440[3]	33	P/RC	3,700	3,700	1,840
Nazareth College of Rochester; Rochester, N.Y. 14610	212[3]	1,063[3]	125	P	3,420	3,420	2,010
Nebraska, University of; Lincoln, Neb. 68588	10,324[3]	7,566[3]	1,200	S	959	2,312	1,550
Univ. of Nebraska at Omaha; Omaha, Neb. 68182	3,532	2,811	500	S	800	2,400	—
Nebraska, Univ. of, Medical Center; Omaha, Neb. 68105	883[3]	851[3]	552	S	n.a.	n.a.	—
Nebraska Wesleyan University; Lincoln, Neb. 68504	554[3]	611[3]	80	P/UM	3,050	3,050	1,524
Neumann College; Aston, Pa. 19014	82	619	36	P	2,500	2,500	—
Nevada, University of; Reno, Nev. 89557							
Univ. of Nevada, Las Vegas; Las Vegas, Nev. 89154	2,331	1,707	350	S	720	2,220	1,925
Univ. of Nevada—Reno; Reno, Nev. 89557	4,160	3,705	335	S	736	2,236	1,520
Newberry College; Newberry, S.C. 29108	483	353	53	P	3,265	3,265	1,485
New Church College, Academy of the; Bryn Athyn, Pa. 19009	72	49	23	P/Sw	1,005	1,005	1,227
Newcomb College. *See* Tulane University							
New England, University of; Biddeford, Me. 04005							
New England College of Osteopathic Medicine; Biddeford, Me. 04005	80	17	11	P	10,000	10,000	2,010
Saint Francis College; Biddeford, Me. 04005	245	122	22	P	3,660	3,660	1,895
New England Aeronautical Institute, N.H. *See* Daniel Webster College							
New England College; Henniker, N.H. 03242	835[3]	685[3]	n.a.	P	4,680[11]	4,680[11]	1,800[11]
New England College of Optometry; Boston, Mass. 02115	290	71	39	P	8,970	8,970	—
New England Conservatory of Music; Boston, Mass. 02115	381	273	100	P	4,700	4,700	2,675
New England School of Law; Boston, Mass. 02116	653	327	22	P	3,575	3,575	—
New Hampshire, University of; Durham, N.H. 03908	5,573	6,093	494	S	1,150	3,700	1,600
New Hampshire College; Manchester, N.H. 03104	1,917[3]	1,143[3]	76	P	4,234	4,234	2,480
New Haven, University of; West Haven, Conn. 06516	1,921[3]	749[3]	140	P	3,094	3,094	1,870
New Jersey Institute of Technology; Newark, N.J. 07102	2,814[3]	305[3]	n.a.	S	n.a.	n.a.	n.a.
New Mexico, The University of; Albuquerque, N.M. 87131	7,332[3]	6,761[3]	988	S	666	2,040	1,650
New Mexico Highlands University; Las Vegas, N.M. 87701	645	722	96	S	453	1,430	1,360
New Mexico Institute of Mining and Technology; Socorro, N.M. 87801	848[3]	357[3]	78	S	330	1,573	1,750

Institution and location	Enrollment		Faculty	Control	Tuition		Rm/Bd
	Male	Female			Res.	Nonres.	
New Mexico State University; Las Cruces, N.M. 88003	6,074	5,107	550	S	708	2,082	1,294
New Orleans, University of; New Orleans, La. 70122[57]	4,572[3]	4,226[3]	459	S	524	1,454	1,860
Newport College, The—Salve Regina; Newport, R.I. 02840	398[3]	1,321[3]	60	P/RC	2,940	2,940	1,800
New Rochelle, College of; New Rochelle, N.Y. 10801	258	3,002	100	P	3,150	3,150	2,320
New School for Social Research; New York, N.Y. 10011	244[3]	237[3]	54	P	3,700	3,700	—
Parsons School of Design; New York, N.Y. 10011	599[3]	893[3]	109	P	3,980	3,980	1,470
New School of Music, The; Philadelphia, Pa. 19103	36	42	6	P	3,000	3,000	2,100
New York, City University of; New York, N.Y. 10001	50,974[3]	65,661[3]	7,000	Mun/S	925	1,425	—
Bernard M. Baruch College; New York, N.Y. 10010	6,708	6,741	470	Mun/S	925	1,425	—
Brooklyn College; Brooklyn, N.Y. 11210	5,569	6,375	949	Mun/S	925	1,425	—
City College; New York, N.Y. 10031	5,016	3,509	690[8]	Mun	1,000	1,500	—
College of Staten Island; Staten Island, N.Y. 10301	4,963	5,443	379	Mun	925	1,425	—
Graduate School and University Center; New York, N.Y. 10036	1,320[3]	1,212[3]	1,351	Mun	750	1,000	—
Herbert H. Lehman College; Bronx, N.Y. 10468	2,090	3,562	n.a.	Mun	925	1,425	—
Hunter College; New York, N.Y. 10021	2,328	7,006	678	Mun/S	942	1,442	—
John Jay College of Criminal Justice; New York, N.Y. 10019	2,453[3]	1,851[3]	263	Mun/S	925	1,425	—
Mount Sinai School of Medicine, New York, N.Y. 10029	309	144	968	P	7,500	7,500	3,000
Queens College; Flushing, N.Y. 11367	5,119	6,146	839	Mun/S	775	925	—
York College; Jamaica, N.Y. 11451	1,101	1,581	150	Mun	935	1,425	—
New York, State University of; Albany, N.Y. 12246							
SUNY at Albany; Albany, N.Y. 12222	5,560	5,233	654	S	900	1,500	1,510
SUNY at Binghamton; Binghamton, N.Y. 13901	5,276[3]	5,360[3]	477	S	900	1,500	1,875
SUNY at Buffalo; Buffalo, N.Y. 14214	10,239[3]	6,738[3]	1,404	S	900	1,500	1,612
SUNY at Stony Brook; Stony Brook, N.Y. 11794	10,147		1,000	S	750	1,200	1,600
SUNY College at Brockport; Brockport, N.Y. 14420	3,491[3]	3,481[3]	449	S	900	1,500	1,715
SUNY College at Buffalo; Buffalo, N.Y. 14787	4,259	6,387	550	S	900	1,500	1,700
SUNY College at Cortland; Cortland, N.Y. 13045	2,058	3,133	272	S	900	1,500	1,554
SUNY College at Fredonia; Fredonia, N.Y. 14063	4,229[3]	2,114[3]	264	S	1,150	1,650	1,660
SUNY College at Geneseo; Geneseo, N.Y. 14454	1,709[3]	3,129[3]	268	S	900	1,500	1,680
SUNY College at New Paltz; New Paltz, N.Y. 12561	1,920	2,307	340	S	900	1,500	1,760
SUNY College at Old Westbury; Old Westbury, N.Y. 11568	1,175	1,671	113	S	900	1,500	1,200
SUNY College at Oneonta; Oneonta, N.Y. 13820	2,557[3]	3,647[3]	337	S	900	1,500	1,570
SUNY College at Oswego; Oswego, N.Y. 13126	3,322	2,829	442	S	900	1,500	1,625
SUNY College of Arts and Science at Plattsburgh; Plattsburgh, N.Y. 12901	2,340[3]	2,987[3]	302	S	900	1,500	1,670
SUNY College of Arts and Science at Potsdam; Potsdam, N.Y. 13676	1,727[3]	1,990[3]	291	S	900	1,500	1,650
SUNY College at Purchase; Purchase, N.Y. 10577	785[3]	1,122[3]	138	S	900	1,500	832
SUNY College of Environmental Science and Forestry; Syracuse, N.Y. 13210	1,061	326	113	S	1,150	1,650	2,100
SUNY College of Optometry; New York, N.Y. 10010	180	71	38	S	3,300	4,400	—
SUNY College of Technology; Utica, N.Y. 13502	567[3]	565[3]	84	S	900	1,500	n.a.
SUNY Downstate Medical Center; Brooklyn, N.Y. 11203	761[9]	547[9]	441	S	3,100	4,500	2,800
SUNY Empire State College; Saratoga Springs, N.Y. 12866	1,297	1,867	104	S	2,438	3,337	—
SUNY Maritime College; Fort Schuyler, Bronx, N.Y. 10465	871	42	68	S	900	1,500	1,380
SUNY Upstate Medical Center; Syracuse, N.Y. 13210	491[3]	347[3]	n.a.	S	900	1,500	2,000
New York, University of the State of, Regents External Degree Program; Albany, N.Y. 12230	10,050	9,328	—	S	75[58]	75[58]	—
New York Chiropractic College; Glen Head, N.Y. 11545	520	130	50	P	3,750	3,750	—
New York College of Podiatric Medicine; New York, N.Y. 10035	405	48	25	P	7,095	7,095	n.a.
New York Institute of Technology; Old Westbury, N.Y. 11568	7,689[3]	2,754[3]	200	P	2,560	2,560	n.a.
New York Law School; New York, N.Y. 10013	563	249	34	P	4,280	4,280	—
New York Medical College; Valhalla, N.Y. 10595	578	223	527	P	9,100	9,100	—
New York University; New York, N.Y. 10003	8,655[3]	8,365[3]	n.a.	P	5,062[11]	5,062[11]	2,624[11]
Niagara University; Niagara University, N.Y. 14109	1,397	1,605	174	RC	3,300	3,300	2,200
Nicholls State University; Thibodaux, La. 70301	2,086	2,172	220	S	535	1,165	1,280
Nichols College; Dudley, Mass. 01570	637	208	35	P	3,490	3,490	2,040
Norfolk State University; Norfolk, Va. 23504	2,202[3]	3,163[3]	406	S	550	975	1,448
North Adams State College; North Adams, Mass. 01247	1,093[3]	1,193[3]	97	S	600	2,100	1,520
North Alabama, University of; Florence, Ala. 35630	1,814[3]	2,158[3]	183	S	680	680	1,374

	Enrollment				Tuition		
Institution and location	Male	Female	Faculty	Control	Res.	Nonres.	Rm/Bd
North Carolina, University System of; Chapel Hill, N.C. 27514							
Appalachian State University; Boone, N.C. 28608	3,935[3]	4,142[3]	585	S	614	2,334	1,330
East Carolina University; Greenville, N.C. 27834	4,624[3]	5,701[3]	619	S	310	2,030	1,524
Elizabeth City State University; Elizabeth City, N.C. 27909	681[3]	843[3]	100	S	250	1,734	1,370
Fayetteville State University; Fayetteville, N.C. 28301	1,842	1,150	127	S	270	1,772	1,139
North Carolina Agricultural and Technical State University; Greensboro, N.C. 27411	2,162	1,779	340	S	310	2,015	1,219
North Carolina Central University; Durham, N.C. 27707	1,749	2,642	325	S	615	2,353	1,449
North Carolina School of the Arts; Winston–Salem, N.C. 27107	319[3]	363[3]	85	S	568	2,020	1,562
N.C. State Univ. at Raleigh; Raleigh, N.C. 27650	9,912[3]	4,094[3]	1,249	S	582[11]	2,294[11]	1,700[11]
Pembroke State University; Pembroke, N.C. 28372	729[3]	960[3]	121	S	470	1,960	1,020
Univ. of N.C. at Asheville; Asheville, N.C. 28814	838	1,055	76	S	490	2,260	1,130
Univ. of N.C. at Chapel Hill; Chapel Hill, N.C. 27514	9,463	10,559	1,873	S	529	2,239	1,721
Univ. of N.C. at Charlotte; Charlotte, N.C. 28223	3,293[3]	2,775[3]	417	S	536	2,268	1,370
Univ. of N.C. at Greensboro; Greensboro, N.C. 27412	2,929[3]	6,661[3]	615	S	603	2,082	1,400
Univ. of N.C. at Wilmington; Wilmington, N.C. 28403	1,680[3]	1,609[3]	193	S	560	2,315	1,560
Western Carolina University; Cullowhee, N.C. 28723	2,534[3]	2,374[3]	311	S	578	2,316	1,480
Winston–Salem State University; Winston–Salem, N.C. 27102	699	1,140	150	S	2,107	3,636	1,475
North Carolina Wesleyan College; Rocky Mount, N.C. 27801	301	285	40	P	2,300	2,300	1,390
North Central Bible College; Minneapolis, Minn. 55404	296	214	18	P/AG	1,392	1,392	1,190
North Central College; Naperville, Ill. 60540	618[3]	493[3]	53	P/UM	3,360	3,360	n.a.
North Dakota, University of; Grand Forks, N.D. 58202	5,180[3]	4,528[3]	485	S	660	1,428	1,290
North Dakota State University; Fargo, N.D. 58105	4,400[3]	3,200[3]	383	S	633	1,401	1,257
Northeastern Bible College; Essex Fells, N.J. 07021	141	89	18	P/ID	2,592	2,592	1,669
Northeastern Illinois University; Chicago, Ill. 60625	1,958[3]	2,837[3]	348	S	558	1,674	—
Northeastern Oklahoma State University; Tahlequah, Okla. 74464	2,250	2,837	206	S	375	550	1,500
Northeastern University; Boston, Mass. 02115	11,100[3]	6,400[3]	777	P	3,637	3,637	2,505
Northeast Louisiana University; Monroe, La. 71209	3,055	3,475	368	S	450	1,100	1,564
Northeast Missouri State University; Kirksville, Mo. 63501	2,685[3]	3,356[3]	273	S	340	760	1,020
Northern Arizona University; Flagstaff, Ariz. 86011	5,406[3]	5,194[3]	523	S	600	2,100	836
Northern Colorado, University of; Greeley, Colo. 80639	4,581[3]	6,401[3]	519	S	805	2,665	1,620
Northern Illinois University; DeKalb, Ill. 60115	7,525	8,809	1,105	S	846	1,942	1,640
Northern Iowa, University of; Cedar Falls, Iowa 50613	3,343	4,216	572	S	774	1,460	1,348
Northern Kentucky University; Highland Heights, Ky. 41076	2,220	1,829	234	S	480	1,300	—
Northern Michigan University; Marquette, Mich. 49855	3,683[3]	3,279[3]	375	S	944	2,112	1,750
Northern Montana College; Havre, Mont. 59501	585	460	72	S	435	1,461	1,471
Northern State College; Aberdeen, S.D. 57401	900[3]	1,100[3]	n.a.	S	708	1,430	1,150
North Florida, University of; Jacksonville, Fla. 32216	631	727	160	S	744	2,340	—
North Georgia College; Dahlonega, Ga. 30533	652[3]	752[3]	93	S	459	1,245	1,230
Northland College; Ashland, Wis. 54806	319	241	40	P	3,290	3,290	1,790
North Park College; Chicago, Ill. 60625	504[3]	649[3]	80	P/EC	3,540	3,540	1,845
Northrop University; Inglewood, Calif. 90306	1,879	81	122	P	3,936	3,936	2,892
North Texas State University; Denton, Tex. 76203	8,898	8,690	700	S	420	1,500	1,900
Northwest Bible College; Minot, N.D. 58701	96	86	10	P/CG	900	900	1,230
Northwest Christian College; Eugene, Ore. 97401	145[3]	110[3]	14	DC	2,520[11]	2,520[11]	1,674
Northwest College; Kirkland, Wash. 98033	362	272	21	P/AG	1,740	1,740	1,427
Northwestern College; Orange City, Iowa 51041	374[3]	457[3]	53	P/RCA	3,220[11]	3,220[11]	1,310
Northwestern College; Roseville, Minn. 55113	301	291	33	P/ND	3,000	3,000	1,710
Northwestern Coll. of Chiropractic; St. Paul, Minn. 55116	320	41	26	P	1,490	1,490	—
Northwestern Oklahoma State University; Alva, Okla. 73717	714[3]	523[3]	71	S	430	1,060	960
Northwestern State University of Louisiana; Natchitoches, La. 71457	1,262	1,789	n.a.	S	442	1,072	n.a.
Northwestern University; Evanston, Ill. 60201	8,423[3]	7,006[3]	1,700	P	5,000	5,000	2,300
Northwest Missouri State University; Maryville, Mo. 64468	2,127[2]	2,274[2]	220	S	490	890	1,250
Northwest Nazarene College; Nampa, Idaho 83651	556[3]	684[3]	71	P/Naz	2,520	2,520	1,590
Northwood Institute; Midland, Mich. 48640	1,198[3]	537[3]	45	P	2,520	2,520	1,590
Norwich University; Northfield, Vt. 05663	1,279	203	148	P	n.a.	n.a.	n.a.
Vermont College; Montpelier, Vt. 05602	38	395	203	P	6,200	6,200	n.a.
Notre Dame, College of; Belmont, Calif. 94002	207	327	63	RC	3,200[11]	3,200[11]	2,150[11]
Notre Dame, University of; Notre Dame, Ind. 46556	6,568[3]	2,200[3]	683	P	4,175	4,175	1,535
Notre Dame College; Manchester, N.H. 03104	33[3]	367[3]	39	P/RC	2,500	2,500	1,600
Notre Dame College of Ohio; Cleveland, Ohio 44121	—	367[3]	32	P/RC	2,375	2,375	1,600

Institution and location	Enrollment Male	Enrollment Female	Faculty	Control	Tuition Res.	Tuition Nonres.	Rm/Bd
Notre Dame of Maryland, College of; Baltimore, Md. 21210	—	590	50	P/RC	3,150	3,150	2,000
Nova University; Ft. Lauderdale, Fla. 33314	2,548[3]	2,108[3]	94	P	—	2,000	—
Nyack College; Nyack, N.Y. 10960	277[3]	325[3]	39	P/CMA	2,496	2,496	1,340
Oakland City College; Oakland City, Ind. 47660	274	173	32	P/B	2,500	2,500	1,500
Oakland University; Rochester, Mich. 48063	4,343	6,747	365	S	872	2,144	1,720
Oakwood College; Huntsville, Ala. 35805	388	439	70	P/SDA	5,085	5,085	1,725
Oberlin College; Oberlin, Ohio 44074	1,430[3]	12[3]	197	P	4,725	4,725	2,000
Occidental College; Los Angeles, Calif. 90041	755	710	114	P	4,944	4,944	2,100
Oglethorpe University; Atlanta, Ga. 30319	316	360	38	P	2,760	2,760	1,460
Ohio College of Podiatric Medicine; Cleveland, Ohio 44106	520	62	n.a.	P	6,200	6,200	—
Ohio Dominican College; Columbus, Ohio 43219	311[3]	538[3]	45	P/RC	3,280[11]	3,280[11]	1,830[11]
Ohio Institute of Technology; Columbus, Ohio 43209	2,089[3]	148[3]	37	P	2,425	2,425	—
Ohio Northern University; Ada, Ohio 45810	1,597[3]	989[3]	161	P/UM	3,276	3,276	1,440
Ohio State University, The; Columbus, Ohio 43210	28,051	21,630	2,616	S	1,005	2,280	1,908
Columbus Campus; Columbus, Ohio 43210	28,608	52,733	n.a.	S	1,080	1,380	2,037
Lima Campus; Lima, Ohio 45804	308[3]	334[3]	40	S	960	2,235	—
Mansfield Campus; Mansfield, Ohio 44906	405	450	39	S	960	2,235	—
Marion Campus; Marion, Ohio 43302	269	265	25	S	960	2,235	—
Newark Campus; Newark, Ohio 43055	476[3]	344[3]	28	S	960	2,235	—
Ohio University; Athens, Ohio 45701	7,569[3]	6,285[3]	706	S	1,071	2,481	1,869
Ohio Wesleyan University; Delaware, Ohio 43015	1,218[3]	1,071[3]	155	P/M	4,315	4,315	1,840
Oklahoma, University of; Norman, Okla. 73019	9,599	6,415	756	S	613	1,682	1,393
Oklahoma, University of Science and Arts of; Chickasha, Okla. 73018	445	687	54	S	434	1,056	1,140
Oklahoma Baptist University; Shawnee, Okla. 74801	615	733	92	P/SB	1,800	1,900	1,300
Oklahoma Christian College; Oklahoma City, Okla. 73111	733[3]	902[3]	55	P/CC	1,760	1,760	1,370
Oklahoma City Southwestern College; Oklahoma City, Okla. 73127	386	119	25	P/PH	1,094	1,094	1,320
Oklahoma City University; Oklahoma City, Okla. 73106	628	473	90	P	2,140	2,140	3,800
Oklahoma College of Osteopathic Medicine and Surgery; Tulsa, Okla. 74101	200	35	30	S	2,500	5,100	—
Oklahoma State University; Stillwater, Okla. 74074	11,805	8,542	1,041	S	600	1,600	1,284
Old Dominion University; Norfolk, Va. 23508	4,762[3]	4,461	581	S	840	1,440	1,690
Olivet College; Olivet, Mich. 49076	349	217	40	P/UCC	3,390	3,390	1,730
Olivet Nazarene College; Kankakee, Ill. 60901	734[3]	1,022[3]	95	P/Naz	2,448	2,448	1,504
Open Bible College; Des Moines, Iowa 50321	66	39	10	P/OBS	1,600	1,600	2,000
Oral Roberts University; Tulsa, Okla. 74171	2,191[3]	1,841[3]	272	P	2,950	2,950	1,875
Oregon, University of; Eugene, Ore. 97403	7,427[3]	6,689[3]	689	S	884	3,008	1,589
Oregon College of Education; Monmouth, Ore. 97361	1,148	1,963	280	S	921	2,921	1,795
Oregon Graduate Center; Beaverton, Ore. 97006	34	3	23	P	4,000	4,000	—
Oregon Institute of Technology; Klamath Falls, Ore. 97601	1,391[3]	716[3]	144	S	867	2,991	2,300
Oregon State University; Corvallis, Ore. 97331	9,524[3]	6,329[3]	1,662	S	924	3,237	1,740
Osteopathic Medicine, College of, of the Pacific; Pomona, Calif. 91766	77	14	16	P	10,000	10,000	—
Osteopathic Medicine and Surgery, College of; Des Moines, Iowa 50312	477	60	50	P	5,450	5,450	—
Otis Art Institute of Parsons School of Design; Los Angeles, Calif. 90057	76	136	10	P	2,900	2,900	—
Ottawa University; Ottawa, Kan. 66067	334	200	30	P/AB	2,400	2,400	1,433
Otterbein College; Westerville, Ohio 43081	579	694	88	P/UM	4,428	4,428	1,713
Ouachita Baptist University; Arkadelphia, Ark. 71923	727	782	102	P/B	1,910	1,910	1,360
Our Lady of Angels College. *See* Neumann College							
Our Lady of Holy Cross College; New Orleans, La. 70114	72	160	232	P/RC	1,640	1,640	—
Our Lady of the Elms, College of; Chicopee, Mass. 01013	—	439	33	P/RC	3,000	3,000	1,800
Our Lady of the Lake University of San Antonio; San Antonio, Tex. 78285	562[3]	1,182[3]	95	P/RC	2,400	2,400	2,400
Ozarks, The College of the; Clarksville, Ark. 72830	234	210	30	P/Pres	1,050	1,050	1,175
Ozarks, The School of the; Point Lookout, Mo. 65726	550	650	81	P	2,400	2,400	2,322
Pace University; New York, N.Y. 10038	2,024	2,003	772	P	3,264	3,264	2,225
College of White Plains of Pace University; White Plains, N.Y. 10603	208	350	30	P	3,060	3,060	2,350
Pace University, Pleasantville/Briarcliff; Pleasantville, N.Y. 10570	1,180[3]	1,620[3]	125	P	3,200	3,200	2,350
Pacific, University of the; Stockton, Calif. 95211	3,201	2,231	367	P	5,682	5,682	2,522
Pacific Christian College; Fullerton, Calif. 92631	112	101	25	P/CC	2,230	2,230	1,250
Pacific Coll. of Fresno, Calif. *See* Fresno Pacific Coll.							
Pacific Lutheran University; Tacoma, Wash. 98447	1,100[3]	1,559[3]	196	P	3,810	3,810	1,835
Pacific Oaks College; Pasadena, Calif. 91103	36	287	22	P	2,880	2,880	—
Pacific Union College; Angwin, Calif. 94508	862[11]	804[11]	119	P/SDA	4,125[11]	4,125[11]	2,140[11]

Institution and location	Enrollment		Faculty	Control	Tuition		Rm/Bd
	Male	Female			Res.	Nonres.	
Pacific University; Forest Grove, Ore. 97116	618	407	70	P/UCC	3,800	3,800	1,600
Paine College; Augusta, Ga. 30910	264	501	71	P/M	2,175	2,175	1,365
Palm Beach Atlantic College; West Palm Beach, Fla. 33401	206[3]	196[3]	32	P/B	1,400	1,400	1,450
Pan American University; Edinburg, Tex. 78539	2,508	2,764	286	S	270	1,350	1,330
Paper Chemistry, The Institute of; Appleton, Wis. 54911	64	9	42	P	3,000	3,000	787
Park College; Parkville, Mo. 64152	186	206	21	P/LDS	1,495	1,495	740
Parks College of Saint Louis University; Cahokia, Ill. 62206	803	69	45	P/RC	2,560	2,560	1,710
Parsons School of Design. *See* New School for Social Research							
Paul Quinn College; Waco, Tex. 76704	537[8]		n.a.	P/AME	1,350	n.a.	1,600
Peabody Institute of the Johns Hopkins University, Conservatory of Music; Baltimore, Md. 21202	152	162	48	P	4,575	4,575	2,195
Pembroke State University. *See* North Carolina, University System of							
Pennsylvania, University of; Philadelphia, Pa. 19104	10,060[3]	6,434[3]	6,270	P	6,000[11]	6,000[11]	2,386
Pennsylvania College of Podiatric Medicine; Philadelphia, Pa. 19107	378	73	130	P	6,620	6,900	3,540
Pennsylvania State University, The; University Park, Pa. 16802	29,765[3]	18,970[3]	3,002	S	1,485	2,982	1,830
Behrend College; Erie, Pa. 16563	925	650	n.a.	P/S	1,281	2,982	1,665
Capitol Campus; Middletown, Pa. 17057	1,197[9]	520[9]	130	S	1,233	2,748	1,566
Radnor Center for Graduate Studies; Radnor, Pa. 19087	204	154	6	S	([59])	([60])	—
Pepperdine University; Malibu, Calif. 90265	2,825	1,731	179	P/CC	5,088	5,088	2,400
Peru State College; Peru, Neb. 68421	343[3]	423[3]	48	S	570	1,020	1,545
Pfeiffer College; Misenheimer, N.C. 28109	397[3]	366[3]	55	P/UM	2,345	2,345	1,450
Philadelphia College of Art; Philadelphia, Pa. 19102	468	670	70	P	4,500	4,500	2,050
Philadelphia College of Bible; Langhorne, Pa. 19047	325	256	37	P	2,150	2,150	1,620
Philadelphia College of Osteopathic Medicine; Philadelphia, Pa. 19131	734[3]	88[3]	96	P	6,250	6,550	—
Philadelphia College of Pharmacy and Science; Philadelphia, Pa. 19104	620[3]	483[3]	71	P	3,500	3,500	1,000[4]
Philadelphia College of Textiles and Sciences; Philadelphia, Pa. 19111	669	812	86	P	3,200	3,200	1,150
Philadelphia College of the Performing Arts; Philadelphia, Pa. 19102	169	146	13	P	3,400	3,400	—
Philadelphia Musical Academy. *See* Philadelphia College of the Performing Arts							
Philander Smith College; Little Rock, Ark. 72203	351	259	n.a.	UM	1,000	1,000	1,475
Phillips University; Enid, Okla. 73701	446	365	79	P	2,080	2,080	1,620
Phoenix, University of; Phoenix, Ariz. 85004	307		30[51]	P	2,700	2,700	4,000
Piedmont Bible College; Winston–Salem, N.C. 27101	235	146	16	P/B	1,570	1,570	1,090
Piedmont College; Demorest, Ga. 30535	209	150	22	P	1,485	1,485	1,905
Pikeville College; Pikeville, Ky. 41501	253	233	42	P/Pres	2,150	2,150	1,275
Pine Manor College; Chestnut Hill, Mass. 02167	—	471	25	P	4,280	4,280	2,675
Pittsburgh, University of; Pittsburgh, Pa. 15260	11,638[3]	9,110[3]	2,285	P/S	1,590	3,180	1,810
U. of Pittsburgh at Bradford; Bradford, Pa. 16701	400[3]	310[3]	42	P/S	1,520	2,970	1,850
U. of Pittsburgh at Greensburg; Greensburg, Pa. 15601	343[3]	175[3]	31	P/S	1,400	2,800	—
U. of Pittsburgh at Johnstown; Johnstown, Pa. 15904	1,301[22]	889[22]	150	P/S	1,410	2,820	1,440
Pittsburg State University; Pittsburg, Kan. 66762	2,829[3]	2,731[3]	222	S	580	1,230	1,636
Pitzer College. *See* Claremont Colleges							
Plymouth State College; Plymouth, N.H. 03264	1,387[3]	1,287[3]	143	S	800	2,700	1,760
Point Loma College; San Diego, Calif. 92106	662	817	74	P/Naz	2,880	2,880	1,425
Point Park College; Pittsburgh, Pa. 15222	655	577	77	P	3,500	3,500	1,800
Polytechnic Institute of New York; Brooklyn, N.Y. 11201	4,271[3]	423[3]	180	P	4,800	4,800	1,050
Pomona College. *See* Claremont Colleges							
Portland, University of; Portland, Ore. 97203	1,050[3]	960[3]	110	P	1,650	1,650	1,800
Portland School of Art; Portland, Me. 04101	80[3]	148[3]	14	P	2,980	2,980	—
Portland State University; Portland, Ore. 97207	8,158[3]	8,683[3]	765	S	890	3,022	2,000
Post College; Waterbury, Conn. 06705	243[3]	467[3]	35	P	3,000	3,000	2,000
Prairie View A&M University; Prairie View, Tex. 77445	2,581[3]	2,645[3]	279	S	([61])	([62])	1,590
Pratt Institute; Brooklyn, N.Y. 11205	2,493[3]	1,929[3]	130	P	3,808	3,808	1,300[4]
Presbyterian College; Clinton, S.C. 29325	476	399	52	P/Pres	4,950	4,950	1,640
Princeton University; Princeton, N.J. 08544	3,891[3]	2,040[3]	683	P	5,585	5,585	2,226
Principia College; Elsah, Ill. 62028	391[3]	477[3]	45	P	4,239[11]	4,239[11]	2,400[11]
Providence College; Providence, R.I. 02918	1,835	1,633	206	P	4,017	4,017	2,550
Puerto Rico, University of; Río Piedras, P.R. 00931	5,509[3]	9,541[3]	1,195	S	200	2,100	1,200
Cayey University College; Cayey, P.R. 00633	1,007	1,516	123	S	1,900	1,900	1,200
Mayaguez Campus; Mayaguez, P.R. 00708	4,969	3,370	479	S	212	212	—
Río Piedras Campus; Río Piedras, P.R. 00931	8,228	13,566	1,185	S	200	2,100	1,200

Institution and location	Enrollment		Faculty	Control	Tuition		
	Male	Female			Res.	Nonres.	Rm/Bd
Puget Sound, University of; Tacoma, Wash. 98416	1,186	1,452	170	P/UM	4,280	4,280	2,000
Purdue University; West Lafayette, Ind. 47907	18,157	11,948	1,945	S	1,008	2,600	1,785
Calumet Campus; Hammond, Ind. 46323	1,191	1,035	210	S	955	2,013	—
Indiana University–Purdue University at Indianapolis. *See* Indiana University							
Queens College; Charlotte, N.C. 28274	19[3]	442[3]	42	P/PUS	3,175	3,175	1,740
Queens College (NYC). *See* New York, City University of							
Quincy College; Quincy, Ill. 62301	402[3]	462[3]	67	P/RC	3,200	3,200	1,690
Quinnipiac College; Hamden, Conn. 06518	1,350	2,083	165	P	3,800	3,800	1,420
Radcliffe College. *See* Harvard University							
Radford University; Radford, Va. 24142	1,635[3]	4,048[3]	281	S	876	1,476	1,698
Ramapo College of New Jersey; Mahwah, N.J. 07430	1,195	1,196	154	S	950	1,654	662
Rand Graduate Institute for Policy Studies; Santa Monica, Calif. 90406	36	7	33	P	3,300	3,300	—
Randolph–Macon College; Ashland, Va. 23005	544	367	55	P	3,870[11]	3,870[11]	1,620[11]
Randolph–Macon Woman's College; Lynchburg, Va. 24503	—	764	65	P/UM	4,500[11]	4,500[11]	2,000[11]
Redlands, University of; Redlands, Calif. 92373	1,368[3]	1,253[3]	170	P	4,470	4,470	2,000
Reed College; Portland, Ore. 97202	621	427	78	P	5,560[11]	5,560[11]	2,050[11]
Reformed Bible College; Grand Rapids, Mich. 49506	105	95	14	P	1,500	1,500	1,300
Regis College; Denver, Colo. 80221	581	420	75	P/RC	3,910	3,910	6,210
Regis College; Weston, Mass. 02193	—	1,270[3]	55	P/RC	3,375	3,375	2,230
Rensselaer Polytechnic Institute; Troy, N.Y. 12181	4,679[3]	860[3]	355	P	5,415	5,415	2,508
Rhode Island, University of; Kingston, R.I. 02881	5,506	5,074	900	S	872	2,508	1,084
Rhode Island College; Providence, R.I. 02903	1,053[3]	2,306[3]	350	S	820	2,420	2,015
Rhode Island School of Design; Providence, R.I. 02903	652	825	91	P	5,200[11]	5,200[11]	2,230[11]
Rice University; Houston, Tex. 77001	2,253	1,215	463	P	2,900	2,900	2,520
Richmond, University of; Richmond, Va. 23173	1,756[3]	1,266[3]	188	P/B	4,100	4,100	1,670
Rider College; Lawrenceville, N.J. 08638	1,825[3]	1,535[3]	188	P	3,250	3,250	1,780
Rio Grande College; Rio Grande, Ohio 45674	523[3]	621[3]	49	P	600	2,230	1,635
Ripon College; Ripon, Wis. 54971	506	412	70	P	4,690	4,690	1,535
Rivier College; Nashua, N.H. 03060	37	486	40	P/RC	2,750	2,750	1,850
Roanoke College; Salem, Va. 24153	658[3]	699[3]	67	P	3,600	3,600	1,700
Robert Morris College; Coraopolis, Pa. 15108	1,350	1,227	88	P	2,160	2,160	1,400
Roberts Wesleyan College; Rochester, N.Y. 14624	179	400	59[8]	P/FM	2,945	2,945	1,750
Rochester, The University of; Rochester, N.Y. 14627	3,695	2,315	1,328[8]	P	5,300	5,300	2,473
Rochester Institute of Technology; Rochester, N.Y. 14623	4,834[3]	2,005[3]	560[8]	P	3,879	3,879	2,368
Rockford College; Rockford, Ill. 61101	243	321	60	P	3,590[2]	3,590[2]	1,575
Rockhurst College; Kansas City, Mo. 64110	706	472	78	P/RC	2,560	2,560	1,810
Rocky Mountain College; Billings, Mont. 59102	255	239	31	P[63]	2,490	2,490	1,512
Roger Williams College; Bristol, R.I. 02809	1,248	642	82	P	3,100	3,100	2,000
Rollins College; Winter Park, Fla. 32789	600	685	110	P	4,350	4,350	2,200
Roosevelt University; Chicago, Ill. 60605	1,767[3]	2,385[3]	248	P	3,000	3,000	n.a.
Rosary College; River Forest, Ill. 60305	165[3]	629[3]	86	P/RC	3,400	3,400	2,000
Rosary Hill College, N.Y. *See* Daemen College							
Rose–Hulman Institute of Technology; Terre Haute, Ind. 47803	1,200	—	80	P	3,600	3,600	1,650
Rosemead Graduate School of Professional Psychology[64]; La Mirada, Calif. 90639	98	41	14	P/ND	3,974	3,974	1,920
Rosemont College; Rosemont, Pa. 19010	—	585[3]	29	P/RC	3,800[11]	3,800[11]	2,400[11]
Rush University; Chicago, Ill. 60612	390[3]	615[3]	636	P	1,150	1,150	700
Russell Sage College; Troy, N.Y. 12180	—	1,358	129	P	3,600	3,600	2,090
Rust College; Holly Springs, Miss. 38635	237	303	40	P/UM	2,125	2,125	1,100
Rutgers University; New Brunswick, N.J. 08903	16,743[3]	15,780[3]	2,476	S	1,007	1,841	1,872
Sacred Heart, Univ. of the; Santurce, P.R. 00914	1,704[3]	2,760[3]	85	P/RC	1,250	1,250	1,425
Sacred Heart College; Belmont, N.C. 28012	103	372	18	P/RC	2,564[11]	2,564[11]	1,540[11]
Sacred Heart University; Bridgeport, Conn. 06606	553[3]	717[3]	65	P/RC	2,800	2,800	—
Saginaw Valley State College; University Center, Mich. 48710	873[3]	834[3]	109	S	899	1,891	1,800
St. Ambrose College; Davenport, Iowa 52803	1,059	802	77	P/RC	3,300	3,300	1,850
St. Andrews Presbyterian College; Laurinburg, N.C. 28352	328[3]	299[3]	49	P/Pres	2,850	2,850	1,495
St. Anselm's College; Manchester, N.H. 03102	922[3]	691[3]	n.a.	P/RC	3,600	3,600	1,880
St. Augustine's College; Raleigh, N.C. 27610	782[3]	983[3]	72	P/E	1,450	1,450	1,100[8]
St. Benedict, College of; St. Joseph, Minn. 56374	6[3]	2,017[3]	114	P/RC	3,350	3,350	1,450
St. Bonaventure University; St. Bonaventure, N.Y. 14778	1,216[3]	1,117[3]	167	P	3,075	3,075	1,765
St. Catherine, The College of; St. Paul, Minn. 55105	—	1,850[3]	121	P/RC	3,260[11]	3,260[11]	1,650[11]
St. Cloud State University. *See* Minnesota State College System							

Institution and location	Enrollment		Faculty	Control	Tuition		
	Male	Female			Res.	Nonres.	Rm/Bd
St. Edward's University; Austin, Tex. 78704	1,280	945	129	P	2,428	2,428	2,700
St. Elizabeth, College of; Convent Station, N.J. 07961	2[3]	523[3]	49	P/RC	3,000	3,000	1,800
St. Francis, College of; Joliet, Ill. 60435	217[3]	367[3]	41	P	2,870	2,870	1,760
St. Francis College; Brooklyn, N.Y. 11201	1,179	795	65	P	2,798	2,798	—
St. Francis College; Fort Wayne, Ind. 46808	556[3]	808[3]	35	P/RC	2,176	2,176	1,700
St. Francis College; Loretto, Pa. 15940	932	738	68	P/RC	2,976	2,976	1,800
St. Francis de Sales College; Milwaukee, Wis. 53207	55	1	16	P/RC	700	700	500
St. John Fisher College; Rochester, N.Y. 14618	877	622	100	P	3,573[11]	3,573[11]	2,110[11]
St. John's College; Annapolis, Md. 21404	200	185	52	P	5,400	5,400	2,000
St. John's College; Sante Fe, N.M. 87501	149	123	27	P	5,400	5,400	2,000
Saint John's University; Collegeville, Minn. 56321	1,924[3]	50[3]	132	RC	3,375[11]	3,375[11]	1,800[11]
St. John's University; Jamaica, N.Y. 11439	10,767[3]	7,045[3]	518	P/RC	2,900[11]	2,900[11]	—
St. Joseph College; West Hartford, Conn. 06117	3	613	71	P	3,450	3,450	2,000
St. Joseph's College; Brooklyn, N.Y. 11205	135	760	70	P	2,400[2]	2,400[2]	—
St. Joseph's College; North Windham, Me. 04062	107	348	35	P/RC	2,800	2,800	1,700
St. Joseph's College; Rensselaer, Ind. 47978	558	390	51	P/RC	2,700	2,700	1,580
St. Joseph's University; Philadelphia, Pa. 19131	1,380[3]	911[3]	123	P/RC	3,250	3,250	2,160
St. Joseph the Provider, College of; Rutland, Vt. 05701	37	147	9	P/RC	2,825	2,825	1,775
St. Lawrence University; Canton, N.Y. 13617	1,178	1,073	152	P	4,995	4,995	1,990
St. Leo College; St. Leo, Fla. 33574	588[3]	467[3]	50	P/RC	2,700	2,700	1,250
St. Louis Christian College; Florissant, Mo. 63033	84	63	9	P/CC	1,270[11]	1,270[11]	1,500[11]
St. Louis College of Pharmacy; St. Louis, Mo. 63110	413[3]	296[3]	35	P	2,740	2,740	1,750
St. Louis Conservatory of Music; St. Louis, Mo. 63130	30[8]	25[8]	5	P	2,700	2,700	—
St. Louis University; St. Louis, Mo. 63103	4,530[3]	3,474[3]	852	P	3,700	3,700	2,000
St. Martin's College; Lacey, Wash. 98503	228[3]	172[3]	40	P/RC	3,422	3,422	1,800
St. Mary, College of; Omaha, Neb. 68124	38	574	44	P/RC	([65])	([11])	1,410[11]
St. Mary College; Leavenworth, Kan. 66048	188	604	40	P/RC	2,400	2,400	1,600
St. Mary of the Plains College; Dodge City, Kan. 67801	435	225	48	P/RC	2,550	2,550	825
St. Mary–of–the–Woods College; St.–Mary–of–the–Woods, Ind. 47876	—	559[3]	47	P/RC	3,050	3,050	1,575
St. Mary's College of California; Moraga, Calif. 94575[42]	1,151[3]	1,267[3]	102	P/RC	3,922	3,922	2,133
St. Mary's College; Notre Dame, Ind. 46556	17	1,737	113	P/RC	3,950	3,950	2,090
St. Mary's College; Orchard Lake, Mich. 48033	109	103	5	P/RC	1,600	1,600	1,200
St. Mary's College; Winona, Minn. 55987	634[3]	595[3]	72	P/RC	3,379	3,379	1,830
St. Mary's Coll. of Maryland; St. Mary's City, Md. 20686	498[3]	626[3]	69	S	675	1,650	1,950
St. Mary's Dominican College; New Orleans, La. 70118	50	750	n.a.	P/RC	2,900	2,900	2,500
St. Mary's University of San Antonio; San Antonio, Tex. 78284	1,968	1,308	120	P/RC	2,340	2,340	1,520
St. Michael's College; Winooski, Vt. 05404	921[3]	654[3]	95	P	3,660	3,660	1,888
St. Norbert College; De Pere, Wis. 54115	783[3]	787[3]	80	P/RC	3,150	3,150	1,600
St. Olaf College; Northfield, Minn. 55057	1,375	1,483	190	P/AL	3,595	3,595	1,455
St. Patrick's College; Mountain View, Calif. 94042	49	—	13	P/RC	1,800	1,800	700
St. Paul's College; Lawrenceville, Va. 23868	313	338	34	P/E	2,040	2,040	1,520
St. Peter's College; Jersey City, N.J. 07306	1,355	1,114	125	P/RC	2,800	2,800	—
St. Rose, The College of; Albany, N.Y. 12203	217	926	105	P	2,500	2,500	1,600
St. Scholastica, College of; Duluth, Minn. 55811	210[3]	852[3]	100	P	3,219	3,219	1,716
St. Teresa, College of; Winona, Minn. 55987	20[3]	720[3]	70	P/RC	3,100	3,100	1,500
St. Thomas, College of; St. Paul, Minn. 55105	3,043	1,638	137[8]	P	3,080	3,080	1,500
St. Thomas, University of; Houston, Tex. 77006	625[3]	1,140[3]	87	P/RC	2,250	2,250	1,400
St. Thomas Aquinas College; Sparkill, N.Y. 10976	500	650	50	P	2,375[11]	2,375[11]	825[4]
St. Xavier College; Chicago, Ill. 60655	585	1,515	109	P	3,270	3,270	1,018
Salem College; Salem, W. Va. 26426	516	407	63	P	2,960	2,960	1,630
Salem College; Winston–Salem, N.C. 27108	1[3]	527[3]	60	P	3,400	3,400	2,075
Salem State College; Salem, Mass. 01970	1,966[3]	2,947[3]	266	S	740	2,240	1,610
Salisbury State College; Salisbury, Md. 21801	1,259	1,514	185	S	620	1,520	1,670
Salve Regina College. *See* Newport College							
Samford University; Birmingham, Ala. 35229	1,791[3]	1,588[3]	218	P/B	2,464	2,560	1,600
Sam Houston State University; Huntsville, Tex. 77341	4,738	4,889	395[8]	S	328	1,188	1,552
San Diego, University of; San Diego, Calif. 92110	1,070[3]	1,383[3]	175	P/RC	4,050[11]	4,050[11]	2,500[11]
San Diego State University; San Diego, Calif. 92182[18]	9,249	9,625	1,029	S	202	1,800	2,700
San Francisco, University of; San Francisco, Calif. 94117	3,180	3,204	250	P/RC	3,850	3,850	2,175
San Francisco Art Institute; San Francisco, Calif. 94133	303	238	32	P	3,900	3,900	3,600
San Francisco Conservatory of Music, The; San Francisco, Calif. 94122	99[3]	73[3]	12	P	4,100	4,100	—
San Francisco State Univ.; San Francisco, Calif. 94132[18]	5,713[3]	6,984[3]	900	S	234	2,160	1,914
Sangamon State University; Springfield, Ill. 62708	3,640		175	S	596	1,788	1,000
San Jose Bible College; San Jose, Calif. 95108	87	40	7	P/ND	1,680	1,680	1,260
San Jose State University; San Jose, Calif. 95192[18]	12,333	12,546	1,071	S	210	2,160	1,800
Santa Clara, University of; Santa Clara, Calif. 95053	2,471	1,973	237[8]	P/RC	3,990[11]	3,990[11]	2,175[11]
Santa Fe, College of; Santa Fe, N.M. 87501	375	386	56	P/RC	2,700	2,700	1,600
Sarah Lawrence College; Bronxville, N.Y. 10708	202[3]	727[3]	69	P	6,200[11]	6,200[11]	2,650[11]

Institution and location	Enrollment		Faculty	Control	Tuition		Rm/Bd
	Male	Female			Res.	Nonres.	
Savannah State College; Savannah, Ga. 31404	867	965	120	S	800	1,728	1,600
Scranton, University of; Scranton, Pa. 18510	1,593	1,047	153	P/RC	2,784[11]	2,784[11]	1,640[11]
Scripps College. *See* Claremont Colleges							
Seattle Pacific University; Seattle, Wash. 98119	758[3]	1,253[3]	103	P/FM	3,525	3,525	1,929
Seattle University; Seattle, Wash. 98122	1,169[3]	1,302[3]	207	P/RC	3,555	3,555	1,980
Seton Hill College; Greensburg, Pa. 15601	—	770[3]	47	P	3,200	3,200	1,740
Shaw University; Raleigh, N.C. 27611	736[3]	594[3]	57	P/B	2,500	2,500	1,300
Sheldon Jackson College; Sitka, Alaska 99835	63	46	21	P	2,500	2,500	2,500
Shepherd College; Shepherdstown, W. Va. 25443	1,173[3]	1,689[3]	104	S	366	1,306	1,351
Sherwood Music School; Chicago, Ill. 60605	90	110	25	P	2,260	2,260	3,380
Shimer College; Waukegan, Ill. 60085	60	90	20	P	3,500	3,500	2,300
Shippensburg State College; Shippensburg, Pa. 17257	2,200[3]	2,428[3]	277	S	950	1,780	1,204
Shorter College; Rome, Ga. 30161	329[3]	436[3]	55	P/SB	1,550	2,150	1,350
Siena College; Loudonville, N.Y. 12211	1,716	1,192	125	P/RC	3,150	3,150	2,100
Siena Heights College; Adrian, Mich. 49221	247	428	59	P/RC	2,520	2,520	1,650
Sierra Nevada College; Incline Village, Nev. 89450	90	80	39	P	2,000	2,000	3,000[20]
Silver Lake College; Manitowoc, Wis. 54220	40[3]	170[3]	30	P/RC	2,600	2,600	1,485
Simmons College; Boston, Mass. 02115	2,088		155	P	4,928	4,928	2,440
Simon's Rock of Bard College; Great Barrington, Mass. 01230	81	126	30	P	4,265	5,265	1,985
Simpson College; Indianola, Iowa 50125	412	363	57	P	3,565	3,565	1,315
Simpson College; San Francisco, Calif. 94134	111[3]	102[3]	22	CMA	2,000	2,000	1,420
Sioux Falls College; Sioux Falls, S.D. 57101	257[3]	271[3]	41	P/B	2,700	2,700	1,540
Skidmore College; Saratoga Springs, N.Y. 12866	412[3]	1,659[3]	157	P	5,580[11]	5,580[11]	2,620[11]
Slippery Rock State College; Slippery Rock, Pa. 16057	2,165	2,287	338	S	1,100	1,930	1,210
Smith College; Northampton, Mass. 01063	3	2,605	254	P	5,900	5,900	2,300
Sonoma State University; Rohnert Park, Calif. 94928[18]	1,429[3]	1,851[3]	251	S	194	1,994	2,135
South, The University of the; Sewanee, Tenn. 37375	548	403	93	P/E	4,070	4,070	1,450
South Alabama, University of; Mobile, Ala. 36688	2,735[3]	2,648[3]	394	S	930	930	1,458
South Carolina, University of; Columbia, S.C. 29208	12,054	12,332	1,066[8]	S	740	1,700	1,520
USC at Aiken; Aiken, S.C. 29801	478	631	87	S	710	1,700	—
Coastal Carolina College; Conway, S.C. 29526	999[3]	889[3]	111	S	710	1,700	n.a.
USC at Spartanburg; Spartanburg, S.C. 29303	1,042[3]	1,382[3]	137	S	710	1,700	n.a.
South Carolina State College; Orangeburg, S.C. 29117	1,284	1,636	244	S	640	1,340	1,226
South Dakota, University of; Vermillion, S.D. 57069	2,612[3]	2,266[3]	358	S	730	1,600	1,370
University of South Dakota at Springfield; Springfield, S.D. 57062	578	172	60	S	592	1,265	1,320
South Dakota School of Mines and Technology; Rapid City, S.D. 57701	1,500	400	100	S	765	1,685	1,350
South Dakota State University; Brookings, S.D. 57007	3,131[3]	2,560[3]	399	S	625	1,425	1,150
Southeastern Bible College; Birmingham, Ala. 35205	170	139	20	P/Ind	2,240	2,240	1,740
Southeastern College of the Assemblies of God; Lakeland, Fla. 33801	696	481	41	P/AG	([66])	([66])	600
Southeastern Louisiana University; Hammond, La. 70402	2,994	4,193	269	S	518	1,148	1,242
Southeastern Massachusetts University; North Dartmouth, Mass. 02740	2,695[3]	2,613[3]	300	S	664	2,400	2,635
Southeastern Oklahoma State Univ.; Durant, Okla. 74701	2,088[3]	2,072[3]	138	S	432	1,055	1,420
Southeastern University; Washington, D.C. 20024	496[3]	269[3]	105[8]	P	2,250	2,250	—
Southeast Missouri State University; Cape Girardeau, Mo. 63701	3,274[3]	3,792[3]	383	S	360	860	1,250
Southern Arkansas University; Magnolia, Ark. 71753	702	764	115	P	630	980	1,056
Southern Bible College; Houston, Tex. 77078	73	58	9	P/CG	1,080	1,080	1,300
Southern California, Univ. of; Los Angeles, Calif. 90007	10,379[3]	6,793[3]	1,601	P	5,310	5,310	2,500
Southern California College; Costa Mesa, Calif. 92626	358	318	32	P/AG	1,990	1,990	1,745
Southern California College of Optometry; Fullerton, Calif. 92631	294[3]	77[3]	40	P	4,725	4,725	3,400
Southern California Institute of Architecture; Santa Monica, Calif. 90404	255	66	42	P	2,800	2,800	6,000[67]
Southern College of Optometry; Memphis, Tenn. 38104	540[3]	40[3]	39	P	5,423	9,423	5,000
Southern Colorado, University of; Pueblo, Colo. 81001	2,167[3]	1,493[3]	190	S	581	2,555	1,840
Southern Connecticut State College; New Haven, Conn. 06515	2,647[3]	4,450[3]	426	S	390	1,030	1,648
Southern Illinois University at Carbondale; Carbondale, Ill. 62901	11,578	6,635	1,760	S	942	2,186	1,801
Southern Illinois University at Edwardsville; Edwardsville, Ill. 62026	2,945[3]	3,463[3]	692	S	615	1,845	1,810
Southern Methodist University; Dallas, Tex. 75275	3,452	2,905	445	P	3,840[11]	3,840[11]	2,330[11]
Southern Missionary College; Collegedale, Tenn. 37315	687[3]	846[3]	125	P/SDA	3,390	3,390	1,720
Southern Mississippi, Univ. of; Hattiesburg, Miss. 39401	4,593[3]	5,491[3]	542	S	776	1,626	1,450
Southern Oregon State College; Ashland, Ore. 97520	1,710[3]	1,610[3]	207	S	858	2,673	1,800
Southern Tech. Inst. *See* Georgia Inst. of Tech.							

Institution and location	Enrollment		Faculty	Control	Tuition		Rm/Bd
	Male	Female			Res.	Nonres.	
Southern University and A&M College System; Baton Rouge, La. 70813							
Southern University and A&M College; Baton Rouge, La. 70813	3,711[3]	4,390[3]	381	S	450	1,080	1,724
Southern University in New Orleans; New Orleans, La. 70126	980[22]	1,642[22]	111	S	195	315	—
Southern Utah State College; Cedar City, Utah 84720	885	692	102	S	462	1,320	1,518
Southern Vermont College; Bennington, Vt. 05201	136	134	16	P	2,550	2,550	2,180
South Florida, The University of; Tampa, Fla. 33620	7,214[3]	6,991[3]	1,050	S	785	2,292	2,459
New College Campus; Sarasota, Fla. 33580	240	260	42	S	870	2,158	1,730
St. Petersburg Campus; St. Petersburg, Fla. 33701	980	1,123	30	S	792	2,184	—
South Texas, University System of:							
Corpus Christi State Univ.; Corpus Christi, Tex. 78412	380	524	99	S	360	1,440	800
Laredo State University; Laredo, Tex. 78040	111	181	24	S	100	960	—
Texas A&I University; Kingsville, Tex. 78363	2,122	1,598	236	S	363	1,443	1,394
South Texas College of Law; Houston, Tex. 77002	861	335	19	P	2,924	2,924	4,583
Southwest Baptist College; Bolivar, Mo. 65613	588	677	70	P/B	2,050	2,050	1,150
Southwestern Adventist College; Keene, Tex. 76059	338	393	49	P/SDA	1,575	1,575	910
Southwestern Assemblies of God College; Waxahachie, Tex. 75165	371	311	19	P/AG	1,200	1,200	1,535
Southwestern at Memphis; Memphis, Tenn. 38112	517	487	n.a.	P	4,000	4,000	1,970
Southwestern Baptist Bible College; Phoenix, Ariz. 85032	77	48	12	P/B	1,742	1,742	1,650
Southwestern College; Winfield, Kan. 67156	256	270	44	P/UM	2,400[11]	2,400[11]	1,566[11]
Southwestern Louisiana, University of; Lafayette, La. 70504	6,648[3]	6,693[3]	584	S	440	1,070	1,000
Southwestern Oklahoma State University; Weatherford, Okla. 73096	1,819[3]	1,887[3]	260	S	415	1,095	1,060
Southwestern Union College, Tex. *See* Southwestern Adventist College							
Southwestern University; Georgetown, Tex. 78626	445[3]	556[3]	60	P	2,600	2,600	1,800
Southwestern University School of Law; Los Angeles, Calif. 90005	730	317	51	P	([68])	([68])	—
Southwest Minnesota State University. *See* Minnesota State College System							
Southwest Missouri State Univ.; Springfield, Mo. 65802	4,746	4,849	520	S	420	900	1,230
Southwest Texas State Univ.; San Marcos, Tex. 78666	5,763[3]	6,073[3]	564	S	340	1,200	1,650
Spalding College; Louisville, Ky. 40203	33	433	60	P/RC	2,400	2,400	1,600
Spelman College; Atlanta, Ga. 30314	—	1,257[3]	92	P	2,350	2,350	1,850
Spertus College of Judaica; Chicago, Ill. 60605	28	48	10	P	2,700	2,700	—
Spring Arbor College; Spring Arbor, Mich. 49283	582	460	39	P/FM	3,600	3,600	1,550
Springfield College; Springfield, Mass. 01109	1,058	1,122	127	P	3,366	3,366	1,683
Spring Garden College; Philadelphia, Pa. 19118	581[3]	100[3]	55	P	2,924	2,924	—
Spring Hill College; Mobile, Ala. 36608	458[3]	382[3]	52	P/RC	3,200[11]	3,200[11]	1,960
Stanford University; Stanford, Calif. 94305	3,792[3]	2,846[3]	1,205	P	6,285	6,285	2,636
Staten Island, College of (NYC). *See* New York, City University of							
Steed College; Johnson City, Tenn. 37601	312	104	14	P	1,920	1,920	—
Stephen F. Austin State Univ.; Nacogdoches, Tex. 75962	4,100[3]	5,900[3]	440	S	400	1,408	1,650
Stephens College; Columbia, Mo. 65201	—	1,400	130	P	6,075[21]	6,075[21]	—
Sterling College; Sterling, Kan. 67579	240	249	43	P/UP	2,770	2,770	1,430
Stetson University; DeLand, Fla. 32720	1,531[3]	1,416[3]	128	P/SB	3,065	3,065	1,565
Stetson Univ. College of Law; St. Petersburg, Fla. 33707	335	132	21	P	3,600	3,600	1,850
Steubenville, University of; Steubenville, Ohio 43952	250	325	70	P/RC	2,860	2,860	1,800
Stevens Institute of Technology; Hoboken, N.J. 07030	1,629	239	130	P	4,800	4,800	2,520
Stillman College; Tuscaloosa, Ala. 35403	245	390	38	P	1,800	1,800	1,825
Stockton State College; Pomona, N.J. 08241	1,992	1,516	163	S	736	1,440	1,464
Stonehill College; North Easton, Mass. 02356	850	850	77	P	3,725	3,725	2,200
Suffolk University; Boston, Mass. 02114	1,298	1,164	103	P	2,900	2,900	—
Sul Ross State University; Alpine, Tex. 79830	746	514	76	S	272	1,424	1,540
Susquehanna University; Selinsgrove, Pa. 17870	824[3]	633[3]	88	P/LCA	4,066	4,066	1,884
Swarthmore College; Swarthmore, Pa. 19081	692	563	136	P	5,400	5,400	2,295
Sweet Briar College; Sweet Briar, Va. 24595	—	633	71	P	5,200	5,200	1,750
Syracuse University; Syracuse, N.Y. 13210	10,803	9,370	846	P	4,500	4,500	900
Utica College of Syracuse Univ.; Utica, N.Y. 13502	609	726	90	P	4,015[3]	4,015[3]	1,886
Tabor College; Hillsboro, Kan. 67063	197	211	30	P/MB	2,560	2,560	1,671
Talladega College; Talladega, Ala. 35160	214[8]	428[3]	49	P	1,615	1,615	1,360
Tampa, The University of; Tampa, Fla. 33606	1,013[3]	642[3]	84	P	3,826	3,826	2,000
Tampa College; Tampa, Fla. 33607	1,000[8]		10	P	1,458	1,458	—
Tarkio College; Tarkio, Mo. 64491	129	111	31	P	2,825	2,825	1,475
Tarleton State University[69]; Stephenville, Tex. 76402	1,889	1,514	165	S	120	1,200	1,292

Institution and location	Enrollment: Male	Enrollment: Female	Faculty	Control	Tuition: Res.	Tuition: Nonres.	Rm/Bd
Taylor University; Upland, Ind. 46989	699	775	82	P/ND	3,544	3,544	1,750
Temple University; Philadelphia, Pa. 19122	17,311[3]	16,282[3]	1,761	S	1,810	3,374	1,960
Tennessee State University; Nashville, Tenn. 37203	4,074	4,539	402	S	—	1,008	1,384
Tennessee System, University of; Knoxville, Tenn. 37916							
U. of Tennessee at Chattanooga; Chattanooga, Tenn. 37402	3,606[3]	3,933[3]	248	S	546	1,546	—
U. of Tennessee at Knoxville; Knoxville, Tenn. 37916	16,626[3]	13,764[3]	1,304	S	744	2,080	2,092
U. of Tennessee at Martin; Martin, Tenn. 38238	1,870	1,831	215	S	588	1,590	1,554
U. of Tennessee at Nashville; Nashville, Tenn. 37203	2,687[9]	2,972[9]	120	S	450	1,386	—
U. of Tennessee Center for the Health Sciences; Memphis, Tenn. 38163	1,324[3]	746[3]	n.a.	S	1,095[8]	1,995[8]	2,025
Tennessee Technological Univ.; Cookeville, Tenn. 38501	4,433[3]	3,416[3]	300	S	483	1,485	1,400
Tennessee Wesleyan College; Athens, Tenn. 37303	200	180	26	P/UM	2,160	2,160	1,560
Texas, Univ. of, at Tyler[70]; Tyler, Tex. 75701	212[3]	326[3]	76	S	345	1,425	—
Texas, Univ. of, Health Science Center at Dallas; Dallas, Tex. 75235	687	144	650	S	300	900	—
Texas, Univ. of, Health Science Center at Houston; Houston, Tex. 77025	393	112	332	S	300	900	—
Texas, Univ. of, Health Science Center at San Antonio; San Antonio, Tex. 78284	1,145	873	490	S	400	1,200	—
Texas, Univ. of, Medical Branch; Galveston, Tex. 77550	789[3]	765[3]	525	S	400	1,200	3,500[20]
Texas, Univ. of Permian Basin; Odessa, Tex. 79762	799[3]	798[3]	64	S	120	1,200	585[4]
Texas, University of, System; Austin, Tex. 78701							
U. of Texas at Arlington; Arlington, Tex. 76019	7,438[3]	4,825[3]	607	S	440	1,480	2,060
U. of Texas at Austin; Austin, Tex. 78712	24,388[3]	19,714[3]	1,763	S	452	1,532	2,096
U. of Texas at Dallas; Dallas, Tex. 75080	936	855	210	S	382	1,242	—
U. of Texas at El Paso; El Paso, Tex. 79968	8,387[3]	7,358[3]	428	S	360	1,440	1,310
U. of Texas at San Antonio; San Antonio, Tex. 78285	3,129	3,199	252	S	150	1,440	—
Texas A&I University at Corpus Christi. *See* South Texas, University System of							
Texas A&I University at Laredo. *See* South Texas, University System of							
Texas A&I University in Kingsville. *See* South Texas, University System of							
Texas A&M University; College Station, Tex. 77843	18,105[3]	9,701[3]	1,879	S	128	1,280	1,500
Texas A&M Univ. at Galveston; Galveston, Tex. 77553	444	133	n.a.	S	180	1,440	1,863
Texas Chiropractic College; Pasadena, Tex. 77505	305[3]	62[3]	20[8]	P	2,905	2,905	—
Texas Christian University; Fort Worth, Tex. 76129	2,730[3]	3,200[3]	329	P/CC	3,200	3,200	1,885
Texas College; Tyler, Tex. 75702	210	224	39	P/M	1,620	1,620	1,485
Texas Coll. of Osteopathic Medicine; Fort Worth, Tex. 76107	257[3]	55[3]	120	S	300	900	—
Texas Eastern Univ. *See* Texas, Univ. of, at Tyler							
Texas Lutheran College; Seguin, Tex. 78155	503[3]	476[3]	58	P/L	2,410	2,410	1,535
Texas Southern University; Houston, Tex. 77004	4,552[9]	4,274[9]	450	S	400	1,600	1,600
Texas Tech University; Lubbock, Tex. 79409	10,580[3]	7,881[3]	975	S	120	1,200	1,200
Texas Wesleyan College; Fort Worth, Tex. 76105	491[3]	538[3]	75	P/M	2,300	2,300	1,600
Texas Woman's University; Denton, Tex. 76204	520[3]	7,236[3]	485	S	120	1,200	1,428
Thiel College; Greenville, Pa. 16125	536[3]	472[3]	61	P/L	3,438	3,438	1,609
Thomas A. Edison College of New Jersey; Trenton, N.J. 08625	2,400	1,600	—	S	—	—	—
Thomas College; Waterville, Me. 04901	440		22	P	3,560	3,560	1,990
Thomas Jefferson University; Philadelphia, Pa. 19107	1,528		372	P	4,000	4,000	n.a.
Thomas M. Cooley Law School; Lansing, Mich. 48901	813[3]	257[3]	20	P	2,700	3,000	—
Thomas More College; Fort Mitchell, Ky. 41017	411[3]	340[3]	65	P/RC	2,665	2,665	1,860
Tiffin University; Tiffin, Ohio 44883	175	120	12	P	2,080	2,080	1,380
Tift College; Forsyth, Ga. 31029	613		34	P	1,700	1,700	1,415
Toccoa Falls College; Toccoa Falls, Ga. 30598	244	215	34	P/ID	1,900	1,900	1,630
Toledo, The University of; Toledo, Ohio 43606	4,857[3]	4,278[3]	643	S	972	2,427	1,854
Tougaloo College; Tougaloo, Miss. 39174	279	468	65	P	2,025	2,025	1,225
Touro College; New York, N.Y. 10036	624	1,138	61	P	3,050	3,050	1,900
Towson State College; Towson, Md. 21204	3,887	5,152	508	S	655	1,610	1,760
Transylvania University; Lexington, Ky. 40508	369[3]	380[3]	57	P	3,600	3,600	1,690
Trenton State College; Trenton, N.J. 08625	4,178[3]	6,349[3]	378	S	736	1,440	1,650
Trevecca Nazarene College; Nashville, Tenn. 37210	408[3]	413[3]	50	P/Naz	2,085	2,085	1,350
Trinity Christian College; Palos Heights, Ill. 60463	150	233	26	P	2,570	2,570	1,650
Trinity College; Burlington, Vt. 05401	109	565	26	P/RC	3,150	3,150	1,880
Trinity College; Deerfield, Ill. 60015	357	423	43	P	3,410	3,410	1,686
Trinity College; Hartford, Conn. 06106	964	773	137	P	5,350	5,350	2,220
Trinity College; Washington, D.C. 20017	4[3]	531[3]	50	P	4,050	4,050	2,425
Trinity University; San Antonio, Tex. 78284	1,333	1,427	202	P/Pres	3,000	3,000	1,565
Tri-State University; Angola, Ind. 46703	987	274	76	P	3,015	3,015	1,590

Institution and location	Enrollment		Faculty	Control	Tuition		
	Male	Female			Res.	Nonres.	Rm/Bd
Troy State University; Troy, Ala. 36081	2,293[3]	2,070[3]	183	S	630	885	1,179
Tufts University; Medford, Mass. 02155[71]	3,465[2]	2,791[2]	413	P	5,850	5,850	3,031
Tulane University; New Orleans, La. 70118	4,797	2,538	683	P	5,046	5,046	2,333
Newcomb College; New Orleans, La. 70118	—	1,598	n.a.	P	5,056	5,056	1,100
Tulsa, The University of; Tulsa, Okla. 74104	2,312[3]	1,792[3]	309	P/UP	2,380	2,380	1,365
Turabo University College. *See* Ana G. Méndez Educational Foundation							
Tusculum College; Greeneville, Tenn. 37743	157	165	29	P	2,340	2,340	1,650
Tuskegee Institute; Tuskegee Institute, Ala. 36088	1,625	1,652	289	P	2,200	2,200	1,890
Union College; Barbourville, Ky. 40906	133	185	48	P	2,700	2,700	1,390
Union College; Lincoln, Neb. 68506	356	360	59	P/SDA	3,600	3,600	1,500
Union College; Schenectady, N.Y. 12308	1,363[3]	688[3]	140	P	5,520[11]	5,520[11]	2,030[11]
Union University; Jackson, Tenn. 38301	382	586	61	P/B	1,900	1,900	1,100
U.S. Air Force Academy; USAF Academy, Colo. 80840	4,081	502	560	Fed	—	—	—
U.S. Coast Guard Academy; New London, Conn. 06320	707	79	111	Fed	—	—	
U.S. International University; San Diego, Calif. 92131	1,898[3]	1,022[3]	85	P	3,690	3,690	2,295
U.S. Merchant Marine Academy; Kings Point, N.Y. 11024	1,015	72	82	Fed	—	—	—
U.S. Military Academy; West Point, N.Y. 10996	3,749	313	639	Fed	—	—	—
U.S. Naval Academy; Annapolis, Md. 21402	4,105	264	550	Fed	—	—	—
United Wesleyan College; Allentown, Pa. 18103	117[3]	69[3]	11	P/W	2,150[11]	2,150[11]	1,740[11]
Unity College; Unity, Me. 04988	337[3]	90[3]	27	P	3,670[11]	3,670[11]	1,950[11]
Upper Iowa University; Fayette, Iowa 52142	224	143	32	P	2,800	2,800	5,350
Upsala College; East Orange, N.J. 07019	656[3]	474[3]	67	P/LCA	3,430	3,430	2,000
Urbana College; Urbana, Ohio 43078	490[3]	259[3]	22	P/Sw	2,898	2,898	1,948
Ursinus College; Collegeville, Pa. 19426	975[3]	796[3]	71	P	4,000	4,000	1,750
Ursuline College; Cleveland, Ohio 44124	8[3]	504[3]	43	P/RC	2,570	2,570	1,500
Utah, University of; Salt Lake City, Utah 84121	9,560[3]	6,213[3]	1,396	S	642	1,890	2,300
Utah State University; Logan, Utah 84322	4,440[3]	3,244[3]	470	S	702	1,860	1,245
Utica College. *See* Syracuse University.							
Valdosta State College; Valdosta, Ga. 31601	2,066[3]	2,786[3]	250	S	579	1,365	1,100
Valley City State College; Valley City, N.D. 58072	408[3]	512[3]	52	S	471	1,040	1,380
Valley Forge Christian College; Phoenixville, Pa. 19460	364	262	17	P/AG	976[8]	976[8]	1,400[8]
Valparaiso University; Valparaiso, Ind. 46383	1,812[3]	1,951[3]	273	P/L	3,500	3,500	1,840
Vanderbilt University; Nashville, Tenn. 37240	4,554	3,700	1,125	P	4,700	4,700	2,285
VanderCook College of Music; Chicago, Ill. 60616	73	17	14	P	2,780	2,780	2,000
Vassar College; Poughkeepsie, N.Y. 12601	946	1,314	189	P	5,375	5,375	7,800
Vennard College; University Park, Iowa 52595	102	99	10	P/ID	1,186	1,186	1,388
Vermont, University of; Burlington, Vt. 05405	3,828[3]	4,527[3]	716	S	1,500	4,150	1,887
Vermont College. *See* Norwich University							
Villa Maria College; Erie, Pa. 16505	3	428	49	P/RC	3,000	3,000	1,750
Villanova University; Villanova, Pa. 19085	5,804		430	P	3,850	3,850	2,400
Virginia, University of; Charlottesville, Va. 22903	8,165	6,197	1,593	S	555	1,800	1,700
Clinch Valley College; Wise, Va. 24293	308	359	43	S	750	1,110	480
Virginia Commonwealth University; Richmond, Va. 23284	8,146	11,282	1,469	S	745	1,490	1,742
Virginia Intermont College; Bristol, Va. 24201	84	524	41	P/B	2,750	2,750	1,800
Virginia Military Institute; Lexington, Va. 24450	1,300[3]	—	91	S	600	1,800	1,095
Virginia State University; Petersburg, Va. 23803	1,582[3]	1,896[3]	231	S	995	1,570	1,683
Virginia Union University; Richmond, Va. 23220	544[3]	568[3]	81	P/B	2,390	2,390	1,600
Virginia Wesleyan College; Norfolk, Va. 23502	416[3]	388[3]	43	P/UM	3,175	3,175	1,625
Virgin Islands, College of the; St. Thomas, V.I. 00801	160[3]	325[3]	61	S	360	1,080	1,570
Visual Arts, School of; New York, N.Y. 10010	1,289	1,180	196	P/Ind	3,600	3,600	—
Viterbo College; La Crosse, Wis. 54601	136	609	80	Ind/RC	2,970	2,970	1,700
Voorhees College; Denmark, S.C. 29042	254	432	40	P/E	2,118	2,118	1,774
Wabash College; Crawfordsville, Ind. 47933	806[3]	—	64	P	4,100	4,100	1,950
Wagner College; Staten Island, N.Y. 10301	892[3]	1,021[3]	97	P	3,828[11]	3,828[11]	2,240[11]
Wake Forest University; Winston–Salem, N.C. 27109	2,917	1,585	568	P/B	3,600	3,600	1,465
Walla Walla College; College Place, Wash. 99324	881[3]	832[3]	125	P/SDA	4,177	4,177	1,650
Walsh College; Canton, Ohio 44720	262	203	31	P/RC	3,000	3,000	1,550
Walsh College; Troy, Mich. 48084	115	59	9	P	1,128	1,128	—
Warner Pacific College; Portland, Ore. 97215	230	231	28	CG	1,040	1,040	1,200
Warner Southern College; Lake Wales, Fla. 33853	128	122	16	P/CG	1,935	1,935	1,335
Warren Wilson College; Swannanoa, N.C. 28778	220	270	36	P/UP	2,800	2,800	1,320
Wartburg College; Waverly, Iowa 50677	476	585	76	P/AL	3,574	3,574	1,552
Washburn University of Topeka; Topeka, Kan. 66621	1,869	1,493	180	Mun	740	1,370	1,600
Washington, University of; Seattle, Wash. 98105	15,780[3]	12,782[3]	2,150	S	687	2,394	1,600
Washington and Jefferson College; Washington, Pa. 15301	655	343	89	P	4,055	4,055	1,550
Washington and Lee University; Lexington, Va. 24450	1,556[3]	92[3]	155	P	4,050	4,050	1,850

Institution and location	Enrollment Male	Enrollment Female	Faculty	Control	Tuition Res.	Tuition Nonres.	Rm/Bd
Washington Bible College; Lanham, Md. 20801	281	187	18	P/ND	1,890	1,890	1,880
Washington College; Chestertown, Md. 21620	382	274	60	P	3,150	3,150	1,550
Washington State University; Pullman, Wash. 99164	9,629[3]	7,363[3]	754	S	686	2,394	1,620
Washington University in St. Louis; St. Louis, Mo. 63130	4,800	3,200	1,278	P	5,350	5,350	2,600
Wayland Baptist College; Plainview, Tex. 79072	279	264	49	SB	1,700	1,700	1,730
Waynesburg College; Waynesburg, Pa. 15370	425	311	53	P	3,700	3,700	1,690
Wayne State College; Wayne, Neb. 68787	711	930	108	S	852	1,215	1,380
Wayne State University; Detroit, Mich. 48202	17,137[3]	17,200[3]	2,200	S	1,344	2,763	1,800
Webb Institute of Naval Architecture; Glen Cove, N.Y. 11542	67	5	15	P	—	—	2,200
Weber State College; Ogden, Utah 84408	5,974	4,337	420	S	633	1,524	1,465
Webster College; St. Louis, Mo. 63119	936[3]	575[3]	75	P	3,300	3,300	1,650
Wellesley College; Wellesley, Mass. 02181	—	2,089	218	P	5,400	5,400	2,840
Wells College; Aurora, N.Y. 13026	—	495	50[8]	P	4,500	4,500	2,000
Wentworth Institute of Technology; Boston, Mass. 02115	2,100	200	120	P	3,050	3,050	2,300
Wesleyan College; Macon, Ga. 31201	2	385	36	P/M	2,400	3,370	1,600
Wesleyan University; Middletown, Conn. 06457	1,250[2]	1,250[2]	235	P	5,950[11]	5,950[11]	2,360[11]
Wesley College; Dover, Del. 19901	666	603	48	P/UM	3,500	3,500	1,720
Westbrook College; Portland, Me. 04103	97	498	48	P	3,400	3,400	1,750
West Chester State College; West Chester, Pa. 19380	2,415[3]	3,428[3]	505	S	1,100	1,930	1,254
West Coast University; Los Angeles, Calif. 90020	1,207[9]	210[9]	250	P	2,100	2,100	—
Western Baptist College; Salem, Ore. 97302	198[3]	196[3]	21	P/B	2,580[11]	2,580[11]	1,755[11]
Western Bible College; Morrison, Colo. 80465	127[3]	83[3]	9	P	1,680	1,680	1,300
Western Carolina University. *See* North Carolina, University System of							
Western Connecticut State College; Danbury, Conn. 06810	1,233[3]	1,556[3]	176	S	760	1,750	1,656
Western Illinois University; Macomb, Ill. 61455	5,646[3]	4,709[3]	702	S	606	1,722	1,623
Western Kentucky University; Bowling Green, Ky. 42101	5,813	6,932	655	S	520	1,240	1,300
Western Maryland College; Westminster, Md. 21157	590	665	88	P	3,875[11]	3,875[11]	1,750[11]
Western Michigan University; Kalamazoo, Mich. 49001	10,454[3]	10,235[3]	840	Mun	1,020	2,180	1,780
Western Montana College; Dillon, Mont. 59725	233	241	35	S	474	1,482	1,522
Western New England College; Springfield, Mass. 01119	1,742[3]	842[3]	130	P	2,850[11]	2,850[11]	1,700[11]
Western New Mexico University; Silver City, N.M. 88061	633	784	60	S	274	1,250	1,200
Western State College of Colorado; Gunnison, Colo. 81230	1,881[3]	1,309[3]	134	S	657	2,262	1,430
Western State University College of Law of Orange County; Fullerton, Calif. 92631	1,221[3]	525[3]	61	P	2,490	2,490	3,875
Western State University College of Law of San Diego; San Diego, Calif. 92101	650	257	13	P	2,800	2,800	—
Western Washington University; Bellingham, Wash. 98225	4,196[3]	4,451[3]	446	S	618	1,983	1,545
Westfield State College; Westfield, Mass. 01086	1,200	1,500	150[8]	S	600	2,100	1,700
West Florida, The University of; Pensacola, Fla. 32504	2,538[3]	2,647[3]	232	S	([72])	([73])	1,570
West Georgia College; Carrollton, Ga. 30118	2,050[3]	3,001[3]	255	S	597	1,383	1,455
West Liberty State College; West Liberty, W. Va. 26074	980[3]	1,078[3]	135	S	370	1,310	1,558
Westmar College; LeMars, Iowa 51031	318	287	46	P/UM	3,170	3,170	1,535
Westminster Choir College; Princeton, N.J. 08540	209[3]	261[3]	38	P	4,100	4,100	2,050
Westminster College; Fulton, Mo. 65251	572[3]	33[3]	51	P	3,800[11]	3,800[11]	1,750[11]
Westminster College; New Wilmington, Pa. 16142	753[3]	754[3]	115	P/UP	3,730	3,730	1,630
Westminster College; Salt Lake City, Utah 84105	427[3]	521[3]	53	P	2,400	2,400	1,565
Westmont College; Santa Barbara, Calif. 93108	475[3]	553[3]	55	P/ID	4,250	4,250	2,100
West Texas State University; Canyon, Tex. 79016	2,237[3]	2,288[3]	217	S	120	1,200	1,274
West Virginia College of Graduate Studies; Institute, W. Va. 25112	1,179[3]	2,048[3]	55	S	250	1,270	—
West Virginia Institute of Technology; Montgomery, W. Va. 25136	1,563[3]	632[3]	136	S	371	1,311	1,640
West Virginia School of Osteopathic Medicine; Lewisburg, W. Va. 24901	182	36	32	S	250	750	—
West Virginia State College; Institute, W. Va. 25112	1,566	1,824	132	S	396	1,336	1,674
West Virginia University; Morgantown, W. Va. 26506	8,000	8,000	1,600	S	482	1,502	1,850
West Virginia Wesleyan College; Buckhannon, W. Va. 26201	680[3]	965[3]	105	P/UM	2,950	2,950	1,850
Wheaton College; Norton, Mass. 02766	—	1,206[3]	90	P	6,040	6,040	2,400
Wheaton College; Wheaton, Ill. 60187	1,165	1,193	140	P/ID	3,534	3,534	2,070
Wheeling College; Wheeling, W. Va. 26003	438[3]	443[3]	68	P/RC	3,240[11]	3,240[11]	1,880[11]
Wheelock College; Boston, Mass. 02215	28	923	56	P	4,240	4,240	2,100
Whitman College; Walla Walla, Wash. 99362	570	511	79	P	4,510	4,510	1,950
Whittier College; Whittier, Calif. 90602	544	614	85	P	4,250	4,250	1,885
Whitworth College; Spokane, Wash. 99251	548[3]	660[3]	70	P/Pres	3,950[11]	3,950[11]	1,775[11]
Wichita State University; Wichita, Kan. 67208	3,580[3]	3,188[3]	516	S	780	1,860	1,725

Institution and location	Enrollment: Male	Enrollment: Female	Faculty	Control	Tuition: Res.	Tuition: Nonres.	Rm/Bd
Widener College; Chester, Pa. 19013	1,191[3]	905[3]	139	P	3,980	3,980	1,970
Wilberforce University; Wilberforce, Ohio 45384	307	332	50	P/AME	2,360	2,360	1,310
Wiley College; Marshall, Tex. 75670	270	297	33	P/UM	1,890	1,890	1,448
Wilkes College; Wilkes–Barre, Pa. 18766	1,078	877	146	P	3,750	3,750	1,900
Willamette University; Salem, Ore. 97301	1,082[3]	747[3]	125	P/M	4,110[11]	4,110[11]	1,900
William and Mary in Virginia, College of; Williamsburg, Va. 23185	3,006[3]	3,381[3]	389	S	1,184	2,928	1,833
William Carey College; Hattiesburg, Miss. 39401	344	477	81	P/SB	1,800	1,800	1,370
William Jewell College; Liberty, Mo. 64068	800	600	92	P/B	2,720	2,720	1,410
William Mitchell College of Law; St. Paul, Minn. 55105	740	387	26	P	1,025	1,025	—
William Paterson Coll. of New Jersey; Wayne, N.J. 07470	2,922	3,302	380	S	690	1,350	1,750
William Penn College; Oskaloosa, Iowa 52577	336	206	34	P/SOF	4,100	4,100	1,380
Williams College; Williamstown, Mass. 01267	1,100[3]	850[3]	175	P	5,950[11]	5,950[11]	2,330
William Smith College. *See* Hobart and William Smith Colleges							
William Woods College; Fulton, Mo. 65251	—	996[3]	72	P/DC	3,725[11]	3,725[11]	1,735
Wilmington College; New Castle, Del. 19720	408	277	10	P	([74])	([74])	1,205
Wilmington College; Wilmington, Ohio 45177	180	390	55	P/SOF	3,045	3,045	1,980
Wilson College; Chambersburg, Pa. 17201	—	127	31	P/Pres	4,050[11]	4,050[11]	1,850
Winona State Univ. *See* Minnesota State Univ. System							
Winston–Salem State University. *See* North Carolina, University System of							
Winthrop College; Rock Hill, S.C. 29733	954	2,288	266	S	913	1,613	1,210
Wisconsin, University of; Madison, Wis. 53706	21,986[3]	18,247[3]	2,350	S	1,006	3,491	1,475
U. of Wisconsin—Eau Claire; Eau Claire, Wis. 54701	3,669	4,861	448	S	839	2,860	1,400
U. of Wisconsin—Green Bay; Green Bay, Wis. 54302	1760[3]	2,082[3]	163	S	850	2,950	1,800
U. of Wisconsin—La Crosse; La Crosse, Wis. 54601	3,048	3,823	395	S	855	2,876	1,354
U. of Wisconsin—Madison; Madison, Wis. 53706	19,020[3]	14,448[3]	2,350	S	877	3,176	1,475
U. of Wisconsin—Milwaukee; Milwaukee, Wis. 53201	6,789[3]	6,607[3]	815	S	898	3,197	2,034
U. of Wisconsin—Oshkosh; Oshkosh, Wis. 54901	4,812	5,556	521	S	830	2,851	1,440
U. of Wisconsin—Parkside; Kenosha, Wis. 53141	2,744	2,548	196	S	803	2,824	—
U. of Wisconsin—Platteville; Platteville, Wis. 53818	2,766	1,606	n.a.	S	862	2,883	1,448
U. of Wisconsin—River Falls; River Falls, Wis. 54022	2,653[3]	2,475[3]	250	S	870	2,910	1,620
U. of Wisconsin—Stevens Point; Stevens Point, Wis. 54481	3,816[3]	3,720[3]	475	S	842	2,864	1,506
U. of Wisconsin—Stout; Menomonie, Wis. 54751	3,173[3]	3,173[3]	334	S	839	2,860	1,500
U. of Wisconsin—Superior; Superior, Wis. 54880	885[3]	654[3]	145	S	895	3,050	1,895
U. of Wisconsin—Whitewater; Whitewater, Wis. 53190	3,503[3]	3,595[3]	507	S	853	2,874	1,462
Wittenberg University; Springfield, Ohio 45501	1,058[3]	1,224[3]	126	P/LCA	3,987	3,987	1,785
Wofford College; Spartanburg, S.C. 29301	798	222	57	P/UM	3,140	3,140	1,735
Woodbury University; Los Angeles, Calif. 90017[42]	697[3]	512[3]	42	P	3,048	3,048	n.a.
Wooster, The College of; Wooster, Ohio 44691	895[3]	814[3]	140	P	6,950[21]	6,950[21]	—
Worcester Art Museum, School of the; Worcester, Mass. 01608	36	63	11	P	2,500[11]	2,500[11]	1,700
Worcester Polytechnic Institute; Worcester, Mass. 01609	2,100	300	180	P	4,350	4,350	2,130
Worcester State College; Worcester, Mass. 01602	1,162[3]	1,549[3]	181	S	600	2,100	1,624
Wright Institute; Berkeley, Calif. 94704	3,135[8]	3,092[8]	575	S	960	1,950	n.a.
Wright State University; Dayton, Ohio 45435	6,798[3]	7,076[3]	587	S	1,020	2,010	1,644
Wyoming, University of; Laramie, Wyo. 82071	4,520[3]	3,118[3]	850	S	596	1,878	1,540[8]
Xavier University; Cincinnati, Ohio 45207	1,543[3]	1,048[3]	192	P	2,990	2,990	1,860
Xavier University of Louisiana; New Orleans, La. 70125	677	1,039	140	P	2,350	2,350	875
Yale University; New Haven, Conn. 06520	9,700		1,300	P	6,210	6,210	2,900
Yankton College; Yankton, S.D. 57078	127	115	30	P/UCC	3,340	3,340	1,530
Yeshiva University; New York, N.Y. 10033	3,431[3]	2,062[3]	1,200	P	3,880[11]	3,880[11]	1,995
York College (NYC). *See* New York, City University of							
York College of Pennsylvania; York, Pa. 17405	796	1,097	95	P	1,998	1,998	1,392
Youngstown State Univ.; Youngstown, Ohio 44555	5,237[3]	4,499[3]	434	S	855	1,575	1,350

1. $95 per unit. 2. Fall 1980. 3. Fall 1979. 4. Room only. 5. $165 per course. 6. Includes SUNY College of Ceramics. 7. Part time, 60. 8. Spring 1979. 9. Fall 1978. 10. Part time, 130. 11. 1980–81. 12. $90 per semester hour. 13. Non-dorm students. 14. Comprehensive fee, including room and board, for dorm students. 15. Georgia residents qualify for Grant Tuition, $600 per year. 16. LDS members. 17. Non-LDS members. 18. Member California State University and Colleges. 19. Plus $40 per unit. 20. Off campus. 21. Comprehensive fee, including room and board. 22. Spring 1978. 23. $145 per semester hour. 24. Continued as Member on Probation. 25. $165 per point of credit as of fall 1980. 26. Includes SUNY statutory colleges. 27. Tax assisted. 28. UCC/M. 29. $70 per credit. 30. $116 per credit hour. 31. Under SUNY supervision. 32. $16.50 per credit hour. 33. $51.50 per credit hour. 34. Academic programs will terminate on Jan. 1, 1982. 35. $49 per credit hour. 36. $66 per unit. 37. $13 per credit hour. 38. $33 per credit hour. 39. $145 per credit hour. 40. Member University of Hawaii System.

41. Protestant. 42. Accreditation on probation. 43. $60 per semester hour. 44. $45 per credit. 45. $40 per credit unit, spring 1979. 46. $44 per week, spring 1978. 47. $34 per hour. 48. $750 per trimester, fall 1978. 49. $590–$1,200, variable. 50. $1,070–$4,450, variable. 51. Part time. 52. $41 per semester hour. 53. Affiliated academically with the University of Minnesota. 54. First year; $6,500 others. 55. $75 per credit. 56. Formerly Our Lady of Angels College. 57. Part of Louisiana State University System. 58. Maintenance fee. 59. $60 per credit. 60. $131 per credit. 61. $4 per semester credit hour. 62. $40 per semester credit hour. 63. UM/UP/UCC. 64. A graduate school of Biola College. 65. Fall 1980, $96 per credit hour. 66. $42 per credit hour. 67. Living expenses; no dorm or eating facilities. 68. $153 per unit. 69. Member Texas A&M System. 70. Formerly Texas Eastern University. 71. Jackson College for Women is part of Tufts University. 72. $16.50 per quarter hour. 73. $51.50 per quarter hour. 74. $240 per 3-credit course (tri-semester). NOTE: A dash means the information does not apply; n.a. = not available.

Complaining About Educational Discrimination

If you think you or your child has been discriminated against by a public school, school system, or University, or a private school, college, or university which gets federal benefits, write to the appropriate regional office of the Department of Health, Education, and Welfare.

Complaints to HEW should be in writing, signed, and filed within 180 days after the discriminatory act takes place. Your complaint should include your name, your address, and telephone number at home and at work. Give the name and address of the person(s) and/or establishment you believe to have discriminated against you. Also give a description of the action or actions of discrimination. This should include the date and place of the action, what you believe to be the basis for discrimination (race, sex, etc.) and the names of the persons who have information concerning your complaint.

When your complaint is investigated, you also may be asked for copies of receipts, contracts, or other records supporting your claim of discrimination. Do not send materials which you want returned with your initial complaint.

According to a 1974 Supreme Court decision, discrimination may also include failure to provide instruction to non-English-speaking students.

Certain kinds of complaints should also be sent to the U.S. Attorney General, who may bring suit after receiving a written and signed complaint from: a parent (or group of parents), stating that his or her child is one of a group being discriminated against by a school board; an individual, or his or her parent, stating that he or she has been denied admission to or dismissed from a public college, university, or postsecondary vocational or technical school because of race, color, religion, sex, or national origin.

These should be sent to: Assistant Attorney General, Civil Rights Division, U.S. Department of Justice, Washington, D.C. 20530.

Teen-Agers Seek Traditional Marriage Values

The 10th annual survey of high school juniors and seniors listed in "Who's Who Among American High School Students" revealed a swing back toward traditional home and marriage values.

Only 8% of the students polled favored living together before marriage as compared to 47% of students surveyed in 1971. Seventy-six percent said that they had not had sexual relations and 86% said they would not have a child without being married.

More than half of the students surveyed said that they were opposed to abortion. Nine years ago, 69% said that they were in favor of it. The poll also found that only 32% of the students felt that a woman should experience both career and marriage to be fulfilled, where only three years ago, 43% felt that this was so.

French Academy Elects First Woman

Marguerite Yourcenar, a naturalized American citizen and long-time resident of Maine, became the first woman to be elected to the French Academy in its 345-year history. The 40-member Academy was founded in 1635 by Cardinal Richelieu to supervise France's language and intellectual life. Miss Yourcenar received the honor in recognition of her work as novelist, poet, and translator.

Freedom of Information

The Freedom of Information Act of 1966 established that Americans have a "right to know" much of the information in their government's files. In 1974, Congress amended the FOIA, providing for even more disclosure, and also passed the Privacy Act, which is intended to assist individuals to obtain information about themselves.

The Freedom of Information Act applies to documents held by administrative agencies of the executive branch of the federal government—for example, surveys of food and drugs, automobile safety, nursing homes, consumer products, etc. The Privacy Act applies to personal records maintained by the executive branch—for example, by the Armed Services, the FBI, VA, etc.

Records that will *not* be supplied fall under specific categories, such as those classified un defense and foreign policy, confidential business information, etc.

A Citizen's Guide on How to Use the Freedom of Information Act and the Privacy A Government Documents is available from the Superintendent of Documents, U.S. Go Office, Washington, D.C. 20402 for $3.00 (Stock No. 052–071–00540–4).

Population

Colonial Population Estimates (in round numbers)

Year	Population	Year	Population	Year	Population	Year	Population
1610	350	1660	75,100	1710	331,700	1760	1,593,600
1620	2,300	1670	111,900	1720	466,200	1770	2,148,100
1630	4,600	1680	151,500	1730	629,400	1780	2,780,400
1640	26,600	1690	210,400	1740	905,600		
1650	50,400	1700	250,900	1750	1,170,800		

National Censuses[1]

Year	Resident population[2]	Land area, sq mi.	Pop. per sq mi.	Year	Resident population[2]	Land area, sq mi.	Pop. per sq mi.
1790	3,929,214	864,746	4.5	1890	62,947,714	2,969,640	21.2
1800	5,308,483	864,746	6.1	1900	75,994,575	2,969,834	25.6
1810	7,239,881	1,681,828	4.3	1910	91,972,266	2,969,565	31.0
1820	9,638,453	1,749,462	5.5	1920	105,710,620	2,969,451	35.6
1830	12,866,020	1,749,462	7.4	1930	122,775,046	2,977,128	41.2
1840	17,069,453	1,749,462	9.8	1940	131,669,275	2,977,128	44.2
1850	23,191,876	2,940,042	7.9	1950	150,697,361	2,974,726	50.7
1860	31,443,321	2,969,640	10.6	1960	179,323,175	3,540,911	50.6
1870	39,818,449	2,969,640	13.4	1970	203,235,298	3,536,855	57.5
1880	50,155,783	2,969,640	16.9				

1. Beginning with 1960, figures include Alaska and Hawaii. 2. Excludes armed forces overseas. *Source:* Department of Commerce, Bureau of the Census.

Population Projections, 1982–2000[1]
(in millions)

Sex, race, age group	1982	1984	1986	1988	1990	1992	1994	1996	1998	2000
MALE, WHITE	95.1	96.7	98.2	99.8	101.2	102.6	103.9	105.0	106.0	106.9
Up to 19 years	29.5	29.3	29.5	29.9	30.3	30.7	31.4	31.9	32.2	32.3
20 to 39 years	32.1	33.0	33.5	33.2	33.1	32.8	32.0	31.1	30.2	29.6
40 to 59 years	19.8	20.3	20.6	21.8	22.7	23.9	25.3	26.7	28.2	29.6
60 to 79 years	12.2	12.6	12.9	13.1	13.2	13.3	13.2	13.2	13.2	13.2
80 years and over	1.6	1.6	1.7	1.8	1.9	1.9	2.0	2.1	2.2	2.3
FEMALE, WHITE	99.5	101.2	102.8	104.5	106.0	107.5	108.8	109.9	111.0	112.0
Up to 19 years	28.2	28.0	28.1	28.5	28.8	29.2	29.8	30.2	30.6	30.7
20 to 39 years	31.8	32.6	33.2	32.9	32.8	32.5	31.7	30.9	30.0	29.3
40 to 59 years	20.8	21.2	21.4	22.5	23.5	24.7	26.1	27.5	29.0	30.4
60 to 79 years	15.6	16.1	16.5	16.7	16.8	16.9	16.8	16.7	16.7	16.6
80 years and over	3.3	3.4	3.6	3.8	4.0	4.2	4.4	4.6	4.7	4.9
[illegible]	12.8	13.2	13.5	13.9	14.2	14.5	14.8	15.1	15.4	15.6
[illegible]	5.2	5.2	5.2	5.3	5.3	5.4	5.4	5.5	5.5	5.5
[illegible]	4.1	4.3	4.6	4.7	4.7	4.8	4.8	4.8	4.8	4.7
[illegible]	2.2	2.3	2.3	2.4	2.6	2.8	3.0	3.2	3.4	3.7
[illegible]	1.2	1.2	1.3	1.3	1.4	1.4	1.4	1.4	1.5	1.5
[illegible]	0.1	0.1	0.1	0.2	0.2	0.2	0.2	0.2	0.2	0.2

Sex, race, age group	1982	1984	1986	1988	1990	1992	1994	1996	1998	2000
FEMALE, BLACK	14.1	14.5	14.9	15.2	15.6	16.0	16.3	16.6	16.9	17.2
Up to 19 years	5.1	5.1	5.2	5.1	5.2	5.2	5.2	5.2	5.3	5.3
20 to 39 years	4.7	4.9	5.1	5.3	5.4	5.4	5.5	5.4	5.3	5.3
40 to 59 years	2.5	2.6	2.7	2.8	3.0	3.2	3.4	3.7	4.0	4.3
60 to 79 years	1.5	1.6	1.7	1.7	1.8	1.8	1.8	1.9	1.9	2.0
80 years and over	0.3	0.3	0.3	0.3	0.3	0.4	0.4	0.4	0.4	0.4
Total white	194.6	197.8	201.1	204.2	207.3	210.1	212.6	214.9	217.0	218.9
Total black	26.9	27.6	28.4	29.1	29.8	30.5	31.1	31.7	32.3	32.8
Total United States[2]	**226.3**	**230.7**	**235.1**	**239.4**	**243.5**	**247.4**	**251.1**	**254.4**	**257.5**	**260.4**
Median age	30.7	31.2	31.7	32.3	32.8	33.3	33.9	34.5	35.0	35.5

1. Based on average of 2.1 lifetime births per woman. 2. Includes all races. *Source:* Department of Commerce, Bureau of the Census, report issued July 1977.

Population of Large Metropolitan Areas
(in thousands)

	Population				Population change					
					1970–1977			1960–1970		
	July 1, 1978									
Standard metropolitan statistical area	Total	Rank	April 1970	April 1960	Number	Percent	Net migration	Number	Percent	Net migration
Akron, Ohio	657	57	679	605	−18	−2.7	−50	74	12.2	1
Abany–Schnectady–Troy, N.Y.	792	49	778	715	16	2.1	−2	63	8.8	9
Abuquerque, N.M.	409	93	333	276	69	20.6	39	57	20.6	17
Allentown–Bethlehem–Easton, Pa.–N.J.	626	63	594	545	30	5.0	19	49	9.0	16
Anaheim–Santa Ana–Garden Grove, Calif.	1,833	19	1,421	704	380	26.7	272	717	101.9	553
Ann Arbor, Mich.	255	145	234	172	16	6.9	−2	62	35.8	32
Appleton–Oshkosh, Wis.	291	128	277	232	13	4.5	−2	45	19.4	9
Atlanta	1,852	18	1,596	1,169	236	14.8	113	426	36.5	233
Augusta, Ga.–S.C.	291	127	276	230	12	4.2	−8	46	19.9	12
Austin, Tex.	478	81	360	267	114	31.6	82	93	34.9	51
Bakersfield, Calif.	365	103	330	292	33	9.9	9	38	13.1	−5
Baltimore	2,145	14	2,071	1,804	76	3.7	4	267	14.8	54
Baton Rouge, La.	445	87	376	300	60	15.9	25	76	25.3	21
Beaumont, Port Arthur–Orange, Tex.	364	104	348	331	16	4.7	−1	17	5.1	−25
Binghamton, N.Y.–Pa.	303	117	303	284	3	1.0	−7	19	6.7	−12
Birmingham, Ala.	818	46	767	747	38	5.0	5	21	2.8	−52
Boston	n.a.	—	2,899	2,688	n.a.	n.a.	n.a.	211	7.9	n.a.
Boston–Lowell–Brockton–Lawrence–Haverhill, Mass.–N.H.[2]	3,888	6	3,849	3,457	49	1.3	−52	392	11.3	61
Bridgeport, Conn.	n.a.	—	402	350	n.a.	n.a.	n.a.	52	14.7	n.a.
Bridgeport–Stamford–Norwalk–Danbury, Conn.[2]	808	47	793	654	14	1.8	−8	139	21.3	72
Buffalo, N.Y.	1,303	29	1,349	1,307	−36	−2.7	−69	42	3.2	−82
Canton, Ohio	404	94	394	361	7	1.8	−10	33	9.0	−3
Charleston–North Charleston, S.C.	389	97	336	279	49	14.7	17	57	20.5	−1
Charleston, W. Va.	261	140	257	276	4	1.5	−6	−19	−7.0	46
Charlotte–Gastonia, N.C.	606	66	558	444	39	7.0	2	114	25.7	45
Chattanooga, Tenn.–Ga.	401	95	371	340	32	8.7	11	31	9.1	−7
Chicago	7,030	3	6,977	6,221	40	.6	−317	756	12.2	16
Cincinnati, Ohio–Ky.–Ind.	1,389	26	1,387	1,268	−12	−.9	−77	119	9.4	−32
Cleveland	1,939	17	2,064	1,909	−114	−5.5	−186	154	8.1	−44
Colorado Springs, Colo.	291	126	239	146	49	20.5	19	93	63.6	62
Columbia, S.C.	380	98	323	261	51	15.9	26	62	23.8	24
Columbus, Ga.–Ala.	228	154	239	218	−9	−3.9	−28	21	9.5	−22
Columbus, Ohio	1,089	35	1,018	845	69	6.8	3	173	20.4	52
Corpus Christi, Tex.	302	118	285	267	18	6.4	−12	18	6.8	−33
Dallas–Ft. Worth	2,720	9	2,378	1,738	296	12.4	121	640	36.8	368
Davenport–Rock Island–Moline, Iowa–Ill.	374	102	363	319	12	3.4	−6	43	13.5	6
Dayton, Ohio	834	45	853	727	−19	−2.3	−66	125	17.2	27
Daytona Beach, Fla.	218	158	169	125	44	26.1	49	44	32.5	43
Denver–Boulder, Colo.	1,505	21	1,240	935	225	18.1	138	305	32.6	165
Des Moines, Iowa	334	110	314	287	20	6.3	3	26	9.2	−8
Detroit	4,386	5	4,435	3,950	−65	−1.5	−293	485	12.3	−17
Duluth–Superior, Minn.–Wis.	266	138	265	277	2	.7	−4	−11	−4.1	−30

Standard metropolitan statistical area	Population				Population change					
	July 1, 1978				1970–1977			1960–1970		
	Total	Rank	April 1970	April 1960	Number	Percent	Net migration	Number	Percent	Net migration
El Paso	443	88	359	314	75	21.0	25	45	14.4	−29
Erie, Pa.	269	136	264	251	8	3.0	−5	13	5.2	−13
Eugene–Springfield, Ore.	258	143	215	163	34	15.6	21	53	32.2	29
Evansville, Ind.–Ky.	295	123	285	272	6	2.0	−3	13	4.7	−9
Fayetteville, N.C.	233	153	212	148	19	9.1	−9	64	42.9	21
Flint, Mich.	521	74	509	428	6	1.1	−32	81	18.9	6
Fort Lauderdale–Hollywood, Fla.	882	42	620	334	244	39.4	241	286	85.7	257
Fort Wayne, Ind.	376	101	362	306	8	2.3	−16	56	18.2	12
Fresno, Calif.	479	80	413	366	59	14.2	29	47	12.9	−3
Gary–Hammond–East Chicago, Ind.	648	59	633	574	11	1.7	−33	60	10.4	−24
Grand Rapids, Mich.	585	69	539	462	36	6.7	3	77	16.7	11
Greensboro–Winston–Salem–High Point, N.C.	779	52	724	622	50	6.9	14	102	16.4	20
Greenville–Spartanburg, S.C.	541	73	473	413	53	11.2	25	61	14.7	7
Hamilton–Middletown, Ohio	256	144	226	199	24	10.8	10	27	13.6	1
Harrisburg, Pa.	430	91	411	372	18	4.5	5	39	10.5	7
Hartford, Conn.	n.a.	—	721	588	n.a.	n.a.	n.a.	132	22.5	n.a.
Hartford–New Britain–Bristol, Conn.[2]	1,045	36	1,035	847	17	1.6	−19	188	22.2	83
Honolulu, Hawaii	720	55	631	500	93	14.7	22	130	26.0	18
Houston	2,595	11	1,999	1,430	513	25.7	322	569	39.8	317
Huntington–Ashland, W. Va.–Ky.–Ohio	300	120	287	284	11	3.7	−1	3	1.0	−24
Huntsville, Ala.	293	124	282	202	8	2.9	−10	81	39.9	38
Indianapolis	1,156	32	1,111	944	32	2.9	−34	167	17.7	38
Jackson, Miss.	299	122	259	221	37	14.2	15	38	17.0	(1)
Jacksonville, Fla.	702	56	622	530	72	11.6	31	92	17.4	13
Jersey City, N.J.	554	71	608	611	−44	−7.2	−58	−3	−.5	−46
Johnson City–Kingsport–Bristol, Tenn.–Va.	411	92	374	347	35	9.3	18	26	7.6	−11
Johnstown, Pa.	265	139	263	281	5	1.9	−1	−18	−6.4	−33
Kalamazoo–Portage, Mich.	270	135	258	218	10	4.0	−4	40	18.2	12
Kansas City, Mo.–Kan.	1,325	28	1,274	1,109	19	1.5	−49	165	14.9	31
Killeen–Temple, Tex.	209	161	160	118	49	30.5	23	42	35.4	15
Knoxville, Tenn.	456	85	409	377	40	7.9	24	33	8.7	−7
Lakeland–Winter Haven, Fla.	278	130	229	195	49	21.2	38	33	17.1	12
Lancaster, Pa.	351	109	320	278	28	8.7	11	42	15.0	11
Lansing–East Lansing, Mich.	458	84	424	342	31	7.3	—	82	24.0	28
Las Vegas, Nev.	377	99	273	127	87	31.7	61	146	115.2	110
Lawrence–Haverhill, Mass.–N.H.	n.a.	—	259	218	n.a.	n.a.	n.a.	40	18.4	n.a.
Lexington–Fayette, Ky.	300	121	267	212	28	10.4	10	55	25.8	26
Lima, Ohio	212	159	210	197	(1)	.1	−12	13	6.6	−10
Little Rock–North Little Rock, Ark.	376	101	323	272	46	14.2	20	51	18.9	12
Long Branch–Asbury Park, N.J.	500	76	462	334	30	6.4	14	127	38.1	89
Lorain–Elyria, Ohio	271	134	257	218	7	2.8	−12	39	18.1	6
Los Angeles–Long Beach, Calif.	7,081	2	7,042	6,039	−11	−.2	−389	1,003	16.6	269
Louisville, Ky.–Ind.	887	41	867	754	16	1.8	−30	113	15.0	21
Lowell, Mass.	n.a.	—	218	176	n.a.	n.a.	n.a.	51	30.8	n.a.
Lubbock, Tex.	200	163	179	156	21	11.6	3	23	14.7	−11
Macon, Ga.	243	148	227	197	15	6.7	—	30	15.2	(1)
Madison, Wis.	319	113	290	222	23	7.8	6	68	30.7	29
Manchester–Nashua, N.H.[2]	260	141	224	178	31	14.0	20	45	25.7	24
McAllen–Pharr–Edinburg, Tex.	236	149	182	181	51	28.0	16	1	.4	−43
Melbourne–Titusville–Cocoa, Fla.	234	151	230	111	3	1.3	−7	119	106.4	87
Memphis, Tenn.–Ark.–Miss.	889	40	834	727	52	6.3	−5	107	14.7	−4
Miami, Fla.	1,451	23	1,268	935	173	13.7	147	333	35.6	255
Milwaukee	1,417	24	1,404	1,279	23	1.6	−40	125	9.8	−37
Minneapolis–St. Paul	2,063	15	1,965	1,598	72	3.6	−43	368	23.0	118
Mobile, Ala.	435	90	377	363	48	12.9	21	13	3.7	42
Modesto, Calif.	246	146	195	157	41	21.3	29	37	23.7	19
Montgomery, Ala.	258	142	226	218	29	12.6	15	7	3.4	−18
Nashville–Davidson, Tenn.	786	51	699	597	74	10.5	36	102	17.2	30
Nassau–Suffolk, N.Y.	2,690	10	2,556	1,967	132	5.2	46	589	29.9	359
Newark, N.J.	1,951	16	2,057	1,833	−88	−4.3	−151	224	12.2	47
New Bedford–Fall River, Mass.[2]	472	82	444	398	24	5.3	10	46	11.5	15
New Brunswick–Perth Amboy–Sayreville, N.J.	591	67	584	434	10	1.7	−16	150	34.6	87
New Haven–West Haven, Conn.	n.a.	—	411	359	n.a.	n.a.	n.a.	52	14.4	n.a.
New Haven–West Haven–Waterbury–Meriden, Conn.[2]	755	54	745	660	14	1.9	−7	85	12.8	20

Standard metropolitan statistical area	Population: July 1, 1978 Total	Rank	April 1970	April 1960	Population change 1970–1977: Number	Percent	Net migration	1960–1970: Number	Percent	Net migration
New London–Norwich, Conn.–R.I.	n.a.	—	242	196	n.a.	n.a.	n.a.	46	23.2	n.a.
New London–Norwich, Conn.[2]	245	147	231	186	14	6.2	2	45	24.2	15
New Orleans	1,141	33	1,046	907	87	8.3	19	139	15.4	11
Newport News–Hampton, Va.	361	105	333	255	31	9.3	6	78	30.8	31
New York, N.Y.–N.J.	9,222	1	9,974	9,540	−587	−5.9	−849	434	4.5	−319
Norfolk–Virginia Beach–Portsmouth, Va.–N.C.	800	48	733	629	70	9.6	16	104	16.5	−2
Northeast Pa.	629	61	622	621	7	1.1	10	1	.1	−13
Oklahoma City	789	50	699	566	69	9.9	21	133	23.5	54
Omaha, Neb.–Iowa	582	70	543	458	38	7.0	—	85	18.5	9
Orlando, Fla.	610	65	453	338	140	30.8	112	116	34.3	70
Oxnard–Simi Valley–Ventura, Calif.	485	79	378	199	89	23.6	56	179	90.1	134
Paterson–Clifton–Passaic, N.J.	445	86	461	407	1	.2	−18	54	13.3	13
Pensacola, Fla.	276	132	243	203	31	12.9	11	40	19.5	([1])
Peoria, Ill.	361	106	342	313	20	5.8	—	29	9.1	−8
Philadelphia, Pa.–N.J.	4,770	4	4,824	4,343	−30	−.6	−179	481	11.1	57
Phoenix, Ariz.	1,293	30	971	664	282	29.1	203	307	46.2	190
Pittsburgh	2,277	13	2,401	2,405	−107	−4.5	−135	−4	−.2	−166
Portland, Me.[2]	234	151	216	206	16	7.3	8	10	5.1	−9
Portland, Ore.–Wash.	1,140	34	1,007	822	114	11.4	72	185	22.5	117
Poughkeepsie, N.Y.	233	152	222	176	10	4.3	1	46	26.3	26
Providence–Warwick–Pawtucket, R.I.–Mass.	n.a.	—	909	821	n.a.	n.a.	n.a.	88	10.7	n.a.
Providence–Warwick–Pawtucket, R.I.[2]	853	43	855	778	−4	−.4	−22	78	10.0	12
Raleigh–Durham, N.C.	494	77	419	324	68	16.2	44	95	29.4	49
Reading, Pa.	306	116	296	275	6	1.9	1	21	7.6	6
Richmond, Va.	612	64	548	462	56	10.2	34	86	18.6	35
Riverside–San Bernardino–Ontario, Calif.	1,385	27	1,139	810	166	14.6	103	329	40.6	214
Roanoke, Va.	211	160	203	179	13	6.3	6	24	13.6	9
Rochester, N.Y.	970	38	962	801	9	.9	−32	161	20.1	68
Rockford, Ill.	269	137	272	230	−4	−1.6	−21	42	18.2	8
Sacramento, Calif.	951	39	804	626	126	15.6	83	178	28.5	89
Saginaw, Mich.	228	155	220	191	7	3.1	−9	29	15.2	2
Salem, Ore.	230	156	187	147	30	16.3	22	39	26.6	26
Salinas–Seaside–Monterey, Calif.	276	131	247	198	27	11.1	6	49	24.8	16
Salt Lake City, Utah	843	44	705	576	117	16.5	17	129	22.4	8
San Antonio	1,038	37	888	736	137	15.4	51	152	20.7	18
San Diego, Calif.	1,744	20	1,358	1,033	325	23.9	237	325	31.4	169
San Francisco–Oakland, Calif.	3,184	7	3,109	2,649	73	2.3	−27	460	17.4	184
San Jose, Calif.	1,232	31	1,065	642	152	14.3	76	423	65.9	285
Santa Barbara–Santa Maria– Lompoc, Calif.	292	125	264	169	23	8.7	11	95	56.4	23
Santa Rosa, Calif.	274	133	205	147	58	28.5	51	58	39.0	45
Savannah, Ga.	219	157	208	205	7	3.4	−6	3	1.6	47
Seattle–Everett, Wash.	1,468	22	1,425	1,107	3	.2	−54	317	28.7	188
Shreveport, La.	356	107	336	321	21	6.1	−4	15	4.6	−32
South Bend, Ind.	281	129	280	271	−3	−1.1	−15	9	3.3	−18
Spokane, Wash.	320	112	287	278	23	7.9	8	9	3.3	−14
Springfield–Chicopee–Holyoke, Mass.–Conn.	n.a.	—	542	504	n.a.	n.a.	n.a.	38	7.5	n.a.
Springfield–Chicopee–Holyoke, Mass.[2]	587	68	583	533	6	1.1	−10	50	9.4	n.a.
St. Louis, Mo.–Ill.	2,386	12	2,411	2,144	−31	−1.3	−134	266	12.4	24
Stamford, Conn.	n.a.	—	206	178	n.a.	n.a.	n.a.	28	15.7	n.a.
Stockton, Calif.	313	115	291	250	20	7.0	7	41	16.4	16
Syracuse, N.Y.	650	58	637	564	11	1.7	−17	73	12.9	2
Tacoma, Wash.	437	89	412	322	11	2.7	−17	91	28.2	46
Tampa–St. Petersburg, Fla.	1,396	25	1,089	809	292	26.8	302	279	34.5	253
Todedo, Ohio–Mich.	776	53	763	695	15	1.9	−26	67	9.7	−8
Trenton, N.J.	317	114	304	266	13	4.2	3	38	14.2	12
Tucson, Ariz.	462	83	352	266	103	29.3	76	86	32.3	48
Tulsa, Okla.	629	62	549	475	61	11.0	30	74	15.5	25
Utica–Rome, N.Y.	326	111	340	331	−14	−4.0	−24	10	2.9	−21
Vallejo–Fairfield–Napa, Calif.	301	119	251	200	43	17.0	27	51	25.3	20
Washington, D.C.–Md.–Va.	3,017	8	2,910	2,097	123	4.2	−58	813	38.3	427
Waterbury, Conn.	n.a.	—	217	191	n.a.	n.a.	n.a.	26	13.7	n.a.
West Palm Beach–Boca Raton, Fla.	487	78	349	228	128	36.7	126	121	53.0	101
Wichita, Kan.	398	96	389	382	6	1.4	−19	8	2.0	−46

Standard metropolitan statistical area	Population				Population change					
	July 1, 1978				1970–1977			1960–1970		
	Total	Rank	April 1970	April 1960	Number	Percent	Net migration	Number	Percent	Net migration
Wilmington, Del.–N.J.–Md.	516	75	499	415	17	3.3	−8	85	20.5	28
Worcester, Mass.	n.a.	—	372	354	n.a.	n.a.	n.a.	18	5.1	n.a.
Worcester–Fitchburg–Leominster, Mass.[2]	645	60	637	583	6	1.0	−11	54	9.2	4
York, Pa.	356	108	330	290	22	6.7	9	39	13.5	10
Youngstown–Warren, Ohio	546	72	537	509	3	.6	−18	28	5.5	−18
STANDARD CONSOLIDATED STATISTICAL AREA										
Boston–Lawrence–Lowell, Mass–N.H.	3,888	7	3,849	3,457	49	1.3	−52	392	11.3	n.a.
Chicago–Gary, Ill.–Ind.	7,678	3	7,611	6,794	51	.7	−350	817	12.0	−9
Cincinnati–Hamilton, Ohio–Ky.–Ind.	1,646	12	1,613	1,468	13	.8	−66	146	9.9	−31
Cleveland–Akron–Lorain, Ohio	2,867	8	3,000	2,732	−126	−4.2	−247	267	9.8	−36
Detroit–Ann Arbor, Mich.	4,641	6	4,669	4,122	−49	−1.0	−294	547	13.3	14
Houston–Galveston, Tex.[3]	2,793	9	2,169	1,571	538	24.8	337	598	38.1	328
Los Angeles–Long Beach–Anaheim, Calif.[4]	10,784	2	9,981	7,752	624	6.3	43	2,231	28.8	624
Miami–Fort Lauderdale, Fla.	2,333	10	1,888	1,269	418	22.1	388	619	48.8	512
Milwaukee–Racine, Wis.	1,594	13	1,575	1,421	29	1.8	43	154	10.9	−29
New York–Newark–Jersey City, N.Y.–N.J.–Conn.[5]	16,761	1	7,494	15,779	−533	−3.0	−1,038	1,715	10.9	349
Philadelphia–Wilmington–Trenton, Pa.–Del.–Md.–N.J.	5,603	4	5,628	5,024	−670	—	−184	604	12.0	98
San Francisco–Oakland–San Jose Calif.[6]	4,717	5	4,426	3,492	268	6.0	77	934	26.8	490
Seattle–Tacoma, Wash.	1,905	11	1,837	1,429	14	.7	−71	408	28.6	235

1. Less than 500 or .05 percent. 2. New England County Metropolitan Area; not included in rank. 3. Includes Galveston–Texas City SMSA. 4. Includes Oxnard–Simi Valley–Ventura SMSA and Riverside–San Bernardino–Ontario SMSA. 5. Includes Nassau–Suffolk SMSA, Long Beach–Asbury Park SMSA, New Brunswick–Perth Amboy–Sayreville SMSA, Paterson–Clifton–Passaic SMSA, and Stamford and Norwalk SMSAs. 6. Includes Vallejo–Fairfield–Napa SMSA. NOTE: Covers 162 large SMSAs with estimated population of 200,000 or more as of July 1, 1978. Rank based on unrounded figures. n.a. = not available. *Source:* Department of Commerce, Bureau of the Census.

Population by Age, Sex, and Race, 1979

(in thousands)

Age	White		Black		Other races		All persons	
	Male	Female	Male	Female	Male	Female	Male	Female
Under 5	6,585	6,262	1,208	1,179	210	205	8,003	7,646
Under 1	1,391	1,320	245	238	44	42	1,680	1,601
1–4	5,194	4,942	963	940	166	164	6,323	6,046
5–9	6,950	6,621	1,265	1,242	209	206	8,424	8,069
10–14	7,669	7,335	1,355	1,341	187	184	9,212	8,859
15–19	8,957	8,631	1,468	1,457	207	197	10,633	10,285
20–24	8,923	8,703	1,293	1,373	219	216	10,435	10,292
25–29	7,986	7,892	1,003	1,142	192	226	9,181	9,260
30–34	7,233	7,198	807	949	182	215	8,221	8,362
35–39	5,886	6,017	657	790	117	147	6,661	6,954
40–44	4,949	5,104	566	682	97	122	5,612	5,909
45–49	4,822	4,990	556	634	99	122	5,476	5,746
50–54	5,053	5,359	527	603	86	106	5,667	6,068
55–59	4,888	5,315	471	546	69	78	5,428	5,939
60–64	4,071	4,599	367	447	49	52	4,487	5,098
65–69	3,453	4,293	370	492	42	38	3,865	4,823
70–74	2,520	3,486	221	289	36	32	2,777	3,807
75–79	1,529	2,410	115	153	33	34	1,678	2,596
80–84	886	1,663	72	120	20	20	977	1,803
85 and over	637	1,455	70	140	14	17	720	1,612
All ages	92,996	97,333	12,391	13,578	2,069	2,218	107,457	113,128
14 and over	73,454	78,711	8,857	10,107	1,500	1,659	83,811	90,478
18 and over	66,504	72,052	7,667	8,941	1,341	1,507	75,512	82,500
21 and over	60,965	66,672	6,803	8,062	1,210	1,386	68,978	76,120
65 and over	9,024	13,306	848	1,194	145	141	10,017	14,641
Median age	29.6	32.2	23.5	25.9	25.0	27.2	28.8	31.3

NOTE: Figures represent resident population of the 50 states and the District of Columbia plus Armed Forces overseas.

Population by State

State	1970	Percent change, 1960–70	Pop. per sq mi., 1970	Pop. rank, 1970	1960	1950	1900	1790
Alabama	3,444,165	5.4	67.9	21	3,266,740	3,061,743	1,828,697	—
Alaska	302,173	33.6	0.5	50	226,167	128,643	63,592	—
Arizona	1,772,482	36.1	15.6	33	1,302,161	749,587	122,931	—
Arkansas	1,923,295	7.7	37.0	32	1,786,272	1,909,511	1,311,564	—
California	19,953,134	27.0	127.6	1	15,717,204	10,586,223	1,485,053	—
Colorado	2,207,259	25.8	21.3	30	1,753,947	1,325,089	539,700	—
Connecticut	3,032,217	19.6	623.7	24	2,535,234	2,007,280	908,420	237,946
Delaware	548,104	22.8	276.5	46	446,292	318,085	184,735	59,096
D.C.	756,510	−1.0	12,401.8	—	763,956	802,178	278,718	—
Florida	6,789,443	37.1	125.5	9	4,951,560	2,771,305	528,542	—
Georgia	4,589,575	16.4	79.0	15	3,943,116	3,444,578	2,216,331	82,548
Hawaii	769,913	21.7	119.8	40	632,772	499,794	154,001	—
Idaho	713,008	6.9	8.6	42	667,191	588,637	161,772	—
Illinois	11,113,976	10.2	199.4	5	10,081,158	8,712,176	4,821,550	—
Indiana	5,193,669	11.4	143.9	11	4,662,498	3,934,224	2,516,462	—
Iowa	2,825,041	2.4	50.5	25	2,757,537	2,621,073	2,231,853	—
Kansas	2,249,071	3.2	27.5	28	2,178,611	1,905,299	1,470,495	—
Kentucky	3,219,311	6.0	81.2	23	3,038,156	2,944,806	2,147,174	73,677
Louisiana	3,643,180	11.9	81.1	20	3,257,022	2,683,516	1,381,625	—
Maine	993,663	2.5	32.1	38	969,265	913,774	694,466	96,540
Maryland	3,922,399	26.5	396.6	18	3,100,689	2,343,001	1,188,044	319,728
Massachusetts	5,689,170	10.5	727.0	10	5,148,578	4,690,514	2,805,346	378,787
Michigan	8,875,083	13.4	156.2	7	7,823,194	6,371,766	2,420,982	—
Minnesota	3,805,069	11.5	48.0	19	3,413,864	2,982,483	1,751,394	—
Mississippi	2,216,912	1.8	46.9	29	2,178,141	2,178,914	1,551,270	—
Missouri	4,677,399	8.3	67.8	13	4,319,813	3,954,653	3,106,665	—
Montana	694,409	2.9	4.8	43	674,767	591,024	243,329	—
Nebraska	1,483,791	5.1	19.4	35	1,411,330	1,325,510	1,066,300	—
Nevada	488,738	71.3	4.4	47	285,278	160,083	42,335	—
New Hampshire	737,681	21.5	81.7	41	606,921	533,242	411,588	141,885
New Jersey	7,168,164	18.2	953.1	8	6,066,782	4,835,329	1,883,669	184,139
New Mexico	1,016,000	6.8	8.4	37	951,023	681,187	195,310	—
New York	18,241,266	8.4	381.3	2	16,782,304	14,830,192	7,268,894	340,120
North Carolina	5,082,059	11.5	104.1	12	4,556,155	4,061,929	1,893,810	393,751
North Dakota	617,761	−2.3	8.9	45	632,446	619,636	319,146	—
Ohio	10,652,017	9.7	260.0	6	9,706,397	7,946,627	4,157,545	—
Oklahoma	2,559,253	9.9	37.2	27	2,328,284	2,233,351	790,391[1]	—
Oregon	2,091,385	18.2	21.7	31	1,768,687	1,521,341	413,536	—
Pennsylvania	11,793,909	4.2	262.3	3	11,319,366	10,498,012	6,302,115	434,373
Rhode Island	949,723	10.5	905.4	39	859,488	791,896	428,556	68,825
South Carolina	2,590,516	8.7	85.7	26	2,382,594	2,117,027	1,340,316	249,073
South Dakota	666,257	−2.2	8.8	44	680,514	652,740	401,570	—
Tennessee	3,924,164	10.0	95.0	17	3,567,089	3,291,718	2,020,616	35,691
Texas	11,196,730	16.9	42.7	4	9,579,677	7,711,194	3,048,710	—
Utah	1,059,273	18.9	12.9	36	890,627	688,862	276,749	—
Vermont	444,732	14.1	48.0	48	389,881	377,747	343,641	85,425
Virginia	4,648,494	17.2	116.9	14	3,966,949	3,318,680	1,854,184	747,610[2]
Washington	3,409,169	19.5	51.2	22	2,853,214	2,378,963	518,103	—
West Virginia	1,744,237	−6.2	72.5	34	1,860,421	2,005,552	958,800	—
Wisconsin	4,417,933	11.8	81.1	16	3,951,777	3,434,575	2,069,042	—
Wyoming	332,416	0.7	3.4	49	330,066	290,529	92,531	—
Total U.S.	**203,235,298**	**13.3**	**57.4**	**—**	**179,323,175**	**151,325,798**	**76,212,168**	**3,929,214**

1. Includes population of Indian Territory: 1900, 392,960. 2. Until 1863, Virginia included what is now West Virginia. NOTE: In April 1973, the Census Bureau reported that it had overlooked 5,300,000 people in the 1970 Census. However, by law, the total figure listed above is official. For provisional 1979 population and rank, *see* the individual states. *Source:* Department of Commerce, Bureau of the Census.

Population Shifts

From 1970 to 1975, the population in *non*-metropolitan areas climbed from 53.5 million to 57 million. During this period, about 400,000 Americans left the larger cities to live in rural areas. By 1978, non-metro areas contained 28% of the U.S. population, according to the Conference Board.

The return to the country is not a stampede, but it does represent a significant shift from the 1960s, when the primary flow was from rural to metropolitan areas.

Although the rate of growth has slowed considerably since 1970, the most rapid population gains continue to be in the suburbs and areas ringing metropolitan areas.

Population of Cities Over 50,000

Asterisk denotes more than one ZIP code for a city and refers to general delivery. To find the ZIP code for a particular address, consult the ZIP code directory available in every post office. NOTE: U = unincorporated area; T = town. For latest population figures of many cities, see listing for individual states in The United States section.

City and major ZIP code	1970 census	1970 rank	1960 census	% change 1960–70	1940 census	1920 census
Abilene, Tex. (79604*)	89,653	181	90,368	−0.8	26,612	10,274
Akron, Ohio (44309*)	275,425	52	290,351	−5.1	244,791	208,435
Alameda, Calif. (94501)	70,968	260	63,855	11.1	36,256	28,806
Albany, Ga. (31706*)	72,263	249	55,890	29.9	19,055	11,555
Albany, N.Y. (12201*)	115,781	127	129,726	−10.8	130,577	113,344
Albuquerque, N.M. (87101*)	243,751	60	201,189	21.2	35,449	15,157
Alexandria, Va. (22313*)	110,927	134	91,023	21.9	33,523	18,060
Alhambra, Calif. (91802*)	62,125	310	54,807	13.4	38,935	9,096
Allentown, Pa. (18105*)	109,871	139	108,347	1.4	96,904	73,502
Altoona, Pa. (16603*)	63,115	305	69,407	−9.1	80,214	60,331
Amarillo, Tex. (79105*)	127,010	116	137,969	−7.9	51,686	15,494
Anaheim, Calif. (92803*)	166,408	82	104,184	59.7	11,031	5,526
Anderson, Ind. (46011*)	70,787	261	49,061	44.3	41,572	29,767
Ann Arbor, Mich. (48106*)	100,035	157	67,340	48.5	29,815	19,516
Appleton, Wis. (54911)	57,143	342	48,411	18.0	28,436	19,561
Arden, Calif. (U) (95825)	82,492	209	73,352	12.5	—	—
Arlington, Tex. (76010*)	90,032	180	44,775	101.0	4,240	3,031
Arlington, Va. (U) (22210*)	174,284	78	163,401	6.9	26,615	—
Arlington Heights, Ill. (60004*)	64,884	294	27,878	132.7	5,668	2,250
Asheville, N.C. (28801*)	57,681	336	60,192	−4.2	51,310	28,504
Atlanta, Ga. (30301*)	495,039	27	487,455	1.6	302,288	200,616
Augusta, Ga. (30903*)	59,864	344	70,626	−15.2	65,919	52,548
Aurora, Colo. (80010*)	74,974	237	48,548	54.5	3,437	983
Aurora, Ill. (60507*)	74,182	241	63,715	16.4	47,710	36,397
Austin, Tex. (78767*)	251,808	57	186,545	35.0	87,930	34,876
Bakersfield, Calif. (93302*)	69,515	268	56,848	22.3	29,252	18,638
Baltimore, Md. (21233*)	905,787	7	939,024	−3.5	859,100	733,826
Baton Rouge, La. (70821*)	165,921	83	152,419	8.9	34,719	21,782
Bayonne, N.J. (07002)	72,743	245	74,215	−2.0	79,198	76,754
Beaumont, Tex. (77704*)	117,548	125	119,175	−1.4	59,061	40,422
Bellevue, Wash. (98009*)	61,102	317	12,809	377.0	—	—
Bellflower, Calif. (90706)	51,454	380	45,909	12.1	—	—
Berkeley, Calif. (94701*)	114,091	128	111,268	2.5	85,547	56,036
Berwyn, Ill. (60402)	52,502	376	54,224	−3.2	48,451	14,150
Bethesda, Md. (U) (20014)	71,621	255	56,527	26.7	—	—
Bethlehem, Pa. (18015*)	72,686	247	75,408	−3.6	58,490	50,358
Billings, Mont. (59101*)	61,581	314	52,851	16.5	23,261	15,100
Binghamton, N.Y. (13902*)	64,123	297	75,941	−15.6	78,309	66,800
Birmingham, Ala. (35203*)	300,910	48	340,887	−11.7	267,583	178,806
Bloomington, Minn. (55420)	81,970	211	50,498	62.3	—	—
Boise, Idaho (83707*)	74,990	236	34,481	117.5	26,130	21,393
Boston, Mass. (02109*)	641,071	16	697,197	−8.1	770,816	748,060
Boulder, Colo. (80302*)	66,870	287	37,718	77.3	12,958	11,006
Bridgeport, Conn. (06601*)	156,542	88	156,748	−0.1	147,121	143,555
Bristol, Conn. (06010)	55,487	355	45,499	22.0	30,167	20,620
Brockton, Mass. (02403)	89,040	184	72,813	22.3	62,343	66,254
Brownsville, Tex. (78520*)	52,522	375	48,040	9.3	22,083	11,791
Buena Park, Calif. (90622*)	63,646	301	46,401	37.2	—	—
Buffalo, N.Y. (14240*)	462,768	28	532,759	−13.1	575,901	506,775
Burbank, Calif. (91505*)	88,871	185	90,155	−1.4	34,337	2,913
Cambridge, Mass. (02138*)	100,361	155	107,716	−6.8	110,879	109,694
Camden, N.J. (08101*)	102,551	150	117,159	−12.5	117,536	116,309
Canton, Ohio (44711*)	110,053	137	113,631	−3.1	108,401	87,091
Carson, Calif. (90749)	71,150	259	38,059	89.6	—	—
Cedar Rapids, Iowa (52401*)	110,642	135	92,035	20.2	62,120	45,566
Champaign, Ill. (61820)	56,532	346	49,583	14.0	23,302	15,873
Charleston, S.C. (29401*)	66,945	284	65,925	1.5	71,275	67,957
Charleston, W. Va. (25301*)	71,505	257	85,796	−16.7	67,914	39,608
Charlotte, N.C. (28202*)	274,784	53	201,564	36.2	100,899	46,338
Chattanooga, Tenn. (37401*)	141,904	97	130,009	9.1	128,163	57,895
Chesapeake, Va. (23320*)	89,580	182	—	—	—	—
Chester, Pa. (19013*)	56,331	348	63,658	−11.5	59.285	58,030
Chicago, Ill. (60607*)	3,369,357	2	3,550,404	−5.1	3,396,808	2,701,705
Chicopee, Mass. (01021*)	66,676	288	61,553	8.3	41,664	36,214
Chula Vista, Calif. (92010*)	67,901	280	42,034	61.5	5,138	1,718

City and major ZIP code	1970 census	1970 rank	1960 census	% change 1960–70	1940 census	1920 census
Cicero, Ill. (60650)	67,058	283	69,130	−3.0	64,712	44,995
Cincinnati, Ohio (45202*)	453,514	30	502,550	−9.8	455,610	401,247
Clearwater, Fla. (33515*)	52,074	379	34,653	50.3	10,136	2,427
Cleveland, Ohio (44101*)	750,879	10	876,050	−14.3	878,336	796,841
Cleveland Heights, Ohio (44118)	60,767	318	61,813	−1.7	54,992	15,236
Clifton, N.J. (07015*)	82,437	210	82,084	0.4	48,827	26,470
Colorado Springs, Colo. (80901*)	135,060	107	70,194	92.4	36,789	30,105
Columbia, Mo. (65201)	58,804	330	36,650	60.4	18,399	10,392
Columbia, S.C. (29201*)	113,542	129	97,433	16.5	62,396	37,524
Columbus, Ga. (31908*)	155,028	90	116,779	32.7	53,280	31,125
Columbus, Ohio (43215*)	540,025	21	471,316	14.6	306,087	237,031
Compton, Calif. (90220*)	78,611	223	71,812	9.5	16,198	1,478
Concord, Calif. (94520*)	85,164	205	36,000	136.5	1,373	912
Corpus Christi, Tex. (78408*)	204,525	62	167,690	22.0	57,301	10,522
Costa Mesa, Calif. (92626*)	72,660	248	37,550	93.5	—	—
Council Bluffs, Iowa (51501)	60,348	320	55,641	8.5	41,439	36,162
Covington, Ky. (41011*)	52,535	374	60,376	−13.0	62,018	57,121
Cranston, R.I. (02910)	74,287	240	66,766	11.3	47,085	29,407
Dallas, Tex. (75221*)	844,401	8	679,684	24.2	294,734	158,976
Daly City, Calif. (94015*)	66,922	285	44,791	49.4	9,625	3,779
Danbury, Conn. (06810)	50,781	384	22,928	121.5	22,339	18,943
Davenport, Iowa (52802*)	98,469	160	88,981	10.7	66,039	56,727
Dayton, Ohio (45401*)	244,564	59	262,332	−6.8	210,718	152,559
Dearborn, Mich. (48120*)	104,199	148	112,007	−7.0	63,584	2,470
Dearborn Heights, Mich. (48127)	80,069	215	—	—	—	—
Decatur, Ill. (62521*)	90,397	177	78,004	15.9	59,305	43,818
Denver, Colo (80201*)	514,678	25	493,887	4.2	322,412	256,491
Des Moines, Iowa (50318*)	201,404	64	208,982	−3.9	159,819	126,468
Des Plaines, Ill. (60018*)	57,239	341	34,886	64.1	9,518	3,451
Detroit, Mich. (48226*)	1,514,063	5	1,670,144	−9.4	1,623,452	993,678
Downey, Calif. (90241*)	88,445	187	82,505	7.2	—	—
Duluth, Minn. (55806*)	100,578	154	106,884	−5.9	101,065	98,917
Dundalk, Md. (U) (21222)	85,377	203	82,428	3.6	—	—
Durham, N.C. (27701*)	95,438	165	78,302	21.9	60,195	21,719
East Los Angeles, Calif. (U) (90022)	105,033	146	104,270	0.7	—	—
East Orange, N.J. (07019*)	75,471	234	77,259	−2.3	68,945	50,710
East St. Louis, Ill. (62201*)	69,996	266	81,712	−14.3	75,609	66,767
El Cajon, Calif. (92020*)	52,273	377	37,618	39.0	1,471	469
El Monte, Calif. (91734*)	69,852	267	13,163	430.7	4,746	1,283
El Paso, Tex. (79940*)	322,261	45	276,687	16.5	96,810	77,560
Elgin, Ill. (60120)	55,691	353	49,447	12.6	38,333	27,454
Elizabeth, N.J. (07207*)	112,654	131	107,698	4.6	109,912	95,783
Elyria, Ohio (44035*)	53,427	367	43,782	22.0	25,120	20,474
Erie, Pa. (16501*)	129,231	114	138,440	−6.7	116,955	93,372
Euclid, Ohio (44117)	71,552	256	62,998	13.6	17,866	3,363
Eugene, Ore. (97401*)	78,389	224	50,977	53.8	20,838	10,593
Evanston, Ill. (60204*)	79,808	216	79,283	0.7	65,389	37,234
Evansville, Ind. (47708*)	138,764	103	141,543	−2.0	97,062	85,264
Everett, Wash. (98201*)	53,622	365	40,304	33.0	30,224	27,644
Fall River, Mass. (02722*)	96,898	162	99,942	−3.0	115,428	120,485
Fargo, N.D. (58102)	53,365	368	46,662	14.4	32,580	21,961
Fayetteville, N.C. (28302*)	53,510	366	47,106	13.6	17,428	8,877
Flint, Mich. (48502*)	193,317	67	196,940	−1.8	151,543	91,599
Florissant, Mo. (63033*)	65,908	290	38,166	72.7	1,369	682
Fort Lauderdale, Fla. (33310*)	139,590	101	83,648	66.9	17,996	2,065
Fort Smith, Ark. (72901*)	62,802	308	52,991	18.5	36,584	28,870
Fort Wayne, Ind. (46802*)	178,021	74	161,776	10.0	118,410	86,549
Fort Worth, Tex. (76101*)	393,455	33	356,268	10.4	177,662	106,482
Framingham, Mass. (T) (01701)	64,048	299	44,526	43.8	23,214	17,033
Fremont, Calif. (94538*)	100,869	153	43,790	130.3	—	—
Fresno, Calif. (93706*)	165,655	84	133,929	23.6	60,685	45,086
Fullerton, Calif. (92631*)	85,987	199	56,180	53.1	10,442	4,415
Gadsden, Ala. (35901*)	53,928	362	58,088	−7.2	36,975	14,737
Gainesville, Fla. (32601*)	64,510	295	29,701	117.2	13,757	6,860
Galveston, Tex (77553*)	61,809	311	67,175	−8.0	60,862	44,255
Garden Grove, Calif. (92640*)	121,155	121	84,238	43.8	—	—
Garland, Tex. (75040*)	81,437	213	38,501	111.5	2,233	1,421
Gary, Ind. (46401*)	188,398	69	178,320	5.6	111,719	55,378
Glendale, Calif. (91209*)	132,664	111	119,442	11.1	82,582	13,536
Grand Prairie, Tex. (75051*)	50,904	382	30,386	67.5	14,595	1,595
Grand Rapids, Mich. (49501*)	197,649	65	177,313	11.5	164,292	137,634

City and major ZIP code	1970 census	1970 rank	1960 census	% change 1960–70	1940 census	1920 census
Great Falls, Mont. (59401*)	60,091	321	55,244	8.8	29,928	24,121
Green Bay, Wis. (54305*)	87,809	191	62,888	39.6	46,235	31,017
Greensboro, N.C. (27420*)	144,076	96	119,574	20.5	59,319	19,861
Greenville, S.C. (29602*)	61,436	315	66,188	−7.2	34,734	23,127
Hamilton, Ohio (45012*)	67,865	281	72,354	−6.2	50,592	39,675
Hammond, Ind. (46320*)	107,983	143	111,698	−3.3	70,184	36,004
Hampton, Va. (23669*)	120,779	122	89,258	35.3	5,898	6,138
Harrisburg, Pa. (17105*)	68,061	277	79,697	−14.6	83,893	75,917
Hartford, Conn. (06101*)	158,017	87	162,178	−2.6	166,267	138,036
Hawthorne, Calif. (90250)	53,304	369	33,035	61.4	8,263	—
Hayward, Calif. (94544*)	93,058	169	72,700	28.0	6,736	3,487
Hialeah, Fla. (33010*)	102,452	151	66,972	52.9	3,958	—
High Point, N.C. (27260*)	63,259	304	62,063	4.2	38,495	14,302
Hollywood, Fla. (33022*)	106,873	144	35,237	203.3	6,239	—
Holyoke, Mass. (01040)	50,112	390	52,689	−4.9	53,750	60,203
Honolulu, Hawaii (96820*)	324,871	44	294,194	10.4	179,326	83,327
Houston, Tex. (77052*)	1,233,535	6	938,219	31.5	384,514	138,276
Huntington, W. Va. (25701*)	74,315	239	83,627	−11.1	78,836	50,177
Huntington Beach, Calif. (92647*)	115,960	126	11,492	909.0	3,738	1,687
Huntsville, Ala. (35804*)	139,282	102	72,365	90.9	13,050	8,018
Independence, Mo. (64050*)	111,630	132	62,328	79.2	16,066	11,686
Indianapolis, Ind. (46206*)	742,925	11	476,258	55.9	386,972	314,194
Inglewood, Calif. (90306*)	89,985	179	63,390	42.0	30,114	3,286
Irving, Tex. (75061*)	98,961	159	45,985	115.2	1,089	357
Jackson, Miss. (39205*)	162,380	86	144,422	12.4	62,107	22,817
Jacksonville, Fla. (32203*)	528,865	23	201,030	163.1	173,065	91,558
Jersey City, N.J. (07303*)	260,350	55	276,101	−5.7	301,173	298,103
Joliet, Ill. (60431*)	78,887	221	66,780	18.0	42,365	38,442
Kalamazoo, Mich. (49003*)	85,555	202	82,089	4.2	54,097	48,487
Kansas City, Kan. (66110*)	178,561	73	121,901	46.4	121,458	101,177
Kansas City, Mo. (64108*)	507,330	26	475,539	6.7	399,178	324,410
Kenosha, Wis. (53141*)	78,805	222	67,899	16.1	48,765	40,472
Kettering, Ohio (45429)	71,864	252	54,462	32.0	—	—
Knoxville, Tenn. (37901*)	174,587	77	111,827	56.1	111,580	77,818
La Crosse, Wis. (54601)	51,153	381	47,575	7.5	42,707	30,421
Lafayette, La. (70502*)	68,908	273	40,400	70.6	19,210	7,855
Lake Charles, La. (70601*)	77,998	228	63,392	23.0	21,207	13,088
Lakewood, Calif. (90714*)	82,973	208	67,126	23.6	—	—
Lakewood, Colo. (80215)	92,743	170	19,338	379.8	—	—
Lakewood, Ohio (44107)	70,173	264	66,154	6.1	69,160	41,732
Lancaster, Pa. (17604*)	57,690	335	61,055	−5.5	61,345	53,150
Lansing, Mich. (48924*)	131,403	113	107,807	21.8	78,753	57,327
Laredo, Tex. (78040*)	69,024	272	60,678	13.8	39,274	22,710
Las Vegas, Nev. (89114*)	125,787	118	64,405	95.3	8,422	2,304
Lawrence, Mass. (01842*)	66,915	286	70,933	−5.7	84,323	94,270
Lawton, Okla. (73501*)	74,470	238	61,697	20.7	18,055	8,930
Lexington, Ky. (40507*)	108,137	141	62,810	72.2	49,304	41,534
Lima, Ohio (45801*)	53,734	364	51,037	5.3	44,711	41,326
Lincoln, Neb. (68501*)	149,518	92	128,521	16.3	81,984	54,948
Lincoln Park, Mich. (48146)	52,984	372	53,933	−1.8	15,236	—
Little Rock, Ark. (72201*)	132,483	112	107,813	22.9	88,039	65,142
Livonia, Mich. (48150*)	110,109	136	66,702	65.1	8,728	—
Long Beach, Calif. (90801*)	358,879	40	344,168	4.3	164,271	55,593
Lorain, Ohio (44052*)	78,185	226	68,932	13.4	44,125	37,295
Los Angeles, Calif. (90055*)	2,811,801	3	2,479,015	13.4	1,504,277	576,673
Louisville, Ky. (40202*)	361,706	38	390,639	−7.4	319,077	234,891
Lowell, Mass. (01853*)	94,239	168	92,107	2.3	101,389	112,759
Lubbock, Tex. (79408*)	149,101	93	128,691	15.9	31,853	4,051
Lynchburg, Va. (24505*)	54,083	361	54,790	−1.3	44,541	30,070
Lynn, Mass. (01901*)	90,294	178	94,478	−4.4	98,123	99,148
Macon, Ga. (31201*)	122,423	120	69,764	75.5	57,865	52,995
Madison, Wis. (53714*)	171,809	80	126,706	35.6	67,447	38,378
Malden, Mass. (02148)	56,127	350	57,676	−2.7	58,010	49,103
Manchester, N.H. (03103*)	87,754	192	88,282	−0.6	77,685	78,384
Mansfield, Ohio (44901*)	55,047	358	47,325	16.3	37,154	27,824
Medford, Mass. (02155)	64,397	296	64,971	−0.9	63,083	39,038
Memphis, Tenn. (38101*)	623,530	17	497,524	25.3	292,942	162,351
Meriden, Conn. (06450)	55,959	351	51,850	7.9	39,494	29,867
Mesa, Ariz. (85201*)	62,853	307	33,772	86.1	7,222	3,036
Mesquite, Tex. (75149*)	55,131	356	27,526	100.3	1,045	674
Metairie, La. (U) (70002*)	136,477	106	—	—	—	—

City and major ZIP code	1970 census	1970 rank	1960 census	% change 1960–70	1940 census	1920 census
Miami, Fla. (33101*)	334,859	42	291,688	14.8	172,172	29,571
Miami Beach, Fla. (33139)	87,072	196	63,145	37.9	28,012	644
Midland, Tex. (79702*)	59,463	327	62,625	−5.0	9,352	1,795
Milford, Conn. (06460)	50,858	383	41,662	22.1	—	—
Milwaukee, Wis. (53201*)	717,372	12	741,324	−3.2	587,472	457,147
Minneapolis, Minn. (55440*)	434,400	32	482,872	−10.0	492,370	380,582
Mobile, Ala. (36601*)	190,026	68	194,856	−2.5	78,720	60,777
Modesto, Calif. (95350*)	61,712	312	36,585	68.7	16,379	9,241
Monroe, La. (71201*)	56,374	347	52,219	8.0	28,309	12,675
Monterey Park, Calif. (91754)	49,166	395	37,821	30.0	8,531	4,108
Montgomery, Ala. (36104*)	140,102	99	134,393	4.2	78,084	43,464
Mount Vernon, N.Y. (10551*)	72,778	244	76,010	−4.3	67,632	42,726
Mountain View, Calif. (94042*)	54,206	359	30,889	75.5	3,946	1,888
Muncie, Ind. (47302*)	69,082	271	68,603	0.7	49,720	36,524
Nashua, N.H. (03061)	55,820	352	39,096	42.8	32,927	23,379
Nashville, Tenn. (37202*)	447,877	31	170,874	162.1	167,402	118,342
New Bedford, Mass. (02741*)	101,777	152	102,477	−0.7	110,341	121,217
New Britain, Conn. (06050*)	83,441	207	82,201	1.5	68,685	59,316
New Haven, Conn. (06510*)	137,707	105	152,048	−9.4	160,605	162,537
New Orleans, La. (70140*)	593,471	19	627,525	−5.4	494,537	387,219
New Rochelle, N.Y. (10802*)	75,385	235	76,812	−1.9	58,408	36,213
New York, N.Y.	7,895,563	1	7,781,984	1.1	7,454,995	5,620,048
Bronx borough (10451*)	1,471,701	—	1,424,815	3.3	1,394,711	732,016
Brooklyn borough (11201*)	2,602,012	—	2,627,319	−1.0	2,698,285	2,018,356
Manhattan borough (10001*)	1,539,233	—	1,698,281	10.2	1,889,924	2,284,103
Queens borough[1]	1,987,174	—	1,809,578	9.1	1,297,634	469,042
Staten Island borough (10314)	295,443	—	221,991	33.1	174,441	116,531
Newark, N.J. (07101*)	381,930	35	405,220	−5.7	429,760	414,524
Newport News, Va. (23607*)	138,177	104	113,662	21.6	37,067	35,596
Newton, Mass. (02158)	91,263	176	92,384	−1.2	69,873	46,054
Niagara Falls, N.Y. (14302*)	85,615	201	102,394	−16.4	78,029	50,760
Norfolk, Va. (23501*)	307,951	47	304,869	1.0	144,332	115,777
Norman, Okla. (73070*)	52,117	378	33,412	56.0	11,429	5,004
North Little Rock, Ark. (72114*)	60,040	322	58,032	3.5	21,137	14,048
Norwalk, Calif. (90650)	91,827	173	88,739	3.5	—	—
Norwalk, Conn. (06856*)	79,113	217	67,775	16.7	39,849	27,743
Oak Park, Ill. (60303*)	62,511	309	61,093	2.3	66,015	39,858
Oakland, Calif. (94617*)	361,561	39	367,548	−1.6	302,163	216,261
Odessa, Tex. (79760*)	78,380	225	80,338	−2.4	9,573	—
Ogden, Utah (84401*)	69,478	269	70,197	−1.0	43,688	32,804
Oklahoma City, Okla. (73125*)	368,164	37	324,253	13.5	204,424	91,295
Omaha, Neb. (68108*)	358,452	41	301,598	15.9	223,844	191,601
Ontario, Calif. (91761*)	64,118	298	46,617	37.5	14,197	7,280
Orange, Calif. (92667*)	77,365	231	26,444	192.6	7,901	4,884
Orlando, Fla. (32802*)	99,006	158	88,135	12.3	36,736	9,282
Oshkosh, Wis. (54901)	53,221	370	45,110	18.0	39,089	33,162
Overland Park, Kan. (66204)	79,034	219	21,110	274.4	—	—
Owensboro, Ky. (42301)	50,329	387	42,471	18.5	30,245	17,424
Oxnard, Calif. (93030)	71,225	258	40,265	76.9	8,519	4,417
Palo Alto, Calif. (94303*)	56,181	349	52,287	7.4	16,774	5,900
Parma, Ohio (44129)	100,216	156	82,845	21.0	16,365	—
Pasadena, Calif. (91109*)	112,951	130	116,407	−2.9	81,864	45,354
Pasadena, Tex. (77501*)	89,277	183	58,737	52.0	3,436	—
Passaic, N.J. (07055)	55,124	357	53,963	2.2	61,394	63,841
Paterson, N.J. (07510*)	144,824	95	143,663	0.8	139,656	135,875
Pawtucket, R.I. (02860*)	76,984	232	81,001	−5.0	75,797	64,248
Pensacola, Fla. (32502*)	59,507	326	56,752	4.9	37,449	31,035
Peoria, Ill. (61601*)	126,963	117	103,162	23.1	105,087	76,121
Philadelphia, Pa. (19104*)	1,949,996	4	2,002,512	−2.6	1,931,334	1,823,779
Phoenix, Ariz. (85026*)	589,016	20	439,170	34.1	65,414	29,053
Pico Rivera, Calif. (90660)	54,170	360	49,150	10.2	—	—
Pine Bluff, Ark. (71601*)	57,389	338	44,037	30.3	21,290	19,280
Pittsburgh, Pa. (15230*)	520,089	24	604,332	−13.9	671,659	588,343
Pittsfield, Mass. (01201)	57,020	343	57,879	−1.5	49,684	41,763
Pomona, Calif. (91766*)	87,384	195	67,157	30.1	23,539	13,505
Pontiac, Mich. (48056*)	85,279	204	82,233	3.7	66,626	34,273
Port Arthur, Tex. (77640)	57,371	340	66,676	−14.0	46,140	22,251
Portland, Me (04101*)	65,116	293	72,566	−10.3	73,643	69,272
Portland, Ore. (97208*)	382,352	36	372,676	2.6	305,394	258,288
Portsmouth, Va. (23705*)	110,963	133	114,773	−3.3	50,745	54,387
Providence, R.I. (02940*)	179,116	72	207,498	−13.6	253,504	237,595

City and major ZIP code	1970 census	1970 rank	1960 census	% change 1960–70	1940 census	1920 census
Provo, Utah (84601)	53,131	371	36,047	47.4	18,071	10,303
Pueblo, Colo. (81002*)	97,774	160	91,181	7.2	52,162	43,050
Quincy, Mass. (02169)	87,966	190	87,409	0.6	75,810	47,876
Racine, Wis. (53401*)	95,162	167	89,144	6.8	67,195	58,593
Raleigh, N.C. (27611*)	123,793	119	93,931	31.7	46,897	24,418
Reading, Pa. (19603*)	87,643	194	98,177	−10.7	110,568	107,784
Redondo Beach, Calif. (90277*)	57,425	337	46,986	22.2	13,092	4,913
Redwood City, Calif. (94063*)	55,686	354	46,290	20.3	12,453	4,020
Reno, Nev. (89501*)	72,863	242	51,470	41.6	21.317	12,016
Richmond, Calif. (94802*)	79,043	218	71,854	10.0	23,642	16,843
Richmond, Va. (23232*)	249,431	58	219,958	13.4	193,042	171,667
Riverside, Calif. (92502*)	140,089	100	84,332	66.1	34,696	19,341
Roanoke, Va. (24022*)	92,115	171	97,110	−5.1	69,287	50,842
Rochester, Minn. (55901*)	53,766	363	40,663	32.2	26,312	13,722
Rochester, N.Y. (14692*)	295,011	49	318,611	−7.4	324,925	295,750
Rock Island, Ill. (61201)	50,166	388	51,863	−3.3	42,775	35,177
Rockford, Ill. (61125*)	147,370	94	126,706	16.3	84,637	65,651
Rome, N.Y. (13440)	50,148	389	51,646	−2.9	34,214	26,341
Roseville, Mich. (48066)	60,529	319	50,195	20.6	9,023	—
Royal Oak, Mich. (48067*)	86,238	198	80,612	7.0	25,087	6,007
Sacramento, Calif. (95814*)	257,105	56	191,667	34.1	105,958	65,908
Saginaw, Mich. (48605*)	91,849	172	98,265	−6.5	82,794	61,903
St. Clair Shores, Mich. (48080*)	88,093	189	76,657	14.9	10,405	—
St. Joseph, Mo. (64501*)	72,691	246	79,673	−8.8	75,711	77,939
St. Louis, Mo. (63166*)	622,236	18	750,026	−17.0	816,048	772,897
St. Paul, Minn. (55101*)	309,866	46	313,411	−1.1	287,736	234,698
St. Petersburg, Fla. (33733*)	216,159	61	181,298	19.3	60,812	14,237
Salem, Ore. (97301*)	68,856	274	49,142	40.1	30,908	17,679
Salinas, Calif. (93901*)	58,896	328	28,957	103.4	11,586	4,308
Salt Lake City, Utah (84101*)	175,885	76	189,454	−7.2	149,934	118,110
San Angelo, Tex. (76902*)	63,884	300	58,815	8.6	25,802	10,050
San Antonio, Tex. (78205*)	708,582	14	587,718	20.6	253,854	161,379
San Bernadino Calif. (92401*)	106,869	145	91,922	16.2	43,646	18,721
San Diego, Calif. (92101*)	697,471	15	573,224	21.7	203,341	74,361
San Francisco, Calif. (94101*)	715,674	13	740,316	−3.3	634,536	506,676
San Jose, Calif. (95113*)	461,212	29	204,196	125.9	68,457	39,642
San Leandro, Calif. (94577*)	68,698	275	65,962	4.1	14,601	5,703
San Mateo, Calif. (94402*)	78,991	220	69,870	13.1	19,403	5,979
Santa Ana, Calif. (92711*)	155,710	89	100,350	55.1	31,921	15,485
Santa Barbara, Calif. (93102*)	70,215	263	58,768	19.5	34,958	19,441
Santa Clara, Calif. (95050*)	87,717	193	58,880	49.0	6,650	5220
Santa Monica, Calif. (90406*)	88,289	188	83,249	6.1	53,500	15,252
Santa Rosa, Calif. (95402*)	50,006	391	31,027	61.2	12,605	8,758
Savannah, Ga. (31402*)	118,349	124	149,245	−20.7	95,996	83,252
Schenectady, N.Y. (12305*)	77,958	229	81,682	−4.6	87,549	88,723
Scottsdale, Ariz. (85251*)	67,823	282	10,026	576.5	—	—
Scranton, Pa. (18501*)	103,564	149	111,443	−7.1	140,404	137,783
Seattle, Wash. (98101*)	530,831	22	557,087	−4.7	368,302	315,312
Shreveport, La. (71101*)	182,064	70	164,372	10.8	98,167	43,874
Silver Spring, Md. (U) (20907*)	77,496	230	66,348	16.8	—	—
Simi Valley, Calif. (93065*)	59,832	325	—	—	—	—
Sioux City, Iowa (51101*)	85,925	200	89,159	−3.6	82,364	71,227
Sioux Falls, S.D. (57101*)	72,488	251	65,466	10.7	40,832	25,202
Skokie, Ill. (60076*)	68,627	276	59,364	15.6	7,172	763
Somerville, Mass. (02143)	88,779	186	94,697	−6.2	102,177	93,091
South Bend, Ind. (46624*)	127,328	115	132,445	−3.8	101,268	70,983
South Gate, Calif. (90280)	56,909	344	53,831	5.7	26,945	—
Southfield, Mich. (48037*)	69,285	270	31,501	119.9	—	—
Spokane, Wash. (99210*)	170,516	81	181,608	−6.1	122,001	104,437
Springfield, Ill. (62708*)	91,753	174	83,271	10.2	75,503	59,183
Springfield, Mass. (01101*)	163,905	85	174,463	−6.1	149,554	129,614
Springfield, Mo. (65801*)	120,096	123	95,865	25.3	61,238	39,631
Springfield, Ohio (45501*)	81,941	212	82,723	−1.0	70,662	60,840
Stamford, Conn. (06904*)	108,798	140	92,713	17.3	47,938	35,096
Sterling Heights, Mich. (48077)	61,365	316	—	—	—	—
Stockton, Calif. (95208*)	109,963	138	86,321	27.4	54,714	40,296
Sunnyvale, Calif. (94088*)	95,976	164	52,898	81.4	4,373	1,675
Syracuse, N.Y. (13220*)	197,297	66	216,038	−8.7	205,967	171,717
Tacoma, Wash. (98402*)	154,407	91	147,979	4.3	109,408	96,965
Tallahassee, Fla. (32301*)	72,586	250	48,174	50.1	16,240	5,637
Tampa, Fla. (33602*)	277,714	50	274,970	1.0	108,391	51,608

City and major ZIP code	1970 census	1970 rank	1960 census	% change 1960–70	1940 census	1920 census
Taylor, Mich. (48180)	70,020	265	—	—	—	—
Tempe, Ariz. (85282*)	63,550	302	24,897	155.3	2,906	1,963
Terre Haute, Ind. (47808*)	70,335	262	72,500	−3.1	62,693	66,083
Toledo, Ohio (43601*)	383,062	34	318,003	20.4	282,349	243,164
Topeka, Kan. (66601*)	132,952	110	119,484	11.2	67,833	50,022
Torrance, Calif. (90510*)	134,968	108	100,991	33.3	9,950	—
Towson, Md. (21204)	77,999	227	19,090	307.6	—	—
Trenton, N.J. (08650*)	104,786	147	114,167	−8.2	124,697	119,289
Troy, N.Y. (12180*)	62,918	306	67,492	−6.8	70,304	71,996
Tucson, Ariz. (85702*)	267,464	54	212,892	25.6	35,752	20,292
Tulsa, Okla. (74101*)	330,350	43	261,685	26.2	142,157	72,075
Tuscaloosa, Ala. (35403*)	65,773	291	63,370	3.8	27,493	11,996
Tyler, Tex. (75702*)	57,770	334	51,230	12.8	28,279	12,085
Union City, N.J. (07087)	58,537	332	52,180	12.2	56,173	20,651
Utica, N.Y. (13503*)	91,611	175	100,410	−8.8	100,518	94,156
Vallejo, Calif. (94590)	71,710	253	60,877	17.8	20,072	21,107
Ventura, Calif. (93001*)	57,964	333	29,114	99.0	—	—
Virginia Beach, Va. (23458*)	172,106	78	8,091	1.000+	2,600	846
Waco, Tex. (76703*)	95,326	166	97,808	−2.5	55,982	38,500
Waltham, Mass. (02154)	61,582	313	55,413	11.1	40,020	30,915
Warren, Mich. (48089*)	179,260	71	89,246	100.9	582	—
Warren, Ohio (44482*)	63,494	303	59,648	6.4	42,837	27,500
Warwick, R.I. (02887*)	83,694	206	68,504	22.2	28,757	13,481
Washington, D.C. (20013*)	756,668	9	763,956	−1.0	663,091	437,571
Waterbury, Conn. (06720*)	108,033	142	107,130	0.8	99,314	91,715
Waterloo, Iowa (50703*)	75,533	233	71,755	5.3	51,743	36,230
Waukegan, Ill. (60085)	65,269	292	55,719	17.1	34,241	19,226
Wauwatosa, Wis. (53213*)	58,676	331	56,923	3.1	27,769	5,818
West Allis, Wis. (53214)	71,649	254	68,157	5.1	36,364	13,745
West Covina, Calif. (91793*)	68,034	278	50,645	34.3	1,072	—
West Hartford, Conn. (T) (06107)	68,031	279	62,382	9.1	33,776	8,854
West Haven, Conn. (06516)	52,851	373	—	—	—	—
West Palm Beach, Fla. (33401*)	57,375	339	56,208	2.1	33,693	8,659
Westland, Mich. (48185)	86,749	197	—	—	—	—
Westminster, Calif. (92683)	59,874	323	25,750	132.5	—	—
Wheaton, Md. (U) (20902)	66,247	289	54,635	21.3	—	—
White Plains, N.Y. (10602*)	50,346	385	50,485	−0.3	40,327	21,031
Whittier, Calif. (90605*)	72,863	243	33,663	116.4	16,115	7,995
Wichita, Kan. (67209*)	276,554	51	254,698	8.6	114,966	72,217
Wichita Falls, Tex. (76307*)	96,265	163	101,724	−5.3	45,112	40,079
Wilkes-Barre, Pa. (18703*)	58,856	329	63,551	−7.4	86,236	73,833
Wilmington, Del. (19899*)	80,386	214	95,827	−16.1	112,504	110,168
Winston-Salem, N.C. (27102*)	133,683	109	111,135	21.2	79,815	48,395
Worcester, Mass. (01613*)	176,572	75	186,587	−5.4	193,694	179,754
Wyoming, Mich. (49509)	56,560	345	45,829	23.4	—	—
Yonkers, N.Y. (10701*)	204,297	63	190,634	7.2	142,598	100,176
York, Pa. (17405*)	50,335	386	54,504	−7.6	56,712	47,512
Youngstown, Ohio (44501*)	140,909	98	166,689	−15.5	167,720	132,358

1. Queens has four major ZIP codes: 11690*—Far Rockaway; 11352*—Flushing; 11431*—Jamaica; 11101*—Long Island City. *Sources:* Department of Commerce, Bureau of the Census; *1980 National ZIP Code & Post Office Directory.*

Income of Households by Age of Head, 1978

		Income (per cent)						
Age of head	Households (thousands)	Under $4,000	$4,000 to $6,999	$7,000 to $9,999	$10,000 to $14,999	$15,000 to $24,999	$25,000 and over	Total
14–24 years	6,342	10.2	10.3	12.8	11.6	7.6	2.2	8.2
25–34 years	16,996	12.0	14.3	19.7	26.0	30.1	19.0	22.0
35–44 years	13,328	7.6	8.6	11.5	15.2	21.3	25.5	17.2
45–54 years	12,585	8.7	8.9	9.9	12.6	17.4	27.9	16.3
55–64 years	12,284	15.2	13.4	14.9	15.4	15.3	19.0	15.9
65 years and over	15,795	46.3	44.5	31.2	19.2	8.3	6.4	20.4
Total	**77,330**	**100.0**	**100.0**	**100.0**	**100.0**	**100.0**	**100.0**	**100.0**

Source: Department of Commerce, Bureau of the Census.

Territorial Expansion

Accession	Date	Area[1]
United States	—	3,615,122
Territory in 1790	—	888,685
Louisiana Purchase	1803	827,192
Florida	1819	58,560
By treaty with Spain	1819	13,443
Texas	1845	390,143
Oregon	1846	285,580
Mexican Cession	1848	529,017
Gadsden Purchase	1853	29,640
Alaska	1867	586,412
Hawaii	1898	6,450
Other territory	—	12,944
Philippines	1898	115,600[2]
Puerto Rico	1899	3,435
Guam	1899	212
American Samoa	1900	76
Canal Zone	1904	553
Corn Islands[3]	1914	4
Virgin Islands of U.S.	1917	133
Trust Territory of Pacific Islands	1947	8,489
All other	—	42
Total, 1970	—	**3,628,066**

1. Total land and water area in square miles. 2. Became independent in 1946; area not included in total. 3. Leased from Nicaragua for 99 years in 1914, but returned April 25, 1971; area included in total. *Source:* Department of Commerce, Bureau of the Census.

Total Population

Area	1940	1960	1970
50 states of U.S.	—	179,323,175	203,235,298
48 coterminous	131,669,275	178,464,236	202,163,212
Alaska	72,524	226,167	302,173
Hawaii	422,770	632,772	769,913
American Samoa	12,908	20,051	27,159
Canal Zone	51,827	42,122	44,198
Canton Island	40	320	—
Corn Islands	1,523	1,872	(4)
Guam	22,290	67,044	84,996
Johnston Island	69	156	1,007
Midway	437	2,356	2,220
Philippines	16,356,000	—	—
Puerto Rico	1,869,255	2,349,544	2,712,033
Swan Islands	(1)	28	22
Trust Ter. of Pac. Is.	—	70,724	90,940
Virgin Is. of U.S.	24,889	32,099	62,468
Wake Island	(1)	1,097	1,647
Population abroad	118,933	1,374,421	1,737,836
Armed forces	(2)	609,720	1,057,776
Other[3]	14	—	—
Total	150,622,754	183,285,009	207,999,824

1. Not enumerated. 2. Not available. 3. Includes Baker Island (3), Enderbury Island (4), Howland Island (4), and Jarvis Island (3) these islands uninhabited in 1960 and 1970. 4. Returned to Nicaragua April 25, 1971. *Source:* Department of Commerce, Bureau of the Census.

Estimated Population by Race, 1976
(in thousands)

State	White	Black	Other
Alabama	2,617	959	13
Alaska	274	15	56
Arizona	2,095	58	121
Arkansas	1,747	366	12
California	18,479	1,648	869
Colorado	2,427	89	21
Connecticut	2,836	213	16
Delaware	494	77	5
D.C.	178	497	18
Florida	7,122	1,319	56
Georgia	3,539	1,336	35
Hawaii	254	6	582
Idaho	814	(1)	14
Illinois	9,189	1,688	16
Indiana	4,868	355	38
Iowa	2,794	35	7
Kansas	2,085	125	18
Kentucky	3,062	296	16
Louisiana	2,660	1,070	15
Maine	1,049	2	5
Maryland	3,166	842	50
Massachusetts	5,518	192	41
Michigan	7,989	1,017	70
Minnesota	3,790	51	48
Mississippi	1,489	829	11
Missouri	4,133	555	18
Montana	721	3	23
Nebraska	1,469	47	13
Nevada	545	38	18
New Hampshire	812	2	3
New Jersey	6,377	782	85
New Mexico	1,017	20	118
New York	15,256	2,234	343
North Carolina	4,045	1,206	131
North Dakota	607	2	12
Ohio	9,584	1,003	46
Oklahoma	2,408	179	94
Oregon	2,209	30	53
Pennsylvania	10,596	1,021	52
Rhode Island	877	25	11
South Carolina	1,887	881	17
South Dakota	644	1	27
Tennessee	3,490	687	8
Texas	10,799	1,428	80
Utah	1,199	8	14
Vermont	467	1	1
Virginia	4,072	779	63
Washington	3,338	67	98
West Virginia	1,753	37	3
Wisconsin	4,409	147	14
Wyoming	364	3	9
Total	**183,637**	**24,297**	**3,583**

1. Less than 1,000. NOTE: Data are latest available. *Source:* Department of Commerce, Bureau of the Census.

Want to Stop Smoking?

A new booklet, "Clearing the Air," contains a variety of sensible approaches. It can be obtained free by writing to: Clearing the Air, Box A, National Cancer Institute, Bethesda, Md. 20205.

Population Distribution by Age, Race, Nativity, and Sex

Year	Total	Age: Under 5	Age: 5–19	Age: 20–44	Age: 45–64	Age: 65 and over	Race and nativity: White: Total	White: Native born	White: Foreign born	Nonwhite
PERCENT DISTRIBUTION										
1860[1]	100.0	15.4	35.8	35.7	10.4	2.7	85.6	72.6	13.0	14.4
1870[1]	100.0	14.3	35.4	35.4	11.9	3.0	87.1	72.9	14.2	12.9
1880[1]	100.0	13.8	34.3	35.9	12.6	3.4	86.5	73.4	13.1	13.5
1890[2]	100.0	12.2	33.9	36.9	13.1	3.9	87.5	73.0	14.5	12.5
1900	100.0	12.1	32.3	37.8	13.7	4.1	87.9	74.5	13.4	12.1
1910	100.0	11.6	30.4	39.1	14.6	4.3	88.9	74.4	14.5	11.1
1920	100.0	11.0	29.8	38.4	16.1	4.7	89.7	76.7	13.0	10.3
1930	100.0	9.3	29.5	38.3	17.5	5.4	89.8	78.4	11.4	10.2
1940	100.0	8.0	26.4	38.9	19.8	6.9	89.8	81.1	8.7	10.2
1950[3]	100.0	10.7	23.2	37.7	20.3	8.1	89.5	82.8	6.7	10.5
1960[3]	100.0	11.3	27.1	32.4	20.0	9.2	88.6	83.4	5.2	11.4
1970[3]	100.0	8.4	29.4	31.7	20.6	9.9	87.7	83.4	4.3	12.3
1977[4]	100.0	7.0	26.5	35.4	20.2	10.8	86.6	n.a.	n.a.	13.4
1978[4]	100.0	7.0	25.9	36.0	20.1	11.0	86.4	n.a.	n.a.	13.6
1979[4]	100.0	7.1	25.2	36.7	19.9	11.2	86.3	n.a.	n.a.	13.7
MALES PER 100 FEMALES										
1860[1]	104.7	102.4	101.2	107.9	111.5	98.3	105.3	103.7	115.1	101.2
1870[1]	102.2	102.9	101.2	99.2	114.5	100.5	102.8	100.6	115.3	98.4
1880[1]	103.6	103.0	101.3	104.0	110.2	101.4	104.0	102.1	115.9	100.7
1890[2]	105.0	103.6	101.4	107.3	108.3	104.2	105.4	102.9	118.7	102.2
1900	104.4	102.1	100.9	105.8	110.7	102.0	104.9	102.8	117.4	101.0
1910	106.0	102.5	101.3	108.1	114.4	101.1	106.6	102.7	129.2	101.3
1920	104.0	102.5	100.8	102.8	115.2	101.3	104.4	101.7	121.7	100.9
1930	102.5	103.0	101.4	100.5	109.1	100.5	102.9	101.1	115.8	99.1
1940	100.7	103.2	102.0	98.1	105.2	95.5	101.2	100.1	111.1	96.7
1950[3]	99.0	103.9	102.9	97.0	100.2	89.6	99.4	99.0	103.9	96.2
1960[3]	97.1	103.4	103.0	96.9	95.8	82.9	97.9	97.5	94.2	95.1
1970[3]	94.8	104.0	103.3	95.1	91.4	72.2	95.7	95.9	83.8	91.6
1977[4]	95.1	104.6	103.8	98.4	92.0	68.7	95.7	n.a.	n.a.	91.7
1978[4]	95.1	104.6	103.8	98.4	92.1	68.5	95.6	n.a.	n.a.	91.6
1979[4]	95.0	104.7	103.9	98.4	92.2	68.4	95.5	n.a.	n.a.	91.6

1. Excludes Indians in Indian Territory and on Indian reservations. 2. The age figures exclude all persons residing on Indian reservations, whether white or nonwhite; these persons are included in the race and nativity distributions. 3. Data by age and race include, and data by nativity exclude, Armed Forces overseas and other persons abroad. 4. Total population including Armed Forces overseas. NOTE: For 1860, the data in the census reports at ages 40–49 and 60–69 are published in 10-year age groupings; these were subdivided into 5-year age groupings by the author. n.a. = not available. *Sources:* Mortimer Spiegelman, *Introduction to Demography;* Department of Commerce, Bureau of the Census.

Distribution of Population by Race

Year[1]	White	Black	Indian	Japanese	Chinese	All other	Total nonwhite
1850	19,553,068	3,638,808	—	—	—	—	3,638,808
1860	26,922,537	4,441,830	44,021	—	34,933	—	4,520,784
1870	33,589,377	4,880,009	25,731	55	63,199	—	4,968,994
1880	43,402,970	6,580,793	66,407	148	105,465	—	6,752,813
1890	55,101,258	7,488,676	248,253	2,039	107,488	—	7,846,456
1900	66,809,196	8,833,994	237,196	24,326	89,863	—	9,185,379
1910	81,731,957	9,827,763	265,683	72,157	71,531	3,175	10,240,309
1920	94,820,915	10,463,131	244,437	111,010	61,639	9,488	10,889,705
1930	110,286,740	11,891,143	332,397	138,834	74,954	50,978	12,488,306
1940	118,214,870	12,865,518	333,969	126,947	77,504	50,467	13,454,405
1950	134,942,028	15,042,286	343,410	141,768	117,629	110,240	15,755,333
1960	158,831,732	18,871,831	523,591	464,332	237,292	394,397	20,491,443
1970	177,748,975	22,580,289	792,730	591,290	435,062	1,063,580	25,462,951
Urban	128,773,240	18,367,318	355,738	523,651	418,779	886,204	20,551,690
Rural	48,975,735	4,212,971	436,992	67,639	16,283	177,376	4,911,261

1. Beginning with 1960, data include Alaska and Hawaii. *Source:* Department of Commerce, Bureau of the Census.

Distribution of Population According to Size of Place

Census year	Total population	Population distribution (total for year = 100%): Total urban	Places of 2,500 or more: 1,000,000 or more	Places of 2,500 or more: 100,000 to 1,000,000	Places of 2,500 or more: Under 100,000	Total rural	Number of places of 2,500 or more: 1,000,000 or more	Number of places of 2,500 or more: 100,000 to 1,000,000	Number of places of 2,500 or more: Under 100,000
1790	3,929,214	5.1	—	—	5.1	94.9	—	—	24
1800	5,308,483	6.1	—	—	6.1	93.9	—	—	33
1810	7,239,881	7.3	—	—	7.3	92.7	—	—	46
1820	9,638,453	7.2	—	1.3	5.9	92.8	—	1	60
1830	12,866,020	8.8	—	1.6	7.2	91.2	—	1	89
1840	17,069,453	10.8	—	3.0	7.8	89.2	—	3	128
1850	23,191,876	15.3	—	5.1	10.2	84.7	—	6	230
1860	31,443,321	19.8	—	8.4	11.4	80.2	—	9	383
1870	39,818,449	25.7	—	10.7	15.0	74.3	—	14	649
1880	50,155,783	28.2	2.4	10.0	15.8	71.8	1	19	919
1890	62,947,714	35.1	5.8	9.6	19.7	64.9	3	25	1,320
1900	75,994,575	39.7	8.5	10.2	21.0	60.3	3	35	1,699
1910	91,972,266	45.7	9.2	12.9	23.6	54.3	3	47	2,212
1920	105,710,620	51.2	9.6	16.3	25.3	48.8	3	65	2,654
1930	122,775,046	56.2	12.3	17.3	26.6	43.8	5	88	3,072
1940	131,669,275	56.5	12.1	16.8	27.6	43.5	5	87	3,372
1950[1]	150,697,361	59.0	11.5	18.0	29.5	41.0	5	102	3,916
1950[2]	150,697,361	64.0	11.5	17.9	34.6	36.0	5	101	4,635
1960[2,3]	179,323,175	69.9	9.8	18.7	41.4	30.1	5	127	5,909
1970[2,3]	203,235,298	73.5	9.2	18.5	45.8	26.5	6	150	6,279

1. Old urban definition. 2. New urban definition. 3. Includes Alaska and Hawaii. *Source:* Department of Commerce, Bureau of the Census.

Population of Races Other Than White or Black, 1970

State	Indian	Japanese	Chinese	Filipino	All other[1]
Alabama	2,443	1,079	626	540	2,179
Alaska	16,276	916	228	1,498	35,786
Arizona	95,812	2,394	3,878	1,253	9,271
Arkansas	2,014	587	743	289	1,302
Calif.	91,018	213,280	170,131	138,859	178,671
Colorado	8,836	7,831	1,489	1,068	9,272
Conn.	2,222	1,621	2,209	2,177	6,845
Delaware	656	359	559	392	1,403
D.C.	956	651	2,582	1,662	3,675
Florida	6,677	4,090	3,133	5,092	9,457
Georgia	2,347	1,836	1,584	1,253	4,164
Hawaii	1,126	217,307	52,039	93,915	98,441
Idaho	6,687	2,255	498	206	1,989
Illinois	11,413	17,299	14,474	12,654	32,081
Indiana	3,887	2,279	2,115	1,365	6,235
Iowa	2,992	1,009	993	614	3,410
Kansas	8,672	1,584	1,233	758	5,286
Kentucky	1,531	1,095	558	612	2,351
Louisiana	5,294	1,123	1,340	1,249	3,970
Maine	2,195	348	206	453	770
Maryland	4,239	3,733	6,520	5,170	8,370
Mass.	4,475	4,393	14,012	2,361	10,488
Michigan	16,854	5,221	6,407	3,657	18,404
Minnesota	23,128	2,603	2,422	1,456	4,456
Miss.	4,113	461	1,441	475	1,369
Missouri	5,405	2,382	2,815	2,010	6,222
Montana	27,130	574	289	236	1,142
Nebraska	6,624	1,314	551	324	1,902
Nevada	7,933	1,087	955	817	2,007
N.H.	361	360	420	157	772
N.J.	4,706	5,681	9,233	5,623	22,721
N.M.	72,788	940	563	386	5,953
New York	28,355	20,351	81,378	14,279	89,565
N.C.	44,406	2,104	1,255	905	5,144
N.D.	14,369	239	165	204	805
Ohio	6,654	5,555	5,305	3,490	13,539
Oklahoma	98,468	1,408	999	612	5,488
Oregon	13,510	6,843	4,814	1,633	6,198
Pa.	5,533	5,461	7,053	4,560	17,056
R.I.	1,390	629	1,093	1,761	1,757
S.C.	2,241	826	521	1,222	2,235
S.D.	32,365	221	163	83	715
Tenn.	2,276	1,160	1,610	846	2,604
Texas	17,957	6,537	7,635	3,442	45,026
Utah	11,273	4,713	1,281	392	3,071
Vermont	229	134	173	53	427
Virginia	4,853	3,500	2,805	7,496	6,958
Wash.	33,386	20,335	9,201	11,462	12,422
W. Va.	751	368	373	722	1,201
Wisconsin	18,924	2,648	2,700	1,209	5,067
Wyoming	4,980	566	292	108	878
Total	**792,730**	**591,290**	**435,062**	**343,060**	**720,520**

1. Aleuts, Asian Indians, Eskimos, Hawaiians, Indonesians, Koreans, Polynesians, and other races not shown separately. NOTE: As of April 1, resident population. *Source:* Department of Commerce, Bureau of the Census.

Immigration to U.S. by Country of Origin

(Figures are totals, not annual averages, and were tabulated as follows: 1820–67, alien passengers arrived; 1868–91 and 1895–97, immigrant aliens arrived; 1892–94 and 1898 to present, immigrant aliens admitted. Data before 1906 relate to country whence alien came; since 1906, to country of last permanent residence.)

Countries	1978	1820–1978	1961–70	1951–60	1941–50	1931–40	1921–30	1820–1920
Europe: Albania[1]	68	2,583	98	59	85	2,040	—	
Austria[2]	467	4,314,979	20,621	67,106	24,860	3,563	32,868	3,626,110
Belgium	439	202,246	9,192	18,575	12,189	4,817	15,846	137,542
Bulgaria[3]	202	67,894	619	104	375	938	2,945	61,973
Czechoslovakia[1]	744	137,335	3,273	918	8,347	14,393	102,194	3,426
Denmark	409	364,170	9,201	10,984	5,393	2,559	32,430	300,036
Estonia[1]	17	1,139	163	185	212	506	—	—
Finland[1]	358	33,486	4,192	4,925	2,503	2,146	16,691	756
France	1,844	749,527	45,237	51,121	38,809	12,623	49,610	532,765
Germany[2]	6,739	6,976,915	190,796	477,765	226,578	114,058	412,202	5,495,691
Great Britain: England	12,076	3,175,652	174,452	156,171	112,252	21,756	157,420	2,462,015
Scotland	1,458	820,566	29,849	32,854	16,131	6,887	159,781	567,106
Wales	211	95,204	2,052	2,589	3,209	735	13,012	72,647
Not specified[4]	500	804,968	3,675	3,884	—	—	—	793,741
Greece	7,035	654,927	85,969	47,608	8,973	9,119	51,084	370,405
Hungary[2]	941	—	5,401	36,637	3,469	7,861	30,680	442,693
Ireland	1,180	4,723,801	37,461	57,332	26,967	13,167	220,591	4,358,350
Italy	7,415	5,294,801	214,111	185,491	57,661	68,028	455,315	4,195,880
Latvia[1]	52	2,591	510	352	361	1,192	—	—
Lithuania[1]	93	3,915	562	242	683	2,201	—	—
Luxembourg[1]	21	2,864	556	684	820	565	—	—
Netherlands	1,153	359,612	30,606	52,277	14,860	7,150	26,948	219,661
Norway[5]	423	856,469	15,484	22,935	10,100	4,740	68,531	731,584
Poland[6]	5,053	515,054	53,539	9,985	7,571	17,026	227,734	169,995
Portugal	10,445	445,282	76,065	19,588	7,423	3,329	29,994	222,721
Romania[7]	2,037	171,300	2,531	1,039	1,076	3,871	67,646	85,428
Spain	2,297	257,582	44,659	7,894	2,898	3,258	28,958	137,907
Sweden[5]	638	1,271,919	17,116	21,697	10,665	3,960	97,249	1,116,239
Switzerland	706	348,949	18,453	17,675	10,547	5,512	29,676	260,492
U.S.S.R.[8]	5,161	3,373,798	2,336	584	548	1,356	61,742	3,280,249
Yugoslavia[3]	2,621	113,943	20,381	8,225	1,576	5,835	49,064	1,888
Other Europe	395	55,593	4,203	8,155	3,983	2,361	22,983	10,716
Total Europe	73,198	36,200,005	1,123,363	1,325,640	621,124	347,552	2,463,194	29,658,016
Asia: China[9]	21,315	534,587	34,764	9,657	16,709	4,928	29,907	347,338
India	20,753	165,306	27,189	1,973	1,761	496	1,886	7,491
Japan[10]	4,010	405,948	39,988	46,250	1,555	1,948	33,462	242,181
Turkey	1,578	386,111	10,142	3,519	798	1,065	33,824	326,347
Other Asia	202,120	1,367,988	315,688	88,707	11,537	7,644	12,980	22,915
Total Asia[11]	249,776	2,859,940	427,771	150,106	32,360	16,081	112,059	946,272
America: Canada and Newfoundland[12]	16,863	4,098,225	413,310	377,952	171,718	108,527	924,515	1,972,686
Central America	20,153	312,535	101,330	44,751	21,665	5,861	15,769	27,524
Mexico[13]	92,367	2,123,412	453,937	299,811	60,589	22,319	459,287	296,649
South America	41,764	712,708	257,954	91,628	21,831	7,803	42,215	71,284
West Indies	91,361	1,690,445	470,213	123,091	49,725	15,502	74,899	356,570
Other America[13]	34	109,458	19,630	59,711	29,276	25	31	—
Total America	262,542	9,046,783	1,716,374	996,944	354,804	160,037	1,516,716	2,724,713
Africa	11,524	133,247	28,954	14,092	7,367	1,750	6,286	18,024
Australia and New Zealand	2,184	118,027	19,562	11,506	13,805	2,231	8,299	44,002
Pacific Islands[14]	137	24,571	1,769	4,698	5,437	780	427	9,938
Countries not specified[15]	2,081	282,392	3,884	12,493	142	—	228	253,838
Total all countries	**601,442**	**48,664,965**	**3,321,677**	**2,515,479**	**1,035,039**	**528,431**	**4,107,209**	**33,654,803**

1. Countries established since beginning of World War I are included with countries to which they belonged. 2. Data for Austria-Hungary not reported until 1861. Austria and Hungary recorded separately after 1905, Austria included with Germany 1938–45. 3. Bulgaria, Serbia, Montenegro first reported in 1899. Bulgaria reported separately since 1920. In 1920, separate enumeration for Kingdom of Serbs, Croats, Slovenes; since 1922, recorded as Yugoslavia. 4. United Kingdom not specified; for 1901–51, included in "Other Europe." 5. Norway included with Sweden 1820–68. 6. Included with Austria-Hungary, Germany, and Russia 1899–1919. 7. No record of immigration until 1880. 8. From 1931–63, the U.S.S.R. was broken down into European U.S.S.R. and Asian U.S.S.R. Since 1964, total U.S.S.R. has been reported in Europe. 9. Beginning in 1957, China includes Taiwan. 10. No record of immigration until 1861. 11. From 1952, Asia included Philippines. From 1934–51, Philippines were included in Pacific Islands; before 1934, recorded in separate tables as insular travel. 12. Includes all British North American possessions, 1820–98. 13. No record of immigration, 1886–93. 14. Included with "Countries not specified" prior to 1925. 15. Includes 32,897 persons returning in 1906 to their homes in U.S. *Source:* Department of Justice, Immigration and Naturalization Service. NOTE: Data are latest available.

Population of Largest Indian Reservations, 1977

Navajo (Ariz., N.M., Utah)	154,748	Papago (Ariz.)	10,542	Standing Rock (N.D., S.D.)	6,957
Creek (Okla.)[1]	26,562	Osage (Okla.)[1]	10,499	Chickasaw (Okla.)[1]	6,800
Cherokee (Okla.)[1]	23,500	Yakima (Wash.)	9,802	Wind River (Wyo.)	6,742
Southern Pueblos (N.M.)	20,080	Gila River (Ariz.)	8,777	Blackfeet (Mont.)	6,269
Choctaw (Okla.)[1]	17,313	Turtle Mountain (N.D.)	7,850	Zuni (N.M.)	6,266
Pine Ridge (S.D.)	12,260	Fort Apache (Ariz.)	7,706	San Carlos (N.M.)	5,979
Rosebud (S.D.)	12,186	Hopi (Ariz.)	7,177		

1. Includes Indians living in former reservation areas. NOTE: The Bureau of Indian Affairs lists 648,700 Indians residing on or near Federal reservations. *Source:* Department of the Interior, Bureau of Indian Affairs.

Immigrant and Nonimmigrant Aliens Admitted to U.S.

Period[1]	Immigrants	Non-immigrants	Total	Period[1]	Immigrants	Non-immigrants	Total
1901–10	8,795,386	1,007,909	9,803,295	1971	370,478	4,403,761	4,774,239
1911–20	5,735,811	1,376,271	7,112,082	1972	384,685	5,171,460	5,556,145
1921–30	4,107,209	1,774,896	5,882,090	1973	400,063	5,977,324	6,377,387
1931–40	528,431	1,574,071	2,102,502	1974	394,861	6,908,708	7,303,569
1941–50	1,035,039	2,461,359	3,496,398	1975	386,194	7,083,937	7,470,131
1951–55	1,087,638	2,654,461	3,742,009	1976	398,613	7,654,491	8,053,104
1956–60	1,427,841	4,458,562	5,886,403	1976, TQ[2]	103,676	2,673,652	2,777,328
1961–65	1,450,312	7,879,564	9,329,876	1977[3]	462,315	8,036,916	8,499,231
1966–70	1,871,365	16,227,660	18,099,025	1978	601,442	9,343,710	9,945,152

1. Fiscal year ending June 30, except as noted. 2. Transition Quarter, July–Sept. 1976. 3. Starting 1977, for fiscal year ending Sept. 30. *Source:* Department of Justice, Immigration and Naturalization Service. NOTE: Nonimmigrant aliens include visitors for business or pleasure, students, foreign government officials, and others temporarily in the U.S.

Persons Naturalized Since 1907

Period[1]	Civilian	Military	Total	Period[1]	Civilian	Military	Total
1907–30	2,713,389	300,506	3,013,895	1974	124,807	6,848	131,655
1931–40	1,498,573	19,891	1,518,464	1975	135,323	6,214	141,537
1941–50	1,837,229	149,799	1,987,028	1976	136,873	5,631	142,504
1951–60	1,148,241	41,705	1,189,946	1976, TQ[2]	46,705	1,513	48,218
1961–70	1,084,195	36,068	1,120,263	1977[3]	154,568	5,305	159,873
1972	107,740	8,475	116,215	1978	168,409	5,126	173,535
1973	112,944	7,796	120,740	1907–78	9,367,854	604,426	9,972,280

1. Fiscal year ending June 30, except as noted. 2. Transition Quarter, July-Sept. 1976. 3. Fiscal year, Oct. 1976–Sept. 1977. *Source:* Department of Justice, Immigration and Naturalization Service. NOTE: Data are latest available.

Marriage and Divorce

In December 1978, the Bureau of the Census issued its new study of American husbands and wives. Among its highlights were:

Most men and women marry at some time during their lives. In 1977, only about 6% of men and 4% of women in their early fifties had never married.

Most married men and women have been married only once—85% of the men and 88% of the women.

The number of interracial couples has been increasing (a one-third increase between 1970 and 1977), but that number still comprises only about 1% of all married couples.

Husbands and wives tend to have similar levels of education. Among men who had completed high school but no college, about two thirds of their wives had the same amount of education.

Young children living with two parents are likely to have the company of at least one brother or sister.

Both the husband and the wife are likely to vote in a presidential election; among two thirds of all married couples, both the husband and wife voted in 1976.

Most married men (81%) and nearly half of the married women (47%) were in the labor force in 1977.

Among a minority of married couples (about 1 in every 6) both spouses work at year-round full-time jobs.

The median family income in 1976 for families with two earners (the husband and wife) was $17,570.

The earnings of the wife were about equal to or greater than the husband's earnings among 1 married couple in 3 in which the wife had earnings.

Marriage Information by State

State	Legal minimum marriage age: With parental consent[3] M	With parental consent[3] F	Without parental consent M	Without parental consent F	Blood test required	Waiting period[1] Before license	Waiting period[1] After license	Marriages[2] 1979[4]	Marriages[2] 1978
Alabama	14	14	18	18	yes	none	none	48,807	47,881
Alaska	16	16	18	18	yes	3 d	none	5,071	5,102
Arizona	18	18	18	18	yes	none	none	29,549	28,228
Arkansas	18	16	18	18	yes	3 d	none	24,947	23,461
California	18	16	18	18	yes	none	none	159,172	149,152
Colorado	16[19]	16[19]	18	18	yes[17]	none	none	31,889	30,362
Connecticut	16	16	18	18	yes	4 d	none	24,675	23,731
Delaware	18[25]	16[25]	18	18	yes[11]	none	24 h[5]	4,418	4,260
D. C.	16–17	16–17	18	18	yes[7]	5 d[6]	none	4,974	4,618
Florida	18	16	18	18	yes	3 d	none	103,406	94,423
Georgia	16	16[26]	18	18[26]	yes[21]	3 d	none	65,898	67,593
Hawaii	16	16	18	18	yes	none	none	11,658	10,675
Idaho	18	16	18	18	yes	3 d[24]	none	13,568	13,768
Illinois	16	16	18	18	yes	none	1 d	108,443	105,605
Indiana	17	17[20]	18	18	yes	3 d	none	59,613	58,197
Iowa	16	16	18	18	yes	3 d	none	27,731	28,089
Kansas	([23])	([23])	18	18	yes	3 d	none	24,867	23,901
Kentucky	([18])	([18])	18	18	yes	3 d	none	36,513	34,104
Louisiana	18	16	18	18	yes	none	72 h	41,816	39,232
Maine	16	16	18	18	no	5 d	none	11,944	11,629
Maryland	16[15]	16[15]	18	18	no	48 h	none	45,903	44,376
Massachusetts	14–17[12]	12–15[12]	18	18	yes	3 d	none	42,652	46,290
Michigan	18	16[8]	18	18	yes	3 d	none	86,660	86,672
Minnesota	18	16	21	18	no	5 d	none	35,758	33,832
Mississippi	17	15	21	21	yes	3 d	none	26,718	26,807
Missouri	15[12]	15[12]	18	18	yes	3 d	none	52,336	54,197
Montana	18	18	16[22]	16[22]	yes	5 d	3 d	8,246	8,137
Nebraska	17	17	19	19	yes	2 d	none	14,032	13,439
Nevada	16	16	18	18	no	none	none	121,874	114,156
New Hampshire	14[12 15]	13[12 15]	18	18	yes[11]	5 d	none	9,189	9,049
New Jersey	18	16	18	18	yes	72 h	none	54,844	53,079
New Mexico	16	16	18	18	yes	none	none	16,785	17,047
New York	16	14[9]	21	18	yes	none	([10])	141,350	135,988
North Carolina	16	16	18	18	yes	none	none	45,233	44,149
North Dakota	16	16	18	18	yes	none	none	5,977	5,664
Ohio	18	16	18	18	yes	5 d	none	102,539	104,340
Oklahoma	16[19]	16[19]	18	18	yes	none[14]	none	44,452	43,115
Oregon	17	17	18	18	yes	7 d	none	21,907	20,961
Pennsylvania	16	16	18	18	yes	3 d	none	89,417	94,030
Rhode Island	18	16[9]	18	18	yes	none	none	7,350	7,247
South Carolina	16	14	18	18	no	24 h	none	53,968	53,173
South Dakota	16	16	18	18	yes	none	none	9,098	10,570
Tennessee	16	16	18	18	yes	none[14]	none	59,407	57,733
Texas	16[13]	16[13]	18	18	yes	none	none	174,743	164,278
Utah	14	14	16	16	yes	none	none	16,823	16,522
Vermont	16	16	18	18	yes	none	5 d[16]	5,228	4,899
Virginia	16	16	18	18	yes	none	none	58,739	59,013
Washington	17	17	18	18	no	3 d	none	45,809	43,612
West Virginia	18	16	18	18	yes	3 d	none	17,733	17,299
Wisconsin	16	16	18	18	yes	5 d	none	39,551	38,010
Wyoming	16[19]	16[19]	19	19	yes	none	none	6,032	6,205

1. In some states, waiting period may be waived or reduced by court order. 2. By place of occurrence. 3. In most states, persons younger than the age shown may be married by court permission. 4. Provisional figures; data represent marriages reported, marriage intentions filed, or marriage licenses issued. 5. 96 hours if nonresidents. 6. Day of application and day of pickup are included in 5-day waiting period. 7. No exceptions granted under this age. 8. Consent of one parent or guardian necessary for female only. 9. Females 14 to 16 years old must also have consent of judge of Family Court. 10. Marriage may not be solemnized within 10 days from date on which specimen was taken for serological test, and not until 24 hours after issuance of marriage license. Waiting period may be waived by court order. 11. Blood test may be waived by court order. 12. Need court order. 13. Parent must appear in person or provide doctor's affidavit of his or her illness. 14. 3 days if either party is under legal age. 15. If pregnant. 16. After date on which marriage application has been filed with town clerk, excluding date of filing. 17. Blood test for rubella and RH type not required of females over 45 years or found by physician to be incapable of bearing children. 18. No age limit. 19. If under 16 need court order. 20. 15 for pregnancy or maternity. 21. Prior to issuance of license, a medical examination for rubella is required. 22. With judicial approval. 23. Under 18 with parental consent only. 24. Only for those under 18. 26. May marry at any age with proof of pregnancy signed by physician or if marrying father of child born out of wedlock. *Sources:* Legal information, *Information Please* questionnaires to states; marriage statistics, Department of Health and Human Services, National Center for Health Statistics.

Divorce Information by State

State	Residence for divorce	Period before parties may remarry		Divorces[1]	
		Plaintiff	Defendant	1979[2]	1978
Alabama	6 mo	60 d	60 d	26,900	25,271
Alaska	([25])	none	none	3,513	3,353
Arizona	90 d	none	none	19,917	17,370
Arkansas	90 d	none	none	19,337	19,389
California	6 mo	none	none	137,714	133,232
Colorado	90 d[20]	none	none	16,688	17,524
Connecticut	1 yr	none	none	12,780	12,678
Delaware	1 yr[20]	none[12]	none[12]	3,166	3,246
D.C.	6 mo	60 d	60	4,173	3,492
Florida	6 mo	none	none	70,155	66,011
Georgia	6 mo	none	none	32,842	31,421
Hawaii	6 mo	none	none	5,035	4,837
Idaho	6 wk	none	none	6,519	6,386
Illinois	1 yr	none	none	53,842	47,676
Indiana	6 mo[4 6]	none	none	n.a.	n.a.
Iowa	1 yr[11]	1 yr	1 yr	11,403	11,083
Kansas	60 d	30 d	30 d	13,017	12,737
Kentucky	6 mo[4 23]	none	none	16,913	14,043
Louisiana	1 yr	none[8]	none[8]	n.a.	n.a.
Maine	6 mo	none	none	6,110	6,244
Maryland	1 yr[24]	none	none	15,541	15,711
Massachusetts	1 yr	none	none	17,405	17,777
Michigan	1 yr	none	none	45,951	44,804
Minnesota	1 yr	6 mo	6 mo	14,526	14,127
Mississippi	6 mo	([10])	([10])	12,901	12,893
Missouri	90 d	none	none	28,467	26,366
Montana	1 yr	none	none	5,159	4,874
Nebraska	1 yr[5]	none	none	6,021	6,108
Nevada	6 wk	none	none	10,465	9,989
New Hampshire	1 yr	none	none	5,056	4,471
New Jersey	1 yr	none	none	24,667	26,029
New Mexico	6 mo[13]	none	none	9,329	9,249
New York	([14])	none	none	59,898	57,021
North Carolina	6 mo	none	none	27,523	26,630
North Dakota	1 yr	([9])	([9])	2,076	2,083
Ohio	6 mo[6]	none	none	60,108	58,149
Oklahoma	6 mo[22]	6 mo[21]	6 mo[21]	22,823	22,507
Oregon	6 mo	60 d	60 d	17,709	16,882
Pennsylvania	6 mo	none	none[15]	39,689	39,061
Rhode Island	2 yr	none	none	3,599	3,471
South Carolina	1 yr	none	none	13,965	12,151
South Dakota	([7])	none	none	2,635	2,446
Tennessee	1 yr	none[16]	none[16]	32,349	28,816
Texas	6 mo	30 d[16]	30 d[16]	91,454	86,533
Utah	3 mo	3 mo[12]	3 mo[12]	7,542	7,128
Vermont	6 mo[19]	none	none	2,296	2,284
Virginia	6 mo	none	none	23,648	22,629
Washington	none[20]	none	none	26,802	26,062
West Virginia	1 yr[17]	([18])	([18])	10,066	9,729
Wisconsin	6 mo	6 mo	6 mo	16,880	15,831
Wyoming	60 d	none	none	3,654	3,117

1. By place of occurrence, including reported annulments. 2. Provisional. 3. Data not available. 4. Only one party must have resided in the state for 180 days. 5. Decree not final until 6 months after trial and decision. 6. 6-month residence in state; 90-day residence in county. 7. Physical presence plus intent to make state the place of residence. 8. In case of adultery, guilty party cannot marry correspondent. 9. At discretion of court. 10. Until court that grants the divorce is adjourned. 11. No time required if both parties are residents of state and intend to make state their place of residence. 12. 30 days between first and final judgment. 13. Servicemen acquire residence by being continuously stationed at military base in state for 6 months. 14. Action for divorce may be maintained only where (1) parties were married in the state and either has been a resident for one year preceding the action; (2) parties have resided in the state as husband and wife and either has been a resident for one year preceding the action; (3) cause for divorce occurred in the state and either party has been a resident for one year preceding the action; (4) cause for divorce occurred in the state and both parties are residents at time of the action; (5) either party is a resident for at least 2 years preceding the action. 15. Party guilty of adultery may not marry the correspondent during lifetime of former spouse. 16. Parties may remarry each other at any time. 17. 2 years if residence is acquired after cause of divorce action arose. 18. Court can lengthen waiting period if desired. 19. Court must find resumption of marital relations not reasonably probable. 20. Must be domiciled in state. 21. 30 days from date of judgment of appeal. 22. 5 years if on grounds of insanity and insane spouse is in institution. 23. No decree shall be entered until parties have lived apart for 60 days. 24. When cause for divorce occurred out of state. 25. No residency requirement but action will not be heard by court until 30 days after filing for divorce. *Sources:* Legal information, *Information Please* questionnaires to states; divorce statistics, Department of Health and Human Services, National Center for Health Statistics.

Grounds for Divorce

State	Adultery	Cruelty	Desertion	Alcoholism	Impotence	Felony conviction	Neglect to provide	Insanity	Pregnancy at marriage[1]	Bigamy	Separation	Indignities	Drug addiction	Violence	Fraudulent contract	Others
Alabama	yes	yes	yes[2]	yes	yes	yes[16]	yes[3]	yes[6]	yes[1]	—	yes[3]	—	yes	yes	—	(27 29 34)
Alaska	yes	yes	yes[2]	yes	yes	yes	yes	yes[9]	—	—	—	yes	yes	yes	—	—
Arizona	—	—	—	—	—	—	—	—	—	—	—	—	—	—	—	(29)
Arkansas	yes	yes	yes[2]	yes	yes	yes	yes	yes	—	yes	yes[4]	yes	—	yes	yes	(12 31 48)
California	—	—	—	—	—	—	—	—	—	—	—	—	—	—	—	(28)
Colorado	—	—	—	—	—	—	—	—	—	—	—	—	—	—	—	(29 52)
Connecticut	yes	yes	yes[2]	yes	—	yes[20]	—	yes[6]	—	—	—	—	—	—	yes	(13 23 30 42 46)
Delaware	yes	yes	yes[2]	yes[3]	—	yes	yes	yes[6]	—	yes	yes[9]	—	—	—	—	(27 68)
D.C.	yes	yes[53]	—	—	—	—	—	—	—	—	yes[2]	—	—	—	—	(63)
Florida	—	—	—	—	—	—	—	—	—	—	—	—	—	—	—	(49 52)
Georgia	yes	yes	yes[2]	yes	yes	yes[15]	yes	yes	yes	yes	yes	yes	yes	yes	yes	(27 31 44 49)
Hawaii	—	—	—	—	—	—	—	—	—	—	yes[3]	—	—	—	—	(29)
Idaho	yes	yes	yes	—	—	yes	yes	yes[4]	—	yes	—	—	—	—	—	(26 28 42)
Illinois	yes	yes	yes[2]	yes[3]	yes	yes	—	—	—	yes[51]	—	—	yes[3]	yes	—	(32 37 56)
Indiana	—	—	—	—	yes	—	—	yes[3]	—	—	—	—	—	—	—	(29 33 52)
Iowa	—	—	—	—	—	—	—	—	—	—	—	—	—	—	—	(49)
Kansas	yes	yes	yes[2]	yes	—	yes	yes	yes[6]	—	—	—	—	—	—	yes	(31 48)
Kentucky	—	—	—	—	—	—	—	—	—	—	—	—	—	—	—	(49)
Louisiana	yes	yes	yes	yes	—	yes	yes	—	—	yes	yes[3]	—	yes	yes	—	(37 58)
Maine	yes	yes	yes	yes	yes	yes[20]	yes	—	—	—	—	—	yes	—	—	(28)
Maryland[65]	yes	—	—	—	yes	yes[18]	—	yes[66]	—	—	yes[10]	—	—	—	—	(28 35 67)
Massachusetts	yes	yes	yes[2]	yes	yes	yes[19]	yes	—	—	—	—	—	yes	—	—	(29 35 49)
Michigan	—	—	—	—	—	—	—	—	—	—	—	—	—	—	—	(29)
Minnesota	yes	—	yes[2]	yes[2]	yes	yes	—	yes[4]	—	—	yes[3]	—	—	—	—	(36 49)
Mississippi	yes	yes	yes	yes	yes	yes[22]	—	yes[47]	yes	yes	yes[2]	—	yes	yes	—	(10 28 31 49)
Missouri	yes	yes	yes	yes	yes	yes	—	—	yes	yes	—	yes		—	—	(10 30 32 52)
Montana	—	—	—	—	—	—	—	—	—	—	—	—	—	—	—	(29)
Nebraska	—	—	—	—	—	—	—	—	—	—	—	—	—	—	—	(49)
Nevada	—	—	—	—	—	—	—	yes[3]	—	—	yes[2]	—	—	—	—	(27)
New Hampshire	yes	yes	yes[3]	yes[3]	yes	yes[14]	yes[3]	—	—	—	—	—	—	yes	—	(25 28 40 57 60)
New Jersey	yes	yes	yes[2]	yes[2]	yes[51]	yes[44]	—	yes[3]	—	yes[51]	yes[9]	—	yes[2]	—	yes[51]	(34 49)
New Mexico	yes	yes	yes	—	—	—	—	—	—	—	—	—	—	—	—	(27)
New York	yes	yes	yes[2]	—	—	yes[17]	—	—	—	—	yes[2]	—	—	—	—	—
North Carolina	yes	—	—	—	yes	—	—	yes[6]	yes	—	yes[2]	—	—	—	—	(34)
North Dakota	yes	yes	yes[2]	yes[2]	—	yes	yes[2]	yes[6]	—	—	—	—	—	—	—	(28)
Ohio	yes	yes	yes	yes[4]	yes	yes	yes	yes[5]	—	yes	yes[2]	—	—	—	yes	(12 24 41 55)
Oklahoma	yes	yes	yes[2]	yes	yes	yes[21]	yes	yes[6]	yes	yes	—	—	—	—	yes	(27 41 55)
Oregon	—	—	—	—	—	—	—	—	—	—	—	—	—	—	—	(49)
Pennsylvania	yes	yes	yes[2]	—	yes[45]	yes[15]	—	yes	—	yes	yes[4]	yes	—	yes	yes	(31)
Rhode Island	yes	yes	yes[6]	yes	yes	yes[7]	yes[2]	yes[48]	—	yes	yes[3]	—	yes	yes	yes	(13 38)
South Carolina	yes	yes[39]	yes[2]	yes	—	—	—	—	—	—	yes[2]	—	yes	—	—	(50)
South Dakota	yes	yes	yes[2]	yes[2]	—	yes	yes[2]	yes[6]	—	yes[61]	—	—	—	—	yes[61]	—
Tennessee	yes	yes	yes[2]	yes[43]	yes	yes	yes	—	yes	yes	—	yes	—	—	—	(28 32 37 59)
Texas	yes	yes	yes[2]	—	—	yes[54]	—	yes[4]	—	—	yes[4]	yes	—	—	—	(28)
Utah	yes	yes	yes[2]	yes	yes	yes	yes	yes	—	—	yes[4]	—	—	—	—	—
Vermont	yes	yes	yes[7]	—	—	yes[17]	yes	yes[6]	—	—	yes[8]	—	—	—	—	(29)
Virginia	yes	yes	yes[2]	—	yes[51]	yes	—	—	yes[51]	yes[51]	yes[2]	—	—	—	yes[51]	—
Washington	—	—	—	—	—	—	—	—	—	—	—	—	—	—	—	(29)
West Virginia	yes	yes	yes[2]	yes	—	yes	—	yes	—	—	yes[3]	—	yes	—	—	(62)
Wisconsin	—	—	—	—	—	—	—	—	—	—	—	—	—	—	—	(29 64)
Wyoming	yes	yes	yes[2]	yes	yes	yes	yes[2]	yes[3]	yes	—	yes[3]	yes	—	—	—	(11 25 28)

1. If unknown to husband. 2. 1 year. 3. 2 years. 4. 3 years. 5. 4 years. 6. 5 years. 7. 7 years. 8. 6 months. 9. 18 months. 10. Absence of 1 year. 11. Absence of 1 year voluntarily, or under legal separation judgment. 12. Absence of 3 years. 13. Absence of one spouse; presumption of death. 14. With imprisonment of 1 year. 15. With imprisonment of 2 years. 16. With imprisonment of 2 years, sentence being for 7 years or more. 17. With imprisonment of 3 years. 18. With imprisonment of three years, twelve months of which have been served. 19. With imprisonment of 5 years. 20. With imprisonment for life. 21. Imprisonment of other party in state or federal penal institution under sentence thereto for commission of felony at time the petition is filed. 22. Unless pardoned before beginning sentence. 23. Noncohabitation for 18 months. 24. Court of Common Pleas may grant a dissolution of marriage—6 months residency required. 25. Noncohabitation for 2 years. 26. Noncohabitation for 5 years. 27. Incompatibility. 28. Irreconcilable differences. 29. Irretrievable breakdown of marriage relationship. 30. Irretrievably broken upon proof, decree of dissolution. 31. Relationship within prohibited degree. 32. Infamous crime. 33.

(Footnotes continued on next page)

Infamous crime subsequent to marriage. 34. Crime against nature. 35. Excessively vicious conduct; any cause which, by laws of state, renders marriage null and void at its inception. 36. A course of conduct detrimental to the marriage relationship of the party seeking the divorce. 37. Attempt by one party on life of other. 38. Any other gross misbehavior or wickedness. 39. Physical cruelty only. 40. Treatment such as to injure health or endanger reason. 41. Gross neglect of duty. 42. Habitual intemperance. 43. Habitual drunkenness contracted after marriage. 44 With imprisonment of 18 months. 45. If at time of marriage and incurable. 46. Infamous crime involving violation of conjugal duty and punishable by imprisonment of more than 1 year. 47. Incurable, regardless when it occurs. 48. Insanity at time of marriage. 49. No-fault divorce. 50. No-fault divorce after 1 year's separation. 51. Grounds for nullity. 52. The term divorce is no longer used. The term now used is Dissolution of Marriage. 53. Limited divorce; may be enlarged into absolute divorce after separation of 1 year. 54. Suit for divorce cannot be sustained until 12 months after final judgment of conviction. Divorce cannot be obtained if plaintiff's testimony contributed toward conviction. 55. Defendant obtained divorce from plaintiff in any other state or country. 56. Infected other party with communicable venereal disease. 57. Joining a religious cult disbelieving in marriage. 58. Public defamation. 59. Wife's refusal to remove with husband to this state and willfully absenting herself for 2 years. 60. Wife gone to reside outside state and absent 10 years. 61. Annulment. 62. Abuse of a child. 63. Modified "no-fault" law enacted April 6, 1977. 64. Voluntary noncohabitation for 1 year. 65. Maryland grants two types of divorce—vinculo and mensa. The information here applies to vinculo divorce. 66. Only after confined 3 years, plus other requirements. 67. Abandonment after 12 months, or living separately for 3 years. 68. If wife was under 16 or husband was under 18 at time of marriage, unless marriage was confirmed by each after arriving at such age. *Source: Information Please* questionnaires to the states.

Marriages and Divorces

	Marriage		Divorce[1]			Marriage		Divorce[1]	
Year	Number	Rate[2]	Number	Rate[2]	Year	Number	Rate[2]	Number	Rate[2]
1900	709,000	9.3	55,751	.7	1956	1,585,000	9.5	382,000	2.3
1905	842,000	10.0	67,976	.8	1957	1,518,000	8.9	381,000	2.2
1910	948,166	10.3	83,045	.9	1958	1,451,000	8.4	368,000	2.1
1915	1,007,595	10.0	104,298	1.0	1959	1,494,000	8.5	395,000	2.2
1920	1,274,476	12.0	170,505	1.6	1960	1,523,000	8.5	393,000	2.2
1925	1,188,334	10.3	175,449	1.5	1961	1,548,000	8.5	414,000	2.3
1930	1,126,856	9.2	195,961	1.6	1962	1,577,000	8.5	413,000	2.2
1935	1,327,000	10.4	218,000	1.7	1963	1,654,000	8.8	428,000	2.3
1940	1,595,879	12.1	264,000	2.0	1964	1,725,000	9.0	450,000	2.4
1941	1,695,999	12.7	293,000	2.2	1965	1,800,000	9.3	479,000	2.5
1942	1,772,132	13.2	321,000	2.4	1966	1,857,000	9.5	499,000	2.5
1943	1,577,050	11.7	359,000	2.6	1967	1,927,000	9.7	523,000	2.6
1944	1,452,394	10.9	400,000	2.9	1968	2,069,258	10.4	584,000	2.9
1945	1,612,992	12.2	485,000	3.5	1969	2,145,438	10.6	639,000	3.2
1946	2,291,045	16.4	610,000	4.3	1970	2,158,802	10.6	708,000	3.5
1947	1,991,878	13.9	483,000	3.4	1971	2,190,481	10.6	773,000	3.7
1948	1,811,155	12.4	408,000	2.8	1972	2,282,154	11.0	845,000	4.1
1949	1,579,798	10.6	397,000	2.7	1973	2,284,108	10.9	915,000	4.4
1950	1,667,231	11.1	385,144	2.6	1974	2,229,667	10.5	977,000	4.6
1951	1,594,694	10.4	381,000	2.5	1975	2,152,662	10.1	1,036,000	4.9
1952	1,539,318	9.9	392,000	2.5	1976	2,154,807	10.0	1,083,000	5.0
1953	1,546,000	9.8	390,000	2.5	1977	2,178,367	10.1	1,091,000	5.0
1954	1,490,000	9.2	379,000	2.4	1978	2,282,272	10.5	1,130,000	5.2
1955	1,531,000	9.3	377,000	2.3	1979[3]	2,317,000	10.5	1,170,000	5.3

1. Includes annulments. 2. Per 1,000 population. Divorce rates for 1941–46 are based on population including armed forces overseas. Marriage rates are based on population excluding armed forces overseas. 3. Provisional. NOTE: Marriage and divorce figures for most years include some estimated data. Alaska is included beginning 1959, Hawaii beginning 1960. *Source:* Department of Health and Human Services, National Center for Health Statistics.

Percent of Population Ever Married

Age group, years	1979	1975	1970	1960	1950	1940	1930	1920	1910	1900
Males: 14 to 19	2.2	2.7	2.6	3.3	2.9	1.5	1.5	1.8	1.0	0.9
20 to 24	32.6	40.1	45.3	46.9	41.0	27.8	29.0	29.1	24.7	22.2
25 to 29	69.8	77.7	80.9	79.2	76.2	64.0	63.2	60.5	57.1	54.1
30 to 34	85.1	88.9	90.6	88.1	86.8	79.3	78.8	75.8	73.9	72.3
35 to 44	91.7	92.1	93.3	91.9	90.4	86.0	85.7	83.8	83.3	83.0
45 to 54	93.1	93.7	92.5	92.6	91.5	88.9	88.6	88.0	88.8	89.7
Females: 14 to 19	1.2	9.3	9.7	13.5	14.4	10.0	10.9	10.8	9.8	9.4
20 to 24	50.6	59.7	64.2	71.6	67.7	52.8	53.9	54.4	51.5	48.4
25 to 29	80.4	86.2	89.5	89.5	86.7	77.2	78.3	76.9	75.0	72.4
30 to 34	90.5	92.5	93.8	93.1	90.7	85.3	86.8	85.1	83.8	83.4
35 to 44	94.1	95.1	94.8	93.9	91.7	89.6	90.0	88.6	88.6	88.9
45 to 54	95.6	95.4	95.1	93.0	92.2	91.3	90.9	90.4	91.4	92.2

Source: Department of Commerce, Bureau of the Census.

Median Age at First Marriage

Year	Males	Females	Year	Males	Females	Year	Males	Females	Year	Males	Females
1890	26.1	22.0	1920	24.6	21.2	1950	22.8	20.3	1975	23.5	21.1
1900	25.9	21.9	1930	24.3	21.3	1960	22.8	20.3	1978	24.2	21.8
1910	25.1	21.6	1940	24.3	21.5	1970	23.2	20.8	1979	24.4	22.1

Source: Department of Commerce, Bureau of the Census.

Marriage Prospects of Single Men and Women

Age	Percent of population single[1]		Percent who ever marry[2]		Age	Percent of population single[1]		Percent who ever marry[2]	
	Male	Female	Male	Female		Male	Female	Male	Female
15	99.4	97.6	95.8	97.4	33	10.9	6.3	63.5	49.7
16	99.0	94.3	95.9	97.4	34	10.3	6.4	60.2	46.0
17	98.1	87.9	96.0	97.3	35	9.9	6.4	57.2	42.9
18	94.6	75.5	96.0	97.0	36	9.0	6.1	54.1	40.0
19	87.3	59.6	95.9	96.4	37	8.7	6.0	51.0	37.3
20	75.8	45.8	95.6	95.5	38	8.1	5.7	48.0	34.7
21	63.3	35.1	95.0	94.2	39	8.1	6.2	45.1	32.2
22	51.4	25.8	94.1	92.2	40	7.6	6.1	42.3	29.9
23	40.5	19.4	92.8	89.4	41	7.5	6.0	39.7	27.6
24	33.5	15.6	91.1	86.1	42	6.9	5.9	37.2	25.5
25	27.8	13.1	89.1	82.5	43	7.1	6.0	34.8	23.6
26	23.9	11.5	86.6	78.4	44	7.4	6.5	32.7	21.7
27	19.6	9.9	83.6	74.2	45	7.1	6.1	30.6	20.0
28	17.3	9.3	80.3	70.3	50	7.6	7.4	21.6	12.8
29	15.9	8.7	77.3	65.7	55	7.9	7.9	13.9	7.7
30	14.2	7.9	73.8	61.2	60	8.0	7.8	8.2	4.4
31	12.9	7.2	70.4	57.3	65 and over	7.7	8.5	—	—
32	11.7	6.6	67.1	53.3					

1. Percent single within specified year of age in 1960, in 5% sample of population (latest available data). 2. Percent of white persons single at beginning of year of age who marry during that year and all later years, based on data for 1958–60. NOTE: "Single" excludes widowed and divorced. *Source:* Department of Commerce, Bureau of the Census.

Persons Living Alone, by Sex and Age

(numbers in thousands)

Sex and age	1979		1975		1970		1965		1960	
	Number	Percent	Number	Percent	Number	Percent	Number	Percent	Number	Percent
BOTH SEXES										
14 to 24 years	1,621	9.4	1,111	8.0	556	5.1	305	3.5	234	3.3
25 to 44 years	4,160	24.2	2,744	19.7	1,604	14.8	1,281	14.9	1,212	17.2
45 to 64 years	4,354	25.3	4,076	29.2	3,622	33.4	3,073	35.7	2,720	38.5
65 years and over	7,067	41.1	6,008	43.1	5,071	46.7	3,943	45.8	2,898	41.0
Total, 14 years and over	**17,202**	**100.0**	**13,939**	**100.0**	**10,851**	**100.0**	**8,602**	**100.0**	**7,063**	**100.0**
MALE										
14 to 24 years	870	5.1	610	4.4	274	2.5	141	1.6	124	1.8
25 to 44 years	2,563	14.9	1,689	12.1	933	8.6	737	8.6	686	9.7
45 to 64 years	1,558	9.1	1,329	9.5	1,152	10.6	1,013	11.8	965	13.7
65 years and over	1,472	8.6	1,290	9.3	1,174	10.8	1,033	12.0	853	12.1
Total, 14 years and over	**6,464**	**37.6**	**4,918**	**35.3**	**3,532**	**32.5**	**2,923**	**34.0**	**2,628**	**37.2**
FEMALE										
14 to 24 years	751	4.4	501	3.6	282	2.6	164	1.9	110	1.6
25 to 44 years	1,597	9.3	1,055	7.6	671	6.2	544	6.3	526	7.4
45 to 64 years	2,796	16.3	2,747	19.7	2,470	22.8	2,060	23.9	1,755	24.8
65 years and over	5,595	32.5	4,718	33.8	3,897	35.9	2,910	33.8	2,045	29.0
Total, 14 years and over	**10,738**	**62.4**	**9,021**	**64.7**	**7,319**	**67.5**	**5,679**	**66.0**	**4,436**	**62.8**

Source: Department of Commerce, Bureau of the Census.

Households, Families, and Married Couples

	Households		Families		Married couples
Date	Number	Average population per household	Number	Average population per family	Number
June 1890	12,690,000	4.93	—	—	—
April 1930	29,905,000	4.11	—	—	25,174,000
April 1940	34,949,000	3.67	32,166,000	3.76	28,517,000
April 1950	43,554,000	3.37	39,303,000	3.54	36,091,000
April 1955	47,874,000	3.33	41,951,000	3.59	37,556,000
March 1960[1]	52,799,000	3.33	45,111,000	3.67	40,200,000
March 1965	57,436,000	3.29	47,956,000	3.70	42,478,000
March 1970	63,401,000	3.14	51,586,000	3.58	45,373,000
March 1975	71,120,000	2.94	55,712,000	3.42	47,547,000
March 1978	76,030,000	2.81	57,215,000	3.33	47,920,000
March 1979	77,330,000	2.78	57,804,000	3.31	48,258,000

1. First year in which figures for Alaska and Hawaii are included. *Source:* Department of Commerce, Bureau of the Census.

Families Maintained by Women
(numbers in thousands)

	1979		1975		1970		1965		1960	
	Number	Percent	Number	Percent	Number	Percent	Number	Percent	Number	Percent
Age of women:										
Under 35 years	2,929	34.6	2,356	32.5	1,364	24.4	958	19.1	796	17.7
35 to 44 years	1,851	21.9	1,510	20.9	1,074	19.2	1,146	22.9	940	20.9
45 to 64 years	2,481	29.3	2,266	31.3	2,021	36.1	1,813	36.2	1,731	38.5
65 years and over	1,196	14.1	1,108	15.3	1,131	20.2	1,091	21.8	1,027	22.9
Median age	42.0	—	43.4	—	48.5	—	49.0	—	50.1	—
Presence of children:										
No own children under 18 years	3,170	37.5	2,838	39.2	2,665	47.7	2,527	50.5	2,397	53.3
With own children under 18 years	5,288	62.5	4,404	60.8	2,926	52.3	2,480	49.5	2,097	46.7
Total own children under 18 years	9,822	—	9,227	—	6,694	—	6,007	—	4,674	—
Average per family	1.16	—	1.27	—	1.20	—	1.20	—	1.04	—
Average per family with children	1.86	—	2.10	—	2.29	—	2.42	—	2.24	—
Race:										
White	5,918	70.0	5,212	72.0	4,165	74.5	3,882	77.5	3,547	78.9
Black[1]	2,390	28.3	1,940	26.8	1,382	24.7	1,125	22.5	947	21.1
Other	150	1.8	90	1.2	44	0.8	n.a.	n.a.	n.a.	n.a.
Marital status:										
Married, husband absent	1,770	20.9	1,647	22.7	1,326	23.7	1,392	27.8	1,099	24.5
Widowed	2,465	29.1	2,559	35.3	2,396	42.9	2,307	46.1	2,325	51.7
Divorced	2,807	33.2	2,110	29.1	1,259	22.5	903	18.0	694	15.4
Single	1,416	16.7	926	12.8	610	10.9	404	8.1	376	8.4
Total families maintained by women	**8,458**	**100.0**	**7,242**	**100.0**	**5,591**	**100.0**	**5,006**	**100.0**	**4,494**	**100.0**

1. Includes other races in 1960 and 1965. NOTE: n.a. = not available. *Source:* Department of Commerce, Bureau of the Census.

Many X-Ray Machines Found Hazardous

A Congressional investigative agency reported that federal and state regulations are not adequate to protect the public from radiation hazards. In a voluntary program, the FDA's Bureau of Radiological Health examined readings from dental machines in 38 states and breast machines in 48 states. Of the 35,224 dental X-ray units looked at, exposures from 36% appeared excessively high, and out of 3,253 breast X-ray units, 46% had excessively high or unusually low X-ray exposures. Low exposures can be dangerous because they could require the operator to use more radiation than necessary to get an acceptable picture.

It was reported that in the year ending October 1978 more than 11,700 new medical X-ray units were installed in this country. After testing 3,152 of them, investigators found that 61% were not in compliance with federal standards.

Families in the U.S.

State	1976 Total families (in thousands)	1976 Percent with own children under 18	1976 Percent increase, 1970–76	1970 Total families (in thousands)	1970 Percent with own children under 18	1970 Percent increase, 1960–70	1960 Total families (in thousands)	1960 Percent with own children under 18	1960 Percent increase 1950–60
Alabama	970	54	11.5	870	55	10.0	791	59	8.2
Alaska	82	66	24.2	66	67	41.1	47	69	96.9
Arizona	592	54	34.9	439	56	40.6	312	62	71.1
Arkansas	585	51	16.5	502	51	11.0	452	55	−4.1
California	5,574	54	11.7	4,988	55	25.0	3,992	58	42.4
Colorado	660	57	21.1	545	58	24.3	439	60	30.2
Connecticut	820	53	6.9	767	55	17.3	654	57	26.0
Delaware	153	56	12.5	136	58	21.6	112	59	38.4
D. C.	158	51	−3.1	163	51	6.4	174	46	−11.5
Florida	2,361	47	30.7	1,806	47	39.3	1,297	52	79.9
Georgia	1,292	56	12.9	1,144	57	20.5	949	59	14.2
Hawaii	201	57	18.2	170	62	30.2	131	70	35.7
Idaho	222	55	24.0	179	57	7.9	166	63	12.1
Illinois	2,849	53	2.3	2,784	55	7.4	2,592	55	13.2
Indiana	1,422	56	7.9	1,318	56	10.0	1,198	57	13.4
Iowa	751	53	5.3	713	54	.2	712	56	3.7
Kansas	619	50	6.9	579	53	1.8	569	56	11.0
Kentucky	909	54	10.7	821	54	9.1	753	56	5.3
Louisiana	944	57	8.8	868	58	12.5	771	59	18.7
Maine	279	54	13.4	246	54	2.2	240	57	7.4
Maryland	1,066	55	9.7	972	57	27.3	763	59	29.5
Massachusetts	1,483	52	6.8	1,388	54	7.4	1,292	55	9.9
Michigan	2,399	56	9.9	2,182	58	12.2	1,944	59	17.3
Minnesota	994	56	8.4	917	57	9.5	837	59	11.4
Mississippi	597	56	12.6	530	55	5.9	501	57	−1.6
Missouri	1,276	51	6.3	1,200	52	5.9	1,133	52	7.8
Montana	193	53	13.5	170	57	2.6	166	61	13.7
Nebraska	401	54	7.8	372	54	1.8	366	56	5.3
Nevada	159	54	28.2	124	56	70.9	72	58	75.3
New Hampshire	218	56	19.1	183	55	19.3	153	56	11.8
New Jersey	1,927	53	5.1	1,833	55	16.0	1,581	56	24.8
New Mexico	297	59	22.7	242	62	9.0	222	67	39.3
New York	4,676	53	2.0	4,585	53	5.7	4,336	54	11.7
North Carolina	1,504	54	17.0	1,286	56	17.8	1,092	60	15.6
North Dakota	159	57	8.2	147	57	1.8	150	62	1.4
Ohio	2,833	54	5.6	2,683	56	8.8	2,465	57	16.9
Oklahoma	749	50	10.6	677	52	10.4	613	55	5.3
Oregon	615	52	13.5	542	53	17.8	460	57	12.0
Pennsylvania	3,076	49	2.6	2,999	53	3.3	2,903	55	9.1
Rhode Island	242	51	3.0	235	53	7.0	220	55	7.1
South Carolina	731	53	17.1	624	58	15.3	541	61	12.2
South Dakota	177	54	10.6	160	56	4.0	167	60	3.7
Tennessee	1,162	53	13.9	1,020	54	14.2	894	56	10.5
Texas	3,258	54	15.9	2,810	56	17.4	2,393	59	21.3
Utah	303	62	21.7	249	63	19.0	209	67	23.3
Vermont	122	59	15.1	106	56	12.7	94	57	2.9
Virginia	1,318	53	13.7	1,159	56	21.4	955	59	21.8
Washington	924	54	7.2	862	56	18.9	725	59	16.4
West Virginia	495	49	9.5	452	52	2.2	462	57	−4.4
Wisconsin	1,182	54	10.3	1,072	56	8.7	987	57	12.3
Wyoming	100	54	19.0	84	57	0.8	84	63	16.5
United States	**56,080**	**53**	**10.0**	**50,969**	**55**	**12.9**	**45,128**	**57**	**17.0**

NOTE: Data are latest available. *Source:* Department of Commerce, Bureau of the Census.

Family Planning

A recent survey conducted by the Alan Guttmacher Institute found that about 4 in 10 married couples have sterilizations within five years after the birth of their last wanted child. Sterilization prevents about 270,000 unwanted births per year.

Births

Registered Live Births and Birth Rates

State	1979[1] Number	1978[2] Number	1978[2] Rate	State	1979[1] Number	1978[2] Number	1978[2] Rate
Alabama	60,628	60,227	16.2	Montana	13,803	13,545	17.4
Alaska	8,912	8,861	21.6	Nebraska	26,093	25,112	16.0
Arizona	45,707	43,112	18.2	Nevada	11,830	10,990	16.5
Arkansas	35,008	34,793	16.1	New Hampshire	12,829	12,429	14.3
California	363,463	356,310	16.0	New Jersey	91,896	93,535	12.8
Colorado	47,813	44,107	16.3	New Mexico	25,570	23,932	19.7
Connecticut	36,959	37,294	12.0	New York	231,787	233,954	13.2
Delaware	9,123	8,685	14.9	North Carolina	84,388	82,442	14.8
D.C.	17,339	9,383	14.0	North Dakota	12,769	11,299	17.3
Florida	120,839	113,343	13.1	Ohio	164,111	160,863	15.0
Georgia	89,446	84,140	16.6	Oklahoma	47,214	45,905	16.1
Hawaii	17,429	16,753	18.6	Oregon	42,984	38,974	15.9
Idaho	19,686	19,391	22.0	Pennsylvania	157,783	152,248	12.9
Illinois	181,218	174,509	15.5	Rhode Island	12,235	11,522	12.4
Indiana	87,452	83,598	15.5	South Caroina	49,956	49,671	17.1
Iowa	47,083	44,584	15.3	South Dakota	12,623	12,239	17.7
Kansas	37,100	36,735	15.7	Tennessee	72,261	66,607	15.4
Kentucky	60,182	57,334	16.4	Texas	265,066	236,952	18.2
Louisiana	79,413	74,928	18.8	Utah	42,304	38,808	29.5
Maine	15,755	15,847	14.5	Vermont	7,396	7,120	14.6
Maryland	50,043	55,329	13.3	Virginia	73,812	73,443	14.2
Massachusetts	73,104	68,657	11.9	Washington	55,077	58,726	15.5
Michigan	142,127	139,149	15.2	West Virginia	30,263	29,280	15.7
Minnesota	64,997	61,993	15.4	Wisconsin	72,818	68,669	14.7
Mississippi	45,913	44,399	18.4	Wyoming	8,946	8,661	20.4
Missouri	78,505	72,892	15.0	**Total**	**3,461,058**	**3,333,279**	**15.3**

1. Provisional. 2. Final. NOTE: Based on 100% of births in selected states and 50% sample in others. Rates are per 1,000 population. *Source:* Department of Health and Human Services, National Center for Health Statistics.

Live Births and Birth Rates

Year	Births[1]	Rate[2]	Year	Births[1]	Rated[2]	Year	Births[1]	Rates[2]
1910	2,777,000	30.1	1948	3,637,000	24.9	1964[3]	4,027,490	21.0
1915	2,965,000	29.5	1949	3,649,000	24.5	1965[3]	3,760,358	19.4
1920	2,950,000	27.7	1950	3,632,000	24.1	1966[3]	3,606,274	18.4
1925	2,909,000	25.1	1951[3]	3,823,000	24.9	1967	3,520,959	17.8
1930	2,618,000	21.3	1952[3]	3,913,000	25.1	1968	3,501,564	17.5
1935	2,377,000	18.7	1953[3]	3,965,000	25.1	1969	3,600,206	17.8
1938	2,496,000	19.2	1954[3]	4,078,000	25.3	1970	3,731,386	18.4
1939	2,466,000	18.8	1955	4,104,000	25.0	1971	3,555,970	17.2
1940	2,559,000	19.4	1956[3]	4,218,000	25.2	1972	3,258,411	15.6
1941	2,703,000	20.3	1957[3]	4,308,000	25.3	1973	3,136,965	14.9
1942	2,989,000	22.2	1958[3]	4,255,000	24.5	1974	3,159,958	14.9
1943	3,104,000	22.7	1959[3]	4,295,000	24.3	1975	3,144,198	14.8
1944	2,939,000	21.2	1960[3]	4,257,850	23.7	1976	3,167,788	14.8
1945	2,858,000	20.4	1961[3]	4,268,326	23.3	1977	3,326,632	15.4
1946	3,411,000	24.1	1962[3]	4,167,362	22.4	1978	3,333,279	15.3
1947	3,817,000	26.6	1963[3]	4,098,020	21.7	1979[4]	3,473,000	15.8

1. Figures through 1959 include adjustment for underregistration; beginning 1960, figures represent number registered. For comparison, the 1959 registered count was 4,245,000. 2. Rates are per 1,000 population estimated as of July 1 for each year except 1940, 1950, 1960, and 1970, which are as of April 1, the census date; for 1941–46 based on population including armed forces overseas. 3. Based on 50% sample of births. 4. Provisional. NOTE: Alaska is included beginning 1959 Hawaii beginning 1960. Since 1972, based on 100% of births in selected states and on 50% sample in all other states. *Sources:* Department of Commerce, Bureau of the Census; and Department of Health and Human Services, National Center for Health Statistics.

Births to Unmarried Women

(in thousands, except as indicated)

Age and race	1978	1975	1970	1965	1960	1955	1950	1945	1940
By age of mother:									
Under 15 years	9.4	11.0	9.5	6.1	4.6	3.9	3.2	2.5	2.1
15–19 years	239.7	222.5	190.4	123.1	87.1	68.9	56.0	49.2	40.5
20–24 years	186.5	134.0	126.7	90.7	68.0	55.7	43.1	39.3	27.2
25–29 years	70.0	50.2	40.6	36.8	32.1	28.0	20.9	14.1	10.5
30–34 years	26.5	19.8	19.1	19.6	18.9	16.1	10.8	7.1	5.2
35–39 years	9.4	8.1	9.4	11.4	10.6	8.3	6.0	4.0	3.0
40 years and over	2.3	2.3	3.0	3.7	3.0	2.4	1.7	1.2	1.0
By race:									
White	233.6	186.4	175.1	123.7	82.5	64.2	53.5	56.4	40.3
Black and other	310.2	261.6	223.6	167.5	141.8	119.2	88.1	60.9	49.2
Total of above births	**543.9**	**447.9**	**398.7**	**291.2**	**224.3**	**183.4**	**141.6**	**117.3**	**89.5**
Percent of all births[1]	16.3	14.2	10.7	7.7	5.3	4.5	3.9	4.1	3.5
Rate[2]	26.2	24.8	26.4	23.4	21.8	19.3	14.1	10.1	7.1

1. Through 1955, based on data adjusted for underregistration; thereafter, registered births. 2. Rate per 1,000 unmarried (never married, widowed, and divorced) women, 15–44 years old. *Sources:* Department of Commerce, Bureau of the Census; and Department of Health and Human Services, National Center for Health Statistics.

Live Births by Age of Mother

Year[1] and race	Total	Age of mother: Under 15 yr	15–19 yr	20–24 yr	25–29 yr	30–34 yr	35–39 yr	40–44 yr	45 yr and over
1940	2,558,647	3,865	332,667	799,537	693,268	431,468	222,015	68,269	7,558
1945	2,858,449	4,028	298,868	832,746	785,299	554,906	296,852	78,853	6,897
1950	3,631,512	5,413	432,911	1,155,167	1,041,360	610,816	302,780	77,743	5,322
1955	4,014,112	6,181	493,770	1,290,939	1,133,155	732,540	352,320	89,777	5,430
1960	4,257,850	6,780	586,966	1,426,912	1,092,816	687,722	359,908	91,564	5,182
1965	3,760,358	7,768	590,894	1,337,350	925,732	529,376	282,908	81,716	4,614
1970	3,731,386	11,752	644,708	1,418,874	994,904	427,806	180,244	49,952	3,146
1972	3,258,411	12,082	616,280	1,174,183	900,392	375,001	141,328	36,861	2,284
1974	3,159,958	12,529	595,449	1,108,051	923,318	372,907	118,115	27,878	1,711
1975	3,144,198	12,642	582,238	1,093,676	936,786	375,500	115,409	26,319	1,628
1976	3,167,788	11,928	558,744	1,091,602	972,130	391,896	115,662	24,383	1,443
1977	3,326,632	11,455	559,154	1,146,491	1,016,231	446,939	120,900	24,117	1,345
1978	3,333,279	10,772	543,407	1,139,524	1,015,183	474,318	126,196	22,627	1,252
White	2,681,116	4,512	380,060	914,772	860,209	401,221	101,880	17,521	941
Black	551,540	6,068	151,001	196,731	121,613	53,491	18,340	4,048	248
Other	100,623	192	12,346	28,021	33,361	19,606	5,976	1,058	63

1. Data for 1940–55 are adjusted for underregistration. Beginning 1960, registered births only are shown. Data for 1960–70 based on a 50% sample of births. Since 1972, based on 100% of births in selected states and on 50% sample in all other states. Beginning 1960, including Alaska and Hawaii. NOTE: Data refer only to births occurring within the U.S. Figures are shown to the last digit as computed for convenience in summation. They are not assumed to be accurate to the last digit. Figures for age of mother not stated are distributed. *Sources:* Department of Commerce, Bureau of the Census; and Department of Health and Human Services, National Center for Health Statistics.

Live Births and Birth Rates by Race

Race	Births 1978[1]	Rates 1978	Rates 1950	Rates 1940	Race	Births 1978[1]	Rates 1978	Rates 1950	Rates 1940
White	2,681,116	14.2	23.0	18.6	Chinese	11,224	n.a.	43.9	14.5
Black	551,540	21.6	33.1	26.5	Filipino	13,753	n.a.	n.a.	n.a.
Indian	33,160	n.a.	45.8	42.0	Other	30,559	n.a.	19.1	22.0
Japanese	8,094	n.a.	24.5	15.0	**All races**	**3,333,279**	**15.3**	**24.1**	**19.4**

1. Based on all births in selected states and on a 50% sample of births in all other states. NOTES: Rates per 1,000 population in each specified group. Rates for 1940 and 1950 based on births adjusted for under-registration; n.a. = not available. *Source:* Department of Health and Human Services, National Center for Health Statistics.

Live Births by Sex and Sex Ratio[1]

Year	Total[2]			White			Black		
	Male	Female	Males per 1,000 females	Male	Female	Males per 1,000 females	Male	Female	Males per 1,000 females
1970[3]	1,915,378	1,816,008	1,055	1,590,140	1,501,124	1,059	290,508	281,854	1,031
1971[3]	1,822,910	1,733,060	1,052	1,499,958	1,419,788	1,056	286,430	278,530	1,028
1972[4]	1,669,927	1,588,484	1,051	1,364,578	1,290,980	1,057	268,842	262,487	1,024
1973[4]	1,608,326	1,528,639	1,052	1,311,032	1,239,998	1,057	259,877	252,720	1,028
1974[4]	1,622,114	1,537,844	1,055	1,325,019	1,250,773	1,059	257,277	249,885	1,030
1975[4]	1,613,135	1,531,063	1,054	1,312,308	1,239,688	1,059	259,610	251,971	1,030
1976[4]	1,624,436	1,543,352	1,053	1,319,717	1,247,897	1,058	260,661	253,818	1,027
1977[4]	1,705,916	1,620,716	1,053	1,383,440	1,307,630	1,058	275,556	268,665	1,026
1978[4]	1,709,394	1,623,885	1,053	1,378,222	1,302,894	1,058	279,598	271,942	1,028

1. Excludes births to nonresidents of U.S. 2. Includes races other than white and black. 3. Based on 50% sample of births. 4. Based on 100% of births for selected states and 50% sample in all others. *Source:* Department of Health and Human Services, National Center for Health Statistics.

Mortality

Accidental Death Rates, 1977

(per 100,000 population by place of residence)

State	Total accidents	Motor vehicle		Falls	Fires and flames	Drownings[1]	Firearms	All others
		Total	Pedestrian					
Alabama	66.7	33.7	3.7	5.7	5.6	4.1	2.1	15.5
Alaska	96.4	29.8	5.8	5.8	6.8	9.9	(2)	44.1
Arizona	67.1	38.8	8.6	7.4	2.5	3.8	1.0	13.6
Arkansas	55.3	25.5	3.0	6.2	4.0	3.7	2.0	13.9
California	47.6	24.1	4.0	5.0	1.8	2.7	0.7	13.3
Colorado	52.8	26.9	3.4	7.8	1.4	1.7	1.2	13.8
Connecticut	31.1	15.0	2.6	5.5	1.7	1.8	(2)	7.1
Delaware	41.2	19.8	3.4	4.1	(2)	(2)	(2)	17.3
D.C.	45.5	12.7	5.0	11.7	5.3	(2)	(2)	15.8
Florida	48.4	23.7	5.3	6.2	2.4	4.3	0.7	11.1
Georgia	60.3	28.9	3.8	6.0	4.3	4.0	2.3	14.8
Hawaii	29.5	16.0	3.8	2.9	(2)	3.6	(2)	7.0
Idaho	74.2	36.7	4.3	5.8	2.8	4.9	(2)	24.0
Illinois	42.7	19.8	3.2	5.6	3.1	2.5	0.6	11.1
Indiana	48.6	24.4	2.2	6.4	3.1	2.4	0.7	11.6
Iowa	46.1	22.8	1.8	8.5	2.3	2.0	0.9	9.6
Kansas	51.5	25.3	1.8	7.9	2.4	2.5	(2)	13.4
Kentucky	61.9	27.2	3.0	7.6	6.2	3.0	1.7	16.2
Louisiana	61.5	27.2	3.9	5.3	4.1	4.9	2.7	17.3
Maine	40.8	17.6	2.7	7.2	3.4	2.7	(2)	9.9
Maryland	36.9	16.5	3.3	5.7	2.7	2.8	(2)	9.2
Massachusetts	36.7	14.2	3.4	9.6	2.2	2.0	(2)	8.7
Michigan	43.2	21.9	3.8	6.1	3.2	2.5	0.7	8.8
Minnesota	46.4	22.4	3.4	7.5	2.5	1.9	0.6	11.5
Mississippi	65.7	31.9	3.8	5.4	5.7	4.6	3.1	15.0
Missouri	51.4	24.6	3.2	7.6	3.3	2.1	0.7	13.1
Montana	74.5	38.9	2.7	8.6	3.5	3.7	3.0	16.8
Nebraska	51.0	23.9	2.2	8.4	2.4	2.0	(2)	14.3
Nevada	65.5	34.4	4.1	6.1	(2)	5.0	(2)	20.1
New Hampshire	38.2	17.8	2.8	5.5	2.6	2.4	(2)	9.9
New Jersey	33.7	14.8	3.4	6.8	2.6	1.5	0.3	7.7
New Mexico	76.3	47.1	7.3	5.7	2.4	2.9	(2)	18.2
New York	32.0	13.8	3.7	6.4	1.9	1.5	0.4	8.0
North Carolina	56.2	26.1	4.6	5.3	4.6	4.0	1.5	14.7
North Dakota	59.1	29.4	(2)	8.3	3.1	(2)	(2)	18.3
Ohio	40.2	17.4	2.5	7.0	3.0	1.7	0.6	10.5
Oklahoma	60.0	31.9	3.1	5.1	3.4	2.8	1.5	15.3
Oregon	57.7	28.5	3.9	6.8	2.9	4.2	0.8	14.5
Pennsylvania	42.3	18.2	3.2	7.6	2.9	1.8	0.5	11.3
Rhode Island	38.3	17.0	3.8	7.3	2.3	2.5	(2)	9.2
South Carolina	62.8	33.1	5.1	4.5	5.1	4.6	2.0	13.5

State	Total accidents	Motor vehicle Total	Motor vehicle Pedestrian	Falls	Fires and flames	Drownings[1]	Firearms	All others
South Dakota	64.5	31.1	3.3	7.6	3.2	(2)	3.5	19.1
Tennessee	57.4	28.7	3.2	6.0	4.7	3.6	1.5	12.9
Texas	53.9	28.3	4.0	5.3	2.7	3.8	1.4	13.4
Utah	50.8	26.2	4.6	8.0	1.7	2.0	(2)	12.9
Vermont	45.2	21.0	(2)	8.9	(2)	(2)	(2)	15.3
Virginia	51.1	23.4	3.6	7.2	3.9	3.1	1.1	12.4
Washington	54.9	26.8	3.1	6.6	2.5	3.5	0.6	14.9
West Virginia	57.2	27.1	2.5	6.6	4.1	3.7	(2)	15.7
Wisconsin	40.8	20.4	2.6	6.3	2.0	2.0	0.5	9.6
Wyoming	85.2	49.5	(2)	6.7	(2)	(2)	(2)	29.0
United States	**47.7**	**22.9**	**3.6**	**6.4**	**2.9**	**2.8**	**0.9**	**11.8**

1. Exclusive of deaths in water transportation. 2. Fewer than 20 deaths; rate not computed. NOTE: Data are latest available. *Source:* Statistical Bureau, Metropolitan Life Insurance Company.

Death Rates for Selected Causes

Cause of death	1979	1978	1950	1945–49	1940–44	1920–24	1900–04
	Death rates per 100,000						
Typhoid fever	0.0	0.0	0.1	0.2	0.6	7.3	26.7
Communicable diseases of childhood	0.0	0.0	1.3	2.3	4.6	33.8	65.2
Measles	0.0	0.0	0.3	0.6	1.1	7.3	10.0
Scarlet fever	0.0	0.0	0.2	0.1	0.4	4.0	11.8
Whooping cough	0.0	0.0	0.7	1.0	2.2	8.9	10.7
Diphtheria	0.0	0.0	0.3	0.7	1.0	13.7	32.7
Enteritis and other diarrheal diseases	n.a.	0.8	5.1	6.5	9.8	42.8	115.3
Pneumonia and influenza	20.0	26.7	31.3	41.3	63.7	140.3	184.3
Influenza	0.3	1.8	4.4	5.0	13.0	34.8	22.8
Pneumonia	19.7	24.9	26.9	37.2	50.7	105.5	161.5
Tuberculosis	0.9	1.3	22.5	33.3	43.4	96.7	184.7
Cancer	183.5	181.9	139.8	134.0	123.1	86.9	67.7
Diabetes mellitus	15.0	15.0	16.2	24.1	26.2	17.1	12.2
Major cardiovascular diseases	431.6	440.3	510.8	493.1	490.4	369.9	359.5
Diseases of the heart	330.4	333.0	356.8	325.1	303.2	169.8	153.0
Cerebrovascular diseases	76.5	79.1	104.0	93.8	91.7	93.5	106.3
Nephritis and nephrosis	7.3	3.7	16.4	48.4	72.1	81.5	84.3
Syphilis	0.1	0.1	5.0	8.4	12.7	17.6	12.9
Appendicitis	0.3	n.a.	2.0	3.5	7.2	14.0	9.4
Accidents, all forms	47.0	47.8	60.6	67.6	73.0	70.8	79.2
Motor vehicle accidents	23.6	23.6	23.1	22.3	22.7	12.9	n.a.
Infant mortality[1]	n.a.	10.3	29.2	33.3	42.4	76.7	n.a.
Neonatal mortality[1]	n.a.	n.a.	20.5	22.9	26.2	39.7	n.a.
Fetal mortality[1]	n.a.	n.a.	22.9	24.3	28.5	39.2[2]	n.a.
Maternal mortality[1]	n.a.	n.a.	0.8	1.4	2.8	6.9	n.a.
All causes	**866.2**	**882.5**	**963.8**	**1,003.3**	**1,062.0**	**1,196.6**	**1,621.6**

1. Rates per 1,000 live births. 2. 1922–24. NOTE: Includes only deaths occurring within the registration areas. Beginning with 1940, area includes the entire United States; beginning with 1960, Alaska and Hawaii were included. Rates per 100,000 population residing in areas, enumerated as of April 1 for 1940 and 1950 and estimated as of July 1 for all other years. Due to changes in statistical methods, death rates are not strictly comparable. n.a. = not available. *Source:* Department of Health and Human Services, National Center for Health Statistics.

Free Breast Cancer Manual

The Women's Breast Cancer Advisory Center has published "If You've Thought About Breast Cancer," a "how-to" manual for women who have symptoms of possible breast cancer. The manual contains information from detection and diagnosis to surgical procedures, prevention and where to call for help.

To obtain a free copy, write to: The Office of Cancer Communications, National Cancer Institute, Bethesda, MD 20205, or call toll-free (800) 638-6694.

Accident Rates, 1978

(twelve accidental deaths every hour)

Class of accident		One every		Class of accident		One every	
All accidents	Deaths	5	minutes	Workers off-job	Deaths	13	minutes
	Injuries	3	seconds		Injuries	10	seconds
Motor-vehicle	Deaths	10	minutes	Home	Deaths	23	minutes
	Injuries	16	seconds		Injuries	9	seconds
Work	Deaths	40	minutes	Public non-motor-vehicle	Deaths	24	minutes
	Injuries	14	seconds		Injuries	12	seconds

Source: National Safety Council.

Transportation-Accident Death Rates

Kind of transportation	1978			1976–78 average death rate[1]
	Passenger miles	Passenger deaths	Death rate[1]	
Passenger automobiles and taxis[2]	2,190,000,000,000	28,450	1.30	1.33
Passenger automobiles on turnpikes[2]	53,500,000,000	370	0.69	0.65
Buses	78,100,000,000	135	0.17	0.16
Intercity buses	16,400,000,000	2	0.01	0.02
Railroad passenger trains	10,200,000,000	13	0.13	0.07
Scheduled air transport planes (domestic)	188,000,000,000	13	0.01	0.02

1. Per 100 million passenger miles. 2. Drivers of passenger automobiles are considered passengers. *Source:* National Safety Council.

Motor-Vehicle Traffic Deaths

State	1978 Number	1978 Rate[1]	1977 Number	1977 Rate[1]
Alabama	1,169	4.2	1,122	4.0
Alaska	127	4.7	136	3.6
Arizona	1,026	5.3	933	5.1
Arkansas	571	3.6	551	3.6
California	5,296	3.4	4,942	3.4
Colorado	713	3.5	701	3.9
Connecticut	456	2.3	454	2.3
Delaware	126	3.3	125	3.1
Dist. of Col.	51	1.6	58	1.8
Florida	2,305	3.2	2,066	3.1
Georgia	1,490	3.3	1,462	3.4
Hawaii	195	4.0	154	3.4
Idaho	330	4.8	330	5.1
Illinois	2,166	3.0	2,170	3.3
Indiana	1,310	2.9	1,255	3.0
Iowa	650	3.0	640	3.1
Kansas	572	3.5	562	3.4
Kentucky	893	3.2	958	3.5
Louisiana	1,092	4.6	1,042	4.5
Maine	235	3.1	218	2.9
Maryland	728	2.5	674	2.5
Massachusetts	655	2.7	743	2.2
Michigan	2,076	3.2	1,950	3.1
Minnesota	980	3.3	856	3.1
Mississippi	764	4.8	690	4.3
Missouri	1,213	3.5	1.211	3.6
Montana	271	4.0	320	5.0
Nebraska	350	2.9	350	2.8
Nevada	312	5.6	255	5.1
New Hampshire	171	2.8	150	2.5
New Jersey	1,157	2.2	1,108	2.1
New Mexico	661	5.8	674	5.9
New York	2,525	3.6	2,471	3.6
North Carolina	1,510	3.6	1,442	3.5
North Dakota	185	3.7	180	3.7
Ohio	2,048	2.9	1,873	2.7
Oklahoma	920	3.5	860	3.2
Oregon	721	3.9	673	3.7
Pennsylvania	2,137	3.0	2,071	2.9
Rhode Island	108	1.7	136	2.2
South Carolina	898	3.8	949	4.1
South Dakota	194	3.4	211	3.7
Tennessee	1,252	3.3	1,218	3.4
Texas	3,970	4.0	3,696	3.9
Utah	374	3.9	356	3.9
Vermont	127	3.4	118	3.1
Virginia	1,080	2.7	1,145	3.0
Washington	1,004	3.5	927	3.4
West Virginia	467	4.0	528	4.3
Wisconsin	998	3.1	945	3.0
Wyoming	241	5.4	250	5.4
Total	**51,500**	**3.4**	**49,510**	**3.4**

1. Number of deaths per 100 million vehicle-miles. *Source:* National Safety Council.

Motor-Vehicle Deaths by Type of Accident

Year	Deaths from collisions with— Pedestrians	Other motor vehicles	Railroad trains	Street cars	Pedalcycles	Animal-drawn vehicle or animal	Fixed objects	Deaths from non-collision accidents	Total deaths[1]
1937	15,500	10,320	1,810	264	700	200	1,160	9,690	39,643
1939	12,400	8,700	1,330	150	710	200	1,000	7,900	32,386
1941	13,550	12,500	1,840	118	910	250	1,350	9,450	39,969
1943	9,900	5,300	1,448	171	450	160	700	5,690	23,823
1945	11,000	7,150	1,703	163	500	130	800	6,600	28,076
1947	10,450	9,900	1,736	102	550	150	1,000	8,800	32,697
1949	8,800	10,500	1,452	56	550	140	1,100	9,100	31,701
1951	9,150	13,100	1,573	46	390	100	1,400	11,200	36,996
1953	8,750	13,400	1,506	26	420	120	1,500	12,200	37,955
1955	8,200	14,500	1,490	15	410	90	1,600	12,100	38,426
1957	7,850	15,400	1,376	13	460	80	1,700	11,800	38,702
1959	7,850	14,900	1,202	6	480	70	1,600	11,800	37,910
1961	7,650	14,700	1,267	5	490	80	1,700	12,200	38,091
1963	8,200	17,600	1,385	10	580	80	1,900	13,800	43,564
1965	8,900	20,800	1,556	5	680	120	2,200	14,900	49,163
1967	9,400	22,000	1,620	3	750	100	2,350	16,700	52,924
1969	10,100	23,700	1,495	2	800	100	3,900	15,700	55,791
1970	9,900	23,200	1,459	3	780	100	3,800	15,400	54,633
1971	9,900	23,100	1,378	2	800	100	3,800	15,300	54,381
1972	10,300	23,900	1,260	2	1,000	100	3,900	15,800	56,278
1973	10,200	23,600	1,194	2	1,000	100	3,800	15,600	55,511
1974	8,500	19,700	1,209	1	1,000	100	3,100	12,800	46,402
1975	8,400	19,550	979	1	1,000	100	3,130	12,700	45,853
1976	8,600	20,100	1,033	2	1,000	100	3,200	13,000	47,038
1977	9,100	21,200	902	3	1,100	100	3,400	13,700	49,510
1978	9,300	22,900	1,100	—	1,000	100	3,500	13,600	51,500

1. Yearly totals do not quite equal sums of various types because totals for most types are estimated, and these have been made to nearest 10 deaths for some types and to nearest 50 deaths for others. *Source:* National Safety Council.

Deaths and Death Rates

State	Total deaths 1979[1] number	Total deaths 1978 rate	Infant mortality 1979[1] number	Infant mortality 1978 rate
Alabama	34,304	9.2	872	16.4
Alaska	1,639	4.4	137	16.3
Arizona	20,385	8.3	671	15.0
Arkansas	21,554	9.9	442	14.3
California	169,954	7.7	4,052	11.6
Colorado	19,057	7.1	542	11.9
Connecticut	26,124	8.4	416	9.6
Delaware	5,048	8.7	144	12.0
D.C.	9,042	13.0	392	23.1
Florida	100,757	11.4	1,811	14.2
Georgia	42,646	8.5	1,264	14.7
Hawaii	5,128	5.4	191	11.8
Idaho	6,061	7.0	155	9.7
Illinois	100,218	8.9	2,750	14.7
Indiana	47,153	8.8	1,126	12.2
Iowa	26,237	9.4	476	11.8
Kansas	20,552	8.9	385	11.5
Kentucky	35,552	9.6	710	12.0
Louisiana	34,918	9.0	1,177	17.8
Maine	10,367	9.3	152	9.2
Maryland	32,002	7.8	623	14.4
Massachusetts	52,624	9.3	764	9.7
Michigan	72,480	8.0	1,916	13.4
Minnesota	32,592	8.5	644[2]	12.3
Mississippi	22,720	9.5	819	17.1
Missouri	48,558	10.7	1,165	16.0
Montana	6,407	8.2	136	10.0
Nebraska	14,116	9.3	305	13.8
Nevada	5,842	7.9	153	11.3
New Hampshire	7,287	8.3	131	8.3
New Jersey	64,126	8.8	1,089	11.8
New Mexico	8,596	7.0	344	14.5
New York	160,937	9.3	3,661	16.3
North Carolina	47,168	8.5	1,292	16.3
North Dakota	5,566	8.8	161	13.1
Ohio	93,197	8.7	1,966	13.0
Oklahoma	27,204	9.3	527	13.8
Oregon	21,071	8.6	477	13.2
Pennsylvania	117,269	10.2	2,099	14.8
Rhode Island	9,295	9.7	186	15.7
South Carolina	23,736	8.1	859	18.5
South Dakota	6,236	9.2	126	12.0
Tennessee	41,264	9.5	1,094	16.1
Texas	107,493	7.9	3,257	13.8
Utah	8,546	6.3	534	12.0
Vermont	4,364	9.4	57	11.4
Virginia	40,183	7.8	1,049	13.3
Washington	29,496	8.0	599	11.5
West Virginia	19,140	10.8	413	15.1
Wisconsin	38,873	8.7	568	9.2
Wyoming	2,929	7.1	80	9.0
United States	**1,905,013**	**8.8**	**44,959**	**13.4**

1. Provisional. By place of occurrence. 2. Excluding December. NOTE: Data exclude fetal deaths. Rates for total deaths are per 1,000 population in each area. Infant mortality rates are deaths under 1 year per 1,000 live births in each area. *Source:* Department of Health and Human Services, National Center for Health Statistics.

Death Rates

Year	Rate	Year	Rate	Year	Deaths	Rate
1900	17.2	1934	11.1	1958	1,647,886	9.5
1905	15.9	1935	10.9	1959	1,656,814	9.4
1910	14.7	1936	11.6	1960	1,711,982	9.5
1915	13.2	1937	11.3	1961	1,701,522	9.3
1916	13.8	1938	10.6	1962	1,756,720	9.5
1917	14.0	1939	10.6	1963	1,813,549	9.6
1918	18.1	1940	10.8	1964	1,798,051	9.4
1919	12.9	1941	10.5	1965	1,828,136	9.4
1920	13.0	1942	10.3	1966	1,863,149	9.5
1921	11.5	1943	10.9	1967	1,851,323	9.4
1922	11.7	1944	10.6	1968	1,930,082	9.7
1923	12.1	1945	10.6	1969	1,921,990	9.5
1924	11.6	1946	10.0	1970[1]	1,921,031	9.5
1925	11.7	1947	10.1	1971	1,927,542	9.3
1926	12.1	1948	9.9	1972	1,963,944	9.4
1927	11.3	1949	9.7	1973	1,973,003	9.4
1928	12.0	1950	9.6	1974	1,934,388	9.2
1929	11.9	1951	9.7	1975	1,892,879	8.9
1930	11.3	1952	9.6	1976	1,909,440	8.9
1931	11.1	1953	9.6	1977	1,899,597	8.8
1932	10.9	1954	9.2	1978	1,927,788	8.8
1933	10.7	1955	9.3	1979[2]	1,906,000	8.7

1. First year for which deaths of nonresidents are excluded. 2. Provisional. NOTE: Includes only deaths occurring within the registration area. Beginning with 1933, area includes entire U.S.; with 1959 includes Alaska, and with 1960 includes Hawaii. Excludes fetal deaths. Rates per 1,000 population residing in area, as of April 1 for 1940, 1950, 1960, and 1970, and estimated as of July 1 for all other years. *Sources:* Department of Commerce, Bureau of the Census; and Department of Health and Human Services, National Center for Health Statistics.

Death Rates by Age, Color, and Sex

Age[1]	1978[2]	1975[2]	1970[2]	1960	1940	1920	1978[2]	1975[2]	1970[2]	1960	1940	1920
	White males						White females					
Under 1	13.5	15.9	21.1	26.9	56.7	98.1	10.6	12.2	16.1	20.1	43.6	76.1
1–4	0.7	0.7	0.8	1.0	2.8	9.8	0.5	0.6	0.8	0.9	2.4	9.0
5–14	0.4	0.4	0.5	0.5	1.1	2.7	0.2	0.3	0.3	0.3	0.8	2.3
15–24	1.7	1.7	1.7	1.4	2.0	4.2	0.6	0.6	0.6	0.5	1.4	4.3
25–34	1.7	1.7	1.8	1.6	2.8	5.9	0.7	0.7	0.8	0.9	2.2	6.5
35–44	2.7	3.0	3.4	3.3	5.1	7.7	1.4	1.6	1.9	1.9	3.7	7.3
45–54	7.2	7.9	8.8	9.3	11.4	12.0	3.9	4.1	4.6	4.6	7.5	10.9
55–64	18.1	19.5	22.0	22.3	25.2	24.2	9.1	9.4	10.1	10.8	16.8	21.7
65–74	41.3	43.6	48.1	48.5	54.0	54.2	20.6	21.5	24.7	27.8	41.5	49.9
75–84	94.2	96.1	101.0	103.0	122.0	122.5	58.1	60.3	67.0	77.0	104.8	116.4
85 and over	181.0	182.6	185.5	217.5	251.4	253.6	141.0	144.9	159.8	194.8	235.0	247.0
	All other males						All other females					
Under 1	27.0	30.0	40.2	51.9	101.2	167.7	22.0	25.2	31.7	40.7	77.4	131.1
1–4	10.8	1.1	1.4	2.1	5.3	15.0	0.9	0.9	1.2	1.7	4.4	14.2
5–14	0.5	0.6	0.6	0.8	1.6	3.7	0.3	0.3	0.4	0.5	1.4	3.9
15–24	2.0	2.4	3.0	2.1	5.0	9.9	0.8	0.9	1.1	1.1	5.0	10.8
25–34	3.8	4.5	5.0	3.9	8.5	12.2	1.4	1.6	2.2	2.6	7.4	13.5
35–44	6.6	7.4	8.7	7.3	13.2	14.4	3.0	3.6	4.9	5.5	11.7	16.0
45–54	13.0	14.2	16.5	15.5	24.5	20.1	7.1	7.8	9.8	11.4	21.1	23.4
55–64	27.3	28.1	30.5	31.5	37.1[3]	31.1	15.3	16.4	18.9	24.1	33.2[3]	35.8
65–74	46.3	49.7	54.7	56.6	62.8[3]	60.2	28.2	31.7	36.8	39.8	52.3[3]	60.4
75–84	89.9	86.0	89.8	86.6	108.8	116.0	65.1	59.8	63.9	67.1	84.1	106.4
85 and over	101.0	116.9	114.1	152.4	199.7	247.1	84.4	91.8	102.9	128.7	159.7	221.2

1. In years. 2. Excludes deaths of nonresidents of U.S. 3. Based on enumerated population adjusted for age bias in nonwhite population at ages 55–69 years. NOTE: For 1920, data are from only 10 selected states and the District of Columbia; for 1940, from D.C. and the former 48 states; for 1960, from D.C. and all 50 states. Excludes fetal deaths. Rates are per 1,000 population in each group, enumerated as of April 1 for 1940, 1950, and 1960, and estimated as of July 1 for all other years. *Sources:* Department of Commerce, Bureau of the Census; and Department of Health and Human Services, National Center for Health Statistics.

Expectation of Life

Expectation of Life in the United States

Calendar period	Age 0	10	20	30	40	50	60	70	80
WHITE MALES									
1850[1]	38.3	48.0	40.1	34.0	27.9	21.6	15.6	10.2	5.9
1890[1]	42.50	48.45	40.66	34.05	27.37	20.72	14.73	9.35	5.40
1900–1902[2]	48.23	50.59	42.19	34.88	27.74	20.76	14.35	9.03	5.10
1909–1911[2]	50.23	51.32	42.71	34.87	27.43	20.39	13.98	8.83	5.09
1919–1921[3]	56.34	54.15	45.60	37.65	29.86	22.22	15.25	9.51	5.47
1929–1931	59.12	54.96	46.02	37.54	29.22	21.51	14.72	9.20	5.26
1930–1939	60.62	55.86	46.77	38.06	29.57	21.71	14.86	9.29	5.30
1939–1941	62.81	57.03	47.76	38.80	30.03	21.96	15.05	9.42	5.38
1949–1951	66.31	58.98	49.52	40.29	31.17	22.83	15.76	10.07	5.88
1959–1961	67.55	59.78	50.25	40.98	31.73	23.22	16.01	10.29	5.89
1969–1971	67.94	59.69	50.22	41.07	31.87	23.34	16.07	10.38	6.18
1977	70.0	61.3	51.9	42.7	33.4	24.7	17.1	11.1	6.8
WHITE FEMALES									
1850[1]	40.5	47.2	40.2	35.4	29.8	23.5	17.0	11.3	6.4
1890[1]	44.46	49.62	42.03	35.36	28.76	22.09	15.70	10.15	5.75
1900–1902[2]	51.08	52.15	43.77	36.42	29.17	21.89	15.23	9.59	5.50
1909–1911[2]	53.62	53.57	44.88	36.96	29.26	21.74	14.92	9.38	5.35
1919–1921[3]	58.53	55.17	46.46	38.72	30.94	23.12	15.93	9.94	5.70
1929–1931	62.67	57.65	48.52	39.99	31.52	23.41	16.05	9.98	5.63
1930–1939	64.52	58.98	49.71	40.90	32.24	23.96	16.44	10.19	5.76
1939–1941	67.29	60.85	51.38	42.21	33.25	24.72	17.00	10.50	5.88
1949–1951	72.03	64.26	54.56	45.00	35.64	26.76	18.64	11.68	6.59
1959–1961	74.19	66.05	56.29	46.63	37.13	28.08	19.69	12.38	6.67
1969–1971	75.49	66.97	57.24	47.60	38.12	29.11	20.79	13.37	7.59
1977	77.7	68.8	59.1	49.4	39.8	30.7	22.3	14.8	8.8
ALL OTHER MALES[4]									
1900–1902[2]	32.54	41.90	35.11	29.25	23.12	17.34	12.62	8.33	5.12
1909–1911[2]	34.05	40.65	33.46	27.33	21.57	16.21	11.67	8.00	5.53
1919–1921[3]	47.14	45.99	38.36	32.51	26.53	20.47	14.74	9.58	5.83
1929–1931	47.55	44.27	35.95	29.45	23.36	17.92	13.15	8.78	5.42
1930–1939	50.06	46.56	38.05	31.11	24.65	18.98	14.13	9.53	6.01
1939–1941	52.33	48.54	39.74	32.25	25.23	19.18	14.38	10.06	6.46
1949–1951	58.91	52.96	43.73	35.31	27.29	20.25	14.91	10.74	7.07
1959–1961	61.48	55.19	45.78	37.05	28.72	21.28	15.29	10.81	6.87
1969–1971	60.98	53.67	44.37	36.20	28.29	21.24	15.35	10.68	7.57
1977	64.6	56.6	47.2	38.6	30.2	22.7	16.5	11.4	8.7
ALL OTHER FEMALES[4]									
1900–1902[2]	35.04	43.02	36.89	30.70	24.37	18.67	13.60	9.62	6.48
1909–1911[2]	37.67	42.84	36.14	29.61	23.34	17.65	12.78	9.22	6.05
1919–1921[3]	46.92	44.54	37.15	31.48	25.60	19.76	14.69	10.25	6.58
1929–1931	49.51	45.33	37.22	30.67	24.30	18.60	14.22	10.38	6.90
1930–1939	52.62	48.29	39.90	32.88	26.11	20.09	15.28	10.88	7.18
1939–1941	55.51	50.83	42.14	34.52	27.31	21.04	16.14	11.81	8.00
1949–1951	62.70	56.17	46.77	38.02	29.82	22.67	16.95	12.29	8.15
1959–1961	66.47	59.72	50.07	40.83	32.16	24.31	17.83	12.46	7.66
1969–1971	69.05	61.49	51.85	42.61	33.87	25.97	19.02	13.30	9.01
1977	73.1	65.0	55.2	45.8	36.7	28.3	21.0	14.5	11.3

1. Massachusetts only; white and nonwhite combined, the latter being about 1% of the total. 2. Original Death Registration States. 3. Death Registration States of 1920. 4. Data for periods 1900–1902 to 1929–1931 relate to blacks only. *Sources:* Metropolitan Life Insurance Company; Department of Health and Human Services, National Center for Health Statistics; Department of Commerce, Bureau of the Census.

Accidents

According to the National Safety Council there are, on the average, 12 accidental deaths and about 1,200 disabling injuries every hour during the year. About one half of the deaths occur in motor vehicle accidents and more than one third of the injuries occur in the home.

Expectation of Life and Mortality Rates, 1977

Age	Expectation of life in years					Mortality rate per 1,000				
	Total persons	White		All other		Total Persons	White		All other	
		Male	Female	Male	Female		Male	Female	Male	Female
0	73.2	70.0	77.7	64.6	73.1	14.2	14.0	10.8	23.9	19.7
1	73.2	70.0	77.6	65.2	73.6	0.9	1.0	0.7	1.4	1.1
2	72.3	69.1	76.6	64.3	72.7	0.7	0.7	0.6	1.1	0.9
3	71.3	68.1	75.7	63.4	71.7	0.6	0.6	0.5	0.9	0.7
4	70.4	67.2	74.7	62.4	70.8	0.5	0.5	0.4	0.8	0.6
5	69.4	66.2	73.7	61.5	69.8	0.4	0.5	0.3	0.7	0.5
6	68.4	65.2	72.8	60.5	68.9	0.4	0.4	0.3	0.6	0.4
7	67.5	64.3	71.8	59.6	67.9	0.3	0.4	0.3	0.5	0.3
8	66.5	63.3	70.8	58.6	66.9	0.3	0.4	0.2	0.5	0.3
9	65.5	62.3	69.8	57.6	65.9	0.3	0.3	0.2	0.4	0.2
10	64.5	61.3	68.8	56.6	65.0	0.2	0.3	0.2	0.4	0.2
11	63.5	60.4	67.9	55.7	64.0	0.2	0.3	0.2	0.4	0.2
12	62.6	59.4	66.9	54.7	63.0	0.3	0.3	0.2	0.5	0.3
13	61.6	58.4	65.9	53.7	62.0	0.4	0.5	0.3	0.6	0.3
14	60.6	57.4	64.9	52.8	61.0	0.6	0.8	0.4	0.8	0.4
15	59.6	56.5	63.9	51.8	60.0	0.8	1.1	0.4	1.0	0.5
16	58.7	55.5	62.9	50.8	59.1	0.9	1.3	0.5	1.2	0.6
17	57.7	54.6	62.0	49.9	58.1	1.1	1.5	0.6	1.5	0.6
18	56.8	53.7	61.0	49.0	57.1	1.2	1.7	0.6	1.7	0.7
19	55.9	52.8	60.1	48.1	56.2	1.2	1.8	0.6	2.0	0.8
20	54.9	51.9	59.1	47.2	55.2	1.3	1.8	0.6	2.3	0.9
21	54.0	51.0	58.1	46.3	54.3	1.3	1.9	0.6	2.5	0.9
22	53.1	50.1	57.2	45.4	53.3	1.4	2.0	0.6	2.8	1.0
23	52.1	49.1	56.2	44.5	52.4	1.4	1.9	0.6	3.1	1.1
24	51.2	48.2	55.2	43.6	51.4	1.4	1.9	0.6	3.3	1.1
25	50.3	47.3	54.3	42.8	50.5	1.3	1.8	0.6	3.5	1.2
26	49.3	46.4	53.3	41.9	49.5	1.3	1.7	0.6	3.7	1.3
27	48.4	45.5	52.3	41.1	48.6	1.3	1.7	0.6	3.9	1.3
28	47.5	44.6	51.4	40.2	47.7	1.3	1.6	0.6	4.0	1.4
29	46.5	43.6	50.4	39.4	46.7	1.3	1.6	0.7	4.0	1.4
30	45.6	42.7	49.4	38.6	45.8	1.3	1.6	0.7	4.0	1.5
31	44.7	41.8	48.5	37.7	44.9	1.4	1.6	0.7	4.0	1.5
32	43.7	40.8	47.5	36.9	43.9	1.4	1.6	0.8	4.1	1.6
33	42.8	39.9	46.5	36.0	43.0	1.5	1.7	0.8	4.3	1.8
34	41.8	39.0	45.6	35.2	42.1	1.6	1.8	0.9	4.5	1.9
35	40.9	38.0	44.6	34.3	41.2	1.7	1.9	1.0	4.9	2.1
36	40.0	37.1	43.6	33.5	40.3	1.8	2.0	1.0	5.2	2.3
37	39.0	36.2	42.7	32.6	39.3	1.9	2.2	1.1	5.6	2.5
38	38.1	35.3	41.7	31.8	38.4	2.1	2.3	1.3	6.0	2.8
39	37.2	34.3	40.8	31.0	37.5	2.3	2.5	1.4	6.4	3.1
40	36.3	33.4	39.8	30.2	36.7	2.5	2.8	1.5	6.9	3.4
41	35.4	32.5	38.9	29.4	35.8	2.8	3.0	1.7	7.4	3.7
42	34.5	31.6	38.0	28.6	34.9	3.0	3.3	1.9	7.9	4.0
43	33.6	30.7	37.0	27.9	34.1	3.3	3.7	2.1	8.4	4.4
44	32.7	29.8	36.1	27.1	33.2	3.6	4.1	2.3	9.0	4.7
45	31.8	29.0	35.2	26.3	32.4	4.0	4.6	2.5	9.5	5.1
46	30.9	28.1	34.3	25.6	31.5	4.4	5.0	2.8	10.1	5.5
47	30.0	27.2	33.4	24.8	30.7	4.8	5.6	3.1	10.8	5.9
48	29.2	26.4	32.5	24.1	29.9	5.2	6.2	3.4	11.7	6.5
49	28.3	25.5	31.6	23.4	29.1	5.8	6.9	3.7	12.7	7.1
50	27.5	24.7	30.7	22.7	28.3	6.3	7.6	4.0	13.8	7.8
51	26.7	23.9	29.8	22.0	27.5	6.9	8.4	4.4	15.0	8.4
52	25.9	23.1	29.0	21.3	26.7	7.5	9.2	4.8	16.2	9.1
53	25.0	22.3	28.1	20.7	26.0	8.2	10.1	5.2	17.3	9.8
54	24.2	21.5	27.2	20.0	25.2	8.8	10.9	5.6	18.6	10.5
55	23.5	20.8	26.4	19.4	24.5	9.5	11.8	6.0	19.7	11.2
56	22.7	20.0	25.5	18.8	23.7	10.3	12.9	6.5	21.0	11.9
57	21.9	19.3	24.7	18.2	23.0	11.2	14.1	7.1	22.6	12.8
58	21.2	18.5	23.9	17.6	22.3	12.3	15.6	7.9	24.5	14.0
59	20.4	17.8	23.1	17.0	21.6	13.6	17.4	8.7	26.8	15.3
60	19.7	17.1	22.3	16.5	21.0	15.1	19.3	9.6	29.5	16.9
61	19.0	16.4	21.5	15.9	20.3	16.6	21.3	10.6	32.2	18.5
62	18.3	15.8	20.7	15.4	19.7	17.9	23.3	11.5	34.2	19.5
63	17.6	15.2	19.9	15.0	19.1	19.1	25.2	12.3	35.1	19.8
64	16.9	14.5	19.2	14.5	18.4	20.2	27.1	13.1	35.1	19.6
65	16.3	13.9	18.4	14.0	17.8	21.3	29.1	13.9	34.6	19.0

Age	Expectation of life in years: Total persons	White: Male	White: Female	All other: Male	All other: Female	Mortality rate per 1,000: Total Persons	White: Male	White: Female	All other: Male	All other: Female
66	15.6	13.3	17.7	13.5	17.1	22.6	31.2	14.8	34.5	18.8
67	15.0	12.7	16.9	13.0	16.4	24.2	33.7	16.0	35.6	20.0
68	14.3	12.2	16.2	12.4	15.8	26.3	36.5	17.5	38.8	22.9
69	13.7	11.6	15.5	11.9	15.1	28.8	39.7	19.2	43.8	27.5
70	13.1	11.1	14.8	11.4	14.5	31.5	43.2	21.1	49.7	32.8
71	12.5	10.5	14.1	11.0	14.0	34.4	46.8	23.1	55.6	37.9
72	11.9	10.0	13.4	10.6	13.6	37.6	50.9	25.6	61.3	42.9
73	11.4	9.6	12.7	10.3	13.2	41.3	53.5	28.7	66.4	47.6
74	10.9	9.1	12.1	10.0	12.8	45.4	60.7	32.4	70.8	51.8
75	10.4	8.6	11.5	9.7	12.5	49.8	66.3	36.4	74.9	55.8
76	9.9	8.2	10.9	9.5	12.2	54.6	72.2	40.8	79.1	59.7
77	9.4	7.8	10.4	9.2	11.9	59.5	78.5	45.3	83.5	63.5
78	9.0	7.5	9.8	9.0	11.7	64.5	85.1	50.0	88.2	67.2
79	8.6	7.1	9.3	8.9	11.5	69.7	91.8	54.9	92.8	70.1
80	8.2	6.8	8.8	8.7	11.3	75.1	98.7	60.2	96.3	71.7
81	7.8	6.5	8.4	8.6	11.1	80.5	105.6	66.0	97.3	70.9
82	7.4	6.2	7.9	8.4	10.9	85.9	112.2	72.4	93.9	66.5
83	7.1	5.9	7.5	8.2	10.7	91.1	118.1	79.7	83.1	56.8
84	6.7	5.6	7.1	7.9	10.2	96.0	122.6	88.2	61.6	40.1
85	6.4	5.3	6.8	7.3	9.6	1000.0	1000.0	1000.0	1000.0	1000.0

Sources: Metropolitan Life Insurance Company; Department of Health and Human Services, National Center for Health Statistics. NOTE: Data are latest available.

Law Enforcement and Crime

Full-Time Law Enforcement Employees

City	Officers	Civilians	Total
Atlanta	1,118	261	1,379
Baltimore	3,337	575	3,912
Birmingham, Ala.	702	180	882
Boston	2,102	832	2,934
Buffalo, N.Y.	1,093	117	1,210
Chicago	13,020	1,304	14,324
Cincinnati	888	166	1,054
Cleveland	1,906	155	2,061
Columbus, Ohio	883	257	1,140
Dallas	1,997	577	2,574
Denver	1,390	276	1,666
Detroit	5,688	683	6,371
El Paso	673	150	823
Ft Worth	684	195	879
Honolulu	1,472	366	1,838
Houston	2,988	885	3,873
Indianapolis	1,046	313	1,359
Jacksonville	958	650	1,608
Kansas City, Mo.	1,192	465	1,657
Long Beach, Calif.	591	204	795
Los Angeles	6,979	2,670	9,649
Louisville, Ky.	716	200	916
Memphis, Tenn.	1,240	414	1,654
Miami, Fla.	698	314	1,012
Milwaukee	2,028	236	2,264
Minneapolis	765	105	870
New Orleans	1,532	366	1,898
New York	24,408	5,035	29,443
Newark, N.J.	1,453	269	1,722
Norfolk, Va.	601	107	708
Oakland, Calif.	642	233	875
Oklahoma City	693	180	873
Omaha, Neb.	550	127	677
Philadelphia	8,209	1,046	9,255
Phoenix, Ariz.	1,528	523	2,051
Pittsburgh	1,400	31	1,431
Portland, Ore.	699	191	890
Rochester, N.Y.	617	140	757
St. Louis	1,997	591	2,588
St. Paul	547	131	678
San Antonio	1,100	286	1,386
San Diego, Calif.	1,193	364	1,557
San Francisco	1,658	228	1,886
San Jose, Calif.	787	189	976
Seattle	970	318	1,288
Tampa, Fla.	588	205	793
Toledo, Ohio	564	113	677
Tucson, Ariz.	538	178	716
Tulsa, Okla.	650	131	781
Washington, D.C.	4,078	573	4,651

NOTE: As of Oct. 31, 1978. *Source:* Department of Justice, Federal Bureau of Investigation. *Uniform Crime Reports for the United States, 1978.*

Arrests by Race, 1978
(in thousands)

Offense	White	Black	Other	Total
Serious Crimes	1,362.4	732.1	66.2	2,160.7
Murder[1]	8.7	9.2	0.8	18.7
Forcible rape	13.6	13.6	0.9	28.2
Robbery	53.3	82.8	5.0	141.1
Aggravated assault	148.2	100.1	8.7	257.0
Burglary	328.7	140.4	14.3	483.4
Larceny—theft	705.3	344.5	30.2	1,079.9
Motor vehicle theft	104.6	41.4	6.4	152.4
All Other				
Other assaults	284.0	147.4	12.1	443.5
Arson	13.6	3.9	0.4	18.0
Forgery and counterfeiting	48.0	23.7	1.3	73.0
Fraud	158.8	86.3	3.7	248.7
Embezzlement	5.7	1.9	0.1	7.7
Stolen property—buying, receiving, possessing	71.4	37.1	3.2	111.6
Vandalism	180.4	37.1	5.2	222.7
Weapons—carrying, possessing, etc.	86.7	56.8	5.1	148.6
Prostitution and commercial vice	40.0	47.2	2.1	89.2
Sex offenses, except forcible rape and prostitution	49.1	14.3	1.9	65.4
Drug abuse violations	452.7	127.3	12.2	592.2
Gambling	14.1	36.7	2.2	53.0
Offenses against family and children	34.8	18.1	1.0	53.9
Driving under the influence	979.4	148.4	32.2	1,160.0
Liquor laws	316.0	26.1	10.6	352.7
Drunkenness	876.5	200.6	34.7	1,111.8
Disorderly conduct	433.2	215.7	28.0	676.9
Vagrancy	27.8	18.2	0.9	46.8
All other offenses, except traffic	1,137.8	538.6	103.4	1,779.7
Curfew and loitering law violations	58.8	18.6	1.4	78.8
Runaways	147.7	19.8	4.5	172.0
Total	**6,778.8**	**2,555.7**	**332.3**	**9,666.8**

1. Includes non-negligent manslaughter. NOTE: Figures represent arrests reported by 11,852 agencies with a total 1978 population of 206,610,000 estimated by FBI. *Source:* Department of Justice, Federal Bureau of Investigation, *Uniform Crime Reports for the United States, 1978.*

Total Estimated Arrests, 1978[1]

Criminal homicide:	
Murder and nonnegligent manslaughter	19,840
Forcible rape	29,660
Robbery	148,930
Aggravated assault	271,270
Burglary—breaking or entering	511,600
Larceny—theft	1,141,800
Motor vehicle theft	161,400
Other assaults	468,600
Arson	19,000
Forgery and counterfeiting	77,200
Fraud	262,500
Embezzlement	8,100
Stolen property—buying, receiving, possessing	118,200
Vandalism	235,300
Weapons; carrying, possessing, etc.	157,900
Prostitution and commercialized vice	94,200
Sex offenses (except forcible rape and prostitution)	69,100
Drug abuse violations	628,700
Opium or cocaine and their derivatives	83,100
Marijuana	445,800
Synthetic or manufactured narcotics	17,200
Other—dangerous nonnarcotic drugs	82,500
Gambling	55,800
Bookmaking	5,400
Numbers and lottery	8,200
All other gambling	42,200
Offenses against family	56,900
Driving under the influence	1,268,700
Liquor laws	376,400
Drunkenness	1,176,600
Disorderly conduct	715,200
Vagrancy	49,300
All other offenses (except traffic)	1,883,800
Suspicion (not included in total)	22,900
Curfew and loitering law violations	83,100
Runaways	182,100
Total	**10,271,000**

1. Arrest totals based on all reporting agencies and estimates for unreported areas. *Source:* Department of Justice, Federal Bureau of Investigation, *Uniform Crime Reports for the United States, 1978.*

Total Arrests, by Age Groups, 1978

Age	Arrests	Age	Arrests	Age	Arrests	Age	Arrests	Age	Arrests
Under 15	728,198	18	589,767	22	420,821	30–34	827,948	50–54	302,276
15	432,078	19	540,790	23	382,602	35–39	586,293	55 & over	411,994
16	542,459	20	499,585	24	352,854	40–44	450,570	Not Known	8,898
17	576,630	21	471,078	25–29	1,283,448	45–49	366,798	Total	**9,775,087**

NOTE: Based on reports furnished to the FBI by 11,872 agencies covering a 1978 estimated population of 207,060,000. *Source:* Department of Justice, Federal Bureau of Investigation, *Uniform Crime Reports for the United States, 1978.*

Number of Arrests by Sex and Age

	Male				Female			
	Total		Under 18		Total		Under 18	
Offense	**1978**	**1977**	**1978**	**1977**	**1978**	**1977**	**1978**	**1977**
Serious Crimes	1,418,343	1,390,403	599,089	601,064	369,142	358,692	139,005	138,813
Murder[1]	12,736	12,558	1,197	1,321	2,234	2,240	149	135
Forcible rape	22,608	22,087	3,526	3,618	186	231	58	84
Robbery	88,928	88,123	27,272	27,294	6,911	7,184	1,985	2,144
Aggravated assault	172,849	161,795	26,452	25,669	25,033	23,557	4,618	4,550
Burglary—breaking or entering	376,982	376,233	199,105	198,758	24,977	24,465	13,070	12,766
Larceny—theft	636,550	626,194	285,416	287,981	299,371	291,513	112,794	113,338
Motor vehicle theft	107,690	103,413	56,121	56,423	10,430	9,502	6,331	5,796
All Other								
Other assaults	332,081	318,511	56,607	56,144	53,266	51,210	14,359	14,540
Arson	13,400	13,231	6,866	6,853	1,786	1,637	719	695
Forgery and counterfeiting	42,682	42,753	5,734	5,435	18,626	17,813	2,520	2,192
Fraud	122,039	113,120	3,941	3,962	83,087	69,717	1,681	1,551
Embezzlement	4,951	4,698	574	576	1,693	1,365	207	159
Stolen property—buying, receiving, possessing	79,367	80,577	27,762	27,887	10,276	9,949	2,819	2,707
Vandalism	178,336	166,698	104,265	101,924	16,287	15,368	8,533	8,351
Weapons—carrying, possessing, etc.	115,927	112,339	18,727	18,564	9,978	10,001	1,190	1,268
Prostitution and commercialized vice	21,967	19,366	891	895	46,812	45,755	2,031	1,987
Sex offenses, except forcible rape and prostitution	47,825	48,039	8,953	9,195	4,116	4,664	897	1,053
Drug abuse violations	426,682	430,585	101,855	101,000	69,347	69,410	20,774	20,086
Gambling	37,566	39,426	1,547	1,756	3,782	3,976	74	99
Offenses against family and children	45,127	46,211	1,711	1,887	5,169	5,216	953	1,131
Driving under the influence	993,468	930,421	22,789	20,986	92,076	84,583	2,432	2,115
Liquor laws	272,604	261,068	89,991	90,724	47,291	45,521	25,392	25,069
Drunkenness	919,200	1,008,105	33,949	39,706	74,897	80,551	5,381	6,336
Disorderly conduct	518,816	485,983	93,452	90,655	99,505	98,273	19,582	21,180
Vagrancy	17,954	20,125	3,849	4,237	7,092	6,149	808	1,002
All other offenses except traffic	1,023,489	987,070	201,172	208,913	198,449	197,337	55,600	59,655
Curfew and loitering law violations	57,048	64,176	57,048	64,176	15,687	17,743	15,687	17,743
Runaways	66,515	74,370	66,515	74,370	89,984	101,192	89,984	101,192
Total	**6,755,387**	**6,657,275**	**1,507,287**	**1,530,909**	**1,318,348**	**1,296,122**	**410,628**	**428,924**

1. Includes non-negligent manslaughter. NOTE: 1978 figures represent arrests reported by 10,319 agencies with a total 1978 population of 179,569,000 as estimated by FBI. *Source:* Department of Justice, Federal Bureau of Investigation, *Uniform Crime Reports for the United States, 1978.*

National Crime, Rate, and Percent Change

	Estimated crime 1978		Percent change over 1977		Percent change over 1974		Percent change over 1969	
Crime index offenses	**Number**	**Rate per 100,000 inhabitants**	**Number**	**Rate**	**Number**	**Rate**	**Number**	**Rate**
Murder	19,560	9.0	+2.3	+2.3	−5.6	−8.2	+32.5	+23.3
Forcible rape	67,130	30.8	+6.5	+5.8	+21.2	+17.6	+80.6	+66.5
Robbery	417,040	191.3	+3.0	+2.2	−5.7	−8.6	+39.5	+28.9
Aggravated assault	558,100	255.9	+6.8	+6.0	+22.3	+18.6	+79.4	+65.6
Burglary	3,104,500	1,423.7	+1.7	+.9	+2.1	−1.0	+56.6	+44.7
Larceny—theft	5,983,400	2,743.9	+1.3	+.5	+13.7	+10.2	+53.9	+42.1
Motor vehicle theft	991,600	454.7	+2.4	+1.6	+1.5	−1.6	+12.9	+4.2
Violent	1,061,830	486.9	+5.2	+4.4	+8.9	+5.6	+60.4	+48.1
Property	10,079,500	4,622.4	+1.5	+.7	+8.6	+5.3	+49.3	+37.9
Total[1]	**11,141,300**	**5,109.3**	**+1.9**	**+1.1**	**+8.7**	**+5.3**	**+50.3**	**+38.8**

Source: Department of Justice, Federal Bureau of Investigation, *Uniform Crime Reports for the United States, 1978.*

Crime Rates for Population Groups and Selected Cities, 1978

(offenses known to the police per 100,000 population)

Group and city	Violent crime					Property crime				Total all crimes
	Murder	Forcible rape	Robbery	Aggravated assault	Total	Burglary—breaking or entering	Larceny—theft	Motor vehicle theft	Total	
Cities over 250,000	20.3	65	601	435	1,121	2,215	3,589	956	6,760	7,881
100,000—249,999	10.3	44	244	329	627	1,961	3,969	624	6,554	7,181
50,000—99,999	6.9	30	176	273	486	1,656	3,488	532	5,676	6,162
25,000—49,999	4.9	23	111	225	364	1,363	3,260	416	5,039	5,403
10,000—24,999	4.3	16	69	186	276	1,094	2,801	310	4,205	4,480
Under 10,000	3.7	13	42	186	245	953	2,602	230	3,785	4,030
Total, 7,980 cities	**10.1**	**36**	**263**	**293**	**602**	**1,622**	**3,305**	**572**	**5,497**	**6,100**
Suburbs, 4,801 agencies[2]	5.2	23	89	206	4,498	1,255	2,571	350	4,175	4,498
Rural areas, 2,714 agencies	7.9	15	21	141	185	796	1,021	133	1,950	2,136
Total, 11,627 agencies	**9.3**	**32**	**203**	**264**	**508**	**1,471**	**2,827**	**474**	**4,772**	**5,280**
Selected cities:										
New York	20.8	54	1,022	597	1,694	2,270	2,763	1,147	6,181	7,875
Chicago	25.5	43	494	334	897	1,107	3,208	970	5,285	6,182
Los Angeles	23.4	89	614	595	1,320	2,507	3,237	1,307	7,051	8,371
Philadelphia	18.6	38	375	224	656	1,016	1,575	622	3,213	3,869
Detroit	38.5	100	949	582	1,669	2,517	2,846	1,506	6,869	8,538
Houston	32.6	74	495	129	730	2,549	4,429	1,172	8,150	8,880
Baltimore	25.2	71	1,036	743	1,875	2,020	4,239	751	7,011	8,886
Dallas	26.4	94	440	573	1,134	2,772	5,340	684	8,796	9,930
Washington, D.C.	28.0	66	940	378	1,412	1,854	3,820	474	6,148	7,559
Cleveland	34.7	83	1,034	427	1,578	2,316	2,337	2,060	6,713	8,291
Indianapolis	14.8	66	382	264	727	1,702	3,642	716	6,060	6,787
Milwaukee	7.7	46	194	143	391	1,156	3,296	580	5,032	5,423
San Francisco	17.9	89	988	501	1,596	2,741	4,992	1,358	9,091	10,687
San Diego, Calif.	8.5	40	317	201	567	2,528	4,419	869	7,816	8,383
San Antonio	16.7	37	176	192	422	2,056	3,503	450	6,009	6,431
CRIME INDEX TRENDS										
(percent change, 1978–79)										
Cities over 1,000,000 (total population 17,783,000)	+14	+ 9	+11	+ 7	+ 9	+ 9	+ 4	+11	+ 7	+ 7
Cities 500,000 to 999,999 (total population 11,846,000)	+17	+12	+10	+11	+11	+ 2	+ 7	+ 9	+ 6	+ 6
Cities 250,000 to 499,999 (total population 11,712,000)	+14	+13	+17	+12	+15	+ 5	+10	+12	+ 8	+ 9
Cities 100,000 to 249,999 (total population 16,603,000)	+ 9	+11	+13	+ 9	+10	+ 7	+ 9	+ 6	+ 8	+ 8
Cities 50,000 to 99,999 (total population 18,343,000)	+ 1	+18	+ 9	+ 8	+ 9	+ 6	+ 9	+10	+ 8	+ 8
Cities 25,000 to 49,999 (total population 22,185,000)	+13	+17	+15	+11	+13	+ 7	+10	+11	+ 9	+10
Cities 10,000 to 24,999 (total population 24,120,000)	+ 6	+13	+12	+12	+12	+ 8	+11	+15	+10	+10
Cities under 10,000 (total population 21,600,000)	+ 2	+16	+13	+13	+13	+ 6	+12	+14	+11	+11
Suburban areas (total population 34,076,000)	+ 6	+10	+13	+ 7	+ 9	+ 4	+10	+ 9	+ 8	+ 8
Rural areas (total population 28,577,000)	− 2	+ 5	+ 6	+ 9	+ 8	+ 3	+12	+11	+ 9	+ 9
All areas (total population 206,845,000)	+ 9	+12	+12	+ 9	+11	+ 6	+ 9	+10	+ 8	+ 8

1. Includes manslaughter by negligence, not shown separately. 2. Agencies also included in other city groups. NOTE: Population in 1978 as estimated by FBI. *Sources:* Department of Justice, Federal Bureau of Investigation, *Uniform Crime Reports for the United States, 1978* and *1979 Preliminary Annual Release.*

Domestic Production and Imports of Civilian Firearms

(in thousands)

Item	1978	1977	1976	1975	1974	1973	1972	1970	1965	1960
Domestic production	4,866	5,016	5,225	5,768	5,639	4,844	n.a.	n.a.	2,355	1,508
Handguns	1,889	1,868	1,833	2,024	1,715	1,734	n.a.	n.a.	666	475
Rifles	1,781	1,923	2,091	2,123	2,099	1,830	n.a.	n.a.	790	469
Shotguns	1,196	1,225	1,301	1,621	1,825	1,280	n.a.	n.a.	899	564
Imports for consumption	869	782	895	1,084	903	914	1,200	826	766	655
Handguns	273	316	270	462	259	299	468	227	347	128
Rifles	223	170	157	166	188	195	197	237	245	402
Shotguns	373	296	468	457	456	420	535	363	174	125
Total	**5,735**	**5,798**	**6,120**	**6,852**	**6,542**	**5,758**	n.a.	n.a.	**3,121**	**2,163**

NOTE: Beginning 1972, fiscal-year data. Includes firearms sold under civilian marksmanship program of Department of Defense. n.a.=not available. *Source:* 1960–1970, Department of Commerce, Bureau of the Census; beginning 1972, Department of the Treasury, Bureau of Alcohol, Tobacco, and Firearms.

Prisoners Under Sentence of Death

Characteristic	1978	1977	1975
White	261	244	214
Black and other	184	199	265
Under 20 years	22	16	43
20–24 years	113	135	139
25–34 years	210	199	204
35–54 years	97	88	83
55 years and over	3	5	10
Schooling completed:			
7 years or less	55	49	71
8 years	46	46	50
9–11 years	158	137	167
12 years	99	88	93
More than 12 years	28	25	21
Unknown	59	98	77

Characteristic	1978	1977	1975
Marital status:			
Never married	187	192	217
Married	136	143	167
Divorced or separated[1]	122	108	95
Time elapsed since sentencing:			
6 months or less }	162	123	166
7–12 months }			130
1–3 years	237	314	155
4–8 years	46	6	13
More than 8 years	0	0	15
Legal status at arrest:			
Not under sentence	277	253	293
On parole or probation	60	60	51
In prison or escaped	35	20	27
Unknown	73	110	108
Total	**445**	**443**	**479**

1. Includes widows, widowers, and unknown. NOTE: As of Dec. 31. Excludes prisoners under sentence of death confined in local correctional systems pending appeal or who had not been committed to prison. *Source:* Department of Justice, Law Enforcement Assistance Administration.

Methods of Execution[1]

State	Method
Alabama[2]	Electrocution
Alaska	No death penalty
Arizona[2]	Lethal gas
Arkansas[2]	Electrocution
California	Lethal gas
Colorado[2]	Lethal gas
Connecticut[2]	Electrocution
Delaware	Hanging
D.C.	No death penalty
Florida	Electrocution
Georgia[2]	Electrocution
Hawaii	No death penalty
Idaho[2]	Lethal injection
Illinois	Electrocution
Indiana[2]	Electrocution
Iowa	No death penalty
Kansas	No death penalty
Kentucky[2]	Electrocution
Louisiana[2]	Electrocution
Maine	No death penalty
Maryland[2]	Lethal gas
Massachusetts	Electrocution
Michigan	No death penalty
Minnesota	No death penalty
Mississippi[2]	Lethal gas
Missouri	Lethal gas
Montana[2]	Hanging
Nebraska[2]	Electrocution
Nevada[2]	Lethal gas
New Hampshire[2]	Hanging
New Jersey[5]	No death penalty
New Mexico	Lethal injection
New York	No death penalty
North Carolina[2]	Lethal gas
North Dakota	No death penalty
Ohio[2]	Electrocution
Oklahoma	Lethal injection
Oregon	Lethal gas
Pennsylvania[2]	Electrocution
Rhode Island[2]	(3)
South Carolina[2]	Electrocution
South Dakota	Electrocution
Tennessee[2]	Electrocution
Texas[2]	Lethal injection
Utah[2]	Shooting
Vermont	Electrocution
Virginia	Electrocution
Washington[2]	Hanging
West Virginia	No death penalty
Wisconsin	No death penalty
Wyoming	Lethal gas
U.S. (Fed. Govt.)	(4)
American Samoa	(5)
Canal Zone	Hanging
Guam	No death penalty
Puerto Rico	No death penalty
Virgin Islands	No death penalty

1. On July 1, 1976, by a 7–2 decision, the U.S. Supreme Court upheld the death penalty as not being "cruel or unusual." However, in another ruling the same day, the Court, by a 5–4 vote, stated that states may not impose, "mandatory" capital punishment on every person convicted of murder. These decisions left uncertain the fate of condemned persons throughout the U.S. On Oct. 4, the Court refused to reconsider its July ruling, which allows some states to proceed with executions of condemned prisoners. The first execution in this country since 1967 was in Utah on Jan. 17, 1977. Gary Mark Gilmore was executed by shooting. 2. Voted to restore death penalty after June 29, 1972, Supreme Court decision ruling capital punishment unconstitutional. 3. Person shall be executed by gas if he commits murder while serving a prison term. 4. Method shall be that used by state in which sentence is imposed. If state does not have death penalty, federal judge shall prescribe method for carrying out sentence. 5. New criminal code re-establishes death penalty but at this time prescribes no method. *Source: Information Please* questionnaires to the states.

Law Enforcement Officers Killed in Line of Duty

(beginning 1972, includes federal officers)

Area	1978	1977	1976	1975	1974	1973	1972	1971	1970	1965	1960
New England	3	2	4	4	2	7	2	5	2	3	3
Middle Atlantic	9	12	15	24	18	21	22	31	29	10	7
East North Central	5	10	19	32	43	21	23	32	38	10	9
West North Central	5	14	11	8	8	6	12	13	6	3	3
South Atlantic	15	31	34	31	42	37	38	28	23	15	13
East South Central	13	11	14	18	12	13	12	13	5	9	2
West South Central	19	21	21	22	23	30	27	23	15	14	6
Mountain	5	3	4	14	9	16	7	11	4	7	0
Pacific	15	15	13	22	18	21	12	22	24	12	5
Puerto Rico	4	1	4	8	4	4	2	3	n.a.	n.a.	n.a.
CAUSE											
By felons	93	93[3]	111	129[1]	132	134	116	129	100	53	n.a.
In accidents	53	30[3]	29	56	47	42	41	52	46	30	n.a.
Total	**146**	**123[3]**	**140[2]**	**185[1]**	**179**	**176**	**157**	**181**	**146**	**83**	**48**

1. Includes one officer each in Virgin Islands and Guam. 2. Includes one officer killed in Bogota, Colombia. 3. Includes one officer killed in Virgin Islands and two FBI agents accidentally killed. NOTE: n.a. = not available. *Source:* Department of Justice, Federal Bureau of Investigation, *Uniform Crime Reports for the United States, 1978.*

One of Five Assault Victims Knows Attacker

A four-year Bureau of Justice Statistics report on crime reported that 21%, or 3.8 million cases out of an estimated 17.9 million attempted or completed violent incidents, happened between friends or relatives.

In one of every five rapes, robberies and assaults covered in the report, the victim knew his or her attacker.

Murder Victims by Weapons Used

Year	Murder victims, total	Weapons used or cause of death: Guns						
		Total	Percent	Cutting or stabbing	Blunt object[1]	Strangulation and hands, fists, feet	Drownings, arson, etc.	All other[2]
1965	8,773	5,015	57.2	2,021	505	894	226	112
1966	9,552	5,660	59.3	2,134	516	896	203	143
1967	11,114	6,998	63.0	2,200	589	957	211	159
1968	12,503	8,105	64.8	2,317	713	936	294	138
1969	13,575	8,876	65.4	2,534	613	1,039	322	191
1970	13,649	9,039	66.2	2,424	604	1,031	353	198
1971	16,183	10,712	66.2	3,017	645	1,295	314	200
1972	15,832	10,379	65.6	2,974	672	1,291	331	185
1973	17,123	11,249	65.7	2,985	848	1,445	173[3]	423
1974	18,632	12,474	66.9	3,228	976	1,417	153[3]	384
1975	18,642	12,061	64.7	3,245	1,001	1,646	193[3]	496
1976	16,605	10,592	63.8	2,956	806	1,330	227[3]	694
1977	18,033	11,274	62.5	3,440	849	1,431	252[3]	787
1978	18,714	11,910	63.6	3,526	896	1,422	255[3]	705

1. Refers to club, hammer, etc. 2. Includes poison, explosives, unknown, and not stated; for 1973 to 1976, includes drowning. 3. Arson only. *Source:* Department of Justice, Federal Bureau of Investigation, *Uniform Crime Reports for the United States, 1978.*

Motor Vehicle Laws, 1980

State	Date new license plates can be used	Age for driver's license[1]			State gasoline tax	Percent state tax[2]	Annual inspection required
		Regular	Learner's	Restrictive			
Alabama	Oct. 1	16	15[5]	14[15]	$.07	1½	no[19]
Alaska	On issue	18		16[3]	.08	—	no[19]
Arizona	On issue	18	15 & 7 mos.[3 5]	16[3]	.08	4	no[23]
Arkansas	On issue	18	(5)	14[3]	.085	3	yes
California	On issue	18	15[4 10]	16[4]	.07	6[23]	no[19]
Colorado	On issue	21	15½[5]	16[4]	.07	3	yes
Connecticut	On issue	18		16[4]	.11	7[6]	no[24]
Delaware	On issue	18	(5)	16[4]	.09	(18)	yes
D. C.	On issue	18	(5)	16[3]	.10	(21)	yes
Florida	30 days before exp. of old	16	(5)	15[3]	.08	4	yes
Georgia	Jan. 1	18	15	16[3]	.075	3	yes
Hawaii	Jan. 1	18	(5)	15[3]	(8)	(9)	yes[12]
Idaho	On issue	16	(5)	14[4]	.095	3	no
Illinois	administratively determined	18	(5)	16[3 4]	.075	4	no
Indiana	On issue	18	15[20]	16 & 1 mo.[3 4]	.08	4	yes
Iowa	Jan. 1	18	14	16[4]	.085	3	(7)
Kansas	On issue	16	(5)	14	.08	3	no
Kentucky	On issue	18	(5)	16[3]	.09	5	no
Louisiana	On issue	17		15[11]	.08	3	yes
Maine	On issue	17	(5)	15[4]	.09	5	6 mos.
Maryland	Mar. 1	18	(5)	15 & 9 mo.[3 4]	.09	5	no[26]
Massachusetts	On issue	18	(5)	16½[3 4]	.085	5	6 mos.
Michigan	On issue	18		16[3 4]	.11	4	no[19]
Minnesota	On issue	18	(5)	16[4]	.09	4	no[19]
Mississippi	On issue	15	(5)		.09	3	yes
Missouri	On issue	16		15[4]	.07	3	yes
Montana	On issue	18	(5)	15[3 4]	.09	1½[13]	no
Nebraska	On issue	16	15[5]	14	.105	3	yes
Nevada	On issue	18	15½[5]	16[3]	.06	2[14]	no
New Hampshire	On issue	18		16[4]	.11	—	6 mos.
New Jersey	On issue	17		16	.08	5	yes
New Mexico	Dec. 15	16	15	15[4]	.08	2	no
New York	On issue	17[4]		16[3]	.08	4	yes
North Carolina	Jan. 1	18		16[3 4]	.09	2[16]	yes
North Dakota	Apr. 1	16	(5)	14[3 4]	.08	3	no[19]
Ohio	1st day/mo. of exp.	18	16[3 5]	14[27]	.07	4	no[19]
Oklahoma	On issue	16		15½[4]	.0658	2	yes
Oregon	On issue	16	15[5]	14	.07	—	no[19]
Pennsylvania	On issue	17[4]	(5)	16[3]	.11	6	6 mos.
Rhode Island	Mar. 1	18	(5)	16[4]	.10	6	yes
South Carolina	On issue	16	15[10]	15	.09	4	yes
South Dakota	Jan. 1	16	(5)	14	.08	3[17]	no
Tennessee	On issue	16	(5)	15	.08	4½[28]	no
Texas	On issue	16[4]	15[10]	15[27]	.05	4	yes
Utah	On issue	16[4]	(5)		.09	4¾	yes
Vermont	On issue	18	15[5]	16	.09	4	6 mos.
Virginia	On issue	18	15 & 8 mos.[3 5]	16[3 4]	.09	2	yes
Washington	On issue	18	15[20]	16[4]	(22)	4.5	no[19]
West Virginia	On issue	18	(5)	16[3]	.105	5	yes
Wisconsin	On issue	18	(5)	16[4]	.07	4	no
Wyoming	Jan. 1	18	15[3 10]	16[3]	.08	3	no

1. Full driving privileges at age given in "Regular" column. A license restricted or qualified in some manner may be obtained at age given in "Restricted" column. 2. Applicable to car sales (local and county sales taxes extra where applicable). 3. Guardian's or parent's consent required. 4. Must have completed approved Driver Education course. 5. Learner's Permit required. 6. Sales or use tax on first registration of new or used cars. 7. Prior to first registration and transfers. 8. 8.5—13.5¢ varies by county. 9. 4% on cars purchased out of state only. 10. Driver with Learner's Permit must be accompanied by locally licensed operator 18 years or older. 11. All persons under 17 are prohibited from operating vehicles between 11 p.m. and 5 a.m. 12. If car is 10 years or older, every 6 months. 13. Periodic reductions for cars purchased later in year. 14. Plus 1% school support tax and 1/2% city and county relief tax in selected counties. 15. Restricted to Mopeds. 16. $120 maximum. 17. Tax on first registration. 18. Document fee of 2% of cost of car. 19. State troopers are authorized to inspect at their discretion. 20. Must be enrolled in a Driver Education course. 21. 4–7%, depending on weight of car. 22. Variable 9–12¢. Based on the average weighted retail sales price of fuel. 23. Arizona emission inspection, fee $5. 24. 6½% in some special districts. 25. Used motor vehicles being registered in Connecticut from out-of-state are required to be inspected and approved and Connecticut cars 10 years old or more must be inspected upon being sold or transferred. 26. Used passenger cars upon resale or transfer. 27. Upon proof of hardship. 28. Some counties have an additional 1 to 1¾% county tax. NOTES: A driver's license is required in every state. The national speed limit is 55 miles per hour. All states have an *implied consent* Chemical Test Law for alcohol. *Source:* American Automobile Association.

Minimum Legal Age for Purchase of Liquor, Wine, and Beer

State	Liquor	Wine	Beer
Alabama	19	19	19
Alaska	19	19	19
Arizona	19	19	19
Arkansas	21	21	21
California	21	21	21
Colorado	21	21	21[1]
Connecticut	18	18	18
Delaware	20	20	20
D.C.	21	21[2]	18
Florida	18	18	18
Georgia	19	19	19
Hawaii	18	18	18
Idaho	19	19	19
Illinois	21	21	21
Indiana	21	21	21
Iowa	19	19	19
Kansas	21	21	21[1]
Kentucky	21	21	21
Louisiana	18	18	18
Maine	20	20	20
Maryland	21	21[2]	18
Massachusetts	20	20	20
Michigan	21	21	21
Minnesota	19	19	19
Mississippi	21	21[2]	21[3]
Missouri	21	21	21
Montana	19	19	19
Nebraska	20	20	20
Nevada	21	21	21
New Hampshire	20	20	20
New Jersey	19	19	19
New Mexico	21	21	21
New York	18	18	18
North Carolina	21	21[4]	18
North Dakota	21	21	21
Ohio	21	21	21[1]
Oklahoma	21	21	21
Oregon	21	21	21
Pennsylvania	21	21	21
Rhode Island	18	18	18
South Carolina	21	18	18
South Dakota	21	21	21[1]
Tennessee	19	19	19
Texas	18	18	18
Utah	21	21	21
Vermont	18	18	18
Virginia	21	21	18
Washington	21	21	21
West Virginia	18	18	18
Wisconsin	18	18	18
Wyoming	19	19	19

1. 3.2 beer: 18. 2. Light wine: 18. 3. Up to 4% alcohol by weight: 18. 4. Up to 14% alcohol by weight: 18. *Source:* Distilled Spirits Council of the United States.

Selected Family Characteristics

Characteristics	1978 Number (thousands)	1978 Median income	1976 Median income
ALL RACES			
All families	57,804	$17,640	$14,958
Type of residence			
Nonfarm	55,753	17,732	15,065
Farm	2,051	15,284	11,663
Inside metropolitan areas	38,581	18,910	16,001
1,000,000 or more	21,586	19,835	16,771
Inside central cities	7,991	15,893	13,700
Outside central cities	13,595	21,746	18,419
Under 1,000,000	16,995	17,976	15,154
Inside central cities	7,642	16,625	14,198
Outside central cities	9,353	18,940	15,908
Outside metropolitan areas	19,223	15,287	12,831
Region			
Northeast	12,895	18,190	15,405
North Central	15,390	18,599	15,942
South	19,037	15,944	13,419
West	10,482	18,410	15,484
Type of family			
Male head	49,346	19,229	16,095
Married, wife present	47,692	19,340	16,203
Wife in paid labor force	23,005	22,109	18,731
Wife not in paid labor force	24,686	16,156	13,931
Other marital status	1,655	15,996	12,860
Female head	8,458	8,537	7,211
Number of earners[1]	57,095	17,710	15,001
No earners	7,028	6,718	5,689
1 Earner	18,346	14,239	12,436

Characteristics	1978 Number (thousands)	1978 Median income	1976 Median income
2 Earners	23,333	20,468	17,341
3 Earners	5,454	25,741	21,680
4 Earners or more	2,934	29,103	25,696
Size of family			
2 Persons	22,485	14,165	12,091
3 Persons	12,975	18,073	15,085
4 Persons	12,037	20,428	17,315
5 Persons	6,089	20,868	17,756
6 Persons	2,524	20,791	17,760
7 Persons or more	1,694	20,132	16,521
Employment status and occupation of head[2]			
Head in civilian labor force	44,561	20,144	16,853
Head employed	42,871	20,400	17,194
White-collar workers	20,133	23,683	20,163
Professional, technical and kindred workers	7,078	25,414	21,888
Salaried	6,359	25,100	21,423
Self-employed	719	31,417	28,565
Managers and administrators, except farm	6,883	25,722	21,563
Salaried	5,695	26,521	22,747
Self-employed	1,188	19,064	15,593
Sales workers	2,494	22,535	18,898
Clerical & kindred workers	3,678	17,640	15,377
Blue-collar workers	17,840	18,944	15,928
Craft and kindred workers	8,832	20,369	17,419
Operatives, incl. transport	7,146	18,155	14,835
Operatives, exc. transport	4,814	17,826	14,447
Transport equip. oper.	2,333	18,945	15,714
Laborers, except farm	1,861	15,522	13,455
Service workers	3,441	14,008	11,999
Private household workers	142	5,691	4,937
Service Workers, exc. private household	3,299	14,387	12,550
Farm workers	1,459	13,109	9,951
Farmers and farm managers	1,070	14,410	10,580
Farm lab. and supervisors	388	11,298	8,754
Head unemployed	1,689	11,342	10,120
Head not in civilian labor force	13,243	9,177	7,850
Tenure status[3]			
Owner occupied	43,037	20,017	16,897
Renter occupied	13,287	11,802	10,324
Occupier paid no cash rent	1,174	11,779	9,999
Total	57,498	17,707	15,003
Educational attainment of head			
Elementary	9,770	10,465	9,223
High school	26,002	17,434	14,907
College	18,195	23,766	20,499
1 to 3 years	8,150	20,421	17,759
4 Years or more	10,046	26,458	23,134
4 Years	5,422	25,529	22,019
5 Years or more	4,623	27,751	24,676
Total, 25 years and over	53,967	18,178	15,454
WHITE			
All families	50,910	18,368	15,537
Type of residence			
Nonfarm	48,951	18,471	15,646
Farm	1,959	15,562	12,129
Location of residence			
Inside metropolitan areas	33,265	19,862	16,767
1,000,000 or more	18,173	20,792	17,693
Inside central cities	5,544	17,486	15,083
Outside central cities	12,629	22,049	18,778
Under 1,000,000	15,092	18,657	15,646
Inside central cities	6,317	17,869	15,089
Outside central cities	8,774	19,206	16,068

Characteristics	1978 Number (thousands)	1978 Median income	1976 Median income
Outside metropolitan areas	17,645	15,792	13,318
Region			
Northeast	11,592	18,765	15,825
North Central	14,049	19,044	16,335
South	15,899	17,149	14,414
West	9,370	18,859	15,741
Type of family			
Male head	44,992	19,561	16,418
Married, wife present	43,636	19,638	16,501
Wife in paid labor force	20,624	22,372	19,047
Wife not in paid labor force	23,012	16,533	14,288
Other marital status	1,355	16,914	13,530
Female head	5,918	9,911	8,226
Number of earners[1]	50,312	18,432	15,571
No earners	5,937	7,395	6,184
1 Earner	15,940	15,223	13,123
2 Earners	20,913	20,745	17,643
3 Earners	4,883	26,150	22,265
4 Earners or more	2,640	29,430	25,986
BLACK			
All families	5,906	10,879	9,242
Type of residence			
Nonfarm	5,827	10,940	9,355
Farm	78	6,813	5,181
Location of residence			
Inside metropolitan areas	4,551	11,819	9,984
1,000,000 or more	2,913	12,274	10,501
Inside central cities	2,179	11,299	9,850
Outside central cities	733	15,668	12,343
Under 1,000,000	1,638	10,868	9,085
Inside central cities	1,202	9,869	8,294
Outside central cities	437	13,397	11,414
Outside metropolitan areas	1,355	8,814	7,435
Region			
Northeast	1,141	11,674	9,727
North Central	1,209	13,695	10,883
South	3,006	9,853	8,526
West	549	10,815	9,853
Type of family			
Male head	3,516	15,578	12,873
Married, wife present	3,244	15,913	13,137
Wife in paid labor force	1,934	19,073	15,703
Wife not in paid labor force	1,310	11,180	9,219
Other marital status	272	12,080	10,277
Female head	2,390	5,888	5,069
Number of earners[1]	5,824	10,820	9,264
No earners	1,002	3,870	3,699
1 Earner	2,111	8,462	7,394
2 Earners	2,016	16,798	14,275
3 Earners	474	19,723	15,946
4 Earners or more	222	25,398	18,933
SPANISH ORIGIN OF HEAD[4]			
All families	2,741	12,566	10,259
Type of residence			
Nonfarm	2,720	12,589	10,304
Farm	21	(B)	—
Location of residence			
Inside metropolitan areas	2,332	12,700	10,603
1,000,000 or more	1,504	12,712	10,775
Inside central cities	868	10,861	9,197
Outside central cities	635	15,509	13,187
Under 1,000,000	829	12,674	10,298
Inside central cities	531	12,439	9,757
Outside central cities	298	13,388	11,084
Outside metropolitan areas	409	11,675	9,069
Region			
Northeast	556	9,754	8,057

Characteristics	1978 Number (thousands)	1978 Median income	1976 Median income
North Central	239	14,460	12,679
South	847	12,400	10,138
West	1,099	13,709	11,220
Type of family			
Male head	2,199	14,528	11,820
Married, wife present	2,089	14,720	11,905
Wife in paid labor force	961	17,888	14,898
Wife not in paid labor force	1,128	11,812	9,908
Other marital status	110	12,051	9,350
Female head	542	5,578	5,118
Number of earners[1]	2,715	12,611	10,278
No earners	366	4,390	3,946
1 Earner	947	10,068	8,753
2 Earners	1,000	15,627	13,692
3 Earners	271	21,088	17,439
4 Earners or more	131	25,685	17,860

1. Excludes families with members in Armed Forces. 2. Employment status and occupation of householder as of March 1979. 3. Restricted to primary families. 4. Persons of Spanish origin may be of any race. *Source:* Department of Commerce, Bureau of the Census.

The Changing Family

The myth of the typical American family—white, middle-class, monogamous, father-at-work, mother-and-children-at-home family living in a suburban one-family house—is beginning to be confronted by the reality. It now effectively excludes more than half the population. With 8,236,000 families maintained by women in 1978, 16,715,000 persons living alone in 1978, and 42,002,000 women in the work force in 1978, it is obvious that the stereotype no longer fits the majority of Americans.

What is the reality?

Increasingly, single women are becoming responsible for maintaining their own families. Of the 8.2 million families maintained by women in 1978, 1.3 million have never been married. Between 1970 and 1978 the total number of female family households rose by 2.7 million, and single women accounted for one quarter of this growth.

More mothers work and so do more wives. By March 1978, more than half of all women with children under 18 years of age were in the labor force. The number of multi-earner husband-wife families has increased substantially. In March 1978, 27.5 million or 58% of all husband-wife families had more than one earner—a record 47.6% of all wives were working or looking for work.

The single population has risen as young people are postponing marriage and opting for alternative life-styles. Since 1970 the number of single men soared by 4.6 million, while that of single women rose by 3.3 million.

Alcohol and Accidents

Drinking is indicated as a factor in at least half of the fatal motor vehicle accidents, according to special studies. Males comprise nearly 80% of all fatalities involving drinking drivers, while females comprise over 20%. For persons of all ages injured in alcohol-related accidents, males represent almost three fourths of the total and females one fourth.

Door-to-Door Sales Regulations

The Federal Trade Commission (FTC) has a regulation that requires a "cooling off" period for door-to-door sales.

This rule requires that the sales person (1) inform consumers of their right to cancel the contract, (2) give consumers two copies of the cancellation form, and (3) give consumers a dated receipt or contract that shows the name and address of the seller.

Should a consumer decide to cancel the purchase, he or she must sign and date one copy of the form and mail it to the address given for cancellation any time before midnight of the third business day after the contract date.

This rule not only includes sales made at home, but also sales agreements made anywhere other than the seller's normal place of business, such as "parties" hosted in homes, and sales made in rented hotel rooms. It does not cover sales made totally by mail or phone; under $25.00; for real estate, insurance or securities; or for emergency home repairs.

The Year in Classical Music

Jacob Stern, Editor

In 1980, there were over 5,000 performances of standard operas in the U.S., testimony to the growing popularity of that musical form. Of perhaps greater significance, however, was the fact that, in addition, over 2,700 performances of contemporary American opera took place, demonstrating the increasing vitality of American music.

Important operatic "firsts" included the long-awaited premiere at the Metropolitan Opera of Kurt Weill's *Mahagonny*, the New York City Opera's production of his *Silverlake*, and the Santa Fe Opera's programming of three works by Arnold Schoenberg. The Santa Fe Opera gave Nino Rota (the composer of most of the music in Fellini's films) his premiere of *Italian Straw Hat*. A sensitive and gifted composer, Rota died during the year.

Opera on television became almost standard fare. The Metropolitan's telecast of *Manon Lescaut* was seen in 20 countries, thanks to satellite transmission. Weill's *Mahagonny* was also televised, and the Chicago Lyric Opera's *Faust* was a TV first for that fine company.

While Vladimir Horowitz continued to be the most popular concert artist, Luciano Pavarotti—yes, 1980 *was* an operatic year—conducted a master class on national television, appeared in a free concert in Central Park in New York before tens of thousands, and had even more recording best sellers. Isaac Stern recorded a major new violin concerto by Penderecki, the renowned contemporary Polish composer.

In conducting, there were significant changes: John Williams, composer of the music for *Star Wars, Jaws, Close Encounters*, and other movies, became conductor of the Boston Pops. Lorin Maazel became administrative and artistic director of the Vienna State Opera, the first American to hold the post. Eugene Ormandy retired as conductor of the Philadelphia Orchestra after 44 years.

And several famous conductors died: André Kostelanetz, Paul Paray, and Richard Franko Goldman. Nadia Boulanger, the great teacher who according to Aaron Copland, "knew all there was to know about music," died in France at the age of 92.

Finally, the secret autobiography of Dmitri Shostakovitch was smuggled out of the Soviet Union. It revealed the frustrations and difficulties faced by a great composer under an autocratic government.

The Year in Popular Music

Clive Davis

President, Arista Records

No modern decade in popular music has begun very auspiciously—in terms of era-defining trends—and 1980 was no exception. New ground was not broken, and no one style emerged as a dominant force. Nevertheless, the year proved very exciting in its transitional diversity. After waiting periods of up to four years, significant artists like Paul Simon, The Rolling Stones, Bruce Springsteen, Rod Stewart, Pink Floyd, The Allman Brothers Band, The Doobie Brothers, and Barbra Streisand released albums that ranked with their careers' finest. R&B stars such as Michael Jackson, Smokey Robinson, Aretha Franklin, George Benson, and Teddy Pendergrass hit new and important peaks. New wave rock gained an impressive foothold, melodic pop staged a renaissance, film drew on music to a greater extent than ever, country music took a giant step forward, and improved technology in the form of digital discs gave "high fidelity" meaning beyond all expectations.

In short, pop music has rarely been less focused, more pluralistic, or more challenging. Without one mass sound, all music is splintering, and innovating. The Commodores coexist with The B-52's; Dylan finds The Lord; Olivia Newton-John and ELO find Xanadu; John Lennon finds his way back to the recording studio; Linda Ronstadt goes from Elvis Costello to Gilbert & Sullivan; a 50-year-old country crooner with a beard and braids—Willie Nelson—becomes a cinematic sex symbol; and The Village People discover that you *can* stop the music, no matter how elaborately packaged and promoted.

One 1980 story was the superstar syndrome. At one point in midyear, more than 75% of the top-selling albums were by artists who had been in the record-making business for more than a decade. In a time of shrinking buying power, the consumer gravitated toward the familiar: to Paul McCartney, Elton John, The Jacksons (Michael and Jermaine), Kenny Rogers, The Eagles, Barry Manilow, Bob Seger, Billy Joel, Diana Ross, The Who's Peter Townshend, The Kinks, and the Grateful Dead. Even Frank Sinatra, with his first newly recorded album in many years, found a place in the top twenty.

At the same time, it was possible, if you had the

right sound, to make an immediate impact from left field. Blondie parlayed a blend of new wave, dance music and old-fashioned sex appeal into stardom. Tom Petty and The Heartbreakers broke through to album sales of over two million. Bluesrocker George Thorogood scored a gold LP on a small "independent" record label. Christopher Cross, Air Supply, Lipps Inc., Robbie Dupree, S.O.S. Band, Willie Nile, Benny Mardones, Gary Numan, The Clash, The Pretenders, Angela Bofill, and Shalamar—all virtually unknown in 1979—ended 1980 with their careers in high gear.

So there is cause for optimism. The record business is in the midst of change, both creatively and financially, and the process will mean surmounting pervasive industry-wide problems. But there is no need for the industry to panic, to get jittery, or to look to such outside stimuli as the videodisk to inject more vitality into the music. Music can, and will, speak for itself by itself.

Dance

Larry White

The year 1980 saw a number of firsts in the dance world. The Peking Opera of the People's Republic of China toured the U.S. for the first time, delighting audiences with its highly stylized performance. American Ballet Theatre presented the first complete production in the West of *La Bayadere*, the 19th century ballet by Marius Petipa, set on the company by Natalia Makarova.

The large list of Soviet defections by dancers was headed by Bolshoi Ballet principal Alexander Godunov, who left that company in New York, gained political asylum, and joined American Ballet Theatre, the reins of which were taken over by another Soviet defector, Mikhail Baryshnikov.

It was also a year for revivals. Two musicals in which dance plays a large role were revived on Broadway this year to critical and box-office success. One was *Oklahoma*, in which Agnes De Mille's dances are crucial in developing characters and relationships and in forwarding the action. The other, *West Side Story*, in which choreographer Jerome Robbins' blend of ethnic dance, jazz, and ballet catches the energy of an earlier period in New York, seems to speak equally well to today's audiences.

The Paul Taylor Dance Company premiered a major modern work, *Le Sacre du Printemps*, subtitled *The Rehearsal*, in which Stravinsky's music, reduced to a score for two pianos, hurtles forward the action of a murder mystery, as well as the rehearsal of a dance of that murder mystery by a dance company—all the while referring the audience back to the ritual events of the original, primitive choreography by Nijinsky.

Martha Graham presented a new work, *Judith*, at her company's season at the Metropolitan Opera. This is her third development of the story of the biblical heroine.

A number of new films took dance or dancers as their subject or as a background for the action. *All That Jazz* was choreographer-director Bob Fosse's confessional film autobiography. *Nijinsky*, starring George de la Pena, explored that great dancer's life and loves. And *Fame* took as its subject the lives of young dancers, actors, and musicians at New York's High School for the Performing Arts.

1981 The Year of Pavlova

The month of January 1981 marks the centenary of Anna Pavlova's birth and the 50th anniversary of her death. This legendary dancer, whose name means ballet even to those who have never seen a dance performance (as does the name Nijinsky), was born in St. Petersburg on January 31, 1881, and died in The Hague in the early hours of January 23, 1931.

The double anniversary is expected to launch many homages to her. In fact they had already begun before 1980 ended. The first was "Tribute to Pavlova" produced by George Daugherty for the Pendleton Festival Ballet and premiered at Indiana's Pendleton Festival during the summer, after which it toured major American cities.

A centenary that the dance world overlooked in 1980 was the birth of Michel Fokine, the father of modern ballet, who was born in St. Petersburg on April 22, 1880. He was responsible for Pavlova's signature piece, "The Dying Swan." Since the stage undoubtedly will be awash with dying swans during the Pavlova centenary, it must serve as a tribute to Fokine as well.

Museum Attendance Soars for Tut Exhibit

More than eight million people saw the King Tutankhamen exhibit before it ended its U.S. tour on September 30, 1979. Participating museums reported attendance as follows: National Gallery of Art, Washington, D.C. 832, 853; Field Museum of Natural History, Chicago, 1,349,724; New Orleans Museum of Art, 870,855; Los Angeles County Museum of Art, 1,250,629; Seattle Art Museum 1,293,203; Metropolitan Museum of Art, New York, 1,267,000; and The Fine Arts Museum of San Francisco M.H. de Young Memorial Museum, 1,360,000.

Top 10 Classical Albums, 1979

1. **Annie's Song,** James Galway, National Philharmonic Orchestra (Gerhardt), (RCA)
2. **Bravo Pavarotti,** Luciano Pavarotti (London)
3. **Hits from Lincoln Center,** Luciano Pavarotti (London)
4. **Suite for Violin & Jazz Piano,** Claude Bolling Zukerman/ Hediguer (Columbia)
5. **Pachalbel: Kanon,** Paillard Chamber Orchestra (Andre) (RCA)
6. **Suite for Flute & Jazz Piano,** Jean-Pierre Rampal & Claude Bolling (Columbia)
7. **Up in Central Park,** Beverly Sills, Milnes (Angel)
8. **Rampal: Japanese Melodies for Flute & Harp,** Jean-Pierre Rampal & Laskine (Columbia)
9. **Rachmaninoff: Concerto #3,** Horowitz, N.Y. Philharmonic (Ormandy) (RCA)
10. **Donizetti: Don Pasquale,** Sills, Kraus, Gramm, Caldwell (Angel)

Source: Billboard. © Billboard Publications, Inc., 1979. Dec. 22, 1979. Reprinted by permission.

Top 10 Country Single Recordings, 1979

1. **I Just Fall In Love Again,** Anne Murray (Capitol)
2. **If I Said You Had a Beautiful Body Would You Hold It Against Me,** Bellamy Brothers (Warner/ Curb)
3. **Amanda,** Waylon Jennings (RCA)
4. **Every Which Way But Loose,** Eddie Rabbitt (Elektra)
5. **Golden Tears,** Dave & Sugar (RCA)
6. **She Believes In Me,** Kenny Rogers (United Artists)
7. **The Gambler,** Kenny Rogers (United Artists)
8. **You're the Only One,** Dolly Parton (RCA)
9. **Sleeping Single in a Double Bed,** Barbara Mandrell (ABC)
10. **Why Have You Left the One You Left Me For,** Crystal Gayle (United Artists)

Source: Billboard. © Billboard Publications, Inc., 1979. Dec. 22, 1979. Reprinted by permission.

Top 10 Pop Albums, 1979

1. **52nd Street,** Billy Joel (Columbia)
2. **Spirits Having Flown,** Bee Gees (RSO)
3. **Minute By Minute,** Doobie Brothers (Warner Bros.)
4. **Cars,** Cars (Elektra)
5. **Breakfast in America,** Supertramp (A&M)
6. **Live and More,** Donna Summer (Casablanca)
7. **Pieces of Eight,** Styx (A&M)
8. **Bad Girls,** Donna Summer (Casablanca)
9. **Parallel Lines,** Blondie (Chrysalis)
10. **Blondes Have More Fun,** Rod Stewart (Warner Bros.)

Source: Billboard. © Billboard Publications, Inc., 1979. Dec. 22, 1979. Reprinted by permission.

Top 10 Pop Single Recordings, 1979

1. **My Sharona,** The Knack (Capitol)
2. **Bad Girls,** Donna Summer (Casablanca)
3. **Le Freak,** Chic (Atlantic)
4. **Do Ya Think I'm Sexy,** Rod Stewart (Warner Bros.)
5. **Reunited,** Peaches & Herb (Polydor/MVP)
6. **I Will Survive,** Gloria Gaynor (Polydor)
7. **Hot Stuff,** Donna Summer (Casablanca)
8. **Y.M.C.A.,** Village People (Casablanca)
9. **Ring My Bell,** Anita Ward (Juana)
10. **Sad Eyes,** Robert John (EMI-America)

Source: Billboard. © Billboard Publications, Inc., 1979. Dec. 22, 1979. Reprinted by permission.

Artists of the Year, 1979

Based on combined singles and albums chart performance—through sales and radio play—during the year.

Single of the Year: My Sharona, The Knack
Album of the Year: 52nd Street, Billy Joel
Female Artist of the Year: Donna Summer
Male Artist of the Year: Billy Joel
Group of the Year: Bee Gees
New Artist of the Year: The Knack
Soul Artist of the Year: Chic
Country Artist of the Year: Kenny Rogers
Disco Artist of the Year: Donna Summer
Adult Contemporary Artist of the Year: Al Stewart
Jazz Artist of the Year: The Crusaders
Soundtrack of the Year: Grease

Source: Billboard. © Billboard Publications, Inc., 1979. Dec. 22, 1979. Reprinted by permission.

Manufacturers' Dollar Shipments of Phonograph Records

(in millions)

	Singles		Albums	
Year	Units	Dollars[1]	Units	Dollars[1]
1974	204	$194	276	$1,356
1975	164	212	257	1,485
1976	190	245	273	1,663
1977	190	245	344	2,195
1978	190	260	341	2,473
1979	212	354	290	2,058

1. List price value. *Source:* Recording Industry Association of America, Inc.

Earth's Population Reaches 4.5 Billion

According to the Environmental Fund's population clock in Washington, D.C., the world's population reached 4.5 billion at 2:42 p.m. on March 14, 1980. It took over a million years for the world's population to reach a billion, 120 years to reach a second billion, 32 years for the third, and 15 years for the fourth billion.

Audience Composition of Selected Prime Time Program Types

(in millions)[1]

	General drama	Suspense and mystery drama	Situation comedy	Feature films	All regular network programs 8–11 p.m.[2]
Women (18 years old and over)	14.06	11.07	13.29	12.36	12.03
Men (18 and over)	9.34	8.79	9.66	10.13	10.05
Teens (12–17)	2.44	2.37	3.34	3.00	2.84
Children (2–11)	3.77	2.47	4.67	2.52	3.46
Total	**29.61**	**24.70**	**30.96**	**28.01**	**28.38**

1. All figures are estimated for the period November 1979. 2. 7–11 p.m. Sunday (EST). *Source:* A. C. Nielsen Company, Nielsen Television Index Audience Estimates.

Top 15 Regular Prime Time TV Programs of 1979–80[1]

Program name (network)	Total percent of TV households
60 Minutes (CBS)	28.8
Three's Company (ABC)	27.0
Alice (CBS)	26.1
M*A*S*H (CBS)	25.1
The Jeffersons (CBS)	24.9
Dallas (CBS)	24.5
One Day at a Time (CBS)	24.4
Eight is Enough (ABC)	23.7
Taxi (ABC)	23.6
Dukes of Hazzard (CBS)	23.4
Archie Bunker's Place (CBS)	23.1
Little House on the Prairie (NBC)	23.1
Charlie's Angels (ABC)	22.4
Trapper John, M.D. (CBS)	22.3
Happy Days (ABC)	21.9
Total U.S. TV Households	**76,300,000**

1. September 17, 1979 through January 27, 1980. NOTE: Percentages are calculated from average audience viewings. 15 minutes or longer and 4 or more telecasts. *Source:* A. C. Nielsen Company, Nielsen Television Index Audience Estimates.

1979–80 Season Miniseries Ratings

(Sept. 1, 1979 Through Aug. 31, 1980)

Rank	Title	Rating
1.	Guyana Tragedy: The Story Of Jim Jones (CBS)	30.3
2.	Scruples (CBS)	26.0
3.	Breaking Up Is Hard To Do (ABC)	21.0
4.	Flesh & Blood (CBS)	19.9
5.	The Martian Chronicles (NBC)	19.7
6.	The Last Convertible (NBC)	19.5
7.	Salem's Lot (CBS)	18.2
8.	Power (NBC)	17.0
	The Golden Moment: An Olympic Love Story (NBC)	17.0
10.	Freedom Road (NBC)	16.7
11.	The Awakening Land (R) (NBC)	16.6
12.	Holocaust (R) (NBC)	15.5
	Little Women (R) (NBC)	15.5
14.	Moviola (NBC)	15.3
15.	Jesus Of Nazareth (R) (NBC)	14.9

Source: Variety.

Television Network Addresses

American Broadcasting Company (ABC)
1330 Avenue of the Americas
New York, N.Y. 10019

Canadian Broadcasting Corporation (CBC)
1500 Bronson Avenue
Ottawa, Ontario, Canada K1G 3J5

Columbia Broadcasting System (CBS)
51 W. 52nd Street
New York, N.Y. 10019

Metromedia, Inc. (WNEW)
655 3rd Avenue
New York, N.Y. 10017

National Broadcasting Company (NBC)
30 Rockefeller Plaza
New York, N.Y. 10020

Public Broadcasting Service (PBS)
475 L'Enfant Plaza West, S.W.
Washington, D.C. 20024

Westinghouse Broadcasting (Group W)
90 Park Avenue
New York, N.Y. 10016

Weekly TV Viewing by Age
(in hours and minutes)

	Time per week 1979	1980
Women 18–24 years old	30 h 59 min	31 h 30 min
Women 25–54	35 h 21 min	36 h 02 min
Women 55 and over	40 h 28 min	41 h 04 min
Men 18–24	23 h 53 min	23 h 42 min
Men 25–54	27 h 06 min	28 h 46 min
Men 55 and over	35 h 35 min	37 h 54 min
Female Teens	24 h 11 min	24 h 10 min
Male Teens	24 h 03 min	25 h 28 min
Children 6–11	29 h 03 min	28 h 14 min
Children 2–5	32 h 47 min	29 h 35 min
Total Persons	**31 h 19 min**	**32 h 00 min**

NOTE: All figures are estimates based on National Audience Demographics Report, February 1979 and 1980. *Source:* A. C. Nielsen Company, Nielsen Television Index Audience Estimates.

Persons Viewing Nightly Prime Time TV[1]
(in millions)

	Total persons[2]
Monday	92.06
Tuesday	86.68
Wednesday	87.63
Thursday	83.89
Friday	84.69
Saturday	86.77
Sunday	104.70
Total average	**89.74**

1. Average minute audiences. 2. Based on National Demographics Report (November 1979). NOTE: Prime time is 8-11 p.m. (EST), except 7-11 p.m. Sunday. *Source:* A. C. Nielsen Company, Nielsen Television Index Audience Estimates.

Average Hours of Household TV Usage
(in hours and minutes per day)

	Yearly average	February	July
1978–79	6 h 26 min	7 h 11 min	5 h 46 min
1977–78	6 h 13 min	7 h 00 min	5 h 32 min
1976–77	6 h 13 min	6 h 55 min	5 h 13 min
1975–76	6 h 11 min	6 h 49 min	5 h 33 min
1970–71	6 h 01 min	6 h 53 min	5 h 08 min

NOTE: Estimates are based on total U.S. TV households, excluding unusual days; September-August 1979 average. *Source:* A. C. Nielsen Company, Nielsen Television Index Audience Estimates.

TOP RENTAL FILMS OF 1979

1. Superman (Warner Bros.)	$81,000,000
2. Every Which Way But Loose (Warner Bros.)	48,000,000
3. Rocky II (United Artists)	43,049,274
4. Alien (20th Century-Fox)	40,086,573
5. The Amityville Horror (American International Pictures)	35,000,000
6. Star Trek (Paramount)	35,000,000
7. Moonraker (United Artists)	33,934,074
8. The Muppet Movie (Associated Film Distribution)	32,000,000
9. California Suite (Columbia)	29,200,000
10. The Deer Hunter (Universal)	26,927,000
11. The Main Event (Warner Bros.)	26,000,000
12. The China Syndrome (Columbia)	25,425,000
13. 10 (Orion)	25,000,000
14. Apocalypse Now (United Artists)	22,855,657
15. Escape From Alcatraz (Paramount)	21,014,000
16. Meatballs (Paramount)	19,674,000
17. Love at First Bite (American International Pictures)	18,100,000
18. The In-Laws (Warner Bros.)	18,000,000
19. Manhattan (United Artists)	16,908,439
20. Starting Over (Paramount)	15,201,000
21. North Dallas Forty (Paramount)	14,062,000
22. The Jerk (Universal)	14,000,000
23. Lord of the Rings (United Artists)	13,487,243
24. Magic (20th Century-Fox)	13,081,000
25. The Champ (United Artists)	12,500,000

NOTE: United States and Canada only. *Source: Variety.*

Terrorist Attacks on U.S. Business Rise Sharply

Business and its employees have become the major target of international terrorism. Between 1970 and 1978, 55% of Americans kidnapped overseas were business executives. Diplomats represented 28% of those kidnapped, followed by military and police officers (8%), and news personnel (4%).

Ransom demands have risen from under $1 million in 1972 to 12 cases in 1978 where ransom demands reached $1 million or over. A $5-million to $10-million ransom is now the norm.

Kidnap victims stand a fairly high chance of survival. Most victims are released within a month after their abduction.

Major Emmy Awards for TV, 1980

Drama series: *Lou Grant* (CBS)
Actress: Barbara Bel Geddes, *Dallas* (CBS)
Actor: Ed Asner, *Lou Grant* (CBS)
Supporting actress: Nancy Marchand, *Lou Grant* (CBS)
Supporting actor: Stuart Margolin, *Rockford Files* (NBC)
Comedy series: *Taxi* (ABC)
Actress: Cathryn Damon, *Soap* (ABC)
Actor: Richard Mulligan, *Soap* (ABC)
Comedy, comedy-variety, or music series, supporting actress: Loretta Swit, *M*A*S*H* (CBS)
Supporting actor: Harry Morgan, *M*A*S*H* (CBS)
Limited series or special: *Edward & Mrs. Simpson* (syndicated by Mobil Showcase Network)
Actress: Patty Duke Astin, *The Miracle Worker* (NBC)
Actor: Powers Boothe, *Guyana Tragedy* (CBS)
Supporting actress: Mare Winningham, *Amber Waves* (ABC)
Supporting actor: George Grizzard, *The Oldest Living Graduate* (NBC)
Drama or comedy special: *The Miracle Worker* (NBC)
Comedy-variety or music program: *IBM Presents Baryshnikov on Broadway* (ABC)
Animated program: *Carlton Your Doorman* (CBS)
Information program: *The Body Human: The Magic Sense* (CBS)
Classical program in the performing arts: *Live from Studio 8H; A Tribute to Toscanini* (NBC)
Special events program: *The 34th Annual Tony Awards* (CBS)
Special class program: *Fred Astaire: Change Partners and Dance* (PBS)
Information program, Individual Achievement: *Dive to the Edge of Creation—A National Geographic Special* (PBS) *Mysteries of the Sea, and The Body Human: The Body Beautiful* (CBS)

Plays and Movies

LONGEST BROADWAY RUNS[1]

1. Grease (M) (1972–80)	3,388
2. Fiddler on the Roof (M) (1964–72)	3,242
3. Life With Father (1939–47)	3,224
4. Tobacco Road (1933–41)	3,182
5. Hello, Dolly! (M) (1964–71)	2,844
6. My Fair Lady (M) (1956–62)	2,717
7. Man of La Mancha (M) (1965–71)	2,329
8. Abie's Irish Rose (1922–27)	2,327
9. Oklahoma! (M) (1943–48)	2,212
10. A Chorus Line (M) (1975–)	2,139
11. South Pacific (M) (1949–54)	1,925
12. Pippin (M) (1971–77)	1,908
13. The Magic Show (M) (1974–78)	1,859
14. Harvey (1944–49)	1,775
15. Hair (M) (1968–72)	1,742
16. The Wiz (M) (1975–79)	1,672
17. Born Yesterday (1946–49)	1,642
18. Mary, Mary (1961–64)	1,572
19. Voice of the Turtle (1943–48)	1,557
20. Barefoot in the Park (1963–67)	1,532
21. Mame (M) (1966–70)	1,503
22. Annie (M) (1977–)	1,445
23. Same Time, Next Year (1975–78)	1,444
24. Arsenic and Old Lace (1941–44)	1,444
25. The Sound of Music (M) (1959–63)	1,443

TOP MONEY-MAKING FILMS[2]

1. Star Wars (1977)	$175,849,013
2. Jaws (1975)	133,429,000
3. Grease (1978)	93,292,000
4. The Exorcist (1973)	88,100,000
5. The Godfather (1972)	86,275,000
6. Superman (1978)	81,000,000
7. The Sound of Music (1965)	79,000,000
8. The Sting (1973)	78,889,000
9. Close Encounters of the Third Kind (1977)	77,000,000
10. Gone With the Wind (1939)	76,700,000
11. Saturday Night Fever (1977)	73,522,000
12. National Lampoon Animal House (1978)	63,471,000
13. Smokey and the Bandit (1977)	61,017,000
14. One Flew Over the Cuckoo's Nest (1975)	59,000,000
15. American Graffiti (1973)	55,886,000
16. Rocky (1976)	54,000,000
17. Jaws II (1978)	50,569,000
18. Love Story (1970)	50,000,000
19. The Towering Inferno (1975)	50,000,000
20. The Graduate (1968)	49,078,000
21. Every Which Way But Loose (1978)	48,000,000
22. Heaven Can Wait (1978)	47,552,000
23. Doctor Zhivago (1965)	46,550,000
24. Butch Cassidy and the Sundance Kid (1969)	46,039,000
25. Airport (1970)	45,300,000

1. As of Oct. 5, 1980. M = musical. Years are those of opening and closing. 2. Figures are rentals collected by film distributors in the U.S. and Canada as of Dec. 31, 1979. *Source: Variety.*

Hollywood on the Hudson

After years of neglect by the film industry, movie-making has made a comeback to New York City, where it all began. The historic Astoria Studios in Queens, reopened in 1977, are now the largest such facility on the East Coast. More recently the old Vitagraph Studios in Brooklyn have been restored to use.

In 1977, 26 feature films were shot in New York. In 1978, the number has grown to 40; in 1979, to 59. In the first six months of 1980, 39 films had been filmed in the city.

Notable Books, 1979

This list has been compiled by the Notable Books Council of the American Library Association for use by the general reader and by librarians who work with adult readers. The titles were selected for their significant contribution to the expansion of knowledge or for the pleasure they can provide to adult readers. Criteria include wide general appeal and literary merit.

Adams, Alice. **Beautiful Girl: Stories.** Knopf.
Blythe, Ronald. **The View in Winter: Reflections on Old Age.** Harcourt.
Conot, Robert. **A Streak of Luck.** Seaview.
Drucker, Peter F. **Adventures of a Bystander.** Harper.
Edel, Leon. **Bloomsbury: A House of Lions.** Lippincott & Crowell.
Epstein, Helen. **Children of the Holocaust: Conversations with Sons and Daughters of Survivors.** Putnam.
Epstein, Leslie. **King of the Jews.** Coward, McCann.
Ferlinghetti, Lawrence. **Landscapes of Living & Dying.** New Directions.
Fraser, Antonia. **Royal Charles: Charles II and the Restoration.** Knopf.
Haviaras, Stratis. **When the Tree Sings.** Simon & Schuster.
Hendricks, Gordon. **The Life and Work of Winslow Homer.** Abrams.
Hoagland, Edward. **African Calliope: A Journey to the Sudan.** Random.
Hoffman, Alice. **The Drowning Season.** Dutton.
Hoffman, Daniel, Ed. **Harvard Guide to Contemporary American Writing.** Harvard.
Kendall, Elizabeth. **Where She Danced: American Dancing 1880–1930.** Knopf.
Keneally, Thomas. **Passenger.** Harcourt.
Kunitz, Stanley. **The Poems of Stanley Kunitz, 1928–1978.** Atlantic-Little, Brown.
Lasch, Christopher. **The Culture of Narcissism: American Life in an Age of Diminishing Expectations.** Norton.
Le Roy Ladurie, Emmanuel. **Carnival in Romans.** Braziller.
Levine, Philip. **7 Years from Somewhere: Poems.** Atheneum.
Lewis, Norman. **Naples '44.** Pantheon.
Litwack, Leon. **Been in the Storm So Long: The Aftermath of Slavery.** Knopf.
Lorenz, Konrad. **The Year of the Greylag Goose.** Harcourt.
Lottman, Herbert. **Albert Camus: Biography.** Doubleday.
Mailer, Norman. **The Executioner's Song.** Little, Brown.
Malamud, Bernard. **Dubin's Lives.** Farrar.
Morgan, Dan. **Merchants of Grain.** Viking.
Morowitz, Harold J. **The Wine of Life and Other Essays on Societies, Energy, and Living Things.** St. Martin's.
Morris, Edmund. **The Rise of Theodore Roosevelt.** Coward, McCann.
Munro, Alice. **The Beggar Maid: Stories of Flo and Rose.** Knopf.
Oates, Joyce Carol. **Unholy Loves: A Novel.** Vanguard.
O'Connor, Flannery. **The Habit of Being: Letters.** Farrar.
Pearson, John. **The Sitwells: A Family's Biography.** Harcourt.
Pritchett, V.S. **The Myth Makers: Literary Essays.** Random.
Puig, Manuel. **Kiss of the Spider Woman.** Knopf.
Roth, Philip. **The Ghost Writer.** Farrar.
Ryan, Cornelius and Ryan, Kathryn Morgan. **A Private Battle.** Simon & Schuster.
Shawcross, William. **Sideshow: Kissinger, Nixon and the Destruction of Cambodia.** Simon & Schuster.
Spencer, Scott. **Endless Love.** Knopf.
Steinfels, Peter. **The Neoconservatives: The Men Who Are Changing America's Politics.** Simon & Schuster.
Stobaugh, Robert and Yergin, Daniel, Ed. **Energy Future: Report of the Energy Project at the Harvard Business School.** Random.
Tafel, Edgar. **Apprentice to Genius: Years with Frank Lloyd Wright.** McGraw-Hill.
Thomas, Gordon and Morgan-Witts, Max. **The Day the Bubble Burst: A Social History of the Wall Street Crash of 1929.** Doubleday.
Updike, John. **The Coup.** Knopf.
Problems and Other Stories. Knopf.
Vonnegut, Kurt. **Jailbird: A Novel.** Delacorte.
Walcott, Derek. **The Star-Apple Kingdom.** Farrar.
Wolfe, Tom. **The Right Stuff.** Farrar.

Source: Reprinted by permission of the American Library Association. Issued as a pamphlet by ALA, 50 E. Huron St., Chicago, Ill. 60611, annually in the spring for the preceding year.

Major U.S. Symphony Orchestras and Their Conductors

Source: American Symphony Orchestra League.

Atlanta Symphony: Robert Shaw
Baltimore Symphony: Sergiu Comissiona
Boston Symphony: Seiji Ozawa
Buffalo Philharmonic: Julius Rudel[1]
Chicago Symphony: Georg Solti
Cincinnati Symphony: Walter Susskind
Cleveland Orchestra: Lorin Maazel
Dallas Symphony: Eduardo Mata
Denver Symphony: Gaetano Delogu
Detroit Symphony: Antal Dorati
Honolulu Symphony: Donald Johanos
Houston Symphony: Sergiu Comissiona[2]
Indianapolis Symphony: John Nelson
Kansas City Philharmonic: Maurice Peress
Los Angeles Philharmonic: Carlo Maria Giulini
Milwaukee Symphony: Kenneth Schermerhorn
Minnesota Orchestra: Neville Marriner[1]
National Symphony (Washington, D.C.): Mstislav Rostropovich
New Jersey Symphony: Thomas Michalak
New Orleans Philharmonic Symphony Orchestra: Philippe Entremont[3]
New York Philharmonic: Zubin Mehta
North Carolina Symphony: John Gosling
Philadelphia Orchestra: Riccardo Muti[1]
Pittsburgh Symphony: André Previn
Rochester Philharmonic: David Zinman
Saint Louis Symphony: Leonard Slatkin
San Antonio Symphony: Lawrence Smith[1]
San Francisco Symphony: Edo de Waart
Seattle Symphony: Rainer Miedel
Syracuse Symphony: Christopher Keene
Utah Symphony: Varujan Kojian[1]

1. Musical director. 2. Artistic advisor. 3. Musical advisor.

Major Public Libraries

(City (branches)	Volumes	Circulation	Budget (in millions)
Akron, Ohio (18)	940,184	2,091,196	$ 3.9
Albuquerque, N.M. (6)	327,392	1,384,732	1.9
Annapolis, Md. (12)	526,592	3,063,780	3.5
Atlanta (27)	979,195	2,248,313	5.0
Austin, Tex. (14)	638,655	2,205,537	3.8
Baltimore (34)	2,251,953	2,348,178	9.8
Baton Rouge, La. (8)	360,259	1,011,353	1.3
Birmingham, Ala. (18)	1,017,570	2,047,866	3.6
Buffalo, N.Y. (60)	3,205,191	5,455,117	11.1
Charleston, W.Va.	492,537	991,136	1.5
Charlotte, N.C. (15)	680,656	1,785,669	3.5
Chicago (85)	6,163,240	6,608,290	28.0
Cincinnati (37)	3,242,497	5,654,005	8.7
Cleveland (34)	2,541,876	2,929,777	15.0
Columbus, Ohio (21)	1,217,545	3,084,857	6.6
Dallas (17)	1,893,553	3,573,391	7.9
Dayton, Ohio (19)	1,354,488	4,441,967	4.6
Des Moines, Iowa (5)	427,445	1,139,141	1.6
Denver (21)	1,709,563	2,840,061	7.6
Detroit (26)	2,507,495	2,022,007	15.5
D.C. (28)	1,413,275	1,371,084	9.9
El Paso (8)	428,912	976,830	2.1
Erie, Pa. (6)	383,644	1,138,535	1.3
Evansville, Ind. (7)	491,063	1,355,116	1.5
Fort Wayne, Ind. (12)	1,615,133	1,364,273	3.4
Fort Worth (7)	758,452	2,259,338	2.5
Grand Rapids, Mich. (5)	593,076	753,957	1.8
Greenville, S.C. (10)	429,442	1,102,501	2.4
Honolulu (21)	1,297,306	3,487,439	4.5
Houston (30)	2,282,945	5,503,313	11.8
Independence, Mo. (24)	1,099,953	3,015,276	3.7
Indianapolis (24)	1,343,669	3,495,641	7.0
Jackson, Miss.	810,644	1,393,843	2.3
Jacksonville, Fla. (10)	848,264	1,747,943	3.0
Kansas City, Mo. (13)	1,204,000	698,429	3.9
Knoxville, Tenn. (19)	532,904	1,558,981	1.8
Lincoln, Neb. (10)	450,077	1,044,438	1.8
Long Beach, Calif. (10)	734,009	1,722,600	5.3
Los Angeles	4,000,214	9,200,000	25.3
Louisville, Ky. (23)	995,170	1,894,736	5.2

City (branches)	Volumes	Circulation	Budget (in millions)
Madison, Wis. (7)	531,572	1,870,507	$ 3.0
Memphis, Tenn. (21)	1,608,845	2,593,506	6.1
Miami, Fla. (20)	1,587,079	2,926,625	10.6
Milwaukee (12)	2,322,999	2,790,124	9.5
Minneapolis (14)	1,520,085	2,288,991	8.5
Nashville, Tenn. (15)	505,595	1,536,522	2.9
New Orleans (11)	760,664	1,099,425	3.2
New York City (83)	3,698,008	9,164,156	30.8
Research	6,419,353	0	21.1
Brooklyn (58)	3,573,673	6,915,959	17.1
Queens (56)	3,853,469	6,128,948	20.3
Newark, N.J. (12)	1,187,479	1,790,291	4.2
Norfolk, Va. (11)	634,455	1,146,468	2.4
Oklahoma City (11)	611,087	1,701,453	2.5
Omaha, Neb. (9)	543,627	1,691,598	2.5
Philadelphia (52)	2,913,935	4,840,059	19.4
Phoenix, Ariz. (9)	1,125,653	3,245,847	5.3
Pittsburgh (21)	1,984,239	2,942,141	6.9
Portland, Ore. (16)	1,110,186	2,945,611	4.8
Providence, R.I. (8)	625,004	549,059	2.3
Richmond, Va. (6)	614,981	1,047,915	1.6
Rochester, N.Y. (11)	885,214	1,495,655	4.6
Sacramento, Calif.			
St. Louis (18)	1,364,930	1,540,820	4.9
St. Paul (10)	760,009	1,727,639	2.6
St. Petersburg, Fla. (2)	415,671	1,203,157	1.3
Salt Lake City, Utah (13)	655,773	2,339,302	4.1
San Antonio (9)	1,496,128	3,302,402	3.3
San Diego, Calif. (29)	1,612,786	3,936,594	5.0
San Francisco (26)	1,667,139	2,424,949	7.8
San Jose, Calif. (16)	930,000	2,375,000	4.2
Seattle (22)	1,515,680	4,270,197	8.3
Springfield, Mass. (8)	690,056	942,174	2.5
Tampa, Fla. (14)	891,825	1,985,474	4.5
Tucson, Ariz. (15)	800,000	3,200,000	5.5
Tulsa, Okla. (20)	779,673	1,672,242	2.6
Wichita, Kan. (11)	396,043	1,015,799	2.1
Winston–Salem, N.C.	320,000	1,313,000	1.8
Worcester, Mass. (6)	899,165	814,595	2.3
Youngstown, Ohio (23)	730,006	1,511,345	3.1

Source: Information Please questionnaires to the libraries.

Glossary of Art Movements

Abstract Expressionism. American art movement of the 1940s that emphasized form and color within a nonrepresentational framework. Jackson Pollock initiated the revolutionary technique of splattering the paint directly on canvas to achieve the subconscious interpretation of the artist's inner vision of reality.

Art Deco. A 1920s style characterized by setbacks, zigzag forms, and the use of chrome and plastic ornamentation. New York's Chrysler Building is an architectural example of the style.

Art Nouveau. An 1890s style in architecture, graphic arts, and interior decoration characterized by writhing forms, curving lines, and asymmetrical organization. Some critics regard the style as the first stage of modern architecture.

Ashcan School. A group of New York realist artists, formed in 1908, who abandoned decorous subject matter and portrayed the more common as well as the sordid aspects of city life.

Assemblage (Collage). Forms of modern sculpture and painting utilizing readymades, found objects, and pasted fragments to form an abstract composition. Louise Nevelson's boxlike enclosures, each with its own composition of assembled objects, illustrate the style in sculpture. Pablo Picasso developed the technique of cutting and pasting natural or manufactured materials to a painted or unpainted surface.

Barbizon School (Landscape Painting). A group of painters who, around the middle of the 19th century, reacted against classical landscape and advocated a direct study of nature. They were influenced by English and Dutch landscape masters. Theodore Rousseau, one of the principal figures of the group, led the fight for outdoor painting. In this respect, the school was a forerunner of Impressionism.

Baroque. European art and architecture of the 17th and 18th centuries. Giovanni Bernini, a major exponent of the style, believed in the union of the arts of architecture, painting, and sculpture to overwhelm the spectator with ornate and highly dramatized themes. Although the style originated in Rome as the instrument of the Church, it spread throughout Europe in such monumental creations as the Palace of Versailles.

Beaux Arts. Elaborate and formal architectural style characterized by symmetry and an abundance of sculptured ornamentation. New York's old Custom House at Bowling Green is an example of the style.

Black or Afro-American Art. The work of American artists of African descent produced in various styles characterized by a mood of protest and a search for identity and historical roots.

Classicism. A form of art derived from the study of Greek and Roman styles characterized by harmony, balance, and serenity. In contrast, the Romantic Movement gave free rein to the artist's imagination and to the love of the exotic.

Constructivism. A form of sculpture using wood, metal, glass, and modern industrial materials expressing the technological society. The mobiles of Alexander Calder are examples of the movement.

Cubism. Early 20th-century French movement marked by a revolutionary departure from representational art. Pablo Picasso and Georges Bracque penetrated the surface of objects, stressing basic abstract geometric forms that presented the object from many angles simultaneously.

Dada. A product of the turbulent and cynical post-World War I period, this anti-art movement extolled the irrational, the absurd, the nihilistic, and the nonsensical. The reproduction of *Mona Lisa* adorned with a mustache is a famous example. The movement is regarded as a precursor of Surrealism. Some critics regard HAPPENINGS as a recent development of Dada. This movement incorporates environment and spectators as active and important ingredients in the production of random events.

Expressionism. A 20th-century European art movement that stresses the expression of emotion and the inner vision of the artist rather than the exact representation of nature. Distorted lines and shapes and exaggerated colors are used for emotional impact. Vincent Van Gogh is regarded as the precursor of this movement.

Fauvism. The name "wild beasts" was given to this group of early 20th-century French painters because their work was characterized by distortion and violent colors. Henri Matisse and Georges Rouault were leaders of this group.

Futurism. This early 20th-century movement originating in Italy glorified the machine age and attempted to represent machines and figures in motion. The aesthetics of Futurism affirmed the beauty of technological society.

Genre. This French word meaning "type" now refers to paintings that depict scenes of everyday life without any attempt at idealization. Genre paintings can be found in all ages, but the Dutch productions of peasant and tavern scenes are typical.

Impressionism. Late 19th-century French school dedicated to defining transitory visual impressions painted directly from nature, with light and color of primary importance. If the atmosphere changed, a totally different picture would emerge. It was not the object or event that counted but the visual impression as caught at a certain time of day under a certain light. Claude Monet and Camille Pissarro were leaders of the movement.

Mannerism. A 17th-century movement, Italian in origin, although El Greco was a major practitioner of the style. The human figure, distorted and elongated, was the most frequent subject.

Neoclassicism. An 18th-century reaction to the excesses of Baroque and Rococo, this European art movement tried to recreate the art of Greece and Rome by imitating the ancient classics both in style and subject matter.

Op Art. The 1960s movement known as Optical Painting is characterized by geometrical forms that create an optical illusion in which the eye is required to blend the colors at a certain distance.

Pop Art. In this return to representational art, the artist returns to the world of tangible objects in a reaction against abstraction. Materials are drawn from the everyday world of popular culture—comic strips, canned goods, and science fiction.

Rococo. A French style of interior decoration developed during the reign of Louis XV consisting mainly of asymmetrical arrangements of curves in paneling, porcelain, and gold and silver objects. The characteristics of ornate curves, prettiness, and gaiety can also be found in the painting and sculpture of the period.

Surrealism. A further development of Collage, Cubism, and Dada, this 20th-century movement stresses the weird, the fantastic, and the dreamworld of the subconscious. Salvador Dali's distorted timepiece in the desert is typical.

Picasso Exhibit A Sell-Out

From the time the Pablo Picasso retrospective exhibition opened at the Museum of Modern Art in New York City on May 22, 1980, until it closed on September 30, approximately 700,000 people had viewed it. All of the tickets for the showing had been sold before the closing date.

Museums of the United States

Source: Information Please questionnaires to museums

New York City

American Academy and Institute of Arts and Letters: 633 W. 155th St., NYC 10032. Open: Tues.-Sun. 1–4 during exhibitions (closed Mon. and natl. hldys.). Free.
Annual exhibitions of work of recipients of awards and honors, and paintings eligible for purchase under Hassam and Speicher Funds. Memorial exhibition of work of deceased members.

American Museum of Natural History: Central Park West at 79th St., NYC 10024. Open: Mon., Tues., Thurs., Fri. 10–4:45, Wed. 10–9, Sat., Sun., and hldys. 10–5 (closed Thanksgiving, Dec. 25).
All branches of natural sciences with exhibits including astronomy at American Museum-Hayden Planetarium.

Brooklyn Museum, The: 188 Eastern Pkwy., Brooklyn, N.Y. 11238. Open: Wed.-Sat. 10–5, Sun. 12–5, hldys. 1–5 (closed Jan. 1, Dec. 25). Suggested voluntary admission fee, $1.50; children under 12 and senior citizens, free.
Egyptian and classical art, American and European paintings, decorative arts and period rooms, prints, drawings, costumes, and textiles. Arts of Africa, Oceania, Orient, Middle East, Islam, and New World. Two reference libraries, sculpture garden.

Cloisters, The: Ft. Tryon Pk., NYC 10040. Open: wkdys. 10–4:45 (closed Mon.), Sun. and hldys. 1–4:45 (May-Sept. 12–4:45). Suggested voluntary admission fee.
Cloisters, chapel, chapter house, apse. The various cloisters are reconstituted from elements of 12–15th-century French cloisters. Apse has been relocated here in its entirety. Frescoes, polychromed statues, stained glass, tapestries, paintings, ivories, precious metalwork. Medieval branch of The Metropolitan Museum of Art.

Cooper-Hewitt Museum, the Smithsonian Institution's National Museum of Design: 2 E. 91st St., NYC 10028. Open: Tues. 10–9, Wed.-Sat. 10–5, Sun. 12–5 (closed Mon.; also Jan. 1, July 4, Thanksgiving, Dec. 25). Adm. $1.50 (free on Tues. after 5:30).
Over 300,000 decorative arts objects and related library housed in 64-room former Carnegie mansion.

Frick Collection: 1 E. 70th St., NYC 10021. Open: Sept.-May—Tues.-Sat. 10–6, Sun. and most hldys. 1–6 (closed Mon.; also Jan. 1, Thanksgiving, Dec. 24–25); June-Aug.—Sun. 1–6, Wed.-Sat. 10–6 (closed Mon. and Tues.; also July 4). Adm. Tues.-Sat. $1 (students and senior citizens, 50¢); Sun. $2. Children under 10 not admitted.
Paintings, prints, drawings of 14th to 19th centuries, Italian Renaissance and French sculpture and furniture. Chinese and French porcelain. Concerts, lectures.

Guggenheim Museum, The Solomon R.: 1071 Fifth Ave. at 88th St., NYC 10028. Open: Tues. 11–8; Wed.-Sun. and hldys. 11–5 (closed Mon., except hldys., and Dec. 25). Adm. $1.50 (children under 7, free). Tues. 5–8 free. College students with ID's, and senior citizens, 75¢; school children in groups of 10 with a teacher, 50¢.
Works of leading 20th-century foreign and American painters and sculptors.

Hayden Planetarium. *See* American Museum of Natural History.

Hispanic Society of America, The (Museum and Library): Broadway and W. 155th St., NYC 10032. Museum open: Tues.-Sat. 10–4:30, Sun. 1–4 (closed Mon.; also Jan. 1, Feb. 12, Feb. 22, Good Friday, Easter, May 30, July 4, Oct. 12, Thanksgiving, Dec. 25). During Christmas Week, museum is open for three consecutive days from Dec. 26 through Dec. 31. Library open: Tues.-Fri. 1–4:30, Sat. 10:30–4:30 (closed Sun., Mon.; also hldys., Good Friday, month of Aug., and for two weeks beginning Tues. before Christmas Eve). Free.
Paintings, sculpture, decorative arts, manuscripts, and incunabula, representative of Hispanic culture. Works on Hispanic art, history, literature.

Jewish Museum, The: 1109 Fifth Ave. at 92nd St., NYC 10028. Open: Mon.-Thurs., 12–5, Sun. 11–6 (closed Fri. and Sat., also Jewish hldys.). Adm. $2 (children 6–16 and students with ID's, $1). Members, free; senior citizens, pay what you wish.
Former Warburg mansion and adjoining Albert A. List building house most extensive collection of Jewish ceremonial objects in U.S. Changing exhibitions of sculpture, paintings, photography and architecture illuminate Jewish experience, culture, and tradition. Also children's programs.

Metropolitan Museum of Art, The: Fifth Ave. at 82nd St., NYC 10028. Open: Tues. 10–8:45, Wed.-Sat. 10–4:45, Sun. and hldys. 11–4:45 (closed Mon.). Discretionary admission fee.
Comprehensive collection of European and American paintings, drawings, sculpture, decorative arts, prints. Egyptian, Greek, Roman, Islamic, and Near and Far Eastern art. Musical instruments, arms and armor. European period rooms. Costumes and textiles. See also *Cloisters.*

Museum of the American Indian, Heye Foundation: Broadway at 155th St., NYC 10032. Open: Tues.-Sat. 10–5; Sun. 1–5 (closed Mon., also Jan. 1, Easter, July 4, Thanksgiving, Dec. 25). Adm. $1.50 (students and senior citizens, 75¢); groups of 10 or more, 25¢ per person.
Archeology, ethnology, and primitive-to-20th-century arts and artifacts of North, Central, and South America.

Museum of the City of New York: 1220 Fifth Ave. at 103rd St., NYC 10029. Open: Tues.-Sat. 10–5, Sun. and hldys. 1–5 (closed Mon.; also Dec. 25). Free.
History and life of New York City. Period costumes, furniture, miniature scenes, portraits, paintings, prints, manuscripts, theater and music collection, silver, dolls and doll houses.

Museum of Modern Art, The: 11 W. 53rd St., NYC 10019. Open: Mon., Tues., Fri., Sat. and Sun. 11–6, Thurs. 11–9 (closed Wed.; also Dec. 25). Adm. $2.50 (full-time students with ID's, $1.50; children and senior citizens, 75¢; members, free). Tuesday, pay what you wish.
Founded 1929 to help people enjoy and understand the art of our times. Changing exhibitions of contemporary painting, sculpture, drawings, prints, photography, architecture, industrial and graphic design, films.

National Academy of Design: 1083 Fifth Ave. at 89th St., NYC 10028. Open: Tues.-Sun. 12–5.

Exhibitions from permanent collection of American paintings, sculptures and graphics; exhibitions of contemporary art.

New-York Historical Society: 170 Central Park West at 77th St., NYC 10024. Museum open; Tues.-Fri. 11–5, Sat. 10–5, Sun. 1–5. Library open to adults: Tues.-Sat. 10–5. (Both closed Mon.; also Jan. 1, July 4, Thanksgiving, Dec. 25). Library adm. $1 to nonmembers; museum, discretionary fee of $1.50 for adults, 75¢ for children.

New York city and state historical exhibits. Early American paintings and portraits. Period rooms. Audubon watercolors. Gallery of American silver.

Pierpont Morgan Library: 29 E. 36th St. NYC 10016. Open: Tues.-Sat. 10:30–5, Sun. 1–5 (closed Mon.; also legal hldys., Sundays in July, and month of August).

Medieval and Renaissance illuminated manuscripts, rare books, music and autograph manuscripts, old master drawings, bindings, early children's books, ancient written records.

Whitney Museum of American Art: 945 Madison Ave. at 75th St., NYC 10021. Open: Wed.-Sat. 11–6, Tues. 11–8 (free 5–8), Sun. and hldys. 12–6 (closed Mon.; also Dec. 25). Adm. $2 (senior citizens, college students with ID, and children under 12 accompanied by an adult, free).

Sculpture, paintings, watercolors, drawings, and prints by 20th-century American artists. Exhibitions of contemporary and historical American art. Daily film and video showings; occasional performing arts programs in spring.

Chicago

Art Institute of Chicago, The: Michigan Ave. at Adams St., Chicago, Ill. 60603. Open: Mon.-Wed. and Fri. 10:30–4:30, Thurs. 10:30–8, Sat. 10–5, Sun. and hldys. 12–5 (Closed Dec. 25). Voluntary admission fee.

Paintings, sculpture, prints, drawings, textiles, photography. Oriental arts; European, American decorative arts; primitive art. Thorne Miniature Rooms. Junior Museum. Goodman Theatre, School of Art.

Beverly Art Center: 2153 W. 111th St., Chicago, Ill. 60643. Open: daily 9 a.m.-10 p.m.

Exhibitions change monthly.

Chicago Academy of Sciences, Museum of Ecology: Lincoln Park—2001 North Clark St., Chicago, Ill. 60614. Open: daily 10–5 (closed Dec. 25). Free.

Exhibits of ecology of animal and plant life, minerals and fossils of Chicago region. Walk-through coal forest, cave, and canyon. Lectures, field trips, movies.

Chicago Historical Society: Clark St. and North Ave., Chicago, Ill. 60614. Open: Mon.-Sat. 9:30–4:30, Sun. 12–5 (closed Jan. 1, Thanksgiving, Dec. 25). Adults, $1; children 6–17, 50¢; senior citizens, 25¢. Free admission Monday. Research collection open Tues.-Sat. 9:30–4:30.

Exhibits and collections relating to Chicago and Illinois history, Illinois pioneer crafts, American history, Lincoln, Civil War.

Field Museum of Natural History: Roosevelt Rd. at Lake Shore Dr., Chicago, Ill. 60605. Open: Daily at 9 a.m. to as early as 4 p.m. in winter and as late as 9 p.m. in summer (closed Jan. 1, Dec. 25). Adm: families, $3.50; adults, $1.50; children (6–17) and students with ID's, 50¢; senior citizens, 35¢. Free on Fri. (9–9). Free at all times to members, teachers, members of the armed forces, and children under 6.

Dioramas of plants, animals and fossils, rocks and geological fragments, and artifacts of early civilizations.

Museum of Science and Industry: 57th St. and Lake Shore Dr., Chicago, Ill. 60637. Open: Memorial Day-Labor Day 9:30–5:30; rest of year, Mon.-Fri. 9:30–4, Sat., Sun. and hldys. 9:30–5:30 (closed Dec. 25). Free (small fee to four exhibits).

Operating coal mine, captured German submarine, giant heart, Paul Bunyan house, Colleen Moore's Fairy Castle, The Farm, the Apollo 8 spacecraft, Sears' Cinema Circus, computerized "Food for Life," historic and advanced forms of planes, ships, trains, and cars.

Oriental Institute Museum of the University of Chicago: 1155 E. 58th St., Chicago, Ill. 60637. Open: Tues.-Sat. 10–4, Sun. 12–4 (closed Mon. and hldys.). Free.

Ancient Near Eastern objects, including 40-ton human-headed winged bull from Khorsabad in Assyria, 16-ft. statue of Tutankhamen from Egypt, colossal bull's head from Persepolis; glyptic, bronze, and ivory artifacts.

Vanderpoel (John H.) Memorial Art Gallery: 2135 W. 111th St., Chicago, Ill. 60643. Open: Tues.-Thurs. and Sun. 1–4 (closed Mon., Fri., Sat. and hldys.).

Paintings, watercolors, etchings, scuplture contributed by the artists in tribute to Mr. Vanderpoel.

Washington, D.C.

Anacostia Neighborhood Museum, Smithsonian Institution: 2405 Martin Luther King, Jr., Ave. SE, Washington, D.C. 20020. Open: Mon.-Fri. 10–6, Sat. and Sun. 1–6 (closed Dec. 25). Free.

Exhibits on Afro-American history, urban problems, art. Programs for children.

Arts and Industries Building, Smithsonian Institution: 900 Jefferson Dr. SW, Washington, D.C. 20560. Open: daily 10–5:30; summer 10–9 (closed Dec. 25). Free.

Constructed to house exhibits from 1876 Centennial Exhibition, building has been restored as nearly as possible to original appearance.

Corcoran Gallery of Art: 17th St. and New York Ave. NW, Washington, D.C. 20006. Open: Tues.-Sun. 10–4:30 (closed Mon.; also Jan. 1, July 4, Thanksgiving, Dec. 25). Free.

Comprehensive collection of American paintings, sculpture, graphics. Choice selection of European art.

Freer Gallery of Art, Smithsonian Institution: Jefferson Dr. at 12th St. SW, Washington, D.C. 20560. Open: daily 10–5:30 (closed Dec. 25). Free.

Oriental paintings, sculpture, bronzes, pottery, and metal work. Early Christian manuscripts. One of largest Whistler collections.

Hirshhorn Museum and Sculpture Garden, Smithsonian Institution: Eighth St. at Independence Ave. SW, Washington, D.C. 20560. Open: daily, 10–5:30; summer, 10–9 (closed Dec. 25). Free.

More than 7,000 works tracing development of modern painting and sculpture since 19th century. Rodin, Moore, Picasso, Calder, Miró, and Matisse among those represented.

National Air and Space Museum, Smithsonian Institution: Independence Ave. bet. 4th and 7th Sts. SW, Washington, D.C. 20560. Open: daily 10–5:30, summer 10–9 (closed Dec. 25). Free.

Exhibits on aviation and space age; Wright Brothers' Kitty Hawk Flyer, *Lindbergh's* Spirit of St. Louis.

National Collection of Fine Arts, Smithsonian Institution: Eighth and G Sts. NW, Washington, D.C. 20560. Open: daily 10–5:30 (closed Dec. 25). Free.

Collections survey 300 years of American art. Over 23,000 paintings, sculptures, and graphics.

National Gallery of Art: Constitution Ave. bet. 3rd and 7th Sts. NW, Washington, D.C. 20565. Open: Mon.-Sat. 10–5, Sun. 12–9[1] (closed Jan. 1, Dec. 25). Free.

Paintings, sculpture, drawings, prints, decorative arts given by Mellon, Kress, Widener, Rosenwald, Dale, Harriman, and others. Index of American Design.

National Museum of History and Technology, Smithsonian Institution: 12th St. and Constitution Ave. NW, Washington, D.C. 20560. Open: daily 10–5:30, summer 10–9 (closed Dec. 25). Free.

Exhibits showing scientific, technological, and cultural development feature original Star-Spangled Banner, costumes and furnishings, gowns of First Ladies, inventions, stamps, coins, musical instruments, ceramics, and crafts.

National Museum of Natural History and National Museum of Man, Smithsonian Institution: 10th St. and Constitution Ave. NW, Washington, D.C. 20560. Open: daily 10–5:30, summer 10–9. (closed Dec. 25). Free.

Origin, development, and physical characteristics of man. Dioramas of peoples and animals in natural settings. Land and sea mammals, birds, fish, reptiles, and gems, minerals, meteorites, volcanoes, prehistoric animals, fossils. Hope Diamond. Insect Zoo.

National Portrait Gallery, Smithsonian Institution: Eighth and F Sts. NW, Washington, D.C. 20560. Open: daily 10–5:30 (closed Dec. 25). Free.

Only major museum in hemisphere devoted exclusively to portraiture. Exhibits likenesses in all media of persons who have made significant contributions to U.S. history, development, and culture.

Renwick Gallery, Smithsonian Institution: 17th St. and Pennsylvania Ave. NW, Washington, D.C. 20560. Open: daily 10–5:30 (closed Dec. 25). Free.

American crafts, decorative arts, and design, housed in a mid-19th-century building restored to its original appearance.

Smithsonian Institution Building: 1000 Jefferson Dr. SW, Washington, D.C. 20560. Open: daily 10–5:30, summer 10–9 (closed Dec. 25). Free.

Information center and James Smithson's tomb are in original building. Institution maintains the museums and art galleries indicated above; also Cooper-Hewitt Museum in New York City, National Zoological Park in Washington, D.C., and research facilities elsewhere.

Philadelphia

Academy of Natural Sciences of Philadelphia: 19th St. and the Parkway, Philadelphia, Pa. 19103. Natural History Museum open: daily 10–4 (closed Jan. 1, Thanksgiving, Dec. 25). Adm. $2.25 (students, senior citizens, military personnel, $1.75; children $1.50).

Exhibits on dinosaurs and extinct species; animal, bird, and gem displays. Live animal shows daily.

Franklin Institute, The: 20th St. and the Parkway, Philadelphia, Pa. 19103. Open: Mon.-Sat. 10–5, Sun. 12–5 (closed Jan. 1, Thanksgiving, Dec. 24–25). Adm: $2.75 (senior citizens, $1.50; students and children 5–11, $2; children under 5, 50¢).

Nonprofit educational and research institution operating science museum, planetarium, library, and research laboratories.

Pennsylvania Academy of the Fine Arts: Broad and Cherry Sts., Philadelphia, Pa. 19102. Open: Tues.-Sat. 10–5, Sun. 1–5 (closed Jan. 1, Dec. 25). Adm. $1 (children under 12, students and senior citizens, 50¢).

Oldest art museum and school in U.S. Collection devoted to American art. Lectures, concerts. Multi-media exhibitions.

Philadelphia Museum of Art: 26th St. and the Parkway, Philadelphia, Pa. 19101. Open: Wed.-Sun. 10–5 (closed major hldys.). Adm. $1.50 (children and senior citizens, 75¢), (free Sun. 9–1).

Paintings, drawings, prints, from old masters to present. Sculpture, decorative arts, period rooms and armor. Oriental collections. New American Wing open. Rodin Museum at Parkway and 22nd St. Colonial Houses in Fairmont Park. Samuel S. Fleisher Art Memorial, 715–19 Catharine St.

Museums In Other Cities

Addison Gallery of American Art: Phillips Academy, Andover, Mass. 01810. Open: Tues.-Sat. 10–5, Sun. 2:30–5 (closed Mon.; also natl. hldys.). Free.

Paintings, sculpture, graphics, photographs of 18th, 19th, and 20th centuries. Changing contemporary exhibitions.

Alabama, Museum of Natural History of: Smith Hall, on campus of U. of Alabama, Tuscaloosa, Ala. 35486. Open: Mon.-Fri. 8–5. Free.

All phases of natural history. See also *Mound State Monument Museum.*

Albright-Knox Art Gallery: 1285 Elmwood Ave., Buffalo, N.Y. 14222. Open: Tues.-Sat. 10–5; Sun. 12–5 (closed Mon.; also Jan. 1, Thanksgiving, Dec. 25). Voluntary admission fee.

Comprehensive collection of contemporary paintings; 18th-19th-century English, French, and American paintings. Sculpture since 3000 B.C.

Atomic Energy, American Museum of: *See* Science and Energy, American Museum of.

Baltimore Museum of Art: Art Museum Dr., Baltimore, Md. 21218. Open: Tues.-Sat. 11–5, Thurs. evening 7–10 (except in summer). Sun. 1–5 (closed Mon.). Free.

Paintings, sculpture, graphics, 2nd-6th-century mosaics from Antioch. Concerts, dance recitals, educational programs for all ages.

Baseball Hall of Fame and Museum, National: Main St., Cooperstown, N.Y. 13326. Open: May-Oct. 9–9, Nov.-Apr. 9–5 (closed Jan. 1, Thanksgiving, Dec. 25). Adm. $3.50 (children 7–15, $1.50).

Relics, pictures, documents of baseball history. Bronze plaques of game's immortals. Baseball movies shown daily. See also *Hall of Fame in index.*

Berkshire Museum, The: 39 South St., Pittsfield, Mass. 01201. Open: Tues.-Sat. 10–5, Sun. 2–5 (closed Mon.; also Jan. 1, July 4, Thanksgiving, Dec. 25). Open Mon. in July and Aug. Free.

Painting, sculpture, decorative arts—ancient to modern. Loan exhibits. Galleries on biology, birds, man, minerals, and American history. Live exhibits. Junior Department. Movies, lectures.

Birmingham Museum of Art: 2000 Eighth Ave. North, Birmingham, Ala. 35203. Open: Tues.-Wed., Fri. and Sat. 10–5, Thurs. 10–9, Sun. 2–6 (closed Mondays; also Jan. 1, Dec. 25). Free.

Kress Collection of Italian art; 17th-century Dutch, Flemish, and English paintings; Beeson Wedgwood Collection; art of Old West, including

Remington bronzes; modern American paintings; silver, porcelain.

(Boston) Museum of Fine Arts: Huntington Ave., Boston, Mass. 02115. Open: Wed.-Sun. 10–5, Tues. 10–9 (closed Mon.; also Jan. 1, July 4, Labor Day, Thanksgiving, and Dec. 24–25). Adm. $1.75 (Tues. 5–9, free; Sun. $1.25; free to senior citizens on Fri.; members and children 16 and under, free).

European and American paintings, sculpture, furniture, interiors, tapestries, textiles, silver, costumes, musical instruments. Prints, drawings, watercolors. Egyptian, Asiatic, contemporary collections.

Buffalo Museum of Science: Humboldt Parkway, Buffalo, N.Y. 14211. Open: Mon.-Thurs. and Sat. 10–5; Fri. 10–10; Sun. and hldys. 1–5 (closed Dec. 25). Free.

Exhibits of astronomy, geology, zoology, botany, anthropology. Kellogg Observatory.

California Academy of Sciences: Golden Gate Park, San Francisco, Calif. 94118. Open: daily 10–5. Adm. $1 (children 12–17, 50¢; under 12 and senior citizens, 25¢). Free adm. first day of month.

North American and African habitat groups. Astronomical exhibits, clocks, watches, lamps, minerals, fossils, plants. Steinhart Aquarium, Morrison Planetarium, Wattis Hall of Man.

California Palace of the Legion of Honor: 34th Ave. and Clement St., Lincoln Park, San Francisco, Calif. 94121. Open: daily 10–5. Adm. $1 (youths 12–18, 50¢; under 12 and senior citizens, free). Free adm. first day of month.

Devoted to arts of France: paintings, sculpture, and decorative arts; prints and drawings of all periods.

Carnegie Institute: 4400 Forbes Ave., Pittsburgh, Pa. 15213. Open: Tues.-Sat. 10–5, Sun. 1–6 (closed Mon. and major hldys.). Suggested contributions: Adults, $1.50; children and students, 75¢. Sat. free.

Museum of Art: European and American paintings, sculpture, and decorative arts. Carnegie Museum of Natural History: exhibits in natural history and science.

Cincinnati Art Museum: Eden Park, Cincinnati, Ohio 45202. Open: wkdys. 10–5, Sun. and hldys. 1–5 (closed Mon. and major hldys.). Adm. $1 (children 12–18, 50¢; 11 and under, free). Free to everyone on Sat.

European and American painting, prints, photographs, decorative arts, sculpture, costumes. Egyptian, Greco-Roman, Medieval, Near and Far Eastern arts. Ancient musical instruments.

Clark (Sterling and Francine) Art Institute: Williamstown, Mass. 01267. Open: daily except Monday, 10–5 (closed Jan. 1, Thanksgiving, Dec. 25). Free.

Paintings from 14th to 19th centuries, including works by Corot, Renoir, Degas, Toulouse-Lautrec, Homer; sculpture, antique silver, prints and drawings.

Cleveland Museum of Art: 11150 East Boulevard, Cleveland, Ohio 44106. Open: Tues. 10–6, Wed. 10–10, Thurs. and Fri. 10–6, Sat. 9–5, Sun. 1–6 (closed Mon.; also Jan. 1, July 4, Thanksgiving, Dec. 25). Free.

Paintings, sculpture, graphic arts, furniture, silver, gold, arms, armor, textiles, ceramics from all cultures and periods.

Cleveland Museum of Natural History: Wade Oval, University Circle, Cleveland, Ohio 44106. Open: Mon.-Sat. 10–5, Sun. 1–5:30 (closed Jan. 1, Memorial Day, July 4, Labor Day, Thanksgiving, Dec. 24–25). Adm. $2 (children 6–18 and senior citizens, 50¢). Free Tues. after 1.

Dinosaurs, area fossils, minerals, birds, mammals, insects, reptiles, plants. American Indian and Eskimo displays. Planetarium, observatory. Hall of Man's Ecology, Hall of Earth Science.

Colonial Williamsburg: Williamsburg, Va. 23185. Open: daily. Tickets for one day, adults $8.50, children (6–12) $4.25; 2 days, adults, $13, children $6.50; 3 days, adults $16, children $8.

Restored 18th-century capital of Colonial Virginia; 173 acres of colonial city with more than 40 exhibition homes, craft shops, and public buildings; 90 acres of gardens; outdoor events; colonial lodging and dining.

Colorado Springs Fine Arts Center: 30 W. Dale St., Colorado Springs, Colo. 80903. Open: Tues.-Sat. 10–5; Sun. 1:30–5 (closed Mon.; also Jan. 1, Thanksgiving, Dec. 25). Free.

Art produced within limits of U.S. from prehistoric to contemporary, including decorative and fine arts. Survey of arts of world. Drama, dance, and music programs.

Columbus Museum of Art: 480 E. Broad St., Columbus, Ohio 43215. Open: Tues., Thurs., Fri., and Sun. 11–5; Wed. 11–8:30; Sat. 10–5 (closed Mon.). Adm. $1.50 (children 6–17, students, and senior citizens, 50¢). Tues. free.

European paintings from 16th to 20th century; 19th- and 20th-century American and European paintings, sculpture, and works on paper. Chinese and Japanese ceramics. European and American decorative arts. Sculpture Park and Garden.

Corning Glass Center: Dept. IP, Corning, N.Y. 14830. Open daily 9–5 (closed Jan. 1, Thanksgiving, Dec. 24–25). Adm.: $2; youths 11–17, $1; children with adult free.

New museum building has comprehensive collection of glass dating from 1500 B.C. Demonstrations of making of glass and its uses in Hall of Science and Industry. Artisans handcraft and engrave crystal in Steuben factory.

Currier Gallery of Art: 192 Orange St., Manchester, N.H. 03104. Open: Tues., Wed., Fri., and Sat. 10–4; Sun. 2–5; Thurs. 10–10 (closed Mon. and major hldys.). Free.

European and American paintings, 13th-20th century. American decorative arts, 18th-19th century, including New England furniture, silver, pewter, and early glass.

Delaware Art Museum, The: 2301 Kentmere Pkwy., Wilmington, Del. 19806. Open: Mon.-Sat. 10–5, Sun. 1–5. Adm.: $1 (youths 12–18 and students, 50¢; children under 12, members, and senior citizens, free).

English pre-Raphaelite; 19th- and 20th-century American art; complete set of John Sloan's graphic work; Paintings by Wyeth, Homer and Hooper; American photography. Art reference library.

Denver Art Museum, The: 100 W. 14th Ave. Parkway, Denver, Colo. 80204. Open: Tues.-Sat. 9–5, Sun. 1–5; also Wed. 9–9 p.m.

Art from nearly every culture and period.

Denver Museum of Natural History: City Park, Denver, Colo. 80205. Open: Mon.-Sat. 9–4:30, Sun. and hldys. 12–4:30 (closed Jan. 1, Thanksgiving, Dec. 24–25, Dec. 31). Free.

Sixty-six life-size ecological habitat dioramas. Animals from four continents, earth-science exhibits, dinosaurs, displays of fossil mammals and historic native Americans. Planetarium (small charge).

Des Moines Art Center: Greenwood Park, 45th St. and Grand Ave., Des Moines, Iowa 50312. Open:

Tues.-Sat. 11–5, Sun. 12–5. Free.

Permanent collection includes Calder, Rodin, Arp, Bellows, Johns, Hopper, Giacometti, David Smith, and Morris Louis, among others.

Detroit Historical Museum: 5401 Woodward Ave., Detroit, Mich. 48202. Open: Tues., Thurs., Fri., Sat. 9:30–5; Wed. 1–9; Sun. 1–5 (closed Mon. and legal hldys.).

Detroit-related industrial, transportation, social history, and ethnic exhibits. Detroit streets of 1840–50, 1870–80, 1895–1905. Urban history. Corridor of Costumes. Marine exhibits at Dossin Great Lakes Museum on Belle Isle; military history exhibits at historic Ft. Wayne, West Jefferson at foot of Livernois.

Detroit Institute of Arts, The: 5200 Woodward Ave., Detroit, Mich. 48202. Open: Tues.-Sun. 9:30–5:30 (closed Mon.; also legal hldys.). Voluntary admission fee.

Paintings, sculpture, decorative arts from ancient times to modern.

Dickson Mounds Museum: off Route 97–78 near Lewistown, Ill. 61542. Open: Daily 8:30–5 (closed Jan. 1, Easter, Thanksgiving, Dec. 25). Free.

Museum of prehistoric Indians. Branch of Illinois State Museum.

Farmers' Museum: Lake Rd., Route 80, Cooperstown, N.Y. 13326. Open: summer season, daily. 9–5; winter season, Tues.-Sat. 9–5, Sun. 1–5 (closed Mon.; also Jan. 1, Thanksgiving, Dec. 25). Adm. $3[3] (children $1.25).

Re-created village crossroads. Early farm and handicraft tools. School house, country store, smithy, print shop, doctor's and lawyer's offices, pharmacy, tavern, church, farm unit. Cardiff Giant. Operated by New York State Historical Association.

Fenimore House: Lake Rd., Route 80, Cooperstown, N.Y. 13326. Open: summer season, daily 9–5; Nov., Dec., and April, Tues.-Sat. 9–5, Sun. 1–5 (closed Mon.; also Jan., Feb., March, Dec. 25). Adm: $2.50[3] (children $1.25).

American portraits, genre paintings. Browere life masks of Founding Fathers. James Fenimore Cooper memorabilia. Folk art. Library. Operated by New York State Historical Association.

Florida State Museum, University of Florida: Museum Road, Gainesville, Fla. 32611. Open: Mon.-Fri. 9–5, Sat. 9–5, Sun. 1–5 (closed Dec. 25). Free.

State and University museum with research and exhibition emphasis on natural and social history of Florida, southeastern United States, and Caribbean area.

Fogg Art Museum: Harvard University, 32 Quincy St., Cambridge, Mass. 02138. Open: Mon.-Fri. 9–5, Sat. 10–5, Sun. 1–4 (closed weekends from July 1 to Labor Day; also natl. hldys.). Free.

Collections illustrate evolution of Eastern and Western art from ancient to modern times. Chinese sculpture and bronzes; Romanesque sculpture; Italian primitives; French 19th-century paintings; European drawings and prints.

Gardner (Isabella Stewart) Museum: 2 Palace Road, Boston, Mass. 02115. Open: Tues., 1–9:30, Wed.-Sun. 1–5:30. July-Aug., Tues.-Sun. 1–5:30 (closed natl. hldys.). Adm.: Suggested contribution, $1, lesser amount acceptable.

Paintings, 14th-20th centuries, in building of Venetian palace style. Sculpture, tapestries, furniture. Flowering courtyard. Free tours on Thursday at 2:30 p.m.

Getty (J. Paul) Museum, The: 17985 Pacific Coast Hgwy., Malibu, Calif. 90265. Open: Mon.-Fri. 10–5 (June-Sept.), Tues.-Sat. 10–5 (Oct.-May), (closed Jan. 1, Feb. 22, Memorial Day, July 4, Labor Day, Thanksgiving, Dec. 25). Free. Parking reservations for guaranteed admission are required (213 454-6541).

Re-creation of Roman seaside villa destroyed by Vesuvius in 79 A.D. Greek and Roman antiquities, Western European paintings, 18th-century French decorative arts. Research library.

Heard Museum: 22 East Monte Vista Rd., Phoenix, Ariz. 85004. Open: Mon.-Sat. 10–5, Sun. 1–5 (closed hldys.). Adm.: $1.50; (senior citizens, $1; children and students, 50¢).

Anthropology and primitive arts, with emphasis on rich heritage of Southwest.

High Museum of Art, The: 1280 Peachtree St. NE, Atlanta, Ga. 30309. Open: Mon.-Sat. 10–5, Sun. 12–5 (closed natl. hldys.). Free.

Paintings and sculpture from 14th to 18th century in Samuel H. Kress Collection. Ralph K. Uhry Print Collection; decorative arts; Richman Collection of African Art; 18th-century European porcelains; photography, contemporary art.

(Houston) Museum of Fine Arts, The: 1001 Bissonnet at Main, Houston, Tex. 77005. Open: Tues.-Sat. 10–5, Sun. 12–6 (closed Mon.; also Jan. 1, July 4, Thanksgiving, Dec. 25). Free.

American and European art through 20th century; Southwest American Indian art and artifacts; early American furniture and decorative arts; pre-Columbian and Far Eastern art; native arts from Africa, Australia, South Pacific. Impressionist and post-Impressionist paintings. 20th-century photography.

Huntington Library, Art Gallery, and Botanical Gardens: 1151 Oxford Rd., San Marino, Calif. 91108. Open: Tues.-Sun. 1–4:30; (free Sun. tickets required) (closed Mon.; also month of Oct., Jan. 1, Easter, Memorial Day, July 4, Labor Day, Thanksgiving, Dec. 25). Free.

18th-century British paintings, including Gainsborough's "Blue Boy" and Lawrence's "Pinkie." Manuscript and rare-book exhibits include Gutenberg Bible, Franklin's Autobiography *in his handwriting. Botanical gardens. Research library.*

Illinois State Museum: Spring and Edwards Sts., Springfield, Ill. 62706. Open: Mon.-Sat. 8:30–5, Sun. 1:30–5 (closed Jan. 1, Easter, Thanksgiving, Dec. 25). Free.

Museum of natural science, anthropology, and art.

Indianapolis Museum of Art: 1200 W. 38th St., Indianapolis, Ind. 46208. Krannert and Clowes Pavilions open: Tues.-Sun. and hldys. 11–5 (closed Mon.; also Jan. 1, Thanksgiving, Dec. 25). Free. Lilly Pavilion of Decorative Arts open Tues.-Sun. 1–4 (closed Mon. and major hldys.). Free.

Pre-Columbian through contemporary art in all media. British and American paintings of 19th century; J.M.W. Turner collection. Dutch and Flemish paintings of 17th century; textiles, decorative arts of 18th-century Germany, England, France, and Italy. Oriental collection. Clowes Fund Collection of old masters.

Los Angeles County Museum of Art: 5905 Wilshire Blvd., Los Angeles, Calif. 90036. Open: Tues.-Fri. 10–5; second Tues. of month 12–9; Sat.-Sun. 10–6 (closed Mon.; also Jan. 1, Thanksgiving, Dec. 25). Adm.: $1 (members free; students with ID, senior citizens, and children 5–17, 50¢). Free to all second Tues. of month.

Ahmanson Gallery houses permanent collections covering entire range of history of art. Special Exhibitions Gallery.

(Los Angeles County) Natural History Museum: Exposition Park, 900 Exposition Blvd., Los Angeles, Calif. 90007. Open: Tues.-Sun. 10–5 (closed Mon.; also Jan. 1, Thanksgiving, Dec. 25). Adm.: $1 (children 5–17, 50¢).

Exhibits in Pre-Columbian archeology, Pacific Islands and African ethnology, Southern California botany, evolution of life, marine biology, insects, mineralogy. Dinosaur and Cenozoic fossil reconstructions. North American and African animal habitat groups. U.S., California, Western, Plains, and West Coast Indian history. Rancho La Brea tar pits, a designated natural history landmark, are at 5801 Wilshire Blvd., Hancock Park, with satellite George C. Page Museum of La Brea. Pleistocene fossil reconstructions. Open: same as parent museum.

Milwaukee Art Center: Milwaukee County War Memorial Bldg., 750 North Lincoln Memorial Dr., Milwaukee, Wis. 53202. Open: Tues., Wed., Fri., and Sat. 10–5; Thurs. 12–9; Sun. 1–6 (closed Mon.). Adm. $1 (students, senior citizens, 50¢; children under 12, free).

Paintings, sculpture, graphics, and decorative arts from ancient to modern; Bradley Collection of 19th- and 20th-century American art. Villa Terrace, Branch Museum for Decorative Arts, 2220 North Terrace Ave.; seasonal hours.

Milwaukee Public Museum: 800 W. Wells St., Milwaukee, Wis. 53233. Open: daily 9–5 (closed Jan. 1, Thanksgiving, Dec. 25). Adm.: $1 (children under 18, 25¢) for Milwaukee County residents; $2 (children, 75¢) for nonresidents.

American Indian and West African art, pre-Columbian collections. Natural history and history displays that include Streets of Old Milwaukee, the Urban Habitat, and European Village.

Minneapolis, Institute of Arts, The: 2400 Third Ave. South, Minneapolis, Minn. 55404. Open: Tues., Wed., Fri., Sat. 10–5; Thurs. 10–9; Sun. 12–5 (closed Mon.; also Dec. 25). Adm. $1 (Thurs. 5–9, free) (students 12–18, 50¢; senior citizens, and children under 12, free).

European and American paintings, sculpture, decorative arts, period rooms, prints and drawings, photography; Oriental, African, Oceanic, ancient and native North and South American arts.

Mint Museum, Art Museum: 501 Hempstead Pl., Charlotte, N.C. 28207. Open: Tues.-Fri. 10–5, Sat.-Sun. 2–5 (closed Mon. and hldys.). Free.

Paintings, sculpture, decorative arts, prints (Renaissance-20th century), pre-Columbian Collection, Delhom Gallery and Institute for Study and Research in Ceramics. Coins and artifacts from 19th-century Charlotte branch of U.S. Mint.

Mound State Monument Archaeological Museum: Rte. 69, Moundville, Ala. 35474. Open: daily 9–5 (closed Dec. 25). Adm. $2 (children $1).

Twenty prehistoric Indian mounds, excavated artifacts, re-created temple and village of Moundville Indians. Trailer and tent campgrounds. Operated by Alabama Museum of Natural History, The University of Alabama.

Mystic Seaport: Mystic, Conn. 06355. Open: daily. Dec.-March 10–4, April-Nov. 9–5 (mid-May to mid-Sept. open until 8) (closed Dec. 25). Adm. Dec.-March $6 (children 5–15, $3; April-Nov. $7 (children, $3.50). Two-day tickets and group rates available.

Maritime museum emphasizing Age of Sail. Tall ships, including Charles W. Morgan, 1841 whaling ship. Waterfront village with working craftsmen and demonstrations of maritime skills. Small boat collection and exhibits of figureheads and marine art. Working shipyard; planetarium. Summer steamboat rides at additional charge.

Nelson (William Rockhill) Gallery—Atkins Museum of Fine Arts: 4525 Oak St., Kansas City, Mo. 64111. Open: Tues.-Sat. 10–5, Sun. 2–6 (closed Mon.; also Jan. 1, Memorial Day, July 4, Thanksgiving, Dec. 25). Adm. $1.50 (children 6–12, 75¢). Free on Sun.

Egyptian, Oriental, classic, and European art. American paintings and decorative arts; five Early American rooms. Pre-Columbian and Indian art. Children's Museum, lectures, films, musical programs.

New Mexico, Museum of: Admin. bldg. at 113 Lincoln St., P.O. Box 2087, Santa Fe, N.M. 87503. Museum of Fine Arts, Museum of International Folk Art, Palace of the Governors. Open: daily 9–4:45 (closed Mon. Oct. 15-March 15; also state hldys). Laboratory of Anthropology. Open: Mon.-Fri. 8–12, 1–5 (closed Sat., Sun., and hldys.).

Exhibits of fine arts, folk arts; history of Southwest and of American Indian; archeology; ethnology.

New Orleans Museum of Art: Lelong Ave., City Park, New Orleans, La. 70179. Open: Tues., Wed., Fri., Sat., Sun. 10–5; Thurs. 1–9 (closed Mon.).

Old master paintings from 14th to 19th centuries, including Kress Collection of Italian Art; 20th-century European and American art; African, Oriental and pre-Columbian collections; Latin American Colonial painting and sculpture; prints and photographs.

New York State Historical Association; Lake Rd., Rte. 80, Cooperstown, N.Y. 13326.

Administers Farmers' Museum and Fenimore House. See those entries. Also, Cooperstown Graduate Program in history museum studies and art conservation.

Newark Museum: 49 Washington St., Newark, N.J. 07101. Open: daily 12–5 (closed Jan. 1, July 4, Thanksgiving, Dec. 25). Free.

Collections: American painting, sculpture; Tibetan, Chinese, Japanese arts; decorative arts, ancient glass and ceramics; natural science, ethnology. Planetarium. Ballantine House restoration. Fire Museum. Sculpture garden. Junior Museum.

Norton Simon Museum of Art at Pasadena: Colorado Blvd. at Orange Grove, Pasadena, Calif. 91105. Open: Thurs.-Sun. 12–6. Adm. $2 (students and senior citizens, 75¢; children under 12, free).

Paintings by old masters and from Italian Renaissance; Dutch 17th-century school; paintings and sculpture by Impressionist and early 20th-century masters; Southeast Asian stone sculptures and bronzes.

Putnam Museum: 1717 W. 12th St., Davenport, Iowa 52804. Open: Tues.-Sat. 9–5, Sun. 1–5 (closed Mon.; also Jan. 1, Easter, Memorial Day, July 4, Labor Day, Thanksgiving, Dec. 25). Adm. 75¢ (children 25¢).

Art, history and natural history collections from the Orient, Africa, and North, Central, and South America.

Ringling Museums: P.O. Box 1838, Sarasota, Fla. 33578. John and Mable Ringling Museum of Art, Asolo Theater, Ringling Residence, Museum of the Circus. Open: Mon.-Fri. 9 a.m.-10 p.m., Sat. 9–5, Sun. 11–6. Adm.: $3.50 (groups, $3; children under 12, free).

Extensive collection of Rubens and Baroque art. Asolo is only 18th-century Italian theater in America. Circus Museum contains gilded wagons and memorabilia.

Rosicrucian Egyptian Museum and Art Gallery: Park and Naglee Aves., San Jose, Calif. 95191. Open: Tues.-Fri. 9–5, Sat.-Mon. 12–5 (closed Jan. 1, July 4, Aug. 2, Thanksgiving, Dec. 25). Free.
Egyptian and Oriental antiquities. Mummies, statuary, jewelry, utensils, clothing. Reproduction of Egyptian rock tomb. Babylonian collection. Art gallery.

St. Louis Art Museum: Forest Park, St. Louis, Mo. 63110. Open: Tues. 2:30–9:30, Wed.-Sun. 10–5 (closed Mon.; also Jan. 1, Dec. 25). Free.
American, European, and Asian painting, sculpture, and decorative arts. African, Oceanic, pre-Columbian, and American Indian arts.

San Diego Museum of Art: Balboa Park, San Diego, Calif. 92101. Open: Tues.-Sun. 10–5 (closed Mon.; also Jan. 1, Thanksgiving, Dec. 25). Adm.: $1. Free adm. Tuesday.
European paintings of Renaissance and Baroque periods. American paintings; Oriental and modern art.

San Diego Museum of Man: 1350 El Prado, Balboa Park, San Diego, Calif. 92101. Open: daily 10–4:30 (closed Jan. 1, Thanksgiving, Dec. 25). Adm. $1 (children 6–16, 25¢; under 6, free). Free adm. on Wed.
Exhibits on Man of the Western Americas, early man, Indians' life style, and Mayan civilization.

San Diego Society of Natural History—Natural History Museum: Balboa Park, San Diego, Calif. 92112. Open: wkdys. and Sun. 10–4:30 (closed Jan. 1, Dec. 25). Adm. $1 (children, free).
Mammals, birds, fossils, shells, plants, insects, minerals, marine biology. Emphasis on Southwestern U.S., Sonora, and Lower California.

San Francisco, The Fine Arts Museums of, M.H. de Young Memorial Museum: Kennedy Dr. and Eighth Ave., Golden Gate Park, San Francisco, Calif. 94118. Open: Daily 10–5. Adm. $1 (children 12–18, 50¢; under 12 and over 65, free). Free adm. first day of month.
Art of Europe, America, Ancient Egypt, Greece, and Rome; traditional arts of Africa, Oceania, and the Americas. Paintings, sculpture, and decorative arts. See also *California Palace of the Legion of Honor.*

San Francisco Museum of Modern Art: Van Ness at McAllister, San Francisco, Calif. 94102. Open: Tues., Wed., and Fri. 10–6, Thurs. 10–10, Sat. and Sun. 10–5 (closed Mon.; also Jan. 1, Memorial Day, July 4, Labor Day, Thanksgiving, Dec. 25). Adm. $2 (senior citizens and children under 16, $1).
Contemporary American and international paintings, sculpture, graphics, photography, and ceramics.

Science and Energy, American Museum of: 300 South Tulane, Oak Ridge, Tenn. 37830. Open: Sept-May, Mon.-Sat. 9–5, Sun. 12:30–5; June-Aug., Mon.-Sat. 9–6, Sun. 12:30–6 (closed Jan. 1, Thanksgiving, Dec. 25). Free.
Demonstrations, exhibits, motion pictures, models, etc., relating to all forms of energy. Traveling exhibits available free to qualified exhibitors in U.S.[2]

Seattle Art Museum: Volunteer Park, Seattle, Wash. 98112. Open: Tues.-Sat. 10–5, Thurs. 10–9 p.m., Sun. 12–5 (closed Mon.; also Jan. 1, Thanksgiving, Dec. 25). Adm. $1 (50¢ for students and senior citizens; children under 12 with adult, free). Free on Thurs.
Asian art and jade; Greek and Roman art; 14th-20th century European paintings; tribal art. Samuel H. Kress Collection of 14th-18th century. European painting and sculpture. Modern Art Pavilion is in Seattle Center. (Hours same as above.)

Southwest Museum: Marmion Way at Museum Dr., Highland Pk., Los Angeles, Calif. 90065. Open: Tues.-Sun. 1–4:45 (closed mid-Aug.-mid-Sept., Mon., Jan. 1, Easter, July 4, Thanksgiving, Dec. 25). Free.
American Indian exhibits, ancient and modern. Research library. Casa de Adobe, reproduction of adobe hacienda, at 4605 N. Figueroa St.; open Wed., Sat., and Sun. 1–4:45 (closed same as Southwest Museum).

Toledo Museum of Art, The: Monroe St. at Scottwood Ave., Toledo, Ohio 43697. Open: Tues.-Sat. 9–5, Sun. 1–6 (closed Mon. and legal hldys.). Free.
European and American paintings and decorative arts. Ancient and medieval art; books, manuscripts, prints, graphics. Ancient and American glass.

Virginia Museum of Fine Arts: Boulevard and Grove Ave., Richmond, Va. 23221. Open: Tues.-Sat. 11–5, Sun. 1–5 (closed Mon.; also Jan. 1, July 4, Thanksgiving, Dec. 25). Adm. Suggested donation of 50¢.
World art of all periods, Lillian Thomas Pratt Collection of Fabergé jewelry, Art Nouveau Gallery.

Wadsworth Atheneum: 600 Main St., Hartford, Conn. 06103. Open: Tues.-Fri. 11–3 (Thurs. to 8), Sat. and Sun. 11–5 (closed Mon.; also Jan. 1, July 4, Thanksgiving, Dec. 25). Suggested contribution: adults, $1; teenagers, 50¢ (children free).
European and American paintings and drawings. Sculpture. Bronzes, silver, porcelain, American period furniture, firearms.

Walker Art Center: Vineland Pl., Minneapolis, Minn. 55403. Open: Tues.-Sat. 10–5 (special exhibition galleries, 5–8), Sun. 11–5 (closed Mon.; also major hldys.). Free.
Collection of major 20th-century art styles. Music, dance, film, theater, and educational programs.

Walters Art Gallery: 600 North Charles St., Baltimore, Md. 21201. Open: Mon. 1–5, Tues.-Sat. 11–5 (July-Aug. Mon. 1–4, Tues.-Sat. 11–4), Sun. and hldys. 2–5 (closed Jan. 1, July 4, Thanksgiving, Dec. 24–25). Free.
Art from ancient empires through 19th-century Europe. Collections of paintings, sculpture, decorative arts, and manuscripts.

Wheelwright Museum, The: 704 Camino Lejo, Santa Fe, N.M. 87502. Open: May-Oct., Mon.-Sat. 10–5, Sun. 1–5; Nov.-April, same as above except closed Mon. (closed Jan. 1, Thanksgiving, Dec. 25). Free.
Baskets, textiles, pottery, jewelry. Historic and contemporary Indian art. (Formerly the Museum of Navajo Ceremonial Art.)

Worcester Art Museum: 55 Salisbury St., Worcester, Mass. 01608. Open: Tues.-Sat. 10–5, Sun. 2–5 (closed Mon.; also Jan. 1, July 4, Thanksgiving, Dec. 25). Adm. $1 (children under 14 and senior citizens, 50¢; children under 5, free).
Art from Egyptian to modern times, with emphasis on painting and sculpture.

1. Summer hours (April 1-Labor Day), Mon.-Sat. 10–9, Sun. 12–9. 2. Send inquiries to Museum Division, Oak Ridge Associated Universities, P.O. Box 117, Oak Ridge, Tenn. 37830. 3. Combination rates are available for Farmers' Museum and Fenimore House.

SPORTS

Sports Personalities

A name in parentheses is the original name or form of name. Localities are places of birth. Dates of birth appear as month/day/year. **Boldface** years in parentheses are dates of **(birth-death).**
Information has been gathered from many sources, including the individuals themselves. However, the *Information Please Almanac* cannot guarantee the accuracy of every individual item.

Aaron, Hank (Henry) (baseball); Mobile, Ala., 2/5/1934
Abdul-Jabbar, Kareem (Lewis Ferdinand Alcindor, Jr.) (basketball); New York City, 4/16/1947
Adderly, Herbert A. (football); Philadelphia, 6/8/1939
Alcindor, Lew. *See* Abdul-Jabbar
Ali, Muhammad (Cassius Clay) (boxing); Louisville, Ky., 1/18/1942
Allen, Dick (Richard Anthony) (baseball); Wampum, Pa., 3/8/1942
Allison, Bobby (Robert Arthur) (auto racing); Hueytown, Ala., 12/3/1937
Alworth, Lance (football); Houston, 8/3/1940
Anderson, Donny (Gary Donny) (football); Brooklyn, N.Y., 4/3/1949
Anderson, Ken (football); Batavia, Ill., 2/15/1949
Anderson, Sparky (George) (baseball); Bridgewater, S.D., 2/22/1934
Andretti, Mario (auto racing); Montona, Trieste, Italy, 2/28/1940
Anthony, Earl (bowling); Kent, Wash. 4/27/1938
Arcaro, Eddie (George Edward) (jockey); Cincinnati, 2/19/1916
Arfons, Arthur Eugene (auto racing); Akron, Ohio, 2/3/1926
Ashe, Arthur (tennis); Richmond, Va., 7/10/1943
Austin, Tracy (tennis); Rolling Hills, Calif., 12/2/1962
Axelrod, Albert (fencing); New York City, 2/21/1921
Babashoff, Shirley (swimming); Whittier, Calif., 1/31/1957
Baer, Max (boxer); Omaha, Neb. **(1909–1959)**
Bakken, Jim (James Leroy) (football); Madison, Wis., 11/2/1940
Ball, Catherine (Catie) (swimming); Jacksonville, Fla., 9/30/1951
Banks, Ernie (baseball); Dallas, 1/31/1931
Bannister, Roger (runner); Harrow, England, 3/24/1929
Barry, Rick (Richard) (basketball); Elizabeth, N.J., 3/28/1944
Bauer, Hank (Henry) (baseball); East St. Louis, Ill., 7/31/1922
Baugh, Sammy (football); Temple, Tex., 3/17/1914
Bayi, Filbert (runner); Karratu, Tanganyika, 6/23/1953
Baylor, Elgin (basketball); Washington, D.C., 9/16/1934
Beamon, Bob (long jumper); New York City, 8/2/1946
Beard, Frank (golf); Dallas, 5/1/1939
Beliveau, Jean (hockey); Three Rivers, Quebec, Canada, 8/31/1931
Beman, Deane (golf); Washington, D.C., 4/22/1938
Bench, Johnny (Johnny Lee) (baseball); Oklahoma City, 12/7/1947
Berg, Patty (Patricia Jane) (golf); Minneapolis, 2/13/1918
Berning, Susie Maxwell (golf); Pasadena, Calif., 7/22/1941
Berra, Yogi (Lawrence) (baseball); St. Louis, 5/12/1925
Biletnikoff, Frederick (football); Erie, Pa., 2/23/1943
Bird, Larry (basketball); French Lick, Ind., 12/7/1956
Blaik, Earl H. (football); Detroit, 2/15/1897
Blanda, George Frederick (football); Youngwood, Pa., 9/17/1927
Blue, Vida (baseball); Mansfield, La., 7/28/1949
Borg, Björn (tennis); Stockholm, 6/6/1956
Boros, Julius (golf); Fairfield, Conn., 3/3/1920
Boston, Ralph (long jumper); Laurel, Miss., 5/9/1939
Bradley, Bill (William Warren) (basketball); Crystal City, Mo., 7/28/1943
Bradshaw, Terry (football); Shreveport, La., 9/2/1948
Breedlove, Craig (Norman) (speed driving); Los Angeles, 3/23/1938
Brock, Louis Clark (baseball); El Dorado, Ark., 6/18/1939
Brown, Doris (runner); Tacoma, Wash., 9/17/1942
Brown, Jimmy (football); St. Simon Island, Ga., 2/17/1936
Brown, Larry (football); Clairton, Pa., 9/19/1947
Brumel, Valeri (high jumper); Tolbuzino, Siberia, 4/14/1942
Bryant, Rosalyn Evette (track); Chicago, 1/7/1956
Burton, Michael (swimming); Des Moines, Iowa, 7/3/1947
Butkus, Dick (Richard Marvin) (football); Chicago, 12/9/1942
Campanella, Roy (baseball); Homestead, Pa., 11/19/1921
Campbell, Earl (football); Tyler, Tex., 3/29/1955
Caponi, Donna Maria. *See* Young, Donna
Cappelletti, Gino (football); Keewatin, Minn., 3/26/1934
Carew, Rod (Rodney Cline) (baseball); Gatun, Panama, 10/1/1945
Carlos, John (sprinter); New York City, 6/5/1945
Carlton, Steven Norman (baseball); Miami, Fla., 12/22/1944
Carner, Joanne Gunderson (Mrs. Don) (golf); Kirkland, Wash., 3/4/1939
Casals, Rosemary (tennis); San Francisco, 9/16/1948
Casper, Billy (golf); San Diego, Calif., 6/24/1931
Caulkins, Tracy (swimming); Wimona, Minn., 1/11/63
Cauthen, Steve (jockey); Covington, Ky., 5/1/1960
Cawley, Evonne; *see* Goolagong
Chamberlain, Wilt (Wilton) (basketball); Philadelphia, 8/21/1936
Chinaglia, Giorgio (soccer); Carrara, Italy 1/24/1947
Chapot, Frank (equestrian); Camden, N.J., 2/24/1934
Clarke, Bobby (Robert Earle) (hockey); Flin Flon, Manitoba, Canada, 8/13/1949
Clay, Cassius. *See* Ali, Muhammad
Clemente, Roberto Walker (baseball); Carolina, Puerto Rico **(1934–1972)**
Cobb, Tyrus Raymond (Ty) (baseball); Narrows, Ga. **(1886–1961)**
Cochran, Barbara Ann (skiing); Claremont, N.H., 1/4/1951
Cochran, Marilyn (skiing); Burlington, Vt., 2/7/1950
Cochran, Robert (skiing); Claremont, N.H., 12/11/1951
Coe, Sebastian Newbold (track); London, England, 9/29/1956
Colavito, Rocky (Rocco Domenico) (baseball); New York City, 8/10/1933
Comaneci, Nadia (gymnast); Onesti, Romania, 11/12/1961
Connors, Jimmy (James Scott) (tennis); East St. Louis, Ill., 9/2/1952
Cordero, Angel (jockey); Santurce, Puerto Rico, 5/8/1942
Cournoyer, Yvan Serge (hockey); Drummondville, Quebec, Canada, 11/22/1943
Court, Margaret Smith (tennis); Albury, New South Wales, Australia, 7/16/1942
Cousy, Bob (basketball); New York City, 8/9/1928
Crenshaw, Ben (golf); Austin, Tex., 1/11/1952
Cronin, Joe (baseball executive); San Francisco, 10/12/1906
Cruyff, Johan (soccer); Amsterdam, Netherlands, 4/25/47
Csonka, Larry (Lawrence Richard) (football); Stow, Ohio, 12/25/1946
Dancer, Stanley (harness racing); New Egypt, N.J., 7/25/1927
Dark, Alvin (baseball); Comanche, Okla., 1/7/1922
Davenport, Willie (track); Troy, Ala., 6/6/1943
Dawson, Leonard Ray (football); Alliance, Ohio, 6/20/1935
Dean, Dizzy (Jay Hanna) (baseball player); Lucas, Ark. **(1911–1974)**
DeBusschere, Dave (basketball); Detroit, 10/16/1940
Delvecchio, Alex Peter (hockey); Fort William, Ontario, Canada, 12/4/1931
Demaret, Jim (golf); Houston, 5/10/1910
Dempsey, Jack (William H.) (boxing); Manassa, Colo., 6/24/1895
DeVicenzo, Roberto (golf); Buenos Aires, 4/14/1923
Dibbs, Edward George (tennis); Brooklyn, N.Y., 2/23/1951
Dietz, James W. (rowing); New York, N.Y., 1/12/1949
DiMaggio, Joe (baseball); Martinez, Calif., 11/25/1914
Dionne, Marcel (hockey); Drummondville, Quebec, Canada, 8/3/1951
Dominguín, Luis Miguel (matador); Madrid, 12/9/1926
Dorsett, Tony (football); Rochester, Pa., 4/7/1954
Douglass, Bobby (football); Manhattan, Kan., 6/22/1947
Dryden, Kenneth (hockey); Hamilton, Ontario, Canada, 8/4/1947
Drysdale, Don (baseball); Van Nuys, Calif., 7/23/1936
Duran, Roberto (boxing); Panama City 6/16/1951
Durocher, Leo (baseball); West Springfield, Mass., 7/27/1906
Durr, François (tennis); Algiers, Algeria, 12/25/1942
El Cordobés, (Manuel Benítez Pérez) (matador); Palma del Río, Córdoba, Spain, 5/4/1936(?)
Elder, Lee (golf); Dallas, 7/14/1934
Emerson, Roy (tennis); Kingsway, Australia, 11/3/1936
Ender, Kornelia (swimming); Plauen, East Germany, 10/25/1958
Erving, Julius (Dr. J) (basketball); Roosevelt, N.Y., 2/22/1950
Esposito, Phil (Philip Anthony) (hockey); Sault Ste. Marie, Ontario, Canada, 2/20/1942
Evans, Lee (runner); Mandena, Calif., 2/25/1947
Evert, Chris; *see* **Lloyd**
Ewbank, Weeb (football); Richmond, Ind., 5/6/1907
Feller, Robert (Bobby) (baseball); Van Meter, Iowa, 11/3/1918
Feuerbach, Allan Dean (track); Preston, Iowa, 1/12/1948
Finley, Charles O. (sportsman); Ensley, Ala., 2/22/1918
Fischer, Bobby (chess); Chicago, 3/9/1943
Fittipaldi, Emerson (auto racer); Sao Paulo, Brazil, 12/12/1946
Fitzsimmons, Bob (Robert Prometheus) (boxer); Cornwall, England **(1862–1917)**
Fleming, Peggy Gale (ice skating); San Jose, Calif., 7/27/1948
Ford, Whitey (Edward) (baseball); New York City, 10/28/1928
Foreman, George (boxing); Marshall, Tex., 1/10/1949
Fosbury, Richard (high jumper); Portland, Ore., 3/6/1947
Fox, Nellie (Jacob Nelson) (baseball); St. Thomas, Pa. **(1927–1975)**
Foxx, James Emory (baseball); Sudlersville, Md., **(1907–1967)**

Foyt, A. J. (auto racing); Houston, 1/16/1935
Francis, Emile (hockey); North Battleford, Sask., 9/13/1926
Fratianne, Linda (figure skating), Los Angeles 8/2/1960
Frazier, Joe (boxing); Beauford, S.C., 1/17/1944
Frazier, Walt (basketball); Atlanta, 3/29/1945
Frick, Ford C. (baseball); Wawaka, Ind., **(1894–1978)**
Furniss, Bruce (swimming); Fresno, Calif., 5/27/1957
Gable, Dan (wrestling); Waterloo, Iowa; 10/25/1945
Gabriel, Roman (football); Wilmington, N.C., 8/5/1940
Gallagher, Michael Donald (skiing); Yonkers, N.Y., 10/3/1941
Gehrig, Lou (Henry Louis Gehrig) (baseball); New York City **(1903–1941)**
Gehringer, Charlie (baseball); Fowlerville, Mich., 5/11/1903
Geoffrion, Bernie (Boom Boom) (hockey); Montreal, 2/14/1931
Gerulaitis, Vitas (tennis); Brooklyn, N.Y., 7/26/1954
Giacomin, Ed (hockey); Sudbury, Ontario, Canada, 6/6/1939
Gibson, Bob (baseball); Omaha, Neb., 11/9/1935
Gifford, Frank (football); Santa Monica, Calif., 8/16/1930
Gilbert, Rod (Rodrique) (hockey); Montreal, 7/1/1941
Giles, Warren (baseball executive); Tiskilwa, Ill., **(1896–1979)**
Gilmore, Artis (basketball); Chipley, Fla., 9/21/1949
Glance, Harvey (track); Phenix City, Ala., 3/28/1957
Gonzalez, Pancho (tennis); Los Angeles, 5/9/1928
Goodell, Brian Stuart (swimming); Stockton, Calif., 4/2/1959
Goodrich, Gail (basketball); Los Angeles, 4/23/1943
Goolagong Cawley, Evonne (tennis); Griffith, Australia, 7/31/1951
Gottfried, Brian (tennis); Baltimore, Md., 1/27/1952
Graham, David (golf); Windson, Australia; 5/23/1946
Graham, Otto Everett (football); Waukegan, Ill., 12/6/1921
Grange, Red (Harold) (football); Forksville, Pa., 6/13/1904
Green, Hubert (golf); Birmingham, Ala., 12/28/1946
Greene, Charles E. (sprinter); Pine Bluff, Ark., 3/21/1945
Griese, Bob (Robert Allen) (football); Evansville, Ind., 2/3/1945
Grove, Lefty (Robert Moses) (baseball); Lonaconing, Md., **(1900–1975)**
Groza, Lou (football); Martins Ferry, Ohio, 1/25/1924
Guidry, Ronald Ames (baseball); Lafayette, La., 8/28/1950
Gunter, Nancy Richey (tennis); San Angelo, Tex., 8/23/1942
Halas, George (football); Chicago, 2/2/1895
Hall, Gary (swimming); Fayetteville, N.C., 8/7/1951
Hamill, Dorothy (figure skater); Chicago, 1956(?)
Hammond, Kathy (runner); Sacramento, Calif., 11/2/1951
Harris, Franco (football); Ft. Dix, N.J., 3/7/1950
Hartack, William, Jr. (jockey); Colver, Pa., 12/9/1932
Haughton, William (harness racing); Gloversville, N.Y., 11/2/1923
Havlicek, John (basketball); Martins Ferry, Ohio, 4/8/1940
Hayes, Elvin (basketball); Rayville, La., 11/17/1945
Haynie, Sandra (golf); Fort Worth, 6/4/1943
Heiden, Eric (speed skating), Madison, Wis., 6/14/1958
Hencken, John (swimming); Culver City, Calif., 5/29/1954
Henie, Sonja (ice skater); b. Oslo **(1912–1969)**
Hickcox, Charles (swimming); Phoenix, Ariz., 2/6/1947
Hines, James (sprinter); Dumas, Ark., 9/10/1946
Hodges, Gil (baseball); Princeton, Ind. **(1924–1972)**
Hogan, Ben (golf); Dublin, Tex., 8/13/1912
Holmes, Larry (boxing); Cuthert, Ga., 11/3/1949
Hornsby, Rogers (baseball); Winters, Tex. **(1896–1963)**
Hornung, Paul (football); Louisville, Ky., 12/23/1935
Houk, Ralph (baseball); Lawrence, Kan., 8/9/1919
Howard, Elston (baseball); St. Louis, 2/23/1930
Howe, Gordon (hockey); Floral, Sask., Canada, 3/31/1928
Howell, Jim Lee (football); Lonoke, Ark., 9/27/1914
Hubbell, Carl (baseball); Carthage, Mo., 6/22/1903
Huff, Sam (Robert Lee) (football); Morgantown, W. Va., 10/4/1934
Hull, Bobby (hockey); Point Anne, Ontario, Canada, 1/3/1939
Hunter, Jim (Catfish) (baseball); Hertford, N.C., 4/8/1946
Huntley, Joni (track); McMinnville, Ore., 8/4/1956
Hutson, Donald (football); Pine Bluff, Ark., 1/31/1913
Insko, Del (harness racing); Amboy, Minn., 7/10/1931
Irwin, Hale (golf); Joplin, Mo., 6/3/1945
Jackson, Reggie (baseball); Wyncote, Pa., 5/18/1946
Jeffries, James J. (boxer); Carroll, Ohio **(1875–1953)**
Jenkins, Ferguson Arthur (baseball); Chatham, Ontario, Canada, 12/13/1943
Jenner, (W.) Bruce (track); Mt. Kisco, N.Y., 10/28/1949
Jezek, Linda (swimming); Palo Alto, Calif., 3/10/1960
Job, Brian (swimming); Warren, Ohio, 11/29/1951
Johnson, Anthony (rowing); Washington, D.C., 11/16/1940
Johnson, Jack (John Arthur Johnson) (boxer); Galveston, Tex. **(1876–1946)**
Johnson, Rafer (decathlon); Hillsboro, Tex., 8/18/1935
Jones, Deacon (David) (football); Eatonville, Fla., 12/9/1938
Juantoreno, Alberto (track); Santiago, Cuba, 12/3/1951
Jurgensen, Sonny (football); Wilmington, N.C., 8/23/1934
Kaline, Al (Albert) (baseball); Baltimore, 12/19/1934
Keino, Kipchoge (runner); Kapchemoiymo, Kenya, 1/1940
Kelly, Leroy (football); Philadelphia, 5/20/1942
Kelly, Red (Leonard Patrick) (hockey); Simcoe, Ontario, Canada, 7/9/1927
Killebrew, Harmon (baseball); Payette, Idaho, 6/29/1936
Killy, Jean-Claude (skiing); Saint-Cloud, France, 8/30/1943
Kilmer, Bill (William Orland) (football); Topeka, Kan., 9/5/1939
King, Billie Jean (Billie Jean Moffitt) (tennis); Long Beach, Calif., 11/22/1943
Kinsella, John (swimming); Oak Park, Ill., 8/26/1952
Kodes, Jan (tennis); Prague, 3/1/1946
Kolb, Claudia (swimming); Hayward, Calif., 12/19/1949
Koosman, Jerry Martin (baseball); Appleton, Minn., 12/23/1942
Korbut, Olga (gymnast); Grodno, Byelorussia, U.S.S.R., 5/16/1955
Koufax, Sandy (Sanford) (baseball); Brooklyn, N.Y., 12/30/1935
Kramer, Jack (tennis); Las Vegas, Nev., 8/1/1921
Kramer, Jerry (football); Jordan, Mont., 1/23/1936
Kuhn, Bowie Kent (baseball); Takoma Park, Md., 10/28/1926
Kwalik, Ted (Thaddeus John) (football); McKees Rocks, Pa., 4/15/1947
Lafleur, Guy Damien (hockey); Thurson, Quebec, Canada, 8/20/1951
Laird, Ronald (walker); Louisville, Ky., 5/31/1935
Lamonica, Daryle (football); Fresno, Calif., 7/17/1941
Landis, Kenesaw Mountain (1st baseball commissioner); Millville, Ohio **(1866–1944)**
Landry, Tom (football); Mission, Tex., 9/11/1924
Landy, John (runner); Australia, 4/4/1930
Larrieu, Francie (track); Palo Alto, Calif., 11/28/1952
Laver, Rod (tennis); Rockhampton, Australia, 8/9/1938
Leonard, Benny (Benjamin Leiner) (boxer); New York City **(1896–1947)**
Leonard, Sugar Ray (boxing); Wilmington, N.C. 5/17/1956
Linehan, Kim (swimming); Bronxville, N.Y., 12/11/1962
Liquori, Marty (runner); Montclair, N.J., 9/11/1949
Little, Floyd Douglas (football); New Haven, Conn., 7/4/1942
Little, Lou (football); Leominster, Mass., **(1893–1979)**
Littler, Gene (golf); San Diego, Calif., 11/16/1920
Lloyd, Chris Evert (Christine Marie) (tennis); Fort Lauderdale, Fla., 12/21/1954
Lombardi, Vince (football); Brooklyn, N.Y. **(1913–1970)**
Longden, Johnny (horse racing); Wakefield, England, 2/14/1907
Lopez, Al (baseball); Tampa, Fla., 8/20/1908
Lopez, Nancy (golf); Torrance, Calif., 1/6/1957
Louis, Joe (Joe Louis Barrow) (boxing); Lexington, Ala., 5/13/1914
Lynn, Frederic Michael (baseball); Chicago, Ill., 2/3/1952
Lynn, Janet (figure skating); Rockford, Ill., 4/6/1953
Mack, Connie (Cornelius Alexander McGillicuddy) (baseball executive); East Brookfield, Mass. **(1862–1956)**
Mackey, John (football); New York City, 9/24/1941
Mahovlich, Frank (Francis William) (hockey); Timmins, Ontario, Canada, 1/10/1938
Mann, Carol (golf); Buffalo, N.Y., 2/3/1941
Manning, Madeline (runner); Cleveland, 1/11/1948
Mantle, Mickey Charles (baseball); Spavinaw, Okla., 10/20/1931
Marichal, Juan (baseball); Laguna Verde, Montecristi, Dominican Republic, 10/20/1937
Maris, Roger (baseball); Hibbing, Minn., 9/10/1934
Martin, Billy (Alfred Manuel) (baseball); Berkeley, Calif., 5/16/1928
Martin, Rick (Richard Lionel) (hockey); Verdun, Quebec, Canada, 7/26/1951
Mathews, Ed (Edwin) (baseball); Texarkana, Tex., 10/13/1931
Matson, Randy (shot putter); Kilgore, Tex., 3/5/1945
Mays, Willie (baseball); Westfield, Ala., 5/6/1931
Melton-Lopez, Nancy; *See* Lopez, Nancy
McAdoo, Bob (basketball); Greensboro, N.C., 9/25/1951
McCarthy, Joe (Joseph Vincent) (baseball); Philadelphia **(1887–1978)**
McCovey, Willie Lee (baseball); Mobile, Ala., 1/10/1938
McEnroe, John Patrick, Jr. (tennis); Wiesbaden, Germany, 2/16/1959
McGraw, John Joseph (baseball); Truxton, N.Y. **(1873–1934)**
McIngvale, Cynthia Potter (diving); Houston, 8/27/1950
McLain, Dennis (baseball); Chicago, 3/24/1944
McMillan, Kathy Laverne (track); Raeford, N.C., 11/7/1957
Merrill, Janice (track); New London, Conn., 6/18/1962
Meyer, Deborah (swimming); Haddonfield, N.J., 8/14/1952
Middlecoff, Cary (golf); Halls, Tenn., 1/6/1921
Mikita, Stan (hockey); Sokolce, Czechoslovakia, 5/20/1940
Milburn, Rodney, Jr. (hurdler); Opelousas, La., 5/18/1950
Miller, Johnny (golf); San Francisco, 4/29/1947
Montgomery, Jim (swimming); Madison, Wis., 1/24/1955
Moore, Archie (boxing); Benoit, Miss., 12/13/1916
Morgan, Joe Leonard (baseball); Bonham, Tex., 9/19/1943
Morrall, Earl (football); Muskegon, Mich., 5/17/1934
Morris, Mercury (Eugene) (football); Pittsburgh, 1/5/1947
Morton, Craig L. (football); Flint, Mich., 2/5/1943
Mosconi, Willie (pocket billiards); Philadelphia, 6/27/1913
Moser, Annemarie; *see* Proell, Annemarie
Moses, Edward Corley (track); Dayton, Ohio, 8/31/1958
Munson, Thurman (baseball); Akron, Ohio, **(1947–1979)**
Murphy, Calvin (basketball), Norwalk, Conn., 5/9/1948
Musial, Stan (baseball); Donora, Pa., 11/21/1920
Myers, Linda (archery); York, Pa., 6/19/1947
Naber, John (swimming); Evanston, Ill., 1/20/1956

Namath, Joe (Joseph William) (football); Beaver Falls, Pa., 5/31/1943
Nastase, Ilie (tennis); Bucharest, 7/19/1946
Navratilova, Martina (tennis); Prague, 10/10/1956
Nehemiah, Renaldo (track); Newark, N.J., 3/24/1959
Nelson, Cindy (skiing); Lutsen, Minn. 8/19/1955
Newcombe, John (tennis); Sydney, Australia, 5/23/1943
Nicklaus, Jack (golf); Columbus, Ohio, 1/21/1940
North, Lowell (yachting); Springfield, Mo., 12/2/1929
Oerter, Al (discus thrower); New York City, 9/19/1936
Okker, Tom (tennis); Amsterdam, 2/22/1944
Oldfield, Barney (racing driver); Fulton County, Ohio **(1878–1946)**
Oliva, Tony (Pedro) (baseball); Pinar Del Rio, Cuba, 7/20/1940
Olsen, Merlin Jay (football); Logan, Utah, 9/15/1940
O'Malley, Walter (baseball executive); New York City, **(1903–1979)**
Orantes, Manuel (tennis); Granada, Spain, 2/6/1949
Orr, Bobby (hockey); Parry Sound, Ontario, Canada, 3/20/1948
Ovett, Steve (track); Brighton, England, 10/9/1955
Owens, Jesse (track); Decatur, Ala., **(1914–1980)**
Pace, Darrell (archery); Cincinnati, 10/23/1956
Paige, Satchel (Leroy) (baseball); Mobile, Ala., 7/7/1906
Palmer, Arnold (golf); Latrobe, Pa., 9/10/1929
Palmer, James Alvin (baseball); New York City, 10/15/1945
Parent, Bernard Marcel (hockey); Montreal, 4/3/1945
Park, Brad (Douglas Bradford) (hockey); Toronto, Ontario, Canada, 7/6/1948
Parseghian, Ara (football); Akron, Ohio, 5/21/1923
Pasarell, Charles (tennis); San Juan, Puerto Rico, 2/12/1944
Patterson, Floyd (boxing); Waco, N.C., 1/4/1935
Pearson, David Gene (auto racing); 12/22/1934
Pelé (Edson Arantes do Nascimento) (soccer); Tres Coracoes, Brazil, 10/23/1940
Perry, Gaylord (baseball); Williamston, N.C., 9/13/1938
Pettit, Bob (basketball); Baton Rouge, La., 12/12/1932
Petty, Richard Lee (auto racing); Randleman, N.C., 7/2/1937
Pincay, Laffit, Jr. (jockey); Panama City, Panama, 12/29/1946
Plante, Jacques (hockey); Shawinigan Falls, Quebec, Canada, 1/17/1929
Player, Gary (golf); Johannesburg, South Africa, 11/1/1935
Plunkett, Jim (football); San Jose, Calif., 12/5/1947
Potter, Cynthia. *See* McIngvale
Potvin, Denis Charles (hockey); Hull, Quebec, Canada, 10/29/1953
Powell, Boog (John) (baseball); Lakeland, Fla., 8/17/1941
Prefontaine, Steve Roland (runner); Coos Bay, Ore. **(1951–1975)**
Proell, Annemarie Moser (Alpine skier); Kleinarl, Austria, 3/27/1953
Ralston, Dennis (tennis); Bakersfield, Calif., 7/27/1942
Rankin, Judy Torluemke (golf); St. Louis, Mo., 2/18/1945
Ratelle, Jean (Joseph Gilbert Yvon Jean) (hockey); St. Jean, Quebec, Canada, 10/29/1953
Rawls, Betsy (Elizabeth Earle) (golf); Spartanburg, S.C., 5/4/1928
Reed, Willis (basketball); Hico, La., 6/25/1942
Reese, Pee Wee (Harold) (baseball); Ekron, Ky., 7/23/1919
Reid, Kerry Melville (tennis); Mosman, Australia, 8/7/1947
Richard, Maurice (hockey); Montreal, 8/14/1924
Riessen, Martin (tennis); Hinsdale, Ill., 12/4/1941
Rigney, William (baseball); Alameda, Calif., 1/29/1918
Rizzuto, Phil (baseball); New York City, 9/25/1918
Roark, Helen Wills Moody (tennis); Centerville, Calif., 10/6/1922
Robertson, Oscar (basketball); Charlotte, Tenn., 11/24/1938
Robinson, Arnie (track); San Diego, Calif., 4/7/1948
Robinson, Brooks (baseball); Little Rock, Ark., 5/18/1937
Robinson, Frank (baseball); Beaumont, Tex., 8/31/1935
Robinson, Jackie (baseball); Cairo, Ga. **(1919–1972)**
Robinson, Larry Clark (hockey); Marvelville, Ontario, Canada, 6/2/1951
Robinson, (Sugar) Ray (boxing); Detroit, 5/3/1920
Rockne, Knute Kenneth (football); Voss, Norway **(1888–1931)**
Rockwell, Martha (skiing); Providence, R.I., 4/26/1944
Rono, Harry (track); Kiptaragon, Kenya, 2/12/1952
Rose, Pete (Peter Edward) (baseball); Cincinnati, 4/14/1942
Rosenbloom, Maxie (boxing); New York City **(1904–1976)**
Rosewall, Ken (tennis); Sydney, Australia, 11/2/1934
Rote, Kyle (football); San Antonio, 10/27/1928
Rozelle, Pete (Alvin Ray) (commissioner of National Football League); South Gate, Calif., 3/1/1926
Rudolph, Wilma Glodean (sprinter); St. Bethlehem, Tenn., 6/23/1940
Russell, Bill (basketball); Monroe, La., 2/12/1934
Ruth, Babe (George Herman Ruth) (baseball); Baltimore **(1895–1948)**
Rutherford, Johnny (auto racing); Fort Worth, 3/12/1938
Ryan, Nolan (Lynn Nolan, Jr.) (baseball); Refugio, Tex., 1/31/1947
Ryon, Luann (archery); Long Beach, Calif., 1/13/1953
Ryun, Jim (runner); Wichita, Kan., 4/29/1947
Santana, Manuel (Manuel Santana Martinez) (tennis); Chamartin, Spain, 5/10/1938
Sayers, Gale (football); Wichita, Kan., 5/30/1943
Schoendienst, Al (Albert) (baseball); Germantown, Ill., 2/2/1923
Schollander, Donald (swimming); Charlotte, N.C., 4/30/1946
Seagren, Bob (Robert Lloyd) (pole vaulter); Pomona, Calif., 10/17/1946
Seaver, Tom (baseball); Fresno, Calif., 11/17/1944
Seidler, Marem (track); Brooklyn, N.Y., 6/11/1962
Sherman, Allie (football); Brooklyn, N.Y., 2/10/1923
Shoemaker, Willie (jockey); Fabens, Tex., 8/19/1931
Shorter, Frank (runner); Munich, Germany, 10/31/1947
Shula, Don (Donald Francis) (football); Grand River, Ohio, 1/4/1930
Silvester, Jay (discus thrower); Tremonton, Utah, 2/27/1937
Simpson, O. J. (Orenthal James) (football); San Francisco, 7/9/1947
Sims, Billy (football); St. Louis, 9/18/1955
Smith, Bubba (Charles Aaron) (football); Orange, Tex., 2/28/1945
Smith, Ronnie Ray (sprinter); Los Angeles, 3/28/1949
Smith, Stanley Roger (tennis); Pasadena, Calif., 12/14/1946
Smith, Tommie (sprinter); Clarksville, Tex., 6/5/1944
Smoke, Marcia Jones (canoeing); Oklahoma City, 7/18/1941
Snead, Sam (golf); Hot Springs, Va., 5/27/1912
Sneva, Tom (auto racing); Spokane, Wash., 6/1/1948
Snider, Duke (Edwin) (baseball); Los Angeles, 9/19/1926
Solomon, Harold (tennis); Washington, D.C., 9/17/1952
Spahn, Warren (baseball); Buffalo, N.Y., 4/23/1921
Spassky, Boris (chess); Leningrad, 1/30/1937
Speaker, Tristram (baseball); Hubbard City, Tex. **(1888–1958)**
Spinks, Leon (boxing); St. Louis, 7/11/1953
Spitz, Mark (swimming); Modesto, Calif., 2/10/1950
Stabler, Kenneth (football); Foley, Ala., 12/25/1945
Stagg, Amos Alonzo (football); West Orange, N.J. **(1862–1965)**
Stapleton, Pat (hockey); Sarnia, Ontario, Canada, 7/4/1940
Stargell, Willie (Wilver Dornell) (baseball); Earlsboro, Okla., 3/6/1941
Starr, Bart (football); Montgomery, Ala., 1/9/1934
Staubach, Roger (football); Cincinnati, 2/5/1942
Steinkraus, William C. (equestrian); Cleveland, 10/12/1925
Stenerud, Jan (football); Fetsund, Norway, 11/26/1942
Stengel, Casey (Charles Dillon) (baseball); Kansas City, Mo. **(1891–1975)**
Stenmark, Ingemar (Alpine skier); Tarnaby, Sweden, 3/18/1956
Stockton, Richard LaClede (tennis); New York City, 2/18/1951
Stones, Dwight Edwin (track); Los Angeles, 12/6/1953
Sullivan, John Lawrence (boxer); Boston **(1858–1918)**
Sutton, Don (Donald Howard) (baseball); Clio, Ala., 4/2/1945
Tanner, Leonard Roscoe III (tennis); Chattanooga, Tenn., 10/15/1951
Tarkenton, Fran (Francis) (football); Richmond, Va., 2/3/1940
Tebbetts, Birdie (George R.) (baseball); Nashua, N.H., 11/10/1914
Thoeni, Gustavo (Alpine skier); Trafoi, Italy, 2/28/1951
Thompson, David (basketball); Shelby, N.C., 7/13/1954
Thorpe, Jim (James Francis Thorpe) (all-around athlete); nr. Prague, Okla. **(1888–1953)**
Tilden, William Tatem II (tennis); Philadelphia **(1893–1953)**
Tittle, Y. A. (Yelberton Abraham) (football); Marshall, Tex., 10/24/1926
Toomey, William (decathlon); Philadelphia, 1/10/1939
Trevino, Lee (golf); Dallas, 12/1/1939
Tunney, Gene (James J.) (boxing); New York City, **(1898–1978)**
Tyus, Wyomia (runner); Griffin, Ga., 8/29/1945
Unitas, John (football); Pittsburgh, 5/7/1933
Unser, Al (auto racing); Albuquerque, N. Mex., 5/29/1939
Unser, Bobby (auto racing); Albuquerque N. Mex., 2/20/1934
Van Brocklin, Norm (football); Eagle Butte, S. Dak. 3/15/1926
Vilas, Guillermo (tennis); Mar del Plata, Argentina, 8/17/1952
Viren, Lasse (track); Myrskyla, Finland, 7/12/1949
Wade, Virginia (tennis); Bournemouth, England; 7/10/1945
Wagner, Honus (John Peter Honus) (baseball); Carnegie, Pa. **(1867–1955)**
Walcott, Jersey Joe (Arnold Cream) (boxing); Merchantville, N.J., 1/31/1914
Walton, Bill (basketball); La Mesa, Calif., 11/5/1952
Watson, Martha Rae (track); Long Beach, Calif., 8/19/1946
Watson, Tom (golf); Kansas City, Mo., 9/4/1944
Weaver, Earl (baseball); St. Louis, 8/14/1930
Webster, Alex (football); Kearny, N.J., 4/19/1931
Weiskopf, Tom (golf); Massillon, Ohio, 11/9/1942
Weiss, George (baseball executive); New Haven, Conn. **(1895–1972)**
Weissmuller, Johnny (swimmer and actor); Windber, Pa., 6/2/1904
West, Jerry (basketball); Cheylan, W. Va., 5/28/1938
White, Willye B. (long jumper); Money, Miss., 1/1/1936
Whitworth, Kathy (golf); Monahans, Tex., 9/27/1939
Wilbur, Doreen (archery); Jefferson, Iowa, 1/8/1930
Wilkens, Mac Maurice (track); Eugene, Ore., 11/15/1950
Wilkins, Lennie (basketball); 11/25/1937
Wilkinson, Bud (football); Minneapolis, 4/23/1916
Williams, Dick (baseball); St. Louis, 5/7/1929
Williams, Ted (baseball); San Diego, Calif., 8/30/1918
Wills, Maury (baseball); Washington, D.C., 10/2/1932
Wohlhuter, Richard C. (runner); Geneva, Ill. 12/23/1945
Woodhead, Cynthia (swimming); Riverside, Calif., 2/7/1964
Wottle, David James (runner); Canton, Ohio, 8/7/1950
Wright, Mickey (Mary Kathryn) (golf); San Diego, Calif., 2/14/1935
Yarborough, Cale (William Caleb) (auto racing); Timmonsville, S.C., 3/27/1939
Yastrzemski, Carl (baseball); Southampton, N.Y., 8/22/1939
Young, Cy (Denton True Young) (baseball); Gilmore, Ohio **(1867–1955)**
Young, Donna Caponi (golf); Detroit, 1/29/1945
Young, Sheila (speed skater, bicycle racer); Detroit, 10/14/1950

The Olympics: Contest, Crisis, and Controversy

The 1980 Moscow Summer Olympics, which the Soviet Union hoped to use as a hallmark for acceptance of its system among the nations of the world, were shrouded in political controversy for several months before they got under way on July 19.

An American-led boycott by more than 50 nations who objected to the Soviet military intervention in Afghanistan in February, prevented many of the best athletes from competing. The Soviet move into Afghanistan had come shortly before the start of the Winter Olympics in Lake Placid, N.Y., and while American hostages were being held in Iran.

The boycott created confusion and doubt among athletes who had trained long and hard for a chance to compete for medals, and now had to relinquish that opportunity. It was spearheaded by President Carter as a protest against the intervention and was designed to reduce Soviet luster in its efforts to conduct the world's biggest athletic event. There had been much clamor among the Western bloc nations to shift the site of the Games or to cancel them altogether as a rebuff to the Soviet military action. The Soviet had spent $300 million in preparations, sparing no cost to put on its best face as a host. It proudly presented the Olympic mascot, Misha the Bear, as a symbol of friendly good will to the world.

The boycott proved costly for television also. The National Broadcasting Company, which had bought the rights to televise the Games for $87 million, decided not to in deference to the boycott. Although NBC was insured for 90% of the sum, its loss was estimated at $20 million after expenses for moving equipment and personnel to and from Moscow were totaled.

Despite the boycott, 81 nations (the lowest number since the 1956 Games at Melbourne) sent 5,687 athletes to Moscow. Controversy arose from the start. President Carter had forbidden the display of the American flag at any of the events by officials or tourists attending the Games. Lord Killanin of Ireland, president of the International Olympic Committee, in remarks aimed primarily at the United States, warned that future Olympics could suffer "if politicians continue to make use of sport for their own ends."

On the day of the opening ceremonies, tens of thousands of uniformed Soviet soldiers and policemen ringed the huge Lenin Stadium, virtually sealed off the Capital, and swept all traffic off the streets, creating a stern security atmosphere. In the stadium, two Americans unfurled a 6-foot American flag as the crowd of 103,000, mostly Russians, cheered wildly. Sixteen nations paraded without their nations' flags, preferring to display 5-ringed Olympic flags instead.

The day before, thousands of Muscovites line the streets to welcome the runner bearing the Olympic flame. A two-week festival seemed under way for city-dwellers and their nearby rural neighbors. Food stuffs, such as oranges and bananas, cheese and sausages, normally in short supply in Moscow, were trucked in to impress citizens and tourists. Prices soared in stores and shops. According to reports, however, little friendly intermingling took place.

Because of the absence of the world's best performers in certain esoteric disciplines, such as horsemanship, rowing, canoeing, etc., competition suffered. But in general quality was not lacking. Thirty-six world records were broken, significantly several in swimming and track and field, events considered the province of Western athletes.

Russians and East Germans dominated the gold-medal victories. Soviet athletes accounted for 80 (197 over all) and East Germans 47 (126 over all), prompting some to observe that they were engaging in a private Spartakiade.

There were incidents that begged for sportsmanship. Cuban boxers were booed by Russian spectators, who also jeered some of their own athletes. Vasily Alekseyev, the defending Olympic weight-lifting champion regarded for a long time as the "world's strongest man," was jeered and whistled by the Soviet crowd after his failure to retain his title. Allegations were made that some Eastern bloc judges showed favoritism in track and gymnastics events. In women's gymnastics, a Romanian coach charged that an East German committee official had ordered the lowering of a score by Nadia Comaneci of Romania to assure a Soviet gold medal in the all-around competition.

In track, officials of the International Amateur Athletic Federation, the world governing body, at the outset were not permitted on the field to observe the events close at hand. Eventually they took the field, but not before allegations that Eastern bloc judges favored athletes by making improper measurements and allowing violations that normally might have led to disqualifications. There were also charges that athletes were using drugs to improve performances, but an inquiry by the Olympic Medical Commission proved the charges unwarranted.

For the first time, Soviet Olympic swimmers won gold medals in a sport dominated for decades by Americans, Australians, and Japanese. The most significant one was by Vladimir Salnikov, who broke the 15-minute barrier in the 1,500-meter freestyle on his way to winning three gold medals. East German women swimmers once again were dominant. A Russian, an East German, and a Pole shattered world records in the hammer throw, high jump, and pole vault, respectively, and an East German's long jump became the best at sea level.

Some Western athletes, averse to mixing politics and sport, chose not to honor the boycott and competed on their own. Among them were Sebastian Coe, Steve Ovett, Allan Wells, and Daley Thompson of Britain, who each won gold medals. An Ethiopian, Miruts Yifter, took two gold medals in the long-distance races, and two Italians also won track gold medals.

Cubans dominated boxing, with Teofilo Stevenson winning a heavyweight gold medal for the third time. The Russian basketball team, favored in the absence of the Americans, failed to make the final as Yugoslavia gained the title.

At the closing ceremonies Aug. 3, instead of the Stars and Stripes, the flag of Los Angeles, the host city for the 1984 Games, was unfurled in a gesture of compromise that hopefully would help heal the political rift that surrounded the 1980 Olympics.

THE OLYMPIC GAMES

(W)—Site of Winter Games. (S)—Site of Summer Games

1896	Athens
1900	Paris
1904	St. Louis
1906	Athens
1908	London
1912	Stockholm
1920	Antwerp
1924	Chamonix (W)
1924	Paris (S)
1928	St. Moritz (W)
1928	Amsterdam (S)
1932	Lake Placid (W)
1932	Los Angeles (S)
1936	Garmisch-Partenkirchen (W)
1936	Berlin (S)
1948	St. Moritz (W)
1948	London (S)
1952	Oslo (W)
1952	Helsinki (S)
1956	Cortina d'Ampezzo, Italy (W)
1956	Melbourne (S)
1960	Squaw Valley, Calif. (W)
1960	Rome (S)
1964	Innsbruck, Austria (W)
1964	Tokyo (S)
1968	Grenoble, France (W)
1968	Mexico City (S)
1972	Sapporo, Japan (W)
1972	Munich (S)
1976	Innsbruck, Austria (W)
1976	Montreal (S)
1980	Lake Placid (W)
1980	Moscow (S)
1984	Sarajevo, Yugoslavia (W)
1984	Los Angeles (S)

The first Olympic Games of which there is record occurred in 776 B.C. and consisted of one event, a great foot race of about 200 yards held on a plain by the River Alpheus (now the Ruphia) just outside the little town of Olympia in Greece. It was from that date that the Greeks began to keep their calendar by "Olympiads," the four-year spans between the celebrations of the famous games.

The modern Olympic Games, which started in Athens in 1896, are the result of the devotion of a French educator, Baron Pierre de Coubertin, to the idea that, since young people and athletics have gone together down the ages, education and athletics might well go hand-in-hand toward a better international understanding.

At the top of the organization responsible for the Olympic movement and the staging of the Games every four years is the International Olympic Committee (IOC). Other important roles are played by National Olympic Committees in each participating country, international sports federations, and the Organizing Committee of the host city.

In 1979, the IOC consisted of 89 members, elected by the IOC itself. Its headquarters are in Lausanne, Switzerland. The president of the IOC is Lord Killanin of Ireland.

The Olympic motto is "Citius, Altius, Fortius"—"Faster, Higher, Stronger." The Olympic symbol is five interlocking circles colored blue, yellow, black, green, and red, on a white background, representing the five continents. At least one of these colors appears in the national flag of every country.

Summer Games

TRACK AND FIELD—MEN

100-Meter Dash

1896	Thomas Burke, United States	12s
1900	Francis W. Jarvis, United States	10.8s
1904	Archie Hahn, United States	11s
1906	Archie Hahn, United States	11.2s
1908	Reginald Walker, South Africa	10.8s
1912	Ralph Craig, United States	10.8s
1920	Charles Paddock, United States	10.8s
1924	Harold Abrahams, Great Britain	10.6s
1928	Percy Williams, Canada	10.8s
1932	Eddie Tolan, United States	10.3s
1936	Jesse Owens, United States	10.3s[1]
1948	Harrison Dillard, United States	10.3s
1952	Lindy Remigino, United States	10.4s
1956	Bobby Morrow, United States	10.5s
1960	Armin Hary, Germany	10.2s
1964	Robert Hayes, United States	10s
1968	James Hines, United States	9.9s
1972	Valery Borzov, U.S.S.R.	10.14s
1976	Hasely Crawford, Trinidad and Tebago	10.06s
1980	Allan Wells, Britain	10.25s

1. Wind assisted.

200-Meter Dash

1900	John Tewksbury, United States	22.2s
1904	Archie Hahn, United States	21.6s
1908	Robert Kerr, Canada	22.6s
1912	Ralph Craig, United States	21.7s
1920	Allan Woodring, United States	22s
1924	Jackson Scholz, United States	21.6s
1928	Percy Williams, Canada	21.8s
1932	Eddie Tolan, United States	21.2s
1936	Jesse Owens, United States	20.7s
1948	Melvin E. Patton, United States	21.1s
1952	Andrew Stanfield, United States	20.7s
1956	Bobby Morrow, United States	20.6s
1960	Livio Berruti, Italy	20.5s
1964	Henry Carr, United States	20.3s
1968	Tommie Smith, United States	19.8s
1972	Valery Borzov, U.S.S.R.	20s
1976	Don Quarrie, Jamaica	20.23s
1980	Pietro Mennea, Italy	20.19s

400-Meter Dash

1896	Thomas Burke, United States	54.2s
1900	Maxwell Long, United States	49.4s
1904	Harry Hillman, United States	49.2s
1906	Paul Pilgrim, United States	53.2s
1908	Wyndham Halswelle, Great Britain (walkover)	50s
1912	Charles Reidpath, United States	48.2s
1920	Bevil Rudd, South Africa	49.6s
1924	Eric Liddell, Great Britain	47.6s
1928	Ray Barbuti, United States	47.8s
1932	William Carr, United States	46.2s
1936	Archie Williams, United States	46.5s
1948	Arthur Wint, Jamaica, B.W.I.	46.2s
1952	George Rhoden, Jamaica, B.W.I.	45.9s
1956	Charles Jenkins, United States	46.7s
1960	Otis Davis, United States	44.9s
1964	Mike Larrabee, United States	45.1s
1968	Lee Evans, United States	43.8s
1972	Vincent Matthews, United States	44.66s
1976	Alberto Juantorena, Cuba	44.26s
1980	Viktor Markin, U.S.S.R.	44.60s

800-Meter Run

1896	Edwin Flack, Australia	2m11s
1900	Alfred Tysoe, Great Britain	2m1.4s
1904	James Lightbody, United States	1m56s
1906	Paul Pilgrim, United States	2m1.2s
1908	Mel Sheppard, United States	1m52.8s
1912	Ted Meredith, United States	1m51.9s

1920	Albert Hill, Great Britain	1m53.4s
1924	Douglas Lowe, Great Britain	1m52.4s
1928	Douglas Lowe, Great Britain	1m51.8s
1932	Thomas Hampson, Great Britain	1m49.8s
1936	John Woodruff, United States	1m52.9s
1948	Malvin Whitfield, United States	1m49.2s
1952	Malvin Whitfield, United States	1m49.2s
1956	Tom Courtney, United States	1m47.7s
1960	Peter Snell, New Zealand	1m46.3s
1964	Peter Snell, New Zealand	1m45.1s
1968	Ralph Doubell, Australia	1m44.3s
1972	David Wottle, United States	1m45.9s
1976	Alberto Juantorena, Cuba	1m43.5s
1980	Steve Ovett, Britain	1m45.4s

1,500-Meter Run

1896	Edwin Flack, Australia	4m33.2s
1900	Charles Bennett, Great Britain	4m6s
1904	James Lightbody, United States	4m5.4s
1906	James Lightbody, United States	4m12s
1908	Mel Sheppard, United States	4m3.4s
1912	Arnold Jackson, Great Britain	3m56.8s
1920	Albert Hill, Great Britain	4m1.8s
1924	Paavo Nurmi, Finland	3m53.6s
1928	Harry Larva, Finland	3m53.2s
1932	Luigi Beccali, Italy	3m51.2s
1936	Jack Lovelock, New Zealand	3m47.8s
1948	Henri Eriksson, Sweden	3m49.8s
1952	Joseph Barthel, Luxembourg	3m45.2s
1956	Ron Delany, Ireland	3m41.2s
1960	Herb Elliott, Australia	3m35.6s
1964	Peter Snell, New Zealand	3m38.1s
1968	Kipchoge Keino, Kenya	3m34.9s
1972	Pekka Vasala, Finland	3m36.3s
1976	John Walker, New Zealand	3m39.17s
1980	Sebastian Coe, Britain	3m38.4s

5,000-Meter Run

1912	Hannes Kolehmainen, Finland	14m36.6s
1920	Joseph Guillemot, France	14m55.6s
1924	Paavo Nurmi, Finland	14m31.2s
1928	Willie Ritola, Finland	14m38s
1932	Lauri Lehtinen, Finland	14m30s
1936	Gunnar Hockert, Finland	14m22.2s
1948	Gaston Reiff, Belgium	14m17.6s
1952	Emil Zatopek, Czechoslovakia	14m6.6s
1956	Vladimir Kuts, U.S.S.R.	13m39.6s
1960	Murray Halberg, New Zealand	13m43.4s
1964	Bob Schul, United States	13m48.8s
1968	Mohamed Gammoudi, Tunisia	14m.05s
1972	Lasse Viren, Finland	13m26.4s
1976	Lasse Viren, Finland	13m24.76s
1980	Miruts Yifter, Ethiopia	13m21s

5-Mile Run

1906	H. Hawtrey, Great Britain	26m26.2s
1908	Emil Voigt, Great Britain	25m11.2s

10,000-Meter Run

1912	Hannes Kolehmainen, Finland	31m20.8s
1920	Paavo Nurmi, Finland	31m45.8s
1924	Willie Ritola, Finland	30m23.2s
1928	Paavo Nurmi, Finland	30m18.8s
1932	Janusz Kusocinski, Poland	30m11.4s
1936	Ilmari Salminen, Finland	30m15.4s
1948	Emil Zatopek, Czechoslovakia	29m59.6s
1952	Emil Zatopek, Czechoslovakia	29m17s
1956	Vladimir Kuts, U.S.S.R.	28m45.6s
1960	Peter Bolotnikov, U.S.S.R.	28m32.2s
1964	Billy Mills, United States	28m24.4s
1968	Naftali Temu, Kenya	29m27.4s
1972	Lasse Viren, Finland	27m38.4s
1976	Lasse Viren, Finland	27m40.38s
1980	Miruts Yifter, Ethiopia	27m42.7s

Marathon

1896	Spiridon Loues, Greece	2h58m50s
1900	Michel Teato, France	2h59m45s
1904	Thomas Hicks, United States	3h28m53s
1906	William J. Sherring, Canada	2h51m23.65s
1908	John J. Hayes, United States	2h55m18.4s
1912	Kenneth McArthur, South Africa	2h36m54.8s
1920	Hannes Kolehmainen, Finland	2h32m35.8s
1924	Albin Stenroos, Finland	2h41m22.6s
1928	A. B. El Ouafi, France	2h32m57s
1932	Juan Zabala, Argentina	2h31m36s
1936	Kitei Son, Japan	2h29m19.2s
1948	Delfo Cabrera, Argentina	2h34m51.6s
1952	Emil Zatopek, Czechoslovakia	2h23m3.2s
1956	Alain Mimoun, France	2h25m
1960	Abebe Bikila, Ethiopia	2h15m16.2s
1964	Abebe Bikila, Ethiopia	2h12m11.2s
1968	Mamo Wold, Ethiopia	2h20m26.4s
1972	Frank Shorter, United States	2h12m19.8s
1976	Walter Cierpinski, East Germany	2h09m55s
1980	Walter Cierpinski, East Germany	2h11m3s

110-Meter Hurdles

1896	Thomas Curtis, United States	17.6s
1900	Alvin Kraenzlein, United States	15.4s
1904	Frederick Schule, United States	16s
1906	R. G. Leavitt, United States	16.2s
1908	Forrest Smithson, United States	15s
1912	Frederick Kelly, United States	15.1s
1920	Earl Thomson, Canada	14.8s
1924	Daniel Kinsey, United States	15s
1928	Sydney Atkinson, South Africa	14.8s
1932	George Saling, United States	14.6s
1936	Forrest Towns, United States	14.2s
1948	William Porter, United States	13.9s
1952	Harrison Dillard, United States	13.7s
1956	Lee Calhoun, United States	13.5s
1960	Lee Calhoun, United States	13.8s
1964	Hayes Jones, United States	13.6s
1968	Willie Davenport, United States	13.3s
1972	Rodney Milburn, United States	13.24s
1976	Guy Drut, France	13.30s
1980	Thomas Munkett, East Germany	13.39s

200-Meter Hurdles

1900	Alvin Kraenzlein, United States	25.4s
1904	Harry Hillman, United States	24.6s

400-Meter Hurdles

1900	John Tewksbury, United States	57.6s
1904	Harry Hillman, United States	53s
1908	Charles Bacon, United States	55s
1920	Frank Loomis, United States	54s
1924	F. Morgan Taylor, United States	52.6s
1928	Lord David Burghley, Great Britain	53.4s
1932	Robert Tisdall, Ireland	51.8s[1]
1936	Glenn Hardin, United States	52.4s
1948	Roy Cochran, United States	51.1s
1952	Charles Moore, United States	50.8s
1956	Glenn Davis, United States	50.1s
1960	Glenn Davis, United States	49.3s
1964	Rex Cawley, United States	49.6s
1968	David Hemery, Great Britain	48.1s
1972	John Akii-Bua, Uganda	47.8s
1976	Edwin Moses, United States	47.64
1980	Volker Beck, East Germany	48.70s

1. Record not allowed.

2,500-Meter Steeplechase

1900	George Orton, United States	7m34s
1904	James Lightbody, United States	7m39.6s

3,000-Meter Steeplechase

1920	Percy Hodge, Great Britain	10m0.4s
1924	Willie Ritola, Finland	9m33.6s
1928	Toivo Loukola, Finland	9m21.8s
1932	Volmari Iso-Hollo, Finland	10m33.4s[1]
1936	Volmari Iso-Hollo, Finland	9m3.8s
1948	Thure Sjoestrand, Sweden	9m4.6s
1952	Horace Ashenfelter, United States	8m45.4s
1956	Chris Brasher, Great Britain	8m41.2s
1960	Zdzislaw Krzyskowiak, Poland	8m34.2s
1964	Gaston Roelants, Belgium	8m30.8s
1968	Amos Biwott, Kenya	8m51s
1972	Kipchoge Keino, Kenya	8m23.6s
1976	Anders Gardervd, Sweden	8m08.02s
1980	Bronislaw Malinowski, Poland	8m9.7s

1. About 3,450 meters—extra lap by error.

Cross-Country

1912	Hannes Kolehmainen, Finland (8,000 meters)	45m11.6s
1920	Paavo Nurmi, Finland (10,000 meters)	27m15s
1924	Paavo Nurmi, Finland (10,000 meters)	32m54.8s

Cross-Country Team Races

		Pts.
1912	Sweden (8,000 meters)	10
1920	Finland (10,000 meters)	10
1924	Finland (10,000 meters)	11

1,500-Meter Walk

1906	George V. Bonhag, United States	7m12.6s

3,000-Meter Walk

1920	Ugo Frigerio, Italy	13m14.2s

10,000-Meter Walk

1912	George Goulding, Canada	46m28.4s
1920	Ugo Frigerio, Italy	48m6.2s
1924	Ugo Frigerio, Italy	47m49s
1948	John Mikaelsson, Sweden	45m13.2s
1952	John Mikaelsson, Sweden	45m2.8s

20,000-Meter Walk

1956	Leonid Spirin, U.S.S.R.	1h31m27.4s
1960	Vladimir Golubnichy, U.S.S.R.	1h34m7.2s
1964	Ken Mathews, Great Britain	1h29m34s
1968	Vladimir Golubnichy, U.S.S.R.	1h33m58.4s
1972	Peter Frenkel, East Germany	1h26m42.4s
1976	Daniel Bautista, Mexico	1h24m40.6s
1980	Maurizio Damiliano, Italy	1h23m35.5s

50,000-Meter Walk

1932	Thomas W. Green, Great Britain	4h50m10s
1936	Harold Whitlock, Great Britain	4h30m41.1s
1948	John Ljunggren, Sweden	4h41m52s
1952	Giuseppe Dordoni, Italy	4h28m7.8s
1956	Norman Read, New Zealand	4h30m42.8s
1960	Donald Thompson, Great Britain	4h25m30s
1964	Abdon Pamich, Italy	4h11m12.4s
1968	Christoph Hohne, East Germany	4h20m13.6s
1972	Bern Kannernberg, West Germany	3h56m11.6s
1980	Hartwig Gauder, East Germany	3h49m24s

400-Meter Relay (4 x 100)

1912	Great Britain	42.4s
1920	United States	42.2s
1924	United States	41s
1928	United States	41s
1932	United States	40s
1936	United States	39.8s
1948	United States	40.6s
1952	United States	40.1s
1956	United States	39.5s
1960	Germany	39.5s
1964	United States	39s
1968	United States	38.2s
1972	United States	38.19s
1976	United States	38.33s
1980	U.S.S.R.	38.26s

1,600-Meter Relay (200–200–400–800)

1908	United States	3m29.4s

1,600-Meter Relay (4 x 400)

1912	United States	3m16.6s
1920	Great Britain	3m22.2s
1924	United States	3m16s
1928	United States	3m14.2s
1932	United States	3m8.2s
1936	Great Britain	3m9s
1948	United States	3m10.4s
1952	Jamaica, B.W.I.	3m3.9s
1956	United States	3m4.8s
1960	United States	3m2.2s
1964	United States	3m0.7s
1968	United States	2m56.1s
1972	Kenya	2m59.8s
1976	United States	2m58.65s
1980	U.S.S.R.	3m01.1s

Team Race

		Pts.
1900	Great Britain (5,000 meters)	26
1904	United States (4 miles)	27
1908	Great Britain (3 miles)	6
1912	United States (3,000 meters)	9
1920	United States (3,000 meters)	10
1924	Finland (3,000 meters)	9

Standing High Jump

1900	Ray Ewry, United States	5 ft 5 in.
1904	Ray Ewry, United States	4 ft 11 in.
1906	Ray Ewry, United States	5 ft 1⅝ in.
1908	Ray Ewry, United States	5 ft 2 in.
1912	Platt Adams, United States	5 ft 4⅛ in.

Running High Jump

1896	Ellery Clark, United States	5 ft 11¼ in.
1900	Irving Baxter, United States	6 ft 2¾ in.
1904	Samuel Jones, United States	5 ft 11 in.
1906	Con Leahy, Ireland	5 ft 9⅞ in.
1908	Harry Porter, United States	6 ft 3 in.
1912	Alma Richards, United States	6 ft 4 in.
1920	Richmond Landon, United States	6 ft 4¼ in.
1924	Harold Osborn, United States	6 ft 5 15/16 in.
1928	Robert W. King, United States	6 ft 4⅜ in.
1932	Duncan McNaughton, Canada	6 ft 5⅝ in.
1936	Cornelius Johnson, United States	6 ft 7 15/16 in.
1948	John Winter, Australia	6 ft 6 in.
1952	Walter Davis, United States	6 ft 8 5/16 in.
1956	Charles Dumas, United States	6 ft 11¼ in.
1960	Robert Shavlakadze, U.S.S.R.	7 ft 1 in.
1964	Valeri Brumel, U.S.S.R.	7 ft 1¾ in.
1968	Dick Fosbury, United States	7 ft 4¼ in.
1972	Yuri Tarmak, U.S.S.R.	7 ft 3¾ in.
1976	Jacek Wszola, Poland	(2.25m) 7 ft 4½ in.
1980	Gerd Wessig, East Germany	7ft 8¾ in.

Standing Long Jump

1900	Ray Ewry, United States	10 ft 6⅖ in.
1904	Ray Ewry, United States	11 ft 4⅞ in.
1906	Ray Ewry, United States	10 ft 10 in.
1908	Ray Ewry, United States	10 ft 11¼ in.
1912	Constantin Tsicilitiras, Greece	11 ft ¼ in.

Long Jump

1896	Ellery Clark, United States	20 ft 9¾ in.
1900	Alvin Kraenzlein, United States	23 ft 6⅞ in.
1904	Myer Prinstein, United States	24 ft 1 in.
1906	Myer Prinstein, United States	23 ft 7½ in.
1908	Frank Irons, United States	24 ft 6½ in.
1912	Albert Gutterson, United States	24 ft 11¼ in.
1920	William Petterssen, Sweden	23 ft 5½ in.
1924	DeHart Hubbard, United States	24 ft 5⅛ in.
1928	Edward B. Hamm, United States	25 ft 4¾ in.
1932	Edward Gordon, United States	25 ft ¾ in.
1936	Jesse Owens, United States	26 ft 5 5/16 in.
1948	Willie Steele, United States	25 ft 8 in.
1952	Jerome Biffle, United States	24 ft 10 in.
1956	Gregory Bell, United States	25 ft 8¼ in.
1960	Ralph Boston, United States	26 ft 7¾ in.
1964	Lynn Davies, Great Britain	26 ft 5¾ in.
1968	Bob Beamon, United States	29 ft 2½ in.
1972	Randy Williams, United States	27 ft ½ in.
1976	Arnie Robinson, United States	(8.35m) 24 ft 7¾ in.
1980	Lutz Dombrowski, Poland	28 ft ¼ in.

Standing Triple Jump

1900	Ray Ewry, United States	34 ft 8½ in.
1904	Ray Ewry, United States	34 ft 7¼ in.

Triple Jump

1896	James B. Connolly, United States	45 ft
1900	Myer Prinstein, United States	47 ft 4¼ in.
1904	Myer Prinstein, United States	47 ft
1906	P. G. O'Connor, Ireland	46 ft 2 in.
1908	Timothy Ahearne, Great Britain	48 ft 11¼ in.
1912	Gustaf Lindblom, Sweden	48 ft 5⅛ in.
1920	Vilho Tuulos, Finland	47 ft 6⅞ in.
1924	Archie Winter, Australia	50 ft 11⅛ in.
1928	Mikio Oda, Japan	49 ft 10 13/16 in.
1932	Chuhei Nambu, Japan	51 ft 7 in.
1936	Naoto Tajima, Japan	52 ft 5⅞ in.
1948	Arne Ahman, Sweden	50 ft 6¼ in.
1952	Adhemar da Silva, Brazil	53 ft 2½ in.
1956	Adhemar da Silva, Brazil	53 ft 7½ in.
1960	Jozef Schmidt, Poland	55 ft 1¾ in.
1964	Jozef Schmidt, Poland	55 ft 3¼ in.
1968	Viktor Saneyev, U.S.S.R.	57 ft ¾ in.
1972	Viktor Saneyev, U.S.S.R.	56 ft 11 in.
1976	Viktor Saneyev, U.S.S.R.	(17.29m) 56 ft 8¾ in.
1980	Jaak Uudmae, U.S.S.R.	56 ft 11⅛ in.

Pole Vault

1896	William Hoyt, United States	10 ft 9¾ in.
1900	Irving Baxter, United States	10 ft 9⅞ in.
1904	Charles Dvorak, United States	11 ft 6 in.
1906	Fernand Gouder, France	11 ft 6 in.
1908	Alfred Gilbert, United States, and Edward Cook, United States (tie)	12 ft 2 in.
1912	Harry Babcock, United States	12 ft 11½ in.
1920	Frank Foss, United States	13 ft 5 9/16 in.
1924	Lee Barnes, United States	12 ft 11½ in.
1928	Sabin W. Carr, United States	13 ft 9⅜ in.
1932	William Miller, United States	14 ft 1⅞ in.
1936	Earle Meadows, United States	14 ft 3¼ in.
1948	Guinn Smith, United States	14 ft 1¼ in.
1952	Robert Richards, United States	14 ft 11⅛ in.
1956	Robert Richards, United States	14 ft 11½ in.
1960	Don Bragg, United States	15 ft 5⅛ in.
1964	Fred Hansen, United States	16 ft 8¾ in.
1968	Bob Seagren, United States	17 ft 8½ in.
1972	Wolfgang Nordwig, East Germany	18 ft ½ in.
1976	Tadeusz Slusarski, Poland	(5.50m) 18 ft ½ in.
1980	Wladyslaw Kozakiewicz, Poland	18 ft 11½ in.

16-lb Shot-Put

1896	Robert Garrett, United States	36 ft 9¾ in.
1900	Richard Sheldon, United States	46 ft 3⅛ in.
1904	Ralph Rose, United States	48 ft 7 in.
1906	Martin Sheridan, United States	40 ft 4⅘ in.
1908	Ralph Rose, United States	46 ft 7½ in.
1912	Pat McDonald, United States	50 ft 4 in.
1920	Ville Porhola, Finland	48 ft 7⅛ in.
1924	Clarence Houser, United States	49 ft 2½ in.
1928	John Kuck, United States	52 ft 11 11/16 in.
1932	Leo Sexton, United States	52 ft 6 3/16 in.
1936	Hans Woellke, Germany	53 ft 1¾ in.
1948	Wilbur Thompson, United States	56 ft 2 in.
1952	Parry O'Brien, United States	57 ft 1½ in.
1956	Parry O'Brien, United States	60 ft 11 in.
1960	Bill Nieder, United States	64 ft 6¾ in.
1964	Dallas Long, United States	66 ft 8¼ in.
1968	Randy Matson, United States	67 ft 4¾ in.
1972	Wladyslaw Komar, Poland	69 ft 6 in.
1976	Udo Beyer, East Germany	(21.05m) 69 ft ¾ in.
1980	Vladimir Kiselyov, U.S.S.R.	70 ft ½ in.

16-lb Shot-Put (Both Hands)

1912	Ralph Rose, United States	90 ft 5⅜ in.

Discus Throw

1896	Robert Garrett, United States	95 ft 7½ in.
1900	Rudolf Bauer, Hungary	118 ft 2⅞ in.
1904	Martin Sheridan, United States	128 ft 10½ in.
1906	Martin Sheridan, United States	136 ft ⅓ in.
1908	Martin Sheridan, United States	134 ft 2 in.
1912	Armas Taipale, Finland	145 ft 9/16 in.
1920	Elmer Niklander, Finland	146 ft 7 in.
1924	Clarence Houser, United States	151 ft 5¼ in.
1928	Clarence Houser, United States	155 ft 2⅖ in.
1932	John Anderson, United States	162 ft 4⅞ in.
1936	Ken Carpenter, United States	165 ft 7⅜ in.
1948	Adolfo Consolini, Italy	173 ft 2 in.
1952	Simeon Iness, United States	180 ft 6½ in.
1956	Al Oerter, United States	184 ft 10½ in.
1960	Al Oerter, United States	194 ft 2 in.
1964	Al Oerter, United States	200 ft 1½ in.
1968	Al Oerter, United States	212 ft 6 in.
1972	Ludvik Danek, Czechoslovakia	211 ft 3 in.
1976	Mac Wilkins, United States	(67.5m) 221 ft 5 in.
1980	Viktor Rashchupkin, U.S.S.R.	218 ft 8 in.

Discus Throw—Greek Style

1906	Werner Jaervinen, Finland	115 ft 4 in.
1908	Martin Sheridan, United States	124 ft 8 in.

Discus Throw (Both Hands)

1912	Armas Taipale, Finland	271 ft 10⅛ in.

Javelin Throw

1906	Eric Lemming, Sweden	175 ft 6 in.
1908	Eric Lemming, Sweden	179 ft 10½ in.
1912	Eric Lemming, Sweden	198 ft 11¼ in.
1920	Jonni Myyra, Finland	215 ft 9¾ in.
1924	Jonni Myyra, Finland	206 ft 6¾ in.
1928	Eric Lundquist, Sweden	218 ft 6⅛ in.
1932	Matti Jarvinen, Finland	238 ft 7 in.
1936	Gerhard Stoeck, Germany	235 ft 8 5/16 in.
1948	Kaj Rautavaara, Finland	228 ft 10½ in.
1952	Cy Young, United States	242 ft ¾ in.
1956	Egil Danielsen, Norway	281 ft 2¼ in.
1960	Viktor Tsibulenko, U.S.S.R.	277 ft 8⅜ in.
1964	Pauli Nevala, Finland	271 ft 2¼ in.
1968	Janis Lusis, U.S.S.R.	295 ft 7 in.
1972	Klaus Wolfermann, West Germany	296 ft 10 in.
1976	Miklos Nemeth, Hungary	(94.58m) 310 ft 4 in.
1980	Dainis Kula, U.S.S.R.	299 ft 2⅜ in.

Javelin Throw—Free Style

1908	Eric Lemming, Sweden	178 ft 7½ in.

Javelin Throw (Both Hands)

1912	Julius Saaristo, Finland	358 ft 11½ in.

16-lb Hammer Throw

1900	John Flanagan, United States	167 ft 4 in.
1904	John Flanagan, United States	168 ft 1 in.
1908	John Flanagan, United States	170 ft 4¼ in.
1912	Matt McGrath, United States	179 ft 7⅛ in.
1920	Pat Ryan, United States	173 ft 5⅝ in.
1924	Fred Tootell, United States	174 ft 10¼ in.
1928	Patrick O'Callaghan, Ireland	168 ft 7½ in.
1932	Patrick O'Callaghan, Ireland	176 ft 11⅛ in.
1936	Karl Hein, Germany	185 ft 4 in.
1948	Imre Nemeth, Hungary	183 ft 11½ in.
1952	Jozsef Csermak, Hungary	197 ft 11$\frac{9}{16}$ in.
1956	Harold Connolly, United States	207 ft 2¾ in.
1960	Vasily Rudenkov, U.S.S.R.	220 ft 1⅝ in.
1964	Romuald Klim, U.S.S.R.	228 ft 9½ in.
1968	Gyula Zsivotzky, Hungary	240 ft 8 in.
1972	Anatoly Bondarchuk, U.S.S.R.	247 ft 8½ in.
1976	Yuri Sedykh, U.S.S.R.	(77.52m) 254 ft 4 in.
1980	Yuri Sedykh, U.S.S.R.	(81.80m) 268 ft 4½ in.

Throwing the Stone (14 lbs.)

1906	Nicolas Georgantas, Greece	65 ft 4⅕ in.

56-lb Weight Throw

1904	Etienne Desmarteau, Canada	34 ft 4 in.
1920	Pat McDonald, United States	36 ft 11⅝ in.

All-Around

1904	Thomas Kiely, Great Britain	6,036 pts.

Pentathlon

1906	H. Mellander, Sweden	24 pts.
1912	Ferdinand Bie, Norway	21 pts.
1920	Eero Lehtonen, Finland	14 pts.
1924	Eero Lehtonen, Finland	16 pts.

Decathlon

1912	Hugo Wieslander, Sweden	7,724.495 pts.
1920	Helge Lovland, Norway	6,804.35 pts.
1924	Harold Osborn, United States	7,710.775 pts.
1928	Paavo Yrjola, Finland	8,053.29 pts.
1932	James Bausch, United States	8,462.23 pts.
1936	Glenn Morris, United States	7,900 pts.[1]
1948	Robert B. Mathias, United States	7,139 pts.
1952	Robert B. Mathias, United States	7,887 pts.
1956	Milton Campbell, United States	7,937 pts.
1960	Rafer Johnson, United States	8,392 pts.
1964	Willi Holdorf, Germany	7,887 pts.[1]
1968	Bill Toomey, United States	8,193 pts.
1972	Nikolai Avilov, U.S.S.R.	8,454 pts.
1976	Bruce Jenner, United States	8,618 pts.
1980	Daley Thompson, Britain	8,495 pts.

1. Point system revised.

Tug of War

1904	United States	1912	Sweden
1906	Germany	1920	Great Britain
1908	Great Britain		

TRACK AND FIELD—WOMEN

100-Meter Dash

1928	Elizabeth Robinson, United States	12.2s
1932	Stella Walsh, Poland	11.9s
1936	Helen Stephens, United States	11.5s
1948	Fanny Blankers-Koen, Netherlands	11.9s
1952	Marjorie Jackson, Australia	11.5s
1956	Betty Cuthbert, Australia	11.5s
1960	Wilma Rudolph, United States	11s
1964	Wyomia Tyus, United States	11.4s
1968	Wyomia Tyus, United States	11s
1972	Renate Stecher, East Germany	11.07s
1976	Annegret Richter, West Germany	11.08s
1980	Lyudmila Kondratyeva, U.S.S.R.	11.06s

200-Meter Dash

1948	Fanny Blankers-Koen, Netherlands	24.4s
1952	Marjorie Jackson, Australia	23.7s
1956	Betty Cuthbert, Australia	23.4s
1960	Wilma Rudolph, United States	24s
1964	Edith McGuire, United States	23s
1968	Irena Szewinska, Poland	22.5s
1972	Renate Stecher, East Germany	22.4s
1976	Baerbel Eckert, East Germany	22.37s
1980	Barbara Wockel, East Germany	22.03s

400-Meter Dash

1964	Betty Cuthbert, Australia	52s
1968	Colette Besson, France	52s
1972	Monika Zehrt, East Germany	51.08s
1976	Irena Szewinska, Poland	49.29s
1980	Marita Koch, East Germany	48.88s

800-Meter Run

1928	Lina Radke, Germany	2m16.8s
1960	Ljudmila Shevcova, U.S.S.R.	2m4.3s
1964	Ann Packer, Great Britain	2m1.1s
1968	Madeline Manning, United States	2m0.9s
1972	Hildegard Falck, West Germany	1m58.6s
1976	Tatiana Kazankina, U.S.S.R.	1m54.94s
1980	Nadezhda Olizarenko, U.S.S.R.	1m53.5s

1,500-Meter Run

1972	Ludmila Bragina, U.S.S.R.	4m01.4s
1976	Tatiana Kazankina, U.S.S.R.	4m05.48s

80-Meter Hurdles

1932	Mildred Didrikson, United States	11.7s
1936	Trebisonda Valla, Italy	11.7s
1948	Fanny Blankers-Koen, Netherlands	11.2s
1952	Shirley S. de la Hunty, Australia	10.9s
1956	Shirley S. de la Hunty, Australia	10.7s
1960	Irina Press, U.S.S.R.	10.8s
1964	Karin Balzer, Germany	10.5s[1]
1968	Maureen Caird, Australia	10.3s

1. Wind assisted.

100-Meter Hurdles

1972	Annelie Ehrhardt, East Garmany	12.59s
1976	Johanna Schaller, East Germany	12.77s
1980	Vera Komisova, U.S.S.R.	12.56s

400-Meter Relay

1928	Canada	48.4s
1932	United States	47s
1936	United States	46.9s
1948	Netherlands	47.5s
1952	United States	45.9s
1956	Australia	44.5s
1960	United States	44.5s
1964	Poland	43.6s
1968	United States	42.8s
1972	West Germany	42.81s
1976	East Germany	42.55s
1980	East Germany	41.60s

1,600-Meter Relay

1972	East Germany	3m23s
1976	East Germany	3m19.23s
1980	U.S.S.R.	3m20.2s

Running High Jump

1928	Ethel Catherwood, Canada	5 ft 3 in.
1932	Jean Shiley, United States	5 ft 5¼ in.
1936	Ibolya Csak, Hungary	5 ft 3 in.
1948	Alice Coachman, United States	5 ft 6⅛ in.
1952	Ester Brand, South Africa	5 ft 5¾ in.
1956	Mildred McDaniel, United States	5 ft 9¼ in.
1960	Iolanda Balas, Romania	6 ft ¾ in.
1964	Iolanda Balas, U.S.S.R.	6 ft 2¾ in.
1968	Miloslava Rezkova, Czechoslovakia	5 ft 11¾ in.
1972	Ulrike Meyfarth, West Germany	6 ft 3⅝ in.
1976	Rosemarie Ackerman, E. Germany	(1.93m) 6 ft 4 in.
1980	Sara Simeoni, Italy	6 ft 5½ in.

Long Jump

1948	Olga Gyarmati, Hungary	18 ft 8¼ in.
1952	Yvette Williams, New Zealand	20 ft 5¾ in.
1956	Elzbieta Krzesinska, Poland	20 ft 9¾ in.
1960	Vera Krepkina, U.S.S.R.	20 ft 10¾ in.
1964	Mary Rand, Great Britain	22 ft 2 in.
1968	Viorica Ciscopoleanu, Romania	22 ft 4½ in.
1972	Heidemarie Rosendahl, West Germany	22 ft 3 in.
1976	Angela Voigt, East Germany	(6.72m) 22 ft ½ in.
1980	Tatiana Kolpakova, U.S.S.R.	23 ft 2 in.

Shot-Put

1948	Micheline Ostermeyer, France	45 ft 1½ in.
1952	Galina Zybina, U.S.S.R.	50 ft 1½ in.
1956	Tamara Tishkyevich, U.S.S.R.	54 ft 5 in.
1960	Tamara Press, U.S.S.R.	56 ft 9⅞ in.
1964	Tamara Press, U.S.S.R.	59 ft 6 in.
1968	Margitta Gummel, East Germany	64 ft 4 in.
1972	Nadezhda Chizhova, U.S.S.R.	69 ft
1976	Ivanka Christova, Bulgaria	(21.16m) 69 ft 5 in.
1980	Ilona Sluplanek, East Germany	73 ft 6 in.

Discus Throw

1928	Helena Konopacka, Poland	129 ft 11⅞ in.
1932	Lillian Copeland, United States	133 ft 2 in.
1936	Gisela Mauermayer, Germany	156 ft 3³⁄₁₆ in.
1948	Micheline Ostermayer, France	137 ft 6½ in.
1952	Nina Romaschkova, U.S.S.R.	168 ft 8⁷⁄₁₆ in.
1956	Olga Fikotova, Czechoslovakia	176 ft 1½ in.
1960	Nina Ponomareva, U.S.S.R.	180 ft 8¼ in.
1964	Tamara Press, U.S.S.R.	187 ft 10¾ in.
1968	Lia Manoliu, Romania	191 ft 2½ in.
1972	Faina Melnik, U.S.S.R.	218 ft 7 in.
1976	Evelin Schlaak, East Germany	(69.0m) 226 ft 4 in.
1980	Evelin Jahl, East Germany	229 ft 6½ in.

Javelin Throw

1932	Mildred Didrikson, United States	143 ft 4 in.
1936	Tilly Fleischer, Germany	148 ft 2¾ in.
1948	Herma Bauma, Austria	149 ft 6 in.
1952	Dana Zatopek, Czechoslovakia	165 ft 7 in.
1956	Inessa Janzeme, U.S.S.R.	176 ft 8 in.
1960	Elvira Ozolina, U.S.S.R.	183 ft 8 in.
1964	Mihaela Penes, Romania	198 ft 7½ in.
1968	Angela Nemeth, Hungary	198 ft 0 in.
1972	Ruth Fuchs, East Germany	209 ft 7 in.
1976	Ruth Fuchs, East Germany	(65.94m) 216 ft 4 in.
1980	Maria Colon, Cuba	224 ft 5 in.

Pentathlon

1964	Irina Press, U.S.S.R.	5,246 pts.
1968	Ingrid Becker, West Germany	5,098 pts.
1972	Mary Peters, Britain	4,801 pts.
1976	Siegrun Siegl, East Germany	4,745 pts.
1980	Nadyezhda Tkachenko, U.S.S.R.	5,083 pts.

SWIMMING—MEN

50-Yard Freestyle

1904	Zoltan de Halmay, Hungary	28s

100 Meters Freestyle

1896	Alfred Hajos, Hungary	1m22.2s
1904	Zoltan de Halmay, Hungary	1m2.8s[1]
1906	Charles Daniels, United States	1m13s
1908	Charles Daniels, United States	1m5.6s
1912	Duke P. Kahanamoku, United States	1m3.4s
1920	Duke P. Kahanamoku, United States	1m1.4s
1924	John Weissmuller, United States	59s
1928	John Weissmuller, United States	58.6s
1932	Yasuji Miyazaki, Japan	58.2s
1936	Ferenc Csik, Hungary	57.6s
1948	Walter Ris, United States	57.3s
1952	Clarke Scholes, United States	57.4s
1956	Jon Henricks, Australia	55.4s
1960	John Devitt, Australia	55.2s
1964	Don Schollander, United States	53.4s
1968	Michael Wenden, Australia	52.2s
1972	Mark Spitz, United States	51.22s
1976	Jim Montgomery, United States	49.99s
1980	Jorg Woithe, East Germany	50.40s

1. 100 yards.

200-Meter Freestyle

1900	Frederick Lane, Australia	2m25.2s
1904	Charles Daniels, United States	2m44.2s[1]
1968	Michael Wenden, Australia	1m55.2s
1972	Mark Spitz, United States	1m52.78s
1976	Bruce Furniss, United States	1m50.29s
1980	Sergei Kopliakov, U.S.S.R.	1m49.81s

1. 220 yards.

400-Meter Freestyle

1896	Paul Neumann, Austria	8m12.6s[1]
1904	Charles Daniels, United States	6m16.2s[2]
1906	Otto Sheff, Austria	6m23.8s
1908	Henry Taylor, Great Britain	5m36.8s
1912	George Hodgson, Canada	5m24.4s
1920	Norman Ross, United States	5m26.8s
1926	Jonn Weissmuller, United States	5m4.2s
1928	Albert Zorilla, Argentina	5m1.6s
1932	Clarence Crabbe, United States	4m48.4s
1936	Jack Medica, United States	4m44.5s
1948	William Smith, United States	4m41s
1952	Jean Boiteux, France	4m30.7s
1956	Murray Rose, Australia	4m27.3s
1960	Murray Rose, Australia	4m18.3s
1964	Don Schollander, United States	4m12.2s
1968	Mike Burton, United States	4m9s
1972	Bradford Cooper, Australia[3]	4m00.27s
1976	Brian Goodell, United States	3m51.93s
1980	Vladimir Salnikov, U.S.S.R.	3m51.31s

1. 500 meters. 2. 440 yards. 3. Rick DeMont, United States, won but was disqualified following day for medical reasons.

1,200-Meter Freestyle

1896	Alfred Hajos, Hungary	18m22.2s

1,500 Meters Freestyle

1904	Emil Rausch, Germany	27m18.2s[1]
1906	Henry Taylor, Great Britain	28m28s[2]
1908	Henry Taylor, Great Britain	22m48.4s
1912	George Hodgson, Canada	22m
1920	Norman Ross, United States	22m23.2s
1924	Andrew Charlton, Australia	20m6.6s
1928	Arne Borg, Sweden	19m51.8s
1932	Kusuo Kitamura, Japan	19m12.4s
1936	Noboru Terada, Japan	19m13.7s

1948	James McLane, United States	19m18.5s
1952	Ford Konno, United States	18m30s
1956	Murray Rose, Australia	17m58.9s
1960	Jon Konrads, Australia	17m19.6s
1964	Robert Windle, Australia	17m1.7s
1968	Michael Burton, United States	16m38.9s
1972	Mike Burton, United States	15m52.58s
1976	Brian Goodell, United States	15m02.4s
1980	Vladimir Salnikov, U.S.S.R.	14m58.27s

1. One mile. 2. 1,600 meters.

4,000-Meter Freestyle

1900	John Jarvis, Great Britain	58m24s

100-Meter Backstroke

1904	Walter Brack, Germany	1m16.8s[1]
1908	Arno Bieberstein, Germany	1m24.6s
1912	Harry Hebner, United States	1m21.2s
1920	Warren Kealoha, United States	1m15.2s
1924	Warren Kealoha, United States	1m13.2s
1928	George Kojac, United States	1m8.2s
1932	Masaji Kiyokawa, Japan	1m8.6s
1936	Adolph Kiefer, United States	1m5.9s
1948	Allen Stack, United States	1m6.4s
1952	Yoshinobu Oyakawa, United States	1m5.4s
1956	David Thiele, Australia	1m2.2s
1960	David Thiele, Australia	1m1.9s
1968	Roland Matthes, East Germany	58.7s
1972	Roland Matthes, East Germany	56.58s
1976	John Naber, United States	55.49s
1980	Bengt Baron, Sweden	56.53s

1. 100 yards

200-Meter Backstroke

1900	Ernst Hoppenberg, Germany	2m47s
1964	Jed Graef, United States	2m10.3s
1968	Roland Matthes, East Germany	2m9.6s
1972	Roland Matthes, East Germany	2m2.82s
1976	John Naber, United States	1m59.19s
1980	Sandor Wladar, Hungary	2:01.93s

100-Meter Breaststroke

1968	Donald McKenzie, United States	1m7.7s
1972	Nobutaka Taguchi, Japan	1m4.94s
1976	John Hencken, United States	1m03.11s
1980	Duncan Goodhew, Britain	1m03.34s

200-Meter Breaststroke

1908	Frederick Holman, Great Britain	3m9.2s
1912	Walter Bathe, Germany	3m1.8s
1920	Haken Malmroth, Sweden	3m4.4s
1924	Robert Skelton, United States	2m56.6s
1928	Yoshiyuki Tsuruta, Japan	2m48.8s
1932	Yoshiyuki Tsuruta, Japan	2m45.4s
1936	Tetsuo Hamuro, Japan	2m41.5s
1948	Joseph Verdeur, United States	2m39.3s
1952	John Davies, Australia	2m34.4s
1956	Masura Furukawa, Japan	2m34.7s
1960	Bill Mulliken, United States	2m37.4s
1964	Ian O'Brien, Australia	2m27.8s
1968	Felipe Munoz, Mexico	2m28.7s
1972	John Hencken, United States	2m21.55s
1976	David Willkie, Britain	2m15.11s
1980	Robertas Zulpa, U.S.S.R.	2m15.85s

400-Meter Breaststroke

1904	Georg Zacharias, Germany	7m23.6s[1]
1912	Walter Bathe, Germany	6m29.6s
1920	Haken Malmroth, Sweden	6m31.8s

1. 440 yards

100-Meter Butterfly

1968	Douglas Russell, United States	55.9s
1972	Mark Spitz, United States	54.27s
1976	Matt Vogel, United States	54.35s
1980	Par Arvidsson, Sweden	54.92s

200-Meter Butterfly

1956	Bill Yorzyk, United States	2m19.3s
1960	Mike Troy, United States	2m12.8s
1964	Kevin Berry, Australia	2m6.6s
1968	Carl Robie, United States	2m8.7s
1972	Mark Spitz, United States	2m00.7s
1976	Mike Bruner, United States	1m59.23s
1980	Sergei Fesenko, U.S.S.R.	1m59.76s

200-Meter Individual Medley

1968	Charles Hickcox, United States	2m12s
1972	Gunnar Larsson, Sweden	2m7.17s

400-Meter Individual Medley

1964	Dick Roth, United States	4m45.4s
1968	Charles Hickcox, United States	4m48.4s
1972	Gunnar Larsson, Sweden	4m31.98s
1976	Rod Strachan, United States	4m23.68s
1980	Aleksandr Sidorenko, U.S.S.R.	4m22.8s

60-Meter Underwater

1900	de Vaudeville, France	1m53.4s

200-Meter Obstacle

1900	Frederick Lane, Australia	2m38.4s

Relays

1900	Germany (200 meters, 5 men)	32 pts.
1904	United States (200 yards)	2m4.6s
1906	Hungary (1,000 meters)	16m52.4s

400-Meter Freestyle Relay

1964	United States	3m32.2s
1968	United States	3m31.7s
1972	United States	3m26.42s

800-Meter Freestyle Relay

1908	Great Britain	10m55.6s
1912	Australia	10m11.2s
1920	United States	10m4.4s
1924	United States	9m53.4s
1928	United States	9m36.2s
1932	Japan	8m58.4s
1936	Japan	8m51.5s
1948	United States	8m46s
1952	United States	8m31.1s
1956	Australia	8m23.6s
1960	United States	8m10.2s
1964	United States	7m52.1s
1968	United States	7m52.3s
1972	United States	7m35.78s
1976	United States	7m23.22s
1980	U.S.S.R.	7m23.50s

400-Meter Medley Relay

1960	United States	4m5.4s
1964	United States	3m58.4s
1968	United States	3m54.9s
1972	United States	3m48.16s
1976	United States	3m42.22s
1980	Australia	3m45.70s

Springboard Dive

		Points
1908	Albert Zuerner, Germany	85.5

1912	Paul Guenther, Germany	79.23
1920	Louis Kuehn, United States	675
1924	Albert White, United States	696.4
1928	Pete Desjardins, United States	185.04
1932	Michael Galitzen, United States	161.38
1936	Richard Degener, United States	163.57
1948	Bruce Harlan, United States	163.64
1952	David Browning, United States	205.59
1956	Robert Clotworthy, United States	159.56
1960	Gary Tobian, United States	170.00
1964	Ken Sitzberger, United States	159.90
1968	Bernard Wrightson, United States	170.15
1972	Vladimir Vasin, U.S.S.R.	594.09
1976	Phil Boggs, United States	619.05
1980	Alexsandr Portnov, U.S.S.R.	905.02

Platform Dive

		Points
1904	G. E. Sheldon, United States	12.75
1906	Gottlob Walz, Germany	156
1908	Hialmar Johansson, Sweden	83.75
1912	Erik Adlerz, Sweden	73.94
1920	Clarence Pinkston, United States	100.67
1924	Albert White, United States	487.3
1928	Pete Desjardins, United States	98.74
1932	Harold Smith, United States	124.80
1936	Marshall Wayne, United States	113.58
1948	Samuel Lee, United States	130.05
1952	Samuel Lee, United States	156.28
1956	Joaquin Capilla, Mexico	152.44
1960	Bob Webster, United States	165.56
1964	Bob Webster, United States	148.58
1968	Klaus Dibiasi, Italy	164.18
1972	Klaus Dibiasi, Italy	504.12
1976	Klaus Dibiasi, Italy	600.51
1980	Falk Hoffman, E. Germany	835.65

Plain High Dive

		Points
1912	Erik Adlerz, Sweden	40
1920	Arvid Wallman, Sweden	7
1924	Richard Eve, Australia	160

Plunge for Distance

1904	W. E. Dickey, United States	62 ft 6 in.

SWIMMING—WOMEN

100 Meters Freestyle

1912	Fanny Durack, Australia	1m22.2s
1920	Ethelda Bleibtrey, United States	1m13.6s
1924	Ethel Lackie, United States	1m12.4s
1928	Albina Osipowich, United States	1m11s
1932	Helene Madison, United States	1m6.8s
1936	Hendrika Mastenbroek, Netherlands	1m5.9s
1948	Greta Andersen, Denmark	1m6.3s
1952	Katalin Szoke, Hungary	1m6.8s
1956	Dawn Fraser, Australia	1m2s
1960	Dawn Fraser, Australia	1m1.2s
1964	Dawn Fraser, Australia	59.5s
1968	Marge Jan Henne, United States	1m
1972	Sandra Neilson, United States	58.59s
1976	Kornelia Ender, East Germany	55.65s
1980	Barbara Krause, East Germany	54.79s

200-Meter Freestyle

1968	Debbie Meyer, United States	2m10.5s
1972	Shane Gould, Australia	2m3.56s
1976	Kornelia Ender, East Germany	1m59.26s
1980	Barbara Krause, East Germany	1m58.33s

400-Meter Freestyle

1920	Ethelda Bleibtrey, United States	4m34s[1]
1924	Martha Norelius, United States	6m2.2s
1928	Martha Norelius, United States	5m42.8s
1932	Helene Madison, United States	5m28.5s
1936	Hendrika Mastenbroek, Netherlands	5m26.4s
1948	Ann Curtis, United States	5m17.8s
1952	Valerie Gyenge, Hungary	5m12.1s
1956	Lorraine Crapp, Australia	4m54.6s
1960	Chris von Saltza, United States	4m50.6s
1964	Ginny Duenkel, United States	4m43.3s
1968	Debbie Meyer, United States	4m31.8s
1972	Shane Gould, Australia	4m19.04s
1976	Petra Thumer, East Germany	4m09.89s
1980	Ines Diers, East Germany	4m08.76s

1. 300 meters.

800-Meter Freestyle

1968	Debbie Meyer, United States	9m24s
1972	Keena Rothhammer, United States	8m53.68s
1976	Petra Thumer, East Germany	8m37.14s
1980	Michelle Ford, Australia	8m28.90s

100-Meter Backstroke

1924	Sybil Bauer, United States	1m23.2s
1928	Marie Braun, Netherlands	1m22s
1932	Eleanor Holm, United States	1m19.4s
1936	Dina Senff, Netherlands	1m18.9s
1948	Karen Harup, Denmark	1m14.4s
1952	Joan Harrison, South Africa	1m14.3s
1956	Judy Grinham, Great Britain	1m12.9s
1960	Lynn Burke, United States	1m9.3s
1964	Cathy Ferguson, United States	1m7.7s
1968	Kaye Hall, United States	1m6.2s
1972	Melissa Belote, United States	1m5.78s
1976	Ulrike Richter, East Germany	1m01.83s
1980	Rica Reinisch, East Germany	1m00.86s

200-Meter Backstroke

1968	Pokey Watson, United States	2m24.8s
1972	Melissa Belote, United States	2m19.19s
1976	Ulrike Richter, East Germany	2m13.43s
1980	Rica Reinisch, East Germany	2m11.77s

100-Meter Breaststroke

1968	Djurdjica Bjedov, Yugoslavia	1m15.8s
1972	Catherine Carr, United States	1m13.58s
1976	Hannelore Anke, East Germany	1m11.16s
1980	Ute Geweniger, East Germany	1m10.22s

200-Meter Breaststroke

1924	Lucy Morton, Great Britain	3m33.2s
1928	Hilde Schrader, Germany	3m12.6s
1932	Clare Dennis, Australia	3m6.3s
1936	Hideko Maehata, Japan	3m3.6s
1948	Nel van Vliet, Netherlands	2m57.2s
1952	Eva Székely, Hungary	2m51.7s
1956	Ursala Happe, Germany	2m53.1s
1960	Anita Lonsbrough, Great Britain	2m49.5s
1964	Galina Prozumenschikova, U.S.S.R.	2m46.4s
1968	Sharon Wichman, United States	2m44.4s
1972	Beverly Whitfield, Australia	2m41.71s
1976	Marina Koshevaia, U.S.S.R.	2m33.35s
1980	Lina Kachushite, U.S.S.R.	2m29.54s

100-Meter Butterfly

1956	Shelley Mann, United States	1m11s
1960	Carolyn Schuler, United States	1m9.5s
1964	Sharon Stouder, United States	1m4.7s
1968	Lynn McClements, Australia	1m5.5s
1972	Mayumi Aoki, Japan	1m3.34s
1976	Kornelia Ender, East Germany	1m00.13s
1980	Caren Metschuck, East Germany	1m00.42s

200-Meter Butterfly

1968	Ada Kok, Netherlands	2m24.7s
1972	Karen Moe, United States	2m15.57s
1976	Andrea Pollack, East Germany	2m11.41s
1980	Ines Geissler, East Germany	2m10.44s

200-Meter Individual Medley

1968	Claudia Kolb, United States	2m24.7s
1972	Shane Gould, Australia	2m23.07s

400-Meter Individual Medley

1964	Donna de Varona, United States	5m18.7s
1968	Claudia Kolb, United States	5m8.5s
1972	Gail Neall, Australia	5m2.97s
1976	Ulrike Tauber, East Germany	4m42.77s
1980	Petra Schneider, East Germany	4m36.29s

400-Meter Freestyle Relay

1912	Great Britain	5m52.8s
1920	United States	5m11.6s
1924	United States	4m58.8s
1928	United States	4m47.6s
1932	United States	4m38s
1936	Netherlands	4m36s
1948	United States	4m29.2s
1952	Hungary	4m24.4s
1956	Australia	4m17.1s
1960	United States	4m8.9s
1964	United States	4m3.8s
1968	United States	4m2.5s
1972	United States	3m55.19s
1976	United States	3m44.82s
1980	East Germany	3m42.71s

400-Meter Medley Relay

1960	United States	4m41.1s
1964	United States	4m33.9s
1968	United States	4m28.3s
1972	United States	4m20.75s
1976	East Germany	4m07.95s
1980	East Germany	4m06.67s

Springboard Dive

		Points
1920	Aileen Riggin, United States	539.90
1924	Elizabeth Becker, United States	474.5
1928	Helen Meany, United States	78.62
1932	Georgia Coleman, United States	87.52
1936	Marjorie Gestring, United States	89.27
1948	Victoria M. Draves, United States	108.74
1952	Patricia McCormick, United States	147.30
1956	Patricia McCormick, United States	142.36
1960	Ingrid Kramer, Germany	155.81
1964	Ingrid Kramer Engel, Germany	145.00
1968	Sue Gossick, United States	150.77
1972	Micki King, United States	450.03
1976	Jennifer Chandler, United States	506.19
1980	Irina Kalinina, U.S.S.R.	725.91

Platform Dive

		Points
1912	Greta Johansson, Sweden	39.9
1920	Stefani Fryland, Denmark	34.60
1924	Caroline Smith, United States	166
1928	Elizabeth B. Pinkston, United States	31.60
1932	Dorothy Poynton, United States	40.26
1936	Dorothy Poynton Hill, United States	33.92
1948	Victoria M. Draves, United States	68.87
1952	Patricia McCormick, United States	79.37
1956	Patricia McCormick, United States	84.85
1960	Ingrid Kramer, Germany	91.28
1964	Lesley Bush, United States	99.80
1968	Milena Duchkova, Czechoslovakia	109.59
1972	Ulrika Knape, Sweden	390.00
1976	Elena Vaytsekhovskaia, U.S.S.R.	406.59
1980	Martina Jaschke, East Germany	596.25

DISTRIBUTION OF MEDALS 1980 SUMMER GAMES

	Gold	Silver	Bronze	Total
Soviet Union	80	70	47	197
East Germany	47	36	43	126
Bulgaria	8	16	16	40
Hungary	7	10	15	32
Poland	3	14	14	31
Romania	6	6	13	25
Britain	5	7	9	21
Cuba	8	7	5	20
Italy	8	3	4	15
France	6	5	3	14
Czechoslovakia	2	2	9	13
Sweden	3	3	6	12
Australia	2	2	5	9
Yugoslavia	2	3	4	9
Finland	3	1	4	8
Spain	1	3	2	6
Denmark	2	1	2	5
Austria	1	3	1	5
North Korea	0	3	2	5
Brazil	2	0	2	4
Ethiopia	2	0	2	4
Mongolia	0	2	2	4
Netherlands	0	1	3	4
Mexico	0	1	3	4
Greece	1	0	2	3
Jamaica	0	0	3	3
Switzerland	2	0	0	2
Tanzania	0	2	0	2
Ireland	0	1	1	2
Belgium	1	0	0	1
India	1	0	0	1
Zimbabwe	1	0	0	1
Venezuela	1	0	0	1
Uganda	0	1	0	1
Guyana	0	0	1	1
Lebanon	0	0	1	1

BOXING

(U.S. winners only)

(U.S. boycotted Olympics in 1980)

Flyweight—112 Pounds (51 kilograms)

1904 George V. Finnegan
1920 Frank De Genaro
1924 Fidel La Barba
1952 Nate Brooks
1976 Leo Randolph

Bantamweight—119 pounds (54 kg)

1904 O.L. Kirk

Featherweight—126 pounds (57 kg)

1904 O.L. Kirk
1924 Jackie Fields

Lightweight—132 Pounds (60 kg)

1904 H.J. Spanger
1920 Samuel Mosberg
1968 Ronnie Harris
1976 Howard Davis

Light Welterweight—140 Pounds (63.5 kg)

1952 Charles Adkins
1972 Ray Seales
1976 Ray Leonard

Welterweight—148 Pounds (67 kg)

1904	Al Young	1932	Edward Flynn

Light Middleweight—157 Pounds (71 kg)

1960	Wilbert McClure

Middleweight—165 Pounds (75 kg)

1904	Charles Mayer	1960	Eddie Crook
1932	Carmen Barth	1976	Mike Spinks
1952	Floyd Patterson		

Light Heavyweight—179 Pounds (81 kg)

1920	Edward Eagan	1960	Cassius Clay
1952	Norvel Lee	1976	Leon Spinks
1956	James Boyd		

Heavyweight (unlimited)

1904	Sam Berger	1964	Joe Frazier
1952	Edward Sanders	1968	George Foreman
1956	Pete Rademacher		

BASKETBALL—MEN

1904	United States	1960	United States
1936	United States	1964	United States
1948	United States	1968	United States
1952	United States	1972	U.S.S.R.
1956	United States	1976	United States
		1980	Yugoslavia

BASKETBALL—WOMEN

1976	U.S.S.R.
1980	U.S.S.R.

Winter Games

FIGURE SKATING—MEN

1908	Ulrich Salchow, Sweden
1920	Gillis Grafstrom, Sweden
1924	Gillis Grafstrom, Sweden
1928	Gillis Grafstrom, Sweden
1932	Karl Schaefer, Austria
1936	Karl Schaefer, Austria
1948	Richard Button, United States
1952	Richard Button, United States
1956	Hayes Alan Jenkins, United States
1960	David Jenkins, United States
1964	Manfred Schnelldorfer, Germany
1968	Wolfgang Schwartz, Austria
1972	Ondrej Nepela, Czechoslovakia
1976	John Curry, Great Britain
1980	Robin Cousins, Great Britain

FIGURE SKATING—WOMEN

1908	Madge Syers, Britain
1920	Magda Julin-Maurey, Sweden
1924	Herma Szabo-Planck, Austria
1928	Sonja Henie, Norway
1932	Sonja Henie, Norway
1936	Sonja Henie, Norway
1948	Barbara Ann Scott, Canada
1952	Jeannette Altwegg, Great Britain
1956	Tenley Albright, United States
1960	Carol Heiss, United States
1964	Sjoukje Dijkstra, Netherlands
1968	Peggy Fleming, United States
1972	Beatrix Schuba, Austria
1976	Dorothy Hamill, United States
1980	Anett Poetzsch, East Germany

SPEED SKATING—MEN

(U.S. winners only)

500 Meters

1924	Charles Jewtraw	44.0
1932	John A. Shea	43.4
1952	Kenneth Henry	43.2
1964	Terrence McDermott	40.1
1980	Eric Heiden	38.03

1,000 Meters

1976	Peter Mueller	1:19.32
1980	Eric Heiden	1:15.18

1,500 Meters

1932	John A. Shea	2:57.5
1980	Eric Heiden	1:55.44

5,000 Meters

1932	Irving Jaffee	9:40.8
1980	Eric Heiden	7:02.29

10,000 Meters

1932	Irving Jaffee	19:13.6
1980	Eric Heiden	14:28.13

SPEED SKATING—WOMEN

500 Meters

1972	Anne Henning	43.33
1976	Sheila Young	42.76

1,500 Meters

1972	Dianne Holum	2:20.85

HEIDEN FIRST ATHLETE TO WIN 5 GOLD MEDALS IN WINTER GAMES

Eric Heiden of Madison, Wis., became the first athlete to win five gold medals in the Winter Olympics when he swept the 1980 speed skating events at Lake Placid, N.Y. The 21-year-old Heiden captured the 500-, 1,000-, 1,500-, 5,000-, and 10,000-meter events. He set an Olympic record in each event and capped his performance on Feb. 23 with a world record of 14 minutes 28.13 seconds in the 10,000-meter race, breaking the mark set in 1977 by Viktor Leskin of the Soviet Union by 16.20 seconds.

Lydia Skoblikova of the Soviet Union was the only other athlete to sweep an Olympic speed skating program. She captured all four female events in the 1964 Winter Games at Innsbruck, Austria.

The weekend after his gold-medal sweep, Heiden failed in his attempt to win a fourth straight world title, at Heerenveen, the Netherlands. He was dethroned by 22-year-old Hilbert van der Duim of the host country.

SKIING, ALPINE—MEN

Downhill

1948	Henri Oreiller, France	2m55.0s
1952	Zeno Colo, Italy	2m30.8s
1956	Anton Sailer, Austria	2m52.2s
1960	Jean Vuarnet, France	2m06.2s
1964	Egon Zimmermann, Austria	2m18.16s
1968	Jean-Claude Killy, France	1m59.85s
1972	Bernhard Russi, Switzerland	1m51.43s
1976	Franz Klammer, Austria	1m45.72s
1980	Leonhard Stock, Austria	1m45.50s

Slalom

1948	Edi Reinalter, Switzerland	2m10.3s
1952	Othmar Schneider, Austria	2m00.0s
1956	Anton Sailer, Austria	194.7 pts.
1960	Ernst Hinterseer, Austria	2m08.9s
1964	Josef Stiegler, Austria	2m10.13
1968	Jean-Claude Killy, France	1m39.73s
1972	Francisco Fernandez Ochoa, Spain	1m49.27s
1976	Piero Gros, Italy	2m03.29s
1980	Ingemar Stenmark, Sweden	1m44.26s

Giant Slalom

1952	Stein Eriksen, Norway	2m25.0s
1956	Anton Sailer, Austria	3m00.1s
1960	Roger Staub, Switzerland	1m48.3s
1964	Francois Bonlieu, France	1m46.71s
1968	Jean-Claude Killy, France	3m29.28s
1972	Gustavo Thoeni, Italy	3m09.52s
1976	Heini Hemmi, Switzerland	3m26.97s
1980	Ingemar Stenmark, Sweden	2m40.74s

SKIING, ALPINE—WOMEN

Downhill

1948	Hedi Schlunegger, Switzerland	2m28.3s
1952	Trude Jochum-Beiser, Austria	1m47.1s
1956	Madeleine Berthod, Switzerland	1m40.1s
1960	Heidi Biebl, Germany	1m37.6s
1964	Christl Haas, Austria	1m55.39s
1968	Olga Pall, Austria	1m40.87s
1972	Marie-Therese Nadig, Switzerland	1m36.68s
1976	Rosi Mittermeier, West Germany	1m46.16s
1980	Annemarie Proell Moser, Austria	1m37.52s

Slalom

1948	Gretchen Fraser, United States	1m57.2s
1952	Andrea Mead Lawrence, United States	2m10.6s
1956	Renee Colliard, Switzerland	112.3 pts.
1960	Anne Heggtveigt, Canada	1m49.6s
1964	Christine Goitschel, France	1m29.86s
1968	Marielle Goitschel, France	1m25.86s
1972	Barbara Cochran, United States	1m31.24s
1976	Rosi Mittermeier, West Germany	1m30.54s
1980	Hanni Wenzel, Liechtenstein	1m25.09s

Giant Slalom

1952	Andrea M. Lawrence, United States	2m06.8s
1956	Ossi Reichert, Germany	1m56.5s
1960	Yvonne Ruegg, Switzerland	1m39.9s
1964	Marielle Goitschel, France	1m52.24s
1968	Nancy Greene, Canada	1m51.97s
1972	Marie-Therese Nadig, Switzerland	1m29.90s
1976	Kathy Kreiner, Canada	1m29.13s
1980	Hanni Wenzel, Liechtenstein	2m41.66s

ICE HOCKEY

1920	Canada	1956	U.S.S.R.
1924	Canada	1960	United States
1928	Canada	1964	U.S.S.R.
1932	Canada	1968	U.S.S.R.
1936	Great Britain	1972	U.S.S.R.
1948	Canada	1976	U.S.S.R.
1952	Canada	1980	United States

SKIING, NORDIC, JUMPING

90-Meter Hill

		Points
1924	Jacob T. Thams, Norway	227.5
1928	Alfred Andersen, Norway	230.5
1932	Birger Ruud, Norway	228.0
1936	Birger Ruud, Norway	232.0
1948	Peter Hugsted, Norway	228.1
1952	A. Bergmann, Norway	226.0
1956	Antti Hyvarinen, Finland	227.0
1960	Helmut Recknagel, Germany	227.2
1964	Toralf Engan, Norway	230.7
1968	Vladimir Beloussov, U.S.S.R.	231.3
1972	Wojciech Fortuna, Poland	219.9
1976	Karl Schnabl, Austria	234.8
1980	Jouko Tormanen, Finland	271.0

Small Hill (70 meters)

1964	Veikko Kankkonen, Finland	229.9
1968	Jiri Raska, Czechoslovakia	216.5
1972	Yukio Kasaya, Japan	244.2
1976	Hans-Georg Aschenbach, East Germany	252.0
1980	Anton Innauer, Austria	266.3

AMERICAN HOCKEY TEAM SCORES BIGGEST UPSET IN GAMES

The United States hockey team, made up of college and minor-league players, stunned the hockey world and stirred patriotic fervor among Americans everywhere with a 4–3 upset triumph in the Winter Olympics over the Soviet Union, considered by experts as the finest hockey team in the world—amateur or professional.

The Soviet team was heavily favored to win the Olympic gold medal at Lake Placid, N.Y., for a fifth straight time. The Americans were rated seventh among the 12 national teams and were given virtually no chance of gaining the final round. The 20-man American squad was coached by Herb Brooks, the coach of the University of Minnesota team. He instituted a new style for the Americans, stressing speed and puck control, tactics generally employed by European teams. The Americans opened their unbeaten streak with a 2–2 tie against Sweden in the first round, then stormed to victories over Romania, Czechoslovakia, West Germany, and Norway. Their upset of the Russians came in the first game of the final round on a goal by Mike Eruzione, the team captain from Winthrop, Mass.

They captured the gold medal with a 4–2 victory over Finland and touched off a national celebration and a surge of patriotism seldom seen in American sports. The triumph came at a time when the Olympic movement was under fire and the United States threatened to boycott the Summer Games in Moscow because of the Soviet invasion of Afghanistan. Only once before, in 1960 at Squaw Valley, Calif., had an American team won an Olympic hockey gold medal.

HOW U.S. HOCKEY ADVANCED TO OLYMPIC TITLE
FINAL STANDING

	W	L	T	Pts	GF	GA
United States	2	0	1	5	10	7
Soviet Union	2	1	0	4	16	8
Sweden	0	2	2	2	7	14
Finland	0	2	1	1	7	11

(The top two teams in the Red Division and the two top teams in the Blue Division of the preliminary round-robin advanced to the final, where the Red Division teams played the Blue Division teams. The records of the teams who played each other in their own divisions were counted in the final standing.)

Results of Final Round Games

United States 4, Soviet Union 3
Sweden 3, Finland 3
United States 4, Finland 2
Soviet Union 9, Sweden 2

Consolation for Fifth Place

Czechoslovakia 6, Canada 1

PRELIMINARY ROUND STANDING
Red Division

	W	L	T	Pts	GF	GA
Soviet Union	5	0	0	10	51	11
Finland	3	2	0	6	26	18
Canada	3	2	0	6	28	12
Poland	2	3	0	4	15	23
Holland	1	3	1	3	16	43
Japan	0	4	1	1	7	36

Blue Division

	W	L	T	Pts	GF	GA
Sweden	4	0	1	9	26	7
United States	4	0	1	9	25	10
Czechoslovakia	3	2	0	6	34	16
Romania	1	3	1	3	13	29
West Germany	1	4	0	2	21	30
Norway	0	4	1	1	9	36

(Top two teams in each division advanced to final round. Third place teams played for fifth.)

Results of Preliminary Round Games Involving U.S.

United States 2, Sweden 2
United States 7, Czechoslovakia 3
United States 5, Norway 1
United States 7, Romania 2
United States 4, West Germany 2

DISTRIBUTION OF MEDALS 1980 WINTER GAMES

	Gold	Silver	Bronze	Total
Soviet Union	10	6	6	22
East Germany	9	7	7	23
United States	6	4	2	12
Norway	1	3	6	10
Finland	1	5	3	9
Austria	3	2	2	7
West Germany	0	2	3	5
Switzerland	1	1	3	5
Liechtenstein	2	2	0	4
Netherlands	1	2	1	4
Sweden	3	0	1	4
Italy	0	2	0	2
Canada	0	1	1	2
Britain	1	0	0	1
Hungary	0	1	0	1
Japan	0	1	0	1
Bulgaria	0	0	1	1
Czechoslovakia	0	0	1	1
France	0	0	1	1

Total countries competing: 37.

Scoring of U.S. Victory Over Soviet Union

United States	2	0	2	—	4
Soviet Union	2	1	0	—	3

FIRST PERIOD—1, Soviet Union, Krutov (Kasatonov), 9:12; 2, United States, Schneider (Pavelich), 14:03; 3, Soviet Union, Makarov (A. Golikov), 17:34; 4, United States, Johnson (Christian, Silk), 19:59

SECOND PERIOD—5, Soviet Union, Maltsev (Krutiv), power-play goal, 2:18

THIRD PERSON—6, United States, Johnson (Silk), power-play goal, 8:39; 7, United States, Eruzione (Pavelich, Harrington), 10:00

SHOTS ON GOAL—United States on Tretiak, Myshkin, 8, 2, 6—16. Soviet Union on Craig, 18, 12, 9—39

Scoring of U.S. Gold Medal Victory Over Finland

United States	0	1	3	—	4
Finland	1	1	0	—	2

FIRST PERIOD—1, Finland, Porvari (Leinonen, Litma), 9:20

SECOND PERIOD—2, United States, Christoff (unassisted), 4:39; 3, Finland, Leinonen (Haapalainen, Kimalainen), power-play goal, 6:30

THIRD PERIOD—4, United States, Verchota (Christian), 2:25; 5, McClanahan (Johnson, Christian), 6:05; 6, United States, Johnson, (Christoff), shorthanded goal, 16:25

SHOTS ON GOAL—United States on Valtonen, 14, 8, 7—29. Finland on Craig, 7, 6, 10—23.

AMERICAN SWIMMERS RACE AGAINST OLYMPIC CLOCK

Forty-eight hours after the Olympic swimming competition in Moscow ended, United States swimmers, who had boycotted the Games, protesting the Soviet intervention in Afghanistan, took to the water at Irvine, Calif., hoping to shatter records in the United States Championships and Olympic Trials. Organizers erected a huge scoreboard showing the Olympic times in each event so swimmers and spectators could make comparisons as to how the Americans would have fared had they chosen to go to Moscow.

In a sport they usually dominated, the Americans registered three world records, and on a basis of comparative times, showed they would have won six of 11 gold medals in men's events and four of 11 in women's events had they competed in the Olympics. The world records shattered at Irvine were by Craig Beardsley of Gainesville, Fla., in the 200-meter butterfly (1:58.46); Bill Barrett of Alpharetta, Ga., in the 200 individual medley (2:03.24); and Mary T. Meagher, a 15-year-old from Cincinnati, in the 200 butterfly (2:06.37).

Other 1980 Olympic Games Champions

SUMMER

Archery
Men—Tomi Polkolainen, Finland
Women—Keto Losaberodze, U.S.S.R.

Boxing
106 lb—Shamil Sabyrov, U.S.S.R.
112 lb—Petar Lessov, U.S.S.R.
119 lb—Juan Hernandez, Cuba
126 lb—Rudi Fink, E. Ger.
132 lb—Angel Herrera, Cuba
140 lb—Patrizio Oliva, Italy
148 lb—Andres Aldama, Cuba
157 lb—Armando Martinez, Cuba
165 lb—Jose Gomez, Cuba
179 lb—Slobodan Kacar, Yugoslavia
Heavyweight—Teofilo Stevenson, Cuba

Canadian Canoeing
500 m—Sergei Postrekhin, U.S.S.R.
1,000 m—Lubomir Lubenov, Bulgaria
500–m pairs—Laszlo Foltan and Istvan Vaskutl, Hungary
1,000–m pairs—Ivan Potzalchin and Toma Simionov, Romania

Kayak—Men
500 m—Vladimir Parfenovich, U.S.S.R.
1,000 m—Rudiger Helm, E. Ger.
500–m pairs—Vladimir Parfenovich and Sergei Chukhrai, U.S.S.R.
1,000–m pairs—Vladimir Parfenovich and Sergei Chukhrai, U.S.S.R.
1,000–m fours—E. Ger.

Kayak—Women
500 m—Birgit Fischer, E. Ger.
500–m pairs—Carsta Genauss and Martina Dischof, E. Ger.

Cycling
1,000 m—Lothar Thoms, E. Ger.
Sprint—Lutz Hesslich, E. Ger.
Pursuit—Robert Dill–Bondi, Switzerland
Team pursuit—U.S.S.R.
Road Race—Sergei Soukhoroutchenkov, U.S.S.R.
Team road race—U.S.S.R.

Equestrian
Dressage—Elisabeth Theurer, Austria
Dressage team—U.S.S.R.
Jumping—Jan Kowalczky, Poland
Team jumping—U.S.S.R.
3–Day event—Federico Euro Roman, Italy
Team 3–day event—U.S.S.R. (Aleksandr Blinov, Yuri Salnikov, Valeri Volkov)

Fencing
Foil—Vladimir Smirnov, U.S.S.R.
Team foil—France
Epee—Johan Harmenberg, Sweden
Team epee—France
Saber—Viktor Krovopuskov, U.S.S.R.
Team saber—U.S.S.R.
Women's foil—Pascale Trinquet, France
Women's team foil—France

Gymnastics—Men
All–around—Aleksandr Dityatin, U.S.S.R.
Floor exercises—Roland Bruckner, E. Ger.
Horizontal bar—Stoyan Deltchev, Bulgaria
Parallel bars—Aleksandr Tkachyov, U.S.S.R.
Pommel horse—Zoltan Magyar, Hungary
Rings—Aleksandr Dityatin, U.S.S.R.
Vault—Nikolai Andrianov, U.S.S.R.
Team all–around—U.S.S.R.

Gymnastics—Women
All–around—Yelena Davydova, U.S.S.R.
Balance beam—Nadia Comaneci, Romania
Floor exercises—Nelli Kim, U.S.S.R., and Nadia Comaneci, Romania, tie
Uneven bars—Maxi Gnauck, E. Ger.
Vault—Natalya Shaposhnikova, U.S.S.R.
Team all–round—U.S.S.R.

Judo
132 lb—Thierry Rey, France
143 lb—Nikolai Solodukhin, U.S.S.R.
157 lb—Ezio Gamba, Italy
172 lb—Shota Khabarell, U.S.S.R.
190 lb—Juerg Roethilsberger, Switzerland
209 lb—Robert Van De Walle, Belgium
Over 209 lb—Angelo Parisi, France
Open—Dietmar Lorenz, East Germany

Modern Pentathlon
Individual—Anatoly Starostin, U.S.S.R.
Team—U.S.S.R.

Rowing—Men
Singles—Pertti Karppinen, Finland
Doubles—Joachim Dreifke and Klaus Kroppelien, E. Ger.
Pairs—Bernd and Jorg Landvoigt, E. Ger.
Pairs with coxswain—Harald Jahrling–Friedrich-Wilhelm Ulrich–Georg Spohr, E. Ger.
Fours—Jurgen Thiele–Andreas Decker–Stefan Semmier–Siegfried Brietzke, E. Ger.
Fours with coxswains—Dieter Wemdisch–Ullrich Diessner–Walter Diessner–Gottfried Dohn–Andreas Gregor, E. Ger.
Quadruple sculls—Frank Dunba–Karstn Bunk–Uwe Heppner–Martin Winter, E. Ger.
Eights—Bernd Krauss–Hans-Peter Koppe–Ulrich Kons–Jorg Friedrich–Jens Doberschutz–Ulrich Karnatz–Uwe Duhring–Bernd Hoing–Klaus-Dieter Ludwig, E. Ger.

Rowing—Women
Singles—Sanda Toma, Romania
Doubles—Yelena Khloptseva and Larisa Popova, U.S.S.R.
Pairs—Ute Steindorf and Cornelia Klier, E. Ger.
Fours with coxswains—Romona Kapheim–Silvia Frohlich–Angelika Noack–Romy Saalfeld–Kirsten Wenzel, E. Ger.
Quadruple sculls—Sybille Reinhardt–Jutta Ploch–Jutta Lau–Roswietha Zobelt–Liane Buhr, E. Ger.
Eights—Martina Boesler–Kersten Neisser–Christiane Kopke–Brigit Schutz–Gabriele Kuhn–Ilona Richter–Marita Sandig–Karin Metze–Marina Wilke, E. Ger.

Shooting
Free pistol—Aleksandr Melentev, U.S.S.R.
Rapid–fire pistol—Corneliu Ion, Romania
Small–bore rifle, prone—Karoly Varga, Hungary
Small–bore rifle, 3 positions—Viktor Vlasov, U.S.S.R.
Rifle, running game target—Igor Sokolov, U.S.S.R.
Trap—Luciano Giovannetti, Italy
Skeet—Hans Kjeld Rasmussen, Denmark

Weight Lifting
114 lb—Kanybek Osmonalieu, U.S.S.R.
123 lb—Daniel Nunez, Cuba
132 lb—Viktor Mazin, U.S.S.R.
149 lb—Yanko Roussev, Bulgaria
165 lb—Assen Zlatev, Bulgaria
182 lb—Yurik Vardanyan, U.S.S.R.
198 lb—Peter Baczako, Hungary
220 lb—Ata Zaremba, Czechoslovakia
242 lb—Leonid Taranenko, U.S.S.R.

Wrestling—Freestyle
106 lb—Claudio Pollio, Italy
115 lb—Anatoly Belogiazov, U.S.S.R.
126 lb—Sergei Belogiazov, U.S.S.R.
137 lb—Magomrdgasan Abushev, U.S.S.R.
149 lb—Salpulla Absaidov, U.S.S.R.
163 lb—Valentin Raitchev, Bulgaria
181 lb—Ismail Abilov, Bulgaria
198 lb—Sanasar Oganesyan, U.S.S.R.
220 lb—Ilya Mate, U.S.S.R.
Over 220 lb—Sosian Andlev, U.S.S.R.

Wrestling—Greco-Roman
106 lb—Saksylik Ushkempirov, U.S.S.R.
114 lb—Vakhtang Blagidze, U.S.S.R.
125 lb—Shamil Sherikov, U.S.S.R.
136 lb—Stillanos Migiakis, Greece
150 lb—Stefan Rusu, Romania
163 lb—Ferenc Kocsis, Hungary
180 lb—Gennady Korban, U.S.S.R.
198 lb—Norbert Nottny, Hungary
220 lb—Gheorghi Raikov, Bulgaria
Over 220 lb—Aleksandr Kolchinsky, U.S.S.R.

Yachting
Finn—Esko Rechardt, Finland
Flying Dutchman—Alesandro Abascal and Miguel Noguer, Spain
470 Class—Marcos Soares and Eduardo Penido, Brazil
Soling—Poul Richard, Erik Hansen and

Valdemar Bandolowski, Denmark
Star—Valentin Mankin and Aleksandr Muzyschenko, U.S.S.R.
Tornado—Alexandre Welter and Lars Bjorkstrom, Brazil

Team Champions

Field hockey, men—India
Field hockey, women—Zimbabwe
Handball, men—E. Ger.
Handball, women—U.S.S.R.
Soccer—Czechoslovakia
Volleyball, men—U.S.S.R.
Volleyball, women—U.S.S.R.
Water polo—U.S.S.R.

WINTER

Biathlon

Individual—(10 km): Frank Ullrich, East Germany (20 km): Anatoly Alabyev, Soviet Union
Relay—Soviet Union (Vladimir Aliken, Aleksandr Tikhonov, Vladimir Barnaschov, and Anatoly Alabyev)

Bobsledding

2-Man—Erich Schaerer and Josef Benz, Switzerland
4-Man—East Germany (Meinhard Nehmer, Bogdan Musiol, Bernhard Germeshausen, and Hans Jurgen Gerhardt)

Figure Skating

Men—Robin Cousins, Great Britain
Women—Anett Poetzsch, East Germany
Pairs—Irina Rodnina and Aleksandr Zaitsev, Soviet Union
Dance—Natalya Linichuk and Gennadi Karponosov, Soviet Union

Speed Skating—Men

500 m—Eric Heiden, Madison, Wis.
1,000 m—Eric Heiden, Madison, Wis.
1,500 m—Eric Heiden, Madison, Wis.
5,000 m—Eric Heiden, Madison, Wis.
10,000 m—Eric Heiden, Madison, Wis.

Speed Skating—Women

500 m—Karin Enke, East Germany
1,000 m—Natalya Petruseva, Soviet Union
1,500 m—Annie Borckink, Netherlands
3,000 m—Bjoerg Eva Jensen, Norway

Hockey

Team—United States

Luge

Men—Bernhard Glass, East Germany
Doubles—Hans Rinn and Norbert Hahn, East Germany
Women—Vera Zozulya, Soviet Union

Skiing, Nordic—Men

Combined—Ulrich Wehling, East Germany
70–m jump—Anton Innauer, Austria
90–m jump—Jouko Tormanen, Finland

Cross-Country Skiing—Men

15 km—Thomas Wassberg, Sweden
30 km—Nikolai Zimyatov, Soviet Union
50 km—Nikolai Zimyatov, Soviet Union
40–km relay—Soviet Union (Vasily Rochev, Nikolai Bazhukov, Yevgeny Beliaev, and Nikolai Zimyatov)

Cross-Country Skiing—Women

5 km—Raisa Smetanina, Soviet Union
10 km—Barbara Petzold, East Germany
20–km relay—East Germany (Marlies Rostock, Carola Anding, Veronika Hesse, and Barbara Petzold)

JAMES E. SULLIVAN MEMORIAL AWARD WINNERS

(Amateur Athlete of Year Chosen in Amateur Athletic Union Poll)

1930	Robert Tyre Jones, Jr.	Golf
1931	Bernard E. Berlinger	Track and field
1932	James A. Bausch	Track and field
1933	Glenn Cunningham	Track and field
1934	William R. Bonthron	Track and field
1935	W. Lawson Little, Jr.	Golf
1936	Glenn Morris	Track and field
1937	J. Donald Budge	Tennis
1938	Donald R. Lash	Track and field
1939	Joseph W. Burk	Rowing
1940	J. Gregory Rice	Track and field
1941	Leslie MacMitchell	Track and field
1942	Cornelius Warmerdam	Track and field
1943	Gilbert L. Dodds	Track and field
1944	Ann Curtis	Swimming
1945	Felix (Doc) Blanchard	Football
1946	Y. Arnold Tucker	Football
1947	John B. Kelly, Jr.	Rowing
1948	Robert B. Mathias	Track and field
1949	Richard T. Button	Figure skating
1950	Fred Wilt	Track and field
1951	Robert E. Richards	Track and field
1952	Horace Ashenfelter	Track and field
1953	Major Sammy Lee	Diving
1954	Malvin Whitfield	Track and field
1955	Harrison Dillard	Track and field
1956	Patricia McCormick	Diving
1957	Bobby Jo Morrow	Track and field
1958	Glenn Davis	Track and field
1959	Parry O'Brien	Track and field
1960	Rafer Johnson	Track and field
1961	Wilma Rudolph Ward	Track and field
1962	Jim Beatty	Track and field
1963	John Pennel	Track and field
1964	Don Schollander	Swimming
1965	Bill Bradley	Basketball
1966	Jim Ryun	Track and field
1967	Randy Matson	Track and field
1968	Debbie Meyer	Swimming
1969	Bill Toomey	Decathlon
1970	John Kinsella	Swimming
1971	Mark Spitz	Swimming
1972	Frank Shorter	Marathon
1973	Bill Walton	Basketball
1974	Rick Wohlhuter	Track
1975	Tim Shaw	Swimming
1976	Bruce Jenner	Track and field
1977	John Naber	Swimming
1978	Tracy Caulkins	Swimming
1979	Kurt Thomas	Gymnastics

Sports Terminology

This concise list does not contain words that most sports followers know, such as "double" in baseball or "touchdown" in football. Rather, it defines those middle-ground terms that somehow are neither simple nor technical—terms that are often used by sports writers and commentators.

A (worn on shirt in hockey): Alternate captain of team; has right to discuss issues with referee if captain is off ice.
Ace (golf): A hole-in-one shot; **(tennis):** Ball placed so well opponent cannot not get to it; if on service, it is a service ace.
Add in, add out (tennis): Score following first point after deuce. If won by server it is advantage, or add in; if won by receiver it is advantage, or add out.
All court press (basketball): Close guarding by defense at all points, trying to force misplays.
Anchor (relay racing): Fourth and last runner or swimmer.
Around-the-horn (baseball): Double play initiated by third baseman who throws to second where relay goes to first.
At bats (baseball): Times in which player bats officially. Does not include bases on balls, hits by pitched ball, sacrifices, sacrifice flies, or bases awarded for interference.
Audible (football): Quarterback's vocal signals at scrimmage line, changing play called in huddle.
Axel (figure skating): To jump from outer forward edge of one skate and land on outer backward edge of other skate after one and one half body turns in air.
Back check (hockey): Delaying or stopping player with puck by opponent in defensive zone.
Back court (basketball): Area between center line and basket which offensive team leaves as it moves toward own basket.
Balanced line (football): Offensive line with guard, tackle, and end on each side of center.
Balk (baseball): Illegal move by pitcher intended to deceive baserunner; runners allowed to advance one base.
Ball control (basketball, football): Prolonged possession of ball on attack, seeking good scoring chance.
Baltimore chop (baseball): Ball batted down into fair territory near plate that bounces high, usually allowing runner to reach first base before infielder's throw.
Bean ball (baseball): Pitched ball thrown near batter's head. Pitch is illegal and can cause pitcher's removal from game if judged deliberate.
Blind side (football, hockey): Side opposite direction player is looking.
Blitz (football): Concentrated charge, usually on passer, by linebackers and defensive backs.
Board check (hockey): Illegal knocking or riding of opponent into boards.
Body check (hockey): Blocking or hitting opponent with body; legal when opponent has puck or has just released it.
Bogey (golf): One stroke over par figure allotted to hole; **double bogey:** two strokes over par.
Bomb (football): Long pass to receiver speeding toward goal line; intended for quick score.
Bonus free throw (basketball): Second throw allowed if first is made on foul committed when team has exceeded limit for fouls in the period.
Bootleg (football): Quarterback's run to side opposite to direction blockers have moved, usually with ball held near hip in effort of concealment.
Break point (tennis): Point being contested that, if won by receiver, will win game and break service.
Breakaway (football, hockey): Play in which player gets free behind defense with good chance to score.
Breather: Game that appears to be an easy victory during hard schedule.
Broken field runner (football): Back who is adept at getting past widely spaced defensemen.
Brush back (baseball): A pitch intended to move batter from position close to plate.
Buttonhook pass (football): Receiver goes downfield and U-turns sharply to catch ball.
Caber (Scotch games): Tapered, heavy tree trunk thrown in competition. It is usually 16 to 20 feet long and weighs around 90 pounds.
Clipping (football): Throwing body across back of legs of non-ball-carrying opponent.
Conversion (basketball): Sinking of free-throw attempt; **(football):** score of point or points after touchdown.
Corner kick (soccer): Kick from corner of field at opponent's goal line awarded offensive team when ball is knocked over line at side of goal by defenders.
Crab, catch a (rowing): Dropping of oar into water on recovery from stroke; can cause injury to oarsman or throw him out of boat.
Crack back (football): Illegal blind-side block usually of defender in secondary by a pass receiver.
Cripple (baseball): Straightaway throw aimed at center of plate when pitcher is in danger of walking batter.
Cross-checking (hockey): Hitting of opponent with both hands on stick and no part of stick on ice; subject to penalty.
Double dribble (basketball): Starting to dribble again after grasping ball with both hands; a violation.
Double fault (tennis): Second failure to hit ball into service court on serve.
Double-team: Method of defense by which two defenders converge on one player, usually a top scorer.
Draw (football): Quarterback fakes as if to pass but hands ball off to another back for running play.
Dribble (soccer): Advancing ball by series of short taps with one or both feet.
Dunking (basketball): Reaching above rim and thrusting ball into basket.
Duster (baseball): Pitch that forces batter to drop to ground.
Eagle (golf): Two shots under par; **double eagle:** three shots under par.
Elbowing (hockey): Striking of opponent with elbow; subject to penalty.
Encroachment (football): Charging of player into neutral zone at line of scrimmage before ball is snapped.
End-around (football): Play in which end takes ball on handoff and races around other end.
E.R.A. (baseball): Earned run average of pitchers; earned run is one scored without errors, passed balls, wild pitches, or interference.
Fair catch (football): Signal, with upraised arm, by kick receiver for chance to make catch unmolested; he cannot advance ball, and a tackler is penalized.
Fast break (basketball): Attempt to get into scoring position before defensive team can regain back court posts.
Fielder's choice (baseball): Scorer's term to show how batter reached first base when batted ball is played to another base.

Flanker (football): Back stationed wide right or left as a pass receiver.
Flare (football): Pass to receiver swinging wide or flaring out of backfield.
Fore checking (hockey): Stopping or delaying opponent with puck in his own zone.
Freestyle (skiing): Style that is innovative and imaginative in the use of acrobatics, tricks, and fancy strides. It has three disciplines—aerials, moguls, and ballet.
Freezing (hockey): Pinning puck against boards with feet or stick to force face-off.
Front court (basketball): Area from center line to offensive team's basket where most of play occurs; area must be reached within 10 seconds after gaining possession of ball and play cannot go to back court unless ball is touched by opponent.
Front four (football): Tackles and ends of defensive line.
Goal crease (hockey): Area in front of goal cage, outlined by lines, which can be occupied only by goalkeeper.
Goal tending (basketball): Touching or knocking ball back when ball is above the basket.
Grand slam (baseball): A home run with the bases full; **(golf):** Winning of United States Amateur, United States Open, British Amateur, and British Open in same year. (Achieved by Bobby Jones in 1930.) **Pro golf:** Winning of United States Open, British Open, Professional Golfers' Association championship, and Masters in one season; **(tennis):** Winning of French, Wimbledon, United States, and Australian championships in one year.
Hat trick (hockey): Scoring of three goals in one game by one player is present conception of term. However, the National Hockey League Guide says that most accepted definition for term, which originated for bowlers in cricket, is the scoring of three successive goals with none scored in between by either team.
Heading (soccer): Method of passing, scoring, or controlling ball with the head.
High post (basketball): Position near outer circle of free-throw line.
High-sticking (hockey): Carrying of stick above shoulder level, sometimes for whacking opponent. It is always illegal and subject to penalty.
Hit for cycle (baseball): Player who hits single, double, triple, and home run in one game. Hits don't have to be in order.
Hooking (hockey): Holding or delaying opponent with blade of stick; subject to penalty.
Icing (hockey): Shooting of puck from behind red line, or length of ice, into opponent's zone; it is illegal unless team is short-handed and play is restarted in zone where puck was hit.
Illegal procedure (football): Usually applies to backfield man in motion before ball was snapped. Calls for penalty.
Infield fly (baseball): Fair ball hit above infielders' territory with men on first and second or first, second, and third with less than two out. Umpire must declare it, saying so, and raising hand. The batter is automatically out.
Interference (hockey): Impeding of opponent who does not have puck; subject to penalty.
Jump ball (basketball): Ball put into play by tossing it up between two players in one of circles marked on floor, usually after held ball.
Jump shot (basketball): Field-goal attempt by player with both feet off floor, shooting over an opponent.
Lateral (football): Pass tossed parallel with goal line or back toward opponent's goal.
Lay-up (basketball): An easy shot, usually banked off backboard from side of basket. It is pushed up with one hand rather than thrown.
Let (tennis): Ball to be served over, usually a net ball, which hits top of net and falls into service court. Lets are called for any interference and are used in most other racquet games.
Let-up pitch (baseball): Ball that is thrown with less speed but usually with same motion as fast ball; a change of pace.
Lob (tennis): Ball stroked high, but not hard, in a loop; usually used as a defensive move to get opponent back from net; **(soccer):** high soft kick taken on the volley.
Love (tennis): Term for zero, or nothing, in counting score.
Low post (basketball): Position at side of basket outside free-throw lane.
Major penalty (hockey): Five-minute penalty assessed for fighting or drawing blood in rough play that would normally be a minor.
Man-to-man defense (basketball): Player guards only the man he is assigned unless switch is called on cross-over plays.
Match penalty (hockey): Banning of player from remainder of game, often for unkind words to an official.
Match play (golf): Two players compete against each other on each hole. Victor is one who wins most holes, and match may end before 18 holes are played. A player ahead by three holes after 16, or two more to go, is winner 3 and 2.
Medal play (golf): Competition decided on fewest strokes taken among group of players for number of holes in tournament.
Medalist (golf): Player with lowest score in qualifying round for match-play tournament.
Metric mile (track): The 1,500-meter run, so called because it is the closest distance to the one-mile run (1,608.84 meters).
Middle-distance races (track): Races from 800 meters to 1,500 yards, or one mile.
Minor penalty (hockey): Penalty of two minutes given for most infractions.
Misconduct penalty (hockey): Ten-minute penalty assessed player for certain violations during which team can use a substitute; usually given for arguing too heatedly with official. Game misconduct is same as match penalty, assessed most often for being third man in fight.
Nassau (golf): Scoring system allowing one point for best score on first nine, one for best on second nine, and one for best on the 18 holes.
Neutral corner (boxing): One of two corners not being used by contestants between rounds. After knocking opponent down, boxer must go to one of neutral corners during count.
Nose guard (football): Defensive lineman, usually the middle guard in some formations. He plays opposite offensive center.
Offside (football): Movement of player over line of scrimmage or kicking line before ball is put into play; **(hockey):** illegal procedure of player with puck or by teammate in preceding puck across opponent's blue line; calls for face-off; **(soccer):** often when player gets between defender and goalkeeper before ball is played.
Onside kick (football): Short, usually angled kickoff, which kicking team hopes to recover after it travels required 10 yards.
Option (football): Choice of ball carrier to run, pass, or hand off.
Overtime: Game in which extra periods are played to dissolve tie existing at end of regular time; **Sudden death:** overtime play which ends as soon as score is made.

Pass rush (football): Charge of lineman against passer.
Pattern (football): Manner in which receiver runs and maneuvers to gain position against defenders.
Penalty kick (soccer): Free kick allowed for flagrant violations from mark 12 yards from goal with only goalkeeper to defend.
Penalty killer (hockey): Player adept at defensive play, who is used when team is short-handed.
Penalty shot (hockey): Shot awarded player when checked illegally while going in alone on opposing goalie; he has only goalie to beat on shot as he skates in on goal from center.
Pick (basketball): Block of defender by player that sets up teammate for shot at basket.
Pitch-out (baseball): Pitch thrown high or wide to enable catcher to make fast throw to second or third when it is thought baserunner might try to steal.
Pivot, pivotman (basketball): Player stationed at strategic point, low post or high post, who stands with back to basket and hands off or passes to others in motion about him, or pivots and uses hook shots to score.
Pocket (football): Small area amid blockers where passer stands while looking for receivers.
Poke-check (hockey): Poking of puck away from opponent with stick.
Power play (hockey): Offensive maneuver in effort to score when opponents have man in penalty box; usually four forwards and a good defenseman shooter are used.
Prevent defense (football): Stratagem of lessening front-line strength for deep defense, allowing short yardage but defending against long gain or score.
Punt (football): Ball dropped from hands by player and kicked before it strikes ground.
Pursuit race (cycling): A relay race by teams of four riders.
Quarterback sneak (football): Play in which quarterback carries ball himself, often through center for short gain to get first down.
Rebound (basketball): Carom of ball off basket after field goal attempt.
Red light (hockey): Indication of score by goal judge who pushes button lighting goal light.
Red shirt (football): Designation for college player who is remaining out of competition during current season in order to have another year of eligibility. He may be working out with squad.
Repechage (rowing): Second chance heats to qualify for semifinals for oarsmen beaten in first heats of regatta.
Reverse (football): Running play in which ball is carried in direction opposite to that in which play started; **naked reverse:** play in which second carrier has no blockers in front of him.
Roll-out (football): Quarterback runs laterally behind blockers, keeping or passing.
Roughing (hockey): Scuffling or show of fists; subject to penalty.
Safety (football): Occurrence in which ball becomes dead behind goal line of player in possession when impetus came from his own team.
Salchow (figure skating): Jump from inside back edge of one skate, landing on outside back edge of other skate after one body revolution.
Save (hockey, soccer): Shot on goal stopped by goalkeeper.
Scratch (racing): Individual or boat that has no handicap.
Screen (basketball): Legal action taken by player to delay opponent from reaching desired position.
Screen pass (football): Pass to receiver stationed behind wall of blockers as defenders harass passer.
Service break (tennis): Loss of game while serving.
Set shot (basketball): Field goal attempt taken with deliberation by player with both feet on floor.
Setbacks (football): Other backs lined up at side or to rear of quarterback.
Skip (curling): Captain of rink or team.
Slalom (skiing): A zigzag race through a series of gates (pairs of poles) so placed as to create sharp turns; **(canoeing):** race through pairs of poles set in water, some at sides of course, some in which the paddler comes in at reverse.
Slap-shot (hockey): Hard shot hit with snap of wrists.
Slashing (hockey): Swinging of stick at opponent; subject to penalty.
Slot back (football): Player placed at least one yard behind line of scrimmage between wide receiver and interior lineman.
Spearing (hockey): Using butt-end of stick to jab opponent; subject to penalty.
Spike (volleyball): To hit ball down hard into opponent's court, often by a leap after ball is set up high for spiker by teammate.
Stick-handling (hockey): Moving of puck around the ice.
Striker (soccer): A central forward player whose responsibility is to score.
Strong side (football): Overbalance of linemen to one side of center.
Sweep check (hockey): Swinging of stick, low along ice, to dislodge puck from stick of opponent or to intercept pass.
Sweeper (soccer): Player who roams either in front or behind defender line to pick up stray passes.
Tackling (soccer): Attempting to take ball away from opponent when both are playing ball with feet, sometimes by sliding under opponent.
Ten-second rule (basketball): Limit of time offensive team has to clear ball from from back court.
Three-point goal (basketball): Field goal from 25 feet out or farther used in certain leagues. It counts 3 points instead of 2.
Three-point play (basketball): Maximum score by player fouled while shooting field goal and who converts free throw.
Three-second rule (basketball): Limit of time an offensive player can stay in free-throw lane unless battling for rebound.
Throw-in (basketball): Method of putting ball into play after score or out of bounds; player must throw to teammate on court within five seconds.
Touchback (football): Occurrence in which ball becomes dead behind goal line of team in possession when impetus came from other team, such as kick. There are no points for touchback.
Trap (football): Maneuver permitting defender into backfield to be blocked from side by another player.
Traveling (basketball): Extra steps taken by player with ball who is allowed one full step after receiving ball.
Turnover: Loss of ball or puck to opponents without scoring.
Weak side (football): Opposite strong side.
Wide receiver (football): Split end or flanker set wide of scrimmage line.
Zone defense (basketball): Method by which player guards an area instead of one man. It is barred in National Basketball Association play.

FOOTBALL

The pastime of kicking around a ball goes back beyond the limits of recorded history. Ancient savage tribes played football of a primitive kind. There was a ball-kicking game played by Athenians, Spartans, and Corinthians 2500 years ago, which the Greeks called *Episkuros*. The Romans had a somewhat similar game called *Harpastum* and are supposed to have carried the game with them when they invaded the British Isles in the First Century, B.C.

Undoubtedly the game known in the United Stated as Football traces directly to the English game of Rugby, though the modifications have been many. Informal football was played on college lawns well over a century ago, and an annual Freshman-Sophomore series of "scrimmages" began at Yale in 1840. The first formal intercollegiate football game was the Princeton-Rutgers contest at New Brunswick, N.J., on Nov. 6, 1869, with Rutgers winning by 6 goals to 4.

In those days, games were played with 25, 20, 15, or 11 men on a side. In 1880, there was a convention at which Walter Camp of Yale persuaded the delegates to agree to a rule calling for 11 players on a side. The game grew so rough that it was attacked as brutal, and some colleges abandoned the sport. Conditions were so bad in 1906 that President Theodore Roosevelt called a meeting of Yale, Harvard, and Princeton representatives at the White House in the hope of reforming and improving the game. The outcome was that the game, with the forward pass introduced and some other modifications of the rules inserted, became faster and cleaner.

The first professional game was played in 1895 at Latrobe, Pa. The National Football League was founded in 1921. The All-American Conference went into action in 1946. At the end of the 1949 season the two circuits merged, retaining the name of the older league. In 1960, the American Football League, began operations. In 1970, the leagues merged.

College Football

NATIONAL COLLEGE FOOTBALL CHAMPIONS

The "National Collegiate A. A. Football Guide" recognizes as unofficial national champion the team selected each year by press association polls. Where The Associated Press poll (of writers) does not agree with the United Press International poll (of coaches), the guide lists both teams selected.

1937	Pittsburgh
1938	Texas Christian
1939	Texas A & M
1940	Minnesota
1941	Minnesota
1942	Ohio State
1943	Notre Dame
1944	Army
1945	Army
1946	Notre Dame
1947	Notre Dame
1948	Michigan
1949	Notre Dame
1950	Oklahoma
1951	Tennessee
1952	Michigan State
1953	Maryland
1954	Ohio State and U.C.L.A.
1955	Oklahoma
1956	Oklahoma
1957	Auburn and Ohio State
1958	Louisiana State
1959	Syracuse
1960	Minnesota
1961	Alabama
1962	So. California
1963	Texas
1964	Alabama
1965	Alabama and Michigan State
1966	Notre Dame
1967	So. California
1968	Ohio State
1969	Texas
1970	Texas and Nebraska
1971	Nebraska
1972	So. California
1973	Notre Dame
1974	Oklahoma and So. California
1975	Oklahoma
1976	Pittsburgh
1977	Notre Dame
1978	Alabama and So. California
1979	Alabama

ARMY-NAVY SERIES RECORD SINCE 1962

1962	Navy 34, Army 14
1963	Navy 21, Army 15
1964	Army 11, Navy 8
1965	Army 7, Navy 7
1966	Army 20, Navy 7
1967	Navy 19, Army 14
1968	Army 21, Navy 14
1969	Army 27, Navy 0
1970	Navy 11, Army 7
1971	Army 24, Navy 23
1972	Army 23, Navy 15
1973	Navy 51, Army 0
1974	Navy 19, Army 0
1975	Navy 30, Army 6
1976	Navy 38, Army 10
1977	Army 17, Navy 14
1978	Navy 28, Army 0
1979	Navy 31, Army 7

RECORD OF ANNUAL MAJOR BOWL COLLEGE FOOTBALL GAMES

Rose Bowl

(At Pasadena, Calif.)

1902	Michigan 49, Stanford 0
1916	Washington State 14, Brown 0
1917	Oregon 14, Pennsylvania 0
1918	Mare Island Marines 19, Camp Lewis 7
1919	Great Lakes 17, Mare Island Marines 0
1920	Harvard 7, Oregon 6
1921	California 28, Ohio State 0
1922	Washington and Jefferson 0, California 0
1923	So. California 14, Penn State 3
1924	Navy 14, Washington 14
1925	Notre Dame 27, Stanford 10
1926	Alabama 20, Washington 19
1927	Alabama 7, Stanford 7
1928	Stanford 7, Pittsburgh 6
1929	Georgia Tech 8, California 7
1930	So. California 47, Pittsburgh 14
1931	Alabama 24, Washington State 0
1932	So. California 21, Tulane 12
1933	So. California 35, Pittsburgh 0
1934	Columbia 7, Stanford 0
1935	Alabama 29, Stanford 13
1936	Stanford 7, So. Methodist 0
1937	Pittsburgh 21, Washington 0
1938	California 13, Alabama 0
1939	So. California 7, Duke 3
1940	So. California 14, Tennessee 0
1941	Stanford 21, Nebraska 13
1942	Oregon State 20, Duke 16[1]
1943	Georgia 9, U.C.L.A. 0
1944	So. California 29, Washington 0
1945	So. California 25, Tennessee 0
1946	Alabama 34, So. California 14
1947	Illinois 45, U.C.L.A. 14
1948	Michigan 49, So. California 0
1949	Northwestern 20, California 14
1950	Ohio State 17, California 14
1951	Michigan 14, California 6
1952	Illinois 40, Stanford 7
1953	So. California 7, Wisconsin 0
1954	Michigan State 28, U.C.L.A. 20
1955	Ohio State 20, So. California 7
1956	Michigan State 17, U.C.L.A. 14
1957	Iowa 35, Oregon State 19

1958 Ohio State 10, Oregon 7
1959 Iowa 38, California 12
1960 Washington 44, Wisconsin 8
1961 Washington 17, Minnesota 7
1962 Minnesota 21, U.C.L.A. 3
1963 So. California 42, Wisconsin 37
1964 Illinois 17, Washington 7
1965 Michigan 34, Oregon State 7
1966 U.C.L.A. 14, Michigan State 12
1967 Purdue 14, So. California 13
1968 So. California 14, Indiana 3
1969 Ohio State 27, So. California 16
1970 So. California 10, Michigan 3
1971 Stanford 27, Ohio State 17
1972 Stanford 13, Michigan 12
1973 So. California 42, Ohio State 17
1974 Ohio State 42, So. California 21
1975 So. California 18, Ohio State 17
1976 U.C.L.A. 23, Ohio State 10
1977 So. California 14, Michigan 6
1978 Washington 27, Michigan 20
1979 So. California 17, Michigan 10
1980 So. California 17, Ohio State 16

1. Played at Durham, N.C.

Orange Bowl

(At Miami)

1933 Miami (Fla.) 7, Manhattan 0
1934 Duquesne 33, Miami (Fla.) 7
1935 Bucknell 26, Miami (Fla.) 0
1936 Catholic 20, Mississippi 19
1937 Duquesne 13, Mississippi State 12
1938 Auburn 6, Michigan State 0
1939 Tennessee 17, Oklahoma 0
1940 Georgia Tech 21, Missouri 7
1941 Mississippi State 14, Georgetown 7
1942 Georgia 40, Texas Christian 26
1943 Alabama 37, Boston College 21
1944 Louisiana State 19, Texas A&M 14
1945 Tulsa 26, Georgia Tech 12
1946 Miami (Fla.) 13, Holy Cross 6
1947 Rice 8, Tennessee 0
1948 Georgia Tech 20, Kansas 14
1949 Texas 41, Georgia 28
1950 Santa Clara 21, Kentucky 13
1951 Clemson 15, Miami (Fla.) 14
1952 Georgia Tech 17, Baylor 14
1953 Alabama 61, Syracuse 6
1954 Oklahoma 7, Maryland 0
1955 Duke 34, Nebraska 7
1956 Oklahoma 20, Maryland 6
1957 Colorado 27, Clemson 21
1958 Oklahoma 48, Duke 21
1959 Oklahoma 21, Syracuse 6
1960 Georgia 14, Missouri 0
1961 Missouri 21, Navy 14
1962 Louisiana State 25, Colorado 7
1963 Alabama 17, Oklahoma 0
1964 Nebraska 13, Auburn 7
1965 Texas 21, Alabama 17
1966 Alabama 39, Nebraska 28
1967 Florida 27, Georgia Tech 12
1968 Oklahoma 26, Tennessee 24
1969 Penn State 15, Kansas 14
1970 Penn State 10, Missouri 3
1971 Nebraska 17, Louisiana State 12
1972 Nebraska 38, Alabama 6
1973 Nebraska 40, Notre Dame 6
1974 Penn State 16, Louisiana State 9
1975 Notre Dame 13, Alabama 11
1976 Oklahoma 14, Michigan 6
1977 Ohio State 27, Colorado 10
1978 Arkansas 31, Oklahoma 6
1979 Oklahoma 31, Nebraska 24
1980 Oklahoma 24, Florida State 7

Sugar Bowl

(At New Orleans)

1935 Tulane 20, Temple 14
1936 Texas Christian 3, Louisiana State 2
1937 Santa Clara 21, Louisiana State 14
1938 Santa Clara 6, Louisiana State 0
1939 Texas Christian 15, Carnegie Tech 7
1940 Texas A & M 14, Tulane 13
1941 Boston College 19, Tennessee 13
1942 Fordham 2, Missouri 0
1943 Tennessee 14, Tulsa 7
1944 Georgia Tech 20, Tulsa 18
1945 Duke 29, Alabama 26
1946 Oklahoma A & M 33, St. Mary's (Calif.) 13
1947 Georgia 20, North Carolina 10
1948 Texas 27, Alabama 7
1949 Oklahoma 14, North Carolina 6
1950 Oklahoma 35, Louisiana State 0
1951 Kentucky 13, Oklahoma 7
1952 Maryland 28, Tennessee 13
1953 Georgia Tech 24, Mississippi 7
1954 Georgia Tech 42, West Virginia 19
1955 Navy 21, Mississippi 0
1956 Georgia Tech 7, Pittsburgh 0
1957 Baylor 13, Tennessee 7
1958 Mississippi 39, Texas 7
1959 Louisiana State 7, Clemson 0
1960 Mississippi 21, Louisiana State 0
1961 Mississippi 14, Rice 6
1962 Alabama 10, Arkansas 3
1963 Mississippi 17, Arkansas 13
1964 Alabama 12, Mississippi 7
1965 Louisiana State 13, Syracuse 10
1966 Missouri 20, Florida 18
1967 Alabama 34, Nebraska 7
1968 Louisiana State 20, Wyoming 13
1969 Arkansas 16, Georgia 2
1970 Mississippi 27, Arkansas 22
1971 Tennessee 34, Air Force Academy 13
1972 Oklahoma 40, Auburn 22
1973 Oklahoma 14, Penn State 0
1974 Notre Dame 24, Alabama 23
1975 Nebraska 13, Florida 10
1976 Alabama 13, Penn State 6
1977 Pittsburgh 27, Georgia 3
1978 Alabama 35, Ohio State 6
1979 Alabama 14, Penn State 7
1980 Alabama 24, Arkansas 9

Cotton Bowl

(At Dallas)

1937 Texas Christian 16, Marquette 6
1938 Rice 28, Colorado 14
1939 St. Mary's (Calif.) 20, Texas Tech. 13
1940 Clemson 6, Boston College 3
1941 Texas A & M 13, Fordham 12
1942 Alabama 29, Texas A & M 21
1943 Texas 14, Georgia Tech 7
1944 Randolph Field 7, Texas 7
1945 Oklahoma A & M 34, Texas Christian 0
1946 Texas 40, Missouri 27
1947 Louisiana State 0, Arkansas 0
1948 So. Methodist 13, Penn State 13
1949 So. Methodist 21, Oregon 13
1950 Rice 27, North Carolina 13
1951 Tennessee 20, Texas 14
1952 Kentucky 20, Texas Christian 7
1953 Texas 16, Tennessee 0
1954 Rice 28, Alabama 6
1955 Georgia Tech 14, Arkansas 6
1956 Mississippi 14, Texas Christian 13
1957 Texas Christian 28, Syracuse 27
1958 Navy 20, Rice 7
1959 Air Force 0, Texas Christian 0
1960 Syracuse 23, Texas 14
1961 Duke 7, Arkansas 6
1962 Texas 12, Mississippi 7
1963 Louisiana State 13, Texas 0
1964 Texas 28, Navy 6
1965 Arkansas 10, Nebraska 7
1966 Louisiana State 14, Arkansas 7
1967 Georgia 24, So. Methodist 9
1968 Texas A & M 20, Alabama 16
1969 Texas 36, Tennessee 13
1970 Texas 21, Notre Dame 17
1971 Notre Dame 24, Texas 11
1972 Penn State 30, Texas 6
1973 Texas 17, Alabama 13
1974 Nebraska 19, Texas 3
1975 Penn State 41, Baylor 20
1976 Arkansas 31, Georgia 10
1977 Houston 30, Maryland 21
1978 Notre Dame 38, Texas 10
1979 Notre Dame 35, Houston 34
1980 Houston 17, Nebraska 14

Gator Bowl

(At Jacksonville, Fla. Played on Saturday nearest New Year's Day of year indicated)

1953 Florida 14, Tulsa 13
1954 Texas Tech 35, Auburn 13
1955 Auburn 33, Baylor 13
1956 Vanderbilt 25, Auburn 13
1957 Georgia Tech 21, Pittsburgh 14
1958 Tennessee 3, Texas A & M 0
1959 Mississippi 7, Florida 3
1960 Arkansas 14, Georgia Tech 7
1961 Florida 13, Baylor 12
1962 Penn State 30, Georgia Tech 15
1963 Florida 17, Penn State 7
1964 No. Carolina 35, Air Force 0
1965 Florida State 36, Oklahoma 19
1966 Georgia Tech 31, Texas Tech 21
1967 Tennessee 18, Syracuse 12
1968 Penn State 17, Florida State 17
1969 Missouri 35, Alabama 10
1970 Florida 14, Tennessee 13
1971 Auburn 35, Mississippi 28
1972 Georgia 7, North Carolina 3
1973 Auburn 24, Colorado 3
1974 Texas Tech 28, Tennessee 19
1975 Auburn 27, Texas 3
1976 Maryland 13, Florida 0
1977 Notre Dame 20, Penn State 9
1978 Pittsburgh 34, Clemson 3
1979 Clemson 17, Ohio State 15
1980 North Carolina 17, Michigan 15

RESULTS OF OTHER 1979 SEASON BOWL GAMES

Bluebonnet (Houston)—Purdue 27, Tennessee 22
Fiesta (Tempe, Ariz.)—Pittsburgh 16, Arizona 10
Hall of Fame (Birmingham, Ala.)—Missouri 24, South Carolina 14
Holiday (San Diego)—Indiana 38, Brigham Young 37
Independence (Shreveport, La.)—Syracuse 31, McNesse State 7
Liberty (Memphis)—Penn State 9, Tulane 6
Garden State (East Rutherford, N.J.)—Temple 28, California 17
Peach (Atlanta)—Baylor 24, Clemson 18
Sun (El Paso)—Washington 14, Texas 7
Tangerine (Orlando, Fla.)—Louisiana State 34, Wake Forest 10

HEISMAN MEMORIAL TROPHY WINNERS

The Heisman Memorial Trophy is presented annually by the Downtown Athletic Club of New York City to the nation's outstanding college football player, as determined by a poll of sportswriters and sportscasters.

1935	Jay Berwanger, Chicago
1936	Larry Kelley, Yale
1937	Clinton Frank, Yale
1938	Davey O'Brien, Texas Christian
1939	Nile Kinnick, Iowa
1940	Tom Harmon, Michigan
1941	Bruce Smith, Minnesota
1942	Frank Sinkwich, Georgia
1943	Angelo Bertelli, Notre Dame
1944	Leslie Horvath, Ohio State
1945	Felix Blanchard, Army
1946	Glenn Davis, Army
1947	Johnny Lujack, Notre Dame
1948	Doak Walker, So. Methodist
1949	Leon Hart, Notre Dame
1950	Vic Janowicz, Ohio State
1951	Dick Kazmaier, Princeton
1952	Billy Vessels, Oklahoma
1953	Johnny Lattner, Notre Dame
1954	Alan Ameche, Wisconsin
1955	Howard Cassady, Ohio State
1956	Paul Hornung, Notre Dame
1957	John Crow, Texas A & M
1958	Pete Dawkins, Army
1959	Billy Cannon, Louisiana State
1960	Joe Bellino, Navy
1961	Ernie Davis, Syracuse
1962	Terry Baker, Oregon State
1963	Roger Staubach, Navy
1964	John Huarte, Notre Dame
1965	Mike Garrett, Southern California
1966	Steve Spurrier, Florida
1967	Gary Beban, U.C.L.A.
1968	O. J. Simpson, Southern California
1969	Steve Owens, Oklahoma
1970	Jim Plunkett, Stanford
1971	Pat Sullivan, Auburn
1972	Johnny Rodgers, Nebraska
1973	John Cappelletti, Penn State
1974–75	Archie Griffin, Ohio State
1976	Tony Dorsett, Pittsburgh
1977	Earl Campbell, Texas
1978	Billy Sims, Oklahoma
1979	Charles White, Southern California

COLLEGE FOOTBALL HALL OF FAME

(Kings Island, Interstate 71, Kings Mills, Ohio)
(Date given is player's last year of competition)

Players
Abell, Earl—Colgate, 1915
Agase, Alex—Purdue/Illinois, 1946
Agganis, Harry—Boston Univ., 1952
Albert, Frank—Stanford, 1941
Aldrich, Chas. (Ki)—T.C.U., 1938
Aldrich, Malcolm—Yale, 1921
Alexander, John—Syracuse, 1920
Ameche, Alan (Horse)—Wisconsin, 1954
Anderson, H. (Hunk)—Notre Dame, 1921
Bacon, C. Everett—Wesleyan, 1912
Bagnell, Francis (Reds)—Penn, 1950
Baker, Hobart (Hobey)—Princeton, 1913
Ballin, Harold—Princeton, 1914
Banker, Bill—Tulane, 1929
Barnes, Stanley—S. California, 1921
Barrett, Charles—Cornell, 1915
Baston, Bert—Minnesota, 1916
Battles, Cliff—W. Va. Wesleyan, 1931
Baugh, Sammy—Texas Christian U., 1936
Bausch, James—Kansas, 1930
Beckett, John—Oregon, 1913
Bednarik, Chuck—Pennsylvania, 1948
Bellini, Joe—Navy, 1960
Benbrook, A.—Michigan, 1911
Bertelli, A.—Notre Dame, 1943
Berry, Charlie—Lafayette, 1924
Berwanger, John (Jay)—Chicago, 1935
Bettencourt, Larry—St. Mary's, 1927
Blanchard, Felix (Doc)—Army, 1946
Bock, Ed—Iowa State, 1938
Bomar, Lynn—Vanderbilt, 1924
Bomeisler, Doug (Bo)—Yale, 1913
Booth, Albie—Yale, 1931
Borries, Fred—Navy, 1934
Boynton, Ben—Williams, 1920
Brewer, Charles—Harvard, 1895
Brooke, George—Pennsylvania, 1895
Brown, Gordon—Yale, 1900
Brown, John, Jr.—Navy, 1913
Brown, Johnny Mack—Alabama, 1925
Brown, Raymond (Tay)—So. California, 1932
Bunker, Paul—Army, 1902
Butler, Robert—Wisconsin, 1912
Cafego, George—Tennessee, 1939
Cagle, Chris—SW La./Army, 1929
Cain, John—Alabama, 1932
Cameron, Eddie—Wash. & Lee, 1924
Campbell, David C.—Harvard, 1901
Cannon, Jack—Notre Dame, 1929
Carideo, Frank—Notre Dame, 1930
Caroline, J.C.—Illinois, 1954
Carney, Charles—Illinois, 1921
Carpenter, C. Hunter—VPI, 1905
Carroll, Charles—Washington, 1928
Casey, Edward L.—Harvard, 1919
Cassady, Howard—Ohio State, 1955
Chamberlain, Guy—Nebraska, 1915
Christman, Paul—Missouri, 1940
Clark, Earl (Dutch)—Colo. College, 1929
Clevenger, Zora—Indiana, 1903
Cochran, Gary—Princeton, 1895
Cody, Josh—Vanderbilt, 1920
Coleman, Don—Mich. State, 1951
Conerly, Chuck—Mississippi, 1947
Connor, George—Notre Dame, 1947
Corbin, W.—Yale, 1888
Corbus, William—Stanford, 1933
Cowan, Hector—Princeton, 1889
Coy, Edward H. (Tad)—Yale, 1909
Crawford, Fred—Duke, 1933
Crow, John D.—Texas A&M, 1957
Crowley, James—Notre Dame, 1924
Cutter, Slade—Navy, 1934
Czarobski, Ziggie—Notre Dame, 1947
Dalrymple, Gerald—Tulane, 1931
Daniell, James—Ohio State, 1941
Dawkins, Pete—Army, 1958
Dalton, John—Navy, 1912
Daly, Charles—Harvard/Army, 1902
Daniell, Averell—Pittsburgh, 1936
Davies, Tom—Pittsburgh, 1921
Davis, Ernest—Syracuse, 1961
Davis, Glenn—Army, 1946
Davis, Robert T.—Georgia Tech, 1947
DesJardien, Paul—Chicago, 1914
Devine, Aubrey—Iowa, 1921
DeWitt, John—Princeton, 1903
Dobbs, Glenn—Tulsa, 1942
Dodd, Bobby—Tennessee, 1930
Donchess, Joseph—Pittsburgh, 1929
Dougherty, Nathan—Tennessee, 1909
Driscoll, Paddy—Northwestern, 1917
Drury, Morley—So. California, 1927
Dudley, William (Bill)—Virginia, 1941
Eckersall, Walter—Chicago, 1906
Edwards, Turk—Washington State, 1931
Edwards, William—Princeton, 1900
Eichenlaub, R.—Notre Dame, 1913
Evans, Ray—Kansas, 1947
Exendine, Albert—Carlisle, 1908
Falaschi, Nello—Santa Clara, 1937
Fears, Tom—Santa Clara/UCLA, 1947
Feathers, Beattie—Tennessee, 1933
Fenimore, Robert—Oklahoma State, 1947
Fenton, G.E. (Doc)—La. State U., 1910
Ferraro, John—So. California, 1944
Fesler, Wesley—Ohio State, 1930
Fincher, Bill—Georgia Tech, 1920
Fish, Hamilton—Harvard, 1909
Fisher, Robert—Harvard, 1911
Flowers, Abe—Georgia Tech, 1920
Fortmann, Daniel—Colgate, 1935
Francis, Sam—Nebraska, 1936
Franco, Edmund (Ed)—Fordham, 1937
Frank, Clint—Yale, 1937

Franz, Rodney—California, 1949
Friedman, Benny—Michigan, 1926
Gain, Bob—Kentucky, 1950
Garbisch, Edgar—Army, 1924
Gelbert, Charles—Pennsylvania, 1896
Geyer, Forest—Oklahoma, 1915
Giel, Paul—Minnesota, 1953
Gifford, Frank—So. California, 1951
Gilbert, Walter—Auburn, 1936
Gipp, George—Notre Dame, 1920
Gladchuk, Chet—Boston College, 1940
Goldberg, Marshall—Pittsburgh, 1938
Gordon, Walter—California, 1918
Graham, Otto—Northwestern, 1943
Grange, Harold (Red)—Illinois, 1925
Grayson, Robert—Stanford, 1935
Gulick, Merel—Hobart, 1929
Guyon, Joe—Georgia Tech, 1919
Hale, Edwin—Mississippi Col, 1921
Hamilton, Robert (Bones)—Stanford, 1935
Hamilton, Tom—Navy, 1925
Hanson, Vic—Syracuse, 1926
Hardwick, H. (Tack)—Harvard, 1914
Hare, T. Truxton—Pennsylvania, 1900
Harley, Chick—Ohio State, 1919
Harmon, Tom—Michigan, 1940
Harpster, Howard—Carnegie Tech, 1928
Hart, Edward J.—Princeton, 1911
Hart, Leon—Notre Dame, 1949
Hazel, Homer—Rutgers, 1924
Healey, Ed—Dartmouth, 1916
Heffelfinger, W. (Pudge)—Yale, 1891
Hein, Mel—Washington State, 1930
Henry, Wilber—Wash. & Jefferson, 1919
Herschberger, Clarence—Chicago, 1899
Herwig, Robert—California, 1937
Heston, Willie—Michigan, 1904
Hickman, Herman—Tennessee, 1931
Hickok, William—Yale, 1895
Hill, Dan—Duke, 1938
Hillebrand, A.R. (Doc)—Princeton, 1900
Hinkey, Frank—Yale, 1894
Hinkle, Carl—Vanderbilt, 1937
Hinkle, Clark—Bucknell, 1932
Hirsch, Elroy—Wis./Mich., 1943
Hitchcock, James—Auburn, 1932
Hoffman, Frank—Notre Dame, 1931
Hogan, James J.—Yale, 1904
Holland, Jerome (Brud)—Cornell, 1938
Hollenbeck, William—Penn., 1908
Holovak, Michael—Boston College, 1942
Horrell, Edwin—California, 1924
Horvath, Les—Ohio State, 1944
Howe, Arthur—Yale, 1911
Howell, Millard (Dixie)—Alabama, 1934
Hubbard, Cal—Centenary, 1926
Hubbard, John—Amherst, 1906
Hubert, Allison—Alabama, 1925
Huff, Robert Lee (Sam)—W. Va., 1955
Humble, Weldon G.—Rice, 1946
Hunt, Joel—Texas A&M, 1927
Huntington, Ellery—Colgate, 1914
Hutson, Don—Alabama, 1934
Ingram, James—Navy, 1906
Isbell, Cecil—Purdue, 1937
Jablonsky, Harvey—Wash. U./Army, 1933
Janowicz, Vic—Ohio State, 1951
Jenkins, Darold—Missouri, 1941
Joesting, Herbert—Minnesota, 1927
Johnson, James—Carlisle, 1903
Jones, Calvin—Iowa, 1955
Jones, Gomer—Ohio State, 1935
Juhan, Frank—Univ. of South, 1910

Justice, Charlie—North Carolina, 1949
Kaer, Mort—So. California, 1926
Kavanaugh, Kenneth—La. State U., 1939
Kaw, Edgar—Cornell, 1922
Kazmaier, Richard—Princeton, 1951
Keck, James—Princeton, 1921
Kelley, Larry—Yale, 1936
Kelly, William—Montana, 1926
Ketcham, Henry—Yale, 1913
Killinger, William—Penn State, 1922
Kimbrough, John—Texas A&M, 1940
Kinard, Frank—Mississippi, 1937
King, Phillip—Princeton, 1893
Kinnick, Nile—Iowa, 1939
Kipke, Harry—Michigan, 1923
Kirkpatrick, John Reed—Yale, 1910
Kitzmiller, John—Oregon, 1929
Koch, Barton—Baylor, 1931
Kitner, Malcolm—Texas, 1942
Kramer, Ron—Michigan, 1956
Lach, Steve—Duke, 1941
Lane, Myles—Dartmouth, 1927
Lattner, Joseph J.—Notre Dame, 1953
Lautenschlaeger—Tulane, 1925
Layden, Elmer—Notre Dame, 1924
Layne, Bobby—Texas, 1947
Lea, Langdon—Princeton, 1895
LeBaron, Eddie—Univ. of Pacific, 1949
Leech, James—Va. Mil. Inst., 1920
Lio, Augie—Georgetown, 1940
Locke, Gordon—Iowa, 1922
Lourie, Don—Princeton, 1921
Luckman, Sid—Columbia, 1938
Lujack, John—Notre Dame, 1947
Lund, J.L. (Pug)—Minnesota, 1934
Macomber, Bart—Illinois, 1915
MacLeod, Robert—Dartmouth, 1938
Maegle, Dick—Rice, 1954
Mahan, Edward W.—Harvard, 1915
Mallory, William—Yale, 1893
Mann, Gerald—So. Methodist, 1927
Markov, Vic—Washington, 1937
Marshall, Robert—Minnesota, 1907
Matson, Ollie—San Fran. U., 1952
Matthews, Ray—Texas Christ. U., 1928
Maulbetsch, John—Michigan, 1914
Mauthe, J.L. (Pete)—Penn State 1912
Maxwell, Robert—Chi./Swarthmore, 1906
McAfee, George—Duke, 1939
McColl, William F.—Stanford, 1951
McCormick, James B.—Princeton, 1907
McDowall, Jack—No. Car. State, 1927
McEver, Gene—Tennessee, 1931
McEwan, John—Minn./Army, 1916
McFadden, J.B.—Clemson, 1939
McClung, Thomas L.—Yale, 1891
McGinley, Edward—Pennsylvania, 1924
McGovern, J.—Minnesota, 1910
McLaren, George—Pittsburgh, 1918
McMillan, Dan—U.S.C./Calif., 1922
McMillan, Bob—Centre, 1921
McWhorter, Robert—Georgia, 1913
Mercer, Leroy—Pennsylvania, 1912
Mickal, Abe—La. State U., 1935
Miller, Creighton—Notre Dame, 1943
Miller, Don—Notre Dame, 1925
Miller, Edgar (Rip)—Notre Dame, 1924
Miller, Eugene—Penn State, 1913
Milstead, Century—Wabash, Yale 1923
Minds, John—Pennsylvania, 1897
Moffatt, Alex—Princeton, 1884
Montgomery, Cliff—Columbia, 1933
Moomaw, Donn—U.C.L.A., 1952

Morley, William—Columbia, 1903
Morton, William—Dartmouth, 1931
Muller, Harold (Brick)—Calif., 1922
Nagurski, Bronko—Minnesota, 1929
Nevers, Ernie—Stanford, 1925
Newell, Marshall—Harvard, 1893
Newman, Harry—Michigan, 1932
Nomellini, Leo—Minnesota, 1949
Oberlander, Andrew—Dartmouth, 1925
O'Brien, Davey—Texas Christ. U., 1938
O'Dea, Pat—Wisconsin, 1899
O'Hearn, J.—Cornell, 1915
Oliphant, Elmer—Purdue/Army, 1917
Olsen, Merlin—Utah State, 1961
Oosterbaan, Ben—Michigan, 1927
O'Rourke, Charles—Boston College, 1940
Osgood, W.D.—Cornell/Penn, 1895
Osmanski, William—Holy Cross, 1938
Parker, Clarence (Ace)—Duke, 1936
Parker, Jackie—Miss. State, 1953
Parker, James—Ohio State, 1956
Pazzetti, V.J.—Wes./Lehigh, 1912
Peabody, Endicott—Harvard, 1941
Peck, Robert—Pittsburgh, 1916
Pennock, Stanley B.—Harvard, 1914
Pfann, George—Cornell, 1923
Phillips, H.D.—U. of South, 1904
Pingel, John—Michigan State, 1938
Pihos, Pete—Indiana, 1945
Pinckert, Ernie—So. California, 1931
Poe, Arthur—Princeton, 1899
Pollard, Fritz—Brown, 1916
Poole, Barney—Miss./Army, 1947
Pund, Henry—Georgia Tech, 1928
Ramsey, Gerrard—Wm. & Mary, 1942
Reeds, Claude—Oklahoma, 1913
Reid, William—Harvard, 1900
Rentner, Ernest—Northwestern, 1932
Reynolds, Robert—Stanford, 1935
Rinehart, Charles—Lafayette, 1897
Rodgers, Ira—West Virginia, 1919
Rogers, Edward L.—Minnesota, 1903
Rosenberg, Aaron—So. California, 1934
Rote, Kyle—So. Methodist, 1950
Routt, Joe—Texas A&M., 1937
Salmon, Louis—Notre Dame, 1904
Sauer, George—Nebraska, 1933
Sayers, Gale—Kansas, 1964
Scarlett, Hunter—Pennsylvania, 1909
Schoonover, Wear—Arkansas, 1929
Schreiner, Dave—Wisconsin, 1942
Schultz, Adolf (Germany)—Mich., 1908
Schwab, Frank—Lafayette, 1922
Schwartz, Marchmont—Notre Dame, 1931
Schwegler, Paul—Washington, 1931
Scott, Clyde—Arkansas, 1949
Scott, Tom—Virgina, 1953
Seibels, Henry—Sewanee, 1899
Shelton, Murray—Cornell, 1915
Shevlin, Tom—Yale, 1905
Simons, Claude—Tulane, 1934
Sington, Fred—Alabama, 1930
Sinkwich, Frank—Georgia, 1942
Skladany, Joe—Pittsburgh, 1933
Slater, F.F. (Duke)—Iowa, 1921
Smith, Bruce—Minnesota, 1941
Smith, Ernie—So. California, 1932
Smith, Harry—So. California, 1939
Smith, John (Clipper)—Notre Dame, 1927
Smith, Vernon—Georgia, 1931
Snow, Neil—Michigan, 1901
Spears, Clarence W.—Dartmouth, 1915
Spears, W.D.—Vanderbilt, 1927

Sprackling, William—Brown, 1911
Sprague, M. (Bud)—Texas/Army, 1928
Stafford, Harrison—Texas, 1932
Stagg, Amos Alonzo—Yale, 1889
Steffen, Walter—Chicago, 1908
Stein, Herbert—Pittsburgh, 1921
Steuber, Robert—Missouri, 1943
Stevens, Mal—Yale, 1923
Stinchcomb, Gaylord—Ohio State, 1920
Stevenson, Vincent—Pennsylvania, 1905
Strong, Ken—New York Univ., 1928
Strupper, George—Georgia Tech, 1917
Stuhldreher, Harry—Notre Dame, 1924
Stydahar, Joe—West Virginia, 1935
Suffridge, Robert—Tennessee, 1940
Sundstrom, Frank—Cornell, 1923
Swanson, Clarence—Nebraska, 1921
Swiacki, Bill—Holy Cross/Colombia. 1947
Swink, Jim—Texas Christian, 1956
Thompson, Joe—Pittsburgh, 1907
Thorne, Samuel B.—Yale, 1906
Thorpe, Jim—Carlisle, 1912
Ticknor, Ben—Harvard, 1930
Tigert, John—Vanderbilt, 1904
Tinsley, Gaynell—La. State U., 1936
Tipton, Eric—Duke, 1938
Tonnemaker, Clayton—Minnesota, 1949
Torrey, Robert—Pennsylvania, 1906
Travis, Ed Tarkio—Missouri, 1920
Trippi, Charles—Georgia, 1946
Tryon, J. Edward—Colgate, 1925
Utay, Joe—Texas A&M, 1907
Van Brocklin, Norm—Oregon, 1948
Van Sickel, Dale—Florida, 1929
Van Surdam, Henderson—Wesleyan, 1905
Very, Dexter—Penn State, 1912
Vessels, Billy—Oklahoma, 1931
Wagner, Huber—Pittsburgh, 1913
Walker, Doak—So. Methodist, 1949
Wallace, Bill—Rice, 1935
Walsh, Adam—Notre Dame, 1924
Warburton, I. (Cotton)—So. Calif., 1934
Ward, Robert (Bob)—Maryland, 1951
Warner, William—Cornell, 1903
Washington, Ken—U.C.L.A., 1939
Wedemeyer, Herman J.—St. Mary's, 1947
Weekes, Harold—Columbia, 1902
Weir, Ed—Nebraska, 1925
Welch, Gus—Carlisle, 1914
Weller, John—Princeton, 1935
Wendell, Percy—Harvard, 1913
West, D. Belford—Colgate, 1919
Weyand, Alex—Army, 1915
Wharton, Charles—Pennsylvania, 1896
Wheeler, Arthur—Princeton, 1894
White, Byron (Whizzer)—Colorado, 1937
Whitmire, Don—Alabama/Navy, 1944
Wickhorst, Frank—Navy, 1926
Widseth, Ed—Minnesota, 1936
Wildung, Richard—Minnesota, 1942
Williams, James—Rice, 1949
Willis, William—Ohio State, 1945
Wilson, George—Washington, 1925
Wilson, Harry—Penn State/Army, 1923
Wistert, Albert A.—Michigan, 1942
Wistert, Frank (Whitey)—Mich., 1933
Wood, Barry—Harvard, 1931
Wojciechowicz, Alex—Fordham, 1936
Wyant, Andrew—Bucknell/Chicago, 1894
Wyatt, Bowden—Tennessee, 1938
Wyckoff, Clint—Cornell, 1896
Young, Claude (Buddy)—Illinois, 1946
Young, Harry—Wash. & Lee, 1916
Zarnas, Gus—Ohio State, 1937

Coaches

Bill Alexander
Dr. Ed Anderson
Ike Armstrong
Matty Bell
Hugo Bezdek
Dana X. Bible
Bernie Bierman
Earl (Red) Blaik
Charles W. Caldwell
Walter Camp
Len Casanova
Frank Cavanaugh
Fritz Crisler
Gil Dobie
Michael Donohue
Gus Dorais
Charles (Rip) Engle
Don Faurot
Jake Gaither
Ernest Godfrey
Jack Harding
Edward K. Hall
Richard Harlow
Jesse Harper
Percy Haughton
John W. Heisman
R. A. (Bob) Higgins
Orin E. Hollingberry
William Ingram
Morley Jennings
Howard Jones
L. (Biff) Jones
Thomas (Tad) Jones
Andy Kerr
Frank Leahy
George E. Little
Lou Little
El (Slip) Madigan
Herbert McCracken
Daniel McGugin
DeOrmond (Tuss) McLaughry
L. R. (Dutch) Meyer
Bernie Moore
Scrappy Moore
Ray Morrison
George A. Munger
Clarence Munn
William Murray
Ed (Hooks) Mylin
Earle (Greasy) Neale
Jess Neely
Robert Neyland
Homer Norton
Frank (Buck) O'Neill
Bennie Owen
Ara Parseghian
James Phalea
E. N. Robinson
Knute Rockne
E. L. (Dick) Romney
William W. Roper
George F. Sanford
Francis A. Schmidt
Clark Shaughnessy
Buck Shaw
Andrew L. Smith
Carl Snavely
Amos A. Stagg
Jock Sutherland
Frank W. Thomas
John H. Vaught
Wallace Wade
Lynn Waldorf
Glenn (Pop) Warner
E. E. (Tad) Wieman
John W. Wilce
Bud Wilkinson
Henry L. Williams
George W. Woodruff
Fielding H. Yost
Robert Zuppke

MAJOR COLLEGE FOOTBALL RECORDS (1940–1979)

(Opposing teams are listed in parentheses. *Source:* National Collegiate Sports Services, compiled by Steve Boda, Jr.)

LONGEST PLAYS

Rushing

	Yards
Kelsey Finch, Tennessee (Florida) 1977	99
Ralph Thompson, W. Tex. State (Wichita State) 1970	99
Max Anderson, Arizona State (Wyoming) 1967	99
Gale Sayers, Kansas (Nebraska) 1963	99
Granville Amos, Virginia M. I. (Wm. & Mary) 1964	98
Jim Thacker, Davidson (George Washington) 1952	98
Bill Powell, California (Oregon State) 1951	98
Al Yannelli, Bucknell (Delaware) 1946	98
Meredith Warner, Iowa State (Iowa Pre-Flight) 1943	98
Stanley Howell, Miss. State (Southern Miss.) 1979	98
Mark Malone, Arizona State (Utah State) 1979	98

Passing

	Yards
Chris Collingsworth–Derrick Gaffney, Florida (Rice) 1977	99
Terry Peel–Robert Ford, Houston (San Diego St.) 1972	99
Terry Peel–Robert Ford, Houston (Syracuse) 1970	99
Colin Clapton–Eddie Jenkins, Holy Cross (Boston U.) 1970	99
Bo Burris–Warren McVea, Houston (Wash. St.) 1966	99
Fred Owens–Jack Ford, Portland (St. Mary's) 1947	99
Jeff Martin–Mark Flaker, Drake (N.M. State) 1976	98
Pete Woods–Joe Stewart, Missouri (Nebraska) 1976	98
Dan Hagemann–Jack Steptoe, Utah (New Mexico) 1976	98
Bruce Shaw–Pat Kenny, N.C. State (Penn State) 1972	98
Jerry Rhome–Jeff Jordan, Tulsa (Wichita State) 1963	98
Bob Dean–Norman Dawson, Cornell (Navy) 1947	98

Punt Returns

	Yards
Jimmy Campagna, Georgia (Vanderbilt) 1952	100
Hugh McElhenny, Washington (So. Cal.) 1951	100
Frank Brady, Navy (Maryland) 1951	100
Bert Rechichar, Tennessee (Wash. & Lee) 1950	100
Eddie Macon, Pacific (Boston U.) 1950	100
Richie Luzzi, Clemson (Georgia) 1968	100[1]
Don Guest, California (Washington State) 1966	100[1]

1. Return of a field goal attempt.

Punts

	Yards
Pat Brady, Nevada (Loyola, L. A.) 1950	99
George O'Brien, Wisconsin (Iowa) 1952	96

John Hadl, Kansas (Oklahoma) 1959	94
Carl Knox, Texas Christian (Oklahoma State) 1947	94
Preston Johnson, SMU (Pittsburgh) 1940	94

Field Goals

	Yards
Joe Williams, Wichita State (So. Illinois) 1978	67
Steve Little, Arkansas (Texas) 1977	67
Russell Erxleben, Texas (Rice) 1977	67
Tony Franklin, Texas A&M (Baylor) 1976	65
Russell Erxleben, Texas (Oklahoma) 1977	64
Tony Franklin, Texas A&M (Baylor) 1976	64
Clark Kemble, Colorado State (Arizona) 1975	63
Dan Christopulos, Wyoming (Colorado State) 1977	62
Iseed Khoury, North Texas State (Richmond) 1977	62
Dave Lawson, Air Force Academy (Iowa State) 1975	62
Steve Little, Arkansas (Tulsa) 1976	61
Wayne Latimer, Virginia Tech (Florida State) 1975	61
Ray Guy, Southern Mississippi (Utah State) 1972	61

Kickoff Returns

123 players have returned kickoffs 100 yards since 1941. The most recent:

James Collier, Southern Methodist (Baylor)	1979
Charlie Crews, San Diego State (Texas-El Paso)	1979
Reggie Evans, Richmond (V.M.I.)	1979
Derek Hughes, Michigan State (Oregon)	1979
Norman Warren, Kent State (Eastern Ky.)	1979
Howard Ballage, Colorado (Nebraska)	1978
Ronnie Horton, East Tennessee (Middle Tennessee)	1978
Drew Hill, Georgia Tech (Georgia)	1978
Ottis Anderson, Miami, Fla. (Utah State)	1978
Ottis Anderson, Miami, Fla. (Tulane)	1978
Nathan Johnson, NE Louisiana (SE Louisiana)	1978
Jesse Williams, Richmond (Villanova)	1978
Lam Jones, Texas (Southern Methodist Univ.)	1978
Phillip Epps, Texas Christian Univ. (Rice)	1978
Larry Fallen, Virginia Tech (Clemson)	1978
Ken Hill, Yale (Cornell)	1978

BEST SINGLE-GAME PERFORMANCES

Most yards, rushing—356, Eddie Lee Ivery, Georgia Tech (Air Force) 1978
Most yards, total offense—599, Virgil Carter, Brigham Young (Texas-El Paso) 1966
Most yards, passing—571, Marc Wilson, Brigham Young (Utah) 1977
Most yards, pass receiving—349, Chuck Hughes, Texas-El Paso (North Texas State) 1965
Most points scored—43, Jim Brown, Syracuse (Colgate) 1956
Most passes attempted—69, Chuck Hixson, Southern Methodist (Ohio State) 1968
Most passes completed—42, Bill Anderson, Tulsa (Southern Illinois) 1965
Most passes caught—22, Jay Miller, Brigham Young (New Mexico) 1973

CAREER LEADERS

Rushing

	Years	Plays	Yds	Avg
Tony Dorsett, Pittsburgh	1973–76	1,074[1]	6,082[1]	5.66
Charles White, So. Calif.	1976–79	1,023	5,598	5.47
Archie Griffin, Ohio State	1972–75	845	5,177	6.13
Ed Marinaro, Cornell	1969–71	918	4,715	5.14
Ted Brown, North Carolina State	1975–78	860	4,602	5.35
Terry Miller, Oklahoma State	1974–77	847	4,582	5.41
Earl Campbell, Texas	1974–77	765	4,443	5.81
Jerome Persell, Western Mich.	1976–78	842	4,190	4.98
Charles Alexander, L.S.U.	1975–78	855	4,035	4.72
Joe Washington, Oklahoma	1972–75	656	3,995	6.09
Mike Voight, North Carolina	1973–76	826	3,971	4.81
Ron Po James, New Mexico St.	1968–71	818	3,884	4.75

1. Record.

Passing

	Years	Cmp	Pct	Yds	Td
Chuck Hixson, Southern Methodist	1968–70	642[1]	.576	7,179	40
John Reaves, Florida	1969–71	603	.535	7,549	54
Jack Thompson, Washington State	1975–78	601	.553	7,818[1]	53
Ed Luther, San Jose State	1976–79	600	.537	7,190	47
Gene Swick, Toledo	1972–75	556	.593	7,267	44
Marc Wilson, Brigham Young	1977–79	535	.571	7,637	61
Jim Plunkett, Stanford	1968–70	530	.551	7,544	52
Tommy Kramer, Rice	1973–76	507	.489	6,197	37
Roch Hontas, Tulane	1976–79	504	.588	5,664	39
Lynn Dickey, Kansas State	1968–70	501	.504	6,208	29
Mark Hermann, Purdue	1977–79	497	.566	6,265	43
Steve Ramsey, North Texas State	1967–69	491	.484	7,076	69[1]

1. Record.

Total Offense

	Years	Plays	Yds	Tdr[1]
Gene Swick, Toledo	1972–75	1,579[2]	8,074[2]	63
Jim Plunkett, Stanford	1968–70	1,174	7,887	62
Jack Thompson, Washington State	1975–78	1,345	7,698	n.a.
Marc Wilson, Brigham Young	1977–79	1,183	7,602	68
John Reaves, Florida	1969–71	1,258	7,283	58
Ed Luther, San Jose State	1976–79	1,230	6,981	n.a.
Chuck Hixson, So. Methodist	1968–70	1,358	6,884	50
Pat Sullivan, Auburn	1969–71	968	6,884	71
Tony Adams, Utah State	1970–72	1,132	6,587	62
Steve Ramsey, N. Texas St.	1967–69	1,132	6,568	71
Danny White, Arizona State	1971–73	813	6,453	73[2]

1. Touchdowns responsible for—scored or passed for. 2. Record. NOTE: n.a. = not available.

Pass Receiving

	Years	Rec	Yds	Td
Howard Twilley, Tulsa	1963–65	261[1]	3,343	32
Ron Sellers, Florida State	1966–68	212	3,598	23
Phil Odle, Brigham Young	1965–67	181	2,548	25
Tim Delaney, San Diego State	1968–70	180	2,535	22
Hugh Campbell, Washington State	1960–62	176	2,453	22

1. Record.

Scoring

	Years	Td	Pat	Fg	Pts
Tony Dorsett, Pittsburgh	1973–76	59[1]	2	0	356[1]
Glenn Davis, Army	1943–46	59[1]	0	0	354
Art Luppino, Arizona	1953–56	48[1]	49	0	337
Steve Owens, Oklahoma	1967–69	56	0	0	336
Wilford White, Arizona State	1947–50	48	27	4	327
Ed Marinaro, Cornell	1969–71	52	6	0	318
Pete Johnson, Ohio State	1973–76	53	0	0	318
Ted Brown, North Carolina State	1975–78	51	6	0	312
Eddie Talboom, Wyoming	1948–50	34	99	0	303

1. Record.

N.C.A.A. DIVISION II AND III FOOTBALL RECORDS (1942–79)

LONGEST PLAYS

Rushing

	Yards
Fred Deutsch, Springfield (Wagner) 1977	99
Sam Hallston, Albany State, N.Y. (Norwich) 1977	99
Sammy Croom, San Diego (Azusa Pacific) 1972	99
John Stenger, Swarthmore (Widener) 1970	99
Jed Knuttila, Hamline (St. Thomas) 1968	99
Dave Lanoha, Colorado College (Texas Lutheran) 1967	99
Tom Pabst, Cal–Riverside (Cal. Tech) 1965	99
George Phillips, Concord (Davis and Elkins) 1961	99
Gerry White, Connecticut (Rhode Island) 1960	99
Leo Williams, St. Augustine's (Morris) 1960	99
George Phelps, Cornell College (Monmouth) 1959	99
Mark Lydon, Tufts (Bowdoin) 1958	99
David Wells, Tufts (Williams) 1956	99
Jack Moskal, Western Reserve (Case Tech) 1954	99
Lou Mariano, Kent State (Western Reserve) 1954	99
Ron Temple, Chico State (Southern Oregon) 1963	99
Ellis Horton, Eureka, (Rose–Hulman) 1952	99
Pat Abbruzzi, Rhode Island (New Hampshire) 1951	99

Field Goals

Joe Duren, Arkansas State (McNeese State) 1974	63
Dom Antonini, Glassboro State (Salisbury State) 1976	62
Mike Flater, Colorado Mines (Western State) 1973	62
Duane Christian, Cameron (Southwestern Oklahoma) 1976	61
Mike Wood, Southeast Missouri (Lincoln) 1975	61
Bill Shear, Cortland State (Hobart) 1966	61

Passing

	Yards
Mike Moroski–Calvin Ellison, California-Davis (Puget Sound) 1978	99
Rich Boling–Lewis Borsellino, DePauw (Valparaiso) 1976	99
John Wicinski–Donnell Lipford, John Carroll (Allegheny) 1975	99
Jack Berry–Mercer West, Washington and Lee (Hampden–Sydney) 1974	99
Gary Shope–Rick Rudolph, Juniata (Moravian) 1973	99
Gary Dusenberg–Harvey King, North Park (Illinois Wesleyan) 1970	99
Bob Janesko–Frank Stankiewicz, Emporia (Pittsburg State) 1969	99
John Williams–Bill Carter, N.M. Highlands (North Colorado) 1964	99
Carl Meyers–Roger Sayers, Nebraska-Omaha (Drake) 1963	99

Punts

Earl Hurst, Emporia State (Central Missouri) 1964	97
Gary Frens, Hope (Olivet) 1966	96
Jim Jarrett, North Dakota (South Dakota) 1957	96
Elliot Mills, Carleton (Monmouth) 1970	93
Kaspar Fitins, Taylor (Georgetown, Ky.) 1966	93
Leeroy Sweeney, Pomona (Cal–Riverside) 1960	93

CAREER LEADERS

Rushing

	Years	Plays	Yds	Avg
Chris Cobb, Eastern Illinois	1976–79	930	5,042[1]	5.42
Jerry Linton, Panhandle State	1959–62	648	4,839	7.47
John VanWagner, Mich. Tech.	1973–76	958	4,788	5.00
Rich Kowalski, Hobart	1972–75	907	4,631	5.11
Don Aleksiewicz, Hobart	1969–72	819	4,525	5.53
Dale Mills, NE Missouri	1957–60	751	4,502	5.99
Leo Lewis, Lincoln (Mo.)	1951–54	623	4,458	7.16
Bernie Peeters, Luther	1968–71	1,072	4,435	4.14
Larry Schreiber, Tenn. Tech.	1966–69	878	4,421	5.04
Brad Rowland, McMurry	1947–50	683	4,347	6.36
Vincent Allen, Indiana State	1973–77	832	4,335	5.21
Bill Rhodes, Colorado Western	1953–56	506	4,294	8.49[1]
Lem Harkey, Col. of Emporia	1951–54	502	4,232	8.43

Scoring

	Years	Td	Pat	Fg	Pts
Walter Payton, Jackson State	1971–74	66[1]	53	5	464[1]
Dale Mills, NE Missouri	1957–60	64	23	0	407
Garney Henley, Huron	1956–59	63	16	0	394
Leo Lewis, Lincoln (Mo.)	1951–54	64	0	0	384
Billy Johnson, Widener	1971–73	62	0	0	372
Tank Younger, Grambling	1945–48	60	9	0	369

Passing

	Years	Cmp	Pct	Yds	Td
Jim Lindsey, Abilene Chr.	1967–70	642[1]	.519	8,521[1]	61
Bob Caress, Bradley	1962–65	610	.528	7,115	64
Dan Miles, So. Oregon	1964–67	577	.662[1]	6,531	52
George Bork, N. Illinois	1960–63	577	.640	6,782	60
Craig Soloman, SW Tennessee	1975–78	542	.530	7,314	71
Kim McQuilken, Lehigh	1971–73	516	.558	6,996	37
Tim Von Dulm, Portland St.	1969–70	500	.541	5,967	51
Doug Williams, Grambling	1974–77	484	.480	8,411	99[1]

1. Record.

Pass Receiving

	Years	Rec	Yards	Td
Chris Myers, Kenyon	1967–70	253[1]	3,897	33
Bruce Cerone, Yankton–Emporia St.	1966–67, 1968–1969	241[1]	4,354[1]	49[1]
Harold Roberts, Austin Peay	1967–70	232	3,005	31
Jerry Hendren, Idaho	1967–69	230	3,435	27
Terry Fredenberg, Wis.–Milwaukee	1965–68	206	2,789	24
Rick Fry, Occidental	1974–77	200	3,073	18
Bill Wick, Carroll (Wis.)	1966–69	190	2,967	20
Don Hutt, Boise State	1971–73	187	2,716	30

1. Record

Total Offense

	Years	Plays	Yds
Jim Lindsey, Abilene Christian	1967–70	1,510	8,385
Doug Williams, Grambling	1974–77	1,072	8,195
Donald Smith, Langston	1958–61	998	7,376
Bruce Upstill, Coll. Emporia	1960–63	922	7,122
Craig Solomon, SW Tennessee	1975–78	1,261	7,055
Kim McQuilken, Lehigh	1971–73	991	6,878
Bob Caress, Bradley	1962–65	1,361	6,757
Ken Anderson, Augustana (Ill.)	1967–70	1,135	6,682

MOST POINTS IN SEASON

	Yards	Tds	PAT	Fg	Pts
Terry Metcalf, Long Beach St.	1971	29[1]	4	0	178
Jim Switzer, Coll. Emporia	1963	28	0	0	168
Carl Herakovich, Rose Polytech	1958	25	18	0	168
Ted Scown, Sul Ross State	1948	28	0	0	168
Eddie McGovern, Rose Polytech	1942	23	27	0	165
Leon Burns, Long Beach State	1969	27	2	0	164

1. Record.

N.C.A.A. 1979 CHAMPIONSHIP PLAYOFFS

DIVISION II
First Round

Delaware 58, Virginia Union 28
Youngstown (Ohio) State 50, South Dakota State 7
Alabama A&M 27, Oregon State 7
Mississippi College 35, North Dakota 15

Semifinals

Delaware 60, Mississippi College 10
Youngstown State 52, Alabama A&M 0

Championship

Delaware 38, Youngstown State 21

DIVISION III
First Round

Wittenberg 21, Millersville (Pa.) State 14
Carnegie–Mellon 31, Minnesota–Morris 25 (double overtime)
Ithaca 27, Dubuque 7
Widener 29, Baldwin–Wallace 8

Semifinals

Wittenberg 17, Wagner 14
Ithaca 15, Carnegie–Mellon 6

Championship

Ithaca 14, Wittenberg 10

NATIONAL ASSOCIATION OF INTERCOLLEGIATE ATHLETICS 1979 CHAMPIONSHIPS

DIVISION I
Semifinals

Texas A & I 22, Angelo State (Texas) 19
Central State (Okla.) 28, Presbyterian (S.C.) 6

Championship

Texas A & I 20, Central State 14

DIVISION II
Semifinals

Findlay (Ohio) 9, Pacific Lutheran (Wash.) 0
Northwestern (Iowa) 49, Bethany (Kan.) 21

Championship

Findlay 51, Northwestern 6

Professional Football

NATIONAL FOOTBALL LEAGUE FINAL STANDING 1979

AMERICAN CONFERENCE

Eastern Division

	W	L	T	Pct	Pts	OP
Miami	10	6	0	.625	341	257
New England	9	7	0	.563	411	326
New York Jets	8	8	0	.500	337	383
Buffalo	7	9	0	.438	268	279
Baltimore	5	11	0	.313	271	351

Central Division

	W	L	T	Pct	Pts	OP
Pittsburgh	12	4	0	.750	416	262
Houston[1]	11	5	0	.688	362	331
Cleveland	9	7	0	.563	359	352
Cincinnati	4	12	0	.250	337	421

Western Division

	W	L	T	Pct	Pts	OP
San Diego	12	4	0	.750	411	246
Denver[1]	10	6	0	.625	289	262
Oakland	9	7	0	.563	365	337
Seattle	9	7	0	.563	378	372
Kansas City	7	9	0	.438	238	262

1. Wild card qualifier for playoffs.

Playoffs: Houston 13, Denver 7; Houston 17, San Diego 14; Pittsburgh 34, Miami 14.
Conference championship: Pittsburgh 27, Houston 13.

NATIONAL CONFERENCE

Eastern Division

	W	L	T	Pct	Pts	OP
Dallas	11	5	0	.688	371	313
Philadelphia[1]	11	5	0	.688	339	282
Washington	10	6	0	.625	348	295
New York Giants	6	10	0	.375	237	323
St. Louis	5	11	0	.313	307	358

Central Division

	W	L	T	Pct	Pts	OP
Tampa Bay	10	6	0	.625	273	237
Chicago[1]	10	6	0	.625	306	249
Minnesota	7	9	0	.438	259	337
Green Bay	5	11	0	.313	246	316
Detroit	2	14	0	.125	219	365

Western Division

	W	L	T	Pct	Pts	OP
Los Angeles	9	7	0	.563	323	309
New Orleans	8	8	0	.500	370	360
Atlanta	6	10	0	.375	300	388
San Francisco	2	14	0	.125	308	416

1. Wild card qualifier for playoffs.

Playoffs: Philadelphia 27, Chicago 17; Tampa Bay 24, Philadelphia 17; Los Angeles 21, Dallas 19.
Conference championship: Los Angeles 9, Tampa Bay 0.

LEAGUE CHAMPIONSHIP—SUPER BOWL XIV

(Jan. 20, 1980; at Rose Bowl, Pasadena; Attendance 103,985)

Scoring

	1st Q	2nd Q	3rd Q	4th Q	Final
Los Angeles Rams (NFC)	7	6	6	0	19
Pittsburgh Steelers (AFC)	3	7	7	14	31

Scoring—Pittsburgh: Touchdowns: Harris, 1–yard run; Swann, 24–yard pass from Bradshaw; Stallworth, 73–yard pass from Bradshaw; Harris, 1–yard run. Conversions: Bahr 4 (kicks). Field goal: Bahr, 41 yards. Los Angeles: Touchdowns: Bryant, 1–yard run; Smith, 24–yard pass from McCutcheon. Conversions: Corral 1 (kick). Field goals: Corral 2, 31 yards and 45 yards.

Statistics of the Game

	Pittsburgh	Los Angeles
First downs	19	16
Yards gained rushing	84	107
Yards gained passing	309	194
Passes completed	14	16
Passes intercepted by	1	3
Punts	2–42.5	5–44
Ball lost, fumbles	0	0
Yards penalized	65	26

SUPER BOWLS V–XIV (N.F.L. CHAMPIONSHIPS)

National Conference champion vs. American Conference champion

Season	Site	Date	Attendance	Winner	Loser
1970	Orange Bowl, Miami	Jan. 17, 1971	79,204	Baltimore Colts, A.C., 16	Dallas Cowboys, N.C., 13
1971	Tulane Stadium, New Orleans	Jan. 16, 1972	80,591	Dallas Cowboys, N.C., 24	Miami Dolphins, A.C., 3
1972	Memorial Coliseum, Los Angeles	Jan. 14, 1973	90,182	Miami Dolphins A.C., 14	Wash. Redskins, N.C., 7
1973	Rice Stadium, Houston	Jan. 13, 1974	68,142	Miami Dolphins, A.C., 24	Minnesota Vikings, N.C., 7
1974	Tulane Stadium, New Orleans	Jan. 12, 1975	80,997	Pittsburgh Steelers, A.C., 16	Minnesota Vikings N.C., 6
1975	Orange Bowl, Miami	Jan. 18, 1976	80,187	Pittsburgh Steelers, A.C., 21	Dallas Cowboys N.C., 17
1976	Rose Bowl, Pasadena	Jan. 9, 1977	100,421	Oakland Raiders, A.C., 32	Minnesota Vikings, N.C., 14
1977	Superdome, New Orleans	Jan. 15, 1978	75,583	Dallas Cowboys, N.C., 27	Denver Broncos, A.C., 10
1978	Orange Bowl, Miami	Jan. 21, 1979	79,484	Pittsburgh Steelers, A.C., 35	Dallas Cowboys, N.C., 31
1979	Rose Bowl, Pasadena	Jan. 20, 1980	103,985	Pittsburgh Steelers, A.C., 31	Los Angeles Rams, N.C., 19

SUPER BOWLS I–IV (INTER-LEAGUE CHAMPIONSHIPS)

National League champion vs. American League champion

Season	Site	Date	Attendance	Winner	Loser
1966	Memorial Coliseum, Los Angeles	Jan. 15, 1967	63,036	Green Bay Packers, N.L., 35	Kansas City Chiefs, A.L., 10
1967	Orange Bowl, Miami	Jan. 14, 1968	75,546	Green Bay Packers, N.L., 33	Oakland Raiders, A.L., 14
1968	Orange Bowl, Miami	Jan. 12, 1969	75,377	New York Jets, A.L., 16	Baltimore Colts, N.L., 7
1969	Tulane Stadium, New Orleans	Jan. 11, 1970	80,562	Kansas City Chiefs, A.L., 23	Minnesota Vikings, N.L., 7

NATIONAL LEAGUE CHAMPIONS

Year	Champion (W-L-T)
1921	Chicago Bears (Staley's) (10–1–1)
1922	Canton Bulldogs (10–0–2)
1923	Canton Bulldogs (11–0–1)
1924	Cleveland Indians (7–1–1)
1925	Chicago Cardinals (11–2–1)
1926	Frankford Yellow Jackets (14–1–1)
1927	New York Giants (11–1–1)
1928	Providence Steamrollers (8–1–2)
1929	Green Bay Packers (12–0–1)
1930	Green Bay Packers (10–3–1)
1931	Green Bay Packers (12–2–0)
1932	Chicago Bears (7–1–6)

Year	Eastern Conference winners (W-L-T)	Western Conference winners (W-L-T)	League champion playoff results
1933	New York Giants (11–3–0)	Chicago Bears (10–2–1)	Chicago Bears 23, New York 21
1934	New York Giants (8–5–0)	Chicago Bears (13–0–0)	New York 30, Chicago Bears 13
1935	New York Giants (9–3–0)	Detroit Lions (7–3–2)	Detroit 26, New York 7
1936	Boston Redskins (7–5–0)	Green Bay Packers (10–1–1)	Green Bay 21, Boston 6
1937	Washington Redskins (8–3–0)	Chicago Bears (9–1–1)	Washington 28, Chicago Bears 21
1938	New York Giants (8–2–1)	Green Bay Packers (8–3–0)	New York 23, Green Bay 17
1939	New York Giants (9–1–1)	Green Bay Packers (9–2–0)	Green Bay 27, New York 0
1940	Washington Redskins (9–2–0)	Chicago Bears (8–3–0)	Chicago Bears 73, Washington 0
1941	New York Giants (8–3–0)	Chicago Bears (10–1–1)[2]	Chicago Bears 37, New York 9
1942	Washington Redskins (10–1–1)	Chicago Bears (11–0–0)	Washington 14, Chicago Bears 6
1943	Washington Redskins (6–3–1)[2]	Chicago Bears (8–1–1)	Chicago Bears 41, Washington 21
1944	New York Giants (8–1–1)	Green Bay Packers (8–2–0)	Green Bay 14, New York 7
1945	Washington Redskins (8–2–0)	Cleveland Rams (9–1–0)	Cleveland 15, Washington 14
1946	New York Giants (7–3–1)	Chicago Bears (8–2–1)	Chicago Bears 24, New York 14
1947	Philadelphia Eagles (8–4–0)[2]	Chicago Cardinals (9–3–0)	Chicago Cardinals 28, Philadelphia 21
1948	Philadelphia Eagles (9–2–1)	Chicago Cardinals (11–1–0)	Philadelphia 7, Chicago Cardinals 0
1949	Philadelphia Eagles (11–1–0)	Los Angeles Rams (8–2–2)	Philadelphia 14, Los Angeles 0
1950[1]	Cleveland Browns (10–2–0)[2]	Los Angeles Rams (9–3–0)[2]	Cleveland 30, Los Angeles 28
1951[1]	Cleveland Browns (11–1–0)	Los Angeles Rams (8–4–0)	Los Angeles 24, Cleveland 17
1952[1]	Cleveland Browns (8–4–0)	Detroit Lions (9–3–0)[2]	Detroit 17, Cleveland 7
1953	Cleveland Browns (11–1–0)	Detroit Lions (10–2–0)	Detroit 17, Cleveland 16

1954	Cleveland Browns (9–3–0)	Detroit Lions (9–2–1)	Cleveland 56, Detroit 10
1955	Cleveland Browns (9–2–1)	Los Angeles Rams (8–3–1)	Cleveland 38, Los Angeles 14
1956	New York Giants (8–3–1)	Chicago Bears (9–2–1)	New York 47, Chicago Bears 7
1957	Cleveland Browns (9–2–1)	Detroit Lions (8–4–0)[3]	Detroit 59, Cleveland 14
1958	New York Giants (9–3–0)[2]	Baltimore Colts (9–3–0)	Baltimore 23, New York 17[3]
1959	New York Giants (10–2–0)	Baltimore Colts (9–3–0)	Baltimore 31, New York 16
1960	Philadelphia Eagles (10–2–0)	Green Bay Packers (8–4–0)	Philadelphia 17, Green Bay 13
1961	New York Giants (10–3–1)	Green Bay Packers (11–3–0)	Green Bay 37, New York 0
1962	New York Giants (12–2–0)	Green Bay Packers (13–1–0)	Green Bay 16, New York 7
1963	New York Giants (11–3–0)	Chicago Bears (11–1–2)	Chicago 14, New York 10
1964	Cleveland Browns (10–3–1)	Baltimore Colts (12–2–0)	Cleveland 27, Baltimore 0
1965	Cleveland Browns (11–3–0)	Green Bay Packers (11–3–1)[2]	Green Bay 23, Cleveland 12
1966	Dallas Cowboys (10–3–1)	Green Bay Packers (12–2–0)	Green Bay 34, Dallas 27
1967	Dallas Cowboys (9–5–0)[2]	Green Bay Packers (9–4–1)[2]	Green Bay 21, Dallas 17
1968	Cleveland Browns (10–4–0)[2]	Baltimore Colts (13–1–0)[2]	Baltimore 34, Cleveland 0
1969	Cleveland Browns (10–3–1)[2]	Minnesota Vikings (12–2–0)[2]	Minnesota 27, Cleveland 7

1. League was divided into American and National Conferences, 1950–52 and again in 1970, when leagues merged. 2. Won divisional playoff. 3. Won at 8:15 of sudden death overtime period.

PRO FOOTBALL HALL OF FAME

(National Football Museum, Canton, Ohio)

Teams named are those with which player is best identified; figures in parentheses indicate number of playing seasons.

Adderley, Herb, defensive back, Packers, Cowboys (12)	1961–72
Alworth, Lance, wide receiver, Chargers, Cowboys (11)	1962–72
Battles, Cliff, back, Redskins (6)	1932–37
Baugh, Sammy, quarterback, Redskins (16)	1937–52
Bednarik, Chuck, center-lineback, Eagles (14)	1949–62
Bell, Bert, N.F.L. founder, owner Eagles and Steelers, N.F.L. Commissioner	1946–59
Berry, Raymond, end, Colts (13)	1955–67
Bidwell, Charles W., owner Chicago Cardinals	1933–47
Brown, Jim, fullback, Browns (9)	1957–65
Brown, Paul E., coach, Browns (1946–62), Bengals (1968–75)	1946–75
Brown, Roosevelt, tackle, Giants (13)	1953–65
Butkus, Dick, linebacker, Bears (19)	1965–73
Canadeo, Tony, back, Packers (11)	1941–52
Carr, Joe, president N.F.L. (18)	1921–39
Chamberlin, Guy, end 4 teams (9)	1919–27
Christiansen, Jack, defensive back, Lions (8)	1951–58
Clark, Earl (Dutch), Qback, Spartans, Lions (7)	1931–38
Connor, George, tackle, linebacker, Bears (8)	1948–55
Conzelman, Jimmy, Qback 5 teams (10), owner	1921–48
Donovan, Art, defensive tackle, Colts (12)	1950–61
Driscoll, John (Paddy), Qback, Cards, Bears (11)	1919–29
Dudley, Bill, back, Steelers, Lions, Redskins (9)	1942–53
Edwards, Albert Glen (Turk), tackle, Redskins (9)	1932–40
Ewbank, Weeb, coach Colts, Jets (20)	1954–73
Fears, Tom, end, Rams (9); coach, Saints	1948–56
Flaherty, Ray, end, Yankees, Giants (9); coach, Redskins, Yankees (14)	1928–49
Ford, Len, end, def. end, Browns, Packers (11)	1948–58
Fortmann, Daniel J., guard, Bears (8)	1936–43
George, Bill, linebacker, Bears, Rams (15)	1952–66
Gifford, Frank, back, Giants (12)	1952–64
Graham, Otto, quarterback, Browns (10)	1946–55
Grange, Harold (Red), back, Bears, Yankees (9)	1925–34
Gregg, Forrest, tackle, Packers (15)	1956–71
Groza, Lou, place-kicker, tackle, Browns (21)	1946–67
Guyon, Joe, back, 6 teams (8)	1919–27
Halas, George, N.F.L. founder, owner and coach, Staleys and Bears, end (11)	1919–67
Healey, Ed, tackle, Bears (8)	1920–27
Hein, Mel, center, Giants (15)	1931–45
Henry, Wilbur (Pete), tackle, Bulldogs, Giants (8)	1920–28
Herber, Arnie, Qback, Packers, Giants (13)	1930–45
Hewitt, Bill, end, Bears, Eagles (9)	1932–43
Hinkle, Clarke, fullback, Packers (10)	1932–41
Hirsch, Elroy (Crazy Legs), back, end, Rams (12)	1946–57
Hubbard, R. (Cal), tackle, Giants, Packers (9)	1927–36
Hunt, Lamar, Founder A.F.L., owner Texans, Chiefs	1959– —
Hutson, Don, end, Packers (11)	1935–45
Jones, David (Deacon), defensive end, Rams, Chargers, Redskins (14)	1961–74
Kiesling, Walt, guard 6 teams (13)	1926–38
Kinard, Frank (Bruiser), tackle, Dodgers (9)	1938–47
Lambeau, Earl (Curly), N.F.L. founder, coach, end, back, Packers (11)	1919–53
Lane, Richard (Night Train), defensive back, Rams, Cardinals, Lions (14)	1952–65
Lary, Yale, defensive back, punter, Lions (11)	1952–64
Lavelli, Dante, end, Browns (11)	1946–56
Layne, Bobby, Qback, Bears, Lions, Steelers (15)	1948–62
Leemans, Alphonse (Tuffy), back, Giants (8)	1936–43
Lilly, Bob, defensive tackle, Cowboys (14)	1961–74
Lombardi, Vince, coach, Packers, Redskins (11)	1959–70
Luckman, Sid, quarterback, Bears (12)	1939–50
Lyman, Roy (Link), tackle, Bulldogs, Bears (11)	1922–34
Mara, Tim, N.F.L. founder, owner Giants	1925–59
Marchetti, Gino, defensive end, Colts (14)	1952–66
Marshall, George P., N.F.L. founder, owner Redskins	1932–65
Matson, Ollie, back, Cardinals, Rams, Lions, Eagles (14)	1952–66
McAfee, George, back, Bears (8)	1940–50
McElhenny, Hugh, back, 49ers, Vikings, Giants (13)	1952–64
McNally, John (Blood), back, 7 teams (15)	1925–39
Michalske, August, guard, Yankees, Packers (11)	1926–37
Millner, Wayne, end, Redskins (7)	1936–45
Mix, Ron, tackle, Chargers (11)	1960–71
Moore, Lenny, back, Colts (12)	1956–67
Motley, Marion, fullback, Browns, Steelers (9)	1946–55
Nagurski, Bronko, fullback, Bears (9)	1930–43
Neale, Earle (Greasy), coach, Eagles	1941–50
Nevers, Ernie, fullback, Chicago Cardinals (5)	1926–31
Nitschke, Ray, linebacker, Packers (15)	1958–72
Nomellini, Leo, defensive tackle, 49ers (14)	1950–63
Otto, Jim, center, Raiders (15)	1960–74
Owen, Steve, tackle, Giants (9), coach, Giants (13)	1924–53
Parker, Clarence (Ace), quarterback, Dodgers (7)	1937–46
Parker, Jim, guard, tackle, Colts (11)	1957–67
Perry, Joe, fullback, 49ers, Colts (16)	1948–63
Pihos, Pete, end, Eagles (9)	1947–55
Ray, Hugh, Shorty, N.F.L. advisor	1938–52
Reeves, Dan, owner Rams	1941–71
Robustelli, Andy, def. end, Rams, Giants (14)	1951–64
Rooney, Art, N.F.L. founder, owner Steelers	1933– —
Sayers, Gale, back, Bears (7)	1965–71
Schmidt, Joe, linebacker, Lions (13)	1953–65
Starr, Bart, quarterback, coach, Packers (16)	1956–71
Stautner, Ernie, defensive tackle, Steelers (14)	1950–63
Strong, Ken, back, Giants, Yankees (14)	1929–47
Stydahar, Joe, tackle, Bears (9); coach,	

Rams, Cardinals (5) 1936–54
Taylor, Jim, fullback, Packers, Saints (10) 1958–67
Thorpe, Jim, back, 7 teams (12) 1915–28
Tittle, Y. A., Qback, Colts, 49ers, Giants (17) 1948–64
Trafton, George, center, Bears (13) 1920–32
Trippi, Charley, back, Chicago Cardinals (9) 1947–55
Tunnell, Emlen, def. back, Giants, Packers (14) 1948–61
Turner, Clyde (Bulldog), center, Bears (13) 1940–52
Unitas, John, quarterback, Colts (18) 1956–73
Van Brocklin, Norm, Qback, Rams, Eagles (12) 1949–60
Van Buren, Steve, back, Eagles (8) 1944–51
Waterfield, Bob, quarterback, Rams (8) 1945–52
Willis, Bill, Guard, Browns (8) 1946–53
Wilson, Larry, defensive back, Cardinals (13) 1960–72
Wojciechowicz, Alex, center, Lions, Eagles (13) 1938–50

N.F.L. INDIVIDUAL LIFETIME, SEASON AND GAME RECORDS

(Through 1978 American Football League marks were incorporated in N.F.L. records after merger in 1970)

All-Time Leading Scorers

	Yrs	TD	FG	PAT	Pts
George Blanda	26	9	335	943	2,002
Jim Turner	16	1	304	521	1,439
Jim Bakken	17	0	282	534	1,380
Fred Cox	15	0	282	519	1,365
Lou Groza	17	1	234	641	1,349
Jan Stenerud	13	0	279	394	1,231
Gino Cappelletti	11	42	176	350	1,130[1]
Bruce Gossett	11	0	219	374	1,031
Sam Baker	15	2	179	428	977
Lou Michaels	13	1	187	386	955[2]

1. Includes four 2-point conversions. 2. Includes one safety.

All-Time Leading Touchdown Scorers

	Yrs	Rush	Pass rec	Returns	TD
Jim Brown	9	106	20	0	126
Lenny Moore	12	63	48	2	113
Don Hutson	11	3	99	3	105
Jim Taylor	10	83	10	0	93
Bobby Mitchell	11	18	65	8	91
Leroy Kelly	10	74	13	3	90
Charley Taylor	13	11	79	0	90
Don Maynard	15	0	88	0	88
Lance Alworth	11	2	85	0	87
Paul Warfield	13	0	85	1	86

All-Time Leading Rushers

	Yrs	Att	Yds	Avg
Jim Brown	9	2,359	12,312	5.2
O.J. Simpson	10	2,258	10,643	4.7
Jim Taylor	10	1,941	8,597	4.4
Franco Harris	8	2,012	8,563	4.3
Joe Perry	14	1,737	8,373	4.8
Larry Csonka	10	1,800	7,770	4.3
Leroy Kelly	10	1,727	7,274	4.2
John Henry Johnson	13	1,571	6,803	4.3
Lydell Mitchell	8	1,668	6,518	3.9
Floyd Little	9	1,641	6,323	3.9

All Time Leading Receivers

	Yrs	Pass rec	Yds	Avg
Charley Taylor	13	649	9,110	14.0
Don Maynard	15	633	11,834	18.7
Raymond Berry	13	631	9,275	14.7
Fred Biletnikoff	14	589	8,974	12.7
Lionel Taylor	10	567	7,195	12.7
Lance Alworth	11	542	10,266	18.9
Bobby Mitchell	11	521	7,954	15.3
Billy Howton	12	503	8,459	16.8
Tommy McDonald	12	495	8,410	17.0
Don Hutson	11	488	7,991	16.4

All-Time Leading Passers

	Comp	Pct comp	Yds	TD	Int	Rating
Roger Staubach	1,685	57.0	22,700	153	109	83.5
Sonny Jurgensen	2,433	57.1	32,224	255	189	82.8
Len Dawson	2,136	57.1	28,711	239	183	82.6
Fran Tarkenton	3,686	57.0	47,003	342	266	80.5
Bert Jones	890	55.9	11,435	78	56	80.3
Bart Starr	1,808	57.4	24,718	152	138	80.3
Ken Stabler	1,486	59.9	19,078	150	143	79.9
Ken Anderson	1,570	56.4	20,030	125	101	79.1
Johnny Unitas	2,830	54.6	40,239	290	253	78.2
Otto Graham	872	55.7	13,499	88	94	78.1

The passing ratings are based on performance standards established for completion percentage, interception percentage, touchdown percentage, and average pass gain. Passers are allocated points according to how their marks compare with those standards. This listing is based on 1,500 or more pass attempts.

Scoring

Most points scored, lifetime—2,002, George Blanda, Chicago Bears, 1949–58; Baltimore, 1950; Houston, 1960–66; Oakland, 1967–75 (9tds, 943 pat, 335 fgs).
Most points, season—176, Paul Hornung, Green Bay, 1960 (15 td, 41 pat, 15 fg).
Most points, game—40, Ernie Nevers, Chicago Cardinals, 1929 (6 td, 4 pat).
Most points, per quarter—29, Don Hutson, Green Bay, 1945 (4 td, 5 pat).
Most touchdowns, lifetime—126, Jim Brown, Cleveland, 1957–65.
Most touchdowns, season—23, O.J. Simpson, Buffalo, 1975.
Most touchdowns, game—6, Ernie Nevers, Chicago Cardinals, 1929; William Jones, Cleveland, 1951; Gale Sayers, Chicago Bears, 1965.
Most points after touchdown, lifetime—943, George Blanda, Chicago Bears, 1949–58; Baltimore, 1950; Houston, 1960–66; Oakland, 1967–75.
Most points after touchdown, game—9, Pat Harder, Chicago Cardinals, 1948; Bob Waterfield, Los Angeles, 1950; Charlie Gogolak, Washington, 1966.
Most consecutive points after touchdown—234, Tommy Davis, San Francisco, 1959–65.
Most points after touchdown, no misses, season—56, Danny Villanueva, Dallas, 1966.
Most field goals, lifetime—335, George Blanda, Chicago Bears 1949–58; Baltimore, 1950; Houston, 1960–66; Oakland 1967–75.
Most field goals, season—34, Jim Turner, New York Jets, 1968.
Most field goals, game—7, Jim Bakken, St. Louis, 1967.
Longest field goal—63 yards, Tom Dempsey, New Orleans, 1970.

Rushing

Most yards gained, lifetime—12,312, Jim Brown, Cleveland, 1957–65.
Most yards gained, season—2,003, O. J. Simpson, Buffalo, 1973.
Most yards gained, game—275, Walter Payton, Chicago, 1977.

Most touchdowns, lifetime—106, Jim Brown, Cleveland, 1957–65.
Most touchdowns, season—19, Earl Campbell, Houston, 1979; Jim Taylor, Green Bay, 1962.
Most touchdowns, game—6, Ernie Nevers, Chicago Cardinals, 1929.
Longest run from scrimmage—97 yards, Andy Uram, Green Bay, 1939; Bob Gage, Pittsburgh, 1949 (both for touchdowns).

Passing

Most passes completed, lifetime—3,686, Fran Tarkenton, Minnesota, 1961–66, 72–78; New York Giants, 1967–71.
Most passes completed, season—347, Steve DeBerg, San Francisco, 1979.
Most passed completed, game—37, George Blanda, Houston, 1964 (68 attempts).
Most consecutive passes completed—17, Bert Jones, Baltimore, 1974.
Most yards gained, lifetime—47,003, Fran Tarkenton, Minnesota, 1961–66, 72–78; New York Giants, 1967–71.
Most yards gained, season—4,082, Dan Fouts, San Diego, 1979.
Most yards gained, game—554, Norm Van Brocklin, Los Angeles, 1951
Most touchdown passes, lifetime—342, Fran Tarkenton, Minnesota, 1961–66, 72–78; New York Giants, 1967–71.
Most touchdown passes, season—36, George Blanda, Houston, 1961; Y. A. Tittle, New York Giants, 1963.
Most touchdown passes, game—7, Sid Luckman, Chicago Bears, 1943; Adrian Burk, Philadelphia, 1954; George Blanda, Houston 1961; Y.A. Tittle, New York Giants, 1963; Joe Kapp, Minnesota, 1969.
Most consecutive games, touchdown passes—47, John Unitas, Baltimore.
Most consecutive passes attempted, none intercepted—294, Bart Starr, Green Bay, 1964–65.
Longest pass completion—99 yards, Frank Filchock (to Andy Farkas), Washington, 1939; George Izo (to Bob Mitchell), Washington, 1963; Karl Sweetan (to Pat Studstill), Detroit, 1966; Sonny Jurgensen (to Gerry Allen), Washington, 1968, (all for touchdowns).
Most pass receptions, lifetime—649, Charley Taylor, Washington, 1964–75, 1977.
Most pass receptions, season—101, Charley Hennigan, Houston, 1964.
Most pass receptions, game—18, Tom Fears, Los Angeles, 1950.
Most consecutive games, pass receptions—105, Dan Abramowicz, New Orleans, 1967–73; San Francisco, 1973–74.
Most yards gained, pass receptions, lifetime—11,834, Don Maynard, New York Giants, 1958; New York Jets, 1960–72; St. Louis, 1973.
Most yards gained receptions, season—1,746, Charley Hennigan, Houston, 1961.
Most yards gained receptions, game—303, Jim Benton, Cleveland Rams, 1945.
Most touchdown pass receptions, lifetime—99, Don Hutson, Green Bay, 1935–45.
Most touchdown pass receptions, season—17, Don Hutson, Green Bay, 1942; Elroy Hirsch, Los Angeles, 1951; Bill Groman, Houston, 1961.
Most touchdown pass receptions, game—5, Bob Shaw, Chicago Cards, 1950.
Most consecutive games, touchdown pass receptions—11, Elroy Hirsch, Los Angeles, 1950–51; Buddy Dial, Pittsburgh, 1959–60.
Most pass interceptions, lifetime—79, Emlen Tunnell, New York Giants, 1948–58 (74); Green Bay, 1959–61 (5).
Most pass interceptions, season—14, Richard (Night Train) Lane, Los Angeles, 1952.
Most pass interceptions, game—4, by 15 players.
Longest pass interception return—102 yards, Bob Smith, Chicago Bears, 1949; Erich Barnes, New York Giants, 1961; Gary Barbaro, Kansas City, 1977.

Kicking

Longest punt—98 yards, Steve O'Neal, New York Jets, 1969.
Highest average punting, lifetime—45.10 yards, Sammy Baugh, Washington, 1937–52.
Longest punt return—98 yards, Gil LeFebvre, Cincinnati Reds, 1933; Charlie West, Minnesota, 1968; Dennis Morgan, Dallas, 1974.
Longest kick-off return—106 yards, Roy Green, St. Louis, 1979; Al Carmichael, Green Bay, 1956; Noland Smith, Kansas City, 1967.

TEAM NICKNAMES AND HOME FIELD STADIUM CAPACITIES

AMERICAN CONFERENCE

Eastern Division

Baltimore Colts	Memorial Stadium (G)	60,020
Buffalo Bills	Rich Stadium (AT)	80,020
Miami Dolphins	Orange Bowl (G)	75,449
New England Patriots	Schaefer Stadium (ST)[1]	61,297
New York Jets	Shea Stadium (G)	60,000

1. At Foxboro, Mass.

Central Division

Cincinnati Bengals	Riverfront Stadium (AT)	56,200
Cleveland Browns	Cleveland Stadium (G)	80,385
Houston Oilers	Astrodome (AT)	50,000
Pittsburgh Steelers	Three Rivers Stadium (TT)	50,350

Western Division

Denver Broncos	Mile High Stadium (G)	75,087
Kansas City Chiefs	Arrowhead Stadium (TT)	78,094
Oakland Raiders	County Coliseum (G)	54,615
San Diego Chargers	San Diego Stadium (G)	52,552
Seattle Seahawks	Kingdome (AT)	64,752

NOTE: Stadium playing surfaces in parentheses: AT = Astro-Turf; G = grass; ST = Super Turf; TT = TartanTurf.

NATIONAL CONFERENCE

Eastern Division

Dallas Cowboys	Texas Stadium (TT)	65,101
New York Giants	Giants Stadium (AT)[2]	76,500
Philadelphia Eagles	Veterans Stadium (AT)	66,052
St. Louis Cardinals	Busch Mem. Stadium (AT)	51,392
Washington Redskins	R. F. Kennedy Stadium (G)	55,031

2. At East Rutherford, N.J.

Central Division

Chicago Bears	Soldier Field (AT)	58,064
Detroit Lions	Pontiac Silverdome (AT)	80,638
	Lambeau Field (G)	56,267
Green Bay Packers	Milwaukee Stadium (G)	55,958
Minnesota Vikings	Metropolitan Stadium (G)	48,446
Tampa Bay Buccaneers	Tampa Stadium (G)	72,112

Western Division

Atlanta Falcons	Atlanta-Fulton Stadium (G)	60,489
Los Angeles Rams[1]	Anaheim Stadium (G)	43,250
New Orleans Saints	Louisiana Superdome (AT)	71,330
San Francisco 49ers	Candlestick Park (G)	61,246

1. Moved to Anaheim Stadium for 1980 season.

NATIONAL CONFERENCE CHAMPIONS

Year	Eastern Division	Central Division	Western Division	Champion
1970	Dallas Cowboys (10–4–0)	Minnesota Vikings (12–2–0)	San Francisco 49ers (10–3–1)	Dallas
1971	Dallas Cowboys (11–3–0)	Minnesota Vikings (11–3–0)	San Francisco 49ers (9–5–0)	Dallas
1972	Washington Redskins (11–3–0)	Green Bay Packers (10–4–0)	San Francisco 49ers (8–5–1)	Washington
1973	Dallas Cowboys (10–4–0)	Minnesota Vikings (12–2–0)	Los Angeles Rams (12–2–0)	Minnesota
1974	St. Louis Cardinals (10–4–0)	Minnesota Vikings (10–4–0)	Los Angeles Rams (10–4–0)	Minnesota
1975	St. Louis Cardinals (11–3–0)	Minnesota Vikings (12–2–0)	Los Angeles Rams (10–4–0)	Dallas
1976	Dallas Cowboys (11–3–0)	Minnesota Vikings (11–2–1)	Los Angeles Rams (10–3–1)	Minnesota
1977	Dallas Cowboys (12–2–0)	Minnesota Vikings (9–5–0)	Los Angeles Rams (10–4–0)	Dallas
1978	Dallas Cowboys (12–4–0)	Minnesota Vikings (8–7–1)	Los Angeles Rams (12–4–0)	Dallas
1979	Dallas Cowboys (11–5–0)	Tampa Bay Buccaneers (10–6–0)	Los Angeles Rams (9–7–0)	Los Angeles

AMERICAN CONFERENCE CHAMPIONS

Year	Eastern Division	Central Division	Western Division	Champion
1970	Baltimore Colts (11–2–1)	Cincinnati Bengals (8–6–0)	Oakland Raiders (8–4–2)	Baltimore
1971	Miami Dolphins (10–3–1)	Cleveland Browns (9–5–0)	Kansas City Chiefs (10–3–1)	Miami
1972	Miami Dolphins (14–0–0)	Pittsburgh Steelers (11–3–0)	Oakland Raiders (10–3–1)	Miami
1973	Miami Dolphins (12–2–0)	Cincinnati Bengals (10–4–0)	Oakland Raiders (9–4–1)	Miami
1974	Miami Dolphins (11–3–0)	Pittsburgh Steelers (10–3–1)	Oakland Raiders (12–2–0)	Pittsburgh
1975	Baltimore Colts (10–4–0)	Pittsburgh Steelers (12–2–0)	Oakland Raiders (12–2–0)	Pittsburgh
1976	Baltimore Colts (11–3–0)	Pittsburgh Steelers (10–4–0)	Oakland Raiders (13–1–0)	Oakland
1977	Baltimore Colts (10–4–0)	Pittsburgh Steelers (9–5–0)	Denver Broncos (12–2–0)	Denver
1978	New England Patriots (11–5–0)	Pittsburgh Steelers (14–2–0)	Denver Broncos (10–6–0)	Pittsburgh
1979	Miami Dolphins (10–6–0)	Pittsburgh Steelers (12–4–0)	San Diego Chargers (12–4–0)	Pittsburgh

AMERICAN LEAGUE CHAMPIONS

Year	Eastern Division (W-L-T)	Western Division (W-L-T)	League champion, playoffs results
1960	Houston Oilers (10–4–0)	Los Angeles Chargers (10–4–0)	Houston 24, Los Angeles 16
1961	Houston Oilers (10–3–1)	San Diego Chargers (12–2–0)	Houston 10, San Diego 3
1962	Houston Oilers (11–3–0)	Dallas Texans (11–3–0)	Dallas 20, Houston 17[1]
1963	Boston Patriots (8–6–1)[2]	San Diego Chargers (11–3–0)	San Diego 51, Boston 10
1964	Buffalo Bills (12–2–0)	San Diego Chargers (8–5–1)	Buffalo 20, San Diego 7
1965	Buffalo Bills (10–3–1)	San Diego Chargers (9–2–3)	Buffalo 23, San Diego 0
1966	Buffalo Bills (9–4–1)	Kansas City Chiefs (11–2–1)	Kansas City 31, Buffalo 7
1967	Houston Oilers (9–4–1)	Oakland Raiders (13–1–0)	Oakland 40, Houston 7
1968	New York Jets (11–3–0)	Oakland Raiders (12–2–0)[2]	New York 27, Oakland 23
1969	New York Jets (10–4–0)	Oakland Raiders (12–1–1)	Kansas City 17, Oakland 7[3]

1. Won at 2:45 of second sudden death overtime period. 2. Won divisional playoff. 3. Kansas City defeated New York, 13–6, and Oakland defeated Houston, 56–7, in interdivisional playoffs.

NATIONAL FOOTBALL LEAGUE GOVERNMENT

Commissioner's Office: Pete Rozelle, commissioner; Don Weiss, executive director; Bill Ray, treasurer; Jan Van Duser, director of player personnel; Jim Heffernan, director of public relations; Joe Browne, director of information; Val Pinchbeck, Jr., director of broadcasting.

American Conference: Lamar Hunt, president; Al Ward, assistant to the president; Fran Connors, director of information.

National Conference: George Halas, president; Joe Rhein, assistant to the president; Dick Maxwell, director of information.

COLLEGE COLORS AND NICKNAMES

Abilene Christian—Purple, white; Wildcats
Adelphi—Brown, gold; Panthers
Air Force—Silver, blue; Falcons
Akron—Blue, gold; Zips
Alabama—Crimson, white; Crimson Tide
Alcorn State—Purple, gold; Braves
Alfred—Purple, gold; Saxon Warriors
Amherst—Purple, white; Lord Jeffs
Arizona—Red, navy blue; Wildcats
Arizona State—Maroon, gold; Sun Devils
Arkansas—Cardinal, white; Razorbacks
Army—Black, gold, gray; Cadets
Auburn—Orange, navy blue; Tigers
Bates—Garnet; Bobcats
Baylor—Green, gold; Bears
Boston Coll.—Maroon, gold; Eagles
Boston—Scarlet, white; Terriers
Bowdoin—White; Polar Bears
Bowling Green—Brown, orange; Falcons
Bradley—Cardinal, white; Braves
Brigham Young—Blue, white; Cougars
Brooklyn—Maroon, gold; Kingsmen
Brown—Brown, white; Bruins
Bucknell—Orange, blue; Bisons
Buffalo—Blue, white; Bulls
Butler—Blue, white; Bulldogs
California at Berkeley—Blue, gold; Golden Bears
Cal, Irvine—Blue, gold; Anteaters
Cal, Davis—Navy, gold; Mustangs
Cal, Northridge—Red, white; Matadors
Cal, San Diego—Blue, gold; Tritons
Cal, Santa Barbara—Blue, gold; Gauchos
Canisius—Blue, gold; Golden Griffins
Carnegie-Mellon—Tartan plaid; Tartans
Catholic—Red, black; Cardinals
Centre—Gold, white; Colonels
Chicago—Maroon; Maroons
Chico State—Cardinal, white; Wildcats
Cincinnati—Red, black; Bearcats
Citadel—Blue, white; Bulldogs
City Coll. of N.Y.—Lavender; Beavers
Clemson—Purple, orange; Tigers
Coast Guard—Blue, white; Cadets
Colgate—Maroon; Red Raiders
Colorado—Silver, gold; Buffaloes
Colorado State—Green, gold; Rams
Columbia—Blue, white; Lions
Connecticut—Blue, white; Huskies
Cornell—Carnelian, white; Big Red

Cortland State—Red, white; Red Dragons
Creighton—White, blue; Blue Jays
C.W. Post—Green, gold; Pioneers
Dartmouth—Green; Big Green
Davidson—Red, black; Wildcats
Dayton—Red, blue; Flyers
Delaware—Blue, gold; Blue Hens
Denver—Red, gold; Pioneers
DePaul—Scarlet, blue; Blue Demons
Detroit—Cardinal, white; Titans
Drake—White, blue; Bulldogs
Duke—Blue, white; Blue Devils
Duquesne—Red, blue; Dukes
East Carolina—Purple, gold; Pirates
Eastern Kentucky—Maroon, white; Maroons
Fairleigh Dickinson—Maroon, white, blue; Knights
Florida—Orange, blue; Gators
Florida State—Garnet, gold; Seminoles
Fordham—Maroon; Rams
Franklin and Marshall—Blue, white; Diplomats
Fresno State—Cardinal, blue; Bulldogs
Fullerton State—Royal blue, orange; Titans
Furman—Purple, white; Paladines
Georgetown—Blue, gray; Hoyas
George Washington—Buff, blue; Colonials
Georgia—Red, black; Bulldogs
Georgia Tech—White, gold; Yellow Jackets
Gonzaga—Blue, white; Bulldogs
Grambling—Black, gold; Tigers
Hamilton—Buff, blue; Continentals
Hampden-Sydney—Garnet, gray; Tigers
Hardin-Simmons—Purple, gold; Cowboys
Harvard—Crimson; The Crimson
Hayward—Red, white, black; Pioneers
Hobart—Orange, purple; Statesmen
Hofstra—Blue, gold; Flying Dutchmen
Holy Cross—Purple; Crusaders
Houston—Scarlet, white; Cougars
Howard—Blue, white; Bisons
Hunter—Purple, white; Hawks
Idaho—Silver, gold; Vandals
Illinois—Orange, blue; Illini
Indiana—Cream, crimson; Hoosiers
Indiana State—Blue, white; Sycamores
Iowa—Gold, black; Hawkeyes
Iowa State—Cardinal, gold; Cyclones
Jackson State—Blue, white; Tigers
Johns Hopkins—Blue, black; Blue Jays
Kansas—Crimson, blue; Jayhawks
Kansas State—Purple, white; Wildcats
Kent State—Blue, gold; Golden Flashes
Kentucky—Blue, white; Wildcats
Lafayette—Maroon, white; Leopards
LaSalle—Blue, gold; Explorers
Lehigh—Brown, white; Engineers
Long Beach State—Brown, gold; 49ers
Los Angeles State—Black, gold; Diablos
Louisiana State—Purple, gold; Tigers
Louisville—Cardinal, black; Cardinals
Loyola (Ill.)—Maroon, gold; Ramblers
Maine—Blue, white; Black Bears
Manhattan—Green, white; Jaspers
Marquette—Blue, gold; Warriors
Maryland—Red, white; Terrapins
Massachusetts—Maroon, white; Redmen
Merchant Marine—Blue, gray; Mariners
Miami (Fla.)—Orange, green, white; Hurricanes
Miami (Ohio)—Red, white; Redskins
Michigan—Maize, blue; Wolverines
Michigan State—Green, white; Spartans
Mid Tennessee—Blue, white; Blue Raiders
Middlebury—Blue, white; Panthers
Minnesota—Maroon, gold; Gophers
Mississippi—Red, blue; Rebels
Mississippi State—Maroon, white; Maroons
Missouri—Black, gold; Tigers
M.I.T.—Cardinal, gray; Beavers
Montana—Copper, silver, gold; Grizzlies
Montana State—Gold, royal blue; Bobcats
Morgan State—Blue, orange; Bears
Navy—Blue, gold; Midshipmen
Nebraska—Scarlet, cream; Cornhuskers
Nebraska-Omaha—Red, black; Mavericks
Nevada—Silver, blue; Wolfpack
New Hampshire—Blue, white; Wildcats
New Mexico—Cherry, silver; Lobos
New York—Violet; Violets
Niagara—Purple, white; Purple Eagles
North Carolina—Blue, white; Tar Heels
North Carolina State—Scarlet, white; Wolfpack
North Dakota—Green, white; Sioux
North Texas State—Green, white; Eagles
Northeastern—Red, black; Huskies
Northwestern—Purple, white; Wildcats
Notre Dame—Blue, gold; Fighting Irish
Occidental—Orange, black; Bengals
Ohio State—Scarlet, gray; Buckeyes
Ohio—Green, white; Bobcats
Oklahoma—Maroon, white; Sooners
Okla. State—Orange, black; Cowboys
Oneonta State—Red, white; Red Dragons
Oregon—Yellow, green; Webfoots
Oregon State—Orange, black; Beavers
Penn State—Blue, white; Nittany Lions
Pennsylvania—Red, blue; Quakers
Pepperdine—Blue, orange, white; Waves
Pittsburgh—Blue, gold; Panthers
Princeton—Orange, black; Tigers
Providence—Black, white; Friars
Purdue—Gold, black; Boilermakers
Rhode Island—Blue, white; Rams
Rice—Blue, gray; Owls
Richmond—Red, blue; Spiders
Rider—Purple, gold; Braves
Rochester—Yellow; Yellowjackets
Rollins—Blue, gold; Tars
R.P.I.—Cherry, white; Engineers
Rutgers—Scarlet; The Scarlet
St. Bonaventure—Brown, white; Bonnies
St. Francis (N.Y.)—Red, blue; Terriers
St. John's (N.Y.)—Red, white; Redman
St. Joseph's (Pa.)—Crimson, gray; Hawks
St. Lawrence—Scarlet, brown; Larries
St. Louis—Blue, white; Billikens
St. Mary's (Calif.)—Red, blue; Gaels
San Diego State—Red, black; Aztecs
San Francisco—Green, gold; Dons
San Jose State—Gold, white; Spartans
Santa Clara—Cardinal, white; Broncos
Seattle—Maroon, white; Chieftains
Seton Hall—Blue, white; Pirates
Sewanee—Purple, gold; Tigers
So. Carolina—Garnet, black; Gamecocks
South Dakota—Scarlet, white; Coyotes
So. California—Cardinal, gold; Trojans
So. Illinois—Maroon, white; Salukis
So. Methodist—Red, blue; Mustangs
Southern—Blue, gold; Jaguars
Springfield—Maroon, white; Maroons
Stanford—Cardinal, white; Cardinals
Stony Brook—Scarlet, white; Patriots
Swarthmore—Garnet; Little Quakers
Syracuse—Orange; Orangemen
Temple—Cherry, white; Owls
Tennessee—Orange, white; Vols
Tennessee A. & I.—Blue, white; Tigers
Texas—Orange, white; Longhorns
Texas A. & M.—Maroon, white; Aggies
Texas Christian—Purple, white; Horned Frogs
Texas, El Paso—Orange, white; Miners
Texas Southern—Maroon, gray; Tigers
Texas Tech—Scarlet, black; Red Raiders
Toledo—Blue, gold; Rockets
Trinity (Conn.)—Blue, gold; Bantams
Tufts—Blue, brown; Jumbos

COLLEGE ATHLETIC CONFERENCES

Atlantic Coast: Clemson, Duke, Georgia Tech, Maryland, North Carolina, North Carolina State, Virginia, Wake Forest

Big Eight: Colorado, Iowa State, Kansas, Kansas State, Missouri, Nebraska, Oklahoma, Oklahoma State

Big Ten: Illinois, Indiana, Iowa, Michigan, Michigan State, Minnesota, Northwestern, Purdue, Ohio State, Wisconsin

Ivy League: Brown, Columbia, Cornell, Dartmouth, Harvard, Pennsylvania, Princeton, Yale

Pacific Ten: Arizona, Arizona State, California, Oregon, Oregon State, Stanford, California–Los Angeles (UCLA), Southern California (USC), Washington, Washington State

Southeastern: Alabama, Auburn, Georgia, Florida, Kentucky, Louisiana State, Mississippi, Mississippi State, Tennessee, Vanderbilt

Southwest: Arkansas, Baylor, Houston, Rice, Southern Methodist, Texas, Texas A&M, Texas Christian, Texas Tech

Southwestern: Alcorn State, Grambling, Jackson State, Mississippi Valley, Prairie View, Southern, Texas Southern

Western Athletic: Brigham Young, Colorado State, Hawaii, Nevada–Las Vegas, New Mexico, San Diego State, Texas–El Paso, Utah, Wyoming

Tulane—Green, blue; Green Wave
Tulsa—Crimson, blue, gold; Golden Hurricane
Tuskegee—Gold, crimson; Golden Tigers
U.C.L.A.—Blue, gold; Bruins
Utah—Crimson, white; Utes
Utah State—Blue, white; Aggies
Vanderbilt—Gold, black; Commodores
Vermont—Green, gold; Catamounts
Villanova—Blue, white; Wildcats
Virginia—Blue, orange; Cavaliers
V.M.I.—Red, white, yellow; Keydets
V.P.I.—Orange, maroon; Gobblers
Wagner—Green, white; Seahawks
Wake Forest—Gold, black; Deacons
Washington & Lee—Blue, white; Generals
Washington (Mo.)—Myrtle, maroon; Bears
Washington (Wash.)—Purple, gold; Huskies
Washington State—Crimson, gray; Cougars
Wesleyan—Cardinal, black; Cardinals
Western Kentucky—Red, white; Hilltoppers
W. Virginia—Gold, blue; Mountaineers
Wichita—Black, gold; Wheatshockers
William and Mary—Green, gold, silver; Indians
Williams—Royal purple; Ephmen
Wisconsin—Cardinal; Badgers
Wyoming—Brown, yellow; Cowboys
Yale—Blue; Bulldogs, Elis

FISHING

WORLD ALL-TACKLE FISHING RECORDS

Caught With Rod and Reel in Fresh Water

Source: International Game Fish Association

Species	lb–oz	Length	Girth	Where caught	Year	Angler
Bass, Largemouth	22–4	32½″	28½″	Montgomery Lake, Ga.	1932	George W. Perry
Bass, Redeye	8–3	23″	16½″	Flint River, Ga.	1977	David A. Hubbard
Bass, Rock	3	13½″	10¾″	York River, Ontario	1974	Peter Gulgin
Bass, Smallmouth	11–15	27″	21⅔″	Dale Hollow Lake, Ky.	1955	David L. Hayes
Bass, Spotted	8–15	—	—	Smith Lake, Ala.	1978	Philip C. Terry Jr.
Bass, White	5–5	19½″	17″	Ferguson Lake, Calif	1972	Norman W. Mize
	5–5	—	—	Theodosia, Mo.	1980	Bernice Morello
	5–6	—	—	Grenada, Miss.	1979	William C. Mulvihill
Bass, Whiterock	20	—	—	Savannah River, Ga.	1977	Ron Raley
Bass, Yellow	2–4	16¼″	12¾″	Lake Monroe, Ind.	1977	Donald L. Stalker
Bluegill	4–12	15″	18¼″	Ketona Lake, Ala.	1950	T. S. Hudson
Bowfin	21–8	—	—	Florence, N.C.	1980	Robert L. Harmon
Buffalo, Bigmouth	56	44¾″	33″	Lock Loma Lake, Mo.	1976	W. J. Long
Buffalo, Smallmouth	51	—	—	Lawrence, Kan.	1979	Scott Butler
Bullhead, Black	8	24″	17¾″	Lake Waccabuc, N.Y.	1951	Kani Evans
Carp	55–5	42″	31″	Clearwater Lake, Minn.	1952	Frank J. Ledwein
Catfish, Blue	97	57″	37″	Missouri River, S.D.	1959	Edward B. Elliott
Catfish, Channel	58	47¼″	29⅛″	Santee-Cooper Res., S.C.	1964	W. B. Whaley
Catfish, Flathead	79–8	44″	27″	White River, Ind.	1966	Glenn T. Simpson
Catfish, White	10–5	25″	17½″	Raritan River, N.J.	1976	L. W. Lomerson
Char, Arctic	29–11	39¾″	26″	Arctic River, N.W.T.	1968	Jeanne P. Branson
Crappie, Black	5	19¼″	18⅝″	Santee-Cooper Res., S.C.	1957	Paul E. Foust
Crappie, White	5–3	21″	19″	Enid Dam, Miss.	1957	Fred L. Bright
Dolly Varden	32	40½″	29¾″	Lake Pend Oreille, Idaho	1949	N. L. Higgins
Drum, Freshwater	54–8	31½″	29″	Nickajack Lake, Tenn.	1972	Benny E. Hull
Gar, Alligator	279	93″	—	Rio Grande River, Tex.	1951	Bill Valverde
Gar, Longnose	50–5	72¼″	22½″	Trinity River, Tex.	1954	Townsend Miller
Grayling, Arctic	5–15	29⅞″	15⅛″	Katseyedie River, N.W.T.	1967	Jeanne P. Branson
Kokanee	6–9	24½″	14½″	Priest Lake, Idaho	1975	Jerry Verge
Muskellunge	69–15	64½″	31¾″	St. Lawrence River, N.Y.	1957	Arthur Lawton
Perch, White	4–12	19½″	13″	Messalonskee Lake, Me.	1949	Mrs. Earl Small
Perch, Yellow	4–3	—	—	Bordentown, N.J.	1865	Dr. C. C. Abbot
Pickerel, Eastern chain	9–6	31″	14″	Homerville, Ga.	1961	Baxley McQuaig, Jr.
Pike, Northern	46–2	52½″	25″	Sacandaga Reservoir, N.Y.	1940	Peter Dubuc
Redhorse, Silver	4–2	20½″	14″	Gasconade River, Mo.	1974	C. L. McKinney
Salmon, Atlantic	79–2	—	—	Tana River, Norway	1928	Henrik Henriksen
Salmon, Chinook	93	50″	39″	Kelp Bay, Alaska	1977	Howard C. Rider
Salmon, Chum	27–3	39⅜″	24½″	Raymond Cove, Alaska	1977	Robert A. Jahnke
Salmon Landlocked	22–8	36″	—	Sebago Lake, Me.	1907	Edward Blakely
Salmon CoHo	31	—	—	Cowichan Bay, B.C.	1947	Mrs. Lee Hallberg
Sauger	8–12	28″	15″	Lake Sakakawea, N.D.	1971	Mike Fischer
Shad, American	9–4	—	—	Delaware River, Pa.	1979	J. Edward Whitman
Sturgeon, White	360	111″	86″	Snake River, Idaho	1956	Willard Cravens
Sunfish, Green	2–2	14¾″	14″	Stockton Lake, Mo.	1971	Paul M. Dilley
Sunfish, Refbreast	1–8½	11″	12⅝″	Suwannee River, Fla.	1977	Tommy D. Cason, Jr.
Sunfish, Redear	4–8	16¼″	17¾″	Chase City, Va.	1970	Maurice E. Ball
Trout, Brook	14–8	31½″	11½″	Nipigon River, Ontario	1916	Dr. W. J. Cook
Trout, Brown	35–15	—	—	Nahuel Haupi, Argentina	1952	Eugenio Cavalia
Trout, Cutthroat	41	39″	—	Pyramid Lake, Nev.	1925	John Skimmerhorn
Trout, Golden	11	28″	16″	Cook's Lake, Wyo.	1948	Charles S. Reed
Trout, Lake	65	52″	38″	Great Bear Lake, N.W.T.	1970	Larry Daunis
Trout, Rainbow or Steelhead	42–2	43″	23½″	Bell Island, Alaska	1970	David R. White
Trout, Sunapee	11–8	33″	17¼″	Lake Sunapee, N.H.	1954	Ernest Theoharis

Trout, Tiger	17	31"	21"	Lake Michigan, Wis.	1977	Edward Rudnicki
Walleye	25	41"	29"	Old Hickory Lake, Tenn.	1960	Mabry Harper
Warmouth	2	12"	12½"	Sylvania, Ga.	1974	Carlton Robbins
Whitefish, Lake	13	32¼"	19"	Great Bear Lake, N.W.T.	1974	Robert L. Stintsman
Whitefish, Mountain	5	19"	14"	Athabasca River, Alberta, Can.	1963	Orville Welch

Caught With Rod and Reel in Salt Water

Source: International Game Fish Association

Species	lb–oz	Length	Girth	Where caught	Year	Angler
Albacore	88–2	—	—	Canary Islands	1977	Siegfried Dickemann
Amberjack	149	71"	41¾"	Bermuda	1964	Peter Simons
Barracuda	83	72¼"	29"	Lagos, Nigeria	1952	K. J. W. Hackett
Bass, Black Sea	8–12	—	—	Oregon Inlet, N.C.	1979	Joe W. Mizelle Sr.
Bass, Giant Sea	563–8	89"	72"	Anacapa Island, Calif.	1968	J. D. McAdam, Jr.
Bass, Striped	72	54½"	31"	Cuttyhunk, Mass.	1969	Edward J. Kirker
Blackfish (Tautog)	21–6	31½"	23½"	Cape May, N.J.	1954	R. N. Sheafer
Bluefish	31–12	47"	23"	North Carolina	1972	James M. Hussey
Bonefish	19	—	—	Zululand, S. Africa	1962	Brian W. Batchelor
Bonito, Atlantic	13–3	—	—	Fuerteventura Is., Canary Islands	1979	Renate Reichel
Bonito, Pacific	23–8	35¼"	23¼"	Victoria, Mahe	1975	Mrs. Anne Cochain
Cod	98–12	63"	41"	Isle of Shoals, N.H.	1969	Alphonse Bielevich
Dolphin	87	81⅔"	28"	Papapagalio Gulf, Costa Rica	1976	Manual Salazar
Drum, Black	113–1	53⅛"	43½"	Lewes, Del.	1975	G. M. Townsend
Drum, Red	90	55½"	38¼"	Rodanthe, N.C.	1973	Elvin Hooper
Flounder, Summer	22–7	—	—	Montauk, N.Y.	1975	Charles Nappi
Halibut, California	37–8	—	—	San Diego, Calif.	1979	William E. Williams
Jack, Horse-eye	21–5	—	—	Arcus Bank, Bermuda	1979	Tom Smith
Jack, Crevalle	51	—	—	Lake Worth, Fla.	1978	Stephen Schwenk
Jewfish	680	85½"	66"	Fernandina Beach, Fla.	1961	Lynn Joiner
Kawakawa	21	34"	22"	Kilauea, Kauai, Hawaii	1975	E. John O'Dell
Mackerel, King	90	—	—	Key West, Florida	1976	Norton I. Thomton
Marlin, Black	1560	174"	81"	Cabo Blanco, Peru	1953	A. C. Glassel, Jr.
Marlin, Atlantic Blue	1282	176"	76½"	St. Thomas, Virgin Islands	1977	Larry Martin
Marlin, Pacific Blue	1153	176"	73"	Ritidian Point, Guam	1969	Greg G. Perez
Marlin, Striped	417–8	139½"	52½"	Cavalli Island, New Zealand	1977	Phillip Bryers
Marlin, White	18–14	—	—	Victoria, Brazil	1979	Evandro Luiz Caser
Permit	51–8	—	—	Lake Worth, Fla.	1978	William M. Kenney
Pollock	46–7	50½"	30"	Brielle, N.J.	1975	John T. Holton
Pompano, African	41–8	—	—	Fort Lauderdale, Fla.	1979	Wayne Sommers
Roosterfish	114	64"	33"	La Paz, Mexico	1960	Abe Sackheim
Runner, Rainbow	33–10	55¼"	22½"	Clarion Island, Mexico	1976	R. A. Mikkelsen
Sailfish, Atlantic	128–1	106¼"	34¼"	Luanda, Angola, Africa	1974	Harm Steyn
Sailfish, Pacific	221	129"	—	Santa Cruz Is., Galapagos Is.	1947	C. W. Stewart
Seabass, White	83–12	65½"	34"	San Felipe, Mexico	1953	L. C. Baumgardner
Seatrout, Spotted	16	32½"	21¾"	Mason's Beach, Va.	1977	William G. Katko
Shark, Blue	437	—	—	Catherine Bay, Australia	1976	Peter Hyde
Shark, Hammerhead	703	172"	63"	Jacksonville, Fla.	1975	H. B. Reasor
Shark, Mako	1080	—	—	Montauk, N.Y.	1979	James L. Melanson
Shark, Porbeagle	465	111"	56"	Padstow, Cornwall, England	1976	Jorge Potier
Shark, Thresher	739	106"	68"	Tutukaka, New Zealand	1975	Brian Galvin
Shark, Tiger	1780	166½"	103"	Cherry Grove, S.C.	1964	Walter Maxwell
Shark, White	2664	202"	114"	South Australia	1959	Alfred Dean
Skipjack, Black	14–8	—	—	Baja, Mexico	1977	Lorraine Carlton
Snook	53–10	—	—	Costa Rica	1978	Gilbert Ponzi
Spearfish	79–5	—	—	Madiera Islands	1979	Ronald Eckert
Swordfish	1182	179¼"	78"	Iquique, Chile	1953	L. E. Marron
Tanguigue	85–6	—	—	Western Australia	1978	Barry Wrightson
Tarpon	283	85⅗"	—	Lake Maracaibo, Venezuela	1956	M. Salazar
Tautog (See Blackfish)						
Trevally, Lowly	116	—	—	American Samoa	1978	William G. Foster
Tuna, Yellowfin	388–12	—	—	Mexico	1977	Curt Wiesenhutter
Tuna, Altantic Bigeye	375–8	—	—	Ocean City, Md.	1977	Cecil Browne
Tuna, Blackfin	42	—	—	Bermuda	1978	Alan J. Card
Tuna, Bluefin	1496	—	—	Nova Scotia, Canada	1979	Ken Fraser
Tuna, Dog-tooth	189–2	—	—	Tanzania	1978	Luke John Samaras
Tuna, Longtail	65	—	—	Port Stephens, Australia	1978	Michael James
Tuna, Pacific Big-Eyed	435	93"	63½"	Cabo Blanco, Peru	1957	R.V. A. Lee
Tuna, Skipjack	39–15	39"	28"	Walker City, Bahamas	1952	R. Drawley
	40	38¾"	27½"	Baie du Tambeau, Mauritius	1971	Joseph R. Cabache
Tuna, Southern Bluefin	256–13	—	—	Mexico	1979	Rodney James Beard
Tunny, Little	27	39"	22"	Key Largo, Fla.	1976	William E. Allison
Weakfish	19–8	37"	23¾"	Trinidad, West Indies	1962	Dennis B. Hall
Yellowtail	111	62"	38"	Bay of Islands, New Zealand	1961	A. F. Plim

BASKETBALL

Basketball may be the one sport whose exact origin is definitely known. In the winter of 1891–92, Dr. James Naismith, an instructor in the Y.M.C.A. Training College (now Springfield College) at Springfield, Mass., deliberately invented the game of basketball in order to provide indoor exercise and competition for the students between the closing of the football season and the opening of the baseball season. He affixed peach baskets overhead on the walls at opposite ends of the gymnasium and organized teams to play his new game in which the purpose was to toss an association (soccer) ball into one basket and prevent the opponents from tossing the ball into the other basket. The game is fundamentally the same today, though there have been improvements in equipment and some changes in rules.

Because Dr. Naismith had eighteen available players when he invented the game, the first rule was: "There shall be nine players on each side." Later the number of players became optional, depending upon the size of the available court, but the five-player standard was adopted when the game spread over the country. United States soldiers brought basketball to Europe in World War I, and it soon became a world-wide sport.

College Basketball

NATIONAL COLLEGIATE A.A. CHAMPIONS

1939	Oregon	1948	Kentucky	1957	North Carolina	1966	Texas Western
1940	Indiana	1949	Kentucky	1958	Kentucky	1967–73	U.C.L.A.
1941	Wisconsin	1950	C.C.N.Y.	1959	California	1974	No. Carolina State
1942	Stanford	1951	Kentucky	1960	Ohio State	1975	U.C.L.A.
1943	Wyoming	1952	Kansas	1961	Cincinnati	1976	Indiana
1944	Utah	1953	Indiana	1962	Cincinnati	1977	Marquette
1945	Oklahoma A & M	1954	La Salle	1963	Loyola (Chicago)	1978	Kentucky
1946	Oklahoma A & M	1955	San Francisco	1964	U.C.L.A.	1979	Michigan State
1947	Holy Cross	1956	San Francisco	1965	U.C.L.A.	1980	Louisville

NATIONAL INVITATION TOURNAMENT (NIT) CHAMPIONS

1939	Long Island U.	1951	Brigham Young	1962	Dayton	1973	Virginia Tech
1940	Colorado	1952	La Salle	1963	Providence	1974	Purdue
1941	Long Island U.	1953	Seton Hall	1964	Bradley	1975	Princeton
1942	West Virginia	1954	Holy Cross	1965	St. John's (Bklyn.)	1976	Kentucky
1943–44	St. John's (Bklyn.)	1955	Duquesne	1966	Brigham Young	1977	St. Bonaventure
1945	DePaul	1956	Louisville	1967	So. Illinois	1978	Texas
1946	Kentucky	1957	Bradley	1968	Dayton	1979	Indiana
1947	Utah	1958	Xavier (Cincinnati)	1969	Temple	1980	Virginia
1948	St. Louis	1959	St. John's (Bklyn.)	1970	Marquette		
1949	San Francisco	1960	Bradley	1971	North Carolina		
1950	C.C.N.Y.	1961	Providence	1972	Maryland		

N.C.A.A. MAJOR COLLEGE INDIVIDUAL SCORING RECORDS

Single Season Averages

Player, Team	Year	G	FG	FT	Pts	Avg
Pete Maravich, Louisiana State	1969–70	31	522[1]	337	1381[1]	44.5[1]
Pete Maravich	1968–69	26	433	282	1148	44.2
Pete Maravich	1967–68	26	432	274	1138	43.8
Frank Selvy, Furman	1953–54	29	427	355[1]	1209	41.7
Johnny Neumann, Mississippi	1970–71	23	366	191	923	40.1
Freeman Williams, Portland State	1976–77	26	417	176	1010	38.8
Billy McGill, Utah	1961–62	26	394	221	1009	38.8
Calvin Murphy, Niagara	1967–68	24	337	242	916	38.2
Austin Carr, Notre Dame	1969–70	29	444	218	1106	38.1

1. Record.

LONGEST FIELD GOAL IN COLLEGE BASKETBALL

What was the longest field goal ever scored in a college basketball game? Would you believe 89 ft 3 in.? That's only 4 ft 9 in. short of the regulation length of a court. It happened on January 21, 1980, at Tallahassee, Fla., and the shooter was Les Henson, a 6-ft-6-in. senior forward for Virginia Tech. He took the shot with only two seconds left in the game against Florida State and gave the Gobblers a 79–77 victory. Henson had just grabbed a rebound off the Florida State boards about a foot from the baseline. The normally left-handed-shooting Henson unleashed a right-handed shot in desperation and it went in. At first the shot was reported as 93 ft, but a later measurement established it at 89–3. "It was eerie while the ball was in the air," Henson later recalled. "Everything was quiet, you couldn't hear a thing in the arena. At first, I thought it was going to hit one of the light fixtures, but it didn't, and then it just swished through the hoop." It bettered the previous longest scoring shot of 88 ft by Rudy Williams of Providence College against Rhode Island on February 17, 1979.

N.C.A.A. CAREER SCORING TOTALS

Division I

Player, Team	Last year	G	FG	FT	Pts	Avg
Pete Maravich, Louisiana State	1970	83	1387[1]	893[1]	3667[1]	44.2[1]
Austin Carr, Notre Dame	1971	74	1017	526	2560	34.6
Oscar Robertson, Cincinnati	1960	88	1052	869	2973	33.8
Calvin Murphy, Niagara	1970	77	947	654	2548	33.1
Dwight Lanar[2]	1973	57	768	326	1862	32.7
Frank Selvy, Furman	1954	78	922	694	2538	32.5
Rick Mount, Purdue	1970	72	910	503	2323	32.3
Darrel Floyd, Furman	1956	71	868	545	2281	32.1
Nick Werkman, Seton Hall	1964	71	812	649	2273	32.0

1. Record. 2. Also played two seasons in college division.

Division II

Player, Team	Last year	G	FG	FT	Pts	Avg
Travis Grant, Kentucky State	1972	121	1760[1]	525	4045[1]	33.4[1]
John Rinka, Kenyon	1970	99	1261	729	3251	32.8
Florindo Vierira, Quinnipiac	1957	69	761	741	2263	32.8
Willie Shaw, Lane	1964	76	960	459	2379	31.3
Mike Davis, Virginia Union	1969	89	1014	730	2758	31.0
Henry Logan, Western Carolina	1968	107	1263	764	3290	30.7
Willie Scott, Alabama State	1969	103	1277	601	3155	30.6
Gregg Northington, Alabama State	1972	75	894	403	2191	29.2
Bob Hopkins, Grambling	1956	126	1403	953	3759	29.8

1. Record.

TOP SINGLE-GAME SCORING MARKS

Player, Team (Opponent)	Yr	Pts
Selvy, Furman (Newberry)	1954	100[1]
Williams, Portland State (Rocky Mtn.)	1978	81
Mikvy, Temple (Wilkes)	1951	73
Williams, Portland State (So. Oregon)	1977	71
Maravich, LSU (Alabama)	1970	69
Murphy, Niagara (Syracuse)	1969	68

1. Record.

Player, Team (Opponent)	Yr	Pts
Floyd, Furman (Morehead)	1955	67
Maravich, LSU (Tulane)	1969	66
Handlan, W & L (Furman)	1951	66
Roberts, Oral Roberts (N.C. A&T)	1977	66
Williams, Portland State (Geo. Fox Coll.)	1978	66
Roberts, Oral Roberts (Oregon)	1977	65

NATIONAL COLLEGIATE ATHLETIC ASSOCIATION (N.C.A.A.)—1980

DIVISION I

First Round—East

Villanova 77, Marquette 59
Iowa 86, Virginia Commonwealth 72
Iona 84, Holy Cross 78
Tennessee 80, Furman 69

First Round—Mideast

Florida State 94, Toledo 91
Pennsylvania 62, Washington State 55
Purdue 90, La Salle 82
Virginia Tech 89, Western Kentucky 85

First Round—Midwest

Alcorn State 70, South Alabama 62
Missouri 61, San Jose State 51
Texas A&M 55, Bradley 53
Kansas State 71, Arkansas 53

First Round—West

U.C.L.A. 87, Old Dominion 74
Arizona State 99, Loyola (Calif.) 71
Clemson 76, Utah State 73
Lamar 87, Weber State 86

Second Round—East

Syracuse 97, Villanova 83
Iowa 77, North Carolina State 64
Georgetown 74, Iona 71
Maryland 86, Tennessee 75

Second Round—Mideast

Kentucky 97, Florida State 78
Duke 52, Pennsylvania 42
Purdue 87, St. John's 72
Indiana 68, Virginia Tech 59

Second Round—Midwest

Louisiana State 98, Alcorn State 88
Missouri 87, Notre Dame 84 (overtime)
Texas A&M 78, North Carolina 61
Louisville 71, Kansas State 69

Second Round—West

U.C.L.A. 77, De Paul 71
Ohio State 89, Arizona State 75
Clemson 71, Brigham Young 66
Lamar 81, Oregon State 77

Third Round—East

Iowa 88, Syracuse 77
Georgetown 74, Maryland 68

Third Round—Mideast

Duke 55, Kentucky 54
Purdue 76, Indiana 69

Third Round—Midwest
Louisiana State 68, Missouri 63
Louisville 66, Texas A&M 55

Third Round—West
U.C.L.A. 72, Ohio State 68
Clemson 74, Lamar 66

Regional Finals
Iowa 81, Georgetown 80
Purdue 68, Duke 60
Louisville 86, Louisiana State 66
U.C.L.A. 85, Clemson 74

National Semifinals
(Indianapolis, March 22, 1980)
Louisville 80, Iowa 72
U.C.L.A. 67, Purdue 62

Third Place
Purdue 75, Iowa 58

National Final
(Indianapolis, March 24, 1980)
Louisville 59, U.C.L.A. 54

DIVISION II
Semifinals
Virginia Union 78, Florida Southern 71 (overtime)
New York Tech 72, North Alabama 66

Third Place
Florida Southern 68, North Alabama 67

Championship
(Springfield, Mass., March 15, 1980)
Virginia Union 80, New York Tech 74

DIVISION III
(Rock Island, Ill., March 15, 1980)

Semifinals
Upsala (N.J.) 67, Wittenberg (Ohio) 63
North Park (Ill.) 57, Longwood (Va.) 55

Third Place
Wittenberg (Ohio) 48, Longwood (Va.) 47 (overtime)

Championship
North Park (Ill.) 83, Upsala (N.J.) 76

ASSOCIATION FOR INTERCOLLEGIATE ATHLETICS FOR WOMEN
(A.I.A.W.—1980)

EASTERN SECTION
Semifinals
Tennessee 84, Kansas State 64
Maryland 68, Texas 63

Final
Tennessee 93, Maryland 76

CENTRAL SECTION
Semifinals
South Carolina 64, Northwestern 61
Stephen F. Austin 76, Oregon 53

Final
South Carolina 63, Stephen F. Austin 56

SOUTHERN SECTION
Semifinals
Old Dominion 88, Brigham Young 66
Rutgers 70, Providence 54

Final
Old Dominion 84, Rutgers 62

WESTERN SECTION
Semifinals
Louisiana Tech 81, Kansas 73
Long Beach State 86, North Carolina State 72

Final
Louisiana Tech 96, Long Beach State 70

NATIONAL SEMIFINALS
(Mount Pleasant, Mich., March 21, 1980)
Tennessee 75, South Carolina 72
Old Dominion 73, Louisiana Tech 59

THIRD PLACE
South Carolina 77, Louisiana Tech 69

CHAMPIONSHIP
(Mount Pleasant, Mich., March 23, 1980)
Old Dominion 68, Tennessee 53

DIVISION II
Semifinals
(Dayton, Ohio, March 21–23, 1980)
Dayton 77, Louisiana College 52
Charleston (S.C.) 67, William Penn (Iowa) 49

Final
Dayton 83, Charleston (S.C.) 53

Third Place
William Penn (Iowa) 77, Louisiana College 71 (overtime)

DIVISION III
Semifinals
(Spokane, Wash., March 20–22, 1980)
Worcester State 81, University of Scranton 60
University of Wisconsin–LaCrosse 66, Mount Mercy College 63

Final
Worcester State 76, University of Wisconsin–LaCrosse 73

Third Place
University of Scranton 78, Mount Mercy College 68

LEADING SCORERS—1979–80

N.C.A.A.—Division I

	FG	FT	Pts	Avg
Tony Murphy, Southern	377	178	932	32.1
Lewis Lloyd, Drake	324	167	815	30.2
Harry Kelly, Texas Southern	313	127	753	29.0
Kenny Page, New Mexico	314	156	784	28.0
James Tillman, Eastern Kentucky	288	158	734	27.2
Earl Belcher, St. Bonaventure	241	164	646	26.9

N.C.A.A.—Division II

	FG	FT	Pts	Avg
Bill Fennelly, Central Missouri	337	189	863	30.8

Greg Jackson, St. Paul's	249	199	697	30.3
Reginald Gaines, Winston-Salem	309	126	744	28.6
Dave Zeigler, Youngstown State	282	101	665	27.7
Ricky Mahorn, Hampton Institute	352	151	855	27.6
Otto Porter, Southeastern Missouri	228	83	539	27.0

N.C.A.A.—Division III

Ray Buckland, Boston State	271	153	695	27.8
Mike Carroll, Nebraska Wesleyan	225	124	574	27.3
Vin Miller, Nichols	301	104	706	27.2
Clinton Wheeler, William Paterson	283	139	705	26.1
Scott Rogers, Kenyon	233	112	578	25.1
John Jordan, Southern Maine	226	114	566	24.6

NATIONAL ASSOCIATION OF INTERCOLLEGIATE ATHLETICS—1980

Round of 16

LeMoyne–Owen (Tenn.) 56, Abilene Christian 55
Central Washington 66, Biola (Calif.) 64
Alabama State 103, South Carolina–Aiken 78
Cameron (Okla.) 120, St. Augustine's (N.C.) 86
Huron (S.D.) 73, Franklin (Ind.) 71
Central Arkansas 54, Rockhurst (Mo.) 53
Wisconsin–Eau Claire 56, Marymount (Kan.) 49
Clarion State (Pa.) 79, Loras (Iowa) 71

Quarterfinals

Cameron (Okla.) 76, LeMoyne–Owen (Tenn.) 65
Alabama State 67, Central Arkansas 53
Wisconsin–Eau Claire 68, Central Washington 61 (overtime)
Huron (S.D.) 61, Clarion State (Pa.) 52

Semifinals

Cameron (Okla.) 71, Wisconsin–Eau Claire 64
Alabama State 72, Huron (S.D.) 58

Third Place

Huron (S.D.) 59, Wisconsin–Eau Claire 54

Championship

Cameron (Okla.) 84, Alabama State 77

A.A.U. CHAMPIONSHIP—WOMEN

(Allentown, Pa., March 17–22, 1980)

(Double-elimination tournament)

New York All–Stars 81, Magic of Sports 75
Detroit Cobras 72, 20th Century Blazers 68
Detroit Cobras 93, Armed Forces 72
Crest Sporting Goods (Allentown) 67, New York Jazz 59
Roberto Clemente State Park (N.Y.) 78, Armed Forces 60
Crest Sporting Goods 81, Shamrocks (North Tonawanda, N.Y.) 79
20th Century Blazers (Phila.) 78, Snitz Manufacturing (Troy, Wis.) 71
Snitz Manufacturing 99, New York All–Stars 87
Detroit Cobras 84, Allentown Crestettes 56
Roberto Clemente State Park 67, New York All–Stars 67
20th Century Blazers 81, New York All–Stars 70
Snitz Manufacturing 67, Roberto Clemente State Park 49
20th Century Blazers 86, Allentown Crestettes 84
Allentown Crestettes 77, Whitey's Hot Shots (Corpus Christi, Tex.) 59
Roberto Clemente State Park 69, New York All–Stars 67
20th Century Blazers 67, Snitz Manufacturing 49
20th Century Blazers 72, Choate Ford (Hennessey, Okla.) 60
20th Century Blazers 80, Detroit Cobras 73

Championship

20th Century Blazers 78, Detroit Cobras 68
Most valuable player—Yolanda Laney, 20th Century Blazers

NATIONAL INVITATION TOURNAMENT

Semifinals (March 17, 1980)

(Madison Square Garden, New York)
Minnesota 65, Illinois 63
Virginia 90, Nevada–Las Vegas 71
Championship (March 19, 1980)
Virginia 58, Minnesota 55

Third Place

Illinois 84, Nevada–Las Vegas 74

A.A.U. CHAMPIONSHIP—MEN

(St. Augustine, Fla., March 27–30, 1980)

Quarterfinals

Capital Insulation, Los Angeles 96, Christian Youth, Joliet, Ill. 95
McGills, Omaha, Neb. 91, Brewster Packing, Seattle, Wash. 78
Airliner, Iowa City 98, Unity Savings, Chicago 87
Sims Insulation, Lake Charles, La. 105, Armed Forces All-Stars 99

Semifinals

Sims Insulation 107, McGills 94
Airliner 113, Capital Insulation 94

Third Place

McGillis 112, Capital Insulation 110

Championship

Airliner 94, Sims Insulation 89
Most valuable player—William Mayfield, Airliner Basketball Club

Professional Basketball

NATIONAL BASKETBALL ASSOCIATION CHAMPIONS

Source: Matt Winick, Director of Media Information, National Basketball Association

The National Basketball Association was originally the Basketball Association of America. It took its current name in 1949 when it merged with the National Basketball League.

Season	Eastern Conference (W-L)	Western Conference (W-L)	Playoff Champions[1]
1946–47	Washington Capitols (49–11)	Chicago Stags (39–22)	Philadelphia Warriors
1947–48	Philadelphia Warriors (27–21)	St. Louis Bombers (29–19)	Baltimore Bullets
1948–49	Washington Capitols (38–22)	Rochester Royals (45–15)	Minneapolis Lakers
1949–50	Syracuse Nationals (51–13)	Indianapolis Olympians (39–25)	Minneapolis Lakers
1950–51	Philadelphia Warriors (40–26)	Minneapolis Lakers (44–24)	Rochester Royals
1951–52	Syracuse Nationals (40–26)	Rochester Royals (41–25)	Minneapolis Lakers
1952–53	New York Knickerbockers (47–23)	Minneapolis Lakers (48–22)	Minneapolis Lakers

Season	Eastern Conference (W-L)	Western Conference (W-L)	Playoff Champions[1]
1953–54	New York Knickerbockers (44–28)	Minneapolis Lakers (46–26)	Minneapolis Lakers
1954–55	Syracuse Nationals (43–29)	Ft. Wayne Pistons (43–29)	Syracuse Nationals
1955–56	Philadelphia Warriors (45–27)	Ft. Wayne Pistons (37–35)	Philadelphia Warriors
1956–57	Boston Celtics (44–28)	St. Louis Hawks (34–38)	Boston Celtics
1957–58	Boston Celtics (48–23)	St. Louis Hawks (41–31)	St. Louis Hawks
1958–59	Boston Celtics (52–20)	St. Louis Hawks (49–23)	Boston Celtics
1959–60	Boston Celtics (59–16)	St. Louis Hawks (46–29)	Boston Celtics
1960–61	Boston Celtics (57–22)	St. Louis Hawks (51–28)	Boston Celtics
1961–62	Boston Celtics (60–20)	Los Angeles Lakers (54–26)	Boston Celtics
1962–63	Boston Celtics (58–22)	Los Angeles Lakers (53–27)	Boston Celtics
1963–64	Boston Celtics (59–21)	San Francisco Warriors (48–32)	Boston Celtics
1964–65	Boston Celtics (62–18)	Los Angeles Lakers (49–31)	Boston Celtics
1965–66	Philadelphia 76ers (55–25)	Los Angeles Lakers (45–35)	Boston Celtics
1966–67	Philadelphia 76ers (68–13)	San Francisco Warriors (44–37)	Philadelphia 76ers
1967–68	Philadelphia 76ers (62–20)	St. Louis Hawks (56–26)	Boston Celtics
1968–69	Baltimore Bullets (57–25)	Los Angeles Lakers (55–27)	Boston Celtics
1969–70	New York Knickerbockers (60–22)	Atlanta Hawks (48–34)	New York Knicks
1970–71	Baltimore Bullets (42–40)	Milwaukee Bucks (66–16)	Milwaukee Bucks
1971–72	New York Knickerbockers (48–34)	Los Angeles Lakers (69–13)	Los Angeles Lakers
1972–73	New York Knickerbockers (57–25)	Los Angeles Lakers (69–22)	New York Knicks
1973–74	Boston Celtics (56–26)	Milwaukee Bucks (59–23)	Boston Celtics
1974–75	Washington Bullets (60–22)	Golden State Warriors (48–34)	Golden State Warriors
1975–76	Boston Celtics (54–28)	Phoenix Suns (42–40)	Boston Celtics
1976–77	Philadelphia 76ers (50–32)	Portland Trail Blazers (49–33)	Portland Trail Blazers
1977–78	Washington Bullets (44–38)	Seattle Super Sonics (47–35)	Washington Bullets
1978–79	Washington Bullets (54–28)	Seattle Super Sonics (52–30)	Seattle Super Sonics
1979–80	Philadelphia 76ers (59–23)	Los Angeles Lakers (60–22)	Los Angeles Lakers

1. Playoffs may involve teams other than conference winners.

INDIVIDUAL N.B.A. SCORING CHAMPIONS

Season	Player, Team	G	FG	FT	Pts	Avg
1953–54	Neil Johnston, Philadelphia Warriors	72	591	577	1759	24.4
1954–55	Neil Johnston, Philadelphia Warriors	72	521	589	1631	22.7
1955–56	Bob Pettit, St. Louis Hawks	72	646	557	1849	25.7
1956–57	Paul Arizin, Philadelphia Warriors	71	613	591	1817	25.6
1957–58	George Yardley, Detroit Pistons	72	673	655	2001	27.8
1958–59	Bob Pettit, St. Louis Hawks	72	719	667	2105	29.2
1959–60	Wilt Chamberlain, Philadelphia Warriors	72	1065	577	2707	37.6
1960–61	Wilt Chamberlain, Phildelphia Warriors	79	1251	531	3033	38.4
1961–62	Wilt Chamberlain, Philadelphia Warriors	80	1597	835	4029	50.4
1962–63	Wilt Chamberlain, San Francisco Warriors	80	1463	660	3586	44.8
1963–64	Wilt Chamberlain, San Francisco Warriors	80	1204	540	2948	36.9
1964–65	Wilt Chamberlain, San Francisco Warriors-Phila. 76ers	73	1063	408	2534	34.7
1965–66	Wilt Chamberlain, Philadelphia 76ers	79	1074	501	2649	33.5
1966–67	Rick Barry, San Francisco Warriors	78	1011	753	2775	35.6
1967–68	Dave Bing, Detroit Pistons	79	835	472	2142	27.1
1968–69	Elvin Hayes, San Diego Rockets	82	930	467	2327	28.4
1969–70	Jerry West, Los Angeles Lakers	74	831	647	2309	31.2
1970–71	Lew Alcindor,[1] Milwaukee Bucks	82	1063	470	2596	31.7
1971–72	Kareem Abdul-Jabbar, Milwaukee Bucks	81	1159	504	2822	34.8
1972–73	Nate Archibald, Kansas City-Omaha Kings	80	1028	663	2719	34.0
1973–74	Bob McAdoo, Buffalo Braves	74	901	459	2261	30.8
1974–75	Bob McAdoo, Buffalo Braves	82	1095	641	2831	34.5
1975–76	Bob McAdoo, Buffalo Braves	78	934	559	2427	31.1
1976–77	Pete Maravich, New Orleans Jazz	73	886	501	2273	31.1
1977–78	George Gervin, San Antonio Spurs	82	864	504	2232	27.2
1978–79	George Gervin, San Antonio	80	947	471	2365	29.6
1979–80	George Gervin, San Antonio	78	1024	505	2585	33.1

1. (Kareem Abdul-Jabbar).

N.B.A. MOST VALUABLE PLAYERS

1956	Bob Pettit
1957	Bob Cousy
1958	Bill Russell
1959	Bob Pettit
1960	Wilt Chamberlain
1961–63	Bill Russell
1964	Oscar Robertson
1965	Bill Russell
1966–68	Wilt Chamberlain
1969	Wes Unseld
1970	Willis Reed
1971–72	Lew Alcindor (Kareem Abdul-Jabbar)
1973	Dave Cowens
1974	Kareem Abdul-Jabbar, Milwaukee
1975	Bob McAdoo, Buffalo
1976–77	Kareem Abdul-Jabbar, Los Angeles
1978	Bill Walton, Portland
1979	Moses Malone, Houston
1980	Kareem Abdul–Jabbar, Los Angeles

N.B.A. LIFETIME LEADERS

(Through June 1980)

Scoring

	Yrs	FG	FT	Pts
Wilt Chamberlain	14	12,681	6,057	31,419
Oscar Robertson	14	9,508	7,694	26,710
John Havlicek	16	10,513	5,394	26,395
Jerry West	14	9,016	7,160	25,192
Kareem Abdul-Jabbar	11	9,979	4,217	24,175
Elgin Baylor	14	8,693	5,763	23,149
Elvin Hayes	12	9,291	4,523	23,108
Hal Greer	15	8,504	4,578	21,586
Walt Bellamy	14	7,914	5,113	20,941
Bob Pettit	11	7,349	6,182	20,880

Scoring Average

(400 games or 10,000 minimum points)

	Games	Pts	Avg
Wilt Chamberlain	1,045	31,419	30.1
Kareem Abdul-Jabbar	855	24,175	28.3
Elgin Baylor	846	23,149	27.4
Jerry West	932	25,192	27.0
Bob McAdoo	583	15,627	26.8
Bob Pettit	792	20,880	26.4
Oscar Robertson	1,040	26,710	25.7
Pete Maravich	658	15,948	24.2
Elvin Hayes	978	23,108	23.6
Rick Barry	794	18,395	23.2

Field Goal Percentage

(2,000 field goals minimum)

	Att	FG	Pct
Artis Gilmore	4,174	2,332	.559
Kareem Abdul-Jabbar	17,983	9,979	.555
Walter Davis	4,022	2,207	.549
Wilt Chamberlain	23,497	12,681	.540
Marques Johnson	3,962	2,137	.539
George Gervin	6,635	3,561	.537
Adrian Dantley	4,174	2,226	.533
Clifford Ray	4,298	2,269	.528
Walt Ballamy	15,340	7,914	.516
Paul Westphal	8,384	4,310	.514

Free Throw Percentage

(2,000 free throws made minimum)

	Att	FT	Pct
Rick Barry	4,243	3,818	.900
Calvin Murphy	3,389	3,001	.886
Bill Sharman	3,557	3,413	.884
Mike Newlin	2,843	2,465	.867
Fred Brown	1,716	1,477	.861
Larry Siegfried	1,945	1,662	.854
Flynn Robinson	1,881	1,597	.849
Dolph Schayes	8,273	6,979	.844
Jack Marin	2,852	2,405	.843
Rickey Sobers	1,458	1,229	.843

Assists

Oscar Robertson	9,887
Lenny Wilkens	7,211
Bob Cousy	6,955
Guy Rodgers	6,917
Jerry West	6,238
John Havlicek	6,114
Dave Bing	5,397
Norm Van Lier	5,217
Walt Frazier	5,040
Gail Goodrich	4,805

Rebounds

Wilt Chamberlain	23,924
Bill Russell	21,620
Nate Thurmond	14,464
Walt Bellamy	14,241
Elvin Hayes	13,867
Wes Unseld	13,096
Jerry Lucas	12,942
Bob Pettit	12,849
Paul Silas	12,357
Kareem Abdul–Jabbar	12,346

N.B.A. INDIVIDUAL RECORDS

Most points, game—100, Wilt Chamberlain, Philadelphia vs. New York at Hershey, Pa., 1962
Most points, quarter—33, George Gervin, San Antonio, 1978
Most points, half—59, Wilt Chamberlain, Philadelphia, 1962
Most free throws, game—28, Wilt Chamberlain, Philadelphia, vs. New York at Hershey, Pa. 1962
Most free throws, quarter—13, David Thompson, Denver, 1978
Most free throws, half—19, Oscar Robertson, Cincinnati, 1964
Most field goals, game—28, Wilt Chamberlain, Philadelphia, 1962
Most consecutive field goals—18, Wilt Chamberlain, San Francisco, 1963; Wilt Chamberlain, Philadelphia, 1967
Most assists, game—29, Kevin Porter, New Jersey Nets, 1978
Most rebounds, game—55, Wilt Chamberlain, Philadelphia, 1963

N.B.A. TEAM RECORDS

Most points, game—173, Boston vs. Minneapolis, 1959
Most points, quarter—58, Buffalo vs. Boston, 1968
Most points, half—97, Atlanta vs. San Diego, 1970
Most points, overtime period—22, Detroit vs. Cleveland, 1973
Most field goals, game—72, Boston, 1959
Most field goals, quarter—23, Boston, 1959, 1972
Most field goals, half—40, Boston, 1959; Syracuse, 1963
Most assists, game—53, Milwaukee, 1978
Most rebounds, game—112, Philadelphia, 1959
Most points, both teams, game—316 (Philadelphia 169, New York 147), Hershey, Pa. 1962; (Cincinnati 165, San Diego 151), Cincinnati, 1970
Most points, both teams, quarter—96 (Boston 52, Minneapolis 44), 1959; (Detroit 53, Cincinnati 43), 1972
Most points, both teams, half—170 (Philadelphia 90, Cincinnati 80), Philadelphia, 1971
Longest winning streak—33, Los Angeles, 1971–72
Longest losing streak—20, Philadelphia, 1973
Longest winning streak at home—36, Philadelphia, 1966–67
Most games won, season—69, Los Angeles, 1971–72
Most games lost, season—73, Philadelphia, 1972–73
Highest average points per game—125.4, Philadelphia, 1961–62

NATIONAL BASKETBALL ASSOCIATION
FINAL STANDING OF THE CLUBS—1979–1980

EASTERN CONFERENCE
Atlantic Division

	W	L	Pct	Scoring For	Scoring Agst
Boston Celtics	61	21	.744	113.5	105.7
Philadelphia 76ers	59	23	.720	109.1	104.9
Washington Bullets	39	43	.476	107.0	109.5
New York Knicks	39	43	.476	114.0	115.1
New Jersey Nets	34	48	.415	108.3	109.5

Central Division

	W	L	Pct	Scoring For	Scoring Agst
Atlanta Hawks	50	32	.610	104.5	101.6
Houston Rockets	41	41	.500	110.8	110.6
San Antonio Spurs	41	41	.500	119.4	119.7
Indiana Pacers	37	45	.451	111.2	111.9
Cleveland Cavaliers	37	45	.451	114.1	113.8
Detroit Pistons	16	66	.195	108.9	117.2

WESTERN CONFERENCE
Midwest Division

	W	L	Pct	Scoring For	Scoring Agst
Milwaukee Bucks	49	33	.598	110.1	106.1
Kansas City Kings	47	35	.573	108.0	104.9
Chicago Bulls	30	52	.366	107.5	110.2
Denver Nuggets	30	52	.366	108.3	112.7
Utah Jazz	24	58	.293	102.4	108.4

Pacific Division

	W	L	Pct	Scoring For	Scoring Agst
Los Angeles Lakers	60	22	.732	115.1	109.2
Seattle SuperSonics	56	26	.683	108.5	103.8
Phoenix Suns	54	27	.671	111.1	107.5
Portland Trail Blazers	38	44	.463	102.5	103.3
San Diego Clippers	35	47	.427	107.6	111.7
Golden State Warriors	24	58	.293	103.6	108.0

PLAYOFFS

EASTERN CONFERENCE
First Round

Philadelphia defeated Washington, 2 games to 0
Houston defeated San Antonio, 2 games to 1

Semifinal Round

Philadelphia defeated Atlanta, 4 games to 1
Boston defeated Houston, 4 games to 0

Conference Final

Philadelphia defeated Boston, 4 games to 1
April 18—Philadelphia 96, Boston 93[1]
April 20—Boston 96, Philadelphia 90[1]
April 23—Philadelphia 99, Boston 97
April 25—Philadelphia 102, Boston 90
April 27—Philadelphia 105, Boston 94[1]
1. At Boston.

WESTERN CONFERENCE
First Round

Seattle defeated Portland, 2 games to 1
Phoenix defeated Kansas City, 2 games to 1

Semifinal Round

Los Angeles defeated Phoenix, 4 games to 1
Seattle defeated Milwaukee, 4 games to 3

Conference Final

Los Angeles defeated Seattle, 4 games to 1
April 22—Seattle 108, Los Angeles 107[1]
April 23—Los Angeles 108, Seattle 99[1]
April 25—Los Angeles 104, Seattle 100
April 27—Los Angeles 98, Seattle 93
April 30—Los Angeles 111, Seattle 105[1]
1. At Los Angeles.

Championship

Los Angeles defeated Philadelphia, 4 games to 2
May 4—Los Angeles 109, Philadelphia 102[1]
May 7—Philadelphia 107, Los Angeles 104[1]
May 10—Los Angeles 111, Philadelphia 101[2]
May 11—Philadelphia 105, Los Angeles 102[2]
May 14—Los Angeles 108, Philadelphia 103[1]
May 16—Los Angeles 123, Philadelphia 107[2]
1. At Los Angeles. 2. At Philadelphia. Most valuable player—Earvin (Magic) Johnson, Los Angeles.

LEADING SCORERS

	G	FG	FT	Pts	Pct
George Gervin, San Antonio	78	1,024	505	2,585	33.1
Lloyd Free, San Diego	68	737	572	2,055	30.2
Adrian Dantley, Utah	68	730	443	1,903	28.0
Julius Erving, Philadelphia	78	838	420	2,100	26.9
Moses Malone, Houston	82	778	563	2,119	25.8
Kareem Abdul-Jabbar, L.A.	82	835	364	2,034	24.8
Dan Issel, Denver	82	715	517	1,951	23.8
Elvin Hayes, Washington	81	761	334	1,859	23.0
Otis Birdsong, Kansas City	82	781	286	1,858	22.7
Mike Mitchell, Cleveland	82	775	270	1,820	22.2
Gus Williams, Seattle	82	739	331	1,816	22.1
Paul Westphal, Phoenix	82	692	382	1,792	21.9
Bill Cartwright, New York	82	665	451	1,781	21.7
Marques Johnson, Milwaukee	77	689	291	1,671	21.7
Walter Davis, Phoenix	75	657	299	1,613	21.5
Larry Bird, Boston	82	693	301	1,745	21.3
Mike Newlin, New Jersey	78	611	367	1,634	20.9
Ray Williams, New York	82	687	333	1,714	20.9
Reggie Theus, Chicago	82	566	500	1,660	20.2
Larry Kenon, San Antonio	78	647	270	1,565	20.1

FIELD GOAL LEADERS
(Minimum 300 FG made)

	FG	Att	Pct
Cedric Maxwell, Boston	457	750	.609
Kareem Abdul-Jabbar, Los Angeles	835	1,383	.604
Artis Gilmore, Chicago	305	513	.595
Adrian Dantley, Utah	730	1,267	.576
Tom Boswell, Utah	346	613	.564
Walter Davis, Phoenix	657	1,166	.563
Swen Nater, San Diego	443	761	.554
Kermit Washington, Portland	421	761	.553
Bill Cartwright, New York	665	1,215	.547
Marques Johnson, Milwaukee	689	1,267	.544

FREE THROW LEADERS
(Minimum 125 FT made)

	FT	Att	Pct
Rick Barry, Houston	143	153	.935
Calvin Murphy, Houston	271	302	.897
Ron Boone, Utah	175	196	.893
Paul Silas, San Antonio	339	382	.887
Mike Newlin, New Jersey	367	415	.884
Terry Furlow, Utah	171	196	.872

Roger Phegley, New Jersey	177	203	.872
Mike Bratz, Phoenix	141	162	.870
Kevin Grevey, Washington	216	249	.867
John Roche, Denver	175	202	.866

N.B.A. ALL-STAR TEAM—1980

First Team	Pos.	Second Team
Julius Erving, Philadelphia	F	Dan Roundfield, Atlanta
Larry Bird, Boston	F	Marques Johnson, Milwaukee
Kareem Abdul–Jabbar, Los Angeles	C	Moses Malone, Houston
George Gervin, San Antonio	G	Dennis Johnson, Seattle
Paul Westphal, Phoenix	G	Gus Williams, Seattle

ASSISTS LEADERS

(Minimum 70 games or 400 assists)

	G	No.	Avg
Michael Ray Richardson, N.Y.	82	832	10.1
Nate Archibald, Boston	80	671	8.4
Clarence Walker, Cleveland	76	607	8.0
Norman Nixon, Los Angeles	82	642	7.8
John Lucas, Golden State	80	602	7.5
Phil Ford, Kansas City	82	610	7.4
Earvin Johnson, Los Angeles	77	563	7.3
Maurice Cheeks, Philadelphia	79	556	7.0
Ed Jordan, New Jersey	82	557	6.8
Kevin Porter, Washington	70	457	6.5

BLOCKED SHOTS LEADERS

(Minimum 70 games or 100 blocked shots)

	G	No.	Avg
Kareem Abdul–Jabbar, L.A.	82	280	3.41
George Johnson, New Jersey	81	258	3.19
Wayne Rollins, Atlanta	82	244	2.98
Terry Tyler, Detroit	82	220	2.68
Elvin Hayes, Washington	81	189	2.33
Harvey Catchings, Milwaukee	72	162	2.25
Caldwell Jones, Philadelphia	80	162	2.03
Ben Poquette, Utah	82	162	1.98

J.C. Meriweather, New York	65	120	1.85
Julius Erving, Philadelphia	78	140	1.79

REBOUND LEADERS

(Minimum 70 games or 800 rebounds)

	G	Off	Def	Total	Avg
Swen Nater, San Diego	81	352	864	1,216	15.0
Moses Malone, Houston	82	573	617	1,190	14.5
Wes Unseld, Washington	82	334	760	1,094	13.3
Caldwell Jones, Philadelphia	80	219	731	950	11.9
Jack Sikma, Seattle	82	198	710	908	11.1
Elvin Hayes, Washington	81	269	627	896	11.1
Robert Parish, Golden State	72	247	536	783	10.9
Kareem Abdul–Jabbar, Los Angeles	82	190	696	886	10.8
Kermit Washington, Portland	80	325	517	842	10.5
Larry Bird, Boston	82	216	636	852	10.4

STEALS LEADERS

(Minimum 70 games or 125 steals)

	G	No.	Avg
Michael Ray Richardson, N.Y.	82	265	3.23
Ed Jordan, New Jersey	82	223	2.72
Dudley Bradley, Indiana	82	211	2.57
Gus Williams, Seattle	82	200	2.44
Earvin Johnson, Los Angeles	77	187	2.43
Maurice Cheeks, Philadelphia	79	183	2.32
Julius Erving, Philadelphia	78	170	2.18
Sonny Parker, Golden State	82	173	2.11
Clarence Walker, Cleveland	76	155	2.04
Ray Williams, New York	82	167	2.04

THREE-POINT FIELD GOAL LEADERS

(Minimum 25 made)

	FG	FGA	Pct
Fred Brown, Seattle	39	88	.443
Chris Ford, Boston	70	164	.427
Larry Bird, Boston	58	143	.406
John Roche, Denver	49	129	.380
Brian Taylor, San Diego	90	239	.377
Brian Winters, Milwaukee	38	102	.373
Kevin Grevey, Washington	34	92	.370
Joe Hassett, Indiana	69	198	.348
Rick Barry, Houston	73	221	.330
Freeman Williams, San Diego	42	128	.328

NATIONAL BASKETBALL ASSOCIATION GOVERNMENT

Commissioner's Office: Lawrence F. O'Brien. Commissioner; Simon P. Gourdine, Deputy Commissioner; Norman F. Drucker, Supervisor of Officials; Matt Winick, Director of Media Information.

WOMEN'S BASKETBALL LEAGUE (Professional league) FINAL STANDING OF THE TEAMS—1980

Eastern Division

	W	L	Pct
New York	28	7	.800
New Orleans	22	13	.629
New Jersey	19	17	.528
St. Louis	15	21	.417

Midwest Division

Iowa	24	12	.667
Minnesota	22	12	.647
Chicago	17	19	.472
Milwaukee	10	24	.294

Western Division

Houston	19	14	.576
San Francisco	18	18	.500
California	11	17	.393
Dallas	7	28	.200

PLAYOFFS

Semifinal Round

New York defeated San Francisco, 2 games to 0
Iowa defeated Minnesota, 2 games to 1

Championship Series

New York 128, Iowa 96
New York 119, Iowa 99
Iowa 119, New York 112
New York 125, Iowa 114
New York won series, 3 games to 1

HOCKEY

Ice hockey, by birth and upbringing a Canadian game, is an offshoot of field hockey. Some historians say that the first ice hockey game was played in Montreal in December 1879 between two teams composed almost exclusively of McGill University students, but others assert that earlier hockey games took place in Kingston, Ontario, or Halifax, Nova Scotia. In the Montreal game of 1879, there were fifteen players on a side, who used an assortment of crude sticks to keep the puck in motion. Early rules allowed nine men on a side, but the number was reduced to seven in 1886 and later to six.

The first governing body of the sport was the Amateur Hockey Association of Canada, organized in 1887. In the winter of 1894–95, a group of college students from the United States visited Canada and saw hockey played. They became enthused over the game and introduced it as a winter sport when they returned home. The first professional league was the International Hockey League, which operated in northern Michigan in 1904–06.

Until 1910, professionals and amateurs were allowed to play together on "mixed teams," but this arrangement ended with the formation of the first "big league," the National Hockey Association, in eastern Canada in 1910. The Pacific Coast League was organized in 1911 for western Canadian hockey. The league included Seattle and later other American cities. The National Hockey League replaced the National Hockey Association in 1917. Boston, in 1924, was the first American city to join that circuit. The league expanded to include western cities in 1967. The Stanley Cup was competed for by "mixed teams" from 1894 to 1910, thereafter by professionals. It was awarded to the winner of the N.H.L. playoffs from 1926–67 and now to the league champion. The World Hockey Association was organized in October 1972 and was dissolved after the 1978–79 season when the N.H.L. absorbed four of the teams.

STANLEY CUP WINNERS

Emblematic of World Professional Championship; N.H.L. Championship after 1967

1894	Montreal A.A.A.
1895	Montreal Victorias
1896	Winnipeg Victorias
1897–99	Montreal Victorias
1900	Montreal Shamrocks
1901	Winnipeg Victorias
1902	Montreal A.A.A.
1903–05	Ottawa Silver Seven
1906	Montreal Wanderers
1907	Kenora Thistles[1]
1907	Mont. Wanderers[2]
1908	Montreal Wanderers
1909	Ottawa Senators
1910	Montreal Wanderers
1911	Ottawa Senators
1912–13	Quebec Bulldogs
1914	Toronto
1915	Vancouver Millionaires
1916	Montreal Canadiens
1917	Seattle Metropolitans
1918	Toronto Arenas
1919	No champion
1920–21	Ottawa Senators
1922	Toronto St. Patricks
1923	Ottawa Senators
1924	Montreal Canadiens
1925	Victoria Cougars
1926	Montreal Maroons
1927	Ottawa Senators
1928	N.Y. Rangers
1929	Boston Bruins
1930–31	Montreal Canadiens
1932	Toronto Maple Leafs
1933	N.Y. Rangers
1934	Chicago Black Hawks
1935	Montreal Maroons
1936–37	Detroit Red Wings
1938	Chicago Black Hawks
1939	Boston Bruins
1940	N.Y. Rangers
1941	Boston Bruins
1942	Toronto Maple Leafs
1943	Detroit Red Wings
1944	Montreal Canadiens
1945	Toronto Maple Leafs
1946	Montreal Canadiens
1947–49	Toronto Maple Leafs
1950	Detroit Red Wings
1951	Toronto Maple Leafs
1952	Detroit Red Wings
1953	Montreal Canadiens
1954–55	Detroit Red Wings
1956–60	Montreal Canadiens
1961	Chicago Black Hawks
1962–64	Toronto Maple Leafs
1965–66	Montreal Canadiens
1967	Toronto Maple Leafs
1968–69	Montreal Canadiens
1970	Boston Bruins
1971	Montreal Canadiens
1972	Boston Bruins
1973	Montreal Canadiens
1974–75	Philadelphia Flyers
1976–79	Montreal Canadiens
1980	New York Islanders

1. January. 2. March.

NATIONAL HOCKEY LEAGUE YEARLY TROPHY WINNERS

The Hart Trophy—Most Valuable Player

1924	Frank Nighbor, Ottawa
1925	Billy Burch, Hamilton
1926	Nels Stewart, Montreal Maroons
1927	Herb Gardiner, Montreal Canadiens
1928	Howie Morenz, Montreal Canadiens
1929	Roy Worters, New York Americans
1930	Nels Stewart, Montreal Maroons
1931–32	Howie Morenz, Montreal Canadiens
1933	Eddie Shore, Boston
1934	Aurel Joliat, Montreal Canadiens
1935–36	Eddie Shore, Boston
1937	Babe Siebert, Montreal Canadiens
1938	Eddie Shore, Boston
1939	Toe Blake, Montreal Canadiens
1940	Ebbie Goodfellow, Detroit
1941	Bill Cowley, Boston
1942	Tom Anderson, New York Americans
1943	Bill Cowley, Boston
1944	Babe Pratt, Toronto
1945	Elmer Lach, Montreal Canadiens
1946	Max Bentley, Chicago
1947	Maurice Richard, Montreal Canadiens
1948	Buddy O'Connor, New York Rangers
1949	Sid Abel, Detroit
1950	Chuck Rayner, New York Rangers
1951	Milt Schmidt, Boston
1952–53	Gordon Howe, Detroit
1954	Al Rollins, Chicago
1955	Ted Kennedy, Toronto
1956	Jean Beliveau, Montreal Canadiens
1957–58	Gordon Howe, Detroit
1959	Andy Bathgate, New York Rangers
1960	Gordon Howe, Detroit
1961	Bernie Geoffrion, Montreal Canadiens
1962	Jacques Plante, Montreal Canadiens
1963	Gordon Howe, Detroit
1964	Jean Beliveau, Montreal Canadiens
1965–66	Bobby Hull, Chicago
1967–68	Stan Mikita, Chicago
1969	Phil Esposito, Boston

1970–72	Bobby Orr, Boston
1973	Bobby Clarke, Philadelphia
1974	Phil Esposito, Boston
1975–76	Bobby Clarke, Philadelphia
1977–78	Guy Lafleur, Montreal
1979	Bryan Trottier, N.Y. Islanders
1980	Wayne Gretzky, Edmonton

Vezina Trophy—Leading Goalkeeper

1956–60	Jacques Plante, Montreal
1961	Johnny Bower, Toronto
1962	Jacques Plante, Montreal
1963	Glenn Hall, Chicago
1964	Charlie Hodge, Montreal
1965	Terry Sawchuk–Johnny Bower, Toronto
1966	Lorne Worsley–Charlie Hodge, Montreal
1967	Glenn Hall–Denis DeJordy, Chicago
1968	Lorne Worsley–Rogatien Vachon, Montreal
1969	Glenn Hall–Jacques Plante, St. Louis
1970	Tony Esposito, Chicago
1971	Ed Giacomin–Gilles Villemure, New York
1972	Tony Esposito–Gary Smith, Chicago
1973	Ken Dryden, Montreal
1974	Bernie Parent, Philadelphia, and Tony Esposito, Chicago
1975	Bernie Parent, Philadelphia
1976	Ken Dryden, Montreal
1977–79	Ken Dryden–Michel Larocque, Montreal
1980	Bob Sauve–Don Edwards, Buffalo

James Norris Trophy—Defenseman

1954	Red Kelly, Detroit
1955–58	Doug Harvey, Montreal
1959	Tom Johnson, Montreal
1960–62	Doug Harvey, Montreal, New York (62)
1963–65	Pierre Pilote, Chicago
1966	Jacques Laperriere, Montreal
1967	Harry Howell, New York
1968–75	Bobby Orr, Boston
1976	Denis Potvin, N.Y. Islanders
1977	Larry Robinson, Montreal
1978	Denis Potvin, N.Y. Islanders
1980	Larry Robinson, Montreal

Lady Byng Trophy—Sportsmanship

1960	Don McKenney, Boston
1961	Red Kelly, Detroit
1962–63	Dave Keon, Toronto
1964	Ken Wharram, Chicago
1965	Bobby Hull, Chicago
1966	Alex Delvecchio, Detroit
1967–68	Stan Mikita, Chicago
1969	Alex Delvecchio, Detroit
1970	Phil Goyette, St. Louis
1971	John Bucyk, Boston
1972	Jean Ratelle, New York
1973	Gil Perreault, Buffalo
1974	John Buyck, Boston
1975	Marcel Dionne, Detroit
1976	Jean Ratelle, N.Y. Rangers–Boston
1977	Marcel Dionne, Los Angeles
1978	Butch Goring, Los Angeles
1979	Bob MacMillan, Atlanta
1980	Wayne Gretzky, Edmonton

Calder Trophy—Rookie

1962	Bobby Rousseau, Montreal
1963	Kent Douglas, Toronto
1964	Jacques Laperriere, Montreal
1965	Roger Crozier, Detroit
1966	Brit Selby, Toronto
1967	Bobby Orr, Boston
1968	Derek Sanderson, Boston
1969	Danny Grant, Minnesota
1970	Tony Esposito, Chicago
1971	Gilbert Perreault, Buffalo
1972	Ken Dryden, Montreal
1973	Steve Vickers, New York Rangers
1974	Denis Potvin, N.Y. Islanders
1975	Eric Vail, Atlanta
1976	Bryan Trottier, N.Y. Islanders
1977	Willi Plett, Atlanta
1978	Mike Bossy, N.Y. Islanders
1979	Bobby Smith, Minnesota
1980	Ray Bourque, Boston

N.H.L. CAREER SCORING LEADERS

(Listed in order of total points scored; figures in parentheses indicate ranking in goals scored)

	Yrs	Games	G	A	Pts
Gordie Howe (1)	26	1,767	801	1,049	1,850
Phil Esposito (2)[1]	17	1,241	710	860	1,570
Stan Mikita (6)	21	1,407	541	926	1,467
John Bucyk (4)	23	1,540	556	813	1,369
Alex Delvecchio (11)	23	1,549	456	825	1,281
Jean Ratelle (10)[1]	18	1,234	480	750	1,230
Norm Ullman (9)	20	1,410	490	739	1,229
Jean Beliveau (8)	18	1,125	507	712	1,219
Bobby Hull (3)[1]	16	1,063	610	560	1,170
Frank Mohovlich (7)	17	1,181	533	570	1,103
Henri Richard (23)	20	1,256	358	688	1,046
Rod Gilbert (13)	16	1,065	406	615	1,021
Andy Bathgate (24)	16	1,069	349	624	973
Maurice Richard (5)	18	978	544	421	965
Guy Lafleur (14)[1]	9	677	405	536	941
Bobby Clarke (36)[1]	11	849	282	655	937
Marcel Dionne (18)[1]	9	699	380	548	928
Dave Keon (20)[1]	16	1,138	375	545	920
Bobby Orr (44)	11	651	270	645	915
Gilbert Perreault (25)[1]	10	753	340	529	869

1. Still active in N.H.L.

Art Ross Trophy—Leading scorer

1955	Bernie Geoffrion, Montreal
1956	Jean Beliveau, Montreal
1957	Gordie Howe, Detroit
1958–59	Dickie Moore, Montreal
1960	Bobby Hull, Chicago
1961	Bernie Geoffrion, Montreal
1962	Bobby Hull, Chicago
1963	Gordie Howe, Detroit
1964–65	Stan Mikita, Chicago
1966	Bobby Hull, Chicago
1967–68	Stan Mikita, Chicago
1969	Phil Esposito, Boston
1970	Bobby Orr, Boston
1971–74	Phil Esposito, Boston
1975	Bobby Orr, Boston
1976–78	Guy Lafleur, Montreal
1979	Bryan Trottier, N.Y. Islanders
1980	Marcel Dionne, Los Angeles

N.H.L. CHAMPIONS

Prince of Wales Trophy

1939	Boston
1940	Boston
1941	Boston
1942	New York
1943	Detroit
1944–47	Montreal
1948	Toronto
1948–55	Detroit
1956	Montreal
1957	Detroit
1958–62	Montreal
1963	Toronto
1964	Montreal
1965	Detroit
1966	Montreal
1967	Chicago

Eastern Division

1968–69	Montreal
1970	Chicago
1971	Boston
1972	Boston
1973	Montreal
1974	Boston

Prince of Wales Conference

1975	Buffalo
1976–79	Montreal
1980	Buffalo

CAMPBELL BOWL
Western Division

1968	Philadelphia
1969	St. Louis
1970	St. Louis
1971–73	Chicago
1974	Philadelphia

Clarence Campbell Conference

1975	Philadelphia
1976–77	Philadelphia
1978–79	N.Y. Islanders
1980	Philadelphia

WORLD HOCKEY ASSOCIATION YEARLY LEADERS

Most Valuable Player

1973	Bobby Hull, Winnipeg
1974	Gordie Howe, Houston
1975	Bobby Hull, Winnipeg
1976	Marc Tardif, Quebec
1977	Robbie Ftorek, Phoenix
1978	Marc Tardif, Quebec
1979	Dave Dryden, Edmonton

Best Defenseman

1973	J. C. Tremblay, Quebec
1974	Pat Stapleton, Chicago
1975	J. C. Tremblay, Quebec
1976	Paul Shmyr, Cleveland
1977	Ron Plumb, Cincinnati
1978	Lars-Erik Sjoberg, Winnipeg
1979	Rick Ley, New England

Best Goaltender

1973	Gerry Cheevers, Cleveland
1974	Don McLeod, Houston
1975	Ron Grahame, Houston
1976	Michel Dion, Indianapolis
1977	Ron Grahame, Houston
1978	Al Smith, New England
1979	Dave Dryden, Edmonton

Scoring Champion

1973	Andre Lacroix, Philadelphia
1974	Mike Walton, Minnesota
1975	Andre Lacroix, San Diego
1976	Marc Tardif, Quebec
1977	Real Cloutier, Quebec
1978	Marc Tardif, Quebec
1979	Real Cloutier, Quebec

Most Gentlemanly

1973	Ted Hampson, Minnesota
1974	Ralph Backstrom, Chicago
1975	Mike Rogers, Edmonton
1976	Vaclav Nedomansky, Toronto
1977–78	Dave Keon, New England
1979	Kent Nillson, Winnipeg

W.H.A. LEAGUE CHAMPIONS

Winners of AVCO Trophy

1972–73	New Eng. Whalers
1973–74	Houston Aeros
1974–75	Houston Aeros
1975–76	Winnipeg Jets
1976–77	Quebec Nordiques
1977–79	Winnipeg Jets

NATIONAL HOCKEY LEAGUE

(Source: John Halligan, Publicity Director, New York Rangers)

Final Standing of the Clubs—1979–80

CLARENCE CAMPBELL CONFERENCE
Patrick Division

	W	L	T	GF	GA	Pts
Philadelphia Flyers	48	12	20	327	254	116
New York Islanders	39	28	13	281	247	91
New York Rangers	38	32	10	308	284	86
Atlanta Flames	35	32	13	282	269	83
Washington Capitals	27	40	13	261	293	67

Smythe Division

	W	L	T	GF	GA	Pts
Chicago Black Hawks	34	27	19	241	250	87
St. Louis Blues	34	34	12	266	278	80
Vancouver Canucks	27	37	16	256	281	70
Edmonton Oilers	28	39	13	301	322	69
Colorado Rockies	19	48	13	234	308	51
Winnipeg Jets	20	49	11	214	314	51

PRINCE OF WALES CONFERENCE
Norris Division

	W	L	T	GF	GA	Pts
Montreal Canadiens	47	20	13	328	240	107
Los Angeles Kings	30	36	14	290	313	74
Pittsburgh Penguins	30	37	13	251	303	73
Hartford Whalers	27	34	19	303	312	73
Detroit Red Wings	26	43	11	268	306	63

Adams Division

	W	L	T	GF	GA	Pts
Buffalo Sabres	47	17	16	318	201	110
Boston Bruins	46	21	13	310	234	105
Minnesota North Stars	36	28	16	311	253	88
Toronto Maple Leafs	35	40	5	304	327	75
Quebec Nordiques	25	44	11	248	313	61

Stanley Cup Playoffs

Preliminary Round

New York Islanders defeated Los Angeles, 3 games to 1
New York Rangers defeated Atlanta, 3 games to 1
Boston defeated Pittsburgh, 3 games to 2
Buffalo defeated Vancouver, 3 games to 1
Chicago defeated St. Louis, 3 games to 0
Philadelphia defeated Edmonton, 3 games to 0
Montreal defeated Hartford, 3 games to 0
Minnesota defeated Toronto, 3 games to 0

Quarterfinal Round

New York Islanders defeated Boston, 4 games to 1
Philadelphia defeated New York Rangers, 4 games to 1
Buffalo defeated Chicago, 4 games to 0
Minnesota defeated Montreal, 4 games to 3

Semifinal Round

Islanders defeated Buffalo, 4 games to 2
- April 29—Islanders 4, Buffalo 1[1]
- May 1—Islanders 2, Buffalo 1 (2 overtimes)[1]
- May 3—Islanders 7, Buffalo 4
- May 6—Buffalo 7, Islanders 4
- May 8—Buffalo 2, Islanders 0[1]
- May 10—Islanders 5, Buffalo 2

1. At Buffalo.

Philadelphia defeated Minnesota, 4 games to 1
- April 29—Minnesota 6, Philadelphia 5[1]
- May 1—Philadelphia 7, Minnesota 0[1]
- May 4—Philadelphia 5, Minnesota 3
- May 6—Philadelphia 3, Minnesota 2
- May 8—Philadelphia 7, Minnesota 3[1]

1. At Philadelphia.

Championship

New York Islanders defeated Philadelphia, 4 games to 2
- May 13—Islanders 4, Philadelphia 3 (overtime)[1]
- May 15—Philadelphia 8, Islanders 3[1]
- May 17—Islanders 6, Philadelphia 2
- May 19—Islanders 5, Philadelphia 2
- May 22—Philadelphia 6, Islanders 3[1]
- May 24—Islanders 5, Philadelphia 4 (overtime)

1. At Philadelphia.

N.H.L. LEADING SCORERS—1979-80

	GP	G	A	Pts
Marcel Dionne, Los Angeles	80	53	84	137*
Wayne Gretzky, Edmonton	79	51	86	137
Guy Lafleur, Montreal	75	50	75	125
Gil Perreault, Buffalo	80	40	66	106
Mike Rogers, Hartford	80	44	61	105
Bryan Trottier, Islanders	78	42	62	104
Charlie Simmer, Los Angeles	64	56	44	100
Blaine Stoughton, Hartford	80	56	44	100
Darryl Sittler, Toronto	73	40	57	97
Blair MacDonald, Edmonton	80	46	48	94
Bernie Federko, St. Louis	79	38	56	94
Al MacAdam, Minnesota	80	42	51	93
Kent Nilsson, Atlanta	80	40	53	93
Mike Bossy, Islanders	75	51	41	92
Rick Middleton, Boston	80	40	52	92
Dave Taylor, Los Angeles	61	38	53	91
Pierre Larouche, Montreal	73	50	40	90

*Won scoring title for getting more goals than Gretzky.

N.H.L. LEADING GOALTENDERS—1979-80

	G	Min	GA	Avg
Bob Sauve, Buffalo	32	1,880	74	2.36
Dennis Herron, Montreal	34	1,909	80	2.51
Don Edwards, Buffalo	49	2,920	125	2.57
Pete Peeters, Philadelphia	40	2,373	108	2.73
Gilles Gilbert, Boston	33	1,933	88	2.73
Gerry Cheevers, Boston	42	2,479	116	2.81
Billy Smith, Islanders	38	2,114	104	2.95
Tony Esposito, Chicago	69	4,140	205	2.97
Glenn Resch, Islanders	45	2,606	132	3.04
Gilles Meloche, Minnesota	54	3,141	160	3.06
Top Team Scores				
Buffalo (Sauve, Edwards)	80	4,800	201	2.51
Boston (Gilbert, Cheevers, Yves Belanger, Marco Baron, Jim Stewart)	80	4,800	234	2.93

N.H.L. ALL-STAR TEAMS—1980

First Team	Pos.	Second Team
Tony Esposito, Chicago	G	Don Edwards, Buffalo
Larry Robinson, Montreal	D	Borje Salming, Toronto
Ray Borque, Boston	D	Jim Schoenfeld, Buffalo
Marcel Dionne, Los Angeles	C	Wayne Gretzky, Edmonton
Charlie Simmer, Los Angeles	LW	Steve Shutt, Montreal
Guy Lafleur, Montreal	RW	Danny Gare, Buffalo

OTHER N.H.L. AWARDS—1980

Selke (Best defensive forward)—Bob Gainey, Montreal
Smythe (Most valuable in playoffs)—Bryan Trottier, New York Islanders

Amateur Leagues

International League—Regular season: North Division: Kalamazoo; South: Fort Wayne. Playoffs: Kalamazoo defeated Fort Wayne, 4 games to 2.

Eastern League—Regular season: Erie. Playoffs: Erie defeated Baltimore, 4 games to 1.

Western League—Regular season: West Division: Portland; East: Regina. Playoffs: Regina defeated Victoria, 4 games to 1.

Ontario Major League—Regular season: Leyden Division: Peterborough; Emms Division: Windsor. Playoffs: Peterborough defeated Windsor, 4 games to 0.

Quebec Major League—Regular season: Lebel Division: Cornwall; Dilio Division: Sherbrooke. Playoffs: Cornwall defeated Sherbrooke, 4 games to 2.

Memorial Cup (Canada juniors)—Cornwall.

WORLD HOCKEY ASSOCIATION

Final Standing of the Clubs—1978-79

	W	L	T	GF	GA	Pts
Edmonton Oilers	48	30	2	340	266	98
Quebec Nordiques	41	34	5	288	271	87
Winnipeg Jets	39	35	6	307	306	84
New England Whalers	37	34	9	298	287	83
Cincinnati Stingers	33	41	6	274	284	72
Birmingham Bulls	32	42	6	286	311	70

Avco Trophy Playoffs

Preliminary Round

New England defeated Cincinnati, 2 games to 1

Semifinal Round

Edmonton defeated New England, 4 games to 3
Winnipeg defeated Quebec, 4 games to 0

Championship

Winnipeg defeated Edmonton, 4 games to 2
- May 11—Winnipeg defeated Edmonton, 3–1[1]
- May 13—Winnipeg defeated Edmonton, 3–2[1]
- May 15—Edmonton defeated Winnipeg, 8–3
- May 16—Winnipeg defeated Edmonton, 3–2
- May 18—Edmonton defeated Winnipeg, 10–2[1]
- May 20—Winnipeg defeated Edmonton, 7–3

1. At Edmonton.

W.H.A. LEADING SCORERS—1978-79

	GP	G	A	Pts
Real Cloutier, Quebec	77	75	54	129
Robbie Ftorek, Cincinnati	80	39	77	116
Wayne Gretzky, Edmonton	80	46	64	110
Mark Howe, New England	77	42	65	107
Kent Nilsson, Winnipeg	78	39	68	107
Morris Lukowich, Winnipeg	80	65	34	99
Marc Tardif, Quebec	74	41	55	96
Andre Lacroix, New England	78	32	56	88
Peter Sullivan, Winnipeg	80	46	40	86
Terry Ruskowski, Winnipeg	75	20	66	86
Serge Bernier, Quebec	65	36	46	82
Rich Leduc, Quebec	74	35	41	76
Mike Rogers, New England	80	27	45	72
Blair MacDonald, Edmonton	80	34	37	71
Reg Thomas, Cincinnati	80	32	39	71

W.H.A. LEADING GOALTENDERS—1978-79

	G	Min	GA	Avg
Dave Dryden, Edmonton	63	3,531	170	2.89
Richard Brodeur, Quebec	42	2,633	126	3.11
Jim Corsi, Quebec	40	2,291	126	3.30
Al Smith, New England	40	2,396	132	3.31
Michel Dion, Cincinnati	30	1,681	93	3.32
Mike Liut, Cincinnati	54	3,181	184	3.47
John Garrett, New England	41	2,496	149	3.58

W.H.A. ALL-STAR TEAMS—1979

First Team	Pos.	Second Team
Dave Dryden, Edmonton	G	Richard Brodeur, Quebec
Rick Ley, New England	D	Paul Shmyr, Edmonton
Rob Ramage, Birmingham	D	Dave Langevin, Edmonton
Robbie Ftorek, Cincinnati	C	Wayne Gretzky, Edmonton
Real Cloutier, Quebec	RW	Blair MacDonald, Edmonton
Mark Howe, New England	LW	Morris Lukowich, Winnipeg

OTHER 1979 AWARDS

Most valuable player—Dave Dryden, Edmonton
Rookie of year—Wayne Gretzky, Cincinnati
Most gentlemanly—Kent Nillson, Winnipeg
Best defenseman—Rick Ley, New England
Leading scorer—Real Cloutier, Quebec
Most valuable in playoffs—Rich Preston, Winnipeg

AMATEUR CHAMPIONS—1980

N.C.A.A. Division I (Providence, R.I., March 27–29)—Final: North Dakota defeated Northern Michigan, 5–2. Third place: Dartmouth defeated Cornell, 8–4. Semifinals: North Dakota defeated Dartmouth, 4–1; Northern Michigan defeated Cornell, 5–4.

N.C.A.A. Division II (Elmira, N.Y., March 14–16)—Final: Mankato State (Minn.) defeated Elmira College, 5–2. Third place: Lowell (Mass.) defeated Merrimack, 8–7.

E.C.A.C. Division I—Final: Cornell defeated Dartmouth, 5–1. Third place: Providence defeated Clarkson, 6–5, (overtime). Semifinals: Cornell defeated Providence, 6–5; Dartmouth defeated Clarkson, 6–4. Quarterfinals: Clarkson defeated Vermont, 8–3; Cornell defeated Boston College, 5–1; Dartmouth defeated R.P.I., 8–0; Providence defeated Colgate, 8–3.

N.A.I.A.—Final: Bemidji State (Minn.) defeated Michigan–Dearborn, 4–3. Third place: Wisconsin–Superior defeated Wisconsin–River Falls, 11–4.

C.C.H.A.—Final: Northern Michigan defeated Ferris State, Big Rapids, Mich., 8–6.

W.C.H.A.—Final: North Dakota defeated Minnesota.

MINOR LEAGUE HOCKEY CHAMPIONS
American League—1980

	W	L	T	GF	GA	Pts
Northern Division						
New Brunswick Hawks*	44	27	8	325	271	96
Nova Scotia Voyageurs*	43	29	7	331	271	93
Maine Mariners	41	28	11	307	266	93
Adirondack Red Wings	32	37	11	297	309	75
Springfield Indians	31	37	12	292	302	74
Southern Division						
New Haven Nighthawks	46	24	9	350	305	101
Hershey Bears	35	39	6	289	273	76
Syracuse Firebirds	31	42	7	303	364	69
Rochester Americans	28	42	10	260	327	66
Binghamton Dusters	24	49	7	268	334	55

*New Brunswick–Nova Scotia game postponed earlier not played because it did not affect standing.

CALDER CUP PLAYOFFS
Quarterfinals

Maine defeated Nova Scotia, 4 games to 2
New Brunswick defeated Adirondack, 4 games to 1
Hershey defeated Syracuse, 4 games to 0
New Haven defeated Rochester, 4 games to 0

Semifinals

Hershey defeated New Haven, 4 games to 2
New Brunswick defeated Maine, 4 games to 2

Final

Hershey defeated New Brunswick, 4 games to 2

Central League—1980

	W	L	T	GF	GA	Pts
Salt Lake City Golden Eagles	49	24	7	342	259	105
Indianapolis Checkers	40	33	7	275	238	87
Fort Worth Texans	37	34	9	312	398	83
Birmingham Bulls	36	39	5	260	295	77
Tulsa Oilers	34	37	9	339	256	77
Houston Apollos	32	38	10	300	319	74
Oklahoma City Stars	30	44	3	261	268	69
Dallas Black Hawks	29	43	8	291	334	66

ADAMS CUP PLAYOFFS
Semifinals

Fort Worth defeated Indianapolis, 3 games to 1
Salt Lake defeated Houston, 4 games to 2

Final

Salt Lake defeated Fort Worth, 4 games to 3

STANDARD MEASUREMENTS IN SPORTS

BASEBALL

Home plate to pitcher's box: 60 feet 6 inches.
Plate to second base: 127 feet 3 3/8 inches.
Distance from base to base (home plate included): 90 feet.
Size of bases: 15 inches by 15 inches.
Pitcher's plate: 24 inches by 6 inches.
Batter's box: 3 feet by 4 feet.
Home plate: 17 inches by 17 inches, cut to a point at rear.
Home plate to backstop: Not less than 60 feet (recommended).
Weight of ball: Not less than 5 ounces nor more than 5 1/4 ounces.
Circumference of ball: Not less than 9 inches nor more than 9 1/4 inches.
Bat: Must be round, not over 2 3/4 inches in diameter at thickest part, nor more than 42 inches in length, and of solid wood in one piece or laminated.

FOOTBALL

Length of field: 120 yards. (including 10 yards of end zone at each end).
Width of field: 53 1/3 yards (160 feet).
Height of goal posts: At least 20 feet.
Height of crossbar: 10 feet.
Width of goal posts (above crossbar): 23 feet 4 inches, inside to inside, and not more than 24 feet, outside to outside.
Length of ball: 11 to 11.25 inches (long axis).
Circumference of ball: 21.25 to 21.50 inches (middle); 28 to 28.5 inches (long axis).

LAWN TENNIS

Size of court: Rectangle 78 feet long and 27 feet wide (singles); 78 feet long and 36 feet wide (doubles).
Height of net: 3 feet in center, gradually rising to reach 3-foot 6-inch posts at a point 3 feet outside each side of court.
Ball: Shall be more than 2 1/2 inches and less than 2 5/8 inches in diameter and weight more than 2 ounces and less than 2 1/16 ounces.
Service line: 21 feet from net.

HOCKEY

Size of rink: 200 feet long by 85 feet wide surrounded by a wooden wall not less than 40 inches and not more than 48 inches above level of ice.
Size of goal: 6 feet wide by 4 feet in height.
Puck: 1 inch thick and 3 inches in diameter; made of vulcanized rubber; weight 5 1/2 to 6 ounces.
Length of stick: Not more than 55 inches from heel to end of shaft nor 12 1/2 inches from heel to end of blade. Blade should not be more than 3 inches in width but not less than 2 inches, except goal keeper's stick, which shall not exceed 3 1/2 inches in width except at the heel, where it must not exceed 4 1/2 inches.

BOWLING

Lane dimensions: Overall length 62 feet 10 3/16 inches, measuring from foul line to pit (not including tail plank), with 1/2 inch tolerance permitted. Foul line to center of No. 1 pinspot 60 feet, with 1/2 inch tolerance permitted. Lane width, 41 1/2 inches with a tolerance of 1/2 inch permitted. Approach, not less than 15 feet. Gutters, 9 5/16 inches wide with 3/16 plus or 5/16 minus tolerances permitted.
Ball: Circumference, not more than 27 inches. Weight, 16 pounds maximum.

GOLF

Weight of ball: Not greater than 1.620 ounces avoirdupois.
Size of ball: Not less than 1.680 inches in diameter.
Velocity of ball: Not greater than 250 feet per second when tested on U.S.G.A. apparatus, with 2 percent tolerance.
Hole: 4 1/4 inches in diamater and at least 4 inches deep.
Clubs: 14 is the maximum number permitted.

BASKETBALL

(National Collegiate A.A. Rules)
Playing court: College: 94 feet long by 50 feet wide (ideal dimensions). High School: 84 feet long by 50 feet wide (ideal inside dimensions).
Baskets: Rings 18 inches in inside diameter, with white cord 12–mesh nets, 15 to 18 inches in length. Each ring is made of metal, is not more than 5/8 of an inch in diameter, and is bright orange in color.
Height of basket: 10 feet (upper edge).
Weight of ball: Not less than 20 ounces nor more than 22.
Circumference of ball: No greater than 30 inches and not less than 29½.
Free-throw line: 15 feet from the face of the backboard, 2 inches wide.

BOXING

Ring: Professional matches take place in an area not less than 18 nor more than 24 feet square including apron. It is enclosed by four covered ropes, each not less than one inch in diameter. The floor has a 2–inch padding of Ensolite (or equivalent) underneath ring cover that extends at least 6 inches beyond the roped area in the case of elevated rings. For A.A.U. boxing, not less than 16 nor more than 20 feet square within the ropes. The floor must extend beyond the ring ropes not less than 2 feet. The ring posts shall be connected to the ring ropes with the extension not shorter than 18 inches and must be properly padded.
Gloves: In professional fights, not less than 8–ounce gloves generally are used. A.A.U., not less than 10 ounces for all divisions; for international competition not less than 8 ounces.

LUGE

WORLD CHAMPIONSHIPS

(Moso in Pessiria, Italy, Feb. 1–3, 1980)

Men—Erich Graber, Italy
Women—Delia Vaudin, Italy
Doubles—Poernbacher–Pineter, Italy

BILLIARDS

WORLD CHAMPIONS—1980

Men's pocket—Nick Varner, Owensboro, Ky.
Women's pocket—Jean Balukas, Brooklyn, N.Y.
Snooker—Cliff Thorborn, Canada

FIGURE SKATING

WORLD CHAMPIONS

Men

1960	Alain Giletti, France
1961	No competition
1962	Donald Jackson, Canada
1963	Don McPherson, Canada
1964	Manfred Schnelldorfer, West Germany
1965	Alain Calmat, France
1966–68	Emmerich Danzer, Austria
1969–70	Tim Wood, United States
1971–73	Ondrej Nepela, Czechoslovakia
1974	Jan Hoffman, East Germany
1975	Sergei Yolkov, U.S.S.R.
1976	John Curry, Britain
1977	Vladimir Kovelov, U.S.S.R.
1978	Charles Tickner, United States
1979	Vladimir Kovalev, U.S.S.R.
1980	Jan Hoffmann, East Germany

Women

1956–60	Carol Heiss, United States
1961	No competition
1962–64	Sjoukje Dijkstra, Netherlands
1965	Petra Burka, Canada
1966–68	Peggy Fleming, United States
1969–70	Gabriele Seyfert, East Germany
1971–72	Beatrix Schuba, Austria
1973	Karen Magnusson, Canada
1974	Christine Errath, East Germany
1975	Dianne de Leeuw, Netherlands
1976	Dorothy Hamill, United States
1977	Linda Fratianne, United States
1978	Anett Poetzsch, East Germany
1979	Linda Fratianne, United States
1980	Anett Poetzsch, East Germany

U.S. CHAMPIONS

Men

1946–52	Richard Button
1953–56	Hayes Jenkins
1957–60	David Jenkins
1961	Bradley Lord
1962	Monty Hoyt
1963	Tommy Litz
1964	Scott Allen
1965	Gary Visconti
1966	Scott Allen
1967	Gary Visconti
1968–70	Tim Wood
1971	John M. Petkevich
1972	Ken Shelley
1973–75	Gordon McKellen
1976	Terry Kubicka
1977–80	Charles Tickner

Women

1943–48	Gretchen Merrill
1949–50	Yvonne Sherman
1951	Sonya Klopfer
1952–56	Tenley Albright
1957–60	Carol Heiss
1961	Laurence Owen
1962	Barbara Roles Pursley
1963	Lorraine Hanlon
1964–68	Peggy Fleming
1969–73	Janet Lynn
1974–76	Dorothy Hamill
1977–80	Linda Fratianne

WORLD CHAMPIONS—1980

(Dortmund, West Germany, March 11–15, 1980)

Men's singles—Jan Hoffmann, East Germany
Women's singles—Anett Poetzsch, East Germany
Pairs—Marina Chersekova and Sergei Shakrai, U.S.S.R.
Dance—Krisztina Regoeczy and Andras Sallay, Hungary

UNITED STATES CHAMPIONS—1980

(Atlanta, Ga., Jan. 18–20, 1980)

Men's singles—Charles Tickner, Littleton, Colo.
Women's singles—Linda Fratianne, Northridge, Calif.
Pairs—Tai Babilonia, Mission Hills, Calif., and Randy Gardner, Los Angeles
Dance—Stacey Smith, Wilmington, Del., and John Summers, Vienna, Va.

BOWLING

AMERICAN BOWLING CONGRESS CHAMPIONS

Year	Singles	All-events
1959	Ed Lubanski	Ed Lubanski
1960	Paul Kulbaga	Vince Lucci
1961	Lyle Spooner	Luke Karen
1962	Andy Renaldo	Billy Young
1963	Fred Delello	Bus Owalt
1964	Jim Stefanich	Les Zikes, Jr.
1965	Ken Roeth	Tom Hathaway
1966	Don Chapman	John Wilcox
1967	Frank Perry	Gary Lewis
1968	Wayne Kowalski	Vince Mazzanti
1969	Greg Campbell	Eddie Jackson
1970	Jake Yoder	Mike Berlin
1971	Al Cohn	Al Cohn
1972	Bill Pointer	Mac Lowry
1973	Ed Thompson	Ron Woolet
1974	Gene Krause	Bob Hart
1975	Jim Setser	Bobby Meadows
1976	Mike Putzer	Jim Lindquist
1977	Frank Gadaleto	Bud Debenham
1978	Rich Mersek	Chris Cobus
1979	Ed Bird	Nelson Burton, Jr.
1980	Mike Eaton	Steve Fehr

BOWLING PROPRIETORS' ASSOCIATION OF AMERICA—MEN

United States Open[1]

1971	Mike Lemongello
1972	Don Johnson
1973	Mike McGrath
1974	Larry Laub
1975	Steve Neff
1976	Paul Moser
1977	Johnny Petraglia
1978	Nelson Burton, Jr.
1979	Joe Berardi
1980	Steve Martin

1. Replaced All-Star tournament and is rolled as part of B.P.A. tour.

PROFESSIONAL BOWLERS ASSOCIATION

National Championship Tournament

1960	Don Carter	1966	Wayne Zahn	1972	Johnny Guenther	1978	Warren Nelson
1961	Dave Soutar	1967	Dave Davis	1973	Earl Anthony	1979	Mike Aulby
1962	Carmen Salvino	1968	Wayne Zahn	1974	Earl Anthony	1980	Johnny Petraglia
1963	Billy Hardwick	1969	Mike McGrath	1975	Earl Anthony		
1964	Bob Strampe	1970	Mike McGrath	1976	Paul Colwell		
1965	Dave Davis	1971	Mike Lemongello	1977	Tommy Hudson		

WOMEN'S INTERNATIONAL BOWLING CONGRESS CHAMPIONS

Year	Singles	All-events	Year	Singles	All-events
1959	Mae Ploegman	Pat McBride	1970	Dorothy Fothergill	Dorothy Fothergill
1960	Marge McDaniels	Judy Roberts	1971	Ginny Younginer	Lorrie Koch
1961	Elaine Newton	Evelyn Teal	1972	D. D. Jacobson	Mildred Martorella
1962	Martha Hoffman	Flossie Argent	1973	Bobby Buffaloe	Toni Calvery
1963	Dot Wilkinson	Helen Shablis	1974	Shirley Garms	Judy C. Soutar
1964	Jean Havlish	Jean Havlish	1975	Barbara Leicht	Virginia Park
1965	Doris Rudell	Donna Zimmerman	1976	Bev Shonk	Betty Morris
1966	Gloria Bouvia	Kate Helbig	1977	Akiko Yamaga	Akiko Yamaga
1967	Gloria Paeth	Carol Miller	1978	Mae Bolt	Annese Kelly
1968	Norma Parks	Susie Reichley	1979	Betty Morris	Betty Morris
1969	Joan Bender	Helen Duval	1980	Betty Morris	Cheryl Robinson

W.I.B.C. QUEENS TOURNAMENT CHAMPIONS

1961	Janet Harman	1966	Judy Lee	1971	Mildred Martorella	1976	Pamela Rutherford
1962	Dorothy Wilkinson	1967	Mildred Martorella	1972	Dorothy Fothergill	1977	Dana Stewart
1963	Irene Monterosso	1968	Phyllis Massey	1973	Dorothy Fothergill	1978	Loa Boxberger
1964	D.D. Jacobson	1969	Ann Feigel	1974	Judy Soutar	1979	Donna Adamek
1965	Betty Kuczynski	1970	Mildred Martorella	1975	Cindy Powell	1980	Donna Adamek

BOWLING PROPRIETORS' ASSOCIATION OF AMERICA—WOMEN

United States Open[1]

1971	Paula Carter	1974	Pat Costello	1977	Betty Morris	1980	Pat Costello
1972	Lorrie Nichols	1975	Paula Carter	1978	Donna Adamek		
1973	Mildred Martorella	1976	Pat Costello	1979	Diana Silva		

1. Replaced All-Star tournament.

AMERICAN BOWLING CONGRESS TOURNAMENT

(Louisville, Ky., March 1–May 19, 1980)

Regular Division

Singles—Mike Eaton, Grand Rapids, Mich.	782
Doubles—Ron Thacker–Bob Bures, Cleveland, Ohio	1,378
All events—Steve Fehr, Cincinatti, Ohio	2,076
Team—Stroh's Beer, Detroit, Mich.	3,119
Team All events—Chadwick Studio, San Antonio, Tex.	9,628
Booster Team—Aqua Lanes, Edgerton, Minn.	2,837

MASTERS

(Louisville, Ky., May 20–25, 1980)

Singles—Neil Burton, St. Louis, (defeated Mark Roth, North Arlington, N.J., 204–192, in final)

Classic Division competition was discontinued following the 1979 event.

WOMEN'S INTERNATIONAL BOWLING CONGRESS

(Seattle, Wash., April 3-June 11, 1980)

Open Division

Singles—Betty Morris, Stockton, Calif.	674
Doubles—Carole Lee, Hempstead, N.Y., and Dawn Raddatz, East Northport, N.Y.	1,247
All events—Cheryl Robinson, Van Nuys, Calif.	1,848
Team—All Japan, Tokyo	3,014

Division I

Singles—Cheri Mason, Lansing, Ill.	651
Doubles—Katherine Alexander, Los Angeles, and Marie Fouche, Los Angeles	1,176
All events—Verlda Morris, Del City, Okla.	1,711
Team—Walker Body Shop, Aurora, Ill.	2,703

Division II

Singles—Connie Deasy, Ephrata, Wash.	583
Doubles—Pauline Gullion, Toledo, Ohio, and Cindy Ortiz, San Jose, Calif.	1,070
All events—Nadine Collins, Peotone, Ill.	1,592
Team—Erie Jr., Detroit Lakes, Minn.	2,414

QUEENS TOURNAMENT

(Seattle, Wash., May 13–17, 1980)

Winner—Donna Adamek, Duarte, Calif. (defeated Cheryl Robinson, Van Nuys, Calif., 213–165, in one-game final match)

COLLEGIATE

Association of College Unions-International

(Seattle, Wash., April 7, 1980)

Singles—Terry Yoshihara, Hillsborough Community College	608
Doubles—Terry Yoshihara–Michele Sullivan, West Texas State	1,193
All events—Terry Yoshihara	1,784

SKIING

ALPINE WORLD CUP OVERALL WINNERS

	Men	Women	Team
1967	Jean-Claude Killy, France	Nancy Greene, Canada	France
1968	Jean-Claude Killy, France	Nancy Greene, Canada	France
1969	Karl Schranz, Austria	Gertrude Gabl, Austria	Austria
1970	Karl Schranz, Austria	Michel Jacot, France	France
1971	Gustavo Thoeni, Italy	Annemarie Proell, Austria	France
1972	Gustavo Thoeni, Italy	Annemarie Proell, Austria	France
1973	Gustavo Thoeni, Italy	Annemarie Proell Moser, Austria	Austria
1974	Piero Gros, Italy	Annemarie Proell Moser, Austria	Austria
1975	Gustavo Thoeni, Italy	Annemarie Proell Moser, Austria	Austria
1976	Ingemar Stenmark, Sweden	Rosi Mittermaier, West Germany	Austria
1977	Ingemar Stenmark, Sweden	Lise-Marie Morerod, Switzerland	Austria
1978	Ingemar Stenmark, Sweden	Hanni Wenzel, Liechtenstein	Austria
1979	Peter Luescher, Switzerland	Annemarie Proell Moser, Austria	Austria
1980	Andreas Wenzel, Liechtenstein	Hanni Wenzel, Liechtenstein	Liechtenstein

CANADIAN ALPINE CHAMPIONSHIPS—1980

Men's Events

Downhill—Ken Read, Calgary, Alta.	1:47.80
Slalom—Peter Monod, Banff, Alta.	1:26.82
Giant Slalom—Peter Monad	1:58.61
Combined—Cesare Percini	

Women's Events

Downhill—Laurie Graham	1:42.60
Slalom—Lynn Lacasse	1:31.42
Giant Slalom—Ann Blackburn	2:12.11
Combined—Ann Blackburn	

UNITED STATES CHAMPIONSHIPS—1980

ALPINE
Men's Events

Downhill—Dave Irwin, Vernon, British Columbia	1:04.87
Slalom—Steve Mahre, White Pass, Wash.	1:24.79
Giant Slalom—Peter Monod, Banff, Alberta	2:24.30
Combined—Jim Kirby, Canada	

Women's Events

Downhill—Cindy Nelson, Lutsen, Minn.	1:08.54
Slalom—Christin Cooper, Ketchum, Idaho	1:30.10
Giant slalom—Christin Cooper	2:25.95
Combined—Christin Cooper	

NORDIC
Men's Cross-Country

15 kilometers—Bill Koch, Guilford, Vt.	41:47.41
30 kilometers—Stan Dunklee, Brattleboro, Vt.	1:27:10.04
50 kilometers—Jim Galanes, Brattleboro, Vt.	2:11:28.84
Relay—Dan Simoneau, Livermore Falls, Me., Tim Caldwell, Putney, Vt., Stan Dunklee	1:24:18.9
Veterans 15 km—James Fredericks, Essex Junction, Vt.	48:16.70
Veterans 30 km—James Fredericks	1:39:44.67
Veterans relay—James Fredericks, Eric Evans, Putney, Vt., Fred Fayette, Colchester, Vt.	1:42:43.90

Women's Cross-Country

7.5 kilometers—Alison Owen-Spencer, East Wenatchee, Wash.	23:46.80
10 kilometers—Alison Owen-Spencer	31:54.79
20 kilometers—Betsy Haines, Anchorage, Alaska	59:19.10
Relay—Leslie Bancroft, Paris, Me., Jennifer Caldwell, Putney, Vt., Ruth Baxter, Aspen, Colo.	50:20.98
Veterans 7.5 km—Jane Parrish, Fairbanks, Alaska	31:41.91
Veterans 10 km—Jane Parrish	42:48.07

COLLEGIATE
Men—N.C.A.A.

(Stowe, Vt., March 6–8, 1980)

Slalom—Bret Williams, Northern Michigan U.	1:17.70
Giant Slalom—John Teague, Vermont	1:01.60
Cross-country (15 km)—Pal Sjustad, Vermont	44:05.6
Jumping—Jorn Stromberg, Wyoming	233.7 pts
Team—Vermont	171 pts

Women—A.I.A.W.

(Lake Placid, N.Y., March 6–8, 1980)

Slalom—Mary Seaton, Vermont	1:25.62
Giant slalom—Becky Simning, Wyoming	1:49.51
Cross-country (7.5 km)—Sissel Bjerkenas, Wyoming	25:40.21
Cross-country relay (20 km)—Middlebury (Toni Jorgensen, Keli McMenamy, Tara McMenamy, Alice Tower)	1:23:29.27
Team—Middlebury	286.7 pts

HANNI AND ANDREAS WENZEL STARS OF WORLD CUP SKIING

Rarely in sport do a brother and sister excel the way Hanni and Andreas Wenzel of Liechtenstein did during the 1980 skiing season. They emerged as the world's top all-round skiers by winning the overall World Cup titles and excelling in the Winter Olympics.

It was the first time a brother and sister took the overall World Cup crowns. Hanni won her title with 311 points and Andreas won with 204. The 23-year-old Hanni also won two gold and one silver medal at the Winter Olympics. Andreas captured two gold medals at the Games at Lake Placid, N.Y.

Their triumphs put tiny Liechtenstein, a country with only seven ski lifts and 6,000 skiers, on the world sports map and placed it fourth in the overall standings of World Cup nations behind Austria, Switzerland, and the United States.

The Wenzels are an active family. There is another sister, Petra, 19, who is a World Cup skier of great promise. Hanni is also a brilliant tennis player, sports car buff, and motorcyclist. Andreas also enjoys tennis and motorcycling.

CANADIAN NORDIC CHAMPIONSHIPS—1980

Men's Cross-Country

15 kilometers—Doug Gudwer, British Colombia	43:04.75
30 kilometers—Doug Gudwer	1:27:54
50 kilometers—Reno Keski–Salmi, British Colombia	2:36:49.88
Veterans 15 km—Mike Miskow, Alberta	52:13.08
Veterans 30 km—Risto Santala, Ontario	1:43:25
Relay—British Colombia (Marvin Strimbold, Reno Keski–Salmi, Doug Gudwer)	1:33:19.45

Women's Cross-Country

5 kilometers—Esther Miller, British Colombia	15:44.41
10 kilometers—Shirley Firth, Northwest Territories	32:24.90
20 kilometers—Angela Schmidt, Ontario	1:08:37.61
Relay—Ontario (Angela Schmidt, Cheryl Niemuller, Dasha Cejnar)	55:32.26

ALPINE WORLD CUP—1980

Overall—Men

	Pts
Andrea Wenzel, Liechtenstein	204
Ingemar Stenmark, Sweden	200
Phil Mahre, White Pass, Wash.	132

Overall—Women

	Pts
Hanni Wenzel, Liechtenstein	311
Annemarie Proell–Moser, Austria	259
Marie–Theres Nadig, Switzerland	221
Perrine Pelen, France	192
Irene Epple, West Germany	141
10—Cindy Nelson, Lutsen, Minn.	94
12—Heidi Preuss, Lakeport, N.H.	78
14—Tamara McKinney, Olympic Valley, Calif.	65
18—Christin Cooper, Sun Valley, Idaho	44

Event Leaders—Men

	Pts
Downhill—Peter Mueller, Switzerland	96
2—Ken Read, Calgary, Alta.	87
3—Herbert Plank, Italy	81
Slalom—Ingemar Stenmark, Sweden	125
2—Bojan Krizaj, Yugoslavia	88
3—Christian Neureuther, West Germany	69
Giant Slalom—Ingemar Stenmark, Sweden	125
2—Hans Enn, Austria	87
3—Jacques Luethy, Switzerland	82

Event Leaders—Women

	Pts
Downhill—Marie–Theres Nadig, Switzerland	125
Annemarie Proell–Moser	100
Hanni Wenzel, Liechtenstein	66
Slalom—Perrine Pelen, France	120
Hanni Wenzel, Liechtenstein	100
Annemarie Proell–Moser	83
Giant Slalom—Hanni Wenzel, Liechtenstein	125
Marie–Theres Nadig, Switzerland	95
Perrine Pelen, France	95

ALPINE NATIONS CUP—1980

	Pts
Overall—Austria	1,289
Switzerland	928
United States	716
Liechtenstein	618
West Germany	618
Italy	615
France	396
9. Canada	262
Men's Events—Austria	741
3. United States	307
8. Canada	185
Women's Events—Austria	548
4. United States	409
9. Canada	77

NORTH AMERICA TROPHY SERIES—1980

	Pts
Men's overall champion—Mark Tache, Aspen, Colo.	100
Women's overall champion—Noel Lyons, East Burke, Vt.	78

EUROPA CUP

	Pts
Men's overall champion—Siegfried Kerschbaumer, Italy	152
55th, Mark Tache, Aspen, Colo.	26
Women's overall champion—Erika Gfrerer, Austria	198
22nd, Noel Lyons, East Burke, Vt.	41

WATER POLO

UNITED STATES CHAMPIONS—1980

Men, Outdoor—Concord, Calif.
Women, Outdoor—Industry Hills, Calif.
Women, Indoor—Industry Hills, Calif.

HANDBALL

U.S.H.A. NATIONAL FOUR-WALL CHAMPIONS

Singles

1960	Jimmy Jacobs
1961	John Sloan
1962–63	Oscar Obert
1964–65	Jimmy Jacobs
1966–67	Paul Haber
1968	Simon (Stuffy) Singer
1969–71	Paul Haber
1972	Fred Lewis
1973	Terry Muck
1974	Fred Lewis
1975	Jay Bilyeu
1976	Vern Roberts, Jr.
1977	Naty Alvarado
1978	Fred Lewis
1979	Naty Alvarado
1980	Naty Alvarado

Doubles

1960	Jimmy Jacobs-Dick Weisman
1961	John Sloan-Vic Hershkowitz
1962–63	Jimmy Jacobs-Marty Decatur
1964	John Sloan-Phil Elbert
1965	Jimmy Jacobs-Marty Decatur
1966	Pete Tyson-Bob Lindsay
1967–68	Jimmy Jacobs-Marty Decatur
1969	Lou Kramberg-Lou Russo
1970	Karl and Ruby Obert
1971	Ray Neveau-Simie Fein
1972	Kent Fusselman-Al Drews
1973–74	Ray Neveau-Simie Fein
1975	Marty Decatur-Steve Lott
1976	Gary Rohrer-Dan O'Connor
1977	Skip McDowell-Matt Kelly
1978	Stuffy Singer-Marty Decatur
1979	Stuffy Singer-Marty Decatur
1980	Skip McDowell-Harry Robertson

HANDBALL

U.S. HANDBALL ASSOCIATION FOUR WALL CHAMPIONS

(Tucson, Ariz., June 13–21, 1980)

Open singles—Naty Alvarado, Hesperia, Calif. (defeated Fred Lewis, Tucson, Ariz., 21–13, 18–21, 11–3, in final)
Open doubles—Skip McDowell and Harry Robertson, Long Beach, Calif. (defeated Vern Roberts and Dave Dohman, Chicago, 21–10, 14–21, 11–1, in final)
Masters singles—Pat Kirby, Shannon, Ireland (defeated Rene Zamorano, Tucson, Ariz., 21–13, 21–1, in final)
Masters doubles—Tom Natale, Lindenhurst, N.Y., and Bill Kennedy, Glen Ridge, N.J., (defeated Mike Dau, Lake Forest, Ill., and Joe Bukant, Kalamazoo, Mich., 21–16, 21–10, in final)
Golden masters singles—Jack Briscoe, St. Louis (defeated Del Mora, Santa Barbara, Calif., 21–11, 21–15, in final)
Golden masters doubles—Arnie Aguilar, Los Angeles, and Del Mora, Santa Barbara, Calif. (defeated Ken Schneider and Bob Peters, Chicago, 19–21, 21–9, 11–7, in final)
Super masters singles—Steve Subak, Edina, Minn. (defeated Ralph Stapper, Austin, Tex., 21–19, 21–5, in final)
Super masters doubles—Lee Shinn, Salem, Ore., and Ralph Stapper, Austin, Tex., (defeated Rod Rodriquez, Los Angeles, and Joe Kaloustian, Whittier, Calif., 21–16, 21–15, in final)
Challenger singles—Steve King, Garden Grove, Calif. (defeated Jaime Parades, San Diego, Calif., 14–21, 21–19, 11–8, in final)

WEIGHT LIFTING

A.A.U. NATIONAL CHAMPIONSHIPS—1980

(Philadelphia, Pa., May 30-June 1, 1980)

	Snatch	C&J[1]	Total
114½ lb—Leslie Sewall, Plymouth, Mass.	182	220	402
123¼ lb—Joe Widdel, Dewar, Iowa	204	259	463
132¼ lb—Philip Sanderson, Billings, Mont.	237	298	535
148¾ lb—Callen Schake, Butler, Pa.	288	353	641
165¼ lb—Myron Davids, Overland, Mo.	281	375	656
181¼ lb—Mike Karchut, Calumet City, Ill.	320	402	722
198¼ lb—James Curry Jr., Berkeley, Calif.	314	408	722
220¼ lb—Brian Derwin, Cresskill, N.J.	331	457	788
242¼ lb—Mark Cameron, Colorado Springs	358	463	821
Super heavyweight—Tom Stock, Belleville, Ill.	380	485	865

1. Clean and jerk.

CANOE RACING

AMERICAN CANOE ASSOCIATION

Source: Marcia Smoke, Buchanan, Mich.

NATIONAL FLATWATER CHAMPIONSHIPS

(Lake Sebago, N.Y., Aug. 21–24, 1980)

Men's Kayak

500 m—Greg Barton, Homer, Mich.
1,000 m—Greg Barton
10,000 m—Greg Barton
500–m tandem—Terry White, Arlington, Vt., and Dave Gilman, Berkeley, Calif.
1,000–m tandem—Terry White and Dave Gilman
10,000–m tandem—Terry White and Dave Gilman
500–m fours—Terry White, Dave Gilman, Steve Kelly, Bronx, New York, Brent Turner, Craftsbury, Vt.
1,000–m fours—Terry White, Dave Gilman, Steve Kelly, Brent Turner
10,000–m fours—Terry White, Dave Gilman, Steve Kelly, Brent Turner

Women's Kayak

500 m—Ann Turner, St. Charles, Ill.
5,000 m—Ann Turner
500–m tandem—Ann Turner and Leslie Klein, Lexington, Ky.
5,000–m tandem—Ann Turner and Leslie Klein
500–m fours—Ann Turner, Leslie Klein, Mary Alice Ross, Yonkers, N.Y., Bonnie McManus, St. Charles, Ill.
5,000–m fours—Ann Turner, Leslie Klein, Mary Alice Ross, Bonnie McManus

Men's Canoe

500 m—Barry Merritt, Washington, D.C.
1,000 m—Kurt Doberstein, Lombard, Ill.
10,000 m—Bruce Merritt, Washington, D.C.
500–m tandem—Barry Merritt and Bruce Merritt, Washington, D.C.
1,000–m tandem—Barry Merritt and Bruce Merritt
10,000–m tandem—Barry Merritt and Bruce Merritt
1,000–m fours—Barry Merritt, Bruce Merritt, D. Havens, K. Havens, Washington, D.C.
Team—Black Anvil Boat Club, Ventura, Calif.

NATIONAL WHITEWATER CHAMPIONSHIPS—1980

Men's kayak—Chuck Stanley.
Women's kayak—Linda Harrison, Newark, Del.
Men's canoe—David Hearn, Garrett Park, Md.
Men's doubles—Paul Grabow and Jeff Huey, Washington, D.C.

NATIONAL WILDWATER CHAMPIONSHIPS—1980

Men's kayak—Dan Schnurrenberger, Washington, D.C.
Women's kayak—Cathy Hearn, Garrett Park, Md.
Men's canoe—David Hearn, Garrett Park, Md.
Men's canoe doubles—Paul Grabow and Jeff Huey, Washington, D.C.
Internatonal open—Mike Stroble, Munich, West Germany

RUGBY—1980

United States—Old Blues, Berkeley, Calif.
Monterey Peninsula—James Bay, Vancouver, British Columbia
Boston 350—Dublin Wanderers
Test Match—Canada 16, United States 0

BIATHLON

UNITED STATES CHAMPIONS—1980

Men's 10 kilometers—Ken Alligood, Anchorage, Alaska
Men's 20 kilometers—Don Nielsen, South Stratford, Vt.
Women's 10 kilometers—Betty Stroock, Jackson, Wyo.
Women's 15 kilometers—Holly Beatie, Squaw Valley, Calif.
Junior 10 kilometers—Tom McElroy, Minneapolis
Junior 15 kilometers—Tom McElroy

SPEED SKATING

U.S. OUTDOOR CHAMPIONS

Men

1959–60	Ken Bartholomew
1961	Ed Rudolph
1962	Floyd Bedbury
1963	Tom Gray
1964	Neil Blatchford
1965–66	Rich Wurster
1967	Mike Passarella
1968–70	Peter Cefalu
1971	Jack Walters
1972	Barth Levy
1973	Mike Woods
1974	Leigh Barczewski, Mike Passarella
1975	Rich Wurster
1976	John Wurster
1977	Jim Chapin
1978	Bill Heinkel
1979	Erik Henriksen
1980	Greg Oly

Women

1960	Mary Novak
1961	Jean Ashworth
1962	Jean Omelenchuk
1963	Jean Ashworth
1964	Diane White
1965	Jean Omelenchuk
1966	Diane White
1967	Jean Ashworth
1968	Helen Lutsch
1969	Sally Blatchford
1970–71	Sheila Young
1972	Ruth Moore, Nancy Thorne
1973	Nancy Class
1974	Kris Garbe
1975	Nancy Swider
1976	Connie Carpenter
1977	Liz Crowe
1978	Paula Class, Betsy Davis
1979	Gretchen Byrnes
1980	Shari Miller

World Speed Skating Records

Men

Distance	Time	Skater	Place	Year
500 m	0:37.00	Evgeny Kulikov, U.S.S.R.	Medeo, U.S.S.R.	1975
1,000 m	1:13.60	Eric Heiden, U.S.	Davos, Switzerland	1980
1,500 m	1:55.18	Jan Egil Storholt, Norway	Medeo, U.S.S.R.	1977
3,000 m	4:04.01	Eric Heiden, U.S.	Inzell, Austria	1978
5,000 m	6:56.90	Kay Arne Stenshjemmet, Norway	Medeo, U.S.S.R.	1977
10,000 m	14:25.71	Dmitri Ogloblin, U.S.S.R.	Alma Ata, U.S.S.R.	1980

Women

Distance	Time	Skater	Place	Year
500 m	0:40.68	Sheila Young, U.S.	Inzell, Austria	1976
1,000 m	1:23.46	Tatiana Averina, U.S.S.R.	Medeo, U.S.S.R.	1975
1,500 m	2:07.18	Halida Vorobieva, U.S.S.R.	Medeo, U.S.S.R.	1978
3,000 m	4:31.00	Galina Stepanskaya, U.S.S.R.	Medeo, U.S.S.R.	1976

WORLD CHAMPIONSHIPS

Men

(Heerenveen, the Netherlands, March 2–3, 1980)

Champion—Hilbert van der Duim, the Netherlands	171.747 pts
500 m—Eric Heiden, Madison, Wis.	0:39.82
1,500 m—Hilbert van der Duim	2:0259
5,000 m—Tom Erik Oxholm, Norway	7:14.51
10,000 m—Mike Woods, Madison, Wis.	15:02.39

Women

(Hamar, Norway, Jan. 13–14, 1980)

Champions—Natalya Petruseva, Soviet Union	179.046 pts
500 m—Natalya Petruseva	0:43.6
1,000 m—Natalya Petruseva	1:25.54
1,500 m—Natalya Petruseva	2:15.98
3,000 m—Bjoerg Eva Jensen, Norway	4:37.35

WORLD SPRINT CHAMPIONSHIPS

(West Allis, Wis., Feb. 9–10, 1980)

Men's Events

Champion—Eric Heiden, Madison, Wis.	154.905 pts
500 m (first race)—Tom Plant, West Allis, Wis.	0:38.66
1,000 m (first race)—Eric Heiden	1:17.23
500 m (second race)—Eric Heiden	0:38.61
1,000 m (second race)—Eric Heiden	1:17.98

Women's Events

Champion—Karin Enke, East Germany	171.120 pts
500 m (first race)—Karin Enke	0:42.06
1,000 m (first race)—Karin Enke	1:25.83
500 m (second race)—Leah Poulos Mueller, West Allis, Wis.	0:42.25
1,000 m (second race)—Karin Enke	1:27.19

U.S. OUTDOOR CHAMPIONS

(St. Paul, Minn., Jan. 26–27, 1980)

Men—Greg Oly, Minneapolis, Minn.
Women—Shari Miller, Butte, Mont.
Intermediate boys—Tom Grannes, Minneapolis, Minn.
Intermediate girls—Sandra Chobot, West Allis, Wis.
Junior boys—Mike Jansen, West Allis, Wis.
Junior girls—Angela Zuckerman, Whitefish Bay, Wis.

U.S. INDOOR CHAMPIONS

(Wyandotte, Mich., March 21–23, 1980)

Men—Barth Levy, Lakewood, Ohio
Women—Tie between Pam Mercer, Wyandotte, Mich., and Debbie Carlstrom, Des Plaines, Ill.
Intermediate boys—Charles Riddle, Wyandotte, Mich.
Intermediate girls—Ann Klopp, St. Paul, Minn.
Junior boys—Tom Carter, Park Ridge, Ill.
Junior girls—Lisa Parfitt, Alpena, Mich.

NORTH AMERICAN OUTDOOR CHAMPIONS

(Saratoga Spring, N.Y., Feb. 2–3, 1980)

Men—Barth Levy, Lakewood, Ohio
Women—Shari Miller, Butte, Mont.
Intermediate boys—Tom Grannes, Minneapolis, Minn.
Intermediate girls—Katie Class, St. Paul, Minn.
Junior boys—Paul Grannes, Minneapolis, Minn.
Junior girls—Angela Zuckerman, Whitefish Bay, Wis.

NORTH AMERICAN INDOOR CHAMPIONS

(Esquimalt, British Columbia, March 28–30, 1980)

Men—Gaetan Boucher, Quebec, Canada
Women—Cathy Turnbull, Saskatchewan, Canada
Intermediate boys—Michael Desisle, Quebec, Canada
Intermediate girls—Louise Begin, Quebec, Canada
Junior boys—Randy Ljuden, British Columbia, Canada
Junior girls—Maryse Perreault, Quebec, Canada

ROLLER SKATING

NATIONAL CHAMPIONSHIPS—1980

Men's singles—Michael Glatz, San Diego, Calif.
Women's singles—Kathleen O'Brien DiFelice, Cherry Hill, N.J.
Men's figures—Tony St. Jacques, Virginia Beach, Va.
Women's figures—Anna Conklin, Bakersfield, Calif.
Junior men—Rick Monturo, Cleveland
Junior women—Gerry Goodman, Chula Vista, Calif.
Junior men's figures—Dallas Oskey, Flint, Mich.
Junior women's figures—Tammy DeWulf, Brighton, Mich.
Pairs—Paul Price and Tina Kneisley, Brighton, Mich.
Junior pairs—Rick Monturo and Valerie Acree, Cleveland
Dance—Harvey White and Beth Wahlig, Newark, Del.
Junior dance—Curt Cherry and Rae Marie Bonacci, Fountain Valley, Calif.
Free dance—Scott Oakley and Gladys Smith, East Meadow, N.Y.
International-style dance—Charles Kirchner and Linda Todd, Cherry Hill, N.J.
Esquire dance—Ralph Crews and Jean Meyers, Decatur, Ga.

Speed

Men—Robb Dunn, Farmington Hills, Mich.
Women—Linda Swaim, High Point, N.C.
2-man relay—Robb Dunn and Chuck Jackson, Farmington Hills, Mich.
2-woman relay—Sandra Dulaney and Karen Johnson, Santa Ana, Calif.
4-man relay—Chris Snyder, Mark Sutton, Marty Sutton, Mike Vouklizas, Irving, Tex.
4-woman relay—Kathy Katovich, Denise McLeod, Tammy Griffith, Sue Dooley, Farmington Hills, Mich.
Mixed couples relay—Robb Dunn, Denise McLeod, Farmington Hills, Mich.
Mixed-4 relay—Robb Dunn, Chuck Jackson, Kathy Katovich, Denise McLeod, Farmington Hills, Mich.

PADDLE TENNIS

Source: Murray Geller, Executive-Secretary, U.S. Paddle Tennis Association

NATIONAL OPEN CHAMPIONSHIPS—1980

(New York City, June 7–8, 1980)

Men's singles—Nels Van Patten, Los Angeles
Men's doubles—Jeff Fleitman and Sol Hauptman, Brooklyn, N.Y.
Women's singles—Kathy May Teacher, Los Angeles

NATIONAL BEACH CHAMPIONSHIPS—1980

(St. Augustine, Fla., Aug. 30-Sept. 1, 1980)

Men's doubles—Jeff Fleitman and Sol Hauptman, Brooklyn, N.Y.
Women's doubles—Donna Sweeney, St. Augustine, Fla., and Jeannie Hall, Los Angeles

HORSESHOE PITCHING

WORLD CHAMPIONSHIPS—1980

(Huntsville, Ala.)

Men	W	L	Ringers No.	Ringers %
Walter Ray Williams, Chino, Calif.	31	0	1,732	85.7
Elmher Hohl, Canada	26	5	1,952	79.6
Carl Steinfeldt, Rochester, N.Y.	26	5	1,883	78.5
Ralph Simon, Waterloo, Iowa	26	5	1,788	77.7
Mark Seibold, Huntington, Ind.	26	5	1,776	76.3
Women				
Opal Reno, Lucasville, Ohio	11	0	542	78.8
Bonnie Seibold, Huntington, Ind.	10	1	560	75.7
Ruth Hangen, Getzville, N.Y.	9	2	541	72.7
Phyllis Negaard, St. Joseph's, Minn.	8	3	527	72.2
Vickie Winston, LaMonte, Mo.	7	4	515	74.0

Other Champions

Senior—Glen Portt, Georgia
Boys—Mark Dyson, Taylorsville, N.C.
Girls—Sue Williams, Diamondale, Mich.
Men's Class B—Victor Pfaff, Indiana
Men's Class C—Jeff Williams, Nebraska
Women's Class B—Juanita Phelps, Virginia
Women's Class C—Connie Cool, Ohio

DOG SHOWS

WESTMINSTER KENNEL CLUB

(Madison Square Garden, New York, Feb. 12, 1980)

Best in show—Ch. Innisfree's Sierra Cinnar, Siberian husky, owned by Kathleen Kanzler, Accokeek, Md.

INTERNATIONAL KENNEL CLUB

(Chicago, Ill., March 31, 1980)

Best in Show—Ch. Thrumpton's Lord Brady, Norwich terrier, owned by Ruth Cooper, Glenview, Ill.

TABLE TENNIS

U.S. OPEN CHAMPIONSHIPS

(Fort Worth, Tex., June 26–29, 1980)

Men's singles—Mikael Appelgren, Sweden
Women's singles—Kayoko Kawahigashi, Japan
Men's doubles—Danny Seemiller–Ricky Seemiller, Pittsburgh, Pa.
Women's doubles—Kyung-Ja Kim–Soo-Ja Lee, South Korea
Mixed doubles—Si-Hung Yoo–Soo-Ja Lee, South Korea
Men's team—United States
Women's team—South Korea
Senior men over 40—George Brathwaite
Senior women over 40—Yvonne Kronlage
Senior men over 50—Norm Schless
Senior men over 60—George Rocker
Senior men over 70—C.H. McCallister
Boys under 17—Dean Wong
Girls under 17—Becky McKnight

BADMINTON

WORLD CHAMPIONS—1980

Men—Rudy Hartono, Indonesia
Women—Wiharjo Verawaty, Indonesia

U.S. BADMINTON ASSOCIATION CHAMPIONSHIPS—1980

(Offutt Air Force Base, Neb., April 16–19, 1980)

Men's singles—Gary Higgins, Alhambra, Calif.
Women's singles—Cheryl Carton, San Diego, Calif.
Men's doubles—Matt Fogarty, Duxbury, Mass., Mike Walker, Manhattan Beach, Calif.
Women's doubles—Pam Brady, Flint, Mich., Judianne Kelly, Costa Mesa, Calif.
Mixed doubles—Mike Walker, Manhattan Beach, Calif., Judianne Kelly, Costa Mesa, Calif.

Seniors

Men's singles—Jim Poole, Westminster, Calif.
Men's doubles—Don Paup, Washington D.C., Jim Poole, Westminster, Calif.
Women's doubles—Claire Bowyer, Canada, Ethel Marshall, Williamsville, N.Y.
Mixed doubles—Don Paup, Washington, D.C., Sondra Fogarty, Duxbury, Mass.

Masters

Men's singles—Ted Moehlmann, Warson Woods, Mo.
Men's doubles—James McQuie, Kirkwood, Mo., Ted Moehlmann, Warson Woods, Mo.
Mixed doubles—Jim Bell, Ypsilanti, Mich., Ethel Marshall, Williamsville, N.Y.

Grand Masters

Men's singles—Waldo Lyon, San Diego, Calif.
Men's doubles—Taylor Caffery, New Orleans, La., Roy Nusbaum, Granger, Ind.

ALL-ENGLAND CHAMPIONSHIPS—1980

(Wembley, England, March 19–22, 1980)

Men's singles—Prakash Padukone, India
Women's singles—Lene Koppen, Denmark
Men's doubles—Johan Wahjudi and Tjun Tjun, Indonesia
Women's doubles—Nora Perry and Gillian Gilks, England
Mixed doubles—Mike Tredgett and Nora Perry, England

WORLD CHAMPIONSHIPS—1980

(Jakarta, Indonesia, May 27–June 1, 1980)

Men's singles—Rudy Hartono, Indonesia
Women's singles—Wiharjo Verawaty, Indonesia
Men's doubles—Ade Chandra and Christian Hadinata, Indonesia
Women's doubles—Nora Perry and Jane Webster, England
Mixed doubles—Christian Hadinata and Imelda Wigoeno, Indonesia

BOBSLEDDING

U.S. CHAMPIONSHIPS—1980

Two man—Brent Rushlaw and Joe Tyler, Saranac Lake, N.Y.
Four man—United States No. 1, Bob Hickey, Keene, N.Y.

NORTH AMERICAN CHAMPIONSHIP—1980

Two man—Bill Renton and Rick Peters, Marionville, Pa.

DUCKPIN BOWLING

NATIONAL CHAMPIONSHIPS—1980

Men's singles—Jim Dion, Westport, Mass.	597
Women's singles—Brenda Wachtell, Hagerstown, Md.	500
Men's doubles—Doug Gosewisch—Kent Schwartz, Glen Burnie, Md.	989
Women's doubles—Dawn Healey—Bonnie Myers, Baltimore, Md.	875
Championship Team—Adams Five, Alexandria, Va.	2,089
Class A Teams—Norwich Duckpin, Norwich, Conn.	2,139
Class B Teams—Kelleher Realty, Waldorf, Md.	2,010
Class C Teams—4 Spares and A Strike, Bethesda, Md.	1,994
Class D Teams—Dean Construction, California, Md.	1,737

TUMBLING

UNITED STATES CHAMPIONS—1980

Men—Jerry Hardy, Detroit
Women—Julie Beatty, Roy, Utah

SQUASH TENNIS

U.S. CHAMPION—1980

Singles—Pedro Baccallao, Miami, defeated Bill Reubin, White Plains, N.Y., 15–11, 15–13, 15–12.

PADDLEBALL

UNITED STATES CHAMPIONS—1980

Men's open—Dick Jury, Williamston, Mich.
Men's doubles—Greg Grambeau and Bob Sterken, Ann Arbor, Mich.
Women's doubles—Grace Louwsma and Judy Shirley, Ann Arbor, Mich.
Men's seniors—Dick Jury
Men's senior doubles—Max Calhoun and Joe Roberson, Flint, Mich.
Men's masters—Don Taylor, Allen Park, Mich.
Men's masters doubles—Rod Grambeau and Steve Galetti, Ann Arbor, Mich.
Men's golden masters doubles—Gale Greenland and Dick Tanner, Kalamazoo, Mich.

MOTORCYCLE RACING

WORLD CHAMPIONSHIPS—1980

Men's 500 cc—Kenny Roberts, Modesto, Calif.
Motocross 500 cc—Andre Malherbe, Belgium

COURT TENNIS

UNITED STATES CHAMPIONS—1980

Men's open—Chris Ronaldson, England
Men's amateur—Gene Scott, New York
Men's seniors—William Vogt, Philadelphia
College—George de Bell, Harvard

SPORTS ORGANIZATIONS AND INFORMATION BUREAUS

Amateur Athletic Union of the U.S. 3400 West 86th St., Indianapolis, Indiana 46862

Amateur Bicycle League of America. *See* United States Cycling Federation

Amateur Hockey Association of the U.S. 10 Lake Circle, Colorado Springs, Colo. 80906

Amateur Skating Union of the U.S. 4423 West Deming Place, Chicago, Ill. 60639

Amateur Softball Association. 2801 N.E. 50th St., P.O. Box 11437, Oklahoma City, Okla. 73111

Amateur Trapshooting Association of America. Vandalia, Ohio 45377

American Amateur Baseball Congress. Box 4, Battle Creek, Mich. 49016

American Association (baseball). P.O. Box 382, Wichita, Kan. 67201

American Bowling Congress. 5301 South 76th St., Greendale, Wis. 53129

American Canoe Association. 4260 East Evans Ave., Denver, Colo. 80222

American Fencers League of America. 249 Eton Place, Westfield, N.J. 07090

American Hockey League. P.O. Box 100, West Springfield, Mass. 01089

American Horse Shows Association. 527 Madison Ave., New York, N.Y. 10022

American Kennel Club. 51 Madison Ave., New York, N.Y. 10010

American League (baseball). 280 Park Ave., New York, N.Y. 10017

American Motorcycle Association. P.O. Box 141, Westerville, Ohio 43081

American Power Boat Association. 415 Burns Drive, Detroit, Mich. 48214

American Water Ski Association. State Route 550 at Carl Floyd Road, P.O. Box 191, Winter Haven, Fla. 33880

Association of Intercollegiate Athletics for Women. 1201 16th St. N.W., Washington, D.C.

Baseball Commissioner. 75 Rockefeller Plaza, New York, N.Y. 10019

Baseball Hall of Fame. Cooperstown, N.Y.

Bowling Proprietors' Association of America. P.O. Box 5802, Arlington, Texas 76011

Central Hockey League. 5740 Oakland Ave., St. Louis, Mo. 63110

Championship Auto Racing Teams (CART). 12626 US 12, Brooklyn, Mich., 49230

Eastern College Athletic Conference. P.O. Box 3, Centerville, Mass. 02632

Elias Sports Bureau. 500 Fifth Ave., New York, N.Y. 10036

Fish and Wildlife Service. Department of the Interior, Washington, D.C. 20240

Football Hall of Fame (college). Kings Mills, Ohio 45034

Football Hall of Fame (pro). Canton, Ohio 44708

International Amateur Athletic Federation. Halton House, 23 Holborn, London, E. C. 1, England

Intercollegiate (Big Ten) Conference (1896). 1111 Plaza Dr., Schaumburg, Ill. 60195

International Game Fish Association. 3000 East Las Olas Blvd., Fort Lauderdale, Fla. 33316

International League (baseball). Box 608, Grove City, Ohio 43123

International Motor Sports Association. P.O. Box 805, Fairfield, Conn. 06430

International Olympic Committee. Chateau de Vidy, Lausanne, Switzerland

The Jockey Club. 300 Park Ave., New York, N.Y. 10022

Ladies Professional Golf Association. 919 Third Ave., New York, N.Y. 10022

Little League Baseball. Williamsport, Pa. 17701

National Archery Association. 1951 Geraldson Drive, Lancaster, Pa. 17601

National Association for Girls and Women in Sports. 1201 16th St. N.W., Washington, D.C.

National Association of Amateur Oarsmen. 4 Boathouse Row, Philadelphia, Pa. 19130

National Association of Intercollegiate Athletics. 1221 Baltimore St., Kansas City, Mo. 64105

National Association of Professional Baseball Leagues (minors). P.O. Box A, St. Petersburg, Fla. 33731

National Association for Stock Car Auto Racing. P.O. Box K, Daytona Beach, Fla. 32015

National Baseball Congress. Wichita, Kan. 67201

National Basketball Association. Olympic Tower, 645 Fifth Ave., New York, N.Y. 10022

National Collegiate Athletic Association. P.O. Box 1906, Shawnee Mission, Kan. 66222

National Duck Pin Bowling Congress. 711–14th St. N.W., Washington, D.C. 20005

National Field Archery Association. Rt. 2, Box 514, Redlands, Calif. 92373

National Football Foundation. 201 East 42nd St., New York, N.Y. 10017. *See also:* Football Hall of Fame (college)

National Football League. 410 Park Ave., New York, N.Y. 10022

National Hockey League. 922 Sun Life Bldg., Montreal, Que., Canada

National Horseshoe Pitchers Association. Route 5, Lucasville, Ohio 45648

National Hot Rod Association. P.O. Box 150, North Hollywood, Calif. 91603

National Junior College Athletic Association. P.O. Box 1586, Hutchinson, Kan. 67501

National Lawn Tennis Hall of Fame. Newport Casino, Newport, R.I., 02840

National League (baseball). 1 Rockefeller Plaza, New York, N.Y. 10019

National Rifle Association of America. 1600 Rhode Island Ave., N.W., Washington, D.C. 20036

National Skeet Shooting Association. P.O. Box 28188, San Antonio, Tex. 78228

New York Racing Association. P.O. Box 90, Jamaica, N.Y. 11417

New York State Athletic Commission (boxing). 226 W. 47th St., New York, N.Y. 10036

National Shuffleboard Association. 5612 Plattsburg Road, Springfield, Ohio, 45505

North American Yacht Racing Union. *See* United States Yacht Racing Union

North American Soccer League. 1133 Avenue of the Americas, New York, N.Y. 10036

Pacific Coast League (baseball). 2509 South Shannon Drive, Tempe, Ariz., 85282

Professional Bowlers Association. 1720 Merriman Road, Akron, Ohio 44313

Professional Golfers' Association of America. Box 12458, Lake Park, Fla. 33403

Rodeo Cowboys Association. 2929 W. 19th Ave., Denver, Colo. 80204

Roller Skating Rink Operators Association. P.O. Box 81846, Lincoln, Neb. 68501

Sports Car Club of America. 6750 So. Emporia St., Englewood, Colo. 80112

Tennis Hall of Fame. *See* National Lawn Tennis Hall of Fame

Thoroughbred Racing Associations of the U.S. 3000 Marcus Ave., Lake Success, N.Y. 11040

Track and Field Association of the USA. 10920 Ambassador Drive, Kansas City, Mo., 64153

Track and Field Hall of Fame. Charleston, W.Va.

United States of America Roller Skating Confederation. 7700 "A" Street, Lincoln, Neb. 68501

United States Auto Club. 4910 West 16th Street, Speedway, Indiana, 46224

United States Badminton Association. 787 South Orange Grove Blvd., Unit 9, Pasadena, Calif. 91105

U.S. Chess Federation. 186 Route 9W, New Windsor, N.Y. 12550

U.S. Cycling Federation. Box 669, Wall Street Station, New York, N.Y. 10005

U.S. Figure Skating Association. 575 Boylston St., Boston, Mass. 02116

U.S. Golf Association. Far Hills, N.J. 07931

U.S. Handball Association. 4101 Dempster St., Skokie, Ill. 60077

U.S. Men's Curling Association. 12822 Water Street, Duluth, Minn., 55008

U.S. Olympic Committee. 1750 East Boulder Street, Colorado Springs, Colo. 80909

U.S. Olympic Training Center. P.O. Box 4000, Colorado Springs, Colo. 80930

U.S. Parachute Association. 806–15th St. N.W., Washington, D.C. 20005

U.S. Polo Association. 1301 W. 22nd St., Oak Brook, Ill. 60521

U.S. Ski Association. 1726 Champa St., Denver, Colorado 80202

U.S. Ski Team. P.O. Box 100, Park City, Utah 84060

U.S. Soccer Federation. 350 Fifth Ave., New York, N.Y. 10001

U.S. Squash Racquets Association. 211 Ford Road, Bala-Cynwyd, Pa., 19004

U.S. Table Tennis Association. 3466 Bridgeland Drive, Bridgeland Square Building, St. Louis, Mo. 63044

U.S. Tennis Association. 51 E. 42nd St., New York, N.Y. 10017

U.S. Touch and Flag Football Association. 2705 Normandy Drive, Youngstown, Ohio, 49511

U.S. Trotting Association. 750 Michigan Ave., Columbus, Ohio 43215

U.S. Volleyball Association. 557 Fourth Street, San Francisco, Calif. 94107

U.S. Women's Curling Association. 635 Chatham Road, Glenview, Ill. 60025

U.S. Yacht Racing Union. P.O. Box 209, Goat Island, Newport, R.I. 02840

Women's International Bowling Congress. 5301 S. 76th St., Greendale, Wis. 53129

WATER SKIING

NATIONAL CHAMPIONSHIPS—1980

(Tyler, Tex., Aug. 20–24, 1980)

Men's Open

Overall—Carl Roberge, Orlando, Fla.	3,159 pts
Slalom—Carl Roberge	58 buoys
Tricks—Cory Pickos, Eagle Lake, Fla.	7,600 pts
Jumping—Bob LaPoint, Castro Valley, Calif.	179 ft

Women's Open

Overall—Karin Roberge, Orlando, Fla.	3,379 pts
Slalom—Cyndi Benzel, Newberry Springs, Calif.	57 buoys
Tricks—Karin Roberge	6,040 pts
Jumping—Linda Giddens, Eastman, Ga.	120 ft

Men's Division I

Overall—Barry Horton, Arcadia, Calif.	2,332 pts
Slalom—Darin Hayes, Napa, Calif.	50 buoys
Tricks—Scott Green, Longwood, Fla.	5,850 pts
Jumping—Ric McCaa, Montgomery, Ala.	154 ft

Women's Division

Overall—Tish Fain, Clemson, S.C.	2,529 pts
Slalom—Jackie Murguia, Key West, Fla.	51¼ buoys
Tricks—Joyce Phelps, Long Beach, Calif.	3,270 pts
Jumping—Tish Fain	105 ft

Senior Men's Division

Overall—Dr. J.D. Morgan, Lake Wales, Fla.	2,985 pts
Slalom—Dr. J.D. Morgan	52 buoys
Tricks—Robert Hurm, St. Marys, Ohio	4,410 pts
Jumping—Dr. J.D. Morgan	124 ft

Senior Women's Division

Overall—Thelma Salmas, Lake Worth, Fla.	3,200 pts
Slalom—Gun Evans, Hollywood, Fla.	46½ buoys
Tricks—Thelma Salmas	4,260 pts
Jumping—Gun Evans	109 ft

Veterans Division

Overall—John Roach, Roswell, Ga.	2,933 pts
Slalom—John Roach	45 buoys
Tricks—Bob Moore, Louisville, Ky.	3,460 pts
Jumping—Lloyd Meredith, Reddick, Ill.	125 ft

MASTERS TOURNAMENT

(Callaway Gardens, Ga., July 12–13, 1980)

Men's Division

Overall—Mike Hazelwood, London, England	2,798 pts
Slalom—Bob LaPoint, Castro Valley, Calif.	53 buoys
Tricks—Cory Pickos, Eagle Lake, Fla.	8,190 pts
Jumping—Sammy Duvall, Greenville, S.C.	183 ft

Women's Division

Overall—Karin Roberge, Orlando, Fla.	2,661 pts
Slalom—Karin Roberge	49 buoys
Tricks—Ana Marie Carrasco, Caracas, Venezuela	5,070 pts
Jumping—Linda Giddens, Eastman, Ga.	117 ft

DOG RACING

1980 CHAMPIONS

World Greyhound Classic—Banker Hap
Flagler International Classic—Bold Mission
Irish-American Classic—Millie's Special
Hecht Marathon—Placid Ace
World Spring—K's Queen Bee
Tom Benner Super Marathon—Irish Company
Great Greyhound Race—Zagger

TRAPSHOOTING

1980 GRAND AMERICAN TOURNAMENT

Grand American Handicap

Men—William Hazlett, Sarven, Pa.
Women—Indika Morris, Wahpeton, S.D.
Junior—Todd Overstreet, St. Charles, Mo.
Veteran—Williard Koch, Upland, Neb.
Sub-Junior—Randy Wilhelm, Mt. Vernon, Ohio

All-Around

Men—Steve Carmichael, Raytown, Mo.
Women—Nyla Johnson, Chattaroy, Wash.
Junior—Stuart Welton, Meridian, Idaho

Overall

Men—Leo Harrison II, Hannibal, Mo.
Women—Nyla Johnson, Chattaroy, Wash.
Junior—Stuart Welton, Meridian, Idaho

Doubles

Men—Brian Robinson, Tahoka, Tex.
Women—Nyla Johnson, Chattaroy, Wash.
Junior—Stuart Welton, Meridian, Idaho

SKEET SHOOTING

NATIONAL SKEET SHOOTING ASSOCIATION WORLD CHAMPIONSHIPS—1980

(Savannah, Ga., July 24-Aug. 1, 1980)

High Overall

Men—Al Magyar Jr., Taylor, Mich.	549
Women—Carla Brundage, San Antonio, Tex.	544
Senior—Jesse L. Vint, Tulsa, Okla.	541
Veteran—Barbee Ponder, Amite, La.	541
Junior—Bobby Wren, Punta Gorda, Fla.	544
Junior women—Vicky Cool, Louisville, Ky.	351
Collegiate—John Shima, San Antonio, Tex.	547

Individual Gun

12–gauge, men—Tito Killian, San Antonio, Tex.	250
12–gauge, women—Barbara Thomas, Brooklyn, N.Y.	250
20–gauge, men—Bruce Evans, Burnet, Tex.	100
20–gauge, women—Sandra McCurley, Mobile, Ala.	100
28–gauge, men—George Desatoff, Hacienda, Calif.	100
28–gauge, women—Ila Hill, Birmingham, Mich.	98
.410–gauge, men—Wayne Mayes, Cleveland, Tenn.	100
.410–gauge, women—Carla Brundage, San Antonio, Tex.	99

Champion of Champions

Men—Todd Bender, San Antonio, Tex.	100
Women—Sheri Confer, Warren, Mich.	98

TAE KWON DO

A.A.U. NATIONAL CHAMPIONS—1980

Men

Finweight—Dae Sung Lee, Honolulu
Flyweight—Michael Vasquez, Port Huron, Mich.
Bantamweight—Chung Sik Choi, Honolulu
Featherweight—Marvin McMillion, Florida
Lightweight—Tom Marshall, Ohio
Welterweight—Mike O'Malley, Boston
Light middleweight—Michael Canada, Oregon
Middleweight—Richard Warwick, Montana
Light heavyweight—Scott Rohr, Portland, Ore.
Heavyweight—Tom Seabourne, Allentown, Pa.

Women

Finweight—Dianna Hill, Florida
Flyweight—Cheryl Kalanoc, Indiana
Bantamweight—Jodene Goldenring, Pacific
Featherweight—Theresa Jun, Florida
Lightweight—Belinda Davis, Pacific
Welterweight—Monique Heckler, Florida
Middleweight—Marcia Hall, Mountainview, Calif.
Heavyweight—Lynette Love, Detroit

JUDO

A.A.U. NATIONAL CHAMPIONSHIPS

(East Lansing, Mich., April 24–26, 1980)

Men

132 lb—Maurice DeLa Torriente, Arlington Heights, Ill.
143 lb—Fred Glock, Minnesota
156 lb—Steve Seck, Los Angeles
172 lb—Brett Barron, San Mateo, Calif.
189 lb—Tommy Martin, Stockton, Calif.
Under 209 lb—Miguel Tudela, Los Angeles
Over 209 lb—John Saylor, Westfield, N.Y.
Open—Dewey Mitchell, Seven Springs, Fla.

Women

106 lb—Jan Zakarzecki, East Lansing, Mich.
114 lb—Eve Aronoff, unattached
123 lb—Geri Bindell, New Milford, N.J.
134 lb—Sandra Coons, Rochelle, Ill.
145 lb—Christine Penick, San Jose, Calif.
158 lb—Amy Kublin, Boston, Mass.
Heavyweight—Margie Castro, New York, N.Y.

PLATFORM TENNIS

UNITED STATES CHAMPIONS—1980

Men's singles—Doug Russell, New York
Women's singles—Robin Rich, Fairfield, Conn.
Men's doubles—Steve Baird, Port Chester, N.Y., and Rich Maier, Allendale, N.J.
Women's doubles—Yvonne Hackenberg, Kalamazoo, Mich., and Hilary Hilton, Glen Ellyn, Ill.
Mixed doubles—Hilary Hilton, Glen Ellyn, Ill., and Doug Russell, New York

RACQUETBALL

U.S. RACQUETBALL ASSOCIATION CHAMPIONS—1980

Men's Events

Open singles—Brett Harnett, Las Vegas, Nev. (defeated Ed Andrews, Bonita, Calif., 21–3, 21–8, in final)
Open doubles—K. Garrigus and K. Fleming, Phoenix, Ariz.
Senior singles, 35 and over—Jay Jones, Sherman Oaks, Calif.
Masters singles, 45 and over—Bud Muehleisen, San Diego, Calif.
Masters doubles, 40 and over—Bud Muehleisen and S. Karp, San Diego, Calif.
Golden masters singles, 55 and over—Kal Gladstone, Glendale, Calif.
Golden masters doubles, 55 and over—Burt Morrow and L. Skelton, Los Angeles
Veterans open singles, 30 and over—Peter Wright, Dallas, Tex.
Veterans open doubles, 30 and over—Mike Romano and Gary Lusk, Chula Vista, Calif.
Veterans senior singles, 40 and over—Charles Garfinkel, Buffalo, N.Y.
Veteran masters singles, 50 and over—Bill Tanner, Memphis, Tenn.
Veterans golden masters singles, 60 and over—Fred Vetter, Elm Grove, Wis.
Professional—Marty Hogan, San Diego, Calif. (defeated Mike Yellen, Southfield, Mich., 21–12, 21–16, in final)
Pro tour—Jerry Hilecher, San Diego, Calif.

Women's Events

Open singles—Susie Dugan, Dallas, Tex. (defeated Peggy Gardner, San Diego, Calif., 21–8, 21–15, in final)
Open doubles—Peggy Gardner, San Diego, Calif., and C. Pool, San Marcos, Calif.
Senior singles, 35 and over—Sue Carow, Chicago
Veterans singles, 30 and over—Camille McCarthy, Indianapolis
Veterans senior singles, 40 and over—Sue Carow, Chicago
Women's pro—Heather McKay, Toronto

PARACHUTING

U.S. CHAMPIONS—1980

Men's overall—Matt O'Gwynn, Langley Air Force Base, Va.
Women's overall—Cheryl Stearns, Fort Bragg, N.C.

POLO

1980 CHAMPIONSHIPS

Gold Cup (18–22 goals)—Retama, San Antonio, Tex.
World Cup—Hallal of Nigeria
Cup of the Americas—Argentina
America Cup—Macondo, Colombia
Silver Cup—Retama
Delegate's Cup (8 goals)—Tennessee
North American Cup—Kingsville, Tex.
Men's college—York University, Toronto
Women's college—University of California—Davis

1979 CHAMPIONSHIPS

United States open—Retama, San Antonio
United States Handicap—Tulsa, Okla.
Gold Cup (18–22 goals)—Retama
Silver Cup—Retama
Butler Handicap—Oak Brook, Ill.
North American Cup—Las Tejas, Tulsa, Okla.
America Cup—Boca Raton, Fla.
Continential Cup (14 goals)—Oak Brook
Copper Cup (20 goals)—Twelve Oaks
Chairman's Cup—Gone Away Farms
Delegate's Cup (8 goals)—Twin Cities, Minneapolis
National President's Cup (8 goals)—Joy Farm
International Open and Palm Beach Handicap—Retama
Retama Cup—Tulsa, Okla.
Oak Brook Cup—Abercrombie and Kent
Abercrombie and Kent Handicap—Milwaukee
Men's college—University of California–Davis
Women's college—Cornell
Women's national handicap—Carmel Valley, Calif.

CURLING

NATIONAL CHAMPIONS

1966	Fargo, N.D. (Joe Zbacnik, skip; Bruce Roberts, Mike O'Leary, Gerald Toutant)
1967	Seattle (Bruce Roberts, skip; Doug Walker, Tom Fitzpatrick, John Wright)
1968–69	Superior, Wis. (Bud Somerville, skip; Bill Strum, Al Gagne, Thomas Wright)
1970	Grafton, N.D. (Art Tallackson, skip; Trueman Thompson, Raymond Holt, Glenn Gilleshammer)
1971	Edmore, N.D. (Dal Dalziel, skip; Rodney Melland, Dennis Melland, Clark Sampson)
1972	Grafton, N.D. (Robert L. LaBonte, skip; Frank L. Aasand, John O. Aasand, Ray Morgan)
1973	Winchester, Mass. (Charles Reeves, Jr., skip; Barry Blanchard, Henry Shean, Douglas Carlson)
1974	Superior, Wis. (Bud Somerville, skip; Tom Locken, Bill Strum, Bob Nichols)[1]
1975	Seattle Granite Club (Ed Risling, skip; Chuck Lundgren, Gary Schnee, Dave Tellvik)
1976	Hibbing, Minn. (Bruce Roberts, skip; Jerry Scott, Gary Kieffmall, Joe Roberts)[1]
1977	Hibbing, Minn. (Bruce Roberts, skip; Paul Pustovar, Gary Kleffman, Jerry Scott)
1978	Superior, Wis. (Bob Nichols, skip; Bob Christman, Tom Lochen, Bill Strum)[1]
1979	Bemidji, Minn. (Scotty Baird, skip)
1980	Hibbing, Minn. (Paul Pustovar, skip; John Jankila, Gary Kleffman, Jerry Scott)

1. Won World Championship.

U.S. CHAMPIONSHIPS—1980

Men—Hibbing, Minn. (Paul Pustovar, skip; John Jankila, Gary Kleffman, Jerry Scott) defeated Wisconsin, 7–5.
Women—Washington State (Sharon Kozai, skip; Aija Edwards, Betty Kozai, Joan Fish)

OTHER MAJOR BONSPIELS—1980

Canadian Championship (Alberta)—Saskatoon, Saskatchewan (Rick Folk, skip)
Gordon Medal (Schenectady, N.Y.)—Schenectady, N.Y. (Chic Hequembourg, skip)

WORLD CHAMPIONSHIPS

Men

(Moncton, New Brunswick; March 24–30, 1980)

Final—Canada (Rick Folk, skip; Ron Mills, Tom Wilson, Jim Wilson) defeated Norway (Kristian Soerum, skip), 7–6

Women

(Perth, Scotland; March 22, 1980)

Final—Canada (Marg Mitchell, skip; Nancy Kerr, Shirley McKendry, Wendy Leach) defeated Sweden, 7–6

LACROSSE

NATIONAL INTERCOLLEGIATE CHAMPIONS

1946	Navy	1958	Army	1970	Johns Hopkins, Navy, Virginia
1947–48	Johns Hopkins	1959	Army, Johns Hopkins, Maryland	1971[1]	Cornell
1949	Johns Hopkins, Navy	1960	Navy	1972	Virginia
1950	Johns Hopkins	1961	Army, Navy	1973	Maryland
1951	Army, Princeton	1962–66	Navy	1974	Johns Hopkins
1952	Virginia, R.P.I.	1967	Johns Hopkins, Maryland, Navy	1975	Maryland
1953	Princeton	1968	Johns Hopkins	1976–77	Cornell
1954	Navy	1969	Army, Johns Hopkins	1978–80	Johns Hopkins
1955–56	Maryland				
1957	Johns Hopkins				

1. First year of N.C.A.A. Championship Tournaments.

NATIONAL COLLEGIATE A.A.

DIVISION I
Final

(Ithaca, N.Y., May 31, 1980)
Johns Hopkins 9, Virginia 8 (overtime)

Semifinals

Johns Hopkins 18, Syracuse 11
Virginia 11, North Carolina 10 (overtime)

Quarterfinals

Johns Hopkins 16, Harvard 12
North Carolina 18, Navy 11
Syracuse 12, Washington & Lee 4
Virginia 9, Cornell 8 (overtime)

ALL-AMERICA TEAM

Attackmen—Mike Buzzell, Navy; Tim O'Hara, Syracuse; Stan Cockerton, North Carolina State
Midfield—Brendan Schneck, Johns Hopkins; John Driscoll, Virginia; Kevin Griswold, North Carolina; Peter Worstell, Maryland
Defense—Mark Greenberg, Johns Hopkins; Kevin O'Shea, Virginia; Mike McLaughlin, Navy
Goal—Mike Frederico, Johns Hopkins; Bob Clements, Washington and Lee

DIVISION II
Final

(Baltimore, May 18, 1980)
Maryland–Baltimore County 23, Adelphi 14
Title decided in playoff between 2 top teams in final coaches' rankings.

DIVISION III
Final

(Geneva, N.Y., May 25, 1980)
Hobart 11, Cortland (N.Y.) State 8

Semifinals

Hobart 21, Salisbury State 5
Cortland State 11, Ithaca 9

Quarterfinals

Hobart 37, M.I.T. 1
Cortland State 13, Ohio Wesleyan 9
Salisbury State 15, St. Lawrence 11
Ithaca 15, Washington (Md.) 14 (overtime)

U.S. WOMEN'S LACROSSE ASSOCIATION NATIONAL COLLEGIATE CHAMPIONSHIP

Final

(Princeton, N.J., May 11, 1980)
Penn State 3, Maryland 1

Semifinals

Penn State 8, Massachusetts 3
Maryland 5, Pennsylvania 4

Quarterfinals

Penn State 12, Harvard 6
Maryland 6, New Hampshire 1
Massachusetts 7, Temple 4
Pennsylvania 8, William and Mary 6

Darts

U.S. OPEN—1980

Rick Ney, Pine Grove, Pa.
World champion—Stefan Lord, Sweden

Frisbee

WORLD CHAMPIONSHIPS

(Pasadena, Calif., Aug. 21–24, 1980)

Men's overall—Scott Zimmerman, McLean, Va.
Women's overall—Cyndi Birch, Santa Barbara, Calif.
Dog "catch-and-fetch"—Kona, Irish Setter, owned by Frank Allen, Phoenix, Ariz.

RODEO

PROFESSIONAL RODEO COWBOY ASSOCIATION, ALL AROUND COWBOY

1953	Bill Linderman	1961	Benny Reynolds	1973	Larry Mahan
1954	Buck Rutherford	1962	Tom Nesmith	1974	Tom Ferguson
1955	Casey Tibbs	1963–65	Dean Oliver	1975	Leo Camarillo and Tom Ferguson
1956–59	Jim Shoulders	1966–70	Larry Mahan	1976–79	Tom Ferguson
1960	Harry Tompkins	1971–72	Phil Lyne		

TENNIS

Lawn tennis is a comparatively modern modification of the ancient game of court tennis. Major Walter Clopton Wingfield thought that something like court tennis might be played outdoors on lawns, and in December, 1873, at Nantclwyd, Wales, he introduced his new game under the name of *Sphairistike* at a lawn party. The game was a success and spread rapidly, but the name was a total failure and almost immediately disappeared when all the players and spectators began to refer to the new game as "lawn tennis." In the early part of 1874, a young lady named Mary Ewing Outerbridge returned from Bermuda to New York, bringing with her the implements and necessary equipment of the new game, which she had obtained from a British Army supply store in Bermuda. Miss Outerbridge and friends played the first game of lawn tennis in the United States on the grounds of the Staten Island Cricket and Baseball Club in the spring of 1874.

For a few years, the new game went along in haphazard fashion until about 1880, when standard measurements for the court and standard equipment within definite limits became the rule. In 1881, the U.S. Lawn Tennis Association (whose name was changed in 1975 to U.S. Tennis Association) was formed and conducted the first national championship at Newport, R.I. The international matches for the Davis Cup began with a series between the British and United States players on the courts of the Longwood Cricket Club, Chestnut Hill, Mass., in 1900, with the home players winning.

Professional tennis, which got its start in 1926 when the French star Suzanne Lenglen was paid $50,000 for a tour, received full recognition in 1968. Staid old Wimbledon, the London home of what are considered the world championships, let the pros compete. This decision ended a long controversy over open tennis and changed the format of the competition. The United States championships were also opened to the pros and the site of the event, long held at Forest Hills, N.Y., was shifted to the National Tennis Center in Flushing Meadows, N.Y., in 1978. Pro tours for men and women became worldwide in play that continued throughout the year.

DAVIS CUP CHAMPIONSHIPS

No matches in 1901, 1910, 1915–18, and 1940–45.

1900	United States 3, British Isles 0
1902	United States 3, British Isles 2
1903	British Isles 4, United States 1
1904	British Isles 5, Belgium 0
1905	British Isles 5, United States 0
1906	British Isles 5, United States 0
1907	Australasia 3, British Isles 2
1908	Australasia 3, United States 2
1909	Australasia 5, United States 0
1911	Australasia 5, United States 0
1912	British Isles 3, Australasia 2
1913	United States 3, British Isles 2
1914	Australasia 3, United States 2
1919	Australasia 4, British Isles 1
1920	United States 5, Australasia 0
1921	United States 5, Japan 0
1922	United States 4, Australasia 1
1923	United States 4, Australasia 1
1924	United States 5, Australasia 0
1925	United States 5, France 0
1926	United States 4, France 1
1927	France 3, United States 2
1928	France 4, United States 1
1929	France 3, United States 2
1930	France 4, United States 1
1931	France 3, Great Britain 2
1932	France 3, United States 2
1933	Great Britain 3, France 2
1934	Great Britain 4, United States 1
1935	Great Britain 5, United States 0
1936	Great Britain 3, Australia 2
1937	United States 4, Great Britain 1
1938	United States 3, Australia 2
1939	Australia 3, United States 2
1946	United States 5, Australia 0
1947	United States 4, Australia 1
1948	United States 5, Australia 0
1949	United States 4, Australia 1
1950	Australia 4, United States 1
1951	Australia 3, United States 2
1952	Australia 4, United States 1
1953	Australia 3, United States 2
1954	United States 3, Australia 2
1955	Australia 5, United States 0
1956	Australia 5, United States 0
1957	Australia 3, United States 2
1958	United States 3, Australia 2
1959	Australia 3, United States 2
1960	Australia 4, Italy 1
1961	Australia 5, Italy 0
1962	Australia 5, Mexico 0
1963	United States 3, Australia 2
1964	Australia 3, United States 2
1965	Australia 4, Spain 1
1966	Australia 4, India 1
1967	Australia 4, Spain 1
1968	United States 4, Australia 1
1969	United States 5, Romania 0
1970	United States 5, West Germany 0
1971	United States 3, Romania 2
1972	United States 3, Romania 2
1973	Australia 5, United States 0
1974	South Africa (Default by India)
1975	Sweden 3, Czechoslovakia 2
1976	Italy 4, Chile 1
1977	Australia 3, Italy 1
1978	United States 4, Britain 1
1979	United States 5, Italy 0

FEDERATION CUP CHAMPIONSHIPS

World team competition for women conducted by International Lawn Tennis Federation

1963	United States 2, Australia 1
1964	Australia 2, United States 1
1965	Australia 2, United States 1
1966	United States 3, West Germany 0
1967	United States 2, Britain 0
1968	Australia 3, Netherlands 0
1969	United States 2, Australia 1
1970	Australia 3, West Germany 0
1971	Australia 3, Britain 0
1972	South Africa 2, Britain 1
1973	Australia 3, South Africa 0
1974	Australia 2, United States 1
1975	Czechoslovakia 3, Australia 0
1976	United States 2, Australia 1
1977	United States 2, Australia 1
1978	United States 2, Australia 1
1979	United States 3, Australia 0
1980	United States 3, Australia 0

FOUR PLAYERS WIN GRAND SLAM OF TENNIS

Only four players, two men and two women, have won the Grand Slam of Tennis by winning the Australian, French, Wimbledon, and United States singles championships. Rod Laver of Australia did it twice, in 1962 and again in 1969 when the tourneys were opens. Don Budge, an American, was the first to complete the slam in 1938. Maureen Connolly of California in 1953 was the first woman to take the four titles. Margaret Smith Court of Australia won them all in 1970.

U.S. CHAMPIONS

Singles—Men

NATIONAL

1881–87	Richard D. Sears
1888–89	Henry Slocum, Jr.
1890–92	Oliver S. Campbell
1893–94	Robert D. Wrenn
1895	Fred H. Hovey
1896–97	Robert D. Wrenn
1898–1900	Malcolm Whitman
1901–02	William A. Larned
1903	Hugh L. Doherty
1904	Holcombe Ward
1905	Beals C. Wright
1906	William J. Clothier
1907–11	William A. Larned
1912–13	Maurice McLoughlin[1]
1914	R. N. Williams II
1915	William Johnston
1916	R. N. William II
1917–18	R. Lindley Murray[2]
1919	William Johnston
1920–25	Bill Tilden
1926–27	Jean Rene Lacoste
1928	Henri Cochet
1929	Bill Tilden
1930	John H. Doeg
1931–32	Ellsworth Vines
1933–34	Fred J. Perry
1935	Wilmer L. Allison
1936	Fred J. Perry
1937–38	Don Budge
1939	Robert L. Riggs
1940	Donald McNeill
1941	Robert L. Riggs
1942	Fred Schroeder
1943	Joseph Hunt
1944–45	Frank Parker
1946–47	Jack Kramer
1948–49	Richard Gonzales
1950	Arthur Larsen
1951–52	Frank Sedgman
1953	Tony Trabert
1954	Vic Seixas
1955	Tony Trabert
1956	Ken Rosewall
1957	Mal Anderson
1958	Ashley Cooper
1959–60	Neale Fraser
1961	Roy Emerson
1962	Rod Laver
1963	Rafael Osuna
1964	Roy Emerson
1965	Manuel Santana
1966	Fred Stolle
1967	John Newcombe
1968	Arthur Ashe[3]
1969	Stan Smith[3]

OPEN

1968	Arthur Ashe
1969	Rod Laver
1970	Ken Rosewall
1971	Stan Smith
1972	Ilie Nastase
1973	John Newcombe
1974	Jimmy Connors
1975	Manuel Orantes
1976	Jimmy Connors
1977	Guillermo Vilas
1978	Jimmy Connors
1979	John McEnroe
1980	John McEnroe

Singles—Women

NATIONAL

1887	Ellen F. Hansel
1888–89	Bertha Townsend
1890	Ellen C. Roosevelt
1891–92	Mabel E. Cahill
1893	Aline M. Terry
1894	Helen R. Helwig
1895	Juliette P. Atkinson
1896	Elisabeth H. Moore
1897–98	Juliette P. Atkinson
1899	Marion Jones
1900	Myrtle McAteer
1901	Elisabeth H. Moore
1902	Marion Jones
1903	Elisabeth H. Moore
1904	May Sutton
1905	Elisabeth H. Moore
1906	Helen Homans
1907	Evelyn Sears
1908	Maud Bargar-Wallach
1909–11	Hazel V. Hotchkiss
1912–14	Mary K. Browne
1915–18	Molla Bjurstedt
1919	Hazel Hotchkiss Wightman
1920–22	Molla Bjurstedt Mallory
1923–25	Helen N. Wills
1926	Molla B. Mallory
1927–29	Helen N. Wills
1930	Betty Nuthall
1931	Helen Wills Moody
1932–35	Helen Jacobs
1936	Alice Marble
1937	Anita Lizana
1938–40	Alice Marble
1941	Sarah Palfrey Cooke
1942–44	Pauline Betz
1945	Sarah Cooke
1946	Pauline Betz
1947	Louise Brough
1948–50	Margaret Osborne duPont
1951–53	Maureen Connolly
1954–55	Doris Hart
1956	Shirley Fry
1957–58	Althea Gibson
1959	Maria Bueno
1960–61	Darlene Hard
1962	Margaret Smith
1963–64	Maria Bueno
1965	Margaret Smith
1966	Maria Bueno
1967	Billie Jean King
1968–69	Margaret Smith Court[3]

OPEN

1968	Virginia Wade
1969–70	Margaret Court
1971–72	Billie Jean King
1973	Margaret Court
1974	Billie Jean King
1975–78	Chris Evert
1979	Tracy Austin
1980	Chris Evert Lloyd

Doubles—Men

NATIONAL

1920	Bill Johnston–C. J. Griffin
1921–22	Bill Tilden–Vincent Richards
1923	Bill Tilden–B. I. C. Norton
1924	H. O. Kinsey–R. G. Kinsey
1925–26	Vincent Richards–R. N. Williams II
1927	Bill Tilden–Frank Hunter
1928	G. M. Lott, Jr.–V. Hennessy
1929–30	G. M. Lott, Jr.–J. H. Doeg
1931	W. L. Allison–John Van Ryn
1932	E. H. Vines, Jr.–Keith Gledh
1933–34	G. M. Lott, Jr.–L. R. Stoefen
1935	W. L. Allison–John Van Ryn
1936	Don Budge–Gene Mako
1937	G. von Cramm–H. Henkel
1938	Don Budge–Gene Mako
1939	A. K. Quist–J. E. Bromwich
1940–41	Jack Kramer–F. R. Schroeder
1942	Gardnar Mulloy–Bill Talbert
1943	Jack Kramer–Frank Parker
1944	Don McNeill–Bob Falkenburg
1945	Gardnar Mulloy–Bill Talbert
1946	Gardnar Mulloy–Bill Talbert
1947	Jack Kramer–Fred Schroeder
1948	Gardnar Mulloy–Bill Talbert
1949	John Bromwich–William Sidwell
1950	John Bromwich–Frank Sedgman
1951	Frank Sedgman–Ken McGregor
1952	Vic Seixas-Mervyn Rose
1953	Mervyn Rose–Rex Hartwig
1954	Vic Seixas–Tony Trabert
1955	Kosei Kamo–Atsushi Miyagi
1956	Lewis Hoad–Ken Rosewall
1957	Ashley Cooper–Neale Fraser
1958	Ham Richardson–Alex Olmedo
1959–60	Neale Fraser–Roy Emerson
1961	Chuck McKinley–Dennis Ralston
1962	Rafael Osuna–Antonio Palafox
1963–64	Chuck McKinley–Dennis Ralston
1965–66	Fred Stolle–Roy Emerson
1967	John Newcombe–Tony Roche
1968	Stan Smith–Bob Lutz[3]
1969	Richard Crealy–Allan Stone[3]

OPEN

1968	Stan Smith–Bob Lutz
1969	Fred Stolle–Ken Rosewall
1970	Nikki Pilic–Fred Barthes

1. Challenge round abandoned in 1912. 2. Patriotic Tournament in 1917. 3. With the inaugural of the Open Tournament in 1968, the United States Lawn Tennis Association held a national championship at Longwood, Chestnut Hill, Mass. which barred contract professionals in 1968 and 1969.

1971 John Newcombe–Roger Taylor
1972 Cliff Drysdale–Roger Taylor
1973 John Newcombe–Owen Davidson
1974 Bob Lutz–Stan Smith
1975 Jimmy Connors–Ilie Nastase
1976 Marty Riessen–Tom Okker
1977 Frew McMillan–Bob Hewitt
1978 Bob Lutz–Stan Smith
1979 John McEnroe–Peter Fleming
1980 Stan Smith–Bob Lutz

Doubles—Women

NATIONAL

1924	G. W. Wightman–Helen Wills
1925	Mary K. Browne–Helen Wills
1926	Elizabeth Ryan–Eleanor Goss
1927	L. A. Godfree–Ermyntrude Harvey
1928	Hazel Hotchkiss Wightman–Helen Wills
1929	Phoebe Watson–L. R. C. Michell
1930	Betty Nuthall–Sarah Palfrey
1931	Betty Nuthall–E. B. Wittingstall
1932	Helen Jacobs–Sarah Palfrey
1933	Betty Nuthall–Freda James
1934	Helen Jacobs–Sarah Palfrey
1935	Helen Jacobs–Sarah Palfrey Fabyan
1936	Marjorie G. Van Ryn–Carolin Babcock
1937–40	Sarah Palfrey Fabyan–Alice Marble
1941	Sarah Palfrey Cooke–Margaret Osborne
1942–47	A. Louise Brough–Margaret Osborne
1948–50	A. Louise Brough–Margaret O. duPont
1951–54	Doris Hart–Shirley Fry
1955–57	A. Louise Brough–Margaret O. duPont
1958–59	Darlene Hard–Jeanne Arth
1960	Darlene Hard–Maria Bueno
1961	Darlene Hard–Lesley Turner
1962	Darlene Hard–Maria Bueno
1963	Margaret Smith–Robyn Ebbern
1964	Karen Hantze Susman–Billie Jean Moffitt
1965	Nancy Richey–Carole Caldwell Graebner
1966	Nancy Richey–Maria Bueno
1967	Billie Jean King–Rosemary Casals
1968	Margaret Court–Maria Bueno[3]
1969	Margaret Court–Virginia Wade[3]

OPEN

1968	Maria Bueno–Margaret Court
1969	Darlene Hard–Francoise Durr
1970	Margaret Court–Judy Dalton
1971	Rosemary Casals–Judy Dalton
1972	Francoise Durr–Betty Stove
1973	Margaret Court–Virginia Wade
1974	Billie Jean King–Rosemary Casals
1975	Margaret Court–Virginia Wade
1976	Linky Boshoff–Ilana Kloss
1977	Martina Navratilova–Betty Stove
1978	Billie Jean King–Martina Navratilova
1979	Betty Stove–Wendy Turnbull
1980	Billie Jean King–Martina Navratilova

1. Challenge round abandoned in 1912. 2. Patriotic Tournament in 1917. 3. With the inaugural of the Open Tournament in 1968, the United States Lawn Tennis Association held a national championship at Longwood, Chestnut Hill, Mass. which barred contract professionals in 1968 and 1969.

U.S. INDOOR CHAMPIONS

Singles—Men

1964	Charles McKinley	1971	Clark Graebner
1965	Erik Lundquist	1972	Stan Smith
1966	Charles Pasarell	1973–75	Jimmy Connors
1967	Charles Pasarell	1976	Ilie Nastase
1968	Cliff Richey	1977	Bjorn Borg
1969	Stan Smith	1978–79	Jimmy Connors
1970	Ilie Nastase	1980	John McEnroe

Singles—Women

1964	Mary Ann Eisel	1971	Billie Jean King
1965	Nancy Richey	1972	Not held
1966	Billie Jean King	1973	Evonne Goolagong
1967	Billie Jean King	1974	Billie Jean King
1968	Billie Jean King	1975	Martina Navratilova
1969	Mary Ann Eisel	1976	Virginia Wade
1970	Mary Ann Curtis	1977–80	Not held

Doubles—Men

1967	Arthur Ashe–Charles Pasarell
1968	Thomas Koch–Tom Okker
1969	Stan Smith–Bob Lutz
1970	Arthur Ashe–Stan Smith
1971	Manuel Orantes–Juan Gisbert
1972	Manuel Orantes–Andres Gimeno
1973	Juan Gisbert–Jurgen Fassbender
1974	Jimmy Connors–Frew McMillan
1975	Jimmy Connors–Ilie Nastase
1976–77	Sherwood Stewart–Fred McNair
1978	Brian Gottfried–Raul Ramirez
1979	Wojtek Fibak–Tom Okker
1980	John McEnroe–Brian Gottfried

Doubles—Women

1967	Carol Aucamp–Mary Ann Eisel
1968	Rosemary Casals–Billie Jean King
1969	Mary Ann Eisel–Valerie Ziegenfuss
1970	Peaches Bartkowicz–Nancy Richey
1971	Billie Jean King–Rosemary Casals
1972	Not held
1973	Olga Morozova–Marina Kroshina
1974	Not held
1975	Billie Jean King–Rosemary Casals
1976	Rosemary Casals–Francoise Durr
1977–80	Not held

SOARING

U.S. CHAMPIONSHIPS—1980

Open division—Dick Butler, Tullahoma, Tenn.
15 meters—Karl Striedieck, Port Matilda, Pa.
Standard division—Karl Striedieck

CASTING

U.S. CHAMPIONSHIPS—1980

Men's all-round—Steve Rajeff, San Francisco
Men's all-accuracy—Steve Rajeff
Women's all-accuracy—Brenda MacSporran, Toronto

BRITISH (WIMBLEDON) CHAMPIONS

(Amateur from inception in 1877 through 1967)

Singles—Men

1908–09	Arthur Gore	1929	Jean Cochet	1950	Budge Patty	1964–65	Roy Emerson
1910–13	A. F. Wilding	1930	Bill Tilden	1951	Richard Savitt	1966	Manuel Santana
1914	N. E. Brookes	1931	S. B. Wood	1952	Frank Sedgman	1967	John Newcombe
1919	G. L. Patterson	1932	Ellsworth Vines	1953	Vic Siexas	1968–69	Rod Laver
1920–21	Bill Tilden	1933	J. H. Crawford	1954	Jaroslav Drobny	1970–71	John Newcombe
1922	G. L. Patterson	1934–36	Fred Perry	1955	Tony Trabert	1972	Stan Smith
1923	William Johnston	1937–38	Don Budge	1956–57	Lewis Hoad	1973	Jan Kodes
1924	Jean Borotra	1939	Robert L. Riggs	1958	Ashley Cooper	1974	Jimmy Connors
1925	Rene Lacoste	1946	Yvon Petra	1959	Alex Olmedo	1975	Arthur Ashe
1926	Jean Borotra	1947	Jack Kramer	1960	Neale Fraser	1976–80	Bjorn Borg
1927	Henri Cochet	1948	R. Falkenburg	1961–62	Rod Laver		
1928	Rene Lacoste	1949	Fred Schroeder	1963	Chuck McKinley		

Singles—Women

1919–23	Lenglen	1937	D. E. Round	1959–60	Maria Bueno	1972–73	Billie Jean King
1924	Kathleen McKane	1938	Helen Wills Moody	1961	Angela Mortimer	1974	Chris Evert
1925	Lenglen	1939	Alice Marble	1962	Karen Susman	1975	Billie Jean King
1926	Godfree	1946	Pauline M. Betz	1963	Margaret Smith	1976	Chris Evert
1927–29	Helen Wills	1947	Margaret Osborne	1964	Maria Bueno	1977	Virginia Wade
1930	Helen Wills Moody	1948–50	A. Louise Brough	1965	Margaret Smith	1978–79	Martina Navratilova
1931	Frl. C. Aussen	1951	Doris Hart	1966–67	Billie Jean King		
1932–33	Helen Wills Moody	1952–54	Maureen Connolly	1968	Billie Jean King	1980	Evonne Goolagong Cawley
1934	D. E. Round	1955	A. Louise Brough	1969	Ann Jones		
1935	Helen Wills Moody	1956	Shirley Fry	1970	Margaret Court		
1936	Helen Jacobs	1957–58	Althea Gibson	1971	Evonne Goolagong		

Doubles—Men

1953	K. Rosewall–L. Hoad	1963	Rafael Osuna–Antonio Palafox	1974	John Newcombe–Tony Roche
1954	R. Hartwig–M. Rose	1964	Fred Stolle–Bob Hewitt	1975	Vitas Gerulaitis–Sandy Mayer
1955	R. Hartwig–L. Hoad	1965	John Newcombe–Tony Roche	1976	Brian Gottfried–Raul Ramirez
1956	L. Hoad–K. Rosewall	1966	John Newcombe–Ken Fletcher	1977	Ross Case–Geoff Masters
1957	Gardnar Mulloy–Budge Patty	1967	Bob Hewitt–Frew McMillan	1978	Frew McMillan–Bob Hewitt
1958	Sven Davidson–Ulf Schmidt	1968–70	John Newcombe–Tony Roche	1979	Peter Fleming–John McEnroe
1959	Roy Emerson–Neale Fraser	1971	Rod Laver–Roy Emerson	1980	Peter McNamara–Paul McNamee
1960	Dennis Ralston–Rafael Osuna	1972	Bob Hewitt–Frew McMillan		
1961	Roy Emerson–Neale Fraser	1973	Jimmy Connors–Ilie Nastase		
1962	Fred Stolle–Bob Hewitt				

Doubles—Women

1956	Althea Gibson–Angela Buxton	1965	Billie Jean Moffitt–Maria Bueno	1974	Evonne Goolagong–Peggy Michel
1957	Althea Gibson–Darlene Hard	1966	Nancy Richey–Maria Bueno	1975	Ann Kiyomura–Kazuko Sawamatsu
1958	Althea Gibson–Maria Bueno	1967–68	Billie Jean King–Rosemary Casals	1976	Chris Evert–Martina Navratilova
1959	Darlene Hard–Jeanne Arth	1969	Margaret Court–Judy Tegart	1977	Helen Cawley–JoAnne Russell
1960	Darlene Hard–Maria Bueno	1970–71	Billie Jean King–Rosemary Casals	1978	Wendy Turnbull–Kerry Reid
1961	Karen Hantze–Billie Jean Moffitt	1972	Billie Jean King–Betty Stove	1979	Billie Jean King–Martina Navratilova
1962	Karen Hantze Susman–Billie Jean Moffitt	1973	Billie Jean King–Rosemary Casals	1980	Kathy Jordan–Anne Smith
1963	Darlene Hard–Maria Bueno				
1964	Margaret Smith–Les Turnerley				

U.S. CHAMPIONSHIPS—1980

Open

(Flushing Meadows, N.Y., Aug. 26–Sept. 7, 1980)

Men's singles—Final: John McEnroe, Douglaston, N.Y., defeated Bjorn Borg, Sweden, 7–6, 6–1, 6–7, 5–7, 6–4. Semifinals: McEnroe defeated Jimmy Connors, Miami Beach, Fla., 6–4, 5–7, 0–6, 6–3, 7–6; Borg defeated Johan Kriek, South Africa, 4–6, 4–6, 6–1, 6–1, 6–1.

Women's singles—Final: Chris Evert Lloyd, Palm Springs, Calif. defeated Hana Mandlikova, Czechoslovakia, 5–7, 6–1, 6–1. Semifinals: Mrs. Lloyd defeated Tracy Auston, Rolling Hills, Calif., 4–6, 6–1, 6–1; Miss Mandlikova defeated Andrea Jaeger, Lincolnshire, Ill., 6–1, 3–6, 7–6.

Men's doubles—Final: Bob Lutz, San Clemente, Calif., and Stan Smith, Hilton Head Island, S.C., defeated McEnroe and Peter Fleming, Seabrook Island, S.C., 7–6, 3–6, 6–1, 3–6, 6–3.

Women's doubles—Final: Billie Jean King, New York City, and Martina Navratilova, Charlottesville, Va., defeated Pam Shriver, Lutherville, Md., and Betty Stove, Netherlands, 7–6, 7–5.

Mixed doubles—Final: Wendy Turnbull, Australia, and Marty Riessen, Boca West, Fla., defeated Miss Stove and Frew McMillan, South Africa, 7–6, 6–2.

Junior boys singles—Final: Mike Falberg, Santa Barbara, Calif., defeated Eric Wilborts, Netherlands, 6–7, 6–3, 6–3.

Junior girls singles—Final: Sue Mascarin, Grosse Point Shores, Mich., defeated Kathrine Keil, Albuquerque, N.M., 6–3, 6–4.

National Clay Court

(Indianapolis, Aug. 6-10, 1980)

Men's singles—Final: Jose-Luis Clerc, Argentina, defeated Mel Purcell, Murray, Ky., 7–5, 6–3.

Women's singles—Final: Chris Evert Lloyd, Palm Springs, Calif., defeated Andrea Jaeger, Lincolnshire, Ill., 6–4, 6–3.

Men's doubles—Final: Kevin Curren, South Africa, and Steve Denton, Kingsville, Tex., defeated Wojtek Fibak, Poland, and Ivan Lendl, Czechoslovakia, 3–6, 7–6, 6–4.

Women's doubles—Final: Anne Smith, Dallas, and Paula Smith, La Jolla, Calif., defeated Virginia Ruzici, Romania, and Renata Tomanova, Czechoslovakia, 4–6, 6–3, 6–4.

World Championship Tennis—Final: Jimmy Connors, Miami Beach, Fla., defeated John McEnroe, Douglaston, N.Y., 2–6, 7–6, 7–4, 6–1, 6–2.

U.S. National Indoor (Memphis)—Final: John McEnroe defeated Jimmy Connors, 7–6, 7–6. Doubles: McEnroe and Brian Gottfried, Fort Lauderdale, Fla., defeated Rod Frawley, Australia, and Tomas Smid, Czechoslovakia, 6–4, 6–7, 7–6.

U.S. Pro Indoor (Philadelphia)—Final: Jimmy Connors defeated John McEnroe, 6–3, 2–6, 6–3, 3–6, 6–4. Doubles: McEnroe and Peter Fleming, Seabrook Island. S.C., defeated Brian Gottfried and Raul Ramirez, Mexico, 6–3, 7–6.

U.S. Pro (Brookline, Mass.)—Final: Eddie Dibbs, Miami Beach, Fla., defeated Gene Mayer, Woodmere, N.Y., 6–2, 6–1. Doubles: Frew McMillan, South Africa, and Colin Dowdeswell, Switzerland, defeated John Yuill, South Africa, and Chris Lewis, New Zealand, 6–3, 6–4.

OTHER 1980 CHAMPIONSHIPS

Wimbledon Open

Men's singles—Bjorn Borg, Sweden, defeated John McEnroe, Douglaston, N.Y., 1–6, 7–5, 6–3, 6–7, 8–6.

Women's singles—Evonne Goolagong Cawley, Australia, defeated Chris Evert Lloyd, Fort Lauderdale, Fla., 6–1, 7–6.

Men's doubles—Peter McNamara and Paul McNamee, Australia, defeated Bob Lutz and Stan Smith, United States, 7–6, 6–3, 6–7, 6–4.

Women's doubles—Kathy Jordan and Anne Smith, United States, defeated Rosemary Casals, United States, and Wendy Turnbull, Australia, 4–6, 7–5, 6–1.

Mixed doubles—John Austin and Tracy Austin, United States, defeated Mark Edmondson and Dianne Fromholtz, Australia, 4–6, 7–6, 6–3.

French Open

Men's singles—Bjorn Borg, Sweden, defeated Vitas Gerulaitis, United States, 6–4, 6–1, 6–2.

Women's singles—Chris Evert Lloyd, United States, defeated Virginia Ruzici, Romania, 6–0, 6–3.

Men's doubles—Henry Pfister and Victor Amaya, United States, defeated Brian Gottfried, United States, and Raul Ramirez, Mexico, 1–6, 6–4, 6–4, 6–3.

Women's doubles—Kathy Jordan and Anne Smith, United States, defeated Ivanna Madruga and Adriana Villagran, Argentina, 6–1, 6–0.

Australian Open

(Melbourne, Dec. 27, 1979-Jan. 2, 1980)

Men's singles—Guillermo Vilas, Argentina, defeated John Sadri, United States, 7–6, 6–3, 6–2.

Women's singles—Barbara Jordan, United States, defeated Sharon Walsh, United States, 6–3, 6–3.

Men's doubles—Peter McNamara and Paul McNamee, Australia, defeated Paul Kronk and Cliff Letcher, Australia, 7–6, 6–2.

Women's doubles—Judy Chaloner, New Zealand, and Dianne Evers, Australia, defeated Leanne Harrison, Australia, and Marcella Mesker, Netherlands, 6–1, 3–6, 6–0.

1980 DAVIS CUP

Zone Competition

(Eliminations started in 1979)

American Zone—South Section: Uruguay defeated Peru, 4–1; Chile defeated Uruguay, 4–1; Brazil won from Ecuador; Brazil defeated Chile, 3–1; Argentina defeated Brazil, 4–1. North Section: Canada defeated Commonwealth Carribean, 5–0; Mexico defeated Canada, 4–1; Venezuela defeated Colombia, 4–1; Mexico defeated Venezuela, 4–1; United States defeated Mexico, 3–2. Zone final: Argentina defeated United States, 4–1.

Eastern Zone—Thailand won from Philippines; Korea defeated Pakistan, 3–2; Taiwan defeated Thailand, 3–2; Korea defeated Indonesia, 5–0; Japan defeated Taiwan, 5–0; Korea defeated India, 3–2; Australia defeated Japan, 5–0; New Zealand defeated Korea, 5–0. Zone final: Australia defeated New Zealand, 3–1.

European Zone A—Turkey defeated Luxembourg, 4–1; Israel defeated Monaco, 4–1; Bulgaria defeated Ireland, 3–2; Netherlands defeated Denmark, 3–2; Norway defeated Turkey, 4–1; Switzerland defeated Israel, 4–1; Hungary defeated Bulgaria, 4–1; Spain defeated Netherlands, 4–1; West Germany defeated Norway, 4–0; Switzerland defeated Hungary, 3–2; West Germany defeated Spain, 3–2; Italy defeated Switzerland, 5–0; Sweden defeated West Germany, 4–1. Zone final: Italy defeated Sweden, 4–1.

European Zone B—Morocco defeated Algeria, 4–1; Belgium defeated Morocco, 4–1; Yugoslavia defeated Portugal, 5–0; Soviet Union defeated Greece, 5–0; Finland defeated Egypt, 5–0; Austria defeated Belgium, 3–2; Romania defeated Yugoslavia, 5–0; France defeated Soviet Union, 3–2; Finland defeated Poland, 5–0; Romania defeated Austria, 3–2; France defeated Finland, 3–2; Romania defeated Britain, 3–2; Czechoslovakia defeated France, 5–0. Zone final: Czechoslovakia defeated Romania, 4–1.

TENNIS EARNINGS—MEN—1980

(Through September 19)

Player	Total
Bjorn Borg	$472,200
John McEnroe	414,945
Jimmy Connors	383,347
Vitas Gerulaitis	270,415
Guillermo Vilas	185,886
Brian Gottfried	173,632
Ivan Lendl	163,131
Gene Mayer	161,844
Harold Solomon	153,743
Eddie Dibbs	150,841

TENNIS EARNINGS—WOMEN—1980

(Through September 19)

Player	Total
Martina Navratilova	$471,400
Tracy Austin	437,853
Billie Jean King	264,680
Chris Evert Lloyd	260,257
Evonne Goolagong Cawley	177,880
Wendy Turnbull	144,288
Kathy Jordan	122,176
Hana Mandlikova	105,805
Andrea Jaeger	104,414
Pam Shriver	101,149

BOXING

Whether it be called pugilism, prize fighting or boxing, there is no tracing "the Sweet Science" to any definite source. Tales of rivals exchanging blows for fun, fame or money go back to earliest recorded history and classical legend. There was a mixture of boxing and wrestling called the "pancratium" in the ancient Olympic Games and in such contests the rivals belabored one another with hands fortified with heavy leather wrappings that were sometimes studded with metal. More than one Olympic competitor lost his life at this brutal exercise.

There was little law or order in pugilism until Jack Broughton, one of the early champions of England, drew up a set of rules for the game in 1743. Broughton, called "the father of English boxing," also is credited with having invented boxing gloves. However, these gloves—or "mufflers" as they were called—were used only in teaching "the manly art of self-defense" or in training bouts. All professional championship fights were contested with "bare knuckles" until 1892, when John L. Sullivan lost the heavyweight championship of the world to James J. Corbett in New Orleans in a bout in which both contestants wore regulation gloves.

The Broughton rules were superseded by the London Prize Ring Rules of 1838. The 8th Marquis of Queensberry, with the help of John G. Chambers, put forward the "Queensberry Rules" in 1866, a code that called for gloved contests. Amateurs took quickly to the Queensberry Rules, the professionals slowly.

HISTORY OF WORLD HEAVYWEIGHT CHAMPIONSHIP FIGHTS

(Bouts in which a new champion was crowned)

Source: Nat Fleischer's Ring Boxing Encyclopedia and Record Book, published and copyrighted by The Ring Book Shop, Inc., 120 West 31st St., New York, N.Y. 10001.

Date	Where held	Winner, weight, age	Loser, weight, age	Rounds	Referee
Sept. 7, 1892	New Orleans, La.	James J. Corbett, 178 (26)	John L. Sullivan, 212 (33)	21	Prof. John Duffy
March 17, 1897	Carson City, Nev.	Bob Fitzsimmons, 167 (34)	James J. Corbett, 183 (30)	KO 14	George Siler
June 9, 1899	Coney Island, N.Y.	James J. Jeffries, 206 (24)[1]	Bob Fitzsimmons, 167 (37)	KO 11	George Siler
Feb. 23, 1906	Los Angeles	Tommy Burns, 180 (24)[2]	Marvin Hart, 188 (29)	20	James J. Jeffries
Dec. 26, 1908	Sydney, N.S.W.	Jack Johnson, 196 (30)	Tommy Burns, 176 (27)	KO 14	Hugh McIntosh
April 5, 1915	Havana, Cuba	Jess Willard, 230 (33)	Jack Johnson, 205½ (37)	KO 26	Jack Welch
July 4, 1919	Toledo, Ohio	Jack Dempsey, 187 (24)	Jess Willard, 245 (37)	KO 3	Ollie Pecord
Sept. 23, 1926	Philadelphia	Gene Tunney, 189 (28)[3]	Jack Dempsey, 190 (31)	10	Pop Reilly
June 12, 1930	New York	Max Schmeling, 188 (24)	Jack Sharkey, 197 (27)	WF 4	Jim Crowley
June 21, 1932	Long Island City	Jack Sharkey, 205 (29)	Max Schmeling, 188 (26)	15	Gunboat Smith
June 29, 1933	Long Island City	Primo Carnera, 260½ (26)	Jack Sharkey, 201 (30)	KO 6	Arthur Donovan
June 14, 1934	Long Island City	Max Baer, 209½ (25)	Primo Carnera, 263¼ (27)	KO 11	Arthur Donovan
June 13, 1935	Long Island City	Jim Braddock, 193¾ (29)	Max Baer, 209½ (26)	15	Jack McAvoy
June 22, 1937	Chicago	Joe Louis, 197¼ (23)	Jim Braddock, 197 (31)	KO 8	Tommy Thomas
June 22, 1949	Chicago	Ezzard Charles, 181¾ (27)[4]	Joe Walcott, 195½ (35)	15	Davey Miller
Sept. 27, 1950	New York	Ezzard Charles, 184½ (29)[5]	Joe Louis, 218 (36)	15	Mark Conn
July 18, 1951	Pittsburgh	Joe Walcott, 194 (37)	Ezzard Charles, 182 (30)	KO 7	Buck McTiernan
Sept. 23, 1952	Philadelphia	Rocky Marciano, 184 (29)[6]	Joe Walcott, 196 (38)	KO 13	Charley Daggert
Nov. 30, 1956	Chicago	Floyd Patterson, 182¼ (21)	Archie Moore, 187[illegible] (42)	KO 5	Frank Sikora
June 26, 1959	New York	Ingemar Johansson, 196 (26)	Floyd Patterson, 182 (24)	KO 3	Ruby Goldstein
June 20, 1960	New York	Floyd Patterson, 190 (25)	Ingemar Johansson, 194¾ (27)	KO 5	Arthur Mercante
Sept. 25, 1962	Chicago	Sonny Liston, 214 (28)	Floyd Patterson, 189 (27)	KO 1	Frank Sikora
Feb. 25, 1964	Miami Beach, Fla.	Cassius Clay, 210 (22)[7]	Sonny Liston, 218 (30)	KO 7	Barney Felix
March 4, 1968	New York	Joe Frazier, 204½ (24)[8]	Buster Mathis, 243½ (23)	KO 11	Arthur Mercante
April 27, 1968	Oakland, Calif.	Jimmy Ellis, 197 (28)[9]	Jerry Quarry, 195 (22)	15	Elmer Costa
Feb. 16, 1970	New York	Joe Frazier, 205 (26)[10]	Jimmy Ellis, 201 (29)	KO 5	Tony Perez
Jan. 22, 1973	Kingston, Jamaica	George Foreman, 217½ (24)	Joe Frazier, 214 (29)	KO 2	Arthur Mercante
Oct. 30, 1974	Kinshasa, Zaire	Muhammad Ali, 216½ (32)	George Foreman, 220 (26)	KO 8	Zack Clayton
Feb. 15, 1978	Las Vegas, Nev.	Leon Spinks, 197 (25)	Muhammad Ali, 224½ (36)	15	Howard Buck
June 9, 1978	Las Vegas, Nev.	Larry Holmes, 212 (28)[11]	Ken Norton, 220 (32)	15	Mills Lans
Sept. 15, 1978	New Orleans	Muhammad Ali, 221 (36)[12]	Leon Spinks, 201 (25)	15	Lucien Joubert
Oct. 20, 1979	Pretoria, S. Africa	John Tate, 240 (24)[13]	Gerrie Coetzee, 222 (24)	15	Carlos Berrocal
March 31, 1980	Knoxville, Tenn.	Mike Weaver, 207½ (27)	John Tate, 232 (25)	KO 15	Ernesto Magana Ansorena

1. Jeffries retired as champion in March 1905. He named Marvin Hart and Jack Root as leading contenders and agreed to referee their fight in Reno, Nev., on July 3, 1905, with the stipulation that he would term the winner the champion. Hart, 190 (28), knocked out Root, 171 (29), in the 12th round. 2. Burns claimed the title after defeating Hart. 3. Tunney retired as champion after defeating Tom Heeney on July 26, 1928. 4. After Louis announced his retirement as champion on March 1, 1949, Charles won recognition from the National Boxing Association as champion by defeating Walcott. 5. Charles gained undisputed recognition as champion by defeating Louis, who came out of retirement. 6. Retired as champion April 27, 1956. 7. The World Boxing Association later withdrew its recognition of Clay as champion and declared the winner of a bout between Ernie Terrell and Eddie Machen would gain its version of the title. Terrell, 199 (25), won a 15-round decision from Machen, 192 (32), in Chicago on March 5, 1965. Clay, 212¼ (25) and Terrell, 212½ (27) met in Houston on Feb. 6, 1967, Clay winning a 15-round decision. 8. Winner recognized by New York, Massachusetts, Maine, Illinois, Texas and Pennsylvania to fill vacated title when Clay was stripped of championship for failing to accept U. S. Induction. 9. Bout was final of eight-man tournament to fill Clay's place and is recognized by World Boxing Association. 10. Bout settled controversy over title. 11. Holmes won World Boxing Council title after W.B.C. had withdrawn recognition of Spinks, March 18, 1978, and awarded its title to Norton. W.B.C. said Spinks had reneged on agreement to fight Norton 12. Ali regained World Boxing Association championship. 13. Tate won W.B.A. title after Ali retired and left it vacant.

BARE KNUCKLE HEAVYWEIGHT CHAMPIONS

1719 Jim Figg
1734 George Taylor
1740 Jack Broughton
1750 Jack Slack
1760 Bill Stevens
1761 George Meggs
1765 Bill Darts
1777 Harry Sellers
1780 Jack Harris
1785 Tom (Jackling) Johnson
1790 Big Ben Brain
1792 Daniel Mendoza
1795 John Jackson (retired)
1802 Jem Belcher
1805 Henry Pearce (Game Chicken)
1808 John Gully (declined title)
1809 Tom Cribb received belt, not transferable, and cup
1824 Tom Spring received four cups; resigned title
1825 Jem Ward received belt, not transferable
1838 James (Deaf) Burke claimed title
1839 William Thompson (Bendigo) beat Burke; claimed championship; received belt from Jem Ward
1841 Nick Ward (Jem's brother) beat Ben Caunt, Feb. 2. In return match Caunt beat Nick Ward and received belt by subscription. It was transferable.
1845 Thompson beat Caunt and got belt
1850 Bill Perry (The Tipton Slasher), after fight with Paddock, claimed title
1851 Harry Broome won title from Perry
1853 Perry claimed title when Broome forfeited £200 to him in a match; retired from ring on Aug. 13
1857 Tom Sayers beat Perry for £200 a side and new belt
1860 Sayers retired after 42-round draw with John C. Heenan (The Benicia Boy), leaving old belt open for competition
1860 Sam Hurst (The Stalybridge Infant) beat Paddock and received belt
1861 Jem Mace beat Hurst
1862 Mace beat Tom King for £200 a side and the belt
1862 King beat Mace and claimed belt. Subsequently gave it up. Declined to meet Mace again. Mace claimed belt.
1863 King beat Heenan for £1,000 a side
1865 Joe Wormald beat Andrew Marsden for £200 a side and belt, which had been claimed by both. Belt was given to Wormald, who forfeited £120 to Mace
1866 Mace and Joe Goss fought draw with £200 a side and belt at stake
1867 Wormald received £200 forfeit from Ned O'Baldwin and claimed belt when O'Baldwin failed to appear at starting place
1867 Mace and O'Baldwin drew; £200 a side; title and belt in abeyance
1869 Mike McCoole defeated Tom Allen and claimed American championship
1870 Mace claimed world title by knocking out Allen in 10 rounds
1873 Mace retired and Allen claimed title of world champion by defeating McCoole
1876 Allen fought Joe Goss, ranked next to Mace in England. Allen was disqualified in the 27th round for fouling and Goss was recognized as world champion under London Prize Ring Rules
1880 Paddy Ryan knocked out Goss in the 87th round on May 30, near Colliers Station, W. Va., and became the first American to hold the undisputed world's bare knuckle championship
1882 John L. Sullivan knocked out Ryan in the 9th round at Mississippi City, Miss., on Feb. 7 and became the last bare knuckle champion
1889 Sullivan defeated Jake Kilrain in the last bare knuckle championship fight. The bout, on July 8 at Richburg, Miss., went 75 rounds.

BOXING'S BIGGEST GATES

Date	Winner, weight Loser, weight	Rounds	Site	Receipts	Attendance
Oct. 2, 1980	Holmes (211½)—Ali (217½)	KO 15	Las Vegas, Nev.	$6,000,000	24,790
Sept. 15, 1978	Ali (221)—Spinks (201)	15	Superdome, New Orleans	4,806,675	65,370
Sept. 22, 1927	Tunney (189½)—Dempsey (192½) (2d)	10	Soldier Field, Chicago	2,658,660	104,943
Sept. 28, 1976	Ali (221)—Norton (217½) (2d)	15	Yankee Stadium, New York	2,400,000	30,289
June 19, 1946	Louis (207)—Conn (187) (2d)	KO 8	Yankee Stadium, New York	1,925,564	45,266
Sept. 23, 1926	Tunney (189½)—Dempsey (190) (1st)	10	Sesquicentennial Stdm., Phila.	1,895,733	120,757
July 2, 1921	Dempsey (188)—Carpentier (172)	KO 4	Boyle's 30 Acres, Jersey City	1,789,238	80,183
Oct. 1, 1975	Ali (224½)—Frazier (214½) (3d)	KO 14	Manila, Philippines	1,600,000	25,000
March 8, 1971	Joe Frazier (205½)—Muhammad Ali (215)	15	New Madison Square Garden	1,352,951	20,455
Oct. 30, 1974	Ali (216½)—Foreman (220)	KO 8	Kinshasa, Zaire	1,200,000	65,000
Sept. 14, 1923	Dempsey (192½)—Firpo (216½)	KO 2	Polo Grounds, New York	1,188,603	82,000
July 21, 1927	Dempsey (194½)—Sharkey (196)	KO 7	Yankee Stadium, New York	1,083,530	75,000
Jan. 28, 1974	Ali (212) Frazier (209) (2d)	12	New Madison Square Garden	1,053,688	20,748
June 22, 1938	Louis (198¾)—Schmeling (193) (2d)	KO 1	Yankee Stadium, New York	1,015,012	70,043
Sept. 24, 1935	Louis (199¼)—Max Baer (210½)	KO 4	Yankee Stadium, New York	1,000,832	88,150
Sept. 21, 1955	Marciano (188¼)—Moore (188)	KO 9	Yankee Stadium, New York	948,117	61,574
June 25, 1948	Louis (213½)—Walcott (194¾) (2d)	KO 11	Yankee Stadium, New York	841,739	42,667
June 20, 1960	Patterson (190)—Johansson (194¾) (2d)	KO 5	Polo Grounds, New York	824,814	31,892
Sept. 12, 1951	Robinson (157½)—Turpin (159) (2d)	KO 10	Polo Grounds, New York	767,626	61,370
June 12, 1930	Schmeling (188)—Sharkey (197) (1st)	WF 4	Yankee Stadium, New York	749,935	79,222
June 22, 1937	Louis (197¼)—Braddock (197)	KO 8	Comiskey Park, Chicago	715,470	45,500
July 26, 1928	Tunney (192)—Heeney (203½)	KO 11	Yankee Stadium, New York	691,014	45,890
Sept. 25, 1962	Liston (214)—Patterson (189) (1st)	KO 1	Comiskey Park, Chicago	665,420	18,894
March 4, 1968	Frazier (206)—Mathis Benvenuti (160)—Griffith (154½)	KO 11 15	New Madison Square Garden	658,503	18,096
Feb. 16, 1970	Joe Frazier (205)—Jimmy Ellis (201)	KO 5	New Madison Square Garden, N.Y.	647,997	18,079
Feb. 25, 1964	Clay (210½)—Liston (218) (1st)	KO 7	Miami Beach, Fla.	625,000	8,927
Dec. 7, 1970	Ali (212)—Bonavena (204)	KO 15	New Madison Square Garden, New York	615,401	19,417
Sept. 29, 1941	Louis (202¼)—Nova (202½)	KO 6	Polo Grounds, New York	583,711	56,549
Sept. 23, 1957	Basilio (153½)—Robinson (160) (1st)	15	Yankee Stadium, New York	556,467	38,072
June 19, 1936	Schmeling (192)—Louis (198) (1st)	KO 12	Yankee Stadium, New York	547,541	42,088

June 17, 1954	Marciano (187½)—Charles (185½) (1st)		15	Yankee Stadium, New York	543,092	47,585
June 17, 1974	Frazier (212)—Quarry (197½) (2d)	KO	5	New Madison Square Garden, N.Y.	517,006	14,611
Sept. 20, 1972	Ali (218)—Patterson (188½) (2d)	KO	7	New Madison Square Garden, N.Y.	512,361	17,378

NOTES: KO—won by knockout; WF—won on foul; ND—no decision; 1st—first bout; 2d—second bout; 3rd—third bout.

OTHER WORLD BOXING TITLEHOLDERS

Light Heavyweight

1903	Jack Root, George Gardner
1903–05	Bob Fitzsimmons
1905–12	Philadelphia Jack O'Brien[1]
1912–16	Jack Dillon
1916–20	Battling Levinsky
1920–22	Georges Carpentier
1923	Battling Siki
1923–25	Mike McTigue
1925–26	Paul Berlenbach
1926–27	Jack Delaney[2]
1927	Mike McTigue
1927–29	Tommy Loughran
1930	Jimmy Slattery
1930–34	Maxie Rosenbloom
1934–35	Bob Olin
1935–39	John Henry Lewis
1939	Melio Bettina
1939–41	Billy Conn[2]
1941	Anton Christoforidis (NBA)
1941–48	Gus Lesnevich
1948–50	Freddie Mills
1950–52	Joey Maxim
1952–61	Archie Moore[3]
1961–63	Harold Johnson
1963–65	Willie Pastrano
1965–66	José Torres
1966–67	Dick Tiger
1968	Dick Tiger, Bob Foster
1969–70	Bob Foster
1971	Vicente Rondon (WBA), Bob Foster (WBC)
1972–73	Bob Foster (WBA, WBC)
1974	John Conteh (WBA), Bob Foster (WBC)[1 4]
1975–76	Victor Galindez (WBA), John Conteh (WBC)
1977	Victor Galindez (WBA), John Conteh (WBC)[4], Miguel Cuello (WBC)
1978	Victor Galindez (WBA), Mike Rossman (WBA), Miguel Cuello (WBC), Mate Parlov (WBC), Marvin Johnson (WBC)
1979	Mike Rossman (WBA), Victor Galindez (WBA), Marvin Johnson (WBC), Matthew (Franklin) Saad Muhammad (WBC)
1980	Matthew Saad Muhammad (WBC), Marvin Johnson (WBA), Eddie (Gregory) Mustafa Muhammad (WBA)

1. Retired. 2. Abandoned title. 3. NBA withdrew recognition in 1961, New York Commission in 1962; recognized thereafter only by California and Europe. 4. WBC withdrew recognition.

Middleweight

1867–72	Tom Chandler
1872–81	George Rooke
1881–82	Mike Donovan[1]
1884–91	Jack (Nonpareil) Dempsey
1891–97	Bob Fitzsimmons[2]
1908	Stanley Ketchel, Billy Papke
1908–10	Stanley Ketchel[3]
1913	Frank Klaus
1913–14	George Chip
1914–17	Al McCoy
1917–20	Mike O'Dowd
1920–23	Johnny Wilson
1923–26	Harry Greb
1926	Tiger Flowers
1926–31	Mickey Walker[2]
1931–41	Gorilla Jones, Ben Jeby, Marcel Thil, Lou Brouillard, Vince Dundee, Teddy Yarosz, Babe Risko, Freddy Steele, Al Hostak, Solly Kreiger, Fred Apostoli, Ceferino Garcia, Ken Overlin, Billy Soose, Tony Zale[4]
1941–47	Tony Zale
1947–48	Rocky Graziano
1948	Tony Zale
1948–49	Marcel Cerdan
1949–51	Jake LaMotta
1952	Ray Robinson, Randy Turpin
1951–52	Ray Robinson[1]
1953–55	Carl Olson
1955–57	Ray Robinson[5]
1957	Gene Fullmer, Ray Robinson
1957–58	Carmen Basilio
1958–60	Ray Robinson[6]
1960–61	Paul Pender[7]
1959–62	Gene Fullmer (NBA)
1961–62	Terry Downes[1]
1962	Paul Pender[1]
1962–63	Dick Tiger
1963–65	Joey Giardello
1965–66	Dick Tiger
1966	Emile Griffith
1967	Nino Benvenuti, Emile Griffith
1968	Emile Griffith, Nino Benvenuti
1969	Nino Benvenuti
1970	Nino Benvenuti, Carlos Monzon
1971–73	Carlos Monzon
1974–75	Carlos Monzon (WBA), Rodrigo Valdez (WBC)
1976	Carlos Monzon (WBA, WBC), Rodrigo Valdez (WBC)
1977	Carlos Monzon (WBA, WBC)[1], Rodrigo Valdez (WBA, WBC)
1978	Rodrigo Valdez, Hugo Corro
1979	Hugo Corro, Vito Antuofermo
1980	Vito Antuofermo, Alan Minter, Marvin Hagler

1. Retired. 2. Abandoned title. 3. Died. 4. National Boxing Association and New York Commission disagreed on champions. Those listed were accepted by one or the other until Zale gained world-wide recognition. 5. Ended retirement in 1954. 6. NBA withdrew recognition. 7. Recognized by New York, Massachusetts, and Europe.

Welterweight

1892–94	Mysterious Billy Smith
1894–96	Tommy Ryan
1896	Kid McCoy[2]
1896–1900	Mysterious Billy Smith
1900	Rube Ferns
1900–01	Matty Matthews
1901	Ruby Ferns
1901–04	Joe Walcott
1904	Dixie Kid[2]
1904–06	Joe Walcott
1906–07	Honey Mellody
1907	Mike (Twin) Sullivan[2]
1915–19	Ted Lewis
1919–22	Jack Britton
1922–26	Mickey Walker
1926–27	Pete Latzo
1927–29	Joe Dundee
1929–30	Jackie Fields
1930	Young Jack Thompson
1930–31	Tommy Freeman
1931	Young Jack Thompson
1931–32	Lou Brouillard
1932–33	Jackie Fields
1933	Young Corbett 3rd
1933–34	Jimmy McLarnin, Barney Ross
1934–35	Jimmy McLarnin
1935–38	Barney Ross
1938–40	Henry Armstrong
1940–41	Fritzie Zivic
1941–46	Freddie Cochrane
1946	Marty Servo[1]
1946–51	Ray Robinson[2]
1951	Johnny Bratton (NBA)
1951–54	Kid Gavilan
1954–55	Johnny Saxton
1955	Tony DeMarco
1955–56	Carmen Basilio
1956	Johnny Saxton
1956–57	Carmen Basilio[2]
1958	Virgil Akins
1959–60	Don Jordan

1960–61	Benny (Kid) Paret
1961	Emile Griffith
1961–62	Benny (Kid) Paret
1962–63	Emile Griffith, Luis Rodriguez
1963–66	Emile Griffith[2]
1966–69	Curtis Cokes
1969	Curtis Cokes, José Napoles
1970	José Napoles, Billy Backus
1971	Billy Backus, José Napoles
1972–74	José Napoles
1975	José Napoles (WBA, WBC)[3], Angel Espada (WBA), John Stracey (WBC)
1976	Angel Espada (WBA), José Cuevas (WBA), John Stracey (WBC), Carlos Palomino (WBC)
1977–78	José Cuevas (WBA), Carlos Palomino (WBC)
1979	José Cuevas (WBA), Carlos Palomino (WBC), Wilfredo Benitez (WBC)
1980	Jose Cuevas (WBA), Sugar Ray Leonard (WBC), Roberto Duran (WBC), Thomas Hearns (WBA)

1. Retired. 2. Abandoned title. 3. WBA withdrew recognition.

Lightweight

1869–99	Kid Lavigne
1899–1902	Frank Erne
1902–08	Joe Gans
1908–10	Battling Nelson
1910–12	Ad Wolgast
1912–14	Willie Ritchie
1914–17	Freddy Welsh
1917–25	Benny Leonard[1]
1925	Jimmy Goodrich
1925–26	Rocky Kansas
1926–30	Sammy Mandell
1930	Al Singer
1930–33	Tony Canzoneri
1933–35	Barney Ross[2]
1935–36	Tony Canzoneri
1936–38	Lou Ambers
1938–39	Henry Armstrong
1939–40	Lou Ambers
1940–41	Lew Jenkins
1941–42	Sammy Angott[1]
1943–47	Beau Jack (N.Y.), Bob Montgomery (N.Y.), Sammy Angott (NBA), Juan Zurita (NBA), Ike Williams (NBA)
1947–51	Ike Williams
1951–52	James Carter
1952	Lauro Salas
1952–54	James Carter
1954	Paddy DeMarco
1954–55	James Carter
1955–56	Wallace Smith
1956–62	Joe Brown
1962–65	Carlos Ortiz
1965	Ismael Laguna
1965–68	Carlos Ortiz
1968	Teo Cruz
1969	Teo Cruz, Mando Ramos
1970	Mando Ramos, Ismael Laguna, Ken Buchanan
1971	Ken Buchanan (WBA), Mando Ramos (WBC), Pedro Carrasco (WBC)
1972	Ken Buchanan (WBA), Roberto Duran (WBA), Pedro Carrasco (WBC), Mando Ramos (WBC), Chango Carmona (WBC), Rodolfo Gonzalez (WBC)
1973	Roberto Duran (WBA), Rodolfo Gonzalez (WBC)
1974	Roberto Duran (WBA), Rodolfo Gonzalez (WBC), Guts Ishimatsu (WBC)
1975	Roberto Duran (WBA), Guts Ishimatsu (WBC)
1976	Roberto Duran (WBA), Guts Ishimatsu (WBC), Esteban De Jesus (WBC)
1977	Roberto Duran (WBA), Esteban De Jesus (WBC)
1978	Roberto Duran (WBA, WBC)
1979	Roberto Duran[2]; Jim Watt (WBC), Ernesto Espana (WBA)
1980	Ernesto Espana (WBA), Hilmer Kenty (WBA), Jim Waat (WBC)

1. Retired. 2. Abandoned title.

Featherweight

1889	Dal Hawkins[1]
1890	Billy Murphy
1892–1900	George Dixon
1900–01	Terry McGovern
1901	Young Corbett[1]
1901–12	Abe Attell
1912–23	Johnny Kilbane
1923	Eugene Criqui
1923–25	Johnny Dundee[1]
1925–27	Louis (Kid) Kaplan[1]
1927–28	Benny Bass
1928	Tony Canzoneri
1928–29	Andre Routis
1929–32	Battling Battalino[1]
1932	Tommy Paul (NBA), Kid Chocolate (N.Y.)
1933–36	Freddie Miller
1936–37	Petey Sarron
1937–38	Henry Armstrong[1]
1938–40	Joey Archibald
1940–41	Harry Jefra, Joey Archibald
1941–42	Chalky Wright
1942–48	Willie Pep
1948–49	Sandy Saddler[2]
1949–50	Willie Pep
1950–57	Sandy Saddler
1957–59	Kid Bassey
1959–63	Davey Moore
1963–64	Sugar Ramos
1964–67	Vicente Saldivar[2]
1968	Howard Winstone, José Legra,[3] Paul Rojas (WBA), Sho Saijo (WBA)
1969	Sho Saijo (WBA), Johnny Famechon[3]
1970	Sho Saijo (WBA), Johnny Famechon,[3] Vicente Salvidar,[3] Kuniaki Shibata[3]
1971	Sho Saijo (WBA), Antonio Gomez (WBA), Kuniaki Shibata (WBC)
1972	Antonio Gomez (WBA), Ernesto Marcel (WBA), Kuniaki Shibata (WBC), Clemente Sanchez (WBC),[2] José Legra (WBC)
1973	Ernesto Marcel (WBA), José Legra (WBC), Eder Jofre (WBC)
1974	Ernesto Marcel (WBA)[2], Ruben Olivares (WBA), Alexis Arguello (WBA), Eder Jofre (WBC), Bobby Chacon (WBC)
1975	Alexis Arguello (WBA), Bobby Chacon (WBC), Ruben Olivares (WBC), David Kotey (WBC)
1976	Alexis Arguello (WBA),[2] David Kotey (WBC), Danny Lopez (WBC)
1977	Rafael Ortega (WBA), Danny Lopez (WBC)
1978	Rafael Ortega (WBA), Cecilio Lastra (WBA), Eusebio Pedrosa (WBA), Danny Lopez (WBC)
1979	Eusebio Pedrosa (WBA), Danny Lopez (WBC)
1980	Eusebio Pedroza (WBA), Danny Lopez (WBC), Salvador Sanchez (WBC)

1. Abandoned title. 2. Retired. 3. Recognized in Europe, Mexico, and Orient.

Bantamweight

1890–92	George Dixon[1]
1894–99	Jimmy Barry[2]
1899–1900	Terry McGovern[1]
1901	Harry Harris[1]
1902–03	Harry Forbes
1903–04	Frankie Neil
1904	Joe Bowker[1]
1905–07	Jimmy Walsh[1]
1910–14	Johnny Coulon
1914–17	Kid Williams
1917–20	Pete Herman
1920	Joe Lynch
1920–21	Joe Lynch, Pete Herman, Johnny Buff

1922	Johnny Buff, Joe Lynch
1923	Joe Lynch
1924	Joe Lynch, Abe Goldstein
1924	Abe Goldstein, Eddie (Cannonball) Martin
1925	Eddie (Cannonball) Martin, Charlie (Phil) Rosenberg[3]
1927–28	Bud Taylor (NBA)[1]
1929–34	Al Brown
1935	Al Brown, Baltazar Sangchili
1936	Baltazar Sangchili, Tony Marino, Sixto Escobar
1937	Sixto Escobar, Harry Jeffra
1938	Harry Jeffra, Sixto Escobar
1939–40	Sixto Escobar[2]
1940–42	Lou Salica
1942–46	Manuel Ortiz
1947	Manuel Ortiz, Harold Dade
1948–50	Manuel Ortiz
1950–52	Vic Toweel
1952–54	Jimmy Carruthers[2]
1954–55	Robert Cohen
1956	Robert Cohen, Mario D'Agata, Raul Macias (NBA)
1957	Mario D'Agata, Alphonse Halimi
1958–59	Alphonse Halimi
1959–60	Jose Becerra[2]
1960–61	Alphonse Halimi[4]
1961–62	Johnny Caldwell[4]
1961–65	Eder Jofre
1965–68	Masahika (Fighting) Harada
1968	Masahika (Fighting) Harada, Lionel Rose
1969	Lionel Rose, Ruben Olivares
1970	Ruben Olivares, Chucho Castillo
1971	Chucho Castillo, Ruben Olivares
1972	Ruben Olivares, Rafael Herrera, Enrique Pinder
1973	Enrique Pinder (WBA), Romeo Anaya (WBA), Arnold Taylor (WBA) Rodolfo Martinez (WBC), Rafael Herrera (WBC)
1974	Arnold Taylor (WBA), Soo Hwan Hong (WBA), Rafael Herrera (WBC), Rodolfo Martinez (WBC)
1975	Soo Hwan Hong (WBA), Alfonso Zamora (WBA), Rodolfo Martinez (WBC)
1976	Alfonso Zamora (WBA), Rodolfo Martinez (WBC), Carlos Zarate (WBC)
1977	Alfonso Zamora (WBA), Jorge Lujan (WBA), Carlos Zarate (WBC)
1978	Jorge Lujan (WBA), Carlos Zarate (WBC)
1979	Jorge Lujan (WBA), Carlos Zarate (WBC), Lupe Pintor (WBC)
1980	Jorge Lujan (WBA), Lupe Pintor (WBC), Julian Solis (WBA)

1. Abandoned title. 2. Retired. 3. Deprived of title for failing to make weight. 4. Recognized in Europe.

Flyweight

1916–23	Jimmy Wilde
1923–25	Pancho Villa[1]
1925	Frankie Genaro
1925–27	Fidel La Barba[2]
1927–31	Corporal Izzy Schwartz, Frankie Genaro, Emile (Spider) Pladner, Midget Wolgast, Young Perez[3]
1932–35	Jackie Brown
1935–38	Bennie Lynch[4]
1939	Peter Kane[4]
1943–47	Jackie Paterson[1]
1947–50	Rinty Monaghan[2]
1950	Terry Allen
1950–52	Dado Marino
1952–54	Yoshio Shirai
1954–60	Pascual Perez
1960–62	Pone Kingpetch
1962–63	Masahika (Fighting) Harada
1963–64	Hiroyuki Ebihara
1964–65	Pone Kingpetch
1965–66	Salvatore Burrini
1966	Walter McGown, Chartchai Chionoi
1966–68	Charchai Chionoi
1969	Bernabe Villacampa, Efran Torres (WBA)
1970	Bernabe Villacampa, Chartchai Chionoi, Erbito Salavarria, Berkrerk Chartvanchai (WBA), Masao Ohba (WBA)
1971	Masao Ohba (WBA), Erbito Salavarria (WBC)
1972	Masao Ohba (WBA), Erbito Salavarria (WBC), Betulio Gonzalez (WBC), Venice Borkorsor (WBC)
1973	Masao Ohba (WBA), Chartchai Chionoi (WBA), Venice Borkorsor (WBC), Betulio Gonzalez (WBC)
1974	Chartchai Chionoi (WBA), Susumu Hanagata (WBA), Betulio Gonzalez (WBC), Shoji Oguma (WBC)
1975	Susumu Hanagata (WBA), Erbito Salavarria (WBA), Shoji Oguma (WBC), Miguel Canto (WBC)
1976	Erbito Salavarria (WBA), Alfonso Lopez (WBA), Guty Espadas (WBA), Miguel Canto (WBC)
1977	Guty Espadas (WBA), Miguel Canto (WBC)
1978	Guty Espadas (WBA), Betulio Gonzalez (WBA), Miguel Canto (WBC)
1979	Betulio Gonzalez (WBA), Miguel Canto (WBC), Park Chan-Hee (WBC)
1980	Luis Ibarra (WBA), Kim Tae Shik (WBA), Park Chan-Hee (WBC), Shoji Oguma (WBC)

1. Died. 2. Retired. 3. Claimants to NBA and New York Commission titles. 4. Abandoned title.

PROFESSIONAL WEIGHT LIMITS

Flyweight	112	Featherweight	126	Welterweight	147	Light heavyweight	175
Bantamweight	118	Lightweight	135	Middleweight	160	Heavyweight	over 175

MARCIANO WAS UNBEATEN AS A PRO

Rocky Marciano, heavyweight boxing champion of the world and winner of each of his 49 fights as a professional, announced his retirement from the ring on Apr. 27, 1956. He was the only heavyweight champion ever to retire without losing a professional fight.

Marciano won the title on Sept. 23, 1952, in Philadelphia, by knocking out Joe Walcott in the 13th round.

Marciano, born in Brockton, Mass., on Sept. 1, 1924, was killed in a plane crash, Aug. 31, 1969.

These were Marciano's championship fights:

Sept. 23, 1952[1]	Joe Walcott, Philadelphia	KO	13
May 15, 1953	Joe Walcott, Chicago	KO	1
Sept. 24, 1953	Roland LaStarza, Polo Grounds	KO	11
June 17, 1954	Ezzard Charles, Yankee Stad.	W	15
Sept. 17, 1954	Ezzard Charles, Yankee Stad.	KO	8
May 16, 1955	Don Cockell, San Francisco	KO	9
Sept. 21, 1955	Archie Moore, Yankee Stad.	KO	9

1. Won title.

CHAMPIONSHIP BOUTS—1980

Junior Flyweight

(108 pound limit)

Shigeo Nakajima, of Japan, captured the World Boxing Council championship on Jan. 3 when he outpointed Kim Sung Jun of South Korea in a 15-round bout in Tokyo.

Yoko Gushiken, of Japan, retained his World Boxing Association title on Jan. 27, in Osaka, Japan, with a unanimous decision over Kim Yong Hyun, of South Korea. There were no knockdowns.

Hilario (Sugar) Zapata, of Panama, took the W.B.C. crown away from Shigeo Nakajima, of Japan, with an unpopular 15-round decision in Tokyo on March 24. Nakajuma had held the title only since January, when he dethroned Kim Sung Jun.

On June 1, the 24-year-old Gushiken held on to his title with a knockout victory over Martin Vargas, of Chile, at 1 minute 42 seconds of the 8th round. Gushiken remained undefeated in 22 bouts and he set a record for the division with his 12th defense of the title. Gushiken floored the Chilean three times in the 8th before the referee stopped the bout. Each fighter weighed 107¾ pounds.

In his first defense of the title Zapata, 107 pounds, scored a unanimous 15-round decision over Kim Chi-Bok, of South Korea, in Seoul on June 7. Zapata lifted his record to 12–1–0. There were no knockdowns. Kim weighed 106 pounds.

Zapata again retained his crown on Aug. 4, gaining a unanimous decision over Hector Melendez, of the Dominican Republic, in a bout fought in a bullfight arena in Caracas, Venezuela. Again there were no knockdowns.

In September, Zapata stopped Nakajima in a rematch of their title bout of Jan. 3. The end came in the 11th round, in Gifu, Japan.

Flyweight

(112 pound limit)

Kim Tae Shik, of South Korea, dethroned Luis Ibarra, of Panama, on Feb. 17 in Seoul, South Korea, with a 2nd-round knockout to win the W.B.A. title. It was Ibarra's first defense. Kim scored his 10th straight knockout. Each fighter weighed 100¼ pounds.

Park Chan Hee, of South Korea, retained his W.B.C. crown on April 13 in Taegu, South Korea, by gaining a unanimous decision over Alberto Morales, of Mexico. There were no knockdowns, but Park piled up points and opened a severe cut over Morales's eye. It was Park's 5th defense since winning the title in 1975 from Miguel Canto, of Mexico.

Shoji Oguma, of Japan, who had held the title in 1974 and lost it a year later, dethroned Park Chun Hee on May 18 with a 9th-round knockout in Seoul and regained the W.B.C. title.

In his 1st defense, Kim Tae Shik kept his W.B.A. crown by scoring a unanimous decision over Arnel Arrozal, of the Philippines, before a crowd of 10,000 in Seoul on June 29. Kim remained unbeaten in 15 bouts. Arrozal had a 27–5–4 record.

Oguma made his 1st defense on July 28 and won a majority decision from Sung Jun Kim, of South Korea. The referee and one judge voted for Oguma, with one judge voting for Sung, who announced his retirement after the bout. The victory for Oguma, a southpaw, was his 34th in 43 fights.

Junior Bantamweight

(115 pound limit)

Rafael Orono, of Venezuela, outpointed Ramon Soria, on April 14, in Caracas, Venezuela, in a 15-round bout to keep his W.B.C. title. Orono weighed 112¾ pounds. Soria, from Argentina, weighed 114¾.

Orono was held to a draw on July 28 by Willie Jensen, of Detroit, but still held the title. Orono weighed 114½ and Jensen 115, the limit, for the bout in Caracas, Venezuela.

Bantamweight

(118 pound limit)

Jorge Lujan, of Panama, retained his W.B.A. championship on April 2 in Tokyo, by knocking out Shuichi Isogami, of Japan, at 2 minutes 45 seconds of the 9th round, when the American referee, Larry Rozadilla, stopped the fight after the ring physician examined Isogami's eyes and declared he could not continue. There were no knockdowns, but Lujan was well ahead on points on the cards of all three officials. It was the 5th defense for Lujan, 118 pounds, since he took the title from Alfonso Zamora, of Mexico, in 1977 in Los Angeles. Isogami weighed 117¾.

On Feb. 9 in Los Angeles, Lupe Pintor, of Mexico City, stopped Alberto Sandoval, of Pomona, Calif., in the 12th round to keep his W.B.C. crown. There were no knockdowns, but in the 12th Pintor hit Sandoval at will. Referee Lou Filippo was about to halt the bout when Sandoval's manager threw in the towel at 1:19 of the round.

Pintor retained the title by battling to a draw with Eijiro Murara, of Japan, in Tokyo on June 11. It was Pintor's 1st draw and his 2nd defense since he took the title from Carlos Zarate, of Mexico, in June of 1979. Referee Martin Denkin of the U.S. scored it 144–144; Takeaki Kanaya, of Japan, scored it 146–144 for Murata, and Marcial Sosa Villamil, the Mexican judge, scored it 147–142 for Pintor, who has a record of 41 victories and 5 defeats.

In August, Lujan, who had held the W.B.A. crown since 1977, lost it on a split decision to Julian Solis, of Puerto Rico, in a 15-round bout at Miami Beach, Fla.

Pintor retained his title on Sept. 19 in Los Angeles when he stopped Johnny Owen, of Wales, in the 12th round. Owen, the British Commonwealth champion, was carried from the ring unconscious and was taken to the California Hospital Medical Center where he underwent surgery to remove a blood clot on the brain. He remained in critical condition following the operation.

Junior Featherweight

(122 pound limit)

Wilfredo Gomez, of Puerto Rico, scored his 11th straight knockout, when he stopped Rubin (Cobra) Valdez, an unbeaten Colombian, in the 6th round to retain his W.B.C. title on Feb. 3 in Las Vegas, Nev. Valdez was unable to answer the bell for the 7th round. Gomez had weighed in three times before the bout and finally made the division limit at 11 p.m. on Feb. 2.

Leo Randolph, of Tacoma, Wash., a 1976 Olympic gold medalist, took the W.B.A. crown on a decision from Ricardo Cordona, of Colombia, on May 4 in Seattle, Wash. Cardona had held the title since May of 1978.

In his 1st defense, Randolph lost the title when he was knocked out in 5th round by Sergio Palma, of Argentina, on Aug. 9 in Spokane, Wash. Palma floored the champion twice in the 1st round and stopped him at 1:12 of the 5th. The following day, Randolph announced his retirement from boxing at the age of 22, saying he wanted "to settle down with my family and have a normal life." His pro record was 17–2.

Gomez kept his title on Aug. 23 with a 5th-round knockout of Derrick Holmes in Las Vegas, Nev.

Featherweight

(128 pound limit)

Eusebio Pedroza, of Panama, retained his W.B.A. title by outpointing Spider Nemoto on Jan. 22 in Tokyo. Pedroza, weighing 126 pounds, won a unanimous decision over the popular Japanese, who scaled 125½. There were no knockdowns.

The W.B.C. title changed hands on Feb. 3 in Phoeniz, Ariz., when Salvador Sanchez, of Mexico, stopped Danny (Little Red) Lopez, of Los Angeles, in the 13th round.

In March, Pedroza retained the title with knockout of Juan

Malvarez in Panama City.

Sanchez made a successful defense of his title on April 12 in Tucson, Ariz., by taking a unanimous decision over top-ranked contender Ruben Castillo, of Bakersfield, Calif. The bout was close until the 11th round when Sanchez began to pile up points. Sanchez weighed 126 pounds. Castillo, who suffered only his 2nd loss in 48 bouts, scaled 125½.

In a rematch against Lopez, the 21-year-old Sanchez retained his title with a 14th-round knockout on June 21 in Las Vegas, Nev. Referee Mills Lane stopped the fight at 1:42 of the round at the same time that Lopez's corner threw in the towel. Lopez, who had held the title for five years before Sanchez dethroned him in February suffered only the 4th knockout of a career that began in 1971 and earned him more than $1 million. The 28-year-old Lopez said he was "pretty sure" he would retire after the bout. Sanchez lifted his record to 35–1–1. Lopez's pro record was 41–5.

Pedroza, making his 9th defense since winning the title in 1978 from Cecilio Lastra, scored an 8-round knockout over Kim Sa Wang, of South Korea, in Seoul on July 20.

Sanchez fought again in September and retained his title with a 15-round split decision over Patrick Ford, of Guyana, in San Antonio, Tex.

Junior Lightweight

(130 pound limit)

Alexis Arguello, of Nicaragua, knocked out Ruben Castillo, of Bakersfield, Calif., who had moved up a weight division, in the 11th round of their bout in Tuscon, Ariz., on Jan. 20 to retain the W.B.C. title he first won in 1978. Arguello trailed on the scorecards of all three judges through 9 rounds. The knockout came at 2:03 of the 11th.

Sammy Serrano, of Puerto Rico, scored with quick sharp punches throughout and stopped Kiyoshi Kazama, 129¾, of Japan, in the 13th round and retained the W.B.A. crown in Nara, Japan, on April 3. The knockout came at 45 seconds of the 13th and Serrano, 129½, won in his 10th defense since he captured the title from Ben Villaflor, of the Philippines, on Oct. 16, 1976.

Arguello made his 2nd defense of the year on April 27 in San Juan, Puerto Rico, and stopped Rolando Navarrete, of the Philippines after 4 rounds. The bout was stopped after the ring doctor examined the cuts Arguello had opened over Navarete's eyes. It was Arguello's 8th defense.

On Aug. 2, Yasutsune Uehara, of Japan, stopped Sammy Serrano, of Puerto Rico, in the 6th round to take the W.B.A. title. The bout was one of three championships fights on a card in Detroit.

Lightweight

(135 pound limit)

Hilmer Kenty, of Detroit, a 24-year-old boxer in only his 17th pro fight, knocked out Ernesto Espana, of Venezuela, in the 9th round at Detroit on March 2 and became the W.B.A. champion. Kenty weighed 134 pounds, and Espana, 134¾, suffered only his 2nd defeat in 30 bouts.

Jim Waat, of Scotland, retained the W.B.C. crown on March 14 in Glasgow, Scotland, by stopping Charles Nash, of Northern Ireland, in the 4th round. Waat, 134¾, floored Nash four times in the 4th round before the referee stopped the fight. Nash, 134¼, floored Waat in the 2nd round, but the champion got up without a count.

In Glasgow, Scotland, a crowd of 15,000 saw Waat make his 3rd defense and gain a unanimous decision over Howard Davis, 133, of Glen Cove, N.Y. Waat, 31 years old, dominated the bout with his left-handed style. Waat, who has been unbeaten since 1976, posted his 37th victory in 44 fights that span 12 years. Waat earned $1 million for the fight, the first outdoors in Glasgow in 20 years. Davis earned $300,000 as his share of the purse. Davis, an ex-Olympic champion, had been unbeaten in 13 previous fights.

Kenty stopped Oh Yong Ho, of Japan, on a TKO in the 9th round and retained his title in Detroit. The bout was one of three championship fights on the Detroit card on Aug. 2.

In a rematch of the title bout in which Kenty wrested the title from Espana, the two fought again in San Juan, Puerto Rico, in September with Kenty retaining the crown on a 4th-round knockout.

Junior Welterweight

(140 pound limit)

Antonio (Kid Pambele) Cervantes, of Colombia, retained W.B.A. title with a 7th-round knockout of Miguel Montilla, of the Dominican Republic, on March 29, in Cartagena, Colombia. Cervantes had floored Montilla in the 5th and the referee stopped the bout when Montilla took a barrage of blows while against the ropes in the 7th.

Saoul Mamby, of New York City, knocked out Kim Sang Hyun, of South Korea, to win the W.B.C. title on Feb. 23 in Seoul, South Korea. Kim was ahead on points until the 12th round. The 37-year-old Mamby staggered Kim with a flurry in the 13th and knocked him out at 1:44 of the 14th with a lightning right.

Unbeaten Aaron Pryor, from Cincinnati, scored a 4th-round knockout over Cervantes and captured the W.B.A. title before a hometown crowd. Pryor opened a one-inch cut over Cervantes's right eye in the 3rd round and a flurry ended it at 1:13 of the 4th. The 34-year-old Cervantes, 137½, had held the title for most of the last eight years. Pryor, 138¼, was knocked to one knee in the 1st round, but got up and remained the aggressor thereafter. The victory was Pryor's 25th. Cervantes's record is 86–10–3, but in the last eight years he had won 31 of 32 bouts.

Mamby, 139, stopped Esteban DeJesus, 140, of Puerto Rico, in the 13th round to retain his title. The bout was on the same card as the heavyweight title fight between Larry Holmes and Scott LeDoux in Bloomington, Minn., on July 7.

Welterweight

(147 pound limit)

Jose (Pipino) Cuevas, of Mexico, knocked out Harold Volbrecht, of South Africa, a southpaw, in the 5th round to keep the W.B.A. title he won on July 17, 1976 by stopping Angel Espada, of Mexico. Cuevas's 12th defense, in Houston, Tex., on April 6 made Volbrecht his 10th knockout victim in a title fight.

Sugar Ray Leonard, of Palmer Park, Md., easily disposed of Davey (Boy) Green, the British champion, with a 4th-round knockout to keep the W.B.C. crown on March 31 in Landover, Md. The 23-year-old Leonard, unbeaten in 23 fights, tore into the challenger with a barrage of rights to score the knockout at 2:27 of the 4th.

Cuevas lost his title on Aug. 2, suffering a knockout at 2:39 of the 2nd round at the hands of Thomas Hearns, of Detroit. Cuevas could not muster a defense against the devastating punching of Hearns. The bout was one of three championship fights held on a card in Detroit.

In one of the most publicized fights in boxing history, Roberto Duran, of Panama, who had relinquished the lightweight title in February of 1979 to fight in a heavier division, scored a unanimous decision over Sugar Ray Leonard and took the W.B.C. title. The bout was held on June 20 in Montreal's Olympic Stadium and drew a crowd of 46,317. Leonard had been unbeaten in 27 previous fights. Duran raised his record to 72–1, with 56 knockouts. From the fight purse, closed TV money, and other ancillary rights Leonard earned $7.5 million and Duran $1.5 million from the bout.

Junior Middleweight

(154 pound limit)

Ayub Kalule, of Uganda, retained the W.B.A. title with a knockout after the 11th round of Emiliano Villa, of Colombia, in Copenhagen, Denmark, on April 17. Kalule had opened a cut over Villa's left eye in the 7th. The cut was examined by the ring physician after the 7th, 8th and 10th rounds but Villa was allowed to continue. But in the 11th he was advised to quit, and he did not answer the bell for the 12th.

Maurice Hope, 153, of Britain, stopped Rocco Mattioli, 151

¾, of Italy in the 11th round and retained his W.B.C. crown on July 12 in Wembley, England.

At Randers, Denmark, Kalule, 153½, outpointed Marjan Benes, 153, of Yugoslavia, in a 15-round bout to retain his title.

Middleweight

(160 pound limit)

Alan Minter, of England, won the undisputed title from Vito Antuofermo, an Italian living in Brooklyn, N.Y., on a split decision in Las Vegas, Nev., on March 16. Minter, a southpaw, won on the cards of Charles Minker, of Las Vegas, (144–141) and Roland Bakin, of Britain, (149–147), and Antuofermo was scored the winner by Vladisas Sanchez, of Venezuela (145–143).

Minter retained his title on June 28 in Wembley, England, stopping Antuofermo in the 8th round of a rematch. Minter, 26 years old, won every round. Antuofermo's manager stopped the bout after the 7th round when his fighter couldn't see because of cuts over his eyes. After the bout Antuofermo needed 15 stitches to close the cuts. A crowd of 10,300 saw the bout at Empire Pool.

Minter suffered almost the same fate on Sept. 27 in the same ring in Wembley when he was knocked out by Marvin Hagler, of Brockton, Mass., at 1:45 of the 3rd round. Minter's face was a mask of blood when the referee, Carlos Berrocal, of Panama, stopped the bout. Hagler opened two cuts over Minter's left eye in the 1st round, rocked him in the 2nd, and opened another cut under the Briton's nose. When the fight was stopped, the sellout crowd of 12,000, mostly Minter backers, threw beer cans and bottles into the ring. The 26-year-old Hagler raised his record to 50–2–2, with 41 by knockout.

Light Heavyweight

(175 pound limit)

Matthew Saad Muhammad, of Philadelphia, floored John Conteh, of England, five times in the 4th round and won on a knockout to retain the W.B.C. title in Atlantic City, N.J., on March 29. The referee stopped the bout at 2 minutes 27 seconds of the 4th.

Eddie Gregory, of Brooklyn, N.Y., scored an upset when he knocked out Marvin Johnson, of Indianapolis, in the 11th round to win the W.B.A. championship in Knoxville, Tenn., on March 31. The 27-year-old Gregory, 174 pounds, had floored Johnson, 174½, who fought southpaw style, in the 3rd round.

Saad Muhammad retained his title on May 11 in Halifax, Nova Scotia, with a 5th-round knockout of Louis Pergaud, of Cameroon. Pergaud suffered his first knockout when Saad Muhammad floored him at 1:19 of the 5th.

Saad Muhammad retained his title on July 12 in McAfee, N.J., at the Playboy Resorts and Country Club, by stopping Alvaro (Yaqui) Lopez, 173¾, of Stockton, Calif., in the 14th round.

In his first fight since changing his name from Eddie Gregory to Eddie Mustafa Muhammad, Muhammad knocked out Jerry Martin, of Antiqua, in the 10th round at the Playboy Club in McAfee, N.J. An overhand right after a left jab dropped Martin for the second time in the fight in the 10th. He got up but the referee halted the action.

Heavyweight

Larry Holmes, of Easton, Pa., stopped Lorenzo Zanon, of Italy, at 2 minutes 39 seconds of the 6th round and retained the W.B.C. title on Feb. 3 in Las Vegas, Nev. It was an easy victory for Holmes who stayed unbeaten in 33 fights as a pro, winning 24 of those by a knockout.

In a big upset, Mike Weaver, of Gatesville, Tex., stunned John Tate, of Knoxville, Tenn., with a hook in the 15th round and won the W.B.A. crown. Tate, who had been unbeaten in 20 previous bouts, was well ahead on the scorecards of the ring officials until Weaver unleashed the punch that knocked him out. The 25-year-old Tate weighed 232 pounds. Weaver scaled 207½ for the bout held in Knoxville on March 31.

Holmes continued to stay unbeaten on March 31 when he stopped Leroy Jones, 254½, in the 8th round in Las Vegas, Nev. Holmes weighed 211 for the fight, handing Jones, from Denver, his 1st defeat in 26 bouts.

Holmes scored his 7th straight knockout in a title defense on July 7 in Bloomington, Minn., by stopping Scott LeDoux, of Anoka, Minn., in the 7th round. The referee halted the bout because LeDoux was bleeding heavily and could not see out of his left eye. Only 8,000 attended the bout in the 16,800-seat Metropolitan Center. Holmes weighed 214¼, and LeDoux 226.

FIGHTER OF THE YEAR

Selected by *The Ring* Magazine.

1928	Gene Tunney	1940	Billy Conn	1953	Bobo Olson	1966	No award
1929	Tommy Loughran	1941	Joe Louis	1954	Rocky Marciano	1967	Joe Frazier
1930	Max Schmeling	1942	Ray Robinson	1955	Rocky Marciano	1968	Nino Benvenuti
1931	Tommy Loughran	1943	Fred Apostoli	1956	Floyd Patterson	1969	Jose Napoles
1932	Jack Sharkey	1944	Beau Jack	1957	Carmen Basilio	1970–71	Joe Frazier
1933	No award	1945	Willie Pep	1958	Ingemar Johansson	1972	Carlos Monzon and Muhammad Ali
1934	Barney Ross and Tony Canzoneri	1946	Tony Zale	1959	Ingemar Johansson		
		1947	Gus Lesnevich	1960	Floyd Patterson	1973	George Foreman
1935	Barney Ross	1948	Ike Williams	1961	Joe Brown	1974–75	Muhammad Ali
1936	Joe Louis	1949	Ezzard Charles	1962	Dick Tiger	1976	George Foreman
1937	Henry Armstrong	1950	Ezzard Charles	1963	Cassius Clay	1977	Carlos Zarate
1938	Joe Louis	1951	Ray Robinson	1964	Emile Griffith	1978	Muhammand Ali
1939	Joe Louis	1952	Rocky Marciano	1965	Dick Tiger	1979	Sugar Ray Leonard

RACQUETS

UNITED STATES CHAMPIONS—1980

Men's open—John Prenn, England
Men's amateur—Willie Boone, England

CANADIAN CHAMPION—1980

Men's open—Willie Boone

TITLE BOUTS OF MUHAMMAD ALI (CASSIUS CLAY)

Feb. 25, 1964[1]	Sonny Liston, Miami Beach	KO	7
(Liston failed to come out for seventh round)			
May 25, 1965	Sonny Liston, Lewiston, Me.	KO	1
Nov. 22, 1965	Floyd Patterson, Las Vegas	KO	12
March 29, 1966	George Chuvalo, Toronto	W	15
May 21, 1966	Henry Cooper, London	KO	6
Aug. 6, 1966	Brian London, London	KO	3
Sept. 10, 1966	Karl Mildenberger, Frankfurt, Ger.	KO	12
Nov. 14, 1966	Cleveland Williams, Houston	KO	3
Feb. 6, 1967	Ernie Terrell, Houston	W	15
March 22, 1967	Zora Folley, New York	KO	7
March 8, 1971[2]	Joe Frazier, New York	L	15
Oct. 30, 1974[1]	George Foreman, Zaire	KO	8
March 24, 1975	Chuck Wepner, Richfield, Ohio	KO	15
May 16, 1975	Ron Lyle, Las Vegas, Nev.	KO	11
July 1, 1975	Joe Bugner, Kuala Lumpur	W	15
Sept. 30, 1975	Joe Frazier, Manila	KO	14
Feb. 20, 1976	Jean-Pierre Coopman, San Juan	KO	5
April 30, 1976	Jimmy Young, Landover, Md.	W	15
May 24, 1976	Richard Dunn, Munich	KO	5
Sept. 28, 1976	Ken Norton, New York	W	15
May 16, 1977	Alfredo Evangelista, Landover, Md.	W	15
Sept. 29, 1977	Earnie Shavers, New York	W	15
Feb. 15, 1978[3]	Leon Spinks, Las Vegas, Nev.	L	15
Sept. 15, 1978[4]	Leon Spinks, New Orleans	W	15
Oct. 2, 1980[5]	Larry Holmes, Las Vegas, Nev.	L KO	11

1. Won world heavyweight championship. 2. Lost title officially. When Ali (Clay) refused induction into the United States armed services, April 18, 1967, the New York State Athletic Commission stripped him of his title and other official groups followed suit. He was convicted of draft evasion June 20, 1967, by a Federal Court and was inactive awaiting results of appeal. Ali regained license to fight in autumn of 1970, after resigning as titleholder. After losing to Frazier, United States Supreme Court reversed Federal court decision on technicalities in Justice Department's presentation of case, June 28, 1971. 3. Lost title. 4. Regained W.B.A. title. 5. Ended 2-year retirement to challenge Holmes for W.B.C. title.

MUHAMMAD ALI FAILS IN COMEBACK ATTEMPT

Muhammad Ali, who had announced his retirement on June 26, 1979, after winning the world heavyweight title for an unprecedented third time from Leon Spinks on Sept. 15, 1978, attempted a comeback against Larry Holmes, the World Boxing Council champion, on Oct. 2, 1980. Ali's long layoff from training had caused him to gain a lot of weight. When he went into training for the Holmes bout, he weighed 254 pounds. He trimmed down to 217½ for the bout in Las Vegas, Nev. But against the 30-year-old Holmes, the 38-year-old Ali was no match. He was defeated on a technical knockout in the 11th round, being unable to answer the bell for the start of that round. Throughout the fight Ali hardly threw a punch, some ringsiders attesting that he only threw 15. The knockout by Holmes was his eighth straight in a title defense, surpassing the record of seven held by Joe Louis. The match set a record of $6 million at the gate. Ali received $8 million from the purse, closed-circuit television, and other ancillary rights.

BOXING—AMATEUR

A.A.U. NATIONAL CHAMPIONSHIPS

(Las Vegas, Nev., May 6–10, 1980)

106 lb—Robert Shannon, Edmonds, Wash.
112 lb—Richard Sandoval, Pomona, Calif.
119 lb—Jackie Beard, Jackson, Tenn.
125 lb—Clifford Gray, Boynton Beach, Fla.
132 lb—Melvin Paul, New Orleans, La.
139 lb—Johnny Bumphus, Nashville, Tenn.
147 lb—Gene Hatcher, Fort Worth, Tex.
156 lb—Don Bowers, Jackson, Tenn.
165 lb—Martin Pierce, Flint, Mich.
178 lb—Jeff Lampkin, Youngstown, Ohio
Heavyweight—Marvis Frazier, Philadelphia, Pa.

NATIONAL GOLDEN GLOVES

(Shreveport, La., March 26–29, 1980)

106 lb—Steven McCrory, Detroit
112 lb—Jerome Coffee, Knoxville, Tenn.
119 lb—Myron Taylor, Pennsylvania
125 lb—Bernard Taylor, Knoxville, Tenn.
132 lb—Melvin Paul, Lafayette, La.
139 lb—Terry Silver, Louisville, Ky.
147 lb—Don Curry, Fort Worth, Tex.
156 lb—James Shuler, Pennsylvania
165 lb—Lamont Kirkland, Omaha, Neb.
178 lb—Steve Eden, Des Moines, Iowa
Heavyweight—Michael Arms, Milwaukee

BOXING DEATHS SINCE 1945 TOTAL 331

The death of Cleveland Denny, a lightweight boxer, a week after he had been knocked out in a bout in Montreal on June 20, 1980, brought to six the number of fighters to die of ring injuries in North America since November of 1979. Denny, a native of Guyana and a former Canadian champion, was stopped in the last seconds of a bout with Gaetan Hart of Buckingham, Quebec. Denny was carried unconscious from the ring. He did not regain consciousness although he was kept alive for a week by a respirator.

On Jan. 1, 1980, Tony Thomas died 10 days after he had been knocked out by Sammy Horne in a bout in Spartanburg, S.C. Thomas had collapsed in the dressing room after the fight. On Jan. 17, Charles Newell died of injuries suffered nine days earlier in a match against Marlon Starling in Hartford, Conn. On Jan. 18, Harlan Hoosier, an amateur boxer, died in a Kentucky hospital after scoring a victory six days earlier in Lenore, W. Va. Shortly after the fight, Hoosier had complained of headaches. Victor Romero, a 20-year-old boxer who had only 10 pro fights, collapsed after a sparring session in Albuquerque, N.M. and died on Aug. 21 from a brain clot.

On Nov. 23, 1979, Willie Classen, Jr., was knocked out by Wilford Scypion in a middleweight bout at the Felt Forum in New York. He died five days later, never regaining consciousness.

Romero's death brought to 331 the total of professional and amateur boxers who have died since 1945 from injuries suffered in the ring, according to The Associated Press.

HORSE RACING

Ancient drawings on stone and bone prove that horse racing is at least 3000 years old, but Thoroughbred Racing is a modern development. Practically every thoroughbred in training today traces its registered ancestry back to one or more of three sires that arrived in England about 1728 from the Near East and became known, from the names of their owners, as the Byerly Turk, the Darley Arabian, and the Godolphin Arabian. The Jockey Club (English) was founded at Newmarket in 1750 or 1751 and became the custodian of the Stud Book as well as the court of last resort in deciding turf affairs.

Horse racing took place in this country before the Revolution, but the great lift to the breeding industry came with the importation in 1798, by Col. John Hoomes of Virginia, of Diomed, winner of the Epsom Derby of 1780. Diomed's lineal descendants included such famous stars of the American turf as American Eclipse and Lexington. From 1800 to the time of the Civil War there were race courses and breeding establishments plentifully scattered through Virginia, North Carolina, South Carolina, Tennessee, Kentucky, and Louisiana.

The oldest stake event in North America is the Queen's Plate, a Canadian fixture that was first run in the Province of Quebec in 1836. The oldest stake event in the United States is The Travers, which was first run at Saratoga in 1864. The gambling that goes with horse racing and trickery by jockeys, trainers, owners, and track officials caused attacks on the sport by reformers and a demand among horse racing enthusiasts for an honest and effective control of some kind, but nothing of lasting value to racing came of this until the formation in 1894 of The Jockey Club.

"TRIPLE CROWN" WINNERS IN THE UNITED STATES[1]

(Kentucky Derby, Preakness and Belmont Stakes)

Year	Horse	Owner	Year	Horse	Owner
1919	Sir Barton	J. K. L. Ross	1946	Assault	Robert J. Kleberg
1930	Gallant Fox	William Woodward	1948	Citation	Warren Wright
1935	Omaha	William Woodward	1973	Secretariat	Meadow Stable
1937	War Admiral	Samuel D. Riddle	1977	Seattle Slew	Karen Taylor
1941	Whirlaway	Warren Wright	1978	Affirmed	Louis Wolfson
1943	Count Fleet	Mrs. John Hertz			

KENTUCKY DERBY

Churchill Downs; 3-year-olds; 1 1/4 miles.

Year	Winner	Jockey	Wt.	Win val.	Year	Winner	Jockey	Wt.	Win val.
1875	Aristides	O. Lewis	100	$2,850	1909	Wintergreen	V. Powers	117	$ 4,850
1876	Vagrant	R. Swim	97	2,950	1910	Donau	F. Herbert	117	4,850
1877	Baden Baden	W. Walker	100	3,300	1911	Meridian	G. Archibald	117	4,850
1878	Day Star	J. Carter	100	4,050	1912	Worth	C. H. Shilling	117	4,850
1879	Lord Murphy	C. Schauer	100	3,550	1913	Donerail	R. Goose	117	5,475
1880	Fonso	G. Lewis	105	3,800	1914	Old Rosebud	J. McCabe	114	9,125
1881	Hindoo	J. McLaughlin	105	4,410	1915	Regret	J. Notter	112	11,450
1882	Apollo	B. Hurd	102	4,560	1916	George Smith	J. Loftus	117	9,750
1883	Leonatus	W. Donohue	105	3,760	1917	Omar Khayyam	C. Borel	117	16,600
1884	Buchanan	I. Murphy	110	3,990	1918	Exterminator	W. Knapp	114	14,700
1885	Joe Cotton	E. Henderson	110	4,630	1919	Sir Barton	J. Loftus	112½	20,825
1886	Ben Ali	P. Duffy	118	4,890	1920	Paul Jones	T. Rice	126	30,375
1887	Montrose	I. Lewis	118	4,200	1921	Behave Yourself	C. Thompson	126	38,450
1888	Macbeth II	G. Covington	115	4,740	1922	Morvich	A. Johnson	126	46,775
1889	Spokane	T. Kiley	118	4,970	1923	Zev	E. Sande	126	53,600
1890	Riley	I. Murphy	118	5,460	1924	Black Gold	J. D. Mooney	126	52,775
1891	Kingman	I. Murphy	122	4,680	1925	Flying Ebony	E. Sande	126	52,950
1892	Azra	A. Clayton	122	4,230	1926	Bubbling Over	A. Johnson	126	50,075
1893	Lookout	E. Kunze	122	4,090	1927	Whiskery	L. McAtee	126	51,000
1894	Chant	F. Goodale	122	4,020	1928	Reigh Count	C. Lang	126	55,375
1895	Halma	J. Perkins	122	2,970	1929	Clyde Van Dusen	L. McAtee	126	53,950
1896	Ben Brush	W. Simms	117	4,850	1930	Gallant Fox	E. Sande	126	50,725
1897	Typhoon II	F. Garner	117	4,850	1931	Twenty Grand	C. Kurtsinger	126	48,725
1898	Plaudit	W. Simms	117	4,850	1932	Burgoo King	E. James	126	52,350
1899	Manuel	F. Taral	117	4,850	1933	Brokers Tip	D. Meade	126	48,925
1900	Lieut. Gibson	J. Boland	117	4,850	1934	Cavalcade	M. Garner	126	28,175
1901	His Eminence	J. Winkfield	117	4,850	1935	Omaha	W. Saunders	126	39,525
1902	Alan-a-Dale	J. Winkfield	117	4,850	1936	Bold Venture	I. Hanford	126	37,725
1903	Judge Himes	H. Booker	117	4,850	1937	War Admiral	C. Kurtsinger	126	52,050
1904	Elwood	F. Prior	117	4,850	1938	Lawrin	E. Arcaro	126	47,050
1905	Agile	J. Martin	122	4,850	1939	Johnstown	J. Stout	126	46,350
1906	Sir Huon	R. Troxler	117	4,850	1940	Gallahadion	C. Bierman	126	60,150
1907	Pink Star	A. Minder	117	4,850	1941	Whirlaway	E. Arcaro	126	61,275
1908	Stone Street	A. Pickens	117	4,850	1942	Shut Out	W. D. Wright	126	64,225

1. Statistics relative to thoroughbred racing in this publication are reproduced from the *American Racing Manual*, by special permission of the copyright owners, TRIANGLE PUBLICATIONS, INC. Reproduction prohibited.

Year	Winner	Jockey	Wt.	Win val.	Year	Winner	Jockey	Wt.	Win val.
1943	Count Fleet	J. Longden	126	$ 60,725	1962	Decidedly	W. Hartack	126	$119,650
1944	Pensive	C. McCreary	126	64,675	1963	Chateauguay	B. Baeza	126	108,900
1945	Hoop Jr.	E. Arcaro	126	64,850	1964	Northern Dancer	W. Hartack	126	114,300
1946	Assault	W. Mehrtens	126	96,400	1965	Lucky Debonair	W. Shoemaker	126	112,000
1947	Jet Pilot	E. Guerin	126	92,160	1966	Kauai King	D. Brumfield	126	120,500
1948	Citation	E. Arcaro	126	83,400	1967	Proud Clarion	R. Ussery	126	119,700
1949	Ponder	S. Brooks	126	91,600	1968	Forward Pass[1]	I. Valenzuela	126	122,600
1950	Middleground	W. Boland	126	92,650	1969	Majestic Prince	W. Hartack	126	113,200
1951	Count Turf	C. McCreary	126	98,050	1970	Dust Commander	M. Manganello	126	127,800
1952	Hill Gail	E. Arcaro	126	96,300	1971	Canonero II	G. Avila	126	145,500
1953	Dark Star	H. Moreno	126	90,050	1972	Riva Ridge	R. Turcotte	126	140,300
1954	Determine	R. York	126	102,050	1973	Secretariat	R. Turcotte	126	155,050
1955	Swaps	W. Shoemaker	126	108,400	1974	Cannonade	A. Cordero, Jr.	126	274,000
1956	Needles	D. Erb	126	123,450	1975	Foolish Pleasure	J. Vasquez	126	209,600
1957	Iron Liege	W. Hartack	126	107,950	1976	Bold Forbes	A. Cordero, Jr.	126	165,200
1958	Tim Tam	I. Valenzuela	126	116,400	1977	Seattle Slew	J. Cruguet	126	214,700
1959	Tomy Lee	W. Shoemaker	126	119,650	1978	Affirmed	S. Cauthen	126	186,900
1960	Venetian Way	W. Hartack	126	114,850	1979	Spectacular Bid	R. Franklin	126	228,650
1961	Carry Back	J. Sellers	126	120,500	1980	Genuine Risk	J. Vasquez	126	250,550

1. Dancer's Image finished first but was disqualified after traces of drug were found in system.

PREAKNESS STAKES

Pimlico; 3-year-olds; $1\frac{3}{16}$ miles; first race 1873.

Year	Winner	Jockey	Wt.	Win val.	Year	Winner	Jockey	Wt.	Win Val.
1919	Sir Barton	J. Loftus	126	$ 24,500	1955	Nashua	E. Arcaro	126	$ 67,550
1930	Gallant Fox	E. Sande	126	51,925	1956	Fabius	W. Hartack	126	84,250
1931	Mate	G. Ellis	126	48,225	1957	Bold Ruler	E. Arcaro	126	65,250
1932	Burgoo King	E. James	126	50,375	1958	Tim Tam	I. Valenzuela	126	97,900
1933	Head Play	C. Kurtsinger	126	26,850	1959	Royal Orbit	W. Harmatz	126	136,200
1934	High Quest	R. Jones	126	25,175	1960	Bally Ache	R. Ussery	126	121,000
1935	Omaha	W. Saunders	126	25,325	1961	Carry Back	J. Sellers	126	126,200
1936	Bold Venture	G. Woolf	126	27,325	1962	Greek Money	J. Rotz	126	135,800
1937	War Admiral	C. Kurtsinger	126	45,600	1963	Candy Spots	W. Shoemaker	126	127,500
1938	Dauber	M. Peters	126	51,875	1964	Northern Dancer	W. Hartack	126	124,200
1939	Challedon	G. Seabo	126	53,710	1965	Tom Rolfe	R. Turcotte	126	128,100
1940	Bimelech	F.A. Smith	126	53,230	1966	Kauai King	D. Brumfield	126	129,000
1941	Whirlaway	E. Arcaro	126	49,365	1967	Damascus	W. Shoemaker	126	141,500
1942	Alsab	B. James	126	58,175	1968	Forward Pass	I. Valenzuela	126	142,700
1943	Count Fleet	J. Longden	126	43,190	1969	Majestic Prince	W. Hartack	126	129,500
1944	Pensive	C. McCreary	126	60,075	1970	Personality	E. Belmonte	126	151,300
1945	Polynesian	W.D. Wright	126	66,170	1971	Canonero II	G. Avila	126	137,400
1946	Assault	W. Mehrtens	126	96,620	1972	Bee Bee Bee	E. Nelson	126	135,300
1947	Faultless	D. Dodson	126	98,005	1973	Secretariat	R. Turcotte	126	129,900
1948	Citation	E. Arcaro	126	91,870	1974	Little Current	M. Rivera	126	156,000
1949	Capot	T. Atkinson	126	79,985	1975	Master Derby	D. McHargue	126	158,100
1950	Hill Prince	E. Arcaro	126	56,115	1976	Elocutionist	J. Lively	126	129,700
1951	Bold	E. Arcaro	126	83,110	1977	Seattle Slew	J. Cruguet	126	138,600
1952	Blue Man	C. McCreary	126	86,135	1978	Affirmed	S. Cauthen	126	136,200
1953	Native Dancer	E. Guerin	126	65,200	1979	Spectacular Bid	R. Franklin	126	165,300
1954	Hasty Road	J. Adams	126	91,600	1980	Codex	A. Cordero	126	180,600

BELMONT STAKES

Belmont Park; 3-year-olds; $1\frac{1}{2}$ miles.

Run at Jerome Park 1867 to 1890; at Morris Park 1890–94; at Belmont Park 1905–62; at Aqueduct 1963–67. Distance $1\frac{5}{8}$ miles prior to 1874; reduced to $1\frac{1}{2}$ miles, 1874; reduced to $1\frac{1}{4}$ miles, 1890; reduced to $1\frac{1}{8}$ miles, 1893; increased to $1\frac{1}{4}$ miles, 1895; increased to $1\frac{3}{8}$ miles, 1896; reduced to $1\frac{1}{4}$ miles in 1904; increased to $1\frac{1}{2}$ miles, 1926.

Year	Winner	Jockey	Wt.	Win val.	Year	Winner	Jockey	Wt.	Win val.
1919	Sir Barton	J. Loftus	126	$ 11,950	1941	Whirlaway	E. Arcaro	126	$ 39,770
1930	Gallant Fox	E. Sande	126	66,040	1942	Shut Out	E. Arcaro	126	44,520
1931	Twenty Grand	C. Kurtsinger	126	58,770	1943	Count Fleet	J. Longden	126	35,340
1932	Faireno	T. Malley	126	55,120	1944	Bounding Home	G.L. Smith	126	55,000
1933	Hurryoff	M. Garner	126	49,490	1945	Pavot	E. Arcaro	126	56,675
1934	Peace Chance	W.D. Wright	126	43,410	1946	Assault	W. Mehrtens	126	75,400
1935	Omaha	W. Saunders	126	35,480	1947	Phalanx	R. Donoso	126	78,900
1936	Granville	J. Stout	126	29,800	1948	Citation	E. Arcaro	126	77,700
1937	War Admiral	C. Kurtsinger	126	38,020	1949	Capot	T. Atkinson	126	60,900
1938	Pasteurized	J. Stout	126	34,530	1950	Middleground	W. Boland	126	61,350
1939	Johnstown	J. Stout	126	37,020	1951	Counterpoint	D. Gorman	126	82,000
1940	Bimelech	F.A. Smith	126	35,030	1952	One Count	E. Arcaro	126	82,400

Year	Winner	Jockey	Wt.	Win val.
1953	Native Dancer	E. Guerin	126	$ 82,500
1954	High Gun	E. Guerin	126	89,000
1955	Nashua	E. Arcaro	126	83,700
1956	Needles	D. Erb	126	83,600
1957	Gallant Man	W. Shoemaker	126	77,300
1958	Cavan	P. Anderson	126	73,440
1959	Sword Dancer	W. Shoemaker	126	93,525
1960	Celtic Ash	W. Hartack	126	96,785
1961	Sherluck	B. Baeza	126	104,900
1962	Jaipur	W. Shoemaker	126	109,550
1963	Chateauguay	B. Baeza	126	101,700
1964	Quadrangle	M. Ycaza	126	110,850
1965	Hail to All	J. Sellers	126	104,150
1966	Amberoid	W. Boland	126	117,700
1967	Damascus	W. Shoemaker	126	$ 104,950
1968	Stage Door Johnny	H. Gustines	126	117,700
1969	Arts and Letters	B. Baeza	126	104,050
1970	High Echelon	J. Rotz	126	115,000
1971	Pass Catcher	R. Blum	126	97,710
1972	Riva Ridge	R. Turcotte	126	93,540
1973	Secretariat	R. Turcotte	126	90,120
1974	Little Current	M. Rivera	126	101,970
1975	Avatar	W. Shoemaker	126	116,160
1976	Bold Forbes	A. Cordero, Jr.	126	117,000
1977	Seattle Slew	J. Cruguet	126	109,080
1978	Affirmed	S. Cauthen	126	110,580
1979	Coastal	R. Hernandez	126	161,400
1980	Temperence Hill	E. Maple	126	176,220

LEADING MONEY-WINNING JOCKEYS

Laffit Pincay, Jr., set a single-season record for purse earnings in 1979 when his mount won The Jockey Club Gold Cup on Oct. 6. His total purses of $8,183,535 broke the mark set in 1978 of $6,188,353 by Darrel McHargue. Pincay rode 420 winners from a total of 1,708 mounts. McHargue finished eighth on the list with $4,197,256 in 1979. The list of annual leaders:

Year	Jockey	Mts.	1st	Amt. won
1956	Bill Hartack	1,387	347	$2,343,955
1957	Bill Hartack	1,238	341	3,060,501
1958	Willie Shoemaker	1,133	300	2,961,693
1959	Willie Shoemaker	1,285	347	2,843,133
1960	Willie Shoemaker	1,227	274	2,123,961
1961	Willie Shoemaker	1,256	304	2,690,819
1962	Willie Shoemaker	1,126	311	2,916,844
1963	Willie Shoemaker	1,203	271	2,526,925
1964	Willie Shoemaker	1,056	246	$ 2,649,553
1965	Braulio Baeza	1,245	270	2,582,702
1966	Braulio Baeza	1,341	298	2,951,022
1967	Braulio Baeza	1,064	256	3,088,888
1968	Braulio Baeza	1,089	201	2,835,108
1969	Jorge Velasquez	1,442	258	2,542,315
1970	Laffit Pincay, Jr.	1,328	269	2,626,526
1971	Laffit Pincay, Jr.	1,627	380	3,784,377
1972	Laffit Pincay, Jr.	1,388	289	3,225,827
1973	Laffit Pincay, Jr.	1,444	350	4,093,492
1974	Laffit Pincay, Jr.	1,278	341	4,251,060
1975	Braulio Baeza	1,190	196	3,674,398
1976	Angel Cordero, Jr.	1,534	274	4,709,500
1977	Steve Cauthen	2,075	487	6,151,750
1978	Darrel McHargue	1,762	375	6,188,353
1979	Laffit Pincay, Jr.	1,708	420	8,183,535

SPECTACULAR BID BREAKS MONEY-EARNINGS RECORD

Spectacular Bid, the 3-year-old champion of 1979 who won the Kentucky Derby and Preakness, became the biggest money-winning horse in history in 1980 and was syndicated on March 11, 1980, for a record $22 million. Earlier in March, the 4-year-old became only the second horse in thoroughbred racing annals to earn more than $2 million, surpassing Affirmed. Spectacular Bid turned in a spectacular campaign in 1980 winning nine straight races through Sept. 20, and zooming his total career earnings to $2,781,607. Syndicated for breeding purposes and scheduled to enter stud in 1981, Spectacular Bid went over the $2-million mark by winning the Santa Anita Handicap on March 2. His syndication called for 40 shares at $550,000 each, with his owner Harry Meyerhoff retaining 20 shares. Spectacular Bid's eighth victory in eight starts in 1980 came in the Amory L. Haskell Handicap at Monmounth Park, Oceanport, N.J., on Aug. 16 and brought his earnings for the year to $1,044,490, and his career racing record to 25 victories in 29 starts. On Sept. 20 at Belmont in the Woodward, the colt ran alone in a walkover when trainers withdrew their horses. He finished out of the money only once. In 1979 the colt earned $1,279,333, winning 10 of 12 races. He missed becoming the 12th horse to win the Triple Crown—Kentucky Derby, Preakness, and Belmont Stakes—when he finished third in the Belmont. The previous record for syndication of a thoroughbred was $16.5 million for Troy, the 1979 European champion. Exceller was syndicated for $15 million in 1979 and Affirmed for $14.4 million. Affirmed was the previous top money-earner with $2,393,818.

Horse	Starts	1st	2nd	3rd	Earnings
Spectacular Bid	30	26	2	1	$2,781,607
Affirmed	29	22	5	1	2,393,818
Kelso	63	39	12	2	1,977,896
Forego	57	34	9	7	1,938,957
Round Table	66	43	8	5	1,749,869
Exceller	33	15	5	6	1,654,002
Dahlia[1]	48	15	3	7	1,543,139
Buckpasser	31	25	4	1	1,462,014
Allez France[1]	21	13	3	1	1,386,146
Secretariat	21	16	3	1	1,316,808
Nashua	30	22	4	1	1,288,565
Ancient Title	57	24	11	9	1,252,791
Susan's Girl[1]	63	29	14	11	1,251,667
Carry Back	61	21	11	11	1,241,165
Foolish Pleasure	26	16	4	3	1,216,705
Seattle Slew	17	14	2	0	1,208,726
Damascus	32	21	7	3	1,176,781
Cougar II	50	20	7	17	1,162,725
Spectacular Bid[2]	17	14	1	1	1,155,867
Riva Ridge	30	17	3	1	1,111,497
Fort Marcy	75	21	18	14	1,109,791
Citation	45	32	10	2	1,085,760
Native Diver	81	37	7	12	1,026,500
Royal Glint	52	21	9	4	1,004,815
Dr. Fager	22	18	2	1	1,002,642
Swoon's Son	51	30	10	3	970,605
Alydar	26	14	9	1	957,195

1. Female.

1980 TRIPLE CROWN RACES

(For 3-year-olds, carrying 126 pounds; jockeys in parentheses)

Kentucky Derby (Churchill Downs, Louisville, Ky., May 3; gross purse $339,300; 1¼ miles)—1. Genuine Risk (Jacinto Vasquez), owned by Bert and Diana Firestone; mutuel returns: $28.60, 10.60, 4.80. 2. Rumbo (Laffit Pincay) $5.20, 3.40. 3. Jaklin Klugman (Darrel McHargue) $4.40. 4. Super Moment (Pierce). 5. Rockhill Native (Oldham). 6. Bold 'n Rulling (Valenzuela). 7. Plugged Nickle (Thornburg). 8. Degenerate Jon (Hernandez). 9. Withholding (Morgan). 10. Tonka Wakhan (Holland). 11. Execution's Reason (Romero). 12. Gold Stage (Cordero). 13. Hazard Duke (Brumfield). Time: 2:02. Winner's purse: $250,550. Margin of victory: 1 length. Attendance: 131,859.

Preakness Stakes (Pimlico, Baltimore, Md., May 17; gross purse $250,600; 1³⁄₁₆ miles)—1. Codex (Angel Cordero), owned by Tartan Stable of James and Virginia Binger; mutuel returns: $7.40, 3.60, 3.80. 2. Genuine Risk (Vasquez) $3.60, 2.80. 3. Colonel Moran (Velasquez) $3.40. 4. Jaklin Klugman (McHargue). 5. Bing (Wright). Time: 1:54⅕. Winner's purse: $180,600. Margin of victory: 4¾ lengths. Attendance: 83,455.

Belmont Stakes (Elmont, N.Y., June 7; gross purse: $293,700; 1½ miles)—1. Temperence Hill (Eddie Maple), owned by John Anthony, Loblolly Farm; mutuel returns: $108.80, 32.80, 15.20. 2. Genuine Risk (Vasquez) $7.80, 5.20. 3. Rockhill Native (Oldham) $10.40. 4. Comptroller (Encinas). 5. Rumbo (Shoemaker). 6. Super Moment (Pincay). 7. Codex (Cordero). 8. Joanie's Chief (Santiago). 9. Bing (Cruguet). 10. Pikotazo (Hernandez). Time: 2:29⅘. Winner's purse: $176,220. Margin of victory: 2 lengths. Attendance: 58,090.

ARCHERY

NATIONAL ARCHERY ASSOCIATION CHAMPIONSHIPS

(Oxford, Ohio, Aug. 6–9, 1980)

Men's Division

	Pts
Richard McKinney, Glendale, Ariz.	2,558
Darrel Pace, Cincinnati	2,536
Larry Smith, Shrewsbury, Pa.	2,527
Rodney Baston, Bossier City, La.	2,517
Scott Kertson, Phoenix, Ariz.	2,503

Women's Division

Judi Adams, Phoenix, Ariz.	2,506
Irene Daubenspeck, Glendale, Ariz.	2,499
Ruth Rowe, Pittsburgh	2,473
N. Fairhall, Christchurch, New Zealand	2,451
Luann Ryon, Riverside, Calif.	2,434

Other Champions

Intermediate boys—Kevin Duffy, San Pablo, Calif., 2,417 points
Intermediate girls—Patty McMinds, Phoenix, Ariz., 2,317
Junior boys—Johnny Kazak, Aurora, Ill., 2,608
Junior girls—Debra Ochs, Howell, Mich., 2,285
Cadet boys—Brian Blum, Cincinnati, 2,642
Cadet girls—Katie Blum, 2,428

Crossbow

Men's Division—Erv Myers, Dallastown, Pa., 3,390 points
Women's Division—Carol Pelosi, Greenbelt, Md., 3,100
Kings Round—Erv Myers
Queens Round—Carol Pelosi

WRESTLING

A.A.U. NATIONAL CHAMPIONSHIPS

Freestyle

(Madison, Wis., April 17–19, 1980)
105.5 lb—Bob Weaver, New York Athletic Club
114.5 lb—Joe Gonzales, Sunkist Kits Wrestling Club
125.5 lb—Joe Corso, Hawkeye W.C.
136.5 lb—Ricky Dellagatta, New York A.C.
149.5 lb—Jim Humphrey, Oklahoma Underdogs W.C.
163 lb—Bruce Kinseth, Hawkeye W.C.
180.5 lb—Chris Campbell, Cyclone W.C.
198 lb—Ben Peterson, Wisconsin W.C.
220 lb—Russ Hellickson, Wisconsin W.C.
Heavyweight—Bruce Baumgartner, New York A.C.
Team—New York A.C.
Outstanding wrestler—Jim Humphrey

Greco-Roman

(Mount Pleasant, Mich., April 4–5, 1980)
105.5 lb—Mark Fuller, San Francisco Peninsula Grapplers
114.5 lb—John Hartupee, Michigan Wrestling Club
125.5 lb—Bruce Thompson, Rosemount, Minn.
136.5 lb—Abdurrahim Kuzu, Nebraska Olympic Club
149.5 lb—Doug Keats, Canada
163 lb—John Matthews, Michigan W.C.
180.5 lb—Louis Santerre, Canada
198 lb—Laurent Soucie, Wisconsin W.C.
220 lb—Brad Rheingans, Minnesota W.C.
Heavyweight—Jeff Blatnick, Adirondack Three–Style W.C.

NATIONAL COLLEGIATE ATHLETIC ASSOCIATION

(Corvallis, Ore., March 13–15, 1980)
118 lb—Joe Gonzales, California State
126 lb—Joe Azevedo, California State
134 lb—Randy Lewis, Iowa
142 lb—Lee Roy Smith, Oklahoma State
150 lb—Andy Rein, Wisconsin
158 lb—Ricky Stewart, Oklahoma State
167 lb—Matt Reiss, North Carolina State
177 lb—Ed Banach, Iowa
190 lb—Noel Loban, Clemson
Heavyweight—Howard Harris, Oregon State
Team—Iowa (110.75 pts)

NATIONAL ASSOCIATION OF INTERCOLLEGIATE ATHLETICS

(Hays, Kan., March 6–8, 1980)
118 lb—Rudy Glur, Huron (S.D.)
126 lb—Scott Ritzen, Adams State (Colo.)
134 lb—David James, Central State (Okla.)
142 lb—Genard Zamudio, Southern Oregon
150 lb—James Morkel, Huron (S.D.)
158 lb—Daniel Morrison, Messiah (Pa.)
167 lb—John Dwyer, Simon Fraser, Canada
177 lb—Jeff Laube, Wisconsin–Superior
190 lb—Tony Huck, Valley City State (N.D.)
Heavyweight—Ron Essink, Grand Valley State (Mich.)
Team—Adams State (Colo.)

QUARTER HORSE RACING—1980

All–American Futurity—Higheasterjet
All–American Derby—Native Gambler

TRACK AND FIELD

Running, jumping, hurdling and throwing weights—track and field sports, in other words—are as natural to young people as eating, drinking and breathing. Unorganized competition in this form of sport goes back beyond the Cave Man era. Organized competition begins with the first recorded Olympic Games in Greece, 776 B.C., when Coroebus of Elis won the only event on the program, a race of approximately 200 yards. The Olympic Games, with an ever-widening program of events, continued until "the glory that was Greece" had faded and "the grandeur that was Rome" was tarnished, and finally were abolished by decree of Emperor Theodosius I of Rome in A.D. 394. The Tailteann Games of Ireland are supposed to have antedated the first Olympic Games by some centuries, but we have no records of the specific events and winners thereof.

Professional contests of speed and strength were popular at all times and in many lands, but the widespread competition of amateur athletes in track and field sports is a comparatively modern development. The first organized amateur athletic meet of record was sponsored by the Royal Military Academy at Woolwich, England, in 1849. Oxford and Cambridge track and field rivalry began in 1864, and the English amateur championships were established in 1866. In the United States such organizations as the New York Athletic Club and the Olympic Club of San Francisco conducted track and field meets in the 1870s, and a few colleges joined to sponsor a meet in 1874. The success of the college meet led to the formation of the Intercollegiate Association of Amateur Athletes of America and the holding of an annual set of championship games beginning in 1876. The Amateur Athletic Union, organized in 1888, has been the ruling body in American amateur athletics since that time. In 1980, The Athletics Congress of the U.S.A. took over the governing of track and field from the A.A.U.

WORLD RECORDS—MEN

Recognized by the International Athletic Federation in January 1977

The I.A.A.F. decided late in 1976 not to recognize records in yards except for the one-mile run. The I.A.A.F. began in 1975 to recognize two sets of records for races of 400 meters or less—hand-timed and automatically timed. General usage now goes with electrically timed records, which are used in the following tables.

Running

Event	Record	Holder	Home Country	Where Made	Date
100 m	0:09.95	Jim Hines	U.S.	Mexico City	Oct. 14, 1968
200 m	0:19.72	Pietro Mennea	Italy	Mexico City	Sept. 17, 1979
400 m	0:43.86	Lee Evans	U.S.	Mexico City	Oct. 18, 1968
800 m	1:42.4	Sebastian Coe	Britain	Oslo, Norway	July 5, 1979
1,000 m	2:13.4	Sebastian Coe	Britain	Oslo	July 1, 1980
1,500 m	3:31.4	Steve Ovett	Britain	Koblenz, W. Ger.	Aug. 27, 1980
1 mile	3:48.8	Steve Ovett	Britain	Oslo	July 1, 1980
2,000 m	4:51.4	John Walker	New Zealand	Oslo	June 30, 1976
3,000 m	7:32.1	Henry Rono	Kenya	Oslo	June 27, 1978
3,000 m steeplechase	8:05.4	Henry Rono	Kenya	Seattle, Washington	May 13, 1978
5,000 m	13:08.4	Henry Rono	Kenya	Berkeley, Calif.	April 8, 1978
10,000 m	27:22.4	Henry Rono	Kenya	Vienna, Austria	June 11, 1978
25,000 m	1:14:12	Bill Rodgers	U.S.	Saratoga, Calif.	Feb. 21, 1979
30,000 m	1:31:31	Jim Alder	Britain	London	Sept. 5, 1970
20,000 m	57:24.2	Jos Hermans	Netherlands	Papandal, Neth.	May 1, 1976
1 hour	13 mi. 24 yd	Jos Hermans	Netherlands	Papandal, Neth.	May 1, 1976

Walking

Event	Record	Holder	Home Country	Where Made	Date
20,000 m	1:20:59	Domingo Colin	Mexico	Bergen, Norway	May 26, 1979
	1:20:07p	Daniel Bautista	Mexico	Montreal	Oct. 17, 1979
2 hours	17 mi. 881 yd	Jose Marin	Spain	Barcelona	Aug. 4, 1979
30,000 m	2:08:00	Jose Marin	Spain	Barcelona	Aug. 4, 1979
50,000 m	3:41:39	Raul Gonzales	Mexico	Bergen, Norway	May 25, 1979

Hurdles

Event	Record	Holder	Home Country	Where Made	Date
110 m	0:13.16	Renaldo Nehemiah	U.S.	San Jose, Calif.	April 14, 1979
	0:13.00p	Renaldo Nehemiah	U.S.	Westwood, Calif.	May 6, 1979
400 m	0:47.13	Edwin Moses	U.S.	Milan, Italy	July 3, 1980

Relay Races

Event	Record	Holder	Home Country	Where Made	Date
400 m (4x100)	0:38.03	National Team	U.S.	Dusseldorf, W. Ger.	Sept. 3, 1977
800 m (4x200)	1:20.3	So. California	U.S.	Tempe, Ariz.	May 27, 1978

		(Joel Andrews, James Sanford, Billy Mullins, Clancy Edwards)			
1,600 m (4x400)	2:56.1	National Team	U.S.	Mexico City	Oct. 20, 1968
		(Vince Matthews, Ron Freeman, Larry James, Lee Evans)			
3,200 m (4x800)	7:08.1	National Team	U.S.S.R.	Podolsk, U.S.S.R.	Aug. 12, 1978

Field Events

High jump	7 ft 8¾ in. (2.36 m)	Gerd Wessig	East Germany	Moscow	Aug. 1, 1980
Long jump	29 ft 2½ in. (8.90 m)	Bob Beamon	U.S.	Mexico City	Oct. 18, 1976
Triple jump	58 ft. 8¼ in. (17.89 m)	Joao Oliveira	Brazil	Mexico City	Oct. 15, 1975
Pole vault	18 ft. 11½ in. (5.78 m)	Wladyslaw Kozakiewicz	Poland	Moscow	July 30, 1980
Shotput	72 ft 8 in. (22 m)	Udo Beyer	East Germany	Göteborg, Sweden	July 6, 1978
Discus throw	233 ft 5 in. (71.16m)	Wolfgang Schmidt	East Germany	East Berlin	Aug. 9, 1978
Javelin throw	317 ft 4 in. (96.72 m)	Ferenc Paragi	Hungary	Tata, Hungary	April 23, 1980
Hammer throw	268 ft 4 in. (81.80m)	Yuri Sedyky	U.S.S.R.	Moscow	July 31, 1980
Decathlon	8,649 pts	Guido Kratschmer	West Germany	Filderstadt, W. Ger.	July 13–14, 1980

p=mark is pending.

WORLD RECORDS—WOMEN

Running

Event	Record	Holder	Home Country	Where Made	Date
100 m	0:10.88	Marlies Goehr	East Germany	Dresden, E. Ger.	July 1, 1977
	0:10.87p	Lyudmila Kondratyeva	U.S.S.R.	Leningrad	June 2, 1980
200 m	0:21.71	Marita Koch	East Germany	Karl Marx Stadt	June 10, 1979
400 m	0:48.89	Marita Koch	East Germany	Potsdam, E. Ger.	July 29, 1979
	0:48.60p	Marita Koch	East Germany	Turin, Italy	Aug. 4, 1979
800 m	1:53.42	Nadezhda Olizaryenko	U.S.S.R.	Moscow	July 27, 1980
1,500 m	3:52.47	Tatyana Kazankina	U.S.S.R.	Zurich, Switz.	Aug. 13, 1980
1 mile	4:21.7	Mary Decker	U.S.	Auckland, New Zealand	Jan. 26, 1980
3,000 m	8:27.2	Lyudmila Bragina	U.S.S.R.	College Park, Md.	Aug. 7, 1976
5,000 m	15:08.8	Loa Olafsson	Denmark	Copenhagen	May 31, 1978
10,000 m	31:45.4	Loa Olafsson	Denmark	Copenhagen	April 6, 1978

Hurdles

100 m	0:12.36	Grazyna Rabsztyn	Poland	Warsaw	June 13, 1980
400 m	0:54.28	Karin Rossley	East Germany	Jena, E. Ger.	May 17, 1980

Relay Races

400 m (4x100)	0:41.60	National Team	East Germany	Moscow	Aug. 1, 1980
		(Romy Mueller, Barbel Woeckel, Ingrid Auerswald, Marlies Goehr)			
800 m (4x200)	1:28.1	National Team	East Germany	Jena, E. Ger.	July 9, 1980
		(Marlies Goehr, Romy Mueller, Barbel Woeckel, Marita Koch)			
1,600 m (4x400)	3:19.2	National Team	East Germany	Montreal	July 31, 1976
		(Doris Maletzki, Brigitte Rohda, Ellen Streidt, Christine Bremer)			
3,200 m (4x800)	7:52.3	National Team	U.S.S.R.	Podolsk, U.S.S.R.	Aug. 16, 1976
		(Tatyana Providokhina, Vera Gerasimova, Svetlana Styrkina, Tatyana Kazankina)			

Field Events

High jump	6 ft 7 in. (2.01 m)	Sara Simeoni	Italy	Brescia	Aug. 4, 1978
	6 ft 7 in. (2.01 m)	Sara Simeoni	Italy	Prague, Czech.	Aug. 31, 1978
Long jump	23 ft 3¼ in. (7.09 m)	Vilma Bardauskiene	U.S.S.R.	Prague, Czech.	Aug. 29, 1978
Shot-put	73 ft 4¼ in. (22.36 m)	Ilona Slupianek	East Germany	Celje, Yugoslavia	May 2, 1980
Discus throw	235 ft 7 in. (71.80 m)	Maria Vergova	Bulgaria	Sofia, Bulgaria	July 13, 1980
Javelin throw	229 ft 11 in. (70.08 m)	Tatyana Biryulina	U.S.S.R.	Podolsk, U.S.S.R.	July 12, 1980
Pentathlon	5,083 pts	Nadezhda Tkachenko	U.S.S.R.	Moscow	July 24, 1980

FLYERS SET N.H.L. RECORD FOR UNBEATEN GAMES

The Philadelphia Flyers fashioned a remarkable unbeaten streak of 35 games during the 1979–80 National Hockey League season, breaking the record of 28 set in 1977–78 by the Montreal Canadiens. The Flyers won 25 games and tied 10 during the streak that began on Oct. 14 with a 4–3 victory over Toronto. They had lost, 9–2, to Atlanta in their second game of the season before embarking on their spree. They didn't lose again until early in January when the Minnesota North Stars stopped them, 7–1, at Bloomington, Minn. The Flyers finished the season with the best overall record in the N.H.L., but they were eliminated in the Stanley Cup playoffs, won by the New York Islanders.

AMERICAN RECORDS—MEN

Officially approved by The Athletics Congress as of Oct. 1, 1980; all listings are for automatic timing.

Running

Event	Record	Holder	Where made	Date
100 m	0:09.95	Jim Hines	Mexico City	Oct. 14, 1968
200 m	0:19.83	Tommie Smith	Mexico City	Oct. 16, 1968
400 m	0:43.86	Lee Evans	Mexico City	Oct. 16, 1968
800 m	1:43.9	Richard Wohlhuter	Stockholm	July 18, 1974
1,000 m	2:13.9	Richard Wohlhuter	Oslo	July 30, 1974
1,500 m	3:33.1	Jim Ryun	Los Angeles	July 18, 1967
1 mile	3:51.1	Jim Ryun	Bakersfield, Calif.	June 23, 1967
2,000 m	5:01.4	Steve Prefontaine	Coos Bay, Ore.	May 10, 1975
3,000 m	7:37.7	Rudy Chappa	Eugene, Ore.	May 12, 1979
5,000 m	13:15.1	Martin Liquori	Dusseldorf, W. Ger.	Sept. 4, 1977
10,000 m	27:29.16	Craig Virgin	Paris	July 17, 1980
20,000 m	59:15	Bill Rodgers	Boston	Aug. 9, 1977
25,000 m	1:14:12	Bill Rodgers	Saratoga, Calif.,	Feb. 21, 1979
30,000 m	1:31:50	Bill Rodgers	Saratoga, Calif.	Feb. 21, 1979
1 hour	12 mi. 997 yds	Bill Rodgers	Saratoga, Calif	Feb. 21, 1979
3,000 m steeplechase	8:15.68	Henry Marsh	Eugene, Ore.	June 28, 1980

Hurdles

110 m	0:13.0	Renaldo Nehemiah	Westwood, Calif.	May 6, 1979
400 m	0:47.13	Edwin Moses	Milan, Italy	July 3, 1980

Relay Races

400 m (4x100)	0:38.03	U.S. team (Bill Collins, Steve Riddick, Cliff Wiley, Steve Williams)	Dusseldorf, W. Ger.	Sept. 3, 1977
800 m (4x200)	1:20.3	Southern California (Joe Andrews, James Sanford, Billy Mullins, Clancy Edwards)	Tempe, Ariz.	May 27, 1978
1,600 m (4x400)	2:56.1	U.S. Team (Vince Matthews, Ron Freeman, Larry James, Lee Evans)	Mexico City	Oct. 20, 1968
3,200 m (4x800)	7:10.4	U. of Chicago T.C.	Durham, N.C.	May 12, 1973

Field Events

High jump	7 ft 7¼ in.	Dwight Stones	Philadelphia	Aug. 4, 1976
Long jump	29 ft 2¼ in.	Robert Beamon	Mexico City	Oct. 18, 1968
Triple jump	56 ft 5¼ in.	Tommy Haynes	Mexico City	Oct. 15, 1975
	56 ft 5½ in.[1]	James Butts	Westwood, Calif.	May 7, 1978
	56 ft 6¾ in.[1]	James Butts	Helsinki, Finland	June 29, 1978
Pole vault	18 ft 8¼ in.	Dave Roberts	Eugene, Ore.	June 22, 1976
Shot put	71 ft 8½ in.	Terry Albritton	Honolulu	Feb. 2, 1976
Discus throw	232 ft 10 in.	Mac Wilkins	Helsinki, Finland	July 9, 1980
Javelin throw	300 ft	Mark Murro	Tempe, Ariz.	March 27, 1970
Hammer throw	235 ft 11 in.	Edward Burke	Bakersfield, Calif.	June 22, 1967

FIELD HOCKEY

CHAMPIONS TROPHY—1980

Men—Pakistan

ROQUE—1980

United States Champion—C.B. Smith, Decatur, Ill.

ASTROS WIN PLAYOFF FOR N.L. WESTERN TITLE

The Houston Astros defeated the Los Angeles Dodgers, 7–1, in a playoff for the National League Western Division crown after the Dodgers had swept three straight games from Houston and deadlocked the standing at the end of the regular season. It was Houston's first title since the franchise was started in 1962. It was only the fifth pennant or division playoff in more than 100 years in the National League.

AMERICAN RECORDS—WOMEN

Running

Event	Record	Holder	Where made	Date
100 m	0:10.97	Evelyn Ashford	Walnut, Calif.	June 10, 1979
200 m	0:22.45	Evelyn Ashford	San Juan, P.R.	July 9, 1979
400 m	0:50.62	Rosalyn Bryant	Montreal	July 28, 1976
800 m	1:57.9	Madeline Jackson	College Park, Md.	Aug. 7, 1976
1,500 m	3:59.43	Mary Decker	Zurich	Aug. 13, 1980
1 mi.	4:28.61	Mary Decker	Auckland, N.Z.	Jan. 26, 1980
3,000 m	8:58.73	Mary Decker	Philadelphia	July 17, 1980
5,000 m	15:35.5	Kathy Mills	Knoxville, Tenn	May 26, 1978
	15:33.8[1]	Jan Merrill	Durham, N.C.	May 19, 1979
10,000 m	33:15.1	Peg Neppel	Westwood, Calif.	June 9, 1977
	32:52.5[1]	Mary Shea	Walnut, Calif.	June 15, 1979

Hurdles

Event	Record	Holder	Where made	Date
100 m	0:12.86	Deby LaPlante	Walnut, Calif.	July 16, 1979
400 m	0:56.16	Esther Mahr	Sittard, Holland	Aug. 15, 1979

Relay Races

Event	Record	Holder	Where made	Date
400 m (4x100)	0:42.87	U.S. team (Barbara Ferrell, Margaret Bailes, Mildrette Netter, Wyomia Tyus)	Mexico City	Oct. 20, 1968
800 m (4x200)	1:32.6	National Team (Wanda Hooker, Karen Hawkins, Chandra Cheeseborough, Brenda Morehead)	Bourges, France	June 23, 1979
1,600 m (4x400)	3:22.8	U.S. team (Debra Sapenter, Sheila Ingram, Pam Jiles, Rosalyn Bryant)	Montreal	July 31, 1976

Field Events

Event	Record	Holder	Where made	Date
High jump	6 ft 4¾ in.	Louise Ritter	Wichita, Kans.	May 30, 1980
Long jump	22 ft 11½ in.	Jodi Anderson	Eugene, Ore.	June 28, 1980
Shot put	62 ft 7¾ in.	Maren Seidler	Walnut, Calif.	June 16, 1979
Discus throw	207 ft 5 in.	Lorna Griffin	Long Beach, Calif.	May 24, 1980
Javelin throw	227 ft 5 in.	Kathy Schmidt	Furth, W. Ger.	Sept. 11, 1977
Long jump	22 ft 7½ in.	Jodi Anderson	Westwood, Calif.	June 10, 1979
Pentathlon	4,708 pts	Jane Frederick	Gotzis, Austria	May 26–27, 1979

1. Betters listed record.

HISTORY OF THE RECORD FOR THE MILE RUN

Time	Athlete	Country	Year	Location
4:36.5	Richard Webster	England	1865	England
4:29.0	William Chinnery	England	1868	England
4:28.8	Walter Gibbs	England	1868	England
4:26.0	Walter Slade	England	1874	England
4:24.5	Walter Slade	England	1875	London
4:23.2	Walter George	England	1880	London
4:21.4	Walter George	England	1882	London
4:18.4	Walter George	England	1884	Birmingham, England
4:18.2	Fred Bacon	Scotland	1894	Edinburgh, Scotland
4:17.0	Fred Bacon	Scotland	1895	London
4:15.6	Thomas Conneff	United States	1895	Travers Island, N.Y.
4:15.4	John Paul Jones	United States	1911	Cambridge, Mass.
4:14.4	John Paul Jones	United States	1913	Cambridge, Mass.
4:12.6	Norman Taber	United States	1915	Cambridge, Mass.
4:10.4	Paavo Nurmi	Finland	1923	Stockholm
4:09.2	Jules Ladoumegue	France	1931	Paris
4:07.6	Jack Lovelock	New Zealand	1933	Princeton, N.J.
4:06.8	Glenn Cunningham	United States	1934	Princeton, N.J.
4:06.4	Sydney Wooderson	England	1937	London

4:06.2	Gundar Hägg	Sweden	1942	Göteborg, Sweden
4:06.2	Arne Andersson	Sweden	1942	Stockholm
4:04.6	Gunder Hägg	Sweden	1942	Stockholm
4:02.6	Arne Andersson	Sweden	1943	Göteborg, Sweden
4:01.6	Arne Andersson	Sweden	1944	Malmö, Sweden
4:01.4	Gunder Hägg	Sweden	1945	Malmö, Sweden
3:59.4	Roger Bannister	England	1954	Oxford, England
3:58.0	John Landy	Australia	1954	Turku, Finland
3:57.2	Derek Ibbotson	England	1957	London
3:54.5	Herb Elliott	Australia	1958	Dublin
3:54.4	Peter Snell	New Zealand	1962	Wanganui, N.Z.
3:54.1	Peter Snell	New Zealand	1964	Auckland, N.Z.
3:53.6	Michel Jarzy	France	1965	Rennes, France
3:51.3	Jim Ryun	United States	1966	Berkeley, Calif.
3:51.1	Jim Ryun	United States	1967	Bakersfield, Calif.
3:51.0	Filbert Bayi	Tanzania	1975	Kingston, Jamaica
3:49.4	John Walker	New Zealand	1975	Göteborg, Sweden
3:49.0	Sebastian Coe	England	1979	Oslo
3:48.8	Steve Ovett	England	1980	Oslo

WORLD'S FASTEST INDOOR MILES

Time	Athlete	Country	Date	Location
3:52.6	Eamonn Coghlan	Ireland	Feb. 16, 1979	San Diego
3:52.9	Eamonn Coghlan	Ireland	Feb. 15, 1980	Los Angeles
3:53.0	Steve Scott[1]	United States	Feb. 15, 1980	Los Angeles
3:54.1	Steve Scott[1]	United States	Feb. 16, 1979	San Diego
3:54.7	Steve Lacy[2]	United States	Feb. 16, 1979	San Diego
3:54.9	Dick Buerkle	United States	Jan. 13, 1978	College Park, Md.
3:55.0	Tony Waldrop	United States	Feb. 17, 1974	San Diego
3:55.0	Eamonn Coghlan	Ireland	Feb. 9, 1979	New York
3:55.4	Neil O'Shaughnessy	Ireland	Jan. 28, 1977	Columbia, Md.
3:55.5	Filbert Bayi[2]	Tanzania	Feb. 15, 1980	Los Angeles
3:55.5	Filbert Bayi[2]	Tanzania	Feb. 22, 1980	San Diego
3:55.6	Steve Lacy[3]	United States	Feb. 15, 1980	Los Angeles
3:55.7	Wilson Waigwa	Kenya	Feb. 8, 1977	San Diego
3:55.7	Eamonn Coghlan[1]	Ireland	Feb. 22, 1980	San Diego
3:55.8	Marty Liquori	United States	Feb. 7, 1975	Philadelphia
3:55.8	John Walker[2]	New Zealand	Feb. 22, 1980	San Diego
3:56.0	Eamonn Coghlan	Ireland	Feb. 17, 1978	San Diego
3:56.1	Filbert Bayi	Tanzania	Feb. 27, 1976	New York
3:56.1	Eamonn Coghlan	Ireland	Jan. 20, 1979	Los Angeles
3:56.2	Ben Jipcho (pro)	Kenya	March 22, 1975	Los Angeles
3:56.3	Wilson Waigwa[1]	Kenya	Feb. 9, 1979	New York
3:56.3	Ben Jipcho (pro)	Kenya	May 31, 1975	Atlanta
3:56.4	Thomas Wessighage[3]	W. Germany	Feb. 22, 1980	San Diego
3:56.4	Tom O'Hara	United States	March 6, 1964	Chicago
3:56.4	Jim Ryun	United States	Feb. 19, 1971	San Diego
3:56.4	Tony Waldrop	United States	Feb. 23, 1974	College Park, Md.
3:56.4	Filbert Bayi	Tanzania	Feb. 15, 1975	San Diego
3:56.5	Steve Scott	United States	Feb. 18, 1975	San Diego
3:56.6	Tom O'Hara	United States	Feb. 13, 1964	New York
3:56.7	Steve Scott[1]	United States	Jan. 20, 1979	Los Angeles
3:56.8	Rod Dixon	New Zealand	Feb. 21, 1976	San Diego
3:56.8	John Walker	New Zealand	Feb. 11, 1979	Montreal
3:56.9	John Walker	New Zealand	Feb. 15, 1975	San Diego
3:57.0	Wilson Waigwa	Kenya	Feb. 15, 1975	Oklahoma City

1. Finished second. 2. Finished third. 3. Finished fourth.

GAELIC SPORTS

IRISH CHAMPIONSHIPS—1979

Football—Kerry
Hurling—Kilkenny

SLED DOG RACING—1980

World champion—Debbie Molburg, Center Harbor, N.H.

WORLD'S FASTEST OUTDOOR MILES

Time	Athlete	Country	Date	Location
3:48.8	Steve Ovett	England	July 1, 1980	Oslo
3:49.0	Sebastian Coe	England	July 17, 1979	Oslo
3:49.4	John Walker	New Zealand	Aug. 12, 1975	Gotesborg, Sweden
3:49.6	Steve Ovett	England	Aug. 31, 1979	London
3:50.6	Thomas Wessinghage[1]	West Germany	Aug. 31, 1979	London
3:51.0	Filbert Bayi	Tanzania	May 17, 1975	Kingston, Jamaica
3:51.1	Jim Ryun	United States	June 23, 1967	Bakersfield, Calif.
3:51.2	Steve Scott[1]	United States	July 17, 1979	Oslo
3:51.3	Jim Ryun	United States	July 17, 1966	Berkeley, Calif.
3:52.0	Ben Jipcho	Kenya	July 2, 1973	Stockholm
3:52.0	John Walker	New Zealand	July 11, 1977	Dublin
3:52.1	Craig Masback[2]	United States	July 17, 1977	Oslo
3:52.2	Marty Liquori[1]	United States	May 17, 1975	Kingston, Jamaica
3:52.2	John Walker	New Zealand	June 30, 1975	
3:52.5	Thomas Wessinghage	West Germany	July 3, 1978	Stockholm
3:52.5	Eamonn Coghlan[3]	Ireland	July 17, 1979	Oslo
3:52.6	Filbert Bayi[1]	Tanzania	July 2, 1973	Stockholm
3:52.6	Jozef Plachy[1]	Czechoslovakia	July 3, 1978	Stockholm
3:52.8	Jim Ryun	United States	July 28, 1972	Toronto
3:52.8	Steve Ovett	England	Sept. 20, 1978	Oslo
3:52.8	John Robson[4]	England	July 17, 1979	Oslo
3:52.9	Steve Scott[2]	United States	July 3, 1978	Stockholm
3:52.9	Eamonn Coghlan	Ireland	June 30, 1979	Philadelphia
3:52.9	John Walker[5]	New Zealand	July 17, 1979	Oslo
3:53.1	Kipchoge Keino	Kenya	Sept. 10, 1967	Kisumu, Kenya
3:53.1	John Walker	New Zealand	Aug. 9, 1976	Stockholm
3:53.1	Thomas Wessinghage[1]	West Germany	Aug. 9, 1976	Stockholm
3:53.2	Jim Ryun	United States	June 2, 1967	Los Angeles
3:53.2	Tony Waldrop	United States	April 22, 1974	Philadelphia
3:53.2	Wilson Waigwa	Kenya	June 27,1978	Oslo
3:53.2	Graham Williamson[6]	England	July 17, 1979	Oslo
3:53.3	Dave Wottle	United States	June 30, 1973	Eugene, Ore.
3:53.3	Eamonn Coghlan[2]	Ireland	May 17, 1975	Kingston, Jamaica
3:53.3	Thomas Wessinghage[7]	West Germany	July 17, 1979	Oslo
3:53.4	Kipchoge Keino	Kenya	Aug. 20, 1966	London
3:53.4	Marty Liquori[1]	United States	June 30, 1975	Stockholm
3:53.4	Steve Scott[1]	United States	June 30, 1979	Philadelphia
3:53.5	Filbert Bayi[1]	Tanzania	June 27, 1978	Oslo
3:53.5	John Robson[2]	England	Aug. 31, 1979	London

1. Finished second. 2. Finished third. 3. Finished fourth. 4. Finished fifth. 5. Finished sixth. 6. Finished seventh. 7. Finished eighth.
NOTE: Professional marks not included.

HISTORY OF THE POLE VAULT

(Some of early dates are the winning heights of A.A.U. champion for that year, used to show progression from one foot level to the next. Figures from A.A.U. records and *Track & Field News.*)

Bamboo Poles

1877	G. McNichol	9 ft 7 in.
1879	W. J. Van Houten	10 ft 4¾ in.
1883	Hugh Baxter	11 ft 0½ in.
1904	Norman Dole	12 ft 1³⁄₁₀ in.
1912	Robert Gardner	13 ft 1 in.
1927	Sabin Carr	14 ft 0 in.
1940	Cornelius Warmerdam	15 ft 1 in.
1942	Cornelius Warmerdam	15 ft 7¾ in.

Metal Poles

1957	Bob Gutowski	15 ft 8¼ in.
1960	Don Bragg	15 ft 9¼ in.

Fiberglas Poles

1961	George Davis	15 ft 10¼ in.
1962	John Uelses	16 ft 0¾ in.
1962	Dave Tork	16 ft 2 in.
1962	Pentti Nikula	16 ft 2½ in.
1963	John Pennel	16 ft 4 in.
1963	Brian Sternberg	16 ft 5 in.
1963	John Pennel	16 ft 6¾ in.
1963	Brian Sternberg	16 ft 8 in.
1963	John Pennel	16 ft 10 in.
1963	John Pennel	17 ft 0¾ in.
1964	Fred Hansen	17 ft 4 in.
1966	Bob Seagren	17 ft 5½ in.
1966	John Pennel	17 ft 6¼ in.
1967	Bob Seagren	17 ft 7 in.
1967	Paul Wilson	17 ft 7¾ in.
1968	Bob Seagren	17 ft 9 in.
1969	John Pennel	17 ft 10¼ in.
1970	Wolfgang Norwig	17 ft 10½ in.
1970	Chris Papanicolaou	18 ft 0¼ in.
1972	Kjell Isaksson	18 ft 1 in.
1972	Kjell Isaksson	18 ft 2 in.
1972	Kjell Isaksson, Bob Seagren	18 ft 4¼ in.
1972	Bob Seagren	18 ft 5¾ in.
1975	Dave Roberts	18 ft 6½ in.
1976	Earl Bell	18 ft 7¼ in.
1976	Dave Roberts	18 ft 8¼ in.
1980	Thierry Vigneron	18 ft 10¼ in.
1980	Philippe Houvion	18 ft 11 in.
1980	Wladyslaw Kozakiewicz	18 ft 11½ in.

UNITED STATES MARATHON CHAMPIONS

(26 miles, 385 Yards)

Boston Marathon

1970	Ron Hill, England	2:10:30
1971	Alvaro Meija, Colombia	2:18:45
1972	Olavi Suomalainen, Finland	2:15:39
1973	Jon Anderson, Eugene, Ore.	2:16:03
1974	Neil Cusack, Ireland	2:13:39
1975	William H. Rodgers, Boston	2:09:55
1976	Jack Fultz, Arlington, Va.	2:20:19
1977	Jerome Drayton, Toronto	2:14:46
1978	William H. Rodgers, Melrose, Mass.	2:10:13
1979	William H. Rodgers, Melrose, Mass.	2:09.27
1980	William H. Rodgers, Melrose, Mass.	2:12:11

Amateur Athletic Union

1970	Bob Fitts, Wisconsin	2:24:11
1971	Ken Moore, Portland, Ore.	2:16:49
1972	Edmund Norris, Brockton, Mass.	2:24:42.8
1973	Doug Schmenk	2:15:48
1974	Ron Wayne, Eugene, Ore.	2:18:52
1975	Gary Tuttle, Beverly Hills Strider	2:17:27
1976	Gary Tuttle, Los Angeles	2:15:15
1977	Not Held	
1978	Carl Hatfield, West Va. T.C.	2:17.20
1979	Tom Antczak, Rockford, Ill.	2:15.28

The Athletics Congress

1980	Paul Richardson, Ames, Iowa	2:13:54*

*Time not recognized because course was too short.

CROSS COUNTRY RACE CHAMPIONS

Amateur Athletic Union

(10,000 Meters)

1971 Frank Shorter, Gainesville, Fla.; Florida T.C.
1972 Frank Shorter, Gainesville, Fla.; Florida T.C.
1973 Frank Shorter, Gainesville, Fla.; Florida T.C.
1974 John Ngeno, Kenya; Colorado T.C.
1975 Greg Fredericks, Philadelphia; Colorado T.C.
1976 Rick Rojas, San Diego; Jamul Toads
1977 Nick Rose, England; Colorado T.C.
1978 Greg Meyer, Boston; Mason Dixon A.C.
1979 Alberto Salazar, Boston; Greater Boston T.C.

N.C.A.A. (University)

(6 Miles)

1973 Steve Prefontaine, Oregon; Oregon
1974 Nick Rose, Western Kentucky; Oregon
1975 Craig Virgin, Illinois; Texas-El Paso
1976 Henry Rono, Wash. State; Texas-El Paso
1977 Henry Rono, Wash. State; Oregon
1978 Alberto Salazar, Oregon; Texas-El Paso
1979 Henry Rono, Washington State; Texas-El Paso

N.C.A.A. (College)

(5 Miles; 4 miles prior to 1968)

1975 Div. II: Ralph Serna, Calif.-Irvine; Calif.-Irvine
Div. III: Vin Fleming, Lowell; N. Central Illinois
1976 Div. II: Ralph Serna, Calif.-Irvine; Calif.-Irvine
Div. III: Dale Cramer, Carleton; N. Central Illinois
1977 Div. II: Michael Bollman, N.D. State; E. Illinois
Div. III: Dale Kramer, Carleton; Occidental
1978 Div. II: Jim Schankel, Cal Poly, San Luis Obispo; Cal Poly, San Luis Obispo
Div. III: Dan Henderson, Wheaton; N. Cent. Illinois
1979 Div. II: Jim Schankel, Cal Poly, San Luis Obispo
Div. III: Steve Hunt, Boston State; North Central, Ill.

N.A.I.A.

(5 Miles)

1973 Tony Brien, Marymount; Eastern New Mexico
1974 Mike Boit, Eastern New Mexico; Eastern New Mexico
1975 Mike Boit, Eastern New Mexico; Edinboro State
1976 John Kebiro, Eastern New Mexico; Edinboro State
1977 Garry Henry, Pembroke State; Adams State
1978 Kelly Jensen, So. Oregon; Pembroke State
1979 Sam Montoya, Adams State; Adams State

CROSS-COUNTRY WORLD CHAMPIONSHIPS

(Paris, France March 9, 1980)

Men—Craig Virgin, United States	37:1.1
Women—Grete Waitz, Norway	15:05
Junior men—Jorge Garcia, Spain	22:17
Men's team—England	100 points
Women's team—Soviet Union	15 points
Junior men's team—Soviet Union	50 points

WORLD AND AMERICAN BEST PERFORMANCES IN INDOOR TRACK

The International Amateur Athletic Union does not recognize indoor records. The following best performances, often called world records, are from lists provided by the Amateur Athletic Union and The Athletics Congress of the United States and *Track and Field News*, published in Los Altos, Calif., Bert Nelson, editor and publisher.

MEN

Running

50 yards—Houston McTear, Toronto, 1978	0:05.25
60 yards—Houston McTear, New York, 1978	0:06.05
70 yards—Herb McFarland, Louisville, Ky.	0:06.7
100 yards—Don Quarrie, Pocatello, Idaho, 1971	0:09.3
Carl Lawson, Pocatello, Idaho, 1971	0:09.3
Cliff Branch, Pocatello, Idaho, 1972	0:09.3
300 yards—William Snoody, Lincoln, Neb., 1978	0:29.47
440 yards—Tommie Smith, Louisville, Ky., 1967	0:46.2
Tim Dale, Princeton, N.J., 1978	0:47.69
500 yards—Lee Evans, College Park, Md., 1971	0:54.4
Pro—Larry James, Salt Lake City, Utah, 1973	0:53.9
600 yards—Martin McGrady, New York, 1970	1:07.6
880 yards—Ralph Doubell, Albuquerque, N.M., 1969	1:47.9
Mark Belger (Am.), College Park, Md., 1978	1:48.1
Tom Von Ruden (Am.), College Park, Md., 1971	1:48.5
1,000 yards—Mark Winzenreid, Louisville, Ky., 1972	2:05.1
Mile—Eamonn Coghlan, San Diego, 1979	3:52.6
Steve Scott (Am.), San Diego, 1979	3:54.1
2 miles—Emiel Puttemans, Berlin, 1973	8:13.2
Terry O'Brien (Am.), San Diego, 1971	8:15.2
Steve Prefontaine (Am.), San Diego, 1974	8:20.4
3 miles—Emiel Puttemans, Pentin, Belgium, 1976	12:54.6
Tracy Smith, (Am.), New York, 1973	13:07.2

Running—Metric Distances

50 meters—Manfred Koket, East Germany, 1971	0:05.4
Bill Gaines (Am.), Highland Park, N.J., 1968	0:05.4
60 meters—Houston McTear, New York, 1978	0:06.11
70 meters—Helmut Kornig, Germany, 1932	0:07.5
Ira Murchison (Am.), United States	0:07.5
Pro—John Carlos, Pocatello, Idaho, 1974	0:07.3
100 meters—Eugen Ray, East Berlin, 1976	0:10.16

Pro—Warren Edmonson, Pocatello, Idaho, 1973 0:10.2
200 meters—Karlh Wiesenseel, West Germany, 1978 0:21.11
Pietro Mennea, Italy, 1978 0:21.11
300 meters—Pietro Mennea, Italy, 1978 0:32.83
400 meters—Karel Kolar, Vienna, 1979 0:46.21
Herman Frazier (Am.), Italy, 1978 0:46.48
500 meters—Herman Frazier, Long Beach, Calif., 1979 1:01.2
Pro—Lee Evans, Pocatello, Idaho, 1973 1:02
600 meters—Martin Bilham, England, 1969 1:17.7
Mark Winzenreid (Am.), England, 1975 1:18.3
Pro—Lee Evans, Pocatello, Idaho, 1977 1:16.7
800 meters—Carlo Grippo, Italy, 1977 1:46.4
Ted Nelson (Am.), Berlin, 1965 1:47.4
1,000 meters—Paul-Heinz Wellmann, West Germany, 1976 2:19.1
Tom Von Ruden (Am.), New York, 1971 2:20.4
Pro—Chris Fisher, Daly City, Calif., 1973 2:19.7
1,500 meters—John Walker, Long Beach, Calif., 1979 3:37.4
Paul Cummings (Am.), Long Beach, Calif., 1979 3:37.6
2,000 meters—Emiel Puttemans, Berlin, 1973 5:00.0
3,000 meters—Emiel Puttemans, Berlin, 1973 7:39.2
Steve Scott (Am.), Long Beach, Calif., 1980 7:45.2
5,000 meters—Emiel Puttemans, Paris, 1976 13:20.8
Glen Harold (Am.), Louisville, Ky., 1975 13:41.0

Hurdles

50 yards—Renaldo Nehemiah, Toronto, 1979 0:06.04
60 yards—Renaldo Nehemiah, New York, 1979 0:06.89
50 meters—Renaldo Nehemiah, Edmonton, 1979 0:06.36
60 meters—Andrey Prokofyev, Vilnius, 1979 0:07.54
Renaldo Nehemiah (Am.), Montreal, 1979 0:07.62

Walking

1,500 meters—Todd Scully, New York, 1979 5:40.0
Mile—Neal Pyke, 1978 6:04.0
3,000 meters—Yevginy Yavsyukov, Montreal, 1979 11:31.1
2 miles—Vittorio Visini, Italy, 1978 12:51.5
Todd Scully (Am.), New York, 1977 13:02.5
3 miles—Antoli Soloman, Toronto, 1978 19:40.0

Relays

880-yards—Idaho State, Pocatello, Idaho, 1979 1:26.9
Mile—Pacific Coast Club, Pocatello, Idaho, 1971 3:09.4
2 miles—Univ. of Chicago T.C., Louisville, Ky., 1974 7:20.8
4 miles—Villanova, Hanover, N.H., 1976 16:19
Sprint medley—Philadelphia T.C., New York, 1980 2:01.1
Distance medley—Villanova, Louisville, Ky., 1980 9:38.4

Field Events

High jump—Dietmar Mogenburg, West Germany, 1980 7 ft 8¾ in.
Franklin Jacobs (Am.) New York, 1978 7 ft 7¼ in.
Long jump—Larry Myricks, San Diego, 1980 27 ft 6 in.
Triple jump—Gennadi Valyukevich, Minsk, 1979 56 ft 8¾ in.
Ron Livers (Am.), Albuquerque, 1980 56 ft 0 in.
Pole vault—Konstantin Volkov, Moscow, 1980 18 ft 8¼ in.
Dan Ripley (Am.), Fort Worth, Tex., 1979 18 ft 5½ in.
Steve Smith (pro), New York, 1975 18 ft 5 in.
Shotput—George Woods, Inglewood, Calif., 1974 72 ft 2¾ in.
Brian Oldfield (pro) El Paso, Tex., 1975 72 ft 6½ in.
35-pound weight throw—Yuri Syedikh, Montreal, 1979 76 ft 11¾ in.
George Frenn (Am.), Boston, 1969 73 ft 3½ in.

WOMEN

Running

50 yards—Andrea Lynch, Toronto, 1978 0:05.80
Deandra Carney (Am.), Toronto, 1978 0:05.68
60 yards—Lyudmilla Storozhkoya, Fort Worth, Tex., 1979 0:06.63
Chandra Cheesborough (Am.), Fort Worth Tex., 1979 0:06.68
100 yards—Marita Koch, East Berlin, 1979 0:10.40
Wilma Rudolph, (Am.), Tennessee State, 1960 0:10.70
220 yards—Rosalyn Bryant, New York, 1977 0:23.40
300 yards—Rita Bottiglieri, Italy, 1978 0:34.20
Liz Young (Am.), Columbia, Md., 1975 0:34.50
440 yards—Rosalyn Bryant, New York, 1977 0:53.20
500 yards—Rosalyn Bryant, San Diego, 1977 1:03.30
600 yards—Yvonne Saunders, Toronto, 1974 1:18.40
Robin Campbell (Am.), Toronto, 1974 1:19.30
880 yards—Mary Decker, San Diego, 1980 1:59.70
1,000 yards—Mary Decker, Inglewood, Calif., 1978 2:23.80
Mile—Francie Larrieu, Richmond, Va., 1975 4:28.50
2 miles—Jan Merrill, New London, Conn., 1979 9:31.70

Running—Metric Distances

50 meters—Renate Stecher, Berlin, 1974 0:06.19
Evelyn Ashfrod (Am.), San Francisco, 1980 0:06.26
60 meters—Marlies Gohr, Senftenburg, East Germany, 1980 0:07.10
Brenda Moorehead (Am.), Louisville, Ky., 1980 0:07.28
100 meters—Marlies Gohr, East Berlin, 1979 0:11.30
Mamie Rallins (Am.), San Diego, 1975 0:12.40
200 meters—Angella Taylor, Dowdsville, Ontario, 1980 0:23.15
300 meters—Rita Wilden East Germany, 1974 0:35.30
Lori Green (Am.), Oklahoma City 1979 0:35.32
400 meters—Marita Koch, Spain, 1977 0:51.14
Sharon Dabney (Am.), Italy, 1978 0:53.27
500 meters—Lorna Forde, Hanover, N.H., 1978 1:10.50
600 meters—Anita Weiss, East Berlin, 1980 1:26.20
Chris Muller (Am.), Columbia, Mo., 1980 1:28.80
800 meters—Olga Vakrusheva, Moscow, 1980 1:58.40
Mary Decker (Am.), San Diego, 1980 1:58.90
1,000 meters—Bridgette Kraus, Dortmund, West Germany, 1978 2:34.80
Francie Larrieu (Am.), Los Angeles, 1975 2:40.20
1,500 meters—Mary Decker, New York, 1980 4:00.80
3,000 meters—Jan Merrill, Montreal, 1978 8:57.60

Hurdles

50 yards—Johanna Klier, Toronto, 1978 0:06.20
Deby LaPlante (Am.), Toronto, 1978 0:06.37
60 yards—Stephanie Hightower, New York, 1980 0:07.47
70 yards—Mamie Rallins, Chicago, 1970 0:08.80
Deby LaPlante, Louisville, Ky., 1976 0:08.80
50 meters—Annelie Ehrhardt, Berlin, 1973 0:06.74
Candy Young (Am.), Edmonton, Alberta, 1979 0:06.95
60 meters—Sofia Brelczyk, Poland, 1980 0:07.77
Stephanie Hightower (Am.), San Diego, 1980 0:08.17
100 meters—Annelie Ehrhardt, East Germany, 1976 0:13.12
Patty van Wolvelaere (Am.), New York, 1974 0:13.20

Walking

Mile—Susan Brodock, New York, 1978 7:01.70
1,500 meters—Susan Brodock, Toronto, 1976 6:42.90

Relays

640 yards—Tennessee State, New York, 1978 1:09.40
880 yards—Tennessee State, Louisville, 1980 1:37.80
Mile—Muhammad Ali T.C., New York, 1980 3:41.00
880 Yard Medley—Tennessee State, New York, 1978 1:38.50
2 Miles—U.S.S.R., 1972 8:41.60

Field Events

Long jump—Angela Voigt, East Berlin, 1976 22 ft 2¼ in.
Martha Watson (Am.), 1973 21 ft 4¾ in.
High jump—Andrea Matay, Budapest, 1979 6 ft 6 in.
Joni Huntley (Am.), New York, 1980 6 ft 4¼ in.
Shotput—Helena Fibingerova, Czechoslovakia, 1977 73 ft 9¾ in.
Maren Seidler (Am.), West Germany, 1978 61 ft 2¼ in.

ATHLETICS CONGRESS NATIONAL CHAMPIONSHIPS*

(June 13–15, 1980, Walnut, Calif.)

OUTDOOR

Men's Events

100 m—Stanley Floyd, Auburn Track Club 0:10.19
200 m—LaMonte King, Stars and Stripes Track Club 0:20.08
400 m—Willie Smith, Auburn T.C. 0:45.36
800 m—James Robinson, Inner City Athletic Club 1:46.3
1,500 m—Steve Lacy, Southern California Striders 3:40.86
3,000–m steeplechase—Doug Brown, Athletics West 8:26.2
5,000 m—Matt Centrowitz, Oregon Track Club 13:33.61
10,000 m—Rodolfo Gomez, Mexico 28:44.0
5,000–m walk—Ray Sharp, unattached 20:27.8
110–m hurdles—Renaldo Nehemiah, D.C. International 0:13.49
400–m hurdles—David Lee, Southern Illinois 0:49.38
High jump—Franklin Jacobs, Athletic Attic 7 ft 4½ in.
Pole vault—Tom Hintnaus, Southern California Striders 18 ft 2½ in.
Long jump—Larry Myricks, Athletic Attic 27 ft 1¼ in.
Triple jump—Willie Banks, American Council of Athletics 56 ft 11½ in.
Shot–put—Brian Oldfield, Univ. of Chicago Track Club 71 ft 7 in.
Discus—Mac Wilkins, Athletics West 224 ft 3 in.
Hammer—Gian Paolo Urlando, Italy 251 ft 3 in.
Javelin—Duncan Atwood, Athletics West 273 ft 10 in.

*Previously under the sponsorship of the Amateur Athletic Union (A.A.U.).

Women's Events

100 m—Alice Brown, Los Angeles Naturite 0:11.21
200 m—Karen Hawkins, Texas Southern 0:22.80
400 m—Sherri Howard, Ali Track Club 0:51.51
800 m—Madeline Manning Mims, Oral Roberts Track Club 1:58.75
1,500 m—Francie Larrieu, Pacific Coast Club 4:12.72
3,000 m—Julie Brown, Los Angeles Naturite 9:07.90
10,000 m—Judi St. Hilare, Vermont 33:31.02
100–m hurdles—Stephanie Hightower, Ohio State 0:13.14
400–m hurdles—Esther Mahr, KCBQ Track Club 0:56.3
5,000–m walk—Sue Brodock, Southern California Road Runners 23:19.1[1]
10,000–m walk—Sue Brodock 51:01.0
400–m relay—Los Angeles Naturite (Jeanette Bolden, Jodi Anderson, Alice Brown, Florence Griffith) 0:43.81
800–m relay—Ali Track Club (Adrienne Lair, Ros Bryant, Jackie Pusey, Denean Howard) 1:37.40
1,600–m relay—Ali Track Club (Ros Bryant, Tina Howard, Yolanda Rich, Sherri Howard) 3:34.16
3,200–m relay—Los Angeles Naturite (Regina Jacobs, Roma Antoniewicz, Lauri Mullins, Julie Brown) 8:32.3
High jump—Coleen Rienstra, Sun Devil Sports 6 ft 4 in.
Long jump—Jodi Anderson, Los Angeles Naturite 21 ft 9¾ in.
Shot–put—Maren Seidler, San Jose Stars 59 ft 1 in.
Discus—Lorna Griffin, American Council of Athletics 191 ft 9 in.
Javelin—Karin Smith, American Council of Athletics 199 ft. 1 in.

1. Betters American record.

AMATEUR ATHLETIC UNION (A.A.U.) NATIONAL CHAMPIONSHIPS

INDOOR

(Madison Square Garden, New York, Feb. 29, 1980)

Men's Events

60 yd—Curtis Dickey, Texas A&M 0:06.09
600 yd—Mark Enyeart, Logan, Utah 1:09.2
1,000 yd—Bill Martin, Iona 2:07.7
Mile—Craid Masback, New York Pioneer Club 4:02.2
3 Miles—Eamonn Coghlan, New York Athletic Club 13:02.8[1]
60–yd hurdles—Rod Milburn, Houston Track Club 0:07.09
2–mile walk—Todd Scully, Shore Athletic Club 12:35.1[2]
Sprint medley relay (1,180 yds)—Philadelphia Pioneer Club (Tony Darden, Steve Riddick, Herm Frazier, William Collins) 2:01[3]
Mile relay—Philadelphia Pioneer Club (Cliff McKenzie, Tim Dale, Tony Darden, Herm Frazier) 3:19.9[3]
2–mile relay—Virginia Tech (Mike Burns, Bruce Merritt, Ray Ackenbor, Ray McDaniels) 7:29.2
Long jump—Larry Myricks, Athletic Attic Track Club 26 ft 11¼ in.
Triple jump—Ron Livers, Norristown, Pa. 55 ft 1½ in.
High jump—Franklin Jacobs, Fairleigh Dickinson Univ. 7 ft 4½ in.
Pole vault—Earl Bell, New York Athletic Club 18 ft 2¼ in.[3]
Shot–put—Jessie Stuart, Univ. of Chicago Track Club 66 ft 5 in.[3]
35–lb weight—Ed Kanla, Hanover, N.H. 72 ft 8 in.
Team—Philadelphia Pioneer Club 25 pts

1. Betters all–comers indoor record. 2. Meet record and betters listed American record. 3. Meet record.

Women's Events

60 yd—Evelyn Ashford, American Council of Athletes 0:06.76
200 yd—Wanda Hooker, Memphis State 0:24
440 yd—Rosalyn Bryant, Muhammad Ali Track Club 0:53.92[1]
880 yd—Madeline Manning, Oral Roberts Univ. Track Club 2:04.5[2]
Mile—Maggie Keyes, Maccabi Union Track Club 4:39.3
2 miles—Cindy Bremser, Wisconsin–United Track Club 9:45[2]
60–yd hurdles—Stephanie Hightower, Ohio State 0:07.4
Mile walk—Susan Brodock, Southern California Roadrunners 7:06.9
640–yd relay—D.C. International (Alice Jackson, Janice Bernard, Carolyn McRoy, Rose Allwood) 1:09.5[3]
880–yd medley relay—Los Angeles Mercurettes (Faye Paige, Yvette Evans, Marbella Washington, Gwen Gardner) 1:45
Mile relay—Muhammad Ali Track Club (Yolanda Rich, Dengan Howard, Sherri Howard, Rosalyn Bryant) 3:41[3]
High jump—Louise Ritter, Texas Women's Univ. 6 ft 3 in.
Long jump—Pat Johnson, Univ. of Wisconsin 20 ft 11½ in.
Shot–put—Maren Seidler, San Jose Stars 57 ft ¼ in.
Team—Tennessee State 13 pts

1. Indoor record for automatic timing. 2. Meet record. 3. Betters listed American indoor record.

NATIONAL COLLEGIATE ATHLETIC ASSOCIATION

Indoor

(Detroit, March 14–15, 1980)

60 yd—Curtis Dickey, Texas A&M 0:06.12
440 yd—Bert Cameron, Texas, El Paso, and Anthony Blair, Tennessee, tie 0:48.7
600 yd—Mike Ricks, Kansas 1:10.06
800 yd—Evans White, Prairie View 1:52.32
1,000 yd—Don Paige, Villanova 2:05.80

Mile—Suleiman Nyambui, Texas, El Paso 4:05.26
2 miles—Suleiman Nyambui 8:36.82
3 miles—Solomon Chebor, Fairleigh Dickinson 13:20.94
60-yd hurdles—Rodney Wilson, Villanova 0:07.15
Mile relay—Florida State (Reginald Ross, Mel Boodie, Palmer Simmons, Walter McCoy) 3:16.64
2-mile relay—Oklahoma (Mahlon Erickson, Jody Jimerson, Dyrk Dahl, John Rohde) 7:32.68
Distance medley relay—Villanova (John Hunter, Tim Robinson, Mike England, Sydney Maree) 9:42.22
Long Jump—Carl Lewis, Houston 26 ft 4½ in.
High jump—Franklin Jacobs, Fairleigh Dickinson 7 ft 4¼ in.
Pole vault—Randy Hall, Texas A&M 17 ft 9½ in.
Triple jump—Sanya Owolabi, Kansas 54 ft 3¾ in.
35-lb weight—David Pellegrini, Princeton 69 ft 3¼ in.
Shot-put—Mike Carter, Southern Methodist 67 ft 7½ in.
Team—Texas, El Paso 76 pts

Outdoor

(Austin, Tex., June 5–7, 1980)

100 m—Stanley Floyd, Auburn 0:10.10
200 m—Mike Roberson, Florida State 0:19.96
400 m—Bert Cameron, Texas–El Paso 0:45.23
800 m—Don Paige, Villanova 1:45.81
1,500 m—Sydney Maree, Villanova 3:38.64
3,000 steeplechase—Randy Jackson, Wisconsin 8:22.81
5,000 m—Suleiman Nyambui, Texas–El Paso 13:44.43
10,000 m—Suleiman Nyambui 29:21.85
110-m hurdles—Greg Foster, U.C.L.A. 0:13.43
400-m hurdles—David Lee, Southern Illinois 0:48.87
400-m relay—Southern California (Kevin Williams, Mike Sanford, James Sanford, Bill Green) 0:39.16
1,600-m relay—Tennessee (Al Horne, Darryl Wilson, Lamar Preyor, Anthony Blair) 3:03.94
Discus—Goran Svensson, Brigham Young 202 ft 6 in.
Javelin—Curt Ransford, San Jose State 269 ft 3 in.
Shot-put—Mike Carter, Southern Methodist 66 ft 11¼ in.
Hammer—Thommie Sjoholm, Texas–El Paso 225 ft
Pole vault—Randy Hall, Texas A&M 18 ft 2 in.
High jump—Jeff Woodard, Alabama 7 ft 7¼ in.
Triple jump—Steve Hanna, Texas–El Paso 55 ft 1 in.
Long jump—Carl Lewis, Houston 27 ft 4¾ in.
Team—Texas–El Paso 69 pts

NATIONAL ASSOCIATION OF INTERCOLLEGIATE ATHLETICS

Indoor

(Kansas City, Mo., Feb. 14–16, 1980)

60 yd—Alvin Matthias, Adams State, Colo. 0:06.1
440 yd—Kenneth Brown, Jackson State, Miss. 0:48.79
600 yd—Joe Johnson, Prairie View A&M, Texas 1:12.23
880 yd—Evans White, Prairie View A&M 1:51.34
1,000 yd—Michael Watson, Jackson State 2:11.17
Mile—John Esquibel, Adams State 4:11.60
2 miles—Kregg Einspahr, Concordia, Neb. 9:01.64
3 miles—Tim Terrill, Adams State 14:03.33
2-mile walk—Jeff Ellis, Wisconsin–Stevens Point 13:53.35
60-yd hurdles—Steve Parker, Abilene Christian, Tex. 0:07.2
Mile relay—Prairie View A&M (Alvin Scott, Clifton Terrell, Evans White, Joe Johnson) 3:17.09
2-mile relay—Prairie View A&M (Ray Roberts, Jody Cleveland, Terrence Ross, Evans White) 7:42.02
Distance medley relay—Jackson State (Ronnie Jackson, Alvin Jackson, Anthony Appoy, Michael Watson) 10:12.48
Long jump—Ricky Smith, Alabama State 23 ft 11 in.
Triple jump—Larry Perkins, Jackson State 49 ft 7¾ in.
High jump—Vic White, Eastern Washington 7 ft 2 in.
Pole vault—Billy Olson, Abilene Christian 17 ft 6½ in.
Shot-put—Harold Leday, Angelo State, Tex. 59 ft 8½ in.
Team—Jackson State 81 pts

Outdoor

(Abilene, Tex., May 22–24, 1980)

100 m—Ellison Portis, Angelo State, Tex. 0:10.15
200 m—Charles Pickins, Mississippi Valley 0:20.77
400 m—Kevin Jones, Northwood, Mich. 0:45.74
800 m—Herman Sanders, Mississippi Valley 1:48.53
1,500 m—Mike Watson, Jackson State, Miss. 3:46.86
3,000-m steeplechase—Kregg Einstahr, Western Washington 8:58.4
110-m hurdles—Steve Parker, Abilene Christian, Tex. 0:13.84
400-m hurdles—James Baldwin, Texas Southern 0:50.48
Marathon—Bill Langhout, Wisconsin–Eau Claire 2:30:33.30
10,000-m walk—Jeff Ellis, Wisconsin–Stevens Point 47:35.1
Decathlon—Gary Wise, Azusa Pacific, Calif. 7,331 pts
High jump—Bruce Beckel, Wisconsin–River Falls 7 ft 2 in.
Pole Vault—Billy Olson, Abilene Southern, Tex. 18 ft 2 in.
Triple jump—Vic White, East Washington 52 ft 8 in.
Long jump—Carl Hanns, Cumberland, Ky. 25 ft 3½ in.
Shot-put—Harold Ledet, Angelo State, Tex. 60 ft 11⅛ in.
Javelin—Mike Barnett, Azusa Pacific, Calif. 242 ft 5 in.
Hammer—Harold Willers, Simon Fraser, Canada 195 ft 5 in.
Discus—Martin Guerrero, Abilene Christian, Tex. 195 ft 7 in.
400-m relay—Mississippi Valley (Fred Johnson, Larry White, Reginald Williamson, Charles Pickins) 0:40.22
Mile relay—Texas Southern (Mike Joseph, Ken Williams, Robert Bullard, Tyrone Cross) 3:07.2
Team—Mississippi Valley 66 pts

ASSOCIATION FOR INTERCOLLEGIATE ATHLETICS FOR WOMEN (A.I.A.W.)

(Eugene, Ore., May 23–24, 1980)

100 m—Alice Brown, California State–Northridge 0:11.27
200 m—Merlene Ottey, Nebraska 0:22.86
400 m—Yolanda Rich, California State–Los Angeles 0:52.7
800 m—Delisa Walton, Tennessee 2:04.88
1,500 m—Maggie Keyes, California Poly–San Luis Obispo 4:15.85
3,000 m—Julie Shea, North Carolina State 9:13.15
5,000 m—Julie Shea 15:41.28
10,000 m—Julie Shea 33:02.32
100-m hurdles—Stephanie Hightower, Ohio State 0:13.07
400-m hurdles—Sandra Myers, California State–Northridge 0:56.40
400-m relay—California State–Northridge (Bolden, Lynch-Saunders, Brown, Griffith) 0:44.79
800-m relay—California State–Los Angeles (Innis, Lair, Pusey, Rich) 1:38.4
Mile relay—Oregon (Batiste, Massey, Waren, Bakari) 3:37.44
2-mile relay—University of California, Los Angeles (Ward, Ralston, Warner, Goen) 8:41.64
Javelin—Jacqueline Nelson, California State–Long Beach 173 ft 11 in.
Shot-put—Meg Ritchie, Arizona 54 ft 2 in.
Discus—Meg Ritchie 211 ft 1 in.
High jump—Coleen Rienstra, Arizona State 6 ft 1¼ in.
Long jump—Sandra Myers, California State–Northridge 20 ft 7¾ in.
Team—California State–Northridge 59 pts

SNOWMOBILE RACING—1980

World champion—Jacques Villeneauve, St. Cuthbert, Quebec
World series champion—Brad Hulings, Crosby, Minn.
International pro—Bruce Olson, Mondovi, Wis.
High-point champion (Formula Snopro)—Brad Hulings, 307 points

U.S. OLYMPIC TRIALS

(Eugene, Ore., June 21–29, 1980)

Men's Events

100 m—Stanley Floyd, Putney, Ga.	0:10.26
200 m—James Butler, Stillwater, Okla.	0:20.49
400 m—Bill Green, Palo Alto, Calif.	0:45.85
800 m—Don Paige, Marcy, N.Y.	1:44.53
1,500 m—Steve Scott, Tempe, Ariz.	3:35.15
3,000–m steeplechase—Henry Marsh, Eugene, Ore.	8:15.68
5,000–m—Matt Centrowitz, Eugene, Ore.	13:30.62
10,000 m—Craig Virgin, Lebanon, Ill.	27:45.61
Marathon—Tony Sandoval, Los Alamos, N.M.	2:10:18.6
110–m hurdles—Renaldo Nehemiah, Scotch Plains, N.J.	0:13.26
400–m hurdles—Edwin Moses, Mission Viejo, Calif.	0:47.90
High jump—Benn Fields, Salibury Mills, N.Y.	7 ft 5 in.
Pole vault—Tom Hintnaus, San Jose, Calif.	18 ft 4½ in.
Long jump—Larry Myricks, Tallahassee, Fla.	27 ft 2 in.
Triple jump—Willie Banks, Los Angeles	55 ft 1½ in.
Shot–put—Peter Shmock, Cupertino, Calif.	68 ft 4 in.
Discus—Mac Wilkins, Soquel, Calif.	225 ft 4 in.
Hammer—Andy Bessette, Vernon, Conn.	232 ft 10 in.
Javelin—Rod Ewaliko, Seattle, Wash.	291 ft
Decathlon—Bob Coffman, Houston, Tex.	8,184 pts
20–km walk—James Heiring, San Bernardino, Calif. and Marco Evoniuk, Boulder, Colo.	1:27:12
50–km walk—Carl Schueler, Silver Spring, Md.	—

Women's Events

100 m—Alice Brown, Anaheim, Calif.	0:11.32
200 m—Chandra Cheeseborough, Jacksonville, Fla.	0:22.70
400 m—Sherri Howard, Granada Hills, Calif.	0:51.48
800 m—Madeline Manning, Tulsa, Okla.	1:58.30
1,500 m—Mary Decker, Eugene, Ore.	4:04.91
100–m hurdles—Stephanie Hightower, Columbus, Ohio	0:12.90
High jump—Louise Ritter, Denton, Tex.	6 ft 1¼ in.
Long jump—Jodi Anderson, Los Angeles	22 ft 11½ in.
Shot–put—Maren Seidler, Los Gatos, Calif.	58 ft 9 in.
Discus—Lorna Griffin, San Diego, Calif.	197 ft 6 in.
Javelin—Karin Smith, LaJolla, Calif.	208 ft 5 in.
Pentathlon—Jodi Anderson, Los Angeles	4,697 pts

A.A.U. RELAY CHAMPIONSHIPS

(New York, July 1, 1979)

400 meters—LeMans T.C. (Brian Denman, Brady Crain, Bill Henderson, Barry Gambrell)	0:40.3
800 meters—LeMans T.C. (Andre Cooper, Brady Crain, Barry Gambrell, Brian Denman)	1:24.4
1,600 meters—New York Pioneers (Mark Hurst, Dennis Dyce Bill Austin, Mike Sands)	3:12.5
2 miles—New York A.C. (Bob Moffatt, Vince Coiro, Don Lockerbie, Ross Donoghue)	7:48
4 miles—Renaissance All-Sports Club (Bill Blewett, Karsten Schultz, Jay Simonetta, Mike Sheely)	17:15.5
Distance medley—New York A.C. (Jim DiRienzo, Harold Schwab, Luis Ostolozaga, Ross Donoghue)	10:09.4
Sprint medley—New York Pioneers (Mervyn Lewis, Steve Hackman Mike Sands, Craig Masback)	3:25.2
440-meter shuttle hurdles—Shore A.C. (Leon Devero, Joe Kraus, Payton Hines, John Charniga)	0:58.5

SWIMMING

WORLD RECORDS—MEN

Approved September 1979 by International Swimming Federation (F.I.N.A.)
(F.I.N.A. discontinued acceptance of records in yards in 1968)

Freestyle

Distance	Record	Holder	Country	Where made	Date
Distance	Record	Holder	Country	Where made	Date
100 Meters	0:49.44	Jonty Skinner	South Africa	Philadelphia	Aug. 14, 1976
200 Meters	1:49.16	Rowdy Gaines	U.S.	Austin, Tex.	April 11, 1980
400 Meters	3:50.49	Peter Szmidt	Canada	Toronto	July 15, 1980
800 Meters	7:56.49	Vladimir Salnikov	U.S.S.R.	Minsk	March 23, 1979
1,500 Meters	14:58.27	Vladimir Salnikov	U.S.S.R.	Moscow	July 22, 1980
Backstroke					
100 Meters	0:55.49	John Naber	U.S.	Montreal	July 19, 1976
200 Meters	1:59.19	John Naber	U.S.	Montreal	July 24, 1976
Breaststroke					
100 meters	1:02.86	Gerald Moerken	West Germany	Jonkoping, Sweden	Aug. 17, 1977
200 Meters	2:15.11	David Wilkie	Britain	Montreal	July 24, 1976
Butterfly					
100 Meters	0:54.15	Par Arvidsson	Sweden	Austin, Tex.	April 11, 1980
200 Meters	1:58.21	Craig Beardsley	U.S.	Irvine, Calif.	July 30, 1980
Individual Medley					
200 Meters	2:03.24	Bill Barrett	U.S.	Irvine, Calif.	Aug. 1, 1980
400 Meters	4:20.05	Jesse Vassallo	U.S.	West Berlin	Aug. 22, 1978
Freestyle Relays					
400 Meters	3:19.74	National Team	U.S.	West Berlin	Aug. 26, 1978
(Jack Babashoff, Rowdy Gaines, Jim Montgomery, David McCagg)					

800 Meters	7:20.82	National Team	U.S.	West Berlin	Aug. 24, 1978
(Bruce Furniss, Bill Forrester, Bobby Hackett, Rowdy Gain)					

Medley Relay

(Backstroke, breaststroke, butterfly, freestyle)

400 Meters	3:42.22	National Team	U.S.	Montreal	July 22, 1976

WORLD RECORDS—WOMEN

Freestyle					
100 Meters	0:54.79	Barbara Krause	East Germany	Moscow	July 21, 1980
200 Meters	1:58.43	Cynthia Woodhead	U.S.	San Juan, P.R.	July 3, 1979
400 Meters	4:06.28	Tracey Wickham	Australia	West Berlin	Aug. 24, 1978
800 Meters	8:24.62	Tracey Wickham	Australia	Edmonton, Can.	Aug. 6, 1978
1,500 Meters	16:04.49	Kim Linehan	U.S.	Ft. Lauderdale, Fla.	Aug. 19, 1979
Backstroke					
100 Meters	1:00.86	Rica Reinisch	East Germany	Moscow	July 23, 1980
200 Meters	2:11.77	Rica Reinisch	East Germany	Moscow	July 28, 1980
Breaststroke					
100 Meters	1:10.11	Ute Geweniger	East Germany	Moscow	July 26, 1980
200 Meters	2:28.36.	Line Kachusite	U.S.S.R.	Potsdam, Germany	March 6, 1979
Butterfly					
100 Meters	0:59.26	Mary T. Meagher	U.S.	Austin, Tex.	April 11, 1980
200 Meters	2:06.37	Mary T. Meagher	U.S.	Irvine, Calif.	July 30, 1980
Individual Medley					
200 Meters	2:13.00	Petra Schneider	East Germany	Magdeburg	May 24, 1980
400 Meters	4:36.29	Petra Schneider	East Germany	Moscow	July 26, 1980
Freestyle Relay					
400 Meters	3:43.43	National Team	U.S.	West Berlin	Aug. 24, 1978
	(Tracy Caulkins, Stephanie Elkins, Jill Sterkel, Cynthia Woodhead)				

Medley Relay

(Backstroke, breaststroke, butterfly, freestyle)

400 Meters	4:07.95	National Team	East Germany	Montreal	July 18, 1976
	(Ulrike Tauber, Hannelore Anke, Andrea Pollack, Korenlia Ender)				

U.S. SHORT-COURSE SWIMMING RECORDS

(Listed by Amateur Athletic Union)

MEN

Freestyle	
100 yards—Rowdy Gaines, 1980	0:43.16
100 yards—Andy Coan, 1979	0:43.25
100 yards—Jonty Skinner, 1978	0:43.29[1]
100 yards—Joe Bottom, 1977	0:43.49
200 yards—Rowdy Gaines, 1980	1:34.57
200 yards—Andy Coan, 1979	1:35.62
200 yards—Jim Montgomery, 1977	1:35.67
500 yards—Brian Goodell, 1978	4:16.40
1,650 yards—Brian Goodell, 1979	14:47.27
1,650 yards—Brian Goodell, 1979	14:54.13
1,650 yards—Brian Goodell, 1978	14:54.54
Backstroke	
100 yards—John Naber, 1977	0:49.31
200 yards—John Naber, 1977	1:46.09
Breaststroke	
100 yards—Steve Lundquist, 1980	0:53.59
100 yards—Steve Lundquist, 1979	0:54.08
100 yards—Graham Smith, 1977	0:54.91[1]
100 yards—Scott Spann, 1977	0:55.19
200 yards—Bill Barrett, 1980	1:58.43
200 yards—Steve Lundquist, 1979	1:59.18
200 yards—Graham Smith, 1977	2:00.05[1]
200 yards—Nick Nevid, 1978	2:00.53
Butterfly	
100 yards—Par Arvidsson, 1980	0:47.34[1]
100 yards—Par Arvidsson, 1979	0:47.76[1]
100 yards—Joe Bottom, 1977	0:47.77
200 yards—Par Arvidsson, 1980	1:44.43[1]
200 yards—Mike Bruner, 1977	1:45.27
Individual Medley	
200 yards—Bill Barrett, 1980	1:46.25
200 yards—Scott Spann, 1977	1:48.26
400 yards—Jesse Vassallo, 1979	3:48.24
400 yards—Brian Goodell, 1979	3:50.80
400 yards—Jesse Vassallo, 1978	3:51.69
Relays	
400-yard freestyle—Tennessee, 1979	2:54.54
400-yard freestyle—Gatorade S.C., 1978	2:55.27
800-yard freestyle—Florida A.C., 1979	6:25.42
800-yard freestyle—Florida A.C., 1978	6:29.81
400-yard medley—California-Berkeley, 1979	3:15.22[1]

400–yard medley—Indiana, 1977	3:17.14[1]
400–yard medley—Auburn, 1977	3:17.62

WOMEN

Freestyle

100 yards—Jill Sterkel, 1980	0:48.76
100 yards—Cynthia Woodhead, 1979	0:49.39
100 yards—Jill Sterkel, 1979	0:49.55
100 yards—Tracy Caulkins, 1978	0:49.58
200 yards—Cynthia Woodhead, 1979	1:44.10
200 yards—Stephanie Elkins, 1978	1:45.91
500 yards—Tracy Caulkins, 1979	4:36.25
500 yards—Cynthia Woodhead, 1978	4:39.94
1,650 yards—Kim Linehan, 1979	15:49.10
1,650 yards—Cynthia Woodhead, 1978	15:55.15

Backstroke

100 yards—Linda Jezek, 1978	0:54.94
200 yards—Linda Jezek, 1978	1:57.79

Breaststroke

100 yards—Tracy Caulkins, 1979	1:01.82
100 yards—Tracy Caulkins, 1979	1:02.06
100 yards—Tracy Caulkins, 1978	1:02.20
200 yards—Tracy Caulkins, 1980	2:11.46
200 yards—Tracy Caulkins, 1978	2:14.07

Butterfly

100 yards—Mary T. Meagher, 1980	0:53.18
100 yards—Jill Sterkel, 1979	0:53.76
100 yards—Diane Johannigman, 1978	0:54.11
200 yards—Mary T. Meagher, 1980	1:53.21
200 yards—Nancy Hogshead, 1978	1:55.74

Individual Medley

200 yards—Tracy Caulkins, 1979	1:57.86
200 yards—Tracy Caulkins, 1978	1:59.33
400 yards—Tracy Caulkins, 1979	4:08.09
400 yards—Tracy Caulkins, 1978	4:11.38

Relays

400–yard freestyle—Nashville A.C., 1979	3:20.51
400–yard freestyle—Nashville A.C., 1978	3:20.69
800–yard freestyle—Mission Viejo S.C., 1979	7:15.14
800–yard freestyle—U.S. Team, 1976	7:15.64
400–yard medley—Nashville A.C., 1978	3:42.54

1. Open American record by non-U.S. competitors.

A.A.U. NATIONAL CHAMPIONSHIPS

(Austin, Tex., April 9–12, 1980)

*Indoor—Men

t50–m freestyle—Gary Schatz, Houston	0:22.86
100–m freestyle—Ambrose (Rowdy) Gaines, Florida Aquatic	0:49.61[1]
200–m freestyle—Ambrose (Rowdy) Gaines	1:49.16[2]
400–m freestyle—Mike Bruner, Stockton, Calif.	3:52.24
1,500–m freestyle—Mike Bruner	15:19.76
800–m freestyle—Djan Madruga, Brazil	7:59.85[3]
100–m backstroke—Peter Rocca, Orinda, Calif.	0:56.66
200–m backstroke—Peter Rocca	2:00.73[4]
100–m breaststroke—Steve Lundquist, Jonesboro, Ga.	1:03.08[1]
200–m breaststroke—Glenn Mills, North Ridgeville, Ohio	2:18.03[4]
100–m butterfly—Par Arvidsson, Sweden (Arvidsson set world record of 0:54.15 in qualifier)	0:54.20
200–m butterfly—Mike Bruner	1:59.48
200–m ind. medley—Chris Cavanaugh, Cupertino, Calif.	2:04.77
400–m ind. medley—Djan Madruga	4:25.30
400–m freestyle relay—Florida Aquatic (Ambrose (Rowdy) Gaines, Davis McCagg, David Larson, Bill Forrester)	3:21.93[5]
800–m freestyle relay—Concord Pleasant Hills A (Pelle Holmertz, Pallo Revelli, Todd Trowbridge, Rich Thorton)	7:29.29
400–m medley relay—Concord Pleasant Hills A (Peter Rocca, Tom McMullen, Par Arvidsson, Pelle Holmertz)	3:46.06[4]
Team—Florida Aquatics	304.0 pts

*Event contested at metric distances during Olympic year. t. New event. 1. American record. 2. World record. 3. U.S. open record. 4. Meet record. 5. American club record.

*Indoor—Women

(Austin, Tex., April 9–12, 1980)

t50–m freestyle—Jill Sterkel, Hacienda Heights, Calif.	0:25.96[1]
100–m freestyle—Jill Sterkel	0:56.12
200–m freestyle—Marybeth Linzmeier, Mission Viejo, Calif.	2:21.0
400–m freestyle—Kim Linehan, Austin, Tex.	4:09.58
1,500–m freestyle—Kim Linehan	16:15.56
800–m freestyle—Kim Linehan	8:27.82
100–m backstroke—Sue Walsh, Hamburg, N.Y.	1:03.34
200–m backstroke—Libby Kinkead, Wayne, Pa.	2:14.59
100–m breaststroke—Tracy Caulkins, Nashville, Tenn.	1:11.34
200–m breaststroke—Tracy Caulkins	2:33.06[1]
100–m butterfly—Mary T. Meagher, Louisville, Ky.	0:59.26[2]
200–m butterfly—Mary T. Meagher	2:08.69
200–m ind. medley—Tracy Caulkins	2:14.73[3]
400–m ind. medley—Anne Tweedy, Santa Barbara, Calif.	4:49.69
400–m freestyle relay—Longhorn Aquatic (Jill Sterkel, Carol Borgmann, Becky Kast, Kim Linehan)	3:48.23
800–m freestyle relay—Longhorn Aquatic (Kim Linehan, Becky Kast, Linda Irish, Jill Sterkel)	8:14.76[4]
400–m medley relay—Cincinnati Pepsi Marlin A (Kim Carlisle, Kim Rhodenbaugh, Mary T. Meagher, Stephani Elkins)	4:11.59[3]
Team—Cincinnati Pepsi Marlins	364.5 pts

*Event contested at metric distances during Olympic year. t. New event. 1. American record. 2. World record. 3. Meet record. 4. U.S. and American record.

A.A.U. NATIONAL CHAMPIONSHIPS AND OLYMPIC TRIALS—1980

Long Course, Outdoor—Men

(Irvine, Calif., July 29–Aug. 2, 1980)

50–m freestyle—Joe Bottom, Walnut Creek, Calif.	0:23.07
100–m freestyle—Ambrose (Rowdy) Gaines, Winter Haven, Fla. (Gaines tied American record in heats at 0:49.61)	0:50.19
200–m freestyle—Rowdy Gaines	1:50.02
400–m freestyle—Mike Bruner, Mesa, Ariz.	3:52.19
800–m freestyle—Brian Goodell, Mission Viejo, Calif.	7:59.66[1]
1,500–m freestyle—Mike Bruner	15:19.80
100–m breaststroke—Steve Lundquist, Jonesboro, Ga.	1:02.88[1]
200–m breaststroke—Glenn Mills, Cincinnati	2:18.78
100–m backstroke—Peter Rocca, Pleasant Hill, Calif.	0:56.64
200–m backstroke—Steve Barnicoat, Mission Viejo, Calif.	2:01.06
100–m butterfly—William Paulus, Austin, Tex.	0:54.34
200–m butterfly—Craig Beardsley, Gainsville, Fla.	1:58.46[2]
200–m ind. medley—Bill Barrett, Alpharetta, Ga.	2:03.24[2]

400–m ind. medley—Jesse Vassallo, Mission Viejo, Calif. 4:21.51
400–m freestyle relay—Florida Aquatic Club (Rowdy Gaines, David Larson, Steve Wood, Bill Forrester) 3:22.24
800–m freestyle relay—Florida Aquatic Club (Rowdy Gaines, David Larson, Steve Wood, Bill Forrester) 7:26.67
400–m medley relay—Dr. Pepper, Dallas, Tex. 3:47.13

Long Course, Outdoor—Women

50–m freestyle—Jill Sterkel, Austin, Tex. 0:26.21
100–m freestyle—Cynthia Woodhead, Cupertino, Calif. 0:56.57
200–m freestyle—Cynthia Woodhead 1:59.44
400–m freestyle—Kim Linehan, Austin, Tex. 4:07.77
800–m freestyle—Kim Linehan 8:27.86
1,500–m freestyle—Kim Linehan 16:21.74
100–m breaststroke—Tracy Caulkins, Nashville, Tenn. 1:10.40[1]
200–m breaststroke—Tracy Caulkins and Terri Baxter, Menlo Park, Calif., tie 2:34.66
100–m backstroke—Linda Jezek, Palo Alto, Calif. 1:03.16
200–m backstroke—Linda Jezek 2:14.52
100–m butterfly—Mary T. Meagher, Cincinnati, Ohio 0:59.41
200–m butterfly—Mary T. Meagher 2:06.37[2]
200–m ind. medley—Tracy Caulkins 2:14.64
400–m ind. medley—Tracy Caulkins 4:40.61[1]
400–m freestyle relay—Cincinnati Pepsi Marlins (Mary T. Meagher, Lisa Busese, Kim Carlisle, Stephani Elkins) 3:48.83
800–m freestyle relay—Cincinnati Pepsi Marlins (Mary T. Meagher, Lisa Busese, Diane Johannigman, Stephanie Elkins) 8:13.07[1]
400–m medley relay—Cincinnati Pepsi Marlins 4:17.81

1. American record. 2. World record.

A.A.U. NATIONAL DIVING CHAMPIONSHIPS—1980

INDOOR

(Milwaukee, Wis., April 17–19, 1980)

Men's Events

	Pts
1 meter—Greg Louganis, El Cajon, Calif.	508.68
3 meter—Greg Louganis	963.30
Platform—Bruce Kimball, Ann Arbor, Mich.	816.975
High point winner—Greg Louganis	
Team—Mission Viejo Nadadores	

Women's Events

	Pts
1 meter—Karen Gorham, Razorback Diving Club	647.77
3 meter—Carrie Finneran, Columbus, Ohio	678.17
Platform—Christine Loock, Dallas	—
High point winner—Cynthia Potter, Dallas	
Team—Mission Viejo Nadadores	

OUTDOOR

(Bartlesville, Okla., Aug. 20–23, 1980)

Men's Events

1–meter—Greg Louganis, Mission Viejo, Calif. 781.53
3–meter—Greg Louganis 843.8
Platform—Greg Louganis 840.33

Women's Events

1–meter—Kelly McCormick, Mission Viejo, Calif. n.a.
3–meter—Chris Seufert, Ann Arbor, Mich. 651.85
Platform—Barbara Weinstein, Cincinnati 549.705

n.a. = not available

NATIONAL COLLEGIATE ATHLETIC ASSOCIATION (N.C.A.A.)

(Cambridge, Mass., March 27–29, 1980)

50–yd freestyle—Andy Coan, Tennessee 0:19.92
100–yd freestyle—Ambrose (Rowdy) Gaines, Auburn 0:43.36
(Gaines set American, N.C.A.A., and meet record of 0:43.16 in trials)
200–yd freestyle—Ambrose (Rowdy) Gaines, Auburn 1:34.57[1]
500–yd freestyle—Brian Goodell, U.C.L.A. 4:17.81
1,650–yd freestyle—Brian Goodell, U.C.L.A. 14:54.07[2]
100–yd backstroke—Clay Britt, Texas 0:49.52
200–yd backstroke—Jamie Fowler, Southern California 1:47.76
100–yd breaststroke—Steve Lundquist, Southern Methodist 0:53.59[1]
200–yd breaststroke—Bill Barrett, U.C.L.A. 1:58.43[3]
100–yd butterfly—Par Arvidsson, California 0:47.36[4]
200–yd butterfly—Par Arvidsson 1:44.43[5]
200–yd ind. medley—Bill Barrett, U.C.L.A. 1:46.25
400–yd ind. medley—Brian Goodell, U.C.L.A. 3:51.38
400–yd freestyle relay—Auburn (David McCagg, Rick Morley, Bill Forrester, Ambrose (Rowdy) Gaines) 2:55.16
880–yd freestyle relay—Auburn (Rick Morley, Bill Forrester, David McCagg, Ambrose (Rowdy) Gaines) 6:28.07
400–yd medley relay—Texas (Clay Britt, Scott Spann, Bill Paulus, Kris Kirchner) 3:14.39[6]
1–m dive—Greg Louganis, Miami (Fla.) 557.20 pts
3–m dive—Greg Louganis 608.10 pts
Team—California 234 pts

1. Betters American and N.C.A.A. record. 2. Betters N.C.A.A. and meet record. 3. Betters American, N.C.A.A., and meet record. 4. Betters N.C.A.A. record. 5. Betters U.S. Open and N.C.A.A. record. 6. Betters U.S. Open, American, and N.C.A.A. record.

NATIONAL ASSOCIATION OF INTERCOLLEGIATE ATHLETICS

(Whitewater, Wis., March 6–8, 1980)

50–yd freestyle—Jeff S. Walker, Central Washington U. 0:21.47
100–yd freestyle—Steve Koga, Willamette University (Ore.) 0:46.57
200–yd freestyle—Gary B. Davis, Simon Fraser, Canada 1:42.54
500–yd freestyle—Gary B. Davis, Simon Fraser 4:36.99
1,650–yd freestyle—Gary B. Davis, Simon Fraser 16:20.69
100–yd backstroke—Nick Borelli, Simon Fraser 0:54.24
200–yd backstroke—Nick Borelli, Simon Fraser 1:55.67
100–yd breaststroke—David Guthrie, Hendrix College (Ark.) 0:59.58
200–yd breaststroke—David Guthrie, Hendrix College 2:10.35
100–yd butterfly—Mark Hartung, Drury College (Mo.) 0:51.82
200–yd butterfly—Mark Hahto, Simon Fraser 1:52.61
200–yd ind. medley—Mark Hartung, Drury 1:52.96
400–yd ind. medley—Victor Batchelor, Simon Fraser 4:09.50
400–yd freestyle relay—Drury College (B. Rogers, D. Sullivan, M. Hartung, J. Yount) 3:09.20
400–yd medley relay—Drury College (S. Allison, R. Markel, D. Ladd, J. Yount) 3:31.35
800–yd freestyle relay—Simon Fraser (K. Franks, R. Barton, G. Davis, B. Batchelor) 6:53.90
1–meter dive—Mike Lewis, Drury College 428.45 pts
3–meter dive—Gore Peterson, Simon Fraser 467.40 pts
Team—Simon Fraser, Burnby, British Colombia, Canada 442 pts

ASSOCIATION OF INTERCOLLEGIATE ATHLETICS FOR WOMEN (A.I.A.W.)

(Las Vegas, Nev., March 19–22, 1980)

50–yd freestyle—Jill Sterkel, University of Texas	0:22.83[1]
100–yd freestyle—Jill Sterkel	0:48.76[1]
200–yd freestyle—Nancy Garapick, Southern California	1:48.25
500–yd freestyle—Maura Walsh, Southern California	4:48.62
1,650–yd freestyle—Kimberly Black, University of Texas (Austin)	16:33.82
50–yd backstroke—Kim Carlisle, Stanford	0:26.26
100–yd backstroke—Linda Jezek, Stanford	0:55.75
200–yd backstroke—Linda Jezek	1:58.61
50–yd breaststroke—Anatte Fredericksson, Southern California	0:29.59
100–yd breaststroke—Anne Gagnon, Arizona State	1:03.57
200–yd breaststroke—Anne Gagnon	2:15.81
50–yd butterfly—Jill Sterkel	0:24.26[1]
100–yd butterfly—Jill Sterkel	0:53.24[1]
200–yd butterfly—Diane Johannignan, Univ. of Houston	1:57.88
100–yd ind. medley—Joan Pennington, University of Texas	0:56.51
200–yd ind. medley—Nancy Garapick	2:02.35
400–yd ind. medley—Janet Puchan, Stanford	4:16.66
200–yd medley relay—Stanford (L. Jezek, P. Spees, K. Asplund, B. Major)	1:43.74[1]
440–yd medley relay—University of Texas (T. Fisher, J. Kubik, J. Sterkel, C. Borgmann)	3:22.56
200–yd freestyle relay—Stanford (N. Thompson, C. Procter, B. Major, K. Asplund)	1:32.65[1]
400–yd freestyle relay—University of Texas (C. Graham, B. Johnson, R. Kast, J. Sterkel)	3:22.56
800–yd freestyle relay—Arizona State (G. Amundrud, M. Hoeflich, A. Gagnon, C. Weinkopsky)	7:19.60
1–meter dive—Amy McGrath, University of Indiana	398.30 pts
3–meter dive—Denis Christenson, University of Texas	453.80 pts
Team—Stanford	629 pts
Top performer (Broderick Award)—Jill Sterkel	97 pts

1. Betters American record.

ROWING

Rowing goes back so far in history that there is no possibility of tracing it to any particular aboriginal source. The oldest rowing race still on the calendar is the "Doggett's Coat and Badge" contest among professional watermen of the Thames (England) that began in 1715. The first Oxford-Cambridge race was held at Henley in 1829. Competitive rowing in the United States began with matches between boats rowed by professional oarsmen of the New York water front. They were oarsmen who rowed the small boats that plied as ferries from Manhattan Island to Brooklyn and return, or who rowed salesmen down the harbor to meet ships arriving from Europe. Since the first salesman to meet an incoming ship had some advantage over his rivals, there was keen competition in the bidding for fast boats and the best oarsmen. This gave rise to match races.

Amateur boat clubs sprang up in the United States between 1820 and 1830 and seven students of Yale joined together to purchase a four-oared lap-streak gig in 1843. The first Harvard-Yale race was held Aug. 3, 1852, on Lake Winnepesaukee, N.H. The first time an American college crew went abroad was in 1869 when Harvard challenged Oxford and was defeated on the Thames. There were early college rowing races on Lake Quinsigamond, near Worcester, Mass., and on Saratoga Lake, N.Y., but the Intercollegiate Rowing Association in 1895 settled on the Hudson, at Poughkeepsie, as the setting for the annual "Poughkeepsie Regatta." In 1950 the I.R.A. shifted its classic to Marietta, Ohio, and in 1952 it was moved to Syracuse, N.Y. The National Association of Amateur Oarsmen, organized in 1872, has conducted annual championship regattas since that time.

INTERCOLLEGIATE ROWING ASSOCIATION REGATTA

(Varsity Eight-Oared Shells)

Rowed at 4 miles, Poughkeepsie, N.Y., 1895–97, 1899–1916, 1925–32, 1934–41. Rowed at 3 miles, Saratoga, N.Y., 1898; Poughkeepsie, 1921–24, 1947–49; Syracuse, N.Y., 1952–1963, 1965–67. Rowed at 2,000 meters, Syracuse, N.Y., 1964 and from 1968 on. Rowed at 2 miles, Ithaca, N.Y., 1920; Marietta, Ohio, 1950–51. Suspended 1917–19, 1933, 1942–46.

Year	Time	First	Second
1895	21:25	Columbia	Cornell
1896	19:59	Cornell	Harvard
1897	20:47 4/5	Cornell	Columbia
1898	15:51 1/2	Pennsylvania	Cornell
1899	20:04	Pennsylvania	Wisconsin
1900	19:44 3/5	Pennsylvania	Wisconsin
1901	18:53 1/5	Cornell	Columbia
1902	19:03 3/5	Cornell	Wisconsin
1903	18:57	Cornell	Georgetown
1904	20:22 3/5	Syracuse	Cornell
1905	20:29	Cornell	Syracuse
1906	19:36 4/5	Cornell	Pennsylvania
1907	20:02 2/5	Cornell	Columbia
1908	19:24 1/5	Syracuse	Columbia
1909	19:02	Cornell	Columbia
1910	20:42 1/5	Cornell	Pennsylvania
1911	20:10 4/5	Cornell	Columbia
1912	19:31 2/5	Cornell	Wisconsin
1913	19:28 3/5	Syracuse	Cornell
1914	19:37 4/5	Columbia	Pennsylvania
1915	19:36 3/5	Cornell	Stanford
1916	20:15 2/5	Syracuse	Cornell
1920	11:02 3/5	Syracuse	Cornell
1921	14:07	Navy	California
1922	13:33 3/5	Navy	Washington
1923	14:03 1/5	Washington	Navy
1924	15:02	Washington	Wisconsin
1925	19:24 4/5	Navy	Washington
1926	19:28 3/5	Washington	Navy
1927	20:57	Columbia	Washington
1928	18:35 4/5	California	Columbia
1929	22:58	Columbia	Washington

Year	Time	First	Second
1930	21:42	Cornell	Syracuse
1931	18:54 1/5	Navy	Cornell
1932	19:55	California	Cornell
1934	19:44	California	Washington
1935	18:52	California	Cornell
1936	19:09 3/5	Washington	California
1937	18:33 3/5	Washington	Navy
1938	18:19	Navy	California
1939	18:12 3/5	California	Washington
1940	22:42	Washington	Cornell
1941	18:53 3/10	Washington	California
1947	13:59 1/5	Navy	Cornell
1948	14:06 2/5	Washington	California
1949	14:42 3/5	California	Washington
1950	8:07.5	Washington	California
1951	7:50.5	Wisconsin	Washington
1952	15:08.1	Navy	Princeton
1953	15:29.6	Navy	Cornell
1954	16:04.4	Navy[1]	Cornell
1955	15:49.9	Cornell	Pennsylvania
1956	16:22.4	Cornell	Navy
1957	15:26.6	Cornell	Pennsylvania
1958	17:12.1	Cornell	Navy
1959	18:01.7	Wisconsin	Syracuse
1960	15:57	California	Navy
1961	16:49.2	California	Cornell
1962	17:02.9	Cornell	Washington
1963	17:24	Cornell	Navy
1964	6:31.1	California	Washington
1965	16:51.3	Navy	Cornell
1966	16:03.4	Wisconsin	Navy
1967	16:13.9	Pennsylvania	Wisconsin
1968	6:15.6	Pennsylvania	Washington
1969	6:30.4	Pennsylvania	Dartmouth
1970	6:39.3	Washington	Wisconsin
1971	6:06	Cornell	Washington
1972	6:22.6	Pennsylvania	Brown
1973	6:21	Wisconsin	Brown
1974	6:33	Wisconsin	Mass. Inst. of Technology
1975	6:08.2	Wisconsin	M.I.T.
1976	6:31	California	Princeton
1977	6:32.4	Cornell	Pennsylvania
1978	6:39.5	Syracuse	Brown
1979	6:26.4	Brown	Wisconsin
1980	6:46	Navy	Northeastern

1. Disqualified.

U.S. MEN'S CHAMPIONSHIPS

National Association of Amateur Oarsmen

(Cooper River, Cherry Hill, N.J., July 19–20, 1980)

Lightweight 1/4-mile dash—Scott Roop, New York Athletic Club 1:14.2
Intermediate doubles—Mike Corboy and Nate Trinsey, Fairmount 6:44
Intermediate fours with coxswain—Northeastern (Greg Rottuno, Dave McCabe, Bill Sussman, John Wilhelm, John Lacouture) 6:54.6
Elite lightweight fours with coxswain—National Lightweight Camp (Tom Perry, Minnesota; John Reichenback, Yale; Dale Emery, California–Berkeley; Scott Carter, Washington; John Stillings, Washington, coxswain) 6:34.5
Elite fours with coxswain—Pennsylvania and M.I.T. (Tim Watentaugh, Sean Calgan, John Everett [M.I.T.], Darrell Vreugdenhil, John Hartigan, coxswain) 6:37.5
Elite lightweight pairs without coxswain—John Sonberg and Bruce Shea, N.Y.A.C. 7:12.2
Senior eights—Vesper Boat Club, Philadelphia 5:49
Elite quads—Larry Klecatsky, Scott Roop, Bill Belden, Jim Dietz, N.Y.A.C. 6:01.5
Elite eight—National Lightweight Camp 5:47.2
Senior quads—Mike Corboy, Jack Frackleton, Nat Trinsey, Charlie Bracken, Fairmount R.C. 6:07.7
Senior pairs without coxswain—Gerry Houlihan and John Brison, N.Y.A.C. 7:02.8
Elite doubles—Bill Belden and Jim Dietz, N.Y.A.C. 6:30.3
Elite pairs with coxswain—Mike Teti, Craig Leads, George Meck, Vesper B.C. 7:28.6
Elite lightweight doubles—Scott Roop, Larry Klecatsky, N.Y.A.C. 6:33.3
Senior singles—Doug Hamilton, Kingston Rowing Club, Canada 7:10.8
Elite lightweight fours without coxswain—Matt Broder, Yale; Frank Neczypor, Vesper; Dave Vogel, Yale; Anthony Johnson, Cornell; National Lightweight Camp 6:27.4
Intermediate pairs without coxswain—Bill Donoho and Bill Thiese, University of Minnesota 7:11.3
Elite lightweight singles—Bill Belden, N.Y.A.C. 7:17.3
Intermediate singles—Doug Hamilton, Kingston R.C., Canada 7:12.4
Elite pairs without coxswain—Gerry Houlihan and John Brison, N.Y.A.C. 6:51.1
Elite lightweight eights—National Lightweight Camp 5:54.2
Lightweight quads—Larry Klecatsky, Scott Roop, John Sonberg, Bill Belden, N.Y.A.C. 6:11.6
Elite singles—Christopher (Tiff) Wood, Harvard 7:04.3
Intermediate eights—N.Y.A.C. 5:59.4
Elite fours without coxswain—Harvard, Penn and M.I.T. (Tom Watentaugh, Tiff Wood, John Everett, Darrell Vreagdenhil) 6:25.4
Team—N.Y.A.C. 223.5 pts

COLLEGIATE—1980

Intercollegiate Rowing Association

(Lake Onondaga, Syracuse, N.Y., May 30-June 1, 1980)
(All races at 2,000 meters)

Eights—1. Navy, 6 minutes 46 seconds. 2. Northeastern, 6:47.5. 3. Brown, 6:48.2. 4. Wisconsin, 6:52.4. 5. Cornell, 6:53.9. 6. Syracuse, 6:58.5.
Junior varsity eights—Cornell 6:53.6
Freshman eights—Orange Coast 7:21.9
Pairs with coxswain—Washington State 9:13.4
Pairs without coxswain—Wisconsin
Fours with coxswain—Wisconsin 7:57.6
Fours without coxswain—Dartmouth 8:05.5
Freshman fours—Brown 8:32.6

WORLD CHAMPIONS

(Bled, Yugoslavia, Sept. 6–9, 1979)

Heavyweight

Singles sculls—Pertti Karppinen, Finland 6:58.27
Double sculls—Frank and Alf Hansen, Norway 6:28.98
Pairs without coxswain—Jorg and Bernd Landvoigt, East Germany 6:42.63
Pairs with coxswain—Gerd Uebler, Juergen Pfeiffer, Georg Spohr, coxswain, East Germany 7:06.35
Fours with coxswain—East Germany 6:27.24
Fours without coxswain—East Germany 6:00.64
Eights—East Germany 5:36.41

SKATEBOARDING—1980

World freestyle pro—Rodney Mullin, Gainesville, Fla.

CYCLING

NATIONAL AMATEUR CHAMPIONS

1951	Gus Gatto	1965	Jack Simes 3rd	1971–72	Gary Campbell
1952	Steve Hromjak	1966	Jack Disney	1973	Roger Young
1953	Ronald Rhoads	1967	Jack Simes, 3rd	1975–75	Steve Woznick
1954–58	Jack Disney	1968	Jack Disney	1976–78	Leigh Barszewski
1959–63	James Rossi	1969	Tim Mountford	1979	Leigh Barszewski
1964	Jack Simes, 3rd	1970	Harry Cutting	1980	Mark Gorski

NATIONAL CHAMPIONSHIPS

Road Racing

(Bisbee, Ariz., Aug. 15–17, 1980)

Senior men—Dale Stetina, Indianapolis, Ind.
Senior women—Beth Heiden, Madison, Wis.
Veteran men—James Montgomery, Herndon, Va.
Veteran women—Joyce Sulanke, Boise, Idaho
Junior men—Sterling McBride, Palo Alto, Calif.
Junior women—Sarah Docter, Madison, Wis.
Intermediate boys—John Gerken, Hanover, Pa.
Intermediate girls—Dedra Chamberlain, El Cajon, Calif.

Time Trials

(Bisbee, Ariz., Aug. 10–14, 1980)

Senior men—Tom Doughty, Indianapolis, Ind.	52:25.9[1]
Senior women—Beth Heiden, Madison, Wis.	59:14.9[1]
Veteran men—Lindsay Crawford, Woodside, Calif.	56:03.7
Veteran women—Joyce Sulanke, Boise, Idaho	1:01:56.4
Junior men—Andy Hampsten, Madison, Wis.	55:28.1[1]
Junior women—Sarah Docter, Madison, Wis.	1:00:00.0[1]
Team—Indiana (Dale Stetina, Wayne Stetina, Joel Stetina, Tom Doughty)	2:06:24.58

Track Racing

(San Diego, Calif., Aug. 20–23, 1980)

Kilometer—Brent Emery, Milwaukee	1:09.26
Pursuit—Leonard Nitz, Pennsylvania	4:57.434
Women's pursuit—Elizabeth Davis, New Jersey	4:12.42

Sprint—Mark Gorski, Illinois
Women's sprint—Sue Novara, Flint, Mich.
Points—Scott Hembree, California
Women's points—Mary Jane Reoch, Philadelphia
Junior men—John Butler, Pennsylvania
Junior women—Maria Wisser, Pennsylvania
Intermediate boys—Tim Volker, Ames, Iowa
Intermediate girls—Sue Schaugg, St. Claire Shores, Mich.

Motocross

N.B.A. champion—Scott Clark, San Jose, Calif.
A.B.A. champion—Stu Thomson, Whittier, Calif.
World champion—Bob Wears, Van Nuys, Calif.

Tour de France

Joop Zoetemelk, Netherlands

WORLD PROFESSIONAL CHAMPIONSHIPS—1980

Sprint—Koichi Nakano, Japan
Pursuit—Tony Doyle, England
Road—Bernard Hinault, France
Kieren—Danny Clark, Australia
Motorpast—Wilfried Peffgen, West Germany
Points—Stan Tourne, Belgium

BARREL JUMPING—1980

World—Yvon Jolin, Anjou City, Quebec

KARATE

A.A.U. NATIONAL CHAMPIONSHIPS

(Akron, Ohio, July 7–8, 1979)

Men's Kata

Advanced—Albert Pena, Haverstraw, N.Y.
Intermediate—Dennis Zamudio, Florida Gold Coast
Novice—Kevin Cyr, New England

Men's Weapon Kata

Champion—Glen Hart, New England

Men's Kumite

Open—Tokay Hill, Chillicothe, Ohio
Advanced Heavyweight—Mike Powell, New Jersey
Advanced middleweight—Bill Blanks, Allegheny Mountain
Advanced lightweight—Mike Sledge, Metropolitan
Intermediate—Patrick Gentempo, New Jersey
Novice—Frederick Fritsch, Virginia

Women's Kata

Advanced—Vicki Johnson, Central
Intermediate—Gwen Hoffman, New Jersey
Novice—Judith Murphy, New Jersey

Women's Kumite

Advanced—Andrea Clark, Metropolitan
Intermediate—Rhonda Hansen, New Jersey
Novice—Melinda Gallop, Florida Gold Coast

Women's Weapon Kata

Champion—Katherine Loakopolos, Metropolitan

SURFING—1980

Australian men's pro—Mark Richards, Australia
Australian women's pro—Margo Oberg, Koloa, Hawaii

SHUFFLEBOARD

NATIONAL SHUFFLEBOARD ASSOCIATION NATIONAL TOURNAMENT

(Lakeside, Ohio, July 23–27, 1979)

Men's open—Lary Faris, Cincinnati
Women's open—June Angeroth, Council Bluffs, Iowa
Men's closed—Henry Rutschow, Toledo, Ohio
Women's closed—Dolores Norman, Utterson, Canada
Men's doubles—Kenneth Worden, Coldwater, Mich.–Virgil Pfisterer, Canton, Ohio
Womens doubles—Mildred Davis, Newcastle, Ind.–Virginia Worden, Coldwater, Mich.

HARNESS RACING

Oliver Wendell Holmes, the famous Autocrat of the Breakfast Table, wrote that the running horse was a gambling toy but the trotting horse was useful and, furthermore, "horse-racing is not a republican institution; horse-trotting is." Oliver Wendell Holmes was a born-and-bred New Englander, and New England was the nursery of the harness racing sport in America. Pacers and trotters were matters of local pride and prejudice in Colonial New England, and, shortly after the Revolution, the Messenger and Justin Morgan strains produced many winners in harness racing "matches" along the turnpikes of New York, Connecticut, Rhode Island, Massachusetts, Vermont, and New Hampshire.

There was English thoroughbred blood in Messenger and Justin Morgan, and, many years later, it was blended in Rysdyk's Hambletonian, foaled in 1849. Hambletonian was not particularly fast under harness but his descendants have had almost a monopoly of prizes, titles, and records in the harness racing game. Hambletonian was purchased as a foal with its dam for a total of $124 by William Rysdyk of Goshen, N.Y., and made a modest fortune for the purchaser.

Trotters and pacers often were raced under saddle in the old days, and, in fact, the custom still survives in some places in Europe. Dexter, the great trotter that lowered the mile record from 2:19¾ to 2:17¼ in 1867, was said to handle just as well under saddle as when pulling a sulky. But as sulkies were lightened in weight and improved in design, trotting under saddle became less common and finally faded out in this country.

WORLD RECORDS

Established in a Race or Against Time at One Mile

Source: Martin J. Evans, Research Specialist, United States Trotting Association

Trotting on Mile Track

	Record	Holder	Driver	Where Made	Year
All Age	1:54 4/5*	Nevele Pride	Stanley Dancer	Indianapolis	1969
2-year-old	1:56 3/5*	Star Investment, f	William Herman	Lexington, Ky.	1979
3-year-old	1:55[1]	Speedy Somolli	Howard Beissinger	DuQuoin, Ill.	1978
		Florida Pro	George Sholty	DuQuoin, Ill.	1978
4-year-old	1:54 4/5*	Nevele Pride	Stanley Dancer	Indianapolis	1969

Trotting on Five-Eighths Mile Track

	Record	Holder	Driver	Where Made	Year
All Age	1:57 3/5[1]	Dream of Glory	Stan Bayless	Cicero, Ill.	1976
		Green Speed	William Haughton	Cicero, Ill.	1978
2-year-old	2:01[1]	Starlark Hanover	David Wade	Wilkes–Barre, Pa.	1973
		Green Speed	William Haughton	Philadelphia	1976
3-year-old	1:58 1/5[1]	Speedy Somolli	Howard Beissinger	Meadow Lands, Pa.	1978
		Florida Pro	George Sholty	Philadelphia	1978
4-year-old	1:57 3/5[1]	Green Speed	William Haughton	Cicero, Ill.	1978

Trotting on Half-Mile Track

	Record	Holder	Driver	Where Made	Year
All Age	1:56 4/5[1]	Nevele Pride	Stanley Dancer	Saratoga Springs, N.Y.	1969
2-year-old	2:00 1/5[1]	Ayres	John Simpson Sr.	Delaware, Ohio	1963
3-year-old	1:58 3/5[1]	Songcan	George Sholty	Delaware, Ohio	1972
4-year-old	1:56 4/5[1]	Nevele Pride	Stanley Dancer	Saratoga Springs, N.Y.	1969

1. Record made in race. f = filly.

Pacing on Mile Track

	Record	Holder	Driver	Where Made	Year
All Age	1:52 4/5[1]	Niatross	Clint Galbraith	Syracuse, N.Y.	1980
	1:49 1/5*	Niatross	Clint Galbraith	Lexington, Ky.	1980
2-year-old	1:54 1/5[1]	Jade Prince	Jack Kopas	Lexington, Ky.	1976
		Fulla Strikes	Joe O'Brien	Inglewood, Calif.	1976
3-year-old	1:52 4/5[1]	Niatross	Clint Galbraith	Syracuse, N.Y.	1980
	1:49 1/5*	Niatross	Clint Galbraith	Lexington, Ky.	1980
4-year-old	1:52*	Steady Star	Joe O'Brien	Lexington, Ky.	1971

Pacing on Five-Eighths Mile Track

	Record	Holder	Driver	Where Made	Year
All Age	1:53 2/5[1]	Storm Damage	Joe O'Brien	Meadow Lands, Pa.	1980
2-year-old	1:57[1]	Wellwood Hanover	Peter Haughton	Philadelphia	1977
3-year-old	1:53 2/5[1]	Storm Damage	Joe O'Brien	Meadow Lands, Pa.	1980
4-year-old	1:54 2/5[1]	Direct Scooter	Warren Cameron	Windsor, Ontario	1980

Pacing on Half-Mile Track

	Record	Holder	Driver	Where Made	Year
All Age	1:55[1]	Niatross	Clint Galbraith	Batavia Downs, N.Y.	1980

2-year-old	1:57⅘[1]	Whamo	Charles Clark	Louisville, Ky.	1979
3-year-old	1:55[1]	Niatross	Clint Galbraith	Batavia Downs, N.Y.	1980
4-year-old	1:55⅗[1]	Albatross	Stanley Dancer	Delaware, Ohio	1972

1. Record made in race. * Time trials.

HARNESS RACING RECORDS FOR THE MILE

Trotters

Time	Trotter, age, driver	Year
2:00	Lou Dillon, 5, Millard Sanders	1903
1:58½	Lou Dillon, 5, Millard Sanders	1903
1:58	Uhlan, 8, Charles Tanner	1912
1:58	Peter Manning, 5, T. W. Murphy	1921
1:57¾	Peter Manning, 5, T. W. Murphy	1921
1:57	Peter Manning, 6, T. W. Murphy	1922
1:56¾	Peter Manning, 6, T. W. Murphy	1922
1:56¾	Greyhound, 5, Sep Palin	1937
1:56	Greyhound, 5, Sep Palin	1937
1:55¼	Greyhound, 6, Sep Palin	1938
1:54⅘	Nevele Pride, 4, Stanley Dancer	1969

Pacers

Time	Pacer, age, driver	Year
2:00½	John R. Gentry, 7, W.J. Andrews	1896
1:59¼	Star Pointer, 8, D. McClary	1897
1:59	Dan Patch, 7, M. E. McHenry	1903
1:56¼	Dan Patch, 7, M. E. McHenry	1903
1:56	Dan Patch, 8, H. C. Hersey	1904
1:55	Billy Direct, 4, Vic Fleming	1938
1:55	Adios Harry, 4, Luther Lyons	1955
1:54⅗	Adios Butler, 4, Paige West	1960
1:54	Bret Hanover, 4, Frank Ervin	1966
1:53⅗	Bret Hanover, 4, Frank Ervin	1966
1:52	Steady Star, 4, Joe O'Brien	1971
1:49⅕	Niatross, 3, Clint Galbraith	1980

HARNESS HORSE OF THE YEAR

Chosen in poll conducted by United States Trotting Association in conjunction with the U.S. Harness Writers Assn.

1959	Bye Bye Byrd, Pacer
1960	Adios Butler, Pacer
1961	Adios Butler, Pacer
1962	Su Mac Lad, Trotter
1963	Speedy Scot, Trotter
1964	Bret Hanover, Pacer
1965	Bret Hanover, Pacer
1966	Bret Hanover, Pacer
1967	Nevele Pride, Trotter
1968	Nevele Pride, Trotter
1969	Nevele Pride, Trotter
1970	Fresh Yankee, Trotter
1971	Albatross, Pacer
1972	Albatross, Pacer
1973	Sir Dalrae, Pacer
1974	Delmonica Hanover, Trotter
1975	Savoir, Trotter
1976	Keystone Ore, Pacer
1977	Green Speed, Trotter
1978	Abercrombie, Pacer
1979	Niatross, Pacer

HISTORY OF TRADITIONAL HARNESS RACING STAKES

The Hambletonian

Three-year-old trotters. One mile. Guy McKinney won first race at Syracuse in 1926; held at Goshen, N.Y., 1930–1942, 1944–1956; at Yonkers, N.Y., 1943; at Du Quoin, Ill., since 1957.

Year	Winner	Driver	Best time	Total purse
1967	Speedy Streak	Del Cameron	2:00	122,650
1968	Nevele Pride	Stanley Dancer	1:59⅖	116,190
1969	Lindy's Pride	Howard Beissinger	1:57⅗	124,910
1970	Timothy T.	John Simpson, Jr.	1:58⅖[1]	143,630
1971	Speedy Crown	Howard Beissinger	1:57⅖	129,770
1972	Super Bowl	Stanley Dancer	1:56⅖	119,090
1973	Flirth	Ralph Baldwin	1:57⅕	144,710
1974	Christopher T	Billy Haughton	1:58⅗	160,150
1975	Bonefish	Stanley Dancer	1:59[2]	232,192
1976	Steve Lobell	Billy Haughton	1:56⅖	263,524
1977	Green Speed	Billy Haughton	1:55⅗	284,131
1978	Speedy Somolli	Howard Beissinger	1:55	241,280
1979	Legend Hanover	George Sholty	1:56	300,000
1980	Burgomeister	Billy Haughton	1:56⅗	293,570

1. By Formal Notice. 2. By Yankee Bambino.

Little Brown Jug

Three-year-old pacers. One Mile. Raced at Delaware County Fair Grounds, Delaware, Ohio.

1967	Best of All	Jim Hackett	1:59[1]	84,778
1968	Rum Customer	William Haughton	1:59⅗	104,226
1969	Laverne Hanover	William Haughton	2:00⅖	109,731
1970	Most Happy Fella	Stanley Dancer	1:57⅕	100,110
1971	Nansemond	Herve Filion	1:57⅖	102,994
1972	Strike Out	Keith Waples	1:56⅗	104,916
1973	Melvin's Wo	Joe O'Brien	1:57⅗	120,000
1974	Ambro Omaha	Billy Haughton	1:57	132,630
1975	Seatrain	Ben Webster	1:57	147,813
1976	Keystone Ore	Stanley Dancer	1:56⅘[2]	153,799
1977	Governor Skipper	John Chapman	1:56⅕	150,000
1978	Happy Escort	William Popfinger	1:55⅖[3]	186,760
1979	Hot Hitter	Herve Filion	1:55⅗	226,455
1980	Niatross	Clint Galbraith	1:54⅘	104,717

1. By Nardin's Byrd. 2. By Armbro Ranger. 3. By Falcon Almahurst.

GOLF

It may be that golf originated in Holland—historians believe it did—but certainly Scotland fostered the game and is famous for it. In fact, in 1457 the Scottish Parliament, disturbed because football and golf had lured young Scots from the more soldierly exercise of archery, passed an ordinance that "futeball and golf be utterly cryit doun and nocht usit." James I and Charles I of the royal line of Stuarts were golf enthusiasts, whereby the game came to be known as "the royal and ancient game of golf."

The golf balls used in the early games were leather-covered and stuffed with feathers. Clubs of all kinds were fashioned by hand to suit individual players. The great step in spreading the game came with the change from the feather ball to the gutta-percha ball about 1850. In 1860, formal competition began with the establishment of an annual tournament for the British Open championship. There are records of "golf clubs" in the United States as far back as colonial days but no proof of actual play before John Reid and some friends laid out six holes on the Reid lawn in Yonkers, N.Y., in 1888 and played there with golf balls and clubs brought over from Scotland by Robert Lockhart. This group then formed the St. Andrews Golf Club of Yonkers, and golf was established in this country.

However, it remained a rather sedate and almost aristocratic pastime until a 20-year-old ex-caddy, Francis Ouimet of Boston, defeated two great British professionals, Harry Vardon and Ted Ray, in the United States Open championship at Brookline, Mass., in 1913. This feat put the game and Francis Ouimet on the front pages of the newspapers and stirred a wave of enthusiasm for the sport. The greatest feat so far in golf history is that of Robert Tyre Jones, Jr., of Atlanta, who won the British Open, the British Amateur, the U.S. Open, and the U.S. Amateur titles in one year, 1930.

U.S. OPEN CHAMPIONS

Year	Winner	Score	Where played
1895	Horace Rawlins	173	Newport
1896	James Foulis	152	Shinnecock Hills
1897	Joe Lloyd	162	Chicago
1898[3]	Fred Herd	328	Myopia
1899	Willie Smith	315	Baltimore
1900	Harry Vardon	313	Chicago
1901	Willie Anderson[1]	331	Myopia
1902	Laurie Auchterlonie	307	Garden City
1903	Willie Anderson[1]	307	Baltusrol
1904	Willie Anderson	303	Glen View
1905	Willie Anderson	314	Myopia
1906	Alex Smith	295	Onwentsia
1907	Alex Ross	302	Philadelphia
1908	Fred McLeod[1]	322	Myopia
1909	George Sargent	290	Englewood
1910	Alex Smith[1]	298	Philadelphia
1911	John McDermott[1]	307	Chicago
1912	John McDermott	294	Buffalo
1913	Francis Ouimet[1, 2]	304	Brookline
1914	Walter Hagen	290	Midlothian
1915	Jerome D. Travers[2]	297	Baltusrol
1916	Charles Evans, Jr.[2]	286	Minikahda
1917–18	No tournaments[4]		
1919	Walter Hagen[2]	301	Brae Burn
1920	Edward Ray	295	Inverness
1921	Jim Barnes	289	Columbia
1922	Gene Sarazen	288	Skokie
1923	R. T. Jones, Jr.[1, 2]	296	Inwood
1924	Cyril Walker	297	Oakland Hills
1925	Willie Macfarlane[1]	291	Worcester
1926	R. T. Jones, Jr.[2]	293	Scioto
1927	Tommy Armour[1]	301	Oakmont
1928	Johnny Farrell[1]	294	Olympia Fields
1929	R. T. Jones, Jr.[1, 2]	294	Winged Foot
1930	R. T. Jones, Jr.[2]	287	Interlachen
1931	Billy Burke[1]	292	Inverness
1932	Gene Sarazen	286	Fresh Meadow
1933	John Goodman[2]	287	North Shore
1934	Olin Dutra	293	Merion
1935	Sam Parks, Jr.	299	Oakmont
1936	Tony Manero	282	Baltusrol
1937	Ralph Guldahl	281	Oakland Hills
1938	Ralph Guldahl	284	Cherry Hills
1939	Byron Nelson[1]	284	Philadelphia
1940	Lawson Little[1]	287	Canterbury
1941	Craig Wood	284	Colonial
1942–45	No tournaments[5]		
1946	Lloyd Mangrum[1]	284	Canterbury
1947	Lew Worsham[1]	282	St. Louis
1948	Ben Hogan	276	Riviera
1949	Cary Middlecoff	286	Medinah
1950	Ben Hogan[1]	287	Merion
1951	Ben Hogan	287	Oakland Hills
1952	Julius Boros	281	Northwood
1953	Ben Hogan	283	Oakmont
1954	Ed Furgol	284	Baltusrol
1955	Jack Fleck[1]	287	Olympic
1956	Cary Middlecoff	281	Oak Hill
1957	Dick Mayer[1]	298	Inverness
1958	Tommy Bolt	283	Southern Hills
1959	Bill Casper, Jr.	282	Winged Foot
1960	Arnold Palmer	280	Cherry Hills
1961	Gene Littler	281	Oakland Hills
1962	Jack Nicklaus[1]	283	Oakmont
1963	Julius Boros[1]	293	Country Club
1964	Ken Venturi	278	Congressional
1965	Gary Player[1]	282	Bellerive
1966	Bill Casper[1]	278	Olympic
1967	Jack Nicklaus	275	Baltusrol
1968	Lee Trevino	275	Oak Hill
1969	Orville Moody	281	Champions G. C.
1970	Tony Jacklin	281	Hazeltine
1971	Lee Trevino[1]	280	Merion
1972	Jack Nicklaus	290	Pebble Beach
1973	Johnny Miller	279	Oakmont
1974	Hale Irwin	287	Winged Foot
1975	Lou Graham[1]	287	Medinah
1976	Jerry Pate	277	Atlanta A.C.
1977	Hubert Green	278	Southern Hills
1978	Andy North	285	Cherry Hills
1979	Hale Irwin	284	Inverness
1980	Jack Nicklaus	272	Baltusrol

1. Winner in playoff. 2. Amateur. 3. In 1898, competition was extended to 72 holes. 4. In 1917, Jock Hutchison, with a 292, won an Open Patriotic Tournament for the benefit of the American Red Cross at Whitemarsh Valley Country Club. 5. In 1942, Ben Hogan, with a 271 won a Hale American National Open Tournament for the benefit of the Navy Relief Society and USO at Ridgemoor Country Club.

U.S. AMATEUR CHAMPIONS

1895	Charles B. Macdonald	1919	S. D. Herron	1940	R. D. Chapman	1963	Deane Beman
1896–97	H. J. Whigham	1920	Charles Evans, Jr.	1941	Marvin H. Ward	1964	Bill Campbell
1898	Findlay S. Douglas	1921	Jesse P. Guilford	1946	Ted Bishop	1965[2]	Robert Murphy, Jr.
1899	H. M. Harriman	1922	Jess W. Sweetser	1947	Robert Riegel	1966	Gary Cowan[1]
1900–01	Walter J. Travis	1923	Max R. Marston	1948	Willie Turnesa	1967	Bob Dickson
1902	Louis N. James	1924–25	R. T. Jones Jr.	1949	Charles Coe	1968	Bruce Fleisher
1903	Walter J. Travis	1926	George Von Elm	1950	Sam Urzetta	1969	Steven Melnyk
1904–05	H. Chandler Egan	1927–28	R. T. Jones Jr.	1951	Billy Maxwell	1970	Lanny Wadkins
1906	Eben M. Byers	1929	H. R. Johnston	1952	Jack Westland	1971	Gary Cowan
1907–08	Jerome D. Travers	1930	R. T. Jones, Jr.	1953	Gene Littler	1972	Vinny Giles 3d
1909	Robert A. Gardner	1931	Francis Ouimet	1954	Arnold Palmer	1973[3]	Craig Stadler
1910	W. C. Fownes, Jr.	1932	Ross Somerville	1955–56	Harvie Ward	1974	Jerry Pate
1911	Harold H. Hilton	1933	G. T. Dunlap, Jr.	1957	Hillman Robbins	1975	Fred Ridley
1912–13	Jerome D. Travers	1934–35	Lawson Little	1958	Charles Coe	1976	Bill Sander
1914	Francis Ouimet	1936	John W. Fischer	1959	Jack Nicklaus	1977	John Fought
1915	Robert A. Gardner	1937	John Goodman	1960	Deane Beman	1978	John Cook
1916	Charles Evans, Jr.	1938	Willie Turnesa	1961	Jack Nicklaus	1979	Mark O'Meara
		1939	Marvin H. Ward	1962	Labron Harris, Jr.	1980	Hal Sutton

1. Winner in playoff. 2. Tourney switched to medal play through 1972. 3. Return to match play.

U.S. P.G.A. CHAMPIONS

1916	Jim Barnes	1938	Paul Runyan	1953	Walter Burkemo	1967	Don January[1]
1919	Jim Barnes	1939	Henry Picard	1954	Chick Harbert	1968	Julius Boros
1920	Jock Hutchison	1940	Byron Nelson	1955	Doug Ford	1969	Ray Floyd
1921	Walter Hagen	1941	Victor Ghezzi	1956	Jack Burke, Jr.	1970	Dave Stockton
1922–23	Gene Sarazen	1942	Sam Snead	1957	Lionel Hebert	1971	Jack Nicklaus
1924–27	Walter Hagen	1944	Bob Hamilton	1958[2]	Dow Finsterwald	1972	Gary Player
1928–29	Leo Diegel	1945	Byron Nelson	1959	Bob Rosburg	1973	Jack Nicklaus
1930	Tommy Armour	1946	Ben Hogan	1960	Jay Hebert	1974	Lee Trevino
1931	Tom Creavy	1947	Jim Ferrier	1961	Jerry Barber[1]	1975	Jack Nicklaus
1932	Olin Dutra	1948	Ben Hogan	1962	Gary Player	1976	Dave Stockton
1933	Gene Sarazen	1949	Sam Snead	1963	Jack Nicklaus	1977	Lanny Wadkins[1]
1934	Paul Runyan	1950	Chandler Harper	1964	Bobby Nichols	1978	John Mahaffey
1935	Johnny Revolta	1951	Sam Snead	1965	Dave Marr	1979	David Graham[1]
1936–37	Denny Shute	1952	Jim Turnesa	1966	Al Geiberger	1980	Jack Nicklaus

1. Winner in playoff. 2. Switched to medal play.

THE MASTERS TOURNAMENT WINNERS

Augusta National Golf Club, Augusta, Ga.

Year	Winner	Score	Year	Winner	Score	Year	Winner	Score
1934	Horton Smith	284	1951	Ben Hogan	280	1966	Jack Nicklaus[1]	288
1935	Gene Sarazen[1]	282	1952	Sam Snead	286	1967	Gay Brewer, Jr.	280
1936	Horton Smith	285	1953	Ben Hogan	274	1968	Bob Goalby	277
1937	Byron Nelson	283	1954	Sam Snead[1]	289	1969	George Archer	281
1938	Henry Picard	285	1955	Cary Middlecoff	279	1970	Billy Casper[1]	279
1939	Ralph Guldahl	279	1956	Jack Burke	289	1971	Charles Coody	279
1940	Jimmy Demaret	280	1957	Doug Ford	283	1972	Jack Nicklaus	286
1941	Craig Wood	280	1958	Arnold Palmer	284	1973	Tommy Aaron	283
1942	Byron Nelson[1]	280	1959	Art Wall, Jr.	284	1974	Gary Player	278
1943–45	No Tournaments		1960	Arnold Palmer	282	1975	Jack Nicklaus	276
1946	Herman Keiser	282	1961	Gary Player	280	1976	Ray Floyd	271
1947	Jimmy Demaret	281	1962	Arnold Palmer[1]	280	1977	Tom Watson	276
1948	Claude Harmon	279	1963	Jack Nicklaus	286	1978	Gary Player	277
1949	Sam Snead	282	1964	Arnold Palmer	276	1979	Fuzzy Zoeller[1]	280
1950	Jimmy Demaret	283	1965	Jack Nicklaus	271	1980	Severiano Ballesteros	275

1. Winner in playoff.

U.S. WOMEN'S AMATEUR CHAMPIONS

1916	Alexa Stirling	1926	Helen Stetson	1937	Mrs. J. A. Page, Jr.	1949	Mrs. D. G. Porter
1919–20	Alexa Stirling	1927	Mrs. M. B. Horn	1938	Patty Berg	1950	Beverly Hanson
1921	Marion Hollins	1928–30	Glenna Collett	1939–40	Betty Jameson	1951	Dorothy Kirby
1922	Glenna Collett	1931	Helen Hicks	1941	Mrs. Frank Newell	1952	Jacqueline Pung
1923	Edith Cummings	1932–34	Virginia Van Wie	1946	Mildred Zaharias	1953	Mary Lena Faulk
1924	Dorothy Campbell Hurd	1935	Glenna Collett Vare	1947	Louise Suggs	1954	Barbara Romack
1925	Glenna Collett	1936	Pamela Barton	1948	Grace Lenczyk	1955	Patricia Lesser
						1956	Marlene Stewart

1957	JoAnne Gunderson	1963	Anne Quast Welts	1970	Martha Wilkinson	1977	Beth Daniel
1958	Anne Quast	1964	Barbara McIntire	1971	Laura Baugh	1978	Cathy Sherk
1959	Barbara McIntire	1965	Jean Ashley	1972	Mary Ann Budke	1979	Carolyn Hill
1960	JoAnne Gunderson	1966	JoAnne Gunderson	1973	Carol Semple	1980	Juli Inkster
1961	Anne Quast Decker	1967	Lou Dill	1974	Cynthia Hill		
		1968	JoAnne G. Carner	1975	Beth Daniel		
1962	JoAnne Gunderson	1969	Catherine Lacoste	1976	Donna Horton		

U.S. WOMEN'S OPEN CHAMPIONS

Year	Winner	Score	Year	Winner	Score	Year	Winner	Score
1946	Patty Berg (match play)	—	1958	Mickey Wright	290	1970	Donna Caponi	287
1947	Betty Jameson	295	1959	Mickey Wright	287	1971	JoAnne Carner	288
1948	Mildred D. Zaharias	300	1960	Betsy Rawls	291	1972	Susie Berning	299
1949	Louise Suggs	291	1961	Mickey Wright	293	1973	Susie Berning	290
1950	Mildred D. Zaharias	291	1962	Murle Lindstrom	301	1974	Sandra Haynie	295
1951	Betsy Rawls	293	1963	Mary Mills	289	1975	Sandra Palmer	295
1952	Louise Suggs	284	1964	Mickey Wright[1]	290	1976	JoAnne Carner	292
1953	Betsy Rawls[1]	302	1965	Carol Mann	290	1977	Hollis Stacy	292
1954	Mildred D. Zaharias	291	1966	Sandra Spuzich	297	1978	Hollis Stacy	289
1955	Fay Crocker	299	1967	Catherine LaCoste	294	1979	Jerilyn Britz	284
1956	Katherine Cornelius[1]	302	1968	Susie Berning	289	1980	Amy Alcott	280
1957	Betsy Rawls	299	1969	Donna Caponi	294			

1. Winner in playoff. 2. Amateur.

BRITISH OPEN CHAMPIONS

(First tournament, held in 1860, was won by Willie Park, Sr.)

Year	Winner	Score	Year	Winner	Score	Year	Winner	Score
1920	George Duncan	303	1939	R. Burton	290	1964	Tony Lema	279
1921	Jock Hutchison[1]	296	1946	Sam Snead	290	1965	Peter Thomson	285
1922	Walter Hagen	300	1947	Fred Daly	294	1966	Jack Nicklaus	282
1923	A. G. Havers	295	1948	Henry Cotton	283	1967	Roberto de Vicenzo	278
1924	Walter Hagen	301	1949	Bobby Locke[1]	283	1968	Gary Player	289
1925	Jim Barnes	300	1950	Bobby Locke	279	1969	Tony Jacklin	280
1926	R. T. Jones, Jr.	291	1951	Max Faulkner	285	1970	Jack Nicklaus[1]	283
1927	R. T. Jones, Jr.	285	1952	Bobby Locke	287	1971	Lee Trevino	278
1928	Walter Hagen	292	1953	Ben Hogan	282	1972	Lee Trevino	278
1929	Walter Hagen	292	1954	Peter Thomson	283	1973	Tom Weiskopf	276
1930	R. T. Jones, Jr.	291	1955	Peter Thomson	281	1974	Gary Player	282
1931	Tommy Armour	296	1956	Peter Thomson	286	1975	Tom Watson[1]	279
1932	Gene Sarazen	283	1957	Bobby Locke	279	1976	Johnny Miller	279
1933	Denny Shute[1]	292	1958	Peter Thomson[1]	278	1977	Tom Watson	268
1934	Henry Cotton	283	1959	Gary Player	284	1978	Jack Nicklaus	281
1935	A. Perry	283	1960	Kel Nagle	278	1979	Severiano Ballesteros	283
1936	A. H. Padgham	287	1961	Arnold Palmer	284	1980	Tom Watson	271
1937	Henry Cotton	290	1962	Arnold Palmer	276			
1938	R. A. Whitcombe	295	1963	Bob Charles[1]	277			

1. Winner in playoff.

U.S. OPEN—MEN

(Baltusrol Club, Springfield, N.J., June 12–15, 1980)

Jack Nicklaus	63	71	70	68—272	$55,000
Isao Aoki	68	68	68	70—274	29,500
Tom Watson	71	68	67	70—276	17,400
Keith Fergus	66	70	70	70—276	17,400
Lon Hinkle	66	70	69	71—276	17,400
Mark Hayes	66	71	69	74—280	11,950
Mike Reid	69	67	75	69—280	11,950
Ed Sneed	72	70	70	70—282	8,050
Hale Irwin	70	70	73	69—282	8,050
Andy North	68	75	72	67—282	8,050
Mike Morley	73	68	69	72—282	8,050

Leaders—18 holes: Jack Nicklaus and Tom Weiskopf 63; 36 holes: Jack Nicklaus 134; 54 holes: Jack Nicklaus and Isao Aoki 204.

P.G.A. CHAMPIONSHIP

(Oak Hill C.C., Rochester, N.Y.; Aug. 7–10, 1980)

Jack Nicklaus	70	69	66	69—274	$60,000
Andy Bean	72	71	68	70—281	40,000
Lon Hinkle	70	69	69	75—283	22,500
Gil Morgan	68	70	73	72—283	22,500
Howard Twitty	68	74	71	71—284	14,500
Curtis Strange	68	72	72	72—284	14,500
Lee Trevino	74	71	71	69—285	11,000
Bobby Walzel	68	76	71	71—286	8,500
Bill Rogers	71	71	72	72—286	8,500

MASTERS TOURNAMENT—MEN

(Augusta, Ga., April 10–13, 1980)

Severiano Ballesteros	66	69	68	72—275	$55,000
Gibby Gilbert	70	74	68	67—279	35,500
Jack Newton	68	74	69	68—279	35,500
Hubert Green	68	74	71	67—280	15,750
David Graham	66	73	72	70—281	13,200
Jerry Pate	72	68	76	67—283	9,958
Larry Nelson	69	72	73	69—283	9,958
Tom Kite	69	71	74	69—283	9,958
Gary Player	71	71	71	70—283	9,958
Ben Crenshaw	76	70	68	69—283	9,958
Ed Fiori	71	70	69	73—283	9,958
Tom Watson	73	69	71	71—284	7,250
Andy Bean	74	72	68	70—284	7,250

BRITISH OPEN

(Muirfield, Scotland, July 17–20, 1980)

Tom Watson	68	70	64	69—271	$59,250
Lee Trevino	68	67	71	69—275	41,475
Ben Crenshaw	70	70	68	69—277	31,995
Jack Nicklaus	73	67	71	69—280	21,623
Carl Mason	72	69	70	69—280	21,623
Andy Bean	71	69	70	72—282	17,181
Ken Brown	70	68	68	76—282	17,181
Hubert Green	77	69	64	72—282	17,181
Craig Stadler	72	70	69	71—282	17,181
Gil Morgan	70	70	71	72—283	13,625
Jack Newton	69	71	73	70—283	13,625

U.S. WOMEN'S OPEN

(Nashville, Tenn., July 10–13, 1980)

Amy Alcott	70	70	68	72—280	$20,047
Hollis Stacy	75	71	70	73—289	11,346
Kathy McMullen	74	73	71	73—291	8,547
Judy Clark	75	73	73	71—292	6,347
Donna Young	72	72	75	73—292	6,347
Louise Bruce	73	74	73	73—293	4,847
Lori Garbacz	72	76	72	71—294	3,964
Nancy Lopez-Melton	74	72	71	77—294	3,964
Jane Blalock	76	71	71	76—294	3,964
JoAnne Carner	74	72	74	75—295	3,085
Patty Hayes	75	72	74	74—295	3,085
Eva Chang	74	74	72	75—295	3,085
Beth Daniel	76	72	69	78—295	3,085

L.P.G.A. CHAMPIONSHIP

(Jack Nicklaus G.C., Kings Island, Ohio, June 5–8, 1980)

Sally Little	69	70	73	73—285	$22,500
Jane Blalock	70	69	75	74—288	14,700
Barbara Moxness	70	71	74	74—289	6,810
JoAnne Carner	71	75	70	73—289	6,810
Beth Daniel	72	70	73	74—289	6,810
Donna C. Young	72	73	72	72—289	6,810
Dot Germain	76	70	72	71—289	6,810
Jo Ann Washam	72	72	71	74—290	4,350
Vicki Gergon	73	74	70	74—291	4,050

P.G.A. EARNINGS—1980

(Through September 17)

Player	Amount	Player	Amount
Tom Watson	$513,408	George Burns	204,628
Lee Trevino	340,814	Craig Stadler	199,391
Curtis Strange	269,100	Ray Floyd	192,993
Andy Bean	264,083	Mike Reid	191,658
Jerry Pate	217,776	Ben Crenshaw	182,802

L.P.G.A. EARNINGS—1980

(Through September 17)

Player	Amount	Player	Amount
Beth Daniel	$202,108	Pat Bradley	158,597
Donna C. Young	192,766	Sally Little	131,249
Amy Alcott	190,095	Jane Blalock	123,249
Nancy Lopez-Melton	186,185	Jo Ann Washam	104,248
JoAnne Carner	173,315	Sandra Post	97,730

OTHER 1980 MEN'S TOURNAMENTS

American Classic—Randy Sonnier, Houston 288
Canadian Open—Bob Gilder, Corvallis, Ore. 274
Canadian P.G.A.—Arnold Palmer, Latrobe, Pa. 271
British Amateur—Duncan Evans, Wales, defeated David Suddards, South Africa, 4 and 3
N.C.A.A. Division I—Jay Don Blake, Utah State 283
N.C.A.A. Division II—Paul Perini, Troy State 288
N.C.A.A. Division III—Mike Bender, California State–Stanislaus 286
New England Amateur—Brad Faxon Jr., Furman University
New England P.G.A.—Paul Moran, Mount Snow, Vt.
North and South—Hal Sutton, Shreveport, La.
Northeastern—Hal Sutton
U.S.G.A. Junior—Eric Johnson, Eugene, Ore.
Porter Cup—Tony DeLuca, Vienna, Va.
Public Links—Jodie Mudd, Louisville, Ky., defeated Richard Gordon, Santa Clara, Calif., 9 and 8
Southern—Bob Tway, Marietta, Ga.
Trans-Mississippi—Ray Barr, University of Houston
Western Amateur—Hal Sutton
Western Open—Scott Simpson, San Diego, Calif. 281

MEN'S AMATEUR

(The Country Club of North Carolina, Pinehurst, N.C., Aug. 26–31, 1980)

Final (36 holes)—Hal Sutton, Shreveport, La., defeated Bob Lewis, Warren, Ohio, 9 and 8

Semifinals—Sutton defeated Jim Holtgrieve, Kirkwood, Mo., 3 and 2; Lewis defeated Dick Von Tacky, Titusville, Ga., 4 and 2

Quarterfinals—Holtgrieve defeated Fred Couples, Seattle, Wash., 5 and 3; Sutton defeated Jodie Mudd, Louisville, Ky., 2 up; Von Tacky defeated Clarence Rose, Goldsboro, N.C., 3 and 1; Lewis defeated Jay Sigel, Berwyn, Pa., 4 and 3

WOMEN'S AMATEUR

(Prairie Dunes, C.C., Hutchinson, Kan., Aug. 13–17, 1980)

Final—Juli Simpson Inkster, Santa Cruz, Calif., defeated Patti Rizzo, Hialeah, Fla., 2 up

Semifinals—Mrs. Inkster defeated Carol Semple, Sewickley, Pa., 2 and 1; Miss Rizzo defeated Mary McKenna, Ireland, 3 and 2

Quarterfinals—Miss Semple defeated Kathy Hanlon, Palos Verde Estates, Calif., 20 holes; Mrs. Inkster defeated Jennifer Davis, Northridge, Calif., 3 and 2; Miss McKenna defeated Kim Bauer, Conroe, Tex., 5 and 4; Miss Rizzo defeated Pam Miller, Libertyville, Ill., 5 and 4

SENIORS

American Senior G.A.—Edward Ervasti, Canada
P.G.A. Senior—Don January, Houston
U.S. Senior Open—Roberto de Vicenzo, Argentina
U.S. Senior G.A.—Bill Johnston, Scottsdale, Ariz.

1980 COLLEGIATE GOLF CHAMPIONS

N.C.A.A. Division I—Oklahoma State, 1,173
N.C.A.A. Division II—Columbus (Ga.) College, 1,178
N.C.A.A. Division III—California State–Stanislaus, 1,156
A.I.A.W.—Tulsa University, 1,188

OTHER 1980 WOMEN'S TOURNAMENTS

Broadmoor Invitational—Mary Beth Zimmerman, Miami–Dade Junior College
Curtis Cup—United States 13, Britain 5
North and South—Barbara Montgomery, Stockholm, Sweden
Public Links—Lori Castillo, Honolulu, defeated Pam Miller, Libertyville, Ill., 2 and 1
Southern—Martha Jones, Houston
Trans–National—Patrice Rizzo, Hialeah, Fla.
U.S.G.A. Girls' Junior—Laurie Rinker, Stuart, Fla.
Western Amateur—Kathy Baker, Tulsa, Okla.

U.S.G.A. SENIORS CHAMPIONSHIP—1980

(Mamaroneck, N.Y., June 26–29, 1980)
(For professionals and amateurs 55 and older)

Roberto de Vicenzo	74	73	68	70—285	$20,000
William Campbell[1]	76	68	76	69—289	—
Art Wall Jr.	74	71	72	73—290	10,000
Charles Sifford	72	77	71	75—295	6,000
Hampton Auld	75	73	74	74—296	4,750
Ed Tutwiler[1]	81	72	68	75—296	—
Mike Fetchick	72	77	78	69—296	4,750
Julius Boros	73	73	74	77—297	3,800
Ted Kroll	72	77	71	77—297	3,800
Gaylon Simon	76	74	76	72—298	3,200

1. Denotes amateur. Tournament held for first time.

SALARIES AND EARNINGS OF PROFESSIONAL ATHLETES

In the major sports the terms of contracts between the clubs and the players are not made public. The figures used in the following tables are those reported by news sources, based on general information brought about by the new era of free agents.

Baseball Earnings

Fielders

Player/Team	Amount
George Brett, Kansas City	$1,000,000
Dave Parker, Pittsburgh	1,000,000
Rod Carew, California	900,000
Pete Rose Philadelphia	810,000
Keith Hernandez, St. Louis	760,000
Jim Rice, Boston	700,000
Ken Griffey, Cincinnati	700,000
Garry Maddox, Philadelphia	675,000
Ted Simmons, St. Louis	650,000
Garry Templeton, St. Louis	600,000
Reggie Jackson, N.Y. Yankees	580,000
Don Baylor, California	580,000
Mike Schmidt, Philadelphia	560,000
Larry Hisle, Milwaukee	525,000
Jim Sundberg, Texas	500,000
Oscar Gamble, N.Y. Yankees	475,000
Joe Rudi, California	440,000
Lee Mazzilli, N.Y. Mets	400,000
Rennie Stennett, Pittsburgh	400,000
Johnny Bench, Cincinnati	400,000
Bob Horner, Atlanta	400,000
Carl Yastrzemski, Boston	400,000
Jeff Burroughs, Atlanta	350,000
Steve Garvey, Los Angeles	335,000
Dave Winfield, San Diego	320,000
Larry Bowa, Philadelphia	300,000

Pitchers

Player/Team	Amount
Nolan Ryan, Houston	$1,000,000
J.R. Richards, Houston	800,000
Phil Niekro, Atlanta	800,000
Bruce Sutter, Chicago Cubs	700,000
Vida Blue, San Francisco	700,000
Craig Swan, N.Y. Mets	600,000
Steve Carlton, Philadelphia	500,000
Sparky Lyle, Philadelphia	500,000
Kent Tekulve, Pittsburgh	500,000
Dave Goltz, Los Angeles	425,000

Basketball Salaries[1]

Player/Team	Amount
Kareem Abdul–Jabbar, Los Angeles	$1,000,000
Bill Walton, San Diego	1,000,000
David Thompson, Denver	800,000
Larry Bird, Boston	750,000
Marvin Webster, New York Knicks	600,000
Bob Lanier, Milwaukee	500,000
Julius Erving, Philadelphia	500,000
Bob McAdoo, Detroit	500,000
Maurice Lucas, New York Nets	450,000
George McGinnis, Indiana	450,000
George Gervin, San Antonio	380,000

1. Terms of contracts between clubs and players are not made public. These figures are estimates and are compiled from news sources, based on general information.

Football Earnings

O.J. Simpson, who retired after the 1979 season from the San Francisco 49ers after being traded by the Buffalo Bills, is reported to have received the top annual salary of $806,668. The N.F.L. Management Council has released the results of a survey of players' salaries for the 1979 season. The survey covered 1,517 players who were under contract to N.F.L. clubs at the end of the regular season. It concluded that the average salary was $68,893.

The Top Salaries in 1979

O.J. Simpson, San Francisco	$806,668
Walter Payton, Chicago	450,000
Bob Griese, Miami	400,025
Archie Manning, New Orleans	379,000
Dan Pastorini, Houston[1]	358,333
Chuck Foreman, Minnesota	300,000
John Riggins, Washington	300,000
Ken Stabler, Oakland[2]	282,000
Bert Jones, Baltimore	275,000
Franco Harris, Pittsburgh	275,000
Delvin Williams, Miami	275,000
Craig Morton, Denver	241,667
Richard Todd, New York Jets	235,000
Dan Fouts, San Diego	225,000
Earl Campbell, Houston	206,667
Tony Dorsett, Dallas	200,500

1. Traded to Oakland at end of season. 2. Traded to Houston at end of season.

Leading Salaries by Position

Quarterback—Bob Griese, Miami, $400,025

Running Back—O.J. Simpson[1]	806,668
Receiver—Russ Francis, New England	202,333
Offensive linemen—Art Shell and Gene Upshaw, Oakland,	150,000
Defensive lineman—Lee Roy Selmon, Tampa Bay	218,000
Linebacker—Jack Ham, Pittsburgh	230,000
Defensive back—Willie Buchanon, San Diego	175,000
Kicker—Russell Erxleben, New Orleans	110,714

1. Retired after 1979 season.

Career Earnings—P.G.A.

(Through 1979)

Player	Amount	Player	Amount
Jack Nicklaus	$3,408,827	Gene Littler	1,509,870
Lee Trevino	2,088,178	Miller Barber	1,457,096
Arnold Palmer	1,840,963	Bruce Crampton	1,374,294
Tom Weiskopf	1,741,155	Hubert Green	1,326,213
Billy Casper	1,683,618	Ray Floyd	1,239,635
Tom Watson	1,671,433	Johnny Miller	1,210,771
Gary Player	1,581,124	Al Geiberger	1,169,074
Hale Irwin	1,580,064		

P.G.A. Earnings—1979

Official money earned in Professional Golfers' Association major tournaments and such other events its Tournament Policy Board designates.

Player	Amount	Player	Amount
Tom Watson	$462,636	Lee Trevino	238,732
Larry Nelson	281,022	Ben Crenshaw	236,770
Lon Hinkle	247,693	Bill Rogers	230,500
Andy Bean	208,253	Jack Renner	182,808
Bruce Lietzke	198,439	Howard Twitty	179,619
Fuzzy Zoeller	196,951	David Graham	177,684
Lanny Wadkins	195,710	Tom Kite	166,878
Jerry Pate	193,707	Jerry McGee	166,735
Lou Graham	190,827	Hale Irwin	154,168
Hubert Green	183,111	Wayne Levi	141,612

L.P.G.A. Earnings—1979

Player	Amount	Player	Amount
Nancy Lopez–Melton	$197,488	Judy Rankin	108,511
		JoAnne Carner	98,218
Sandra Post	178,750	Beth Daniel	97,026
Amy Alcott	144,838	Hollis Stacy	81,265
Pat Bradley	132,428	Jo Ann Washam	77,303
Donna C. Young	125,493	Silvia Bertolaccini	76,244
Sally Little	119,500	Donna H. White	70,796
Jane Blalock	115,226	Jan Stephenson	69,519

Career Earnings—L.P.G.A.

(Through 1979)

Player	Amount	Player	Amount
Kathy Whitworth	$858,461	Sandra Haynie	498,387
Judy Rankin	761,130	Pat Bradley	452,617
Jane Blalock	708,936	Nancy Lopez–Melton	410,440
JoAnne Carner	649,980	Marlene Hagge	372,252
Donna C. Young	602,808	Mickey Wright	368,215
Sandra Palmer	596,021	Amy Alcott	366,435
Sandra Post	525,590	Jo Ann Prentice	358,299
Carol Mann	498,532		

SOCCER

WORLD CUP

1930	Uruguay
1934	Italy
1938	Italy
1942	No competition
1946	No competition
1950	Uruguay
1954	West Germany
1958	Brazil
1962	Brazil
1966	England
1970	Brazil
1974	West Germany
1978	Argentina

MAJOR INDOOR SOCCER LEAGUE

Atlantic Division

	W	L	Pct	GB
New York	27	5	.844	—
Pittsburgh	18	14	.563	9
Buffalo	17	15	.531	10
Philadelphia	17	15	.531	10
Hartford	6	26	.188	21

Central Division

	W	L	Pct	GB
Houston	20	12	.625	—
Whichita	16	16	.500	4
Detroit	15	17	.469	5
Cleveland	12	20	.375	8
St. Louis	12	20	.375	8

CHAMPIONSHIP PLAYOFFS

Atlantic Division Semifinals

New York 5, Pittsburgh 3
New York 11, Pittsburgh 3 (New York won series, 2–0)

Central Division Semifinals

Houston 5, Wichita 4 (overtime)
Houston 4, Wichita 3 (Houston won series, 2–0)

Final

New York 7, Houston 4

NORTH AMERICAN SOCCER LEAGUE

Final Standing—1980

NATIONAL CONFERENCE

Eastern Division

	W	L	GF	GA	BP[1]	Pts
Cosmos	24	8	87	41	68	213
Washington Diplomats	17	15	72	61	57	159
Toronto Metros	14	18	49	64	44	128
Rochester Lancers	12	20	42	67	37	109

Central Division

	W	L	GF	GA	BP[1]	Pts
Dallas Tornado	18	14	57	58	49	157
Minnesota Kicks	16	16	66	56	51	147
Tulsa Roughnecks	15	17	56	62	49	139
Atlanta Chiefs	7	25	34	84	32	74

Western Division

	W	L	GF	GA	BP[1]	Pts
Seattle Sounders	25	7	74	31	57	207
Los Angeles Aztecs	20	12	61	52	54	174
Vancouver Whitecaps	16	16	52	47	43	139
Portland Timbers	15	17	50	53	43	133

PLAYOFFS

Quarterfinals

Seattle defeated Vancouver, 2 games to 0
Los Angeles defeated Washington, 2 games to 1

Cosmos defeated Tulsa, 2 games to 0
Dallas defeated Minnesota, 2 games to 0

Semifinals

Cosmos defeated Dallas, 2 games to 1
Los Angeles defeated Seattle, 2 games to 1

Final

Cosmos defeated Los Angeles, 2 games to 0

AMERICAN CONFERENCE
Eastern Division

	W	L	GF	GA	BP[1]	Pts
Tampa Bay Rowdies	19	13	61	50	54	168
Fort Lauderdale Strikers	18	14	61	55	55	163
New England Tea Men	18	14	54	56	46	154
Philadelphia Fury	10	22	42	68	38	98
Central Division						
Chicago Sting	21	11	80	50	61	187
Houston Hurricane	14	18	56	69	46	130
Detroit Express	14	18	51	52	45	129
Memphis Rogues	14	18	49	57	42	126
Western Division						
Edmonton Drillers	17	15	58	51	47	149
California Surf	15	17	61	67	54	144
San Diego Sockers	16	16	53	51	44	140
San Jose Earthquake	9	23	45	68	41	95

1. Bonus points—awarded for each goal to a maximum of three per team per game; teams receive 6 points for each victory.

PLAYOFFS
Quarterfinals

San Diego defeated Chicago, 2 games to 1
Tampa Bay defeated New England, 2 games to 0
Edmonton defeated Houston, 2 games to 1
Fort Lauderdale defeated California, 2 games to 1

Semifinals

Fort Lauderdale defeated Edmonton, 2 games to 1
San Diego defeated Tampa Bay, 2 games to 1

Final

Fort Lauderdale defeated San Diego, 2 games to 1

CHAMPIONSHIP BOWL

(R.F.K. Stadium, Washington, D.C., Sept. 21, 1980)
Cosmos 3, Fort Lauderdale 0
(Scoring: Chinaglia 2, Romero)

LEADING N.A.S.L. SCORERS—1980

	GP	G	A	Pts
Giorgio Chinaglia, Cosmos	32	32	13	77
Karl–Heinz Granitza, Chicago	31	19	26	64
Roger Davies, Seattle	29	24	11	61
Luis Fernando, Los Angeles	28	28	4	60
Alan Green, Washington	31	25	9	59
Lauri Abrams, California	28	17	15	49
Julio Romero, Cosmos	32	14	19	47
Arno Steffenhagen, Chicago	28	15	15	45
Ace Ntsoelengoe, Minnesota	32	13	17	43
Edi Kirschner, Edmonton	31	15	12	42
Teofilo Cubillas, Fort Lauderdale	27	14	14	42

1980 N.A.S.L. AWARDS

Most valuable player—Roger Davies, Seattle
Offensive player—Johann Cruyff, Los Angeles
Defensive player—Carlos Alberto, Cosmos
Rookie—Jeff Durgan, Cosmos
Top scorer—Giorgio Chinaglia, Cosmos
Top goalkeeper—Jack Brand, Seattle
Top North American player—Jack Brand, Seattle
Coach of the year—Alan Hinton, Seattle

N.C.A.A.

Division I—Southern Illinois–Edwardsville defeated Clemson, 3–2, in final
Division II—Alabama A & M defeated Eastern Illinois, 2–0, in final
Division III—Babson defeated Glassboro State, 2–1, in final

FENCING

WORLD CHAMPIONSHIPS

(Melbourne, Australia, 1979)

Men's foil—Aleksandr Romankov, U.S.S.R.
Men's foil, team—U.S.S.R.
Men's saber—Vladimir Lazlymov, U.S.S.R.
Men's saber, team—U.S.S.R.
Men's epée—Phillippe Riboud, France
Men's epée, team—U.S.S.R.
Women's foil—Cornelia Hanisch, West Germany
Women's foil, team—U.S.S.R.

INTERCOLLEGIATE CHAMPIONSHIPS
National Collegiate Athletic Association

(University Park, Pa., March 13–15, 1980)

Foil—Ernie Simon, Wayne State
Epee—Gil Pezza, Wayne State
Saber—Paul Friedberg, Pennsylvania
Team—Wayne State

National Intercollegiate Women's Fencing Association

Individual—Gina Farkashazy, Wayne State University
Team—Penn State (Judy Smith, Cathy McClellan, Nancy Anderson, Phyllis Wert)

AMATEUR FENCERS LEAGUE OF AMERICA—U.S. CHAMPIONSHIPS

(New York City, June 21–29, 1980)

Men's foil—Greg Massialas, Salle D'Asaro, San Jose, Calif.
Women's foil—Nikki Franke, Salle Caiszar, Philadelphia
Men's epee—Leonid Dervbinsky, New York Athletic Club
Women's epee—Jane Littman, Palmetto Fencers Club, Columbia, S.C.
Men's saber—Peter Westbrook, Fencers Club of New York
Men's foil team—Fencers Club of New York (John Nonna, Mike McCahey, Jack Tichackek, Neil Cohen)
Men's epee team—United States Modern Penthathlon, Fort Sam Houston, Tex. (Robert Nieman, John Moreau, Greg Losey, John Fitzgerald)

Men's saber team—New York Athletic Club (Phil Reilly, Stan Lekach, Tom Losonczy, Edgar House)

Under 19

Men's foil—Demetrios Valsamis, Fencers Club of New York

Women's foil—Jana Angelakis, Tanner City Fencers Club, Peabody, Mass.

Men's epee—Adam Meyers, Philadelphia

Men's saber—Rick Blum, University of Pennsylvania

NATIONAL SPORTS FESTIVAL

(Colorado Springs, Colo., July 27-Aug. 1, 1979)

ARCHERY

Men—Rodney Baston, Bossier City, La.
Women—Lynette Johnson, Cypress, Calif.

SWIMMING

Men's Events

100–m freestyle—Art Griffith, Arvada, Colo.	0:52.22
200–m freestyle—Chuck Sharpe, Omaha, Neb.	1:54.92
400–m freestyle—John Spald, Ann Arbor, Mich.	4:04.80
1,500–m freestyle—Brian Roney, Woodland Hills, Calif.	16:27.93
100–m backstroke—Mark Gordin, Cerritos, Calif.	1:00.44
200–m backstroke—Paul Sigfusson, Bloomington, Ind.	2:12.33
100–m breaststroke—Bob McAdam, Decatur, Ill.	1:06.88
200–m breaststroke—John Moffet, Newport Beach, Calif.	2:29.11
100–m butterfly—Jim Halliburton, Bloomington, Ind.	0:55.55
200–m butterfly—David Santos, Walnut Creek, Calif.	2:06.84
200–m ind. medley—Roger VanJouanne, Carbondale, Ill.	2:09.47
400–m ind. medley—David Santos	4:40.56
400–m relay—Midwest	3:56.38
400–m freestyle relay—Midwest	3:29.07
800–m freestyle relay—Midwest	7:46.19

Women's Events

100–m freestyle—Sippy Woodhead, Riverside, Calif.	0:57.36
200–m freestyle—Bonnie Glasgow, Glen Arm, Md.	2:06.21
400–m freestyle—Sippy Woodhead	4:21.89
800–m freestyle—Ann Stier, Alameda, Calif.	9:09.64
100–m backstroke—Diane Johanningman, Houston, Tex.	1:06.16
200–m backstroke—Kaili Chun, Honolulu	2:22.61
100–m breaststroke—Terri Baxter, Palo Alto, Calif.	1:15.08
200–m breaststroke—Jeanne Childs, Englewood, Colo.	2:45.34
100–m butterfly—Dian Johanningman	1:03.22
200–m butterfly—Sippy Woodhead	2:17.42
200–m ind. medley—Bonnie Glasgow	2:25.42
400–m ind. medley—Sippy Woodhead	5:07.33
400–m medley relay—West	4:24.94
400–m freestyle relay—Midwest	3:56
800–m freestyle relay—West	8:35.51
Team—Midwest	370.5 pts

SYNCHRONIZED SWIMMING

Solo—Brenda Florio, Hamden, Conn.
Figures—Candy Costio, Seattle
Duet—Brenda Florio and Janine Sacramone, Hamden Conn.
Team—West

TRACK

Men's Events

100 m—Harvey Glance, Auburn, Ala.	0:10.41
200 m—James Sanford, Los Angeles	0:20.64
400 m—Tony Darden, Philadelphia	0:45.02
800 m—Evans White, Prairie View, Tex.	1:48.88
1,500 m—Tom Duits, Kalamazoo, Mich.	3:45.44
3,000–m steeplechase—Randy Jackson, Madison, Wis.	9:01.22
5,000 m—Herb Lindsay, Lansing, Mich.	14:25.30
10,000 m—Frank Shorter, Boulder, Colo.	29:29.9
Marathon—Barney Klecker, Chaska, Minn.	2:28:36.5
20,000–m walk—Marco Evoniuk, Longmont, Colo.	1:35:10
50,000–m walk—Dan O'Connor, Wantaugh, N.Y.	4:34:52
110–m hurdles—Charles Foster, Durham, N.C.	0:13.79
400–m hurdles—James Walker, Auburn, Ala.	0:49.1
400–m relay—South	0:38.30
1,600–m relay—South	3:03.72
Hammer throw—Emmitt Berry, El Paso, Tex.	213 ft 4 in.
Javelin—Scott Sorchik, Sussex, N.J.	266 ft 3 in.
Long jump—Larry Myricks, Clinton, Miss.	27 ft 1½ in.
Pole vault—Jeff Buckingham, Gardner, Kan.	17 ft 4¾ in.
Discus—John Powell, San Jose, Calif.	214 ft
High jump—Nat Page, Columbia, Mo.	7 ft 5½ in.
Shot-put—Ian Pyka, College Park, Md.	65 ft 10¼ in.
Triple jump—Willie Banks, Los Angeles	56 ft 10½ in.
Decathlon—Wes Herbst, Houston	7,635 pts
Team—West	235 pts

Women's Events

100 m—Brenda Morehead, Toledo, Ohio	0:11.40
200 m—Liz Young, Washington, D.C.	0:23.6
400 m—Sheri Howard, Los Angeles	0:52.09
800 m—Joetta Clark, Maplewood, N.J.	2:05.43
1,500 m—Darlene Beckford, West Orange, N.J.	4:27.34
3,000 m—Cindy Bremser, Madison, Wis.	9:41.3
100–m hurdles—Stephanie Hightower, Columbus, Ohio	0:13.43
High jump—Paula Girven, Dale City, Va.	6 ft 1 in.
Javelin—Lynn Cannon, Chico, Calif.	182 ft 1 in.
Shot-put—Jill Stenwall, Winside, Neb.	51 ft 1½ in.
Discus—Julie Hansen, Seattle	158 ft 7 in.
Long jump—Jodi Anderson, Van Nuys, Calif.	22 ft 7½ in.
Pentathlon—Linda Waltman, College Staton, Tex.	3,865 pts
400–m relay—South	0:43.80
1,600–m relay—West	3:30.79
Team—West	157 pts
Combined team—West	392 pts

EQUESTRIAN EVENTS—1980

World Cup jumping—Conrad Homfeld, Pinehurst, N.C.
International 3–day festival—Nils Haagensen, Denmark

BASEBALL

The popular tradition that baseball was invented by Abner Doubleday at Cooperstown, N.Y., in 1839 has been enshrined in the Hall of Fame and National Museum of Baseball erected in that town, but research has proved that a game called "Base Ball" was played in this country and England before 1839. The first team baseball as we know it was played at the Elysian Fields, Hoboken, N.J., on June 19, 1846, between the Knickerbockers and the New York Nine. The next fifty years saw a gradual growth of baseball and an improvement of equipment and playing skill.

Historians have it that the first pitcher to throw a curve was William A. (Candy) Cummings in 1867. The Cincinnati Red Stockings were the first all-professional team, and in 1869 they played 64 games without a loss. The standard ball of the same size and weight, still the rule, was adopted in 1872. The first catcher's mask was worn in 1875. The National League was organized in 1876. The first chest protector was worn in 1885. The three-strike rule was put on the books in 1887, and the four-ball ticket to first base was instituted in 1889. The pitching distance was lengthened to 60 feet 6 inches in 1893, and the rules have been modified only slightly since that time.

The American League, under the vigorous leadership of B. B. Johnson, became a major league in 1901. Judge Kenesaw Mountain Landis, by action of the two major leagues, became Commissioner of Baseball in 1921, and upon his death (1944), Albert B. Chandler, former United States Senator from Kentucky, was elected to that office (1945). Chandler failed to obtain a new contract and was succeeded by Ford C. Frick (1951), the National League president. Frick retired after the 1965 season, and William D. Eckert, a retired Air Force lieutenant general, was named to succeed him. Eckert resigned under pressure in December, 1968. Bowie Kuhn, a New York attorney, became interim commissioner for one year in February. His appointment was made permanent with two seven-year contracts until August 1983.

PROFESSIONAL BASEBALL GOVERNMENT

MAJOR LEAGUES

Bowie Kuhn, *Commissioner*
Alexander Hadden, *Secretary-Treasurer*
Joseph L. Reichler, Monte Irvin, *Special Assistants to Commissioner*
George E. Pfister, *Assistant to Administrative Officer*
Bob Wirz, *Director of Information*
75 Rockefeller Plaza, New York, N.Y. 10019

NATIONAL LEAGUE

Charles S. Feeney, *President*
1 Rockefeller Plaza
New York, N.Y. 10020
John J. McHale, *Vice President*
Blake Cullen, *Public Relations Director*

AMERICAN LEAGUE

Leland S. MacPhail, *President*
280 Park Avenue
New York, N.Y. 10017
Robert Holbrook, *Secretary*
Robert O. Fishel, *Assistant to President*
Phyllis Merhige, *Public Relations Assistant*

NATIONAL ASSOCIATION OF PROFESSIONAL BASEBALL LEAGUES (MINOR LEAGUES)

John H. Johnson, *President-Treasurer*
201 Bayshore Drive, P. O. Box A, St. Petersburg, Fla. 33731

RECORD OF WORLD SERIES GAMES

Source: The Book of Baseball Records, published by Seymour Siwoff, New York City.

Figures in parentheses for winning pitchers (WP) and losing pitchers (LP) indicate the game number in the series

1903—Boston A.L. 5 (Jimmy Collins); Pittsburgh N.L. 3 (Fred Clarke). WP—Bos.: Dinneen (2, 6, 8), Young (5, 7); Pitts.: Phillippe (1, 3, 4). LP—Bos.: Young (1), Hughes (3), Dinneen (4); Pitts.: Leever (2, 6), Kennedy (5), Phillippe (7, 8).

1904—No series.

1905—New York N.L. 4 (John J. McGraw); Philadelphia A.L. 1 (Connie Mack). WP—N.Y.: Mathewson (1, 3, 5); McGinnity (4); Phila.: Bender (2). LP—N.Y.: McGinnity (2); Phila.: Plank (1, 4), Coakley (3), Bender (5).

1906—Chicago A.L. 4 (Fielder Jones); Chicago N.L. 2 (Frank Chance). WP—Chi.: A.L.: Altrock (1), Walsh (3, 5), White (6); Chi.: N.L.: Reulbach (2), Brown (4). LP—Chi. A.L.: White (2), Altrock (4); Chi.: N.L.: Brown (1, 6), Pfeister (3, 5).

1907—Chicago N.L. 4 (Frank Chance); Detroit A.L. 0 (Hugh Jennings). First game tied 3–3, 12 innings. WP—Pfeister (2), Reulbach (3), Overall (4), Brown (5). LP—Mullin (2, 5), Siever (3), Donovan (4).

1908—Chicago N.L. 4 (Frank Chance); Detroit A.L. 1 (Hugh Jennings). WP—Chi.: Brown (1, 4), Overall (2, 5); Det.: Mullin (3). LP—Chi.: Pfeister (3); Det.: Summers (1, 4), Donovan (2, 5).

1909—Pittsburgh N.L. 4 (Fred Clarke); Detroit A.L. 3 (Hugh Jennings). WP—Pitts.: Adams (1, 5, 7), Maddox (3); Det.: Donovan (2), Mullin (4, 6). LP—Pitts.: Camnitz (2), Leifield (4), Willis (6); Det.: Mullin (1), Summers (3, 5), Donovan (7).

1910—Philadelphia A.L. 4 (Connie Mack); Chicago N.L. 1 (Frank Chance). WP—Phila.: Bender (1), Coombs (2, 3, 5); Chi.: Brown (4). LP—Phila.: Bender (4); Chi.: Overall (1), Brown (2, 5), McIntyre (3).

1911—Philadelphia A.L. 4 (Connie Mack); New York N.L. 2 (John J. McGraw). WP—Phila.: Plank (2), Coombs (3), Bender (4, 6); N.Y.: Mathewson (1), Crandall (5). LP—Phila.: Bender (1), Plank (5); N.Y.: Marquard (2), Mathewson (3, 4), Ames (6).

1912—Boston A.L. 4 (J. Garland Stahl); New York N.L. 3 (John J. McGraw). Second game tied, 6–6, 11 innings. WP—Bos.: Wood (1, 4, 8), Bedient (5); N.Y.: Marquard (3, 6), Tesreau (7). LP—Bos.: O'Brien (3, 6), Wood (7); N.Y.: Tesreau (1, 4), Mathewson (5, 8).

1913—Philadelphia A.L. 4 (Connie Mack); New York N.L. 1 (John J. McGraw). WP—Phila.: Bender (1, 4), Bush (3), Plank (5); N.Y.: Mathewson (2); LP—Phila.: Plank (2); N.Y.: Marquard (1), Tesreau (3), Demaree (4), Mathewson (5).

1914—Boston N.L. 4 (George Stallings); Philadelphia A.L. 0 (Connie Mack). WP—Rudolph (1, 4), James (2, 3). LP—Bender (1), Plank (2), Bush (3), Shawkey (4).

1915—Boston A.L. 4 (Bill Carrigan); Philadelphia N.L. 1 (Pat Moran). WP—Bos.: Foster (2, 5), Leonard (3), Shore (4); Phila.: Alexander (1). LP—Bos.: Shore (1); Phila.: Mayer (2), Alexander (3), Chalmers (4), Rixey (5).

1916—Boston A.L. 4 (Bill Carrigan); Brooklyn N.L. 1 (Wilbert Robinson). WP—Bos.: Shore (1, 5), Ruth (2), Leonard (4); Bklyn.: Coombs (3). LP—Bos.: Mays (3); Bklyn.: Marquard (1, 4), Smith (2), Pfeffer (5).

1917—Chicago A.L. 4 (Clarence Rowland); New York N.L. 2 (John J. McGraw). WP—Chi.: Cicotte (1), Faber (2, 5, 6); N.Y.: Benton (3), Schupp (4). LP—Chi.: Cicotte (3), Faber (4); N.Y.: Sallee (1, 5), Anderson (2), Benton (6).

1918—Boston A.L. 4 (Ed Barrow); Chicago N.L. 2 (Fred Mitchell). WP—Bos.: Ruth (1, 4), Mays (3, 6); Chi.: Tyler (2), Vaughn (5). LP—Bos.: Bush (2), Jones (5); Chi.: Vaughn (1, 3), Douglas (4), Tyler (6).

1919—Cincinnati N.L. 5 (Pat Moran); Chicago A.L. 3 (William Gleason). WP—Cin.: Ruether (1), Sallee (2), Ring (4), Eller (5, 8); Chi.: Kerr (3, 6), Cicotte (7). LP—Cin.: Fisher (3), Ring (6), Sallee (7); Chi.: Cicotte (1, 4), Williams (2, 5, 8).

1920—Cleveland A.L. 5 (Tris Speaker); Brooklyn N.L. 2 (Wilbert Robinson). WP—Cleve.: Coveleski (1, 4, 7), Bagby (5), Mails (6); Bklyn.: Grimes (2), Smith (3). LP—Cleve.: Bagby (2), Caldwell (3). Bklyn.: Marquard (1), Cadore (4), Grimes (5, 7), Smith (6).

1921—New York N.L. 5 (John J. McGraw); New York A.L. 3 (Miller Huggins). WP—N.Y. N.L.: Barnes (3, 6), Douglas (4, 7), Nehf (8); N.Y. A.L.: Mays (1), Hoyt (2, 5). LP—N.Y. N.L.: Nehf (2, 5), Douglas (1). N.Y. A.L.: Quinn (3), Mays (4, 7), Shawkey (6), Hoyt (8).

1922—New York N.L. 4 (John J. McGraw); New York A.L. 0 (Miller Huggins). Second game tied 3–3, 10 innings. WP—Ryan (1), Scott (3), McQuillan (4), Nehf (5); LP—Bush (1, 5), Hoyt (3), Mays (4).

1923—New York A.L. 4 (Miller Huggins); New York N.L. 2 (John J. McGraw). WP—N.Y. A.L.: Pennock (2, 6), Shawkey (4), Bush (5); N.Y. N.L.:Ryan (1), Nehf (3). LP—N.Y. A.L.: Bush (1), Jones (3); N.Y. N.L.: McQuillan (2), Scott (4), Bentley (5), Nehf (6).

1924—Washington A.L. 4 (Bucky Harris); New York N.L. 3 (John J. McGraw). WP—Wash.: Zachary (2, 6), Mogridge (4), Johnson (9); N.Y.: Nehf (1), McQuillan (3), Bentley (5). LP—Wash.: Johnson (1, 5), Marberry (3); N.Y.: Bentley (2, 7), Barnes (4), Nehf (6).

1925—Pittsburgh N.L. 4 (Bill McKechnie); Washington A.L. 3 (Bucky Harris). WP—Pitts.: Aldridge (2, 5), Kremer (6, 7); Wash.: Johnson (1, 4), Ferguson (3). LP—Pitts.: Meadows (1), Kremer (3), Yde (4); Wash.: Coveleski (2, 5), Ferguson (6), Johnson (7).

1926—St. Louis N.L. 4 (Rogers Hornsby); New York A.L. 3 (Miller Huggins). WP—St. L.: Alexander (2, 6), Haines (3, 7); N.Y.: Pennock (1, 5), Hoyt (4). LP—St. L.: Sherdel (1, 5), Reinhart (4); N.Y.: Shocker (2), Ruether (3), Shawkey (6), Hoyt (7).

1927—New York A.L. 4 (Miller Huggins); Pittsburgh N.L. 0 (Donie Bush). WP—Hoyt (1), Pipgras (2), Pennock (3), Moore (4). LP—Kremer (1), Aldridge (2), Meadows (3), Miljus (4).

1928—New York A.L. 4 (Miller Huggins); St. Louis N.L. 0 (Bill McKechnie). WP—Hoyt (1, 4), Pipgras (2), Zachary (3). LP—Sherdel (1, 4), Alexander (2), Haines (3).

1929—Philadelphia A.L. 4 (Connie Mack); Chicago N.L. 1 (Joe McCarthy). WP—Phila.: Ehmke (1), Earnshaw (2), Rommel (4), Walberg (5); Chi.: Bush (3). LP—Phila.: Earnshaw (3); Chi.: Root (1), Malone (2, 5), Blake (4).

1930—Philadelphia A.L. 4 (Connie Mack); St. Louis N.L. 2 (Gabby Street). WP—Phila.: Grove (1, 5), Earnshaw (2, 6); St. L.: Hallahan (3), Haines (4). LP—Phila.: Walberg (3), Grove (4); St. L.: Grimes (1, 5), Rhem (2), Hallahan (6).

1931—St. Louis N.L. 4 (Gabby Street); Philadelphia A.L. 3 (Connie Mack). WP—St. L.: Hallahan (2, 5), Grimes (3, 7); Phila.: Grove (1, 6), Earnshaw (4). LP—St. L.: Derringer (1, 6), Johnson (4); Phila.: Earnshaw (2, 7), Grove (3), Hoyt (5).

1932—New York A.L. (Joe McCarthy); Chicago N.L. 0 (Charles Grimm). WP—Ruffing (1), Gomez (2), Pipgras (3), Moore (4). LP—Bush (1), Warneke (2), Root (3), May (4).

1933—New York N.L. 4 (Bill Terry); Washington A.L. 1 (Joe Cronin.). WP—N.Y.: Hubbell (1, 4), Schumacher (2), Luque (5); Wash.: Whitehill (3). LP—N.Y.: Fitzsimmons (3); Wash.: Stewart (1), Crowder (2), Weaver (4), Russell (5).

1934—St. Louis N.L. 4 (Frank Frisch); Detroit A.L. 3 (Mickey Cochrane). WP—St. L.: J. Dean (1, 7), P. Dean (3, 6); Det.: Rowe (2), Auker (4), Bridges (5). LP—St. L.: W. Walker (2, 4), J. Dean (5); Det.: Crowder (1), Bridges (3), Rowe (6), Auker (7).

1935—Detroit A.L. 4 (Mickey Cochrane); Chicago N.L. 2 (Charles Grimm). WP—Det.: Bridges (2, 6), Rowe (3), Crowder (4); Chi.: Warneke (1, 5); LP—Det.: Rowe (1, 5); Chi.: Root (2), French (3, 6), Carleton (4).

1936—New York A.L. 4 (Joe McCarthy); New York N.L. 2 (Bill Terry). WP—N.Y. A.L.: Gomez (2, 6), Hadley (3), Pearson (4); N.Y. N.L.: Hubbell (1), Schumacher (5); LP—N.Y. A.L.: Ruffing (1), Malone (5); N.Y. N.L.: Schumacher (2), Fitzsimmons (3, 6), Hubbell (4).

1937—New York A.L. 4 (Joe McCarthy); New York N.L. 1 (Bill Terry). WP—N.Y. A.L.: Gomez (1, 5), Ruffing (2), Pearson (3); N.Y. N.L.: Hubbell (4). LP—N.Y. A.L.: Hadley (4); N.Y. N.L.: Hubbell (1), Melton (2, 5), Schumacher (3).

1938—New York A.L. 4 (Joe McCarthy); Chicago N.L. 0 (Gabby Hartnett). WP—Ruffing (1, 4), Gomez (2), Pearson (3). LP—Lee (1, 4), Dean (2), Bryant (3).

1939—New York A.L. 4 (Joe McCarthy); Cincinnati N.L. 0 (Bill McKechnie). WP—Ruffing (1), Pearson (2), Hadley (3), Murphy (4). LP—Derringer (1), Walters (2, 4), Thompson (3).

1940—Cincinnati N.L. 4 (Bill McKechnie); Detroit A.L. 3 (Del Baker). WP—Cin.: Walters (2, 6), Derringer (4, 7); Det.: Newsom (1, 5), Bridges (3). LP—Cin.: Derringer (1), Turner (3), Thompson (5); Det.: Rowe (2, 6), Trout (4), Newsom (7).

1941—New York A.L. 4 (Joe McCarthy); Brooklyn N.L. 1 (Leo Durocher). WP—N.Y.: Ruffing (1), Russo (3), Murphy (4), Bonham (5); Bklyn: Wyatt (2). LP—N.Y.: Chandler (2); Bklyn: Davis (1), Casey (3, 4), Wyatt (5).

1942—St. Louis N.L. 4 (Billy Southworth); New York A.L. 1 (Joe McCarthy). WP—St. L.: Beazley (2, 5), White (3), Lanier (4); N.Y.: Ruffing (1). LP—St. L.: Cooper (1); N.Y.: Bonham (2), Chandler (3), Donald (4), Ruffing (5).

1943—New York A.L. 4 (Joe McCarthy); St. Louis N.L. 1 (Billy Southworth). WP—N.Y.: Chandler (1, 5), Borowy (3), Russo (4); St. L.: Cooper (2). LP—N.Y.: Bonham (2); St. L.: Lanier (1), Brazle (3), Brecheen (4), Cooper (5).

1944—St. Louis N.L. 4 (Billy Southworth); St. Louis A.L. 2 (Luke Sewell). WP—St. L. N.L.: Donnelly (2), Brecheen (4), Cooper (5), Lanier (6); St. L. A.L.: Galehouse (1), Kramer (3). LP—St. L. N.L.: Cooper (1), Wilks (3); St. L. A.L.: Muncrief (2), Jakucki (4), Galehouse (5), Potter (6).

1945—Detroit A.L. 4 (Steve O'Neill); Chicago N.L. 3 (Charles Grimm). WP—Det.: Trucks (2), Trout (4), Newhouser (5, 7); Chi.: Borowy (1, 6), Passeau (3). LP—Det.: Newhouser (1), Overmire (3), Trout (6); Chi.: Wyse (2), Prim (4), Borowy (5, 7).

1946—St. Louis N.L. 4 (Eddie Dyer); Boston A.L. 3 (Joe Cronin). WP—St. L.: Brecheen (2, 6, 7), Munger (4); Bos.: Johnson (1), Ferriss (3), Dobson (5). LP—St. L.: Pollet (1), Dickson (3), Brazle (5); Bos.: Harris (2, 6), Hughson (4), Klinger (7).

1947—New York A.L. 4 (Bucky Harris); Brooklyn N.L. 3 (Burt Shotton). WP—N.Y.: Shea (1, 5), Reynolds (2), Page (7); Bklyn.: Casey (3, 4), Branca (6). LP—N.Y.: Newsom (3), Bevens (4), Page (6); Bklyn.: Branca (1), Lombardi (2), Barney (5), Gregg (7).

1948—Cleveland A.L. 4 (Lou Boudreau); Boston N.L. 2 (Billy Southworth). WP—Cleve.: Lemon (2, 6), Bearden (3), Gromek (4); Bos.: Sain (1), Spahn (5). LP—Cleve.: Feller (1, 5); Bos.: Spahn (2), Bickford (3), Sain (4), Voiselle (6).

1949—New York A.L. 4 (Casey Stengel); Brooklyn N.L. 1 (Burt Shotton). WP—N.Y.: Reynolds (1), Page (3), Lopat (4), Raschi (5); Bklyn.: Roe (2). LP—N.Y.: Raschi (2); Bklyn.: Newcombe (1, 4), Branca (3), Barney (5).

1950—New York A.L. 4 (Casey Stengel); Philadelphia N.L. 0 (Eddie Sawyer). WP—Raschi (1), Reynolds (2), Ferrick (3), Ford (4). LP—Konstanty (1), Roberts (2), Meyer (3), Miller (4).

1951—New York A.L. 4 (Casey Stengel); New York N.L. 2 (Leo Durocher). WP—N.Y. A.L.: Lopat (2, 5), Reynolds (4), Raschi (6); N.Y. N.L.: Koslo (1), Hearn (3). LP—N.Y. A.L.: Reynolds (1), Raschi (3); N.Y. N.L.: Jansen (2, 5), Maglie (4), Koslo (6).

1952—New York A.L. 4 (Casey Stengel); Brooklyn N.L. 3 (Chuck Dressen). WP—N.Y.: Raschi (2, 6), Reynolds (4, 7); Bklyn.: Black (1), Roe (3), Erskine (5). LP—N.Y.: Reynolds (1), Lopat (3), Sain (5); Bklyn.: Erskine (2), Black (4, 7), Loes (6).

1953—New York A.L. 4 (Casey Stengel); Brooklyn N.L. 2 (Chuck Dressen). WP—N.Y.: Sain (1), Lopat (2), McDonald (5), Reynolds (6); Bklyn.: Erskine (3), Loes (4). LP—N.Y.: Raschi (3), Ford (4); Bklyn.: Labine (1, 6), Roe (2), Podres (5)

1954—New York N.L. 4 (Leo Durocher); Cleveland A.L. 0 (Al Lopez). WP—Grissom (1), Antonelli (2), Gomez (3), Liddle (4). LP—Lemon (1, 4), Wynn (2), Garcia (3).

1955—Brooklyn N.L. 4 (Walter Alston); New York A.L. 3 (Casey Stengel). WP—Bklyn.: Podres (3, 7), Labine (4), Craig (5); N.Y.: Ford (1, 6), Byrne (2). LP—Bklyn.: Newcombe (1), Loes (2), Spooner (6); N.Y.: Turley (3), Larsen (4), Grim (5), Byrne (7).

1956—New York A.L. 4 (Casey Stengel); Brooklyn N.L. 3 (Walter Alston). WP—N.Y.: Ford (3), Sturdivant (4), Larsen (5), Kucks (7); Bklyn.: Maglie (1), Bessent (2), Labine (6). LP—N.Y.: Ford (1), Morgan (2), Turley (6); Bklyn.: Craig (3), Erskine (4), Maglie (5), Newcombe (7).

1957—Milwaukee N.L. 4 (Fred Haney); New York A.L. 3 (Casey Stengel). WP—Mil.: Burdette (2, 5, 7), Spahn (4); N.Y.: Ford (1), Larsen (3), Turley (6). LP—Mil.: Spahn (1), Buhl (3), Johnson (6); N.Y.: Shantz (2), Grim (4), Ford (5), Larsen (7).

1958—New York A.L. 4 (Casey Stengel); Milwaukee N.L. 3 (Fred Haney). WP—N.Y.: Larsen (3), Turley (5, 7), Duren (6); Mil.: Spahn (1, 4), Burdette (2). LP—N.Y.: Duren (1), Turley (2), Ford (4); Mil.: Rush (3), Burdette (5, 7), Spahn (6).

1959—Los Angeles N.L. 4 (Walter Alston); Chicago A.L. 2 (Al Lopez). WP—L.A.: Podres (2), Drysdale (3), Sherry (4, 6); Chi.: Wynn (1), Shaw (5). LP—L.A.: Craig (1), Koufax (5); Chi.: Shaw (2), Donovan (3), Staley (4), Wynn (6).

1960—Pittsburgh N.L. 4 (Danny Murtaugh); New York A.L. 3 (Casey Stengel). WP—Pitts.: Law (1, 4), Haddix (5, 7); N.Y.: Turley (2), Ford (3, 6). LP—Pitts.: Friend (2, 6), Mizell (3); N.Y.: Ditmar (1, 5), Terry (4, 7).

1961—New York A.L. 4 (Ralph Houk); Cincinnati N.L. 1 (Fred Hutchinson). WP—N.Y.: Ford (1, 4), Arroyo (3), Daley (5); Cin.: Jay (2). LP—N.Y.: Terry (2); Cin.: O'Toole (1, 4), Purkey (3), Jay (5).

1962—New York A.L. 4 (Ralph Houk); San Francisco N.L. 3 (Al Dark). WP—N.Y.: Ford (1), Stafford (3), Terry (5, 7); S.F.: Sanford (2), Larsen (4), Pierce (6). LP—N.Y.: Terry (2), Coates (4), Ford (6); S.F.: O'Dell (1), Pierce (3), Sanford (5, 7).

1963—Los Angeles N.L. 4 (Walter Alston); New York A.L. 0 (Ralph Houk). WP—Koufax (1, 4), Podres (2), Drysdale (3). LP—Ford (1, 4), Downing (2), Bouton (3).

1964—St. Louis N.L. 4 (Johnny Keane); New York A.L. 3 (Yogi Berra). WP—St. L.: Sadecki (1), Craig (4), Gibson (5, 7); N.Y.: Stottlemyre (2), Bouton (3, 6). LP—St. L.: Gibson (2), Schultz (3), Simmons (6); N.Y.: Ford (1), Downing (4), Mikkelsen (5), Stottlemyre (7).

1965—Los Angeles N.L. 4 (Walter Alston); Minnesota A.L. 3 (Sam Mele). WP—L.A.: Osteen (3), Drysdale (4), Koufax (5, 7); Minn.: Grant (1, 6), Kaat (2). LP—L.A.: Drysdale (1), Koufax (2), Osteen (6); Minn.: Pascual (3), Grant (4), Kaat (5, 7).

1966—Baltimore A.L. 4 (Hank Bauer); Los Angeles N.L. 0 (Walter Alston). WP—Drabowsky (1), Palmer (2), Bunker (3), McNally (4). LP—Drysdale (1, 4), Koufax (2), Osteen (3).

1967—St. Louis N.L. 4 (Red Schoendienst); Boston A.L. 3 (Dick Williams). WP—St. L.: Gibson (1, 4, 7), Briles (3); Bos.: Lonborg (2, 5); Wyatt (6). LP—St. L.: Hughes (2), Carlton (5), Lamabe (6); Bos.: Santiago (1, 4), Bell (3), Lonborg (7).

1968—Detroit A.L. 4 (Mayo Smith); St. Louis N.L. 3 (Red Schoendienst). WP—Det.: Lolich (2, 5, 7), McLain (6); St. L.: Gibson (1, 4), Washburn (3), LP—Det.: McLain (1, 4), Wilson (3); St. L.: Briles (2), Hoerner (5), Washburn (6), Gibson (7).

1969—New York N.L. 4 (Gil Hodges); Baltimore A.L. 1 (Earl Weaver). WP—N.Y.: Koosman (2, 5), Gentry (3), Seaver (4); Balt.: Cuellar (1). LP—N.Y.: Seaver (1); Balt.: McNally (2), Palmer (3), Hall (4), Watt (5).

1970—Baltimore A.L. 4 (Earl Weaver); Cincinnati N.L. 1 (Sparky Anderson) 1. WP—Balt.: Palmer (1), Phoebus (2), McNally (3), Cuellar (5); Cin.: Carroll (4). LP—Cin.: Nolan (1), Wilcox (2), Cloninger (3), Merritt (5); Balt.: Watt (4).

1971—Pittsburgh N.L. 4 (Danny Murtaugh); Baltimore A.L. 3 (Earl Weaver). WP—Pitts.: Blass (3, 7), Kison (4), Briles (5); Balt.: McNally (1, 6), Palmer (2). LP—Pitts.: Ellis (1), R. Johnson (2), Miller (6); Balt.: Cuellar (3, 7), Watt (4) McNally (5).

1972—Oakland A.L. 4 (Dick Williams); Cincinnati N.L. (Sparky Anderson) 3. WP—Oakland: Holtzman (1), Hunter (2, 7), Fingers (4); Cincinnati: Billingham (3), Grimsley (5, 6). LP—Oakland: Odom (3), Fingers (5), Blue (6); Cincinnati: Nolan (1), Grimsley (2), Carroll (4), Bordon (7).

1973—Oakland A.L. 4 (Dick Williams): New York N.L. 3 (Yogi Berra). WP—Oakland: Holtzman (1, 7), Lindblad (3), Hunter (6). New York: McGraw (2), Matlack (4), Koosman (5). LP—Oakland: Fingers (2), Holtzman (4), Blue (5). New York: Matlack (1, 7) Parker (3), Seaver (6).

1974—Oakland A.L. 4 (Al Dark); Los Angeles N.L. 1 (Walter Alston). WP—Oakland: Fingers (1), Hunter (3), Holtzman (4), Odom (5). Los Angeles: Sutton (2). LP—Oakland: Blue (2), Los Angeles: Messersmith (1, 4), Downing (3), Marshall (5).

1975—Cincinnati N.L. 4 (Sparky Anderson); Boston A.L. 3 (Darrell Johnson). WP—Cincinnati: Eastwick (2-3), Gullett (5), Carroll (7); Boston: Tiant (1–4), Wise (6). LP—Cincinnati: Gullett (1), Norman (4), Darcy (6); Boston: Drago (2), Willoughby (3), Cleveland (5), Burton (7).

1976—Cincinnati N.L. 4 (Sparky Anderson); New York A.L. 0 (Billy Martin). WP—Gullett (1), Billingham (2), Zachry (3), Nolan (4). LP—Alexander (1), Hunter (2), Ellis (3), Figueroa (4).

1977—New York A.L. 4 (Billy Martin); Los Angeles N.L. 2 (Tom Lasorda). WP—New York: Lyle (1), Torrez (3,6), Guidry (4); Los Angeles: Hooton (2), Sutton (5). LP—New York: Hunter (2), Gullett (5); Los Angeles: Rhoden (1), John (3), Rau (4), Hooton (6).

1978—New York A.L. 4 (Bob Lemon), Los Angeles N.L. 2 (Tom Lasorda); WP—New York: Guidry (3), Gossage (4); Beattie (5), Hunter (6); Los Angeles: John (1), Hooton (2). LP—New York: Figuero (1), Hunter (2); Los Angeles: Sutton (3-6), Welch (4), Hooton (5).

1979—Pittsburgh N.L. 4 (Chuck Tanner), Baltimore A.L. 3 (Earl Weaver); WP—Pittsburgh: D. Robinson (2), Blyleven (5), Candelaria (6), Jackson (7); Baltimore: Flanagan (1), McGregor (3), Stoddard (4). LP—Pittsburgh: Kison (1), Candelaria (3), Tekulve (4); Baltimore: Stanhouse (2), Flanagan (5), Palmer (6), McGregor (7).

WORLD SERIES CLUB STANDING (THROUGH 1979)

	Series	Won	Lost	Pct.
Oakland (A)	3	3	0	1.000
Pittsburgh (N)	7	5	2	.714
New York (A)	33	23	10	.697
St. Louis (N)	12	8	4	.667
Cleveland (A)	3	2	1	.667
Boston (A)	8	5	3	.625
Philadelphia (A)	8	5	3	.625
Los Angeles (N)	8	3	5	.375
New York (N-Mets)	2	1	1	.500
Milwaukee (N)	2	1	1	.500
Boston (N)	2	1	1	.500
Chicago (A)	4	2	2	.500
Cincinnati (N)	8	4	4	.500
Baltimore (A)	5	2	3	.400
Detroit (A)	8	3	5	.375
New York (N-Giants)	14	5	9	.357
Washington (A)	3	1	2	.333
Chicago (N)	10	2	8	.200
Brooklyn (N)	9	1	8	.111
St. Louis (A)	1	0	1	.000
San Francisco (N)	1	0	1	.000
Minnesota (A)	1	0	1	.000
Philadelphia (N)	2	0	2	.000

Recapitulation

	Won
American League	45
National League	31

SINGLE GAME AND SINGLE SERIES RECORDS*

Most hits game—4, held by many players.
Most hits inning—2, held by many players.
Most hits series—13 (7 games) Bobby Richardson, New York A.L., 1964; Lou Brock, St. Louis N.L., 1968; 12 (6 games) Billy Martin, New York A.L., 1953; 12 (8 games) Buck Herzog, New York N.L., 1912; Joe Jackson, Chicago A.L., 1919; 10 (4 games) Babe Ruth, New York A.L., 1928; 9 (5 games) held by 8 players.
Most home runs, series—5 (6 games) Reggie Jackson, New York A.L., 1977; 4 (7 games) Babe Ruth, New York A.L., 1926; Duke Snider, Brooklyn N.L., 1952, 1955; Hank Bauer, New York A.L., 1958; Gene Tenace, Oakland A.L., 1972; 4 (4 games) Lou Gehrig, New York A.L., 1928; 3 (6 games) Babe Ruth, New York A.L., 1923; Ted Kluszewski, Chicago A.L., 1959; 3 (5 games) Donn Clendenon, New York Mets N.L., 1969; 2 (8 games) Patrick Dougherty, Boston A.L., 1903.
Most home runs, game—3, Babe Ruth, New York A.L., 1926 and 1928; Reggie Jackson, New York A.L., 1977.
Most strikeouts, series—11 (7 games) Ed Mathews, Milwaukee N.L., 1958; Wayne Garrett, New York N.L., 1973; 10 (8 games) George Kelly, New York N.L., 1921; 9 (6 games) Jim Bottomley, St. Louis N.L., 1930; 8 (5 games) Rogers Hornsby, Chicago N.L., 1929; Duke Snider, Brooklyn N.L., 1949; 7 (4 games) Bob Meusel, New York A.L., 1927.
Most stolen bases, game—3, Honus Wagner, Pittsburgh N.L., 1909; Willie Davis, Los Angeles N.L., 1965; Lou Brock, St. Louis N.L., 1967 and 1968.
Most strikeouts by pitcher, game—17, Bob Gibson, St. Louis N.L. 1968.
Most strikeouts by pitcher in succession—6, Horace Eller, Cincinnati N.L., 1919; Moe Drabowsky, Baltimore A.L., 1966.
Most strikeouts by pitcher, series—35 (7 games) Bob Gibson, St. Louis N.L., 1968; 28 (8 games) Bill Dinneen, Boston A.L., 1903; 23 (4 games) Sandy Koufax, Los Angeles, 1963; 20 (6 games) Chief Bender, Philadelphia A.L., 1911; 18 (5 games) Christy Mathewson, New York N.L., 1905.
Most bases on balls, series—11 (7 games) Babe Ruth, New York A.L., 1926; Gene Tenace, Oakland A.L., 1973; 8 (6 games) Babe Ruth, New York A.L., 1923; 7 (5 games) James Sheckard, Chicago N.L., 1910; Mickey Cochrane, Philadelphia A.L., 1929; Joe Gordon, New York A.L. 1941.
Most consecutive scoreless innings, one series—27, Christy Mathewson, New York N.L., 1905.

* Through 1979.

LIFETIME WORLD SERIES RECORDS

Most hits—71, Yogi Berra, New York A.L., 1947, 1949–53, 1955–58, 1960–63.
Most runs—42, Mickey Mantle, New York A.L., 1951–53, 1955–58, 1960–64.
Most runs batted in—40, Mickey Mantle, New York A.L., 1951–53, 1955–58, 1960–64..
Most home runs—18, Mickey Mantle, New York A.L., 1951–53, 1955–58, 1960–64.
Most bases on balls—43, Mickey Mantle, New York A.L., 1951–53, 1955–58, 1960–64.
Most strikeouts—54, Mickey Mantle, New York A.L., 1951–53, 1955–58, 1960–64.
Most stolen bases—34, Ed Collins, Philadelphia A.L., (10), 1910–11, 1913–14; Chicago A.L. (6), 1917, 1919.
Most victories, pitcher—10, Whitey Ford, New York A.L., 1950, 1953, 1955–58, 1960–64.
Most times member of winning team—10, Yogi Berra, New York A.L., 1947, 1949–53, 1956, 1958, 1961–62.
Most victories, no defeats—6, Vernon Gomez, New York A.L., 1932, 1936(2), 1937(2), 1938.
Most shutouts—4, Christy Mathewson, New York N.L., 1905 (3), 1913.
Most innings pitched—146, Whitey Ford, New York A.L., 1950, 1953, 1955–58, 1960–1964.
Most consecutive scoreless innings—33⅔, Whitey Ford, New York A.L., 1960 (18), 1961 (14), 1962 (1⅔).
Most strikeouts by pitcher—94, Whitey Ford, New York A.L., 1950, 1953, 1955–58, 1960–64.

AMERICAN LEAGUE HOME RUN CHAMPIONS

Year,	Player, team	No.
1901	Nap Lajoie, Phila.	13
1902	Ralph Seybold, Phila.	16
1903	Buck Freeman, Bost.	13
1904	Harry Davis, Phila.	10
1905	Harry Davis, Phila.	8
1906	Harry Davis, Phila.	12
1907	Harry Davis, Phila.	8
1908	Sam Crawford, Det.	7
1909	Ty Cobb, Det.	9
1910	J. Garland Stahl, Bost.	10
1911	Franklin Baker, Phila.	9
1912	Franklin Baker, Phila.	10
1913	Franklin Baker, Phila.	12
1914	Franklin Baker, Phila., and Sam Crawford, Det.	8
1915	Robert Roth, Chi.-Cleve.	7
1916	Wally Pipp, N.Y.	12
1917	Wally Pipp, N.Y.	9
1918	Babe Ruth, Bost., and Clarence Walker, Phila.	11
1919	Babe Ruth, Bost.	29
1920	Babe Ruth, N.Y.	54
1921	Babe Ruth, N.Y.	59
1922	Ken Williams, St. L.	39
1923	Babe Ruth, N.Y.	41
1924	Babe Ruth, N.Y.	46
1925	Bob Meusel, N.Y.	33
1926	Babe Ruth, N.Y.	47
1927	Babe Ruth, N.Y.	60
1928	Babe Ruth, N.Y.	54
1929	Babe Ruth, N.Y.	46
1930	Babe Ruth, N.Y.	49
1931	Lou Gehrig, N.Y., and Babe Ruth, N.Y.	46
1932	Jimmy Foxx, Phila.	58
1933	Jimmy Foxx, Phila.	48
1934	Lou Gehrig, N.Y.	49
1935	Jimmy Foxx, Phila., and Hank Greenberg, Det.	36
1936	Lou Gehrig, N.Y.	49
1937	Joe DiMaggio, N.Y.	46
1938	Hank Greenberg, Det.	58
1939	Jimmy Foxx, Bost.	35
1940	Hank Greenberg, Det.	41
1941	Ted Williams, Bost.	37
1942	Ted Williams, Bost.	36
1943	Rudy York, Det.	34
1944	Nick Etten, N.Y.	22
1945	Vern Stephens, St. L.	24
1946	Hank Greenberg, Det.	44
1947	Ted Williams, Bost.	32
1948	Joe DiMaggio, N.Y.	39
1949	Ted Williams, Bost.	43
1950	Al Rosen, Cleve.	37
1951	Gus Zernial, Chi.-Phila.	33
1952	Larry Doby, Cleve.	32
1953	Al Rosen, Cleve.	43
1954	Larry Doby, Cleve.	32
1955	Mickey Mantle, N.Y.	37
1956	Mickey Mantle, N.Y.	52
1957	Roy Sievers, Wash.	42
1958	Mickey Mantle, N.Y.	42
1959	Rocky Colavito, Cleve., and Harmon Killebrew, Wash.	42
1960	Mickey Mantle, N.Y.	40
1961	Roger Maris, N.Y.	61
1962	Harmon Killebrew, Minn.	48
1963	Harmon Killebrew, Minn.	45
1964	Harmon Killebrew, Minn.	49
1965	Tony Conigliaro, Bost.	32
1966	Frank Robinson, Balt.	49
1967	Carl Yastrzemski, Bost., and Harmon Killebrew, Minn.	44
1968	Frank Howard, Wash.	44
1969	Harmon Killebrew, Minn.	49
1970	Frank Howard, Wash.	44
1971	Bill Melton, Chicago	33
1972	Dick Allen, Chicago	37
1973	Reggie Jackson, Oak.	32
1974	Dick Allen, Chicago	32
1975	Reggie Jackson, Oak., and George Scott, Mil.	36
1976	Graig Nettles, N.Y.	32
1977	Jim Rice, Boston	39
1978	Jim Rice, Boston	46
1979	Gorman Thomas, Milwaukee	45
1980	Reggie Jackson, N.Y., and Ben Oglivie, Mil.	41

AMERICAN LEAGUE BATTING CHAMPIONS

Year,	Player, team	Avg.
1901	Nap Lajoie, Phila.	.422
1902	Ed Delahanty, Wash.	.376
1903	Nap Lajoie, Cleve.	.355
1904	Nap Lajoie, Cleve.	.381
1905	Elmer Flick, Cleve.	.306
1906	George Stone, St. L.	.358
1907	Ty Cobb, Det.	.350
1908	Ty Cobb, Det.	.324
1909	Ty Cobb, Det.	.377
1910	Ty Cobb, Det.	.385
1911	Ty Cobb, Det.	.420
1912	Ty Cobb, Det.	.410
1913	Ty Cobb, Det.	.390
1914	Ty Cobb, Det.	.368
1915	Ty Cobb, Det.	.369
1916	Tris Speaker, Cleve.	.386
1917	Ty Cobb, Det.	.383
1918	Ty Cobb, Det.	.382
1919	Ty Cobb, Det.	.384
1920	George Sisler, St. L.	.407
1921	Harry Heilmann, Det.	.394
1922	George Sisler, St. L.	.420
1923	Harry Heilmann, Det.	.403
1924	Babe Ruth, N.Y.	.378
1925	Harry Heilmann, Det.	.393
1926	Heinie Manush, Det.	.378
1927	Harry Heilmann, Det.	.398
1928	Goose Goslin, Wash.	.379
1929	Lew Fonseca, Cleve.	.369
1930	Al Simmons, Phila.	.381
1931	Al Simmons, Phila.	.390
1932	Dale Alexander, Det.-Bost.	.367
1933	Jimmy Foxx, Phila.	.356
1934	Lou Gehrig, N.Y.	.363
1935	Buddy Myer, Wash.	.349
1936	Luke Appling, Chi.	.388
1937	Charley Gehringer, Det.	.371
1938	Jimmy Foxx, Bost.	.349
1939	Joe DiMaggio, N.Y.	.381
1940	Joe DiMaggio, N.Y.	.352
1941	Ted Williams, Bost.	.406
1942	Ted Williams, Bost.	.356
1943	Luke Appling, Chi.	.328
1944	Lou Boudreau, Cleve.	.327
1945	George Sternweiss, N.Y.	.309
1946	Mickey Vernon, Wash.	.353
1947	Ted Williams, Bost.	.343
1948	Ted Williams, Bost.	.369
1949	George Kell, Det.	.343
1950	Billy Goodman, Bost.	.354
1951	Ferris Fain, Phila.	.344
1952	Ferris Fain, Phila.	.327
1953	Mickey Vernon, Wash.	.337
1954	Bobby Avila, Cleve.	.341
1955	Al Kaline, Det.	.340
1956	Mickey Mantle, N.Y.	.353
1957	Ted Williams, Bost.	.388
1958	Ted Williams, Bost.	.328
1959	Harvey Kuenn, Det.	.353
1960	Pete Runnels, Bost.	.320
1961	Norman Cash, Det.	.361
1962	Pete Runnels, Bost.	.326
1963	Carl Yastrzemski, Bost.	.321
1964	Tony Oliva, Minn.	.323
1965	Tony Oliva, Minn.	.321
1966	Frank Robinson, Balt.	.316
1967	Carl Yastrzemski, Bost.	.326
1968	Carl Yastrzemski, Bost.	.301
1969	Rod Carew, Minn.	.332
1970	Alex Johnson, Calif.	.329
1971	Tony Oliva, Minn.	.337
1972	Rod Carew, Minn.	.318
1973	Rod Carew, Minn.	.350
1974	Rod Carew, Minn.	.364
1975	Rod Carew, Minn.	.359
1976	George Brett, Kansas City	.333
1977	Rod Carew, Minn.	.388
1978	Rod Carew, Minn.	.333
1979	Fred Lynn, Boston	.333
1980	George Brett, Kansas City	.390

CONSECUTIVE NO-HITTERS BY VANDER MEER

Johnny Vander Meer, a 23-year-old lefthander with the Cincinnati Reds, pitched consecutive no-hitters in June 1938, setting a mark of 18 innings of no-hit hurling. On June 11, in Cincinnati, he set down Boston without a hit as the Reds won, 3–0. Four days later, June 15, in the first night game in Brooklyn, he again held the opposition hitless as the Reds triumphed, 6–0. He was nicknamed Johnny (Double No-Hitter) Vander Meer.

NATIONAL LEAGUE HOME RUN CHAMPIONS

Year	Player, team	No.
1876	George Hall, Phila. Athletics	5
1877	George Shaffer, Louisville	3
1878	Paul Hines, Providence	4
1879	Charles Jones, Bost.	9
1880	James O'Rourke, Bost., and Harry Stovey, Worcester	6
1881	Dan Brouthers, Buffalo	8
1882	George Wood, Det.	7
1883	William Ewing, N.Y.	10
1884	Ed Williamson, Chi.	27
1885	Abner Dalrymple, Chi.	11
1886	Arthur Richardson, Det.	11
1887	Roger Connor, N.Y., and Wm. O'Brien, Wash.	17
1888	Roger Connor, N.Y.	14
1889	Sam Thompson, Phila.	20
1890	Tom Burns, Bklyn., and Mike Tiernan, N.Y.	13
1891	Harry Stovey, Bost., and Mike Tiernan, N.Y.	16
1892	Jim Holliday, Cin.	13
1893	Ed Delahanty, Phila.	19
1894	Hugh Duffy, Bost., and Robert Lowe, Bost.	18
1895	Bill Joyce, Wash.	17
1896	Ed Delahanty, Phila., and Sam Thompson, Phila.	13
1897	Nap Lajoie, Phila.	10
1898	James Collins, Bost.	14
1899	John Freeman, Wash.	25
1900	Herman Long, Bost.	12
1901	Sam Crawford, Cin.	16
1902	Tom Leach, Pitts.	6
1903	James Sheckard, Bklyn.	9
1904	Harry Lumley, Bklyn.	9
1905	Fred Odwell, Cin.	9
1906	Tim Jordan, Bklyn.	12
1907	David Brain, Bost.	10
1908	Tim Jordan, Bklyn.	12
1909	John Murray, N.Y.	7
1910	Fred Beck, Bost., and Frank Schulte, Chi.	10
1911	Frank Schulte, Chi.	21
1912	Henry Zimmerman, Chi.	14
1913	Cliff Cravath, Phila.	19
1914	Cliff Cravath, Phila.	19
1915	Cliff Cravath, Phila.	24
1916	Davis Robertson, N.Y., and Fred Williams, Chi.	12
1917	Davis Robertson, N.Y., and Cliff Cravath, Phila.	12
1918	Cliff Cravath, Phila.	8
1919	Cliff Cravath, Phila.	12
1920	Cy Williams, Phila.	15
1921	George Kelly, N.Y.	23
1922	Rogers Hornsby, St. L.	42
1923	Cy Williams, Phila.	41
1924	Jacques Fournier, Bklyn.	27
1925	Rogers Hornsby, St. L.	39
1926	Hack Wilson, Chi.	21
1927	Hack Wilson, Chi., and Cy Williams, Phila.	30
1928	Hack Wilson, Chi., and Jim Bottomley, St. L.	31
1929	Chuck Klein, Phila.	43
1930	Hack Wilson, Chi.	56
1931	Chuck Klein, Phila.	31
1932	Chuck Klein, Phila., and Mel Ott, N.Y.	38
1933	Chuck Klein, Phila.	28
1934	Mel Ott, N.Y., and Rip Collins, St. L.	35
1935	Wally Berger, Bost.	34
1936	Mel Ott, N.Y.	33
1937	Mel Ott, N.Y., and Joe Medwick, St. L.	31
1938	Mel Ott, N.Y.	36
1939	John Mize, St. L.	28
1940	John Mize, St. L.	43
1941	Dolph Camilli, Bklyn.	34
1942	Mel Ott, N.Y.	30
1943	Bill Nicholson, Chi.	29
1944	Bill Nicholson, Chi.	33
1945	Tommy Holmes, Bost.	28
1946	Ralph Kiner, Pitts.	23
1947	Ralph Kiner, Pitts., and John Mize, N.Y.	51
1948	Ralph Kiner, Pitts., and John Mize, N.Y.	40
1949	Ralph Kiner, Pitts.	54
1950	Ralph Kiner, Pitts.	47
1951	Ralph Kiner, Pitts.	42
1952	Ralph Kiner, Pitts., and Hank Sauer, Chi.	37
1953	Ed Mathews, Mil.	47
1954	Ted Kluszewski, Cin.	49
1955	Willie Mays, N.Y.	51
1956	Duke Snider, Bklyn.	43
1957	Henry Aaron, Mil.	44
1958	Ernie Banks, Chi.	47
1959	Ed Mathews, Mil.	46
1960	Ernie Banks, Chi.	41
1961	Orlando Cepeda, San Fran.	46
1962	Willie Mays, San Fran.	49
1963	Henry Aaron, Mil., and Willie McCovey, San Fran.	44
1964	Willie Mays, San Fran.	47
1965	Willie Mays, San Fran.	52
1966	Henry Aaron, Atlanta	44
1967	Henry Aaron, Atlanta	39
1968	Willie McCovey, San Fran.	36
1969	Willie McCovey, San Fran.	45
1970	Johnny Bench, Cin.	45
1971	Willie Stargell, Pitts.	48
1972	Johnny Bench, Cin.	40
1973	Willie Stargell, Pitts.	44
1974	Mike Schmidt, Phila.	36
1975	Mike Schmidt, Phila.	38
1976	Mike Schmidt, Phila.	38
1977	George Foster, Cin.	52
1978	George Foster, Cin.	40
1979	Dave Kingman, Chicago	48
1980	Mike Schmidt, Phila.	48

NATIONAL LEAGUE BATTING CHAMPIONS

Year	Player/Team	Avg
1876	Roscoe Barnes, Chicago	.404
1877	Jim White, Boston	.385
1878	Abner Dalrymple, Mil.	.356
1879	Cap Anson, Chicago	.407
1880	George Gore, Chicago	.365
1881	Cap Anson, Chicago	.399
1882	Dan Brouthers, Buffalo	.367
1883	Dan Brouthers, Buffalo	.371
1884	James O'Rourke, Buffalo	.350
1885	Roger Connor, N. Y.	.371
1886	King Kelly, Chicago	.388
1887	Cap Anson, Chicago	.421
1888	Cap Anson, Chicago	.343
1889	Dan Brouthers, Boston	.373
1890	John Glasscock, N. Y.	.336
1891	William Hamilton, Phila.	.338
1892	Dan Brouthers, Bklyn., and Clarence Childs, Cleve.	.335
1893	Hugh Duffy, Boston	.378
1894	Hugh Duffy, Boston	.438
1895	Jesse Burkett, Cleveland	.423
1896	Jesse Burkett, Cleveland	.410
1897	Willie Keeler, Baltimore	.432
1898	Willie Keeler, Baltimore	.379
1899	Ed Delahanty, Phila.	.408
1900	Honus Wagner, Pittsburgh	.381
1901	Jesse Burkett, St. Louis	.382
1902	Clarence Beaumont, Pitts.	.357
1903	Honus Wagner, Pittsburgh	.355
1904	Honus Wagner, Pittsburgh	.349
1905	Cy Seymour, Cincinnati	.377
1906	Honus Wagner, Pittsburgh	.339
1907	Honus Wagner, Pittsburgh	.350
1908	Honus Wagner, Pittsburgh	.354
1909	Honus Wagner, Pittsburgh	.339
1910	Sherwood Magee, Philadelphia	.331
1911	Honus Wagner, Pittsburgh	.334
1912	Henry Zimmerman, Chicago	.372
1913	Jake Daubert, Brooklyn	.350
1914	Jake Daubert, Brooklyn	.329
1915	Larry Doyle, New York	.320
1916	Hal Chase, Cincinnati	.339
1917	Edd Roush, Cincinnati	.341
1918	Zack Wheat, Brooklyn	.335
1919	Edd Roush, Cincinnati	.321
1920	Rogers Hornsby, St. Louis	.370
1921	Rogers Hornsby, St. Louis	.397
1922	Rogers Hornsby, St. Louis	.401
1923	Rogers Hornsby, St. Louis	.384
1924	Rogers Hornsby, St. Louis	.424
1925	Rogers Hornsby, St. Louis	.403
1926	Gene Hargrave, Cincinnati	.353
1927	Paul Waner, Pittsburgh	.380
1928	Rogers Hornsby, Boston	.387
1929	Lefty O'Doul, Phila.	.398
1930	Bill Terry, N. Y.	.401
1931	Chick Hafey, St. Louis	.349
1932	Lefty O'Doul, Brooklyn	.368
1933	Chuck Klein, Phila.	.368
1934	Paul Waner, Pittsburgh	.362
1935	Arky Vaughan, Pittsburgh	.385
1936	Paul Waner, Pittsburgh	.373
1937	Joe Medwick, St. Louis	.374
1938	Ernie Lombardi, Cin.	.342
1939	John Mize, St. Louis	.349
1940	Debs Garms, Pittsburgh	.355
1941	Pete Reiser, Brooklyn	.343
1942	Ernie Lombardi, Boston	.330
1943	Stan Musial, St. Louis	.357
1944	Dixie Walker, Brooklyn	.357
1945	Phil Cavarretta, Chicago	.355

Year	Player/Team	Avg	Year	Player/Team	Avg	Year	Player/Team	Avg
1946	Stan Musial, St. Louis	.365	1958	Richie Ashburn, Phila.	.350	1970	Rico Carty, Atlanta	.366
1947	Harry Walker, St. L.-Phila.	.363	1959	Henry Aaron, Mil.	.355	1971	Joe Torre, St. Louis	.363
1948	Stan Musial, St. Louis	.376	1960	Dick Groat, Pittsburgh	.325	1972	Billy Williams, Chicago	.333
1949	Jackie Robinson, Brooklyn	.342	1961	Roberto Clemente, Pitts.	.351	1973	Pete Rose, Cincinnati	.338
1950	Stan Musial, St. Louis	.346	1962	Tommy Davis, L. A.	.346	1974	Ralph Garr, Atlanta	.353
1951	Stan Musial, St. Louis	.355	1963	Tommy Davis, L. A.	.326	1975	Bill Madlock, Chicago	.354
1952	Stan Musial, St. Louis	.336	1964	Roberto Clemente, Pitts.	.339	1976	Bill Madlock, Chicago	.339
1953	Carl Furillo, Brooklyn	.344	1965	Roberto Clemente, Pitts.	.329	1977	Dave Parker, Pittsburgh	.338
1954	Willie Mays, N. Y.	.345	1966	Matty Alou, Pittsburgh	.342	1978	Dave Parker, Pittsburgh	.334
1955	Richie Ashburn, Phila.	.338	1967	Roberto Clemente, Pitts.	.357	1979	Keith Hernandez, St. Louis	.344
1956	Henry Aaron, Mil.	.328	1968	Pete Rose, Cincinnati	.335	1980	Bill Buckner, Chicago	.324
1957	Stan Musial, St. Louis	.351	1969	Pete Rose, Cincinnati	.348			

AMERICAN LEAGUE PENNANT WINNERS

Year	Club	Manager	Won	Lost	Pct.	Year	Club	Manager	Won	Lost	Pct.
1901	Chicago	Clark C. Griffith	83	53	.610	1942	New York	Joseph V. McCarthy	103	51	.669
1902	Philadelphia	Connie Mack	83	53	.610	1943[1]	New York	Joseph V. McCarthy	98	56	.636
1903[1]	Boston	Jimmy Collins	91	47	.659	1944	St. Louis	Luke Sewell	89	65	.578
1904[2]	Boston	Jimmy Collins	95	59	.617	1945[1]	Detroit	Steve O'Neill	88	65	.575
1905	Philadelphia	Connie Mack	92	56	.622	1946	Boston	Joseph E. Cronin	104	50	.675
1906[1]	Chicago	Fielder A. Jones	93	58	.616	1947[1]	New York	Stanley R. Harris	97	57	.630
1907	Detroit	Hugh A. Jennings	92	58	.613	1948[1]	Cleveland	Lou Boudreau	97	58	.626
1908	Detroit	Hugh A. Jennings	90	63	.588	1949[1]	New York	Casey Stengel	97	57	.630
1909	Detroit	Hugh A. Jennings	98	54	.645	1950[1]	New York	Casey Stengel	98	56	.636
1910[1]	Philadelphia	Connie Mack	102	48	.680	1951[1]	New York	Casey Stengel	98	56	.636
1911[1]	Philadelphia	Connie Mack	101	50	.669	1952[1]	New York	Casey Stengel	95	59	.617
1912[1]	Boston	J. Garland Stahl	105	47	.691	1953[1]	New York	Casey Stengel	99	52	.656
1913[1]	Philadelphia	Connie Mack	96	57	.627	1954	Cleveland	Al Lopez	111	43	.721
1914	Philadelphia	Connie Mack	99	53	.651	1955	New York	Casey Stengel	96	58	.623
1915[1]	Boston	William F. Carrigan	101	50	.669	1956[1]	New York	Casey Stengel	97	57	.630
1916[1]	Boston	William F. Carrigan	91	63	.591	1957	New York	Casey Stengel	98	56	.636
1917[1]	Chicago	Clarence H. Rowland	100	54	.649	1958[1]	New York	Casey Stengel	92	62	.597
1918[1]	Boston	Ed Barrow	75	51	.595	1959	Chicago	Al Lopez	94	60	.610
1919	Chicago	William Gleason	88	52	.629	1960	New York	Casey Stengel	97	57	.630
1920[1]	Cleveland	Tris Speaker	98	56	.636	1961[1]	New York	Ralph Houk	109	53	.673
1921	New York	Miller J. Huggins	98	55	.641	1962[1]	New York	Ralph Houk	96	66	.593
1922	New York	Miller J. Huggins	94	60	.610	1963	New York	Ralph Houk	104	57	.646
1923[1]	New York	Miller J. Huggins	98	54	.645	1964	New York	Yogi Berra	99	63	.611
1924[1]	Washington	Stanley R. Harris	92	62	.597	1965	Minnesota	Sam Mele	102	60	.630
1925	Washington	Stanley R. Harris	96	55	.636	1966[1]	Baltimore	Hank Bauer	97	63	.606
1926	New York	Miller J. Huggins	91	63	.591	1967	Boston	Dick Williams	92	70	.568
1927[1]	New York	Miller J. Huggins	110	44	.714	1968[1]	Detroit	Mayo Smith	103	59	.636
1928[1]	New York	Miller J. Huggins	101	53	.656	1969	Baltimore[3]	Earl Weaver	109	53	.673
1929[1]	Philadelphia	Connie Mack	104	46	.693	1970[1]	Baltimore[3]	Earl Weaver	108	54	.667
1930[1]	Philadelphia	Connie Mack	102	52	.662	1971	Baltimore[4]	Earl Weaver	101	57	.639
1931	Philadelphia	Connie Mack	107	45	.704	1972[1]	Oakland[5]	Dick Williams	93	62	.600
1932[1]	New York	Joseph V. McCarthy	107	47	.695	1973[1]	Oakland[6]	Dick Williams	94	68	.580
1933	Washington	Joseph E. Cronin	99	53	.651	1974[1]	Oakland[6]	Alvin Dark	90	72	.556
1934	Detroit	Gordon Cochrane	101	53	.656	1975	Boston[4]	Darrell Johnson	95	65	.594
1935[1]	Detroit	Gordon Cochrane	93	58	.616	1976	New York[7]	Billy Martin	97	62	.610
1936[1]	New York	Joseph V. McCarthy	102	51	.667	1977[1]	New York[7]	Billy Martin	100	62	.617
1937[1]	New York	Joseph V. McCarthy	102	52	.662	1978	New York[7]	Billy Martin			
1938[1]	New York	Joseph V. McCarthy	99	53	.651			and Bob Lemon	100	63	.613
1939[1]	New York	Joseph V. McCarthy	106	45	.702	1979	Baltimore[8]	Earl Weaver	102	57	.642
1940	Detroit	Delmar D. Baker	90	64	.584	1980	Kansas City[9]	Jim Frey	97	65	.599
1941[1]	New York	Joseph V. McCarthy	101	53	.656						

1. World Series winner. 2. No World Series. 3. Defeated Minnesota, Western Division winner, in playoff. 4. Defeated Oakland, Western Division Leader, in playoff. 5. Defeated Detroit, Eastern Division winner, in playoff. 6. Defeated Baltimore, Eastern Division winner, in playoff. 7. Defeated Kansas City, Western Division winner, in playoff. 8. Defeated California, Western Division winner, in playoff. 9. Defeated New York, Eastern Division winner, in playoff.

ICEBOATING—1980

World DN Class—Matti Kleman, Soviet Union
United States DN Class—Meade Geougon, Bay City, Mich.

NATIONAL LEAGUE PENNANT WINNERS

Year	Club	Manager	Won	Lost	Pct
1876	Chicago	Albert G. Spalding	52	14	.788
1877	Boston	Harry Wright	31	17	.646
1878	Boston	Harry Wright	41	19	.683
1879	Providence	George Wright	55	23	.705
1880	Chicago	Adrian C. Anson	67	17	.798
1881	Chicago	Adrian C. Anson	56	28	.667
1882	Chicago	Adrian C. Anson	55	29	.655
1883	Boston	John F. Morrill	63	35	.643
1884	Providence	Frank C. Bancroft	84	28	.750
1885	Chicago	Adrian C. Anson	87	25	.777
1886	Chicago	Adrian C. Anson	90	34	.726
1887	Detroit	W. H. Watkins	79	45	.637
1888	New York	James J. Mutrie	84	47	.641
1889	New York	James J. Mutrie	83	43	.659
1890	Brooklyn	William H. McGunnigle	86	43	.667
1891	Boston	Frank G. Selee	87	51	.630
1892	Boston	Frank G. Selee	102	48	.680
1893	Boston	Frank G. Selee	86	44	.662
1894	Baltimore	Edward H. Hanlon	89	39	.695
1895	Baltimore	Edward H. Hanlon	87	43	.669
1896	Baltimore	Edward H. Hanlon	90	39	.698
1897	Boston	Frank G. Selee	93	39	.705
1898	Boston	Frank G. Selee	102	47	.685
1899	Brooklyn	Edward H. Hanlon	88	42	.677
1900	Brooklyn	Edward H. Hanlon	82	54	.603
1901	Pittsburgh	Fred C. Clarke	90	49	.647
1902	Pittsburgh	Fred C. Clarke	103	36	.741
1903	Pittsburgh	Fred C. Clarke	91	49	.650
1904	New York[2]	John J. McGraw	106	47	.693
1905	New York[1]	John J. McGraw	105	48	.686
1906	Chicago	Frank L. Chance	116	36	.763
1907	Chicago[1]	Frank L. Chance	107	45	.704
1908	Chicago[1]	Frank L. Chance	99	55	.643
1909	Pittsburgh[1]	Fred C. Clarke	110	42	.724
1910	Chicago	Frank L. Chance	104	50	.675
1911	New York	John J. McGraw	99	54	.647
1912	New York	John J. McGraw	103	48	.682
1913	New York	John J. McGraw	101	51	.664
1914	Boston[1]	George T. Stallings	94	59	.614
1915	Philadelphia	Patrick J. Moran	90	62	.592
1916	Brooklyn	Wilbert Robinson	94	60	.610
1917	New York	John J. McGraw	98	56	.636
1918	Chicago	Fred L. Mitchell	84	45	.651
1919	Cincinnati[1]	Patrick J. Moran	96	44	.686
1920	Brooklyn	Wilbert Robinson	93	61	.604
1921	New York[1]	John J. McGraw	94	59	.614
1922	New York[1]	John J. McGraw	93	61	.604
1923	New York	John J. McGraw	95	58	.621
1924	New York	John J. McGraw	93	60	.608
1925	Pittsburgh[1]	William B. McKechnie	95	58	.621
1926	St. Louis[1]	Rogers Hornsby	89	65	.578
1927	Pittsburgh	Donie Bush	94	60	.610
1928	St. Louis	William B. McKechnie	95	59	.617
1929	Chicago	Joseph V. McCarthy	98	54	.645
1930	St. Louis	Gabby Street	92	62	.597
1931	St. Louis[1]	Gabby Street	101	53	.656
1932	Chicago	Charles J. Grimm	90	64	.584
1933	New York[1]	William H. Terry	91	61	.599
1934	St. Louis[1]	Frank F. Frisch	95	58	.621
1935	Chicago	Charles J. Grimm	100	54	.649
1936	New York	William H. Terry	92	62	.597
1937	New York	William H. Terry	95	57	.625
1938	Chicago	Gabby Hartnett	89	63	.586
1939	Cincinnati	William B. McKechnie	97	57	.630
1940	Cincinnati[1]	William B. McKechnie	100	53	.654
1941	Brooklyn	Leo E. Durocher	100	54	.649
1942	St. Louis[1]	William H. Southworth	106	48	.688
1943	St. Louis	William H. Southworth	105	49	.682
1944	St. Louis[1]	William H. Southworth	105	49	.682
1945	Chicago	Charles J. Grimm	98	56	.636
1946	St. Louis[1]	Edwin H. Dyer	98	58	.628
1947	Brooklyn	Burton E. Shotton	94	60	.610
1948	Boston	William H. Southworth	91	62	.595
1949	Brooklyn	Burton E. Shotton	97	57	.630
1950	Philadelphia	Edwin M. Sawyer	91	63	.591
1951	New York	Leo E. Durocher	98	59	.624
1952	Brooklyn	Charles W. Dressen	96	57	.630
1953	Brooklyn	Charles W. Dressen	105	49	.682
1954	New York[1]	Leo E. Durocher	97	57	.630
1955	Brooklyn[1]	Walter Alston	98	55	.641
1956	Brooklyn	Walter Alston	93	61	.604
1957	Milwaukee[1]	Fred Haney	95	59	.617
1958	Milwaukee	Fred Haney	92	62	.597
1959	Los Angeles[1]	Walter Alston	88	68	.564
1960	Pittsburgh[1]	Danny Murtaugh	95	59	.617
1961	Cincinnati	Fred Hutchinson	93	61	.604
1962	San Francisco	Alvin Dark	103	62	.624
1963	Los Angeles[1]	Walter Alston	99	63	.611
1964	St. Louis[1]	Johnny Keane	93	69	.574
1965	Los Angeles[1]	Walter Alston	97	65	.599
1966	Los Angeles	Walter Alston	95	67	.586
1967	St. Louis[1]	Red Schoendienst	101	60	.627
1968	St. Louis	Red Schoendienst	97	65	.599
1969	New York[1, 3]	Gil Hodges	100	62	.617
1970	Cincinnati[4]	Sparky Anderson	102	60	.630
1971	Pittsburgh[1, 5]	Danny Murtaugh	97	65	.599
1972	Cincinnati	Sparky Anderson	95	59	.617
1973	New York[6]	Yogi Berra	82	79	.509
1974	Los Angeles[6]	Walter Alston	102	60	.630
1975	Cincinnati[1, 6]	Sparky Anderson	108	54	.667
1976	Cincinnati[7]	Sparky Anderson	102	60	.630
1977	Los Angeles[7]	Tom Lasorda	98	64	.605
1978	Los Angeles[7]	Tom Lasorda	95	67	.586
1979	Pittsburgh[6]	Chuck Tanner	98	64	.605
1980	Philadelphia[8]	Dallas Green	91	71	.562

1. World Series winner. 2. No World Series. 3. Defeated Atlanta, Western Division winner, in playoff. 4. Defeated Pittsburgh, Eastern Division winner, in playoff. 5. Defeated San Francisco, Western Division winner, in playoff. 6. Defeated Cincinnati, Western Division winner, in playoff. 7. Defeated Philadelphia, Eastern Division winner, in playoff. 8. Defeated Houston, Western Division winner, in playoff.

Ted Williams' Major League Batting Record

(All games with Boston Red Sox)

	G	R	H	HR	RBI	Avg
1939	149	131	185	31	145[1]	.327
1940	144	134[1]	193	23	113	.344
1941	143	135[1]	185	37[1]	120	.406[1]
1942	150	141[1]	186	36[1]	137[1]	.356[1]
1946	150	142[1]	176	38	123	.342
1947	156	125[1]	181	32[1]	114[1]	.343[1]
1948	137	124	188	25	127	.369[1]
1949	155	150[1]	194	43[1]	159[2]	.343
1950	89	82	106	28	97	.317
1951	148	109	169	30	126	.318
1952	6	2	4	1	3	.400
1953	37	17	37	13	34	.407
1954	117	93	133	29	89	.345
1955	98	77	114	28	83	.356
1956	136	71	138	24	82	.345
1957	132	96	163	38	87	.388[1]
1958	129	81	135	26	85	.328[1]
1959	103	32	69	10	43	.254
1960	113	56	98	29	72	.316
Total	**2292**	**1798**	**2654**	**521**	**1839**	**.344**

1. Led league. 2. Tied for league lead. NOTE: The years 1943–45 were spent in military service.

MAJOR LEAGUE ALL-STAR GAME

Year	Date	Winning league and manager	Runs	Losing league and manager	Runs	Winning pitcher	Losing pitcher	Site	Paid attendance
1933	July 6	A.L. (Mack)	4	N.L. (McGraw)	2	Gomez	Hallahan	Chicago A.L.	47,595
1934	July 10	A.L. (Cronin)	9	N.L. (Terry)	7	Harder	Mungo	New York N.L.	48,363
1935	July 8	A.L. (Cochrane)	4	N.L. (Frisch)	1	Gomez	Walker	Cleveland A.L.	69,831
1936	July 7	N.L. (Grimm)	4	A.L. (McCarthy)	3	J. Dean	Grove	Boston N.L.	25,556
1937	July 7	A.L. (McCarthy)	8	N.L. (Terry)	3	Gomez	J. Dean	Washington A.L.	31,391
1938	July 6	N.L. (Terry)	4	A.L. (McCarthy)	1	Vander Meer	Gomez	Cincinnati N.L.	27,067
1939	July 11	A.L. (McCarthy)	3	N.L. (Hartnett)	1	Bridges	Lee	New York A.L.	62,892
1940	July 9	N.L. (McKechnie)	4	A.L. (Cronin)	0	Derringer	Ruffing	St. Louis N.L.	32,373
1941	July 8	A.L. (Baker)	7	N.L. (McKechnie)	5	E. Smith	Passeau	Detroit A.L.	54,674
1942	July 6	A.L. (McCarthy)	3	N.L. (Durocher)	1	Chandler	Cooper	New York N.L.	34,178
1943	July 13[1]	A.L. (McCarthy)	5	N.L. (Southworth)	3	Leonard	Cooper	Philadelphia A.L.	31,938
1944	July 11[1]	N.L. (Southworth)	7	A.L. (McCarthy)	1	Raffensberger	Hughson	Pittsburgh N.L.	29,589
1946	July 9	A.L. (O'Neill)	12	N.L. (Grimm)	0	Feller	Passeau	Boston A.L.	34,906
1947	July 8	A.L. (Cronin)	2	N.L. (Dyer)	1	Shea	Sain	Chicago N.L.	41,123
1948	July 13	A.L. (Harris)	5	N.L. (Durocher)	2	Raschi	Schmitz	St. Louis A.L.	34,009
1949	July 12	A.L. (Boudreau)	11	N.L. (Southworth)	7	Trucks	Newcombe	Brooklyn N.L.	32,577
1950	July 11	N.L. (Shotton)	4	A.L. (Stengel)	3[3]	Blackwell	Gray	Chicago A.L.	46,127
1951	July 10	N.L. (Sawyer)	8	A.L. (Stengel)	3	Maglie	Lopat	Detroit A.L.	52,075
1952	July 8	N.L. (Durocher)	3	A.L. (Stengel)	2[4]	Rush	Lemon	Philadelphia N.L.	32,785
1953	July 14	N.L. (Dressen)	5	A.L. (Stengel)	1	Spahn	Reynolds	Cincinnati N.L.	30,846
1954	July 13	A.L. (Stengel)	11	N.L. (Alston)	9	Stone	Conley	Cleveland A.L.	68,751
1955	July 12	N.L. (Durocher)	6	A.L. (Lopez)	5[5]	Conley	Sullivan	Milwaukee N.L.	45,643
1956	July 10	N.L. (Alston)	7	A.L. (Stengel)	3	Friend	Pierce	Washington A.L.	28,843
1957	July 9	A.L. (Stengel)	6	N.L. (Alston)	5	Bunning	Simmons	St. Louis N.L.	30,693
1958	July 8	A.L. (Stengel)	4	N.L. (Haney)	3	Wynn	Friend	Baltimore A.L.	48,829
1959[2]	July 7	N.L. (Haney)	5	A.L. (Stengel)	4	Antonelli	Ford	Pittsburgh N.L.	35,277
	Aug. 3	A.L. (Stengel)	5	N.L. (Haney)	3	Walker	Drysdale	Los Angeles N.L.	55,105
1960[1]	July 11	N.L. (Alston)	5	A.L. (Lopez)	3	Friend	Monbouquette	Kansas City A.L.	30,619
	July 13	N.L. (Alston)	6	A.L. (Lopez)	0	Law	Ford	New York A.L.	38,362
1961[2]	July 11	N.L. (Murtaugh)	5	A.L. (Richards)	4[6]	Miller	Wilhelm	San Francisco N.L.	44,115
	July 31	N.L. (Murtaugh)	1	A.L. (Richards)	1[7]	—	—	Boston A.L.	31,851
1962[2]	July 10	N.L. (Hutchinson)	3	A.L. (Houk)	1	Marichal	Pascual	Washington A.L.	45,480
	July 30	A.L. (Houk)	9	N.L. (Hutchinson)	4	Herbert	Mahaffey	Chicago N.L.	38,359
1963	July 9	N.L. (Dark)	5	A.L. (Houk)	3	Jackson	Bunning	Cleveland A.L.	44,160
1964	July 7	N.L. (Alston)	7	A.L. (Lopez)	4	Marichal	Radatz	New York N.L.	50,850
1965	July 13	N.L. (March)	6	A.L. (Lopez)	5	Koufax	McDowell	Minnesota A.L.	46,706
1966	July 12	N.L. (Alston)	2	A.L. (Mele)	1[6]	Perry	Richert	St. Louis N.L.	49,926
1967	July 11	N.L. (Alston)	2	A.L. (Bauer)	1[8]	Drysdale	Hunter	Anaheim A.L.	46,309
1968	July 9	N.L. (Schoendienst)	1	A.L. (Williams)	0	Drysdale	Tiant	Houston N.L.	48,321
1969	July 23	N.L. (Schoendienst)	9	A.L. (M. Smith)	3	Carlton	Stottlemyre	Washington A.L.	45,259
1970	July 14	N.L. (Hodges)	5	A.L. (Weaver)	4[5]	Osteen	Wright	Cincinnati N.L.	51,838
1971	July 13	A.L. (Weaver)	6	N.L. (Anderson)	4	Blue	Ellis	Detroit A.L.	53,559
1972	July 25	N.L. (Murtaugh)	4	A.L. (Weaver)	3[6]	McGraw	McNally	Atlanta N.L.	53,107
1973	July 24[1]	N.L. (Anderson)	7	A.L. (Williams)	1	Wise	Blyleven	Kansas City A.L.	40,849
1974	July 23[1]	N.L. (Berra)	7	A.L. (Williams)	2	Brett	Tiant	Pittsburgh N.L.	50,706
1975	July 15[1]	N.L. (Dark)	6	A.L. (Alston)	3	Matlack	Hunter	Milwaukee A.L.	51,540
1976	July 13	N.L. (Anderson)	7	A.L. (D. Johnson)	1	R. Jones	Fidrych	Philadelphia N.L.	63,974
1977	July 19[1]	N.L. (Anderson)	7	A.L. (Martin)	5	Sutton	Palmer	New York A.L.	56,683
1978	July 11[1]	N.L. (Lasorda)	7	A.L. (Martin)	3	Sutter	Gossage	San Diego N.L.	51,549
1979	July 17[1]	N.L. (Lasorda)	7	A.L. (Lemon)	6	Sutter	Kern	Seattle A.L.	58,905
1980	July 8[1]	N.L. (Tanner)	4	A.L. (Weaver)	2	Reuss	John	Los Angeles N.L.	56,088

1. Night game. 2. Two games. 3. Fourteen innings. 4. Five innings, rain. 5. Twelve innings. 6. Ten innings. 7. Called because of rain after nine innings. 8. Fifteen innings. NOTE: No game in 1945.

BASEBALL'S PERFECTLY PITCHED GAMES[1]

(no opposing runner reached base)

John Richmond—Worcester vs. Cleveland (NL) June 12, 1880	1–0
John M. Ward—Providence vs. Buffalo (NL) June 17, 1880	5–0
Cy Young—Boston vs. Philadelphia (AL) May 5, 1904	3–0
Addie Joss—Cleveland vs. Chicago (AL) Oct. 2, 1908	1–0
Ernest Shore[2]—Boston vs. Washington (AL) June 23, 1917	4–0
Charles Robertson—Chicago vs. Detroit (AL) April 30, 1922	2–0
Don Larsen[3]—New York (AL) vs. Brooklyn (NL) Oct. 8, 1956	2–0
Jim Bunning—Philadelphia vs. New York (NL) June 21, 1964	6–0
Sandy Koufax—Los Angeles vs. Chicago (NL) Sept. 9, 1965	1–0
Jim Hunter—Oakland vs. Minnesota (AL) May 8, 1968	4–0

1. Harvey Haddix, of Pittsburgh, pitched 12 perfect innings against Milwaukee (NL), May 26, 1959 but lost game in 13th on error and hit. 2. Shore, relief pitcher for Babe Ruth who walked first batter before being ejected by umpire, retired 26 batters who faced him and baserunner was out stealing. 3. World Series.

NATIONAL BASEBALL HALL OF FAME

Cooperstown, N.Y.

Fielders

Member	Active years
Anson, Adrian (Cap)	1876–1897
Appling, Lucius (Luke)	1930–1950
Averill, H. Earl	1929–1941
Baker, J. Frank (Home Run)	1908–1922
Bancroft, David	1915–1930
Banks, Ernest	1953–1971
Beckley, Jacob	1888–1907
Bell, James (Cool Papa)[1]	1920–1947
Berra, Lawrence (Yogi)	1946–1965
Bottomley, James	1922–1937
Boudreau, Louis	1938–1952
Bresnahan, Roger	1897–1915
Brouthers, Dennis	1879–1896
Burkett, Jesse	1890–1905
Campanella, Roy	1948–1957
Carey, Max	1910–1929
Chance, Frank	1898–1914
Charleston, Oscar[1]	1915–1954
Clarke, Fred	1894–1915
Clemente, Roberto	1955–1972
Cobb, Tyrus	1905–1928
Cochrane, Gordon (Mickey)	1925–1937
Collins, Edward	1906–1930
Collins, James	1895–1908
Comiskey, Charles	1882–1894
Combs, Earle	1924–1935
Connor, Roger	1880–1897
Crawford, Samuel	1899–1917
Cronin, Joseph	1926–1945
Cuyler, Hazen (Kiki)	1921–1938
Delahanty, Edward	1888–1903
Dickey, William	1928–1946
Dihigo, Martin[1]	1923–1945
DiMaggio, Joseph	1936–1951
Duffy, Hugh	1888–1906
Evers, John	1902–1919
Ewing, William	1880–1897
Flick, Elmer	1898–1910
Foxx, James	1925–1945
Frisch, Frank	1919–1937
Gehrig, H. Louis (Lou)	1923–1939
Gehringer, Charles	1924–1942
Gibson, Josh[1]	1929–1946
Goslin, Leon (Goose)	1921–1938
Greenberg, Henry (Hank)	1933–1947
Hafey, Charles (Chick)	1924–1937
Hamilton, William	1888–1901
Hartnett, Charles (Gabby)	1922–1941
Heilmann, Harry	1914–1932
Herman, William	1931–1947
Hooper, Harry	1909–1925
Hornsby, Rogers	1915–1937
Irvin, Monford (Monte)[1]	1939–1956
Hugh Jennings	1891–1918
Johnson, William (Judy)[1]	1921–1937
Kaline, Albert W.	1953–1974
Keeler, William (Wee Willie)	1892–1910
Kelley, Joseph	1891–1908
Kelly, George	1915–1932
Kelly, Michael (King)	1878–1893
Kiner, Ralph	1946–1955
Klein, Charles H. (Chuck)	1928–1944
Lajoie, Napoleon	1896–1916
Leonard, Walter (Buck)[1]	1933–1955
Lindstrom, Frederick	1924–1936
Lloyd, John Henry[1]	1905–1931
Mantle, Mickey	1951–1968
Manush, Henry (Heinie)	1923–1939
Maranville, Walter (Rabbit)	1912–1935
Mathews, Edwin	1952–1968
Mays, Willie	1951–1973
McCarthy, Thomas	1884–1896
McGraw, John J.	1891–1906
Medwick, Joseph (Ducky)	1932–1948
Musial, Stanley	1941–1963
O'Rourke, James	1876–1894
Ott, Melvin	1926–1947
Rice, Edgar (Sam)	1915–1934
Robinson, Jack	1947–1956
Robinson, Wilbert	1886–1902
Roush, Edd	1913–1931
Ruth, George (Babe)	1914–1935
Schalk, Raymond	1912–1929
Sewell, Joseph	1920–1933
Simmons, Al	1924–1944
Sisler, George	1915–1930
Snider, Edwin D. (Duke)	1947–1964
Speaker, Tristram	1907–1928
Terry, William	1923–1936
Thompson, Samuel	1885–1906
Tinker, Joseph	1902–1916
Traynor, Harold (Pie)	1920–1937
Wagner, John (Honus)	1897–1917
Wallace, Roderick (Bobby)	1894–1918
Waner, Lloyd	1927–1945
Waner, Paul	1926–1945
Ward, John (Monte)	1878–1894
Wheat, Zachariah	1909–1927
Williams, Theodore	1939–1960
Wilson, Lewis R. (Hack)	1923–1934
Youngs, Ross (Pep)	1917–1926

Pitchers

Member	Active years
Alexander, Grover	1911–1930
Bender, Charles (Chief)	1903–1925
Brown, Mordecai (3-Finger)	1903–1916
Chesbro, John	1899–1909
Clarkson, John	1882–1894
Coveleski, Stanley	1912–1928
Dean, Jerome (Dizzy)	1930–1947
Faber, Urban (Red)	1914–1933
Feller, Robert	1936–1956
Ford, Edward (Whitey)	1950–1967
Galvin, James (Pud)	1876–1892
Gomez, Vernon (Lefty)	1930–1943
Griffith, Clark	1891–1914
Grimes, Burleigh	1916–1934
Grove, Robert (Lefty)	1925–1941
Haines, Jesse	1918–1937
Hoyt, Waite	1918–1938
Hubbell, Carl	1928–1943
Johnson, Walter	1907–1927
Joss, Adrian	1902–1910
Keefe, Timothy	1880–1893
Koufax, Sanford (Sandy)	1955–1966
Lemon, Robert	1946–1958
Lyons, Theodore	1923–1946
Marquard, Richard (Rube)	1908–1925
Mathewson, Christopher	1900–1916
McGinnity, Joseph	1899–1908
Nichols, Charles (Kid)	1890–1906
Paige, LeRoy (Satchel)[1]	1926–1965
Pennock, Herbert	1912–1934
Plank, Edward	1901–1917
Radbourn, Charles (Hoss)	1880–1891
Rixey, Eppa	1912–1933
Roberts, Robert (Robin)	1948–1966
Ruffing, Charles (Red)	1924–1947
Rusie, Amos	1889–1901
Spahn, Warren	1942–1965
Vance, Arthur (Dazzy)	1915–1935
Waddell, George	1897–1910
Walsh, Edward	1904–1917
Welch, Michael (Mickey)	1880–1892
Wynn, Early	1939–1963
Young, Denton (Cy)	1890–1911

Officials and Others

Barrow, Edward[2, 3]
Bulkeley, Morgan G.[3]
Cartwright, Alexander[3]
Chadwick, Henry[4]
Conlan, John[5]
Connolly, Thomas[5]
Cummings, William A.[6]
Evans, William G.[5, 3]
Frick, Ford C.[7, 3]
Giles, Warren C.[3]
Harridge, William[3]
Harris, Stanley R.[8]
Hubbard, R. Calvin[5]
Higgins, Miller J.[2]
Johnson, B. Bancroft[3]
Klem, William[5]
Landis, Kenesaw M.[7]
Lopez, Alfonso R.[8]
Mack, Connie[2, 3]
MacPhail, Leland S.[3]
McCarthy, Joseph V.[2]
McKechnie, William B.[2]
Rickey, W. Branch[2, 3]
Spalding, Albert G.[6]
Stengel, Charles D.[8]
Weiss, George M.[3]
Wright, George[6]
Wright, Harry[6, 2]
Yawkey, Thomas[3]

1. Negro league player selected by special committee. 2. Manager. 3. Executive. 4. Writer-statistician. 5. Umpire. 6. Early player. 7. Commissioner. 8. Player-manager

MOST VALUABLE PLAYERS

(Baseball Writers Association selections)

American League

1931 Lefty Grove, Philadelphia
1932–33 Jimmy Foxx, Philadelphia
1934 Mickey Cochrane, Detroit
1935 Hank Greenberg, Detroit
1936 Lou Gehrig, New York
1937 Charlie Gehringer, Detroit
1938 Jimmy Foxx, Boston
1939 Joe DiMaggio, New York
1940 Hank Greenberg, Detroit
1941 Joe DiMaggio, New York
1942 Joe Gordon, New York
1943 Spurgeon Chandler, New York
1944–45 Hal Newhouser, Detroit
1946 Ted Williams, Boston
1947 Joe DiMaggio, New York
1948 Lou Boudreau, Cleveland
1949 Ted Williams, Boston
1950 Phil Rizzuto, New York
1951 Yogi Berra, New York
1952 Bobby Shantz, Philadelphia
1953 Al Rosen, Cleveland
1954–55 Yogi Berra, New York
1956–57 Mickey Mantle, New York
1958 Jackie Jensen, Boston
1959 Nellie Fox, Chicago
1960–61 Roger Maris, New York
1962 Mickey Mantle, New York
1963 Elston Howard, New York
1964 Brooks Robinson, Baltimore
1965 Zoilo Versalles, Minnesota
1966 Frank Robinson, Baltimore
1967 Carl Yastrzemski, Boston
1968 Dennis McLain, Detroit
1969 Harmon Killebrew, Minnesota
1970 John (Boog) Powell, Baltimore
1971 Vida Blue, Oakland
1972 Dick Allen, Chicago
1973 Reggie Jackson, Oakland
1974 Jeff Burroughs, Texas
1975 Fred Lynn, Boston
1976 Thurman Munson, New York
1977 Rod Carew, Minnesota
1978 Jim Rice, Boston
1979 Don Baylor, California

National League

1931 Frank Frisch, St. Louis
1932 Chuck Klein, Philadelphia
1933 Carl Hubbell, New York
1934 Dizzy Dean, St. Louis
1935 Gabby Hartnett, Chicago
1936 Carl Hubbell, New York
1937 Joe Medwick, St. Louis
1938 Ernie Lombardi, Cincinnati
1939 Bucky Walters, Cincinnati
1940 Frank McCormick, Cincinnati
1941 Dolph Camilli, Brooklyn
1942 Mort Cooper, St. Louis
1943 Stan Musial, St. Louis
1944 Marty Marion, St. Louis
1945 Phil Cavarretta, Chicago
1946 Stan Musial, St. Louis
1947 Bob Elliott, Boston
1948 Stan Musial, St. Louis
1949 Jackie Robinson, Brooklyn
1950 Jim Konstanty, Philadelphia
1951 Roy Campanella, Brooklyn
1952 Hank Sauer, Chicago
1953 Roy Campanella, Brooklyn
1954 Willie Mays, New York
1955 Roy Campanella, Brooklyn
1956 Don Newcombe, Brooklyn
1957 Henry Aaron, Milwaukee
1958–59 Ernie Banks, Chicago
1960 Dick Groat, Pittsburgh
1961 Frank Robinson, Cincinnati
1962 Maury Wills, Los Angeles
1963 Sandy Koufax, Los Angeles
1964 Ken Boyer, St. Louis
1965 Willie Mays, San Francisco
1966 Roberto Clemente, Pittsburgh
1967 Orlando Cepeda, St. Louis
1968 Bob Gibson, St. Louis
1969 Willie McCovey, San Francisco
1970 Johnny Bench, Cincinnati
1971 Joe Torre, St. Louis
1972 Johnny Bench, Cincinnati
1973 Pete Rose, Cincinnati
1974 Steve Garvey, Los Angeles
1975–76 Joe Morgan, Cincinnati
1977 George Foster, Cincinnati
1978 Dave Parker, Pittsburgh
1979 Willie Stargell, Pittsburgh
1979 Keith Hernandez, St. Louis

CY YOUNG AWARD

1956 Don Newcombe, Brooklyn N.L.
1957 Warren Spahn, Milwaukee N.L.
1958 Bob Turley, New York A.L.
1959 Early Wynn, Chicago A.L.
1960 Vernon Law, Pittsburgh, N.L.
1961 Whitey Ford, New York A.L.
1962 Don Drysdale, Los Angeles N.L.
1963 Sandy Koufax, Los Angeles N.L.
1964 Dean Chance, Los Angeles A.L.
1965 Sandy Koufax, Los Angeles N.L.
1966 Sandy Koufax, Los Angeles N.L.
1967 Jim Lonborg, Boston A.L.; Mike McCormick, San Francisco N.L.
1968 Dennis McLain, Detroit A.L.; Bob Gibson, St. Louis N.L.
1969 Mike Cuellar, Baltimore, and Dennis McLain, Detroit, tied in A.L.; Tom Seaver, N.Y. N.L.
1970 Jim Perry, Minnesota A.L.; Bob Gibson, St. Louis N.L.
1971 Vida Blue, Oakland A.L.; Ferguson Jenkins, Chicago N.L.
1972 Gaylord Perry, Cleveland A.L.; Steve Carlton, Phila. N.L.
1973 Jim Palmer, Baltimore A.L.; Tom Seaver, New York N.L.
1974 Catfish Hunter, Oakland A.L.; Mike Marshall, Los Angeles N.L.
1975 Jim Palmer, Baltimore A.L.; Tom Seaver, New York N.L.
1976 Jim Palmer, Baltimore A.L.; Randy Jones, San Diego N.L.
1977 Sparky Lyle, N.Y., A.L.; Steve Carlton, Philadelphia N.L.
1978 Ron Guidry, N.Y., A.L.; Gaylord Perry, San Diego N.L.
1979 Mike Flanagan, Baltimore, A.L.; Bruce Sutter, Chicago, N.L.

ROOKIE OF THE YEAR

(Baseball Writers Association selections)

American League

1949 Roy Sievers, St. Louis
1950 Walt Dropo, Boston
1951 Gil McDougald, New York
1952 Harry Byrd, Philadelphia
1953 Harvey Kuenn, Detroit
1954 Bob Grim, New York
1955 Herb Score, Cleveland
1956 Luis Aparicio, Chicago
1957 Tony Kubek, New York
1958 Albie Pearson, Washington
1959 Bob Allison, Washington
1960 Ron Hansen, Baltimore
1961 Don Schwall, Boston
1962 Tom Tresh, New York
1963 Gary Peters, Chicago
1964 Tony Oliva, Minnesota
1965 Curt Blefary, Baltimore
1966 Tommy Agee, Chicago
1967 Rod Carew, Minnesota
1968 Stan Bahnsen, New York
1969 Lou Piniella, Kansas City
1970 Thurman Munson, New York
1971 Chris Chambliss, Cleveland
1972 Carlton Fisk, Boston
1973 Alonzo Bumbry, Baltimore
1974 Mike Hargrove, Texas
1975 Fred Lynn, Boston
1976 Mark Fidrych, Detroit
1977 Eddie Murray, Baltimore
1978 Lou Whitaker, Detroit
1979 Alfredo Griffin, Toronto
1979 John Castino, Minnesota

National League

1949 Don Newcombe, Brooklyn
1950 Sam Jethroe, Boston
1951 Willie Mays, New York
1952 Joe Black, Brooklyn
1953 Jim Gilliam, Brooklyn
1954 Wally Moon, St. Louis
1955 Bill Virdon, St. Louis
1956 Frank Robinson, Cincinnati
1957 Jack Sanford, Philadelphia
1958 Orlando Cepeda, San Francisco
1959 Willie McCovey, San Francisco
1960 Frank Howard, Los Angeles
1961 Billy Williams, Chicago
1962 Ken Hubbs, Chicago
1963 Pete Rose, Cincinnati
1964 Richie Allen, Philadelphia
1965 Jim Lefebvre, Los Angeles
1966 Tommy Helms, Cincinnati
1967 Tom Seaver, New York
1968 Johnny Bench, Cincinnati

1969	Ted Sizemore, Los Angeles	1973	Gary Matthews, San Francisco	1977	Andre Dawson, Montreal
1970	Carl Morton, Montreal	1974	Bake McBride, St. Louis	1978	Bob Horner, Atlanta
1971	Earl Williams, Atlanta	1975	John Montefusco, San Francisco	1979	Rick Sutcliffe, Los Angeles
1972	Jon Matlack, New York	1976	Pat Zachry, Cincinnati		

MAJOR LEAGUE LIFETIME RECORDS

Source: The Book of Baseball Records, published and copyrighted by Seymour Siwoff, New York, N.Y. 10036.

Leading Batters

(Over 2,000 Hits)

	Years	At bat	Hits	Avg.
Ty Cobb	24	11,429	4,191	.367
Rogers Hornsby	23	8,173	2,930	.358
Ed Delahanty	16	7,493	2,593	.346
Dan Brouthers	19	6,725	2,349	.349
Willie Keeler	19	8,564	2,955	.345
Ted Williams	19	7,706	2,654	.344
Tris Speaker	22	10,196	3,515	.345
Billy Hamilton	14	6,262	2,157	.344
Harry Heilmann	17	7,787	2,660	.342
Babe Ruth	22	8,399	2,873	.342
Jesse Burkett	16	8,389	2,872	.342
Bill Terry	14	6,428	2,193	.341
Lou Gehrig	17	8,001	2,721	.340
George Sisler	15	8,267	2,812	.340
Nap Lajoie	21	9,589	3,251	.339
Cap Anson	22	9,084	3,081	.339
Sam Thompson	15	6,005	2,016	.336
Al Simmons	20	8,761	2,927	.334
Rod Carew	14	6,775	2,261	.334
Eddie Collins	25	9,952	3,313	.333
Paul Waner	20	9,459	3,152	.333
Stan Musial	22	10,972	3,630	.331
Heinie Manush	17	7,653	2,524	.330
Hugh Duffy	17	6,999	2,307	.330
Honus Wagner	21	10,427	3,430	.329
Joe DiMaggio	13	6,821	2,214	.325
Jimmy Foxx	20	8,134	2,646	.325

Leading Pitchers

(Over 250 Victories)

	Years	W	L	Pct.
Cy Young	22	511	315	.619
Walter Johnson	21	416	279	.599
Grover Alexander	20	373	208	.642
Christy Mathewson	17	373	188	.665
James Galvin	15	365	309	.542
Warren Spahn	21	363	245	.597
Charles Nichols	15	360	202	.641
Tim Keefe	14	346	225	.606
John Clarkson	12	328	175	.652
Eddie Plank	17	325	190	.631
Mickey Welch	13	316	214	.596
Hoss Radbourne	11	308	191	.617
Lefty Grove	20	300	141	.680
Early Wynn	23	300	244	.551
Robin Roberts	19	286	245	.539
Tony Mullane	14	282	221	.561
Red Ruffing	22	273	225	.548
Burleigh Grimes	19	270	212	.560
Gaylord Perry	19	289	230	.557
Bob Feller	18	266	162	.621
Eppa Rixey	21	266	251	.515
Gus Weyhing	14	265	236	.529
Jim McCormick	10	264	217	.549
Jim Kaat	22	272	227	.545
Ted Lyons	21	260	230	.531
Carl Hubbell	16	253	154	.622
Red Faber	20	254	212	.545

BASEBALL'S TRIPLE CROWN WINNERS

(Players leading league for season in batting, runs batted in, and home runs)

Two-Time Winners

1922, 1925 Rogers Hornsby, St. Louis (N.L.)
1942, 1947 Ted Williams, Boston (A.L.)

Others

1909 Ty Cobb, Detroit (A.L.)
1912 Heinie Zimmerman, Chicago (N. L.)
1933 Jimmy Foxx, Philadelphia (A. L.)
1933 Chuck Klein, Philadelphia (N. L.)
1934 Lou Gehrig, New York (A. L.)
1937 Joe Medwick, St. Louis (N.L.)
1956 Mickey Mantle, New York (A. L.)
1966 Frank Robinson, Baltimore (A. L.)
1967 Carl Yastrzemski, Boston (A.L.)

SANDY KOUFAX'S MAJOR LEAGUE PITCHING RECORD

(1955–57, with Brooklyn Dodgers; 1958–66, with Los Angeles Dodgers)

	G	IP	H	BB	SO	W	L	ERA
1955	12	42	33	28	30	2	2	3.00
1956	16	59	66	29	30	2	4	4.88
1957	34	104	83	51	122	5	4	3.89
1958	40	159	132	105	131	11	11	4.47
1959	35	153	136	92	173	8	6	4.06
1960	37	175	133	100	197	8	13	3.91
1961	42	256	212	96	269[1]	18	13	3.52
1962	28	184	134	57	216	14	7	2.54[1]
1963	40	311	214	58	306[1]	25[2]	5	1.88[1]
1964	29	223	154	58	223	19	5	1.74[1]
1965	43	336[1]	216	71	382[1]	26[1]	8	2.04[1]
1966	41	323[1]	241	77	317	27[1]	9	1.73[1]
Totals	397	2,325[1]	1,754	817	2,396	165	87	2.76

1. Led league. 2. Tied for league lead.

World Series Record

	G	IP	H	BB	SO	W	L	ERA
1959	2	9	5	1	7	0	1	1.00
1963	2	18	12	3	23	2	0	1.50
1965	3	24	13	5	29	2	1	0.38
1966	1	6	6	2	2	0	1	1.50
Totals	8	57	36	11	61	4	3	0.95

Koufax pitched four no-hit games, more than any other man. They came in consecutive years—1962, 1963, 1964, and 1965. The 1965 no-hitter, against the Chicago Cubs, was a perfect game. Koufax won the Cy Young Award three times—more than any other pitcher.

MAJOR LEAGUE INDIVIDUAL ALL-TIME RECORDS

Highest Batting Average—.438, Hugh Duffy, Boston N.L., 1894 (Since 1900—.424, Rogers Hornsby, St. Louis N.L., 1924.)
Most Times at Bat—12,364, Henry Aaron, Milwaukee N.L., 1954–65; Atlanta N.L., 1966–74; Milwaukee A.L., 1975–76.
Most Years Batted .300 or Better—23, Ty Cobb, Detroit A.L., 1906–26, Philadelphia A.L., 1927–28.
Most hits—4,191, Ty Cobb, Detroit A.L., 1905–26, Philadelphia A.L., 1927–28.
Most Hits, Season—257, George Sisler, St. Louis A.L., 1920.
Most Hits, Game (9 innings)—7, Wilbert Robinson, Baltimore N.L., 6 singles, 1 double, 1892. Rennie Stennett, Pittsburgh N.L., 4 singles, 2 doubles, 1 triple, 1975.
Most Hits, Game (extra innings)—9, John Burnett, Cleveland A.L., 18 innings, 7 singles, 2 doubles, 1932.
Most Hits in Succession—12, Mike Higgins, Boston A.L., in four games, 1938; Walt Dropo, Detroit A.L., in three games, 1952.
Most Consecutive Games Batted Safely—56, Joe DiMaggio, New York A.L., 1941.
Most Runs—2,244, Ty Cobb, Detroit A.L., 1905–26, Philadelphia A.L., 1927–28.
Most Runs, Season—196, William Hamilton, Philadelphia N.L., 1894. (Since 1900—177, Babe Ruth, New York A.L., 1921.)
Most Runs, Game—7, Guy Hecker, Louisville A.A., 1886. (Since 1900—6, by Mel Ott, New York N.L., 1934, 1944; Johnny Pesky, Boston A.L., 1946; Frank Torre, Milwaukee N.L., 1957.)
Most Runs Batted In—2,297, Henry Aaron, Milwaukee N.L., 1954–1965; Atlanta N.L., 1966–74; Milwaukee A.L., 1975–76.
Most Runs Batted in, Season—190, Hack Wilson, Chicago N.L., 1930.
Most Runs Batted In, Game—12, Jim Bottomley, St. Louis N.L., 1924.
Most Home Runs—755, Henry Aaron, Milwaukee N.L., 1954–1965; Atlanta N.L., 1966–74; Milwaukee A.L., 1975–76.
Most Home Runs, Season—61, Roger Maris, New York A.L., 1961 (162-game season); 60, Babe Ruth, New York A.L., 1927 (154-game season)
Most Home Runs, Game—4 (see table on page 968).
Most Home Runs with Bases Filled—23, Lou Gehrig, New York A.L., 1927–39.
Most 2-Base Hits—793, Tris Speaker, Boston A.L., 1907–15, Cleveland A.L., 1916–26, Washington A.L., 1927, Philadelphia A.L., 1928.
Most 2-Base Hits, Season—67, Earl Webb, Boston A.L., 1931.
Most 2-base Hits, Game—4, by many.
Most 3-Base Hits—312, Sam Crawford, Cincinnati N.L., 1899–1902, Detroit A.L., 1903–17.
Most 3-Base Hits, Season—36, Owen Wilson, Pittsburgh N.L., 1912.
Most 3-Base Hits, Game—4, George Strief, Philadelphia A.A., 1885; William Joyce, New York N.L., 1897. (Since 1900—3, by many.)
Most Games Played—3,218. Henry Aaron, Milwaukee N.L., 1954–1965; Atlanta, N.L., 1966–74; Milwaukee A.L., 1975–76.
Most Consecutive Games Played—2,130, Lou Gehrig, New York A.L., 1925–39.
Most Bases on Balls—2,056, Babe Ruth, Boston A.L., 1914–19; New York A.L., 1920–34, Boston N.L., 1935.
Most Bases on Balls, Season—170, Babe Ruth, New York A.L., 1923.
Most Bases on Balls, Game—6, Walter Wilmot, Chicago N.L., 1891; Jimmy Foxx, Boston A.L., 1938.
Most Strikeouts—1,710, Mickey Mantle, New York A.L., 1951–68.
Most Strikeouts, Season—189, Bobby Bonds, San Francisco N.L., 1970.
Most Strikeouts, Game (9 innings)—5, by many.
Most Strikeouts, Game (extra innings)—6, Carl Weilman, St. Louis A.L., 15 innings, 1913; Don Hoak, Chicago N.L., 17 innings, 1956; Fred Reichardt, California A.L., 17, innings, 1966; Billy Cowan, California A.L., 20, 1971; Cecil Cooper, Boston A.L., 15, 1974.
Most pinch-hits, lifetime—144, Forrest Burgess, Chi.-Mil.-Cin.-Pitts., N.L., 1949, 1951–64; Chi., A.L., 1964–67.
Most Pinch-hits, season—25, Jose Morales, Montreal N.L., 1976.
Most consecutive pinch-hits—9, Dave Philley, Phil., N.L., 1958 (8), 1959 (1).
Most pinch-hit home runs, lifetime—18, Gerald Lynch, Pitt.-Cin. N.L., 1957–66.
Most pinch-hit home runs, season—6, Johnny Frederick, Brooklyn, N.L., 1932.
Most stolen bases, lifetime (since 1900)—938, Lou Brock, Chicago N.L. 1961–64; St. Louis, N.L. 1964–79.
Most stolen bases, season—156, Harry Stovey, Philadelphia, American Assn., 1888. Since 1900: 96, Ty Cobb, Detroit A.L. (156 games 1915); 118, Lou Brock, St. Louis, N.L. (162 games, 1974).
Most stolen bases, game—7, George Gore, Chicago N.L. 1881; William Hamilton, Philadelphia N.L. 1894. (Since 1900—6, Eddie Collins, Philadelphia A.L., 1912.)
Most times stealing home, lifetime—35, Ty Cobb, Detroit-Phil. A.L., 1905–28.

MAJOR LEAGUE ALL-TIME PITCHING RECORDS

Most Games Won—511, Cy Young, Cleveland N.L., 1890–98, St. Louis N.L., 1899–1900, Boston A.L., 1901–08, Cleveland A.L., 1909–11, Boston N.L., 1911.
Most Games Won, Season—60, Hoss Radbourne, Providence N.L., 1884. (Since 1900—41, Jack Chesbro, New York A.L., 1904.)
Most Consecutive Games Won—24, Carl Hubbell, New York N.L., 1936 (16) and 1937 (8).
Most Consecutive Games Won, Season—19, Tim Keefe, New York N.L., 1888; Rube Marquard, New York N.L., 1912.
Most Years Won 20 or More Games—16, Cy Young, Cleveland N.L., 1891–98, St. Louis N.L., 1899–1900, Boston A.L., 1901–04, 1907–08.
Most Shutouts—113, Walter Johnson, Wash. A.L., 1907–27.
Most Shutouts, Season—16, Grover Alexander, Philadelphia N.L., 1916.
Most Consecutive Shutouts—6, Don Drysdale, Los Angeles, N.L., 1968.
Most Consecutive Scoreless Innings—58, Don Drysdale, Los Angeles, N.L., 1968.
Most Strikeouts—3,508, Walter Johnson, Washington A.L. 1907–27.
Most Strikeouts, Season—505, Matthew Kilroy, Baltimore A.A., 1886. (Since 1900—383, Nolan Ryan, California, A.L., 1973.)
Most Strikeouts, Game—21, Tom Cheney, Washington A.L. 1962, 16 innings. Nine innings: 19, Charles McSweeney, Providence N.L., 1884; Hugh Dailey, Chicago U.A., 1884. (Since 1900—19, Steve Carlton, St. Louis N.L. vs. New York, Sept. 15, 1969; Tom Seaver, New York N.L. vs. San Diego, April 22, 1970; Nolan Ryan, California A.L. vs. Boston, Aug. 12, 1974.)
Most Consecutive Strikeouts—10, Tom Seaver, New York N.L. vs. San Diego, April 22, 1970.
Most Games, Season—106, Mike Marshall, Los Angeles, N.L., 1974.
Most Complete Games, Season—74, William White, Cincinnati N.L., 1879. (Since 1900—48, Jack Chesbro, New York A.L., 1904.)

OTHER LIFETIME BATTING, PITCHING, AND BASE-RUNNING RECORDS

Source: Baseball Record Book, published and copyrighted by The Sporting News, St. Louis, Mo. 63166

Hits

Ty Cobb	4,191
Henry Aaron	3,771
Stan Musial	3,630
Pete Rose[1]	3,557
Tris Speaker	3,515
Honus Wagner	3,430
Eddie Collins	3,311
Willie Mays	3,283
Nap Lajoie	3,251
Paul Waner	3,152
Carl Yastrzemski[1]	3,109
Cap Anson	3,081
Lou Brock	3,023
Al Kaline	3,007
Roberto Clemente	3,000
Edgar Rice	2,987
Sam Crawford	2,964
Willie Keeler	2,995
Frank Robinson	2,943
Jacob Beckley	2,930
Rogers Hornsby	2,930
Al Simmons	2,927
Zach Wheat	2,884
Frank Frisch	2,880
Mel Ott	2,876

Earned-Run Average

Walter Johnson	2.37
Grover Alexander	2.56
Tom Seaver[1]	2.56
Jim Palmer[1]	2.70
Whitey Ford	2.74
Stanley Coveleski	2.88
Juan Marichal	2.89
Wilbur Cooper	2.89
Bob Gibson	2.91
Carl Mays	2.92
Gaylord Perry[1]	2.93
Don Drysdale	2.95

Runs

Ty Cobb	2,244
Henry Aaron	2,174
Babe Ruth	2,174
Willie Mays	2,062
Stan Musial	1,949
Lou Gehrig	1,888
Tris Speaker	1,881
Mel Ott	1,859
Pete Rose[1]	1,843
Frank Robinson	1,829
Eddie Collins	1,818
Ted Williams	1,798
Charley Gehringer	1,773
Jimmy Foxx	1,751
Honus Wagner	1,740
Willie Keeler	1,720
Cap Anson	1,712
Jesse Burkett	1,708
Billy Hamilton	1,690
Mickey Mantle	1,677
John McPhee	1,674
George Van Haltren	1,650

Strikeouts, Pitching

Walter Johnson	3,508
Gaylord Perry[1]	3,276
Bob Gibson	3,117
Nolan Ryan[1]	3,109
Tom Seaver[1]	2,988
Steve Carlton[1]	2,969
Ferguson Jenkins[1]	2,899
Jim Bunning	2,853
Cy Young	2,819
Mickey Lolich	2,812
Warren Spahn	2,583
Bob Feller	2,581
Tim Keefe	2,538

Home Runs

Henry Aaron	755
Babe Ruth	714
Willie Mays	660
Frank Robinson	586
Harmon Killebrew	573
Mickey Mantle	536
Jimmy Foxx	534
Ted Williams	521
Willie McCovey	521
Ernie Banks	512
Ed Mathews	512
Mel Ott	511
Lou Gehrig	493
Stan Musial	475
Willie Stargell[1]	472
Billy Williams	426
Carl Yastrzemski[1]	419
Duke Snider	407
Al Kaline	399
Frank Howard	382
Orlando Cepeda	379
Norm Cash	377
Rocky Colavito	374

Shutouts

Walter Johnson	113
Grover Alexander	90
Christy Mathewson	83
Cy Young	77
Eddie Plank	64
Warren Spahn	63
Ed Walsh	58
James Galvin	57
Bob Gibson	56
Tom Seaver[1]	53
Juan Marichal	52

Strikeouts, Batting

Willie Stargell[1]	1,851[2]
Lou Brock	1,730
Mickey Mantle	1,710
Harmon Killebrew	1,699
Bobby Bonds[1]	1,639[2]
Reggie Jackson[1]	1,606[2]
Dick Allen	1,556
Tony Perez[1]	1,535
Frank Robinson	1,532
Willie Mays	1,526
Ed Mathews	1,487
Frank Howard	1,460

Bases on Balls

Babe Ruth	2,056
Ted Williams	2,018
Mickey Mantle	1,734
Mel Ott	1,708
Carl Yastrzemski[1]	1,639[2]
Eddie Yost	1,614
Stan Musial	1,599
Harmon Killebrew	1,559
Lou Gehrig	1,508
Joe Morgan[1]	1,466[2]
Willie Mays	1,464
Jimmy Foxx	1,452
Ed Mathews	1,444

Stolen Bases

Lou Brock	938
Billy Hamilton	937
Ty Cobb	892
Walter Latham	791
Harry Stovey	744
Eddie Collins	743
Max Carey	738
Honus Wagner	720
Tom Brown	697
George Davis	632

1. Active player. 2. Through 1979.

MICKEY MANTLE'S MAJOR LEAGUE BATTING RECORD

(All games with New York Yankees)

Year	G	R	H	HR	RBI	Avg
1951	96	61	91	13	65	.267
1952	142	94	171	23	87	.311
1953	127	105	136	21	92	.295
1954	146	129[1]	163	27	102	.300
1955	147	121	158	37[1]	99	.306
1956	150	132[1]	188	52[1]	130[1]	.353[1]
1957	144	121[1]	173	34	94	.365
1958	150	127[1]	158	42[1]	97	.304
1959	144	104	154	31	75	.285
1960	153	119[1]	145	40[1]	94	.275
1961	153	132[1]	163	54	128	.317
1962	123	96	121	30	89	.321
1963	65	40	54	15	35	.314
1964	143	92	141	35	111	.303
1965	122	44	92	19	46	.255
1966	108	40	96	23	56	.288
1967	144	63	108	22	55	.245
1968	144	57	103	18	54	.237
Total	**2401**	**1677**	**2415**	**536**	**1509**	**.298**

1. Led league.

World Series Record

Year	G	R	H	HR	RBI	Avg
1951	2	1	1	0	0	.200
1952	7	5	10	2	3	.345
1953	6	3	5	2	7	.208
1955	3	1	2	1	1	.200
1956	7	6	6	3	4	.250
1957	6	3	5	1	2	.263
1958	7	4	6	2	3	.250
1960	7	8	10	3	11	.400
1961	2	0	1	0	0	.167
1962	7	2	3	0	0	.120
1963	4	1	2	1	1	.133
1964	7	8	8	3	8	.333
Total	**65**	**42[1]**	**59**	**18[1]**	**40[1]**	**.257**

1. Series record.

MAJOR LEAGUE ATTENDANCE RECORDS

Single game—78,672, San Francisco at Los Angeles (N.L.), April 18, 1958. (At Memorial Coliseum.)
Doubleheader—84,587, New York at Cleveland (A.L.), Sept. 12, 1954.
Night—78,382, Chicago at Cleveland (A.L.), Aug. 20, 1948.
Season, home—3,347,845, Los Angeles (N.L.), 1978.
Season, road—2,320,693, Cincinnati (N.L.), 1978.
Season, league—22,371,979, American League, 1979.
Season, both leagues—43,550,398, 1979.
World Series, single game—92,706, Chicago (A.L.) at Los Angeles (N.L.), Oct. 6, 1959.
World Series, all games (6)—420,784, Chicago (A.L.) and Los Angeles (N.L.), 1959.

MOST HOME RUNS IN ONE SEASON

HR	Player/Team	Year
61	Roger Maris, New York (AL)	1961
60	Babe Ruth, New York (AL)	1927
59	Babe Ruth, New York (AL)	1921
58	Jimmy Foxx, Philadelphia (AL)	1932
58	Hank Greenberg, Detroit (AL)	1938
56	Hack Wilson, Chicago (NL)	1930
54	Babe Ruth, New York (AL)	1920
54	Babe Ruth, New York (AL)	1928
54	Ralph Kiner, Pittsburgh (NL)	1949
54	Mickey Mantle, New York (AL)	1961
52	Mickey Mantle, New York (AL)	1956
52	Willie Mays, San Francisco (NL)	1965
52	George Foster, Cincinnati (NL)	1977
51	Ralph Kiner, Pittsburgh (NL)	1947
51	John Mize, New York (NL)	1947
51	Willie Mays, New York (NL)	1955
50	Jimmy Foxx, Boston (AL)	1938
49	Babe Ruth, New York (AL)	1930
49	Lou Gehrig, New York (AL)	1934
49	Lou Gehrig, New York (AL)	1936
49	Ted Kluszewski, Cincinnati (NL)	1954
49	Willie Mays, San Francisco (NL)	1962
49	Harmon Killebrew, Minnesota (AL)	1964
49	Frank Robinson, Baltimore (AL)	1966
49	Harmon Killebrew, Minnesota (AL)	1969

HOME RUN RECORDS OF HENRY AARON AND BABE RUTH

Henry Aaron broke Babe Ruth's career home run record, April 8, 1974, by hitting the ball over the left-center field fence at Atlanta for his 715th homer. He had tied Ruth's mark, April 4, at Cincinnati. Aaron, of the Atlanta Braves, hit 20 homers during the 1974 season, raising the mark to 733. Playing for Milwaukee, he added 22 in the next two seasons for a 755 total. He made 3,771 hits and scored 2,174 runs.

HENRY AARON'S RECORD

Year	Club	HR
1954	Milwaukee (NL)	13
1955	Milwaukee (NL)	27
1956	Milwaukee (NL)	26
1957	Milwaukee (NL)	44
1958	Milwaukee (NL)	30
1959	Milwaukee (NL)	39
1960	Milwaukee (NL)	40
1961	Milwaukee (NL)	34
1962	Milwaukee (NL)	45
1963	Milwaukee (NL)	44
1964	Milwaukee (NL)	24
1965	Milwaukee (NL)	32
1966	Atlanta (NL)	44
1967	Atlanta (NL)	39
1968	Atlanta (NL)	29
1969	Atlanta (NL)	44
1970	Atlanta (NL)	38
1971	Atlanta (NL)	47
1972	Atlanta (NL)	34
1973	Atlanta (NL)	40
1974	Atlanta (NL)	20
1975	Milwaukee (AL)	12
1976	Milwaukee (AL)	10

Totals

Regular Season	755
World Series	2
Playoff Games	3
All-Star Games	2
	762

Aaron also set numerous other major league records as well as National League marks. They include:

Major League Records

Most games	3,298
Most times at bat	12,364
Most runs batted in	2,297
Total bases	6,856
Most extra-base hits	1,475

National League Records

Most runs	2,107
Most games	2,503
Most times at bat	8,399

BABE RUTH'S RECORD

Year	Club	HR
1914	Boston (AL)	0
1915	Boston (AL)	4
1916	Boston (AL)	3
1917	Boston (AL)	2
1918	Boston (AL)	11
1919	Boston (AL)	29
1920	New York (AL)	54
1921	New York (AL)	59
1922	New York (AL)	35
1923	New York (AL)	41
1924	New York (AL)	46
1925	New York (AL)	25
1926	New York (AL)	47
1927	New York (AL)	60
1928	New York (AL)	54
1929	New York (AL)	46
1930	New York (AL)	49
1931	New York (AL)	46
1932	New York (AL)	41
1933	New York (AL)	34
1934	New York (AL)	22
1935	Boston (NL)	6

World Series

1915	Boston (AL)	0
1916	Boston (AL)	0
1918	Boston (AL)	0
1921	New York (AL)	1
1922	New York (AL)	0
1923	New York (AL)	3
1926	New York (AL)	4
1927	New York (AL)	2
1928	New York (AL)	3
1932	New York (AL)	2

Totals

Regular season	714
World Series	15
All-Star	1

(Ruth was a pitcher mainly until 1918, when he also played outfield. That was the first year he appeared at bat over 150 times. He became a regular outfielder in 1919.)

MAJOR LEAGUE BALL PARK STATISTICS

lf—Left-field foul line; cf—center field; rf—right-field foul line. (2)—Indicates double-header.

American League

Club, nickname and grounds	Distance, feet lf	cf	rf	Seating capacity	Record attendance[1]	Visiting club	Date
Baltimore Orioles—Memorial Stadium	309	405	309	52,137	51,195	Kansas City (night)	May 8, 1976
Boston Red Sox—Fenway Park	315	420	302	33,524	41,766	New York (2)	Aug. 12, 1934
California Angels—Anaheim Stadium	333	404	333	43,204	44,631	Oakland	July 4, 1971
Chicago White Sox—Comiskey Park	352	400	352	46,550	55,555	Minnesota (2)	May 2, 1973
Cleveland Indians—Municipal Stadium	320	400	320	76,997	84,587	New York (2)	Sept. 12, 1954
Detroit Tigers—Tiger Stadium	340	440	325	54,220	58,369	New York (2)	July 20, 1947
Kansas City Royals—Royals Stadium	330	410	330	40,762	40,435	New York (night)	Aug. 9, 1976
Milwaukee Brewers—County Stadium	320	402	315	46,000	55,120	Baltimore	April 12, 1977
Minnesota Twins—Metropolitan Stadium	330	410	330	45,921	46,963	Chicago	June 26, 1977
New York Yankees—Yankee Stadium (old)	301	461	296	65,010	81,841	Boston (2)	May 30, 1938
New York Yankees—Yankee Stadium (new)	312	430	310	54,208	55,269	Boston (night)	Sept. 13, 1977
New York Yankees—Shea Stadium[2]	341	410	330	55,300	53,631	Boston (2)	July 27, 1975
Oakland Athletics—Oakland Coliseum	330	400	330	50,000	50,182	Balitmore (night)	June 12, 1972
Seattle Mariners—Kingdome	316	405	316	59,059	57,762	California (night)	April 6, 1977
Texas Rangers—Arlington Stadium	330	400	330	35,698	40,854	California (night)	May 21, 1976
Toronto Blue Jays—Exhibition Stadium	330	400	330	40,000	44,649	Chicago	April 6, 1977

National League

Club, nickname and grounds	lf	cf	rf	Seating capacity	Record attendance	Visiting club	Date
Atlanta Braves—Atlanta Stadium	330	400	330	52,744	53,775	Los Angeles (night)	April 8, 1974
Chicago Cubs—Wrigley Field	355	400	353	37,741	46,965	Pittsburgh (2)	May 31, 1948
Cincinnati Reds—Riverfront Stadium	330	404	330	51,786	53,390	Houston (day)	April 11, 1976
Houston Astros—Astrodome	340	406	340	45,000	50,908	Los Angeles (night)	June 22, 1966
Los Angeles Dodgers—Dodger Stadium	330	395	330	56,000	55,110	San Diego (night)	June 26, 1970
Montreal Expos—Jarry Park (old)	340	420	340	28,000	34,331	Philadelphia	Sept. 13, 1973
Montreal Expos—Olympic Stadium	325	404	325	60,000	57,592	Philadelphia	April 15, 1977
New York Mets—Shea Stadium	341	410	341	55,300	57,175	Los Angeles (2)	June 13, 1965
Philadelphia Phillies—Veterans Stadium	330	408	330	56,581	63,283	New York (night)	July 4, 1977
Pittsburgh Pirates—Three Rivers Stadium	335	400	335	50,230	51,726	San Diego (day)	June 6, 1976
St. Louis Cardinals—Busch Mem'l Stadium	330	404	330	50,101	50,340	Chicago (night)	July 2, 1977
San Diego Padres—San Diego Stadium	330	410	330	48,460	50,569	St. Louis (night)	April 24, 1976
San Francisco Giants—Candlestick Park	335	410	335	58,000	56,103	Los Angeles	May 28, 1978

1. Regular season in listed park. 2. Yankees played in New York National League Shea Stadium in 1974–75 while Yankee Stadium was being rebuilt.

MAJOR LEAGUE FRANCHISE SHIFTS AND ADDITIONS

1953—Boston Braves (N.L.) became Milwaukee Braves. Home attendance, last season in Boston (1952), 281,278; first season in Milwaukee (1953), 1,826,397.

1954—St. Louis Browns (A.L.) became Baltimore Orioles. Home attendance, last season in St. Louis (1953), 297,238; first season in Baltimore (1954), 1,060,910.

1955—Philadelphia Athletics (A.L.) became Kansas City Athletics. Home attendance, last season in Phila. (1954), 627,100; first season in K.C. (1955), 1,393,054.

1958—New York Giants (N.L.) became San Francisco Giants. Home attendance, last season in New York (1957), 653,923; first season in San Francisco (1958), 1,272,625.

1958—Brooklyn Dodgers (N.L.) became Los Angeles Dodgers. Home attendance, last season in Brooklyn (1957), 1,028,258; first season in Los Angeles (1958), 1,845,556.

1961—Washington Senators (A.L.) became Minnesota Twins. Home attendance, last season in Washington (1960), 743,404; first season in Minneapolis-St. Paul (1961), 1,256,722.

1961—Los Angeles Angels (later renamed the California Angels) enfranchised by the American League.

1961—Washington Senators enfranchised by the American League (a new team, replacing the former Washington club, whose franchise was moved to Minneapolis-St. Paul).

1962—Houston Colt .45's (later renamed the Houston Astros) enfranchised by the National League.

1962—New York Mets enfranchised by the National League. Home attendance, first season (1962), 922,530.

1966—Milwaukee Braves (N.L.) became Atlanta Braves. Home attendance, last season in Milwaukee (1965), 555,584; first season in Atlanta (1966), 1,539,801.

1968—Kansas City Athletics (A.L.) became Oakland Athletics.

1969—Two major leagues each added two teams for totals of 12 and split into two divisions. American League additions: Kansas City Royals and Seattle Pilots; National League additions: Montreal Expos and San Diego Padres. The Division leaders met for the league championship and the two league winners met in the World Series.

1970—Seattle franchise was shifted to Milwaukee, with final court approval coming on March 31. Club was renamed Milwaukee Brewers.

1971—Washington franchise shifted at end of season to Dallas-Fort Worth Texas Rangers with field at Arlington, Tex.

1977—Seattle and Toronto began play in American League.

LARSEN'S PERFECT GAME IN 1956 WORLD SERIES

Don Larsen of the New York Yankees pitched the only no-run no-hit game in World Series history in 1956 and hurled a perfect game in so doing. Facing the Brooklyn Dodgers at the Yankee Stadium in the fifth game before 64,519 on Oct. 8, Larsen retired 27 batters in a row. The Yankees won, 2 to 0.

AMERICAN LEAGUE (Final Standing—1980)

EAST DIVISION

Team	W	L	Pct	GB
New York Yankees	103	59	.636	—
Baltimore Orioles	100	62	.617	3
Milwaukee Brewers	86	76	.531	17
Boston Red Sox	83	77	.519	19
Detroit Tigers	84	78	.519	19
Cleveland Indians	79	81	.494	23
Toronto Blue Jays	67	95	.414	36

WEST DIVISION

Team	W	L	Pct	GB
Kansas City Royals	97	65	.599	—
Oakland A's	83	79	.512	14
Minnesota Twins	77	84	.478	19½
Texas Rangers	76	85	.472	20½
Chicago White Sox	70	90	.438	26
California Angels	65	95	.406	31
Seattle Mariners	59	103	.364	38

AMERICAN LEAGUE PLAYOFFS

1st game, Kansas City, Oct. 8

New York	020	000	000—2	10	1
Kansas City	022	000	12X—7	10	0

Guidry, Davis (4), Underwood (8); Gura. Winner: Gura; Loser: Guidry. Home runs: New York: Cerone, Piniella. Kansas City: G. Brett. Attendance: 42,598.

2nd game, Kansas City, Oct. 9

New York	000	200	000—2	8	0
Kansas City	003	000	00X—3	6	0

May; Leonard, Quisenberry (9). Winner: Leonard; Loser: May. Home runs: New York: Nettles. Kansas City: None. Attendance: 42,633.

3rd game, New York, Oct. 10

Kansas City	000	010	300—4	12	1
New York	000	002	000—2	8	0

Splittorff, Quisenberry (6); John, Gossage (7), Underwood (8). Winner: Quisenberry; Loser: Gossage. Home runs: Kansas City: White, G. Brett. New York: None. Attendance: 56,588.

AMERICAN LEAGUE LEADERS

Batting—George Brett, Kansas City	.390
Runs—Willie Wilson, Kansas City	134
Hits—Willie Wilson, Kansas City	230
Runs batted in—Cecil Cooper, Milwaukee	122
Doubles—Robin Yount, Milwaukee	49
Triples—Alfredo Griffin, Toronto	15
Home Runs—Ben Oglivie, Milwaukee	41
Reggie Jackson, New York	41
Stolen Bases—Rick Henderson, Oakland	100

Pitching

Victories—Steve Stone, Baltimore	25
Earned–run average—Rudy May, New York	2.46
Strikeouts—Len Barker, Cleveland	188
Shutouts—Tommy John, New York	6

NATIONAL LEAGUE (Final standing—1980)

EAST DIVISION

Team	W	L	Pct	GB
Philadelphia Phillies	91	71	.562	—
Montreal Expos	90	72	.556	1
Pittsburgh Pirates	83	79	.512	8
St. Louis Cardinals	74	88	.457	17
New York Mets	67	95	.414	24
Chicago Cubs	64	98	.395	27

WEST DIVISION

Team	W	L	Pct.	GB
*Houston Astros	93	70	.571	—
Los Angeles Dodgers	92	72	.564	1
Cincinnati Reds	89	73	.549	3½
Atlanta Braves	81	80	.503	11
San Francisco Giants	75	86	.466	17
San Diego Padres	73	89	.451	19½

*Won one-game playoff for division title.

NATIONAL LEAGUE PLAYOFFS

1st game, Philadelphia, Oct. 7

Houston	001	000	000—1	7	0
Philadelphia	000	000	21X—3	8	1

Forsch; Carlton, McGraw (8). Winner: Carlton; Loser: Forsch. Home runs: Philadelphia: Luzinski. Attendance: 65,277.

2nd game, Philadelphia, Oct. 8

Houston	001	000	110	4—7	8	1
Philadelphia	000	200	010	1—4	14	2

Ryan, Sambito (7), D. Smith (8), LaCorte (9), Andular (10); Ruthven, McGraw (8), Reed (9), Saucier (10). Winner: LaCorte; Loser: Reed. Home runs: None. Attendance: 65,476.

3rd game, Houston, Oct. 10

Philadelphia	000	000	000	00—0	7	1
Houston	000	000	000	01—1	6	1

Christenson, Noles (7), McGraw (8); Niekro, D. Smith (11). Winner: D. Smith; Loser: McGraw. Home runs: None. Attendance: 44,443.

4th game, Houston, Oct. 11

Philadelphia	000	000	030	2—5	13	0
Houston	000	110	001	0—3	5	1

Carlton, Noles (6), Saucier (7), Reed (7), Brusstar (8), McGraw (10); Ruhle, D. Smith (8), Sambito (8). Winner: Brusstar; Loser: Sambito. Home runs: None. Attendance: 44,952.

5th game, Houston, Oct. 12

Philadelphia	020	000	050	1—8	13	2
Houston	100	001	320	0—7	14	0

Bystrom, Brussat (6), Christenson (7), Reed (7), McGraw (8), Ruthven (9); Ryan, Sambito (8), K. Forsch (8), LaCorte (9). Winner: Ruthven; Loser: LaCorte. Home runs: None. Attendance: 44,802.

NATIONAL LEAGUE LEADERS

Batting—Bill Buckner, Chicago	.324
Runs—Keith Hernandez, St. Louis	111
Hits—Steve Garvey, Los Angeles	200
Runs batted in—Mike Schmidt, Philadelphia	121
Doubles—Pete Rose, Philadelphia	42
Triples—Rod Scott, Montreal	13
Oscar Moreno, Pittsburgh	13
Home runs—Mike Schmidt, Philadelphia	48
Stolen bases—Ron LeFlore, Montreal	97

Pitching

Victories—Steve Carlton, Philadelphia	24
Earned–run average—Don Sutton, Los Angeles	2.20
Strikeouts—Steve Carlton, Philadelphia	286
Shutouts—Jerry Reuss, Los Angeles	6

AMERICAN LEAGUE AVERAGES—1980

(Unofficial)

Batting—Club

	AB	R	H	HR	RBI	PCT
Kansas City	5,715	811	1,634	115	767	.286
Texas	5,690	756	1,616	124	720	.284
Boston	5,606	757	1,589	160	717	.283
Cleveland	5,471	737	1,516	89	692	.277
Milwaukee	5,656	811	1,555	204	772	.275
Detroit	5,618	824	1,534	142	764	.273
Baltimore	5,558	797	1,513	155	742	.272
New York	5,555	821	1,485	189	773	.267
Minnesota	5,531	670	1,467	98	637	.265
California	5,443	698	1,442	106	655	.265
Oakland	5,495	687	1,424	133	635	.259
Chicago	5,440	587	1,408	91	547	.259
Toronto	5,571	625	1,398	125	579	.251
Seattle	5,492	610	1,359	104	565	.247

Batting Leaders

Player/team	AB	R	H	HR	RBI	PCT
G. Brett, Kansas City	449	87	175	24	118	.390
Cooper, Milwaukee	622	96	219	25	122	.352
Dilone, Cleveland	528	87	180	0	40	.341
Rivers, Texas	630	96	210	7	60	.333
Carew, California	540	74	179	3	59	.331
B. Bell, Texas	489	76	161	17	83	.329
Wilson, Kansas City	705	134	230	3	50	.326
Stapleton, Boston	449	61	144	7	45	.321
Bumbry, Baltimore	641	117	205	9	53	.320
Oliver, Texas	656	96	209	19	117	.319
Hassey, Cleveland	390	42	124	8	65	.318
Watson, New York	469	62	144	13	68	.307
Wathan, Kansas City	453	57	138	6	58	.305
Molitor, Milwaukee	450	81	137	9	37	.304
Oglivie, Milwaukee	592	94	180	41	117	.304
Hargrove, Cleveland	589	86	179	11	85	.304
Henderson, Oakland	591	111	179	9	53	.303
Singleton, Baltimore	579	84	175	24	103	.302
Castino, Minnesota	546	67	165	13	64	.302
Murray, Baltimore	620	100	187	32	115	.302
Lynn, Boston	415	67	125	12	61	.301
Woods, Toronto	373	54	112	15	47	.300
Bochte, Seattle	520	62	156	13	78	.300
Staub, Texas	340	42	102	9	55	.300
R. Jackson, New York	514	94	154	41	111	.300
Hurdle, Kansas City	395	49	118	10	60	.299

Leading Pitchers

(15 or more decisions)

Player/team	IP	H	BB	SO	W	L	ERA
R. May, New York	175	144	39	133	15	5	2.46
M. Norris, Oakland	284	215	83	181	22	9	2.53
Darwin, Texas	109	98	50	103	13	4	2.63
Burns, Chicago	238	213	63	133	15	13	2.84
Keough, Oakland	250	218	93	122	16	13	2.92
Gura, Kansas City	283	271	76	112	18	10	2.95
Proly, Chicago	146	136	58	54	5	10	3.07
Quisenberry, Kansas City	128	129	27	37	12	7	3.09
Haas, Milwaukee	252	246	56	146	16	15	3.14
Clear, California	106	82	65	104	11	11	3.21
Stone, Baltimore	250	224	101	149	25	7	3.23
Erickson, Minnesota	191	198	56	97	7	13	3.25
Farmer, Chicago	99	92	56	54	7	9	3.25
Langford, Oakland	290	276	64	100	19	12	3.26
Clancy, Toronto	250	217	128	152	13	16	3.30
B. Stanley, Boston	179	186	52	71	10	8	3.32
McGregor, Baltimore	252	254	58	119	20	8	3.32
John, New York	265	270	56	78	22	9	3.43
F. Bannister, Seattle	217	200	66	154	9	13	3.47
Jenkins, Texas	198	190	52	129	12	12	3.55
Trout, Chicago	199	229	49	89	9	16	3.56
Guidry, New York	219	215	80	166	17	10	3.56
T. Underwood, New York	187	163	66	116	13	9	3.66
Sorensen, Milwaukee	195	242	45	54	12	10	3.68
Stied, Toronto	242	232	83	108	12	15	3.71

NATIONAL LEAGUE AVERAGES—1980

(Unofficial)

Batting—Club

	AB	R	H	HR	RBI	PCT
St. Louis	5,607	738	1,538	101	689	.274
Philadelphia	5,625	728	1,517	117	674	.270
Pittsburgh	5,518	666	1,466	117	625	.266
Los Angeles	5,570	663	1,461	148	635	.262
Cincinnati	5,518	704	1,446	112	667	.262
Houston	5,566	637	1,456	76	599	.262
Montreal	5,466	696	1,413	114	648	.259
New York	5,478	611	1,407	61	554	.257
San Diego	5,540	591	1,411	67	546	.255
Chicago	5,627	617	1,415	108	579	.252
Atlanta	5,396	629	1,354	144	597	.251
San Francisco	5,368	573	1,308	79	539	.244

Batting Leaders

Player/team	AB	R	H	HR	RBI	PCT
L. Smith, Philadelphia	298	69	101	3	20	.339
Easler, Pittsburgh	393	66	133	21	74	.338
Lacy, Pittsburgh	278	45	93	7	33	.335
Buckner, Chicago	578	69	187	10	68	.324
R. Smith, Los Angeles	311	47	100	15	55	.322
K. Hernandez, St. Louis	595	111	191	16	99	.321
Templeton, St. Louis	504	83	161	4	43	.319
Valentine, Montreal	311	40	99	13	67	.318
McBride, Philadelphia	554	68	171	9	87	.309
Cedeno, Houston	499	70	154	10	73	.309
Dawson, Montreal	577	96	178	17	87	.308
Johnstone, Los Angeles	251	31	77	2	20	.307
Garvey, Los Angeles	658	78	200	26	106	.304
Oberkfell, St. Louis	422	58	128	3	47	.303
Simmons, St. Louis	495	84	150	21	98	.303
Collins, Cincinnati	551	94	167	3	34	.303
Hendrick, St. Louis	572	73	173	25	109	.302
J. Cruz, Houston	612	79	185	11	91	.302
Richards, San Diego	642	91	193	4	41	.301
Walling, Houston	284	30	85	3	28	.299
Iorg, St. Louis	251	33	75	3	36	.299
Vail, Chicago	312	29	93	6	47	.298
Mumphry, San Diego	564	31	168	4	59	.298
Whitfield, San Francisco	321	38	95	4	26	.296
Parker, Pittsburgh	581	71	153	18	79	.295
Griffey, Cincinnati	544	90	160	13	85	.294
Baker, Los Angeles	579	80	170	29	97	.294

Leading Pitchers

(15 or more decisions)

Player/team	IP	H	BB	SO	W	L	ERA
Sutton, Los Angeles	212	163	47	128	13	5	2.20
Carlton, Philadelphia	304	243	90	286	24	9	2.34
Ruhle, Houston	158	148	30	54	12	4	2.39
Shone, Los Angeles	84	83	22	40	7	9	2.44
Reuss, Los Angeles	229	193	40	111	18	6	2.51
Hume, Cincinnati	137	121	38	64	9	10	2.56
Reardon, New York	110	96	47	104	8	7	2.61
Fingers, San Diego	103	101	32	68	11	9	2.80
Blue, San Francisco	224	202	61	129	14	10	2.97
Rogers, Montreal	281	247	85	147	16	11	2.98
Zachry, New York	165	145	58	88	6	10	2.99
Gullickson, Montreal	141	127	50	119	10	5	3.00
Soto, Cincinnati	190	126	84	181	10	8	3.07
Whitson, San Francisco	211	222	56	91	11	13	3.10
Sanderson, Montreal	211	206	56	124	16	11	3.11
Sosa, Montreal	94	106	21	58	9	6	3.16

Player/team	IP	H	BB	SO	W	L	ERA
K. Forsch, Houston	223	230	42	84	12	13	3.18
Pastore, Cincinnati	184	161	42	110	13	7	3.27
Welch, Los Angeles	213	190	79	141	14	9	3.28
Bibby, Pittsburgh	238	209	88	141	19	6	3.29
Tekulve, Pittsburgh	93	96	40	47	8	12	3.29
Ryan, Houston	233	205	98	200	11	10	3.35
Reuschel, Chicago	257	281	76	140	11	13	3.40
Vuckovich, St. Louis	222	203	68	131	12	9	3.40
Boggs, Atlanta	192	180	46	84	12	9	3.42

WORLD SERIES—1980

Philadelphia Phillies (NL) defeated Kansas City Royals (AL), 4 games to 2

1st Game—Philadelphia, Oct. 14

PHILADELPHIA (N)	AB	R	H	BI	KANSAS CITY (A)	AB	R	H	BI
Smith, lf	4	0	2	0	Wilson, lf	5	0	0	0
Gross, lf	1	0	0	0	McRae, dh	3	1	1	0
Rose, 1b	3	1	0	0	G. Brett, 3b	4	1	1	0
Schmidt, 3b	2	2	1	0	Aikens, 1b	4	2	2	4
McBride, rf	4	1	3	3	Porter, c	2	1	0	0
Luzinski, dh	3	0	0	0	Otis, cf	4	1	3	2
Maddox, cf	3	0	0	1	Hurdle, rf	3	0	1	0
Trillo, 2b	4	1	1	0	Wathan, rf	1	0	0	0
Bowa, ss	4	1	1	0	White, 2b	4	0	1	0
Boone, c	4	1	3	2	Washington, ss	4	0	0	0
Total	32	7	11	6	Total	34	6	9	6

Kansas City	022 000 020—6
Philadelphia	005 110 00X—7

E—Leonard. DP—Philadelphia. LOB—Kansas City 4, Philadelphia 6. 2B—Boone 2, G. Brett. HR—Otis, Aikens 2, McBride. SB—Bowa, White. SF—Maddox.

	IP	H	R	ER	BB	SO
Kansas City						
Leonard (L)	3⅔	6	6	6	1	3
Martin	4	5	1	1	1	1
Quisenberry	⅓	0	0	0	0	0
Philadelphia						
Walk (W)	7	8	6	6	3	3
McGraw	2	1	0	0	0	1

WP—Walk. HBP—by Leonard (Rose), by Martin (Luzinski). Walk pitched to 2 batters in 8th. Times of game—3:01. Attendance—65,791.

2nd Game—Philadelphia, Oct. 15

KANSAS CITY (A)	AB	R	H	BI	PHILADELPHIA (N)	AB	R	H	BI
Wilson, lf	4	1	1	0	Smith, lf	3	0	0	0
Washington, ss	4	0	1	0	Unser, cf	1	1	1	1
G. Brett, 3b	2	0	2	0	Rose, 1b	4	0	0	0
Chalk, 3b	0	1	0	0	McBride, rf	3	1	1	1
Porter, ph	1	0	0	0	Schmidt, 3b	4	1	2	1
McRae, dh	4	1	3	0	Moreland, dh	4	1	2	1
Otis, cf	5	1	2	2	Maddox, cf	3	1	1	0
Wathan, c	3	0	0	1	Gross, lf	1	0	0	0
Aikens, 1b	3	0	1	0	Trillo, 2b	2	0	0	1
LaCock, 1b	0	0	0	0	Bowa, ss	3	0	1	1
Cardenal, rf	4	0	0	0	Boone, c	1	1	0	0
White, 2b	4	0	1	0	Total	29	6	8	6
Total	34	4	11	3					

Kansas City	000 001 300—4
Philadelphia	000 020 04X—6

E—Trillo. DP—Kansas City 2, Philadelphia 4. LOB—Kansas City 11, Philadelphia 3. 2B—Maddox, Otis, Unser, Schmidt. SB—Wilson, Chalk. S—Washington. SF—Trillo, Wathan.

	IP	H	R	ER	BB	SO
Kansas City						
Gura	6	4	2	2	2	2
Quisenberry (L)	2	4	4	4	1	0
Philadelphia						
Carlton (W)	8	10	4	3	6	10
Reed	1	1	0	0	0	2

WP—Carlton. Time of game—3:01. Attendance—65,775.

3rd Game—Kansas City, Oct. 17

PHILADELPHIA (N)	AB	R	H	BI	KANSAS CITY (A)	AB	R	H	BI
L. Smith, lf	4	0	2	1	Wilson, lf	4	1	0	0
Gross, lf	0	0	0	0	White, 2b	5	0	0	0
Rose, 1b	4	0	1	1	G. Brett, 3b	4	1	2	1
Schmidt, 3b	5	1	1	1	Aikens, 1b	5	1	2	1
McBride, rf	5	0	2	0	McRae, dh	4	0	2	1
Moreland, dh	5	0	1	0	Otis, cf	4	1	2	1
Maddox, cf	4	0	1	0	Hurdle, rf	4	0	2	0
Trillo, 2b	5	1	2	0	Concepcion, pr	0	0	0	0
Bowa, ss	5	1	3	0	Cardenal, rf	0	0	0	0
Boone, c	4	0	1	0	Porter, c	4	0	0	0
Total	41	3	14	3	Washington, ss	4	0	1	0
					Total	38	4	11	4

Philadelphia	010 010 010 0—3
Kansas City	100 100 100 1—4

DP—Philadelphia 1, Kansas City 2. LOB—Philadelphia 15, Kansas City 7. 2B—Trillo, G. Brett. 3B—Aikens. HRs—G. Brett, Schmidt, Otis. SB—Hurdle, Bowa, Wilson. S—Gross.

	IP	H	R	ER	BB	SO
Philadelphia						
Ruthven	9	9	3	3	0	7
McGraw (L)	*⅔	2	1	1	2	1
Kansas City						
Gale	4⅓	7	2	2	3	3
Martin	3⅓	5	1	1	1	1
Quisenberry (W)	2⅓	2	0	0	2	0

*Two outs when winning run was scored. Time of game—3:19. Attendance—42,380.

1980 WORLD SERIES MATCHED CLUBS WHO HAD NEVER WON

The Kansas City Royals in 1980 competed in their first World Series since the franchise was started in 1968. Their opponents, the Philadelphia Phillies, had not appeared in the Series in 30 years, losing in four straight games to the New York Yankees in 1950. The confrontation between the Royals and Phillies marked the first time since 1920, when Cleveland met Brooklyn, that two teams that had not won a World Series faced each other. In Philadelphia's only other appearance in a Series, in 1915 against the Boston Red Sox, the Phillies won the first game with Grover Alexander pitching, then lost four in a row.

4th Game—Kansas City, Oct. 18

PHILADELPHIA (N)	AB	R	H	BI	KANSAS CITY (A)	AB	R	H	BI
L. Smith, dh	4	0	0	0	Wilson, lf	4	1	1	0
Rose, 1b	4	1	2	0	White, 2b	5	0	0	0
McBride, rf	3	0	1	0	G. Brett, 3b	5	1	1	1
Schmidt, 3b	3	0	1	1	Aikens, 1b	3	2	2	3
Unser, lf	4	0	1	0	McRae, dh	4	1	2	0
Maddox, cf	4	0	1	0	Otis, cf	4	0	2	1
Trillo, 2b	4	2	1	0	Hurdle, rf	2	0	1	0
Bowa, ss	4	0	2	1	Porter, c	3	0	0	0
Boone, c	3	0	1	1	Washington, ss	4	0	1	0
Total	**33**	**3**	**10**	**3**	**Total**	**34**	**5**	**10**	**5**

Philadelphia	**010 000 110—3**
Kansas City	**410 000 00X—5**

E—White, Christenson, Washington. DP—Kansas City 1. LOB—Philadelphia 5, Kansas City 10. 2B—McRae 2, Otis, Hurdle, McBride, Trillo, Rose. 3B—G. Brett. HR—Aikens 2. SB—Bowa. SF—Schmidt.

	IP	H	R	ER	BB	SO
Philadelphia						
Christenson (L)	⅓	5	4	4	0	0
Noles	4⅔	5	1	1	2	6
Saucier	⅔	0	0	0	2	0
Brusstar	2⅓	0	0	0	1	0
Kansas City						
Leonard (W)	7	9	3	2	1	2
Quisenberry	2	1	0	0	0	0

Time of game—2:37. Attendance—42,363.

5th Game—Kansas City, Oct. 19

PHILADELPHIA (N)	AB	R	H	BI	KANSAS CITY (A)	AB	R	H	BI
Rose, 1b	4	0	0	0	Wilson, lf	5	0	2	0
McBride, rf	4	1	0	0	White, 2b	3	0	0	0
Schmidt, 3b	4	2	2	2	G. Brett, 3b	5	0	1	1
Luzinski, lf	2	0	0	0	Aikens, 1b	3	0	1	0
L. Smith, lf	0	0	0	0	Concepcion, pr	0	0	0	0
Unser, lf	1	1	1	1	McRae, dh	5	0	1	0
Moreland, dh	3	0	1	0	Otis, cf	3	1	2	1
Maddox, cf	4	0	0	0	Hurdle, rf	3	1	1	0
Trillo, 2b	4	0	1	1	Cardenal, rf	2	0	0	0
Bowa, ss	4	0	1	0	Porter, c	4	0	2	0
Boone, c	3	0	1	0	Washington, ss	3	1	2	1
Total	**33**	**4**	**7**	**4**	**Total**	**36**	**3**	**12**	**3**

Philadelphia	**000 200 002—4**
Kansas City	**000 012 000—3**

E—Aikens, G. Brett. DP—Kansas City 2. LOB—Philadelphia 4, Kansas City 13. 2B—Wilson, McRae, Unser. HRs—Schmidt, Otis. SB—G. Brett. S—White, Moreland. SF—Washington.

	IP	H	R	ER	BB	SO
Philadelphia						
Bystrom	5	10	3	3	1	4
Reed	1	1	0	0	0	0
McGraw (W)	3	1	0	0	4	5
Kansas City						
Gura	6⅓	4	2	1	1	2
Quisenberry (L)	2⅔	3	2	2	0	0

Time of game—2:51. Attendance—42,369.

6th Game—Philadelphia, Oct. 21

KANSAS CITY (A)	AB	R	H	BI	PHILADELPHIA (N)	AB	R	H	BI
Wilson, lf	4	0	0	0	L. Smith, lf	4	2	1	0
Washington, ss	3	0	1	1	Gross, lf	0	0	0	0
G. Brett, 3b	4	0	2	0	Rose, 1b	4	0	3	0
McRae, dh	4	0	0	0	Schmidt, 3b	3	0	1	2
Otis, cf	3	0	0	0	McBride, rf	4	0	0	1
Aikens, 1b	2	0	0	0	Luzinski, dh	4	0	0	0
Concepcion, pr	0	0	0	0	Maddox, cf	4	0	2	0
Wathan, c	3	1	2	0	Trillo, 2b	4	0	0	0
Cardenal, rf	4	0	2	0	Bowa, ss	4	1	1	0
White, 2b	4	0	0	0	Boone, c	2	1	1	1
Total	**31**	**1**	**7**	**1**	**Total**	**33**	**4**	**9**	**4**

Kansas City	**000 000 010—1**
Philadelphia	**002 011 00X—4**

E—White, Aikens. DP—Kansas City 1, Philadelphia 2. LOB—Kansas City 9, Philadelphia 7. 2B—Maddox, L. Smith, Bowa. SF—Washington.

	IP	H	R	ER	BB	SO
Kansas City						
Gale (L)	2	4	2	1	1	1
Martin	2⅓	1	1	1	1	0
Splittorff	1⅔	4	1	1	0	0
Pattin	1	0	0	0	0	2
Quisenberry	1	0	0	0	0	0
Philadelphia						
Carlton (W)	7	4	1	1	3	7
McGraw	2	3	0	0	2	2

Time of game—3:00. Attendance—65,838.

1916 NEW YORK GIANTS HOLD WINNING STREAK RECORD AT 26

The longest winning streak in major-league history was registered by the New York Giants of the National League in 1916 when they reeled off 26 in a row, all at home. The American League record is held by the Chicago White Sox who posted 19 straight victories in 1906, 11 at home and 8 on the road. In the losing streak category, the American League mark is held by the 1906 Boston Red Sox who dropped 20 in order, 19 of them before the home fans. Cleveland lost 24, only 3 at home, in 1899 when it was a member of the National League.

STEVE CARLTON TOP LEFT-HANDER IN STRIKEOUTS

Steve Carlton, who led the Philadelphia Phillies to the National League pennant in 1980 with 24 victories, became the major leagues' leading left-hander in career strikeouts, when he registered 286 for the season. That gave him a lifetime total of 2,969 and moved him ahead of Mickey Lolich among left-handers. Lolich was the leading left-hander, with 2,812. Carlton's strikeout total moved him up to fourth place on the career list, just behind Walter Johnson (3,508), Gaylord Perry (3,276), and Bob Gibson (3,117). Perry moved up to second place ahead of Gibson during the 1980 season.

Carlton also distinguished himself with the sixth one-hitter of his career, putting him in third place and breaking a tie he shared with five other hurlers. Bob Feller holds the record for one-hitters in a career, with 12. Among the active pitchers, Tom Seaver and Don Sutton have each thrown five one-hitters.

BASEBALL—AMATEUR

1980 CHAMPIONS

N.C.A.A. Division I—Arizona
N.C.C.A. Division II—California–Poly, Pomona
N.C.A.A. Division III—Ithaca (N.Y.) College
N.A.I.A.—Grand Canyon College, Phoenix, Ariz.
Connie Mack League—Saginaw Township, Mich.
Little League—Taiwan
Babe Ruth League (16–18) Nashville, Tenn.
(13–15) Rotterdam, N.Y.
(13 and under) Miami, Fla.

BASEBALL—MINOR LEAGUES—1980

CLASS AAA

AMERICAN ASSOCIATION

Eastern Division

	W	L	Pct.
Springfield (Cardinals)	75	61	.551
Evansville (Tigers)	61	74	.452
Iowa (White Sox)	59	77	.434
Indianapolis (Reds)	58	77	.430

Western Division

	W	L	Pct.
Denver (Expos)	92	44	.676
Oklahoma City (Phillies)	70	65	.519
Omaha (Royals)	66	70	.485
Wichita (Cubs)	61	74	.452

Playoff—Springfield defeated Denver, 4 games to 1

INTERNATIONAL LEAGUE

	W	L	Pct.
Columbus (Yankees)	83	57	.593
Toledo (Twins)	77	63	.550
Rochester (Orioles)	74	65	.532
Richmond (Braves)	69	71	.493
Charleston (Rangers)	67	71	.486
Tidewater (Mets)	67	72	.482
Pawtucket (Red Sox)	62	77	.446
Syracuse (Blue Jays)	58	81	.417

Playoffs

Semifinals—Columbus defeated Richmond, 3 games to 2
Toledo defeated Rochester, 3 games to 1
Final—Columbus defeated Toledo, 4 games to 1

PACIFIC COAST LEAGUE

North Division

First half winner—Hawaii (Padres)
Second half winner—Vancouver (Brewers)
Playoff—Hawaii defeated Vancouver

South Division

First half winner—Tucson (Rangers)
Second half winner—Albuquerque (Dodgers)
Playoff—Albuquerque defeated Tucson
Championship playoff—Albuquerque defeated Hawaii, 3 games to 2

MEXICAN LEAGUE[1]

Southeastern Division—Puebla
Southwestern Division—Mexico City
Northeastern Division—Aquascalientes
Northwestern Division—Juarez

1. Players' strike canceled regular season after July 3.

CLASS AA

Eastern League—Northern Division, first half: Buffalo (Pirates); second half: Holyoke (Brewers); playoff: Holyoke. Southern Division, first half: Waterbury (Reds); second half: Reading (Phillies); playoff: Waterbury. League championship: Holyoke defeated Waterbury, 2 games to 1

Southern League—Eastern Division, first half: Charlotte (Orioles); second half: Savannah (Braves); playoff: Charlotte. Western Division, first half: Memphis (Expos); second half: Nashville (Yankees); playoff: Memphis. League champion: Charlotte defeated Memphis, 3 games to 1

Texas League—Eastern Division, first half: Arkansas (Cardinals); second half: Jackson (Mets); playoff: Arkansas. Western Division, first half: San Antonio (Dodgers); second half: Amarillo (Padres); playoff: San Antonio. League championship: Arkansas defeated San Antonio, 3 games to 0

CLASS A

California League—Southern Division, first half: Fresno (Giants); second half: Visalia (Twins); playoff: Visalia. Northern Division, first half: Stockton (Brewers); second half: Stockton. League championship: Stockton defeated Visalia, 3 games to 0

Midwest League—Northern Division, first half, Waterloo (Indians); second half: Wisconsin Rapids (Twins); playoff: Waterloo. Southern Division, first half: Quad–Cities (Cubs); second half: Burlington (Brewers); playoff: Quad–Cities. League championship: Waterloo defeated Quad–Cities, 2 games to 1

New York–Penn League—Eastern Division, Oneonta (Yankees); Western Division, Geneva (Cubs). League championship: Oneonta defeated Geneva, 2 games to 1

Northwest League—Northern Division: Bellingham (Mariners). Southern Division: Eugene (Reds). Playoff: Teams declared co–champions after third game of two–of–three series was rained out. Seattle parent club refused extension of series. Each team had won a game.

South Atlantic League—Northern Division: Greensboro (Yankees) won first and second half. Southern Division: Charleston (Royals) won first and second half. League championship: Greensboro defeated Charleston, 3 games to 0

ROOKIE LEAGUES

Appalachian—Paintsville (Yankees)
Pioneer—Northern Division: Lethbridge (Dodgers). Southern Division: Billings (Reds)

BRETT's .390 BATTING AVERAGE HIGHEST IN MAJORS SINCE 1941

George Brett, who led the Kansas City Royals to their first pennant, won the American League batting championship in 1980 with a .390 average, the highest since Ted Williams of the Boston Red Sox finished with .406 in 1941.

For much of the last month of the season, Brett flirted with becoming the first batter since Williams to bat .400 or better. He reached .408, then suffered a case of tendinitis in the wrist and was sidelined for several games. He made another attempt when he returned, but faltered in the final week of the campaign.

Only 19 men have batted .400 or better in the history of baseball, with several of those accomplishing it more than once. Williams was the last to do it in the majors and the American League. Bill Terry of the New York Giants, with .401 in 1930, was the last National League batter to attain the mark.

LITTLE LEAGUE WORLD SERIES

1947	Williamsport, Pa.	1958	Monterrey, Mexico	1969	Taiwan (Nationalist China)
1948	Lock Haven, Pa.	1959	Hamtramck, Mich.	1970	Wayne, N.J.
1949	Hammonton, N.J.	1960	Levittown, Pa.	1971	Taiwan (Nationalist China)
1950	Houston, Tex.	1961	El Cajon, Calif.	1972	Taiwan (Nationalist China)
1951	Stamford, Conn.	1962	San Jose, Calif.	1973	Taiwan (Nationalist China)
1952	Norwalk, Conn.	1963	Granada Hills, Calif.	1974	Taiwan (Nationalist China)
1953	Birmingham, Ala.	1964	Staten Island, N.Y.	1975	Lakewood Township, N.J.
1954	Schenectady, N.Y.	1965	Windsor Locks, Conn.	1976	Tokyo, Japan
1955	Morrisville, Pa.	1966	Houston, Tex.	1977	Tapei, Taiwan
1956	Roswell, N.M.	1967	West Tokyo, Japan	1978–79	Pintung, Taiwan
1957	Monterrey, Mexico	1968	Wakayama, Japan	1980	Hua Lian, Taiwan

SOFTBALL

Source: Amateur Softball Association.

Amateur Champions

1959	Aurora (Ill.) Sealmasters	1968	Clearwater (Fla.) Bombers	1975	Rising Sun Hotel, Reading, Pa.
1960	Clearwater (Fla.) Bombers	1969	Raybestos Cardinals, Stratford, Conn.	1976	Raybestos Cardinals, Stratford, Conn.
1961	Aurora (Ill.) Sealmasters	1971	Welty Way, Cedar Rapids, Iowa	1977	Billard Barbell, Reading, Pa.
1962–63	Clearwater (Fla.) Bombers	1972	Raybestos Cardinals, Stratford, Conn.	1978	Reading, Pa.
1964	Burch Gage & Tool, Detroit	1973	Clearwater (Fla.) Bombers	1979	Midland, Mich.
1965	Aurora (Ill.) Sealmasters	1974	Santa Rosa (Calif.)	1980	Peterbuilt Western, Seattle
1966	Clearwater (Fla.) Bombers				
1967	Aurora (Ill.) Sealmasters				

AMATEUR SOFTBALL ASSOCIATION CHAMPIONS—1980

Men's major fast pitch—Peterbuilt Western, Seattle, Wash.
Women's major fast pitch—Raybestos Brakettes, Stratford, Conn.
Women's Class A fast pitch—Astros, San Diego, Calif.
Men's major slow pitch—Campbell's Carpets, Concord, Calif.
Women's major slow pitch—Rubi–Otts, Graham, N.C.
Men's major industrial slow pitch—Sikorsky, Stratford, Conn.
Men's Class A slow pitch—Wreckers, Houston, Tex.
Women's Class A slow pitch—Encore, Brandywine, Md.
Men's Class A industrial slow pitch—Local 761, Louisville, Ky.
Women's Class A industrial slow pitch—Provident Vets, Chattanooga, Tenn.
Modified—Cadillac, Atlanta, Ga.
Men's church slow pitch—West End Baptist, Houston, Tex.
Women's church slow pitch—Rock Creek Methodist, Snow Camp, N.C.

YOUTH TOURNAMENTS—1980

Boys 16–18 fast pitch—Schlitz Bulls, Springfield, Mo.
Boys 16–18 slow pitch—Gills's Insurance, Tifton, Ga.
Boys 13–15 fast pitch—Universal Corp., Baton Rouge, La.
Boys 13–15 slow pitch—The Mavericks, Tifton, Ga.
Girls 16–18 fast pitch—Nor–cal Tremors, Fairfield, Calif.
Girls 16–18 slow pitch—Chem–Nut Tom Boys, Tifton, Ga.
Girls 13–15 fast pitch—Aces, Eugene, Ore.
Girls 13–15 slow pitch—The Mets, Satellite Beach, Fla.

WORLD CHAMPION—1980

Men's fast pitch—Home Savings, Aurora, Ill.

SQUASH RACQUETS

1980 U.S. SQUASH RACQUETS ASSOCIATION CHAMPIONS

Men's Events

Singles—Michael Desaulniers, Montreal
Singles, 35–40—Thomas Poor, Boston
Singles, 40–45—Raul Sanchez, Mexico City
Singles, 45–50—George H. Bostwick, Jr., Locust Valley, N.Y.
Singles, 50–55—Henri Salaun, Boston
Singles, 55–60—Delbert O. Fuller, Chicago
Singles, 60–65—Calvin MacCracken, Englewood, N.J.
Class B singles—Thomas Fortson, White Plains, N.Y.
Class C singles—David Boyum, Brooklyn, N.Y.
Doubles—John Bottger, Philadelphia–Gilbert Mateer, Cleveland
Veterans doubles—Helmut Meertz–Christian Spahr, Philadelphia
Seniors doubles—Darwin P. Kingsley–Alfred R. Hunter, Philadelphia
College singles A—Michael Desaulniers, Harvard
College singles B—Murray Shaw, Univ. of Western Ontario
College singles C—Patrick Murray, Pennsylvania
United States teams—New York No. 1
College team—Univ. of Western Ontario
Lapham Cup (singles)—Canada 8, United States 7
Grant Trophy (doubles)—Canada 4, United States 3
North American open—Sharif Khan, Toronto
U.S. Pro singles—Sharif Khan, Toronto

Women's Events

Singles—Barbara Maltby, Philadelphia
Singles, 35 and over—Joyce Davenport, King of Prussia, Pa.
Singles, 40 and over—Marigold Edwards, Pittsburgh
Class B singles—Annette Seegers, Chicago
Class C singles—Aileen White, Chatham, N.J.
Doubles—Joyce Davenport, King of Prussia, Pa.–Carol Thesieres, Broomall, Pa.
Doubles, 40 and over—Irma Brogan, Wynnewood, Pa.–Carol Thesieres, Broomall, Pa.
Mixed doubles—Ralph E. Howe, Cold Spring Harbor, N.Y.–Joyce Davenport, King of Prussia, Pa.

1980 WORLD CHAMPION—MEN

Pro—Clive Caldwell, Toronto

YACHTING

AMERICA'S CUP RECORD

First race in 1851 around Isle of Wight, Cowes, England. First defense and all others through 1920 held 30 miles off New York Bay. Races since 1930 held 30 miles off Newport, R.I. Conducted as one race only in 1851 and 1870; best four-of-seven basis, 1871; best two-of-three, 1876–1887; best three-of-five, 1893–1901; best four-of-seven, since 1930. Figures in parentheses indicate number of races won.

Year	Winner and owner	Loser and owner
1851	AMERICA (1), John C. Stevens, U.S.	AURORA, T. Le Marchant, England[1]
1870	MAGIC (1), Franklin Osgood, U.S.	CAMBRIA, James Ashbury, England[2]
1871	COLUMBIA (2), Franklin Osgood, U.S.[3]	LIVONIA (1), James Ashbury, England
	SAPPHO (2), William P. Douglas, U.S.	
1876	MADELEINE (2), John S. Dickerson, U.S.	COUNTESS OF DUFFERIN, Chas. Gifford, Canada
1881	MISCHIEF (2), J. R. Busk, U.S.	ATALANTA, Alexander Cuthbert, Canada
1885	PURITAN (2), J. M. Forbes-Gen. Charles Paine, U.S.	GENESTA, Sir Richard Sutton, England
1886	MAYFLOWER (2), Gen. Charles Paine, U.S.	GALATEA, Lt. William Henn, England
1887	VOLUNTEER (2), Gen. Charles Paine, U.S.	THISTLE, James Bell et al, Scotland
1893	VIGILANT (3), C. Oliver Iselin et al., U.S.	VALKYRIE II, Lord Dunraven, England
1895	DEFENDER (3), C. O. Iselin-W. K. Vanderbilt-E. D. Morgan, U.S.	VALKYRIE III, Lord Dunraven-Lord Lonsdale-Lord Wolverton, England
1899	COLUMBIA (3), J. P. Morgan-C. O. Iselin, U.S.	SHAMROCK I, Sir Thomas Lipton, Ireland
1901	COLUMBIA (3), Edwin D. Morgan, U.S.	SHAMROCK II, Sir Thomas Lipton, Ireland
1903	RELIANCE (3), Cornelius Vanderbilt et al., U.S.	SHAMROCK III, Sir Thomas Lipton, Ireland
1920	RESOLUTE (3), Henry Walters et al., U.S.	SHAMROCK IV (2), Sir Thomas Lipton, Ireland
1930	ENTERPRISE (4), Harold S. Vanderbilt et al., U.S.	SHAMROCK V, Sir Thomas Lipton, Ireland
1934	RAINBOW (4), Harold S. Vanderbilt, U.S.	ENDEAVOUR (2), T. O. M. Sopwith, England
1937	RANGER (4), Harold S. Vanderbilt, U.S.	ENDEAVOUR II, T. O. M. Sopwith, England
1958	COLUMBIA (4), Henry Sears et al., U.S.	SCEPTRE, Hugh Goodson et al., England
1962	WEATHERLY (4), Henry D. Mercer et al., U.S.	GRETEL (1), Sir Frank Packer et al., Australia
1964	CONSTELLATION (4), New York Y.C. Syndicate, U.S.	SOVEREIGN (0), J. Anthony Bowden, England
1967	INTREPID (4), New York Y.C. Syndicate, U.S.	DAME PATTIE (0), Sydney (Aust.) Syndicate
1970	INTREPID (4), New York Y.C. Syndicate, U.S.	GRETEL II (1), Sydney (Aust.) Syndicate
1974	COURAGEOUS (4), New York, N.Y. Syndicate, U.S.	SOUTHERN CROSS (0), Sydney (Aust.) Syndicate
1977	COURAGEOUS (4), New York, N.Y. Syndicate, U.S.	AUSTRALIA (0), Sun City (Aust.) Syndicate
1980	FREEDOM (4), New York, N.Y. Syndicate, U.S.	AUSTRALIA (1), Alan Bond et al, Australia

1. Fourteen British yachts started against America; Aurora finished second. 2. Cambria sailed against 23 U.S. yachts and finished tenth. 3. Columbia was disabled in the third race, after winning the first two; Sappho substituted and won the fourth and fifth.

SOUTHERN OCEAN RACING CONFERENCE

(6 races, 72 Grand Prix yachts, 6 classes)

St. Petersburg to Boca Grande (138 miles)—Kialoa (Class A), John Kilroy
St. Petersburg to Fort Lauderdale (359 miles)—Tatoosh (Class B), Robert Hutton
Ocean Triangle (176 miles)—Kialoa (Class A), John Kilroy
Lipton Cup (135 miles)—Intuition (Class B), Pat Malloy
Miami to Nassau (176 miles)—Thunderbird (Class F), Rodney Wallace
Nassau Cup (27 miles, Olympic course)—Tatoosh (Class B), Robert Hutton

FINAL FLEET STANDING

(Fleet position for 6 races in parentheses)

Overall winner—Acadia (Class C), Burt Keenan, (12–2–16–7–22–16), 1,985 points
Tatoosh (Class B), Robert Hutton, (16–1–15–15–34–1), 1,962.5
Forte (Class C), Tom Tobin, (9–20–22–2–26–12), 1,936
Merrythought (Class B), Jack King, (15–14–17–19–32–3), 1,929.5
Pegasus (Class B), David Fenix, (25–4–10–21–38–6), 1,929.5

U.S.Y.R.A. YOUTH CHAMPIONSHIPS

(Port Townsend, Wash., June 28, 1980)

Single-handed—Russ Silvestri, Tiburon, Calif.
Double-handed—Allen and Peter Lindsey, Miami, Fla.

OCEAN AND DISTANCE RACING

(Newport, R.I., to Bermuda, 635 miles)

Class A—Tenacious, J.R. Mattingly, skipper
Class B—Merrythought, J.W. King
Class C—Acadia, B.H. Keenan
Class D—Hilaria, C.F. Chapin–G.H. Schryver
Class E—Katrinka, F., and M. Winder
Class F—Holger Danske, J.J. Wilson
Overall winner (corrected time)—Holger Danske
First to finish—Bumblebee 4, placed 143rd on corrected time

HANG GLIDING

1979 World Champion—Malcolm Jones, Tampa, Fla.

CRICKET—1980

West Indies–England—West Indies

LAWN BOWLING

NATIONAL OPEN TOURNAMENT—1980

Men's singles—Richard Folkins, Mission Viejo, Calif.
Women's singles—Harriett Bauer, Seattle
Men's pairs—Ross Brown, Chicago, and Ron Veitch, Portland, Ore.
Men's triples—John Stewart, Roy Webb, and Derrick Stewart, Cleveland

AUTO RACING

INDIANAPOLIS 500

Year	Winner	Car	Time	mph	Second place
1911	Ray Harroun	Marmon	6:42:08	74.59	Ralph Mulford
1912	Joe Dawson	National	6:21:06	78.72	Teddy Tetzloff
1913	Jules Goux	Peugeot	6:35:05	75.93	Spencer Wishart
1914	René Thomas	Delage	6:03:45	82.47	Arthur Duray
1915	Ralph DePalma	Mercedes	5:33:55.51	89.84	Dario Resta
1916[1]	Dario Resta	Peugeot	3:34:17	84.00	Wilbur D'Alene
1919	Howard Wilcox	Peugeot	5:40:42.87	88.05	Eddie Hearne
1920	Gaston Chevrolet	Monroe	5:38:32	88.62	René Thomas
1921	Tommy Milton	Frontenac	5:34:44.65	89.62	Roscoe Sarles
1922	Jimmy Murphy	Murphy Special	5:17:30.79	94.48	Harry Hartz
1923	Tommy Milton	H. C. S. Special	5:29.50.17	90.95	Harry Hartz
1924	L. L. Corum–Joe Boyer	Dusenberg Special	5:05:23.51	98.23	Earl Cooper
1925	Peter DePaolo	Dusenberg Special	4:56:39.45	101.13	Dave Lewis
1926[2]	Frank Lockhart	Miller Special	4:10:14.95	95.904	Harry Hartz
1927	George Souders	Dusenberg Special	5:07:33.08	97.54	Earl DeVore
1928	Louis Meyer	Miller Special	5:01:33.75	99.48	Lou Moore
1929	Ray Keech	Simplex Special	5:07:25.42	97.58	Louis Meyer
1930	Billy Arnold	Miller–Hartz Special	4:58:39.72	100.448	Shorty Cantlon
1931	Louis Schneider	Bowes Special	5:10:27.93	96.629	Fred Frame
1932	Fred Frame	Miller–Hartz Special	4:48:03.79	104.144	Howard Wilcox
1933	Louis Meyer	Tydol Special	4:48:00.75	104.162	Wilbur Shaw
1934	Bill Cummings	Boyle Products Special	4:46:05.20	104.863	Mauri Rose
1935	Kelly Petillo	Gilmore Special	4:42:22.71	106.240	Wilbur Shaw
1936	Louis Meyer	Ring Free Special	4:35:03.39	109.069	Ted Horn
1937	Wilbur Shaw	Shaw–Gilmore Special	4:24:07.80	113.580	Ralph Hepburn
1938	Floyd Roberts	Burd Piston Ring Special	4:15:58.40	117.200	Wilbur Shaw
1939	Wilbur Shaw	Boyle Special	4:20:47.39	115.035	Jimmy Snyder
1940	Wilbur Shaw	Boyle Special	4:22:31.17	114.277	Rex Mays
1941	Floyd Davis–Mauri Rose	Noc-Out Hose Clamp Special	4:20:36.24	115.117	Rex Mays
1946	George Robson	Thorne Engineering Special	4:21:26.71	114.820	Jimmy Jackson
1947	Mauri Rose	Blue Crown Special	4:17:52.17	116.338	Bill Holland
1948	Mauri Rose	Blue Crown Special	4:10:23.33	119.814	Bill Holland
1949	Bill Holland	Blue Crown Special	4:07:15.97	121.327	Johnny Parsons
1950[3]	Johnnie Parsons	Wynn's Friction Proof Special	2:46:55.97	124.002	Bill Holland
1951	Lee Wallard	Belanger Special	3:57:38.05	126.244	Mike Nazaruk
1952	Troy Ruttman	Agajanian Special	3:52:41.88	128.922	Jim Rathmann
1953	Bill Vukovich	Fuel Injection Special	3:53:01.69	128.740	Art Cross
1954	Bill Vukovich	Fuel Injection Special	3:49:17.27	130.840	Jim Bryan
1955	Bob Sweikert	John Zink Special	3:53:59.13	128.209	Tony Bettenhausen
1956	Pat Flaherty	John Zink Special	3:53:28.84	128.490	Sam Hanks
1957	Sam Hanks	Belond Exhaust Special	3:41:14.25	135.601	Jim Rathmann
1958	Jimmy Bryan	Belond A–P Special	3:44:13.80	133.791	George Amick
1959	Rodger Ward	Leader Card 500 Roadster	3:40:49.20	135.857	Jim Rathmann
1960	Jim Rathmann	Ken–Paul Special	3:36:11.36	138.767	Rodger Ward
1961	A. J. Foyt	Bowes Special	3:35:37.49	139.130	Eddie Sachs
1962	Rodger Ward	Leader Card Special	3:33:50.33	140.293	Len Sutton
1963	Parnelli Jones	Agajanian Special	3:29:35.40	143.137	Jim Clark
1964	A. J. Foyt	Offenhauser Special	3:23:35.83	147.350	Rodger Ward
1965	Jim Clark	Lotus–Ford	3:19:05.34	150.686	Parnelli Jones
1966	Graham Hill	Lola–Ford	3:27:52.53	144.317	Jim Clark
1967[4]	A. J. Foyt	Coyote–Ford	3:18:24.22	151.207	Al Unser
1968	Bobby Unser	Eagle–Offenhauser	3:16:13.76	152.882	Dan Gurney
1969	Mario Andretti	STP Hawk–Ford	3:11:14.71	156.867	Dan Gurney
1970	Al Unser	P. J. Colt–Ford	3:12:37.04	155.749	Mark Donohue
1971	Al Unser	P. J. Colt–Ford	3:10:11.56	157.735	Peter Revson
1972	Mark Donohue	McLaren–Offenhauser	3:04:05.54	162.962	Al Unser
1973[5]	Gordon Johncock	Eagle–Offenhauser	2:05:26.59	159.036	Bill Vukovich
1974	Johnny Rutherford	McLaren–Offenhauser	3:09:10.06	158.589	Bobby Unser
1975[6]	Bobby Unser	Eagle–Offenhauser	2:54:55.08	149.213	Johnny Rutherford
1976[7]	Johnny Rutherford	McLaren–Offenhauser	1:42:52.48	148.725	A. J. Foyt
1977	A. J. Foyt	Coyote–Foyt	3:05:57.16	161.331	Tom Sneva
1978	Al Unser	Lola–Cosworth	3:05:54.99	161.363	Tom Sneva
1979	Rick Mears	Penske–Cosworth	3:08:27.97	158.899	A. J. Foyt
1980	Johnny Rutherford	Chaparral–Cosworth	3:29:59.56	142.862	Tom Sneva

1. 300 miles. 2. Race ended at 400 miles because of rain. 3. Race ended at 345 miles because of rain. 4. Race, postponed after 18 laps because of rain on May 30, was finished on May 31. 5. Race postponed May 28 and 29 was cut to 332.5 miles because of rain, May 30. 6. Race ended at 435 miles because of rain. 7. Race ended at 255 miles because of rain.

U.S. AUTO CLUB NATIONAL CHAMPIONS

1910	Ray Harroun	1925	Peter DePaolo	1946–48	Ted Horn	1963–64	A. J. Foyt
1911	Ralph Mulford	1926	Harry Hartz	1949	Johnnie Parsons	1965–66	Mario Andretti
1912	Ralph DePalma	1927	Peter DePaolo	1950	Henry Banks	1967	A. J. Foyt
1913	Earl Cooper	1928–29	Louis Meyer	1951	Tony Bettenhausen	1968	Bobby Unser
1914	Ralph DePalma	1930	Billy Arnold			1969	Mario Andretti
1915	Earl Cooper	1931	Louis Schneider	1952	Chuck Stevenson	1970	Al Unser
1916	Dario Resta	1932	Bob Carey	1953	Sam Hanks	1971–72	Joe Leonard
1917	Earl Cooper	1933	Louis Meyer	1954	Jimmy Bryan	1973	Roger McCluskey
1918	Ralph Mulford	1934	Bill Cummings	1955	Bob Sweikert	1974	Bobby Unser
1919	Howard Wilcox	1935	Kelly Petillo	1956–57	Jimmy Bryan	1975	A. J. Foyt
1920	Gaston Chevrolet	1936	Mauri Rose	1958	Tony Bettenhausen	1976	Gordon Johncock
1921	Tommy Milton	1937	Wilbur Shaw			1977–78	Tom Sneva
1922	James Murphy	1938	Floyd Roberts	1959	Rodger Ward	1979	A. J. Foyt
1923	Eddie Hearne	1939	Wilbur Shaw	1960–61	A. J. Foyt		
1924	James Murphy	1940–41	Rex Mays	1962	Rodger Ward		

NATIONAL ASSOCIATION FOR STOCK CAR AUTO RACING (NASCAR) GRAND NATIONAL CHAMPIONS

1949	Red Byron	1955	Tim Flock	1964	Richard Petty	1971–72	Richard Petty
1950	Bill Rexford	1956–57	Buck Baker	1965	Ned Jarrett	1973	Benny Parsons
1951	Herb Thomas	1958–59	Lee Petty	1966	David Pearson	1974–75	Richard Petty
1952	Tim Flock	1960	Rex White	1967	Richard Petty	1976–78	Cale Yarborough
1953	Herb Thomas	1961	Ned Jarrett	1968–69	David Pearson	1979	Richard Petty
1954	Lee Petty	1962–63	Joe Weatherly	1970	Bobby Isaac		

WORLD GRAND PRIX DRIVER CHAMPIONS

1950	Giuseppe Farina, Italy, Alfa Romeo
1951	Juan Fangio, Argentina, Alfa Romeo
1952	Alberto Ascari, Italy, Ferrari
1953	Alberto Ascari, Italy, Ferrari
1955	Juan Fangio, Argentina, Maserati, Mercedes-Benz
1955	Juan Fangio, Argentina, Mercedes-Benz
1956	Juan Fangio, Argentina, Lancia-Ferrari
1957	Juan Fangio, Argentina, Masserati
1958	Mike Hawthorn, England, Ferrari
1959	Jack Brabham, Australia, Cooper
1960	Jack Brabham, Australia, Cooper
1961	Phil Hill, United States, Ferrari
1962	Graham Hill, England, BRM
1963	Jim Clark, Scotland, Lotus-Ford
1964	John Surtees, England, Ferrari
1965	Jim Clark, Scotland, Lotus-Ford
1966	Jack Brabham, Australia, Brabham-Repco
1967	Denis Hulme, New Zealand, Brabham-Repco
1968	Graham Hill, England, Lotus-Ford
1969	Jackie Stewart, Scotland, Matra-Ford
1970	Jochen Rindt, Austria, Lotus-Ford
1971	Jackie Stewart, Scotland, Tyrrell-Ford
1972	Emerson Fittipaldi, Brazil, Lotus-Ford
1973	Jackie Stewart, Scotland, Tyrrell-Ford
1974	Emerson Fittipaldi, Brazil, McLaren-Ford
1975	Niki Lauda, Austria, Ferrari
1976	James Hunt, Britain, McLaren-Ford
1977	Niki Lauda, Austria, Ferrari
1978	Mario Andretti, Nazareth, Pa., Lotus
1979	Jody Scheckter, South Africa
1980	Alan Jones, Australia

THE ONE-MILE SPEED MARK

The first recorded effort for one mile was made on Jan. 12, 1904, by Henry Ford, driving a Ford "999." He established a record of 39.40 sec or 91.370 mph. All prior records were established over the flying kilometer. The first man to travel better than 100 mph was Rigolly, on July 2, 1904, at 103.56 mph. The first over 200 mph was Major H.O.D. Segrave, who drove a Sunbeam at 203.79 mph on March 29, 1927, at Daytona, Fla.

In 1947, John Cobb of London became the first person to travel more than 400 mph on land. The Englishman accomplished the feat on Sept. 16 at Bonneville, Utah, and raised the world mile record to 394.2 mph and the world kilometer mark to 393.8 mph. His car was a Railton-Mobil Special. Cobb's average speed was 9.1325 seconds per mile.

The record held by Cobb was surpassed by Britain's Donald Campbell at Lake Eyre in Australia on July 17, 1964. He drove his 30-foot, 4,250-horsepower Bluebird to two runs of 403.1 mph each. This record was beaten by Bob Summers of Ontario, Calif., who drove his 32-foot, four-engined Goldenrod to a speed of 409.227 mph at Bonneville on Nov. 12, 1965.

Craig Breedlove of Los Angeles, driving "Spirit of America," a three-wheeled, jet-powered car, at Bonneville on Aug. 5, 1963, attained a speed of 8.8355 seconds per mile, or 407.45 mph. The U.S. Auto Club created a new category for the record—jet unlimited class. The record was broken a number of times in 1964, Breedlove lifting it above 500 mph to 526.277 on Oct. 15. Again, in 1965, the mark was topped frequently—Breedlove and Art Arfons of Akron, Ohio, beating one another's records; finally, on Nov. 15, Breedlove surpassed 600 mph, achieving a standard of 600.601 at Bonneville. Gary Gabelich, driving the Blue Flame, raised the record to 622.407 mph on Oct. 23, 1970, at Bonneville. The rocket car, powered by a mixture of peroxide and natural gas, hit 617.602 on the first run and 627.287 on the second.

Stan Barrett, of Hollywood, Calif., drove a 48,000-horsepower rocket car to a record of 638.637 mph at Bonneville, Sept. 9, 1979.

U.S. AUTO CLUB

1980 Triple Crown Races

Indianapolis 500 (Indianapolis Motor Speedway, May 26, 500 miles)—1, Johnny Rutherford, Fort Worth, Tex.; Chaparral–Cosworth; 200 laps; 3 hours, 29 minutes, 59.56 seconds; average speed: 142.862 mph; first-place prize: $318,019. 2, Tom Sneva, Spokane, Wash.; McLaren–Cosworth; 200 laps; $128,945. 3, Gary Bettenhausen, Monrovia, Ind., Wildcat–DGS; 200 laps; $86,945. 4, Gordon Johncock, Phoenix, Ariz.; Penske–Cosworth; 200 laps; $56,495. 5, Rick Mears, Bakersfield, Calif.; Penske–Cosworth; 199 laps; $45,505.

Music 500 (Pocono International Raceway, Long Pond, Pa., June 22, 500 miles)—Bobby Unser, Albuquerque, N.M.; PC-9 Cosworth; 200 laps; 3:18:04.81; 151.454 mph; $74,880. 2, Johnny Rutherford, Fort Worth, Tex.; Chaparral–Cosworth; 200 laps; $38,580. 3, Tom Sneva, Spokane, Wash.; McLaren–Cosworth; 198 laps; $24,605. 4, Bill Alsup, PC–7 Cosworth; 194 laps; $15,680. 5, Vern Schuppan, Wildcat DGS; 193 laps; $11,430.

California 500 (Ontario, Calif., Aug. 31, 500 miles)—Bobby Unser, Albuquerque, N.M.; Penske–Cosworth; 200 laps; 3 hours, 11 minutes, 51 seconds; average speed: 156.372 mph; $72,600. 2, Johnny Rutherford, Fort Worth, Tex.; Chaparral–Cosworth; 200 laps; $41,450. 3, Rick Mears, Bakersfield, Calif.; Penske–Cosworth; 199 laps; $24,475. 4, Al Unser, Albuquerque, N.M.; Cosworth, $14,550. 5, Tom Gloy, Lafayette, Calif., Penske–Cosworth, $11,050.

LEADING NASCAR MONEY-WINNERS

(Through Sept. 22, 1980)

Dale Earnhardt	$358,250	Bobby Allison	$302,470
Cale Yarborough	337,355	Buddy Baker	212,725
Darrell Waltrip	320,115	Neil Bonnett	176,755
Richard Petty	313,940	Terry Labonte	162,225
Benny Parsons	303,275	Jody Ridley	138,025

GRAND PRIX—1980

Formula One Competition

Argentina (Buenos Aires, 198 miles, Jan. 13)—Alan Jones, Australia; driving a Saudi–Williams; 1 hour, 43 minutes, 24.38 seconds

Brazil (Sao Paulo, 197.85 miles, Jan. 27)—Rene Arnoux, France; Renault; 1:40:01.35; 117.138 mph

South Africa (Kyalami, 192.8 miles, March 1)—Rene Arnoux, France; Renault; 126.8 mph

United States West (Long Beach, Calif., March 20)—Nelson Piquet, Brazil; Brabham Ford; 88.44 mph

Belgium (Zolder, 190.68 miles, May 4)—Didier Pironi, France; Ligier; 1:38:46.51; 115.75 mph

Monaco (Monte Carlo, May 18)—Carlos Reutemann, Argentina; Williams

Spain (Madrid, 164.4 miles, June 1)—Alan Jones, Australia; Saudi–Williams; 1:43:14.076; 95.692 mph

France (Le Castellet, 196.1 miles, June 29)—Alan Jones, Australia; Saudi–Williams; 1:32:43.42; 126.072 mph

Britain (Brands Hatch, July 13)—Alan Jones, Australia; Saudi–Williams; 1:34:49.228; 125.690 mph

Germany (Hockenheim, 190 miles, Aug. 10)—Jacques Laffite, Jr., France; Ligier-Ford; 1:22:59.73;

Austria (Zeltweg, 199.391 miles, Aug. 17)—Pierre Jabouille, France; Renault; 1:26:15.77; 139.50 mph

Dutch (Zandvoort, Aug. 31)—Nelson Piquet, Brazil; Brabham.

Canada (Montreal, 191.8 miles, Sept. 28)—Alan Jones, Australia; Saudi–Williams; 1:46:45.53; 106.2 mph

United States East (Watkins Glen, N.Y., 199.243 miles, Oct. 5)—Alan Jones, Williams–Ford, 1:34:36.05; 125.37 mph

WINSTON CUP GRAND NATIONAL LEADERS

(Through Sept. 22, 1980)

	Pts
Dale Earnhardt	3,847
Cale Yarborough	3,757
Richard Petty	3,741
Benny Parsons	3,708
Darrell Waltrip	3,662
Bobby Allison	3,532
Jody Ridley	3,273
Harry Gant	3,242
Richard Childress	3,125
Dave Marcis	3,099

OTHER 1980 CHAMPIONSHIP CAR RACES

Twin 200 (Ontario, Calif., April 13, 200 miles)—Johnny Rutherford, Fort Worth, Tex.; Chaparral–Cosworth; 1 hour, 14 minutes, 4 seconds; Average speed: 162.016 mph; $15,550.

Rey Mays Classic (Milwaukee, June 8, 150 miles)—Bobby Unser, Albuquerque, N.M.; Penske PC–9; 112,773 mph; $14,-300.

Tony Bettenhausen 200 (Milwaukee, Aug. 10, 200 miles)—Johnny Rutherford, Fort Worth, Tex.; Chaparral–Cosworth; 1:54:13; 105.063 mph; $20,150.

Norton 200 (Brooklyn, Mich., July 20, 200 miles CART)—Johnny Rutherford, Fort Worth, Tex.; Chaparral–Cosworth; 1:20:48; 148.515 mph; $21,850.

Kent Oil 150 (Watkins Glen, N.Y., Aug. 3, 150 miles CART)—Bobby Unser, Albuquerque, N.M.; Penske PC–9; $19,000.

Gould Grand Prix (Brooklyn, Mich., Sept. 20, 150 miles, CART)—Mario Andretti, Nazareth, Pa.; Penske PC–9 Cosworth; 167.494 mph.

NATIONAL ASSOCIATION FOR STOCK CAR AUTO RACING (NASCAR)—1980

Winston Western 500 (Riverside, Calif., Jan. 19, 500 kilometers, 311.78 miles)—Darrell Waltrip, Franklin, Tenn., Chevrolet, 3 hours, 16 minutes, 58 seconds; average speed: 94.974 mph; winner's purse: $24,700.

Daytona 500 (Daytona Beach, Fla., Feb. 17, 500 miles)—Buddy Baker, Charlotte, N.C.; Oldsmobile; 2:48:55; 177.602 mph (record); $102,175.

Richmond 400 (Richmond, Va., Feb. 24, 216.8 miles)—Darrell Waltrip; 3:12:08; 67.703 mph; $17,800.

Carolina 500 (Rockingham, N.C., March 9, 500 miles)—Cale Yarborough, Timmonsville, S.C.; Oldsmobile; 4:36:06; 108.735 mph; $19,280.

Atlanta 500 (Atlanta, Ga., March 16, 500 miles)—Dale Earnhardt; Kannapolis, N.C.; Chevrolet; 3:42:32; 134.808 mph; $36,200.

Virginia 500 (Martinsville, Va., April 27, 262.5 miles)—Darrell Waltrip; 3:48.06; 69.049 mph; $26,850.

Winston 500 (Talladega, Ala., May 4, 500 miles)—Buddy Baker; 2:56; 170.481 mph; $32,150.

Music City 420 (Nashville, Tenn., May 10, 250 miles)—Richard Petty, Randleman, N.C.; Chevrolet; 2:47:52; 89.471 mph; $15,350.

Mason–Dixon 500 (Dover, Del., May 18, 500 miles)—Bobby Allison, Hueytown, Ala.; Ford; 4:23:28; 113.866 mph; $21,900.

World 600 (Charlotte, N.C., May 25, 600 miles)—Benny Parsons, Ellerbe, N.C.; Chevrolet; 5:01:51; 119.265 mph; $44,850.

Nascar 400 (College Station, Tex., June 1, 400 miles)—Cale Yarborough; 2:30:54; 159.046 mph (record); $21,000.

Hodgdon 400 (Riverside, Calif., June 8, 248.9 miles)—Darrell Waltrip; 2:26:38; 101.846 mph; $22,100.

Gabriel 400 (Brooklyn, Mich., June 15, 400 miles)—Benny

Parsons; 3:02:05; 131.808 mph; $24,800.
Firecracker 400 (Daytona Beach, Fla., July 4, 400 miles)—Bobby Allison; Mercury; 2:18:21; 173.473 mph (record); $24,-805.
Coca-Cola 500 (Pocono, Pa., July 27, 500 miles)—Neil Bonnett, Hueytown, Ala.; Mercury; 4:01:10; 124.395 mph; $19,-915.
Talladega 500 (Talladega, Ala., Aug. 3, 500 miles)—Neil Bonnett; 2:59:47; 166.894; $35,675.
Southern 500 (Darlington, S.C., Sept. 1, 500 miles)—Terry Labonte, Corpus Christi, Tex.; Chevrolet; 4:21:05; 115.210 mph; $27,325.
Capital City 400 (Richmond, Va., Sept. 7, 216.8 miles)—Bobby Allison; Ford; 2:43.10; 79.722 mph; $17,175.
CRC Chemicals 500 (Dover, Del., Sept. 14, 500 miles)—Darrell Waltrip; 4:18:34; 116.024 mph; $22,900.

GYMNASTICS

WORLD CHAMPIONSHIPS—1979

(Fort Worth, Tex., Dec. 7–9, 1979)

Men's Events

	Pts
All around—Aleksandr Dityatin, Soviet Union	118.25
Floor exercises—Kurt Thomas, Indiana State	19.80
Pommel horse—Zoltan Magyar, Hungary	19.82
Still rings—Aleksandr Dityatin	19.80
Vault—Aleksandr Dityatin	19.72
Parallel bars—Bart Conner, United States	19.72
Horizontal bar—Kurt Thomas	19.77
Team—Soviet Union	587.50

Women's Events

All around—Nelli Kim, Soviet Union	78.65
Floor exercises—Emilia Eberle, Romania	19.80
Balance beam—Vera Cerna, Czechoslovakia	19.80
Uneven parallel bars—Yanhons Ma, China	19.82
Vault—Dumitrita, Turner, Romania	19.77
Team—Romania	389.55

ASSOCIATION OF INTERCOLLEGIATE ATHLETICS FOR WOMEN (A.I.A.W.)

(Baton Rouge, La., April 3–5, 1980)

DIVISION I

	Pts
All around—Sharon Shapiro, U.C.L.A.	n.a.
Balance beam—Sharon Shapiro, U.C.L.A.	18.850
Floor exercise—Sharon Shapiro, U.C.L.A.	18.98
Vault—Sharon Shapiro, U.C.L.A.	19.350
Uneven parallel bars—Sharon Shapiro, U.C.L.A.	19.00
Team—Penn State	145.50

DIVISION II

(Shreveport, La., March 27–30, 1980)

	Pts
All around—Beth Johnson, Centenary	37.00
Balance beam—Jill Brown, Centenary	18.45
Floor exercise—Margo Todd, Centenary	18.75
Vault—Beth Johnson, Centenary	18.30
Uneven parallel bars—Beth Johnson, Centenary	18.55
Team—Centenary	144.85

DIVISION III

	Pts
All-around—Sheila Ewer, Wisconsin-Oshkosh	34.05
Team—Wisconsin-Oshkosh	132.00

NATIONAL COLLEGIATE ATHLETIC ASSOCIATION

(Lincoln, Neb., April 3–5, 1980)

Division I

	Pts
All around—Jim Hartung, Nebraska	115.02
Floor exercises—Steve Elliott, Nebraska	19.55
Pommel horse—Dave Stoldt, Illinois	19.45
Still rings—Jim Hartung, Nebraska	19.45
Vault—Ron Galimore, Iowa State	19.75
Parallel bars—Phil Cahoy, Nebraska	19.55
Horizontal bar—Phil Cahoy, Nebraska, and Darroll Kerbel, Louisiana State (tie)	19.55
Team—Nebraska	563.30

WORLD CUP

(Tokyo, June 2-4, 1979)

Men's Events

	Pts
Combined—Alexandre Ditiatin, U.S.S.R.	57.65
Floor exercises—Tie between Shigeru Kasamatsu, Japan and Stoian Deltchev, Bulgaria	19.45
Horizontal bar—Eberhard Gienger, East Germany	19.525
Still rings—Alexandre Dititian	19.40
Pommel horse—Bart Conner, Norman, Okla.	19.35
Parallel bars—Eizo Kennetsu, Japan	19.60
Vault—Ralph Bathel, East Germany	19.525

Women's Events

Combined—Stella Zakharova, U.S.S.R.	39.30
Floor exercises—Nadia Comaneci, Romania	20.00
Balance beam—Emilia Eberle, Romania	15.70
Vault—Nadia Comaneci	19.70
Uneven parallel bars—Tie between Emilia Eberle and Steffi Kraker, East Germany	19.60

KURT THOMAS FIRST GYMNAST TO WIN SULLIVAN AWARD

Kurt Thomas, a graduate assistant gymnastics coach at Arizona State University, became the first gymnast to be named the outstanding amateur athlete in America in 1979. The 24-year-old Thomas won the James A. Sullivan Award by excelling in a sport generally dominated by Europeans and Japanese. The showing by the 5-ft-5-in., 127-lb Thomas in the world championships in December 1979 at Fort Worth, Tex., put him in the forefront. He won the gold medal in the horizontal bar, shared a gold in the floor exercises, took a silver medal in the pommel horse, shared a silver medal on the parallel bars, and won the second-place silver in the all-around championship. Thomas has a gymnastic trick named after him—"The Thomas Flair." He does it on the pommel horse. His legs whirl and then he goes into a scissors, a move that has been described as seeming to resemble a helicopter in action.

Tennis Earnings—1979

These figures from the United States Tennis Association include prize money from recognized tournaments, recognized bonuses, and recognized national team competition. They do not include challenge matches, exhibition, or special events involving fewer than eight players.

Men

Player	Amount	Player	Amount
Bjorn Borg	$1,019,345	Sherwood Stewart	219,675
John McEnroe	1,005,238	Gene Mayer	219,018
Jimmy Connors	701,340	Jose Higueras	211,180
Vitas Gerulaitis	414,515	Victor Pecci	209,636
Guillermo Vilas	374,195	Brian Gottfried	196,915
Peter Fleming	353,315	Stan Smith	190,314
Roscoe Tanner	263,433	Marty Riessen	184,124
Eddie Dibbs	249,293	Victor Amaya	139,112
Wojtek Fibak	234,452	Pat DuPre	138,480
Harold Solomon	222,078		

Women

Player	Amount	Player	Amount
Martina Navratilova	$747,548	Betty Stove	182,006
Chris Evert Lloyd	564,398	Sue Barker	175,452
Tracy Austin	541,676	Evonne Goolagong Cawley	171,573
Wendy Turnbull	317,463	Virginia Wade	146,283
Dianne Fromholtz	265,990		
Billie Jean King	185,804		

Tennis Career Earnings (Through 1979)

Men

Player	Amount
Jimmy Connors 1972–79	$2,742,621
Bjorn Borg 1973–79	2,416,016
Guillermo Vilas 1972–79	2,161,454
Ilie Nastase 1969–79	2,102,861
Raul Ramirez 1973–79	1,776,100
Arthur Ashe 1969–79	1,711,373
Ken Rosewall 1957–79	1,602,300
Eddie Dibbs 1972–79	1,572,683
Rod Laver 1963–79	1,564,331
Brian Gottfried 1972–79	1,564,213
Stan Smith 1969–79	1,505,249
John McEnroe 1978–79	1,450,262
Manuel Orantes 1968–79	1,325,574
Harold Solomon 1972–79	1,309,611
Roscoe Tanner 1972–79	1,256,924
Vitas Gerulaitis 1974–79	1,225,603
Tom Okker 1968–79	1,222,854
Wojtek Fibak 1974–79	1,148,673
John Newcombe 1968–79	1,062,408

Women

Player	Amount
Chris Evert Lloyd 1973–79	2,398,622
Martina Navratilova 1973–79	1,791,567
Billie Jean King 1968–79	1,369,644
Virginia Wade 1968–79	1,336,031
Evonne Goolagong Cawley 1970–79	979,404
Rosemary Casals 1968–79	903,157

CHESS

WORLD CHAMPIONS

1894–1921	Emanuel Lasker, Germany
1921–27	Jose R. Capablanca, Cuba
1927–35	Alexander A. Alekhine, U.S.S.R.
1935–37	Dr. Max Euwe, Netherlands
1937–46	Alexander A. Alekhine, U.S.S.R.[1]
1948–57	Mikhail Botvinnik, U.S.S.R.
1957–58	Vassily Smyslov, U.S.S.R.
1958–60	Mikhail Botvinnik, U.S.S.R.
1960–61	Mikhail Tal, U.S.S.R.
1961–63	Mikhail Botvinnik, U.S.S.R.
1963–68	Tigran Petrosian, U.S.S.R.
1969–71	Boris Spassky, U.S.S.R.
1972–74	Bobby Fischer, Los Angeles
1975	Bobby Fischer[2]; Anatoly Karpov, U.S.S.R.
1976–79	Anatoly Karpov, U.S.S.R.[3]

1. Alekhine, a French citizen, died while champion. 2. Relinquished title. 3. In 1978, Karpov defeated Viktor Korchnoi 6 games to 5.

UNITED STATES CHAMPIONS

1909–36	Frank J. Marshall, New York
1936–44	Samuel Reshevsky, New York[1]
1944–46	Arnold S. Denker, New York
1946	Samuel Reshevsky, Boston
1948	Herman Steiner, Los Angeles
1951–52	Larry Evans, New York
1954–57	Arthur Bisguier, New York
1958–61	Bobby Fischer, Brooklyn, N.Y.
1962	Larry Evans, New York
1963–67	Bobby Fischer, New York
1968	Larry Evans, New York
1969–71	Samuel Reshevsky, Spring Valley, N.Y.
1972	Robert Byrne, Ossining, N.Y.
1973	Lubomir Kavelek, Washington; John Grefe, San Francisco
1974–77	Walter Browne, Berkeley, Calif.
1978–79	Lubomir Kavalek, New York

1. In 1942, Isaac I. Kashdan of New York was co-champion for a while because of a tie with Reshevsky in that year's tournament. Reshevsky won the play-off.

VOLLEYBALL

U.S. VOLLEYBALL ASSOCIATION CHAMPIONSHIPS

(Portland, Ore., May 13–17, 1980)

National Champions

Men—Olympic Club, San Francisco; runnerup: Chuck's Steak House, Los Angeles

Women—ANVA, Fountain Valley, Calif.; runnerup: Renegades, Los Angeles

Senior women—South Bay Spoilers, Hermosa Beach, Calif.; runnerup: Mavericks, Manhattan Beach, Calif.

NATIONAL COLLEGIATE ATHLETIC ASSOCIATION CHAMPIONSHIPS

(Muncie, Ind., May 9–10, 1980)

Final—Southern California defeated U.C.L.A.

Third place—Ohio State defeated Rutgers

N.A.I.A. CHAMPIONSHIPS—1979

Final—Graceland College defeated George Williams College in final (Championships not held in 1980)

A.I.A.W. CHAMPIONSHIPS—1979

Division I—Univ. of Hawaii defeated Utah State in final

Division II—Univ. of Hawaii–Hilo defeated Florida Institute in final

Division III—Azusa Pacific College defeated Sacramento State Univ. in final

COMPREHENSIVE INDEX

A

B

C

D

E

F

G

H

J

K

N

O

P

Q

R

S

T

U

V

W

X

Y

Z

TRIVIA (Continued from page 52)

Canadian farmer John Duncan MacKay thought he was simply being kind to his animals, but Ontario law enforcement authorities didn't see it quite that way.

MacKay received a 30-day jail sentence for growing marijuana on his farm—and feeding the evil weed to his five beef cattle.

Before he was sentenced, MacKay told the judge: "The cattle are in the bar eating grain all winter. It's monotonous. A few leaves of marijuana on their food really lives them up."

●

In Tempe, Ariz., two scientists—Ross Consaul and George Seperich—began a study of the effects that diet and jogging have on the human heart.

But instead of observing people, they're studying pigs. It turns out that pigs and people have a number of biological similarities. But there's an even more compelling reason for using pigs. As Seperich pointed out: "We can be fairly sure no one is going to invite our pigs out for beer and pizza in the middle of our study."

●

If you want to make an educated guess as to what part of the British Isles a woman lives in, ask her to show you her underwear.

According to a survey by a British magazine, *Women's World*, the higher the waistband on a lady's undergarment, the farther north she lives.

The publication noted that women who dwell in the south of England have a decided preference for bikini underwear. But Scottish females seem to opt for the type of high-waisted undies the magazine calls "passion killers."

●

In order to prevent unauthorized entry into its Institute of Material Sciences and to reduce thefts from the building, the University of Connecticut installed an ultrasophisticated $16,000 computerized security system.

It worked perfectly—until someone stole it.

●

The U.S. Postal Service announced a program to transfer some of its letter carriers from vehicular to foot delivery.

As one might have expected, they came up with a non-bureaucratic name for the project: "Route Demotorization."

●

Colorado Springs, Colo., police arrived at the home of James and Mary Seals after their domestic dispute had gone well beyond the name-calling stage.

According to Mrs. Seals, the husband punctuated the argument they were having in their kitchen by slapping her in the face. She retaliated by stabbing him with a fork. She told the police that he then went to the garage, returned with a tire iron and struck her with it.

The cops arrested both of them. They were charged with . . . dueling.

●

We don't know how seriously Swedish parents react when they catch their kids with a hand in the cookie jar.

But, judging from what happened to Swen-Ove Borgstroem, a Swedish man, it's not healthy for mommies and daddies to temper with their children's financial assets.

Police arrested the 30-year-old father and charged him with robbing his three-year-old son's piggy bank.

●

Thanks to a California courtroom verdict, happiness continued to reign supreme throughout the Magic Kingdoms of Disneyland.

The jury dismissed charges against Robert L. Hill, a Disneyland employee who earns his living by walking around the park clad in a large, furry Winnie-the-Pooh costume. Hill had been accused of striking a nine-year-old Disneyland visitor with his paw. The suit claimed that the little girl suffered a bruise that turned green, and her attorneys demanded $15,000 in damages.

Hill denied striking the youngster with his paw. He said he hit her with his fur-covered, wiggling plastic car. Unintentionally, of course. He claimed that he was shoved from behind and that he hit her by accident. After the jury acquitted Hill, Superior Court judge Jerrold Oliver observed: "Winnie-the-Pooh has been vindicated."